D1606689

TESTS IN PRINT VII

EARLIER PUBLICATIONS IN THIS SERIES

TESTS
IN PRINT VII

AN INDEX TO TESTS, TEST REVIEWS, AND THE LITERATURE ON SPECIFIC TESTS

Edited by

LINDA L. MURPHY
ROBERT A. SPIES
BARBARA S. PLAKE

The Buros Institute of Mental Measurements
The University of Nebraska-Lincoln
Lincoln, Nebraska

2006
Distributed by The University of Nebraska Press

Note to Users

TABLE OF CONTENTS

INTRODUCTION

The *Tests in Print* (TIP) series consists of descriptive listings of commercially published tests. This volume also serves as a comprehensive index to all editions of the *Mental Measurements Yearbook* series (MMY) published to date.

There are key differences between the *Tests in Print* series and the *Mental Measurements Yearbook* series. In contrast to TIP, the MMY series contains both descriptive entries and critical reviews of commercially published tests available in the English language. Each MMY, of which there are now 16, includes reviews and descriptions of only those tests that are new or substantially revised since the previous MMY. The MMY series is, therefore, sequential and cumulative in nature.

Each TIP, of which there are now seven, is a comprehensive volume describing, to the best of our ability, every test that is currently commercially available. *TIP VII*, therefore, supersedes *TIP VI*. Although it is necessary to have the entire MMY series to be sure of finding a descriptive entry or a review of a particular test, only the latest addition to the TIP series is needed for comprehensive coverage of currently available testing products.

To complement these two publications, Tests Reviews Online (www.unl.edu/buros) has been developed to permit users instant access to test descriptions and reviews from the Buros Institute of Mental Measurements. Test information and reviews available from Tests Reviews Online appear exactly as in the *The Ninth* through *The Sixteenth Mental Measurements Yearbooks*. In addition, regular updates are provided from our current database. For a small fee, users may download descriptive testing information and test critiques for over 2,500 tests.

TIP VII may be best used as a means to locate and learn about commercially available testing products. Because *TIP VII* indexes all 16 books in the MMY series (for tests still in print), it is an invaluable guide to both descriptive and analytical information. As a directory of commercially available tests, *TIP VII* is not designed to include all known tests. Specifically, the TIP series does not include research or proprietary instruments. Research instruments are often published in journals and serve the limited uses of test authors. Proprietary instruments are frequently designed for specialized audiences (e.g., admissions, licensure, certification) or for highly secured markets (e.g., government, industry) and are not considered "commercially available" tests.

In the Preface of the first *Tests in Print* volume (1961), Oscar Buros noted that this work had been in preparation for over 20 years. The first two volumes of *The Mental Measurements Yearbook* were published in 1938 and 1940. It became increasingly apparent that a comprehensive bibliography of tests and an index to the contents of the MMY volumes was needed. The initial delay in *Tests in Print* was due to World War II, and then various other financial and production limitations postponed its publication. *Tests in Print II* was published in 1974. After the death of Oscar Buros in 1978, the Buros Institute was established at the University of Nebraska-Lincoln. The first publication from the new Institute was *Tests in Print III* in 1983. *Tests in Print IV* was published in 1994, *Tests in Print V* in 1999, and *Tests in Print VI* in 2002.

The need for a comprehensive bibliography of tests has never been more essential. Because of the proliferation of commercially available tests, we have adopted a policy of reviewing in *The Mental Measurements Yearbook* series only those tests with at least a minimum of technical and development information. This policy was implemented with tests reviewed in the *14th MMY*. Therefore, not all commercially available tests will be reviewed in the MMY. However, we continue to include descriptive information for all known in-print commercially available tests in the *Tests in Print* series. With the more rapid publication of *The Mental Measurements Yearbook* series (approximately every 24 months), it also became necessary to update our listing of commercially available tests on a more frequent basis. Beginning with *Tests in Print VI*, we embarked on a plan to publish TIP every 3 years.

Our efforts in this massive enterprise have been consistent with those initially proposed by Oscar K. Buros, that is, to improve the science and practice of testing by offering information and evaluative reviews of commercial products to informed consumers. *Tests in Print VII* is a continuation of our efforts to provide a product for people who develop, evaluate, study, and/or buy tests.

TESTS IN PRINT VII

The contents of *Tests in Print VII* include: (a) a comprehensive bibliography of commercially available tests published as separates for use with English-speaking individuals; (b) a list of contributing reviewers for the entire MMY series; (c) a test title index that includes all in-print tests, tests that have gone out of print since the publication of *TIP VI*, and alternative or superseded titles for some tests; (d) a separate listing of the tests that have gone out of print since the publication of *TIP III* (1983); (e) a list of test acronyms; (f) a classified subject index that also describes the population for which each test is intended; (g) a publishers directory and index, including contact information and test listings by publisher; (h) a name index, which includes the names of all authors of tests or of reviews; and (i) a score index listing all scores generated by tests listed in *TIP VII*.

The organization of the volume is encyclopedic in nature, with tests being ordered alphabetically by title. Thus, if the title of a test is known, the reader can locate the test description immediately without having to consult the Index of Titles. Test classifications appear in the Classified Subject Index.

TABLE 1

Test Entries in *TIP VII* by Major Classification

Classification	Number of Test Entries
Achievement	81
Behavior Assessment	134
Developmental	135
Education	110
English and Language	161
Fine Arts	17
Foreign Language	45
Intelligence and General Aptitude	202
Mathematics	70
Miscellaneous	254
Neuropsychological	120
Personality	615
Reading	118
Science	45
Sensory-Motor	58
Social Studies	31
Speech and Hearing	86
Vocations	564

The page headings reflect the encyclopedic organization. The page heading of the left-hand page cites the number and title of the first test listed on that page, and the page heading of the right-hand page cites the number and title of the last test listed on that page. All numbers presented in the various indexes are test numbers, not page numbers. Page numbers, important only for the Table of Contents, are indicated at the bottom of each page.

TESTS

Tests in Print VII contains 2,846 test entries. The in-print status of these tests was confirmed by direct correspondence with publishers. Table 1 presents the number of test entries included in each major classification of the Classified Subject Index. Any classification system is to some degree dependent on human judgment, but broad comparisons between categories are often useful. It is interesting to note, for example, that once again the Personality test category continues to include the greatest number of tests of any category in *TIP VII*.

REVIEWS AND EXCERPTS

Tests in Print VII serves as a master index of in-print tests that refers the reader to all the original test reviews and excerpted test reviews that appeared for these tests in all of the *Mental Measurements Yearbooks* to date. In addition, it provides references to entries and reviews in earlier Yearbooks for all tests that have gone out of print since *TIP III*. Authors of reviews and excerpts are named following the test entries in cross references to the appropriate MMY. Although *TIP VII* will serve a very useful function by providing a comprehensive bibliography of tests in print, the cross references to the critical reviews are also of great importance if tests are to be used wisely. Thus TIP and the MMYs are inseparable partners in the cause of promoting effective selection and use of tests.

A total of 3,068 individuals have contributed reviews to one or more MMYs. Because of their important contributions to the *Mental Measurements Yearbooks*, a complete listing of MMY test reviewers is presented in the index section of *TIP VII*.

REFERENCES

Earlier volumes have included specific test references selected by Buros staff who searched through hundreds of professional journals. Because of the availability of online search features that allow users to do independent reference searches, it was our decision to discontinue providing these references in the MMY and TIP series. Cross references for a number of test descriptions will still indicate when references were provided in previous publications (e.g., "See T5:326 [10 references]").

INDEXES

As mentioned earlier, *TIP VII* includes eight indexes invaluable as aids to effective use: (a) Index of MMY test reviewers, (b) Index of Titles, (c) Index of Recently-Out-of-Print Tests, (d) Index of Acronyms, (e) Classified Subject Index, (f) Publishers Directory and Index, (g) Index of Names, and (h) Score Index. Additional comment on these indexes is presented below.

Index of MMY Test Reviewers. This listing represents all test reviewers who have had their reviews published in *The Mental Measurements Yearbook* series and the volume number of their test reviews.

Index of Titles. Because the organization of TIP is comprehensive in nature, with the tests ordered alphabetically by title throughout the volume, the test title index does not have to be consulted to find a test for which the title is known. However, the title index has some features that make it useful beyond its function as a complete title listing. First, it includes cross-reference information useful for tests with superseded or alternative titles or tests commonly (and sometimes inaccurately) known by multiple titles. Second, it lists the 292 tests that have gone out of print since being listed in *TIP VI* or the *15th* or *16th MMY*. To differentiate between in-print and out-of-print tests in the title index, it is important to read carefully the instructions on the use of the test title index that precede the title listing. It is important to keep in mind that the numbers in this index, like those for all TIP and MMY indexes, are test numbers and not page numbers.

Index of Recently-Out-of-Print Tests. This index is a comprehensive listing of all tests that have gone out of print since the publication of *Tests in Print III* (1983). The number following the title indicates the last Buros publication in which the test was listed as an in-print test.

Index of Acronyms. Some tests seem to be better known by their acronyms than by their full titles. The Index of Acronyms can help in these instances; it refers the reader to the full title of the test and to the relevant descriptive information and reviews.

Classified Subject Index. The Classified Subject Index classifies all tests listed in *TIP VII* into 18 major categories: Achievement, Behavior Assessment, Developmental, Education, English and Language, Fine Arts, Foreign Languages, Intelligence and General Aptitude, Mathematics, Miscellaneous, Neuropsychological, Personality, Reading, Science, Sensory-Motor, Social Studies, Speech and Hearing, and Vocations. Each test entry includes test title, population for which the test is intended, and test number. The Classified Subject Index is of great help to readers who seek a listing of tests in given subject areas. The Classified Subject Index represents a starting point for readers who know their area of interest but do not know how to further focus that interest in order to identify the best test(s) for their particular purposes. A descriptive listing of the categories precedes the Classified Subject Index.

Publishers Directory and Index. The Publishers Directory and Index includes the names and addresses of the publishers of all tests included in *TIP VII* plus a listing of test numbers for each individual publisher. This index also includes telephone and FAX numbers and addresses for electronic access (email and web pages). Publishers were given an opportunity to provide this information as they wanted it listed. For those not providing contact information, only a mailing address is included. This index can be particularly useful in obtaining addresses for specimen sets or catalogs after the test descriptions have been read and evaluated. It can also be useful when a reader knows the publisher of a certain test but is uncertain about the test title, or when a reader is interested in the range of tests published by a given publisher. A few publishers are listed as "Status Unknown" because recent correspondence has been returned by the Post Office and we have been unable to obtain a current address.

Index of Names. The Index of Names provides a comprehensive list of names, indicating authorship of a test or a test review.

Score Index. The Score Index is an index to all scores generated by the tests in *TIP VII*. Test titles are sometimes misleading or ambiguous, and test content may be difficult to define with precision. Test scores represent operational definitions of the variables the test author is trying to measure, and as such they often define test purpose and content more adequately than other descriptive information. A search for a particular test is most often a search for a test that measures some specific variables. Test scores and their associated labels can often be the best definitions of the variables of interest. It is, in fact, a detailed subject index based on the most critical operational features of any test—the scores and their associated labels.

HOW TO USE TIP VII

A reference work like *TIP VII* can be of far greater benefit to a reader if a little time is taken to become familiar with what it has to offer and how one might use it most effectively to obtain the information wanted. The first step in this process is to read the Introduction to *TIP VII*. The second step is to become familiar with the eight indexes and particularly with the instructions preceding each index listing. The third step is to make actual use of the book by looking up needed information. This third step is simple if one keeps in mind the following possibilities:

1. If you know the title of the test, use the alphabetical page headings to go directly to the test entry.

2. If you do not know, cannot find, or are unsure of the title of a test, consult the Index of Titles for possible variants of the title or consult the appropriate subject area of the Classified Subject Index for other possible leads or for similar or related tests in the same area. (Other uses for both of these indexes were described earlier.)

3. If you know the author of a test but not the title or publisher, consult the Index of Names and look up the author's titles until you find the test you want.

4. If you know the test publisher but not the title or author, consult the Publishers Directory and Index and look up the publisher's titles until you find the test you want.

5. If you are looking for a test that yields a particular kind of score, but have no knowledge of which test that might be, look up the score in the Score Index and locate the test or tests that include the score variable of interest.

6. Once you have found the test or tests you are looking for, read the descriptive entries for these tests carefully so that you can take advantage of the information provided. A description of the information available in these test entries will be presented later in this section.

7. After you have read the descriptive information, you may want to order a specimen set for a particular test so that you can examine it firsthand. The Publishers Directory and Index has the address information needed to obtain specimen sets or catalogs.

Making Effective Use of the Test Entries. The test entries include extensive information. For each test, descriptive information is presented in the following order:

a) TITLES. Test titles are printed in boldface type. Secondary or series titles are set off from main titles by a colon.

b) PURPOSE. For each test we have included a brief, clear statement describing the purpose of the test. Often these statements are quotations from the test manual.

c) POPULATION. This is a description of the groups for which the test is intended. The grade, chronological age, semester range, or employment category is usually given. "Grades 1.5–2.5, 2–3, 4–12, 13–17" means that there are four test booklets: a booklet for the middle of first grade through the middle of the second grade, a booklet for the beginning of the second grade through the end of third grade, a booklet for Grades 4 through 12 inclusive, and a booklet for undergraduate and graduate students in colleges and universities.

d) PUBLICATION DATE. The inclusive range of publication dates for the various forms, accessories, and editions of a test is reported.

e) ACRONYM. When a test is often referred to by an acronym by the test publisher, the acronym is given in the test entry immediately following the publication date.

f) SCORES. The number of part scores is presented along with their titles or descriptions of what they are intended to represent or measure.

g) ADMINISTRATION. Individual or group administration is indicated. A test is considered a group test unless it may be administered only individually.

h) FORMS, PARTS, AND LEVELS. All available forms, parts, and levels are listed.

i) MANUAL. Notation is made if no manual is available. All other manual information is included under Price Data.

j) RESTRICTED DISTRIBUTION. This is noted only for tests that are put on a special market by the publisher. Educational and psychological restrictions are not noted (unless a special training course is required for use).

k) PRICE DATA. Price information is reported for test packages (usually 20 to 35 tests), answer sheets, all other accessories, and specimen sets. The statement "$17.50 per 35 tests" means that all accessories are included unless otherwise indicated by the reporting of separate prices for accessories. The statement also means 35 tests of one level, one edition, or one part unless stated otherwise. Because test prices can change very quickly, the year that the listed test prices were obtained is also given. Foreign currency is assigned the appropriate symbol. When prices are given in foreign dollars, a qualifying symbol is added (e.g., A$16.50 refers to 16 dollars and 50 cents in Australian currency). Along with cost, the publication date and number of pages on which print occurs is reported for manuals and technical reports (e.g., 1995, 102 pages). All types of machine-scorable answer sheets available for use with a specific test are also re-

ported in the descriptive entry. Scoring and reporting services provided by publishers are reported along with information on costs. In a few cases, special computerized scoring and interpretation services are given in separate entries immediately following the test.

l) FOREIGN LANGUAGE AND OTHER SPECIAL EDITIONS. This section concerns foreign language editions published by the same publisher who sells the English edition. It also indicates special editions (e.g., Braille, large type) available from the same or a different publisher.

m) TIME. The number of minutes of actual working time allowed examinees and the approximate length of time needed for administering a test are reported whenever obtainable. The latter figure is always enclosed in parentheses. Thus, "50(60) minutes" indicates that the examinees are allowed 50 minutes of working time and that a total of 60 minutes is needed to administer the test. A time of "40–50 minutes" indicates an untimed test that takes approximately 45 minutes to administer, or—in a few instances—a test so timed that working time and administration time are very difficult to disentangle. When the time necessary to administer a test is not reported or suggested in the test materials but has been obtained through correspondence with the test publisher or author, the time is enclosed in brackets.

n) COMMENTS. Some entries contain special notations, such as: "for research use only"; "revision of the ABC Test"; "tests administered monthly at centers throughout the United States"; "subtests available as separates"; and "verbal creativity." A statement such as "verbal creativity" is intended to further describe what the test claims to measure. Some of the test entries include factual statements that may imply criticism of the test, such as "1990 test identical with test copyrighted 1970."

o) AUTHOR. For most tests, all authors are reported. In the case of tests that appear in a new form each year, typically only authors of the most recent forms are listed. Names are reported exactly as printed on test booklets. Names of editors generally are not reported.

p) PUBLISHER. The name of the publisher or distributor is reported for each test. Foreign publishers are identified by listing the country in brackets immediately following the name of the publisher. The Publishers Directory and Index must be consulted for a publisher's address and other contact information.

q) FOREIGN ADAPTATIONS. Revisions and adaptations of tests for foreign use are listed in a separate paragraph following the original edition.

r) SUBLISTINGS. Levels, editions, subtests, or parts of a test available in separate booklets are sometimes presented as sublistings with titles set in small capitals. Sub-sublistings are indented and titles are set in italic type.

s) CROSS REFERENCES. For tests that have been listed previously in a Buros Institute publication, a test entry includes—if relevant—a final paragraph containing a cross reference to the reviews, excerpts, and references for that test in those volumes. For example, in the cross references, "T3:467" refers to test 467 in *Tests in Print III*, "8:1023" refers to test 1023 in *The Eighth Mental Measurements Yearbook*, "T2:144" refers to test 144 in Tests in Print II, "7:637" refers to test 637 in *The Seventh Mental Measurements Yearbook*, "P:262" refers to test 262 in *Personality Tests and Reviews I*, "2:1427" refers to test 1427 in *The 1940 Yearbook*, and "1:1110" refers to test 1110 in *The 1938 Yearbook*. In the case of batteries and programs, the paragraph also includes cross references—from the battery to the separately listed subtests and vice versa—to entries in this volume and to entries and reviews in earlier editions of TIP and the MMY.

ACKNOWLEDGEMENTS

The publication of a volume of this kind is only accomplished with the effort and cooperation of many people. The editors are grateful to all who have given of their time and expertise in the publication process.

Staff members of the Buros Institute have been major contributors and vital to the success of gathering and compiling the information to be included in *TIP VII*. It has truly been a team effort. Gary Anderson, Assistant Editor, and Rosemary Sieck, Word Processing Specialist, have worked long and hard in helping to organize, proofread, and present the information included. Their careful and conscientious efforts are very important to our final product. The administrative support of Rasma Strautkalns, Institute Secretary, has also been very important and helpful. The Buros Institute for Assessment Consultation and Outreach professional staff of Chad W.

Buckendahl, Susan L. Davis, and James C. Impara have provided valuable assistance and insights into a range of testing products that has made this publication a better product. Finally, we would like to thank Kurt F. Geisinger, Director of the Buros Center for Testing, for his leadership during the final stages required to complete *TIP VII*.

The Buros Institute is part of the Department of Educational Psychology of the University of Nebraska-Lincoln and many students from the department and the university have contributed to the publication of this volume. We thank the following graduate research assistants who helped with the preparation of *TIP VII:* Jeff Babl, Stacey DeSchane, Kelly Haack, Wei Huang, Michael Lemberger, Tabethah Mack, Brad Merker, Alejandro Morales, Erin Rhoads, Anja Römhild, Michelle Simpson, Rhonda Turner, and Georgette Yetter.

Appreciation is also extended to our National Advisory Committee for their willingness to assist in the operation of the Buros Institute. The members of the National Advisory Committee during the time of preparation of this volume were Angee Baker, Jane Close Conoley, Greg Cizek, Terry Gutkin, Milton Hakel, Gail Latta, Larry Rudner, Paul Sackett, and Jeffrey Smith.

Most of the publishers of the tests listed have been extremely cooperative in providing us with their materials and information to make these listings comprehensive and accurate. We appreciate their timely assistance. A small minority of publishers refuse to provide information and materials. We sincerely regret that we were not able to list their products. Some others did not respond to our requests for an accuracy check of information, so we have included the information we have for their tests and addresses. We have made every effort to stay alert to new tests, publishers, and publisher addresses. We apologize for any oversights and hope that the test authors or publishers will make us aware of omissions and discrepancies so that their entries can be corrected in future editions.

And finally, we thank our friends and families for their patience and encouragement during the publication process.

Linda L. Murphy
Robert A. Spies
Barbara S. Plake
September 2006

Tests in Print

[1]
A-4 Police Officer Video Test.

Purpose: Designed as an entry-level test to "assess both cognitive and non-cognitive competencies that new police officers need to perform successfully on the job."

Population: Candidates for entry-level police officer positions.

Publication Date: 1999.

Scores: 3 abilities: Ability to Observe/Listen to/ and Remember Information, Ability to Use Situational Judgment and Interpersonal Skills, Ability to Learn and Apply Police Information.

Administration: Individual or group.

Price Data: Available from publisher.

Time: 155 minutes.

Comments: Administered via videotaped scenarios as an alternative to traditional multiple-choice tests; all instructions as well as count down timer are included on the video to facilitate test administration.

Authors: International Public Management Association for Human Resources.

Publisher: International Public Management Association for Human Resources (IPMA-HR).

[2]
AAMR Adaptive Behavior Scale—Residential and Community, Second Edition.

Purpose: To determine "an individual's strengths and weaknesses among adaptive domains and factors."

Population: Persons with disabilities in residential and community settings.

Publication Dates: 1969–1993.

Acronym: ABS-RC:2.

Scores, 23: 18 domain scores (10 part one domain scores: Independent Functioning, Physical Development, Economic Activity, Language Development, Numbers and Time, Domestic Activity, Prevocational/Vocational Activity, Self-Direction, Responsibility, Socialization; 8 part two domain scores: Social Behavior, Conformity, Trustworthiness, Stereotyped and Hyperactive Behavior, Sexual Behavior, Self-Abusive Behavior, Social Engagement, Disturbing Interpersonal Behavior); 5 factor scores (Personal Self-Sufficiency, Community Self-Sufficiency, Personal-Social Responsibility, Social Adjustment, Personal Adjustment).

Administration: Individual.

Price Data, 2006: $150 per complete kit including examiner's manual (1993, 76 pages), 25 examination booklets, and 25 profile/summary forms; $225 per 100 examination booklets; $30 per 25 profile/summary forms; $63 per examiner's manual.

Time: Administration time varies but ranges between 25–30 minutes.

Authors: Kazuo Nihira, Henry Leland, and Nadine Lambert.

Publisher: PRO-ED.

Cross References: For reviews by Karen T. Carey and Patti L. Harrison, see 13:1.

[3]
AAMR Adaptive Behavior Scale—School, Second Edition.

Purpose: "Used to assess adaptive behavior."

Population: Ages 3–21.

Publication Dates: 1981–1993.

Acronym: ABS-S:2.

Scores, 21: 16 domain scores (9 part one domain scores: Independent Functioning, Physical Development, Economic Activity, Language Development, Numbers and Time, Prevocational/Vocational Activity, Self-Direction, Responsibility, Socialization; 7 part two domain scores: Social Behavior, Conformity, Trustworthiness, Stereotyped and Hyperactive Behavior, Self-

Abusive Behavior, Social Engagement, Disturbing Interpersonal Behavior), 5 factor scores (Personal Self-Sufficiency, Community Self-Sufficiency, Personal-Social Responsibility, Social Adjustment, Personal Adjustment).
Administration: Individual.
Price Data, 2006: $150 per complete kit including examiner's manual (1993, 118 pages), 25 examination booklets, and 25 profile/summary forms; $63 per 25 examination booklets; $30 per 25 profile/summary forms; $60 per examiner's manual.
Time: (15–30) minutes
Comments: Previously called AAMD Adaptive Behavior Scale.
Authors: Nadine Lambert, Kazuo Nihira, and Henry Leland.
Publisher: PRO-ED.
Cross References: See T5:2 (2 references); for reviews by Robert G. Harrington and Terry A. Stinnett, see 13:2 (6 references); see also T4:2 (42 references); for a review of an earlier edition by Stephen N. Elliott, see 9:3 (9 references); see also T3:6 (55 references); for reviews of an earlier edition by Morton Bortner and by C. H. Ammons and R. B. Ammons, see 8:493 (25 references); see also T2:1092 (3 references); for reviews of an earlier edition by Lovick C. Miller and Melvyn I. Semmel, see 7:37 (9 references).

[4]
Abbreviated Torrance Test for Adults.
Purpose: To assess creative thinking ability.
Population: Adults.
Publication Date: 2002.
Acronym: ATTA.
Scores, 23: Norm-Referenced Measures (Fluency, Originality, Elaboration, Flexibility, Total Scaled Score), Criterion-Referenced Creativity Indicators (Richness and Colorfulness of Imagery, Emotions/Feelings, Future Orientation, Humor: Conceptual Incongruity, Provocative Questions, Verbal Responses Total, Openness: Resistance to Premature Closure, Unusual Visualization/Different Perspective, Movement and/or Sound, Richness and/or Colorfulness of Imagery, Abstractness of Titles, Articulateness in Telling Story, Combination/Synthesis of Two or More Figures, Internal Visual Perspective, Expressions of Feelings and Emotions, Fantasy, Figural Responses Total), Creativity Index.
Administration: Group.
Price Data, 2005: $15.45 per nonreturnable sample set including manual (39 pages) and 1 booklet; $27.55 per starter set including 10 booklets and manual; $16.75 per 10 booklets; $12.70 per manual.
Time: 15 minutes.
Comments: Based on 1980 Demonstration Form of the Torrance Tests; may be self-administered; norm- and criterion-referenced.

Authors: Kathy Goff and E. Paul Torrance.
Publisher: Scholastic Testing Service, Inc.

[5]
Aberrant Behavior Checklist.
Purpose: Constructed to rate "inappropriate and maladaptive behavior of mentally retarded individuals in residential and community settings, and developmental centers."
Population: Mentally retarded adolescents and adults.
Publication Date: 1986.
Acronym: ABC.
Scores, 5: Irritability, Lethargy, Stereotypy, Hyperactivity, Inappropriate Speech.
Administration: Individual.
Price Data, 2002: $63 per Residential complete kit including manual (32 pages) and Community supplemental manual; $70 per Community complete kit including manual, supplementary manual, and 50 Residential/Community forms/score sheets; $33 per 50 Residential/Community forms/score sheets; $33 per manual; $12 per Community supplemental manual.
Time: (5) minutes.
Comments: Ratings by direct care or professional staff member acquainted with individual.
Authors: Michael G. Aman and Nirbhay N. Singh.
Publisher: Slosson Educational Publications, Inc.
Cross References: See T5:4 (23 references); for reviews by Lena R. Gaddis and by J. Jeffrey Grill, see 12:1 (5 references); see T4:4 (2 references).

[6]
Abortion Scale.
Purpose: To measure attitudes toward abortion.
Population: Older adolescents and adults.
Publication Dates: 1972–1988.
Scores: Total score only.
Manual: No manual.
Price Data, 2002: $2 per scale.
Time: [10] minutes.
Comments: Supplementary article available.
Author: Panos D. Bardis.
Publisher: Donna Bardis.
Cross References: See T4:4 (2 references).

[7]
Abuse Disability Questionnaire.
Purpose: "Designed to assess both the extent of exposure to partner abuse, as well as its associated consequences."
Population: Women ages 18 years and older.
Publication Date: 2005.
Acronym: ADQ.
Scores, 8: Relationship Disability, Psychological Dysfunction, Substance Abuse, Anxiety, Life Restriction,

Health Status Issues, Inadequate Life Control, Concern with Physical Harm.
Administration: Individual or group.
Price Data, 2006: $70 per complete kit including 50 questionnaires/profile forms and manual (27 pages); $45 per 50 questionnaires/profile forms; $30 per manual.
Time: (5-15) minutes.
Comments: Includes a self-report questionnaire/profile form and an information/diagnostics form to be completed via an interview.
Author: John R. McNamara.
Publisher: Stoelting Co.

[8]
Abuse Risk Inventory for Women, Experimental Edition.

Purpose: To identify women who are current victims of abuse or who are at risk for abuse by their male intimate partners or ex-partners.
Population: Women seeking medical or mental health services.
Publication Date: 1989.
Acronym: ARNN.
Scores: Total score only.
Administration: Group and individual.
Price Data: Available from publisher (www.mindgarden.com).
Time: (10–15) minutes.
Comments: Test booklet title is Interpersonal Relationship Survey; self-administered; workbook available.
Author: Bonnie L. Yegidis.
Publisher: Mind Garden, Inc.
Cross References: For reviews by Cynthia A. Rohrbeck and Janice G. Williams, see 11:1.

[9]
Academic Advising Inventory.

Purpose: "Designed to measure three aspects of academic advising: (1) the nature of advising relationships, seen along a developmental-prescriptive continuum, (2) the frequency of activities taking place during advising sessions, and (3) satisfaction with advising."
Population: Undergraduate students.
Publication Dates: 1984–1986.
Acronym: AAI.
Scores, 3: Developmental-Prescriptive Advising, Advisor-Advisee Activity Scales, Student Satisfaction with Advising.
Administration: Group.
Price Data: Available from publisher.
Time: (20) minutes.
Comments: Manual entitled Evaluating Academic Advising; scoring service available from publisher.

Authors: Roger B. Winston, Jr. and Janet A. Sandor.
Publisher: Student Development Associates, Inc. [No reply from publisher; status unknown].
Cross References: See T5:8 (1 reference) and T4:7 (2 references); for a review by Robert D. Brown, see 10:3.

[10]
Academic Aptitude Test: Non-Verbal Intelligence: Acorn National Aptitude Tests.

Purpose: "Designed to evaluate that aspect of intelligence related to the aptitude for abstract academic work required in mathematical, engineering, designing and other physical sciences."
Population: Grades 7–16 and adults.
Publication Dates: 1943–1957.
Scores, 4: Spatial Relations, Physical Relations, Graphic Relations, Total.
Administration: Group.
Price Data: Available from publisher.
Time: 26 minutes.
Authors: Andrew Kobal, J. Wayne Wrightstone, and Karl R. Kunze.
Publisher: Psychometric Affiliates.
Cross References: For a review by William B. Schrader, see 4:274.

[11]
Academic Aptitude Test: Verbal Intelligence: Acorn National Aptitude Tests.

Purpose: "Designed to evaluate mental abilities and capacities that are important in academic work."
Population: Grades 7–16 and adults.
Publication Dates: 1943–1952.
Scores, 4: General Information, Mental Alertness, Comprehension of Relations, Total.
Administration: Group.
Price Data: Available from publisher.
Time: 40 minutes.
Authors: Andrew Kobal, J. Wayne Wrightstone, and Karl R. Kunze.
Publisher: Psychometric Affiliates.
Cross References: For a review by William B. Schrader, see 4:275; for a review by Marion A. Bills, see 3:215.

[12]
Academic Competence Evaluation Scales.

Purpose: "Measures academic skills (reading/language arts, mathematics, critical thinking) as well as academic enablers (motivation, study skills, engagement, interpersonal skills)."
Population: Grades K–12, Grades 6–12, 2- or 4-year college.
Publication Date: 2000.
Acronym: ACES.

Scores, 9: Academic Skills (Reading/Language Arts, Mathematics, Critical Thinking, Total), Academic Enablers (Interpersonal Skills, Motivation, Study Skills, Engagement, Total).
Administration: Group.
Forms, 3: Teacher (Grades K–12), Student (Grades 6–12), College (2- or 4-year college).
Price Data, 2001: $119 per K–12 basic kit including manual, 25 each of student and teacher record forms, boxed; $195 per K–12 complete kit including manual (154 pages), 25 each of student and teacher record forms, scoring assistant (disk or CD-ROM version); $165 per college complete kit including manual, 25 college record forms, scoring assistant (disk or CD-ROM version); $65 per K–12 manual or college manual; $34 per 25 record forms (specify Student, Teacher, or College), quantity discounts available; $91 per scoring assistant software (disk or CD-ROM version).
Time: (10–15) minutes.
Comments: Standardized; indicates confidence intervals for each subscale; allows ranking of scale and subscale scores into one of three competence levels (developing, competent, advanced); Assistant software (version 2.0) scores, monitors change in scores over time, graphs data, generates descriptive reports; system requirements: Windows 95/98/2000/NT 4.0/ME, 32 MB RAM, 100 MHz processor or higher, CD-ROM and 3.5-inch floppy diskette drive (CD-ROM version) or 3.5-diskette drive only (diskette version), 2 MB video card, 800 x 600 resolution, 256 colors, 25 MB free disk space.
Authors: James C. DiPerna and Stephen N. Elliott.
Publisher: PsychCorp, A brand of Harcourt Assessment, Inc.
Cross References: For reviews by Ronald K. Hambleton and by Darrell L. Sabers and Sarah Bonner, see 16:1.

[13]
Academic Freedom Survey.

Purpose: "Attempted to measure academic freedom" at college level.
Population: College students and faculty.
Publication Date: 1954.
Scores, 3: Student, Faculty, Total.
Administration: Group.
Price Data, 2001: $4 per specimen set.
Time: Administration time not reported.
Authors: Paul Slivnick and Academic Freedom Committee, Illinois Division, American Civil Liberties Union.
Publisher: Psychometric Affiliates.

[14]
Academic Intervention Monitoring System.

Purpose: Guidebook and intervention planning questionnaires "designed to provide teachers and other school-based professionals with the resources they need for developing, monitoring, and evaluating classroom-based, empirically supported interventions for academic difficulties."
Population: Grades K–12.
Publication Date: 2001.
Acronym: AIMS.
Scores: Not scored.
Administration: Individual.
Forms, 3: Student, Parent, Teacher.
Price Data, 2004: $133 per complete kit including manual (147 pages), 25 each of Student, Parent, and Teacher forms; $19 per 25 Student forms; $19 per 25 Parent forms; $36 per 25 Teacher forms; $95 per manual.
Time: (10–15) minutes.
Comments: Developed in conjunction with the Academic Competence Evaluation Scales (16:1); student and parent forms available in Spanish.
Authors: Stephen N. Elliott, James C. DiPerna, with Edward Shapiro.
Publisher: PsychCorp, A brand of Harcourt Assessment, Inc.

[15]
Academic Perceptions Inventory [2000 Revision].

Purpose: "Developed to assess a profile of the academic self in various classrooms and in the learning environment ... with perceptions of the self as a person, as a student, and at school."
Population: Grades K–16.
Publication Dates: 1979–2000.
Acronym: API.
Administration: Group.
Price Data, 2002: $20 per packet of 25 scales (specify level); $25 per test manual (specify Primary Level [2000, 83 pages], Intermediate Level [2000, 76 pages], Advanced Level [2000, 79 pages], or College Level [2000, 73 pages]); $40 per composite test manual (2000, 146 pages); $.40 per answer sheet; $.30 per scale for scoring.
Foreign Language Editions: Available in Spanish, Italian, and French.
Time: (5–20) minutes per test.
Comments: Ratings by self and others; previous edition entitled The Affective Perception Inventory.
Authors: Louise M. Soares and Anthony T. Soares.
Publisher: Castle Consultants.
a) PRIMARY LEVEL.
Population: Grades K–3.
Scores: 9 Scales: Self Concept, Student Self, School, Reading, Social Studies, Science, Arithmetic, Fine Arts, Sports and Games.
b) INTERMEDIATE LEVEL.
Population: Grades 4–8.

Scores: 11 scales: Self Concept, Student Self, School, Language Arts, Reading, Foreign Languages, History and Geography, Science, Mathematics, Fine Arts, Physical Education.
c) ADVANCED LEVEL.
Population: Grades 9–12.
Scores: 13 scales: Self Concept, Student Self, School, English, Foreign Languages, American History, Mathematics, Biology, Chemistry, Earth Sciences, Physics, Fine Arts, Sports.
d) COLLEGE LEVEL.
Population: Grades 13–16.
Scores: 15 scales: Self Concept, Student Self, Campus, English, Foreign Languages, World History, Political Science, Business, Mathematics, Biology, Chemistry, Physics, Humanities, Fine Arts, Sports.
Cross References: For reviews by Carol E. Kessler and Aimin Wang, see 15:1; see T4:130 (3 references); for reviews by Rosa A. Hagin and Gerald R. Smith of The Affective Perception Inventory, see 9:59.

[16]

ACCESS—A Comprehensive Custody Evaluation Standard System.

Purpose: Constructed as a "total system for conducting child custody evaluations."
Population: Children, parents, and others involved in child custody evaluations.
Publication Dates: 1997–2002.
Administration: Individual.
Price Data, 2002: $1,495 per complete kit including Bricklin Perceptual Scales Comprehensive Starting Kit with 3.5-inch unlimited use computer scoring profile, Perception-of-Relationships Test Comprehensive Starting Kit with 3.5-inch unlimited use computer scoring profile, Parent Awareness Skills Survey Comprehensive Starting Kit; Parent Perception-of-Child Profile Comprehensive Starting Kit, Custody Evaluation Questionnaires Kit, Custody Evaluation Interview Kit, Custody Evaluation Observation Kit, Custody Evaluation Aggregation Kit, Discipline Index Kit with 3.5-inch unlimited use computer scoring profiles, Home-Visit Kit, and Assessment of Parenting Skills: Infant and Preschooler.
Time: Administration time not reported.
Comments: Ratings by parents, children, teachers, and health/mental health professionals.
Authors: Barry Bricklin and Gail Elliot.
Publisher: Village Publishing.
a) BRICKLIN PERCEPTUAL SCALES.
Comments: See 342.
b) PERCEPTION-OF-RELATIONSHIPS TEST.
Comments: See 1881.

c) PARENT AWARENESS SKILLS SURVEY.
Comments: See 1837.
d) PARENT PERCEPTION OF CHILD PROFILE.
Comments: See 1843.
e) CUSTODY EVALUATION QUESTIONNAIRES KIT.
Purpose: "Designed to gather self-report data … in every single area that are considered important in model custody statutes."
Population: Children, parents, grandparents, and collateral informants involved in a custody evaluation.
Scores: No scores, ratings only.
Forms, 6: Parent Self-Report Questionnaire, "Would" Questionnaire, Child Data Questionnaire, Child Self-Report Questionnaire, Child's Access to Parental Strengths Questionnaire, Child's Sexual Abuse Questionnaire.
f) CUSTODY EVALUATION INTERVIEW KIT.
Purpose: Designed for conducting custody evaluation interviews.
Population: Professionals conducting custody evaluation interviews.
Scores: No scores, structured interviews only.
Forms, 5: Parent Interview, Physician Interview, Teacher Interview, Mental Health Professional Interview, Corroborative Source Interview.
g) CUSTODY EVALUATION OBSERVATION KIT.
Purpose: Constructed to "discriminate among the different ways, positive and negative, a child responds to parental communications."
Population: Professionals conducting custody evaluations.
Scores: No scores, ratings by observers.
Forms, 2: Adult Observation Form, Child Observation Form.
h) CUSTODY EVALUATION AGGREGATION KIT.
Purpose: "Designed to aggregate the enormous amount of information gathered" in custody evaluations.
Population: Professionals conducting custody evaluations.
Scores: No scores.
Comments: Also includes phone logs, critical targets forms, and model contracts.
i) DISCIPLINE INDEX.
Comments: See 844.
j) HOME-VISIT KIT.
Comments: See 1193.
k) ASSESSMENT OF PARENTING SKILLS: INFANT AND PRESCHOOLER.
Comments: See 210.
Cross References: For a review by Mark W. Roberts, see 14:1.

[17]
Access Management Survey.

Purpose: Designed to measure the extent to which a manager provides opportunities and support for employee involvement, and the necessary resources for people to influence work-life issues.
Population: Adults.
Publication Dates: 1989–1995.
Acronym: AMS.
Scores, 5: Access to the Problem, Access to People, Access to Information and Resources, Access to Support, Access to the Solution.
Administration: Group.
Price Data, 2001: $8.95 per instrument.
Time: Untimed.
Comments: Self-assessment survey.
Author: Jay Hall.
Publisher: Teleometrics International, Inc.
Cross References: For reviews by Thomas M. Haladyna and Mary A. Lewis, see 12:2.

[18]
Accountant Staff Selector.

Purpose: Designed "to evaluate the administrative, intellectual and analytical skills necessary for successful performance as an accountant."
Population: Adult applicants for accounting positions.
Publication Dates: 1982–2002.
Scores, 7: Numerical Skills, Attention to Detail, Problem Solving Ability, Reading Comprehension, Spreadsheet Simulation, Verbal Fluency, Bookkeeping Skills.
Administration: Individual or group.
Price Data: Available from publisher.
Foreign Language Edition: French edition available.
Time: (66) minutes.
Comments: Scoring available by mail, courier service, fax, or telephone.
Author: Walden Personnel Testing and Consulting, Inc.
Publisher: Walden Personnel Performance, Inc. [Canada].
Cross References: For a review by JoEllen V. Carlson, see 16:2.

[19]
Accounting Aptitude Test.

Purpose: Designed to assess aptitude for an accounting career.
Population: First-year college students.
Publication Dates: 1982–1992.
Scores, 3: Communication Skills, Quantitative Skills, Problem-Solving Skills.
Administration: Group or individual.

Price Data, 2002: $53 per examination kit including Form Z test booklet, Ready-Score answer document, and administrator's handbook (1992, 22 pages); $30 per 10 test booklets; $64 per 20 answer documents; $37.50 per administrator's handbook.
Time: 50(55) minutes.
Author: The Psychological Corporation.
Publisher: PsychCorp, A brand of Harcourt Assessment, Inc.
Cross References: For reviews by JoEllen Carlson and Bikkar S. Randhawa, see 13:3.

[20]
Accounting Program Admission Test.

Purpose: Designed as "an objective measure of student achievement in elementary accounting."
Population: College level elementary accounting students.
Publication Date: 1988.
Acronym: APAT.
Scores, 3: Financial Accounting, Managerial Accounting, Total.
Administration: Group or individual.
Price Data: Available from publisher.
Time: 100(110) minutes.
Comments: Formerly called the AICPA Accounting Program Admission Test; no longer affiliated with the AICPA.
Author: American Institute of Certified Public Accountants.
Publisher: PsychCorp, A brand of Harcourt Assessment, Inc.
Cross References: For reviews by JoEllen Carlson and William R. Koch, see 12:3.

[21]
ACCUPLACER: Computerized Placement Tests.

Purpose: Designed to assist colleges in determining student entry skills in reading, writing, mathematics, and levels of English proficiency; scores aid in the appropriate placement of students into entry level higher education courses.
Population: Entry level students in 2-year and 4-year institutions.
Publication Date: 1985–2005.
Acronym: CPTs.
Administration: Individual.
Price Data: Price information for student fee available from publisher.
Time: Untimed.
Comments: Administered through the internet adaptively.
Authors: The College Board.
Publisher: The College Board.

a) READING COMPREHENSION.
Scores: Total score only.
Comments: Each student is administered a fixed number of items which are selected adaptively depending on student responses to prior items.
b) SENTENCE SKILLS.
Comments: Each student is administered a fixed number of items which are adaptively delivered; diagnostic information is available.
c) ARITHMETIC.
Scores: Total score only.
Comments: Each student is administered a fixed number of items which are adaptively delivered.
d) ELEMENTARY ALGEBRA.
Scores: Total score only.
Comments: Each student is administered a fixed number of items which are adaptively delivered.
e) COLLEGE LEVEL MATHEMATICS.
Comments: Each student is administered a fixed number of items covering the areas of College Algebra and Precalculus, which are adaptively delivered.
f) LEVELS OF ENGLISH PROFICIENCY.
Scores: 3 modules: Language Usage, Sentence Meaning, Reading Skills.
Comments: Designed to identify the English proficiency levels of students; each student takes a fixed number of items; the 3 tests are administered separately and adaptively delivered.
g) WRITERPLACER PLUS.
Comments: Examinees are asked to provide a writing sample in response to a specific prompt; measures writing skill at the level expected of an entering level college student; can be delivered by computer with essays scored electronically by artificial intelligence or by paper and pencil with essays scored by two trained readers.
Cross References: For reviews by Martin A. Fischer and Steven V. Owen, see 13:4.

[22]
ACDI-Corrections Version and Corrections Version II.

Purpose: "Designed for troubled youth screening and assessment."
Population: Troubled youth between the ages of 12 and 18 years in juvenile probation, parole, and corrections programs.
Publication Dates: 1988–1995.
Acronym: ACDI.
Administration: Group.
Price Data: Available from publisher.
Time: (15–25) minutes.

Comments: Both computer version and paper-pencil format are scored on IBM-PC compatibles.
Author: Risk & Needs Assessment, Inc.
Publisher: Risk & Needs Assessment, Inc.
a) VERSION I.
Scores, 5: Truthfulness, Alcohol, Drug, Adjustment, Distress.
b) VERSION II.
Scores, 6: Truthfulness, Alcohol, Drug, Adjustment, Distress, Violence.
Cross References: For reviews by Carol Collins and Mark Pope, see 14:2.

[23]
ACER Advanced Test B40.

Purpose: Intended to assess general intellectual ability at the advanced adult level.
Population: Ages 15 and over.
Publication Dates: 1945–1983.
Acronym: B40.
Scores: Total score only.
Administration: Group.
Price Data, 2005: A$11.55 per 10 test booklets; $4.95 per scoring key; $19 per manual (1983, 7 pages); $24.20 per specimen set.
Time: 55(65) minutes.
Authors: Australian Council for Educational Research Ltd.
Publisher: Australian Council for Educational Research Ltd. [Australia].
Cross References: For a review by Harriet C. Cobb, see 9:4; see also T2:323 (6 references) and 7:328 (4 references); for a review by C. Sanders, see 5:296 (3 references).

[24]
ACER Advanced Test B90: New Zealand Edition.

Purpose: "Designed to measure general intellectual ability."
Population: College students and adults.
Publication Date: 1991.
Scores: Total score only.
Administration: Group.
Price Data: Available from publisher for test materials including administrator's manual (5 pages).
Time: 50(55) minutes.
Comments: "Selected items from the ACER Advanced Test B40 and the ACER Test of Cognitive Ability."
Authors: Australian Council for Educational Research and manual by Neil Reid and Cedric Croft.
Publisher: New Zealand Council for Educational Research [New Zealand].
Cross References: For a review by John Rust, see 12:4; for a review of ACER Advanced Test B40

by Harriet C. Cobb, see 9:4; see also T2:323 (6 references) and 7:328 (4 references); for a review of ACER Advanced Test B40 by C. Sanders, see 5:296 (3 references).

[25]
ACER Advanced Tests AL and AQ (Second Edition) and BL-BQ.

Purpose: "To measure general intellectual ability at advanced secondary and college levels."
Population: College and senior high.
Publication Dates: 1953–1982.
Acronym: AL-AQ (2nd Edition), BL-BQ.
Administration: Group.
Price Data, 2005: A$14.55 per 10 test booklets; A$4.95 per scoring key.
Authors: Australian Council for Educational Research Ltd.
Publisher: Australian Council for Educational Research Ltd. [Australia].
  a) TEST AL-BL.
  Scores: Linguistic.
  Forms, 2: A, B.
  Time: 15(25) minutes.
  b) TEST AQ-BQ.
  Scores: Quantitative.
  Forms, 2: A, B.
  Time: 20(30) minutes.
Cross References: See T5:23 (1 reference); for reviews by Harriet C. Cobb and Leland K. Doebler, see 9:5; see also T3:21 (1 reference) and T2:324 (3 references); for a review by Duncan Howie, see 5:295.

[26]
ACER Applied Reading Test.

Purpose: Designed to measure ability to read and understand technical material.
Population: Apprentices, trainees, technical and trade personnel.
Publication Dates: 1989–1990.
Scores: Total score only.
Administration: Group.
Forms, 2: A, B.
Price Data, 2005: A$9.95 per test booklet; A$9.95 per 10 answer sheets; A$9.95 per score key; A$34.95 per manual (1990, 24 pages); A$54.95 per specimen set A–Personnel only or B–Personnel or Technical and Further Education Colleges.
Time: 40–45 minutes.
Authors: J. M. van den Berg and I. R. Woff.
Publisher: Australian Council for Educational Research Ltd. [Australia].
Cross References: For reviews by Mark H. Daniel and Michael S. Trevisan, see 12:5.

[27]
ACER Mechanical Comprehension Test.

Purpose: "Designed to test understanding of mechanical problems."
Population: Ages 13.5 and over.
Publication Dates: 1942–1956.
Scores: Total score only.
Administration: Group.
Price Data, 2005: A$3.85 per test booklet; A$4.95 per scoring key; A $7.70 per 10 answer sheets.
Time: 30 minutes.
Comments: The publisher advises that this test is only available while current stock lasts; has been replaced by ACER Mechanical Reasoning Test (28).
Author: Australian Council for Educational Research Ltd.
Publisher: Australian Council for Educational Research Ltd. [Australia].
Cross References: See T3:37 (1 reference); for reviews by John R. Jennings and Hayden S. Williams, see 5:874 (2 references); for a review by D. W. McElwain, see 4:756.

[28]
ACER Mechanical Reasoning Test [Revised 1997].

Purpose: "Designed to assess a person's aptitude for solving problems requiring the understanding of mechanical ideas."
Population: Ages 15 and over.
Publication Dates: 1951–1997.
Scores: Total score only.
Administration: Group.
Forms, 2: Parallel Forms A and B.
Price Data, 2005: A$10.95 per test booklet; A$9.95 per scoring key; A$19.95 per 10 answer sheets; A$55.95 per manual (1997, 58 pages); A$89.95 per specimen set.
Time: 20(25) minutes.
Comments: Revision of ACER Mechanical Comprehension Test (27).
Authors: Australian Council for Educational Research Ltd.
Publisher: Australian Council for Educational Research Ltd. [Australia].
Cross References: For a review by Gerald R. Schneck, see 15:2; see T2:2238 (3 references); for reviews by John R. Jennings and Hayden S. Williams of an earlier edition, see 5:875.

[29]
ACER Short Clerical Test.

Purpose: Designed to measure aptitudes for speed and accuracy in routine clerical work.
Population: Age 15 and over.
Publication Date: 1953–2001.
Scores, 2: Checking, Arithmetic.

Administration: Group.
Price Data, 2005: A$15 per 10 test booklets; A$5.95 per score key; A$29.95 per manual; A$36 per specimen set.
Time: 5(10) minutes per test.
Authors: Australian Council for Educational Research.
Publisher: Australian Council for Educational Research Ltd. [Australia].

[30]
ACER Test of Employment Entry Mathematics.

Purpose: "A group test of basic mathematical ability ... used for the selection of apprentices, trainees, and any other technical and trades personnel."
Population: Apprentice, trainee, technical and trade applicants.
Publication Date: 1992.
Acronym: TEEM.
Scores: Total score only.
Administration: Group.
Price Data, 2006: A$9.95 per test booklet; A$9.95 per score key; A$9.95 per 10 answer sheets; A$69.95 per specimen set.
Time: 25(40) minutes.
Comments: Can be hand scored or scored by testing service.
Authors: John Izard, Ian Woff, and Brian Doig.
Publisher: Australian Council for Educational Research Ltd. [Australia].
Cross References: For reviews by Jay R. Stewart and Patricia H. Wheeler, see 15:3.

[31]
ACER Tests of Basic Skills—Orchid Series.

Purpose: Developed to assess skills in literacy and numeracy.
Population: Students, year 4 to 6 in Australian school system.
Publication Dates: 1990–1997.
Administration: Group.
Price Data, 2006: A$26.40 per 10 nonreusable Level A & B test booklets for Literacy; A$30.80 per 10 nonreusable Level A & B test booklets with press-out shapes and tiles for Numeracy; A$33 per stimulus material; A$22 per audio tape; A$66 per Level A manual (1997, 73 pages); A$66 per Level B manual (1997, 82 pages); A$93.50 per specimen set; A$26.40 per nonreusable Level C test booklets for Literacy; A$30.80 per 10 nonreusable Level C test booklets with press-out shape and tiles for Numeracy; A$33 per stimulus material; A$66 per Level C manual (1997, 60 pages); A$71.50 per specimen set.
Comments: Earlier versions called Blue and Green Series; requires a cassette tape player.

Authors: Australian Council for Educational Research, Joy McQueen, and Brian Doig.
Publisher: Australian Council for Educational Research Ltd. [Australia].
a) LEVEL A.
Scores, 6: Aspects of Literacy (Reading, Proofreading and Editing, Listening, Writing), Aspects of Numeracy (Number, Measurement and Space).
Time: (222–245) minutes.
b) LEVEL B.
Scores, 6: Same as Level A.
Time: (248–271) minutes.
c) LEVEL C.
Scores, 4: Aspects of Literacy (Reading and Viewing, Proofreading and Editing, Writing), Aspects of Numeracy (Number/Measurement/Space).
Time: (165–181) minutes.
Cross References: For a review by Lisa F. Smith, see 15:4; for reviews by Lewis R. Aiken and Delwyn L. Harnisch of an earlier edition, see 12:88.

[32]
ACER Word Knowledge Test.

Purpose: Designed to obtain a quick assessment of verbal or language ability.
Population: Australian years 9–12 and job applicants.
Publication Dates: 1984–1990.
Scores: Total score only.
Administration: Group.
Editions, 2: E, F.
Restricted Distribution: Distribution of Form E restricted to personnel use.
Price Data, 2005: A$9.95 per reusable test booklet; A$9.95 per 10 answer sheets; A$9.95 per score key; A$30 per manual (1990, 44 pages); A$49.95 per specimen set (specify Form E or F).
Time: 10(20) minutes.
Comments: Replacement for the ACER Adult Form B.
Author: Marion M. de Lemos.
Publisher: Australian Council for Educational Research Ltd. [Australia].
Cross References: See T5:34 (6 references); for reviews by Douglas Ayers and William R. Merz, Sr., see 11:2.

[33]
Achenbach System of Empirically Based Assessment.

Purpose: "An integrated ... [approach] designed to provide standardized descriptions of ... competencies, adaptive functioning, and problems."
Population: Ages 18 months to 90+ years.
Publication Dates: 1980–2004.

Acronym: ASEBA.
Administration: Individual or group.
Levels, 4: Preschool, School-Age, Adult, Older Adult.
Price Data, 2005: $150 per Preschool hand-scoring starter kit including 50 each of CBCL/1 1/2-5 & LDS forms, C-TRF forms, CBCL/1 1/2-5 hand-scoring profiles, C-TRF hand-scoring profiles, LDS hand-scoring forms, CBCL/1 1/2-5 and C-TRF templates, and Manual for the Preschool Forms & Profiles (2000, 189 pages); $230 per Preschool computer-scoring starter kit including 50 CBCL/1 1/2-5 & LDS forms, 50 C-TRF forms, Ages 1 1/2-5 entry scoring module, Manual for the Preschool Forms & Profiles; $325 per School-Age computer-scoring starter kit including 50 CBCL forms, 50 TRF forms, 50 YSR forms, Ages 6–18 entry scoring module, and Manual for the School-Age Forms & Profiles (2001, 238 pages); $35 per Manual for the Preschool Forms and Profiles, Manual for the School-Age Forms and profiles, or Manual for the SCICA (2001, 164 pages); $35 per Manual for the ASEBA Adult Forms and Profiles (2003, 216 pages); $35 per Manual for the ASEBA Older Adult Forms and Profiles (2004, 190 pages); $10 per Mental Health Practitioners' Guide for the ASEBA (2004, 42 pages), School-Based Practitioners' Guide for the ASEBA (2004, 48 pages), Child and Family Service Workers' Guide for the ASEBA (2003, 37 pages), Medical Practitioners' Guide for the ASEBA (2003, 33 pages), Guide for ASEBA Instruments for Adults/18-59 and Older Adults/60-90+ (2004, 39 pages); $695 per full set of ADM Software Modules including Ages 1 1/2-5, 6–18, 18–59, 60–90+, SCICA, and Test Observation Form (TOF); $170 per ADM Software Modules for Ages 1 1/2-5, 18–59, 60–90+, SCICA, or TOF; $250 per ADM Software Module for Ages 6–18; $220 per Scanning Module or Client Entry Module for CBCL/6–18, TRF/6–18, and YSR/11–18; $220 per ASEBA Web-Link (following purchase of any ADM Module) including E-package of 100 E-units; $25 per 50 CBCL/1 1/2-5 & LDS, C-TRF, CBCL/6–18, TRF/6–18, YSR, DOF, SCICA, ASR, ABCL, OASR, OABCL, or TOF forms; $25 per 50 Profiles for hand scoring profiles for any of CBCL/ 1 1/2-5, C-TRF, CBCL/6–18 (specify gender), TRF (specify gender), YSR, DOF, SCICA, ASR, ABCL, OASR, OABCL, or TOF; $25 per 50 forms for hand-scoring LDS; $25 per 50 Combined SCICA Observation and Self-Report scoring forms; $25 per 50 CBCL, TRF, YSR, SCICA, ASR, ABCL, OASR, or OABCL DSM-Oriented Profiles; $7 per reusable templates for hand scoring CBCL/1 1/2-5, C-TRF, CBCL/ 6–18, TRF, YSR, ASR, ABCL, OASR, or OABCL Profiles.
Foreign Language Editions: One or more forms have been translated into 74 languages, check website (www.ASEBA.org) for availability.

Comments: Revised version of the Child Behavior Checklist; includes both empirically based syndrome scales and DSM-oriented scales for scoring consistent with DSM-IV categories; designed to be usable in diverse contexts, including schools, mental health, medical, child and family service, and other settings; all forms except DOF and SCICA are parallel, facilitating comparisons across informants; hand- or computer-scorable; reusable hand-scoring templates available; data processed by Assessment Data Manager (ADM); cross-informant bar graphs; minimum system requirements Windows 95/98/NT/2000, 64 MB RAM, 65 MB free hard disk space, Pentium recommended; can be completed using paper forms (hand- or machine-readable), by direct client-entry on computer, or via Web-Link; LDS, Preschool and School-Age manuals.
Authors: Thomas M. Achenbach (all forms and manuals), Leslie A. Rescorla (all forms and Mental Health Practitioners' Guide for the ASEBA), Stephanie H. McConaughy (SCICA, SCICA manual, and School-Based Practitioners' Guide for the ASEBA), Peter J. Pecora and Kathleen M. Wetherbee (Child and Family Service Workers' Guide for the ASEBA), Thomas M. Ruffle (Medical Practitioners' Guide for the ASEBA), Paul A. Newhouse (older adult forms, manual, and Guide for Adult and Older Adult Forms).
Publisher: ASEBA Research Center for Children, Youth, and Families

a) PRESCHOOL FORMS AND PROFILES.
Purpose: To provide "systematic assessment of maladaptive behavior among preschoolers."
Comments: DSM-Oriented Scales rated as very consistent with the following DSM-IV categories: Affective Problems consistent with Dysthymia, Major Depressive Disorder; Anxiety Problems consistent with Generalized Anxiety Disorder, Separation Anxiety Disorder, Specific Phobia; Pervasive Developmental Problems consistent with Asperger's Disorder and Autistic Disorder; Attention Deficit/Hyperactivity Problems consistent with Hyperactive-Impulsive and Inattentive types of ADHD.

1) *Child Behavior Checklist for Ages 1 1/2-5.*
Population: Ages 18 months to 5 years.
Publication Dates: 1988–2000.
Acronym: CBCL/1 1/2-5.
Scores: 7 Syndrome scales (Emotionally Reactive, Anxious/Depressed, Somatic Complaints, Withdrawn, Sleep Problems, Attention Problems, Aggressive Behavior), plus Internalizing, Externalizing, Total Problems; Language Development Survey (LDS) scored (for children age 18–35 months); 5 DSM-Oriented scales (Affective Problems, Anxiety Problems, Pervasive Developmental Problems,

Attention Deficit/Hyperactivity Problems, Oppositional Defiant Problems).

Time: (10) minutes.

Comments: Designed to be completed by parents and others who see children in home-like settings; includes the Language Development Survey (LDS) for evaluating language delays in children under age 3 as well as those over age 3 suspected of having language delays.

2) Caregiver-Teacher Report Form for Ages 1 1/2-5.

Population: Ages 18 months to 5 years.

Publication Dates: 1997–2000.

Acronym: C-TRF.

Scores: 6 Syndrome scales (Emotionally Reactive, Anxious/Depressed, Somatic Complaints, Withdrawn, Attention Problems, Aggressive Behavior), plus Internalizing, Externalizing, Total Problems.

Time: (10) minutes.

Comments: Designed to be completed by daycare providers and preschool teachers who have known a child in daycare, preschool, or similar settings for at least 2 months.

b) SCHOOL-AGE FORMS AND PROFILES.

Comments: DSM-Oriented Scales rated as very consistent with the following DSM-IV categories: Affective Problems consistent with Dysthymia, Major Depressive Disorder; Anxiety Problems consistent with Generalized Anxiety Disorder, Separation Anxiety Disorder, Specific Phobia; Attention Deficit/Hyperactivity Problems consistent with Hyperactive-Impulsive and Inattentive types of ADHD; Somatic Problems consistent with Somatization Disorder and Somatoform Disorder.

1) Child Behavior Checklist for Ages 6–18.

Population: Ages 6–18.

Publication Dates: 1981–2001.

Acronym: CBCL/6–18.

Scores: 4 Competence scales (Activities, Social, School, Total Competence); 8 Syndrome scales (Anxious/Depressed, Withdrawn/Depressed, Somatic Complaints, Social Problems, Thought Problems, Attention Problems, Rule-Breaking Behavior, Aggressive Behavior), plus Internalizing, Externalizing, Total Problems; 6 DSM-Oriented scales (Affective Problems, Anxiety Problems, Somatic Problems, Attention Deficit/Hyperactivity Problems, Oppositional Defiant Problems, Conduct Problems).

Time: (15–20) minutes.

2) Teacher's Report Form for Ages 6–18.

Purpose: "Quickly obtain[s] a picture of children's functioning in school, as seen by teachers and other personnel."

Population: Teachers of children ages 6–18.

Publication Dates: 1981–2001.

Acronym: TRF.

Scores: 6 Adaptive Functioning scales (Academic Performance, Working Hard, Behaving Appropriately, Learning, Happy, Total); same Syndrome and DSM-Oriented scales as CBCL/6–18; yields separate scores for Inattention and Hyperactivity-Impulsivity.

Time: (15–20) minutes.

3) Youth Self-Report for Ages 11–18.

Purpose: To obtain youths' reports of their own problems and competencies in a standardized format.

Population: Ages 11–18.

Publication Dates: 1981–2001.

Acronym: YSR.

Scores: 2 Competence scales (Activities, Social) plus Total Competence; same Syndrome and DSM-Oriented scales as CBCL/6–18.

4) Direct Observation Form for Ages 5–14.

Purpose: "Used to record and rate behavior in group settings."

Publication Dates: 1983–1986.

Acronym: DOF.

Comments: Used to obtain 10-minute samples of children's behavior in classrooms and other group settings; enables users to compare an observed child with 2 control children for on-task, Internalizing, Externalizing, and Total Problems, averaged for up to 6 observation sessions; 6 syndrome scales available (computer-scored profiles only).

5) Semistructured Clinical Interview for Children and Adolescents.

Purpose: "Used to record and rate children's behavior and self-reports during an interview."

Population: Ages 6–18.

Publication Dates: 1989–2001.

Acronym: SCICA.

Scores: 8 Syndrome scales (Anxious, Anxious/Depressed, Withdrawn/Depressed, Language/Motor Problems, Aggressive/Rule-Breaking Behavior, Attention Problems, Self-Control Problems, Somatic Complaints (ages 12–18 only), plus Internalizing, Externalizing, Total Problems; same DSM-Oriented scales as CBCL/6–18.

Time: (60–90) minutes.

Comments: Designed for use by experienced clinical interviewers; protocol form includes topic questions and activities, such as kinetic family drawing and tasks for screening fine and gross motor functioning; observation and self-report form for rating what a child does and says during interview.

c) ADULT FORMS AND PROFILES.
Publication Dates: 1997–2003.
  1) *Adult Self-Report for Ages 18–59.*
Population: Ages 18–59.
Acronym: ASR.
Scores: 5 Adaptive Functioning scales (Education, Friends, Job, Family, Spouse or Partner), 3 Substance Use scales (Tobacco, Alcohol, Drugs) plus Mean Substance Use score, 6 DSM-oriented scales (Depressive Problems, Anxiety Problems, Somatic Problems, Avoidant Personality Problems, Attention Deficit/Hyperactivity Problems, Antisocial Personality Problems), same Syndrome scales as CBCL/6–18, plus Intrusive, Internalizing, Externalizing, Total Problems.
Time: (15–20) minutes.
Comments: Upward extension of YASR.
  2) *Adult Behavior Checklist for Ages 18–59.*
Population: Ages 18–59.
Acronym: ABCL.
Scores: 2 Adaptive Functioning scales (Friends, Spouse/Partner), other scales same as ASR.
Time: (10–15) minutes.
Comments: Upward extension of YABCL. Ratings by parents, surrogates, friends, and spouses of adults.
d) OLDER ADULT FORMS AND PROFILES.
Publication Date: 2004.
  1) *Older Adult Self-Report for Ages 60-90+.*
Population: Ages 60-90+.
Acronym: OASR.
Scores: 3 Adaptive Functioning scales (Friends, Spouse/Partner, Personal Strengths), 7 Syndrome scales (Anxious/Depressed, Worries, Somatic Complaints, Functional Impairment, Memory/Cognition Problems, Thought Problems, Irritable/Disinhibited), 6 DSM-oriented scales (Depressive Problems, Anxiety Problems, Somatic Problems, Dementia Problems, Psychotic Problems, Antisocial Personality Problems), plus Total Problems.
Time: (15-20) minutes.
  2) *Older Adult Behavior Checklist for Ages 60-90+.*
Population: Ages 60-90+.
Acronym: OABCL.
Scores: Same scales as OASR.
Time: (15-20) minutes.
Comments: Ratings by people who know the older adult well.
Cross References: For reviews by Rosemary Flanagan and T. Steuart Watson, see 16:3; see also T5:451 (292 references); for reviews by Beth Doll and by Michael J. Furlong and Michelle Wood of an earlier edition, see 13:55 (556 references); see also T4:433 (135 references); for reviews by Sandra L. Christenson and by Stephen N. Elliott and R. T. Busse of the Teacher's Report Form and the Youth Self-Report, see 11:64 (216 references); for additional information and reviews by B. J. Freeman and Mary Lou Kelley, see 9:213 (5 references).

[34]
Achievement Identification Measure.

Purpose: Developed to provide a measure of the characteristics that distinguish achieving students from underachievers.
Population: School age children.
Publication Date: 1985.
Acronym: AIM.
Scores, 6: Competition, Responsibility, Control, Achievement, Communication, Respect.
Administration: Individual.
Price Data, 2005: $120 per 30 tests, manual for administration (8 pages), manual for interpretation of scores (7 pages), and computer scoring of 30 tests; $15 per specimen set.
Foreign Language Edition: Spanish edition available.
Time: (20) minutes.
Comments: Parent report inventory.
Author: Sylvia B. Rimm.
Publisher: Educational Assessment Service, Inc.
Cross References: See T5:35 (1 reference); for reviews by Howard M. Knoff and Sharon B. Reynolds, see 10:5.

[35]
Achievement Identification Measure— Teacher Observation.

Purpose: Identify underachievers.
Population: School-age children.
Publication Date: 1988.
Acronym: AIM-TO.
Scores: 5 dimension scores: Competition, Responsibility, Achievement Communication, Independence/Dependence, Respect/Dominance.
Administration: Individual.
Price Data, 2005: $120 per set of 30 test booklets/answer sheets (scoring by publisher included); $15 per specimen set.
Foreign Language Edition: Spanish edition available.
Time: (20) minutes.
Comments: Ratings by teacher.
Author: Sylvia B. Rimm.
Publisher: Educational Assessment Service, Inc.
Cross References: For reviews by William P. Erchul and Geoffrey F. Schultz, see 11:3.

[36]
Achievement Motivation Inventory.

Purpose: Designed to evaluate "all major aspects of job-related achievement motivation."
Population: Adults.
Publication Date: 2004.
Acronym: AMI.
Scores: 17 scales: Compensatory Effort, Competitiveness, Confidence in Success, Dominance, Eagerness to Learn, Engagement, Fearlessness, Flexibility, Flow, Goal Setting, Independence, Internality, Persistence, Preference for Difficult Tasks, Pride in Productivity, Self-Control, Status Orientation.
Administration: Individual or group.
Price Data, 2006: $188 per complete kit including manual (60 pages), questionnaire, 20 score sheets, 20 score profiles, and case; $18 per questionnaire; $68 per 20 response sheets; $12 per 20 score profiles; $98 per manual.
Time: Administration time not reported.
Authors: Heinz Schuler, George C. Thornton III, Andreas Frintrup, Rose Mueller-Hanson.
Publisher: Hogrefe & Huber Publishers.

[37]
Achievement Motivation Profile.

Purpose: "Designed to be a measure of a student's motivation to achieve" and related personality characteristics.
Population: Ages 10 to 14 for AMP Juniors; 14 years and older in high school, junior college, and college.
Publication Dates: 1995–1996.
Acronym: AMP.
Scores, 18: Response style (Inconsistent Responding, Self-Enhancing, Self-Critical), Motivation for Achievement (Achiever, Motivation, Competitiveness, Goal Orientation), Inner Resources (Relaxed Style, Happiness, Patience, Self-Confidence), Interpersonal Strengths (Assertiveness, Personal Diplomacy, Extroversion, Cooperativeness), Work Habits (Planning and Organization, Initiative, Team Player).
Administration: Group.
Price Data, 2006: $150 per complete kit including 25 AutoScore™ forms for High School; 25 College Student AutoScore forms, and manual (1996, 93 pages); $47 per 25 AutoScore™ forms; $58 per manual; $45 each for 1–9 AMP mail-in answer sheets; $231 per 25-use microcomputer disk (PC with Microsoft Windows); $16.50 per 100 microcomputer answer sheets; $9 per fax service scoring.
Time: (20–30) minutes.
Authors: Jotham G. Friedland, Harvey P. Mandel, and Sander I. Marcus.
Publisher: Western Psychological Services.

[38]
Achievement Test for Accounting Graduates.

Purpose: Constructed to assess achievement in accounting for use in selecting applicants or placing and training of current personnel.
Population: Accounting job applicants or employees.
Publication Dates: 1989–1992.
Acronym: ATAG.
Scores, 6: Financial Accounting, Auditing, Cost and Managerial Accounting, Information Systems, Taxation, Total.
Administration: Group or individual.
Forms, 2: T, V.
Restricted Distribution: Distribution restricted and test administered at licensed testing centers; details may be obtained from publisher.
Price Data, 2002: $53.50 per examination kit including Form V test booklet, Ready-Score answer document, and administrator's handbook (1992, 20 pages); $40.50 per 10 test booklets (specify Form T or V); $85.50 per 20 answer documents; $37.50 per administrator's handbook.
Time: 120(125) minutes.
Author: The Psychological Corporation.
Publisher: PsychCorp, A brand of Harcourt Assessment, Inc.
Cross References: For reviews by JoEllen Carlson and Thomas F. Donlon, see 13:5.

[39]
Achieving Behavioral Competencies.

Purpose: To develop a program of instruction in social/emotional skills.
Population: "Students who are seriously emotionally disturbed, closed head injured, juvenile offenders, learning disabled, or at-risk for school drop-out" and "adults served by voc rehab programs."
Publication Date: 1992.
Acronym: ABC.
Scores, 24: Relating to Others (Building Friendships, Maintaining Friendships, Apologizing, Compromising/Negotiating, Giving/Accepting Praise or Criticism, Total), Personal Responsibility (Goal Setting, Decision Making, Assuming Responsibility, Promptness, Asking for Assistance, Total), Coping with Stress (Handling Frustration, Coping with Anger, Dealing with Stress, Accepting Authority, Resisting Peer Pressure, Total), Personal/Affective Development (Building Self-Esteem, Coping with Depression, Coping with Anxiety, Controlling Impulsivity, Sensitivity to Others, Total).
Administration: Group.
Editions, 2: Individual Student Report, Class Report.
Price Data, 2006: $150 per set including curriculum, 25 rating forms, and computer program (Windows or Macintosh).

Time: Administration time not reported.
Comments: Computer reports generated from teacher ratings.
Authors: Lawrence T. McCarron, Kathleen McConnell Fad, and Melody B. McCarron.
Publisher: McCarron-Dial Systems.
Cross References: For reviews by Sally Kuhlenschmidt and Robert A. Leark, see 13:6.

[40]
Ackerman-Banks Neuropsychological Rehabilitation Battery.

Purpose: Designed as a comprehensive neuropsychological screening instrument.
Population: Adult clients referred for psychological or neuropsychological assessment and/or cognitive rehabilitation.
Publication Dates: 1991–2006.
Acronym: ABNRB.
Scores, 40: Alertness (Attention/Concentration), Prosody (Receptive Prosody, Expressive Prosody), Memory (Long-Term Memory, Short-Term Interference Memory, Short-Term Input Memory, Short-Term Retrieval Memory), Sensorimotor (Auditory Input, Auditory Discrimination, Tactile Input, Tactile Output, Visual Input, Visual Discrimination, Visual-Spatial Construction, Proprioception, Motor Quality, Motor Writing), Speech (Speech Production, Dysarthria, Dysnomia, Neologisms, Confabulation, Perseveration, Lisping), Academic Abilities (Mathematics, Reading, Writing), Cognitive Problem Solving (Concreteness, Integration, Judgment, Speed), Organic Emotions (Depression, Anxiety, Impulsivity), Asymmetry (Left-Right Confusion, Left-Brain Controlled Balance, Right-Brain Controlled Balance), Treatment Problems (Peripheral Control, Awareness of Deficits, Socially Appropriate Comments, Frustration Tolerance).
Administration: Individual.
Price Data, 2006: $800 per complete kit including professional manual (2006, 192 pages), stimulus card book, 10 administration protocols, 10 response booklets, 10 scoring forms, and processing fee for web-based, mail-in, or faxed computer score submission; $500 per administration package including 10 administration protocols, 10 response booklets, 10 scoring forms, and processing fee for web-based, mail-in, or faxed computer score submission; $300 per professional manual; student, volume, and research discounts available.
Time: (45–120) minutes.
Authors: Rosalie J. Ackerman and Martha E. Banks.
Publisher: ABackans DCP, Inc.
Cross References: For reviews by Surendra P. Singh and by Wilfred G. Van Gorp and Colleen A. Ewing, see 15:5.

[41]
Ackerman-Schoendorf Scales for Parent Evaluation of Custody.

Purpose: "A clinical tool designed to aid mental health professionals in making child custody recommendations."
Population: Parents engaged in a dispute over custody of their children.
Publication Date: 1992.
Acronym: ASPECT.
Scores: 3 scales (Observational, Social, Cognitive-Emotional) yielding 1 score: Parental Custody Index (PCI).
Administration: Individual.
Price Data, 2006: $152 per kit including 20 parent questionnaires, 10 AutoScore™ answer forms, manual (77 pages), and 2 prepaid mail-in WPS test report answer sheets for computer scoring and interpretation; $40 per 20 answer forms; $32.50 per 20 parent questionnaires; $58 per manual; $19 or less per mail-in answer sheet; $13.75 each for test report fax service.
Time: Administration time varies.
Comments: For complete set of information to score, need results of each parent's MMPI or MMPI-2, Rorschach, WAIS-R, and WRAT-R or NEAT tests.
Authors: Marc J. Ackerman and Kathleen Schoendorf.
Publisher: Western Psychological Services.
Cross References: See T5:41 (1 reference); for reviews by Joyce A. Arditti and Gary R. Melton, see 12:9.

[42]
ACS Examination in Analytical Chemistry.

Purpose: Designed to measure a student's achievement in analytical chemistry.
Population: 1 year college.
Publication Dates: 1944–2001.
Scores: Total score only.
Administration: Group.
Manual: No specific manual; general directions (no date, 4 pages).
Price Data: Available from publisher.
Time: 90(100) minutes.
Comments: ACS test program is continually updated by retiring an older form of the test upon release of a new form; separate answer sheet must be used; exam carries secure copyright.
Author: ACS DivCHED Examinations Institute.
Publisher: ACS DivCHED Examinations Institute.
Cross References: See 7:836 (1 reference) and 6:907 (1 reference); for an excerpted review by H. E. Wilcox of an earlier form, see 5:735; for reviews by William B. Meldrum and William Rieman III, see 3:563.

[43]
ACS Examination in Biochemistry.

Purpose: Designed to measure a student's achievement in biochemistry.
Population: 1 year college.
Publication Dates: 1947–2003.
Scores: Total score only.
Administration: Group.
Manual: No specific manual; general directions (no date, 4 pages).
Price Data: Available from publisher.
Time: 120(130) minutes.
Comments: ACS test program is continually updated by retiring an older form of the test upon release of a new form; separate answer sheet must be used; exam carries secure copyright.
Authors: ACS DivCHED Examinations Institute.
Publisher: ACS DivCHED Examinations Institute.
Cross References: See 7:823 (1 reference); for an excerpted review by Wilhelm R. Frisell of an earlier form, see 6:898 (2 references).

[44]
ACS Examination in General Chemistry.

Purpose: Designed to measure a student's achievement in general chemistry.
Population: 1 year college.
Publication Dates: 1934– 2005.
Scores: Total score only.
Administration: Group.
Manual: No specific manual; general directions (no date, 4 pages).
Price Data: Available from publisher.
Time: 110(120) minutes.
Comments: ACS test program is continually updated by retiring an older form of the test upon release of a new form; separate answer sheet must be used; exam carries secure copyright.
Authors: ACS DivCHED Examinations Institute.
Publisher: ACS DivCHED Examinations Institute.
Cross References: For a review by Frank J. Fornoff of an earlier edition, see 8:837 (3 references); see also T2:1819 (1 reference) and 7:826 (5 references); for reviews by J. A. Campbell and William Hered and an excerpted review by S. L. Burson, Jr., see 6:902 (3 references); for reviews by Frank P. Cassaretto and Palmer O. Johnson, see 5:732 (2 references); for a review by Kenneth E. Anderson, see 4:610 (1 reference); for reviews by Sidney J. French and Florence E. Hooper, see 3:557 (3 references); see also 2:1593 (5 references).

[45]
ACS Examination in General Chemistry (Brief Test).

Purpose: Designed to measure a student's achievement in general chemistry.

Population: 1 year college.
Publication Dates: 1981–2002.
Scores: Total score only.
Administration: Group.
Manual: No specific manual; general directions (no date, 4 pages).
Price Data: Available from publisher.
Time: 55(60) minutes.
Comments: ACS test program is continually updated by retiring an older form of the test upon release of a new form; separate answer sheet must be used; exam carries secure copyright.
Authors: ACS DivCHED Examinations Institute.
Publisher: ACS DivCHED Examinations Institute.

[46]
ACS Examination in General-Organic-Biological Chemistry.

Purpose: Designed to measure a student's achievement in general, organic, and biological chemistry.
Population: Nursing and other paramedical and home economics students.
Publication Dates: 1979–2000.
Scores, 10: General (Part A, Part B, Total), Organic (Part A, Part B, Total), Biological (Part A, Part B, Total), Part A Total.
Administration: Group.
Manual: No specific manual; general directions (no date, 4 pages).
Price Data: Available from publisher.
Time: 165(180) minutes.
Comments: ACS test program is continually updated by retiring an older form of the test upon release of a new form; separate answer sheet must be used; exam carries secure copyright.
Authors: ACS DivCHED Examinations Institute.
Publisher: ACS DivCHED Examinations Institute.

[47]
ACS Examination in High School Chemistry [Advanced Level].

Purpose: To measure achievement in high school chemistry.
Population: Advanced high school chemistry students.
Publication Dates: 1963– 2004.
Scores: Total score only.
Administration: Group.
Price Data: Available from publisher.
Time: 110(120) minutes.
Comments: ACS test program is continually updated by retiring an older form of the test upon release of a new form; exam carries secure copyright.
Authors: ACS DivCHED Examinations Institute.
Publisher: ACS DivCHED Examinations Institute.
Cross References: See T5:48 (1 reference) and T4:57 (1 reference); for reviews by Peter A. Dahl and

John P. Penna of an earlier form, see 8:844 (1 reference); for a review by Irvin J. Lehmann, see 7:838 (3 references); for reviews by Frank J. Fornoff and William Hered, see 6:909.

[48]
ACS Examination in High School Chemistry [Lower Level].

Purpose: To measure achievement in high school chemistry.
Population: High school first year chemistry students.
Publication Dates: 1957–2005.
Scores, 3: Part I, Part II, Total.
Administration: Group.
Price Data: Available from publisher.
Time: 80(90) minutes.
Comments: ACS test program is continually updated by retiring an older form of the test upon release of a new form; exam carries secure copyright.
Authors: ACS DivCHED Examinations Institute.
Publisher: ACS DivCHED Examinations Institute.
Cross References: See T5:49 (1 reference), T4:59 (1 reference) and 9:41 (1 reference); for a review by Edward F. DeVillafranca of an earlier form, see 8:845 (11 references); see also T2:1830 (3 references); for reviews by William R. Crawford and Irvin J. Lehmann, see 7:837 (9 references); for reviews by Frank J. Fornoff and William Hered and excerpted reviews by Christine Jansing and Joseph Schmuckler, see 6:908 (5 references); for reviews by Edward G. Rietz and Willard G. Warrington, see 5:729.

[49]
ACS Examination in Inorganic Chemistry.

Purpose: Designed to measure a student's achievement in inorganic chemistry.
Population: 1 year college.
Publication Dates: 1961– 2002.
Scores: Total score only.
Administration: Group.
Manual: No specific manual; general directions (no date, 4 pages).
Price Data: Available from publisher.
Time: 120(130) minutes.
Comments: ACS test program is continually updated by retiring an older form of the test upon release of a new form; separate answer sheet must be used; exam carries secure copyright.
Authors: ACS DivCHED Examinations Institute.
Publisher: ACS DivCHED Examinations Institute.
Cross References: See T3:64 (1 reference), 8:838 (2 references), T2:1820 (1 reference), and 7:827 (2 references); for a review by Frank J. Fornoff and an excerpted review by George B. Kauffman of an earlier form, see 6:903 (1 reference).

[50]
ACS Examination in Instrumental Methods.

Purpose: Designed to measure a student's achievement in instrumental determinations.
Population: 1 year college.
Publication Dates: 1966–2001.
Scores: Total score only.
Administration: Group.
Manual: No specific manual; general directions (no date, 4 pages).
Price Data: Available from publisher.
Time: 110(120) minutes.
Comments: ACS test program is continually updated by retiring an older form of the test upon release of a new form; separate answer sheet must be used; exam carries secure copyright.
Authors: ACS DivCHED Examinations Institute.
Publisher: ACS DivCHED Examinations Institute.
Cross References: See 7:830 (1 reference).

[51]
ACS Examination in Organic Chemistry.

Purpose: Designed to measure a student's achievement in organic chemistry.
Population: 1 year college.
Publication Dates: 1942–1986.
Scores: Total score only.
Administration: Group.
Manual: No specific manual; general directions (no date, 4 pages).
Price Data: Available from publisher.
Time: 115(125) minutes.
Comments: ACS test program is continually updated by retiring an older form of the test upon release of a new form; separate answer sheet must be used; Exam carries secure copyright.
Authors: ACS DivCHED Examinations Institute.
Publisher: ACS DivCHED Examinations Institute.
Cross References: See 8:840 (3 references), 7:831 (3 references), and 6:905 (4 references); for a review by Shailer Peterson of an earlier form, see 3:558.

[52]
ACS Examination in Physical Chemistry.

Purpose: Designed to measure a student's mastery of physical chemistry.
Population: 1 year college.
Publication Dates: 1946–2001.
Administration: Group.
Manual: No specific manual.
Price Data: Available from publisher.
Comments: ACS test program is continually updated by retiring an older form of the test upon release of a new form; subtests may be administered separately or together; separate answer sheet must be

used; includes a comprehensive exam and three subject matter exams.
Author: ACS DivCHED Examinations Institute.
Publisher: ACS DivCHED Examinations Institute.

a) THERMODYNAMICS.
Scores, 3: Part A, Part B, Total.
Time: 90(100) minutes.
b) CHEMICAL DYNAMICS.
Scores, 3: Part A, Part B, Total.
Time: 90(100) minutes.
c) QUANTUM CHEMISTRY.
Scores, 3: Part A, Part B, Total.
Time: 100(110) minutes.
Cross References: For a review by Gerald R. Van Hecke of an earlier form, see 8:842 (2 references); see also T2:1826 (2 references), 7:833 (2 references), and 6:904 (1 reference); for a review by Alfred S. Brown, see 3:559.

[53]
ACS Examination in Physical Chemistry for Life Sciences.

Purpose: Designed to measure a student's achievement in physical chemistry for life sciences.
Population: 1 year college.
Publication Date: 1982.
Scores: Total score only.
Administration: Group.
Manual: No specific manual; general directions (no date, 4 pages).
Price Data: Available from publisher.
Time: 100(110) minutes.
Comments: ACS test program is continually updated by retiring an older form of the test upon publication of a new form; separate answer sheet must be used.
Author: ACS DivCHED Examinations Institute.
Publisher: ACS DivCHED Examinations Institute.

[54]
ACS Examination in Polymer Chemistry.

Purpose: Designed to measure a student's achievement in polymer chemistry.
Population: 1 year college.
Publication Dates: 1978–1990.
Scores: Total score only.
Administration: Group.
Price Data: Available from publisher.
Time: 75(85) minutes.
Comments: ACS test program is continually updated by retiring an older form of the test upon release of a new form; separate answer sheet must be used; exam carries secure copyright.
Author: ACS DivCHED Examinations Institute.
Publisher: ACS DivCHED Examinations Institute.

[55]
ACS Toledo Chemistry Placement Examination.

Purpose: Designed to measure a student's achievement in general chemistry.
Population: 1 year college.
Publication Dates: 1959–1998.
Scores: 4: General Mathematics, General Chemical Knowledge, Specific Chemical Knowledge, Total.
Administration: Group.
Manual: No specific manual; general directions (no date, 4 pages).
Price Data: Available from publisher.
Time: 55(65) minutes.
Comments: ACS test program is continually updated by retiring an older form of the test upon release of a new form; separate answer sheet must be used; exam carries secure copyright.
Author: ACS DivCHED Examinations Institute.
Publisher: ACS DivCHED Examinations Institute.
Cross References: For a review by Frank J. Fornoff of an earlier form, see 8:853 (3 references); see also T2:1847 (2 references); for reviews by Kenneth E. Anderson and William R. Crawford, see 6:920 (1 reference).

[56]
ACT Survey Services.

Purpose: Designed to help educational institutions obtain reliable survey information that can be used to evaluate and enhance their programs.
Population: Secondary and postsecondary students and alumni.
Publication Dates: 1979–2006.
Acronym: ESS.
Administration: Group or individual.
Comments: For measurement of groups, not individuals.
Author: ACT, Inc.
Publisher: ACT, Inc.

a) SECONDARY SCHOOL LEVEL.
Population: High school.
Publication Dates: 1979–2006.
Price Data, 2005: $17.50 per 25 survey instruments; $9.20 per User's Guide; $46 per normative data reports; $8.70 per item catalog; $72 per institutional processing/handling fee; $1 per instrument scanning fee; $210-$350 per report fee.
Time: (15–25) minutes.
1) *High School Student Opinion Survey.*
Publication Dates: 1980–2006.
Acronym: HSSOS.
Scores: Student's perceptions in 6 areas: High School Environment, Occupational Preparation, Educational Preparation, High

School Characteristics, Additional Questions, Comments and Suggestions.

2) *Student Needs Assessment Questionnaire.*
Publication Dates: 1979–2006.
Acronym: SNAQ.
Scores: Student's personal and educational needs in 4 areas: Importance and Life Goals, Individual Growth/Development/Planning, Additional Questions, Comments and Suggestions.

3) *High School Follow-Up Survey.*
Publication Dates: 1990–2006.
Acronym: HSFS.
Scores: Student's satisfaction with high school in 5 areas: Continuing Education, Employment History, High School Experiences, Additional Questions, Comments and Suggestions.
Comments: Administered to recent graduates.

b) POSTSECONDARY SCHOOL LEVEL.
Population: College.
Publication Dates: 1981–2006.
Price Data: $17.50 per 25 survey instruments; $9.20 per User's Guide; $46 per normative data reports; $8.70 per item catalog; $72 per institutional processing/handling fee; $1 per instrument scanning fee; $210-$350 per report fee.
Time: (15–25) minutes.

1) *Adult Learner Needs Assessment Survey.*
Publication Dates: 1981–2006.
Acronym: ALNAS.
Scores: Adult student's educational and personal needs in 4 areas: Personal and Educational Needs, Educational Plans and Preferences, Additional Questions, Comments and Suggestions.

2) *Alumni Survey.*
Publication Dates: 1981–2006.
Acronym: AS.
Scores: Impact of college on graduates in 5 areas: Continuing Education, College Experiences, Employment History, Additional Questions, Comments and Suggestions.

3) *Alumni Survey (2-Year College Form).*
Publication Dates: 1981–2006.
Scores: Same as 2 above but for 2-year colleges.

4) *Alumni Outcomes Survey.*
Publication Dates: 1993–2006.
Acronym: AOS.
Scores: Alumni outcomes in 7 areas: Employment History and Experiences, Educational Outcomes, Educational Experiences, Activities and Organizations, Additional Questions, Comments and Suggestions, Mailing Address.

5) *College Outcomes Survey.*
Publication Dates: 1992–2006.
Acronym: COS.
Scores: Student's perception of their college experience in 4 areas: College Outcomes, Satisfaction with Experiences at College, Additional Questions, Comments and Suggestions.

6) *College Student Needs Assessment Survey.*
Acronym: CSNAS.
Scores: Student's educational and personal needs in 4 areas: Career and Life Goals, Educational and Personal Needs, Additional Questions, Comments and Suggestions.

7) *Entering Student Survey.*
Publication Dates: 1982–2006.
Acronym: ESS.
Scores: Student's expectations for college in 4 areas: Educational Plans and Preferences, College Impressions, Additional Questions, Comments and Suggestions.

8) *Financial Aid Student Services Survey.*
Publication Dates: 1997-2006.
Acronym: FASSS.
Scores: Students' Perceptions of Financial Aid Services Received at Their College or University.

9) *Student Opinion Survey.*
Publication Dates: 1981–2006.
Acronym: SOS.
Scores: Student's perceptions of the institution in 4 areas: College Services, College Environment, Additional Questions, Comments and Suggestions.
Comments: Available via paper/pencil and online.

10) *Student Opinion Survey (2-Year College Form).*
Publication Dates: 1981–2006.
Scores: Student's perceptions of the 2-year college in 5 areas: College Impressions, College Services, College Environment, Additional Questions, Comments and Suggestions.
Comments: Available via paper/pencil and online.

11) *Survey of Academic Advising.*
Publication Dates: 1990-2006.
Acronym: SAA.
Scores: Student's perception of academic advising services in 6 areas: Advising Information, Academic Advising Needs, Impressions of Your Advisor, Additional Advising Information, Additional Questions, Comments and Suggestions.

12) *Survey of Current Activities and Plans.*
Publication Dates: 1988–2006.
Acronym: SCAP.

Scores: Student's current educational status in 5 areas: Impressions of This College, Educational Plans and Activities, Employment Plans, Additional Questions, Comments and Suggestions.

13) *Survey of Postsecondary Plans.*
Publication Dates: 1982–2006.
Acronym: SPP.
Scores: Student's educational plans in 4 areas: Educational Plans After High School, Impressions of This College, Additional Questions, Comments and Suggestions.

14) *Withdrawing/Nonreturning Student Survey.*
Publication Dates: 1979–2006.
Acronym: WNSS.
Scores: Student's reasons for leaving an institution in 4 areas: Reasons for Leaving This College, College Services and Characteristics, Additional Questions, Comments and Suggestions.

15) *Withdrawing/Nonreturning Student Survey (short form).*
Publication Dates: 1981–2006.
Acronym: WNSS-Short Form.
Scores: Student's reasons for leaving an institution in 2 areas: Reasons for Leaving This College, Additional Questions.

16) *Faces of the Future.*
Publication Dates: 1998–2006.
Acronym: FFS.
Scores: 6 areas: Employment Background, Education Background, Current College Experience, ID Number, Additional Questions, Comments and Suggestions.

Cross References: For reviews by Marcia J. Belcher and Claudia J. Morner of an earlier edition, see 12:10; see T4:61 (5 references); for a review by Rodney T. Hartnett of an earlier edition, see 9:44.

[57]

ACT Test.

Purpose: "Contains five curriculum-based tests (four multiple-choice tests and an optional Writing Test) that measure academic achievement in English/Writing, mathematics, reading, and science as well as noncognitive components (high school course/grade information, ACT interest inventory, and the student profile section). Results of the cognitive section are used by high schools and post-secondary institutions to understand what students are likely to know and ready to learn next in preparation for, and the transition to, post-secondary education. Results from the ACT Test are used in admissions, scholarship determination, academic advising, course placement, and career counseling."
Population: Grades 11–12.

Publication Dates: 1959–2005.
Administration: Group.
Price Data: Available from publisher.
Time: 175(190) minutes; 205(220) with the Optional Writing Test.
Comments: Tests administered nationally 6 times per year (February, April, June, September [in some states], October, December) at centers established by the publisher; also offered up to 5 times per year at international test centers outside the U.S.; special testing with extended time and alternate test formats are available for students who receive special accommodations in school due to professionally diagnosed and documented disabilities; a previous version was entitled Enhanced ACT Assessment.
Author: ACT, Inc.
Publisher: ACT, Inc.

a) ACT ENGLISH TEST.
Purpose: "Measures the student's understanding of the conventions of standard written English."
Scores, 3: Usage/Mechanics, Rhetorical Skills, Total.
Time: 45 minutes.

b) ACT MATHEMATICS TEST.
Purpose: "Measures reasoning and mathematical skills."
Scores, 4: Pre-Algebra/Elementary Algebra, Intermediate Algebra/Coordinate Geometry, Plane Geometry/Trigonometry, Total.
Time: 60 minutes.

c) ACT READING TEST.
Purpose: "Measures reading comprehension as a product of skill in referring and reasoning."
Scores, 3: Social Studies/Sciences, Arts/Literature, Total.
Time: 35 minutes.

d) ACT SCIENCE TEST.
Purpose: "Measures the interpretation, analysis, evaluation, reasoning, and problem-solving skills required in the natural sciences."
Scores: Total score only.
Time: 35 minutes.

e) ACT WRITING TEST (Optional).
Purpose: "Measures writing skills emphasized in high school English classes and in college-level composition courses."
Scores, 2: Writing Test subscore, Combined English/Writing Test score.
Time: 30 minutes.

Cross References: See T5:56 (19 references); for reviews by A. Harry Passow and James S. Terwilliger of the Enhanced ACT Assessment, see 12:139 (35 references); see also T4:913 (71 references); for reviews by Lewis R. Aiken and Edward Kifer of the ACT Assessment Program, see 9:42 (27 references); see also T3:76 (76 references); for a review by John R. Hills, see 8:469

(208 references); see also T2:1044 (97 references); for a review by Wimburn L. Wallace of an earlier program, see 7:330 (265 references); for reviews by Max D. Engelhart and Warren G. Findley and an excerpted review by David V. Tiedeman, see 6:1 (14 references).

[58]
Adaptability Test.
Purpose: "Designed to measure mental adaptability or mental alertness."
Population: Job applicants.
Publication Dates: 1942–1994.
Scores: Total score only.
Administration: Individual or group.
Forms, 2: A, B.
Price Data, 2002: $79 per start-up kit including 25 test booklets (specify Form A or Form B) and examiner's manual; $61 per 25 test booklets (specify Form A or Form B); $28 per examiner's manual.
Time: 15 minutes.
Authors: Joseph Tiffin and C. H. Lawshe.
Publisher: Pearson Performance Solutions [No reply from publisher; status unknown].
Cross References: See T4:80 (2 references), T3:111 (1 reference), T2:337 (3 references), and 7:333 (6 references); for a review by John M. Willits, see 5:305 (13 references); for reviews by Anne Anastasi and Marion A. Bills, see 3:216 (3 references).

[59]
Adaptive Behavior Assessment System®— Second Edition.
Purpose: Designed to provide a comprehensive norm-referenced assessment of adaptive skills.
Population: Birth to 89 years.
Publication Dates: 2002–2003.
Acronym: ABAS-Second Edition.
Scores, 14: 10 skill areas, 3 adaptive domains, 1 overall score: Conceptual (Communication, Functional Academics, Self-Direction, Composite), Social (Leisure, Social, Composite), Practical (Community Use, Home Living, Health and Safety, Self-Care, Work, Composite), Motor, General Adaptive Composite.
Administration: Individual.
Forms, 5: Parent/Primary Caregiver Form (Ages Birth–5), Parent Form (Ages 5–21), Teacher/Day Care Form (Ages 2–5), Teacher Form (Ages 5–21), Adult Form (Ages 16–89).
Price Data, 2006: $175 per examination kit including manual, 5 Parent/Primary Caregiver Forms (Ages 0–5), 5 Teacher/Daycare Provider Forms (Ages 2–5), 5 Parent Forms (Ages 5–21), 5 Teacher Forms (Ages 5–21), and 5 Adult Forms; $120 per manual; $59 per 25 Forms (specify respondent and age); $175 per Infant and Preschool kit including manual, 25 Parent/Primary Caregiver Forms, and 25 Teacher/Daycare Provider Forms; $175 per School kit including manual, 25 Parent Forms, and 25 Teacher Forms; $175 per Adult kit including manual and 25 Adult Forms; $199 per Scoring Assistant Windows CD-ROM.
Time: (15–20) minutes.
Comments: Personal computer scoring software available; incorporates current AAMR and DSM-IV diagnostic guidelines.
Authors: Patti Harrison and Thomas Oakland.
Publisher: PsychCorp, A brand of Harcourt Assessment, Inc.
Cross References: For reviews by Matthew K. Burns and by Joyce Meikamp and Carolyn H. Suppa, see 16:4; for a review by James K. Benish of the original edition, see 15:6.

[60]
Adaptive Behavior Evaluation Scale, Revised.
Purpose: Designed to assist in "making diagnostic, placement, and programming decisions for mentally retarded and emotionally disturbed/behaviorally disordered children and adolescents."
Population: Ages 5-0 to 18-0.
Publication Dates: 1983–1995.
Acronym: ABES-R.
Scores, 10: Communication, Self-Care, Home Living, Social, Community Use, Self-Direction, Health and Safety, Functional Academics, Leisure, Work.
Administration: Individual.
Forms, 2: Adaptive Behavior Evaluation Scale, School Version; Adaptive Behavior Evaluation Scale, Home Version.
Price Data: Available from publisher.
Time: (15–20) minutes.
Comments: Publisher advises that ABES-R2 replaces this test.
Author: Stephen B. McCarney.
Publisher: Hawthorne Educational Services, Inc.
Cross References: For reviews by John H. Kranzler and by Mark D. Shriver and Merilee McCurdy, see 14:4; for reviews by Mary Ross Moran and Harvey N. Switzky of an earlier edition, see 12:14.

[61]
Adaptive Behavior Inventory.
Purpose: Designed to evaluate functional daily living skills.
Population: Mentally retarded students ages 6-0 through 18-11 years and normal students ages 5-0 through 18-11 years.
Publication Date: 1986.
Acronym: ABI.
Scores, 6: Self-Care Skills, Communication Skills, Social Skills, Academic Skills, Occupational Skills, Composite Quotient.
Administration: Individual.

Price Data, 2006: $89 per complete kit including 25 profile and response sheets, 25 short form response sheets, and examiner's manual (69 pages); $34 per 25 profile and response sheets; $14 per 25 short form response sheets; $44 per examiner's manual.
Time: (20–25) minutes.
Comments: Inventory is completed by classroom teacher or other professional having regular contact with the student; ABI-Short Form available for research and screening purposes.
Authors: Linda Brown and James E. Leigh.
Publisher: PRO-ED.
Cross References: For a review by Corinne Roth Smith, see 10:9 (2 references).

[62]
Adaptive Behavior Inventory for Children.

Purpose: Designed to "measure the child's social role performance in the family, the peer group, and the community."
Population: Ages 5–11.
Publication Dates: 1977–1982.
Acronym: ABIC.
Scores, 6: Family, Community, Peer Relations, Non-academic School Roles, Earner/Consumer, Self-Maintenance.
Administration: Individual.
Price Data, 2002: $149 per basic kit including manual (1982, 121 pages), 6 keys, and 25 record forms; $44 per 6 scoring keys; $40 per 25 record forms.
Time: (45) minutes.
Comments: A component of the System of Multicultural Pluralistic Assessment (2520); the manual includes the ABIC questions in Spanish as well as in English.
Authors: Jane R. Mercer and June F. Lewis.
Publisher: PsychCorp, A brand of Harcourt Assessment, Inc.
Cross References: See T5:61 (2 references) and T4:85 (10 references); for reviews by James E. Jirsa and Benson P. Low, see 9:48 (1 reference); see T3:2387 (9 references) for ABIC and related references.

[63]
Adaptive Behavior: Street Survival Skills Questionnaire.

Purpose: "To assess fundamental community living and prevocational skills of mentally disabled adolescents and adults."
Population: Ages 9.5 and over.
Publication Date: 1979–1993.
Acronym: SSSQ.
Scores, 10: Basic Concepts, Functional Signs, Tools, Domestics, Health and Safety, Public Services, Time, Monetary, Measurements, Total.
Administration: Individual.

Price Data, 2006: $400 per complete kit including 9 picture volumes (1993, 50 pages each), 50 scoring forms, 50 planning charts, Curriculum Guide (1982, 272 pages), and manual (1993, 95 pages); $29.50 per 50 scoring forms; $19 per 50 planning charts; $59.75 per Curriculum Guide; $42.50 per manual; $250 per computer software (Windows or Macintosh) offered by publisher.
Time: [45] minutes.
Authors: Dan Linkenhoker and Lawrence McCarron.
Publisher: McCarron-Dial Systems.
Cross References: See T4:139 (1 reference); for a review by Thomas G. Haring, see 11:6.

[64]
Adaptive Functioning Index.

Purpose: "Training and assessment tool to be used by those working with the developmentally handicapped adolescent and adult."
Population: Ages 14 and over in rehabilitation or special education settings.
Publication Dates: 1971–1978.
Acronym: AFI.
Administration: Individual.
Price Data: Price information available from publisher for complete kit, administration manual (1976, 43 pages), standardization manual (1977, 42 pages), program manual (1978, 198 pages), Program Workbooks (1977, 19 pages), and Target Workbooks (1977, 12 pages).
Time: Administration time not reported.
Comments: Ratings by staff; 3 subtests: Social Education Test, Vocational Check List, Residential Check List, plus Adaptive Functioning of the Dependent Handicapped; Training Package available, includes Training Manual, Program Workbook, and Target Workbook; Program manual and workbooks not necessary for test administration; no norms.
Authors: Nancy J. Marlett and E. Anne Hughson (Program Workbook and Target Workbook).
Publisher: Vocational and Rehabilitation Research Institute [Canada].

a) SOCIAL EDUCATION TEST.
Scores, 9: Reading, Writing, Communication, Concept Attainment, Number Concepts, Time, Money Handling, Community Awareness, Motor Movements.
b) VOCATIONAL CHECK LIST.
Scores, 12: Basic Work Habits (Independence, Making Decisions, Use and Care of Equipment and Materials, Taking Direction), Work Skills (Speed of Movement, Ability to Follow Instructions, Competence, Skill Level), Acceptance Skills (Appearance, Attendance/Punctuality, Self-Expressions, Relation with Co-workers).

c) RESIDENTIAL CHECK LIST.
Scores, 15: Personal Routines (Cleanliness, Appearance and Eating, Room Management, Time Management, Health), Community Awareness (Transportation, Shopping, Leisure, Budgeting, Cooking and Home Management), Social Maturity (Communication, Consideration, Getting Friends, Keeping Friends, Handling Problems).
d) ADAPTIVE FUNCTIONING OF THE DEPENDENT HANDICAPPED.
Population: Profoundly handicapped of all ages.
Scores, 20: Nursing Care (Medications, Body Tone, Medical Care, Observation for Injury, Feeding), Physical Development (Head, Legs, Body, Hands or Feet, Movement), Awareness (Eye Contact, Contact with His World, Contact with People, Communication, Contact with Things), Self Help (Feeding, Eating, Washing, Dressing, Toileting).
Cross References: See T5:63 (1 reference) and T4:87 (2 references); for reviews by Nadine M. Lambert and David J. Mealor, see 9:49 (1 reference).

[65]
Adaptive Style Inventory.

Purpose: "Designed to assess individuals' ability to adapt to different learning situations."
Population: Junior high through adult.
Publication Date: 1993.
Acronym: ASI.
Scores, 16: 4 scores: Concrete Experience, Reflective Observation, Abstract Conceptualization, Active Experimentation in each of 4 situations: Acting Situation, Deciding Situation, Thinking Situation, Valuing Situation.
Administration: Group or individual.
Price Data, 2006: $69 per complete kit including 10 questionnaires, 10 profiles and interpretive notes (14 pages), and 10 scoring booklets.
Time: [30–40] minutes.
Comments: Self-scored inventory.
Authors: Richard E. Boyatzis and David A. Kolb.
Publisher: Hay Group.
Cross References: For reviews by Thomas R. Knapp and Erich P. Prien, see 13:7.

[66]
Addiction Severity Index—Multimedia Version.

Purpose: "An interactive, multimedia administration of the Addiction Severity Index," "a measure of addiction severity."
Population: Adults seeking substance abuse treatment.
Publication Date: 1999.
Acronym: ASI-MV.

Scores, 7: Composite scores and severity ratings provided for 7 domains: Medical Status, Employment/Support Status, Alcohol Use, Drug Use, Legal Status, Family/Social Relationships, Psychiatric Status.
Administration: Individual or group.
Price Data: Available from publisher.
Time: (45) minutes.
Comments: Same clinical interview as Addiction Severity Index (5th edition) adapted for self-report, multimedia format; clients are guided through a series of on-screen offices and meet with virtual interviewers; produces narrative report, severity profile, utilization report; customized reports available; personal computer or mouse-driven computer kiosk versions available; PC system requirements: Windows 95/98/NT 4.0, 6 MB hard drive, 12 MB RAM, 100 MHz processor, SVGA monitor (256 colors), 4X CD-ROM, sound card, speakers with headphones, mouse, keyboard, printer; kiosk information available from publisher.
Author: Innovative Training Systems, Inc.
Publisher: PsychCorp, A brand of Harcourt Assessment, Inc.

[67]
AD/HD Comprehensive Teacher's Rating Scale, Second Edition [1998 Revision].

Purpose: "Designed to help identify attention disorder, with or without hyperactivity."
Population: Grades K–adult.
Publication Dates: 1986–2000.
Acronym: ACTeRS.
Administration: Individual.
Editions, 2: Paper-and-pencil; microcomputer.
Price Data, 2006: $62 per Teacher and Parent Form examiner's kit including manual (2000, 31 pages) and 50 rating/profile forms; $43 per 50 rating/profile forms; $67 per Self-Report examiner's kit including manual and 50 rating/profile forms; $48 per 50 rating/profile forms; $19 per introductory kit including manual, sample Parent rating/profile Form, sample Teacher rating/profile Form, sample Self-Report Form, and annotated bibliography of research; $19 per manual.
Time: [5–15] minutes.
Comments: Parent forms available in Spanish.
Authors: Rina K. Ullmann, Esther K. Sleator, Robert L. Sprague, and MetriTech staff.
Publisher: MetriTech, Inc.
a) ACTeRS TEACHER FORM.
Population: Grades K–8.
Scores, 4: Attention, Hyperactivity, Social Skills, Oppositional Behavior.
Price Data: $62 including manual and 50 forms; $43 per 50 forms.
Time: Untimed.

b) ACTeRS PARENT FORM.
Scores, 5: Attention, Hyperactivity, Social Skills, Oppositional Behavior, Early Childhood.
Price Data: $62 including manual and 50 forms; $43 per 50 forms.
Time: Untimed.
c) ACTeRS SELF-REPORT.
Population: Adolescence through adulthood.
Scores, 3: Attention, Hyperactivity/Impulsivity, Social Adjustment.
Price Data: $67 including manual and 50 forms; $48 per 50 forms.
Time: Untimed [10–15 minutes].
Cross References: For reviews by Cederick O. Lindskog and Janet V. Smith and by Everett V. Smith, Jr., see 14:5; for reviews by Robert J. Miller and Judy Oehler-Stinnett of an earlier edition, see 12:15 (2 references); see also T4:89 (1 reference); for reviews by Ellen H. Bacon and Ayres G. D'Costa of an earlier edition, see 11:7 (2 references).

[68]
ADHD Rating Scale-IV.
Purpose: Designed to help identify the frequency of ADHD symptoms of a child as reported by a parent or educator.
Population: Ages 5–18 years.
Publication Date: 1998.
Scores, 3: Inattention, Hyperactivity-Impulsivity, Total.
Administration: Individual.
Forms, 2: Home, School.
Price Data, 2001: $29.75 per scale including manual (79 pages) and photocopiable scales.
Foreign Language Edition: Spanish questionnaires available.
Time: Administration time not reported.
Comments: Symptom criteria based on the DSM-IV; 18-item rating scale.
Authors: George J. DuPaul, Thomas J. Power, Arthur D. Anastopolous, and Robert Reid.
Publisher: Guilford Publications, Inc.
Cross References: For reviews by Jill Ann Jenkins and Cederick O. Lindskog, see 15:7.

[69]
ADHD Symptom Checklist—4.
Purpose: Designed as "a screening instrument for the behavioral symptoms of attention-deficit/hyperactivity disorder (AD/HD) and oppositional defiant disorder (ODD)."
Population: Ages 3–18.
Publication Date: 1997.
Acronym: ADHD-SC4.
Scores, 3: Screening Cutoff, Symptom Count, Symptom Severity.
Administration: Individual.
Forms, 1: Same checklist completed by parent and teacher.
Price Data, 2006: $52 per kit including 50 checklists, 50 symptom count score sheets, 50 symptom severity profile score sheets, and manual (1997, 200 pages); $26 per 50 checklists.
Time: (5) minutes.
Authors: Kenneth D. Gadow and Joyce Sprafkin.
Publisher: Checkmate Plus, Ltd.
Cross References: For reviews by James C. DiPerna and Robert J. Volpe and by Cynthia A. Rohrbeck, see 15:8.

[70]
ADHD Symptoms Rating Scale.
Purpose: Designed "to assess behaviors symptomatic of Attention Deficit Hyperactivity Disorder in children and adolescents."
Population: Ages 5–18 years.
Publication Date: 2001.
Acronym: ADHD-SRS.
Scores, 4: Hyperactive, Impulsive, Inattentive, Total.
Administration: Individual.
Price Data, 2006: $85 per starter set including manual (100 pages), 25 English forms, and 5 Spanish forms; $38 per 25 rating forms (specify English or Spanish); $50 per manual.
Foreign Language Edition: Spanish edition available.
Time: (10–15) minutes.
Authors: Melissa Lea Holland, Gretchen A. Gimpel, and Kenneth W. Merrell.
Publisher: Psychological Assessment Resources, Inc.
Cross References: For reviews by Kevin M. Jones and Ronald A. Madle, see 15:9.

[71]
The Adjective Check List.
Purpose: Designed to identify personal characteristics of individuals.
Population: High school and over.
Publication Dates: 1952–1980.
Acronym: ACL.
Scores, 37: Number of Adjectives Checked, Number of Favorable Adjectives, Number of Unfavorable Adjectives, Commonality, Achievement, Dominance, Endurance, Order, Intraception, Nurturance, Affiliation, Heterosexuality, Exhibition, Autonomy, Aggression, Change, Succorance, Abasement, Deference, Counseling Readiness, Self-Control, Self-Confidence, Personal Adjustment, Ideal Self, Creative Personality, Military Leadership, Masculine Attributes, Feminine Attributes, Critical Parent, Nurturing Parent, Adult, Free Child, Adapted Child, High Origence-Low

Intellectence, High Origence-High Intellectence, Low Origence-Low Intellectence, Low Origence-High Intellectence.

Administration: Group.

Price Data, 2001: $23 per 25 profiles; $72.10 per manual (1980, 110 pages); scoring service available from publisher; $106.7 per 10 prepaid profile/answer sheets; $26.70 per nonprepaid combined item booklet/answer sheet.

Foreign Language Edition: Spanish edition available.

Time: [15–20] minutes.

Authors: Harrison G. Gough and Alfred B. Heilbrun, Jr. (manual and bibliography).

Publisher: CPP, Inc.

Cross References: See T5:68 (62 references) and T4:93 (92 references); for reviews by Phyllis Anne Teeter and John A. Zarske, see 9:52 (39 references); see also T3:116 (117 references), 8:495 (202 references), and T2:1094 (85 references); for reviews by Leonard G. Rorer and Forrest L. Vance, see 7:38 (131 references); see also P:4 (102 references).

[72]
Adjustment Scales for Children and Adolescents.

Purpose: "Designed to assess through teacher observation behavior pathology in youths."

Population: Ages 5–17.

Publication Dates: 1993–1994.

Acronym: ASCA.

Scores, 10: Overactivity, Underactivity, Attention-Deficit Hyperactive, Solitary Aggressive-Provocative, Solitary Aggressive-Impulsive, Oppositional Defiant, Diffident, Avoidant, Delinquent, Lethargic-Hypoactive.

Administration: Individual.

Price Data, 2006: $87 per complete kit including 25 male and 25 female self-scoring forms and profiles and manual (1994, 68 pages); $26.20 per 25 self-scoring forms and profiles (specify male or female); $34.95 per manual.

Time: (10–20) minutes.

Comments: Behavior checklist to be completed by a teacher about a student; scored by a psychologist or assessment specialist.

Authors: Paul A. McDermott, Neville C. Marston, and Denis H. Stott.

Publisher: Ed & Psych Associates.

Cross References: For reviews by Gary L. Canivez and Richard V. Schowengerdt, see 14:6; see also T5:69 (1 reference).

[73]
Administrative Series Modules.

Purpose: Designed to assess skills needed in various administrative positions.

Population: Candidates for administrative positions.

Publication Dates: 1975-1997.

Administration: Individual or group.

Price Data: Available from publisher.

Comments: "Designed in module format so test users can select the modules that best suit their testing needs"; "hand scoring is available for all individual and combined modules"; "machine scoring is available for all modules except I, K, and L"; previous version listed as SCC Clerical Skills Series.

Authors: International Public Management Association for Human Resources.

Publisher: International Public Management Association for Human Resources (IPMA-HR).

    a) INDIVIDUAL ADMINISTRATIVE MODULE TESTS.

    1) *Grammar (A).*
    Score: Total score only.
    Time: 15 minutes.
    2) *Punctuation (B).*
    Score: Total score only.
    Time: 11 minutes.
    3) *Vocabulary (C).*
    Score: Total score only.
    Time: 9 minutes.
    4) *Spelling (D).*
    Score: Total score only.
    Time: 6 minutes.
    5) *Basic Filing Skills (E).*
    Score: Total score only.
    Time: 18 minutes.
    6) *Reasoning (F).*
    Score: Total score only.
    Time: 9 minutes.
    7) *Following Oral Instructions (G).*
    Score: Total score only.
    Time: 33 minutes.
    8) *Following Written Instructions (H).*
    Score: Total score only.
    Time: 25 minutes.
    9) *Forms, Completion/Listening (I).*
    Score: Total score only.
    Time: 30 minutes.
    10) *Data Proofing (J).*
    Score: Total score only.
    Time: 13 minutes.
    11) *Document Proofing-Part A (K).*
    Score: Total score only.
    Time: 15 minutes.
    12) *Document Proofing-Part B (L).*
    Score: Total score only.
    Time: 20 minutes.
    13) *Mathematical Reasoning (M).*
    Score: Total score only.
    Time: 35 minutes.
    14) *Basic Math Calculations (N).*
    Score: Total score only.
    Time: 20 minutes.

b) COMBINED ADMINISTRATIVE MODULE TESTS.

   1) *Clerical Series 1-A.*
Acronym: CS1-A.
Scores: 5 modules: Grammar, Punctuation, Vocabulary, Spelling, Basic Filing.
Time: 59 minutes.
   2) *Clerical Series 1-B.*
Acronym: CS1-B.
Scores: 3 modules: Reasoning, Following Written Instructions, Basic Math Calculations.
Time: 54 minutes.
Cross References: For a review by Lorraine D. Eyde of a previous version, see 9:1074.

[74]
Adolescent/Adult Sensory Profile.

Purpose: Designed "to promote self-evaluation of behavioral responses to everyday sensory experiences."
Population: Ages 11–65+.
Publication Date: 2002.
Scores, 4: Low Registration, Sensation Seeking, Sensory Sensitivity, Sensation Avoiding.
Administration: Individual.
Price Data, 2003: $85 per complete kit including user's manual (144 pages) and 25 self-questionnaire/summary reports; $65 per user's manual; $27 per 25 self-questionnaire/summary reports.
Time: (10–15) minutes.
Comments: Self-report inventory based on the Sensory Profile (2306), a measure developed for children.
Authors: Catana E. Brown and Winnie Dunn.
Publisher: PsychCorp, A brand of Harcourt Assessment, Inc.
Cross References: For reviews by Corine Fitzpatrick and Janet V. Smith, see 16:5.

[75]
Adolescent American Drug and Alcohol Survey with Prevention Planning Survey.

Purpose: Designed to survey youth about their experiences with alcohol, tobacco and other drugs, and "about various risk and protective factors associated with the Prevention Planning Model."
Population: Grades 6–12.
Publication Dates: 1999-2005.
Acronym: ADAS/PPS.
Scores: Not scored.
Administration: Group.
Price Data, 2003: $1.90 per booklet with Prevention Planning Survey (volume discount available for orders of 1,000 booklets or more); $450 per detailed report on both ADAS and PPS.
Time: (20–30) minutes.
Comments: For information about the Children's ADAS, see 149.

Authors: Ruth Edwards, Fred Beauvais, and Eugene R. Oetting.
Publisher: Rocky Mountain Behavioral Science Institute, Inc.
Cross References: For reviews by Jody L. Kulstad and by Nathaniel J. Pallone and James J. Hennessy, see 16:6.

[76]
Adolescent and Adult Psychoeducational Profile: Volume IV.

Purpose: Assesses skills and behaviors of moderately to severely retarded and autistic individuals.
Population: Adolescents and adults with moderate to severe mental retardation or autism.
Publication Date: 1988.
Acronym: AAPEP.
Scores: 3 scales (Direct Observation, Home, School/Work); 6 scores for each: Vocational Skills, Independent Functioning, Leisure Skills, Vocational Behavior, Functional Communication, Interpersonal Behavior.
Administration: Individual.
Price Data, 2001: $69 per manual (Vol. IV; 119 pages); price data for testing kit available from Residential Services, Inc., Day Program, P.O. Box 487, Carrboro, NC 27510.
Time: (60–90) minutes per scale.
Comments: Title on manual is Individualized Assessment and Treatment for Autistic and Developmentally Disabled Children, Volume IV; other materials (e.g., ball, magazines, playing cards) necessary for test administration may be supplied by examiner or purchased from Residential Services, Inc.
Authors: Gary Mesibov, Eric Schopler, Bruce Schaffer, and Rhoda Landrus.
Publisher: PRO-ED.
Cross References: See T5:70 (1 reference); for reviews by Lena R. Gaddis and J. Jeffrey Grill, see 11:8.

[77]
Adolescent Anger Rating Scale.

Purpose: Developed to "assess the intensity and frequency of anger expression in adolescents."
Population: Ages 11–19.
Publication Date: 2001.
Acronym: AARS.
Scores, 4: Instrumental Anger, Reactive Anger, Anger Control, Total Anger.
Administration: Individual or group.
Price Data, 2006: $142 per introductory kit including professional manual (69 pages) and 50 test booklets.
Time: (5–10) minutes for individuals; (10–20) minutes per group.
Comments: Self-rating scale.
Author: DeAnna McKinnie Burney.

Publisher: Psychological Assessment Resources, Inc.
Cross References: For reviews by Carlen Henington and Hugh Stephenson, see 15:10.

[78]
Adolescent Apperception Cards.

Purpose: "Intended to suggest themes and evoke narratives that include … family, sibling, and peer relationships; abuse and neglect."
Population: Ages 12–19.
Publication Date: 1993.
Acronym: AAC.
Scores: No scores.
Administration: Individual.
Forms, 2: Black, White.
Price Data, 2006: $109.50 per kit including Adolescent Apperception Cards (Black and White versions included); $64 per cards (specify version).
Time: [45–60] minutes.
Comments: Publisher recommends (a) training and experience in projective testing and in working with adolescents, and (b) that the test be used as one component of a comprehensive battery of measures.
Authors: Leigh Silverton; illustrated by Laurie Harden.
Publisher: Western Psychological Services.
Cross References: For reviews by David M. Kaplan and Molly L. Vanduser and by Jody L. Swartz-Kulstad, see 14:7.

[79]
Adolescent Coping Scale.

Purpose: Assesses 18 possible coping strategies used by adolescents and young adults in dealing with stress.
Population: Ages 12–18.
Publication Dates: 1993–1997.
Acronym: ACS.
Scores, 18: Seek Social Support, Focus on Solving the Problem, Work Hard and Achieve, Worry, Invest in Close Friends, Seek to Belong, Wishful Thinking, Not Coping, Tension Reduction, Social Action, Ignore the Problem, Self-Blame, Keep to Self, Seek Spiritual Support, Focus on the Positive, Seek Professional Help, Seek Relaxing Diversions, Physical Recreation.
Administration: Group.
Price Data, 2005: A$121 per complete kit including manual (48 pages) and all required material in a notebook; A$24.95 per 10 questionnaires (short form); A$24.95 per 10 questionnaires (long form); A$11.55 per 10 scoring sheets; A$11.55 per 10 profile charts; A$51.80 per manual.
Time: 10 minutes for Long Form; 3 minutes for Short Form.
Authors: Erica Frydenberg and Ramon Lewis.
Publisher: Australian Council for Educational Research Ltd. [Australia].

Cross References: See T5:72 (3 references); for reviews by Frederick T. L. Leong and Judy J. Oehler-Stinnett, see 13:8.

[80]
Adolescent Diagnostic Interview.

Purpose: "Assesses psychoactive substance use disorders."
Population: Ages 12–18.
Publication Date: 1993.
Acronym: ADI.
Scores: 8 sections to indicate presence or absence of a DSM-III-R diagnosis of psychoactive substance use disorder: Sociodemographic Factors, Psychosocial Stressors, Substance Use/Consumption History, Alcohol Use Symptoms, Cannabis Use Symptoms, Additional Drug Use Symptoms, Level of Functioning Domains, Orientation and Memory Screen; plus 8 psychiatric status screens: Depression, Mania, Eating Disorder, Delusional Thinking, Hallucinations, Attention Deficit Disorder, Anxiety Disorder, Conduct Disorder.
Administration: Individual.
Price Data, 2002: $78 per complete kit including 5 administration booklets and manual (46 pages); $35 per 5 administration booklets; $45 per manual.
Time: (45–55) minutes.
Comments: Structured interview for use with adolescents; complements the Personal Experience Inventory (1896).
Authors: Ken C. Winters and George A. Henly.
Publisher: Western Psychological Services.
Cross References: See T5:73 (1 reference); for reviews by Tony Toneatto and by Logan Wright, Donna Ford, and Karyll Kiser, see 12:16.

[81]
Adolescent Dissociative Experiences Scale.

Purpose: Designed as a "screening measure for pathological dissociation during adolescence."
Population: Ages 11–17.
Publication Date: 1996.
Acronym: A-DES.
Scores, 5: Dissociative Amnesia, Absorption and Imaginative Involvement, Depersonalization and Derealization, Passive Influence, Total.
Administration: Individual or group.
Price Data: Available from publisher
Time: (10–15) minutes.
Comments: A 30-item self-report measure, derived from the Dissociative Experiences Scale (original adult version) (846).
Authors: Judith Armstrong, Frank Putnam, and Eve Carlson.
Publisher: The Sidran Foundation.
Cross References: For reviews by Rosemary Flanagan and Ramasamy Manikam, see 14:8.

[82]
Adolescent Drinking Index.

Purpose: Constructed to "assess alcohol abuse in adolescents with psychological, emotional, or behavioral problems; identify referred adolescents who need further evaluation or treatment; and define the type of drinking problem the adolescent is experiencing."
Population: Ages 12–17.
Publication Dates: 1985–1989.
Acronym: ADI.
Scores, 3: Self-Medicated Drinking (MED), Aggressive/Rebellious Behavior (REB), Total.
Administration: Group or individual.
Price Data, 2005: $85 per Introductory Kit including manual (1989, 34 pages) and 25 test booklets.
Time: (5) minutes.
Comments: Test booklet title is Drinking & You.
Authors: Adele V. Harrell and Philip W. Wirtz.
Publisher: Psychological Assessment Resources, Inc.
Cross References: See T5:75 (1 reference); for reviews by Thomas F. Donlon and by Kevin J. McCarthy and Penelope W. Dralle, see 12:17.

[83]
Adolescent Language Screening Test.

Purpose: "Developed to screen for deficits in the dimensions of language use, content, and form" in adolescents.
Population: Ages 11–17.
Publication Date: 1984.
Acronym: ALST.
Scores: 7 subtests: Pragmatics, Receptive Vocabulary, Concepts, Expressive Vocabulary, Sentence Formulation, Morphology, Phonology.
Administration: Individual.
Price Data, 2006: $140 per complete kit including 50 test booklets, picture book, and examiner's manual (26 pages); $40 per 50 test booklets; $70 per picture book; $40 per examiner's manual.
Time: (10–15) minutes.
Authors: Denise L. Morgan and Arthur M. Guilford.
Publisher: PRO-ED.
Cross References: For reviews by Linda Crocker and by Robert T. Williams and Amy Finch-Williams, see 10:10.

[84]
Adolescent Psychopathology Scale.

Purpose: Designed to "evaluate symptoms of psychological disorders and distress in adolescents … measures psychopathology, personality, and social-emotional problems and competencies."
Population: Ages 12–19.
Publication Date: 1998.
Acronym: APS.
Scores: 40 scales in 4 domains: Clinical Disorders Domain (Attention-Deficit/Hyperactivity Disorder, Conduct Disorder, Oppositional-Defiant Disorder, Adjustment Disorder, Substance Abuse Disorder, Anorexia Nervosa, Bulimia Nervosa, Sleep Disorder, Somatization Disorder, Panic Disorder, Obsessive-Compulsive Disorder, Generalized Anxiety Disorder, Social Phobia, Separation Anxiety Disorder, Posttraumatic Stress Disorder, Major Depression, Dysthymic Disorder, Mania, Depersonalization Disorder, Schizophrenia); Personality Disorder Domain (Avoidant, Obsessive-Compulsive, Borderline, Schizotypal, Paranoid); Psychosocial Problem Content Domain (Self-Concept, Psycho-social Substance Use Difficulties, Introversion, Alienation-Boredom, Anger, Aggression, Interpersonal Problems, Emotional Lability, Disorientation, Suicide, Social Adaptation; Response Style Indicators (Lie, Consistency, Infrequency, Critical Item Endorsement); Factor Scales (Internalizing Disorder Factor, Externalizing Disorder Factor, Personality Disorder Factor).
Administration: Individual or group.
Price Data, 2006: $360 per introductory kit including CD ROM based scoring program, administration and interpretation manual, psychometric and technical manual, and 25 test booklets.
Time: (45–60) minutes.
Comments: A 346-item self-report scale; developed to be consistent with the DSM-IV disorders; test form is entitled Adolescent Mental Health Questionnaire; software for computerized (Windows) scoring program included.
Author: William M. Reynolds.
Publisher: Psychological Assessment Resources, Inc.
Cross References: For reviews by Timothy R. Konold and Wayne C. Piersel, see 14:9.

[85]
Adolescent Psychopathology Scale—Short Form.

Purpose: Constructed as a "multidimensional measure of psychopathology and personality characteristics derived from the APS to evaluate symptoms of psychological disorder and distress consistent with DSM-IV symptom specifications."
Population: Ages 12–19 years.
Publication Dates: 1998–2000.
Acronym: APS-SF.
Scores, 14: Defensiveness, Consistency Response, Conduct Disorder, Oppositional Defiant Disorder, Substance Abuse Disorder, Anger/Violence Proneness, Academic Problems, Generalized Anxiety Disorder, Posttraumatic Stress Disorder, Major Depression, Eating Disturbance, Suicide, Self-Concept, Interpersonal Problems.
Administration: Group or individual.

Price Data, 2006: $235 per Introductory kit including CD ROM based unlimited use scoring program with on-screen user's guide, professional manual, and 25 test booklets.

Time: (15–20) minutes.

Comments: Derived from the Adolescent Psychopathology Scale (APS; 84).

Authors: William M. Reynolds.

Publisher: Psychological Assessment Resources, Inc.

Cross References: For reviews by Janet F. Carlson and Steven I. Pfeiffer, see 15:11.

[86]
Adolescent Separation Anxiety Test.

Purpose: "Provides a measure of emotional and personality patterns which adolescents show in reaction to separation experiences."

Population: Ages 11–18.

Publication Dates: 1972–1980.

Scores, 28: 18 association responses (Rejection, Impaired Concentration, Phobic Feeling, Anxiety, Loneliness, Withdrawal, Somatic, Adaptive Reaction, Anger, Projection, Empathy, Evasion, Fantasy, Well-Being, Sublimation, Intrapunitive, Identify Stress, Total), plus 10 derived response patterns (Attachment, Individuation, Hostility, Painful Tension, Reality Avoidance, Concentration Impairment and Sublimation, Self-Love, Identity Stress, Absurd Responses, Attachment-Individuation Balance).

Administration: Individual.

Forms: Separate forms for boys and girls.

Price Data: Not available.

Time: Administration time not reported.

Comments: Formerly titled Separation Anxiety Test.

Author: Henry G. Hansburg.

Publisher: Krieger Publishing Company [No reply from publisher; status unknown].

Cross References: See T5:78 (1 reference) and T4:100 (1 reference); for reviews by Brenda Bailey-Richardson and Carolyn S. Hartsough, see 9:53.

[87]
Adolescent Symptom Inventory-4.

Purpose: Designed as a "screening instrument for the behavioral, affective, and cognitive symptoms of a variety of adolescent psychiatric disorders."

Population: Ages 12–18.

Publication Dates: 1997–1998.

Acronym: ASI-4.

Scores, 15: 11 scores shared on both Parent and Teacher Forms: AD/HD Inattentive, Hyperactive-Impulsive, Combined, Conduct Disorder, Oppositional Defiant, Generalized Anxiety Disorder, Schizoid Personality, Schizophrenia, Major Depressive Disorder, Dysthymic Disorder, Bipolar Disorder; 4 additional scores on the Parent Form: Antisocial Personality Disorder, Separation Anxiety, Anorexia Nervosa, Bulimia Nervosa.

Administration: Individual.

Forms, 2: Teacher Checklist, Parent Checklist.

Price Data, 2006: $102 per deluxe kit including 25 parent checklists, 25 teacher checklists, 50 symptom count score sheets, 50 parent and teacher symptom severity profile score sheets, , screening manual (1997, 145 pages), and norms manual (1998, 168 pages); $52 per 50 parent checklists; $38 per 50 teacher checklists.

Time: [10–15] minutes.

Comments: Checklists completed by teachers and caregivers about adolescents; scores are not intended for diagnostic purposes, only screening purposes.

Authors: Kenneth D. Gadow and Joyce Sprafkin.

Publisher: Checkmate Plus, Ltd.

Cross References: For reviews by Stephen N. Axford and Patti L. Harrison, see 15:12.

[88]
Adult Attention Deficit Disorders Evaluation Scale.

Purpose: Designed to provide a measure of inattention and hyperactivity-impulsivity in adults.

Population: Adults.

Publication Dates: 1996–1997.

Scores, 3: Inattentive, Hyperactive-Impulsive, Total Percentile Rank.

Administration: Individual.

Price Data, 2006: $175 per complete kit including 50 self-report rating forms, 50 Home Version rating forms, 50 Work Version rating forms, Self-Report technical manual (1996, 43 pages), Home Version technical manual (1996, 41 pages), Work Version technical manual (1996, 40 pages), and Adult Attention Deficit Disorders Intervention manual (1997, 183 pages); $35 per 50 rating forms (specify Self-Report, Home Version, or Work Version); $22 per 50 ADDES/DSM-IV forms; $15 per technical manual (specify Self-Report, Home Version, or Work Version); $25 per Adult Attention Deficit Disorders Intervention manual; $2 per Comparing the Technical Aspects of Adult Attention-Deficit/Hyperactivity Disorder Rating Scales review.

Time: Untimed.

Comments: Behavioral rating system with three

Forms: Home, Work, and Self-Report; may be completed in one sitting or over a period of days.

Authors: Stephen B. McCarney and Paul D. Anderson.

Publisher: Hawthorne Educational Services, Inc.

   a) HOME VERSION.

   Comments: To be completed by a spouse or other close relative/friend who observes daily behavior in the home; best when used in conjunction with Work and Self-Report versions.

b) WORK VERSION.
Comments: To be completed by an employer, supervisor, or fellow employee who can closely observe the subject's work behaviors; best when used in conjunction with Work and Self-Report versions.
Cross References: For reviews by Helen Kitchens and James C. Reed, see 14:10.

[89]
Adult Basic Learning Examination, Second Edition.

Purpose: "Designed to measure the educational achievement of adults who may or may not have completed twelve years of schooling . . . also useful in evaluating efforts to raise the educational level of these adults."
Population: Adults with less than 12 years of formal schooling.
Publication Dates: 1986–1990.
Acronym: ABLE.
Administration: Group.
Levels, 3: 1, 2, 3 and placement test (SelectABLE).
Forms, 2: E, F (equivalent forms).
Price Data, 2002: $67 per examination kit containing test booklets and directions for administering for 1 form of each of the 3 levels, hand-scorable answer sheet, Ready Score® Answer Sheet and group record for Level 2, and SelectABLE Ready Score® Answer Sheet; $43.50 per Handbook of Instructional Techniques and Materials (1986, 67 pages); $51.90 per norms booklet (specify level); $13.80 per Reading Supplement.
Foreign Language Edition: Spanish edition (1990) ABLE Screening Battery available for Level 2 Reading and Mathematics subtests only.
Authors: Bjorn Karlsen and Eric F. Gardner.
Publisher: PsychCorp, A brand of Harcourt Assessment, Inc.

a) SELECTABLE.
Purpose: A screening test to determine which level of ABLE is most suitable for use with a particular individual.
Price Data: $72.60 per 25 Ready Score® Answer Sheets; $44.50 per 50 hand-scorable test sheets; $37.60 per scoring key; $12.70 per SelectABLE Handbook (1986, 15 pages).
Time: (15) minutes.
b) LEVEL 1.
Population: Adults with 1–4 years of formal education.
Scores, 5: Vocabulary, Reading Comprehension, Spelling, Number Operations, Problem Solving.
Price Data: $89 per 25 hand-scorable test booklets and directions for administering including

group record (specify Form E or F); $77.40 per scoring key (specify Form E or F); $10.60 per directions for administering (1986, 38 pages).
Time: (130–165) minutes.
c) LEVEL 2.
Population: Adults with 5–8 years of formal education.
Scores: Same as *b* plus Language.
Price Data: $89 per 25 hand-scorable or reusable test booklets (specify Form E or F); $77.40 per scoring key (specify Form E or F); $79.50 per 25 Ready Score® Answer Sheets (specify Form E or F); $66.80 per 50 hand-scorable answer sheets and 2 group records; $10.60 per directions for administering Levels 2 and 3.
Time: (175–215) minutes.
d) LEVEL 3.
Population: Adults with 9–12 years of formal schooling who may or may not have completed 12 years of schooling.
Scores: Same as *c* above.
Price Data: Same as *c* above.
Time: Same as *c* above.
Cross References: See T5:82 (1 reference); for reviews by Anne R. Fitzpatrick and Robert T. Williams, see 11:9 (1 reference); see also T3:121 (6 references), 8:2 (4 references), and T2:3 (3 references); for a review by A. N. Hieronymus of the earlier edition and excerpted reviews by Edward B. Fry and James W. Hall of Levels 1 and 2 of the earlier edition, see 7:3.

[90]
Adult Language Assessment Scales.

Purpose: "Designed to provide complete information about language proficiency of adults who speak English as a Second or Foreign Language.
Population: Adults.
Publication Date: 1991.
Acronym: A-LAS®.
Scores, 10: Listening (Conversations, Same/Different, Total), Speaking (Vocabulary, Making Sentences, Newscast, Sounds, Total), Pronunciation, Total.
Administration: Individual.
Forms, 2: A, and B.
Price Data, 2002: $201.95 per complete kit (Form A) including oral administration manual (28 pages) (Forms A and B), oral scoring and interpretation manual (53 pages) (Forms A and B), cue picture book (Form A), audiocassette for the oral language component (Form A), audiocassette for the additional pronunciation section (Form A), audiocassette holder, and 50 answer booklets (Form A); $142.55 per augmentation kit (Form B including cue picture book (Form B), audiocassette for oral language component (Form B), audiocassette for pronunciation section (Form B), and 50 answer booklets (Form B); $110.15 per 25 reading

and mathematics booklets (specify level and Form); $75.60 per 50 writing booklets (specify Form); $43.20 per 50 reading and mathematics answer sheets (specify level); $51.85 per 50 oral answer booklets (specify form); $45.35 per 50 oral profile sheets (specify form); $31.30 per oral administration manual; $32.40 per oral scoring and interpretation manual; $45.35 per cue picture book (specify form); $20.55 per audiocassette (specify form and story).

Time: (25–30) minutes.

Comments: Includes equivalent forms, A and B.

Authors: Sharon E. Duncan and Edward A. DeAvila.

Publisher: CTB/McGraw-Hill.

Cross References: For reviews by Roger A. Richards and Wayne H. Slater, see 14:11.

[91]
Adult Level of Care Index-2R.

Purpose: "To provide assessment summation and documentation for addictions treatment planning."

Population: Adults.

Publication Date: 2001.

Acronym: LOCI-2R.

Scores: 56 ratings: 5 Acute Intoxication/Withdrawal (Outpatient Detoxification, Ambulatory Detoxification with Extended On-Site Monitoring, Clinically Managed Residential Detoxification, Medically Monitored Inpatient Detoxification, Medically Managed Intensive Inpatient Detoxification); 8 Biomedical Conditions/Complications (Outpatient Treatment, Intensive Outpatient Treatment, Partial Hospitalization, Clinically Managed Low-/Medium-/High-Intensity Residential Treatment, Medically Monitored Intensive Inpatient, Medically Managed Inpatient Services); 9 Emotional, Behavioral, or Cognitive Conditions and Complications (Early Intervention, Outpatient Services, Intensive Outpatient, Partial Hospitalization, Clinically Managed Low-/Medium-/High-Intensity Residential Treatment, Medically Monitored Intensive Inpatient Services, Medically Managed Inpatient Services); 9 Readiness to Change (Early Intervention, Outpatient Services, Intensive Outpatient Treatment, Partial Hospitalization, Clinically Managed Low-/Medium-/High-Intensity Residential Treatment, Medically Monitored Inpatient Treatment, Medically Managed Inpatient Treatment); 9 Relapse, Continued Use, or Continued Problem Potential (Early Intervention, Outpatient Treatment, Intensive Outpatient Treatment, Partial Hospitalization, Clinically Managed Low-/Medium-/High-Intensity Residential Treatment, Medically Monitored Intensive Inpatient, Medically Managed Inpatient Treatment); 9 Recovery Environment (Early Intervention, Outpatient Treatment, Intensive Outpatient Treatment, Partial Hospitalization, Clinically Managed Low-/Medium-/High-Intensity Residential Treatment, Medically Monitored Inpatient Treatment, Medi-

cally Managed Inpatient Treatment); 6 Opioid Maintenance Therapy (Acute Intoxication/Withdrawal; Biomedical Conditions and Complications; Emotional, Behavioral, or Cognitive Conditions and Complications; Readiness to Change; Relapse, Continued Use, or Continued Problem Potential; Recovery Environment); Level of Care Indicated.

Administration: Individual.

Price Data: Available from publisher.

Time: Variable.

Comments: Not a psychometric instrument; summary checklist provides an estimate of the likelihood that an individual meets the criteria for substance abuse or dependency on six dimensions in accordance with the criteria of the American Society of Addiction Medicine; also indicates overall level of care needed.

Authors: Norman G. Hoffmann, David Mee-Lee, and Gerald D. Shulman.

Publisher: Change Companies.

[92]
The Adult Manifest Anxiety Scale.

Purpose: Used to evaluate the level of anxiety experienced by individuals across the age spectrum from early adulthood to elderly.

Population: Ages 19–59, college students, ages 60 and over.

Publication Date: 2003.

Administration: Group.

Levels, 3: AMAS-A, AMAS-C, AMAS-E.

Price Data, 2006: $102 per kit including 30 AutoScore™ answer forms (10 for each subtest) and manual (44 pages); $37.95 per 20 AutoScore™ answer forms; $49.50 per manual.

Time: 10 minutes.

Comments: All three scales together represent an upward extension of the Revised Children's Manifest Anxiety Scale (2159); the original CMAS was a downward extension of the Taylor Manifest Anxiety Scale.

Authors: Cecil R. Reynolds, Bert O. Richmond, and Patricia A. Lowe.

Publisher: Western Psychological Services.

a) AMAS-A.

Population: Ages 19–59.

Acronym: AMAS-A.

Scores, 5: Worry/Oversensitivity, Physiological Anxiety, Social Concerns/Stress, Lie, Worry.

b) AMAS-C.

Population: College students.

Acronym: AMAS-C.

Scores, 6: Worry/Oversensitivity, Physiological Anxiety, Social Concerns/Stress, Test Anxiety, Lie, Total.

c) AMAS-E.

Population: Ages 60 and over.

Acronym: AMAS-E.

Scores, 5: Worry/Oversensitivity, Physiological Anxiety, Fear of Aging, Lie, Total.
Cross References: For a review by Ashraf Kagee, see 16:7.

[93]
Adult Personality Inventory [Revised].

Purpose: Designed as a "tool for analyzing and reporting differences in personality, interpersonal style, and career preferences."
Population: Ages 16–adult.
Publication Dates: 1982–1996.
Acronym: API.
Scores, 25: Personality Scores (Extroverted, Adjusted, Tough-Minded, Independent, Disciplined, Creative, Enterprising); Interpersonal Style Scores (Caring, Adapting, Withdrawn, Submissive, Uncaring, Non-Conforming, Sociable, Assertive); Career/Life-style Scores (Practical, Scientific, Aesthetic, Social, Competitive, Structured); Validity Scores (Good Impression, Bad Impression, Infrequency, Uncertainty).
Administration: Group or individual.
Time: (45–60) minutes.
Comments: Self-report; computer scored and interpreted.
Author: Samuel E. Krug.
Publisher: MetriTech, Inc.
  a) API NARRATIVE REPORTS.
  Purpose: "Oriented to the test taker, provides users with scores, extensive interpretive information in narrative form, and a series of questions that systematically guide the reader toward a practical application of assessment data."
  Price Data, 2005: $49 per Narrative Report kit including Interpretive and Technical Guide (1996, 53 pages), processing of 5 reports, 2 reusable test booklets, and 5 answer sheets; $48.75 per 5 reports; $89.50 per 10 reports; $196.25 per 25 reports; $337.50 per 50 reports; $16.50 per manual; $16 per 10 reusable test booklets.
  b) API/PC.
  Purpose: "Administers, scores, and generates immediate test results for the same 21 scales and validity checks as the API Narrative Report."
  Price Data: $54 per API/PC Introductory kit including manual (1996, 21 pages), and 5-report demo disk; $18 per manual; $105 per 10 administrations disk; $237.50 per 25 administrations disk; $400 per 50 administrations disk; [off-line assessment support materials: $16 per 10 reusable test booklets; $14 per 50 answer sheets; $20 per 50 scannable answer sheets; $36 per 50 decision model worksheets].
  Comments: Supports both on-line or off-line testing; IBM version only (3.5-inch DD); optional

189-item short version requires 25–35 minutes for administration.
  c) API/CAREER PROFILE.
  Purpose: Oriented to the test administrator and compares the individual test taker with Occupational Decision Models and user created models.
  Forms, 2: Form E "includes expanded descriptions of the 6 career/lifestyle factors;" Form M offers "automatic comparisons of the individual test taker to each of the decision models."
  Price Data: $59 per API/Career Profile Introductory Kit (Form E or M) including API/Career Profile manual (n.d., 71 pages), and 5-report demo disk; $120 per 10 administrations disk; $275 per 25 administrations disk; $475 per 50 administrations disk; $20 per manual.
  Comments: Supports both on-line or off-line testing; IBM version only; optional 189-item short version requires 25–35 minutes for administration.
Cross References: For a review by Kevin Lanning, see 14:12; for a review by Rik Carl D'Amato of an earlier edition, see 12:20; see also T4:106 (4 references); for a review by Brian Bolton of an earlier edition, see 9:54.

[94]
Adult Rating of Oral English.

Purpose: "Designed to assess the oral English language skills of secondary and adult students" who speak English as a second language.
Population: Adult and secondary students in vocational education and employment training programs.
Publication Date: 1995.
Acronym: AROE.
Scores, 15: Pronunciation, Grammar, General Vocabulary, Vocational Vocabulary, Building Blocks Subscore; Listener and Speaker scores for Conversation, Instructions, Explanations, Clarification/Verification; Discourse Subscore; Mean Proficiency Score; Total Score.
Administration: Individual.
Price Data, 2006: $75 per training kit including 5 user's handbooks (43 pages) and 25 matrix scoring sheets; $20 per set of 25 matrix scoring sheets; $15 per user's handbook; $10 per technical manual (16 pages); $15 per supplementary video explaining use and purpose.
Time: Untimed.
Comments: A rating scale completed by teachers about individual students' skills; supplementary video explaining use and purpose is available.
Authors: Annette M. Zehler and Patricia A. DiCerbo.
Publisher: Development Associates, Inc.
Cross References: For reviews by Roger A. Richards and Gerald Tindal, see 14:13.

[95]
The Adult Self Expression Scale.

Purpose: Assesses the assertiveness level of the respondent.
Population: Adults.
Publication Dates: 1974-1975.
Acronym: ASES.
Scores: Total score only.
Administration: Group or individual.
Price Data: Available from publisher.
Time: Administration time not reported.
Authors: Melvin L. Gay, James G. Hollandsworth, Jr., and John P. Galassi.
Publisher: Adult Self Expression Scale.
Cross References: See T5:88 (2 references) and T4:107 (1 reference); for reviews by Philip H. Dreyer and Goldine C. Gleser, see 9:55 (15 references).

[96]
Adult Suicidal Ideation Questionnaire.

Purpose: "Designed to evaluate the presence and frequency of suicidal thoughts."
Population: Ages 18 and over.
Publication Dates: 1987–1991.
Acronym: ASIQ.
Scores: Total score only.
Administration: Individual or group.
Price Data, 2006: $78 per introductory kit including manual (1991, 62 pages) and 25 respondent forms.
Time: (5–10) minutes.
Author: William M. Reynolds.
Publisher: Psychological Assessment Resources, Inc.
Cross References: See T5:89 (1 reference); for reviews by Debra E. Cole and Isadore Newman, see 12:21.

[97]
Advanced Measures of Music Audiation.

Purpose: Developed to measure music aptitude.
Population: Junior high school through college.
Publication Date: 1989.
Scores, 3: Tonal, Rhythm, Total.
Administration: Group.
Price Data, 2006: $70 per complete kit including compact disc, 100 answer sheets, and manual (54 pages); $20 per 100 answer sheets; $10 per manual; $20 per set of scoring stencils (scoring stencils not part of complete kit); $25 per compact disc; scoring service available from publisher at $1 per student.
Time: 16(20) minutes.
Comments: CD player necessary for administration; upward extension of the Intermediate Measures of Music Audiation (1260).
Author: Edwin E. Gordon.
Publisher: GIA Publications, Inc.
Cross References: For reviews by Rudolf E. Radocy and James W. Sherbon, see 12:22.

[98]
Advanced Placement Examination in Art History.

Purpose: Designed to measure college-level achievement of students in art history.
Population: High school students desiring credit for college-level courses and admission to advanced courses.
Publication Dates: 1972–2005.
Scores: Total score only.
Administration: Group.
Price Data: Available from publisher.
Time: 180 minutes.
Comments: Available to secondary schools for annual administration on specific days in May; inactive form and previous free-response questions available; program sponsored by the College Board with exams administered by Educational Testing Service.
Authors: Educational Testing Service.
Publisher: The College Board.
Cross References: For additional information concerning an earlier edition, see 8:83. For reviews of the AP® Program, see 8:471 (2 reviews) and 7:662 (2 reviews).

[99]
Advanced Placement Examination in Biology.

Purpose: Designed to measure college-level achievement of students in biology.
Population: High school students desiring credit for college-level courses and admission to advanced courses.
Publication Dates: 1956–2005.
Scores: Total score only.
Administration: Group.
Price Data: Available from publisher.
Time: 180 minutes.
Comments: Available to secondary schools for annual administration on specific days in May; inactive form and previous free-response questions available; program sponsored by the College Board with exams administered by Educational Testing Service.
Authors: Educational Testing Service.
Publisher: The College Board.
Cross References: See T5:92 (1 reference), T4:110 (1 reference), 8:381 (1 reference), and 7:807 (1 reference); for a review by Clarence H. Nelson of earlier forms, see 6:893 (1 reference); for a review by Clark W. Horton, see 5:724. For reviews of the AP® Program, see 8:471 (2 reviews) and 7:662 (2 reviews).

[100]
Advanced Placement Examination in Calculus.

Purpose: Designed to measure college-level achievement of students in calculus.

Population: High school students desiring credit for college-level courses and admission to advanced courses.
Publication Dates: 1954–2005.
Scores: Total score only.
Administration: Group.
Levels, 2: AB, BC (candidate elects only one).
Price Data: Available from publisher.
Time: 195 minutes.
Comments: Available to secondary schools for annual administration on specific days in May; inactive form and previous free-response questions available; program sponsored by the College Board with exams administered by Educational Testing Service.
Author: Educational Testing Service.
Publisher: The College Board.
   a) CALCULUS AB.
   Scores: Total score only.
   Comments: Covers differential and integral calculus topics typically included in an introductory Calculus I college course.
   b) CALCULUS BC.
   Scores: Total score plus an AB subscore.
   Comments: Covers the Calculus AB topics, as well as additional topics in differential and integral calculus, and series.
Cross References: See T5:93 (1 reference), 8:309 (1 reference), T2:742 (1 reference), 7:451 (2 references), and 6:570 (4 references); for a review by Paul L. Dressel of an earlier form, see 5:419. For reviews of the AP® Program, see 8:471 (2 reviews) and 7:662 (2 reviews).

[101]
Advanced Placement Examination in Chemistry.

Purpose: Designed to measure college-level achievement of students in chemistry.
Population: High school students desiring credit for college-level courses and admission to advanced courses.
Publication Dates: 1954–2005.
Scores: Total score only.
Administration: Group.
Price Data: Available from publisher.
Time: 180 minutes.
Comments: Available to secondary schools for annual administration on specific days in May; inactive form and previous free-response questions available; program sponsored by the College Board with exams administered by Educational Testing Service.
Author: Educational Testing Service.
Publisher: The College Board.
Cross References: See T5:94 (3 references) and T4:111 (1 reference); for a review by J. Arthur Campbell, see 8:846; see also T2:1832 (1 reference) and 6:915 (1 reference); for a review by Theo A. Ashford of an

earlier form, see 5:743. For reviews of the AP® Program, see 8:471 (2 reviews) and 7:662 (2 reviews).

[102]
Advanced Placement Examination in Comparative Government and Politics.

Purpose: Designed to measure college-level achievement of students in comparative government and politics.
Population: High school students desiring credit for college-level courses and admission to advanced courses.
Publication Dates: 1987–2005.
Scores: Total score only.
Administration: Group.
Price Data: Available from publisher.
Time: 145 minutes.
Comments: Available to secondary schools for annual administration on specific days in May; inactive forms and previous free-response questions available; program sponsored by the College Board with exams administered by Educational Testing Service.
Author: Educational Testing Service.
Publisher: The College Board.

[103]
Advanced Placement Examination in Computer Science.

Purpose: Designed to measure college-level achievement of students in computer science.
Population: High school students desiring credit for college-level courses and admission to advanced courses.
Scores: Total score only.
Administration: Group.
Levels, 2: A, AB (candidate elects only one).
Price Data: Available from publisher.
Comments: Available to secondary schools for annual administration on specific days in May; inactive forms and previous free-response questions available; program sponsored by the College Board with exams administered by Educational Testing Service.
Author: Educational Testing Service.
Publisher: The College Board.
   a) COMPUTER SCIENCE A.
   Publication Dates: 1988–2005.
   Time: 180 minutes.
   Comments: Covers topics in a first-semester introductory college course in computer science; emphasizes programming in C++, programming methodology (including recursion), and procedural abstraction; also includes algorithms, data structures, and data abstraction.
   b) COMPUTER SCIENCE AB.
   Publication Dates: 1984–2005.
   Time: 180 minutes.
   Comments: Covers topics in a full-year introductory college course in computer science; in-

cludes all the topics in Computer Science A as well as more in-depth algorithm analysis (Big-Oh notation) and dynamic data structures.

[104]
Advanced Placement Examination in English—Language and Composition.
Purpose: Designed to measure college-level achievement of students in English language and composition. **Population:** High school students desiring credit for college-level courses and admission to advanced courses. **Publication Dates:** 1981–2005. **Scores:** Total score only. **Administration:** Group. **Price Data:** Available from publisher. **Time:** 180 minutes. **Comments:** Available to secondary schools for annual administration on specific days in May; inactive form and previous free-response questions available; program sponsored by the College Board with exams administered by Educational Testing Service. **Author:** Educational Testing Service. **Publisher:** The College Board. **Cross References:** See T5:97 (1 reference); for additional information and a review by Ellis Batten Page of an earlier edition, see 8:39; see also T2:51 (2 references) and 7:184 (1 reference); for a review by Robert C. Pooley of an earlier form of the English composition test, see 5:205. For reviews of the AP® Program, see 8:471 (2 reviews) and 7:662 (2 reviews).

[105]
Advanced Placement Examination in English—Literature and Composition.
Purpose: Designed to measure college-level achievement of students in English literature and composition. **Population:** High school students desiring credit for college-level courses and admission to advanced courses. **Publication Dates:** 1956–2005. **Scores:** Total score only. **Administration:** Group. **Price Data:** Available from publisher. **Time:** 180 minutes. **Comments:** Available to secondary schools for annual administration on specific days in May; inactive form and previous free-response questions available; program sponsored by the College Board with exams administered by Educational Testing Service. **Author:** Educational Testing Service. **Publisher:** The College Board. **Cross References:** See T4:112 (2 references); for a review by Ellis Batten Page of an earlier edition, see 8:39; see also T2:51 (2 references) and 7:184 (1 reference); for a review by Robert C. Pooley of an earlier form of the English composition test, see 5:205; for a review by John S. Diekhoff of an earlier form of the

literature test, see 5:211. For reviews of the AP® Program, see 8:471 (2 reviews) and 7:662 (2 reviews).

[106]
Advanced Placement Examination in Environmental Science.
Purpose: Designed to measure college-level achievement of students in environmental science. **Population:** High school students desiring credit for college-level courses and admission to advanced courses. **Publication Dates:** 1998–2005. **Scores:** Total score only. **Administration:** Group. **Price Data:** Available from publisher. **Time:** 180 minutes. **Comments:** Available to secondary schools for annual administration on specific days in May; inactive forms and previous free-response questions available; program sponsored by the College Board with exams administered by Educational Testing Service. **Author:** Educational Testing Service. **Publisher:** The College Board.

[107]
Advanced Placement Examination in European History.
Purpose: Designed to measure college-level achievement of students in European history. **Population:** High school students desiring credit for college-level courses and admission to advanced courses. **Publication Dates:** 1956–2005. **Scores:** Total score only. **Administration:** Group. **Price Data:** Available from publisher. **Time:** 185 minutes. **Comments:** Available to secondary schools for annual administration on specific days in May; inactive form and previous free-response questions available; program sponsored by the College Board with exams administered by Educational Testing Service. **Author:** Educational Testing Service. **Publisher:** The College Board. **Cross References:** See T5:100 (1 reference), T4:114 (1 reference), 8:908 (1 reference), and 6:1001 (2 references). For reviews of the AP® Program, see 8:471 (2 reviews) and 7:662 (2 reviews).

[108]
Advanced Placement Examination in French Language.
Purpose: Designed to measure college-level achievement of students in the French language. **Population:** High school students desiring credit for college-level courses and admission to advanced courses. **Publication Dates:** 1971–2005. **Scores:** Total score only.

Administration: Group.
Price Data: Available from publisher.
Time: 165 minutes.
Comments: Available to secondary schools for annual administration on apecific days in May; inactive form and previous free-response questions available; program sponsored by the College Board with exams administered by Educational Testing Service.
Author: Educational Testing Service.
Publisher: The College Board.
Cross References: See T3:131 (1 reference); for additional information and a review by Michio Peter Hagiwara, see 8:112. For reviews of the AP® Program, see 8:471 (2 reviews).

[109]
Advanced Placement Examination in French Literature.

Purpose: Designed to measure college-level achievement of students in French literature.
Population: High school students desiring credit for college-level courses and admission to advanced courses.
Publication Dates: 1954–2005.
Scores: Total score only.
Administration: Group.
Price Data: Available from publisher.
Time: 180 minutes.
Comments: Available to secondary schools for annual administration on specific days in May; inactive form and previous free-response questions available; program sponsored by the College Board with exams administered by Educational Testing Service.
Author: Educational Testing Service.
Publisher: The College Board.
Cross References: For additional information and reviews by Michio Peter Hagiwara and Joseph A. Murphy, see 8:113 (3 references); see also 7:268 (1 reference) and 6:368 (3 references). For a review of the AP® Program, see 8:471 (2 reviews) and 7:662 (2 reviews).

[110]
Advanced Placement Examination in German Language.

Purpose: Designed to measure college-level achievement of students in German language.
Population: High school students desiring credit for college-level courses and admission to advanced courses.
Publication Dates: 1956–2005.
Scores: Total score only.
Administration: Group.
Price Data: Available from publisher.
Time: 150 minutes.
Comments: Available to secondary schools for annual administration on specific days in May; inactive form and previous free-response questions available;

program sponsored by the College Board with exams administered by Educational Testing Service.
Author: Educational Testing Service.
Publisher: The College Board.
Cross References: For reviews of the AP® Program, see 8:471 (2 reviews) and 7:662 (2 reviews).

[111]
Advanced Placement Examination in Human Geography.

Purpose: Designed to measure college-level achievement of students in human geography.
Population: High school students desiring credit for college-level courses and admission to advanced courses.
Publication Dates: 2001–2005.
Scores: Total score only.
Administration: Group.
Price Data: Available from publisher.
Time: 135 minutes.
Comments: Available to secondary schools for annual administration on specific days in May; inactive form and previous free-response questions available; program sponsored by the College Board with exams administered by Educational Testing Service.
Author: Educational Testing Service.
Publisher: The College Board.

[112]
Advanced Placement Examination in Latin Literature.

Purpose: Designed to measure college-level achievement of students in Latin literature.
Population: High school students desiring credit for college-level courses and admission to advanced courses.
Publication Dates: 1980–2005.
Scores: Total score only.
Administration: Group.
Price Data: Available from publisher.
Time: 180 minutes.
Comments: Available to secondary schools for annual administration on specific days in May; inactive form and previous free-response questions available; program sponsored by the College Board with exams administered by Educational Testing Service.
Author: Educational Testing Service.
Publisher: The College Board.
Cross References: For additional information concerning an earlier edition of the Classics examination, see 8:144 (3 references). For reviews of the AP® Program, see 8:471 (2 reviews) and 7:662 (2 reviews).

[113]
Advanced Placement Examination in Latin— Vergil.

Purpose: Designed to measure college-level achievement of students in Latin (Vergil).

Population: High school students desiring credit for college-level courses and admission to advanced courses.
Publication Dates: 1972–2005.
Scores: Total score only.
Administration: Group.
Price Data: Available from publisher.
Time: 180 minutes.
Comments: Available to secondary schools for annual administration on specific days in May; inactive form and previous free-response questions available; program sponsored by the College Board with exams administered by Educational Testing Service.
Author: Educational Testing Service.
Publisher: The College Board.
Cross References: For additional information concerning an earlier edition of the classics examination, see 8:144 (3 references). For reviews of the AP® Program, see 8:471 (2 reviews) and 7:662 (2 reviews).

[114]

Advanced Placement Examination in Macroeconomics.

Purpose: Designed to measure college-level achievement of students in macroeconomics.
Population: High school students desiring credit for college-level courses and admission to advanced courses.
Publication Dates: 1989–2005.
Scores: Total score only.
Administration: Group.
Price Data: Available from publisher.
Time: 130 minutes.
Comments: Available to secondary schools for annual administration on specific days in May; inactive forms and previous free-response questions available; program sponsored by the College Board with exams administered by Educational Testing Service.
Author: Educational Testing Service.
Publisher: The College Board.

[115]

Advanced Placement Examination in Microeconomics.

Purpose: Designed to measure college-level achievement of students in microeconomics.
Population: High school students desiring credit for college-level courses and admission to advanced courses.
Publication Dates: 1989–2005.
Scores: Total score only.
Administration: Group.
Price Data: Available from publisher.
Time: 130 minutes.
Comments: Available to secondary schools for annual administration on specific days in May; inactive forms and previous free-response questions available; program sponsored by the College Board with exams administered by Educational Testing Service.

Author: Educational Testing Service.
Publisher: The College Board.

[116]

Advanced Placement Examination in Music Theory.

Purpose: Designed to measure college-level achievement of students in music theory.
Population: High school students desiring credit for college-level courses and admission to advanced courses.
Publication Dates: 1978–2005.
Scores, 3: Aural, Nonaural, Total.
Administration: Group.
Price Data: Available from publisher.
Time: 180 minutes.
Comments: Available to secondary schools for annual administration on specific days in May; inactive form and previous free-response questions available; program sponsored by the College Board with exams administered by Educational Testing Service.
Author: Educational Testing Service.
Publisher: The College Board.
Cross References: For additional information regarding an earlier edition of the Music Examination, see 8:90. For reviews of the AP® Program, see 8:471 (2 reviews).

[117]

Advanced Placement Examination in Physics.

Purpose: Designed to measure college-level achievement of students in physics.
Population: High school students desiring credit for college-level courses and admission to advanced courses.
Publication Dates: 1954–2005.
Administration: Group.
Levels, 2: B, C (candidate elects only one).
Price Data: Available from publisher.
Comments: Available to secondary schools for annual administration on specific days in May; inactive forms and previous free-response questions available; program sponsored by the College Board with exams administered by Educational Testing Service.
Author: Educational Testing Service.
Publisher: The College Board.
a) PHYSICS B.
Scores: Total score only.
Comments: Equivalent of 1-year terminal course in noncalculus-based college physics.
Time: 180 minutes.
b) PHYSICS C.
Scores: 1 or 2 scores: Mechanics (Part 1), Electricity and Magnetism (Part 2).
Comments: Equivalent of 1-year nonterminal course in calculus-based college physics; 2 parts in each test booklet (candidate elects either one or both parts).
Time: 90 minutes for each part.

Cross References: See T3:143 (1 reference); for a review by Mario Iona, see 8:862 (3 references); see also 6:927 (2 references); for a review by Leo Nedelsky of an earlier form, see 5:750. For reviews of the AP® Program, see 8:471 (2 reviews) and 7:662 (2 reviews).

[118]
Advanced Placement Examination in Psychology.

Purpose: Designed to measure college-level achievement of students in psychology.
Population: High school students desiring credit for college-level courses and admission to advanced courses.
Publication Dates: 1992–2005.
Scores: Total score only.
Administration: Group.
Price Data: Available from publisher.
Time: 120 minutes.
Comments: Available to secondary schools for annual administration on specific days in May; inactive forms and previous free-response questions available; program sponsored by the College Board with exams administered by Educational Testing Service.
Author: Educational Testing Service.
Publisher: The College Board.

[119]
Advanced Placement Examination in Spanish Language.

Purpose: Designed to measure college-level achievement of students in Spanish language.
Population: High school students desiring credit for college-level courses and admission to advanced courses.
Publication Dates: 1976–2005.
Scores: Total score only.
Administration: Group.
Price Data: Available from publisher.
Time: 170 minutes.
Comments: Available to secondary schools for annual administration on specific days in May; inactive form and previous free-response questions available; program sponsored by the College Board with exams administered by Educational Testing Service.
Author: Educational Testing Service.
Publisher: The College Board.
Cross References: See T3:139 (1 reference); for a review by George W. Ayer of an earlier edition, see 8:153 (1 reference); see also 7:313 (2 references) and 6:421 (1 reference). For reviews of the AP® Program, see 8:471 (2 reviews) and 7:662 (2 reviews).

[120]
Advanced Placement Examination in Spanish Literature.

Purpose: Designed to measure college-level achievement of students in Spanish literature.

Population: High school students desiring credit for college-level courses and admission to advanced courses.
Publication Dates: 1956–2005.
Scores: Total score only.
Administration: Group.
Price Data: Available from publisher.
Time: 190 minutes.
Comments: Available to secondary schools for annual administration on specific days in May; inactive form and previous free-response questions available; program sponsored by the College Board with exams administered by Educational Testing Service.
Author: Educational Testing Service.
Publisher: The College Board.
Cross References: For a review by George W. Ayer of an earlier edition, see 8:153 (1 reference); see also 7:313 (2 references) and 6:421 (1 reference). For reviews of the AP® Program, see 8:471 (2 reviews) and 7:662 (2 reviews).

[121]
Advanced Placement Examination in Statistics.

Purpose: Designed to measure college-level achievement of students in statistics.
Population: High school students desiring credit for college-level courses and admission to advanced courses.
Publication Dates: 1997–2005.
Scores: Total score only.
Administration: Group.
Price Data: Available from publisher.
Time: 180 minutes.
Comments: Available to secondary schools for annual administration on specific days in May; inactive forms and previous free-response questions available; program sponsored by the College Board with exams administered by Educational Testing Service.
Author: Educational Testing Service.
Publisher: The College Board.

[122]
Advanced Placement Examination in Studio Art.

Purpose: Designed to measure college-level achievement of students in studio art.
Population: High school students desiring credit for college-level courses and admission to advanced courses.
Publication Dates: 1972–2005.
Scores: Total score only.
Administration: Group.
Price Data: Available from publisher.
Comments: Candidate submits materials (original works, written commentary, slides) for evaluation of quality, concentration, and breadth; available to secondary schools for annual submission of materials on specific days in May; program sponsored by the College

Board with exams administered by Educational Testing Service.
Author: Educational Testing Service.
Publisher: The College Board.
Cross References: For additional information concerning an earlier edition, see 8:83. For reviews of the AP® Program, see 8:471 (2 reviews).

[123]
Advanced Placement Examination in U.S. History.

Purpose: Designed to measure college-level achievement of students in U.S. history.
Population: High school students desiring credit for college-level courses and admission to advanced courses.
Publication Dates: 1956–2005.
Scores: Total score only.
Administration: Group.
Price Data: Available from publisher.
Time: 185 minutes.
Comments: Available to secondary schools for annual administration on specific days in May; inactive form and previous free-response questions available; program sponsored by the College Board with exams administered by Educational Testing Service.
Author: Educational Testing Service.
Publisher: The College Board.
Cross References: See T5:117 (4 references), T4:127 (1 reference) and T2:1980 (1 reference); for a review by Harry D. Berg of an earlier form, see 6:1000 (1 reference); for reviews by James A. Field, Jr. and Christine McGuire, see 5:812. For reviews of the AP® Program, see 8:471 (2 reviews) and 7:662 (2 reviews).

[124]
Advanced Placement Examination in United States Government and Politics.

Purpose: Designed to measure college-level achievement of students in United States government and politics.
Population: High school students desiring credit for college-level courses and admission to advanced courses.
Publication Dates: 1987–2005.
Scores: Total score only.
Administration: Group.
Price Data: Available from publisher.
Time: 145 minutes.
Comments: Available to secondary schools for annual administration on specific days in May; inactive forms and previous free-response questions available; program sponsored by the College Board with exams by Educational Testing Service.
Author: Educational Testing Service.
Publisher: The College Board.

[125]
Advanced Placement Examination in World History.

Purpose: Designed to measure college-level achievement of students in world history.
Population: High school students desiring credit for college-level courses and admission to advanced courses.
Publication Dates: 2002–2005.
Scores: Total score only.
Administration: Group.
Price Data: Available from publisher.
Time: 185 minutes.
Comments: Available to secondary schools for annual administration on specific days in May; inactive form and previous free-response questions available; program sponsored by the College Board with exams administered by Educational Testing Service.
Author: Educational Testing Service.
Publisher: The College Board.

[126]
Advanced Placement Examinations.

Purpose: Designed to measure college-level achievement of students in various subject areas.
Population: High school students desiring credit for college-level courses and admission to advanced courses.
Publication Dates: 1954–1999.
Acronym: AP®.
Scores: 32 tests in 18 subject areas: Art History, Studio Art (2 portfolios: Drawing and General), Biology, Calculus AB, Calculus BC, Chemistry, Computer Science A, Computer Science AB, English Language and Composition, English Literature and Composition, Environmental Science, European History, French Language, French Literature, German Language, Government & Politics—Comparative, Government & Politics—United States, International English Language, Latin Literature, Latin—Vergil, Macroeconomics, Microeconomics, Music Theory, Physics B., Physics C (2 tests: Electricity and Magnetism, Mechanics), Psychology, Spanish Language, Spanish Literature, Statistics, United States History.
Administration: Group.
Price Data: Available from publisher.
Time: 120–200 minutes.
Comments: Available to secondary schools for annual administration on specified days in May; inactive forms and previous essay/free-response sections available; program administered by the College Board and Educational Testing Service.
Author: Educational Testing Service.
Publisher: Educational Testing Service.
Cross References: See T5:118 (1 reference) and T3:124 (1 reference); for additional information and reviews by Paul L. Dressel and David A. Frisbie, see 8:471 (5 references); see also T2:1045 (4 references); for

reviews by Warren G. Findley and Alexander G. Wesman of an earlier program, see 7:662 (3 references); see also 6:761 (5 references). For reviews of individual tests, see 8:112 (1 review), 8:113 (2 reviews), 8:126 (1 review), 8:153 (1 review), 8:846 (1 review), 8:862 (1 review), 6:893 (1 review), 6:1000 (1 review), 5:205 (1 review), 5:211 (1 review), 5:273 (1 review), 5:419 (1 review), 5:724 (1 review), 5:743 (1 review), 5:750 (1 review), and 5:812 (2 reviews).

[127]
Advanced Test Battery.
Purpose: "Designed for use in the selection, development, or guidance of personnel at graduate level or in management positions."
Population: Personnel at graduate level or in management positions.
Publication Dates: 1979–1983.
Acronym: ATB.
Administration: Group.
Levels, 2: Higher order aptitudes, Higher order aptitudes in a work setting.
Restricted Distribution: Restricted to persons who have completed the publisher's training course or members of the Division of Occupational Psychology of the British Psychological Society.
Price Data: Available from publisher.
Comments: Subtests available as separates; separate answer sheets must be used.
Authors: Roger Holdsworth (VA3, NA4, manual); Peter Saville (VA1, NA2, manual), Gill Nyfield (manual), Dave Hawkey (DA5, ST7, DT8), Steve Blinkhorn (VA3), and Alan Iliff (NA4).
Publisher: SHL Group plc [United Kingdom].
a) LEVEL 1. 1979–1980; HIGHER ORDER APTITUDES, 3 TESTS.
1) *Verbal Concepts.*
Publication Date: 1980.
Acronym: VA1.
Time: 15(20) minutes.
2) *Number Series.*
Publication Date: 1980.
Acronym: NA2.
Time: 15(20) minutes.
3) *Diagramming.*
Publication Date: 1980.
Acronym: DA5.
Time: 20(25) minutes.
b) LEVEL 2. 1979–1980; HIGHER ORDER APTITUDES IN A WORK CONTEST; 4 TESTS.
1) *Verbal Critical Reasoning.*
Publication Date: 1983.
Acronym: VA3.
Time: 30(35) minutes.
2) *Numerical Critical Reasoning.*
Publication Dates: 1979–1983.

Acronym: NA4.
Time: 35(40) minutes.
3) *Spatial Reasoning.*
Publication Dates: 1979–1981.
Acronym: ST7.
Time: 20(25) minutes.
4) *Diagrammatic Reasoning.*
Publication Dates: 1979–1981.
Acronym: DT8.
Time: 15(20) minutes.

[128]
Age Projection Test.
Purpose: Designed as "an imagery test aimed at revealing self-images at various age [and self] levels and their associated structures of imagery functioning useful toward the understanding of a presented problem or a symptom."
Population: Adults.
Publication Date: 1988.
Acronym: APT.
Scores: No scores.
Administration: Individual.
Price Data: Available from publisher.
Time: [60–120] minutes.
Author: Akhter Ahsen.
Publisher: Brandon House, Inc. [No reply from publisher; status unknown].
Cross References: For reviews by Edward Aronow and Michael D. Botwin, see 12:23.

[129]
Ages & Stages Questionnaires: A Parent-Completed, Child-Monitoring System, Second Edition.
Purpose: Designed to screen "infants and young children for developmental delays."
Population: Ages 4–60 months.
Publication Dates: 1995–1999.
Acronym: ASQ.
Scores, 5: Communication, Gross Motor, Fine Motor, Problem Solving, Personal-Social.
Administration: Individual.
Levels, 19: 4, 6, 8, 10, 12, 14, 16, 18, 20, 22, 24, 27, 30, 33, 36, 42, 48, 54, and 60 months.
Price Data, 2005: $190 per complete kit including user's guide (1999, 195 pages) and set of 19 master questionnaires for photocopying; $165 per set of 19 master questionnaires; $45 per user's guide; $44 per The Ages & Stages Questionnaires on a Home Visit (VHS video); $49.95 per ASQ Scoring and Referral (video).
Foreign Language Editions: Spanish, French, and Korean editions available; contact publisher for availability in additional languages.
Time: (10–20) minutes.

Comments: Parent-completed questionnaire.
Authors: Diane Bricker and Jane Squires, with assistance from Linda Mounts, LaWanda Potter, Robert Nickel, Elizabeth Twombly, and Jane Farrell.
Publisher: Brookes Publishing Co., Inc.
Cross References: For reviews by B. Ann Boyce and G. Michael Poteat, see 16:8; for reviews by Dorothy M. Singleton and Rhonda H. Solomon of the original edition, see 14:14.

[130]
Ages & Stages Questionnaires: Social-Emotional: A Parent-Completed, Child-Monitoring System for Social-Emotional Behaviors.

Purpose: Designed to assess "children's social-emotional development."
Population: Ages 3–66 months.
Publication Dates: 2002–2003.
Acronym: ASQ-SE.
Scores, 7: Self-Regulation, Compliance, Communication, Adaptive Functioning, Autonomy, Affect, Interaction with People.
Administration: Individual.
Levels, 8: 6, 12, 18, 24, 30, 36, 48, and 60 month questionnaires.
Price Data, 2003: $125 per complete kit including user's guide (2003, 192 pages), and a boxed set of 8 photocopiable master questionnaires and corresponding scoring sheets; $100 per boxed set of 8 photocopiable master questionnaires and corresponding scoring sheets; $40 per user's guide.
Foreign Language Edition: Questionnaires available in Spanish.
Time: (10–15) minutes.
Comments: Parent-completed questionnaires.
Authors: Jane Squires, Diane Bricker, Elizabeth Twombly, Suzanne Yockelson, Maura Schoen Davis, and Younghee Kim.
Publisher: Brookes Publishing Co., Inc.
Cross References: For a review by John J. Vacca, see 16:9.

[131]
Aggression Questionnaire.

Purpose: Designed to aid in evaluating an individual's aggressive responses and ability to channel those responses in a safe and constructive manner.
Population: Ages 9–88.
Publication Date: 2000.
Scores, 7: Physical Aggression, Verbal Aggression, Anger, Hostility, Indirect Aggression, Inconsistent Responding, Total Score.
Administration: Individual or group.
Price Data, 2006: $99 per complete kit; $43.50 per 25 AutoScore™ answer forms; $199 per computer disk; $16.50 per 100 answer sheets; $57.75 per manual (2000, 95 pages).
Time: (10) minutes.
Comments: Updated version of the Buss-Durkee Hostility Inventory; computer scoring is available from publisher.
Authors: Arnold H. Buss and W. L. Warren.
Publisher: Western Psychological Services.
Cross References: For reviews by Johnnie A. Brown and Mary Lou Kelley, see 15:13.

[132]
AH4: Group Test of General Intelligence.

Purpose: "Designed as a group test of general intelligence."
Population: Ages 10 and over.
Publication Dates: 1955–1984.
Scores: Total score only.
Administration: Group.
Price Data: Price information available from publisher for tests, answer sheets, marking key, data supplement, manual (1970, 17 pages), and specimen set.
Time: 20(30–45) minutes.
Authors: A. W. Heim, K. P. Watts (test), V. Simmonds (test), and Anne Walters (data supplement).
Publisher: NFER-Nelson Publishing Co., Ltd. [England].
Cross References: See T5:127 (5 references), T4:137 (5 references), and T2:331 (20 references); for a review by John Nisbet, see 7:331 (12 references); for a review by John Liggett of the original edition, see 6:506; for a review by George A. Ferguson, see 5:390 (11 references).

[133]
AH5 Group Test of High Grade Intelligence.

Purpose: Designed as a test of general intelligence "for use with selected, highly intelligent subjects."
Population: Ages 13 and over.
Publication Dates: 1968–1984.
Scores, 3: Verbal and Numeric, Diagrammatic, Total.
Administration: Group.
Price Data: Price information available from publisher for tests, answer sheets, manual (1983, 21 pages), and for specimen set including test, key, answer sheet, and manual.
Time: 40(60) minutes.
Author: A. W. Heim.
Publisher: NFER-Nelson Publishing Co., Ltd. [England].
Cross References: See T5:128 (3 references), T4:138 (2 references), and 9:66 (1 reference).

[134]
Air Conditioning Specialist (Form SWA-C).

Purpose: For selecting candidates with knowledge of air conditioning.

Population: Applicants and incumbents for jobs requiring air conditioning knowledge and skills.
Publication Dates: 1992–2002.
Scores, 7: Print Reading/Electrical/and Test Equipment, Controls, Welding/Piping and Plumbing, Mechanical Maintenance and Machines & Equipment, Heating & Ventilation and Combustion, Air Conditioning and Refrigeration, Total.
Administration: Group.
Price Data, 2006: $20 per consumable self-scoring test booklet (minimum order of 20); $24.95 per manual (2002, 16 pages).
Time: (60) minutes.
Author: Roland T. Ramsay.
Publisher: Ramsay Corporation.

[135]
The Alcadd Test, Revised Edition.

Purpose: "Designed to: a) provide an objective measurement of alcoholic addiction that could identify individuals whose behavior and personality structure indicated that they were alcoholic addicts or had serious alcoholic problems; b) identify specific areas of maladjustment in alcoholics to facilitate therapeutic and rehabilitation activities; and c) obtain better insight into the psychodynamics of alcoholic addiction."
Population: Adults.
Publication Dates: 1949–1988.
Scores, 6: Regularity of Drinking, Preference for Drinking over Other Activities, Lack of Controlled Drinking, Rationalization of Drinking, Excessive Emotionality, Total.
Administration: Individual or group.
Editions, 2: Paper-and-pencil, microcomputer.
Price Data, 2002: $60 per complete kit including 25 AutoScore™ test/profile forms (1988, 4 pages) and manual (1988, 24 pages); $32.50 per 25 AutoScore™ test booklets; $32.50 per manual; $139.50 per microcomputer edition (IBM) including diskette (tests up to 25) and user's guide; $9.50 or less per mail-in answer sheet.
Time: (5–15) minutes.
Comments: Self-administered.
Authors: Morse P. Manson, Lisa A. Melchior, and G. J. Huba.
Publisher: Western Psychological Services.
Cross References: For reviews by William L. Curlette and Paul Retzlaff, see 11:12 (1 reference); see also T3:152 (3 references), T2:1098 (1 reference), and P:7 (3 references); for a review by Dugal Campbell, see 6:60 (6 references); for reviews by Charles H. Honzik and Albert L. Hunsicker, see 4:30.

[136]
Alcohol Dependence Scale.

Purpose: "Provides a brief measure of the extent to which the use of alcohol has progressed from psychological involvement to impaired control."

Population: Problem drinkers.
Publication Date: 1984.
Acronym: ADS.
Scores: Total score only.
Administration: Group.
Price Data: Available from publisher.
Foreign Language Edition: Questionnaire available in French.
Time: (5–10) minutes.
Comments: Test booklet title is Alcohol Use Questionnaire.
Authors: Harvey A. Skinner and John L. Horn.
Publisher: Centre for Addiction and Mental Health [Canada].
Cross References: See T5:134 (41 references) and T4:145 (5 references); for reviews by Robert E. Deysach and Nick J. Piazza, see 10:12 (1 reference).

[137]
Alcohol Use Disorders Identification Test.

Purpose: A screening procedure "to identify persons whose alcohol consumption has become hazardous or harmful to their health."
Population: Adults.
Publication Dates: 1992–1993.
Acronym: AUDIT.
Scores: Total score only.
Administration: Individual or group.
Price Data, 2001: Test and manual (88 pages) are free; $75 per training module.
Foreign Language Editions: English, Japanese, Spanish, Norwegian, Romanian, Portuguese, German, Indian, French, Swedish, Russian, Catalan, and Italian.
Time: [2] minutes.
Comments: Developed by World Health Organization and validated on primary care patients in six countries.
Authors: Thomas F. Babor, Juan Ramon de la Fuente, John Saunders, O. G. Aasland, and Marcus Grant.
Publisher: World Health Organization [Switzerland].
Cross References: For reviews by Philip Ash and Herbert Bischoff, see 14:15; see T5:135 (6 references).

[138]
Alcohol Use Inventory.

Purpose: "To assess the nature of an individual's alcohol use pattern, and problems associated with that pattern."
Population: Adults and adolescents suspected of problem drinking.
Publication Date: 1987.
Acronym: AUI.
Scores, 24: Social Improvement, Mental Improvement, Manage Moods, Marital Coping, Gregarious, Compulsive, Sustained, Loss of Control, Role Maladaptation, Delirium, Hangover, Marital Problems, Quantity, Guilt and Worry, Help Before, Receptivity, Aware-

ness, Enhanced, Obsessed, Disruption 1, Disruption 2, Anxious Concern, Receptive Awareness, Alcohol Involvement.

Administration: Group.

Price Data, 2006: $38 per 10 reusable test booklets; $38 per hand-scoring key; $43 per manual (1987, 95 pages); $31 per User's Guide: $145 per hand score starter kit including manual, test booklets, answer sheets, profile forms, and answer keys; $111 per Q Local starter kit; $116 per mail-in scoring starter kit; $16.75 per Q Local interpretive report; $8.50 per Q Local profile report; $19.75 per mail-in interpretive report; $11.50 per mail-in profile report.

Time: (35–60) minutes.

Comments: Reports are available via Q Local Assessment System Software as well as through a mail-in scoring service.

Authors: John L. Horn, Kenneth W. Wanberg, and F. Mark Foster.

Publisher: Pearson Assessments.

Cross References: See T5:136 (12 references); for reviews by Robert J. Drummond and Sharon McNeely, see 12:25 (3 references); see also T4:146 (6 references).

[139]
Algebra Test for Engineering and Science: National Achievement Tests.

Purpose: Designed to screen proficiency in trigonometry and geometry.

Population: College entrants.

Publication Dates: 1958–1961.

Scores, 2: Test 1, Total.

Administration: Group.

Price Data: Available from publisher.

Time: 50(55) minutes for Test 1; 80(85) minutes for total test.

Author: A. B. Lonski.

Publisher: Psychometric Affiliates.

Cross References: For a review by Peter A. Lappan, Jr., see 6:595.

[140]
Alleman Leadership Development Questionnaire.

Purpose: "Measures the amount of mentoring activity between individuals or in an organization or work unit."

Population: Mentors and protégés.

Publication Dates: 1982–1985.

Acronym: ALDQ.

Scores, 12: Teach the Job, Teach Politics, Assign Challenging Tasks, Career Counseling, General Counseling, Career Help, Demonstrated Trust, Endorse Acts/Views, Sponsor, Protect, Associate Socially, Friendship.

Administration: Group.

Restricted Distribution: Available for use only by those trained and certified by Leadership Development Consulting Co.

Price Data, 2002: $10 per manual (1985, 35 pages); $5 per questionnaire.

Time: (10–15) minutes.

Author: Elizabeth Alleman.

Publisher: Silverwood Enterprises, LLC.

Cross References: See T4:149 (1 reference).

[141]
Alleman Mentoring Activities Questionnaire.

Purpose: "Measures the amount, quality and impact of mentoring activity."

Population: Mentors and protégés.

Publication Dates: 1987–2000.

Acronym: AMAQ.

Scores, 10: Teach the Job, Provide Challenge, Teach Politics, Career Help, Protect, Sponsor, Counsel, Friendship, Demonstrate Trust, Total.

Administration: Group or individual.

Price Data, 2002: $10 per form; report costs and research discounts available from publisher.

Time: (10–15) minutes.

Comments: Previously listed as Alleman Mentoring Scales Questionnaire; available in paper-and-pencil or electronic format.

Authors: Elizabeth Alleman and Diana Clarke.

Publisher: Silverwood Enterprises, LLC.

Cross References: See T5:139 (1 reference).

[142]
Alleman Relationship Value Questionnaire.

Purpose: "Designed to measure the quality of mentoring activity."

Population: Mentors and protégés.

Publication Date: 1985.

Acronym: ARVQ.

Scores, 10: Information, Politics, Counsel, Tough Job, Career Moves, Trust, Achievements, Protection, Friendship, Overall Relationship.

Administration: Group.

Forms, 2: Mentor, Protégé.

Manual: No manual.

Price Data, 2002: $4 per questionnaire.

Time: Administration time not reported.

Author: Elizabeth Alleman.

Publisher: Silverwood Enterprises, LLC.

[143]
Allied Health Professions Admission Test.

Purpose: Developed to measure general academic ability and scientific knowledge.

Population: Applicants to 4-year allied health programs.

Publication Dates: 1979–1999.

Acronym: AHPAT.

Scores, 5: Verbal Ability, Quantitative Ability, Biology, Chemistry, Reading Comprehension.
Administration: Group.
Restricted Distribution: Distribution restricted and test administered at licensed testing centers; details may be obtained from publisher.
Price Data: Available from publisher.
Time: 165 minutes.
Author: The Psychological Corporation.
Publisher: PsychCorp, A brand of Harcourt Assessment, Inc.
Cross References: For reviews by Alan C. Bugbee, Jr. and Richard C. Pugh, see 12:26

[144]
Alternate Uses.

Purpose: "Designed to represent an expected factor of 'flexibility of thinking' in an investigation of creative thinking."
Population: Grades 6–16 and adults.
Publication Dates: 1960–1978.
Scores: Total score only.
Administration: Group.
Forms, 2: Form B, C.
Price Data: Available from publisher.
Time: 12(20) minutes.
Authors: Paul R. Christensen, J. P. Guilford, Philip R. Merrifield, and Robert C. Wilson.
Publisher: Charlotte Mackley [No reply from publisher; status unknown].
Cross References: See T5:142 (8 references) and T4:154 (4 references); for a review by Edys S. Quellmalz, see 9:71 (3 references); see also T3:157 (21 references), 8:235 (32 references), T2:542 (94 references), and 6:542 (7 references).

[145]
Alzheimer's Disease Caregiver's Questionnaire.

Purpose: Designed to "evaluate the likelihood that a specific individual has a dementia suggestive of Alzheimer's Disease."
Population: Ages 40 and over.
Publication Dates: 1998–2002.
Acronym: ADCQ.
Scores, 7: Likelihood of a Dementia Consistent with or Suggestive of Alzheimer's Disease (Memory, Confusion and Disorientation, Geographic Disorientation, Behavior, Reasoning and Judgment, Language Abilities, Total).
Administration: Individual.
Price Data, 2005: $299 per introductory kit on a 3.5-inch disk including 25 paper-and-pencil versions, software program, on-screen user's manual, installation guide, and 25 caregiver's report generations; $350 per 50 record forms with 50-use key disk.

Time: (5–10) minutes.
Comments: Symptom checklist completed by caregiver; can be administered on-line, on desk-top computer, or in paper-and-pencil format; software requires Windows 95/98/ME/NT/2000/XP and standard 3.5-inch, 1.44 MB disk.
Authors: Paul R. Solomon and Cynthia A. Murphy (manual).
Publisher: Psychological Assessment Resources, Inc.
Cross References: For reviews by Mark A. Albanese and Matthew E. Lambert, see 16:10.

[146]
Alzheimer's Quick Test: Assessment of Parietal Function.

Purpose: Designed to "screen adolescents and adults for parietal lobe dysfunctions indicative of mild cognitive impairments, acquired neurogenic disorders of language and communication … or degenerative neurological disorders such as Alzheimer's or Parkinson's disease."
Population: Adolescents and adults.
Publication Date: 2002.
Acronym: AQT.
Scores, 5: Color-Form, Color-Number, Color-Letter, Color-Animal, Color-Object.
Administration: Individual.
Price Data, 2004: $249 per complete kit including examiner's manual (88 pages), stimulus manual, and 25 record forms; $75 per examiner's manual; $150 per stimulus manual; $50 per 25 record forms.
Foreign Language Edition: Spanish and French-Canadian directions included in examiner's manual.
Time: [3–5] minutes.
Comments: "Criterion-referenced."
Authors: Elisabeth H. Wiig, Niels Peter Nielsen, Lennart Minthon, and Siegbert Warkentin.
Publisher: PsychCorp, A brand of Harcourt Assessment, Inc.
Cross References: For reviews by Shawn K. Acheson and Joan C. Ballard, see 16:11.

[147]
Am I Musical? Music Audiation Games.

Purpose: Designed to objectively reveal a general estimate of the extent of music potential a child or adult possess.
Population: Ages 7–12, 13–adult.
Publication Date: 2003.
Scores: Total score only.
Administration: Group.
Levels, 2: Youth Game, Adult Game.
Price Data: Available from publisher.
Time: (12) minutes.
Comments: Test administered via CD; CD player needed; self-administered, self-scored.

Author: Edwin E. Gordon.
Publisher: GIA Publications, Inc.
Cross References: For reviews by Christopher M. Johnson and James W. Sherbon, see 16:12.

[148]
The AMA DISC Survey.

Purpose: Personal styles survey that focuses on the ways in which people approach their work and relate to others within their organization.
Population: Adults.
Publication Date: 2000.
Scores: 4 styles of behavior: Directing, Influencing, Supportive, Contemplative.
Administration: Individual or group.
Price Data: Price data for test materials including Facilitator's Manual (84 pages) and Debriefing Guide (47 pages) available from Human Synergistics International.
Time: 20–25 minutes.
Author: Robert A. Cooke.
Publisher: American Management Association [distributed by Human Synergistics International].

[149]
The American Drug and Alcohol Survey.

Purpose: Designed to estimate levels of drug use in youth populations.
Population: Schools and school districts.
Publication Dates: 1989–2005.
Scores: Item scores, High/Moderate/Low Drug Involvement.
Administration: Group.
Levels, 2: Grades 4–6, Grades 6–12.
Price Data: Available from publisher.
Time: (20–30) minutes.
Comments: Results tabulated by publisher.
Authors: Eugene R. Oetting, Frederick Beauvais, and Ruth Edwards.
Publisher: Rocky Mountain Behavioral Science Institute, Inc.
Cross References: See T5:143 (1 reference); for reviews by Jeffrey Jenkins and Steven Schinke, see 12:27; see also T4:155 (1 reference).

[150]
The American Home Scale.

Purpose: "Designed to measure the socioeconomic status of individuals and groups."
Population: Grades 8–16.
Publication Date: 1942.
Scores, 5: Cultural, Aesthetic, Economic, Miscellaneous, Total.
Administration: Group.
Price Data: Available from publisher.
Time: (35–50) minutes.

Author: W. A. Kerr.
Publisher: Psychometric Affiliates.
Cross References: See T2:1039 (5 references) and 5:596 (2 references); for reviews by Henry S. Maas and Verner M. Sims, see 3:417 (7 references).

[151]
American Invitational Mathematics Examination.

Purpose: "Provides challenge and recognition to high school students in the United States and Canada who have exceptional mathematical ability."
Population: American and Canadian high school students.
Publication Dates: 1983–2002.
Acronym: AIME.
Score: Total score only.
Administration: Group.
Manual: No manual.
Price Data: Price information available from publisher for practice examination set including past exam (specify year desired 1983–present) and solution pamphlet; other price data available from publisher.
Time: 180 minutes.
Comments: Administered annually, three weeks after the American Mathematics Competitions 12 (AMC12; 154) to students attaining a predetermined cutoff score on the AMC12.
Authors: Sponsored jointly by the Mathematical Association of America, Society of Actuaries, Mu Alpha Theta, National Council on Teachers of Mathematics, Casualty Actuarial Society, American Statistical Association, and American Mathematical Association of Two Year Colleges, and others.
Publisher: Mathematical Association of America; American Mathematics Competitions.
Cross References: For reviews by Robert W. Lissitz and Claudia R. Wright, see 11:14.

[152]
American Literacy Test.

Purpose: Constructed to assess literacy based on vocabulary.
Population: Adults.
Publication Date: 1962.
Scores: Total score only.
Administration: Group.
Price Data: Available from publisher.
Time: 4 minutes.
Author: John J. McCarty.
Publisher: Psychometric Affiliates.
Cross References: For a review by Victor H. Noll, see 6:328.

[153]
American Mathematics Competitions, Contest 8 (AMC8).

Purpose: "To increase interest in mathematics and to develop problem solving ability through a friendly competition."

Population: American and Canadian students in grade 8 or below.

Publication Dates: 1985–2001.

Acronym: AMC8.

Scores: Total score only.

Administration: Group.

Price Data, 2001: $25 per school registration fee; $10 per 10 exam booklets.

Special Editions: Braille and large-print editions available.

Time: 40 minutes.

Comments: Test administered annually in December at participating schools; test previously called American Junior High School Mathematics Examination.

Authors: Sponsored jointly by Mathematical Association of America, Society of Actuaries, Mu Alpha Theta, National Council of Teachers of Mathematics, Casualty Actuarial Society, American Statistical Association, and American Mathematical Association of Two Year Colleges.

Publisher: Mathematical Association of America; American Mathematics Competitions.

Cross References: For reviews by John M. Enger and Darrell Sabers, see 11:15.

[154]
American Mathematics Competitions, Contest 12.

Purpose: "To identify, through friendly competition, students with an interest and a talent for mathematical problem solving."

Population: High school students competing for individual and school awards.

Publication Dates: 1950–2002.

Acronym: AMC12.

Score: Total score only.

Administration: Group.

Price Data, 2002: $30 per school registration fee; $1.40 per exam (specify English or Spanish); $4 per 10 solutions pamphlets; $.51 per specimen set of prior year exams (specify year and English or Spanish); price data available from publisher for additional study aids and supplementary materials.

Foreign Language and Special Editions: Spanish, Braille, and large-print editions available.

Time: (75) minutes.

Comments: Test administered annually in February or March at participating secondary schools; test previously called American High School Mathematics Examination (AHSME).

Authors: Sponsored jointly by the Mathematical Association of America, Society of Actuaries, Mu Alpha Theta, National Council of Teachers of Mathematics, Casualty Actuarial Society, American Statistical Association, and American Mathematical Association of Two-Year Colleges, and others.

Publisher: Mathematical Association of America; American Mathematics Competitions.

Cross References: For reviews by Camilla Persson Benbow and Randy W. Kamphaus of the American High School Mathematics Examination, see 11:13; for a review by Thomas P. Hogan, see 8:252 (1 reference); see also T2:598 (3 references).

[155]
American Numerical Test.

Purpose: Designed to assess "numerical alertness and adaptation."

Population: Adults in "vocations which emphasize shop and white collar skills."

Publication Date: 1962.

Scores: Total score only.

Administration: Group.

Price Data: Available from publisher.

Time: 4 minutes.

Author: John J. McCarty.

Publisher: Psychometric Affiliates.

Cross References: For reviews by Marvin D. Glock and Richard T. Johnson, see 6:604.

[156]
The American Occupational Therapy Association, Inc. Fieldwork Evaluation for the Occupational Therapist.

Purpose: Constructed to evaluate "student competence at the completion of each Level II fieldwork experience."

Population: Occupational therapy students.

Publication Dates: 1973–1987.

Scores, 3: Performance, Judgment, Attitude.

Administration: Individual.

Price Data: Available from publisher.

Time: Administration time not reported.

Comments: Ratings by supervisor; revision of the Field Work Performance Report (T3:885).

Author: The American Occupational Therapy Association, Inc.

Publisher: The American Occupational Therapy Association, Inc.

Cross References: For reviews by James T. Austin and Brian Bolton, see 12:28; for information on the Field Work Performance Report, see T3:885 (2 references) and 8:1107 (1 reference).

[157]
Amsterdam Short-Term Memory Test.
Purpose: Designed to be used in "neuropsychological evaluation of persons who claim to have memory and/or concentration problems, but in whom these problems are not clinically obvious, while the possibility exists that they are exaggerating or simulating their problems."
Population: Individuals who claim to have memory and/or concentration problems, but do not have clinical symptoms.
Publication Dates: 1999-2005.
Acronym: ASTM.
Scores: Total score only.
Administration: Individual.
Price Data, 2006: EURO350 per complete kit including manual (2005, 75 pages), computer program for administration, and 100 record forms; EURO49.50 per manual; EURO29.95 per 100 record forms.
Foreign Language Editions: Manual and record forms are also available in German and Dutch.
Time: (10-30) minutes.
Comments: Test is administered via computer; computer program is available on a CD.
Authors: Ben Schmand and Jaap Lindeboom with collaboration of Thomas Merten and Scott R. Millis.
Publisher: PITS: Psychologische Instrumenten, Tests en Services [The Netherlands]

[158]
Analytic Learning Disability Assessment.
Purpose: Designed to match student learning style with instructional strategies.
Population: Ages 8-14.
Publication Date: 1982.
Acronym: ALDA.
Scores: Fail, Weak, or Solid in 77 unit skill subtests.
Administration: Individual.
Price Data, 2005: $174.25 per complete kit; $55.75 per 20 test forms including test score formulation sheet and student worksheets.
Time: (75) minutes.
Authors: Thomas D. Gnagey and Patricia A. Gnagey.
Publisher: Slosson Educational Publications, Inc.
Cross References: For a review by Marcia B. Shaffer, see 9:72.

[159]
Analytical Aptitude Skills Evaluation.
Purpose: To evaluate aptitude and potential for analyzing business problems.
Population: Entry-level and experienced candidates for positions requiring the ability to analyze business problems.
Publication Date: 1993.
Acronym: AASE.
Scores: Total Score, Narrative Evaluation, Rating, Recommendation.
Administration: Group.
Price Data, 2001: $235 per candidate; quantity discounts available.
Foreign Language Edition: French version available.
Time: (60) minutes.
Comments: Scored by publisher; must be proctored.
Author: Bruce A. Winrow.
Publisher: Walden Personnel Performance, Inc.
Cross References: For a review by John S. Geisler, see 15:14.

[160]
Analytical Reasoning Skills Battery.
Purpose: Measures high level analytical reasoning skills.
Population: Adults.
Publication Date: 1998.
Acronym: ANAL.
Scores: Total Score, Narrative Evaluation, Ranking, Recommendation.
Administration: Group.
Price Data, 2001: $150 per candidate; quantity discount available.
Time: (68) minutes.
Comments: Scored by publisher; must be proctored.
Author: Bruce A. Winrow.
Publisher: Walden Personnel Performance, Inc. [Canada].

[161]
Analytical Thinking Test.
Purpose: Designed as a self-assessment exercise in analytical thinking.
Population: Adults.
Publication Dates: 1992–1994.
Scores, 2: Situations, Proposals.
Administration: Group.
Manual: No manual.
Price Data: Available from publisher.
Time: [30–40] minutes.
Comments: Self-administered, self-scored.
Author: Training House, Inc.
Publisher: Training House, Inc.

[162]
Analyzing the Communication Environment.
Purpose: "An inventory of ways to encourage communication in functional activities."
Population: Preschool to adolescent children with severe disabilities.
Publication Date: 1993.
Acronym: ACE.

Scores: Total score only.
Administration: Individual.
Price Data: Price data available from publisher for complete kit including 90-minutes VHS videotape and softbound instructor's guide (85 pages).
Time: Administration time not reported.
Authors: Charity Rowland and Philip Schweigert.
Publisher: Harcourt Assessment, Inc.
Cross References: For reviews by Pat Mirenda and Sheila Pratt, see 14:16.

[163]
Anger Disorders Scale.

Purpose: "Designed to help practitioners identify clinically dysfunctional anger."
Population: Ages 18 and over.
Publication Date: 2004.
Administration: Individual or group.
Forms, 2: Anger Disorders Scale; Anger Disorders Scale: Short.
Price Data, 2006: $135 per ADS complete kit including technical manual (2004, 184 pages), 10 reusable item booklets, and 25 each ADS and ADS:S QuikScore forms; $64 per technical manual; $42 per 25 ADS QuikScore forms; $40 per 25 ADS:S Quikscore forms; $23 per 10 reusable item booklets.
Authors: Raymond DiGiuseppe and Raymond Chip Tafrate.
Publisher: Multi-Health Systems, Inc.
  a) ANGER DISORDERS SCALE.
  Acronym: ADS.
  Scores, 22: Reactivity/Expression (Scope of Anger Provocations, Physiological Arousal, Duration of Anger Problems, Rumination, Impulsivity, Coercion, Verbal Expression, Total), Anger-In (Hurt/Social Rejection, Episode Length, Suspiciousness, Resentment, Tension Reduction, Brooding, Total), Vengeance (Revenge, Physical Aggression, Relational Aggression, Passive Aggression, Indirect Aggression, Total), Total.
  Time: (20) minutes.
  b) ANGER DISORDERS SCALE; SHORT.
  Acronym: ADS:S.
  Scores, 4: Reactivity/Expression, Anger-In, Vengeance, Total.
  Time: (5-10) minutes.

[164]
Ann Arbor Learning Inventory [1996 Edition].

Purpose: To evaluate competencies in visual, memory, auditory, and comprehension skills.
Population: Grades K-1, Grades 2-4, Grades 5-8.
Publication Dates: 1977-1996.
Acronym: AALI.
Administration: Group.

Price Data, 2006: $20 per manual (specify Level A, B, or C); $15 per 10 student booklets (specify level); $10 per Level C stimulus cards.
Foreign Language Editions: All levels available in Spanish.
Time: Administration time not reported.
Comments: These are informal criterion-referenced tools.
Authors: Barbara Meister Vitale and Waneta B. Bullock.
Publisher: Ann Arbor Publishers, division of Academic Therapy Publications.
  a) SKILL LEVEL A.
  Population: Grades K-1.
  Scores, 7: Body Image, Visual Discrimination, Visual Motor Coordination, Visual Sequential Memory, Auditory Discrimination, Auditory Sequential Memory, Auditory Conceptual Memory.
  b) SKILL LEVEL B.
  Population: Grades 2-4.
  Scores, 6: Visual Discrimination, Visual Motor Coordination, Visual Sequential Memory, Auditory Sequential Memory, Auditory Discrimination, Auditory Comprehension.
  c) SKILL LEVEL C.
  Population: Grades 5-8.
  Comments: In process of revision; information available from publisher.
Cross References: For reviews by June Ellen Shepherd and Ruth E. Tomes of an earlier edition, see 11:16.

[165]
The ANSER System-Aggregate Neurobehavioral Student Health and Educational Review [Revised 1997].

Purpose: Designed as a system of collecting and integrating information from several sources about children suspected of having developmental and/or behavioral problems.
Population: Children ages 3+, suspected of having learning difficulties.
Publication Dates: 1980-1997.
Acronym: The ANSER System.
Scores: Not scored; questionnaires cover the following areas: Parent Questionnaires (Identifying Information, Initial Background Information, Possible Pregnancy Problems, Newborn Infant Problems, Health Problems or Conditions, Early Life Problems, Early Development, Family History), Attention Control Inventory (Skills and Interests, Attention Problems, Additional Behavior Traits, Behavioral Strengths, Open-Ended Comments), School Questionnaires (Identifying Information, Difficulties and Strengths, Specific Questions, School Facilities and Programs, Previous Reports and Assessments, Developmental Functions, Attention

Control Inventory, Additional Behavior Traits, Open-Ended Comments), Self-Administered Student Profile (Attention, Language Function, Spatial Motor Function, Graphomotor Function, Gross Motor Function, Memory Function, Temporal-Sequential Ordering, Efficiency, Affect, Outlook, Academic Skills, Social Function, Weekend Activities, Strengths and Weaknesses, Open-Ended Comments), Self-Administered Follow-Up Profile ("How I Think I'm Doing").
Administration: Individual.
Forms, 6: Form 1 (Ages 3–5), Form 2 (Ages 6–11), Form 3 (Ages 12+), Form 4 (Ages 9+), Form 5 (All ages), Form 6 (Ages 9+).
Price Data, 2006: $18.60 per Interpreter's Guide (1997, 56 pages); $18.60 per specimen set; $36 each per Forms 1–3 (Parent Questionnaire); $30.40 each per Forms 1–3 (School Questionnaire); $29.25 each per Form 4; $29.60 per 24 each of Forms 5P and 5S or Form 6; quantity discounts available.
Time: Administration time not reported.
Comments: A series of questionnaires to be completed by parents, school personnel, and students.
Author: Melvin D. Levine.
Publisher: Educators Publishing Service, Inc.
Cross References: For reviews by Robert G. Harrington and Kenneth W. Howell of an earlier edition, see 9:74.

[166]
Antisocial Process Screening Device.

Purpose: Designed to assess personality processes related to antisocial behavior in young populations.
Population: Ages 6–13.
Publication Date: 2001.
Acronym: APSD.
Scores, 4: Callous/Unemotional, Impulsivity, Narcissism, Total.
Administration: Individual.
Price Data, 2006: $145 per complete kit including technical manual (84 pages), and 25 Quikscore forms for each of APSD-T, APSD-P, and APSD-C; $59 per technical manual; $38 per 25 Quikscore forms.
Time: 10 minutes per rater for Parent and Teacher forms.
Comments: Individual Parent and Teacher ratings.
Authors: Paul J. Frick and Robert D. Hare.
Publisher: Multi-Health Systems, Inc.
Cross References: For reviews by Arthur S. Ellen and Mary Lou Kelley, see 16:13.

[167]
Aphasia Diagnostic Profiles.

Purpose: "Provides a systematic method of assessing language and communication impairment associated with aphasia."
Population: Adults with acquired brain damage.

Publication Date: 1992.
Acronym: ADP.
Scores: Behavioral Profile Score plus 9 subtests: Personal Information, Writing, Reading, Fluency, Naming, Auditory Comprehension, Repetition, Elicited Gestures, Singing.
Administration: Individual.
Price Data, 2006: $164 per complete kit including 25 record forms, manual (55 pages), stimulus cards/letterboard/pointer, and carrying case; $49 per 25 record forms; $64 per manual; $54 per stimulus cards/letterboard/pointer.
Time: (40–50) minutes.
Author: Nancy Helm-Estabrooks.
Publisher: PRO-ED.
Cross References: See T5:159 (2 references); for reviews by Wilfred G. Van Gorp and Richard G. Whitten, see 13:11.

[168]
Applicant Potential Inventory.

Purpose: Designed as a pre-employment screening assessment to help determine the employability of applicants.
Population: Job applicants.
Publication Date: 1996.
Acronym: API™.
Scores, 11: Candidness, Accuracy, Customer Service, Honesty, Drug Avoidance, Employee Relations, Safety Attitudes, Work Values, Supervision Attitudes, Tenure, Employability.
Administration: Group.
Price Data: Available from publisher.
Time: (15) minutes.
Author: National Computer Systems, Inc.
Publisher: Pearson Performance Solutions [No reply from publisher; status unknown].

[169]
Applicant Productivity Profile.

Purpose: Designed "to help screen applicants with limited reading abilities for low-skill positions."
Population: Age 18 and over.
Publication Dates: 1994–1997.
Acronym: APP.
Scores: 3 scores (Validity, Reading Ease, Employability Index), and 7 supplementary scores (Honesty II, Drug Avoidance II, Employee/Customer Relations II, Safety Attitude II, Work Values II, Supervision Attitudes II, Tenure II).
Administration: Individual or group.
Price Data, 2005: $22 for 1–999 Internet scoring with booklets $22 for 1–999 Internet scoring without booklets; $22 for 1–999 Scan scoring; $22 for 1–999 Quanta-TouchTest™ scoring; $22 for 1–999 Quanta® Fax scoring; $22 for 1–999 Quanta® software for Win-

dows with booklets; $22 for 1–999 Quanta® software for Windows without booklets.
Foreign Language Editions: Spanish and Mexican Spanish versions available.
Time: (15) minutes.
Comments: Test can be scored online, by fax, optical screening; software is available.
Author: Reid London House.
Publisher: Pearson Performance Solutions [No reply from publisher; status unknown].

[170]
Applicant Risk Profiler.

Purpose: "Designed to assist companies in determining which applicants are a potential risk or threat to their supervisors, coworkers and/or themselves."
Population: Job applicants.
Publication Date: 2001.
Acronym: ARP.
Scores, 5: Deception, Integrity, Illegal Drug Use, Workplace Policy Compliance, Workplace Aggression.
Administration: Individual.
Price Data, 2005: $99.99 per starter kit including manual (44 pages), 5 tests, and 1 test log; $34.99 per manual; $13.29 per paper-and-pencil version test (sold in quantities of 10; quantity discounts available); $13.29 per on-line test.
Time: (30) minutes.
Comments: Online and paper-and-pencil administration available; online version includes interpretive reports and follow-up interview questions.
Author: J. M. Llobet.
Publisher: G. Neil.

[171]
Appraise Your World™.

Purpose: Constructed "to measure the complexity and richness of the way individuals develop their personal worlds and make life choices."
Population: Adults.
Publication Dates: 1983-2001.
Acronym: AYW.
Scores: 29 dimensions: Emphasis (Career, Economic, Community, Interpersonal, Recreation, Travel, Nature, Palate, Arts, Practical Arts, Home, Romance, Family, Intellectual, Ideological, Physical, Emotional, Spiritual), World Dynamics (Level of Security, Level of Insecurity, Level of Satisfaction, Level of Dissatisfaction, Internal Focus of World, External Focus of World, Flexibility of Boundaries, Level of Growth, Balance of World, Level of Public Success, Level of Present Support).
Administration: Group.
Price Data: Available from publisher.
Time: (45) minutes.
Comments: Purchase and use requires training by publisher.

Authors: James T. Mahoney, Joan W. Chadbourne (test), and Robert I. Kabacoff (manual).
Publisher: Management Research Group.

[172]
Apraxia Battery for Adults, Second Edition.

Purpose: Designed to "verify the presence of apraxia in the adult patient and to estimate the severity of the disorder."
Population: Adults.
Publication Dates: 1979–2000.
Acronym: ABA-2.
Scores: 6 subtests: Diadochokinetic Rate, Increasing Word Length, Limb Apraxia and Oral Apraxia, Latency Time and Utterance Time for Polysyllabic Words, Repeated Trials, Inventory of Articulation Characteristics of Apraxia.
Administration: Individual.
Price Data, 2006: $130 per complete kit including 25 profile/examiner record forms, picture book, and manual (2000, 46 pages); $45 per 25 profile/examiner record forms; $50 per manual; $40 per picture book.
Time: (20) minutes.
Comments: Publisher states that the "vocabulary and conceptual structure of the six subtests allows administration of the battery to adolescents and children down to about age 9"; however, the norming group included only adults.
Authors: Barbara L. Dabul.
Publisher: PRO-ED.
Cross References: For reviews by Elaine Clark and by Raymond S. Dean and John J. Brinkman, Jr., see 15:15; see T5:163 (3 references) and T4:179 (4 references); for a review by Norma Cooke of an earlier edition, see 9:77 (1 reference).

[173]
Aprenda®: La prueba de logros en español—Segunda edición.

Purpose: Designed to measure the academic achievement of Spanish-speaking students.
Publication Dates: 1990–1998.
Acronym: Aprenda 2.
Administration: Group.
Price Data, 2002: $33.90 per multiple-choice assessment kit (Preprimer–Advanced) including test booklet and directions for administering (1997, 68 pages), practice test and directions, answer document, and reviewer's edition; $17.50 per 25 practice tests and directions (Preprimer–Intermediate 3); $5.30 per single copy directions for administering practice tests (Preprimer–Intermediate 3); $13.80 per directions for administering (Preprimer–Advanced); $102 per 25 reusable test booklets (Intermediate 1–Advanced); $42.90 each per overlay keys for scoring machine-scorable answer documents (Intermediate 1–Advanced); $28.60

each per response keys (Preprimer-Advanced); $125 per 25 machine-scorable test booklets (Preprimer-Primary 3); $79.50 per 100 type 1 machine-scorable answer documents (Intermediate 1–Advanced) $6.50 per package of 25 markers/rulers (Preprimer-Advanced); $64.60 per technical manual (1998, 331 pages); $71.55 per spring or fall multilevel norms book (all levels); $21.70 per 25 preview for parents (Preprimer–Advanced, in Spanish); $21.70 per 25 understanding test results (Preprimer–Advanced); $22.80 per compendium of instructional objectives (all levels); $33.40 per guide for classroom planning (all levels); $11 per open-ended assessment kit per level across Reading, Mathematics, and Writing (Primary 1–Advanced) including one open-ended directions for administering (1997, 68 pages), and reviewer's edition; $26 per 25 open-ended test booklets for Reading, Mathematics, or Writing (Primary 1–Advanced); $32.30 per single copy scoring guides for open-ended assessments for Reading, Mathematics (Primary 1–Advanced); $9 per single copy open-ended directions for administering Reading, Mathematics, Writing (Primary 1–Advanced); $23.30 per single copy manual for Interpreting Writing (Primary 1–Advanced); Information on optional score/reporting services, package services and electronic services can be obtained by contacting the publisher.

Foreign Language Edition: Test booklets written in Spanish; content mirrors Stanford Achievement Test Series (Stanford 9; 13:292).

Author: Harcourt Brace Educational Measurement.

Publisher: Harcourt Assessment, Inc.

a) PREPRIMER (PREPRIMARIO).
Population: Grades K.5–1.5.
Scores, 6: Sounds and Letters, Word Reading, Sentence Reading, Total Reading, Mathematics, Listening to Words and Stories.
Time: (140) minutes.

b) PRIMARY 1 (PRIMARIO 1).
Population: Grades 1.5–2.5
Scores, 11: 8 multiple-choice scores (Word Reading, Reading Comprehension, Total Reading, Mathematics: Problem Solving, Mathematics: Procedures, Total Mathematics, Language, Listening), and 3 open-ended scores (Reading, Mathematics, Writing).
Time: (265) minutes.

c) PRIMARY 2 (PRIMARIO 2).
Population: Grades 2.5–3.5.
Scores, 11: 8 multiple-choice scores (Reading Vocabulary, Reading Comprehension, Total Reading, Mathematics: Problem Solving, Mathematics: Procedures, Total Mathematics, Language, Listening), and 3 open-ended scores (Reading, Mathematics, Writing).
Time: (260) minutes.

d) PRIMARY 3 (PRIMARIO 3).
Population: Grades 3.5–4.5.
Scores, 11: 8 multiple-choice scores (Reading Vocabulary, Reading Comprehension, Total Reading, Mathematics: Problem Solving, Mathematics: Procedures, Total Mathematics, Language, Listening), and 3 open-ended scores (Reading, Mathematics, Writing).
Time: (280) minutes.

e) INTERMEDIATE 1 (INTERMEDIO 1).
Population: Grades 4.5–5.5.
Scores, 12: 9 multiple-choice scores (Reading Vocabulary, Reading Comprehension, Total Reading, Mathematics: Problem Solving, Mathematics: Procedures, Total Mathematics, Language, Listening, English), and 3 open-ended scores (Reading, Mathematics, Writing).
Time: (320) minutes.

f) INTERMEDIATE 2 (INTERMEDIO 2).
Population: Grades 5.5–6.5.
Scores, 12: 9 multiple-choice scores (Reading Vocabulary, Reading Comprehension, Total Reading, Mathematics: Problem Solving, Mathematics: Procedures, Total Mathematics, Language, Listening, English), and 3 open-ended scores (Reading, Mathematics, Writing).
Time: (330) minutes.

g) INTERMEDIATE 3 (INTERMEDIO 3).
Population: Grades 6.5–8.9.
Scores, 12: 9 multiple-choice scores (Reading Vocabulary, Reading Comprehension, Total Reading, Mathematics: Problem Solving, Mathematics: Procedures, Total Mathematics, Language, Listening, English), and 3 open-ended scores (Reading, Mathematics, Writing).
Time: (330) minutes.

h) ADVANCED (AVANZADO).
Population: Grades 9.0–12.9.
Scores, 9: 6 multiple-choice scores (Reading Vocabulary, Reading Comprehension, Total Reading, Mathematics, Language, English), and 3 open-ended scores (Reading, Mathematics, Writing).
Time: (265) minutes.

Cross References: For reviews by Joseph O. Prewitt and by Maria Prendes Lintel and Francisca Esteban Peterson, see 14:18; for reviews by Maria Medina-Diaz and Salvador Hector Ochoa of an earlier edition, see 13:12.

[174]
The APT Inventory.
Purpose: Designed to measure an individual's relative strength on each of ten personal traits.
Population: Adults.
Publication Date: 1992.

Scores, 10: Communication, Analytical Thinking, Administrative, Relating to Others, Influencing, Achieving, Empowering, Developing, Leadership, Ethics.
Administration: Individual or group.
Manual: No manual.
Price Data: Price information per set available from publisher (each set includes assessment, response sheet, and interpretation booklet).
Time: (40) minutes.
Comments: Self-administered; self-scored.
Author: Training House, Inc.
Publisher: Training House, Inc.
Cross References: For reviews by E. Scott Huebner and Jayne E. Stake, see 13:13.

[175]

Aptitude Assessment Battery: Programming.
Purpose: Designed to measure programming aptitude.
Population: Programmers and trainees.
Publication Date: 1967.
Acronym: AABP.
Scores: Total score only.
Administration: Group.
Restricted Distribution: Restricted to employers of programmers, not available to school personnel.
Price Data, 2001: $290 per candidate.
Foreign Language and Special Editions: French, Spanish, Braille, and left-handed editions available.
Time: Untimed.
Comments: Percentile and qualitative information provided in detailed report.
Author: Jack M. Wolfe.
Publisher: Rose Wolfe Family Partnership LLP [Canada].
Cross References: See 7:1087 (1 reference).

[176]

Aptitude Profile Test Series.
Purpose: Designed to assess a range of core cognitive abilities relevant to and known to predict success in many occupations and areas of study.
Population: Years 9–11 in Australian school system to adults.
Publication Date: 2000.
Acronym: APTS and APTS-E.
Scores, 4: Abstract Reasoning, Quantitative Reasoning, Spatial-Visual Reasoning, Verbal Reasoning.
Administration: Individual or group.
Price Data, 2006: A$19.80 per Occupational Verbal Reasoning test book; $19.80 per Occupational Quantitative Reasoning test book; $19.80 per Occupational Abstract Reasoning test book; $19.80 per Occupational Spatial Reasoning test book; $13.20 per 10 Occupational answer sheets; $25.30 per score keys; $119.90 per Occupational manual; $225.50 per Occupational specimen set (incl. one each of the above); $7.70 per Educational Verbal Reasoning test book; $7.70 per Educational Quantitative Reasoning test book; $8.80 per Educational Abstract Reasoning test book; $9.90 per Educational Spatial Reasoning test book; $10.90 per 10 Educational answer sheets; $25.30 per score keys; $105 per Educational manual (incl. score keys); $137.50 per Educational specimen set (incl. one each of the above).
Time: 30(45) minutes per test.
Authors: George Morgan, Andrew Stephanou, and Brian Simpson.
Publisher: Australian Council for Educational Research Ltd. [Australia].
a) APTITUDE PROFILE TEST SERIES.
Purpose: "Developed for use … with assessing people's abilities in relation to employment and to occupational needs of organisations and industry."
Population: Adults.
Acronym: APTS.
b) APTITUDE PROFILE TEST SERIES—EDUCATIONAL.
Purpose: "Developed for … assessing students' abilities in an educational context."
Population: Years 9–11 in Australian school system.
Acronym: APTS-E.
Cross References: For a review by Robert M. Thorndike, see 15:16.

[177]

Aptitude Tests for School Beginners.
Purpose: "Obtain a differentiated picture of certain aptitudes of school beginners."
Population: Grade 1 entrants.
Publication Dates: 1974–1994.
Acronym: ASB.
Scores, 8: Perception, Spatial, Reasoning, Numerical, Gestalt, Co-ordination, Memory, Verbal Comprehension.
Administration: Group.
Price Data: Available from publisher.
Time: (390–450) minutes for full battery, (180–240) minutes for abbreviated battery.
Comments: An abbreviated battery (Reasoning, Numerical, and Gestalt subtests) may be administered to obtain total score only; revised 1994 norms include norms for all South-Africans, norms for nonenvironmentally disadvantaged children, and norms for environmentally disadvantaged children.
Authors: D. J. Swart (manuals), T. M. Coetzee (manual), Margaretha Tredoux (manual), and N. M. Oliver (manual).
Publisher: Human Sciences Research Council [South Africa].

Cross References: See T5:169 (1 reference) and T4:186 (1 reference).

[178]

Aptitudes Associates Test of Sales Aptitude: A Test for Measuring Knowledge of Basic Principles of Selling, Revised.

Purpose: Designed to aid in the appraisal of one aspect of sales aptitude, understanding and appreciation of sales techniques.
Population: Applicants for sales positions and general population.
Publication Dates: 1947–1983.
Scores: Total score only.
Administration: Group.
Price Data, 2006: $94.20 per package; $52.20 per specimen set; $12.95 per manual; $3.75 per scoring key.
Time: (20–30) minutes.
Author: Martin M. Bruce.
Publisher: Martin M. Bruce, Ph.D.
Cross References: See 6:1169 (6 references); for reviews by Milton E. Hahn and Donald G. Paterson, see 4:824.

[179]

Arabic Proficiency Test.

Purpose: "Designed to assess the general proficiency in listening and reading attained by English-speaking learners of Arabic."
Population: Postsecondary to adult.
Publication Date: 1994.
Acronym: APT.
Scores, 2: Listening Comprehension, Reading Comprehension.
Administration: Group.
Price Data, 2005: $25 per test; quantity discounts available; $6 per official score report.
Time: 110(150) minutes.
Comments: Multiple-choice, machine-scorable test.
Authors: University of Michigan and Center for Applied Linguistics.
Publisher: Center for Applied Linguistics.
Cross References: For reviews by James D. Brown and Atiqa Hachimi and by Antony John Kunnan, see 16:14.

[180]

Arithmetic Skills Assessment Test.

Purpose: "Designed to quickly determine the approximate mathematical abilities of students with unknown math skills."
Population: High school and adults.
Publication Dates: 1993–1999.
Scores, 3: Whole Numbers, Fractions/Mixed Numbers, Decimals.
Administration: Group.

Price Data, 2006: $89 per computer application including 1 CD-ROM, management, and documentation; $445 per site license version.
Time: (15) minutes.
Comments: Computerized, self-administered; available in Macintosh Version and Windows Version.
Author: Howard Behrns.
Publisher: Educational Activities Software.
Cross References: For reviews by Michael B. Bunch and Kevin D. Crehan, see 14:19.

[181]

Arithmetic Test (Fundamentals and Reasoning): Municipal Tests: National Achievement Tests.

Purpose: Constructed to assess arithmetic skills.
Population: Grades 3–6, 6–8.
Publication Dates: 1938–1962.
Scores, 6: Computation, Number Comparisons, Comparisons, Problem Analysis, Problems, Total.
Administration: Group.
Forms, 2: A, B.
Price Data: Available from publisher.
Time: 60 minutes over 2 sessions
Comments: Subtest of Municipal Battery.
Authors: Robert K. Speer and Samuel Smith.
Publisher: Psychometric Affiliates.
Cross References: For reviews by Foster E. Grossnickle and Charles S. Ross, see 4:406. For reviews of the complete battery, see 5:18 (1 review), 4:20 (1 review), and 2:1191 (2 reviews).

[182]

Arithmetic Test: National Achievement Tests.

Population: Grades 3–8.
Publication Dates: 1936–1961.
Administration: Group.
Forms, 2: A, B.
Manual: No manual.
Price Data: Available from publisher.
Authors: Robert K. Speer and Samuel Smith.
Publisher: Psychometric Affiliates.
   a) FUNDAMENTALS.
   Purpose: Constructed to assess "speed, knowledge, and accuracy in computation."
   Scores, 4: Fundamentals-Speed, Number Comparisons, Fundamentals-Skills, Total.
   Time: (55–85) minutes.
   b) REASONING.
   Purpose: Designed to measure ability to compare, comprehend, analyze, and solve problems.
   Scores, 5: Comparisons, Problem Analysis, Finding the Key to a Problem, Problems, Total.
   Time: (40) minutes.

Cross References: For reviews by R. L. Morton and Leroy H. Schnell, see 2:1449; for reviews by William A. Brownell and W. J. Osburn, see 1:889.

[183]
Arizona Articulation Proficiency Scale, Third Revision.

Purpose: An "assessment measure of articulatory proficiency in children, adolescents, and adults."
Population: Ages 1.5–18 years.
Publication Dates: 1963–2000.
Acronym: Arizona-3.
Scores: Total score only.
Administration: Individual.
Price Data, 2006: $147 per kit including 42 picture cards, 25 test booklets, and manual (2000, 60 pages); $70.50 per picture cards; $28.50 per 25 test booklets, quantity discounts available; $54.50 per manual.
Time: (3) minutes.
Comments: Replaces the Arizona Articulation Proficiency Scale, Second Edition (AAPS); has updated picture cards, new gender-specific norms.
Author: Janet Barker Fudala.
Publisher: Western Psychological Services.
Cross References: For reviews by Steven Long and Roger L. Towne, see 16:15; see also T5:175 (12 references) and T4:191 (4 references); for reviews by Penelope K. Hall and Charles Wm. Martin of a previous edition, see 11:17 (12 references); see also T3:200 (8 references); for reviews by Raphael M. Haller and Ronald K. Sommers, and an excerpted review by Barton B. Proger, see 8:954 (6 references); see also T2:2065 (2 references), 7:948 (2 references), and 6:307a (2 references).

[184]
The Arizona Battery for Communication Disorders of Dementia.

Purpose: To measure "the effects and severity of Alzheimer's Disease."
Population: Alzheimer's patients.
Publication Dates: 1991–1993.
Acronym: ABCD.
Scores, 6: Mental Status, Episodic Memory, Linguistic Expression, Linguistic Comprehension, Visuospatial Construction, Total.
Administration: Individual.
Price Data, 2006: $225 per complete kit including manual (77 pages), scoring and interpretation card, 25 response record forms, stimulus book A, stimulus book B, and nail and envelope; $35 per 25 response record forms; $55 per stimulus book A; $65 per stimulus book B; $20 per scoring and interpretation card; $60 per manual.
Time: (45–90) minutes.
Authors: Kathryn A. Bayles and Cheryl K. Tomoeda.
Publisher: PRO-ED.

Cross References: For reviews by Charles J. Long and Kenneth Sakauye, see 12:31.

[185]
Arlin Test of Formal Reasoning.

Purpose: Designed to assess "individual's ability to use the eight specific concepts associated with (Piaget's) stages of formal operations"; profiles individual as "concrete, high concrete, transitional, low formal, or high formal."
Population: Grades 6-12 and adults.
Publication Date: 1984.
Acronym: ATFR.
Scores, 9: Volume, Probability, Correlations, Combinations, Propositions, Momentum, Mechanical Equilibrium, Frames of Reference, Total.
Administration: Group.
Price Data, 2002: $69 per complete kit; $37 per 35 test question booklets; $12 per 35 answer sheets; $5 per hand-scoring template; $15 per manual (28 pages).
Time: (45–50) minutes.
Author: Patricia Kennedy Arlin.
Publisher: Slosson Educational Publications, Inc.
Cross References: See T5:178 (1 reference) and T4:194 (3 references); for a review by Toni E. Santmire, see 9:80 (5 references).

[186]
Armed Services-Civilian Vocational Interest Survey.

Purpose: Designed to assess interest in careers in the armed-services and related civilian jobs.
Population: Grades 11–12.
Publication Date: 1983.
Acronym: ASCVIS.
Scores: Ratings in 8 occupational groups: Administrative/Clerical/Personnel, Communications, Computer and Data-Processing, Construction/Engineering/Craft, Mechanical/Repairer/Machining, Service and Transportation, Health and Health Care, Scientific/Technical/Electronic.
Administration: Group.
Price Data: Available from publisher.
Time: (30) minutes.
Comments: Self-administering and self-scoring; may be used in conjunction with the ASVAB (187).
Author: Robert Kauk.
Publisher: CFKR Career Materials.
Cross References: For reviews by Bruce W. Hartman and Frederick A. Schrank, see 10:13.

[187]
Armed Services Vocational Aptitude Battery [Forms 18/19].

Purpose: Intended "for use in educational and vocational counseling and to stimulate interest in job and training opportunities in the Armed Forces."

Population: High school, junior college, and young adult applicants to the Armed Forces.
Publication Dates: 1967–1992.
Acronym: ASVAB.
Scores: 3 composite scores: Academic Ability, Verbal Ability, Math Ability.
Subtests, 10: General Science, Arithmetic Reasoning, Word Knowledge, Paragraph Comprehension, Numerical Operations, Coding Speed, Auto-Shop Information, Math Knowledge, Mechanical Comprehension, Electronics Information.
Administration: Group.
Price Data: Administered free of charge at participating high schools by Department of Defense personnel.
Time: 144(180) minutes.
Comments: Several supplemental publications provide support for counseling: Counselor Manual, an interpretive guide; Technical Manual; Exploring Careers: The ASVAB Workbook; Military Careers.
Author: United States Military Entrance Processing Command.
Publisher: United States Military Entrance Processing Command.
Cross References: See T5:180 (37 references) and T4:196 (27 references); for a review by R. A. Weitzman, see 9:81 (3 references); see also T3:202 (8 references); for a review by David J. Weiss, see 8:483 (4 references); see also T2:1067 (1 reference).

[188]
Arousal Seeking Tendency Scale.

Purpose: Designed to "assess individual differences in preference for change, novelty, and risk taking."
Population: Ages 15 and older.
Publication Dates: 1978–1994.
Acronym: MAST.
Scores: Total score only.
Administration: Group or individual.
Price Data: Available from publisher for test kit including scale, scoring directions, norms, and manual (1994, 6 pages).
Time: (10–15) minutes.
Comments: Previously listed as Measure of Arousal Seeking Tendency.
Author: Albert Mehrabian.
Publisher: Albert Mehrabian.
Cross References: For a review by Gregory J. Boyle, see 13:15; for reviews by Norman S. Endler and Jon D. Swartz of an earlier edition, see 9:677; see also T3:1438 (1 reference).

[189]
Ashland Interest Assessment.

Purpose: "A career interest inventory for individuals with restricted abilities developed in response to a need for a career measure to accommodate individuals with

barriers to employment due to educational, physical, emotional, cognitive, or psychiatric conditions."
Population: Adults and adolescents.
Publication Date: 1997.
Acronym: AIA.
Scores: 12 scales: Arts and Crafts, Sales, Clerical, Protective Service, Food Service, Personal Service, Health Care, General Service, Plant or Animal Care, Construction, Transportation, Mechanical.
Administration: Group or individual.
Price Data, 2006: $75 per examination kit including manual (1997, 94 pages), 5 hand-scorable question and answer booklets, 5 profile sheets, 5 scoring sheets, one set of templates, and one machine-scorable question and answer booklet for a Mail-in Extended Report; $34 per test manual; $50 per 25 hand-scorable question and answer booklets; $60 per 25 response sheets (includes 25 scoring sheets and 25 profile sheets); $30 per set of templates; $66–$75 (depending on volume) per 10 machine-scorable question and answer documents for Mail-in Extended Reports; $105 per software package including disks, software manual for Windows, test manual, and 10 coupons for computer report.
Foreign Language Edition: Hand-scorable and machine-scorable question and answer booklets and extended reports available in French.
Time: 35 minutes.
Comments: Scored by self, publisher, or computer.
Authors: Douglas N. Jackson and Connie W. Marshall.
Publisher: Sigma Assessment Systems, Inc.
Cross References: For reviews by Richard J. McCowan and Sheila C. McCowan and by Mary Roznowski, see 14:20.

[190]
ASIST: A Structured Addictions Assessment Interview for Selecting Treatment.

Purpose: To assess alcohol and drug use for the purpose of selecting treatment.
Population: Adults.
Publication Dates: 1984–1990.
Acronym: ASIST.
Scores: 12 sections: Identifying Information, Basic Information, Alcohol Use, Psychoactive Drug Use, Health Screening, Other Life Areas, Previous Treatment, Client Preference for Treatment, Treatment Assessment Summary, Treatment Plan, Actual Referrals, Assessment Worker's Observation.
Administration: Individual.
Price Data, 2002: C$25 per 10 questionnaires; C$35 per Assessment Handbook (1990, 200 pages).
Time: Administration time not reported.
Author: Addiction Research Foundation.
Publisher: Centre for Addiction and Mental Health [Canada].

Cross References: For reviews by Wesley E. Sime and by Nicholas A. Vacc and Gerald A. Juhnke, see 13:16.

[191]
Asperger Syndrome Diagnostic Scale.

Purpose: "Designed to assess individuals who manifest the characteristics of Asperger syndrome."
Population: Ages 5–18.
Publication Date: 2001.
Acronym: ASDS.
Scores, 6: Language, Social, Maladaptive, Cognitive, Sensorimotor, Total.
Administration: Individual.
Price Data, 2006: $100 per complete kit including 50 summary/response forms, and examiner's manual (39 pages); $50 per 50 summary response forms; $55 per examiner's manual.
Time: (10–15) minutes.
Comments: Ratings by parents, teachers, and professionals at home and school.
Authors: Brenda Smith Myles, Stacey Jones Bock, and Richard L. Simpson.
Publisher: PRO-ED.
Cross References: For reviews by Kimberly Ann Blair and Pat Mirenda, see 15:17.

[192]
The Assertiveness Skills Inventory.

Purpose: Developed to measure an individual's level of assertiveness.
Population: Adults.
Publication Date: 1997.
Acronym: ASI.
Scores: Total score only.
Administration: Group.
Manual: No manual; scoring/instruction sheet available.
Price Data: Available from publisher.
Time: Administration time not reported.
Author: Millard J. Bienvenu.
Publisher: Millard J. Bienvenu, Northwest Publications.

[193]
ASSESS Expert Assessment System Internet Version 1.3.

Purpose: "A web-based assessment system, which incorporates intellectual abilities and work personality characteristics for selection and development of professionals and managers."
Population: Potential employees and candidates for promotion in professional, managerial, and sales positions, as well as employee development applications.
Publication Date: 1997.
Scores: Updated and shortened versions of the Guilford Zimmerman Temperament Survey (GZTS)

and Dynamic Factors Opinion Survey (DFOS) provide normative results on 23 characteristics grouped in the areas of Thinking, Working, and Relating; Intellectual Ability Tests: 7 possible scores: Watson-Glaser Critical Thinking, Raven's Standard Progressive Matrices (Abstract Reasoning), Thurstone Test of Mental Alertness, Arithmetic Reasoning, Employee Aptitude Survey 1 (EAS1)—Verbal Comprehension, EAS2—Numerical Ability, EAS7—Verbal Reasoning and SHL Numerical Critical Thinking Battery.
Administration: Group or individual.
Price Data, 2002: $1,095 per one-time purchase of the initial HASP key preloaded with units for 5 administrations, ASSESS software, user's guide (85 pages), technical manual (83 pages), 1 reusable personality survey booklet, 5 personality survey answer sheets, 1 Raven test booklet, 5 Raven answer sheets, 1 Watson-Glaser appraisal booklet, 5 Watson-Glaser answer sheets, 5 Thurstone self-scoring tests, scoring keys, samples of additional ability tests; report costs vary from $42.50 to $125 depending on report type and volume; additional consulting services available to customize the report.
Time: Administration time varies for each test.
Comments: "Detailed competency-based narrative reports or general assessment narrative reports provide profile level interpretation of personality and ability scores in comparison with a professional database of 33,000 people"; graphic profile results allow for additional comparison to specific subgroups; selection reports include interview and reference probes; developmental reports include specific developmental suggestions; career manager reports provide job search and job fit suggestions; onsite scoring; administration via paper or Internet.
Author: Bigby, Havis, & Associates, Inc.
Publisher: Bigby, Havis, & Associates, Inc.
Cross References: For reviews by Peter F. Merenda and Stephen Olejnik of an earlier edition, see 14:21.

[194]
Assessing and Teaching Phonological Knowledge.

Purpose: Designed to assess children's reading readiness and diagnose a child's reading difficulty.
Population: Young children.
Publication Date: 1998.
Scores: 5 ratings: Acquiring Implicit Awareness of Sound Patterns in Words, Segmenting Words into Sounds, Sound Blending, Manipulating Sounds Within Words, Phonemic Recoding: Bridging to Written Words.
Administration: Individual.
Forms, 3: Screening Checklist, Parental Referral Form, Profile Sheet.
Price Data, 2006: A$133.00 per starter set including manual (144 pages), record book, checklist, and

task sheets; A$69.95 per manual; A$25.95 per record book; A$17.60 per checklist (10); A$19.80 per set of task sheets.
Time: Administration time not reported.
Author: John Munro.
Publisher: Australian Council for Educational Research Ltd. [Australia].
Cross References: For reviews by Rebecca McCauley and Steven A. Stahl, see 14:22.

[195]
Assessing Motivation to Communicate.

Purpose: Designed to assess communication apprehension and willingness to communicate.
Population: Postsecondary students.
Publication Date: 1994.
Acronym: AMTC.
Scores, 5: Group Discussions, Meetings, Interpersonal Conversations, Public Speaking, Total.
Administration: Group.
Price Data: Available from publisher.
Time: Administration time not reported.
Comments: Instrument consists of two assessment tools (The Personal Report of Communication Apprehension and The Willingness to Communicate) administered on a Macintosh computer, Operating System 7.0 or higher.
Author: Speech Communication Association.
Publisher: National Communication Association.
Cross References: For reviews by Ric Brown and Claudia R. Wright, see 14:23.

[196]
Assessing Your Team: Seven Measures of Team Success.

Purpose: Intended to give insight and understanding in assessing a team.
Population: Teams.
Publication Date: 1994.
Scores, 7: Purpose, Role, Strategy, Processes, People, Feedback, Interfaces.
Administration: Group.
Price Data: Available from publisher.
Time: [.5] day.
Authors: Dick Richards and Susan Smyth.
Publisher: Jossey-Bass, A Wiley Company.
Cross References: For a review by Peter F. Merenda, see 14:24.

[197]
Assessment for Persons Profoundly or Severely Impaired.

Purpose: Designed to measure the responsiveness of a preverbal individual's communicative functioning.

Population: Infants through adults who are preverbal and functioning with a mental age between approximately 0 and 8 months.
Publication Dates: 1984–1998.
Acronym: APPSI.
Administration: Individual.
Price Data, 2006: $185 per complete kit including examiner's manual (1998, 31 pages), 25 record booklets, 25 profile/summary forms, set of cards, and other manipulatives; $50 per examiner's manual; $50 per 25 record booklets; $30 per 25 profile/summary forms; $60 per object kit.
Time: Untimed.
Comments: A revision of the Preverbal Assessment—Intervention Profile (T4:2093).
Authors: Patricia Connard and Sharon Bradley-Johnson.
Publisher: PRO-ED.
   a) STAGE I.
   Population: Mental age 0–1 month.
   Scores: 4 domains: Visual Responsiveness, Auditory Responsiveness, Tactile Responsiveness, Interaction with Others.
   b) STAGE II.
   Population: Mental age 1–4 months.
   Scores: Same as *a* above.
   c) STAGE III.
   Population: Mental age 4–8 months.
   Scores: 2 domains: Responsiveness to Objects, Interaction with Others.
Cross References: For reviews by Carolyn Mitchell-Person and Lawrence J. Ryan, see 15:18; for reviews by Karen T. Carey and Joe Olmi of the earlier edition, see 11:301.

[198]
Assessment Inventory for Management.

Purpose: "For screening candidates for insurance field sales management positions."
Population: Managers.
Publication Dates: 1991–1993.
Acronym: AIM.
Scores, 19: 7 Job Task Areas [Basic Task Areas (Staffing/Recruiting and Selection, Training, Performance Management—Supervision, Total); Advanced Task Areas (Business Management, Field Office Development, Total)]; 12 Job Behaviors [Interpersonal Relations (Communicating, Counseling, Supporting), Leadership (Delegating, Motivating, Rewarding, Team Building, Networking), Organization (Coordinating, Monitoring, Planning, Problem-Solving and Decision-Making)].
Administration: Group.
Price Data: Available from publisher.
Foreign Language Edition: French Canadian edition (1992) available.
Time: (120–180) minutes.

Comments: Mail-in scoring.
Author: LIMRA International.
Publisher: LIMRA International.
Cross References: For reviews by Connie Kubo Della-Piana and Gabriel M. Della-Piana and by Cyril J. Sadowski, see 13:17.

[199]
Assessment of Adaptive Areas.

Purpose: Designed to identify deficits in 10 adaptive skill areas of mental retardation.
Population: Ages 3–60+ years.
Publication Date: 1996.
Acronym: AAA.
Scores: Communication, Self-Care, Home-Living, Social, Community Use, Self-Direction, Health and Safety, Functional Academics, Leisure, Work.
Administration: Individual.
Price Data, 2006: $108 per complete kit including examiner's manual (143 pages) and 25 profile/examiner record booklets; $53 per examiner's manual; $59 per 25 profile/examiner record booklets.
Time: (30) minutes.
Comments: The AAA is a system of reassigning the items from the Adaptive Behavior Scale—Residential and Community: Second Edition (2) and the Adaptive Behavior Scale—School: Second Edition (3) into the 10 adaptive skill areas delineated by the American Association on Mental Retardation.
Authors: Brian R. Bryant, Ronald L. Taylor, and Diane Pedrotty Rivera.
Publisher: PRO-ED.
Cross References: For reviews by Jack A. Cummings and by Mark D. Shriver and Merilee McCurdy, see 14:25.

[200]
Assessment of Chemical Health Inventory.

Purpose: "Designed to evaluate the nature and extent of adolescent and adult chemical use and associated problems."
Population: Adolescents, adults.
Publication Dates: 1988–1992.
Acronym: ACHI.
Scores: 9 factors (Chemical Involvement, Alienation, Family Estrangement, Personal Consequence, Depression, Family Support, Social Impact, Self Regard, Family Chemical Use) yielding Total score.
Administration: Individual.
Price Data: Price available from publisher for starter set including microcomputer disk containing 25 administrations and user manual (1992, 119 pages), response forms, microcomputer disk (sold in multiples of 50) to administer and score ACHI, and manual.
Time: (15–25) minutes.

Comments: Requires 4th grade reading level; may be taken and scored on computer (or administered on paper); mail-in service available.
Authors: Daniel Krotz, Richard Kominowski, Barbara Berntson, and James W. Sipe.
Publisher: RENOVEX Corporation.
Cross References: For reviews by Philip Ash and Betsy Waterman, see 13:18.

[201]
Assessment of Classroom Communication and Study Skills.

Purpose: Designed to "provide classroom teachers and specialists with a tool that efficiently comments on the quality of a student's school language skills."
Population: Grades 5-12.
Publication Dates: 1998-2000.
Acronym: ACCSS.
Scores, 2: Total Score, Vocabulary Score.
Administration: Group or individual.
Forms, 3: ACCSS-Long Form, ACCSS-Short Form, ACCSS-esl.
Price Data, 2006: $40 per test and manual (1998, 211 pages).
Time: (40-60) minutes.
Comments: Criterion-referenced measure; includes an audio cassette containing the administration scenario; revised and expanded edition of the Classroom Communication Screening Procedure.
Author: Charlann S. Simon.
Publisher: Thinking Publications.

[202]
Assessment of Competencies for Instructor Development.

Purpose: To measure six competencies important to being an effective instructor in an industrial setting.
Population: Instructors in industrial settings.
Publication Date: 1986.
Scores, 7: Analyzing the Needs and "Entering Behavior" of the Learner, Specifying Outcomes and "Terminal Behaviors" for a Course, Designing Instructional Sequences and Learning Materials, Instructing in Both the Inductive and Deductive Modes, Maintaining Adult-to-Adult (not "Parent-Child") Relationships in Class, Staying Learner-Centered not Information-Centered, Overall Instructional Competency.
Administration: Individual or group.
Manual: No manual.
Price Data: Price information available from publisher for 20 tests, 20 interpretation brochures, and 20 response sheets.
Time: (45) minutes.
Comments: Self-administered, self-scored.

Author: Training House, Inc.
Publisher: Training House, Inc.
Cross References: For a review by Stephen F. Davis, see 11:20.

[203]
Assessment of Comprehension and Expression 6–11.

Purpose: Designed to "assess language development."
Population: Ages 6-0 to 11-11.
Publication Date: 2002.
Acronym: ACE 6–11.
Administration: Individual.
Price Data: Available from publisher.
Comments: Subtests may be administered individually although it is recommended that a minimum of three subtests be employed.
Authors: Catherine Adams, Rosanne Cooke, Alison Crutchley, Anne Hesketh, and David Reeves.
Publisher: NFER-Nelson Publishing Co., Ltd. [England].
    a) MAIN TEST.
    Scores, 6: Sentence Completion, Inferential Comprehension, Naming, Syntactic Formulation, Semantic Decisions, Total.
    Time: (26–32) minutes.
    b) EXTENDED TEST.
    Scores, 10: Same as above with the addition of Non-Literal Comprehension, Narrative Propositions, Narrative Syntax/Discourse, Total.
    Time: (46–59) minutes.
Cross References: For reviews by Cleborne D. Maddux and Sheila Pratt, see 16:16.

[204]
Assessment of Conceptual Organization (ACO): Improving Writing, Thinking, and Reading Skills.

Purpose: Developed to assess "understanding of conceptual organization in written language."
Population: Grades 4-6, 7-12, 10-adult.
Publication Date: 1991.
Acronym: ACO.
Scores: 3 criteria: Correct Superordinate Word Chosen, Appropriateness of Topic Sentence, Relatedness of Topic Sentence and Three Other Sentences.
Administration: Group.
Price Data, 2001: $4.99 per set of 20 assessment and 20 scoring forms (select level); $9.99 per manual (57 pages).
Time: (15-20) minutes.
Comments: Optional administration and scoring procedures available for "reluctant" writers.
Author: Christian Gerhard.

Publisher: Research for Better Schools, Inc.
Cross References: For reviews by Deborah L. Bandalos and Dale P. Scannell, see 12:34.

[205]
Assessment of Core Goals.

Purpose: Constructed to define core goals and to identify activities that will lead to satisfaction of these goals.
Population: High school and over.
Publication Date: 1991.
Acronym: ACG.
Scores: No scores, workbook developmental format.
Administration: Group or individual.
Price Data: Available from publisher (www.mindgarden.com).
Time: (60-600) minutes.
Comments: Method and length of administration depends on desired depth of information.
Author: C. W. Nichols.
Publisher: Mind Garden, Inc.
Cross References: For reviews by Gary J. Dean and Carol Kehr Tittle, see 12:35.

[206]
Assessment of Individual Learning Style: The Perceptual Memory Task.

Purpose: "To provide measures of the individual's perception and memory for spatial relationships; visual and auditory sequential memory; intermediate term memory; and discrimination of detail."
Population: Ages 4 and over.
Publication Dates: 1984–1993.
Acronym: PMT.
Scores: 7 scores, 3 alternate scores: Spatial Relations, Visual Designs Recognition, Visual Designs-Sequencing, Auditory-Visual Colors Recognition, Auditory-Visual Colors Sequencing, Discrimination Recall, Total PMT, Visual-Visual (alternate), Auditory-Auditory (alternate), Visual-Auditory (alternate).
Administration: Individual.
Price Data, 2006: $470 per complete kit including carrying case containing various subtest components, 25 scoring forms, 25 alternate forms, and manual (129 pages); $36.75 per 25 scoring forms; $20.25 per 25 alternate forms; $63 per manual; $350 per PMT computer (Windows or Macintosh) report.
Time: (30–40) minutes.
Comments: PMT Computer Report (1993) is available for IBM or Macintosh and for use in profiling PMT scores for ages 14 through adult.
Author: Lawrence McCarron.
Publisher: McCarron-Dial Systems.
Cross References: For reviews by Steven Ferrara and Arlene Coopersmith Rosenthal, see 11:21 (1 reference).

[207]
Assessment of Intelligibility of Dysarthric Speech.

Purpose: Designed "to provide clinicians and researchers with a means of measuring intelligibility and speaking rate of dysarthric individuals."
Population: Adult and adolescent dysarthric speakers.
Publication Dates: 1981–1984.
Scores, 6: Single Word Intelligibility (Transcription, Multiple Choice), Sentence Intelligibility (Transcription, Speaking Rate, Rate of Intelligible Speech, Communication Efficiency Ratio).
Administration: Individual.
Price Data, 2006: $98 per complete kit including examiner's manual (60 pages) and picture book of stimulus words and sentences.
Time: Administration time not reported.
Authors: Kathryn M. Yorkston, David R. Beukelman, and Charles Traynor.
Publisher: PRO-ED.
Cross References: See T5:209 (5 references) and T4:217 (3 references); for reviews by Katharine G. Butler and C. Dale Carpenter, see 10:19.

[208]
Assessment of Language-Related Functional Activities.

Purpose: Designed to answer the question, "Despite this person's impairment, is he or she able to integrate skills adequately to perform selected functional daily activities?"
Population: People with suspected language or cognitive compromise, aged 16 to 95.
Publication Date: 1999.
Acronym: ALFA.
Scores, 10: Telling Time, Counting Money, Addressing an Envelope, Solving Daily Math Problems, Writing a Check and Balancing a Checkbook, Understanding Medicine Labels, Using a Calendar, Reading Instructions, Using the Telephone, Writing a Phone Message.
Administration: Individual.
Price Data, 2006: $159 per complete kit including 25 profile/examiner record forms, picture book, examiner's manual (39 pages), and an additional materials kit; $35 per materials kit including 10 tokens, clock, medicine chart, and 25 envelopes; $27 per 25 profile/examiner record forms; $56 per picture book; $45 per examiner's manual.
Time: (30–120) minutes.
Authors: Kathleen Anderson Baines, Heidi McMartin Heeringa, and Ann W. Martin.
Publisher: PRO-ED.
Cross References: For reviews by Steven R. Shaw and by T. Steuart Watson and R. Anthony Doggett, see 15:19.

[209]
Assessment of Living Skills and Resources.

Purpose: Assesses "daily tasks that require a high level of cognitive function," or Instrumental Activities of Daily Living (IADLs), "in community-dwelling elders."
Population: Community-dwelling elders.
Publication Date: 1991.
Acronym: ALSAR.
Scores: 11 task scores: Telephoning, Reading, Leisure, Medication Management, Transportation, Shopping, Meal Preparation, Laundering, Housekeeping, Home Maintenance.
Administration: Individual.
Price Data: Price data available from publisher for master of the reproducible ALSAR, and each of two instructional videotapes ("An Overview of IADL Assessment" and "Administration of the ALSAR"); master of the ALSAR included in the latter videotape.
Time: (15–20) minutes.
Comments: Incorporates assessment of Instrumental Activities of Daily Living (IADL); administered by health professionals from any discipline.
Authors: Theresa J. K. Drinka, Jane H. Williams, Martha Schram, Jean Farrell-Holtan, and Reenie Euhardy.
Publisher: Madison Geriatric Research, Education, and Clinical Center, VA Medical Center.
Cross References: For reviews by Cameron J. Camp and Anita M. Hubley, see 13:20.

[210]
Assessment of Parenting Skills: Infant and Preschooler.

Purpose: Designed to "evaluate the parenting skills of parents of children between birth and five years of age."
Population: Parents of children between birth and 5 years of age.
Publication Dates: 1998–2002.
Acronym: APSIP.
Scores, 13: Discipline, Fears (Stranger Anxiety, Mobility Fears, Separation Fears, Nightmares and Night Terrors, Fears of Real Events, Abstract Fears, Doctors and Dentists), Tantrums, Crying, Individual Differences and Temperament, Daily Routine, Parental Strengths and Weaknesses.
Administration: Individual.
Price Data, 2002: $189 per complete kit including 8 booklets, 8 summary sheets, and instruction manual (21 pages); $99 per 8 booklets with summary sheets; $159 per 16 booklets with summary sheets; $199 per 24 booklets with summary sheets; $119 per instruction manual.
Time: [45] minutes.
Author: Gail Elliot.

Publisher: Village Publishing.
Cross References: For a review by T. Steuart Watson, see 14:26.

[211]
The Assessment of Personal Goals.

Purpose: Designed to assist the individual "to seriously consider life goals based on the APG Taxonomy of Human Goals, and organize them according to importance."
Population: Adults.
Publication Dates: 1988–2004.
Scores, 24: Task Goals (Mastery, Task Creativity, Management, Material Gain, Safety), Self-Assertive Social Relationship Goals (Individuality, Self-Determination, Superiority, Resource Acquisition), Integrative Social Relationship Goals (Belongingness, Social Responsibility, Equity, Resource Provision), Cognitive Goals (Curiosity, Understanding, Intellectual Creativity, Positive Self-Evaluations), Affective Goals (Excitement, Tranquility, Happiness, Bodily Sensations, Physical Well-Being), Subjective Organization Goals (Unity, Transcendence).
Administration: Individual
Price Data: Available from publisher.
Time: Administration time not reported.
Comments: Self-administered and self-scored; web-based administration and reporting available (www.mindgarden.com).
Authors: Martin E. Ford and Charles W. Nichols.
Publisher: Mind Garden, Inc.

[212]
Assessment of Practices in Early Elementary Classrooms.

Purpose: "Designed to evaluate the use of developmentally appropriate practices in early elementary classrooms … that include children with disabilities."
Population: Kindergarten through Grade 3 classrooms.
Publication Date: 2001.
Acronym: APEEC.
Scores: Total score only.
Administration: Group or individual.
Manual: No manual.
Price Data, 2006: $13.95 per booklet (39 pages).
Time: Administration time not reported.
Comments: Assesses three domains of classroom practices: physical environment, curriculum and instruction, social context.
Authors: Mary Louise Hemmeter, Kelly L. Maxwell, Melinda Jones Ault, and John W. Schuster.
Publisher: Teachers College Press.
Cross References: For reviews by Edward J. Daly III and Michael Persampieri and by Kathleen A. Dolgos, see 15:20.

[213]
Assessment of Qualitative and Structural Dimensions of Object Representations, Revised Edition.

Purpose: Designed to measure aspects of an individual's conceptualization of others.
Population: Adolescents and adults (patients and normals).
Publication Dates: 1981–1992.
Acronym: AQSDOR.
Scores: Ratings in 4 areas: Personal Qualities, Degree of Ambivalence in Description, Length of Description, Conceptual Level.
Administration: Group.
Price Data: Available from publisher.
Time: (5) minutes per description.
Comments: Subjects' descriptions of significant figures (e.g., parent) rated by judges; no reading by examinees.
Authors: Sidney J. Blatt, Eve S. Chevron, Donald M. Quinlan, Carrie E. Schaffer, and Steven Wein.
Publisher: Sidney J. Blatt.
Cross References: For a review by C. H. Swensen, see 9:92.

[214]
Assessment of School Needs for Low-Achieving Students: Staff Survey.

Purpose: Designed to measure "staff perceptions as to whether certain behaviors are occurring in their school."
Population: Teachers and administrators.
Publication Dates: 1988–1989.
Acronym: ASNLAS.
Scores, 9: School Programs and Policies, Classroom Management, Instruction, Teacher Expectations, Principal Leadership, Staff Development, Student Involvement in Learning, School Climate, Parent Involvement.
Administration: Group.
Price Data, 2001: $2 per survey booklet; $.25 per scoring form; $18.95 per manual (1989, 44 pages).
Time: (45–50) minutes.
Authors: Francine S. Beyer and Ronald L. Houston.
Publisher: Research for Better Schools, Inc.
Cross References: For a review by Dean H. Nafziger and Ann M. Muench, see 11:22.

[215]
Assessor Employment Values Inventory.

Purpose: "A measure of personal values associated with work and the working environment."
Population: Adults.
Publication Dates: 1988–2001.
Scores, 14: Work Ethic, Social Outgoingness, Risk-Taking, Stability, Responsibility, Need For Achieve-

ment, Task Orientation, Leadership, Training and Development, Innovation, Intellectual Demands, Status, Structure, Inclusion.
Administration: Individual or group.
Price Data: Available from publisher.
Time: (30–40) minutes.
Comments: Computer administration and scoring available; test previously listed as Employment Values Inventory.
Author: Selby MillSmith Limited.
Publisher: Penna Assessment [England] [No reply from publisher; status unknown].
Cross References: For reviews by Julie A. Allison and Nambury S. Raju, see 14:139.

[216]
Assessor Occupational Relationships Profile.
Purpose: Designed to assess a person's preferred styles of working with colleagues.
Population: Adults.
Publication Dates: 1991–2001.
Scores, 18: Core Scales (Contact at Work, Membership, Power, Responsiveness, Openness, Shyness); Composite Scales (Sociability, Proactivity); Special Scales (Team, Individual, Leadership Overall, Leadership-Coach, Leadership-Fighter, Leadership-Expert, Preferred Style of Leader Overall, Preferred Style of Leader-Coach, Preferred Style of Leader-Fighter, Preferred Style of Leader-Expert).
Administration: Individual or group.
Price Data: Available from publisher.
Time: (30) minutes.
Comments: Computer administration and scoring available; previously listed as Occupational Relationships Profile.
Author: Selby MillSmith, Ltd.
Publisher: Penna Assessment [England] [No reply from publisher; status unknown].
Cross References: For a review by Robert W. Hiltonsmith, see 13:215.

[217]
Assessor Occupational Type Profile.
Purpose: Designed to measure individual's preferences related to the manner in which they acquire information and make decisions based on that information.
Population: Adults.
Publication Dates: 1991–2001.
Scores, 5: Extraversion/Introversion, Sensing/Intuition, Thinking/Feeling, Judgement/Perception, Uncertainty.
Administration: Individual or group.
Price Data: Available from publisher.
Time: (20) minutes.

Comments: Computer administration and scoring available; previously listed as Occupational Type Profile.
Author: Selby MillSmith Ltd.
Publisher: Penna Assessment [England] [No reply from publisher; status unknown].
Cross References: For a review by Steven J. Lindner, see 14:261.

[218]
Association Adjustment Inventory.
Purpose: "Designed for use as a screening instrument for maladjustment and immaturity."
Population: Normal and institutionalized adults.
Publication Dates: 1959–1984.
Acronym: AAI.
Scores, 3: Juvenility, Psychotic Responses, Depressed-Optimistic, Hysteric-Non-Hysteric, Withdrawal-Sociable, Paranoid-Naive, Rigid-Flexible, Schizophrenic-Objective, Impulsive-Restrained, Sociopathic-Empathetic, Psychosomapathic-Physical Contentment, Anxious-Relaxed, Total.
Administration: Group.
Price Data, 2006: $98.75 per test package; $65.25 per IBM answer sheet/profile sheet package; $56.50 per set of IBM scoring stencils; $25 per set of fan type keys; $43.50 per manual (15 pages) and manuals supplement (1984, 17 pages); $76.50 per IBM format specimen set with keys; $26.50 per IBM format specimen set without keys; $49.50 per fan key specimen set.
Foreign Language Editions: Spanish and German editions available.
Time: (10) minutes.
Comments: Adaptation of the Kent-Rosanoff Word List.
Author: Martin M. Bruce.
Publisher: Martin M. Bruce, Ph.D.
Cross References: For reviews by W. Grant Dahlstrom and Bertram R. Forer and an excerpted review by Edward S. Bordin, see 6:201.

[219]
Athletic Motivation Inventory.
Purpose: Constructed to measure the personality and motivation of athletes participating in competitive sports.
Population: Male and female athletes ages 13 and older and coaches.
Publication Dates: 1969–1995.
Acronym: AMI.
Scores, 14: Drive, Aggressiveness, Determination, Responsibility, Leadership, Self-Confidence, Emotional Control, Mental Toughness, Coachability, Conscientiousness, Trust, Validity Scales (Accuracy, Desirability, Completion Rate).
Administration: Group or individual.
Price Data: Available from publisher.

Foreign Language Editions: French and Spanish editions available.
Time: (40–50) minutes.
Comments: May be used for individual self-assessment.
Authors: Thomas A. Tutko, Leland P. Lyon, and Bruce C. Oglive.
Publisher: Athletic Success Institute.
  a) ATHLETIC SUCCESS PROFILE.
  Publication Dates: 1968–1995.
  Acronym: ASP.
  Price Data: Available from publisher.
  Manual: No manual.
  Time: (20) minutes.
  Comments: Shortened version of the Athletic Motivation Inventory.
Cross References: For a review by John W. Shepard, see 12:37; for a review by Andrew L. Comrey of an earlier edition, see 8:409 (19 references).

[220]
Attention Deficit Disorder Checklist.

Purpose: Designed "to collect behavioral data" as a preliminary assessment for further in-depth evaluation.
Population: School-aged children.
Publication Dates: 1990–1995.
Scores: Not scored.
Administration: Individual or group.
Price Data, 2002: $10 per 25 checklists.
Time: Administration time not reported.
Comments: "This checklist is designed to collect behavioral data. It is not intended for diagnosis. It should be completed by adults familiar with the child's behavior in various settings—preferably the parent/guardian and the classroom teacher. It may be used for educational intervention or as a prereferral tool for further in-depth testing."
Authors: Academic Consulting & Testing Service.
Publisher: Academic Consulting & Testing Service.

[221]
Attention Deficit Disorders Evaluation Scale Secondary-Age Student.

Purpose: "Designed to provide a measure of those characteristics of Attention-Deficit/Hyperactivity Disorder."
Population: Ages 11.5–19.
Publication Date: 1996.
Acronym: ADDES-S.
Scores, 3: Inattentive, Hyperactive/Impulsive, Total Percentile Rank.
Administration: Individual or group.
Forms, 3: Home, School, DSM-IV.
Price Data, 2006: $232 per complete kit including 50 Pre-Referral Attention Deficit Checklists, 50 Intervention Strategies documentation forms, 50 School Version rating forms, 50 Home Version rating forms, 50 ADDES/DSM-IV forms, School Version technical manual, Home Version technical manual, Attention Deficit Disorders Intervention Manual: Secondary-Age Student, and Parent's Guide; $30 per 50 Pre-Referral Attention Deficit Checklists; $30 per 50 intervention Strategies documentation forms; $35 per 50 rating forms (specify School Version or Home Version); $22 per 50 ADDES/DSM-IV forms; $15 per technical manual (specify School Version or Home Version); $30 per Attention Deficit Disorders Intervention Manual: Secondary-Age Student; $20 per Parent's Guide; $35 per computerized Quick Score (Windows).
Time: (15–20) minutes.
Comments: Ratings by parents/guardians and/or teachers.
Author: Stephen B. McCarney.
Publisher: Hawthorne Educational Services, Inc.
Cross References: For reviews by Helen Kitchens and Joseph G. Law, Jr., see 14:28.

[222]
Attention Deficit Disorders Evaluation Scale—Third Edition.

Purpose: Designed "to provide a measure of the ADHD characteristics of inattention and hyperactivity-impulsivity in the DSM-IV."
Population: Ages 4-18.
Publication Dates: 1989-2004.
Acronym: ADDES-3.
Scores, 3: Inattentive, Hyperactive-Impulsive, Total Score.
Administration: Individual.
Forms, 2: School Version, Home Version.
Price Data, 2006: $232 per complete kit including 50 Pre-Referral Attention Deficit checklists, 50 Intervention Strategies Documentation forms, School Version technical manual (2004, 48 pages), 50 School Version rating forms, Home Version technical manual (2004, 48 pages), 50 Home Version rating forms, 50 ADDES-3/DSM-IV forms, Attention Deficit Disorders Intervention manual, and the Parent's Guide to Attention Deficit Disorders; $15 per technical manual (specify School or Home Version); $30 per Attention Deficit Disorders Intervention manual; $35 per 50 rating forms (specify School or Home Version); $30 per 50 Intervention Strategies Documentation forms; $30 per 50 Pre-Referral Attention Deficit checklists; $22 per 50 ADDES-3/DSM-IV forms; $20 per Parent's Guide to Attention Deficit Disorders; $35 per Quick Score computerized Windows program (specify English or Spanish); $35 per 50 Spanish rating forms (specify School or Home Version).
Foreign Language Edition: Spanish edition available.
Time: (20) minutes.

Comments: Scale is rated by parent/caregiver or an educator.
Authors: Stephen B. McCarney and Tamara J. Arthaud.
Publisher: Hawthorne Educational Services, Inc.
Cross References: For reviews by Hugh W. Glenn and Beverly M. Klecker of the second edtion, see 14:27; for reviews by Deborah Collins and Stephen Olejnik of the original edition, see 12:38 (1 reference).

[223]
Attention-Deficit/Hyperactivity Disorder Test.

Purpose: Designed to "contribute to the diagnosis of students with Attention-Deficit/Hyperactivity Disorder."
Population: Ages 3–23.
Publication Date: 1995.
Acronym: ADHDT.
Scores: 3 subtests (Hyperactivity, Impulsivity, Inattention), plus ADHD Quotient.
Administration: Individual.
Price Data, 2006: $110 per complete kit including manual (46 pages) and 50 summary/response forms in storage box; $50 per 50 summary/response forms; $65 per manual.
Time: (5–10) minutes.
Comments: Ratings by teacher, teacher's aide, or parent.
Author: James E. Gilliam.
Publisher: PRO-ED.
Cross References: For reviews by Robert S. Miller and Anthony W. Paolitto, see 14:30.

[224]
Attention-Deficit Scales for Adults.

Purpose: Designed as an objective measure of attention deficit in adults.
Population: Adults.
Publication Date: 1996.
Acronym: ADSA.
Scores, 11: Attention-Focus/Concentration, Interpersonal, Behavior-Disorganized Activity, Coordination, Academic Theme, Emotive, Consistency/Long Term, Childhood, Negative-Social, Internal Consistency, Total.
Administration: Individual.
Price Data: Available from publisher.
Time: Untimed.
Comments: A 54-item, Likert-scale questionnaire to be administered in a clinical setting; self-report.
Authors: Santo James Triolo and Kevin Richard Murphy.
Publisher: Taylor & Francis [No reply from publisher; status unknown].
Cross References: For reviews by Joseph G. Law, Jr. and James C. Reed, see 14:29.

[225]
The Attentional and Interpersonal Style Inventory.

Purpose: "Developed to measure the critical concentration and interpersonal determinants of performance."
Population: Adults and adolescents.
Publication Dates: 1993–1996.
Acronym: TAIS.
Scores: 18 scales: Attentional (Broad External Awareness, External Distractibility, Conceptual/Analytical, Internal Distractibility, Narrow/Focused, Reduced Flexibility), Interpersonal (Information Processing, Orientation Toward Rules and Risk/Impulse Control, Need for Control, Self Esteem, Physical Competitiveness, Decision Making Speed, Extroversion, Introversion, Expression of Ideas, Expression of Criticism, Expression of Support, Self Critical).
Administration: Individual or group.
Price Data: Certification and test pricing available from publisher.
Time: [20–25] minutes.
Comments: Can be administered via pencil and paper, computer, or the internet.
Author: Robert M. Nideffer.
Publisher: Enhanced Performance Systems, Inc.
Cross References: For reviews by Phillip L. Ackerman and Eugene V. Aidman, see 14:31; see also T5:226 (2 references).

[226]
Attitudes Toward Working Mothers Scale.

Purpose: "Designed to assess attitudes toward the . . . dual role of mother and worker."
Population: Adults.
Publication Date: No date on test materials.
Acronym: AWM.
Scores: Total score only.
Administration: Group.
Price Data: Free of charge for inventory, scoring instructions, and mimeographed paper on construction validation of scale (23 pages).
Time: Administration time not reported.
Authors: Toby J. Tetenbaum, Jessica Lighter, and Mary Travis.
Publisher: Toby J. Tetenbaum.
Cross References: See T4: 229 (1 reference); for reviews by Mark W. Roberts and Charles Wenar, see 9:99 (1 reference).

[227]
Attitudes Towards Guns and Violence Questionnaire.

Purpose: Designed to measure "attitudes concerning guns, physical aggression, and interpersonal conflict."
Population: Ages 6–29.
Publication Date: 2000.

Acronym: AGVQ.
Scores, 6: Total (Favorable or Unfavorable to Violence and Guns), Inconsistent Responding, Aggressive Response to Shame, Comfort with Aggression, Excitement, Power/Safety.
Administration: Group.
Price Data, 2006: $99 per kit including 25 score forms, manual, and 50 Aggressive Behavior checklists (25 teacher forms and 25 student forms); $37.95 per 25 answer forms; $49.50 per manual; $27.50 per 100 Aggressive Behavior checklists (teacher or student form); $105 per Windows scoring computer disk (good for 50 uses); $16.50 per 100 PC answer sheets.
Time: (5–10) minutes.
Author: Jeremy P. Shapiro.
Publisher: Western Psychological Services.
Cross References: For reviews by Stephen E. Trotter and Delores D. Walcott, see 15:22.

[228]
Auditory Continuous Performance Test.

Purpose: "Designed to help ... identify children who have auditory attention disorders ... Also yields information that will help diagnose children as having Attention Deficit/Hyperactivity Disorder."
Population: Ages 6 to 11.
Publication Date: 1994.
Acronym: ACPT.
Scores, 4: Inattention Errors, Impulsivity Errors, Total Error Score, Vigilance Decrement.
Administration: Individual.
Price Data, 2002: $109 per complete kit including examiner's manual (52 pages), test audiocassette, and 12 record forms; $16 per 12 record forms; $48 per examiner's manual; $59 per 1 test audiocassette.
Time: (15) minutes.
Author: Robert W. Keith.
Publisher: PsychCorp, A brand of Harcourt Assessment, Inc.
Cross References: See T5:229 (1 reference); for reviews by Nadeen L. Kaufman and Alan S. Kaufman and by Joseph G. Law, Jr., see 13:22.

[229]
Auditory Processing Abilities Test.

Purpose: Designed to assess auditory processing.
Population: Ages 5-0 through 12-11.
Publication Date: 2004.
Acronym: APAT.
Scores, 20: Phonemic Awareness, Word Sequences, Semantic Relationships, Sentence Memory, Cued Recall, Content Memory, Complex Sentences, Sentence Absurdities, Following Directions, Passage Comprehension, Global Index, Auditory Memory Index, Linguistic Processing Index, Auditory Discrimination Index (optional), Auditory Sequencing Index (optional), Auditory Cohesion Index (optional), Immediate Recall Index (optional), Delayed Recall Index (optional), Sequential Recall Index (optional), Cued Recall Index (optional).
Administration: Individual.
Price Data, 2006: $112 per complete kit including examiner's manual (95 pages), 25 test booklets, 25 summary sheets in portfolio; $42 per manual; $45 per 25 test booklets; $25 per 25 summary sheets.
Time: (30–45) minutes.
Authors: Deborah Ross-Swain and Nancy Long.
Publisher: Academic Therapy Publications.
Cross References: For reviews by Jeffery P. Braden and Kelly M. Laugle and by Christopher A. Sink and Rick Eigenbrood, see 16:17.

[230]
Auditory Selective Attention Test.

Purpose: Designed as "a measure of auditory selective attention."
Population: Adults.
Publication Date: 1993.
Acronym: ASAT.
Scores: Total Errors.
Administration: Individual.
Price Data, 2002: $100 per test (cassette tape); $5 per manual (15 pages).
Time: 30(35) minutes.
Comments: Stereo tape player and a pair of stereo headphones must be supplied by the examiner.
Authors: Winfred Arthur, Jr., Gerald V. Barrett, and Dennis Doverspike.
Publisher: Barrett and Associates, Inc.
Cross References: See T5:231 (1 reference); for reviews by William W. Deardorff and Judy R. Dubno, see 13:23.

[231]
Australian Developmental Screening Checklist.

Purpose: Designed to "provide a brief screening measure of early developmental delay."
Population: Ages 6 months–5 years.
Publication Dates: 1968–1994.
Acronym: ADSC.
Scores, 5: Personal/Social, Language, Cognition, Fine Motor, Gross Motor.
Administration: Individual.
Price Data, 2006: A$288.05 per complete kit; A$118.40 per 25 record forms.
Time: (10–15) minutes.
Author: Barry Burdon.
Publisher: Harcourt Assessment Australia and New Zealand [Australia].
Cross References: For a review by James A. Athanasou, see 15:23.

[232]
Australian Developmental Screening Test.

Purpose: Designed to provide a brief screening measure of early developmental delay.
Population: Ages 6 months–5 years.
Publication Date: 1993.
Acronym: ADST.
Scores, 5: Personal-Social, Language, Cognitive, Fine Motor, Gross Motor.
Administration: Individual.
Price Data, 2006: A$675.15 per complete kit including manual (135 pages), stimulus cards, 25 record forms, and a set of toys; A$115 per 25 record forms.
Time: (15–20) minutes.
Author: Barry Burdon.
Publisher: Harcourt Assessment Australia and New Zealand [Australia].
Cross References: For a review by Koressa Kutsick Malcolm, see 15:24.

[233]
Australian Second Language Proficiency Ratings.

Purpose: "Designed to measure general proficiency by matching observed language behavior against global descriptions."
Population: Adolescents and adults.
Publication Dates: 1982–1984.
Acronym: ASLPR.
Scores, 4: Speaking, Listening, Reading, Writing.
Administration: Individual.
Price Data: Available from publisher.
Foreign Language Editions: French, Italian, and Japanese versions available.
Time: Administration time not reported.
Authors: D. E. Ingram and Elaine Wylie.
Publisher: Australian Department of Immigration and Multicultural Affairs [Australia].
Cross References: See T5:233 (2 references).

[234]
Autism Screening Instrument for Educational Planning, Second Edition.

Purpose: "Designed to help professionals identify individuals with autism and to provide information needed to develop appropriate educational plans."
Population: Autistic individuals ages 18 months to adult.
Publication Dates: 1978–1993.
Acronym: ASIEP-2.
Administration: Individual.
Price Data, 2006: $230 per complete kit including examiner's manual (1993, 81 pages), 25 summary booklets, 25 Autism Behavior Checklist Forms, 25 Sample of Vocal Behavior Record Forms, 25 Interaction Assessment Record Forms, 25 Educational Assessment Forms, 25 Prognosis of Learning Rate Forms, toys, manipulatives, stand, and coding audiotape for Interaction Assessment; $30 per 25 summary booklets; $51 per toys, manipulatives, and stand; $15 per coding audiotape for Interaction Assessment; $51 per examiner's manual.
Time: Administration time varies.
Comments: Subtests administered depends on results of Autism Behavior Checklist and purpose of assessment.
Authors: David A. Krug, Joel R. Arick, and Patricia J. Almond.
Publisher: PRO-ED.
a) AUTISM BEHAVIOR CHECKLIST.
Scores, 6: Sensory, Relating, Body and Object Use, Language, Social and Self Help, Total.
Price Data: $20 per 25 record forms.
b) SAMPLE OF VOCAL BEHAVIOR.
Scores, 5: Repetitive, Noncommunicative, Babbling, Unintelligible, Total.
Price Data: $20 per 25 record forms.
c) INTERACTION ASSESSMENT.
Scores, 4: Interaction, Independent Play, No Response, Negative.
Price Data: $20 per 25 record forms.
d) EDUCATIONAL ASSESSMENT.
Scores, 6: In Seat, Receptive Language, Expressive Language, Body Concept, Speech Imitation, Total.
Price Data: $20 per 25 record forms.
e) PROGNOSIS OF LEARNING RATE.
Scores, 5: Hand-Shaping, Random Position–A, Fixed Position–B, Fixed Position–C, Random Position–D.
Price Data: $20 per 25 record forms.
Cross References: See T5:234 (3 references); for reviews by D. Joe Olmi and Donald P. Oswald, see 13:24 (3 references); see also T4:235 (1 reference); for reviews by Lawrence J. Turton and Richard L. Wikoff of an earlier edition, see 9:105 (1 reference).

[235]
The Autistic Continuum: An Assessment and Intervention Schedule.

Purpose: Designed to indicate the presence of autistic features and to aid in developing educational and therapeutic programs.
Population: Ages 2–8.
Publication Dates: 1987–1992.
Scores: Item scores only in 8 areas: General Observations, Attention Control, Sensory Function, Non-Verbal Symbolic Function, Concept Formation, Sequencing and Rhythmic Abilities, Speech and Language, Educational Attainments and Intelligence.
Administration: Individual.

Price Data, 1998: £60 per manual (1992, 78 pages) incorporating schedule; sample sheets are free.
Time: Untimed.
Comments: Revision of Is This Autism? A Checklist of Behaviours and Skills for Children Showing Autistic Features.
Authors: Maureen Aarons and Tessa Gittens.
Publisher: NFER-Nelson Publishing Co., Ltd. [England].
Cross References: For reviews by Doreen W. Fairbank and Pat Mirenda, see 15:25; for reviews by William M. Bart and Doreen Ward Fairbank of the earlier edition, see 12:197.

[236]
The Autobiographical Memory Interview.

Purpose: "Provides an assessment of a subject's personal remote (retrograde) memory."
Population: Ages 18–80.
Publication Date: 1990.
Acronym: AMI.
Scores, 8: Personal Semantic (Childhood, Young Adult, Recent, Total), Autobiographical Incidents (Childhood, Young Adult, Recent, Total).
Administration: Individual.
Price Data, 2006: £84 per complete kit including manual (24 pages) and 25 scoring sheets; £104 per 50 scoring sheets.
Time: Untimed.
Comments: Semistructured interview format.
Authors: Michael Kopelman, Barbara Wilson, and Alan Baddeley.
Publisher: Harcourt Assessment [England].

[237]
Automated Office Battery.

Purpose: Aptitude tests designed for the selection of staff to work in offices with a high degree of automation.
Population: Student and employed clerical staff.
Publication Dates: 1985–1986.
Acronym: AOB.
Scores: 3 tests: Numerical Estimation, Computer Checking, Coded Instructions.
Administration: Group.
Price Data: Available from publisher.
Time: 40(60) minutes for entire battery.
Comments: "Tests may be used individually or as a complete battery as particular requirements dictate."
Authors: Bill Mabey and Hazel Stevenson.
Publisher: SHL Group plc [United Kingdom].
  a) NUMERICAL ESTIMATION.
  Purpose: A test to measure the ability to estimate the answer to a calculation.
  Acronym: NE-1.
  Time: 10(15) minutes.

b) COMPUTER CHECKING.
Purpose: A test to measure the ability to check machine input information with the corresponding output.
Acronym: CC-2.
Time: 12(17) minutes.
c) CODED INSTRUCTIONS.
Purpose: A test to measure the ability to comprehend and follow written instructions when a form of coded language is used.
Time: 18(23) minutes.
Cross References: For a review by Philip Ash, see 11:24.

[238]
The Awareness of Social Inference Test.

Purpose: To test "the ability of the viewer to recognize basic emotions shown by other people" and to test "the ability of the viewer to determine speaker intention, attitude, and meaning."
Population: Ages 14–60.
Publication Date: 2002.
Acronym: TASIT.
Scores: Emotion Evaluation Test (Happy, Surprised, Neutral, Sad, Angry, Anxious, Revolted, Total Positive Emotions, Total Negative Emotions, Total Positive and Negative Emotions), Social Inference [Minimal] Test (Sincere, Sarcasm, Total), Social Inference [Enriched] Test (Lies, Sarcasm, Total).
Administration: Individual.
Forms, 2: A, B.
Price Data, 2006: £215 per complete kit including manual (16 pages), 2 packs of 25 scoring sheets, 2 video tapes, and 2 stimulus books; £64.50 per 2 packs of 25 scoring sheets.
Time: (30–45) minutes.
Authors: Skye McDonald, Sharon Flanagan, and Jennifer Rollins.
Publisher: Harcourt Assessment [England].

[239]
B-3R, B-4R, B-5, B-5a Firefighter Tests.

Purpose: Designed to assess critical abilities necessary for the successful job performance of entry-level firefighters.
Population: Candidates for entry-level firefighter positions.
Publication Dates: 1994-2001
Administration: Individual or group.
Price Data: Available from publisher.
Comments: Previous versions listed as Firefighter Exams (T6:1273) and IPMA Fire Service Tests (9:538); no prior taining or experience as a firefighter is assumed of candidates taking the tests.
Authors: International Public Management Association for Human Resources & Bruce Davey Associates.

Publisher: International Public Management Association for Human Resources (IPMA-HR).

a) B-3R and B-4R FIREFIGHTER TESTS.

Scores: 10 knowledge areas: Reading Comprehension, Interpreting Tables, Situational Judgment, Logical Reasoning, Reading Gauges, Applying Basic Math Rules, Mechanical Aptitude, Spatial Sense, Map Reading, Vocabulary.

Time: 120 minutes.

Comments: B-3R and B-4R are parallel forms.

b) B-5 and B-5a FIREFIGHTER TESTS.

Scores: 5 knowledge areas: Ability to Learn/Remember and Apply Information, Reading Comprehension, Interests (B-5 only), Situational Judgment, Logical and Mathematical Reasoning Ability.

Time: 140 minutes for B-5; 125 minutes for B-5a.

Comments: The B-5 assesses a wider range of characteristics than typical entry-level firefighter tests and includes a noncognitive component that measures personal traits.

Cross References: For a review by Lawrence Allen of an earlier version, see 9:538.

[240]
Balanced Assessment in Mathematics.

Purpose: Designed to improve the teaching and learning of mathematics in schools by introducing goals and curricula based on national and international standards.

Population: Grades 3–10.

Publication Dates: 2001–2003.

Scores: Total score only.

Administration: Group.

Levels, 8: 3, 4, 5, 6, 7, 8, 9, 10.

Forms: 2 forms at all 8 levels for 2001-2002; one form for 2003.

Price Data: Available from publisher.

Foreign Language Edition: Spanish edition available.

Time: (40) minutes per form.

Comments: Two forms per grade each year (practice and secure tests) are published; scoring is done locally; performance is reported at four levels and cut scores are determined each year; no norms.

Author: Mathematics Assessment Resource Service.

Publisher: CTB/McGraw-Hill.

Cross References: For reviews by Matthew K. Burns and Joseph C. Ciechalski, see 16:18.

[241]
The Balanced Emotional Empathy Scale.

Purpose: To measure an individual's vicarious emotional response to perceived emotional experiences of others.

Population: Ages 15 and older.

Publication Dates: 1972–1996.

Acronym: BEES.

Scores: Total score only.

Administration: Group or individual.

Price Data: Available from publisher for test kit including scale, scoring directions, norms, manual (1996, 12 pages), and literature review.

Time: (10–15) minutes.

Comments: Replaces The Emotional Empathic Tendency Scale.

Author: Albert Mehrabian.

Publisher: Albert Mehrabian.

Cross References: For reviews by Richard W. Johnson and Susana Urbina, see 13:25.

[242]
The Balloons Test.

Purpose: "Designed to detect visual inattention following brain injury."

Population: Adults.

Publication Date: 1998.

Scores, 4: Total A, Total B, Generalized Inattention Index, Lateralized Inattention Index.

Administration: Individual.

Price Data, 2006: £130 per complete kit including manual (10 pages), test cards, and 20 scoring sheets; £39.50 per 50 scoring sheets.

Time: [5-10] minutes.

Authors: Jennifer A. Edgeworth, Ian H. Robertson, and Thomas M. McMillan.

Publisher: Harcourt Assessment [England].

[243]
Bankson-Bernthal Test of Phonology.

Purpose: "Designed for use by speech-language clinicians to assess the phonology of preschool and school-age children."

Population: Ages 3-9.

Publication Dates: 1989–1990.

Acronym: BBTOP.

Scores, 3: Word Inventory, Consonants Composite, Phonological Processes Composite.

Administration: Individual.

Price Data, 2006: $170 per complete kit; $80 per picture book; $45 per 25 record forms; $50 per manual (1990, 111 pages).

Time: (10-15) minutes.

Authors: Nicholas W. Bankson and John E. Bernthal.

Publisher: PRO-ED.

Cross References: See T5:240 (4 references); for reviews by Lynn S. Bliss and Lawrence J. Turton, see 12:41.

[244]
Bankson Language Test—2.

Purpose: Constructed "to establish the presence of a language disorder and identify areas in need of further, in-depth testing."

Population: Ages 3-0 to 6-11.
Publication Dates: 1977–1990.
Acronym: BLT-2.
Scores, 4: Semantic Knowledge, Morphological and Syntactic Rules, Language Quotient, Pragmatic Knowledge (optional).
Administration: Individual.
Forms, 2: BLT-2; BLT-2 Screen.
Price Data, 2006: $139 per complete kit including 25 profile/examiner's record booklets, 25 screen record forms, picture book, and examiner's manual (1990, 32 pages); $49 per picture book; $34 per 25 profile/examiner's record booklets; $16 per 25 screen record forms; $44 per examiner's manual.
Time: (30) minutes.
Comments: Revision of Bankson Language Screening Test.
Author: Nicholas W. Bankson.
Publisher: PRO-ED.
Cross References: See T5:241 (4 references) and T4:241 (3 references); for reviews by Ronald B. Gillam and Roger L. Towne, see 11:26 (4 references); for a review of an earlier edition by Barry W. Jones, see 9:107 (1 reference).

[245]
Bar-Ilan Picture Test for Children.

Purpose: "A semi-projective device to pinpoint the child's perception of his place in society, in his formal educational setting, and in his home, as well as his perception of his weaker points and of his potential for coping with life."
Population: Ages 4–16.
Publication Dates: 1982–1989.
Scores: Guidelines for analysis in 8 areas: Emotional Makeup, Motivation, Interpersonal Behavior and Areas of Conflict, Attitudes of Teachers-Parents Toward Testee, Attitudes of Peers and Siblings Towards Testee, Degree of Mastery and Feeling of Competence, Quality of Thinking Process, Activity.
Administration: Individual.
Forms, 1: 9 drawings (6 of which have different versions for boys and girls).
Price Data, 2005: $50 per set of 15 drawings; $25 per manual (1982, 49 pages).
Time: Administration time not reported.
Comments: 1989 edition is identical to 1982 edition except Appendix II was added.
Authors: Rivkah Itskowitz and Helen Strauss.
Publisher: Dansk psykologisk Forlag [Denmark].
Cross References: See T5:242 (1 reference) and T4:242 (1 reference).

[246]
BarOn Emotional Quotient-360.

Purpose: Designed to provide a "multiperspective view of [an] individual's emotional functioning."

Population: Ages 16 and over.
Publication Date: 2003.
Acronym: EQ-360.
Scores, 21: Intrapersonal (Self-Regard, Emotional Self-Awareness, Assertiveness, Independence, Self-Actualization, Total), Interpersonal (Empathy, Social Responsibility, Interpersonal Relationship, Total), Stress Management (Stress Tolerance, Impulse Control, Total), Adaptability (Reality Testing, Flexibility, Problem Solving, Total), General Mood (Optimism, Happiness, Total), Total.
Administration: Individual.
Price Data, 2006: $62 per technical manual; $38 per 10 reusable item booklets; $32 per 10 additional rater response sheets; $193 per online multirater kit including technical manual and 1 multirater feedback report.
Time: (30) minutes.
Comments: Designed for use in conjunction with the BarOn EQ-i (932); multi-informant rating scale available for paper-and-pencil or on-line administration.
Authors: Reuven Bar-On and Rich Handley.
Publisher: Multi-Health Systems, Inc.

[247]
Barrier to Employment Success Inventory, Second Edition.

Purpose: Designed to help identify personal barriers to getting or keeping a job.
Population: Adult and teenage job seekers and career planners.
Publication Date: 2002.
Acronym: BESI.
Scores, 5: Personal and Financial, Emotional and Physical, Career Decision-Making and Planning, Job Seeking Knowledge, Training and Education.
Administration: Group or individual.
Price Data, 2006: $39.95 per 25 inventories including copy of instructor's guide (12 pages).
Time: (10–15) minutes.
Comments: Self-administered and self-scored; revised version features simplified language, and color-coded response and scoring tables.
Author: John J. Liptak.
Publisher: JIST Publishing, Inc.
Cross References: For reviews by Wayne J. Camara and Kathy E. Green, see 16:22.

[248]
Barsch Learning Style Inventory-Revised.

Purpose: Designed to assess an individual's learning style.
Population: 14 through adult.
Publication Date: 1980–1996.
Scores, 4: Visual Preference, Auditory Preference, Tactile Preference, Kinesthetic Preference.
Administration: Group.

Manual: No manual.

Price Data, 2006: $14 per kit (10 Inventories & 10 Effective Study Tips).

Time: Administration time not reported.

Comments: Intended as an "informal survey, such as would be used by teachers or education specialists to guide them in setting up an appropriate educational plan."

Authors: Jeffrey R. Barsch.

Publisher: Academic Therapy Publications.

Cross References: For reviews by John Biggs and Jayne A. Parker, see 9:11.

[249]
BASC Monitor for ADHD.

Purpose: Designed to survey the primary symptoms of ADHD in a format suited to repeated assessments in order to see relationships between treatments and symptoms overtime.

Population: Ages 4–18.

Publication Date: 1998.

Acronym: BASC Monitor for ADHD.

Scores: 4 scales: Attention Problems, Hyperactivity, Internalizing Problems, Adaptive Skills; plus Student Observation System (13 adaptive and maladaptive behavior categories).

Administration: Group.

Forms, 2: Teacher Monitor Ratings, Parent Monitor Ratings.

Price Data, 2006: $135.99 per hand-scoring set including 25 Teacher Monitor rating forms, 25 Parent Monitor rating forms, scoring templates, and manual (112 pages); $33.99 per 25 Teacher Monitor rating forms or 25 Parent Monitor rating forms; $34.99 per 25 Student Observation System forms; $68.99 per manual; $277.99 per single-user complete software kit including 25 Teacher Monitor rating forms, 25 Parent Monitor rating forms, manual, and software disks (network version also available).

Time: (5–10) minutes.

Comments: Instrument is designed to supplement the BASC (283) or to be used independently; questionnaires are completed by parents and teachers; Parent Monitor Ratings form available in Spanish; BASC Monitor software available for Windows 95 or Windows NT, single-user or network versions.

Authors: Randy W. Kamphaus and Cecil R. Reynolds.

Publisher: Pearson Assessments (originally published by AGS Publishing, acquired by Pearson in 2005).

Cross References: For reviews by Hugh W. Glenn and Kevin M. Jones, see 14:33.

[250]
Basic Achievement Skills Individual Screener.

Purpose: "Designed to provide norm-referenced and criterion-referenced information for reading, mathematics, and spelling."

Population: Grades 1–12 and post high school.

Publication Date: 1983.

Acronym: BASIS.

Scores, 3 or 4: Mathematics, Reading, Spelling, Writing Exercise (optional).

Administration: Individual.

Price Data, 2002: $92.20 per content booklet; $81 per 25 record forms; $92.20 per manual (1983, 232 pages); $181 per examiner's kit.

Time: (50–60) minutes.

Author: The Psychological Corporation.

Publisher: PsychCorp, A brand of Harcourt Assessment, Inc.

Cross References: See T5:246 (7 references) and T4:244 (6 references); for reviews by Robert E. Floden and Richard E. Schutz, see 9:112.

[251]
Basic Achievement Skills Inventory.

Purpose: Designed "to measure reading, written language, and math skills among children and adults."

Population: Grades 3 & 4, 5 & 6, 7 & 8, 9–12, and ages 8 to 80.

Publication Date: 2004.

Acronym: BASI.

Administration: Individual or group.

Tests, 2: Comprehensive, Survey.

Price Data, 2006: $109 per Comprehensive starter kit including manual (382 pages), 1 test booklet for each level (Levels 1–4, Forms A and B), and 12 hand-scored answer sheets (3 for each level); $173.50 per Mail-in Scoring Service Comprehensive starter kit with Student Summary Report, includes same materials as hand-scored starter kit but with scannable answer sheets; $151 per Q Local Comprehensive starter kit with Student Summary Report, includes same materials as hand-scored starter kit but with scannable answer sheets and 12 Q Local administrations, which require separate purchase of Q Local Software of $89 (desktop version) or $250 (network version) annual license fee; $51.50 per Survey starter kit including manual (146 pages), 1 test booklet (Math and Verbal), and 3 hand-scored answer sheets; $63 per Q Local Survey starter kit with Summary Report, includes same materials as hand-scored starter kit but with scannable answer sheets, and 12 Q Local administrations, which require separate purchase of Q Local Software; quantity discounts available for the reports.

Comments: Form A is for August-December testing; Form B is for January-July testing.

Author: Achilles N. Bardos.

Publisher: Pearson Assessments.

a) BASI COMPREHENSIVE.

Population: Grades 3 & 4, 5 & 6, 7 & 8, 9–12.

Scores, 9: Reading (Vocabulary, Reading Comprehension, Total), Written Language (Spelling, Language Mechanics, Total), Math (Math Comprehension, Math Application, Total).

Subtests, 6: Vocabulary, Spelling, Language Mechanics, Reading Comprehension, Math Computation, Math Application.

Levels, 4: Grades 3 & 4, Grades 5 & 6, Grades 7 & 8, Grades 9–12.

Forms, 2: A, B at each level.

Time: 115 minutes.

b) BASI SURVEY.

Population: Ages 8 to 80.

Scores, 7: Verbal Skills (Vocabulary, Language Mechanics, Reading Comprehension, Total), Math Skills (Math Computation, Math Application, Total).

Subtests, 5: Vocabulary, Language Mechanics, Reading Comprehension, Math Computation, Math Application.

Price Data: $36.05 per 10 test booklets (Math and Verbal).

Time: 50 minutes.

Comments: Brief version of the Comprehensive Test.

[252]
Basic Banking Skills Battery.

Purpose: Designed to "measure skills and abilities for financial services jobs."

Population: Age 18 and over.

Publication Dates: 1987–1995.

Acronym: BBSB.

Scores, 14: Number Comparison, Name Comparison, Arithmetic Computation, Error Recognition, Drive, School Achievement, Interpersonal Skills, Cognitive Skills, Motor Ability, Math Ability, Self Discipline, Leadership, Perceptual Skills, Error Perception.

Administration: Group.

Forms, 2: Timed, Untimed.

Price Data, 2005: $22 for 1–999 Internet scoring with booklets; $22 for 1–999 Internet scoring without booklets; $22 for 1–999 Scan scoring; $22 for 1–999 Quanta-TouchTest™ scoring (timed); $22 for 1–999 Quanta-TouchTest™ scoring (untimed); $22 for 1–999 Quanta® Fax scoring; $22 for 1–999 Quanta® software for Windows with booklets; $22 for 1–999 for Quanta® software for Windows without booklets.

Time: (45) minutes.

Comments: Test can be scored online, by fax, optical screening; software is available.

Author: Reid London House.

Publisher: Pearson Performance Solutions [No reply from publisher; status unknown].

[253]
Basic Early Assessment of Reading™.

Purpose: Designed "to assess young students' acquisition of the essential components of reading—phonemic awareness, phonics, vocabulary, comprehension, and oral reading fluency."

Population: Grades K–3.

Publication Date: 2002.

Acronym: BEAR®.

Levels, 4: K, 1, 2, 3.

Price Data, 2005: $280.75 per complete kit (specify Levels K and 1 or Levels 2 and 3) including 25 Initial-Skills Analysis student booklets for each level, 1 Initial-Skills Analysis administration and scoring guide for each level, 1 Specific-Skill Analysis—Reading Basics black-line master for each level, 1 Specific-Skill Analysis—Language Arts black-line master for each level, 1 Specific-Skill Analysis—Comprehension black-line master for each level, 1 Specific-Skill Analysis administration and scoring guide for each level, 13 Oral Reading Fluency Assessment Passage Sheets for Levels K–3, 1 Oral Reading Fluency Assessment administration and scoring guide for Levels K–3, 25 Summative Assessment—Reading Basics student booklets for each level, 25 Summative Assessment—Language Arts student booklets for each level, 25 Summative Assessment—Comprehension student booklets for each level, 1 Summative Assessment administration guide for each level, 1 Summative Assessment scoring guide for each level, and Scoring and Reporting Software; $23 per 25 Initial-Skills Analysis test booklets (specify level); $74.50 per set of 3 Specific-Skill Analysis black-line masters (specify Levels K and 1, or 2 and 3); $34.25 per 13 Oral Reading Fluency Assessment Passage sheets; $19.50 per 25 Summative Assessment test booklets (specify level and content area); $5.75 per administration and scoring guide—Initial-Skills Analysis (specify level); $5.75 per administration and scoring guide—Specific-Skill Analysis (specify Levels K and 1 or 2 and 3); $28.50 per administration and scoring guide—Oral Reading fluency Assessment; $5.75 per administration guide—Summative Assessment (specify level); $17.25 per scoring guide—Summative Assessment (specify level); $31.75 per technical manual; $86.25 per scoring and reporting software; $209 per computer-administered BEAR.

Comments: Criterion-referenced testing program with modules designed for use in conjunction with classroom activities; computer-scoring and reporting available for PC.

Author: Riverside Publishing.

Publisher: Riverside Publishing.

a) INITIAL-SKILLS ANALYSIS.

Purpose: Designed to provide a quick overview of students' skills in Reading Basics, Comprehension, and Language Arts.

Scores, 4: Reading Basics, Comprehension, Language Arts, Total.
Administration: Individual or group.
Time: (45–60) minutes.
b) SPECIFIC-SKILL ANALYSIS.
Purpose: Designed to provide diagnostic information about students' specific skills in Reading Basics, Comprehension, and Language Arts.
Scores, 4: Reading Basics, Comprehension, Language Arts, Total.
Administration: Individual or group.
Time: (30–40) minutes per content area.
c) ORAL READING FLUENCY ASSESSMENT.
Purpose: Designed to provide information about students' accuracy, ability to retell what was read, oral reading skills, and reading rate (for Levels 1–3).
Scores, 3: Letter Recognition, Informational, Narrative.
Administration: Individual.
Forms: 6 (8 at Level K).
Time: (15–30) minutes per passage or list.
d) SUMMATIVE ASSESSMENT.
Purpose: Designed to assess early reading and language arts skills for placement and instructional planning.
Scores, 4: Reading Basics, Comprehension, Language Arts, Total.
Administration: Individual or group.
Time: (30–40) minutes per content area.
Cross References: For reviews by Zandra S. Gratz and Annita Marie Ward, see 16:23.

[254]
Basic Economics Test, Second Edition.

Purpose: "An updated economics achievement test for curriculum development, for the assessment of student understanding, and for determining the effectiveness of educational materials and teaching strategies."
Population: Grades 5–6.
Publication Dates: 1980–1990.
Acronym: BET.
Scores: Total score only.
Administration: Group.
Forms, 2: A, B.
Price Data, 2001: $19.95 per 25 test booklets (specify Form A or B); $14.95 per examiner's manual (1990, 54 pages) which includes scoring keys and model answer sheet which may be duplicated locally.
Time: 30 minutes.
Authors: William B. Walstad and Denise Robson.
Publisher: National Council on Economic Education.
Cross References: For reviews by Irvin J. Lehmann and A. Harry Passow of an earlier edition, see 11:27; for reviews by Mary Friend Adams and James O. Hodges of an earlier edition, see 8:901 (1 reference).

[255]
Basic English Literacy Skills Test.

Purpose: To measure the skills needed for a basic knowledge of the English language.
Population: Candidates for any position requiring a basic knowledge of the English language.
Publication Date: 1996.
Acronym: ENGLIT.
Scores: Total Score, Narrative Evaluation, Rating, Recommendation.
Administration: Group.
Price Data, 2001: $130 per candidate; quantity discounts available.
Time: (77) minutes.
Comments: Scored by publisher; must be proctored.
Author: Walden Personnel Performance, Inc.
Publisher: Walden Personnel Performance, Inc. [Canada].

[256]
Basic English Skills Test.

Purpose: Designed to test listening comprehension, speaking, reading, and writing skills at a basic level when information on the attainment of basic functional language skills is needed.
Population: Limited-English-speaking adults.
Publication Dates: 1982–1988.
Acronym: B.E.S.T.
Scores, 9: Oral Interview Section (Listening Comprehension, Communication, Fluency, Pronunciation, Reading/Writing, Total) and Literacy Skill Section (Reading Comprehension, Writing, Total).
Subtests, 2: Oral Interview Section, Literacy Skills Section.
Administration: Individual in part.
Parts: 4 forms (Forms B and C only in current circulation).
Price Data, 2002: $150 per complete test kit; $12 per picture cue book (1988, 15 pages); $13 per 5 interviewer's booklets (1988, 13 pages); $30 per 100 interview scoring sheets (1988, 2 pages); $45 per literacy skills testing package including 20 literacy skills test booklets (1988, 20 pages) and 20 literacy skills scoring sheets (1988, 2 pages); $25 per manual (1988, 79 pages); $50 per training video and guide.
Time: [75] minutes.
Comments: Orally administered in part; subtests available as separates; other test materials (e.g., 3 $1 bills, 2 dimes, etc.) must be supplied by examiner.
Authors: Center for Applied Linguistics (test), Dorry Kenyon (revised manual), and Charles W. Stansfield (revised manual) with assistance from Dora Johnson, Allene Grognet, and Dan Dreyfus.
Publisher: Center for Applied Linguistics.
Cross References: For reviews by Alan Garfinkel and Patsy Arnett Jaynes, see 11:28.

[257]
Basic Number Diagnostic Test [2001 Revision].

Purpose: Designed to "show what a child can do (and cannot do) so that teaching objectives for that child can be determined."

Population: Ages 5–7.

Publication Dates: 1980–2001.

Scores, 13: Reciting Numbers, Naming Numerals, Copying Over Numerals, Copying Underneath Numerals, Counting Bricks, Selecting Bricks, Writing Numerals in Sequence, Writing Numerals to Dictation, Addition with Objects, Addition with Numerals, Subtraction with Objects, Subtraction with Numerals, Total.

Administration: Individual.

Forms, 2: A, B.

Price Data, 2002: £8.99 per set of 10 copies; £13.99 per manual (2001, 30 pages); £14.99 per specimen set.

Time: (15–25) minutes.

Comments: "Criterion-referenced."

Author: Bill Gillham.

Publisher: Hodder & Stoughton Educational [England].

Cross References: For reviews by Cleborne D. Maddux and Jeffrey K. Smith, see 15:27; for a review by Mary Montgomery Lindquist of an earlier edition, see 9:117.

[258]
Basic Number Screening Test [2001 Edition].

Purpose: "Quick assessment of a child's understanding of ... number concepts and number skills."

Population: Ages 7–12.

Publication Dates: 1976–2001.

Scores: No scores.

Administration: Group.

Forms, 2: A, B.

Price Data, 2002: £9.99 per 20 tests (Form A or B); £10.99 per manual; £11.99 per specimen set.

Time: (20–35) minutes.

Comments: May be orally administered.

Authors: Bill Gillham and Kenneth Heese.

Publisher: Hodder & Stoughton Educational [England].

Cross References: For reviews by Kevin D. Crehan and Thanos Patelis, see 16:24; for reviews by John O. Anderson and Suzanna Lance of the 1996 edition, see 15:28; for reviews by Mary Montgomery Lindquist and Marilyn N. Suydam of an earlier edition, see 9:118.

[259]
Basic Personality Inventory.

Purpose: Constructed to be a "measure of personality and psychopathology."

Population: Adult and adolescent.

Publication Dates: 1988-1997.

Acronym: BPI.

Scores, 12: Hypochondriasis, Depression, Denial, Interpersonal Problems, Alienation, Persecutory Ideas, Anxiety, Thinking Disorder, Impulse Expression, Social Introversion, Self Depreciation, Deviation.

Administration: Individual or group.

Price Data, 2001: $66 per examination kit including 5 reusable test booklets, scoring template, 10 hand-scorable answer sheets, 10 profile sheets, answer sheet and coupon for BPI Basic Report, and manual (1996, 120 pages); $38 per manual; $30.50–$45 (depending on volume) per 25 test booklets; $10–$12 (depending on volume) per 25 hand-scorable answer sheets; $10–$12 (depending on volume) per 25 profile sheets (select adult or adolescent); $14 per scoring template; $59–$66 (depending on volume) per 10 machine-scorable answer sheets and coupons for Basic Reports; $99 per software package including disks, software manual for Windows, test manual, and 10 coupons for computer report; $14 per online password; volume discounts available.

Foreign Language Editions: Test booklets available in French and Spanish.

Time: 35 minutes.

Authors: Douglas N. Jackson.

Publisher: Sigma Assessment Systems, Inc.

Cross References: See T5:256 (4 references); for reviews by Susana Urbina and Tamela Yelland, see 12:42 (1 reference); see also T4:254 (16 references).

[260]
Basic Reading Inventory, Eighth Edition.

Purpose: Designed as an informal measure of students' reading behavior.

Population: Pre-primer through Grade 12.

Publication Dates: 1978–2001.

Scores, 9–16: 3 reading scores (Independent, Instructional, Frustration, Word Recognition in Isolation, Word Recognition in Context, Comprehension—Oral, Comprehension—Silent, Listening Level); Rate of Reading (Optional); 9 informal Early Literacy Assessment ratings (Alphabet Knowledge, Writing, Literacy Knowledge, Wordless Picture Reading, Caption Reading, Auditory Discrimination, Phoneme Awareness, Phoneme Segmentation, Basic Word Knowledge).

Administration: Individual.

Levels, 2: Pre-primer through Grade 12; Grades 3–12.

Forms, 6: A, B, C, D, LN, LE.

Price Data: Price data available from publisher for manual with paper-and-pencil materials (2001, 472 pages), including CD-ROM (with videos, Performance Booklets, and Record Booklet, and demo disk for recording and tracking software); a training video is available to train administrators.

Time: [20] minutes.
Comments: Optional Basic Reading Inventory Tracking Software available to assist with advanced qualitative analysis available from publisher. System requirements: Windows or Macintosh, CD-ROM drive, 20 MB RAM, 20 MB hard drive, sound and video options.
Author: Jerry L. Johns.
Publisher: Kendall/Hunt Publishing Company.
Cross References: For reviews by Matthew K. Burns and Zandra S. Gratz of the eighth edition, see 15:29; for reviews by Michael Harwell and Steven A. Stahl of the seventh edition, see 14:34 (6 references); see also T5:257 (4 references); for reviews by Jerrilyn V. Andrews and Robert T. Williams of the fifth edition, see 12:43 (3 references); see also T4:255 (4 references); for a review by Gus Plessas of the second edition, see 9:119.

[261]
Basic School Skills Inventory, Third Edition.
Purpose: Designed to locate children who are at-risk for school failure, who need more in-depth assessment, and who should be referred for additional study.
Population: Ages 4-0 to 8-11.
Publication Dates: 1975–1998.
Acronym: BSSI-3.
Scores, 7: Spoken Language, Reading, Writing, Mathematics, Classroom Behavior, Daily Living Skills, Overall Skill Level.
Administration: Individual.
Price Data, 2006: $105 per complete kit including examiner's manual (1998, 77 pages), and 25 profile/response forms; $60 per examiner's manual; $50 per 25 profile/response forms.
Time: (5–8) minutes.
Comments: Replaces the Basic School Skills Inventory—Diagnostic (T4:256).
Authors: Donald D. Hammill, James E. Leigh, Nils A. Pearson, and Taddy Maddox.
Publisher: PRO-ED.
Cross References: For reviews by R. W. Kamphaus and Leah M. Nellis, see 14:35; see also T5:258 and T4:256 (1 reference); for a review by William J. Webster of the Basic School Skills Inventory—Diagnostic, see 9:120; for reviews by Byron R. Egeland and Lawrence M. Kasdon of an earlier edition, see 8:424 (2 references).

[262]
Basic Skills Locater Test.
Purpose: "Designed to assess a person's functional skill levels in math and language."
Population: Ages 15 to adult who are functioning below a 12th grade level.
Publication Date: 1998.

Scores, 2: Language, Math.
Administration: Group or individual.
Price Data, 2002: $195 per Basic Skills Locater Test (software version) including 1 guide, 1 reproducible test master, and software; $195 per Basic Skills Locater Test (print version) including 1 user's guide, 10 reusable test booklets, 100 answer sheets, 1 test key, and a Windows scoring disk; $995 per Network Version.
Time: (30–60) minutes.
Comments: Test results place test-takers into four levels corresponding to GED and grade levels: GED Level 1 (grades 1–3); GED Level 2 (grades 4–6); GED Level 3 (grades 7–8) and GED Level 4 (grades 9–12). Bar graphs representing competency in each level in the two domains of Language and Math yield 8 levels of competency for each test-taker.
Author: Helena Hendrix-Frye.
Publisher: Piney Mountain Press, Inc.
Cross References: For a review by Hoi K. Suen, see 15:30.

[263]
Basic Tests Series.
Purpose: To assess basic skills and knowledge relevant to the world of work or postsecondary education.
Population: High school seniors and college entrants and job applicants.
Publication Dates: 1981–1993.
Scores: Total scores only.
Administration: Group.
Restricted Distribution: Distribution restricted and tests administered at licensed testing centers.
Price Data, 2001: £9 entry fee per candidate per test; £1 per Basic Tests booklet containing syllabus and specimen papers (specify test); price data for additional supplementary materials available from publisher.
Comments: Tests administered each May at centers established by the publisher; tests available as separates.
Author: The Assessment and Qualifications Alliance.
Publisher: The Assessment and Qualifications Alliance [England].
   a) BASIC TEST IN LIFE SKILLS.
   Time: 90(100) minutes.
   b) BASIC TEST IN GRAPHICACY.
   Time: 90(100) minutes.
   c) BASIC TEST IN HEALTH, HYGIENE AND SAFETY.
   Time: 75(85) minutes.
Cross References: For reviews by Steven Ferrara and Anne R. Fitzpatrick, see 11:29.

[264]
BASIS-A Inventory [Basic Adlerian Scales for Interpersonal Success—Adult].
Purpose: Designed "to help understand how an individual's life-style, based on beliefs developed in

early childhood, contributes to one's effectiveness in social, work, and intimate relationships."
Population: Adults.
Publication Dates: 1993–1997.
Acronym: BASIS-A.
Scores, 10: BASIS scales (Belonging-Social Interest, Taking Charge, Going Along, Wanting Recognition, Being Cautious); HELPS scales (Harshness, Entitlement, Liked By All, Striving for Perfection, Softness).
Administration: Group or individual.
Price Data, 2001: $95 per introductory kit including 15 test booklets, technical manual (1997, 87 pages), interpretive manual (1997, 61 pages), and 15 copies of interpretive guide; $85 per 25 test booklets; $34 per technical manual and interpretive manual; $7 per sampler kit including test booklet and BASIS-A interpretive guide; $35 per 25 BASIS-A interpretive guides.
Foreign Language Editions: Test items and instructions available in Spanish and German.
Time: (10–15) minutes.
Comments: Self-scored.
Authors: Mary S. Wheeler, Roy M. Kern, and William L. Curlette.
Publisher: TRT Associates, Inc.
Cross References: For reviews by James P. Choca and Peggy E. Gallaher, see 13:26.

[265]
Bass Orientation Inventory.

Purpose: Designed to measure kinds of satisfactions and rewards sought in jobs.
Population: College and industry.
Publication Dates: 1962–1977.
Acronym: RNVT.
Scores, 3: Self-Orientation, Interaction-Orientation, Task-Orientation.
Administration: Group.
Price Data: Available from publisher (www.mindgarden.com).
Time: (20–25) minutes.
Comments: Previously listed as The Orientation Inventory.
Author: Bernard M. Bass.
Publisher: Mind Garden, Inc.
Cross References: See T3:1748 (1 reference); for a review by Thomas J. Bouchard, Jr., see 8:636 (15 references); see also T2:1306 (26 references) and P:187 (13 references); for reviews by Richard S. Barrett and H. Bradley Sagen, see 6:153 (2 references).

[266]
Batería III Woodcock-Muñoz™.

Purpose: Designed to "measure intellectual abilities and academic achievement" in Spanish-speaking individuals.

Population: Ages 2–90+.
Publication Dates: 1982–2005.
Acronym: Bateria III.
Price Data, 2006: $1,233.50 per complete Bateria III with 2 carrying cases including Cognitive standard and extended test books, examiner's manual (158 pages), examiner's training workbook, audio recording, 25 test records with 25 subject response booklets, 5 BIA test records, scoring guides, Achievement standard and extended test books, examiner's manual (180 pages), examiner's training workbook, audio recording, 25 test records with 25 subject response booklets, Bateria III Compuscore® and Profiles Program (Windows), and scoring guides; $746.50 per Bateria III Cognitive Battery with carrying case including Cognitive standard and extended test books, examiner's manual, examiner's training workbook, audio recording, 25 test records with 25 subject response booklets, 5 BIA test records, Bateria III Compuscore and Profiles Program (Windows), and scoring guides; $359.50 per Diagnostic Supplement including test book, examiner's manual (151 pages), 25 test records, audio recording, Bateria III Compuscore and Profile Program (Windows), and scoring guides; $574 per Bateria III Achievement Battery with carrying case including Achievement standard and extended test books, examiner's manual, examiner's training workbook, audio recording, 25 test records with 25 subject response booklets, Bateria III Compuscore and Profiles Program (Windows), and scoring guides.
Foreign Language Editions: All of the materials are in Spanish including the examiner's manuals and the technical manual.
Time: (5–10) minutes per test.
Comments: The Batería III Woodcock-Muñoz is the parallel Spanish adaption/translation of the Woodcock-Johnson III (2795).
Authors: Ana F. Muñoz-Sandoval, Richard W. Woodcock, Kevin S. McGrew, and Nancy Mather (test); Fredrick A. Schrank, Kevin S. McGrew, Mary L. Ruef, Griselda G. Alvarado, Ana F. Muñoz-Sandoval, and Richard W. Woodcock (manual).
Publisher: Riverside Publishing.
  a) Pruebas de habilidades cognitivas (Test of Cognitive Abilities).
Acronym: Batería III COG.
Scores: 20 tests: Comprensión verbal, Aprendizaje visual-auditivo, Relaciones espaciales, Integración de sonidos, Formación de conceptos, Pareo visual, Inversión de números, Palabras incompletas, Memoria de trabajo auditiva, Memoria diferida—aprendizaje visual-auditivo, Información general, Fluidez de recuperación, Reconocimiento de dibujos, Atención auditiva, Análisis-síntesis, Rapidez en la decisión, Memoria

para palabras, Rapidez en la idenificación de dibujos, Planeamiento, Cancelación de pares.

1) *Suplemento Diagnóstico (Diagnostic Supplement)*.

Acronym: Bateria III SD.

Scores: 11 tests: Memoria para nombres, Integración visual, Configuración de sonidos—vocalizada, Series numéricas, Números matrices, Tachar, Memoria para frases, Rotación de bloques, Configuración de sonidos—musical, Memoria diferida—Memoria para nombes, Comprensión verbal bilingüe—español/inglés.

b) Pruebas de aprovechamiento (Tests of Achievement).

Acronym: Bateria III APROV.

Scores: 22 tests: Standard Battery (Identificación de letras y palabras, Fluidez en la lectura, Rememoración de cuentos, Comprensión de indicaciones, Cálculo, Fluidez en matemáticas, Ortografiá, Fluidez en la escritura, Comprensión de textos, Problemas aplicados, Muestras de redacción, Memoria diferida—Rememoración de cuentos), Extended Battery (Análisis de palabras, Vocabulario sobre dibujos, Comprensión oral, Corrección de textos, Vocabulario de lectura, Conceptos cuantitativos, Conocimientos academicos, Análisis de sonidos, Discernimiento de sonidos, Puntuación y mayúsculas.

Cross References: For reviews by Robert B. Frary and Maria Prendes Lintel of a previous edition, see 13:27; for reviews by Jack A. Cummings and by Steven W. Lee and Elaine Flory Stefany of the Woodcock-Johnson Psycho-Educational Battery—Revised, see 12:415 (36 references); see also T4:2973 (90 references) and T3:2639 (3 references); for reviews by Jack A. Cummings and Alan S. Kaufman of an earlier edition of the Woodcock-Johnson Psycho-Educational Battery, see 9:1387 (6 references).

[267]
Battelle Developmental Inventory, 2nd Edition.

Purpose: "Screening, diagnosis, and evaluation of early development."

Population: Birth to 7 years, 11 months.

Publication Dates: 1984–2005.

Acronym: BDI-2.

Administration: Individual.

Forms, 2: Full Assessment, Screening Test.

Foreign Language Editions: Test items available in Spanish translation/adaptation for use by bilingual examiner or with a Spanish monolingual examiner.

Comments: Screening Test available as separate; hand-scoring, web-based, or standalone computer scoring and Palm Powered Electronic Record Form available for full Assessment and Screening Test in English and Spanish.

Author: Jean Newborg.

Publisher: Riverside Publishing.

a) FULL ASSESSMENT.

Purpose: Assess and identify "strengths and opportunities for learning of typically developing infants, preschoolers, kindergarteners, and early primary school students, as well as those who are advanced," and "children who have a disability or delay in any area of development."

Scores, 19: Self-Care, Personal Responsibility, Adaptive Total, Adult Interaction, Peer Interaction, Self-Concept and Social Role, Personal-Social Total, Receptive Communication, Expressive Communication, Communication Total, Gross Motor, Fine Motor, Perceptual Motor, Motor Total, Attention and Memory, Reasoning and Academic Skills, Perception and Concepts, Cognitive Total, Total.

Domains, 5: Adaptive, Personal-Social, Communication, Motor, Cognitive.

Administration Methods, 3: Structured Procedure, Observation Procedure, Interview Procedure.

Price Data, 2006: $427.50 per complete kit including 5 test item books, examiner's manual (256 pages), stimulus book, set of presentation cards, 15 scoring booklets, 15 workbooks, the screening test item book with 30 screening test booklets, set of screening visuals, and carrying case; $480.50 per manipulatives kit; $867.50 per complete kit with manipulatives; $67.50 per examiner's manual; $42 per 15 scoring booklets; $42 per 15 workbooks; $229 per ScoringPro™ software kit (PC); $229 per ScoringPro™ software kit (Web) single; $57 per Palm Application Kit.

Time: (60–90) minutes.

b) SCREENING TEST.

Purpose: Provides "method for determining in which areas of development, if any, a comprehensive assessment is needed for a given child."

Scores, 6: Adaptive, Personal-Social, Communication, Motor, Cognitive, Total.

Price Data: $171.50 per Screener Kit including the screening test item book with 30 screening test booklets, and set of screening visuals (must purchase BDI-2 examiner's manual separately); $67.50 per examiner's manual; $49.50 per 30 screening test booklets.

Time: (10-30) minutes.

Cross References: See T5:265 (15 references) and T4:263 (4 references); for reviews by Judy Oehler-Stinnett and Kathleen D. Paget of an earlier edition, see 10:25 (1 reference); for information about the Screening Test, see T5:266 (4 references) and T4:264 (1 reference); for reviews by David W. Barnett and by Joan Ershler and Stephen N. Elliott of an earlier edition of the Screening Test, see 11:30.

[268]
Battery for Health Improvement 2.

Purpose: A psychomedical assessment designed "to provide relevant information and treatment recommendations to professionals who treat injured patients in a variety of settings."

Population: Ages 18–65, individuals who are being treated for a physical injury.

Publication Dates: 1996–2003.

Acronym: BHI 2.

Scores: 18 scales: Validity (Self-Disclosure, Defensiveness), Physical Symptoms (Somatic Complaints, Pain Complaints, Functional Complaints, Muscular Bracing), Affective Scales (Depression, Anxiety, Hostility), Character Scales (Borderline, Symptom Dependency, Chronic Maladjustment, Substance Abuse, Perseverance), Psychosocial Scales (Family Dysfunction, Survivor of Violence, Doctor Dissatisfaction, Job Dissatisfaction).

Administration: Group or individual.

Price Data, 2006: $101 per Q Local scoring starter kit with enhanced interpretive reports including manual (2003, 291 pages), 1 soft-cover test booklet, and answer sheets; $91 per Q Local scoring starter kit with basic interpretive reports; $69 per Q Local scoring starter kit with profile reports; $110 per mail-in starter kit with enhanced interpretive reports including manual, 1 soft-cover test booklet, and answer sheets; $99 per mail-in starter kit with basic interpretive reports; $77 per mail-in starter kit with profile reports; $89 per Desktop Version Q Local Software (requires annual license fee); $250 per Network Version Q Local Software (requires annual license); $46 per manual; $10.25 per 5 test booklets; $21 per 25 answer sheets; $51.50 per compact disc; quantity discounts available for the reports.

Foreign Language Editions: Spanish forms available.

Time: (30–45) minutes.

Comments: Computer administration and audio CD; mail-in scoring, Q Local software, fax-scoring.

Authors: Daniel Bruns and John Mark Disorbio.

Publisher: Pearson Assessments.

Cross References: For reviews by Gregory J. Boyle and Ephrem Fernandez of an earlier edition, see 14:36.

[269]
Bay Area Functional Performance Evaluation, Second Edition.

Purpose: Developed to assess "general components of functioning that are needed to perform activities of daily living."

Population: Psychiatric patients.

Publication Dates: 1978–1987.

Acronym: BaFPE.

Administration: Individual.

Price Data: Available from publisher.

Comments: Task-Oriented Assessment and Social Interaction Scale may be used separately.

Authors: Susan Lang Williams and Judith Bloomer.

Publisher: Maddak Inc.

a) TASK-ORIENTED ASSESSMENT.

Acronym: TOA.

Scores, 138: 16 Component scores: Cognitive (Memory for Written/Verbal Instruction, Organization of Time and Materials, Attention Span, Evidence of Thought Disorder, Ability to Abstract, Total), Performance (Task Completion, Errors, Efficiency, Total), Affective (Motivation/Compliance, Frustration Tolerance, Self-Confidence, General Affective Impression, Total), Total for the following 11 Parameters: Sorting Shells, Money/Marketing, Home Drawing, Block Design, Kinetic Person Drawing, Total; also 11 Qualitative Signs and Referral Indicators ratings: Language, Comprehension, Hemispatial Neglect, Memory, Abstraction, Task-Specific Observations, Total for the above parameters.

Time: (30–45) minutes.

b) SOCIAL INTERACTION SCALE.

Acronym: SIS.

Scores, 13: Parameter scores (Verbal Communication, Psychomotor Behavior, Socially Appropriate Behavior, Response to Authority Figures, Degree of Independence/Dependence, Ability to Work with Others, Participation in Group Activities), Social Situations (One-to-One, Mealtime, Unstructured Group, Structured Task or Activity Group, Structured Verbal Group), Total Interaction.

Time: [50–60] minutes.

Cross References: See T5:268 (1 reference); for reviews by Deborah D. Roman and Orest E. Wasyliw, see 12:44; see also T4:265 (1 reference).

[270]
Bayley Infant Neurodevelopmental Screener.

Purpose: "Designed to identify infants between the ages of 3 and 24 months who are developmentally delayed or have neurological impairments."

Population: Ages 3–24 months.

Publication Dates: 1992–1995.

Acronym: BINS.

Scores: 4 areas: Basic Neurological Functions/Intactness, Auditory and Visual Receptive Functions, Verbal and Motor Expressive Functions, Cognitive Processes; total score for each level.

Administration: Individual.

Levels, 6: 3–4 months, 5–6 months, 7–10 months, 11–15 months, 16–20 months, 21–24 months.

Price Data, 2002: $265 per complete kit including 25 record forms, manual (1995, 105 pages), stimulus cards, and necessary manipulables in soft-sided carrying case; $33 per 25 record forms; $80 per manual; $17 per stimulus card; $50 per training video.

Time: (10–15) minutes.

Comments: Includes a subset of items from the Bayley Scales of Infant Development—Second Edition (BSID–II; T5:271), but is not an abbreviated form of the BSID-II.

Author: Glen P. Aylward.

Publisher: PsychCorp, A brand of Harcourt Assessment, Inc.

Cross References: For reviews by James K. Benish and by Damon Krug and Brandon Davis, see 13:28.

[271]
Bayley Scales of Infant and Toddler Development-Third Edition.

Purpose: Designed to "assess the developmental functioning of infants and young children."

Population: Ages 1-42 months.

Publication Dates: 1969-2006.

Acronym: Bayley-III.

Scores, 19: Cognitive, Language (Receptive Communication, Expressive Communication, Total), Motor (Fine Motor, Gross Motor, Total), Social-Emotional, Adaptive Behavior (Communication, Community Use, Functional Pre-Academics, Home Living, Health and Safety, Leisure, Self-Care, Self-Direction, Social, Motor, Total).

Administration: Individual.

Price Data, 2006: $895 per complete kit including administration manual (2006, 266 pages), technical manual (2006, 163 pages), 25 Cognitive, Language, and Motor record forms, stimulus booklet, picture book, manipulative set, 25 Social-Emotional/Adaptive Behavior Questionnaires, 25 Caregiver Report forms, rolling case, and PDA Administrative Assistant; $98 per 25 Cognitive, Language, and Motor record forms; $75 per 25 Social-Emotional/Adaptive Behavior Questionnaires; $225 per stimulus booklet; $15 per picture book; $150 per administration manual; $150 per technical manual.

Time: (30-60) minutes.

Comments: Hand scored or scored with use of a PDA.

Author: Nancy Bayley.

Publisher: PsychCorp, A brand of Harcourt Assessment, Inc.

Cross References: See T5:270 (48 references); for reviews by Carl J. Dunst and Mark H. Fugate of a previous edition, see 13:29 (130 references); see also T4:266 (58 references); for reviews by Michael J. Roszkowski and Jane A. Rysberg of an earlier edition, see 10:26 (80 references); see also 9:126 (42 references) and T3:270 (101 references); for a review by Fred Damarin, see 8:206 (28 references); see also T2:484 (11 references); for reviews by Roberta R. Collard and Raymond H. Holden, see 7:402 (20 references).

[272]
Bayley Scales of Infant and Toddler Development, Third Edition, Screening Test.

Purpose: Designed to "briefly assess the cognitive, language, and motor functioning of infants and young children."

Population: Ages 1-42 months.

Publication Date: 2006.

Acronym: Bayley-III Screening Test.

Scores, 5: Cognitive, Receptive Communication, Expressive Communication, Fine Motor, Gross Motor.

Administration: Individual.

Price Data, 2006: $225 per screening test kit including screening test manual (138 pages), 25 screening record forms, screening stimulus book, picture book, and screening manipulative set; $35 per 25 screening record forms; $100 per stimulus booklet; $15 per picture book; $50 per manual.

Time: (15-30) minutes.

Author: Nancy Bayley.

Publisher: PsychCorp, A brand of Harcourt Assessment, Inc.

[273]
BDI-FastScreen for Medical Patients.

Purpose: Designed to screen for depression in patients reporting somatic and behavioral symptoms that may be attributable to biological, medical, alcohol, and/or substance abuse problems.

Population: Ages 12–82.

Publication Date: 2000.

Acronym: BDI-FastScreen.

Scores: Total score only.

Administration: Group.

Price Data, 2003: $67 per complete kit including manual and 50 score forms; $39 per manual; $39 per 50 record forms; $43 per 50 scannable record forms; quantity discounts available.

Time: (5) minutes.

Comments: Formerly called Beck Depression Inventory for Primary Care; based upon Beck Depression Inventory—II (275).

Authors: Aaron T. Beck, Robert A. Steer, and Gregory K. Brown.

Publisher: PsychCorp, A brand of Harcourt Assessment, Inc.

Cross References: For reviews by James J. Hennessy and Nathaniel J. Pallone and by Susan C. Whiston and Kelly Eder, see 16:25.

[274]
Beck Anxiety Inventory [1993 Edition].

Purpose: "Measures the severity of anxiety in adults and adolescents."

Population: Adults and adolescents ages 17 and over.

Publication Dates: 1987–1993.

Acronym: BAI.

Scores: Total score only.

Administration: Group or individual.

Price Data, 2002: $66 per complete kit including 25 record forms and manual (1993, 23 pages); $34.50 per 25 record forms; $34 per manual.

Foreign Language Edition: Available in Spanish.

Time: (5–10) minutes.

Comments: Computer scoring and interpretation available.

Authors: Aaron T. Beck and Robert A. Steer.

Publisher: PsychCorp, A brand of Harcourt Assessment, Inc.

Cross References: See T5:271 (18 references); for reviews by E. Thomas Dowd and Niels G. Waller, see 13:30 (73 references); see also T4:267 (2 references).

[275]
Beck Depression Inventory—II.

Purpose: "Developed for the assessment of symptoms corresponding to criteria for diagnosing depressive disorders listed in the … DSM IV."

Population: Ages 13 and over.

Publication Dates: 1961–1996.

Acronym: BDI-II.

Scores: Total score only.

Administration: Group or individual.

Price Data, 2002: $66 per complete kit including manual (1996, 38 pages) and 25 recording forms; $34 per manual; $34.50 per 25 recording forms; $130 per 100 recording forms; $34.50 per 25 Spanish recording forms; $130 per 100 Spanish recording forms.

Foreign Language Edition: Available in Spanish.

Time: (5–10) minutes.

Comments: Hand-scored or computer-based administration, scoring, and interpretation available; "revision of BDI based upon new information about depression."

Authors: Aaron T. Beck, Robert A. Steer, and Gregory K. Brown.

Publisher: PsychCorp, A brand of Harcourt Assessment, Inc.

Cross References: For reviews by Paul A. Arbisi and Richard F. Farmer, see 14:37; see also T5:272 (384 references); for reviews by Janet F. Carlson and Niels G. Waller of an earlier edition, see 13:31 (1026 references); see also T4:268 (660 references); for

reviews by Collie W. Conoley and Norman D. Sundberg of an earlier edition, see 11:31 (286 references).

[276]
Beck Hopelessness Scale [Revised].

Purpose: Measures "the extent of negative attitudes about the future (pessimism) as perceived by adolescents and adults."

Population: Adolescents and adults ages 17 and over.

Publication Dates: 1978–1993.

Acronym: BHS.

Scores: Total score only.

Administration: Group or individual.

Price Data, 2002: $66 per complete kit including 25 record forms and manual (1993, 29 pages); $34.50 per 25 record forms; $34 per manual; $8.50 per scoring key.

Foreign Language Edition: Available in Spanish.

Time: (5–10) minutes.

Comments: Computer scoring and interpretation available.

Authors: Aaron T. Beck and Robert A. Steer.

Publisher: PsychCorp, A brand of Harcourt Assessment, Inc.

Cross References: See T5:273 (34 references); for a review by Ephrem Fernandez, see 13:32 (83 references); see also T4:269 (37 references); for reviews by E. Thomas Dowd and Steven V. Owen of an earlier edition, see 11:32 (13 references).

[277]
Beck Scale for Suicide Ideation.

Purpose: "To detect and measure the severity of suicidal ideation in adults and adolescents."

Population: Adults and adolescents ages 17 and over.

Publication Dates: 1991–1993.

Acronym: BSS.

Scores: Total score only; item score ranges.

Administration: Group or individual.

Price Data, 2002: $66 per complete kit including 25 record forms and manual (1993, 24 pages); $34.50 per 25 record forms; $34 per manual.

Foreign Language Edition: Spanish forms available.

Time: (5–10) minutes.

Comments: Computer scoring and interpretation available.

Authors: Aaron T. Beck and Robert A. Steer.

Publisher: PsychCorp, A brand of Harcourt Assessment, Inc.

Cross References: For reviews by Karl R. Hanes and Jay R. Stewart, see 13:33 (14 references).

[278]
Beck Youth Inventories of Emotional & Social Impairment.

Purpose: To "evaluate children's emotional and social impairment."
Population: Ages 7–14.
Publication Date: 2001.
Administration: Group or individual.
Forms, 5: Beck Depression Inventory for Youth, Beck Anxiety Inventory for Youth, Beck Anger Inventory for Youth, Beck Disruptive Behavior Inventory for Youth, Beck Self-Concept Inventory for Youth.
Price Data, 2001: $108 per starter kit including manual (59 pages) and 25 combination inventory booklets: $70 per combination inventory including 25 booklets (quantity discounts available); $34.50 per 25 inventories (specify BDI-Y, BAI-Y, BANI-Y, BDBI-Y, or BSCI-Y) (quantity discounts available); $54 per manual.
Time: (5–10) minutes per inventory.
Comments: Brief self-report measures of behavior, cognitions, and feelings; consistent with IDEA requirements; inventories can be administered alone or in combination.
Authors: Judith S. Beck (tests and manual) and Aaron T. Beck (tests and manual) with John Jolly (manual).
Publisher: PsychCorp, A brand of Harcourt Assessment, Inc.

  a) BECK DEPRESSION INVENTORY FOR YOUTH.
  Acronym: BDI-Y.
  Score: Total.
  Comments: Consistent with DSM-IV depression criteria.
  b) BECK ANXIETY INVENTORY FOR YOUTH.
  Acronym: BAI-Y.
  Score: Total.
  Comments: Reflects specific worries about school performance, the future, others' negative reactions; fears; physiological symptoms.
  c) BECK ANGER INVENTORY FOR YOUTH.
  Acronym: BANI-Y.
  Score: Total.
  Comments: Evaluates thoughts of being treated unfairly by others; feelings of anger, hatred.
  d) BECK DISRUPTIVE BEHAVIOR INVENTORY FOR YOUTH.
  Acronym: BDBI-Y.
  Score: Total.
  Comments: Identifies thoughts and behaviors associated with conduct disorder, oppositional-defiant behavior.
  e) BECK SELF-CONCEPT INVENTORY FOR YOUTH.
  Acronym: BSCI-Y.
  Score: Total.

Comments: Taps cognitions of competence, potency, positive self-worth.
Cross References: For reviews by Mike Bonner and Hugh Stephenson, see 15:31.

[279]
Becker Work Adjustment Profile: 2.

Purpose: Designed to "assess work habits, attitudes, and skills of people with special needs."
Population: Individuals ages 13 and over, who are mentally retarded, physically disabled, emotionally disturbed, learning disabled, and/or economically disadvantaged.
Publication Dates: 1989-2005.
Acronym: BWAP:2.
Scores, 5: Work Habits/Attitudes, Interpersonal Relations, Cognitive Skills, Work Performance Skills, Broad Work Adjustment.
Administration: Individual.
Price Data, 2005: $67.50 per value kit including 25 test booklets and manual (2005, 76 pages); $31.50 per 25 test booklets; $39 per manual; $39.75 per starter set including 2 test booklets and manual; quantity discounts available.
Time: (15) minutes.
Comments: Ratings by teachers, counselors, or other vocational professionals.
Author: Ralph L. Becker.
Publisher: Elbern Publications.
Cross References: See T5:275 (1 reference); for reviews by Brian Bolton and Elliot L. Gory of an earlier form, see 11:33.

[280]
Bedside Evaluation of Dysphagia, Revised Edition.

Purpose: Designed to assess swallowing abilities and the factors that may influence those abilities.
Population: Adults neurologically impaired.
Publication Date: 1995.
Acronym: BED.
Scores, 13: Behavioral Characteristics, Cognition and Communication Screening (Cognition, Receptive Language, Expressive Language/Speech Production), Oral Motor Examination (Lips, Tongue, Soft Palate, Cheeks, Mandible, Larynx), Oral-Pharyngeal Dysphagia Symptoms Assessment (Oral State, Pharyngeal State, Additional Observations).
Administration: Individual.
Price Data, 2006: $92 per complete kit including 25 evaluation forms, manual (54 pages), 25 evaluation forms, and 25 screening forms; $69.75 per manual; $41 per 25 standard evaluation forms.
Time: (15–45) minutes.
Author: Edward Hardy.
Publisher: PRO-ED.

Cross References: For reviews by Carlos Inchaurralde and Steven B. Leder, see 14:38.

[281]
Bedside Evaluation Screening Test, Second Edition.

Purpose: "Designed to assess and quantify language disorders in adults resulting from aphasia."
Population: Patients with language deficits.
Publication Dates: 1987–1998.
Acronym: BEST-2.
Scores, 8: Conversational Expression, Naming Objects, Describing Objects, Repeating Sentences, Pointing to Objects, Pointing to Parts of a Picture, Reading, Total.
Administration: Individual.
Price Data, 2006: $143 per complete kit including examiner's manual (1998, 49 pages), picture book, 25 record forms, and 25 profile/summary sheets; $45 per examiner's manual; $51 per picture book; $40 per 25 record forms; $15 per 25 profile/summary sheets.
Time: (20–30) minutes.
Comments: Replaces the Bedside Evaluation and Screening Test of Aphasia (T4:272).
Authors: Joyce Fitch West, Elaine S. Sands, and Deborah Ross-Swain.
Publisher: PRO-ED.
Cross References: For reviews by Pamilla Morales and Carolyn Mitchell-Person, see 14:39; for a review by Malcolm R. McNeil of an earlier edition, see 11:34.

[282]
The Beery-Buktenica Developmental Test of Visual-Motor Integration, 5th Edition.

Purpose: "Designed to assess the extent to which individuals can integrate their visual and motor abilities (eye-hand coordination)."
Publication Dates: 1967-2004.
Acronym: BEERY VMI.
Scores, 3: Beery VMI, Visual Perception [optional], Motor Coordination [optional].
Administration: Group or individual.
Forms, 2: Full, Short.
Price Data, 2006: $105.65 per starter kit including manual (2004, 207 pages), 10 Full forms, 10 Short forms, 10 Visual Perception forms, and 10 Motor Coordination forms; $52.50 per manual; $86.75 per 25 Full forms; $64.25 per 25 Short forms; $14.25 per 25 Visual Perception forms; $14.25 per 25 Motor Coordination forms (bulk discounts available for forms); $135 per Teaching Materials starter kit including My Book of Shapes, My Book of Letters and Numbers, Developmental Teaching Activities, Developmental Wall Chart, and 25 Stepping Stones Parent Checklists; $35 per My Book of Shapes; $35 per My Book of Letters and Numbers; $45 per Developmental Teaching Activities;

$25 per Stepping Stones Parent Checklist; $19.75 per Developmental Wall Chart for Visual-Motor Integration.
Comments: The subtests must be given in the appropriate sequence.
Authors: Keith E. Beery and Natasha A. Beery.
Publisher: Pearson Assessments.
  a) BEERY VMI.
    1) *Full form.*
    Population: Ages 2-80.
    Time: (10-15) minutes.
    2) *Short form.*
    Population: Ages 2-8.
    Time: (5-15) minutes.
  b) VISUAL PERCEPTION [OPTIONAL].
  Population: Ages 2-80.
  Time: (3-7) minutes.
  c) MOTOR COORDINATION [OPTIONAL].
  Population: Ages 2-80.
  Time: (3-7) minutes.
Cross References: For a review by Jan Visser of an earlier version, see 14:119; see also T5:815 (52 references); for reviews by Darrell L. Sabers and James E. Ysseldyke of the Third Revision, see 12:111 (25 references); see also T4:768 (42 references), 9:329 (15 references), and T3:701 (57 references; for reviews by Donald A. Leton and James A. Rice of an earlier edition, see 8:870 (24 references); see also T2:1875 (6 references); for a review by Brad S. Chissom of an earlier edition, see 7:867 (5 references).

[283]
Behavior Assessment System for Children [Second Edition].

Purpose: Designed "to facilitate the differential diagnosis and educational classification of a variety of emotional and behavioral disorders of children and to aid in the design of treatment plans."
Population: Ages 2-25.
Publication Dates: 1992–2004.
Acronym: BASC-2.
Administration: Individual.
Forms, 11: Teacher Rating Scale–Preschool, Teacher Rating Scale–Child, Teacher Rating Scale–Adolescent, Parent Rating Scale–Preschool, Parent Rating Scale–Child, Parent Rating Scale–Adolescent, Self-Report of Personality—Child, Self-Report of Personality—Adolescent, Self-Report of Personality—College, Structured Developmental History, Student Observation System.
Price Data, 2006: $109.99 per starter set including manual (2004, 606 pages), and 1 sample each of the hand-scored forms for all levels of the Teacher Rating Scale, Parent Rating Scale, and Self-Report of Personality, Parent Feedback Report, the Structured Developmental History, and the Student Observation Scale;

$249.99 per ASSIST software for Windows and Macintosh (nonscannable version); $549.99 per AS-SIST software for Windows and Macintosh (scanning version); $79.99 per BASC-2 Training Video (DVD or VHS); $79.99 per manual; additional price data available on publisher's website (www.agsnet.com).

Foreign Language Editions: Spanish edition available for the Parent Rating scales and the Self-Report of Personality forms.

Comments: Student Observation System includes Parent Feedback Reports for the Teacher Rating Scales, Parent Rating Scales, and Self-Report of Personality forms; computer programs (BASC-2 ASSIST and BASC-2 ASSIST Plus, which includes optional content scales) to score and report results are also available; computer version of the Structured Observation System (BASC Portable Observation Program) is available for use with Windows (Win 98 SE, 4.0 NT, 2000, ME, XP), Macintosh (OS 9.2, 10.x), Palm (OS 3.x, 4.x, 5.x), and Pocket PC (2000, 2002); audiorecordings are available for administration of the Parent Rating Scales and Self-Report of Personality forms.

Authors: Cecil R. Reynolds and Randy W. Kamphaus.

Publisher: Pearson Assessments (originally published by AGS Publishing, acquired by Pearson in 2005).

a) TEACHER RATING SCALES.

Price Data: $29.99 per 25 hand-scored forms; $24.99 per 25 computer-scored forms; $39.99 per 25 scannable forms; $38.99 per 25 Parent Feedback Reports.

Time: (10–15) minutes.

1) *Teacher Rating Scales—Preschool.*

Population: Ages 2–5.

Scores, 9: Externalizing Problems (Aggression, Hyperactivity), Internalizing Problems (Anxiety, Depression, Somatization), Adaptive Skills (Adaptability, Social Skills, Functional Communication), Behavior Symptoms Index.

2) *Teacher Rating Scales—Child.*

Population: Ages 6–11.

Scores, 14: Externalizing Problems (Aggression, Hyperactivity, Conduct Problems), Internalizing Problems (Anxiety, Depression, Somatization), School Problems (Attention Problems, Learning Problems), Adaptive Skills (Adaptability, Social Skills, Leadership, Study Skills, Functional Communication), Behavioral Symptoms Index.

3) *Teacher Rating Scales—Adolescent.*

Population: Ages 12–21.

Scores, 14: Externalizing Problems (Aggression, Hyperactivity, Conduct Problems), Internalizing Problems (Anxiety, Depression, Somatization), School Problems (Attention Problems, Learning Problems), Adaptive Skills (Adaptability, Social Skills, Leadership, Study Skills, Functional Communication), Behavioral Symptoms Index.

b) PARENT RATING SCALES.

Price Data: $29.99 per 25 hand-scored forms; $24.99 per 25 computer-scored forms; $39.99 per 25 scannable forms; $38.99 per 25 Parent Feedback Reports.

Time: (10–20) minutes.

1) *Parent Rating Scales—Preschool.*

Population: Ages 2–5.

Scores, 10: Externalizing Problems (Aggression, Hyperactivity), Internalizing Problems (Anxiety, Depression, Somatization), Adaptive Skills (Adaptability, Social Skills, Activities of Daily Living, Functional Communication), Behavioral Symptoms Index.

2) *Parent Rating Scales—Child.*

Population: Ages 6–11.

Scores, 12: Externalizing Problems (Aggression, Hyperactivity, Conduct Problems), Internalizing Problems (Anxiety, Depression, Somatization), Adaptive Skills (Adaptability, Social Skills, Leadership, Activities of Daily Living, Functional Communication), Behavioral Symptoms Index.

3) *Parent Rating Scales—Adolescent.*

Population: Ages 12–21.

Scores, 12: Externalizing Problems (Aggression, Hyperactivity, Conduct Problems), Internalizing Problems (Anxiety, Depression, Somatization), Adaptive Skills (Adaptability, Social Skills, Leadership, Activities of Daily Living, Functional Communication), Behavioral Symptoms Index.

c) SELF-REPORT OF PERSONALITY.

Price Data: $29.99 per 25 hand-scored forms; $24.99 per 25 computer-scored forms; $39.99 per 25 scannable forms; $38.99 per 25 Parent Feedback Reports.

Time: (20–30) minutes.

1) *Self-Report of Personality—Child.*

Population: Ages 8–11.

Scores, 20: School Problems (Attitude to School, Attitude to Teachers), Internalizing Problems (Atypicality, Locus of Control, Social Stress, Anxiety, Depression, Sense of Inadequacy), Inattention/Hyperactivity (Attention Problems, Hyperactivity), Emotional Symptoms Index (Social Stress, Anxiety, Depression, Sense of Inadequacy, Self-Esteem, Self-Reliance), Personal Adjustment (Relations with Parents, Interpersonal Relations, Self-Esteem, Self-Reliance).

2) *Self-Report of Personality—Adolescent.*
Population: Ages 12–21.
Scores, 22: School Problems (Attitude to School, Attitude to Teachers, Sensation Seeking), Internalizing Problems (Atypicality, Locus of Control, Social Stress, Anxiety, Depression, Sense of Inadequacy, Somatization), Inattention/Hyperactivity (Attention Problems, Hyperactivity), Emotional Symptoms Index (Social Stress, Anxiety, Depression, Sense of Inadequacy, Self-Esteem, Self-Reliance), Personal Adjustment (Relations with Parents, Interpersonal Relations, Self-Esteem, Self-Reliance).
3) *Self-Report of Personality—College.*
Population: Ages 18–25.
Scores, 18: Internalizing Problems (Atypicality, Locus of Control, Social Stress, Anxiety, Depression, Sense of Inadequacy), Inattention/Hyperactivity (Attention Problems, Hyperactivity), Emotional Symptoms Index (Social Stress, Anxiety, Depression, Sense of Inadequacy, Self-Esteem, Self-Reliance), Personal Adjustment (Relations with Parents, Interpersonal Relations, Self-Esteem, Self-Reliance).
d) STRUCTURED DEVELOPMENTAL HISTORY.
Price Data: $38.99 per 25 history forms.
e) STUDENT OBSERVATION SYSTEM.
Price Data: $32.99 per 25 observation forms.
Time: (15) minutes.
Cross References: for reviews by James Clyde DiPerna and by Robert Spies and Christina Finley Jones of an earlier version, see 14:40; see also T5:280 (6 references); for reviews by Jonathon Sandoval and by Joseph C. Witt and Kevin M. Jones of an earlier edition, see 13:34 (6 references).

[284]
Behavior Dimensions Rating Scale.

Purpose: Developed to screen for emotional/behavior disorders and for monitoring behavior change.
Population: Ages 5–adult.
Publication Date: 1989.
Acronym: BDRS.
Scores, 5: Aggressive/Acting Out, Irresponsible/Inattentive, Socially Withdrawn, Fearful/Anxious, Total.
Administration: Individual.
Price Data, 2006: $134 per complete kit including examiner's manual (77 pages) and 25 record forms; $93.50 per examiner's manaul; $50.50 per 25 test records
Time: [5–10] minutes.
Comments: Ratings by teachers, parents, and psychologists.
Authors: Lyndal M. Bullock and Michael J. Wilson.

Publisher: Riverside Publishing.
Cross References: For reviews by Martha W. Blackwell and Rosemary O. Nelson-Gray, see 11:37 (1 reference).

[285]
Behavior Dimensions Scale.

Purpose: Designed to categorize and document existing behavior patterns into recognized areas of behavior disorders to assist in making diagnostic, placement, and programming decisions.
Population: Ages 3–19.
Publication Date: 1995.
Acronym: BDS.
Scores, 7: Inattentive, Hyperactive-Impulsive, Oppositional Defiant, Conduct, Avoidant Personality, Anxiety, Depression.
Administration: Individual.
Price Data, 2006: $130 per complete kit including School Version (59 pages) and Home Version (55 pages) manuals, 50 rating forms (School and Home), intervention manual (323 pages); $15 per manual (School or Home); $35 per 50 rating forms (School or Home); $35 per 50 Home Version Spanish rating forms; $30 per intervention manual; $35 per computerized scoring disk (Windows).
Time: (20–25) minutes.
Author: Stephen B. McCarney.
Publisher: Hawthorne Educational Services, Inc.
Cross References: For reviews by Kevin M. Jones and Beverly M. Klecker, see 14:41.

[286]
Behavior Disorders Identification Scale— Second Edition.

Purpose: "To document the existence of behaviors which meet the criteria for identifying the student as behaviorally disordered."
Population: Ages 4.5-21.
Publication Dates: 1988–2000.
Acronym: BDIS-2 SV (School Version); BDIS-2 HV (Home Version).
Scores, 5: Learning Problems, Interpersonal Relations, Inappropriate Behavior, Unhappiness/Depression, Physical Symptoms/Fears.
Administration: Individual.
Forms, 2: School Version, Home Version.
Price Data, 2006: $190 per complete kit including 50 Pre-Referral Behavior Checklists, 50 Intervention Strategies Documentation forms, 50 School Version Rating forms, 50 Home Version Rating forms, School Version Technical Manual, Home Version Technical Manual, and Teacher's Guide to Behavioral Interventions; $30 per 50 Pre-Referral Behavior Checklists; $30 per 50 Intervention Strategies Documentation forms; $15 per Technical Manual (School Version or Home

Version); $35 per 50 rating forms (School Version, Home Version, or Home Version Spanish); $30 per Teacher's Guide to Behavioral Interventions; $35 per BDIS-2 Quick Score; $225 per Teacher's Guide to Behavioral Interventions computer version (Windows®).

Time: [20] minutes for School Version; [15] minutes for Home Version.

Comments: Completed by adult observers; based on federal definitions of serious emotional disturbance (PL 94-142 and IDEA Amendments of 1997); available in paper or computer version; system requirements: IBM-compatible computer, 30 MB of drive space, 32–64 MB of free RAM, Windows 98 or newer, and a 2X CD-ROM drive, 580K memory; Quick Score computer scoring of school and Home Versions available, system requirements Windows 95 or newer, 8 MB RAM, 10 MB hard disk space, 2X CD-ROM drive; Quick Score provides individualized goals, objectives, interventions; Spanish language Home Version rating forms available.

Authors: Stephen B. McCarney and Tamara J. Arthaud (Technical Manuals, Home Version and School Version), and Kathy Cummins Wunderlich (Teacher's Guide to Behavioral Interventions).

Publisher: Hawthorne Educational Services, Inc.

Cross References: For reviews by Judy Oehler-Stinnett and by Stephanie Stein and Phil Diaz, see 16:26; for reviews by Doreen Ward Fairbank and Harlan J. Stientjes of an earlier edition, see 12:46.

[287]
Behavior Evaluation Scale—Third Edition.

Purpose: Designed "to contribute to the early identification and service delivery for students with serious emotional disturbance or behavior disorders."

Population: Ages 4-19.

Publication Dates: 1990-2005.

Acronym: BES-3:L, BES-3:S.

Scores, 6: Learning Problems, Interpersonal Difficulties, Inappropriate Behavior, Unhappiness/Depression, Physical Symptoms/Fears, Total Score.

Administration: Individual.

Forms, 4: Long-School Version, Long-Home Version, Short-School Version, Short-Home Version.

Price Data, 2006: LONG VERSION: $208.50 per complete kit including Long-School Version technical manual (2005, 77 pages), 50 Long-School Version rating forms, Long-Home Version technical manual (2005, 75 pages), 50 Long-Home Version rating forms, 50 Intervention Strategies Documentation forms, 50 Long-Pre-Referral checklists, Long-Intervention manual, and one Parent's Guide; $20 per Long-technical manual (specify School or Home Version); $30 per Long-Intervention manual; $35 per 50 Long-rating forms (specify School or Home Version); $35 per 50 Long-Home Version Spanish rating forms; $30 per 50 Intervention Strategies Documentation forms; $30 per 50 Long-Pre-Referral checklists; $8.50 per the Parent's Guide; $35 per Long-Quick Score computerized Windows program; SHORT VERSION: $206.50 per complete kit including Short-School Version technical manual (2005, 83 pages), 50 Short-School Version rating forms, Short-Home Version technical manual (2005, 77 pages), 50 Short-Home Version rating forms, 50 Intervention Strategies Documentation forms, 50 Long-Pre-Referral checklists, Short-Intervention manual, and one Parent's Guide; $20 per Short-technical manual (specify School or Home Version); $28 per Short-Intervention manual; $35 per 50 Short-rating forms (specify School or Home Version); $35 per 50 Short-Home Version Spanish rating forms; $30 per 50 Intervention Strategies Documentation forms; $30 per 50 Short-Pre-Referral checklists; $8.50 per the Parent's Guide; $35 per Short-Quick Score computerized Windows program.

Foreign Language Editions: Long-Home and Short-Home Version Spanish rating forms available.

Time: (20) minutes.

Comments: Includes Home Version and School Version; scale is completed by parent/caregiver or an educator.

Authors: Stephen B. McCarney and Tamara J. Arthaud.

Publisher: Hawthorne Educational Services, Inc.

Cross References: See T5:284 (1 reference); for reviews by Bert A. Goldman and D. Joe Olmi of a previous edition, see 12:47; for reviews by J. Jeffrey Grill, Lester Mann, and Leonard Kenowitz of an earlier edition, see 9:128.

[288]
Behavior Rating Instrument for Autistic and Other Atypical Children, 2nd Edition.

Purpose: Designed to evaluate the status of autistic, atypical, and other developmentally delayed children by assessing their present levels of functioning and measuring changes in their behavior.

Population: Autistic children.

Publication Dates: 1977–1991.

Acronym: BRIAAC.

Scores, 9: Relationship to an Adult, Communication, Drive for Mastery, Vocalization and Expressive Speech, Sound and Speech Reception, Social Responsiveness, Psychobiological Development, Expressive Gesture and Sign Language, Receptive Gesture and Sign Language.

Administration: Individual.

Price Data, 2005: $130 per complete kit including manual (1991, 140 pages) and report form masters with permission to reproduce 50 copies; $50 per manual; $80 per reproducible masters and permission to make 50 copies.

Time: Untimed.

Authors: Bertram A. Ruttenberg, Enid G. Wolf-Schein, and Charles Wenar.
Publisher: Stoelting Co.
Cross References: For a review by Doreen Ward Fairbank, see 13:35; see also T4:280 (1 reference); for a review by Edward Workman of an earlier edition, see 9:129; see also T3:272 (1 reference).

[289]
Behavior Rating Inventory of Executive Function.

Purpose: Designed to assess impairment of executive function behaviors in the home and school environments using parent and teacher questionnaires.
Population: Ages 5–18.
Publication Dates: 1996–2000.
Acronym: BRIEF.
Scores, 11: Inhibit, Shift, Emotional Control, Behavioral Regulation Index, Initiate, Working Memory, Plan/Organize, Organization of Materials, Monitor, Metacognition Index, Global Executive Composite.
Administration: Individual or group.
Forms, 2: Parent Form, Teacher Form.
Price Data, 2006: $196 per introductory kit including professional manual (2000, 150 pages), 25 Parent Form Questionnaires, 25 Teacher Form Questionnaires, 50 Parent Form Scoring Summary/Profile Forms, and 50 Teacher Form Scoring Summary/Profile Forms; $525 per Scoring Program including unlimited scoring and reports for both BRIEF forms on CD-ROM.
Time: (10–15) minutes.
Comments: Ratings by teachers, parents, or guardians; CD-ROM-based Software Portfolio is also available for scoring and report generation.
Authors: Gerard A. Gioia, Peter K. Isquith, Steven C. Guy, and Lauren Kenworthy.
Publisher: Psychological Assessment Resources, Inc.
Cross References: For reviews by Corine Fitzpatrick and Gregory Schraw, see 15:32.

[290]
Behavior Rating Inventory of Executive Function—Adult Version.

Purpose: Designed to capture "adults' views of their own executive functions, or self-regulation, in their everyday environment."
Population: Ages 18-90.
Publication Dates: 1996-2005.
Acronym: BRIEF-A.
Scores, 12: 9 subscales: Inhibit, Shift, Emotional Control, Self-Monitor, Initiate, Working Memory, Plan/Organize, Task Monitor, Organization of Materials; 3 composite scores: Behavioral Regulation Index, Metacognition Index, Global Executive Composite.
Administration: Individual.

Price Data, 2006: $189 per introductory kit including professional manual (2005, 147 pages), 25 self-report forms, 25 informant report forms, 25 self-report scoring summary/profile forms, and 25 informant report scoring summary/profile forms; $55 per professional manual; $45 per 25 self-report forms; $45 per 25 informant report forms; $30 per 25 self-report scoring summary/profile forms; $30 per 25 informant report scoring summary/profile forms.
Time: (15) minutes.
Comments: It is preferable to administer the informant report form to a knowledgeable informant such as a spouse, adult child, caregiver, or other person who has frequent face-to-face interaction with the individual completing the self-report form.
Authors: Robert M. Roth, Peter K. Isquith, and Gerard A. Gioia.
Publisher: Psychological Assessment Resources, Inc.

[291]
Behavior Rating Inventory of Executive Function—Preschool Version.

Purpose: Designed to "assess executive function behaviors of preschool aged children in the home and preschool environments using the observations of parents, teachers, and daycare providers."
Population: Ages 2-0 to 5-11.
Publication Dates: 1996–2003.
Acronym: BRIEF-P™.
Scores, 9: Inhibit, Shift, Emotional Control, Working Memory, Plan/Organize, Inhibitory Self-Control Index, Flexibility Index, Emergent Metacognition Index, Global Executive Composite.
Administration: Individual.
Price Data, 2006: $125 per introductory kit including manual (2003, 111 pages), 25 rating forms, and 25 scoring summary/profile forms.
Time: (10–15) minutes.
Comments: Behavior rating scale is completed by parent or teacher/child care worker who is familiar with the child.
Authors: Gerard A. Gioia, Kimberly Andrews Espy, and Peter K. Isquith.
Publisher: Psychological Assessment Resources, Inc.
Cross References: For reviews by R. Anthony Doggett and Carl J. Sheperis and by Leah M. Nellis, see 16:27.

[292]
Behavior Rating Inventory of Executive Function—Self-Report Version.

Purpose: Designed to assess children's and adolescents' "views of their own executive functions, or self-regulation, in their everyday environment."
Population: Ages 11–18.
Publication Dates: 1996–2004.

Acronym: BRIEF-SR.
Scores, 15: Behavioral Regulation Index (Inhibit, Shift, Emotional Control, Monitor, Total), Metacognition Index (Working Memory, Plan/Organize, Organization of Materials, Task Completion, Total), Global Executive Composite, Behavioral Shift, Cognitive Shift, Inconsistency, Negativity.
Administration: Individual.
Price Data, 2006: $142 per introductory kit including professional manual (2004, 204 pages), 25 rating forms, and 50 scoring summary/profile forms.
Time: (10-15) minutes.
Authors: Steven C. Guy, Peter K. Isquith, and Gerard A. Gioia.
Publisher: Psychological Assessment Resources, Inc.
Cross References: For reviews by Stephen L. Benton and Sheryl Benton and by Manuel Martinez-Pons, see 16:28.

[293]
Behavior Rating Profile, Second Edition.

Purpose: "To evaluate students' behaviors at home, in school, and in interpersonal relationships."
Population: Ages 6-6 to 18-6.
Publication Dates: 1978–1990.
Acronym: BRP-2.
Scores: 5 checklists: Student Rating Scales (Home, School, Peers), Teacher Rating Scale, Parent Rating Scale, plus Sociogram score.
Administration: Individual.
Price Data, 2006: $204 per complete kit; $40 per 50 rating scale booklets (specify student, parent, or teacher form); $40 per 50 profile forms; $48 per examiner's manual (1990, 75 pages).
Time: (15–30) minutes per scale.
Authors: Linda Brown and Donald D. Hammill.
Publisher: PRO-ED.
Cross References: See T5:286 (3 references); for reviews by Sarah J. Allen and Lisa A. Bloom, see 12:48 (1 reference); see also T4:281 (1 reference); for reviews by Thomas R. Kratochwill and Joseph C. Witt of an earlier edition, see 9:130 (1 reference); see also T3:273 (1 reference).

[294]
Behavior Rating Scale.

Purpose: Designed to sample teachers' perceptions about their pupils' behavior in the classroom.
Population: Grades K–8.
Publication Dates: 1970–1975.
Score: Total score only.
Administration: Group.
Forms, 3: Forms differ only in number of rating categories.
Manual: No manual.
Price Data, 2001: Now free upon request from publisher.

Time: Administration time not reported.
Comments: Ratings by teachers; research instrument; may be used with or separately from Characteristics Scale (445).
Authors: Patricia B. Elmore and Donald L. Beggs.
Publisher: Patricia B. Elmore.
Cross References: See T5:287 (1 reference) and T4:282 (2 references); for a review by Jayne A. Parker, see 9:131 (2 references).

[295]
Behavioral Analysis Forms for Clinical Intervention.

Purpose: To gather client interview data in a structured manner.
Population: Behavior therapy clients.
Publication Dates: 1977–1981.
Scores: Volume 1: 36 plans, questionnaires, scales, forms, schedules, and data forms in areas such as Client History, Motivation for Change, Reinforcement, Social Performance; Volume 2: 59 questionnaires, scales, forms, schedules, and data forms in areas such as Reinforcers for Specific Populations, Survey of Phobic or Relationship Reactions, and Guidelines for Clients.
Administration: Group or individual.
Price Data, 2001: $79.95 for each volume.
Time: Administration times vary.
Author: Joseph R. Cautela.
Publisher: Cambridge Center for Behavioral Studies.
Cross References: For reviews by Mary Lou Kelley and Francis E. Lentz, Jr., see 9:127.

[296]
Behavioral and Emotional Rating Scale, Second Edition.

Purpose: Designed to "measure the personal strengths and competencies of children."
Population: Ages 5-0 to 18-11.
Publication Dates: 1998–2004.
Acronym: BERS-2.
Scores, 6: 5 subscales: Interpersonal Strength, Family Involvement, Intrapersonal Strength, School Functioning, Affective Strength, plus Strength Index .
Administration: Individual.
Price Data, 2006: $165 per complete kit including examiner's manual (2004, 112 pages), 25 teacher rating scales, 25 parent rating scales, 25 youth rating scales, and 50 summary forms; $57 per examiner's manual; $30 per 25 teacher rating scales; $30 per parent rating scales; $30 per youth rating scales; $30 per 50 summary forms.
Time: (10) minutes.
Comments: Revised edition adds Parent and Youth Rating Scales.
Author: Michael H. Epstein.

Publisher: PRO-ED.
Cross References: For reviews by John D. King and by Mark E. Swerdlik and W. Joel Schneider, see 16:29; for reviews by Beth Doll and D. Joe Olmi of an earlier edition, see 14:42.

[297]

Behavioral Assessment of Pain Questionnaire.

Purpose: "Used for gaining a better understanding of factors which may be maintaining the subacute and chronic noncancerous pain experience."
Population: Subacute and chronic pain patients.
Publication Dates: 1990-1992.
Administration: Individual.
Price Data, 2001: $30 per sample kit including manual (1992, 44 pages); answer sheet and Mercury scoring with interpretive clinical profile, general information, scale descriptions, sample BAP clinical profile, and reprint of journal article; $10 per manual.
Foreign Language Editions: Spanish and French editions available.
Time: (60) minutes.
Authors: Michael J. Lewandowski and Blake H. Tearnan.
Publisher: Pain Assessment Resources [No reply from publisher; status unknown].
a) BEHAVIORAL ASSESSMENT OF PAIN.
Acronym: BAP.
Scores, 34: Demographic Information, Activity Interference Scale (Domestic/Household Activities, Heavy Activities, Social Activities, Personal Care Activities, Personal Hygiene Activities), Avoidance Scale, Spouse/Partner Influence Scale (Reinforcement of Pain, Discouragement/Criticism of Pain, Reinforcement of Wellness, Discouragement/Criticism of Wellness), Physician Influence Scale (Discouragement/Criticism of Pain, Reinforcement of Wellness, Discouragement/Criticism of Wellness, Reinforcement of Pain), Physician Qualities Scale, Pain Beliefs Scale (Catastrophizing, Fear of Reinjury, Expectation for Cure, Blaming Self, Entitlement, Future Despair, Social Disbelief, Lack of Medical Comprehensiveness), Perceived Consequences Scale (Social Interference, Physical Harm, Psychological Harm, Pain Exacerbation, Productivity Interference), Coping Scale, Negative Mood Scale (Depression, Anxiety, Muscular Discomfort, Change in Weight).
Price Data: $21.50 per on-site scored interpretive report; $23.50 per Mercury scored interpretive report; $5 per BAP booklet.
b) POST BEHAVIORAL ASSESSMENT OF PAIN.
Acronym: P-BAP.
Scores, 23: Avoidance, Spouse/Partner Influence Scale (Reinforcement of Pain, Discourage-

ment/Criticism of Pain, Reinforcement of Wellness, Discouragement/Criticism of Wellness), Pain Beliefs Scale (Catastrophizing, Fear of Reinjury, Expectation for Cure, Blaming Self, Entitlement, Future Despair, Social Disbelief, Lack of Medical Comprehensiveness), Perceived Consequences Scale (Social Interference, Physical Harm, Psychological Harm, Pain Exacerbation, Productivity Interference), Coping Scale, Negative Mood Scale (Depression, Anxiety, Muscular Discomfort, Change in Weight).
Price Data: $21.50 per on-site scored P-BAP report; $23.50 per Mercury scored P-BAP report; $5 per P-BAP booklet.
Cross References: For reviews by Gerald E. DeMauro and Ronald J. Ganellen, see 12:49.

[298]

Behavioral Characteristics Progression (BCP) Assessment Record.

Purpose: Assesses developmental skills/behaviors.
Population: Children and adults with mental and physical disabilities.
Publication Dates: 1973-1997.
Acronym: BCP.
Scores: Item scores only.
Administration: Individual.
Price Data, 2006: $5 per record booklet (1997, 64 pages); $59.95 per BCP Instructional Activities resource book (1997, 400 pages).
Time: Administration time not reported.
Comments: "Criterion-referenced" assessment for developmental ages 1-14 years.
Author: VORT Corporation.
Publisher: VORT Corporation.
Cross References: See T5:292 (1 reference); for reviews by Rosemery O. Nelson-Gray and Harvey N. Switzky of an earlier edition, see 11:38.

[299]

Behavioral Objective Sequence.

Purpose: Designed to "assist special educators and other professionals assess behavioral competencies of students with emotional and behavioral disorders."
Population: Students (grades 1-12) with emotional and behavioral disorders.
Publication Date: 1998.
Acronym: BOS.
Scores, 6: Adaptive Behaviors, Self-Management Behaviors, Communication Behaviors, Interpersonal Behaviors, Task Behaviors, Personal Behaviors.
Administration: Individual.
Price Data, 2006: $39.95 per manual (1998, 104 pages), recording forms, and test; $150 per report generating software (for Windows) Behavioral Objective Sequence Reports (BOSR) including BOS manual.

Time: Administration time not reported.

Comments: "Can be used as a bank of (behavioral) objectives, as a rating scale, or as a structured observational system"; completed by educational/psychological professionals about a student; software program available.

Authors: Sheldon Braaten (test and software program) and John B. Merbler (software program).

Publisher: Research Press.

Cross References: For reviews by M. David Miller and Stephanie Stein, see 15:33.

[300]
Behaviors and Experiences Inventory.

Purpose: "An initial screen for Attention-Deficit/Hyperactivity Disorder (ADHD), Conduct Disorder (CD), and Antisocial Personality Disorder (ASPD)."

Population: Adults.

Publication Dates: 1998–1999.

Acronym: BEI.

Scores, 24: ADHD: Inattention (Difficulty Sustaining Attention, Fails to Finish Assignments, Inattention to Details/Careless, Difficulty Organizing Tasks/Activities, Tendency to Lose Things, Distractible), Hyperactivity, Impulsivity, Conduct Disorder as a Child/Adolescent (Aggression, Destruction of Property, Deceitfulness or Theft, Serious Violation of Rules, Cruelty to Animals and Fire-Setting), Antisocial Personality Disorder (Failure to Conform to Social Norms, Deceitfulness, Impulsivity, Irritability/Aggressiveness, Reckless Disregard for Safety, Irresponsibility, Lack of Remorse), History of Abuse as a Child/Adolescent (Physical, Sexual, Emotional).

Administration: Individual.

Price Data: Available from publisher.

Time: (15–20) minutes.

Comments: Can be administered as paper-and-pencil questionnaire or as a structured interview; screens for DSM-IV diagnostic criteria, providing an estimate of the likelihood that an individual meets the criteria for ADHD, CD, and ASPD; covers current problems only.

Authors: Norman G. Hoffmann, David Mee-Lee, and Gerald D. Shulman.

Publisher: Change Companies.

Cross References: For a review by Mark R. Cooper, see 15:34.

[301]
Behaviour Problems: A System of Management.

Purpose: "A systematic means of recording and analysing information on children's problem behaviour."

Population: Problem behavior children in a classroom situation.

Publication Date: 1984.

Scores: 8 areas of behavior: Classroom Conformity, Task Orientation, Emotional Control, Acceptance of Authority, Self-Worth, Peer Relationships, Self Responsibility/Problem Solving, Other.

Administration: Individual.

Price Data: Price information available from publisher for complete set including manual (15 pages), pad of 50 Daily Records, and pack of 10 Behaviour Checklist/Monthly Progress Charts.

Time: Administration time not reported.

Authors: Peter P. Galvin and Richard M. Singleton.

Publisher: NFER-Nelson Publishing Co., Ltd. [England].

Cross References: For reviews by Kathryn M. Benes and Terry Overton, see 11:39.

[302]
Behavioural Assessment of the Dysexecutive Syndrome.

Purpose: "A test battery aimed at predicting everyday problems arising from the Dysexecutive Syndrome."

Population: Ages 16–87.

Publication Date: 1996.

Acronym: BADS.

Scores, 7: Rule Shift Card, Action Program, Key Search, Temporal Judgement, Zoo Map, Modified Six Elements, Total.

Administration: Individual.

Price Data, 2006: £319.50 per complete kit including manual, 25 scoring sheets, 5 stimulus books, stimulus cards, three-dimensional plastic materials, timer, 25 self-rater dex questionnaires, and 25 independent rater questionnaires; £26 per 2 packs of 25 dex questionnaires (self-rater and independent rater).

Time: 40 minutes.

Comments: Subtest scores "may be used individually, although validation studies have indicated that the overall battery score is the most sensitive predictor of executive problems"; useful with brain-injured and schizophrenic patients for identifying general or specific deficits in executive functions; supplemental information about patients can be gathered using the self-rating and caregiver rating forms included in the test kit.

Authors: Barbara A. Wilson, Nick Alderman, Paul W. Burgess, Hazel Emslie, and Jonathan J. Evans.

Publisher: Harcourt Assessment [England].

Cross References: For reviews by Rik Carl D'Amato and Sandra D. Haynes, see 14:43.

[303]
Behavioural Assessment of the Dysexecutive Syndrome in Children.

Purpose: Tests the executive functioning of children and adolescents.

Population: Children and adolescents ages 8 to 16.

Publication Date: 2003.
Acronym: BADS-C.
Scores, 8: Playing Cards Test, Water Test, Key Search Test, Zoo Map Test 1, Zoo Map Test 2, Six Parts Test, Dysexecutive Questionnaire for Children, Total Score.
Administration: Individual.
Price Data, 2006: £367 per complete kit including manual (41 pages), 25 scoring sheets, stimulus cards, three-dimensional plastic materials, timer, 25 Dysexecutive Questionnaire for Children (DEX-C), independent rater questionnaires, beads, nuts, bolts, and washers; £37.50 per 50 record sheets; £26 per 50 DEX-C questionnaires.
Time: (35–45) minutes.
Comments: Adaptation of Behavioural Assessment of the Dysexecutive Syndrome (302); examinee IQ-score must be available to determine scaled score and percentile rank.
Authors: Hazel Emslie, F. Colin Wilson, Vivian Burden, Ian Nimmo-Smith, and Barbara A. Wilson.
Publisher: Harcourt Assessment [England].

[304]
Behavioural Inattention Test.

Purpose: Developed to measure unilateral visual neglect.
Population: Ages 19-83.
Publication Date: 1987.
Acronym: BIT.
Scores, 17: Conventional Subtest Scores (Line Crossing, Letter Cancellation, Star Cancellation, Figure and Shape Copying, Line Bisection, Representational Drawing, Total), Behavioural Subtests (Picture Scanning, Telephone Dialling, Menu Reading, Article Reading, Telling and Setting the Time, Coin Sorting, Address and Sentence Copying, Map Navigation, Card Sorting, Total).
Administration: Individual.
Price Data, 2006: £229.50 per complete kit including manual (19 pages), various stimuli, test, playing cards, and clock face; £60.50 per 50 scoring sheets.
Time: (40) minutes.
Authors: Barbara Wilson, Janet Cockburn, and Peter Halligan.
Publisher: Harcourt Assessment [England].

[305]
Belbin Team-Roles Self-Perception Inventory.

Purpose: Designed to determine which contributions each team member can make best.
Population: Teams.
Publication Date: 1994.
Scores: 9 Profiles: Plant, Coordinator, Resource Investigator, Monitor Evaluator, Implementer, Team Worker, Completer-Finisher, Specialist, Shaper.
Administration: Group.
Price Data: Available from publisher
Time: [1 day].
Author: Meredith Belbin.
Publisher: Jossey-Bass, A Wiley Company.
Cross References: For reviews by Keith Hattrup and by Kristin O. Prien and Erich P. Prien, see 14:44.

[306]
Bell Object Relations and Reality Testing Inventory.

Purpose: Designed to assess "dimensions of object relations and reality testing ego functioning."
Population: Ages 18 and older.
Publication Date: 1995.
Acronym: BORRTI.
Scores, 8: Object Relations (Alienation, Insecure Attachment, Egocentricity, Social Incompetence); Reality Testing (Reality Distortion, Uncertainty of Perception, Hallucinations and Delusions); Inconsistent Responding; plus two validity indexes: FREQ, INFREQ.
Administration: Group.
Price Data, 2002: $99.50 per complete kit including 2 prepaid Full Form mail-in answer sheets, 2-use clinical disk, 2 Full Form PC answer sheets, and manual; $47.50 per manual; $17.50 per Full Form mail-in answer sheet; $16.50 per Form O mail-in answer sheet; $215 per 20-use clinical disk (Full Form or Form O; PC with Microsoft Windows) including interpretive report; $72.50 per 20-use clinical disk for scoring only; $15 per 100 PC answer sheets (specify Full Form or Form O); $41.50 per FAX Scoring service for Full Form; $10.50 per FAX Scoring Service for Form O.
Time: (15–20) minutes.
Comments: Form O including only items measuring object relations also available.
Author: Morris D. Bell.
Publisher: Western Psychological Services.
Cross References: For reviews by Glen Fox and Steven I. Pfeiffer, see 14:45; see also T5:297 (2 references).

[307]
Bem Sex-Role Inventory.

Purpose: Provides independent assessments of masculinity and femininity in terms of the respondent's self-reported possession of socially desirable, stereotypically masculine and feminine personality characteristics; can also be used as a measurement of the extent to which respondents spontaneously sort self-relevant information into distinct masculine and feminine categories; measures masculinity, femininity, androgyny, and undifferentiated, using the Masculinity and Femininity scales.
Population: High school and college and adults.

Publication Dates: 1978-1981.
Acronym: BSRI.
Scores, 4: Femininity, Masculinity, Androgeny, Undifferentiated.
Administration: Group.
Price Data: Available from publisher (www.mindgarden.com).
Time: (10-15) minutes.
Comments: Test is titled Bem Inventory; self-administered; short and long form available (short form consists of first 30 items only).
Author: Sandra Lipsitz Bem.
Publisher: Mind Garden, Inc.
Cross References: See T5:298 (167 references) and T4: 288 (204 references); for reviews by Richard Lippa and Frank D. Rayne, see 9:137 (121 references).

[308]
Bench Mark Measures.

Purpose: Measures a student's general knowledge of phonics.
Population: Ungraded.
Publication Date: 1977.
Scores: 3 levels in 4 areas: Alphabet and Dictionary Skills, Reading, Handwriting, Spelling.
Administration: Individual in part.
Price Data, 2006: $77.60 per complete kit including administrator's guide (16 pages), test booklet (26 pages), 24 summary sheets (6 pages), graph of concepts and multisensory introductions (16 pages), sheet of block capitals, set of three-dimensional letters, skeleton dictionary (Anna Gillingham and Bessie Stillman, 1956, 79 pages), test cards (56), spirit duplicating master (1 page); $18 per 12 summary sheets; $8.20 per graph; $9.70 per skeleton dictionary; quantity discounts available.
Time: (30–60) minutes.
Comments: "Criterion-referenced"; follows the sequence of the Alphabetic Phonics curriculum developed in the Language Research and Training Laboratory of the Texas Scottish Rite Hospital for its remedial language training program.
Author: Aylett R. Cox.
Publisher: Educators Publishing Service, Inc.
Cross References: For a review by David J. Carroll, see 9:138.

[309]
Benchmark of Organizational Emotional Intelligence.

Purpose: "Designed to measure the level of emotional intelligence in an organization as a whole and across departments, teams, or divisions."
Population: Ages 18 and over.
Publication Date: 2005.
Acronym: BOEI.

Scores, 24: 7 scale scores (Job Happiness, Compensation, Work/Life Stress Management, Organizational Cohesiveness, Supervisory Leadership, Diversity and Anger Management, Organizational Responsiveness), 14 subscale scores (Pay, Benefits, Stability, Stress Management, Work/Life Balance, Coworker Relationships, Teamwork, Diversity Climate, Gender/Racial Acceptance, Anger Management, Training and Innovation, Optimism and Integrity, Courage and Adaptability, Top Management Leadership), 2 validity scale scores (Positive Impression, Negative Impression), Total Score.
Administration: Group or individual.
Price Data, 2006: $330 per Online Organizational Report kit including technical manual (176 pages) and 1 Organizational Report; $300 per Online Organizational Report; $50 per technical manual; $50 per Online Group Report comparing up to 5 groups; $12 per Online Individual Report; $35 per 10 item booklets; $20 per 25 faxable response sheets.
Time: (30) minutes.
Comments: Test can be administered over the internet.
Authors: Steven J. Stein and Multi-Health Systems Staff.
Publisher: Multi-Health Systems, Inc.

[310]
Benchmarks [Revised].

Purpose: "Assesses skills and perspectives that leaders can learn from experience; also, potential flaws that can derail a career."
Population: Middle- to upper-level managers and executives with at least 3–5 years of managerial experience.
Publication Dates: 1990–2001.
Scores, 21: 3 Skill Areas: Meeting Job Challenges (Resourcefulness, Doing Whatever It Takes, Being A Quick Study, Decisiveness), Leading People (Leading Employees, Confronting Problem Employees, Participative Management, Change Management), Respecting Self and Others (Building And Mending Relationships, Compassion And Sensitivity, Straightforwardness And Composure, Balance Between Personal Life And Work, Self-Awareness, Putting People At Ease, Differences Matter, Career Management), Potential for Derailment (Problems With Interpersonal Relationships, Difficulty Building And Leading A Team, Difficulty Changing Or Adapting, Failure To Meet Business Objectives, Too Narrow Functional Orientation).
Administration: Group.
Restricted Distribution: The publisher requires a 2-day certification program for those who wish to give feedback from Benchmarks in their own organization or as a consultant.
Price Data, 2006: $275 per set including 13 survey questionnaires (paper-and-pencil or internet), Feed-

back Reports, Developmental Learning Guide, and a Facilitators Guide; $40 handling fee charged per set; quantity discounts available; $300 per group profile (2005, 13 pages).

Foreign Language Editions: Translations available include British English, French, French-Canadian, Dutch, German, Italian, and Spanish; normative comparisons are available for Belgium and the United Kingdom.

Time: (30–40) minutes.

Comments: Available in paper-and-pencil and online; hard copy Feedback Report is generated providing mean scores and normative comparisons for all items and the 21 scores as rated by all observers, self, boss, superior, peer, direct report, other; Developmental Learning Guide "suggests strategies for change" including exercises to help analyze feedback, presentation of "tactics and strategies."

Authors: Michael Lombardo, Cynthia McCauley, Dana McDonald-Mann, and Jean Brittain Leslie.

Publisher: Center for Creative Leadership.

> *a)* BENCHMARKS GROUP PROFILE.
> **Purpose:** "To assess the caliber and potential of management to fulfill … objectives, and to develop more appropriate and effective management and organizational development strategies."
> **Price Data:** $300 per group profile.
> **Comments:** Provides group-level mean scores and normative comparisons for the 21 scores as rated by all observers, self, boss/superior, peer, direct report, other.

Cross References: For reviews by Heidi M. Carty and Michael Spangler, see 15:35; for a review by Sheldon Zedeck of an earlier edition, see 12:50.

[311]
Bender® Visual-Motor Gestalt Test, Second Edition.

Purpose: Designed to measure visual-motor integration skills in children and adults.

Population: Ages 4–85+.

Publication Dates: 1938–2003.

Acronym: Bender®-Gestalt II.

Scores, 4: Copy Score, Recall Score, Motor Test Score, Perception Test Score.

Administration: Individual.

Price Data, 2006: $130.50 per complete kit including manual (2003, 181 pages), cards, 25 observation forms, 25 motor test booklets, and 25 perception test booklets; $68.50 per manual; $13 per 25 observation forms; $13 per 25 motor test booklets; $13 per 25 perception test booklets.

Time: Untimed; typically (10-15) minutes.

Comments: Revision of the Visual Motor Gestalt Test [Bender-Gestalt Test].

Authors: Gary G. Brannigan and Scott L. Decker.

Publisher: Riverside Publishing.

Cross References: For reviews by D. Joe Olmi and by Darrell L. Sabers and Sarah Bonner, see 16:30; see also T5:301 (61 references) and T4:291 (34 references); for reviews by Jack A. Naglieri and by John E. Obrzut and Carol A. Boliek of an earlier edition, see 11:40 (92 references) for reviews by Kenneth W. Howell and Jerome M. Sattler, see 9:139 (65 references); see also T3:280 (159 references), 8:506 (253 references), and T2:1447 (144 references); for a review by Phillip M. Kitay, see 7:161 (192 references); see also P:415 (170 references); for a review by C. B. Blakemore and an excerpted review by Fred Y. Billingslea, see 6:203 (99 references); see also 5:172 (118 references); for reviews by Arthur L. Benton and Howard R. White, see 4:144 (34 references); see also 3:108 (8 references).

[312]
Bennett Mechanical Comprehension Test, Second Edition.

Purpose: "Designed to measure the ability to perceive and understand the relationship of physical forces and mechanical elements in practical situations."

Population: Industrial employees and high school and adult applicants for mechanical positions or engineering schools.

Publication Dates: 1940–1994.

Acronym: BMCT.

Scores: Total score only.

Administration: Group.

Forms, 2: S, T (equivalent forms).

Price Data, 2006: $275 per complete starter kit including 10 forms test booklet, 50 answer booklets for both forms, and manual (1994, 89 pages); $195 per 25 test booklets; $100 per 10 test booklets; $115 per 50 answer documents; $35 per hand-scoring keys; $45 per manual; $135 per taped recordings of test questions.

Time: (30) minutes.

Comments: Tape recordings of test questions read aloud are available for use with examinees who have limited reading abilities; total assessment score and percentile score provided; available online and via pencil-and-paper; Spanish version available.

Author: George K. Bennett.

Publisher: Harcourt Assessment, Inc.

Cross References: For reviews by Joseph C. Ciechalski and Michael Spangler, see 16:31; see also T5:302 (4 references) and T4:292 (2 references); for a review by Hilda Wing of an earlier edition, see 11:41 (3 references); see also T3:282 (7 references) and T2:2239 (9 references); for reviews by Harold P. Bechtoldt and A. Oscar H. Roberts, and an excerpted review by Ronald K. Hambleton of the first edition, see 7:1049 (22 references); see also 6:1094 (15 references) and 5:889 (46 references); for a review by N. W. Morton of earlier forms, see 4:766 (28 references); for reviews by

Charles M. Harsh, Lloyd G. Humphreys, and George A. Satter, see 3:683 (19 references).

[313]

Benton Visual Retention Test, Fifth Edition.

Purpose: "To assess visual perception, visual memory, and visuoconstructive abilities."
Population: Age 8–adults.
Publication Dates: 1946–1991.
Acronym: BVRT.
Scores, 9: Omissions, Distortions, Perseverations, Rotations, Misplacements, Size Errors, Total Left, Total Right, Total.
Administration: Individual.
Forms, 3: C, D, E in a single booklet.
Price Data, 2002: $168 per complete set including stimulus booklet (all 30 designs), scoring template, 25 response booklets, record form, and manual (1992, 108 pages); $76per stimulus booklet; $45 per 25 response booklets-record form; $10 per scoring template; $67 per manual.
Time: (15–20) minutes.
Author: Arthur L. Benton.
Publisher: PsychCorp, A brand of Harcourt Assessment, Inc.
Cross References: See T5:303 (32 references); for reviews by Anita M. Hubley and Cynthia A. Rohrbeck, see 13:36 (66 references); see also T4:293 (62 references), 9:140 (30 references), T3:283 (27 references), 8:236 (32 references), T2:543 (71 references), and 6:543 (22 references); for a review by Nelson G. Hanawalt, see 5:401 (5 references); for reviews by Ivan Norman Mensh, Joseph Newman, and William Schofield of the original edition, see 4:360 (3 references); for an excerpted review, see 3:297.

[314]

The Benziger Thinking Styles Assessment.

Purpose: Designed to "help individuals increase their general effectiveness, collaborative skills and overall well-being through enhanced self-awareness and understanding."
Population: Working adults, aged 18 or older.
Publication Dates: 1988–2004.
Acronym: BTSA, E-BTSA.
Scores: Frontal Left, Basal Left, Basal Right, Frontal Right, Introversion/Extraversion.
Administration: Individual or group.
Restricted Distribution: Administrators must be persons (licensees) who have completed the publisher's training course.
Price Data, 2004: $100 per E-BTSA (electronic version); $25 per book Thriving in Mind (2003, 326 pages); North American and European licensee prices: $45 per BTSA and book Thriving in Mind; $15 per workbook, Thriving in Mind: The Workbook (specify English or Spanish); $75 per hour telephone feedback from author; price information for other countries available from publisher.
Time: (30–45) minutes.
Comments: Not intended as a psychometric measure; paper and electronic versions available.
Author: Katherine Benziger.
Publisher: KBA, LLC.
Cross References: For reviews by Richard E. Harding and Mark L. Pope, see 16:32.

[315]

The Ber-Sil Spanish Test.

Purpose: Screening and evaluation of Spanish-speaking children.
Population: Ages 5–12, 13–17.
Publication Dates: 1972–1987.
Administration: Individual.
Price Data: Available from publisher.
Author: Marjorie L. Beringer.
Publisher: Ber-Sil Co.
a) ELEMENTARY LEVEL.
Population: Ages 5–12.
Publication Date: 1987.
Scores, 7: Vocabulary, Response to Directions, Writing, Geometric Figures, Draw a Boy or Girl, Math Skills, English Vocabulary.
Foreign Language Editions: Cantonese, Mandarin, Ilokano, Tagalog, Korean, and Persian translations available.
Time: (45–55) minutes.
b) SECONDARY LEVEL.
Population: Ages 13–17.
Publication Date: 1984.
Scores, 4: Vocabulary, Dictation in Spanish, Draw a Person, Mathematics.
Foreign Language Editions: Philippine, Tagalog, and Ilokano translations available.
Time: (45) minutes.
Cross References: For reviews by J. Manuel Casas and David Strand and by Giuseppe Costantino, see 10:30; for reviews by Giuseppe Costantino and Jaclyn B. Spitzer of an earlier edition, see 9:141.

[316]

BEST Instruments.

Purpose: A series of learning instruments designed to help managers and employees understand their behavior.
Population: Adults.
Publication Dates: 1989–1994.
Acronym: BEST.
Administration: Group.
Price Data: Available from publisher.
Comments: Subtests available as separates.
Author: James H. Brewer.
Publisher: Associated Consultants in Education.

a) MY BEST PROFILE.
Purpose: "To promote positive interpersonal relations."
Publication Date: 1989.
Scores: 4 personality types: Bold, Expressive, Sympathetic, Technical.
Time: (15–20) minutes.

b) MY BEST COMMUNICATION STYLE.
Purpose: "To improve communication skills."
Publication Dates: 1989–1990.
Scores: 4 styles: Bold, Expressive, Sympathetic, Technical.
Time: (15–20) minutes.

c) MY BEST LEADERSHIP STYLE.
Purpose: "To improve leadership skills."
Publication Dates: 1989–1994.
Scores: Same as *a* above.
Time: (15–20) minutes.

d) LEADERSHIP/PERSONALITY COMPATIBILITY INVENTORY.
Purpose: "To promote more productive leadership in organizations."
Acronym: L/PCI.
Scores: Same as *a* above plus 4 Leadership Role Characteristics: Active/Competitive, Persuasive/Interactive, Precise/Systematic, Willing/Steady.
Publication Dates: 1990–1994.
Time: (15–20) minutes.

e) WORKING WITH MY BOSS.
Purpose: "To improve the productive relationship between employee and supervisor."
Publication Date: 1989.
Scores: Same as *a* above.
Time: (10–15) minutes.

f) PRE-EVALUATION PROFILE.
Purpose: "To prepare supervisors for performance evaluations of employees without personality type bias."
Acronym: PEP.
Publication Date: 1989.
Scores: Same as *a* above.
Time: (15–20) minutes.
Comments: Supervisor completes profile for self and employee.

g) OUR BEST TEAM.
Purpose: "To build a more productive team."
Publication Date: 1989.
Scores: Same as *a* above.
Time: (20–30) minutes.
Comments: Ratings of all team members are combined for a composite profile.

h) MY TIMESTYLE.
Purpose: "To develop more productive time usage."
Publication Date: 1990.
Scores: 4 timestyles: Road Runner, Race Horse, New Pup, Tom Cat.
Time: (10–15) minutes.

i) MY BEST PRESENTATION STYLE.
Purpose: "To assist individuals in making more effective presentations."
Publication Date: 1989.
Scores: Same as *a* above.
Time: (15–20) minutes.

j) SALES STYLE.
Purpose: "To sharpen sales skills."
Publication Date: 1990.
Scores: 4 sales styles: Quick-Sell, Persistent-Sell, Talkative-Sell, Precise-Sell.
Time: (10–15) minutes.

k) MY TEACHING STYLE.
Purpose: "To help teachers understand learning style."
Publication Date: 1989.
Scores: Bold, Expressive, Sympathetic, Technical.
Time: (15–20) minutes.

l) NEGOTIATING STYLE.
Purpose: "To build productive negotiating strategies."
Publication Date: 1991.
Scores: 4 negotiating styles: Pushy, Stand Pat, Buddy, Check All.
Time: (10–15) minutes.

m) CAREER/PERSONALITY COMPATIBILITY INVENTORY.
Purpose: "To improve career selection."
Publication Date: No date on materials.
Acronym: C/PCI.
Scores: Bold, Expressive, Sympathetic, Technical.
Time: (20–30) minutes.
Cross References: For reviews by Mary A. Lewis and Frank Schmidt, see 13:37.

[317]
BEST Plus: Oral English Proficiency Test.

Purpose: Designed "to assess the oral language proficiency of adult" nonnative speakers of English "who need to use English to function in day-to-day life in the United States."
Population: Adults.
Publication Date: 2005.
Acronym: BEST Plus.
Scores: 3 subscales: Listening Comprehension, Language Complexity, Communication, Total.
Administration: Individual.
Levels, 3: 1 (low proficiency), 2 (middle proficiency), 3 (high proficiency).
Versions, 2: Computer-adaptive version, Print-based version.

Forms, 3: A, B, C (all for Print-based version).
Price Data, 2006: $30 per 20 Print-based test administrations; $15 per picture cue book; $15 per replacement test administrator guide (without CD); $10 per replacement BEST Plus Test CD; $5 per replacement practice CD; $25 per technical report; $1.50 per administration for 20-280 computer administrations; bulk discounts are available for computer administrations.
Time: (5-15) minutes.
Comments: An adaptation of the Basic English Skills Test (256); computer administrations must be ordered in multiples of 20 or 50.
Authors: The Best Plus Development Team.
Publisher: Center for Applied Linguistics.

[318]

Beta III.

Purpose: "Provides a quick ... measure of nonverbal intellectual ability."
Population: Ages 16–89.
Publication Dates: 1934–1999.
Scores, 6: Coding, Picture Completion, Clerical Checking, Picture Absurdities, Matrix Reasoning, IQ Score.
Administration: Group or individual.
Price Data, 2002: $145 per complete kit including manual (1999, 58 pages), 25 response booklets, and scoring key; $42 per manual; $104 per 25 response booklets; $299 per 100 response booklets; quantity discounts available; $16 per scoring key.
Time: 15(25–30) minutes including 10–15 minutes of instruction and practice.
Comments: Revision of the Revised Beta Examination, Second Edition.
Authors: C. E. Kellogg and N. W. Morton.
Publisher: PsychCorp, A brand of Harcourt Assessment, Inc.
Cross References: For reviews by C. G. Bellah and Louise M. Soares, see 16:33; for information regarding the previous edition, see T5:2212 (3 references) and T4:2255 (4 references); see also T2:447 (29 references); for a review by Bert A. Goldman, see 6:494 (13 references); see also 5:375 (14 references); for reviews by Raleigh M. Drake and Walter C. Shipley, see 3:259 (5 references); for reviews by S. D. Porteus and David Wechsler, see 2:1419 (4 references).

[319]

Bilingual Syntax Measure [medida de Sintaxis Bilingüe].

Purpose: Designed to measure second-language oral proficiency with respect to syntactic structures in English and Spanish.
Population: Grades PK–2, 3–12.
Publication Dates: 1975–1980.

Acronym: BSM I, BSM II.
Scores: Scores consist of assigned levels of proficiency.
Administration: Individual.
Price Data, 2002: $476 per complete set including picture booklet, 35 English response booklets, 35 Spanish response booklets, class record, technical handbook, English manual, and Spanish manual (specify BSM I or BSM II); $133.50 per picture booklet (specify BSM I or BSM II); $118 per 35 BSM I response booklets (specify English or Spanish); $135 per 35 BSM II response booklets (specify English or Spanish); $10 per class record (specify BSM I or BSM II); $40.30 per BSM I technical handbook (1976, 53 pages); $40.30 per BSM II technical handbook (1980, 33 pages); $24.50 per BSM I manual (1975, 15 pages) (specify English or Spanish); $24.50 per BSM II manual (1978, 11 pages) (specify English or Spanish); $26 per English-Spanish reference handbook for educators.
Foreign Language Editions: English, Spanish (both of which may be administered as an indicator of language dominance).
Time: (10–15) minutes for each edition.
Comments: BSM II is an upward extension of the Bilingual Syntax Measure (BSM I).
Authors: Marina K. Burt, Heidi C. Dulay, and Eduardo Hernandez Ch.
Publisher: PsychCorp, A brand of Harcourt Assessment, Inc.
Cross References: See T5:307 (3 references) and T4:298 (2 references); for reviews of BSM II by Eugene E. Garcia and Sylvia Shellenberger, see 9:147 (1 reference); for reviews of BSM I by Isaac I. Bejar and C. Ray Graham, and an excerpted review by John W. Oller, Jr., see 8:156 (4 references); for information on BSM I, see T3:290 (5 references).

[320]

Bilingual Two-Language Assessment Battery of Tests.

Purpose: Designed to reveal "levels of language proficiency" and to determine language skills, acquisition, and loss.
Population: Students, adults, and potential employees with a language proficiency at second grade or higher level.
Publication Dates: 1983-2005.
Scores, 13: First Letter Recognition, Second Letter Recognition, Spelling, Opposites, Similarities, Comparisons, Reading, Listening, Items, Actions, Relationships, Total, Oral Proficiency.
Administration: Individual or group.
Forms, 5: Spanish-English, Portuguese-English, Vietnamese-English, Italian-English, French-English.
Price Data, 2005: $99 per battery including manual (2005, 104 pages), profile cards, one language test,

student's test work pages, and test answers; $594 per complete battery including manual, profile cards, six language tests, student's test work pages, and test answers.

Foreign Language Editions: Spanish, Portuguese, Vietnamse, Italian, and French.

Time: (20-30) minutes per language.

Comments: "Criterion-referenced"; each session consists of a Native language sitting followed by an English language sitting within 2 weeks; the battery is prerecorded and requires access to a CD player; optimal administration frequency is every 6 to 8 months.

Author: Adolph Caso.

Publisher: Branden Publishing Co.

[321]
Bilingual Verbal Ability Tests.

Purpose: "Provides a measure of overall verbal ability, and an unique combination of cognitive/academic language abilities for bilingual individuals."

Population: Ages 5 and older.

Publication Date: 1998.

Acronym: BVAT.

Scores, 5: Bilingual Verbal Ability, English Language Proficiency, Picture Vocabulary, Oral Vocabulary, Verbal Analogies.

Administration: Individual.

Price Data, 2006: $817.50 per complete kit including test book with English test pages, 16 sets of tests in languages (Arabic, Chinese Simplified, Chinese Traditional, French, German, Haitian-Creole, Hindi, Italian, Japanese, Korean, Polish, Portuguese, Russian, Spanish, Turkish, and Vietnamese), software (Windows and Mac), comprehensive manual (110 pages), and package of 25 assorted test records; $79.80 for Hmong or Navajo test pages; $199 per English test kit; $309 per Spanish test kit; $35 per 25 test records.

Time: (20–30) minutes.

Comments: Yields an aptitude measure that can be used in conjunction with the WJ-R® Tests of Achievement; an optional training video with administration procedures is available.

Authors: Ana F. Muñoz-Sandoval, Jim Cummins, Criselda G. Alvarado, and Mary L. Ruef.

Publisher: Riverside Publishing.

Cross References: For reviews by Alan Garfinkel and Charles W. Stansfield, see 14:46.

[322]
Biofeedback Certification Examination.

Purpose: A certification examination covering "the knowledge needed by providers of biofeedback services at the time they begin practice."

Population: Entry-level biofeedback service providers.

Publication Dates: 1980–1984.

Scores: 11 Blueprint Areas: Introduction to Biofeedback, Preparing for Clinical Intervention, Neuromuscular Intervention: General, Neuromuscular Intervention: Specific, Central Nervous System Interventions: General, Autonomic Nervous System Interventions: General, Autonomic Nervous System Interventions: Specific, Biofeedback and Distress, Instrumentation, Adjunctive Techniques and Cognitive Interventions, Professional Conduct.

Administration: Group.

Manual: No manual.

Price Data: Available from BCIA.

Time: (180) minutes.

Comments: Administration schedule available from BCIA.

Author: Biofeedback Certification Institute of America.

Publisher: Biofeedback Certification Institute of America.

[323]
Biographical Inventory Form U.

Purpose: "To obtain and analyze information about an individual's characteristics and background."

Population: Grades 7–12.

Publication Dates: 1976–1978.

Acronym: BI.

Scores, 6: Academic Performance, Creativity, Artistic Potential, Leadership, Career Maturity, Educational Orientation.

Administration: Group.

Price Data: Available from publisher.

Time: (60–65) minutes.

Comments: Replaces earlier Alpha Biographical Inventory (7:975).

Author: Institute for Behavioral Research in Creativity.

Publisher: Institute for Behavioral Research in Creativity.

Cross References: See T5:311 (1 reference); for reviews by Christopher Borman and Courtland C. Lee, see 9:150.

[324]
The Birkman Method.

Purpose: "Developed as a self-report questionnaire eliciting responses about perception of self, perception of social context and perception of occupational opportunities."

Population: Ages 25-65.

Publication Dates: 1992-2001.

Scores, 33: Esteem Usual, Esteem Need, Acceptance Usual, Acceptance Need, Structure Usual, Structure Need, Authority Usual, Authority Need, Advantage Usual, Advantage Need, Activity Usual, Activity Need, Challenge Usual, Challenge Need,

Empathy Usual, Empathy Need, Change Usual, Change Need, Freedom Usual, Freedom Need, Thought Usual, Thought Need, Persuasive Interest, Social Service Interest, Scientific Interest, Mechanical Interest, Outoor Interest, Numerical Interest, Clerical Interest, Artistic Interest, Literacy Interest, Musical Interest, Stress Behaviors.
Administration: Group.
Price Data, 2003: $45 per Birkman Method reliability and validity report.
Time: Administration time not reported.
Author: Roger W. Birkman.
Publisher: Birkman International, Inc.

[325]
Birmingham Object Recognition Battery.

Purpose: Designed to assess neuropsychological disorders of visual object recognition.
Population: Available from publisher.
Publication Date: 1993.
Acronym: BORB.
Scores: Available from publisher.
Administration: Individual.
Price Data, 2001: $250 per book.
Time: Administration time not reported.
Authors: M. Jane Riddoch and Glyn W. Humphreys.
Publisher: Psychology Press.

[326]
Birth to Three Assessment and Intervention System, Second Edition.

Purpose: Designed to "identify children who are developmentally at risk in the areas of language and learning."
Population: Birth to 3 years.
Publication Dates: 1986–2000.
Acronym: BTAIS-2.
Scores, 5: Language Comprehension, Language Expression, Nonverbal Thinking, Social/Personal Behaviors, Motor Behaviors.
Administration: Individual.
Price Data, 2006: $246 per complete kit including screening test kit, comprehensive test kit, and teaching manual (2000, 163 pages); $71 per teaching manual.
Time: Untimed.
Authors: Jerome J. Ammer and Tina E. Bangs.
Publisher: PRO-ED.
  a) SCREENING TEST OF DEVELOPMENTAL ABILITIES.
  Purpose: Designed "to identify young children who may have developmental delays."
  Price Data: $81 per complete dcreening yest kit including manual (2000, 93 pages) and 25 record forms; $59 per manual; $25 per 25 record forms.

  b) COMPREHENSIVE TEST OF DEVELOPMENTAL ABILITIES.
  Purpose: Designed "to identify each child's specific strengths and weaknesses and to guide the preparation of instructional plans."
  Price Data: $101 per complete comprehensive test kit including manual (2000, 107 pages) and 25 record forms; $59 per manual; $45 per 25 record forms.
Cross References: For reviews by Kimberly A. Blair and Leah M. Nellis, see 15:36; see T5:315; for a review by Donna Spiker of an earlier edition, see 11:45; for a review by Bonnie W. Camp of an earlier edition, see 9:152.

[327]
Bloomer Learning Test—Neurologically Enhanced.

Purpose: Designed as a "diagnostic, focused process assessment of cognitive processes and neurological substrates underlying academic learning."
Population: Grades 1–11 and adults.
Publication Dates: 1978–1998.
Acronym: BLT-NE.
Scores: 56 scores in 5 domains: Cognitive Processing Speed (Activity Persistence, Automaticity, Arousal Need, Association Index, Language/Abstract Processing Ratio), Processing in Short Term Memory (Visual Short Term Memory, Auditory Short Term Memory, Visual Apprehension Span, Short Term Memory Composite, Stimulus Complexity Ratio, Working Memory for Letters, Working Memory for Words, Impulsivity, Rehearsal Effects, Cross Modal Efficiency, Stimulus Mode, Response Mode, Memory Response Sequencing, Working Memory Sequencing Stimulus Number Effects, Stimulus Number Sequencing Effects), Learning and Retention Processes (Serial Learning, Learning Set Ratio, Acquisition, Seriation, Auditory Serial Learning, Auditory Acquisition, Auditory Seriation, Free Association, Verbal Response Association, Verbal Written Association Ratio, Free Spelling Error Ratio, Idiosyncratic Language Ratio, Language Complexity Ratio, Cortical Arousal, Paired Associate Index, Paired Associate Learning, Paired Associate Decrement, Recall, Relearning, Recall Ratio, Savings Ratio), Complex Conceptual Processes (Concept Recognition, Concept Production, Concept Synthesis, Problem Solving, Familiarity, Multiordinality), Emotional Mediating Processes (Emotional Passivity, Intensity, Lability, Valence, Emotional Ratio, Verbal Emotional Ratio, Suppression Index).
Administration: Individual or group.
Price Data: Available from publisher.
Time: (10–25) minutes per domain; (70–95) minutes total.
Author: Richard H. Bloomer.

Publisher: Brador Publications, Inc. [No reply from publisher; status unknown].
Cross References: For a review by Edward Earl Gotts of an earlier edition, see 9:154.

[328]
Blox Test.
Purpose: Designed to measure the individual's perceptual ability for spatial relations.
Population: Job applicants with at least 10 years of education.
Publication Dates: 1961–1963.
Scores: Total score only.
Administration: Group.
Manual: No manual.
Price Data: Available from publisher.
Time: 30(35) minutes.
Comments: Test previously known as Perceptual Battery (T3:1777).
Author: National Institute for Personnel Research of the Human Sciences Research Council.
Publisher: Human Sciences Research Council [South Africa].

[329]
The Boder Test of Reading-Spelling Patterns.
Purpose: Designed as a diagnostic screening test for developmental dyslexia.
Population: Grades K–12 and adult.
Publication Date: 1982.
Scores, 5: Reading (Level, Age, Quotient), Spelling (Known Words/Correct, Unknown Words/Phonetic Equivalence).
Administration: Individual.
Price Data, 2002: $175 per complete kit including 25 reading test record forms, 25 spelling test record forms, 25 alphabet tasks record forms, 25 diagnostic summary record forms, and manual (175 pages); $55 per 25 reading test record forms; $39 per 25 spelling test record forms; $39 per 25 alphabet tasks record forms; $39 per 25 diagnostic summary forms; $82 per manual.
Time: (10–30) minutes.
Authors: Elena Boder and Sylvia Jarrico.
Publisher: PsychCorp, A brand of Harcourt Assessment, Inc.
Cross References: See T5:322 (7 references) and T4:312 (5 references); for reviews by Frederick A. Schrank and Timothy Shanahan, see 9:155 (2 references).

[330]
Boehm Test of Basic Concepts—Third Edition.
Purpose: Designed to "assess ... [school] readiness or [to] identify students who may be at risk for learning difficulty."

Population: Grades K–2.
Publication Dates: 1967–2001.
Acronym: Boehm-3.
Scores: Total score only.
Administration: Group or individual.
Forms, 2: E, F.
Price Data, 2004: $62 per examination set including examiner's manual (2001, 145 pages), 1 Form E booklet, 1 Form F booklet, 1 Form E class key, 1 Form F class key, and 1 directions for administration (Forms E and F, English and Spanish); $83 per testing kit (Form E or F) including directions for administration (English and Spanish), 1 package of 25 booklets, and 1 class key; $57 per examiner's manual (Fall norms manual); $7 per class key (Form E or F); $18 per directions for administration (English and Spanish).
Foreign Language Edition: Directions for administering in Spanish are available for both forms.
Time: 30(45) minutes if administered in one session; 45(60) minutes if administered in two test sessions.
Comments: Revision of the Boehm Test of Basic Concepts—Revised; yields raw scores, percent correct, performance range, and percentiles by grade.
Author: Ann E. Boehm.
Publisher: PsychCorp, A brand of Harcourt Assessment, Inc.
Cross References: For reviews by Sherry K. Bain and James Hawkins and by Harold R. Keller, see 16:34; for information regarding previous editions, see T5:324 (12 references) and T4:314 (5 references); for reviews by Robert L. Linn and by Colleen Fitzmaurice and Joseph C. Witt, see 10:32 (16 references); see also T3:302 (18 references); for an excerpted review by Theodore A. Dahl, see 8:178 (22 references); se also T2:344 (1 reference); for reviews by Boyd R. McCandless and Charles D. Smock, and excerpted reviews by Frank S. Freeman, George Lawlor, Victor H. Noll, and Barton B. Proger, see 7:335 (1 reference).

[331]
Boehm Test of Basic Concepts—3 Preschool.
Purpose: "Designed to assess young children's understanding of the basic relational concepts" ("quality, spatial, temporal, quantity") "important for language and cognitive development."
Population: Ages 3-0 to 5-11.
Publication Dates: 1986–2001.
Scores: Total score only.
Administration: Individual.
Price Data, 2006: $159 per complete kit including examiner's manual (2001, 111 pages), picture manual, and 25 record forms; $52 per examiner's manual; $116 per picture manual; $34 per 25 record forms.

Foreign Language Edition: Spanish version available.
Time: (15–20) minutes.
Comments: Revision of Boehm Test of Basic Concepts—Preschool Version; norms extended upward; provides Parent Report Form, Ongoing Observation and Intervention Planning Form (Spanish versions included); includes directions for Spanish administration and scoring; separate English and Spanish norms available.
Authors: Ann E. Boehm.
Publisher: PsychCorp, A brand of Harcourt Assessment, Inc.
Cross References: For reviews by Theresa Graham and Koressa Kutsick Malcolm, see 16:35; see also T5:323 (1 reference) and T4:313 (1 reference); for reviews by Judy Oehler-Stinnett and Stephanie Stein of an earlier edition, see 11:46 (1 reference).

[332]
Booker Profiles in Mathematics: Numeration and Computation.

Purpose: "Designed to pinpoint strengths and weaknesses in basic mathematical knowledge."
Population: Ages 7–16.
Publication Date: 1994.
Scores, 2: Numeration, Computation.
Administration: Individual.
Price Data, 2006: A$132 per kit including manual.
Time: (45) minutes.
Author: George Booker.
Publisher: Australian Council for Educational Research Ltd. [Australia].
Cross References: For reviews by Richard C. Pugh and James P. Van Haneghan, see 13:38.

[333]
Booker Profiles in Mathematics: Problem Solving.

Purpose: Designed "to be used to gauge an individual's capacity to think, reason, and problem solve in mathematics."
Population: Early school learners through adults.
Publication Date: 2001.
Scores, 5: Relatively Obvious Answers, Less Obvious Answers, Too Much Information, Too Little Information, Strategic Thinking.
Administration: Individual or group.
Price Data, 2006: A$198 per kit including manual (2001, 60 pages), easel, and photocopy masters.
Time: Levels 1 and 2: 20–30 minutes depending on reading ability; Level 3: 20–30 minutes; Level 4: 30–40 minutes.
Authors: George Booker and Denise Bond.
Publisher: Australian Council for Educational Research Ltd. [Australia].

[334]
The Booklet Category Test, Second Edition.

Purpose: Designed to "distinguish individuals with brain damage from normal individuals by measuring concept formation and abstract reasoning."
Population: Ages 15 and older.
Publication Dates: 1979–1997.
Acronym: BCT.
Scores: Total score only.
Administration: Individual.
Price Data, 2006: $460 per introductory kit including professional manual, 2-volume set of stimulus books, and 50 response forms.
Time: (30–60) minutes.
Authors: Nick A. DeFilippis and Elizabeth McCampbell.
Publisher: Psychological Assessment Resources, Inc.
Cross References: For reviews by Carolyn M. Callahan and David C. S. Richard, see 14:47; see also T5:326 (10 references) and T4:315 (4 references); for reviews by Raymond S. Dean and Thomas A. Hammeke of an earlier edition, see 9:156.

[335]
Borromean Family Index.

Purpose: Developed to measure "attitudes and feelings about one's family."
Population: Adolescents and adults.
Publication Dates: 1975–1988.
Scores, 2: Internal (forces that attract toward family), External (forces that pull away).
Subtests, 2: For Married Persons, For Single Persons.
Administration: Group.
Manual: No manual.
Price Data, 2005: $2 per test.
Time: [10] minutes.
Comments: Supplementary article available.
Author: Panos D. Bardis.
Publisher: Donna Bardis.
Cross References: For additional information, see 8:332 (1 reference).

[336]
Boston Assessment of Severe Aphasia.

Purpose: Developed to identify "preserved abilities that might form the beginning steps of rehabilitation programs for severely aphasic patients."
Population: Aphasic adults.
Publication Date: 1989.
Acronym: BASA.
Scores, 5: Auditory Comprehension, Praxis, Oral-Gestural Expression, Reading Comprehension, Other.
Administration: Individual.
Price Data, 2006: $277 per complete kit; $66 per package of manipulatives; $45 per set of stimulus cards;

$41 per custom aluminum clipboard; $40 per 25 record forms; $56 per manual (96 pages).

Time: (30–40) minutes.

Comments: See T5:328 (1 reference); for reviews by Steven B. Leder and Roger L. Towne, see 12:52 (3 references).

Authors: Nancy Helm-Estabrooks, Gail Ramsberger, Alisa R. Morgan, and Marjorie Nicholas.

Publisher: PRO-ED.

Cross References: See T5:328 (1 reference); for reviews by Steven B. Leder and Roger L. Towne, see 12:52 (3 references).

[337]
Boston Diagnostic Aphasia Examination—Third Edition.

Purpose: Designed to help "identify and distinguish among disorders of language function and neurologically recognized aphasic syndromes."

Population: Individuals with aphasia.

Publication Dates: 1972-2001.

Acronym: BDAE-3.

Scores, 59: Conversational and Expository Speech (Simple Social Responses, Free Conversation, Picture Description [Discourse Analysis-Segmentation into Utterances], Severity Rating and Profile of Speech Characteristics), Auditory Comprehension (Word Comprehension [Basic Word Discrimination, Supplemental Test], Commands and Complex Ideational Material Test), Oral Expression (Oral Agility [Nonverbal Agility and Verbal Agility], Automatized Sequences, Recitation, Melody, and Rhythm [Recitation, Melody and Rhythm], Repetition [Single Word Repetition and Repetition of Sentences], Naming [Responsive Naming, Boston Naming Test-Visual Confrontation Naming, Screening for Naming of Special Categories]), Reading (Basic Symbol Recognition [Matching Across Cases and Scripts and Number Matching], Word Identification [Picture-Word Match], Phonics [Homophone Matching], Derivational and Inflectional Morphology [Free Grammatical Morphemes], Oral Reading [Basic Oral Word Reading and Oral Reading of Special Word Lists (Mixed Morphological Types and Semantic Paralexia-Prone Words)], Oral Reading of Sentences with Comprehension, Reading Comprehension-Sentences and Paragraphs), Writing (Mechanics of Writing, Basic Encoding Skills [Primer Word Vocabulary, Regular Phonics and Common Irregular Forms], Written Picture Naming and Narrative Writing) and Apraxia Assessment (Natural Gestures, Conventional Gestures, Use of Pretend Objects without an Action Goal, Use of Pretend Objects with an Action Goal and Bucco-Facial Respiratory Movements).

Administration: Individual.

Forms, 3: Short, Standard (Long), Boston Naming Test (Short and Long combined).

Price Data, 2006: $400 per complete kit including manual (2001, 136 pages), 147 long form stimulus cards picture book, 25 long form record booklets, 27 short form stimulus cards picture book, 25 short form record booklets, Boston Naming Test stimulus cards picture book, 25 Boston Naming Test record booklets, and videotape; $90 per manual; $40 per videotape; $90 per Boston Naming Test kit including Boston Naming Test stimulus cards picture book and 25 Boston Naming Test record booklets; $35 per 25 Boston Naming Test record booklets; $65 per Boston Naming Test stimulus cards picture book.

Time: (35-45) minutes.

Comments: Previously listed as The Assessment of Aphasia and Related Disorders and that is the title of the manual.

Authors: Harold Goodglass with the collaboration of Edith Kaplan and Barbara Barresi.

Publisher: PRO-ED.

a) SHORT FORM.

Purpose: Designed "to provide a comprehensive, but brief sampling of the performances necessary for an informed quantitative assessment" of individuals with aphasia.

Price Data: $42 per short form kit including 27 short form stimulus cards picture book and 25 short form record booklets; $15 per 25 short form record booklets; $30 per short form stimulus cards picture book.

Time: (30-45) minutes.

Comments: The short form consists of shortened or omitted sections that are included in the standard form.

b) STANDARD (Long) FORM.

Purpose: Designed to be a "more probing evaluation of particular language functions within each area of testing."

Scores, 18: Aesop's Fables, Word Comprehension in Categories, Syntactic Processing (Touching A with B, Reversible Possessives, Embedded Sentences), Repetition of Nonsense Words, Naming in Categories, Advanced Phonic Analysis–Pseudo-Homophone Matching, Bound Grammatical Morphemes, Derivational Morphemes, Uncommon Irregularities, Nonsense Words, Oral Spelling, and Cognitive/Grammatical Influences (Part of Speech Effects: Dictated Words, Subtest 2: "Dictated Functor Loaded Sentences").

Price Data: $148 per long form kit including manual, 147 long form stimulus cards picture book, and 25 long form record booklets; $20 per 25 long form record booklets; $61 per long form stimulus cards picture book.

Time: Administration time not reported.

Comments: All scores included in the standard form are also included in the extended form.

c) BOSTON NAMING TEST, SECOND EDITION.
Population: Ages 55-59.
Scores: Total score only.
Time: Administration time not reported.
Authors: Edith Kaplan, Harold Goodglass, and Sandra Weintraub.
Cross References: See T5:199 (18 references) and T4:207 (105 references); for reviews by Rita Sloan Berndt and Malcolm R. McNeil of an earlier edition, see 10:15 (3 references); see also 9:86 (2 references) and T3:308 (28 references); for reviews by Daniel R. Boone and Manfred J. Meier of an earlier edition, see 8:955 (1 reference).

[338]

The Boston Qualitative Scoring System for the Rey-Osterrieth Complex Figure.

Purpose: Designed as a quantifiable approach to rating the qualitative features of the ROCF (which was designed to assess visuoconstructional ability and visual memory performance in brain-impaired patients).
Population: Ages 18–94.
Publication Dates: 1994–1999.
Acronym: BQSS.
Scores, 23: Qualitative (Configural Presence, Configural Accuracy, Cluster Presence, Cluster Accuracy, Cluster Placement, Detail Presence, Detail Placement, Fragmentation, Planning, Neatness, Vertical Expansion, Horizontal Expansion, Reduction, Rotation, Perseveration, Confabulation, Asymmetry), Summary (Copy Presence and Accuracy, Immediate Presence and Accuracy, Delayed Presence and Accuracy, Immediate Retention, Delayed Retention, Organization).
Administration: Individual.
Price Data, 2005: $202 per introductory kit including professional manual, 50 scoring booklets, 50 response sheets, stimulus card, reference guide, scoring templates, and metric ruler.
Time: (45) minutes, including a (20–30) minute delay interval.
Authors: Robert A. Stern, Debbie J. Javorsky, Elizabeth A. Singer, Naomi G. Singer Harris, Jessica A. Somerville, Lisa M. Duke, Jodi A. Thompson, and Edith Kaplan.
Publisher: Psychological Assessment Resources, Inc.
Cross References: For reviews by D. Ashley Cohen and Robert A. Leark, see 15:37.

[339]

Bracken Basic Concept Scale—Revised.

Purpose: Designed to measure relevant educational concepts and receptive language skills.
Population: Ages 2 1/2 to 8.
Publication Dates: 1984–1998.
Acronym: BBCS-R.

Scores, 11: Colors, Letters, Numbers/Counting, Sizes, Comparisons, Shapes, Direction/Position, Self-/Social Awareness, Texture/Material, Quantity, and Time/Sequence.
Administration: Individual.
Price Data, 2006: $315 per complete program including examiner's manual (1998, 223 pages), stimulus manual (276 pages), 15 diagnostic scale record forms, and one screening test; $32 per 15 English record forms; $80 per 50 English record forms; $32 per 15 Spanish record forms; $80 per 50 Spanish record forms.
Time: (30) minutes.
Comments: May be used diagnostically or as a screening test by scoring the first six subtests called the School Readiness Composite (SRC); may be used for norm-referenced, criterion referenced, or curriculum-based assessments.
Authors: Bruce A. Bracken.
Publisher: PsychCorp, A brand of Harcourt Assessment, Inc.
Cross References: For reviews by Leah M. Nellis and Rhonda H. Solomon, see 14:48; see also T5:331 (6 references) and T4:319 (4 references); for reviews by Timothy L. Turco and James E. Ysseldyke of an earlier edition, see 10:33.

[340]

Bracken School Readiness Assessment.

Purpose: Designed to "assess academic readiness by evaluating a child's understanding of 88 important fundamental concepts in the categories of Colors, Letters, Numbers/Counting, Sizes, Comparisons and Shapes."
Population: Ages 2:6 to 7:11.
Publication Date: 2002.
Acronym: BSRA.
Scores, 7: Colors, Letters, Numbers/Counting, Sizes, Comparisons, Shapes, School Readiness Composite.
Administration: Individual.
Price Data, 2003: $119 per complete kit including administration manual (104 pages), stimulus manual, and 25 record forms (specify English or Spanish); $39 per administration manual; $89 per stimulus manual; $25 per 25 record forms (specify English or Spanish).
Foreign Language Edition: Spanish edition available.
Time: (10–15) minutes.
Comments: The subtests in this test are the first 6 of 11 subtests of the Bracken Basic Concept Scale—Revised (339); national norms not available for Spanish edition.
Author: Bruce A. Bracken.
Publisher: PsychCorp, A brand of Harcourt Assessment, Inc.
Cross References: For reviews by Thomas McKnight and Gene Schwarting, see 16:36.

[341]
The BrainMap™.

Purpose: "A tool for determining the world-building (or thinking/information-processing) style of individuals and of groups."
Population: Adults.
Publication Dates: 1981–1986.
Scores: 4 scales: Posterior Brain Scale, Anterior Brain Scale, Left Brain Scale, Right Brain Scale.
Administration: Group.
Price Data: Available from publisher.
Time: [30–40] minutes.
Comments: Self-administered, self-scored.
Author: Dudley Lynch.
Publisher: Brain Technologies Corporation.
Cross References: For a review by Manfred J. Meier, see 11:47.

[342]
Bricklin Perceptual Scales.

Purpose: Yields information on a child's unconscious or nonverbal perception of his or her parents; for determining which of the parents would make the better primary caretaker for a particular child in child-custody decisions.
Population: Ages 6 and over.
Publication Dates: 1984–2002.
Acronym: BPS.
Scores, 10: 5 scores each for mother and father: Perception of Competency, Perception of Supportiveness, Perception of Follow-Up Consistency, Perception of Admirable Character Traits, Total.
Administration: Individual.
Price Data, 2002: $199 per complete kit including 8 sets of response cards, 8 scoring sheets, stylus-pen, placement dots, test box with foam insert, manual (1992, 141 pages), instructions, and Bricklin Updates; $99 per 8 additional sets of response cards; $159 per 16 sets of response cards with summaries; $199 per 24 sets of response cards with summaries; $198 per IBM computer scoring profile (3.5-inch disk).
Time: (40) minutes.
Comments: IBM or compatible computer required for computer scoring profile (unlimited uses).
Author: Barry Bricklin.
Publisher: Village Publishing.
Cross References: For reviews by Rosa A. Hagin and Marcia B. Shaffer, see 11:48.

[343]
Brief Battery for Health Improvement 2.

Purpose: Designed for "assessing medical patients who may be experiencing problems with pain, functioning, somatization, depression, anxiety, or other factors relevant to rehabilitation and recovery."
Population: 18–65 years.
Publication Date: 2002.
Acronym: BBHI 2.
Scores, 6: Validity Scale (Defensiveness), Physical Symptom Scales (Somatic Complaints, Pain Complaints, Functional Complaints), Affective Scales (Depression, Anxiety).
Administration: Individual.
Parts, 4: Part I (Pain Complaints scale), Part II (Somatic Complaints scale), Part III (Functional Complaints scale), Part IV (Depression, Anxiety, and Defensiveness scales).
Price Data, 2006: $115 per starter kit with Standard or Extended Reports including manual (151 pages) and 10 fax-in answer sheets and scoring; $85 per starter kit with Standard or Extended Reports including manual, 10 answer sheets, and 10 Q Local administrations; $35.50 per manual; $51 per compact disk administration; $25.50 per 25 fax-in answer sheets; $9.15 per fax-in service of 2 fax-in answer sheets; $5.15 per 5–9 Patient Assessment Device Reports; $89 per Q Local Software Desktop version (annual license fee); $6 per 25 Q Local answer sheets; $7.25 per 5–9 Q Local Standard or Extended Reports; no charge for Q Local Progress Reports; $10.25 per 5–9 mail-in answer sheets and Standard or Extended Reports; quantity discounts available for the reports.
Foreign Language Editions: Spanish materials available.
Time: (7–10) minutes.
Comments: Shorter version of the Battery for Health Improvement 2 (BHI 2; 343); mail-in and fax-in scoring available from publisher along with on-site computer (Q Local software) and hand-held electronic device (Patient Assessment Device) scoring; three automated reports available (Standard Report, Extended Report, Progress Report).
Authors: John Mark Disorbio and Daniel Bruns.
Publisher: Pearson Assessments.

[344]
Brief Derogatis Psychiatric Rating Scale.

Purpose: To obtain clinical observors' ratings on nine personality dimensions.
Population: Psychiatric and medical patients.
Publication Dates: 1974–1978.
Acronym: B-DPRS™.
Scores: 9 dimensions: Somatization, Obsessive-Compulsive, Interpersonal Sensitivity, Depression, Anxiety, Hostility, Phobic Anxiety, Paranoid Ideation, Psychoticism.
Administration: Individual.
Manual: No manual.
Price Data, 2006: $50 per 100 tests.
Time: (5) minutes.
Comments: Formerly the Brief Hopkins Psychiatric Rating Scale; short form of the Derogatis Psychiatric

Rating Scale; self-report; can also be used with Symptom Checklist-90-Revised or Brief Symptom Inventory.
Author: Leonard R. Derogatis.
Publisher: Pearson Assessments.
Cross References: See T5:335 (15 references) and T4:323 (5 references).

[345]
Brief Neuropsychological Cognitive Examination.

Purpose: Constructed as "an assessment of the severity and nature of cognitive impairment" for psychiatric and neurological patients.
Population: Ages 18 and older.
Publication Date: 1997.
Acronym: BNCE.
Scores, 4: Validity Index, Part I, Part II, Total.
Administration: Individual.
Price Data, 2006: $137.50 per complete kit including manual (58 pages), stimulus booklet, 20 response booklets, and 20 administration and scoring forms; $42.50 per 20 response booklets; $30 per 20 administration and scoring forms; $38.50 per stimulus booklet; $50.50 per manual.
Time: (30) minutes.
Author: Joseph Tonkonogy.
Publisher: Western Psychological Services.
Cross References: For reviews by Eugene V. Aidman and Sheila Mehta, see 14:50.

[346]
Brief Symptom Inventory.

Purpose: "Designed to reflect the psychological symptom patterns of psychiatric and medical patients as well as non-patients."
Population: Adults and adolescents age 13 or older.
Publication Date: 1975.
Acronym: BSI®.
Scores: 9 primary dimensions: Somatization, Obsessive-Compulsive, Interpersonal Sensitivity, Depression, Anxiety, Hostility, Phobic Anxiety, Paranoid Ideation, Psychoticism; plus 3 global indices: Global Severity Index, Positive Symptom Distress Index, Positive Symptom Total.
Administration: Group or individual.
Price Data, 2006: $100 per hand-scoring starter kit including manual, 50 answer sheets, 50 profile forms, 2 worksheets, and answer keys (specify Nonpatient Adult, Nonpatient Adolescent, Outpatient Psychiatric, or Inpatient Psychiatric); $52.50 per 50 hand-scoring answer sheets; $24.50 per answer keys; $24.50 per 50 profile forms and 2 worksheets (specify Nonpatient Adult, Nonpatient Adolescent, Outpatient Psychiatric, or Inpatient Psychiatric); $34 per manual; price information for Interpretive Report and Profile Report scoring and software available from publisher.; quantity discounts available for the reports; price information for Spanish materials available from publisher.
Foreign Language Editions: Spanish materials available.
Time: (8–10) minutes.
Comments: Essentially the brief form of the Symptom Checklist-90-Revised (2674); self-report; useful in initial evaluation and measurement of patient progress during treatment to monitor change and after treament for assessment of treatment outcome; companion clinician and observer rating forms are also available.
Author: Leonard R. Derogatis.
Publisher: Pearson Assessments.
Cross References: See T5:337 (198 references) and T4:324 (59 references); for reviews by Bert C. Cundick and Charles A. Peterson, see 10:35 (7 references); see also 9:160 (1 reference).

[347]
Brief Symptom Inventory 18.

Purpose: Designed to "screen for psychological distress and psychiatric disorders in medical and community populations."
Population: Age 18 and older.
Publication Dates: 2000–2001.
Acronym: BSI 18.
Scores, 4: Somatization, Depression, Anxiety, Total (Global Severity Index).
Administration: Individual or group.
Price Data, 2006: $44.50 per Q Local starter kit with profile reports including manual (2001, 54 pages), 3 answer sheets with test items to conduct and receive 3 Q local administrations; $26 per 25 answer sheets; $4.15 per profile report (quantity discounts available); $97.75 per hand-scoring starter kit including manual, 50 answer sheets with test items, and 50 profile forms (specify Community or Oncology norms); $52.50 per 50 answer sheets; $25.50 per 50 profile forms (specify Community or Oncology norms); $34 per manual; quantity discounts available for the reports; price information for Spanish materials available from publisher.
Foreign Language Editions: Spanish materials available.
Time: (4–5) minutes.
Comments: Abbreviated adaptation of Brief Symptom Inventory (346); self-report; may be administered in paper-and-pencil format or online.
Author: Leonard R. Derogatis.
Publisher: Pearson Assessments.
Cross References: For reviews by Roger A. Boothroyd and William E. Hanson, see 15:38; for information on the Brief Symptom Inventory, see T5:337 (198 references); for reviews by Bert C. Cundick and Charles A. Peterson of an earlier edition, see 10:35 (7 references); see also 9:160 (1 reference).

[348]
Brief Test of Attention.

Purpose: Designed "to assess the severity of attentional impairment among nonaphasic hearing adult patients."
Population: Ages 17–82.
Publication Date: 1997.
Acronym: BTA.
Scores: Total score only.
Administration: Individual.
Forms, 2: N (Numbers), L (Letters).
Price Data, 2006: $78 per introductory kit including professional manual (34 pages), stimulus audiotape, and 50 scoring forms.
Time: (10) minutes.
Author: David Schretlen.
Publisher: Psychological Assessment Resources, Inc.
Cross References: For reviews by Elizabeth Kelley Boyles and Steven R. Shaw, see 15:39.

[349]
Brief Test of Head Injury.

Purpose: Designed to provide information about cognitive, linguistic, and communicative abilities of patients with severe head trauma.
Population: Acute and long-term head-injured adults.
Publication Dates: 1989–1991.
Acronym: BTHI.
Scores, 8: Orientation/Attention, Following Commands, Linguistic Organization, Reading Comprehension, Naming, Memory, Visual-Spatial Skills, Total.
Administration: Individual.
Price Data, 2006: $180 per complete kit including 25 record forms, examiner's manual (1991, 85 pages), manipulatives package, stimulus cards and letter board, and carrying case; $51 per 25 record forms; $35 per manipulatives package; $76 per stimulus cards and letter board; $76 per examiner's manual.
Time: (25–30) minutes.
Authors: Nancy Helm-Estabrooks and Gillian Hotz.
Publisher: PRO-ED.
Cross References: For reviews by Deborah D. Roman and Michael Lee Russell, see 13:39.

[350]
Brief Visuospatial Memory Test—Revised.
Purpose: Designed as an equivalent, multiple-test form assessment of visuospatial memory.
Population: Ages 18–79.
Publication Dates: 1988–1997.
Acronym: BVMT-R.
Scores, 12: Trial 1, Trial 2, Trial 3, Total Recall, Learning, Delayed Recall, Percent Retained, Recognition Hits, Recognition False Alarms, Recognition Discrimination Index, Recognition Response Bias, Copy (Optional).
Administration: Individual.

Forms, 6: 1, 2, 3, 4, 5, 6.
Price Data, 2006: $255 per introductory kit including professional manual (1997, 131 pages), recognition stimulus booklet, reusable recall stimulus booklet, and 25 response forms.
Time: (45) minutes including 25-minute delay.
Comments: Can be administered bed-side by appropriately trained personnel.
Author: Ralph H. B. Benedict.
Publisher: Psychological Assessment Resources, Inc.
Cross References: For review by Anita M. Hubley and Terry A. Stinnett, see 15:40.

[351]
BRIGANCE® Diagnostic Comprehensive Inventory of Basic Skills, Revised.

Purpose: Designed for diagnostic and classroom assessment in basic reading skills, reading comprehension, math calculation, math reasoning, written language, listening comprehension, and information-processing.
Population: Pre K–Grade 9 (Criterion Testing); Grades 1–6 (Readiness Standardized Testing).
Publication Dates: 1976–1999.
Acronym: CIBS-R.
Scores: 154 scores in 8 areas: Readiness, Speech, Listening, Research and Study Skills, Reading, Spelling, Writing, Math.
Administration: Individual and group.
Forms, 2: Form A (pretesting), Form B (posttesting).
Price Data, 2005: $185 per Inventory tests with standardization and validation manual (1999, 143 pages) (U.S. or Canadian versions); $159 per inventory only tests (U.S. or Canadian versions); $35 per 10 student record books; $329 per 100 student record books; $14 per class record book; $22 per 10 student profile test booklets; $40 per manual; $70 per 120 readiness or Grades 1–6 scoring sheets; $20 per 30 readiness or Grades 1–6 scoring sheets; $99.95 standardized scoring conversion CD w/standardization and validation manual; $59.95 Goals and Objectives Writer CD; customized prices for web-based CIBS-R Management System available from publisher.
Time: Specific time limits are listed for some normed/standardized tests.
Comments: "Criterion-referenced"; normed/standardized option for key tests; web-based data management system generates goals and objectives for IEP development and reports standardized scores available.
Authors: Albert H. Brigance and Frances Page Glascoe (standardization and validation manual).
Publisher: Curriculum Associates, Inc.
Cross References: For reviews by Gregory J. Cizek and Mary J. McLellan, see 14:51; see also T5:340 (1 reference); for reviews by Craig N. Mills and Mark E. Swerdlik of an earlier edition, see 9:162.

[352]
BRIGANCE® Diagnostic Employability Skills Inventory

Purpose: Designed to assess employability and basic skills in the "context of job-seeking or employment situations."

Population: Secondary Special Education, Vocational, ESL students.

Publication Date: 1995.

Scores: 8 skills: Reading Grade-Placement Assessments; Career Awareness and Self-Understanding; Job-Seeking Skills and Knowledge; Rating Scales; Reading Skills; Speaking and Listening Skills; Pre-Employment Writing; Math and Concepts.

Administration: Group.

Price Data, 2005: $89.95 per manual (233 pages); $24.95 per 10 Learner Record Books; $229 per 100 Learner Record Books; $12.95 per Program Record Book; $59.95 per Goals and Objectives Writer CD; customized pricing for web-based ESI Data Management System available from publisher.

Time: Administration time varies.

Author: Albert H. Brigance.

Publisher: Curriculum Associates, Inc.

Cross References: For reviews by JoEllen V. Carlson and William C. Tirre, see 14:52.

[353]
Brigance® Diagnostic Inventory of Early Development-II.

Purpose: Designed to "determine readiness for school; track developmental progress; provide a range of scores needed for documenting eligibility for special education service; enable a comparison of children's skills within and across developmental domains in order to view strengths and weaknesses; determine entry points for instruction; and assist with program evaluation."

Population: Developmental ages birth to age 7.

Publication Dates: 1978–2004.

Acronym: IED-II.

Scores, 24: Fine Motor (Drawing/Visual Motor, Writing, Total), Gross Motor (Nonlocomotor, Locomotor, Total), Total Motor, Receptive Language (Nouns and Early Listening, Actions, Total), Expressive Language (Isolated Skills, Contextual Skills, Total), Total Language, Academic/Cognitive (Quantitative/General, Prereading/Reading, Total), Daily Living (Self-Help, Prevocational, Total), Social-Emotional (Play Skills and Behaviors, Engagement and Initiative, Total), Total Adaptive Behavior.

Administration: Individual.

Price Data, 2005: $185 per complete inventory including standardization and validation manual (2004, 248 pages); $35 per 10 record books; $159 per inventory only; $40 per standardization and validation manual;

$329 per 100 record books; $14 per class record book; $65 per testing accessories kit; $35 per 10 standardized record books; $329 per 100 standardized record books; $99.95 per scoring software with standardization and validation manual; $59.95 per Goals and Objective Writer software on CD-ROM; customized price information for web-based Screens Data Management System available from publisher.

Time: (20–35) minutes.

Comments: Criterion-referenced and norm-referenced; previous edition entitled Revised BRIGANCE® Diagnostic Inventory of Early Development (12:326).

Authors: Albert H. Brigance (test) and Frances Page Glascoe (standardization and validation manual).

Publisher: Curriculum Associates, Inc.

Cross References: For reviews by C. Dale Carpenter and Douglas A. Penfield of the previous edition, see 12:326; see also T4:2256 (3 references); for reviews by Stephen J. Bagnato and Elliot L. Gory of an earlier edition, see 9:164.

[354]
BRIGANCE® Diagnostic Inventory of Essential Skills.

Purpose: Designed to assess skills seen as necessary for successful functioning as an adult.

Population: Grade 6-adult.

Publication Date: 1981.

Acronym: IES.

Scores: 191 tests in 26 areas: Word Recognition Grade Placement (1 test), Oral Reading (5 tests), Reading Comprehension (9 tests), Functional Word Recognition (6 tests), Word Analysis (9 tests), Reference Skills (5 tests), Schedules and Graphs (3 tests), Writing (7 tests), Forms (2 tests), Spelling (8 tests), Math Grade Placement (2 tests), Numbers (4 tests), Number Facts (4 tests), Computations of Whole Numbers (6 tests), Fractions (9 tests), Decimals (6 tests), Percents (4 tests), Measurement (15 tests), Metrics (16 tests), Math Vocabulary (3 tests), Health and Safety (6 tests), Vocational (23 tests), Money and Finance (11 tests), Travel and Transportation (10 tests), Food and Clothing (10 tests), Oral Communication and Telephone Skills (7 tests).

Administration: Individual in part.

Price Data, 2005: $169 per manual (391 pages); $36.95 per 10 student record books; $12.95 per class record book.

Time: Specific time limits are listed on many tests; others are untimed.

Author: Albert Brigance.

Publisher: Curriculum Associates, Inc.

Cross References: See T4: 329 (2 references); for reviews by Paula Matuszek and Philip A. Saigh, see 9:165.

[355]

BRIGANCE® Diagnostic Life Skills Inventory.

Purpose: Designed to evaluate "listening, speaking, reading, writing, comprehending, and computing skills within the context of everyday situations."

Population: Grades 2–8.

Publication Date: 1994.

Scores: 9 skills: Speaking and Listening Skills, Functional Writing Skills, Words on Common Signs and Warning Labels, Telephone Skills, Money and Finance, Food, Clothing, Health, Travel and Transportation.

Administration: Individual or group.

Price Data, 2005: $89.95 per manual (239 pages); $24.95 per 10 Learner Record Books; $229 per 100 Learner Record Books; $12.95 per Program Record Book; $59.95 per Goals and Objectives Writer CD; customized pricing for web-based LSI Data Management System available from publisher.

Time: Administration time varies.

Author: Albert H. Brigance.

Publisher: Curriculum Associates, Inc.

Cross References: For reviews by Cleborne D. Maddux and Rhoda Cummings and by James A. Wollack, see 14:53; see also T5:344 (1 reference).

[356]

Brigance Early Preschool Screen-II.

Purpose: Criterion-referenced and norm-referenced screen designed to identify "those who may have developmental problems such as language impairments, learning disabilities, or cognitive delays"; also used to "identify children who may have academic talent or intellectual giftedness."

Population: Ages 2-0 to 2-11.

Publication Dates: 1990–2005.

Administration: Individual.

Price Data, 2005: $110 per manual (2005, 73 pages) with building blocks; $58 per technical report (2005, 262 pages); $38 per 30 data sheets; $148 per 120 data sheets; $48 per 10 class folders; $25 per Spanish directions booklet; $117.95 per Screens Scoring Software CD with technical report; customized price information for web-based Screens Data Management System available from publisher.

Foreign Language Edition: Spanish directions available, contains reproducible data sheets.

Time: (15) minutes.

Comments: Can be used to identify a child's strengths and weaknesses to determine what kinds of additional evaluations are needed; includes prompts for behavioral observations, and supplemental rating scales for parents and teachers; Screens Scoring Software provides percentile ranks, standard scores, and age equivalent scores; web-based Screens Data Man-

agement System reports individual and program-wide progress including growth indicators, cutoff scores, and other standardized scores.

Authors: Albert H. Brigance (test) and Frances Page Glascoe (technical manual).

Publisher: Curriculum Associates, Inc.

> *a)* TWO-YEAR-OLD CHILD.
>
> **Scores, 9:** Identifies Body Parts, Gross-Motor Skills, Picture Vocabulary, Identifies People in Picture by Naming, Knows Use of Objects, Visual Motor Skills, Verbal Fluency, Builds Tower with Blocks, Total.
>
> **Subtests, 5:** Visual/Fine/and Graphomotor, Gross Motor, Receptive Language, Expressive Vocabulary, Articulation/Verbal/Fluency/Syntax.
>
> *b)* TWO-AND-A-HALF-YEAR-OLD CHILD.
>
> **Scores, 12:** Personal Data Response, Identifies Body Parts, Gross-Motor Skills, Knows Use of Objects, Repeats Sentences, Visual Motor Skills, Quantitative Concepts, Builds Tower with Blocks, Matches Colors, Picture Vocabulary, Plural s and -ing, Total.
>
> **Subtests, 5:** Visual/Fine/and Graphomotor, Gross Motor, Receptive Language, Expressive Vocabulary, Articulation/Verbal/Fluency/Syntax, Quantitative Concepts, Personal Information, Prereading/Reading Skills.

Cross References: For reviews by William M. Bart and Joseph M. Ryan of an earlier edition, see 11:49.

[357]

BRIGANCE® Infant & Toddler Screen.

Purpose: Designed to obtain a broad sampling of a very young child's development and skills; … enables professionals to monitor children's developmental progress, advise parents on how to promote a child's development, initiate individualized instruction, and recommend special services to facilitate learning needs and/or family adjustments.

Population: Infants (birth through 11 months) and toddlers (12 months through 23 months).

Publication Date: 2002.

Administration: Individual or group.

Price Data, 2006: $110 per manual (89 pages); $38 per 30 Infant or Toddler data sheets; $148 per 120 copies of data sheet; $48 per 10 Infant or Toddler record folders (English or Spanish); $59.95 per box of materials; $58 per technical report (232 pages); $59.95 per Screens Scoring Software; $25 per Spanish Directions booklet with reproducible data sheets.

Time: (15) minutes.

Comments: Screens Scoring Software provides percentile ranks, standard scores, and age equivalent scores; Spanish directions available, contains reproducible data sheets.

Authors: Albert H. Brigance (Screen) and Frances Page Glascoe (Screen and Technical Report).
Publisher: Curriculum Associates, Inc.

a) INFANT.

Scores, 7: Fine-Motor Skills, Receptive Language Skills, Expressive Language Skills, Gross Motor Skills, Self-Help Skills, Social-Emotional Skills, Total Score.

b) TODDLER.

Scores, 12: Fine-Motor Skills, Receptive Language Skills—General, Receptive Language Skills—Body Parts, Receptive Language Skills—Picture Naming, Receptive Language Skills—Environmental Sounds, Expressive Language Skills—General, Expressive Language Skills—Object Naming, Expressive Language Skills—Phrases, Gross Motor Skills, Self-Help Skills, Social-Emotional Skills, Total Score.

Cross References: For reviews by Theresa Graham and Loraine J. Spenciner, see 15:41.

[358]
Brigance K & 1 Screen-II.

Purpose: Criterion-referenced and norm-referenced screen designed to "identify quickly and accurately those who may have developmental problems such as language impairments, learning disabilities, or cognitive delays"; also used to "identify children who may have academic talent or intellectual giftedness."
Population: Grades K, 1.
Publication Dates: 1982-2005.
Administration: Individual.
Price Data, 2006: $110 per manual with building blocks; $58 per technical report; $38 per 30 data sheets; $48 per 10 class folders; $25 per Spanish directions booklet; $117.95 per Screens Scoring Software CD with technical report; customized price information for web-based Screens Data Management System available from publisher.
Foreign Language Edition: Spanish directions available, contains reproducible data sheets.
Time: (15) minutes.
Comments: Can be used to identify a child's strengths and weaknesses in order to determine what kinds of additional evaluations are needed; includes prompts for behavioral observations, and supplemental rating scales for parents and teachers; Screens Scoring Software provides percentile ranks, standard scores, and age equivalent scores; Web-based Screens Data Management System reports individual and program-wide progress including growth indicators, cutoff scores, and other standardized scores.
Authors: Albert H. Brigance (test) and Frances Page Glascoe (technical report).
Publisher: Curriculum Associates, Inc.

a) KINDERGARTEN.

Scores, 14: Personal Data Response, Identifies Body Parts, Gross-Motor Skills, Color Recognition, Visual Motor Skills, Draws a Person (Body Image), Prints Personal Data, Rote Counting, Numeral Comprehension, Number Readiness, Reads Uppercase Letters, Alternate-Reads Lowercase Letters, Syntax and Fluency, Total.

b) FIRST GRADE.

Scores, 13: Personal Data Response, Recites Alphabet, Visual Discrimination-Lowercase Letters and Words, Reads Lowercase Letters, Auditory Discrimination, Phonemic Awareness and Decoding, Listening Vocabulary Comprehension, Word Recognition, Draws a Person (Body Image), Prints Personal Data, Computation, Numerals in Sequence, Total.

Cross References: For reviews by Ronald A. Berk and T. Steuart Watson of the previous edition, see 12:53 (1 reference); see also T4:331 (3 references); for reviews by Ann E. Boehm and Dan Wright of an earlier edition, see 9:166.

[359]
Brigance Preschool Screen-II.

Purpose: Identifies children who may have "developmental problems such as language impairments, learning disabilities, or cognitive delays" or "academic talent or intellectual giftedness."
Population: Ages 3–4.
Publication Dates: 1985–2005.
Administration: Individual.
Price Data, 2005: $110 per manual (2005, 104 pages); $38 per 30 data sheets; $148 per 120 data sheets; $48 per 10 class folders; $58 per technical report (2005, 262 pages); $25 per Spanish directions booklet; $117.95 per Screens Scoring Software CD with technical report; customized price information for web-based Screens Data Management System available from publisher.
Foreign Language Edition: Spanish directions available, contains reproducible data sheets.
Time: (10–15) minutes.
Comments: Screens Scoring Software provides percentile ranks, standard scores, and age equivalent scores; Web-based Screens Data Management System reports individual and program-wide progress including growth indicators, cutoff scores, and other standardized scores.
Authors: Albert H. Brigance (test) and Frances Page Glascoe (technical report).
Publisher: Curriculum Associates, Inc.

a) AGE 3.

Scores: 11 skills: Personal Data Response, Color Recognition, Picture Vocabulary, Knows Use of Objects, Visual Motor Skills, Gross Motor Skills, Number Concepts, Builds Tower with Blocks,

Identifies Body Parts, Repeats Sentences, Prepositions and Irregular Plural Nouns.
b) AGE 4.
Scores: 11 skills: Personal Data Response, Color Recognition, Picture Vocabulary, Visual Discrimination-Forms and Uppercase Letters, Visual Motor Skills, Gross Motor Skills, Rote Counting, Identifies Body Parts, Follows Verbal Direction, Number Concepts, Syntax and Fluency.
Cross References: For reviews by Edith S. Heil and Timothy L. Turco of an earlier edition, see 10:36.

[360]
British Ability Scales: Second Edition.

Purpose: Designed as a battery to assess "cognitive abilities and educational achievement."
Population: Ages 2.6 to 17.11.
Publication Dates: 1977–1997.
Acronym: BAS II.
Scores: Early Years Core Scales (Block Building, Verbal Comprehension, Picture Similarities, Naming Vocabulary, Pattern Construction, Early Number Concepts, Copying), School Age Core Scales (Recall of Designs, Word Definitions, Pattern Construction, Matrices, Verbal Similarities, Quantitative Reasoning), Diagnostic Scales (Speed of Information Processing, Recall of Digits Forward, Recall of Objects—Immediate, Recall of Objects—Delayed, Matching Letter-Like Forms, Recognition of Pictures, Recall of Digits Backward), Achievement Scales (Number Skills, Spelling, Word Reading).
Administration: Individual.
Forms, 2: Early Years, School Age.
Price Data, 2005: £810 per full age range complete set including stimulus books, 10 relevant record forms and consumable booklets; £575 per early years complete set including stimulus books, 10 record forms and consumable booklets; £495 per school age complete set including stimulus books, 10 record forms and consumable booklets; £40.50 per 25 early years record booklets; £52.50 per 25 school age record booklets; £10.90 per 25 achievement scales record forms; £12 per 10 Speed of Information Processing booklets A, B, or C; £12 per 10 Quantitative Reasoning booklets set A; £6 per 100 sheets copying paper; £6 per 100 recall of designs sheets; £17.50 per 25 number skills/spelling worksheets; £8.75 per 25 number skills worksheets; $8.75 per 25 spelling worksheets; £87.25 per administration and scoring manual (1996, 544 pages); £70 per technical manual (1997, 341 pages); £168.80 per BAS II Scoring and Reporting Software.
Time: Administration time varies.
Comments: Considerations for testing special populations detailed in manual.

Authors: Colin D. Elliott with Pauline Smith and Kay McCulloch.
Publisher: NFER-Nelson Publishing Co., Ltd. [England].
Cross References: For reviews by Colin Cooper and Robert W. Hiltonsmith, see 16:37; see also T5:349 (39 references) and T4:336 (25 references); for reviews by Susan Embretson (Whitely), Benjamin D. Wright, and Mark H. Stone of an earlier edition, see 9:172 (5 references); for reviews by Steve Graham and William D. Schafer of an earlier edition of the British Ability Scales: Spelling Scale, see 12:55.

[361]
The British Picture Vocabulary Scale, Second Edition.

Purpose: Designed to serve as a "norm referenced wide-range test of hearing vocabulary for Standard English."
Population: Ages 3.0 to 15.8.
Publication Dates: 1982–1997.
Acronym: BPVS-II.
Scores: Total score only.
Administration: Individual.
Price Data: Available from publisher.
Time: (5–8) minutes.
Comments: Manual is incorporated in the easeled test book.
Authors: Lloyd M. Dunn, Leota M. Dunn, Chris Whetton, and Juliet Burley.
Publisher: NFER-Nelson Publishing Co., Ltd. [England].
Cross References: For reviews by Alfred P. Longo and Dolores Kluppel Vetter, see 16:38; for information regarding the original edition, see T5:350 (53 references) and T4:338 (16 references).

[362]
British Spelling Test Series.

Purpose: Developed to serve as a "comprehensive screening test that delivers detailed information about the spelling ability of groups or individuals."
Population: Ages 5–adult.
Publication Date: 1997.
Acronym: BSTS.
Administration: Individual or group.
Levels, 5: 1, 2, 3, 4, 5.
Forms, 2: X and Y, alternate forms.
Price Data: Available from publisher.
Time: (30–40) minutes.
Authors: Denis Vincent and Mary Crumpler.
Publisher: NFER-Nelson Publishing Co. Ltd. [England].
Cross References: For reviews by Timothy Z. Keith and S. Kathleen Krach, see 16:39.

[363]
Brown Attention-Deficit Disorder Scales.

Purpose: Designed to "elicit cognitive and affective indications of Attention-Deficit Disorder."

Publication Dates: 1996–2001.

Acronym: Brown ADD Scales.

Scores, 6: Organizing and Activating to Work, Sustaining Attention and Concentration, Sustaining Energy and Effort, Managing Affective Interference, Utilizing "Working Memory" and Assessing Recall, Total.

Administration: Individual or group.

Price Data, 2002: $270 per complete kit for Children and Adolescents including 25 Ready Score® Parent and Teacher forms for ages 3–7, 25 Ready Score® Parent, Teacher and self-report forms for ages 8–12, 25 Ready Score® answer documents for ages 12–18, diagnostic forms (10 each, Children and Adolescents), and manual for Children and Adolescents; $160 per complete kit for Adolescents and Adults including treatment monitoring worksheet, 50 Ready Score® answer documents (25 each for ages 12–18 and 18+), diagnostic forms (10 each for ages 12–18 and 18+), and manual for Adolescents and Adults; $40 per 25 Ready Score® parent forms (specify ages 3–7 or ages 8–12); $40 per 25 Ready Score® teacher forms (specify ages 3–7 or ages 8–12); $40 per 25 Ready Score® self-report forms/answer documents (specify ages 8–12, or ages 12–18, or ages 18+); $20 per 10 diagnostic forms (specify ages 3–12, ages 12–18, or ages 18+); $79 per manual for Children and Adolescents or manual for Adolescents and Adults; $150 per Scoring Assistant (3.5-inch diskette or CD-ROM Windows).

Time: (10–20) minutes.

Author: Thomas E. Brown.

Publisher: PsychCorp, A brand of Harcourt Assessment, Inc.

a) PRIMARY/PRESCHOOL.
Population: Ages 3–7.
b) SCHOOL-AGE.
Population: Ages 8–12.
c) ADOLESCENT SCALE.
Population: Ages 12 to 18.
d) ADULT SCALE.
Population: Ages 18 and over.

Cross References: For reviews by Nadeen L. Kaufman and Alan S. Kaufman, by E. Jean Newman, and by Judy Oehler-Stinnett, see 14:54.

[364]
Brown Attention-Deficit Disorder Scales for Children and Adolescents.

Purpose: "Designed to elicit … [information] that may indicate impairment in executive functions related to Attention-Deficit/Hyperactivity Disorders (AD/HD)."

Population: Ages 3–18.

Publication Date: 2001.

Acronym: Brown ADD Scales for Children.

Scores, 7: 6 cluster scores (Organizing/Prioritizing/and Activating to Work, Focusing/Sustaining/and Shifting Attention to Tasks, Regulating Alertness/Sustaining Effort/and Processing Speed, Managing Frustration and Modulating Emotions, Utilizing Working Memory and Accessing Recall, Monitoring and Self-Regulating Action), Total Score.

Administration: Group or individual.

Price Data, 2001: $270 per complete kit including manual (149 pages), 25 each Ready Score Parent Forms and Teacher Forms (ages 3–7), 25 each Ready Score Parent Forms, Teacher Forms, and Self-Report Forms (ages 8–12), 25 Ready Score Answer Documents (ages 12–18), and 10 each Child Diagnostic Forms (ages 3–12) and Adolescent Diagnostic Forms (ages 12–18); $79 per manual; $40 per 25 Ready Score Parent Forms (ages 3–7 or 8–12); $40 per 25 Ready Score Teacher Forms (ages 3–7 or 8–12); $40 per 25 Ready Score Self-Report Forms/Answer Documents (child, ages 8–12; or adolescent, ages 12–18); $20 per 10 Diagnostic Forms (child, ages 3–12; or adolescent, ages 12–18); $350 per Scoring Assistant kit including manual, 25 each Parent Forms (ages 3–7 and 8–12), 25 each Teacher Forms (ages 3–7 and 8–12), 25 each Self-Report Forms (ages 8–12 and 12–18), Brown ADD Scoring Assistant CD-ROM (3.5-inch diskette version available); $40 per 25 Parent or Teacher Forms (ages 3–7 or 8–12); $40 per 25 Self-Report Forms/Answer Documents (child, ages 8–12; or adolescent, ages 12–18).

Time: (10–20) minutes.

Comments: Downward extension of the Brown Attention Deficit Disorder Scales for Adolescents and Adults; describes cognitive, affective, behavioral symptoms beyond DSM-IV diagnostic criteria to assess executive function impairments; optional Brown ADD Scales Scoring Assistant software scores, analyzes results, maintains records, generates graphical and narrative reports; system requirements: Windows 95/98/2000/ME/NT 4.0, 100 MHz Pentium processor, 32 MB RAM, 2 MB video card capable of 800 x 600 resolution (256 colors), 20 MB free hard disk space, 3.5-inch floppy drive, 50 MB temporary disk space.

Author: Thomas E. Brown.

Publisher: PsychCorp, A brand of Harcourt Assessment, Inc.

a) PRIMARY/PRESCHOOL LEVEL.
Population: Ages 3–7.
Forms, 2: Parent Form, Teacher Form.
Comments: Elicits parent and teacher reports of symptoms.
b) SCHOOL-AGE LEVEL.
Population: Ages 8–12.

Forms, 3: Self-Report Form, Parent Form, Teacher Form.
Comments: Elicits parent, teacher and self-reports of symptoms.
c) ADOLESCENT LEVEL.
Population: Ages 13–18.
Form, 1: Ready-Score Answer Document.
Comments: Elicits parent and self-reports of symptoms.
Cross References: For reviews by Karen E. Jennings and William K. Wilkinson, see 15:42.

[365]
Bruce Vocabulary Inventory.

Purpose: Constructed to measure vocabulary.
Population: Business and industry and general population.
Publication Dates: 1959–1984.
Scores: Total score only.
Administration: Group.
Price Data, 2006: $96 per test package; $36 per IBM answer sheet package; $12.50 per set of IBM scoring stencils; $5.50 per set of fan keys; $35 per manual (1959, 4 pages) and manual supplement (1984, 17 pages); $39 per IBM specimen set; $33.50 per fan key specimen set.
Time: (15–20) minutes.
Author: Martin M. Bruce.
Publisher: Martin M. Bruce, Ph.D.
Cross References: See T5:352 (1 reference); for reviews by Fred H. Borgen and Robert Fitzpatrick, see 7:231.

[366]
Bruininks-Oseretsky Test of Motor Proficiency (Second Edition).

Purpose: Designed to measure gross and fine motor skills of children.
Population: Ages 4–21.
Publication Dates: 1978–2005.
Acronym: BOT-2.
Scores: 3 scores: Gross Motor Composite, Fine Motor Composite, Battery Composite, for 8 subtests: Fine Motor Precision, Fine Motor Integration, Manual Dexterity, Bilateral Coordination, Balance, Running Speed and Agility, Upper-Limb Coordination, Strength.
Administration: Individual.
Price Data, 2006: $699.99 per kit including a manual, administration easel, 25 record forms, 25 examinee booklets, scoring transparency, balance beam, blocks with string, penny box, penny pad, plastic pennies, knee pad, peg board and pegs, 2 red pencils, scissors, target, tennis ball, shape cards, and shuttle block; $38.99 per 25 record forms for complete battery/short form; $38.99 per 25 examinee booklets.

Time: (45–60) minutes for complete battery; (15–20) minutes for short form.
Comments: Second revised edition of the Oseretsky Tests of Motor Proficiency.
Author: Robert H. Bruininks.
Publisher: Pearson Assessments (originally published by AGS Publishing, acquired by Pearson in 2005).
Cross References: See T5:353 (22 references) and T4:340 (18 references); for a review by David A. Sabatino of an earlier edition, see 9:174 (7 references); see also T3:324 (3 references) and T2:1898 (15 references); for a review by Anna Espenschade, see 4:650 (10 references); for an excerpted review, see 3:472 (6 references).

[367]
Burks' Behavior Rating Scales

Purpose: Identify "particular behavior problems and patterns of problems shown by children."
Population: Preschool–grade 9.
Publication Dates: 1968–1977.
Acronym: BBRS.
Administration: Individual.
Price Data: Available from publisher.
Time: Administration time not reported.
Comments: Ratings of problem children by teachers or parents; this version is no longer available and will be replaced with BBRS-2 in Spring 2006.
Author: Harold F. Burks.
Publisher: Western Psychological Services.
  a) PRESCHOOL AND KINDERGARTEN.
  Population: Ages 3–6.
  Scores, 18: Excessive Self-Blame, Excessive Anxiety, Excessive Withdrawal, Excessive Dependency, Poor Ego Strength, Poor Physical Strength, Poor Coordination, Poor Intellectuality, Poor Attention, Poor Impulse Control, Poor Reality Contact, Poor Sense of Identity, Excessive Suffering, Poor Anger Control, Excessive Sense of Persecution, Excessive Aggressiveness, Excessive Resistance, Poor Social Conformity.
  b) GRADES 1–9.
  Population: Grades 1–9.
  Scores, 19: Same scores as *a* above plus Poor Academics.
Cross References: See T5:355 (1 reference) and T4:342 (5 references); for reviews by Lisa G. Bischoff and Leland C. Zlomke and Brenda R. Bush, see 11:50 (7 references); see also T3:328 (1 reference), T2:1115 (1 reference), and 7:46 (2 references).

[368]
Burns Brief Inventory of Communication and Cognition.

Purpose: Designed to "assist in determining which of a client's cognitive or communication skills are impaired as a result of a neurological lesion or other

disease process, and to assist in selecting appropriate treatment targets and functional treatment goals."
Population: Adults with neurological impairment.
Publication Date: 1997.
Acronym: Burns Inventory.
Scores: Left Hemisphere Inventory: 16 scores in 5 domains: Auditory Comprehension (Yes/No Questions, Comprehension of Words and Sentences, Comprehension of Paragraphs), Verbal Expression (Automatic Speech, Verbal Repetition, Responsive Naming-Nouns, Responsive Naming-Verbs, Confrontation Naming), Reading (Oral Reading of Words and Sentences, Reading Comprehension of Words and Sentences, Reading Comprehension of Functional Paragraphs), Writing (Writing to Dictation, Functional Writing), Numerical Reasoning (Time, Money, Calculation); Right Hemisphere Inventory: 12 scores in 3 domains: Scanning and Tracking (Functional Scanning and Tracking, Scanning and Tracking of Single Words), Visuo-Spatial Skills (Functional Spatial Distribution of Attention, Spatial Distribution of Attention, Recognition of Familiar Faces, Gestalt Perception, Visuo-Spatial Construction-Clock, Visuo-Spatial Organization for Writing), Prosody and Abstract Language (Spontaneous Expressive Prosody, Receptive Prosody, Inferences, Metaphorical Language); Complex Neuropathology Inventory: 15 scores in 4 domains: Orientation to Factual Memory (Orientation to Person/Place/Time, Factual Current and Remote Memory), Auditory Attention and Memory (Auditory Attention/Vigilance, Immediate Auditory Recall of Digits, Immediate Auditory Recall of Digits with Distractions, Immediate Auditory Recall of Functional Information); Visual Perception (Color Recognition, Picture Matching, Word Matching); Visual Attention and Memory (Functional Short-Term Recognition, Short-Term Recognition of Pictures, Short-Term Recognition of Words, Divided Visual Attention, Delayed Recognition of Pictures, Delayed Recognition of Words).
Administration: Individual.
Forms, 3: Inventories: Left Hemisphere Inventory, Right Hemisphere Inventory, Complex Neuropathology Inventory.
Price Data, 2002: $159 per complete kit; $23 per 15 Right Hemisphere record forms; $23 per 15 Complex Neuropathology record forms; $23 per 15 Left Hemisphere record forms; $52 per stimulus plates; $53 per examiner's manual (116 pages); $6 per 3-minute audiocassette.
Time: (30) minutes per inventory.
Comments: For use by speech pathologists; each inventory can be used separately or all three can be used as a battery.
Author: Martha S. Burns.

Publisher: PsychCorp, A brand of Harcourt Assessment, Inc.
Cross References: For reviews by Joan C. Ballard and Richard I. Frederick, see 14:55.

[369]
Burns/Roe Informal Reading Inventory: Preprimer to Twelfth Grade, Sixth Edition.
Purpose: Provides information about the reading skills, abilities, and needs of individual students in order to plan an appropriate program of reading intervention.
Population: Beginning readers–Grade 12.
Publication Dates: 1985–2002.
Acronym: IRI.
Scores, 2: Word Recognition, Comprehension.
Administration: Individual.
Levels, 14: Preprimer, Primer, First Reader, Second Grade, Third Grade, Fourth Grade, Fifth Grade, Sixth Grade, Seventh Grade, Eighth Grade, Ninth Grade, Tenth Grade, Eleventh Grade, Twelfth Grade.
Price Data, 2005: $55.56 per Informal Reading Inventory manual including reproducible teacher pages.
Time: (40–50 minutes).
Authors: Betty D. Roe and Paul C. Burns.
Publisher: Houghton Mifflin Company.
Cross References: For reviews by Felice J. Green and Timothy Shanahan of the Fifth Edition, see 14:56; see also T5:357 (1 reference) and T4:343; for reviews by Carolyn Colvin Murphy and Roger H. Bruning and by Edward S. Shapiro of an earlier edition, see 10:37.

[370]
Burt Word Reading Test, New Zealand Revision.
Purpose: Designed to provide an estimate of word recognition skills for 110 words.
Population: Ages 6-0 to 12-11 years.
Publication Date: 1981.
Scores: 1 overall performance score.
Administration: Individual.
Price Data, 2001: NZ$3.60 per 20 record forms; $.99 per test card; $6.30 per manual (10 pages); $8.10 per specimen set.
Time: [5] minutes.
Comments: Revision and New Zealand standardization of the Burt Word Reading Test; identical to 1974 revision except for word order.
Authors: Alison Gilmore, Cedric Croft, and Neil Reid.
Publisher: New Zealand Council for Educational Research [New Zealand].
Cross References: See T5:358 (13 references) and T4:344 (4 references); for reviews by Mark W. Aulls and John Elkins, see 9:175 (2 references).

[371]
Bury Infant Check.
Purpose: To aid in identifying children with special needs.
Population: Children in second term of infant school.
Publication Date: 1986.
Acronym: BIC.
Administration: Individual.
Price Data: Price information available from publisher for Full Check record booklets, Quick Check record forms, and for teacher's set including Full Check record booklet, Quick Check record form, and manual (36 pages).
Authors: Lea Pearson and John Quinn.
Publisher: NFER-Nelson Publishing Co., Ltd. [England].
    a) QUICK CHECK.
    Scores, 3: Language Expression, Learning Style, Total.
    Time: (3–4) minutes.
    Comments: Teacher-rated.
    b) FULL CHECK.
    Scores, 12: Language Skills (Comprehension, Expression, Total), Learning Style, Memory Skills (Visual, Auditory, Total), Number Skills, Perceptual Motor Skills (Copying Shapes, Visual Discrimination, Total), Total.
    Time: (20) minutes.
Cross References: For a review by Stephan A. Henry, see 9:38.

[372]
Business Analyst Skills Evaluation [One-Hour].
Purpose: Measures practical and analytical skills for the position of Business Systems Analyst.
Population: Candidates for Business Analyst positions.
Publication Dates: 1984–1998.
Acronym: BUSAN.
Scores: Total Score, Narrative Evaluation, Ranking, Recommendation.
Administration: Group.
Price Data, 2001: $225 per candidate, quantity discounts available.
Foreign Language Edition: Available in French.
Time: (60) minutes.
Comments: Available in booklet and Internet formats; scored by publisher; must be proctored.
Author: Bruce A. Winrow.
Publisher: Walden Personnel Performance, Inc. [Canada].
Cross References: For reviews by Charles K. Parsons and Michael Spangler, see 16:40.

[373]
Business Analyst Skills Evaluation—2 Hour.
Purpose: "Measures practical and analytical skills required for the position of Business Systems Analyst."
Population: Candidates for business analyst positions.
Publication Date: 1984.
Acronym: PRBUSAN.
Score: Total score, narrative evaluation, rating, recommendation.
Administration: Group.
Price Data, 2001: $350 per candidate; quantity discounts available.
Time: (120) minutes.
Comments: Also available with interpersonal skills; graded by publisher; must be proctored.
Author: Bruce A. Winrow.
Publisher: Walden Personnel Performance, Inc. [Canada].
Cross References: For a review by Lenore W. Harmon, see 10:39.

[374]
Business Judgment Test, Revised.
Purpose: "Designed to be a measure of empathy or 'feel' for the generally accepted ideas and opinions on desirable courses of action in interpersonal relationships."
Population: Adults.
Publication Dates: 1953–1984.
Acronym: BJT.
Scores: Total score only.
Administration: Group.
Price Data, 2006: $119.50 per test package; $3.25 per scoring key; $49.50 per manual (1965, 12 pages) and manual supplement (1984, 17 pages); $55.50 per specimen set.
Foreign Language Edition: French edition available.
Time: (10–20) minutes.
Author: Martin M. Bruce.
Publisher: Martin M. Bruce, Ph.D.
Cross References: See T2:2275 (1 reference); for a review by Jerome E. Doppelt, and an excerpted review by Kenneth D. Orton, see 7:1059 (1 reference); see also 6:1101 (4 references); for a review by Edward B. Greene, see 5:893.

[375]
Butcher Treatment Planning Inventory.
Purpose: Designed to provide psychotherapists with "relevant personality and symptomatic information early in the treatment process."
Population: Adults in therapy.
Publication Date: 1998.
Acronym: BTPI.
Administration: Individual or group.

Price Data, 2002: $147 per starter kit including manual (236 pages), 10 full form reusable question booklets, 25 full form answer/profile sheets, scoring templates, 1 free sample symptom monitoring form reusable question booklet, 1 free sample symptom monitoring ready score answer document; $74 per symptom monitoring supplement hand scoring kit including 10 reusable question booklets and 25 ready score answer booklets; $20 per 10 full form question booklets; $14 per 10 symptom monitoring form reusable question booklets; $32 per 25 full form answer sheets; $67 per 25 symptom monitoring ready score answer documents; $67 per manual; $39 per full form scoring templates.

Comments: Normed on ages 18 and over; hand- or computer-scored; paper-and-pencil or computerized administration; computer-generated interpretive reports available.

Author: James N. Butcher.

Publisher: PsychCorp, A brand of Harcourt Assessment, Inc.

   a) FULL FORM.

   Scores, 16: Validity Scales (Inconsistent Responding, Overly Virtuous Self-Views, Exaggerated Problem Presentation, Closed-Mindedness), Treatment Issues Scales (Problems in Relationship Formation, Somatization of Conflict, Low Expectation of Benefit, Self-Oriented/Narcissism, Perceived Lack of Environmental Support), Current Symptom Scales (Depression, Anxiety, Anger-Out, Anger-In, Unusual Thinking), General Pathology Composite, Treatment Difficulty Composite.

   Time: [30] minutes.

   b) SYMPTOM MONITORING FORM.

   Scores: Includes only Current Symptom Scales from *a* above.

   Time: [12] minutes.

   c) TREATMENT PROCESS/SYMPTOM FORM.

   Scores: Includes only Treatment Issues Scales and Current Symptom Scales from *a* above.

   Time: Administration time not reported.

   d) TREATMENT ISSUES FORM.

   Scores: Includes only Validity Scales and Treatment Issues Scales from *a* above.

   Time: Administration time not reported.

Cross References: For reviews by Wiliam E. Hanson and Samuel Juni, see 14:57.

[376]
C-BDQ Correctional Officer Background Data Questionnaire.

Purpose: Developed to assess background and personal characteristics.

Population: Candidates for entry-level correctional officer positions.

Publication Date: 1995.

Acronym: C-BDQ.

Scores: 7 biodata subtypes: Unscored Demographic Information, Background, Lifestyle, Interest, Personality, Ability, Opinion-Based.

Administration: Individual or group.

Price Data: Available from publisher.

Time: 60 minutes.

Comments: "It is recommended that this test be given in conjunction with one of IPMA-HR's other entry-level correctional officer tests."

Authors: International Public Management Association for Human Resources & Bruce Davey Associates.

Publisher: International Public Management Association for Human Resources (IPMA-HR).

[377]
C-1 and C-2 Correctional Officer Tests.

Purpose: Designed as entry-level tests for correctional officers.

Population: Candidates for entry-level correctional officer positions.

Publication Dates: 1991-1995.

Scores: 4 knowledge areas: Reading Comprehension, Counting Accuracy, Inductive Reasoning, Deductive Reasoning.

Administration: Individual or group.

Forms, 2: C-1, C-2.

Price Data: Available from publisher.

Time: 120 minutes per test.

Comments: No prior training or experience as a correctional officer is assumed of candidates taking these tests.

Authors: International Public Management Association for Human Resources.

Publisher: International Public Management Association for Human Resources (IPMA-HR).

[378]
California Achievement Tests, Fifth Edition.

Purpose: "Designed to measure achievement in the basic skills taught in schools throughout the nation."

Population: Grades K–12.

Publication Dates: 1957–1993.

Acronym: CAT/5.

Administration: Group.

Levels: 13.

Forms, 4: Complete Battery A, B; Survey A, B.

Price Data, 2006: $44 per 30 locator tests with directions and answer sheets (specify Grades 1–6 or Grades 6–12); $26 per 30 practice tests; $22 per Form A Complete Battery Examiner's Manual (1993, 45 pages); $209 per 30 Form A Complete Battery reflective machine-scorable booklets; $218 per 30 Form A Complete Battery (Trans-Optic) booklets; $61 per 50 CompuScan answer sheets, Levels 14–21/22 (specify Complete Battery or Survey tests); $1,488 per 1,250 continuous form (Trans-Optic) answer sheets (specify form and indicate Level 14–21/22); $2.30 per class record sheet for hand-recording; $63 per test coordinator's handbook; $59 per technical report; $45 per Class Management Guide; $20 per Multi-Level Norms book (specify Fall, Winter, or Spring); scoring service available from publisher.

Comments: California Achievement Tests, Sixth Edition is now the same as TerraNova, The Second Edition (2563); additional information available from publisher.

Author: CTB Macmillan/McGraw-Hill.

Publisher: CTB/McGraw-Hill.

Cross References: See T5:364 (28 references); for reviews by Anthony J. Nitko and by Robert F. McMorris, Wei-Ping Liu, and Elizabeth L. Bringsjord, see 13:40 (113 references); see also T4:352 (52 references); for reviews by Peter W. Airasian and James L. Wardrop of the 1985 edition, see 10:41 (68 references); for reviews by Bruce G. Rogers and Victor L. Willson of the 1978 edition, see 9:180 (19 references); see also T3:344 (68 references); for reviews by Miriam M. Bryan and Frank Womer of the 1970 edition, see 8:10 (33 references); for reviews by Jack C. Merwin and Robert D. North of the 1957 edition, see 6:3 (19 references); for a review by Charles O. Neidt, see 5:2 (10 references); for reviews by Warren G. Findley, Alvin W. Schindler, and J. Harlan Shores of the 1950 edition, see 4:2 (8 references); for a review by Paul A. Witty of the 1943 edition, see 2:1193 (1 reference); for a review by D. Welty Lefever and an excerpted review by E. L. Abell, see 7:876. For reviews of subtests, see 8:45 (2 reviews), 8:257 (1 review), 8:719 (2 reviews), see 6:251 (1 review), 5:177 (2 reviews), 5:468 (1 review), 4:151 (2 reviews), 4:411 (1 review), 4:530 (2 reviews, 1 excerpt), 2:1292 (2 reviews), 2:1459 (2 reviews), 2:1563 (1 review), 1:893 (1 review), and 1:1110 (2 reviews).

[379]
The California Child Q-Set.

Purpose: "Designed to describe a child's behavior and personality."

Population: Children.

Publication Date: 1980.

Acronym: CAQC.

Scores: Q-sort rating of children by teachers and counselors in 9 categories ranging from extremely uncharacteristic to extremely characteristic.

Administration: Group.

Price Data: Available from publisher (www.mindgarden.com).

Time: (35-60) minutes.

Comments: For an upward extension see The California Q-Sort (386).

Authors: Jeanne Block and Jack Block.

Publisher: Mind Garden, Inc.

Cross References: See T5:365 (11 references) and T4:354 (6 references); for a review by Alfred B. Heilbrun, Jr., see 9:181; see also T3:348 (2 references).

[380]
California Computerized Assessment Package.

Purpose: Designed as a "standardized assessment of reaction time and speed of information processing."

Population: Ages 10–90.

Publication Dates: 1986–1999.

Acronym: CalCAP.

Scores, 7: Simple Reaction Time, Choice Reaction Time for Single Digits, Serial Pattern Matching, Lexical Discrimination, Visual Selective Attention, Response Reversal and Rapid Visual Scanning, Form Discrimination.

Administration: Individual.

Forms, 2: Standard, Abbreviated.

Price Data, 2005: $495 per complete kit including manual (2001, 80 pages), standard battery and abbreviated battery; $10 per demonstration program; $15 per manual.

Foreign Language Editions: Danish, Flemish, French, Norwegian, and Spanish editions available.

Time: (20–25) minutes-Standard battery; (8-10) minutes-Abbreviated battery.

Comments: DOS or Windows PC running MS-DOS 3.1 or greater, Windows 95/98 required; see CalCAP web site (www.calcaprt.com) for workarounds if using Windows 2000/XP.

Author: Eric N. Miller.

Publisher: Norland Software.

Cross References: For reviews by Howard A. Lloyd and by Goran Westergren and Ingela Westergren, see 14:58.

[381]
The California Critical Thinking Dispositions Inventory.

Purpose: "Measures one's disposition or inclination toward critical thinking."

Population: High school, college, and adult.

Publication Date: 1992.

Acronym: CCTDI.

Scores, 8: Truth-Seeking, Inquisitiveness, Open-Mindedness, Confidence in One's Own Reasoning, Analyticity, Systematicity, Cognitive Maturity, Total.

Administration: Group or individual. On-line e-testing or paper-and-pencil.

Price Data, 2006: $45 per specimen kit including inventory and test manual; information available from publisher (www.insightassessment.com) for current educational and retail prices; available on-line with immediate scoring, or in paper-and-pencil lots of 25 bundled with CapScore scoring service; doctoral student discounts available.

Foreign Language Editions: Available in English and in several other languages including: Arabic, Chinese (Hong Kong), Finnish, French (Canada), Hebrew, Japanese, Korean, Portuguese, Spanish (Mexico), and Thai.

Comments: Inventory is available on-line with immediate scoring, or via paper and pencil.

Time: (15–20) minutes.

Authors: Peter A. Facione and Noreen C. Facione.

Publisher: Insight Assessment—The California Academic Press LLC.

Cross References: For reviews by Carolyn M. Callahan and Salvador Hector Ochoa, see 12:57.

[382]
California Critical Thinking Skills Test.

Purpose: Designed to be "a standardized assessment instrument targeting core critical thinking skills at the post-secondary level."

Population: College and adult

Publication Dates: 1990-2000.

Acronym: CCTST.

Scores, 6: Analysis, Evaluation, Inference, Inductive Reasoning, Deductive Reasoning, Total.

Administration: Group or individual.

Forms, 3: Forms A, B (alternative forms) and Form 2000.

Price Data, 2005: $45 per specimen kit including Form A, Form B, Form 2000, and most recent edition of test manual, plus sample CapScore answer sheet; educational and retail prices available from publisher at www.insightassessment.com; doctoral student discounts available.

Foreign Language Editions: All forms available in English; Form A is available in Chinese (Taiwan), Hebrew, Korean, Spanish (Mexico), and Thai; Form B is available in Portuguese; Form 2000 is available in French (Canadian), Korean, and Spanish (Spain).

Time: 45 minutes.

Comments: Available online with immediate scoring, or in paper-and-pencil lots of 25 bundled with CapScore scoring service.

Author: Peter A. Facione.

Publisher: Insight Assessment—The California Academic Press LLC.

Cross References: For reviews by Robert F. McMorris and William B. Michael, see 12:58.

[383]
California Diagnostic Mathematics Tests.

Purpose: Developed to assess mathematics achievement for use in instructional planning and program evaluation.

Publication Date: 1988.

Acronym: CDMT.

Administration: Group.

Price Data, 2002: $20.55 per 35 practice tests (select Levels A, B–C, D–F); $35.55 per 35 locator tests (select Levels A–C, D–F); $30.15 per 50 locator test answer sheets (Levels D–F); $140.65 per 35 scannable test bookes (specify Level A, B, or C); $64.90 per 35 reusable test books (specify Level D, E, or F); $23.15 per 50 CompuScore or Scantron answer sheets (for use with scanning); $29.25 per 25 SCOREZE answer sheets (for use with handscoring); $16.90 per set of hand scoring stencils (select Levels D, E, F); $49.55 per 100 student diagnostic profiles; $2.70 per class report form; $11.20 per locator test directions; $14.65 per examiner's manual and answer keys (select level); $20.40 per teacher's guide (select Levels A–B, C–D, or E–F); $64.85 per specimen set; price information for norms book and technical report available from publisher; scoring service available from publisher.

Time: Administration time not reported.

Author: CTB/McGraw-Hill.

Publisher: CTB/McGraw-Hill.

a) LEVEL A.

Population: Grades 1.1–2.9.

Scores, 3: Number Concepts, Computation, Applications.

b) LEVEL B.

Population: Grades 2.6–3.9.

Scores, 3: Same as *a* above.

c) LEVEL C.

Population: Grades 3.6–4.9.

Scores, 3: Same as *a* above.

d) LEVEL D.

Population: Grades 4.6–6.9.

Scores, 3: Same as *a* above.

e) LEVEL E.

Population: Grades 6.6–8.9.

Scores, 3: Same as *a* above.

f) LEVEL F.

Population: Grades 8.6–12.

Scores, 3: Same as *a* above plus Life Skills.

Cross References: For reviews by Michael B. Bunch and Jerry Johnson, see 11:52.

[384]
California Diagnostic Reading Tests.

Purpose: Developed to assess reading achievement for use in instructional planning and program evaluation.

Publication Date: 1989.

Acronym: CDRT.

Administration: Group.

Price Data, 2002: $20.55 per 35 practice books (select Levels A, B–C, D–F); $35.55 per 35 locator tests (select Levels A–C, D–F); $140.65 per 35 scannable test books (specify Level A, B, or C); $64.90 per 35 reusable test books (specify Level D, E, or F);

$40.65 per 50 CompuScan answer sheets (use for scanning) (specify Level D, E, or F); $46.15 per 50 Scantron answer sheets (use for scanning) (specify Level D, E, or F); $58.50 per 25 SCOREZE answer sheets (use for handscoring) (specify Level D, E, or F); $30.15 per 50 locator test answer sheets (Levels D–F only); $50.95 per set of scoring stencils (Levels D–F only); $49.55 per 100 student diagnostic profiles; $2.70 per class record sheet for handscoring (select level); $11.20 per locator test directions; $14.55 per examiner's manual including answer keys (select level); $20.40 per teacher's guide (select Levels A–B, C–D, E–F); $14.55 per norms book (32 pages); $14.55 per technical report; $64.85 per review kit; scoring service available from publisher.
Time: Tests are untimed.
Author: CTB/McGraw-Hill.
Publisher: CTB/McGraw-Hill.

   a) LEVEL A.
   Population: Grades 1.1–2.9.
   Scores, 3: Word Analysis, Vocabulary, Comprehension.
   b) LEVEL B.
   Population: Grades 2.6–3.9.
   Scores, 3: Same as *a* above.
   c) LEVEL C.
   Population: Grades 3.6–4.9.
   Scores, 3: Same as *a* above.
   d) LEVEL D.
   Population: Grades 4.6–6.9.
   Scores, 4: Same as *a* above plus Applications.
   e) LEVEL E.
   Population: Grades 6.6–8.9.
   Scores, 4: Same as *d* above.
   f) LEVEL F.
   Population: Grades 8.6–12.
   Scores, 3: Vocabulary, Comprehension, Applications.
Cross References: For a review by T. Steuart Watson, see 11:53.

[385]
California Psychological Inventory™, Third Edition.

Purpose: Designed to assess personality characteristics and to predict what people will say and do in specified contexts.
Population: Ages 13 years and over.
Publication Dates: 1956–1996.
Acronym: CPI.
Scores, 36: 20 Folk Scales: Dominance (Do), Capacity for Status (Cs), Sociability (Sy), Social Presence (Sp), Self-Acceptance (Sa), Independence (In), Empathy (Em), Responsibility (Re), Socialization (So), Self-Control (Sc), Good Impression (Gi), Communality (Cm), Well-Being (Wb), Tolerance (To), Achievement via Conformance (Ac), Achievement via Inde-

pendence (Ai), Intellectual Efficiency (Ie), Psychological-Mindedness (Py), Flexibility (Fx), Femininity/Masculinity (Fm); 3 Vector Scales: v. 1 (Internality/Externality), v. 2 (Norm Questioning/Norm Favoring), v. 3 (Self-Realization), plus 13 Special Purpose scales: Managerial Potential, Work Orientation, Creative Temperament, Leadership, Amicability, Law Enforcement Orientation, Tough-mindedness, Baucom Scale for Masculinity, Baucom Scale for Femininity, Leventhal Scale for Anxiety, Wink-Gough Scale for Narcissism, Dicken Scale for Social Desirability, Dicken Scale for Aquiescence.
Administration: Group.
Price Data, 2001: $18.50 per preview kit including prepaid answer sheet and item booklet; $70 per 25 reusable item booklets; $176.50 per 10 prepaid answer sheets (for mail-in scoring, for use with item booklets); $16.50 per 25 scannable answer sheets (specify for use with NCS Sentry 300 scanner or Scantron 8000 series scanners); $76 per manual (1996, 431 pages); $60.10 per A Practical Guide to CPI Interpretation, Third Edition.
Foreign Language Editions: French, German, Italian, and Spanish editions available in an earlier edition.
Time: (45–60) minutes.
Comments: Previous edition still available; 1 form; reports available: Narrative, Configural Analysis; Scoring Options: Prepaid (mail-in), CPP Software System, skillsone.com
Authors: Harrison G. Gough and Pamela Bradley (manual).
Publisher: CPP, Inc.
Cross References: For reviews by Mark J. Atkinson and Keith Hattrup, see 15:43; see T5:372 (118 references) and T4:361 (57 references); for reviews by Brian Bolton and George Engelhard, Jr., see 11:54 (108 references); for reviews by Donald H. Baucom and H. J. Eysenck, see 9:182 (61 references); see also T3:354 (195 references); for a review by Malcolm D. Gynther, see 8:514 (452 references); see also T2:1121 (166 references); for reviews by Lewis R. Goldberg and James A. Walsh and an excerpted review by John O. Crites, see 7:49 (370 references); see also P:27 (249 references); for a review by E. Lowell Kelly, see 6:71 (116 references); for reviews by Lee J. Cronbach and Robert L. Thorndike and an excerpted review by Laurance F. Shaffer, see 5:37 (33 references).

[386]
California Q-Sort (Revised Adult Set).

Purpose: Designed as "a systematic way of comparing different [intra-individual] personalities with one another."
Population: Adults.
Publication Dates: 1961–1990.
Acronym: CAQR.

Scores: Ratings in 9 categories ranging from most uncharacteristic to most characteristic.
Administration: Individual.
Price Data: Available from publisher (www. mindgarden.com).
Time: (30–40) minutes.
Comments: For an adaptation for children, see The California Child Q-Set (379).
Author: Jack Block.
Publisher: Mind Garden, Inc.
Cross References: For a review by George Domino, see 14:59; see also T5:373 (43 references); T4:362 (20 references), and T3:356 (1 reference); for reviews by Allen L. Edwards and David T. Lykken of an earlier edition and excerpted reviews by Samuel J. Beck and John E. Exner, Jr., see 6:72 (2 references); see also P:28 (1 reference).

[387]
California Verbal Learning Test, Children's Version.

Purpose: "Designed to assess multiple components of verbal learning/memory, interference effects on memory and recall strategy/control."
Population: Ages 5–16.
Publication Dates: 1989–1994.
Acronym: CVLT-C.
Scores: List A Trials 1–5 Total, List B Free-Recall Trial, Short Delay Free Recall, Short-Delay Cued Recall, Long-Delay Free Recall, Long-Delay Cued Recall, Semantic Cluster Ratio, Perseverations, Free-Recall Intrusions, Cued-Recall Intrusions, Recognition Hits, Discriminability, False Positives.
Administration: Individual
Price Data, 2006: $168 per set including manual (1994, 147 pages) and 25 record forms; $58 per 25 record forms or $220 per 100 record forms; $349 per scoring assistant including CD-ROM, user's guide, and keyboard overlay (Macintosh or Windows).
Time: (55) minutes with 20 minute interval between short and long delay.
Authors: Dean C. Delis, Joel H. Kramer, Edith Kaplan, and Beth A. Ober; Alan J. Fridlund, and Dean C. Delis (Scoring Assistant User's Guide).
Publisher: PsychCorp, A brand of Harcourt Assessment, Inc.
Cross References: See T5:375 (8 references); for reviews by Billy T. Ogletree and LeAdelle Phelps, see 13:41 (2 references).

[388]
California Verbal Learning Test, Second Edition, Adult Version.

Purpose: To "assess multiple cognitive components of verbal learning and memory functioning including recall strategy/organization, interference effects, recall accuracy and effort."

Population: 16–89 years.
Publication Dates: 1983–2000.
Acronym: CVLT-II (Standard); CVLT-II SF (Short Form).
Scores: Immediate Recall (Trial 1, Trials 2–5, Trials 1–5 Total), Learning Slope, Semantic Clustering, Serial Clustering, Subjective Clustering, Primacy/Recency Recall, Percentage of Recall Consistency, List B Trial, Proactive Interference, Short-Delay Free Recall, Retroactive Interference, Short-Delay Cued Recall, Long-Delay Free Recall, Long-Delay Free Recall Retention, Long-Delay Cued Recall, Repetition Errors, Synonym/Subordinate Intrusions, Across-List Intrusions, Categorical Intrusions, Non-Categorical Intrusions, Yes/No Recognition Testing, False-Positive Errors, Total Recognition Discriminability, Source Recognition Discriminability, Semantic Recognition Discriminability, Novel Recognition Discriminability, Response Bias, Critical Item Analysis, Forced-Choice Recognition [optional].
Administration: Individual.
Forms, 3: Standard Form, Alternate Form, Short Form.
Price Data, 2006: $525 per complete kit including software package (CD-ROM or diskette version), manual (2000, 287 pages), 25 Standard Record Forms, 1 Alternate Record Form, and 25 Short Record Forms; $58 per 25 Standard or Alternate Record Forms (quantity discounts available); $47 per 25 Short Record Forms (quantity discounts available).
Time: (30) minutes plus 30 minutes of delay for Standard and Alternate Forms; (15) minutes plus 15 minutes of delay for Short Form.
Comments: Comprehensive Scoring System software generates Core Report (generates 27 scores), Expanded Report (generates 66 scores), Research Report (generates over 260 scores); computer system requirements: Windows 95/98/NT 4.0, 100 MHz processor, 32 MB RAM, CD-ROM and 3.5-inch floppy diskette drive (CD-ROM version) or 3.5-inch diskette drive (diskette version), 2 MB video card with 800 x 600 resolution (256 colors), and 25 MB free disk space.
Authors: Dean C. Delis, Joel H. Kramer, Edith Kaplan, and Beth A. Ober.
Publisher: PsychCorp, A brand of Harcourt Assessment, Inc.
Cross References: For reviews by Anita M. Hubley and Cederick O. Lindskog, see 16:41; see also T5:376 (35 references); for a review by Ray Fenton of the previous edition, see 13:42 (57 references); see also T4:364 (12 references).

[389]
Call Center Skills Test.

Purpose: Measures practical and intellectual skills for call center positions.
Population: Candidates for call center positions.

Publication Date: 2001.
Acronym: CCTR.
Scores: Total Score, Narrative Evaluation, Ranking, Recommendation.
Administration: Group.
Price Data, 2001: $150 per candidate; quantity discounts available.
Foreign Language Edition: Available in French.
Time: (60) minutes.
Comments: Available in booklet and internet versions; scored by publisher; must be proctored.
Author: Bruce A. Winrow.
Publisher: Walden Personnel Performance, Inc. [Canada].
Cross References: For reviews by Theodore L. Hayes and Judith A. Rein, see 16:42.

[390]
The Callier-Azusa Scale: G Edition.

Purpose: A developmental scale "designed to aid in the assessment of deaf-blind and severely and profoundly handicapped children."
Population: Deaf-blind and severely/profoundly handicapped children.
Publication Date: 1978.
Scores: 18 subscales in 5 areas: Motor Development (Postural Control, Locomotion, Fine Motor, Visual Motor), Perceptual Development (Vision, Auditory, Tactile), Daily Living Skills (Dressing, Personal Hygiene, Feeding, Toileting), Cognition, Communication and Language (Cognition, Receptive, Expressive, Speech), Social Development (Adults, Peers, Environment).
Administration: Individual.
Price Data: Available from publisher.
Time: Administration time not reported.
Comments: Criterion-referenced.
Author: Robert Stillman (Editor).
Publisher: Callier Center for Communication Disorders.
Cross References: See T5:377 (1 reference).

[391]
Cambridge Prospective Memory Test.

Purpose: Designed to "assess prospective memory" (remembering to do previously planned actions).
Population: Ages 16 and over.
Publication Date: 2005.
Acronym: CAMPROMPT.
Score: Total score only.
Administration: Individual.
Forms, 2: Parallel Forms A and B.
Price Data, 2006: £171.50 per complete kit including manual (44 pages), 25 record forms, quiz question cards, puzzle cards, message card, clock, and two timers; £36.50 per 25 record forms.

Time: 20(25) minutes.
Authors: Barbara A. Wilson, Hazel Emslie, Jennifer Foley, Agnes Shiel, Peter Watson, Kari Hawkins, Yvonne Groot, and Jonathan J. Evans.
Publisher: Harcourt Assessment [England].

[392]
The Camden Memory Tests.

Purpose: Designed "to fulfill a clinical need that was not met by existing memory tests."
Population: Available from publisher.
Publication Date: 1996.
Scores: 5 tests: Pictorial Recognition Memory Test, Topographical Recognition Memory Test, Paired Associate Learning Test, Short Recognition Memory Test for Words, Short Recognition Memory Test for Faces.
Administration: Available from publisher.
Price Data, 2001: $182 per Pictorial Recognition Memory Test; $182 per Topographical Recognition Memory Test; $59.95 per Paired Associate Learning Test; $59.95 per Short Recognition Memory Test for Words; $59.95 per Short Recognition Memory Test for Faces; $21.95 per test manual; $395 per set of all 5 tests including 1 manual and 5 packs of scoring sheets; and $16.95 plus postage per 25 scoring sheets.
Time: Administration time not reported.
Author: Elizabeth Warrington.
Publisher: Psychology Press.

[393]
Campbell-Hallam Team Development Survey.

Purpose: "Designed to give teams standardized feedback on their strengths and weaknesses."
Population: Members of intact working teams.
Publication Date: 1994.
Acronym: TDS.
Scores, 19: Resources (Time and Staffing, Information, Material Resources, Organizational Support, Skills, Commitment), Efficiency (Mission Clarity, Team Coordination, Team Unity, Individual Goals, Empowerment), Improvement (Team Assessment, Innovation, Feedback, Rewards, Leadership), Success (Satisfaction, Performance, Overall Index).
Administration: Group.
Price Data, 1999: $180 per preview package including 10 individual survey booklets, team report, individual report for each team member, manual (216 pages), administrator's guide (15 pages), and facilitator's guide (16 pages); $15 per individual survey and report; $10 per 10 observer survey forms; $60 per team report including scoring of one team report, narrative summary profile, miniature profile, and item response summary; $35 plus $10 per item per supplemental items summary reports; $30 per manual; $10 per administrator's guide; $20 per facilitator's guide; $50

per set of manual, administrator's guide, and facilitator's guide.
Time: (20–25) minutes.
Authors: Glenn Hallam and David Campbell.
Publisher: Pearson Performance Solutions [No reply from publisher; status unknown].
Cross References: For reviews by Frederick T. L. Leong and Mary A. Lewis, see 14:60; see also T5:379 (1 reference).

[394]
Campbell™ Interest and Skill Survey.
Purpose: "Measures self-reported interests and skills."
Population: Ages 15 years to adult.
Publication Dates: 1989–1992.
Acronym: CISS™.
Scores, 99: 7 Orientation Scales (Influencing, Organizing, Helping, Creating, Analyzing, Producing, Adventuring), 29 Basic Scales (Leadership, Law/Politics, Public Speaking, Sales, Advertising/Marketing, Supervision, Financial Services, Office Practices, Adult Development, Child Development, Counseling, Religious Activities, Medical Practice, Art/Design, Performing Arts, Writing, International Activities, Fashion, Culinary Arts, Mathematics, Science, Mechanical Crafts, Woodworking, Farming/Forestry, Plants/Gardens, Animal Care, Athletics/Physical Fitness, Military/Law Enforcement, Risks/Adventure), 58 Occupational Scales (Attorney, Financial Planner, Hotel Manager, Manufacturer's Representative, Marketing Director, Realtor, CEO/President, Human Resources Director, School Superintendent, Advertising Account Executive, Media Executive, Public Relations Director, Corporate Trainer, Secretary, Bank Manager, Insurance Agent, Retail Store Manager, Hospital Administrator, Accountant/CPA, Bookkeeper, Child Care Worker, Guidance Counselor, Religious Leader, Teacher K–12, Social Worker, Psychologist, Nursing Administrator, Commercial Artist, Fashion Designer, Liberal Arts Professor, Librarian, Musician, Translator/Interpreter, Writer/Editor, Restaurant Manager, Chef, Physician, Chemist, Medical Researcher, Math/Science Teacher, Computer Programmer, Statistician, Systems Analyst, Carpenter, Electrician, Veterinarian, Airline Mechanic, Agribusiness Manager, Landscape Architect, Architect, Police Officer, Military Officer, Ski Instructor, Test Pilot, Athletic Coach, Athletic Trainer, Emergency Medical Technician, Fitness Instructor), 2 Special Scales (Academic Focus, Extraversion), 3 Procedural Checks (Response Percentage Check, Inconsistency Check, Omitted Items Check).
Administration: Group.
Price Data, 2006: $2.30 per Career Planner; $51.50 per hardcover (ring-binder) manual; $33 per softcover manual; $12.50 per 50 interest/skill pattern worksheets; $21 per 25 Q Local answer sheets; $7.60 per Q Local

report; $30.75 per 100 report cover sheets; $55 per Q Local starter kit including softcover manual, 3 career planners, interest/skill pattern worksheets, 3 answer sheets with test items, and 3 Q Local administrations; $60 per mail-in socring starter kit including softcover manual, 3 career planners, interest/skill pattern worksheets, 3 answer sheets with test items, and all materials necessary to generate 3 reports using mail-in scoring service; $10.95 per internet vouchers including profile report, career planner, and career web resources; quantity discounts available for the reports; price information for Spanish materials available from publisher.
Time: (35) minutes.
Comments: Each scale contains both an interest and a skill score; combined gender scales allow for broadest interpretation of survey results; workshops available.
Author: David Campbell.
Publisher: Pearson Assessments.
Cross References: See T5:380 (1 reference); for reviews by Richard C. Pugh and Michael J. Roszkowski, see 13:43; see also T4:368 (1 reference).

[395]
Campbell Leadership Index.
Purpose: "An adjective checklist designed to be used in the assessment of leadership characteristics."
Population: Leaders.
Publication Date: 1991.
Acronym: CLI.
Scores, 22: Ambitious, Daring, Dynamic, Enterprising, Experienced, Farsighted, Original, Persuasive, Energy, Affectionate, Considerate, Empowering, Entertaining, Friendly, Credible, Organized, Productive, Thrifty, Calm, Flexible, Optimistic, Trusting.
Administration: Group or individual.
Price Data: Available from publisher.
Time: (45–60) minutes.
Comments: Self-ratings plus 3–5 observer ratings.
Author: David Campbell.
Publisher: Pearson Performance Solutions [No reply from publisher; status unknown].
Cross References: See T5:381 (1 reference); for reviews by George Domino and Charles Houston, see 12:59; see also T4:369 (1 reference).

[396]
Campbell Organizational Survey.
Purpose: Designed to measure attitudes of employees regarding the organization.
Population: Working adults.
Publication Dates: 1988–1990.
Acronym: COS.
Scores, 14: The Work Itself, Working Conditions, Freedom from Stress, Co-Workers, Supervision, Top Leadership, Pay, Benefits, Job Security, Promotional Opportunities, Feedback/Communications, Organiza-

tional Planning, Support for Innovation, Overall Satisfaction Index.
Administration: Group.
Price Data: Available from publisher.
Time: (15–25) minutes.
Comments: A component of Campbell Development Surveys (CDS); scoring and reporting discounts for 50, 250, 1,000 or 2,500+ examinees.
Author: David Campbell.
Publisher: Pearson Performance Solutions [No reply from publisher; status unknown].
Cross References: For reviews by Ralph O. Mueller and Kevin R. Murphy, see 12:60; see T4:370 (1 reference).

[397]
Canadian Achievement Survey Tests for Adults.

Purpose: "Designed to measure achievement in reading, language, and mathematics ... subject areas commonly found in adult basic education curricula."
Population: Adults.
Publication Date: 1994.
Acronym: CAST.
Scores, 6: Reading (Vocabulary, Comprehension), Language (Language Mechanics, Language Expression), Mathematics (Mathematics Computation, Mathematics Concepts and Applications).
Administration: Group.
Levels, 3: Completed up to Grade 6, completed Grades 7 to 9, completed Grades 10 and above.
Price Data, 2005: $67 per 25 test booklets (specify level); $34 per 25 hand-scorable answer sheets; $65 per 50 machine scorable answer sheets; $46 per manual (53 pages); $25 per review kit including brochure, 1 copy each of Levels 1, 2, and 3 test booklets, hand-scorable answer sheet, machine-scorable answer sheet, and directions for administering.
Time: (90) minutes.
Authors: Canadian Test Centre.
Publisher: Canadian Test Centre, Educational Assessment Services [Canada].
Cross References: For reviews by John O. Anderson and Mark H. Daniel, see 14:61.

[398]
Canadian Achievement Tests, Third Edition.

Purpose: Designed to measure achievement in the basic skills of reading, language, spelling, mathematics, and writing.
Population: Grades 1.6–postsecondary.
Publication Dates: 1981–2002.
Acronym: CAT-3.
Administration: Group.
Parts, 3: Basic Battery, Supplemental Tests, Constructed-Response Tests.

Levels, 10: 11 (Grades 1.6–2.5), 12 (Grades 2.6–3.5), 13 (Grades 3.6–4.5), 14 (Grades 4.6–5.5), 15 (Grades 5.6–6.5), 16 (Grades 6.6–7.5), 17 (Grades 7.6–8.5), 18 (Grades 8.6–9.5), 19 (Grades 9.6–11.5), 20 (Grades 11.6–postsecondary).
Price Data, 2002: C$205 per Teacher Resource Kit including 3 Student Books at each of Levels 11–13, 1 Student Book at each of Levels 14–19/20, 1 Test Directions for Teachers for each level, 3 Practice Tests for each level, 3 U-Score answer sheets each (Levels 14–19/20), 3 Student Diagnostic Profiles for each level, 9 each of Locator Tests 1 and 2, 1 Locator Test Directions, 18 Locator Test answer sheets, 1 scoring key at each of Levels 11–13, 1 scoring mask at each of Levels 14–18, 1 Norms Book (2001, 101 pages), 1 Teacher Resource Manual for CAT-3 (2002, 242 pages), 1 Parents' Guide to Understanding CAT Results, and 1 carrying bag; $105 per 30 Basic Battery Plus test books (Levels 11–13, specify level); $120 per 30 Basic Battery Plus test books (Levels 14–19/20, specify level); $90 per 30 Basic Battery test books (Levels 12, 13, specify level); $65 per 50 machine-scorable answer sheets (Levels 14–19/20, specify level); $42 per 30 hand-scorable answer sheets (Levels 14–19/20, specify level); $1 per machine-scoring Directions for Test Coordinators; $8 per Test Directions for Teachers (Levels 11–18) or Administering Directions (Levels 19/20), specify level; $40 per Norms Book; $48 per Technical Manual (2002, 156 pages); $35 per Teacher Resource Manual for CAT-3; $1.50 per Parents' Guide to CAT Results; $15 per 30 Student Diagnostic Profiles (Levels 11–19/20, specify level); $12 per 30 Practice Tests (Levels 11–19/20, specify level); $1.50 per scoring key (Levels 11–19/20, specify level); $21 per Locator Test 1 or 2 (specify Test 1 or 2) including directions and 35 answer sheets; $8 per additional directions for Locator Tests 1–2; $21 per 50 additional answer sheets for Locator Tests 1–2; $1.50 per Constructed Response Dictation Worksheet Photocopy Master (Levels 14–16, specify level); $22.50 per Constructed Response Writing Directions including 30 Student Worksheets Narrative Prompts (Levels 12–16), Informational Prompts (Levels 14–16), Letter Prompts (Levels 17–19/20), or Persuasive Prompts (Levels 17–19/20), specify level and prompt; $22.50 per Constructed Response Mathematics directions including 30 Student Worksheets (Levels 11–18), specify level and task; $50 per scoring binder for Constructed-Response Writing or Mathematics including blackline masters for scoring manual, rubrics, and anchor papers (Levels 12–19/20, specify level); $.44 per Administrator's Summary/Graphic Frequency Distribution (per student); $2.90 per Class Record Sheet (per student, Level 11); $4 per Class Record Sheet (per student, Levels 12–13, specify level), $2.10 per Class Record Sheet (per student, Levels 14–19/20, specify level); $.61 per Ob-

jective Competency Report (per student); $.91 per Parent Report or Student Test Record (per student); additional price information available from publisher.
Time: Varies by level; (85–115) minutes for Basic Battery, (55–75) minutes for Supplemental Tests, (40–230) minutes for Constructed Response Test.
Comments: Revision of the CAT/2; hand- or machine-scored by the Canadian Test Centre; machine-scoring recommended when testing 30 or more students; Supplemental and Constructed Response Tests optional.
Author: Canadian Test Centre, Educational Assessment Services.
Publisher: Canadian Test Centre, Educational Assessment Services [Canada].

a) LOCATOR TESTS.
Population: Grades 2–12.
Scores, 2: Vocabulary, Mathematics.
Levels, 2: 1 (Grades 2–6), 2 (Grades 6–12).
Time: (10) minutes.
b) LEVEL 11.
Population: Grades 1.6–2.5.
Scores, 6: 2 Basic Battery Tests (Reading/Language, Mathematics), 3 Supplemental Tests (Word Analysis, Vocabulary, Computation), 1 Constructed Response Test (Mathematics).
Time: (85) minutes for Basic Battery, (55) minutes for Supplemental Tests, (40) minutes for Constructed Response Test.
c) LEVEL 12.
Population: Grades 2.6–3.5.
Scores, 9: 2 Basic Battery Tests (Reading/Language, Mathematics), 4 Supplemental Tests (Word Analysis, Vocabulary, Language/Writing, Computation), 3 Constructed Response Tests (Dictation, Mathematics, Writing-Narrative).
Time: (115) minutes for Basic Battery, (70) minutes for Supplemental Tests, (110) minutes for Constructed Response Test.
d) LEVEL 13.
Population: Grades 3.6–4.5.
Scores, 9: 2 Basic Battery Tests (Reading/Language, Mathematics), 4 Supplemental Tests (Word Analysis, Vocabulary, Language/Writing, Computation), 3 Constructed Response Tests (Dictation, Mathematics, Writing-Narrative).
Time: (110) minutes for Basic Battery, (70) minutes for Supplemental Tests, (110) minutes for Constructed Response Test.
e) LEVEL 14.
Population: Grades 4.6–5.5.
Scores, 10: 2 Basic Battery Tests (Reading/Language, Mathematics), 4 Supplemental Tests (Vocabulary, Spelling, Language/Writing, Computation), 4 Constructed Response Tests (Dictation, Mathematics, Writing-Narrative, Writing-Informational).

Time: (110) minutes for Basic Battery, (75) minutes for Supplemental Tests, (230) minutes for Constructed Response Test.
f) LEVEL 15.
Population: Grades 5.6–6.5.
Scores, 10: 2 Basic Battery Tests (Reading/Language, Mathematics), 4 Supplemental Tests (Vocabulary, Spelling, Language/Writing, Computation), 4 Constructed Response Tests (Dictation, Mathematics, Writing-Narrative, Writing-Informational).
Time: (110) minutes for Basic Battery, (75) minutes for Supplemental Tests, (220) minutes for Constructed Response Test.
g) LEVEL 16.
Population: Grades 6.6–7.5.
Scores, 10: 2 Basic Battery Tests (Reading/Language, Mathematics), 4 Supplemental Tests (Vocabulary, Spelling, Language/Writing, Computation), 4 Constructed Response Tests (Dictation, Mathematics, Writing-Narrative, Writing-Informational).
Time: (110) minutes for Basic Battery, (75) minutes for Supplemental Tests, (220) minutes for Constructed Response Test.
h) LEVEL 17.
Population: Grades 7.6–8.5.
Scores, 10: 2 Basic Battery Tests (Reading/Language, Mathematics), 4 Supplemental Tests (Vocabulary, Spelling, Language/Writing, Computation), 3 Constructed Response Tests (Mathematics, Writing-Letter, Writing-Persuasive).
Time: (110) minutes for Basic Battery, (75) minutes for Supplemental Tests, (220) minutes for Constructed Response Test.
i) LEVEL 18.
Population: Grades 8.6–9.5.
Scores, 10: 2 Basic Battery Tests (Reading/Language, Mathematics), 4 Supplemental Tests (Vocabulary, Spelling, Language/Writing, Computation), 3 Constructed Response Tests (Mathematics, Writing-Letter, Writing-Persuasive).
Time: (110) minutes for Basic Battery, (75) minutes for Supplemental Tests, (220) minutes for Constructed Response Test.
j) LEVEL 19.
Population: Grades 9.6–11.5.
Scores, 10: 2 Basic Battery Tests (Reading/Language, Mathematics), 4 Supplemental Tests (Vocabulary, Spelling, Language/Writing, Computation), 2 Constructed Response Tests (Writing-Letter, Writing-Persuasive).
Time: (110) minutes for Basic Battery, (75) minutes for Supplemental Tests, (180) minutes for Constructed Response Test.
k) LEVEL 20.
Population: Grades 11.6-postsecondary.

Scores, 10: 2 Basic Battery Tests (Reading/Language, Mathematics), 4 Supplemental Tests (Vocabulary, Spelling, Language/Writing, Computation), 2 Constructed Response Tests (Writing-Letter, Writing-Persuasive).
Time: (110) minutes for Basic Battery, (75) minutes for Supplemental Tests, (180) minutes for Constructed Response Test.
Cross References: For reviews by John O. Anderson and Louise M. Soares, see 16:43; see T5:384; for reviews by John Hattie and Leslie Eastman Lukin of the second edition, see 13:44 (2 references); see also T4:371 (3 references); for a review by L. A. Whyte of an earlier edition, see 9:187.

[399]
Canadian Cognitive Abilities Test, Form K.

Purpose: "Designed to assess the development of cognitive abilities related to verbal, quantitative, and nonverbal reasoning and problem solving."
Population: Grades K–2, 3–12.
Publication Dates: 1970–1997.
Acronym: CCAT.
Scores, 4: Verbal, Quantitative, Nonverbal, Composite.
Administration: Group.
Time: 90 minutes for Grades 3-12.
Comments: Canadian version of Cognitive Abilities Test, Form 5 (T4:537); statistical information for CCAT is available from publisher.
Authors: Original edition by Robert L. Thorndike and Elizabeth P. Hagen; Canadian version by Edgar N. Wright.
Publisher: Nelson, A Thomson Company [Canada].
  a) PRIMARY BATTERIES.
  Population: Grades K–1, 2–3.
  Levels, 2: 1, 2.
  Price Data, 2005: $4.20 per test booklet; $8.70 per Directions for Administration; $9.20 per scoring key; $40.10 per norms booklet; $40.10 per Teacher's Handbook; $12.10 per 10 class record folders; $181.10 per score conversion software; $13.80 per preview kit; scoring service available from publisher.
  b) MULTILEVEL EDITION.
  Population: Grades 3–12.
  Levels, 8: A, B, C, D, E, F, G, and H.
  Price Data: $5.20 per test booklet; $31.40 per 35 answer sheets; $76.50 per 100 answer sheets; $8.70 per Directions for Administration; $21.80 per scoring mask; $40.10 per norms booklet; $40.10 per Teacher's Handbook; $12.10 per 10 class record folders; $246 per score conversion software; $14.80 per preview kit; scoring service available from publisher.
Cross References: See T5:385 (3 references); for reviews by John O. Anderson and John Hattie of an earlier edition, see 12:61 (3 references); for reviews by Giuseppe Costantino and Jack A. Cummings of an earlier edition, see 10:42 (3 references); see also T3:361 (5 references) and 8:180 (2 references).

[400]
Canadian Dental Aptitude Test.

Purpose: "Designed to measure general academic achievement, comprehension of scientific information, perceptual ability, and manual dexterity."
Population: Canadian dental school applicants.
Publication Dates: 1946-2005.
Scores: 7: Reading Comprehension, Natural Sciences (Biology, General Chemistry, Total), Perceptual Ability Test, Chalk Carving Test, Academic Average.
Administration: Group.
Price Data: Available from publisher.
Time: 235(330) minutes in 2 sessions.
Comments: Based on the Dental Admission Testing program (772).
Authors: Department of Testing Services, American Dental Association.
Publisher: American Dental Association.

[401]
Canadian Test of Cognitive Skills.

Purpose: Designed to assess the academic aptitude important for scholastic success of students in grades 2 through 12.
Population: Grades 2–12.
Publication Dates: 1992–1996.
Acronym: Canadian TCS.
Scores, 4: Sequences, Memory, Analogies, Verbal Reasoning.
Administration: Group.
Levels, 5: Level 1 (Grades 2–3); Level 2 (Grades 4–5); Level 3 (Grades 6–7); Level 4 (Grades 8–9); Level 5 (Grades 10–12+).
Price Data, 2005: C$85 per 35 consumable test booklets (Level 1); $105 per 35 reusable test booklets (specify Level 2–5); $12 per 35 practice tests including directions; $65 per 50 machine-scorable answer sheets (specify level); $28 per 25 U-Score answer sheets; $1.50 per scoring keys (specify level); $17 per 50 individual record sheets; $1.50 per class record sheet; $8 per examiner's manual (1992, 26 pages; specify level); $32 per norms book (1992, 154 pages); $21 per handbook and technical bulletin (1996, 87 pages); $50 per Multi-Level specimen set; $25 per Primary, Junior, or Senior specimen set.
Time: (52) minutes for Level 1; (55) minutes for Level 2–5.
Comments: A Practice Test (15–20 minute administration time) is available and is recommended to be administered at least one day prior to the actual testing session; adapted from Test of Cognitive Skills, Second Edition (T5:2677).

Authors: Canadian Test Centre, Educational Services.
Publisher: Canadian Test Centre, Educational Assessment Services [Canada].
Cross References: For reviews by Martine Hébert and Susan J. Maller, see 13:45.

[402]
Canadian Tests of Basic Skills, Forms K and L.

Purpose: Constructed to measure growth in the fundamental skills crucial to day-to-day learning.
Population: Grades K–2, 3–8, and 9–12.
Publication Dates: 1955–1997.
Acronym: CTBS.
Scores, 12: Vocabulary, Reading Comprehension, Spelling, Capitalization, Punctuation, Usage, Reference Materials, Math Concepts & Estimation, Math Problems & Data, Math Computation, Science, Maps & Diagrams.
Administration: Group.
Time: (280) minutes for Grades 3-8 Form K; (100) for Grades 3-8 Form L.
Comments: Scoring service available from publisher; statistical information available from publisher.
Authors: A. N. Hieronymus, H. D. Hoover, E. F. Lindquist, and others (original Level 5–14 tests); Dale P. Scannell and others (original Level 15–18 tests); Ethel King-Shaw and others (Canadian adaptation).
Publisher: Nelson, A Thomson Company [Canada].
a) PRIMARY BATTERY FORM K.
Population: Grades K.1–1.5, K.8–1.9, 1.7–2.6, 2.5–3.5.
Levels, 4: 5, 6, 7, 8.
Price Data, 2005: $4 per test booklet; $11 per Directions for Administration; $13.40 per scoring key and skill guide; $40.10 per norms booklet; $40.10 per Teacher's Handbook; $12.10 per 10 class record folders; $12.10 per 10 profile charts; $17.50 per 35 student profile charts (K and L); $181.10 per score conversion software; $13.80 per preview kit.
b) LEVELS 9–14 FORM K.
Population: Grades 3–8.
Levels, 6: 9, 10, 11, 12, 13, 14.
Price Data: $4.20 per test booklet (Language Arts, or Math & Science); $31.10 per 35 answer sheets (select level); $8.70 per Directions for Administration; $21.80 per scoring mask (select level); $40.10 per norms booklet; $40.10 per Teacher's Handbook; $12.10 per 10 class record folders; $12.10 per 10 profile charts; $17.50 per 35 student profile charts; $246 per score conversion software; $21.20 per preview kit.
c) LEVELS 15–18 FORM K.
Population: Grades 9–12.

Levels, 3: 15, 16, 17/18.
Price Data: $4.20 per test booklet (English, or Math & Science); $31.10 per 35 answer sheets; $8.70 per Directions for Administration; $17.95 per scoring mask (select level); $40.10 per norms booklet; $40.10 per Teacher's Handbook; $12.10 per 10 class record folders; $12.10 per 10 profile charts; $17.50 per 35 student profile charts; $181.10 per score conversion software; $17.60 per preview kit.
d) LEVELS 9–14 FORM L.
Population: Grades 3–8.
Levels, 6: 9, 10, 11, 12, 13, 14.
Price Data: $5.20 per test booklet; $31.10 per 35 answer sheets; $8.70 per Directions for Administration; $21.80 per scoring mask (select level); $40.10 per norms booklet; $40.10 per Teacher's Handbook; $12.10 per 10 class record folders; $12.10 per 10 profile charts; $17.50 per 35 student profile charts; $246 per score conversion software; $14.80 per preview kit.
Cross References: See T5:389 (14 references) and T4:375 (5 references); for reviews by John O. Anderson and by Jean-Jacques Bernier and Martine Hébert of an earlier edition, see 11:55 (9 references); see also T3:363 (15 references) and 8:11 (1 reference); for a review by L. B. Birch of an earlier edition, see 7:6.

[403]
Cardall Test of Practical Judgement— Revised.

Purpose: To measure problem-solving ability in everyday life.
Population: Adults in business and industry.
Publication Dates: 1942–1999.
Scores, 3: Factual, Empathetic, Total.
Administration: Group.
Price Data, 2005: $22 per review set including manual (1961, 4 pages); $55 per 25 test booklets.
Foreign Language Edition: French edition available.
Time: (30) minutes.
Author: Alfred J. Cardall.
Publisher: Institute of Psychological Research, Inc. [Canada].
Cross References: See 6:1102 (4 references) and 4:784 (6 references); for reviews by Glen U. Cleeton and Howard R. Taylor of an earlier edition, see 3:694.

[404]
Career Ability Placement Survey.

Purpose: Designed to measure abilities as they relate to careers.
Population: Junior high, high school, college, and adults.
Publication Dates: 1976–1995.

Acronym: CAPS.

Scores: Scores in 14 COPSystem Career Clusters: Science-Professional, Science-Skilled, Technology-Professional, Technology-Skilled, Consumer Economics, Outdoor, Business-Professional, Business-Skilled, Clerical, Communication, Arts-Professional, Arts-Skilled, Service-Professional, Service-Skilled; and 8 ability scores: Mechanical Reasoning, Spatial Relations, Verbal Reasoning, Numerical Ability, Language Usage, Word Knowledge, Perceptual Speed and Accuracy, Manual Speed and Dexterity.

Administration: Group.

Price Data: Available from publisher.

Time: (5) minutes per test; (50) minutes for entire battery.

Authors: Lila F. Knapp and Robert R. Knapp.

Publisher: EdITS/Educational and Industrial Testing Service.

Cross References: See T5:395 (1 reference) and T4:382 (1 reference).

[405]
Career Anchors: Discovering Your Real Values, Revised Edition.

Purpose: Designed to help a person identify their career anchor, uncover their real values, and use them to make better career choices.

Population: Adults.

Publication Date: 1990.

Scores, 8: Technical/Functional Competence, General Managerial Competence, Autonomy/Independence, Security/Stability, Entrepreneurial Creativity, Service/Dedication to a Cause, Pure Challenge, Lifestyle.

Administration: Group.

Price Data: Price information available from publisher for complete kit including instrument (67 pages) and trainer's manual (20 pages).

Time: (180–240) minutes.

Comments: Self-rating plus interview with a partner.

Author: Edgar H. Schein.

Publisher: Jossey-Bass, A Wiley Company.

Cross References: See T5:396 (1 reference); for reviews by Michael B. Bunch and Gary J. Robertson, see 13:46.

[406]
Career & Life Explorer.

Purpose: Designed to "engage youths in thinking about themselves and in planning their future."

Population: Grades 5-12.

Publication Date: 2002.

Acronym: CLE.

Scores: No formal scores; 6 interest groups: Realistic, Investigative, Artistic, Social, Enterprising, Conventional.

Administration: Individual or group.

Price Data, 2006: $29.95 per complete kit includint 25 test booklets and 1 administrator's guide (12 pages).

Time: (55-65) minutes.

Comments: Self-guided, self-scored, and self-interpreted; includes a "My Ideal Job" poster.

Author: Michael Farr.

Publisher: JIST Publishing, Inc.

[407]
Career Assessment Inventory™—The Enhanced Version.

Purpose: A vocational interest assessment tool focusing on careers requiring "various amounts of post-secondary education."

Population: Grade 9 through adult.

Publication Dates: 1975–1994.

Scores, 142: 6 themes (Realistic, Investigative, Artistic, Social, Enterprising, Conventional), 25 basic interest (Mechanical/Fixing, Electronics, Carpentry, Manual/Skilled Trades, Protective Service, Athletics/Sports, Nature/Outdoors, Animal Service, Mathematics, Scientific Research/Development, Medical Science, Writing, Creative Arts, Performing/Entertaining, Educating, Community Service, Medical Service, Religious Activities, Public Speaking, Law/Politics, Management/Supervision, Sales, Office Practices, Clerical/Clerking, Food Service), 111 occupational (Accountant, Advertising Artist/Writer, Advertising Executive, Aircraft Mechanic, Architect, Athletic Trainer, Author/Writer, Auto Mechanic, Bank Manager, Bank Teller, Barber/Hairstylist, Biologist, Bookkeeper, Bus Driver, Buyer/Merchandiser, Cafeteria Worker, Camera Repair Technician, Card/Gift Shop Manager, Carpenter, Caterer, Chef, Chemist, Child Care Assistant, Chiropractor, Computer Programmer, Computer Scientist, Conservation Officer, Cosmetologist, Counselor-Chemical Dependency, Court Reporter, Data Input Operator, Dental Assistant, Dental Hygienist, Dental Lab Technician, Dentist, Dietitian, Drafter, Economist, Elected Public Official, Electrician, Electronic Technician, Elementary School Teacher, Emergency Medical Technician, Engineer, Executive Housekeeper, Farmer/Rancher, Firefighter, Florist, Food Service Manager, Forest Ranger, Guidance Counselor, Hardware Store Manager, Hospital Administrator, Hotel/Motel Manager, Insurance Agent, Interior Designer, Janitor/Janitress, Lawyer, Legal Assistant, Librarian, Machinist, Mail Carrier, Manufacturing Representative, Mathematician, Math-Science Teacher, Medical Assistant, Medical Lab Technician, Military Enlisted, Military Officer, Musical Instrument Repair, Musician, Newspaper Reporter, Nurse Aide, Nurse/LPN, Nurse/RN, Occupational Therapist, Operating Room Technician, Orthotist/Prosthetist, Painter, Park Ranger, Personnel Manager, Pharmacist, Pharmacy Technician, Photographer, Physical Therapist, Physician, Piano Technician, Pipefitter/Plumber, Police Officer, Printer, Private Investigator, Psychologist, Purchasing Agent, Radio/TV Repair, Radiologic Technician, Real Estate Agent, Religious Leader, Reservation Agent, Respiratory Therapy Technician, Restaurant Manager, Secretary, Security Guard, Sheet Metal Worker, Surveyor, Teacher Aide, Telephone Repair Technician, Tool and Die Maker, Travel Agent, Truck Driver, Veterinarian, Waiter/Waitress.

Administration: Group or individual.

Price Data, 2006: $33 per manual; $55 per mail-in starter kit including manual and 3 answer sheets with test items to conduct and receive 3 interpretive reports; $52 per Q Local starter kit including manual, 3 answer sheets with test items, and 3 Q Local administrations; $21 per 25 Q Local answer sheets with test items; $8.65 per Q Local interpretive reports; $5.30 per Q Local profile reports; $10.65 per mail-in interpretive answer sheets with test items; $7.30 per mail-in profile reports; quantity discounts available for the reports; price information available from publisher for Spanish/French Canadian materials.

Time: (35–40) minutes.

Author: Charles B. Johansson.

Publisher: Pearson Assessments.

Cross References: See T5:398 (4 references); for a review by James B. Rounds, see 10:43 (2 references); see also T3:367 (1 reference); for reviews by Jack L. Bodden and Paul R. Lohnes of an earlier edition, see 8:993.

[408]
Career Assessment Inventory™—Vocational Version.

Purpose: "A vocational interest assessment tool for individuals planning to enter occupations requiring 0-2 years of post-secondary training."

Population: Grade 9 through adult.

Publication Dates: 1973–1994.

Scores, 125: 2 Administrative Indices (Total Responses, Response Patterning), 4 Nonoccupational (Fine Arts-Mechanical, Occupational Extroversion-Introversion, Educational Orientation, Variability of Interests), 6 General Themes (Realistic, Investigative, Artistic, Social, Enterprising, Conventional), 22 Basic Interest Area Scales (Mechanical/Fixing, Electronics, Carpentry, Manual/Skilled Trades, Agriculture, Nature/Outdoors, Animal Service, Science, Numbers, Writing, Performing/Entertaining, Arts/Crafts, Social Service, Teaching, Child Care, Medical Service, Religious Activities, Business, Sales, Office Practices, Clerical/Clerking, Food Service), 91 Occupational Scales (Aircraft Mechanic, Auto Mechanic, Bus Driver, Camera Repair Technician, Carpenter, Conservation Officer, Dental Laboratory Technician, Drafter, Electrician, Emergency Medical Technician, Farmer/Rancher, Firefighter, Forest Ranger, Hardware Store Manager, Janitor/Janitress, Machinist, Mail Carrier, Musical Instrument Repair, Navy Enlisted, Orthodontist/Prosthetist, Painter, Park Ranger, Pipefitter/Plumber, Police Officer, Printer, Radio/TV Repair, Security Guard, Sheet Metal Worker, Telephone Repair, Tool/Die Maker, Truck Driver, Veterinary Technician, Chiropractor, Computer Programmer, Dental Hygienist, Electronic Technician, Math-Science Teacher, Medical Laboratory Technician, Radiological Technician, Respiratory Therapeutic Technician, Surveyor, Advertising Artist/Writer, Advertising Executive, Author/Writer, Counselor-Chemical Dependency, Interior Designer, Legal Assistant, Librarian, Musician, Newspaper Reporter, Photographer, Piano Technician, Athletic Trainer, Child Care Assistant, Cosmetologist, Elementary School Teacher, Licensed Practical Nurse, Nurse Aide, Occupational Therapist Assistant, Operating Room Technician, Physical Therapist Assistant, Registered Nurse, Barber/Hairstylist, Buyer/Merchandiser, Card/Gift Shop Manager, Caterer, Florist, Food Service Manager, Hotel/Motel Manager, Insurance Agent, Manufacturing Representative, Personnel Manager, Private Investigator, Purchasing Agent, Real Estate Agent, Reservation Agent, Restaurant Manager, Travel Agent, Accountant, Bank Teller, Bookkeeper, Cafeteria Worker, Court Reporter, Data Entry Operator, Dental Assistant, Executive Housekeeper, Medical Assistant, Pharmacy Technician, Secretary, Teacher Aide, Waiter/Waitress).

Administration: Group.

Price Data, 2006: $55 per manual (1984, 152 pages); $55 per mail-in starter kit including manual and 3 answer sheets with test items to conduct and receive 3 interpretive reports; $52 per Q Local starter kit including manual, 3 answer sheets with test items, and 3 Q Local administrations; $21 per 25 Q Local answer sheets with test items; $8.65 per Q Local interpretive reports; $5.30 per Q Local profile reports; $10.65 per mail-in interprtive answer sheets with test items; $7.30 per mail-in profile reports; quantity discounts available for the reports; price information for Spanish/French Canadian materials available from publisher.

Foreign Language Editions: Spanish and French editions available.

Time: (30–45) minutes.

Author: Charles B. Johansson.

Publisher: Pearson Assessments.

Cross References: See T5:399 (5 references) and T4:385 (4 references); for reviews by Jerard F. Kehoe and Nicholas A. Vacc, see 11:59 (1 reference); see also T3:367 (1 reference); for reviews by Jack L. Bodden and Paul R. Lohnes of an earlier edition, see 8:993.

[409]
Career Attitudes and Strategies Inventory: An Inventory for Understanding Adult Careers.

Purpose: "Developed to assess some common attitudes, feelings, experiences, and obstacles that influence the careers of employed and unemployed adults."
Population: Adults seeking vocational counseling.
Publication Dates: 1992–1994.
Acronym: CASI.
Scores: 9 scales: Job Satisfaction, Work Involvement, Skill Development, Dominant Style, Career Worries, Interpersonal Abuse, Family Commitment, Risk-Taking Style, Geographical Barriers.
Administration: Individual.
Price Data, 2005: $117 per introductory kit including professional manual (1994, 53 pages), 25 inventory booklets, 25 hand-scorable answer sheets, and 25 interpretive summary booklets.
Time: (35) minutes.
Comments: Also includes Career Obstacles Checklist designed to assess "personal problems that may influence an individual's job situation."
Authors: John L. Holland and Gary D. Gottfredson.
Publisher: Psychological Assessment Resources, Inc.
Cross References: For reviews by Michael B. Brown and Richard T. Kinnier, see 13:47.

[410]
Career Beliefs Inventory.

Purpose: Designed to assist people to identify career beliefs that may influence their career goals.
Population: 13 years and above.
Publication Dates: 1991–1998.
Acronym: CBI.
Scores, 26: Administrative Index, Employment Status, Career Plans, Acceptance of Uncertainty, Openness, Achievement, College Education, Intrinsic Satisfaction, Peer Equality, Structured Work Environment, Control, Responsibility, Approval of Others, Self-Other Comparisons, Occupation/College Variation, Career Path Flexibility, Post-Training Transition, Job Experimentation, Relocation, Improving Self, Persisting While Uncertain, Taking Risks, Learning Job Skills, Negotiating/Searching, Overcoming Obstacles, Working Hard.
Administration: Group.
Price Data, 2001: $60.60 per 25 test booklets; $78.20 per 10 prepaid answer sheets (price includes scoring by publisher); $49.40 per 10 self-scorable booklets; $47.80 per manual (46 pages); $69.60 per preview kit including item booklet, answer sheet, manual, and Exploring Your Career Beliefs workbook.
Time: (20–30) minutes.
Comments: Available in self-scorable booklets.

Author: John D. Krumboltz.
Publisher: CPP, Inc.
Cross References: See T5:401 (3 references); for reviews by David L. Bolton and Robert M. Guion, see 12:64 (9 references).

[411]
Career Counseling Personal Data Form.

Purpose: "Designed to provide [background] information useful in career counseling."
Population: Vocational counselees
Publication Date: 1962.
Scores: No scores.
Administration: Group.
Manual: No manual.
Price Data, 2006: $94.20 per package of forms; $43.50 per specimen set.
Time: (30-40) minutes.
Author: John B. Ahrens.
Publisher: Martin M. Bruce, Ph.D.

[412]
Career Decision Scale.

Purpose: Developed to provide "an estimate of career indecision and its antecedents."
Population: Grades 9–12 and college.
Publication Dates: 1976–1987.
Scores, 2: Certainty, Career Indecision.
Administration: Group or individual.
Price Data, 2006: $65 per introductory kit including 50 test booklets and manual (1987, 28 pages).
Time: (10-15) minutes.
Authors: Samuel H. Osipow, Clarke G. Carney (test), Jane Winer (test), Barbara Yanico (test), and Maryanne Koschier (test).
Publisher: Psychological Assessment Resources, Inc.
Cross References: See T5:404 (47 references) and T4:390 (49 references); for reviews by Lenore W. Harmon and David O. Herman, see 9:194 (4 references).

[413]
Career Decision Self-Efficacy Scale.

Purpose: "Measures an individual's degree of belief that he/she can successfully complete tasks necessary to making career decisions."
Population: College students.
Publication Dates: 1983–1994.
Acronym: CDMSE.
Scores, 6: Self-Appraisal, Occupational Information, Goal Selection, Planning, Problem Solving, Total.
Administration: Group.
Price Data: Available from publisher (now free of charge).
Time: Administration time not reported.

Comments: A 25-item short form is also available.
Authors: Nancy E. Betz and Karen M. Taylor.
Publisher: Nancy E. Betz (the author).
Cross References: For reviews by James K. Benish and Richard W. Johnson, see 14:62; see also T5:403 (1 reference).

[414]
Career Directions Inventory [Second Edition].

Purpose: "Designed to identify areas of greater or lesser interest from among a wide variety of occupations."
Population: Adolescents and adults ages 15 years or older.
Publication Dates: 1986–2003.
Acronym: CDI.
Scores: 15 Basic Interest Scales (Administration, Art, Clerical, Food Service, Industrial Art, Health Service, Outdoors, Personal Service, Sales, Science, Teaching/Social Service, Writing, Assertive, Persuasive, Systematic); 7 General Occupational Themes (Realistic/Practical, Enterprising, Artistic/Communicative, Social/Helping, Investigative/Logical, Conventional, Serving); 27 Job Clusters (Computer and Mathematical Science, Science and Engineering, Electronic Technology, Medical and Health Care, Health Record Technology, Social Science, Banking and Accounting, Funeral Services, Architectural Technology/Drafting and Design, Word Processing and Administrative Assistant, Public and Protective Services, Art, Social Services, Sales, Administration, Performing Arts, Communication Arts, Food Services, Education, Hospitality and Travel Services, Law Enforcement, Agriculture and Animal Science, Personal Care, Renewable Resource Technology, Marketing and Merchandising, Skilled Trades, Library Science).
Administration: Group.
Price Data, 2006: $25 per examination kit including manual on CD (2003, 116 pages) and question and answer document for the Mail-in Extended Report; $15 per manual on CD; $85-$95 per 10 Mail-in Extended Reports; $105 per SigmaSoft CDI for Windows Software including complete installation package and 10 coupons; $8 per online password.
Time: 30 minutes.
Comments: Test may be administered through mail-in scoring, SigmaSoft for Windows Software, or via the internet at www.sigmatesting.com.
Author: Douglas N. Jackson.
Publisher: Sigma Assessment Systems, Inc.
Cross References: For reviews by Darrell L. Sabers and Fredrick A. Schrank of an earlier edition, see 9:44.

[415]
Career Exploration Inventory: A Guide for Exploring Work, Leisure, and Learning, Third Edition.

Purpose: Designed to help participants explore and plan three major areas in their lives-work, leisure activities, and education or learning.
Population: Employed and unemployed youth and adults.
Publication Dates: 1992-2006.
Acronym: CEI.
Scores: 17 occupational categories: Agriculture and Natural Resources, Architecture and Construction, Arts and Communication, Business and Administration, Education and Training, Finance and Insurance, Government and Public Administration, Health Science, Hospitality, Tourism and Recreation, Human Service, Information Technology, Law and Public Safety, Manufacturing, Retail and Wholesale Sales, Scientific Research/Engineering and Mathematics, Transportation/Distribution and Logistics.
Administration: Group or individual.
Price Data, 2006: $36.95 per 25 inventories including free administrator's guide.
Time: (30) minutes.
Comments: Occupational categories correspond to the U.S. Department of Education Career Clusters; 12-panel foldout; self-scoring and self-interpreting; no other components needed.
Author: John J. Liptak.
Publisher: JIST Publishing, Inc.
Cross References: For reviews by Bert A. Goldman and Douglas J. McRae of an earlier edition, see 13:49.

[416]
Career Exploration Series, 1992 Revision.

Purpose: Designed for career guidance using "a series of six job interest inventories that focus on specific occupational fields."
Population: Grades 7–12 and college and adults.
Publication Dates: 1979–1992.
Acronym: CES.
Scores: 6 areas: Agriculture–Forestry–Conservation, Science–Mathematics–Health, Business, Industrial, Consumer Economics, Design–Art–Communications.
Administration: Group.
Price Data: Available from publisher.
Time: (50–60) minutes.
Comments: Self-administered and self-scored interest inventories.
Authors: Arthur Cutler, Francis Ferry, Robert Kauk, and Robert Robinett.
Publisher: CFKR Career Materials.
Cross References: For a review by Herbert C. Rudman, see 13:50; for reviews by Mark Pope and

William I. Sauser, Jr. of an earlier edition, see 11:60; for reviews by Bruce R. Fretz and Robert B. Slaney of the original edition, see 9:196.

[417]
Career Factors Inventory.

Purpose: Designed to provide an understanding of career decision-making readiness.
Population: Ages 13 and over.
Publication Date: 1997.
Acronym: CFI.
Scores, 4: Need for Career Information, Need for Self-Knowledge, Career Choice Anxiety, Generalized Indecisiveness.
Administration: Group.
Price Data, 2001: $33.30 per kit including self-scorable item booklet and answer sheet, interpretation, and Applications and Technical Guide (37 pages); $19.10 per 10 self-scorable booklets; $2.70 per single self-scorable booklet; $34.50 per Applications and Technical Guide.
Time: (5–10) minutes.
Comments: Inventory is untimed; also part of the skillsone.com website.
Authors: Judy M. Chartrand, Steven B. Robbins, and Weston H. Morrill.
Publisher: CPP, Inc.
Cross References: For a review by Ayres D'Costa, see 14:63.

[418]
Career Guidance Inventory.

Purpose: "Designed to provide measures of relative interest in postsecondary instructional programs."
Population: Students and prospective students at trade, vocational, or technical school, or at community college.
Publication Dates: 1972–1989.
Acronym: CGI.
Scores, 47: Agribusiness and Agricultural Production, Renewable Natural Resources, Business (Accounting and Finance, Data Processing, Clerical/Typing/Word Processing, Office Supervision and Management, Secretarial), Marketing and Distribution (General Marketing, Financial Services, Hospitality/Recreation/Tourism, Real Estate), Communications and Communications Technologies, Computer and Information Sciences, Cosmetology and Barbering, Engineering and Related Technologies (Architectural, Civil, Electrical and Electronic, Environmental Control, Industrial Production, Mechanical Engineering, Mining and Petroleum), Allied Health (Dental Services, Diagnostic and Treatment Services, Miscellaneous Services, Medical Laboratory Technologies, Mental Health/Human Services, Nursing and Related Services, Rehabilita-tion Services), Vocational Home Economics (Child Care and Guidance, Clothing/Apparel/Textiles, Food Production/Management/Services, Institutional/Home Management/Supporting Services), Protective Services, Construction Trades (Brickmason/Stonemason/Tile Setting, Carpentry, Electrical and Power Transmission Installation, Plumbing/Pipefitting/Steamfitting), Mechanics and Repairers (Electrical and Electronic Equipment Repair, Heating/Air Conditioning/Refrigeration Mechanics, Industrial Equipment Maintenance and Repair, Vehicle and Mobile Equipment), Precision Production (Drafting, Graphic and Printing Communications, Precision Metal Work, Woodworking), Transportation and Material Moving, Visual Arts (Fine Arts).
Administration: Group.
Price Data: Price information available from publisher for reusable test booklet, answer sheet/interpretation guides, administrator's manual (1989, 43 pages), and specimen set of all Career Guidance Inventory and Educational Interest Inventory (859) components.
Time: [45–60] minutes.
Comments: Self-administered, self-scored.
Author: James E. Oliver.
Publisher: Wintergreen/Orchard House, Inc.
Cross References: For reviews by E. Jack Asher, Jr., and Michael B. Bunch, see 11:61; for a review by James B. Rounds, Jr., of an earlier edition, see 9:197; for a review by Bert W. Westbrook, see 8:996.

[419]
Career Interest Inventory.

Purpose: "Designed to assist students in making decisions concerning their educational and vocational plans."
Publication Dates: 1989–1996.
Administration: Group or individual.
Price Data, 2002: $18 per examination kit including Level 1 machine-scorable answer document, Level 2 hand-scorable booklet, directions for administering, and student profile; $51 per counselor's manual (1991, 120 pages); $18 per 25 Exploring Interests: An Introduction to the Career Interest Inventory; $7 per directions for administering 1990, 29 pages); $2.65 scoring charge per Level 1 answer document; $1 for first copy and $.27 per each additional copy of individual report; $.92 for first copy and $.06 per each additional copy of counselor's report (by Teacher/Counselor or School); $.86 for first copy and $.28 per each additional copy of student record label; $.68 for first copy and $.16 per each additional copy of occupational interest report (by School); $.44 for first copy and $29.75 per set of career planning summary (by Teacher/Counselor); $.35 for first copy and $26.50 per set of career planning summary (by

School); $.24 for first copy and $22.05 per set of career planning summary (by District); $.61 per pupil for student data diskette; $25 for first 1,000 and $10 per each additional 1,000 for return of test booklets; $25 for first 1,000 plus $10 per each additional 1,000 for return of answer documents; $25 for first 1,000 plus $10 per each additional 1,000 for return of mixed documents.

Time: (30–40) minutes.

Author: The Psychological Corporation.

Publisher: PsychCorp, A brand of Harcourt Assessment, Inc.

a) LEVEL 1.

Population: Grades 7–9.

Scores, 47: 15 Occupational Interests (Social Science, Clerical Services, Health Services, Agriculture, Customer Services, Fine Arts, Mathematics and Science, Building Trades, Educational Services, Legal Services, Transportation, Sales, Management, Benchwork, Machine Operation), 16 High School Subject Interests (Speech or Drama, Metal Shop or Woodworking, Mathematics, Auto Repair, Science, Cooking or Sewing, Art or Music, Farming or Livestock Care, Newspaper Writing, Typing or Office Machines, Social Studies, Health Care, Creative Writing, Computers, English or Literature, Bookkeeping or Office Practices), 16 High School Activity Interests (Mathematics Club, Farming Club, Speech or Debate Team, School Library Aide, School Play, Automobile Club, Science Fair, Teacher's Aide, Student Government, Office Helper or Assistant, School Literary Magazine, School Officer, Photography Club, Business Club, School Newspaper, Computer Club).

Price Data: $59 per 25 hand-scorable booklets; $59 per 25 Type 1 machine-scorable answer documents; Type 2 machine-scorable answer documents available from publisher by special arrangement.

b) LEVEL 2.

Population: Grades 10–12 and adults.

Scores, 35: 15 Occupational Interests (same as Level 1), 20 Post-High School Course Interests (Marketing or Sales, Computer Programming, Electronics or Electrical Trades, Plumbing or Welding, Automotive Repair, Carpentry or Home Building, Word Processing or Typing, Haircutting or Styling, Bookkeeping or Office Practices, Cooking or Sewing, Music or Art, Farming or Livestock Care, Mathematics or Science, English or Foreign Language, Business Law or Management, Creative Writing, Speech or Drama, Photography, Health Care, Newspaper Writing).

Price Data: $64 per 25 hand-scorable booklets; $64 per 25 Type 1 machine-scorable answer documents; Type 2 machine-scorable answer documents available from publisher by special arrangement.

Cross References: For reviews by William D. Schafer and Sheldon Zedeck, see 13:51.

[420]
Career Occupational Preference System, Interest Inventory, Form R.

Purpose: Designed to measure interests as they relate to careers using simplified language.

Population: Grade 6 through high school.

Publication Dates: 1984–1992.

Acronym: COPS-R.

Scores: Scores in the 14 COPSystem Career Clusters: Science-Professional, Science-Skilled, Technology-Professional, Technology-Skilled, Consumer Economics, Outdoor, Business-Professional, Business-Skilled, Clerical, Communication, Arts-Professional, Arts-Skilled, Service-Professional, Service-Skilled.

Administration: Group.

Price Data: Available from publisher.

Time: (20) minutes.

Authors: Lila F. Knapp and Robert R. Knapp.

Publisher: EdITS/Educational and Industrial Testing Service.

Cross References: See T5:414 (2 references and T4:399 (12 references).

[421]
Career Occupational Preference System, Intermediate Inventory.

Purpose: To measure career interests and provide a rating of interests based on knowledge of school subjects and activities familiar to elementary and intermediate grade students.

Population: Elementary through high school with 4th grade reading level.

Publication Dates: 1981–1997.

Acronym: COPS-II.

Scores: Scores in 14 COPSystem Career Clusters: Science-Professional, Science-Skilled, Technology-Professional, Technology-Skilled, Consumer Economics, Outdoor, Business-Professional, Business-Skilled, Clerical, Communication, Arts-Professional, Arts-Skilled, Service-Professional, Service-Skilled.

Administration: Group.

Price Data: Available from publisher.

Time: (15–20) minutes.

Authors: Robert R. Knapp and Lila F. Knapp.

Publisher: EdITS/Educational and Industrial Testing Service.

Cross References: See T5:415 (1 reference).

[422]
Career Occupational Preference System—Professional Level Interest Inventory.

Purpose: Designed to measure career interest for those wanting to focus on the professional level careers.

Population: College and adult professionals, college-bound senior high school students.

Publication Dates: 1982–1989.

Acronym: COPS-P.

Scores: Scores in the 16 COPSystem Career Clusters: Service-Social, Service-Instructional, Science-Physical, Science-Medical/Life, Technology-Civil, Technology-Electrical, Technology-Mechanical, Outdoor-Agribusiness, Outdoor-Nature, Business-Management, Business-Finance, Computation, Communication-Written, Communication-Oral, Arts-Design, Arts-Performing.

Administration: Group.

Price Data: Available from publisher.

Time: (15–20) minutes.

Authors: Lisa Knapp-Lee, Lila F. Knapp, Robert R. Knapp.

Publisher: EdITS/Educational and Industrial Testing Service.

Cross References: For reviews by Mark A. Albanese and Jeffrey A. Jenkins, see 14:65; see also T5:416 (1 reference).

[423]
Career Orientation Placement and Evaluation Survey.

Purpose: Designed to measure values having a demonstrated effect on vocational motivation.

Population: Grade 7 through high school, college, and adult.

Publication Dates: 1981–1995.

Acronym: COPES.

Scores: Scores in 8 work values dimensions: Investigative v. Accepting, Practical v. Carefree, Independence v. Conformity, Leadership v. Supporting, Orderliness v. Flexibility, Recognition v. Privacy, Aesthetic v. Realistic, Social v. Reserved; and 14 COPSystem Career Clusters: Science-Professional, Science-Skilled, Technology-Professional, Technology-Skilled, Consumer Economics, Outdoor, Business-Professional, Business-Skilled, Clerical, Communication, Arts-Professional, Arts-Skilled, Service-Professional, Service-Skilled.

Administration: Group.

Price Data: Available from publisher.

Time: (15–20) minutes.

Authors: Robert R. Knapp and Lila F. Knapp.

Publisher: EdITS/Educational and Industrial Testing Service.

[424]
Career Planning Survey.

Purpose: Intended "to help students in grades 8–10 identify and explore personally relevant occupations and high school courses ... to provide students with a general sense of direction for career exploration ... show students how occupations relate to each other, thus giving students a context in which to explore their career options."

Population: Grades 8–10.

Publication Dates: 1997–2001.

Scores, 4: (UNIACT) Interest Inventory, Inventory of Work-Relevant Abilities, and 2 ability measures (Reading Skills, Numerical Skills).

Administration: Group.

Price Data, 2006: $4.10 per Assessment Set Option A (with ability measures); $3.50 per Assessment Set Option B (without ability measures) (each set includes an answer sheet [scored by ACT], a student guidebook, prepaid scoring, and two copies of the student report); $13.00 per examination kit (with detailed information and sample materials for the preview of Career Planning Survey, including test booklet, Directions for Administration, Counselor's Manual [2001, 48 pages], and student guidebook [2001, 24 pages]); $.75 per reusable test booklet; $8.60 per Counselor's Manual; $2.35 per Directions for Administration; volume discounts available.

Time: (90) minutes (Option A); (45) minutes (Option B).

Authors: ACT, Inc.

Publisher: ACT, Inc.

Cross References: For a review by Sandra A. Loew, see 15:44.

[425]
Career Profile +.

Purpose: "Predicts an individual's probability of success in an insurance sales career."

Population: Candidates for financial services sales representative positions.

Publication Dates: 1983-2000.

Administration: Individual.

Price Data: Available from publisher.

Foreign Language Editions: English-speaking Canada and French-speaking Canada editions available; U.S. Spanish and Chinese editions of nonstudent version are available.

Time: Untimed.

Comments: Profiles processed by publisher.

Authors: LIMRA International.

Publisher: LIMRA International.

a) STUDENT CAREER PROFILE.
Population: High school–college student.
Scores: Career Profile rating.

Comments: Career Profile rating indicates probability of success in financial services sales; versions available for Financial Services Sales, Life and Health Sales, and Multiple-Line & Property-Casualty Sales.

1) *Personality Assessment.*

Scores: 4 personality characteristics: Persuasiveness, Energy, Achievement Drive, Initiative & Persistence.

b) NONSTUDENT CAREER PROFILE.

Population: Inexperienced candidates.

Scores: Same as above.

Comments: Versions available for Financial Services Sales, Life and Health Sales, and Multiple-Line & Property-Casualty Sales.

1) *Personality Assessment.*

Scores: Same as *a*-1 above.

Cross References: For reviews by Ayres G. D'Costa and Michael S. Trevisan, see 13:52.

[426]
Career Thoughts Inventory.

Purpose: Constructed to " identify an individual who is likely to need career counseling and identify the nature of the individual's career problems."

Population: Adults, college students, and high school students.

Publication Dates: 1994–1996.

Acronym: CTI.

Scores, 4: Decision Making Confusion, Commitment Anxiety, External Conflict, Total.

Administration: Group.

Price Data, 2006: $185 per introductory kit including manual (1996, 99 pages), 25 test booklets, and 10 workbooks (1996, 39 pages).

Time: (7–15) minutes.

Authors: James P. Samson, Jr., Gary W. Peterson, Janet G. Lenz, Robert C. Reardon, and Denise E. Saunders.

Publisher: Psychological Assessment Resources, Inc.

Cross References: For a review by Janet H. Fontaine, see 14:66.

[427]
Career Transitions Inventory.

Purpose: "Designed to assess the resources and barriers" experienced "in making a career transition."

Population: Adults.

Publication Date: 1991.

Acronym: CTI.

Scores, 5: Readiness, Confidence, Personal Control, Support, Independence.

Administration: Group.

Manual: No manual.

Price Data: Available from author.

Time: Administration time not reported.

Author: Mary J. Heppner.

Publisher: Mary J. Heppner (the author).

Cross References: For reviews by Robert J. Drummond and Jean Powell Kirnan, see 15:45.

[428]
Career Values Card Sort.

Purpose: Defines factors that affect career satisfaction, the intensity of feelings about these factors, determines areas of value conflict and congruence, helps make career decisions.

Population: Adults.

Publication Dates: 1993–2002.

Scores: No scores.

Administration: Group or individual.

Price Data: Available from publisher

Time: (20–30) minutes.

Comments: Self-administered.

Author: Richard L. Knowdell.

Publisher: CareerTrainer.

Cross References: For reviews by Esther E. Diamond and Richard T. Kinnier, see 13:53.

[429]
Caregiver-Teacher Report Form.

Purpose: Designed "to assess behavioral/emotional problems and identify syndromes of problems that tend to occur together."

Population: Ages 1.5–5.

Publication Dates: 1997– 2000.

Acronym: C-TRF.

Scores: 10 Syndromes: Emotionally Reactive, Anxious/Depressed, Somatic Complaints, Withdrawn, Attention Problems, Aggressive Behavior; Internalizing, Externalizing, Total; DMS oriented scales: Affective Problems, Anxiety Problems, Attention Deficit/Hyperactivity Problems, Oppositional Defiant Problems, Pervasive Developmental Problems.

Administration: Group.

Price Data: Available from publisher.

Time: [10] minutes.

Comments: Ratings by daycare providers and preschool teachers.

Author: Thomas M. Achenbach.

Publisher: ASEBA Research Center for Children, Youth, and Families

Cross References: For reviews by Karen T. Carey and by Michael Furlong and Renee Pavelski, see 14:67.

[430]
Carey Temperament Scales.

Purpose: Designed to assess "temperamental characteristics in infants and children."

Population: Ages 1 month to 12 years-11 months.

Publication Dates: 1996–1998.

Acronym: CTS.

Scores: 9 categories of temperament: Activity, Rhythmicity, Approach, Adaptability, Intensity, Mood, Persistence, Distractibility, Threshold.

Administration: Individual.

Price Data: Price information available from publisher for questionnaires with hand scoring, software (diskette or CD), and online scoring are available or online at www.b-di.com.

Time: [15–20] minutes for administration; 2-3 minutes for software scoring; 10-15 minutes for hand scoring.

Comments: Parent/caregiver ratings of infant and child temperament; also assesses the caregiver's overall general impression of each category of temperament and provides a general manageability score; measures the nine NYLS temperament dimensions; or use in research and in clinical work with parents of preadolescent children; five separate questionnaires are included in the series, based on age levels in early infancy, infancy, toddlerhood, early childhood and middle childhood; computer scoring software on diskette, CDs and internet scoring are available (CDs are available for PC and Macintosh).

Authors: William B. Carey, Sean C. McDevitt, Barbara Medoff-Cooper, William Fullard, and Robin L. Hegvik.

Publisher: Behavioral-Developmental Initiatives.

Cross References: For reviews by Aimée Langlois and E. Jean Newman, see 14:68.

[431]
Caring Relationship Inventory.

Purpose: Designed to "measure the ... elements of love or caring in human relationships."

Population: Premarital and marital counselees.

Publication Dates: 1966–1975.

Acronym: CRI.

Scores, 7: Affection, Friendship, Eros, Empathy, Self-Love, Being Loved, Deficiency Love.

Administration: Individual.

Price Data: Available from publisher.

Time: (40) minutes.

Author: Everett L. Shostrom.

Publisher: EdITS/Educational and Industrial Testing Service.

Cross References: See T4:408 (3 references); for reviews by Donald L. Mosher and Robert F. Stahmann, see 8:333 (5 references); for a review by Albert Ellis, see 7:561; see also P:31 (1 reference).

[432]
Carlson Psychological Survey.

Purpose: Developed to assess and classify offenders quickly and accurately.

Population: Adult and adolescent offenders.

Publication Dates: 1982–1997.

Acronym: CPS.

Scores: 5 scale scores: Chemical Abuse, Thought Disturbance, Anti-Social Tendencies, Self-Depreciation, Validity.

Administration: Group or individual.

Price Data, 2006: $70 per examination kit including manual on CD (1982, 28 pages), 5 question and answer booklets, 5 scoring sheets, 5 profile sheets, and one machine-scorable question-and-answer document for an Extended Report; $15 per test manual on CD; $50 per 25 question-and-answer booklets; $50 per 25 response sheets (including 25 scoring sheets and 25 profile sheets); $65-$75 (depending on volume) per 10 machine-scorable question-and-answer booklets for Extended Reports; $105 per software package including disks, software manual for Windows, test manual, and 10 coupons for computer reports.

Foreign Language Editions: Psicologico Texto (PT) designed specifically for use with Spanish-literate offenders; question and answer booklets available in French and Spanish.

Time: 15 minutes.

Author: Kenneth A. Carlson.

Publisher: Sigma Assessment Systems, Inc.

Cross References: See T4:409 (2 references); for a review by H. C. Ganguli, see 9:203.

[433]
The Carolina Curriculum.

Purpose: Designed as an assessment and intervention program for use with young children who have mild to severe disabilities.

Population: Birth to age 5.

Publication Date: 2004.

Scores: 5 domains: Cognition, Communication, Social Adaptation, Fine Motor, Gross Motor.

Administration: Individual.

Price Data, 2004: $80 per 2-book set; $25 per 10 assessment and development progress charts; $125 per printable masters on CD-ROM; $44.95 per special bound book (specify level).

Time: Administration time not reported.

Comments: A criterion-referenced system that links assessment with intervention.

Authors: Nancy M. Johnson-Martin, Susan M. Attermeier, and Bonnie J. Hacker.

Publisher: Brookes Publishing Co., Inc.

a) THE CAROLINA CURRICULUM FOR INFANTS & TODDLERS WITH SPECIAL NEEDS, THIRD EDITION.

Population: Birth to 36 months.

Acronym: CCITSN.

Price Data: $44.95 per special-bound book (512 pages).

b) THE CAROLINA CURRICULUM FOR PRESCHOOLERS WITH SPECIAL NEEDS, SECOND EDITION.

Population: 24–60 months.

Acronym: CCPSN.
Price Data: $44.95 per special-bound book (448 pages).

[434]
Carolina Developmental Profile.

Purpose: "Designed to assist the teacher in establishing long-range objectives to increase developmental abilities in six areas: fine motor, gross motor, visual perception, reasoning, receptive language, and expressive language."
Population: Ages 2–5.
Publication Date: 1980.
Acronym: CDP.
Scores, 7: Fine Motor, Gross Motor, Visual Perception, Reasoning, Receptive Language, Expressive Language, Social/Emotional.
Administration: Individual.
Manual: No manual.
Price Data, 2003: $199.95 per complete kit including 10 scoring booklets, toy, supplies, and manipulatives; $14.95 per 10 scoring booklets.
Time: Administration time not reported.
Comments: "Criterion referenced" behavior checklist.
Authors: David L. Lillie and Gloria L. Harbin.
Publisher: Kaplan Early Learning Company.

[435]
Carolina Picture Vocabulary Test (for Deaf and Hearing Impaired).

Purpose: "To measure the receptive sign vocabulary in individuals where manual signing [is] the primary mode of communication."
Population: Deaf and hearing-impaired children ages 4–11.5 years.
Publication Date: 1985.
Acronym: CPVT.
Scores: Total score only.
Administration: Individual.
Price Data, 2006: $135 per complete program; $69 per picture book; $33 per 50 record forms; $43 per manual (38 pages).
Time: (10–15) minutes.
Authors: Thomas L. Layton and David W. Holmes.
Publisher: PRO-ED.
Cross References: For additional information, see 11:62 (1 reference).

[436]
Carroll Depression Scales.

Purpose: Designed as a measure of depression; providing diagnostic as well as level of severity information.
Population: Ages 18 and older.
Publication Date: 1998.
Scores, 5: Major Depression, Dysthymic Disorder, Melancholic and Atypical Features, HDRS, Total.

Administration: Group.
Price Data, 2006: $138 per complete kit including 25 CDS-R QuikScore™ forms, 25 Brief CDS QuikScore™ forms, and technical manual (96 pages); $50 per CDS-R 25 QuikScore™ forms (English or French-Canadian); $40 per 25 Brief QuikScore™ forms (English or French-Canadian); $71 per technical manual; computer version also available.
Foreign Language Editions: Arabic, Chinese, Dutch, French, French-Canadian, German, Greek, Italian, Japanese, Russian, Slovakian, and Spanish.
Comments: Interpretation by qualified professionals only.
Author: Bernard Carroll.
Publisher: Multi-Health Systems, Inc.
a) CARROLL DEPRESSION SCALES.
Acronym: CDS-R.
Time: (20) minutes.
Comments: A 52-item self-report measure.
b) CARROLL DEPRESSION SCALE—REVISED.
Acronym: CDS-R.
Time: (10) minutes.
Comments: A 52-item self-report measure; includes diagnostic index in addition to severity score provided by CDS.
c) BRIEF CARROLL DEPRESSION INVENTORY.
Acronym: Brief CDS-R.
Time: (2) minutes.
Comments: A 12-item self-report rapid screening measure of depressive symptoms.
Cross References: For a review by Susan M. Swearer, see 14:69.

[437]
The Category-Specific Names Test.

Purpose: Designed to detect category-specific deficits both in naming and in comprehension of the spoken or written name within four semantic categories: animals, fruits and vegetables, praxic objects, and non-praxic objects.
Population: Children and adults.
Publication Date: Unavailable.
Scores: Available from publisher.
Administration: Individual.
Price Data, 2001: $415 per complete test.
Time: Administration time not reported.
Author: Pat McKenna.
Publisher: Psychology Press.

[438]
Cattell Infant Intelligence Scale.

Purpose: Designed to measure the infant's developmental progress.
Population: Ages 3–30 months.
Publication Dates: 1946–1960.
Acronym: CIIS.

Scores: Ratings in 4 areas: Willingness, Self-Confidence, Social-Confidence, Attention.
Administration: Individual.
Price Data, 2002: $795 per basic set including all necessary equipment, 25 record forms, and carrying case (manual not included); $113 per manual entitled The Measurement of Intelligence of Infants and Young Children (1960, 274 pages); $40 per 25 record forms.
Time: (20-30) minutes.
Comments: Downward extension of Stanford-Binet Intelligence Scale, Second Revision.
Author: Psyche Cattell.
Publisher: PsychCorp, A brand of Harcourt Assessment, Inc.
Cross References: See T5:433 (14 references), T4:423 (13 references) and T3:381 (19 references); for a review by Fred Damarin, see 8:209 (7 references); see also T2:487 (27 references) and 6:515 (22 references); for reviews by Florence M. Teagarden and Beth L. Wellmann and excerpted reviews by Rachel Stutsman Ball, C. M. Louttit, T. L. McCulloch, Norma V. Schneidmann, and Helen Speyer, see 3:281.

[439]
CERAD Behavior Rating Scale for Dementia, Second Edition.

Purpose: Designed to "assess the behavioral problems and psychiatric symptoms of individuals with no history of mental retardation who have or are suspected to have acquired cognitive deficits."
Population: Adults who have, or are suspected to have, acquired cognitive deficits.
Publication Dates: 1991–2001.
Acronym: BRSD.
Scores, 7: Depressive Symptoms, Inertia, Vegetative Symptoms, Irritability/Aggression, Behavioral Dysregulation, Psychotic Symptoms, Total Weighted Score.
Administration: Individual.
Price Data, 2003: $85 per test kit including manual; $75 per training video.
Time: [20–40] minutes.
Comments: Informant report interview; short form available; may be administered via telephone.
Authors: James L. Mack and Marion Patterson.
Publisher: CERAD Administrative CORE, Duke University Medical Center.
Cross References: For a review by Pamilla Ramsden, see 16:44.

[440]
CERAD (Consortium to Establish a Registry for Alzheimer's Disease) Assessment Battery.

Purpose: "To develop brief, standardized instruments for the assessment of patients with probable Alzheimer's disease."

Population: Patients with mild to moderate dementia.
Publication Date: 1987.
Acronym: CERAD.
Scores: Information gathered in 19 areas: Demographic, Drug Inventory, Informant History (Clinical, Blessed Dementia Rating Scale), Subject History, Short Blessed Test, Depression and Calculation and Language, Examinations (Physical, Neurological), Laboratory Studies, Diagnostic Impression, Neuropsychological Battery (Neuropsychology Battery Status, Verbal Fluency Categories, Boston Naming Test, Mini-Mental State Exam, Word List Memory, Constructional Praxis, Word List Recall, Word List Recognition), Constructional Praxis Recall.
Administration: Individual.
Restricted Distribution: Current use only with permission of CERAD.
Price Data: Price information available from publisher.
Foreign Language Editions: Forms available in French, Spanish, Italian, Chinese, Japanese, and Korean.
Time: 50–70] minutes.
Comments: Manual title is Instruction Manual for Assessment of Patient and Control Subjects Entered into the CERAD Study.
Authors: Consortium to Establish a Registry for Alzheimer's Disease, Albert Heyman (Principal Investigator).
Publisher: CERAD Administrative CORE, Duke University Medical Center.
Cross References: For reviews by Frank M. Bernt and Gabrielle Stutman, see 12:66 (1 reference).

[441]
Certified Picture Framer Examination.

Purpose: "To provide professional recognition to competent individuals who are engaged in the business of picture framing."
Population: Individuals actively involved in the business of picture framing for one year.
Publication Dates: 1986–1993.
Acronym: CPF.
Scores: Total score only.
Administration: Group.
Price Data: Available from publisher.
Time: (210) minutes.
Comments: Test administered on specific dates at centers established by the publisher.
Author: Certification Board of the Professional Picture Framers Association.
Publisher: Professional Picture Framers Association.

[442]
Change Abilitator.
Purpose: Designed to identify six types of concerns people experience when change is introduced into their organization.
Population: Teams.
Publication Date: 1995.
Scores, 6: Information, Personal, Operational, Impact, Collaboration, Transforming.
Administration: Group.
Price Data: Available from publisher.
Time: (15) minutes.
Comments: Revision of the Stages of Concern Questionnaire.
Author: LHE, INC.
Publisher: HRD Press, Inc.
Cross References: For a review by Cynthia A. Larson-Daugherty, see 14:70.

[443]
Change Agent Questionnaire.
Purpose: Assesses "the underlying assumptions and practical strategies employed by agents of change as they seek to influence others."
Population: Adults.
Publication Dates: 1969-1995.
Acronym: CAQ.
Scores, 20: Client-Centered Change (Philosophy, Strategy, Evaluation, Total), Charismatic Change (Philosophy, Strategy, Evaluation, Total), Custodial Change (Philosophy, Strategy, Evaluation, Total), Compliance Change (Philosophy, Strategy, Evaluation, Total), Credibility Change (Philosophy, Strategy, Evaluation, Total).
Administration: Group.
Manual: No manual.
Price Data, 2001: $8.95 per instrument.
Time: Administration time not reported.
Authors: Jay Hall and Martha S. Williams.
Publisher: Teleometrics International, Inc.

[444]
Chapin Social Insight Test.
Purpose: Designed to "assess the perceptiveness and accuracy with which an individual can appraise others and forecast what they might say and do."
Population: Ages 13 and over.
Publication Dates: 1967–1993.
Acronym: SCLT.
Scores: Total score only.
Administration: Group.
Price Data: Available from publisher (www.mindgarden.com).
Time: (20–30) minutes.
Authors: F. Stuart Chapin (test) and Harrison G. Gough (manual).

Publisher: Mind Garden, Inc.
Cross References: For reviews by Frank M. Bernt and by Collie W. Conoley and Linda Castillo, see 16:45; see also T3:384 (5 references); for reviews by Richard I. Lanyon and David B. Orr of an earlier edition, see 7:51; see also P:34 (3 references).

[445]
Characteristics Scale.
Purpose: To determine teachers' views of important pupil characteristics and behaviors.
Population: Grades K-8.
Publication Dates: 1970-1975.
Scores: Total score only.
Administration: Group.
Manual: No manual.
Price Data, 2001: Now free upon request from publisher.
Time: Administration time not reported.
Comments: Ratings by teachers; research instrument; may be used with or separately from Behavior Rating Scale.
Authors: Patricia B. Elmore and Donald L. Beggs.
Publisher: Patricia B. Elmore.

[446]
Checking Individual Progress in Phonics.
Purpose: Designed to "assess pupils' progress in phonics, identify their learning strategies and improve their skills."
Population: Ages 6 to 7.
Publication Date: 2001.
Acronym: ChIPPs.
Scores: Total words read correctly.
Administration: Individual.
Forms: 2 parallel forms: Version 1 and Version 2.
Price Data: Price data for complete set including teacher's manual (106 pages), test materials, and reproducible Individual, Class, and Pupil record sheets available from publisher.
Time: Administration time not reported.
Authors: Sue Palmer and Rea Reason.
Publisher: NFER-Nelson Publishing Co., Ltd. [England].

[447]
Checklist for Child Abuse Evaluation.
Purpose: Designed as a "tool for investigating and evaluating children and adolescents who may have been neglected or abused."
Population: Children and adolescents.
Publication Dates: 1988–1990.
Acronym: CCAE.
Scores: 24 sections: Identification and Case Description, The Child's Status, Accuracy of Allegations by the Reporter, Interview with the Child (Physical/Behavioral Observations, Disclosure, Emotional Abuse, Sexual

Abuse, Physical Abuse, Neglect), Events Witnessed or Reported by Others (Neglect, Emotional Abuse, Sexual Abuse, Physical Abuse), The Child's Psychological Status, History and Observed/Reported Characteristics of the Accused, Credibility of the Child—Observed/Reported, Competence of the Child—Observed/Reported, Conclusions (Consistency of Other Information, Allegation Motives, Substantiation of Allegations, Competence of the Child as a Witness, Level of Stress Experienced by the Child, Protection of the Child), Treatment Recommendations.
Administration: Individual.
Price Data, 2006: $138 per introductory kit including manual (1990, 19 pages) and 25 checklists.
Time: Untimed.
Author: Joseph Petty.
Publisher: Psychological Assessment Resources, Inc.
Cross References: For reviews by Denise M. DeZolt and Janice G. Williams, see 12:68.

[448]
Checklist of Adaptive Living Skills.

Purpose: "A criterion-referenced measure of adaptive living skills and a tool for program planning."
Population: Infants to adults.
Publication Date: 1991.
Acronym: CALS.
Scores: 4 areas: Personal Living Skills, Home Living Skills, Community Living Skills, Employment Skills; and 24 subscales: Socialization, Eating, Grooming, Toileting, Dressing, Health Care, Sexuality, Clothing Care, Meal Planning and Preparation, Home Cleaning and Organization, Home Maintenance, Home Safety, Home Leisure, Social Interaction, Mobility and Travel, Time Management, Money Management and Shopping, Community Safety, Community Leisure, Community Participation, Job Search, Job Performance and Attitudes, Employee Relations, Job Safety.
Administration: Individual.
Price Data, 2006: $117.50 per complete kit including manual (62 pages) and 25 checklists; $75.50 per manual; $82 per 25 checklists.
Time: [60] minutes.
Comments: "Designed to be completed by a respondent who has had the opportunity to observe the learner in natural environments for a period of three or more months"; conceptually and statistically linked to two normative measures of adaptive behavior: Scales of Independent Behavior—Revised (SIB-R; 2240) and Inventory for Client and Agency Planning (ICAP; 1272); companion publication is the Adaptive Living Skills Curriculum.
Authors: Lanny E. Morreau and Robert H. Bruininks.
Publisher: Riverside Publishing.
Cross References: See T5:443 (1 reference); for reviews by Patricia A. Bachelor and James P. Van Haneghan, see 12:69.

[449]
ChemTest (Form AC).

Purpose: For selecting candidates with basic chemical knowledge.
Population: Applicants and incumbents for jobs requiring knowledge of chemical principles.
Publication Dates: 2001–2002.
Scores, 9: Physical Knowledge, Acids/Bases & Salts, Compounds, Elements, Miscellaneous, Chemical Knowledge, Mechanical Principles, gases & Fluids, Total.
Administration: Group.
Price Data, 2006: $20 per consumable self-scoring test booklet (minimum order of 20); $24.95 per manual (2002, 13 pages).
Time: (60) minutes.
Comments: Self-scoring instrument.
Author: Roland T. Ramsay.
Publisher: Ramsay Corporation.

[450]
Child Abuse/Husband Abuse/Wife Abuse.

Purpose: Designed to compile an individual's history of abuse.
Population: Children, husbands, wives.
Publication Date: 1991.
Administration: Individual or group.
Forms, 3: Child Abuse, Husband Abuse, Wife Abuse.
Manual: No manual.
Price Data, 2001: $10 per 20 record forms (specify Child, Husband, or Wife).
Time: Administration time not reported.
Author: Allan Roe.
Publisher: Diagnostic Specialists, Inc.

[451]
The Child Abuse Potential Inventory, Form VI.

Purpose: "To assist in the screening of suspected physical child abuse cases."
Population: Male and female parents or primary caregivers who are suspected of physical child abuse.
Publication Dates: 1980–1993.
Acronym: CAP Inventory.
Scores: 12 scale scores: Abuse scale (Distress, Rigidity, Unhappiness, Problems With Child and Self, Problems With Family, Problems With Others, Total Physical Child Abuse), Validity scales (Lie Scale, Random Response Scale, Inconsistency Scale), Loneliness, Ego-Strength, and 3 Response Distortion Indexes (Faking-Good, Faking-Bad, Random Response).
Administration: Individual administration recommended.
Price Data: Available from publisher.
Time: (12–20) minutes.
Author: Joel S. Milner.

Publisher: Psytec Inc.

Cross References: See T5:448 (30 references) and T4:429 (10 references); for reviews by Stuart N. Hart and Gary B. Melton, see 10:50 (5 references).

[452]
Child and Adolescent Risk Evaluation: A Measure of the Risk for Violent Behavior.

Purpose: Designed to screen "for violence risk and protective factors in childhood and adolescence."
Population: Ages 2–19.
Publication Date: 2003.
Acronym: CARE.
Scores, 3: Risk, Resiliency, Total.
Administration: Individual.
Price Data, 2005: $75 per complete kit including manual (37 pages), 25 assessment forms, and 25 case management planning forms; $19.95 per manual; $29.95 per 25 assessment forms; $29.95 per 25 case management planning forms: $9.95 per optional Tabulation Software (for Windows, 24 uses).
Time: Administration time not reported.
Comments: Assessment includes record review and interviews with subject, family, and caregivers.
Author: Kathryn Seifert.
Publisher: Research Press.

[453]
Child Care Inventory.

Purpose: Developed to evaluate child care programs in order to improve program effectiveness or to determine the level of program implementation.
Population: Child care programs.
Publication Date: 1986.
Scores: 11 performance areas: Classroom Arrangement, Safety, Curriculum, Interacting, Scheduling, Child Assessment, Health, Special Needs, Parent Involvement, Outdoor Play, Infant Programs.
Administration: Individual.
Price Data, 2002: $22.95 per complete kit including test booklet and manual (32 pages); 11.95 per test booklet; $12.95 per manual.
Time: Administration time not reported.
Authors: Martha S. Abbott-Shim and Annette M. Sibley.
Publisher: Humanics Learning.
Cross References: For reviews by Lisa G. Bischoff and Annette M. Iverson, see 12:71.

[454]
Child Development Inventory.

Purpose: "Designed to provide systematic ways of obtaining in depth developmental information from parents."
Population: Ages 1–3 to 6–3.
Publication Dates: 1968–1992.

Acronym: CDI.
Scores, 9: Social, Self Help, Gross Motor, Fine Motor, Expressive Language, Language Comprehension, Letters, Numbers, General Development.
Administration: Individual.
Price Data, 2005: $72 per complete set including 10 test booklets, 25 answer sheets, 25 CDI profiles, and manual (2005, 44 pages) with scoring template; $18 per 10 test booklets; $12.50 per 25 answer sheets; $12.50 per 25 CDI profiles; $33 per manual with scoring template.
Time: [30–50] minutes.
Comments: Parent-completed questionnaire; formerly called the Minnesota Child Development Inventory.
Author: Harold Ireton.
Publisher: Child Development Review - Behavior Science Systems, Inc.
Cross References: For reviews by Jean Powell Kirnan and Diana Crespo and by Stephanie Stein, see 13:56; see also T4:436 (14 references); for a review of an earlier edition by Jane A. Rysberg, see 9:712; see also T3:1492 (6 references); for a review by William L. Goodwin, see 8:220 (3 references).

[455]
Child Development Review Parent Questionnaire.

Purpose: A brief screening inventory "designed to help identify children with developmental, behavioral, or health problems."
Population: 18 months to age 5.
Publication Date: 1994.
Acronym: CDR.
Scores, 5: Development (Social, Self-Help, Gross Motor, Fine Motor, Language), Possible Problems, Child Description, Parents' Questions/Concerns, Parents' Functioning.
Administration: Individual.
Price Data, 2005: $12.50 per 25 parent questionnaire/child development charts; $33 per manual (22 pages).
Time: [5–10] minutes.
Comments: Parent-completed questionnaire; scores reflect parents' report of child's present functioning-development; Child Development Chart on back, can be used for observation or for parent report.
Author: Harold Ireton.
Publisher: Child Development Review - Behavior Science Systems, Inc.
Cross References: For reviews by Terry Overton and Gary J. Stainback, see 14:71.

[456]
Child Language Ability Measures.

Purpose: "Designed to measure language development."

Population: Ages 2–8.
Publication Date: 1979.
Acronym: CLAM.
Scores: 6 tests: Vocabulary Comprehension, Grammar Comprehension, Inflection Production, Grammar Imitation, Grammar Formedness Judgment, Grammar Equivalence Judgment.
Administration: Individual.
Price Data: Available from publisher.
Time: (15) minutes per test.
Comments: Tests may be administered separately or in any of 11 combinations.
Authors: Christy Moynihan and Albert Mehrabian.
Publisher: Albert Mehrabian.
Cross References: For a review by Allen Jack Edwards, see 10:51.

[457]
Child Sexual Behavior Inventory.

Purpose: Designed as a "measure of sexual behavior in children"; used in the identification of sexual abuse.
Population: Ages 2–12.
Publication Dates: 1986–1997.
Acronym: CSBI.
Scores, 3: Developmentally Related Sexual Behaviors, Sexual Abuse Specific Items, Total.
Administration: Individual.
Price Data, 2006: $155 per introductory kit including manual (1997, 61 pages) and 50 test booklets.
Time: [10–15] minutes.
Comments: Completed by a child's primary caregiver.
Author: William N. Friedrich.
Publisher: Psychological Assessment Resources, Inc.
Cross References: For reviews by Frank M. Bernt and Thomas McKnight, see 14:72; see also T5:457 (1 reference).

[458]
Child Symptom Inventory-4 [2002 Update].

Purpose: Designed as a "screening instrument for the behavioral, affective, and cognitive symptoms" of childhood psychiatric disorders.
Population: Ages 5–12.
Publication Dates: 1994–2002.
Acronym: CSI-4.
Scores, 13: AD/HD Inattentive, AD/HD Hyper-Impulsive, AD/HD Combined, Oppositional Defiant Disorder, Conduct Disorder, Generalized Anxiety Disorder, Schizophrenia, Major Depressive Disorder, Dysthymic Disorder, Autistic Disorder, Asperger's Disorder, Social Phobia, Separation Anxiety Disorder.
Administration: Individual.
Forms, 2: Parent Checklist, Teacher Checklist.
Price Data, 2006: $98 per deluxe kit including screening and norms manual (2002, 179 pages), 25 parent checklists, 25 teacher checklists, 50 symptom count score sheets, and 50 symptom severity profile score sheets; $358 per deluxe kit also including scoring CD; $44 per screening and norms manual; $32 per 50 parent checklists; $60 per 100 parent checklists; $32 per 50 Spanish parent checklists; $32 per 50 teacher checklists; $13 per 50 profiles for parent or teacher checklists; $290 per computer scoring software.
Time: [10–15] minutes.
Comments: Instrument is designed to correspond to the DSM-IV classification system.
Authors: Kenneth D. Gadow and Joyce Sprafkin.
Publisher: Checkmate Plus Ltd.
Cross References: For a review by Kathryn E. Hoff and W. Joel Schneider, see 16:46; for reviews by James C. DiPerna and Robert J. Volpe and by Rosemary Flanagan based on an earlier edition of the manual for this test, see 15:47.

[459]
Child Well-Being Scales and Rating Form.

Purpose: Designed for the assessment of children's welfare.
Population: Child welfare practitioners.
Publication Date: 1987.
Scores: No scores.
Administration: Group.
Manual: No manual.
Price Data: Price information available from publisher for test booklet.
Time: Administration time not reported.
Comments: Ratings by child welfare practitioners.
Authors: Stephen Magura and Beth Silverman Moses.
Publisher: Child Welfare League of America, Inc.
Cross References: See T5:458 (2 references).

[460]
The Childhood Autism Rating Scale.

Purpose: "To identify children with autism, and to distinguish them from developmentally handicapped children without the autism syndrome."
Population: Ages 2 and over.
Publication Dates: 1986–1988.
Acronym: CARS.
Scores: 16 rating scores: Relating to People, Imitation, Emotional Response, Body Use, Object Use, Adaptation to Change, Visual Response, Listening Response, Taste/Smell/Touch Response and Use, Fear or Nervousness, Verbal Communication, Nonverbal Communication, Activity Level, Level and Consistency of Intellectual Response, General Impressions, Total.
Administration: Individual.
Price Data, 2002: $65 per complete kit including 25 rating scales and manual (1988, 20 pages); $22.50 per 25 rating scales; $45 per manual; $182.50 per training video (Demonstration tape using the CARS or Practice Tape on Using the CARS).

Time: Administration time not reported.
Comments: Revision of the Childhood Psychosis Rating Scale; ratings by professionals trained to administer the CARS.
Authors: Eric Schopler, Robert J. Reichler, and Barbara Rochen Renner.
Publisher: Western Psychological Services.
Cross References: See T5:459 (40 references) and T4:439 (6 references); for reviews by Barry M. Prizant and J. Steven Welsh, see 11:65 (4 references).

[461]
Childhood Trauma Questionnaire.

Purpose: Designed as a self-report inventory for "screening for histories of abuse and neglect."
Population: Ages 12 and up.
Publication Dates: 1997–1998.
Acronym: CTQ.
Scores, 5: Emotional Abuse, Physical Abuse, Sexual Abuse, Emotional and Physical Neglect and Minimization/Denial of Abuse.
Administration: Individual.
Price Data, 2002: $99 per complete kit including 25 READYSCORE answer documents and manual (1998, 76 pages); $40 per 25 READYSCORE answer documents; $73 per manual.
Time: (5) minutes.
Comments: A 28-item, self-report inventory.
Authors: David P. Bernstein and Laura Fink.
Publisher: PsychCorp, A brand of Harcourt Assessment, Inc.
Cross References: For reviews by Michael Furlong and Renee Pavelski and by Jonathan Sandoval, see 14:73; see also T5:460 (2 references).

[462]
Children of Alcoholics Screening Test.

Purpose: Measures children's and adults' attitudes, feelings, perceptions, and experiences related to their parents' drinking behavior; also identifies probable children of alcoholics (CoAs) and adult children of alcoholics (ACoAs).
Population: School-age children through adults.
Publication Dates: 1981–1993.
Acronym: CAST.
Scores: Total score only.
Administration: Group or individual.
Price Data: Available from publisher.
Time: (5–10) minutes.
Comments: Reduced rate is available for additional forms used in research or mass testing.
Author: John W. Jones.
Publisher: Camelot Unlimited.
Cross References: See T5:462 (33 references) and T4:440 (8 references); for reviews by Stuart N.

Hart and Steven P. Schinke, see 10:52; for reviews by Susanna Maxwell and Barrie G. Stacey, see 9:217.

[463]
Children's Academic Intrinsic Motivation Inventory.

Purpose: "To measure academic intrinsic motivation ... defined as enjoyment of school learning characterized by an orientation toward mastery, curiosity, persistence, and the learning of challenging, difficult, and novel tasks."
Population: Grades 4–8.
Publication Date: 1986.
Acronym: CAIMI.
Scores: 5 scales: Reading, Math, Social Studies, Science, General.
Administration: Individual or group.
Price Data, 2006: $162 per introductory kit including 50 test booklets, 50 profile forms, and manual (24 pages).
Time: (20–30) minutes for individual administration; (60) minutes for group administration.
Comments: Self-report inventory.
Author: Adele Gottfried.
Publisher: Psychological Assessment Resources, Inc.
Cross References: See T5:464 (5 references); for a review by C. Dale Posey, see 10:54.

[464]
Childrens Adaptive Behavior Scale, Revised.

Purpose: Provides a means to gather information on the relevant knowledge and concepts requisite to adaptive functioning.
Population: Ages 5–11.
Publication Dates: 1980–2002.
Acronym: CABS.
Scores, 6: Language Development, Independent Functioning, Family Role Performance, Economic-Vocational Activity, Socialization, Total.
Administration: Individual.
Price Data, 2002: $1 per student booklet; $14.95 per manual (1983, 42 pages); $35.95 per specimen set including 5 student booklets, picture book, and manual.
Time: (45–50) minutes.
Comments: Other test materials (e.g., coins, blocks, scissors, paper) must be supplied by examiner.
Authors: Richard H. Kicklighter and Bert O. Richmond.
Publisher: Humanics Learning.
Cross References: See T4:442 (1 reference); for reviews by Kenneth A. Kavale and Esther Sinclair, see 10:55 (1 reference); for reviews by Thomas R. Kratochwill and Corinne R. Smith of the original edition, see 9:218; see also T3:395 (1 reference).

[465]
Children's Apperception Test [1991 Revision].

Purpose: A projective "method of investigating personality by studying the dynamic meaningfulness of the individual differences in perception of standard stimuli."

Population: Ages 3–10.

Publication Dates: 1949–1992.

Acronym: C.A.T.

Scores: No scores.

Administration: Individual.

Editions, 3: Animal, Human, Supplement, plus Short Form.

Price Data, 2001: $95 per C.A.T.–A, C.A.T.–S, C.A.T.–H, manual (1991, 24 pages), 25 recording and analysis blanks (short form), and 10 copies of Haworth's Schedule of Adaptive Mechanisms in C.A.T. Responses; $86 per C.A.T.–A or C.A.T.–H; $32 per C.A.T.–S; $9.25 per 25 recording and analysis blanks (short form); $9 per 30 Haworth's Schedules; $9 per 10 psychodiagnostic test reports.

Time: (15–20) minutes.

Authors: Leopold Bellak and Sonya Sorel Bellak.

Publisher: C.P.S., Inc.

Cross References: See T5:466 (1 reference); for reviews by Howard M. Knoff and Robert C. Reinehr, see 13:58 (4 references); see also T4:444 (4 references); for reviews by Clifford V. Hatt and Marcia B. Shaffer of an earlier edition, see 9:219 (1 reference); see also T3:396 (1 reference), T2:1451 (23 references), and P:419 (18 references); for reviews by Bernard L. Murstein and Robert D. Wirt, see 6:206 (19 references); for reviews by Douglas T. Keeny and Albert I. Rabin, see 5:126 (15 references); for reviews by John E. Bell and L. Joseph Stone and excerpted reviews by M. M. Genn, Herbert Herman, Robert R. Holt, Laurance F. Shaffer, and Adolf G. Woltmann, see 4:103 (2 references).

[466]
Children's Articulation Test.

Purpose: Designed to "assess child's ability to produce consonants, vowels and diphthongs in an in-depth relationship to other consonants and vowels."

Population: Ages 3–11.

Publication Date: 1989.

Acronym: CAT.

Scores, 7: Medial Vowels/Diphthongs, Final Consonants, Initiating Consonants, Abutting Consonants, Abutting Consonants and Vowels/Diphthongs, Connected Speech, Language Concepts.

Administration: Individual.

Price Data: Available from publisher.

Time: [15] minutes.

Author: George S. Haspiel.

Publisher: Dragon Press [No reply from publisher; status unknown].

Cross References: For reviews by Kathryn W. Kenney and Lawrence J. Turton, see 12:74.

[467]
Children's Attention and Adjustment Survey.

Purpose: "Designed to measure the diagnostic criteria of inattention, impulsivity, hyperactivity, and aggressiveness or conduct problems."

Population: Ages 5–13.

Publication Date: 1990.

Acronym: CAAS.

Scores, 7: Inattention, Impulsivity, ADD, Hyperactivity, ADHD, Conduct Problems, DSM III-R ADHD.

Administration: Individual.

Editions, 2: School, Home.

Price Data, 2006: $49.99 per 25 self-scorable booklets (select School or Home form); $19.99 per 25 scoring profiles; $45.99 per manual (75 pages); $154.99 per starter set including manual and 25 each of Home Form, School Form, and Scoring Profile.

Time: (5–10) minutes per form.

Comments: Ratings by teacher or parent.

Authors: Nadine Lambert, Carolyn Hartsough, and Jonathan Sandoval.

Publisher: Pearson Assessments (originally published by AGS Publishing, acquired by Pearson in 2005).

Cross References: See T5:469 (3 references); for reviews by Claire B. Ernhart and Stephen L. Koffler, see 12:75 (1 reference).

[468]
Children's Auditory Verbal Learning Test-2.

Purpose: Constructed to "measure auditory verbal learning and memory abilities" in children.

Population: Ages 6-6 to 17-11.

Publication Dates: 1988–1993.

Acronym: CAVLT-2.

Scores, 6: Immediate Memory Span, Level of Learning, Immediate Recall, Delayed Recall, Recognition Accuracy, Total Intrusions.

Administration: Individual.

Price Data, 2005: $106 per introductory kit including 25 test booklets and professional manual (1993, 68 pages).

Time: (25–30) minutes.

Comments: Orally administered.

Author: Jack L. Talley.

Publisher: Psychological Assessment Resources, Inc.

Cross References: For reviews by John O. Anderson and Sherwyn Morreale, see 12:76.

[469]
Children's Category Test.

Purpose: "Designed to assess non-verbal concept formation, ability to benefit from verbal feedback to alter problem solving behavior and abstract reasoning."
Population: Ages 5-0 to 16-11.
Publication Date: 1993.
Acronym: CCT.
Scores, 6: Subtest I, Subtest II, Subtest III, Subtest IV, Subtest V, Total.
Administration: Individual.
Levels, 2: Level 1 (Ages 5 to 8), Level 2 (Ages 9 to 16).
Price Data, 2006: $399 per complete kit including manual (72 pages), 25 Level 1 record forms, 25 Level 2 record forms, stimulus booklets, and color response cards (1 for each level); $37 per 25 record forms.
Time: (15–20) minutes.
Author: Thomas Boll.
Publisher: PsychCorp, A brand of Harcourt Assessment, Inc.
Cross References: For reviews by Mark D. Shriver and Nicholas A. Vacc, see 13:59.

[470]
Children's Color Trails Test.

Purpose: "Designed to provide an easily administered and objectively scored measure of alternating and sustained visual attention, sequencing, psychomotor speed, cognitive flexibility, and inhibition-disinhibition."
Population: Ages 8–16.
Publication Dates: 1989–2003.
Acronym: CCTT.
Scores, 6: Time Scores, Prompt Scores, Near-Miss Scores, Error Scores (Number Sequence Errors, Color Sequence Errors), Interference Index.
Subtests, 2: CCTT-1, CCTT-2.
Administration: Individual.
Forms, 4: K, X, Y, Z.
Price Data, 2006: $145 per Introductory kit including professional manual (2003, 81 pages), 50 record forms, and 50 copies of Form K, Parts 1 & 2.
Time: (5–7) minutes.
Comments: Also called Kid's Color Trails, Kiddie Color Trails, K Color Trails; modeled after Color Trails Test.
Authors: Antolin M. Llorente, Jane Williams, Paul Satz, and Louis F. D'Elia.
Publisher: Psychological Assessment Resources, Inc.
Cross References: For reviews by Andrew S. Davis and W. Holmes Finch and by Shawn Powell and Michelle A. Butler, see 16:47.

[471]
Children's Depression Inventory [Revised].

Purpose: "Evaluates the presence and severity of depressive symptoms in children."

Population: Ages 7-17.
Publication Dates: 1977–2003.
Price Data, 2006: $187 per complete user's package including technical manual (2003, 170 pages), 25 CDI QuikScore forms, 25 CDI:S Quikscore forms, 25 CDI:P QuikScore forms, and 25 CDI:T QuikScore forms; $62 per technical manual; $43 per 25 CDI Quikscore forms; $41 per 25 CDI:S QuikScore forms; $39 per 25 CDI:P or CDI:T QuikScore forms; $90 per CDI V.5 Software kit including technical manual, CDI V.5 Getting Started Guide, and 25 Profile Report uses.
Foreign Language Editions: Translation of the CDI available in Afrikaans, Arabic, Bulgarian, Cantonese, Czech, Dutch, French (European), French (Canadian), German, Hebrew, Italian, Japanese, Lithuanian, Malay, Norwegian, Polish, Portugese (South American), Russian, Spanish (European), Spanish (South American), Swedish, Turkish, and Ukrainian.
Time: [10–30] minutes.
Comments: New edition adds parent and teacher report forms; paper-and-pencil or computer formats available.
Author: Maria Kovacs.
Publisher: Multi-Health Systems, Inc.
a) CHILDREN'S DEPRESSION INVENTORY.
   Acronym: CDI.
   Scores, 6: Negative Mood, Interpersonal Problems, Ineffectiveness, Anhedonia, Negative Self Esteem, Total.
b) CHILDREN'S DEPRESSION INVENTORY: SHORT VERSION.
   Acronym: CDI:S.
   Scores: Total score only.
c) CHILDREN'S DEPRESSION INVENTORY: PARENT VERSION.
   Acronym: CDI:P.
   Scores, 3: Emotional Problems, Functional Problems, Total.
d) CHILDREN'S DEPRESSION INVENTORY: TEACHER VERSION.
   Acronym: CDI:T.
   Scores, 3: Same as *c* above.
Cross References: See T5:472 (235 references) and T4:450 (71 references); for reviews by Michael G. Kavan and Howard M. Knoff of an earlier edition, see 11:66 (63 references).

[472]
Children's Depression Rating Scale, Revised.

Purpose: Constructed as a "screening instrument, diagnostic tool, and severity measure of depression in children."
Population: Ages 6–12.
Publication Date: 1996.
Acronym: CDRS-R.
Scores: Total score only.

Administration: Group.
Price Data, 2002: $72 per complete kit including manual (91 pages), and 25 administration booklets; $27.50 per 25 administration booklets; $49.50 per manual.
Time: (15–20) minutes.
Comments: Ratings by health care professionals.
Authors: Elva O. Poznanski and Hartmut B. Mokros.
Publisher: Western Psychological Services.
Cross References: For reviews by E. Thomas Dowd and Donald Lee Stovall, see 14:74; see also T5:473 (8 references).

[473]
Children's Interview for Psychiatric Syndromes.

Purpose: Designed to identify "symptoms of 20 common Axis I psychiatric disorders in children and adolescents."
Population: Ages 6–18.
Publication Date: 1999.
Acronym: ChIPS.
Scores, 20: Attention-Deficit/Hyperactivity Disorder, Oppositional Defiant Disorder, Conduct Disorder, Substance Abuse, Specific Phobia, Social Phobia, Separation Anxiety Disorder, Generalized Anxiety Disorder, Obsessive-Compulsive Disorder, Acute Stress Disorder, Posttraumatic Stress Disorder, Anorexia, Bulimia, Depressive Episode, Dysthymic Disorder, Manic Episode, Hypomanic Episode, Enuresis, Encopresis, Schizophrenia/Psychosis.
Administration: Individual.
Price Data, 2006: $34.95 per administration manual (60 pages); $59 per reusable interview administration booklet (30 pages); $33.95 per 20 scoring forms; $28.50 per 20 report forms; $236 per starter kit.
Time: Administration time not reported.
Authors: Elizabeth B. Weller, Ronald A. Weller, Mary A. Fristad, and Marijo Teare Rooney.
Publisher: American Psychiatric Publishing, Inc.
Cross References: For reviews by Janet F. Carlson and R. Joel Farrell II, see 15:48.

[474]
Children's Inventory of Anger.

Purpose: Designed "to measure aspects of a youngster's experience of anger."
Population: Ages 6–16.
Publication Date: 2000.
Acronym: CIA.
Scores, 5: Frustration, Physical Aggression, Peer Relationship, Authority Relations, Total.
Administration: Group or individual.
Price Data, 2006: $93.50 per complete kit including 25 autoscore answer forms, and manual; $42.50 per 25 autoscore answer forms; $54.50 per manual; $105

per disk that offers scoring for 25 uses; $16.50 per PC answer sheet pads of 100.
Time: 10 minutes.
Comments: Self-report inventory.
Authors: W. Michael Nelson III and A. J. Finch, Jr.
Publisher: Western Psychological Services.
Cross References: For reviews by Theresa Volpe-Johnstone and Delores D. Walcott, see 15:49.

[475]
Children's Inventory of Self-Esteem, Second Edition.

Purpose: "Provides … a quick way to assess the relative strength of a child's self-worth."
Population: Ages 5–12.
Publication Dates: 1987–2001.
Acronym: CISE.
Scores, 7: 4 components of self-esteem: Belonging (B), Purpose (P), Control (C), Self (S); Total (T); 2 favored coping styles: Defensive (TD), Aggressive (TA).
Administration: Individual.
Price Data, 2006: $99 per an individual lifetime license for individuals, including examiner's manual (2001, 24 pages), CISE for girls, CISE for boys, answer form, Exploring Your Child's Self-Esteem form, Your Child's Sense of Self form, Your Child's Sense of Purpose form, Your Child's Sense of Control form, Your Child's Sense of Belonging form (all forms personalized with unlimited copying privileges); $125 per school or agency lifetime license; $110 per lifetime license for each school when purchased by school district (minimum 2 schools); $4.95 shipping/handling fee.
Time: (10) minutes.
Comments: 64-item behavior rating scale completed by parents and teachers of child; provides strategies for helping improve self-esteem.
Author: Richard A. Campbell.
Publisher: Brougham Press.
Cross References: For reviews by R. Joel Farrell II and Jacqueline Johnson, see 15:50; for reviews by Kathy E. Green and Nicholas A. Vacc of a previous edition, see 12:78.

[476]
Children's Memory Scale.

Purpose: "Comprehensive assessment of visual/verbal learning and memory skills" in children and adolescents.
Population: Ages 5–16.
Publication Dates: 1997–1998.
Acronym: CMS.
Scores, 34: 14 Core Battery Subtest scores: Dot Locations (Learning, Total Score, Long Delay); Stories (Immediate, Delayed, Delayed Recognition); Faces (Immediate, Delayed); Word Pairs (Learning, Total Score,

Long Delay, Delayed Recognition); Numbers (Total Score); Sequences (Total Score); 6 supplemental scores: Dot Locations (Short Delay), Stories (Immediate Thematic, Delayed Thematic), Word Pairs (Immediate), Numbers (Forward, Backward); 6 Supplemental scores from 3 Supplemental Subtests: Word Lists (Learning, Delayed, Delayed Recognition), Picture Locations (Total Score), Family Pictures (Immediate, Delayed); 8 Indexes: Visual Immediate, Visual Delayed, Verbal Immediate, Verbal Delayed, General Memory, Attention/Concentration, Learning, Delayed Recognition.
Administration: Individual.
Levels, 2: 5–8, 9–16.
Price Data, 2006: $499 per complete kit including manual (1997, 288 pages), 25 record forms for both age levels, 2 stimulus booklets, 5 family picture cards, and response grid in a box along with 8 chips in a pouch; $549 per complete kit available in soft-sided carrying case; $62 per record forms (specify level); $210 per computer Scoring Assistant (available for Windows or Macintosh).
Time: (20–50) minutes.
Author: Morris J. Cohen.
Publisher: PsychCorp, A brand of Harcourt Assessment, Inc.
Cross References: For reviews by Scott A. Napolitano and Margot B. Stein, see 14:75.

[477]
Children's Personality Questionnaire.

Purpose: Designed to measure personality traits to predict and evaluate the course of personal, social, and academic development.
Population: Ages 8–12.
Publication Dates: 1959–1992.
Acronym: CPQ.
Scores, 18: 14 primary factors [Cool vs. Warm (A), Concrete Thinking vs. Abstract Thinking (B), Affected by Feelings vs. Emotionally Stable (C), Phlegmatic vs. Excitable (D), Obedient vs. Dominant (E), Sober vs. Enthusiastic (F), Expedient vs. Conscientious (G), Shy vs. Bold (H), Tough-Minded vs. Tender-Minded (I), Vigorous vs. Guarded (J), Forthright vs. Shrewd (N), Self-Assured vs. Apprehensive (O), Undisciplined Self-Conflict vs. Controlled (Q3), Relaxed vs. Tense (Q4)]; 4 optional secondary factors (Extraversion, Anxiety, Tough Poise, Independence).
Administration: Group or individual.
Forms, 4: A, B, C, D.
Price Data, 2005: $40 per handscoring introductory kit including test booklet (Form A), technical handbook (1992, 84 pages) with norms, answer/profile sheet, second-order worksheet, and scoring keys; $20 per technical handbook; $20 per 25 reusable test booklets (Form A or B); $25 per 25 reusable test booklets (Form C or D); $18 per 50 handscoring answer sheets; $20 per 50 answer-profile sheets; $18 per 50 second-order worksheets; $18

per scoring key (separate scoring keys required for Forms A/C and B/D); $22 per 25 machine-scorable answer sheets; $23 per computer interpretation introductory kit including test booklet (Form A), technical handbook, machine-scorable answer sheet, and report processing form; $7 to $30 per computer interpretation.
Foreign Language Editions: Information regarding several non-English-language adaptations available from publisher.
Time: (30–60) minutes per form.
Comments: Test booklet is entitled "What You Do and What You Think."
Authors: Rutherford B. Porter and Raymond B. Cattell.
Publisher: Institute for Personality and Ability Testing, Inc. (IPAT).
Cross References: For reviews by Rosa A. Hagin and Terry A. Stinnett, see 13:60 (3 references); see also T4:454 (9 references); for reviews by Steven Klee and Howard M. Knoff of an earlier edition, see 9:222 (11 references); for a review by Harrison G. Gough, see 8:520 (46 references); see also T3:1129 (60 references) and P:38 (14 references); for reviews by Anne Anastasi, by Wilbur L. Layton, and by Robert D. Wirt of the 1963 edition, see 6:122 (2 references).

[478]
Children's Problems Checklist.

Purpose: "To identify relevant problems, establish rapport, and provide written documentation of presenting problems consistent with community standards of care."
Population: Ages 5-12.
Publication Date: 1985.
Acronym: CPC.
Scores: 11 areas: Emotions, Self-Concept, Peers and Play, School, Language and Thinking, Concentration and Organization, Activity Level and Motor Control, Behavior, Values, Habits, Health.
Administration: Individual or group.
Manual: No manual.
Price Data, 2005: $49 per package of 50.
Time: (10-20) minutes.
Comments: Ratings by parent or guardian.
Author: John A. Schinka.
Publisher: Psychological Assessment Resources, Inc.
Cross References: For a review by Wayne C. Piersel, see 10:56.

[479]
Children's PTSD Inventory: A Structured Interview for Diagnosing Posttraumatic Stress Disorder.

Purpose: "Designed for the identification and assessment of posttraumatic stress disorder in children and adolescents."

Population: Ages 6–18.
Publication Date: 2004.
Scores, 7: Exposure, Situational Reactivity, Reexperiencing, Avoidance and Numbing, Increased Arousal, Significant Distress, Total.
Administration: Individual.
Price Data, 2004: $104 per complete kit including manual (52 pages) and 25 inventory forms; $43 per 25 inventory forms; $167 per 100 inventory forms; $66 per manual.
Time: (5–20) minutes.
Comments: Inventory forms also available in Spanish and Canadian French; five overall diagnostic categories (PTSD Negative, Acute PTSD, Chronic PTSD, Delayed Onset PTSD, or No Diagnosis) provided.
Author: Phillip A. Saigh.
Publisher: PsychCorp, A brand of Harcourt Assessment, Inc.

[480]
Children's Speech Intelligibility Measure.

Purpose: "Designed to provide clinicians with an objective measure of single-word intelligibility of children ages 3.0 to 10.11 whose speech is considered unintelligible."
Population: Ages 3.0–10.11.
Publication Date: 1999.
Acronym: CSIM.
Scores: Total score only.
Administration: Individual.
Price Data, 2004: $94 per complete kit including manual (140 pages), 15 record forms, and microphone switch; $15 per 15 record forms; $50 per manual.
Time: (10-20) minutes.
Authors: Kim Wilcox and Sherrill Morris.
Publisher: PsychCorp, A brand of Harcourt Assessment, Inc.

[481]
The Children's Test of Nonword Repetition.

Purpose: To assess short term memory in children.
Population: Ages 4–8.
Publication Date: 1996.
Acronym: CN REP.
Scores: Total score only.
Administration: Individual.
Price Data, 2006: £74 per complete set including record forms, cassette tape, and manual (29 pages).
Time: [15] minutes.
Authors: Susan Gathercole and Alan Baddeley.
Publisher: Harcourt Assessment [England].
Cross References: For reviews by Patrick Grehan and Manuel Martinez-Pons, see 16:48.

[482]
Children's Version of the Family Environment Scale.

Purpose: "Provides a measure of young children's subjective appraisal of their family environment."
Population: Ages 5–12.
Publication Date: 1984.
Acronym: CV/FES.
Scores, 10: Cohesion, Expressiveness, Conflict, Independence, Achievement Orientation, Intellectual-Cultural Orientation, Active-Recreational Orientation, Moral-Religious Emphasis, Organization, Control.
Administration: Group.
Price Data, 2002: $64 per complete kit; $14 per manual (15 pages); $34 per 10 (reusable) test answer booklets; $19 per 50 profiles; $19 per 50 examiner's worksheets; $19 per 50 individual student answer sheets.
Time: Administration time not reported.
Comments: Downward extension of the Family Environment Scale (9:408).
Authors: Christopher J. Pino, Nancy Simons, and Mary Jane Slawinowski.
Publisher: Slosson Educational Publications, Inc.
Cross References: For a review by Nancy A. Busch-Rossnagel, see 10:57.

[483]
Chinese Proficiency Test.

Purpose: "Designed to evaluate the proficiency in Chinese listening and reading comprehension attained by Americans and other English-speaking learners of Chinese."
Population: Postsecondary to adults.
Publication Dates: 1986–1992.
Scores, 4: Listening Comprehension, Structure, Reading Comprehension, Total.
Administration: Group.
Price Data, 2002: $25 per test (quantity discounts available); $6 per official score report.
Time: 120(180) minutes.
Comments: Mail-in scoring.
Author: Center for Applied Linguistics.
Publisher: Center for Applied Linguistics.
   a) PRELIMINARY CHINESE PROFICIENCY TEST.
   Publication Date: 1991.
   Acronym: Pre-CPT.
   Comments: "Designed to be most appropriate for students who are completing at least one year of language study at the college level or three or four years of instruction at the high school level.
   b) CHINESE PROFICIENCY TEST.
   Publication Dates: 1986–1992.
   Acronym: CPT.

Comments: Available in Cantonese and Mandarin; "designed to be most appropriate for students who have completed two or more years of study at the college level."
Cross References: For reviews by Chi-wen Kao and Antony John Kunnan, see 13:62.

[484]
Choosing Outcomes and Accommodations for Children (COACH): A Guide to Educational Planning for Students with Disabilities, Second Edition.

Purpose: A tool to assist in educational planning.
Population: Preschool and school-aged learners with moderate, severe, or profound handicap.
Publication Date: 1998.
Acronym: COACH.
Scores: Item scores only.
Administration: Individual.
Price Data, 2002: $23.95 per 3 student record forms; $39.95 per manual (1998, 400 pages).
Time: (60) minutes (part 1 of 3 parts).
Comments: "Criterion-referenced"; ratings by a team including a parent, student (where appropriate), educators, related service personnel, and family advocate; previous versions available on microfiche from ERIC; previously listed as C.O.A.C.H.: Cayuga-Onondaga Assessment for Children with Handicaps.
Authors: Michael F. Giangreco, Chigee J. Cloninger, and Virginia S. Iverson.
Publisher: Brookes Publishing Co., Inc.
Cross References: See T5:553 (1 reference); for a review by Jay Kuder and David E. Kapel, see 11:73.

[485]
Chronic Pain Battery.

Purpose: Constructed to assess chronic pain by collecting "medical, psychological, behavioral, social, demographic and pain data."
Population: Patients ages 18 and over.
Publication Dates: 1983–1986.
Acronym: CPB.
Scores: 10 topics: Demographic and Social History, Past and Present Pain History, Past Treatment, Medications, Medical History, Personality-Pain Coping Style, Patient Expectations and Goals, Behavioral-Learning Factors, Psychosocial Factors, Patient Problem Ratings.
Administration: Group or individual.
Manual: No manual.
Price Data, 1994: $20 per specimen set including question book, answer sheet, and sample report.
Time: (30–60) minutes.
Comments: Comprises the Pain Assessment—Revised and the Symptom Checklist-90—Revised (2518);

self-administered; self-report; symptom inventory questionnaire.
Author: Stephen R. Levitt.
Publisher: Pain Resource Center, Inc.

[486]
Chronicle Career Quest.

Purpose: Designed to "help individuals identify careers related to personal interests and preferences and move independently from assessment through awareness to career exploration."
Population: Grades 7–10, Grades 9–16 and adult.
Publication Dates: 1989–2005.
Acronym: CCQ.
Scores: 12 G.O.E. clusters: Artistic, Scientific, Plants and Animals, Protective, Mechanical, Industrial, Business Detail, Selling, Accommodating, Humanitarian, Leading Influencing, Physical Performing.
Administration: Group or individual.
Forms, 2: S and L.
Price Data, 2005: $15 per specimen set including 1 each Form S and L (each Form includes Interest Inventory, Interest Profile & Career Paths; 2001, 16 pages each), 1 Reuseable Occupations Booklet (2005, 24 pages), Administrator's Guide (2001, 10 pages), 1 Technical Manual (2001, 10 pages); $30.75 per 25 Form S Booklets; $31 per 25 Form L Booklets; $32 per 25 Reuseable Occupations Booklets; $7.50 per Administrator's Guide; $18 per Technical Manual; quantity and package pricing available.
Time: (10–15) minutes for Interest Inventory (Form S and Form L); (10–15) minutes for Interpretation Guide (Form S and Form L); (20–45) minutes for Career Paths (Form S); (180–240) minutes for Career Paths (Form L).
Comments: Available online at www.MyeCareers.com.
Authors: Chronicle Guidance Publications, Inc.
Publisher: Chronicle Guidance Publications, Inc.
Cross References: For reviews by Larry G. Daniel and Donald Thompson, see 12:79.

[487]
CID Phonetic Inventory.

Purpose: To evaluate the hearing-impaired "child's speech ability at the phonetic level."
Population: Hearing-impaired children.
Publication Date: 1988.
Scores, 7: Suprasegmental Aspects, Vowels and Diphthongs, Initial Consonants, Consonants with Alternating Vowels, Final Consonants, Alternating Consonants, Average.
Administration: Individual.
Price Data, 2005: $50 per complete kit including manual (24 pages), 25 rating forms, and 166 stimulus cards; $12 per 25 additional rating forms.

Time: (30-35) minutes.
Author: Jean S. Moog.
Publisher: Central Institute for the Deaf.
Cross References: See T5:486 (3 references); for a review by Vincent J. Samar, see 11:67.

[488]
CID Picture SPINE (SPeech INtelligibility Evaluation).

Purpose: To "provide a measure of speech intelligibility for severely and profoundly hearing-impaired children and adolescents."
Population: Hearing-impaired children ages 6–13.
Publication Date: 1988.
Scores: Total score only.
Administration: Individual.
Price Data, 2005: $110 per complete kit including 300 picture cards, 25 response forms (4 pages), and test manual (31 pages); $12 per 25 additional response forms.
Time: (20-30) minutes.
Authors: Randall Monsen, Jean S. Moog, and Ann E. Geers.
Publisher: Central Institute for the Deaf.
Cross References: See T5:487 (2 references) and T4:465 (1 reference); for a review by Vincent J. Samar, see 11:68.

[489]
CID Preschool Performance Scale.

Purpose: Designed to measure the intelligence of hearing-impaired and language-impaired children.
Population: Hearing- and language-impaired and normal children ages 2 to 6.
Publication Date: 1984.
Scores, 7: Manual Planning, Manual Dexterity, Form Perception, Perceptual-Motor Skills, Preschool Skills, Part/Whole Relations, Total.
Administration: Individual.
Price Data, 2005: $850 per complete kit including manipulatives for subtests, manual (29 pages), and 30 recording booklets; $30 per manual; $35 per 30 recording booklets.
Time: (40) minutes.
Comments: Adaptation of the Randall's Island Performance Series.
Authors: Ann E. Geers, Helen S. Lane, and Central Institute for the Deaf.
Publisher: Stoelting Co.
Cross References: For reviews by Bruce A. Bracken and Albert C. Oosterhof, see 12:80.

[490]
The City University Colour Vision Test, Second Edition 1980.

Purpose: To assess defects of color vision.

Population: Adults and children.
Publication Date: 1980.
Scores, 3: Chroma Four, Chroma Two, Overall.
Administration: Individual.
Manual: No manual (introductory notes and instructions included in binder of test plates).
Price Data, 2001: $268 per complete kit including profile sheets, 10 test pages, and instructions.
Time: Administration time not reported.
Author: Robert Fletcher.
Publisher: Keeler Instruments Inc.
Cross References: For a review by Karen T. Carey, see 13:65.

[491]
Clark-Beck Obsessive-Compulsive Inventory.

Purpose: Developed to "provide an efficient, yet comprehensive and precise self-report screening instrument for obsessive and compulsive symptoms."
Population: Adolescents and adults suspected of having Obsessive Compulsive Disorder.
Publication Date: 2002.
Acronym: CBOCI.
Scores, 3: Obsessions, Compulsions, Total.
Administration: Individual.
Price Data, 2003: $80 per complete kit including manual (68 pages) and 25 record forms; $55 per manual; $35 per 25 record forms; $133 per 100 record forms.
Time: (10–30) minutes.
Comments: Requires eighth grade reading level.
Authors: David A. Clark and Aaron T. Beck.
Publisher: PsychCorp, A brand of Harcourt Assessment, Inc.
Cross References: For a review by Tony Cellucci, see 16:49.

[492]
The Clark Wilson Group Multi-Level Feedback Instruments and Development Programs.

Purpose: Designed to identify group or individual training needs, assess the effects of training, support interactive and participatory management, and to be used in organizational and management studies.
Population: Organizations, executives, managers, and employees.
Publication Dates: 1973–2002.
Administration: Group.
Price Data: Available from publisher.
Time: (12–18) minutes.
Comments: Paper-and-pencil or web-based administration; publisher suggests allowing 6 weeks to administer surveys and give feedback.
Authors: Clark L. Wilson and others noted below.
Publisher: The Clark Wilson Group.

a) LEADERSHIP SERIES.

1) *Executive Leadership.*

Purpose: Assesses executive competencies such as strategic foresight and oversight.
Population: Executives.
Publication Date: 1988.
Acronym: EXEC.
Scores, 17: Leadership Vision, Risk-Taking, Financial and Operational Analysis, Marketplace Savvy, Organizational Savvy, Judgement, Decisiveness, Team Growth and Development, Cultural Appreciation, Standards of Performance, Executive Energy, Push/Pressure, Coping with Stress, Sharing Credit, Effectiveness/Outcomes, Temporary Sources of Power, Lasting Sources of Power.
Authors: Paul M. Connolly and Clark L. Wilson.

2) *Leadership Practices.*

Purpose: Designed to provide feedback on an individual's vision, influence, and drive for change.
Population: Managers and executives.
Publication Date: 1986.
Acronym: SLP.
Scores, 17: Vision/Imagination, Risk-Taking, Organizational Sensitivity, Encouraging Participation, Persuasiveness, Teaming, Standards of Performance, Perseverance, Push/Pressure, Effectiveness/Outcomes, Coping with Stress, Feedback, Energy, Sharing Credit, Trustworthiness, Temporary Sources of Power, Lasting Sources of Power.
Authors: Clark L. Wilson and Paul M. Connolly.

3) *Project Leadership Practices.*

Purpose: Designed to assess leadership skills for project managers.
Population: Project managers and project leaders.
Publication Date: 1995.
Acronym: PLP.
Scores, 19: Clarification of Goals and Objectives, Organization Courage, Judgement, Planning, Adaptation, Problem Solving, Teaming, Coaching, Manager Relations, Customer Relations, Feedback, Push/Pressure, Delegation/Permissiveness, Recognition/Reinforcement, Approachability, Building Trust, Sources of Power, Effectiveness, Belief in Project.
Authors: Clark L. Wilson, Paul M. Connolly, and David B. Gillespie.

4) *Leadership in Health Services.*

Purpose: Designed to assess leadership and management skills for health administration.

Population: VPs, directors, senior and middle administrators.
Acronym: LHS.
Scores, 21: Vision and Imagination, Strategic and Operational Goals, Understanding the Changing Environment, Managing Financial Drivers, Expertise, Risk-Taking, Empowering Employees, Building a Team Environment, Coaching for Performance, Openness to Feedback, Valuing Diversity, Standards of Performance, Clarity of Communications, Persuasiveness, Managing Conflict, Delegation/Permissiveness, Goal Pressure, Recognizing and Reqarding Others, Building Trust, Tension Level, Overall Effectiveness.
Authors: Eugene P. Buccini, Richard L. Dowall, and Clark L. Wilson.

b) MANAGEMENT SERIES.

1) *Management Practices.*

Purpose: Assesses basic managerial competencies.
Population: Managers.
Publication Date: 1973.
Acronym: SMP.
Scores, 23: Clarification of Goals and Objectives, Upward Communication, Orderly Work Planning, Expertise, Work Facilitation, Feedback, Time Emphasis, Control of Details, Goal Pressure, Delegation (Permissiveness), Recognition for Good Performance, Approachability, Teambuilding, Interest in Subordinate Growth, Building Trust, Work Involvement, Coworker Competence, Team Atmosphere, Opportunity for Growth, Tension Level, Organization Climate, General Morale, Commitment.
Author: Clark L. Wilson.

2) *Peer Relations.*

Purpose: Assesses organizational skills for specialists.
Population: Managers and individual contributors.
Publication Date: 1974.
Acronym: SPR.
Scores, 22: Clarity of Your Own Goals, Clarity of Communications, Encouraging Peer Participation, Orderly Work Planning, Problem Solving, Expertise, Teamwork/Cooperation, Feedback to Peers, Time Emphasis, Attention to Details, Pressure on Peers, Acknowledging Peer Contributions, Approachability, Dependability, Work Involvement, Coworker Competence, Team Atmosphere, Opportunity for Growth, Tension Level, Organization Climate, General Morale, Commitment.
Author: Clark L. Wilson.

3) *Working with Others.*

Purpose: Assesses supervisory skills for the first-time or prospective manager.

Publication Date: 1991.

Acronym: WWO.

Scores, 13: Commitment to Work, Assertiveness, Problem Solving/Resourcefulness, Teamwork, Willingness to Listen, Attention to Details, Push/Pressure, Recognizing Co-worker Performance, Effectiveness/Outcomes, Friendliness, Dependability, Working with Diversity, Future Promise.

Author: Clark L. Wilson.

4) *Coaching Practices.*

Purpose: Assesses coaching and appraising skills for performance management.

Population: Managers and executives.

Publication Date: 1993.

Acronym: SCP.

Scores, 14: Commitment to Coaching, Planning for Personal Growth, Coaching Skills, Coaching for Teamwork, Technical/Functional Expertise, Organization Awareness, Assessment Skills, Responding to Defensiveness, Control of Details, Delegation (Permissiveness), Recognizing Good Performance, Approachability, Trust, Overall Effectiveness.

Authors: Richard L. Dowall and Clark L. Wilson.

5) *Leadership Competencies for Managers.*

Population: Managers.

Publication Date: 1998.

Acronym: LCM.

Scores, 21: Vision/Imagination, Clarification of Goals, Risk-Taking, Decision Making/Problem Solving, Managing Costs, Encouraging Participation, Clarity of Communications, Teambuilding, Coaching, Managing Conflict, Feedback, Standards of Performance, Personal Drive, Persuasiveness, Delegation, Goal Pressure, Recognition for Good Performance, Building Trust, Managing Diversity, Tension Level, Overall Effectiveness.

Authors: Clark L. Wilson, Paul Connolly, and Richard L. Dowell.

c) SALES SERIES.

1) *Sales Management Practices.*

Purpose: Assesses managerial competencies for field sales managers.

Population: Sales managers.

Publication Date: 1975.

Acronym: SSMP.

Scores, 23: Clarification of Goals and Objectives, Upward Communication, Orderly Work Planning, Expertise, Work Facilitation, Feedback, Time Emphasis, Control of Details, Goal Pressure, Delegation (Permissiveness), Recognition of Good Performance, Approachability, Teambuilding, Interest in Subordinate Growth, Building Trust, Work Involvement, Coworker Competence, Team Atmosphere, Opportunity for Growth, Tension Level, Organization Climate, General Morale, Commitment.

Author: Clark L. Wilson.

2) *Sales Relations.*

Purpose: Provides feedback on skills of sales representatives from customers and prospects.

Population: Sales representatives.

Publication Date: 1975.

Acronym: SSR.

Scores, 11: Understanding Us, Communicating Effectively, Account Service, Analyzing Needs, Presenting Benefits, Asking for the Order, Answering Objections, Selling Pressure, Professionalism, Approachability, Overall Satisfaction.

Author: Clark L. Wilson.

3) *Client Relations.*

Purpose: Assesses internal and external consulting skills.

Population: Consultants and client service representatives.

Publication Date: 1998.

Acronym: SCR.

Scores, 13: Understanding Us, Communicating Effectively, Account Service, Analyzing Needs, Presenting Benefits, Making Recommendations, Answering Objections, Personal Enthusiasm, Personal Pressure, Acknowledging Client Responses, Professionalism, Approachability, Overall Satisfaction.

d) TEAM SERIES.

1) *Executive Team.*

Purpose: Coordinates efforts of top management groups.

Population: Executive teams.

Publication Date: 1993.

Acronym: XT.

Scores, 16: Clarity of Mission/Strategic Goals, Leadership for Growth/Productivity, Resistance to Change, Marketing Focus, Organization Awareness, Consensus Planning, Team Atmosphere, Information/Data Support, Human Resource Development, Organization Stretch, Monitoring Executive Plans, Satisfying, Internal Problems, Sharing Credit, Coping with Stress, Effectiveness/Outcomes.

Authors: Paul M. Connolly and Clark L. Wilson.

2) *Our Team.*

Purpose: Provides feedback from team members on team negotiating skills and conflict resolution.

Population: Teams (Work Groups, Task Forces, Quality Circles, Project Teams, Design Teams, Teams with or without Leaders).

Publication Date: 1989.

Acronym: OT.

Scores, 14: Clarity of Goals and Priorities, Coworker Competence, Consensus Planning, Team Atmosphere, Newcomer Support, Conflict Resolution, Management Support, Management Feedback, Monitoring the Team's Work, Tension/Stress Level, Domination, Satisfying, Recognition/Satisfaction, Effectiveness/Outcomes.

Author: Clark L. Wilson.

3) *My Team Mates.*

Purpose: Provides feedback from team mates on a member's teaming skills.

Population: Team members.

Publication Date: 1989.

Acronym: MTM.

Scores, 13: Clarity of Personal Goals, Innovativeness, Functional Expertise, Teamwork, Leadership for Consensus, Negotiating Skills, Monitoring Personal Output, Coping with Stress and Ambiguity, Personal Drive, Pressure on Team Mates, Acknowledging Others' Efforts, Personal Values, Personal Effectiveness.

Author: Clark L. Wilson.

Cross References: See T4:469 (1 reference).

[493]
Clarke Sex History Questionnaire for Males—Revised.

Purpose: Designed "to evaluate a sex offender's sexual preference profile as well as evaluating their potential for sexually conventional behavior."

Population: Sex offenders.

Publication Date: 1999.

Acronym: SHQ-R.

Scores: 23 scales: Childhood and Adolescent Sexual Experiences and Sexual Abuse, Sexual Dysfunction, Female Adult Frequency, Female Pubescent Frequency, Female Child Frequency, Male Adult Frequency, Male Pubescent Frequency, Male Child Frequency, Child Identification, Fantasy Activities with Females, Fantasy Activities with Males, Exposure to Pornography, Transvestism, Fetishism, Feminine Gender Identity, Voyeurism, Exhibitionism Frequency, Exhibiting Behavior, Obscene Phone Calls, Toucheurism and Frotteurism, Sexual Aggression, Lie, Infrequency.

Administration: Individual.

Price Data, 2006: $63 per preview kit including technical manual (2002, 76 pages), 1 item booklet, and 1 comprehensive report; $46 per 3 item booklets; $141 per 10 item booklets; $57 per technical manual; $20 per mail-in or fax-in individual summary report.

Time: Administration time not reported.

Comments: Self-report paper-and-pencil inventory that is scored electronically by publisher.

Authors: Ron Langevin and Dan Paitch.

Publisher: Multi-Health Systems, Inc.

Cross References: For reviews by Roger A. Boothroyd and Delores D. Walcott, see 16:50.

[494]
The Class Activities Questionnaire.

Purpose: Developed to provide "a measure of the instructional climate."

Population: Students and teachers Grades 6–12.

Publication Date: 1982.

Acronym: CAQ.

Scores: 5 dimensions: Lower Thought Processes, Higher Thought Processes, Classroom Focus, Classroom Climate, Student Opinions.

Administration: Group.

Price Data: Available from publisher.

Time: (20–30) minutes.

Author: Joe M. Steele.

Publisher: Creative Learning Press, Inc.

Cross References: See T5:493 (1 reference); for a review by Robert W. Hiltonsmith, see 9:226 (1 reference).

[495]
The Classroom Communication Skills Inventory: A Listening and Speaking Checklist.

Purpose: Evaluates "oral communication skills that have been determined to be important for listening and speaking in the school setting and are essential for classroom learning."

Population: Students.

Publication Date: 1993.

Acronym: CCSI.

Scores: 10 ratings: Basic Speech and Hearing Processes (Auditory Perception, Speech), Classroom Communication (Attention, Class Participation), Language Content and Structure (Vocabulary, Grammar, Organization of Language), Interpersonal Classroom Communication (Using Language for a Variety of Purposes, Conversing Effectively, Using Appropriate Nonverbal Communication Skills).

Administration: Individual.

Price Data, 2002: $40.30 per teacher's manual (51 pages) and 25 record forms.

Time: (10–15) minutes.

Author: The Psychological Corporation.

Publisher: PsychCorp, A brand of Harcourt Assessment, Inc.

Cross References: For reviews by Linda Crocker and Dolores Kluppel Vetter, see 13:66.

[496]
Classroom Environment Scale, Second Edition.

Purpose: Designed to "assess the social climate of junior high and high school classrooms. It focuses on teacher-student and student-student relationships and on the organizational structure of a classroom."

Population: Junior high and senior high teachers and students.

Publication Dates: 1974–1987.

Acronym: CES.

Scores, 9: Relationship dimensions (Involvement, Affiliation, Teacher Support), Personal Growth/Goal Orientation dimensions (Task Orientation, Competition), System Maintenance and Change dimensions (Order and Organization, Rule Clarity, Teacher Control, Innovation).

Administration: Group.

Forms, 3: Real Form (Form R), Ideal Form (Form I), Expectations Form (Form E), and a Short Form (Form S) by administering and scoring the first 36 items of Form R.

Price Data, 2006: $40 per sampler set including third edition manual; $120 per 150-copy duplication set; quantity discounts for bulk permissions bundles.

Time: [15–20] minutes.

Comments: One of ten Social Climate Scales (T5:2445).

Authors: Rudolf H. Moos and Edison J. Trickett.

Publisher: Mind Garden, Inc.

Cross References: See T5:495 (16 references) and T4:475 (5 references); for reviews by Richard A. Saudargas and Corinne Roth Smith, see 10:60 (16 references); see also T3:409 (9 references); for reviews by Maurice J. Eash and C. Robert Pace of an earlier edition, see 8:521 (3 references). For a review of the Social Climate Scales, see 8:681.

[497]
Classroom Reading Inventory, Seventh Edition.

Purpose: To identify the student's reading skills and/or abilities.

Population: Grades 2–8, high school and adults.

Publication Dates: 1965–1994.

Acronym: CRI.

Scores, 6: Word Recognition, Comprehension, Independent Reading Level, Instructional Reading Level, Frustration Reading Level, Hearing Capacity Level.

Administration: Individual in part.

Forms: Form A (elementary, subskills format); Form B (elementary, literature format); Form C (junior high or middle school students); Form D (for use with high school and adults).

Price Data: Available from publisher.

Time: (24) minutes.

Author: Nicholas J. Silvaroli.

Publisher: Brown and Benchmark Publishers, a Division of Wm. C. Brown Communications [No reply from publisher; status unknown].

Cross References: See T5:496 (4 references) and T4:476 (4 references); for reviews by Ira E. Aaron and Sylvia M. Hutchinson and by Janet A. Norris, see 10:61 (4 references); for a review of an earlier edition by Marjorie S. Johnson, see 8:749; see also T2:1618 (1 reference); for an excerpted review by Donald L. Cleland, see 7:715.

[498]
CLEP Examination in American Government.

Purpose: For college accreditation, advanced placement, or assessment of educational attainment.

Population: Persons entering college or already in college.

Publication Dates: 1965–2002.

Scores: Total score only.

Administration: Group.

Price Data: Available from publisher.

Time: (90) minutes.

Comments: Tests administered at centers throughout the United States and internationally; program administered by the College Board and Educational Testing Service.

Author: Educational Testing Service.

Publisher: Educational Testing Service.

Cross References: For additional information and a review by Howard D. Mehlinger, see 8:919. For reviews of the CLEP program, see 8:473 (3 reviews) and 7:664 (3 reviews).

[499]
CLEP Examination in American Literature.

Purpose: For college accreditation, advanced placement, or assessment of educational attainment.

Population: Persons entering college or already in college.

Publication Dates: 1971–2002.

Scores: Total score only; optional essay, locally scored.

Administration: Group.

Price Data: Available from publisher.

Time: (90) minutes.

Comments: Tests administered at centers throughout the United States and internationally; program administered by the College Board and Educational Testing Service.

Author: Educational Testing Service.
Publisher: Educational Testing Service.
Cross References: For additional information and a review by Leo P. Ruth, see 8:64. For reviews of the CLEP program, see 8:473 (3 reviews).

[500]
CLEP Examination in Analyzing and Interpreting Literature.
Purpose: For college accreditation, advanced placement, or assessment of educational attainment.
Population: Persons entering college or already in college.
Publication Dates: 1964–2002.
Scores: Total score only; optional essay, locally scored.
Administration: Group.
Price Data: Available from publisher.
Time: (90) minutes.
Comments: Tests administered at centers throughout the United States and internationally; program administered by the College Board and Educational Testing Service.
Author: Educational Testing Service.
Publisher: Educational Testing Service.
Cross References: For additional information and a review by John C. Sherwood, see 8:65 (1 reference). For reviews of the CLEP program, see 8:473 (3 reviews) and 7:664 (3 reviews).

[501]
CLEP Examination in Calculus with Elementary Functions.
Purpose: For college accreditation, advanced placement, or assessment of educational attainment.
Population: Persons entering college or already in college.
Publication Dates: 1974–2002.
Scores: Total score only.
Administration: Group.
Price Data: Available from publisher.
Time: (90) minutes.
Comments: Tests administered at centers throughout the United States and internationally; program administered by the College Board and Educational Testing Service.
Author: Educational Testing Service.
Publisher: Educational Testing Service.
Cross References: For a review by J. Phillip Smith, see 8:255. For reviews of the CLEP program, see 8:473 (3 reviews).

[502]
CLEP Examination in College Algebra.
Purpose: For college accreditation, advanced placement, or assessment of educational attainment.

Population: Persons entering college or already in college.
Publication Dates: 1968-1999.
Scores: Total score only.
Administration: Group.
Price Data: Available from publisher.
Time: (90) minutes.
Comments: Tests administered at centers throughout the United States and internationally; program administered by the College Board and Educational Testing Service.
Author: Educational Testing Service.
Publisher: Educational Testing Service.
Cross References: For additional information and a review by J. Philip Smith, see 8:297. For reviews of the CLEP program, see 8:473 (3 reviews) and 7:664 (3 reviews).

[503]
CLEP Examination in College Algebra–Trigonometry.
Purpose: For college accreditation, advanced placement, or assessment of educational attainment.
Population: Persons entering college or already in college.
Publication Dates: 1968-1999.
Scores: Total score only.
Administration: Group.
Price Data: Available from publisher.
Time: (90) minutes.
Comments: Tests administered at centers throughout the United States and internationally; program administered by the College Board and Educational Testing Service.
Author: Educational Testing Service.
Publisher: Educational Testing Service.
Cross References: For a review by Peter A. Lappan, Jr., see 8:256 (1 reference); for a review by Carl G. Willis, see 7:454. For reviews of the CLEP program, see 8:473 (3 reviews) and 7:664 (3 reviews).

[504]
CLEP Examination in College-Level French Language, Levels 1 and 2.
Purpose: For college accreditation, advanced placement, or assessment of educational attainment.
Population: Persons entering college or already in college.
Publication Dates: 1975–2002.
Scores, 3: Reading Comprehension, Listening Comprehension, Total.
Administration: Group.
Price Data: Available from publisher.
Time: (90) minutes.

Comments: Tests administered at centers throughout the United States and internationally; program administered by the College Board and Educational Testing Service.
Author: Educational Testing Service.
Publisher: Educational Testing Service.
Cross References: For a review by Michio Peter Hagiwara, see 8:115. For reviews of the CLEP program, see 8:473 (3 reviews).

[505]
CLEP Examination in College-Level German Language, Levels 1 and 2.

Purpose: For college accreditation, advanced placement, or assessment of educational attainment.
Population: Persons entering college or already in college.
Publication Dates: 1975–2002.
Scores, 3: Reading Comprehension, Listening Comprehension, Total.
Administration: Group.
Price Data: Available from publisher.
Time: (90) minutes.
Comments: Tests administered at centers throughout the United States and internationally; program administered by the College Board and Educational Testing Service.
Author: Educational Testing Service.
Publisher: Educational Testing Service.
Cross References: For reviews by Stefan R. Fink and Herbert Lederer, see 8:127. For reviews of the CLEP program, see 8:473 (3 reviews).

[506]
CLEP Examination in College-Level Spanish Language, Levels 1 and 2.

Purpose: For college accreditation, advanced placement, or assessment of educational attainment.
Population: Persons entering college or already in college.
Publication Dates: 1975–2002.
Scores, 3: Reading Comprehension, Listening Comprehension, Total.
Administration: Group.
Price Data: Available from publisher.
Time: (90) minutes.
Comments: Tests administered at centers throughout the United States and internationally; program administered by the College Board and Educational Testing Service.
Author: Educational Testing Service.
Publisher: Educational Testing Service.
Cross References: For reviews of the CLEP program, see 8:473 (3 reviews).

[507]
CLEP Examination in Educational Psychology.

Purpose: For college accreditation, advanced placement, or assessment of educational attainment.
Population: Persons entering college or already in college.
Publication Dates: 1967–2002.
Scores: Total score only.
Administration: Group.
Price Data: Available from publisher.
Time: (90) minutes.
Comments: Tests administered at centers throughout the United States and internationally; program administered by the College Board and Educational Testing Service.
Author: Educational Testing Service.
Publisher: Educational Testing Service.
Cross References: For reviews of the CLEP program, see 8:473 (3 reviews) and 7:664 (3 reviews).

[508]
CLEP Examination in English Literature.

Purpose: For college accreditation, advanced placement, or assessment of educational attainment.
Population: Persons entering college or already in college.
Publication Dates: 1970–2002.
Scores: Total score only; optional essay, locally scored.
Administration: Group.
Price Data: Available from publisher.
Time: (90) minutes.
Comments: Tests administered at centers throughout the United States and internationally; program administered by the College Board and Educational Testing Service.
Author: Educational Testing Service.
Publisher: Educational Testing Service.
Cross References: For additional information and a review by Edward M. White, see 8:66. For reviews of the CLEP program, see 8:473 (3 reviews).

[509]
CLEP Examination in General Biology.

Purpose: For college accreditation, advanced placement, or assessment of educational attainment.
Population: Persons entering college or already in college.
Publication Dates: 1970–2002.
Scores: Total score only.
Administration: Group.
Price Data: Available from publisher.
Time: (90) minutes.
Comments: Tests administered at centers throughout the United States and internationally; program

administered by the College Board and Educational Testing Service.
Author: Educational Testing Service.
Publisher: Educational Testing Service.
Cross References: For additional information and a review by Clarence H. Nelson, see 8:832. For reviews of the CLEP program, see 8:473 (3 reviews) and 7:664 (3 reviews).

[510]

CLEP Examination in General Chemistry.

Purpose: For college accreditation, advanced placement, or assessment of educational attainment.
Population: Persons entering college or already in college.
Publication Dates: 1964–2002.
Scores: Total score only.
Administration: Group.
Price Data: Available from publisher.
Time: (90) minutes.
Comments: Tests administered at centers throughout the United States and internationally; program administered by the College Board and Educational Testing Service.
Author: Educational Testing Service.
Publisher: Educational Testing Service.
Cross References: For additional information and a review by J. Arthur Campbell, see 8:847. For reviews of the CLEP program, see 8:473 (3 reviews) and 7:664 (3 reviews).

[511]

CLEP Examination in History of the United States: Early Colonizations to 1877.

Purpose: For college accreditation, advanced placement, or assessment of educational attainment.
Population: Persons entering college or already in college.
Publication Dates: 1980–2002.
Scores: Total score only.
Administration: Group.
Price Data: Available from publisher.
Time: (90) minutes.
Comments: Tests administered at centers throughout the United States and internationally; program administered by the College Board and Educational Testing Service.
Author: Educational Testing Service.
Publisher: Educational Testing Service.

[512]

CLEP Examination in History of the United States II: 1865 to the Present.

Purpose: For college accreditation, advanced placement, or assessment of educational attainment.

Population: Persons entering college or already in college.
Publication Dates: 1980–2002.
Scores: Total score only.
Administration: Group.
Price Data: Available from publisher.
Time: (90) minutes.
Comments: Tests administered at centers throughout the United States and internationally; program administered by the College Board and Educational Testing Service.
Author: Educational Testing Service.
Publisher: Educational Testing Service.

[513]

CLEP Examination in Human Growth and Development.

Purpose: For college accreditation, advanced placement, or assessment of educational attainment.
Population: Persons entering college or already in college.
Publication Dates: 1969–2002.
Scores: Total score only.
Administration: Group.
Price Data: Available from publisher.
Time: (90) minutes.
Comments: Tests administered at centers throughout the United States and internationally; program administered by the College Board and Educational Testing Service.
Author: Educational Testing Service.
Publisher: Educational Testing Service.
Cross References: For reviews of the CLEP program, see 8:473 (3 reviews) and 7:664 (3 reviews).

[514]

CLEP Examination in Information Systems and Computer Applications.

Purpose: For college accreditation, advanced placement, or assessment of educational attainment.
Population: Persons entering college or already in college.
Publication Dates: 1968–2002.
Scores: Total score only.
Administration: Group.
Price Data: Available from publisher.
Time: (90) minutes.
Comments: Tests administered at centers throughout the United States and internationally; program administered by the College Board and Educational Testing Service; previously entitled CLEP Subject Examination in Computers and Data Processing.
Author: Educational Testing Service.
Publisher: Educational Testing Service.
Cross References: For reviews of the CLEP program, see 8:473 (3 reviews) and 7:664 (3 reviews).

[515]
CLEP Examination in Introductory Business Law.

Purpose: For college accreditation, advanced placement, or assessment of educational attainment.

Population: Persons entering college or already in college.

Publication Dates: 1970–2002.

Scores: Total score only.

Administration: Group.

Price Data: Available from publisher.

Time: (90) minutes.

Comments: Tests administered at centers throughout the United States and internationally; program administered by the College Board and Educational Testing Service.

Author: Educational Testing Service.

Publisher: Educational Testing Service.

Cross References: For reviews of the CLEP program, see 8:473 (3 reviews) and 7:664 (3 reviews).

[516]
CLEP Examination in Introductory Psychology.

Purpose: For college accreditation, advanced placement, or assessment of educational attainment.

Population: Persons entering college or already in college.

Publication Dates: 1967–2002.

Scores: Total score only.

Administration: Group.

Price Data: Available from publisher.

Time: (90) minutes.

Comments: Tests administered at centers throughout the United States and internationally; program administered by the College Board and Educational Testing Service; previously entitled CLEP Subject Examination in General Psychology.

Author: Educational Testing Service.

Publisher: Educational Testing Service.

Cross References: See T3:442 (2 references); for additional information and a review by Alfred E. Hall of an earlier edition, see 8:460. For reviews of the CLEP program, see 8:473 (3 reviews) and 7:664 (3 reviews).

[517]
CLEP Examination in Introductory Sociology.

Purpose: For college accreditation, advanced placement, or assessment of educational attainment.

Population: Persons entering college or already in college.

Publication Dates: 1965–2002.

Scores: Total score only.

Administration: Group.

Price Data: Available from publisher.

Time: (90) minutes.

Comments: Tests administered at centers throughout the United States and internationally; program administered by the College Board and Educational Testing Service.

Author: Educational Testing Service.

Publisher: Educational Testing Service.

Cross References: For reviews of the CLEP program, see 8:473 (3 reviews) and 7:664 (3 reviews).

[518]
CLEP Examination in Principles of Accounting.

Purpose: For college accreditation, advanced placement, or assessment of educational attainment.

Population: Persons entering college or already in college.

Publication Dates: 1970–2002.

Scores: Total score only.

Administration: Group.

Price Data: Available from publisher.

Time: (90) minutes.

Comments: Tests administered at centers throughout the United States and internationally; program administered by the College Board and Educational Testing Service.

Author: Educational Testing Service.

Publisher: Educational Testing Service.

Cross References: For reviews of the CLEP program, see 8:473 (3 reviews).

[519]
CLEP Examination in Principles of Macroeconomics.

Purpose: For college accreditation, advanced placement, or assessment of educational attainment.

Population: Persons entering college or already in college.

Publication Dates: 1974–2002.

Scores: Total score only.

Administration: Group.

Price Data: Available from publisher.

Time: (90) minutes.

Comments: Tests administered at centers throughout the United States and internationally; program administered by the College Board and Educational Testing Service.

Author: Educational Testing Service.

Publisher: Educational Testing Service.

Cross References: For reviews of the CLEP program, see 8:473 (3 reviews).

[520]
CLEP Examination in Principles of Management.

Purpose: For college accreditation, advanced placement, or assessment of educational attainment.
Population: Persons entering college or already in college.
Publication Dates: 1969–2002.
Scores: Total score only.
Administration: Group.
Price Data: Available from publisher.
Time: (90) minutes.
Comments: Tests administered at centers throughout the United States and internationally; program administered by the College Board and Educational Testing Service.
Author: Educational Testing Service.
Publisher: Educational Testing Service.
Cross References: For reviews of the CLEP program, see 8:473 (3 reviews) and 7:664 (3 reviews).

[521]
CLEP Examination in Principles of Marketing.

Purpose: For college accreditation, advanced placement, or assessment of educational attainment.
Population: Persons entering college or already in college.
Publication Dates: 1968–2002.
Scores: Total score only.
Administration: Group.
Price Data: Available from publisher.
Time: (90) minutes.
Comments: Tests administered at centers throughout the United States and internationally; program administered by the College Board and Educational Testing Service.
Author: Educational Testing Service.
Publisher: Educational Testing Service.
Cross References: For reviews of the CLEP program, see 8:473 (3 reviews) and 7:664 (3 reviews).

[522]
CLEP Examination in Principles of Microeconomics.

Purpose: For college accreditation, advanced placement, or assessment of educational attainment.
Population: Persons entering college or already in college.
Publication Dates: 1974–2002.
Scores: Total score only.
Administration: Group.
Price Data: Available from publisher.
Time: (90) minutes.

Comments: Tests administered at centers throughout the United States and internationally; program administered by the College Board and Educational Testing Service.
Author: Educational Testing Service.
Publisher: Educational Testing Service.
Cross References: For reviews of the CLEP program, see 8:473 (3 reviews).

[523]
CLEP Examination in Trigonometry.

Purpose: For college accreditation, advanced placement, or assessment of educational attainment.
Population: Persons entering college or already in college.
Publication Dates: 1968–2002.
Scores: Total score only.
Administration: Group.
Price Data: Available from publisher.
Time: (90) minutes.
Comments: Tests administered at centers throughout the United States and internationally; program administered by the College Board and Educational Testing Service.
Author: Educational Testing Service.
Publisher: Educational Testing Service.
Cross References: For reviews of the CLEP program, see 8:473 (3 reviews) and 7:664 (3 reviews).

[524]
CLEP Examination in Western Civilization I: Ancient Near East to 1648.

Purpose: For college accreditation, advanced placement, or assessment of educational attainment.
Population: Persons entering college or already in college.
Publication Dates: 1964–2002.
Scores: Total score only.
Administration: Group.
Price Data: Available from publisher.
Time: (90) minutes.
Comments: Tests administered at centers throughout the United States and internationally; program administered by the College Board and Educational Testing Service.
Author: Educational Testing Service.
Publisher: Educational Testing Service.
Cross References: For reviews of the CLEP program, see 8:473 (3 reviews) and 7:664 (3 reviews).

[525]
CLEP Examination in Western Civilization II: 1648 to Present.

Purpose: For college accreditation, advanced placement, or assessment of educational attainment.

Population: Persons entering college or already in college.
Publication Dates: 1964–2002.
Scores: Total score only.
Administration: Group.
Price Data: Available from publisher.
Time: (90) minutes.
Comments: Tests administered at centers throughout the United States and internationally; program administered by the College Board and Educational Testing Service.
Author: Educational Testing Service.
Publisher: Educational Testing Service.
Cross References: For reviews of the CLEP program, see 8:473 (3 reviews) and 7:664 (3 reviews).

[526]
CLEP Examinations in English Composition and English Composition Test with Essay.

Purpose: For college accreditation, advanced placement, or assessment of educational attainment.
Population: Persons entering college or already in college.
Publication Dates: 1964–2002.
Scores: Total score only.
Administration: Group.
Price Data: Available from publisher.
Time: (45) minutes per composition test; (45) minutes per essay.
Comments: English Composition Test with Essay administered via computer at any time per a test site's schedule; English Composition test administered at centers throughout the United States and internationally; program administered by the College Board and Educational Testing Service.
Author: Educational Testing Service.
Publisher: Educational Testing Service.
Cross References: See T3:412 (1 reference); for additional information, see 8:42 (4 references) and T2:58 (1 reference); for reviews of the CLEP program, see 8:473 (3 reviews) and 7:664 (3 reviews).

[527]
CLEP Examinations in Humanities.

Purpose: For college accreditation, advanced placement, or assessment of educational attainment.
Population: Persons entering college or already in college.
Publication Dates: 1964–2002.
Scores: Total score only.
Administration: Group.
Price Data: Available from publisher.
Time: (90) minutes.
Comments: Tests administered at centers throughout the United States and internationally; program administered by the College Board and Educational Testing Service.

Author: Educational Testing Service.
Publisher: Educational Testing Service.
Cross References: For additional information and a review by William E. Kline, see 8:254 (1 reference); for reviews of the CLEP program, see 8:473 (3 reviews) and 7:664 (3 reviews).

[528]
CLEP Examinations in Mathematics.

Purpose: For college accreditation, advanced placement, or assessment of educational attainment.
Population: Persons entering college or already in college.
Publication Dates: 1964–2002.
Scores: Total score only.
Administration: Group.
Price Data: Available from publisher.
Time: (90) minutes.
Comments: Tests administered at centers throughout the United States and internationally; program administered by the College Board and Educational Testing Service.
Author: Educational Testing Service.
Publisher: Educational Testing Service.
Cross References: For a review by William E. Kline, see 8:254 (1 reference).

[529]
CLEP Examinations in Natural Sciences.

Purpose: For college accreditation, advanced placement, or assessment of educational attainment.
Population: Persons entering college or already in college.
Publication Dates: 1964–2002.
Scores: Total score only.
Administration: Group.
Price Data: Available from publisher.
Time: (90) minutes.
Comments: Tests administered at centers throughout the United States and internationally; program administered by the College Board and Educational Testing Service.
Author: Educational Testing Service.
Publisher: Educational Testing Service.
Cross References: For additional information by George G. Mallinson, see 8:824 (2 references); for reviews of the CLEP program, see 8:473 (3 reviews) and 7:664 (3 reviews).

[530]
CLEP Examinations in Social Sciences and History.

Purpose: For college accreditation, advanced placement, or assessment of educational attainment.
Population: Persons entering college or already in college.

Publication Dates: 1964–2002.
Scores: Total score only.
Administration: Group.
Price Data: Available from publisher.
Time: (90) minutes.
Comments: Tests administered at centers throughout the United States and internationally; program administered by the College Board and Educational Testing Service.
Author: Educational Testing Service.
Publisher: Educational Testing Service.
Cross References: For additional information and a review by Richard E. Gross, see 8:886 (1 reference); for reviews of the CLEP program, see 8:473 (3 reviews) and 7:664 (3 reviews).

[531]
CLEP Examination in Freshman College Composition.

Purpose: For college accreditation, advanced placement, or assessment of educational attainment.
Population: Persons entering college or already in college.
Publication Dates: 1994–2002.
Scores: Total score only; optional essay, scored locally.
Administration: Group.
Price Data: Available from publisher.
Time: (90) minutes.
Comments: Tests administered at centers throughout the United States and internationally; program administered by the College Board and Educational Testing Service; replaces College Composition (T4:491) and Freshman English (T4:498) examinations.
Author: Educational Testing Service.
Publisher: Educational Testing Service.
Cross References: For a review by Leonard S. Feldt of the CLEP Freshman English Examination, see 8:44 (1 reference). For a review by Charlotte Croon Davis of the CLEP College Composition Examination, see 8:43 (2 references).

[532]
Clerical Abilities Battery.

Purpose: Assesses clerical abilities "for use in hiring and promoting clerical personnel."
Population: Clerical applicants and employees and business school students.
Publication Dates: 1985–1987.
Acronym: CAB.
Scores: 7 tests: Filing, Comparing Information, Copying Information, Using Tables, Proofreading, Addition and Subtraction, Reasoning with Numbers.
Administration: Group or individual.
Forms, 2: A, B.

Restricted Distribution: Distribution of Form A restricted to personnel departments in business and industry.
Price Data, 2006: $180 per starter kit including 5 test booklets of each of 7 tests, 7 keys, and manual; $55 per 25 test booklets (specify form: Filing, Copying Information, Comparing Information, Using Tables, Proofreading, Addition and Subtraction, Reasoning with Numbers); $207 per 100 test booklets (specify form); $84 per set of scoring stencils; $36 per manual.
Time: 70(105) minutes for the battery; 5(10) minutes each for first four tests, 15(20) minutes each for next two tests, 20(25) minutes for last test.
Comments: Tests available as separates.
Authors: The Psychological Corporation.
Publisher: Harcourt Assessment, Inc.
Cross References: For reviews by Joseph C. Ciechalski and Bikkar S. Randhawa, see 11:71.

[533]
Clerical Aptitude Test: Acorn National Aptitude Tests.

Purpose: Designed to measure qualities associated with good clerical performance.
Population: Grades 7–12 and adult clerks.
Publication Dates: 1943–1950.
Scores, 4: Business Practice, Number Checking, Date and Name and Address Checking, Total.
Administration: Group.
Price Data: Available from publisher.
Time: 40(50) minutes.
Authors: Andrew Kobal, J. Wayne Wrightstone, and Karl R. Kunze.
Publisher: Psychometric Affiliates.
Cross References: See T3:464 (2 references); see also 5:847 (1 reference); for reviews by Marion A. Bills, Donald G. Paterson, Henry Weitz, and E. F. Wonderlic, see 3:623.

[534]
Clerical Aptitudes.

Purpose: "Designed to indicate ability to learn the tasks usually performed in various clerical jobs."
Population: Applicants for office personnel positions.
Publication Dates: 1947–1982.
Scores, 4: Office Vocabulary, Office Arithmetic, Office Checking, Total.
Administration: Individual or group.
Price Data: Available from publisher.
Time: 25 minutes.
Comments: Previously listed as SRA Clerical Aptitudes.
Author: Richardson, Bellows, Henry & Co., Inc.
Publisher: Pearson Performance Solutions [No reply from publisher; status unknown].

Cross References: See T2:791 (2 references); for reviews by Edward N. Hay and G. A. Satter, see 4:732.

[535]
Clerical Skills Series.

Purpose: "Designed to measure proficiency in paper work tasks typical of . . . clerical occupations."
Population: Clerical worker.
Publication Date: 1966-1986.
Administration: Group.
Price Data, 2006: $65 per complete kit; $33 per profile sheet package; $49.50 per manual (1966, 20 pages) and manuals supplement (1984, 17 pages).
Author: Martin M. Bruce.
Publisher: Martin M. Bruce, Ph.D.

a) ALPHABETIZING-FILING.
Time: 8(13) minutes.
Price Data: $39 per specimen set; $44 per test package; $3.25 per scoring key.
b) ARITHMETIC.
Time: 8(13) minutes.
Price Data: Same as *a* above.
c) CLERICAL SPEED AND ACCURACY.
Time: 3(5) minutes.
Price Data: Same as *a* above.
d) CODING.
Time: 2(7) minutes.
Price Data: Same as *a* above.
e) EYE-HAND ACCURACY.
Time: 5(10) minutes.
Price Data: $39 per specimen set; $44 per test package; no key required.
f) GRAMMAR AND PUNCTUATION.
Time: (5-10) minutes.
Price Data: Same as *a* above.
g) SPELLING.
Time: (15-20) minutes.
Price Data: Same as *a* above.
h) SPELLING-VOCABULARY.
Time: (15-20) minutes.
Price Data: Same as *a* above.
i) VOCABULARY.
Time: (10-15) minutes.
Price Data: Same as *a* above.
j) WORD FLUENCY.
Time: 5(10) minutes.
Price Data: Same as *e* above.
Cross References: For a review by Robert Fitzpatrick, see 7:988.

[536]
Clerical Skills Test.

Purpose: "Designed to assist companies in identifying individuals who have strong reading, mathematical and analytical skills."
Population: Current and prospective employees.

Publication Date: 1999–2001.
Acronym: CST.
Scores: 7: Writing, Analyzing, Proofreading, Filing, Math, Checking, Total.
Administration: Group.
Price Data, 2005: $79.99 per starter kit including administrator's manual (2001, 28 pages), 5 tests, and 1 test log; $29.99 per administrator's manual; $9.25 per test (online or paper-and-pencil version; paper-and-pencil version sold in quantities of 10).
Time: 21(26) minutes.
Comments: Paper-and-pencil and online versions available.
Author: J. M. Llobet.
Publisher: G. Neil.

[537]
Clerical Skills Test Series [Scored By Client].

Purpose: Measures 16 different clerical-administrative skills.
Population: Adults.
Publication Date: 1990.
Scores: 16 skills: Alphabetizing—Filing, Attention to Detail With Words & Numbers, Bookkeeping Skills, Coding, Grammar & Punctuation, Manual Dexterity, Mechanical Comprehension, Numerical Skills, Problem Solving, Proofreading Skills, Reading Comprehension, Receptionist Skills, Spatial Perception, Spelling, Verbal Fluency, English Vocabulary, plus Total Score.
Administration: Group.
Price Data, 2001: $300 per 20 of the same test; quantity discounts available.
Time: (5) minutes per subtest.
Comments: Scored by the client; includes scoring keys; must be proctored.
Author: Stephen Berke.
Publisher: Walden Personnel Performance, Inc. [Canada].
Cross References: For reviews by Phillip L. Ackerman and Eleanor E. Sanford, see 16:51.

[538]
Client/Server Skills Test.

Purpose: To evaluate the candidate's general client/server knowledge.
Population: Information technology professionals who possess some basic knowledge or experience in a client/server environment.
Publication Date: 1994.
Scores: Total Score, Narrative Evaluation, Ranking, Recommendation.
Administration: Group.
Price Data, 2001: $240 per candidate.
Time: (80) minutes.
Comments: Scored by publisher; must be proctored.

Author: Bruce A. Winrow.
Publisher: Walden Personnel Performance, Inc.

[539]
Clifton Assessment Procedures for the Elderly.

Purpose: Designed to assess cognitive and behavioral competence of the elderly.
Population: Ages 60 and over.
Publication Dates: 1979–1981.
Acronym: CAPE.
Administration: Group.
Price Data, 2002: £8.99 per 20 report forms; £9.50 per manual (1979, 34 pages); £11.99 per specimen set.
Time: Administration time not reported.
Comments: Distributed in the U.S.A. by The Psychological Corporation; 2 tests plus combination short version; authors recommend administering both tests concurrently, however, they can be used separately.
Authors: A. H. Pattie and C. J. Gilleard.
Publisher: Hodder & Stoughton Educational [England].

a) COGNITIVE ASSESSMENT SCALE.
Acronym: CAS.
Scores, 4: Information/Orientation, Mental Ability, Psychomotor (adaptation of Gibson Spiral Maze), Total.
Price Data: £8.99 per 20 tests (CAS); £13.99 per 20 mazes.

b) BEHAVIOUR RATING SCALE.
Acronym: BRS.
Scores, 5: Physical Disability, Apathy, Communication Difficulties, Social Disturbance, Total.
Price Data: £8.99 per 20 tests.
Comments: Shortened version of Stockton Geriatric Rating Scale.
Cross References: See T5:537 (4 references) and T4:518 (19 references); for reviews by Alicia Skinner Cook and K. Warner Schaie, see 9:231 (2 references); see also T3:471 (1 reference).

[540]
Clinical Analysis Questionnaire.

Purpose: Designed to assess both normal and pathological personality traits.
Population: Ages 16 and over.
Publication Dates: 1949–1978.
Acronym: CAQ.
Administration: Group or individual.
Price Data, 2005: $33 per computer interpreted introductory kit including test booklet, answer sheet, prepaid processing form, and manual; $40 (Standard Form) or $35 (Short Form) per 25 reusable test booklets; $32 per 2 short form scoring keys or 4 standard form scoring keys; $18 per 25 hand-scorable or 25 machine-scorable answer sheets (specify short or standard form); $22 per 25 individual record folders (specify short or standard form); $19.50 to $30 per report for scoring and interpretive services.
Foreign Language Editions: Information regarding several non-English-language adaptations available from publisher.
Time: (120) minutes for both parts of standard form; (100) minutes for both parts of short form.
Authors: Samuel E. Krug and Raymond B. Cattell.
Publisher: Institute for Personality and Ability Testing, Inc. (IPAT).

a) PART I (NORMAL PERSONALITY TRAITS).
Scores, 21: 16 primary factor scores: Warmth (A), Intelligence (B), Emotional Stability (C), Dominance (E), Impulsivity (F), Conformity (G), Boldness (H), Sensitivity (I), Suspiciousness (L), Imagination (M), Shrewdness (N), Insecurity (O), Radicalism (Q), Self-Sufficiency (Q2), Self-Discipline (Q3), Tension (Q4), plus 5 second-order factor scores: Extraversion (Ex), Anxiety (Ax), Tough Poise (C+), Independence (In), Super-ego Strength (Se).
Comments: Normal personality traits from the 16PF.

b) PART II (THE CLINICAL FACTORS).
Scores, 16: 12 primary factor scores: Hypochondriasis (D1), Suicidal Depression (D2), Agitation (D3), Anxious Depression (D4), Low Energy Depression (D5), Guilt and Resentment (D6), Boredom and Withdrawal (D7), Paranoia (Pa), Psychopathic Deviation (Pp), Schizophrenia (Sc), Psychasthenia (As), Psychological Inadequacy (Ps), plus 4 second-order factor scores: Socialization (So), Depression (D), Psychoticism (P), Neuroticism (Ne).
Cross References: See T5:538 (8 references) and T4:519 (7 references); for a review by George Guthrie, see 9:232 (4 references); see also T3:472 (11 references); for a review by Douglas McNair, see 8:522 (7 references); see also T2:1131 (1 reference) and 7:54 (1 reference).

[541]
Clinical Assessment of Articulation and Phonology.

Purpose: Designed to "assess English articulation and phonology in preschool and school aged children."
Population: Ages 3 to 9 years.
Publication Date: 2002.
Acronym: CAAP.
Administration: Individual.
Price Data, 2006: $219 per complete kit including examiner's manual (2002, 136 pages), 50 Articulation Inventory forms, 30 Phonological Checklists forms, stimulus easel, 5 Clinical Assessment of Articulation and Phonology Pals, and Clinical Assessment of Articulation and Phonology Stickers; $29.99 per 50 Ar-

ticulation Inventory forms; $29.95 per 30 Phonological Checklists forms; $45 for examiner's manual.
Comments: This is a norm-referenced instrument.
Authors: Wayne A. Secord and JoAnn S. Donohue.
Publisher: Super Duper Publications.
a) ARTICULATION INVENTORY.
Scores, 2: Consonant Inventory Score, School Age Sentence Score.
Time: (15-20) minutes.
b) PHONOOLOGICAL PROCESS CHECKLISTS I AND II.
Scores, 10: Final Consonant Deletion, Cluster Reduction, Syllable Reduction, Gliding, Vocalization, Fronting, Deaffrication, Stopping, Prevocalic Voicing, Postvocalic Devoicing.
Time: (20) minutes.

[542]
Clinical Assessment of Attention Deficit–Adult.

Purpose: Designed to provide a "comprehensive assessment of attention deficit with and without hyperactivity (ADD/ADHD)" in adults.
Population: Ages 19-79.
Publication Dates: 1994-2005.
Acronym: CAT-A.
Scores, 17: Clinical Index, Childhood Memories Clinical Index (Inattention, Impulsivity, Hyperactivity), Childhood Memories Context Clusters (Personal, Academic/Occupational, Social), Childhood Memories Locus Clusters (Internal, External), Current Symptoms Clinical Index (Inattention, Impulsivity, Hyperactivity), Current Symptoms Context Clusters (Personal, Academic/Occupational, Social), Current Symptoms Locus Clusters (Internal, External).
Administration: Group or individual.
Price Data, 2006: $152 per introductory kit including professional manual (2005, 139 pages), 25 rating forms, and 25 score summary/profile forms; $65 per professional manual; $68 per 25 rating forms; $26 per 25 score summary/profile forms; $185 per unlimited use scoring software CD (CAT-SP).
Time: (20-25) minutes.
Comments: Can be computer scored; a child and adolescent form (CAT-C; 543) is also available and shares the same professional manual.
Authors: Bruce A. Bracken and Barbara S. Boatwright.
Publisher: Psychological Assessment Resources, Inc.

[543]
Clinical Assessment of Attention Deficit–Child.

Purpose: Designed to provide a "comprehensive assessment of attention deficit with and without hyperactivity (ADD/ADHD)" in children and adolescents.
Population: 8-18 years.

Publication Date: 1994-2005.
Acronym: CAT-C.
Scores: 12: Clinical (Inattention, Impulsivity, Hyperactivity), Clinical Index, Context (Personal, Academic/Occupational, Social), Locus (Internal, External), Validity (Negative Impression, Infrequency, Positive Impression)
Administration: Individual.
Parts, 3: Self-Report, Parent Report, Teacher Report.
Price Data, 2006: $265 per introductory kit including professional manual (2005, 251 pages), 25 Self-Rating Forms, 25 Parent Rating Forms, 25 Teacher Rating Forms, 25 Self-Rating Score Summary/Profile Forms, 25 Parent Score Summary/Profile Forms, and 25 Teacher Score Summary/Profile Forms; $65 per professional manual; $52 per 25 Parent Rating Forms; $52 per 25 Teacher Rating Forms; $22 per 25 Parent Score Summary/Profile Forms; $22 per 25 Self-Rating Score Summary/Profile Forms; $22 per 25 Teacher Score Summary/Profile Forms; $185 per unlimited use CAT C SP scoring software CD.
Time: (10-20) minutes.
Comments: An adult form (CAT-A; 542) is also available and shares the same professional manual.
Authors: Bruce A. Bracken and Barbara S. Boatwright.
Publisher: Psychological Assessment Resources, Inc.

[544]
Clinical Assessment of Behavior.

Purpose: "Assists in the identification of children and adolescents across a wide age range who are in need of behavioral, educational, or psychiatric treatment or intervention."
Population: Ages 2–18.
Publication Dates: 1996–2004.
Acronym: CAB.
Scores, 21: Internalizing Behaviors, Externalizing Behaviors, Critical Behaviors, Social Skills, Competence, Adaptive Behaviors, CAB Behavioral Index, Anxiety, Depression, Anger, Aggression, Bullying, Conduct Problems, Attention-Deficit/Hyperactivity, Autistic Spectrum Behaviors, Learning Disability, Mental Retardation, Executive Function, Gifted and Talented, Emotional Disturbance, Social Maladjustment.
Administration: Individual.
Forms, 3: Parent Extended Rating Form, Parent Rating Form, Teacher Rating Form.
Price Data, 2006: $229 per introductory kit including CD ROM-based scoring program with on-screen professional manual, installation guide, and professional manual (2004, 309 pages), 25 Parent Rating Forms, 25 Parent Extended Forms, and 25 Teacher Rating Forms.
Time: (10–30) minutes.

Comments: Informant-completed behavior rating scale.
Authors: Bruce A. Bracken and Lori K. Keith.
Publisher: Psychological Assessment Resources, Inc.
Cross References: For reviews by Mike Bonner and Metta K. Volker-Fry and by John Hattie, see 16:52.

[545]
Clinical Assessment of Depression.

Purpose: "Developed to aid in the clinical assessment and diagnosis of depression."
Population: Ages 8 to 79.
Publication Dates: 1994–2004.
Acronym: CAD.
Scores, 14: Symptom Scale Scores (Depressed Mood, Anxiety/Worry, Diminished Interest, Cognitive and Physical Fatigue, Total), Validity Scale Scores (Inconsistency, Negative Impression, Infrequency), Critical Item Cluster Scores (Hopelessness, Self-Devaluation, Sleep/Fatigue, Failure, Worry, Nervous).
Administration: Group.
Price Data, 2006: $125 per introductory kit including professional manual (2004, 96 pages), 25 rating forms, and 25 score summary/profile forms; $205 per scoring program (CD-ROM) including unlimited scoring and reports.
Time: 10 minutes.
Authors: Bruce A. Bracken and Karen Howell.
Publisher: Psychological Assessment Resources, Inc.

[546]
Clinical Assessment Scales for the Elderly and Clinical Assessment Scales for the Elderly—Short Form.

Purpose: "A comprehensive measure of acute psychopathology in the elderly" and to "screen for acute psychopathology in the elderly."
Population: Ages 55–90.
Publication Dates: 1999–2001.
Scores, 10: Anxiety, Cognitive Competence, Depression, Fear of Aging, Mania, Obsessive-Compulsive, Paranoia, Psychoticism, Somatization, Substance Abuse.
Administration: Individual or group.
Forms, 2: R (caregiver rating), S (self-rating).
Comments: Addresses selected DSM-IV Axis I disorders.
Authors: Cecil R. Reynolds (test and manual) and Erin D. Bigler (test).
Publisher: Psychological Assessment Resources, Inc.
  a) CLINICAL ASSESSMENT SCALES FOR THE ELDERLY.
  Purpose: "A comprehensive measure of acute psychopathology in the elderly."
  Acronym: CASE.

Price Data, 2006: $210 per introductory kit including CASE/CASE-SF professional manual (2001, 140 pages), 25 CASE Form S item booklets, 25 CASE Form R item booklets, 25 CASE Form S hand-scorable answer sheets, 25 CASE Form R hand-scorable answer sheets, and 50 CASE profile forms.
Time: 20–40(30–50) minutes.
  b) CLINICAL ASSESSMENT SCALES FOR THE ELDERLY—SHORT FORM.
  Purpose: To "screen for acute psychopathology in the elderly."
  Acronym: CASE-SF.
  Price Data: $160 per Short Form introductory kit including CASE/CASE-SF professional manual, 25 CASE-SF Form S test booklets, 25 CASE-SF Form R test booklets, and 50 CASE profile forms.
  Time: 10–20(20–30) minutes.
Cross References: For reviews by Stephen J. DePaola and Iris Phillips, see 15:51.

[547]
Clinical Evaluation of Language Fundamentals—4 Screening Test.

Purpose: "Designed to screen school age children, adolescents, and young adults for language disorders."
Population: Ages 5-0 to 21-11.
Publication Dates: 1995–2004.
Acronym: CELF-4 Screening Test.
Scores: Total score only.
Administration: Individual.
Price Data, 2006: $225 per kit including examiner's manual (2004, 55 pages), stimulus manual, and 25 record forms; $59 per 25 record forms; $220 per 100 record forms.
Time: 15 minutes.
Comments: A test in the CELF series of language testing instruments; administered orally with visual stimuli; not for diagnostic use; "criterion-referenced."
Authors: Eleanor Semel, Elisabeth H. Wiig, and Wayne A. Secord.
Publisher: PsychCorp, A brand of Harcourt Assessment, Inc.
Cross References: See T5:542 (2 references); for reviews by Billy T. Ogletree and Marcel O. Ponton of an earlier edition, see 13:69 (1 reference); for reviews by Linda M. Crocker and Jon F. Miller of an earlier edition, see 9:234.

[548]
Clinical Evaluation of Language Fundamentals, Fourth Edition.

Purpose: Constructed as "a clinical tool for the identification, diagnosis and follow-up evaluation of language and communication disorders."

Population: Ages 5–21.
Publication Dates: 1980–2003.
Acronym: CELF-4.
Administration: Individual.
Price Data, 2005: $425 per complete kit including examiner's manual, 2 stimulus manuals, 10 record form1, 10 record form 2, 50 ORS record forms, and 1 luggage tag; $150 per examiner's manual; $215 per 2 stimulus manuals; $110 per stimulus manual 1; $110 per stimulus manual 2; $40 per 50 ORS record forms; $59 per 25 record form 1; $59 per 25 record form 2; $199 per Scoring Assistant; $550 per complete kit/Scoring Assistant Combo.
Time: (30-45) minutes.
Authors: Eleanor Semel, Elisabeth Wiig, and Wayne A. Secord.
Publisher: PsychCorp, A brand of Harcourt Assessment, Inc.

a) CELF-4, AGES 5–8.
Population: Ages 5–8.
Scores, 22: Core Language (Concepts and Following Directions, Word Structure, Recalling Sentences, Formulated Sentences), Receptive Language (Concepts and Following Directions, Word Classes 1 and 2-Receptive, Sentence Structure), Expressive Language (Word Structure, Recalling Sentences, Formulated Sentences, Language Content (Concepts and Following Directions, Word Classes 1 and 2-Total, Expressive Vocabulary), Language Structure (Word Structure, Recalling Sentences, Formulated Sentences, Sentence Structure), Phonological Awareness, Word Associations, Rapid Automatic Naming, Number Repetition 1, Familiar Sequences 1.
b) CELF-4, AGES 9–12.
Population: Ages 9–12.
Scores, 21: Core Language (Concepts and Following Directions, Recalling Sentences, Formulated Sentences, Word Classes 2-Total) Receptive Language (Concepts and Following Directions, Word Classes 2-Receptive), Expressive Language (Recalling Sentences, Formulated Sentences, Word Classes 2-Expressive), Language Content (Word Classes 2-Total, Expressive Vocabulary [Age 9], Word Definitions [Ages 10–12], Understanding Spoken Paragraphs), Language Memory (Recalling Sentences, Concepts and Following Directions, Formulated Sentences), Phonological Awareness, Word Associations, Rapid Automatic Naming, Number Repetition 1, Familiar Sequences 1.
c) CELF-4, AGES 13-21.
Population: Ages 13-21.
Scores, 20: Core Language (Recalling Sentences, Formulated Sentences, Word Classes 2-

Total, Word Definitions), Receptive Language (Word Classes 2-Receptive, Semantic Relationships, Understanding Spoken Paragraphs), Expressive Language (Recalling Sentences, Formulated Sentences, Word Classes 2-Expressive), Language Content (Word Definitions, Sentence Assembly, Understanding Spoken Paragraphs), Language Memory (Recalling Sentences, Formulated Sentences, Semantic Relationships), Word Associations, Rapid Automatic Naming, Number Repetition 1 and 2, Familiar Sequences 1 and 2.

Cross References: For reviews by Aimee Langlois and Vincent J. Samar, see 16:53; for reviews by Robert R. Haccoun and David P. Hurford of an earlier edition, see 14:76; see also T5:540 (26 references); for reviews by Ronald B. Gillam and John MacDonald of an earlier edition, see 13:68 (38 references); see also T4:521 (5 references); for reviews by Linda Crocker and David A. Shapiro of an earlier edition, see 11:72; for a review by Dixie D. Sanger of an earlier edition, see 9:233 (2 references); see also T3:474.

[549]
Clinical Evaluation of Language Fundamentals Preschool—Second Edition.
Purpose: Designed as a "clinical tool for identifying, diagnosing, and performing follow-up evaluations of language deficits."
Population: Ages 3–6.
Publication Dates: 1991–2004.
Acronym: CELF Preschool-2.
Scores, 16: 11 subtests (Sentence Structure, Word Structure, Expressive Vocabulary, Concepts and Following Directions, Recalling Sentences, Basic Concepts, Word Classes, Recalling Sentences in Context, Phonological Awareness, Pre-Literacy Rating Scale, Descriptive Pragmatics Profile); 5 Composites (Core Language, Receptive Language, Expressive Language, Language Content, Language Structure).
Administration: Individual.
Price Data, 2005: $295 per complete kit; $80 per examiner's manual (2004, 220 pages); $195 per Stimulus Book #1; $45 per Stimulus Book #2; $59 per 25 record forms.
Time: (30–45) minutes.
Comments: A downward extension of the Clinical Evaluation of Language Fundamentals—Fourth Edition (548).
Authors: Elisabeth H. Wiig, Wayne A. Secord, and Eleanor Semel.
Publisher: PsychCorp, A brand of Harcourt Assessment, Inc.
Cross References: See T5:539 (2 references); for reviews by Janet A. Norris and Nora M. Thompson of an earlier edition, see 13:67 (2 references).

[550]
Clinical Evaluation of Language Fundamentals, Third Edition—Observational Rating Scales.

Purpose: Designed to measure "a student's classroom communication and language learning difficulties."
Population: Ages 6–21.
Publication Date: 1996.
Acronym: CELF-3ORS.
Scores: 4 sections: Listening, Speaking, Reading, Writing.
Administration: Individual or group.
Forms, 4: Parent, Teacher, Student, Summary.
Price Data, 2002: $59 per complete kit including rating scales, summary forms, and guide (86 pages); $15 per Teacher rating forms; $15 per Parent rating forms; $20 per summary forms; $27 per guide.
Time: Administration time not reported.
Comments: Ratings by parents, teachers, and students.
Authors: Eleanor Semel, Elisabeth H. Wiig, and Wayne A. Secord.
Publisher: PsychCorp, A brand of Harcourt Assessment, Inc.
Cross References: For reviews by Robert R. Haccoun and David P. Hurford, see 14:76; see also T5:541 (1 reference).

[551]
Clinical Experience Record for Nursing Students.

Purpose: Evaluates the "performance and progress of nursing students."
Population: Nursing students and nurses.
Publication Dates: 1960–1975.
Acronym: CERNS.
Scores: No scores.
Administration: Individual.
Price Data: Available from publisher.
Time: Administration time not reported.
Comments: Two assessment areas: Clinical Performance Record, Performance/Progress Record.
Authors: John C. Flanagan, Angeline C. Marchese, Grace Fivars, and Shirley A. Tuska (manual).
Publisher: Grace Fivars.
Cross References: For additional information, see 8:1120 (1 reference).

[552]
Clinical Rating Scale for Circumplex Model.

Purpose: Designed to type marital and family systems and identify intervention targets related to Circumplex Model.
Population: Couples and families.
Publication Dates: 1980–2004.
Acronym: CRS.
Scores: 3 rating scales (Cohesion, Flexibility, Communication) yielding Family System Type related to Circumplex Model.
Administration: Group (couple or family).
Price Data, 2006: $30 for CRS and manual (includes unlimited copying privileges).
Time: (5-10) minutes.
Comments: Rating of couple or family system based on interview and/or observation.
Author: David H. Olson.
Publisher: Life Innovations, Inc.
Cross References: For reviews by Stuart N. Hart and Steven W. Lee of an earlier edition, see 12:81 (4 references).

[553]
The Clock Test.

Purpose: "Intended to assess visual-spatial construction, visual perception, and abstract conceptualization in individuals 65 and older using three subtests, clock drawing, clock reading, and clock setting, to determine an individual's level of cognitive impairment."
Population: Ages 65 and older.
Publication Date: 1995.
Scores, 3: Clock Reading, Clock Drawing, Clock Setting.
Administration: Individual.
Price Data, 2006: $215 per test kit including 25 QuikScore™ forms, 25 profile sheets, stimulus cards tent, and manual (85 pages); $92 per 25 QuikScore™ forms; $19 per 25 profile sheets; $90 per administration tent; $68 per manual.
Time: (5-10) minutes.
Authors: H. Tuokko, T. Hadjistavropoulos, J. A. Miller, A. Horton, and B. L. Beattie.
Publisher: Multi-Health Systems, Inc.
Cross References: For reviews by Howard A. Lloyd and Antony M. Paolo, see 14:78.

[554]
Closed Head Injury Screener.

Purpose: "Designed to help medical doctors and psychologists assess whether patient symptoms are suggestive of closed-head injuries."
Population: English-speaking adults.
Publication Date: 1994.
Acronym: CHIS.
Scores: 3 ratings: Medical Facts, Presenting Complaints, Response Validity.
Administration: Individual.
Price Data: Available from publisher (www.mindgarden.com).
Time: Approximately 30 minutes.
Comments: To be used as a supplement to a full face-to-face patient interview; partial paper and pencil/

partial oral interview; results interpreted by administrator; not to be used with patients with cognitive deficits that are explainable by a previous diagnosis.
Author: Michael Ivan Friedman.
Publisher: Mind Garden, Inc.
Cross References: For reviews by Thomas J. Cullen, Jr. and Scott A. Napolitano, see 14:79.

[555]
Closed High School Placement Test.

Purpose: Designed as a measure of cognitive and basic skills to assist in placement decisions for entering freshmen.
Population: Eighth grade students.
Publication Dates: 1985-2005.
Acronym: HSPT.
Scores: 8: Cognitive Skills (Verbal, Quantitative, Total), Basic Skills (Reading, Mathematics, Language, Total), Composite.
Administration: Group.
Price Data, 2005: Available only through Lease/ Score program including school rental of test materials and scoring service; $6.55 per student, minimum scoring service charge of $43.65 required.
Time: 150 minutes plus (15–25) minutes per optional test.
Comments: Optional tests include science, mechanical aptitude, and Catholic religion; new form is developed each year.
Authors: Scholastic Testing Service, Inc.
Publisher: Scholastic Testing Service, Inc.
Cross References: For reviews by George Engelhard, Jr. and Ernest Kimmel, see 14:80; see also T5:547 (1 reference) and T3:2324 (1 reference); for reviews by Leonard S. Cahen and Irvin J. Lehmann of an earlier edition, see 8:26 (1 reference); see also 7:21 (2 references); for reviews by Marion F. Shaycoft and James R. Hayden of an earlier series, see 6:6; for reviews by William C. Cottle and Robert A. Jones of the 1955 "open" test, see 5:15.

[556]
Closure Flexibility (Concealed Figures).

Purpose: "To measure the ability to hold a configuration in mind despite distracting irrelevancies."
Population: Wide range of higher level occupations personnel.
Publication Dates: 1956–1965.
Scores: Total score only.
Administration: Individual or group.
Price Data, 2002: $91 per start-up kit including 25 test booklets, score key, and interpretation and research manual (1965, 20 pages); $54 per 25 tests (quantity discounts available); $20 per score key; $28 per interpretation and research manual.
Time: (10) minutes.

Authors: L. L. Thurstone and T. E. Jeffrey.
Publisher: Pearson Performance Solutions [No reply from publisher; status unknown].
Cross References: See T5:548 (1 reference), T3:477 (5 references), T2:547 (9 references), and 7:435 (9 references); for a review by Leona E. Tyler, see 6:545 (4 references).

[557]
Closure Speed (Gestalt Completion).

Purpose: "To measure the ability to see apparently disorganized or unrelated parts as a meaningful whole."
Population: Employees in wide range of occupations.
Publication Date: 1959.
Scores: Total score only.
Administration: Individual or group.
Price Data, 2002: $91 per start-up kit including 25 test booklets, score key, and interpretation and research manual (1966, 18 pages); $54 per 25 test booklets (quantity discounts available); $20 per score key; $28 per interpretation and research manual.
Time: 3 minutes.
Authors: L. L. Thurstone and T. E. Jeffrey.
Publisher: Pearson Performance Solutions [No reply from publisher; status unknown].
Cross References: See T4:530 (2 references), T3:478 (2 references), T2:548 (1 reference), and 7:436 (2 references); for a review by Leona E. Tyler, see 6:546 (3 references).

[558]
Cloze Reading Tests 1-3, Second Edition.

Purpose: Designed to provide a method of testing reading skills.
Population: Ages 8-0 to 10-6, 8-5 to 11-10, 9-5 to 12-6.
Publication Dates: 1982–1992.
Scores: Overall performance score.
Administration: Individual or group.
Levels, 3: Level 1 (Ages 8-0 to 10-6), Level 2 (Ages 8-5 to 11-10), Level 3 (Ages 9-5 to 12-6).
Price Data, 2002: £5.99 per 10 tests (specify Test 1, 2, or 3); £11.99 per manual (16 pages); £12.99 per specimen set.
Time: 35(45) minutes.
Author: D. Young.
Publisher: Hodder & Stoughton Educational [England].
Cross References: See T5:550 (5 references) and T4:531 (3 references); for a review by Esther Geva, see 9:237.

[559]
CNS Vital Signs Screening Battery.

Purpose: Designed to "assess neurocognitive state."
Population: Children, adults.

Publication Date: 2003.
Scores: 5: Memory, Mental Speed, Reaction Time, Attention, Cognitive Flexibility.
Subtest: 7: Verbal Memory, Visual Memory, Finger Tapping, Symbol Digit Coding, Stroop, Shifting Attention, Continuous Performance.
Administration: Individual.
Price Data: Available from publisher.
Time: (30) minutes.
Comments: Computer administered and scored; requires Windows 2000 or XP.
Authors: CNS Vital Signs.
Publisher: CNS Vital Signs.
Cross References: For reviews by D. Ashley Cohen and Karl R. Hanes, see 16:54.

[560]
Coaching Effectiveness Survey.

Purpose: Designed as a 360° (self and coachees) measure of coaching skills and coaching style preferences. It is an assessment of executives' coaching skills and developmental needs and it contrasts how executives prefer to coach with how the people they coach prefer to be coached.
Population: Executives in leadership positions.
Publication Date: 1997.
Scores, 5: Coaching Behavior, Coaching Attitude, Coaching Process, Coaching Style, Coaching Effectiveness.
Administration: Group.
Forms, 2: Online Coach Questionnaire, Online Coachee Questionnaire.
Price Data, 2005: $49 per complete kit including questionnaires and answer sheets for 1 self-assessment, 12 coachees, and 1 feedback report.
Foreign Language Edition: Available in English and German.
Time: (30) minutes.
Comments: Assessment is administered online via Lore's Assessment Center. Assessment results are emailed to participant. A paper report may be requested for an additional $50 fee per report.
Authors: Lore International Institute.
Publisher: Lore International Institute.

[561]
Coaching Process Questionnaire.

Purpose: "Provides managers with an assessment of their coaching ability."
Population: Managers and employees.
Publication Date: 1992.
Acronym: CPQ.
Administration: Group or individual.
Foreign Language Editions: Available in French and Spanish.
Time: [30–40] minutes.

Comments: Self-scored instrument.
Authors: Hay Group.
Publisher: Hay Group.
a) PARTICIPANT VERSION.
Population: Managers.
Scores, 5: Diagnostic Skills, Coaching Techniques, Coaching Qualities, Coaching Model, Overall CPQ score.
Price Data, 2006: $79 per complete kit including 10 questionnaires, and 10 profiles and interpretive notes.
b) EMPLOYEE VERSION.
Population: Employees.
Scores, 5: Diagnostic Skills, Coaching Techniques, Coaching Qualities, Coaching Model, Overall Employee score.
Price Data: $29 per 10 questionnaires.
Cross References: For reviews by Patricia A. Bachelor and Geneva D. Haertel, see 13:70.

[562]
Coaching Skills Inventory.

Purpose: Identifies and evaluates "success in performing coaching functions" for organizational leaders.
Population: Adults.
Publication Date: 1991.
Acronym: CSI.
Scores, 5: Contact and Core Skills, Counseling, Mentoring, Tutoring, Confronting and Challenging.
Administration: Group.
Forms, 2: Self, Other.
Price Data: Available from publisher.
Time: Administration time not reported.
Comments: Self-administered; self-scored.
Author: Dennis C. Kinlaw.
Publisher: Jossey-Bass, A Wiley Company.

[563]
Coddington Life Events Scales.

Purpose: "Designed to assess the influence of life events and change in a young person's life, and help determine how these events affect their personal growth and ability to adjust."
Population: Ages 5 and under, ages 6–10, ages 11–19.
Publication Dates: 1981–1999.
Acronym: CLES.
Scores: Total Life Change Unit score only.
Administration: Group.
Forms, 3: Preschool (CLES-P), Child (CLES-C), Adolescent (CLES-A).
Price Data, 2006: $157 per complete kit including technical manual (1999, 58 pages) and 25 Quikscore forms for the CLES-P, CLES-C, and CLES-A; $59 per technical manual; $42 per 25 Quikscore forms (specify CLES-P, CLES-C, or CLES-A); $69 per

specimen set including technical manual and 3 of each Quikscore forms for the CLES-P, CLES-C, CLES-A.
Time: (15) minutes.
Comments: Self-report, assisted self-report.
Author: R. Dean Coddington.
Publisher: Multi-Health Systems, Inc.
Cross References: For reviews by James A. Athanasou and Howard M. Knoff, see 15:52; see T5:557 (7 references) and T4:1453 (3 references).

[564]
Cognistat (The Neurobehavioral Cognitive Status Examination).

Purpose: Designed to assess intellectual functioning.
Population: Adults.
Publication Dates: 1983–1995.
Acronym: Cognistat.
Scores, 11: Level of Consciousness, Orientation, Attention, Language (Comprehension, Repetition, Naming), Constructional Ability, Memory, Calculations, Reasoning (Similarities, Judgment).
Administration: Individual.
Price Data: Available from publisher.
Time: Administration time not reported.
Authors: R. J. Kiernan, J. Mueller, and J. W. Langston.
Publisher: Northern California Neurobehavioral Group, Inc.
Cross References: For reviews by Charles J. Long and Faith Gunning-Dixon and by Steven R. Shaw, see 14:81.

[565]
Cognitive Abilities Scale—Second Edition.

Purpose: Developed to assess the cognitive abilities of infants and young children and to identify children who have delays in cognitive development.
Population: Ages 3-23 months; 24-47 months.
Publication Dates: 1987–2001.
Acronym: CAS-2.
Administration: Individual.
Price Data, 2006: $72 per examiner's manual (2001, 83 pages); $40 per 25 Profile/Examiner Record Booklets (Infant Form); $40 per 25 Profile/Examiner Record Booklets (Preschool Form); $15 per 25 Symbol Reproduction Forms; $41 per 25 Mikey's Favorite Things Book; $29 per Picture Cards; $9 per Ramp; $204 per Manipulatives Kit; $437 per complete kit including examiner's manual, 25 Profile/Examiner Record Booklets (Infant Form), 25 Profile/Examiner Record Booklets (Preschool Form), 25 Symbol Reproduction Forms, 25 copies of "Mikey's Favorite Things," Picture Cards, Ramp, and Manipulatives Kit.
Time: (20–30) minutes.
Authors: Sharon Bradley-Johnson and C. Merle Johnson.
Publisher: PRO-ED.

a) INFANT FORM.
Population: Ages 3–23 months.
Scores, 3: Exploration of Objects, Communication with Others, Initiation and Imitation.
b) PRESCHOOL FORM.
Population: Ages 24–47 months.
Scores, 5: Oral Language, Reading, Math, Writing, Enabling Behaviors.
Cross References: For reviews by Bert A. Goldman and Joyce Meikamp, see 15:53; see T5:559 (1 reference); for reviews by A. Dirk Hightower and Gary J. Robertson of the original edition, see 10:65.

[566]
Cognitive Abilities Test, Form 6.

Purpose: Designed to "assess students' abilities in reasoning and problem solving using verbal, quantitative, and spatial (nonverbal) symbols."
Population: Grades K–12.
Publication Dates: 1954–2002.
Acronym: CogAT.
Scores, 4: Verbal Battery, Quantitative Battery, Nonverbal Battery, Composite.
Administration: Group.
Price Data, 2006: $21.80 per Interpretive Guide for Teachers and Counselors (2001, 174 pages); $21.80 per Interpretive Guide for School Administrators (2001, 140 pages); $63 per Research Handbook (2002, 112 pages); $55.75 per norms booklet; $26.80 per 25 practice tests (specify level); $113.10 per 25 machine-scorable test booklets and 1 Directions for Administration (specify Level K, l, or 2); $88.60 per 25 reusable test booklets and 1 Directions for Administration (specify Level A through H); $16.50 per Directions for Administration (specify level); $45 per 50 answer sheets (Levels A–H); $85 per 100 answer sheets (Levels A–H); $11.85 per scoring key (specify Level K, 1, or 2); $21.80 per scoring key (Levels A—H).
Comments: Scoring service available from publisher.
Authors: David F. Lohman and Elizabeth P. Hagen.
Publisher: Riverside Publishing.
a) PRIMARY BATTERY.
Population: Grades K–2.
Subtests, 6: Oral Vocabulary, Verbal Reasoning, Relational Concepts, Quantitative Concepts, Figure Classification, Matrices.
Levels: 3 overlapping levels, K, 1, and 2.
Time: Untimed, approximately 140 minutes, including administration time (Levels 1 and 2) to 170 minutes (Level K).
b) MULTILEVEL BATTERY.
Population: Grades 3–12.
Subtests, 9: Verbal Classification, Sentence Completion, Verbal Analogies, Quantitative Relations, Number Series, Equation Building, Figure Classification, Figure Analogies, Figure Analysis.

Levels: 8 overlapping Levels, A through H.
Time: Approximately 145 minutes, including administration time.
Cross References: For reviews by James C. DiPerna and Bruce G. Rogers, see 16:55; see also T5:560 (4 references); for reviews by Bert A. Goldman and Stephen H. Ivens of an earlier edition, see 13:71 (23 references); see also T4:537 (19 references); for reviews by Anne Anastasi and Douglas Fuchs of an earlier edition, see 10:66 (13 references); for a review by Charles J. Ansorge of an earlier edition, see 9:240 (5 references); see also T3:483 (32 references); for reviews by Kenneth D. Hopkins and Robert C. Nichols, see 8:181 (12 references); for reviews by Marcel L. Goldschmid and Carol K. Tittle and an excerpted review by Richard C. Cox of the primary batteries, see 7:343.

[567]
Cognitive Behavior Rating Scales.

Purpose: Intended to "evaluate the presence and severity of cognitive impairment" using observations of family and/or significant others.
Population: Patients with possible neurological impairment.
Publication Date: 1987.
Acronym: CBRS.
Scores: 9 scales: Language Deficit, Apraxia, Disorientation, Agitation, Need for Routine, Depression, Higher Cognitive Deficits, Memory Disorder, Dementia.
Administration: Individual.
Price Data, 2005: $123 per introductory kit including manual, 50 reusable item booklets, and 50 rating booklets.
Time: (15-20) minutes.
Comments: Completed by family and/or significant others.
Author: J. Michael Williams.
Publisher: Psychological Assessment Resources, Inc.
Cross References: For reviews by Ron Edwards and David J. Mealor, see 11:74.

[568]
Cognitive Distortion Scales.

Purpose: Designed to measure cognitive/distortions (dysfunctional thinking patterns) that interfere with optimal functioning.
Population: Ages 18 and over.
Publication Date: 2000.
Acronym: CDS.
Scores, 5: Self-Criticism, Self-Blame, Helplessness, Hopelessness, Preoccupation with Danger.
Administration: Individual or group.
Price Data, 2006: $132 per introductory kit including manual (2000, 40 pages), 25 test booklets, and 25 profile forms.

Time: (10–15) minutes.
Authors: John Briere.
Publisher: Psychological Assessment Resources, Inc.
Cross References: For reviews by Sandra D. Haynes and Timothy J. Makatura, see 15:54.

[569]
Cognitive Linguistic Quick Test.

Purpose: "To assess the relative status of five cognitive domains in adults with known or suspected neurological dysfunction."
Population: Adults ages 18–89 with known or suspected acquired neurological dysfunction.
Publication Date: 2001.
Acronym: CLQT.
Scores, 7: 5 Cognitive Domain Scores (Attention, Memory, Language, Executive Functions, Visuospatial Skills), Total Composite Severity Rating, Clock Drawing Severity Rating.
Administration: Individual.
Price Data, 2002: $150 per complete kit including examiner's manual (146 pages), stimulus manual, 15 English record forms, and 15 response forms; $71 per examiner's manual; $61 per stimulus manual; $53 per 25 English record response forms; $32 per 15 Spanish record/response forms.
Foreign Language Editions: Available in English and Spanish versions.
Time: (15–30) minutes.
Comments: Test is composed of 10 tasks (Personal Facts, Symbol Cancellation, Confrontation Naming, Clock Drawing, Story Retelling, Symbol Trails, Generative Naming, Design Memory, Mazes, Design Generation); includes 5 tasks with minimal language demands; hand-scored.
Author: Nancy Helm-Estabrooks.
Publisher: PsychCorp, A brand of Harcourt Assessment, Inc.
Cross References: For reviews by Tony Cellucci and Thomas McKnight, see 15:55.

[570]
Cognitive Skills Assessment Battery, Second Edition.

Purpose: "To provide teachers with information regarding children's progress relative to teaching goals in the cognitive and physical-motor areas."
Population: PreK–K.
Publication Dates: 1974–1981.
Acronym: CSAB.
Scores: 98 item scores (49 consist of plus or minus) in 18 areas: Basic Information (4 scores), Identification of Body Parts (4 scores), Color Identification (4 scores), Shape Identification (4 scores), Symbol Discrimination (10 scores), Visual-Auditory Discrimination (5 scores), Auditory Discrimination (6 scores), Number Knowl-

edge (10 scores), Letter Naming (2 scores), Vocabulary (6 scores), Information from Pictures (4 scores), Picture Comprehension (4 scores), Story Comprehension (4 scores), Multiple Directions (4 scores), Large Muscle Coordination (4 scores), Visual-Motor Coordination (6 scores), Memory (8 scores), Response During Assessment (8 scores).
Administration: Individual.
Price Data, 2006: $51.95 per testing materials including 30 response sheets (1981, 4 pages); $8.95 per refill (1 class record, 30 pupil response sheets); $3.50 per assessors manual (1981, 61 pages); $3.95 per specimen set (including 1 sample easel page).
Time: (20-25) minutes.
Comments: "Criterion-referenced."
Authors: Ann E. Boehm and Barbara R. Slater.
Publisher: Teachers College Press.
Cross References: See T5:565 (1 reference) and T4:542 (3 references); for reviews by Esther E. Diamond and Susan Embretson (Whitely), see 9:242; see also T3:484 (2 references); for reviews by Kathryn Hoover Calfee and Barbara K. Keogh, see 8:797.

[571]
Cognitive Symptom Checklists.
Purpose: "Developed to assist in the identification and treatment of problems in five basic cognitive areas."
Population: Ages 16 and older.
Publication Date: 1993.
Acronym: CSC.
Scores: 5 checklists: Attention/Concentration, Memory, Visual Processes, Language, Executive Functions.
Administration: Individual or group.
Price Data, 2006: $86 per introductory kit including Clinician's Guide (26 pages), and 25 each of Attention/Concentration, Memory, Visual Processes, Language, and Executive Functions checklists.
Time: (10–20) minutes per checklist.
Comments: Checklists can be used separately or in any combination.
Authors: Christina O'Hara, Minnie Harrell, Eileen Bellingrath, and Katherine Lisicia.
Publisher: Psychological Assessment Resources, Inc.
Cross References: For reviews by Thomas J. Cullen, Jr. and Michael Lee Russell, see 14:82.

[572]
CogScreen Aeromedical Edition.
Purpose: "Designed to rapidly assess deficits or changes in" various cognitive abilities associated with flying.
Population: Aviators ages 25–73 with 12 or more years of education.
Publication Date: 1995.
Acronym: CogScreen-AE.

Scores, 65: 19 Speed Measures (Math Speed, Visual Sequence Comparison Speed, Matching-to-Sample Speed, Manikin Speed, Divided Attention Sequence Comparison Speed, Divided Attention Indicator Alone Speed, Divided Attention Indicator Dual Speed, Auditory Sequence Comparison Speed, Pathfinder Number Speed, Pathfinder Letter Speed, Pathfinder Combined Speed, Shifting Attention Arrow Direction Speed, Shifting Attention Arrow Color Speed, Shifting Attention Instruction Speed, Shifting Attention Discovery Speed, Dual Task Previous Number Alone Speed, Dual Task Previous Number Dual Speed, Dual Task Tracking Alone Error, Dual Task Tracking Dual Error), 19 Accuracy Measures (Backward Digit Span Accuracy, Math Accuracy, Visual Sequence Comparison Accuracy, Symbol Digit Coding Accuracy, Symbol Digit Coding Immediate Recall Accuracy, Symbol Digit Coding Delayed Recall Accuracy, Matching-to-Sample Accuracy, Manikin Accuracy, Divided Attention Sequence Comparison Accuracy, Auditory Sequence Comparison Accuracy, Pathfinder Number Accuracy, Pathfinder Letter Accuracy, Pathfinder Combined Accuracy, Shifting Attention Arrow Direction Accuracy, Shifting Attention Arrow Color Accuracy, Shifting Attention Instruction Accuracy, Shifting Attention Discovery Accuracy, Dual Task Previous Number Alone Accuracy, Dual Task Previous Number Dual Accuracy), 16 Thruput Measures (Math Thruput, Visual Sequence Comparison Thruput, Symbol Digit Coding Thruput, Matching-to-Sample Thruput, Manikin Thruput, Divided Attention Sequence Comparison Thruput, Auditory Sequence Comparison Thruput, Pathfinder Number Thruput, Pathfinder Letter Thruput, Pathfinder Combined Thruput, Shifting Attention Arrow Direction Thruput, Shifting Attention Arrow Color Thruput, Shifting Attention Instruction Thruput, Shifting Attention Discovery Thruput, Dual Task Previous Number Alone Thruput, Dual Task Previous Number Dual Thruput), 11 Process Measures (Divided Attention Indicator Alone Premature Responses, Divided Attention Indicator Dual Premature Responses, Pathfinder Number Coordination, Pathfinder Letter Coordination, Pathfinder Combined Coordination, Shifting Attention Discovery Rule Shifts Completed, Shifting Attention Discovery Failures to Maintain Set, Shifting Attention Discovery Nonconceptual Responses, Shifting Attention Discovery Perseverative Errors, Dual Task Tracking Alone Boundary Hits, Dual Task Tracking Dual Boundary Hits).
Administration: Individual.
Price Data, 1996: $849 per software kit including manual (148 pages), quick start guide, internal light pen package, and Testkey with 10 administrations (specify 3.5-inch or 5.25-inch disk); $69 per manual; $29.50 per administration with Testkey unlock; $75 per extra Testkey

(with no administration); $375 per internal light pen package.

Time: (45–60) minutes.

Comments: Requires IBM or compatible 640K, EGA or VGA graphics card, color monitor, and light pen.

Author: Gary G. Kay.

Publisher: CogScreen LLC [No reply from publisher; status unknown].

Cross References: For reviews by Robert W. Elliott and Hilda Wing, see 14:83.

[573]
Coitometer.

Purpose: Designed to "measure knowledge of the physical aspects of human coitus."

Population: Adults.

Publication Dates: 1974–1988.

Scores: Total score only.

Administration: Group.

Manual: No manual.

Price Data, 2005: $2 per test.

Time: [10] minutes.

Comments: Supplementary article available.

Author: Panos D. Bardis.

Publisher: Donna Bardis.

[574]
College ADHD Response Evaluation.

Purpose: Designed to assess ADHD in postsecondary students.

Population: College students, Parents of college students.

Publication Date: 2002.

Acronym: CARE.

Scores: Inattention, Hyperactivity, Impulsivity, Total Score, DSM-IV Inattentive, DSM-IV Hyperactive/Impulsive.

Administration: Individual.

Forms, 2: Student Response Inventory, Parent Response Inventory.

Price Data, 2006: $135 per complete kit including manual (144 pages), 25 each of student inventory, parent inventory, student profile, and parent profile; $50 per manual; $55 per 25 inventories and 25 profiles (specify student or parent).

Time: 10–15 minutes.

Comments: Oral administration permitted.

Authors: Joseph Glutting, David Sheslow, and Wayne Adams.

Publisher: Psychological Assessment Resources, Inc.

  a) STUDENT RESPONSE INVENTORY.

  Population: College students.

  Scores, 6: Inattention, Hyperactivity, Impulsivity, Total Score, DSM-IV Inattentive, DSM-IV Hyperactive/Impulsive.

  b) PARENT RESPONSE INVENTORY.

  Population: Parents of college students.

  Scores, 5: Inattention, Hyperactivity, Total Score, DSM-IV Inattentive, DSM-IV Hyperactive/Impulsive.

Cross References: For reviews by Mary "Rina" M. Chittooran and William K. Wilkinson, see 16:57.

[575]
College Adjustment Scales.

Purpose: Identifies psychological and adjustment problems experienced by college students.

Population: College and university students.

Publication Date: 1991.

Acronym: CAS.

Scores, 9: Anxiety, Depression, Suicidal Ideation, Substance Abuse, Self-Esteem Problems, Interpersonal Problems, Family Problems, Academic Problems, Career Problems.

Administration: Individual or group.

Price Data, 2006: $130 per introductory kit including professional manual (25 pages), 25 reusable item booklets, and 25 answer sheets.

Time: (15–20) minutes.

Authors: William D. Anton and James R. Reed.

Publisher: Psychological Assessment Resources, Inc.

Cross References: For reviews by William E. Martin, Jr. and Edward R. Starr, see 13:72 (3 references); see also T4:544 (1 reference).

[576]
College Basic Academic Subjects Examination.

Purpose: Designed to assess skills and competencies achieved through the general education component of a college curriculum.

Population: College students having completed the general education component of a college curriculum.

Publication Dates: 1989–2006.

Acronym: College BASE, CBASE.

Scores, 40: Competency (Interpretive Reasoning, Strategic Reasoning, Adaptive Reasoning), Skill (Social Science Procedures, Political/Economic Structures, Geography, Significance of U.S. Events, Significance of World Events, Physical Sciences, Life Sciences, Interpreting Results, Laboratory/Field Techniques, Observation/Experimental Design, Geometrical Calculations, 2- & 3-Dimensional Figures, Equations & Inequalities, Evaluating Expressions, Using Statistics, Properties and Notations, Practical Applications, Expository Writing Sample, Conventions of Written English, Writing as a Process, Understanding Literature, Reading Analytically, Reading Critically), Cluster (Social Sciences, History, Fundamental Concepts, Laboratory & Field Work, Geometry, Algebra, General Mathematics, Writing, Reading & Literature), Subject (Social Studies, Science, Mathematics, English), Composite.

Administration: Group.

Price Data, 2006: $72 per 50 test booklets; $48 per 50 answer booklets (includes examiner's manual); Scoring: $21.90 per student for four subjects with essay, and $10.90 per student for four subjects without essay. Includes institutional summary and student score reports.

Time: 45 minutes per subject; 40 minutes for optional essay; plus 20 minutes for administration time.

Comments: "Criterion-referenced"; 180 multiple-choice items, optional essay assignment; All four subjects may be administered or any combination of 1-3 subjects; accommodations packages are available for students with special needs; additional technical reports and data files may be ordered by special request.

Author: Steven J. Osterlind.

Publisher: Assessment Resource Center, University of Missouri-Columbia.

Cross References: See T5:570 (1 reference); for reviews by William E. Coffman and Delwyn L. Harnisch, see 11:76.

[577]
College Board Institutional SAT Subject Test in Biology E/M.

Purpose: To measure content knowledge in biology.

Population: Entering college freshmen.

Publication Dates: 1962–2005.

Scores: Total (200–800).

Administration: Group or individual.

Price Data: Rental fee per student available from publisher.

Time: 60 minutes.

Comments: Available for local administration and scoring by higher educational institutions; student chooses an Ecological (E) or Molecular (M) emphasis; previously known as College Board One-Hour Achievement Test in Biology.

Authors: Educational Testing Service.

Publisher: The College Board.

Cross References: See T5:573 (1 reference) and 8:834 (1 reference); for a review by Elizabeth Hagen of an earlier form, see 5:723; for a review by Clark W. Horton of an earlier form, see 4:600; for a review of an earlier form of the program, see 7:665.

[578]
College Board Institutional SAT Subject Test in Chemistry.

Purpose: To measure content knowledge in chemistry.

Population: Entering college freshmen.

Publication Dates: 1962–2005.

Scores: Total (200–800).

Administration: Group or individual.

Price Data: Rental fee per student available from publisher.

Time: 60 minutes.

Comments: Available for local administration and scoring by higher educational institutions; previously known as College Board One-Hour Achievement Test in Chemistry.

Authors: Educational Testing Service.

Publisher: The College Board.

Cross References: See T5:574 (1 reference); for a review by William Hered of earlier forms, see 6:914; for a review by Max D. Engelhart of an earlier form, see 5:742; for a review by Evelyn Raskin of an earlier form, see 4:617; for a review of an earlier form of the program, see 7:665.

[579]
College Board Institutional SAT Subject Test in Chinese with Listening Subject.

Purpose: To measure content knowledge in Chinese.

Population: Entering college freshmen.

Publication Dates: 1997–2005.

Scores, 4: Subscores in Listening, Usage, Reading (20–80), and Total (200–800).

Administration: Group or individual.

Price Data: Rental fee per student available from publisher.

Time: 60 minutes.

Comments: Available for local administration and scoring by higher educational institutions; CD player and earphones required; program previously known as College Board One-Hour Achievement Test.

Authors: Educational Testing Service.

Publisher: The College Board.

Cross References: For a review of an earlier form of the program, see 7:665

[580]
College Board Institutional SAT Subject Test in English Language Proficiency.

Purpose: To measure spoken and written standard American English, and the ability to use English in the classroom and in daily life.

Population: Entering college freshmen.

Publication Dates: 1997–2005.

Acronym: ELPT.

Scores: 3: Listening, Reading (1–50), and Total (901–999).

Administration: Group or individual.

Price Data: Rental fee per student available from publisher.

Time: 60 minutes.

Comments: Available for local administration and scoring by higher educational institutions.

Authors: Educational Testing Service.

Publisher: The College Board.
Cross References: For a review of an earlier form of the program, see 7:665.

[581]
College Board Institutional SAT Subject Test in French.

Purpose: To measure content knowledge in French.
Population: Entering college freshmen.
Publication Dates: 1962–2005.
Scores: Total (200–800).
Administration: Group or individual.
Price Data: Rental fee per student available from publisher.
Time: 60 minutes.
Comments: Available for local administration and scoring by higher educational institutions; previously known as College Board One-Hour Achievement Test in French Reading.
Author: Educational Testing Service.
Publisher: The College Board.
Cross References: For a review of an earlier form of the program, see 7:665.

[582]
College Board Institutional SAT Subject Test in French with Listening.

Purpose: To measure content knowledge in French.
Population: Entering college freshmen.
Publication Dates: 1971–2005.
Scores: 3: Subscores in Listening, Reading (20–80), Total (200–800).
Administration: Group or individual.
Price Data: Rental fee per student available from publisher.
Time: 60 minutes.
Comments: Available for local administration and scoring by higher educational institutions; CD player and earphones required; previously known as College Board One-Hour Achievement Test in French with Listening and College Placement Test.
Authors: Educational Testing Service.
Publisher: The College Board.
Cross References: For a review of an earlier form of the program, see 7:665.

[583]
College Board Institutional SAT Subject Test in German.

Purpose: To measure content knowledge in German.
Population: Entering college freshmen.
Publication Dates: 1962–2005.
Scores: Total (200–800).
Administration: Group or individual.
Price Data: Rental fee per student available from publisher.

Time: 60 minutes.
Comments: Available for local administration and scoring by higher educational institutions; previously known as College Board One-Hour Achievement Test in German Reading and College Placement Test.
Author: Educational Testing Service.
Publisher: The College Board.
Cross References: See 7:285 (2 references); for a review by Gilbert C. Kettelkamp of earlier forms, see 6:383; for a review by Harold B. Dunkel, see 5:272; for a review by Herbert Schueler, see 4:244. For a review of an earlier form of the program, see 7:665.

[584]
College Board Institutional SAT Subject Test in German with Listening.

Purpose: To measure content knowledge in German.
Population: Entering college freshmen.
Publication Dates: 1971–2005.
Scores, 3: Subscores in Listening, Reading (20–80), Total (200–800).
Administration: Group or individual.
Price Data: Rental fee per student available from publisher.
Time: 60 minutes.
Comments: Available for local administration and scoring by higher educational institutions; CD player and headphones required; previously known as College Board One-Hour Achievement Test in German with Listening and College Placement Test.
Author: Educational Testing Service.
Publisher: The College Board.
Cross References: See 8:130 (1 reference). For a review of an earlier form of the program, see 7:665.

[585]
College Board Institutional SAT Subject Test in Italian.

Purpose: To measure content knowledge in Italian.
Population: Entering college freshmen.
Publication Dates: 1962–2005.
Scores: Total (200-800) score only.
Administration: Group or individual.
Price Data: Rental fee per student available from publisher.
Time: 60 minutes.
Comments: Available for local administration and scoring by higher educational institutions; previously known as College Board One-Hour Achievement Test in Italian and College Placement Test.
Author: Educational Testing Service.
Publisher: The College Board.
Cross References: For a review by Paolo Valesio of earlier forms, see 7:300. For a review of an earlier form of the program, see 7:665.

[586]

College Board Institutional SAT Subject Test in Japanese with Listening.

Purpose: To measure content knowledge in Japanese.

Population: Entering college freshmen.

Publication Dates: 1997–2005.

Scores: 4: Subscores in Listening, Usage, Reading (20–80), and Total (200–800).

Administration: Group or individual.

Price Data: Rental fee per student available from publisher.

Time: 60 minutes.

Comments: Active forms of College Board SAT Subject Test in Japanese with Listening available for local administration and scoring by colleges, universities, and other appropriate organizations; CD player and earphones required; program previously known as College Board One-Hour Achievement Test.

Author: Educational Testing Service.

Publisher: The College Board.

Cross References: For a review of an earlier form of the program, see 7:665.

[587]

College Board Institutional SAT Subject Test in Latin.

Purpose: To measure content knowledge in Latin.

Population: Entering college freshmen.

Publication Dates: 1962–2005.

Scores: Total (200–800).

Administration: Group or individual.

Price Data: Rental fee per student available from publisher.

Time: 60 minutes.

Comments: Available for local administration and scoring by higher educational institutions; previously known as College Board One-Hour Achievement Test in Latin Reading and College Placement Test.

Author: Educational Testing Service.

Publisher: The College Board.

Cross References: For a review by Konrad Gries of an earlier form, see 5:280; for a review by Harold B. Dunkel, see 4:250. For a review of an earlier form of the program, see 7:665.

[588]

College Board Institutional SAT Subject Test in Literature.

Purpose: To measure content knowledge in literature.

Population: Entering college freshmen.

Publication Dates: 1968–2005.

Scores: Total (200–800).

Administration: Group or individual.

Price Data: Rental fee per student available from publisher.

Time: 60 minutes.

Comments: Available for local administration and scoring by higher educational institutions; previously known as College Board One-Hour Achievement Test in Literature.

Author: Educational Testing Service.

Publisher: The College Board.

Cross References: For a review of an earlier form of the program, see 7:665.

[589]

College Board Institutional SAT Subject Test in Modern Hebrew.

Purpose: To measure content knowledge in Hebrew.

Population: Entering college freshmen.

Publication Dates: 1962–2005.

Scores: Total (200–800) score only.

Administration: Group or individual.

Price Data: Rental fee per student available from publisher.

Time: 60 minutes.

Comments: Available for local administration and scoring by higher educational institutions; previously known as College Board One-Hour Achievement Test in Modern Hebrew and College Placement Test.

Author: Educational Testing Service.

Publisher: The College Board.

Cross References: For a review of an earlier form of the program, see 7:665.

[590]

College Board Institutional SAT Subject Test in Physics.

Purpose: To measure content knowledge in physics.

Population: Entering college freshmen.

Publication Dates: 1962–2005.

Scores: Total (200–800).

Administration: Group or individual.

Price Data: Rental fee per student available from publisher.

Time: 60 minutes.

Comments: Available for local administration and scoring by higher educational institutions; previously known as College Board One-Hour Achievement Test in Physics.

Author: Educational Testing Service.

Publisher: The College Board.

Cross References: See T5:587 (1 reference); for a review of an earlier form of the program, see 7:665.

[591]

College Board Institutional SAT Subject Test in Spanish.

Purpose: To measure content knowledge in Spanish.

Population: Entering college freshmen.
Publication Date: 1962–2005.
Scores: Total (200–800).
Administration: Group or individual.
Price Data: Rental fee per student available from publisher.
Time: (60) minutes.
Comments: Available for local administration and scoring by higher educational institutions; previously known as College Board One-Hour Achievement Test in Spanish Reading.
Author: Educational Testing Service.
Publisher: The College Board.
Cross References: See 8:161 (1 reference) and 7:316 (1 reference); for a review of an earlier form of the program, see 7:665.

[592]
College Board Institutional SAT Subject Test in Spanish with Listening.

Purpose: To measure content knowledge in Spanish.
Population: Entering college freshmen.
Publication Dates: 1971–2005.
Scores, 3: Subscores in Listening, Reading (20–80), Total (200–800).
Administration: Group or individual.
Price Data: Rental fee per student available from publisher.
Time: (60) minutes.
Comments: Available for local administration and scoring by higher educational institutions; CD player and earphones required; previously known as College Board One-Hour Achievement Test in Spanish with Listening and College Placement Test.
Author: Educational Testing Service.
Publisher: The College Board.
Cross References: For a review of an earlier form of the program, see 7:665.

[593]
College Board Institutional SAT Subject Test in U.S. History.

Purpose: To measure content knowledge in American History.
Population: Entering college freshmen.
Publication Dates: 1965–2005.
Scores: Total (200–800).
Administration: Group or individual.
Price Data: Rental fee per student available from publisher.
Time: (60) minutes.
Comments: Available for local administration and scoring by higher educational institutions; previously known as College Board One-Hour Achievement Test in American History and Social Studies.
Author: Educational Testing Service.

Publisher: The College Board.
Cross References: For a review by Howard R. Anderson of an earlier form, see 6:966; for a review by Ralph W. Tyler, see 5:786; for a review by Robert L. Thorndike, see 4:662; for a review of an earlier form of the program, see 7:665.

[594]
College Board Institutional SAT Subject Test in World History.

Purpose: To measure content knowledge in World History.
Population: Entering college freshmen.
Publication Dates: 1963–2005.
Scores: Total (200–800).
Administration: Group or individual.
Price Data: Rental fee per student available from publisher.
Time: 60 minutes.
Comments: Available for local administration and scoring by higher educational institutions; previously known as College Board One-Hour Achievement Test in World History.
Author: Educational Testing Service.
Publisher: The College Board.
Cross References: For a review by David K. Heenan of an earlier form, see 6:967; for a review of an earlier form of the program, see 7:665.

[595]
College Board Institutional SAT Subject Test in Writing.

Purpose: To measure students' writing skills.
Population: Entering college freshmen.
Publication Dates: 1962–2005.
Scores: Subscores in Multiple Choice, Writing Sample (20–80), Total (200–800).
Administration: Group or individual.
Price Data: Rental fee per student available from publisher.
Time: 60 minutes (20-minute essay and 40-minute multiple-choice).
Comments: Administration and scoring by higher educational institutions; previously known as College Board One-Hour Achievement Test in Writing and College Placement Test; includes a writing sample and multiple-choice questions.
Author: Educational Testing Service.
Publisher: The College Board.
Cross References: See 8:48 (20 references); for a review by John C. Sherwood of an earlier form, see 7:190 (3 references); for reviews by Charlotte Croon Davis, Robert C. Pooley, and Holland Roberts of earlier forms, see 6:287; for a review by Charlotte Croon Davis with Frederick B. Davis, see 4:178. For a review of an earlier form of the program, see 7:665.

[596]
College Board Institutional SAT Subject Tests in Mathematics Level 1 and Level 2.

Purpose: To measure content knowledge in mathematics.
Population: Entering college freshmen.
Publication Dates: 1964–2005.
Scores: Total (200–800).
Administration: Group or individual.
Price Data: Rental fee per student available from publisher.
Time: 60 minutes for each level.
Comments: Available for local administration and scoring by higher educational institutions; a calculator at least at the level of a scientific calculator is required to solve some, but not all, of the questions; previously known as College Board One-Hour Achievement Test in Mathematics.
Author: Educational Testing Service.
Publisher: The College Board.
Cross References: See T5:585 (1 reference); for a review of an earlier form of the program, see 7:665.

[597]
College Board On-Campus Tests.

Purpose: A portfolio of assessments, programs, and services designed to help higher education personnel determine the placement levels and remediation requirements of incoming, as well as continuing, students.
Population: Entering and continuing college students.
Publication Dates: 1989-2001.
Scores: Provides data in the following assessment areas: Course Placement, Remediation, Selection, Instruction, Guidance, and Counseling. Also used for Exemption by some institutions of higher education.
Administration: Group or individual.
Price Data: Available from publisher.
Comments: Through its On-Campus Testing Program, the College Board offers institutions of higher education the following: Descriptive Tests System (DTS), Institutional SAT Program, Test of Standard Written English (two forms), Essay Reading Service, and special contracts for state departments of education and consortia of higher education institutions; previously entitled Multiple Assessments, Programs, and Services (MAPS) of the College Board.
Author: Educational Testing Service.
Publisher: Educational Testing Service and the College Board.
Cross References: See T5:1746 (1 reference).

[598]
College Board SAT II: English Language Proficiency Test.

Purpose: To measure understanding of spoken and written standard American English and ability to use English in the classroom and in daily life.
Population: Candidates for college entrance
Publication Dates: 1997–2005.
Acronym: ELPT.
Scores: 3 subscores in Listening, Reading (1–50), and Total (901–999); in addition proficiency ratings (below intermediate to advanced high or higher) are provided for Listening and Reading.
Administration: Group.
Price Data: Available from publisher.
Time: Administration time not reported.
Comments: Test administered once annually (November) at centers established by the publisher; also administered once annually (April) in participating high schools; test takers are required to bring a cassette player with earphones for use on the Listening section of the test; available for local administration and scoring by higher-educational institutions through the College Entry-Level Assessment (CELA) Program; the final administration of this test was in January 2005.
Authors: Program administered by the College Board and Educational Testing Service.
Publisher: The College Board.

[599]
College Board SAT Program.

Purpose: To provide "tests and related educational services for students who plan to continue their education beyond high school."
Population: Candidates for college entrance.
Publication Dates: 1901–2005.
Acronym: SAT Program.
Administration: Group.
Price Data: Price data is available from the publisher for priced and free materials including technical report (1984, 225 pages), supervisor's manual (1998, 69 pages), student bulletins, test familiarization material for students, score use and interpretation booklets for counselors and admissions officers, summary report guides for high schools and for colleges, state and national reports on college-bound seniors, guide to the College Board Admitted Student Evaluation Service (formerly Validity Study Service), and test and technical data; examination fees include reporting of scores to the candidate's secondary school and 1–4 colleges and/or scholarship services.
Comments: Formerly called the College Board Admissions Testing Program; the SAT I: Reasoning Test is administered 7 times annually (January, March or April, May, June, October, November, December) at centers established by the publisher; The SAT II:

Subject Tests are administered 6 times annually (January, May, June, October, November, December) at centers established by the publisher, though not all tests are available at each administration; English Language Proficiency Test (ELPT) is also offered in April in participating secondary schools; Student Descriptive Questionnaire provides background information to colleges and scholarship services; special administration arrangements available for students with disabilities, including Braille, cassette tape, regular type, and large-type formats, individualized testing, and additional testing time. The SAT I and SAT II score scales were rescaled in 1995; equivalence tables are available for converting scores from the original scale to the new recentered scale. SAT I and SAT II forms are available for local administration and scoring by higher educational institutions through the College Entry-Level Assessment (CELA) Program.

Author: Educational Testing Service.

Publisher: The College Board.

a) COLLEGE BOARD SAT REASONING TEST.

Publication Dates: 1926–1999.

Price Data: Examination fee per candidate available from publisher. Price data for guidelines on the uses of College Board test scores and related data, guide to the College Board Admitted Student Evaluation Service (formerly the Validity Study Service), Technical Handbook, SAT Program Handbooks, Student Bulletins, Taking the SAT I, test preparation materials and software, SAT I Question and Answer Service, SAT I Student Answer Service, SAT Score Verification Service, and clerical scoring service are all available from the publisher.

Time: (180) minutes.

Comments: The SAT I: Reasoning Test replaced the College Board Scholastic Aptitude Test and the Test of Standard Written English in 1994. Scores are reported for Verbal and Mathematical sections of the SAT I. No subscores are provided. Performance data by item type/content available for Verbal and Mathematics beginning in 1994.

b) COLLEGE BOARD SAT SUBJECT TESTS.

Publication Dates: 1901–1999.

Scores: 21 tests in 18 subjects: Writing (including an essay at every national administration), Literature, American History & Social Studies, World History, Mathematics [Math Level IC, Math Level IIC], Biology E/M [Ecological/Molecular], Chemistry, Physics, French (reading only), French (reading and listening), German (reading only), German (reading and listening), Spanish (reading only), Spanish (reading and listening), Modern Hebrew, Italian, Latin, Japanese (reading and listening), Chinese (reading and listening), Korean (reading and listening), and English Language Proficiency.

Price Data: Examination fees per candidate available from publisher. Price data for guidelines on the uses of College Board test scores and related data, guide to the College Board Admitted Student Evaluation Service (formerly the Validity Study Service), Writing Sample Copy Service, technical handbook, SAT Program Handbooks, student bulletins, Taking the SAT II, test and preparation materials, and clerical scoring service are all available from the publisher.

Time: (60) minutes.

Comments: Formerly called the College Board Achievement Tests; candidate elects 1 to 3 tests as specified by individual college or scholarship program requirments; candidates have the option of reviewing their SAT II scores prior to deciding whether or not to have these scores reported to colleges or scholarship services. The administration schedule of each Subject Test is available from the publisher.

Cross References: See T5:615 (55 references), T3:500 (3 references), 8:472 (6 references), T2:1048 (9 references), and 7:663 (16 references); for reviews by Benno G. Fricke and Dean K. Whitla of an earlier program, see 6:760 (12 references); see also 5:599 (3 references) and 4:526 (9 references). For reviews of individual tests, see 8:46 (2 reviews), 8:128 (1 review), 8:147 (1 review), 8:258 (2 reviews), 7:344 (2 reviews), 6:287 (3 reviews, 6:289 (1 review), 6:383 (1 review), 6:384 (2 reviews), 6:449 (2 reviews), 6:568 (1 review), 6:569 (1 review), 6:914 (1 review), 6:966 (1 review), 6:967 (1 review), 5:272 (1 review), 5:277 (1 review), 5:280 (1 review), 5:318 (1 review), 5:723 (1 review), 5:742 (1 review), 5:749 (1 review), 5:786 (1 review), 4:178 (1 review), 4:237 (1 review), 4:244 (1 review), 4:250 (1 review), 4:285 (1 review), 4:367 (1 review), 4:368 (1 review), 4:600 (1 review), 4:617 (1 review), 4:633 (1 review), and 4:662 (1 review).

[600]

College Board SAT Reasoning Test.

Purpose: To measure "the developed verbal and mathematical reasoning abilities related to successful performance in college."

Population: Candidates for college entrance.

Publication Dates: 1926–2005.

Acronym: SAT.

Scores, 2: Critical Reading, Mathematics, and Writing reported on the College Board 200–800 scale.

Administration: Group.

Forms: Forms issued annually.

Price Data: Examination fees per candidate available from publisher; price data for guidelines on the uses of

College Board test scores and related data, guide to the College Board Admitted Student Evaluation Service (formerly the Validity Study Service), technical handbook, SAT Program handbooks, student bulletins, Taking the SAT, test and technical data, SAT Question and Answer Service, SAT Student Answer Service, SAT Score Verification Service, and clerical scoring service are all available from the publisher.

Time: 225 minutes.

Comments: The SAT I is administered 7 times annually (January, March or April, May, June, October, November, and December) at centers established by the publisher. The SAT Reasoning Test replaced the College Board Scholastic Aptitude Test and Test of Standard Written English in 1994. Scores are reported for Verbal, Mathematical, and Writing sections of the SAT. Performance data by item type/content are available for Verbal and Math beginning in 1994. The SAT I scale was rescaled in 1995; equivalence tables are available for converting scores from one scale to another. SAT forms are available for local administration and scoring through the College Entry-Level Assessment (CELA) Program. Special administration arrangements available for students with disabilities, including Braille, cassette tape, regular type and large-type formats, individualized testing, and additional testing time.

Authors: The College Board and Educational Testing Service.

Publisher: The College Board.

Cross References: See T5:592 (107 references) and T4:564 (167 references); for reviews by Sanford J. Cohn and Lee J. Cronbach of an earlier edition, see 9:244 (31 references); see T3:501 (152 references), 8:182 (217 references), and T2:357 (148 references); for reviews by Philip H. Dubois and Wimburn L. Wallace of an earlier form, see 7:344 (298 references); for reviews by John E. Bowers and Wayne S. Zimmerman, see 6:449 (79 references); for a review by John T. Dailey, see 5:318 (20 references); for a review by Frederick B. Davis, see 4:285 (22 references). For reviews of the testing program, see 6:760 (2 reviews).

[601]
College Board SAT Subject Test in American History and Social Studies.

Purpose: To measure content knowledge in American history and social studies.

Population: Candidates for college entrance with one-year American history course at the college-preparatory level.

Publication Dates: 1937–2005.

Scores: Total scores reported on the College Board 200–800 scale, subscores reported on a 20–80 scale; ELPT total score reported on a 901–999 scale; ELPT subscores reported on a 1–50 scale.

Administration: Group.

Price Data: Available from publisher.

Time: Administration time not reported.

Comments: Test administered 6 times annually (January, May, June, October, November, December) at centers established by publisher; available for local administration and scoring by higher educational institutions through the College Entry-Level Assessment (CELA) programs; replaces College Board Achievement Test in American History and Social Studies.

Authors: Program administered by The College Board and Educational Testing Service.

Publisher: The College Board.

Cross References: See T4:565 (1 reference) and T2:1939 (1 reference); for a review by Howard R. Anderson of earlier forms, see 6:966; for a review by Ralph W. Tyler, see 5:786 (3 references); for a review by Robert L. Thorndike, see 4:662 (6 references). For reviews of an earlier form of the testing program, see 6:760 (2 reviews).

[602]
College Board SAT Subject Test in Biology.

Purpose: To measure content knowledge in biology.

Population: Candidates for college entrance with one-year courses in biology and algebra.

Publication Dates: 1915–2005.

Scores: Total (200–800).

Administration: Group.

Price Data: Available from publisher.

Time: Administration time not reported.

Comments: Test administered for the last time in May 1999 at centers established by publisher; available for local administration and scoring by higher educational institutions through the College Entry-Level Assessment (CELA) Program; replaces College Board Achievement Test in Biology.

Authors: Program administered by the College Board and Educational Testing Service.

Publisher: The College Board.

Cross References: See 8:833 (1 reference), 7:813 (2 references), and 6:892 (3 references); for a review by Elizabeth Hagen of an earlier form, see 5:723; for a review by Clark W. Horton, see 4:600. For reviews of an earlier form of the testing program, see 6:760 (2 reviews).

[603]
College Board SAT Subject Test in Biology E/M.

Purpose: To measure content knowledge in biology.

Population: Candidates for college entrance with one-year courses in biology and algebra.

Publication Dates: 1998–2005.

Scores: Total score only.

Administration: Group.

Price Data: Available from publisher.
Time: 60 minutes
Comments: Administered 6 times annually beginning in 1999 (October, November, December, January, May, and June) at centers established by publisher; candidates take a core set of questions and then select a specialized section of questions in either ecological or molecular biology; available for local administration and scoring by higher educational institutions through the College Entry-Level Assessment (CELA) Program; replaces College Board SAT II: Subject Test in Biology.
Authors: Program administered by the College Board and Educational Testing Service.
Publisher: The College Board.

[604]
College Board SAT Subject Test in Chemistry.

Purpose: To measure content knowledge in chemistry.
Population: Candidates for college entrance with one-year course in introductory chemistry at the college-preparatory level.
Publication Dates: 1937–2005.
Scores: Total (200–800) score only.
Administration: Group.
Price Data: Available from publisher.
Time: 60 minutes.
Comments: Test administered 6 times annually (January, May, June, October, November, December) at centers established by publisher; available for local administration and scoring by higher educational institutions through the College Entry-Level Assessment (CELA) Program.
Authors: Program administered by the College Board and Educational Testing Service.
Publisher: The College Board.
Cross References: See T4:567 (1 reference) and 7:844 (3 references); for a review by William Hered of earlier forms, see 6:914 (4 references); for a review by Max D. Engelhart, see 5:742 (2 references); for a review by Evelyn Raskin, see 4:617 (4 references). For reviews of an earlier form of the testing program, see 6:760 (2 reviews).

[605]
College Board SAT Subject Test in Chinese with Listening.

Purpose: To measure content knowledge in Chinese.
Population: Candidates for college entrance with 2–4 years high school Chinese (Mandarin).
Publication Dates: 1994–2005.
Scores, 4: Usage, Listening, Reading, Total.
Administration: Group.
Price Data: Available from publisher.

Comments: Test administered once annually (November) at centers established by publisher; test takers are required to bring a CD player with earphones for use on the Listening section of the test; available for local administration and scoring by higher educational institutions through the College Entry-Level Assessment (CELA) Program.
Authors: Program administered by the College Board and Educational Testing Service.
Publisher: The College Board.

[606]
College Board SAT Subject Test in French.

Purpose: To measure content knowledge in French.
Population: Candidates for college entrance with 2–4 years of high school French.
Publication Dates: 1937–2005.
Scores: Total (200–800) score only.
Administration: Group.
Price Data: Available from publisher.
Time: 60 minutes
Comments: Test administered 6 times annually (January, May, June, October, November, December) at centers established by publisher; available for local administration and scoring by higher educational institutions through the College Entry-Level Assessment (CELA) Program; replaces College Board Achievement Test in French.
Authors: Program administered by the College Board and Educational Testing Service.
Publisher: The College Board.
Cross References: For a review by Helen L. Jorstad of an earlier form, see 8:116; see also 6:366 (4 references) and 5:263 (2 references); for a review by Walter V. Kaulfers of earlier forms, see 4:237 (7 references). For reviews of an earlier form of the testing program, see 6:760 (2 reviews).

[607]
College Board SAT Subject Test in French with Listening.

Purpose: To measure content knowledge in French.
Population: Candidates for college entrance with 3–4 years high school French.
Publication Dates: 1994–2005.
Scores: 3: subscores in Listening, Reading (20–80), and Total (200–800).
Administration: Group.
Price Data: Available from publisher.
Time: Administration time not reported.
Comments: Test administered once annually (November) at centers established by publisher; test takers are required to bring a CD player with earphones for use on the Listening section of the test; available for local administration and scoring by higher educational

institutions through the College Entry-Level Assessment (CELA) Program.
Authors: Program administered by the College Board and Educational Testing Service.
Publisher: The College Board.

[608]
College Board SAT Subject Test in German.
Purpose: To measure content knowledge in German.
Population: Candidates for college entrance with 2–4 years high school German.
Publication Dates: 1937–2005.
Scores: Total (200–800) score only.
Administration: Group.
Price Data: Available from publisher.
Time: 60 minutes.
Comments: Test administered once annually (June) at centers established by publisher; available for local administration and scoring by higher educational institutions through the College Entry-Level Assessment (CELA) Program; replaces College Board Achievement Test in German.
Authors: Program administered by the College Board and Educational Testing Service.
Publisher: The College Board.
Cross References: For a review by Randall L. Jones of an earlier form, see 8:128; for a review by Gilbert C. Kettelkamp of earlier forms, see 6:383; for a review by Harold B. Dunkel, see 5:272 (3 references); for a review by Herbert Shueler, see 4:244 (3 references). For reviews of an earlier form of the testing program, see 6:760 (2 reviews).

[609]
College Board SAT Subject Test in German with Listening.
Purpose: To measure content knowledge in German.
Population: Candidates for college entrance with 2–4 years in high school German.
Publication Dates: 1994–2005.
Scores: 3: subscores in Listening, Reading (20–80), and Total (200–800).
Administration: Group.
Price Data: Available from publisher.
Time: 60 minutes.
Comments: Test administered once annually (November) at centers established by publisher; test takers are required to bring a CD player with earphones for use on the Listening section of the test; available for local administration and scoring by higher educational institutions through the College Entry-Level Assessment (CELA) Program.
Authors: Program administered by the College Board and Educational Testing Service.
Publisher: The College Board.

[610]
College Board SAT Subject Test in Italian.
Purpose: To measure content knowledge in Italian.
Population: Candidates for college entrance with 2–4 years high school Italian.
Publication Dates: 1990–2005.
Scores: Total score only (200–800).
Administration: Group.
Price Data: Available from publisher.
Comments: Test administered 6 times annually (January, May, June, October, November, December) at centers established by publisher; available for local administration and scoring by higher educational institutions through the College Entry-Level Assessment (CELA) Program; replaces College Board Achievement Test in Italian.
Authors: Program administered by the College Board and Educational Testing Service.
Publisher: The College Board.

[611]
College Board SAT Subject Test in Japanese with Listening.
Purpose: To measure content knowledge in Japanese.
Population: Candidates for college entrance with 2–4 years high school Japanese.
Publication Dates: 1993–2005.
Scores, 4: Usage, Listening, Reading, Total.
Administration: Group.
Price Data: Available from publisher.
Comments: Test administered once annually (November) at centers established by the publisher; test takers required to bring a CD player with earphones for use on the Listening section of the test; available for local administration and scoring by higher educational institutions through the College Entry-Level Assessment (CELA) Program.
Authors: Program administered by the College Board and Educational Testing Service.
Publisher: The College Board.

[612]
College Board SAT Subject Test in Korean with Listening.
Purpose: To measure content knowledge in Korean.
Population: Candidates for college entrance with 2–4 years high school Korean
Publication Dates: 1994–2005.
Scores, 4: Usage, Listening, Reading (20–80), Total (200–800).
Administration: Group.
Price Data: Available from publisher.
Time: 60 minutes.
Comments: Test administered once annually (November) at centers established by publisher; test takers

are required to bring a CD player with earphones for use on the Listening section of the test; available for local administration and scoring by higher educational institutions through the College Entry-Level Assessment (CELA) Program.
Authors: Program administered by the College Board and Educational Testing Service.
Publisher: The College Board.

[613]
College Board SAT Subject Test in Latin.
Purpose: To measure content knowledge in Latin.
Population: Candidates for college entrance with 2–4 years high school Latin.
Publication Dates: 1937–2005.
Scores: Total scores only.
Administration: Group.
Price Data: Available from publisher.
Time: 60 minutes.
Comments: Test administered 6 times annually (January, May, June, October, November, December) at centers established by publisher; available for local administration and scoring by higher educational institutions through the College Entry-Level Assessment (CELA) Program; replaces College Board Achievement Test in Latin.
Authors: Program administered by the College Board and Educational Testing Service.
Publisher: The College Board.
Cross References: For a review by Konrad Gries of an earlier form, see 5:280 (1 reference); for a review by Harold B. Dunkel, see 4:250 (2 references). For reviews of an earlier form of the testing program, see 6:760 (2 reviews).

[614]
College Board SAT Subject Test in Literature.
Purpose: To measure content knowledge in Literature.
Population: Candidates for college entrance.
Publication Dates: 1968–2005.
Scores: Total (200–800) score only.
Administration: Group.
Price Data: Available from publisher.
Time: 60 minutes.
Comments: Test administered 6 times annually (January, May, June, October, November, December) at centers established by publisher; available for local administration and scoring by higher educational institutions through the College Entry-Level Assessment (CELA) Program; replaces College Board Achievement Test in Literature.
Authors: Program administered by the College Board and Educational Testing Service.
Publisher: The College Board.

Cross References: See T5:604 (1 reference) and 7:217 (2 references). For reviews of an earlier form of the testing program, see 6:760 (2 reviews).

[615]
College Board SAT Subject Test in Modern Hebrew.
Purpose: To measure content knowledge in Modern Hebrew.
Population: Candidates for college entrance with 2–4 years high school Hebrew.
Publication Dates: 1989–2005.
Scores: Total (200–800) score only.
Administration: Group.
Price Data: Available from publisher.
Time: 60 minutes.
Comments: Test administered 6 times annually (January, May, June, October, November, December) at centers established by publisher; available for local administration and scoring by higher educational institutions through the College Entry-Level Assessment (CELA) Program; replaces College Board Achievement Test in Hebrew.
Authors: Program administered by the College Board and Educational Testing Service.
Publisher: The College Board.
Cross References: For reviews of an earlier form of the testing program, see 6:760 (2 reviews).

[616]
College Board SAT Subject Test in Physics.
Purpose: To measure content knowledge in physics.
Population: Candidates for college entrance with one-year course in introductory physics at the college-preparatory level.
Publication Dates: 1937–2005.
Scores: Total (200–800) score only.
Administration: Group.
Price Data: Available from publisher.
Time: 60 minutes.
Comments: Test administered 6 times annually (January, May, June, October, November, December) at centers established by publisher; available for local administration and scoring by higher educational institutions through the College Entry-Level Assessment (CELA) Program; replaces College Board Achievement Test in Physics.
Authors: Program administered by the College Board and Educational Testing Service.
Publisher: The College Board.
Cross References: See T4:574 (2 reference, 8:863 (1 reference), 7:855 (2 references), and 6:926 (4 references); for a review by Theodore G. Phillips of an earlier form, see 5:749 (2 references); for a review by Palmer O. Johnson, see 4:633 (3 references). For reviews of an earlier form of the testing program, see 6:760 (2 reviews).

[617]
College Board SAT Subject Test in Spanish.

Purpose: To measure content knowledge in Spanish.
Population: Candidates for college entrance with 2–4 years high school Spanish.
Publication Dates: 1937–2005.
Scores: Total (200–800) score only.
Administration: Group.
Price Data: Available from publisher.
Time: 60 minutes.
Comments: Test administered 6 times annually (January, May, June, October, November, December) at centers established by publisher; available for local administration and scoring by higher educational institutions through the College Entry-Level Assessment (CELA) Program; replaces College Board Achievement Test in Spanish.
Authors: Program administered by the College Board and Educational Testing Service.
Publisher: The College Board.
Cross References: See 6:419 (1 reference), 5:287 (1 reference), and 4:259 (3 references) for information on earlier forms. For reviews of an earlier form of the testing program, see 6:760 (2 reviews).

[618]
College Board SAT Subject Test in Spanish with Listening.

Purpose: To measure content knowledge in Spanish.
Population: Candidates for college entrance with 3–4 years high school Spanish.
Publication Dates: 1994–2005.
Scores, 3: Subscores in Listening, Reading (20–80), Total (200–800).
Administration: Group.
Price Data: Available from publisher.
Time: 60 minutes.
Comments: Test administered once annually (November) at centers established by publisher; test takers required to bring a CD player with earphones for use on the Listening section of the test; available for local administration and scoring by higher educational institutions through the College Entry-Level Assessment (CELA) Program.
Authors: Program administered by the College Board and Educational Testing Service.
Publisher: The College Board.

[619]
College Board SAT Subject Test in World History.

Purpose: To measure content knowledge in world history.
Population: Candidates for college entrance.
Publication Dates: 1937–2005.
Scores: Total (200–800) only.

Administration: Group.
Price Data: Available from publisher.
Time: 60 minutes
Comments: Test administered 2 times annually (June, December) at centers established by publisher; available for local administration and scoring by higher educational institutions through the College Entry-Level Assessment (CELA) Program; replaces College Board Achievement Test in European History and World Cultures.
Authors: Program administered by the College Board and Educational Testing Service.
Publisher: The College Board.
Cross References: For a review by David K. Heenan of an earlier form, see 6:967. For reviews of an earlier form of the testing program, see 6:760 (2 reviews).

[620]
College Board Subject Test in Mathematics Level I and Mathematics Level II.

Purpose: To measure content knowledge in mathematics.
Population: Candidates for college entrance.
Publication Dates: 1937–2005.
Scores: Total (200–800) score only.
Administration: Group.
Price Data: Available from publisher.
Time: 60 minutes.
Comments: For Math Level I, administered to candidates with 3 years of college-preparatory math (2 years algebra, 1 year of geometry); for Math Level II, administered to candidates with more than 3 years of college-preparatory Math (2 years algebra, 1 year geometry, and precalculus and/or trigonometry); test administered 6 times annually (January, May, June, October, November, December) at centers established by publisher; available for local administration and scoring by higher educational institutions through the College Entry-Level Assessment (CELA) Program; a calculator at least at the level of a scientific calculator is required to solve some, but not all, of the questions; replaces College Board Achievement Tests in Mathematics, the final administration of the Math Level 2 test was January 1994; it was replaced by the Math Level IIC Subject Test at all administrations beginning in May 1994; the final administration of Math Level 1 test was January 1998; it was replaced by the Math Level IC Subject Test at all administrations beginning May 1998.
Authors: Program administered by the College Board and Educational Testing Service.
Publisher: The College Board.
Cross References: See T4:578 (2 references); for reviews by Jeremy Kilpatrick and Peter A. Lappan, Jr. of Level 1, see 8:258 (4 references); see also 7:456 (4 references). For additional information concerning Level

2, see 8:259 (1 reference); see also 7:457 (1 reference). For reviews of an earlier form of the testing program, see 6:760 (2 reviews).

[621]
College English Test: National Achievement Tests.

Purpose: Designed to measure the student's mastery of elements of the English language.
Population: High school and college freshmen.
Publication Dates: 1937–1943.
Scores, 7: Punctuation, Capitalization, Language Usage, Sentence Structure, Modifiers, Miscellaneous Principles, Total.
Administration: Group.
Forms, 2: A, B.
Price Data: Available from publisher.
Time: 45(50) minutes.
Author: A. C. Jordan.
Publisher: Psychometric Affiliates.
Cross References: For a review by Osmond E. Palmer, see 5:178; for reviews by Constance M. McCullough and Robert W. Howard, see 2:1269.1.

[622]
College Level Examination Program.

Purpose: Designed as a way for college accreditation, advanced placement, or assessment of educational attainment.
Population: 1–2 years of college or equivalent.
Publication Dates: 1964–2002.
Acronym: CLEP.
Price Data: Available from publisher.
Time: (90) minutes per test.
Comments: Tests administered at 1,100 centers throughout the United States as well as internationally; as of July, 2001 administered as a computer-based program; program administered by the College Board and Educational Testing Service.
Author: Educational Testing Service.
Publisher: Educational Testing Service.

a) BUSINESS.
   1) *Information Systems and Computer Applications.*
   2) *Principles of Management.*
   3) *Principles of Accounting.*
   4) *Introductory Business Law.*
   5) *Principles of Marketing.*

b) COMPOSITION AND LITERATURE.
Comments: Composition and Literature tests have optional essay supplement that is scored by the college.
   1) *American Literature.*
   2) *Analyzing and Interpreting Literature.*
   3) *Freshman College Composition.*
   4) *English Literature.*
   5) *English Composition (with and without essay).*
Comments: English Composition with Essay scored by faculty for CLEP.
   6) *Humanities.*

c) FOREIGN LANGUAGES.
   1) *College French, Levels 1 and 2.*
   2) *College German, Levels 1 and 2.*
   3) *College Spanish, Levels 1 and 2.*

d) HISTORY AND SOCIAL SCIENCES.
   1) *American Government.*
   2) *History of the United States I: Early Colonization to 1877.*
   3) *History of the United States II: 1865 to the Present.*
   4) *Educational Psychology.*
   5) *Introductory Psychology.*
   6) *Human Growth and Development.*
   7) *Principles of Macroeconomics.*
   8) *Principles of Microeconomics.*
   9) *Introductory Sociology.*
   10) *Western Civilization I: Ancient Near East to 1648.*
   11) *Western Civilization II: 1648 to the Present.*
   12) *Social Sciences and History.*

e) SCIENCE AND MATHEMATICS.
   1) *Calculus with Elementary Functions.*
   2) *College Algebra.*
   3) *College Algebra—Trigonometry.*
   4) *General Biology.*
   5) *General Chemistry.*
   6) *Trigonometry.*
   7) *Mathematics.*
   8) *Natural Sciences.*

Cross References: See 9:245 (1 reference) and T3:506 (7 references); for reviews by Paul L. Dressel, David A. Frisbie, and Wimburn L. Wallace of an earlier program, see 8:473 (15 references); for reviews of the General Examinations, see 8:8 (2 reviews); for reviews of the separate Subject Examinations, see 8:43 (1 review), 8:44 (1 review), 8:64 (1 review), 8:65 (1 review), 8:66 (1 review), 8:255 (1 review), 8:256 (1 review), 8:297 (1 review), 8:365 (1 review), 8:460 (1 review), 8:832 (1 review), 8:847 (1 review), 8:911 (1 review), , 8:919 (1 review), 8:1119 (1 review), and 8:1120 (1 review); see also T2:1050 (4 references); for reviews by Alexander W. Astin, Benjamin S. Bloom, and Warren G. Findley, see 7:664 (7 references).

[623]
College Student Expectations Questionnaire, Second Edition.

Purpose: Designed to evaluate new students' expectations for college including their goals, motivations, and future plans for various college experiences.
Population: Precollege students and first-year students at the beginning of the first semester.

Publication Dates: 1997–2005.
Acronym: CSXQ.
Scores, 16: Background Information, College Activities Scales (Library and Information Technology, Experiences with Faculty, Course Learning, Writing, Campus Facilities, Clubs, Organizations, Service Projects, Student Acquaintances, Scientific and Quantitative Experiences, Conversations), Reading/Writing, Satisfaction, The College Environment, Additional Questions.
Administration: Group.
Price Data, 2005: $200–$500 administration fee depending on mode of administration (paper or an online mode) includes all survey processing/setup, one customized institutional report containing means, frequency and descriptive information of survey results arrayed by gender, and an electronic data file containing all student responses; $2 per paper survey; $2.75 per student in a self-service online administration where the institution sends all invitations and communications to students; $3 per student in a full-service online administration where CSEQ sends all invitations and communications to students; $25 per Norms for the Fourth Edition (2003, 178 pages); $150 per hour for special additional analysis.
Time: (10–15) minutes.
Comments: Adapted from the College Student Experiences Questionnaire (CSEQ; 624); longitudinal assessments are possible by comparing results from the CSXQ with data from the CSEQ completed by the same students near the end of the first year or later in the college experience.
Authors: George D. Kuh and C. Robert Pace.
Publisher: Indiana University Center for Postsecondary Research.

[624]

College Student Experiences Questionnaire, Fourth Edition.

Purpose: Designed to measure (a) the quality of effort undergraduate students invest in using educational resources and opportunities provided for their learning and development, (b) the students' perceptions of how much the campus environment emphasizes a diverse set of educational priorities, and (c) how the students' efforts and perceptions relate to personal estimates of progress made toward a holistic set of learning outcomes.
Population: Undergraduate college students.
Publication Dates: 1979-2003.
Acronym: CSEQ.
Scores, 19: Background Information, College Activities Scales (Library, Computer and Information Technology, Course Learning, Writing Experiences, Experiences with Faculty, Art, Music and Theater, Campus Facilities, Clubs and Organizations, Personal

Experiences, Student Acquaintances, Scientific and Quantitative Experiences, Conversations), Reading/Writing, Satisfaction, The College Environment, Estimate of Gains, Additional Questions.
Administration: Group.
Price Data, 2005: $200–$500 administration fee depending on mode of administration (paper or an online mode) includes all survey processing/setup, one customized institutional report containing means, frequency and descriptive information of survey resulsts arrayed by gender, and an electronic data file containing all student responses; $2 per paper survey; $2.75 per student in a self-service online administration where the institution sends all invitations and communications to students; $3 per student in a full-service online administration where CSEQ sends all invitations and communications to students; $25 per Norms for the Fourth Edition (2003, 178 pages); $150 per hour for special additional analysis.
Time: (30) minutes.
Authors: C. Robert Pace and George D. Kuh.
Publisher: Indiana University Center for Postsecondary Research.
Cross References: For reviews by Kurt F. Geisinger and by M. David Miller and J. Monroe Miller, see 16:58; see also T5:620 (6 references) and T4:588 (4 references); for reviews by David A. Decoster and Susan McCammon of an earlier edition, see 10:67; for reviews by Robert D. Brown and John K. Miller, see 9:246 (1 reference).

[625]

College Student Inventory [part of the Retention Management System].

Purpose: Designed to assess "a variety of motives and background information related to college success," improved student retention, and enhancing student advising effectiveness.
Population: First-year undergraduate college students.
Publication Date: 1988.
Acronym: CSI.
Scores: 4 Domains: Academic Motivation (Study Habits, Intellectual Interests, Academic Confidence, Desire to Finish College, Attitude Toward Educators), Social Motivation (Self-Reliance, Sociability, Leadership), General Coping Ability (Ease of Transition, Family Emotional Support, Openness, Career Planning, Sense of Financial Security), Receptivity to Support Services (Academic Assistance, Personal Counseling, Social Enhancement, Career Counseling).
Administration: Group.
Price Data: Available from publisher.
Time: (60) minutes.
Author: Michael L. Stratil.
Publisher: Noel-Levitz.

Cross References: For reviews by Michael H. Campbell and Thomas P. Hogan, see 16:59.

[626]
College Survival and Success Scale.

Purpose: Designed to "identify the concerns college students are experiencing or the concerns that prospective college students can anticipate."
Population: Individuals interested in attending college, or agencies that work with individuals interested in attending college.
Publication Date: 2006.
Acronym: CSSS.
Scores, 5: Commitment to Education, Self-/Resource-Management Skills, Interpersonal/Social Skills, Academic Success Skills, Career Planning Skills.
Administration: Individual or group.
Price Data, 2006: $37.95 per complete kit including 25 test booklets and 1 administrator's guide (8 pages).
Time: (15-25) minutes.
Author: John Liptak.
Publisher: JIST Publishing, Inc.

[627]
Collegiate Assessment of Academic Proficiency.

Purpose: Designed to assess selected academic skills typically obtained in a core general education curriculum.
Population: Freshmen–Seniors in college.
Publication Dates: 1989–1991.
Acronym: CAAP.
Administration: Group.
Restricted Distribution: Available to institutions signing a participation agreement and paying a participation fee
Price Data, 2005: $350 per year institutional participation fee; test module prices (including scoring and reporting) available from publisher.
Time: 40 minutes per test.
Authors: ACT, Inc.
Publisher: ACT, Inc.
a) WRITING SKILLS.
Publication Date: 1998.
Scores, 3: Usage/Mechanics, Rhetorical Skills, Total.
b) MATHEMATICS.
Publication Date: 1989.
Scores, 3: Basic Algebra, College Algebra, Total.
c) READING.
Publication Date: 1989.
Scores, 3: Arts/Literature, Social Studies/Sciences, Total.
d) CRITICAL THINKING.
Publication Date: 1989.
Scores: Total score only.

e) SCIENCE REASONING.
Publication Date: 1989.
Scores: Total score only.
f) WRITING (ESSAY).
Publication Date: 1990.
Scores: Total score only.
Comments: Total of 3 individual essays.
Cross References: See T5:621 (2 references); for reviews by Steven V. Owen and Jeffrey K. Smith, see 13:74 (3 references); see also T4:589 (1 reference).

[628]
Collis-Romberg Mathematical Problem Solving Profiles.

Purpose: Assesses student progress through a variety of mathematical problem-solving skills.
Population: Ages 9–13, 13–17.
Publication Date: 1992.
Scores, 6: Number, Algebra, Space, Measurement, Chance and Data, Total.
Administration: Group.
Levels, 2: Junior, Senior.
Price Data, 2006: A$66 per complete set including profiles A and B, and manual (72 pages); A$20.90 per manual.
Time: (40–50) minutes.
Comments: Junior version (ages 9–13) uses Parts A to C of each question; Senior version (ages 13–17) uses Parts A to D of each question.
Authors: K. F. Collis and T. A. Romberg.
Publisher: Australian Council for Educational Research Ltd. [Australia].
Cross References: For reviews by John W. Fleenor and Judith A. Monsaas, see 12:85.

[629]
Color Trails Test.

Purpose: Designed as a test of sustained visual attention and simple sequencing.
Population: Ages 18 and over.
Publication Dates: 1994–1996.
Acronym: CTT.
Scores, 10: Color Trails 1, Color Trails 1 Errors, Color Trails 1 Near-Misses, Color Trails 1 Prompts, Color Trails 2, Color Trails 2 Color Errors, Color Trails 2 Number Errors, Color Trails 2 Near-Misses, Color Trails 2 Prompts, Interference Index.
Administration: Individual.
Forms, 8: Color Trails 1: A, B, C, D; Color Trails 2: A, B, C, D.
Price Data, 2006: $110 per introductory kit including professional manual (1996, 88 pages), 25 record forms, and 25 administrations of the CCT Form A, Parts 1 and 2.
Time: (10) minutes

Comments: The CTT was developed to be free from the influence of language, and is an analogue of the Trail Making Test (TMT). Administration instructions in Spanish and English are provided in the manual. Respondents must be able to recognize Arabic numerals 1–25.

Authors: Louis F. D'Elia, Paul Satz, Craig Lyons Uchiyama, and Travis White.

Publisher: Psychological Assessment Resources, Inc.

Cross References: For reviews by James C. Reed and Surendra P. Singh, see 15:56.

[630]
Colored Overlay Assessment Kits.

Purpose: Designed to help determine the effectiveness of each colored overlay in improving the ease and accuracy of seeing the printed word while reading.

Population: Individuals experiencing reading and writing problems due to suspected visual perception problems.

Publication Date: 1993.

Scores: Not scored.

Administration: Individual.

Price Data, 2005: $29.95 per each 8-color pack (there are 24 assorted colors in all); packets of 4 individual colored overlays are available; An assessment video is also available at www.nrsi.com; additional price information available at www.dyslexiacure.com.

Time: Administration time varies from student to student.

Author: Marie Carbo.

Publisher: National Reading Styles Institute, Inc.

[631]
Columbia Mental Maturity Scale, Third Edition.

Purpose: Designed to provide "an estimate of the general reasoning ability of children."

Population: 3.5–10 years.

Publication Dates: 1954–1972.

Acronym: CMMS.

Scores: Total score only.

Administration: Individual.

Price Data, 2002: $678 per complete kit including 95 item cards, Guide for Administering and Interpreting (1972, 61 pages); $72 per 35 individual record forms; $25 per English-Spanish Reference Handbook for Educators; $75 per Guide for Administering and Interpreting including Spanish Directions.

Time: (15-20) minutes.

Comments: Requires no verbal response and a minimal motor response.

Authors: Bessie B. Burgemeister, Lucille Hollander Blum, and Irving Lorge.

Publisher: PsychCorp, A brand of Harcourt Assessment, Inc.

Cross References: See T5:624 (31 references), T4:591 (20 references), and T3:534 (15 references); for reviews by Byron R. Egeland and Alan S. Kaufman, and an excerpted review by Joseph M. Petrosko, see 8:210 (18 references); see also T2:489 (43 references); for reviews by Marshall S. Hiskey and T. Earnest Newland of the 1959 edition, see 6:517 (22 references); see also 5:402 (13 references).

[632]
Combined Basic Skills (Form LCS-C & Form B-C).

Purpose: To evaluate literacy and cognitive skills.

Population: Applicants and incumbents for jobs requiring literacy and cognitive skills.

Publication Dates: 1998–2003.

Scores, 4: Reading, Arithmetic, Inspection and Measurement, Process Monitoring & Problem Solving.

Administration: Group.

Price Data, 2006: $15 per consumable self-scoring test booklet (minimum order of 20); $24.95 per manual (2003, 30 pages).

Foreign Language Edition: Available in Spanish.

Time: (48) minutes.

Comments: Self-scoring instrument; two alternate equivalent forms.

Author: Roland T. Ramsay.

Publisher: Ramsay Corporation.

[633]
Combined Cognitive Preference Inventory.

Purpose: Designed to measure how a student processes information intellectually.

Population: Students.

Publication Date: [no date on materials].

Acronym: CCPI.

Scores: 4 cognitive preference areas: Recall, Principles, Questioning, Application.

Administration: Group.

Manual: No manual.

Price Data: Available from publisher.

Time: (20) minutes.

Author: Pinchas Tamir.

Publisher: Israel Science Teaching Center [Israel] [No reply from publisher; status unknown].

Cross References: See T5:626 (1 reference).

[634]
The Common-Metric Questionnaire.

Purpose: "Designed to describe, analyze, and evaluate jobs of all types from both public and private sector organizations."

Population: Job incumbents, supervisors, job analysts.

Publication Dates: 1990–1992.

Acronym: CMQ.
Scores: 6 sections: General Background, Contacts With People, Making Decisions, Physical and Mechanical Activities, Work Setting, Selection Test Scores.
Administration: Group.
Price Data: Available from publisher.
Time: (180–240) minutes.
Comments: When individually administered, the CMQ is mailed to the rater who completes it on his/her own time and returns it; The CMQ should only be individually administered to executive, managerial, and professional level employees; small group administration is recommended.
Authors: Robert J. Harvey (questionnaire) and The Psychological Corporation (manuals).
Publisher: Robert J. Harvey (the author) [No reply from publisher; status unknown].
Cross References: For a review by Gerald A. Rosen, see 13:75.

[635]
Communication Activities of Daily Living, Second Edition.

Purpose: "To assess the functional communication skills of adults with neurogenic communication disorders."
Population: Aphasic adults.
Publication Dates: 1980–1999.
Acronym: CADL-2.
Scores: Total score only.
Administration: Individual.
Price Data, 2006: $195 per complete kit; $25 per patient response forms; $40 per examiner record booklets; $78 per picture book; $56 per examiner's manual.
Time: (25–35) minutes.
Comments: Previous edition entitled Communicative Abilities in Daily Living.
Authors: Audrey Holland, Carol Frattali, and David Fromm.
Publisher: PRO-ED.
Cross References: For reviews by Carolyn Mitchell Person and Katharine Snyder, see 14:84; for a review by Rita Sloan Berndt of an earlier edition, see 10:69 (2 references).

[636]
Communication and Symbolic Behavior Scales Developmental Profile: First Normed Edition.

Purpose: Designed to "evaluate communication and symbolic abilities of children whose functional communication is between 6 months and 2 years."
Population: Ages 6–24 months.
Publication Dates: 1995–2002.
Acronym: CSBS DP.
Scores, 11: Social Composite (Emotion and Eye Gaze, Communication, Gestures, Total); Speech Composite (Sounds, Words, Total); Symbolic Composite (Understanding, Object Use, Total); Total.
Administration: Individual.
Levels, 3: Infant-Toddler Checklist, Caregiver Questionnaire, Behavior Sample.
Price Data, 2003: $399 per complete kit including manual (2002, 188 pages), 25 infant-toddler checklists, 25 caregiver questionnaires, 25 caregiver questionnaire scoring worksheets, 25 behavior sample scoring worksheets, 25 caregiver perception rating forms, 1 of each (Part 1 and Part 2) VHS sampling and scoring videos, and toy kit; $199.95 per test kit including manual, 25 infant-toddler checklists, 25 caregiver questionnaires, 25 caregiver questionnaire scoring worksheets, 25 behavior sample scoring worksheets, 25 caregiver perception rating forms, and 1 of each (Part 1 and Part 2) VHS sampling and scoring videos; $259.95 per toy kit; $65 per manual; $35 per 25 of each infant-toddler checklists, caregiver questionnaires, caregiver questionnaire scoring worksheets, behavior sample scoring worksheets, and caregiver perception rating forms; $25 per 50 caregiver questionnaires; $50 per VHS sampling and scoring video (specify Part 1 or Part 2).
Comments: May be used with children "up to 5–6 years if their developmental level of functioning is younger than 24 months."
Authors: Amy M. Wetherby and Barry M. Prizant.
Publisher: Brookes Publishing Co., Inc.
a) INFANT-TODDLER CHECKLIST.
Time: (5–10) minutes.
Comments: A screening tool completed by a caregiver; computer scoring available; may be administered independent of other components.
b) CAREGIVER QUESTIONNAIRE.
Time: (15–20) minutes.
Comments: Companion to the behavior sample completed by caregiver.
c) BEHAVIOR SAMPLE.
Time: (30) minutes.
Comments: A "face to face evaluation tool" conducted by professional evaluator with the caregiver present. The caregiver questionnaire is designed to "determine whether a child has a developmental delay or disability in the areas measured."
Cross References: For a review by Karen T. Carey, see 16:60; see also T5:630 (1 reference); for reviews by Steven H. Long and Dolores Kluppel Vetter of the original edition, see 13:76 (3 references).

[637]
Communication Response Style: Assessment.

Purpose: To assess an individual's communication response style.
Population: Adults.

Publication Dates: 1981–1987.
Scores, 4: Empathic Response Score, Critical Response Score, Searching Response Score, Advising Response Score.
Administration: Group or individual.
Manual: No manual.
Price Data: Price information available from publisher for set including test, answer sheets, and interpretation sheets.
Time: (20) minutes.
Comments: Self-administered, self-scored.
Author: Madelyn Burley-Allen.
Publisher: Training House, Inc.
Cross References: For reviews by Janet Norris and Gargi Roysircar Sodowsky, see 11:78.

[638]
Communication Skills Profile.

Purpose: "Designed to help people who want to gain a thorough knowledge of the processes of communication and to improve their effectiveness as communicators."
Population: Individuals or teams within organizations.
Publication Date: 1997.
Scores: 6 scales: Slowing My Thought Processes, Making Myself Understood, Testing My Conclusions, Listening Constructively, Getting to the Essence, Exploring Disagreement.
Administration: Group.
Price Data: Available from publisher.
Time: Administration time not reported.
Author: Elena Tosca.
Publisher: Jossey-Bass, A Wiley Company.
Cross References: For reviews by Robert Brown and Thomas P. Hogan, see 14:86.

[639]
Community-Based Social Skill Performance Assessment Tool.

Purpose: Designed to assess students' social skill performance in the home and in the community.
Population: Ages 14–21 years, with emotional or behavioral disorders.
Publication Date: Not dated.
Acronym: CBSP.
Scores, 5: Positive Social Behavior, Social Skills Mechanics, Anti-Social Behavior, Self-Control, Total.
Administration: Group.
Forms, 2: Male, Female.
Price Data: Price data available from publisher for set including teaching guide and script (no date, 34 pages), male and female testing materials, response form, and response interpretation/scoring guide.
Time: (45) minutes.
Author: Michael Bullis.
Publisher: James Stanfield Co., Inc.

[640]
Community College Student Experiences Questionnaire, Second Edition.

Purpose: Designed to assess community college students' "quality of effort" toward maximizing college opportunities and achieving their goals.
Population: Community college students.
Publication Dates: 1990–2001.
Acronym: CCSEQ-2.
Scores: 9 scales: Quality of Effort (Course Activities, Library Activities, Faculty-Student Acquaintances, Art, Music and Theater, Writing Activities, Science Activities, Vocational Skills), Satisfaction.
Administration: Group.
Price Data, 2006: $1 per copy of questionnaire; $1.50 per copy for scoring and processing; $12 per test manual (2001, 111 pages); $150 per diskette containing results and summary computer report.
Time: (20–30) minutes.
Comments: For use with students fluent in English.
Authors: C. Robert Pace, Patricia H. Murrell, Jack Friedlander, Penny W. Lehman; Corinna A. Ethington, Anne Marie Guthrie, and Penny W. Lehman (test manual, 3rd edition).
Publisher: Center for the Study of Higher Education, The University of Memphis.
Cross References: For reviews by Candice Haas Hollingsead and James P. Van Haneghan, see 14:87; for reviews by Charles Houston and by Rosemary E. Sutton and Hinsdale Bernard of the original edition, see 12:87.

[641]
Community Improvement Scale.

Purpose: Designed as "a device for measuring neighborhood morale" and "obtaining a diagnostic analysis of principal areas of neighborhood morale maintenance."
Population: Citizens in a neighborhood.
Publication Date: No date.
Scores: Total score only.
Administration: Individual or group.
Price Data, 2001: $3 per specimen set.
Time: (10) minutes.
Author: Inez Fay Smith.
Publisher: Psychometric Affiliates.
Cross References: For a review by Jody L. Kulstad, see 15:57.

[642]
Community Opinion Inventory, Revised Edition.

Purpose: "To identify areas the public sees as being done well, and areas seen as not done well" in the local school.
Population: Adults who do not have children enrolled in school.
Publication Dates: 1990–2003.

Scores: 6 subscales: Quality of the Instructional Program, Program Awareness, Responsiveness to the Community, Support for Student Learning, Environment for Learning, Resource Management.

Administration: Group.

Parts, 2: A (Likert-scale items), B (customize up to 20 local questions).

Price Data, 2006: $25 per 25 inventories; administrator's manual (26 pages) may be downloaded free from publisher website.

Time: Untimed.

Author: National Study of School Evaluation.

Publisher: National Study of School Evaluation.

[643]

Community Oriented Programs Environment Scale, Third Edition.

Purpose: Designed to "assess the social environments of community-based psychiatric treatment programs, day programs, sheltered workshops, rehabilitation centers and community care homes."

Population: Patients and staff of community oriented psychiatric facilities.

Publication Dates: 1974–1996.

Acronym: COPES.

Scores, 10: Involvement, Support, Spontaneity, Autonomy, Practical Orientation, Personal Problem Orientation, Anger and Aggression, Order and Organization, Program Clarity, Staff Control.

Administration: Group.

Price Data: Available from publisher (www.mindgarden.com).

Time: Administration time not reported.

Comments: A part of the Social Climate Scales (T5:2445).

Author: Rudolf H. Moos.

Publisher: Mind Garden, Inc.

Cross References: See T5:637 (3 references), T4:605 (11 references) and T3:542 (6 references); for a review by Richard I. Lanyon, see 8:525 (17 references). For a review of the Social Climate Scales, see 8:681.

[644]

Competency-Based Performance Improvement: Organizational Assessment Package.

Purpose: Used to assess an organization's performance improvement program/s and to improve planning for future programs.

Population: Business managers.

Publication Date: 1995.

Scores, 7: 6 categories (Strategic Goals and Business Objectives, Needs Analysis/Assessment/Planning, Competency Modeling, Curriculum Planning, Learning Intervention Design and Development, Evaluation), Total.

Administration: Group.

Price Data: Available from publisher.

Time: Administration time not reported.

Author: David D. Dubois.

Publisher: HRD Press, Inc.

Cross References: For reviews by Stephen F. Davis and Jerry M. Lowe, see 14:88.

[645]

The Competent Speaker Speech Evaluation Form.

Purpose: Designed to measure public speaking competency.

Population: Post-secondary students.

Publication Date: 1993.

Scores, 9: Chooses and Narrows a Topic Appropriately for the Audience and Occasion, Communicates the Thesis/Specific Purpose in a Manner Appropriate for Audience and Occasion, Uses an Organizational Pattern Appropriate to Topic/Audience/Occasion and Purpose, Provides Appropriate Supporting Material Based on the Audience and Occasion, Uses Language That is Appropriate to the Audience/Occasion and Purpose, Uses Vocal Variety in Rate/Pitch and Intensity to Heighten and Maintain Interest, Uses Pronunciation/Grammar and Articulation Appropriate to the Designated Audience, Uses Physical Behaviors that Support the Verbal Message, Total.

Administration: Individual.

Price Data: Available from publisher.

Time: Administration time not reported.

Author: Speech Communication Association.

Publisher: National Communication Association.

Cross References: For reviews by Sandra M. Ketrow and Julia Y. Porter, see 14:89.

[646]

Complex Figure Test.

Purpose: To serve as an index of brain damage.

Population: Ages 16 and over.

Publication Dates: 1970–1973.

Acronym: CFT.

Scores, 4: Interruption, Omission, Sequence, Total.

Administration: Individual.

Price Data: Available from publisher.

Time: Administration time not reported.

Comments: Originally published in Dutch in 1970 as a revision of Test de Copie d'une Figure Complexe (1959) by André Rey.

Author: R. S. H. Visser.

Publisher: Harcourt Assessment [England].

Cross References: See T5:641 (8 references) and T4:606 (8 references); for an excerpted review by C. H. Ammons and R. B. Ammons, see 8:528 (1 reference).

[647]

Comprehensive Ability Battery.

Purpose: "Features 5 tests that measure 20 primary abilities and basic skills important in industrial settings and career and vocational counseling."

Population: Ages 15 and over.
Publication Date: 1975.
Acronym: CAB.
Administration: Group or individual.
Price Data, 2005: $25 per 10 test booklets (CAB-1, CAB-2, CAB-3/4 are reusable; CAB-5 is not reusable); $20 per 50 answer sheets (CAB-1/2, CAB-3/4); $18 per 50 profile sheets; $20 per audio cassette tape (required for AA and Ms tests); $18 per scoring key and instructions (specify Level CAB-1/2/3/4); $32 per 2 scoring keys and instructions (CAB-5).
Foreign Language Editions: Contact publisher regarding non-English-language versions.
Authors: A. Ralph Hakstian and Raymond B. Cattell.
Publisher: Institute for Personality and Ability Testing, Inc. (IPAT).

a) CAB-1.
Scores: 4 test scores: Verbal Ability, Numerical Ability, Spatial Ability, Perceptual Completion.
Time: 21.75(30) minutes.

b) CAB-2.
Scores: 5 test scores: Clerical Speed and Accuracy, Reasoning, Hidden Shapes, Rote Memory, Mechanical Knowledge.
Time: 28(35) minutes.

c) CAB-3/4.
Scores: 5 test scores: Memory Span, Meaningful Memory, Spelling, Auditory Ability, Aesthetic Judgment.
Time: (25–30) minutes.
Comments: MS and AA administered by audio cassette tape.

d) CAB-5.
Scores: 6 test scores: Organizing Ideas, Production of Ideas, Verbal Fluency, Originality, Tracking, Drawing.
Time: 32(40) minutes.
Comments: Test booklets are reusable for Batteries 1, 2, and 3/4; not reusable for Battery 5; non-machine-scorable tests.
Cross References: See T5:644 (7 references) and T4:609 (11 references); for reviews by Robert C. Nichols and Karl R. White, see 9:255; see also T3:547 (5 references); for reviews by John B. Carroll and Robert M. Thorndike, see 8:484 (3 references).

[648]
Comprehensive Adult Student Assessment System—Third Edition.

Purpose: Designed to provide a measure to "place students in the appropriate program, level or test, diagnose student learning needs, monitor student progress and certify student proficiency levels."
Population: Adults.
Publication Dates: 1980-2004.
Acronym: CASAS.
Administration: Group.
Restricted Distribution: Agency training is required before test can be provided.
Price Data: Available from publisher.
Time: Administration times vary.
Comments: Third edition includes new technical manual; Computer scoring and individual and class score profiles available.
Author: CASAS.
Publisher: CASAS.

a) APPRAISAL TESTS.
1) *ESL Appraisal (English as a Second Language).*
Scores: 4 tests: Listening, Reading, Speaking, Writing.
Comments: Appraisal determines level of pretests of CASAS Life Skills Series to be administered.
2) *Life Skills Appraisal.*
Scores: 2 tests: Reading, Math.
Comments: Appraisal determines level of CASAS Life Skills Series Pre-Test to be administered.
3) *ECS Appraisal (Employability Competency System).*
Scores: 2 tests: Reading, Math.
Forms, 2: 120, 130.
Comments: Appraisal determines level of CASAS Basic Skills for Employability Pre-Test to be administered.

b) CASAS TESTS FOR MONITORING PROGRESS.
Comments: All test serve as pre/post tests.
1) *Employability Competency Series.*
(a) Reading.
Levels, 4: A, B, C, and D each with 2 forms.
(b) Math.
Levels, 4: A, B, C, and D each with 2 forms.
(c) Listening.
Levels, 3: A, B, and C each with 2 forms.
2) *Life Skills Series.*
(a) Reading.
Levels, 5: (Beginning Literacy, A, B, C, D), Beginning Literacy, Levels C and D each have 2 forms; Levels A and B have 3 forms.
(b) Math.
Levels, 4: A, B, C, and D each with 2 forms.
(c) Listening.
Levels, 3: A, B, and C each with 2 forms.
Cross References: For reviews by Terri Flowerday and Carol S. Parke, see 16:61; see also T5:645 (1 reference); for reviews by Ralph O. Mueller and Patricia

K. Freitag and by William D. Schafer of a previous edition, see 13:78 (2 references).

[649]
Comprehensive Affair Worksheets.

Purpose: Designed to "analyze the reasons for the affair, the affair behaviors and relationship, the impact on the marriage and all the individuals involved, decisions that need to be made and what needs to be done to solve the problems caused by the affair."
Population: Individuals who have had an affair.
Publication Date: 1995.
Scores: 19 sections: Therapy, Marriage Before the Affair, Pre-Affair Involvement, Activities, Relationship, Religion, Communication, Feelings, Sex, Cheating Opinions, Keeping It Secret, Spouse's Reaction, Effects on the Person, Effects on the Spouse, Others Finding Out, Decisions and Planning, Repairing the Marriage, Marital Sex, Other Problems.
Administration: Individual.
Manual: No manual.
Price Data, 2001: $16 per 5 worksheets.
Time: Administration time not reported.
Author: Allan Roe.
Publisher: Diagnostic Specialists, Inc.

[650]
Comprehensive Assessment of Mathematics Strategies.

Purpose: Designed to "identify and assess a student's level of mastery in each of 12 mathematics strategies."
Population: Grades 1–8.
Publication Dates: 2000-2006.
Acronym: CAMS.
Scores, 12: Building Number Sense, Using Estimation, Applying Addition, Applying Subtraction, Applying Multiplication, Applying Division, Converting Time and Money, Converting Customary and Metric Measures, Using Algebra, Using Geometry, Determining Probability and Averages, Interpreting Graphs and Charts.
Administration: Group.
Levels, 8: Grade 1, Grade 2, Grade 3, Grade 4, Grade 5, Grade 6, Grade 7, Grade 8.
Price Data, 2006: $24.90 per 10 student books; $4.95 per teacher guide (for each level); $25.95 per CD Management Software.
Time: (60) minutes.
Comments: Testing materials include practice lessons, self-assessments, and teacher assessments; self-assessments (both of which are completed after the student is exposed to and practices lessons 1–5, and again after the student is exposed to each practices lessons 6–10); class performance chart available; Teacher Assessment 1 "assesses a student's performance for each of the 12 mathematics' strategies"; Teacher Assessment

2 compares a student's level of mastery in the criteria for the 12 mathematics' strategies.
Author: Robert G. Forest.
Publisher: Curriculum Associates, Inc.

[651]
Comprehensive Assessment of Mathematics Strategies II.

Purpose: Designed to measure "improvement in mathematics comprehension after instruction," identify "level of mastery" of mathematics strategies, and provide "practice with self-assessment."
Population: Grades 1–8.
Publication Dates: 2001–2006.
Administration: Group.
Levels, 8: Books 1–8.
Manual: No comprehensive manual. A Teacher's guide is provided for each level (2001–2003, 13 pages each).
Price Data, 2006: $17.90 per 10 student booklets (specify level); $4.95 per Teacher Guide (specify level).
Time: 45 minutes per lesson (5 lessons per book); 20 minutes per self-assessment.
Comments: Intended for use "after students have been diagnosed with Comprehensive Assessment of Mathematics Strategies and have been instructed with Strategies to Achieve Mathematics Success"; Teacher and Self-Assessments also included.
Author: Robert G. Forest.
Publisher: Curriculum Associates, Inc.
  a) BOOK 1.
  Scores, 8: Building Number Sense, Applying Addition, Applying Subtraction, Applying Multiplication, Converting Time and Money, Converting Measures, Using Geometry, Reading Math Pictures.
  b) BOOK 2.
  Scores, 12: Building Number Sense, Using Estimation, Applying Addition, Applying Subtraction, Applying Multiplication, Applying Division, Converting Time and Money, Converting Customary and Metric Measures, Using Algebra, Using Geometry, Determining Probability and Averages, Interpreting Graphs and Charts.
  c) BOOK 3.
  Scores, 12: Same as Book 2.
  d) BOOK 4.
  Scores, 12: Same as Book 2.
  e) BOOK 5.
  Scores, 12: Same as Book 2.
  f) BOOK 6.
  Scores, 12: Same as Book 2.
  g) BOOK 7.
  Scores, 12: Same as Book 2.
  h) BOOK 8.
  Scores, 12: Same as Book 2.

[652]
Comprehensive Assessment of Reading Strategies.

Purpose: Designed to "identify and assess a student's level of mastery with each of 12 reading strategies."
Population: Grades 1-8.
Publication Dates: 1998–2006.
Acronym: CARS.
Scores, 13: Finding Main Idea, Recalling Facts and Details, Understanding Sequence, Recognizing Cause and Effect, Comparing and Contrasting, Making Predictions, Finding Word Meaning in Context, Drawing Conclusions and Making Inferences, Distinguishing Between Fact and Opinion, Identifying Author's Purpose, Interpreting Figurative Language, Distinguishing Between Real and Make-Believe [Books 1-4], Summarizing [Books 5–8].
Administration: Group.
Levels, 8: Grade 1, Grade 2, Grade 3, Grade 4, Grade 5, Grade 6, Grade 7, Grade 8.
Price Data, 2006: $24.90 per 10 student books; $4.95 per teacher's guide; $25.95 per CD Management Software.
Time: (45) minutes.
Comments: Testing materials include practice lessons, self-assessments, and teacher assessments; self-assessment and teacher assessment are completed after student is exposed to and practices the lessons presented in the test materials; class performance charts available; computer software available for generating interpretive reports; assessment consists of 2 assessments to be given at separate times.
Authors: Deborah Adcock and Courtney Bolser (contributing author to test booklet).
Publisher: Curriculum Associates, Inc.

[653]
Comprehensive Assessment of Reading Strategies II.

Purpose: Designed to "measure improvement in reading comprehension after instruction," identify "level of mastery" for specified reading strategies, and provide "practice with self-assessment."
Population: Grades 1-8.
Publication Dates: 2000–2006.
Administration: Group.
Levels, 8: Grades 1–8.
Price Data, 2006: $17.90 per 10 student books (specify level); $4.95 per teacher's guide (specify level).
Time: (45) minutes per lesson, (20) minutes per self-assessment.
Comments: Designed as a follow-up measure for use with the Comprehensive Assessment of Reading Strategies (T6:634; a diagnostic measure) and Strategies to Achieve Reading Success (focused instructional system).
Authors: Deborah Adcock (Teacher Guides 1–8, and Student Books 1–8), Christopher Forest (contributing author on Student Books 1, 3, 4, 6, and 7).
Publisher: Curriculum Associates, Inc.

a) BOOK 1.
Population: Grade 1.
Scores, 8: Finding Main Idea, Recalling Facts and Details, Understanding Sequence, Recognizing Cause and Effect, Making Predictions, Finding Word Meaning in Context, Drawing Conclusions and Making Inferences, Reading Pictures.
b) BOOK 2.
Population: Grade 2.
Scores, 12: Same as Book 1, with the deletion of Reading Pictures and the addition of Comparing and Contrasting, Distinguishing Between Fact and Opinion, Identifying Author's Purpose, Interpreting Figurative Language, and Distinguishing Between Real and Make-believe.
c) BOOK 3.
Population: Grade 3.
Scores, 12: Same as Book 2.
d) BOOK 4.
Population: Grade 4.
Scores, 12: Same as Book 2.
e) BOOK 5.
Population: Grade 5.
Scores, 12: Same as Book 2, with the deletion of Distinguishing Between Real and Make-believe, and the addition of Summarizing.
f) BOOK 6.
Population: Grade 6.
Scores, 12: Same as Book 5.
g) BOOK 7.
Population: Grade 7.
Scores, 12: Same as Book 5.
h) BOOK 8.
Population: Grade 8.
Scores, 12: Same as Book 5.

[654]
Comprehensive Assessment of School Environments.

Purpose: Developed to assess perceptions of the school climate and student, teacher, and parent satisfaction with each individual's personal environment in order "to foster data-based decision making for school improvement."
Population: Junior and senior high schools.
Publication Dates: 1986–1989.
Acronym: CASE.
Administration: Group.
Price Data: Available from publisher.
Time: Administration time not reported.

Comments: Test booklet titles are School Climate Survey, Parent Satisfaction Survey, Teacher Satisfaction Survey, and Student Satisfaction Survey.

Authors: Cynthia Halderson (manuals and climate survey), Edgar A. Kelley (manuals and climate survey), James W. Keefe (manuals and climate survey), Paul S. Berge (technical manual), John A. Glover (climate survey), Carrie Sorenson (climate survey), Carol Speth (climate survey), Neal Schmitt (satisfaction surveys), and Brian Loher (satisfaction surveys).

Publisher: National Association of Secondary School Principals.

a) SCHOOL CLIMATE SURVEY.

Scores: Student, Teacher, and Parent scores for the following 10 subscales: Teacher-Student Relationships, Security and Maintenance, Administration, Student Academic Orientation, Student Behavioral Values, Guidance, Student-Peer Relationships, Parent & Community-School Relationships, Instructional Management, Student Activities.

b) PARENT SATISFACTION SURVEY.

Scores, 9: Parent Involvement, Curriculum, Student Activities, Teachers, Support Services, School Building/Supplies/Maintenance, Student Discipline, School Administrators, School Information Services.

c) TEACHER SATISFACTION SURVEY.

Scores, 9: Administration, Compensation, Opportunities for Advancement, Student Responsibility & Discipline, Curriculum and Job Tasks, Co-workers, Parents and Community, School Building/Supplies/Maintenance, Communication.

d) STUDENT SATISFACTION SURVEY.

Scores, 8: Teachers, Fellow Students, Schoolwork, Student Activities, Student Discipline, Decision-Making Opportunities, School Building/Supplies/Upkeep, Communication.

Cross References: For reviews by Nancy L. Allen and Frederick T. L. Leong, see 11:80.

[655]
Comprehensive Assessment of School Environments Information Management System.

Purpose: Designed to facilitate and encourage the use of data-based planning for school improvement projects.

Population: Secondary schools.

Publication Dates: 1991–1995.

Acronym: CASE-IMS.

Scores, 9: Principal Questionnaire, Teacher Report Form, Student Report Form, Teacher Satisfaction Survey, Student Satisfaction Survey, Parent Satisfaction Survey (optional), School Climate Survey for Teachers, School Climate Survey for Students, School Climate Survey for Parents (optional).

Administration: Group.

Price Data: Available from publisher.

Time: Administration time not reported.

Comments: Computer administered; available in MS/DOS (3.5-inch or 5.25-inch disks) or Macintosh (3.5-inch disk) format.

Author: National Association of Secondary School Principals Task Force on Effective School Environments.

Publisher: National Association of Secondary School Principals.

Cross References: For reviews by Joseph R. Manduchi and Daniel L. Yazak, see 14:90.

[656]
Comprehensive Assessment of Spoken Language.

Purpose: Designed to measure the processes of comprehension, expression, and retrieval in oral language.

Population: Ages 3–21.

Publication Date: 1999.

Acronym: CASL.

Scores: 15 tests: Basic Concepts, Antonyms, Synonyms, Sentence Completion, Idiomatic Language, Syntax Construction, Paragraph Comprehension, Grammatical Morphemes, Sentence Comprehension, Grammaticality Judgment, Nonliteral Language, Meaning from Context, Inference, Ambiguous Sentences, and Pragmatic Judgment; plus Core Composite scores, Category Index scores (Lexical/Semantic, Syntactic, Supralinguistic); Processing Index scores (Expressive, Receptive).

Administration: Individual.

Forms, 2: 1, 2.

Price Data, 2005: $339.99 per complete kit, including manual (164 pages), three test books, 12 Record Form 1 and 12 Record Form 2, norms book (168 pages), and carry bag; $24.99 per 12 Record Form 1; $29.99 per 12 Record Form 2; $199.99 per AGS computer ASSIST™ CD for CASL (Mac/Win).

Author: Elizabeth Carrow-Woolfolk.

Publisher: Pearson Assessments (originally published by AGS Publishing, acquired by Pearson in 2005).

Cross References: For reviews by Katharine A. Snyder and Gabrielle Stutman, see 15:58.

[657]
Comprehensive Assessment of Symptoms and History.

Purpose: "Designed as a structured interview and recording instrument for documenting the signs, symptoms, and history of subjects evaluated in research studies of the major psychoses and affective disorders."

Population: Psychiatric patients.

Publication Date: 1987.

Acronym: CASH.

Scores: Interview divided into 3 major sections: Present State (Sociodemographic Data, Evaluation of Current Condition, Psychotic Syndrome, Manic Syndrome, Major Depressive Syndrome, Treatment, Cognitive Assessment, Global Assessment Scale, Diagnosis for Current Episode), Past History (History of Onset and Hospitalization, Past Symptoms of Psychosis, Characterization of Course, Past Symptoms of Affective Disorder), Lifetime History (History of Somatic Therapy, Alcoholism, Drug Use and Abuse and Dependence, Modified Premorbid Adjustment Scale, Premorbid or Intermorbid Personality, Functioning During Past Five Years, Global Assessment Scale, Diagnosis for Lifetime).
Administration: Individual.
Price Data: Available from publisher.
Time: [60–180] minutes.
Comments: The CASH is one component of a modular assessment battery available from the publisher.
Author: Nancy C. Andreasen.
Publisher: Nancy C. Andreasen.
Cross References: See T5:650 (16 references); for reviews by Patricia A. Bachelor and Barbara J. Kaplan, see 12:88 (12 references); see also T4:612 (4 references).

[658]
Comprehensive Behavior Rating Scale for Children.

Purpose: A teacher rating scale designed to measure various dimensions of a child's school functioning.
Population: Ages 6–14.
Publication Date: 1990.
Acronym: CBRSC.
Scores: 9 scales: Inattention-Disorganization, Reading Problems, Cognitive Deficits, Oppositional-Conduct Disorders, Motor Hyperactivity, Anxiety, Sluggish Tempo, Daydreaming, Social Competence.
Administration: Individual.
Price Data, 2002: $118 per complete kit including manual (10 pages), 25 profile and questionnaire forms, and scoring key; $26 per 25 profile and questionnaire forms; $65 per manual; $39 per scoring key.
Time: (10–15) minutes.
Authors: Ronald Neeper, Benjamin B. Lahey, and Paul J. Frick.
Publisher: PsychCorp, A brand of Harcourt Assessment, Inc.
Cross References: See T5:651 (2 references); for a review by Wayne C. Piersel, see 13:79 (1 reference).

[659]
Comprehensive Identification Process [Revised].

Purpose: "Designed to identify children who may have medical, psychological or learning problems that could interfere with their success in school."

Population: Ages 2–6.5.
Publication Dates: 1975–1997.
Acronym: CIP.
Administration: Individual.
Price Data, 2005: $310.00 per complete kit including Symbol booklet, Screening booklet, Parent Interview forms, Observation of Behavior forms, Speech and Expressive Language Record forms, Child Record Folders, Interviewer's manual (1997, 40 pages), Administrator's Manual (1997, 54 pages), and manipulatives in carrying case.
Foreign Language Edition: Earlier edition available in Spanish.
Time: Varies.
Comments: CIP screening team should include at least one member who has a background in early childhood education of the disabled and is skilled in screening and evaluation; alternatives to the standard screening, such as in-home screening or bilingual screening available.
Authors: R. Reid Zehrbach (test), and Joan Good Erickson (Speech and Expressive Language Record Form).
Publisher: Scholastic Testing Service, Inc.
　　a) CHILD: RECORD FOLDER.
　　Scores, 5: Hearing, Vision, Perceptual Motor, Cognitive-Verbal, Gross Motor.
　　Comments: Materials for hearing and vision screening must be obtained locally.
　　b) SPEECH AND EXPRESSIVE LANGUAGE RECORD FORM.
　　Scores, 6: Articulation/Phonology, Voice, Fluency, Expressive Language, Associated Factors, Total.
　　Author: Joan Good Erickson.
　　c) OBSERVATION OF BEHAVIOR FORM.
　　Scores, 7: Hearing, Vision, Physical/Motor Speech and Expressive Language, Social Behavior (Responses, Interaction), Affective Behavior.
　　d) PARENT INTERVIEW FORM.
　　Scores, 7: Pregnancy/Birth/Hospitalization, Walking/Toilet Training, Hearing, Vision, Speech and Expressive Language, Medical, Social Affect.
　　Comments: History and ratings by parent.
Cross References: For a review by J. Jeffrey Grill, see 14:91; see also T4:616 (1 reference); for reviews by Robert P. Anderson and Phyllis L. Newcomer of an earlier version, see 8:425 (1 reference).

[660]
Comprehensive Mathematical Abilities Test.

Purpose: Developed to "assess a broad spectrum of mathematical abilities in the areas of comprehension (reasoning), calculation and application."
Population: Ages 7:0 to 18:11.
Publication Date: 2003.

Acronym: CMAT.

Scores, 18: General Mathematics (Basic Calculations, composed of Addition, Subtraction, Multiplication, Division, and Mathematical Reasoning, composed of Problem Solving, Charts/Tables/and Graphs); Advanced Calculations (Algebra, Geometry, Rational Numbers) [supplemental]; Practical Applications (Time, Money, Measurement) [supplemental]; Global Mathematics Ability.

Administration: Individual.

Price Data, 2006: $285 per complete kit including examiner's manual (199 pages), picture book, 25 profile/examiner record booklets, 25 student response booklet I, and 25 student response booklet II; $81 per examiner's manual; $66 per picture book.

Time: 45–60 minutes.

Comments: Computer scoring available.

Authors: Wayne P. Hresko, Paul L. Schlieve, Shelley R. Herron, Colleen Swain, and Rita J. Sherbenou.

Publisher: PRO-ED.

Cross References: For reviews by George Engelhard, Jr. and Suzanne Lane, see 16:62.

[661]
Comprehensive Personality Profile.

Purpose: Designed to provide a comprehensive assessment of job-relevant personality characteristics that impact the successful fulfillment of job requirements; used within organizations to identify individuals whose personality characteristics are compatible with job demands.

Population: Ages 15 and up.

Publication Dates: 1985–2002.

Acronym: CPP.

Scores, 48: Primary Scales (Emotional Intensity, Intuition, Recognition Motivation, Sensitivity, Assertiveness, Trust, Exaggeration), Secondary Traits (Ego Drive, Interpersonal Warmth, Stability, Empathy, Objectivity, Independence, Aggressiveness, Decisiveness, Tolerance, Efficiency), Interaction Traits (Temperament, Ego Style, Social Style), Management Performance Traits (Ability To Make Unpopular Decisions, Decisiveness To Act Without Precedent, Ingenuity To Create New Ideas, Ability To Motivate Others To Act, Vision To Plan Ahead On A Large Scale, Self-Discipline To Efficiently Manage Time, Communicates With Frankness And Humility, Tolerance For Corporate Red Tape Or Politics, Delegates Responsibility Or Authority, Caution In Making Policy Commitments), Sales Performance Traits (Goal Oriented Drive Toward Immediate Results, Insight To Perceive The Buyer's Need, Ability To Close Sales Without Hesitation, Ability To Make New Contacts (Call Courage), Overcomes Objections With Tact And Diplomacy, Desire To Provide After-The-Sale Service, Desire To Compete And Win At All Costs, Ability To Keep Positive Attitude (Optimism), Ability To Control Emotional Ups And Downs, Ability To Handle Sales Rejection), Administrative Performance Traits (Tolerance To Stay At One Work Station, Desire To Conform To Management Objectives, Ability To Cope With Change And Disruption, Satisfaction To Stay At Job Level Attained, Ability To Be Diplomatic And Cooperative, Patience To Follow Detailed Instructions, Capacity To Follow Systems), Summary Profile.

Administration: Group or individual.

Price Data: Available from publisher.

Foreign Language Editions: Available in French and Spanish.

Time: (15–25) minutes.

Comments: Title on questionnaire is CPP Compatibility Questionnaire; online administration available.

Authors: Wonderlic, Inc. and Larry L. Craft (questionnaire).

Publisher: Wonderlic, Inc.

Cross References: For reviews by Sanford J. Cohn and Ira Stuart Katz, see 14:92; see also T4:617 (1 reference). For reviews by Sanford J. Cohn and Ira Stuart Katz, see 14:92; see also T4:617 (1 reference).

[662]
Comprehensive Receptive and Expressive Vocabulary Test—Second Edition.

Purpose: "To identify ... deficiencies in oral vocabulary ... discrepancies between receptive and expressive vocabulary, [and] ... progress in instructional programs."

Population: Ages 4-0 through 89-11, ages 5-0 through 89-11.

Publication Dates: 1994–2002.

Acronym: CREVT-2.

Scores, 3: Receptive Vocabulary, Expressive Vocabulary, General Vocabulary.

Administration: Individual.

Forms, 2: A, B.

Price Data, 2006: $243 per complete kit; $45 per forms (A or B); $80 per photo album picture book; $80 per examiner's manual (2002, 141 pages).

Time: Untimed.

Comments: Combines the CREVT and CREVT-A; old editions still available.

Authors: Gerald Wallace and Donald D. Hammill.

Publisher: PRO-ED.

Cross References: For reviews by Luanne Andersson and Gretchen Owens, see 15:59; see T5:655 (CREVT, 1 reference) and T5:656 (CREVT); for reviews by Alan S. Kaufman and Mary J. McLellan of the CREVT, see 13:80 (1 reference); for reviews by Margaret E. Malone and Wayne H. Slater of the CREVT-A, see 14:93 (1 reference).

[663]
Comprehensive Sex History.

Purpose: Designed to compile an individual's complete sexual history.
Population: Adults.
Publication Date: 1995.
Administration: Individual.
Forms, 2: Male, Female.
Manual: No manual.
Price Data, 2001: $12 for one set of reusable question sheets for all 5 parts (specify Male or Female).
Time: Administration time not reported.
Author: Allan Roe.
Publisher: Diagnostic Specialists, Inc.
a) SEXUAL EXPERIENCES.
Population: General adult.
b) DATING EXPERIENCES.
Population: Those who have dated.
c) NON-MARITAL INTERCOURSE.
Population: Those who have had intercourse outside of marriage.
d) MARITAL OR LIVING TOGETHER SEXUAL EXPERIENCES.
Population: Those who have been married or lived together.
e) INAPPROPRIATE SEXUAL BEHAVIORS.
Population: Those who have done inappropriate criminal sexual activities.

[664]
Comprehensive Spouse's Worksheets.

Purpose: Designed to "analyze the spouse's reaction to [an] affair, the impact on the marriage and everyone involved, decisions that need to be made and what needs to be done to solve the problems caused by the affair."
Population: Spouses of persons who had an affair.
Publication Date: 1996.
Scores: 14 sections: Therapy, Marriage Before the Affair, Pre-Affair, Spouse's Relationship with the Lover, Cheating Opinions, Keeping It Secret, Reaction to the Affair, Others Finding Out, Spouse's Reaction, Effects on the Person, Sex After the Affair, Decisions and Planning, Repairing the Marriage, Other Problems.
Administration: Individual.
Manual: No manual.
Price Data, 2001: $10 per 5 worksheets.
Time: Administration time not reported.
Author: Allan Roe.
Publisher: Diagnostic Specialists, Inc.

[665]
Comprehensive Test of Nonverbal Intelligence.

Purpose: Constructed to measure "nonverbal intellectual abilities."

Population: Ages 6-0 to 90-11.
Publication Date: 1996.
Acronym: CTONI.
Scores, 9: 6 subtest scores (Pictorial Analogies, Geometric Analogies, Pictorial Categories, Geometric Categories, Pictorial Sequences, Geometric Sequences), 3 composite scores (Nonverbal Intelligence Quotient, Pictorial Nonverbal Intelligence Quotient, Geometric Nonverbal Intelligence Quotient).
Administration: Individual.
Price Data, 2006: $350 per complete kit including examiner's manual (92 pages), analogies picture book, categories picture book, sequences picture book, and 25 profile/examiner record forms in storage box; $45 per 25 profile/examiner record forms; $90 per examiner's manual; $75 per picture book (specify Analogies, Categories, or Sequences).
Time: (40–60) minutes.
Authors: Donald D. Hammill, Nils A. Pearson, and J. Lee Wiederholt.
Publisher: PRO-ED.
Cross References: See T5:662 (1 reference); for reviews by Glen P. Aylward and Gabriele van Lingen, see 13:82.

[666]
Comprehensive Test of Phonological Processing.

Purpose: Designed to measure "phonological awareness, phonological memory, and rapid naming."
Population: Ages 5–6, ages 7–24.
Publication Date: 1999.
Administration: Individual.
Price Data, 2006: $254 per complete kit including examiner's manual (159 pages), 25 each profile/examiner record booklets for ages 5 to 6 and ages 7 to 24, picture book, and audiocassette; $55 per 25 profile/examiner record booklets for ages 5 to 6; $65 per 25 profile/examiner record booklets for ages 7 to 24; $40 per picture book; $81 per manual; $20 per audio CD.
Time: (30) minutes.
Authors: Richard K. Wagner, Joseph K. Torgesen, and Carol A. Rashotte.
Publisher: PRO-ED.
a) 5- AND 6-YEAR-OLD VERSION.
Population: Ages 5–6.
Scores, 11: Phonological Awareness (Elision, Blending Words, Sound Matching), Phonological Memory (Memory for Digits, Nonword Repetition), Rapid Naming (Rapid Color Naming, Rapid Object Naming), Blending Nonwords (Supplemental Subtest).
b) 7- THROUGH 24-YEAR-OLD VERSION.
Population: Ages 7–24.
Scores, 17: Phonological Awareness (Elision, Blending Words), Phonological Memory (Memory

for Digits, Nonword Repetition), Rapid Naming (Rapid Digit Naming, Rapid Letter Naming), Alternate Phonological Awareness (Blending Nonwords, Segmenting Nonwords), Alternate Rapid Naming (Rapid Color Naming, Rapid Object Naming), Phoneme Reversal (Supplemental Subtest), Segmenting Words (Supplemental Subtest).

Cross References: For reviews by David P. Hurford and Claudia R. Wright, see 15:60.

[667]
Comprehensive Test of Visual Functioning.

Purpose: Designed to identify and differentiate type of visual perceptual dysfunction.

Population: Ages 8 and over.

Publication Date: 1990.

Acronym: CTVF.

Scores, 9: Visual/Letter Integration, Visual/Writing Integration, Nonverbal Visual Closure, Nonverbal Visual Reasoning/Memory, Spatial Orientation/Memory/Motor, Spatial Orientation/Motor, Visual Design/Motor, Visual Design/Memory/Motor, Total.

Administration: Individual.

Price Data, 2002: $108 per complete kit including manual (64 pages), stimulus cards/easel, and stimulus items; $28 per manual; $42 per examiner's directions and scoring protocol (18 pages); $29 per 25 examinee test booklets; $29 per stimulus cards/easel.

Time: (25) minutes.

Comments: "Norm-referenced"; includes 4 additional subtests (Visual Acuity, Visual Processing/Figure-Ground, Visual Tracking, Reading Word Analysis) which do not contribute to the overall visual performance quotient.

Authors: Sue L. Larson, Evelyn Buethe, and Gary J. Vitali.

Publisher: Slosson Educational Publications, Inc.

Cross References: For reviews by Stephen R. Hooper and Douglas J. McRae, see 12:89.

[668]
Comprehensive Testing Program 4.

Purpose: "Designed to provide instructionally useful information about student performance in key areas of the school curriculum: listening, reading, vocabulary, writing, and mathematics"; beginning with the spring of Grade 3, includes verbal and quantitative reasoning tests to measure higher order thinking skills.

Population: Grades 1–2, 2–3, 3–4, 4–5, 5–6, 6–7, 7–8, 8–9, 9–10, 10–11.

Publication Dates: 1974–2004.

Acronym: CTP 4.

Administration: Group.

Levels, 10: 1–10.

Price Data: Available from publisher.

Time: (300) minutes for total battery.

Comments: Machine scoring by the publisher; provides "Independent," "Suburban Public," and "National" norms; hand-scoring keys and norms booklets are also available from the publisher; partial battery is an option; allows for nonstandard administration.

Author: Educational Records Bureau.

Publisher: Educational Records Bureau.

a) LEVEL 1.
Population: Grade 1 spring or Grade 2 fall.
Scores, 4: Auditory Comprehension, Reading Comprehension, Word Analysis, Mathematics Achievement.

b) LEVEL 2.
Population: Grade 2 spring or Grade 3 fall.
Scores, 5: Same as for Level 1 plus Writing Mechanics.

c) LEVEL 3.
Population: Grade 3 spring or Grade 4 fall.
Scores, 7: Verbal Reasoning, Auditory Comprehension, Reading Comprehension, Writing Mechanics, Writing Concepts and Skills, Mathematics Achievement, Quantitative Reasoning.

d) LEVEL 4.
Population: Grade 4 spring or Grade 5 fall.
Scores, 7: Verbal Reasoning, Vocabulary, Reading Comprehension, Writing Mechanics, Writing Concepts and Skills, Mathematics Achievement, Quantitative Reasoning.

e) LEVEL 5.
Population: Grade 5 spring or Grade 6 fall.
Scores, 7: Same as for Level 4.

f) LEVEL 6.
Population: Grade 6 spring or Grade 7 fall.
Scores, 7: Same as for Levels 4 and 5.

g) LEVEL 7.
Population: Grade 7 spring or Grade 8 fall.
Scores, 7: Same as for Levels 4, 5, and 6.

h) LEVEL 8.
Population: Grade 8 spring or Grade 9 fall.
Scores, 8: Same as for Levels 4, 5, 6, and 7 plus Algebra 1.

i) LEVEL 9.
Population: Grade 9 spring or Grade 10 fall.
Scores, 8: Same as for Level 8.

j) LEVEL 10.
Population: Grade 10 spring or Grade 11 fall.
Scores, 7: Same as for Levels 8 and 9 except for omission of Algebra 1.

[669]
Comprehensive Trail-Making Test.

Purpose: Developed for the evaluation and diagnosis of brain injury and other forms of central nervous system compromise.

Population: Ages 11 to 74-11.

Publication Date: 2002.
Acronym: CTMT.
Scores, 6: Trail 1, Trail 2, Trail 3, Trail 4, Trail 5, Composite Index.
Administration: Individual.
Price Data, 2006: $115 per complete kit; $55 per 10 record booklets; $65 per examiner's manual (79 pages).
Time: (5–12) minutes.
Author: Cecil R. Reynolds.
Publisher: PRO-ED.
Cross References: For a review by Nora M. Thompson, see 15:61.

[670]
Computer Career Assessment Test.

Purpose: Measures aptitude for work in the computer field.
Population: Any adult without prior computer experience.
Publication Date: 2000.
Acronym: CCAT.
Scores: Total Score, Narrative Evaluation, Ranking.
Administration: Group.
Price Data, 2001: $99 for industry; $65 for educational institutions; quantity discounts available.
Time: (60) minutes.
Comments: Available in booklet and internet versions; scored by publisher; must be proctored.
Author: Bruce A. Winrow.
Publisher: Walden Personnel Performance, Inc. [Canada].
Cross References: For reviews by Michael B. Bunch and Thomas R. O'Neill, see 16:63.

[671]
Computer Literacy Skills Profile.

Purpose: To evaluate computer literacy potential.
Population: Candidates whose job responsibilities will include utilizing common software packages.
Publication Date: 1996.
Acronym: COMPLIT.
Scores: Total Score, Narrative Evaluation, Ranking, Recommendation.
Administration: Group.
Price Data, 2001: $235 per candidate; quantity discounts available.
Time: (110) minutes.
Comments: Scored by publisher; must be proctored.
Author: Bruce A. Winrow.
Publisher: Walden Personnel Performance, Inc.

[672]
Computer Operator Aptitude Battery.

Purpose: Predict "ability to perform computer operator job and potential for learning computer programming."

Population: Experienced computer operators and trainees.
Publication Dates: 1973–1974.
Acronym: COAB.
Scores, 4: Sequence Recognition, Formal Checking, Logical Thinking, Total.
Administration: Individual or group.
Price Data, 2002: $193 per Start-up kit including 5 test booklets, 25 answer sheets, and examiner's manual (1974, 19 pages); $112 per 5 test booklets; $76 per 25 answer sheets (quantity discounts available); $28 per examiner's manual.
Time: 45 minutes.
Author: Pearson Reid London House.
Publisher: Pearson Performance Solutions [No reply from publisher; status unknown].

[673]
Computer Programmer Aptitude Battery.

Purpose: To "measure abilities related to success in computer programmer and systems analysis fields."
Population: Students, programmer trainees, entry-level and experienced.
Publication Dates: 1964–1993.
Acronym: CPAB.
Scores, 6: Verbal Meaning, Reasoning, Letter Series, Number Ability, Diagramming, Total.
Administration: Individual or group.
Forms, 2: A, B.
Price Data, 2002: $193 per start-up kit including 5 test reusable booklets (specify Form A or Form B), 25 answer sheets (specify Form A or Form B) and examiner's manual; $166 per Short Form start-up kit; $158 per 25 Short Form A tests (with carbon answer sheets); $112 per 5 test booklets (quantity discount available; specify Form A or Form B); $76 per 25 answer sheets (quantity discount available; specify Form A or Form B); $28 per examiner's manual.
Time: 79 minutes; 55 minutes for short form.
Comments: Short form contains the Reasoning and Diagramming sections and can be used for all levels of programmers but norms for short form available only for entry level.
Author: Science Research Associates.
Publisher: Pearson Performance Solutions [No reply from publisher; status unknown].
Cross References: For reviews by Roderick K. Mahurin and William D. Schafer, see 11:85; see also T3:557 (1 reference); for additional information and a review by Nick L. Smith, see 8:1079 (3 references); see also T2:2334 (2 references); for reviews by Richard T. Johnson and Donald J. Veldman, see 7:1089 (2 references).

[674]
Computerized Assessment of Response Bias: Revised Edition.

Purpose: "To quantitatively assess a given patient's attitude (response bias) in taking neuropsychological or neurocognitive tests."

Population: Severely impaired neurologic patients, mild traumatic brain injury patients, non-neurologic simulators.

Publication Dates: 1992–2000.

Acronym: CARB.

Scores, 24: 4 actions (Block 1, 2, 3, Total) each with 6 scores: Total Correct, Number of Correct Responses Obtained with Left Hand, Number of Correct Responses Obtained with Right Hand, Reaction Time Average, Reaction Time Average for Correct Responses, Reaction Time Average for Incorrect Responses.

Administration: Individual

Forms, 4: Standard or Quick form, each with or without item-specific feedback.

Price Data, 2002: $300 for disk and comprehensive manual (63 pages).

Foreign Language Edition: Spanish language version available.

Time: (22–40) minutes.

Comments: Typically, this is a test of motivation, not ability or impairment; instructions for installing and operating CARB (DOS based) software are included in the manual.

Authors: Robert L. Conder, Jr., Lyle M. Allen, III, David R. Cox, and Carol M. King.

Publisher: CogniSyst, Inc.

Cross References: For reviews by M. Allan Cooperstein and Edward E. Gotts, see 14:95.

[675]
Computerized Lifestyle Assessment.

Purpose: Designed to identify lifestyle behaviors such as substance use, health maintenance, preventive activities, social issues, and emotional well-being to provide a basis for individuals to discuss their lifestyles with a health professional.

Population: 14 years and older.

Publication Date: 1994.

Scores, 16: Nutrition, Eating Habits, Caffeine Use, Physical Activity, Body Weight, Sleep, Social Relationships, Family Interactions, Tobacco Use, Alcohol Use, Non-Medical Drug Use, Medical/Dental Care, Motor Vehicle Safety, Sexual Activities, Work & Leisure, Emotional Health.

Administration: Individual.

Price Data, 2003: $195 per MS-DOS disk for 100 uses; $895 per MS-DOS disk for 500 uses; $25 per preview version MS-DOS for 3 uses.

Time: (20–30) minutes.

Comments: Self-Report; designed to run on most IBM-compatible computers; minimum requirements include a color graphics adapter card (CGA, EGA, VGA, or SVGA), DOS ver. 3.3 or later, 640K free RAM, and 2 floppy drives or 1 hard disk and 1 floppy disk drive; registered users receive all program upgrades free for the first year after purchase.

Author: Harvey A. Skinner.

Publisher: Multi-Health Systems, Inc.

Cross References: For reviews by F. Felicia Ferrara and Chockalingam Viswesvaran, see 15:63.

[676]
Comrey Personality Scales.

Purpose: Developed to measure major personality characteristics.

Population: Ages 16 and over.

Publication Date: 1970.

Acronym: CPS.

Scores, 10: Trust vs. Defensiveness (T), Orderliness vs. Lack of Compulsion (O), Social Conformity vs. Rebelliousness (C), Activity vs. Lack of Energy (A), Emotional Stability vs. Neuroticism (S), Extraversion vs. Introversion (E), Mental Toughness vs. Sensitivity (M), Empathy vs. Egocentrism (P), Validity Check (V), Response Bias (R).

Administration: Group.

Price Data: Available from publisher.

Time: (35–50) minutes.

Comments: Comrey Personality Scales, Short Form is also available with same scales and prices.

Author: Andrew L. Comrey.

Publisher: EdITS/Educational and Industrial Testing Service.

Cross References: See T5:672 (6 references), T4:628 (21 references), 9:261 (8 references), and T3:558 (22 references); for a review by Edgar Howarth, see 8:527 (27 references); for reviews by R. G. Demaree and M. Y. Quereshi, see 7:59 (20 references).

[677]
Comrey Personality Scales—Short Form.

Purpose: To provide a comprehensive, multidimensional assessment instrument for measuring eight personality dimensions.

Population: High school, college, and adults.

Publication Dates: 1993–1995.

Acronym: CPS Short Form.

Scores, 10: Trust vs. Defensiveness, Orderliness vs. Lack of Compulsion, Social Conformity vs. Rebelliousness, Activity vs. Lack of Energy, Emotional Stability vs. Neuroticism, Extraversion vs. Introversion, Mental Toughness vs. Sensitivity, Empathy vs. Egocentrism, Validity Check, Response Bias.

Administration: Group.

Price Data: Available from publisher.

Time: Administration time not reported.
Comments: Includes same scales as the Comrey Personality Scales (676) but has fewer items per scale.
Author: Andrew L. Comrey.
Publisher: EdITS/Educational and Industrial Testing Service.

[678]
Concept Assessment Kit—Conservation.

Purpose: To "determine child's level of conservation by his conservation behavior and his comprehension of the principle involved."
Population: Ages 4–7.
Publication Date: 1968.
Acronym: CAK.
Administration: Individual.
Price Data: Available from publisher.
Authors: Marcel L. Goldschmid and Peter M. Bentler.
Publisher: EdITS/Educational and Industrial Testing Service.

a) FORMS A AND B.
Scores, 13: 2 scores (Behavior, Explanation) in each of 6 areas (2-Dimensional Space, Number, Substance, Continuous Quantity, Weight, Discontinuous Quantity), Total.
Time: (15) minutes per form.
b) FORM C.
Scores, 13: 2 scores (Behavior, Explanation) in each of 3 areas and 3 lengths, Total.
Cross References: See T5:674 (5 references), T4:630 (11 references), T3:559 (17 references), 8:238 (32 references), and T2:549 (5 references); for a review by J. Douglas Ayers, and excerpted reviews by Rheta DeVries and Lawrence Kohlberg, by Vernon C. Hall and Michael Mery, and by Charles D. Smock, see 7:437 (5 references).

[679]
Conditional Reasoning Test of Aggression.

Purpose: "To identify people who have a high probability of engaging in aggressive, harmful behavior."
Population: Employees ages 18 and over.
Publication Date: 2000.
Acronym: CRTA.
Scores: Total score only.
Administration: Group or individual.
Price Data, 2006: $175 per complete kit including manual (63 pages), 25 test booklets, answer sheet, scoring key, and score interpretation; $45 per manual; $135 per 25 test booklets, answer sheet, and score interpretation.
Time: (25) minutes.
Comments: Provides an indirect measure of "potential for aggressive tendencies"; paper-and-pencil format only; hand-scored.
Authors: Lawrence R. James and Michael D. McIntyre.

Publisher: Harcourt Assessment, Inc.
Cross References: For a review by Jayne E. Stake, see 15:64.

[680]
Conduct Disorder Scale.

Purpose: "To identify persons with Conduct Disorder by evaluating the characteristic behaviors that define this condition."
Population: Ages 5–22 years.
Publication Date: 2002.
Acronym: CDS.
Scores: 5: 4 subscales (Aggressive Conduct, Hostility, Deceitfulness/Theft, Rule Violations), Conduct Disorder Quotient.
Administration: Group or individual.
Price Data, 2006: $89 per complete kit including examiner's manual (41 pages), 50 summary/response forms, and storage box; $51 per examiner's manual; $40 per 50 summary/response forms.
Time: (5–10) minutes.
Comments: Based on the diagnostic criteria for conduct disorder specified by the Diagnostic and Statistical Manual of Mental Disorders—Fourth Edition—Text Revision (DSM-IV-TR); provides interpretation guide for classifying degree of severity of conduct disorder (severe, moderate, mild, not applicable).
Author: James E. Gilliam.
Publisher: PRO-ED.
Cross References: For reviews by Michael J. Furlong and Jenne Simental and by Steven I. Pfeiffer, see 16:64.

[681]
Conference Meeting Rating Scale.

Purpose: Designed as "an overall rating procedure for observers in evaluating both the effectiveness of the conference leader and the conference group, conferees in evaluating leader portion of the meeting, and for the conference leader in measuring the reactions of the conference group."
Population: Employees.
Publication Date: No date.
Scores: Total score only.
Administration: Group.
Price Data: Available from publisher.
Time: Administration time not reported.
Author: B. J. Speroff.
Publisher: Psychometric Affiliates.

[682]
Conflict Analysis Battery.

Purpose: Designed to "assess a person's conflict resolution process, qualitatively, quantitatively and graphically along a range of four relational modalities and a symbolic system consisting of a six step dialectic of formal and energetic intertransformations."

Population: School age and adults.
Publication Date: 1988.
Acronym: CAB.
Scores: 11 subtests: The personality inventory (Relational Modality Evaluation Scale), projective tests (Balloon Portraits and Story, Conflictual Memories Test, Dream Analysis), Transparent Mask Test, Animal Metaphor Test, Fairy Tale Metaphor Test, Short Story Metaphor, Intensified Animal Metaphor Test, House-Tree-Person Metaphor Test, Scribble Metaphor.
Administration: Individuals and group.
Price Data, 2006: $ 40 per volume (packages of 12); $60 per textbook entitled "Conflict Analysis, the Formal Theory of Behavior."
Time: Administration time not reported.
Comments: Self-administered inventory and projective test battery; developed for use with Conflict Analysis Training: A Concise Program of Emotional Education.
Author: Albert J. Levis.
Publisher: The Institute of Conflict Analysis.
Cross References: For reviews by Susan M. Brookhart and Carl Isenhart, see 16:65.

[683]
Conflict Management Appraisal.

Purpose: "Designed to provide information about the various ways people react to and try to manage the differences between themselves and others."
Population: Adults.
Publication Dates: 1986–1995.
Acronym: CMA.
Scores, 20: 5 conflict management styles (9/1 Win-Lose, 1/9 Yield-Lose, 1/1 Lose-Leave, 5/5 Compromise, 9/9 Synergistic) for each of 4 contexts (Personal Orientation, Interpersonal Relationships, Small Group Relationships, Intergroup Relationships).
Administration: Individual.
Price Data, 2001: $7.95 per instrument.
Time: (30) minutes.
Comments: Adaptation of the Conflict Management Survey (684); to be used in conjunction with the Conflict Management Survey; ratings by person well acquainted with subject.
Author: Jay Hall.
Publisher: Teleometrics International, Inc.
Cross References: For reviews by William L. Curlette and David N. Dixon, see 12:90.

[684]
Conflict Management Survey.

Purpose: "Designed to provide information about the various ways people react to and try to manage the differences between themselves and others."
Population: Adults.
Publication Dates: 1969–1996.

Acronym: CMS.
Scores, 20: 5 conflict management styles (9/1 Win-Lose, 1/9 Yield-Lose, 1/1 Lose-Leave, 5/5 Compromise, 9/9 Synergistic) for each of 4 contexts (Personal Orientation, Interpersonal Relationships, Small Group Relationships, Intergroup Relationships).
Administration: Group.
Price Data, 2001: $8.95 per instrument.
Time: Administration time not reported.
Comments: Self-ratings.
Author: Jay Hall.
Publisher: Teleometrics International, Inc.
Cross References: For reviews by Frederick Bessai and Douglas J. McRae, see 12:91; for a review by Frank J. Landy of an earlier edition, see 8:1173 (2 references).

[685]
Conflict Style Inventory.

Purpose: Designed to assess an individual's approach to conflict resolution.
Population: Adults.
Publication Dates: 1990–1995.
Acronym: CSI.
Scores, 15: Total Score, Individual [one-on-one] Conflict Situations, Group/Team Conflict Situations on 5 styles: (Avoiding, Smoothing, Bargaining, Forcing, Problem Solving).
Administration: Group.
Price Data: Available from publisher.
Time: (20) minutes.
Comments: Self-scored.
Author: Marshall Sashkin.
Publisher: HRD Press, Inc.
Cross References: For reviews by Trenton R. Ferro and Scott T. Meier, see 14:96.

[686]
Conners' Adult ADHD Diagnostic Interview for DSM-IV.

Purpose: Empirically based structured interview that assists the process of diagnosing ADHD.
Population: Age 18 and older.
Publication Date: 2001.
Acronym: CAADID.
Scores: Childhood and Adult ADHD Diagnosis (specifies Inattentive vs. Hyperactive Impulsive).
Administration: Individual.
Price Data, 2006: $112 per complete kit including technical manual (2001, 64 pages), 10 patient history forms, and 10 diagnostic criteria interview forms; $53 per specimen set including technical manual, 1 patient history form, and 1 diagnostic criteria interview form; $47 per technical manual; $46 per 10 patient history forms; $46 per 10 diagnostic criteria interview forms.
Time: (60–90) minutes for Interview; (30–60) minutes for Self-Report.

Comments: Interview format.
Authors: Jeff Epstein, Diane Johnson, and C. Keith Conners.
Publisher: Multi-Health Systems, Inc.
Cross References: For reviews by George J. Demakis and Timothy J. Makatura, see 16:66.

[687]
Conners' Adult ADHD Rating Scales.

Purpose: Designed to assess "psychopathology and problem behaviors associated with adult ADHD."
Population: Ages 18 and over.
Publication Date: 1999.
Administration: Individual.
Forms, 6: Self-Report: Long (CAARS-S:L); Self-Report: Short (CAARS-S:S); Self-Report: Screening (CAARS-S:SV); Observer: Long (CAARS-O:L); Observer: Short (CAARS-O:S); Observer: Screening (CAARS-O: SV).
Price Data, 2006: $262 per complete kit including manual (144 pages) and 25 QuikScore™ forms for each of the 6 forms; $63 per manual; $43 per 25 of any one of the 6 QuikScore™ forms; $75 per specimen set including manual, and 1 QuikScore™ form for each of the 6 forms; $65 per online profile report kit including manual and 3 online profile reports; $70 per online interpretive report kit including manual and 3 online interpretive reports.
Comments: Observer rating and/or self-report.
Authors: C. Keith Conners, Drew Erhardt, and Elizabeth Sparrow.
Publisher: Multi-Health Systems, Inc.
   a) CAARS—SELF-REPORT: LONG; CAARS—OBSERVER: LONG.
   Scores, 9: Inattention/Memory Problems, Hyperactivity/Restlessness, Impulsivity/Emotional Lability, Problems with Self-Concept, DSM-IV Inattentive Symptoms, DSM-IV Hyperactive-Impulsive Symptoms, DSM-IV Total ADHD Symptoms, ADHD Index, Inconsistency Index.
   Time: (30) minutes.
   b) CAARS—SELF-REPORT: SHORT; CAARS—OBSERVER: SHORT.
   Scores, 6: Inattentive/Memory Problems, Hyperactivity/Restlessness, Impulsivity/Emotional Lability, Problems with Self-Concept, ADHD Index, Inconsistency Index.
   Time: (10) minutes.
   c) CAARS—SELF-REPORT: SCREENING; CAARS—OBSERVER: SCREENING.
   Scores, 4: DSM-IV Inattentive Symptoms, DSM-IV Hyperactive/Impulsivity Symptoms, DSM-IV Total ADHD Symptoms, ADHD Index.
   Time: (10) minutes.

Cross References: For reviews by Andrew S. Davis and Rik Carl D'Amato and by Ronald J. Ganellen, see 15:65.

[688]
Conners' Continuous Performance Test II.

Purpose: A computerized assessment tool used to assess attention problems and to measure treatment effectiveness.
Population: Ages 6 to adult.
Publication Dates: 1992–1996.
Acronym: CPT II.
Scores, 12: Omissions, Commissions, Hit Reaction Time, Hit Reaction Time Standard Error, Variability of Standard Error, Attentiveness (d prime), Perseverations, Hit Reaction Time Block Change (Vigilance Measure), Hit Standard Error Block Change (Vigilance Measure), Hit Reaction Time Inter-Stimulus Interval Change (Adjusting to Presentation Speed), Hit Standard Error Inter-Stimulus Change (Adjusting to Presentation Speed), Confidence Index.
Administration: Individual.
Price Data, 2006: $645 per Psychmanager Lite CD kit and Correction Manager CD kit with manual; $50 per preview version.
Time: (14) minutes.
Comments: Self-report performance measure; includes CD-ROM and 3.5-inch disk; requires Windows 95 or higher.
Authors: C. Keith Conners and the MHS staff.
Publisher: Multi-Health Systems Inc.
Cross References: For reviews by Beverly M. Klecker and Wesley E. Sime, see 15:66; for a review by James Ysseldyke of an earlier version, see 14:97; see also T5:679 (2 references).

[689]
Conners' Kiddie Continuous Performance Test.

Purpose: Software programs designed to identify attention problems and measure treatment effectiveness in very young children.
Population: Age 4–5.
Publication Date: 2001.
Acronym: K-CPT.
Scores: Omissions, Comissions, Hit RT, Hit RT Standard Error, Variability, Detectability (d), Response Style, Perseverations, Hit RT Block Change, Hit SE Block Change, Hit RT ISI Change, Hit SE ISI Change, and Confidence Index.
Administration: Individual.
Price Data, 2006: $215 per unlimited-use software kit, including manual (2001, 156 pages); $50 per preview version (3 uses).
Time: 7.5 minutes.
Comments: Self-completed; administered and scored on computer running Windows 95 or higher.

Authors: C. Keith Conners and Multi-Health Systems, Inc. staff.
Publisher: Multi-Health Systems, Inc.
Cross References: For reviews by Brian F. French and by Scott A. Napolitano and Courtney Miller, see 16:67.

[690]
Conners-March Developmental Questionnaire.

Purpose: To gather personal history information about a child from the parents prior to meeting with a physician or psychologist.
Population: Children.
Publication Date: 1994.
Scores: Not scored.
Administration: Group.
Manual: No manual.
Price Data, 2006: $39 per 25 questionnaires.
Time: Administration time not reported.
Comments: Completed by parent.
Authors: C. Keith Conners and John S. March.
Publisher: Multi-Health Systems, Inc.

[691]
Conners' Rating Scales—Revised.

Purpose: Designed to assess psychopathology and problem behaviors.
Population: Ages 3–17; self-report scales can be completed by 12- to 17-year-olds.
Publication Dates: 1989–1997.
Acronym: CRS-R.
Administration: Group.
Price Data, 2006: $267 per CRS-R starter kit including technical manual (1997, 226 pages), 25 Quikscore forms for each of the CPRS-R:L, CPRS-R:S, CTRS-R:L, CTRS-R:S, CASS:L, and CASS:S; $198 per CRS-R Parent and Teacher Rating Scale kit including technical manual and 25 Quikscore forms for each of the CPRS–R:L, CPRS-R:S, CTRS-R:L, and CTRS-R:S; $166 per CRS-R Long Version kit including technical manual and 25 Quikscore forms for each of CPRS–R:L, CTRS–R:L, and CASS:L; $161 per CRS–R Short Version kit including technical manual and 25 Quikscore forms for each of CPRS–R:S, CTRS–R:S, and CASS:S; $79 per specimen set including technical manual, 1 Quikscore form for each of CPRS–R:L, CPRS-R:S, CTRS-R:L, CTRS-R:S, CASS:L, CASS:S, CADS-P, CADS-T, CADS-A, CGI-T, and CGI-P, 1 CRS-R Treatment Progress ColorPlot Form, 1 Feedback Handout, and 1 CTIF; $41 per 25 CPRS–R:L, CTRS–R:L, or CASS:L; Quikscore forms; $39 per 25 CPRS–R:S, CTRS–R:S, or CASS:S Quikscore forms; $74 per technical manual; $47 per user's manual; $12.50 per 25 Conners' Teacher Information Forms (CTIF); $33 per 15 CRS-R Treatment Progress ColorPlot Forms.
Comments: Ratings by parents and teachers and adolescent self-report.
Author: C. Keith Conners.
Publisher: Multi-Health Systems, Inc.
a) CONNERS' PARENT RATING SCALE—REVISED.
Acronym: CPRS-R.
Scores, 13: Oppositional, Cognitive Problems/Inattention, Hyperactivity, Anxious-Shy, Perfectionism, Social Problems, Psychosomatic, ADHD Index, Conners' Global Index: Restless-Impulsive and Emotional Lability, DSM-IV Inattentive, DSM-IV Hyperactive-Impulsive, DSM-IV Total.
Forms, 2: Long, Short.
Time: (15–20) minutes.
b) CONNERS' TEACHER RATING SCALE—REVISED.
Acronym: CTRS-R.
Scores: Same as *a* above.
Forms, 2: Long, Short.
Time: (15) minutes.
c) CONNERS-WELLS' ADOLESCENT SELF-REPORT SCALE.
Acronym: CASS.
Scores, 10: Conduct Problems, Cognitive Problems/Inattention, Hyperactivity, ADHD Index, Family Problems, Anger Control Problems, Emotional Problems, DSM-IV Inattentive, DSM-IV Hyperactive-Impulsive, DSM-IV Total.
Forms, 2: Long, Short.
Time: (15–20) minutes.
d) CONNERS' GLOBAL INDEX.
Acronym: CGI.
Scores, 3: Emotional Lability, Restless-Impulsive, Total.
Forms, 2: Parent, Teacher.
Time: (5) minutes.
e) CONNERS' ADHD/DSM-IV™ SCALES.
Acronym: CADS.
Scores, 4: Conners' ADHD Index, DSM-IV: Inattentive, DSM-IV: Hyperactive/Impulsive, DSM-IV Total.
Forms, 3: Parent, Teacher, Adolescent.
Time: (5–10) minutes.
Cross References: For reviews by Allen K. Hess and Howard M. Knoff, see 14:98; see also T5:681 (99 references) and T4:636 (50 references); for reviews by Brian K. Martens and Judy Oehler-Stinnett of the original edition, see 11:87 (83 references).

[692]
Consequences.

Purpose: Measure ideational fluency and originality.
Population: Grades 9–16.

Publication Date: 1958.
Scores, 2: Originality, Ideational Fluency.
Administration: Group.
Forms, 2: A1, A2.
Price Data: Available from publisher.
Time: 10(13) minutes.
Comments: Mimeographed manual, third edition (8 pages); Form A1 consists of first 5 items and Form A2 consists of last 5 items of the original 1958 (single-form) 10-item test.
Authors: Paul R. Christensen, P. R. Merrifield, and J. P. Guilford.
Publisher: Charlotte Mackley [No reply from publisher; status unknown].
Cross References: See T5:682 (5 references), T4:637 (2 references) and T2:551 (71 references); for a review by Goldine C. Gleser of the 10-item test, see 6:547 (13 references).

[693]
Constructive Thinking Inventory.

Purpose: "Evaluates an individual's experiential intelligence and coping skills."
Population: Ages 18–81 years.
Publication Date: 2001.
Acronym: CTI.
Scores: Emotional Coping (Self-Acceptance, Absence of Negative Overgeneralization, Nonsensitivity, Absence of Dwelling), Behavioral Coping (Positive Thinking, Action Orientation, Conscientiousness), Personal Superstitious Thinking, Categorical Thinking (Polarized Thinking, Distrust of Others, Intolerance), Esoteric Thinking (Belief in the Unusual, Formal Superstitious Thinking), Naive Optimism (Over-Optimism, Stereotypical Thinking, Polyanna-ish Thinking), Defensiveness, Validity, Global Constructive Thinking.
Administration: Individual or group.
Price Data, 2006: $145 per introductory kit including CD ROM-based scoring program with on-screen user's manual, professional manual (59 pages), 25 test booklets, and 25-report uses.
Time: (15–30) minutes.
Comments: Administered in paper-and-pencil format only; responses are manually entered into scoring program; software generates raw scores, T-scores, and profile; system requirements: Windows 95/98/NT/2000/ME/XP; 8 MB hard disk, 16 MB RAM (Windows 95/98/ME) or 24 MB RAM (Windows NT/2000/XP), CD ROM with internet and telephone.
Authors: Seymour Epstein.
Publisher: Psychological Assessment Resources, Inc.

[694]
Contextual Memory Test.

Purpose: Designed to assess awareness of memory capacity, strategy use, and recall in adults with memory dysfunction.

Population: Adults.
Publication Date: 1993.
Acronym: CMT.
Scores, 12: Recall Score (Immediate Recall, Delayed Recall, Total Recall), Cued Recall, Recognition, Awareness Score (Prediction, Estimation of Performance Following Recall, Response to General Questioning [Prior to Recall, Following Recall]), Strategy Use (Effect of Context, Order of Recall, Total Strategy Score).
Administration: Individual.
Price Data, 2002: $105 per complete kit including manual (138 pages), 2 test cards, 14 cut-apart sheets of 80 picture cards, 25 score sheets (12 pages), and carrying case; $37 per 25 score sheets.
Time: (10–20) minutes.
Author: Joan P. Toglia.
Publisher: Harcourt Assessment, Inc.
Cross References: For reviews by Karen Mackler and Alan J. Raphael, see 14:99.

[695]
Contextual Test of Articulation.

Purpose: "Designed to ... identify phonetic contexts that facilitate correct production of phonemes incorrectly produced by children ... who display speech sound production disorders."
Population: Ages 4-9.
Publication Date: 2000.
Acronym: CTA.
Scores: 6 subtests: Consonant Singleton /s/, Consonant Singleton /l/, Consonant Singleton /k/, Consonant Singleton /r/, Semivowel, Consonant Clusters.
Administration: Individual.
Price Data, 2006: $129 per complete kit including manual (46 pages), easel-style spiral, and 195 full-color picture plates.
Time: (15-25) minutes per subtest.
Comments: This test should be administered "after a child's phonemes production errors have been identified."
Authors: Dawn Aase, Charity Hovre, Karleen Krause, Sarah Schelfhout, Jennifer Smith, and Linda J. Carpenter.
Publisher: Thinking Publications.

[696]
Continuous Visual Memory Test [Revised].

Purpose: Constructed to assess visual memory.
Population: Ages 7–80+.
Publication Date: 1983–1997.
Acronym: CVMT.
Scores: 6: Acquisition (Hits, False Alarms, d-Prime, Total), Delayed Recognition, Visual Discrimination.
Administration: Individual.
Price Data, 2006: $170 per kit including manual (1988, 22 pages), norms manual (1997, 51 pages), stimulus cards, and 50 scoring forms.

Time: (45–50) minutes.
Authors: Donald E. Trahan and Glenn J. Larrabee.
Publisher: Psychological Assessment Resources, Inc.
Cross References: For reviews by Michael B. Brown and Alice J. Corkill, see 14:100; see also T5:687 (4 references); for reviews by Nancy B. Bologna and Stephen F. Davis of an earlier edition, see 12:93; see also T4:642 (4 references).

[697]
Controller Staff Selector.

Purpose: To evaluate the bookkeeping and analytical reasoning skills necessary for the position of controller.
Population: Candidates for the position of controller.
Publication Date: 1988.
Acronym: COCON.
Scores: Total Score, Narrative Evaluation, Ranking, Recommendation.
Administration: Group.
Price Data, 2001: $500 per candidate; quantity discounts available.
Time: (319) minutes.
Comments: Scored by publisher; must be proctored; previously listed as Controller/Accountant Staff Selector.
Author: Walden Personnel Performance, Inc.
Publisher: Walden Personnel Performance, Inc. [Canada]

[698]
The Conversational Skills Rating Scale: An Instructional Assessment of Interpersonal Competence.

Purpose: "To assess the skills domain of conversational competence."
Population: Secondary and post-secondary students.
Publication Date: 1995.
Acronym: CSRS.
Scores, 5: Altercentricism, Composure, Expressiveness, Interaction Management, Total.
Administration: Group.
Forms, 7: Rating of Partner Form, Rating of Self Form, Instructor Rating of Student Form, Self Frequency Version, Partner Frequency Version, Self Trait Rating Form, Other Trait Rating Form.
Price Data: Available from publisher.
Time: (5–15) minutes.
Author: Brian H. Spitzberg.
Publisher: National Communication Association.
Cross References: For reviews by Sandra M. Ketrow and Julia Y. Porter, see 14:101.

[699]
Coolidge Assessment Battery.

Purpose: Designed to assess personality disorders and neuropsychological functioning.
Population: Ages 15 and older.
Publication Date: 1999.
Acronym: CAB.
Scores, 46: 7 Axis I scales (Anxiety, Depression, Post-Traumatic Stress, Psychotic Thinking, Schizophrenia, Social Phobia, Withdrawal); 14 Axis II scales (Antisocial, Avoidant, Borderline, Dependent, Depressive, Histrionic, Narcissistic, Obsessive-Compulsive, Paranoid, Passive-Aggressive, Sadistic, Schizoid, Schizotypal, Self-Defeating); 4 Neuropsychological Dysfunction scales (Overall Neuropsychological, Language Functions, Memory and Concentration, Neurosomatic Functions); 4 Executive Functions of the Frontal Lobe scales (Overall Executive Functions, Decision Difficulty, Planning Problems, Task Completion Difficulty); 5 Personality Change due to Medical Condition scales (Aggression, Apathy, Disinhibition, Emotional Lability, Paranoid); 3 Hostility scales (Anger, Dangerousness, Impulsiveness); 5 Normative scales (Apathy, Emotional Lability, Indecisiveness, Maladjustment, Introversion-Extroversion); 4 Validity scales (Answer Choice Frequency, Random Responding, Tendency to Look Good or Bad, Tendency to Deny Blatant Pathology).
Administration: Group or individual.
Price Data, 2006: $40 per manual (1999, 54 pages); $105 per Windows software package including disks, software manual, test manual, and 10 coupons.
Time: 40 minutes.
Comments: Originally published as the Coolidge Axis II Inventory (14:102); mail-in or software scoring.
Authors: Frederick L. Coolidge.
Publisher: Sigma Assessment Systems, Inc.
Cross References: For reviews by Mark A. Staal and Peter Zachar, see 15:68; for reviews by Kevin L. Moreland and Paul Retzlaff of an earlier edition, see 14:102; see also T5:690 (3 references).

[700]
The Cooperative Institutional Research Program.

Purpose: "A national longitudinal study of the American higher educational system" based on freshman survey data.
Population: First-time, full-time entering college freshmen.
Publication Dates: 1966–1994.
Acronym: CIRP.
Scores: No scores.
Administration: Group.
Price Data: Available from publisher.
Time: (40) minutes.
Comments: Test entitled Student Information Form (T3:2333); national norms reported annually.
Authors: Alexander W. Astin, William S. Korn, and Ellyne R. Riggs.

Publisher: Higher Education Research Institute, University of California-Los Angeles [No reply from publisher; status unknown].

Cross References: See T5:692 (1 reference) and T4:645 (8 references); for a review by Harvey Resnick, see 9:266. For a review by Albert B. Hood of the Student Information Form, see 8:397 (15 references).

[701]
Coopersmith Self-Esteem Inventories.

Purpose: "Designed to measure evaluative attitudes toward the self in social, academic, family, and personal areas of experience."

Population: Ages 8–15, 16 and above.

Publication Date: 1981.

Acronym: SEI.

Administration: Group.

Price Data, 2006: $30 per sampler set including manual; $120 per 150-copy duplication set (specify Adult Form or School Form); quantity discounts available for bulk permissions bundles; $10 per scoring key (specify form); $25 per 25 booklets (specify form).

Time: (10) minutes.

Author: Stanley Coopersmith.

Publisher: Mind Garden, Inc.

a) SCHOOL FORM.

Population: Ages 8–15.

Scores, 6: General Self, Social Self-Peers, Home-Parents, School-Academic, Total Self Score, Lie.

Comments: Separate answer sheets may be used; school short form also available.

b) ADULT FORM.

Population: Ages 16 and above.

Cross References: See T5:694 (134 references) and T4:647 (106 references); for reviews by Christopher Peterson and James T. Austin and by Trevor E. Sewell, see 9:267 (32 references).

[702]
Coping Inventory: A Measure of Adaptive Behavior.

Purpose: "Assess the behavior patterns and skills used to meet personal needs and to adapt to the demands of the environment."

Population: Ages 3–16; Ages 15-Adult.

Publication Date: 1985.

Scores, 9: 3 scores (Productive, Active, Flexible) for Coping with Self, Coping with Environment, plus Adaptive Behavior Index.

Administration: Individual.

Levels: 2.

Time: Administration time not reported.

Authors: Shirley Zeitlin.

Publisher: Scholastic Testing Service, Inc.

a) SELF-RATED FORM.

Population: Ages 15-Adult.

Price Data, 2006: $35.55 per starter set including manual (6 pages) and 10 forms; $18.85 per 10 inventories; $16.90 per manual; $16.20 per sample set.

Comments: Self-report ratings of adaptive behavior.

b) OBSERVATION FORM.

Population: Ages 3–16.

Price Data: $54.60 per starter set including manual (75 pages) and 20 forms; $35.55 per 20 inventories; $29.15 per manual; $26.75 per sample set.

Comments: Ratings of adaptive behavior by adult informant.

Cross References: See T5:695 (3 references) and T4:648 (1 reference).

[703]
Coping Inventory for Stressful Situations, Second Edition.

Purpose: Designed as a "scale for measuring coping styles."

Population: Adolescents ages 13–18, adults age 18 and over.

Publication Date: 1990–1999.

Acronym: CISS.

Scores, 5: Task, Emotion, Avoidance, Distraction, Social Diversion.

Administration: Individual or group.

Forms, 3: Adult, Adolescent, Situation-Specific.

Price Data, 2006: $94 per CISS Adult Version Complete Kit including 25 Adult QuikScore™ forms, 25 SSC QuikScore™ forms, and manual (1999, 87 pages); $64 per CISS Adolescent Version Complete Kit including 25 Adolescent QuikScore™ forms and manual (1999, 87 pages); $35 per 25 QuikScore™ forms (specify Adult or Adolescent); $41 per manual. Foreign Language Editions: French (European), French (Quebec), Arabic, Armenian, Danish, German, Greek, Hebrew, Icelandic, Italian, Japanese, Korean, Malaysian, Norwegian, Polish, Russion, Spanish (U.S.), and Spanish (European) translations available.

Time: (10) minutes.

Comments: Self-report.

Authors: Norman S. Endler and James D. A. Parker.

Publisher: Multi-Health Systems, Inc.

Cross References: For a review by William C. Tirre, see 15:69; for reviews by E. Thomas Dowd and Stephanie Stein of an earlier edition, see 14:104, see also T5:696 (2 references).

[704]
Coping Resources Inventory.

Purpose: Developed to assess a person's resources for coping with stress.

Population: Middle school-age to adult.

Publication Dates: 1987–1988.
Acronym: CRI.
Scores, 6: Cognitive, Social, Emotional, Spiritual/Philosophical, Physical, Total.
Administration: Group.
Price Data, 2006: $40 per sampler set including manual (1988, 30 pages); $120 per 150-copy duplication set; quantity discounts available for bulk permissions bundles.
Time: (10) minutes.
Comments: For research use only; also available as part of www.careerhub.org website; mail-in or hand scoring available.
Authors: Allen L. Hammer and M. Susan Marting.
Publisher: Mind Garden, Inc.
Cross References: See T5:697 (6 references); for reviews by Roger A. Boothroyd and Larry Cochran, see 12:95 (1 reference); see also T4:649 (2 references).

[705]
Coping Resources Inventory for Stress.

Purpose: "Designed to measure coping resources which are believed to help lessen the negative effects of stress."
Population: Adults.
Publication Dates: 1988–1993.
Acronym: CRIS.
Scores, 16: Self-Disclosure, Self-Directedness, Confidence, Acceptance, Social Support, Financial Freedom, Physical Health, Physical Fitness, Stress Monitoring, Tension Control, Structuring, Problem Solving, Cognitive Restructuring, Functional Beliefs, Social Ease, Coping Resource Effectiveness.
Administration: Group or individual.
Price Data: Available from publisher.
Foreign Language Editions: Spanish, French, Russian, Chinese, Portugese, and Korean editions available.
Time: (45–90) minutes.
Comments: Computer (PC-CRIS) administration and software package available.
Authors: Kenneth B. Matheny, William L. Curlette, David W. Aycock, James L. Pugh, and Harry F. Taylor.
Publisher: Health Prisms, Inc. [No reply from publisher; status unknown].
Cross References: See T5:698 (1 reference); for reviews by Sharon L. Weinberg and Paul D. Werner, see 13:84; see also T4:650 (3 references).

[706]
Coping Responses Inventory—Adult and Youth.

Purpose: Constructed to "identify and monitor coping strategies in adults and adolescents."
Population: Ages 12–18, 18 and older.

Publication Date: 1993.
Acronym: CRI.
Scores: 8 scales: Logical Analysis, Positive Reappraisal, Seeking Guidance and Support, Problem Solving, Cognitive Avoidance, Acceptance or Resignation, Seeking Alternative Rewards, Emotional Discharge.
Administration: Group.
Levels, 2: Adult and Youth.
Forms, 2: Ideal, Actual.
Price Data, 2006: $158 per CRI-Adult introductory kit including CRI-Adult professional manual (44 pages), 10 reusable item booklets, 50 answer sheets, and "Coping Responses Inventory"; $158 per CRI-Youth introductory kit including CRI-Adult professional manual, 10 reusable item booklets, 50 answer sheets, and "Coping Responses Inventory."
Time: (10–15) minutes.
Author: Rudolf H. Moos.
Publisher: Psychological Assessment Resources, Inc.
Cross References: For reviews by Ashraf Kagee and Everett V. Smith, Jr., see 14:105; see also T5:699 (5 references).

[707]
Coping Scale for Adults.

Purpose: Designed as a self-report inventory that examines coping behavior and facilitates development of coping strategies.
Population: Ages 18 and over.
Publication Date: 1997.
Acronym: CSA.
Scores, 19: Seek Social Support, Focus on Solving the Problem, Work Hard, Worry, Improve Relationships, Wishful Thinking, Tension Reduction, Social Action, Ignore the Problem, Self-Blame, Keep to Self, Seek Spiritual Support, Focus on the Positive, Seek Professional Help, Seek Relaxing Diversions, Physical Recreation, Protect Self, Humor, Not Cope.
Administration: Group.
Forms, 2: Short Form, Long Form.
Price Data, 2006: A$129.95 per complete kit; A$24.95 per 10 short forms; A$29.95 per 10 long forms; A$12.95 per 10 scoring sheets; A$12.95 per 10 profile charts; A$54.95 per manual (60 pages).
Time: Administration time not reported.
Authors: Erica Frydenberg and Ramon Lewis.
Publisher: Australian Council for Educational Research Ltd. [Australia].
Cross References: For reviews by Peter Miles Berger and M. Allan Cooperstein, see 15:70.

[708]
Coping With Health Injuries and Problems.

Purpose: Designed to assess coping with physical health problems.
Population: Adults.

Publication Dates: 1992–2000.
Acronym: CHIP.
Scores: 4 dimensions: Distraction, Palliative, Instrumental, Emotional Preoccupation.
Administration: Group.
Price Data, 2006: $68 per complete kit including technical manual (2000, 76 pages) and 25 Quikscore forms; $35 per 25 Quikscore forms; $47 per technical manual.
Time: (15) minutes.
Comments: Self-report.
Authors: Norman S. Endler and James D. A. Parker.
Publisher: Multi-Health Systems, Inc.
Cross References: For reviews by Linda K. Bunker and by Leonard Handler and Amanda Jill Clements, see 15:71.

[709]
Coping With Stress.

Purpose: Constructed as a self-assessment tool to identify sources of stress and responses to stress.
Population: Adults.
Publication Date: 1989.
Scores, 9: Reaction to Stress (Obsessive, Hysteria, Anxiety, Phobia, Total, Normal), Adjustment to Stress (Healthy, Unhealthy), Sources of Stress.
Administration: Group.
Price Data: Price information available from publisher for complete kit including 20 test folders, 20 response sheets, and 20 interpretation sheets.
Time: [20] minutes administration; [10] minutes scoring; [30] minutes interpretation.
Comments: Self-administered, self-scored.
Author: Training House, Inc.
Publisher: Training House, Inc.
Cross References: For a review by Bert W. Westbrook and Suzanne Markel-Fox, see 12:96.

[710]
COPSystem Picture Inventory of Careers.

Purpose: To measure career interest for persons with reading or language difficulties.
Population: Elementary through adult-non-verbal.
Publication Date: 1993.
Acronym: COPS-PIC.
Scores: Interest scores in 14 COPSystem Career Clusters: Science—Professional, Science—Skilled, Technology—Professional, Technology—Skilled, Consumer Economics, Outdoor, Business—Professional, Business—Skilled, Clerical, Communication, Arts—Professional, Arts—Skilled, Service—Professional, Service—Skilled.
Administration: Group.
Price Data: Available from publisher.
Time: (30) minutes.
Author: Lisa Knapp-Lee.

Publisher: EdITS/Educational and Industrial Testing Service.

[711]
The Cornell Class-Reasoning Test, Form X.

Purpose: "A multiple-choice deductive logic class-reasoning test."
Population: Grades 4–12.
Publication Date: 1964.
Scores: Deductive Logic.
Administration: Group.
Manual: No manual.
Price Data: Available from publisher.
Time: Untimed.
Comments: Subtitle on test booklet is Cornell Critical Thinking Test Series.
Authors: Robert H. Ennis, William L. Gardiner, Richard Morrow, Dieter Paulus, and Lucille Ringel.
Publisher: Illinois Critical Thinking Project.
Cross References: See T2:1753 (1 reference).

[712]
The Cornell Conditional-Reasoning Test.

Purpose: Designed as "a multiple-choice deductive logic conditional-reasoning test."
Population: Grades 4–12.
Publication Date: 1964.
Scores: Deductive Logic.
Administration: Group.
Manual: No manual.
Price Data: Available from publisher.
Time: Untimed.
Comments: Subtitle on test booklet is Cornell Critical Thinking Test Series.
Authors: Robert H. Ennis, William L. Gardiner, John Gazzetta, Richard Morrow, Dieter Paulus, and Lucille Ringel.
Publisher: Illinois Critical Thinking Project.
Cross References: See T2:1754 (1 reference).

[713]
Cornell Critical Thinking Tests.

Purpose: Assesses general critical thinking ability including "induction, deduction, evaluation, observation, credibility (of statements made by others), assumption identification, and meaning."
Publication Dates: 1961-1985.
Acronym: CCTT.
Scores: Total score only for each level.
Administration: Group.
Levels, 2: X, Z.
Price Data, 2001: $21.99 per 10 test booklets (specify level); $8.99 per 10 machine-gradable answer sheets; $8.99 per manual (1985, 32 pages); $17.99 per specimen set including both tests, answer sheet, and manual; $39.99 per software (specify Level X or Level

Z and Macintosh or Windows; quantity licenses available); includes 10 free tests (any combination of X and Z levels); $.99 per additional per student license.
Time: (50) minutes.
Comments: Identical to 1971 edition except for minor format and wording changes and 1999 publication of software; 1 form.
Authors: Robert H. Ennis, Jason Millman, and Thomas N. Tomko (manual).
Publisher: The Critical Thinking Co.
　a) LEVEL X.
　Population: Grade 5–college.
　Comments: Software version for Grade 7–college population.
　b) LEVEL Z.
　Population: Advanced and gifted high school students and college students and adults.
Cross References: See T5:705 (10 references) and T4:655 (1 reference); for reviews by Jan N. Hughes and Koressa Kutsick Malcolm, see 11:88 (3 references); see also 9:269 (1 reference), T3:606 (7 references), T2:1755 (2 references), and 7:779 (10 references).

[714]
Cornell Index—Form N2.

Purpose: For collecting pertinent medical and psychiatric data from patients.
Population: Ages 14 and over.
Publication Dates: 1949–1956.
Acronym: C.I.
Scores: Total score only.
Administration: Group or individual.
Price Data, 2006: $60 per 100 copies; $30 per specimen set.
Foreign Language Editions: French Canadian and Spanish editions available.
Time: (5–15) minutes.
Comments: Title on test is C.I. Form N2.
Authors: Arthur Weider.
Publisher: Arthur Weider and James Weider.
Cross References: See T5:708 (9 references), T4:658 (16 references), 9:270 (15 references), T3:609 (33 references), 8:530 (46 references), and T2:1145 (42 references); for reviews by Eugene E. Levitt and David T. Lykken, see 7:61 (32 references); see also P:49 (77 references).

[715]
The Cornell Inventory for Student Appraisal of Teaching and Courses.

Purpose: "Provides teachers with feedback of student opinion."
Population: College teachers.
Publication Dates: 1972–1973.
Scores: Item norms only.
Administration: Group.

Price Data: Not available.
Time: (15–20) minutes.
Authors: James B. Maas and Thomas R. Owen (manual).
Publisher: James B. Maas [No reply from publisher; status unknown].
Cross References: For a review by Wilbert J. McKeachie, see 8:367.

[716]
Cornell Word Form 2.

Purpose: "To assess mental health adjustment using a forced choice word association technique."
Population: Adults.
Publication Dates: 1946–1955.
Acronym: C.W.F.-2.
Scores: Total score only.
Administration: Group or individual.
Price Data, 2006: $60 per 100 copies; $30 per specimen set.
Time: [5–15] minutes.
Comments: Title on test is C.W.F.
Author: Arthur Weider.
Publisher: Arthur Weider and James Weider.
Cross References: See T2:1146 (1 reference), P:50 (2 references), and 5:44 (11 references); for a review by S. B. Sells, see 6:80 (1 reference).

[717]
Correctional Institutions Environment Scale, Second Edition.

Purpose: Designed to measure the "social climate of juvenile and adult correctional programs."
Population: Residents and staff of correctional facilities.
Publication Dates: 1974–1987.
Acronym: CIES.
Scores, 9: Involvement, Support, Expressiveness, Autonomy, Practical Orientation, Personal Problem Orientation, Order and Organization, Clarity, Staff Control.
Administration: Group.
Forms, 4: Real (R), Ideal (I), Expectations (E), Short (S).
Price Data: Available from publisher (www.mindgarden.com).
Foreign Language Editions: Versions adapted for use in French Quebec, Slovenia, Sweden, Spain, and the United Kingdom.
Time: Administration time not reported.
Comments: Part of the Social Climate Scales (T5:2445).
Authors: Rudolf H. Moos.
Publisher: Mind Garden, Inc.
Cross References: For reviews by Kevin J. McCarthy and M. David Miller, see 14:106; see also

T4:660 (3 references) and T3:612 (1 reference); for a review by Kenneth A. Carlson of an earlier version, see 8:531 (16 references). For a review of the Social Climate Scales, see 8:681.

[718]
Correctional Officers' Interest Blank.

Purpose: Designed for research in the development of selection techniques for correctional officers.
Population: Correctional officer applicants.
Publication Dates: 1953-2001.
Acronym: COIB.
Scores: Total score only or 19 scales: Dominance, Capacity for Status, Sociability, Social Presence, Self-Acceptance, Well-Being, Responsibility, Socialization, Self-Control, Tolerance, Good Impression, Communality, Achievement via Conformance, Achievement via Independence, Intellectual Efficiency, Psychological-Mindedness, Flexibility, Femininity, Empathy.
Administration: Group or individual.
Price Data: Available from publisher (www.mindgarden.com).
Time: (10) minutes.
Authors: Harrison G. Gough.
Publisher: Mind Garden, Inc.
Cross References: For reviews by Robert J. Howell and R. Lynn Richards and by Samuel Roll, see 10:75.

[719]
Correctional Policy Inventory: A Survey of Correctional Philosophy and Characteristic Methods of Dealing with Offenders.

Purpose: Developed to identify the correctional philosophies utilized in particular situations.
Population: Correctional managers.
Publication Date: 1970.
Scores, 4: Reintegration, Rehabilitation, Reform, Restraint.
Administration: Group.
Price Data: Available from publisher.
Time: [20] minutes.
Author: Vincent O'Leary.
Publisher: National Council on Crime and Delinquency.
Cross References: See 8:1092 (2 references).

[720]
Cortical Vision Screening Test.

Purpose: "Designed to detect visual impairments in individuals with normal (corrected) or near-normal vision."
Population: Ages 18–80.
Publication Date: 2001.
Acronym: CORVIST.
Scores, 10: Symbol Acuity, Shape Discrimination, Size Discrimination, Shape Detection, Hue Discrimi-

nation, Scattered Dot Counting, Fragmented Numbers, Word Reading, Face Perception, Crowding.
Administration: Individual.
Price Data, 2006: £119.50 per complete kit including manual/stimulus book (40 pages) and 25 scoring sheets; £26.50 per 50 scoring sheets.
Time: Untimed.
Authors: Merle James, Gordon T. Plant, and Elizabeth K. Warrington.
Publisher: Harcourt Assessment [England].

[721]
The Couples BrainMap™

Purpose: "To help partners gain new perspective of, and value for, their relationship."
Population: Couples.
Publication Dates: 1981-1986.
Scores, 4: I-Organize, I-Explore, I-Pursue, I-Preserve.
Administration: Group.
Price Data: Available from publisher.
Time: 40(50) minutes.
Comments: Self-administered, self-scored.
Authors: Sherry Lynch, Dudley Lynch, Phyllis Miller, and Sherod Miller.
Publisher: Brain Technologies Corporation.
Cross References: For a review by Alicia Skinner Cook and Richard E. Guest, see 11:91.

[722]
Course Finder.

Purpose: Assesses "students' interests and preferences, and identifies suitable higher education courses at appropriate universities/colleges in Great Britain."
Population: Students entering higher education.
Publication Dates: 1992–1993.
Acronym: CF.
Administration: Group.
Price Data: Available from publisher.
Time: (45–60) minutes.
Comments: For use in Great Britain; was listed in a previous MMY as Course Finder 2000, however, is updated each year. Now also available online at www.ukcoursefinder.com.
Authors: Malcolm Morrisby, Glen Fox, and Mark Parkinson.
Publisher: The Morrisby Organisation [England].
Cross References: For a review by Colin Cooper, see 13:85.

[723]
CPF [Second Edition].

Purpose: "To assess extroversion and preference for social contact."
Population: Ages 16–adult.
Publication Dates: 1954–1992.
Acronym: CPF.

Scores, 3: Validity Scores (Uncertainty, Good Impression), Total Extroversion.
Administration: Group or individual.
Price Data, 2005: $30 per introductory kit including manual (1992, 10 pages), 20 test booklets, and scoring key; $26 per 20 test booklets; $10 per manual.
Time: (5–10) minutes.
Comments: Previously listed as a subtest of the Employee Attitude Series of the Job Tests Program (T3:1219).
Authors: Samuel E. Krug.
Publisher: Industrial Psychology International Ltd.
Cross References: For reviews by Michael R. Harwell and Allen K. Hess, see 12:97.

[724]
Crane Oral Dominance Test: Spanish/English.

Purpose: "To determine if the student has a dominant language, if the student is bilingual ..., or if the student needs concentrated language, concept, and memory development to function adequately in either language."
Population: Ages 4-8.
Publication Date: 1976.
Acronym: CODT.
Scores, 4: Spanish Dominant, English Dominant, Bilingual, Indeterminable.
Administration: Individual.
Price Data, 2001: $34.64 per 30 test booklets and manual (11 pages).
Time: (20) minutes.
Comments: Both English and Spanish used in administration and in pupil responses.
Author: Barbara J. Crane.
Publisher: Bilingual Educational Services, Inc.
Cross References: For excerpted reviews by Protase E. Woodford and Porfirio Sanchez, see 8:162 (1 reference).

[725]
Crawford Small Parts Dexterity Test.

Purpose: "A performance test designed to measure fine eye-hand coordination."
Population: High school and adults.
Publication Dates: 1946–1981.
Acronym: CSPDT.
Scores, 2: Pins and Collars, Screws.
Administration: Individual.
Price Data, 2002: $446 per complete set including manual (1981, 22 pages) and spare parts; $18 per manual; replacement parts are available by calling the publisher.
Time: (8–15) minutes.
Authors: John E. Crawford and Dorothea M. Crawford.
Publisher: PsychCorp, A brand of Harcourt Assessment, Inc.

Cross References: See T4:679 (2 references), T3:627 (4 references), and T2:2223 (12 references); for a review by Neil D. Warren, see 5:871 (8 references); for a review by Raymond A. Katzell, see 4:752; for a review by Joseph E. Moore, see 3:667.

[726]
Creative Behavior Inventory.

Purpose: Designed to measure "behavioral characteristics associated with creativity."
Population: Grades 1–6, 7–12.
Publication Date: 1989.
Acronyms: CBI1, CBI2.
Scores, 5: Contact, Consciousness, Interest, Fantasy, Total.
Administration: Individual.
Levels, 2: I (elementary), II (secondary).
Price Data: Price data for materials including manual (70 pages) available from publisher.
Time: Administration time not reported.
Comments: Ratings by teachers; manual title is Understanding the Creative Activity of Students.
Author: Robert J. Kirschenbaum.
Publisher: Creative Learning Press, Inc.
Cross References: For a review by Richard M. Clark, see 11:93.

[727]
Creativity Assessment Packet.

Purpose: To assess creative potential.
Population: Ages 6 through 18.
Publication Date: 1980.
Acronym: CAP.
Administration: Group.
Price Data, 2006: $120 per complete kit including 25 of each test and manual (1980, 24 pages); $30 per manual; $25 per test form.
Authors: Frank Williams.
Publisher: PRO-ED.
a) TEST OF DIVERGENT THINKING.
Scores, 6: Fluency, Flexibility, Originality, Elaboration, Titles, Total.
Forms, 2: A, B.
Price Data: $25 per 25 tests (specify Form A or Form B).
Time: 20(25) minutes for grades 6-12; 25(30) minutes for grades 3-5.
b) TEST OF DIVERGENT FEELING.
Scores, 5: Curiosity, Imagination, Complexity, Risk-Taking, Total.
Price Data: $25 per 25 tests.
Time: 10(20) minutes.
c) THE WILLIAMS SCALE.
Scores, 9: Fluency, Flexibility, Originality, Elaboration, Curiosity, Imagination, Complexity, Risk-Taking, Total.

Price Data: $25 per 25 tests.
Time: Administration time not reported.
Comments: Ratings by parents and teachers.
Cross References: See T5:724 (6 references) and T4:682 (3 references); for reviews by Fred Damarin and Carl L. Rosen, see 9:280.

[728]
The Creatrix Inventory [Revised].

Purpose: Determines a person's "creative risk-taking propensity."
Population: Members of organizations.
Publication Dates: 1971–2006.
Scores, 2: Creativity, Risk Taking; plotted on matrix to determine 1 of 8 orientations: Sustainer, Modifier, Challenger, Practicalizer, Innovator, Synthesizer, Dreamer, Planner.
Administration: Group.
Price Data: Available from publisher.
Time: Administration time not reported.
Comments: Online administration and scoring; designed for self-assessment and educational purposes.
Authors: Richard E. Byrd and Jacqueline L. Byrd.
Publisher: Creatrix.
Cross References: For reviews by Harrison G. Gough and John F. Wakefield of an earlier version, see 11:95.

[729]
Cree Questionnaire.

Purpose: "To measure an individual's overall creative potential."
Population: Individuals in a variety of occupations; clients in vocational and career counseling.
Publication Dates: 1957–1995.
Acronym: CQ.
Scores, 11: Overall Creative Potential, plus 10 factorially determined dimension scores grouped under 4 broad headings: Social Orientation, Work Orientation, Internal Functioning, and Interests.
Administration: Individual or group.
Price Data, 2002: $114 per start-up kit including 25 test booklets, 25 score sheets, and interpretation and research manual; $54 per 25 test booklets (quantity discounts available); $45 per 25 score sheets; $28 per interpretation and research manual.
Time: No limit (approximately 20 minutes).
Authors: T. G. Thurstone and J. Melinger.
Publisher: Pearson Performance Solutions [No reply from publisher; status unknown].
Cross References: See T5:728 (1 reference); for a review by Janet M. Stoppard, see 9:282; see also T2:1149 (1 reference) and P:53 (3 references); for reviews of an earlier edition by Allyn Miles Munger and Theodor F. Naumann, see 6:84.

[730]
Crichton Vocabulary Scale.

Purpose: Designed to provide an index of a child's "acquired fund of verbal information."
Population: Ages 4.5–11.
Publication Dates: 1950–1988.
Acronym: CVS.
Scores, 3: Definitions of Set One, Definitions of Set Two, Total.
Administration: Individual.
Price Data: Available from publisher.
Time: Administration time not reported.
Comments: Designed for use with Raven's Progressive Matrices (2122).
Author: J. C. Raven.
Publisher: Oxford Psychologists Press, Ltd. [England].
Cross References: See T4:687 (3 references), T3:632 (2 references), and T2:491 (3 references); for a review by Morton Bortner, see 6:518 (1 reference); for reviews by Charlotte Banks and W. D. Wall, see 4:337.

[731]
Criterion Test of Basic Skills [2002 Edition].

Purpose: Developed to assess "the basic reading and arithmetic skills of individual students."
Population: Ages 6 through 11-11
Publication Dates: 1976–2002.
Acronym: CTOBS-2.
Administration: Individual.
Price Data, 2006: $112 per test kit including manual (2002, 136 pages), 25 Arithmetic recording forms, 25 Reading recording forms, 25 Math problem sheets, and test plates in vinyl folder; $25 per manual; $25 per 25 Arithmetic recording forms; $25 per 25 Reading recording forms; $12 per 25 Math problem sheets; 25 per set of test plates.
Time: (15–20) minutes.
Comments: "Criterion referenced."
Authors: James Evans, Kerth Lundell, and William Brown.
Publisher: Academic Therapy Publications
a) READING.
Scores, 7: Letter Recognition, Letter Sounding, Blending and Sequencing, Phonics Patterns, Multisyllable Words, Sight Words, Letter Writing.
b) ARITHMETIC.
Scores, 14: Correspondence, Numbers and Numerals, Addition, Subtraction, Multiplication, Division, Measurement, Telling Time, Symbols, Fractions, Decimals and Percents, Geometric Concepts, Pre-Algebra, Rounding and Estimations.
Cross References: See T3:635 (1 reference).

[732]
Criterion Validated Written Test for Emergency Medical Practitioner.

Purpose: Intended for the selection of paramedic personnel.
Population: Prospective paramedics.
Publication Dates: 1995-1999.
Scores: 7 subtests and total: Interest, Teamwork, Problem Solving—Common Sense, Problem Solving—Map Reading, Problem Solving—Logical Thinking, Problem Solving—Relevancy, Attentiveness, Total.
Administration: Group.
Form, 1: EMP 90.
Restricted Distribution: Distribution restricted to civil service commissions and qualified municipal officials.
Price Data: Available from publisher.
Time: 110 minutes.
Comments: Practice test, candidate study guide, and technical manual are available.
Author: McCann Associates, Inc.
Publisher: Vantage McCann Associates.

[733]
Criterion Validated Written Test for Fire Medic.

Purpose: Intended for the selection of cross-trained firefighter/fire medic candidates.
Population: Prospective firefighter/fire medic candidates.
Publication Dates: 1995-1999.
Scores: 7 subtests and total: Interest, Teamwork, Problem Solving—Common Sense, Problem Solving—Mechanical, Problem Solving—Logical Thinking, Problem Solving—Relevancy, Attentiveness, Total.
Administration: Group.
Form, 1: ESV-100.
Restricted Distribution: Distribution restricted to civil service commissions and qualified municipal officials.
Price Data: Available from publisher.
Time: 135 minutes.
Comments: Practice test, candidate study guide, and technical manual are available.
Author: McCann Associates, Inc.
Publisher: Vantage McCann Associates.

[734]
Criterion Validated Written Tests for Firefighter [Revised].

Purpose: For the selection of firefighter candidates.
Population: Prospective firefighters.
Publication Dates: 1976–1998.
Scores: 7 subtests and total: Interest in Firefighting, Compatibility, Map Reading, Spatial Visualization, Visual Pursuit, Understanding and Interpreting Table and Text Material About Firefighting, Mechanical Aptitude, Total.
Administration: Group.
Forms, 2: Form ESV-100, M-100.
Restricted Distribution: Distribution restricted to civil service commissions and qualified municipal officials.
Price Data: Available from publisher.
Time: 131(141) minutes.
Comments: Practice test and candidate study guide available.
Author: McCann Associates, Inc.
Publisher: Vantage McCann Associates, Inc.

[735]
Criterion Validated Written Tests for Police Officer [Revised].

Purpose: Designed for the selection of police officer candidates.
Population: Prospective police officers.
Publication Dates: 1980–2003.
Scores: 7 subtests and total: Observational Ability, Ability to Exercise Judgment and Common Sense, Interest in Police Work, Ability to Exercise Judgment—Map Reading, Ability to Exercise Judgment—Dealing With People, Ability to Read and Comprehend Police Test Material, Reasoning Ability, Total.
Administration: Group.
Forms, 2: Form ESV 100, Form N-100.
Restricted Distribution: Distribution restricted to civil service commissions and qualified municipal officials.
Price Data: Available from publisher.
Time: 170(180) minutes.
Comments: Practice test and candidate study guide available.
Author: McCann Associates, Inc.
Publisher: Vantage McCann Associates.

[736]
Critical Reasoning Test Battery.

Purpose: To assist students in subject and career choices and employers with the selection of job candidates.
Population: Students and employees ages 15 and over.
Publication Dates: 1981–1983.
Acronym: CRTB.
Administration: Group.
Restricted Distribution: Distribution restricted to persons who have completed the publisher's training course or members of the Division of Occupational Psychology of the British Psychological Society.
Price Data: Available from publisher.
Comments: 3 subtests available as separates.
Authors: Peter Saville, Roger Holdsworth, Gill Nyfield, David Hawkey, Susan Bawtree, and Ruth Holdsworth.
Publisher: SHL Group plc [United Kingdom].

a) VERBAL EVALUATION.
Publication Dates: 1982–1983.
Acronym: VC1.
Time: 30(35) minutes.
b) INTERPRETING DATA.
Publication Dates: 1982–1983.
Acronym: NC2.
Time: 30(35) minutes.
c) DIAGRAMMATIC SERIES.
Publication Dates: 1982–1983.
Acronym: DC3.
Time: 20(25) minutes.

[737]
Cross-Cultural Adaptability Inventory.

Purpose: "Designed to provide information to an individual about his or her potential for cross-cultural effectiveness."
Population: Trainers and professionals who work with culturally diverse and cross-culturally oriented populations.
Publication Dates: 1987–1995.
Acronym: CCAI.
Scores: 4 scales: Emotional Resilience, Flexibility/ Openness, Perceptual Acuity, Personal Autonomy.
Administration: Group.
Price Data: Available from publisher.
Time: (15–30) minutes.
Comments: Observer-rating survey is optional.
Authors: Colleen Kelley and Judith Meyers.
Publisher: Pearson Performance Solutions [No reply from publisher; status unknown].
Cross References: For reviews by Lynn L. Brown and Wendy Naumann, see 14:107.

[738]
Cross Reference Test.

Purpose: Constructed to assess "skill in routine checking tasks."
Population: Clerical job applicants.
Publication Date: 1959.
Scores: Total score only.
Administration: Group.
Price Data: Available from publisher.
Time: 5(10) minutes.
Author: James W. Curtis.
Publisher: Psychometric Affiliates.
Cross References: For a review by Philip H. Kriedt, see 6:1039.

[739]
CRS Placement/Diagnostic Test.

Purpose: Designed to diagnose and locate the student's CRS (Crane Reading System) level.
Population: Grades Preprimer-2.
Publication Dates: 1977-1978.
Scores: Total score only.

Administration: Group.
Price Data: Price information for test materials including general directions (1977, 7 pages) available from publisher.
Foreign Language Edition: Spanish version available.
Time: Administration time not reported.
Authors: Barbara J. Crane.
Publisher: Bilingual Educational Services, Inc.
a) ENGLISH VERSION.
1) *Level A.*
Population: Grade Preprimer.
Subtests, 4: Rhyming, Words That Begin Alike, Long Vowel Recognition, Consonant Sounds.
2) *Levels B, C, and D (Beginning Consonant Sounds).*
Population: Preprimer-primer.
Comments: Levels determined by number of errors.
3) *Level E (Blends).*
Population: Grade 1.
4) *Level F (Vowel Recognition).*
Population: Grade 1.
5) *Level G (Digraphs).*
Population: Grade 1.
6) *Levels H, I, and J (Special Vowel Patterns).*
Population: Grades 1-2.
Comments: Levels determined by number of errors.
b) SPANISH VERSION.
1) *Level A.*
Subtests, 2: Rhyming, Words That Begin Alike.
2) *Level B (Beginning Consonant Sounds—S, M, F, R, N, L, Z).*
3) *Level C (Beginning Consonant Sounds—B, P, T, D, V, CH).*
4) *Level D (Beginning Consonant Sounds—C, G, LL, Q, J, Y).*
5) *Level E (Special Patterns).*

[740]
CTB Writing Assessment System.

Purpose: "Includes direct and indirect writing measures to aid educators in evaluating writing programs and students' writing abilities."
Population: Grades 2.0–12.9.
Publication Date: 1993.
Scores, 6: Holistic, Analytic (Content, Organization, Sentence Construction, Vocabulary/Grammar, Spelling/Capitalization).
Administration: Group.
Levels, 4: 12–13 (grades 2.0–4.2), 14–16 (grades 3.6–7.2), 17–19 (grades 6.6–10.2), and 20–22 (grades 9.6–12.9 and adults).

Price Data, 2002: $53.35 per 30 consumable Writing books including administration and scoring manual (specify Narrative, Descriptive, Informative, or Persuasive and specify level); $41.80 per 30 Writing books with independent prompts only (Specify Narrative, Descriptive, Informative, or Persuasive and specify level); $23.10 per 50 Student Information and Score Sheets; additional price information and information regarding scoring services available from publisher.
Comments: Includes books 1–32 with a writing assignment called a "prompt"; each book comes with its own manual; books are available as separates; overall guide is entitled Writing Assessment Guide.
Author: CTB Macmillan/McGraw-Hill.
Publisher: CTB/McGraw-Hill.
> *a)* LEVEL 12–13.
> **Population:** Grades 2.0–4.2
> **Time:** 30–35(35–40) minutes.
> **Comments:** 4 books (Personal Expression—Descriptive [Books 1 & 4], Personal Expression—Narrative [Books 2 & 3]) available as separates.
> *b)* LEVEL 14–16.
> **Population:** Grades 3.6–7.2.
> **Time:** 30–35(35–40) minutes.
> **Comments:** 8 books (Personal Expression—Descriptive [Books 5 & 8], Personal Expression—Narrative [Books 6 & 7], and Informative [Books 9–12]) available as separates.
> *c)* LEVEL 17–19.
> **Population:** Grades 6.6–10.2.
> **Time:** 40–45(45–50) minutes.
> **Comments:** 10 books (Personal Expression—Narrative [Books 13 & 14], Informative [Books 15–18], Persuasive [Books 19–22]) available as separates.
> *d)* LEVEL 20–22.
> **Population:** Grades 9.6–12.9.
> **Time:** 40–45(45–50) minutes.
> **Comments:** 10 books (Personal Expression—Narrative [Books 23 & 24], Informative [Books 25–28], Persuasive [Books 29–32]) available as separates.
Cross References: For reviews by George Engelhard, Jr. and Joe B. Hansen, see 13:88.

[741]
Cultural Competence Self-Assessment Instrument.
Purpose: Designed "to help agencies measure their cultural competency in agency policymaking, administrative procedures, and practices."
Population: Business staff and clients of child welfare agencies.
Publication Date: 1993.
Scores: Not scored.
Administration: Group.

Price Data: Price information available from publisher for instrument including manual (48 pages).
Time: Administration time not reported.
Author: Child Welfare League of America, Inc.
Publisher: Child Welfare League of America, Inc.

[742]
Culture Fair Intelligence Test.
Purpose: Designed to measure individual intelligence with minimal influence from verbal fluency, educational level, and ethnic/racial group membership.
Publication Dates: 1950-1973.
Acronym: CFIT.
Scores: Total scores only.
Administration: Group or individual.
Foreign Language Editions: Information regarding many non-English-language adaptations available from publisher.
Comments: Formerly called Culture Free Intelligence Test; test booklet title is Test of "g": Culture Fair.
Authors: Raymond B. Cattell and A. Karen S. Cattell (Scales 2 and 3).
Publisher: Institute for Personality and Ability Testing, Inc. (IPAT).
> *a)* SCALE 1.
> **Population:** Ages 4–8 and developmentally delayed persons.
> **Administration:** Individual.
> **Price Data, 2005:** $64 per introductory kit including 25 test booklets, scoring key, reusable classification cards, and handbook (1950, 15 pages); $27 per 25 test booklets; $8 per scoring key: $22 per reusable classification test cards; $7 per handbook; $16 per specimen set including test booklet, scoring key, and handbook.
> **Time:** (22) minutes (untimed).
> **Comments:** Identical to Cattell Intelligence Tests, Scale O: Dartington Scale; materials for Test 5 (Following Directions) must be assembled locally.
> *b)* SCALE 2.
> **Population:** Ages 8–14 and adults.
> **Forms, 2:** A, B.
> **Price Data:** $51 per introductory kit including test booklet, scoring keys, answer sheets, manual (1973, 27 pages), and technical supplement (1973, 30 pages); $27 per 25 test booklets (specify Form A or B); $8 per scoring keys for answer sheets; $8 per scoring keys for test booklets; $18 per 50 answer sheets; $15 per manual; $15 per technical supplement.
> **Time:** 12.5 minutes.
> *c)* SCALE 3.
> **Population:** Adults.
> **Forms, 2:** A, B.

Price Data: Same as *b* above.
Time: 12.5 minutes.
Cross References: See T5:745 (25 references), T4:699 (34 references), 9:290 (13 references), T3:643 (51 references), 8:184 (38 references), and T2:364 (61 references); for reviews by John E. Milholland and Abraham J. Tannenbaum, see 6:453 (15 references); for a review by I. MacFarlane Smith of *a*, see 5:343 (11 references); for reviews by Raleigh M. Drake and Gladys C. Schwesinger, see 4:300 (2 references).

[743]
Culture-Free Self-Esteem Inventories, Third Edition.

Purpose: "A set of self-report inventories used to determine the level of self-esteem in students ages 6-0 through 18-11."
Population: Ages 6-0 through 8-11.
Publication Dates: 1981–2002.
Acronym: CFSEI-3.
Administration: Group.
Levels, 3: Primary, Intermediate, Adolescent.
Price Data, 2006: $184 per complete kit including manual (2002, 60 pages); $28 per 50 primary examiner/record forms; $28 per 50 intermediate profile/scoring forms; $28 per 50 intermediate student response forms; $28 per 50 adolescent profile/scoring forms; $28 per 50 adolescent student response forms; $51 per manual.
Time: (15–20) minutes.
Comments: Newly normed revision of Culture-Free Self-Esteem Inventories, Second Edition; all levels include Defensiveness Score (a lie scale); previous editions entitled Culture-Free Self-Esteem Inventories for Children and Adults; derivative entitled North American Depression Inventories for Children and Adults (T5:1803).
Author: James Battle.
Publisher: PRO-ED.
　a) PRIMARY.
　Population: Ages 6–8.
　Score: Global Self-Esteem Quotient.
　Price Data: $28 per 50 primary examiner/record forms.
　b) INTERMEDIATE.
　Population: Ages 9–12.
　Scores, 5: Academic, General, Parental/Home, Social, Global Self-Esteem Quotient.
　Price Data: $28 per 50 intermediate profile/scoring forms; $28 per 50 intermediate student response forms.
　c) ADOLESCENT.
　Population: Ages 13–18.
　Scores, 6: Academic, General, parental/Home, Social, Personal, Global Self-Esteem Quotient.
　Price Data: $28 per 50 adolescent profile/scoring forms, $28 per 50 adolescent student response forms.

Cross References: For reviews by Bethany A. Brunsman and Y. Evie Garcia, see 15:72; see T5:746 (4 references); for reviews by Michael G. Kavan and Michael J. Subkoviak of a previous edition, see 12:100 (7 references); see also T4:700 (9 references); for reviews by Gerald R. Adams and Janet Morgan Riggs of the original edition, see 9:291 (1 reference); see also T3:644 (1 reference). For reviews by Patricia A. Bachelor and Michael G. Kavan of the North American Depression Inventories for Children and Adults, see 11:265 (1 reference).

[744]
Curtis Interest Scale.

Purpose: Developed to identify vocational interest patterns.
Population: Grades 9–16 and adults.
Publication Date: 1959.
Scores, 10: Business, Mechanics, Applied Arts, Direct Sales, Production, Science, Entertainment, Interpersonal, Computation, Farming; 1 rating: Desire for Responsibility.
Administration: Group.
Price Data: Available from publisher.
Time: (6–12) minutes.
Comments: Self-administered.
Author: James W. Curtis.
Publisher: Psychometric Affiliates.
Cross References: See T2:2177 (1 reference); for reviews by Warren T. Norman and Leona E. Tyler, see 6:1052.

[745]
[Curtis Object Completion and Space Form Tests].

Purpose: "Devised to provide estimates of individual competence in two basic areas of mechanical aptitude and pattern visualization."
Population: Applicants for mechanical and technical jobs.
Publication Dates: 1960–1961.
Scores: Total scores only.
Administration: Group.
Price Data: Available from publisher.
Time: 1(6) minutes per test.
Author: James W. Curtis.
Publisher: Psychometric Affiliates.
　a) OBJECT-COMPLETION TEST.
　b) SPACE FORM TEST.
Cross References: For reviews by Richard S. Melton and I. Macfarlane Smith, see 6:1085.

[746]
Curtis Verbal-Clerical Skills Tests.

Purpose: "Devised to provide estimates of individual competence in ... verbal skill usually identified with office and clerical work."

Population: Applicants for clerical positions.
Publication Dates: 1963–1965.
Acronym: CVCST.
Scores: 4 tests: Computation, Checking, Comprehension, Capacity.
Administration: Group.
Price Data: Available from publisher.
Time: 8(10) minutes.
Author: James W. Curtis.
Publisher: Psychometric Affiliates.

[747]
Customer Reaction Survey.

Purpose: Assesses customers' perceptions of salespeople's interpersonal skills.
Population: Salespeople.
Publication Dates: 1972-1995.
Acronym: CRS.
Scores, 4: Observed Exposure, Observed Feedback, Preferred Exposure, Preferred Feedback.
Administration: Group.
Price Data, 2006: $9.95 per instrument.
Time: Administration time not reported.
Comments: Ratings by customers; also called Customer Reaction Index; based on the Johari Window Model of interpersonal relations.
Authors: Jay Hall and C. Leo Griffith.
Publisher: Teleometrics International, Inc.

[748]
Customer Service Applicant Inventory.

Purpose: "Evaluates skills and attitudes to help hire customer service oriented, honest, safe, and productive employees."
Population: Job applicants.
Publication Date: 1996.
Acronym: CSAI.
Scores, 12: Validity Scales (Candidness, Accuracy), Interpersonal Scales (Customer Service, Teamwork, Communication, Stress Tolerance), Core Values (Honesty, Drug Avoidance, Safety), Supplemental Scales (Applied Math, Training Readiness), Composite (Employability Index).
Administration: Group or individual.
Price Data: Available from publisher.
Time: (45) minutes.
Comments: Paper-and-pencil or computer administration available.
Author: Pearson Performance Solutions [No reply from publisher; status unknown].
Publisher: Pearson Reid London House.

[749]
Customer Service Profile.

Purpose: Designed to "identify qualified people for service positions by measuring important attitudes and aptitudes."

Population: Ages 18 and over.
Publication Date: 1994.
Acronym: CSP.
Scores, 6: Validity-Candidness, Validity-Accuracy, Customer Service Attitude, Customer Service Aptitude, Sales Aptitude, Customer Service Index.
Administration: Individual or group.
Price Data, 2005: $16 including 1–999 reports for Internet scoring with booklets; $16 including 1–999 reports for Internet scoring without booklets; $16 including 1–999 reports for QuantaTouch Test; $16 including 1–999 reports for QUANTA Software for Windows with booklets; $16 including 1–999 reports for QUANTA Software for Windows without booklets.
Time: (20–25) minutes.
Comments: Test can be scored using operator-assisted telephone scoring, touch-test telephone scoring, Quanta-based scoring, or mail-in scoring.
Authors: Reid London House.
Publisher: Pearson Performance Solutions [No reply from publisher; status unknown].

[750]
Customer Service Simulator.

Purpose: "Designed to identify individuals who can solve problems while projecting responsiveness and sensitivity, and who avoid making common interpersonal errors in dealing with customers."
Population: Any position requiring public contact.
Publication Dates: 1993–2006.
Acronym: CSS.
Scores, 3: Customer Service Orientation, Interpersonal Sensitivity, Total.
Administration: Group or individual.
Forms, 2: Private and public sector forms: Clerical/Customer Service Representative Version, Supervision Version.
Restricted Distribution: Clients may be required to pay a nominal one-time overhead/sign-up fee.
Price Data, 2006: $90 per candidate for rental/scoring and feedback report of Clerical/Customer Service Representative Version; and $110 per candidate for the Supervisor Version.
Time: 90 minutes.
Author: Richard C. Joines.
Publisher: Management & Personnel Systems, Inc.

[751]
Customer Service Skills Inventory.

Purpose: Designed to "assess customer service skills across a variety of customer-contact jobs."
Population: Ages 18 and over.
Publication Dates: 1993–1995.
Acronym: CSSI.
Scores, 8: Pressure Tolerance, Realistic Orientation, Time Appraisal, Independent Judgment, Responsive-

ness, Sensitivity, Balanced Judgment, Precision Orientation.
Administration: Group or individual.
Price Data, 2005: $139 per start-up kit including examiner's manual (1995, 34 pages) and 10 test booklets; $139 per QUANTA start-up kit including examiner's manual and 10 administrations and scoring (does not include QUANTA software); $28 per examiner's manual; $127 per 10 tests (quantity discounts available).
Time: (25–30) minutes.
Comments: Test can be administered over the Internet or via paper and pencil; can be scored via Internet, QUANTA software, or self-scoring.
Authors: Juan I. Sanchez and Simon L. Fraser.
Publisher: Pearson Performance Solutions [No reply from publisher; status unknown].

[752]
Customer Service Skills Test.

Purpose: To evaluate technical and interpersonal skills of persons for the customer service position; available also to measure computer use skills.
Population: Candidates for customer service positions.
Publication Date: 1992.
Acronym: BASLCUS.
Scores: Total Score, Narrative Evaluation, Ranking, Recommendation.
Administration: Group.
Price Data, 2001: $150 per candidate; quantity discounts available.
Foreign Language Edition: Available in French.
Time: (70) minutes.
Comments: Scored by publisher; available in booklet and internet versions; must be proctored.
Author: Walden Personnel Performance, Inc.
Publisher: Walden Personnel Performance, Inc. [Canada].
Cross References: For reviews by Wayne J. Camara and Jean Powell Kirnan, see 16:68.

[753]
D-1, D-2, and D-3 Police Officer Tests.

Purpose: "Designed to assess the basic abilities identified as being important for successful performance as a police officer."
Population: Candidates for entry-level police officer positions.
Publication Dates: 1999-2006.
Scores: 5 job dimensions: Observation and Memory [Wanted Posters], Ability to Learn Police Material, Police Interest Questionnaire [Non-Cognitive], Verbal and Reading Comprehension (all but D-1), Situational Judgment and Problem Solving.
Administration: Individual or group.
Forms, 3: D-1, D-2, D-3.

Price Data: Available from publisher.
Time: 130 minutes per test.
Comments: D-1, D-2, D-3 are comparable forms; no prior training or experience as a police officer is assumed of candidates taking any of the three forms.
Authors: International Public Management Association for Human Resources & Bruce Davey Associates.
Publisher: International Public Management Association for Human Resources (IPMA-HR).

[754]
d2 Test of Attention.

Purpose: Designed to measure processing speed, rule compliance, and quality of performance, allowing for a neuropsychological estimation of individual attention and concentration performance.
Population: Children, adolescents, and adults.
Publication Date: 1998.
Acronym: d2 Test.
Scores: Score information available from publisher.
Administration: Individual and group.
Price Data, 2006: $68 per complete test including 20 recording blanks, set of 2 scoring keys, and manual (1998, 80 pages); $12.50 per 50 recording blanks; $18 per set of 2 scoring keys; $45 per manual.
Time: (8) minutes.
Comments: Originally conceived to assess individuals' suitability for driving, the test has also been used as a part of personnel selection in other workplace environments where high levels of visual attention and concentration are demanded.
Authors: Rolf Brickenkamp and Eric Zillmer.
Publisher: Hogrefe & Huber Publishers.
Cross References: For reviews by Phillip L. Ackerman and Elaine Clark, see 15:87.

[755]
DABERON-2: Screening for School Readiness, Second Edition.

Purpose: Developed to provide a standardized assessment of school readiness.
Population: Ages 3-0 to 7-11.
Publication Dates: 1972–1991.
Scores: Total score only.
Administration: Individual.
Price Data, 2006: $170 per complete kit including 24 presentation cards, 25 screen forms, 25 readiness reports, 5 classroom summary forms, object kit of manipulatives, and administration manual (1991, 38 pages); $15 per set of presentation cards; $35 per 25 screen forms; $35 per 25 readiness reports; $15 per 5 classroom summary forms; $35 per object kit of manipulatives; $50 per administration manual.
Time: (20-40) minutes.
Authors: Virginia A. Danzer, Mary Frances Gerber, Theresa M. Lyons, and Judith K. Voress.

Publisher: PRO-ED.
Cross References: For reviews by Stephen N. Axford and Selma Hughes, see 11:100 (1 reference).

[756]
Das•Naglieri Cognitive Assessment System.

Purpose: "To provide a cognitive processing measure of ability that is fair to minority children, effective for differential diagnosis, and related to intervention."
Population: Ages 5 to 17-11.
Publication Date: 1997.
Levels, 2: Ages 5–7, ages 8–17.
Price Data, 2006: $800.50 per complete kit including stimulus book, administration and scoring manual (305 pages), interpretive handbook, 10 record forms, 5 response booklets ages 5-7, 5 response booklets ages 8-17, 10 figure memory response booklets, scoring templates, and red pencil all in a canvas bag; $65.50 per administration and scoring manual; $65.50 per interpretive manual; $38.50 per 25 record forms; $24.50 per 25 response booklets; $24.50 per figure memory response booklets.
Comments: PASS theory reconceptualizes intelligence as cognitive processes.
Authors: Jack A. Naglieri and J. P. Das.
Publisher: Riverside Publishing.
   a) STANDARD BATTERY.
   Scores: 4 scales with 13 subtests: Planning (Matching Numbers, Planned Codes, Planned Connections), Simultaneous (Nonverbal Matrices, Verbal-Spatial Relations, Figure Memory), Attention (Expressive Attention, Number Detection, Receptive Attention), Successive (Word Series, Sentence Repetition, Speech Rate, Sentence Questions).
   Time: [60] minutes.
   b) BASIC BATTERY.
   Scores: 4 scales with 8 subtests: Planning (Matching Numbers, Planned Codes), Simultaneous (Nonverbal Matrices, Verbal-Spatial Relations), Attention (Expressive Attention, Number Detection), Successive (Word Series, Sentence Repetition).
   Time: [40] minutes.
Cross References: For reviews by Joyce Meikamp and Donald Thompson, see 14:109; see also T5:763 (5 references).

[757]
Database Analyst Staff Selector.

Purpose: To evaluate the analytical reasoning and detail skills necessary for successful performance as a database analyst.
Population: Candidates for database positions.
Publication Date: 1992.
Acronym: DBPRDF.
Scores: Total Score, Narrative Evaluation, Ranking, Recommendation.

Administration: Group.
Price Data, 2001: $340 per candidate.
Time: (85) minutes.
Comments: Scored by publisher; must be proctored.
Author: Walden Personnel Performance, Inc.
Publisher: Walden Personnel Performance, Inc. [Canada].

[758]
A Dating Scale.

Purpose: To measure "liberalism of attitudes toward dating."
Population: Adolescents and adults.
Publication Dates: 1962–1988.
Scores: Total score only.
Administration: Group.
Manual: No manual.
Price Data, 2005: $2 per scale.
Time: [10] minutes.
Comments: Supplementary article available.
Author: Panos D. Bardis.
Publisher: Donna Bardis.
Cross References: For additional information and a review by Charles F. Warnath, see 8:335 (3 references).

[759]
Davidson Trauma Scale.

Purpose: "Developed to assess post traumatic stress disorder (PTSD) symptoms and aid in treatment."
Population: Adults who have been exposed to a serious trauma.
Publication Date: 1996.
Acronym: DTS.
Scores, 4: Intrusion, Avoidance/Numbing, Hyperarousal, Total.
Administration: Individual or group.
Price Data, 2006: $76 per complete kit including manual (42 pages), and 25 QuikScore™ forms; $36 per 25 QuikScore™ forms; $55 per manual.
Foreign Language Edition: French-Canadian QuikScore™ forms available.
Time: (10) minutes.
Comments: Self-report.
Author: Jonathan Davidson.
Publisher: Multi-Health Systems, Inc.
Cross References: For reviews by Janet F. Carlson and William E. Martin, Jr., see 14:110.

[760]
DCS—A Visual Learning and Memory Test for Neuropsychological Assessment.

Purpose: Designed as "a learning and memory test for detecting memory deficits resulting from neurological disorders."
Population: Ages 6–70.

Publication Date: 1998.
Scores: Score information available from publisher.
Administration: Individual.
Price Data, 2006: $89 per complete kit including folder, 50 record and evaluation sheets, 18 test cards, 5 wooden sticks, and manual (1998, 48 pages); $15 per 50 record and evaluation sheets; $30 per set of 18 test cards and 5 wooden sticks; $39.50 per manual.
Time: (20–60) minutes.
Authors: Georg Lamberti and Sigrid Weidlich.
Publisher: Hogrefe & Huber Publishers.
Cross References: For a review by Andrew S. Davis and Rik Carl D'Amato, see 15:73.

[761]
Dean-Woodcock Neuropsychological Battery.

Purpose: Designed to provide a "comprehensive assessment of sensory-motor functioning."
Population: Ages 4-0 and over.
Publication Date: 2003.
Acronym: DWNB.
Administration: Individual.
Price Data, 2006: $300.50 per complete kit including manual (269 pages), 25 test records, 25 interview forms, 25 emotional status forms, and a plastic storage box containing a comb, scissors, key, candle, nail, paper clip, pen, ball, plastic fork, plastic spoon, stylus, eye occluder, and three blindfolds; $45.50 per 25 test records; $37.50 per 25 interview forms; $54.50 per 25 emotional status forms.
Comments: Examiner's manual provides verbal instructions in Spanish and English.
Authors: Raymond S. Dean and Richard W. Woodcock.
Publisher: Riverside Publishing.
  a) DEAN-WOODCOCK SENSORY-MOTOR BATTERY.
  Acronym: DWSMB.
  Scores, 21: Sensory (Near Point Visual Acuity, Visual Confrontation, Naming Pictures of Objects, Auditory Acuity), Tactile (Palm Writing, Object Identification, Finger Identification, Simultaneous Localization, Total), Motor (Lateral Preference, Gait and Station, Romberg, Construction, Coordination, Mime Movements, Left-Right Movements, Finger Tapping, Expressive Speech, Grip Strength, Total), Impairment Index.
  Time: (30+45) minutes.
  b) DEAN-WOODCOCK STRUCTURED NEUROPSYCHOLOGICAL INTERVIEW.
  Scores: Not scored.
  Time: (30) minutes.
  Comments: Structured interview can be administered to the subject, a parent, or "other informant who knows the subject well."

  c) DEAN-WOODCOCK EMOTIONAL STATUS EXAMINATION.
  Scores: Not scored.
  Time: (30) minutes.
  Comments: May be administered to subject or to an informant.

[762]
Decision Making Inventory.

Purpose: "Designed to assess an individual's preferred style of decision making."
Population: High school and college, working adults.
Publication Dates: 1983–1986.
Acronym: DMI.
Scores, 4: Information Gathering Style (Spontaneous, Systematic), Information Processing Style (Internal, External).
Administration: Group.
Forms, 2: H, I.
Price Data: Available from publisher.
Time: (10) minutes.
Authors: William C. Coscarelli, Richard Johnson (test), and JaDean Johnson (test).
Publisher: Jossey-Bass, A Wiley Company.
Cross References: See T5:768 (2 references); for reviews by George Domino and Barbara A. Kerr, see 10:77 (3 references).

[763]
Decoding Skills Test.

Purpose: Measures the reading levels and decoding skills of elementary school readers and identifies reading disabled children and provides a diagnostic profile of their decoding skill development.
Population: Grades 1.0-5.8+.
Publication Date: 1985.
Acronym: DST.
Scores: 3 subtests yielding 12 scores: Basal Vocabulary (Instructional Level, Frustration Level), Phonic Patterns (Monosyllabic, Polysyllabic), Contextual Decoding (Instructional Level [Reading Rate, Error Rate, Phonic Words, Comprehension], Frustration Level [Reading Rate, Error Rate, Phonic Words, Comprehension]).
Administration: Individual.
Price Data, 2006: $154 per complete kit including reusable Presentation Book, 10 scoring booklets, and manual; $71.50 per 1 reusable Presentation Book; $68.50 per 2+ books; $37.95 per scoring booklet; $50 per manual.
Time: 15-30 minutes.
Comments: "Criterion-referenced."
Authors: Ellis Richardson and Barbara DiBenedetto.
Publisher: Western Psychological Services.
Cross References: See T5:769 (8 references); for reviews by Stephen N. Elliott and Timothy S. Hartshorne, see 10:78.

[764]

Defendant Questionnaire.

Purpose: "Designed for defendant (misdemeanor or felony) assessment in court settings."
Population: Defendants (misdemeanor or felony).
Publication Date: 1997.
Acronym: DQ.
Scores: 7 scales: Truthfulness, Alcohol, Drugs, Substance Abuse/Dependency, Violence (Lethality), Antisocial, Stress Coping Abilities.
Administration: Group.
Price Data: Available from publisher.
Foreign Language Editions: Available in English and Spanish.
Time: Administration time not reported.
Comments: Can be administered via paper and pencil test booklet, directly on computer screen, optically scanned answer sheet, human voice audio via headset and computer.
Author: Risk & Needs Assessment, Inc.
Publisher: Risk & Needs Assessment, Inc.

[765]

Defining Issues Test.

Purpose: "Gives information about the process by which people judge what ought to be done in moral dilemmas."
Population: Grades 9-12 and college and adults.
Publication Dates: 1979-1987.
Acronym: DIT.
Scores, 12: Consistency Check, M (meaningless items) score, P (principled moral thinking) score, U (utilizer) score, D (composite) score, A (antiestablishment) score, and stage scores (2, 3, 4, 5A, 5B, and 6).
Administration: Group.
Forms, 2: Short form, long form.
Price Data, 2001: $25 per manual including both forms and scoring information (1986, 96 pages); scoring service available from publisher; $1.90 or less per prepaid scoring sheet including all reports, handling costs, etc.
Time: (30-40) minutes for short form; (40-50) minutes for long form.
Comments: 2 optional companion booklets available: Development in Judging Moral Issues from the Center for the Study of Ethical Development, and Moral Development: Advances in Theory and Research from Praeger Press.
Authors: James R. Rest, with model computer scoring programs by Steve Thoma, Mark Davison, Stephen Robbins, and David Swanson.
Publisher: Center for the Study of Ethical Development.
Cross References: See T5:771 (28 references) and T4:724 (10 references); for reviews by Rosemary E. Sutton and by Bert W. Westbrook and K. Denise Bane,

see 11:104 (34 references); for reviews by Robert R. McCrae and Kevin L. Moreland, see 9:304 (22 references); see also T3:666 (8 references).

[766]

DeGangi-Berk Test of Sensory Integration.

Purpose: "Designed to overcome problems in detecting sensory integrative dysfunction in the early years."
Population: Ages 3–5.
Publication Date: 1983.
Acronym: TSI.
Scores, 4: Postural Control, Bilateral Motor Integration, Reflex Integration, Total.
Administration: Individual.
Price Data, 2006: $192.50 per complete kit including set of test materials, 25 star design sheets, 25 protocol booklets, and manual (48 pages) in a carrying case; $29 per 100 star designs; $29 per 25 protocol booklets; $42.50 per manual.
Time: (30) minutes.
Comments: Other test materials (e.g., stopwatch, carpeted scooter board, hula hoop) must be supplied by examiner.
Authors: Georgia A. DeGangi and Ronald A. Berk.
Publisher: Western Psychological Services.
Cross References: See T5:772 (2 references); for a review by R. A. Bornstein, see 10:80.

[767]

Degrees of Reading Power [Primary and Standard Test Forms J & K and Advanced Test Forms T & U].

Purpose: Designed to provide direct criterion-referenced, performance measures of reading comprehension.
Population: Grades 1–12 and over.
Publication Dates: 1979–2002.
Acronym: DRP.
Scores: Total DRP score.
Administration: Group.
Levels, 3: Primary, Standard, Advanced.
Price Data, 2006: $53 per Primary/Standard examination set including 1 copy of each J series test form, 5 answer sheets, 1 J & K tests handbook (2000, 124 pages), and 1 norms booklet; $20 per 25 answer sheets (Standard and Advanced tests); $9.50 per 3-year license to use answer sheets per package of test booklets ordered; $36 per J & K tests handbook; $33 per Primary/Standard norms booklet; $20 per 5 test administration procedures (specify Primary, Standard, or Advanced); $32 per Degrees of Reading Power Program technical manual; $19 per scoring key or scoring overlay per test form.
Time: (45) minutes.
Comments: Practice exercises provided; provides readability analysis of instructional material in print; computer or hand scored; group profiles, optional reports, services, and software also available.

Authors: Touchstone Applied Science Associates (TASA), Inc.
Publisher: Touchstone Applied Science Associates (TASA), Inc.

a) PRIMARY.
Purpose: To provide a measure of how well students understand the meaning of text.
Population: Grades 1–3.
Forms, 2: J, K.
Levels, 2: 0, 9.
Price Data: $166 per Primary classroom set including 25 practice exercises, 25 test booklets, 25 answer sheets, test administration procedures, J & K tests handbook, norms booklet, and teacher class profile; $16 per 25 Primary practice exercises; $99 per 25 consumable Primary test booklets including 1 test administration procedures.

b) STANDARD.
Purpose: To provide a measure of how well students understand the meaning of text.
Population: Grades 3–12 and over.
Forms, 2: J, K.
Levels, 5: 8, 7, 6, 4, 2.
Price Data: $166 per Standard classroom set including 25 practice exercises, 25 test booklets, 25 answer sheets, test administration procedures, J & K tests handbook, norms booklet, and teacher class profile; $16 per 25 Standard practice exercises; $79 per reusable Standard test booklets including 1 test administration procedures.

c) ADVANCED.
Purpose: To assess how well students are able to reason with textual materials.
Population: Grades 6–12 and over.
Forms, 2: T, U.
Levels, 2: 4, 2.
Price Data: $45 per Advanced examination set including 1 T4 test booklet, 1 T2 test booklet, 5 answer sheets, and Advanced handbook (2002, 98 pages); $149 per Advanced classroom set including 25 practice exercises, 25 test booklets, 25 answer sheets, test administration procedures, and Advanced handbook; $18 per 25 Advanced practice exercises; $89 per 25 Advanced test booklets; $38 per Advanced handbook (T & U test forms).
Cross References: For reviews by Jeffrey K. Smith and Keith F. Widaman, see 16:69; for reviews by Felice J. Green and Howard Margolis of a previous edition, see 14:111; see also T5:773 (5 references); for reviews by Darrell N. Caulley, Elaine Furniss, and Michael McNamara and by Lawrence Cross of an earlier edition, see 12:101 (9 references); see also T4:726 (14 references); for reviews by Roger Bruning and Gerald S. Hanna of an earlier edition, see 9:305 (1 reference).

[768]
Degrees of Word Meaning.

Purpose: Developed to "assess the size of students' reading vocabularies by measuring their understanding of the meaning of words in naturally occurring contexts."
Population: Grades 3–8+.
Publication Date: 1993.
Acronym: DWM.
Scores: Total score only.
Administration: Group.
Levels: 6 overlapping levels.
Price Data, 2005: $32 per user's manual (96 pages); $17 per 5 test administration procedures; $50 per 30 test booklets (select level); $12.50 per 30 practice booklets; $16 per 30 NCS answer sheets; $14 per scoring key (select level).
Time: Untimed.
Authors: Touchstone Applied Science Associates (TASA), Inc.
Publisher: Touchstone Applied Science Associates (TASA), Inc.
Cross References: For reviews by David P. Hurford and Judith A. Monsaas, see 13:90.

[769]
Delaware County Silent Reading Test, Second Edition.

Purpose: "Designed to measure pupil achievement in typical . . . reading materials."
Population: Grades 1.5, 2, 2.5, 3, 3.5, 4, 5, 6, 7, 8.
Publication Date: 1965.
Scores, 5: Interpretation, Organization, Vocabulary, Structural Analysis, Total.
Administration: Group.
Levels, 10: Grades 1.5, 2, 2.5, 3, 3.5, 4, 5, 6, 7, 8.
Manual: No manual.
Price Data: Available from publisher.
Time: Administration time not reported.
Comments: Teacher's guide for each level.
Authors: Judson E. Newburg and Nicholas A. Spennato.
Publisher: Delaware County Intermediate Unit.
Cross References: For a review by Allen Berger, see 7:686.

[770]
Delis-Kaplan Executive Function System.

Purpose: To "comprehensive assess ... the key components of executive functions believed to be mediated primarily by the frontal lobe."
Population: 8–89 years.
Publication Date: 2001.
Acronym: D-KEFS.
Scores: 9 tests: Trail Making Test, Verbal Fluency Test, Design Fluency Test, Color-Word Interference

Test, Sorting Test, 20 Questions Test, Word Context Test, Tower Test, Proverb Test.

Administration: Individual.

Price Data, 2001: $415 per complete kit in box including manual (388 pages), stimulus booklet, sorting cards (3 sets of 6 cards each), 1 tower stand with 5 color disks, 25 record forms, 25 Design Fluency Response booklets, 25 Trail Making response booklet sets (each set contains 25 response booklets for the 5 Trail Making conditions; $470 per complete kit with soft-side case; $520 per complete kit in box with Scoring Assistant (CD-ROM or diskette, Windows only); $575 per complete kit in a soft-side case with Scoring Assistant; $155 per D-KEFS Scoring Assistant (CD-ROM or diskette); $68 per examiner's and technical manual; $53 per examiner's manual; $42 per technical manual (144 pages); $37 per 25 record forms; $21 per 25 Sorting or Color-Word Interference test record forms; $55 per 25 sets of Trail Making Test response booklets (each set contains 25 different response booklets for the 5 Trail Making conditions); $15 per 25 Trail Making or Design Fluency Test record forms; $22 per 25 Verbal Fluency, 20 Questions, or Word Context test record forms; $18 per 25 Tower or Proverb test record forms; $21 per 25 alternate record forms for Sorting, Verbal Fluency, 20 Questions Tests; $42 per Sorting Test set of cards including 2 sets of standard sorting cards, and 2 practice set; $42 per Sorting Test alternate set of cards including 3 sets of 6 cards each.

Time: (90) minutes for all 9 tests.

Comments: Each test assesses a different executive-function domain; tests may be administered alone or in combination; hand-scorable; D-KEFS Scoring Assistant software available; scoring software generates reports in table or graphical format; for system requirements contact publisher.

Authors: Dean C. Delis, Edith Kaplan, and Joel H. Kramer.

Publisher: PsychCorp, A brand of Harcourt Assessment, Inc.

a) D-KEFS TRAIL MAKING TEST.
Purpose: Assesses "flexibility of thinking on a visual-motor task."
Form, 1: Standard Record Form.
Scores, 6: Visual Scanning, Number Sequencing, Letter Sequencing, Number-Letter Switching, Motor Speed, Composite Score.
b) D-KEFS VERBAL FLUENCY TEST.
Purpose: Assesses "fluent productivity in the verbal domain."
Forms, 2: Standard Record Form, Alternate Record Form.
Scores, 3: Letter Fluency, Category Fluency, Category Switching.
c) D-KEFS DESIGN FLUENCY TEST.
Purpose: Assesses "fluent productivity in the spatial domain."

Form, 1: Standard Record Form.
Scores, 3: Filled Dots, Empty Dots Only, Switching.
d) D-KEFS COLOR-WORD INTERFERENCE TEST.
Purpose: Assesses "verbal inhibition."
Form, 1: Standard Record Form.
Scores, 4: Color Naming, Word Reading, Inhibition, Inhibition/Switching.
e) D-KEFS SORTING TEST.
Purpose: Assesses "problem-solving, verbal and spatial concept formation, flexibility of thinking on a conceptual task."
Forms, 2: Standard Record Form, Alternate Record Form.
Scores, 2: Free Sorting, Sort Recognition.
Comments: Alternate set of scoring cards available.
f) D-KEFS TOWER TEST.
Purpose: Assesses "planning and reasoning in the spatial modality [and] impulsivity."
Form, 1: Standard Record Form.
Score: Total Achievement Score.
g) D-KEFS 20 QUESTIONS TEST.
Purpose: Assesses "hypothesis testing, verbal and spatial abstract thinking, [and] impulsivity."
Forms, 2: Standard Record Form, Alternate Record Form.
Score: Initial Abstraction Score.
h) D-KEFS WORD CONTEXT TEST.
Purpose: Assesses "deductive reasoning [and] verbal abstract thinking."
Form, 1: Standard Record Form.
Score: Total Consecutively Correct.
i) D-KEFS PROVERB TEST.
Purpose: Assesses "metaphorical thinking, generating versus comprehending abstract thought."
Form, 1: Standard Record Form.
Scores, 2: Total Achievement **Scores:** Free Inquiry, Multiple Choice.

Cross References: For reviews by Anthony T. Dugbartey and Pamilla Ramsden, see 15:74.

[771]
Dementia Rating Scale—2.

Purpose: To measure and track "mental status in adults with cognitive impairment."

Population: Adults ages 56–89 and older.

Publication Dates: 1973–2001.

Acronym: DRS-2.

Scores: 6: Attention, Initiation/Perseveration, Construction, Conceptualization, Memory, Total.

Administration: Individual.

Price Data, 2006: $240 per introductory kit including professional manual (2001, 47 pages), 50 scoring booklets, 50 profile forms and set of 32 stimulus

cards; $210 per Alternate Form introductory kit; $350 per CD ROM based software with unlimited use Scoring and Interpretive Reports.
Time: (15–30) minutes.
Comments: Revised version of the DRS; DRS-2 stimulus cards same as for original DRS; can be administered bedside by appropriately trained personnel; alternate form is also available.
Authors: Steven Mattis (professional manual, stimulus cards, scoring booklet), Paul J. Jurica, and Christopher L. Leitten (professional manual).
Publisher: Psychological Assessment Resources, Inc.
Cross References: For reviews by Iris Phillips and Pamilla Ramsden, see 15:75; see T5:776 (63 references); for a review by R. A. Bornstein of an earlier edition, see 11:107 (2 references).

[772]
Dental Admission Test.
Purpose: "Designed to measure general academic achievement, comprehension of scientific information, and perceptual ability."
Population: United States dental school applicants.
Publication Dates: 1950–2006.
Acronym: DAT.
Scores, 8: Natural Sciences (Biology, General Chemistry, Organic Chemistry, Total), Reading Comprehension, Quantitative Reasoning, Perceptual Ability, Academic Average.
Administration: Group.
Price Data: Available from publisher.
Time: 255(270) minutes.
Comments: Formerly called Dental Aptitude Testing Program; computer-based test administered throughout the year at centers approved by publisher.
Authors: Department of Testing Services.
Publisher: American Dental Association.
Cross References: For reviews by Janet Baldwin and Jerry S. Gilmer, see 12:102; for reviews by Henry M. Cherrick and Linda M. DuBois of an earlier edition, see 9:308; see also T3:673 (2 references); for reviews by Robert L. Linn and Christine H. McGuire of an earlier edition, see 8:1085 (7 references); see also T2:2337 (8 references), 7:1091 (28 references), 5:916 (6 references), and 4:788 (2 references).

[773]
Dental Assistant Test.
Purpose: Developed to help screen for dental assistant positions.
Population: Dental assistant applicants.
Publication Date: 1975.
Scores: 8 tests: Attention to Details, Organization Skills, Perception of Objects in Space, Perception of Spatial Perspective, Following Directions, Detail Judgments, Dexterity, Logic and Reasoning.

Administration: Group.
Price Data: Available from publisher.
Time: (40-45) minutes.
Comments: Self-administered.
Authors: Mary Meeker and Robert Meeker.
Publisher: SOI Systems.

[774]
Dental Receptionist Test.
Purpose: Developed to help screen for dental receptionist positions.
Population: Dental receptionist applicants.
Publication Date: 1975.
Scores: 8 tests: Attention to Details, Vocabulary, Verbal Reasoning, Following Directions, Management of Details, Management of Numerical Information, Dexterity, Logic and Reasoning.
Administration: Group.
Price Data: Available from publisher.
Time: (45-50) minutes.
Comments: Self-administered.
Authors: Mary Meeker and Robert Meeker.
Publisher: SOI Systems.

[775]
Denver Articulation Screening Exam.
Purpose: Designed to identify significant developmental delay in the acquisition of speech sounds.
Population: Ages 2.5 to 7.0.
Publication Dates: 1971–1973.
Acronym: DASE.
Scores, 2: DASE Word Score, Intelligibility Rating.
Administration: Individual.
Price Data, 2005: $8 per 25 test forms; $8 per set of picture cards for use with "shy or immature" children; $230 per training videotape; $19 per manual/workbook (1973, 42 pages).
Time: (10–15) minutes.
Comments: Orally administered.
Authors: Amelia F. Drumwright and William K. Frankenburg (manual).
Publisher: Denver Developmental Materials, Inc.
Cross References: See T3:675 (1 reference); for a review by Harold A. Peterson, see 8:958.

[776]
Denver Audiometric Screening Test.
Purpose: Constructed to identify children who have a serious hearing loss.
Population: Ages 3–6.
Publication Date: 1973.
Acronym: DAST.
Scores: 3 ratings for each ear: Pass, Fail, Uncertain.
Administration: Individual.
Price Data, 2005: $6 per 25 test forms; $230 per training videotape; $28 per manual/workbook (30 pages); $23.50 per reference manual.

Time: [5–10] minutes.
Authors: William K. Frankenburg, Marion Downs, and Elynor Kazuk.
Publisher: Denver Developmental Materials, Inc.
Cross References: See T5:784 (1 reference); for a review by Lear Ashmore, see 9:309.

[777]
Denver Eye Screening Test.

Purpose: Developed to detect problems in visual acuity and screen for eye diseases.
Population: Ages 6 months and over.
Publication Date: 1973.
Acronym: DEST.
Scores: 3 ratings for each eye: Normal, Abnormal, Untestable.
Administration: Individual.
Price Data, 2005: $6 per 25 test forms; $24 per set of test materials including picture cards, cord, and spinning toy; $11 per set of picture cards; $3.00 per cord; $6 per spinning toy; $180 per training videotape; $24 per manual/workbook (37 pages); $19 per reference manual.
Time: (5-10) minutes.
Comments: "Criterion-referenced."
Authors: William K. Frankenburg, Arnold D. Goldstein, and John Barker.
Publisher: Denver Developmental Materials, Inc.
 a) VISION TESTS.
  1) *Fixation.*
  Population: Ages 6 months to 2.5 years.
  2) *Picture Card.*
  Population: Ages 2.5 to 3.
  3) *"E."*
  Population: Ages 3 and over.
 b) TESTS FOR NON-STRAIGHT EYES.
 Population: Ages 6 months and over.

[778]
Denver Prescreening Developmental Questionnaire II.

Purpose: "To facilitate earlier identification of children whose development may be delayed."
Population: Ages 0-9 months, 9-24 months, 2-4 years, 4-6 years.
Publication Dates: 1975–1998.
Acronym: PDQII.
Scores: Item scores only.
Administration: Individual.
Levels, 4: Ages 0-9 months, 9-24 months, 2-4 years, 4-6 years.
Manual: No manual.
Price Data, 2005: $22–$25 (English) per 100 questionnaires (specify level); $24-$28 (Spanish) per 100 questionnaires (specify level).
Time: [12.5] minutes.

Comments: Ratings by parents; previous edition entitled Revised Denver Prescreening Developmental Questionnaire.
Authors: William K. Frankenburg.
Publisher: Denver Developmental Materials, Inc.
Cross References: See T5:787 (4 references); for reviews by Stephen N. Axford and William B. Michael of the Revised Denver Prescreening Developmental Questionnaire, see 12:327 (1 reference).

[779]
Denver II (Denver Developmental Screening Test).

Purpose: Designed to screen for developmental delays.
Population: Birth to age 6.
Publication Dates: 1967–1992.
Scores: Item scores in 4 areas (Personal-Social, Fine Motor-Adaptive, Language, Gross Motor) and 5 test behavior ratings (Typical, Compliance, Interest in Surroundings, Fearfulness, Attention Span).
Administration: Individual.
Price Data, 2005: $90 per complete package; $55 per test kit; $25 per 100 test forms; $215 per training videotape (rental price $90); $26 per training manual (1990, 50 pages); $30 per technical manual (1990, 91 pages).
Time: (10–15) minutes for abbreviated version; (20–25) minutes for entire test.
Comments: Revision is intended to be used as a developmental chart designed to give a broad overview of general development in a minimum amount of time.
Authors: W. K. Frankenburg, Josiah Dodds, Phillip Archer, Beverly Bresnick, Patrick Maschka, Norma Edelman, and Howard Shapiro.
Publisher: Denver Developmental Materials, Inc.
Cross References: See T5:788 (3 references); for reviews by Selma Hughes and Pat Mirenda, see 12:103 (3 references); see also T4:740 (18 references).

[780]
Depression and Anxiety in Youth Scale.

Purpose: Designed to help professionals identify depression and anxiety in children and youth.
Population: Ages 6-0 to 19-0.
Publication Date: 1994.
Acronym: DAYS.
Administration: Group.
Price Data, 2006: $150 per complete kit including 50 student rating scales, 50 teacher rating scales, 50 parent rating scales, 50 profile/record forms, scoring keys, and manual (39 pages); $25 per 50 record forms; $25 per 50 profile/record forms; $60 per manual.
Authors: Phyllis L. Newcomer, Edna M. Barenbaum, and Brian R. Bryant.
Publisher: PRO-ED.

a) STUDENT SELF-REPORT SCALE (SCALE S).
Scores, 2: Depression, Anxiety.
Time: (15–20) minutes.
b) TEACHER RATING SCALE (SCALE T).
Scores, 2: Depression, Anxiety.
Time: (5–10) minutes.
c) PARENT RATING SCALE (SCALE P).
Scores, 3: Depression, Anxiety, Social Maladjustment.
Time: (6–10) minutes.
Cross References: For reviews by Gloria Maccow and Janet V. Smith, see 13:91.

[781]
Depressive Experiences Questionnaire.

Purpose: Designed to assess an individual's depressive experience.
Population: Adolescents and adults (patients and normals).
Publication Dates: 1976–1989.
Acronym: DEQ.
Scores, 3: Dependency, Self-Criticism, Efficacy.
Administration: Group.
Forms, 2: DEQ, DEQ-A.
Manual: No manual.
Price Data: Available from publisher.
Time: Administration time not reported.
Authors: Sidney J. Blatt, Carrie E. Schaffer, Susan A. Bers, and Donald M. Quinlan.
Publisher: Sidney J. Blatt.
Cross References: See T5:790 (29 references), T4:744 (30 references), 9:316 (2 references), and T3:682 (1 reference).

[782]
Derogatis Affects Balance Scale [Revised].

Purpose: Designed as a multidimensional mood and affects inventory to "measure the affects profile of community, medical, and psychiatric respondents."
Population: Adults.
Publication Dates: 1975–1996.
Acronym: DABS.
Scores, 13: Joy, Contentment, Vigor, Affection, Anxiety, Depression, Guilt, Hostility, Positive Score Total, Negative Score Total, Affects Balance Index, Affects Expressiveness Index, Positive Affects Ratio.
Administration: Individual.
Forms, 2: DABS, DABS-SF (Short Form).
Price Data, 2002: $50 per 50 tests; $25 per 50 profiles; $29.50 per manual (1996, 58 pages).
Time: (5) minutes (DABS); (2–3) minutes (Short Form).
Comments: Self-report inventory, for clinical or research uses; formerly published as the Affects Balance Scale (ABS); scoring is available online ($1 per scoring) at www.derogatis-tests.com.

Author: Leonard R. Derogatis.
Publisher: Clinical Psychometric Research, Inc.
Cross References: For reviews by Mark J. Atkinson and Carlen Hennington, see 14:112; see also T5:791 (16 references), T4:132 (6 references), and 9:61 (6 references).

[783]
Derogatis Interview for Sexual Functioning.

Purpose: "A brief semistructured interview designed to provide an estimate of the quality of an individual's current sexual functioning in quantitative terms."
Population: Adults.
Publication Dates: 1987–1989.
Scores, 6: Sexual Cognition/Fantasy, Sexual Arousal, Sexual Behavior/Experience, Orgasm, Sexual Drive/Relationship, Total Score.
Administration: Individual.
Price Data, 2006: $62.50 per 50 DISF or DISF-SR (specify gender); $25 per 50 DISF or DISF-SR score sheets (specify gender); additional shipping charges apply.
Foreign Language Editions: Danish, Dutch, English, French, German, Italian, Norwegian, and Spanish editions available.
Time: (15–20) minutes for DISF; (10–15) minutes for DISF-SR.
Author: Leonard R. Derogatis.
Publisher: Clinical Psychometric Research, Inc.
a) DEROGATIS INTERVIEW FOR SEXUAL FUNCTIONING.
Acronym: DISF.
Time: (15–20) minutes.
Comments: Semistructured interview format using a 4-point Likert scale.
b) DEROGATIS INTERVIEW FOR SEXUAL FUNCTIONING—SELF REPORT.
Acronym: DISF-SR.
Time: (10–15) minutes.
Comments: Paper-and-pencil format using Likert scales; may be used to gain evaluations of patient's sexual functioning by the patient or the patient's spouse.
Cross References: For a review by Sheri Bauman, see 15:76.

[784]
Derogatis Psychiatric Rating Scale.

Purpose: Multidimensional psychiatric rating scale for use by clinician to assist in validating patient-reported results.
Population: Adults and adolescents.
Publication Dates: 1974–1992.
Acronym: DPRS.
Administration: Individual.
Comments: Formerly called Hopkins Psychiatric Rating Scale (9:483).

Author: Leonard R. Derogatis.
Publisher: Pearson Assessments.
a) BRIEF DEROGATIS PSYCHIATRIC RATING SCALE.
Acronym: B-DPRS.
Scores, 10: Primary Dimensions (Somatization, Obsessive-Compulsive, Interpersonal Sensitivity, Depression, Anxiety, Hostility, Phobic Anxiety, Paranoid Ideation, Psychoticism) and Global Pathology Index.
Price Data, 2006: $50 per 100 forms.
Time: (1–2) minutes.
b) DEROGATIS PSYCHIATRIC RATING SCALE.
Acronym: DPRS.
Scores, 18: Same as brief edition plus Sleep Disturbance, Psychomotor Retardation, Hysterical Behavior, Abjection-Disinterest, Conceptual Dysfunction, Disorientation, Excitement, Euphoria.
Price Data: $32 per 100 forms.
Time: (2–5) minutes.
Cross References: For reviews by Samuel Juni and Paul Retzlaff, see 13:92 (1 reference); see also T4:745 (6 references) and 9:483 (1 reference).

[785]
Derogatis Sexual Functioning Inventory.
Purpose: Multidimensional assessment of sexual functioning.
Population: Adults.
Publication Dates: 1975–1979.
Acronym: DSFI.
Scores, 12: Information, Experience, Drive, Attitudes, Psychological Symptoms, Affects, Gender Role, Definition, Fantasy, Body Image, Sexual Satisfaction, Total, Patient's Evaluation of Current Functioning.
Administration: Individual.
Price Data, 2006: $3.50 per nonreusable test (1978, 8 pages); $12.50 per manual (1979, 36 pages); $.50 per profile form (specify male or female).
Time: (45–60) minutes.
Comments: Scoring is available online ($5 per scoring) at www.derogatis-tests.com.
Author: Leonard R. Derogatis.
Publisher: Clinical Psychometric Research, Inc.
Cross References: See T5:793 (24 references) and T4:746 (10 references); for reviews by Edward S. Herold and David L. Weis, see 9:317 (3 references); see also T3:683 (6 references).

[786]
Derogatis Stress Profile.
Purpose: "Designed to assess and represent stress at three distinct but related levels of measurement."
Population: Adults.
Publication Dates: 1984–1986.
Acronym: DSP.

Scores: 3 domains: Environmental Events, Emotional Response, Personality Mediators; 11 dimensions: Time Pressure, Driven Behavior, Attitude Posture, Relaxation Potential, Role Definition, Vocational Satisfaction, Domestic Satisfaction, Health Posture, Hostility, Anxiety, Depression; 2 global scores: Subjective Stress, Total Stress.
Administration: Individual.
Price Data, 2006: $55 per 50 tests; $25 per 50 score profile forms; $12.50 per summary report and scoring instructions (1986, 14 pages).
Time: 10(15) minutes.
Comments: Scoring available online ($2 per scoring) at www.derogatis-tests.com.
Author: Leonard R. Derogatis.
Publisher: Clinical Psychometric Research, Inc.
Cross References: See T5:794 (2 references); for reviews by Mariela C. Shirley and Paul D. Werner, see 13:93 (4 references); see also T4:747 (1 reference).

[787]
Detailed Assessment of Posttraumatic Stress.
Purpose: Designed as a comprehensive diagnostic measure of trauma exposure and posttraumatic stress and associated functions, including dissociative symptoms, substance abuse, and suicidality.
Population: Adults 18 and over who have undergone a significant psychological stressor.
Publication Date: 2001.
Acronym: DAPS.
Scores: 2 validity scales (Positive Bias and Negative Bias) and 11 scales in 3 clusters: Trauma Specification (Relative Trauma Exposure, Peritraumatic Distress, Peritraumatic Dissociation), Posttraumatic Stress (Reexperiencing, Avoidance, Hyperarousal, Posttraumatic Stress—Total, Posttraumatic Impairment), Associated Features (Trauma-Specific Dissociation, Substance Abuse, Suicidality).
Administration: Individual or group.
Price Data, 2006: $189 per introductory kit including professional manual (56 pages), 10 item booklets, 50 hand-scorable answer sheets, and 50 male/female profile forms; $360 per DAPS-IR CD ROM based software kit.
Time: (20–30) minutes.
Comments: Self-administered; CD-ROM based software with Interpretive Report also available (DAPS-IR).
Author: John Briere.
Publisher: Psychological Assessment Resources, Inc.
Cross References: For reviews by Roger A. Boothroyd and Larissa Smith, see 15:77.

[788]
Detention Promotion Tests—Complete Service.
Purpose: Designed as a custom-made test to fit duties and responsibilities for promotion of detention personnel.

Population: Detention workers under consideration for promotion.
Publication Dates: 1990–1998.
Scores: 6 subtests: Detention-Related Technical Knowledges, Knowledge of the Behavioral Sciences and Human Relations, Supervisory and Managerial Knowledges, Administrative Knowledges, Knowledge of Inmate Legal Rights, Comprehension Ability, Total.
Administration: Group.
Price Data: Available from publisher.
Time: [210] minutes.
Comments: Candidate study guide available.
Author: McCann Associates, Inc.
Publisher: Vantage McCann Associates.

[789]
Detroit Tests of Learning Aptitude—Adult.
Purpose: Designed to measure both general intelligence and discrete mental ability areas.
Population: Ages 16-0 and over.
Publication Date: 1991.
Acronym: DTLA-A.
Scores, 20: 12 subtest scores: Word Opposites, Story Sequences, Sentence Imitation, Reversed Letters, Mathematical Problems, Design Sequences, Basic Information, Quantitative Relations, Word Sequences, Design Reproduction, Symbolic Relations, Form Assembly and 8 composite scores (Linguistic Verbal, Linguistic Nonverbal, Attention-Enhanced, Attention-Reduced, Motor-Enhanced, Motor-Reduced, General Mental Ability, Optimal).
Administration: Individual.
Price Data, 2006: $295 per complete kit including picture book 1, picture book 2, 25 response forms, 25 examiner record booklets, 25 profile/summary forms, and manual (120 pages); $59 per picture book 1; $27 per picture book 2; $35 per 25 response forms; $50 per 25 examiner record forms; $35 per 25 profile/summary forms; $50 per manual; $51 per manipulatives.
Time: (90–150) minutes.
Comments: Upward extension of the Detroit Tests of Learning Aptitude (Second Edition) (10:85) and (Third Edition) (12:107).
Authors: Donald D. Hammill and Bryan R. Bryant.
Publisher: PRO-ED.
Cross References: For reviews by Thomas E. Dinero and Cynthia Ann Druva-Roush, see 12:105.

[790]
Detroit Tests of Learning Aptitude, Fourth Edition.
Purpose: Designed to measure both general intelligence and discrete ability areas.
Population: Ages 6-0 to 17-11.
Publication Dates: 1935–1998.
Acronym: DTLA-4.

Scores: 10 subtest scores: Word Opposites, Design Sequences, Sentence Imitation, Reversed Letters, Story Construction, Design Reproduction, Basic Information, Symbolic Relations, Word Sequences, Story Sequences; and 16 composite scores: General Mental Ability Composite, Optimal Composite, Domain Composites (Verbal, Nonverbal, Attention-Enhanced, Attention-Reduced, Motor-Enhanced, Motor-Reduced, Total), Theoretical Composites (Fluid Intelligence, Crystallized Intelligence, Associative Level, Cognitive Level, Simultaneous Processing, Successive Processing, Verbal Scale, Performance Scale, Total).
Administration: Individual.
Price Data, 2006: $367 per complete kit including examiner's manual (1998, 247 pages), Picture Books 1 and 2, 25 Profile/Summary forms, 25 Examiner Record Booklets, 25 response forms, Story Sequence Chips, and Design Sequence Cubes; $79 per examiner's manual; $97 per Picture Book 1 (for Design Sequences, Design Reproduction and Symbolic Relations); $50 per Picture Book 2 (for Story Sequences and Story Construction); $30 per 25 Profile/Summary forms; $50 per 25 Examiner Record Booklets; $30 per 25 response forms; $21 per Story Sequence Chips; $40 per Design Sequence Cubes; $112 per software scoring and report system (Windows).
Time: (40–120) minutes.
Authors: Donald D. Hammill.
Publisher: PRO-ED.
Cross References: For reviews by Jeffrey K. Smith and Ross E. Traub, see 14:113; see also T5:798 (27 references); for reviews by William A. Mehrens and Michael Poteat of an earlier edition, see 12:107 (4 references); see also T4:752 (7 references); for reviews by Arthur B. Silverstein and Joan Silverstein of an earlier edition, see 10:85 (15 references); see also 9:320 (11 references), and T3:691 (20 references); for a review by Arthur B. Silverstein of an earlier edition, see 8:213 (14 references); see also T2:493 (3 references), and 7:406 (10 references); for a review by F. L. Wells, see 3:275 (1 reference); for reviews by Anne Anastasi and Henry Feinburg and an excerpted review by D. A. Worcester and S. M. Corey, see 1:1058.

[791]
Detroit Tests of Learning Aptitude— Primary, Third Edition.
Purpose: "Measures general aptitude."
Population: Ages 3–9.
Publication Dates: 1986–2005.
Acronym: DTLA-P:3.
Scores, 7: Verbal-Enhanced, Verbal-Reduced, Attention-Enhanced, Attention-Reduced, Motor-Enhanced, Motor-Reduced, General Ability.
Administration: Individual.
Price Data, 2006: $200 per complete kit including examiner's manual (2005, 128 pages), picture book, 25

examiner record booklets, and 25 response forms; $62 per picture book; $37 per 25 response forms; $50 per 25 examiner record booklets; $60 per manual.

Time: (15–45) minutes.

Comments: Adaptation of the Detroit Tests of Learning Aptitude—Second Edition (T5:779).

Authors: Donald D. Hammill and Bryan R. Bryant.

Publisher: PRO-ED.

Cross References: See T5:799 (2 references); for reviews by Terry A. Ackerman and Robert T. Williams of an earlier edition, see 12:106 (1 reference); for reviews by Cathy F. Telzrow and Stanley F. Vasa of an earlier edition, see 10:84 (1 reference).

[792]
Developing Skills Checklist.

Purpose: Designed to measure skills and behaviors that children typically develop between prekindergarten and the end of kindergarten.

Population: Ages 4–6.

Publication Date: 1990.

Acronym: DSC.

Scores: 9 scales: Mathematical Concepts and Operations, Language, Memory, Auditory, Print Concepts, Motor, Visual, Writing and Drawing Concepts, Social-Emotional.

Administration: Individual.

Price Data, 2006: $424.50 per complete kit; $17.30 per 50 Writing and Drawing books; $49 per 50 Social-Emotional Observational Records; $50 per 50 score sheets (specify hand-recording or machine-scoring); $49 per 50 Parent Conference Forms; $4.77 per Class record book; $91 per set of 3 DSC item books; $11.50 per A Day at School; $25 per administration and score interpretation manual; $16.60 per Concepts of Print and Writing administration manual; $16.60 per Social-Emotional Administration manual; $19.40 per norms book and technical manual (90 pages); $51 per training video (entitled How to Administer and Score DSC); $36 per 5 replacement bunnies; $225 per La Lista test kit.

Foreign Language Editions: Spanish adaptation entitled Lista de Destrezas en Desarrollo (La Lista) available as an all-in-Spanish supplement to the DSC. English DSC kit is also required in order to administer La Lista.

Time: (10–15) minutes per session (untimed).

Author: CTB Macmillan/McGraw-Hill.

Publisher: CTB/McGraw-Hill.

Cross References: For reviews by Elaine Clark and Claire B. Ernhart, see 12:108 (2 references).

[793]
Developing the High-Performance Workplace.

Purpose: "Created to give organizational members a tool for assessing employee opinions about the status of high-performance workplace characteristics in their work environments."

Population: Organizational employees.

Publication Date: 1996.

Scores, 18: Importance Ratings (Training and Continuous Learning, Information Sharing, Employee Participation, Organization Structure, Worker-Management Partnerships, Compensation Linked to Performance and Skills, Employment Security, Supportive Work Environment, Overall HPW Rating), Quality Ratings (Training and Continuous Learning, Information Sharing, Employee Participation, Organization Structure, Worker-Management Partnerships, Compensation Linked to Performance and Skills, Employment Security, Supportive Work Environment, Overall HPW Rating).

Administration: Group.

Price Data: Available from publisher.

Time: Administration time not reported.

Authors: David D. Dubois and William J. Rothwell.

Publisher: HRD Press, Inc.

Cross References: For reviews by M. David Miller and Deniz S. Ones, see 14:114.

[794]
Developing the Leader Within.

Purpose: Assessment of leadership skills by self and others.

Population: Management personnel.

Publication Date: 1995.

Scores: 4 dimensions: Developing Within, Helping Others Excel, Improving Critical Processes, Showing Commitment to the Team.

Administration: Group.

Forms, 4: Leader Form, Direct Manager Form, Higher Manager Form, Colleague Form.

Manual: No manual.

Price Data: Available from publisher (www.mindgarden.com).

Time: Administration time not reported.

Comments: Basic assessment includes leader self-rating and up to six ratings by colleagues; Direct Manager and Higher Manager Forms are optional.

Authors: L. Phillips-Jones.

Publisher: Mind Garden, Inc.

[795]
Developmental Activities Screening Inventory, Second Edition.

Purpose: To provide early detection of developmental disabilities in children functioning between the ages of birth and 60 months.

Population: Ages birth to 60 months.

Publication Dates: 1977–1984.

Acronym: DASI-II.

Scores: Total score only.

Administration: Individual.
Price Data, 2006: $92 per complete kit including 50 record forms, 37 Picture Cards, 5 Set-Configuration Cards, 2 pairs of Numeral Cards, 3 pairs of Word Cards, 4 Shape Cards, and examiner's manual (1984, 103 pages); $25 per 50 record forms; $35 per 56 Picture Cards; $35 per examiner's manual.
Time: (25-30) minutes.
Comments: Behavior checklist; some test materials (form board, bell) must be supplied by examiner.
Authors: Rebecca R. Fewell and Mary Beth Langley.
Publisher: PRO-ED.
Cross References: See T5:803 (3 references); for reviews by Dennis C. Harper and William B. Michael, see 10:87; see also 9:323 (1 reference).

[796]
A Developmental Assessment for Individuals with Severe Disabilities, Second Edition.

Purpose: Designed to aid "in identifying discrete changes in behavior ... in five areas of development."
Population: Individuals of all ages who are functioning within the birth to 7-year developmental range.
Publication Dates: 1980–1999.
Acronym: DASH-2.
Scores, 6: Social-Emotional, Language, Sensory-Motor, Activities of Daily Living, Basic Academics, Overall Developmental Age.
Administration: Individual.
Forms: 5 pinpoint scales: Social-Emotional (17 pages), Language (30 pages), Sensory-Motor (35 pages), Activities of Daily Living (21 pages), Basic Academics (25 pages).
Price Data, 2006: $210 per complete kit including manual (23 pages), 5 each of 5 pinpoint scales, 50 priority intervention worksheets, 50 comprehensive program record forms, and 50 cumulative summary sheets; $45 per 10 pinpoint scales (specify area); $20 per 50 priority intervention worksheets; $20 per 50 comprehensive program record forms; $20 per 50 cumulative summary sheets; $45 per manual.
Time: (120–180) minutes.
Comments: Previously titled Developmental Assessment for the Severely Handicapped; also listed as A Developmental Assessment for Students with Severe Disabilities, Second Edition in Tests in Print V; may administer all or any combination of the pinpoint scales; "criterion-referenced"; criterion performance levels 1–5; ratings by developmental professionals.
Authors: Mary K. Dykes and Jane N. Erin.
Publisher: PRO-ED.
Cross References: See T5:804 (1 reference); for reviews by Harvey N. Switzky and David P. Wacker of the original edition, see 9:324.

[797]
Developmental Assessment of Life Experiences (2000 Edition).

Purpose: Developed to assess daily living, intellectual, and adaptive skills of persons with disabilities.
Population: Individuals with developmental disabilities.
Publication Dates: 1974–2000.
Acronym: D.A.L.E. System.
Scores: 8 categories: Personal Hygiene, Daily Living Skills, Community Skills/Safety Skills, Language and Educational Skills, Personal Management, Gender Specific—Female, Gender Specific—Male, Leisure Skills.
Administration: Individual.
Price Data, 2000: $10.50 per complete set including manual (2000, 64 pages).
Time: Administration time not reported.
Authors: Gertrude A. Barber, Vincent Olewnik, Joanne Haughey, Traci Gardner, Michelle Sosnowski, Jennifer Lawrence, Nia Bell, Daneen Engel, Pam Johns, and Nadine Hornyak.
Publisher: The Barber Center Press, Inc.
Cross References: For reviews by Martin E. Block and Linda K. Bunker and by Elizabeth L. Jones of an earlier edition, see 12:109; for a review by Frank M. Gresham of an earlier edition, see 9:295.

[798]
Developmental Assessment of Young Children.

Purpose: Designed to identify children birth through 5-11 with possible delays in the domains of cognition, communication, social-emotional development, physical development, and adaptive behavior.
Population: Birth to age 5-11.
Publication Date: 1998.
Scores: General Development Quotient.
Administration: Individual.
Price Data, 2006: $215 per complete kit including examiner's manual (67 pages), 25 each of Adaptive, Cognitive, Communication, Physical, and Social-Emotional scoring forms, and 25 profile/summary forms; $30 per 25 scoring forms (specify domain); $20 per 25 profile/summary forms; $55 per manual.
Time: (10–20) minutes per subtest.
Comments: Rating by examiner; subtests may be used alone or in any combination.
Authors: Judith K. Voress and Taddy Maddox.
Publisher: PRO-ED.
a) COGNITIVE SUBTEST.
    Purpose: Designed to measure "skills and abilitiess that are conceptual in nature."
    Scores: Total score only.

b) COMMUNICATION SUBTEST.

Purpose: Constructed to assess "the exchange of ideas, information, and feelings."

Scores: Total score only.

c) SOCIAL-EMOTIONAL SUBTEST.

Purpose: Designed to measure "social awareness, social relationships, and social competence."

Scores: Total score only.

d) PHYSICAL DEVELOPMENT SUBTEST.

Purpose: Designed to measure "motor development."

Scores: Total score only.

e) ADAPTIVE BEHAVIOR SUBTEST.

Purpose: Designed to assess "independent functioning."

Scores: Total score only.

Cross References: For reviews by Billy T. Ogletree and T. Steuart Watson, see 14:115.

[799]
Developmental Assessment Resource for Teachers (DART) English.

Purpose: Designed to "assist teachers of upper primary and middle primary in their assessment of students' viewing, reading, listening, speaking and writing skills."

Population: Australian students in years 3–4, 5–6.

Publication Dates: 1994–1997.

Scores, 5: Viewing, Reading, Listening, Speaking, Writing.

Administration: Group.

Forms, 2: Form A, Form B.

Publisher: Australian Council for Educational Research Ltd. [Australia].

a) DART MIDDLE PRIMARY ENGLISH.

Population: Students in years 3–4 in Australian classrooms.

Publication Date: 1997.

Price Data, 2006: A$169.00 per specimen set including 1 of each test component; A$75.90 per manual (1997, 152 pages); A$14.25 per 10 Viewing answer booklets; A$53.90 per Viewing video; A$21.95 per 10 reusable Reading stimulus booklets (specify Form A or Form B); A$16.45 per 10 Reading answer booklets A; A$14.25 per 10 Reading answer booklets B; A$10.95 per 10 Listening answer booklets; A$14.25 per audio cassette; A$8.75 per 10 reusable Character Review Speaking Guides; A$10.95 per 10 Writing answer booklets.

Time: (40–190) minutes per section.

Authors: Wendy Bodey, Lynne Darkin, Margaret Forster, and Geoff Masters.

b) DART UPPER PRIMARY ENGLISH.

Population: Students in years 5–6 in Australian classrooms.

Publication Date: 1994.

Price Data: A$120 per specimen set including 1 of each test component; A$45 per manual (1994, 159 pages); A$16.95 per 10 Viewing answer booklets; A$49 per Viewing video; A$5 per Viewing poster; A$19.95 per 10 reusable Reading stimulus booklets (specify Form A or Form B); A$9.95 per 10 Reading answer booklets A; A$12.95 per 10 Reading answer booklets B; A$6.95 per 10 Listening answer booklets; A$12.95 per audio cassette; A$9.95 per 10 reusable Speaking poetry booklets; A$9.95 per 10 Writing answer booklets; A$295 per complete package including testing materials for 30 students.

Time: (40–190) minutes per section.

Authors: Margaret Forster, Juliette Mendelovits, and Geoff Masters.

Cross References: For reviews by Valentina McInerney and by Gretchen Owens and Jan Harting-McChesney, see 15:78.

[800]
Developmental Assessment Resource for Teachers (DART) Mathematics.

Purpose: "Provides an estimate of a student's level of achievement on each of four strands of the [Australian] national mathematics profile … and on each of three strands of the national benchmark framework."

Population: Australian students in years 5–6.

Publication Date: 1998.

Acronym: DART MATHEMATICS.

Scores, 5: Number, Space, Measurement, Chance and Data, Data Sense.

Administration: Group.

Forms, 2: Form A, Form B.

Price Data, 2006: A$75 per kit including video, manual (160 pages), 30 grid sheets, 30 measurement sheets, and photocopy master answer booklet and stimulus for all tests; A$54.95 per manual; A$54.95 per video; A$21.95 per each photocopy master answer booklet and stimulus (specify Number, Space, Measurement, Chance and Data or Data Sense; also specify Form A or Form B); A$14.25 per 30 grid sheets; A$14.25 per 30 measurement sheets.

Time: (60) minutes per section.

Authors: Eve Recht, Margaret Forster, and Geoff Masters.

Publisher: Australian Council for Educational Research Ltd. [Australia].

Cross References: For reviews by Carlen Henington and Judith A. Monsaas, see 15:79.

[801]
Developmental History Checklist for Children.

Purpose: To document the developmental history of children.

Population: Ages 5–12.
Publication Date: 1989.
Scores: 7 Content Areas: Presenting Information, Personal Information/Family Background, Early Developmental History, Educational History, Medical History/Health Status, Family History, Current Behavior/Relationships.
Administration: Individual.
Manual: No manual.
Price Data, 2006: $50 per package of 25.
Time: Administration time not reported.
Comments: Designed to be completed by a parent, guardian, or clinician.
Authors: Edward H. Dougherty and John A. Schinka.
Publisher: Psychological Assessment Resources, Inc.

[802]
Developmental Indicators for the Assessment of Learning, Third Edition.

Purpose: A developmental screening test for identifying young children in need of further diagnostic assessment.
Population: Ages 3-0 to 6-11.
Publication Dates: 1983–1998.
Acronym: DIAL-3.
Scores, 7: Motor, Concepts, Language, DIAL-3 Total, Self-Help Development, Social Development, Speed DIAL.
Subtests, 5: Motor, Concepts, Language, Self-Help Development, Social Development.
Administration: Individual.
Price Data, 2005: $469.99 per complete kit including manual (1998, 126 pages), 50 record forms (English), 1 record form (Spanish), 50 cutting cards, 50 parent questionnaires (English), manipulatives, dials, operator's handbooks in English and Spanish for motor, concepts and language areas, Speed DIAL, and training packet; $469.99 per complete kit in Spanish; $64.99 per DIAL-3 administration forms (specify English or Spanish) including 50 record forms, 50 cutting cards, and 50 parent questionnaires; $44.99 per 50 cutting cards and 50 record forms (specify English or Spanish); $29.99 per 50 parent/child activity forms (specify English or Spanish); $79.99 per training video; $199.99 per computer program (specify Windows or Macintosh).
Foreign Language Edition: Spanish edition available.
Time: (30) minutes; Speed DIAL: (15–20) minutes.
Comments: In contrast to DIAL-R, the DIAL-3 has two formats: the full version and the short version (called the Speed DIAL).
Authors: Carol Mardell-Czudnowski and Dorothea S. Goldenberg.
Publisher: Pearson Assessments (originally published by AGS Publishing, acquired by Pearson in 2005).

Cross References: For reviews by Gregory J. Cizek and Doreen Ward Fairbank, see 14:116; see also T5:809 (2 references); for reviews by Darrell L. Sabers and Scott Spreat of an earlier edition, see 12:110 (1 reference); see also T4:762 (6 references); for reviews by David W. Barnett and G. Michael Poteat of an earlier version, see 10:89 (6 references); see also 9:326 (1 reference) and T3:696 (2 references); for reviews by J. Jeffrey Grill and James J. McCarthy of an earlier edition, see 8:428 (3 references).

[803]
Developmental Observation Checklist System.

Purpose: "For the assessment of very young children with respect to general development (DC), adjustment behavior (ABC), and parent stress and support (PSSC)."
Population: Birth through age 6.
Publication Date: 1994.
Acronym: DOCS.
Scores, 12: Developmental Checklist (Cognition, Language, Social, Motor, Total); Adjustment Behavior Checklist (Mother, Father, Both Parents, Teacher); Parental Stress and Support Checklist (Mother, Father, Both Parents).
Administration: Individual.
Parts, 3: Developmental Checklist, Adjustment Behavior Checklist, Parental Stress and Support Checklist.
Price Data, 2006: $165 per complete kit including examiner's manual (91 pages), 25 profile/record forms, 25 DC profile/record forms, 25 ABC profile/record forms, and 25 PSSC profile/record forms; $61 per manual; $20 per 25 profile/record forms; $50 per 25 DC profile/record forms; $20 per ABC or PSSC profile/record forms.
Time: [30] minutes.
Authors: Wayne P. Hresko, Shirley A. Miguel, Rita J. Sherbenou, and Steve D. Burton.
Publisher: PRO-ED.
Cross References: For reviews by Frank M. Bernt and Gene Schwarting, see 13:95.

[804]
Developmental Profile II.

Purpose: "Designed to assess a child's functional, developmental age level."
Population: Birth to age 9.5.
Publication Dates: 1972–1986.
Acronym: DP-II.
Scores: Ratings in 5 areas: Physical Age, Self-Help Age, Social Age, Academic Age, Communication Age.
Administration: Group.
Price Data, 2006: $126.50 per kit including 25 scoring/profile forms and manual (1986, 95 pages); $64.50 per 25 scoring/profile forms; $64.50 per manual;

$240 per 25-use disk (PC with DOS) for administration, scoring, and interpretation; $17 per mail-in answer sheet.
Time: (20–40) minutes.
Authors: Gerald Alpern, Thomas Boll, and Marsha Shearer.
Publisher: Western Psychological Services.
Cross References: See T5:811 (14 references) and T4:764 (1 reference); for reviews by A. Dirk Hightower and E. Scott Huebner, see 10:90 (3 references); for reviews by Dennis C. Harper and Sue White, see 9:327; see also T3:698 (5 references); for a review by Jane V. Hunt of the original edition, see 8:215 (1 reference).

[805]
Developmental Readiness Scale—Revised II.
Purpose: Designed as a screening instrument for school readiness.
Population: Ages 3–6.
Publication Dates: 1982–2003.
Acronym: DRS-R2.
Scores, 9: Fine Motor, Visual Motor, Numbers, Concepts, Body Image, Language, Personal-Social, Gross Motor, Reading.
Administration: Individual.
Price Data: Available from publisher.
Time: (30–40) minutes.
Author: Barbara Ball.
Publisher: Academic Consulting & Testing Service.
Cross References: For reviews by Hoi K. Suen and by Kathryn E. Hoff and Mark E. Swerdlik, see 15:80.

[806]
Developmental Tasks for Kindergarten Readiness—II.
Purpose: Designed to provide "objective data about the school-readiness of pre-kindergarten children so that effective educational programming can be planned for them."
Population: Pre-kindergarten children.
Publication Dates: 1978–1994.
Acronym: DTKR-II.
Scores, 19: Composite Score (Social Interaction, Name Printing, Body Concepts—Awareness, Body Concepts—Use, Auditory Sequencing, Auditory Association, Visual Discrimination, Visual Memory, Visual Motor, Color Naming, Relational Concepts, Number Counting, Number Use, Number Naming, Alphabet Knowledge), Acquired Knowledge, Verbal-Conceptual, Visual Skills.
Administration: Individual.
Price Data, 2006: $134 per kit including manual (1994, 97 pages), materials book (cards), and 25 test booklets; $45 per 25 test booklets; $35 per materials book; $60 per test manual.
Time: (20–40) minutes.

Comments: Administered by school personnel for diagnostic-remedial purposes.
Authors: Walter J. Lesiak and Judi Lucas Lesiak.
Publisher: PRO-ED.
Cross References: For reviews by Joseph O. Prewitt and Theresa Graham, see 14:117; see also T4:766 (1 reference); for reviews by Carol A. Gray and Sue White of an earlier edition, see 9:328.

[807]
Developmental Teaching Objectives and Rating Form—Revised.
Purpose: Designed "for assessing social and emotional development of children and youth."
Population: Ages 0–16 years.
Publication Dates: 1992–1999.
Acronym: DTORF-R.
Scores, 5: Behavior, Communication, Socialization, Academics/Cognition, Total.
Administration: Individual.
Price Data, 2002: $60 per kit including 4 subscale booklets, user's manual (63 pages), technical report (29 pages), and rating forms; $25 per additional packet of 4 subscale booklets; software in revision.
Time: Administration time not reported.
Comments: Rating form filled out by people familiar with the child, following observations; older students (and also their parents) participate in their own team ratings; electronic version is available (DTORF-ONLINE).
Authors: Mary M. Wood; Developmental Therapy Institute, Inc.
Publisher: Developmental Therapy Institute, Inc.
Cross References: For a review by Sharon H. deFur, see 14:118.

[808]
Developmental Test of Visual Perception—Adolescent and Adult.
Purpose: "To document the presence and degree of visual perceptual or visual-motor difficulties in individual adolescents and adults."
Population: Ages 11-0 to 74-11 years.
Publication Date: 2002.
Acronym: DTVP-A.
Scores, 9: Motor-Reduced Visual Perception (Figure-Ground, Visual Closure, Form Constancy, Motor-Reduced Visual Perception Index), Visual-Motor Integration (Copying, Visual-Motor Search, Visual-Motor Speed, Visual-Motor Integration Index), General Visual Perception Index.
Administration: Individual.
Price Data, 2006: $200 per complete kit including examiner's manual (135 pages), picture book, 25 profile/examiner record forms, 25 response booklets, and storage box; $70 per examiner's manual; $55 per picture

book; $53 per 25 profiler/examiner record forms; $30 per 25 response booklets.
Time: (20–30) minutes.
Comments: Upward extension and redevelopment of the Developmental Test of Visual Perception, Second Edition (DTVP-2; 809); designed to identify candidates for referral to special education, cognitive rehabilitation, or occupational therapy; may be used to distinguish true visual-perception deficits from problems solely with complex eye-hand or perceptual-motor actions; may assist in differential diagnosis of various dementias.
Authors: Cecil R. Reynolds, Nils A. Pearson, and Judith K. Voress.
Publisher: PRO-ED.
Cross References: For reviews by James M. Hodgson and Ralph G. Leverett, see 16:70.

[809]
Developmental Test of Visual Perception, Second Edition.

Purpose: Measures visual-perceptual and visual-motor integration skills.
Population: Ages 4-0 to 10-11.
Publication Dates: 1961–1993.
Acronym: DTVP-2.
Scores, 8: Motor-Reduced Visual Perception (Position in Space, Figure Ground, Visual Closure, Form Constancy), Visual-Motor Integration (Eye-Hand Coordination, Copying, Spatial Relations, Visual-Motor Speed), General Visual Perception.
Administration: Individual.
Price Data, 2006: $200 per complete kit including examiner's manual (1993, 73 pages), picture book, 25 profile/examiner record forms, and 25 response booklets; $60 per examiner's manual; $55 per picture book; $30 per 25 profile/examiner record forms; $65 per 25 response booklets.
Time: (35–45) minutes.
Comments: 1993 revision of the Marianne Frostig Developmental Test of Visual Perception (DTVP).
Authors: Donald D. Hammill, Nils A. Pearson, and Judith K. Voress.
Publisher: PRO-ED.
Cross References: See T5:816 (1 reference); for reviews by Nancy B. Bologna and Gerald Tindal, see 12:112 (1 reference); see also T4:767 (2 references); for reviews by Richard E. Darnell and David A. Sabatino of the earlier edition, see 9:650 (4 references); see also T3:1371 (25 references), 8:882 (72 references), and T2:1921 (43 references); for reviews by Brad S. Chissom, Newell C. Kephart, and Lester Mann, see 7:871 (117 references); for reviews by James M. Anderson and Mary C. Austin, see 6:553 (7 references).

[810]
Devereux Behavior Rating Scale—School Form.

Purpose: To evaluate "behaviors typical of children and adolescents with moderate to severe emotional disturbance."
Population: Ages 5–18.
Publication Dates: 1990–1993.
Acronym: BRSS.
Scores, 4: Interpersonal Problems, Inappropriate Behaviors/Feelings, Depression, Physical Symptoms/Fears.
Administration: Individual or group.
Forms, 2: Children, Adolescents.
Price Data, 2002: $149 per complete kit including manual (1993, 142 pages), 25 answer documents 5–12, and 25 ready score answer documents 13–18; $80 per manual; $36 per 25 ready score answer documents 5–12; $36 per 25 ready score answer documents 13–18.
Time: (5–10) minutes.
Comments: Ratings by parents and teachers.
Authors: Jack A. Naglieri, Paul A. LeBuffe, and Steven I. Pfeiffer.
Publisher: PsychCorp, A brand of Harcourt Assessment, Inc.
Cross References: See T5:817 (1 reference); for additional information on the Devereux Adolescent Behavior Rating Scale, see T3:702 (1 reference); for a review by Carl F. Jesness, see 7:66; see also P:60 (1 reference). For reviews by Lisa Bloom and Richard F. Farmer, see 13:96 (8 references). For additional information on the Devereux Child Behavior Rating Scale, see T3:203 (6 references); see also T2:1158 (1 reference); for a review by Allan G. Barclay, see 7:67; see also P:61 (3 references).

[811]
Devereux Early Childhood Assessment.

Purpose: "To assess preschool children's protective factors and behavioral concerns."
Population: Ages 2–5.
Publication Date: 1999.
Acronym: DECA.
Scores, 5: Initiative, Self-Control, Attachment, Total Protective Factors, Behavioral Concerns.
Administration: Individual.
Price Data, 2002: $199.95 per kit including 40 record forms, user's guide (65 pages), technical manual (42 pages), classroom strategies guide, 20 parent guides, and classroom observation journal in a carrying case.
Foreign Language Edition: Parent guides and record forms also available in Spanish.
Time: (10) minutes.
Comments: Ratings by teachers and parents.
Authors: Paul A. LeBuffe and Jack A. Naglieri.
Publisher: Kaplan Early Learning Company.

Cross References: For reviews by Eric S. Buhs and Mary M. Chittooran, see 15:81.

[812]
Devereux Early Childhood Assessment— Clinical Form.

Purpose: Designed to evaluate "behaviors related to both social and emotional resilience as well as social and emotional concerns in preschool children."
Population: Ages 2:0–5:11.
Publication Dates: 2002–2003.
Acronym: DECA-C.
Scores, 9: Protective Factors (Initiative, Self-Control, Attachment, Total), Behavioral Concerns (Withdrawal/Depression, Emotional Control Problems, Attention Problems, Aggression, Total).
Administration: Individual.
Price Data: Prices for the manual, record forms, and norms reference card available from publisher.
Time: Administration time not reported.
Comments: Behavior rating scale may be completed by parent or family member or teacher.
Authors: Paul A. LeBuffe and Jack A. Naglieri.
Publisher: Kaplan Early Learning Company.
Cross References: For reviews by Joan C. Ballard and Sandra A. Loew, see 16:71.

[813]
Devereux Scales of Mental Disorders.

Purpose: Constructed for "evaluating behaviors associated with psychopathology."
Population: Ages 5–12, 13–18.
Publication Dates: 1993–1996.
Acronym: DSMD.
Scores, 10: Conduct, Attention/Delinquency, Anxiety, Depression, Autism, Acute Problems, Internalizing Composite, Externalizing Composite, Critical Pathology Composite, Total.
Administration: Group or individual.
Forms, 2: Child Form, Adolescent Form.
Price Data, 2002: $195 per complete kit including manual (1994, 300 pages), and 25 ReadyScore™ answer documents for each Child Form and Adolescent Form; $64 per ReadyScore™ answer documents (specify form); $80 per manual; $242 per DSMD Scoring Assistant including user's guide (1996, 77 pages), 2 disks, 5 child's record forms, and 5 adolescent record forms.
Time: (15) minutes.
Comments: Revision of Devereux Child Behavior Rating Scale (T3:703) and Devereux Adolescent Behavior Rating Scale (T3:702); ratings by parents, teachers, or other professionals; Scoring Assistant available to provide narrative interpretive reports and other information.
Authors: Jack A. Naglieri, Paul A. LeBuffe, and Steven I. Pfeiffer.

Publisher: PsychCorp, A brand of Harcourt Assessment, Inc.
Cross References: For reviews by Colin Cooper and Charles A. Peterson, see 14:120; see also T5:818 (1 reference).

[814]
The Devine Inventory [Revised].

Purpose: Designed as a comprehensive measure of work-related behaviors to assist in employee selection and development.
Population: Employees and prospective employees.
Publication Dates: 1989–2005.
Scores, 29: Self-Responsibility, Role Clarity, Approaches Problems Realistically, Openness to Change And Experience, Growth And Development/Learning, Response to Crisis, Trust in Self, Trust in Others, Dominance/Leadership, Negotiating, Decisiveness, Thinking, Detail Mindedness, Structure, Follow-Through, Diligence/Work Ethic, Goal Orientation, Response to Change, Mobility, Energy, Quiescence, Assertiveness, Authority Relationships/Loyalty, Following Rules and Procedures, Recognition, Sociability/Gregariousness, Belonging, Intimacy, Dependability.
Administration: Individual.
Price Data: Available from publisher.
Foreign Language Editions: Spanish, French, and German.
Time: (25–30) minutes.
Comments: Administered and scored via the internet.
Authors: Donald W. Devine.
Publisher: The Devine Group, Inc.
Cross References: For reviews by Phillip Benson and William L. Deaton of an earlier edition, see 12:113.

[815]
Diagnosing Organizational Culture.

Purpose: "Designed to help consultants and organizational members identify the shared values and beliefs that constitute an organization's culture."
Population: Adults.
Publication Dates: 1992–1993.
Scores: 5 scores (Power, Role, Achievement, Support, Total) in each of two areas: Existing Culture, Preferred Culture.
Administration: Group.
Price Data: Price information available from publisher for complete kit including trainer's manual (1993, 58 pages) and instrument (1992, 30 pages).
Time: (45–60) minutes.
Authors: Roger Harrison and Herb Stokes (instrument only).
Publisher: Jossey-Bass, A Wiley Company.
Cross References: For a review by John W. Fleenor, see 13:97.

[816]
Diagnostic Achievement Battery, Third Edition.

Purpose: Designed "to assess children's abilities in listening, speaking, reading, writing, and mathematics."
Population: Ages 6-0 to 14-0.
Publication Dates: 1984–2001.
Acronym: DAB-3.
Scores, 22: 14 subtest scores (Story Comprehension, Characteristics, Synonyms, Grammatic Completion, Alphabet/Word Knowledge, Reading Comprehension, Capitalization, Punctuation, Spelling, Writing: Contextual Language, Writing: Story Construction, Mathematics Reasoning, Mathematics Calculation, Phonemic Analysis) and 8 composite scores (Listening, Speaking, Reading, Writing, Mathematics, Spoken Language, Written Language, Total Achievement).
Administration: Individual.
Price Data, 2006: $285 per complete kit including examiner's manual (2001, 152 pages), student booklet, 25 profile/examiner's record booklets, 25 student response booklets, assessment probes, and audiotape; $112 per software kit including manual and CD-ROM; $80 per manual; $45 per 25 student response booklets; $65 per 25 profile/examiner's record booklets; $45 per student booklet; $20 per audiotape; $40 per assessment probes.
Time: (90–120) minutes.
Authors: Phyllis Newcomer.
Publisher: PRO-ED.
Cross References: For reviews by Michael B. Bunch and Cleborne D. Maddux, see 15:82, see T5:821 (2 references); for reviews by Jean-Jacques Bernier and Martine Hebert and by Ric Brown of an earlier edition, see 12:114 (2 references); see also T4:774 (1 reference); for a review by William J. Webster of the original edition, see 9:333.

[817]
Diagnostic Achievement Test for Adolescents, Second Edition.

Purpose: To measure the spoken language ability and academic achievement levels of students.
Population: Ages 12–0 to 18–11.
Publication Dates: 1986–1993.
Acronym: DATA-2.
Scores, 22: 13 subtest scores (Receptive Vocabulary, Receptive Grammar, Expressive Grammar, Expressive Vocabulary, Word Identification, Reading Comprehension, Spelling, Writing Composition, Math Calculation, Math Problem Solving, Science, Social Studies, Reference Skills) and 9 composite scores (Listening, Speaking, Reading, Writing, Math, Spoken Language, Written Language, Achievement Screener, Total Achievement).

Administration: Individual.
Price Data, 2006: $175 per complete kit including examiner's manual (1993, 73 pages), 25 student response forms, 25 profile/examiner record forms, and a student booklet; $60 per examiner's manual; $30 per 25 student response forms; $60 per 25 profile/examiner record forms; $32 per student booklet.
Time: (60–120) minutes.
Authors: Phyllis L. Newcomer and Brian R. Bryant.
Publisher: PRO-ED.
Cross References: For reviews by Jerrilyn V. Andrews and Gerald E. DeMauro, see 13:98 (1 reference); for reviews by Randy W. Kamphaus and James E. Ysseldyke of an earlier edition, see 10:92.

[818]
Diagnostic Assessments of Reading.

Purpose: Assesses skills in reading and language.
Population: Ages 6–adult.
Publication Date: 1992.
Acronym: DAR.
Scores: Mastery level scores in 6 areas: Word Recognition, Word Analysis, Oral Reading, Silent Reading Comprehension, Spelling, Word Meaning.
Administration: Individual.
Price Data: Available from publisher.
Time: Untimed; approximately 20–30 minutes.
Comments: Part of the DARTTS testing and teaching program.
Authors: Florence G. Roswell and Jeanne S. Chall.
Publisher: Riverside Publishing.
Cross References: For reviews by Kevin D. Crehan and Gene Schwarting, see 12:115.

[819]
Diagnostic English Language Tests

Purpose: Designed to measure "ability to cope with the English language demands of upper secondary school in Australia."
Population: Non-English-speaking students entering Australian secondary schools at years 10 and 11.
Publication Date: 1994.
Acronym: DELTA.
Scores, 3: Reading, Writing, Listening.
Administration: Group.
Price Data, 2006: A$139.95 per complete set; A$21.95 per 10 copies Reading Test; A$21.95 per 10 copies Listening Test.
Time: (180) minutes.
Authors: Joy McQueen and Cecily Aldous.
Publisher: Australian Council for Educational Research Ltd. [Australia]
Cross References: For a review by Alfred Longo, see 15:83.

[820]
Diagnostic Evaluation of Language Variation-Norm Referenced.

Purpose: Designed "to be used by clinicians to identify speech and language disorders (or delays) in children."
Population: Ages 4-0 to 9-11.
Publication Date: 2005.
Acronym: DELV-Norm Referenced.
Scores, 5: Total Language Composite, Syntax, Pragmatics, Semantics, Phonology.
Administration: Individual.
Price Data, 2006: $145 per complete test kit including examiner's manual (209 pages), picture manual, and 25 record forms; $85 per examiner's manual; $85 per stimulus book; $59 per 25 record forms.
Time: (45) minutes.
Comments: Appropriate for use with children for whom English is their first and primary language.
Authors: Harry N. Seymour, Thomas W. Roeper, and Jill de Villiers.
Publisher: PsychCorp, A brand of Harcourt Assessment, Inc.

[821]
Diagnostic Evaluation of Language Variation™—Screening Test.

Purpose: Designed to "distinguish variations due to normal developmental language changes or to regional and cultural patterns of language difference from true markers of language disorder or delay."
Population: Ages 4-0 to 12-11.
Publication Date: 2003.
Acronym: DELV—Screening Test.
Administration: Individual.
Parts, 2: Part I, Part II.
Price Data, 2005: $135 per complete test; $80 per examiner's manual (122 pages), $80 per stimulus manual; $59 per 25 record forms; $195 per 100 record forms.
Time: (15–20) minutes.
Comments: "Criterion-referenced."
Authors: Harry N. Seymour, Thomas W. Roeper, and Jill de Villiers with contributions by Peter A. de Villiers.
Publisher: PsychCorp, A brand of Harcourt Assessment, Inc.
    a) PART I.
    Population: Ages 4-0 to 12-11.
    Scores: Language Variation Status.
    b) PART II.
    Population: Ages 4-0 to 9-11.
    Scores: Diagnostic Risk Status.
Cross References: For reviews by Aimee Langlois and Sheila Pratt, see 16:72.

[822]
Diagnostic Interview for Borderline Patients.

Purpose: Designed to discriminate borderline patients from patients with schizophrenia, neurotic depression, and mixed diagnoses.
Population: Patients.
Publication Dates: [1982–1983].
Scores, 6: Social Adaptation, Impulse Action Patterns, Affects, Psychosis, Interpersonal Relations, Total.
Administration: Individual.
Price Data: Available from publisher.
Time: (50–90) minutes.
Authors: John G. Gunderson (interview), Pamela S. Ludolph (manual), Kenneth R. Silk (manual), Naomi E. Lohr (manual), and Dewey G. Cornell (manual).
Publisher: Pamela S. Ludolph [No reply from publisher; status unknown].
Cross References: See T5:824 (6 references) and T4:779 (19 references); for reviews by Robert E. Deysach and Charles A. Peterson, see 10:95 (12 references).

[823]
Diagnostic Interview for Children and Adolescents–IV.

Purpose: "Designed to assess psychiatric problems in children and adolescents."
Population: Ages 6–17.
Publication Dates: 1997–1999.
Acronym: DICA-IV.
Scores: 28 diagnostic categories: Attention Deficit/Hyperactivity Disorder, Oppositional/Defiant Disorder, Conduct Disorder, Alcohol, Tobacco, Inhalant Use, Marijuana, Street Drugs, Major Depressive Disorder, Mania or Hypomania, Dysthymic Disorder, Separation Anxiety Disorder, Panic Disorder, Generalized Anxiety Disorder, Phobias (Social and Specific), Obsessions, Compulsions, Posttraumatic Stress Disorder, Eating Disorders, Elimination Disorders, Menstruation, Gender Identity, Psychotic Symptoms, Somatization, Psychosocial Stressors, Observation (Clinician Use), Pregnancy/Birth (Parent Version), Early Development (Parent Version).
Administration: Individual.
Price Data, 2006: $535 per Child/Adolescent Version (unlimited use); $535 per Parent Version (unlimited use); $859 per both versions (unlimited use); $50 per preview version including 3 Child/Adolescent Version uses and 3 Parent Version uses.
Time: (5–20) minutes per category.
Comments: 2 versions: Child/Adolescent, Parent; must be used in conjunction with MHS's PsycManager; Windows compatible computer-administered interview format.
Authors: Wendy Reich, Zila Welner, Barbara Herjanic, and MHS Staff.
Publisher: Multi-Health Systems, Inc.

[824]
Diagnostic Mathematics Profiles.

Purpose: Constructed to diagnose problems in addition, subtraction, multiplication, and division.
Population: Australian school years 3–6.
Publication Date: 1990.
Scores: Item scores only.
Administration: Group or individual.
Parts, 4: Addition, Subtraction, Multiplication, Division.
Price Data, 2006: A$40.70 per test package including 30 copies of each part; A$15.30 per manual (23 pages).
Time: Administration time not reported.
Authors: Brian Doig.
Publisher: Australian Council for Educational Research Ltd. [Australia].
Cross References: For reviews by John M. Enger and Arlen R. Gullickson, see 12:116.

[825]
Diagnostic Screening Test: Achievement.

Purpose: Designed "for estimating practical data about student's overall school achievement level in general, and achievement in Science, Social Studies, and Literature and the Arts more specifically."
Population: Grades K–12.
Publication Date: 1977.
Acronym: DSTA.
Scores, 5: Science, Social Studies, Literature and the Arts, Practical Knowledge, Total Achievement.
Administration: Group.
Price Data, 2002: $58 per complete kit including manual (12 pages) and 50 test forms; $33 per 50 test forms.
Time: (5–10) minutes.
Authors: Thomas D. Gnagey and Patricia A. Gnagey.
Publisher: Slosson Educational Publications, Inc.
Cross References: For a review by Edward F. Iwanicki, see 9:339.

[826]
Diagnostic Screening Test: Language, Second Edition.

Purpose: Designed "for estimating over-all achievement level in written language."
Population: Grades 1–12.
Publication Date: 1977.
Acronym: DSTL.
Scores, 8: Punctuation, Grammar, Spelling Rules, Sentence Structure, Capitalization, Formal Knowledge of Language, Applied Knowledge of Language, Total Language.
Administration: Group.
Price Data, 2005: $65.25 per complete kit including manual (12 pages) and 50 test forms; $33 per 50 test forms.

Time: (5–10) minutes.
Authors: Thomas D. Gnagey and Patricia A. Gnagey.
Publisher: Slosson Educational Publications, Inc.
Cross References: For reviews by Janice Arnold Dole and Edward J. Iwanicki, see 9:340.

[827]
Diagnostic Screening Test: Math, Third Edition.

Purpose: Designed for estimating practical data about students' mathematical skills.
Population: Grades 1–11.
Publication Date: 1980.
Acronym: DSTM.
Scores, 31: Basic Process Scores (Addition, Subtraction, Multiplication, Division, Total), Specialized Process Scores (Money, Time, Percent, U.S. Measurement, Metric Measurement, Total), Concept Scores (Process, Sequencing, Simple Computation, Complex Computation, Special Manipulations, Use of Zero, Decimals, Simple Fractions, Manipulation in Fractions), 11 consolidation index scores.
Administration: Group.
Price Data, 2002: $58 per complete kit including manual (17 pages), 25 test Form A, and 25 test Form B; $29 per 50 test Form A; $29 per 50 test Form B.
Time: (5–20) minutes.
Author: Thomas D. Gnagey.
Publisher: Slosson Educational Publications, Inc.
Cross References: For reviews by Edward F. Iwanicki and Stanley F. Vasa, see 9:341.

[828]
Diagnostic Screening Test: Reading, Third Edition.

Purpose: Designed "for estimating practical data about students' reading skills."
Population: Grades 1–12.
Publication Date: 1979.
Acronym: DSTR.
Scores, 16: Comfort Reading Level, Instructional Reading Level, Frustration Reading Level, Comprehension Reading Level, Listening Level, Phonics/Sight Ratio, Word Attack Skill Analysis (c-v/c, v-r, v-l, v-v, c-v-c, Silent e, Mix, Sight, Total), Consolidation Index.
Administration: Individual.
Price Data, 2005: $65.25 per complete kit including manual (13 pages), 25 test Form A, and 25 test Form B; $36.75 per 50 test Form A; $36.75 per 50 test Form B.
Time: (5–10) minutes.
Authors: Thomas D. Gnagey and Patricia A. Gnagey.
Publisher: Slosson Educational Publications, Inc.
Cross References: For a review by Edward F. Iwanicki, see 9:342; for a review by P. David Pearson of an earlier edition, see 8:755.

[829]
Diagnostic Screening Test: Spelling, Third Edition.

Purpose: Designed to gather diagnostic information regarding spelling skills.
Population: Grades 1–12.
Publication Date: 1979.
Acronym: DSTS.
Scores, 12: 3 scores (Verbal, Written, Total) for each of 3 categories (Phonics, Sight, Total); 3 Consolidation Index scores (Phonics Written, Sight Written, Total Spelling Written).
Administration: Group.
Price Data, 2005: $65.25 per complete kit including manual (13 pages), 25 test Form A, and 25 test Form B; $36.75 per 50 test Form A; $36.75 per 50 test Form B.
Time: (5–10) minutes.
Authors: Thomas D. Gnagey.
Publisher: Slosson Educational Publications, Inc.
Cross References: For reviews by Edward F. Iwanicki and Robert E. Schafer, see 9:343 (4 references).

[830]
Diagnostic Supplement to the WJ III® Tests of Cognitive Abilities.

Purpose: Designed to expand "the diagnostic capabilities of the [Woodcock-Johnson III Tests of Cognitive Abilities] for educational, clinical, or research purposes."
Population: Ages 2–90+.
Publication Date: 2003.
Acronym: WJ III® Diagnostic Supplement to the Tests of Cognitive Abilities.
Scores, 11: Memory for Names, Visual Closure, Sound Patterns—Voice, Number Series, Number Matrices, Cross Out, Memory for Sentences, Block Rotation, Sound Patterns—Music, Memory for Names—Delayed, Bilingual Verbal Comprehension—English/Spanish.
Administration: Individual.
Price Data, 2006: $295.50 per complete kit including test book, examiner's manual (119 pages) 25 test records, audio cassette, WJIII Compuscore and Profiles Program, Version 2.1 (Windows and Mac), and scoring guides; $85 per examiner's manual; $57 per 25 test records; $130.50 per WJIII Compuscore and Profiles Program, Version 2.1 (Windows and Mac).
Time: (5–10) minutes per subtest.
Comments: Tests from the Diagnostic Supplement can be combined with other tests from the Woodcock-Johnson III® (15:281) Tests of Cognitive Abilities Standard and Extended Batteries and the WJIII® Tests of Achievement to provide 14 additional interpretive clusters.

Authors: Richard W. Woodcock, Kevin S. McGrew, Nancy Mather, and Fredrick A. Schrank.
Publisher: Riverside Publishing.
Cross References: For reviews by Timothy Sares and Donald L. Thompson, see 16:275.

[831]
Diagnostic Test of the New Testament.

Purpose: "Measures and assesses New Testament knowledge."
Population: Ages 17 and older.
Publication Date: 1986.
Scores: Total score only.
Subtests, 5: Introduction to New Testament World and Records, Gospels, Acts, Epistles, Revelation.
Administration: Group or individual.
Manual: No manual.
Restricted Distribution: This test is "for the exclusive use of institutions of higher learning, such as Bible colleges, liberal arts colleges, and seminaries."
Price Data, 2005: $1 per test; $.10 per answer sheet; $2 per scoring key; bulk discount pricing is available.
Time: (40-50) minutes.
Author: Fred R. Johnson.
Publisher: The Association for Biblical Higher Education.

[832]
DIBELS: Dynamic Indicators of Basic Early Literacy Skills, Sixth Edition.

Purpose: Designed to assess "growth and development of early literacy skills."
Population: Grades K–6.
Publication Dates: 2002–2003.
Acronym: DIBELS.
Scores, 7: Initial Sound Fluency, Letter Naming Fluency, Phoneme Segmentation Fluency, Nonsense Word Fluency, Oral Reading Fluency, Oral Retelling Fluency, Word Use Fluency.
Administration: Individual.
Levels, 7: K, 1, 2, 3, 4, 5, 6.
Parts, 2: Benchmark Assessment, Progress Monitoring.
Price Data, 2006: $69 per classroom set (Grades K-3); $55 per classroom set (Grades 4-6); $88.95 per implementation video, "Catch Them Early, Watch them Grow! Using DIBELS in Your School"; $88.95 per implementation CD-ROM.
Time: (10–15) minutes.
Comments: Benchmark Assessments administered to whole class three times per year; progress monitoring components used with at-risk students on a week-to-week basis to determine progress.
Authors: Roland H. Good III, Ruth A. Kaminski, and Louisa C. Moats (overview only).
Publisher: Sopris West.

a) LETTER NAMING FLUENCY.
Population: Grades K–1.
Authors: Ruth A. Kaminski and Roland H. Good III.
b) INITIAL SOUND FLUENCY.
Population: Grade K.
Forms: 20 alternate forms.
Authors: Roland H. Good III, Deborah Laimon, Ruth A. Kaminski, and Sylvia Smith.
c) PHONEME SEGMENTATION FLUENCY.
Population: Grades K–1.
Forms: 20 alternate forms.
Authors: Roland H. Good III, Ruth A. Kaminski, and Sylvia Smith.
d) NONSENSE WORD FLUENCY.
Population: Grades K–2.
Forms: 20 alternate forms.
Authors: Roland H. Good III and Ruth A. Kaminski.
e) ORAL READING FLUENCY.
Population: Grades 1–6.
Forms: 20 alternate forms.
Authors: Roland H. Good III, Ruth A. Kaminski, and Sheila Dill.
f) ORAL RETELLING FLUENCY.
Population: Grades 1–6.
Authors: Roland H. Good III, Ruth A. Kaminski, and Sheila Dill.
g) WORD USE FLUENCY.
Population: Grades K–3.
Authors: Roland H. Good III, Ruth A. Kaminski, and Sylvia Smith.
Cross References: For reviews by Bethany A. Brunsman and Timothy Shanahan, see 16:73.

[833]
Differential Ability Scales.

Purpose: Designed to measure cognitive abilities and achievement.
Population: Ages 2-6 to 17-11.
Publication Date: 1990.
Acronym: DAS.
Administration: Individual.
Price Data, 2002: $750 per complete kit with briefcase; $46 per 20 preschool forms; $46 per 20 school-age record forms; $15 per 20 basic number skills and spelling worksheets; $15 per 10 speed of information processing booklets (select A, B, C); $25 per 10 sequential and quantitative reasoning booklets; $94 per administration and scoring manual (1990, 445 pages); $43 per introductory and technical handbook (1990, 379 pages).
Comments: Based on the British Ability Scales (360).
Author: Colin D. Elliott.
Publisher: PsychCorp, A brand of Harcourt Assessment, Inc.

a) COGNITIVE BATTERY.
1) *Preschool.*
Population: Ages 2-6 to 7-11.
Time: (25–65) minutes.
(a) Ages 2-6 to 3-5.
Scores, 7: Block Building, Verbal Comprehension, Picture Similarities, Naming Vocabulary, Total General Conceptual Ability, Recall of Digits, Recognition of Pictures.
(b) Ages 3-6 to 5-11.
Scores, 14: Verbal Ability (Verbal Comprehension, Naming Vocabulary, Total), Nonverbal Ability (Picture Similarities, Pattern Construction, Copying, Total), Early Number Concepts, Total General Conceptual Ability, Block Building, Matching Letter-Like Forms, Recall of Digits, Recall of Objects, Recognition of Pictures.
2) *School-Age.*
Population: Ages 6-0 to 17-11.
Scores, 13: Verbal Ability (Word Definitions, Similarities, Total), Nonverbal Reasoning Ability (Matrices, Sequential and Quantitative Reasoning, Total), Spatial Ability (Recall of Designs, Pattern Construction, Total), Total General Conceptual Ability, Recall of Digits, Recall of Objects, Speed of Information Processing.
Time: (40–65) minutes.
b) SCHOOL ACHIEVEMENT.
Population: Ages 6-0 to 17-11.
Scores, 3: Basic Number Skills, Spelling, Word Reading.
Time: (15–25) minutes.
Cross References: See T5:837 (14 references) and T4:800 (3 references); for reviews by Glen P. Aylward and Robert C. Reinehr, see 11:111 (1 reference).

[834]
Differential Aptitude Tests—Australian and New Zealand Editions [Forms V and W].

Purpose: Provides a battery of tests for personnel selection and rehabilitation counseling with relation to successful job performance.
Population: Grades 8–12.
Publication Dates: 1973–1989.
Scores, 9: Verbal Reasoning, Numerical Ability, Abstract Reasoning, Clerical Speed and Accuracy, Mechanical Reasoning, Space Relations, Spelling, Language Use, Verbal Reasoning + Numerical Ability.
Subtests: Available as separates.
Administration: Individual or group.
Price Data, 2006: A$76.30 per exam kit; A$122.95 per manual (1989, 160 pages; A$272.10 per 25 test booklets (Verbal, Numerical and Abstract Reasoning); A$110.45 per 25 test booklets (Clerical Speed and

Accuracy); A$237.95 per 25 test booklets (Mechanical Reasoning); A$184.45 per 25 test booklets (Space Relations); A$153.70 per 25 test booklets (Spelling and Language Usage); A$76.30 per 25 answer sheets; A$55.80 per SP1; A$67.15 per SP2; A$76.30 per scoring keys.
Time: (60-90) minutes for entire battery.
Comments: New Zealand manual information included; Australian manual same as that for the American version of the Differential Aptitude Tests with norms and revisions for the Australian and New Zealand population.
Authors: Marion M. de Lemos (Australian manual), George K. Bennett, Harold G. Seashore, and Alexander G. Wesman.
Publisher: Harcourt Assessment Australia and New Zealand; Australian Council for Educational Research Ltd. [Australia].
Cross References: For reviews by Lynn Lakota Brown and Jack E. Gebart-Eaglemont, see 15:85.

[835]
Differential Aptitude Tests, Fifth Edition.

Purpose: "Designed to measure students' ability to learn or to succeed in a number of different areas."
Population: Grades 7–9, grades 10–12 and adults.
Publication Dates: 1947–1992.
Acronym: DAT.
Scores: 9 tests (Verbal Reasoning, Numerical Reasoning, Abstract Reasoning, Perceptual Speed and Accuracy [Part 1, Part 2], Mechanical Reasoning, Space Relations, Spelling, Language Usage) and Total Scholastic Aptitude.
Administration: Group.
Levels, 2: 1, 2.
Price Data, 2002: $59 per 25 Form C partial battery test booklets (Levels 1 or 2) including Directions for Administering (1990, 47 pages); $128 per 25 Form C complete battery test booklets (Levels 1 or 2) including Directions for Administering; $128 per 100 Type 1 machine-scorable answer documents with DAT (Levels 1 or 2, Form C), $152 per 100 Type 1 machine-scorable answer documents with DAT (Levels 1 or 2, Form C) and Level 1 or Level 2 Career Interest Inventory; $67 per Ready-Score answer documents with 25 Perceptual Speed and Accuracy—Part 1 answer sheets, Profile Your DAT scores pamphlet, and Levels 1 or 2 of Form C; $34.50 per norms booklet (Fall or Spring); $34.50 per Using the DAT with Adults; $28 per 25 Practice Tests including a practice test for the Career Interest Inventory and Directions; $108.70 per Guide to Careers Student Workbook; $19 per 25 Exploring Aptitudes: An Introduction to the Differential Aptitude Tests; $19 per 25 Using Test Results for Decision-Making; $34.50 per Technical Manual (1992, 192 pages); $5.30 per Directions for Practice Test; $7 per

Directions for Administering; price information for scoring and reporting services available from publisher.
Time: 90(150) minutes.
Comments: 2 forms (C, D) per level; partial battery includes only 2 subtests (Verbal Reasoning and Numerical Reasoning); can be used in conjunction with Career Interest Inventory (419).
Authors: G. K. Bennett, H. G. Seashore, and A. G. Wesman.
Publisher: PsychCorp, A brand of Harcourt Assessment, Inc.
Cross References: See T5:838 (23 references); for reviews by Keith Hattrup and Neal Schmitt, see 12:118 (16 references); see also T4:802 (31 references); for reviews of Forms V and W by Ronald K. Hambleton and Daryl Sander, see 9:352 (19 references); see also T3:732 (26 references); for reviews by Thomas J. Bouchard, Jr., and Robert L. Linn and an excerpted review by Gerald S. Hanna of earlier forms, see 8:485 (56 references); see also T2:1069 (64 references); for a review by M. Y. Quereshi and an excerpted review by Jack C. Merwin of earlier forms, see 7:673 (139 references); for reviews by J. A. Keats and Richard E. Schutz, see 6:767 (52 references); for reviews by John B. Carroll and Norman Frederiksen, see 5:605 (49 references); for reviews by Harold Bechtoldt, Ralph F. Berdie, and Lloyd G. Humphreys, see 4:711 (27 references); for an excerpted review, see 3:620.

[836]
Differential Aptitude Tests for Personnel and Career Assessment.

Purpose: Designed to measure ability to learn in eight aptitude areas.
Population: Adult.
Publication Dates: 1972–1991.
Acronym: DAT for PCA.
Scores, 8: General Cognitive Abilities Tests (Verbal Reasoning, Numerical Ability, Total), Perceptual Abilities Tests (Abstract Reasoning, Mechanical Reasoning, Space Relations), Clerical and Language Tests (Spelling, Language Usage, Clerical Speed and Accuracy).
Administration: Group or individual
Price Data, 2002: $146 per 25 General Cognitive Abilities Battery tests; $146 per 25 Perceptual Abilities Battery tests; $146 per 25 Clerical/Language Battery tests; $74 per 25 tests (select Verbal Reasoning, Numerical Reasoning, Abstract Reasoning, Spelling, Language Usage, or Clerical Speed and Accuracy); $74 per 25 tests (select Mechanical Reasoning or Space Relations); $57 per 25 ready-score answer sheets (select battery); $38 per 50 General Cognitive Abilities Battery hand-scorable answer sheets; $38 per 50 Perceptual Abilities Battery or Clerical/Language Battery hand-scorable answer sheets; $38 per 50 specific test hand-scorable answer sheets (select test); $32 per set of

General Cognitive Abilities Battery scoring keys; $32 per set of Perceptual Abilities Battery or Clerical/Language Battery scoring keys; $19 per set of scoring keys for specific tests (select test); $45 per directions for administering (includes norms); $45 per technical manual; $62 per examination kit.

Time: 114(144) minutes.

Comments: Abbreviated form of the Differential Aptitude Tests, Form V/W.

Authors: George K. Bennett, Harold G. Seashore, and Alexander G. Wesman.

Publisher: PsychCorp, A brand of Harcourt Assessment, Inc.

Cross References: For reviews by Victor L. Willson and Hilda Wing, see 12:119.

[837]
Differential Test of Conduct and Emotional Problems.

Purpose: "Designed to effect differentiations between conduct problem, emotionally disturbed and noninvolved populations."

Population: Grades K–12.

Publication Dates: 1990–1991.

Acronym: DT/CEP.

Scores, 2: Emotional Disturbance Scale, Conduct Problem Scale.

Administration: Group.

Price Data, 2002: $78 per complete set including manual (1990, 58 pages), score forms, and scoring template; $29 per 50 score forms; $9 per set of 2 scoring templates.

Time: (15–20) minutes.

Comments: Ratings by teachers.

Author: Edward J. Kelly.

Publisher: Slosson Educational Publications, Inc.

Cross References: For reviews by Richard Brozovich and Alida S. Westman, see 12:120; see also T4:804 (1 reference).

[838]
Digit Vigilance Test.

Purpose: Designed to measure vigilance during rapid visual tracking and accurate selection of target stimuli.

Population: Ages 20–80.

Publication Date: 1995.

Acronym: DVT.

Scores, 2: Total Time, Total Errors.

Administration: Individual.

Forms, 2: 6s, 9s.

Price Data, 2006: $130 per introductory kit including professional user's guide (12 pages), 25 test booklets, and set of 4 scoring keys.

Time: (10) minutes.

Authors: Ronald F. Lewis.

Publisher: Psychological Assessment Resources, Inc.

Cross References: For reviews by Raymond S. Dean and Scott Kristian Hill and by Daniel C. Miller, see 14:122.

[839]
Dimensions of Excellence Scales [1991 Edition].

Purpose: Designed to identify, describe and validate successful programs and practices of a school district, as well as to forecast future needs.

Population: Schools or districts.

Publication Dates: 1988–1990.

Acronym: DOES.

Administration: Group.

Price Data, 2001: $2 per school staff survey; $1.25 per parent survey; $1.25 per student survey; $23.95 per manual (1990, 71 pages).

Comments: Ratings by students, parents, and school staff.

Authors: Russel A. Dusewicz and Francine S. Beyer.

Publisher: Research for Better Schools, Inc.

    a) STUDENT SCALE.

    Scores: 4 dimensions: School Climate, Teacher Behavior, Monitoring and Assessment, Student Discipline and Behavior.

    Time: (30) minutes.

    b) PARENT SCALE.

    Scores, 8: Same as *a* above plus Leadership, Curriculum, Staff Development, Parent Involvement.

    Time: (20–30) minutes.

    c) SCHOOL STAFF SCALE.

    Scores, 8: Same as *b* above.

    Time: (45) minutes.

Cross References: For a review by Andrew A. McConney, see 14:123; for reviews by Janet F. Carlson and William P. Erchul of an earlier edition, see 11:112.

[840]
Dimensions of Self-Concept.

Purpose: Designed to "measure non-cognitive factors associated with self-esteem or self-concept in a school setting."

Publication Dates: 1976–1989.

Acronym: DOSC.

Administration: Group.

Price Data: Available from publisher.

Comments: Self-report instrument.

Authors: William B. Michael, Robert A. Smith, and Joan J. Michael.

Publisher: EdITS/Educational and Industrial Testing Service.

    a) FORM E.

    Population: Grades 4–6.

    Scores, 5: Level of Aspiration, Anxiety, Academic Interest and Satisfaction, Leadership and Initiative, Identification vs. Alienation.

    Time: (20–40) minutes.

b) FORM S.
Population: Grades 7–12.
Scores: Same as for *a* above.
Time: (15–35) minutes.
c) FORM H.
Population: College.
Scores: Same as for *a* above.
Time: (15–35) minutes.
d) FORM W.
Population: Adult workers.
Scores, 5: Aspiration, Anxiety, Job Interest and Satisfaction, Identification vs. Alienation, Level of Job Stress.
Time: Administration time not reported.
Cross References: See T5:844 (6 references) and T4:806 (1 reference); for a review by Sharon Johnson-Lewis, see 11:113 (10 references); for reviews by Herbert G. W. Bischoff and Alfred B. Heilbrun, Jr., see 9:353 (4 references); see also T3:734 (5 references).

[841]
The Diplomacy Test of Empathy.

Purpose: Constructed to measure empathic ability.
Population: Business and industrial personnel.
Publication Dates: 1960–1962.
Scores: Total score only.
Administration: Group.
Price Data: Available from publisher.
Time: (20–25) minutes.
Comments: Revision of Primary Empathic Abilities; title on test is Diplomacy Test of Empathic Ability.
Author: Willard A. Kerr.
Publisher: Psychometric Affiliates.
Cross References: See T2:1160 (1 reference) and P:64 (2 references); for reviews by Arthur H. Brayfield and Richard S. Hatch, see 6:85 (1 reference); for a review by Robert L. Thorndike of the earlier test, see 5:99.

[842]
DiSC Classic.

Purpose: Designed to "help adults better understand themselves and others."
Population: Adults.
Publication Dates: 1996–2001.
Scores, 4: Dominance, Influence, Steadiness, Conscientiousness.
Administration: Individual or Group.
Price Data: Available from publisher.
Time: (7–10) minutes.
Comments: Update of the Personal Profile System; self-report, self-scored instrument; related scripted seminar available from publisher.
Author: Inscape Publishing.
Publisher: Inscape Publishing.
Cross References: For a review by Collie W. Conoley and Linda Castillo, see 16:74.

[843]
DiSC Indra.

Purpose: Provides "an in-depth understanding of relationship dynamics."
Population: Adults.
Publication Date: 2003.
Scores, 10: Convincing, Sociable, Receptive, Patient, Careful, Serious, Resolute, Competitive, DiSC Vector Angle and Length, Goodness of Fit.
Administration: Individual, dyad, or group.
Price Data: Available from publisher.
Time: (15-20) minutes.
Comments: Self-report rating scale; computerized, on-line assessment.
Authors: Inscape Publishing (test), Pamela Cole and Kathleen Tuzinski (research report).
Publisher: Inscape Publishing.
Cross References: For reviews by Gypsy M. Denzine and Frederick T. L. Leong, see 16:75.

[844]
The Discipline Index.

Purpose: "Systematically obtains information from a child about the child's overall perceptions of each parent's disciplinary practices."
Population: Ages 6–17.
Publication Dates: 1999–2002.
Acronym: DI.
Scores, 6: Mother and Father scores for: Clear Expectations, Effectively Monitors, Consistently Enforces, Fairness, Attunement, Moderates Anger, plus Mother Total, Father Total.
Administration: Individual.
Price Data, 2002: $199 per complete kit including handbook (2000, 140 pages), 8 sets response cards, 8 scoring summaries, stylus-pen, placement dots, updates, and 3-year update service; $99 per 8 response cards with summaries; $159 per 16 response cards with summaries; $199 per 24 response cards with summaries; $198 per computer scoring program (half price when purchased with kit); $129 per handbook.
Time: (35 minutes).
Authors: Anita K. Lampel, Barry Bricklin, and Gail Elliot.
Publisher: Village Publishing.
Cross References: For reviews by Patti L. Harrison and Darrell L. Sabers, see 15:86.

[845]
Dissemination Self-Inventory.

Purpose: "To help people involved in NIDRR-funded disability research and development projects bridge the gap between the creation of disability research outcomes and their use."
Population: Organizations.
Publication Date: 2002.

Scores, 4: Organizational Structure and Policies, Research Design, Dissemination Plan, Evaluation.
Administration: Individual.
Price Data, 2002: $10 per Dissemination Self-Inventory (2002, 24 pages).
Time: [20–35] minutes.
Author: Southwest Educational Development Laboratory.
Publisher: Southwest Educational Development Laboratory.

[846]
Dissociative Experiences Scale.

Purpose: "Developed to serve as a clinical tool to help identify patients with dissociative psychopathology and as a research tool to provide a means of quantifying dissociative experiences."
Population: Late adolescent–adult.
Publication Date: 1986.
Acronym: DES.
Scores: Total score only.
Administration: Group or individual.
Price Data: Available from publisher.
Foreign Language Editions: Available in French, Spanish, Italian, Dutch, Hindi, Cambodian, Czech, Swedish, Norwegian, Japanese, Hebrew, Chinese (Mandarin, Traditional Character, and Simplified Character), Finnish, Korean, Polish, and Turkish.
Time: [10] minutes.
Comments: Self-report inventory; translation also in progress for version of the DES in German; test is in the public domain and is available from publisher for cost of copying, handling, and mailing.
Authors: Eve Bernstein Carlson and Frank W. Putnam.
Publisher: The Sidran Foundation.
Cross References: See T5:846 (26 references); for reviews by Samuel Juni and Niels G. Waller, see 12:122 (16 references); see also T4:809 (1 reference).

[847]
Dissociative Features Profile.

Purpose: Developed to "help uncover dissociative pathology in children and adolescents."
Population: Children and adolescents.
Publication Date: 1996.
Acronym: DFP.
Scores, 22: Part I: Evidence of Amnesia, Staring Episodes, Odd Movements, Fluctuations/Relatedness, Fluctuations/Language, Fearfulness, Anger, Physical Complaints, Dividedness (1), Dividedness (2), Total; Part II: Multiplicity, Malevolent Religiosity, Dissociative Coping, Depersonalized Humans, Explicit Emotional Confusion, Categories of Good and Bad, Mutilation, Torture, Magical Transformations, Total; Combined Part I and Part II Total.

Administration: Individual.
Parts, 2: Behaviors, Markers.
Price Data: Price data available from publisher for set of 5 preliminary DFP forms and scoring manual/reference guide (1996, 4 pages).
Time: Untimed.
Comments: "Developed to be used with a typical psychological testing battery" (at least 2 other psychological tests given in conjunction with this test); profile completed by psychological professionals about juvenile clients.
Author: Joyanna L. Silberg.
Publisher: The Sidran Foundation.

[848]
Diversity Awareness Profile.

Purpose: "Designed to assist people in becoming aware of ways in which they discriminate against, judge, or isolate others."
Population: Employees or managers.
Publication Date: 1991.
Acronym: DAP.
Scores: Total score only.
Administration: Group.
Forms, 2: Employee, Manager.
Price Data: Price information available from publisher.
Time: (90) minutes.
Author: Karen Grote.
Publisher: Jossey-Bass, A Wiley Company.
Cross References: For reviews by Donald B. Pope-Davis and Jonathan G. Dings and by Gargi Roysircar Sodowsky, see 12:123.

[849]
Domestic Situation Inventory.

Purpose: "Designed to provide an objective, research-based, and statistically sound survey of the elements and risk factors that influence and contribute to domestic violence, specifically a male perpetrating violence against a female partner."
Population: Adults.
Publication Date: 2004.
Acronym: DSI.
Scores: DSI Total Score, The Hopelessness/Depression Scale [optional], The Powerlessness/Helplessness Scale [optional], The Threatening Behaviors Scale [optional], The Violent Behaviors Scale [optional].
Administration: Individual or group.
Price Data, 2006: $37.95 per complete kit including 25 test booklets and 1 administrator's guide (8 pages).
Time: (10-15) minutes.
Author: Robert P. Brady.
Publisher: JIST Publishing, Inc.

[850]
Domestic Violence Inventory.

Purpose: "Designed specifically for risk and needs assessment of people who have committed physical, emotional and verbal abuse."
Population: Ages 12–18, adults.
Publication Dates: 1991–1995.
Acronym: DVI.
Scores: 6 scales: Truthfulness, Violence, Alcohol, Drugs, Control, Stress Coping Ability.
Administration: Group.
Forms, 2: Adult, Juvenile.
Price Data: Available from publisher.
Time: (30) minutes.
Comments: Available in English and Spanish; both computer version and paper-pencil format are scored on IBM-PC compatibles.
Author: Risk & Needs Assessment, Inc.
Publisher: Risk & Needs Assessment, Inc.
Cross References: For reviews by Carol Collins and by David M. Kaplan and Molly L. Vanduser, see 14:125.

[851]
Doors and People.

Purpose: Designed to "provide comparable measures of visual and verbal memory" and "test both recall and recognition."
Population: Ages 18–80.
Publication Date: 1994.
Scores, 12: Verbal Recall (People), Visual Recognition (Doors), Visual Recall (Shapes), Verbal Recognition (Names), Overall, Combined Visual, Combined Verbal, Combined Recall, Combined Recognition, Forgetting (Verbal), Forgetting (Visual), Overall Forgetting.
Administration: Individual.
Price Data, 2006: £251 per complete kit including manual (20 pages), 25 scoring sheets, and 3 stimulus books; £39.50 per 50 scoring sheets.
Time: [35–40] minutes.
Authors: Alan Baddeley, Hazel Emslie, and Ian Nimmo-Smith.
Publisher: Harcourt Assessment [England].

[852]
Dos Amigos Verbal Language Scales

Purpose: Designed to assess the level of both English and Spanish language development in children.
Population: Ages 5-0 to 13-5
Publication Dates: 1973–1996.
Scores, 3: English, Spanish, Dominant Language.
Administration: Individual.
Price Data, 2006: $45 per complete test kit including manual (1996, 17 pages), and 25 test forms; $20 per 25 test forms.

Time: (20) minutes.
Comments: No reading by examinees; examiner must read and speak Spanish and English; the 1996 edition is criterion-referenced with scoring based on data used in earlier editions.
Authors: Donald E. Critchlow.
Publisher: Academic Therapy Publications
Cross References: For reviews by Robert B. Frary and Maria Del R. Medina-Diaz, see 14:126.

[853]
Drafter (CAD Operator).

Purpose: For selecting CAD operator candidates.
Population: Applicants for drafter positions.
Publication Date: 2005.
Scores, 3: Print Reading, Computer Aided Design, Total.
Administration: Group.
Price Data, 2006: $20 per consumable self-scoring test booklet (minimum order of 20).
Time: (30) minutes.
Comments: Packet of supplemental sheets included and required for test administration.
Author: Roland T. Ramsay.
Publisher: Ramsay Corporation.

[854]
Draw A Person: A Quantitative Scoring System.

Purpose: "To meet the need for a modernized, recently normed, and objective scoring system to be applied to human figure drawings produced by children and adolescents."
Population: Ages 5-17.
Publication Date: 1988.
Acronym: Draw A Person: QSS.
Scores, 4: Man, Woman, Self, Total.
Administration: Group.
Price Data, 2002: $146 per complete kit including 25 student record/response forms, scoring chart, and manual (1988, 100 pages); $101 per scoring chart and manual; $47 per 25 student record/response forms.
Time: 15(25) minutes.
Author: Jack A. Naglieri.
Publisher: PsychCorp, A brand of Harcourt Assessment, Inc.
Cross References: See T5:854 (2 references) and T4:814 (3 references); for reviews by Merith Cosden and W. Grant Willis, see 11:114 (1 reference).

[855]
Draw-A-Person Intellectual Ability Test for Children, Adolescents, and Adults.

Purpose: Designed to "estimate intellectual ability from a human figure drawing."
Population: Ages 4-0 to 89-11.

Publication Date: 2004.
Acronym: DAP: IQ.
Scores: DAP IQ.
Administration: Individual or group.
Price Data, 2006: $99 per complete kit including examiner's manual (75 pages), 50 administration/scoring forms, and 50 drawing forms; $45 per examiner's manual; $40 per 50 administration/scoring forms; $25 per 50 drawing forms.
Time: (8-15) minutes.
Authors: Cecil R. Reynolds and Julia A. Hickman.
Publisher: PRO-ED.

[856]

Draw A Person: Screening Procedure for Emotional Disturbance.

Purpose: Designed to screen for children who may have emotional disorders and require further evaluation.
Population: Ages 6–17.
Publication Date: 1991.
Acronym: DAP:SPED.
Scores: Total score only.
Administration: Group and individual.
Price Data, 2006: $140 per complete kit including 25 record forms and manual (77 pages); $45 per 25 record forms; $65 per manual; $40 per 10 scoring templates.
Time: 15(20) minutes.
Authors: Jack A. Naglieri, Timothy J. McNeish, and Achilles N. Bardos.
Publisher: PRO-ED.
Cross References: See T5:852 (1 reference); for reviews by Merith Cosden and Gale M. Morrison, see 12:124 (2 references); see also T4:816 (1 reference).

[857]

Driver Risk Inventory—II.

Purpose: "Designed for DUI/DWI offender screening."
Population: Convicted DUI and DWI offenders.
Publication Dates: 1986–1997.
Acronym: DRI-II.
Scores, 6: Truthfulness, Alcohol, Driver Risk, Drug, Stress Coping, Dependency.
Price Data: Available from publisher.
Time: (30–35) minutes.
Comments: Self-administered, computer-scored test.
Author: Behavior Data Systems Ltd.
Publisher: Behavior Data Systems Ltd.
Cross References: For reviews by Tony Cellucci and Kevin J. McCarthy, see 14:127; for a review by Frank Gresham of an earlier version, see 12:125.

[858]

Drug Abuse Screening Test.

Purpose: To assess "potential involvement with drugs."
Population: Clients of addiction treatment.

Publication Date: 1982.
Acronym: DAST-20.
Scores: Total score only.
Administration: Group.
Price Data, 2002: C$9.05 in Ontario (C$12.95 outside Ontario) per test.
Foreign Language Edition: Available in French.
Time: (5–10) minutes.
Comments: Self-report inventory; manual is entitled "Directory of Client Outcome Measures for Addiction Treatment Programs"; has also been listed as Drug Use Questionnaire.
Author: Harvey A. Skinner.
Publisher: Centre for Addiction and Mental Health [Canada].
Cross References: For reviews by Philip Ash and Jeffrey S. Rain, see 13:104.

[859]

Drug-Taking Confidence Questionnaire.

Purpose: "As an assessment tool, the DTCQ identifies a client's coping self-efficacy in relation to 50 drinking or drug-taking situations."
Population: Clients of addiction treatment.
Publication Date: 1997.
Acronym: DTCQ.
Scores: Situation profiles in two areas: Personal States, Situations Involving Other People; 8 subscales: Unpleasant Emotions, Physical Discomfort, Pleasant Emotions, Testing Personal Control, Urges and Temptations to Use, Conflict with Others, Social Pressure to Use, Pleasant Times with Others.
Administration: Group.
Price Data, 2002: C$34.95 per user's guide; C$14.95 per 30 questionnaires (specify alcohol or drug); C$39.95 per sample pack including user's guide and 40 questionnaires (10 alcohol and 30 drug); C$75 per 50 uses of computer-administration software (DOS format); C$100 per 50 uses of software with user's guide; C$250 per 200 uses of software; C$275 per 200 uses of software with user's guide.
Time: (15) minutes.
Comments: User's guide written in both English (160 pages) and French (69 pages); "French versions of DTCQ have not been scientifically validated."
Authors: Helen M. Annis, Sherrilyn M. Sklar, and Nigel E. Turner.
Publisher: Centre for Addiction and Mental Health [Canada].
Cross References: For reviews by Michael H. Campbell and Glenn B. Gelman, see 14:128.

[860]

Drug Use Screening Inventory—Revised.

Purpose: Designed to quantify "severity of problems in multiple domains of health, behavior, and psychosocial development."

Population: Ages 10 to 16; 17 and over.
Publication Dates: 1990–1991.
Acronym: DUSI-R.
Scores: 12 Domains: Drug and Alcohol Use, Substance Use, Behavior Patterns, Health Status, Psychiatric Disorder, Social Competence, Family System, School Performance, Work Adjustment, Peer Relationships, Leisure/Recreation, Overall Problem Density Index.
Administration: Individual.
Levels, 2: Youth, Adult.
Forms, 3: Past Year, Past Month, Past Week.
Price Data, 2004: $199 per Computer System (specify Youth or Adult) including 3.5-inch diskette or CD-ROM; $50 per 25 paper version forms (specify Youth or Adult); $49 annual maintenance fee for software license; volume discounts available.
Foreign Language Edition: Spanish edition available for computer.
Time: [15] minutes.
Comments: Self-report behavior inventory.
Author: Ralph E. Tarter.
Publisher: Gordian Group.
Cross References: For a review by Tony Cellucci, see 16:76.

[861]
DSST/DANTES Subject Standardized Tests.

Purpose: Gives colleges and universities the opportunity to offer non-traditional learners college credit for knowledge acquired outside the traditional classroom.
Population: Non-traditional students wishing to earn college credit by examination.
Publication Dates: 1983–2002.
Acronym: DSST.
Administration: Group.
Price Data, 2002: $40 per exam; test centers may also require an administration fee for each examination; scoring by publisher included in price.
Time: Untimed, requiring approximately (90) minutes per test.
Comments: Paper-and-pencil administration; additional information available at www.getcollegecredit.com.
Author: The Chauncey Group International.
Publisher: The Chauncey Group International.
  a) MATHEMATICS.
  Scores: Total score for each of 2 tests:
    1) *Fundamentals of College Algebra.*
    2) *Principles of Statistics.*
  b) SOCIAL SCIENCE.
  Scores: Total score for each of 14 tests:
    1) *Western Europe Since 1945.*
    2) *Introduction to the Modern Middle East.*
    3) *A History of the Vietnam War.*
    4) *Human/Cultural Geography.*
    5) *Lifespan Developmental Psychology.*
    6) *General Anthropology.*
    7) *Introduction to Law Enforcement.*
    8) *Criminal Justice.*
    9) *Fundamentals of Counseling.*
    10) *Art of the Western World.*
    11) *Drug and Alcohol Abuse.*
    12) *The Civil War and Reconstruction.*
    13) *Foundations of Education.*
    14) *Rise and Fall of the Soviet Union.*
  c) PHYSICAL SCIENCE.
  Scores: Total score for each of 5 tests:
    1) *Astronomy.*
    2) *Here's to Your Health.*
    3) *Environment and Humanity: The Race to Save the Planet.*
    4) *Principles of Physical Science I.*
    5) *Physical Geology.*
  d) BUSINESS.
  Scores: Total score for each of 12 tests:
    1) *Principles of Finance.*
    2) *Principles of Financial Accounting.*
    3) *Human Resource Management.*
    4) *Organizational Behavior.*
    5) *Introduction to Computing.*
    6) *Introduction to Business.*
    7) *Money and Banking.*
    8) *Business Mathematics.*
    9) *Business Law II.*
    10) *Principles of Supervision.*
    11) *Personal Finance.*
    12) *Management Information Systems.*
  e) FOREIGN LANGUAGE.
  f) APPLIED TECHNOLOGY.
    1) *Technical Writing.*
  g) HUMANITIES.
  Scores: Total score for each of 3 tests:
    1) *Ethics in America.*
    2) *Principles of Public Speaking.*
    3) *Introduction to World Religions.*
Cross References: For reviews by Laura L. B. Barnes and William A. Mehrens, see 11:103.

[862]
Durrell Analysis of Reading Difficulty, Third Edition.

Purpose: Designed to screen for reading problems.
Population: Grades 1–6.
Publication Dates: 1937–1980.
Acronym: DARD.
Scores, 16 to 21: Oral Reading, Silent Reading, Listening Comprehension, Word Recognition, Word Analysis, Listening Vocabulary, Sounds in Isolation (Letters, Blends and Digraphs, Phonograms, Initial Affixes, Final Affixes), Spelling, Phonic Spelling of Words, Visual

Memory of Words (Primary, Secondary), Identifying Sounds in Words, Prereading Phonics Abilities Inventories (Optional, Including Syntax Matching, Letter Names in Spoken Words, Phonemes in Spoken Words, Naming Lower Case Letters, Writing Letters from Dictation).
Administration: Individual.
Price Data, 2002: $137 per examiner's kit including tachistoscope, reading booklet, 5 record booklets, and manual (1980, 63 pages); $45.60 per reading booklet; $43 per tachistoscope; $81.60 per 35 record booklets; $23 per manual.
Time: (35–50) minutes.
Authors: Donald D. Durrell and Jane H. Catterson.
Publisher: PsychCorp, A brand of Harcourt Assessment, Inc.
Cross References: See T5:861 (5 references) and T4:822 (14 references); for reviews by Nancy L. Roser and Byron H. Van Roekel, see 9:360 (3 references); see also T3:766 (14 references) and T2:1628 (18 references); for reviews by James Maxwell and George D. Spache of an earlier edition, see 5:660; for a review by Helen M. Robinson of the original edition, see 4:561 (2 references); for reviews by Guy L. Bond and Miles A. Tinker, see 2:1533; for a review by Marion Monroe, see 1:1098.

[863]
Dutch Eating Behaviour Questionnaire.
Purpose: Assesses "the structure of an individual's eating behaviour.
Population: Ages 9–adult.
Publication Date: 2002.
Acronym: DEBQ.
Scores, 3: Emotional Eating, External Eating, Restrained Eating.
Administration: Individual.
Price Data, 2006: £87 per complete kit including manual (24 pages), questionnaire, and 25 scoring sheets; £47 per 50 questionnaires and scoring sheets.
Foreign Language Editions: German, French, Swedish, Portugese, Chinese, Greek, and Korean editions available.
Time: (10) minutes.
Author: Tatjana van Strien.
Publisher: Harcourt Assessment [England].

[864]
Dvorine Color Vision Test.
Purpose: Designed as a "method of identifying individuals with defective color vision."
Population: Ages 3 and over.
Publication Dates: 1944-1958.
Scores, 2: Nomenclature, Color Perception.
Administration: Individual.
Price Data, 2002: $335 per booklet of color plates (1953, 33 pages, manual and 24 color plates); 297 per 35 record forms.

Time: [2] minutes.
Comments: Revision of Dvorine Color Perception Testing Charts; also called Dvorine Pseudo-Isochromatic Plates.
Author: Israel Dvorine.
Publisher: PsychCorp, A brand of Harcourt Assessment, Inc.
Cross References: See T4:823 (1 reference), T3:767 (1 reference), T2:1911 (13 references), and 6:955 (12 references); for excerpted reviews by Elsie Murray, Laurance F. Shaffer, and Miles A. Tinker, see 5:773 (13 references); for excerpted reviews by Knight Dunlap, Carel C. Koch, Elsie Murray (reply by Israel Dvorine), and Miles A. Tinker, see 3:462 (4 references).

[865]
Dyadic Adjustment Scale.
Purpose: Designed to measure the quality of adjustment in marriage and similar dyadic relationships.
Population: People who have any committed couple relationship including unmarried cohabitation.
Publication Date: 1989.
Acronym: DAS.
Scores, 5: Dyadic Consensus, Dyadic Satisfaction, Affectional Expression, Dyadic Cohesion, Total.
Administration: Group or individual.
Price Data, 2006: $62 per complete kit including test manual (55 pages) and 20 QuikScore™ forms; $41 per 20 QuikScore™ forms (for 10 couples); $32 per manual; $2 each (minimum purchase of 50) for Windows software profile reports (with Psychmanager platform).
Time: (5-10) minutes.
Comments: Self-report.
Author: Graham B. Spanier.
Publisher: Multi-Health Systems, Inc.
Cross References: See T5:863 (94 references) and T4:824 (37 references); for reviews by Karen S. Budd and Nancy Heilman and by Richard B. Stuart, see 11:117 (17 references).

[866]
Dyadic Parent-Child Interaction Coding System.
Purpose: For use in assessing the quality of parent-child social interaction, discriminating between parent-child interactions of children with and without disruptive behavior disorders and their parents, and evaluating change after parent training interventions for young children with behavior problems.
Population: Children ages 2-10 and their parents.
Publication Dates: 1981-2005.
Acronym: DPICS.
Scores: 24 behavioral categories that provide frequency scores: parent and child positive and negative verbalization and physical touch categories, child nega-

tive vocalization categories (whine, yell), and child responses to parent commands and questions.
Administration: Individual dyads.
Price Data: Now available free of charge; can be downloaded from www.pcit.org.
Time: 15(20) minutes.
Comments: Behavioral coding by clinician in three standard 5-minute situations that vary in amount of parent control required: child-led play; parent-led play; clean-up; abridged version available for clinical use; workbook to assist coder training available.
Authors: Sheila M. Eyberg, Melanie M. Nelson, Maura Duke, and Stephen R. Boggs.
Publisher: Sheila M. Eyberg.
Cross References: See T5:864 (3 references) and T4:825 (11 references); for reviews by Robert J. McMahon and Phillip S. Strain, see 9:361 (1 reference); see also T3:768 (1 reference).

[867]
Dynamic Assessment of Test Accommodations.

Purpose: "Designed to assist the teacher in determining the appropriate accommodations that will allow students with learning disabilities to demonstrate academic ability independent of their handicapping conditions."
Population: Students with special needs in Grades 2 to 7.
Publication Date: 2003.
Acronym: DATA.
Administration: Individual or group.
Levels, 3: Grades 2–3, Grades 4–5, Grades 6–7.
Price Data, 2003: $150 per complete kit including manual, and 3 test booklets (specify level); $5.50 per Reading Screener card; $14 per 25 Reading Screener score sheets; $5.50 per Workbook Symbols card; $65 per manual, $25 per 25 Math booklets (specify level); $45 per 25 Reading booklets (specify level).
Comments: Student must be capable of reading basic text at a rate of at least 10 words per minute before Reading Comprehension is assessed.
Authors: Lynn Fuchs, Douglas Fuchs, Susan Eaton, and Carol Hamlett.
Publisher: PsychCorp, A brand of Harcourt Assessment, Inc.
  a) READING COMPREHENSION.
  Scores, 4: Large Print Gain, Extended Time Gain, Read Aloud Gain, No Accommodation.
  Time: 40(45) minutes.
  b) MATH COMPUTATION.
  Scores, 2: Extended Time Gain, No Accommodation.
  Time: 24(29) minutes.

  c) MATH APPLICATION.
  Scores, 4: Extended Time Gain, Calculator Condition Gain, Reader Condition Gain, No Accommodation.
  Time: (42) minutes.
Cross References: For reviews by Michelle Athanasiou and Bethany A. Brunsman, see 16:77.

[868]
Dynamic Factors Survey.

Purpose: Measurement of motivational factors related to personality and interest research, personnel selection, and vocational assessment.
Population: Grades 12-16 and adults.
Publication Dates: 1954–1956.
Acronym: DFOS.
Scores, 10: Need for Attention, Liking for Thinking, Adventure vs. Security, Self-Reliance vs. Dependence, Aesthetic Appreciation, Cultural Conformity, Need for Freedom, Realistic Thinking, Need for Precision, Need for Diversion.
Administration: Group.
Price Data: Available from publisher (www.mindgarden.com).
Time: (45) minutes.
Authors: J. P. Guilford, Paul R. Christensen, and Nicholas A. Bond, Jr.
Publisher: Mind Garden, Inc.
Cross References: See T2:1151 (7 references) and P:54 (12 references); for reviews by Andrew R. Baggaley, John W. French, and Arthur W. Meadows, see 5:45.

[869]
Dysarthria Examination Battery.

Purpose: Designed to "assess motor speech disorders."
Population: Children and adults.
Publication Date: 1993.
Scores, 5: Respiration, Phonation, Resonation, Articulation, Prosody.
Administration: Individual.
Price Data: Price data available from publisher for complete kit including test booklet, 3 stimulus cards, 20 scoring forms, and manual (48 pages).
Time: (60) minutes.
Author: Sakina S. Drummond.
Publisher: Harcourt Assessment, Inc.
Cross References: For reviews by Steven B. Leder and Malcolm R. McNeil, see 14:129.

[870]
Dyscalculia Screener.

Purpose: To screen pupil(s) to establish whether a pupil has low attainment because of a dyscalculic deficit.
Population: Ages 6–14.
Publication Date: 2003.

Scores: 4 tests: Dot Enumeration, Number Comparison (Numerical Stroop), Arithmetic Achievement, Simple Reaction Time.
Administration: Group.
Price Data, 2003: £150 for Annual License; £50 for License Renewal.
Time: (15–30) minutes.
Comments: Test administered via microcomputer conforming to the following specification: Pentium class system with at least 32 MB of RAM, 100 MB of free hard drive space, running Windows 98, 98SE, NT4, or 2000, with sound card.
Author: Brian Butterworth.
Publisher: NFER-Nelson Publishing Co., Ltd. [England].
Cross References: For reviews by Cleborne D. Maddux and Gretchen Owens, see 16:78.

[871]
Dyslexia Adult Screening Test.

Purpose: To assess strengths and weaknesses often associated with dyslexia.
Population: 16 years 5 months to adult.
Publication Date: 1998.
Acronym: DAST.
Scores, 12: Rapid Naming, One Minute Reading, Postural Stability, Nonverbal Reasoning, Phonemic Segmentation, Two Minute Spelling, Backwards Span, Verbal Fluency, Semantic Fluency, Nonsense Passage Reading, One Minute Writing, Total.
Administration: Individual.
Price Data, 2006: £140 per complete kit.
Time: 30 minutes.
Authors: Angela J. Fawcett and Rod I. Nicolson.
Publisher: Harcourt Assessment [England].
Cross References: For reviews by Manuela H. Habicht and William K. Wilkinson, see 16:79.

[872]
Dyslexia Determination Test, Second Edition.

Purpose: To identify individuals who exhibit dyslexic patterns of responding in the areas of reading, writing, and spelling.
Population: Grades 2–12.
Publication Dates: 1980-1987.
Acronym: DDT.
Scores: 6 subtests: Dysnemkinesia (Writing of Numbers, Writing of Letters), Dysphonesia (Decoding, Encoding), Dyseidesia (Decoding, Encoding).
Administration: Individual.
Price Data: Available from publisher.
Time: (15–20) minutes.
Authors: John R. Griffin and Howard N. Walton.
Publisher: I-MED, Instructional Materials & Equipment Distributors.

Cross References: For a review by Fred M. Grossman, see 9:362.

[873]
Dyslexia Early Screening Test [Second Edition].

Purpose: "Designed to pick out children who are 'at risk' of reading failure early enough to allow them to be given extra support at school."
Population: Ages 4 years, 6 months to 6 years, 5 months.
Publication Dates: 1996-2004.
Acronym: DEST-2.
Scores, 13: Tests of Attainment (Digit Naming, Letter Naming), Diagnostic Tests (Rapid Naming, Bead Threading, Phonological Discrimination, Postural Stability, Rhyme/First Letter, Forwards Digit Span, Sound Order, Shape Copying, Corsi Frog, Vocabulary), At Risk Quotient.
Administration: Individual.
Price Data, 2006: £125 per complete kit including examiner's manual (2004, 106 pages), envelope 1 (containing 7 subtest cards and sample permission letter), envelope 2 (containing score keys), Forward Digit Span tape, Sound Order tape, Corsi Frog, beads, cord, blindfold, balance tester, scoring software with manual, and 50 score sheets in a carrying case; £83 per upgrade kit including examiner's manual, envelope 1 (containing 7 subtest cards and sample permission letter), envelope 2 (containing score keys), Corsi Frog, scoring software with manual, and 50 score sheets in carrying case; £24.50 per manual; £38.50 per 50 score sheets.
Time: (30) minutes.
Authors: Rod I. Nicolson and Angela J. Fawcett.
Publisher: Harcourt Assessment [England].
Cross References: For reviews by Kathleen M. Johnson and William K. Wilkinson of the earlier edition, see 15:88.

[874]
Dyslexia Screening Instrument.

Purpose: Designed to identify students with dyslexia.
Population: Grades 1–12, ages 6–21.
Publication Date: 1994.
Scores, 4: Passed, Failed, Inconclusive, Cannot Be Scored.
Administration: Individual.
Price Data, 2002: $85 per complete kit including teacher rating scale, manual (40 pages), and scoring program software; $16 per 50 rating forms.
Time: (15–20) minutes.
Comments: Rating form is completed by student's teacher; computer scored, DOS 3.0 or higher.
Authors: Kathryn B. Coon, Mary Jo Polk, and Melissa McCoy Waguespack.

Publisher: PsychCorp, A brand of Harcourt Assessment, Inc.
Cross References: For reviews by Janet E. Spector and Betsy Waterman, see 14:130.

[875]
Dyslexia Screening Test.

Purpose: "A screening instrument … for profil[ing] the strengths and weaknesses often associated with dyslexia."
Population: Ages 6-6 to 16-5.
Publication Date: 2004.
Acronym: DST.
Scores, 11: 3 Tests of Attainment (One Minute Reading, Two Minute Spelling, One Minute Writing), 8 Diagnostic Tests (Rapid Naming, Bead Threading, Postural Stability, Phonemic Segmentation, Backwards Digit Span, Nonsense Passage Reading, Semantic Fluency, Verbal Fluency), At Risk Quotient.
Administration: Individual.
Price Data, 2004: $119 per complete kit including manual (1996, 63 pages), score keys, Backwards Digit Span audiocassette, and carrying case; $55 per 50 record forms.
Time: (30) minutes for entire battery.
Comments: Normed in the United Kingdom.
Authors: Angela J. Fawcett and Rod I. Nicolson.
Publisher: Harcourt Assessment [England].
Cross References: For reviews by Karen T. Carey and James E. Ysseldyke, see 16:80.

[876]
Dysphagia Evaluation Protocol.

Purpose: Developed to "assist in evaluating swallowing functioning in adult patients."
Population: Adult patients.
Publication Date: 1997.
Acronym: DEP.
Scores: 14 ratings: History and Observations (Feeding History, Nutritional Status, Respiratory Status), Clinical Evaluation of Swallowing (Observations, Oral Control, Primitive and Abnormal Reflexes, Pharyngeal Control), Feeding Trial (Appetite/Willingness to Participate, Ability to Swallow Without Food Bolus, Oral State, Pharyngeal Stage), Impressions (Summary, Functional Level, Recommendations/Plan).
Administration: Individual.
Price Data, 2002: $72 per complete kit including 15 record forms, pocket manual (40 pages), and manual (64 pages), $13 per 15 record forms; $36 per pocket manual; $36 per manual.
Time: (30) minutes.
Authors: Wendy Avery-Smith, Abbey Brod Rosen, and Donna M. Dellarosa.
Publisher: Harcourt Assessment, Inc.
Cross References: For a review by Maynard D. Filter, see 14:131.

[877]
Early Child Development Inventory.

Purpose: "A brief screening inventory … designed to help identify children with developmental, behavioral, or health problems."
Population: Ages 1-3 to 3-0.
Publication Date: 1988.
Acronym: ECDI.
Scores: General Development Score, Possible Problems List (24), Child Description, Parent's Questions/Concerns, Parent's Functioning.
Administration: Individual or group.
Price Data, 2005: $12.50 per 25 Parent Questionnaires; $12.50 per manual (15 pages).
Time: (15) minutes.
Comments: Parent-completed questionnaire; scores reflect parent's report of child's present functioning; publisher now recommends using Child Development Review Parent Questionnaire (455) instead of this.
Authors: Harold Ireton.
Publisher: Child Development Review - Behavior Science Systems, Inc.
Cross References: For a review by Robert W. Hiltonsmith, see 11:119.

[878]
Early Childhood Attention Deficit Disorders Evaluation Scale.

Purpose: Designed to document behaviors and measure the characteristics of ADHD in school and home environments.
Population: Males, ages 24–84 months; Females ages 24–83 months.
Publication Date: 1995.
Acronym: ECADDES.
Scores, 3: Inattentive, Hyperactive-Impulsive, Total Percentile Rank.
Administration: Individual.
Forms, 3: Home, School, ECADDES/DSM-IV.
Price Data, 2006: $162 per complete kit including 50 School Version rating forms, 50 Home Version rating forms, 50 ECADDES/DSM-IV forms, School Version technical manual (42 pages), Home Version technical manual (42 pages), ECADDES Intervention manual (147 pages), and Parent's Guide (134 pages); $35 per 50 rating forms (specify School Version or Home Version); $35 per 50 Home Version Spanish rating forms; $22 per 50 ECADDES/DSM-IV forms; $15 per technical manual (specify School Version or Home Version); $25 per ECADDES Intervention manual; $15 per Parent's Guide; $35 per computerized Quick Score program (WIN).
Time: (15–20) minutes.
Comments: Ratings by persons familiar with the child's behavior patterns in home or school settings.

Authors: Stephen B. McCarney and Nancy W. Johnson (Intervention Manual and Parent's Guide).
Publisher: Hawthorne Educational Services, Inc.
Cross References: For reviews by Libby G. Cohen and Harold R. Keller, see 14:132.

[879]
The Early Childhood Behavior Scale.

Purpose: Designed to assess behaviors related to early childhood emotional disturbance and behavior disorder.
Population: 36–72 months.
Publication Dates: 1991–1994.
Acronym: ECBS.
Scores, 4: Academic Progress, Social Relationships, Personal Adjustment, Total Percentile Rank.
Administration: Individual.
Price Data, 2006: $105 per complete kit including technical manual (1994, 36 pages), intervention manual (1991, 130 pages), and 50 ratings forms; $15 per technical manual; $25 per intervention manual; $35 per 50 rating forms.
Time: (15–20) minutes.
Comments: Ratings by teachers.
Authors: Stephen B. McCarney.
Publisher: Hawthorne Educational Services, Inc.
Cross References: For reviews by Kathleen D. Paget and Jonathan Sandoval, see 13:105.

[880]
Early Childhood Environment Rating Scale—Revised Edition.

Purpose: Designed to measure the quality of the environments in early childhood programs.
Population: Early childhood programs or classrooms (excluding infant and toddler programs).
Publication Dates: 1980–1998.
Acronym: ECERS-R.
Scores, 8: Space and Furnishings, Personal Care Routines, Language-Reasoning, Activities, Interaction, Program Structure, Parents and Staff, Total.
Administration: Group.
Price Data, 2006: $12.95 per complete test.
Foreign Language Editions: Translations of the original ECERS in Italian, Swedish, German, Portugese, Spanish, and Icelandic.
Time: (140) minutes.
Comments: Can be completed by an outside observer or as a self-assessment by program staff.
Authors: Thelma Harms, Richard M. Clifford, and Debbie Cryer.
Publisher: Teachers College Press.
Cross References: For reviews by Kathleen D. Paget and Gene Schwarting, see 14:133; see also T5:875 (11 references) and T4:833 (7 references); for reviews by Richard Elardo and Cathy Fultz Telzrow of the original version, see 9:365.

[881]
Early Childhood Inventory–4.

Purpose: Constructed to assess the "behavioral, affective, and cognitive symptoms of childhood psychiatric disorders."
Population: Ages 3–6.
Publication Dates: 1996–1997.
Acronym: ECI-4.
Scores, 25: AD/HD Inattentive, AD/HD Hyperactive-Impulsive, AD/HD Combined, Oppositional Defiant Disorder, Conduct Disorder, Peer Conflict Scale, Separation Anxiety Disorder, Specific Phobia, Obsessions, Compulsions, Motor Tics, Vocal Tics, Generalized Anxiety Disorder, Selective Mutism, Major Depressive Disorder, Dysthymic Disorder, Adjustment Disorder, Social Phobia, Sleep Problems, Elimination Problems, Posttraumatic Stress Disorder, Feeding Problems, Reactive Attachment Disorder, Autistic Disorder, Asperger's Disorder.
Administration: Individual.
Forms, 2: Parent Checklist, Teacher Checklist.
Price Data, 2006: $102 per deluxe kit including screening manual (2000, 117 pages), norms manual (1997, 184 pages), 25 parent checklists, 25 teacher checklists, 50 parent score sheets, and 50 teacher score sheets; $52 per 50 parent checklists and score sheets; 38 per 50 teacher checklists and score sheets; $22 per screening manual; $22 per norms manual.
Time: (10–15) minutes.
Comments: Instrument is designed to correspond to the DSM-IV classification system.
Authors: Kenneth D. Gadow and Joyce Sprafkin.
Publisher: Checkmate Plus, Ltd.
Cross References: For a review by Robert C. Reinehr, see 14:134.

[882]
Early Childhood Physical Environment Observation Schedules and Rating Scales

Purpose: "Intended for the systematic assessment of the quality of the physical environment of child care centers and related early childhood environments."
Population: Directors and staff of child care centers, early childhood teachers.
Publication Dates: 1982–1994.
Scores: 9 scales: Early Childhood Teacher Style and Dimensions of Education Rating Scales (Early Childhood Teacher Style Rating Scale, Early Childhood Dimensions of Education Rating Scale, Teacher Style and Dimensions of Education Validity Check), Early Childhood Physical Environment Scales (Pattern 905: Spatial Organization, Pattern 908: Behavior Settings), Playground and Neighborhood Observation Behavior Maps (Playground Observation Behavior Map, Neighborhood Observation Behavior Map, Neighborhood Observation Supplementary Coding Sheet), Environ-

ment/Behavior Observation Schedule for Early Childhood Environments.
Administration: Group.
Time: [10–30] minutes per scale.
Comments: For research purposes only; the publisher advised in March 2006 that this test is no longer commercially available; it can be downloaded free of charge from the UW-Milwaukee Golda Meir Library e-reserve and is available in hard copy at that library and the Library of Congress.
Authors: Gary T. Moore.
Publisher: Center for Architecture and Urban Planning Research, University of Wisconsin-Milwaukee.
Cross References: For reviews by Lisa G. Bischoff and Patricia B. Keith, see 13:106.

[883]
Early Coping Inventory.

Purpose: Measures coping related behaviors.
Population: Mental age 4–36 months.
Publication Date: 1988.
Scores, 4: Sensorimotor Organization, Reactive Behavior, Self-Initiated Behavior, Total.
Administration: Individual.
Price Data, 2005: $54.60 per complete kit including manual (62 pages) and 20 inventories (9 pages); $35.55 per 20 inventories; $29.15 per manual; $26.75 per sample set.
Time: Administration time varies.
Comments: Downward extension of the Coping Inventory (702); ratings of adaptive behavior by an adult.
Authors: Shirley Zeitlin and G. Gordon Williamson with Margery Szczepanski.
Publisher: Scholastic Testing Service, Inc.
Cross References: See T5:878 (1 reference); for reviews by Harlan J. Stientjes and by Logan Wright and Wade L. Hamil, see 11:120.

[884]
Early Intervention Developmental Profile.

Purpose: Designed to yield information for planning comprehensive developmental programs for children with all types of disabilities.
Population: Children who are at developmental ages of 0–36 months.
Publication Dates: 1977–2006.
Scores, 8: Perceptual/Fine Motor, Cognition, Language, Social/Emotional, Self-Care (Feeding, Toileting, Dressing), Gross Motor.
Administration: Individual.
Price Data: Available from publisher and on the web at www.press.umich.edu.
Time: (50–60) minutes.
Comments: Stimulation activities manual included; see Preschool Developmental Profile (2010) for developmental ages from 36 months to 5 years.

Authors: D. Sue Schafer, Martha S. Moersch, Sally J. Rogers, Diane B. D'Eugenio, Sara L. Brown, Carol M. Donovan, and Eleanor Whiteside Lynch.
Publisher: University of Michigan Press.
Cross References: For reviews by Barbara A. Rothlisberg and Gary J. Stainback, see 13:107 (1 reference); see also T4:835 (1 reference).

[885]
Early Language Milestone Scale, Second Edition.

Purpose: To assess speech and language development during infancy and early childhood.
Population: Birth to 36 months.
Publication Dates: 1983–1993.
Acronym: ELM Scale-2.
Scores, 4: Auditory Expressive, Auditory Receptive, Visual, Global Language.
Administration: Individual.
Price Data, 2006: $160 per complete kit including manual (1993, 95 pages), object kit, and 100 records; $60 per manual; $55 per 100 record forms; $51 per object kit.
Time: (1–10) minutes.
Authors: James Coplan.
Publisher: PRO-ED.
Cross References: See T5:880 (1 reference) for reviews by Philip Backlund and Sherwyn Morreale and by Betsy Waterman, see 13:108; for a review by Ruth M. Noyce of an earlier edition, see 10:99 (2 references).

[886]
Early Language Skills Checklist.

Purpose: Designed as an observation-based checklist for children "whose language development is causing concern."
Population: Ages 3–5.
Publication Date: 1998.
Acronym: ELS.
Scores: No scores; 4 areas: Attention and Listening Skills, Receptive Language, Expressive Language, Social and Intellectual Use of Language.
Administration: Individual.
Price Data, 2002: £9.99 per 10 checklists; £16.99 per specimen set; £15.99 per handbook.
Time: (5–20) minutes.
Authors: James Boyle and Elizabeth McLellan.
Publisher: Hodder & Stoughton Educational [England].

[887]
Early Literacy Skills Assessment.

Purpose: "Designed to provide preschool programs and teachers with an authentic and meaningful way to assess young children's early literacy skills."
Population: Ages 3-5 years.

Publication Date: 2005.

Acronym: ELSA.

Scores: 12 scores in 4 areas: Comprehension (Prediction, Retelling, Connection to Real Life), Phonological Awareness (Rhyming, Segmentation, Phonemic Awareness), Alphabetic Principle (Sense of Word, Alphabet Letter Recognition, Letter-Sound Correspondence), Concepts About Print (Orientation, Story Beginning, Direction of Text).

Administration: Individual.

Price Data, 2006: $149.95 per complete kit including 2 copies of Violet's Adventure or Dante Grows Up, user guide (48 pages), 60 score sheets, 60 Child Summary forms, 12 Class Summary forms, and 60 Family Report forms; $199.95 per Spanish version complete kit including 2 copies of La Aventura de Violeta or El Combio en Dante, user guide, 60 score sheets, 60 Child Summary forms, 12 Class Summary forms, and 60 Family Report forms; $39.95 per Violet's Adventure or La Aventura de Violeta; $39.95 per Dante Grows Up or El Cambio en Dante; $84.95 per DVD Scoring the ELSA: Establishing Reliability.

Foreign Language Edition: Spanish edition (2006) available.

Time: (15-20) minutes.

Author: Andrea DeBruin-Parecki.

Publisher: High/Scope Educational Research Foundation.

[888]

Early Math Diagnostic Assessment.

Purpose: Designed to "screen and identify children at risk for math difficulties."

Population: Prekindergarten to Grade 3.

Publication Date: 2002.

Acronym: EMDA.

Scores: 2 subtests: Math Reasoning, Numerical Operations.

Administration: Individual.

Price Data, 2003: $110 per complete kit including examiner's manual (84 pages), stimulus book, 25 record forms, 25 response booklets, and 30 "Thumbs Up" worm stickers; $25 per examiner's manual; $75 per stimulus book; $50 per 25 record forms and response booklets.

Time: (20–30) minutes.

Comments: Items selected to "address mathematical domains identified by" the Principles and Standards for School Mathematics (2002) set forth by the National Council of Teachers of Mathematics.

Author: The Psychological Corporation.

Publisher: PsychCorp, A brand of Harcourt Assessment, Inc.

Cross References: For reviews by Mark J. Gierl and Xuan Tan and by Arturo Olivarez, Jr., see 16:81.

[889]

Early Memories Procedure.

Purpose: "Method of exploring personality organization, especially current life concerns, based on an individual's memory of the past."

Population: Ages 10 and over with at least a fourth-grade reading level.

Publication Dates: 1989–1992.

Scores: No scores.

Administration: Group.

Price Data: Available from publisher.

Time: (90–240) minutes.

Comments: Instrument may be interpreted according to a Freudian, Adlerian, Ego-Psychological, or Cognitive-Perceptual model.

Author: Arnold R. Bruhn.

Publisher: Arnold R. Bruhn and Associates.

Cross References: For reviews by Karl R. Hanes and LeAdelle Phelps, see 13:109; see also T4:840 (1 reference).

[890]

Early Reading Diagnostic Assessment— Second Edition.

Purpose: Designed to evaluate "the essential components of reading defined by Reading First—phonemic awareness, phonics, fluency, vocabulary and comprehension."

Population: Grades K–3.

Publication Dates: 2002–2003.

Acronym: ERDA Second Edition.

Administration: Individual.

Levels, 4: Grades K, 1, 2, and 3.

Price Data: Available from publisher.

Author: The Psychological Corporation.

Publisher: PsychCorp, A brand of Harcourt Assessment, Inc.

  a) GRADE K.

  Population: Kindergarten.

  Scores, 11: Letter Recognition, Story Retell, Phonological Awareness (Rhyming, Phonemes, Syllables, Composite), Vocabulary (Receptive, Expressive, Composite), Reading Comprehension, Passage Fluency.

  Time: (65–75) minutes.

  b) GRADE 1.

  Population: Grade 1.

  Scores, 14: Word Reading, Pseudoword Decoding, Letter Recognition, Listening Comprehension, Phonological Awareness (Phonemes, Rimes, Syllables, Composite), Reading Comprehension, Vocabulary (Receptive, Expressive, Word Opposites, Composite), Passage Fluency.

  Time: (90–95) minutes.

  c) GRADE 2.

  Population: Grade 2.

Scores, 23: Brief Vocabulary (Receptive, Expressive, Composite), Reading Comprehension, Listening Comprehension, Phonological Awareness (Phonemes, Rimes, Syllables, Comprehension), Word Reading, Pseudoword Decoding, Rapid Automatic Naming (Letters, Words, Digits, Words and Digits, Composite), Full Vocabulary (Brief Vocabulary Composite, Synonyms, Word Definitions, Multiple Meanings, Composite), Passage Fluency (Narrative, Informational).
Time: (110) minutes.
d) GRADE 3.
Population: Grade 3.
Scores, 23: Same as Grade 2.
Time: (110) minutes.
Cross References: For reviews by Marie Miller-Whitehead and Steven R. Shaw, see 16:82.

[891]
Early Reading Success Indicator.
Purpose: "To identify children at risk for developing reading difficulties."
Population: Ages 5–11.
Publication Date: 2004.
Acronym: ERSI.
Scores: RAN-Letters, Phonological Processing, Speeded Naming, Word Reading, Pseudoword Decoding.
Administration: Individual.
Price Data, 2005: $175 per complete kit including manual (89 pages), stimulus book, and 25 record forms; $28 for 25 record forms.
Time: (20–25) minutes.
Comments: A brief battery of cognitive tests composed of subtests selected from various products from this publisher: Process Assessment of the Learner: Test Battery for Reading and Writing (16:199), NEPSY: A Developmental Neuropsychological Assessment (T6:1696), and Wechsler Individual Achievement Test—Second Edition (15:275).
Authors: PsychCorp.
Publisher: PsychCorp, A brand of Harcourt Assessment, Inc.

[892]
Early School Inventory.
Population: Ages 5–7.
Publication Dates: 1986–1987.
Acronym: ESI.
Price Data: Available from publisher.
Time: Administration time not reported.
Authors: Joanne R. Nurss and Mary E. McGauvran.
Publisher: Pearson Early Learning [No reply from publisher; status unknown).
    a) EARLY SCHOOL INVENTORY—DEVELOPMENTAL.
    Purpose: "Provides a systematic method for gathering information about a child's development for use in planning effective instruction."
    Acronym: ESI-D.
    Scores, 4: Physical Development, Language Development, Cognitive Development, Social-Emotional Development.
    Administration: Group.
    b) EARLY SCHOOL INVENTORY—PRELITERACY.
    Purpose: Provides information about "a child's progress in acquiring the preliteracy skills needed when learning to read and write."
    Acronym: ESI-P.
    Scores, 3: Print Concepts, Writing Concepts, Story Structure.
    Administration: Individual.
Cross References: For reviews by Damon Krug and Brandon Davis and by Carol Westby, see 13:110.

[893]
Early School Personality Questionnaire.
Purpose: Measures personality dimensions of young children; useful in the treatment of emotional and conduct problems.
Population: Ages 6–8.
Publication Date: 1966.
Acronym: ESPQ.
Scores: 13 primary factors (Reserved vs. Warmhearted, Dull vs. Bright, Affected by Feelings vs. Emotionally Stable, Undemonstrative vs. Excitable, Obedient vs. Dominant, Sober vs. Enthusiastic, Disregards Rules vs. Conscientious, Shy vs. Venturesome, Tough-Minded vs. Tender-Minded, Vigorous vs. Circumspect Individualism, Forthright vs. Shrewd, Self-Assured vs. Guilt-Prone, Relaxed vs. Tense), and 4 second-order factors (Extraversion, Anxiety, Tough Poise, Independence).
Administration: Group or individual.
Price Data, 2005: $37 per introductory kit including manual with test questions, 2 answer booklets, profile sheet, and scoring keys; $15 per manual with test questions; $14 per 25 child's answer booklets (2 answer booklets needed for each child); $20 per 50 profile sheets/second-order worksheets; $20 per tape recording of items; $18 per scoring keys.
Foreign Language Editions: Information regarding several non-English-language adaptations available from publisher.
Time: (30–50) minutes for each of two parts (untimed).
Authors: Richard W. Coan and Raymond B. Cattell.
Publisher: Institute for Personality and Ability Testing, Inc. (IPAT).
Cross References: See T4:843 (3 references and T3:772 (4 references); for reviews by Jacob O. Sines and Robert L. Thorndike, see 8:540 (8 references); see also T2:1163 (3 references); for a review by Lovick C. Miller, see 7:71 (8 references); see also P:66 (7 references).

[894]

Early Screening Inventory—Revised.

Purpose: Designed to identify children at risk for possible school failure.
Population: Ages 3–6.
Publication Dates: 1976–1997.
Acronym: ESI-R.
Scores, 3: Visual-Motor/Adaptive, Language and Cognition, Gross Motor.
Administration: Individual.
Levels, 2: Preschool (3 to 4 1/2 years old), Kindergarten (4 1/2 to 6 years old).
Price Data: Available from publisher.
Foreign Language Edition: All screening materials available in Spanish.
Time: (15–20) minutes.
Comments: Originally introduced as the Eliot-Pearson Screening Inventory.
Authors: Samuel J. Meisels, Dorothea B. Marsden, Martha Stone Wiske, and Laura W. Henderson.
Publisher: Rebus Inc.
Cross References: For reviews by Ernest Kimmel and Kathleen D. Paget, see 14:135; see also T5:889 (1 reference); for reviews by Denise M. Dezolt and Kevin Menefee of an earlier edition, see 11:122 (1 reference).

[895]

Early Screening Profiles.

Purpose: A comprehensive, brief, multidimensional screening instrument for children.
Population: Ages 2-0 to 6-11.
Publication Date: 1990.
Acronym: ESP.
Scores: 3 Profile scores: Cognitive/Language, Motor, Self-Help/Social (Parent or Teacher), and 4 Survey scores: Articulation, Home, Behavior, Health History.
Administration: Individual.
Price Data, 2006: $313.99 per complete kit including manual (297 pages), Motor administration manual (16 pages), test easel, 25 test records, 25 Self-Help/Social Profile Questionnaires, 25 Score Summaries, Sample Home/Health History Survey, tape measure, beads; $33.99 per 25 test records; $18.99 per 25 Self-Help/Social Profile questionnaires; $18.99 per 25 Home/Health History surveys; $12.99 per 25 score summaries; $67.99 per manual; $99.99 per ESP Training Video.
Time: [15–40] minutes.
Comments: Two levels of scoring: Level I scores are 6 "screening indexes" and 3 descriptive categories; Level II scores are standard scores, percentile ranks, normal curve equivalents (NCEs), stanines, and age equivalents; ecological assessment with ratings by parents and teachers as well as direct assessment of the child; previously listed as AGS Early Screening Profiles.
Authors: Patti L. Harrison (coordinating author and manual author), Alan S. Kaufman (Cognitive/Language Profile), Nadeen L. Kaufman (Cognitive/Language Profile), Robert H. Bruininks (Motor Profile), John Rynders (Motor Profile), Steven Ilmer (Motor Profile), Sara S. Sparrow (Self-Help/Social Profile), and Domenic V. Cicchetti (Self-Help/Social Profile).
Publisher: Pearson Assessments (originally published by AGS Publishing, acquired by Pearson in 2005).
Cross References: See T5:124 (1 reference); for reviews by David W. Barnett and Cathy Telzrow, see 12:24 (1 reference); see also T4:134 (2 references).

[896]

Early Screening Project.

Purpose: "Allows for the cost-effective screening of problem behaviors to aid in the early remediation of behavior disorders."
Population: Ages 3–6.
Publication Date: 1995.
Acronym: ESP.
Scores, 4: Critical Events Index, Aggressive Behavior Scale [Externalizers], Social Interaction Scale [Internalizers], Combined Frequency Index Adaptive Behavior, Combined Frequency Index Maladaptive Behavior.
Administration: Individual and group.
Price Data, 2002: $95 per complete kit including manual (103 pages), instrument packet, social observation training video, and a stopwatch.
Time: [60] minutes total/group.
Authors: Hill M. Walker, Herbert H. Severson, and Edward G. Feil.
Publisher: Sopris West.
Cross References: For a review by J. Jeffrey Grill, see 14:136.

[897]

Early Speech Perception Test.

Purpose: "Developed to obtain increasingly more accurate information about speech discrimination skills as the profoundly hearing-impaired child's verbal abilities develop."
Population: Ages 3–6, ages 6–12.
Publication Date: 1990.
Acronym: ESP.
Administration: Individual.
Price Data, 2005: $200 per ESP kit including manual (32 pages), standard and low verbal scoring forms, box of toys, full-color picture cards, and CD; $15 per alternate randomization CD; $25 per IBM computer disc set.
Time: (15–20) minutes.
Comments: Information regarding specialized hardware and software equipment necessary for administering the computerized version of the ESP test battery can be found in the test manual.
Authors: Jean S. Moog and Ann E. Geers.
Publisher: Central Institute for the Deaf.

a) ESP STANDARD VERSION.
Population: Ages 6–15.
Scores, 4: Pattern Perception, Spondee Identification, Monosyllable Identification, Total.
Price Data: $10 per 25 standard version scoring forms.
b) ESP LOW-VERBAL VERSION.
Population: Ages 3–6.
Scores, 4: Pattern Perception Test, Word Identification Test (Spondee Identification, Monosyllable Identification), Total.
Price Data: $10 per 25 low-verbal version scoring forms.
Cross References: See T5:891 (1 reference); for a review by Arlene E. Carney, see 12:128.

[898]
Early Years Easy Screen.
Purpose: Constructed to screen for strengths and weaknesses in the areas of physical and cognitive development.
Population: Ages 4–5.
Publication Date: 1991.
Acronym: EYES.
Scores, 6: Level of Performance in 6 areas: Pencil Coordination, Active Body, Number, Oral Language, Visual Reading, Auditory Reading.
Administration: Group.
Price Data: Available from publisher.
Time: (160–194) minutes over several sessions.
Comments: Other test materials (e.g., bean bag, beads) must be supplied by examiner.
Authors: Joan Clerehugh, Kim Hart, Rosalind Pither, Kay Rider, and Kate Turner.
Publisher: NFER-Nelson Publishing Co., Ltd. [England].
Cross References: For a review by Martin J. Wiese, see 12:129.

[899]
Eating Disorder Inventory-3.
Purpose: Designed to "provide a standardized clinical evaluation of symptomatology associated with eating disorders."
Population: Females ages 13 to 53 years.
Publication Dates: 1984–2004.
Acronym: EDI-3.
Administration: Group.
Price Data, 2006: $240 per introductory kit including professional manual (2004, 223 pages), referral form manual (2004, 36 pages), 25 item booklets, 25 answer sheets, 25 percentile/T-score profile forms, 25 symptom checklists, and 25 referral forms; $255 per CD-ROM based scoring program.
Authors: David M. Garner.
Publisher: Psychological Assessment Resources, Inc.

a) EATING DISORDER INVENTORY-3.
Population: Females ages 11 to 53 years.
Scores, 21: 6 composite scores (Eating Disorder Risk Composite, Ineffectiveness Composite, Interpersonal Problems Composite, Affective Problems Composite, Overcontrol Composite, General Psychological Maladjustment Composite), 12 primary scores (Drive for Thinness, Bulimia, Body Dissatisfaction, Low Self-Esteem, Personal Alienation, Interpersonal Insecurity, Interpersonal Alienation, Interoceptive Deficits, Emotional Dysregulation, Perfectionism, Asceticism, Maturity Fears), 3 response style indicators (Inconsistency, Infrequency, Negative Impression).
Time: (20) minutes.
Comments: Full battery.
b) EATING DISORDER INVENTORY-3 REFERRAL FORM.
Population: Adolescents and adults ages 13 and older.
Acronym: EDI-3 RF.
Scores, 4: Drive for Thinness, Bulimia, Body Dissatisfaction, BMI.
Time: (10) minutes.
Comments: Abbreviated referral form of Eating Disorder Inventory-3 "used to identify individuals who are at risk for eating disorders."
c) EATING DISORDER INVENTORY-3 SYMPTOM CHECKLIST.
Population: Adolescents and adults.
Acronym: EDI-3 SC.
Scores: Frequency ratings.
Time: (10) minutes.
Comments: Symptom checklist used as an aid in the diagnosis of eating disorders.
Cross References: See T5:893 (54 references); for reviews by Phillip Ash and Steven Schinke of an earlier edition, see 12:130 (38 references); see also T4:847 (38 references); for a review by Cabrini S. Swassing of an earlier edition, see 10:100 (16 references).

[900]
Eating Inventory.
Purpose: To assess "three dimensions of eating behavior found to be important in recognizing and treating eating-related disorders: cognitive control of eating, disinhibition, and hunger."
Population: Ages 17 and older.
Publication Dates: 1983–1988.
Scores, 3: Cognitive Restraint of Eating, Disinhibition, Hunger.
Administration: Group or individual.
Price Data, 2002: $160 per complete kit including 25 questionnaires, 25 answer sheets, and manual (1988, 37 pages); $46 per 25 questionnaires; $67 per 25 answer sheets; $67 per manual.

Time: (15–20) minutes.
Authors: Albert J. Stunkard and Samuel Messick.
Publisher: PsychCorp, A brand of Harcourt Assessment, Inc.
Cross References: For reviews by Lisa Bloom and Sandra D. Haynes, see 13:111 (3 references); see also T4:848 (1 reference).

[901]
Eckstein Audiometers.

Purpose: For the measurement and evaluation of hearing losses.
Population: All ages.
Publication Dates: 1961–1973.
Subtests: 7 models (solid state).
Administration: Individual.
Price Data: Available from publisher.
Time: Administration time not reported.
Author: Eckstein Bros., Inc.
Publisher: Eckstein Bros., Inc.

a) EB-47 MICROPROCESSOR SCREENING AUDIOMETER.
Publication Date: 1998.
Comments: For screening in schools and medical offices; 4 frequencies; 4 hearing classifications.
b) MINIATURE AUDIOMETER MODEL 60.
Publication Date: 1961.
Comments: For air conduction screening and threshold testing in schools and medical offices; 7 frequencies.
c) AUDIOMETER MODEL 350-I.
Publication Dates: 1964–1972.
Comments: Air conduction threshold testing in industry.
d) FULL RANGE PORTABLE AUDIOMETERS.
Publication Dates: 1970–1972.
Comments: 2 models (may be AC operated).
 1) *Model 390.*
 Comments: For pure tone air conducting testing.
 2) *Model 390 MB.*
 Comments: Diagnostic Model for pure tone air and bone conducting testing.
e) DIAGNOSTIC AUDIOMETER, MODEL 400.
Publication Date: 1969.
Comments: Air and bone conduction; calibrated speech and pure tone.
f) EB-23-NOISESTIK II - PEDIATRIC HEARING SCREENER.
Publication Date: 1998.
Comments: A hearing screener for testing of infants, toddlers, and older persons not able to respond manually to auditory stimulus.

[902]
Edinburgh Picture Test.
Purpose: To assess reasoning ability in young children.

Population: Ages 6-6 to 8-3.
Publication Dates: 1985–1991.
Scores, 6: Doesn't Belong, Classification, Reversed Similarities, Analogies, Sequences, Total.
Administration: Group.
Price Data, 2002: £8.99 per specimen set; £12.99 per 20 test booklets; £6.99 per manual (1988, 15 pages).
Time: (30–60) minutes.
Author: Godfrey Thomson Unit, University of Edinburgh.
Publisher: Hodder & Stoughton Educational [England].
Cross References: For reviews by Carole M. Krauthamer and Bruce G. Rogers, see 12:133.

[903]
Edinburgh Reading Tests.
Purpose: To assess pupil progress in reading.
Population: Ages 7-0 to 9-0, 8-6 to 10-6, 10-0 to 12-6, 12-0 to 16-6.
Publication Dates: 1972–2002.
Administration: Group.
Levels, 4: Stages 1, 2, 3, 4.
Publisher: Hodder & Stoughton Educational [England].

a) STAGE 1 [THIRD EDITION].
Population: Ages 7-0 to 9-0.
Publication Dates: 1977–2002.
Scores, 5: Vocabulary, Syntax, Sequences, Comprehension, Total.
Forms, 2: A, B.
Price Data, 2002: £9.99 per 10 copies of test (specify Form A or Form B); £14.99 per manual; £16.99 per specimen set.
Time: (30–55) minutes.
Author: Educational Assessment Unit, University of Edinburgh.
b) STAGE 2 [FOURTH EDITION].
Population: Ages 8-6 to 10-6.
Publication Dates: 1972–2002.
Scores, 5: Vocabulary, Comprehension of Sequences, Use of Context, Comprehension of Essential Ideas, Total.
Price Data: £9.99 per 10 copies of test booklet; £14.99 per manual; £15.99 per specimen set; £39.99 per scorer/profiler CD-ROM.
Time: (40) minutes for part I; (35) minutes for part II.
Author: Educational Assessment Unit, University of Edinburgh
c) STAGE 3 [FOURTH EDITION].
Population: Ages 10-0 to 12-6.
Publication Dates: 1973–2002.
Scores, 5: Reading for facts and Comprehension of Sequences, Main Ideas, Comprehension of Points of View, Vocabulary, Total.

Price Data: £9.99 per 10 test booklets; £14.99 per manual; £15.99 per specimen set; £39.99 per scorer/profiler CD-ROM.

Time: (40) minutes for part I; (35) minutes for part II.

Author: Educational Assessment Unit, University of Edinburgh.

d) STAGE 4 [THIRD EDITION].

Population: Ages 11-7 to 16+.

Publication Dates: 1977–2002

Scores, 6: Skimming, Vocabulary, Reading for Facts, Points of View, Comprehension, Total.

Price Data: £10.99 per 10 test booklets; £15.99 per manual; £16.99 per specimen set; £39.99 per scorer/profiler CD-ROM.

Time: 60(70) minutes.

Author: Educational Assessment Unit, University of Edinburgh.

e) SHORTENED EDINGURGH READING TEST.

Purpose: Designed as a survey and screening instrument of written language attainment.

Population: Ages 10-0 to 11-6.

Scores, 3: Vocabulary, Syntax and Sequence, Comprehension.

Time: (40) minutes.

Price Data: £15.99 per 20 copies of test; £14.99 per manual; £15.99 per specimen set.

Comments: Questions selected from items in the full Edinburgh Reading Tests.

Authors: Godfrey Thomson Unit for Educational Research, Moray House Institute of Education, and the Child Health and Education Study, University of Bristol.

Cross References: See T5:901 (2 references) and T4:855 (1 reference); for reviews by Nancy L. Roser and Byron H. Van Roekel of previous editions, see 9:374 (1 reference); see T3:775 (2 references); for reviews by Douglas A. Pidgeon and Earl F. Rankin of the first editions of Stages 2 and 3, see 8:724.

[904]

Educational Development Series (2000 Edition).

Purpose: A battery of ability and achievement tests and questions on interests and plans.

Population: Grades K-12.

Publication Dates: 1963-2000.

Acronym: EDS.

Administration: Group.

Levels: 13.

Price Data, 2005: $59.40 per 10 test booklets (Levels 13G–16H) and manual (1999, 15–20 pages); $68.25 per 10 test booklets (Levels 17G–18H) and manual; $40.95 per 50 answer sheets (Levels 13G–18H); $4.72 per student for complete battery standard

scoring; $24 per sample set of specified grades (K–2, 3–5, 6–8, 9–12); minimum scoring service is $43.65.

Authors: O. F. Anderhalter, R. H. Bauernfeind, V. M. Cashew, Mary E. Greig, Walter M. Lifton, George Mallinson, Jacqueline Mallinson, Joseph F. Papenfuss, and Neil Vail.

Publisher: Scholastic Testing Service, Inc.

a) LEVEL 10G.

Population: Grade K.

Publication Date: 1999.

Scores, 8: Cognitive Skills (Verbal, Nonverbal, Total), Basic Skills (Reading, Language, Mathematics, Total), Battery Average.

Price Data: $7.50 per student for rental and scoring service.

Time: (190) minutes in 5 sessions.

b) LEVEL 11G.

Population: Grade 1.

Publication Date: 1999.

Scores, 11: Cognitive Skills (Verbal, Quantitative, Total), Basic Skills (Reading, Language, Mathematics, Total), Reference Skills, Science, Social Studies, Battery Average.

Price Data: $8.10 per student for rental and scoring service.

Time: (280-300) minutes in 5 sessions.

c) LEVEL 12G.

Population: Grade 2.

Publication Date: 1999.

Scores, 11: Cognitive Skills (Verbal, Quantitative, Total), Basic Skills (Reading, Language Arts, Mathematics, Total), Reference Skills, Science, Social Studies, Battery Average.

Price Data: $8.10 per student for rental and scoring service.

Time: (310 minutes in 5 sessions.

d) LEVEL 13G.

Population: Grade 3.

Publication Date: 1999.

Scores, 11: Same as for *c* above.

Price Data: $6.55 per student for rental and scoring service.

Time: (360) minutes in 5 sessions.

e) LEVEL 14G.

Population: Grade 4.

Publication Date: 1999.

Scores, 14: Cognitive Skills (Verbal, Quantitative, Total), Basic Skills (Reading, Language Arts, Mathematics, Total), Reference Skills, Science, Social Studies, Battery Average, Career Interests, School Plans, School Interests.

Price Data: Same as for *d* above.

Time: (400) minutes in 3 sessions.

f) LEVEL 15G.

Population: Grade 5.

Publication Date: 1999.

Scores, 14: Same as for *e* above.
Price Data: Same as for *d* above.
Time: (400) minutes in 3 sessions.
g) LEVEL 15H.
Population: Grade 6.
Publication Date: 1999.
Scores, 14: Same as for *e* above.
Price Data: Same as for *d* above.
Time: (400) minutes in 3 sessions.
h) LEVEL 16H.
Population: Grade 7.
Publication Date: 1999.
Scores, 14: Same as for *e* above.
Price Data: Same as for *d* above.
Time: (400) minutes in 3 sessions.
i) LEVEL 16H.
Population: Grade 8.
Publication Date: 1999.
Scores, 14: Same as for *e* above.
Price Data: Same as for *d* above.
Time: (400) minutes in 3 sessions.
j) LEVEL 17G.
Population: Grade 9.
Publication Date: 1999.
Scores, 14: Same as for *e* above.
Price Data: Same as for *d* above.
Time: (410) minutes in 3 sessions.
k) LEVEL 17H.
Population: Grade 9.
Publication Date: 1999.
Details: Same as for *j* above.
l) LEVEL 18G.
Population: Grade 10.
Publication Date: 1999.
Details: Same as for *j* above.
m) LEVEL 18H.
Population: Grade 11.
Publication Date: 1999.
Details: Same as for *j* above.
Cross References: See T4:858 (2 references); for a review by Esther E. Diamond of an earlier edition, see 9:376; see also T3:2325 (1 reference); for reviews by Samuel T. Mayo and William A. Mehrens of forms copyrighted 1976 and earlier see 8:27; see also T2:33 (1 reference); for a review by Robert D. North of forms copyrighted 1968 and earlier see 7:22.

[905]
Educational Interest Inventory.
Purpose: Designed to identify personal preference for different college educational programs.
Population: Prospective college students.
Publication Date: 1989.
Acronym: EII.
Scores: 47 scales: Agriculture (Agribusiness/Agricultural Production, Agricultural Sciences, Renewable Natural Resources), Architecture and Environmental Design, Area/Ethnic Studies, Business/Management (Accounting and Finance, Administration and Management, Human Resources Management, Marketing/Distribution), Communications, Computer and Information Sciences, Education (Pre-Elementary and Elementary, Secondary and Post-Secondary, Special Education, Physical Education, Industrial Arts), Engineering (Chemical, Civil, Electrical/Electronic, Mechanical), Foreign Languages, Health Sciences (General Medicine, Dentistry, Nursing, Pharmacy, Medical Laboratory), Home Economics, Law, Letters, Library and Archival Sciences, Life Sciences/General Biology, Mathematics, Philosophy and Religion, Theology, Physical Sciences (Chemistry, Geological Sciences, Physics), Psychology, Protective Services, Public Affairs/Social Work, Social Sciences (Economics, History, Political Sciences/Government, Sociology), Visual and Performing Arts (Fine Arts, Drama, Music).
Administration: Group.
Price Data: Price information available from publisher for reusable test booklet, answer sheets and profile guides, manual (43 pages), and for specimen set of all Educational Interest Inventory and Career Guidance Inventory components.
Time: [45–60] minutes.
Comments: Self-administered; self-scored; manual is for the EII and the Career Guidance Inventory (418).
Author: James E. Oliver.
Publisher: Wintergreen/Orchard House, Inc.
Cross References: For reviews by Lois T. Strauss and David E. Kapel and by Jim Fortune and Javaid Kaiser, see 11:123.

[906]
Educational Process Questionnaire.
Purpose: "To aid teachers in their own self-development by providing objective information about the processes used in the teacher's own actual classroom."
Population: Grades 4–12.
Publication Dates: 1973–1987.
Acronym: EPQ.
Scores: 5 scale scores: Reinforcement of Self-Concept, Academic Learning Time, Feedback, Expectations, Development of Multiple Talents.
Administration: Group.
Price Data: Available from publisher.
Time: 35(45) minutes.
Comments: Ratings by students.
Author: Institute for Behavioral Research in Creativity.
Publisher: Institute for Behavioral Research in Creativity.
Cross References: For a review by William L. Curlette, see 11:125.

[907]
Edwards Personal Preference Schedule.

Purpose: Developed to measure "a number of relatively independent normal personality variables."
Population: College and adults.
Publication Dates: 1953–1959.
Acronym: EPPS.
Scores, 16: Achievement, Deference, Order, Exhibition, Autonomy, Affiliation, Intraception, Succorance, Dominance, Abasement, Nurturance, Change, Endurance, Heterosexuality, Aggression, Consistency.
Administration: Group or individual.
Price Data, 2002: $91 per 25 schedule booklets; $50 per 50 hand-scorable answer documents; $65 per 50 NCS machine-scorable answer documents; $65 per 50 IBM answer documents; $47 per scoring template for hand-scorable answer documents including manual (1959, 27 pages); $86.50 per keys for IBM answer documents including manual; $42 per manual; $50 per examination kit.
Time: (40–50) minutes.
Author: Allen L. Edwards.
Publisher: PsychCorp, A brand of Harcourt Assessment, Inc.
Cross References: See T5:908 (12 references), T4:862 (44 references), 9:378 (16 references), T3:780 (70 references), 8:542 (334 references), and T2:1164 (226 references); for reviews by Alfred B. Heilbrun, Jr., and Michael G. McKee, see 7:72 (391 references); see also P:67 (363 references); for reviews by John A. Radcliffe and Lawrence J. Stricker and an excerpted review by Edward S. Bordin, see 6:87 (284 references); for reviews by Frank Barron, Ake Bjerstedt, and Donald W. Fiske and excerpted reviews by John W. Gustad and Laurance F. Shaffer, see 5:47 (50 references).

[908]
The Egan Bus Puzzle Test.

Purpose: "Designed to assess language development and some performance skills of young children."
Population: 20 months to 4 years.
Publication Date: No date on test materials.
Scores, 6: Expressive Verbal Labels, Comprehension (Verbal Labels, Recognition of Shape, Orientation of Piece to Recess), Comprehension of Sentences, Expressive Language.
Administration: Individual.
Price Data, 2001: £89.50 per complete set including manual (no date, 36 pages), board, and 25 forms; £73.50 per board and manual; £22.50 per 25 forms.
Time: (7-8) minutes.
Authors: Dorothy F. Egan and Rosemary Brown.
Publisher: The Test Agency Limited [England] [No reply from publisher; status unknown].
Cross References: For a review by Sheldon L. Stick, see 10:105.

[909]
Ego Function Assessment.

Purpose: Designed as a "mental status examination" to assess ego function.
Population: Adults.
Publication Date: 1989.
Acronym: EFA.
Scores, 12: Reality Testing, Judgment, Sense of Reality, Regulation and Control of Drives, Object Relations, Thought Processes, Adaptive Regression in the Service of the Ego, Defensive Functions, Stimulus Barrier, Autonomous Functions, Synthetic Functions, Mastery-Competence.
Administration: Individual.
Price Data, 2001: $12 per manual (64 pages); $9.50 per 10 blanks.
Time: Administration time not reported.
Author: Leopold Bellak.
Publisher: C.P.S., Inc.
Cross References: For reviews by Beth Doll and Samuel Juni, see 13:112.

[910]
The Ego Strength Q-Sort Test.

Purpose: Designed to "assess the general strength of one's ego."
Population: Grades 9–16 and adults.
Publication Dates: 1956–1958.
Acronym: ESQST.
Scores, 6: Ego-Status, Social Status, Goal Setting and Striving, Good Mental Health, Physical Status, Total.
Administration: Individual or group.
Price Data: Available from publisher.
Time: (50–90) minutes.
Author: Russell N. Cassel.
Publisher: Psychometric Affiliates.
Cross References: See T5:913 (1 reference) and T2:1167 (1 reference); for reviews by Allen L. Edwards and Harrison G. Gough, see 6:88 (3 references).

[911]
Eidetic Parents Test.

Purpose: To provide stimuli meant to arouse eidetic images of parents to aid in exploring emotional attachments that affect current functioning.
Population: Clinical patients and marriage and family counselees.
Publication Date: 1972.
Acronym: EPT.
Scores: No scores; verbal reporting by individuals of subjective visual images (called eidetics) of increasingly surrealistic situations.
Administration: Individual.
Price Data: Available from publisher.
Time: (60) minutes for brief report; "many hours" for comprehensive report.

Author: Akhter Ahsen.

Publisher: Brandon House, Inc. [No reply from publisher; status unknown].

Cross References: For additional information and a review by Charles Warnath and excerpted reviews by Gregory Sarmousakis, Barry Bricklin, and Manas Raychaudhuri, see 8:546 (8 references).

[912]

801 Public Safety Telecommunicator First-Line Supervisor Test.

Purpose: Designed "to assist Emergency Communications Centers ... in promoting qualified candidates to the supervisory level."

Population: Candidates for promotion to the public safety telecommunicator first-line supervisor position.

Publication Dates: 2002-2006.

Scores: 6 knowledge areas: Communication Center Operation, Concepts of Supervision, Concepts of Evaluating Subordinate Performance, Concepts of Training, Concepts of Writing and Reviewing Reports and Paperwork, Concepts of Administration.

Administration: Individual or group.

Price Data: Available from publisher.

Time: 150 minutes.

Comments: A reading list is provided to help candidates prepare for the test.

Authors: International Public Management Association for Human Resources.

Publisher: International Public Management Association for Human Resources (IPMA-HR).

[913]

Einstein Assessment of School-Related Skills.

Purpose: "To identify children who are at risk for, or are experiencing, learning difficulties; and who therefore should be referred for a comprehensive evaluation."

Population: Grades K–5.

Publication Date: 1988.

Administration: Individual.

Levels, 6: Kindergarten, First Grade, Second Grade, Third Grade, Fourth Grade, Fifth Grade.

Price Data: Available from publisher.

Time: (10) minutes.

Authors: Ruth L. Gottesman and Frances M. Cerullo.

Publisher: Slosson Educational Publications, Inc.

a) KINDERGARTEN LEVEL.

Scores, 5: Language/Cognition, Letter Recognition, Auditory Memory, Arithmetic, Visual-Motor Integration.

b) FIRST GRADE LEVEL.

Scores, 7: Language/Cognition, Word Recognition, Oral Reading, Reading Comprehension, Auditory Memory, Arithmetic, Visual-Motor Integration.

c) SECOND GRADE LEVEL.

Scores: Same as *b* above.

d) THIRD GRADE LEVEL.

Scores: Same as *b* above.

e) FOURTH GRADE LEVEL.

Scores: Same as *b* above.

f) FIFTH GRADE LEVEL.

Scores: Same as *b* above.

Cross References: See T5:916 (1 reference) and T4:871 (1 reference); for a review by Gloria A. Galvin, see 11:126 (1 reference).

[914]

Ekwall/Shanker Reading Inventory—Third Edition.

Purpose: "Designed to assess the full range of students' reading abilities."

Population: Grades 1–9.

Publication Dates: 1979–1993.

Acronym: ESRI.

Administration: Individual.

Price Data: Available from publisher.

Authors: Eldon E. Ekwall and James L. Shanker.

Publisher: Pearson Allyn & Bacon.

a) GRADED WORD LIST.

Purpose: "To obtain a quick estimate of the student's independent, instructional, and frustration reading levels."

Acronym: GWL.

Scores, 3: Independent Reading Level, Instructional Reading Level, Frustration Level.

Time: (5–10) minutes.

b) ORAL AND SILENT READING.

Purpose: To obtain an assessment of the student's independent, instructional, and frustration reading levels in oral and silent reading.

Scores, 3: 3 scores (Independent Reading Level, Instructional Reading Level, Frustration Level) in each of 2 areas (Oral, Silent Reading).

Time: (10–30) minutes.

c) LISTENING COMPREHENSION.

Purpose: "To obtain the level at which a student can understand material when it is read to him or her."

Score: Listening Comprehension Level.

Time: (5–10) minutes.

d) THE BASIC SIGHT WORDS AND PHRASES TEST.

Purpose: To determine basic sight words and basic sight word phrases that can be recognized and pronounced instantly by the student.

Scores, 2: Basic Sight Words, Basic Sight Phrases.

Time: (5–12) minutes.

e) LETTER KNOWLEDGE.

Purpose: "To determine if the student can associate the letter symbols with the letter names."

Scores, 2: Letters (Auditory), Letters (Visual).
Time: Administration time not reported.

f) PHONICS.
Purpose: "To determine if the student has mastered letter-sound (phonics)."
Scores, 9: Initial Consonants, Initial Blends and Digraphs, Ending Sounds, Vowels, Phonograms, Blending, Substitution, Vowel Pronunciation, Application in Context.
Time: Administration time not reported.

g) STRUCTURAL ANALYSIS.
Purpose: "To determine if the student can use structural analysis skills to aid in decoding unknown words."
Scores, 10: Hearing Word Parts, Inflectional Endings, Prefixes, Suffixes, Compound Words, Affixes, Syllabication, Application in Context (Part I, Part II, Total).
Time: Administration time not reported.

h) KNOWLEDGE OF CONTRACTIONS TEST.
Purpose: "To determine if the student has knowledge of contractions."
Scores, 3: Number of Words Pronounced, Number of Words Known, Total.
Time: Administration time not reported.

i) EL PASO PHONICS SURVEY.
Purpose: "To determine if the student has the ability to pronounce and blend 90 phonic elements."
Scores, 4: Initial Consonant Sounds, Ending Consonant, Initial Consonant Clusters, Vowels, Vowel Teams, and Special Letter Combinations.
Time: Administration time not reported.

j) QUICK SURVEY WORD LIST.
Purpose: "To determine quickly if the student has mastered phonics and structural analysis."
Score: Comments.
Time: Administration time not reported.

k) READING INTEREST SURVEY.
Purpose: "To assess the student's attitude toward reading and school, areas of reading interest, reading experiences, and conditions affecting reading in the home."
Score: Comments.
Time: Administration time not reported.
Cross References: For reviews by Koressa Kutsick Malcolm and by Blaine R. Worthen and Richard R. Sudweeks, see 13:113 (2 references); see also T4:872 (3 references); for reviews by Lynn S. Fuchs and Mary Beth Marr of an earlier edition, see 9:380.

[915]
ElecTest (Form A, Form A-C, & Form B).
Purpose: For selecting electrical repair and maintenance candidates.
Population: Applicants and incumbents for jobs requiring practical electrical knowledge and skills.

Publication Dates: 1997–2004.
Scores, 9: Motors, Digital & Analog, Schematics & Print Reading and Control Circuits, Basic AC/DC Theory and Electrical Maintenance, Computers & PLC and Test Instruments, Power Supplies, Power Distribution and Construction & Installation, Mechanical and Hand & Power Tools, Total.
Administration: Group.
Forms, 3: A, A-C, B.
Price Data, 2006: $20 per consumable self-scoring test booklet (minimum order of 20); $24.95 per manual (2004, 23 pages).
Foreign Language Edition: Available in Spanish.
Time: (60) minutes.
Comments: Self-scoring instrument; on-line version available; Form B is an alternate equivalent of Form A.
Author: Roland T. Ramsay.
Publisher: Ramsay Corporation.

[916]
Electrical and Electronics Test.
Purpose: "Examines knowledge of fundamental laws, symbols and definitions and requires the application of them to familiar equipment."
Population: Students in electrical or electronics programs ages 15 and over.
Publication Date: No date on test materials.
Scores: Total score only.
Administration: Group.
Price Data, 2001: £6.50 per test booklet; £8.50 per answer key; £12.50 per manual; £27 per specimen set.
Time: (15-30) minutes.
Author: The Test Agency Ltd.
Publisher: The Test Agency Limited [England] [No reply from publisher; status unknown].

[917]
Electrical Aptitude Test (Form EA-R-C).
Purpose: For evaluating electrical aptitude skills.
Population: Applicants for jobs that require the ability to learn electrical skills.
Publication Dates: 2003–2004.
Scores: Total score only for 6 areas: Mathematics, Electrical Concepts, Electrical Schematics, Process Flow, Signal Flow, Electrical Sequences.
Administration: Group.
Price Data, 2006: $20 per consumable self-scoring test booklet (minimum order of 20); $24.95 per manual (2004, 10 pages).
Time: (18) minutes.
Comments: Self-scoring instrument.
Author: Roland T. Ramsay.
Publisher: Ramsay Corporation.

[918]
Electrical Maintenance Trainee—Form UKE-1C.

Purpose: To "select or develop electrical trainees with one year of training or experience."

Population: Applicants for jobs requiring electrical knowledge and skills.

Publication Dates: 1991–2001.

Scores, 12: Motors, Digital and Analog Electronics, Schematics and Electrical Print Reading, Control, Power Supplies, Basic AC/DC Theory, Construction Installation and Distribution, Test Instruments, Mechanical/Equipment Operation/Hand and Power Tools, Computers and PLC, Electrical Maintenance, Total.

Administration: Group.

Price Data, 2006: $20 per consumable self-scoring test booklet (20 minimum order); $24.95 per manual (2001, 18 pages).

Time: (60) minutes.

Comments: Self-scoring instrument.

Authors: Roland T. Ramsay.

Publisher: Ramsay Corporation.

Cross References: For a review by David C. Roberts of an earlier edition, see 13:114.

[919]
Electrical Sophistication Test.

Purpose: "Intended to discriminate between persons with substantial knowledges of electricity and those with no, little, and merely chance knowledge."

Population: Job applicants.

Publication Dates: 1963–1965.

Scores: Total score only.

Administration: Group.

Price Data: Available from publisher.

Time: (5–10) minutes.

Author: Stanley G. Ciesla.

Publisher: Psychometric Affiliates.

Cross References: For a review by Charles F. Ward, see 7:1125.

[920]
Electromechanical Vocational Assessment Manuals.

Purpose: Designed to evaluate a variety of work abilities (tasks) of blind or visually impaired persons.

Population: Blind or visually impaired adults.

Publication Date: 1983.

Scores, 6: Fine Finger Dexterity Work Task Unit, Foot Operated Hinged Box Work Task Unit, Hinged Box Work Task Unit, Index Card Work Task Unit, Multifunctional Work Task Unit, Revolving Assembly Table Work Task Unit.

Administration: Individual.

Price Data: Available from publisher.

Time: 50(60) minutes for any one task unit.

Comments: Special administration equipment required.

Author: Rehabilitation Research and Training Center on Blindness and Low Vision.

Publisher: Rehabilitation Research and Training Center on Blindness and Low Vision.

Cross References: For reviews by John Geisler and Robert Johnson, see 13:115.

[921]
Electron Test—Form H-C.

Purpose: To "select or develop candidates for industrial electronics jobs."

Population: Electronics employees and applicants for electronics jobs.

Publication Dates: 1987–2001.

Scores, 7: Digital & Analog Electronics, AC/DC Theory Schematics & Print Reading, Motors/Regulators/Electronic Equipment/Power Distribution, Power Supplies, Test Instruments, Computers and PLC, Total.

Administration: Group.

Price Data, 2006: $20 per consumable self-scoring test booklet (20 minimum order); $24.95 per manual (2001, 15 pages).

Time: (60) minutes.

Comments: Self-scoring instrument.

Authors: Roland T. Ramsay.

Publisher: Ramsay Corporation.

Cross References: For reviews by Keith Hattrup and Eugene (Geno) Pichette, see 13:116.

[922]
Elementary Program Implementation Profile.

Purpose: Designed as an instrument for "evaluating the appropriateness of elementary school programs and for rating the level of implementation of the High/Scope educational approach in a variety of program settings."

Population: Elementary schools.

Publication Date: 1997.

Acronym: PIP.

Scores, 6: Physical Environment, Daily Schedule, Adult-Child Interaction, Instructional Methods/Content and Assessment, Staff Development and Non-School Collaboration, Total.

Administration: Individual.

Price Data, 2001: $6.95 per manual (7 pages); $14.95 per 25 assessment forms.

Time: Administration time not reported.

Comments: Can also be used with non-High/Scope programs.

Author: High/Scope Educational Research Foundation.

Publisher: High/Scope Educational Research Foundation.

[923]
Elementary Student Opinion Inventory.

Purpose: Designed to measure how elementary students feel about their school.
Population: Elementary students.
Publication Date: 2003.
Scores: 4 subscales: Quality of the Instructional Program, Support for Student Learning, School Climate/Environment for Learning, Student/School Relationships.
Administration: Group.
Parts, 2: A (Likert-scale items), B (customize up to 20 local questions).
Price Data, 2006: $25 per 25 inventories; administrative manual may be downloaded free from publisher webpage.
Time: (15) minutes.
Author: National Study of School Evaluation.
Publisher: National Study of School Evaluation.

[924]
Eliot-Price Perspective Test.

Purpose: "Designed to measure the ability to perceive and to imagine object arrangments from different viewpoints."
Population: Grades 2 and over.
Publication Dates: 1974–1975.
Scores: Total score only.
Administration: Group.
Price Data: Available from publisher.
Time: (20) minutes.
Comments: For research use only.
Authors: John Eliot and Lewis Price.
Publisher: John Eliot (the author) [No reply from publisher; status unknown].
Cross References: See T3:792 (1 reference).

[925]
Emo Questionnaire.

Purpose: "Designed to assess an individual's personal-emotional adjustment."
Population: Clinical and research applications.
Publication Dates: 1958–1998.
Scores: 10 diagnostic dimensions: Rationalization, Inferiority Feelings, Hostility, Depression, Fear and Anxiety, Organic Reaction, Projection, Unreality, Sex Problems, Withdrawal, 3 key adjustment factors: Internal, External, Somatic, and 4 normative level adjustment factors: Internal, External, Somatic, General.
Administration: Individual or group.
Forms, 2: A, B.
Price Data, 2002: $97 per start-up kit including 25 test booklets (specify Form A or Form B), 25 score sheets, and interpretation and research manual; $52 per 25 test booklets (quantity discounts available; specify Form A or Form B); $29 per 25 score sheets; $28 per interpretation and research manual.

Time: No limit (approximately 20 minutes).
Authors: George O. Baehr and Melany E. Baehr.
Publisher: Pearson Performance Solutions [No reply from publisher; status unknown].
Cross References: See T5:927 (1 reference) and T4:883 (1 reference); for reviews by Allan L. Lavoie and Paul McReynolds, see 9:383; see also T2:1170 (1 reference); for reviews by Bertram D. Cohen and W. Grant Dahlstrom, see 6:90 (1 reference).

[926]
Emotional and Behavior Problem Scale—Second Edition.

Purpose: "Developed to contribute to the early identification and service delivery for students with behavior disorders/emotional disturbance."
Population: Ages 5–18.
Publication Dates: 1989–2001.
Acronym: EBPS-2.
Scores, 10: Theoretical (Learning Problems, Interpersonal Relations, Inappropriate Behavior, Unhappiness/Depression, Physical Symptoms/Fears), Empirical (Social Aggression/Conduct Disorder, Social-Emotional Withdrawal/Depression, Learning/Comprehension Disorder, Avoidance/Unresponsiveness, Aggressive/Self-Destructive).
Administration: Individual.
Price Data, 2006: $125 per complete kit including technical manual (2001, 47 pages), 50 School Version rating forms, 50 Home Version rating forms, and IEP and intervention manual (2001, 205 pages); $15 per technical manual (specify Home or School); $35 per 50 rating forms; $25 per IEP and intervention manual; $35 per computerized quick score (Windows®); $225 per computerized IEP and intervention manual (Windows®).
Time: (15) minutes.
Comments: Ratings by teachers and/or parents/guardians.
Authors: Stephen B. McCarney and Tamara J. Arthaud.
Publisher: Hawthorne Educational Services, Inc.
Cross References: For reviews by Adrienne Garro and Judy Oehler-Stinnett, see 16:83; for reviews by J. Jeffrey Grill and Robert C. Reinehr of the original edition, see 12:134.

[927]
Emotional Behavioral Checklist.

Purpose: To assess an individual's overt emotional behavior.
Population: Ages 16 and over.
Publication Date: 1986.
Acronym: EBC.
Scores: 8: Impulsivity-Frustration, Anxiety, Depression-Withdrawal, Socialization, Self-Concept, Aggression, Reality Disorientation, Total EBC.

Administration: Individual.
Manual: No manual.
Price Data, 2006: $32 per 25 checklists.
Time: Administration time not reported.
Comments: Included in the Auxiliary Component of the McCarron-Dial System (1555).
Authors: Jack G. Dial, Carolyn Mezger, Theresa Massey, and Lawrence T. McCarron.
Publisher: McCarron-Dial Systems.
Cross References: For reviews by William A. Stock and Hoi K. Suen, see 11:130.

[928]
Emotional Competence Inventory.

Purpose: "Designed to assess emotional intelligence (the ability to recognize and manage emotions [yours and others])."
Population: Coaches, executive coaches, mid to senior level managers.
Publication Dates: 1999–2002.
Acronym: ECI.
Scores: 4 clusters, 18 competencies: Self-Awareness (Emotional Self-Awareness, Accurate Self-Assessment, Self-Confidence); Self-Management (Emotional Self-Control, Transparency, Adaptability, Achievement Orientation, Initiative, Optimism); Social Awareness (Empathy, Organizational Awareness, Service Orientation); Relationship Management (Developing Others, Inspirational Leadership, Influence, Change Catalyst, Conflict Management, Teamwork & Collaboration).
Administration: Group or individual.
Price Data, 2005: $3,000 Accreditation (2-day program); $1,800 Accreditation (one-day master class); once accredited internet assessments are $150 per participant (this includes unlimited raters); online development tool available for $75 annual subscription.
Time: (50–60) minutes.
Comments: Accreditation required; multirater assessment to be administered by accredited consultants only; accreditation programs run approximately every second month.
Authors: Daniel Goleman, Richard Boyatzis, and the Hay Group.
Publisher: Hay Group.

[929]
Emotional Judgment Inventory.

Purpose: "Developed to assess emotional intelligence for use in employee selection and development in organizational contexts."
Population: Ages 16 and over.
Publication Dates: 2000–2003.
Acronym: EJI.
Scores, 8: Being Aware of Emotions, Identifying Own Emotions, Identifying Others' Emotions,

Managing Own Emotions, Managing Others' Emotions, Using Emotions in Problem Solving, Expressing Emotions Adaptively, Impression Management.
Administration: Group.
Price Data, 2005: $41 per introductory kit (for 1 person only) including manual (2003, 56 pages), questionnaire, answer sheet, and prepaid Mail-In report; $38 per manual; $20 per 10 reusable test booklets; $18 per 25 answer sheets.
Time: (15) minutes.
Comments: Onsite software available; NetAssess online administration, mail-in scoring service.
Author: Scott Bedwell.
Publisher: Institute for Personality and Ability Testing, Inc. (IPAT).
Cross References: For reviews by Phillip L. Ackerman and by Deniz S. Ones and Stephan Dilchert, see 16:84.

[930]
Emotional or Behavior Disorder Scale—Revised.

Purpose: "Designed to document those behaviors most indicative of emotional or behavioral disorders and the behavior problems which exceed the norms of any student in the environment."
Population: Ages 5–18.
Publication Dates: 1991–2003.
Acronym: EBDS-R.
Scores, 6: Behavioral Component (Academic Progress, Social Relationships, Personal Adjustment), Vocational Component (Work Related, Interpersonal Relations, Social/Community Expectations).
Administration: Individual.
Price Data, 2006: $80 per complete kit including technical manual (2003, 66 pages), 50 rating forms, and intervention manual (2003, 407 pages); $15 per technical manual; $35 per 50 rating forms; $30 per intervention manual; $35 per Quick Score; $225 per intervention manual (Windows®).
Time: Administration time not reported.
Comments: Behavior rating scale completed by observers familiar with the student; derived from the Emotional or Behavior Disorder Scale School Version and the Work Adjustment Scale (T6:2743); accompanied by Intervention manual; computer scoring software available.
Authors: Stephen B. McCarney (scale and manuals) and Tamara J. Arthaud (technical manual).
Publisher: Hawthorne Educational Services, Inc.
Cross References: For reviews by Amy M. Rees and T. Steuart Watson, see 16:85; for reviews by Patti L. Harrison and Steven W. Lee of the original edition, see 13:117.

[931]
Emotional Problems Scales.

Purpose: "To assess emotional and behavioral problems in individuals with mild mental retardation or borderline intelligence."

Population: Ages 14 and over.

Publication Dates: 1984–1991.

Acronym: EPS.

Price Data, 2006: $154 per introductory kit including manual (1991, 31 pages), 25 BRS test booklets, 25 SRI test booklets, SRI scoring keys, and 25 profile forms.

Comments: Previous editions titled Prout-Strohmer Personality Inventory and Strohmer-Prout Behavior Rating Scale.

Authors: H. Thompson Prout and Douglas C. Strohmer.

Publisher: Psychological Assessment Resources, Inc.

a) BEHAVIOR RATING SCALES.

Acronym: BRS.

Scores, 12: Thought/Behavior Disorder, Verbal Aggression, Physical Aggression, Sexual Maladjustment, Distractibility, Hyperactivity, Somatic Concerns, Depression, Withdrawal, Low Self-Esteem, Externalizing Behavior Problems, Internalizing Behavior Problems.

Administration: Individual.

Time: [20–50] minutes.

b) SELF-REPORT INVENTORY.

Acronym: SRI.

Scores, 7: Positive Impression, Thought/Behavior Disorder, Impulse Control, Anxiety, Depression, Low Self-Esteem, Total Pathology.

Administration: Individual.

Time: (30–35) minutes.

Cross References: For reviews by S. Alvin Leung and John A. Mills, see 13:118. For reviews by Richard Brozovich and Ernest A. Bauer and by Peter F. Merenda of the Prout-Strohmer Personality Inventory, see 11:311.

[932]
Emotional Quotient Inventory.

Purpose: Designed to measure emotional intelligence.

Population: Ages 16 and older.

Publication Date: 1997.

Acronym: EQ-i.

Scores: 21 content scores: Composite Scale Scores (Total EQ, Intrapersonal EQ, Interpersonal EQ, Adaptability EQ, Stress Management EQ, General Mood EQ), Intrapersonal Subscale Scores (Self-Regard, Emotional Self-Awareness, Assertiveness, Independence, Self-Actualization), Interpersonal Subscale Scores (Empathy, Social Responsibility, Interpersonal Relationship), Adaptability Subscale Scores (Reality Testing, Flexibility, Problem Solving), Stress Management Subscale Scores (Stress Tolerance, Impulse ·Control),

General Mood Subscale Scores (Optimism, Happiness), plus 4 validity indicators (Omission Rate, Inconsistency, Positive Impression, Negative Impression).

Administration: Individual or group.

Price Data, 2006: $22 per summary report; $36 per development report; $59 per group report (volume discounts available); $145 per user's set including user's manual, administrator's guide, and facilitator's guide; $40 per user's manual; $23 per administrator's guide; $84 per technical manual (234 pages); $35 per 10 item booklets.

Foreign Language Editions: Translations available in Afrikaans, Chinese, Czech, Dutch, French-Canadian, Korean, German, Hebrew, Norwegian, Russian, Spanish (South American), Swedish, Danish, Finnish, French (Euro), Hindi, Indonesian, Italian, Japanese, Portuguese, Slovakian, and Slovene.

Time: (30–40) minutes.

Comments: Paper-and-pencil and computer administrations available; previously listed as BarOn Emotional Quotient Inventory.

Authors: Reuven Bar-On.

Publisher: Multi-Health Systems, Inc.

Cross References: For reviews by Andrew A. Cox and Robert M. Guion, see 14:32.

[933]
Emotional Quotient Inventory: Short Development Edition.

Purpose: Designed to measure emotionally intelligent behavior in situations where a more detailed assessment is not possible or required.

Population: Age 16 and older

Publication Date: 2002.

Acronym: EQ-i:S.

Scores, 8: Intrapersonal, Interpersonal, Adaptability, Stress Management, General Mood, Positive Impression, Inconsistency Index, Total EQ.

Administration: Group or individual.

Price Data, 2006: $144 per complete kit including technical manual and 10 complete assessment sets; $63 per technical manual; $135 per 10 complete assessment sets; $224 per software kit including technical manual, getting started guide, and 10 feedback reports; $95 per online feedback report kits including technical manual and 3 feedback reports.

Time: 10–15 minutes.

Comments: Self-report; previously listed as BarOn Emotional Quotient Inventory: Short Development Edition.

Author: Reuven Bar-On.

Publisher: Multi-Health Systems, Inc.

Cross References: For reviews by R. Anthony Doggett and Carl J. Sheperis and by John T. Willse, see 16:20.

[934]
Emotional Quotient Inventory: Youth Version.

Purpose: "Designed to measure emotional intelligence in young people aged 7 to 18 years."
Population: Ages 7–18
Publication Date: 2000.
Acronym: EQ-i: YV.
Scores, 8: Intrapersonal Scale, Interpersonal Scale, Adaptability Scale, Stress Management Scale, Total EQ, General Mood Scale, Positive Impression Scale, Inconsistency Index.
Administration: Group.
Forms, 2: BarOn EQ-i:YV Long Form; BarOn EQ-i:YV(S) Short Form.
Price Data, 2006: $124 per complete kit including manual (86 pages) and 25 Quikscore forms for each of EQ-i:YV and EQ-i:YV(S); $63 per manual; $42 per 25 Quikscore forms.
Time: (20–25) minutes.
Comments: Self-report; previously listed as BarOn Emotional Quotient Inventory: Youth Version.
Authors: Reuven Bar-On and James D. A. Parker.
Publisher: Multi-Health Systems, Inc.
Cross References: For reviews by Joan C. Ballard and Frederick T. L. Leong, see 15:26.

[935]
The Empathy Test.

Purpose: Constructed to assess empathy.
Population: Junior high school and over.
Publication Dates: 1947–1962.
Scores: Total score only.
Administration: Group.
Forms, 3: A, B, C.
Price Data: Available from publisher.
Time: (6-15) minutes.
Authors: W. A. Kerr and B. J. Speroff.
Publisher: Psychometric Affiliates.
Cross References: See T4:890 (2 references), T2:1171 (10 references), and P:73 (1 reference); for a review by Wallace B. Hall, see 6:91 (9 references); for a review by Robert L. Thorndike, see 5:50 (20 references)

[936]
Employability Maturity Interview.

Purpose: "Developed to assess readiness for the vocational rehabilitation planning process."
Population: Rehabilitation clients.
Publication Date: 1987.
Acronym: EMI.
Scores: Total score only.
Administration: Individual.
Price Data: Available from publisher.
Time: (15–20) minutes.

Comments: Based upon the Adult Vocational Maturity Assessment Interview.
Authors: Richard Roessler and Brian Bolton.
Publisher: The National Center on Employment & Disability.
Cross References: See T5:936 (1 reference); for a review by William R. Koch, see 11:132.

[937]
Employee Aptitude Survey, Second Edition

Purpose: Designed to predict future job performance.
Population: Ages 16 to adult
Publication Date: 1952–2000.
Acronym: EAS.
Administration: Group or individual.
Price Data: Price data available from publisher for test materials including User's Manual (2005, 64 pages), Technical Manual (1994, 91 pages), Technical Addendum: Fairness of the EAS (2000, 11 pages), and Supplemental Norms Report (1995, 92 pages).
Time: 5-10(10-15) minutes.
Comments: Tests available separately; computerized versions available; transportability procedure available.
Authors: G. Grimsley (a–h), F. L. Ruch (a–g, i, j), N. D. Warren (a–g), and J. S. Ford (a, c, e–g).
Publisher: Psychological Services, Inc.
　a) TEST 1, VERBAL COMPREHENSION.
　Publication Dates: 1956–1984.
　Scores: Total score only.
　b) TEST 2, NUMERICAL ABILITY.
　Publication Dates: 1952–1963.
　Scores: Total score only.
　c) TEST 3, VISUAL PURSUIT.
　Publication Date: 1956.
　Scores: Total score only.
　d) TEST 4, VISUAL SPEED AND ACCURACY.
　Publication Dates: 1952–1980.
　Scores: Total score only.
　e) TEST 5, SPACE VISUALIZATION.
　Publication Dates: 1952–1980.
　Scores: Total score only.
　f) TEST 6, NUMERICAL REASONING.
　Publication Dates: 1957–1985.
　Scores: Total score only.
　g) TEST 7, VERBAL REASONING.
　Publication Dates: 1952–1963.
　Scores: Total score only.
　h) TEST 8, WORD FLUENCY.
　Publication Dates: 1953–1963.
　Scores: Total score only.
　i) TEST 9, MANUAL SPEED AND ACCURACY.
　Publication Dates: 1953–1963.
　Scores: Total score only.
　j) TEST 10, SYMBOLIC REASONING.
　Publication Dates: 1957–1985.
　Scores: Total score only.

Cross References: For reviews by Brian Engdahl and Paul M. Muchinsky, see 14:137; see also T5:937 (4 references), T4:894 (1 reference), T3:799 (4 references), and T2:1071 (14 references); for reviews by Paul F. Ross and Erwin K. Taylor, and an excerpted review by John O. Crites of an earlier edition, see 6:769 (4 references); for reviews by Dorothy C. Adkins and S. Rains Wallace of an earlier edition, see 5:607.

[938]
Employee Assistance Program Inventory.

Purpose: "Designed as an intake or screening tool for professionals who provide counseling and other services in working adults."
Population: Adults seeking vocational counseling.
Publication Date: 1994.
Acronym: EAPI.
Scores: 10 scales: Anxiety, Depression, Self-Esteem Problems, Marital Problems, Family Problems, External Stressors, Interpersonal Conflict, Work Adjustment, Problem Minimization, Effects of Substance Abuse.
Administration: Group.
Price Data, 2006: $120 per introductory kit including manual (44 pages), 25 reusable item booklets, and 25 answer sheet/profiles.
Time: (20) minutes.
Authors: William D. Anton and James R. Reed.
Publisher: Psychological Assessment Resources, Inc.
Cross References: For reviews by Michael G. Kavan and David J. Pittenger, see 14:138.

[939]
Employee Effectiveness Profile.

Purpose: "Designed to assist managers in identifying the overall effectiveness of individual employees."
Population: Managers.
Publication Date: 1986.
Scores: Total score only.
Administration: Individual.
Price Data: Price information available from publisher for profiles (24 pages) or short forms.
Time: No time limit.
Author: J. William Pfeiffer.
Publisher: Jossey-Bass, A Wiley Company.
Cross References: For reviews by Lawrence M. Aleamoni and Daniel E. Vogler, see 12:136.

[940]
Employee Involvement Survey.

Purpose: Assesses employees' actual and desired opportunities for personal involvement and influence in the workplace.
Population: Business and industry employees.
Publication Date: 1988.
Acronym: EIS.
Scores, 5: Basic Creature Comfort, Safety and Order, Belonging and Affiliation, Ego-Status, Actualization and Self-Expression.

Administration: Group.
Price Data, 2001: $7.95 per instrument (14 pages).
Time: Administration time not reported.
Comments: Self-administered, self-scored.
Author: Jay Hall.
Publisher: Teleometrics International, Inc.

[941]
Employee Performance Appraisal.

Purpose: "Designed as a tool to aid in performance appraisal and merit review."
Population: Business and industry.
Publication Dates: 1962-1984.
Acronym: EPA.
Scores: 7 merit ratings: Quantity of Work, Quality of Work, Job Knowledge, Initiative, Interpersonal Relationships, Dependability, Potential.
Administration: Group.
Manual: No manual; included in Manuals Supplement (1984) along with 13 tests from this publisher.
Price Data, 2006: $35.20 per package of forms; $19.25 per specimen set.
Time: [10-20] minutes.
Comments: Ratings by supervisors.
Author: Martin M. Bruce.
Publisher: Martin M. Bruce, Ph.D.
Cross References: For a review by Jean Maier Palormo, see 6:1116.

[942]
Employee Productivity Index.

Purpose: "Designed to aid in hiring productive and responsible employees."
Population: Job applicants.
Publication Date: 1989.
Acronym: EPI.
Scores, 7: Dependability Scale, Interpersonal Cooperation Scale, Drug Avoidance Scale, Safety Scale, Validity/Accuracy Scale, Productivity Index, Significant Behavioral Indicators.
Administration: Individual or group.
Forms, 6: Quanta Touch Test, Quanta Software for Windows, Online, Scan, Quanta-Fax, Optical Scoring.
Price Data, 2005: $18 per 1–999 each Quanta Touch Test, Quanta Software for Windows—administration and scoring (no booklets), Quanta Software for Windows—scoring only (one booklet for every coupon ordered), Internet with booklets, internet without booklets, Scan, Quanta-Fax; volume discounts available.
Foreign Language Editions: Available in Spanish.
Time: [20–40] minutes.
Author: London House.
Publisher: Pearson Performance Solutions [No reply from publisher; status unknown].

[943]
Employee Reliability Inventory.

Purpose: Designed to be used as a preemployment instrument for assessing a number of different dimensions of work behavior skills, each of which are associated with reliable and productive work behavior.
Population: Prospective employees.
Publication Dates: 1986–1998.
Acronym: ERI.
Scores, 7: Freedom from Disruptive Alcohol and Illegal Drug Use, Courtesy, Emotional Maturity, Conscientiousness, Trustworthiness, Long Term Job Commitment, Safe Job Performance.
Administration: Group.
Price Data, 2005: $17 or less (depending on the administration and scoring methods used) per complete kit including questionnaire, user's manual (1998, 52 pages), all documentation, training, toll-free technical support, and consultation; $55 per Americans With Disabilities Act Kit including user's manual addendum (1992, 19 pages), audio version, Braille version, and large print version.
Special Editions: Braille, Large Print, and Audio versions available.
Time: (12–15) minutes.
Comments: Individual applicant scores are compared to a position specific profile; can be administered online, at a stand alone computer terminal, or by paper and pencil; results for online administration are stored in a database, which is user accessible, and can be used to generate a range of reports.
Authors: Gerald L. Borofsky.
Publisher: Bay State Psychological Associates, Inc.
Cross References: See T5:944 (1 reference); for reviews by Robert M. Guion and Lawrence M. Rudner, see 12:137 (3 references); see also T4:899 (2 references).

[944]
Employee Safety Inventory.

Purpose: Designed to "assess the safety attitudes of job applicants and current employees."
Population: Job applicants and employees.
Publication Dates: 1989–1994.
Acronym: ESI.
Scores, 7: Survey Scales (Safety Control, Risk Avoidance, Stress Tolerance), Validity Scales (Validity/Distortion, Accuracy), Composite Score (Safety Index), Supplemental Scale (Driver Attitude).
Administration: Group or individual.
Price Data: Price information for Quanta Touch Test administration and scoring and for Windows administration and scoring available from publisher.
Time: (45) minutes.
Comments: Paper-and-pencil or computer administration available.
Author: London House.
Publisher: Pearson Performance Solutions [No reply from publisher; status unknown].

[945]
Employee Screening Questionnaire.

Purpose: "A personality-based selection measure designed to provide employers with a technique for identifying superior job candidates and to screen out dishonest and unproductive ones."
Population: Ages 16 and over.
Publication Dates: 2001–2002.
Acronym: ESQ.
Scores: 15 Performance Dimensions: Customer Service, Productivity, Accuracy, Commitment/Job Satisfaction, Promotability, Risk of Counter-Productive Behavior, Alcohol and Substance Abuse, Bogus Sick Days, Driving Delinquency, Lateness, Loafing, Sabotage of Employer's Production or Property, Safety Infractions, Theft, Overall Hiring Recommendation.
Administration: Individual or group.
Price Data, 2006: $15 per test manual; $17 per administration; volume discounts available.
Time: 15 minutes.
Comments: Internet administration or fax-in scoring service available through publisher; recommended by publisher for use in conjunction with the Personnel Assessment Form (1932).
Authors: Douglas N. Jackson.
Publisher: Sigma Assessment Systems, Inc.
Cross References: For reviews by Paul M. Muchinsky and Frank Schmidt, see 16:86.

[946]
Endeavor Instructional Rating System.

Purpose: Student ratings of courses and instructors.
Population: College.
Publication Dates: 1973–1979.
Acronym: EIRS.
Scores, 9: 7 item scores (Hard Work, Advanced Planning, Class Discussion, Personal Help, Presentation Clarity, Grade Accuracy, Increased Knowledge), and 2 composite scores (Student Perception of Achievement, Student-Instructor Rapport).
Administration: Group.
Price Data: Available from publisher.
Time: (5–10) minutes.
Author: Peter W. Frey.
Publisher: Endeavor Information Systems, Inc. [No reply from publisher; status unknown].
Cross References: See 9:386 (1 reference), and T3:818 (2 references); for a review by Kenneth O. Doyle, Jr., see 8:370 (5 references).

[947]
Endicott Work Productivity Scale.

Purpose: "Designed to describe types of behavior and subjective feelings that are highly likely to reduce productivity and efficiency in work activities."
Population: Adults.
Publication Dates: 1994–1997.

Acronym: EWPS.
Scores: Total score only.
Administration: Individual.
Manual: No manual.
Price Data, 2001: $1 per questionnaire.
Time: [3–5] minutes.
Author: Jean Endicott.
Publisher: Department of Research Assessment and Training.
Cross References: For reviews by Andrew A. Cox and William C. Tirre, see 14:140.

[948]
Endler Multidimensional Anxiety Scales.

Purpose: Developed to assess state and trait anxiety and the respondent's perception of threat in the immediate situation.
Population: Adolescents and over.
Publication Date: 1991.
Acronym: EMAS.
Administration: Group.
Price Data, 2006: $109 per complete kit including 25 EMAS-S AutoScore™ test forms, 25 EMAS-T/EMAS-P AutoScore™ test forms, and manual; $35.75 per 25 test forms (select EMAS-S or EMAS-T/EMAS-P); $14.95 per prepaid test report answer sheets (select EMAS-S or EMAS-T/EMAS-P); $53 per manual; $170 per 20-use computer disk (PC with MS Windows); $21.95 per 100 PC answer booklets; $8 per FAX service scoring charge.
Time: (25) minutes.
Comments: Tests may be used separately.
Authors: Norman S. Endler, Jean M. Edwards, and Romeo Vitelli.
Publisher: Western Psychological Services.
a) EMAS-STATE.
Acronym: EMAS-S.
Scores, 3: Cognitive-Worry, Autonomic-Emotional, Total.
b) EMAS-TRAIT.
Acronym: EMAS-T.
Scores, 4: Social Evaluation, Physical Danger, Ambiguous, Daily Routines.
c) EMAS-PERCEPTION.
Acronym: EMAS-P.
Scores: Item scores only.
Cross References: See T5:950 (6 references); for reviews by Deborah L. Bandalos and Steven D. Spaner, see 12:138 (2 references); see also T4:905 (7 references).

[949]
English as a Second Language Oral Assessment, Second Edition.

Purpose: Measures the "learner's ability to speak and understand English."

Population: Adult nonnative speakers of English.
Publication Dates: 1978–1996.
Acronym: ESLOA.
Scores, 4: Auditory Comprehension, Basic Vocabulary and Grammatical Structures, Complex Grammatical Structures and Communicating Meaning and Comprehension, Comprehension and Fluency and Pronunciation.
Administration: Individual.
Levels, 4: 1, 2, 3, 4.
Price Data, 2005: $6.50 per 50 answer sheets; $15.00 per manual (1996, 80 pages).
Time: Administration time not reported.
Authors: Joye Coy Shaffer and Teri McLean.
Publisher: ProLiteracy Worldwide.
Cross References: For reviews by James D. Brown and Charlene Rivera of an earlier edition, see 11:136.

[950]
English Placement Test, Revised.

Purpose: Designed to "quickly place English language students into homogenous ability levels."
Population: English language learners.
Publication Dates: 1972–1993.
Acronym: EPT.
Scores: Total score only.
Subtests, 4: Listening Comprehension, Grammar, Vocabulary, Reading.
Administration: Individual or group.
Forms, 3: A, B, C.
Price Data: Price data for examiner's manual (1993, 8 pages), cassette or CD containing Forms A, B, and C of Listening Comprehension items, test booklets for Forms A, B, and C, and answer sheets available from publisher.
Time: (75) minutes.
Authors: Testing and Certification Division, English Language Institute, University of Michigan.
Publisher: English Language Institute, University of Michigan.
Cross References: See T4:908 (3 references); for a review by John L. D. Clark of an earlier form, see 8:102.

[951]
English Skills Assessment.

Purpose: ACER adaptation of STEP Series and DTLS by Educational Testing Service and The College Board.
Population: Grades 11-12 and first year of post-secondary education
Publication Dates: 1969-1982.
Acronym: ESA.
Scores, 11: Part I (Spelling, Punctuation and Capitalization, Comprehension I, Total), Part II (Comprehension II, Usage, Vocabulary, Sentence Structure, Logical Relationships [optional], Total), Total.

Administration: Group.
Price Data, 2006: A\$4.95 per Part I test booklet; A\$4.95 per Part II test booklet; A\$24.20 per 10 answer sheets; A\$4.95 per score key; A\$22 per manual; A\$42.95per specimen set.
Time: 50(70) minutes for Part I; 60(70) minutes for Part II.
Authors: Australian Council for Educational Research (adaptation).
Publisher: Australian Council for Educational Research Ltd. [Australia]
Cross References: See T4:910 (1 reference); for a review by John C. Sherwood, see 9:389.

[952]
English Test: Municipal Tests: National Achievement Tests.

Purpose: "To test ... mastery in language usage (words and sentences), punctuation and capitalization, and expression of ideas."
Population: Grades 3–8.
Publication Dates: 1938–1956.
Scores, 5: Language Usage-Words, Language Usage-Sentences, Punctuation and Capitalization, Expressing Ideas, Total.
Administration: Group.
Forms, 2: A, B.
Levels, 2: Grades 3–6, Grades 6–8.
Price Data: Available from publisher.
Time: 30(35) minutes.
Comments: Subtest of the formerly published Municipal Battery (see 4:20).
Authors: Robert K. Speer and Samuel Smith.
Publisher: Psychometric Affiliates.
Cross References: See T2:77 (1 reference) and 5:190. For reviews of the complete battery, see 5:18 (1 review), 4:20 (1 review), and 2:1191 (2 reviews).

[953]
English Test: National Achievement Tests.

Purpose: To test skills in English language usage.
Population: Grades 3–12.
Publication Dates: 1936–1957.
Administration: Group.
Levels, 2: Grades 3–8, Grades 7–12.
Forms, 2: A, B.
Price Data: Available from publisher.
Time: (40) minutes.
Authors: Robert K. Speer and Samuel Smith.
Publisher: Psychometric Affiliates.
   a) GRADES 3–8.
   Publication Dates: 1936–1938.
   Scores, 7: Capitalization, Punctuation, Language Usage (Sentences), Language Usage (Words), Expressing Ideas, Letter Writing, Total.
   b) GRADES 7–12.
   Publication Dates: 1936–1957.

Scores, 7: Word Usage, Punctuation, Vocabulary, Language Usage (Sentences), Expressing Ideas, Expressing Feeling, Total.
Cross References: See T2:78 (1 reference) and 5:191; for a review by Winifred L. Post, see 4:162; for a review by Harry A. Greene, see 3:126.

[954]
Enneagram Personality Portraits Inventory and Profile.

Purpose: Designed to identify an individual's personality type, work style, and leadership style.
Population: Work team members.
Publication Date: 1997.
Scores, 9: Ones—Perfecters/Quality Performers/Stabilizers, Twos—Carers/Helpers/Supporters, Threes—Achievers/Producers/Motivators, Fours—Creators/Expressionists/Individualists, Fives—Observers/Thinkers/Systematizers, Sixes—Groupists/Relaters/Teamsters, Sevens—Cheerers/Animators/Cheerleaders, Eights—Challengers/Asserters/Directors, Nines—Accepters/Receptionists/Reconcilers.
Administration: Group.
Price Data: Available from publisher.
Time: Administration time not reported.
Comments: Classifies respondents into one of nine "types."
Authors: Patrick J. Aspell and Dee Dee Aspell.
Publisher: Jossey-Bass, A Wiley Company.

[955]
The Ennis-Weir Critical Thinking Essay Test.

Purpose: "To help evaluate a person's ability to appraise an argument and to formulate in writing an argument in response, thus recognizing a creative dimension in critical thinking ability."
Population: High school and college.
Publication Dates: 1983–1985.
Scores: Critical Thinking Ability.
Administration: Group.
Price Data: Now available free of charge from author's website: http://faculty.ed.uiuc.edu/rhennis.
Time: (40) minutes.
Authors: Robert H. Ennis and Eric Weir.
Publisher: Robert H. Ennis (the author).
Cross References: See T5:959 (2 references); for reviews by James A. Poteet and Gail E. Tompkins, see 10:107.

[956]
The Enright Forgiveness Inventory.

Purpose: "To measure the degree to which one person forgives another who has hurt him or her deeply and unfairly."
Population: High school and college and adults.

Publication Dates: 2000-2004.
Acronym: EFI.
Scores, 10: 3 Affect scores (Positive Affect, Negative Affect, Total Affect), 3 Behavior scores (Positive Behavior, Negative Behavior, Total Behavior), 3 Cognition scores (Positive Cognition, Negative Cognition, Total Cognition), Total.
Administration: Group or individual.
Price Data, 2005: $40 per manual/sample set (63 pages); $120 for permission to reproduce 150 copies, other pricing available at www.mindgarden.com/products/efins.htm.
Time: (40) minutes.
Authors: Robert D. Enright and Julio Rique.
Publisher: Mind Garden, Inc.
Cross References: For reviews by Laura L. B. Barnes and by James Fauth and Scott T. Meier, see 15:89.

[957]
Entrepreneurial Quotient.

Purpose: Designed to profile managerial preferences and personality traits to determine whether an individual has a creative, entrepreneurial management style or a more traditional, operational management style; compares an individual's managerial style and personality traits to those of successful entrepreneurs; designed for use in pre-employment testing and worker development.
Population: Adult.
Publication Dates: 1993–1998.
Acronym: EQ.
Scores, 16: Adaptability, Managerial Traits (Risk Tolerance, Time Management, Creativity, Strategic Thinking, Planning, Goal-Orientation, Total), Personality Traits (Extroversion, Intuition, Thinking, Perceiving, Total), EQ Index, Managerial Type, Personality Type.
Administration: Individual or group.
Price Data: Available from publisher.
Time: 25–35 minutes.
Comments: Online administration available; previously listed as EQ Questionnaire.
Authors: Wonderlic, Inc. and Edward J. Fasiska.
Publisher: Wonderlic, Inc.
Cross References: For reviews by James T. Austin and Paul M. Muchinsky, see 14:141.

[958]
Entrepreneurial Style and Success Indicator [Revised].

Purpose: Designed to help individuals identify their preferred entrepreneurial style and its related strengths and weaknesses, as well as comparing their background to the background of other successful entrepreneurs.
Population: Adults.

Publication Dates: 1988-2006.
Acronym: ESSI.
Scores, 4: Behavioral/Action, Cognitive/Analysis, Interpersonal/Harmony, Affective/Expression, plus 28 Entrepreneurial Success Factors.
Administration: Individual or group.
Price Data, 2006: $19.95 per test booklet (2006, 32 pages); $14.95 per Indicator In-Depth Interpretations booklet (2006, 48 pages); $34.95 per code for online version; $69.95 per Professional's Guide (2006, 62 pages); $38 per Trainer's Guidelines (1996, 18 pages); $159.95 per Power Point CD & Binder 126 slides; $23.95 per participant workbook entitled Discovering Your Pathway to Entrepreneurial Success (2006, 64 pages).
Time: [120-180] minutes for Basic; [360-720] minutes for Advanced.
Comments: Test can be self-administered and self-scored.
Authors: Ken Keis, Terry D. Anderson, and Howard Shenson.
Publisher: Consulting Resource Group International, Inc.
Cross References: For a review by Stephen F. Davis of an earlier edition, see 13:120.

[959]
Eosys Word Processing Aptitude Battery.

Purpose: For use in selection, allocation, and development of word processor operators.
Population: Job candidates for work processor operator positions.
Publication Date: 1983.
Acronym: WPAB.
Scores, 5: Verbal Skills (WP1), Checking Skills (WP2), Written Instructions (WP3), Coded Information (WP4), Numerical Computation (WP5).
Administration: Group.
Price Data: Available from publisher.
Time: (10) minutes per WP1, WP2, WP5; (12) minutes per WP3; (15) minutes per WP4.
Authors: Gill Nyfield, Susan Bawtree, Michael Pearn (test), David Hawkey (test), and Emma Bird (manual).
Publisher: SHL Group plc [United Kingdom].

[960]
ERB Writing Assessment [Revised].

Purpose: "Designed to assess six domains of writing proficiency."
Population: Grades 3–4, 5–6, 7–8, 9–10, 11–12.
Publication Dates: 1989–2004.
Acronym: ERB WrAP.
Scores: 6 writing traits: Overall Development, Organization, Support, Sentence Structure, Word Choice, Mechanics.
Administration: Group.

Price Data, 2006: $7.75 per student for test materials and scoring, plus shipping; $35 per electronic data disk (ASCII file); $7 per additional set of anchor papers; $8 per perusal set (per level) including technical manual (2004, 45 pages), writing booklet, rubric, anchor papers, and report of individual student results; $10 per technical manual.
Comments: Writing samples scored by Measurement Incorporated.
Authors: Educational Records Bureau.
Publisher: Educational Records Bureau.
a) ELEMENTARY LEVEL.
Purpose: To assess a student's narrative writing.
Population: Grades 3 and 4.
Time: Two [40–60] minute sessions.
b) INTERMEDIATE LEVEL.
Purpose: To assess a student's descriptive writing.
Population: Grades 5 and 6.
Time: Two [40–50] minute sessions.
c) MIDDLE SCHOOL LEVEL.
Purpose: To assess a student's expository writing.
Population: Grades 7 and 8.
Time: Two [40–50] minute sessions.
d) SECONDARY LEVEL.
Purpose: To assess a student's persuasive writing.
Population: Grades 9 and 10.
Time: Two [40–50] minute sessions.
e) COLLEGE PREP LEVEL.
Purpose: To assess a student's critical thinking.
Population: Grades 11 and 12.
Time: Two [40–50] minute sessions.
Cross References: For reviews by G. Michael Poteat and Wayne H. Slater of an earlier edition, see 13:122.

[961]
Erotometer: A Technique for the Measurement of Heterosexual Love.
Purpose: Designed to measure attitudes toward heterosexual love.
Population: Adults.
Publication Dates: 1971–1988.
Scores: Total score only.
Administration: Group.
Manual: No manual.
Price Data, 2005: $2 per test.
Time: [10] minutes.
Comments: Supplementary article available.
Authors: Panos D. Bardis.
Publisher: Donna Bardis.
Cross References: For additional information, see 8:337 (1 reference).

[962]
ESL/Adult Literacy Scale
Purpose: Developed to identify "the appropriate starting level for ESL and literacy instruction."

Population: Age 16 through adult.
Publication Date: 1989.
Scores, 6: Listening, Grammar, Life Skills, Reading, Composition, Total.
Administration: Individual.
Manual: No manual.
Price Data, 2006: $25 per 25 test booklets; $5 per scoring template; $5 per instruction card.
Time: [15–20] minutes.
Authors: Michael Roddy.
Publisher: Academic Therapy Publications
Cross References: See T5:971 (2 references); for reviews by Anne L. Harvey and by Dianna L. Newman and Kathleen T. Toms, see 11:138.

[963]
Essential Skills Assessments: Information Skills.
Purpose: "Broad measures of achievement set within the Essential skills of the New Zealand Curriculum Framework ... [for the purpose of] formative assessment."
Population: Ages 9–14.
Publication Date: 2001.
Administration: Group.
Levels, 3: Primary, Intermediate, Secondary.
Price Data, 2002: NZ$36 per full specimen set including 1 each of primary, intermediate, and secondary tests, and teacher's manual (71 pages); NZ$22.50 per specimen set including all tests and teacher's manual (primary level); NZ$27 per specimen set including all tests and teacher's manual (intermediate level); NZ$22.95 per specimen set including all tests and teacher's manual (secondary level); NZ$450 per CD-ROM pack including CD-ROM with all tests (PDF format), teacher's manual, 1 set of printed tests, and help sheet; NZ$18 per teacher's manual; NZ$9.90 per 10 Finding Information in Books (all levels, specify level); NZ$9.90 per 10 Finding Information in Graphs and Tables (primary level); NZ$12.60 per 10 Finding Information in Graphs and Tables (intermediate level); NZ$11.70 per 10 Finding Information in Graphs and Tables (secondary level); NZ$9.90 per 10 Finding Information in a Library (primary and intermediate levels, specify level); NZ$12.60 per 10 finding Information in a Library (secondary level); NZ$9.90 per 10 Finding Information in Reference Sources (primary and intermediate levels, specify level); NZ$9.90 per 10 Evaluating Information in Text (intermediate level); NZ12.60 per 10 Evaluating Information in Text (secondary level); NZ$12.60 per 10 finding Information in Prose Text (intermediate and secondary levels, specify level).
Time: (30) minutes per test.
Comments: Replaces the Progressive Achievement Tests of Study Skills (T5:2095); tests include both

constructed-response and selected-response format items; normed on children living in New Zealand; available in print or CD-ROM format; CD-ROM system requirements: 600 dpi laser or inkjet printer, Adobe Acrobat reader version 3 or 4.
Authors: Cedric Croft, Karyn Dunn, and Gavin Brown.
Publisher: New Zealand Council for Educational Research [New Zealand].
a) FINDING INFORMATION IN BOOKS.
Levels, 2: Primary, Intermediate.
Scores: Total score only.
b) FINDING INFORMATION IN GRAPHS AND TABLES.
Levels, 3: Primary, Intermediate, Secondary.
Scores: Total score only.
c) FINDING INFORMATION IN A LIBRARY.
Levels, 3: Primary, Intermediate, Secondary.
Scores: Total score only.
d) FINDING INFORMATION IN PROSE TEXT.
Levels, 2: Intermediate, Secondary.
Scores: Total score only.
e) FINDING INFORMATION IN REFERENCE SOURCES.
Levels, 2: Primary, Intermediate.
Scores: Total score only.
f) FINDING INFORMATION IN TEXT.
Levels, 2: Intermediate, Secondary.
Scores: Total score only.
Cross References: For a review by Robert L. Johnson, see 15:90; see T5:2095 (1 reference); for reviews by Michael D. Hiscox and Ronald C. Rodgers of an earlier edition, see 9:1006; see also T3:1913 (1 reference).

[964]
ETS Tests of Applied Literacy Skills.
Purpose: To measure adult literacy.
Population: Adults.
Publication Date: 1991.
Scores, 3: Total score for each of 3 subtests: Quantitative Literacy, Document Literacy, Prose Literacy.
Administration: Group.
Forms, 2: Forms A and B for each test.
Price Data: Available from publisher.
Time: 6(20) minutes for the battery; 2(20) minutes of any one subtest.
Authors: Educational Testing Service, Irwin J. Kirsch (manual), Anne Jungeblut (manual), and Anne Campbell (manual), with contributions from Norman E. Freeberg, Robert J. Mislevy, Donald A. Rock, and Kentaro Yamamoto.
Publisher: Prentice Hall [No reply from publisher; status unknown].
Cross References: For reviews by Roger A. Richards and Herbert C. Rudman, see 13:124.

[965]
Evaluating Courses for Inclusion of New Scholarship on Women.
Purpose: A student evaluation questionnaire designed to evaluate course content in terms of information presented about women.
Population: Post-secondary students.
Publication Date: 1988.
Scores: 4 ratings: Evaluation of Course Readings, Evaluation of the Syllabus, Evaluation of the Class, Overall Course Evaluation.
Administration: Group.
Manual: No manual.
Price Data: Available from publisher.
Time: Administration time not reported.
Author: Women's Studies Program, Duke University.
Publisher: Association of American Colleges and Universities.

[966]
Evaluating Diversity Training.
Purpose: "Designed to help diversity-training managers evaluate the effectiveness of training, instructors, and vendors."
Population: Diversity-training managers.
Publication Date: 1996.
Scores: 17 checklists: Participant Reactions (rating scale, open ended), Self-Assessment of Learning, Learning Self-Assessment, Knowledge of Diversity Issues, Learning Outcomes Role-Play, Participant Post-Training (open ended, short version, rating scale), Manager's Post training (open ended, satisfaction measure, application estimate), Diversity Behavior, Organizational Results, Vendor Evaluation, Instructor/Facilitator Effectiveness, Experiential Training Evaluation.
Administration: Group.
Price Data: Available from publisher.
Time: Untimed.
Authors: John M. Keller, Andrea Young, and Mary Riley.
Publisher: Jossey-Bass, A Wiley Company.

[967]
Evaluation Aptitude Test.
Purpose: Constructed to assess deductive reasoning.
Population: Candidates for college and graduate school entrance.
Publication Dates: 1951–1952.
Acronym: EAT.
Scores, 5: Neutral Syllogisms, Emotionally Toned Syllogisms, Total, Emotional Bias, Indecision.
Administration: Group.
Price Data: Available from publisher.
Time: 50(55) minutes.
Author: DeWitt E. Sell.

Publisher: Psychometric Affiliates.
Cross References: For reviews by J. Thomas Hastings and Walker H. Hill, see 5:691.

[968]
Evaluation Disposition Toward the Environment.

Purpose: Evaluates "value orientation used to approach environmental experiences and responsibilities."
Population: High school and college.
Publication Date: 1976.
Acronym: EDEN.
Scores, 7: Aesthetic, Experiential, Knowledge Seeking, Prudent, Active, Responsible, Practical.
Administration: Group.
Price Data: Available from publisher.
Time: (45) minutes.
Comments: Scoring must be done by publisher.
Author: Norman J. Milchus.
Publisher: Norman Milchus (the author).

[969]
Evaluation Modality Test.

Purpose: Developed to analyze the characteristics of "the mode in which an individual valuates."
Population: Adults.
Publication Date: 1956.
Acronym: EMT.
Scores, 4: Realism, Moralism, Individualism, Total.
Administration: Individual or group.
Price Data: Available from publisher.
Time: (25–35) minutes.
Author: Hugo O. Engelmann.
Publisher: Psychometric Affiliates.
Cross References: For a review by Wilson H. Guertin, see 5:51.

[970]
Evaluation of Basic Skills.

Purpose: Designed to provide a concept-based measurement of reading, writing, and mathematics.
Population: Ages 3 to 18.
Publication Dates: 1995–1996.
Scores, 3: Reading, Writing, Mathematics.
Administration: Individual.
Price Data, 2005: $89.95 per complete start-up kit including administration manual (1995, 27 pages), 50 test forms, and 25 pre-test/post-test word tests; $15.95 per administration manual; $12 per 2-tape audio cassette set "Administering the Test"; $195 per application fee as test administrator; $50 per 50 test forms; $40 per 50 pre-test/post-test word tests.
Time: (10) minutes for Mathematics section; untimed for Reading and Writing sections.
Authors: Lee Havis.
Publisher: Trust Tutoring.

Cross References: For reviews by Eleanor E. Sanford and Loraine J. Spenciner, see 14:142.

[971]
Evaluation of Competency to Stand Trial—Revised.

Purpose: "Designed for specialized forensic evaluations related to competency to stand trial."
Population: Ages 18 and over.
Publication Date: 2004.
Acronym: ECST-R.
Scores, 8: Competency Scales (Factual Understanding of Courtroom Proceedings, Rational Understanding of Courtroom Proceedings, Consult with Counsel), Atypical Presentation Scales (Realistic, Psychotic, Nonpsychotic Impairment, Both [Psychotic and Nonpsychotic combined]).
Administration: Individual.
Price Data, 2006: $220 per introductory kit including professional manual (2004, 176 pages), binder with interview booklet, 25 record forms, and 25 profile/summary forms in a soft-sided attaché case.
Time: Untimed.
Comments: Semistructured interview format.
Authors: Richard Rogers, Chad E. Tillbrook, and Kenneth W. Sewell.
Publisher: Psychological Assessment Resources, Inc.
Cross References: For reviews by D. Ashley Cohen and Robert A. Leark, see 16:87.

[972]
Everyday Life Activities: Photo Series.

Purpose: Designed as a photo series for "language training, teaching, testing and remediation of word-, sentence-, and text/discourse-level abilities."
Population: Children with delay in language development, autistic children, and adults with a language or speech impairment sequel to brain damage.
Publication Date: 1994.
Acronym: ELA.
Scores: Available from publisher.
Administration: Individual.
Price Data, 2001: $743 per book.
Time: Administration time not reported.
Author: Jacqueline Stark.
Publisher: Psychology Press.

[973]
Examination for the Certificate of Competency in English.

Purpose: "Intended for learners who have acquired an intermediate competence in English language use" who may wish some "external measure of their competence in English for documentation for employment or promotion purposes" in their native countries.
Population: Nonnative speakers of English.

Publication Dates: 1995–2002.
Acronym: ECCE.
Scores, 4: Listening, Grammar/Vocabulary/Reading, Writing, Speaking.
Administration: Group.
Price Data, 2002: $40 per candidate to publisher plus local administrative fees.
Time: (160–180) minutes for complete battery; (25) minutes for Listening; (90) minutes for Grammar/Vocabulary and Reading; (30) minutes for Writing; (10–15) minutes for Speaking.
Comments: Administrative manual for local test centers includes Speaking criteria; not "an academically oriented examination, though it may be a bridge to such an examination, for instance, the ECPE"; 2 forms per year; "administered once a year at approved test centers outside the U.S."; "examinees who pass all sections of the ECCE receive the Michigan Certificate of Competency in English."
Author: The English Language Institute of the University of Michigan, Testing and Certification Division.
Publisher: English Language Institute, University of Michigan.

[974]
Examination for the Certificate of Proficiency in English.

Purpose: Designed to assess language proficiency for advanced English-as-a-Second-Language speakers.
Population: Adults who are advanced level English-as-a-Second-Language speakers and who wish documentation for academic or employment purposes.
Publication Dates: 1953–2002.
Acronym: ECPE.
Scores, 5: Writing, Listening Comprehension, Cloze, Grammar/Vocabulary/Reading, Speaking.
Administration: Group.
Forms: 3 Preliminary, 1 Final each year.
Price Data, 2002: $50 per candidate to publisher plus local administrative fees.
Comments: Administrative manual for local test centers includes Speaking criteria.
Author: English Language Institute of the University of Michigan.
Publisher: English Language Institute, University of Michigan.

a) PRELIMINARY ECPE.
Time: 30 minutes.
Comments: A 35-item preliminary test designed to familiarize the examinee with the examination and serve as an indicator of how they might perform on the Final ECPE.
b) FINAL ECPE.
Time: (160–180) minutes for Final Battery; (10–15) minutes for Speaking; (30) minutes for Writ-

ing; (25–30) minutes for Listening; (25) minutes for Cloze; (60) minutes for Grammar/Vocabulary/Reading.
Comments: "Administered once a year, at approved test centers" throughout the world; "an entirely new ECPE is produced every year"; "examinees who pass all sections of the ECPE receive the Michigan Certificate of Proficiency in English. The CPE is not awarded in recognition of academic studies, nor teaching ability," it is only a recognition of language proficiency. It may be used for entrance to U.S. or Canadian universities, for advanced placement in local university English courses, for evidence of English language ability for teachers of English.

[975]
Examining for Aphasia, Third Edition.

Purpose: "For evaluating possible aphasic language impairments and other acquired impairments that are often closely related to language functions."
Population: Adolescents and adults.
Publication Dates: 1946–1994.
Acronym: EFA-3.
Scores, 41: Agnosias (Common Objects, Pictures, Colors, Geometric Forms, Numerals, Letters, Printed Words, Almost Alike Pictures, Printed Sentences, Nonverbal Noises, Object Identification, Total); Aphasias (Word Identification, Comprehension of Sentences, Comprehension of Multiple Choice, Oral Paragraphs, Silent Reading Sentences, Silent Reading Paragraphs, Total); Apraxias (Body Parts, Simple Skills, Pretend Action, Numerals, Words, Sentences, Total), Aphasios (Automatic Speech, Writing Numerals, Writing Letters, Spelling, Writing from Dictation, Naming Body Parts, Word Finding, Arithmetic Computations, Arithmetic Problems, Total); Composites (Receptive, Expressive, Subaphasic, Aphasia, Total).
Administration: Individual.
Price Data, 2006: $180 per complete kit including 25 examiner record books, 25 Profile/Response forms, picture book, examiner's manual (1994, 35 pages), and object kit; $50 per 25 examiner record booklets; $30 per 25 Profile/Response forms; $49 per picture book; $40 per examiner's manual; $20 per object kit.
Time: (30–120) minutes.
Comments: Shortened version of test may be administered for screening purposes.
Authors: Jon Eisenson.
Publisher: PRO-ED.
Cross References: For a review by Helen Kitchens, see 13:124: see also T4:940 (2 references), T2:2071 (3 references), and P:76 (2 references); for excerpted reviews by Louis M. DiCarlo and Laurance F. Shaffer, see 5:52 (3 references); for a review by D. Russell Davis and excerpted reviews by Nolan D. C. Lewis and one

other, see 4:42; for a review by C. R. Strother and an excerpted review, see 3:39.

[976]
Executive Administrative Assistant Skills Test.

Purpose: To evaluate the suitability of candidates for the position of executive administrative assistant.
Population: Candidates with all levels of experience for the position of executive administrative assistant.
Publication Date: 1977.
Acronym: PRSECTY.
Scores: Total Score, Narrative Evaluation, Ranking, Recommendation.
Administration: Group.
Price Data, 2001: $355 per candidate.
Time: (45) minutes.
Comments: Scored by publisher; must be proctored.
Author: Walden Personnel Performance, Inc.
Publisher: Walden Personnel Performance, Inc.

[977]
The Executive Control Battery.

Purpose: "To document the presence and extent of the 'executive dyscontrol' or 'frontal lobe' syndrome."
Population: Adults.
Publication Date: 1999.
Acronym: ECB.
Administration: Individual.
Price Data: Available from publisher.
Comments: Neuropsychological battery; subtests can be administered independently.
Authors: Elkhonon Goldberg, Kenneth Podell, Robert Bilder, and Judith Jaeger.
Publisher: Psych Press [Australia].
 a) THE GRAPHICAL SEQUENCES TEST.
 Purpose: "Designed to elicit perseverations ... and various behavioural stereotypies."
 Scores, 7: Hyperkinetic Motor Perseverations (Occurrences), Perseveration of Elements (Occurrences, Repetitions), Perseveration of Features (Occurrences, Repetitions), Perseverations of Activities (Occurrences, Repetitions).
 Time: (15–20) minutes.
 b) COMPETING PROGRAMS TEST.
 Purpose: "Designed to elicit various types of echopraxia, behavioural stereotypies, and disinhibition."
 Scores, 8: Simple Go/No-Go (Random, Simple Stereotype, Alternating Stereotype, Total Errors), Simple Conflict—Visual (Random, Simple Stereotype, Alternating Stereotype, Total Errors).
 Time: (12–15) minutes.
 c) MANUAL POSTURES TEST.
 Purpose: "Designed to elicit various types of echopraxia."

Scores: 3 ratings: Correct, Full Mirroring, Other.
Time: (10–15) minutes.
 d) MOTOR SEQUENCES TEST.
 Purpose: "Designed to elicit various types of motor perseverations, stereotypies, and other deficits of sequential motor organisation."
 Parts, 2: Dynamic Praxis, Bimanual Coordination.
 Time: (10–15) minutes.
  1) *Dynamic Praxis.*
  Scores, 6: Two Stage Movement (Imitation, Continuation, Without Model), Reversal of Two State Movement (Imitation, Continuation Without Model), Three Stage Movement (Imitation, Continuation Without Model).
  2) *Bimanual Coordination.*
  Scores, 6: Distal (Imitation, Continuation Without Model), Proximal (Imitation, Continuation Without Model), Mixed (Imitation, Continuation Without Model).
Cross References: For reviews by Anthony T. Dugbartey and by Shawn Powell and David McCone, see 15:92.

[978]
Executive Profile Survey.

Purpose: Constructed to assess whether an individual has the attributes for success by measureing behavioral characteristics in comparison with over 2,000 top-level executives.
Population: Prospective executives.
Publication Dates: 1967–1983.
Acronym: EPS.
Scores: 11 dimensions: Ambitious, Assertive, Enthusiastic, Creative, Spontaneous, Self-Focused, Considerate, Open-Minded, Relaxed, Practical, Systematic.
Administration: Group or individual.
Price Data, 2005: $22 per 10 reusable test booklets; $22 per 25 answer sheets; $30 per manual (1983, 79 pages); $34 per introductory kit; $16.50 to $30 per reports.
Time: (60) minutes.
Comments: Self-administered; manual title is Perspectives on the Executive Personality.
Authors: Virgil R. Lang and Samuel E. Krug (manual).
Publisher: Institute for Personality and Ability Testing, Inc. (IPAT).
Cross References: For reviews by S. David Kriska and Gregory J. Marchant, see 12:146; for a review of an earlier edition by William I. Sauser, Jr., see 9:401.

[979]
Expectations Edition of the Personal Values Inventory.

Purpose: To identify role expectations and compare them with the motivational values of the person in the role.

Population: Adolescents and adults reading at or above sixth grade (U.S.) reading level.
Publication Date: 2001.
Acronym: EE/PVI.
Scores: Blue Motivation, Red-Blue Motivation, Red Motivation, Red-Green Motivation, Green Motivation, Blue-Green Motivation.
Administration: Group or individual.
Manual: No manual.
Price Data, 2002: $4.50 per inventory.
Time: (15–30) minutes.
Comments: For use with the Personal Values Inventory (1919); scores reflect expectations of the person in the role when things are going well and the expected responses when there is conflict or opposition.
Author: Elias H. Porter.
Publisher: Personal Strengths Publishing.

[980]
Expectations Edition of the Strength Development Inventory.

Purpose: To identify role expectations and compare them with the motivational values of the person in the role.
Population: Adults.
Publication Date: 2001.
Acronym: EE/SDI.
Scores: Altruistic-Nurturing Motivation, Assertive-Nurturing Motivation, Assertive-Directing Motivation, Judicious-Competing Motivation, Analytic-Autonomizing Motivation, Cautious-Supporting Motivation.
Administration: Group or individual.
Manual: No manual.
Price Data, 2002: $4.50 per inventory.
Foreign Language Edition: French edition available entitled Édition sur les attentes de l'inventaire du déploiement des forces de la personnalité.
Time: (15–30) minutes.
Comments: For use with the Strength Deployment Inventory (2436); supersedes the Job Interactions Inventory (14:474); scores reflect expectations of the person in the role when things are going well and the expected responses when there is conflict or opposition.
Author: Elias H. Porter.
Publisher: Personal Strengths Publishing.

[981]
Experience and Background Inventory (Form S).

Purpose: "Provides quantitative measures of past performance and experience."
Population: Adults [industry].
Publication Dates: 1980–1996.
Acronym: EBI.

Scores: 9 factors: School Achievement, Choice of a College Major, Aspiration Level, Drive/Career Progress, Leadership and Group Participation, Vocational Satisfaction, Financial Responsibility, General Responsibility, Relaxation Pursuits.
Administration: Group.
Price Data, 2002: $102 per start-up kit including 25 test booklets, 25 score sheets, and interprettion and research manual (1996, 15 pages); $54 per 25 test booklets; $32 per 25 score sheets; $28 per interpretation and research manual.
Time: Administration time not reported.
Authors: Melany E. Baehr and Ernest C. Froemel.
Publisher: Pearson Performance Solutions [No reply from publisher; status unknown].
Cross References: For reviews by F. Felicia Ferrara and Chantale Jeanrie, see 15:93.

[982]
The Experiencing Scale.

Purpose: Assess the degree to which a patient communicates and employs a personal, phenomenological perspective in a therapy session.
Population: Counselors and counselor trainees.
Publication Date: 1969.
Acronym: EXP.
Scores, 2: Mode, Peak; based on a 7-point rating scale.
Administration: Individual.
Price Data, 2001: $26 per Volumes I and II; $42 per Volume III.
Time: Administration time not reported.
Comments: "Evaluating the quality of patient self-involvement in psychotherapy directly from tape recordings or typescripts of the therapy session"; tape or transcript of session required; rated by trained raters from tapes (audio or video).
Authors: M. H. Klein, P. L. Mathieu, E. T. Gendlin, and D. J. Kiesler.
Publisher: Marjorie H. Klein, Ph.D. (the author).
Cross References: See T5:991 (3 references) and T4:943 (1 reference).

[983]
EXPLORE.

Purpose: Measures the academic progress of eighth and ninth graders in four areas: English, mathematics, reading, and science; helps students explore the range of career options; and assists them in developing a high school coursework plan.
Population: Grades 8–9.
Publication Dates: 1995–2000.
Administration: Group.
Price Data: Available from publisher.
Time: (120) minutes for four academics tests; (45–60) minutes for interest inventory, plans and background information, and needs assessment.

Comments: EXPLORE is the initial component of ACT's Educational Planning and Assessment System (EPAS), which also includes PLAN (1962) in Grade 10, and the ACT in Grades 11 or 12. Special testing with extended time and alternate test formats are available for students who receive special accommodations in school due to professionally diagnosed and documented disabilities.
Authors: ACT, Inc.
Publisher: ACT, Inc.

a) EXPLORE ENGLISH TEST.
Purpose: Measures understanding of the conventions of standard written English.
Scores, 3: Usage/Mechanics (Punctuation, Grammar and Usage, Sentence Structure), Rhetorical Skills (Strategy, Organization, Style), Total.
Time: 30 minutes.

b) EXPLORE MATHEMATICS TEST.
Purpose: Measures student's mathematical reasoning skills.
Scores: Total score only.
Time: 30 minutes.

c) EXPLORE READING TEST.
Purpose: Measures reading comprehension as a product of referring and reasoning skills.
Scores: Total score only.
Time: 30 minutes.

d) EXPLORE SCIENCE TEST.
Purpose: Measures scientific reasoning skills.
Scores: Total score only.
Time: 30 minutes.

Cross References: For a review by Sandra A. Loew, see 15:94.

[984]
Explore the World of Work.

Purpose: Designed to stimulate job awareness and exploration for jobs requiring up to 2 years of training.
Population: Elementary and special education.
Publication Dates: 1989–1991.
Acronym: E-WOW.
Scores, 6: Business/Office/Sales, Industry/Mechanics/Transportation/Construction, Art/Communications/Design, Health/Education/Social Service, Forestry/Agriculture/Natural Resources, Scientific/Technical/Health.
Administration: Group.
Price Data: Available from publisher.
Time: (40–70) minutes.
Comments: Children's Occupational Outlook Handbook suggested to complete follow-up activities on the questionnaire; self-scored.
Authors: Lori Constantino, Bob Kauk, and CFKR Career Materials, Inc. (manuals).
Publisher: CFKR Career Materials.

[985]
Expressive One-Word Picture Vocabulary Test: Spanish-Bilingual Edition.

Purpose: Designed to "provide an assessment of an individual's combined Spanish and English vocabulary."
Population: Ages 4-0 through 12-11.
Publication Date: 2001.
Acronym: EOWPVT-SBE.
Scores: Total score only.
Administration: Individual.
Price Data, 2006: $140 per test kit including manual (108 pages), test plates, and 25 record forms in portfolio; $38 per Spanish-Bilingual Edition manual; $27 per Spanish-Bilingual record forms.
Time: (10–15) minutes.
Comments: Adaptation of the English edition of the Expressive One-Word Picture Vocabulary Test (986); co-normed with the Receptive One-Word Picture Vocabulary Test: Spanish-Bilingual Edition (2138).
Authors: Rick Brownell.
Publisher: Academic Therapy Publications.
Cross References: For a review by Jill Ann Jenkins, see 16:88.

[986]
Expressive One-Word Picture Vocabulary Test [2000 Edition].

Purpose: Designed to measure an individual's English-speaking vocabulary.
Population: Ages 2–0 through 18-11.
Publication Dates: 1979–2000.
Acronym: EOWPVT.
Scores: Total score only.
Administration: Individual.
Price Data, 2006: $145 per kit including manual (2000, 128 pages), 25 record forms, and test plates in a vinyl portfolio; $75 per test plates; $30 per 25 record forms; $40 per manual.
Time: (10–15) minutes.
Comments: The editor combines the lower and upper levels in previous editions and extends the use of the test through age 18-11.
Authors: 1990 and earlier edition by Morrison F. Gardner; 2000 edition by Rick Brownell.
Publisher: Academic Therapy Publications.
Cross References: For a review by Alfred Longo, see 15:95; see T5:994 (53 references) and T4:946 (23 references); for reviews by Gregory J. Cizek and Larry B. Grantham of an earlier edition, see 12:147 (6 references); for reviews by Jack A. Cummings and Gilbert M. Spivak of the Lower Level, see 9:403 (2 references).

[987]
Expressive Vocabulary Test.

Purpose: Designed to assess expressive oral vocabulary and word retrieval.

Population: Ages 2.5–90+ years.
Publication Date: 1997.
Acronym: EVT.
Scores: Total score only.
Administration: Individual.
Price Data, 2005: $174.99 per complete kit, including Easel, 25 record forms, and manual (176 pages); $34.99 per 25 record forms; $99.99 for Easel; $69.99 per examiner's manual; $199.99 per AGS Computer ASSIST™ for the EVT (Windows or Macintosh).
Time: (15) minutes.
Comments: Conormed with the Peabody Picture Vocabulary Test—III; comparison between EVT and PPVT-III standard scores yields an evaluation of word retrieval; computer scoring ASSIST™ program provides extended norms below 40 and includes vocabulary-building exercises.
Authors: Kathleen T. Williams.
Publisher: Pearson Assessments (originally published by AGS Publishing, acquired by Pearson in 2005).
Cross References: For reviews by Frederick Bessai and Orest Eugene Wasyliw, see 14:143.

[988]
Extended Complex Figure Test.

Purpose: Designed to measure both perceptual organization and visual memory in persons with brain injury.
Population: Ages 19–85.
Publication Date: 2003.
Acronym: ECFT.
Scores, 14: Copy Total Correct, Copy Time, Immediate Recall Total Correct, Immediate Recall Time, Delayed Recall Total Correct, Delayed Recall Time, Recognition Total Correct, Recognition Global, Recognition Detail, Recognition Left Detail, Recognition Right Detail, Matching Total Correct, Matching Left Detail, Matching Right Detail.
Administration: Individual.
Price Data, 2006: $159.50 per kit including manual (94 pages), stimulus booklet, and administration scoring booklet; $68.50 per stimulus booklet; $47 per 25 administration and scoring booklets; $58 per manual.
Time: (15–20) minutes.
Authors: Philip S. Fastenau.
Publisher: Western Psychological Services
Cross References: For reviews by Mary "Rina" M. Chittooran and Daniel C. Miller, see 16:89.

[989]
Eyberg Child Behavior Inventory and Sutter-Eyberg Student Behavior Inventory—Revised.

Purpose: Designed "to measure conduct problems in children ages 2 through 16 years."
Population: Ages 2–16.

Publication Dates: 1978–1999.
Acronym: ECBI; SESBI-R.
Scores, 2: Intensity, Problem.
Administration: Group or individual.
Forms, 2: Eyberg Child Behavior Inventory; Sutter-Eyberg Student Behavior Inventory—Revised.
Price Data, 2006: $162 per introductory kit including professional manual (1999, 64 pages), 50 ECBI test sheets, and 50 SESBI-R test sheets.
Time: (10) minutes.
Comments: ECBI is a rating form completed by parents; SESBI-R is a rating form completed by teachers.
Authors: Sheila Eyberg (SESBI-R, ECBI, and professional manual), Joseph Sutter (SESBI-R), and Donna Pincus (professional manual).
Publisher: Psychological Assessment Resources, Inc.
Cross References: For reviews by Joyce Meikamp and by Susan C. Whiston and Jennifer C. Bouwkamp, see 15:96; for information on the Eyberg Child Behavior Inventory, see T5:997 (30 references) and T4:948 (26 references); for a review by Michael L. Reed of an earlier edition, see 9:404 (6 references); see also T3:858 (2 references). For information on the Sutter-Eyberg Student Behavior Inventory, see T5:2595 (2 references) and T4:2668 (1 reference); for a review by T. Steuart Watson of an earlier edition, see 11:410 (2 references).

[990]
Eysenck Personality Inventory.

Purpose: Measures two independent dimensions of personality: Extraversion-Introversion and Neuroticism-Stability.
Population: Adults.
Publication Dates: 1963–1969.
Acronym: EPI.
Scores, 3: Extraversion, Neuroticism, Lie.
Administration: Group.
Time: (10–15) minutes.
Comments: Revision of Maudsley Personality Inventory; for revised edition of EPI, see Eysenck Personality Questionnaire—Revised (991); no reliability data for Lie scores; authors recommend use of both forms to obtain adequate reliability for individual measurements; U.S. and British Editions are identical except for three words and directions.
Authors: H. J. Eysenck and Sybil B. G. Eysenck.
   a) UNITED STATES EDITION.
   Population: Grades 9–16 and adults.
   Publication Dates: 1963–1969.
   Forms, 2: A, B.
   Price Data: Available from publisher.
   Foreign Language Edition: Spanish edition (1972) available.
   Comments: A printing with the title Eysenck Personality Inventory is available for industrial use.

Publisher: EdITS/Educational and Industrial Testing Service.
b) BRITISH EDITION.
Population: Adults.
Publication Dates: 1963–1964.
Forms, 2: A, B.
Price Data: Available from publisher.
Comments: This test is now superseded by Eysenck Personality Questionnaire [Revised] (991) except where parallel forms are required.
Publisher: Hodder & Stoughton Educational [England].
Cross References: See T5:998 (135 references), T4:949 (226 references), 9:405 (91 references), and T3:859 (245 references); for a review by Auke Tellegen, see 8:553 (405 references); see also T2:1174 (140 references); for reviews by Richard I. Lanyon and excerpted reviews by A. W. Heim and James Linder, see 7:776 (121 references); see also P:77 (52 references); for a review by James C. Lingoes, see 6:93 (1 reference).

[991]
Eysenck Personality Questionnaire [Revised].

Publication Dates: 1975–1994.
Acronym: EPQ-R.
Scores, 5: Psychoticism or Tough-Mindedness, Extraversion, Neuroticism or Emotionality, Lie, Addiction.
Administration: Group.
Time: (10–15) minutes.
Comments: Revision of the still-in-print Eysenck Personality Inventory (990).
Authors: H. J. Eysenck and Sybil B. G. Eysenck.
a) UNITED STATES EDITION.
Purpose: Designed to measure four dimensions of personality in adults.
Population: College and general adults including those with lower education levels.
Publication Dates: 1975–1994.
Price Data: Available from publisher.
Publisher: EdITS/Educational and Industrial Testing Service.
b) BRITISH EDITION.
Purpose: Measures three main personality factors: Psychoticism, Extraversion, and Neuroticism.
Population: Ages 7–15, 16 and over.
Publication Dates: 1975–1991.
Price Data: Available from publisher.
Publisher: Hodder & Stoughton Educational [England].
Cross References: See T5:999 (195 references), T4:950 (190 references), 9:406 (32 references), and T3:860 (72 references); for reviews by Jack Block, Paul Kline, Lawrence J. Stricker, and Auke Tellegen, see 8:554 (84 references).

[992]
FACES IV (Family Adaptability and Cohesion Evaluation Scale).

Purpose: To determine the structure of the family, in terms of the Circumplex Model.
Population: Families.
Publication Dates: 1985-2006.
Acronym: FACES IV.
Scores: 2 major dimensions: Family Cohesion, Family Flexibility; 6 scales with 2 balanced scales (Balanced Cohesion and Balanced Flexibility) and 4 unbalanced scales (Disengaged and Enmeshed, Rigid and Chaotic).
Administration: Individual or group.
Price Data, 2006: $95 for FACES IV Package, which includes unlimited use (package includes manual, scales, and scoring procedures).
Time: (15-20) minutes.
Comments: FACES II and FACES III are no longer available but are integrated into FACES IV; also known as Family Adaptability & Cohesion Evaluation Scales; self-report instrument; additional information available at www.facesiv.com.
Authors: David H. Olson, Dean Gorall, and Judy Tiesel.
Publisher: Life Innovations, Inc.
Cross References: See T5:1000 (110 references), T4:951 (31 references), and 11:140 (26 references).

[993]
Facial Action Coding System.

Purpose: Constructed to assess facial movements or expressions.
Population: Adults.
Publication Date: 1978.
Acronym: FACS.
Scores: 66 Action Units.
Administration: Individual.
Price Data: Available from publisher.
Time: Administration time not reported.
Authors: Paul Ekman and Wallace V. Friesen.
Publisher: Paul Ekman (the author) [No reply from publisher; status unknown].
Cross References: See T5:1001 (17 references); for reviews by Kathryn M. Benes and Thomas F. Donlon, see 12:149 (7 references); see also T4:952 (11 references).

[994]
Facial Expressions of Emotion—Stimuli and Tests.

Purpose: Designed to "assess recognition of facial expressions of emotion."
Population: Adults.
Publication Date: 2002.
Acronym: FEEST.
Administration: Individual.

Price Data, 2006: £384 per CD-ROM including tests and manual.
Time: Untimed.
Comments: Computer administered; requires Pentium PC running Windows 98, 64 Mb RAM and CD-ROM drive; also runs on Apple Macintosh System 7.5 through 9; 2 tests: Ekman 60 Faces, Emotion Hexagon.
Authors: Andrew Young, David Perrett, Andrew Calder, Reiner Sprengelmeyer, and Paul Ekman.
Publisher: Harcourt Assessment [England].
  a) EKMAN 60 FACES.
  Scores, 7: Anger, Disgust, Fear, Happiness, Sadness, Surprise, Total.
  b) EMOTION HEXAGON.
  Scores, 7: Same as *a* above.
  Comments: Uses computer-morphed expressions to manipulate test difficulty.

[995]
Faculty Morale Scale for Institutional Improvement.

Purpose: Designed "as a diagnostic instrument—an attitudinal fact-finding device."
Population: Faculty members.
Publication Date: No date.
Scores: Total score only.
Administration: Group.
Price Data, 2001: $3 per specimen set.
Time: Administration time not reported.
Author: A Local Chapter Committee, American Association of University Professors.
Publisher: Psychometric Affiliates.
Cross References: For a review by Keith Hattrup, see 15:97.

[996]
A Familism Scale.

Purpose: Measures attitudes related to family.
Population: Adolescents and adults.
Publication Dates: 1959–1988.
Scores, 3: Nuclear, Extended, Total.
Administration: Group.
Manual: No manual.
Price Data, 2005: $2 per scale.
Time: [8] minutes.
Comments: Supplementary article available.
Authors: Panos D. Bardis.
Publisher: Donna Bardis.
Cross References: See T4:957 (1 reference).

[997]
Family Adjustment Test.

Purpose: "Designed to measure feelings of intrafamily homeyness-homelessness."
Population: Ages 12 and over.
Publication Dates: 1952–1954.
Acronym: FAT.
Scores, 11: Attitudes Toward Mother, Attitudes Toward Father, Father-Mother Attitude Quotient, Oedipal, Struggle for Independence, Parent-Child Friction-Harmony, Interparental Friction-Harmony, Family Inferiority-Superiority, Rejection of Child, Parental Qualities, Total.
Administration: Group.
Price Data: Available from publisher.
Time: (35–40) minutes.
Comments: Title on test is Elias Family Opinion Survey.
Author: Gabriel Elias.
Publisher: Psychometric Affiliates.
Cross References: See T4:958 (1 reference), T2:1181 (12 references), and P:80 (1 reference); for a review by John Elderkin Bell, see 6:95; for a review by Albert Ellis, see 5:53 (6 references).

[998]
Family Assessment Form: A Practice-Based Approach to Assessing Family Functioning.

Purpose: Constructed to "standardize the assessment of family functioning and service planning for families receiving home-based services."
Population: Families receiving home-based services.
Publication Date: 1997.
Acronym: FAF.
Scores: 6 scales: Parent-Child Interactions, Living Conditions, Caregiver Interactions, Supports for Parents, Financial Conditions, Developmental Stimulation.
Administration: Group.
Price Data: Price information available from publisher for test booklet/manual (79 pages).
Time: (60–90) minutes.
Comments: Ratings by child welfare practitioners.
Author: Children's Bureau of Southern California.
Publisher: Child Welfare League of America, Inc.
Cross References: For reviews by Cindy Carlson and Mary Lou Kelley, see 14:144; see also T5:1007 (1 reference).

[999]
Family Assessment Measure Version III.

Purpose: "Provides quantitative indices of family strengths and weaknesses."
Population: Families.
Publication Date: 1993–1995.
Acronym: FAM-III.
Scores, 26: General scale (Task Accomplishment, Role Performance, Communication, Affective Expression, Involvement, Control, Values and Norms, Social Desirability, Defensiveness, Total), Dyadic Relationships (Task Accomplishment, Role Performance, Communication, Affective Expression, Involvement, Control, Values and

Norms, Total), Self-Rating (Task Accomplishment, Role Performance, Communication, Affective Expression, Involvement, Control, Values and Norms, Total).

Administration: Individual.

Price Data, 2006: $209 per complete kit including manual (1995, 90 pages), 25 General Scale QuikScore™ forms, 50 Dyadic Relationship Scale QuikScore™ forms, 25 Self-Rating Scale QuikScore™ forms, and 15 MHS ColorPlot Profile of Family Perceptions; $179 per Brief FAM complete kit including manual, 25 Brief General Scale QuikScore™ forms, 25 Brief Dyadic Relationship Scale QuikScore™ forms, 25 Brief Self-Rating Scale QuikScore™ forms, and 15 MHS Progress ColorPlot Profiles; $40 per 25 General Scale QuikScore™ forms (English, Spanish, or French-Canadian); $40 per 25 Dyadic Relationship Scale QuikScore™ forms (English, Spanish, or French-Canadian); $40 per 25 Self-Rating Scale QuikScore™ forms (English, Spanish, or French-Canadian); $35 per 15 Progress Color Plot Profiles; $35 per 15 MHS Color Plot Profile of Family Perceptions; $67 per manual; software also available; $7 per long profile report; $5 per brief profile report; $50 per preview version including 3 profile reports and manual.

Foreign Language Editions: Spanish and French-Canadian QuikScore™ forms available.

Time: (30–40) minutes.

Authors: Harvey A. Skinner, Paul D. Steinhauer, and Jack Santa-Barbara.

Publisher: Multi-Health Systems Inc.

Cross References: For reviews by Kenneth J. Manges and Stephen A. Spilland, see 14:145; see also T5:1008 (3 references).

[1000]
Family Day Care Rating Scale.

Purpose: Assesses the quality of family day care.

Population: Consumers of day care services, day care providers, agency supervisors, and researchers.

Publication Date: 1989.

Acronym: FDCRS.

Scores, 6: Space and Furnishings for Care and Learning, Basic Care, Language and Reasoning, Learning Activities, Social Development, Adult Needs.

Administration: Group.

Price Data, 2006: $15.95 per manual (48 pages); $8.95 per 30 scoring sheets.

Time: (2) hours.

Authors: Thelma Harms and Richard M. Clifford.

Publisher: Teachers College Press.

Cross References: For a review by Annette M. Iverson, see 11:141.

[1001]
Family Environment Scale [Third Edition Manual].

Purpose: Designed to assess family members' perceptions of their social environment.

Population: Ages 11–adult.

Publication Dates: 1974–1994.

Acronym: FES.

Scores, 11: Cohesion, Expressiveness, Conflict, Independence, Achievement, Intellectual-Cultural, Active-Recreational, Moral-Religious, Organization, Control, Incongruence.

Administration: Group.

Forms, 4: Real (Form R), Ideal (Form I), Expectations (Form E), Children's Version.

Price Data, 2006: $40 per sampler set including manual (1994, 96 pages); $120 per 150-copy duplication set; quantity discounts available for bulk permissions; $25 per 25 Real Form booklets; $25 per 25 Ideal Form booklets; $25 per 25 Expected Form booklets; $12.50 per 25 profiles; $12.50 per 25 answer sheets; $10 per scoring key; $20 per bibliography.

Time: (15–20) minutes.

Comments: One component of the Social Climate Scales (T5:2445).

Authors: Rudolf H. Moos and Bernice S. Moos.

Publisher: Mind Garden, Inc.

Cross References: For reviews by Jay A. Mancini and Michael J. Sporakowski, see 14:146; see also T5:1010 (138 references); for reviews by Julie A. Allison and Brenda H. Loyd of an earlier edition, see 12:151 (76 references); see also T4:961 (136 references); for reviews by Nancy A. Busch-Rossnagel and Nadine M. Lambert of an earlier edition, see 9:408 (18 references); see also T3:872 (14 references); for a review by Philip H. Dreyer, see 8:557 (4 references). For a review of the Social Climate Series, see 8:681.

[1002]
Family Relations Test.

Purpose: "Designed to give concrete representation of the subject's childhood family."

Population: Ages 7–12, ages 13–17, adults, married couples.

Publication Dates: 1965–1978.

Acronym: FRT.

Scores: Nobody, Self, Father, Mother, Siblings, and Others scores for 2 areas: Outgoing Feelings, Incoming Feelings.

Administration: Individual.

Time: (20–25) minutes.

Publisher: NFER-Nelson Publishing Co., Ltd. [England].

a) CHILDREN'S VERSION.

Price Data, 1999: £180 per complete set; £98 per set of figures; £36 per manual (1978, 56 pages).

Authors: Eva Bene and James Anthony.

1) *Younger Children.*

Population: Ages 7–12.

Price Data: £18 per 25 record/score sheets.

2) *Older Children.*

Population: Ages 13–17.

Price Data: £31 per 25 record/score sheets.

b) ADULT VERSION.
Population: Adults.
Price Data: £216 per complete set; £51.50 per 25 record/score sheets.
Author: Eva Bene.
c) MARRIED COUPLES VERSION.
Population: Married couples.
Price Data: Same as for *b* above.
Authors: Eva Bene and James Anthony (test).
Cross References: See T5:1011 (4 references), T4:962 (1 reference), 9:409 (3 references), T3:874 (33 references), 8:558 (18 references), and T2:1182 (4 references); for an excerpted review by B. Semeonoff of *a* and *b*, see 7:79 (7 references); see also P:81 (2 references); for reviews by John E. Bell, Dale B. Harris, and Arthur R. Jensen of *a*, see 5:132 (1 reference).

[1003]
Family Relations Test: Children's Version.

Purpose: "To assess the relative importance that different family members have for children" and to explore the child's emotional relations with his family.
Population: Ages 3–15.
Publication Date: 1976.
Administration: Individual.
Levels, 2: Form for Young Children, Form for Older Children.
Price Data: 1999: £180 for complete set including manual (1985, 59 pages), test figures and item cards, scoring and record sheets for older children, and record/score sheets for young children.
Time: 25(40) minutes.
Authors: Eva Bene (test and revised manual) and James Anthony (test).
Publisher: NFER-Nelson Publishing Co., Ltd. [England].
    a) FORM FOR YOUNG CHILDREN.
    Population: Ages 3–7.
    Scores, 8: Outgoing Feelings (Positive Total, Negative Total), Incoming Feelings (Positive Total, Negative Total), Dependency Feelings, Sum of Positive, Sum of Negative, Total Involvement.
    b) FORM FOR OLDER CHILDREN.
    Population: Ages 7–15.
    Scores, 12: Sum of Outgoing Positive, Sum of Outgoing Negative, Sum of Incoming Positive, Sum of Incoming Negative, Total Involvement, Sum of Positive Mild, Sum of Positive Strong, Sum of Negative Mild, Sum of Negative Strong, Maternal Overprotection, Paternal Overindulgence, Maternal Overindulgence.
Cross References: See T5:1012 (2 references); for reviews by Cindy I. Carlson and Steven I. Pfeiffer, see 11:142; for information on the complete test, see 9:409 (3 references), T3:874 (33 references), 8:558 (18 references), and T2:1182 (4 references); for an excerpted

review by B. Semeonoff of the Children's Version and the Adult Version, see 7:79 (7 references); see also P:81 (2 references); for reviews by John E. Bell, Dale B. Harris, and Arthur R. Jensen of the Children's Version, see 5:132 (1 reference).

[1004]
Family Relationship Inventory.

Purpose: "Method of examining family relationships, designed to clarify individual feelings and interpersonal behavior"; within the family, the FRI identifies who feels closest to whom and who feels most distant and provides a Self-Esteem score for each family member.
Population: Young children age 5 and above, adolescents, and adults.
Publication Dates: 1972–1984.
Acronym: FRI.
Scores, 2: Positive, Negative, for each family member.
Administration: Individual or family groups.
Price Data, 2006: $169 per complete kit including item cards, 25 scoring forms, 50 tabulating forms, 50 individual relationship wheel forms, 25 familygram forms, and test manual (1982, 36 pages); $55 per set of item cards; $33.50 per 100 scoring forms; $33.50 per 100 tabulating forms; $33.50 per 100 individual relationship wheels; $33.50 per 100 familygrams.
Time: Administration time not reported.
Comments: Based upon Family Relationship Scale.
Authors: Ruth B. Michaelson, Harry L. Bascom, Louise Nash, W. Lee Morrison, and Robert M. Taylor.
Publisher: Psychological Publications, Inc.
Cross References: See T5:1013 (2 references) and T4:964 (2 references); for a review by Mary Henning-Stout, see 10:112.

[1005]
Family Satisfaction Scale [Revised].

Purpose: Designed to measure satisfaction on the dimensions of family cohesion and family adaptability.
Population: Families.
Publication Dates: 1982-2005.
Scores: Total Family Satisfaction.
Administration: Individual or group.
Price Data, 2006: $30 per manual (7 pages) and scale (unlimited rights for duplication).
Time: (10-15) minutes.
Authors: David H. Olson and Marc Wilson.
Publisher: Life Innovations, Inc.
Cross References: See T5:1014 (7 references).

[1006]
Family System Test.

Purpose: Designed "for representing emotional bonds (cohesion) and hierarchical structures in the family or similar social systems."
Population: Individuals and families.
Publication Dates: 1993–1998.

Acronym: FAST.
Scores: Score information available from publisher.
Administration: Individuals or group.
Price Data, 2006: $298 per complete test including 20 recording blanks, board and schematic figures, and manual (1998, 80 pages); $19.50 per 20 recording blanks; $39.50 per manual.
Time: (5–10) minutes for individuals; (10–30) minutes for groups.
Comments: A "figural technique"; "language independent"; authorized English translation of the 1993 German edition "Familiensystemtest" (FAST).
Authors: Thomas Gehring; translated from the German edition by Anita Arnone-Reitezle.
Publisher: Hogrefe & Huber Publishers.
Cross References: For reviews by Lisa Bischoff and Richard B. Stuart, see 15:98.

[1007]
A Family Violence Scale.

Purpose: To indicate the occurrence of family violence in one's childhood.
Population: Adolescents and adults.
Publication Dates: 1973–1988.
Scores: Total Family Violence Score.
Administration: Group.
Manual: No manual.
Price Data, 2005: $2 per scale.
Time: Administration time not reported.
Comments: Supplementary article available.
Author: Panos D. Bardis.
Publisher: Donna Bardis.
Cross References: See 8:340 (1 reference).

[1008]
The Farnum String Scale: A Performance Scale for All String Instruments.

Purpose: Measurement of ability to play a stringed instrument.
Population: Grades 7–12.
Publication Date: 1969.
Scores, 4: Total score only for each test (Violin, Viola, Cello, String Bass).
Administration: Individual.
Price Data: Available from publisher.
Time: Administration time not reported.
Author: Stephen E. Farnum.
Publisher: Hal Leonard Publishing Corporation [No reply from publisher; status unknown].
Cross References: For additional information and a review by Walter L. Wehner, see 8:94.

[1009]
Fast Health Knowledge Test, 1986 Revision.

Purpose: "To measure discrimination and judgment in matters of health."

Population: High school and college.
Publication Date: 1986.
Scores, 11: Personal Health, Exercise-Relaxation-Sleep, Nutrition, Consumer Health, Contemporary Health Problems, Substance of Abuse, Safety and First Aid, Disease Control, Mental Health, Family Life and Sex Education, Total.
Administration: Group.
Price Data: Available from publisher.
Time: 40(50) minutes.
Author: Charles G. Fast.
Publisher: Charles G. Fast.
Cross References: For a review by Linda K. Bunker, see 10:113.

[1010]
Fast Track.

Purpose: Designed as a "simple screening tool to identify those who have literacy needs below Level 1 and/or numeracy needs below Entry Level of the Basic Skills Standards."
Population: Adults.
Publication Date: 2000.
Scores: Total score only.
Administration: Individual.
Forms, 3: Fast Track 20 Questions, Fast Track Assessment-Written, Fast Track Assessment-Oral.
Price Data, 2000: £15 per complete kit including manual (24 pages), 50 Fast Track 20 Question, 50 Fast Track Assessment-Written, and 50 Fast Track Assessment-Oral; £9 per manual; £3 per 50 Fast Track 20 Questions; £3 per 50 Fast Track Assessment-Written; £3 per 50 Fast Track Assessment-Oral.
Time: (5-15) minutes.
Comments: This test can be completed as part of a 1:1 interview.
Authors: The Basic Skills Agency.
Publisher: The Basic Skills Agency [England].

[1011]
Fear of Appearing Incompetent Scale.

Purpose: Designed "to identify if individuals are concerned about maintaining or saving face around others to the extent of sacrificing tangible rewards in order to do so."
Population: Adults and college-age.
Publication Date: No date.
Scores: Total score only.
Administration: Group.
Price Data, 2001: $3 per specimen set.
Time: Administration time not reported.
Authors: L. R. Good and K. C. Good.
Publisher: Psychometric Affiliates.
Cross References: For a review by William C. Tierre, see 15:99.

[1012]

Fear of Powerlessness Scale.

Purpose: Developed as "a self-report measure of the motive to avoid powerlessness."
Population: College-age and adults.
Publication Date: No date.
Scores: Total score only.
Administration: Group.
Price Data, 2001: $3 per specimen set.
Time: Administration time not reported.
Authors: L. R. Good, K. C. Good, and S. B. Golden, Jr.
Publisher: Psychometric Affiliates.
Cross References: For a review by Nathaniel J. Pallone and James J. Hennessy, see 15:100.

[1013]

Fear of Success Scale.

Purpose: Designed as a self-report measure of fear of success.
Population: College students.
Publication Date: No date.
Scores: Total score only.
Administration: Group.
Price Data, 2001: $3 per specimen set.
Time: Administration time not reported.
Authors: L. R. Good and K. C. Good.
Publisher: Psychometric Affiliates.
Cross References: For a review by Laura L. B. Barnes, see 15:101.

[1014]

Fear Survey Schedule.

Purpose: "Designed to identify and quantify patients' reactions to a variety of sources of maladaptive emotional reactions."
Population: College and adults.
Publication Dates: 1964–1977.
Acronym: FSS.
Scores: Total score only.
Administration: Group.
Price Data: Available from publisher.
Time: (15) minutes.
Comments: Self-rating.
Authors: Joseph Wolpe and Peter J. Lang.
Publisher: EdITS/Educational and Industrial Testing Service.
Cross References: See T5:1021 (48 references), T4:974 (30 references), 9:411 (23 references), and T3:883 (53 references); for a review by Charles D. Spielberger, see 8:559 (32 references); see also T2:1185 (14 references); for a review by R. G. Demaree, see 7:80 (17 references).

[1015]

Feedback Edition of the Strength Deployment Inventory.

Purpose: Designed to elicit feedback to describe how a person uses his/her personal strengths in relationships.

Population: Adults.
Publication Dates: 1973–1996.
Acronym: SDI/PVI.
Scores, 20: 7 Motivational Values (Altruistic-Nurturing, Assertive-Directing, Analytic-Autonomizing, Flexible-Cohering, Assertive-Nurturing, Judicious-Competing, Cautious-Supporting), plus 13 scores reflecting Progression through Conflict.
Administration: Individual or group.
Price Data, 2001: $4.50 per test booklet; $30 per manual (1996, 146 pages).
Time: (20–40) minutes.
Comments: Uses self-ratings and ratings of a significant other person; manual is entitled Relationship Awareness Theory Manual of Administration and Interpretation (9th Ed.).
Author: Elias H. Porter.
Publisher: Personal Strengths Publishing.

[1016]

Feedback Portrait of Overdone Strengths.

Purpose: Designed to elicit feedback to describe how a person uses his/her personal strengths.
Population: Adults.
Publication Date: 1997.
Scores, 3: Profile, Top Overdone Strengths, Least Overdone Strengths.
Administration: Individual or group.
Price Data, 2001: $5.50 per test booklet; $100 per manual.
Time: (20–40) minutes.
Author: Personal Strengths Publishing.
Publisher: Personal Strengths Publishing.

[1017]

Feedback Portrait of Personal Strengths.

Purpose: Designed to elicit feedback to describe how a person uses his/her personal strengths in relationships.
Population: Adults.
Publication Date: 1997.
Scores, 3: Profile, Top Strengths, Least Deployed Strengths.
Administration: Individual or group.
Price Data, 2001: $5.50 per test booklet; $100 per manual.
Time: (20–40) minutes.
Author: Personal Strengths Publishing.
Publisher: Personal Strengths Publishing.

[1018]

Feelings, Attitudes, and Behaviors Scale for Children.

Purpose: "Designed to assess a range of emotional and behavioral problems."
Population: Ages 6–13.

Publication Date: 1996.
Acronym: FAB-C.
Scores, 7: Conduct Problems, Self Image, Worry, Negative Peer Relationships, Antisocial, Lie, Problem Index.
Administration: Group.
Price Data, 2006: $85 per complete kit including manual (59 pages), and 25 QuikScore™ forms; $42 per 25 QuikScore™ forms; $59 per manual; $61 per online profile report kit including manual and 3 profile reports.
Time: (10) minutes.
Comments: Self-report.
Author: Joseph H. Beitchman.
Publisher: Multi-Health Systems, Inc.
Cross References: For reviews by Patti L. Harrison and Mary Lou Kelley, see 14:147.

[1019]
50 Grammar Quizzes for Practice and Review.

Purpose: Designed to "guide students to learn correct grammar, improve their writing skills, and write clearly and effectively."
Population: Students.
Publication Date: 1985.
Scores: No scores.
Administration: Group.
Parts, 6: Part I: Writing Clear, Complete Sentences (15 quizzes); Part II: Correcting Errors in Agreement: Pronouns and Antecedents, Subjects and Verbs (3 study guides and 9 quizzes); Part III: Correcting Pronoun and Verb Shifts (2 sets of instructions and 5 quizzes); Part IV: Correcting Errors in the Use of Modifiers (4 quizzes); Part V: Correcting Errors in the Use of Parallel Structure (study guide and 3 quizzes); Part VI: Writing Precise, Effective Sentences (3 study guides and 14 quizzes).
Price Data: Price information available form publisher for complete set of display copy.
Time: Administration time not reported.
Comments: Reproduction rights limited to purchaser of masters and a single classroom teacher.
Author: Joan R. Markos.
Publisher: Walch Publishing.

[1020]
Figure Classification Test.

Purpose: Designed to "measure abstract reasoning ability."
Population: Applicants for industrial work with 7 to 9 years of schooling.
Publication Date: 1976.
Scores: Total score only.
Administration: Group.
Price Data: Price information available from publisher for test materials including manual (21 pages).
Foreign Language Edition: Manual written in both English and Afrikaans.

Time: 60(70) minutes.
Comments: Separate answer sheets must be used.
Author: T. R. Taylor.
Publisher: Human Sciences Research Council [South Africa].
Cross References: See T4:978 (1 reference).

[1021]
The Filipino Work Values Scale.

Purpose: "Constructed to measure work values."
Population: Filipino employees and students.
Publication Dates: 1987–1988.
Acronym: FWVS.
Scores, 10: Environmental, Familial, Intellectual-Achievement Oriented, Interpersonal, Managerial, Material, Occupational, Organizational, Religious, Variety.
Administration: Group.
Forms, 2: Employee, Student.
Price Data, 2006: $205 per employee edition complete kit including manual (1987, 39 pages), 25 scale booklets, 25 answer sheets, and manual scoring keys; $205 per student edition complete kit including manual, 25 scale booklets, 25 answer sheets, and manual scoring keys.
Foreign Language Editions: English, Thai; Philippine languages editions: Cebuano, Filipino, Pangasinense.
Time: (15–20) minutes.
Author: Vicentita M. Cervera.
Publisher: Vicentita M. Cervera (the author) [Philippines].
Cross References: For reviews by Gary J. Dean and William I. Sauser, Jr., see 14:148.

[1022]
Fine Dexterity Test.

Purpose: To provide "a measure of manual dexterity using a fine test task."
Population: Applicants for jobs involving fine motor dexterity.
Publication Date: 1983.
Acronym: FDT.
Scores, 2: Finger Dexterity, Fine Tool Dexterity.
Administration: Group.
Price Data: Available from publisher.
Time: 6(8) minutes.
Author: Educational & Industrial Test Services Ltd.
Publisher: Educational & Industrial Test Services Ltd. [England].

[1023]
Fire Promotion Tests-—Complete Service [Revised].

Purpose: Custom-made test to fit duties and responsibilities for promotion of firefighters.
Population: Firefighters.

Publication Dates: 1979–2002.
Scores: 8 subtests: Knowledge of Fire Protection/ Prevention Practices, Fire Investigation Knowledge, Fire Attack-Related Technical Knowledge, Extinguishment-Related Technical Knowledge, Emergency Medical Care Knowledge, Supervisory and Managerial Knowledge, Administrative Knowledge, Comprehension Ability, Total.
Administration: Group.
Price Data: Available from publisher.
Time: (210) minutes.
Comments: Candidate study guide available.
Author: McCann Associates, Inc.
Publisher: Vantage McCann Associates.

[1024]
Firefighter Learning Simulation.

Purpose: Designed to "simulate the learning process required of entry-level firefighters in Fire Academies."
Population: Applicants for firefighter trainee positions.
Publication Dates: 1983-1998.
Acronym: FLS.
Scores: Total score only.
Administration: Group or individual.
Price Data: Price information available from publisher for test material including Administration Guide and Technical Manual (11 pages), and Training Manual (26 pages).
Time: 90(95) minutes.
Comments: Simulated training manual is provided to examinees in advance of the test.
Authors: Psychological Services, Inc.
Publisher: Psychological Services, Inc.
Cross References: For reviews by JoEllen V. Carlson and James W. Pinkney, see 15:102.

[1025]
Firefighter Selection Test [Revised].

Purpose: "To rank-order applicants according to their probability of success in training and success on the job" as a firefighter.
Population: Applicants for firefighter trainee positions.
Publication Dates: 1983–1998.
Acronym: FST.
Scores: Total score only.
Administration: Group or individual.
Price Data: Price data available from publisher for test material including Technical Manual (1998, 22 pages), Administrator's Guide (1998, 6 pages), and Study Guide (1998, 16 pages).
Time: 150 (165) minutes.
Comments: Measures mechanical comprehension, reading comprehension, and report interpretation.
Authors: Psychological Services, Inc.

Publisher: Psychological Services, Inc.
Cross References: For reviews by Chantale Jeanrie and Deniz S. Ones, see 15:103; for reviews by David O. Anderson and Cynthia Ann Druva-Roush of an earlier edition, see 11:143.

[1026]
Firestone Assessment of Self-Destructive Thoughts.

Purpose: Constructed "for the clinical assessment of a patient's suicidal potential."
Population: Ages 16–80.
Publication Date: 1996.
Acronym: FAST.
Scores: No scores.
Administration: Group.
Price Data, 2002: $142 per complete kit including manual (176 pages) and 25 ReadyScore® response booklets; $61 per 25 response booklets, $86 per manual.
Time: (20) minutes.
Comments: Includes 11 levels of progressively self-destructive thoughts on a continuum ranging from Social Isolation, Eating Disorders, Substance Abuse, Self-Mutilation, and Suicide.
Authors: Robert W. Firestone and Lisa A. Firestone.
Publisher: PsychCorp, A brand of Harcourt Assessment, Inc.
Cross References: For reviews by William E. Martin and Robert C. Reinehr, see 14:149.

[1027]
FIRO-B™ [Fundamental Interpersonal Relations Orientation–Behavior™].

Purpose: Designed "to measure behavior that derives from interpersonal needs."
Population: Age 13 and over.
Publication Dates: 1957–2000.
Acronym: FIRO-B™.
Scores, 7: 2 Overall Behavior scores (Expressed, Wanted) for each of 3 dimensions (Inclusion, Control, Affection) plus Overall Need score.
Administration: Individual or group.
Price Data, 2001: $60 per 10 FIRO-B™ self-scorable forms; $38 per 10 FIRO-B™ technical guides (2000, 77 pages); $9.35 per Introduction to the FIRO-B™; $160 per 10 prepaid Leadership Reports; $100 per 10 FIRO-B™ Interpretive Reports for Organizations.
Time: (10–15) minutes.
Comments: May be administered via paper-pencil or online at skillsone.com; earlier versions entitled FIRO Awareness Scales.
Authors: Will Schutz (original test), Allen L. Hammer (technical guide), and Eugene R. Schnell (technical guide).
Publisher: CPP, Inc.
Cross References: For reviews by Michelle Athanasiou and Donald Oswald, see 15:104; see T5:1036

(13 references) and T4:982 (18 references); for a review by Peter D. Lifton of an earlier edition, see 9:416 (12 references); see also T3:890 (45 references), 8:555 (147 references), and T2:1176 (58 references); for a review by Bruce Bloxom, see 7:78 (70 references); see also P:79 (30 references) and 6:94 (15 references).

[1028]
First Year Algebra Test: National Achievement Tests.

Purpose: Designed to measure the student's knowledge of first year algebra.
Population: One year high school.
Publication Dates: 1958–1962.
Scores: Total score only.
Administration: Group.
Forms, 2: A, B.
Price Data: Available from publisher.
Time: (40–45) minutes.
Authors: Ray Webb and Julius H. Hlavaty.
Publisher: Psychometric Affiliates.
Cross References: For a review by Donald L. Meyer, see 6:600.

[1029]
FirstSTEP: Screening Test for Evaluating Preschoolers.

Purpose: "Designed to identify preschool children who are at risk for developmental delays in the five areas mandated by IDEA (PL 99-457)."
Population: Preschool children.
Publication Dates: 1990–1993.
Scores, 7: Cognitive, Language, Motor, Composite, Social-Emotional, Adaptive Behavior, Parent/Teacher.
Administration: Individual.
Levels, 3: Ages 1–2, Ages 3–4, Ages 5–7.
Price Data, 2002: $195 per complete kit including 5 record forms each for levels 1, 2, and 3, 25 Social-Emotional/Adaptive Behavior booklets, 25 Parent booklets, manipulatives in a plastic case, and manual (1993, 166 pages); $34 per 25 record forms (specify level); $34 per 25 Social-Emotional Scale/Adaptive Behavior checklists; $17 per 25 Parent/Teacher Scales.
Time: (15–20) minutes.
Author: Lucy J. Miller.
Publisher: PsychCorp, A brand of Harcourt Assessment, Inc.
Cross References: For a review by Terry Overton, see 13:126.

[1030]
The Fisher-Logemann Test of Articulation Competence.

Purpose: "Designed to ... facilitate ... analysis and categorization of articulation errors."
Population: Preschool to adult.

Publication Date: 1971.
Acronym: F-LTOAC.
Scores: No scores.
Administration: Individual.
Price Data, 2006: $195 per complete kit; $30 per manual; $100 per test portfolio; $35 per Picture Test or Sentence Articulation Test record forms.
Time: (40-45) minutes.
Authors: Hilda B. Fisher and Jerilyn A. Logemann.
Publisher: PRO-ED.
  a) PICTURE TEST.
  Population: Preschool to adult.
  Comments: 3 areas are covered: Singleton Consonants, Consonant Blends, Vowel Phonemes and Diphthongs; a shortened screening form consisting of 11 of the Singleton Consonants may be administered.
  b) SENTENCE ARTICULATION TEST.
  Population: Grade 3 to adult.
  Comments: 5 areas are covered: Consonant Pairs, Singleton Consonants, Nasals, Vowel Phonemes, Diphthongs.
Cross References: See T5:1040 (11 references), T4:986 (6 references), and T3:896 (9 references); for reviews by Marie C. Fontana and Lawrence J. Turton, see 8:961.

[1031]
Five Factor Wellness Inventory.

Purpose: Designed to "assess characters of wellness as a basis for helping individuals make choices for healthier living."
Population: Elementary, high school, and adults.
Publication Date: 2005.
Acronym: 5F-WEL.
Scores, 28: Wellness (Creative Self [Thinking, Emotions, Control, Positive Humor, Work], Coping Self [Realistic Beliefs, Stress Management, Self-Worth, Leisure], Social Self [Friendship, Love], Essential Self [Spirituality, Self-Care, Gender Identity, Cultural Identity], Physical Self [Exercise, Nutrition]), Local Context, Institutional Context, Global Context, Chronometrical Context, Life Satisfaction Index.
Administration: Group or individual.
Levels, 3: Elementary, Teen, Adults.
Price Data, 2005: $40 per manual (71 pages); $10 per adult web-based administration; $160 per 20 reports of one version; bulk pricing is available.
Foreign Language Editions: Hebrew, Korean, Turkish.
Time: (10-20) minutes.
Comments: Web-based administration and reporting including a development guide.
Authors: Jane E. Myers and Thomas J. Sweeney.
Publisher: Mind Garden, Inc.

[1032]

The Five P's (Parent/Professional Preschool Performance Profile) [2002 Update].

Purpose: Constructed to collect teacher and parent ratings of child's observed performance across all domains of development to create a comprehensive profile of child's current level of functioning, to link assessment to goal setting and remediation, to monitor change over time, and to promote home/school collaboration.

Population: Children with disabilities between the ages of 6 and 59 months.

Publication Dates: 1982–2004.

Scores: Standard Index and Percentile scores may be prepared separately in five domains of development: Self Help (Toileting and Hygiene, Mealtime Behaviors, Dressing), Language Development (Communicative Competence, Receptive Language, Expressive Language), Social Development (Emerging Self, Relationships to Adults, Relationships to Children, Classroom Adjustment), Motor Development (Gross Motor/Balance/Coordination Skills, Perceptual/Fine Motor Skills), Cognitive Development; Interfering Behaviors for each of the five domains are scored separately.

Administration: Individual.

Price Data, 2004: $150 per materials for class of 10 children including 10 sets of scales, 1 user manual (2002, 40 pages), 10 Information and Directions, 10 graphic profiles, 1 copy of The Five P's Preschool Annual Goals and Short-Term Instructional Objectives; $45 per training video (25 minutes); $10 per user manual; $25 per copy of The Five P's Preschool Annual Goals and Short-Term Instructional Objectives (bound copy); $45 per technical manual, which includes Index and Percentile Score Tables (2004, 132 pages); $85 per sample packet including assessment packet, training video, research papers, and The Five P's Preschool Annual Goals and Short-Term Instructional Objectives.

Foreign Language Edition: Spanish edition available.

Time: (60) minutes.

Comments: Teacher and Parent Observer training protocol and training video available.

Authors: Judith Simon Bloch, John S. Hicks, and Janice L. Friedman.

Publisher: Variety Child Learning Center.

Cross References: For reviews by Kimberly A. Blair and Lisa F. Smith, see 16:91; for reviews by Annie W. Ward and Steven Zucker of an earlier edition, see 13:127; for a review by Barbara Perry-Sheldon, see 10:116.

[1033]

Flanagan Aptitude Classification Tests.

Purpose: Measurement of aptitudes for sixteen on-the-job skills.

Population: Individuals in a variety of lower-level industrial or mechanical positions.

Publication Dates: 1951–1994.

Acronym: FACT.

Scores: Total score only for each test.

Administration: Individual or group.

Price Data, 2002: $85 per start-up kit including 25 test booklets (specify test) and examiner's manual; $67 per 25 test booklets (quantity discounts available; specify test); $28 per examiner's manual.

Author: John C. Flanagan.

Publisher: Pearson Performance Solutions [No reply from publisher; status unknown].

a) FACT 1A, INSPECTION.
Publication Dates: 1953–1956.
Time: 6 minutes.

b) FACT 2A AND 2B, CODING.
Publication Dates: 1953–1956.
Forms, 2: A, B.
Time: 10 minutes.

c) FACT 3A AND 3B, MEMORY.
Publication Dates: 1953–1956.
Forms, 2: A, B.
Time: 4 minutes.

d) FACT 4A, PRECISION.
Publication Dates: 1953–1956.
Time: 8 minutes.

e) FACT 5A, ASSEMBLY.
Publication Dates: 1953–1956.
Time: 12 minutes.

f) FACT 6A, SCALES.
Publication Dates: 1953–1956.
Time: 16 minutes.

g) FACT 7A, COORDINATION.
Publication Dates: 1953–1956.
Time: 2 minutes, 40 seconds.

h) FACT 8A, JUDGEMENT AND COMPREHENSION.
Publication Dates: 1953–1956.
Time: No limit (approximately 35 minutes).

i) FACT 9A, ARITHMETIC.
Publication Dates: 1953–1956.
Time: 10 minutes.

j) FACT 10A, PATTERNS.
Publication Dates: 1953–1956.
Time: 20 minutes.

k) FACT 11A, COMPONENTS.
Publication Dates: 1953–1956.
Time: 20 minutes.

l) FACT 12A, TABLES.
Publication Dates: 1953–1956.
Time: 10 minutes.

m) FACT 13A AND 13B, MECHANICS.
Publication Dates: 1953–1956.
Forms, 2: A, B.
Time: 20 minutes.

n) FACT 14A, EXPRESSION.
Publication Dates: 1953–1956.
Time: No limit (approximately 30 minutes).
o) FACT 15A, REASONING.
Publication Dates: 1957–1960.
Time: 24 minutes.
p) FACT 16A, INGENUITY.
Publication Dates: 1957–1960.
Time: 24 minutes.
Cross References: See T3:899 (2 references), and T2:1072 (1 reference); for an excerpted review by Harold D. Murphy (with John P. McQuary), see 7:675 (10 references); for reviews by Norman Frederiksen and William B. Michael, see 6:770 (7 references); for reviews by Harold P. Bechtoldt, Ralph F. Berdie, and John B. Carroll, see 5:608.

[1034]
Flanagan Industrial Tests.

Purpose: Measurement of aptitudes for eighteen on-the-job skills.
Population: Supervisory, technical, office, skilled labor, and other industrial positions.
Publication Dates: 1960–1975.
Acronym: FIT.
Scores: Total score only for each test.
Administration: Individual or group.
Price Data, 2002: $99 per start-up kit including 25 test booklets, scoring stencil, and examinee's manual (1975, 36 pages); $63 per 25 test booklets (quantity discounts available); $20 per scoring stencil; $28 per examiner's manual.
Author: John C. Flanagan.
Publisher: Pearson Performance Solutions [No reply from publisher; status unknown].
a) ARITHMETIC.
Time: 5(7) minutes.
b) ASSEMBLY.
Time: 10(13) minutes.
c) COMPONENTS.
Time: 10(12) minutes.
d) COORDINATION.
Price Data: $82 per start-up kit.
Time: 5(7) minutes.
e) ELECTRONICS.
Time: 15(17) minutes.
f) EXPRESSION.
Time: 5(8) minutes.
g) INGENUITY.
Time: 15(18) minutes.
h) INSPECTION.
Price Data: $117 per start-up kit; $39 per scoring stencil.
Time: 5(9) minutes.
i) JUDGMENT AND COMPREHENSION.
Time: 15(17) minutes.

j) MATHEMATICS AND REASONING.
Time: 15(18) minutes.
k) MECHANICS.
Time: 15(18) minutes.
l) MEMORY.
Time: 10(19) minutes.
m) PATTERNS.
Time: 5(7) minutes.
n) PLANNING.
Time: 15(18) minutes.
o) PRECISION.
Price Data: $82 per start-up kit.
Time: 5(8) minutes.
p) SCALES.
Time: 5(7) minutes.
q) TABLES.
Time: 5(8) minutes.
r) VOCABULARY.
Time: 15(17) minutes.
Cross References: See T5:1043 (1 reference) and T4:989 (1 reference); for reviews by David O. Herman and Arthur C. MacKinney, see 8:981 (3 references); for reviews by C. J. Adcock and Robert C. Droege and an excerpted review by John L. Horn, see 7:977 (1 reference).

[1035]
Fleishman Job Analysis Survey [Revised].

Purpose: "A means for analyzing the knowledge, skills and abilities needed to perform jobs."
Population: Adults.
Publication Dates: 1992–1996.
Acronym: F-JAS.
Scores: 52 Abilities Scales: Cognitive (Oral Comprehension, Written Comprehension, Oral Expression, Written Expression, Fluency of Ideas, Originality, Memorization, Problem Sensitivity, Mathematical Reasoning, Number Facility, Deductive Reasoning, Inductive Reasoning, Information Ordering, Category Flexibility, Speed of Closure, Flexibility of Closure, Spatial Orientation, Visualization, Perceptual Speed, Selective Attention, Time Sharing), Psychomotor (Control Precision, Multilimb Coordination, Response Orientation, Rate Control, Reaction Time, Arm-Hand Steadiness, Manual Dexterity, Finger Dexterity, Wrist-Finger Speed, Speed of Limb Movement), Physical (Static Strength, Explosive Strength, Dynamic Strength, Trunk Strength, Extent Flexibility, Dynamic Flexibility, Gross Body Coordination, Gross Body Equilibrium, Stamina), Sensory/Perceptual (Near Vision, Far Vision, Visual Color Discrimination, Night Vision, Peripheral Vision, Depth Perception, Glare Sensitivity, Hearing Sensitivity, Auditory Attention, Sound Localization, Speech Recognition, Speech Clarity).
Administration: Group.

Levels, 3: Job-Level Analysis, Job Dimension-Level Analysis, Task-Level Analysis.
Price Data: Available from publisher.
Time: (40) minutes.
Comments: Previously referred to as the Task Assessment Scales, Ability Requirement Scale, Manual for the Ability Requirement Scales (MARS); Handbook of Human Abilities brings together ability definitions, tasks, and jobs requiring each ability, and test descriptions and tests available to measure each ability.
Authors: Edwin A. Fleishman, Maureen E. Reilly, and David P. Costanza.
Publisher: Management Research Institute, Inc.
  a) SOCIAL/INTERPERSONAL ABILITIES.
  Publication Date: 1996.
  Acronym: F-JAS-2.
  Scores: 21 Social/Interpersonal Skill Scales: Agreeableness, Behavior Flexibility, Coordination, Dependability, Assertiveness, Negotiation, Persuasion, Sociability, Social Conformity, Social Sensitivity, Self Control, Social Confidence, Coaching, Oral Fact Finding, Achievement Striving, Openness to Experience, Self Sufficiency, Perseverance, Resistance to Premature Judgment, Oral Defense, Resilience.
  Time: (20) minutes.
  b) KNOWLEDGES/SKILLS.
  Publication Date: 1992.
  Acronym: F-JAS-3.
  Scores: 33 Knowledge Scales: Administration and Management, Clerical, Economics and Accounting, Sales and Marketing, Customer and Personal Service, Personnel and Human Resources, Production and Processing, Food Production, Computers and Electronics, Engineering and Technology, Design, Building and Construction, Mechanical, Mathematics, Physics, Chemistry, Biology, Psychology, Sociology and Anthropology, Geography, Medicine and Dentistry, Therapy and Counseling, Education and Training, English Language, Foreign Language, Fine Arts, History and Archeology, Philosophy and Theology, Public Safety and Security, Law/Government and Jurisprudence, Telecommunications, Communications and Media, Transportation.
  Time: (25) minutes.

[1036]
Flex Style Negotiating.
Purpose: Designed to profile participants' preferred negotiation styles and to define legitimate versus illegitimate behaviors.
Population: Employees and managers.
Publication Date: 1997.
Scores, 3: Social Dimension, Emotional Dimension, Cognitive Dimension.
Administration: Group.

Price Data: Available from publisher.
Time: (25) minutes.
Author: Alexander Watson Hiam.
Publisher: HRD Press, Inc.

[1037]
Fluharty Preschool Speech and Language Screening Test—Second Edition.
Purpose: Designed to identify preschool children whose speech and language skills warrant a comprehensive communication evaluation.
Population: Ages 3-0 to 6-11.
Publication Dates: 1978–2001.
Acronym: FLUHARTY-2.
Scores, 8: Articulation, Repeating Sentences, Following Directives and Answering Questions, Describing Actions, Sequencing Events, Receptive Language, Expressive Language, General Language.
Administration: Individual.
Price Data, 2006: $168 per complete kit including examiner's manual (2001, 65 pages), picture book, 25 profile/examiner record forms, and a set of 12 colored blocks; $35 per 25 profile/examiner record forms; $30 per set of blocks; $55 per picture book; $55 per examiner's manual.
Time: (10) minutes.
Author: Nancy Buono Fluharty.
Publisher: PRO-ED.
Cross References: For reviews by David P. Hurford and Rebecca McCauley, see 15:105; see T5:1047 (7 references) and T4:993 (2 references); for reviews by Nicholas W. Bankson and Harold A. Peterson of an earlier edition, see 9:422 (1 reference).

[1038]
Food Protection Certification Test.
Purpose: "To test persons who have ongoing on-site responsibility for protecting the consumer from foodborne illness in food preparation, serving, or dispensing establishments."
Population: Food industry personnel.
Publication Dates: 1985–1993.
Scores, 3: Purchasing/Receiving/Storing Food, Processing/Serving/Dispensing Food, Employees/Facilities/Equipment.
Administration: Group.
Price Data: Price information available from publisher for registration fee providing for administration and scoring of the test and mailing of results to examinee and for practice test.
Time: (120) minutes.
Comments: Tests administered per request of certified site examiner.
Author: Center for Occupational and Professional Assessment.
Publisher: Educational Testing Service.

[1039]
The Forer Structured Sentence Completion Test.

Purpose: Designed to measure personality variables and attitudes that may be of some value in treatment planning.
Population: Ages 10–18 and adults.
Publication Dates: 1957–1967.
Acronym: FSSCT.
Scores: No scores; 100 items in 18 areas: Interpersonal Figures (Mother, Males, Females, Groups, Father, Authority), Wishes, Causes of Own (Aggression, Anxiety/Fear, Giving Up [Adolescents] or Depression [Adults], Failure, Guilt, Inferiority Feelings [Adolescents]), Reactions To (Aggression, Rejection, Failure, Responsibility, School [Adolescents], Sexual Stimuli [Adults], Love and Marriage [Adults]).
Administration: Group.
Editions, 4: Separate editions for boys, girls, men, and women.
Price Data, 2006: $93.50 per kit including 10 tests, 20 checklists, and manual (1957, 34 pages) for any of each level; $24.75 per 25 tests (specify edition); $24.75 per 25 checklists (specify edition); $32.50 per manual.
Time: [30–45] minutes.
Author: Bertram R. Forer.
Publisher: Western Psychological Services.
Cross References: See T5:1049 (2 references), T2:1461 (3 references), and P:429 (4 references); for reviews by Charles N. Cofer and Percival M. Symonds, see 5:134 (5 references).

[1040]
Forms for Behavior Analysis with Children.

Purpose: A collection of assessment measures "designed to provide a comprehensive portrait of problems with an eye to how the information can be used to design behavioral treatments."
Population: Children and adolescents.
Publication Date: 1983.
Scores: 21 measures: Behavior Analysis History Questionnaire, Behavior Status Checklist, Reinforcement Survey Schedules, Assertive Behavior Survey Schedule, Bodily Cues for Tension and Anxiety, Fear Inventory, Medical History Inventory, Parental Reaction Survey Schedule, Physical Complaint Survey Schedule, School Behavior Status Checklist, Self-Evaluation Scale, Parents' and Children's Reinforcement Survey Schedule, Reinforcement Menu, Response Cost Survey Schedule, School Reinforcement Survey Schedule, Behavior Record Form, Home Visit Observation Form, Behavior Rating Card, Motivation Assessment of Parents and Children, Progress Chart, Session Report.
Administration: Group.
Forms, 5: C (child), A (adolescent), P (parent), S (school personnel), T (therapist).

Price Data: 2001: $39.95 per manual (208 pages) including reproducible forms.
Time: Administration time not reported.
Comments: Forms (C, A, P, S, T) refer to the person who is to complete the form; "Different assessment formats are encompassed, ranging from direct observations and interviews to informant ratings and self-report."
Authors: Joseph R. Cautela, Julie Cautela, and Sharon Esonis.
Publisher: Research Press
Cross References: For reviews by Sarah J. Allen and Karen T. Carey, see 11:144.

[1041]
Four Picture Test, Third Revised Edition.

Purpose: A projective technique "of the Thematic Apperception type" requiring written, rather than verbal, responses.
Population: Ages 10 and over.
Publication Dates: 1948–1983.
Acronym: FPT.
Scores: No scores.
Administration: Group.
Price Data: Price information available from publisher for materials including manual (1983, 26 pages).
Time: (30–45) minutes.
Comments: Projective analysis guidelines provided in manual.
Author: D. J. van Lennep.
Publisher: Harcourt Assessment [England].
Cross References: See P:431 (3 references); for a review by S. G. Lee and Johann M. Schepers of an earlier edition, see 6:213 (3 references); for reviews by John E. Bell, E. G. Bradford, and Ephraim Rosen of the original edition, see 4:105 (3 references, 1 excerpt).

[1042]
Fox Adds Up.

Purpose: Designed to assess mathematics skills.
Population: Grades K-3.
Publication Date: 2005.
Subtests: 5 per level: Number/Operations, Algebra, Geometry, Measurement, Data Analysis/Probability.
Administration: Individual.
Levels, 4: Kindergarten, Grade 1, Grade 2, Grade 3.
Price Data, 2006: $245 per complete kit including teacher's guide, observation and scoring records, Activity Cards, Math Manipulatives, and DVD; $55 per 25 observation and scoring records.
Foreign Language Edition: Parent letter available in Spanish.
Time: Administration time not reported.
Comments: Designed to be administered twice during the school year, including once in the fall and once in the spring; directly connects to benchmarks in Fox

Letters and Numbers (1044) and Fox in a Box-Second Edition (1043).
Author: CTB/McGraw-Hill.
Publisher: CTB/McGraw-Hill.

  a) KINDERGARTEN.
  Scores, 21: Number/Operations (Counting Cubes, Counting Forward/Backward, Representing Numbers, Coins, Modeling Additions, Modeling Subtraction, Adding, Subtracting), Algebra (Sorting, Patterns, Missing Addends), Geometry (Geometric Shapes, Position Words, Finding Shapes), Measurement (Measurement Totals, Time to the Hour, Nonstandard Units), Data Analysis/Probability (Organizing Data, Choosing a Graph, Likely/Unlikely), Kindergarten Total.
  b) GRADE 1.
  Scores, 20: Number/Operations (Two-Digit Numbers, Counting Backward, Composing/Decomposing Numbers, Comparing Two-Digit Numbers, Addition, Subtraction), Algebra (Sorting, Patterns, Commutative Property), Geometry (Comparing/Contrasting Shapes, Arranging Objects, Re-creating a Design), Measurement (Appropriate Measurement Units, Time to the Half-Hour, Nonstandard Units), Data Analysis/Probability (Organizing Data, Choosing Graph, Reading a Graph, Most Likely Outcome), Grade 1 Total.
  c) GRADE 2.
  Scores, 20: Number/Operations (Place Value, Representing Two-Digit Numbers, Modeling Two-Digit Addition, Modeling Two-Digit Subtraction, Adding Two-Digit Numbers, Subtracting Two-Digit Numbers), Algebra (Sorting, Patterns, Using a Pattern in a Table), Geometry (Compares Geometric Shapes, Using a Grid, Redrawing a Design from Memory), Measurement (Appropriate Measurement Tool, Time to 5 Minutes, Standard and Nonstandard Units), Data Analysis/Probability (Organizing Data, Choosing a Graph, Analyzing a Graph, Most and Least Likely Outcomes), Grade 2 Total.
  d) GRADE 3.
  Scores, 18: Number/Operations (Place Value, Fractions, Multiplication, Division), Algebra (Sorting, Patterns in a Table, Equations), Geometry (Combining Shapes, Using a Map, Flips/Sides/Turns, Three-Dimensional Figures), Measurement (Appropriate Measurement Unit, Elapsed Time, Area/Perimeter), Data Analysis/Probability (Organizing Data, Choosing and Analyzing a Graph, Most Likely Outcome on a Spinner), Grade 3 Total.

[1043]

Fox in a Box-Second Edition.

Purpose: Designed to measure "children's literacy skills."

Population: Grades K-3.
Publication Dates: 1998-2005.
Subtests: 4-6 per level: Phonemic Awareness [Levels 1-2 only], Phonics, Vocabulary [Levels 2-8 only], Reading Comprehension, Fluency [Levels 4-8 only], Listening and Comprehension.
Levels, 8: Level 1 (Fall Kindergarten), Level 2 (Spring Kindergarten), Level 3 (Fall Grade 1), Level 4 (Spring Grade 1), Level 5 (Fall Grade 2), Level 6 (Spring Grade 2), Level 7 (Fall Grade 3), Level 8 (Spring Grade 3).
Price Data, 2006: $245 per complete kit including teacher's guide, observation and scoring records, activity cards, window card, reader, fox puppet, "Monday" book, and Staff Development DVD; $55 per 25 observation scoring records.
Foreign Language Edition: Parent letter available in Spanish.
Comments: Designed to be given twice a year, including once in early fall (October/November) and once in early spring (March/April); spelling section of this test is designed to be administered over 2 to 3 days; directly connects to benchmarks in Fox Letters and Numbers (1044) and Fox Adds Up (1042).
Author: CTB/McGraw-Hill.
Publisher: CTB/McGraw-Hill.

  a) LEVEL 1-FALL KINDERGARTEN.
    1) *Phonemic Awareness.*
    Scores, 4: Rhyme Recognition, Rhyme Generation, Syllable Clapping, Initial Consonants.
    Administration: Individual.
    Time: (10-20) minutes.
    2) *Phonics.*
      (a) Alphabet Recognition.
      Administration: Individual.
      Time: (2-7) minutes.
      (b) Alphabet Writing.
      Administration: Individual or group.
      Time: (2-7) minutes.
      (c) Spelling.
      Administration: Individual or group.
      Time: (5-10) minutes for battery; (2-7) minutes for any one test.
    3) *Reading Comprehension.*
    Scores, 2: Listening Comprehension, Writing Development.
    Administration: Individual or group.
    Time: (40-60) minutes.
    4) *Listening and Writing.*
      (a) Timmy Turtle.
      Administration: Individual.
      Time: (2-7) minutes.
  b) LEVEL 2-SPRING KINDERGARTEN.
    1) *Phonemic Awareness.*
    Scores, 3: Final Consonants, Blending, Segmenting.

Administration: Individual.
Time: (5-15) minutes.
2) *Phonics.*
   (a) Alphabet Recognition.
   Administration: Individual.
   Time: (2-7) minutes.
   (b) Alphabet Writing.
   Administration: Individual or group.
   Time: (2-7) minutes.
   (c) Spelling.
   Administration: Individual or group.
   Time: (10-20) minutes for battery; (2-7) minutes for any one test.
   (d) Decoding.
   Administration: Individual.
   Time: (2-7) minutes.
3) *Vocabulary.*
   (a) Sight Words.
   Administration: Individual or group.
   Time: (2-7) minutes.
4) *Reading Comprehension.*
Scores, 2: Emergent Reading, Oral Expression.
Administration: Individual.
Time: (10-20) minutes.
5) *Listening and Writing.*
   (a) The Squirrel, the Eagle, and the Egg.
   Scores, 2: Listening Comprehension, Writing Development.
   Administration: Individual or group.
   Time: (35-55) minutes.
c) LEVEL 3-FALL GRADE 1.
  1) *Phonics.*
   (a) Spelling.
   Administration: Individual or group.
   Time: (20-40) minutes for battery; (5-15) minutes for any one test.
   (b) Decoding.
   Administration: Individual.
   Time: (2-7) minutes.
  2) *Vocabulary.*
   (a) Work Knowledge.
   Administration: Individual or group.
   Time: (10-20) minutes.
   (b) Sight Words.
   Administration: Individual.
   Time: (2-7) minutes.
  3) *Reading Comprehension.*
Scores, 3: Reading Accuracy, Reading Comprehension, Oral Expression.
Administration: Individual.
Time: (10-20) minutes.
  4) *Listening and Writing.*
   (a) Danger Dog.
   Scores, 2: Listening Comprehension, Writing Development.

Administration: Individual or group.
Time: (35-55) minutes.
d) LEVEL 4-SPRING GRADE 1.
  1) *Phonics.*
   (a) Spelling.
   Administration: Individual or group.
   Time: (20-40) minutes for battery; (5-15) minutes for any one test.
   (b) Decoding.
   Administration: Individual.
   Time: (2-7) minutes.
  2) *Vocabulary.*
   (a) Work Knowledge.
   Administration: Individual or group.
   Time: (10-20) minutes.
   (b) Sight Words.
   Administration: Individual.
   Time: (2-7) minutes.
  3) *Reading Comprehension.*
Scores, 3: Reading Accuracy, Reading Comprehension, Oral Expression.
Administration: Individual.
Time: (10-20) minutes.
  4) *Fluency.*
Scores, 2: Reading Rate, Reading Expression.
Administration: Individual.
Time: (1-3) minutes.
  5) *Listening and Writing.*
   (a) Magpie Robbery.
   Scores, 3: Listening Comprehension, Writing Expression, Writing Development.
   Administration: Individual or group.
   Time: (35-55) minutes.
e) LEVEL 5-FALL GRADE 2.
  1) *Phonics.*
   (a) Spelling.
   Administration: Individual or group.
   Time: (35-55) minutes for battery; (10-20) minutes for any one test.
   (b) Decoding.
   Administration: Individual.
   Time: (2-7) minutes.
  2) *Vocabulary.*
   (a) Work Knowledge.
   Administration: Individual or group.
   Time: (10-20) minutes.
   (b) Sight Words.
   Administration: Individual.
   Time: (2-7) minutes.
  3) *Reading Comprehension.*
Scores, 3: Reading Accuracy, Reading Comprehension, Oral Expression.
Administration: Individual.
Time: (15-25) minutes.
  4) *Fluency.*
Scores, 2: Reading Rate, Reading Expression.

Administration: Individual.
Time: (1-3) minutes.
5) *Listening and Writing.*
    (a) Puffin Patrol.
    Scores, 3: Listening Comprehension, Writing Expression, Writing Development.
    Administration: Individual or group.
    Time: (35-55) minutes.
f) LEVEL 6-SPRING GRADE 2.
    1) *Phonics.*
    (a) Spelling.
    Administration: Individual or group.
    Time: (35-55) minutes for battery; (10-20) minutes for any one test.
    (b) Decoding.
    Administration: Individual.
    Time: (2-7) minutes.
    2) *Vocabulary.*
    (a) Work Knowledge.
    Administration: Individual or group.
    Time: (10-20) minutes.
    (b) Sight Words.
    Administration: Individual.
    Time: (2-7) minutes.
    3) *Reading Comprehension.*
    Scores, 3: Reading Accuracy, Reading Comprehension, Oral Expression.
    Administration: Individual.
    Time: (15-25) minutes.
    4) *Fluency.*
    Scores, 2: Reading Rate, Reading Expression.
    Administration: Individual.
    Time: (1-3) minutes.
    5) *Listening and Writing.*
    (a) Dodger's Den Mother.
    Scores, 3: Listening Comprehension, Writing Expression, Writing Development.
    Administration: Individual or group.
    Time: (35-55) minutes.
g) LEVEL 7-FALL GRADE 3.
    1) *Phonics.*
    (a) Spelling.
    Administration: Individual or group.
    Time: (35-55) minutes for battery; (10-20) minutes for any one test.
    2) *Vocabulary.*
    (a) Work Knowledge.
    Administration: Individual or group.
    Time: (10-20) minutes.
    (b) Sight Words.
    Administration: Individual.
    Time: (2-7) minutes.
    3) *Reading Comprehension.*
    Scores, 3: Reading Accuracy, Reading Comprehension, Oral Expression.

Administration: Individual.
Time: (15-25) minutes.
4) *Fluency.*
Scores, 2: Reading Rate, Reading Expression.
Administration: Individual.
Time: (1-3) minutes.
5) *Listening and Writing.*
    (a) Some Jungles are Noisier Than Others.
    Scores, 3: Listening Comprehension, Writing Expression, Writing Development.
    Administration: Individual or group.
    Time: (45-65) minutes.
h) LEVEL 8-SPRING GRADE 3.
    1) *Phonics.*
    (a) Spelling.
    Administration: Individual or group.
    Time: (35-55) minutes for battery; (10-20) minutes for any one test.
    2) *Vocabulary.*
    (a) Work Knowledge.
    Administration: Individual or group.
    Time: (10-20) minutes.
    (b) Sight Words.
    Administration: Individual.
    Time: (2-7) minutes.
    3) *Reading Comprehension.*
    Scores, 3: Reading Accuracy, Reading Comprehension, Oral Expression.
    Administration: Individual.
    Time: (15-25) minutes.
    4) *Fluency.*
    Scores, 2: Reading Rate, Reading Expression.
    Administration: Individual.
    Time: (1-3) minutes.
    5) *Listening and Writing.*
    (a) Rainforest Surprise.
    Scores, 3: Listening Comprehension, Writing Expression, Writing Development.
    Administration: Individual or group.
    Time: (45-65) minutes.

[1044]
Fox Letters and Numbers.

Purpose: Designed as "an observational assessment of literacy and mathematics for the years proceeding kindergarten."
Population: Prekindergarten students.
Publication Date: 2005.
Subtests, 2: Literacy, Mathematics.
Administration: Individual.
Price Data, 2006: $245 per complete kit including teacher's guide, observation and scoring records, activity cards, storybook, math manipulatives, and Product DVD; $55 per 25 observation and scoring records.

Foreign Language Edition: Parent letter available in Spanish.

Time: Administration time not reported.

Comments: Designed to be administered twice during the school year, including one time early in the fall; directly connects to benchmarks in Fox in a Box-Second Edition (1043) and Fox Adds Up (1042).

Author: CTB/McGraw-Hill.

Publisher: CTB/McGraw-Hill.

   a) LITERACY.

   Scores, 15: Oral Language (Identifying Same/Different Sounds, Following Directions, Story Retell, Labeling Objects, Position Words, Opposites), Phonological Awareness (Rhyme Recognition, Syllable Clapping, Identifying Same/Different Words, Blending Phonemes), Alphabet Knowledge (Naming Letters, Naming Letter Sounds), Print Awareness (Differentiates Numbers/Letters/Print, Handling a Book), Literacy Total.

   b) MATHEMATICS.

   Scores, 14: Number and Operations (Finding How many, Numbers to 10, Conservation of Number, More or Fewer), Geometry (Identifies Shape, Matches Shapes), Measurement (Comparing, Time of Day, Conservation of Length, Nonstandard Units), Algebra (Patterns, Sorting), Data Analysis and Probability (Comparing Groups of Objects, Classifying Groups), Mathematics Total.

[1045]
Frenchay Dysarthria Assessment.

Purpose: Developed to diagnose dysarthria.

Population: Ages 12 and over.

Publication Date: 1983.

Scores, 11: Reflex, Respiration, Lips, Jaw, Palate, Laryngeal, Tongue, Intelligibility, Rate, Sensation, Associated Factors.

Administration: Individual.

Price Data, 2001: $56 per complete kit including examiner's manual (59 pages) and scoring form; $30 per 25 scoring forms.

Time: [20] minutes.

Comments: Tongue depressor, stop watch, tape recorder, glass of water, and word cards needed for administration.

Author: Pamela M. Enderby.

Publisher: PRO-ED.

Cross References: See T5:1056 (2 references); for reviews by Steven B. Leder and Malcolm R. McNeil, see 12:154; see also T4:1007 (2 references).

[1046]
Friedman Well-Being Scale.

Purpose: "Designed to assess the level of well-being of an individual."

Population: Adults.

Publication Dates: 1992–1994.

Acronym: FWBS.

Scores: 6: Composite/Total, Sociability, Self-Esteem, Joviality, Emotional Stability, Happiness.

Administration: Group.

Price Data: Available from publisher (www.mindgarden.com).

Time: (2–3) minutes.

Comments: Scale for rating perception of others or for self-rating; self-administered, administrator scored.

Author: Phillip H. Friedman.

Publisher: Mind Garden, Inc.

Cross References: For a review by John W. Fleenor, see 14:152.

[1047]
Frontal Systems Behavior Scale.

Purpose: "Identifies and quantifies behavioral problems associated with frontal lobe lesions."

Population: Ages 18–95.

Publication Date: 2001.

Acronym: FrSBe.

Scores, 4: Apathy (subscale A), Disinhibition (subscale D), Executive Dysfunction (subscale E), Total Score.

Administration: Individual or group.

Forms, 2: Family Rating Form, Self-Rating Form.

Price Data, 2006: $195 per introductory kit including professional manual (109 pages), 25 hand-scorable Self-Rating test booklets, 25 hand-scorable Family Rating test booklets, 25 Self-Rating profile forms, and 25 Family Rating profile forms.

Time: 10 minutes to administer; 10–15 minutes to score.

Comments: Revision of the Frontal Lobe Personality Scale; available in paper-and-pencil form only; obtains ratings of patient's behavior before and after an injury or illness.

Authors: Janet Grace and Paul F. Malloy.

Publisher: Psychological Assessment Resources, Inc.

Cross References: For reviews by Harrison D. Kane and Shawn K. Acheson and by Nora M. Thompson, see 15:106.

[1048]
Fuld Object-Memory Evaluation.

Purpose: Designed to "evaluate memory and learning under conditions that virtually guarantee attention and minimize anxiety."

Population: Ages 70–90 regardless of language and sensory handicaps.

Publication Date: 1977.

Acronym: FOME.

Scores, 5: Total Recall, Storage, Consistency of Retrieval, Ability to Benefit from Reminding, Ability to Say Words in Categories.

Administration: Individual.
Forms, 2: Record Form I, II.
Price Data, 2005: $75 per complete kit; $25 per 30 record forms; $25 per manual (24 pages).
Time: Administration time not reported.
Author: Paula Altman Fuld.
Publisher: Stoelting Co.
Cross References: See T5:1058 (9 references) and T4:1009 (6 references); for a review by Eric F. Gardner, see 9:427.

[1049]
Full Range Test of Visual Motor Integration.

Purpose: Designed to assess the ability of individuals to "accurately relate visual stimuli to motor responses" and "to assist in differentiating normal from pathological aging."
Population: Ages 5-74.
Publication Dates: 1996-2006.
Acronym: FRTVMI.
Scores: Total score only.
Administration: Group or individual.
Price Data, 2006: $169 per complete kit including examiner's manual (2006, 102 pages), 25 profile/examiner record forms for ages 5-10, 25 profile/examiner record forms for ages 11-74, and scoring transparency; $51 per examiner's manual; $59 per 25 profile/examiner record forms for ages 5-10; $59 per 25 profile/examiner record forms for ages 11-74; $6 per scoring transparency.
Time: (15-30) minutes
Comments: Extensive revision and redevelopment of the Test of Visual-Motor Integration.
Authors: Donald D. Hammill, Nils A. Pearson, Judith K. Voress, and Cecil R. Reynolds.
Publisher: PRO-ED.
Cross References: For a review by Deborah Erickson of the Test of Visual-Motor Integration, see 14:395; see also T5:2722 (1 reference).

[1050]
The Fullerton Language Test for Adolescents, Second Edition.

Purpose: Constructed to "distinguish normal from language-impaired adolescents."
Population: Ages 11-18.
Publication Dates: 1980–1986.
Scores, 8: Auditory Synthesis, Morphology Competency, Oral Commands, Convergent Production, Divergent Production, Syllabication, Grammatic Competency, Idioms.
Administration: Individual.
Price Data, 2006: $110 per complete kit including stimulus items, 25 scoring forms and profiles, and manual (1986, 55 pages); $35 per set of stimulus items; $30 per 25 scoring forms and profiles; $45 per manual.

Time: (45) minutes.
Author: Arden R. Thorum.
Publisher: PRO-ED.
Cross References: See T5:1060 (7 references) and T4:1011 (3 references); for a review by Diane J. Sawyer of the experimental edition, see 10:122; for a review by Margaret C. Byrne, see 9:428.

[1051]
Functional Assessment and Intervention System: Improving School Behavior.

Purpose: "Designed to enable interdisciplinary staff (school psychologists, teachers, counselors, and support staff) to systematically identify the intent or function of a student's challenging behaviors and gain a clear understanding of his or her needs."
Population: Early childhood through high school.
Publication Date: 2004.
Acronym: FAIS.
Scores: No scores.
Administration: Individual.
Forms, 2: Social Competence Performance Checklist, Classroom Competence Observation Form.
Price Data, 2004: $85 per complete kit including manual (177 pages) and 25 record forms.
Time: (10) minutes for Social Competence Performance Checklist; (15–30) minutes for observation and support plan development.
Comments: Components of the FAIS can be used with Outcomes: Planning, Monitoring, Evaluating (1821) for planning interventions.
Author: Karen Callan Stoiber.
Publisher: PsychCorp, A brand of Harcourt Assessment, Inc.
Cross References: For reviews by Robert W. Hiltonsmith and Daniel C. Miller, see 16:93.

[1052]
Functional Assessment of Academic Behavior.

Purpose: Designed as an ecological approach to "evaluate learners in context and address needed instructional, home, and home-school supports for learning."
Population: Grades PreK-12.
Publication Dates: 1987-2002.
Acronym: FAAB.
Scores, 23: 12 classroom components: Instructional Math, Instructional Expectations, Classroom Environment, Instructional Presentation, Cognitive Emphasis, Motivational Strategies, Relevant Practice, Informed Feedback, Academic Engaged Time, Adaptive Instruction, Progress Evaluation, Student Understanding; 5 home components: Home Expectations and Attributions, Discipline Orientation, Home-affective Environment, Parent Participation, Structure for Learning; 6 home-school relationship components: Shared Stan-

dards and Expectations, Consistent Structure, Cross-setting Opportunity to Learn, Mutual Support, Positive/Trusting Relationships, Modeling.
Administration: Individual.
Forms, 11: 5 required forms: Instructional Environment Checklist, Instructional Environment Checklist: Annotated Version, Instructional Needs Checklist, Parental Experience With Their Children's Learning and Schoolwork, Intervention Documentation Record; 6 supplemental forms: Observation Record, Student Interview Record, Teacher Interview Record, Parent Interview Record, Supplemental Teacher Interview Questions, Supplemental Student Interview Questions.
Price Data, 2006: $61.95 per Functional Assessment of Academic Behavior book (2002, 105 pages).
Time: Administration time not reported.
Comments: Replaces The Instructional Environment System-III (T6:1223).
Authors: James Ysseldyke and Sandra L. Christenson.
Publisher: Sopris West.
Cross References: See T5:1275 (1 reference); for reviews by Michael J. Furlong and Jennifer A. Rosenblatt and by Jerry Tindal of The Instructional Environment System-II, see 13:150; for reviews by Kenneth W. Howell and by William T. McKee and Joseph C. Witt of an earlier form, see 10:149.

[1053]
Functional Communication Profile.

Purpose: Designed to measure functional language performance in aphasic patients.
Population: Aphasic adults.
Publication Dates: 1956–1969.
Acronym: FCP.
Scores, 6: Movement, Speaking, Understanding, Reading, Other, Total.
Administration: Individual.
Price Data: Available from publisher.
Time: (15–30) minutes for interview.
Comments: Ratings by experienced clinician following nonstructured interview.
Author: Martha Taylor Sarno.
Publisher: Institute of Rehabilitation Medicine, New York University Medical Center [No reply from publisher; status unknown].
Cross References: See T5:1061 (1 reference), T4:1012 (3 references), and T3:925 (3 references); for reviews by Raphael M. Haller and Harvey Halpern, see 8:962 (11 references).

[1054]
Functional Fitness Assessment for Adults Over 60 Years, Second Edition.

Purpose: Developed as a field test to determine the functional capacity of older adults.
Population: Adults over age 60.

Publication Dates: 1990–1996.
Scores, 7: Body Composition (Body Weight, Standing Height Measurement), Flexibility, Agility/Dynamic Balance, Coordination, Strength/Endurance, Endurance.
Administration: Group.
Price Data, 2001: $12 per manual (1996, 60 pages).
Time: Administration time not reported.
Authors: Wayne H. Osness, Marlene Adrian, Bruce Clark, Werner Hoeger, Dianne Raab, and Robert Wiswell.
Publisher: American Association for Active Lifestyles and Fitness.
Cross References: For reviews by Anita M. Hubley and Anthondy M. Paolo, see 15:107; for reviews by Matthew E. Lambert and Cecil R. Reynolds of an earlier edition, see 13:128.

[1055]
Functional Grammar Test.

Purpose: To assess student mastery of English grammar.
Population: High school and college.
Publication Date: 1970.
Acronym: FGT.
Scores: Total score only.
Administration: Group.
Forms, 2: A, B.
Price Data: Available from publisher.
Time: (15–20) minutes.
Author: Joyce E. Lackey.
Publisher: Psychometric Affiliates.

[1056]
Functional Linguistic Communication Inventory.

Purpose: "Designed to quantify the functional linguistic communication skills of moderately and severely demented individuals."
Population: Adults diagnosed with Alzheimer's disease.
Publication Date: 1994.
Acronym: FLCI.
Scores, 11: Greeting and Naming, Question Answering, Writing, Comprehension of Signs and Object-to-Picture Matching, Word Reading and Comprehension, Reminiscing, Following Commands, Pantomime, Gesture, Conversation, Total.
Administration: Individual.
Price Data, 2006: $200 per complete kit including manual (31 pages), 25 response record forms, 25 score forms, stimulus book (50 pages), and 3 objects (comb, pencil, mask); $25 per 25 response record forms; $20 per 25 score sheets; $60 per manual; $100 per stimulus book; $15 per kit including comb, pencil, and mask.
Time: (30) minutes.
Authors: Kathryn A. Bayles and Cheryl K. Tomoeda.

Publisher: PRO-ED.
Cross References: For reviews by Cameron J. Camp and Jennifer A. Brush and by Wilfred G. Van Gorp, see 13:129.

[1057]
Functional Skills Screening Inventory, Individual Edition.

Purpose: "To be used in natural settings to assess critical living and working skills in persons with moderate to severe handicapping conditions."
Population: Age 6 through adult.
Publication Dates: 1984-1986.
Acronym: FSSI.
Scores, 9: Categorized into 3 priority levels: Basic Skills and Concepts, Communication, Personal Care, Homemaking, Work Skills and Concepts, Community Living, Social Awareness, Functional Skills Subtotal, Problem Behaviors.
Administration: Individual.
Price Data, 2006: $190 per master print copy including assessment booklet for unlimited assessments, hand-scoring sheets, and user guide (1986, 117 pages); $450 per Windows interactive computer program; web site provides demo with documentation.
Time: [60-120] minutes per assessment.
Comments: A domain-referenced behavioral checklist; Employment Edition and Environmental Edition are also available in Windows format.
Authors: Heather Becker, Sally Schur, Michele Paoletti-Schelp, and Ed Hammer.
Publisher: Functional Resources.
Cross References: See T5:1067 (1 reference); for reviews by Diane Browder and G. Michael Poteat, see 10:123 (3 references).

[1058]
GAINS: A Pre-test and Post-test for Measuring Career Development Competency Progress.

Purpose: A diagnostic tool for assessing level of competency accrued from career development studies.
Population: Grades 4-7, 8-11.
Publication Date: 1995.
Acronym: GAINS I, GAINS II.
Scores, 2: Pre-Test Total, Post-Test Total, Modified Percent Gain.
Administration: Group.
Price Data: Price information available from publisher for classroom set including 30 tests and teacher's guide (specify GAINS I or GAINS II; volume discounts available).
Time: Testing time specified by teacher based on reading ability; pre-test and post-test must use the same time limit.

Author: Norene Lindsay.
Publisher: Wintergreen/Orchard House, Inc.

[1059]
Gates-MacGinitie Reading Tests, 2nd Canadian Edition.

Purpose: Constructed to assess reading achievement.
Population: Grades K.7-12.
Publication Dates: 1978-1992.
Administration: Group.
Forms, 2: 3, 4.
Price Data, 2005: $60.75 to $63.25 per 35 test booklets (select level); $9.40 per scoring key (select level); $14.20 per 10 class record sheets; $45.60 per Teacher's Guide (select level; includes directions for administration, interpretation, and norms tables); $37.90 per Out-of-Level Norms Booklet; $47.70 per preview kit; $29.95 per technical manual; scoring service available from publisher.
Comments: Levels PRE, R, and A are each available as Form 3; Levels B through F have two parallel forms (3, 4).
Authors: Walter H. MacGinitie and Ruth K. MacGinitie.
Publisher: Nelson, A Thomson Company [Canada].
a) LEVEL PRE.
Population: Grades K.7-1.2.
Scores: Total score only.
Price Data: $60.75 per 35 test booklets.
Time: (90) minutes
b) LEVEL R.
Population: Grades 1.0-1.9.
Scores: Total score only.
Time: (70) minutes.
c) LEVEL A.
Population: Grades 1.3-1.9.
Scores, 3: Vocabulary, Comprehension, Total.
Price Data: $12 per decoding skills analysis forms.
Time: 55 minutes.
d) LEVEL B.
Population: Grade 2.
Scores, 3: Same as for *c* above.
Price Data: Same as for *c* above.
Time: Same as for *c* above.
e) LEVEL C.
Population: Grade 3.
Scores, 3: Same as for *c* above.
Time: Same as for *c* above.
f) LEVEL D 4.
Population: Grade 4.
Scores, 3: Same as for *c* above.
Price Data: $37.80 per 35 hand-scorable answer sheets; $90.25 per 100 hand-scorable answer sheets; $83.75 per 50 machine-scorable answer sheets;

$379.00 per 250 machine-scorable answer sheets; $21.70 per set of scoring stencils.
Time: Same as for *c* above.
g) LEVEL D 5/6.
Population: Grades 5-6.
Scores, 3: Same as for *c* above.
Price Data: Same as for *f* above.
h) LEVEL E.
Population: Grades 7-9.
Scores, 3: Same as for *c* above.
Price Data: Same as for *f* above.
Time: Same as for *c* above.
i) LEVEL F.
Population: Grades 10-12.
Scores, 3: Same as for *c* above.
Price Data: Same as for *f* above.
Time: Same as for *c* above.
Cross References: See T5:1071 (5 references) and T4:1021 (6 references); for reviews by Mariam Jean Dreher and Susanna W. Pflaum of an earlier edition, see 9:431.

[1060]
Gates-MacGinitie Reading Tests®, Fourth Edition, Forms S and T.

Purpose: Designed to assess students' "general level of reading achievement."
Population: Grades K.7–12 and adults.
Publication Dates: 1926–2000.
Acronym: GMRT®.
Scores, 11: Literacy Concepts, Oral Language Concepts, Letters and Letter/Sound Correspondences, Listening Comprehension, Initial Consonants and Consonant Clusters, Final Consonants and Consonant Clusters, Vowels, Basic Story Words, Word Decoding, Vocabulary/Word Knowledge, Comprehension.
Administration: Group.
Levels, 11: PR (Pre-Reading), BR (Beginning Reading), 1, 2, 3, 4, 5, 6, 7/9, 10/12, AR (Adult Reading).
Forms, 2: S, T.
Price Data, 2006: $78.75 per hand-scorable test booklet package (Levels PR–3, specify level and form) including 25 test booklets, one Directions for Administration, one Booklet Scoring Key, one Class Summary Record, and one Decoding Skills Analysis form (for Levels 1 and 2 only); $119.25 per machine-scorable test booklet package (Levels BR–3, specify level and form); $141.50 per Level PR machine-scorable test booklet package (scored by publisher for an additional fee) including 25 test booklets, one Directions for Administration, and materials needed for machine scoring; $78.75 per reusable test booklet package (Levels 4–10/12 and AR) including 25 test booklets, one Directions for Administration, one Booklet Scoring Key, and one Class Summary Record; $113.50 per machine-scorable answer sheet package (Levels 4–10/12 and AR; scored by publisher for an additional fee) including 100 answer sheets and materials for machine scoring (specify level); $42.75 per self-scorable answer sheet package (Levels 4–10/12 and AR) including 25 answer sheets and one Class Summary Record (specify level); $380.75 per self-scorable answer sheet package (Levels 4–10/12 and AR) including 250 answer sheets (specify level); $10.75 per extra copy of Directions for Administration (specify level); $21 per Manual for Scoring and Interpretation (specify level); $14.50 per Linking Testing to Teaching: A Classroom Resource for Reading Assessment and Instruction (specify level); $25.75 per Technical Report; $475 per Score Converting and Reporting Software (for PC only).
Time: (55–100) minutes.
Comments: Norms tables available on CD-ROM.
Authors: Walter H. MacGinitie, Ruth K. MacGinitie, Katherine Maria, and Lois G. Dreyer.
Publisher: Riverside Publishing.
Cross References: For reviews by Kathleen M. Johnson and Patrick P. McCabe, see 16:94; see also T5:1072 (55 references) and T4:1022 (13 references); for a review by Mark E. Swerdlik of the third edition, see 11:146 (78 references); for reviews by Robert Calfee and William H. Rupley of an earlier edition, see 9:430 (15 references); see also T3:932 (77 references) and 8:726A (34 references); for reviews by Carolyn L. Burke and Byron H. Van Roekel and an excerpted review by William R. Powell of an earlier edition, see 7:689.

[1061]
Gates-McKillop-Horowitz Reading Diagnostic Test, Second Edition.

Purpose: "Assess the strengths and weaknesses in reading and related areas of a particular child."
Population: Grades 1-6.
Publication Dates: 1962-1981.
Scores, 23: Omissions, Additions, Repetitions, Mispronunciations (Directional Errors, Wrong Beginning, Wrong Middle, Wrong Ending, Wrong in Several Parts, Accent Errors, Total), Reading Sentences, Words-Flash, Words-Untimed, Word-Attack (Syllabication, Recognizing and Blending Common Word Parts, Reading Words, Giving Letter Sounds, Naming Capital Letters, Naming Lower-Case Letters), Vowels, Auditory (Blending, Discrimination), Spelling.
Administration: Individual.
Price Data, 2006: $2.50 per test materials; $7.50 per 30 pupil record booklets; $1 per manual of directions (1981, 16 pages); $3.95 per manual of directions kit (includes test materials, 1 pupil record booklet, manual of directions).
Time: Administration time not reported.
Comments: Revision of Gates-McKillop Reading Diagnostic Tests.

Authors: Arthur I. Gates, Anne S. McKillop, and Elizabeth Cliff Horowitz.
Publisher: Teachers College Press.
Cross References: See T5:1072 (3 references) and T4:1023 (3 references); for reviews by Priscilla A. Drum and by P. David Pearson and Patricia Herman, see 9:432 (2 references); for a review by Harry Singer of an earlier edition, see 8:759 (8 references); see also T2:1629 (11 references); for reviews by N. Dale Bryant and Gabriel M. Della-Piana, see 6:824 (2 references); for a review by George D. Spache of the earlier edition, see 5:662; for a review by T. L. Torgerson, see 3:510 (3 references).

[1062]
The Geist Picture Interest Inventory .

Purpose: Designed to "assess quantitatively eleven male and twelve female general interest areas and identify motivating forces behind occupational choice."
Population: Grade 8–adulthood.
Publication Dates: 1959–1971.
Acronym: GPII.
Scores: 18 (males) or 19 (females) scores: 11 or 12 Interest scores (Persuasive, Clerical, Mechanical, Musical, Scientific, Outdoor, Literary, Computational, Artistic, Social Service, Dramatic, Personal Service—females only), and 7 Motivation scores (Family, Prestige, Financial, Intrinsic and Personality, Environmental, Past Experience, Could Not Say).
Administration: Group or individual.
Forms, 2: M (male), F (female).
Price Data, 2006: $87.95 per kit including 10 tests of each form (male or female), and manual (1971, 42 pages plus tests and motivation questionnaires); $37.95 per 20 tests of male form; $36 per 20 tests of female form; $57 per manual; $14.95 per 20 motivation questionnaires of male form; $11 per 20 motivation questionnaires of female form.
Time: 10–20 minutes.
Author: Harold Geist.
Publisher: Western Psychological Services.
Cross References: See T2:2180 (18 references); for reviews by Milton E. Hahn and Benjamin Shimberg, and an excerpted review by David V. Tiedeman, see 6:1054 (12 references)

[1063]
General Ability Measure for Adults.

Purpose: "Designed to evaluate intellectual ability using abstract designs."
Population: Ages 18–96.
Publication Date: 1997.
Acronym: GAMA.
Scores, 5: Matching, Analogies, Sequences, Construction, GAMA IQ Score.
Administration: Individual and/or group.

Price Data, 2006: $58 per manual (1997, 97 pages); $153 per 10 softcover test booklets; $73.75 per 25 hand-scored answer sheets (test items included); $21 per 25 Q Local answer sheets (test items included); $5.80 per Q Local report; quantity discounts availabe for the reports; price information for Spanish materials available from publisher.
Time: (25) minutes.
Comments: May be self-administered.
Authors: Jack A. Naglieri and Achilles N. Bardos.
Publisher: Pearson Assessments.
Cross References: For reviews by Robert Fitzpatrick and Bert A. Goldman, see 14:153.

[1064]
General Chemistry Test: National Achievement Tests.

Purpose: Designed to measure students' knowledge in three areas of general chemistry.
Population: Grades 10–16.
Publication Dates: 1958–1959.
Scores, 4: Uses-Processes-Results, Formulae and Valence, Miscellaneous Facts, Total.
Administration: Group.
Manual: No manual.
Price Data: Available from publisher.
Time: 40(45) minutes.
Authors: Lester D. Crow and Roy S. Cook.
Publisher: Psychometric Affiliates.
Cross References: See T4:1025 (1 reference); for a review by J. A. Campbell, see 6:918.

[1065]
General Clerical Test.

Purpose: Developed to assess clerical speed and accuracy, numerical skills, and language-related skills.
Population: Clerical applicants and workers.
Publication Dates: 1972–1988.
Acronym: GCT.
Scores, 4: Clerical, Numerical, Verbal, Total.
Administration: Group or individual.
Price Data, 2006: $151 per 25 Clerical/Numerical/Verbal test booklets; $99 per 25 Clerical/Numerical test booklets; $72 per 25 Verbal test booklets; $555 per 100 Clerical/Numerical/Verbal test booklets; $358 per 100 Clerical/Numerical test booklets; $215 per 100 Verbal only test booklets; $51 per handscoring key; $52 per manual; 57 per examination kit, including 1 complete test booklet and manual (no key).
Time: 60 minutes.
Author: The Psychological Corporation.
Publisher: Harcourt Assessment, Inc.
Cross References: See T5:1078 (1 reference); for reviews by Dianna L. Newman and Alfred L. Smith, Jr., see 12:158.

[1066]
General Management In-Basket.

Purpose: "Designed to assess supervisory/managerial skills independent of any particular job classification; may be used for selection and/or career development."
Population: Supervisors and managers.
Publication Dates: 1985–2006.
Acronym: GMIB.
Scores, 5: Leadership Style and Practices, Handling Priorities and Sensitive Situations, Managing Conflict, Organizational Practices/Management Control, Total.
Administration: Group or individual.
Forms, 4: Private and public sector forms include Executive Version, Engineer Version, Police Versions for each managerial level from Police Sergeant to Police Chief, and Fire Versions for each managerial level from Fire Captain to Fire Chief.
Restricted Distribution: Clients must pay a one-time overhead/sign-up fee of $400.
Price Data, 2006: $325 per candidate for rental/scoring and detailed Career Development Report identifying strengths, weaknesses, and developmental needs with specific learning objectives, for each of the four factors measured by the test.
Time: 165 (175) minutes.
Author: Richard C. Joines.
Publisher: Management & Personnel Systems, Inc.
Cross References: For reviews by S. David Kriska and William J. Waldron, see 12:160.

[1067]
General Physics Test: National Achievement Tests.

Purpose: "Constructed to test the student's basic knowledge of Physics and his ability to apply that knowledge."
Population: Grades 10–16.
Publication Dates: 1958–1962.
Scores, 3: Uses and Application of Principles, Miscellaneous Facts and Scientists, Total.
Administration: Group.
Manual: No manual.
Price Data: Available from publisher.
Time: 40(45) minutes.
Authors: Lester D. Crow and Roy S. Cook.
Publisher: Psychometric Affiliates.
Cross References: For a review by Theodore G. Phillips, see 6:930.

[1068]
General Processing Inventory.

Purpose: Designed to identify learning disabilities.
Population: Ages 5–75 years.
Publication Dates: 1986–2004.
Acronym: GPI.

Scores, 7: Graphomotor, Short Term Memory Retrieval, Long Term Memory Retrieval, Visual (Dyslexia), Auditory, Speech (Dysphasia), Total.
Subtests, 2: General Elementary Inventory of Language Skills (GEILS), General Elementary Inventory of Mathematics and Numeration (GEIMAN).
Administration: Individual.
Levels, 4: One (5 years old), Two (Above 6 years), Three (Above 8 years), Four (Above 10 years).
Price Data, 2005: $350 per test kit; $400 for training required to administer test.
Time: (60–180) minutes.
Comments: Training required; psychologists and other licensed test administrators will learn to tabulate errors and may send their results to publisher for report writing. There is a fee for report writing dependent on volume.
Author: Ruth M. Geiman.
Publisher: Ruth M. Geiman, Ph.D.
Cross References: For reviews by Sherry K. Bain and Stephen A. Spillane, see 14:154.

[1069]
General Science Test: National Achievement Tests.

Purpose: Designed to measure students' knowledge of general science.
Population: Grades 7–9.
Publication Dates: 1936–1950.
Scores, 7: General Concepts, Identifications, Men of Science, Definitions, Uses of Objects, Miscellaneous Facts, Total.
Administration: Group.
Manual: No manual.
Price Data: Available from publisher.
Time: (30–45) minutes.
Authors: Robert K. Speer, Lester D. Crow, and Samuel Smith.
Publisher: Psychometric Affiliates.
Cross References: For a review by Robert M. W. Travers, see 5:712; for reviews by Francis D. Curtis and G. W. Hunter, see 2:1602.

[1070]
The Gesell Developmental Observation.

Purpose: A comprehensive developmental screening that measures physical/neurological growth, language skills, and adaptive behaviors such as thinking, memory, perception, attention to task, ability to follow directions, short term visual and aduitory memory, cognitive-perceptual thinking, organizational skills, logical mathematical thinking skills, and application of what is learned.
Population: Ages 2.5 through 9 years.
Publication Dates: 1964-2005.
Administration: Individual.

Price Data, 2006: $129 per reusable kit; $55.95 per 30 precollated sheets to test 30 children; $4.95 per pad of 75 Assessment Profile Forms (Summary Sheets).
Comments: Earlier version of the test was called The Gesell School Readiness Test.
Author: The Gesell Institute.
Publisher: The Gesell Institute.
Cross References: See T5:1085 (4 references) and T4:1035 (13 references); for reviews by Robert H. Bradley and Everett Waters of an earlier version, see 9:438; see also T3:953 (6 references) and T2:1703 (4 references); for excerpted reviews by L. J. Borstelmann and Edith Meyer Taylor, see 7:750 (5 references).

[1071]
Gesell Preschool Test.

Purpose: "Designed to measure . . . relative maturity ratings in four basic fields of behavior."
Population: Ages 2.5–6.
Publication Date: 1980.
Scores: Ratings in 4 areas: Motor, Adaptive, Language, Personal-Social.
Administration: Group.
Price Data, 2001: $127.30 per kit (reusable materials only); $29 per formboard; $28 per picture vocabulary cards; $10 per color forms; $9 per letters and numbers; $5.50 per pellets and bottles; $12.50 per copy forms; $14.95 per manual (72 pages); $5 per 25 developmental schedules; $9.50 per 10 one-inch cubes; $13.75 per typical response cards for incomplete man test.
Time: (30-45) minutes.
Comments: Abbreviated adaptation of the Gesell Developmental Schedules (see 6:522) and the Gesell Developmental Tests (see 7:750).
Authors: Jacqueline Haines, Louise Bates Ames, and Clyde Gillespie.
Publisher: The Gesell Institute.
Cross References: See T5:1086 (4 references); for reviews by Nadeen L. Kaufman and Jack A. Naglieri, see 9:437 (8 references).

[1072]
Gibson Spiral Maze, Second Edition.

Purpose: Measures "the speed, accuracy, and general style of people's muscular reactions in response to carefully controlled stimuli."
Population: Children and adults.
Publication Dates: 1961–1965.
Scores, 2: Time score, Error score.
Administration: Individual.
Price Data, 2002: £13.99 per test 20 copies; manual and specimen set are now out of print.
Time: (2) minutes.
Comments: Forms part of the Clifton Assessment Procedures for the Elderly (539).
Author: H. B. Gibson.

Publisher: Hodder & Stoughton Educational [England].
Cross References: For reviews by William K. Wilkinson and James Ysseldyke, see 14:155; see also T4:1037 (3 references), T3:955 (1 reference), T2:1191 (3 references), 7:82 (3 references), and P:90 (2 references).

[1073]
Gifted and Talented Evaluation Scales.

Purpose: Designed to help "identify persons who are gifted and talented."
Population: Ages 5-18.
Publication Date: 1996.
Acronym: GATES.
Scores, 5: Intellectual Ability, Academic Skills, Creativity, Leadership, Artistic Talent.
Administration: Individual.
Price Data, 2006: $110 per complete kit including examiner's manual (50 pages) and 50 summary/response forms; $65 per examiner's manual; $50 per 50 summary/response forms.
Time: (5-10) minutes.
Comments: This test is to be completed by a teacher, parent, or guardian of the individual being assessed.
Authors: James E. Gilliam, Betsy O. Carpenter, and Janis R. Christensen.
Publisher: PRO-ED.

[1074]
Gifted Evaluation Scale, Second Edition.

Purpose: Designed to help identify gifted students.
Population: Ages 5–18.
Publication Dates: 1987–2000.
Acronym: GES-2.
Scores, 8: 6 subscales (Intellectual, Creativity, Specific Academic Aptitude, Leadership Ability, Performing and Visual Arts, Motivation [optional]), Quotient Score, Percentile Score.
Administration: Individual.
Price Data, 2006: $75 per complete kit including technical manual (1998, 60 pages), 50 rating forms, and Gifted Intervention Manual (1990, 107 pages); $10 per 50 motivation scoring forms; $15 per technical manual; $35 per 50 rating forms; $25 per Gifted Intervention Manual; $5 per subscale percentile tables; $35 per Quick Score (WIN).
Time: (15–20) minutes.
Comments: Ratings by "anyone familiar with the student's behavior patterns and specific skills ... (e.g., teacher, counselor, etc.)."
Authors: Diana Henage (The Gifted Intervention Manual), Stephen B. McCarney and Paul D. Anderson (technical manual and subscale percentile tables).
Publisher: Hawthorne Educational Services, Inc.
Cross References: For reviews by Douglas K. Smith and John W. Young, see 14:156; see also T5:1089 (2

references); for reviews by Carolyn M. Callahan and Ross E. Traub of an earlier edition, see 12:162 (1 reference).

[1075]
Gifted Rating Scales.

Purpose: Designed to "assess observable student behaviors indicating giftedness."
Publication Date: 2003.
Acronym: GRS.
Administration: Individual.
Price Data, 2003: $125 per complete kit including manual (86 pages), 25 Early Child record forms, and 25 School Age record forms; $75 per manual; $40 per 25 Early Child record forms; $40 per 25 School Age record forms.
Comments: Norm-referenced, teacher-completed rating scale.
Authors: Steven I. Pfeiffer and Tania Jarosewich.
Publisher: PsychCorp, A brand of Harcourt Assessment, Inc.

a) GIFTED RATING SCALE—PRESCHOOL AND KINDERGARTEN.
Population: Ages 4:0 to 6:11.
Acronym: GRS-P.
Scores, 5: Intellectual Ability, Academic Ability, Creativity, Artistic Talent, Motivation.
Time: (10) minutes.
b) GIFTED RATING SCALE—SCHOOL.
Population: Ages: 6:0 to 13:11.
Acronym: GRS-S.
Scores, 6: Same as *a* above with the addition of Leadership Ability.
Time: (15) minutes.
Cross References: For a review by Sandra A. Ward, see 16:95.

[1076]
Gilliam Asperger's Disorder Scale [2003 Update].

Purpose: Designed to evaluate children with unique behavioral problems who may have Asperger's Disorder.
Population: Ages 3–22 years.
Publication Date: 2001.
Acronym: GADS.
Scores, 4: Social Interaction, Restricted Patterns of Behavior, Cognitive Patterns, Pragmatic Skills.
Administration: Individual.
Price Data, 2006: $100 per complete kit including examiner's manual (52 pages) and 25 summary/response forms; $60 per examiner's manual; $45 per 25 summary/response booklets.
Time: (5–10) minutes.
Author: James E. Gilliam.
Publisher: PRO-ED.
Cross References: For reviews by Connie T. England and Carol M. McGregor, see 16:96; for reviews

by Donald Oswald and Theresa Volpe-Johnstone of an earlier edition, see 15:108.

[1077]
Gilliam Autism Rating Scale—Second Edition.

Purpose: Designed to help professionals "identify children with autism from children with other severe behavioral problems."
Population: Ages 3-22.
Publication Dates: 1995-2006.
Acronym: GARS-2.
Scores: 3 subscales: Stereotyped Behaviors, Communication, Social Interaction, plus Autism Index .
Administration: Individual.
Price Data, 2006: $131 per complete kit including examiner's manual (2006, 85 pages), 50 summary/response booklets, and instructional objectives manual (2006, 26 pages); $60 per examiner's manual; $45 per 50 summary/response booklets; $28 per instructional objectives manual.
Time: (5-10) minutes.
Comments: Appropriate raters include parents, teachers, or other caregivers who have had regular, sustained contact with the individual for at least 2 weeks.
Author: James E. Gilliam.
Publisher: PRO-ED.
Cross References: For reviews by Donald P. Oswald and Steven Welsh of an earlier form, see 13:130.

[1078]
Gilmore Oral Reading Test.

Purpose: "Developed to provide ... a means of analyzing the oral reading performance of pupils."
Population: Grades 1–8.
Publication Dates: 1951–1968.
Acronym: GORT.
Scores, 3: Accuracy, Comprehension, Rate.
Administration: Individual.
Forms, 2: C, D.
Price Data, 2002: $24.50 per examination kit including manual (1968, 31 pages) and record blank; $41.25 per reading paragraphs (both forms); $70 per 35 record blanks (specify Form C or D); $22 per manual.
Time: (15-20) minutes.
Author: John V. Gilmore and Eunice C. Gilmore.
Publisher: Harcourt Assessment, Inc.
Cross References: See T5:1092 (18 references), T4:1042 (21 references), and T3:958 (13 references); for an excerpted review by Jerry Stafford, see 8:785 (17 references); see also T2:1679 (5 references); for reviews by Albert J. Harris and Kenneth J. Smith, see 7:737 (17 references); for reviews by Lydia A. Duggins and Maynard C. Reynolds of the original edition, see 5:671.

[1079]

Giotto.

Purpose: To provide a wide-ranging measure of personal integrity for use in staff selection.
Population: Unspecified.
Publication Dates: 1996–1997.
Scores: 7 scales: Prudence, Fortitude, Temperance, Justice, Faith, Charity, Hope.
Administration: Group or individual.
Price Data, 2006: $297 per starter kit including 20 question and answer booklets, scoring software, and manual (1997, 79 pages).
Time: (15) minutes.
Comments: Must be scored by computer on Giotto software using Windows 3.1 or Windows 95.
Author: John Rust.
Publisher: Harcourt Assessment [England].
Cross References: For reviews by Eugene V. Aidman and by Deniz S. Ones and Stephan Dilchert, see 16:97.

[1080]

Global Assessment Scale.

Purpose: "For evaluating the overall functioning of a subject during a specified time period on a continuum from psychological or psychiatric sickness to health."
Population: Psychiatric patients and possible psychiatric patients.
Publication Dates: 1976-1985.
Acronym: GAS.
Scores: Mental Health-Illness rating of individual on a continuum of 1 to 100.
Administration: Individual.
Price Data, 2001: $.50 per scale; $2.50 per case vignettes and keys (1985, 17 pages); $1 per instructions (1978, 8 pages).
Authors: Robert L. Spitzer, Miriam Gibbon, and Jean Endicott.
Publisher: Department of Research Assessment and Training.
Cross References: See T5:1093 (116 references) and T4:1043 (62 references); for a review by Michael J. Subkoviak, see 11:147 (22 references).

[1081]

GOALS®: A Performance-Based Measure of Achievement.

Purpose: A measure of student achievement using open-ended questions requiring reasoning skills.
Population: Grades 1–12.
Publication Dates: 1992–1994.
Administration: Group.
Forms, 3: A, B, C (Form C is secure and not available through the catalog).
Levels, 11: 1–11.
Price Data, 2002: $23.90 per 25 test booklets including directions for administering; $11.70 per scoring guide; $8 per directions for administering; $26.50 per 1991 norms booklet (separate by content area); $80 per 1992 norms booklet (all content areas); $53 per technical manual (1994, 114 pages); $26.50 per interpretive manual; $4.50 per Option 1 computer scoring by publisher of one domain including scoring and two copies of the Student Performance Roster; $3.40 per each additional domain; $.22 per additional copy of Student Performance Roster); $760 set-up charge for Option 2 computer scoring by publisher including scoring and recording of scores in test booklets; $3.41 per domain scored; $.62 per class profile ($43.25 per order each additional copy); $.51 per school profile ($34.25 per order each additional copy); $.44 per district profile ($25.50 per order each additional copy); $.79 per administrator's data summary-school ($34.50 per order each additional copy); $.79 per administrator's data summary-district ($25.50 per order each additional copy); $1.03 per administrator's data summary-school and district ($43.25 per each additional copy); $.87 per student profile ($.25 per additional copy); $.68 per student record label; $.68 per master list of test results ($.22 per additional copy); $.68 per student performance roster ($.22 per additional copy); $.44 per student data diskette; $760 per set-up charge for customer data input (plus cost of additional optional reports ordered).
Time: Approximately one class period.
Comments: Produces norm-referenced and holistic-analytic scores.
Author: Harcourt Brace Educational Measurement.
Publisher: Harcourt Assessment, Inc.

a) MATHEMATICS.
Scores, 5: Content (Problem Solving [All Levels], Procedures [All Levels]), Process (Applying Mathematical Skills and Concepts to Solve Problems [Levels 1–2], Drawing Conclusions Using Mathematical Skills and Concepts [Levels 1–4], Integrating Mathematical Concepts and Skills to Solve Problems [Levels 1–8], Analyzing Problems Using Mathematical Skills and Concepts [Levels 3–11], Creating Solutions Through Synthesis of Mathematical Concepts and Skills [Levels 5–11], Evaluating Problems Using Mathematical Skills and Concepts [Levels 9–11]).

b) LANGUAGE.
Scores, 5: Content (Narrative Writing, Expository Writing), Process (Skill in Composing, Understanding of Usage, Application in Mechanics).

c) READING.
Scores, 5: Content (Narrative Text, Informational Text), Process (Global Understanding, Identification and Application of Strategies, Critical Analysis).

d) SCIENCE.
Scores, 6: Content (Life Science, Physical Science, Earth/Space Science), Process (Collecting

and Recording Scientific Data, Applying Science Concepts, Drawing Conclusions).
e) SOCIAL SCIENCE.
Scores, 5: Content (Geographic/Economic/and Cultural Foundations of Society, Historical and Political Bases of Society), Process (Understanding of Basic Conceptual Social Science Frameworks, Creative Thinking and Problem-Solving Skills, Inquiry and Decision Making Using Social Science Tools).
Cross References: For reviews by C. Dale Carpenter and Darrell L. Sabers, see 13:131.

[1082]
Goldman-Fristoe Test of Articulation— Second Edition.

Purpose: Designed as "a systematic means of assessing an individual's articulation of the consonant sounds of Standard American English."
Population: Ages 2–21.
Publication Dates: 1969–2000.
Acronym: GFTA-2.
Scores: 3 sections: Sounds-in-Words, Sounds-in-Sentences, Stimulability.
Administration: Individual.
Price Data, 2005: $229.99 per complete kit, including test manual (2000, 146 pages), test easel, 25 response forms, supplemental developmental norms booklet, and canvas carrying bag; $29.99 per 25 response forms; $49.99 per test manual.
Time: 5–15 minutes.
Comments: Normative scores are available for the Sounds-in-Words section only.
Authors: Ronald Goldman and Macalyne Fristoe.
Publisher: Pearson Assessments (originally published by AGS Publishing, acquired by Pearson in 2005).
Cross References: For reviews by Steven Long and Katharine A. Snyder, see 15:109; see T5:1095 (48 references) and T4:1045 (15 references); for a review by Donald E. Mowrer of an earlier edition, see 10:126 (7 references); see also T3:960 (21 references); for reviews by Margaret C. Byrne and Ralph L. Shelton, and an excerpted review by Dorothy Sherman, see 7:952 (4 references).

[1083]
Goldman-Fristoe-Woodcock Test of Auditory Discrimination.

Purpose: "Designed to provide measures of speech-sound discrimination ability."
Population: Ages 3-8 through 70+.
Publication Date: 1970.
Acronym: G-F-W.
Scores: 2 subtests: Quiet, Background Noise.
Administration: Individual.
Price Data, 2005: $139.99 per kit, including test easel, 50 response forms, audiocassette, and manual (31 pages); $29.99 per 50 response forms; $24.99 per manual.

Time: [20–30] minutes.
Authors: Ronald Goldman, Macalyne Fristoe, and Richard W. Woodcock.
Publisher: Pearson Assessments (originally published by AGS Publishing, acquired by Pearson in 2005).
Cross References: See T5:1096 (13 references), T4:1046 (8 references), and T3:962 (14 references); for an excerpted review by Alex Bannatyne, see 8:938 (18 references); see also T2:2037 (4 references); for reviews by Eugene C. Sheeley and Ralph L. Shelton and an excerpted review by Barton B. Proger, see 7:938.

[1084]
Goodenough-Harris Drawing Test.

Purpose: Developed for use "as a measure of intellectual maturity."
Population: Ages 3-15.
Publication Dates: 1926-1963.
Scores: Total score only.
Administration: Group or individual.
Price Data, 2002: $70 per 35 test booklets; $67 per set of quality scale cards; $62 per manual (1963, 80 pages); $131 per examiner's kit.
Time: (10-15) minutes.
Comments: Revision and extension of the Goodenough Draw-a-Man Test.
Authors: Florence L. Goodenough and Dale B. Harris (test).
Publisher: PsychCorp, A brand of Harcourt Assessment, Inc.
Cross References: See T5:1097 (14 references), T4:1049 (20 references), 9:441 (6 references), T3:964 (52 references), 8:187 (87 references), and T2:381 (93 references); for reviews by Anne Anastasi and James A. Dunn, and excerpted reviews by M. L. Kellmer Pringle, Marjorie P. Honzik, Carol Hunter, Adolph G. Woltmann, Marvin S. Kaplan, and Mary J. Rouse, see 7:352 (158 references); see also 6:460 (43 references) and 5:335 (34 references); for a review by Naomi Stewart of the original edition, see 4:292 (60 references).

[1085]
The Gordon Diagnostic System.

Purpose: Aids in the evaluation of Attention Deficit Hyperactivity Disorder as well as useful in titrating stimulant medication; is also used in the neuropsychological assessment of disorders such as subclinical hepatic encephalopathy, AIDS dementia complex, post concussion syndrome, closed head injury, and neurotoxicity.
Population: Children, adolescents, and adults.
Publication Dates: [1982–1996].
Acronym: GDS.
Scores: 11 tests: Standard Vigilance Task, Standard Distractibility Test, Delay Task, Preschool Delay Task, Preschool Vigilance "0" Task, Preschool Vigilance "1" Task, Vigilance "3/5" Task, Adult Vigilance Task,

Adult Distractibility Task, Auditory Vigilance Task, Auditory Interference Task.
Administration: Individual.
Price Data, 2005: $1,595 per GDS III microprocessor-based portable unit including all tasks, capacity for automatic output to a printer, instruction manual (1996, 102 pages), interpretive guide, 50 record forms, 4 issues of the ADHD REPORT, and 1-year warranty; $200 plus shipping per 2-month trial rental; $299 plus shipping per optionalGDS compatible printer; $30 per 50 GDS record forms; $225 plus shipping per optional auditory module.
Time: (9) minutes per task.
Comments: A micro-processor-based unit that administers tests of attention and impulse control; FDA approved as a medical device.
Author: Michael Gordon.
Publisher: Gordon Systems, Inc.
Cross References: See T5:1099 (5 references); for reviews by Robert G. Harrington and Judy J. Oehler-Stinnett, see 13:132 (6 references); see also T4:1051 (6 references).

[1086]
Gordon Occupational Check List II.

Purpose: "Designed for persons seeking education and job training below the college level."
Population: Grades 8–12 and adults.
Publication Dates: 1961–1981.
Acronym: GOCL II.
Scores, 6 or 12: Business, Outdoor, Arts, Technology (Mechanical, Industrial), Service, and 6 optional summarization scores (preceding 6 areas).
Administration: Group or individual.
Price Data, 2002: $105 per 35 check lists including manual (1982, 19 pages) and 35 job title supplements; $29 per manual; $36.50 per examination kit including check list, manual, and job title supplement.
Time: (20-25) minutes.
Author: Leonard V. Gordon.
Publisher: PsychCorp, A brand of Harcourt Assessment, Inc.
Cross References: For a review by Donald G. Zytowski, see 9:443; for reviews by John N. McCall and Bert W. Westbrook of an earlier edition, see 7:1019; for reviews by John O. Crites and Kenneth B. Hoyt of an earlier edition, see 6:1056.

[1087]
Gordon Personal Profile—Inventory™ [Revised].

Purpose: Pre-employment assessment for all roles; nine "normal" personality traits are measured.
Population: Grades 9–12 and college and adults.
Publication Dates: 1951–1993.
Acronym: GPP-I.

Administration: Group.
Price Data, 2006: $300 per starter kit including 25 handscorable booklets, 25 machine-scorable booklets, manual, scoring key, and interpretative guide; $85 per package of 25 hand-scorable test booklets; $65 per manual; $45 per score key; $35 per interpretive guide; available online.
Time: (20–25) minutes.
Comments: Combination of Gordon Personal Profile and Gordon Personal Inventory; separate booklet editions still available.
Author: Leonard V. Gordon.
Publisher: Harcourt Assessment, Inc.
  a) GORDON PERSONAL PROFILE.
  Scores, 5: Ascendancy, Responsibility, Emotional Stability, Sociability, Self-Esteem (Total).
  b) GORDON PERSONAL INVENTORY.
  Scores, 4: Cautiousness, Original Thinking, Personal Relations, Vigor.
Cross References: See T5:1101 (2 references); for reviews by Robert M. Guion and Allen K. Hess, see 13:133 (4 references); see also T4:1053 (2 references); for reviews by Douglas Fuchs and Alfred B. Heilbrun, Jr. of an earlier edition, see 10:128 (4 references); see also 9:444 (1 reference), T3:966 (6 references), 8:568 (34 references), 8:569 (52 references), T2:1194 (56 references), and P:93 (23 references); for reviews by Charles F. Dicken and Alfred B. Heilbrun, Jr., see 6:102 (13 references) and 6:103 (25 references); for reviews by Benno G. Fricke and John A. Radcliffe and excerpted reviews by Laurance F. Shaffer and Laurence Siegel, see 5:58 and 5:59 (16 references).

[1088]
Goyer Organization of Ideas Test, Form S (Revised).

Purpose: Intended to assess the ability to organize ideas.
Population: College and adults.
Publication Dates: 1966–1993.
Acronym: GOIT, Form S (Rev.).
Scores: Total score only.
Administration: Individual or group.
Manual: No manual.
Price Data: Available from publisher.
Time: [20–40] minutes.
Author: Robert S. Goyer.
Publisher: Robert S. Goyer.
Cross References: For reviews of an earlier edition by Ric Brown and Robert B. Frary, see 9:445; see also 8:817 (1 reference).

[1089]
Graded Arithmetic-Mathematics Test.

Purpose: Designed to assess overall mathematical attainment.
Population: Ages 5–12.

Publication Dates: 1949–1998.
Scores: Total score only.
Administration: Group.
Price Data, 2002: £9.99 per 20 tests; £9.99 per manual; £10.99 per specimen set.
Time: (30) minutes.
Comments: Oral administration instructions provided.
Authors: P. E. Vernon and K. M. Miller.
Publisher: Hodder & Stoughton Educational [England].
Cross References: For reviews by Kevin D. Crehan and Delwyn L. Harnisch, see 15:110; see T3:972 (3 references) and T2:618 (8 references); for a review by Stanley Nisbet of the original edition, see 5:476.

[1090]
Graded Nonword Reading Test.
Purpose: Designed to "identify reading difficulties associated with impaired phonological skills."
Population: Ages 5-11.
Publication Date: 1996.
Scores: Total score only.
Administration: Individual.
Price Data, 2006: £84 per complete kit including manual (32 pages), 100 scoring sheets, and stimulus book; £26.50 per 100 scoring sheets.
Time: (5) minutes.
Authors: Margaret J. Snowling, Susan E. Stothard, and Janet McLean.
Publisher: Harcourt Assessment [England].

[1091]
Graded Word Spelling Test, Second Edition.
Purpose: Designed to measure spelling achievement.
Population: Ages 6-0 to adults.
Publication Dates: 1977–1998.
Scores: Total Words Correct.
Administration: Group.
Price Data, 2002: £8.99 per test booklet/manual.
Time: (20–30) minutes.
Author: P. E. Vernon.
Publisher: Hodder & Stoughton Educational [England].
Cross References: For a review by Deborah L. Bandalos, see 14:157; see also T5:1105 (1 reference); for a review by Carol E. Westby of an earlier edition, see 12:165 (3 references); see also T4:1056 (2 references).

[1092]
Graduate Management Admission Test.
Purpose: Designed to measure "general verbal and mathmatical skills important in the study of management at the graduate level."
Population: Applicants to study in graduate management education.

Publication Dates: 1954-1994.
Acronym: GMAT.
Scores, 3: Verbal, Quantitative, Total.
Administration: Group.
Price Data: Available from publisher.
Time: 180(210) minutes; 210(235) minutes including Writing Assessment.
Comments: Test administered 4 times annually (January, March, June, October) at centers established by publisher; Analytical Writing Assessment added October 1994.
Author: Graduate Management Admission Council.
Publisher: Pearson VUE.
Cross References: See T5:1107 (10 references) and T4:1058 (6 references); for reviews by Lawrence A. Crosby and James Ledvinka, see 9:447 (1 reference); see also T3:973 (6 references), 8:1074 (11 references), and T2:2325 (5 references); for reviews by Jerome E. Doppelt and Gary R. Hanson of earlier forms, see 7:1080 (10 references).

[1093]
Graduate Program Self-Assessment Service.
Purpose: "To assist colleges and universities that are carrying out departmental or program reviews at the graduate level."
Population: Faculty members, students majoring in the department, and recent graduates.
Publication Date: 1986.
Acronym: GPSA.
Scores, 16: Environment for Learning, Scholarly Excellence, Quality of Teaching, Faculty Concern for Students, Curriculum, Departmental Procedures, Available Resources, Student Satisfaction with Program, Internship/Fieldwork/Clinical Experiences, Resource Accessibility, Employment Assistance, Faculty Work Environment, Faculty Program Involvement, Faculty Research Activities, Faculty Professional Activities, Student Accomplishments.
Administration: Group.
Forms, 6: Faculty, Student, Alumni for both Masters and Doctoral Programs.
Price Data: Available from publisher.
Time: (30–45) minutes.
Author: Educational Testing Service.
Publisher: Educational Testing Service.

[1094]
The Graduate Record Examinations Biochemistry, Cell and Molecular Biology Test.
Purpose: Designed to assess the qualifications of graduate school applicants for advanced study and for fellowships in biochemistry, cell biology, molecular biology, and genetics, along with related programs such as microbiology and genetics.

Population: Graduate school candidates.
Publication Dates: 1990–2006.
Acronym: GRE.
Scores, 4: Biochemistry, Cell Biology, Molecular Biology and Genetics, Total.
Administration: Group.
Price Data: Available from publisher.
Time: (170) minutes.
Comments: Test administered 3 times annually (April, November, December) at centers established by publisher.
Author: Educational Testing Service.
Publisher: Educational Testing Service.
Cross References: For reviews of the GRE program, see 7:667 (1 review) and 5:601 (1 review).

[1095]
The Graduate Record Examinations Biology Test.

Purpose: Designed to assess the qualifications of graduate school applicants for advanced study and for fellowships in Biology.
Population: Graduate school candidates.
Publication Dates: 1939–2006.
Acronym: GRE.
Scores, 4: Cellular and Molecular Biology, Organismal Biology, Ecology and Evolution, Total.
Administration: Group.
Price Data: Available from publisher.
Time: (170) minutes.
Comments: Test administered 3 times annually (April, November, December) at centers established by publisher.
Author: Educational Testing Service.
Publisher: Educational Testing Service.
Cross References: See T5:1110 (1 reference); for a review by Clark W. Horton of an earlier form, see 5:727. For reviews of the GRE program, see 7:667 (1 review) and 5:601 (1 review).

[1096]
The Graduate Record Examinations Chemistry Test.

Purpose: Designed to assess the qualifications of graduate school applicants for advanced study and for fellowships in chemistry.
Population: Graduate school candidates.
Publication Dates: 1939–2006.
Acronym: GRE.
Scores: Total score only.
Administration: Group.
Price Data: Available from publisher.
Time: (170) minutes.
Comments: Test administered 3 times annually (April, November, December) at centers established by publisher.

Author: Educational Testing Service.
Publisher: Educational Testing Service.
Cross References: See T4:1060 (1 reference), 8:852 (1 reference), and 7:848 (1 reference); for a review by Max D. Engelhart of an earlier form, see 6:919. For reviews of the GRE program, see 7:667 (1 review) and 5:601 (1 review).

[1097]
The Graduate Record Examinations Computer Science Test.

Purpose: Designed to assess the qualifications of graduate school applicants for advanced study and for fellowships in computer science.
Population: Graduate school candidates.
Publication Dates: 1976–2006.
Acronym: GRE.
Scores: Total score only.
Administration: Group.
Price Data: Available from publisher.
Time: (170) minutes.
Comments: Test administered 3 times annually (April, November, December) at centers established by publisher.
Author: Educational Testing Service.
Publisher: Educational Testing Service.

[1098]
The Graduate Record Examinations— General Test.

Purpose: "Designed to assess the verbal reasoning, quantitative reasoning, critical thinking, and analytical writing abilities of graduate school applicants."
Population: Graduate school candidates.
Publication Dates: 1949–2006.
Acronym: GRE.
Scores, 3: Verbal Reasoning, Quantitative Reasoning, Analytical Writing.
Administration: Individual.
Price Data: Available from publisher.
Time: (240) minutes for computer-based test.
Comments: Beginning in September 2007, the General Test will be composed of revised Verbal Reasoning, Quantitative Reasoning, and Analytical Writing sections; the same three sections are in the current test; however, each of the sections will be revised to better focus on skills that are necessary for success in graduate school. In addition, the test is changing from an adaptive test, where the questions presented to each examinee vary in part, according to his or her performance, to a linear test, where all examinees testing at the same time receive the same questions.
Author: Educational Testing Service.
Publisher: Educational Testing Service.
Cross References: See T5:1115 (29 references) and T4:1076 (31 references); for reviews by Sanford J.

Cohn and Richard M. Jaeger, see 9:448 (9 references); see also T3:995 (26 references), 8:188 (45 references), T2:382 (15 references), and 7:353 (43 references); for reviews by Robert L. French and Warren W. Willingham of an earlier edition, see 6:461 (17 references); for a review by John T. Dailey, see 5:336 (7 references); for reviews by J. P. Guilford and Carl I. Hovland, see 4:293 (2 references). For reviews of the GRE program, see 7:667 (1 review) and 5:601 (1 review).

[1099]
The Graduate Record Examinations Literature in English Test.

Purpose: Designed to assess the qualifications of graduate school applicants for advanced study and for fellowships in literature in English.
Population: Graduate school candidates.
Publication Dates: 1939–2006.
Acronym: GRE.
Scores: Total score only.
Administration: Group.
Price Data: Available from publisher.
Time: (170) minutes.
Comments: Test administered 3 times annually (April, November, December) at centers established by publisher.
Author: Educational Testing Service.
Publisher: Educational Testing Service.
Cross References: See T5:1118 (1 reference); for a review by Edward M. White, see 8:69; see also 7:219 (1 reference); for a review by Robert C. Pooley of an earlier form, see 5:215. For reviews of the GRE program, see 7:667 (1 review) and 5:601 (1 review).

[1100]
The Graduate Record Examinations Mathematics Test.

Purpose: Designed to assess the qualifications of graduate school applicants for advanced study and for fellowships in mathematics.
Population: Graduate school candidates.
Publication Dates: 1939–2006.
Acronym: GRE.
Scores: Total score only.
Administration: Group.
Price Data: Available from publisher.
Time: (170) minutes.
Comments: Test administered 3 times annually (April, November, December) at centers established by publisher.
Author: Educational Testing Service.
Publisher: Educational Testing Service.
Cross References: See T4:1069 (1 reference) and 8:272 (1 reference); for a review by Paul C. Rosenbloom of an earlier form, see 6:578; for a review by Eric F.

Gardner, see 5:427 (1 reference). For reviews of the GRE program, see 7:667 (1 review) and 5:601 (1 review).

[1101]
The Graduate Record Examinations Physics Test.

Purpose: Designed to assess the qualifications of graduate school applicants for advanced study and for fellowships in physics.
Population: Graduate school candidates.
Publication Dates: 1939–2006.
Acronym: GRE.
Scores: Total score only.
Administration: Group.
Price Data: Available from publisher.
Time: (170) minutes.
Comments: Test administered 3 times annually (April, November, December) at centers established by publisher.
Author: Educational Testing Service.
Publisher: Educational Testing Service.
Cross References: See 8:866 (1 reference); for a review by Theodore G. Phillips, see 6:931; for a review by Leo Nedelsky, see 5:754. For reviews of the GRE program, see 7:667 (1 review) and 5:601 (1 review).

[1102]
The Graduate Record Examinations Psychology Test.

Purpose: Designed to assess the qualifications of graduate school applicants for advanced study and for fellowships in psychology.
Population: Graduate school candidates.
Publication Dates: 1939–2006.
Acronym: GRE.
Scores, 3: Experimental Psychology, Social Psychology, Total.
Administration: Group.
Price Data: Available from publisher.
Time: (170) minutes.
Comments: Test administered 3 times annually (April, November, December) at centers established by publisher.
Author: Educational Testing Service.
Publisher: Educational Testing Service.
Cross References: See T5:1122 (2 references), T4:1073 (3 references), 8:461 (3 references), T2:1005 (2 references), and 7:644 (9 references); for a review by Harold Seashore of an earlier form, see 5:583. For reviews of the GRE program, see 7:667 (1 review) and 5:601 (1 review).

[1103]
Graduate Record Examinations: Subject Tests.

Purpose: Designed to assess the qualifications of graduate school applicants in specific fields of study.
Population: Graduate school candidates.

Publication Dates: 1939–2006.
Acronym: GRE.
Scores: 8 tests: Biochemistry/Cell and Molecular Biology, Biology, Chemistry, Computer Science, Literature in English, Mathematics, Physics, Psychology.
Administration: Group.
Price Data: Available from publisher.
Time: (170) minutes.
Comments: Test administered 3 times annually (April, November, December) at centers established by publisher.
Author: Educational Testing Service.
Publisher: Educational Testing Service.
Cross References: See T4:1075 (2 references), T3:994 (5 references), and 8:476 (6 references); for a review by Leona E. Tyler of an earlier program, see 7:667 (10 references); see also 6:762 (1 reference); for a review by Harold Seashore, see 5:601 (12 references); see also 4:527 (24 references).

[1104]
Grammatical Analysis of Elicited Language—Pre-Sentence Level.

Purpose: Designed to provide in-depth grammatical analysis of children's expressive language.
Population: Hearing-impaired children ages 3–6.
Publication Date: 1983.
Acronym: GAEL-P.
Scores: 3 sections (Readiness Skills, Single Words, Word Combinations) yielding 3 scores: Comprehension, Prompted Production, Imitated Production.
Administration: Individual.
Price Data, 2005: $400 per complete kit including manual (81 pages), scoring forms, videotape, and toys; $10 per videotape; $19.95 per additional manual; $12 per 25 additional record forms.
Time: [60] minutes.
Authors: Jean S. Moog, Victoria J. Kozak, and Ann E. Geers.
Publisher: Central Institute for the Deaf.
Cross References: See T5:1126 (3 references) and T4:1078 (1 reference).

[1105]
Grandparent Strengths and Needs Inventory.

Purpose: "To help grandparents recognize their favorable qualities and identify aspects of their family relationships in which further growth is needed."
Population: Grandparents of children 6 and over.
Publication Date: 1993.
Acronym: GSNI.
Scores, 6: Satisfaction, Success, Teaching, Difficulty, Frustration, Information Needs.
Administration: Group.
Price Data, 2005: $78.75 per complete kit including 20 identification forms and 20 inventory booklets

each: grandparent, parent, and grandchild versions, 20 profiles, and manual (20 pages).
Foreign Language Edition: Spanish version available.
Time: Administration time not reported.
Comments: Parent and grandchild inventories included for comparison purposes.
Authors: Robert D. Strom and Shirley K. Strom.
Publisher: Scholastic Testing Service, Inc.
Cross References: See T5:1128 (4 references); for reviews by Roger A. Boothroyd and Dianna L. Newman, see 13:134 (2 references).

[1106]
Gravidometer.

Purpose: Measures knowledge about human pregnancy.
Population: Adolescents and adults.
Publication Dates: 1974–1988.
Scores: Total score only.
Administration: Group.
Manual: No manual.
Price Data, 2005: $2 per test.
Time: [10] minutes.
Comments: Supplementary article available.
Author: Panos D. Bardis.
Publisher: Donna Bardis.

[1107]
Gray Diagnostic Reading Tests—Second Edition.

Purpose: Designed as "a comprehensive measure of reading skills … to determine strengths and weaknesses, document progress in reading programs, [and] help diagnose specific reading problems."
Population: Ages 6-0 to 13-11.
Publication Dates: 1991-2004.
Acronym: GDRT-2.
Scores: 7 subtests: Letter/Word Recognition, Phonetic Analysis, Reading Vocabulary, Meaningful Reading, Listening Vocabulary, Rapid Naming, Phonological Awareness; and 3 composites: Decoding, Comprehension, General Reading.
Administration: Individual.
Forms: 2 equivalent forms: A, B.
Price Data, 2006: $250 per complete kit including examiner's manual (2004, 113 pages), Adventures in Fancyland Storybook, Student Book Form A, Student Book Form B, 25 record Forms A, 25 record Forms B, and storage box; $73 per examiner's manual; $50 per Student Book Form A; $50 per Student Book Form B; $5 per Adventures in Fancyland Storybook; $47 per 25 record Forms A; $47 per 25 record Forms B.
Time: (45-60) minutes.
Comments: Norm-referenced; revision of the Gray Oral Reading Tests-Diagnostic.

Authors: Brian R. Bryant, J. Lee Wiederholt, and Diane Pedrotty Bryant.
Publisher: PRO-ED.
Cross References: See T5: 1130 (2 references); for reviews by William R. Merz, Sr. and Steven A. Stahl of the original edition, see 11:149 (1 reference).

[1108]
Gray Oral Reading Tests, Fourth Edition.

Purpose: Designed "to provide a measure of growth in oral reading and an aid in the diagnosis of oral reading difficulties."
Population: Ages 6-0 to 18-11.
Publication Dates: 1967–2001.
Acronym: GORT-4.
Scores, 4: Rate, Accuracy, Fluency, Comprehension.
Administration: Individual.
Forms, 2: A, B.
Price Data, 2006: $225 per kit including 25 each of profile/examiner record forms (Form A and Form B), student book, and examiner's manual (2001, 146 pages); $50 per 25 record forms (specify Form A or B); $50 per student book; $80 per examiner's manual.
Time: (20–30) minutes.
Authors: J. Lee Wiederholt and Brian R. Bryant.
Publisher: PRO-ED.
Cross References: For reviews by Nancy L. Crumpton and Marie Miller-Whitehead, see 15:111; see T5:1131 (18 references); for reviews by John D. King and Deborah King Kundert of an earlier edition, see 12:166 (5 references); see also T4:1084 (9 references); for reviews by Julia A. Hickman and Robert J. Tierney of an earlier edition, see 10:131 (15 references).

[1109]
Gray Silent Reading Tests.

Purpose: "Designed to assess silent reading comprehension."
Population: Ages 7–25.
Publication Date: 2000.
Acronym: GSRT.
Scores: Silent Reading Quotient.
Administration: Group.
Forms, 2: A, B.
Price Data, 2006: $160 per complete kit including 25 profile/response forms, 10 each of reading book Forms A and B, and manual (101 pages); $25 per 25 profile/response forms; $35 per 10 reading books (specify Form A or Form B); $71 per manual.
Time: (15–30) minutes.
Comments: Developed to be used as an adjunct to the Gray Oral Reading Tests (1108) or independently.
Authors: J. Lee Wiederholt and Ginger Blalock.
Publisher: PRO-ED.
Cross References: For reviews by Harold R. Keller and Darrell L. Sabers, see 15:112.

[1110]
Greenspan Social-Emotional Growth Chart.

Purpose: Designed to help determine a child's social-emotional development and growth.
Population: Birth to 3-5 years.
Publication Date: 2004.
Scores, 3: Total Growth Chart Score, Sensory Processing Score, Highest Stage Mastered.
Administration: Individual.
Price Data, 2006: $99 per complete kit including manual, 25 caregiver reports, and 25 questionnaires; $80 per manual; $25 per 25 caregiver reports; $35 per 25 questionnaires.
Time: (5-15) minutes.
Comments: It is recommended that the questionnaire be administered at each developmental stage.
Author: Stanley I. Greenspan.
Publisher: PsychCorp, A brand of Harcourt Assessment, Inc.

[1111]
Gregorc Style Delineator.

Purpose: "Designed to aid an individual to recognize and identify the channels through which he/she receives and expresses information."
Population: Adults.
Publication Dates: 1982–2002.
Scores, 4: Concrete Sequential score, Abstract Sequential score, Abstract Random score, Concrete Random score.
Administration: Group.
Price Data, 2002: $69.95 per sample set including An Adult's Guide to Style (2002, 110 pages), Mind Styles Model: Theory Principles and Practice (1998, 28 pages), Mind Styles FAQs Book (2001, 152 pages), Relating with Style (1997, 170 pages), test, Extends Charts, Phoenix bookmark, and Careful Us audio tape; $15.95 per technical manual (1982, 46 pages); $59.50 per 25 instrument packets or $29.95 per 10 instrument packets including guidelines for group administration; $9.95 per audiocassette on careful use; $17.95 per An Adult's Guide to Style; $19.95 per Mind Styles FAQs Book; $19.95 per Relating with Style; $7.50 per Mind Styles Model: Theory, Principles, and Practice.
Time: 3 minutes.
Comments: Self-assessment instrument.
Author: Anthony F. Gregorc.
Publisher: Gregorc Associates, Inc.
Cross References: See T5:1132 (1 reference); for reviews by Stephen L. Benton and Trenton R. Ferro, see 12:167 (3 references); see also T4:1086 (2 references).

[1112]
Grid Test of Schizophrenic Thought Disorder.

Purpose: "Developed to detect the presence of schizophrenic thought disorder."

Population: Adults.
Publication Date: 1967.
Acronym: GTSTD.
Scores, 2: Intensity, Consistency.
Administration: Individual.
Price Data: Available from publisher.
Time: (15–25) minutes.
Comments: 1 form (set of 8 photographs).
Authors: D. Bannister and Fay Fransella.
Publisher: Psychological Test Publications [England] [No reply from publisher; status unknown].
Cross References: See T4:1087 (4 references) and T3:1009 (3 references); for a review by Robert W. Payne, see 8:571 (30 references); see also T2:1198 (8 references); for a review by David Jones, see 7:84 (7 references); see also P:96 (8 references).

[1113]
Griffiths Mental Development Scales [Revised].

Purpose: Designed to measure trends of development that are indicative of intelligence/mental growth.
Publication Dates: 1951–1996.
Administration: Individual.
Forms, 2: Scale 1 (0–2 years), Scale 2 (2–8 years).
Restricted Distribution: Restricted to persons who qualify by attending an approved course; details available from distributor.
Price Data, 2001: £260 per Scale 1; £315 per Scale 2; £2.20 per Scale 2 record book; £1.65 per Scale 1 record form; £24.50 per The Abilities of Babies (1976, 239 pages); £24.50 per The Abilities of Young Children (1996, 114 pages); £39.50 per Scale 1 manual; £29.50 for 8 additional test items for 1996 Revised Scale 1.
Authors: Ruth Griffiths and Michael Huntley (Birth-2 years Scale [Scale 1] and manual, 1996 Revision).
Publisher: The Test Agency Limited [England] [No reply from publisher; status unknown].
a) SCALE 1: BIRTH TO 2 YEARS.
Population: Ages 0–2 years.
Publication Dates: 1951–1996.
Scores, 6: Locomotor, Personal-Social, Hearing and Speech, Eye and Hand, Performance, Total.
Time: (20–40) minutes.
b) SCALE 2: (2 TO 8 YEARS).
Population: Ages 2–8 years.
Publication Dates: 1951–1978.
Scores, 7: Same as Scale 1 above plus Practical Reasoning.
Time: Administration time not reported.
Cross References: See T5:1134 (8 references), T4:1088 (10 references), and 9:450 (1 reference); for a review by C. B. Hindley of an earlier version of Scale 2, see 6:523 (4 references); for a review by Nancy Bayley of Scale 1, see 5:404 (3 references).

[1114]
Grooved Pegboard Test.

Purpose: To assess manipulative dexterity.
Population: Ages 5 to 8-12, 9 to 14-12, 15 to adult.
Publication Date: 1989.
Scores, 3: Total Time, Number of "Drops," Total Pegs Correctly Placed.
Administration: Individual.
Price Data: Available from publisher.
Time: Trial discontinued after 5 minutes.
Comments: Ages 5 to 8-12 only complete first two rows of the Pegboard; "this test requires more complex visual-motor coordination than most pegboards."
Author: Ronald Trites (manual).
Publisher: Lafayette Instrument.
Cross References: See T5:1135 (27 references); for reviews by Roderick K. Mahurin and Erin McClure and Richard K. Stratton, see 12:170 (14 references); see also T4:1089 (2 references).

[1115]
Group Achievement Identification Measure.

Purpose: "To determine the degree to which children exhibit the characteristics of underachievers so that preventative or curative efforts may be administered."
Population: Grades 5-12.
Publication Date: 1986.
Acronym: GAIM.
Scores, 6: Competition, Responsibility, Achievement Communication, Independence/Dependence, Respect/Dominance, Total.
Administration: Group.
Price Data, 2005: $15 per specimen set; $120 per class set of 30 inventories including prepaid computer scoring by publisher; manual for administration and interpretation (12 pages) included with test orders.
Time: (30) minutes.
Comments: Student self-report inventory.
Author: Sylvia B. Rimm.
Publisher: Educational Assessment Service Inc.
Cross References: See T5:1136 (1 reference); for reviews by Robert K. Gable and Jeffrey Jenkins, see 11:151.

[1116]
Group Cohesiveness: A Study of Group Morale.

Purpose: Designed to assess group cohesiveness.
Population: Adults.
Publication Dates: 1957–1958.
Acronym: GC.
Scores, 5: Satisfaction of Individual Motives, Satisfaction of Interpersonal Relations, Homogeneity of Attitude, Satisfaction With Leadership, Total.
Administration: Group.
Price Data: Available from publisher.

Time: (10–15) minutes.
Comments: Self-administered.
Author: Bernard Goldman.
Publisher: Psychometric Affiliates.
Cross References: See T2:1199 (1 reference) and P:97; for reviews by Eric F. Gardner and Cecil A. Gibb, see 6:104 (1 reference).

[1117]
Group Diagnostic Reading Aptitude and Achievement Tests.

Purpose: Diagnose whether children need remedial work in reading.
Population: Grades 3–9.
Publication Date: 1939.
Scores, 15: Reading (Paragraph Understanding, Speed), Word Discrimination (Vowels, Consonants, Reversals, Additions and Omissions), Arithmetic, Spelling, Visual Ability (Letter Memory, Form Memory), Auditory Ability (Letter Memory, Discrimination and Orientation), Motor Ability (Copying Text, Crossing Out Letters), Vocabulary.
Administration: Group.
Manual: No manual.
Price Data: Available from publisher.
Time: (60–70) minutes.
Authors: Marion Monroe and Eva Edith Sherman.
Publisher: C. H. Nevins Printing Co.
Cross References: See T5:1138 (2 references) and T4:1092 (1 reference).

[1118]
Group Diagnostic Reading Aptitude and Achievement Tests, Intermediate Form.

Purpose: Designed to assess reading achievement and to diagnose reading problems.
Population: Grades 3–9.
Publication Date: [Orig. 1937].
Scores, 13: Achievement [Reading (Paragraph Understanding, Speed, Word Discrimination), Arithmetic, Spelling], Diagnostic [Word Discrimination Errors, Visual (Letter Memory, Form Memory), Auditory (Letter Memory, Discrimination and Orientation), Motor (Copying Text, Cross Out Letters), Language-Vocabulary].
Administration: Group.
Price Data: Available from publisher.
Time: (40) minutes (includes both timed and untimed tests).
Authors: Marion Monroe and Eva Edith Sherman.
Publisher: C. H. Nevins Printing Co.
Cross References: For reviews by Deborah King Kundert and Margaret R. Rogers, see 12:170.

[1119]
Group Embedded Figures Test.

Purpose: Developed to evaluate field-dependence.
Population: Older children, adolescents, adults.

Publication Date: 1971.
Acronym: GEFT.
Scores: Total score only.
Administration: Group.
Price Data, 2006: $40 per sampler set including manual (32 pages); $50 per 25 booklets; $10 per scoring key.
Time: (20) minutes.
Comments: Adaptation of the individually administered Embedded Figures Test (T6:900); manual is a combined manual for this test and the Embedded Figures Test.
Authors: Philip K. Oltman, Evelyn Raskin, Herman A. Witkin, and Stephen A. Karp (manual).
Publisher: Mind Garden, Inc.
Cross References: See T5:1140 (60 references), T4:1094 (95 references), 9:452 (41 references), and T3:1013 (88 references); for reviews by Leonard D. Goodstein and Alfred E. Hall, see 8:572 (47 references); see also T2:1201 (3 references); for references to reviews of the individual test, see 8:548.

[1120]
Group Environment Scale, Third Edition.

Purpose: Designed to "measure the actual, preferred, and expected, social environments of task-oriented, social, psychotherapy, and self-help groups."
Population: Group members and leaders; clinicians, consultants, and program evaluators.
Publication Dates: 1974–2002.
Acronym: GES.
Scores, 10: Cohesion, Leader Support, Expressiveness, Independence, Task Orientation, Self-Discovery, Anger and Aggression, Order and Organization, Leader Control, Innovation.
Administration: Group.
Forms, 3: Real (R), Ideal (I), Expectations (E).
Price Data: Available from publisher (www.mindgarden.com).
Time: Administration time not reported.
Comments: A component of the Social Climate Scales.
Author: Rudolf H. Moos.
Publisher: Mind Garden, Inc.
Cross References: See T5:1141 (5 references) and T4:1095 (5 references); for a review by Arthur M. Nezu of an earlier edition, see 10:132 (6 references); for reviews by Michael J. Curtis and Robert J. Illback, see 9:435 (4 references); for reviews by David P. Campbell and Robyn M. Dawes, see 8:573; see also T3:1015 (1 reference); for a review of the Social Climate Scales, see 8:681.

[1121]
Group Inventory for Finding Creative Talent.

Purpose: "Identify students with attitudes and values usually associated with creativity."
Population: Grades K-2, 3-4, 5-6.

Publication Dates: 1976-1980.
Acronym: GIFT.
Scores, 4: Imagination, Independence, Many Interests, Total.
Administration: Group or individual.
Levels, 3: Primary (Grades K-2), Elementary (Grades 3-4), Upper Elementary (Grades 5-6).
Price Data, 2005: $100 per 30 test booklets and scoring service (scoring must be done by publisher); $15 per specimen set.
Foreign Language Edition: Spanish edition available.
Time: (20-45) minutes.
Author: Sylvia B. Rimm.
Publisher: Educational Assessment Service Inc.
Cross References: See T5:1142 (5 references); for reviews by Patricia L. Dwinell and Dan Wright, see 9:454 (1 reference); see also T3:1016 (1 reference).

[1122]
Group Inventory For Finding Interest.

Purpose: "Identify students with attitudes and interests usually associated with creativity."
Population: Grades 6-1.
Publication Dates: 1979-1980.
Acronym: GIFFI.
Scores: 5 dimensional scores: Creative Arts and Writing, Challenge-Inventiveness, Confidence, Imagination, Many Interests.
Administration: Group or individual.
Levels, 2: Level 1: Grades 6-9; Level 2: Grades 9-12.
Price Data, 2005: $120 per 30 test booklets and scoring service (scoring must be done by publisher); $15 per specimen set.
Foreign Language Edition: Spanish edition available.
Time: (20-40) minutes.
Authors: Sylvia B. Rimm and Gary A. Davis.
Publisher: Educational Assessment Service Inc.
Cross References: See T5:1143 (2 references); for a review by M. O'Neal Weeks, see 9:455 (1 reference).

[1123]
Group Literacy Assessment.

Purpose: To sample children's overall skills level with written material.
Population: End of junior school and beginning of secondary school.
Publication Dates: 1981–1999.
Acronym: GLA.
Scores, 3: Proof-Reading, Fill the Gaps, Total.
Administration: Group.
Price Data, 2002: £8.50 per 20 tests; £8.99 per manual (16 pages); £9.99 per specimen set.
Time: 16(30) minutes.

Author: Frank A. Spooncer.
Publisher: Hodder & Stoughton Educational [England].
Cross References: For a review by Gail E. Tompkins of an earlier edition, see 9:456.

[1124]
Group Mathematics Assessment and Diagnostic Evaluation.

Purpose: A group-administered diagnostic mathematics test that measures individual skills in key areas, including concepts, operations, computation, and applications.
Population: Grades K–12.
Publication Date: 2004.
Acronym: G•MADE.
Administration: Group.
Forms: 2 parallel forms, A or B, for each of 9 levels.
Price Data, 2006: $109.99–$182.99 per Form A classroom sets (specify Level) including teacher's manual (102 pages), hand-scoring templates, answer sheets, and 30 student booklets; $200–$300.99 per Forms A & B classroom sets (specify Level); $29.99 per norms supplement (specify age-based or grade-based out-of-level); $32.99 per technical manual (122 pages); $299.99 per Scoring and Reporting Software v. 1.1 Single PC Version; $1,995.99 per Scoring and Reporting Software v. 1.1 Single PC Scanning Version; $109.99 per Resource Library (specify Level).
Time: (50–90) minutes per level.
Author: Kathleen T. Williams.
Publisher: Pearson Assessments (originally published by AGS Publishing, acquired by Pearson in 2005).
    a) LEVEL R.
    Population: Ages 5-0 to 7-11.
    Scores, 3: Concepts and Communication, Process and Applications, Total.
    b) LEVEL 1.
    Population: Ages 6-0 to 8-11.
    Scores, 4: Same as *a* above plus Operations and Computation.
    c) LEVEL 2.
    Population: Ages 6-0 to 9-11.
    Scores, 4: Same as *b* above.
    d) LEVEL 3.
    Population: Ages 7-0 to 10-11.
    Scores, 4: Same as *b*.
    e) LEVEL 4.
    Population: Ages 8-0 to 12-11.
    Scores, 4: Same as *b*.
    f) LEVEL 5.
    Population: Ages 9-0 to 18-0 and above.
    Scores, 4: Same as *b*.
    g) LEVEL 6.
    Population: Ages 10-0 to 18-0 and above.
    Scores, 4: Same as *b*.

h) LEVEL M.
Population: Ages 11-0 to 18-0 and above.
Scores, 4: Same as *b*.
i) LEVEL H.
Population: Ages 12-0 to 18-0 and above.
Scores, 4: Same as *b*.

[1125]
Group Mathematics Test, Third Edition.

Purpose: General assessment of mathematical understanding.
Population: Ages 6.5-8.10 and older underachieving students.
Publication Dates: 1970–1996.
Acronym: GMT.
Scores, 3: Oral, Computation, Total.
Administration: Group.
Forms, 2: A, B.
Price Data, 2002: £7.99 per 20 tests (Form A or B); £8.99 per manual; £9.99 per specimen set.
Time: (40–50) minutes.
Author: D. Young.
Publisher: Hodder & Stoughton Educational [England].
Cross References: See T5:1145 (2 references) and T4:1049 (1 reference); for reviews by Mary Kay Corbitt and Douglas H. Crawford, see 9:457; for a review by John Cook of an earlier edition, see 8:273.

[1126]
Group Process Questionnaire.

Purpose: "Designed to help groups assess how effective they are."
Population: Adults.
Publication Date: 1988.
Scores, 29 to 145: My Rating, Group Rating, and How I Did scores for Behavior Scale (Task Behavior, Maintenance Behavior), for Total Scale, and for 12 optional categories (Initiating, Seeking Information or Opinions, Giving Information or Opinions, Clarifying and Elaborating, Summarizing, Consensus-Testing, Listening, Harmonizing, Gatekeeping, Encouraging, Compromising, Standard Setting/Testing), and My Rating and Group Rating scores for 5 additional optional categories (Leadership, Time Utilization, Results, Acceptance, Inclusion).
Administration: Group.
Price Data: Available from publisher.
Time: (60) minutes.
Comments: Scale for ratings by group members and for self-ratings.
Authors: Richard Hill, D. Joseph Fisher, Tom Webber, and Kathleen A. Fisher.
Publisher: Aviat.

[1127]
Group Reading Assessment and Diagnostic Evaluation.

Purpose: Designed to pinpoint students' individual reading levels.
Population: Pre-K through adult.
Publication Dates: 2001-2002.
Administration: Individual or group.
Levels, 11: P (pre-kindergarten and kindergarten), K (kindergarten and first grade), 1 (kindergarten through second grade), 2, 3, 4, 5, 6, M (middle school, grades 5–9), H (high school, grades 9–12), A (grades 11 to postsecondary).
Forms, 2: Form A, Form B.
Price Data, 2006: $210.99 per Levels 1, 2, or 3 Classroom Set with Forms A and B including 30 each of Form A and Form B student booklets, 1 teacher's administration manual, and 2 scoring and interpretative manual; $222.99 per Levels P and K Classroom Set with Forms A and B; $312.99 per Levels 4, 5, 6, M, H, or A Classroom Set with Forms A and B; $30.99 per 10 student booklets (each of Levels P–A); $9.99 per 10 answer sheets (Levels 4–A); $43.99 per Forms a and B hand-scoring templates (each of Levels 4–A); $11.99 per teacher's administration manual (each of Levels P–A); $19.99 per scoring and interpretative manual (each of Levels P–A); $32.99 per technical manual (for all levels); $32.99 per Out of Level Norms Supplement (205 page book of norm tables); $109.99 per GRADE Resource Library (each of Levels P–A); $299.99 per GRADE Scoring and Reporting Software (single PC version); $1,995.99 per GRADE Scoring and Reporting Software (single PC scanning version).
Time: (45–90) minutes.
Comments: May be hand scored or computer scored.
Author: Kathleen T. Williams.
Publisher: Pearson Assessments (originally published by AGS Publishing, acquired by Pearson in 2005).
a) LEVEL P.
Scores, 8: Picture Matching, Picture Differences, Verbal Concepts, Picture Categories, Sound Matching, Rhyming, Listening Comprehension, Total Score.
b) LEVEL K.
Scores, 9: Sound Matching, Rhyming, Print Awareness, Letter Recognition, Same and Different Words, Phoneme-Grapheme Correspondence, Word Reading, Listening Comprehension, Total Score.
c) LEVEL 1, 2.
Scores, 6: Word Reading, Word Meaning, Sentence Comprehension, Passage Comprehension, Listening Comprehension, Total Score.
d) LEVEL 3.
Scores, 6: Word Reading, Vocabulary, Sentence Comprehension, Passage Comprehension, Listening Comprehension, Total Score.

e) LEVEL 4–A.

Scores, 5: Vocabulary, Sentence Comprehension, Passage Comprehension, Listening Comprehension, Total Score.

Cross References: For reviews by Mark H. Fugate and Betsy B. Waterman, see 15:113.

[1128]
Group Reading Test, Fourth Edition.

Purpose: Designed to measure "the reading of single words and of simple sentences."

Population: Ages 6:4 to 8:11 and less able children 8:0 to 11:11.

Publication Dates: 1968–1999.

Acronym: GRT.

Scores: Total score only.

Administration: Group.

Forms, 2: A, B

Price Data, 2002: £7.99 per 20 Form A or Form B; £9.99 per manual (1999, 27 pages); £4.99 per template A or B; £10.99 per specimen set.

Time: (20) minutes.

Author: Dennis Young.

Publisher: Hodder & Stoughton Educational [England].

Cross References: For reviews by Gretchen Owens and John W. Young, see 14:158; for reviews by William R. Merz, Sr., and Diane J. Sawyer of an earlier edition, see 12:171 (1 reference); see also T4:1102 (4 references); for reviews by Patrick Groff and Douglas A. Pidgeon of the Second Edition, see 9:458 (1 reference); for a review by Ralph D. Dutch of the original edition, see 8:729.

[1129]
Group Reading Test II (6–14).

Purpose: Designed to monitor progress in reading and to screen and identify pupils who require further diagnostic assessment.

Population: Ages 6 years to 15 years 9 months.

Publication Dates: 1985–2000.

Acronym: GRT II(6–14).

Scores, 2: Sentence Completion, Context Comprehension.

Administration: Group.

Forms, 6: Forms A and B, Forms C and D, and Forms X and Y.

Price Data, 2004: Price data for teacher's guide (2000, 75 pages), At-a-Glance Guide, group record sheet, and record forms available from publisher.

Time: (30) minutes.

Comments: Computer and publisher scoring service available; originally published as Macmillan Group Reading Test.

Author: NFER-Nelson Publishing Co., Ltd.

Publisher: NFER-Nelson Publishing Co., Ltd. [England].

Cross References: For reviews by C. Dale Carpenter and Alice J. Corkill, see 16:98; for reviews by Koressa Kutsick and Gail E. Tompkins of the Macmillan Reading Test, see 10:179.

[1130]
Group Shorr Imagery Test.

Purpose: Designed as a projective measure of personality conflict.

Population: Adults.

Publication Date: 1977.

Acronym: GSIT.

Scores, 6: Item scores in 5 areas (Human, Animal, Inanimate, Botanical, Others) plus Total score for Conflict.

Administration: Group.

Price Data: Available from publisher.

Time: Administration time not reported.

Comments: Tape cassette used for administration; group form of the Shorr Imagery Test (2330).

Author: Joseph E. Shorr.

Publisher: Institute for Psychoimagination Therapy.

[1131]
Group Styles Inventory.

Purpose: Designed to "assess the particular style or styles of your work group following a simulated or real problem-solving session or meeting."

Population: Group members.

Publication Dates: 1990–1993.

Acronym: GSI.

Scores: 12 styles in 3 general clusters: Constructive (Achievement, Self-Actualizing, Humanistic-Encouraging, Affiliative), Passive/Defensive (Approval, Conventional, Dependent, Avoidance), Aggressive/Defensive (Oppositional, Power, Competitive, Perfectionistic).

Administration: Group.

Price Data: Price information for test materials including Participant Guide (50 pages) and Leader's Guide (53 pages) available from publisher.

Time: [10–15] minutes.

Authors: Robert A. Cooke and J. Clayton Lafferty.

Publisher: Human Synergistics International.

Cross References: For reviews by Lawrence M. Aleamoni and Bert A. Goldman, see 12:172.

[1132]
Group Tests of Musical Abilities.

Purpose: Developed to measure an individual's musical ability level.

Population: Ages 7–14.

Publication Date: 1988.

Scores, 2: Pitch, Pulse.

Administration: Group.

Price Data: Price information available from publisher for starter pack including cassette tape, 25 answer sheets, and manual (25 pages).

Time: [15–20] minutes.
Comments: A good quality audiocassette player is needed to administer test.
Author: Janet Mills.
Publisher: NFER-Nelson Publishing Co., Ltd. [England].
Cross References: For reviews by J. David Boyle and Annabel J. Cohen, see 12:173.

[1133]
Gudjonsson Suggestibility Scales.

Purpose: "Developed in order to measure objectively the vulnerability or proneness of people to give erroneous accounts when interviewed," particularly in forensic contents.
Population: Ages 6 and over.
Publication Date: 1997.
Scores, 7: Immediate Recall, Delayed Recall, Yield 1, Yield 2, Shift, Total Suggestibility, Confabulation.
Administration: Individual.
Forms: 2 parallel forms: GSS1, GSS2.
Price Data: Available from publisher.
Time: Administration time not reported.
Author: Gisli H. Gudjonsson.
Publisher: Taylor & Francis [England].

[1134]
Guide for Occupational Exploration Interest Inventory, Second Edition

Purpose: Designed to help people identify their interests, then use this information to explore career, learning, and lifestyle alternatives.
Population: High school through adult
Publication Date: 2002.
Acronym: GOEII.
Scores: Arts/Entertainment/Media, Science/Math/Engineering, Plants and Animals, Law/Law Enforcement/Public Safety, Mechanics/Installers/Repairers, Construction/ Mining/Drilling, Transportation, Industrial Production, Business Detail, Sales and Marketing, Recreation/Travel/Other Personal Services, Education and Social Service, General Management and Support, Medical and Health Services.
Administration: Group or individual.
Price Data, 2006: $29.95 per 25 inventories including copy of administrator's guide (12 pages).
Time: (20-40) minutes.
Comments: Self-administered and self-scored.
Author: J. Michael Farr.
Publisher: JIST Publishing, Inc.
Cross References: For reviews by M. David Miller and Jennifer M. Bergeron and by William I. Sauser, Jr., see 16:99.

[1135]
Guide to the Assessment of Test Session Behavior for the WISC-III and the WIAT.

Purpose: Assesses "whether a child's behavior during WISC-III and/or WIAT testing differs substantially from the behavior of other children of the same age."
Population: Ages 6–16.
Publication Date: 1992.
Acronym: GATSB.
Scores: 4 scales: Avoidance, Inattentiveness, Uncooperative Mood, Total Score.
Administration: Individual.
Price Data, 2002: $80 per complete kit including 25 ready-score answer forms and manual (88 pages); $36 per 25 ready-score answer documents; $140 per 100 ready-score answer documents; $44 per manual.
Time: (5–10) minutes.
Authors: Joseph J. Glutting and Tom Oakland.
Publisher: PsychCorp, A brand of Harcourt Assessment, Inc.
Cross References: See T5:1155 (1 reference); for reviews by Alice J. Corkill and Eleanor E. Sanford, see 13:135.

[1136]
Hall Occupational Orientation Inventory, Form II and Young Adult/College/Adult Form (Fourth Edition).

Purpose: Designed to help individuals understand their values, needs, interests, and preferred life-styles, and how these relate to career goals and future educational plans.
Population: Junior high–adults, high school–adults.
Publication Dates: 1968–2002.
Administration: Group or individual.
Price Data, 2005: $20.10 per Choosing: Your Way, a supplementary career reader (2000, 40 pages); $20.10 per Counselor/User's manual (2000, 59 pages); $16.50 per sample set including 1 inventory booklet, 1 interpretive manual, and 1 response sheet (Young Adult/College/Adult Form); $24 per sample set with Choosing: Your Way; $24 per sample set with Counselor/User's Manual(Young Adult/College/Adult Form); $42.20 per sample set with both Choosing: Your Way and Counselor/User's manual (Young Adult/College/Adult Form); $19.50 per sample set (Form II); $26.50 per sample set with Professional Manual (Form II).
Time: (45–60) minutes.
Author: Lacy G. Hall.
Publisher: Scholastic Testing Service, Inc.
    a) YOUNG ADULT/COLLEGE/ADULT FORM.
    Population: High school–adults.
    Publication Dates: 1968–2002.
    Scores, 29: Creativity-Independence, Information-Knowledge, Belongingness, Security, Aspira-

tion, Esteem, Self-Actualization, Personal Satis-faction, Routine-Dependence, People-Social-Ac-commodating, Data-Information, Things-Physi-cal, People-Business-Influencing, Ideas-Scientific, Aesthetics-Arts, Geographic Location, Abilities, Monetary-Compensation, Workplace, Coworkers, Time, Qualifications, Risk, Subjective External Authority, Objective External Authority, Subjec-tive Internal Authority, Shaping/Autonomy/and Self-Empowerment, Interdependent, Procrastina-tion.

b) FORM II.

Population: Junior high students–adults.

Publication Dates: 1968–1989.

Scores, 15: Creativity-Independence, Infor-mation-Knowledge, Belongingness, Security, As-piration, Esteem, Self-Actualization, Personal Satisfaction, Routine-Dependence, People-So-cial-Accommodating, Data-Information, Things-Physical, People-Business-Influencing, Ideas-Scientific, Aesthetics-Arts.

Cross References: For reviews by John S. Geisler and Joseph G. Law, Jr., see 16:100; for reviews by Gregory Schraw and Hilda Wing of an earlier edition, see 12:175 (1 reference); see also T3:1051 (4 refer-ences); for reviews by Robert H. Dolliver and Austin C. Frank of an earlier edition, see 8:1003 (5 references); see also T2:2187 (3 references); for a review by Donald G. Zytowski of the original edition, see 7:104 (4 refer-ences).

[1137]

Halstead-Reitan Neuropsychological Test Battery.

Purpose: "Developed to evaluate the brain-behavior functioning of individuals."

Population: Ages 5-8, 9-14, 15 and over.

Publication Dates: 1979-1993.

Scores: 1 combined score for each battery and for areas of function, plus scores for individual tests.

Price Data: Available from publisher.

Comments: Consists of three neuropsychological test batteries, one for each age level; each battery includes a Neuropsychological Deficit Scale, which provides normative ranges for each test, for areas of function, and for the entire battery in addition to cut-off scores (brain impairment versus normal brain status) for each variable, area, and summary score.

Author: Ralph M. Reitan.

Publisher: Reitan Neuropsychology Laboratory/Press.

a) REITAN-INDIANA NEUROPSYCHOLOGICAL TEST BATTERY FOR YOUNG CHILDREN.

Population: Ages 5-8.

  1) *Category.*

  Comments: Projection box with slide pro-jector and slides necessary for administration.

  2) *Tactual Performance.*

  Scores, 3: Total Time, Memory, Localiza-tion.

  Comments: 6-figure board.

  3) *Finger Tapping.*

  Comments: Electronic finger tapper neces-sary for administration.

  4) *Matching Pictures.*

  5) *Individual Performance.*

  Subtests, 4: Matching Figures, Star, Match-ing V's, Concentric Squares.

  6) *Marching.*

  7) *Progressive Figures.*

  8) *Color Form.*

  Scores, 2: Total Time, Errors.

  9) *Lateral Dominance Examination.*

  10) *Target.*

  11) *Aphasia Screening.*

  12) *Sensory Perceptual.*

  Subtests, 6: Imperception (Tactile, Audi-tory, Visual), Tactile Finger Recognition, Fin-ger-Tip Symbol Writing and Recognition, Tac-tile Form Recognition.

  13) *Grip Strength.*

  Scores, 2: Preferred Grip, Nonpreferred Grip.

  Comments: Hand dynamometer necessary for administration.

  14) *Name Writing.*

b) HALSTEAD-REITAN NEUROPSYCHOLOGI-CAL TEST BATTERY FOR OLDER CHILDREN.

Population: Ages 9-14.

  1) *Category.*

  Comments: Similar to *a* above.

  2) *Tactual Performance.*

  Comments: Same as *a* above.

  3) *Seashore Rhythm Test.*

  4) *Speech-Sounds Perception.*

  5) *Trail Making.*

  6) *Finger Tapping.*

  Comments: Manual finger tapping appara-tus necessary for administration.

  7) *Aphasia Screening.*

  8) *Sensory-Perceptual.*

  Subtests, 5: Sensory Imperception (Tactile, Auditory, Visual), Finger Agnosia, Finger-Tip Number Writing.

  9) *Tactile Form Recognition.*

  10) *Grip Strength.*

  Scores, 2: Preferred Grip, Nonpreferred Grip.

  Comments: Hand dynamometer necessary for administration.

  11) *Lateral Dominance.*

  12) *Name Writing.*

c) HALSTEAD-REITAN NEUROPSYCHOLOGI-CAL TEST BATTERY FOR ADULTS.

Population: Ages 15 and over.

Comments: Battery has 11 tests same as *b* above with a number of changes in equipment, administration, and scoring forms for this level.
Cross References: See T5:1164 (187 references) and T4:1119 (159 references); for reviews by Raymond S. Dean and Manfred J. Meier, see 9:463 (79 references); see also T3:1052 (4 references).

[1138]
Halstead Russell Neuropsychological Evaluation System.

Purpose: Provides "comprehensive measures of the functions relevant to neuropsychological assessment."
Population: Neuropsychological patients.
Publication Date: 1993.
Acronym: HRNES.
Scores, 3: Percent Impaired Score, Average Index Score, Lateralization Key.
Administration: Individual.
Price Data, 2006: $495 per complete kit including manual (99 pages), 10 recording booklets, and unlimited-use HRNES-R disk; $495 per complete kit with CD including manual, 10 recording booklets, and unlimited-use HRNES-R CD; $54.50 per 10 recording booklets; $57 per manual.
Time: Administration time not reported.
Comments: HRNES computer program compiles raw scores from up to 22 tests, corrects them for age and education, and converts them to scaled scores; includes unlimited use disk.
Authors: Elbert W. Russell and Regina I. Starkey.
Publisher: Western Psychological Services.
Cross References: For reviews by Roderick K. Mahurin and Paul Retzlaff, see 12:176 (1 reference).

[1139]
Hamilton Depression Inventory.

Purpose: Designed to "comprehensively screen for symptoms of depression."
Population: Adults.
Publication Date: 1995.
Acronym: HDI.
Scores: Total score only.
Administration: Group or Individual.
Forms, 2: HS and Short Form.
Price Data, 2006: $249 per kit including manual (140 pages), 10 reusable item booklets, 25 summary sheets, 25 answer sheets, 25 short form test booklets, and HDI Scoring Program software (3.5" diskette).
Time: (10) minutes.
Comments: Self-report version of the Hamilton Depression Rating Scale; computer scoring software included; software for administration and interpretation available from publisher.
Authors: William M. Reynolds and Kenneth A. Kobak.

Publisher: Psychological Assessment Resources, Inc.
Cross References: See T5:1166 (230 references); for reviews by Ephrem Fernandez and Carl Isenhart, see 13:136 (43 references).

[1140]
Hammill Multiability Achievement Test.

Purpose: Designed as a "measure of school achievement."
Population: Ages 7-0 to 17-11.
Publication Date: 1998.
Acronym: HAMAT.
Scores, 5: Reading, Writing, Arithmetic, Facts, General Achievement Quotient.
Administration: Individual.
Forms, 2: A, B.
Price Data, 2006: $210 per complete kit including examiner's manual (116 pages), 25 each Form A and Form B response booklets, and 25 each Form A and Form B record forms; $45 per student response booklets (Form A or B); $30 per profile/examiner record forms; $71 per examiner's manual.
Time: (30–60) minutes.
Authors: Donald D. Hammill, Wayne P. Hresko, Jerome J. Ammer, Mary E. Cronin, and Sally S. Quinby.
Publisher: PRO-ED.
Cross References: For reviews by Jeffrey A. Jenkins and Eleanor E. Sanford, see 14:159.

[1141]
The Hand Test [Revised].

Purpose: Designed as "a diagnostic technique that uses pictures of hands as the projective medium."
Population: Ages 5 and older.
Publication Dates: 1959–1991.
Scores, 41: 24 quantitative scores: Interpersonal (Affection, Dependence, Communication, Exhibition, Direction, Aggression, Total), Environmental (Acquisition, Active, Passive, Total), Maladjustive (Tension, Crippled, Fear, Total), Withdrawal (Description, Bizarre, Failure, Total), Experience Ratio, Acting Out Ratio, Pathological, Average Initial Response Time, High Minus Low Score, plus 17 qualitative scores: Ambivalent, Automatic Phrase, Cylindrical, Denial, Emotion, Gross, Hiding, Immature, Inanimate, Movement, Oral, Perplexity, Sensual, Sexual, Original, Repetition.
Administration: Individual.
Price Data, 2006: $164.50 per complete kit including manual (1983, 94 pages), manual supplement: Interpreting Child and Adolescent Responses (1991, 41 pages), 25 scoring booklets, and 1 set of picture cards; $27.50 per 25 scoring booklets; $43.50 per set of picture cards; $53 per manual; $48.95 per manual supplement: Interpreting Child and Adolescent Responses.

Time: (10) minutes.
Author: Edwin E. Wagner.
Publisher: Western Psychological Services.
Cross References: For reviews by Colin Cooper and Susana Urbina, see 14:161; see also T5:1169 (6 references) and T4:1121 (17 references); for a review by Marcia B. Shaffer of an earlier edition, see 10:134 (5 references); see also 9:464 (16 references), T3:1053 (21 references), 8:575 (29 references), T2:1470 (15 references), and P:438 (12 references); for a review by Goldine C. Gleser and an excerpted review by Irving R. Stone of an earlier edition, see 6:216 (6 references).

[1142]
Hand-Tool Dexterity Test.

Purpose: Intended to "provide a measure of proficiency in using ordinary mechanic's tools."
Population: Adolescents and adults.
Publication Dates: 1946–1981.
Acronym: HTDT.
Scores: Total score only.
Administration: Individual.
Price Data, 2006: $390 per complete set including all necessary equipment and manual (1981, 19 pages); $45 per manual.
Time: (5–10) minutes.
Comments: Examinee's score based on time it takes to finish test.
Author: George K. Bennett.
Publisher: Harcourt Assessment, Inc.
Cross References: See T3:1054 (1 reference) and 7:1044 (4 references); for reviews by C. H. Lawshe, Jr. and Neil D. Warren, see 3:649 (2 references).

[1143]
Hanes Sales Selection Inventory.

Purpose: Designed "to help select potentially successful insurance, printing and closely allied salesmen."
Population: Applicants for sales positions.
Publication Date: No date.
Scores: Part II, Part III, Drive Score.
Administration: Group.
Price Data: Available from publisher.
Time: (30) minutes.
Author: Bernard Hanes.
Publisher: Psychometric Affiliates.
Cross References: For a review by Theodore L. Hayes, see 15:114.

[1144]
Haptic Intelligence Scale for Adult Blind.

Purpose: Designed to "measure the intelligence of blind persons on the basis of non-verbal factors."
Population: Blind and partially sighted individuals ages 16 years and older.
Publication Dates: 1964-2004.
Acronym: HIS.

Scores: Digital Symbol, Block Design, Object Assembly, Object Completion, Pattern Board, Bead Arithmetic, Total.
Administration: Individual.
Price Data, 2006: $850 per complete kit including manual (2004, 50 pages), 25 record booklets, and all other necessary materials; $30 per manual; $27 per 25 record booklets.
Time: 91.75(121.75) minutes for the battery.
Comments: It is recommended that this test be used with a verbal test of intelligence for more comprehensive results.
Authors: Harriet C. Shurrager and Phil S. Shurrager.
Publisher: Stoelting Co.
   a) DIGITAL SYMBOL.
   Time: 2(7) minutes.
   b) BLOCK DESIGN.
   Time: 21(26) minutes.
   c) OBJECT ASSEMBLY.
   Time: 20(25) minutes.
   d) OBJECT COMPLETION.
   Time: 15(20) minutes.
   e) PATTERN BOARD.
   Time: 19(24) minutes.
   f) BEAD ARITHMETIC.
   Time: 14.75(19.75) minutes.

[1145]
Hare P-Scan.

Purpose: Designed as a "tool for assessing psychopathy and managing risk for antisocial, criminal, and violent behavior."
Population: Ages 13 and older.
Publication Date: 1999.
Scores, 4: Interpersonal Facet, Affective Facet, Lifestyle Facet, Total.
Administration: Individual.
Price Data, 2006: $65 per complete kit including 25 QuikScore™ forms, 1 manual, and 1 book "Without Conscience"; $27 per 25 QuikScore™ forms; $30 per manual; $48 per kit including manual and 25 QuikScore™ forms.
Time: (10–15) minutes.
Comments: Ratings by evaluator.
Author: Robert D. Hare.
Publisher: Multi-Health Systems, Inc.

[1146]
Hare Psychopathy Checklist–Revised: 2nd Edition.

Purpose: Designed for "the assessment of psychopathy in research, clinical and forensic settings."
Population: Ages 18 and over.
Publication Dates: 1990–2003.
Acronym: PCL-R.
Scores, 7: Factor 1 (Interpersonal, Affective, Total), Factor 2 (Lifestyle, Antisocial, Total), Total.

Administration: Individual.
Forms, 2: Rating Booklet, Interview Guide.
Price Data, 2006: $295 per complete kit including technical manual (2003, 231 pages), 1 rating booklet, 25 QuikScore™ forms, and 25 interview guides; $108 per technical manual; $60 per rating booklet (reusable, hardcover); $68 per 25 QuikScore™ forms; $111 per 25 interview guides; $150 per specimen set including manual, 1 rating booklet, 2 Quikscore forms, and 2 interview guides.
Time: (90–120) minutes for interview; (60) minutes for collateral review.
Comments: Rating scale based on responses to semistructured interview and collateral information review. Expands previous edition for use with female and African American offenders, substance abusers, and offenders in countries other than the U.S.
Author: Robert D. Hare.
Publisher: Multi-Health Systems, Inc.
Cross References: For reviews by Shawn K. Acheson and Joshua W. Payne and by D. Joe Olmi, see 16:101; see also T5:1174 (1 reference); for reviews by Solomon M. Fulero and Gerald L. Stone of a previous edition, see 12:177 (5 references); see also T4:1127 (3 references).

[1147]
Hare Psychopathy Checklist: Screening Version.

Purpose: To screen for psychopathy in forensic and nonforensic settings.
Population: Adults age 18 and over.
Publication Date: 1995.
Acronym: PCL:SV.
Scores, 3: Part 1, Part 2, Total.
Administration: Individual.
Price Data, 2006: $153 per complete kit including 25 interview guides, 25 QuikScore™ forms, and manual (82 pages); $99 per 25 interview guides/QuikScore™ forms; $60 per 25 interview guides; $60 per 25 QuikScore™ forms; $57 per manual.
Time: (30–60) minutes; case history review and scoring require further (20–30) minutes.
Comments: Interview format; shortened version of Hare Psychopathy Checklist—Revised (1146).
Authors: S. D. Hart, D. N. Cox, and R. D. Hare.
Publisher: Multi-Health Systems, Inc.
Cross References: For reviews by Ronald J. Ganellen and by Nathaniel J. Pallone and James J. Hennessy, see 14:162.

[1148]
Hare Psychopathy Checklist: Youth Version.

Purpose: Designed for "the assessment of psychopathic traits in adolescents."
Population: Ages 12–18.

Publication Date: 2003.
Acronym: PCL:YV
Scores, 5: Interpersonal, Affective, Behavioral, Antisocial, Total.
Administration: Individual.
Forms, 2: Interview Guide, QuikScore™ Rating Form.
Price Data, 2006: $277 per kit including technical manual, rating booklet, 25 Quikscore forms, and 25 interview guides; $86 per technical manual; $60 per rating booklet (reusable, hardcover); $68 per 25 Quikscore forms; $111 per 25 interview guides.
Time: (120) minutes for interview.
Comments: Adapted from the Hare Psychopathy Checklist—Revised (1146); expert-completed rating scale based on responses to semistructured interview and collateral information review.
Authors: Adelle E. Forth, David S. Kosson, and Robert D. Hare.
Publisher: Multi-Health Systems, Inc.
Cross References: For a review by John W. Fleenor, see 16:102.

[1149]
Harmonic Improvisation Readiness Record and Rhythm Improvisation Readiness Record.

Purpose: Designed to "help determine objectively whether individual students have the necessary harmonic and rhythmic readiness to learn to improvise" music.
Population: Grades 3 through music graduate school.
Publication Date: 1998.
Scores, 2: Harmonic Readiness, Rhythmic Readiness.
Administration: Group.
Price Data, 2006: $110 per complete kit including 100 harmonic answer sheets, 100 rhythm answer sheets, scoring masks, compact disc, and manual (1998); $20 per 100 answer sheets (specify harmonic or rhythm); $20 per scoring masks; $25 per compact disc.
Time: (20) minutes per test.
Comments: Can be machine scored.
Author: Edwin E. Gordon.
Publisher: GIA Publications, Inc.

[1150]
The Harrington-O'Shea Career Decision-Making System—Revised, 2005 Update.

Purpose: An interest inventory that provides an assessment of career interests, job choices, school subjects, future plans, values, and abilities.
Population: Grade 7 and over.
Publication Dates: 1976-2005.
Acronym: CDM-R.
Administration: Individual or group.
Price Data, 2006: $399.99 per Career Exploration Classroom Set Level 1 or 2, including 25 workbooks,

teacher's guide, and video set; $57.99 per CDM Hand-scored Level 1 or 2, including 25 booklets, directions; $29.99 per manual (156 pages); $199.99 per set of career videos; $199.99 per software for Windows or Macintosh: includes CD-ROM, manual, and 50 administrations; $52.99 per 25 scannable forms and 25 Level 2 Interpretive Folders.

Foreign Language Edition: Available in Spanish.

Comments: Hand scored or computer scored; updated every 2 years to reflect changes in occupational forecasts and titles.

Authors: Thomas F. Harrington and Arthur J. O'Shea.

Publisher: Pearson Assessments (originally published by AGS Publishing, acquired by Pearson in 2005).

a) LEVEL 1.

Population: Middle school students, and other students and adults with reading difficulty.

Publication Dates: 1992–2000.

Scores: 6 Career Interest Areas: Crafts, Scientific, The Arts, Social, Business, Office Operations; 18 Career Clusters: Manual, Skilled Crafts, Technical, Math-Science, Medical-Dental, Literary, Art, Music, Entertainment, Customer Service, Personal Service, Social Service, Education, Sales, Management, Legal, Clerical, Data Analysis.

Time: (20–25) minutes.

b) LEVEL 2.

Population: High school and college students and adults with average or better reading level.

Publication Dates: 1976–2000.

Scores: Same as *a* above and questions in 5 areas: Career Choices, School Subjects, Future Plans, Values, Abilities.

Time: (30–45) minutes.

Cross References: For reviews by Kevin R. Kelly and Mark L. Pope, see 16:103; see also T5:1177 (2 references); for reviews by Debra Neubert and Marcia B. Shaffer of an earlier edition, see 12:179; see also T4:1128 (1 reference); for a review by Caroline Manuele-Adkins of an earlier edition, see 10:136 (1 reference); see also T3:1054 (3 references); for a review by Carl G. Willis of an earlier edition, see 8:1004.

[1151]
The Hartman Value Profile.

Purpose: Assesses the development of the capacity to make certain evaluative judgments.

Population: Age 5 and older.

Publication Dates: 1965-1972.

Acronym: HVP.

Scores: 4 parts: The Development of the Capacities to Make Valuations in the Outside World, The Development of the Capacities to Make Valuations of One's Own Self, The Development of the Balance Between the Capacities to Value the Outside World and to Value One's Own Self, The Development of Certain Selected Value Capacities.

Administration: Group or individual.

Price Data, 2004: $35 per 35 copies Regular Form (individual or group administration); $35 per 35 copies of Research Form; $28 per set of Card Form or Pictorial Form (reuseable for individual administration only); $25 per 35 handscoring forms; $42 per manual (269 pages).

Time: (20-30 minutes).

Authors: Robert S. Hartman and Mario Cardenas Trigos.

Publisher: Research Concepts.

Cross References: See T4:1130 (1 reference), T2:1211 (2 references), and P:106 (2 references).

[1152]
Hassles and Uplifts Scales.

Purpose: To identify sources of stress and positive aspects of daily living that help counteract the damaging effects of stress.

Population: Adults.

Publication Date: 1989.

Acronym: HSUP.

Administration: Group.

Price Data: Available from publisher (www.mindgarden.com).

Time: (10-15) minutes per test.

Comments: Self-administered; tests available as separates.

Authors: Richard S. Lazarus and Susan Folkman.

Publisher: Mind Garden, Inc.

a) THE DAILY HASSLES SCALE.

Scores, 2: Frequency, Severity.

b) THE UPLIFTS SCALE.

Scores, 2: Frequency, Intensity.

c) THE COMBINED HASSLES AND UPLIFTS SCALES.

Scores, 2: Hassles, Uplifts.

Cross References: See T5:1178 (17 references) and T4:1132 (2 references); for reviews by Karen S. Budd and Nancy Heilman and by Barbara A. Reilly, see 11:155 (6 references).

[1153]
Hay Aptitude Test Battery [Revised].

Purpose: Designed to assess perceptual speed and accuracy.

Population: Applicants for positions that place a heavy emphasis on information processing speed and accuracy.

Publication Dates: 1947-2004.

Scores, 2: Number of Correct Responses, Number of Incorrect Responses.

Administration: Group or individual.

Price Data: Available from publisher.
Foreign Language Editions: French and Spanish versions available.
Author: Edward N. Hay.
Publisher: Wonderlic, Inc.

a) WARM-UP TEST.
Purpose: Designed to reduce test-taker anxiety and help acclimate the test taker to the testing setting.
Time: (1) minute.

b) NUMBER PERCEPTION TEST.
Purpose: Designed to assess short-term memory and accuracy with numerical detail.
Time: (4) minutes.

c) NAME FINDING TEST.
Purpose: Assesses short-term memory and accuracy with alphabetical detail.
Time: (4) minutes.

d) NUMBER SERIES COMPLETION TEST.
Purpose: Assesses numerical comprehension, logical thinking, and the ability to perceive patterns and relationships.
Time: (4) minutes.

Cross References: For reviews by Mark A. Albanese and Michael Kane, see 14:164; for reviews by Sue M. Legg and M. David Miller of an earlier edition, see 12:179; for a review by Robert P. Vecchio of an earlier edition, see 9:470; see also T2:2132 (2 references) and 5:849 (2 references); for reviews by Reign H. Bittner and Edward E. Cureton, see 4:725 (8 references).

[1154]
The Hayling and Brixton Tests.
Purpose: Designed to assess executive functions.
Population: Ages 18-80.
Publication Date: 1997.
Administration: Individual.
Price Data, 2006: £136 per complete kit including manual (20 pages), stimulus book, and 25 scoring sheets; £39.50 per 50 scoring sheets.
Authors: Paul W. Burgess and Tim Shallice.
Publisher: Harcourt Assessment [England].

a) HAYLING TEST.
Scores, 4: Response Latency, Error Score, Time Taken to Respond, Total.
Time: [5] minutes.
Comments: Administered verbally; requires no reading or writing.

b) BRIXTON TEST.
Score: Total score only.
Time: [5-10] minutes.

[1155]
HCR-20: Assessing Risk for Violence.
Purpose: Designed as "a broad-band violence risk assessment instrument with potential applicability to a variety of settings."

Population: Adults (Psychiatric and Correctional Settings).
Publication Date: 1997.
Scores, 4: Final Risk Judgment, Historical Items, Clinical Items, Risk Management Items.
Administration: Individual.
Price Data: Available from publisher.
Time: Administration time not reported.
Comments: "Research instrument."
Authors: Christopher D. Webster, Kevin S. Douglas, Derek Eaves, and Stephen D. Hart.
Publisher: Mental Health, Law, and Policy Institute, Simon Fraser University [Canada].
Cross References: For reviews by Paul A. Arbisi and Colin Cooper, see 15:115.

[1156]
Health and Daily Living Form, Second Edition.
Purpose: To examine the influence of extratreatment factors on treatment outcome as well as to explore the social resources and coping processes people use to prevent and adapt to stressful life circumstances.
Population: Students ages 12-18, Adults.
Publication Dates: 1984-1990.
Acronym: HDLF.
Administration: Group.
Forms, 2: Youth Form, Adult Form B.
Price Data: Available from publisher (www. mindgarden.com).
Time: (30-45) minutes.
Comments: May be administered as an interview or as a questionnaire.
Authors: Rudolf H. Moos, Ruth C. Cronkite, and John W. Finney.
Publisher: Mind Garden, Inc.

a) YOUTH FORM.
Population: Students ages 12-18.
Scores: 9 indices: Health-Related (Self-Confidence, Positive Mood, Distressed Mood, Physical Symptoms, Medical Conditions, Health—Risk Behaviors), Social Functioning (Family Activities, Activities with Friends, Social Integration in School).

b) ADULT FORM B.
Population: Adults.
Scores: 41 indices: Health-Related Functioning (Self-Confidence, Physical Symptoms, Medical Conditions, Global Depression, Depressive Mood and Ideation, Endogenous Depression, Depressive Features, Depressed Mood/Past 12 Months, Alcohol Consumption—Quantity, Alcohol Consumption—Quantity/Frequency, Drinking Problems, Smoking Symptoms, Medication Use), Social Functioning and Resources (Social Activities with Friends, Network Contacts, Number of Close

Relationships, Quality of Significant Relationship), Family Functioning and Home Environment (Family Social Activities, Family Task Sharing, Tasks Performed by Self, Tasks Performed by Partner, Family Arguments, Negative Home Environment), Children's Health and Functioning (Children's Physical Health Problems, Children's Psychological Health Problems, Children's Total Health Problems, Children's Behavioral Problems, Children's Health—Risk Behaviors), Life Change Events (Negative Life Change Events, Exit Events, Positive Life Change Events), Help-Seeking (Mental Health Professional [past 12 months], Mental Health Professional [ever gone], Non-Mental Health Professional [past 12 months], Non-Mental Health Professional [ever gone]), Family Level Composite (Quality of Conjugal Relationship, Family Social Activities, Family Agreement on Task Sharing, Family Agreement on Household Tasks, Family Arguments, Negative Home Environment).

Cross References: For reviews by Sandra D. Haynes and Ashraf Kagee, see 15:116; see T5:1181 (28 references) and T4:1135 (19 references); for reviews by Arthur M. Nezu and Steven P. Schinke, see 10:137 (8 references).

[1157]
Health and Safety Education Test: National Achievement Tests.

Purpose: Designed to measure students' knowledge of health and safety.
Population: Grades 3–6.
Publication Dates: 1947–1960.
Scores, 5: Good Habits, Cause and Effect, Facts, Application of Rules, Total.
Administration: Group.
Manual: No manual.
Price Data: Available from publisher.
Time: 40(45) minutes.
Authors: Lester D. Crow and Loretta C. Ryan.
Publisher: Psychometric Affiliates.
Cross References: For a review by Clarence H. Nelson, see 5:555.

[1158]
Health Attribution Test.

Purpose: Constructed to measure "beliefs about the causes and cures of illness"; a constructive measure of the patient's attitude on questions of responsibility for their own health maintenance or treatment.
Population: Age 14 and over.
Publication Date: 1990.
Acronym: HAT.
Scores, 3: Internal Scale, Powerful Others Scale, Chance Scale.

Administration: Group or individual.
Price Data, 2005: $27 per complete kit including 10 combination test booklets/answer sheets/scoring keys, and manual (20 pages); $30 per 25 combined test booklets/answer sheets/scoring keys; $15 per manual.
Foreign Language Edition: Spanish edition available.
Time: (10) minutes.
Authors: Jeanne Achterberg and G. Frank Lawlis.
Publisher: Institute for Personality and Ability Testing, Inc. (IPAT).
Cross References: For reviews by Dianna L. Newman and Stephen Olejnik, see 11:156.

[1159]
Health Dynamics Inventory.

Purpose: Developed to assess mental health status.
Population: Ages 3–18, 16–84.
Publication Date: 2003.
Acronym: HDI.
Scores, 13: Morale, Global Symptoms, Global Impairment, Depression, Anxiety, Attention Problems, Psychotic Thinking, Eating Disorders, Substance Abuse, Behavioral Problems, Occupational/Task Impairment, Relationship Impairment, Self-Care Impairment.
Administration: Group.
Forms, 2: Parent, Self.
Price Data, 2006: $248 per complete kit including technical manual (166 pages), 10 each Parent and Self item booklets, 25 each Parent and Self background information questionnaires, and 25 each Parent and Self response forms; $70 per technical manual; $23 per 10 Parent or Self item booklets; $55 per 25 Parent or Self background information questionnaires; $41 per 25 Parent or Self response forms; $76 per specimen set including technical manual, 1 Parent and 1 Self item booklets, 3 Parent and 3 Self background information questionnaires, and 3 Parent and 3 Self response forms.
Time: (15) minutes.
Comments: Parent form is completed for children ages 3–18 by parent.
Authors: Stephen M. Saunders and James V. Wojcik.
Publisher: Multi-Health Systems, Inc.
Cross References: For reviews by Rik Carl D'Amato and Gregory C. Wochos and by Jeffrey A. Jenkins, see 16:104.

[1160]
Health Education Test: Knowledge and Application: Acorn National Achievement Tests, Revised Edition.

Purpose: Constructed to measure the student's knowledge and application of health information.
Population: Grades 7–13.
Publication Dates: 1946–1956.
Scores, 3: Knowledge, Application, Total.

Administration: Group.
Manual: No manual.
Price Data: Available from publisher.
Time: 40(45) minutes.
Authors: John H. Shaw and Maurice E. Troyer.
Publisher: Psychometric Affiliates.
Cross References: See T2:928 (1 reference) and 5:557 (1 reference); for reviews by H. H. Remmers and Mabel E. Rugen, see 3:421.

[1161]
Health Knowledge Test for College Freshmen: National Achievement Tests.

Purpose: Designed to measure the health knowledge of college freshmen.
Population: College freshmen.
Publication Date: 1956.
Scores: Total score only.
Administration: Group.
Price Data: Available from publisher.
Time: 40(45) minutes.
Author: A. Frank Bridges.
Publisher: Psychometric Affiliates.
Cross References: For a review by James E. Bryan, see 5:558 (3 references).

[1162]
Health Occupations Basic Entrance Test.

Purpose: "A diagnostic instrument [designed] to assist Health Occupation schools evaluate the academic and counseling skills of new applicants to their programs."
Population: Adult applicants to health occupation schools or programs.
Publication Dates: 2000–2001.
Acronym: HOBET.
Scores, 28: 7 Essential Math Skills scores (Whole Numbers, Number System Conversions, Algebra Equations, Percent Operations, Decimal Operations, Fractions Operations, Composite), 3 Reading Comprehension scores (Reading Rate, Reading Rate Placement, Composite), 3 Critical Thinking Appraisal scores (Main Idea of Passage, Inferential Reading, Predicting of Outcomes), Testtaking Skills score, 2 Social Interaction Profile scores (Passive, Aggressive), 5 Stress Level Profile scores (Family, Social, Money/Time, Academic, Work Place), 6 Learning Styles (Auditory Learner, Solitary Learner, Visual Learner, Social Learner, Oral Dependent Learner, Writing Dependent Learner), Composite Percentage.
Administration: Group.
Forms, 2: A, B.
Price Data, 2002: $17 per test by computer; $10.50 per test booklet (36 pages); $8 per answer sheet; $27.50 per Study Guide (150 pages); quantity discounts available.
Time: 150 minutes.

Comments: Generates a Diagnostic Report including Group Report and individual Student Reports; Group Report provides group-level mean percentages and normative comparisons for the 28 scores; optional Study Guide offers test-taking strategy tips and practice tests.
Author: Michael D. Frost.
Publisher: Educational Resources, Inc.
Cross References: For reviews by James T. Austin and Erich C. Fein and by Nambury S. Raju, see 16:105.

[1163]
Health Problems Checklist.

Purpose: To facilitate "the rapid assessment of the health status and potential health problems of clients typically seen in psychotherapy settings."
Population: Adults.
Publication Dates: 1984-1989.
Scores: Items in 13 areas: General Health, Cardiovascular/Pulmonary, Endocrine/Hematology, Gastrointestinal, Dermatological, Visual, Auditory/Olfactory, Mouth/Throat/Nose, Orthopedic, Neurological, Genitourinary, Habits, History; no formal scoring procedure.
Administration: Individual or group.
Manual: No manual.
Price Data, 2006: $50 per package of 50.
Time: (10–20) minutes.
Author: John A. Schinka.
Publisher: Psychological Assessment Resources, Inc.
Cross References: See T5:1186 (1 reference); for a review by Robert M. Kaplan and Michelle T. Toshima of an earlier version, see 10:138.

[1164]
Health Status Questionnaire 2.0.

Purpose: Designed "to measure physical and social functioning and emotional well-being."
Population: Ages 14 and older.
Publication Date: 1994.
Acronym: HSQ® 2.0.
Scores, 8: Health Perception, Physical Functioning, Role Limitations-Physical, Role Limitations-Emotional, Social Functioning, Mental Health, Bodily Pain, Energy/Fatigue.
Administration: Group.
Price Data, 2006: $21 per Q Local answer sheets; $30 per user's guide; $10.25 per 5 test booklets; $1.40 per Q Local single administration report; no charge for progress reports; quantity discounts available for single administration reports.
Time: (5–10) minutes.
Comments: Self-administered; may be administered in paper-and-pencil format or online; contains all items found on the SF-36 Questionnaire (MOS 36-Item Short Form Health Survey) and SF-36 scores are included in the HSQ 2.0 report; scoring via MICROTEST Q Assessment System Software.

Authors: Health Outcomes Institute and the RAND Health Services Program.
Publisher: Pearson Assessments.
Cross References: For reviews by John C. Caruso and Theodore L. Hayes, see 15:117.

[1165]
Health Test: National Achievement Tests.

Purpose: To assess students' information, judgment, and evaluation of health knowledge and habits.
Population: Grades 3–8.
Publication Dates: 1937–1957.
Scores, 5: Recognizing Best Habits, Health Comparisons, Causes and Effects, Health Facts, Total.
Administration: Group.
Forms, 2: A, B.
Manual: No manual.
Price Data: Available from publisher.
Time: (40) minutes.
Authors: Robert K. Speer and Samuel Smith.
Publisher: Psychometric Affiliates.
Cross References: For a review by Benno G. Fricke, see 5:560; for a review by Jacob S. Orleans, see 4:485.

[1166]
Healthcare Customer Service Test.

Purpose: Selects customer service oriented workers for hospitals and healthcare settings.
Population: Hospital employees (service, skilled, professional, nursing, administrative, physician, technicians, environmental services).
Publication Dates: 1996–1997.
Acronym: HCST.
Scores, 5: Collaborate, Accommodate, Respect, Engage, Total.
Administration: Group.
Price Data: Available from publisher.
Time: (25–35) minutes, untimed.
Comments: Used for selection; subtests can be used for interview probes.
Author: Healthcare Testing, Inc.
Publisher: Silverwood Enterprises, LLC.
Cross References: For a review by Ronald A. Berk, see 16:106.

[1167]
Help Desk Support Staff Selector.

Purpose: To evaluate essential skills for the Help Desk position.
Population: Candidates for Help Desk positions.
Publication Date: 1993.
Acronym: HEDCO.
Scores: Total Score; Narrative Evaluation, Ranking, Recommendation.
Administration: Group.

Price Data, 2001: $300 per candidate; quantity discounts available.
Time: (180) minutes.
Comments: Scored by publisher; must be proctored.
Authors: Walden Personnel Testing & Training, Inc. and R. Label.
Publisher: Walden Personnel Performance, Inc. [Canada].

[1168]
Help for Preschoolers Assessment Strands: Ages 3-6.

Purpose: Assesses developmental skills/behaviors.
Population: Ages 3-6 years.
Publication Dates: 1987-1995.
Scores: Item scores only; 6 developmental areas: Cognitive, Language, Gross Motor, Fine Motor, Social, Self-Help.
Administration: Individual.
Price Data, 2006: $3.25 per child; price information regarding quantity discounts available from publisher (www.vort.com).
Time: Administration time not reported.
Comments: Adaptation of Behavioral Characteristics Progression (BCP; 298); upward extension of Hawaii Early Learning Profile (Ages 0-3; 1169); "criterion-referenced"; previous version entitled Help for Special Preschoolers ASSESSMENT CHECKLIST: Ages 3-6.
Author: VORT Corporation.
Publisher: VORT Corporation.
Cross References: For reviews by Harlan J. Stientjes and Gerald Tindal of an earlier edition, see 11:158.

[1169]
HELP Strands (Hawaii Early Learning Profile): Ages Birth-3.

Purpose: Assesses developmental skills/behaviors.
Population: Ages birth-3 years.
Publication Dates: 1984-2004.
Acronym: HELP Strands.
Scores: Item scores only; 6 developmental areas: Cognitive, Language, Gross Motor, Fine Motor, Social, Self-Help.
Administration: Individual.
Price Data, 2006: $3.25 per child; price information for quantity discounts available from publisher (www.vort.com).
Time: Administration time not reported.
Comments: Ratings by professionals; previous version entitled HELP Checklist (Hawaii Early Learning Profile).
Authors: Stephanie Parks (based on original work by Setsu Furuno, Katherine A. O'Reilly, Carol M. Hosaka, Takayo T. Inatsuka, Barbara Zeisloft-Falbey, and Toney Allman).

Publisher: VORT Corporation.
Cross References: For reviews by William Steven Lang and Koressa Kutsick Malcolm of an earlier edition, see 11:157.

[1170]

Herrmann Brain Dominance Instrument [Revised].

Purpose: Designed to measure "a person's preference both for right-brained or left-brained thinking and for conceptual or experiential thinking."
Population: Adults.
Publication Dates: 1981–1995.
Acronym: HBDI.
Scores, 12: Left Mode Dominance, Right Mode Dominance, Quadrant (Upper Left, Lower Left, Upper Right, Lower Right), Adjective Pairs (subset of 4 Quadrant Scores), Cerebral Mode Dominance, Limbic Mode Dominance.
Administration: Group.
Manual: No manual.
Price Data: Available from publisher.
Time: (15–20) minutes.
Comments: Self-administered; must be scored by publisher or certified practitioner.
Author: Ned Herrmann.
Publisher: Herrmann International.
Cross References: For reviews by F. Felicia Ferrara and Gabriele van Lingen, see 14:165; see also T5:1197 (1 reference); for a review by Rik Carl D'Amato of an earlier edition, see 11:159 (7 references).

[1171]

High Level Battery: Test A/75.

Purpose: To provide "measures of general intelligence, arithmetical ability and certain language abilities."
Population: Adults with at least 12 years of education.
Publication Dates: 1960–1972.
Scores: Total scores only for 4 tests in a single booklet: Mental Alertness, Arithmetical Problems, Reading Comprehension (English, Afrikaans), Vocabulary (English, Afrikaans).
Administration: Group.
Price Data: Available from publisher.
Time: 197(215) minutes.
Comments: Formerly listed as National Institute for Personnel Research High Level Battery.
Author: D. P. M. Beukes (manual).
Publisher: Human Sciences Research Council [South Africa].
Cross References: See 6:778 (1 reference).

[1172]

High Level Figure Classification Test.

Purpose: Designed to assess intellectual ability.
Population: Grades 10–12.

Publication Date: 1983.
Acronym: HL FCT.
Scores: Total score only.
Administration: Group.
Price Data: Available from publisher.
Foreign Language Edition: Test printed in both English and Afrikaans.
Time: 30(40) minutes.
Authors: M. Werbeloff and T. R. Taylor.
Publisher: Human Sciences Research Council [South Africa].

[1173]

High School Career-Course Planner.

Purpose: Designed "to develop a high school course plan that is consistent with self-assessed career goals."
Population: Grades 8 and 9.
Publication Dates: 1983–1990.
Acronym: HSCCP.
Scores: Total score only.
Administration: Group.
Price Data: Available from publisher.
Time: (50) minutes; (5–8) minutes for computer version.
Comments: Computer version also available.
Author: CFKR Career Materials, Inc.
Publisher: CFKR Career Materials.
Cross References: For reviews by Mary Henning-Stout and James W. Pinkney, see 12:181.

[1174]

High School Personality Questionnaire.

Purpose: Measures primary personality characteristics in adolescents.
Population: Ages 12–18.
Publication Dates: 1958–1984.
Acronym: HSPQ.
Scores, 18: 14 primary factor scores (Warmth, Abstract Thinking, Emotional Stability, Excitability, Dominance, Enthusiasm, Conformity, Boldness, Sensitivity, Withdrawal, Apprehension, Self-Sufficiency, Self-Discipline, Tension), 4 second-order factor scores (Extraversion, Anxiety, Tough Poise, Independence).
Administration: Group or individual.
Price Data, 2005: $35 per 25 reusable test booklets; $18 per scoring keys; $18 per 25 machine-scorable answer sheets; $18 per 50 hand-scoring answer sheets; $20 per 50 hand-scoring answer-profile sheets; $18 per 50 profile sheets; $18 per 50 second-order worksheets; $20 per manual (1984, 98 pages); $23 per computer interpretation introductory kit including manual, reusable test booklet, answer sheet, and prepaid processing form for computer interpretive report; $41 per hand-scoring introductory kit including test booklet, scoring keys, answer sheet, and profile sheet; computer scoring and interpretive services available from publisher for $7 to $30 per individual report depending upon quantity requested.

Foreign Language Editions: Information regarding several non-English-language adaptations available from publisher.

Time: (45-60) minutes.

Comments: Previously listed as Jr.-Sr. High School Personality Questionaire.

Authors: Raymond B. Cattell, Mary D. Cattell, and Edgar Johns (manual and norms).

Publisher: Institute for Personality and Ability Testing, Inc. (IPAT).

Cross References: See T5:1201 (6 references) and T4:1159 (4 references); for reviews by Richard I. Lanyon and Steven V. Owen, see 11:188 (17 references); see also 9:559 (8 references), T3:1233 (22 references), 8:597 (68 references), and T2:1253 (37 references); for reviews by Robert Hogan and Douglas N. Jackson, see 7:97 (53 references); see also P:136 (29 references); for reviews by C. J. Adcock and Philip E. Vernon of an earlier edition, see 6:131 (17 references); see also 5:72 (4 references).

[1175]
High School Placement Test-Open Edition.

Purpose: Designed as a measure of cognitive and basic skills to assist in placement decisions for entering freshmen.

Population: Eighth grade students.

Publication Dates: 1982–2004.

Acronym: HSPT.

Scores, 5: Verbal Skills, Quantitative Skills, Reading, Mathematics, Language.

Administration: Group.

Restricted Distribution: Available for school purchase only.

Price Data, 2005: $131 per starter set including manual (1995, 15 pages), and 35 test booklets; $47.50 per 35 optional test booklets (specify subject); $6.95 per large-print test booklet; $38.55 per 50 answer sheets; $31.20 per scoring kit including manual for hand scoring and interpreting results, 1 answer key, and 2 class record sheets; $7.50 per manual; $8.40 per manual for handscoring and interpreting results; $9.30 per technical supplement; $.59 per student score folder; $11.05 per 20 practice tests; $24 per specimen set.

Time: 150 minutes plus (15–25) minutes per optional test.

Comments: Optional tests available including Science, Mechanical Aptitude, and Catholic Religion.

Author: Scholastic Testing Service, Inc.

Publisher: Scholastic Testing Service, Inc.

Cross References: For reviews by John O. Anderson and Geneva D. Haertel, see 14:166.

[1176]
High School Reading Test: National Achievement Tests.

Purpose: Designed to measure the student's mastery and application of factual material in English, reading, literature, and vocabulary.

Population: Grades 7–12.

Publication Dates: 1939–1952.

Scores, 6: Vocabulary, Word Discrimination, Sentence Meaning, Noting Details, Interpreting Paragraphs, Total.

Administration: Group.

Forms, 2: A, B.

Price Data: Available from publisher.

Time: (40) minutes.

Authors: Robert K. Speer and Samuel Smith.

Publisher: Psychometric Affiliates.

Cross References: For a review by Victor H. Noll, see 5:634; for a review by Holland Roberts, see 4:536; for a review by Robert L. McCaul, see 3:488.

[1177]
Higher Education Learning Profile.

Purpose: "Designed primarily as a diagnostic instrument to assist educational programs evaluate the academic processing skills of new applicants."

Population: Adult applicants to college automotive, business, computer, electronics, legal, technology, and telecommunication programs.

Publication Date: 2001.

Acronym: HELP.

Scores, 28: Essential Math Skills (Whole Numbers, Number System Conversions, Algebra Equations, Percent Operations, Decimal Operations, Fractions Operations, Composite), Reading Comprehension (Reading Rate, Reading Rate Placement, Composite), Critical Thinking Appraisal (Main Idea of Passage, Inferential Reading, Predicting of Outcomes), Testtaking Skills, Social Interaction Profile (Passive, Aggressive), Stress Level Profile (Family, Social, Money/Time, Academic, Work Place), Learning Styles (Auditory Learner, Solitary Learner, Visual Learner, Social Learner, Oral Dependent Learner, Writing Dependent Learner), Composite Percentage.

Administration: Group.

Forms, 3: A, B, C.

Price Data, 2002: $17 per test by computer; $10.50 per test booklet; $8 per answer sheet; $27.50 per Student Study Guide; quantity discounts available.

Time: (150) minutes.

Comments: Generates a Diagnostic Report including the test Group Report, and Individual Student Reports; Group Report provides group-level mean percentages and normative comparisons for the 28 scores; optional Study Guide offers test-taking strategy tips and practice tests.

Author: Educational Resources, Inc.

Publisher: Educational Resources, Inc.

[1178]
Hill Interaction Matrix.

Purpose: "To study group development, group composition, and therapist style."

Population: Prospective members, members, and leaders of psychotherapy groups.

Publication Dates: 1954–1994.
Acronym: HIM.
Scores: Matrix of 4 columns (Topics, Groups, Personal, Relationship) and 4 rows (Conventional, Assertive, Speculative, Confrontive) produces 16 scores, 8 marginal Total scores, Grand Total, and other derivative scores.
Administration: Group or individual.
Price Data: Available from publisher.
Time: (20) minutes.
Author: Wm. Fawcett Hill.
Publisher: Howdah Press [No reply from publisher; status unknown].

    a) HIM A AND B.
    Population: Prospective members and members of psychotherapy groups.
    Publication Dates: 1954–1968.
    Editions, 2: HIM-A, HIM-B.
    b) HIM-G.
    Population: Observers and leaders of psychotherapy groups.
    Publication Dates: 1967–1968.
    Manual: No manual.
Cross References: See T5:1205 (1 reference), T4:1162 (25 references), T3:1099 (9 references), 8:577 (35 references), and T2:1214 (29 references).

[1179]
Hilson Adolescent Profile.

Purpose: "Designed as a screening tool to assess the presence and extent of adolescent behavior patterns and problems."
Population: Ages 10 to 19.
Publication Dates: 1984–1987.
Acronym: HAP.
Scores, 16: Guarded Responses, Alcohol Use, Drug Use, Educational Adjustment Difficulties, Law Violations, Frustration Tolerance, Antisocial/Risk-Taking, Rigidity/Obsessiveness, Interpersonal/Assertiveness Difficulties, Homelife Conflicts, Social/Sexual Adjustment, Health Concerns, Anxiety/Phobic Avoidance, Depression/Suicide Potential, Suspicious Temperament, Unusual Responses.
Administration: Individual or group.
Price Data: Available from publisher.
Special Edition: Audiotape edition available.
Time: (45–55) minutes.
Comments: Self-administered; computer-scored.
Authors: Robin E. Inwald.
Publisher: Hilson Research, Inc.
Cross References: See T5:1207 (1 referfence); for a review by Allen K. Hess, see 11:161.

[1180]
Hilson Adolescent Profile—Version S.

Purpose: "Designed as a screening tool to identify adolescent emotional difficulties, depression and/or suicidal tendencies, homelife conflicts, and other behavior patterns."
Population: Ages 10–19.
Publication Date: 1993.
Acronym: HAP-S.
Scores, 7: Guarded Responses, Educational Adjustment Difficulties, Frustration Tolerance, Homelife Conflicts, Social/Sexual Adjustment, Depression/Suicide Potential, Unusual Responses.
Administration: Individual or group.
Price Data: Available from publisher.
Time: (15–25) minutes.
Comments: Short version of the Hilson Adolescent Profile (1179).
Authors: Robin Inwald.
Publisher: Hilson Research, Inc.

[1181]
Hilson Career Satisfaction Index.

Purpose: To aid in employee "fitness-for-duty" evaluations, promotion, and special assignment decisions.
Population: Public safety/security officers.
Publication Date: 1989.
Acronym: HCSI.
Scores, 13: Stress Patterns, Stress Symptoms, Drug/Alcohol Abuse, Lack of Interpersonal Support, Anger/Hostility Patterns, Disciplinary History, Excusing Attitudes, Aggression/Hostility, Dissatisfaction with Career, Dissatisfaction with Supervisor, Relationship with Co-Workers, Dissatisfaction with Job, Defensiveness.
Administration: Individual or group.
Price Data: Available from publisher.
Time: (25–35) minutes.
Authors: Robin Inwald.
Publisher: Hilson Research, Inc.
Cross References: See T4:1166 (1 reference).

[1182]
Hilson Personnel Profile/Success Quotient.

Purpose: To identify individual "strengths," behavior patterns, and personality characteristics "leading to success in a variety of work settings."
Population: High school through adult.
Publication Date: 1988.
Acronym: HPP/SQ.
Scores, 13: Candor, Achievement History, Social Ability (Extroversion, Popularity/"Charisma," Sensitivity to Approval), "Winner's" Image (Competitive Spirit, Self-Worth, Family Achievement Expectations), Initiative (Drive, Preparation Style, Goal Orientation, Anxiety About Organization), Success Quotient.
Administration: Individual or group.
Price Data: Available from publisher.
Time: (20–30) minutes.
Author: Robin E. Inwald.
Publisher: Hilson Research, Inc.

Cross References: For a review by Joseph G. Law, Jr., see 11:162.

[1183]
Hines Functional Dysphagia Scale.
Purpose: A quick scale for measuring swallowing behavior "to distill the results of a videofluoroscopic swallow study."
Population: Ages 20-86.
Publication Date: 2005.
Acronym: HFDS.
Scores, 6: Food, Liquid, Aspiration, Efficiency, Compensations, Total Score.
Administration: Individual.
Price Data, 2006: $85 per complete kit including examiner's manual (41 pages) and 50 evaluation and summary forms; $57 per examiner's manual; $35 per 50 evaluation and summary forms.
Time: (3-5) minutes.
Authors: Barry M. Klor, Mary J. Bacon, Barbara S. Cook, and Franklin J. Milianti.
Publisher: PRO-ED.

[1184]
Hodson Assessment of Phonological Patterns—Third Edition.
Purpose: Designed to "assess and analyze phonological deviations of children with highly unintelligible speech."
Population: Ages 3 to 8.
Publication Dates: 1986-2004.
Acronym: HAPP-3.
Scores, 14: Word/Syllable Structures Omissions (Syllables, Consonant Sequences/Clusters, Prevocalic Singletons, Intervocalic Singletons, Postvocalic Singletons, Total), Consonant Category Deficiencies (Liquids, Nasals, Glides, Stridents, Velars, Anterior Nonstridents, Total), Total Occurrences of Major Phonological Deviations.
Administration: Individual.
Levels, 3: Comprehensive Phonological Evaluation, Preschool Phonological Screening, Multisyllabic Word Screening.
Price Data, 2006: $189 per complete kit including examiner's manual (2004, 64 pages); $35 per 25 Comprehensive Phonological Evaluation Record Forms; $30 per 25 Major Phonological Deviations Analysis Forms; $30 per 25 Substitutions and Other Strategies Analysis Forms; $20 per 50 Preschool Phonological Screening Record Forms; $20 per 50 Multisyllabic Word Screening Record Forms; $9 per 1 Multisyllabic Word Screening Picture Sheet; $50 per 30-piece object kit and 13 picture cards; $71 per examiner's manual.
Time: (15–20) minutes.
Comments: Norm referenced and "criterion referenced"; formerly called The Assessment of Phonological Processes.

Author: Barbara Williams Hodson.
Publisher: PRO-ED.
Cross References: See T5:214 (19 references); for reviews of an earlier version by Allen O. Diefendorf, Michael K. Wynne, and Kathy Kessler and by Kathryn W. Kenney, see 12:36; see also T4:220 (4 references); for a review by Sheldon L. Stick, see 9:91 (1 reference).

[1185]
Hogan Development Survey.
Purpose: "Designed to assess eleven common dysfunctional dispositions."
Population: Ages 16 and older.
Publication Dates: 1995–1997.
Acronym: HDS.
Scores: 11 scales: Excitable, Skeptical, Cautious, Reserved, Leisurely, Bold, Mischievous, Colorful, Imaginative, Diligent, Dutiful.
Administration: Group.
Price Data, 2006: Selection Reports starting at $20; Development Reports starting at $35.
Time: (20) minutes.
Comments: Web-based administration.
Authors: Robert Hogan and Joyce Hogan (manual).
Publisher: Hogan Assessment Systems, Inc.
Cross References: For reviews by Glen Fox and E. Scott Huebner, see 14:168.

[1186]
Hogan Personality Inventory [Revised].
Purpose: Measure of normal personality designed for use in personnel selection, individualized assessment, and career-related decision making.
Population: College students and adults.
Publication Dates: 1985–1995.
Acronym: HPI.
Scores: 7 primary scale scores (Inquisitive, Adjustment, Ambition, Sociability, Interpersonal Sensitivity, Prudence, Learning Approach), 6 occupational scale scores (Service Orientation, Stress Tolerance, Reliability, Clerical Potential, Sales Potential, Managerial Potential), and Validity scale score.
Administration: Group.
Price Data, 2006: Selection Reports starting at $20; Development Reports starting at $40.
Time: (15–20) minutes.
Comments: Web-based administration.
Authors: Robert Hogan and Joyce Hogan (manual).
Publisher: Hogan Assessment Systems, Inc.
Cross References: See T5:1212 (1 reference); for reviews by Stephen N. Axford and Steven G. LoBello, see 13:138 (2 references); see also T4:1169 (7 references); for reviews by James J. Hennessy and Rolf A. Peterson of an earlier edition, see 10:140.

[1187]
Holden Psychological Screening Inventory.

Purpose: "To provide a very brief measure of psychiatric symptomatology, social symptomatology, and depression."
Population: Ages 14 and older.
Publication Date: 1996.
Acronym: HPSI.
Scores, 4: Psychiatric Symptomatology, Social Symptomatology, Depression, Total.
Administration: Individual or group.
Price Data, 2006: $75 per complete kit including manual (50 pages) and 25 QuikScore™ forms; $39 per 25 QuikScore™ forms (English or French-Canadian); $51 per manual; $56 per online profile report kit including manual and 3 profile reports.
Foreign Language Edition: French-Canadian QuikScore™ forms available.
Time: (5–7) minutes.
Comments: Self-report; Windows™ version computer administration and scoring available on CD or 3.5-inch disk.
Author: Ronald R. Holden.
Publisher: Multi-Health Systems, Inc.
Cross References: For reviews by Stephen N. Axford and Janet F. Carlson, see 14:169; see also T5:1213 (1 reference).

[1188]
Holtzman Inkblot Technique.

Purpose: Designed as a projective personality test.
Population: Ages 5 and over.
Publication Dates: 1958–1972.
Acronym: HIT.
Scores, 20–22: Reaction Time (*a* only), Rejection, Location, Space, Form Definiteness, Form Appropriateness, Color, Shading, Movement, Pathognomic Verbalization, Integration, Content (Human, Animal, Anatomy, Sex, Abstract), Anxiety, Hostility, Barrier, Penetration, Balance (*a* only), Popular.
Administration: Group or individual.
Price Data, 2002: $11 per 25 or $40 per 100 Hill clinical summary forms; $31.50 per Workbook for the Holtzman Inkblot Technique.
Author: Wayne H. Holtzman.
Publisher: PsychCorp, A brand of Harcourt Assessment, Inc.
  a) INDIVIDUAL TEST.
  Publication Dates: 1958–1972.
  Forms, 2: A, B.
  Price Data: $687 per complete set for Forms A and B combined including 47 inkblots, 25 record forms with summary sheets, and scoring guide; $369 per complete set (specify Form A or B).
  b) GROUP TEST.
  Publication Dates: 1958–1972.

Manual: No manual.
Price Data: $21 per 50 Gorham-Holtzman group record forms; $11 per normative item statistics.
Comments: Administration slides for either form must be constructed locally.
Author: Donald R. Gorham (record form).
Cross References: See T4:1170 (12 references); for reviews by Bert P. Cundick and David M. Dush, see 9:480 (17 references); see also T3:1106 (25 references); for a review by Rolf A. Peterson, see 8:578 (96 references); see also T2:1471 (42 references); for excerpted reviews by Raymond J. McCall and David G. Martin, see 7:169 (106 references); see also P:439 (90 references); for reviews by Richard N. Coan, H. J. Eysenck, Bertram R. Forer, and William N. Thetford, see 6:217 (22 references).

[1189]
Home & Community Social Behavior Scales.

Purpose: Designed to evaluate social competence and antisocial behavior.
Population: Ages 5–18 (Grades K-12).
Publication Date: 2002.
Acronym: HCSBS.
Scores, 6: Peer Relations, Self-Management/Compliance, Social Competence Total, Defiant/Disruptive, Antisocial/Aggressive, Antisocial Behavior Total.
Administration: Individual.
Price Data, 2006: $49 per user's guide (116 pages); $36 per 25 test forms.
Time: (5–10) minutes.
Comments: Companion to the School Social Behavior Scales (2262); rated by parent or other home- or community-based rater.
Authors: Kenneth W. Merrell and Paul Caldarella.
Publisher: Assessment-Intervention Resources.
Cross References: For reviews by Theodore Coladarci and by Stephanie Stein and Phil Diaz, see 16:107.

[1190]
Home Environment Questionnaire, HEQ-2R and HEQ-1R.

Purpose: Measures "dimensions of the child's psychological environment that exert specific types of pressure on the child."
Population: Grades 4–6.
Publication Date: 1983.
Acronym: HEQ.
Scores, 10: P(ress) Achievement, P Aggression-External, P Aggression-Home, P Aggression-Total, P Supervision, P Change, P Affiliation, P Separation, P Sociability, P Socioeconomic Status.
Administration: Individual or group.
Forms, 2: HEQ-2R for use with two-parent families and HEQ-1R for use with single-parent families.
Price Data: Available from publisher.

Time: Administration time not reported.
Comments: Ratings by child's mother.
Author: Jacob O. Sines.
Publisher: Jacob O. Sines (the author).
Cross References: See T5:1215 (4 references) and T4:1171 (1 reference); for a review by Steven I. Pfeiffer and Julia Pettiette-Doolin, see 10:141 (1 reference).

[1191]
Home Observation for Measurement of the Environment.

Purpose: Designed to measure the quality and quantity of stimulation and support available to a child in the home environment.
Population: Birth to age 3, early childhood, middle childhood, early adolescent.
Publication Dates: 1978–2003.
Acronym: HOME Inventory.
Administration: Individual.
Price Data, 2003: $50 per comprehensive manual; $40 per standard manual (without Disability Adapted or Child Care HOME); $30 per Child Care HOME Manual; $15.00 per pad of Infant Toddler forms; $25 per 50 Early Childhood forms; $12.50 per 25 Middle and Early Adolescent forms.
Time: (60) minutes.
Comments: Focus is on the child in the home environment as a recipient of inputs from objects, events, and transactions occurring in connection with the family surroundings.
Authors: Bettye M. Caldwell and Robert H. Bradley.
Publisher: Home Inventory LLC.
a) INFANT/TODDLER HOME INVENTORY.
Population: Birth-3 years.
Scores, 7: Responsivity, Acceptance, Organization, Learning Materials, Involvement, Variety, Total.
b) EARLY CHILDHOOD HOME INVENTORY.
Population: 3-6 years.
Scores, 9: Learning Materials, Language Stimulation, Physical Environment, Responsivity, Academic Stimulation, Modeling, Variety, Acceptance, Total.
c) MIDDLE CHILDHOOD HOME INVENTORY.
Population: 6-10 years.
Scores, 8: Responsivity, Encouragement of Maturity, Acceptance, Learning Materials, Enrichment, Family Companionship, Paternal Involvement, Total.
*d)*EARLY ADOLESCENT HOME INVENTORY.
Population: Early adolescents.
Scores, 7: Physical Environment, Learning Materials, Modeling, Instructional Activities, Regular Activities, Variety of Experience and Acceptance, Responsivity.
Cross References: See T5:1216 (113 references), T4:1172 (42 references), 9:481 (13 references), and T3:1108 (14 references).

[1192]
Home Screening Questionnaire.

Purpose: Constructed to screen the home environment for factors related to the child's growth and development.
Population: Birth to age 3, ages 3–6.
Publication Date: 1981.
Acronym: HSQ.
Scores, 3: Questions, Toy Checklist, Total.
Administration: Individual.
Price Data, 2005: $17 per 25 questionnaires; $18 per reference manual (29 pages).
Time: (15–20) minutes.
Comments: Ratings by parents; abbreviated adaptation of the Home Observation for Measurement of the Environment (1191).
Authors: Cecilia E. Coons, Elizabeth C. Gay, Alma W. Fandal, Cynthia Ker, and William K. Frankenburg.
Publisher: Denver Developmental Materials, Inc.
Cross References: See T5:1217 (1 reference).

[1193]
Home-Visit Kit.

Purpose: Yields information regarding home safety and life-style issues necessary in child custody evaluations.
Population: Families involved in child custody situations.
Publication Dates: 1997–2002.
Scores: Unscored.
Administration: Group.
Price Data, 2002: $189 per kit including 8 Home-Visit booklets, instruction booklet (42 pages), and update service; $99 per 8 Home-Visit booklets; $159 per 16 Home-Visit booklets; $199 per 24 Home-Visit booklets; $119 per Home-Visit instruction booklet.
Time: Administration time not reported.
Comments: Previously listed as The Bricklin/Elliot Child Custody Evaluation.
Authors: Barry Bricklin and Gail Elliot.
Publisher: Village Publishing.

[1194]
The Hooper Visual Organization Test.

Purpose: Measures an individual's ability to organize visual stimuli.
Population: Ages 5 years and over.
Publication Dates: 1957–1983.
Acronym: VOT.
Scores: Total score only.
Administration: Group or individual.
Price Data, 2006: $207 per complete kit including 4 reusable test pictures booklets, manual (1983, 39 pages), 25 test booklets, 100 answer sheets, and scoring key; $27.50 per 25 test booklets; $40 per reusable test pictures booklet; $16.50 per scoring key; $27.50 per 100 answer sheets; $47 per manual.

Time: (15) minutes.
Author: H. Elston Hooper.
Publisher: Western Psychological Services.
Cross References: See T5:1218 (19 references); for reviews by Kathy E. Green and Wilfred G. VanGorp, see 12:182 (7 references); see also T4:1174 (28 references), T3:1109 (6 references), T2:1216 (5 references), and P:111 (7 references); for reviews by Ralph M. Reitan and Otfried Spreen of an earlier edition, see 6:116 (4 references).

[1195]
Hopkins Verbal Learning Test—Revised.

Purpose: A "brief assessment of verbal learning and memory (immediate recall, delayed recall, delayed recognition)."
Population: Ages 16 years and older.
Publication Dates: 1991–2001.
Acronym: HVLT-R.
Scores, 4: Total Recall, Delayed Recall, Retention, Recognition Discrimination Index.
Administration: Individual.
Forms, 6: 1–6.
Price Data, 2006: $255 per introductory kit including professional manual (2001, 55 pages) and 25 each of 6 test booklets (Forms 1–6).
Time: (5–10) minutes with a 25-minute delay.
Comments: Forms 1–6 are very similar psychometrically and can be used to eliminate practice effects on repeated administration.
Authors: Jason Brandt and Ralph H. B. Benedict.
Publisher: Psychological Assessment Resources, Inc.
Cross References: For reviews by Timothy Z. Keith and Wendy J. Steinberg, see 16:108.

[1196]
The Hospital Anxiety and Depression Scale with the Irritability-Depression-Anxiety Scale and the Leeds Situational Anxiety Scale.

Purpose: Designed to detect and distinguish "between anxiety and depression and measures the severity of emotional disorder."
Population: Adults.
Publication Date: 1994.
Acronym: HADS.
Scores, 3: Irritability, Anxiety, Depression.
Administration: Group.
Price Data: Available from publisher.
Time: (5) minutes.
Authors: R. P. Snaith and A. S. Zigmond.
Publisher: NFER-Nelson Publishing Co., Ltd. [England]
Cross References: For reviews by Michael H. Campbell and William E. Martin, Jr., see 15:118.

[1197]
House-Tree-Person and Draw-A-Person as Measures of Abuse in Children: A Quantitative Scoring System.

Purpose: Developed to "evaluate possible child sexual abuse."
Population: Ages 7–11.
Publication Date: 1994.
Acronym: H-T-P/D-A-P.
Scores, 4: Preoccupation with Sexually Relevant Concepts, Aggression and Hostility, Withdrawal and Guarded Accessibility, Alertness for Danger/Suspiciousness and Lack of Trust.
Administration: Individual.
Price Data, 2005: $102 per H-T-P/D-A-P Quantitative Scoring System Kit including "H-T-P/D-A-P as Measures of Abuse in Children," and 25 scoring booklets.
Time: Administration time not reported.
Comments: A projective drawing instrument; for related instruments see The Draw-A-Person, Draw A Person: A Quantitative Scoring System, Draw-A-Person Quality Scale, and Draw A Person: Screening Procedure for Emotional Disturbance.
Author: Valerie Van Hutton.
Publisher: Psychological Assessment Resources, Inc.
Cross References: See T5:1219 (1 reference); for reviews by E. Thomas Dowd and Howard M. Knoff, see 13:139 (2 references).

[1198]
How Am I Doing? A Self-Assessment for Child Caregivers.

Purpose: Designed to identify areas of strength and skill development needs of caregivers of children with disabilities.
Population: Caregivers of children with disabilities.
Publication Date: 1993.
Scores: 8 sections: Arrival and Departure, Free Choice Play, Structured Group Activities, Outside Play, Meal Time, Toileting, Nap Time, Throughout the Day.
Administration: Group.
Price Data: Price data available from publisher.
Time: Administration time not reported.
Author: Irene Carney.
Publisher: Child Development Resources.
Cross References: For reviews by Lisa G. Bischoff and by Frederic J. Medway and Karen Fay, see 13:140.

[1199]
How I Think Questionnaire.

Purpose: Designed to "measure self-serving cognitive distortion."
Population: Ages 12–21.
Publication Date: 2001.

Acronym: HIT.
Scores, 11: Hit Questionnaire, Overt, Covert, Self-Centered, Blaming Others, Minimizing/Mislabeling, Assuming the Worst, Opposition-Defiance, Physical Aggression, Lying, Stealing, Anomalous Responding.
Administration: Individual.
Price Data, 2006: $25.95 per 20 questionnaires and manual (44 pages); $23.95 per 20 additional questionnaires.
Time: (5–15) minutes.
Authors: John C. Gibbs, Alvaro Q. Barriga, Granville Bud Potter, and Albert K. Kiau.
Publisher: Research Press.
Cross References: For reviews by Jack E. Gebart-Eaglemont and Joseph C. Kush, see 15:119.

[1200]

How Supervise?

Purpose: Designed to assess the knowledge of practices affecting worker efficiency.
Population: Supervisors.
Publication Dates: 1943–1971.
Scores: Total score only.
Administration: Group or individual.
Forms, 3: A, B, M.
Price Data, 2006: $77 per 25 test booklets (specify form); $26 per manual (1971, 17 pages); $30 per examination kit including test booklets for all three forms and manual.
Time: [40] minutes.
Authors: Quentin W. File and H. H. Remmers.
Publisher: Harcourt Assessment, Inc.
Cross References: See T4:1177 (2 references) and T2:2448 (11 references); for a review by Joel T. Campbell, see 6:1189 (9 references); see also 5:926 (18 references); for a review by Milton M. Mandell, see 4:774 (8 references); for reviews by D. Welty Lefever, Charles I. Moiser, and C. H. Ruedisili, see 3:687 (5 references).

[1201]

H.R.R. Pseudoisochromatic Plates for Detecting, Classifying and Estimating the Degree of Defective Color Vision.

Purpose: Designed to test for color vision; distinguishes those with normal color vision from those with defective color vision; for those with defective color vision, indicates the type (Protan, Deutan, or Tritan) and the degree of defect (mild, medium, or strong).
Population: People who may have color vision deficiency and occupational settings where the work requires a known level of color vision.
Publication Dates: 1991-2002.
Scores, 3: Normal Color Vision, Defective Color Vision (Red-Green Deficiency, Blue-Yellow Deficiency).
Administration: Individual.

Price Data, 2005: $219 per H.R.R. 4th Edition book including 4 demonstration plates, 20 test pages, Directions (in English) and laminated score sheet; other versions available with laminated plates for longer wear; additional options include directions in Spanish, French, Korean, Japanese, and Traditional Chinese; additional price information available from publisher.
Time: (1–3) minutes.
Authors: Richmond Products, Inc.; LeGrand H. Hardy (manual), Gertrude Rand (manual), and M. Catherine Rittler (manual); J. Neitz (Fourth Edition), and J. Bailey (Fourth Edition).
Publisher: Richmond Products, Inc.
Cross References: For a review by Ayres G. D'Costa, see 15:120.

[1202]

H-T-P: House-Tree-Person Projective Drawing Technique.

Purpose: "To provide psychologists and psychiatrists … with an examining procedure with which to acquire diagnostically and prognostically significant data concerning a subject's total personality."
Population: Ages 3 and over.
Publication Dates: 1946–1993.
Acronym: H-T-P.
Scores: Total score only.
Administration: Individual.
Price Data, 2002: $168 per complete kit including 1 copy of The House-Tree-Person Projective Drawing Technique: Manual and Interpretive Guide (1993, 165 pages), 1 copy of H-T-P Drawings: An illustrated Diagnostic Handbook (108 pages), 1 copy of Catalog for the Qualitative Interpretation of the H-T-P (191 pages), 25 interpretation booklets, and 25 drawing forms; $37.50 per interpretive catalogue; $39.50 per diagnostic handbook; $65 per revised manual (1993).
Time: (60–90) minutes.
Authors: John N. Buck, W. L. Warren (revision), Isaac Jolles (interpretive catalog), L. Stanley Wenck (diagnostic handbook), and Emmanuel F. Hammer (clinical research manual).
Publisher: Western Psychological Services.
Cross References: See T5:1160 (4 references), T4:1183 (6 references), T2:1469 (61 references), and P:437 (24 references); for a review by Mary R. Haworth of an earlier edition, see 6:215 (32 references); for a review by Philip L. Harriman, see 5:139 (61 references); for reviews by Albert Ellis and Ephraim Rosen and an excerpted review, see 4:107 (14 references); for reviews by Morris Krugman and Katherine N. Wilcox, see 3:47 (5 references).

[1203]

Hughes Basic Gross Motor Assessment.

Purpose: Designed to detect disorders in motor performance.

Population: Ages 6–12 believed to have minor motor dysfunctions.
Publication Date: 1979.
Acronym: BGMA.
Scores: 8 subtests: Static Balance, Stride Jump, Tandem Walking, Hopping, Skipping, Target, Yo-Yo, Ball Handling Skills.
Administration: Individual.
Price Data: Available from publisher.
Time: Administration time not reported.
Author: Jeanne E. Hughes.
Publisher: Nancy Hughes [No reply from publisher; status unknown].
Cross References: See 9:487 (1 reference).

[1204]
Human Figure Drawing Test.

Purpose: "Designed to provide an objective approach ..." to human figure drawings.
Population: Clients in psychotherapy.
Publication Date: 1993.
Acronym: HFDT.
Scores, 4: Impairment, Distortion, Simplification, Organic Factors Index.
Administration: Individual.
Price Data, 2006: $86.50 per complete kit including handbook (189 pages), 25 drawing forms, and 25 AUTOSCORE™ forms; $19.25 per 25 drawing forms; $35.75 per 25 AUTOSCORE™ forms; $54.50 per handbook.
Time: (5–20) minutes.
Authors: Jerry Mitchell, Richard Trent, and Roland McArthur.
Publisher: Western Psychological Services.
Cross References: For reviews by Charles A. Peterson and William K. Wilkinson, see 14:170; see also T5:1226 (4 references).

[1205]
Human Information Processing Survey.

Purpose: "Assesses processing preference—left, right, integrated, or mixed [brain functioning]."
Population: Adults.
Publication Date: 1984.
Acronym: HIP Survey.
Scores, 3: Right, Left, Integrated.
Administration: Group.
Editions, 2: Research Edition, Professional Edition.
Price Data, 2005: $56.90 per professional edition starter set including administrator's manual (44 pages), 10 survey forms, and 10 strategy and tactics profiles booklets; $43.85 per 10 survey forms and strategy and tactics profiles; $22 per manual (professional and research editions); $75.50 per research edition starter set including administrator's manual, 20 reusable survey forms, 20 profile forms, and 20 response sheets; $22.65

per 20 profile forms and response sheets (research edition); $23.10 per sample set for each edition.
Time: [40] minutes.
Authors: E. Paul Torrance, William Taggart (manual), and Barbara Taggart.
Publisher: Scholastic Testing Service, Inc.
Cross References: See T5:1227 (2 references) and T4:1186 (1 reference); for a review by J. P. Das, see 10:144 (1 reference).

[1206]
Human Relations Inventory.

Purpose: Designed to measure social conformity.
Population: Grades 9–16 and adults.
Publication Dates: 1954–1959.
Acronym: HRI.
Scores: Total score only.
Administration: Group.
Price Data: Available from publisher.
Time: (20) minutes.
Author: Raymond E. Bernberg.
Publisher: Psychometric Affiliates.
Cross References: See T2:1221 (4 references), P:114 (1 reference), and 6:119 (6 references); for reviews by Raymond C. Norris and John A. Radcliffe, see 5:68.

[1207]
Humanics National Child Assessment Form [Revised].

Purpose: To serve as developmental checklists of skills and behavior that occur during the first 9 years of life.
Population: Ages 0–3, 3–6, 6–9.
Publication Dates: 1981–2002.
Administration: Group.
Levels, 3: Birth to age 3, ages 3 to 6, ages 6 to 9.
Price Data, 2002: $34.95 per 25 assessment forms (specify level).
Time: Administration time varies.
Comments: Behavior checklists to be completed by parents or teachers.
Publisher: Humanics Learning.
   a) BIRTH TO THREE.
   Scores, 5: Social-Emotional, Language, Cognitive, Gross Motor, Fine Motor.
   Price Data: $23.95 per handbook and 5 assessment forms; $18.95 per handbook.
   Authors: Marsha Kaufman (checklist), T. Thomas McMurrain (checklist), Jane A. Caballero (handbook), and Derek Whordley (handbook).
   b) AGES THREE TO SIX.
   Scores, 5: Same as *a* above.
   Price Data: $39.95 per handbook and 5 assessment forms; $18.95 per handbook.
   Authors: Derek Whordley (handbook) and Rebecca J. Doster (handbook).

c) AGES SIX TO NINE.
Scores, 5: Same as *a* above.
Authors: Jackson Rabbit (checklist), Sylvia B. Booth (checklist), and Marilyn L. Perling (checklist).
Comments: Age level 6 to 9 is not accompanied by a handbook; behavior checklists to be completed by parents or teachers.
Cross References: For reviews by Arthur S. Ellen and David MacPhee of an earlier edition, see 11:170.

[1208]
The Hundred Pictures Naming Test.

Purpose: "A confrontation naming test designed to evaluate rapid naming ability."
Population: Ages 4-6 to 11-11.
Publication Date: 1992.
Acronym: HPNT.
Scores, 3: Error, Accuracy, Time.
Administration: Individual.
Price Data, 2006: A$104.50 per complete kit including manual (84 pages), test book, and 25 response forms; A$13.20 per 25 response forms.
Time: (6) minutes.
Authors: John P. Fisher and Jennifer M. Glenister.
Publisher: Australian Council for Educational Research Ltd. [Australia].
Cross References: For reviews by Jeffrey A. Atlas and Stephen Jurs, see 12:183.

[1209]
Hunter-Grundin Literacy Profiles.

Purpose: Designed to monitor the written and spoken language skills of children.
Population: Ages 6.5–8, 7.10–9.3, 9–10, 9.10–11.5, 10.10–12.7.
Publication Dates: 1979–1989.
Scores: 6 tests: Attitude to Reading (Levels 1 and 2 only), Reading for Meaning, Spelling, Free Writing, Spoken Language, Profile of Personal Interests (Levels 4 and 5 only).
Administration: Individual and group.
Levels: 5 overlapping levels.
Manual: Separate manual for each level.
Price Data: Available from publisher.
Time: (3-10) minutes per test at any one level.
Comments: Ratings by teacher in part.
Authors: Elizabeth Hunter-Grundin and Hans U. Grundin.
Publisher: The Test Agency Limited [England] [No reply from publisher; status unknown].
a) LEVEL 1.
Population: Ages 6.5–8.
b) LEVEL 2.
Population: Ages 7.10–9.3.
c) LEVEL 3.
Population: Ages 9–10.

d) LEVEL 4.
Population: Ages 9.10–11.5.
e) LEVEL 5.
Population: Ages 10.10–12.7.
Cross References: For reviews by Martha C. Beech and Patricia H. Kennedy of a previous edition, see 9:491.

[1210]
I Can Do Maths.

Purpose: Designed "to inform teachers and parents about children's development in numeracy in the early years of schooling."
Population: Children in the first 3 years of Australian and New Zealand school systems.
Publication Date: 2000–2001.
Scores, 4: Number, Measurement, Space, Total.
Administration: Group.
Price Data, 2006: A$58.30 per specimen set including one Level A test booklet, one Level B test booklet, one Level A Ezi-guide, one Level B Ezi-guide, and teacher's guide (36 pages).
Time: (30–40) minutes.
Authors: Brian Doig and Marion de Lemos.
Publisher: Australian Council for Educational Research Ltd. [Australia]
a) LEVEL A.
Population: Children in the first 2 years of school.
Price Data: $27.50 per 10 Level A test booklets.
b) LEVEL B.
Population: Children in the second and third years of school.
Price Data: Same as Level A above.
Cross References: For a review by Theresa Graham, see 16:109.

[1211]
I-SPEAK Your Language™: A Survey of Personal Styles.

Purpose: Designed to teach employees how to identify and modify their communication style to work best with others in a variety of situations.
Population: Employees.
Publication Dates: 1972–1999.
Scores, 8: Favorable Conditions (Intuitor, Thinker, Feeler, Senser), Stress Conditions (Intuitor, Thinker, Feeler, Senser).
Administration: Group or individual.
Price Data, 2002: $50 per 10 questionnaires; $12.95 per Self-Development Exercises manual (1992, 59 pages); $12.95 per manual (1993, 46 pages); $25 per specimen set including questionnaire, manual, and Self-Development Exercises manual.
Time: (20) minutes.
Comments: Also available (except Self-Development Exercises manual) in Spanish, French, German, Portuguese, Arabic, Norwegian, Bhasa Indonesian.

Author: Drake Beam Morin, Inc.
Publisher: Drake Beam Morin, Inc.
Cross References: For reviews by Mary Anne Bunda and Kimberly A. Lawless, see 13:141.

[1212]
IDEA Feedback for Administrators.

Purpose: Designed "to assist in appraising professional functioning and to suggest how that functioning could be improved."
Population: College and university administrators.
Publication Date: 2001.
Scores: Summary Ratings (Quality of Job, Confidence in Administrator), Strengths in Performing Administrative Roles (Planner, Consultant, Communicator, Expert, Community Builder), Administrative Style (Democratic Practice, Structuring, Vigor), Personal Characteristics (Interpersonal Sensitivity, Integrity, Character).
Administration: Group.
Price Data, 2003: $150 per administrator including initial and reminder e-mails to administrator, 3 copies of the report that includes responses to open-ended questions, and shipping plus $1 for each individual notified of survey via e-mail; $25 cancellation fee after e-mail addresses loaded into system; $50 fee assessed to correct undeliverable e-mails.
Time: Administration time not reported.
Comments: Online administration; ratings by faculty members and chairperson; publisher scores and generates interpretive reports.
Author: The IDEA Center.
Publisher: The IDEA Center.

[1213]
IDEA Feedback for Deans.

Purpose: To diagnose and find ways to improve the performance of the dean.
Population: College and university deans.
Publication Date: 2002.
Scores: Summary Ratings (Faculty Confidence in Ability to Manage, Influence in Changing the College's Quality, Overall Effectiveness), Administrative Effectiveness in Specific Activities (Improving College's Major Programs, Developing Resources, Organizational Matters, Program Leadership, Personnel Management), Administrative Style (Democratic Practice, Structuring, Vigor), Personal Characteristics (Interpersonal Sensitivity, Integrity, Character).
Administration: Group.
Price Data, 2003: $150 per dean including initial and reminder e-mails to administrator, 3 copies of the report that includes responses to open-ended questions, and shipping plus $1 for each individual notified of survey via e-mail; $25 cancellation fee after e-mail addresses loaded into system; $50 fee assessed to correct undeliverable e-mails.
Time: Administration time not reported.

Comments: Online administration; ratings by faculty and dean; publisher scores and generates interpreting report.
Author: The IDEA Center.
Publisher: The IDEA Center.

[1214]
IDEA Feedback for Department Chairs.

Purpose: Designed to diagnose administrative performance and discover ways to effectively improve it.
Population: College and university department chairpersons.
Publication Dates: 1977–1998.
Scores: 17 scores in 3 areas: Overall Ratings (Summary Judgement, Effectiveness in Performance, Five Types of Administrative Responsibilities); Effectiveness in Performing Twenty Specific Administrative Responsibilities (Administrative Support, Personnel Management, Program Leadership/Support, Building Image/Reputation, Developing Positive Climate); Description of Administrative Methods and Personal Characteristics (Democratic/Humanistic, Goal-Oriented/Structured, Supports Faculty, Promotes Positive Climate, Promotes Department Advancement, Ability to Resolve Issues, Communication Skills, Steadiness, Trustworthiness, Openness).
Administration: Group.
Price Data: Available from publisher.
Time: (15–30) minutes.
Comments: Available for online administration; previous version entitled Departmental Evaluation of Chairperson Activities for Development; publisher scores and generates interpretive reports; online inventory completed by faculty about their department chairs.
Authors: IDEA Center and Donald D. Hoyt (Technical Report, 1998).
Publisher: The IDEA Center.
Cross References: For reviews by John W. Fleenor and M. David Miller, see 15:121; see T4:741 (1 reference).

[1215]
IDEA Oral Language Proficiency Test.

Purpose: To "assist in the initial identification designation and redesignation of a student as being NES, LES, or FES (Non-Limited-Fluent English Speaking)."
Population: Preschool–grade 12.
Publication Dates: 1983–2006.
Acronym: IPT 2004.
Scores: 3 Modality scores: Oral, Listening, Speaking; 4 Diagnostic scores: Vocabulary, Comprehension, Syntax, Verbal Expression.
Administration: Individual.
Price Data: Available from publisher.
Foreign Language Editions: English and Spanish versions available for each level.
Publisher: Ballard & Tighe, Publishers.

a) PRE-IPT.
Population: Ages 3–5.
Publication Date: 2006.
Time: (8–13) minutes.
Authors: Constance O. Williams, Enrique F. Dalton, and Phyllis L. Tighe.
b) IPT-I.
Population: Grades K–6.
Publication Date: 2006.
Time: (14–19) minutes.
Authors: Wanda S. Ballard, Phyllis L. Tighe, and Enrique F. Dalton.
c) IPT-II.
Population: Grades 7–12.
Publication Date: 2006.
Time: (15–20) minutes.
Authors: Enrique F. Dalton and Beverly A. Amori.
Cross References: For reviews by Emilia C. Lopez and Salvador Hector Ochoa, see 14:171; see also T5:1234 (5 references).

[1216]
IDEA Reading and Writing Proficiency Test.

Purpose: To provide "comprehensive assessment for the initial identification and redesignation of Limited English Proficient (LEP) students."
Population: Grades K–12.
Publication Dates: 1992–2006.
Acronym: IPT R & W 2004.
Scores: 2 skill scores: Reading, Writing; 5 Diagnostic Scores for Reading: Vocabulary, Vocabulary in Context, Reading for Understanding, Reading for Life Skills, Language Usage; 3 Diagnostic Scores for Writing: Conventions, Write a Story, Write Your Own Story; 12 Diagnostic Scores for Early Literacy: Visual Recognition, Letter Recognition, Phonemic Awareness, Phonics, Reading Vocabulary, Reading for Life Skills, Reading for Understanding, Sentences and Stories, Copy Letters, Write Name and Copy Sentence, Descriptive/Narrative Writing, Spelling.
Administration: Group.
Levels, 4: Grades K–1, Grades 2–3, Grades 4–6, Grades 7–12.
Price Data: Available from publisher.
Foreign Language Editions: English and Spanish versions available for each level.
Time: (70–115) minutes.
Comments: Used in conjunction with the IPT Oral Language Proficiency Test (1215) with scoring rules available for deriving both a comprehension and an overall score.
Authors: Beverly A. Amori, Enrique F. Dalton, and Phyllis L. Tighe.
Publisher: Ballard & Tighe, Publishers.
Cross References: For reviews by James Dean Brown and Alan Garfinkel, see 13:142.

[1217]
IDEA Student Ratings of Instruction.

Purpose: Designed to provide student ratings of college instructors.
Population: College faculty.
Publication Dates: 1975–1998.
Scores: 5-part report compiled from ratings data: Overall Measures of Teaching Effectiveness, Student Ratings of Progress in Specific Objectives, Teaching Methods/Style, Course Description/Context, Statistical Detail.
Administration: Group.
Price Data: Available from publisher.
Time: (10–20) minutes.
Comments: Available for use in the classroom and in online classes.
Authors: Donald P. Hoyt, William H. Pallett, Amy B. Gross, Richard E. Owens, William E. Cashin (technical reports), Glenn R. Sixbury (technical reports, numbers 7–10), Yih-Fen Chen (technical report number 11).
Publisher: The IDEA Center.
Cross References: For reviews by Raoul A. Arreola and Jennifer J. Fager, see 14:172; see also T4:1195 (1 reference); for a review by John C. Ory of an earlier edition, see 9:493 (2 references).

[1218]
IDEAS: Interest Determination, Exploration and Assessment System™.

Purpose: "To be used as an introduction to career exploration for students and adults."
Population: Grades 7–12 and adults.
Publication Dates: 1977–1994.
Acronym: IDEAS™.
Scores, 16: Mechanical/Fixing, Protective Services, Nature/Outdoors, Mathematics, Science, Medical, Creative Arts, Writing, Community Service, Educating, Child Care, Public Speaking, Business, Sales, Office Practices, Food Service.
Administration: Group or individual.
Price Data, 2006: $70 per 50 test booklets (Youth or Adult version); $21 per manual (1990, 80 pages); $25 per starter kit with self-scored reports; quantity discounts available for the reports; price information for Spanish materials available from publisher.
Time: (40–45) minutes.
Comments: Self-administered, self-scored.
Author: Charles B. Johansson.
Publisher: Pearson Assessments.
Cross References: For a review by Robert J. Miller, see 11:172; for a review by M. O'Neal Weeks of an earlier edition, see 9:516.

[1219]
Illinois Test of Psycholinguistic Abilities, Third Edition.

Purpose: Designed "to help children who have weakness in various linguistic processes including spoke or written language."

Population: Ages 5-0 to 12-11.

Publication Dates: 1961–2001.

Acronym: ITPA-3.

Scores, 12: Spoken Analogies, Spoken Vocabulary, Morphological Closure, Syntactic Sentences, Sound Deletion, Rhyming Sequences, Sentence Sequencing, Written Vocabulary, Sight Decoding, Sound Decoding, Sight Spelling, Sound Spelling.

Administration: Individual.

Price Data, 2006: $179 per kit including 25 profile/examiner record booklets, 25 student response booklets, manual (2001, 165 pages), and an audio cassette; $50 per 25 profile/examiner record booklets; $45 per 25 student response booklets; $71 per examiner's manual; $20 per audio cassette; $276 print/software combo kit; $112 per software scoring and report system.

Time: (45–60) minutes.

Authors: Donald D. Hammill, Nancy Mather, and Rhia Roberts.

Publisher: PRO-ED.

Cross References: For a review by Roger L. Towne, see 15:122; see T5:1240 (51 references), T4:1201 (53 references), 9:496 (37 references), and T3:1126 (145 references); for reviews by James Lumsden and J. Lee Wiederholt of an earlier edition, and an excerpted review by R. P. Waugh, see 8:431 (269 references); see also T2:981 (113 references); for reviews by John B. Carroll and Clinton I. Chase, see 7:442 (239 references); see also 6:549 (22 references).

[1220]
Illness Behaviour Questionnaire, Third Edition.

Purpose: In the clinical context, to screen for the presence, and "record aspects of illness behaviour, particularly those attitudes that suggest or are associated with inappropriate or maladaptive modes of responding to one's state of health."

Population: Pain clinic, psychiatric, and general practice patients.

Publication Dates: 1983–1994.

Acronym: IBQ.

Scores, 9: 7 factors (General Hypochondriasis, Disease Conviction, Psychological vs. Somatic Perception of Illness, Affective Inhibition, Affective Disturbance, Denial, Irritability) and Discriminant Function Score and Whitely Index of Hypochondriasis.

Administration: Individual or group.

Price Data, 1999: $40 per manual (1994, 95 pages) including test.

Time: (10) minutes.

Comments: Self-report instrument; the Discriminant Function Score indicates likelihood of conversion disorder.

Authors: Issy Pilowsky and Neil Spence.

Publisher: I. Pilowsky [Australia].

Cross References: For reviews by Colin Cooper and M. Allan Cooperstein, see 15:123; see also T5:1241 (6 references) and T4:1203 (6 references).

[1221]
Illness Effects Questionnaire—Multi-Perspective.

Purpose: Designed to assess "the impact of a patient's illness from multiple perspectives."

Population: Ages 18 and over.

Publication Date: 2002.

Acronym: IEQ—MP.

Administration: Individual.

Forms, 4: Self-Report, Professional, Observer, Treatment.

Price Data, 2006: $242 per complete kit including user's manual (91 pages), 25 of each form, and 25 comparative and integrated profile forms; $59 per user's manual; $50 per 25 of any one form; $83 per specimen set including user's manual, 3 of each form, and 3 comparative and integrated profile forms.

Time: (10) minutes.

Authors: Glen D. Greenberg and Rolf A. Peterson.

Publisher: Multi-Health Systems Inc.

Cross References: For reviews by Alan C. Bugbee, Jr. and Beth Doll, see 16:110.

[1222]
Impact Message Inventory, Research Edition.

Purpose: Designed to help clarify interpersonal transactions in any dyad (e.g., friends, teacher-student, employer-employee, therapist-client); provides a method of assessing personality by measuring the attitudes and feelings that the person being studied arouses in the respondent such as dominance, competition, hostility, inhibition, distrust.

Population: Older adolescents, college, and adults.

Publication Dates: 1975–1987.

Acronym: IMI.

Scores, 15: Dominant, Competitive, Hostile, Mistrustful, Detached, Inhibited, Submissive, Succorant, Abasive, Deferent, Agreeable, Nurturant, Affiliative, Sociable, Exhibitionistic.

Administration: Group.

Forms, 2: Male Targets, Female Targets.

Price Data: Available from publisher (www.mindgarden.com).

Time: [15] minutes.

Comments: Self-report inventory; includes original and an updated octant version (which measures 8 scales instead of 15).

Author: Donald J. Kiesler.
Publisher: Mind Garden, Inc.
Cross References: See T4:1205 (13 references); for reviews by Stephen L. Benton and Steven G. LoBello, see 12:186 (4 references); for reviews by Fred H. Borgen and Stanley R. Strong of an earlier edition, see 9:500 (1 reference); see also T3:1130 (1 reference).

[1223]
Incentives Management Index.

Purpose: Designed to make explicit sales managers' "assumptions, theories, and practices in the realm of sales motivation."
Population: Sales managers.
Publication Dates: 1972–1995.
Acronym: IMI.
Scores, 5: Basic Creative Comfort, Safety and Order, Belonging and Affiliation, Ego-Status, Actualization and Self-Expression.
Administration: Group.
Price Data, 2001: $8.95 per instrument (1995, 24 pages).
Time: Administration time not reported.
Comments: Self-administered; self-scored.
Authors: Jay Hall and Norman J. Seim.
Publisher: Teleometrics International, Inc.
Cross References: For reviews by Leslie H. Krieger and Patricia H. Wheeler, see 14:173.

[1224]
Independent Living Scales.

Purpose: Designed to assess adults' competence in instrumental activities of daily living.
Population: Adults with cognitive impairments.
Publication Date: 1996.
Acronym: ILS.
Scores, 6: Memory/Orientation, Managing Money, Managing Home and Transportation, Health and Safety, Social Adjustment, Total.
Administration: Individual.
Price Data, 2002: $248 per complete kit including manual (119 pages), 25 record forms, stimulus booklet, and a pouch containing a facsimile of a driver's license, credit card, and key; $37 per 25 record forms.
Time: (45) minutes.
Comments: Four screening items are used to determine whether the examinee has a vision, speech, or hearing impairment; the stimulus booklet is designed for adults who can hear and those with a hearing impairment.
Author: Patricia Anderten Loeb.
Publisher: PsychCorp, A brand of Harcourt Assessment, Inc.
Cross References: For reviews by Libby G. Cohen and Jack A. Cummings, see 14:174.

[1225]
Independent Mastery Testing System for Math Skills.

Purpose: "To monitor the student's mastery of basic mathematics skills, to diagnose specific student weaknesses, to recommend a program of further study, and to provide the teacher with a comprehensive record of student progress."
Population: Adult students.
Publication Date: 1984.
Acronym: IMTS.
Scores: 13 tests: Adding and Subtracting Whole Numbers, Multiplying and Dividing Whole Numbers, Adding and Subtracting Fractions, Multiplying and Dividing Fractions, Adding and Subtracting Decimals, Multiplying and Dividing Decimals, Percents Skills, Charts and Graphs Skills, Measurement Skills, The Language of Algebra, The Uses of Algebra, Geometry—Angles, Geometry—Plane and Solid Figures.
Administration: Individual.
Forms: 3 parallel forms of each test.
Price Data: Not available.
Time: Administration time not reported.
Comments: Computer-administered instructional management system; Apple II, Apple II+, Apple IIe, or Apple IIc computer necessary for administration.
Authors: Cambridge, The Adult Education Company in association with Moravian College, Bethlehem, PA.
Publisher: Prentice Hall [No reply from publisher; status unknown].
Cross References: For a review by Richard M. Jaeger, see 10:147.

[1226]
Independent Mastery Testing System for Writing Skills.

Purpose: "To monitor the student's mastery of basic grammar and writing skills, to diagnose specific student weaknesses, to recommend a program of further study, and to provide the teacher with a comprehensive record of student progress."
Population: Adult students.
Publication Date: 1984.
Acronym: IMTS.
Scores: 15 tests: Recognizing Sentences, Verb Tenses, Subject-Verb Agreement—Part A, Subject-Verb Agreement—Part B, Pronouns—Part A, Pronouns—Part B, Plurals and Possessives, Adjectives and Adverbs—Part A, Adjectives and Adverbs—Part B, Sentence Structure, Prepositions and Conjunctions, Logic and Organization, Capitalization, Punctuation, Spelling.
Administration: Individual.
Forms: 3 parallel forms (1, 2, 3) of each test.
Price Data: Available from publisher.

Time: Administration time not reported.
Comments: Computer-administered instructional management system; Apple II, Apple II+, Apple IIe, or Apple IIc computer necessary for administration.
Authors: Cambridge, The Adult Education Company, in association with Moravian College, Bethlehem, PA.
Publisher: Prentice Hall [No reply from publisher; status unknown].
Cross References: For a review by Pamela A. Moss, see 11:173.

[1227]
Independent School Entrance Examination.

Purpose: Developed to assess verbal reasoning, quantitative reasoning, reading comprehension, and mathematics achievement for use in admissions into independent schools and to provide independent schools with a candidate's writing sample given under standard conditions.
Population: Grades 4–11, or candidates for grades 5–12.
Publication Dates: 1989–1999.
Acronym: ISEE.
Scores, 4: Verbal Reasoning, Quantitative Reasoning, Reading Comprehension, Mathematics Achievement.
Administration: Group.
Levels, 3: Lower, Middle, Upper.
Forms, 2: A, B.
Price Data, 2006: $73 per large group testing fee; price information for technical manual and additional materials available from publisher.
Time: 130 minutes; 30 minutes for essay component.
Comments: Test book name is ISEE; essay component is not scored but is sent to schools.
Author: Educational Records Bureau.
Publisher: Educational Records Bureau.
Cross References: For reviews by Mary Anne Bunda and Joyce R. McLarty, see 11:174.

[1228]
Index of Teaching Stress.

Purpose: Designed to "assess the effects of a specific student's behavior on a teacher's stress level and self-perception."
Population: Teachers from preschool to 12th grade.
Publication Dates: 2003–2004.
Acronym: ITS.
Scores, 12: Total Stress Score, Attention-Deficit/Hyperactivity Disorder, Student Characteristics (Emotional Lability/Low Adaptability, Anxiety/Withdrawal, Low Ability/Learning Disability, Aggressive/Conduct Disorder, Total); Teacher Characteristics (Sense of Competence/Need for Support, Loss of Satisfaction From Teaching, Disruption of the Teaching Process, Frustration Working With Parents, Total).
Administration: Group.

Price Data, 2006: $125 per introductory kit including manual (2004, 89 pages), 25 reusable item booklets, 25 answer sheets, and 25 profile forms.
Time: (20–25) minutes.
Authors: Richard R. Abidin, Ross W. Greene, and Timothy R. Konold.
Publisher: Psychological Assessment Resources, Inc.

[1229]
Individual Directions Inventory™.

Purpose: Designed to provide insight into a wide range of personal motivations; useful in individual and organizational development.
Population: Adults.
Publication Dates: 1988–2001.
Acronym: IDI.
Scores: 17 dimensions: Types of Emotional Satisfaction (Giving, Receiving, Belonging, Expressing, Gaining Stature, Entertaining, Creating, Interpreting, Excelling, Enduring, Structuring, Maneuvering, Winning, Controlling, Stability, Independence, Irreproachability).
Administration: Group.
Price Data: Available from publisher.
Time: (30) minutes.
Comments: Purchase and use requires training by publisher or credential review.
Authors: James T. Mahoney (test) and Robert I. Kabacoff (manual).
Publisher: Management Research Group.

[1230]
Individual Employment Plan with 84-Item Employability Assessment

Purpose: To help service organizations gather information about clients' employability status and assist clients in creating and completing a training and services plan.
Population: Participants in employment programs.
Publication Date: 2002.
Acronym: IEP.
Scores: Personal Issues and Considerations, Health and Physical Considerations, Work Orientation, Career and Life Planning Skills, Job Seeking Skills, Job Adaptation Skills, Education and Training.
Administration: Individual.
Price Data, 2006: $34.95 per 25 inventories including free administrator's guide (8 pages).
Time: (30) minutes.
Comments: Eight-panel foldout.
Authors: LaVerne L. Ludden and Bonnie R. Maitlen.
Publisher: JIST Publishing, Inc.

[1231]
Individual Outlook Test.

Purpose: Designed to assess codependent orientation.

Population: Adults.
Publication Date: 1993.
Acronym: IOT.
Scores, 6: Codependent Orientation, Externally Derived Sense of Self Worth, Anxiety, Dysfunctional Family of Origin, Dependency within Relationships, Dysfunctional Relationships.
Administration: Group or individual.
Price Data: Available from publisher.
Time: (15–20) minutes.
Authors: Laurie A. Sim and Eugene E. Fox (test and manual); Michelle J. Worth and Donald Macnab (manual).
Publisher: Psychometrics Canada Ltd. [Canada].
Cross References: For reviews by Jeffrey A. Atlas and by Susan C. Whiston and Wendi L. Tai, see 16:111.

[1232]
Individual Style Survey.

Purpose: "Intended to be an educational tool for self and interpersonal development."
Publication Dates: 1989–1990.
Administration: Group.
Price Data: Available from publisher.
Time: (60–90) minutes.
Comments: Self-administered, self-scored survey.
Author: Norman Amundson.
Publisher: Psychometrics Canada Ltd. [Canada] [No reply from publisher; status unknown].
a) INDIVIDUAL STYLE SURVEY.
   Population: Adults.
   Publication Date: 1989.
   Acronym: ISS.
   Scores, 14: 8 categories of behavior (Forceful, Assertive, Outgoing, Spontaneous, Empathetic, Patient, Reserved, Analytical) yielding 4 styles (Dominant, Influencing, Harmonious, Cautious) that combine to form 2 summary scores (People/Task Orientation, Introspective/Interactive Stance).
b) MY PERSONAL STYLE.
   Population: Ages 10–18.
   Publication Date: 1990.
   Acronym: MPS.
   Scores, 14: 8 categories (Carefree, Outgoing, Straight Forward, Forceful, Precise, Reserved, Patient, Sensitive) yielding 4 styles (Influencing, Strong Willed, Cautious, Peaceful) that combine to form 2 summary scores (People/Task Orientation, Expressive/Thoughtful Stance).
   Comments: Simplified version of the Individual Style Survey for use with young people.
Cross References: For reviews by Jeffrey A. Atlas and William I. Sauser, see 13:144.

[1233]
Industrial Reading Test.

Purpose: "Measures an individual's ability to comprehend written technical materials."

Population: Grade 9 and above vocational students and applicants or trainees in technical or vocational training programs.
Publication Dates: 1976-1989.
Acronym: IRT.
Scores: Total score only.
Administration: Group or individual.
Forms, 2: A, B.
Restricted Distribution: Distribution of Form A restricted to business and industry.
Price Data, 2006: $34 per examination kit; $30 per manual; $28 per Form A Test Booklets; $155 per Form B Test Booklets; $49 per Form A Keys; $49 per Form B Keys; $105 per IBM 805/OpScan Answer Sheets.
Time: (40) minutes.
Comments: Test can be scored by hand or with an IBM 805 or OpScan machine.
Author: The Psychological Corporation.
Publisher: Harcourt Assessment, Inc.
Cross References: For a review by Darrell L. Sabers, see 9:504.

[1234]
Industrial Test Battery.

Purpose: Intended to assess an individual's conceptual reasoning and spatial abilities.
Population: Individuals with less than 7 years of formal schooling.
Publication Date: 1986.
Acronym: ITB.
Scores: Total score only for each test.
Subtests, 3: Anomalous Concept Test (ACT), Anomalous Figure Test (AFT), Series Induction Test (SIT).
Administration: Group.
Price Data: Available from publisher.
Foreign Language Edition: Tests printed in both English and Afrikaans.
Time: 20(30) minutes for ACT; 25(35) minutes for AFT; 30(40) minutes for SIT.
Author: T. R. Taylor.
Publisher: Human Sciences Research Council [South Africa].

[1235]
The Infanib.

Purpose: Designed to provide a systematic scorable method to assess the neurological status of infants, especially infants who are premature or have special conditions.
Population: Infants from 4 to 18 months corrected gestational age.
Publication Date: 1994.
Scores, 20: Hands Open, Hands Closed, Scarf Sign, Heel-To-Ear, Popliteal Angle, Leg Abduction, Dorsiflexion of the Foot, The Foot Grasp, Tonic Labyrinthine Supine, Asymmetric Tonic Neck Reflex, Pull-

To-Sitting, Body Denotative, Body Rotative, All-Fours, Tonic Labyrinthine Prone, Sitting, Sideways Parachute, Backwards Parachute, Standing-Positive Support Reaction, Forward Parachute.
Administration: Individual.
Price Data, 2002: $94 per complete kit including 50 screening forms and manual (131 pages); $28 per 50 screening forms.
Time: Untimed.
Comments: "Criterion-referenced" test with ratings determined by therapist.
Author: Patricia H. Ellison.
Publisher: Harcourt Assessment, Inc.
Cross References: For reviews by Jill Ann Jenkins and John J. Vacca, see 14:175.

[1236]
Infant Development Inventory.
Purpose: Designed "for screening or assessing the development of infants in the first eighteen months."
Population: Birth to 18 months.
Publication Dates: 1980–1995.
Acronym: IDI.
Scores, 5: Social, Self-Help, Gross Motor, Fine Motor, Language.
Administration: Individual.
Manual: Brief Instructions only.
Price Data, 2005: $12.50 per 25 parent questionnaires.
Time: [5–10] minutes.
Comments: New version of the Minnesota Infant Development Inventory (T4:1642); observations by mother.
Author: Harold Ireton.
Publisher: Child Development Review - Behavior Science Systems, Inc.
Cross References: For reviews by Alan S. Kaufman and John J. Vacca, see 14:176; see also T5:1259 (2 references); for information on the earlier edition, see T4:1642 (1 reference); for a review by Bonnie W. Camp of the earlier edition, see 9:714.

[1237]
The Infant-Toddler and Family Instrument.
Purpose: Designed as "a relatively short survey of family and child functioning" to "help in making a judgment about whether a child and family need further services and referrals."
Population: Families with infants and toddlers 6–36 months.
Publication Date: 2001.
Acronym: ITFI.
Scores, 4: Caregiver Interview, Developmental Map, Checklist for Evaluating Concern, Plan for the Child and Family.
Administration: Individual.

Price Data: Available from publisher.
Time: (150–165) minutes.
Authors: Nancy H. Apfel and Sally Provence.
Publisher: Paul H. Brookes Publishing Co.

[1238]
Infant-Toddler Developmental Assessment.
Purpose: Constructed as "an integrated family-centered assessment process that addresses the health and development of children." It is designed to improve the early identification of children (birth to 3 years) who are developmentally at risk.
Population: Birth to 36 months.
Publication Date: 1995.
Acronym: IDA.
Scores: 8 developmental domains: Gross Motor, Fine Motor, Relationship to Inanimate Objects (Cognitive), Language Communication, Self-Help, Relationship to Persons, Emotions and Feeling States (Affects), Coping.
Administration: Individual.
Price Data, 2006: $595 per complete kit including administration manual (223 pages), foundations and study guide, readings, 25 parent report forms (English), 25 health record guides, and 25 record forms all in a canvas carrying case along with manipulatives in a separate carrying case; $79.50 per administration manual; $79.50 per foundations and study guide; $32.50 per 25 parent report forms (English or Spanish); $25.50 per 25 health record guides; $58 per 25 record forms.
Time: Varies.
Comments: Ratings by multidisciplinary team.
Authors: Sally Provence, Joanna Erikson, Susan Vater, and Saro Palmeri.
Publisher: Riverside Publishing.
Cross References: For reviews by Melissa M. Groves and E. Jean Newman, see 13:146.

[1239]
Infant/Toddler Environment Rating Scale-Revised Edition.
Purpose: Designed to assess programs for children from birth to 30 months of age in group care settings.
Population: Infant/toddler day care centers.
Publication Dates: 1990-2006.
Acronym: ITERS-R.
Scores, 8: Space and Furnishings, Personal Care Routines, Listening and Talking, Activities, Interaction, Program Structure, Parents and Staff, Total.
Administration: Individual.
Price Data, 2006: $14.95 per rating scale (2006, 79 pages) including administration and scoring instructions and score sheet and profile that may be photocopied.
Time: (180) minutes to observe and rate.
Authors: Thelma Harms, Debby Cryer, and Richard M. Clifford.

Publisher: Teachers College Press.
Cross References: See T5:1264 (6 references); for reviews by Norman A. Constantine and Annette M. Iverson of an earlier edition, see 12:188.

[1240]
Infant/Toddler Symptom Checklist.

Purpose: Designed as a screening instrument for infants and toddlers with regulatory and sensory-integrative disorders.
Population: 7–30 months.
Publication Date: 1995.
Scores, 9: Self-Regulation, Attention, Sleep, Eating or Feeding, Dressing/Bathing or Touch, Movement, Listening and Language, Looking and Sight, Attachment/Emotional Functioning.
Administration: Individual.
Levels, 6: 7–9 months, 10–12 months, 13–18 months, 19–24 months, 25–30 months, General Screening Version (when age specific administration is inconvenient).
Price Data, 2002: $63 per Infant/Toddler Symptom Checklist including manual (58 pages) and 6 sets of 5 score sheets in 25-page pads in a vinyl storage portfolio; $37 per additional score sheets available in 6 sets of five sheets in 25-page pads.
Time: (10) minutes.
Comments: "Criterion-referenced"; checklist completed by parents or caregiver.
Authors: Georgia A. DeGangi, Susan Poisson, Ruth Z. Sickel, and Andrea Santman Wiener.
Publisher: Harcourt Assessment, Inc.
Cross References: For reviews by Deborah Erickson and Ruth E. Tomes, see 14:178.

[1241]
Influence Strategies Exercise.

Purpose: Designed to identify and develop influence techniques.
Population: Managers and employees.
Publication Date: 1993.
Acronym: ISE.
Scores, 9: Empowerment, Interpersonal Awareness, Bargaining, Relationship Building, Organizational Awareness, Common Vision, Impact Management, Logical Persuasion, Coercion.
Administration: Individual or group.
Parts, 3: Participant Version, Profile and Interpretative Notes, and Feedback Version (optional).
Price Data, 2006: $79 per complete kit including 10 exercises and 10 profiles and interpretive notes (19 pages); $29 per 10 feedback version exercises.
Time: (20–25) minutes.
Comments: Self-administered questionnaire.
Author: Hay Group.
Publisher: Hay Group.

Cross References: For reviews by Collie W. Conoley and Paul M. Muchinsky, see 13:147.

[1242]
The Influence Styles Inventory.

Purpose: Designed to identify and examine the styles and strategies used in "day-to-day problems managers face."
Population: Managers.
Publication Dates: 1997–1998.
Scores, 3: Aggressive, Assertive, Passive.
Administration: Group.
Price Data: Available from publisher.
Time: (20) minutes.
Author: Marshall Sashkin.
Publisher: HRD Press, Inc.

[1243]
Informal Reading Comprehension Placement Test [Revised].

Purpose: "Assesses the instructional and independent comprehension levels of students from pre-readiness (grade 1) through level twelve plus (grade 12)."
Population: Grades 1–8 for typical learners and grades 8–12 remedially; adult education students.
Publication Dates: 1983–1999.
Scores, 3: Word Comprehension, Passage Comprehension, Total Comprehension.
Administration: Individual.
Price Data, 2006: $59.95 per test including Mac/Win CD-ROM, management, and guide; $299.75 per site license version.
Time: (35–50) minutes for the battery; (15–20) minutes for Part 1; (20–30) minutes for Part 2.
Comments: Automatically administered, scored, and managed; for use with adults, the placements are correlated with Tests of Adult Basic Education (2636); test administered in two parts; microcomputer (IBM Windows or MAC) necessary for administration.
Authors: Ann Edson and Eunice Insel.
Publisher: Educational Activities Software.
Cross References: For reviews by Diane I. Sawyer and Gabrielle Stutman, see 13:148; for reviews by Gloria A. Galvin and Claudia R. Wright of an earlier edition, see 11:178.

[1244]
Information System Skills.

Purpose: Constructed to predict "a person's success in operating terminal based information systems."
Population: Information processing job applicants.
Publication Date: 1983.
Acronym: ISS.
Scores, 4: Reasoning, Form Recognition, Document Checking, Speed.
Administration: Group.

Price Data: Available from publisher.
Time: 36 minutes and 30 seconds (45 minutes).
Author: Malcolm Morrisby.
Publisher: Educational & Industrial Test Services Ltd. [England].

[1245]
Informeter: An International Technique for the Measurement of Political Information.
Purpose: Designed to measure political information.
Population: Adults.
Publication Date: 1972.
Scores, 5: Local, National, International, Miscellaneous, Total.
Administration: Group.
Manual: No manual.
Price Data, 2005: $2 per scale.
Time: [15] minutes.
Comments: Supplementary article available.
Author: Panos D. Bardis.
Publisher: Donna Bardis.

[1246]
Inquiry Mode Questionnaire: A Measure of How You Think and Make Decisions.
Purpose: Developed to measure "individual preferences in the way people think."
Population: Business and industry.
Publication Dates: 1977–1989.
Acronym: INQ.
Scores, 5: Synthesist, Idealist, Pragmatist, Analyst, Realist.
Administration: Group or individual.
Price Data: Available from publisher.
Time: (20) minutes.
Comments: Manual title is INQ Styles of Thinking.
Authors: Allen F. Harrison and Robert M. Bramson.
Publisher: INQ Educational Materials Inc.
Cross References: For reviews by Philip Benson and Tamela Yelland, see 12:189.

[1247]
Insight: Assessing and Developing Self-Esteem.
Purpose: Designed as a tool to "assess and, where required, improve a (child's) self-esteem."
Population: Ages 3 to 16.
Publication Date: 2002.
Scores, 4: Sense of Self, Sense of Belonging, Sense of Personal Power, Overall.
Administration: Individual or group.
Price Data: Available from publisher.
Time: (10) minutes.
Comments: Reproducible rating scale forms are titled "Self-Esteem Indicator."
Author: Elizabeth Morris.

Publisher: NFER-Nelson Publishing Co., Ltd. [England].
a) INSIGHT: PRE-SCHOOL.
Population: Ages 3 to 5.
Comments: Rating scale completed by adult observer.
b) INSIGHT: PRIMARY.
Population: Ages 5 to 11.
Comments: Rating scale can be completed by adult observer or by adult and student working together.
c) INSIGHT: SECONDARY.
Population: Ages 11 to 16.
Comments: Rating scale completed by adult observer or by adult and student working together.
Cross References: For reviews by Gerald E. DeMauro and Gypsy M. Denzine, see 16:112.

[1248]
INSIGHT Inventory [Revised].
Purpose: Designed to determine how an individual differs from other individuals in his or her style of influencing others, relating to others, responding to people, making decisions and taking action, and structuring time and handling details.
Population: Adults age 21 and over, students age 16–21.
Publication Dates: 1988–2006.
Scores: 4 traits: Getting Your Way (Direct, Indirect), Responding to People (Reserved, Outgoing), Pacing Activity (Urgent, Steady), Dealing with Details (Unstructured, Precise).
Administration: Group or individual.
Forms, 3: INSIGHT Inventory, Teaming Up with INSIGHT, INSIGHT 360 Degree Style Feedback Set.
Price Data, 2006: $12 per INSIGHT Inventory; $16 per Teaming Up with INSIGHT; $16 per Form F, INSIGHT 360 Degree Style Feedback Set; $295 per Training Kit for adult version including video, training guide, technical manual, and CD with digital slides.
Time: (15–20) minutes.
Comments: Users get two profiles, one reflecting how they see themselves in their work (school) environment and the other reflecting how they see themselves in their personal (at home) environment; "has field theory base which takes into account that participants may change their behavior from one environment (field) to another"; utilizes self-perception; supporting feedback sets provide perceptions of how five others see the user; 1993 revision based on a second collection of norms and a factor analysis of the items; online version available at www.insightinstitute.com.
Author: Patrick Handley.
Publisher: Insight Institute, Inc.
Cross References: For reviews by Sanford J. Cohen and Elizabeth L. Jones, see 14:179; for a review by Susana Urbina of an earlier edition, see 13:149.

[1249]
Instructional Leadership Evaluation and Development Program (ILEAD).

Purpose: "Designed to assess instructional leadership behavior, job satisfaction and commitment, and school culture or climate from the teachers' perspective." "Designed to assess school climate from the student perspective." "Designed to simultaneously assess the person, the job, and the culture or climate of the setting in which the person works." "Designed to assess instructional leadership behavior."
Population: School climates and leadership.
Publication Dates: 1985–1988.
Acronym: ILEAD.
Administration: Individual or group.
Price Data: Available from publisher.
Time: Administration time varies with form.
Authors: Larry A. Braskamp (School Climate Inventories, School Administrator Assessment Survey), Martin L. Maehr (same material as above), and MetriTech, Inc. (manual and Instructional Leadership Inventory).
Publisher: MetriTech, Inc.

a) SCHOOL CLIMATE INVENTORY (FORM T).
Purpose: "Designed to assess instructional leadership behavior, job satisfaction and commitment, and school culture or climate from the teachers' perspective."
Scores, 12: Instructional Leadership (Defines Mission, Manages Curriculum, Supervises Teaching, Monitors Student Progress, Promotes Instructional Climate), Climate (Satisfaction, Commitment, Strength, Accomplishment, Recognition, Power, Affiliation).
Comments: Ratings by teachers.

b) SCHOOL CLIMATE INVENTORY (FORM S).
Purpose: "Designed to assess school climate from the student perspective."
Scores, 5: Strength of Climate, Accomplishment, Recognition, Power, Affiliation.
Comments: Ratings by students in grades 3–12.

c) SCHOOL ADMINISTRATOR ASSESSMENT SURVEY.
Purpose: "Designed to simultaneously assess the person, the job, and the culture or climate of the setting in which the person works."
Scores, 19: Personal Incentive (Accomplishment, Recognition, Power, Affiliation), Self-Concept (Self-Reliance, Self-Esteem, Goal-Directedness), Job Opportunity (Accomplishment, Recognition, Power, Affiliation, Advancement), Organizational Culture (Accomplishment, Recognition, Power, Affiliation, Satisfaction, Strength of Culture, Commitment).
Comments: Adaptation of SPECTRUM; self-ratings by administrators.

d) INSTRUCTIONAL LEADERSHIP INVENTORY.
Purpose: "Designed to assess instructional leadership behavior."
Scores, 8: Instructional Leadership (Defines Mission, Manages Curriculum, Supervises Teaching, Monitors Student Progress, Promotes Instructional Climate), Contextual (Staff, School, Community).
Comments: Self-ratings by principals.
Cross References: For reviews by David L. Bolton and Donna L. Sundre, see 12:190; see also T4:1240 (1 reference).

[1250]
Instructional Style Indicator [Revised].

Purpose: Designed to identify "instructional preferences and learning effectiveness with others."
Population: Adults.
Publication Dates: 1996-2006.
Acronym: ISI.
Scores, 4: Behavioral/Action/Independent, Cognitive/Analysis/Visual, Interpersonal/Harmony/Auditory, Affective/Expression/Experiential.
Administration: Individual or group.
Price Data, 2006: $13.95 per test booklet (2006, 16 pages); $13.95 per In-Depth Interpretation booklet (2006, 28 pages); $26.95 per access code online version; $37.95 per Trainer's Guidelines (1996, 28 pages).
Time: (30) minutes (90-180 minutes program options).
Comments: Self-administered and self-scored; can be used in conjunction with the Learning Style Indicator (1432).
Authors: Ken Keis, Everett T. Robinson, and Terry D. Anderson.
Publisher: Consulting Resource Group International, Inc.

[1251]
Instrument for Disability Screening [Developmental Edition].

Purpose: To screen for learning disabilities.
Population: Primary grade children.
Publication Date: 1980.
Acronym: IDS.
Scores, 9: Hyperactive/Aggression, Visual, Speech/Auditory, Reading, Drawing/Writing, Inactivity, Concepts, Psychomotor Development, Total.
Administration: Individual.
Manual: No manual.
Price Data: Not available.
Time: (5-15) minutes.
Author: James R. Beatty.
Publisher: James R. Beatty [No reply from publisher; status unknown].

Cross References: See T3:1161 (3 references); for reviews by Norman A. Buktenica and Stephen J. Pfeiffer, see 9:515.

[1252]
Instrument Timbre Preference Test.

Purpose: "To act as an objective aid to the teacher and the parent in helping a student choose an appropriate woodwind or brass instrument to learn to play in beginning instrumental music and band."
Population: Grades 4-12.
Publication Dates: 1984-1985.
Acronym: ITPT.
Scores, 7: Flute, Clarinet, Saxophone and French Horn, Oboe/English Horn/Bassoon, Trumpet and Cornet, Trombone/Baritone/French Horn, Tuba and Sousaphone.
Administration: Group.
Price Data, 2006: $59 per complete kit including 100 test sheets, scoring masks, compact disc, and manual (1984, 53 pages); $14.50 per 100 test sheets; scoring service available from publisher.
Time: (30) minutes.
Author: Edwin E. Gordon.
Publisher: GIA Publications, Inc.
Cross References: For reviews by Richard Colwell and Paul R. Lehman, see 10:150.

[1253]
InstrumenTest (Form AIT-C).

Purpose: For selecting instrument technicians.
Population: Applicants and incumbents for jobs requiring technical knowledge and skills of instrumentation.
Publication Dates: 2001–2005.
Scores, 8: Mathematics & Basic AC/DC Theory, Analog & Digital Electronics and Power Supplies, Schematics & Electrical Print Reading, Process Control, Test Instruments, Mechanical and Hand & Power Tools, Computers & PLC, Total.
Administration: Group.
Price Data, 2006: $20 per consumable self-scoring test booklet (minimum order of 20); $24.95 per manual (2005, 15 pages).
Time: (60) minutes.
Comments: Self-scoring instrument.
Author: Roland T. Ramsay.
Publisher: Ramsay Corporation.

[1254]
Insurance Selection Inventory.

Purpose: Designed to "evaluate skills and attitudes that are generally appropriate for insurance claims examiner/adjuster, correspondence representative or customer service representative positions."
Population: Ages 18 and over.
Publication Date: 2002.
Acronym: ISI.

Scores, 11: Number Comparison, Verbal Reasoning, Arithmetic Computation, Error Recognition, Applied Arithmetic, Drive, Interpersonal Skills, Cognitive Skills, Self-Discipline, Writing Skills, Work Preference.
Administration: Group.
Forms, 2: Timed, Untimed.
Price Data, 2005: $16 including 1–999 reports for Internet scoring with booklets; $16 including 1–999 reports for Internet scoring without booklets; $16 including 1–999 reports for QuantaTouch Test; $16 including 1–999 reports for QUANTA Software for Windows with booklets; $16 including 1–999 reports for QUANTA Software for Windows without booklets.
Time: (45) minutes.
Comments: Test can be scored via Touch Test, Internet, or Optical Scanning Software.
Author: Pearson Reid London House.
Publisher: Pearson Performance Solutions [No reply from publisher; status unknown].

[1255]
Integrated Assessment System®.

Purpose: "A series of performance tasks that can be used independently or in combination with a norm-referenced achievement test to offer a comprehensive view of student achievement."
Population: Grades 1–9.
Publication Dates: 1990–1992.
Acronym: IAS®.
Subtests: 3.
Administration: Group.
Authors: Roger Farr and Beverly Farr (Language Arts and Spanish only).
Publisher: PsychCorp, A brand of Harcourt Assessment, Inc.
  a) IAS-LANGUAGE ARTS.
  Population: Grades 1–8.
  Scores, 3: Response to Reading, Management of Content, Command of Language.
  Price Data, 2002: $160.60 per complete grade 1 package including 25 each of three student booklets and one directions for administering; $280.40 per complete grades 2–8 package including 25 each of three reading passages, three sets of guided-writing-activity blackline masters, directions for administering, three packages of 25 response forms, and response form directions; $28.10 per grade 1 examination kit including student booklet, directions for administering, and one passage-specific scoring rubric; $35.50 per grades 2–8 examination kit including one each of reading passage, guided-writing-activity blackline master, response form, response form directions, directions for administering, and one passage-specific scoring rubric; $40.30 per grade 1 activity package including 25 of one student booklet and directions

for administering; $100.20 per grades 2–8 activity package including 25 of one reading passage, one directions for administering, and one guided-writing activity blackline master; $9 per grades 2–8 response form package; $10.60 per grades 1–8 directions for administering; $23.30 per grades 1–8 scoring guides; $37.10 per 25 grade 1 reading passage only; $91.20 per 25 grades 2–8 reading passage only; $20.10 per grades 2–8 guided-writing-activity blackline masters; $55 per technical report (1991, 53 pages); $324.90 per scoring workshop kit including videotape, trainer's manual, 25 overhead transparencies, and blackline masters of model papers and training papers; $200.30 per portfolio starter kit including classroom storage box, 25 student portfolios, and teacher's manual; $64.10 per 25 student portfolio folders; $64.10 per teacher's manual; $98.60 per introductory videotape and viewer's guide; $6.60 per basic scoring service including list report and summary.

Time: (120–240) minutes.

1) *IAS—Language Arts, Spanish Edition.*

Scores: Same as *a* above.

Price Data: $28 per grade 1 examination kit including student booklet, directions for administering, and a passage-specific scoring rubric; $33 per grades 2–8 examination kit including one each of reading passage, guided-writing-activity blackline master, response form, response form directions, directions for administering, and passage-specific scoring rubric; $38.70 per grade 1 activity package including 25 copies of one student booklet and one directions for administering; $97 per grades 2–8 activity package including 25 copies of one reading passage, one directions for administering, and one guided-writing-activity blackline master; $9 per grades 2–8 response form package including 25 response forms and one response form directions; $10.60 per grades 1–8 directions for administering; $22.80 per grades 1–8 scoring guides; $36 per 25 grade 1 reading passage; $88 per 25 grades 2–8 reading passage; $18.60 per grades 2–8 guided-writing-activity blackline masters; $6.60 per basic scoring service including list report and summary.

b) IAS-MATHEMATICS.

Population: Grades 1–9.

Scores, 4: Reasoning, Conceptual Knowledge, Communication, Procedures.

Price Data: $28.10 per examination kit including one of each student booklet, directions for administering, and scoring rubric; $40.90 per activity package including 25 student booklets and one directions for administering; $11.70 per direc-

tions for administering; $24.40 per scoring guides; $180.70 per scoring training kit including binder and overhead transparencies; $8 per basic scoring service (holistic only).

Time: (80–90) minutes.

c) IAS-SCIENCE.

Population: Grades 1–8.

Scores, 4: Experimenting, Collecting Data, Drawing Conclusions, Communicating.

Price Data: $27 per examination kit including one each of student booklet, directions for administering, and scoring rubric; $40.90 per activity package including 25 student booklets and one directions for administering; $11.70 per directions for administering; $24.40 per scoring guides; $45.60 per manipulative materials; $179 per scoring workshop kit including trainer's manual; $8 per basic scoring service (holistic only).

Time: (80–90) minutes.

Cross References: For reviews by Gabriel M. Della-Piana and Bikkar S. Randhawa, see 13:152.

[1256]

Integrated Writing Test.

Purpose: "Designed to evaluate major components of good writing in students' writing samples."

Population: Grades 2–12.

Publication Date: 1993.

Acronym: IWT.

Scores, 7: Productivity, Clarity, Vocabulary, Spelling, Punctuation, Legibility, Total Test Language Quotient.

Administration: Group.

Levels, 5: Grades 2/3, Grade 4, Grades 5/6, Grades 7 to 9, Grades 10 to 12.

Price Data, 2001: $131.95 per kit including manual (66 pages) and 35 booklets for each grade level; $22.95 per package of 35 booklets; $22.95 per manual.

Time: 15(20) minutes.

Comments: Academic extension of the Developmental Test of Visual-Motor Integration (119); also based upon the National Assessment of Educational Progress Writing Test.

Authors: Keith E. Beery with assistance from the Integrated Teaching Team.

Publisher: Golden Educational Center.

Cross References: For reviews by C. Dale Carpenter and Richard M. Wolf, see 14:181.

[1257]

Interest-A-Lyzer Family of Instruments.

Purpose: Series of instruments "designed to assess various aspects of student interests."

Publication Dates: 1982–1997.

Administration: Group.

Price Data, 2004: $15.95 per manual (1997, 80 pages); $29.95 per 30 Interest-A-Lyzer Forms (specify

level); $22.95 per 30 Art Interest-A-Lyzer Forms (specify level); $14.95 per My Book of Things and Stuff (1982, 60 pages).
Time: Untimed.
Author: Joseph S. Renzulli.
Publisher: Creative Learning Press, Inc.
a) INTEREST-A-LYZER.
Population: Grades 4–8.
Scores, 10: Performing Arts, Creative Writing and Journalism, Mathematics, Business Management, Athletics, History, Social Action, Fine Arts and Crafts, Science, Technology.
b) PRIMARY INTEREST-A-LYZER.
Population: Grades Kindergarten–3.
Scores, 10: Same as *a* above.
Authors: Joseph S. Renzulli and Mary G. Rizza.
c) SECONDARY INTEREST-A-LYZER.
Population: Grades 7–12.
Scores, 10: Same as *a* above.
Authors: Thomas P. Hebert, Michelle F. Sorensen, and Joseph S. Renzulli.
d) PRIMARY ART INTEREST-A-LYZER.
Purpose: "Invites students to examine their present and potential interest in art."
Population: Grades Kindergarten–3.
Scores, 7: Painting, Drawing, Photography, Sculpture, Printmaking, Commercial Art, Art History.
e) ART INTEREST-A-LYZER.
Purpose: "Invites students to examine their present and potential interest in art."
Population: Grades 4–12.
Scores, 7: Same as *d* above.
f) MY BOOK OF THINGS AND STUFF.
Purpose: Designed to assess students' "special interests and learning styles."
Population: Grades Kindergarten–6.
Publication Date: 1982.
Scores: No scores.
Author: Ann McGreevy.

[1258]
Interest Explorer.

Purpose: Designed "to explore interests combined with academic skills for the purpose of career and educational planning."
Population: Grades 8–12.
Publication Date: 1999.
Scores: Interest Levels in 14 career areas: Animals and Plants, Arts, Business Services, Computer Technology, Customer Services, Educational and Social Services, Engineering Technology, Legal Services, Management and Administration, Mechanical and Craft Technology, Medical Sciences, Physical and Life Sciences and Mathematics, Protective Services, Sales.
Administration: Group.

Levels, 2: 1, 2.
Price Data: Available from publisher.
Time: Less than one class period for Interest Explorer, plus (260) minutes for ITED for complete battery; (160) minutes for ITED Core battery.
Comments: The Interest Explorer is designed to be used in conjunction with The Iowa Tests of Educational Development (1292).
Author: Riverside Publishing.
Publisher: Riverside Publishing.

[1259]
Interference Learning Test.

Purpose: Designed "for detecting and characterizing mild and moderate as well as severe levels of" neuropsychological impairment.
Population: Ages 16 and over.
Publication Date: 1999.
Scores: Learning Performance (List 1 Total Recall, Best Recall, List 2 Total Recall, Added Words, Lost Words, Middle Recall, Recency Minus Primary, Subjective Organization, Category Clustering, Seriation, Intertrial Consistency, New Word Priority, Repeats, Source Errors, Confabulations), Delayed Recall Performance (Short Delay Recall, Long Delay Recall, Cued Recall, Retroactive Inhibition, Cueing Facilitation, Encoding, Rebound), Recognition Performance (Recognition Correct, Overlap Correct, Novel Foil Correct, Indirect Correct), Total.
Administration: Individual.
Price Data, 2006: $165 per kit including manual (186 pages), 5 Response Record Forms, a stimulus booklet, and 5-use disk for computer scoring and interpretation; $55 per stimulus booklet; $55 per manual; $36 per 20 Response Record Forms; $270 per 20-use disk.
Time: (20–30) minutes.
Comments: Computer administration option available.
Authors: Michael M. Schmidt and Frederick L. Coolidge.
Publisher: Western Psychological Services.
Cross References: For reviews by Joan C. Ballard and Shawn Powell, see 15:125.

[1260]
Intermediate Measures of Music Audiation.

Purpose: "To identify children with exceptionally high music aptitude … who can profit from the opportunity to participate in additional group study and special private instruction … to evaluate the comparative tonal and rhythm aptitudes of each child with exceptionally high music aptitude."
Population: Grades 1-4.
Publication Dates: 1978-1982.
Acronym: IMMA.
Scores, 3: Tonal, Rhythm, Composite.

Administration: Group.
Price Data, 2006: $100 per complete kit containing 1 tonal and rhythm compact disc, 100 tonal answer sheets, 100 rhythm answer sheets, 2 sets of scoring masks, 100 profile cards, 4 class record sheets, research monographs, and test manual (1982, 44 pages); $25 per CD; $41.50 per 500 tonal answer sheets; $41.50 per 500 rhythm answer sheets; $5 per set of tonal or rhythm scoring masks; $15.50 per 100 profile cards; $2 per 10 class record sheets; $20 per manual.
Time: (20) minutes per Tonal test; (20) minutes per Rhythm test.
Comments: Advanced version of the Primary Measures of Music Audiation (2024); tests administered by CD.
Author: Edwin E. Gordon.
Publisher: GIA Publications, Inc.

[1261]
Internalized Shame Scale.

Purpose: Developed to measure an individual's feelings of shame and the negative response patterns that result from internalized chance.
Population: Age 13 and older.
Publication Date: 2001.
Acronym: ISS.
Scores, 2: Shame, Self-Esteem.
Administration: Individual.
Price Data, 2006: $92 per complete kit including technical manual (128 pages), 25 Quikscore forms, and 25 patient handouts; $51 per technical manual; $39 per 25 Quikscore forms; $27 per 25 patient handouts.
Time: 15 minutes.
Comments: Self-completed.
Author: David R. Cook.
Publisher: Multi-Health Systems, Inc.
Cross References: For reviews by Sean P. Reilley and by Susan M. Swearer and Kelly Brey Love, see 16:113.

[1262]
International Personality Disorder Examination.

Purpose: To "diagnose personality disorders using DSM-IV or ICD-10 criteria."
Population: Adults.
Publication Dates: 1988–1999.
Acronym: IPDE.
Scores: 11 scores for DSM-IV version: Paranoid, Schizoid, Schizotypal, Antisocial, Borderline, Histrionic, Narcissistic, Avoidant, Dependent, Obsessive-Compulsive, Not Otherwise Specified; 10 scores for ICD-10 version: Paranoid, Schizoid, Dissocial, Emotionally Unstable/Impulsive Type, Emotionally Unstable/Borderline Type, Histrionic, Anankastic, Anxious (Avoidant), Dependent, Unspecified.

Administration: Individual.
Parts, 2: DSM-IV Module, ICD-10 Module.
Price Data, 2006: $185 per introductory kit including professional manual, 25 screening questionnaires (specify for DSM-IV or ICD-10), 15 scoring booklets (specify DSM-IV or ICD-10), and 50 answer sheets (specify DSM-IV or ICD-10).
Time: [60–120] minutes.
Comments: Complete administration includes a self-administered questionnaire as well as a clinical interview with client/subject.
Author: Armand W. Loranger.
Publisher: Psychological Assessment Resources, Inc.
Cross References: For reviews by Felito Aldarondo and Kwong-Liem Karl Kwan and by Gregory J. Boyle, see 15:126.

[1263]
Interpersonal Adjective Scales.

Purpose: "A self-report instrument designed to measure two important dimensions of interpersonal transactions: Dominance and Nurturance."
Population: Ages 18 and up.
Publication Date: 1995.
Acronym: IAS.
Scores, 10: Assured-Dominant, Arrogant-Calculating, Cold-hearted, Aloof-Introverted, Unassured-Submissive, Unassuming-Ingenious, Warm-Agreeable, Gregarious-Extraverted, Dominance, Nurturance.
Administration: Individual or group.
Price Data, 2005: $109 per introductory kit including manual (143 pages), 25 test booklets, 25 scoring booklets, and 25 glossaries.
Time: (15–20) minutes.
Comments: Separate norms are available for college students and adults; glossary is included to be used by subjects during testing.
Author: Jerry S. Wiggins.
Publisher: Psychological Assessment Resources, Inc.
Cross References: For reviews by Steven J. Lindner and Gerald R. Schneck, see 14:184; see also T5:1288 (2 references).

[1264]
Interpersonal Behavior Survey.

Purpose: "Developed to distinguish assertive behaviors from aggressive behaviors."
Population: Grades 9–16 and adults.
Publication Date: 1980.
Acronym: IBS.
Scores, 21: Denial, Infrequency, Impression Management, General Aggressiveness—Rational, Hostile Stance, Expression of Anger, Disregard for Rights, Verbal Aggressiveness, Physical Aggressiveness, Passive Aggressiveness, General Assertiveness—Rational, Self-Confidence, Initiating Assertiveness, Defending Assertiveness, Frankness, Praise, Requesting Help,

Refusing Demands, Conflict Avoidance, Dependency, Shyness, plus additional scores (General Aggressiveness—Empirical, General Assertiveness—Empirical) and 10 short-form scores.
Administration: Group.
Price Data, 2006: $143 per complete kit including 5 reusable administration booklets, 50 profile forms, 50 answer sheets, set of scoring keys, manual (78 pages), and 25 autoscore forms for the short form IBS; $27.50 per 10 administration booklets; $32.50 per set of scoring keys; $27.50 per 100 answer sheets; $27.50 per 100 profiles; $52.25 per manual.
Time: 45 minutes.
Comments: Self-report inventory.
Authors: Paul A. Mauger, David R. Adkinson, Suzanne K. Zoss (test), Gregory Firestone (test), and J. David Hook (test).
Publisher: Western Psychological Services.
Cross References: See T5:1290 (4 references) and T4:1251 (5 references); for reviews by Stephen L. Franzoi and Robert R. Hutzell, see 9:518.

[1265]
Interpersonal Communication Inventory.

Purpose: To assess "a client's interpersonal communication as it provides clues to communication difficulties outside of the family relationship."
Population: Grade 9 to adult.
Publication Dates: 1969-1976.
Acronym: ICI.
Scores, 12: Self-Disclosure, Awareness, Evaluation and Acceptance of Feedback, Self-Expression, Attention, Coping with Feelings, Clarity, Avoidance, Dominance, Handling Differences, Perceived Acceptance, Total.
Administration: Group.
Price Data, 1993: $.75 per inventory; $3.50 per guide (1976, 15 pages).
Time: (20) minutes.
Author: Millard J. Bienvenu.
Publisher: Millard J. Bienvenu, Northwest Publications.
Cross References: See T5:1292 (1 reference), T4:1253 (3 references), and T3:1171 (2 references); see also 8:589 (3 references) and T2:1241 (1 reference).

[1266]
Interpersonal Intelligence Inventory.

Purpose: Intended "to identify the teamwork skills individuals demonstrate" in cooperative learning situations.
Population: Grade 6-adult.
Publication Date: 2002.
Acronym: III.
Scores, 5: Attends to Teamwork, Seeks and Shares Information, Communicates with Teammates, Thinks Critically and Creatively, Gets Along with Team.
Administration: Group.
Price Data, 2005: $38 per starter kit including manual of administration and interpretation (46 pages), 10 definitions of Team skills booklet, 1 pad of 10 Team Skills Profile forms, and 1 pad of 20 Teamwork Skills forms; $21 per additional manual of administration and interpretation; $23 per additional package of 10 booklets, 1 pad each of Team Skills Profile forms, Team Scoring forms, and Teamwork Skills forms; $24 per sample set (nonreturnable) including 1 manual, 1 booklet, 1 Team Skills Profile form, 1 Team Scoring form, and 1 Teamwork Skills form.
Time: Varies.
Comments: Test can be administered in middle school, high school, college, and universities.
Authors: Paris S. Strom and Robert D. Strom.
Publisher: Scholastic Testing Service, Inc.

[1267]
Interpersonal Relations Questionnaire.

Purpose: "To identify specific problems in connection with interpersonal relations and identity formation."
Population: "White pupils" in Standards 5–7 in South African schools.
Publication Dates: 1981–1988.
Acronym: IRQ.
Scores, 13: Self-Confidence, Self-Esteem, Self-Control, Nervousness, Health, Family Influences, Personal Freedom, Sociability A, Sociability T, Sociability D, Moral Sense, Formal Relations, Lie Scale.
Administration: Group.
Price Data: Available from publisher.
Time: (105–120) minutes.
Comments: Supplementary manual in English and Afrikaans.
Authors: Marianne Joubert and Dawn Schlebusch (supplementary manual).
Publisher: Human Sciences Research Council [South Africa].

[1268]
Interpersonal Style Inventory.

Purpose: To measure "an individual's characteristic ways of relating to other people ... also evaluates style of impulse control and characteristic modes of dealing with work and play."
Population: Ages 14 and over.
Publication Dates: 1977–1986.
Acronym: ISI.
Scores: 15 in 5 areas: Interpersonal Involvement (Sociable, Help Seeking, Nurturant, Sensitive), Socialization (Conscientious, Trusting, Tolerant), Autonomy (Directive, Independent, Rule Free), Self-Control (Deliberate, Orderly, Persistent), Stability (Stable, Approval Seeking).

Administration: Group.
Price Data, 2006: $99 per complete kit including 2 reusable administration booklets, 20 AutoScore™ answer forms, and manual (1986, 69 pages); $32.50 per 10 administration booklets; $54.50 per manual; $42.50 per 20 AutoScore™ answer forms; $21.90 per 20 profile sheets for adolescents; $13.75 per mail-in answer sheet; $8.80 per FAX service scoring charge.
Time: 30 minutes.
Authors: Maurice Lorr and Richard P. Youniss.
Publisher: Western Psychological Services.
Cross References: See T5:1294 (4 references) and T4:1256 (6 references); for reviews by Randy W. Kamphaus and Gerald L. Stone, see 10:151 (4 references); for reviews by John Duckitt and Stuart A. Karabenick of an earlier edition, see 9:521; see also T3:1173 (1 reference).

[1269]
Interpersonal Style Questionnaire.

Purpose: Designed "to help educators determine their primary interpersonal style."
Population: Educators at grades K–12.
Publication Dates: 1987–1998.
Scores, 4: Achiever, Persuader, Supporter, Analyst.
Administration: Group.
Manual: No manual.
Price Data, 2002: $25 per 20 test booklets.
Time: Administration time not reported.
Comments: Can be used alone or with Working Together, a tool for collaborative teaching, available from publisher.
Author: Anita DeBoer.
Publisher: Sopris West.

[1270]
Interpersonal Trust Surveys.

Purpose: Designed to measure an individual's "propensity to trust and to build trust with other people."
Population: Adults.
Publication Dates: 1996–1997.
Acronyms: ITS; ITS-O; OTS.
Administration: Group.
Scores, 6: Shares Information, Reduces Control, Allows for Mutual Influences, Clarifies Expectations, Meets Others' Expectations, Total.
Forms, 3: Interpersonal Trust Survey, Interpersonal Trust Survey—Observer, Organizational Trust Survey.
Price Data: Available from publisher.
Time: Administration time not reported.
Comments: Scored for "My Behavior" and "Others' Behavior"; can be used as part of an educational workshop in interpersonal trust or as a tool for counseling; based on the "behavioral model of interpersonal trust"; scoring software available (must be run with Microsoft Excel).
Author: Guy L. DeFuria.

Publisher: Jossey-Bass, A Wiley Company.
Cross References: For a review by Mark E. Sibicky, see 14:185.

[1271]
Intuitive Mechanics (Weights & Pulleys).

Purpose: "To measure the ability to understand mechanical relationships, to visualize internal movement in a mechanical system."
Population: Industrial positions.
Publication Dates: 1956–1984.
Scores: Total score only.
Administration: Individual or group.
Price Data, 2002: $91 per start-up kit including 25 test booklets, score key, and interpretation and research manual; $54 per 25 test booklets (quantity discounts available); $20 per score key; $28 per interpretation and research manual.
Time: (3) minutes.
Authors: L. L. Thurstone and T. E. Jeffrey.
Publisher: Pearson Performance Solutions [No reply from publisher; status unknown].
Cross References: For a review by William A. Owens, see 9:523.

[1272]
Inventory for Client and Agency Planning.

Purpose: Developed "to assess the status, adaptive functioning, and service needs of clients."
Population: Infant to adult.
Publication Date: 1986.
Acronym: ICAP.
Scores, 10: Maladaptive Behavior Indexes (Internalized, Asocial, Externalized, General), Adaptive Behavior (Motor Skills, Social and Communication Skills, Personal Living Skills, Community Living Skills, Total), Broad Independence Service Level Index.
Administration: Individual.
Price Data, 2006: $167.50 per complete kit in English or Spanish including examiner's manual (165 pages) and 25 test records; $106 per examiner's manual; $65 per 25 test records.
Foreign Language Edition: Also available in Spanish.
Time: (20–30) minutes.
Comments: Statistically related to the Scales of Independent Behavior (2240) and the Woodcock-Johnson Psycho-Educational Battery (2795); to be completed by "a respondent who has known a client for at least 3 months and who sees him or her on a day-to-day basis."
Authors: Robert H. Bruininks, Bradley K. Hill, Richard F. Weatherman, and Richard W. Woodcock.
Publisher: Riverside Publishing.
Cross References: See T5:1300 (11 references) and T4:1260 (3 references); for reviews by Ronn Johnson and Richard L. Wikoff, see 10:152.

[1273]
Inventory of Altered Self-Capacities.

Purpose: Designed to assess difficulties in relatedness, identity, and affect control.
Population: Age 18 and above.
Publication Dates: 1998–2000.
Acronym: IASC.
Scores, 11: Interpersonal Conflicts, Idealization—Disillusionment, Abandonment Concerns, Identity Impairment, Self-Awareness, Identity Diffusion, Susceptibility to Influence, Affect Dysregulation, Affect Skill Deficits, Affect Instability, Tension Reduction Activities.
Administration: Group or individual.
Price Data, 2006: $175 per introductory kit including 25 reusable item booklets, 50 hand-scorable answer sheets, 50 profile forms, and professional manual (2000, 49 pages).
Time: [15–20] minutes.
Author: John Briere.
Publisher: Psychological Assessment Resources, Inc.
Cross References: For a review by Rosemary Flanagan, see 15:127.

[1274]
Inventory of Anger Communication.

Purpose: "To identify the subjective and interactional aspects of anger in assessing how one communicates around anger."
Population: High school and adults.
Publication Dates: 1974-1976.
Acronym: IAC.
Scores: Total score only.
Administration: Group.
Price Data, 1993: $.75 per inventory; $2 per manual (1976, 10 pages).
Time: [15-20] minutes.
Author: Millard J. Bienvenu.
Publisher: Millard J. Bienvenu, Northwest Publications.
Cross References: For additional information, see 8:591 (1 reference).

[1275]
Inventory of Drinking Situations.

Purpose: "Designed to assess situations in which a client drank heavily over the past year."
Population: Ages 18 to 75.
Publication Date: 1987.
Acronym: IDS.
Scores, 8: Personal Status (Unpleasant Emotions, Physical Discomfort, Pleasant Emotions, Testing Personal Control, Urges and Temptations), Situations Involving Other People (Conflict with Others, Social Pressure to Drink, Pleasant Times with Others).
Administration: Group.
Forms, 2: IDS-100, IDS-42 (Brief Version).

Price Data, 2002: C$25 per specimen set including user's guide (53 pages), 25 questionnaires, 25 answer sheets, 25 profiles; C$13.50 per user's guide; C$12.75 per 25 IDS-42 (Brief Version) questionnaires, 25 answer sheets, and 25 profile sheets; C$14.75 per 25 IDS-100 questionnaires, 25 answer sheets, and 25 profile sheets.
Foreign Language Edition: Both forms available in French.
Time: (20–25) minutes.
Comments: IDS-42 (Brief Version) is for research use only.
Authors: Helen M. Annis, J. Martin Graham, and Christine S. Davis.
Publisher: Centre for Addiction and Mental Health [Canada].
Cross References: See T5:1304 (1 reference); for reviews by Merith Cosden and Kevin L. Moreland, see 13:155 (3 references); see also T4:1265 (2 references).

[1276]
Inventory of Drug Taking Situations.

Purpose: "Designed primarily as an assessment instrument, the IDTS generates an individualized profile detailing situations in which a client has used alcohol and/or other drugs over the past year."
Population: Drug or alcohol users.
Publication Date: 1997.
Acronym: IDTS.
Scores: Situation profiles in three areas: Negative Situations, Positive Situations, Temptation Situations; 8 subscales: Unpleasant Emotions, Physical Discomfort, Pleasant Emotions, Testing Personal Control, Urges/Temptations to Use, Conflict with Others, Social Pressure to Use, Pleasant Times with Others.
Administration: Group.
Price Data, 2002: C$34.95 per user's guide; C$14.95 per 30 questionnaires (specify alcohol or drug); C$39.95 per sample pack including user's guide, and 40 questionnaires (10 alcohol and 30 drug);C$75 per 50 uses of computer-administration software (DOS format); C$100 per 50 uses of software with user's guide; C$250 per 200 uses of software; C$275 per 200 uses of software with user's guide.
Time: (15) minutes per each drug class.
Comments: User's guide written in both English (150 pages) and French (72 pages); French version of IDTS have not been scientifically validated; "The IDTS is administered separately for each of the client's major substances of abuse, not once for the client's overall use of drugs."
Authors: Helen M. Annis, Nigel E. Turner, and Sherrilyn M. Sklar.
Publisher: Centre for Addiction and Mental Health [Canada].
Cross References: For reviews by Tony Cellucci and Glenn B. Gelman, see 14:186.

[1277]
Inventory of Interpersonal Problems.
Purpose: "A self-report instrument that identifies a person's most salient interpersonal problems."
Population: Adults ages 18 and over.
Publication Date: 2000.
Acronym: IIP.
Scores, 9: Domineering/Controlling, Vindictive/Self-Centered, Cold/Distant, Socially Inhibited, Nonassertive, Overly Accommodating, Self-Sacrificing, Intrusive/Needy, Total.
Administration: Individual or group.
Price Data, 2002: $111 per complete kit including manual (2000, 98 pages), 25 64-item question sheets, 25 64-item scoring sheets, and 25 32-item question scoring sheets; $48 per manual; $42 per 64-item question/scoring sheet combination including 25 64-item question sheets, and 25 64-item scoring sheets; $33 per 25 32-item question/scoring sheets.
Time: (10–15) minutes for Full Version; (5–10) minutes for Short Version.
Comments: Full version (IIP-64) contains 64 items; short version (IIP-32), intended for screening, contains 32 items.
Authors: Leonard M. Horowitz, Lynn E. Alden, Jerry S. Wiggins, and Aaron L. Pincus.
Publisher: PsychCorp, A brand of Harcourt Assessment, Inc.
Cross References: For reviews by Joshua M. Gold and Brian Hess, see 15:128.

[1278]
Inventory of Learning Processes–R.
Purpose: To measure learning styles of college and university students.
Population: College and university students.
Publication Dates: 1977–1992.
Acronym: ILP-R.
Scores, 14: Academic Self-Concept (Intrinsic Motivation, Self-Efficacy, Non-reiterative Processing, Self-Esteem, Total), Reflective Processing (Deep Processing, Elaborative Processing, Self-Expression, Total), Agentic Processing (Conventional, Serial Processing, Fact Retention, Total), Methodical Study.
Administration: Group.
Price Data: Price information available from publisher for test booklet (includes answer sheets).
Time: Administration time not reported.
Authors: Ronald R. Schmeck and Elke Geisler-Bernstein.
Publisher: Ronald R. Schmeck (the author).
Cross References: For reviews by Kusum Singh and Gerald L. Stone, see 13:156 (5 references).

[1279]
Inventory of Perceptual Skills.
Purpose: "Assesses visual and auditory perceptual skills."
Population: Ages 5–10.
Publication Date: 1983.
Acronym: IPS.
Scores, 11: Visual Perception Skills (Visual Discrimination, Visual Memory, Object Recognition, Visual-Motor Coordination, Total), Auditory Perception Skills (Auditory Discrimination, Auditory Memory, Auditory Sequencing, Auditory Blending, Total), Total.
Administration: Individual.
Price Data, 2005: $45 per complete kit including manual (16 pages), stimulus cards, student workbook, and record books; $20 per 10 student record books; $15 per manual; $15 per stimulus cards; $6 per student workbook.
Time: (15) minutes.
Author: Donald R. O'Dell.
Publisher: Stoelting Co.
Cross References: For reviews by Donna Spiker and by Logan Wright, Tim Eck, and Natasha Gwartney, see 12:193.

[1280]
Inventory of Positive Thinking Traits.
Purpose: "Designed to assess the attitudes of individuals in terms of their positivity and negativity."
Population: Adults and adolescents.
Publication Date: 1992.
Scores: Total score only.
Administration: Individual and group.
Price Data, 1998: $.50 per inventory; $1 per guide.
Time: (10) minutes.
Author: Millard J. Bienvenu.
Publisher: Millard J. Bienvenu, Northwest Publications.
Cross References: For a review by Peggy E. Gallaher, see 13:157.

[1281]
An Inventory of Religious Activities and Interests.
Purpose: "Measures interest in activities performed by persons employed in a variety of church-related occupations."
Population: High school and college.
Publication Dates: 1967–1970.
Acronym: IRAI.
Scores: 11 scales: Counselor, Administrator, Teacher, Scholar, Evangelist, Spiritual Guide, Preacher, Reformer, Priest, Musician, Check Scale.
Administration: Group.
Price Data: Available from publisher.
Time: (40–45) minutes for both forms.

Comments: For research use only.
Authors: Sam C. Webb and Richard A. Hunt.
Publisher: Ministry Inventories.
Cross References: See T2:1025A (2 references); for a review by Donald G. Zytowski, see 7:1023.

[1282]
Inventory of School Effectiveness.

Purpose: Designed as a rating by staff of practices and conditions that contribute to improved student performance.
Population: Administrators, teachers, and support staff.
Publication Date: 2005.
Scores: 11 topics: Research-Based Practices (Expect Results, Monitor Performance, Support Student Learning, Maximize Teacher's Effectiveness, Develop a Professional Learning Community, Lead for Improvement), Organizational Conditions for Improving Schools (Quality Teachers, Effective Leadership, Quality Information, Policies and Procedures, Resources and Support Systems).
Administration: Group.
Price Data, 2006: $25 per 25 inventories; administrative manual may be downloaded free from publisher webpage.
Time: (20) minutes.
Comments: Web-based and paper-based; unlimited items can be added to the web-based version; schools can use the "A and B" line to add additional demographic items to the paper version.
Author: National Study of School Evaluation.
Publisher: National Study of School Evaluation.

[1283]
Inventory of Suicide Orientation-30.

Purpose: "To assess and help identify adolescents who are at risk for suicide orientation by measuring the strength of their suicide orientation."
Population: Adolescents.
Publication Dates: 1988–1994.
Acronym: ISO-30.
Scores, 2: Final Raw Score, Final Critical Item Score.
Administration: Group.
Price Data, 2006: $55 per 25 hand-scored answer sheets with test; $25.50 per 25 Q Local answer sheets with test items; $3.95 per Q Local report; quantity discounts available for the reports; price information for Spanish materials available from publisher.
Foreign Language Edition: Hispanic edition available.
Time: [10] minutes.
Authors: John D. King and Brian Kowalchuk.
Publisher: Pearson Assessments.
Cross References: For a review by George Domino, see 13:158.

[1284]
Inventory of Vocational Interests: Acorn National Aptitude Tests.

Purpose: Designed to provide evidence of vocationally significant interests.
Population: Grades 7–16 and adults.
Publication Dates: 1943–1960.
Scores, 5: Mechanical, Academic, Artistic, Business and Economic, Farm-Agricultural.
Administration: Group.
Price Data, 2001: $4 per specimen set.
Time: (35) minutes.
Authors: Andrew Kobal, J. Wayne Wrightstone, and Karl R. Kunze.
Publisher: Psychometric Affiliates.
Cross References: For a review by John W. French, see 6:1060; for reviews by Marion A. Bills, Edward S. Bordin, Harold D. Carter, and Patrick Slater, see 3:638.

[1285]
InView.

Purpose: "A cognitive abilities test ... measur[ing] selected verbal, nonverbal, and quantitative reasoning abilities ... important for success in an educational program."
Population: Grades 2–12.
Publication Date: 2001.
Scores, 8: 5 subtest scores (Sequences, Analogies, Quantitative Reasoning, Verbal Reasoning—Words, Verbal Reasoning—Context); 3 composite scores (Verbal Composite, Nonverbal Composite, Total Test Scale Score).
Administration: Group.
Levels, 6: 1 (Grades 2–3), 2 (Grades 4–5), 3 (Grades 6–7), 4 (Grades 8–9), 5 (Grades 10–11), 6 (Grades 11–12).
Price Data, 2006: $109 per 25 InView-1 consumable test books; $85 per 25 InView 2–6 reusable test books (specify level); $37 per 50 InView 2–6 answer sheets; $1,408 per 2,500 InView continuous form answer sheets; $26 per InView 2–6 stencil set (specify level); $23 per examiner's manual, specify level); $41 per Teacher's Guide to InView, Technical Bulletin 1, Technical Report (CD-ROM version), or Norms Book (all levels); $3.12 per Class Record Sheet for Handscoring.
Time: 95 minutes.
Comments: Replaces the Test of Cognitive Skills, Second Edition (TCS/2); conormed with the Primary Test of Cognitive Skills (PTCS) (see 2025) and with TerraNova, The Second Edition (see 2563); Level 1 students record answers in test books; Levels 2–6 students use separate answer sheets; variety of score report formats available; on-line feedback on test performance available, contact publisher for details.
Author: CTB/McGraw-Hill.
Publisher: CTB/McGraw-Hill.

Cross References: For reviews by Russell N. Carney and Bruce Thompson, see 16:114; see T5:2677 for information on the Test of Cognitive Skills, Second Edition; for a review by Randy W. Kamphaus of an earlier edition, see 13:325 (8 references); see also T4:2745 (4 references); for reviews by Timothy Z. Keith and Robert J. Sternberg of an earlier edition, see 9:1248; for a review by Lynn H. Fox and an excerpted review by David M. Shoemaker of the Short Form Test of Academic Aptitude, see 8:202 (9 references).

[1286]
Inwald Personality Inventory [Revised].

Purpose: "To aid public safety/law enforcement and security agencies in selecting new officers."
Population: Public safety, security, and law enforcement applicants (post-conditional job offer only).
Publication Dates: 1980–1992.
Acronym: IPI.
Scores, 26: Guardedness, Externalized Behavior Measures (Actions [Alcohol, Drugs, Driving Violations, Job Difficulties, Trouble with the Law and Society, Absence Abuse], Attitudes [Substance Abuse, Antisocial Attitudes, Hyperactivity, Rigid Type, Type A]), Internalized Conflict Measures (Illness Concerns, Treatment Programs, Anxiety, Phobic Personality, Obsessive Personality, Depression, Loner, Unusual Experiences/Thoughts), Interpersonal Conflict Measures (Lack of Assertiveness, Interpersonal Difficulties, Undue Suspiciousness, Family Conflicts, Sexual Concerns, Spouse/Mate Conflicts).
Administration: Individual or group.
Price Data: Available from publisher.
Time: (30–45) minutes.
Author: Robin Inwald.
Publisher: Hilson Research, Inc.
Cross References: See T5:1313 (2 references) and T4:1275 (1 reference); for reviews by Brian Bolton and Richard I. Lanyon, see 12:194; for reviews by Samuel Juni and Niels G. Waller of an earlier edition, see 11:183 (2 references); for reviews by Brian Bolton and Jon D. Swartz of an earlier edition, see 9:530.

[1287]
Inwald Survey 5– Revised.

Purpose: "To aid in employee selection."
Population: All occupations including public safety/security, clerical, managerial, sales, and entry-level.
Publication Dates: 1992-2001.
Acronym: IS5-R.
Scores, 12: Lack of Insight/Candor, Frustration/Anger Patterns, Distrust of Others, Work Adjustment Difficulties, Attitudes (Antisocial Behaviors), Behavior Patterns (Integrity Concerns), Lack of Competitive Motivation, Work Effort Concerns, Lack of Sensitivity, Leadership Avoidance, Introverted Personality Style, Domestic Difficulties.
Administration: Individual or group.
Price Data: Available from publisher.
Time: (20-30) minutes.
Comments: "Appropriate under ADA and can be administered pre-employment."
Author: Robin Inwald.
Publisher: Hilson Research, Inc.

[1288]
Iowa Algebra Aptitude Test™, Fifth Edition.

Purpose: Designed to "help teachers and counselors make the most informed decisions possible regarding the initial placement of students in the secondary mathematics curriculum."
Population: Grades 7-8.
Publication Dates: 1931-2006.
Acronym: IAAT.
Scores, 5: Pre-Algebraic Number Skills and Concepts, Interpreting Mathematical Information, Representing Relationships, Using Symbols, Total.
Administration: Group or individual.
Forms, 2: A, B.
Price Data, 2006: $31 per manual Forms A and B; $78 per 25 test booklets (Form A or B); $8 per Directions for Administration booklet (Forms A and B); $35 per 25 self-scoring answer sheets (Forms A and B); $98 per 100 Mark Reflex answer sheets (Forms A and B); $33 per 25 Report to Families booklets (Forms A and B); $1,250 per Licensed Norms (Forms A and B).
Time: 10(40) minutes for the battery; (10) minutes for each subtest.
Comments: "Designed to be used in conjunction with other indicators of student progress, such as grades and teacher evaluations."
Authors: Harold L. Schoen and Timothy N. Ansley.
Publisher: Riverside Publishing.
Cross References: For reviews by John W. Fleenor and Judith A. Monsaas of an earlier edition, see 12:195; see also T2:681 (7 references); for reviews by W. L. Bashaw and Cyril J. Hoyt, and an excerpted review by Russell A. Chadbourn of an earlier edition, see 7:505 (8 references); for reviews by Harold Gulliksen and Emma Spaney of an earlier edition, see 4:393; for a review by David Segel, see 3:327 (2 references); for reviews by Richard M. Drake and M. W. Richardson, see 2:144 (1 reference).

[1289]
Iowa Parent Behavior Inventory.

Purpose: Designed "to measure parental behavior in relation to a child."
Population: Parents.
Publication Dates: 1976–1979.
Acronym: ITBI.

Administration: Group.
Price Data: Price information available from publisher for test and manual (1979, 41 pages including both forms and score sheet).
Time: Administration time not reported.
Authors: Sedahlia Jasper Crase, Samuel G. Clark, and Damaris Pease.
Publisher: Iowa State University Research Foundation, Inc. [No reply from publisher; status unknown].
  a) MOTHER FORM.
    Publication Date: 1977.
    Scores, 6: Parental Involvement, Limit Setting, Responsiveness, Reasoning Guidance, Free Expression, Intimacy.
  b) FATHER FORM.
    Publication Date: 1977.
    Scores, 5: Parental Involvement, Limit Setting, Responsiveness, Reasoning Guidance, Intimacy.
Cross References: See T5:1316 (2 references) and T4:1278 (3 references); for reviews by Verna Hart and Richard L. Wikoff, see 9:531 (1 reference).

[1290]
Iowa Social Competency Scales.

Purpose: To provide an "easily administered and objectively scored individual rating instrument for parents relative to the social behavior (competencies) of normal children."
Population: Ages 3–12.
Publication Dates: 1976–1982.
Acronym: ISCS.
Administration: Group.
Price Data: Available from publisher.
Time: Administration time not reported.
Comments: Ratings by parents.
Authors: Damaris Pease, Samuel G. Clark, and Sedahlia Jasper Crase.
Publisher: Iowa State University Research Foundation, Inc. [No reply from publisher; status unknown].
  a) PRESCHOOL.
    Population: Ages 3–6.
      1) *Mother.*
      Scores, 5: Social Activator, Hypersensitivity, Reassurance, Uncooperativeness, Cooperativeness.
      2) *Father.*
      Scores, 5: Social Activator, Hypersensitivity, Reassurance, Social Ineptness, Attentiveness.
      3) *Combined.*
      Scores, 3: Social Activator, Hypersensitivity, Reassurance.
  b) SCHOOL-AGE.
    Population: Ages 6–12.
    Comments: Adaptation of Devereux Elementary School Behavior Rating Scale.

      1) *Mother.*
      Scores, 6: Task Oriented, Disruptive, Leader, Physically Active, Affectionate Toward Parent, Apprehensive.
      2) *Father.*
      Scores, 5: Capable, Defiant, Leader, Active with Peers, Affectionate Toward Parent.
Cross References: For a review by Gloria E. Miller, see 10:154; see also 9:532 (2 references).

[1291]
Iowa Tests of Basic Skills®, Forms A and B.

Purpose: Designed to measure skills and achievement in fundamental content areas of school curricula: vocabulary, word analysis, reading comprehension, language arts, mathematics, social studies, science, and sources of information.
Population: Grades K–9.
Publication Dates: 1955–2003.
Acronym: ITBS®.
Administration: Group.
Levels, 10: 5–14.
Forms, 2: A and B; 3 batteries: Complete (Levels 5–14), Core (Levels 7–14 only), and Survey (Levels 7–14 only).
Price Data: Available from publisher.
Comments: Provides norm-referenced scores.
Authors: H. D. Hoover, S. B. Dunbar, D. A. Frisbie, K. R. Oberley, V. L. Ordman, R. J. Naylor, G. B. Bray, J. C. Lewis, A. L. Qualls, M. A. Mengeling, G. P. Shannon, and S. von Schrader.
Publisher: Riverside Publishing.
  a) LEVEL 5.
    Population: Grades K.1–1.5.
    Scores, 8: Vocabulary, Word Analysis, Reading Words, Listening, Language, Mathematics, Reading Profile Total, Core Total.
    Time: Untimed, approximately 120-145 minutes.
  b) LEVEL 6.
    Population: Grades K.7–1.9.
    Scores, 10: Same as *a* above, with the addition of Reading Comprehension and Reading Total.
    Time: Untimed, approximately 163 minutes.
  c) LEVELS 7 and 8.
    Population: Grades 1.7–3.2.
    Scores, 18: Vocabulary, Word Analysis, Reading Comprehension, Reading Total, Listening, Spelling, Language, Math Concepts, Math Problems, Math Computation, Math Total, Core Total, Social Studies, Science, Sources of Information, Composite, Reading Profile Total, Survey Battery Total.
    Time: Untimed, approximately 260-284 minutes for Core Battery; approximately 344-374 minutes for Complete Battery; approximately 114-136 minutes for Survey Battery.

d) LEVELS 9–14.

Population: Grades 3.0–9.9.

Scores, 21–23: Vocabulary, Reading Comprehension, Reading Total, Spelling, Capitalization, Punctuation, Usage and Expression, Language Total, Math Concepts and Estimation, Math Problem Solving, Math Computation, Math Total, Core Total, Social Studies, Science, Maps and Diagrams, Reference Materials, Sources of Information Total, Word Analysis (Level 9 only), Listening (Level 9 only), Composite, Survey Battery Total.

Time: 250–360 minutes for Core Battery; 362–515 minutes for Complete Battery; 101–142 minutes for Survey Battery.

Cross References: See T5:1318 (24 references); for reviews by Susan M. Brookhart and Lawrence H. Cross of Forms K, L and M, see 13:159 (110 references); see also T4:1280 (33) references; for reviews by Suzanne Lane and Nambury S. Raju of Form J, see 11:184 (24 references); for reviews by Robert L. Linn and Victor L. Willson of Forms G and H, see 10:155 (45 references); for reviews by Peter W. Airasian and Anthony J. Nitko of Forms 7 and 8, see 9:533 (29 references); see also T3:1192 (97 references); for reviews by Larry A. Harris and Fred Pyrczak of Forms 5-6, see 8:19 (58 references); see T2:19 (87 references) and 6:13 (17 references); for reviews by Virgil E. Herrick, G.A.V. Morgan, and H. H. Remmers, and an excerpted review by Laurence Siegel of Forms 1-2, see 5:16. For reviews of the modern mathematics supplement, see 7:481 (2 reviews).

[1292]
Iowa Tests of Educational Development®, Forms A and B.

Purpose: Designed to "provide objective, norm-referenced information about high school students' development in the skills that are the long-term goals of secondary education."

Population: Grades 9–12.

Publication Dates: 1942–2006.

Acronym: ITED®.

Administration: Group.

Levels, 3: 15, 16, 17/18.

Forms, 2: A, B (parallel forms).

Price Data: Available from publisher.

Special Editions: Braille and large-print editions available.

Authors: R. A. Forsyth, T. N. Ansley, L. S. Feldt, and S. D. Alnot.

Publisher: Riverside Publishing.

a) CORE BATTERY.

Scores, 7: Vocabulary, Reading Comprehension, Language: Revising Written Materials, Spelling, Mathematics: Concepts and Problem Solving, Computation, Total.

Time: (160) minutes.

b) COMPLETE BATTERY.

Scores, 10: Vocabulary, Reading Comprehension, Language: Revising Written Materials, Spelling, Mathematics: Concepts and Problem Solving, Computation, Analysis of Social Studies Materials, Analysis of Science Materials, Sources of Information, Total.

Time: (260) minutes.

Cross References: For reviews by Alan C. Bugbee, Jr. and William D. Schafer, see 16:116; for reviews by William A. Mehrens and Michael J. Subkoviak of an earlier edition, see 13:160 (7 references); see also T4:1281 (4 references); for a review by S. E. Phillips of an earlier edition, see 10:156 (3 references); for reviews by Edward Kifer and James L. Wardrop of an earlier form, see 9:534 (5 references); see also T3:1193 (14 references) for reviews by C. Mauritz Lindvall and John E. Milholland of an earlier form, see 8:20 (15 references); see T2:20 (85 references); for reviews by Ellis Batton Page and Alexander G. Wesman of earlier forms, see 6:14 (23 references); for reviews by J. Murray Lee and Stephen Wiseman, see 5:17 (9 references); for a review by Eric Gardner, see 4:17 (3 references); for reviews by Henry Chauncey, Gustav J. Froelich, and Lavone A. Hanna, see 3:12.

[1293]
Iowa Tests of Music Literacy, Revised.

Purpose: Assesses "a student's comparative strengths and weaknesses in six dimensions of tonal and rhythm audiation and notational audiation" and compares these scores to the student's "music aptitude."

Population: Grades 4–12.

Publication Dates: 1970–1991.

Scores, 9: Tonal Concepts (Audiation/Listening, Audiation/Reading, Audiation/Writing, Total), Rhythm Concepts (Audiation/Listening, Audiation/Reading, Audiation/Writing, Total), Total.

Administration: Group.

Price Data, 2006: $350 per complete kit for all six levels including manual, six cassette tapes, 50 answer sheets, six record folders, and scoring masks; $90 per complete kit for Level One Only including manual, one cassette tape, scoring masks, 50 answer sheets, and 6 record folders; $8 per 50 tonal answer sheets; $8 per 50 rhythm answer sheets; $15 per 50 cumulative record folders; $3 per 6 class record sheets; $15 per manual; $15 per cassette tape (specify level).

Time: 36(45) minutes for Tonal Concepts; 36(45) minutes for Rhythm Concepts.

Author: Edwin E. Gordon.

Publisher: GIA Publications, Inc.

Cross References: For a review by Rudolf E. Radocy, see 13:161; for a review by Paul R. Lehman of an earlier edition, see 8:97 (16 references); see also T2:199 (5 references) and 7:245 (2 references).

[1294]

IPI Job-Tests Program.

Purpose: "Screening, selection, and promotion of job applicants and employees."

Population: Job applicants and employees in industry.

Publication Dates: 1948–1997.

Administration: Group or individual.

Price Data, 2005: Batteries: Sales Personnel, Medical Office Assistant, Clerical Staff, Dental Technician, and Production/Mechanical: $80 per Starter Kit, $12 per Individual Test Package; $18 per 20 scoring worksheets.

Foreign Language Editions: French and Spanish editions available.

Comments: Program is composed of 19 tests "used in different combinations to form specific batteries for each of the job-test fields"; job fields include Sales Personnel, Medical Office Assistant, Clerical Staff, Dental Technician, and Production/Mechanical.

Author: Industrial Psychology International Ltd.

Publisher: Industrial Psychology International Ltd.

a) OFFICE TERMS.

Price Data: $26 per 20 test booklets; $30 per introductory kit including 20 test booklets, technical manual, and scoring key.

Time: (6) minutes.

b) NUMBERS.

Price Data: Same as *a* above.

Time: (6) minutes.

c) PERCEPTION.

Price Data: Same as *a* above.

Time: Same as *a* above.

d) JUDGMENT.

Price Data: Same as *a* above.

Time: Same as *a* above.

e) FLUENCY.

Price Data: Same as *a* above.

Time: Same as *a* above.

f) PARTS.

Price Data: Same as *a* above.

Time: Same as *a* above.

g) MEMORY.

Price Data: $40 per 20 test booklets; $44 per introductory kit including 20 test booklets, technical manual, and scoring key.

Time: Same as *a* above.

h) BLOCKS.

Price Data: Same as *a* above.

Time: Same as *a* above.

i) DEXTERITY.

Price Data: Same as *a* above.

Time: (3) minutes.

j) DIMENSION.

Price Data: Same as *a* above.

Time: Same as *a* above.

k) PRECISION.

Price Data: Same as *a* above.

Time: Same as *a* above.

l) TOOLS.

Price Data: Same as *a* above.

Time: Same as *a* above.

m) MOTOR.

Price Data: $26 per 20 record booklets; $30 per introductory kit including 20 record booklets and technical manual; $150 per motor board.

Time: Same as *a* above.

n) SALES TERMS.

Price Data: Same as *a* above.

Time: (5) minutes.

o) APPLIED MATH.

Price Data: Same as *a* above.

Time: (12) minutes.

p) READING COMPREHENSION.

Price Data: $18 per 10 reusable test booklets; $28 per 20 answer/score sheets; $38 per introductory kit including 5 reusable test booklets, 20 answer/score sheets, and technical manual.

Time: Same as *o* above.

q) CPF SECOND EDITION.

Acronym: CPF.

Price Data: Same as *a* above.

Time: (5-10) minutes.

Author: Samuel E. Krug.

r) NPF SECOND EDITION.

Acronym: NPF.

Price Data: Same as *a* above.

Time: Same as *q* above.

Author: Same as *q* above.

Cross References: For reviews by Laura L. B. Barnes and Mary A. Lewis, see 11:185; see also T2:1078 (12 references); for reviews by William H. Helme and Stanley I. Rubin, see 6:774; for a review by Harold P. Bechtoldt of the Factored Aptitude Series, see 5:602; for a review by D. Welty Lefever and an excerpted review by Laurance F. Shaffer of an earlier edition of this series, see 4:712 (1 reference).

[1295]

IPT Early Literacy Test.

Purpose: Designed to "assess the skill development of English learners in kindergarten and first grade relative to their becoming proficient English language readers and writers."

Population: Grades K-1.

Publication Dates: 2000-2004.

Administration: Group.

Price Data: Available from publisher.

Comments: Measures students' developmental stages of reading and writing and helps educators develop instructional programs tailored to meet students' specific needs.

Authors: Beverly Amori and Enrique F. Dalton.
Publisher: Ballard & Tighe, Publishers.
  a) READING.
  Scores, 9: Visual Recognition, Letter Recognition, Phonemic-Initial Sounds, Phonics-Initial Blends and Digraphs, Reading Vocabulary, Reading for Life Skills, Reading for Understanding Sentences, Reading for Understanding Stories, Total Reading.
  Time: (10-30) minutes.
  b) WRITING.
  Scores, 5: Copy Letters, Write Name and Copy the Sentence, Descriptive or Narrative Writing, Spelling, Total Writing.
  Time: (30-45) minutes.

[1296]
IRAOS: Interview for the Retrospective Assessment of the Onset and Course of Schizophrenia and Other Psychoses.

Purpose: Designed to provide "a retrospective assessment of symptoms, disability and social development in schizophrenic and affective illness."
Population: Adults who have schizophrenia.
Publication Dates: 1987–2003.
Acronym: IRAOS.
Scores: Item scores only.
Subtests, 5: General Information, Socio-Demographic and Case History Information, Episodes and Intervals of Mental Disorder, Indicators of Psychiatric Illness, Evaluation of Success of Information.
Administration: Individual.
Price Data, 2006: $238 per kit including manual (2003, 60 pages), 5 interview booklets, 50 score sheets, 50 IND forms, 50 TREAT forms, 50 EPIS forms, 50 time schedules, and 50 calendars of episodes; $48 per manual; $36 per 5 interview booklets; $54 per 50 score sheets; $14.80 per 50 IND forms; $14.80 per 50 EPIS forms; $14.80 per 50 time schedules; $14.80 per 50 calendars of episodes.
Time: (90–120) minutes.
Authors: Heinz Häfner, Walter Löffler, Kurt Maurer, Anita Riecher-Rössler, and Astrid Stein.
Publisher: Hogrefe & Huber Publishers.
Cross References: For reviews by Allen K. Hess and Janet V. Smith, see 16:117.

[1297]
Irenometer.

Purpose: Measures attitudes toward peace.
Population: Adults.
Publication Dates: 1984–1985.
Scores: Total score only.
Administration: Group.
Manual: No manual.
Price Data, 2005: $2 per scale.

Time: [12] minutes.
Comments: Supplementary article available.
Author: Panos D. Bardis.
Publisher: Donna Bardis.

[1298]
IS Manager/Consultant Skills Evaluation.

Purpose: To assess essential skills needed for the position of IS Manager or IS Consultant.
Population: Candidates for IS Manager or IS Consultant positions.
Publication Date: 1992.
Acronym: BAEDPMC.
Scores: Total Score, Narrative Evaluation, Ranking, Recommendation.
Administration: Group.
Price Data, 2001: $500 per candidate; quantity discounts available.
Time: Administration time not reported.
Comments: Scored by publisher; must be proctored.
Author: Bruce A. Winrow.
Publisher: Walden Personnel Performance, Inc. [Canada].

[1299]
IT Consultant Skills Evaluation.

Purpose: Designed "to evaluate technical, intellectual and supervisory skills required for a senior level IT Consultant, Data Processing Consultant, or IT Trainer."
Population: Candidates for the position of senior level IT Consultant, Data Processing Consultant, or IT Trainer.
Publication Dates: 1988–2002.
Scores, 7: Technical-Analytical Skills (Procedural Ability, Error Recognition, Problem Solving, Business Analysis, Project Management, Planning), Management-Related Skills (Business Judgment).
Administration: Group.
Price Data: Available from publisher.
Foreign Language Editions: Available in French and English.
Time: (180) minutes.
Author: Walden Personnel Performance, Inc.
Publisher: Walden Personnel Performance, Inc. [Canada].

[1300]
ITSEA/BITSEA: Infant-Toddler and Brief Infant-Toddler Social and Emotional Assessment.

Purpose: Designed to identify children "who may have social-emotional and behavioral problems and/or delays, or deficits in social-emotional competence."
Population: Ages 12-0 to 35-1 months.
Publication Date: 2006.
Administration: Individual.

Forms, 2: Brief Infant Toddler Social Emotional Assessment, Infant Toddler Social Emotional Assessment.

Parts, 2: Parent, Childcare Provider.

Price Data, 2006: $275 per ITSEA/BITSEA comprehensive kit including ITSEA/BITSEA Scoring Assistant software, ITSEA manual, BITSEA manual, 10 ITSEA Parent Forms, 10 ITSEA Childcare Provider Forms 25 BITSEA Parent Forms, and 25 BITSEA Childcare Provider Forms.

Foreign Language Editions: Parent and Childcare Provider Forms available in Spanish.

Comments: These tests are to be completed by a parent/guardian and a childcare provider; the parent form may be completed as an interview.

Publisher: PsychCorp, A Brand of Harcourt Assessment, Inc.

a) BRIEF INFANT TODDLER SOCIAL EMOTIONAL ASSESSMENT.

Acronym: BITSEA.

Scores, 2: Problem Total, Competence Total.

Price Data: $99 per complete kit including BITSEA manual (2006, 62 pages), 25 BITSEA Parent Forms, and 25 BITSEA Childcare Provider Forms; $50 per BITSEA manual; $35 per 25 BITSEA Parent Forms; $35 per 25 BITSEA Childcare Provider Forms.

Time: (5-10) minutes.

Authors: Margaret J. Briggs-Gowan and Alice S. Carter.

b) INFANT TODDLER SOCIAL EMOTIONAL ASSESSMENT.

Acronym: ITSEA.

Scores, 20: Externalizing (Activity/Impulsivity, Aggression/Defiance, Peer Aggression), Internalizing (Depression/Withdrawal, General Anxiety, Separation Distress, Inhibition to Novelty), Dysregulation (Sleep, Negative Emotionality, Eating, Sensory Sensitivity), Competence (Compliance, Attention, Imitation/Play, Mastery Motivation, Empathy, Prosocial Peer Relations), Maladaptive Item Cluster, Social Relatedness Cluster, Atypical Item Cluster.

Price Data: $150 per complete kit including ITSEA manual (2006, 180 pages), 10 BITSEA Parent Forms, and 10 ITSEA Childcare Provider Forms; $25 per ITSEA manual; $25 per 10 ITSEA Parent Forms; $25 per 10 ITSEA Childcare Provider Forms; $75 per ITSEA Scoring Assistant.

Time: (20-30) minutes.

Authors: Alice S. Carter and Margaret J. Briggs-Gowan.

[1301]

IVA+Plus [Integrated Visual and Auditory Continuous Performance Test].

Purpose: "Designed primarily to help in the diagnosis and quantification of the symptoms of Attention-Deficit/Hyperactivity Disorders (ADHD)."

Population: Ages 6 to adult.

Publication Dates: 1993–2005.

Acronym: IVA+Plus CPT.

Scores, 28: Auditory Response Control Quotient, Prudence Auditory, Consistency Auditory, Stamina Auditory, Visual Response Control Quotient, Prudence Visual, Consistency Visual, Stamina Visual, Full Scale Response Control Quotient, Auditory Attention Quotient, Vigilance Auditory, Focus Auditory, Speed Auditory, Visual Attention Quotient, Vigilance Visual, Focus Visual, Speed Visual, Full Scale Attention Quotient, Fine Motor Regulation Quotient (Hyperactivity), Balance, Readiness Auditory, Readiness Visual, Comprehension Auditory, Comprehension Visual, Persistence Auditory, Persistence Visual, Sensory/Motor Auditory, Sensory/Motor Visual.

Administration: Individual.

Price Data, 2006: Option 1: $549 per starter kit with Investigator including CD-ROM, interpretation, administration and technical support manuals (included on CD), and 10 testing administrations (licensed for use at one computer); $139 per 10 additional test administrations for starter kit preferred customer; Option 2: $859 per registration kit with Investigator including CD-ROM, interpretation, administration, and technical support manuals (included on CD), and 10 testing administrations; $129 per 25 additional test administrations for registration kit preferred customer; Option 3: $1,795 per unlimited use kit with Investigator including CD-ROM, interpretation, administration, and technical support manuals (included on CD), and unlimited testing administrations at one computer station; $99 per preferred customer plan; $10 per two trial tests (downloadable free from www.braintrain.com); $259 per Interpretive Report Writer Kit; $99 per 10 additional reports; $499 per 100 additional reports.

Foreign Language Editions: Option available to allow the test stimuli to be spoken in a foreign language (Arabic, Danish, Dutch, French, German, Greek, Hebrew, Hindi, Indonesian, Italian, Japanese, Mandarin, Pashto, Polish, Portuguese, Russian, Spanish, Swahili, Swedish, Taiwanese Dialect, Turkish, Vietnamese, and Welsh) for an additional charge of $259.

Time: 13[20] minutes.

Comments: Computer administered; requires IBM computer with a Pentium 166 or higher processor, Windows 98SE, 2000, ME, or XP, Internet Explorer 6.0 or higher, and speakers; optional analyses (Investigator and Special Analyses) and report writers (Standard Report, ADHD Report) may be added to software; the Preferred Customer Plan provides software and normative updates, free technical support for one year, and discounts on the cost of additional testing administrations and Add-Ons.

Authors: Joseph A. Sandford and Ann Turner.

Publisher: BrainTrain.

Cross References: For reviews by Harrison Kane and Susan C. Whiston and by Martin J. Wiese of an earlier edition, see 14:180.

[1302]
Jackson Personality Inventory—Revised.

Purpose: Designed as a "modern measure of normal personality, useful in counseling and business settings."
Population: Adolescents and adults.
Publication Dates: 1976–1997.
Acronym: JPI-R.
Scores: 15 scales in 5 clusters: Analytical (Complexity, Breadth of Interest, Innovation, Tolerance), Emotional (Empathy, Anxiety, Cooperativeness), Extroverted (Sociability, Social Confidence, Energy Level), Opportunistic (Social Astuteness, Risk Taking), Dependable (Organization, Traditional Values, Responsibility).
Administration: Group or individual.
Price Data, 2006: $80 per examination kit including manual on CD (1994, 138 pages), 5 test booklets, 5 Quick Score answer sheets, 5 profile sheets, and coupon and machine-scorable answer sheet for one Basic Report; $15 per manual on CD; $50 per 25 test booklets; $65 per 25 Quick Score answer sheets; $40 per 25 profile sheets; $58–$65 (depending on volume) per 10 machine-scorable answer sheets and coupons for Basic Reports; $105 per software package including disks, software manual for Windows, test manual, and 10 coupons for computer reports; $14 per online password; volume discount available.
Foreign Language Edition: Available in French (booklets only).
Time: 45 minutes.
Author: Douglas N. Jackson.
Publisher: Sigma Assessment Systems, Inc.
Cross References: See T5:1333 (8 references); for reviews by David J. Pittenger and Peter Zachar, see 13:162 921 references); see also T4:1296 (28 references) and T3:1203 (6 references); for reviews by Lewis R. Goldberg and David T. Lykken of an earlier edition, see 8:593 (6 references).

[1303]
Jackson Vocational Interest Survey [1999 Revision].

Purpose: "Designed to yield ... a set of scores representing interests and preferences relevant to work ..., conceptualized as work roles and work styles."
Population: High school and above.
Publication Dates: 1977–2000.
Acronym: JVIS.
Scores, 50: 34 Basic Interest Scales (Creative Arts, Performing Arts, Mathematics, Physical Science, Engineering, Life Science, Social Science, Adventure, Nature—Agriculture, Skilled Trades, Personal Service, Family Activity, Medical Service, Dominant Leadership, Job Security, Stamina, Accountability, Teaching, Social Service, Elementary Education, Finance, Business, Office Work, Sales, Supervision, Human Relations Management, Law, Professional Advising, Author—Journalism, Academic Achievement, Technical Writing, Independence, Planfulness, Interpersonal Confidence); 10 General Occupational Themes (Expressive, Logical, Inquiring, Practical, Assertive, Socialized, Helping, Conventional, Enterprising, Communicative); 3 Administrative Indices (Unscorable Responses, Response Consistency Index, Infrequency Index); Academic Satisfaction; Similarity to College Students; Similarity to Occupational Classifications.
Administration: Group.
Price Data, 2006: $95 per examination kit including manual on CD (2000, 149 pages), JVIS Applications Handbook, JVIS Occupations Guide, machine-scorable answer sheet for Extended Report, reusable test booklet, hand-scorable answer and profile sheets, and jvis.com password; $15 per test manual on CD; $40 per JVIS Applications Handbook; $30 per JVIS Occupations Guide (2005); $50 per 25 reusable test booklets; $40 per 25 hand-scorable answer sheets; $40 per 25 profile sheets; $85-$95 per Mail-in Extended Report including machine-scorable answer sheet and laser-printed report; $58-$65 per Mail-in Basic Report including machine-scorable answer sheet; $105 per SigmaSoft JVIS for Windows start-up package including disks, software manual, test manual, and 10 coupons; $10 per online password; volume discounts available.
Foreign Language Editions: Available in Spanish (booklets only) and in French (booklets and extended reports); also, online administration using SigmaSoft JVIS for Windows and reports).
Time: 45 minutes.
Comments: Former edition no longer available; available in paper-and-pencil format (hand scoring or mail-in scoring), online administration and scoring available using SigmaSoft JVIS for Windows software; system requirements: SigmaSoft JVIS for Windows also can be used for scoring data scanned by an optical mark reader using SigmaSoft Scanning Utility; SigmaSoft JVIS for Windows produces Basic Report, Extended Report, and Data Report.
Authors: Douglas N. Jackson and Marc Verhoeve (applications handbook).
Publisher: Sigma Assessment Systems, Inc.
Cross References: For reviews by Eleanor E. Sanford and Wendy J. Steinberg, see 15:129; see T5:1334 (5 references and T4:1297 (1 reference); for reviews by Douglas T. Brown and John W. Shepard of a previous edition, see 10:158 (1 reference); for reviews by Charles Davidshofer and Ruth G. Thomas, see 9:542; see also T3:1204 (1 reference).

[1304]
Jail Inmate Inventory.

Purpose: "Designed for inmate risk assessment and needs identification"; provides information to "help determine inmate risk, establish supervisory levels and identify readiness for classification or status changes."
Population: Jail inmates with a sixth grade or above reading level.
Publication Dates: 1991–1995.
Acronym: JII.
Scores, 6: Truthfulness, Violence, Antisocial, Adjustment, Alcohol, Drugs.
Administration: Group.
Price Data: Available from publisher.
Foreign Language Edition: Spanish Edition available.
Time: (15–20) minutes.
Comments: Can be administered by paper and pencil or by computer; all scoring is done by computer.
Author: Risk & Needs Assessment, Inc.
Publisher: Risk & Needs Assessment, Inc.

[1305]
James Madison Test of Critical Thinking.

Purpose: "Designed to evaluate the in-depth critical thinking ability of middle school students through adults."
Population: Grades 7-12+.
Publication Date: 2004.
Scores: Total score only.
Administration: Individual or group.
Forms, 2: A, B.
Price Data, 2006: $64.99 per 50-use CD (specify form); $103.99 per 50-use CD including both forms; quantity discounts available; $9.99 per test online administration.
Time: 50 minutes.
Comments: Can be administered online, over a network, or on a stand-alone computer (Windows or Macintosh); both forms can be used as a pretest or posttest; formerly known as the Comprehensive Test of Critical Thinking.
Authors: Don Fawkes, Bill O'Meara, and Dan Flage.
Publisher: The Critical Thinking Co.

[1306]
Jesness Behavior Checklist.

Purpose: "Designed as a multiple rating scale to be used by self and others that measures individuals at risk for antisocial behavior."
Population: Delinquents ages 13-20.
Publication Dates: 1970-1971.
Scores, 14: Unobtrusiveness/Obtrusiveness, Friendliness/Hostility, Responsibility/Irresponsibility, Considerateness/Inconsiderateness, Independence/Dependence, Rapport/Alienation, Enthusiasm/Depression, Sociability/Poor Peer Relations, Conformity/Non-Conformity, Calmness/Anxiousness, Effective Communications/Inarticulateness, Insight/Unawareness and Indecisiveness, Social Control/Attention-Seeking, Anger Control/Hypersensitivity.
Administration: Individual.
Price Data, 2006: $156 per complete kit including 10 Observer item booklets, 25 Observer QuikScore™ forms, 10 Self-Appraisal item booklets, 25 Self-Appraisal QuikScore™ forms, and manual (1971, 32 pages); $32 per 10 Observer item booklets; $31 per 25 Observer QuikScore™ forms; $32 per 10 Self-Appraisal item booklets; $37 per 25 Self-Appraisal QuikScore™ forms; $51 per manual.
Editions, 2: Observer, Self-Appraisal.
Time: (15-20) minutes.
Comments: Self-report and observer rating; Windows™ or MS DOS computer administration and scoring software available on CD or 3.5-inch disk.
Author: Carl F. Jesness.
Publisher: Multi-Health Systems, Inc.
Cross References: See T5:1340 (5 references); for reviews by Dorcas Susan Butt and Edwin I. Megargee, see 8:594 (3 references).

[1307]
Jesness Inventory—Revised.

Purpose: Designed to be used as a personality inventory for delinquent and conduct-disordered youths and adults.
Population: Ages 8 and over.
Publication Dates: 1962–2003.
Acronym: JI-R.
Scores, 24: Randomness Scale, Lie Scale, Asocial Index, Social Maladjustment, Value Orientation, Immaturity, Autism, Alienation, Manifest Aggression, Withdrawal-Depression, Social Anxiety, Repression, Denial, Conduct Disorder, Oppositional Defiant Disorder, Undersocialized/Active [Unsocialized/Aggressive], Undersocialized/Passive [Unsocialized/Passive], Conformist [Immature Conformist], Group Oriented [Cultural Conformist], Pragmatist [Manipulator], Autonomy-Oriented [Neurotic/Acting-Out], Introspective [Neurotic/Anxious], Inhibited [Situational], Adaptive [Cultural Identifier].
Administration: Group.
Price Data, 2006: $182 per complete kit including technical manual, 10 item booklets, 25 response forms, and scoring templates; $71 per technical manual; $22 per 10 item booklets; $50 per 25 response forms; $71 for scoring templates.
Time: (30–45) minutes.
Comments: Mail-in/fax-in scoring service available; software version available; web administration available.
Author: Carl F. Jesness.
Publisher: Multi-Health Systems, Inc.

Cross References: For reviews by Elizabeth Kelley Rhoades and Georgette Yetter, see 16:118; for reviews by Robert M. Guion and Susana Urbina of a previous edition, see 14:188; see also T5:1341 (3 references) and T3:1209 (9 references); for a review by Dorcas Susan Butt of an earlier edition, see 8:595 (14 references); see also T2:1249 (5 references); for a review by Sheldon A. Weintraub of the Youth Edition of the earlier edition, see 7:94 (10 references); see also P:133 (3 references).

[1308]
Job Activity Preference Questionnaire.

Purpose: To obtain a measure of job interests or preferences.
Population: Adults.
Publication Dates: 1972–1981.
Acronym: JAPQ.
Scores, 16: Making Decisions/Communicating and Having Responsibility, Operating Vehicles, Using Machines-Tools-Instruments, Performing Physical Activities, Operating Keyboard and Office Equipment, Monitoring and/or Controlling Equipment and/or Processes, Working Under Uncomfortable Conditions, Working with Art-Decor/Entertainment, Performing Supervisory Duties, Performing Estimating Activities, Processing Written Information, Working With Buyers-Customers-Salespersons, Working Under Hazardous Conditions, Performing Paced and/or Repetitive Activities, Working with Aerial and Aquatic Equipment, Catering/Serving/Smelling/Tasting.
Administration: Group.
Price Data: Available from publisher.
Time: Administration time not reported.
Comments: Restructured and simplified version of Position Analysis Questionnaire (1977).
Authors: Robert C. Mecham, Alma F. Harris (test), Ernest J. McCormick (test), and P. R. Jeanneret (test).
Publisher: PAQ Services, Inc.
Cross References: For reviews by Norman G. Peterson and Paul R. Sackett, see 9:547.

[1309]
Job Attitude Analysis.

Purpose: Devised to "reveal a person's underlying attitudes pertinent for success and satisfaction in his work."
Population: Production and clerical workers.
Publication Dates: 1961–1970.
Acronym: JAA.
Scores: Total score only.
Administration: Group.
Price Data: Available from publisher.
Time: Administration time not reported.
Comments: An inventory for employment interviewing and vocational counseling.
Author: P. L. Mellenbruch.

Publisher: Psychometric Affiliates.
Cross References: For additional information, see 7:980 (1 reference).

[1310]
Job Attitude Scale.

Purpose: Designed to assess intrinsic and extrinsic job orientations.
Population: Adults.
Publication Dates: 1971–1988.
Acronym: JAS.
Scores, 17: Praise and Recognition, Growth in Skill, Creative Work, Responsibility, Advancement, Achievement, Salary, Security, Personnel Policies, Competent Supervision, Relations-Peers, Relations-Subordinates, Relations-Supervisor, Working Conditions, Status, Family Needs-Salary, Total Intrinsic.
Administration: Group.
Forms, 2: Full, Abbreviated.
Price Data: Available from publisher.
Time: (15–20) minutes.
Author: Shoukry D. Saleh.
Publisher: Shoukry D. Saleh [Canada] [No reply from publisher; status unknown].
Cross References: For a review by Gregory J. Boyle, see 11:186; see also 8:1049 (9 references).

[1311]
Job Challenge Profile.

Purpose: "Designed to help managers better understand and see their job assignments as opportunities for learning and growth."
Population: Managers, leaders, and executives.
Publication Date: 1999.
Acronym: JCP.
Scores, 10: Unfamiliar Responsibilities, New Directions, Inherited Problems, Problems with Employees, High Stakes, Scope and Scale, External Pressure, Influence Without Authority, Work Across Cultures, Work Group Diversity.
Administration: Individual.
Price Data, 2006: $30 per Facilitator's Guide (76 pages); $15 per Participant's Workbook/Survey (49 pages); quantity discounts are available.
Time: 15-20 minutes.
Comments: Revision of the Developmental Challenge Profile (DCP; no longer available); self-scored; Facilitator's Guide includes details of workshop procedures, reproducible overheads, and handout masters; Participant's Workbook contains test items and action guide.
Authors: Cynthia D. McCauley (Facilitator's Guide, Participant Workbook/Survey), Patricia J. Ohlott (Facilitator's Guide, Survey), and Marian N. Ruderman (Facilitator's Guide, Survey).
Publisher: Jossey-Bass, A Wiley Company.

Cross References: For reviews by Laura L. B. Barnes and Jean Powell Kirnan, see 16:119; for reviews by Jean Powell Kirnan and Kristen Wojcik and by Eugene P. Sheehan of The Developmental Challenge Profile, see 13:94 (2 references).

[1312]
A Job Choice Decision-Making Exercise.

Purpose: Serves as a behavioral decision theory measurement approach to need for affiliation, need for power, and need for achievement.
Population: High school and college and adults.
Publication Dates: 1981–1986.
Acronym: JCE.
Scores, 3: Affiliation, Power, Achievement.
Administration: Group.
Price Data, 2006: $4 per exercise booklet; $35 per Managerial and Technical Motivation book (1986, 178 pages, available from Praeger Publishers, in lieu of manual).
Time: [15–20] minutes.
Authors: Michael J. Stahl and Anil Gulati (scoring software and scoring manual).
Publisher: Assessment Enterprises.
Cross References: For a review by Nicholas A. Vacc and J. Scott Hinkle, see 11:187.

[1313]
Job Descriptive Index (1997 Revision) and The Job in General Scales (1985 Revision).

Purpose: To measure job satisfaction (facet and/or overall).
Population: Employees
Publication Dates: 1969–1997.
Acronyms: JDI; JIG.
Scores: Five facets (Work on Present Job, Pay, Opportunities for Promotion, Supervision, and People on Your Present Job) and the Job in General.
Administration: Group or individual.
Price Data, 2006: $100 per 100 test booklets; $50 (plus shipping & handling) per paper user's manual (1997, 275 pages); $40 per electronic printable manual(pdf format 340 KB); $25 per electronic nonprintable manual (pdf format 340 KB).
Time: 5-10 minutes.
Authors: Patricia C. Smith, Lorne M. Kendall, and Charles L. Hulin (1969 edition); William K. Balzer, Jenifer A. Kihm, Patricia C. Smith, Jennifer L. Irwin, Peter D. Bachiochi, Chet Robie, Evan F. Sinar, and Luis F. Parra (1997 edition).
Publisher: Bowling Green State University
Cross References: For a review by Michael R. Harwell, see 15:130; see T5:1348 (16 references); for reviews by Charles K. Parsons and Norman D. Sundberg for an earlier edition of the Job Descriptive Index and Retirement Descriptive Index, see 12:199 (33 references); see also T4:1312 (63 references); for reviews by John O. Crites and Barbara A. Kerr of an earlier edition of the Job Descriptive Index, see 9:550 (49 references).

[1314]
JOB-O.

Purpose: "To facilitate self-awareness, career-awareness, and career exploration."
Publication Dates: 1981–1992.
Administration: Group.
Price Data: Price information available from publisher.
Comments: Also known as Judgement of Occupational Behavior-Orientation.
Authors: Arthur Cutler, Francis Ferry, Robert Kauk, and Robert Robinett.
Publisher: CFKR Career Materials.
a) JOB-O (ELEMENTARY).
Population: Grades 4–7.
Scores: 6 ratings: Mechanical/Construction/Agriculture, Scientific/Technical, Creative/Artistic, Social/Legal/Educational, Managers/Sales, Administrative Support.
Time: Administration time not reported.
b) JOB-O.
Population: Junior high school through adult.
Scores, 8: Education, Interest, Inclusion, Control, Affection, Physical Activity, Hands/Tools/Machinery, Problem-Solving, Creative-Ideas.
Foreign Language Editions: Spanish and Vietnamese test booklets and answer sheets available.
Time: (60–65) minutes.
c) JOB-O A (ADVANCED).
Population: Grades 10–12 and adult.
Scores, 16: Occupational Interest, Training Time, Reasoning Skills, Mathematical Skills, Language Skills, Working with Data, Working with People, Working with Things, Working Conditions, Physical Demands, Leadership, Helping People, Problem-Solving, Initiative, Team Work, Public Contact.
Time: [50–55] minutes.
Comments: May be self-administered.
Cross References: For reviews by F. Marion Asche and Lawrence H. Cross, see 12:200; for a review by James W. Pinkney of an earlier edition, see 10:160; for a review by Bruce J. Eberhardt of an earlier edition, see 9:560.

[1315]
Job Observation and Behavior Scale.

Purpose: Designed as "a work performance evaluation for supported and entry level employees."
Population: Ages 15 and above.
Publication Dates: 1998–2000.

Acronym: JOBS.
Scores, 4: Work-Required Daily Living Activities, Work-Required Behavior, Work-Required Job Duties, Quality of Performance Composite/Total.
Administration: Individual.
Price Data, 2005: $75 per complete kit including 25 record forms and manual (1998, 28 pages); $30 per 25 record forms; $50 per job manual.
Time: (30) minutes.
Authors: Howard Rosenberg and Michael Brady.
Publisher: Stoelting Co.
Cross References: For reviews by Ayres G. D'Costa and Sheldon Zedeck, see 15:131.

[1316]
Job Readiness Skills Pre- and Post-Assessment.

Purpose: Designed to assess examinees on skills related to employability and work maturity/job retention.
Population: Individuals seeking employment.
Publication Dates: 1984–2000.
Administration: Group or individual.
Manual: No manual.
Price Data, 2002: $18 per specimen set including 5 copies each of Pre- and Post-Assessment forms; $52 per set of 25 assessments (specify Pre- or Post-Assessment).
Time: (45–55) minutes.
Comments: Earlier version entitled Assessing Specific Competencies.
Author: Education Associates, Inc.
Publisher: Education Associates.
a) PRE-ASSESSMENT.
Scores: 9 areas: Career Goals, Finding a Job, Resumes, Job Applications, Interviews, Positive Attitudes, Good Appearance, Communication, Written Communication.
b) POST-ASSESSMENT.
Scores: Same as *a* above.
Cross References: For reviews by Robert Fitzpatrick and Robert C. Reinehr of an earlier edition, see 12:33.

[1317]
Job Search Attitude Inventory, Second Edition

Purpose: Helps identify personal attitudes about looking for a job.
Population: Adult and teen job seekers and career planners.
Publication Date: 2002.
Acronym: JSAI.
Scores, 4: Luck vs. Planning, Uninvolved vs. Involved, Help from Others vs. Self-Help, Passive vs. Active.
Administration: Group or individual.
Price Data, 2006: $39.95 per 25 inventories including copy of administrator's guide (8 pages).

Time: (10–15) minutes.
Comments: Self-administered and self-scored; revised edition features simplified language and directions, plus added practical advice for becoming more self-directed in a job search.
Author: John J. Liptak.
Publisher: JIST Publishing, Inc.
Cross References: For reviews by John W. Fleenor and Thomas R. O'Neill, see 16:120.

[1318]
Job Search Knowledge Scale.

Purpose: Designed to "measure a person's knowledge about finding a job."
Population: Job seekers.
Publication Date: 2005.
Acronym: JSKS.
Scores, 5: Identifying Job Leads, Direct Application to Employers, Resumes/Cover Letters, Employment Interviews, Following Up.
Administration: Individual or group.
Price Data, 2006: $34.95 per complete kit including 25 test booklets and administrator's guide (8 pages).
Time: (15-25) minutes.
Comments: This test can be self-administered and self-scored.
Author: John Liptak.
Publisher: JIST Publishing, Inc.

[1319]
Job Seeking Skills Assessment.

Purpose: "For assessing clients' ability to complete a job application form and participate in the employment interview, and to serve as a guide for integrating the results into program planning."
Population: Vocational rehabilitation clients.
Publication Date: 1988.
Acronym: JSSA.
Scores, 2: Job Application, Employment Interview.
Administration: Group.
Price Data: Available from publisher.
Time: Administration time not reported.
Comments: Designed as a component of the Diagnostic Employability Profile (DEP).
Authors: Suki Hinman, Bob Means, Sandra Parkerson, and Betty Odendahl.
Publisher: The National Center on Employment & Disability.
Cross References: For reviews by Paul M. Muchinsky and William I. Sauser, Jr., see 12:201.

[1320]
Job Stress Survey.

Purpose: "Designed to assess generic sources of occupational stress encountered by men and women employed in a variety of work settings."
Population: Adults ages 18 and older.

Publication Dates: 1991–1999.
Acronym: JSS.
Scores, 9: Job Stress Index, Job Stress Severity, Job Stress Frequency, Job Pressure Index, Job Pressure Severity, Job Pressure Frequency, Lack of Organizational Support Index, Lack of Organizational Support Severity, Lack of Organizational Support Frequency.
Administration: Group.
Forms, 2: Form HS (Hand-Scorable), Form SP (Scoring Program).
Price Data, 2006: $136 per introductory kit including professional manual (1999, 72 pages), 25 test booklets, 25 profile forms, and scoring software on 3.5-inch disk with 5 free uses of the scoring program.
Time: (10–15) minutes.
Comments: Computer scoring program available; Forms HS and SP are identical in content.
Authors: Charles D. Spielberger and Peter R. Vagg.
Publisher: Psychological Assessment Resources, Inc.
Cross References: For reviews by Peter M. Berger and James W. Pinkney, see 15:132.

[1321]
Job Style Indicator [Revised].

Purpose: Designed to help understand "the work behavioral style and task requirements" of a job and to provide "a job compatibility rating when used with the following CRG Style assessments: Personal, Sales, Instructional, Entrepreneurial, and Quick."
Population: Adults.
Publication Dates: 1988-2006.
Acronym: JSI.
Scores, 4: Behavioral/Action, Cognitive/Analysis, Interpersonal/Harmony, Affective/Expression.
Administration: Individual or group.
Price Data, 2006: $7.95 per test booklet (2006, 12 pages); $7.95 per access code online version; $69.95 per professional's guide (2006, 64 pages).
Time: [30-60] minutes.
Comments: Self-administered and self-scored; may be used in conjunction with Personal Style Indicator (1916), Sales Style Indicator (2219), Quick Style Indicator (2114), Entrepreneurial Style and Success Indicator (958), and the Instructional Style Indicator (1250).
Authors: Ken Keis, Terry D. Anderson, and Everett T. Robinson.
Publisher: Consulting Resource Group International, Inc.
Cross References: For reviews by Neal Schmitt and David M. Williamson of an earlier edition, see 13:164.

[1322]
Job Survival and Success Scale.

Purpose: Designed to "identify a person's attitudes and knowledge about keeping a job and getting ahead in the workplace."

Population: Job seekers.
Publication Date: 2005.
Acronym: JSSS.
Scores, 5: Dependability, Responsibility, Human Relations, Ethical Behavior, Getting Ahead.
Administration: Individual or group.
Price Data, 2006: $37.95 per complete kit including 25 test booklets and administrator's guide (8 pages).
Time: (15-25) minutes.
Comments: This test can be self-administered and self-scored.
Author: John Liptak.
Publisher: JIST Publishing, Inc.

[1323]
Johnston Informal Reading Inventory.

Purpose: "To assess the reading comprehension of junior and senior high school students."
Population: Grades 7–12.
Publication Date: 1982.
Acronym: JIRI.
Scores, 2: Vocabulary Screening, Reading Comprehension.
Administration: Group or individual.
Price Data: Available from publisher.
Time: (20) minutes.
Comments: Forms B and C are approximately parallel and Form L is longer; "high-interest materials utilized."
Author: Michael C. Johnston.
Publisher: Educational Publications [No reply from publisher; status unknown].
Cross References: For reviews by Margaret R. Rogers and Claudia R. Wright, see 12:202.

[1324]
Joliet 3-Minute Preschool Speech and Language Screen.

Purpose: "Differentiates individuals with intact skills from those with suspected problems in phonology, semantics, and grammar."
Population: 2.5–4.5 years.
Publication Date: 1992.
Scores: 3 areas: Grammar, Semantics, Phonology.
Administration: Individual.
Price Data: Price data available from publisher for complete kit including 12 vocabulary plates on card stock, 2 reproducible scoring sheets, recordkeeping manual, and manual (57 pages).
Time: (3) minutes.
Author: Mary C. Kinzler.
Publisher: Harcourt Assessment, Inc.
Cross References: For a review by Carlos Inchaurralde, see 14:189.

[1325]
Joliet 3-Minute Speech and Language Screen (Revised).

Purpose: To "identify children with age-appropriate phonological, grammatical, and semantic structures."
Population: Grades K, 2, 5.
Publication Dates: 1983–1992.
Scores, 5: Receptive Vocabulary, Grammar (Evoked Sentences), Phonology, Voice, Fluency.
Administration: Individual.
Levels, 3: Grades K, 2, 5.
Price Data: Price information available from publisher for complete kit including manual (1992, 39 pages), vocabulary plates on card stock, recordkeeping manual (15 pages), and 2 reproducible scoring sheets.
Time: (2–5) minutes.
Authors: Mary C. Kinzler and Constance Cowing Johnson.
Publisher: Harcourt Assessment, Inc.
Cross References: For reviews by Martin A. Fischer and by Malcolm R. McNeil and Thomas F. Campbell, see 13:165; for a review by Robert E. Owens, Jr. of the original edition, see 9:555 (1 reference).

[1326]
The Jones-Mohr Listening Test.

Purpose: "To provide feedback on listening efficiency and to measure the effect of skill building in this area."
Population: Persons in educational and training programs.
Publication Date: 1976.
Scores: Total score only.
Administration: Group.
Forms, 2: A, B.
Price Data: Price information available from publisher for kit including 50 test forms, audiocassette, and facilitator's guide (26 pages); 25 test forms (specify form).
Time: (25–30) minutes.
Authors: John E. Jones and Lawrence Mohr.
Publisher: Jossey-Bass, A Wiley Company.
Cross References: For reviews by Lear Ashmore and John F. Schmitt, see 9:556 (1 reference).

[1327]
Jordan Left-Right Reversal Test—Revised.

Purpose: Constructed "to measure letter and number reversals in the area of visual receptive functioning."
Population: Ages 5-0 through 12-11.
Publication Dates: 1973–1990.
Scores: Total score only.
Administration: Individual or group.
Levels: 2 overlapping levels (ages 5-12, 9-12) in a single booklet.
Price Data, 2006: $90 per complete kit including 50 test forms, 50 laterality checklists, 50 remedial checklists, and manual (1990, 64 pages); $30 per 50 test forms; $15 per 50 laterality checklists; $15 per 50 remedial checklists; $30 per manual; $30 per specimen set including manual and sample forms.
Time: (20) minutes.
Comments: Norm-referenced.
Author: Brian T. Jordan.
Publisher: Academic Therapy Publications.
Cross References: For reviews by Christine W. Burns and Jeffrey H. Snow, see 12:203 (1 reference); see also T4:1326 (4 references); for reviews by Mary S. Poplin and Joseph Torgesen, see 9:557; see also T3:1224 (2 references); for reviews by Barbara K. Keogh and Richard J. Reisboard, and excerpted reviews by Alex Bannatyne and Alan Krichev, see 8:434 (5 references).

[1328]
Joseph Picture Self-Concept Scale.

Purpose: Designed to measure "self-concept in children" and "identify children whose negative self-appraisals signal that they are at risk for academic and behavioral difficulties."
Publication Date: 2004.
Scores: Total Self-Concept Score.
Administration: Individual.
Parts, 4: Light-Skin Boys, Dark-Skin Boys, Light-Skin Girls, Dark-Skin Girls.
Price Data, 2006: $198 for complete kit for younger children including 2 stimulus booklets, 20 AutoScore forms, and manual (86 pages); $121 for complete kit for older children including 2 stimulus booklets, 20 AutoScore forms, and manual; $44 per manual; $40 per 20 AutoScore forms (specify Form Y [younger] or Form O [older]); $64 for choice of stimulus booklets; $28.50 for either Form O light-skin or Form O dark-skin version stimulus booklet.
Time: (5-10) minutes.
Comments: Both forms of this test allow participants to "respond using pictures rather than words."
Author: Jack Joseph.
Publisher: Western Psychological Services.
   a) FORM Y-YOUNG CHILD INTERVIEW.
   Population: Ages 3-0 to 7-11 years.
   b) FORM O-OLDER CHILD INTERVIEW.
   Population: Ages 7-0 to 13-11 years.

[1329]
Joseph Pre-School and Primary Self-Concept Screening Test.

Purpose: Constructed as an early screen for learning problems.
Population: Ages 3-5 to 9-11.
Publication Date: 1979.
Scores: Global Self Concept.
Administration: Individual.
Price Data, 2005: $150 per complete kit including manual (66 pages), 56 stimulus cards, 100 identity

reference drawings, and 100 record forms; $30 per 50 record forms; $80 per set of stimulus cards; $35 per set of identity drawings; $25 per manual.
Time: (5–7) minutes.
Comments: May be used with non-verbal children.
Author: Jack Joseph.
Publisher: Stoelting Co.
Cross References: See T5:1363 (2 references); for reviews by Kathryn Clark Gerken and Cathy Fultz Telzrow, see 9:558.

[1330]
Jung Personality Questionnaire.
Purpose: "To assist pupils in choosing a career."
Population: Standards 7 and 8 and 10 in South African school system.
Publication Date: 1983.
Acronym: JPQ.
Scores, 4: Extraversion vs. Introversion, Thinking vs. Feeling, Sensation vs. Intuition, Judgement vs. Perception.
Administration: Group.
Price Data: Available from publisher.
Foreign Language Edition: Afrikaans edition available.
Time: (25–35) minutes.
Comments: "Criterion-referenced."
Author: L. B. H. duToit.
Publisher: Human Sciences Research Council [South Africa].

[1331]
Jungian Type Survey: The Gray-Wheelwrights Test (16th Revision).
Purpose: "Designed to delineate types of personality structure."
Population: Adults.
Publication Date: 1964.
Scores, 6: Introversion, Extraversion, Intuition, Sensation, Thinking, Feeling.
Administration: Group.
Price Data: Price information available from publisher for reusable question sheet, answer sheet, and manual (8 pages).
Time: (20) minutes.
Authors: Horace Gray (test only), Joseph B. Wheelwright (test and manual), Jane H. Wheelwright (test and manual), and John A. Bueler (manual only).
Publisher: C. G. Jung Institute of San Francisco.

[1332]
Junior Eysenck Personality Inventory.
Purpose: "Designed to measure … neuroticism or emotionality, and extraversion-introversion in children."
Population: Ages 7–16.
Publication Dates: 1963–1970.

Acronym: JEPI.
Scores, 3: Extraversion, Neuroticism, Lie.
Administration: Group.
Price Data: Available from publisher.
Foreign Language Edition: Spanish edition available.
Time: [15–20] minutes.
Author: Sybil B. G. Eysenck.
Publisher: EdITS/Educational and Industrial Testing Service.
Cross References: See T5:1367 (7 references), T4:1331 (13 references), 9:561 (10 references), T3:1229 (24 references), 8:596 (36 references), and T2:1252 (14 references); for reviews by Maurice Chazan and Robert D. Wirt and excerpted reviews by Gertrude H. Keir and B. Semeonoff, see 7:96 (19 references); see also P:135 (7 references).

[1333]
Junior High School Mathematics Test: Acorn Achievement Tests.
Purpose: Designed to test the pupil's knowledge of junior high level mathematics concepts, skills, and insights.
Population: Grades 7–9.
Publication Dates: 1942–1952.
Scores, 4: Concepts, Problem Analysis, Problems, Total.
Administration: Group.
Price Data: Available from publisher.
Time: 52(57) minutes.
Author: Harry Eisner.
Publisher: Psychometric Affiliates.
Cross References: For a review by Myron F. Rosskopf, see 5:429; for a review by William Betz, see 3:310.

[1334]
Junior Rating Scale.
Purpose: Designed to provide teachers with a framework to record and display visually ratings of pupils' strengths and needs.
Population: Ages 8–11.
Publication Date: 1990.
Acronym: JRS.
Scores: 5 subscale scores: Language/Education, Motor Skills, Behaviour, Social Integration, General Development.
Administration: Individual.
Price Data: Available from publisher.
Time: Untimed.
Comments: Developed from Infant Rating Scale (9:505).
Authors: J. A. Abraham and G. A. Lindsay.
Publisher: NFER-Nelson Publishing Co., Ltd. [England].

[1335]
Junior South African Individual Scales.

Purpose: Measures general intellectual level.
Population: South African children ages 3.0–7.11.
Publication Dates: 1981–1988.
Acronym: JSAIS.
Scores, 27: Verbal (Vocabulary, Reading Knowledge, Story Memory, Picture Riddles, Word Association, Social Reasoning, Picture Analogies, Word Fluency), Numerical (Number and Quantity A, Number and Quantity B, Number and Quantity A & B, Memory for Digits A, Memory for Digits B, Memory for Digits A & B), Visual-Spatial (Form Board, Block Designs, Absurdities A, Absurdities B, Form Discrimination A & B, Grouping, Gestalt Completion, Picture Series, Picture Puzzles, Visual Memory A, Visual Memory B, Visual Memory A & B, Copying).
Administration: Individual.
Price Data: Available from publisher.
Foreign Language Edition: Afrikaans edition available.
Time: (60–90) minutes.
Authors: Elizabeth M. Madge (manuals, Parts 1-3), A. R. vandenBerg (manual, Part 3), Maryna Robinson (manual, Part 3), and J. Landman (appendix to manuals).
Publisher: Human Sciences Research Council [South Africa].
Cross References: See T5:1370 (1 reference) and T4:1335 (1 reference).

[1336]
Just-in-Time Training Assessment Instrument.

Purpose: "Intended to measure ... perceptions of how frequently and how effectively [an] organization has created a work environment that supports JITT."
Population: Adults.
Publication Date: 1996.
Acronym: JITT.
Scores, 2: Frequency, Effectiveness.
Administration: Group.
Price Data: Available from publisher.
Time: (15–20) minutes.
Author: William J. Rothwell.
Publisher: HRD Press, Inc.

[1337]
Juvenile Automated Substance Abuse Evaluation.

Purpose: Intended to "measure adolescent alcohol and drug use/abuse ... attitudes and life-stress issues."
Population: Adolescents.
Publication Dates: 1989–1997.
Acronym: JASAE.

Scores, 6: Test Taking Attitude, Life Circumstance Evaluation, Drinking Evaluation Category, Alcohol Addiction Evaluation, Drug Use Evaluation, Summary.
Administration: Individual or group.
Price Data: Available from publisher.
Time: (20) minutes.
Comments: Self-administered; computer scored, IBM compatible with either DOS or Windows required; provides DSM–IV classification for alcohol and drug use and ASAM patient placement criteria for treatment recommendations; available in English and Spanish.
Author: ADE Incorporated.
Publisher: ADE Incorporated.
Cross References: For reviews by Mark Pope and Jody L. Swartz-Kulstad, see 14:190.

[1338]
Juvenile Justice Policy Inventory.

Purpose: "Designed to assess both individual attitudes toward juvenile justice policies and characteristic methods of dealing with juvenile offenders."
Population: Juvenile justice professionals.
Publication Date: 1973.
Scores, 4: Reintegration, Rehabilitation, Reform, Restraint.
Administration: Group.
Price Data: Available from publisher.
Time: Administration time not reported.
Author: Vincent O'Leary.
Publisher: National Council on Crime and Delinquency.

[1339]
Kaplan Baycrest Neurocognitive Assessment.

Purpose: "Test of neurocognitive functioning."
Population: Ages 20–89.
Publication Date: 2000.
Acronym: KBNA.
Scores: 8 index scores: Attention/Concentration, Immediate Memory Recall, Delayed Memory Recall, Delayed Memory Recognition, Spatial Processing, Verbal Fluency, Reasoning/Conceptual Shifting, Total Index.
Administration: Individual.
Price Data, 2002: $239 per complete kit including manual (188 pages), stimulus book (94 pages), 8 response chips, cassette, 25 response booklets, 25 record forms, and response grid (packaged in a box); $70 per manual; $70 per stimulus book; $43 per 25 response booklets; $43 per 25 record forms; $11 per response grid.
Time: (60–90) minutes.
Comments: Test contains 25 subtests (Orientation, Sequences, Numbers, Word Lists 1, Complex Figure 1, Motor Programming, Auditory Signal Detection, Symbol Cancellation, Clocks, Word Lists 2, Complex Figure 2, Picture Naming, Sentence Reading—Arithmetic,

Reading Single Words, Spatial Location, Verbal Fluency, Praxis, Picture Recognition, Expression of Emotion, Practical Problem Solving, Conceptual Shifting, Picture Description—Oral, Auditory Comprehension, Repetition, Picture Description—Written); detailed analysis of neurocognitive functioning can be obtained through examination of 94 component Process Scores; Process Scores are categorized as below average, equivocal, or average.

Authors: Larry Leach, Edith Kaplan, Dmytro Rewilak, Brian Richards, and Guy-B. Proulx.

Publisher: PsychCorp, A brand of Harcourt Assessment, Inc.

Cross References: For reviews by Raymond S. Dean and John J. Brinkman, Jr., and by Harrison D. Kane and Shawn K. Acheson, see 16:121.

[1340]
Katz Adjustment Scales—Relative Report Form.

Purpose: Designed to assess aspects of community adjustment of psychiatric patients "to identify whether follow-up rehabilitation services are required."

Population: Adults with psychiatric, medical, or neurological disorders.

Publication Dates: 1961–1999.

Acronym: KAS-R.

Administration: Individual.

Parts, 3: General Behavior, Socially Expected Activities, Use of Leisure Time.

Price Data, 2006: $114.50 per complete kit including manual (1998, 94 pages), response card, and 25 AutoScore™ answer forms; $60.50 per manual; $40 per 25 AutoScore™ answer forms; $21.50 per 10 Spanish language test forms; $17 per 5 response cards; $18 per mail-in answer booklet; $265 per 25-use PC disk; $16.50 per 50 PC answer booklets; volume discounts available.

Time: (35–45) minutes; (10–15) minutes for Short Form.

Comments: Informant (relative or close friend) completes behavior rating scale; computer scoring available; formerly a subscale of the Katz Adjustment Scale; Spanish language form available for research purposes; Short Form includes General Psychopathology, Stability, Social Aggression Index, Emotionality Index, Disorientation, Withdrawal Index, and Psychopathology Index.

Authors: Martin M. Katz and W. Louise Warren.

Publisher: Western Psychological Services.

a) GENERAL BEHAVIOR.

Scores, 16: Inconsistent Responding, General Psychopathology, Stability, Social Aggression Index (Belligerence, Negativism, Verbal Expressiveness), Emotionality Index (Anxiety Index [Anxiousness, Nervousness], Depression Index

[Depression, Helplessness]), Disorientation/Withdrawal Index (Confusion, Expressive Deficit, Withdrawal/Retardation), Severe Psychopathology Index (Bizarreness, Hyperactivity, Suspiciousness).

b) SOCIALLY EXPECTED ACTIVITIES.

Scores, 3: Level of Performance of Socially Expected Activities, Level of Expectations for Performance of Socially Expected Activities, Expectation/Performance Discrepancy.

c) USE OF LEISURE TIME.

Scores, 2: Level of Performance of Leisure Activities, Level of Satisfaction with Leisure Activities.

Cross References: For a review by Roger A. Boothroyd, see 16:122; for information on an earlier edition of the Katz Adjustment Scales, see T4:1340 (30 references), T3:1240 (18 references), 8:599 (3 references), T2: 1255 (12 references), and P:138 (10 references).

[1341]
Kaufman Adolescent and Adult Intelligence Test.

Purpose: "An individually administered measure of general intelligence developed from fluid and crystallized theory."

Population: Ages 11 to 85+.

Publication Date: 1993.

Acronym: KAIT.

Scores, 9 to 14: Crystallized Scale (Definitions, Auditory Comprehension, Double Meanings, Famous Faces [alternate subtest], Total), Fluid Scale (Rebus Learning, Logical Steps, Mystery Codes, Memory for Block Designs [alternate subtest], Total), Measures of Delayed Recall [optional] (Rebus Delayed Recall, Auditory Delayed Recall), Mental Status [supplementary subtest], Total.

Administration: Individual.

Price Data, 2006: $709.99 per complete kit including 2 test easels, manual (161 pages), 25 individual test records, 25 Mystery Codes item booklets, Auditory Comprehension audiocassette, set of 6 Memory for Design Blocks with holder, and carrying Case; $64.99 per record set including 25 each, record booklets and mystery code booklets; $70.99 per manual; $199.99 per KAIT ASSIST (IBM); $103.99 per KAIT training video.

Time: 60 minutes for Core Battery; 90 minutes for Expanded Battery.

Authors: Alan S. Kaufman and Nadeen L. Kaufman.

Publisher: Pearson Assessments (originally published by AGS Publishing, acquired by Pearson in 2005).

Cross References: See T5:1378 (14 references); for reviews by Dawn P. Flanagan and Timothy Z. Keith, see 12:204 (6 references); see also T4:1342 (1 reference).

[1342]
Kaufman Assessment Battery for Children, Second Edition.

Purpose: Designed to measure the "processing and cognitive abilities of children and adolescents."
Population: Ages 3-18.
Publication Dates: 1983-2004.
Acronym: KABC-II.
Scores, 7–23: Sequential (Number Recall, Word Order, Hand Movements, Total), Simultaneous (Block Counting, Conceptual Thinking, Face Recognition, Pattern Reasoning [Ages 5 and 6], Rover, Story Completion [Ages 5 and 6], Triangles, Gestalt Closure, Total), Planning [Ages 7–18 only] (Pattern Reasoning, Story Completion, Total), Learning (Atlantis, Rebus, Atlantis Delayed, Rebus Delayed, Total), Knowledge (Expressive Vocabulary, Riddles, Verbal Knowledge, Total), Nonverbal Index, Mental Processing Index, Fluid-Crystallized Index.
Administration: Individual.
Price Data, 2006: $749.99 per complete kit, including 4 easels, manual (2004, 236 pages), all necessary stimulus and manipulative materials, 25 record forms, and soft-sided briefcase; $49.99 per manual; $51.99 per 25 record forms; $199.99 per computer ASSIST scoring software.
Time: (25-70) minutes.
Comments: Nonverbal scale available for hearing impaired, speech-and-language disordered, and non-English-speaking children (an adaptation that examiners can make when verbal concerns are present).
Authors: Alan S. Kaufman and Nadeen L. Kaufman.
Publisher: Pearson Assessments (originally published by AGS Publishing, acquired by Pearson in 2005).
Cross References: For reviews by Jeffery P. Braden and Sandye M. Ouzts and by Robert M. Thorndike, see 16:123; see also T5:1379 (103 references) and T4:1343 (114 references); for reviews by Anne Anastasi, William E. Coffman, and Ellis Batten Page of an earlier edition, see 9:562 (3 references).

[1343]
Kaufman Brief Intelligence Test, Second Edition.

Purpose: Intended as a brief measure of verbal and nonverbal intelligence.
Population: Ages 4-90.
Publication Dates: 1990–2004.
Acronym: KBIT-2.
Scores, 3: Verbal, Nonverbal, IQ Composite.
Subtests, 3: Verbal Knowledge, Riddles, Matrices.
Administration: Individual.
Price Data, 2006: $204.99 per complete kit including easel, manual (2004, 147 pages), 25 individual test record forms, and carry bag; $41.99 per 25 individual

test records; $59.99 per scoring and administration manual.
Time: (15–30) minutes.
Comments: Examiners are encouraged to teach individuals, using teaching items, how to solve the kinds of items included in subtests.
Authors: Alan S. Kaufman and Nadeen L. Kaufman.
Publisher: Pearson Assessments (originally published by AGS Publishing, acquired by Pearson in 2005).
Cross References: See T5:1380 (21 references); for reviews by M. David Miller and John W. Young of an earlier version, see 12:205 (9 references); see also T4:1344 (4 references).

[1344]
Kaufman Developmental Scale.

Purpose: Designed to assess the "level of development ... and an overall level of functioning."
Population: Birth to age 9 and mentally retarded of all ages.
Publication Dates: 1972–1975.
Acronym: KDS.
Scores, 7: Gross Motor, Fine Motor, Receptive, Expressive, Personal Behavior, Inter-Personal Behavior, Total.
Administration: Individual.
Price Data, 2005: $425 per complete kit including test materials, manual (1974, 83 pages), 25 record forms, and carrying case; $55 per 25 evaluation booklets; $30 per 25 record forms; $55 per manual.
Time: (30) minutes.
Author: H. Kaufman.
Publisher: Stoelting Co.
Cross References: For a review by Dorothy H. Eichorn, see 8:218.

[1345]
Kaufman Functional Academic Skills Test.

Purpose: A quick measure of reading and math functional skills designed as a brief, individually administered test to determine performance in reading and mathematics as applied to daily life.
Population: Ages 15–85+.
Publication Date: 1994.
Acronym: K-FAST.
Scores, 3: Arithmetic Subtest, Reading Subtest, Functional Academic Skills Composite.
Administration: Individual.
Price Data, 2006: $144.99 per complete kit including manual (110 pages), test easel, and 25 record forms; $119.99 per test easel; $34.99 per 25 record forms.
Time: (15–25) minutes.
Comments: Examinees may respond in any language
Authors: Alan S. Kaufman and Nadeen L. Kaufman.
Publisher: Pearson Assessments (originally published by AGS Publishing, acquired by Pearson in 2005).

Cross References: See T5:1382 (1 reference); for reviews by Steven R. Shaw and Robert T. Williams, see 13:166 (2 references).

[1346]
Kaufman Infant and Preschool Scale.
Purpose: Designed to measure "early, high-level cognitive thinking, and indicates possible need for intervention."
Population: Ages 1 month–48 months and mentally retarded individuals whose preacademic functioning age does not exceed 48 months.
Publication Date: 1979.
Acronym: KIPS.
Scores: Tasks in 3 areas: General Reasoning, Storage, Verbal Communication.
Administration: Individual.
Price Data, 2005: $300 per complete kit including all manipulatives, stimulus cards, and 10 evaluation booklets; $33 per 10 evaluation booklets; $20 per set of stimulus cards; $28 per manual (40 pages).
Time: (20-30) minutes.
Author: H. Kaufman.
Publisher: Stoelting Co.
Cross References: For reviews by Roy A. Kress and Phyllis Anne Teeter, see 9:563.

[1347]
Kaufman Short Neuropsychological Assessment Procedure.
Purpose: A brief, individually administered measure of the cognitive functioning of adolescents and adults.
Population: Ages 11 through 85+.
Publication Date: 1994.
Acronym: K-SNAP.
Scores, 5: Gestalt Closure, Number Recall, Four-Letter Words, Recall/Closure Composite, K-SNAP Composite.
Administration: Individual.
Price Data, 2006: $219.99 per complete kit including manual (128 pages), easel, and 25 record forms; $34.99 per 25 record forms; $149.99 per easel.
Time: 30 minutes.
Authors: Alan S. Kaufman and Nadeen L. Kaufman.
Publisher: Pearson Assessments (originally published by AGS Publishing, acquired by Pearson in 2005).
Cross References: See T5:1384 (2 references); for reviews by Karen Geller and Martine Hebert, see 13:167 (2 references).

[1348]
Kaufman Survey of Early Academic and Language Skills.
Purpose: Designed as an easy-to-administer measure of children's language skills (expressive and receptive vocabulary), numerical skills, and articulation.

Population: 3-0 to 6-11
Publication Date: 1993.
Acronym: K-SEALS.
Scores, 3: Vocabulary; Numbers, Letters, and Words; Articulation Survey.
Administration: Individual.
Price Data, 2006: $244.99 per complete kit including manual (109 pages), easel, 25 test records, and carrying bag; $34.99 per 25 record booklets; $45.99 per manual.
Time: (15–25) minutes.
Comments: The Early Academic Scales can be interpreted only for ages 5-0 to 6-11.
Authors: Alan S. Kaufman and Nadeen L. Kaufman.
Publisher: Pearson Assessments (originally published by AGS Publishing, acquired by Pearson in 2005).
Cross References: For reviews by Phillip L. Ackerman and by Laurie Ford and Kerri Turk, see 12:206.

[1349]
Kaufman Test of Educational Achievement—Second Edition, Comprehensive Form.
Purpose: Designed to measure "achievement in reading, mathematics, written language, and oral language."
Population: Ages 4.6–25.
Publication Dates: 1985–2004.
Acronym: KTEA-II.
Scores, 23: Reading (Letter and Word Recognition, Reading Comprehension, Composite), Mathematics (Math Concepts & Applications, Math Computation, Composite), Written Language (Written Expression, Spelling, Composite), Oral Language (Listening Comprehension, Oral Expression, Composite), Comprehensive Achievement Composite, Phonological Awareness, Nonsense Word Decoding, Sound-Symbol Composite, Decoding Composite, Word Recognition Fluency, Decoding Fluency, Reading Fluency Composite, Associational Fluency, Naming Facility [RAN], Oral Fluency Composite.
Administration: Individual.
Forms, 2: Parallel forms A and B.
Price Data, 2006: $564.99 per complete form A and B kit including Comprehensive Form A and Form B kits with 2 manuals (2004, 442 pages) and 2 norms books; $309.99 per comprehensive kit (Form A or B) including 2 easels, manual, norms book, 25 record forms, 25 student response booklets, 25 error analysis booklets, 2 each of 3 Written Expression booklets, all necessary stimulus materials, administration CD, puppet, and tote bag; $34.99 per manual; $34.99 per norms book; $59.99 per 25 record forms and 25 student response booklets; $25.99 per 25 error analysis booklets; $9.99 per 10 Written Expression booklets; $199.99 per Computer ASSIST computer scoring program.
Time: (30–85) minutes.
Comments: Computer and hand scoring available.
Authors: Alan S. Kaufman and Nadeen L. Kaufman.

Publisher: Pearson Assessments (originally published by AGS Publishing, acquired by Pearson in 2005).
Cross References: For reviews by Mike Bonner and C. Dale Carpenter, see 16:124; for reviews by John Poggio and William D. Schafer of an earlier edition, see 14:191; see also T5:1386 (26 references) and T4:1348 (5 references); for reviews by Elizabeth J. Doll and Jerome M. Sattler of an earlier edition, see 10:161.

[1350]
Keegan Type Indicator.

Purpose: Measures perception, judgment, and attitude (extraversion/introversion) based on C. G. Jung's theory of psychological types.
Population: Adults.
Publication Dates: 1980–2006.
Acronym: KTI.
Scores, 3: Extraversion vs. Introversion, Sensation vs. Intuition, Thinking vs. Feeling.
Administration: Group.
Price Data: Price data, including user's manual (1980, 12 pages) and instructor's manual (1980, 21 pages), available from publisher.
Time: [20] minutes.
Author: Warren J. Keegan.
Publisher: Keegan (Warren) Associates Press.
Cross References: For a review by Arlene C. Rosenthal, see 10:162.

[1351]
Keirsey Temperament Sorter II.

Purpose: Designed to be used "for assessing temperament, character, and personality."
Population: College and adult.
Publication Dates: 1978–2003.
Acronym: KTS-II.
Scores, 16: Artisan-Promoter (ESTP), Artisan-Crafter (ISTP), Artisan-Performer (ESFP), Artisan-Composer (ISFP), Guardian-Supervisor (ESTJ), Guardian-Inspector (ISTJ), Guardian-Provider (ESFJ), Guardian-Protector (ISFJ), Rational-Fieldmarshal (ENTJ), Rational-Architect (ENFP), Rational-Mastermind(INTJ), Rational-Inventor (INTP), Idealist-Champion (ENFP), Idealist-Header (INFP), Idealist-Counselor (INFJ), Idealist-Teacher (ENFJ).
Administration: Group.
Price Data, 2004: KTS-II may be taken free online; $14.95 per Classic Temperament Report; $19.95 per Career Temperament Report; $27.95 per Career Personality Package; price information available from publisher for Statistical Study (2003, 89 pages) and for Academic Platform or Corporate Platform delivery; $15.95 per "Please Understand Me II" (1998, 352 pages).
Foreign Language Editions: Available in American English, Spanish, French, German, Italian, Polish, Portuguese, and Japanese.

Time: (10–15) minutes.
Authors: David Keirsey (instrument and "Please Understand Me II") and Alpine Media Corporation (Statistical Study).
Publisher: AdvisorTeam, Inc.
Cross References: For a review by Peter Zachar, see 16:125.

[1352]
Kendrick Assessment Scales of Cognitive Ageing.

Purpose: Designed "to provide an accurate and flexible means of screening for and predicting possible dementia."
Population: Ages 40–92.
Publication Dates: 1979–1999.
Acronym: KOLT.
Administration: Individual.
Price Data, 1999: £125 per complete set including 10 record forms, manual (1999), and material for the four subtests; £15 per 10 record forms.
Time: Untimed.
Comments: Revision of Kendrick Cognitive Tests for the Elderly (T4:1352).
Authors: Don Kendrick and Geoff Watts.
Publisher: NFER-Nelson Publishing Co., Ltd. [England].
  a) OBJECT LEARNING TEST.
  Acronym: KOLT.
  Scores: Total score only.
  Forms, 2: A, B (4 cards).
  Comments: Test of recall of everyday objects.
  b) DIGIT COPYING TEST.
  Acronym: KDCT.
  Scores: Total score only.
  Comments: Test of speed performance.
  c) WATTS VISUO-SPATIAL TEST.
  Acronym: WVST.
  Scores: Total score only.
  Comments: Test of visuo-spatial ability.
  d) KENDRICK ATTENTION AND REASONING TEST.
  Acronym: KART.
  Scores: Total score only.
  Comments: Test of reasoning and attention.
Cross References: See T5:1390 (7 references), T4:1352 (1 reference), and 11:189 (2 references); for reviews by Joseph D. Matarazzo and K. Warner Schaie of an earlier edition, see 9:566 (2 references).

[1353]
Kent Inventory of Developmental Skills [1996 Standardization].

Purpose: Designed to assess the developmental status and progress of healthy infants, infants at risk, and young children with developmental disabilities.

Population: Infants up to 15 months of age and young children whose developmental age is less than 15 months.
Publication Dates: 1978–1999.
Acronym: KIDS.
Scores, 12: Developmental Ages and Standard Scores for: Cognitive, Motor, Language, Self-Help, Social Domains, Full Scale.
Administration: Individual.
Price Data: Price information available from publisher for complete kit including 25 profile sheets, 25 answer sheets, reusable administration and scoring booklet, 5 scoring templates, set of developmental timetables, manual, and 2-use disk for on-site computer scoring and interpretation.
Time: (45) minutes.
Comments: Relies on caregiver report; also yields individualized developmental timetables; includes handscoring materials and an expanded computer report, including a list of developmentally appropriate activities selected to match each child's specific competencies; earlier editions entitled The Kent Infant Development Scale.
Authors: Jeanette Reuter with Lewis Katoff and Jeffrey Wozniak (3rd edition of the test manual and user's guide) and James Whiteman (computer-scoring disk).
Publisher: Western Psychological Services.
Cross References: For reviews by Diane J. Sawyer and Gary J. Stainback, see 14:192; see also T5:1391 (2 references); for reviews by Candice Feiring and Edward S. Shapiro of an earlier edition, see 10:163 (2 references); for a review by Candice Feiring of an earlier version, see 9:567; see also T3:1246 (1 reference).

[1354]
Kent Visual Perceptual Test.

Purpose: Designed to "identify and characterize visual processing deficits in school or neuropsychological settings."
Population: Ages 5–11.
Publication Dates: 1995–2000.
Acronym: KVPT.
Administration: Individual.
Price Data, 2005: $207 per complete kit including 10 copy tests, memory test stimuli, discrimination test stimuli, 10 scoring and error analysis booklets, and professional manual (2000, 128 pages).
Time: (25–30) minutes.
Author: Lawrence E. Melamed.
Publisher: Psychological Assessment Resources, Inc.
a) KENT VISUAL PERCEPTION TEST—DISCRIMINATION.
Purpose: Designed to assess visual discrimination skills.
Acronym: KVPT-D.
Scores, 2: Error Analysis, Total.
b) KENT VISUAL PERCEPTION TEST—COPY.
Purpose: Designed to assess visual reproduction skills.

Acronym: KVPT-C.
Scores, 4: KVPT-C1, KVPT-C2, KVPT-C3, Total.
c) VISUAL PERCEPTION TESTS—IMMEDIATE MEMORY.
Purpose: Designed to assess immediate memory.
Acronym: KVPT-M.
Scores, 2: Error Analysis, Total.
Cross References: For reviews by Ralph G. Leverett and Katharine A. Snyder, see 16:126; for a review by Annie W. Ward of an earlier edition, see 14:193.

[1355]
KeyMath Revised: A Diagnostic Inventory of Essential Mathematics [1998 Normative Update].

Purpose: Designed to assess understanding and applications of mathematics concepts and skills.
Population: Grades K–9, ages 5-0 to 22-11.
Publication Dates: 1971–1998.
Acronym: KeyMath-R.
Scores, 17: Basic Concepts (Numeration, Rational Numbers, Geometry, Total), Operations (Addition, Subtraction, Multiplication, Division, Mental Computation, Total), Applications (Measurement, Time and Money, Estimation, Interpreting Data, Problem Solving, Total), Total.
Administration: Individual.
Forms, 2: A, B.
Price Data, 2006: $532.99 per complete kit including Form A and Form B test easels, 25 each Form A and Form B test records, sample report to parents, normative update manual, and carry bag (1998, 255 pages); $294.99 per single form (A or B) kit including test easels, 25 test records, sample reports to parents, manual, and carry bag; $50.99 per 25 test records (select A or B); $26.99 per 25 reports to parents; $115.99 per manual; $199.99 per complete ASSIST™ reporting software (Macintosh or Windows).
Time: (35–50) minutes.
Comments: Revision of KeyMath Diagnostic Arithmetic Test; computerized reporting software available.
Author: Austin J. Connolly.
Publisher: Pearson Assessments (originally published by AGS Publishing, acquired by Pearson in 2005).
Cross References: For reviews by G. Gage Kingsbury and James A. Wollack, see 14:194; see also T5:1392 (15 references) and T4:1355 (5 references); for reviews by Michael D. Beck and Carmen J. Finley of an earlier edition, see 11:191 (26 references); see also T3:1250 (12 references); for an excerpted review by Alex Bannatyne of an earlier edition, see 8:305 (10 references).

[1356]

Keynotes.

Purpose: Designed to "provide the classroom teacher with a profile of students' strengths and weaknesses in domains considered to be important for most kinds of music learning" and to provide instrumental music teachers and their students with information that may be used to help student select an instrument.
Population: Ages 9–14.
Publication Date: 2000.
Scores, 3: Pitch Discrimination, Patterns Recognition, Music Reading.
Administration: Individual.
Price Data, 2006: A$149.95 per complete kit; A$99.95 per 5 copies CD-ROM.
Time: Administration time not reported.
Comments: Software does not operate on Macintosh computers; requires Windows 95 or higher.
Authors: Jennifer Bryce and Margaret Wu.
Publisher: Australian Council for Educational Research Ltd. [Australia]
Cross References: For reviews by Bethany A. Brunsman and Christopher Johnson, see 15:133.

[1357]

KEYS® to Creativity.

Purpose: Designed to measure how "employees perceive stimulants and barriers to creativity."
Population: Employees.
Publication Date: 1995.
Scores, 10: 8 environment scales (6 environmental stimulants to creativity: Organizational Encouragement of Creativity, Supervisory Encouragement of Creativity, Work Group Supports, Freedom, Sufficient Resources, Challenging Work; 2 obstacles to creativity: Organizational Impediments, Workload Pressure); 2 outcome scales (Creativity, Productivity).
Administration: Group.
Price Data, 2006: $20 per survey booklet (5–50 booklets); quantity discounts available; $75 per group comparisons.
Time: (15–20) minutes.
Comments: Costs of survey booklets includes scoring, standard feedback results, one KEYS User's Guide (205 pages), and one KEYS: Interpreting the Results.
Authors: Teresa M. Amabile and Center for Creative Leadership.
Publisher: Center for Creative Leadership.
Cross References: For a review by Carolyn M. Callahan, see 14:195; see also T5:1393 (1 reference).

[1358]

Khan-Lewis Phonological Analysis—Second Edition.

Purpose: Measures phonological process usage in speech and allows tracking of intervention planning and progress.
Population: Ages 2-0 to 21-11.
Publication Dates: 1986-2002.
Acronym: KLPA-2.
Scores, 11: 5 Reduction Processes (Deletion of Final Consonants, Syllable Reduction, Stopping of Fricatives and Affricates, Cluster Simplification, Liquid Simplification), 3 Place and Manner Processes (Velar Fronting, Palatal Fronting, Deaffrication), 2 Voicing Processes (Initial Voicing, Final Devoicing), Total Score.
Administration: Individual.
Price Data, 2005: $134.99 per kit including manual (2002, 206 pages), 25 analysis forms, Sound Change booklet, and 25 Phonological Summary and Progress Report worksheets; $74.99 per manual; $29.99 per analysis forms.
Time: [10–30] minutes.
Comments: Revision of the Khan-Lewis Phonological Analysis (KLPA), old edition still available; supplements the Goldman-Fristoe Test of Articulation—Second Edition (GFTA-2; 15:109); scores based on responses to the Sounds-in-Words subtest of the GFTA-2; to complete the KLPA-2, examiner needs both complete KLPA-2 kit and complete GFTA-2 kit; is conormed with the Goldman-Fristoe Test of Articulation, Second Edition.
Authors: Linda M. L. Khan and Nancy P. Lewis.
Publisher: Pearson Assessments (originally published by AGS Publishing, acquired by Pearson in 2005).
Cross References: For reviews by Carlos Inchaurralde and Steven Long, see 16:127; see also T5:1394 (13 references) and T4:1356 (1 reference); for a review by Donald E. Mowrer of an earlier edition, see 10:164.

[1359]

Khatena-Morse Multitalent Perception Inventory.

Purpose: Identifies giftedness in music, art, and leadership.
Population: Age 6–adult.
Publication Dates: 1985–1994.
Acronym: KMMPI.
Scores, 6: Artistic, Musical, Creative Imagination, Initiative, Leadership, Versatility.
Administration: Group.
Forms, 2: A, B.
Price Data, 2005: $56.60 per starter set including 35 questionnaires and 35 profile charts (specify Form A or B) and manual (1994, 101 pages); $27.75 per 35 questionnaires and 35 profile charts (specify Form A or B); $31.10 per manual; $30 per sample set.
Time: (30–45) minutes.
Authors: Joe Khatena and David T. Morse.
Publisher: Scholastic Testing Service, Inc.
Cross References: For reviews by Carolyn M. Callahan and William Steve Lang, see 13:169.

[1360]

Khatena-Torrance Creative Perception Inventory.

Purpose: Developed as measures of creative personality.
Population: Age 10–adult.
Publication Dates: 1976–1998.
Acronym: KTCPI.
Administration: Group.
Price Data, 2001: $57.65 per starter set including instruction manual (1998, 96 pages), 35 SAM checklists, 35 WKOPAY? checklists, and 35 scoring worksheets; $32.75 per instruction manual; $38 per package of 35 SAM checklists, 35 WKOPAY? checklists, and 35 scoring worksheets; $18.90 per specimen set including instruction manual (abridged), 1 SAM checklist, and 1 WKOPAY? checklist.
Time: (10–20) minutes per checklist.
Comments: Includes 2 self-report checklists designed to identify candidates for creativity programs.
Publisher: Scholastic Testing Service, Inc.

  a) WHAT KIND OF PERSON ARE YOU?
  Purpose: Designed to "yield an index of the individual's disposition or motivation to function in creative ways."
  Acronym: WKOPAY?
  Scores: 5 factors: Acceptance of Authority, Self-Confidence, Inquisitiveness, Awareness of Others, Disciplined Imagination.
  Author: E. Paul Torrance.

  b) SOMETHING ABOUT MYSELF.
  Purpose: Designed as an autobiographical "screening device for the identification of creative people."
  Acronym: SAM.
  Scores: 6 factors: Environmental Sensitivity, Initiative, Self-Strength, Intellectuality, Individuality, Artistry.
  Author: Joe Khatena.

Cross References: For reviews by Carolyn M. Callahan and Gregory Schraw, see 16:128; see also T5:1396 (5 references); for reviews by David L. Bolton and William Steve Lang of a previous edition, see 13:168 (2 references); for a review by Philip E. Vernon of an earlier edition, see 9:569 (3 references).

[1361]

Kilmann-Saxton Culture-Gap Survey [Revised].

Purpose: Assesses "actual versus desired cultural norms."
Population: Work team members, employees.
Publication Dates: 1983–1991.
Acronym: CGS.
Scores, 4: Task Support, Social Relationships, Task Innovation, Personal Freedom.
Administration: Group.
Price Data, 2001: $8.50 per survey.

Time: (30) minutes.
Authors: Ralph H. Kilmann and Mary J. Saxton.
Publisher: CPP, Inc.
Cross References: For reviews by Russell N. Carney and Norman D. Sundberg, see 13:170; for reviews by Andres Barona and Gargi Roysircar Sodowsky of an earlier edition, see 11:192.

[1362]

Kilmanns Organizational Belief Survey.

Purpose: Assesses beliefs about one's level of control in their organizational surroundings.
Population: Employees.
Publication Date: 1991.
Scores, 8: Control Score, My Work Group, My Department, My Organization, Individual Profile, Work Group Profile, Department Profile, Organizational Profile.
Administration: Group.
Price Data, 2001: $8.50 each questionnaire/booklet.
Time: Administration time not reported.
Comments: A component of the Workshop for Implementing the Five Tracks, part of a completely integrated set of materials for creating and maintaining long-term organizational success; self-scored.
Authors: Ralph H. Kilmann and Ines Kilmann.
Publisher: CPP, Inc.

[1363]

Kindergarten Diagnostic Instrument—Second Edition.

Purpose: "Designed to assess developmental readiness skills in children."
Population: Children ages 4–6 years or older children with known or suspected developmental delays.
Publication Date: 2000.
Acronym: KDI-2.
Scores, 22: 13 subtest scores (Body Awareness, Concept Mastery, Form/Letter Identification, General Information, Gross Motor, Memory for Sentences, Number Skills, Phonemic Awareness, Verbal Associations, Visual Discrimination, Visual Memory, Visual-Motor Integration, Vocabulary), 6 subskills (Form Identification, Letter Identification, Verbal Associations—Similarities, Verbal Associations—Opposites, Visual Discrimination—Similarities, Visual Discrimination—Differences), Nonverbal Factor Score, Verbal Factor Score, Total Test Score.
Administration: Individual.
Price Data, 2004: $175 per complete test kit including administration manual (146 pages), 3 stimulus booklets, 13 1-inch wooden blocks, and 25 student response booklets in a carrying case; $495 per assessment bundle including complete test kit, 50 student response booklets, 50 My Kindergarten Fun Books-II

(40 pages), and scoring program for Windows; $32 per 25 student response booklets; $50 per 25 My Kindergarten Fun Books-II; $275 per KDI-2 Scoring Program for Windows (one-time license fee, additional cost applies for sites screening more than 300 children annually); $30 per training video; quantity discounts available on all items.

Time: (35–45) minutes.

Comments: KDI-2 Scoring Program for Windows stores students' pre-kindergarten and kindergarten data, generates local schoolwide norms, assesses performance compared to local norms, generates individual reports, test-retest reports; contact publisher for KDI-2 Scoring Program system requirements.

Authors: Daniel C. Miller (KDI-2, Training Video, My Kindergarten Fun Book-II) and Michie A. Miller (Training Video, My Kindergarten Fun Book-II).

Publisher: Kindergarten Interventions and Diagnostic Services, Inc.

Cross References: For reviews by Glen P. Aylward and Lisa F. Smith, see 16: 129.

[1364]
Kindergarten Inventory of Social-Emotional Tendencies.

Purpose: "Designed to screen for social skill deficits and signs of emotional immaturity in preschool and kindergarten aged children."

Population: Ages 4–6.

Publication Date: 1997.

Acronym: KIST.

Scores: 7 domains: Communication Skills, Daily Living Skills, Hyperactive/Inattentive Behaviors, Maladaptive Behaviors, Separation Anxiety Behaviors, Socialization or Peer Relation Skills, Sleeping & Eating Behaviors.

Administration: Individual.

Price Data: Available from publisher.

Time: (10) minutes.

Comments: Ratings by child's primary caregiver, or by a teacher who knows the child well.

Authors: Daniel C. Miller and Michie A. Miller.

Publisher: Kindergarten Interventions and Diagnostic Services, Inc.

Cross References: For reviews by Amy M. Rees and Cynthia A. Rohrbeck, see 16:130.

[1365]
Kindergarten Language Screening Test, Second Edition.

Purpose: Designed to help identify children "who need further diagnostic testing to determine whether or not they have language deficits that will accelerate academic failure."

Population: Ages 4-0 through 6-11.

Publication Dates: 1978–1998.

Acronym: KLST-2.

Scores: Total score only.

Administration: Individual.

Price Data, 2006: $130 per complete kit including examiner's manual (1998, 30 pages), 50 profile/examiner record forms, picture book, and 3 picture cards; $40 per examiner's manual; $45 per 50 profile/examiner record forms; $40 per picture book; $12 per 3 picture cards.

Time: (5) minutes.

Authors: Sharon V. Gauthier and Charles L. Madison.

Publisher: PRO-ED.

Cross References: For reviews by Timothy R. Konold and Leslie Eastman Lukin, see 14:196; see also T4:1359 (2 references).

[1366]
Kindergarten Readiness Test.

Purpose: Determines the readiness of children to begin kindergarten.

Population: Ages 4–6.

Publication Date: 1988.

Acronym: KRT.

Scores: Total score only.

Administration: Individual.

Price Data, 2002: $118 per complete kit; $38 per manual (39 pages); $55 per 25 test booklets; $14 per 25 performance grid sheets; $14 per 25 letter to parent; $14 per 25 scoring interpretation; $21 per stimulus items.

Time: (15) minutes.

Authors: Sue L. Larson and Gary J. Vitali.

Publisher: Slosson Educational Publications, Inc.

Cross References: For reviews by Michael D. Beck and by Rosemary E. Sutton and Catharine C. Knight, see 12:207.

[1367]
Kinetic Drawing System for Family and School: A Handbook.

Purpose: Designed "as a projective technique which assesses a child's perceptions of relationships among the child, peers, family, school, and significant others."

Population: Ages 5-20.

Publication Date: 1985.

Scores: 5 diagnostic categories: Actions of and Between Figures, Figure Characteristics, Position/Distance/Barriers, Style, Symbols.

Administration: Individual.

Price Data, 2006: $81.50 per complete kit including 25 scoring booklets and handbook (65 pages); $37.95 per 25 scoring booklets; $48.50 per handbook (including scoring booklet).

Time: (20-40) minutes.

Comments: A combination of the Kinetic Family Drawing and Kinetic School Drawing.

Authors: Howard M. Knoff and H. Thompson Prout (handbook).

Publisher: Western Psychological Services.
Cross References: See T5:1401 (4 references) and T4:1362 (2 references); for reviews by Bert P. Cundick and Richard A. Weinberg, see 10:166 (4 references).

[1368]

Kipnis-Schmidt Profiles of Organizational Influence Strategies.

Purpose: To "measure how people use influence in their organizations."
Population: Organizational members.
Publication Date: 1982.
Acronym: POIS.
Scores, 12 or 14: Friendliness, Bargaining, Reason, Assertiveness, Sanctions (Form S only), Higher Authority, Coalition scores for each of 2 areas (First Attempt to Influence, Attempts to Overcome Resistance to Influence).
Administration: Group.
Forms, 3: M (Influencing Your Manager), C (Influencing Your Co-Workers), S (Influencing Your Subordinates).
Price Data: Price information available from publisher for set of 10 forms (specify Form M, C, S, or respondent's guides); trainer's package including 1 copy of each instrument, respondent's guide, and manual (16 pages).
Time: (20–30) minutes.
Authors: David Kipnis and Stuart M. Schmidt.
Publisher: Jossey-Bass, A Wiley Company.
Cross References: See T5:1402 (3 references) and T4:1363 (2 references).

[1369]

The Kirkpatrick Management and Supervisory Skills Series.

Purpose: Designed to assess "Key management skills and practices."
Publication Date: 1995.
Scores: Total score only.
Administration: Group.
Price Data: Available from publisher.
Time: (20) minutes per inventory.
Author: Donald L. Kirkpatrick.
Publisher: Donald L. Kirkpatrick (the author).
    a) COMMUNICATION INVENTORY.
    Purpose: Constructed to "improve knowledge, attitudes, and skills" related to communication.
    Population: Supervisors and all levels of managers.
    Acronym: CI.
    b) HUMAN RELATIONS INVENTORY.
    Purpose: Constructed to assess "the relationships that exist between supervisor and subordinate."
    Population: Same as *a* above.
    Acronym: HRI.

    c) MANAGING CHANGE INVENTORY.
    Purpose: Designed to "cover principles, facts, and attitudes that are basic to managing change effectively."
    Population: All levels of managers.
    Acronym: MCI.
    d) MODERN MANAGEMENT INVENTORY.
    Purpose: Designed to measure "philosophy, principles, and approaches related to the effective performance of managers."
    Population: Same as *c* above.
    Acronym: MMI.
    e) COACHING AND PERFORMANCE APPRAISAL INVENTORY.
    Purpose: Constructed to assess "concepts, principles, and techniques that are important ingredients" of on-the-job coaching.
    Population: Same as *c* above.
    Acronym: CPAI.
    f) TIME MANAGEMENT INVENTORY.
    Purpose: Constructed to measure "Key factors in better time utilization and delegation."
    Population: Same as *c* above.
    Acronym: TMI.
    g) LEADERSHIP, MOTIVATION, AND DECISION-MAKING INVENTORY.
    Purpose: Constructed to "make managers more conscious of their need to be leaders."
    Population: Same as *c* above.
    Acronym: LMDMI.
Cross References: For a review by L. Carolyn Pearson and Lee Droegemueller, see 14:197.

[1370]

Kirton Adaption-Innovation Inventory [1998 Edition].

Purpose: A measure of a person's preference for, or style of, creativity, problem solving, and decision making.
Population: British and U.S. adults and teenagers over age 14.
Publication Dates: 1976–1998.
Acronym: KAI.
Scores, 4: Sufficiency v. Proliferation of Originality, Efficiency, Rule/Group Conformity, Total.
Administration: Individual or group.
Price Data: Available from publisher.
Time: (5–10) minutes.
Comments: Translations available for Italian, Slovak, French, and Dutch adults and teenagers.
Author: Michael Kirton.
Publisher: Occupational Research Centre [England].
Cross References: For reviews by Lynn L. Brown and Ric Brown, see 14:198; see also T5:1404 (15 references) and T4:1364 (9 references); for reviews by Gregory J. Boyle and Gerald E. DeMauro of an earlier edition, see 11:193 (8 references).

[1371]

Kit of Factor Referenced Cognitive Tests.

Purpose: "To provide research workers with a means of identifying certain aptitude factors in factor-analytic studies."

Population: Various grades 6-college level.

Publication Dates: 1954–1978.

Administration: Group.

Price Data, 2002: $30 per complete set including 72 tests and manual (1976, 230 pages); $10 per manual; a license agreement is required for the use of the tests ($.10 a copy with a minimum of $35 for graduate students, $.20 a copy with a minimum of $50 for other researchers).

Time: Administration time given separately for each test.

Comments: Formerly called the Kit of Reference Tests for Cognitive Factors.

Authors: Tests and manual written by Ruth B. Ekstrom, John W. French, Harry H. Harman, and Diran Dermen.

Publisher: Educational Testing Service.

a) FACTOR CF: FLEXIBILITY OF CLOSURE.
   1) *Hidden Figures Test.*
   2) *Hidden Patterns Test.*
   3) *Copying Test.*

b) FACTOR CS: SPEED OF CLOSURE.
   1) *Gestalt Completion Test.*
   2) *Concealed Words Test.*
   3) *Snowy Pictures.*

c) FACTOR CV: VERBAL CLOSURE.
   1) *Scrambled Words.*
   2) *Hidden Words.*
   3) *Incomplete Words.*

d) FACTOR FA: ASSOCIATIONAL FLUENCY.
   1) *Controlled Associations Test.*
   2) *Opposites Test.*
   3) *Figures of Speech.*

e) FACTOR FE: EXPRESSIONAL FLUENCY.
   1) *Making Sentences.*
   2) *Arranging Words.*
   3) *Rewriting.*

f) FACTOR FF: FIGURAL FLUENCY.
   1) *Ornamentation Test.*
   2) *Elaboration Test.*
   3) *Symbols Test.*

g) FACTOR FI: IDEATIONAL FLUENCY.
   1) *Topics Test.*
   2) *Theme Test.*
   3) *Thing Categories Test.*

h) FACTOR FW: WORD FLUENCY.
   1) *Word Endings Test.*
   2) *Word Beginnings Test.*
   3) *Word Beginnings and Endings Test.*

i) FACTOR I: INDUCTION.
   1) *Letter Sets Test.*

   2) *Locations Test.*
   3) *Figure Classifications.*

j) FACTOR IP: INTEGRATIVE PROCESSES.
   1) *Calendar Test.*
   2) *Following Directions.*

k) FACTOR MA: ASSOCIATIVE MEMORY.
   1) *Picture-Number Test.*
   2) *Object-Number Test.*
   3) *First and Last Names Test.*

l) FACTOR MS: MEMORY SPAN.
   1) *Auditory Number Span Test.*
   2) *Visual Number Span Test.*
   3) *Auditory Letter Span Test.*

m) FACTOR MV: VISUAL MEMORY.
   1) *Shape Memory Test.*
   2) *Building Memory.*
   3) *Map Memory.*

n) FACTOR N: NUMBER.
   1) *Addition Test.*
   2) *Division Test.*
   3) *Subtraction and Multiplication Test.*
   4) *Addition and Subtraction Correction.*

o) FACTOR P: PERCEPTUAL SPEED.
   1) *Finding A's Test.*
   2) *Number Comparison Test.*
   3) *Identical Pictures Test.*

p) FACTOR RG: GENERAL REASONING.
   1) *Arithmetic Aptitude Test.*
   2) *Mathematics Aptitude Test.*
   3) *Necessary Arithmetic Operations Test.*

q) FACTOR RL: LOGICAL REASONING.
   1) *Nonsense Syllogisms Test.*
   2) *Diagramming Relationships.*
   3) *Inference Test.*
   4) *Deciphering Languages.*

r) FACTOR S: SPATIAL ORIENTATION.
   1) *Card Rotations Test.*
   2) *Cube Comparisons Test.*

s) FACTOR SS: SPATIAL SCANNING.
   1) *Maze Tracing Speed Test.*
   2) *Choosing a Path.*
   3) *Map Planning Test.*

t) FACTOR V: VERBAL COMPREHENSION.
   1) *Vocabulary Test I.*
   2) *Vocabulary Test II.*
   3) *Extended Range Vocabulary Test.*
   4) *Advanced Vocabulary Test I.*
   5) *Advanced Vocabulary Test II.*

u) FACTOR VZ: VISUALIZATION.
   1) *Form Board Test.*
   2) *Paper Folding Test.*
   3) *Surface Development Test.*

v) FACTOR XF: FIGURAL FLEXIBILITY.
   1) *Toothpicks Test.*
   2) *Planning Patterns.*
   3) *Storage Test.*

w) FACTOR XU: FLEXIBILITY OF USE.
1) *Combining Objects.*
2) *Substitute Uses.*
3) *Making Groups.*
4) *Different Uses.*

Cross References: See T5:1405 (40 references), T4:1365 (92 references), 9:572 (27 references), T3:1257 (78 references), and T2:561 (103 references).

[1372]
Knox's Cube Test-Revised.

Purpose: A nonverbal mental test designed to measure attention span and memory of children and adults.
Population: Ages 3 and over.
Publication Dates: 1980–2002.
Acronym: KCT-R.
Scores: Total score only.
Administration: Individual.
Price Data, 2005: $105 per complete kit including manual, tapping cubes, and 15 test/record booklets; $25 per 15 report booklets.
Time: (10-15) minutes.
Comments: Items unchanged from previous edition; Junior and Senior forms have been eliminated.
Author: Mark H. Stone.
Publisher: Stoelting Co.
Cross References: For reviews by Carolyn M. Callahan and Anita M. Hubley, see 16:131; see also T5:1407 (5 references) and T4:1367 (7 references); for reviews by Raymond S. Dean and Jerome M. Sattler of the previous edition, see 9:574 (2 references).

[1373]
Kohlberg's Moral Judgment Interview.

Purpose: To identify stages of moral development.
Population: Ages 10 and over.
Publication Date: 1983.
Scores: Moral Development Stages.
Price Data: Available from publisher.
Time: Administration time not reported.
Authors: Anne Colby and Lawrence Kohlberg.
Publisher: Cambridge University Press.
Cross References: See T5:1408 (9 references), T4:1368 (9 references), and T3:1262 (2 references).

[1374]
The Kohlman Evaluation of Living Skills.

Purpose: "An occupational therapy evaluation that is designed to determine a person's ability to function in basic living skills."
Population: Occupational therapy clients with living skill deficits.
Publication Dates: 1981–1992.
Acronym: KELS.
Scores: 5 areas: Self-care, Safety and Health, Money Management, Transportation and Telephone, Work and Leisure.

Administration: Individual.
Price Data: Available from publisher.
Time: (30–45) minutes.
Comments: Evaluation combines interview questions and tasks; can be used with the elderly, with persons who have cognitively disabling conditions, in court for the determination of commitment, and in discharge planning at acute-care hospitals.
Author: Linda Kohlman Thomson.
Publisher: The American Occupational Therapy Association, Inc.
Cross References: For a review by Gabriele van Lingen, see 14:199.

[1375]
The Kohs Block-Design Test.

Purpose: Designed as "performance tests that have been standardized to measure intelligence."
Population: Mental ages 5–20.
Publication Date: [1919].
Scores: Total score only.
Administration: Individual.
Price Data, 2005: $140 per complete kit including cubes, cards, manual (20 pages), and 50 record blanks; $25 per 50 record blanks; $20 per set of design cards; $100 per set of blocks; $25 per manual.
Time: (30-40) minutes.
Comments: Formerly called The Block-Design Test; modifications appear in Arthur Point Scale of Performance Tests, New Guinea Performance Scales, Ohwaki-Kohs Tactile Block Design Intelligence Test for the Blind, and Pacific Design Construction Test.
Author: S. C. Kohs.
Publisher: Stoelting Co.
Cross References: See T5:1410 (4 references), T4:1370 (5 references), T3:1265 (4 references), and T2:545 (74 references).

[1376]
Kolbe Conative Index.

Purpose: Designed to focus on the "predisposition of a subject to respond to specific behavioral settings with certain patterns of behavior."
Publication Dates: 1987–1997.
Administration: Group or individual.
Price Data: Available from publisher.
Comments: A series of instruments designed to enhance personnel selection and increase self-awareness about instructive talent and potential.
Author: Kathy Kolbe.
Publisher: Kolbe Corp.

a) KOLBE A™ INDEX.
Purpose: Designed to measure conative style.
Population: Adults.
Acronym: KCI-A.
Scores, 4: Fact Finder, Follow Thru, Quick Start, Implementor.
Time: (25) minutes.

b) KOLBE B™ INDEX.

Purpose: Designed to "identify the characteristics perceived as necessary to succeed in a given job."

Population: Job applicants.

Acronym: KCI-B.

Time: (15–20) minutes.

c) KOLBE C™ INDEX.

Purpose: Designed to "identify the characteristics necessary to function successfully in a specific job."

Population: Supervisors.

Acronym: KCI-C.

d) KOLBE R™ INDEX.

Purpose: Designed to identify "how you (the respondent) wish another person would take action."

Population: Adults.

Acronym: KCI-R.

e) KOLBE Y™ INDEX.

Purpose: Designed to assist the respondent in identifying his/her "talent for certain types of activities."

Population: Youth (5th grade reading level).

Acronym: KCI-Y.

Cross References: For reviews by Raoul A. Arreola and Chockalingam Visweswaran, see 14:200; for reviews by Collie Wyatt Conoley and Frank Gresham of an earlier edition, see 12:208.

[1377]
Krantz Health Opinion Survey.

Purpose: "To measure attitudes toward different treatment approches."

Population: College, healthy adults, and chronic disease populations.

Publication Date: 1980.

Acronym: KHOS.

Scores, 3: Information, Behavioral Involvement, Total.

Administration: Group.

Manual: No manual.

Price Data: Test materials now available free of charge from author.

Time: (10-15) minutes.

Authors: David S. Krantz, Andrew Baum, and Margaret V. Wideman.

Publisher: David S. Krantz.

Cross References: See T5:1412 (4 references) and T4:1373 (1 reference); for a review by James A. Blumenthal, see 9:578 (1 reference); see also T3:1267 (1 reference).

[1378]
Krug Asperger's Disorder Index.

Purpose: To identify individuals who have Asperger's Disorder, to target goals for intervention on the IEP, and for use in research.

Population: Ages 6-0 to 21-11.

Publication Date: 2003.

Acronym: KADI.

Scores: Total score only.

Administration: Individual.

Price Data, 2006: $90 per complete kit; $54 per examiner's manual (39 pages); $20 per 50 profile/examiner record forms (specify ages 6-11 or ages 12-22).

Time: Untimed.

Comments: Ratings by parents, close relatives, teachers, educational assistants, or counselors.

Authors: David A. Krug and Joel R. Arick.

Publisher: PRO-ED.

Cross References: For reviews by Leah M. Nellis and Stephen E. Trotter, see 16:132.

[1379]
Kuder Career Search.

Purpose: Assesses activity preferences to suggest possible satisfying occupations.

Population: Middle school through adult.

Publication Date: 1999.

Acronym: KCS.

Scores, 6: Outdoor/Mechanical, Science/Technical, Arts/Communication, Social/Personal Services, Sales/Management, Business Operations.

Administration: Individual or group.

Price Data: Available from publisher.

Time: (20–25) minutes including scoring.

Comments: Uses preference profile to find best matches from a database of approximately 2,000 employed adults and yields first-person accounts of their occupations/jobs; with Kuder Skills Assessment (1382) and Super's Work Values Inventory—Revised (2486), plus the Kuder Electronic Career Portfolio constitutes the Kuder Career Planning System.

Authors: Frederic Kuder and Donald G. Zytowski.

Publisher: National Career Assessment Services, Inc. [No reply from publisher; status unknown].

[1380]
Kuder General Interest Survey, Form E.

Purpose: Constructed to assess "broad interest areas" related to occupational choices.

Population: Grades 6–12.

Publication Dates: 1963–1991.

Scores, 11: Outdoor, Mechanical, Computational, Scientific, Persuasive, Artistic, Literary, Musical, Social Service, Clerical, Verification.

Administration: Group.

Price Data: Available from publisher.

Time: [45–60] minutes.

Comments: Extension of the Kuder vocational interest inventories series.

Author: G. Frederic Kuder.

Publisher: National Career Assessment Services, Inc. [No reply from publisher; status unknown].

Cross References: See T5:1413 (1 reference); for reviews by Mark Pope and Donald Thompson, see 12:209; see also T4:1374 (4 references), T3:1269 (4 references), and 8:1009 (16 references); for reviews by Barbara A. Kirk, Paul R. Lohnes, and John N. McCall of an earlier edition, and excerpted reviews by T. R. Husek and Robert F. Stahmann, see 7:1024 (8 references).

[1381]

Kuder Occupational Interest Survey, Revised (Form DD).

Purpose: Measures individual interests in order to "suggest promising occupations and college majors in rank order, based on examinee's interest pattern."
Population: Grade 10 through adult.
Publication Dates: 1956–1985.
Acronym: KOIS.
Scores, 4: Dependability, Vocational Interest Estimates (10 areas), Occupational Scales (approximately 100), College Major Scales (approximately 40).
Administration: Group.
Price Data: Available from publisher.
Time: (30–45) minutes.
Comments: Includes Vocational Interest Estimate scales identical in content to those of the Kuder Preference Record, Form C and the Kuder General Interest Survey, Form E.
Authors: Frederic Kuder, Esther E. Diamond, and Donald G. Zytowski (manual supplement).
Publisher: National Career Assessment Services, Inc. [No reply from publisher; status unknown].
Cross References: See T4:1375 (1 reference); for reviews by Edwin L. Herr and Mary L. Tenopyr, see 10:167 (3 references); see also T3:1270 (12 references), 8:1010 (41 references), and T2: 2194 (13 references); for reviews by Robert H. Dolliver and W. Bruce Walsh, and excerpted reviews by Frederick G. Brown and Robert F. Stahmann, see 7:1025 (19 references).

[1382]

Kuder Skills Assessment.

Purpose: Assesses self-efficacy in six skill areas.
Population: Middle school through adult.
Publication Date: 2001.
Acronym: KSA.
Scores, 6: Outdoor/Mechanical, Science/Technical, Arts/Communication, Social/Personal Services, Sales Management, Business Operations.
Administration: Individual or group.
Price Data: Available from publisher.
Time: (15–20) minutes.
Comments: Online administration; instant scoring; combined report with Kuder Career Search (1379) available; with Kuder Career Search and Super's Work Values Inventory—Revised (2486), plus the Kuder Electronic Career Portfolio, constitutes the Kuder Career Planning System.
Authors: Donald G. Zytowski and Darrell Luzzo.
Publisher: National Career Assessment Services, Inc. [No reply from publisher; status unknown].

[1383]

Kuhlmann-Anderson Tests, Eighth Edition.

Purpose: "Designed to provide a measure of an individual's academic potential through assessing cognitive skills related to the learning process."
Population: Grades K, 1, 2–3, 3–4, 5–6, 7–9, 9–12.
Publication Dates: 1927–1982.
Acronym: KA.
Scores, 6: 3 raw scores (Verbal, Nonverbal, Full) and 3 derived scores.
Administration: Group.
Levels, 7: K, A, BC, CD, EF, G, and H.
Manual: Separate manual of directions for each level.
Authors: F. Kuhlmann (fourth and earlier editions) and Rose G. Anderson.
Publisher: Scholastic Testing Service, Inc.
   a) LEVEL K.
   Population: Kindergarten.
   Price Data, 2005: $42.85 per starter set including manual of directions and 20 machine-scorable test booklets; $34.30 for starter set including manual of directions, 20 hand-scorable test booklets, class record sheet, and answer key; $24 per sample set; $5.60 per student for scoring service ($43.65 minimum scoring service).
   Time: 28(50–75) minutes in 2 days.
   b) LEVEL A.
   Population: Grade 1.
   Price Data: Same as *a* above.
   Time: 28(50–75) minutes in 2 days.
   c) LEVEL BC.
   Population: Grades 2, 3.
   Price Data: Same as *a* above.
   Time: 28(50–75) minutes in 2 days.
   d) LEVEL CD.
   Population: Grades 3, 4.
   Price Data: $34.30 per starter set including manual of directions, 20 test booklets, and class record sheet, $4.30 per student for scoring service, $24 per sample set.
   Time: 35(50–75) minutes.
   e) LEVEL EF.
   Population: Grades 5, 6.
   Price Data: Same as for *d* above.
   Time: 40(50–75) minutes.
   f) LEVEL G.
   Population: Grades 7–9.
   Price Data: Same as for *d* above.
   Time: 40(50–75) minutes.
   g) LEVEL H.
   Population: Grades 9–12.
   Price Data: Same as for *d* above.
   Time: 40(50–75) minutes.
Cross References: See T4:1377 (2 references); for reviews by Michael D. Hiscox and Ronald C. Rodgers, see 9:579 (2 references); see T3:1272 (13 references)

and T2:398 (53 references); for reviews by William B. Michael and Douglas A. Pidgeon, and an excerpted review by Frederick B. Davis of the seventh edition, see 6:466 (11 references); see also 5:348 (15 references); for reviews by Henry E. Garrett and David Segel of an earlier edition, see 5:302 (10 references); for reviews by W. G. Emmett and Stanley S. Maryolf, see 3:236 (25 references); for a review by Henry E. Garrett, see 2:1404 (15 references); for reviews by Psyche Cattell, S. A. Courtis, and Austin H. Turney, see 1:1049.

[1384]
Kundu Introversion Extraversion Inventory.

Purpose: Designed to obtain a measure of the introversion-extraversion dimension of adult behavior to be used for diagnosis, selection, or career guidance.
Population: Adults.
Publication Date: 1976.
Scores: Total score only.
Administration: Group.
Price Data: Available from publisher.
Time: (20–40) minutes.
Author: Ramanath Kundu.
Publisher: Ramanath Kundu [India] [No reply from publisher; status unknown].

[1385]
Kundu Neurotic Personality Inventory.

Purpose: Designed to measure neurotic tendencies.
Population: Adults.
Publication Dates: 1965–1987.
Acronym: KNPI.
Scores: Item scores only.
Administration: Individual or group.
Price Data: Available from publisher.
Foreign Language Edition: Bengali edition available.
Time: (20–30) minutes.
Author: Ramanath Kundu.
Publisher: Ramanath Kundu [India] [No reply from publisher; status unknown].
Cross References: See T2:1257 (2 references) and P:140 (5 references).

[1386]
The Lake St. Clair Incident.

Purpose: To examine group and individual decision-making processes, help individuals and groups perceive and evaluate their interactions and styles of communicating, and utilize the instrument to simply have fun or create an environment.
Population: Adults.
Publication Dates: 1977-1978.
Acronym: LSC.
Scores, 3: Autocratic, Consultative, Consensual.

Administration: Individual in part.
Price Data, 2006: $46.95 per 10 test booklets and 1 manual (1977, 22 pages); $27.50 per manual; $46.95 per 25 test booklets.
Time: (65-80) minutes.
Author: Albert A. Canfield.
Publisher: Western Psychological Services.
Cross References: For a review by Jack L. Bodden, see 9:582.

[1387]
Language Arts Objective Sequence.

Purpose: "Helps evaluate students' current [language arts] performance levels and identify specific goals and objectives."
Population: Grades 1–12.
Publication Date: 2001.
Scores: 9 ratings/objectives: Readiness (Level 3), Listening (Levels 3, 2), Speaking (Levels 3, 2, 1), Reading—Word Recognition (Level 3), Reading—Comprehension (Levels 3, 2, 1), Writing—Handwriting (Level 3), Writing—Spelling (Levels 3, 2), Writing Process (Levels 3, 2, 1), Writing—Grammar (Levels 3, 2, 1).
Administration: Individual.
Levels, 3: 1, 2, 3.
Price Data, 2006: $39.95 per assessment manual (120 pages) including 24 reproducible forms and checklists; $150 per report generating software (for Windows) Language Arts Objective Sequence Reports (LOSR) including LOS manual.
Time: Administration time not reported.
Comments: Intended to be used by teachers as an informal "curriculum guide, bank of objectives, rubric guide, or structured observation system"; some objectives do not include all 3 levels.
Authors: Jacqueline Robertson and Sheldon Braaten.
Publisher: Research Press.

[1388]
Language Assessment Scales, 2nd Edition—Oral.

Purpose: Designed to "measure those English and language skills necessary for functioning in a mainstream academic environment."
Population: Grades 1–6, 7–2.
Publication Dates: 1987–1991.
Acronym: LAS-O.
Scores, 6: Vocabulary, Listening Comprehension, Story Retelling, Minimal Sound Pairs, Phonemes, Total.
Administration: Individual.
Levels, 2: 1, 2.
Parts, 2: Oral Language (for Level 1 & 2), Pronunciation (for Grades 2–12).
Forms, 2: C, D.
Price Data, 2006: $80 per test review kit including administration manual, scoring and interpretation

manual, student test booklet or multicopy scoresheet, and cue picture booklet along with test reviewer's guide (specify level and form); $51 per 50 answer documents; $54 per reusable cue picture booklet; $26 per audiocassette (specify level and form); $40 per administration manual (specify level); $42 per scoring and interpretation manual (specify level); $40 per technical report (1991, 144 pages); $193 per examiner's kit (specify level).

Foreign Language Edition: Spanish edition (1990) available.

Time: [15] minutes.

Comments: Language Proficiency Score also incorporates Language Assessment Scales, Reading and Writing (1389).

Authors: Edward A. DeAvila and Sharon E. Duncan.

Publisher: CTB/McGraw-Hill.

Cross References: See T5:1420 (1 references); for reviews by Natalie L. Hedberg and Pamela S. Tidwell, see 12:210 (1 reference); for a review of the Language Assessment Scales by Lyn Haber, see 9:584 (1 reference).

[1389]
Language Assessment Scales, 2nd Edition, Reading and Writing.

Purpose: Designed to measure "English language skills in reading and writing necessary for functioning in a mainstream academic environment."

Population: Language-minority students in Grades 2–3, 4–6, 7–11.

Publication Dates: 1988–2000.

Acronym: LAW R/W.

Scores, 3: Reading, Writing, Total.

Administration: Group.

Levels, 3: 1, 2, 3.

Forms, 2: A, B.

Price Data, 2006: $125 per 35 Level 1 Reading test booklets and examiner's manual (67 pages); $80 per 35 Level 2 or Level 3 Reading test booklets and Reading/Writing examiner's manual (Level 2, 79 pages; Level 3, 73 pages); $61 per 35 Writing test booklets (specify level); $53 per 50 student answer documents (sepecify Level 2 or Level 3); $188 per 9 Level 1 scoring stencils (Reading only); $22 per Level 2 or Level 3 scoring stencil (Reading only); $19 per administration manual (specify level); materials also available in Spanish; $29 per technical manual (98 pages); $336 for LASSCORE site license.

Time: (50–75) minutes for Level 1; (49–87) minutes for Level 2; (53–86) minutes for Level 3.

Comments: May be used in conjunction with LAS Oral, 2nd Edition (1388).

Authors: Sharon E. Duncan and Edward A. DeAvila.

Publisher: CTB/McGraw-Hill.

Cross References: See T5:1421 (4 references); for reviews by C. Dale Carpenter and Thomas W. Guyette, see 12:211; see also T4:1386 (5 references).

[1390]
Language Assessment Skills Links Benchmark Assessment.

Purpose: Designed to "measure students' skills in speaking, listening, reading and writing."

Population: Grades K-12.

Publication Date: 2005.

Acronym: LAS Links Benchmark Assessment.

Scores, 6: Speaking, Listening, Reading, Writing, Comprehension, Oral.

Administration: Individual or group.

Levels, 5: Grades K-1; Grades 2-3; Grades 4-5; Grades 6-8; Grades 9-12.

Price Data, 2006: $$25 per 10 student books; $15 per student answer documents (specify book number and grades); $14.95 per examiner's guide (99-111 pages, specify level); $17.50 per 10 student profile sheets (specify grades).

Comments: Test is designed for English language learners.

Author: CTB/McGraw-Hill.

Publisher: CTB/McGraw-Hill.

a) SPEAKING.
Time: (2-8) minutes.
Subtests, 4: Speak in Words, Speak in Sentences, Make Conversation, Tell a Story.
b) LISTENING.
Time: (5-15) minutes.
Subtests, 3: Listen for Information, Listen in the Classroom, Listen/Comprehend.
c) READING.
Time: (10-20) minutes.
Subtests, 3: Analyze Words, Read Words, Read for Understanding.
d) WRITING.
Time: (5-15) minutes.
Subtests, 3-4: Use Conventions, Write About, Write Why, Write in Detail (not included in Grades K-1).

[1391]
Language Assessment Skills Links K-12 Assessments.

Purpose: Designed to "measure students' skills in speaking, listening, reading, writing, and comprehension."

Population: Grades K-12.

Publication Date: 2005.

Acronym: LAS Links K-12.

Scores, 7: Speaking, Listening, Reading, Writing, Overall, Comprehension, Oral.

Levels, 5: Grades K-1; Grades 2-3; Grades 4-5; Grades 6-8; Grades 9-12.

Price Data, 2006: $92.45 per classroom kit including consumable student book, cue picture book, examiner's guide (66-69 pages), and audio CD (specify Grades K-1 or 2-3); $43.55 per classroom kit including reusable student book, student answer book, examiner's guide and audio CD (specify Grades 4-5, 6-8, or 9-12); $35 per 10 consumable student books (specify Grades K-1 or 2-3); $42 per 10 reusable student books (specify Grades 4-5, 6-8, or 9-12); $50.40 per cue picture book (specify Grades K-1 or 2-3); $15 pr 10 student answer books (specify Grades 4-5, 6-8, 9-12); $19.95 per examiner's guide (specify grades); $24.95 per audio cassette (specify grades); $24.95 per audio CD (specify grades); $17.50 per student profile sheets; $39.50 per interpretation guide.

Comments: Test is designed for English language learners.

Author: CTB/McGraw-Hill.

Publisher: CTB/McGraw-Hill.

a) SPEAKING.

Administration: Individual.

Time: (5-15) minutes.

Subtests, 4: Speak in Words, Speak in Sentences, Make Conversation, Tell a Story.

b) LISTENING.

Administration: Individual or group.

Time: (10-20) minutes.

Subtests, 3: Listen for Information, Listen in the Classroom, Listen/Comprehend.

c) READING.

Administration: Individual or group.

Time: (35-45) minutes.

Subtests, 3: Analyze Words, Read Words, Read for Understanding.

d) WRITING.

Administration: Individual or group.

Time: (35-45) minutes.

Subtests, 3: Use Conventions, Write About, Write Why, Write in Detail [not included in Grades K-1].

[1392]
Language Processing Test 3: Elementary.

Purpose: Designed to identify "students' language processing strengths and weaknesses in a hierarchical framework."

Population: Ages 5-0 to 11-11.

Publication Dates: 1985-2005.

Acronym: LPT 3.

Scores, 8: Labeling, Stating Functions, Associations, Categorization, Similarities, Differences, Multiple Meanings, Attributes.

Administration: Individual.

Price Data: Available from publisher.

Time: (30) minutes.

Authors: Gail J. Richard and Mary Anne Hanner.

Publisher: LinguiSystems, Inc.

Cross References: See T5:1424 (5 references); for reviews by Thomas W. Guyette and Lyn Haber of an earlier edition, see 10:169.

[1393]
Language Proficiency Test Series.

Purpose: Designed to aid in student placement and the evaluation of student language proficiency in reading, writing, listening, and speaking.

Population: Grades K–12, specifically ELL students.

Publication Dates: 1998-2001.

Acronym: LPTS.

Scores, 3: Reading, Writing, Listening/Speaking.

Administration: Individual or group.

Forms, 24: Listening/Speaking: L/S 1—Grades K–2, L/S 2—Grades 3–5, L/S 3—Grades 6–8, L/S 4—Grades 9–12, Reading: R1—Grades K–2, R2—Grades 3–5, R3—Grades 6–8, R4—Grades 9–12, Writing: W1—Grades K–2, W2—Grades 3–5, W3—Grades 6–8, W4—Grades 9–12; alternate forms available for all subjects and grade clusters.

Price Data, 2005: $32 per administrator's sample set including Administration and Scoring Guide plus one test booklet each for Reading, Writing, and Listening/Speaking at grade level of choice (K-2, 3–5, 6–8, or 9–12); $59.50 per 25 Grades K–2 or for Grades 3–5 (Form A or B) Reading Test booklets; $51.50 per 25 Grades 6–8 or Grades 9–12 (Form A or B) Reading Test booklets; $12.50 per 25 scannable answer sheets for Reading Test (Grades 6–12 only); $1.25 each for scoring Reading Test booklet; $26.50 per 25 Writing Test booklets (Grades K-2, 3–5, 6–8, or 9–12, Form A or B); $1.25–$2.30 each for scoring Writing Test booklet; $26.50 per 25 Listening/Speaking Test booklets (Grades K-2, 3–5, 6–8, or 9–12, Form A or B); $1.25–$2.85 each for scoring Listening/Speaking Test booklet; $59.50 per technical manual (2004, 36 pages).

Time: (25) minutes average per test.

Author: MetriTech, Inc.

Publisher: MetriTech, Inc.

Cross References: For reviews by Marie Miller-Whitehead and Judith A. Monsaas, see 15:134.

[1394]
Language Sampling, Analysis, and Training—Third Edition.

Purpose: "Designed to analyze the syntax and morphology of children who are producing a significant number of utterances containing at least three morphemes."

Population: Children with language delay.

Publication Dates: 1974–1999.

Acronym: LSAT-3.

Scores, 39: Word Morpheme (Sentences Total, Words Total, Morphemes Total, Words/Sentences Means, Morphemes/Sentence Means, Word-Morpheme Index), Noun Phrase Constituents (Pronouns, Prepositions, Possessive Marker, Demonstratives, Articles, Plurals, Locatives, Conjunctions), Verb Phrase Constituents (Modals,

Particles, Copula, Present Progressive Tense, Present Tense-3rd Singular, Past Tense, Irregular), Simple Sentence Constructions (Noun Phrase, Verb Phrase, Verb Phrase + Noun Phrase, Noun Phrase + Verb Phrase + [Noun Phrase], Noun Phrase + Copula + N/Adj, Unclassifiable Constructions), Complex Sentences (Coordination, Subordination-Infinitives, Adverbials, Indirect Questions, Verb + [that] + Sentence, Relatives, Direct Quotations, Complex in More Than One Way, Unclassifiable, Percentage Complex), Questions, Negatives.

Administration: Individual.

Price Data, 2006: $100 per complete kit including manual (1999, 163 pages), analysis forms, and transcription sheets; $40 per manual; $40 per analysis forms; $30 per transcription sheets.

Time: Administration time varies.

Comments: Visual and verbal stimuli for eliciting language sample determined by examiner; tape recording recommended for recording responses; a detailed tutorial with self-checking exercises covering all steps in the procedure, multicultural issues, setting targets, training, measuring and reporting change are new inclusions in the third edition handbook.

Authors: Dorothy Tyack and Gail Portnuff Venable.

Publisher: PRO-ED.

Cross References: For a review by Sheila Pratt, see 14:201; for a review by Margaret C. Byrne of an earlier edition, see 9:590.

[1395]
LARR Test of Emergent Literacy.

Purpose: Designed to provide "a simple measure of young children's level of literacy on entry to compulsory schooling."

Population: Students entering school.

Publication Date: 1993.

Acronym: LARRTEL.

Scores: Total score only.

Administration: Group.

Price Data: Available from publisher.

Time: (25) minutes.

Comments: Based on the Linguistic Awareness in Reading Readiness (LARR) Test (T6:1434).

Author: National Foundation for Educational Research.

Publisher: NFER-Nelson Publishing Co., Ltd. [England].

Cross References: For a review by Jill Ann Jenkins, see 16:133.

[1396]
Law Enforcement Applicant Inventory

Purpose: Designed to "identify individuals who have the integrity and attitudes important to become model law enforcement officers and security personnel."

Population: Ages 18 and over.

Publication Dates: 1991–1996.

Acronym: LEAI.

Scores, 12: Honesty, Nonviolence, Drug Avoidance, Risk Avoidance, Safety, Stress Tolerance, Validity/Distortion, Validity/Accuracy, Candidate Potential Index, Criminal Justice Orientation, Background and Work Experience, Narrative Information.

Administration: Individual or group.

Price Data, 2005: $16 including 1–999 reports for Internet scoring with booklets; $16 including 1–999 reports for Internet scoring without booklets; $16 including 1–999 reports for QuantaTouch Test; $16 including 1–999 reports for QUANTA Software for Windows with booklets; $16 including 1–999 reports for QUANTA Software for Windows without booklets.

Time: (30–45) minutes.

Comments: Test can be scored via Touch Test, Internet, or Optical Scanning Software.

Author: Pearson Reid London House.

Publisher: Pearson Performance Solutions [No reply from publisher; status unknown].

[1397]
Law Enforcement Assessment and Development Report.

Purpose: Intended to evaluate personality implications for performance in law enforcement jobs.

Population: Applicants and incumbents for law enforcement and other public safety positions.

Publication Dates: 1967–1987.

Acronym: LEADR.

Scores, 37: 4 personality dimensions (Emotional Adjustment, Integrity/Control, Intellectual Efficiency, Interpersonal Relations); 16 normal personality primary factor scores; 17 pathological characteristics; Performance Index; Tough Poise; Independence; Leadership, Accident Proneness.

Administration: Group or individual.

Price Data, 2005: $40 per 25 reusable test booklets; $18 per 25 answer sheets; $30 per manual (1987, 43 pages); $33 per introductory kit including manual, test booklet, answer sheet, and prepaid processing form; $19.50 to $30 per individual score report.

Time: (120) minutes.

Comments: Represents a computer-based analysis from the Clinical Analysis Questionnaire (540); on-site software scoring and report options available.

Author: IPAT staff.

Publisher: Institute for Personality and Ability Testing, Inc. (IPAT).

Cross References: For a review by David S. Hargrove, see 10:170; for a review by Lawrence Allen of the earlier edition, see 9:593.

[1398]
The LAW-PSI Adult Life History Questionnaire.

Purpose: Designed to gather a defendant's summary of life history prior to legal investigation or polygraph examination.

Population: Adults.
Publication Date: 1986.
Scores: 17 areas: Personal History, Developmental History, Family History, Educational History, Employment History, Dating History, Marital History, Driving History, Legal History, Financial History, Drug History, Alcohol History, Mental Health History, Health History, Sexual History, Military History, Daily Activity History.
Administration: Individual.
Price Data, 2001: $24.50 each questionnaire booklet (66 pages).
Time: Administration time not reported.
Author: Stephen B. Lawrence.
Publisher: California Counseling Centers.

[1399]
The LAW-PSI Child/Adolescent Life History Questionnaire.

Purpose: Individual life history information gathered prior to verification either by legal investigation or polygraph examination.
Population: Children/adolescents.
Publication Date: [1986].
Scores: 14 areas: Personal History, Developmental History, Family History, Educational History, Employment History, Dating History, Driving History, Legal History, Financial History, Drug History, Alcohol History, Mental Health History, Daily Activity History, Health History.
Administration: Individual.
Price Data, 2001: $24.50 each questionnaire/booklet.
Time: Untimed.
Author: Stephen B. Lawrence.
Publisher: California Counseling Centers.

[1400]
The LAW-PSI Sexual History Questionnaire.

Purpose: "To obtain a comprehensive, accurate sexual history in a wide variety of individuals."
Population: Adults.
Publication Date: 1994.
Scores: 16 areas: Total Sexual Partners, Primary Sexual Partners, Locations for Sex, Use of Erotic Materials, Masturbation History, Visiting Erotic Locations, Commercial Sex Experiences, Sexual Victim History, Sexual Disorders, Homosexual Experiences, Physical Sexual Problems, Sexual Dysfunctions, Child Pornography, Sexual Fantasies, Sexual Offenses, Current Sexual Allegations/Offenses.
Administration: Individual.
Price Data, 2001: $24.50 per sexual history questionnaires; $15 per 5 sexual history worksheets; $35 per sexual offender reports; $24.50 per manual (72 pages);

$25 per 15 minutes for forensic consultation via telephone with author.
Time: Administration time not reported.
Author: Stephen B. Lawrence.
Publisher: California Counseling Centers.

[1401]
Law School Admission Test.

Purpose: "To measure skills that are considered essential for success in law school."
Population: Law school entrants.
Publication Dates: 1948–2006.
Acronym: LSAT.
Scores: Total score plus unscored writing sample.
Administration: Group.
Price Data, 2006: $115 per LSAT; $58 per late registration; $30 per test center change; $30 per test date change; $213 per nonpublished test center (U.S.A., Canada, Puerto Rico); $284 per nonpublished test center (all other countries); $36 per hand scoring;$36 per former registrants score report; $106 per LSDAS subscription (5 years no report); $12 per law school report.
Time: 175 minutes; 35 minutes per writing sample.
Comments: Test administered 4 times annually (June, October, December, February) at centers established by the publisher.
Author: Law School Admission Council, Inc.
Publisher: Law School Admission Council, Inc.
Cross References: See T5:1434 (2 references); for reviews by James B. Erdmann and by Robert F. McMorris, Elizabeth L. Bringsjord, and Wei-Ping Liu, see 13:174 (8 references); see also T4:1400 (4 references); for a review by Gary B. Melton of an earlier edition, see 9:594 (2 references); see also T3:1292 (6 references), 8:1093 (7 references), and T2:2349 (7 references); for a review by Leo A. Munday of earlier forms, see 7:1098 (23 references); see also 5:928 (7 references); for a review by Alexander G. Wesman, see 4:815 (6 references).

[1402]
The Lawrence Psychological Forensic Examination.

Purpose: "A guide for comprehensive psychological assessments and report writing with clients in the criminal, juvenile and civil justice systems."
Population: Juvenile, criminal, and civil justice clients.
Publication Dates: 1978–1983.
Acronym: LAW-PSI.
Scores: No scores as such; ratings and judgments.
Administration: Individual.
Price Data: Available from publisher.
Comments: Ratings by mental health professional; handbook contains descriptive legal information for report writing, and 3 tests.

Author: Stephen B. Lawrence.
Publisher: California Counseling Centers.
  a) LAWRENCE PSYCHOLOGICAL FORENSIC
  EXAMINATION.
  Comments: Guided forensic interview to de-
  termine precise mental states of mind, life history,
  or prediction of future client behavior.
  b) LAWRENCE MENTAL COMPETENCY TEST.
  Acronym: LAW-COMP.
  Comments: To aid clinicians in making judgments needed to determine a client's present legal
  mental competency to stand trial.
  c) LAWRENCE PSYCHOLOGICAL FORENSIC
  EXAMINATION REPORT EVALUATION.
  Acronym: LAW-PSI/EVAL.
  Comments: A rating instrument (175 pages)
  for evaluating written forensic reports.
Cross References: For a review by Samuel Roll,
see 10:171.

[1403]
Leader Behavior Analysis II.

Purpose: Developed to assess leadership style.
Population: Middle and upper level managers.
Publication Date: 1991.
Acronym: LBAII.
Scores, 6: Style Flexibility, Style Effectiveness, Di-
recting Style, Coaching Style, Supporting Style, Del-
egating Style.
Administration: Group.
Editions, 2: Self, Other.
Price Data: Price information available from pub-
lisher for complete kit including 1 LBAII-Self instru-
ment, 8 LBAII-Other instruments, data summary sheet,
and scoring instructions.
Time: [15-20] minutes.
Comments: Ratings by employees and self-ratings.
Authors: Drea Zigarmi, Douglas Forsyth, Kenneth
Blanchard, and Ronald Hambleton (tests).
Publisher: The Ken Blanchard Companies.
Cross References: See T5:1436 (1 reference); for
reviews by H. John Bernardin and Donna K. Cooke
and by Sharon McNeely, see 12:212; see also T4:1402
(1 reference).

[1404]
Leader Behavior Questionnaire, Revised.

Purpose: Constructed as a measure of "organizational
leadership."
Population: Managers and employees.
Publication Dates: 1988–1996.
Acronym: LBQ.
Scores: Visionary Leadership Behavior Scales (Clear
Leadership, Communicative Leadership, Consistent
Leadership, Caring Leadership, Creative Leadership)
Visionary Leadership Characteristics Scales (Confident
Leadership, Empowered Leadership, Visionary Lead-

ership), Visionary Culture Building Scales (Organiza-
tional Leadership, Cultural Leadership).
Administration: Group.
Forms, 2: Self, Other.
Price Data, 1996: $7.95 per self questionnaire;
$2.95 per other questionnaire; $24.95 per trainer's guide
(1996, 63 pages).
Time: (10–20) minutes.
Author: Marshall Sashkin.
Publisher: HRD Press, Inc.
Cross References: For reviews by Janet Barnes-
Farrell and Hilda Wing, see 14:202.

[1405]
Leadership and Self-Development Scale.

Purpose: Measurement of the effectiveness of a lead-
ership workshop for college women.
Population: College.
Publication Dates: 1976-1979.
Scores, 9: Assertiveness, Risk Taking, Self-Concept,
Setting Goals, Decision Making, Obtaining a Followership,
Conflict Resolution, Group Roles, Evaluation.
Administration: Group.
Manual: No manual; mimeographed research report
(1976, 20 pages).
Price Data, 2001: Now free upon request from
publisher.
Time: Administration time not reported.
Authors: Virginia Hoffman and Patricia B. Elmore.
Publisher: Patricia B. Elmore.
Cross References: For a review by Robert R.
McCrae, see 9:597; see also T3:1298 (2 references).

[1406]
Leadership Appraisal Survey.

Purpose: "An assessment of leadership practices and
attitudes as viewed through the eyes of others."
Population: Adults.
Publication Dates: 1971-1997.
Scores, 5: Philosophy, Planning, Implementation,
Evaluation, Total.
Administration: Group.
Manual: No manual.
Price Data, 2001: $7.95 per instrument.
Time: Administration time not reported.
Comments: Self-administered survey.
Author: Jay Hall.
Publisher: Teleometrics International, Inc.
Cross References: See T3:2351 (1 reference); for a
review by Abraham K. Korman of the Styles of Lead-
ership and Management, see 8:1185 (8 references).

[1407]
Leadership Competency Inventory.

Purpose: Measures an individual's use of four competencies related to leadership.
Population: Managers and employees.

Publication Dates: 1993–1996.
Acronym: LCI.
Scores, 4: Information Seeking, Conceptual Thinking, Strategic Orientation, Service Orientation.
Administration: Group or individual.
Price Data, 2006: $69 per complete kit including 10 profiles and interpretive notes (20 pages), and 10 questionnaires; $29 per 10 (employee version) questionnaires; $55 per 10 Development Assistant booklets.
Time: [30–40] minutes.
Comments: Self-scored questionnaire.
Author: Hay Group.
Publisher: Hay Group.
Cross References: For a review by L. Carolyn Pearson, see 13:175.

[1408]
Leadership Development Report.

Purpose: "An expert system providing insight into how a manager's personality affects his or her performance and how to modify a manager's behavior within his or her natural limits."
Population: Adults.
Publication Dates: 1996–2000.
Acronym: LDR.
Scores, 34: Impulsivity, Understanding, Complexity, Risk Taking, Breadth of Interests, Innovation, Endurance, Cognitive Structure, Order, Organization, Play, Self-Esteem, Anxiety, Tolerance, Change, Achievement, Aggression, Responsibility, Abasement, Value Orthodoxy, Energy Level, Harm Avoidance, Affiliation, Dominance, Exhibition, Interpersonal Affect, Succorance, Social Participation, Social Adroitness, Conformity, Defendence, Social Recognition, Nurturance, Autonomy.
Administration: Group.
Price Data, 2006: $15 per test manual; $98 per report available through fax-in scoring system or online at www.sigmatesting.com; volume discounts available.
Time: 40 minutes.
Comments: Includes items from the Jackson Personality Inventory—Revised (1302), The Personality Research Form (1928), and The Survey of Work Styles (2510), all still available for sale. The LDR can be administered in two ways: answer sheets can be faxed to publisher, bound reports are returned via courier or sent by email; or test can be administered and scored directly through a SigmaTesting.com account.
Authors: Douglas N. Jackson and Julie Carswell.
Publisher: Sigma Assessment Systems, Inc.
Cross References: For a review by Mark A. Staal, see 15:135.

[1409]
Leadership Effectiveness Analysis™.

Purpose: Developed to identify leadership skills and behaviors in a 360 degree context.
Population: Managers, supervisors, individual contributors at all levels.

Publication Dates: 1981–2001.
Acronym: LEA.
Scores, 23: Conservative, Innovative, Technical, Self, Strategic, Persuasive, Outgoing, Excitement, Restraint, Structuring, Tactical, Communication, Delegation, Control, Feedback, Management Focus, Dominant, Production, Cooperation, Consensual, Authority, Empathy, Exaggeration.
Administration: Group.
Price Data: Available from publisher.
Foreign Language Editions: English (American), English (British), Chinese (Simplified characters), Chinese (Traditional characters), Danish, Dutch, Finnish, French, German, Italian, Japanese, Portuguese (Brazil), Spanish, and Swedish.
Time: (45) minutes.
Comments: Requires training by publisher before purchase and use.
Authors: James T. Mahoney (test) and Robert I. Kabacoff (manual).
Publisher: Management Research Group.

[1410]
Leadership/Impact.

Purpose: Provides people in leadership with information about their current performance as well as insights into ways they can enhance their effectiveness through the leadership strategies they employ and the impact they have on others.
Population: Leaders at the executive level.
Publication Date: 1996.
Acronym: L/I.
Scores: 3 Dimensions of Effectiveness: Organizational Effectiveness, Personal Effectiveness, Balance; 12 Types of Impact on Others: Impact (Achievement, Self-Actualizing, Humanistic-Encouraging, Affiliative), Passive/Defensive (Approval, Conventional, Dependent, Avoidance), Aggressive/Defensive (Oppositional, Power, Competitive, Perfectionistic); 10 Domains of Leadership: Personal Focus (Envisioning, Role Modeling), Interpersonal Focus (Mentoring, Stimulating Thinking, Referring, Monitoring, Providing Feedback), Organizational Focus (Reinforcing, Influencing, Creating a Setting).
Administration: Individual or group.
Price Data: Price data for test materials including Facilitator's Guide available from publisher.
Time: Administration time not reported.
Comments: Ratings by self and at least three co-workers.
Author: Robert A. Cooke.
Publisher: Human Synergistics International.

[1411]
Leadership Opinion Questionnaire.

Purpose: To measure supervisory leadership dimensions.
Population: Supervisors and prospective supervisors.

Publication Dates: 1960–1989.
Acronym: LOQ.
Scores, 2: Structure, Consideration.
Administration: Individual or group.
Price Data, 2002: $72 per start-up kit including 25 test booklets and examiner's manual; $53 per 25 test booklets (quantity discounts available); $28 per examiner's manual; price data available from publisher for Quanta Computer Administration and Scoring software (Windows); $72 per Quanta start-up kit including examiner's manual and 25 administrations and scoring (does not include Quanta software)
Time: No limit (approximately 10–15 minutes).
Author: Edwin A. Reishman.
Publisher: Pearson Performance Solutions [No reply from publisher; status unknown].
Cross References: See T5:1444 (4 references), T4:1409 (7 references), T3:1300 (10 references), 8:1177 (52 references), and T2:2454 (15 references); for a review by Cecil A. Gibb, see 7:1149 (41 references); for reviews by Jerome E. Doppelt and Wayne K. Kirchner, see 6:1190 (6 references).

[1412]

Leadership Practices Inventory [Pfeiffer & Company International Publishers].

Purpose: Designed to provide ratings of five leadership behaviors.
Population: Managers.
Publication Dates: 1990–1992.
Acronym: LPI.
Scores, 5: Challenging the Process, Inspiring a Shared Vision, Enabling Others to Act, Modeling the Way, Encouraging the Heart.
Administration: Group.
Editions, 2: Self, Other.
Price Data: Price information available from publisher for trainer's package including LPI: Self-Assessment booklet and inventory, LPI: Other inventory, technical manual (1992, 31 pages) and trainer's manual (1990, 39 pages); LPI: Self-Assessment booklet and inventory; LPI: Other inventory; IBM-PC (or compatible) scoring software.
Time: Administration time not reported.
Comments: Scale for ratings by employees and for self-ratings.
Authors: James M. Kouzes and Barry Z. Posner.
Publisher: Jossey-Bass, A Wiley Company.
Cross References: See T5:1448 (1 reference); for reviews by Frederick T. L. Leong and Mary A. Lewis, see 12:213; see also T4:1411 (2 references).

[1413]

Leadership Practices Inventory—Individual Contributor [Second Edition].

Purpose: "Designed to assist a nonmanagerial leader in assessing the extent to which he or she engages in certain leadership behaviors."

Population: Nonmanagerial leaders.
Publication Dates: 1990–1997.
Acronym: LPI-IC.
Scores, 5: Challenging, Inspiring, Enabling, Modeling, Encouraging.
Administration: Group.
Forms, 2: Self, Observer.
Price Data: Available from publisher.
Time: Administration time not reported.
Comments: Nonmanagerial version of the Leadership Practices Inventory (1412); a 30-item Self or Observer rating; hand or computer scored (computer scoring recommended); computer scoring software available.
Authors: James M. Kouzes and Barry Z. Posner.
Publisher: Jossey-Bass, A Wiley Company.
Cross References: For reviews by John M. Enger and L. Carolyn Pearson, see 14:204; for reviews by Frederick T. L. Leong and Mary A. Lewis of an earlier edition of the Leadership Practices Inventory, see 12:213; see also T4:1411 (2 references).

[1414]

The Leadership Q-Sort Test (A Test of Leadership Values).

Purpose: Designed to "assess an individual's values with respect to the leadership role."
Population: Adults.
Publication Date: 1958.
Acronym: LQST.
Scores, 7: Personal Integrity, Consideration of Others, Mental Health, Technical Information, Decision Making, Teaching and Communication, Total.
Administration: Individual or group.
Price Data: Available from publisher.
Time: (40–45) minutes.
Author: Russell N. Cassel.
Publisher: Psychometric Affiliates.
Cross References: For reviews by Joel T. Campbell, Cecil A. Gibb, and William Stephenson, see 6:134 (6 references).

[1415]

Leadership Skills Inventory [Revised] [Consulting Resource Group International, Inc.].

Purpose: Designed to benchmark 60 leadership competencies and skills required for effective leadership; also offers 360° feedback with the LSI-Others version.
Population: Adults.
Publication Dates: 1992-2006.
Acronym: LSI.
Scores, 6: Self-Management Skills, Interpersonal Communication Skills, Coaching/Counseling and Problem Management Skills, Skills for Developing Teams and Organizations, Versatility and Organizational Development Skills, Total Score.

Administration: Individual or group.
Price Data, 2006: $16.95 per Leadership Skills Inventory-Self (2006, 20 pages); $9.95 per Leadership Skills Inventory-Others (2006, 8 pages); $38 per Trainer's Guidelines (1996, 18 pages); $50 per Transforming Leadership Book–Second Edition (1998, 340 pages).
Editions, 3: Self (print), Others (print), Self (online).
Time: (30) minutes.
Comments: Self-administered and self-scored.
Authors: Ken Keis and Terry D. Anderson.
Publisher: Consulting Resource Group International, Inc.

a) LEADERSHIP SKILLS INVENTORY-OTHERS.
Acronym: LSI-O.
Price Data: $9.95 per test booklet.
b) LEADERSHIP SKILLS INVENTORY-SELF.
Acronym: LSI-S.
Price Data: $16.95 per test booklet.
c) ONLINE LEADERSHIP SKILLS INVENTORY-SELF.
Acronym: Online LSI-S.
Price Data: $16.95 per online assessment code.
Cross References: For reviews by Alan D. Moore and Nambury S. Raju of an earlier edition, see 16:134; for reviews by Mary Henning-Stout and George C. Thornton, III of an earlier edition, see 13:176.

[1416]
Leadership Skills Profile.

Purpose: Designed to analyze "the strengths and weaknesses of managerial and executive candidates."
Population: Ages 18 and over.
Publication Date: 2003.
Acronym: LSP.
Scores: 42 Leadership Dimensions: Technical Orientation, Analytical Orientation, Decisiveness, Creativity, Thoroughness, Objectivity, Risk Taking, Open-Mindedness, First Impression, Interpersonal Relations, Sensitivity, Social Astuteness, Conflict Management, Communication, Formal Presentation, Persuasiveness, Negotiation, Listening, Achievement/Motivation, Self Discipline, Flexibility, Independence, Self Esteem, Emotional Control, Dependability, Ambition, General Leadership Effectiveness, Assuming Responsibility, Vision, Emphasizing Excellence, Organizational Spokesperson, Subordinate Involvement, Facilitating Teamwork, Inspirational Role Model, Short-Term Planning, Strategic Planning, Organizing the Work of Others, Delegation, Monitoring and Controlling, Motivating Others, Attracting Staff, Productivity.
Administration: Individual.
Price Data, 2006: $15 per test manual; $225 per administration; volume discounts available.
Time: [40] minutes.
Comments: Publisher scoring services provided via internet or fax.

Author: Douglas N. Jackson.
Publisher: Sigma Assessment Systems, Inc.
Cross References: For reviews by Philip G. Benson and John S. Geisler, see 16:135.

[1417]
Leadership Spectrum Profile.

Purpose: To identify leadership business priorities in a given situation, develop business acumen, improve team effectiveness, enhance strategic thinking, and to reflect that leadership requirements change by context or circumstance.
Population: Senior leaders, teams, and individuals in leadership positions.
Publication Dates: 1998–2000.
Acronym: LSP.
Scores: 6 choices: Inventor (new products/services), Catalyst (market growth), Developer (reduce risk and improve accountabilities), Performer (increase efficiency, quality, and resource utilization), Protector (build culture and develop talent), and Challenger (position for the future, check assumptions and trends) .
Administration: Group.
Price Data, 2005: $24.95 per manual/test booklet (2000, 31 pages), volume discounts available; $45 per Priority Balancing Handbook (110 pages); price information for online version is available from publisher.
Foreign Language Edition: Japanese language version is available.
Time: (12–18) minutes.
Comments: Results reflect the business priorities that are currently driving the leader; online version is available at www.leadershipspectrum.com.
Author: Mary Lippitt.
Publisher: Enterprise Management Ltd.

[1418]
Leadex: Leadership Assessment System.

Purpose: Designed to help "managers at all levels become more effective by increasing their self-awareness and self-understanding."
Population: Managers.
Publication Date: 1990.
Scores, 6: Vision and Values, Direction, Persuasion, Support, Development, Appreciation.
Administration: Individual or group.
Forms, 2: A (Self Rating), B (Feedback Questionnaire).
Price Data: Available from publisher.
Time: Administration time not reported.
Author: Karl Albrecht.
Publisher: Karl Albrecht International.

[1419]
Leading Edge Portrait.

Purpose: Designed as "an assessment of preferences for nine distinctive leadership roles."

Population: Age 13 and over.
Publication Date: 1997.
Scores, 9: Sage, Visionary, Magician, Globalist, Mentor, Ally, Sovereign, Guide, Artisan.
Administration: Group.
Manual: No manual.
Price Data, 2001: $15.25 per client kit; $138.70 per 10 item booklet/answer sheets; $106 per facilitator's guide.
Time: (30) minutes.
Comments: Self-scored instrument; can be accompanied by PowerPoint® software product facilitator's guide.
Author: Stuart Wells.
Publisher: CPP, Inc.

[1420]
Learned Behaviors Profile—Self/Other.

Purpose: "Designed to help people explore their patterns of behavior."
Population: Adults.
Publication Date: 1990.
Acronym: LBP.
Scores, 6: Caretaker, People-Pleaser, Workaholic, Martyr, Perfectionist, Tap Dancer.
Administration: Group.
Editions, 2: Self, Other.
Price Data: Price information available from publisher for LBP: Self inventory (31 pages); LBP: Other inventory (6 pages); each includes administrator's guide (no date, 2 pages).
Time: Administration time not reported.
Comments: Self-administered, self-scored.
Authors: J. William Pfeiffer and Judith A. Pfeiffer.
Publisher: Jossey-Bass, A Wiley Company.
Cross References: For reviews by Diane Billings Findley and John R. Graham, see 11:197.

[1421]
Learning Accomplishment Profile Diagnostic Edition.

Purpose: "Designed to provide the teacher of the young child with a simple criterion-referenced tool for systematic assessment of the child's existing skills."
Publication Dates: 1992–1997.
Administration: Individual or group.
Parts, 4: LAP-D Normed Assessment, LAP-D Screen, LAP (Revised Edition), Early LAP.
Comments: May be administered in station or individual format.
Publisher: Kaplan Early Learning Company.
 a) LEARNING ACCOMPLISHMENT PROFILE DIAGNOSTIC EDITION NORMED ASSESSMENT.
 Purpose: "Facilitates standardized, norm referenced assessment ... of developmental skills."
 Population: Ages 30–60 months.

Publication Date: 1992.
Acronym: LAP-D.
Scores, 8: 4 development areas: Fine Motor (Writing, Manipulation), Language (Comprehension, Naming), Gross Motor (Body Movement, Object Movement), Cognitive (Counting, Matching).
Price Data, 2001: $624.95 per Normed Assessment including examiner's manual (62 pages), technical report, scoring booklets, and training manual (55 pages); $25.95 per 20 scoring protocols; $19.95 per technical report; $9.95 per examiner's manual; $12.95 per 10 Partial Person pads; $9.95 per 10 Plain Paper pads or 10 Diamond Design Cutting pads; $199.95 per single-user software (diskette or CD-ROM); $899.95 per 5-user site license (diskette); $1,799.95 per 10-user site license (diskette).
Time: (45–90) minutes.
Comments: "Designed to assist in making relevant educational decisions with regard to young children and to enable the teacher to develop developmentally appropriate instructional objectives and strategies"; hand or computer scoring available; LAP-D Windows software Version 3.5 system requirements: Windows 3.1, 3.51, or 98, 80486 or higher microprocessor, VGA or higher resolution screen supported by Windows, 8MB or more RAM, Windows-compatible printer.
Authors: Aubrey D. Nehring, Ema F. Nehring, John R. Bruni, Jr., and Patricia L. Randolph.
 b) LEARNING ACCOMPLISHMENT PROFILE DIAGNOSTIC EDITION NORMED SCREEN.
 Purpose: "Quick initial developmental instruments designed as entry level to the diagnostic process."
 Population: Ages 3–5 years.
 Publication Date: 1997.
 Acronym: LAP-D Screen.
 Scores, 6: 4 developmental areas: Fine Motor (Writing, Manipulation), Language (Comprehension, Naming), Gross Motor, Cognitive.
 Price Data: $124.95 per Screen kit (specify age 3, age 4, or Kindergarten) including examiner's manual, 25 scoring booklets, 3 Kindergarten Progress Charts, and screening items (specify English or Spanish); $349.95 per ages 3/4/5 Screen package (specify English or Spanish); $9.95 per 30 scoring profiles (specify age 3, age 4, or Kindergarten, specify English or Spanish); $52.95 per Screen manuals for ages 3, 4, and 5 (specify English or Spanish).
 Time: (12–15) minutes, untimed.
 Comments: Designed to be completed by the child's classroom teacher; items selected from LAP-D Standardized Assessment.
 Author: Kaplan Press.

c) LEARNING ACCOMPLISHMENT PROFILE—REVISED EDITION.

Purpose: "A systematic, ongoing, criterion-referenced assessment of a child's existing skills in fine and gross motor, cognitive/language, personal/social, and self-help skills."

Population: Ages 3–6 years.

Publication Date: 1995.

Acronym: LAP-R.

Ratings, 7: Gross Motor, Fine Motor, Pre-Writing, Cognitive, Language, Self-Help, Personal/Social.

Price Data: $274.95 per kit including manipulatives, supplies, toys for use during assessment, 380 Learning Activities for Young Children cards, 20 scoring booklets, instruction manual (132 pages), and IEP forms; $89.95 per 10 manuals (specify English or Spanish); $6.50 per Social or Self-Help Observation Checklist.

Time: Administration time not reported.

Authors: Anne R. Sanford and Janet G. Zelman.

d) EARLY LEARNING ACCOMPLISHMENT PROFILE.

Purpose: "An ongoing, criterion-referenced assessment system covering gross motor, fine motor, cognitive, language, self-help, and social/emotional domains."

Population: Birth to 36 months.

Publication Date: 1995.

Acronym: E-LAP.

Ratings, 6: Gross Motor, Fine Motor, Cognitive, Language, Self-Help, Social/Emotional.

Price Data: $334.95 per Early Learning kit including manipulatives, toys, supplies, 20 scoring booklets, Early Learning Activity Cards, and instruction manual (111 pages); $89.95 per 10 manuals (specify English or Spanish); $22.95 per 20 scoring booklets (specify English or Spanish); $9.95 per manual.

Time: Administration time not reported.

Authors: M. Elayne Glover, Jodi L. Preminger, and Anne R. Sanford.

Cross References: For a review by Loraine J. Spenciner, see 16:136.

[1422]
Learning and Memory Battery.

Purpose: Used for assessing both specificity and sensitivity to diverse memory problems.

Population: Ages 20 to 80.

Publication Date: 1995.

Acronym: LAMB.

Scores: 7 subtests: Paragraph Learning, Word List, Word Pairs, Digit Span, Supraspan Digit, Simple Figure, Complex Figure.

Administration: Individual.

Price Data, 2006: $370 per complete kit including 25 recording forms, 25 profile/summary sheets, 100 Simple and Complex Figure drawing forms, administration tents, standard score conversion booklet, and manual (171 pages); $93 per manual; $99 per 25 recording forms; $19 per Standard Score Conversion Booklet; $15 per 100 Simple and Complex Figure Drawing Forms; $274 per administration tents (set of 2); $319 per LAMB Score Windows™ CD or 3.5-inch disk (unlimited use); price information available from publisher for Administration Windows™ 3.5-inch (per usage).

Time: (45–60) minutes.

Authors: James P. Schmidt and Tom N. Tombaugh.

Publisher: Multi-Health Systems, Inc.

Cross References: For reviews by Charles J. Long and Michelle L. Ries and by Wilfred G. Van Gorp, see 14:205.

[1423]
Learning and Study Strategies Inventory—High School Version.

Purpose: Designed to assist high school students "in determining their study skills strategies, problems and attitudes, and learning practices."

Population: Grades 9–12.

Publication Date: 1990.

Acronym: LASSI-HS.

Scores, 10: Attitude, Motivation, Time Management, Anxiety, Concentration, Information Processing, Selecting Main Ideas, Study Aids, Self Testing, Test Strategies.

Administration: Group.

Price Data, 2006: $2.75 per self-scored form, internet, or computer-scored form; quantity discounts available.

Time: (25–30) minutes.

Authors: Claire E. Weinstein and David R. Palmer.

Publisher: H & H Publishing Co., Inc.

Cross References: For reviews by Kenneth A. Kiewra and Robert T. Williams, see 13:177 (4 references).

[1424]
Learning and Study Strategies Inventory, Second Edition.

Purpose: Designed to assess "students' awareness about and use of learning and study strategies related to skill, will and self-regulation components of strategic learning."

Population: Grades 9 and over.

Publication Dates: 1987-2002.

Acronym: LASSI.

Scores, 10: Anxiety Scale, Attitude Scale, Concentration Scale, Information Processing Scale, Motivation Scale, Self-Testing Scale, Selecting Main Ideas Scale, Study Aids Scale, Time Management Scale, Test Strategies Scale.

Administration: Individual or group.
Foreign Language Edition: Spanish Version available for college students.
Time: (15-20) minutes.
Comments: This test can be self-administered and self-scored; can be computer administered and scored.
Authors: Claire E. Weinstein, Ann C. Schulte, and David R. Palmer.
Publisher: H&H Publishing Company, Inc.
  a) COLLEGE VERSION.
  Population: College students.
  Price Data: $3.25 per complete kit including test booklet and user's manual (2002, 28 pages).
  b) HIGH SCHOOL VERSION.
  Population: Grades 9-12.
  Price Data: $2.75 per complete kit including test booklet and user's manual (2002, 28 pages).
  c) SPANISH VERSION.
  Population: College students.
  Price Data: $3 per complete kit including test booklet and user's manual (2002, 28 pages).
Cross References: See T5:1455 (13 references) and T4:1417 (1 reference); for reviews by Martha W. Blackwell and Steven C. Hayes of an earlier edition, see 11:198 (3 references).

[1425]
Learning/Behavior Problems Checklist.

Purpose: Designed "to identify children at risk of or already experiencing behavior problems or learning disorders."
Population: Students in the primary grades.
Publication Date: 1990.
Scores: Not scored.
Administration: Individual.
Price Data, 2002: $10 per 25 checklists.
Time: [5–10] minutes.
Comments: Ratings by teachers.
Author: Academic Consulting & Testing Service.
Publisher: Academic Consulting & Testing Service.

[1426]
Learning Disabilities Diagnostic Inventory.

Purpose: Designed to identify specific learning disabilities and to help diagnose dysphasia, dyslexia, dysgraphia, dyscalculia, and disorders in executive function.
Population: Ages 8-0 to 17-11.
Publication Date: 1998.
Acronym: LDDI.
Scores, 6: Listening, Speaking, Reading, Writing, Mathematics, Reasoning.
Administration: Individual.
Price Data, 2006: $120 per complete kit including examiner's manual (106 pages) and 50 rating summary booklets; $50 per examiner's manual; $75 per 50 rating summary booklets.

Time: (10–20) minutes.
Authors: Donald D. Hammill and Brian R. Bryant.
Publisher: PRO-ED.
Cross References: For reviews by Terry B. Gutkin and John MacDonald, see 14:206.

[1427]
Learning Disability Evaluation Scale (Renormed).

Purpose: "Developed to aid in diagnosis, placement, and planning for learning disabled children and adolescents."
Population: Grades K–12.
Publication Dates: 1983–1996.
Acronym: LDES.
Scores, 7: Listening, Thinking, Speaking, Reading, Writing, Spelling, Mathematical Calculations.
Administration: Individual.
Price Data, 2005: $152 per complete kit including 50 Pre-Referral Learning Problem Checklist forms, 50 Pre-Referral Intervention Strategies Documentation forms, 50 LDES rating forms, LDES technical manual (1996, 71 pages), Learning Disability Intervention manual (1995, 223 pages), and Parents' Guide to Learning Disabilities (1991, 200 pages); $30 per 50 Pre-Referral Learning Problem Checklist forms; $30 per 50 Pre-Referral Intervention Strategies Documentation forms; $35 per 50 LDES rating forms; $15 per technical manual; $25 per Learning Disability Intervention manual; $17 per Parents' Guide to Learning Disabilities; $25 per computerized Quick Score (Win); $225 per computerized manual (Win).
Time: (15–20) minutes.
Comments: Ratings by teacher; the 1996 edition is renormed but content is not revised.
Authors: Stephen B. McCarney (test and manual) and Angela Marie Bauer (manual).
Publisher: Hawthorne Educational Services, Inc.
Cross References: For reviews by Patricia B. Keith and Loraine J. Spenciner, see 14:207; for reviews by Glen P. Aylward and Scott W. Brown of an earlier edition, see 12:214 (1 reference).

[1428]
Learning Efficiency Test-II (1998 Revision).

Purpose: "Yields information about a person's preferred modality for learning and provides insights about the impact of interference on memory storage and retrieval, and the kinds of metacognitive strategies used during learning."
Population: Ages 5–75+.
Publication Dates: 1981–1998.
Acronym: LET-II.
Scores, 15: Visual Ordered Recall (Immediate Recall, Short Term Recall, Long Term Recall) Visual Unordered Recall (Immediate Recall, Short Term Re-

call, Long Term Recall), Auditory Ordered Recall (Immediate Recall, Short Term Recall, Long Term Recall), Auditory Unordered Recall (Immediate Recall, Short Term Recall, Long Term Recall), Total Visual Memory, Total Auditory Memory, Global Memory.
Administration: Individual.
Price Data, 2006: $92 per test kit including manual, stimulus cards, and 50 record forms.
Time: (10–15) minutes.
Author: Raymond E. Webster.
Publisher: Academic Therapy Publications.
Cross References: See T5:1462 (3 references); for reviews by Alice J. Corkill and Gregory Schraw of the 1992 Revision, see 12:215; see also T4:1423 (1 reference); for a review by Robert G. Harrington of an earlier form, see 9:601.

[1429]
Learning Organization Practices Profile.

Purpose: Designed "to facilitate a diagnostic process by which an organization can measure its capacity as a learning organization."
Population: Organizations.
Publication Date: 1994.
Acronym: LOPP.
Scores, 12: Vision and Strategy, Executive Practices, Managerial Practices, Climate, Organizational and Job Structure, Information Flow, Individual and Team Practices, Work Processes, Performance Goals and Feedback, Training and Education, Rewards and Recognition, Individual and Team Development.
Administration: Group.
Price Data: Available from publisher.
Time: Administration time not reported.
Author: Michael J. O'Brien.
Publisher: Jossey-Bass, A Wiley Company.
Cross References: For reviews by Neil P. Lewis and Michael J. Zickar, see 14:208.

[1430]
Learning Process Questionnaire.

Purpose: "To assess the extent to which a secondary school student endorses different approaches to learning and the more important motives and strategies comprising those approaches."
Population: Secondary students.
Publication Dates: 1985–1987.
Acronym: LPQ.
Scores, 9: Surface Motive, Surface Strategy, Deep Motive, Deep Strategy, Achieving Motive, Achieving Strategy, Surface Approach, Deep Approach, Achieving Approach.
Administration: Individual or group.
Price Data, 2006: A$11.50 per 10 questionnaires; A$7.70 per 10 answer sheets; A$5.50 per score key; A$34.10 per monograph entitled Student Approaches

to Learning and Studying (1987, 151 pages); A$29.80 per manual (1987, 36 pages); A$51.80 per starter set.
Time: 20(40) minutes.
Comments: Tertiary counterpart of the Study Process Questionnaire (T6:2417).
Author: John Biggs.
Publisher: Australian Council for Educational Research Ltd. [Australia]
Cross References: See T5:1466 (9 references); for reviews by Robert D. Brown and Cathy W. Hall, see 11:202 (1 reference); for a review by Cathy W. Hall of the Study Process Questionnaire, see 11:389.

[1431]
Learning Skills Profile.

Purpose: To assess the gap between personal aptitudes and critical skills required by a job.
Population: Junior high to adults.
Publication Date: 1993.
Acronym: LSP.
Scores, 36: 3 scores: Personal Learning Skill, Job Skill Demand, and Learning Gap in each of 12 skill areas: Interpersonal Skills (Leadership Skill, Relationship Skill, Help Skill), Analytical Skills (Theory Skill, Quantitative Skill, Technology Skill), Information Skills (Sense-Making Skill, Information-Gathering Skill, Information Analysis Skill), Behavioral Skills (Goal Setting Skill, Action Skill, Initiative Skill).
Administration: Group or individual.
Price Data, 2006: $50 per complete kit including 10 workbooks and profiles, and 1 set of reusable LSP cards and instructions; $40 per 10 workbooks; $15 per reusable LSP cards, instructions, and profiles; also available online at $10 per person.
Time: [45–60] minutes.
Comments: Self-scored profile.
Authors: Richard E. Boyatzis and David A. Kolb.
Publisher: Hay Group.
Cross References: See T5:1467 (1 reference); for a review by David O. Herman, see 13:179.

[1432]
Learning Style Indicator [Revised].

Purpose: Designed to identify "preferred learning style and preferences."
Population: Ages 15 years and over.
Publication Dates: 1996-2006.
Acronym: LSI.
Scores, 4: Behavioral/Action/Independent, Cognitive/Analysis/Visual, Interpersonal/Harmony/Auditory, Affective/Expression/Experiential.
Administration: Individual or group.
Price Data, 2006: $12.95 per test booklet (2006, 12 pages); $13.95 per In-Depth Interpretations booklet (2006, 28 pages); $24.95 per access code online version; $37.95 per Trainer's Guidelines (1996, 28 pages).

Time: (30) minutes (90-180 minutes program options).
Comments: Self-administered and self-scored; can be used in conjunction with the Instructional Style Indicator (1250).
Authors: Ken Keis and Everett T. Robinson.
Publisher: Consulting Resource Group International, Inc.

[1433]
Learning Style Inventory [Price Systems, Inc.].

Purpose: Identifies "the conditions under which an individual is most likely to learn, remember, and achieve."
Population: Grades 3–12.
Publication Dates: 1976–1996.
Acronym: LSI.
Scores: 22 areas: Noise Level, Light, Temperature, Design, Motivation, Persistent, Responsible, Structure, Learning Alone/Peer Oriented, Authority Figures Present, Learn in Several Ways, Auditory, Visual, Tactile, Kinesthetic, Requires Intake, Evening/Morning, Late Morning, Afternoon, Needs Mobility, Parent Figure Motivated, Teacher Motivated, plus a Consistency score.
Administration: Group or individual.
Price Data, 2006: $22.50 per 10 answer sheets for Grades 3 & 4 or for Grade 5 thru 12 (includes scoring); $7.50 or less per group and subscale summaries available from publisher only in addition to individual profiles; $.60 per individual interpretative booklet; $12.50 per manual (1997, 100 pages); $3.25 per research report; $395 per computerized self-administered inventory program in English ($495 for multi-language version) with 100 administrations ($60 per 100 additional administrations) (Windows); $495 for Scanwin program permitting schools to scan and profile forms on site (includes multi-language capability); $.60 per answer form to use with Scanwin.
Time: (20–30) minutes.
Comments: PC compatible computer required for (optional) computerized administration; NCS Pearson Optical Mark Reader with dual pencil reader; Scrantron 8000, 8200, 8400, or SCANMARK 2550, 2660, 2800, 4000 orr 5500 Scanner with dual pencil read for Scanwin; may be administered online at www.learningstyle.com.
Authors: Rita Dunn, Kenneth Dunn, and Gary E. Price.
Publisher: Price Systems, Inc.
Cross References: See T5:1470 (5 references); for reviews by Thomas R. Knapp and Craig S. Shwery, see 13:180 (9 references); see also T4:1432 (3 references); for reviews by Jan N. Hughes and Alida S. Westman of an earlier edition, see 11:203 (6 references).

[1434]
Learning Style Inventory, Version 3.1.

Purpose: Identifies an individual's learning preference and explores the opportunities that different learning styles present.
Population: Ages 18-60.
Publication Dates: 1976–2005.
Acronym: LSI3.1.
Scores: 4 scores: Concrete Experience, Active Experimentation, Reflective Observation, Abstract Conceptualization; 4 learning styles: Accommodating, Diverging, Converging, Assimilating.
Administration: Group or individual.
Price Data, 2006: $90 per 10 self-scoring booklets; $50 per facilitator's guide to learning (2000, 81 pages); PowerPoint slides free with purchase; also available online at $15 per person. Free technical manual and bibliography of research.
Foreign Language Editions: French and Spanish versions available.
Time: [20–30] minutes.
Author: David A. Kolb.
Publisher: Hay Group.
Cross References: For reviews by Cecil R. Reynolds and David Shum, see 15:136; see T5:1469 (13 references) and T4:1438 (12 references); for a review by Noel Gregg of an earlier edition, see 10:173 (17 references); see also 9:607 (7 references).

[1435]
Learning Style Profile.

Purpose: Designed to evaluate student learning style as the basis for student advisement and placement, instructional strategy, and the evaluation of learning.
Population: Grades 6–12.
Publication Dates: 1986–1990.
Acronym: LSP.
Scores, 23: Cognitive Skills (Analytic, Spatial, Discrimination, Categorizing, Sequential Processing, Memory), Perceptual Responses (Visual, Auditory, Emotive), Persistence Orientation, Verbal Risk Orientation, Study and Instructional Preferences (Verbal-Spatial, Manipulative, Study Time [Early Morning, Late Morning, Afternoon, Evening], Grouping, Posture, Mobility, Sound, Lighting, Temperature).
Administration: Group.
Price Data: Available from publisher.
Foreign Language Edition: Spanish version available.
Time: (50–60) minutes.
Authors: James W. Keefe (test, Handbook II), John S. Monk (test), Charles A. Letteri (test, Handbook I), Marlin Languis (test), Rita Dunn (test), John M. Jenkins (Handbook I), and Patricia Rosenlund (Handbook I).
Publisher: National Association of Secondary School Principals.

Cross References: For reviews by Sonya Blixt and James A. Jones and by Philip Nagy, see 12:217 (1 reference); see also T4:1433 (1 reference).

[1436]
Learning Style Questionnaire.

Purpose: Developed to "help individuals measure their preferences for learning."
Population: Adults.
Publication Date: 1999.
Acronym: LSQ.
Scores, 4: Participation, Reflecting, Structuring, Experiencing.
Administration: Group.
Price Data, 2001: $6.50 per questionnaire; $29.95 per leader's guide (24 pages).
Time: (20–30) minutes.
Author: Chris Hutcheson.
Publisher: HRD Press, Inc.

[1437]
Learning Styles Inventory [Western Psychological Services].

Purpose: Provides a quick measure of learning preferences.
Population: Junior High School, High School, College, Adults in business settings.
Publication Dates: 1976–1988.
Acronym: LSI.
Scores, 21: Conditions for Learning (Peer, Organization, Goal Setting, Competition, Instructor, Detail, Independence, Authority), Area of Interest (Numeric, Qualitative, Inanimate, People), Mode of Learning (Listening, Reading, Iconic, Direct Experience), Expectation for Course Grade (A-expectation, B-expectation, C-expectation, D-expectation, Total expectation).
Administration: Group.
Forms, 4: A (College), B (High School), C (Junior High School), E (College-Easy).
Price Data, 2006: $109.50 per complete kit including 2 each of Forms A, B, C, and E inventory booklets, 1 Form ABC computer-scorable booklet, 1 Form E computer-scorable booklet, 2 prepaid mail-in booklets for computer scoring and interpretation, and manual (1988, 76 pages); $58 per 10 inventory booklets (specify form); $14 per computer-scorable booklet (price depends on quantity ordered and includes scoring service by publisher); $53.50 per manual.
Time: (15–20) minutes.
Comments: Previously listed as Canfield Learning Styles Inventory.
Author: Albert A. Canfield.
Publisher: Western Psychological Services.
Cross References: See T5:392 (2 references) and T4:378 (5 references); for a review by Stephen L. Benton, see 11:57 (2 references); for reviews by John

Biggs and C. Dean Miller of an earlier edition, see 9:609 (1 reference).

[1438]
Learning Styles Inventory [Educational Activities, Inc.].

Purpose: Designed to assess an individual's learning style of receiving and expressing information.
Population: Intermediate and secondary level students.
Publication Dates: 1993-2000.
Acronym: LSI.
Scores, 9: Visual Language, Visual Numeric, Auditory Language, Auditory Numeric, Tactile Concrete, Social Individual, Social Group, Oral Expressiveness, Written Expressiveness.
Administration: Group.
Price Data, 2006: $98 per CD-ROM, management, and documentation; $490 per site license.
Foreign Language Editions: Available in English and Spanish with audio.
Time: Administration time not reported.
Comments: Pencil-and-paper or computer (Windows/Mac) administered.
Authors: Jerry F. Brown and Richard M. Cooper.
Publisher: Educational Activities Software.
Cross References: For reviews by Robert Brown and Robert J. Drummond, see 14:209.

[1439]
Learning Styles Inventory [Piney Mountain Press, Inc.].

Purpose: Designed to identify learning needs of students.
Population: Grades 6–12.
Publication Dates: 1988–2000.
Scores: 9 subtopics in 2 areas: Learning (Auditory Language, Visual Language, Auditory Numerical, Visual Numerical, Auditory-Visual-Kinesthetic), Working (Group Learner, Individual Learner, Oral Expressive, Written Expressive).
Administration: Individual or group.
Price Data, 2002: $195 per single station software; $395 per multistation software including instructor guide, software, multimedia CD, video, and response sheets; $995 for Network version.
Time: [11] minutes.
Author: Al Babich.
Publisher: Piney Mountain Press, Inc.
Cross References: For reviews by Kevin D. Crehan and Mark H. Fugate, see 12:218.

[1440]
Learning Styles Inventory, Version III.

Purpose: Designed to identify "student preferences for particular instructional techniques."

Population: Elementary and middle school students.
Publication Dates: 1978–2002.
Acronym: LSI-III.
Scores, 9: Direct Instruction, Instruction through Technology, Simulations, Projects, Independent Study, Peer Teaching, Drill and Recitation (Elementary school only), Discussion (Middle school only), Teaching Games (Middle school only).
Administration: Group.
Forms, 3: Elementary school, Middle school, Teacher.
Price Data, 2004: $17.95 per technical and administration manual (2002, 95 pages); $29.95 per class set including 30 student instruments, 1 teacher instrument, and 1 classroom summary sheet.
Time: (15) minutes.
Authors: Joseph S. Renzulli, Mary G. Rizza, and Linda R. Smith.
Publisher: Creative Learning Press, Inc.
Cross References: See T5:1474 (2 references) and T4:1435 (1 reference); for a review by Benson P. Low of a previous edition, see 9:608.

[1441]
Learning Tactics Inventory.

Purpose: "Provides … individuals with information about how they learn and illustrates behaviors that they can adopt to become more versatile learners."
Population: Managers, leaders, executives.
Publication Date: 1999.
Acronym: LTI.
Scores: 4 learning tactics: Action, Thinking, Feeling, Accessing Others.
Administration: Individual.
Price Data, 2006: $32 per Facilitator's Guide (41 pages); $17 per Participant's Workbook/Survey; quantity discounts are available.
Time: 15 minutes.
Comments: An inventory of the behaviors individuals have reported using when engaged in the task of learning from experience; self-scored; Facilitator's Guide includes details of workshop procedures, reproducible overheads, and handout masters.
Author: Maxine Dalton.
Publisher: Jossey-Bass Pfeiffer.
Cross References: For reviews by Kathleen A. Dolgos and William B. Michael, see 15:137.

[1442]
Learning/Working Styles Inventory.

Purpose: "Developed to assess learning styles and preferred working conditions."
Population: Grades 7–12 and adults.
Publication Dates: 1989–2000.
Scores: 25 subtopics in 5 areas: Physical Domain (Kinesthetic, Visual, Tactile, Auditory), Social Domain (Group, Individual), Environmental Domain (Formal Design, Informal Design, Bright Lights, Dim Lights, Warm Temperature, Cool Temperature, With Sound, Without Sound), Mode of Expression Domain (Oral Expressive, Written Expressive), Work Characteristics Domain (Outdoors, Indoors, Sedentary, Non-Sedentary, Lifting, Non-Lifting, Data, People, Things).
Administration: Group and individual.
Price Data, 2002: $195 per single station software, $395 per multistation software including instructor guide, software, multimedia CD, video, and response sheets; $995 for Network version.
Time: [15] minutes.
Comments: Previously entitled Vocational Learning Styles.
Author: Helena Hendrix-Frye.
Publisher: Piney Mountain Press, Inc.
Cross References: For reviews by Leo M. Harvill and Craig N. Mills of the earlier edition (Vocational Learning Styles), see 12:410.

[1443]
Leatherman Leadership Questionnaire [Revised].

Purpose: "To aid in selecting leaders, providing specific feedback to participants on their leadership knowledge for career counseling, conducting accurate needs analysis, and screening for assessment centers or giving pre/post assessment feedback."
Population: Managers, supervisors, team leaders, and potential leaders.
Publication Dates: 1987–1992.
Acronym: LLQ.
Scores, 28: Assigning Work, Career Counseling, Coaching Employees, Oral Communication, Managing Change, Handling Employee Complaints, Dealing with Employee Conflicts, Counseling Employees, Helping an Employee Make Decisions, Delegating, Taking Disciplinary Action, Handling Emotional Situations, Setting Goals/Planning with Employees, Handling Employee Grievances, Conducting Employee Meetings, Giving Positive Feedback, Negotiating, Conducting Performance Appraisals, Establishing Performance Standards, Persuading/Influencing Employees, Making Presentations to Employees, Problem Solving with Employees, Conducting Selection Interviews, Team Building, Conducting Termination Interviews, Helping an Employee Manage Time, One-on-One Training, Total.
Subtests, 2: May be administered in separate parts.
Administration: Group.
Price Data: Available from publisher.
Time: (300–325) minutes for battery; (150–165) minutes per part.
Comments: Complete test administered in 2 parts; machine scored by publisher.
Author: Richard W. Leatherman.

Publisher: International Training Consultants, Inc. [No response from publisher; status unknown].

Cross References: For reviews by Jeffrey S. Rain and Lawrence M. Rudner, see 12:219; for reviews by Walter Katkovsky and William D. Porterfield of an earlier edition, see 11:205.

[1444]
Leeds Scales for the Self-Assessment of Anxiety and Depression.

Purpose: Self-assessment measure of the severity of symptoms of clinical anxiety and depression.

Population: Psychiatric patients.

Publication Date: 1976.

Scores, 4: Depression (General, Specific), Anxiety (General, Specific).

Administration: Group or individual.

Price Data: Available from publisher.

Time: Administration time not reported.

Comments: Self-rating scale.

Authors: R. P. Smith, G. W. K. Bridge, and Max Hamilton.

Publisher: Psychological Test Publications [England] [No reply from publisher; status unknown].

Cross References: See T5:1481 (4 references) and T4:1440 (11 references); for reviews by John Duckitt and H. J. Eysenck, see 9:611 (4 references).

[1445]
Leisure Interest Inventory.

Purpose: Designed to assess "preferred leisure activities."

Population: College students.

Publication Date: 1969.

Acronym: LII.

Scores, 5: Sociability, Games, Art, Mobility, Immobility.

Administration: Group.

Price Data: Available from publisher.

Time: (20-25) minutes.

Author: Edwina E. Hubert.

Publisher: Edwina E. Hubert, Ph.D.

[1446]
Leisure to Occupations Connection Search

Purpose: Designed to allow the user to explore career options based on leisure-time interests.

Population: Seventh-grade students through adults.

Publication Date: 1999.

Acronym: LOCS.

Scores: Scores interests in 100 leisure activities.

Administration: Individual.

Price Data, 2006: $29.95 for two packages of 25 inventories and a professional's manual (6 pages).

Time: (45) minutes.

Comments: Lists related occupations for each leisure activity; 12-panel foldout; self-scoring and self-interpreting; consumable; no other components needed.

Authors: Carl McDaniels and Sue Rife Mullins.

Publisher: JIST Publishing, Inc.

[1447]
Leiter International Performance Scale—Revised.

Purpose: Constructed as a "nonverbal cognitive assessment."

Population: Ages 2.0–20.11, adults.

Publication Dates: 1936–1998.

Acronym: Leiter-R.

Scores, 31: Visualization and Reasoning (Figure Ground, Design Analogies, Form Completion, Matching, Sequential Order, Repeated Patterns, Picture Context, Classification, Paper Folding, Figure Rotation), VR Composite (Fluid Reasoning, Brief IQ, Fundamental Visualization, Spatial Visualization, Full IQ), Attention and Memory Associated Pairs, Immediate Recognition, Forward Memory, Attention Sustained, Reverse Memory, Visual Coding, Spatial Memory, Delayed Pairs, Delayed Recognition, Attention Divided), AM Composite (Memory Screen, Associative Memory, Memory Span, Attention, Memory Process, Recognition Memory).

Administration: Individual.

Price Data, 2005: $895 per complete kit (in rolling backpack) including manual (1997, 378 pages), 3 easel books, VR response cards, AM response cards, manipulatives, 20 each VR and AM record forms, Attention Sustained booklets A, B, and C, and the Growth Profile Booklet and the rating scales; $850 per complete kit (in cloth carrying case); $25 per 20 record forms (specify battery); $15 per 20 Attention Sustained booklets (specify form); $10 per 20 rating scale record forms (specify form); $25 per 20 Growth Profile booklets, $75 per manual.

Time: (90) minutes.

Comments: May calculate growth scores (criterion-referenced scores) to assess improvement in cognitive skills; computer scoring software available requiring Windows 3.1, Windows 95 or Windows 98 operating systems.

Authors: Gale H. Roid and Lucy J. Miller.

Publisher: Stoelting Co.

Cross References: For reviews by Gary L. Marco and Terry A. Stinnett, see 14:211; see also T5:1485 (64 references), T4:1446 (33 references), T3:1319 (16 references), and T2:505 (18 references); for a review by Emmy E. Werner of the original version, see 6:526 (10 references); see also 5:408 (17 references); for a review by Gwen F. Arnold and an excerpted review by Laurance F. Shaffer, see 4:349 (25 references).

[1448]
Level of Service/Case Management Inventory: An Offender Assessment System.
Purpose: Designed to help "determine an offender's risk/needs level so that an appropriate level of service can be provided."
Population: Offenders ages 16 and over.
Publication Date: 2004.
Acronym: LS/CMI.
Scores: 8 Risk/Need factors: Criminal History, Education/Employment, Family/Marital, Leisure/Recreation, Companions, Alcohol/Drug Problem, Procriminal Attitude/Orientation, Antisocial Pattern.
Administration: Individual.
Price Data, 2006: $209 per complete kit including user's manual, scoring guide, and 25 each of interview guides, offender history forms, Quikscore forms, ColorPlot profiles, and case management protocols; $75 per user's manual (228 pages); $81 per 25 interview guides; $16 per 25 offender history forms; $49 per 25 QuikScore forms; $22 per 25 ColorPlot profile forms; $243 per software kit.
Time: (20–30) minutes.
Comments: Computer version available.
Authors: D. A. Andrews, James L. Bonta, and J. Stephen Wormith.
Publisher: Multi-Health Systems, Inc.

[1449]
Level of Service Inventory—Revised: Screening Version.
Purpose: Designed to provide "a risk/needs assessment important to offender treatment planning."
Population: Ages 16 and older.
Publication Date: 1998.
Acronym: LSI-R:SV.
Scores: Total score only.
Administration: Individual.
Price Data, 2006: $117 per complete kit including 25 interview guides, 25 QuikScore™ forms, and manual (1998, 26 pages); $68 per 25 interview guides/QuikScore™ forms; $30 per 25 interview guides; $50 per 25 QuikScore™ forms; $57 per manual; $59 per specimen set including 3 interview guides, 3 QuikScore™ forms, and manual; computer version also available.
Time: (10–15) minutes.
Authors: Don Andrews and James Bonta.
Publisher: Multi-Health Systems, Inc.
Cross References: For reviews by Ira S. Katz and Kevin J. McCarthy, see 15:138.

[1450]
The Level of Service Inventory—Revised [2003 Norms Update].
Purpose: Designed as a "quantitative survey of attributes of offenders and their situations relevant to level of service decisions."

Population: Ages 16 and older.
Publication Dates: 1995–2003.
Acronym: LSI-R.
Scores: Total score only.
Administration: Individual.
Price Data, 2006: $182 per complete kit including manual (2001, 63 pages), 25 Interview guides, 25 QuikScore forms, and 25 ColorPlot profiles; $64 per manual; $124 per 25 each of Interview guides, QuikScore forms, and ColorPlot profiles; $81 per 25 interview guides; $48 per 25 QuikScore forms; $25 per 25 ColorPlot profile forms; $79 per specimen set including manual, 3 interview guides, 3 QuikScore forms, and 3 ColorPlot profiles.
Foreign Language Editions: French-Canadian and Spanish forms, interview guides, and ColorPlot profiles available.
Time: (30–45) minutes.
Comments: Windows computerized version available on CD or 3.5-inch disk.
Authors: Don A. Andrews and James L. Bonta.
Publisher: Multi-Health Systems, Inc.
Cross References: For reviews by Solomon M. Fulero and Romeo Vitelli of an earlier edition, see 14:212.

[1451]
Levine-Pilowsky [Depression] Questionnaire.
Purpose: A questionnaire technique for classifying depression.
Population: Adults.
Publication Date: 1979.
Acronym: LPD.
Scores: 9 subscales: Insomnia (Initial), Sleep (General), Paranoia, Appetite, Insomnia (Late), Crying, Diurnal Variation, Hopelessness, Intensity of Depression.
Administration: Individual or group.
Manual: No manual.
Price Data: Available from publisher.
Time: (10) minutes.
Author: I. Pilowsky.
Publisher: I. Pilowsky [Australia].
Cross References: See T4:1448 (3 references).

[1452]
Lexington Developmental Scales.
Purpose: To "provide an individual graph or profile which depicts the child's developmental age level."
Population: Ages birth-6 years.
Publication Dates: 1973-1977.
Acronym: LDS.
Scores: Contains behavioral and experimental items rated by examiner in 4 areas: Motor, Language, Cognitive, Personal and Social.
Administration: Individual administration to ages birth-2 years.

Price Data: Not available.
Time: (60) minutes in children birth-2 years; time varies for older children.
Comments: Long and Short Forms; may be used by parents and volunteers; "particularly helpful in pre- and post-testing"; additional testing materials must be supplied by the examiner.
Authors: United Cerebral Palsy of the Bluegrass, John V. Irwin, Margaret Norris Ward, Ann B. Greis, Carol C. Deen, Valerie C. Cooley, Alice A. Auvenshine, Rhea A. Taylor, C. A. Coleman.
Publisher: Child Development Centers of the Bluegrass, Inc.
Cross References: See T5:1490 (2 references) and T4:1450 (1 reference); for reviews by Michael J. Roznowski and Zona R. Weeks, see 9:615 (1 reference); see also T3:1322 (1 reference).

[1453]
The Life Adjustment Inventory.
Purpose: Developed to survey "the extent to which a secondary school curriculum meets the needs of all its pupils."
Population: Grades 9–12.
Publication Date: 1951.
Scores, 14: General Feeling of Adjustment to the Curriculum, Reading and Study Skills, Communication and Listening Skills, General Social Skills and Etiquette, Boy-Girl Relationships, Religion/Morals/Ethics, Functional Citizenship, Vocational Orientation and Preparation, Education for Physical and Mental Health, Education for Family Living, Orientation to Science, Consumer Education, Development of Appreciation for and Creativity in the Arts, Education for Wise Use of Leisure Time.
Administration: Group.
Price Data: Available from publisher.
Time: (20–25) minutes.
Authors: Ronald C. Doll and J. Wayne Wrightstone.
Publisher: Psychometric Affiliates.
Cross References: See P:145 (1 reference); for reviews by John W. M. Rothney and Helen Schacter, see 4:67.

[1454]
Life Attitudes Schedule: A Risk Assessment for Suicidal and Life-Threatening Behaviors.
Purpose: Designed to "measure the cognitive, affective, and action-oriented components of suicide proneness."
Population: Ages 15–20.
Publication Date: 2004.
Administration: Individual or group.
Forms, 2: Life Attitudes Schedule, Life Attitudes Schedule: Short.
Price Data, 2006: $118 per complete kit including technical manual (80 pages), 10 item booklets, and 25 Quikscore forms each for LAS and LAS:S; $49 per

technical manual; $25 per 10 item booklets (reusable); $39 per 25 LAS Quikscore forms; $33 per 25 LAS:S Quikscore forms.
Authors: Peter M. Lewinsohn, Jennifer Langhinrichsen-Rohling, Paul Rohde, and Richard A. Langford.
Publisher: Multi-Health Systems, Inc.
a) LIFE ATTITUDES SCHEDULE.
  Acronym: LAS.
  Scores, 12: Composite Scores (Physical, Psychological), Content Scales (Health-Related, Death-Related, Injury-Related, Self-Related), Modality Type Scales (Actions, Thoughts, Feelings), Valence Scales (Negative, Positive), Total.
  Time: (30) minutes.
b) LIFE ATTITUDES SCHEDULE: SHORT.
  Acronym: LAS:S.
  Scores, 3: Physical, Psychological, Total.
  Time: (10) minutes.

[1455]
Life Stressors and Social Resources Inventory—Adult Form.
Purpose: "Provides an integrated picture of an individual's current life context" including "stable life stressors and social resources."
Population: Healthy adults, psychiatric patients, and medical patients.
Publication Dates: 1988–1994.
Acronym: LISRES-A.
Scores: 16 scales: 9 Life Stressor Scales (Physical Health, Home/Neighborhood, Financial, Work, Spouse or Partner, Children, Extended Family, Friends, Negative Life Events); 7 Social Resources Scales (Financial, Work, Spouse or Partner, Children, Extended Family, Friends, Positive Life Events).
Administration: Individual or group.
Price Data, 2006: $165 per introductory kit including manual (1994, 40 pages), 10 reusable item booklets, and 50 hand-scorable answer/profile forms.
Time: [10] minutes.
Comments: May be administered using either a self-report or a structured interview format.
Authors: Rudolf H. Moos (instrument and manual) and Bernice S. Moos (manual).
Publisher: Psychological Assessment Resources, Inc.
Cross References: See T5:1495 (1 reference); for reviews by M. Allan Cooperstein and Richard B. Stuart, see 13:184 (1 reference).

[1456]
Life Stressors and Social Resources Inventory—Youth Form.
Purpose: "Provides an integrated picture of a youth's current life context … assesses stable life stressors and social resources as well as changes in them over time."

Population: Ages 12–18.
Publication Dates: 1990–1994.
Acronym: LISRES-Y.
Scores, 16: 9 Life Stressors Scales (Physical Health, Home and Money, Parents, Siblings, Extended Family, School, Friends, Boyfriend/Girlfriend, Negative Life Events); 7 Social Resources Scales (Parents, Siblings, Extended Family, School, Friends, Boyfriend/Girlfriend, Positive Life Events).
Administration: Individual or Group.
Editions, 2: Youth, Adult.
Price Data, 2006: $165 per introductory kit including manual (1994, 38 pages), 10 item booklets, and 50 hand-scorable answer/profile forms.
Time: (45) minutes for self-report; (45–90) minutes for structured interview.
Comments: Available as self-report or structured interview; structured interview "allows an interviewer to use the inventory with youths whose reading and comprehension skills are below a sixth-grade level."
Authors: Rudolf H. Moos and Bernice S. Moos.
Publisher: Psychological Assessment Resources, Inc.
Cross References: See T5:1496 (1 reference); for reviews by Kevin D. Crehan and Albert Oosterhof, see 13:185 (1 reference).

[1457]
Life Style Questionnaire.

Purpose: To provide information regarding vocational interests and attitudes.
Population: Ages 14 and over.
Publication Date: No date on test materials.
Acronym: LSQ.
Scores: 13 scales: Expressive/Imaginative, Logical/Analytical, Managerial/Enterprising, Precise/Administrative, Active/Concrete, Supportive/Social, Risk Taking/Uncertainty, Perseverance/Determination, Self Evaluation, Sensitivity/Other Awareness, Affiliation, Degree to Which a Vocation is Associated with Self Fulfillment, Degree of Certainty.
Administration: Group or individual.
Price Data, 2001: £35 per specimen set; £4 per answer sheet and graph; £6.50 per questionnaire booklet; £25 per manual (26 pages); £459 per computer software version.
Time: Administration time not reported.
Author: James S. Barrett.
Publisher: The Test Agency Limited [England] [No reply from publisher; status unknown].
Cross References: For a review by Robert B. Slaney, see 9:169.

[1458]
Life Styles Inventory.

Purpose: Designed to assess an individual's thinking and behavioral styles.

Population: Adults.
Publication Dates: 1973–1990.
Acronym: LSI.
Administration: Individual.
Price Data: Price data for test materials including Leader's Guide (1989, 211 pages), Self-Development Guide (1989, 75 pages), and Description by Others Self-Development Guide (1990, 123 pages) available from publisher.
Time: (20-25) minutes.
Author: J. Clayton Lafferty.
Publisher: Human Synergistics International.
 a) LSI1: LIFE STYLES INVENTORY (SELF DESCRIPTION).
 Scores, 12: Constructive Styles (Achievement, Self-Actualizing, Humanistic-Encouraging, Affiliative), Passive/Defensive Styles (Approval, Conventional, Dependent, Avoidance), Aggressive/Defensive Styles (Oppositional, Power, Competitive, Perfectionistic).
 b) LSI2: LIFE STYLES INVENTORY (DESCRIPTION BY OTHERS).
 Scores, 12: Same as for *a* above.
 Comments: Administered to manager and 4 or 5 others.
Cross References: For reviews by Gregory J. Boyle and Patricia Schoenrade, see 12:222; see also T4:1459 (6 references); for reviews by Henry M. Cherrick and Linda M. DuBois, see 9:620 (1 reference).

[1459]
Lifestyle Assessment Questionnaire.

Purpose: Provides individuals with a measurement of their lifestyle status in various wellness categories, offers a health risk appraisal component that lists the individual's top ten risks of death, projects an achievable health age, makes suggestions for lifestyle improvement, and offers a stimulus for positive lifestyle change by providing a guide to successful implementation of that change.
Population: Adults ages 18–60 with a minimum of 12th grade education.
Publication Dates: 1978–1989.
Scores, 16: Physical (Exercise, Nutrition, Self-Care, Vehicle Safety, Drug Usage), Social/Environmental, Emotional (Emotional Awareness and Acceptance, Emotional Management), Intellectual, Occupational, Spiritual, Actual Age, Appraised Health Age, Achievable Health Age, Top 10 Risks of Death, Lifestyle Improvement Suggestions.
Administration: Group.
Price Data: Available from publisher.
Time: (45–60) minutes.
Comments: Scoring by National Wellness Institute; information on up to four wellness areas included in scoring report; individual and group reports available.

Authors: Dennis Elsenrath, Bill Hettler, and Fred Leafgren.
Publisher: National Wellness Institute, Inc.
Cross References: For reviews by Michael B. Brown and William E. Martin, Jr., see 13:186 (3 references); see also T4:1461 (3 references).

[1460]
Light's Retention Scale [Revised Edition 2006].
Purpose: Aids the school professional in determining whether the student would benefit from grade retention.
Population: Ages 6 through 18.
Publication Dates: 1981–1998.
Acronym: LRS.
Scores, 20: Sex of Student, Preschool Attendance, Student's Age, Knowledge of English Language, Physical Size, Present Grade Placement, Previous Grade Retentions, Siblings, Parents' School Participation, Experiential Background, Transiency, School Attendance, Estimate of Intelligence, History of Learning Disabilities, Present Level of Academic Achievement, Student's Attitude About Possible Retention, Motivation to Complete School Tasks, Immature Behavior, Emotional Problems, History of Delinquency, Total.
Administration: Individual.
Price Data, 2006: $95 per complete test kit (includes manual, 50 recording forms, and 50 English parent guides); $32 per manual; $35 per 50 recording forms; $25 per 50 English parent guides; $25 per 50 Spanish parent guides; $20 per optional school administrator's kit.
Time: (10–15) minutes.
Comments: Ratings by teachers and parents; a nonpsychometric instrument used as a counseling tool with a specific retention candidate; Spanish parent guides available.
Author: H. Wayne Light.
Publisher: Academic Therapy Publications.
Cross References: For reviews by Bruce K. Alcorn and Frederic J. Medway of the 1991 Revision, see 11:208 (2 references); for reviews by Michael J. Hannafin and Patti L. Harrison of an earlier edition, see 9:622; see also T3:1328 (1 reference).

[1461]
The Lincoln-Oseretsky Motor Development Scale.
Purpose: "Designed to test the motor ability of children."
Population: Ages 6–14.
Publication Dates: 1948-1956.
Scores: Total score only.
Administration: Individual.
Price Data, 2005: $235 per complete kit including 50 record blanks and manual (1948, 79 pages); $20 per

50 record blanks; $20 per 50 mazes; $20 per 50 concentric circles; $25 per manual.
Time: Administration time not reported.
Comments: Revision of Oseretsky Tests of Motor Proficiency.
Author: William Sloan.
Publisher: Stoelting Co.
Cross References: See T4:1464 (5 references), T3:1331 (5 references), and T2:1895 (27 references); for a review by Anna Espenschade, see 5:767 (10 references).

[1462]
Lindamood Auditory Conceptualization Test—Third Edition.
Purpose: Designed to measure "the ability to (a) discriminate one speech sound or phoneme from another and (b) segment a spoken word into its constituent phonemic units."
Population: Ages 5-0 through 18-11.
Publication Dates: 1971–2004.
Acronym: LAC-3.
Scores, 6: Isolated Phoneme Patterns, Tracking Phonemes, Counting Syllables, Tracking Syllables, Tracking Syllables and Phonemes, Total.
Administration: Individual.
Price Data, 2006: $189 per complete kit including examiner's manual, 25 examiner record booklets, LiPS/KAC blocks, felt kit, and CD; $89 per examiner's manual; $68 per 25 examiner record booklets; $24 per LiPS/KAC blocks; $8 per felt kit; $20 per CD.
Time: (20–30) minutes.
Comments: "Criterion referenced"; requires no reading by examinees.
Authors: Patricia C. Lindamood and Phyllis Lindamood.
Publisher: PRO-ED.
Cross References: See T5:1503 (16 references) and T4:1465 (2 references); for reviews by Nicholas G. Bountress and James R. Cox of a previous edition, see 9:623 (1 reference).

[1463]
Listen Up: Skills Assessment.
Purpose: Designed to measure listening comprehension, interpretation, and ability to follow directions.
Population: Grades 7–12 and adults.
Publication Dates: 1985–1995.
Scores, 6: Evaluating Message Content, Understanding Meaning in Conversations, Understanding and Remembering Lectures, Evaluating Emotional Meanings in Messages, Following Instructions and Directions, Total.
Administration: Group.
Price Data: Available from publisher.
Time: [40–80] minutes.

Authors: Kittie W. Watson and Larry L. Barker.
Publisher: Jossey-Bass, A Wiley Company.
Cross References: For reviews by Cleborne D. Maddux and Sandra J. Wanner, see 14:213.

[1464]
Listening Comprehension Test.

Purpose: To estimate a student's ability to comprehend orally presented basic English structures.
Population: Nonnative speakers of English who wish to pursue academic work at universities where English is the medium of instruction.
Publication Dates: 1972–1986.
Acronym: LCT.
Scores: Total score only.
Administration: Group.
Forms, 3: 4, 5, 6 (equivalent forms).
Price Data, 2005: $125 per complete kit including 20 test booklets, 3 scoring stencils, 100 answer sheets, cassette tape, and manual (17 pages); $5 per 25 test booklets; $20 per scoring stencil; $10 per 100 answer sheets; $30 per cassette; $10 per manual; no charge for specimen set.
Time: 15(20) minutes.
Comments: Created for use as one of the component tests of the former Michigan Battery II.
Authors: J. Upshur, H. Koba, M. Spaan, and L. Strowe.
Publisher: English Language Institute, University of Michigan.
Cross References: See T5:1506 (1 reference); for reviews by James Dean Brown and Phyllis Kuehn, see 12:113.

[1465]
Listening Comprehension Test Series.

Purpose: Designed to "assess the communication skills that enable a child to listen, understand and respond appropriately to information."
Population: Ages 4–14.
Publication Date: 1999.
Scores: Total score only.
Administration: Individual or group.
Levels, 5: A, B, C, D, E.
Price Data: Price data for starter set including teacher's guide group record sheet, 20 pupil booklets, At-a-Glance Guide, and audiocassette available from publisher.
Time: Untimed.
Comments: Linked to the National Curriculum for England and Wales, the Scottish 5–14 Guidelines, and the Northern Ireland Curriculum.
Authors: Neil Hagues, Rifat Siddiqui, and Paul Merwood.
Publisher: NFER-Nelson Publishing Co., Ltd. [England].
Cross References: For a review by Michael D. Beck, see 16:137.

[1466]
The Listening Skills Test.

Purpose: Designed to measure "comprehension monitoring and message appraisal."
Population: 3 years 6 months to 6 years 11 months.
Publication Date: 2001.
Acronym: LIST.
Scores: 4 subtests: Referent Identification, Message Appraisal, Comprehension of Directions, Verbal Message Evaluation.
Administration: Individual.
Price Data, 2006: £81 per complete test kit including 25 record forms, stimulus manual, and manual (101 pages).
Time: (20–30) minutes.
Authors: Peter Lloyd, Ian Peers, and Caroline Foster.
Publisher: Harcourt Assessment [England].
Cross References: For reviews by Pam Lindsey and Gene Schwarting, see 15:139.

[1467]
Listening Styles Profile.

Purpose: "Designed to identify habitual listening responses and to encourage participants to think about how preference traits might be expressed in actual settings."
Population: Adults.
Publication Date: 1995.
Scores, 4: People Oriented, Action Oriented, Content Oriented, Time Oriented.
Administration: Group.
Price Data: Available from publisher.
Time: (5–10) minutes.
Comments: Can be used to evaluate self or another person.
Authors: Kittie W. Watson and Larry L. Barker.
Publisher: Jossey-Bass, A Wiley Company.
Cross References: For reviews by Mildred Murray-Ward and Sandra Ward, see 14:214.

[1468]
Literature Tests/Objective and Essay.

Purpose: To assess students' literal and interpretive comprehension of over 200 works of contemporary and classical literature.
Population: Middle school and high school.
Publication Dates: 1929–1990.
Scores: Total score only.
Administration: Group.
Manual: No manual.
Price Data, 2005: $4.75 per 50-question test; $5.75 per 100-question test; $5.75 per essay test.
Time: Administration time not reported.
Comments: Over 700 tests on specific literary works; formerly called Book Review Tests and Objective Tests in English.

Author: Perfection Learning Corp.
Publisher: Perfection Learning Corp.

[1469]
Living in the Reader's World: Locator Test.
Purpose: Diagnose nonproficient reader's appropriate starting point in a 4-book adult education reading program.
Population: Adults at reading grade levels 2.0–6.0.
Publication Date: 1983.
Administration: Group.
Price Data: Not available.
Time: Administration time not reported.
Comments: Upward extension of the Maryland/Baltimore County Design for Adult Basic Education (1536).
Author: Cambridge, The Adult Education Co.
Publisher: Prentice Hall [No reply from publisher; status unknown].

[1470]
Location Learning Test.
Purpose: To measure visuo-spatial learning and recall.
Population: Elderly adults.
Publication Date: 2000.
Acronym: LLT.
Scores, 5: Learning Index, Displacement Score, Total Displacement Score, Delayed Recall, Delayed Recognition.
Administration: Individual.
Forms, 2: A, B.
Price Data, 2006: £113.50 per complete kit including manual (15 pages), 25 scoring sheets, test grids, practice grids, and picture cards; £35.50 per 50 scoring sheets.
Time: (25) minutes.
Authors: Romola S. Bucks, Jonathan R. Willison, and Lucie M. T. Byrne.
Publisher: Harcourt Assessment [England].

[1471]
LOCO (Learning Opportunities Coordination): A Scale for the Assessment of Coordinated Learning Opportunities in Living Units for People with a Handicap.
Purpose: Designed "for indicating to what extent a Living Unit for people with handicaps is able to contribute significantly to their social and personal development and to maintain a level of reasonable independence."
Population: Residents of any type of living units where people with a handicap live with the assistance of care givers.
Publication Date: 1987.
Acronym: LOCO.

Scores, 4: Basic Training Conditions, Essential Items, Additional Items, Total.
Administration: Group.
Price Data: Available from publisher.
Time: Administration time not reported.
Comments: Can be used in conjunction with P-A-C (Progress Assessment Chart) (2050).
Authors: H. C. Gunzburg and A. L. Gunzburg.
Publisher: SEFA (Publications) Ltd. [England].

[1472]
Loewenstein Occupational Therapy Cognitive Assessment.
Purpose: "A cognitive battery of tests for both primary assessments and ongoing evaluation in the occupational therapy treatment of brain-injured patients."
Population: Ages 6 to 12 and brain-injured adults.
Publication Date: 1990.
Acronym: LOTCA.
Scores: 21 tests in 4 areas: Orientation (Orientation for Place, Orientation for Time), Visual and Spatial Perception (Object Identification, Shapes Identification, Overlapping Figures, Object Constancy, Spatial Perception, Praxis), Visual Motor Organization (Copying Geometric Forms, Reproduction of a Two-Dimensional Model, Pegboard Construction, Colored Block Design, Plain Block Design, Reproduction of a Puzzle, Drawing a Clock), Thinking Operations (Categorization, ROC Unstructured, ROC Structured, Pictorial Sequence A, Pictorial Sequence B, Geometric Sequence).
Administration: Individual.
Price Data: Price data available from publisher for complete kit including manual (56 pages), test booklet, and other materials packed in a plastic carrying case.
Time: (30–45) minutes.
Authors: Loewenstein Rehabilitation Hospital; Malka Itzkovich (manual), Betty Elazar (manual), Sarah Averbuch (manual), Naomi Katz (principal researcher), and Levy Rahmani (advisor).
Publisher: Maddak Inc.
Cross References: For reviews by Elaine Clark and Stephen R. Hooper, see 13:187.

[1473]
Logical Reasoning.
Purpose: Designed to measure sensitivity to logical necessity, consistency and inconsistency, and relationships.
Population: Grades 9–16 and adults.
Publication Date: 1955.
Scores: Total score only.
Administration: Group.
Parts, 2: 1, 2.
Price Data: Available from publisher.
Time: 20(25) minutes.
Comments: Two parallel parts may be administered separately or together.

Authors: Alfred F. Hertzka and J. P. Guilford.
Publisher: Charlotte Mackley [No reply from publisher; status unknown].
Cross References: See T5:1514 (1 reference), T4:1476 (3 references), and T2:1761 (10 references); for reviews by Duncan Howie and Charles R. Langmuir, see 5:694 (1 reference).

[1474]

The Lollipop Test: A Diagnostic Screening Test of School Readiness—Revised.

Purpose: "A screening test to identify the child's deficits (and strengths) in readiness skills."
Population: First grade entrants.
Publication Dates: 1981–2002.
Scores, 5: Identification of Colors and Shapes and Copying Shapes, Picture Description and Position and Spatial Recognition, Identification of Numbers and Counting, Identification of Letters and Writing, Total.
Administration: Individual.
Price Data, 2002: $59.95 per complete kit including 25 test booklets, stimulus cards, and manual (1989, 35 pages); $34.95 per 25 test booklets; $14.95 per set of stimulus cards; $15.95 per manual.
Foreign Language Edition: Available in Spanish.
Time: (15–20) minutes.
Author: Alex L. Chew.
Publisher: Humanics Learning.
Cross References: See T5:1515 (1 reference) and T4:1477 (2 references); for reviews by Sylvia T. Johnson and Albert C. Oosterhof, see 11:210 (5 references); for reviews by Isabel L. Beck and Janet A. Norris of an earlier edition, see 9:629.

[1475]

Looking at MySELF.

Purpose: Designed to help students "build self-esteem."
Population: Grades 3–6, Grades 7–12.
Publication Dates: 1991–1993.
Scores: Total score only.
Administration: Group.
Forms, 2: Form I, Form II.
Price Data: Available from publisher.
Time: (120–180) minutes or in steps in a weekly program.
Author: CFKR Career Materials, Inc.
Publisher: CFKR Career Materials.

[1476]

Lore Leadership Assessment.

Purpose: Measures perceived skill and effectiveness in the five dimensions of the Lore Leadership Model: moral, intellectual, courageous, collaborative, and visionary/inspirational; measures executive's leadership skill levels as well as their impact on the people they are leading.
Population: Executives in leadership positions.
Publication Dates: 1998–2001.
Scores, 6: Overall Leadership Effectiveness, Moral Leadership, Intellectual Leadership, Courageous Leadership, Collaborative Leadership, Visionary/Inspirational Leadership.
Administration: Group.
Forms, 2: Self-Assessment, Assessment of Other.
Manual: No manual.
Price Data, 2005: $49 per online assessment with electronic report.
Foreign Language Editions: Available in English and German.
Time: [30] minutes.
Comments: Test forms are administered online via the internet at Lore's Assessment Center.
Author: Lore International Institute.
Publisher: Lore International Institute.
Cross References: For a review by Connie Kubo Della-Piana of the original edition, see 14:215.

[1477]

Lorimer Braille Recognition Test: A Test of Ability in Reading Braille Contractions.

Purpose: Designed to test blind children's performance in reading Braille contractions.
Population: Students (ages 7–13) in Grade 2 Braille.
Publication Date: 1962.
Scores: Total score only.
Administration: Group.
Price Data: Price data, including manual (27 pages) (available in printed form or Braille), available from publisher.
Time: Administration time not reported.
Author: John Lorimer.
Publisher: Association for the Education and Welfare of the Visually Handicapped [England] [No reply from publisher; status unknown].
Cross References: See 6:854 (1 reference).

[1478]

LSI Conflict.

Purpose: Enables individuals to identify and understand how their thinking patterns and coping behaviors influence their ability to deal with conflict situations.
Population: Adults.
Publication Date: 1990.
Scores: 12 patterns of thinking and behavior: Constructive (Pragmatist, Self-Empowered, Conciliator, Relationship Builder), Passive/Defensive (Accommodator, Regulator, Insulator, Avoider), Aggressive/Defensive (Escalator, Dominator, Competitor, Perfectionist).
Administration: Individual or group.

Price Data: Price data for test materials including Self-Development Guide and Leader's Guide available from publisher.
Time: Administration time not reported.
Author: J. Clayton Lafferty.
Publisher: Human Synergistics International.

[1479]
Luria-Nebraska Neuropsychological Battery: Children's Revision.

Purpose: "To diagnose general and specific cognitive deficits, including lateralization and localization of focal brain impairments, and to aid in the planning and evaluation of rehabilitation programs."
Population: Ages 8–12.
Publication Date: 1987.
Acronym: LNNB-C.
Scores, 16: Clinical scales (Motor Functions, Rhythm, Tactile Functions, Visual Functions, Receptive Speech, Expressive Speech, Writing, Reading, Arithmetic, Memory, Intellectual Processes), Optional scales (Spelling, Motor Writing), Summary scales (Pathognomonic, Left Sensorimotor, Right Sensorimotor).
Administration: Individual.
Price Data, 2006: $549.50 per complete kit including manual (266 pages) and all required materials in a carrying case; $26.95 per 10 patient response booklets; $59.95 per 10 administration and scoring booklets; $93.50 per manual; $21.50 per prepaid WPS Test Report answer sheet; $319.00 per 25-use computer disk (PC with DOS); $12.50 each per FAX scoring service.
Time: (150) minutes.
Comments: Uses the same stimulus materials, with the addition of 3 extra cards and an audiotape, as Form I of the adult version of the Luria-Nebraska Neuropsychological Battery (1480); other test materials (e.g., tape recorder, stopwatch, eraser, door key) must be supplied by examiner.
Author: Charles J. Golden.
Publisher: Western Psychological Services.
Cross References: See T5:1524 (2 references) and T4:1487 (2 references); for a review by Stephen R. Hooper, see 11:211 (3 references).

[1480]
Luria-Nebraska Neuropsychological Battery: Forms I and II.

Purpose: Designed "to diagnose general and specific cognitive deficits, including lateralization and localization of focal brain impairments, and to aid in the planning and evaluation of rehabilitation programs."
Population: Ages 15 and over
Publication Dates: 1980–1985.
Acronym: LNNB.
Scores, 27: Clinical and Summary scales (Motor Functions, Rhythm, Tactile Functions, Visual Functions, Receptive Speech, Expressive Speech, Writing, Reading, Arithmetic, Memory, Intellectual Processes, Intermediate Memory [Form II only], Pathognomonic, Left Hemisphere, Right Hemisphere, Profile Elevation, Impairment), Localization scales (Left Frontal, Left Sensorimotor, Left Parietal-Occipital, Left Temporal, Right Frontal, Right Sensorimotor, Right Parietal-Occipital, Right Temporal), Optional scales (Spelling, Motor Writing), plus 28 Factor scales.
Administration: Individual.
Forms, 2: I, II.
Price Data, 2006: $549.50 per Form I set including manual (1985, 423 pages), test materials, 10 administration and scoring booklets, and 10 patient response booklets; $489.50 per Form II set; $59.95 per 10 administration and scoring booklets (Form I); $54.95 per 10 administration and scoring booklets (Form II); $25 per 10 patient response booklets (Forms I and II); $152 per manual; $319 per 25-use (PC with DOS) disk for LNNB, Forms I, II, and Children's Revision; $12.50 per FAX service scoring charge.
Time: (90-150) minutes.
Comments: Uses cards adapted from Luria's Neuropsychological Investigation by Anne-Lise Christensen (Form II includes improved, spiral-bound stimulus cards); tape provided for rhythm subtest; Form I can be scored by hand or computer; Form II is computer scored only.
Authors: Charles J. Golden, Arnold D. Purisch, and Thomas A. Hammeke.
Publisher: Western Psychological Services.
Cross References: See T5:1525 (25 references) and T4:1488 (16 references); for reviews by Jeffrey H. Snow and Wilfred G. van Gorp, see 11:212 (105 references); for a review by Russell L. Adams, see 9:637 (41 references); see also T3:1346 (8 references).

[1481]
MAC Checklist for Evaluating, Preparing, and/or Improving Standardized Tests for Limited English Speaking Students.

Purpose: Aids in the review, critique, or preparation of ESL assessment instruments.
Population: ESL test developers, reviewers, and users.
Publication Date: 1981.
Scores: 5 criterion categories: Evidence of Validity, Evidence of Examinee Appropriateness, Evidence of Proper Item Construction, Evidence of Technical Merit, Evidence of Administrative Excellence.
Administration: Group.
Price Data: Available from publisher.
Time: Administration time not reported.
Author: Jean D'Arcy Maculaitis.
Publisher: Jean D'Arcy Maculaitis [No reply from publisher; status unknown].
Cross References: For reviews by Eugene E. Garcia and Charles W. Stansfield, see 10:177.

[1482]
Machinist Test—Form AC.

Purpose: "Select or develop journey-level candidates or incumbents for machine shop jobs."
Population: Machinist job applicants or incumbents.
Publication Dates: 1981–2004.
Scores, 10: Heat Treating, Layout/Cutting and Assembly, Print Reading, Steel/ Metals and Materials, Rigging, Mechanical Principles and Repair, Machine Tools, Tools/Material and Equipment, Machine Shop Lubrication, Total.
Administration: Group.
Price Data, 2006: $20 per consumable self-scoring test booklet (20 minimum order); $24.95 per manual (2004).
Time: (60) minutes.
Comments: Self-scoring instrument; previously listed as Ramsay Corporation Job Skills—Machinist Test.
Author: Roland T. Ramsay.
Publisher: Ramsay Corporation.
Cross References: For reviews by John Peter Hudson, Jr. and James W. Pinkney of an earlier edition, see 13:253.

[1483]
Maculaitis Assessment of Competencies II.

Purpose: "A comprehensive assessment of English Language proficiency for students ... whose first language is not English."
Population: Grades K–12.
Publication Dates: 1982–2001.
Acronym: MAC II.
Scores, 5: 4 subtests (Speaking, Listening, Reading, Writing), Total Battery.
Forms, 2: A, B.
Price Data: Available from publisher.
Comments: Updated and revised version of Maculaitis Assessment of Competencies (MAC), subtests can be administered separately; hand- or machine-scorable; machine scoring performed by publisher; variety of score reports available including Roster Reports, Individual Student Labels, Individual Student Record Form Reports, Summary Reports; Green 10-minute screening test for new students also available.
Author: Jean D'Arcy Maculaitis.
Publisher: Touchstone Applied Science Associates (TASA), Inc.
  a) RED LEVEL.
  Population: Grades K–1.
  Administration: Individual.
  Time: (25) minutes.
  b) BLUE LEVEL.
  Population: Grades 2–3.
  Administration: Individual or group.
  Time: (75) minutes.
  c) ORANGE LEVEL.
  Population: Grades 4–5.

  Administration: Individual or group.
  Time: (121) minutes.
  d) IVORY LEVEL.
  Population: Grades 6–8.
  Administration: Individual or group.
  Time: (126) minutes.
  e) TAN LEVEL.
  Population: Grades 9–12.
  Administration: Individual or group.
  Time: (131) minutes.

[1484]
Maintenance Electrician A Test (Form BTA-C).

Purpose: For selecting manufacturing or processing maintenance candidates.
Population: Applicants and incumbents for jobs requiring electrical knowledge and skills at the highest level.
Publication Dates: 2000–2005.
Scores, 8: Motors, Digital Electronics and Analog Electronics, Schematics & Print Reading and Control Circuits, Power Supplies/Power Distribution and Construction & Installation, AC/DC Theory and Electrical Maintenance & Troubleshooting, Test Instruments and Computers & PLC, Mechanical Maintenance, Total.
Administration: Group.
Price Data, 2006: $20 per consumable self-scoring test booklet (minimum order of 20); $24.95 per manual (2000, 17 pages).
Time: (60) minutes.
Comments: Self-scoring instrument.
Author: Roland T. Ramsay.
Publisher: Ramsay Corporation.

[1485]
Maintenance Electrician B Test (Form BTB-C).

Purpose: For selecting manufacturing or processing maintenance candidates.
Population: Applicants and incumbents for jobs requiring electrical knowledge and skills.
Publication Dates: 2000–2005.
Scores, 8: Motors, Digital Electronics and Analog Electronics, Schematics & Print Reading and Control Circuits, Power Supplies/Power Distribution and Construction & Installation, AC/DC Theory and Electrical Maintenance, Test Instruments and Computers & PLC, Mechanical Maintenance and Hand & Power Tools, Total.
Administration: Group.
Price Data, 2006: $20 per consumable self-scoring test booklet (minimum order of 20); $24.95 per manual (2000, 16 pages).
Time: (60) minutes.
Comments: Self-scoring instrument.

Author: Roland T. Ramsay.
Publisher: Ramsay Corporation.

[1486]

MAINTEST (Form NL-1R, Form B, & Form C).

Purpose: Measures practical mechanical and electrical knowledge.
Population: Applicants and incumbents for jobs requiring practical mechanical and electrical knowledge and skills.
Publication Dates: 1991–2005.
Scores, 22: Hydraulics, Pneumatics, Welding, Power Transmission, Lubrication, Pumps, Piping, Rigging, Mechanical Maintenance, Shop Machines and Tools & Equipment, Combustion, Motors, Digital Electronics, Schematics & Print Reading, Control Circuits, Power Supplies, Basic AC & DC Theory, Power Distribution, Test Instruments, Computers & PLC, Electrical Maintenance, Total.
Administration: Group.
Price Data, 2006: $60 per consumable test booklet; no charge for manual (2005, 28 pages).
Time: (150) minutes.
Comments: Tests scored by publisher; Forms B and C are alternate forms of Form NL-1R.
Author: Roland T. Ramsay.
Publisher: Ramsay Corporation.
Cross References: For reviews by Nambury S. Raju and William J. Waldron of an earlier edition, see 13:189.

[1487]

Major Field Tests.

Purpose: Designed to measure the basic knowledge and understanding achieved by students in a major field of study.
Population: Undergraduate students completing an academic major program and MBA.
Publication Dates: 1988–2006.
Acronym: MFT.
Scores: Total score only.
Administration: Group.
Price Data: Available from publisher at www.ETS.org/MFT.
Time: (120) minutes; MBA: 180 minutes.
Comments: Objective, end-of-program content tests in 16 disciplines; yields individual scores and subscores, group mean scores, and "assessment indicators" (group reliable subscores); delivered in two formats: online and paper-and-pencil; because there are no preset test administration dates, institutions and departments may schedule testing at their convenience; colleges and academic departments can choose where to administer the exams, as long as it is in a proctored environment, and with Internet connections for the online tests.

Author: Educational Testing Service.
Publisher: Educational Testing Service.

[1488]

The Major-Minor-Finder, 1986–1996 Edition.

Purpose: Designed to assist students in selecting a college major.
Population: High school and college.
Publication Dates: 1978–1987.
Acronym: MMF.
Scores: No scores; decisions based on number of matches for each major.
Administration: Group.
Price Data: Available from publisher.
Time: (40) minutes per printed version; (10) minutes per microcomputer version.
Authors: Arthur Cutler, Francis Ferry, Robert Kauk, and Robert Robinett.
Publisher: CFKR Career Materials.
Cross References: For a review by James W. Pinkney, see 10:181; for reviews by Rodney L. Lowman and Daryl Sander of an earlier edition, see 9:643.

[1489]

Make A Picture Story.

Purpose: "A projective psychological test" intended "as an aid in inferring psychodynamic interpretations and structural aspects of personality."
Population: Age 6 and over.
Publication Dates: 1947–1952.
Acronym: MAPS.
Scores: Not scored.
Administration: Individual.
Price Data, 2006: $104.50 per complete kit including manual (1952, 92 pages), 22 stimulus cards, 67 cut-out figures, and 25 Location sheets; $27.50 per 100 Location sheets.
Time: Untimed.
Comments: A projective test similar to the Thematic Apperception Test (2645); best when used as a component of a battery of psychological tests; guidelines for qualitative interpreting of subjects' responses provided.
Author: Edwin S. Shneidman.
Publisher: Western Psychological Services.
Cross References: See T3:1361 (66 references), T2:1482 (10 references) and P:452 (4 references); for a review by Arthur R. Jensen, see 6:230 (10 references); see also 5:149 (18 references); for reviews by Albert Rabin and Charles R. Strother, see 4:113 (19 references).

[1490]

Making a Terrific Career Happen.

Purpose: For use in guiding examinees in self-evaluation and exploration of careers.

Population: High school graduates, college students, and adults.
Publication Date: 1992.
Acronym: MATCH.
Scores: Science-Professional, Science-Skilled, Technology-Professional, Technology-Skilled, Consumer Economics, Outdoor, Business-Professional, Business-Skilled, Clinical, Communication, Arts-Professional, Arts-Skilled, Service-Professional, Service-Skilled.
Administration: Group.
Price Data: Available from publisher.
Time: Administration time varies.
Comments: Self-administered and interpreted.
Author: Lisa Knapp-Lee.
Publisher: EdITS/Educational and Industrial Testing Service.

[1491]
Malingering Probability Scale.

Purpose: Designed to "assess whether an individual is attempting to produce false evidence of psychological distress."
Population: Ages 17 and over.
Publication Date: 1998.
Acronym: MPS.
Scores, 6: Depression and Anxiety, Dissociative Disorders, Post-Traumatic Stress, Schizophrenia, Inconsistency, Malingering.
Administration: Individual.
Price Data, 2006: $154 per kit for mail-in computer scoring including reusable administration card, 5 prepaid mail-in answer sheets, and manual; $412.50 per kit for on-site computer scoring including reusable administration card, 20-use disk, 100 PC answer sheets, and manual; $6.60 per reusable administration card; $54.50 per manual; $21.95 per mail-in answer sheet; $363 per 20-use disk (PC with Microsoft Windows); $16.50 per 100 PC answer sheets; $17.60 per FAX Service Scoring charge.
Time: (20) minutes.
Comments: May be administered by paper and pencil or personal computer; computer scored (only) and interpreted locally or by publisher FAX or mail-in service.
Authors: Leigh Silverton and Chris Gruber (manual).
Publisher: Western Psychological Services.
Cross References: For reviews by Solomon M. Fulero and Radhika Krishnamurthy, see 14:216.

[1492]
Management and Graduate Item Bank.

Purpose: "For use in the selection, development or guidance of personnel at graduate level or in management positions."
Population: Graduate level and senior management applicants for the following areas: finance, computing, engineering, corporate planning, purchasing, personnel, and marketing.
Publication Dates: 1985–1987.
Acronym: MGIB.
Scores, 2: Verbal Critical Reasoning, Numerical Critical Reasoning.
Administration: Group.
Price Data: Available from publisher.
Time: 60(65) minutes.
Comments: Abbreviated adaptation of the Advanced Test Battery (127); subtests available as separates.
Authors: Saville & Holdsworth Ltd. and Linda Espey (supplementary norms manual).
Publisher: SHL Group plc [United Kingdom].
Cross References: For reviews by James T. Austin and H. John Bernardin and by R. W. Faunce, see 11:213.

[1493]
Management & Leadership Systems.

Purpose: Designed to assess management and leadership skills and team effectiveness.
Population: Management personnel.
Publication Dates: 1992–2001.
Acronym: MLS.
Administration: Group.
Price Data, 2001: $495 per Facilitator's kit including User's Manual (2001, 230 pages), Guide to Management & Leadership, High-Performing Teams Action Planning Workbook, 6 Management & Leadership Profiles, 6 Team Effectiveness Profiles, 6 Management Candidate Profiles, and transparency masters; $35 per Guide to Management & Leadership; $35 per High-Performing Teams Action Planning workbook; $195 annual licensing fee for scoring software.
Foreign Language Editions: Available in English, Spanish, French, and Portuguese.
Time: (20) minutes per test.
Comments: Inventories may be completed via paper-and-pencil, or on-line via the internet; microcomputer software requirements are Windows 98 or newer, 32 MB RAM, and 10 MB free on hard drive; the option to have the publisher generate the MLP, TEKP, MCP, and SIP is available, thus eliminating licensing of the scoring software; reports can be printed in different languages.
Author: Curtiss S. Peck.
Publisher: Assessment Systems International, Inc.

    a) MANAGEMENT & LEADERSHIP PROFILE.
    Purpose: Designed to measure "both present behavior and desired behavior based on the needs and expectations of the people who are evaluating the manager."
    Acronym: MLP.
    Scores, 15: Clarity of Purpose (Goals, Communication), Planning and Problem Avoidance

(Planning, Involvement, Decision Making), Task Accomplishment (Competence, Motivation, Work Facilitation), Providing Feedback (Feedback), Exercising Control (Managing Performance, Accountability, Delegation), Individual & Team Relationships (Relationships, Linking, Teamwork).

b) TEAM EFFECTIVENESS PROFILE.

Purpose: "Provides a way of measuring and giving feedback to teams on how they manage their processes and projects."

Acronym: TEP.

Scores, 15: Clarity of Purpose (Goals, Communication), Planning and Problem Avoidance (Planning, Involvement, Innovation/Risk, Decision Making), Task Accomplishment (Values, Competence, Motivation, Quality/Continuous Improvement), Providing Feedback (Feedback), Exercising Control (Control, Delegation), Individual & Team Relationships (Linking, Teamwork).

c) MANAGEMENT CANDIDATE PROFILE.

Purpose: "Measures day-to-day behavior that is correlated with effective management and leadership behavior. The MCP helps people understand the skills required to become effective managers and provides a clear picture of the candidate's strengths and softspots in ten important areas."

Acronym: MCP.

Scores, 10: Goals, Communication, Planning, Innovation/Risk, Decision Making, Motivation, Quality/Continuous Improvement, Feedback, Control, Relationships.

d) SELLING WITH INTEGRITY PROFILE.

Purpose: "Measure the perceptions of current behavior and desired behavior of internal and external sales people. The SIP is completed by customers, sales manager, and sales person."

Acronym: SIP.

Scores, 7: Professionalism, Identification of Needs, Partnering, Competence, Negotiation, Close, Service.

Cross References: For reviews by Stephen F. Davis and William J. Waldron, see 14:217.

[1494]
Management and Organizational Skills Test.

Purpose: Measures "an individual's knowledge and understanding of how relatively complex organizations function as well as knowledge of the competencies and skills required for success in management and executive positions."

Population: Job applicants.

Publication Date: 2004.

Acronym: MOST.

Scores: Total score only.

Administration: Group.

Price Data, 2005: $29.95 per manual (10 pages); $50 per 10 test booklets.

Time: (45–60) minutes.

Comments: Web-based test version is self-administering.

Authors: E. P. Prien and Leonard D.Goodstein.

Publisher: HRD Press, Inc.

[1495]
Management Appraisal Survey.

Purpose: "An assessment of managerial practices and attitudes as viewed through the eyes of employees."

Population: Employees.

Publication Dates: 1967-1996.

Scores, 5: Overall Leadership Style, Philosophy, Planning, Implementation, Evaluation.

Administration: No manual.

Price Data, 2001: $7.95 per instrument.

Time: Administration time not reported.

Comments: Self-administered survey.

Authors: Jay Hall, Jerry B. Harvey, and Martha S. Williams.

Publisher: Teleometrics International, Inc.

Cross References: See T3:2351 (1 reference); for a review by Abraham K. Korman of the Styles of Leadership and Management, see 8:1185 (8 references).

[1496]
Management Aptitude Test.

Purpose: Designed to "evaluate critical thinking skills typically relevant to management positions."

Population: Age 18 and over.

Publication Date: 1993.

Acronym: MAT.

Scores, 7: Administrative Skills, Business Control, Communication, Planning/Organizing, Problem Solving, Supervisory Skills, Manager Potential Index.

Administration: Group or individual.

Price Data, 2005: $43 per 1–999 profiles using Inernet without booklets; $43 per 1–999 profiles using Quanta-TouchTest™, $43 per 1–999 profiles using Quanta® software for Windows without booklets.

Time: (90–100) minutes.

Comments: Test can be scored using operator-assisted telephone scoring, touch-test telephone scoring, and Quanta-based scoring.

Author: Reid London House.

Publisher: Pearson Performance Solutions [No reply from publisher; status unknown].

[1497]
Management Development Questionnaire.

Purpose: A personal competence assessment instrument "designed to help managers identify their weakness and strengths and decide what they need to do to develop themselves."

Population: Managers.
Publication Date: 1997.
Acronym: MDQ.
Scores, 20: Initiative, Risk Taking, Innovation, Flexibility/Adaptability, Analytical Thinking, Decision Making, Planning, Quality Focus, Oral Communication, Sensitivity, Relationships, Teamwork, Achievement, Customer Focus, Business Awareness, Learning Orientation, Authority/Presence, Motivating Others, Developing People, Resilience.
Administration: Individual.
Price Data: Available from publisher.
Time: (35) minutes.
Author: Alan Cameron.
Publisher: HRD Press, Inc.
Cross References: For reviews by Samuel Hinton and Eugene P. Sheehan, see 15:140.

[1498]
Management Effectiveness Profile System.
Purpose: "Identifies managers' current strengths and weaknesses and provides direction for individual development."
Population: Managers and coworkers.
Publication Dates: 1983–1993.
Acronym: MEPS.
Scores: 2 scores (Self, Other) in 14 management skill areas: Problem Solving, Time Management, Planning, Goal Setting, Performance Leadership, Organizing, Team Development, Delegation, Participation, Integrating Differences, Providing Feedback, Stress Processing, Maintaining Integrity, Commitment.
Administration: Individual or group.
Forms, 2: Self Description, Description by Others.
Price Data: Available from publisher.
Comments: Originally called Management Practices Audit; administered to manager and 4 or 5 coworkers.
Author: Human Synergistics International.
Publisher: Human Synergistics International.

[1499]
Management Interest Inventory.
Purpose: "To assist both organizations and individuals in making decisions relating to selection, placement, and career development at management level."
Population: Managers.
Publication Dates: 1983–1986.
Scores, 54: Management Functions Preference Scores and Experience Scores (Production Operations, Technical Services, Research and Development, Distribution, Purchasing, Sales, Marketing Support, Personnel and Training, Data Processing, Finance, Legal and Secretarial, Administration, Total, Spread Across Functions); Management Skills Preference Scores and Experience Scores (Information Collecting, Information Processing, Problem-Solving, Decision-Making, Mod-

elling, Communicating Orally, Communicating in Writing, Organising Things, Organising People, Persuading, Developing, Representing, Total).
Administration: Group.
Price Data: Available from publisher.
Time: (20–40) minutes.
Authors: Roger Holdsworth (test), Ruth Holdsworth (test), Lisa Cramp (test), and Miranda Blum (manual).
Publisher: SHL Group plc [United Kingdom].
Cross References: For a review by David M. Saunders, see 11:216.

[1500]
Management Inventory on Leadership, Motivation and Decision-Making.
Purpose: Designed for use in the training and selection of managers.
Population: Managers and manager trainees.
Publication Date: 1991.
Acronym: MILMD.
Scores: Total score only.
Administration: Group.
Price Data, 2001: $40 per 20 test and answer booklets; $5 per Instructor Manual (1991, 8 pages); $10 per Review Set including one test, one answer booklet, and Instructor Manual.
Time: (15-20) minutes.
Author: Donald L. Kirkpatrick.
Publisher: Donald L. Kirkpatrick (the author).
Cross References: For reviews by Kevin R. Murphy and Eugene P. Sheehan, see 12:226.

[1501]
Management Inventory on Managing Change.
Purpose: To assess managers' attitudes, knowledge, and opinions regarding principles and approaches for facilitating change.
Population: Managers.
Publication Dates: 1978-1983.
Acronym: MIMC.
Scores: Total score only.
Administration: Group or individual.
Price Data, 2001: $40 per 20 tests and answer booklets; $5 per instructor's manual (1983, 8 pages); $10 per review set (includes test, answer booklet, and manual).
Time: (15-25) minutes.
Author: Donald L. Kirkpatrick.
Publisher: Donald L. Kirkpatrick (the author).

[1502]
Management Inventory on Modern Management.
Purpose: "Developed to cover eight different topics of importance to managers."

Population: Managers.
Publication Date: 1984.
Acronym: MIMM.
Scores: 8 areas: Leadership Styles, Selecting and Training, Communicating, Motivating, Managing Change, Delegating, Decision Making, Managing Time; Total score is sum of the 8 areas.
Administration: Group or individual.
Price Data, 2001: $40 per 20 tests and answer booklets; $5 per manual (12 pages); $10 per specimen set.
Time: (20) minutes.
Comments: Self-scored training tool.
Author: Donald L. Kirkpatrick.
Publisher: Donald L. Kirkpatrick (the Author).
Cross References: For a review by Lenore W. Harmon, see 10:183.

[1503]

Management Inventory on Performance Appraisal and Coaching.

Purpose: To determine the need for training in "performance appraisal and coaching."
Population: Managers.
Publication Date: 1990.
Acronym: MIPAC.
Scores: Total score only.
Administration: Group.
Price Data, 2001: $40 per 20 tests and answer booklets; $10 per optional audiocassette; $5 per manual (7 pages); $10 per specimen set.
Time: (20-25) minutes.
Comments: Self-administered, self-scored.
Author: Donald L. Kirkpatrick.
Publisher: Donald L. Kirkpatrick (the author).

[1504]

Management Inventory on Time Management.

Purpose: Tests time management ability of managerial personnel.
Population: Managers.
Publication Date: 1980.
Acronym: MITM.
Scores: Total score only.
Administration: Group or individual.
Price Data, 2001: $40 per 20 tests and answer booklets; $5 per instructor's manual (8 pages); $10 per review set (includes test, answer booklet, and manual).
Time: (15-25) minutes.
Author: Donald L. Kirkpatrick.
Publisher: Donald L. Kirkpatrick (the author).

[1505]

Management of Differences Inventory.

Purpose: To provide feedback to an individual concerning his/her manner of handling differences in managerial situations.

Population: Business managers.
Publication Dates: 1981–1994.
Acronym: MODI.
Scores, 9: Maintain, Smooth, Dominate, Decide by Rule, Coexist, Bargain, Yield, Release, Collaborate.
Administration: Group.
Forms, 2: Self, Feedback.
Price Data, 2002: $8.95 per Self form; $8.95 per Feedback form; minimum of 20 (volume discounts available).
Time: (20) minutes.
Comments: Self-administered; self-scored.
Author: Herbert S. Kindler.
Publisher: The Center for Management Effectiveness, Inc.

[1506]

Management Practices Update.

Purpose: To provide individuals with information about managerial behavior in areas of interpersonal relationships, the management of motivation, and personal "style" of management.
Population: Individuals involved in the management of others.
Publication Date: 1987.
Acronym: MPU.
Scores, 12: Section I (Exposure, Feedback), Section II (Basic, Safety, Belonging, Ego Status, Actualization), Section III (Team Management, Middle-of-the-Road Management, Task Management, Country Club Management, Impoverished Management).
Administration: Group.
Levels: 3 parts: I (Interpersonal Relationships), II (Management of Motivation), III (Analysis of Management Style).
Price Data, 2001: $8.95 per instrument (25 pages).
Time: Administration time not reported.
Comments: Represents a shortened version of Personnel Relations Survey (1935), Management of Motives Index, and Styles of Management Inventory (2474).
Author: Jay Hall.
Publisher: Teleometrics International, Inc.

[1507]

Management Readiness Profile.

Purpose: Designed to "measure the attitudes and aptitudes that are commonly critical to management success."
Population: Ages 18 and over.
Publication Dates: 1989–2000.
Acronym: MRP.
Scores, 9: Managerial Interest, Leadership, Energy Level, Practical Thinking, Interpersonal Skills, Business Ethics, Management Readiness Index, Candidness, Accuracy.
Administration: Group or individual.

Price Data, 2005: $20 including 1–999 reports for Internet scoring with booklets; $20 including 1–999 reports for Internet scoring without booklets; $20 including 1–999 reports for QuantaTouch Test; $20 including 1–999 reports for QUANTA Software for Windows with booklets; $20 including 1–999 reports for QUANTA Software for Windows without booklets.
Foreign Language Editions: Available in Spanish and French Canadian.
Time: (20–25) minutes.
Comments: Test can be scored over Touch Test, Internet, and Optical Scanning Software.
Author: Reid London House.
Publisher: Pearson Performance Solutions [No reply from publisher; status unknown].

[1508]
Management Relations Survey.

Purpose: To assess employees' perceptions of their practices toward their managers.
Population: Subordinates to managers.
Publication Dates: 1970-1995.
Acronym: MRS.
Scores, 2: Exposure, Feedback.
Administration: Group.
Price Data, 2001: $7.95 per instrument.
Time: Administration time not reported.
Comments: Companion instrument to Personnel Relations Survey (1935); based on the Johari Window Model of interpersonal relations.
Author: Jay Hall.
Publisher: Teleometrics International, Inc.
Cross References: For a review by Walter C. Borman, see 8:1178 (1 reference).

[1509]
Management Situation Checklist.

Purpose: Designed to help determine how management style matches management demands, to define vulnerabilities from management style and develop strategies for improving vulnerabilities.
Population: Managers.
Publication Date: 1986.
Acronym: MSC.
Scores, 6: Coercive, Authoritative, Affiliative, Democratic, Pacesetting, Coaching.
Administration: Group or individual.
Price Data, 2006: $33 per 10 booklets.
Time: [20–30] minutes.
Comments: Self-rating checklist; self-scored; is a companion to the Managerial Style Questionnaire (1524).
Author: Hay Group.
Publisher: Hay Group.

[1510]
Management Style Inventory [Training House, Inc.].

Purpose: "This exercise is designed to give you some insights into your management style and how it affects others."
Population: Industry.
Publication Dates: 1986–1987.
Scores, 5: Team Builder, Soft, Hard, Middle of Road, Ineffective.
Administration: Group or individual.
Price Data: Price information available from publisher for complete sets including test, answer sheet, and interpretation sheet.
Time: (20) minutes.
Comments: Self-administered, self-scored.
Author: Training House, Inc.
Publisher: Training House, Inc.
Cross References: For reviews by Ernest J. Kozma and Charles K. Parsons, see 11:220.

[1511]
Management Styles Inventory.

Purpose: Assesses individual management style under a variety of conditions.
Population: Adults.
Publication Dates: 1964-1995.
Scores, 5: Philosophy, Planning and Goal Setting, Implementation, Performance Evaluation, Total.
Administration: Group.
Price Data, 2001: $8.95 per instrument.
Time: Untimed.
Comments: Self-administered survey.
Authors: Jay Hall, Jerry B. Harvey, and Martha S. Williams.
Publisher: Teleometrics International, Inc.
Cross References: For reviews by Ralph F. Darr, Jr. and Charles K. Parsons, see 12:227.

[1512]
Management Success Profile.

Purpose: "Provides a standardized measure of potential for success in management and is an ideal instrument for selecting supervisors, unit managers, and team leaders. The MSP assesses the individual's interest in, motivation toward, and knowledge about management positions."
Population: Adults (management position candidates).
Publication Date: 1996.
Acronym: MSP.
Scores: Validity (Candidness, Accuracy), Management Focus (Work Background, Leadership), Motivation and Attitudes (Management Responsibility, Productivity, Customer Service Orientation), Management Style (Practical Thinking, Adaptability, Coaching),

Stability and Risk (Business Ethics, Job Commitment), Overall Management Profile Index.
Administration: Group.
Price Data: Available from publisher.
Time: (45) minutes.
Comments: Toll free customer service hotline for immediate assistance with Profile (1-800-221-8378).
Author: London House.
Publisher: Pearson Performance Solutions [No reply from publisher; status unknown].

[1513]
Management Team Roles—Indicator.
Purpose: "A team roles model and questionnaire [that] identifies the contribution ... made by each individual to the success of [his or her work] team" and "indicates which [of 8 distinct] Jungian function-attitudes are primarily being used at present."
Population: Adults.
Publication Date: 2000.
Acronym: MTR-i.
Scores: 8 team roles: Coach, Crusader, Explorer, Innovator, Sculptor, Curator, Conductor, Scientist.
Administration: Group.
Price Data, 2001: £49.50 per specimen set including technical manual (2000, 95 pages), question card, answer sheet, report, and 360 Degree feedback form; £35 per 10 self-score answer sheets; £35 per 10 report and 360 Degree feedback forms; £42.50 per technical manual.
Time: (10–15) minutes.
Comments: Can be completed online.
Author: Stephen P. Myers.
Publisher: The Test Agency Limited [England] [No reply from publisher; status unknown].
Cross References: For reviews by Gary J. Dean and John Tivendell, see 15:141.

[1514]
Management Transactions Audit.
Purpose: Assesses "one's interpersonal transactions and their implications for managerial effectiveness."
Population: Managers.
Publication Dates: 1973–1997.
Acronym: MTA.
Scores, 9: Transaction Scores (Parent Subsystem, Adult Subsystem, Child Subsystem); Tension Index Scores (Subordinates [Disruptive, Constructive], Colleagues [Disruptive, Constructive], Superiors [Disruptive, Constructive]).
Administration: Group.
Manual: No manual.
Price Data, 2001: $8.95 per instrument.
Time: [15-30] minutes.
Comments: Self-administered survey.
Authors: Jay Hall and C. Leo Griffith.

Publisher: Teleometrics International, Inc.
Cross References: For reviews by Stephan J. Motowidlo and Ronald N. Taylor, see 8:1180.

[1515]
Manager Style Appraisal.
Purpose: A measure of managerial style.
Population: Adults.
Publication Dates: 1967-1995.
Scores, 5: Philosophy, Planning and Goal Setting, Implementation, Performance Evaluation, Total.
Administration: Group.
Price Data, 2001: $7.95 per instrument.
Time: Untimed.
Comments: Self-administered survey.
Authors: Jay Hall, Jerry B. Harvey, and Martha S. Williams.
Publisher: Teleometrics International, Inc.
Cross References: For reviews by Kenneth N. Anchor and Claudia J. Morner, see 12:228.

[1516]
Manager/Supervisor Staff Selector.
Purpose: "Measures important intellectual and personality characteristics needed for the successful manager/supervisor."
Population: Candidates for managerial and supervisory positions.
Publication Dates: 1976–1984.
Scores: 10 tests: Problem Solving Ability, Numerical Skills, Fluency, Business, Judgment, Supervisory Practices, CPF (interest in working with people), NPF (emotional stability), Adult Personality Inventory, Work Motivation Inventory.
Administration: Group.
Price Data, 2001: $500 per person; quantity discounts available.
Foreign Language Edition: French edition available.
Time: (240) minutes.
Comments: Graded by publisher; comprehensive report prepared for each candidate; must be proctored.
Authors: Tests from various publishers compiled, distributed, and scored by Walden Personnel Testing.
Publisher: Walden Personnel Performance, Inc. [Canada].
Cross References: For a review by Eric F. Gardner, see 10:186.

[1517]
Managerial and Professional Job Functions Inventory.
Purpose: "For defining the basic dimensions of jobs and assessing their relative importance for the job" and "assessing one's ability to perform them."
Population: Middle and upper level managers and higher-level professionals.

Publication Dates: 1978–1997.
Acronym: MPJFI.
Scores, 16: Setting Organizational Objectives, Financial Planning and Review, Improving Work Procedures and Practices, Interdepartmental Coordination, Developing and Implementing Technical Ideas, Judgment and Decision-Making, Developing Teamwork, Coping with Difficulties and Emergencies, Promoting Safety Attitudes and Practices, Communications, Developing Employee Potential, Supervisory Practices, Self-Development and Improvement, Personnel Practices, Promoting Community-Organization Relations, Handling Outside Contacts.
Administration: Individual or group.
Price Data, 2002: $101 per start-up kit including 25 test booklets (specify Importance or Ability), 25 score sheets, and interpretation and research manual; $54 per 25 test booklets (specify Importance or Ability); $31 per 25 score sheets; $28 per interpretation and research manual.
Time: No limit (approximately 40–60 minutes).
Authors: Melany E. Baehr, Wallace G. Lonergan, and Bruce A. Hunt.
Publisher: Pearson Performance Solutions [No reply from publisher; status unknown].
Cross References: For reviews by L. Alan Witt and Sheldon Zedeck, see 11:222.

[1518]
Managerial Assessment of Proficiency MAP™.

Purpose: "Shows a participant's strengths and weaknesses in twelve areas of managerial competency and two dimensions of management style."
Population: Managers.
Publication Dates: 1985–1988.
Acronym: MAP.
Scores, 19: Administrative Competencies (Time Management and Prioritizing, Setting Goals and Standards, Planning and Scheduling Work, Administrative Composite), Communication Competencies (Listening and Organizing, Giving Clear Information, Getting Unbiased Information, Communication Composite), Supervisory Competencies (Training/Coaching/Delegating, Appraising People and Performance, Disciplining and Counseling, Supervisory Composite), Cognitive Competencies (Identifying and Solving Problems, Making Decisions/Weighing Risk, Thinking Clearly and Analytically, Cognitive Composite), Proficiency Composite, Theory X Style (Parent-Child), and Theory Y Style (Adult-Adult).
Administration: Group.
Price Data: Available from publisher.
Time: (360–420) minutes.
Comments: May be purchased with licensing agreement, contracted for in-house administration, or used by attending a public workshop provided by publisher; administered in part by videocassette.
Author: Scott B. Parry.
Publisher: Training House, Inc.
Cross References: For a review by Jerard F. Kehoe, see 11:223.

[1519]
Managerial Competence Index.

Purpose: "To assess the probable competence of one's approach to management."
Population: Individuals who manage or are being assessed for their potential to manage others.
Publication Dates: 1980-1989.
Acronym: MCI.
Scores, 5: Team Management, Middle-of-the-Road Management, Task Management, Country Club Management, Impoverished Management.
Administration: Group.
Price Data, 2001: $8.95 per instrument (1989, 21 pages).
Time: Administration time not reported.
Author: Jay Hall.
Publisher: Teleometrics International, Inc.
Cross References: For a review by Kurt F. Geisinger, see 11:224.

[1520]
Managerial Competence Review.

Purpose: To identify a manager's preferred managerial style and assess the relative competence of his/her approach to management.
Population: Subordinates to managers.
Publication Dates: 1980–1989.
Acronym: MCR.
Scores, 5: Relative measures of concern for people and concern for production ("9/9," "1/9," "5/5," "9/1," "1/1").
Administration: Group.
Price Data, 2001: $7.95 per instrument (1989, 17 pages).
Time: Administration time not reported.
Comments: Companion instrument for Managerial Competence Index (1519).
Author: Jay Hall.
Publisher: Teleometrics International, Inc.

[1521]
Managerial Competency Questionnaire.

Purpose: "Developed to measure the use of seven competencies that have been found to be critical for effective managers."
Population: Managers.
Publication Date: 1997.
Acronym: MCQ.
Scores, 7: Achievement Orientation, Developing Others, Directiveness, Impact and Influence, Interper-

sonal Understanding, Organizational Awareness, Team Leadership.
Administration: Individual or group.
Price Data, 2006: $69 per 10 questionnaire, and interpretive notes (24 pages); $29 per 10 questionnaires only; $55 per 10 Development Assistant booklets. Refer to the Manager Competency Portfolio for a more comprehensive on-line alternative.
Time: [30–40] minutes.
Comments: Self-report questionnaire.
Author: Hay Group.
Publisher: Hay Group.

[1522]
Managerial Philosophies Scale.

Purpose: Surveys the "manager's assumptions and working theories about the nature of those whose activities he or she coordinates."
Population: Managers.
Publication Dates: 1975–1995.
Acronym: MPS.
Scores, 2: Theory X (Reductive Management Beliefs), Theory Y (Developmental Management Beliefs).
Administration: Group.
Manual: No manual.
Price Data, 2001: $8.95 per instrument.
Time: [15-30] minutes.
Comments: Self-administered survey.
Authors: Jacob Jacoby and James R. Terborg.
Publisher: Teleometrics International, Inc.
Cross References: See T3:1366 (1 reference).

[1523]
Managerial Scale for Enterprise Improvement.

Purpose: Designed "to measure management morale."
Population: Managers.
Publication Date: No date.
Scores: Total score only.
Administration: Group.
Price Data, 2001: $2 per specimen set.
Time: (12) minutes.
Author: Herbert A. Kaufman.
Publisher: Psychometric Affiliates.
Cross References: For a review by Nambury S. Raju, see 15:142.

[1524]
Managerial Style Questionnaire.

Purpose: Measures individuals' perception of how they manage based on the assessment of six managerial styles.
Population: Persons in managerial situations.
Publication Dates: 1980–1996.
Acronym: MSQ.

Scores, 6: Coercive, Authoritative, Affiliative, Democratic, Pacesetting, Coaching.
Administration: Group or individual.
Forms, 2: Participant, Employee.
Price Data, 2006: $79 per 10 Participant version questionnaires, profiles, and interpretive notes; $29 per 10 Employee version questionnaires; $25 per trainer's guide (1994, 28 pages) hardcopy of free electronic copy with purchase.
Foreign Language Editions: Available in Spanish and French.
Time: [30–40] minutes.
Comments: Self-scored instrument.
Author: Hay Group.
Publisher: Hay Group.
Cross References: For a review by H. John Bernardin and Joan E. Pynes, see 10:185; for a review by Frank L. Schmidt of an earlier edition, see 8:1182 (1 reference).

[1525]
Manchester Personality Questionnaire.

Purpose: Designed to provide an occupational personality test with a focus on traits relevant to creative and innovative behavior.
Population: Adults.
Publication Dates: 1993–1996.
Acronym: MPQ.
Administration: Group.
Author: CIM Test Publishers.
Publisher: The Test Agency Limited [England]; North American Distributor: Human Resource Development Press [No reply from publisher; status unknown].

a) MPQ FACTOR 14.
Purpose: An assessment of 14 personality traits covering the Big Five personality factors.
Scores, 19: Big Five Factors (Creativity, Agreeableness, Achievement, Extroversion, Resilience), Originality, Rule Consciousness, Openness to Change, Assertiveness, Social Confidence, Empathy, Communicativeness, Independence, Rationality, Competitiveness, Conscientiousness, Perfectionism, Decisiveness, Apprehension.
Price Data, 2001: £65 per administration set including user's manual (1996, 72 pages), reusable questionnaire, answer sheet, and profile chart; £55 per user's manual; £6.50 per reusable question booklet; £62.50 per 25 answer sheets; £25 per 25 profile charts; £450 per MPQ Expert System.
Time: (20) minutes.
b) MANCHESTER CREATIVITY QUESTIONNAIRE FACTOR 7.
Purpose: An assessment of the personality attributes of creativity.
Scores, 9: Global Factor (Creativity), Originality, Rule Consciousness, Openness to Change,

Assertiveness, Independence, Achievement, Radicalness, Response Style.
Price Data: £65 per 10 combined question/answer booklets.
Time: Administration time not reported.
Cross References: For reviews by Jack E. Gebart-Eaglemont and Carl Isenhart, see 13:191.

[1526]
Manifestation of Symptomatology Scale.

Purpose: Designed "to identify problems of children and adolescents."
Population: Ages 11–18.
Publication Date: 1999.
Acronym: MOSS.
Scores, 20: Validity Scores (Inconsistent Responding, Random Responding, Faking Good, Faking Bad), Summary Index (Affective State, Home, Acting Out), Content Scales (Sexual Abuse, Alcohol and Drugs, Suspiciousness, Thought Process, Self-Esteem, Depression, Anxiety, Mother, Father, Home Environment, Impulsivity, School, Compliance).
Administration: Group or individual.
Price Data, 2006: $99 per kit including 25 AutoScore forms and manual (69 pages); $48.50 per 25 AutoScore forms; $55 per manual.
Time: (15–20) minutes.
Comments: Self-report inventory.
Author: Neil L. Mogge.
Publisher: Western Psychological Services.
Cross References: For reviews by Ronald A. Berk and Richard B. Stuart, see 15:143.

[1527]
The Manson Evaluation, Revised Edition.

Purpose: Identifies alcoholics and potential alcoholics.
Population: Adults.
Publication Dates: 1948–1987.
Scores, 8: Anxiety, Depressive Fluctuations, Emotional Sensitivity, Resentfulness, Incompleteness, Aloneness, Interpersonal Relations, Total.
Administration: Individual or group.
Editions, 2: Paper-and-pencil, microcomputer.
Price Data, 2006: $82.50 per complete kit including 25 AutoScore™ test profile forms and manual (1987, 28 pages); $37.95 per 25 AutoScore™ test booklets/profiles (1987); $49.50 per manual.
Time: 5–10 minutes.
Comments: Self-administered; computer program and mail-in answer sheets can be used for both the Manson Evaluation and the Alcadd Test (135).
Authors: Morse P. Manson and George J. Huba.
Publisher: Western Psychological Services.
Cross References: For reviews by Tony Toneatto and Jalie A. Tucker, see 11:226; see also T2:1271 (2

references) and P:152 (1 reference); for a review by Dugal Campbell, see 6:137 (5 references); for reviews by Charles H. Honzik and Albert L. Hunsicker, see 4:68 (4 references).

[1528]
Manual Dexterity Test.

Purpose: Designed to provide "a measure of manual speed and skill."
Population: Ages 16 and over.
Publication Date: No date.
Acronym: MDT.
Scores, 4: Speed, Speed and Skill, Manual Speed (average scale score of Speed, Speed and Skill), Manual Skill (difference between Speed, Speed and Skill scale scores).
Administration: Group.
Price Data: Available from publisher.
Time: 2 minutes and 15 seconds (8 minutes).
Author: Educational & Industrial Test Services Ltd.
Publisher: Educational & Industrial Test Services Ltd. [England].

[1529]
MAPP: Motivational Appraisal of Personal Potential.

Purpose: Intended to measure "an individual's potential and motivation for given areas of work."
Population: Employees at all levels.
Publication Date: 1995.
Acronym: MAPP.
Scores, 13: Interest in Job Content, Temperament for the Job, Aptitude for the Job, Orientation to People, Affinity for Objects and Things, Approach to Data and Information, Reasoning and Thinking Style, Mathematical Capability, Language Levels, Personal Style, Personal Traits, Interpersonal and Social Tendencies, Learning Style.
Administration: Group.
Price Data: Available from publisher.
Time: (20–25) minutes.
Comments: Available as paper-and-pencil or computerized version.
Author: International Assessment Network.
Publisher: International Assessment Network.
Cross References: For reviews by Martha E. Hennen and Abbot Packard, see 14:218.

[1530]
A Marital Communication Inventory.

Purpose: Designed to assess the communications dimension of a marital relationship for purposes of counseling and marriage enrichment.
Population: Married couples.
Publication Dates: 1968-1979.
Acronym: MCI.

Scores: Total score only.
Administration: Group.
Price Data, 1993: $1.50 per inventory; $2 per manual (1978, 8 pages).
Time: (20) minutes.
Author: Millard J. Bienvenu.
Publisher: Millard J. Bienvenu, Northwest Publications.
Cross References: See T5:1580 (5 references) and T4:1536 (4 references); for a review by Joseph P. Stokes, see 9:651 (1 reference).

[1531]
Marital Evaluation Checklist.

Purpose: "Provides a brief yet comprehensive survey of the most common characteristics and problem areas in a marital relationship."
Population: Married couples in counseling.
Publication Date: 1984.
Acronym: MEC.
Scores: 3 areas: Reasons for Marrying, Problems of the Current Relationship, Motivation for Counseling.
Administration: Group.
Price Data, 2006: $50 per package of 50.
Time: (30-40) minutes.
Comments: Self-administered checklist.
Author: Leslie Navran.
Publisher: Psychological Assessment Resources, Inc.
Cross References: See T5:1581 (1 reference); for a review by Richard B. Stuart, see 10:187.

[1532]
Marital Satisfaction Inventory—Revised.

Purpose: Designed to "identify, separately for each partner in a relationship, the nature and extent of distress along several key dimensions of their relationship."
Population: Couples who are married or living together.
Publication Dates: 1979–1998.
Acronym: MSI-R.
Scores, 13: Conventionalization, Global Distress, Affective Communication, Problem-Solving Communication, Aggression, Time Together, Disagreement About Finances, Sexual Dissatisfaction, Role Orientation, Family History of Distress, Dissatisfaction with Children, Conflict over Child Rearing, Inconsistency.
Administration: Group.
Price Data, 2006: $121 per complete kit including 40 AutoScore™ answer forms and manual (1997, 126 pages); $42.50 per 20 AutoScore™ answer forms; $54.50 per manual; $18.50 per 6 Spanish research administration booklets; $18.50 per mail-in answer booklet; $265 per 20-use disk (PC with Microsoft Windows); $16.50 per 100 PC answer sheets; $12.50 per FAX Service Scoring charge.

Foreign Language Edition: Spanish research edition administration booklet available but without separate norms.
Time: 20 to 25 minutes.
Comments: 150-item self-report inventory; hand or computer scoring available; computer-generated interpretation available.
Author: Douglas K. Snyder.
Publisher: Western Psychological Services.
Cross References: For reviews by Frank Bernt and Mary Lou Bryant Frank, see 14:219; see also T5:1582 (15 references) and T4:1538 (7 references); for reviews by David N. Dixon and E. M. Waring of an earlier edition, see 9:652 (2 references).

[1533]
The Maroondah Assessment Profile for Problem Gambling.

Purpose: Designed as "an instrument that assists counselors in developing treatment intervention for their clients with gambling problems."
Population: People with gambling problems.
Publication Date: 1999.
Acronym: G-MAP.
Scores, 17: Beliefs About Winning (Control, Prophecy, Uninformed), Feelings (Good Feelings, Relaxation, Boredom, Numbness), Situations (Oasis, Transition, Desperation, Mischief), Attitudes to Self (Low Self-Image, "Winner," Entrenchment, Harm to Self), Social (Shyness, Friendship).
Administration: Group or individual.
Price Data, 2006: A$240.90 per kit including 10 questionnaires, manual (2000, 234 pages), 10 answer sheets, 18 photocopiable action sheet masters, 10 profile sheets, 10 response reports, and computer scoring program disk; $108.90 per manual (including disk); $60.50 per 10 questionnaires; $42.90 per 10 answer sheet; $22 per 10 profile sheets; $5.50 per response form; $29.70 per 18 action sheets.
Time: (20) minutes.
Comments: Self-report inventory; Scoring program calculates scores for all factors and provides unlimited scoring.
Authors: Tim Loughnan, Mark Pierce, and Anastasia Sagris-Desmond.
Publisher: Australian Council for Educational Research Ltd. [Australia].
Cross References: For reviews by George Engelhard, Jr. and Michael G. Kavan, see 15:144.

[1534]
Martin and Pratt Nonword Reading Test.

Purpose: Designed to "investigate the [phonological] recoding skills of students."
Population: Ages 6–16.
Publication Date: 2001.

Scores: Total score only.
Administration: Individual.
Forms, 2: A, B.
Price Data, 2006: A$120 per starter set including record booklet, stimulus book, and manual (60 pages); A$16.50 per 10 record booklets (A or B); A$35 per stimulus book; A$60 per manual.
Time: (5–10) minutes.
Authors: Frances Martin and Chris Pratt.
Publisher: Australian Council for Educational Research Ltd. [Australia].
Cross References: For reviews by Kris L. Baack and Annabel J. Cohen, see 16:139.

[1535]
Maryland Addictions Questionnaire.

Purpose: Intended to survey "issues relevant to the severity of patients' alcohol and drug abuse history."
Population: Ages 17 and older.
Publication Date: 1997.
Acronym: MAQ.
Scores, 15: Validity (Response Inconsistency, Defensiveness), Summary (Emotional Distress, Resistance to Treatment, Admission of Problems), Substance Abuse (Alcoholism Severity, Drug Abuse Severity, Craving, Substance Abuse Control, Resentment), Treatment (Motivation for Treatment, Social Anxiety, Antisocial Behaviors, Cognitive Symptoms, Affective Disturbance).
Administration: Group.
Price Data, 2006: $99 per complete kit including manual (102 pages) and 25 AutoScore™ answer sheets; $47 per 25 AutoScore™ answer sheets; $15.95 per mail-in answer sheet; $16.50 per 100-pad PC answer sheets; $54.95 per manual; $299 per PC disk good for 25 uses (3.5-inch, Microsoft Windows required); $11.50 per FAX Scoring Service.
Time: (15–20) minutes.
Comments: Author suggests should be administered as an intake measure for individuals entering addiction treatment programs.
Authors: William E. O'Donnell, Clinton B. DeSoto, and Janet L. DeSoto.
Publisher: Western Psychological Services.
Cross References: For reviews by Carl Isenhart and John A. Mills, see 14:220.

[1536]
Maryland/Baltimore County Design for Adult Basic Education.

Purpose: "Diagnoses a student's strengths, weaknesses, and deficiencies in skill areas that are prerequisite to literacy."
Population: Adult nonreaders.
Publication Date: 1982.
Scores: 21 subtest scores in 5 areas: Background Knowledge, Alphabet Recognition and Reproduction,

Auditory Perception and Discrimination, Visual Perception and Discrimination, Sight Vocabulary.
Administration: Group and individual.
Price Data: Not available.
Time: (120–180) minutes.
Comments: Commonly called the "BCD Test."
Author: Baltimore County Public Schools Office of Adult Education.
Publisher: Prentice Hall [No reply from publisher; status unknown].
Cross References: For reviews by Mary M. Dupuis and Sharon L. Smith, see 9:658.

[1537]
Maryland Parent Attitude Survey.

Purpose: Designed to measure child-rearing attitudes.
Population: Parents.
Publication Dates: [1957-1966].
Acronym: MPAS.
Scores, 4: Disciplinarian, Indulgent, Protective, Rejecting.
Administration: Group.
Price Data, 2001: $5 per complete package including test, scoring instructions and tables, T scores, and copy of article.
Time: [20–60] minutes.
Comments: For research use only; tests may be reproduced locally.
Author: Donald K. Pumroy.
Publisher: Donald K. Pumroy.
Cross References: See T4:1551 (1 reference).

[1538]
Maslach Burnout Inventory, Third Edition.

Purpose: Constructed to measure three aspects of burnout.
Population: Members of the helping professions including educators and human service professionals.
Publication Dates: 1981–1996.
Scores, 3: Emotional Exhaustion, Depersonalization, Personal Accomplishment.
Administration: Group.
Price Data, 2001: $65 per review kit including Human Services Survey booklet, Educators Survey booklet, General Survey booklet, set of scoring keys, and manual (1996, 56 pages); $28 per 25 nonreusable survey booklets (specify Human Services, Educators, or General); $17.50 per 25 Human Services Survey or Educators Survey demographic data sheets; $14 per 25 scoring keys; $42 per manual.
Authors: Wilmar B. Schaufeli, Michael P. Leiter, Christina Maslach, and Susan E. Jackson.
Publisher: CPP, Inc.
a) HUMAN SERVICES SURVEY.
Acronym: MBI-HSS.

Population: Staff members in the Human Services profession.
Time: (10–15) minutes.
b) EDUCATORS SURVEY.
Acronym: MBI-ES.
Population: Educators.
Time: (5–10) minutes.
c) GENERAL SURVEY.
Acronym: MBI-GS.
Population: Other workers in the service professions.
Time: (10-15) minutes.
Cross References: For reviews by Robert Fitzpatrick and Claudia R. Wright, see 16:140; see also T5:1590 (69 references) and T4:1552 (30 references); for reviews by David S. Hargrove and Jonathan Sandoval of an earlier edition, see 10:189 (34 references).

[1539]
Matching Assistive Technology & CHild.

Purpose: A series of instruments designed to assess "infants' and childrens' need for assistive technology" to determine the most appropriate child-technology match.
Population: Children with disabilities, ages 0–5.
Publication Date: 1997.
Administration: Individual.
Price Data: Available from publisher.
Time: (90) minutes for entire battery.
Comments: To be used by Early Intervention and Special Education professionals with parents.
Author: Marcia J. Scherer.
Publisher: The Institute for Matching Person & Technology, Inc.
a) TECHNOLOGY UTILIZATION WORKSHEET FOR MATCHING ASSISTIVE TECHNOLOGY & CHILD.
Purpose: Designed to "review technologies the child is currently using, has used in the past, and needs."
Scores: No formal scores; examines perceptions in 10 areas: Communication, Mobility/Gross Motor, Vision, Hearing, Fine Motor Skills, Daily Living, Health Maintenance, Play, Self-Care, Learning/Cognition.
Comments: Completed by parent and/or educator.
b) WORKSHEET FOR MATCHING ASSISTIVE TECHNOLOGY & CHILD.
Purpose: Designed to "obtain parent perspectives of a child's particular limitations, goals, and interventions as well as strengths which can be bulit upon in planning interventions."
Scores: No scores; examines perceptions of 10 areas: Communication, Mobility/Gross Motor, Vision, Hearing, Fine Motor Skills, Daily Living, Health Maintenance, Play, Self-Care, Learning/Cognition.
Comments: Completed by the child's parent.
c) SURVEY OF TECHNOLOGY USE.
Purpose: Designed to "help identify technologies and technology functions/features a child is likely to feel comfortable or successful in using."
Acronym: SOTU.
Scores: No formal scores.
Comments: Completed by educator and/or parent.
d) MATCHING ASSISTIVE TECHNOLOGY & CHILD.
Purpose: Designed to help "select the most appropriate assistive technology for a child's use while pinpointing areas for training and further assessment."
Acronym: MATCH.
Scores: No formal scores.
Comments: Completed by caregiver or educator.
Cross References: For reviews by Libby G. Cohen and by T. Steuart Watson and R. Anthony Doggett, see 15:145.

[1540]
Matching Familiar Figures Test.

Purpose: Measurement of constructs of reflection and impulsivity.
Population: Ages 5–12, 13 and over.
Publication Date: 1965.
Acronym: MFF.
Scores: Total score only.
Administration: Individual.
Levels, 2: Elementary, Adolescent/Adult.
Manual: No manual.
Price Data: Available from publisher.
Time: Administration time not reported.
Authors: Jerome Kagan (test) and Neil J. Salkind (norms booklet).
Publisher: Jerome Kagan [No reply from publisher; status unknown].
Cross References: See T5:1592 (28 references), T4:1553 (106 references), and 9:662 (71 references).

[1541]
Matching Person and Technology.

Purpose: Designed for "selecting and evaluating technologies used in rehabilitation, education, the workplace and other settings."
Population: Clients, students, or employees,
Publication Dates: 1991–2005.
Acronym: MPT.
Administration: Individual or group.
Forms, 2: Consumer, Professional.
Price Data: Available from publisher.

421

Time: (15) minutes per test.
Comments: CD version (2005) is available with additional administration tools and supplemental resources.
Author: Marcia J. Scherer.
Publisher: The Institute for Matching Person & Technology, Inc.

a) SURVEY OF TECHNOLOGY USE.
Purpose: Constructed to measure "the consumer's present use of, experiences with, and feelings toward technological devices."
Acronym: SOTU.
Scores: 4 categories: Experience with Current Technologies, Perspectives on Technologies, Typical Activities, Personal/Social Characteristics.

b) ASSISTIVE TECHNOLOGY DEVICE PREDISPOSITION ASSESSMENT.
Purpose: Designed to "help individuals select appropriate assistive technologies."
Acronym: ATD PA.
Scores: 5 categories: Subjective View of Capabilities, Subjective Well-Being/Quality of Life, Temperament and Psychosocial Characteristics, Device and Person Degree of Match.

c) EDUCATIONAL TECHNOLOGY PREDISPOSITION ASSESSMENT.
Purpose: Designed "for teachers who are helping students use technology to reach educational goals."
Acronym: ET PA.
Scores: 4 categories: Educational Goal, The Student, Educational Technology, Educational Environment.

d) WORKPLACE TECHNOLOGY PREDISPOSITION ASSESSMENT.
Purpose: "Designed to assist employers in identifying factors that might inhibit the acceptance or use of a new technology in the workplace."
Acronym: WT PA.
Scores: 4 categories: The Technology, The Employee Being Trained to Use the Technology, The Workplace Environment, Match Between Person and Technology.

e) HEALTH CARE TECHNOLOGY PREDISPOSITION ASSESSMENT.
Purpose: "Developed to assist health care professionals in identifying factors that might inhibit the acceptance or appropriate use of health care technologies."
Acronym: HCT PA.
Scores: 5 categories: Health Problem, Consequences of HCT Use, Characteristics of the Health Care Technology, Personal Issues, Attitudes of Others.
Cross References: For reviews by Patricia A. Bachelor and by Laura L. B. Barnes and Carrie L. Winterowd, see 14:221.

[1542]
MATE [Marital ATtitude Evaluation].

Purpose: "Designed to explore the relation between two people who have close contact with each other."
Population: Couples.
Publication Date: 1989.
Acronym: WET.
Scores: 5 scales: Inclusion Behavior, Inclusion Feelings, Control Behavior, Control Feelings, Affection.
Administration: Group.
Manual: Information included in manual of FIRO Awareness Scales.
Price Data: Available from publisher (www.mindgarden.com).
Time: Administration time not reported.
Comments: Based on FIRO Awareness Scales.
Author: Will Schutz.
Publisher: Mind Garden, Inc.

[1543]
Math-Level Indicator.

Purpose: Designed to survey the basic mathematical skills of students.
Population: Grades 4–12.
Publication Date: 2003.
Acronym: MLI.
Scores: Total score only.
Administration: Group.
Price Data, 2006: $144.99 per starter set including manual, 1 package (25) Red forms, 1 package (25) Blue forms, 2 hand-scoring templates, and 2 scannable answer sheets packages (25 each); $25.99 per manual; $36.99 per 25 forms (specify Red or Blue); $41.99 per 2 hand-scoring templates; $19.99 per 25 scannable answer sheets.
Time: (30) minutes.
Comments: Designed to work with the Group Mathematics Assessment and Diagnostic Evaluation (G·MADE; 1124).
Author: Kathleen T. Williams.
Publisher: Pearson Assessments (originally published by AGS Publishing, acquired by Pearson in 2005).
Cross References: For reviews by Zandra S. Gratz and Dixie McGinty, see 16:141.

[1544]
Mathematical Olympiads.

Purpose: Constructed "to discover and challenge secondary school students with outstanding mathematical talent."
Population: Secondary school.
Publication Dates: 1972-2001.
Scores: Total score only.
Administration: Group.
Manual: No manual.
Price Data: Available from publisher.

Author: Committee on the American Mathematics Competitions.
Publisher: Mathematical Association of America; American Mathematics Competitions.
   a) USA MATHEMATICAL OLYMPIAD.
   Acronym: USAMO.
   Time: 10–20) minutes over 2 sessions.
   Comments: Test administered annually in April; selection to participate is based on both the AMC12 and AIME scores.
   b) INTERNATIONAL MATHEMATICAL OLYMPIAD.
   Acronym: IMO.
   Time: (10–20) minutes over 2 sessions.
   Comments: Test administered annually in July; selection to participate is based on USAMO scores and other scores obtained during the training session.
Cross References: For reviews by Phillip L. Ackerman and William R. Koch, see 11:228.

[1545]
Mathematics Attitude Inventory.
Purpose: "To measure the attitudes toward mathematics of secondary school and college students."
Population: Grades 7-12 and undergraduate students.
Publication Date: 1979.
Acronym: MAI.
Scores, 6: Perception of the Mathematics Teacher, Anxiety Toward Mathematics, Value of Mathematics in Society, Self-Concept in Mathematics, Enjoyment of Mathematics, Motivation in Mathematics.
Administration: Group.
Price Data: Price information available from publisher for tests, scoring key, and manual (26 pages).
Time: 15-20 minutes.
Comments: Tests may be reproduced locally.
Author: Richard S. Sandman.
Publisher: Quantitative Methods in Education, University of Minnesota.
Cross References: See T5:1599 (6 references); for reviews by Harvey Resnick and Richard F. Schmid, see 9:664 (3 references); see also T3:1410 (1 reference).

[1546]
Mathematics Competency Test.
Purpose: Constructed to assess "mathematics achievement."
Population: Ages 11 to adult.
Publication Date: 1996.
Scores: Total score only.
Administration: Group.
Price Data, 2006: A$18.15 per 10 test booklets; $36.30 per manua; $38 per specimen set.
Time: (40) minutes.
Authors: P. E. Vernon, K. M. Miller, and J. F. Izard.

Publisher: Australian Council for Educational Research Ltd. [Australia]; Hodder & Stoughton Educational [England].
Cross References: For reviews by Joseph C. Ciechalski and G. Michael Poteat, see 14:222.

[1547]
Mathematics Self-Efficacy Scale.
Purpose: Intended to measure beliefs regarding ability to perform various math-related tasks and behaviors.
Population: College freshmen.
Publication Date: 1993.
Acronym: MATH.
Scores, 3: Mathematics Task Self-Efficacy, Math-Related School Subjects Self-Efficacy, Total Mathematics Self-Efficacy Score.
Administration: Group.
Forms, 2: A, B.
Price Data: Available from publisher (www.mindgarden.com).
Time: (15) minutes.
Authors: Nancy E. Betz and Gail Hackett.
Publisher: Mind Garden, Inc.
Cross References: For reviews by Joseph C. Ciechalski and Everett V. Smith, Jr., see 14:223; see also T5:1602 (1 reference).

[1548]
Mathematics 7.
Purpose: "Assess the mathematics attainment of children near the end of the school year in which they reach their seventh birthday."
Population: Ages 6-10 to 7-9.
Publication Date: 1987.
Scores: 1 individual total score, 4 item analysis categories: Understanding, Computational Skill, Application, Factual Recall.
Administration: Group.
Price Data: Price information available from publisher for specimen set including Teacher's Guide (24 pages), test booklet, and group record sheet.
Time: (30–50) minutes.
Comments: Downward extension of Mathematics 8–12 Series; no norms for categories; orally administered.
Author: Test Development Unit of the Foundation for Educational Research in England and Wales.
Publisher: NFER-Nelson Publishing Co., Ltd. [England].
Cross References: For reviews by Camilla Persson Benbow and Kevin Menefee, see 11:230.

[1549]
A Mathematics Test for Grades Four, Five and Six.
Purpose: Designed to measure "achievement in modern mathematics."

Population: Grades 4–6.
Publication Date: 1969.
Scores, 13: Understanding Numeration Systems, Set Terminology, Mathematical Structure, Addition and Subtraction of Whole Numbers, Multiplication of Whole Numbers, Division of Whole Numbers, Common Fractions, Decimal Fractions and Per Cent, Measurements, Geometry, Solving Problems with the Use of Number Sentences, Graphs and Scale Drawings, Total.
Administration: Group.
Price Data: Available from publisher.
Time: (120–180) minutes in 2 sessions.
Author: Stanley J. LeJeune.
Publisher: Psychometric Affiliates.
Cross References: For a review by William H. Nibbelink, see 8:280; for a review by Arthur Mittman, see 7:476.

[1550]
Mather-Woodcock Group Writing Tests.
Purpose: "Designed for early identification of problems/weaknesses, measurement of growth in writing skills, instructional planning, and curriculum evaluation."
Population: Grades 2.0–16.9.
Publication Date: 1997.
Acronym: GWT.
Scores: 3 clusters (Total Writing, Basic Writing Skills, Expressive Writing Ability), and 4 subtests (Dictation Spelling, Writing Samples, Editing, Writing Fluency).
Administration: Group.
Price Data, 2006: $229.50 per complete package including 25 writing booklets at selected level, administration instructions (96 pages), scoring key, 25 writing evaluation scales, manual, and scoring software (3.5 disk- Windows/Mac and user's manual); $90 per additional packages of booklets includes 25 writing booklets, 25 writing evaluation scales, and scoring key.
Time: (60) minutes or less.
Authors: Nancy Mather and Richard W. Woodcock.
Publisher: Riverside Publishing.
Cross References: For a review by Bruce Thompson, see 14:224.

[1551]
Matrix Analogies Test.
Purpose: Developed to "measure nonverbal reasoning ability."
Population: Ages 5-0 to 17-11.
Publication Date: 1985.
Author: Jack A. Naglieri.
Publisher: PsychCorp, A brand of Harcourt Assessment, Inc.
   a) SHORT FORM.
   Acronym: MAT-SF.
   Administration: Group.
   Scores: Total score only.

Price Data, 2002: $105 per 15 test booklets; $58 per 25 answer sheets; $43 per manual (1985, 45 pages); $51 per examination kit.
Time: 25(30) minutes.
   b) EXPANDED FORM.
   Acronym: MAT-EF.
   Administration: Individual.
   Scores, 5: Pattern Completion, Reasoning by Analogy, Serial Reasoning, Spatial Visualization, Total.
   Price Data: $218 per complete kit including stimulus book, 50 answer sheets, manual (1985, 82 pages) and case; $98 per stimulus manual; $58 per 50 answer sheets; $73 per examiner's manual.
   Time: (20–25) minutes.
Cross References: See T5:1607 (15 references) and T4:1566 (8 references); for a review by Robert F. McMorris, David L. Rule, and Wendy J. Steinberg, see 10:191 (1 reference).

[1552]
Mayer-Salovey-Caruso Emotional Intelligence Test.
Purpose: Designed to assess emotional intelligence, measuring a person's capacity for reasoning with emotional information.
Population: Age 17 and older.
Publication Date: 2002.
Acronym: MSCEIT.
Scores, 4: Managing Emotions, Understanding Emotions, Using Emotions, Perceiving Emotions.
Administration: Individual or group.
Price Data, 2006: $63 per user kit including user's manual (100 pages), 1 profile summary report, and 1 item booklet; $51 per user's manual; $38 per mail-in/fax-in report; $60 per online personal summary report kit includiong user's manual and 1 personal summary report; $66 per software preview version including getting started guide and 3 personal summary reports.
Time: (25–35) minutes.
Comments: Self-completed.
Authors: John D. Mayer, Peter Salovey, and David R. Caruso.
Publisher: Multi-Health Systems, Inc.
Cross References: For reviews by S. Alvin Leung and by Catherine Cook-Cottone and Scott T. Meier, see 16:143.

[1553]
The MbM Questionnaire: Managing by Motivation, Third Edition.
Purpose: Designed for "helping managers understand their own needs" ... and "to identify the needs of their employees."
Population: Managers and supervisors.
Publication Dates: 1986–1996.

Acronym: The MbM Questionnaire.
Scores: 4 scales: Safety/Security, Social/Belonging, Self-Esteem, Self-Actualization.
Administration: Group.
Price Data: Available from publisher.
Time: (10) minutes.
Author: Marshall Sashkin.
Publisher: HRD Press, Inc.
Cross References: For reviews by John W. Fleenor and Robert K. Gable, see 14:225.

[1554]
McCall-Crabbs Standard Test Lessons in Reading.
Purpose: Measurement of reading progress.
Population: Reading level grades 3-8.
Publication Dates: 1926–1979.
Scores: Item and grade equivalent scores.
Administration: Group.
Levels, 6: Overlapping levels labeled A, B, C, D, E, F.
Price Data, 2006: $3.95 per test booklet (any level); $6.95 per 30 answer sheets; $1.50 per manual/answer key (1979, 16 pages).
Time: 3 minutes for any one test; 180 minutes for each booklet (60 tests per booklet).
Comments: Fourth edition.
Authors: William A. McCall and Lelah Crabbs Schroeder; revision by Robert P. Starr.
Publisher: Teachers College Press.
Cross References: See T4:1568 (1 reference); for a review by Brendan John Bartlett, see 9:669.

[1555]
McCarron-Dial System.
Purpose: A battery of neurometric and behavioral measures to be used for vocational, educational, and neuropsychological assessment particularly in meeting the programming needs of handicapped persons.
Population: Normal and handicapped individuals ages 3 to adult.
Publication Dates: 1973-1986.
Acronym: MDS.
Scores: 5 factors: Verbal-Spatial-Cognitive, Sensory, Motor, Emotional, Integration-Coping.
Administration: Individual.
Parts: 3 components (Auxiliary Component, Haptic Visual Discrimination Test [HVDT], McCarron Assessment of Neuromuscular Development [MAND]).
Price Data, 2006: $3,115 per complete System including Auxiliary, HVDT, and MAND Components; price data for software for computer-assisted programs supporting the MDS available from publisher; price information for workshops and training available from publisher.
Comments: "A commitment to receive training is required for all purchasers of the McCarron-Dial System"; components available as separates.

Authors: Lawrence McCarron and Jack G. Dial.
Publisher: McCarron-Dial Systems.
a) AUXILIARY COMPONENT.
Publication Dates: 1973-1986.
Price Data: $640 per set of materials in carrying case; $49 per 25 forms for Peabody Form III-A; $32 per 50 IEP forms; $32 per 25 IPP forms; $125 per manual (2005, 259 pages).
Comments: Manual title is Revised McCarron-Dial Evaluation System Manual; kit includes Peabody Picture Vocabulary Test-III (1997), Bender Visual Motor Gestalt Test, and Koppitz Scoring Manual for The Bender Gestalt Test for Young Children, the McCarron-Dial System Individual Evaluation Profile (IEP), the McCarron-Dial Individual Program Plan (IPP), the Observational Emotional Inventory, the Emotional Behavioral Checklist, and the Dial Behavior Rating Scale.
1) *Dial Behavior Rating Scale.*
Purpose: To provide an abbreviated assessment of essential personal, social, and work adjustment behaviors that relate to vocational placement, adjustment to work, and personal-social adjustment.
Publication Dates: 1973-1986.
Acronym: BRS.
Price Data: $32 per 25 forms.
Author: Jack G. Dial.
2) *Observational Emotional Inventory.*
Publication Date: 1986.
Acronym: OEI.
Price Data: $32 per 25 forms.
Time: 120 minutes on each of 5 days.
Comments: Behavior checklist.
3) *Emotional Behavioral Checklist.*
Purpose: To assess an individual's overt emotional behavior.
Publication Date: 1986.
Acronym: EBC.
Price Data: $32 per 25 forms.
Comments: Behavior Checklist (alternate to OEI).
b) HAPTIC VISUAL DISCRIMINATION TEST.
Purpose: To measure an individual's haptic-visual integration skills.
Publication Dates: 1976-1979.
Acronym: HVDT.
Scores, 4: Shape, Size, Texture, Configuration.
Price Data: $1125 per complete kit including score forms, photographic plates, folding screen, sets of shapes, sizes, textures, and configurations, manual (1988, 261 forms) in a carrying case; $33.50 per 50 score forms; $50 per manual.
Time: (10-15) minutes per hand.
Comments: Manual title is Sensory Integration: The Haptic Visual Processes.

c) McCARRON ASSESSMENT OF NEUROMUS-CULAR DEVELOPMENT.
Purpose: "A standardized and quantitative procedure for assessing fine and gross motor abilities."
Population: Ages 3.5 to adult.
Publication Dates: 1976–1986.
Acronym: MAND.
Scores, 3: Fine Motor, Gross Motor, Total.
Price Data: $1,350 per complete kit including score forms, a dynamometer, stopwatch-timer, components for fine and gross motor testing, and manual (1982, 221 pages) in carrying case; $44.50 per 25 score forms; $65 per manual.
Time: (15) minutes.
Comments: Manual title is Revised McCarron Assessment of Neuromuscular Development Manual.
Author: Lawrence T. McCarron.
Cross References: For reviews by Calvin P. Garbin and David C. Solly, see 11:231 (1 reference).

[1556]
McCarthy Scales of Children's Abilities.
Purpose: Developed to "determine . . . general intellectual level as well as . . . strengths and weaknesses in important abilities."
Population: Ages 2.6–8.6.
Publication Dates: 1970–1972.
Acronym: MSCA.
Scores, 6: Verbal, Perceptual-Performance, Quantitative, Composite (General Cognitive), Memory, Motor.
Administration: Individual.
Price Data, 2002: $583 per complete set including all necessary equipment, 25 drawing booklets, 25 record forms, and manual (1972, 217 pages); $57 per 25 drawing booklets; $220 per 100 drawing booklets; $43 per 25 record forms; $157 per 100 record forms; $66 per manual.
Time: (45–60) minutes.
Author: Dorothea McCarthy.
Publisher: PsychCorp, A brand of Harcourt Assessment, Inc.
Cross References: See T5:1612 (101 references) and T4:1571 (97 references); for reviews by Kathleen D. Paget and David L. Wodrich, see 9:671 (29 references); see also T3:1424 (60 references); for reviews by Jane V. Hunt, Jerome M. Sattler, and Arthur B. Silverstein, and excerpted reviews by Everett E. Davis, by Linda Hufano and Ralph Hoepfner, by R. B. Ammons and C. H. Ammons, and by Alan Krichev, see 8:219 (29 references).

[1557]
McCarthy Screening Test.
Purpose: Designed to "identify children who are likely to encounter difficulty in coping with schoolwork."

Population: Ages 4–6.5.
Publication Dates: 1970–1978.
Acronym: MST.
Scores, 6: Right-Left Orientation, Verbal Memory, Draw-A-Design, Numerical Memory, Conceptual Grouping, Leg Coordination.
Administration: Individual.
Price Data, 2002: $225 per complete set including all necessary equipment, manual (1978, 71 pages), 25 record forms, 25 drawing booklets, and carrying case: $58 per 25 drawing booklets; $230 per 100 drawing booklets; $37 per 25 record forms; $152 per 100 record forms; $52 per manual.
Time: (20) minutes.
Comments: Adaptation of the McCarthy Scales of Children's Abilities; criterion-referenced; percentile cutoff scores provided for classification as "at risk" for learning problems.
Author: Dorothea McCarthy.
Publisher: PsychCorp, A brand of Harcourt Assessment, Inc.
Cross References: See T5:1613 (2 references) and T4:1572 (9 references); for reviews by Nadeen L. Kaufman and Jack A. Naglieri, see 9:672 (3 references); see also T3:1425 (2 references).

[1558]
McDowell Vision Screening Kit.
Purpose: "Designed for screening children's vision problems."
Population: 2 1/2 to 5 1/2 years.
Publication Date: 1994.
Scores, 15: Distance Vision, Near Point Vision, Ocular Alignment/Motility (Cover/Uncover, Light Reflex), Color Perception, Ocular Function (Pupils, Scanning, Shifts Attention, Blink, Tracking, Convergence, Conjugate Gaze, Visual Fields, Distant/Near Accommodation, Nystagmus).
Administration: Individual.
Price Data, 2006: $154 per kit including all test materials, 100 recording forms, and manual (40 pages); $32.50 per 100 recording forms; $49.50 per manual.
Time: (10–20) minutes.
Comments: Recording form for use in screening young children or disabled students; administrator scored.
Authors: P. Marlene McDowell and Richard L. McDowell.
Publisher: Western Psychological Services.
Cross References: For a review by Cynthia A. Rohrbeck, see 14:226.

[1559]
The mCircle™ Instrument.
Purpose: "Tests for and explores appropriate uses for five strategies routinely used by individuals to solve problems and reach resolution in human interaction."

Population: Business and industry.
Publication Date: 1986.
Scores, 5: Get Out, Give In, Take Over, Trade Off, Breakthrough.
Administration: Group.
Price Data: Available from publisher.
Time: (30-40) minutes.
Comments: Self-administered, self-scored.
Authors: Paul Kordis and Dudley Lynch.
Publisher: Brain Technologies Corporation.
Cross References: For reviews by Stephen Jurs and Rick Lindskog, see 11:232.

[1560]
MD5 Mental Ability Test.

Purpose: "To assess mental ability quickly, easily and over a wide range of educational and ability levels, in staff selection, placement and counselling."
Population: Supervisors to managers.
Publication Date: No date on test materials.
Scores: Total score only.
Administration: Group.
Price Data, 2001: £3.25 per question/answer book; £5 per scoring key; £19.50 per technical manual; £300 per computer system version.
Time: (15) minutes.
Author: The Test Agency.
Publisher: The Test Agency Limited [England] [No reply from publisher; status unknown].
Cross References: For reviews by M. Harry Daniels and David J. Mealor, see 10:193.

[1561]
MDS Vocational Interest Exploration System.

Purpose: "A computer-assisted interest exploration process that facilitates the discovery of personal preferences and job opportunities."
Population: High school–adults.
Publication Date: 1991.
Acronym: VIE.
Scores: 3 steps: Selection of Jobs Based on Work Preferences, Occupational Exploration, Job Review Comparison.
Administration: Individual.
Price Data, 2006: $350 per set including computer program (Windows or Macintosh), 4 VIE job manuals, instructor's manual (135 pages), 25 VIE system guides with work preference questionnaires and job review forms.
Time: Administration time not reported.
Comments: Three supplementary forms are also provided with materials: Pre-Post Job Knowledge Form, Understanding of Self and Job Questionnaire, and Vocational Goal Planning Exercise.
Authors: Lawrence T. McCarron and Harriette P. Spires.

Publisher: McCarron-Dial Systems.
Cross References: For reviews by Douglas J. McRae and Myra N. Womble, see 13:194.

[1562]
Meadow-Kendall Social-Emotional Assessment Inventory for Deaf and Hearing Impaired Students.

Purpose: "Can be used to flag students who need extra attention in particular areas . . . . useful in communicating with parents who are reluctant to admit that their child needs special attention ... helpful in implementing an individualized program so that social and emotional areas are emphasized in the curriculum for the child who needs them."
Population: Ages 3–6, 7–21.
Publication Date: 1983.
Acronym: SEAI.
Administration: Group.
Levels: 2 levels.
Price Data, 2001: $8 per 10 forms; $15 per manual (37 pages).
Time: Administration time not reported.
Comments: Behavior checklist to be completed by adult informant.
Authors: Kathryn P. Meadow and others listed below.
Publisher: Laurent Clerc National Deaf Education Center.
   a) PRE-SCHOOL.
   Population: Ages 3-6.
   Scores, 5: Sociable/Communicative Behaviors, Impulsive Dominating Behaviors, Developmental Lags, Anxious/Compulsive Behaviors, Special Items.
   Authors: Kathryn P. Meadow, Pamela Getson, Chi K. Lee, Linda Stamper, and the Center for Studies in Education and Human Development.
   b) SCHOOL-AGE.
   Population: Ages 7-21.
   Scores, 3: Social Adjustment, Self Image, Emotional Adjustment.
   Authors: Kathryn P. Meadow, Michael A. Karchmer, Linda M. Petersen, and Lawrence Rudner.
Cross References: See T5:1618 (3 references) and T4:1579 (2 references); for reviews by Marilyn E. Demorest and Kenneth L. Sheldon, see 10:194 (1 reference).

[1563]
Measure of Achieving Tendency.

Purpose: Developed to assess achievement motivation.
Population: Ages 15 and older.
Publication Dates: 1969–1993.

Acronym: MACH.
Scores: Total score only.
Administration: Group or individual.
Price Data: Available from publisher for complete kit including scales, scoring directions, norms, manual (1994, 8 pages), and literature review.
Time: (10–15) minutes.
Comments: Current revision also based on previous edition entitled A Questionnaire Measure of Individual Differences in Achieving Tendency.
Author: Albert Mehrabian.
Publisher: Albert Mehrabian.
Cross References: For reviews by James T. Austin and E. Scott Huebner, see 13:195 (1 reference); for a review by Timothy S. Hartshorne of an earlier edition, see 10:301; for a review by Jayne E. Stake of an earlier edition, see 9:682; see also T3:1442 (1 reference).

[1564]
Measure of Child Stimulus Screening and Arousability.

Purpose: Designed to assess child individual differences in positive and/or negative emotionality, emotional sensitivity, or emotional reactivity.
Population: Ages 3 months to 7 years.
Publication Date: 1978.
Scores: Total score only.
Administration: Group or individual.
Manual: No manual.
Price Data: Available from publisher for test kit including scale, scoring directions, norms, and descriptive material.
Time: [15] minutes.
Comments: Ratings by parents.
Authors: Albert Mehrabian and Carol A. Falender.
Publisher: Albert Mehrabian.
Cross References: See T5:1621 (1 reference); for a review by Steven Klee, see 9:678; see also T3:1439 (2 references).

[1565]
Measure of Existential Anxiety.

Purpose: Designed as a measure of existential anxiety.
Population: Adults and college-age.
Publication Date: No date.
Scores: Total score only.
Administration: Group.
Price Data, 2001: $3 per specimen set.
Time: Administration time not reported.
Authors: L. R. Good and K. C. Good.
Publisher: Psychometric Affiliates.
Cross References: For a review by Matthew E. Lambert, see 15:146.

[1566]
Measure of Individual Differences in Dominance-Submissiveness.

Purpose: Constructed as a "general measure of trait dominance-submissiveness—the general feeling of control and influence versus lack of control over one's surroundings and life situations."
Population: Ages 15 and older.
Publication Dates: 1978–1994.
Scores: Total score only.
Administration: Group or individual.
Price Data: Available from publisher for test kit including scale, scoring directions, norms, and manual (1994, 7 pages).
Time: (10–15) minutes.
Authors: Albert Mehrabian and Melissa Hines (original edition).
Publisher: Albert Mehrabian.
Cross References: For reviews by Robert H. Deluty and Douglas N. Jackson of an earlier edition, see 9:679.

[1567]
Measure of Questioning Skills.

Purpose: Designed "to measure the quantity and quality of questions."
Population: Grades 3–10.
Publication Dates: 1986–1993.
Scores, 4: Gathering Information, Organizing Information, Extending Information, Composite.
Administration: Group.
Forms, 2: A, B.
Price Data, 2005: $42.85 per complete kit including manual (1993, 61 pages), 20 activity booklets, 20 tally sheets, 20 result forms, 20 individual profile charts, and 1 class record sheet (specify form); $29 per 20 activity booklets, 20 tally sheets, 20 results forms, 20 individual profile charts, and 1 class record sheet (specify form); $16.55 per manual; $18.80 per sample set.
Time: (20) minutes.
Authors: Ralph Himsl and Garnet W. Millar.
Publisher: Scholastic Testing Service, Inc.
Cross References: For a review by Darrell R. Sabers, see 14:228.

[1568]
A Measure of Self-Esteem.

Purpose: Designed as a "measure of self-esteem ... that was constructed on the assumption that low self-esteem is indicated when someone feels inferior, inadequate, unworthy, disliked, helpless, etc."
Population: College-age and adults.
Publication Date: No date.
Scores: Total score only.
Administration: Group.
Price Data, 2001: $3 per specimen set.
Time: Administration time not reported.

Authors: L. R. Good and K. C. Good.
Publisher: Psychometric Affilates.
Cross References: For a review by Jeffrey A. Atlas, see 15:147.

[1569]
Measure of Self-Evaluation.

Purpose: Developed to measure an individual's need for self-evaluation.
Population: Adults.
Publication Date: No date.
Scores: Total score only.
Administration: Group.
Price Data, 2001: $3 per specimen set.
Time: Administration time not reported.
Comments: Manual is entitled An Objective Measure of the Self-Evaluation Motive.
Authors: L. R. Good and K. C. Good.
Publisher: Psychometric Affilates.
Cross References: For a review by Jody L. Kulstad, see 15:148.

[1570]
Measure of Vindication.

Purpose: Designed to measure the vindication motive.
Population: College-age and adults.
Publication Date: No date.
Scores: Total score only.
Administration: Group.
Price Data, 2001: $3 per specimen set.
Time: Administration time not reported.
Authors: L. R. Good and K. C. Good.
Publisher: Psychometric Affilates.
Cross References: For a review by Dennis Doverspike, see 15:149.

[1571]
The Measurement of Moral Judgment.

Purpose: Measures moral judgment through dilemma interviews.
Population: Ages 10 and over.
Publication Date: 1984.
Scores: 1 score dichotomized as moral stage (I to V) and moral type (A: Heteronomous or B: Autonomous).
Administration: Individual.
Forms, 3: Parallel Forms A, B, and C consist of 3 standard dilemmas each.
Price Data: Available from publisher.
Time: (10-15) minutes.
Authors: Anne Colby, Lawrence Kohlberg, John Gibbs, and Marcus Lieberman.
Publisher: Cambridge University Press.
Cross References: See T5:1625 (1 reference), 9:681 (9 references), and T3:1262 (2 references).

[1572]
Measures in Post Traumatic Stress Disorder: A Practitioner's Guide.

Purpose: A set of tests that may be used to assist in identifying post traumatic stress disorder.
Population: Adults.
Publication Date: 1998.
Administration: Individual and group.
Price Data, 1998: £95 per practitioner's guide (77 pages); sample sheets are free.
Time: Administration time not reported.
Comments: Some of these tests may also have other uses and may be available separately from other sources.
Authors: Stuart Turner and Deborah Lee.
Publisher: NFER-Nelson Publishing Co., Ltd. [England].
a) GENERAL HEALTH QUESTIONNAIRE—28.
Publication Date: 1981.
Acronym: GHQ-28.
Scores: 4 subscales; Somatic Symptoms, Anxiety and Insomnia, Social Dysfunction, Severe Depression.
Comments: Self-report measure; see T6:1038.
b) HOSPITAL ANXIETY AND DEPRESSION SCALE.
Purpose: Designed to detect anxiety and depressive states.
Publication Dates: 1983–1994.
Acronym: HADS.
Scores: 2 subscales; Anxiety, Depression.
Comments: Self-report.
c) THE IMPACT OF EVENT SCALE.
Purpose: Designed as a measure of specific responses to trauma.
Acronym: IES.
Scores: 2 subscales; Intrusion, Avoidance.
Comments: Self-report.
d) DISSOCIATIVE EXPERIENCES SCALE II.
Purpose: A measure of dissociation.
Publication Date: 1993.
Acronym: DES-II.
Comments: Self-report; see 846.
e) INTERNALISED SHAME SCALE.
Purpose: Developed to measure "the extent to which respondents have internalised shame feelings."
Publication Date: 1990.
Acronym: ISS.
Scores, 2: Shame, Positive Self-Esteem.
Comments: Self-administered.
f) TRAUMA, ATTITUDES AND BELIEFS SCALE.
Purpose: A descriptive measure intended to identify feelings of personal change and alienation.
Acronym: TABS.
Comments: Self-administered.

g) TRAUMA INTERVIEW SCHEDULE.
Acronym: TIS.
Comments: A structured interview.
h) CLINICIAN-ADMINISTERED PTSD SCALE FOR DSM-IV.
Acronym: CAPS.
Comments: A structured interview designed to assess the 17 symptoms of PTSD outlined in the DSM-IV.

[1573]
Measures of Affiliative Tendency and Sensitivity to Rejection.

Population: Ages 15 and older.
Publication Dates: 1976–1994.
Administration: Group or individual.
Price Data: Available from publisher for complete kit including scales, scoring directions, norms, manual (1994, 13 pages), and literature review.
Time: (10–15) minutes.
Author: Albert Mehrabian.
Publisher: Albert Mehrabian.
   a) AFFILIATIVE TENDENCY.
   Purpose: "Designed to measure friendliness, sociability, and social skills conducive to positive and comfortable social exchanges."
   Scores: Total score only.
   b) SENSITIVITY TO REJECTION.
   Purpose: "Designed to assess social submissiveness."
   Scores: Total score only.
Cross References: For reviews by Sheila Mehta and Scott T. Meier, see 13:196; for a review by Peter D. Lifton of an earlier edition, see 9:683; see also T3:1443 (1 reference).

[1574]
Measures of Individual Differences in Temperament.

Purpose: Provides three basic temperament scores (Trait Pleasure-Displeasure, Trait Arousability, Trait Dominance-Submissiveness) for a comprehensive description of temperament; includes formulas that can employ these basic temperament scores to compute a variety of personality-scale scores (e.g., Trait Anxiety, Neuroticism, Depression, Exuberance, Dependency, Achievement, Affiliation, Shyness, Dependency).
Population: Ages 15 and older.
Publication Dates: 1978–1994.
Scores: Total scores only.
Administration: Group or individual.
Price Data: Available from publisher for complete kit including scales, scoring directions, norms, computational formulas, four manuals (1994, 10 pages, 8 pages, 7 pages, 5 pages), and literature review.
Time: (30–45) minutes.

Author: Albert Mehrabian.
Publisher: Albert Mehrabian.
Cross References: For a review by John B. Gormly of an earlier edition, see 9:684; see also T3:1444 (1 reference).

[1575]
Measures of Pleasure-, Arousal-, and Dominance-Inducing Qualities of Parental Attitudes.

Purpose: Constructed for "a comprehensive measurement of the emotional climate parents create for their children."
Population: Parents of children ages 3 months to 7 years.
Publication Date: 1980.
Scores, 3: Pleasure-Inducing Parental Attitude, Arousal-Inducing Parental Attitude, Dominance-Inducing Parental Attitude.
Administration: Individual.
Manual: No manual.
Price Data: Available from publisher for complete kit including scale, scoring directions, norms, and descriptive material.
Time: [20] minutes.
Authors: Carol Ann Falender and Albert Mehrabian.
Publisher: Albert Mehrabian.
Cross References: For reviews by Douglas N. Jackson and Charles Wenar, see 9:686; see also T3:1448 (1 reference).

[1576]
Measures of Psychosocial Development.

Purpose: "Assesses personality development through eight stages of life."
Population: Ages 13–86 years.
Publication Dates: 1980-1988.
Acronym: MPD.
Scores, 27: 8 Positive scores (Trust [P1], Autonomy [P2], Initiative [P3], Industry [P4], Identity [P5], Intimacy [P6], Generativity [P7], Ego Integrity [P8]), 8 Negative scores (Mistrust [N1], Shame and Doubt [N2], Guilt [N3], Inferiority [N4], Identity Confusion [N5], Isolation [N6], Stagnation [N7], Despair [N8]), 8 Resolution scale scores (R1, R2, R3, R4, R5, R6, R7, R8), 3 Total scores (Total Positive [TP], Total Negative [TN], Total Resolution [TR]).
Administration: Individual or group.
Price Data, 2006: $153 per introductory kit including 25 reusable item booklets, 50 answer sheets, 25 male profile forms, 25 female profile forms, and manual (1988, 31 pages).
Time: (15-20) minutes.
Comments: Based upon Erikson's theory of human development.
Author: Gwen A. Hawley.

Publisher: Psychological Assessment Resources, Inc.
Cross References: See T5:1631 (4 references); for reviews by James C. Carmer and Robert K. Gable, see 11:233.

[1577]
Mechanic Evaluation Test—Forms AI-C, BI-C, CI-C.

Purpose: To "select or develop industrial mechanics."
Population: Mechanic job applicants.
Publication Dates: 1992–2001.
Administration: Group.
Levels, 3: C Mechanic, B Mechanic, A Mechanic.
Price Data, 2006: $20 per consumable self-scoring booklet (20 minimum order); $24.95 per manual (A: 2001, 20 pages; B: 2001, 18 pages; C: 2001, 18 pages).
Time: [60] minutes.
Comments: Self-scoring instrument.
Author: Roland T. Ramsay.
Publisher: Ramsay Corporation.
  a) A MECHANIC.
  Scores: 6 areas: Welding & HVAC; Pneumatics amd Lubrication; Print Reading and Shop; Electrical; Mechanical & Miscellaneous; Total.
  b) B MECHANIC.
  Scores: 5 areas: Welding, Plumbing & HVAC; Pneumatics and Lubrication; Print Reading, Mechanical & Shop; Electrical; Total.
  c) C MECHANIC.
  Scores: 6 areas: Welding, Plumbing & HVAC; Pneumatics and Lubrication; Mechanical & Print Reading; Electrical; Shop, Tools & Machines; Rigging & Miscellaneous; Total.
Cross References: For reviews by David O. Anderson and Alan C. Bugbee, see 13:254.

[1578]
Mechanical Aptitude Test: Acorn National Aptitude Tests.

Purpose: Designed to measure interests and abilities associated with aptitudes for skilled trades.
Population: Grades 7–16 and adults.
Publication Dates: 1943–1952.
Scores, 5: Verbal (Comprehension of Mechanical Tasks, Use of Tools and Materials, Matching Tools and Operations), Nonverbal (Use of Tools and Materials), Total.
Administration: Group.
Price Data: Available from publisher.
Time: 45(50) minutes.
Authors: Andrew Kobal, J. Wayne Wrightstone, and Karl R. Kunze.
Publisher: Psychometric Affiliates.
Cross References: For reviews by Reign H. Bittner, James M. Porter, Jr., and Alec Rodger, see 3:669.

[1579]
Mechanical Aptitude Test (Form MAT-AR2-C).

Purpose: For evaluating mechanical aptitude.
Population: Applicants for jobs that require the ability to learn mechanical skills.
Publication Dates: 2002–2004.
Scores: Total score only covering 4 areas: Household Objects, Work-Production and Maintenance, School-Science and Physics, Hand and Power Tools.
Administration: Group.
Price Data, 2006: $20 per consumable self-scoring test booklet (minimum order of 20); $24.95 per manual (2004, 12 pages).
Time: (20) minutes.
Comments: Self-scoring instrument.
Author: Roland T. Ramsay.
Publisher: Ramsay Corporation.

[1580]
Mechanical Aptitudes.

Purpose: Measures ability to learn and succeed in an industrial, mechanical or maintenance position.
Population: Applicants for industrial positions, training programs, and vocational counseling.
Publication Dates: 1947–1995.
Scores, 4: Mechanical Knowledge, Space Relations, Shop Arithmetic, Total.
Administration: Individual or group.
Price Data, 2002: $177 per start-up kit including 5 test booklets, 25 answer sheets, 100 profile sheets, and examiner's manual; $91 per 5 test booklets (quantity discounts available); $41 per 25 answer sheets (quantity discounts available); $37 per 100 profile sheets (quantity discounts available); $28 per examiner's manual.
Time: 35 minutes.
Comments: Previously listed as SRA Mechanical Aptitudes.
Author: Richardson, Bellows, Henry & Co., Inc.
Publisher: Pearson Performance Solutions [No reply from publisher; status unknown].
Cross References: See T2:2267 (8 references); for reviews by Alec Rodger and Douglas G. Schultz, see 4:764.

[1581]
Mechanical Maintenance Trainee (Form UKM-1C).

Purpose: Selecting mechanical maintenance trainees.
Population: Applicants with mechanical training and experience necessary for entry into a training program.
Publication Dates: 1998–2005.
Scores, 13: Hydraulics, Pneumatics, Print Reading, Welding, Power Transmission, Lubrication, Pumps,

Piping, Rigging, Maintenance, Shop Machines, Tools/
Material & Equipment, Total.
Administration: Group.
Price Data, 2006: $20 per consumable self-scoring
test booklet (minimum order of 20); $24.95 per manual
(1999, 18 pages).
Time: (60) minutes.
Comments: Self-scoring instrument.
Author: Roland T. Ramsay.
Publisher: Ramsay Corporation.

[1582]
Mechanical Movements.

Purpose: Assesses the ability to visualize a mechanical system where there is internal movement or displacement of parts.
Population: Assesses the ability to visualize a mechanical system where there is internal movement or
displacement of parts.
Publication Dates: 1959–1963.
Scores: Total score only.
Administration: Individual or group.
Price Data, 2002: $91 per start-up kit including 25
test booklets, score key, and interpretation and research
manual (1963, 14 pages); $54 per 25 test booklets
(quantity discounts available); $20 per score key; $28
per interpretation and research manual.
Time: 14 minutes.
Authors: L. L. Thurstone and T. E. Jeffrey.
Publisher: Pearson Performance Solutions [No reply
from publisher; status unknown].
Cross References: For a review by William A.
Owens, see 6:1089.

[1583]
Mechanical Technician A.

Purpose: For selecting mid-journey level mainte-
nance technicians for jobs in the metals or manufactur-
ing industry.
Population: Applicants and incumbents for jobs re-
quiring mechanical maintenance knowledge and skills
at the highest level.
Publication Dates: 2003–2005.
Scores, 6: Hydraulics & Pneumatics, Print Reading,
Power Transmission & Lubrication, Pumps & Piping,
Mechanical Maintenance Principles, Total.
Administration: Group.
Forms, 2: MTA-XC, MTA-YC.
Price Data, 2006: $20 per consumable self-scoring
test booklet (minimum order of 20); $24.95 per manual
(2005, 18 pages).
Time: (60) minutes.
Comments: Self-scoring instrument; Form MTA-
YC is an alternate equivalent of Form MTA-XC.
Author: Roland T. Ramsay.
Publisher: Ramsay Corporation.

[1584]
Mechanical Technician B.

Purpose: For selecting mid-journey level mainte-
nance technicians for jobs in the metals or manufactur-
ing industry.
Population: Applicants and incumbents for jobs re-
quiring mechanical maintenance knowledge and skills.
Publication Dates: 2003–2005.
Scores, 8: Hydraulics & Pneumatics, Print Reading,
Burning/Fabricating/Welding & Rigging, Power Trans-
mission & Lubrication, Pumps & Piping, Mechanical
Maintenance Principles, Shop Equipment & Tools,
Total.
Administration: Group.
Forms, 2: MTB-XC, MTB-YC.
Price Data, 2006: $20 per consumable self-scoring
test booklet (minimum order of 20); $24.95 per manual
(2005, 18 pages).
Time: (60) minutes.
Comments: Self-scoring instrument; Form MTB-
YC is an alternate equivalent of Form MTB-XC.
Author: Roland T. Ramsay.
Publisher: Ramsay Corporation.

[1585]
Mechanical Technician C.

Purpose: For selecting entry-journey level mainte-
nance technicians for jobs in the metals or manufactur-
ing industry.
Population: Applicants and incumbents for jobs re-
quiring mechanical maintenance knowledge and skills.
Publication Dates: 2003–2005.
Scores, 8: Hydraulics & Pneumatics, Print Reading,
Burning/Fabricating/Welding & Rigging, Power Trans-
mission & Lubrication, Pumps & Piping, Mechanical
Maintenance Principles, Shop Equipment & Tools,
Total.
Administration: Group.
Forms, 2: MTC-YC, MTC-XC.
Price Data, 2006: $20 per consumable self-scoring
test booklet (minimum order of 20); $24.95 per manual
(2005, 18 pages).
Time: (60) minutes.
Comments: Self-scoring instrument; Form MTC-
YC is an alternate equivalent of Form MTC-XC.
Author: Roland T. Ramsay.
Publisher: Ramsay Corporation.

[1586]
Mechanical Understanding Test.

Purpose: Designed to assess how well people understand "the basic principles of physics and mechanics
that determine success in handling and manipulating
objects and machines."
Population: Adults.
Publication Date: 2004.

Acronym: MUT.
Scores: Total score only.
Administration: Group.
Price Data: Available from publisher.
Time: (30–40) minutes.
Authors: Erich P. Prien, Leonard D. Goodstein, and Kristin O. Prien.
Publisher: HRD Press, Inc.

[1587]
MecTest (A Test for Maintenance Mechanics)—Form AU-C.

Purpose: Designed to "select or develop journey-level maintenance mechanics."
Population: Applicants and incumbents for maintenance jobs.
Publication Dates: 1991–2004.
Scores, 9: Hydraulics and Pneumatics, Print Reading, Welding and Rigging, Power Transmission, Lubrication, Pumps and Piping, Mechanical Maintenance, Machines/Tools/Equipment, Total.
Administration: Group.
Price Data, 2006: $20 per consumable self-scoring test booklet (20 minimum order); $24.95 per manual (2004).
Time: (60) minutes.
Comments: Self-scoring instrument.
Author: Roland T. Ramsay.
Publisher: Ramsay Corporation.
Cross References: For a review by Robert J. Drummond of an earlier edition, see 13:197.

[1588]
Medical College Admission Test.

Purpose: "Designed primarily to aid members of admissions committees in the . . . selection of applicants" for medical colleges.
Population: Applicants for admission to member colleges of the Association of American Medical Colleges and to other participating institutions.
Publication Dates: 1946-1994.
Acronym: MCAT.
Scores, 4: Verbal Reasoning, Physical Sciences, Biological Sciences, Writing Sample.
Administration: Group.
Price Data: Available from publisher.
Time: (345) minutes.
Comments: Administered 2 times annually (April, August) at centers established by publisher.
Author: Constructed under the direction of the Association of American Medical Colleges.
Publisher: Administered at the direction of the Association of American Medical Colleges.
Cross References: See T5:1638 (3 references), T4:1600 (11 references), 9:691 (9 references), T3:1576 (40 references), 8:1101 (40 references), and T2:2355

(30 references); for reviews by Nancy S. Cole and James M. Richards, Jr. of earlier forms, see 7:1100 (57 references); for reviews by Robert L. Ebel and Philip H. DuBois, see 6:1137 (43 references); for a review by Alexander G. Wesman, see 5:932 (4 references); for a review by Morey J. Wantman, see 4:817 (11 references).

[1589]
Medical Ethics Inventory.

Purpose: Designed to provide "profiles of the value preferences of medical students regarding medical ethical dilemmas."
Population: First year medical students.
Publication Date: 1982.
Acronym: MEI.
Scores, 6: Social, Economic, Theoretical, Political, Religious, Aesthetic.
Administration: Group.
Price Data: Available from publisher.
Time: [30-40] minutes.
Authors: Cynthia J. Stolman and Rodney L. Doran.
Publisher: Rodney L. Doran [No reply from publisher; status unknown].
Cross References: For reviews by Joseph D. Matarazzo and Gary B. Melton, see 10:197.

[1590]
Meeker Behavioral Correlates.

Purpose: Assesses "major dimensions of intellectual abilities and personality characteristics" for management matching of teams.
Population: Industry.
Publication Date: 1981.
Scores: Ratings by self in 6 areas: Comprehension, Memory, Leadership, Convergent Production Skills, Creativity, Team Contributions.
Administration: Group.
Price Data: Available from publisher.
Time: [20] minutes.
Comments: Self-ratings.
Author: Mary Meeker.
Publisher: SOI Systems.

[1591]
Memory and Behavior Problems Checklist and The Burden Interview.

Publication Dates: 1983–1990.
Administration: Individual.
Price Data, 2001: $5.25 per manual including the instruments.
Authors: Steven H. Zarit and Judy M. Zarit.
Publisher: Gerontology Center, The Pennsylvania State University.
  a) MEMORY AND BEHAVIOR PROBLEMS CHECKLIST.
  Purpose: Designed to "determine how frequently a dementia patient engages in problematic behav-

iors and which problems are especially upsetting for family members."
Population: Dementia patients and their families.
Acronym: MBPC.
Scores, 3: Frequency of Problems, Severity of Functional Behavior Problems, Mean Distress.
Comments: Administered by an interviewer to family members of a demential patient.
b) THE BURDEN INTERVIEW.
Purpose: "Designed to assess the stresses experienced by family caregivers of elderly and disabled persons."
Population: Caregivers of elderly and disabled persons.
Scores, 2: Personal Strain, Role Strain.
Comments: Administered by an interviewer or self-administered.
Cross References: For reviews by Sally Kuhlenschmidt and Richard A. Wantz, see 14:229; see also T5:1643 (2 references).

[1592]
Memory Assessment Scales.
Purpose: Developed to provide a comprehensive battery that assesses short- and long-term verbal and visual (nonverbal) memory.
Population: Ages 18 and over.
Publication Date: 1991.
Acronym: MAS.
Scores, 16: Short-Term Memory (Verbal Span, Visual Span, Total), List Acquisition, Delayed List Recall, Delayed Prose Recall, Global Memory Scale (Verbal Memory [List Recall, Immediate Prose Recall, Total], Visual Memory [Visual Reproduction, Immediate Visual Recognition, Total], Total), Delayed Visual Recognition, Names-Faces (Immediate, Delayed) and 7 Verbal Process scores: Total Intrusions, List Clustering (Acquisition, Recall, Delayed Recall), Cued List Recall (Recall, Delayed Recall), List Recognition.
Administration: Individual.
Price Data, 2006: $289 per introductory kit including stimulus card set, 25 record forms, manual (131 pages), and attache case.
Time: [40-45] minutes.
Author: J. Michael Williams.
Publisher: Psychological Assessment Resources, Inc.
Cross References: See T5:1644 (1 reference); for reviews by Ronald A. Berk and John W. Young, see 12:229.

[1593]
Memory Test for Older Adults.
Purpose: Designed as a brief instrument to assess verbal and visuospatial learning and memory in older adults.

Population: Ages 55–84.
Publication Date: 2002.
Acronym: MTOA, MTOA:S, MTOA:L.
Scores, 8: Free Recall Word List Total Score, Free Recall Word List Retention, Free Recall + Cued Recall Word List Total Score, Free Recall + Cued Recall Word List Retention Score, Recognition Score, Geometric Figure Total Score, Geometric Figure Retention Score, Geometric Figure Copy Score.
Administration: Individual.
Forms, 2: Long, Short.
Price Data, 2006: $165 per complete kit including 1 long form (MTOA:L), 1 short form (MTOA:S), geometric cards, 25 short form record forms, 25 long form record forms, and technical manual; $49 per 25 long or short record forms; $59 per technical manual.
Time: Administration time not reported.
Authors: Anita M. Hubley and Tom M. Tombaugh.
Publisher: Multi-Health Systems, Inc.
Cross References: For reviews by Stephen J. Freeman and by W. Joel Schneider and Mark E. Swerdlik, see 16:144.

[1594]
Menometer.
Purpose: Designed to measure "knowledge of the physical aspects of human menstruation."
Population: Adolescents and adults.
Publication Date: 1974–1988.
Scores: Total score only.
Administration: Group.
Manual: No manual.
Price Data, 2005: $2 per scale.
Time: [10] minutes.
Comments: For a supplementary source, see Panos D. Bardis, "Research Instruments for Population Studies," *Society and Culture,* July 1974, *5*(2), 177-191.
Author: Panos D. Bardis.
Publisher: Donna Bardis.

[1595]
Menstrual Distress Questionnaire.
Purpose: Designed as "a self-report inventory for use in the diagnosis and treatment of premenstrual and menstrual distress."
Population: Women who experience strong to severe premenstrual or menstrual distress
Publication Dates: 1968–1991.
Acronym: MDQ.
Scores, 8: Pain, Water Retention, Autonomic Reactions, Negative Affect, Impaired Concentration, Behavior Change, Arousal, Control.
Administration: Group or individual.
Forms, 2: Form C, Form T.
Price Data: Available from publisher.
Time: (15) minutes for Form C; (5) minutes for Form T.

Author: Rudolph H. Moos.
Publisher: Western Psychological Services.
Cross References: See T5:1647 (4 references); for reviews by Jennifer J. Fager and Donna L. Sundre, see 12:230 (12 references); see T4:1608 (7 references), 9:695 (6 references), and T3:1466 (4 references).

[1596]
Mental Status Checklist for Adolescents.

Purpose: To assist professionals in the assessment of adolescents' mental status.
Population: Ages 13–17.
Publication Date: 1988.
Scores: Item scores only.
Administration: Individual.
Price Data, 2006: $50 per package of 25.
Time: Administration time not reported.
Comments: Reliability and validity data not reported; problems checklist.
Authors: Edward H. Dougherty and John A. Schinka.
Publisher: Psychological Assessment Resources, Inc.
Cross References: For a review by Julian Fabry, see 11:234.

[1597]
Mental Status Checklist for Adults, 1988 Revision.

Purpose: "Surveys items that are commonly included in a comprehensive mental status examination."
Population: Adults.
Publication Dates: 1986–1988.
Scores: 10 Content Areas: Presenting Problems, Behavioral/Physical Descriptions, Emotional State, Mental Status, Health and Habits, Legal Issues, Current Living Situation, Diagnoses, Treatment Recommendations, Disposition.
Administration: Individual.
Manual: No manual.
Price Data, 2006: $50 per package of 25.
Time: Administration time not reported.
Author: John A. Schinka.
Publisher: Psychological Assessment Resources, Inc.

[1598]
Mental Status Checklist for Children.

Purpose: Assess childhood problems and plan for treatment approaches.
Population: Ages 5–12.
Publication Date: 1989.
Scores: Item scores only.
Administration: Individual.
Manual: No manual.
Price Data, 2006: $50 per package of 25.
Time: (10–20) minutes.
Comments: Downward extension of the Mental Status Checklist–Adult (1597); scale for ratings by parents, caregivers, or self-ratings.

Authors: Edward H. Dougherty and John A. Schinka.
Publisher: Psychological Assessment Resources, Inc.
Cross References: For reviews by David Lachar and Marcia B. Shaffer, see 11:235.

[1599]
Mentoring Skills Assessment.

Purpose: Provides awareness about successful mentoring or being a successful mentee; feedback report is designed to improve mentoring and mentee skills; the mentor form is designed to rate skills in the areas of quality and frequency of mentoring skills.
Population: Mentors, coaches, and mentees.
Publication Dates: 1995–1998.
Acronym: MSA.
Scores, 27: Importance, Quality, Frequency on each of the following scales: Listening, Encouraging, Inspiring/Instilling Vision, Coaching, Instructing, Managing Risks, Opening Doors, Demonstrating Personal Mastery, Giving Constructive Feedback.
Administration: Group.
Forms, 2: Mentor/Colleague or Mentee/Colleague.
Manual: No manual.
Price Data: Available from publisher (www.mindgarden.com).
Time: Administration time not reported.
Comments: Web-based and paper-based; multirater.
Author: Linda Phillips-Jones.
Publisher: Mind Garden, Inc.

[1600]
Mentoring Style Indicator™.

Purpose: Assesses 4 mentoring styles (Informational, Guiding, Collaborative, Confirming) and associated mentoring behaviors; identifies the style of mentoring that mentors prefer to provide and proteges prefer to receive.
Population: Mentors and proteges.
Publication Dates: 1987–2005.
Acronym: MSI.
Scores: Informational Mentoring, Guiding Mentoring, Collaborative Mentoring, Confirming Mentoring, Preferred Mentoring Style.
Administration: Individual and group.
Price Data: Available from publisher; discounts on bulk orders.
Time: (20-25) minutes.
Comments: Versions available for new hires, career development, leadership development, generic, sales, healthcare, youth, new teachers, college students, college faculty, and educational administrators; can be answered online as part of the web-based Colaboro® Mentoring Management System™; scoring is automatically done online; Preferred Mentoring Style and an interpretation is printed out.
Authors: William A. Gray.
Publisher: Corporate Mentoring Solutions, Inc.

a) MSI FOR MENTORING NEW HIRES.
Population: Mentors and proteges wanting orientation.
b) MSI FOR CAREER DEVELOPMENT.
Population: Mentors and proteges wanting to explore career options.
c) MSI FOR LEADERSHIP DEVELOPMENT.
Population: Mentors and proteges wanting to become leaders.
d) MSI–GENERIC.
Population: Mentors and proteges wanting to handle generic work challenges.
e) MSI FOR SALES.
Population: Mentors and proteges wanting to handle common sales challenges.
f) MSI FOR HEALTHCARE PROFESSIONALS.
Population: Mentors and proteges wanting to handle healthcare challenges.
g) MSI FOR MENTORING NEW TEACHERS.
Population: Mentors and new teachers wanting induction into the profession.
h) MSI FOR EDUCATIONAL ADMINISTRATORS.
Population: Educational administrators and proteges wanting to become administrators.
i) MSI FOR MENTORING COLLEGE/UNIVERSITY STUDENTS.
Population: Mentors and college students wanting to handle freshman and transfer challenges.
j) MSI FOR MENTORING COLLEGE/UNIVERSITY FACULTY.
Population: Mentors and proteges wanting to get tenured and promoted.
k) MSI FOR MENTORING YOUTH.
Population: Mentors and youthful proteges wanting adult assistance.
Cross References: For reviews by Raoul A. Arreola and Russell N. Carney, see 13:198.

[1601]

Merrill-Palmer-Revised Scales of Development.

Purpose: Designed to assess cognitive, social-emotional, self-help, and fine and gross motor development in infants and children.
Population: Ages 0-1 to 6-6 years.
Publication Dates: 1926-2004.
Acronym: M-P-R.
Administration: Individual.
Price Data, 2006: $925 per complete kit including manual (2004, 267 pages), infant stimuli book, easel book, Fido book, choke-safe toys and manipulatives, 20 Cognitive Battery record forms, 20 Social Emotional Development Parent Scales, 20 Social Emotional Temperament Style Parent Forms, 20 Gross Motor record forms, 20 Self-Help/Adaptive Development Scale Par-

ent Forms, 20 Expressive Language Evaluator Forms, 20 Expressive Language Parent Forms, 20 Summary Reports/Growth Score Profiles, 20 Copying Response Sheets A, and 20 Copying Response Sheets B; $55 per manual; $30 per 20 Cognitive Battery record forms; $10 per 20 Social Emotional Development Parent Scales; $20 per 20 Spanish Social Emotional Development Parent Scales; $10 per 20 Social Emotional Temperament Style Parent Forms; $20 per 20 Spanish Social Emotional Temperament Style Parent Forms; $20 per 20 Gross Motor Record Forms; $10 per 20 Self-Help/Adaptive Development Scale Parent Forms; $20 per 20 Spanish Self-Help Parent Report Forms; $10 per 20 Expressive Language Evaluator Forms; $10 per 20 Expressive Language Parent Forms; $20 per 20 Summary Reports/Growth Score Profiles; $2.50 per 20 Copying Response Sheets A; $2.50 per 20 Copying Response Sheets B.
Foreign Language Editions: Spanish editions of parent reports available.
Time: (40-50) minutes.
Comments: Portions of this test are to be completed by a parent/guardian; previous edition entitled Merrill-Palmer Scale of Mental Tests.
Authors: Gale H. Roid and Jackie L. Sampers.
Publisher: Stoeling Co.

a) EXPRESSIVE LANGUAGE-EXAMINER FORM.
  1) *Element of Attire, Body Parts, Verbs.*
  Population: Ages 1-1 years and older.
  2) *Adverbs, Adjectives, Prepositions, Pronouns.*
  Population: Ages 1-6 years and older.
b) EXPRESSIVE LANGUAGE-PARENT REPORT.
Scores: 2 scales, 4 subscales: 0-12 months, 13 months and older (Word Combination, Word Meanings/Semantics, Gestural, Expressive Verbal).
c) SELF-HELP/ADAPTIVE-PARENT.
Forms, 5: 0-11 months, 12-23 months, 24-35 months, 36-37 months, 48-78 months.
d) GROSS MOTOR-EXAMINER.
Scores: 7 scales, 23 subscales: 0-12 months (Lifts Head, Supported Sitting, Reaching, Rolls, Balance Responses, Independent Sitting, Stomach Creep, Hand/Knee Creep), 13-24 months (Pull to Standing, Cruises Furniture, Independent Walking), 25-36 months (Child Squats to Pick Up Toy, Climbing Into Chair, Stairs, Special Walking), 37-48 months (Running, Jumping #1), 49-78 months (Throwing/Catching, Kicking, Dynamic Walking, Static Balance, Jumping #2, Hopping Movements), Quality of Movement, Tone.
e) SOCIAL-EMOTIONAL DEVELOPMENTAL-PARENT.
Forms, 5: Same as *c* above.

f) SOCIAL-EMOTIONAL TEMPERAMENT-PARENT.

Forms, 2: 0-17 months, 18-78 months.

g) COGNITIVE BATTERY-EXAMINER.

Scores, 6: Cognitive, Memmory, Fine Motor, Speed, Receptive Language, Visual Motor; 8 scales, 49 subscales: 1-5 months (Warm-up, Visual Regard, Small Rattle Play, Visual Preference), 6-12 months (Spin Toy, Large Rattle Play, Dangle Toy, Push-Spin Toy, Object Permanence), 13-23 months (Novel Problem, Blocks, Chips in the Box, Round Peg Board (A), Body Parts, Pop Out, Simple Puzzle, Square Peg Board (B), Fido Book), 24-35 months (Ring Stack, Color Matching, Identifies Emotions, Picture Details, Goodnight Baby, Bead Stringing, Two Puzzles, Find It, Goes Together, Square Pegs, Same), 36-47 months (Fingers, Questions, Where Do They Go?, Word Pictures, See It?, Shapes Puzzle), 48-59 momths (Puzzle Fun, Big/Small, Touch Picture, Draw It, Hidden Picture, Different Pictures), 60-78 months (Find 'em, High/Low, Count 'em, Fun with Cards, Touch 'em, What's Next?, Different Pictures, Let's Draw It).

1) *Testing Behaviors-Examiner.*

Scores: 4 scales, 6 subscales: 1-5 months (Emotionality), 6-11 months (Attention), 12-17 months (Fearful/Cautious), 18-78 months (Organized/Cooperative, Active/Eager, Angry/Oppositional).

h) SUMMARY REPORT-EXAMINER.

1) *Developmental Index.*

Scores, 7: Developmental Index, Cognitive, Fine Motor, Receptive Language, Memory (ages 1-4 years and older), Speed (ages 1-4 years and older), Visual Motor.

2) *Gross Motor.*

Score: Gross Motor.

3) *Language.*

Scores, 2: Overall Expressive Language, Overall Language.

4) *Social-Emotional.*

Score: Social-Emotional.

5) *Self-Help.*

Score: Self-Help/Adaptive.

Cross References: See T5:1653 (29 references) and T4:1614 (19 references); for a review by Jack A. Naglieri of an earlier edition, see 9:697 (4 references).

[1602]

Meta-Motivation Inventory.

Purpose: Designed to measure personal and managerial style.

Population: Managers and persons in leadership positions.

Publication Date: 1979.

Acronym: MMI.

Scores, 32: Motivation for Achievement, Perfection, Assertiveness, Independence, Achievement, Meta-Achievement, Deterministic, Approval, Conventional, Dependent, Avoidance, Helplessness, Need for Control, Persuasiveness, Manipulation, Reactive, Authoritarian, Exploitive, Concern for People, Cooperation, Affiliation, Humanistic, Synergy, Meta-Humanistic, Self-Actualization, Stress, Repression, Anger, Judgemental, Creativity, Growth Potential, Fun Scale.

Administration: Group.

Price Data: Available from publisher.

Time: Administration time not reported.

Comments: Self-administered.

Author: John A. Walker.

Publisher: Meta-Visions.

Cross References: For reviews by John K. Butler, Jr. and Denise M. Rousseau, see 9:698.

[1603]

Metaphon.

Purpose: Designed to be "a complete assessment and therapy programme for children with phonological disorders."

Population: Ages 3.5–7.

Publication Date: 1990.

Scores: Total score only.

Administration: Individual.

Parts, 4: Screening, Probing, Intervention, Monitoring.

Price Data: Available from publisher.

Time: (15) minutes.

Authors: Elizabeth Dean, Janet Howell, Ann Hill, and Daphne Waters.

Publisher: NFER-Nelson Publishing Co., Ltd. [England].

Cross References: For a review by Allan O. Diefendorf, Kathy Kessler, and Michael K. Wynne, see 12:231.

[1604]

Metropolitan Achievement Tests, Eighth Edition.

Purpose: Designed to provide assessment of students' achievement in reading, mathematics, language arts, science, and social studies at appropriate levels.

Publication Dates: 1931–2001.

Acronym: METROPOLITAN8.

Administration: Group.

Forms, 2: Complete Battery, Short Form.

Price Data, 2002: $31.50 per multiple-choice Complete Battery examination kit (for preview only) including Complete Battery test booklet, directions for administering, practice test with directions (Preprimer through Intermediate 4 only), separate answer document (Elementary 1 through Secondary 3 only), and

open-ended assessment preview brochure (specify level); $16 per multiple-choice Complete Battery 25 practice tests (specify Level Preprimer through Intermediate 2/ 3/4); $7 per directions for administering practice tests; $122.50 per 25 machine-scorable multiple-choice Complete Battery test booklets (specify preprimer–Elementary 1); $93 per 25 reusable multiple-choice Complete Battery test booklets (specify Elementary 1–Secondary 3); $76 per 100 Complete Battery machine-scorable answer documents (specify Elementary 1–Secondary 3); $11.50 per directions for administering (specify level); $7 per 25 test booklet place markers; $31.50 per multiple-choice Complete Battery response key–list of correct responses (specify level); $16 per 25 multiple-choice Short Form practice tests (specify Primary 1–Intermediate 2/3/4); $7 per directions for administering Short Form practice tests; $104 per 25 multiple-choice Short Form machine-scorable test booklets (specify Primary 1–Elementary 1); $83 per 25 multiple-choice Short Form reusable test booklets (specify Elementary 2–Secondary 3); $11.50 per directions for administering (specify Primary 1–Secondary); $69 per 100 multiple-choice Short Form machine-scorable answer documents (specify Elementary 1–Secondary 3); $31.50 per multiple-choice Short Form response key–list of correct responses (specify level); $14 per 25 Parent Guide to METROPOLITAN8 (specify English or Spanish); $66 per norms book (specify Fall or Spring); $60 per technical manual; $40 per Compendium of Instructional Objectives (also available in CD-ROM version); $25 per Guide for Classroom Planning (specify Primary 1/2, Elementary 1/2, Intermediate 1/ 2/3/4, or Secondary 1/2/3); $21 per Understanding Test Results (specify Primary 1/2–Secondary 1/2/3); price information for scoring and reporting services available from publisher.
Author: Harcourt Educational Measurement.
Publisher: Harcourt Assessment, Inc.
  a) PREPRIMER.
  Population: Grades K.0–K.5.
  Scores, 4: Sounds and Print, Mathematics, Language, Complete Battery.
  Time: (90–100) minutes.
  b) PRIMER.
  Population: Grades K.5–1.5.
  Scores, 4: Same as for Preprimer.
  Time: (90–100) minutes.
  c) PRIMARY 1.
  Population: Grades 1.5–2.5.
  Scores, 12: Sounds and Print, Reading Vocabulary, Reading Comprehension, Total Reading, Mathematics Concepts and Problem Solving, Mathematics Computation, Total Mathematics, Language, Spelling, Science, Social Studies, Complete Battery.
  Time: (265–292) minutes.

  d) PRIMARY 2.
  Population: Grades 2.5–3.5.
  Scores, 12: Same as for Primary 1.
  Time: (270–296) minutes.
  e) ELEMENTARY 1.
  Population: Grades 3.5–4.5.
  Scores, 12: Same as for Primary 1.
  Time: (275–328) minutes.
  f) ELEMENTARY 2.
  Population: Grades 4.5–5.5.
  Scores, 11: Same as for Primary 1 minus Sounds and Print.
  Time: (255–298) minutes.
  g) INTERMEDIATE 1.
  Population: Grades 5.5–6.5.
  Scores, 11: Same as Elementary 2.
  Time: (275–316) minutes.
  h) INTERMEDIATE 2.
  Population: Grades 6.5–7.5.
  Scores, 11: Same as for Elementary 2.
  Time: (275–316) minutes.
  i) INTERMEDIATE 3.
  Population: Grades 7.5–8.5.
  Scores, 11: Same as for Elementary 2.
  Time: (275–316) minutes.
  j) INTERMEDIATE 4.
  Population: Grades 8.5–9.5.
  Scores, 11: Same as for Elementary 2.
  Time: (275–316) minutes.
  k) SECONDARY 1.
  Population: Grade 9.
  Scores, 9: Reading Vocabulary, Reading Comprehension, Sounds and Print/Total Reading, Mathematics, Language, Spelling, Science, Social Studies, Complete Battery.
  Time: (240–288) minutes.
  l) SECONDARY 2.
  Population: Grade 10.
  Scores, 9: Same as for Secondary 1.
  Time: (240–288) minutes.
  m) SECONDARY 3.
  Population: Grades 11–12.
  Scores, 9: Same as for Secondary 1.
  Time: (240–288) minutes.
Cross References: For reviews by Michael R. Harwell and Leslie Eastman Lukin, see 16:146; see also T5:1657 (25 references); for reviews by Carmen J. Finley and Ronald K. Hambleton, see 12:232 (37 references); see also T4:1618 (31 references); for reviews by Anthony J. Nitko and Bruce G. Rogers of an earlier edition, see 10:200 (44 references); for reviews by Edward H. Haertel and Robert L. Linn, see 9:699 (30 references); see also T3:1473 (89 references); for reviews by Norman E. Gronlund and Richard M. Wolf and an excerpted review by Joseph A. Wingard and Peter M. Bentler of an earlier edition, see 8:22 (41

references); see also T2:22 (20 references) and 7:14 (25 references); for reviews by Henry S. Dyer and Warren G. Findley of an earlier edition, see 6:16 (16 references); for a review by Warren G. Findley, see 4:18 (10 references); see also 3:13 (7 references); for reviews by E. V. Pullias and Hugh B. Wood, see 2:1189 (3 references); for reviews by Jack W. Dunlap, Charles W. Odell, and Richard Ledgerwood, see 1:874. For reviews of subtests, see 8:283 (1 review), 8:732 (2 reviews), 6:627 (2 reviews), 6:797 (1 review), 6:877 (2 reviews), 6:970 (2 reviews), 4:416 (1 review), 4:543 (2 reviews), 2:1458.1 (2 reviews), 2:1551 (1 review), 1:892 (2 reviews), and 1:1105 (2 reviews).

[1605]
METROPOLITAN8 Writing Test.

Purpose: Designed to provide a "norm-referenced measure of student achievement in written expression."
Population: Grades 1–12.
Publication Dates: 1931–2001.
Acronym: METROPOLITAN8 Writing.
Scores: Analytical Scoring option yields Content Development, Organizational Strategies, Word Choice, Sentence Formation, Usage, and Writing Mechanics scores; Holistic Scoring option yields total score only.
Administration: Group.
Levels, 11: Primary 1 and 2; Elementary 1 and 2; Intermediate 1, 2, 3, and 4; Secondary 1, 2, and 3.
Forms, 22: 2 forms for each level.
Price Data: Available from publisher.
Time: Untimed (40–50 minutes).
Comments: Scoring and reporting services available from publisher; may be used alone, or in combination with the Metropolitan Achievement Tests (1604) Language Test.
Author: Harcourt Educational Measurement.
Publisher: Harcourt Assessment, Inc.
Cross References: For reviews by Stephen L. Benton and Natalie Rathvon, see 16:147.

[1606]
Metropolitan Performance Assessment: Integrated Performance Tasks.

Purpose: Designed to show progression in the "acquisition of concepts, strategies, and skills needed to perform language/literacy and quantitative/mathematics tasks" usually taught through kindergarten.
Population: Ages 4-4 to 6-3; ages 5-5 to 7-0.
Publication Date: 1995.
Acronym: MPA.
Scores, 3: Holistic, Analytic (Language/Literacy, Quantitative/Mathematics).
Administration: Group.
Levels, 2: 1, 2.
Price Data, 2002: $40 per examination kit including task booklet, set of manipulative sheets, directions

for administering, scoring guide, and teacher observation form (Level 1 or Level 2); $49 per task package including 25 booklets, 25 sets of manipulative sheets, directions for administering, and teacher observation form (Level 1 or Level 2); $26.50 per scoring guide (Level 1 or Level 2); $6.40 per directions for administering (Level 1 or Level 2); $57 per preliteracy inventory including 25 record forms, Homer the Goose Storybook, and directions for administering; $23.85 per developmental inventory; $13.25 per portfolio assessment guidelines with information for interpreting preliteracy and devlopmental inventories; $17 per literacy environment inventory; $65.75 per Handbook of Early Childhood Activities.
Time: Untimed.
Comments: Handbook of Early Childhood Activities covers many areas assessed in the MPA, but may also be used independently of the program.
Author: Joanne R. Nurss.
Publisher: PsychCorp, A brand of Harcourt Assessment, Inc.
Cross References: For reviews by Theodore Coladarci and Delwyn L. Harnisch, see 14:230.

[1607]
Metropolitan Readiness Tests®, Sixth Edition.

Purpose: Designed to assess basic and advanced skills important in beginning reading and mathematics.
Population: PreKindergarten through grade 1.
Publication Dates: 1933–1995.
Acronym: MRT®6.
Administration: Individual (Level 1) or group (Level 2).
Price Data, 2002: $19 per 25 parent-teacher conference reports (specify level); $19 per story comprehension big book.
Time: (85) minutes per level; (10) minutes for the practice items for each level.
Authors: Joanne R. Nurss and Mary E. McGauvran.
Publisher: PsychCorp, A brand of Harcourt Assessment, Inc.
a) LEVEL 1.
Population: PreKindergarten and beginning Kindergarten.
Administration: Individual.
Scores: 5 tests: Beginning Reading Skill Area (Visual Discrimination, Beginning Consonants, Sound-Letter Correspondence), Story Comprehension, Quantitative Concepts and Reasoning, plus Prereading Composite.
Price Data: $121 per complete kit including stimulus manual, story comprehension big book, manual (1995, 43 pages), 25 parent-teacher conference reports, and 25 student record forms; $32 per 25 student record forms; $31 per manual;

$57.25 per stimulus manual; $29 per exam kit including Level I flyer, story comprehension big book flyer, manual, student record form, and parent-teacher conference report.

b) LEVEL 2.

Population: Middle and end of kindergarten and beginning of grade 1.

Administration: Group.

Scores: 5 tests: Beginning Reading Skill Area (Beginning Consonants, Sound-Letter Correspondence, Aural Cloze with Letter), Story Comprehension, Quantitative Concepts and Reasoning, plus Prereading Composite.

Price Data: $164 per starter kit including 25 test booklets, directions for administering, story comprehension big book, 25 practice booklets, class record and analysis chart, norms book, answer keys, parent-teacher conference reports, 25 Birthday Surprise Task booklets, 25 Birthday Surprise manipulative sheets, Birthday Surprise directions for administering, scoring guide, and teacher observation form; $82 per 25 handscorable test booklets also including directions for administration, 25 practice booklets, and class record and analysis chart; $29.50 per answer keys; $41 per manual; $31 per norms book (1995, 72 pages); $17 per exam kit including test booklet, directions for administering, practice booklet, class record and analysis chart, and parent-teacher conference report.

Cross References: For reviews by Randy W. Kamphaus and Christine Novak, see 14:231; see also T5:1659 (14 references) and T4:1619 (35 references); for a review by Michael M. Ravitch of an earlier edition, see 9:700 (11 references); see also T3:1479 (73 references), 8:802 (111 references), and T2:1716 (55 references); for reviews by Robert Dykstra and Harry Singer of an earlier edition, see 7:757 (124 references); for a review by Eric F. Gardner and an excerpted review by Fay Griffith, see 4:570 (3 references); for a review by Irving H. Anderson, see 3:518 (5 references); for a review by W. J. Osburn, see 2:1552 (10 references).

[1608]
Meyer-Kendall Assessment Survey.

Purpose: Constructed to assess work-related personality style.

Population: Business employees and job applicants.

Publication Dates: 1986–1991.

Acronym: MKAS.

Scores, 12: Objectivity, Social Desirability Bias, Dominance, Extraversion, People Concerns, Attention to Detail, Anxiety, Stability, Psychosomatic Tendencies, Determination, Achievement Motivation, Independence.

Administration: Group or individual.

Price Data, 2002: $92.50 per complete kit including 2 prepaid assessment sheets, 2 prepaid pre-assess-

ment sheets, and manual (1991, 72 pages); $29.50 per mail-in assessment sheet (price includes scoring and report by publisher); $8.50 per pre-assessment sheet; $45 per manual.

Time: (15–20) minutes.

Authors: Henry D. Meyer and Edward L. Kendall.

Publisher: Western Psychological Services.

Cross References: For reviews by Mark H. Daniel and Gregory H. Dobbins, see 12:234.

[1609]
Michigan Alcoholism Screening Test.

Purpose: Designed as a screening test for assessing alcohol abuse.

Population: Adults.

Publication Dates: 1971–1980.

Acronym: MAST.

Scores: Total score only.

Administration: Group or individual.

Manual: No manual available.

Price Data, 2006: $40 per copy, which includes scoring key and permission to duplicate the test.

Foreign Language Editions: French, Japanese, Spanish, and Vietnamese versions available.

Time: (10) minutes.

Comments: Can be self-administered.

Author: Melvin L. Selzer.

Publisher: Melvin L. Selzer.

Cross References: For reviews by Jane Close Conoley and Jeff Reese and by Janice W. Murdoch, see 14:232; see also T5:1661 (85 references).

[1610]
Michigan English Language Assessment Battery.

Purpose: Designed "to evaluate the advanced level English language proficiency of adult non-native speakers of English."

Population: Adult non-native speakers of English.

Publication Dates: 1985–2002.

Acronym: MELAB.

Scores, 5: Writing, Listening, GCVR [includes Grammar, Cloze Reading, Vocabulary Synonym, Vocabulary Completion, Reading] Final Score, Speaking Test (optional).

Administration: Group or individual.

Forms: Multiple equivalent forms.

Price Data, 2005: $80 per registration for Standard Individual MELAB; $40 per Oral Interview; additional price information available from publisher.

Time: (135–150) minutes for complete battery; (30) minutes for Writing; (30) minutes for Listening; (75) minutes for Grammar/Cloze/Vocabulary/Reading; (15) minutes for optional oral interview.

Comments: "Used primarily to draw inferences about a test-taker's ability to study in an institution where

English is the medium of instruction" or for test takers who require evidence of English language ability for professional purposes; candidates register to take exam through the publisher, which authorizes every examination (at a group test center or by certified examiner), marks all papers, and issues official score report directly to institutions selected by examinee.

Authors: The English Language Institute Testing and Certification Division.

Publisher: English Language Institute, University of Michigan.

Cross References: For reviews by Ayres D'Costa and Alan Garfinkel, see 14:233.

[1611]
Michigan English Language Institute College English Test—Grammar, Cloze, Vocabulary, Reading.

Purpose: "To provide educational institutions and researchers with information about the English language competencies of their own students, employees, or research participants."

Population: Adult nonnative speakers of English.

Publication Date: 2001.

Acronym: MELICET-GCVR.

Scores: Total score only.

Administration: Group.

Forms, 2: AA, BB.

Price Data, 2005: $170 per complete testing package (specify Form AA or BB) including 20 test booklets, 100 answer sheets, stencil, and user's manual (32 pages); $100 per 20 test booklets (specify Form AA or BB); $20 per 100 answer sheets; $30 per plastic scoring stencil (specify Form AA or BB); $25 per user's manual.

Time: 75 minutes.

Comments: Consists of retired forms of grammar, cloze, vocabulary, and reading components of the Michigan English Language Assessment Battery, Part 3 (MELAB, see 1610); administered and scored by educational institutions or researchers who have purchased the test for use within their institution; test is nonsecure; all items are of multiple-choice format; scoring by punched stencil, purchasers may use their own scannable answer sheets.

Authors: The English Language Institute Testing and Certification Division.

Publisher: English Language Institute, The University of Michigan.

Cross References: For a review by Thomas P. Hogan, see 15:151.

[1612]
Michigan English Language Institute College English Test—Listening.

Purpose: "Designed to provide information about the English language competence of adult non-native speakers of English who have high-intermediate to advanced level English skills."

Population: Adult nonnative speakers of English.

Publication Date: 2003.

Acronym: MELICET-L.

Scores: Total score only.

Administration: Group.

Forms, 2: A1, B1.

Restricted Distribution: Distribution restricted to authorized educational institutions and researchers.

Price Data, 2005: $200 per complete testing package (specify Form A1 or B1) including 20 test booklets, 100 answer sheets, stencil, cassette tape or CD, and user's manual (16 pages); $100 per 20 test booklets (specify Form A1 or B1); $20 per 100 answer sheets; $30 per plastic scoring stencil (specify Form A1 or B1); $30 per cassette tape or CD (specify form A1 or B1), $25 per user's manual.

Time: 30(45) minutes.

Comments: Consists of retired forms of listening component of the Michigan English Language Assessment Battery, Part 2 (MELAB, see 1610); administered and scored by educational institutions or researchers who have purchased the test for use within their institution; test is nonsecure; all items are of multiple-choice format; scoring by punched stencil, purchasers may use their own scannable answer sheets.

Authors: The English Language Institute Testing and Certification Division.

Publisher: English Language Institute, University of Michigan.

Cross References: For reviews by Marsha Bensoussan and by Catherine P. Cook-Cottone and Jennifer Piccolo and by Alan Garfinkel, see 16:148.

[1613]
Michigan Test of English Language Proficiency.

Purpose: "To screen non-native speakers of English who wish to study at universities where English is the medium of instruction."

Population: College applicants from non-English-language countries.

Publication Date: 1979.

Acronym: MTELP.

Scores: Total score only.

Administration: Group.

Forms, 3: P, Q, R.

Price Data, 2005: $60 per complete kit including 20 tests of 1 form, 100 answer sheets, stencil, and manual (1977, 24 pages); $25 per 20 tests (specify form); $10 per 100 answer sheets; $20 per scoring stencil (specify form); $10 per manual (all forms).

Time: 75 minutes.

Comments: Older forms no longer available; a component test of the former "Michigan Battery."

Authors: M. Spaan, A. Corrigan, B. Dobson, E. Kellman, L. Strowe, and S. Tyma (tests), and Division of Testing and Certification (manual).
Publisher: English Language Institute, University of Michigan.
Cross References: See T5:1664 (6 references), T4:1623 (5 references), and T3:1484 (7 references); for a review by Edward J. Cervenka, see 8:106 (5 references); see also T2:233 (1 reference) and 7:264 (2 references); for a review by John B. Carroll, see 6:360.

[1614]
MicroCog: Assessment of Cognitive Functioning.

Purpose: "Assesses important neurocognitive functions in adults."
Population: Ages 18–89.
Publication Dates: 1993–2004.
Scores: 9 areas: Attention/Mental Control, Memory, Reasoning/Calculation, Spatial Processing, Reaction Time, Information Processing Accuracy, Information Processing Speed, General Cognitive Functioning, General Cognitive Proficiency.
Administration: Individual.
Price Data, 2006: $235 per complete kit including manual (1993, 106 pages0, user's guide (2004, 94 pages), CD-ROM Windows software with booklet insert, and 10 report credits; $155 per 10 report credits; bulk discounts available for report credits.
Time: (50–60) minutes for Standard form; (30) minutes for Brief form.
Comments: Computer administered and scored.
Authors: Douglas Powell, Edith Kaplan, Dean Whitla, Sandra Weintraub, Randolph Catlin, and Harris Funkenstein.
Publisher: PsychCorp, A brand of Harcourt Assessment, Inc.
Cross References: For reviews by Charles J. Long and Stephanie L. Cutlan and by Cynthia A. Rohrbeck, see 13:199.

[1615]
The MIDAS: Multiple Intelligences Developmental Assessment Scales [Revised].

Purpose: "A self-report designed to provide an objective measure of the multiple intelligences using a process approach."
Publication Date: 1994-2005.
Acronym: MIDAS.
Administration: Group or individual.
Price Data, 2006: $250 per Professional kit including MIDAS Questionnaire (select 2 age groups-reproducible), 50 MIDAS Profiles (pre-paid bulk scoring), The MIDAS: A Professional Manual (2005, 136 pages), and 1 interpretative workbook (reproducible); $350 per Classroom kit including MIDAS Questionnaire (select 1 age group-reproducible), 100 MIDAS Profiles (bulk pre-paid mail-in scoring included), The MIDAS Teacher's Handbook, Common Miracles in Your School, Select 1 of the two (2) reproducible workbooks above, 1 hour technical support, and discount bulk scoring rate; $900 per Guidance kit including MIDAS Questionnaires for Teens and Adults (reproducible), 200 MIDAS Profiles (pre-paid bulk scoring), The MIDAS: Professional Manual, The Challenge! Guide to Career Development, Student High Impact Project (SHIP) reproducible, and 1 hour technical support; $2,500 per School kit including MIDAS Questionnaires for 2 age groups-reproducible, bulk scoring for 1,000 profiles, on-site DOS scoring program (upon request during checkout), The MIDAS: A Professional Manual, Common Miracles in Your School (bulk pricing available), Student High Impact Project (SHIP) (reproducible), Teacher's Handbook for MI in the Classroom (bulk pricing available), Stepping Stones: A Teacher's Workbook (reproducible), Stepping Stones: Student Workbook for MI (reproducible), The Challenge! Guide to Career Success (reproducible), 2 hours on-site training (plus travel expenses), and 3 hours of telephone (free), Discounted Bulk Scoring Rate; $500 per Staff Development kit including MIDAS Questionnaire for adults (reproducible), 100 MIDAS Profiles (pre-paid bulk scoring), Teacher's Handbook: Multiple Intelligences in the Classroom, Common Miracles in Your School, Stepping Stones Workbook for Teachers (reproducible), 1 hour of technical support, Staff Development Packet (reproducible)-forthcoming, inquire; $40 per MIDAS preview package including 3 profiles, 1 book, interpretative packet, and Teacher's Handbook for MI in the Classroom; $45 per Teacher's Profile Package including Teacher's Handbook for MI in the Classroom, Common Miracles in Your School, and 1 MIDAS Adult Profile; $150 per The Basic Research kit, 100 MIDAS profiles, Professional Manual or Teacher's Handbook, Brief Interpretative Packet, data imported into database (either SPSS or Excel database-upon request), and 1 workbook (upon request); $300 per 100 MIDAS Profiles (with kit purchase); $400 per 100 MIDAS Profiles (without kit purchase); $100 per MIDAS Database; $7 per MIDAS Personal Profile (with purchase of book or package); $15 per MIDAS profile (bulk discounts available); $20 per Teacher's Handbook: Multiple Intelligences in the Classroom; $40 per The MIDAS: A Professional Manual.
Foreign Language Editions: Korean (MIDAS-K) and Chinese (C-MIDAS) and Danish (MIDAS-DK); research editions available: Singaporean, Spanish, Malaysian, German, Romanian, Venezuelan, Persian, Arabic, Turkish, Icelandic, and French.
Time: (25-35) minutes via self-completion using Online MIDAS System (OMS) or paper questionnaire; (60-90) minutes via structured interview.

Comments: This assessment can be administered via self-completion or as a structured interview; can be completed by an individual who is close to the subject; parents complete the MIDAS-KIDS: My Young Child version; the web-based administrative system automatically scores the responses and returns the profile via email within minutes.

Author: C. Branton Shearer.

Publisher: Multiple Intelligences Research and Consulting, Inc.

a) MIDAS.

Population: Ages 20 and up.

Scores: 11 scales and 26 subscales: Basic Scales: Musical (Appreciation, Vocal Ability, Instrumental Skill, Composing), Kinesthetic (Athletics, Dexterity), Logical-Mathematical (Strategy Games, Everyday Skills with Math, Everyday Problem Solving, School Math), Spatial (Spatial Awareness, Artistic Design, Working with Objects), Linguistic (Rhetorical Skill, Expressive Sensitivity, Written/Academic Ability), Interpersonal (Social Sensitivity, Social Persuasion, Interpersonal Work), Intrapersonal (Personal Knowledge/Efficacy, Self/Other Efficacy, Calculations, Spatial Problem-Solving), Naturalist (Animal Care, Plant Care, Science), Intellectual Style Scales: Leadership (Social Adeptness, Communication Skill, Managerial Skill), Innovation (Musical, Kinesthetic, Logical-Mathematical, Spatial, Linguistic, Interpersonal, Intrapersonal), General Logic (Logical-Mathematical, Spatial, Interpersonal, Intrapersonal).

b) TEEN-MIDAS.

Population: Ages 15-19.

Scores: Same as *a* above.

c) MIDAS-KIDS: ALL ABOUT ME.

Population: Ages 9-14.

Scores: 10 scales and 24 subscales: Basic Scales: Musical (Musicality, Vocal, Appreciation, Instrument), Kinesthetic (Physical Ability, Dance, Working with Hands), Logical-Mathematical (Problem Solving, Calculations), Spatial (Artistic, Constructions, Imagery), Linguistic (Linguistic Sensitivity, Writing, Reading), Interpersonal (Leadership, Understanding People, Getting Along with Others), Intrapersonal (Self Knowledge, Managing Feelings, Effective Relationships, Goal Achievement), Naturalist (Animal Care, Earth Science), Intellectual Style Scales: Technical, Innovative.

d) MIDAS-KIDS: MY YOUNG CHILD.

Population: Ages 6-9.

Scores: Same as *c* above, except without Intellectual Style Scales.

Cross References: For reviews by Abbot Packard and Michael S. Trevisan of an earlier version, see 14:234.

[1616]
The Middle Infant Screening Test.

Purpose: Designed to screen for reading and writing difficulties in first year school children.

Population: Ages 5-8 and over.

Publication Date: 1993.

Acronym: MIST.

Scores, 5: Listening Skills, Letter Sounds, Written Vocabulary, Three-Phoneme Words, Sentence Dictation.

Administration: Group.

Price Data: Available from publisher.

Time: (50–60) minutes.

Comments: "Criterion referenced"; designed for use with the Forward Together skills recovery program.

Author: Sybil Hannavy.

Publisher: NFER-Nelson Publishing Co., Ltd. [England].

[1617]
The Middlesex Elderly Assessment of Mental State.

Purpose: "Developed as a screening test to detect gross impairment of specific cognitive skills in the elderly."

Population: Adults.

Publication Date: 1989.

Acronym: MEAMS.

Scores, 12: Orientation, Name Learning, Naming, Comprehension, Remembering Pictures, Arithmetic, Spatial Construction, Fragmented Letter Perception, Unusual Views, Usual Views, Verbal Fluency, Motor Perseveration.

Administration: Individual.

Forms, 2: Version A, Version B.

Price Data, 2006: £175 per complete kit including manual (14 pages), 25 scoring sheets, and 2 stimulus books; £33.50 per 50 scoring sheets.

Time: [10] minutes.

Author: Evelyn Golding.

Publisher: Harcourt Assessment [England].

[1618]
Milani-Comparetti Motor Development Screening Test.

Purpose: "The test provides the clinician with a synopsis of the child's motor development by systematically examining the integration of primitive reflexes and the emergence of volitional movement against gravity."

Population: Ages 1–16 months.

Publication Dates: 1977–1992.

Scores, 27: Body Lying Supine, Hand Grasp, Foot Grasp, Supine Equilibrium, Body Pulled Up From Supine, Sitting Posture, Sitting Equilibrium, Sideways Parachute, Backward Parachute, Body Held Vertical, Head Righting, Downward Parachute, Standing, Standing Equilibrium, Locomotion, Landau Response, For-

ward Parachute, Body Lying Prone, Prone Equilibrium, All Fours, All Fours Equilibrium, Symmetric Tonic Neck Reflex, Body Derotative, Standing Up From Supine, Body Rotative, Asymmetrical Tonic Neck Reflex, Moro Reflex.
Administration: Individual.
Price Data: Price data for test including manual (1992, 48 pages) available from publisher.
Time: (10–15) minutes.
Comments: Behavior checklist.
Authors: Wayne Stuberg (Project Director), Pam Dehne, Jim Miedaner, and Penni White (Content Consultants).
Publisher: Munroe-Meyer Institute for Genetics & Rehabilitation.
Cross References: See T5:1668 (1 reference); for reviews by Linda K. Bunker and Ruth E. Tomes, see 11:236.

[1619]
MILCOM Patient Data Base System.

Purpose: Designed to record a patient's medical history.
Population: Medical patients.
Publication Dates: 1971–1985.
Scores: Item scores only.
Administration: Individual.
Manual: No manual.
Price Data: Available from publisher.
Foreign Language Edition: Spanish version available.
Time: Administration time not reported.
Comments: Questionnaire includes health questionnaire and 18-part physical exam.
Author: MILCOM Systems, A Division of Hollister, Inc.
Publisher: MILCOM Systems, A Division of Hollister, Inc.

[1620]
Military Environment Inventory.

Purpose: "Asesses the social environment of varied types of military contexts."
Population: Military personnel.
Publication Date: 1986.
Acronym: MEIN.
Scores, 7: Involvement, Peer Cohesion, Officer Support, Personal Status, Order and Organization, Clarity, Officer Control.
Administration: Group.
Forms, 4: Real Form (Form R), Short Form (Form S), Ideal Form (Form I), Expectations Form (Form E).
Price Data: Available from publisher (www.mindgarden.com).
Time: Administration time not reported.
Comments: One of 10 Social Climate Scales.

Author: Rudolf H. Moos.
Publisher: Mind Garden, Inc.
Cross References: For reviews by David O. Herman and Alfred L. Smith, Jr., see 11:237 (1 reference).

[1621]
Mill Hill Vocabulary Scale.

Purpose: Provides a measure of acquired verbal knowledge.
Publication Dates: 1943–1998.
Acronym: MHV.
Scores: Total score only.
Administration: Group or individual.
Forms, 2: A, B.
Price Data: Price information available from publisher for test booklets and for specimen set including one of each test booklet, scoring key, and appropriate sections of the Raven's manuals (Section 1–1998, 119 pages; Section 5–1998, 124 pages).
Time: (15–40) minutes.
Comments: To be used in conjunction with the Raven's Progressive Matrices (2122); short-form also available.
Authors: J. C. Raven, J. H. Court, and J. Raven.
Publisher: Oxford Psychologists Press, Ltd. [England].
a) JUNIOR.
Population: Ages 6.5–16.5.
b) SENIOR.
Population: Ages 18–adult.
Cross References: See T5:1671 (8 references); for reviews by Theodore L. Hayes and William K. Wilkinson, see 13:200 (30 references); see also T4:1629 (51 reference), 9:705 (8 references), T3:1485 (29 references), and T2:402 (32 references); for a review by Morton Bortner of an earlier edition, see 6:471 (16 references); see also 4:303 (7 references); for a review by David Wechsler, see 3:239 (3 references).

[1622]
Miller Analogies Test.

Purpose: Measures background knowledge and analytical abilities critical to the commencement of study in graduate school.
Population: Graduate school applicants.
Publication Dates: 1926–2006.
Acronym: MAT.
Scores: Total score only.
Administration: Group or individual.
Price Data: Available from publisher.
Time: 60 minutes.
Comments: Paper-and-pencil or computer-based, on-demand.
Author: Harcourt Assessment, Inc.
Publisher: PsychCorp, A brand of Harcourt Assessment, Inc.

Cross References: See T5:1672 (5 references); for reviews by Robert B. Frary and Stephen H. Ivens, see 12:235 (2 references); see also T4:1630 (1 reference), T3:1486 (16 references), 8:192 (31 references), T2:404 (15 references), and 7:363 (57 references); for reviews by Lloyd G. Humphreys, William B. Schrader, and Warren W. Willingham, see 6:472 (26 references); for a review by John T. Dailey, see 5:352 (28 references); for reviews by J. P. Guilford and Cart I. Hovland, see 4:304 (16 references).

[1623]
Miller Assessment for Preschoolers.

Purpose: Designed "to identify children who exhibit moderate 'preacademic' problems."
Population: Ages 2-9 to 5-8.
Publication Date: 1982.
Acronym: MAP.
Scores, 6: Foundations, Coordination, Verbal, Non-Verbal, Complex Tasks, Total.
Administration: Individual.
Levels: 6 developmental levels (ages 2-9 to 3-2, 3-3 to 3-8, 3-9 to 4-2, 4-3 to 4-8, 4-9 to 5-2, 5-3 to 5-8).
Price Data, 2002: $695 per complete kit including manual (220 pages), score sheets, and all items needed for administration and scoring; $100 per examiner's manual; $299 per training tape; $99 per training tape rental; $72 per workshop set; $36 per 6 cue sheets; $34 per 25 score sheets; $34 per 25 drawing booklets; $34 per 25 record booklets.
Time: (20–30) minutes.
Author: Lucy Jane Miller.
Publisher: PsychCorp, A brand of Harcourt Assessment, Inc.
Cross References: See T5:1673 (11 references) and T4:1631 (6 references); for reviews by Dennis J. Deloria and William B. Michael, see 9:706.

[1624]
Miller Common Sense Scale.

Purpose: "Designed to permit the individual to compare his/her level of common sense with other individuals ... and to determine changes that should be made as a result of this information."
Population: Ages 15 to adult.
Publication Date: 1997.
Scores: Total score only.
Administration: Group.
Price Data, 2001: $35 per administration via webpage (Visa or MasterCard are required to use this test).
Time: (15) minutes.
Comments: Administered and scored on the internet; printout of results is provided. [Editor's note: Since November 2002, the webpage for administration of this test has been unavailable.]

Author: Harold J. Miller.
Publisher: Meta Development LLC [Canada] [No reply from publisher; status unknown].
Cross References: For a review by Carl Isenhart, see 15:152.

[1625]
Miller Depression Scale.

Purpose: Designed to "measure an individual's depression level."
Population: Ages 15 years and over.
Publication Date: 1997.
Scores: Total score only.
Administration: Individual or group.
Manual: No manual.
Price Data, 2001: $35 per administration via webpage (Visa or MasterCard are required to use this test).
Time: (15) minutes.
Comments: "Designed to be given and scored over the internet"; printout of results provided; can be used to monitor treatment effectiveness. [Editor's note: Since November 2002, the webpage for administration of this test has been unavailable.]
Author: Harold J. Miller.
Publisher: Meta Development LLC [Canada] [No reply from publisher; status unknown].
Cross References: For a review by Cederick O. Lindskog, see 15:153.

[1626]
Miller Emotional Maturity Scale.

Purpose: Designed to "measure the individual's emotional maturity."
Population: Adults with reading levels at 7th grade or above.
Publication Date: 1991.
Scores, 8: Secure, Stable, Independent, Optimistic, Responsible, Assertive, Social, Honest.
Administration: Individual or group.
Manual: No manual.
Price Data, 2001: $35 per administration via webpage (Visa or MasterCard are required to use this test).
Time: (30–45) minutes.
Comments: "Designed to be administered and scored on the internet"; printout of results is provided. [Editor's note: Since November 2002, the webpage for administration of this test has been unavailable.]
Author: Harold J. Miller.
Publisher: Meta Development LLC [Canada] [No reply from publisher; status unknown].
Cross References: For reviews by Robert J. Drummond and Jeffrey A. Jenkins, see 15:154.

[1627]

Miller Forensic Assessment of Symptoms Test.

Purpose: Designed to "provide information regarding the probability that an individual is malingering psychiatric illness."
Population: Ages 18 and over.
Publication Dates: 1995–2001.
Acronym: M-FAST.
Scores, 8: Reported vs. Observed, Extreme Symptomatology, Rare Combinations, Unusual Hallucinations, Unusual Symptom Course, Negative Image, Suggestibility, Total.
Administration: Individual.
Price Data, 2006: $135 per introductory kit including professional manual and 25 interview booklets.
Time: (5–10) minutes.
Author: Holly A. Miller.
Publisher: Psychological Assessment Resources, Inc.
Cross References: For reviews by Marc Janoson and by Nathaniel J. Pallone and James J. Hennessy, see 15:155.

[1628]

Miller Getting Along With People Scale.

Purpose: "Designed to help individuals determine how well they get along with other people."
Population: Ages 15 to adult.
Publication Date: 1996.
Scores: Total score only.
Administration: Group.
Price Data, 2001: $35 per administration via webpage (Visa or MasterCard are required to use this test).
Time: (15) minutes.
Comments: Administered and scored on the internet; printout of results provided. [Editor's note: Since November 2002, the webpage for administration of this test has been unavailable.]
Author: Harold J. Miller.
Publisher: Meta Development LLC [Canada] [No reply from publisher; status unknown].
Cross References: For reviews by Albert M. Bugaj and Jean Powell Kirnan, see 15:156.

[1629]

Miller Happiness Scale.

Purpose: "Designed to measure eight areas of an individual's happiness."
Population: Grade 7 reading level or higher.
Publication Date: 1998.
Scores, 8: Personal Happiness, Health Happiness, Spiritual Happiness, Intimate Relationship Happiness, Family Happiness, Friendship Happiness, Work Happiness, Leisure Happiness.
Administration: Group.

Price Data, 2001: $35 per administration via webpage (Visa or MasterCard are required to use this test).
Time: (30–45) minutes.
Comments: Administered and scored on the internet; printout of results is provided. [Editor's note: Since November 2002, the webpage for administration of this test has been unavailable.]
Author: Harold J. Miller.
Publisher: Meta Development LLC [Canada] [No reply from publisher; status unknown].
Cross References: For reviews by Julie A. Allison and Raoul A. Arreola, see 15:157.

[1630]

Miller Love Scale.

Purpose: "Designed to measure eight areas of love."
Population: Ages 16 to adult.
Publication Date: 1998.
Scores, 8: Self-Love, Love Motivation, Value, Perception of Partner, Love Thoughts, Love Feelings, Love Behavior, Spiritual Love.
Administration: Group.
Price Data, 2001: $35 per administration via webpage (Visa or MasterCard are required to use this test).
Time: (30–45) minutes.
Comments: Administered and scored on the internet; printout of results is provided. [Editor's note: Since November 2002, the webpage for administration of this test has been unavailable.]
Author: Harold J. Miller.
Publisher: Meta Development LLC [Canada] [No reply from publisher; status unknown].
Cross References: For reviews by Jill Ann Jenkins and S. Alvin Leung, see 15:158.

[1631]

Miller Marriage Satisfaction Rating Scale.

Purpose: "Designed to compare one's level of marriage satisfaction to the marriage satisfaction of other married people."
Population: Individuals who are dating, living together or who are married.
Publication Date: 1997.
Scores: Total score only.
Administration: Group.
Price Data, 2001: $35 per administration via web page (Visa or MasterCard are required to use this test).
Time: (15) minutes.
Comments: Administered and scored on the internet; online documentation lists as Miller Marriage Satisfaction Scale but test itself is entitled Miller Marriage Satisfaction Rating Scale; printout of results is provided. [Editor's Note: Since November 2002, the webpage for administration of this test has been unavailable.]
Author: Harold J. Miller.

Publisher: Meta Development LCC [Canada] [No reply from publisher; status unknown].
Cross References: For reviews by Frank M. Bernt and Cindy I. Carlson, see 15:159.

[1632]
Miller Motivation Scale.

Purpose: "Designed to measure positive and negative aspects of the individual's motivation."
Population: Individuals who have a grade seven reading level or greater.
Publication Dates: 1986–1988.
Scores, 8: Creative, Innovative, Productive, Cooperative, Attention, Power, Revenge, Give-Up.
Administration: Group.
Price Data, 2001: $35 per administration via webpage (Visa or MasterCard are required to use this test).
Time: (30–45) minutes.
Comments: Administered and scored on the internet; printout of results is provided. [Editor's note: Since November 2002, the webpage for administration of this test has been unavailable.]
Author: Harold J. Miller.
Publisher: Meta Development LLC [Canada] [No reply from publisher; status unknown].
Cross References: For a review by Michael J. Roszkowski, see 15:160.

[1633]
Miller Psychological Independence Scale.

Purpose: Designed to "measure the individual's psychological independence in a dependent-independent continuum."
Population: High school students and athletes.
Publication Date: 1996.
Scores, 8: Independent Behavior, Independence in Relationships, Perfection, Effectiveness, Egocentric, Independent Thoughts, Independent Feelings, Control.
Administration: Group.
Price Data, 2001: $35 per administration via webpage (Visa or MasterCard are required to use this test).
Time: (30–45) minutes.
Comments: "Designed to be given on the internet"; results immediately available in a six-page printout. [Editor's note: Since November 2002, the webpage for administration of this test has been unavailable.]
Author: Harold J. Miller.
Publisher: Meta Development LLC [Canada] [No reply from publisher; status unknown].
Cross References: For a review by Brian F. Bolton, see 15:161.

[1634]
Miller Self-Concept Scale.

Purpose: Designed to "measure components of the individual's self-concept."

Population: Individuals with a seventh-grade or higher reading level.
Publication Date: 1989.
Scores, 8: Intrapsychic, Family, Friendship Self-Concept, Work/School Self-Concept, Locus of Control, Attribution, Courage, Flexibility.
Administration: Group.
Price Data, 2001: $35 per administration via webpage (Visa or MasterCard are required to use this test).
Time: (30–45) minutes.
Comments: "Designed to be given and scored on the internet"; results are immediately available in a six-page printout. [Editor's note: Since November 2002, the webpage for administration of this test has been unavailable.]
Author: Harold J. Miller.
Publisher: Meta Development LLC [Canada] [No reply from publisher; status unknown].
Cross References: For reviews by Trenton R. Ferro and Judith A. Rein, see 15:162.

[1635]
Miller Stress Scale.

Purpose: "Designed to measure the individual's stress in several areas of the individual's life."
Population: Individuals with reading level at or above the 7th grade.
Publication Date: 1992.
Scores, 8: Stressful Behavior, Relationship Stress, Family Stress, Work Stress, Physical Stress, Stressful Thoughts, Stressful Feelings, Coping.
Administration: Group.
Price Data, 2001: $35 per administration via webpage (Visa or MasterCard are required to use this test).
Time: (30–45) minutes.
Comments: "Designed to be given and scored on the internet"; results are available immediately in a six-page printout. [Editor's note: Since November 2002, the webpage for administration of this test has been unavailable.]
Author: Harold J. Miller.
Publisher: Meta Development LLC [Canada] [No reply from publisher; status unknown].
Cross References: For a review by Michael J. Scheel and Brad M. Merker, see 15:163.

[1636]
Millon Adolescent Clinical Inventory.

Purpose: Designed to assess "an adolescent's personality, along with self-reported concerns and clinical syndromes."
Population: Ages 13–19.
Publication Date: 1993.
Acronym: MACI.
Scores: 27 scales: Personality Patterns (Introversive, Inhibited, Doleful, Submissive, Dramatizing, Egotis-

tic, Unruly, Forceful, Conforming, Oppositional, Self-Demeaning, Borderline Tendency), Expressed Concerns (Identify Diffusion, Self-Devaluation, Body Disapproval, Sexual Discomfort, Peer Insecurity, Social Insensitivity, Family Discord, Childhood Abuse), Clinical Syndromes (Eating Dysfunctions, Substance Abuse Proneness, Delinquent Predisposition, Impulsive Propensity, Anxious Feelings, Depressive Affect, Suicidal Tendency), and 3 Modifying Indices (Disclosure, Desirability, Debasement).

Administration: Individual or group.

Price Data, 2006: $41 per manual (123 pages); $5.25 per test booklet; $51 per compact disc; $100 per Q Local starter kit including manual, 3 answer sheets, and 3 Q Local administrations; $26 per 25 Q Local answer sheets; $24 per Q Local interpretive reports; $18 per Q Local profile reports; $108 per mail-in starter kit including manual and 3 answer sheets to conduct 3 assessments and receive 3 interpretive reports using mail-in scoring service; $27 per mail-in interpretive report; $21 per mail-in profile report; $335 per handscoring starter kit including manual, handscoring user's guide, 20 test booklets, 50 answer sheets, 50 work sheets, and 50 profile forms and keys; $144 per reorder kit including 50 answer sheets, 50 worksheets, and 50 profile sheets; quantity discounts available for the reports; price information for Spanish manterials available from publisher.

Foreign Language Edition: Spanish materials available.

Time: (30) minutes.

Comments: Self-report personality inventory; available in paper-and-pencil and on-line administration; Q Local, mail-in scoring, and handscoring available.

Authors: Theodore Millon with Carrie Millon, Roger Davis, and Seth Grossman.

Publisher: Pearson Assessments.

Cross References: See T5:1685 (2 references); for reviews by Paul Retzlaff and Richard B. Stuart, see 12:236 (6 references); see also T4:1633 (14 references); for reviews by Douglas T. Brown and Thomas A. Widiger of the Millon Adolescent Personality Inventory, see 9:707.

[1637]
Millon Adolescent Personality Inventory.

Purpose: Designed to assess an adolescent's personality.

Population: Ages 13-18.

Publication Dates: 1976-1982.

Acronym: MAPI.

Scores: 20 scales: Introversive, Inhibited, Cooperative, Sociable, Confident, Forceful, Respectful, Sensitive, Self-Concept, Personal Esteem, Body Comfort, Sexual Acceptance, Peer Security, Social Tolerance, Family Rapport, Academic Confidence, Impulse Con-

trol, Social Conformity, Scholastic Achievement, Attendance Consistency.

Administration: Group or individual.

Price Data: Available from publisher.

Time: (20-30) minutes.

Authors: Theodore Millon, Catherine J. Green, and Robert B. Meagher, Jr.

Publisher: Pearson Assessments.

Cross References: For reviews by Douglas T. Brown and Thomas A. Widiger, see 9:707.

[1638]
Millon Behavioral Medicine Diagnostic.

Purpose: Designed to "assess psychological factors that can influence the course of treatment of medically ill patients ... especially for patients in which psychosocial factors may play a role in the course of the disease and treatment outcome."

Population: Clinical and rehabilitation patients ages 18–85.

Publication Date: 2001.

Acronym: MBMD.

Scores, 39: Validity Indicator, Response Patterns (Disclosure, Desirability, Debasement), Negative Health Habits (Alcohol, Drug, Eating, Caffeine, Inactivity, Smoking), Psychiatric Indications (Anxiety-Tension, Depression, Cognitive Dysfunction, Emotional Lability, Guardedness), Coping Styles (Introversion, Inhibited, Dejected, Cooperative, Sociable, Confident, Nonconforming, Forceful, Respectful, Oppositional, Denigrated), Stress Moderators (Illness Apprehension, Functional Deficits, Pain Sensitivity, Social Isolation, Future Pessimism, Spiritual Absence), Treatment Prognostics (Interventional Fragility, Medication Abuse, Information Discomfort, Utilization Excess, Problematic Compliance), Management Guides (Adjustment Difficulties, Psych Referral).

Administration: Individual or group.

Price Data, 2006: $110 per Q Local starter kit with interpretive reports including manual, softcover test booklet, 3 answer sheets with test items to conduct and receive 3 interpretive Q Local administrations; $21 per 25 Q Local answer sheets with test items; $51 per manual (183 pages); $51 per compact disc; $24.50 per Q Local interpretive report; $16.75 per Q Local profile report; $117 per mail-in scoring service starter kit with interpretive reports including manual, softcover test booklet, 3 answer sheets with test items to conduct 3 assessments and receive 3 interpretive reports using mail-in socring service; $27.50 per mail-in interpretive report (test items and answer sheets included); $19.75 per mail-in profile reports (test items and answer sheets included); $337 per hand-scoring starter kit including manual, hand-scoring user's guide, 10 test booklets, 50 answer sheets, 50 worksheets, and 50 profile forms and answer keys; $28 per 10 hand-scoring test booklets; $19

per 25 large print answer sheets; quantity discounts available; price information for Spanish materials available from publisher.
Foreign Language Edition: Available in Spanish.
Time: (20–25) minutes.
Comments: Upgrading of the Millon Behavioral Health Inventory (T5:1686); self-administered; may be administered in paper-and pencil format, via computer, or via audiocassette; interpretive reports with healthcare provider summary and profile available; scoring options include handscoring, mail-in, Q Local Assessment System software.
Authors: Theodore Millon, Michael Antoni, Carrie Millon, Sarah Minor, and Seth Grossman.
Publisher: Pearson Assessments.
Cross References: For reviews by Mark J. Atkinson and John C. Caruso, see 15:164; for information regarding the original Millon Behavioral Health Inventory, see T5:1686 (7 references) and T4:1634 (6 references); for reviews of the Millon Behavioral Health Inventory by Mary J. Allen and Richard I. Lanyon, see 9:708 (1 reference).

[1639]
Millon Clinical Multiaxial Inventory—III [Manual Third Edition].

Purpose: Designed to provide diagnostic and treatment information to clinicians in the areas of personality disorders and clinical syndromes.
Population: "Adults [18+] who are seeking [or in] mental health treatment and who have eighth-grade reading skills."
Publication Dates: 1976–2006.
Acronym: MCMI-III.
Scores, 28: Modifying Indices (Disclosure, Desirability, Debasement, Validity), Clinical Personality Patterns (Schizoid, Avoidant, Depressive, Dependent, Histrionic, Narcissistic, Antisocial, Sadistic [Aggressive], Compulsive, Negativistic [Passive-Aggressive], Masochistic [Self-Defeating]), Severe Personality Pathology (Schizotypal, Borderline, Paranoid), Clinical Syndromes (Anxiety, Somatoform, Bipolar: Manic, Dysthymia, Alcohol Dependence, Drug Dependence, Post-Traumatic Stress Disorder), Severe Clinical Syndromes (Thought Disorder, Major Depression, Delusional Disorder).
Administration: Individual or group.
Price Data, 2006: $49 per manual (223 pages); $28 per 10 test booklets; $20 per Corrections Report user's guide (1998, 56 pages); $51 per compact disc; $134 per Q Local starter kit including manual, 1 softcover test booklet with 3 answer sheets and 3 Q Local administrations; $21 per 25 Q Local answer sheets; $35 per interpretive report; $31.50 per corrections interpretive report; $17 per profile report (Q-Local scoring); $140 per mail-in starter kit including manual, 2 softcover test booklet, and 3 answer sheets to conduct 3 assessments

and receive 3 interpretive reports using mail-in scoring service; $38 per prepaid interpretive report; $34.50 per prepaid corrections interpretive report; $20 per prepaid profile report (mail-in scoring); $335 per hand-scoring starter kit including manual, hand-scoring users guide (1994, 9 pages), 10 test booklets, 50 answer sheets, 50 worksheets, 50 profile forms, and answer keys; $146 per kit including 50 answer sheets, 50 worksheets, and 50 profile forms; quantity discounts available for the reports; price data for Spanish materials available from publisher.
Foreign Language Edition: Spanish materials available.
Time: 25-30 minutes.
Comments: Designed to coordinate with DSM-IV categories of clinical syndromes and personality disorders; revision of the Millon Clinical Multiaxial Inventory—III (13:201); includes optional Corrections Report for use with correctional inmates.
Authors: Theodore Millon, Roger Davis, Carrie Millon, and Seth Grossman.
Publisher: Pearson Assessments.
Cross References: For reviews by James P. Choca and Thomas A. Widiger, see 14:236; see also T5:1687 (47 references); for reviews by Allen K. Hess and Paul Retzlaff of the third edition, see 13:201 (81 references); see also T4:1635 (104 references); for reviews by Thomas M. Haladyna and Cecil K. Reynolds of the second edition, see 11:239 (74 references); for reviews by Allen K. Hess and Thomas A. Widiger of the original edition, see 9:709 (1 reference); see also T3:1488 (3 references).

[1640]
Millon Index of Personality Styles Revised.

Purpose: "Designed to measure personality styles of normally functioning adults."
Population: 18 years and older.
Publication Dates: 1994-2004.
Acronym: MIPS Revised.
Scores, 28: 6 Motivating Styles (Pleasure-Enhancing, Pain-Avoiding, Actively Modifying, Passively Accommodating, Self-Indulging, Other-Nuturing), 8 Thinking Styles (Externally Focused, Internally Focused, Realistic/Sensing, Imaginative/Intuiting, Thought-Guided, Feeling-Guided, Conservation-Seeking, Innovation-Seeking), 10 Behavior Styles (Asocial/Withdrawing, Gregarious/Outgoing, Anxious/Hesitating, Confident/Asserting, Unconventional/Dissenting, Dutiful/Conforming, Submissive/Yielding, Dominant/Controlling, Dissatisfied/Complaining, Cooperative/Agreeing), 4 Validity Indices (Positive Impression, Negative Impression, Consistency, Clinical Index).
Administration: Group or individual.
Forms, 2: Interpretive, Profile.
Price Data, 2006: $46 per manual (2004, 176 pages); $21 per 10 test booklets; $21 per 25 answer

sheets; $41.50 per 50 hand-scoring answer sheets; $89 per Q Local desktop software; $250 per Q Local network software; quantity discounts available.
Time: (25-30) minutes.
Comments: Paper-and-pencil or computer administration available.
Author: Theodore Millon.
Publisher: Pearson Assessments.

a) Q LOCAL SCORING AND REPORTING SOFTWARE.
Price Data: $85 per Q Local starter kit with interpretive reports including manual, 3 answer sheets, 1 test booklet, and 3 Q Local administrations (does not include Q Local software); $16.50 per Q Local interpretive report administration; $8.50 per Q Local profile reports administration.
b) MAIL-IN SCORING SERVICE.
Price Data: $92 per mail-in starter kit with profile reports including manual, 3 answer sheets, and 1 test booklet; $19.50 per mail-in interpretive report scoring and answer sheet; $11.50 per mail-in profile report scoring and answer sheet.
c) HAND-SCORING MATERIALS.
Price Data: $163 per hand-scoring starter kit including manual, 10 test booklets, 50 answer sheets, and answer keys.
Cross References: See T5:1688 (1 reference); for reviews by James P. Choca and Peter Zachar of an earlier version, see 13:202.

[1641]
Millon Pre-Adolescent Clinical Inventory.

Purpose: To "identify, predict, and understand a broad range of psychological disorders that are common in 9–12 year olds seen in clinical settings."
Population: Ages 9–12.
Publication Date: 2005.
Acronym: M-PACI.
Scores: 16 scales: Emerging Personality Patterns (Confident, Outgoing, Conforming, Submissive, Inhibited, Unruly, Unstable), Current Clinical Signs (Anxiety/Fears, Attention Deficits, Obsessions/Compulsions, Conduct Disorder, Disruptive Behaviors, Depressive Moods, Reality Distortions), Response Validity Indicators (Invalidity, Response Negativity).
Administration: Individual or group.
Price Data, 2005: $215 per hand-scoring starter kit including manual (115 pages), 50 answer sheets, 50 profile forms, and answer keys; $86 per mail-in scoring starter kit including manual and 3 answer sheets; $81 per Q local starter kit with interpretive reports including manual, 3 answer sheets, and 3 Q local administrations; $89 per Q local software for desktop version; $250 per Q local software for network version; $38 per manual; quantity discounts available.
Time: (15–20) minutes.

Comments: Hand-scored, mail-scored, or computer-based administration, scoring, and interpretation available.
Authors: Theodore Millon, Robert Tringone, Carrie Millon, and Seth Grossman.
Publisher: Pearson Assessments.

[1642]
The Milwaukee Evaluation of Daily Living Skills.

Purpose: "To assess basic daily living skills for use with the chronically mentally ill."
Population: Ages 18 and over.
Publication Date: 1989.
Acronym: MEDLS.
Scores, 20: Basic Communication Skills, Bathing, Brushing Teeth, Denture Care, Dressing, Eating, Eyeglass Care, Hair Care, Maintenance of Clothing, Makeup Use, Medication Management, Nail Care, Personal Health Care, Safety in Community, Safety in Home, Shaving, Time Awareness, Use of Money, Use of Telephone, Use of Transportation.
Administration: Individual.
Price Data: Available from publisher.
Time: (80) minutes.
Author: Carol A. Leonardelli.
Publisher: SLACK Incorporated.

[1643]
Mindex: Your Thinking Style Profile.

Purpose: Designed to measure "thinking style," an individual's "unique way of processing ideas and deriving meaning" from experience.
Population: Adults.
Publication Date: 1983.
Scores, 20: Thinking Style Preference (Red Earth, Blue Earth, Red Sky, Blue Sky), Sensory Mode Preference (Kinesthetic, Visual, Auditory), Structure Preference (Time Orientation, Detail Orientation, Technical Orientation, Goal Orientation), Mental Flexibility (Tolerance for Ambiguity, Opinion Flexibility, Semantic Flexibility, Positive Orientation, Sense of Humor, Investigative Orientation, Resistance to Enculturation), Thinking Fluency (Idea Fluency, Logical Fluency).
Administration: Individual.
Price Data: Available from publisher.
Time: Administration time not reported.
Author: Karl Albrecht.
Publisher: Karl Albrecht International.

[1644]
MindMaker6™.

Purpose: To determine personality or personal style using hemispheric dominance theories for use in training, consulting, and counseling clients.
Population: Adults.
Publication Dates: 1985-1987.

Scores, 6: Kins-Person, Loner, Loyalist, Achiever, Involver, Choice-Seeker.
Administration: Group.
Price Data: Available from publisher.
Time: (30-40) minutes.
Authors: Kenneth L. Adams and Dudley Lynch.
Publisher: Brain Technologies Corporation.
Cross References: For a review by Thomas A. Wrobel, see 11:240.

[1645]
Miner Sentence Completion Scale.

Purpose: Intended for use in "selection, vocational and career guidance, identifying talent supplies, and evaluating training primarily."
Population: Workers and prospective workers in management, professional, and entrepreneurial or task-oriented occupations.
Publication Dates: 1961–1986.
Acronym: MSCS.
Administration: Group.
Forms, 3: Form H (Management domain), Form P (Professional domain), Form T (Task domain).
Price Data, 2002: $30 per 50 tests with scoring sheets; $10 per scoring guide (Form H, 1964, 64 pages, with 1977 supplement, 15 pages, and 1989 supplement, 4 pages; Form P, 1981, 49 pages; Form T, 1986, 56 pages).
Time: (20–30) minutes.
Comments: Form H available as free-response or multiple-choice version; directions included for scoring rare response patterns.
Author: John B. Miner.
Publisher: Organizational Measurement Systems Press.

a) FORM H.
Scores, 9: Authority Figures, Competitive Games, Competitive Situations, Assertive Role, Imposing Wishes, Standing Out from Group, Routine Administrative Functions, Supervisory Job, Total.
b) FORM P.
Scores, 6: Acquiring Knowledge, Independent Action, Accepting Status, Providing Help, Professional Commitment, Total.
c) FORM T.
Scores, 6: Self Achievement, Avoiding Risks, Feedback of Results, Personal Innovation, Planning for the Future, Total.
Cross References: See T5:1689 (4 references) and T4:1637 (1 reference); for reviews by Frederick T. L. Leong and Linda F. Wightman, see 11:241 (2 references); see also T2:1484 (4 references); for a review by C. J. Adcock, see 7:172 (2 references); see also P:450 (3 references) and 6:230a (2 references).

[1646]
Mini-Battery of Achievement.

Purpose: Constructed as a brief, wide-range test of basic skills and knowledge.
Population: Ages 4–adult.
Publication Date: 1994.
Acronym: MBA.
Scores, 5: Basic Skills (Reading, Writing, Mathematics, Total), Factual Knowledge.
Administration: Individual.
Price Data, 2006: $231.50 per complete kit including test book with manual, 25 test records with subject worksheets, and scoring and reporting program (Windows and Mac); $176.50 per test book, $35 per 25 test records with subject worksheets; $28.50 per scoring and reporting program.
Time: (20–30) minutes.
Comments: Previously listed as Woodcock-McGrew-Werder Mini-Battery of Achievement.
Authors: Richard W. Woodcock, Kevin S. McGrew, and Judy K. Werder.
Publisher: Riverside Publishing.
Cross References: See T5:2903 (2 references); for reviews by William B. Michael and Eleanor E. Sanford, see 13:363.

[1647]
Mini Inventory of Right Brain Injury, Second Edition.

Purpose: Designed for "screening neurocognitive deficits associated with right hemisphere lesions."
Population: Ages 20-80.
Publication Dates: 1989–2000.
Acronym: MIRBI-2.
Scores, 10: Visual Scanning, Integrity of Gnosis, Integrity of Body Image, Visuoverbal Processing, Visuosymbolic Processing, Integrity of Visuomotor Praxis, Higher-Level Language Skills, Expressing Emotion, General Affect, General Behavior.
Administration: Individual.
Price Data, 2006: $163 per complete kit; $35 per examiner record booklets; $35 per response forms; $20 per response sheets; $20 per caliper; $60 per manual (2000, 58 pages).
Time: (15–30) minutes.
Authors: Patricia A. Pimental and Jeffrey A. Knight.
Publisher: PRO-ED.
Cross References: For reviews by Daniel C. Miller and David Shum, see 15:165; for reviews of an earlier edition by R. A. Bornstein and by John E. Obrzut and Carol A. Boliek, see 11:242.

[1648]
Mini-Mental State Examination.

Purpose: Designed to "measure cognitive status in adults."

Population: Adults.
Publication Dates: 1975–2001.
Acronym: MMSE.
Scores: Total score only with items in 11 sections: Orientation to Time, Orientation to Place, Registration, Attention and Calculation, Recall, Naming, Repetition, Comprehension, Reading, Writing, Drawing.
Administration: Individual.
Price Data, 2006: $112 per introductory kit including MMSE clinical guide, pocket norms card, user's guide (2001, 11 pages), and 50 test forms; $285 per Mental Status Reporting Software (which incorporates the MMSE and an additional checklist) on CD-ROM providing unlimited scoring, interpretation, and reports.
Time: (5–10) minutes.
Authors: Marshal F. Folstein, Susan E. Folstein, and Paul R. McHugh, and Gary Fanjiang (manual only).
Publisher: Psychological Assessment Resources, Inc.
Cross References: For reviews by Mark A. Albanese and Sandra B. Ward, see 15:166.

[1649]
Minnesota Clerical Test.

Purpose: Designed to measure speed and accuracy in clerical work.
Population: Grades 8–12 and adults.
Publication Dates: 1933–1979.
Acronym: MCT.
Scores, 2: Number Comparison, Name Comparison.
Administration: Group or individual.
Price Data, 2006: $89 per per starter kit, including 25 test booklets key and manual; $30 per key for hand scoring test booklets; $36 per manual;
Time: 15(20) minutes.
Authors: Dorothy M. Andrew, Donald G. Paterson, and Howard P. Longstaff.
Publisher: Harcourt Assessment, Inc.
Cross References: See T5:1693 (3 references) and T4:1640 (3 references); for reviews by Michael Ryan and Ruth G. Thomas, see 9:713 (2 references); see also T3:1493 (5 references), T2:2135 (23 references), and 6:1040 (10 references); for a review by Donald E. Super, see 5:850 (46 references); for reviews by Thelma Hunt, R. B. Selover, Erwin K. Taylor, and E. F. Wonderlic, see 3:627 (22 references); for a review by W. D. Commins, see 2:1644 (18 references).

[1650]
Minnesota Handwriting Assessment.

Purpose: "Used to assess manuscript and D'Nealian handwriting of students."
Population: Grades 1–2.
Publication Date: 1999.
Acronym: MHA.

Scores, 6: Rate, Legibility, Form, Alignment, Size, Spacing.
Administration: Group or individual.
Price Data, 2002: $56 per kit including 25 manuscript sheets, 25 D'Nealian sheets, and manual (99 pages).
Time: (2.5–10) minutes.
Author: Judith Reisman.
Publisher: Harcourt Assessment, Inc.
Cross References: For reviews by Kathy J. Bohan and Andrew A. Cox, see 16:149.

[1651]
Minnesota Importance Questionnaire.

Purpose: "To measure twenty psychological needs and six underlying values that have been found to be relevant to work adjustment, specifically to satisfaction with work."
Population: Ages 16 and over.
Publication Dates: 1967-1981.
Acronym: MIQ.
Scores, 21: Ability Utilization, Achievement, Activity, Independence, Variety, Compensation, Security, Working Conditions, Advancement, Recognition, Authority, Social Status, Co-workers, Social Services, Moral Values, Company Policies, Supervision-Human Relations, Supervision-Technical, Creativity, Responsibility, Autonomy (ranked form only).
Administration: Group.
Forms, 2: Ranked form (1975, 9 pages), paired form (1975, 18 pages).
Price Data, 2001: $39.50 per complete kit including 50 answer sheets, 10 reusable booklets, manual (1981, 73 pages), and Occupational Reinforcer Patterns (1986); $.70 or less per reusable booklet ($7 minimum); $.12 or less per answer sheet ($6 minimum); $8.50 per manual; scoring service offered by publisher.
Foreign Language Edition: Spanish edition available.
Time: (15-25) minutes for ranked form; (30-40) minutes for paired form.
Authors: James B. Rounds, Jr., George A. Henly, René V. Dawis, Lloyd H. Lofquist, and David J. Weiss.
Publisher: Vocational Psychology Research.
Cross References: See T5:1694 (10 references) and T4:1641 (3 references); for reviews by Barbara Lachar and Wilbur L. Layton, see 11:243 (4 references); for reviews by Lewis E. Albright and Sheldon Zedeck, see 8:1050 (40 references); see also T3:1495 (14 references), T2:2283 (8 references), and 7:1063 (29 references).

[1652]
Minnesota Job Description Questionnaire.

Purpose: "Designed to measure the reinforcer characteristics of jobs."

Population: Employees and supervisors.
Publication Dates: 1967-1968.
Acronym: MJDQ.
Scores: 21 reinforcer dimensions: Ability Utilization, Achievement, Activity, Advancement, Authority, Company Policies and Practices, Compensation, Co-Workers, Creativity, Independence, Moral Values, Recognition, Responsibility, Security, Social Service, Social Status, Supervision—Human Relations, Supervision—Technical, Variety, Working Conditions, Autonomy.
Administration: Group.
Forms, 2: E (for employees), S (for supervisors).
Price Data, 2001: $.73-$.75 per copy (Form S); $.78-$.80 per copy (Form E); $6 per manual (1968, 96 pages); $1.75 per person for scoring service.
Time: [20] minutes.
Comments: For research use only; 20 scores parallel scores of the Minnesota Importance Questionnaire (1651) and Minnesota Satisfaction Questionnaire (1656).
Authors: Fred H. Borgen, David J. Weiss, Howard E. A. Tinsley, René V. Dawis, and Lloyd H. Lofquist.
Publisher: Vocational Psychology Research.
Cross References: See T5:1695 (2 references), T4:1643 (3 references), and T3:1497 (4 references); for a review by Sheldon Zedeck, see 8:1051 (15 references); see also T2:2284 (8 references).

[1653]
Minnesota Manual Dexterity Test.

Purpose: "Measures the capacity for simple but rapid eyehand coordination as well as arm-hand dexterity."
Population: Ages 13–adult.
Publication Date: [Undated].
Scores: Total time for each of two tests.
Administration: Group.
Tests, 2: Placing Test, Turning Test.
Price Data: Available from publisher.
Time: Administration time not reported.
Author: Lafayette Instrument.
Publisher: Lafayette Instrument.
Cross References: For reviews by Deborah Erickson and Alida S. Westman, see 12:237.

[1654]
Minnesota Multiphasic Personality Inventory-Adolescent.

Purpose: Designed for use with adolescents to assess a number of the major patterns of personality and emotional disorders.
Population: Ages 14-18
Publication Date: 1992.
Acronym: MMPI-A.
Scores, 68: 8 Validity Scales (Cannot Say (?), Lie (L), Infrequency 1 (F1), Infrequency 2 (F2), Infrequency (F), Defensiveness (K), Variable Response In-

consistency (VRIN), True Response Inconsistency (TRIN); 10 Clinical Scales (Hypochondriasis, Depression, Hysteria, Psychopathic Deviate, Masculinity-Femininity, Paranoia, Psychasthenia, Schizophrenia, Hypomania, Social Introversion); 28 Harris-Lingoes Subscales (Subjective Depression, Psychomotor Retardation, Physical Malfunctioning, Mental Dullness, Brooding, Denial of Social Anxiety, Need for Affection, Lassitude-Malaise, Somatic Complaints, Inhibition of Aggression, Familial Discord, Authority Problems, Social Imperturbability, Social Alienation, Self-Alienation, Persecutory Ideas, Poignancy, Naivete, Social Alienation, Emotional Alienation, Lack of Ego Mastery-Cognitive, Lack of Ego Mastery-Conative, Lack of Ego Mastery-Defective Inhibition, Bizarre Sensory Experiences, Amorality, Psychomotor Acceleration, Imperturbability, Ego Inflation); 3 Si Subscales (Shyness/Self-Consciousness, Social Avoidance, Alienation); 15 Adolescent Content Scales (Anxiety, Obsessiveness, Depression, Health Concerns, Alienation, Bizarre Mentation, Anger, Cynicism, Conduct Problems, Low Self-Esteem, Low Aspirations, Social Discomfort, Family Problems, School Problems, Negative Treatment Indicators); 6 Supplementary Scales (Anxiety, Repression, MacAndrew Alcoholism Scale—Revised, Alcohol/Drug Problem Acknowledgment, Alcohol/Drug Problem Proneness, Immaturity).
Administration: Group or individual.
Price Data, 2006: $50 per manual; $35 per Adolescent Interpretive System User's Guide; $35 per 10 softcover test booklets; $50 per 1 hardcover test booklet; $80 per audiocassette; $86 hand-scoring materials package (50 answer sheets, 50 Validity/Clinical scales profile forms); $46 profile and record forms, 50 per each package for Validity/Clinical scales, clinical subscales, Content scales, Content Component scales, Supplementary scales; price information for scoring and interpretive reports available from Pearson Assessments.
Time: 45–60 minutes.
Comments: May be administered by audiocassette or microcomputer.
Authors: James N. Butcher, Carolyn L. Williams, John R. Graham, Robert P. Archer, Auke Tellegen, Yossef S. Ben-Porath, and Beverly Kaemmer (manual).
Publisher: University of Minnesota Press; distributed by Pearson Assessments.
Cross References: See T5:1698 '(28 references); for reviews by Charles D. Claiborn and Richard I. Lanyon, see 12:238 (4 references); see also T4:1646 (4 references).

[1655]
Minnesota Multiphasic Personality Inventory-2.

Purpose: "Designed to assess a number of the major patterns of personality and emotional disorders."

Population: Ages 18 and over.
Publication Dates: 1942–1990.
Acronym: MMPI-2.
Scores, 75: 7 Validity Indicators: Cannot Say (?), Lie (L), Infrequency (F), Correction (K), Back F (FB), Variable Response Inconsistency (VRIN), True Response Inconsistency (TRIN); 10 Clinical Scales: Hypochondriasis (Hs), Depression (D), Conversion Hysteria (Hy), Psychopathic Deviate (Pd), Masculinity-Femininity (Mf), Paranoia (Pa), Psychasthenia (Pt), Schizophrenia (Sc), Hypomania (Ma), Social Introversion (Si); 15 Supplementary Scales: Anxiety (A), Repression (R), Ego Strength (Es), MacAndrew Alcoholism Scale-Revised (MAC-R), Overcontrolled Hostility (O-H), Dominance (Do), Social Responsibility (Re), College Maladjustment (Mt), Gender Role-Masculine (GM), Gender Role-Feminine (GF), 2 Post-Traumatic Stress Disorder Scales (PK & PS); Marital Distress Scale (MDS), Addiction Potential Scale (APS), Addiction Admission Scale (AAS); 15 Content Scales: Anxiety (ANX), Fears (FRS), Obsessiveness (OBS), Depression (DEP), Health Concerns (HEA), Bizarre Mentation (BIZ), Anger (ANG), Cynicism (CYN), Antisocial Practices (ASP), Type A (TPA), Low Self-Esteem (LSE), Social Discomfort (SOD), Family Problems (FAM), Work Interference (WRK), Negative Treatment Indicators (TRT); 3 Si subscales: Shyness/Self-Consciousness (Si1), Social Avoidance (Si2), Alienation-Self and Others (Si3); 28 Harris-Lingoes Subscales: Subjective Depression (D1), Psychomotor Retardation (D2), Physical Malfunctioning (D3), Mental Dullness (D4), Brooding (D5), Denial of Social Anxiety (Hy1), Need for Affection (Hy2), Lassitude-Malaise (Hy3), Somatic Complaints (Hy4), Inhibition of Aggression (Hy5), Familial Discord (Pd1), Authority Problems (Pd2), Social Imperturbability (Pd3), Social Alienation (Pd4), Self-Alienation (Pd5), Persecutory Ideas (Pa1), Poignancy (Pa2), Naivete (Pa3), Social Alienation (Sc1), Emotional Alienation (Sc2), Lack of Ego Mastery, Cognitive (Sc3), Conative (Sc4), Defective Inhibition (Sc5), Bizarre Sensory Experiences (Sc6), Amorality (Ma1), Psychomotor Acceleration (Ma2), Imperturbability (Ma3), Ego Inflation (Ma4).
Administration: Group or individual.
Price Data, 1999: $27 per 10 reusable softcover test booklets (English or Hispanic); $36 per reusable hardcover test booklet (English); $77 per 100 hand-scorable answer sheets and profile forms; $78 per audiocasette (English or Hispanic); $38.50 per 50 profile forms (specify Supplementary Scales, Content Scales, Content Component Scales, or Harris-Lingoes Subscales); $67 per answer keys (specify scale and for softcover or hardcover test booklets); $43 per manual for administration and scoring (1989, 166 pages); $18 per Adult Clinical System User's Guide (1989, 71 pages); $18 per Revised Personnel System User's Guide

(1989, 76 pages); price data available from publisher for IBM compatible microcomputer edition based on type of score or interpretive report desired; price data available from publisher for scoring service by publisher based on type of score or interpretive report desired.
Time: (90) minutes.
Comments: Revision of the Minnesota Multiphasic Personality Inventory; may be administered by audio-cassette or microcomputer.
Authors: James N. Butcher, W. Grant Dahlstrom, John Graham, Auke Tellegen, and Beverly Kaemmer.
Publisher: Published by University of Minnesota Press; distributed by Pearson Assessments.
Cross References: See T5:1697 (600 references) and T4:1645 (504 references); for reviews by Robert P. Archer and David S. Nichols, see 11:244 (637 references); see also 9:715 (339 references) and T3:1498 (749 references); for reviews by Henry A. Alker and Glen D. King of the original version, see 8:616 (1,188 references); see also T2:1281 (549 references); for reviews by Malcolm D. Gynther and David A. Rodgers, see 7:104 (831 references); see also P:166 (1,066 references); for a review by Arthur L. Benton, see 4:71 (211 references); for reviews by Arthur L. Benton, H. J. Eysenck, L. S. Penrose, and Julian B. Rotter, and an excerpted review, see 3:60 (76 references).

[1656]
Minnesota Satisfaction Questionnaire.

Purpose: "Designed to measure an employee's satisfaction with his/her job."
Population: Business and industry.
Publication Dates: 1963-1977.
Acronym: MSQ.
Administration: Group.
Price Data, 2001: $.38 to $.39 per questionnaire for Short Form; $.64 to $.66 per questionnaire for Long Form; $4.95 per manual (1967, 130 pages); $6.60 per specimen set including MSQ Long Form, MSQ Long Form (1967 revision), MSQ Short Form, and manual; $1.10 per booklet for scoring service (Short Form); $1.65 per booklet for scoring service (Long Form).
Authors: David J. Weiss, René V. Dawis, George W. England, and Lloyd H. Lofquist.
Publisher: Vocational Psychology Research.
a) LONG FORM.
Scores, 21: Ability Utilization, Achievement, Activity, Advancement, Authority, Company Policies and Practices, Compensation, Coworkers, Creativity, Independence, Moral Values, Recognition, Responsibility, Security, Social Service, Social Status, Supervision-Human Relations, Supervision-Technical, Variety, Working Conditions, General Satisfaction.
Editions, 2: 1967 revision, 1977 edition.
Time: (15-20) minutes.

b) SHORT FORM.
Scores, 3: Intrinsic, Extrinsic, General.
Time: (5-10) minutes.
Cross References: See T5:1701 (56 references), T4:1649 (49 references), 9:721 (21 references), and T3:1508 (27 references); for a review by Robert M. Guion, see 8:1052 (82 references); see also T2:2285 (11 references); for reviews by Lewis E. Albright and John P. Foley, Jr., see 7:1064 (18 references).

[1657]

Minnesota Satisfactoriness Scales.

Purpose: "Designed to measure an employee's satisfactoriness on a job."
Population: Employees.
Publication Dates: 1965-1970.
Acronym: MSS.
Scores, 5: Performance, Conformance, Dependability, Personal Adjustment, General Satisfactoriness.
Administration: Group.
Price Data, 2001: $.33-$.35 per test; manual (1970, 53 pages plus test) no longer in print, photocopies available for $3.50; $1.25 per person for scoring service.
Time: (5) minutes.
Comments: Ratings by supervisors.
Authors: Dennis L. Gibson, David J. Weiss, René V. Dawis, and Lloyd H. Lofquist.
Publisher: Vocational Psychology Research.
Cross References: See T5:1702 (4 references), T4:1650 (6 references), and T3:1509 (2 references); for a review by Jerome E. Doppelt, see 8:1061 (9 references).

[1658]

Mirror-Couple Relationship Inventory.

Purpose: To reflect to a couple how each partner sees self and other partner.
Population: Engaged and married couples.
Publication Date: 1980.
Scores: 24 scales: 11 content scales (Parents, Lifestyle, Career, Money, Sex, Leisure, Friends, Religion, Children, Future, Rank Importance), 12 process scales (Personality, Awareness, OK Alone, Freedom, Problem Solving, Fight/Flight, Values Self, Values Partner, Positive Communication, Negative Communication, Stress, Satisfaction), and 1 Attitude scale.
Administration: Group or individual.
Price Data: Available from publisher.
Time: Administration time not reported.
Authors: Joan A. Hunt and Richard A. Hunt.
Publisher: Ministry Inventories.
Cross References: See T5:1705 (4 references).

[1659]

Mirror Edition of the Personal Values Inventory.

Purpose: Designed to describe how a person uses his/her personal strengths in relationships.

Population: Adolescents and adults reading at sixth grade level or above.
Publication Dates: 1973-1997.
Scores, 20: 7 Motivational Values.
Administration: Individual or group.
Price Data, 2001: $4.50 per test booklet; $30 per manual (1996, 146 pages).
Time: (20–40) minutes.
Comments: Manual is entitled Relationship Awareness Theory Manual of Administration and Interpretation (9th Ed.).
Author: Elias H. Porter.
Publisher: Personal Strengths Publishing.
Cross References: For a review by Ric Brown, see 16:150.

[1660]

The Missouri Children's Picture Series.

Purpose: Assessment of personality.
Population: Ages 5–16.
Publication Dates: 1971, c1963–1964.
Acronym: MCPS.
Scores, 8: Conformity, Masculinity-Femininity, Maturity, Aggression, Inhibition, Activity Level, Sleep Disturbance, Somatization.
Administration: Group.
Price Data: Available from publisher.
Time: (25-35) minutes.
Authors: Jacob O. Sines, Jerome D. Pauker, and Lloyd K. Sines.
Publisher: Jacob O. Sines (the author).
Cross References: See T5:1706 (3 references), T4:1655 (6 references), and T3:1515 (3 references); for reviews by Dale B. Harris and Lovick C. Miller, and an excerpted review by George Gilmore, see 8:625 (11 references); see also T2:1287 (4 references).

[1661]

Missouri Kindergarten Inventory of Developmental Skills, Alternate Form.

Purpose: A screening battery providing a comprehensive assessment measure to use at or before kindergarten entrance.
Population: Ages 48-72 months.
Publication Date: 1982.
Acronym: KIDS.
Scores: 6 areas: Number Concepts, Auditory Skills, Language Concepts, Paper and Pencil Skills, Visual Skills, Gross Motor Skills.
Administration: Individual.
Price Data, 2006: $1.13 per Student Packet (including Pupil Record Sheet, Answer Sheets, and Parent/Guardian Questionnaire); $12.58 for Manual Packet (includes Administration and Scoring Manual, Color Cards, and one Student Packet); $4.25 for the

Instructional Guidebook; $15.70 per specimen set (includes Manual Packet and Instructional Guidebook).
Time: 35 minutes.
Comments: Can be given anytime within the year preceding kindergarten as well as at kindergarten entrance.
Authors: Missouri Department of Elementary and Secondary Education.
Publisher: Assessment Resource Center, University of Missouri-Columbia.
Cross References: For reviews by Mary Henning-Stout and James E. Ysseldyke, see 11:246.

[1662]
MKM Binocular Preschool Test.

Purpose: To evaluate "the near point performance of preschool and other nonreading children."
Population: Preschool.
Publication Dates: 1963–1965.
Scores: Item scores only.
Administration: Individual.
Price Data: Available from publisher.
Time: [1–2] minutes.
Comments: Stereoscope necessary for administration.
Authors: Leland D. Michael, James W. King, and Arlene Moorhead (instructions).
Publisher: MKM.

[1663]
MKM Monocular and Binocular Reading Test.

Purpose: "To detect children who are likely to have reading problems associated with poor binocular coordination and macular suppression."
Population: Grades 1–2, 3 and over.
Publication Dates: 1963–1964.
Scores: Item scores only.
Administration: Individual.
Levels, 2: 1, 2.
Price Data: Available from publisher.
Time: [3–10] minutes.
Comments: Stereoscope necessary for administration.
Authors: Leland D. Michael, James W. King, and Arlene Moorhead (instructions).
Publisher: MKM.
Cross References: See T2:1920 (1 reference).

[1664]
MKM Picture Arrangement Test.

Purpose: Tests directionality.
Population: Grades K–6.
Publication Dates: 1963–1965.
Scores: No scores.
Administration: Individual.
Price Data: Available from publisher.
Time: [1–2] minutes.

Authors: Leland D. Michael and James W. King.
Publisher: MKM.

[1665]
Mobile Vocational Evaluation.

Purpose: "Computer assisted testing system that measures vocationally related abilities and interests."
Population: Adults.
Publication Date: 1983.
Acronym: MVE.
Scores, 29: 17 ability factors (Finger Dexterity, Wrist-Finger Speed, Arm-Hand Steadiness, Manual Dexterity, Two-Arm Coordination, Two-Hand Coordination, Perceptual Accuracy, Spatial Perception, Aiming, Reaction Time, Abstract Reasoning, Numerical Reasoning, Verbal Reasoning, Reading and Arithmetic Grade Levels, Leadership Structure and Consideration, Following Directions, Sales Attitude); 12 interest categories (Artistic, Scientific, Plants and Animals, Protective, Mechanical, Industrial, Business Detail, Selling, Accommodating, Humanitarian, Leading-Influencing, Physical Performing).
Administration: Group and individual.
Price Data, 2006: $5,300 for the entire system including 10 each of nine standardized paper-and-pencil tests with manuals, scoring keys, and oral directions, cassette tape with cassette tape player, 10 interest inventory test booklets with scoring forms, system manual, software (IBM or MAC), data processing user's guide, and professional consultation.
Time: (180) minutes.
Author: Edward J. Hester.
Publisher: Hester Evaluation Systems, Inc.

[1666]
Modern Photography Comprehension Test.

Purpose: Developed to assess knowledge of photography.
Population: Photography students.
Publication Dates: 1953-1969.
Scores: Total score only.
Administration: Group.
Price Data, 2006: $49.50 per test package; $2.35 per key; $2 per direction sheet; $10.50 per specimen set.
Time: (15-20) minutes.
Comments: Revision of What Do You Know About Photography?
Author: Martin M. Bruce.
Publisher: Martin M. Bruce, Ph.D.
Cross References: For a review by David P. Campbell, see 7:547.

[1667]
Modified Vygotsky Concept Formation Test.

Purpose: "Measures an individual's ability to think in abstract concepts."

Population: Older children and adolescents and adults.

Publication Dates: 1940–1984.

Scores, 2: Convergent Thinking, Divergent Thinking.

Administration: Individual.

Price Data, 2005: $195 per Kasanin-Hanfmann test kit; $35 per modified manual (1984, 75 pages); $28 per 30 record forms.

Time: (30) minutes.

Comments: Modified manual used in conjunction with Kasanin-Hanfmann Concept Formation Test (Vigotsky Test) (T3:1239).

Author: Paul L. Wang (modified manual).

Publisher: Stoelting Co.

Cross References: For reviews by Kathryn A. Hess and Gregory Schraw, see 12:240; for information on the Kasanin-Hanfmann Concept Formation Test, see also T3:1239 (1 reference), T2:1140 (9 references), P:47 (7 references), and 6:78 (11 references); for a review of an earlier edition by Kate Levine Kogan (with William S. Kogan), see 4:35 (8 references); for a review of an earlier edition by O. L. Zangwill, see 3:27 (21 references).

[1668]
Monitoring Basic Skills Progress—Second Edition.

Purpose: "Designed to monitor students' acquisition of basic skills in one of three academic areas" using curriculum-based measurements.

Population: Grades 1–7.

Publication Dates: 1990–1999.

Administration: Group, via individual personal computers.

Price Data, 2006: $369 per complete program including Basic Reading, Basic Math Computation, and Basic Math Concepts and Applications; $123 per Basic Reading—Second Edition (Mac); $236 per Math Complete kit (Mac); $123 per Basic Math Computation—Second Edition (Mac); $133 per Math Concepts and Applications (Mac); $30 per Basic Math Computation, Second Edition blackline masters; $50 per Math Concepts and Applications blackline masters.

Comments: "Derived from the curriculum-based measurement (CBM) model of student monitoring"; for use in general or special education classrooms; computer administered and scored (requires Macintosh 68020 or higher CPU with System 7.1 or later).

Authors: Lynn S. Fuchs, Carol L. Hamlett, and Douglas Fuchs.

Publisher: PRO-ED.

a) BASIC READING.

Purpose: Designed to "monitor student progress, identify students who require intervention, and improve instructional programs" in reading.

Population: Grades 1–7.

Scores: Total score only.

Time: (2.5) minutes.

b) BASIC MATH COMPUTATION.

Purpose: Designed to "monitor student progress, identify students who require intervention, and improve instructional programs" in mathematics.

Population: Grades 1–6.

Scores: Total score only.

Time: (2–6) minutes.

c) MATH CONCEPTS AND APPLICATIONS.

Population: Grades 1–6.

Cross References: For reviews by Mary J. McLellan and Jeffrey K. Smith of a and b, see 14:238; for a review by Joseph C. Witt and Kevin M. Jones of an earlier edition, see 12:241.

[1669]
The Mooney Problem Check Lists, 1950 Revision.

Purpose: "Intended to help individuals express their personal problems."

Population: Junior high–adults.

Publication Dates: 1941–1950.

Acronym: MPCL.

Administration: Group.

Price Data, 2002: $36 per combined levels examination kit (for use without separate answer documents) including Check Lists and manual (1950, 15 pages); $12 per combined examination kit (for use with separate answer documents) including Check List, answer document, and manual; $4 per 25 checklists (for use without separate answer documents) and manual (specify level); $151 per 100 checklists (for use without separate answer documents) and manual (specify level).

Time: (35) minutes.

Authors: Ross L. Mooney and Leonard V. Gordon (manuals, c, and d).

Publisher: PsychCorp, A brand of Harcourt Assessment, Inc.

a) JUNIOR HIGH SCHOOL FORM.

Population: Grades 7–9.

Publication Dates: 1942–1950.

Scores, 7: Health and Physical Development, School, Home and Family, Money-Work-The Future, Boy and Girl Relations, Relations to People in General, Self-Centered Concerns.

b) HIGH SCHOOL FORM.

Population: Grades 9–12.

Publication Dates: 1941–1950.

Scores, 11: Health and Physical Development, Finances-Living Conditions-Employment, Social and Recreational Activities, Social-Psychological Relations, Personal-Psychological Relations, Courtship-Sex-Marriage, Home and Family, Morals and Religion, Adjustment to School Work,

The Future-Vocational and Educational, Curriculum and Teaching Procedure.
c) COLLEGE FORM.
Population: Grades 13–16.
Publication Dates: 1941–1950.
Scores, 11: Same as for High School Form.
d) ADULT FORM.
Population: Adults.
Publication Date: 1950.
Scores, 9: Health, Economic Security, Self-Improvement, Personality, Home and Family, Courtship, Sex, Religion, Occupation.
Cross References: See T5:1716 (5 references), T4:1667 (14 references), T3:1531 (19 references), 8:626 (48 references), T2:1289 (92 references), and P:173 (55 references); for a review by Thomas C. Burgess, see 6:145 (25 references); see also 5:89 (26 references); for reviews by Harold E. Jones and Morris Krugman, see 4:73 (13 references); for reviews by Ralph C. Bedell and Theodore F. Lentz of an earlier form of *a–c*, see 3:67 (17 references).

[1670]
Morrisby Profile.

Purpose: "Designed to give a complete statement, in objective terms, about the basic mental structure of a person."
Population: Age 14–adults.
Publication Dates: 1955–1992.
Acronym: MP.
Scores: 12 tests: Compound Series, General Abilities-Verbal, General Abilities-Numerical, General Abilities-Perceptual, Shapes, Mechanical Ability, Speed Tests 1–4 (Modal Profile), Speed Tests 5–6 (Dexterity).
Administration: Group.
Price Data: Available from publisher.
Time: (165–180) minutes.
Comments: Although more commonly used as a battery of tests to provide a profile of an individual's attributes, often for vocational guidance; component tests are regularly used in isolation for selection purposes (e.g., the Compound Series test is used to measure Abstract Reasoning, and the three General Ability tests are used together to identify relative strengths in verbal, numerical, and perceptual abilities).
Author: The Morrisby Organisation.
Publisher: The Morrisby Organisation [England].
Cross References: For a review by Patricia A. Bachelor, see 16:151; for information on the Differential Test Battery, see T3:733 (2 references) and T2:1070 (6 references); for reviews by E. A. Peel, Donald E. Super, and Philip E. Vernon, see 5:606.

[1671]
Motivated Skills Card Sort.

Purpose: To identify skills that are central to personal and career satisfaction and success by rank ordering skills on two dimensions: Competency and Motivation.

Population: Adults.
Publication Dates: 1981–2002.
Scores: Skills Ratings Matrix.
Administration: Group or individual.
Price Data: Available from publisher.
Time: (45–60) minutes.
Author: Richard L. Knowdell.
Publisher: CareerTrainer.
Cross References: For reviews by Albert M. Bugaj and Gary J. Robertson, see 13:204.

[1672]
Motivated Strategies for Learning Questionnaire.

Purpose: "To assess college students' motivational orientations and their use of different learning strategies for a college course."
Population: College students.
Publication Date: 1991.
Acronym: MSLQ.
Scores, 15: 3 Motivation Scales [Value Component (Intrinsic Goal Orientation, Extrinsic Goal Orientation, Task Value), Expectancy Component (Control of Learning Beliefs, Self-Efficacy for Learning and Performance), Affective Component (Test Anxiety)]; 2 Learning Strategies Scales [Cognitive and Metacognitive Strategies (Rehearsal, Elaboration, Organization, Critical Thinking, Metacognitive Self-Regulation), Resource Management Strategies (Time and Study Environment, Effort Regulation, Peer Learning, Help Seeking)].
Administration: Group.
Price Data: Available from publisher.
Time: (20–30) minutes.
Authors: Paul R. Pintrich, David A. F. Smith, Teresa Garcia, and Wilbert J. McKeachie.
Publisher: Combined Program in Education and Psychology, University of Michigan.
Cross References: See T5:1720 (5 references); for reviews by Jeri Benson and Robert K. Gable, see 13:205 (5 references).

[1673]
Motivation Assessment Scale.

Purpose: Designed to assess the motivation underlying problem behaviors so as to curb those behaviors.
Population: People with mental disabilities.
Publication Date: 1992.
Scores, 4: Sensory, Escape, Attention, Tangible.
Administration: Individual.
Price Data: Available from publisher.
Time: 10 minutes.
Comments: A rating tool designed and validated to provide results equivalent to a functional assessment of behavior; may be administered to or completed by someone in close contact with the target individual; can be completed by paper and pencil or as an interview;

results identify the maintaining consequence for the target behavior given the particular setting and rater; also available in electronic and Internet subscription versions, which score and summarize results.

Authors: V. Mark Durand and Daniel B. Crimmins.
Publisher: Monaco & Associates Incorporated.
Cross References: For reviews by Roger A. Boothroyd and James P. Van Haneghan, see 14:239; see also T5:1722 (2 references).

[1674]
Motivational Patterns Inventory.

Purpose: "Designed to help members of an organization explore dominant motivations that can affect the way they contribute to the success of that organization."
Population: Organizational members.
Publication Date: 1990.
Scores, 3: Farmer, Hunter, Shepherd.
Administration: Group.
Price Data: Price information available from publisher for inventory (33 pages) including administrator's guide (2 pages).
Time: Administration time not reported.
Comments: Self-scored.
Authors: Richard E. Byrd and William R. Neher.
Publisher: Jossey-Bass, A Wiley Company.
Cross References: For reviews by Larry G. Daniel and Barbara A. Reilly, see 12:245.

[1675]
Motive to Attain Social Power.

Purpose: Designed to evaluate one's "probable enjoyment or dislike (motivational preference) for a variety of socialized power activities."
Population: Undergraduates.
Publication Date: No date.
Scores: Total score only.
Administration: Group.
Price Data, 2001: $3 per specimen set.
Time: Administration time not reported.
Authors: L. R. Good and K. C. Good.
Publisher: Psychometric Affiliates.
Cross References: For a review by Gary J. Dean, see 15:168.

[1676]
Motives, Values, Preferences Inventory.

Purpose: Designed to assess "the fit between an individual and the organizational culture" and "a person's motives."
Population: Adults.
Publication Dates: 1987–1996.
Acronym: MVPI.
Scores: 10 scales: Aesthetics, Affiliation, Altruistic, Commerce, Hedonism, Power, Recognition, Science, Security, Tradition.

Administration: Group.
Price Data, 2006: Selection Reports starting at $20; Development Reports starting at $40.
Time: (20) minutes.
Comments: Web-based administration.
Authors: Joyce Hogan and Robert Hogan (manual).
Publisher: Hogan Assessment Systems, Inc.
Cross References: For reviews by Brent W. Roberts and Sheldon Zedeck, see 14:240.

[1677]
Motor-Free Visual Perception Test, 3rd Edition.

Purpose: Designed to assess an individual's "visual perceptual ability without any motor involvement needed to make a response."
Population: Ages 4–0 through 94+.
Publication Dates: 1972-2003.
Acronym: MVPT-3.
Scores: Total score only.
Administration: Individual.
Price Data, 2006: $120 per test kit including manual (2003, 95 pages), test plates, and 25 recording forms in portfolio; $30 per manual; $65 per set of test plates; $25 per 25 recording forms.
Time: (20-30) minutes.
Comments: Revision includes updated norms and new test items.
Authors: Ronald P. Colarusso and Donald D. Hammill.
Publisher: Academic Therapy Publications.
Cross References: For reviews by Gary L. Canivez and John D. King, see 16:152; for reviews by Nancy B. Bologna and Theresa Volpe-Johnstone of an earlier edition, see 14:241; see also T5:1725 (8 references) and T4:1677 (6 references); for a review by Carl L. Rosen of an earlier edition and an excerpted review by Alan Krichev, see 8:883 (9 references).

[1678]
Motor-Free Visual Perception Test—Vertical.

Purpose: Designed to assess problems in visual perception in individuals with hemispatial visual neglect.
Population: People with brain injuries.
Publication Date: 1997.
Acronym: MVPT-V.
Scores: Total score only.
Administration: Individual.
Price Data, 2006: $80 per complete test kit including manual (35 pages), test plates, and 50 recording forms; $16 per 50 recording forms; $38 per test plates; $23 per manual.
Time: (10) minutes.
Comments: Contents of test based on the Motor-Free Visual Perception Test (1677).

Authors: Louisette Mercier, Rejean Hebert, Ronald Colarusso, and Donald Hammill.
Publisher: Academic Therapy Publications.
Cross References: For a review by Matthew E. Lambert, see 14:242.

[1679]
Motor Skills Acquisition Checklist.

Purpose: "Helps identify the proper milestones ... of [motor] development."
Population: Birth to 12 months.
Publication Date: 2000.
Scores: 47 behavior ratings.
Administration: Individual.
Price Data, 2002: $9 per checklist (48 pages); $40 per 10 checklists.
Time: Untimed.
Comments: Companion to "Motor Skills Acquisition in the First Year."
Author: Lois Bly.
Publisher: Harcourt Assessment, Inc.

[1680]
Movement Assessment Battery for Children.

Purpose: Designed to assess motor skills and motor development difficulties.
Population: Ages 4–12 years.
Publication Dates: 1972–1992.
Acronym: Movement ABC.
Administration: Individual.
Price Data, 2006: £575.50 per complete kit including manual (1992, 260 pages), 50 checklists, 10 of each record form, bibliography, and all manipulatives in briefcase; £17 per 50 checklists; £50.50 per 25 record forms (specify level); £83 per manual.
Authors: Sheila E. Henderson and David A. Sugden.
Publisher: Harcourt Assessment [England].
a) MOVEMENT ABC.
Scores, 3: Manual Dexterity, Ball Skills, Static and Dynamic Balance.
Administration: Individual.
Levels, 4: Age Band 1 (Ages 4–6); Age Band 2 (Ages 7–8); Age Band 3 (Ages 9–10); Age Band 4 (Ages 11–12).
Time: (20–30) minutes.
Comments: Developed from the Test of Motor Impairment (9:1265).
b) MOVEMENT ABC CHECKLIST.
Scores, 5: Child Stationary/Environment Stable, Child Moving/Environment Stable, Child Stationary/Environment Changing, Child Moving/Environment Changing, Behavioral Problems Related to Motor Difficulties.
Administration: Group or individual.
Time: Administration time not reported.

Comments: Behavior Checklist used by teachers, parents, and other professionals.
Cross References: For reviews by Larry M. Bolen and Carol E. Kessler, see 14:243; see also T5:1725 (8 references); for a review by Jerome D. Pauker of an earlier edition, see 8:881 (2 references); see also T2:1904 (4 references).

[1681]
Mullen Scales of Early Learning: AGS Edition.

Purpose: A comprehensive measure of cognitive functioning for infants and preschool children.
Population: Birth to 68 months.
Publication Dates: 1984–1995.
Scores, 6: Gross Motor Scale, Cognitive Scales (Visual Reception, Fine Motor, Receptive Language, Expressive Language), Early Learning Composite.
Administration: Individual.
Price Data, 2002: $635.95 per complete kit; $28.95 per 25 record forms; $199.95 per Mullen ASSIST (Macintosh/Windows CD-ROM).
Time: (15–60) minutes.
Comments: Previous editions entitled Infant Mullen Scales of Early Learning and Preschool Mullen Scales of Early Learning.
Author: Eileen M. Mullen.
Publisher: Pearson Assessments (originally published by AGS Publishing, acquired by Pearson in 2005).
Cross References: For reviews by Mary Mathai Chittooran and Carol E. Kessler, see 14:244; see also T5:1728 (2 references); for a review by Verna Hart of the earlier edition, see 11:177.

[1682]
Multi-Craft Aptitude Test.

Purpose: To evaluate mechanical and electrical aptitude.
Population: Applicants for jobs that require the ability to learn mechanical and electrical skills.
Publication Dates: 2004–2005.
Scores: Total score only covering 9 areas: General Science, Power Tools, Hand Tools, Household Items, Electrical Concepts, Electrical Schematic Maze, Process Flow, Signal Flow, Electrical Sequences.
Administration: Group.
Price Data, 2006: $20 per consumable self-scoring test booklet (minimum order of 20); $24.95 per manual (2005, 12 pages).
Time: (20) minutes.
Author: Roland T. Ramsay.
Publisher: Ramsay Corporation.

[1683]
MultiCraft Trainee Test.

Purpose: For selecting MultiCraft (mechanical and electrical) trainees.

Population: Applicants for jobs where some knowledge and skill in mechanical and electrical areas is needed.
Publication Date: 2004.
Scores, 8: Hydraulics & Pneumatics, Welding/Cutting & Rigging, Power Transmission/Lubrication/Mechanical Maintenance & Shop Machines and Tools & Equipment, Pumps/Piping & Combustion, Motors/Control Circuits and Schematics & Print Reading, Digital & Analog Electronics, Power Supplies/Computers & PLC and Test Instruments, Basic AC/DC Theory/Power Distribution and Electrical Maintenance, Total.
Administration: Group.
Price Data, 2006: $20 per consumable self-scoring test booklet (minimum order of 20); scoring and administration instructions are included with this test at no charge.
Time: Administration time not reported.
Comments: Self-scoring instrument.
Author: Roland T. Ramsay.
Publisher: Ramsay Corporation.

[1684]
Multi-CrafTest.

Purpose: For selecting maintenance employees.
Population: Applicants and incumbents for jobs requiring electrical knowledge and skills.
Publication Dates: 2000–2002.
Scores, 8: Hydraulics & Pneumatics, Welding & Rigging, Power Transmission/Lubrication/Mechanical Maintenance & Shop Machines/Tools and Equipment, Pumps/Piping & Combustion, Motors/Control Circuits & Schematics and Print Reading, Digital Electronics/Power Supplies/Computers & PLC and Test Instruments, Basic AC & DC Theory/Power Distribution and Electrical Maintenance, Total.
Administration: Group.
Forms, 2: MC-C, B.
Price Data, 2006: $20 per consumable self-scoring test booklet (minimum order of 20); $24.95 per manual (2002, 19 pages).
Time: (60) minutes.
Comments: Self-scoring instrument; Form B is an alternate equivalent of Form MC-C.
Author: Roland T. Ramsay.
Publisher: Ramsay Corporation.

[1685]
The Multidimensional Addictions and Personality Profile.

Purpose: Designed as "an objective measure of substance abuse and personal adjustment problems."
Population: Adolescents and adults experiencing substance abuse and mental health disorders.
Publication Dates: 1988–1996.

Acronym: MAPP.
Scores, 15: Substance Abuse Subscales (Psychological Dependence, Abusive/Secretive/Irresponsible Use, Interference, Signs of Withdrawal, Total), Personal Adjustment Subscales (Frustration Problems, Interpersonal Problems, Self-Image Problems, Total), Defensiveness and Inconsistency Scores (Defensiveness, Inconsistency, Total); Minimizing Response Pattern Scales (Substance Abuse, Personal Adjustment, Total).
Administration: Group and individual.
Price Data: Available from publisher.
Foreign Language Editions: French and Spanish translation package available (including printed questions with audio tape).
Time: (20–25) minutes.
Comments: Previous edition entitled The COMPASS; IBM or compatible with 2 disk drives and at least 640K RAM, monitor, and printer required for computer scoring option.
Authors: John R. Craig and Phyllis Craig.
Publisher: Diagnostic Counseling Services, Inc.
Cross References: For reviews by Carl Isenhart and Keith F. Widaman, see 14:245.

[1686]
Multidimensional Anxiety Questionnaire.

Purpose: Designed "for the evaluation of anxiety symptoms in adults."
Population: Ages 18–89.
Publication Date: 1999.
Acronym: MAQ.
Scores, 5: Physiological-Panic, Social Phobia, Worry-Fears, Negative Affectivity, Total.
Administration: Group or individual.
Price Data, 2006: $118 per introductory kit including 25 hand-scorable booklets, professional manual (94 pages), and 50 profile forms.
Time: (10) minutes.
Author: William M. Reynolds.
Publisher: Psychological Assessment Resources, Inc.
Cross References: For reviews by Stephanie Stein and Robert E. Wall, see 15:169.

[1687]
Multidimensional Anxiety Scale for Children.

Purpose: "Designed to assess a variety of anxiety dimensions in children and adolescents."
Population: Ages 8–19.
Publication Date: 1997.
Administration: Group.
Price Data, 2006: $119 per MASC/MASC-10 complete kit including MASC manual (62 pages) and 25 MASC and MASC-10 QuikScore™ forms; $85 per MASC kit including manual and 25 MASC QuikScore™ forms; $59 per manual; $42 per 25 MASC

QuikScore™ forms; $40 per 25 MASC-10 QuikScore™ forms.
Comments: Self-report.
Author: John March.
Publisher: Multi-Health Systems, Inc.
 a) MULTIDIMENSIONAL ANXIETY SCALE FOR CHILDREN.
 Acronym: MASC.
 Scores, 13: Physical Symptoms (Tense Symptom Subscale, Somatic Symptoms Subscale, Total), Harm Avoidance (Perfectionism Subscale, Anxious Coping Subscale, Total), Social Anxiety (Humiliation Fears Subscale, Performance Fears Subscale, Total), Separation/Panic, Total Anxiety, Anxiety Disorders Index, Inconsistency Index.
 Time: (15) minutes.
 Comments: Self-report measure; can be orally administered to young children or poor readers; for use only by psychology professionals with training in assessment.
 b) MASC-10: MULTIDIMENSIONAL ANXIETY SCALE FOR CHILDREN—10 ITEM.
 Acronym: MASC-10.
 Scores, 4: Physical Symptoms, Harm Avoidance, Social Anxiety, Separation/Panic.
 Time: (2–5) minutes.
 Comments: A shortened, 10-item version of the MASC tapping the four basic anxiety scales.
Cross References: For reviews by John C. Caruso and Robert Christopher, see 14:246.

[1688]
Multidimensional Aptitude Battery-II.

Purpose: Designed "to provide a measure of general cognitive ability or intelligence."
Population: Ages 16 and over.
Publication Dates: 1984–1998.
Acronym: MAB-II.
Scores, 13: Verbal (Information, Comprehension, Arithmetic, Similarities, Vocabulary, Total); Performance (Digit Symbol, Picture Completion, Spatial, Picture Arrangement, Object Assembly, Total), Total.
Administration: Group or individual.
Price Data, 2006: $60 per machine-scoring examination kit including Verbal and Performance booklets, manual on CD (1998, 107 pages), Verbal and Performance answer sheets, and one coupon for computerized scoring; $9 per hand-scoring examination scoring kit including Verbal and Performance booklets, manual on CD, Verbal and Performance answer sheets, record form, and set of scoring templates; $15 per test manual on CD; $50 per 10 Verbal or Performance test booklets; $100 per 25 Verbal or Performance test booklets; $50 per 25 Verbal or Performance answer sheets; $40 per 25 record forms; $35 per scoring templates; $65–$75 (depending on volume) per 10 machine-scorable

answer sheets and coupons for Mail-in Extended Reports; $85–$95 (depending on volume) per 10 machine-scorable answer sheets and coupons for Mail-in Clinical Reports; $105 per software package including disks, software manual for Windows, test manual, and 10 coupons for computer reports.
Time: 100 minutes.
Comments: Paper-and-pencil or computer administration available.
Author: Douglas N. Jackson.
Publisher: Sigma Assessment Systems, Inc.
Cross References: For reviews by Donald L. Thompson and Keith F. Widaman, see 15:170; see T5:1731 (3 references), and T4:1678 (13 references); for reviews by Sharon B. Reynolds and Arthur B. Silverstein of an earlier edition, see 10:202 (5 references).

[1689]
Multidimensional Health Profile.

Purpose: Developed to provide a brief but comprehensive assessment of psychosocial and health functioning for general use in health-related settings.
Population: Ages 18–90.
Publication Dates: 1992–1998.
Administration: Group or individual.
Forms, 2: Psychosocial Functioning (MHP-P), Health Functioning (MHP-H).
Price Data, 2006: $149 per introductory kit including professional manual, 25 MHP-P booklets, and 25 MHP-H booklets.
Time: (15) minutes for either form.
Authors: Linda S. Ruehlman, Richard I. Lanyon, and Paul Karoly.
Publisher: Psychological Assessment Resources, Inc.
 a) MULTIDIMENSIONAL HEALTH PROFILE—PSYCHOSOCIAL FUNCTIONING.
 Acronym: MHP-P.
 Scores, 17: Number of Stressful Events, Perceived Stress, Coping Skills, Total Social Support, Emotional Support, Informational Support, Tangible Support, Negative Social Exchange, Total Psychological Distress, Depressed Affect, Guilt, Motor Retardation, Anxious Affect, Somatic Complaints, Cognitive Disturbance, Life Satisfaction, Global Stress.
 Comments: 58-item self-report questionnaire to assess psychosocial functioning.
 b) MULTIDIMENSIONAL HEALTH PROFILE—HEALTH FUNCTIONING.
 Acronym: MHP-H.
 Scores, 20: Self-Help, Professional Help, Help from Friends, Spiritual Help, Positive Health Habits, Negative Health Habits, Self-Efficacy, Health Vigilance, Health Values, Trust in Health Care Personnel, Trust in Health Care System, Hypochondriasis, Overall Health, Recent Health,

Presence of a Chronic Illness, Impairment Due to a Chronic Illness, Office Visits, Overnight Hospital Treatment, Emergency Room Treatment, Over the Counter Medication.

Comments: 69-item self-report questionnaire to assess health functioning.

Cross References: For reviews by Wendy Naumann and Terri L. Weaver, see 14:247.

[1690]
Multidimensional Perfectionism Scale.

Purpose: Designed to assess "different aspects of perfectionism."

Population: Ages 18 and over.

Publication Date: 2004.

Acronym: MPS.

Scores: 3 subscales: Self-Oriented Perfectionism, Other-Oriented Perfectionism, Socially Prescribed Perfectionism.

Administration: Individual or group.

Price Data, 2006: $84 per complete kit including manual (100 pages) and 25 QuikScore forms; $61 per manual; $44 per 25 QuikScore forms; $63 per Profile Report Kit-Web including manual and 3 profile reports; $113 per software kit including manual, Getting Started Guide, and 25 interpretive reports.

Time: (15) minutes.

Comments: Self-report inventory.

Authors: Paul L. Hewitt and Gordon L. Flett.

Publisher: Multi-Health Systems, Inc.

[1691]
Multidimensional Self Concept Scale.

Purpose: Designed to provide a multidimensional assessment of self concept in clinical and research settings.

Population: Grades 5–12.

Publication Date: 1992.

Acronym: MSCS.

Scores, 7: Social, Competence, Affect, Academic, Family, Physical, Total.

Administration: Group or individual.

Price Data, 2006: $110 per complete set; $60 per 50 record booklets; $55 per examiner's manual (82 pages).

Time: (20) minutes.

Author: Bruce A. Bracken.

Publisher: PRO-ED.

Cross References: See T5:1734 (6 references); for reviews by Francis X. Archambault, Jr. and W. Grant Willis, see 12:246 (1 reference); see also T4:1682 (1 reference).

[1692]
The Multidimensional Self-Esteem Inventory.

Purpose: "Measures global self-esteem and its eight components."

Population: Adults.

Publication Dates: 1983–1988.

Acronym: MSEI.

Scores, 11: Competence, Lovability, Likability, Self-Control, Personal Power, Moral Self-approval, Body Appearance, Body Functioning, Identity Integration, Defensive Self-enhancement, Global Self-esteem.

Administration: Individual or group.

Price Data, 2006: $165 per introductory kit including manual (1988, 22 pages), 25 reusable test booklets, 50 rating forms, and 50 profile forms.

Time: (15-30) minutes.

Comments: Originally called Self-Report Inventory.

Authors: Edward J. O'Brien and Seymour Epstein.

Publisher: Psychological Assessment Resources, Inc.

Cross References: See T5:1735 (12 references) and T4:1683 (2 references); for reviews by Barbara J. Kaplan and Joseph G. Ponterotto, see 11:250 (1 reference).

[1693]
Multifactor Leadership Questionnaire for Teams.

Purpose: To assess and develop a plan for enhancing team leadership.

Population: Management personnel.

Publication Date: 1996.

Acronym: MLQT.

Scores, 6: Transformational Leadership, Transactional Leadership, Non-Transactional Leadership, Outcomes of Leadership Styles (Extra Effort, Effectiveness, Satisfaction).

Administration: Group.

Price Data: Available from publisher (www.mindgarden.com).

Time: Administration time not reported.

Comments: Same instrument as MLQTR (1694) but packaged for researchers only.

Authors: Bernard M. Bass and Bruce J. Avolio.

Publisher: Mind Garden, Inc.

[1694]
Multifactor Leadership Questionnaire for Teams Report.

Purpose: To assess and develop a plan for enhancing team leadership.

Population: Management personnel.

Publication Date: 1996.

Acronym: MLQTR.

Scores, 12: Transformational Leadership: Idealized Attributes, Idealized Behaviors, Inspirational Motivation, Intellectual Stimulation, Individualized Consideration, Transactional Leadership: Contingent Reward, Management-by-Exception (Active), Passive/Avoidant: Management-by-Exception (Passive), Laissez-faire, Outcomes of Leadership: Extra Effort, Effectiveness, Satisfaction.

Administration: Group.

Price Data: Available from publisher (www. mindgarden.com).
Time: (20) minutes.
Comments: Web-based administration and reporting available.
Authors: Bernard M. Bass and Bruce J. Avolio.
Publisher: Mind Garden, Inc.

[1695]
Multifactor Leadership Questionnaire, Third Edition.

Purpose: Measures a broad range of leadership types; identifies the characteristics of a transformational leader and helps individuals discover how they measure up in their own eyes and in the eyes of those with whom they work.
Population: Researchers, consultants, leaders, supervisors, colleagues, peers, direct reports.
Publication Dates: 1985–2004.
Acronym: MLQ.
Scores, 12: Transformational Leadership (Idealized Attributes, Idealized Behaviors, Inspirational Motivational, Intellectual, Stimulation, Individualized Consideration), Transactional Leadership (Contingent Reward, Management-by-Exception: Active), Passive-Avoidant Behaviors (Management-by-Exception: Passive, Laissez-Faire), Extra Effort, Effectiveness, and Satisfaction with the Leadership.
Administration: Group.
Forms, 5: Leader 5X-Short, Leader 5X-Long, Rater 5X-Short, Rater 5X-Long, Actual-Ought.
Price Data: Available from publisher (www. mindgarden.com).
Foreign Language Editions: Translations and reports available in English, German, Italian, Swedish, Spanish, Turkish, and Portuguese; MLQ translations only: French, Norwegian, Hebrew, Arabic, Chinese, Thai, Korean, and others.
Time: (15) minutes.
Comments: Both paper form-based and Web-based forms are available; scoring and reporting provided by publisher (including both multirater and an Actual vs Ought Feedback Report); previous edition listed as Multifactor Leadership Questionnaire for Research, Second Edition.
Authors: Bruce J. Avolio and Bernard M. Bass.
Publisher: Mind Garden, Inc.
Cross References: For a review by David J. Pittenger of an earlier edition, see 14:248; see also T5:1736 (5 references); for reviews by Frederick Bessai and Jean Powell Kirnan and Brooke Snyder of an earlier edition, see 12:247 (5 references); see also T4:1684 (5 references).

[1696]
Multilevel Academic Survey Test.

Purpose: Developed "for use by school personnel who make decisions about student performance in reading and mathematics."

Population: K–8 and high school students with reading or mathematics skills deficits.
Publication Date: 1985.
Acronym: MAST.
Scores: Total score only for each test.
Price Data, 2002: $79 per examination kit including Grade Level test booklet, answer sheet, Curriculum Level record form, and manual (189 pages); $52 per 25 grade 1evel test booklets; $33 per 25 grade level self-scoring answer sheets; $51 per 25 curriculum level record forms.
Authors: Kenneth W. Howell, Stanley H. Zucker, and Mada Kay Morehead.
Publisher: PsychCorp, A brand of Harcourt Assessment, Inc.
  a) GRADE LEVEL TEST.
    1) *Primary.*
    Population: Grades K–2.
    Administration: Individual.
    Time: (10–15) minutes.
    2) *Short.*
    Population: Grades 3–12.
    Administration: Group.
    Time: 22(27) minutes.
    3) *Extended.*
    Population: Grades 3-12.
    Administration: Group.
    Time: 30(35) minutes.
    Comments: Administered to students who have taken the short form when a larger sample of performance is required.
  b) CURRICULUM LEVEL TEST.
  Population: Grades K–8.
  Administration: Group.
  Time: 1–5 minutes per test.
  Comments: "Criterion-referenced."
    1) *Reading.*
    Tests, 4: Graded Oral Reading, Graded Comprehension, Diagnostic Oral Reading, Comprehension Problem Profile.
    2) *Mathematics.*
    Tests, 8: Basic Facts Screening, Addition, Multiplication, Division, Fractions, Decimals/Ratios/Percents, Problem Solving, Applications Content.
Cross References: See T5:1738 (1 reference) and T4:1685 (1 reference); for reviews by Ellen H. Bacon and Thomas G. Haring, see 10:203.

[1697]
Multilingual Aphasia Examination, Third Edition.

Purpose: Designed to evaluate the presence, severity, and qualitative aspects of aphasic disorder.
Population: Ages 6–69.
Publication Dates: 1978–1994.

Acronym: MAE.
Scores, 11: Visual Naming, Sentence Repetition, Controlled Word Association, Oral Spelling, Written Spelling, Block Spelling, MAE Token Test, Aural Comprehension of Words and Phrases, Reading Comprehension of Words and Phrases, Rating of Articulation, Rating of Praxic Features of Writing.
Administration: Individual.
Price Data: Not available.
Foreign Language Edition: Spanish edition available.
Time: Administration time not reported.
Authors: A. L. Benton, deS. Hamsher, and A. B. Sivan.
Publisher: AJA Associates [No reply from publisher; status unknown].
Cross References: For reviews by Nancy B. Bologna and by Malcolm R. McNeil and Wiltrud Fassbinder, see 14:249; see also T5:1740 (36 references).

[1698]
Multimodal Life History Inventory.

Purpose: To provide "therapists with an in-depth assessment tool for adult counseling."
Population: Adult counseling clients.
Publication Dates: 1980-1991.
Scores: No scores.
Administration: Group.
Manual: No manual.
Price Data, 2006: $25.95 per set of 20 inventories; price information for Spanish version available from publisher.
Foreign Language Edition: Spanish version available.
Time: Administration time not reported.
Comments: Self-report to be completed in the client's "own time"; previously listed as Multimodal Life History Questionnaire.
Authors: Arnold A. Lazarus and Clifford N. Lazarus.
Publisher: Research Press.

[1699]
Multiphasic Environmental Assessment Procedure.

Purpose: Characterizes the "physical and social environments of residential care settings for older adults."
Population: Nursing home residents, residential care facilities, congregate apartments.
Publication Dates: 1979–1998.
Acronym: MEAP.
Administration: Individual.
Price Data: Available from publisher.
Time: [4–8] hours.
Comments: Administration time dependent on size and complexity of facility.
Authors: Rudolf H. Moos and Sonne Lemke.

Publisher: SAGE Publications [No reply from publisher; status unknown].
a) PHYSICAL AND ARCHITECTURAL FEATURES CHECKLIST.
Acronym: PAF.
Scores, 8: Community Accessibility, Physical Amenities, Social-Recreational Aids, Prosthetic Aids, Orientational Aids, Safety Features, Staff Facilities, Space Availability.
b) POLICY AND PROGRAM INFORMATION FORM.
Acronym: POLIF.
Scores, 9: Expectations for Functioning, Acceptance of Problem Behavior, Policy Choice, Resident Control, Policy Clarity, Provision for Privacy, Availability of Health Services, Availability of Daily Living Assistance, Availability of Social-Recreational Activities.
c) RESIDENT AND STAFF INFORMATION FORM.
Acronym: RESIF.
Scores, 6: Resident Social Resources, Resident Heterogeneity, Resident Functional Abilities, Resident Activity Level, Resident Activities in the Community, Staff Resources.
d) SHELTERED CARE ENVIRONMENT SCALE.
Acronym: SCES.
Scores, 7: Cohesion, Conflict, Independence, Self-Disclosure, Organization, Resident Influence, Physical Comfort.
e) RATING SCALE.
Acronym: RS.
Scores, 4: Physical Attractiveness, Environmental Diversity, Resident Functioning, Staff Functioning.
Cross References: See T5:1743 (2 references); for reviews by Julian Fabry and Kenneth Sakauye, see 12:248; see also T4:1688 (4 references), 9:733 (1 reference), and T3:1546 (4 references).

[1700]
Multiphasic Sex Inventory II.

Purpose: "To assess a wide range of psychosexual characteristics of the sexual offender."
Population: Adult males, ages 18–84.
Publication Dates: 1984–2003.
Acronym: MSI II.
Scores: 42 scales and indices: Suicide, Sexual Ethics, Sex Knowledge and Beliefs, Repeated Items, Infrequency, Social Sexual Desirability, Sexual Obsessions, Dissimulation, Lie, Molester Comparison, Rapist Comparison, Child Molest, Rape, Exhibitionism, Voyeurism, Sex Harassment, Net Sex, Obscene Call, Pornography, Transvestism, Fetishism & NOS Paraphilias, Bondage Discipline, Sexual Sadism, Masochism, Physiologic Dysfunction, Desire, Premature Ejaculation, Body

Image, Social Sexual Inadequacies, Emotional Neediness, Cognitive Distortion and Immaturity, Antisocial Behavior, Conduct Disorder, Sociopathy, Domestic Violence, Substance Abuse, Denial, Justification, Scheming, Superoplimism, Gender Identity, Treatment Attitudes.
Administration: Group.
Price Data: Available from publisher.
Foreign Language Edition: Spanish language version available.
Time: (45–120) minutes.
Comments: May be administered via audio cassette or paper-pencil; computer scoring done by publisher.
Authors: H. R. Nichols and Ilene Molinder.
Publisher: Nichols & Molinder Assessments.
Cross References: For reviews by Paul A. Arbisi and Albert Bugaj, see 16:153; see also T5:1744 (8 references) and T4:1689 (2 references).

[1701]
Multiple Affect Adjective Check List—Revised.

Purpose: "To measure both state and affect traits."
Population: Ages 20–79.
Publication Dates: 1960–1999.
Acronym: MAACL-R.
Scores, 7: Anxiety, Depression, Hostility, Positive Affect, Sensation Seeking, Dysphoria, Positive Affect and Sensation Seeking.
Administration: Group.
Price Data, 2005: $11 per 25 hand-scoring or machine-scoring lists (specify State or Trait) [$41.75 per 100, $166.50 per 500]; $16.50 per scoring key; $28.75 per manual (1999, 71 pages); $26.75 per bibliography (1991, 1,000 references); $31 per specimen set including manual and 1 copy of all forms.
Time: 5(10) minutes.
Comments: Previous edition still available.
Authors: Marvin Zuckerman and Bernard Lubin.
Publisher: EdITS/Educational and Industrial Testing Service.
Cross References: For reviews by Gerald E. DeMauro and Paul Retzlaff, see 16:154; see also T5:1745 (89 references) and T4:1690 (96 references); for a review by John A. Zarske of an earlier edition, see 10:205 (84 references); see also 9:734 (47 references), T3:1547 (108 references), 8:628 (102 references), and T2:1293 (56 references); for reviews by E. Lowell Kelly and Edwin I. Megargee of an earlier edition, see 7:112 (60 references); see also P:176 (28 references).

[1702]
Multiscale Dissociation Inventory.

Purpose: To assess the clinical severity of dissociative disturbance.
Population: Ages 18 and older.
Publication Dates: 1998–2002.

Acronym: MDI.
Scores, 6: Disengagement, Depersonalization, Derealization, Emotional Constriction, Memory Disturbance, Identity Dissociation.
Administration: Individual or group.
Price Data, 2006: $122 per introductory kit including professional manual (2002, 40 pages), 25 test booklets, and 25 profile forms.
Time: (5–10) minutes.
Comments: Self-report; requires 6th grade reading level; normed on 440 adults with a histories of at least one DSM-IV-TR "Criterion A" traumatic event.
Author: John Briere.
Publisher: Psychological Assessment Resources, Inc.
Cross References: For reviews by Frederick T. L. Leong and Paul Retzlaff, see 16:156.

[1703]
Multiscore Depression Inventory for Adolescents and Adults.

Purpose: "To provide an objective measure of the severity of self-reported depression."
Population: Ages 13 through adult.
Publication Date: 1986.
Acronym: MDI.
Scores, 10: Low Energy Level, Cognitive Difficulty, Guilt, Low Self-Esteem, Social Introversion, Pessimism, Irritability, Sad Mood, Instrumental Helplessness, Learned Helplessness.
Administration: Group.
Forms, 2: Short Form version available by administering first 47 items of questionnaire.
Price Data, 2006: $132 per kit including scoring keys, 25 hand-scored test/answer sheets, 25 profile forms, and manual (111 pages); $21.95 per set of scoring keys; $31 per 100 hand-scored test/answer sheets; $20.50 or less per prepaid mail-in WPS Test Report answer sheet; $31 per 100 profile forms; $54.50 per manual; $335.50 per 25-use disk (PC with DOS) for administration, scoring, and interpretation; $16.50 per 100 PC answer sheets; $13.25 per FAX service scoring charge.
Time: (20) minutes; (10) minutes for Short Form.
Comments: Self-report format; IBM PC, XT, or AT or compatible computer required for optional computer administration or scoring.
Author: David J. Berndt.
Publisher: Western Psychological Services.
Cross References: See T5:1748 (1 reference) and T4:1693 (2 references); for reviews by David N. Dixon and Stephen G. Flanagan, see 11:251.

[1704]
Multiscore Depression Inventory for Children.

Purpose: Designed to assess depression and "features related to depression."

Population: Ages 8–17.
Publication Date: 1996.
Acronym: MDI-C.
Scores, 9: Anxiety, Self-Esteem, Sad Mood, Instrumental Helplessness, Social Introversion, Low Energy, Pessimism, Defiance, Total.
Administration: Group.
Price Data, 2006: $115.50 per complete kit including manual (54 pages), 25 AutoScore™ test forms, and 25 profile forms; $42.50 per 25 AutoScore™ test forms; $19.25 per mail-in answer sheet; $26.95 per 50 profile forms; $53 per manual; $335 per MDI-C microcomputer disk including 25 uses (IBM or compatible and Microsoft Windows 3.1 or above; 3.5-inch); $16.50 per 100 microcomputer answer sheets; $13 per FAX service scoring.
Time: (15–20) minutes.
Authors: David J. Berndt and Charles F. Kaiser.
Publisher: Western Psychological Services.
Cross References: For reviews by Jill Ann Jenkins and Michael G. Kavan, see 14:250.

[1705]
Murphy-Meisgeier Type Indicator for Children.

Purpose: Designed to assess "how an individual child best perceives and processes information and how that child prefers to interact socially and behaviorally with others."
Population: Ages 7–12.
Publication Date: 1987.
Acronym: MMTIC.
Scores, 4: Extraversion/Introversion, Sensing/Intuition, Thinking/Feeling, Judging/Perceiving.
Administration: Group.
Price Data, 2005: $110 per stater kit including 25 question booklets, 25 answer sheets, 1 set of scoring templates, 25 Your Report from the MMTIC forms, 25 Your Results from the MMTIC forms, 25 Discovering Your Type forms, and 2 poster Type tables; $8 per sample pack including question booklet, answer sheet, and one each of the following handouts: Your Report from the MMTIC, Your Results from the MMTIC, and Discovering Your Type; $35 per 25 reusable question booklets; $15 per 25 non-prepaid answer sheets; $50 per template scoring key; $10 per 25 Discovering Your Type report forms; $10 per 25 Your Report from the MMTIC forms; $12 per 25 Your Results from the MMTIC forms; $10 per 25 Professonal's Report Forms; $10 per 25 Student Profile sheets; $24.95 per manual (45 pages).
Time: (30) minutes.
Comments: Modeled after the Myers-Briggs Type Indicator™ (1710); scoring options: template (hand) score or prepaid mail-in score.
Authors: Charles Meisgeier and Elizabeth Murphy.
Publisher: Center for Applications of Psychological Type, Inc.

Cross References: See T5:1750 (1 reference); for reviews by Joanne Jensen and Norman A. Constantine and by Hoi K. Suen, see 12:249.

[1706]
Music Achievement Tests 1, 2, 3, and 4.

Purpose: Constructed to measure musical achievement.
Publication Dates: 1968–1986.
Acronym: MAT.
Administration: Group.
Price Data: Available from publisher.
Comments: Record player necessary for administration.
Author: Richard Colwell.
Publisher: MAT [No reply from publisher; status unknown].

a) TEST 1.
Population: Grades 3–12.
Scores, 4: Pitch Discrimination, Interval Discrimination, Meter Discrimination, Total.
Time: (18) minutes.
b) TEST 2.
Population: Grades 4–12.
Scores, 6: Major-Minor Mode Discrimination, Feeling for Tonal Center, Auditory-Visual Discrimination (Pitch, Rhythm, Total), Total.
Time: (28) minutes.
c) TEST 3.
Population: Grades 4–12.
Scores, 5: Tonal Memory, Melody Recognition, Pitch Recognition, Instrument Recognition, Total.
Time: (32) minutes.
d) TEST 4.
Population: Grades 5–12.
Scores, 7: Musical Style (Composers, Texture, Total), Auditory-Visual Discrimination, Chord Recognition, Cadence Recognition, Total.
Time: (38) minutes.
Cross References: For reviews by J. David Boyle and Rudolf E. Radocy, see 12:250; see also T2:207 (5 references); for a review by Paul R. Lehman, see 7:248 (5 references).

[1707]
Musical Aptitude Profile [1995 Revision].

Purpose: Designed to evaluate music aptitude.
Population: Grades 4–12.
Publication Dates: 1965–1995.
Scores, 11: Tonal Imagery (Melody, Harmony, Total), Rhythm Imagery (Tempo, Meter, Total), Musical Sensitivity (Phrasing, Balance, Style, Total), Total.
Administration: Group.
Price Data, 2006: $140 per complete kit; $25 per 100 answer sheets; $30 per 100 profile cards; $2 per

class record sheet; $25 per sensitivity compact disc; $25 per tonal and rhythm compact disc; $20 per scoring masks (with school purchase order only; $20 per manual (1995, 162 pages).
Time: (110) minutes.
Comments: Test must be scored manually.
Author: Edwin E. Gordon.
Publisher: GIA Publications, Inc.
Cross References: For reviews by Christopher M. Johnson and James W. Sherbon, see 16:157; see also T5:1752 (1 reference); for reviews by Annabel J. Cohen and James W. Sherbon of an earlier edition, see 12:251; see also T4:1697 (2 references); T3:1552 (4 references); 8:98 (25 references), and T2:209 (11 references); for reviews by Robert W. Lundin and John McLeish, see 7:249 (33 references).

[1708]
My Vocational Situation.

Purpose: Designed to diagnose difficulties in vocational decision-making.
Population: High school and college and adult.
Publication Date: 1980.
Acronym: MVS.
Scores, 3: Vocational Identity, Occupational Information, Barriers.
Administration: Group.
Price Data, 2001: $14.50 per 25 item booklets (for hand scoring); $5.50 per manual (8 pages).
Time: (5-10) minutes.
Authors: John L. Holland, Denise Daiger, and Paul G. Power.
Publisher: CPP, Inc.
Cross References: See T5:1754 (27 references) and T4:1701 (24 references); for a review by Bert W. Westbrook, see 9:738 (1 reference).

[1709]
My Worst Experience Scale.

Purpose: Designed to "assess youngsters' reports of their most stressful experiences and their thoughts, behaviors, and feelings associated with those experiences."
Population: Ages 9–18.
Publication Date: 2002.
Acronym: MWES.
Scores, 12: DSM IV PTSD Criterion Subscales (Impact of the Event, Re-experience of the Trauma, Avoidance and Numbing, Increased Arousal), Symptoms Subscales (Depression, Hopelessness, Somatic Symptoms, Oppositional Conduct, Hypervigilance, Dissociation and Dreams, General Maladjustment), Total.
Administration: Group or individual.
Price Data, 2006: $126.50 per test kit including 25 AutoScore™ answer forms, manual (78 pages), and 100 school alienation and trauma survey forms; $49.50 per manual; $54.95 per 25 AutoScore™ answer forms;

$26.95 per 100 school alienation and trauma survey forms; $280 per 25-use disk; $16.50 per PC answer booklet; $13.75 per mail-in answer booklet; volume discounts available.
Time: (20–30) minutes.
Comments: Self-report questionnaire; computer administration and scoring available.
Authors: Irwin A. Hyman, and Pamela A. Snook (scale and manual), J. M. Berna, M. A. Kohr, J. DuCette, and G. Britton (scale).
Publisher: Western Psychological Services.
Cross References: For reviews by Frederic J. Medway and Heidi K. Moore, see 16:158.

[1710]
Myers-Briggs Type Indicator®, Form M.

Purpose: Designed for "the identification of basic preferences on each of the four dichotomies specified or implicit in Jung's theory" and "the identification and description of the 16 personality types that result from interactions among the preferences."
Population: Ages 14 and older.
Publication Dates: 1943–1998.
Acronym: MBTI™.
Scores, 4: Extraversion vs. Introversion, Sensing vs. Intuition, Thinking vs. Feeling, Judging vs. Perceiving.
Administration: Group.
Foreign Language Edition: Spanish (Form M Template scoring) edition available.
Price Data, 2001: $70 per 10 MBTI Form M self-scorable; $75 per manual (1998, 420 pages); $6.50 per Introduction to Type, Sixth Edition (1998, 43 pages); $9 per Introduction to Type in Organizations, Third Edition; $90 per 10 Form M prepaid profile combined item booklet/answer sheets; $230 per 10 Form M prepaid interpretive report combined item booklet/answer sheets; $180 per 10 Form M prepaid Interpretive Report for Organizations combined item booklet/answer sheets; $170 per 10 Form M prepaid Team Report answer sheets; $105 per 10 Form M prepaid Career Report combined item booklet/answer sheets; $82.50 per Form M item booklets; $22.50 per 25 nonprepaid answer sheets; $67 per 8 templates (for nonprepaid answer sheets); $90 per 10 prepaid workstyles report.
Time: (15–25) minutes.
Comments: Scoring options: Self-scorable, template scoring, software on-site scoring, mail-in scoring; administration also available via software and internet; Spanish (Form M template scoring) edition available; based on personality theory of C. G. Jung; Forms F and G still available.
Authors: Katharine C. Briggs, Isabel Briggs Myers, Mary H. McCaulley (revised manual), Naomi L. Quenk (revised manual), and Allen L. Hammer (revised manual).
Publisher: CPP, Inc.

Cross References: For reviews by John W. Fleenor and Paul M. Mastrangelo, see 14:251; see also T5:1755 (78 references) and T4:1702 (45 references); for a review by Jerry S. Wiggins of an earlier edition, see 10:206 (42 references); for a review by Anthony J. DeVito of an earlier edition, see 9:739 (19 references); see also T3:1555 (42 references); for a review by Richard W. Coan, of an earlier edition, see 8:630 (115 references); see also T2:1294 (120 references) and P:177 (56 references); for reviews by Gerald A. Mendelson and Norman D. Sundberg and an excerpted review by Laurence Siegel, see 6:147 (10 references).

[1711]
Myers-Briggs Type Indicator® Step II (Form Q).

Purpose: "Provides an in-depth personalized account of personality preferences."
Population: Ages 18 and over.
Publication Date: 2001.
Acronym: MBTI Step II—Form Q.
Scores, 24: Four dichotomies (Extraversion vs. Introversion, Sensing vs. Intuition, Thinking vs. Feeling, Judging vs. Perceiving), 20 facets: 5 Extraversion—Introversion facets (Initiating—Receiving, Expressive—Contained, Gregarious—Intimate, Active—Reflective, Enthusiastic—Quiet), 5 Sensing—Intuition facets (Concrete—Abstract, Realistic—Imaginative, Practical—Conceptual, Experiential—Theoretical, Traditional—Original), 5 Thinking—Feeling facets (Logical—Empathetic, Reasonable—Compassionate, Questioning—Accommodating, Critical—Accepting, Tough—Tender), 5 Judging—Perceiving facets (Systematic—Casual, Planful—Open-Ended, Early Starting—Pressure-Prompted, Scheduled—Spontaneous, Methodical—Emergent).
Administration: Individual or group.
Price Data, 2001: $85 per preview kit including item booklet, prepaid profile answer sheet, and manual (2001, 202 pages); $97 per interpretive (Form Q) preview kit including item booklet, prepaid interpretive answer sheet, and manual; $50 per 25 item booklets; $150 per 10 profile answer sheets; $110 per 5 interpretive answer sheets; $15 per profile web administration; $22 per interpretive web administration; $65 per manual.
Time: (25–35) minutes.
Comments: Includes all items comprising Step I, Form M of MBTI® (1710); can be used to generate all reports produced by Step I, Form M of MBTI®; provides advice for enhancing communication, conflict and change management, and decision making skills; computer or web-administered scoring available.
Authors: Katharine C. Briggs, Isabel Briggs Myers, Naomi L. Quenk (Profile Form, Interpretive Form, MBTI Step II Manual), Jean Kummerow (Profile Form, Interpretive Form), Allen L. Hammer (MBTI Step II Manual), and Mark S. Major (MBTI Step II Manual).

Publisher: CPP, Inc.
Cross References: For reviews by Allen K. Hess and Kevin Lanning, see 15:172; for information about other components of this program, see T5:1755 (78 references) and T4:1702 (45 references); for reviews by John W. Fleenor and Paul M. Mastrangelo of Form M, see 14:251 (1 reference); for a review by Jerry S. Wiggins, see 10:206 (42 references); for a review by Anthony J. DeVito, see 9:739 (19 references); see also T3:1555 (42 references); for a review by Richard Coan, see 8:630 (115 references); see also T2:1294 (120 references) and P:177 (56 references); for reviews by Gerald A. Mendelsohn and Norman D. Sundberg and an excerpted review by Laurence Siegel, see 6:147 (10 references).

[1712]
Naglieri Nonverbal Ability Test.

Purpose: A "measure of nonverbal reasoning and problem solving independent of educational curricula and cultural or language background."
Population: Grades K–12.
Publication Dates: 1996–1997.
Acronym: NNAT.
Scores, 5: Pattern Completion (PC), Reasoning by Analogy (RA), Serial Reasoning (SR), Spatial Visualization (SV), Total (Nonverbal Ability Index—NAI).
Administration: Group.
Levels, 7: A (Kindergarten), B (Grade 1), C (Grade 2), D (Grades 3–4), E (Grades 5–6), F (Grades 7–9), G (Grades 10–12).
Price Data, 2002: $24.90 per examination kit (specify Level A–G) including one copy each machine-scorable or reusable test booklets, multilevel directions for administration, and machine-scorable answer documents (for Levels E–G); $92.80 per 25 machine-scorable test booklets including directions for administering and order for scoring services (specify Level A–D); $67.30 per 25 reusable test booklets for use with machine-scorable and hand-scorable answer documents (specify Level E–G); $67.30 per 25 hand-scorable test booklets including directions and 1 multilevel class record (specify Level A–D); $26 per 25 combined D/E/F/G machine-scorable answer documents; $26 per 25 combined D/E/F/G hand-scorable answer documents; $44.50 per side by side keys for hand-scorable test booklets (specify Level A–D); $22 per stencil keys for hand-scorable answer documents (specify Level D–G); $30 per response keys for all levels (list of correct responses); $60 per fall or spring norms book; $78.50 per technical manual; $9 per additional copy of directions for administering (all levels); price information for scoring and reporting services available from publisheer.
Time: 30 (45) minutes.
Comments: An extension and revision of the Matrix Analogies Test (1551); appropriate for non-English-speaking students, students with hearing, language, or

motor impairment, and impaired color vision; a general measure of ability or identification of students with learning problems.
Author: Jack A. Naglieri.
Publisher: Harcourt Assessment, Inc.
Cross References: For reviews by Terry A. Stinnett and Michael S. Trevisan, see 14:252.

[1713]
Naglieri Nonverbal Ability Test—Individual Administration.

Purpose: Designed to provide a brief nonverbal measure of general ability.
Population: Ages 5-0 to 17-11.
Publication Date: 2003.
Acronym: NNAT-I.
Scores: Total score only.
Administration: Individual.
Price Data, 2004: $233 per complete kit including manual (139 pages), stimulus book, 25 parent reports, and 25 each of record forms A and B; $110 per stimulus book; $5 per manual; $55 per 25 record forms (specify Form A or B); $55 per 25 parent reports.
Time: (25–30) minutes.
Comments: This test and the Naglieri Nonverbal Ability Test (Multilevel Form) (T6:1680) are the second editions of the still in-print Matrix Analogies Test (Expanded Form and Short Form) (T6:1531).
Author: Jack A. Naglieri.
Publisher: PsychCorp, A brand of Harcourt Assessment, Inc.
Cross References: For reviews by Connie T. England and Brian F. French, see 16:159; see also T5:1607 (15 references) and T4:1566 (8 references); for a review by Robert F. McMorris, David L. Rule, and Wendy J. Steinberg of the Matrix Analogies Test, see 10:191 (1 reference).

[1714]
NASA Moon Survival Task.

Purpose: To explore the performance characteristics of a decision-making group and the significance of member contributions to the quality of group production.
Population: Individuals who work, or anticipate working, in a group setting.
Publication Dates: 1963-1989.
Scores, 4: Commitment, Conflict, Creativity, Consensus.
Administration: Individual in part.
Price Data, 2001: $8.95 per instrument (1989, 21 pages).
Time: Administration time not reported.
Author: Jay Hall.
Publisher: Teleometrics International, Inc.
Cross References: See T5:1757 (2 references).

[1715]
National Assessment of Educational Progress—Released Exercises.

Purpose: "A continuing, congressionally mandated national survey of knowledge, skills, and understanding, of young Americans" in the fields of mathematics, science, reading, writing, U.S. history, geography, and other subject areas.
Population: Grades 4, 8, and 12 (main NAEP); Ages 9, 13, and 17 (Long-Term Trend NAEP).
Publication Dates: 1983–2002.
Acronym: NAEP.
Scores: No individual scores, scaled results (average proficiency) are provided for designated reporting subgroups.
Administration: Group.
Price Data: Released items available on the NAEP web-site.
Comments: Released-exercise set, which is approximately one-third to one-half of the complete assessment package; administered to national samples of specified age groups biennially since 1969 (1969–1998 now out of print); released exercises are in the public domain and may be copied without restriction following receipt of permission from the author (NCES); student, teacher, and school questionnaires are also available; details of the assessments, procedures, analyses, and results can be found in a series of reports available from the author and publisher; ETS has served as the primary NAEP contractor since 1983. Available on the web at NCES.ed.gov/nationsreportand/itmrls.
Authors: National Assessment of Educational Progress; National Center for Education Statistics; Office of Educational Research and Improvement; U.S. Dept. of Education.
Publisher: Educational Testing Service.
> *a)* MATHEMATICS.
> **Scores:** 5 content areas (Numbers and Operations, Measurement, Geometry, Data Analysis/Statistics and Probability, Algebra and Functions), Estimation Skills; 3 process areas (Conceptual Understanding, Procedural Knowledge, Problem Solving).
> **Comments:** Assessment dates: 1986, 1990, 1992, 1996.
> *b)* SCIENCE.
> **Scores:** 3 content areas (Life Sciences, Physical Sciences, Earth & Space Sciences); 3 thinking skills/areas (Conducting Inquiries, Solving Problems, Knowing Science).
> **Comments:** Assessment dates: 1986, 1990.
> *c)* READING.
> **Scores:** 3 purposes (Reading for Literary Experience, Reading to Gain Information, Reading to Perform a Task); 4 stances (Initial Understanding, Developing Interpretation, Personal Reflection and Response, Demonstrating a Critical Stance).

Comments: Assessment dates: 1984, 1986, 1988, 1990, 1992, 1994, 1998, 2000, 2002.

d) WRITING.

Scores: 3 purposes (Informative, Narrative, Persuasive).

Comments: Assessment dates: 1984, 1988, 1992, 1998, 2002.

e) U.S. HISTORY.

Scores: 4 themes (Change and Continuity in American Democracy, The Gathering and Interaction of Peoples/Cultures/and Ideas, Economic and Technological Changes and Their Relation to Society/Ideas/and the Environment, The Changing Role of America in the World).

Comments: Assessment dates: 1988, 1994, 2001.

f) GEOGRAPHY.

Scores: 3 content areas (Space and Place, Environment and Society, Spatial Dynamics and Dimensions).

Comments: Assessment dates: 1988, 1994, 2001.

g) FINE ARTS.

Scores: 4 content areas (Music, Dance, Theatre, Visual Arts).

Comments: Assessment date: 1997.

Cross References: See T5:1759 (18 references).

[1716]
National Educational Development Tests.

Purpose: To provide students with information in their development of skills that are necessary to do well on college admissions tests and in college work itself.

Population: Grades 9–10.

Publication Dates: 1983–1984.

Acronym: NEDT.

Scores, 6: English Usage, Mathematics Usage, National Sciences Reading, Social Studies Reading, Composite Score, Educational Ability.

Administration: Group.

Price Data: Available from publisher for combined test materials and standard scoring services, student materials consist of test booklets and answer sheets, Student Handbook, Certificates of Educational Development, and Student Information Bulletin; administrative materials consist of identification sheets, Supervisor's and Examiner's Manuals (1984, 14 pages), and Interpretive Manuals.

Time: 150(180) minutes.

Comments: Tests administered 2 times annually (October and February).

Author: Science Research Associates, Inc.

Publisher: CTB/McGraw-Hill.

Cross References: See T4:1707 (1 reference); for reviews by Patti L. Harrison and Howard M. Knoff, see 11:255.

[1717]
National German Examination for High School Students.

Purpose: To evaluate students' achievement in German study, may be used as a diagnostic tool.

Population: 2, 3, or 4 years high school.

Publication Dates: 1960-2006.

Scores: Total score only.

Administration: Group.

Levels, 3: 2nd year, 3rd year, 4th year.

Price Data, 2006: $5 per test, includes scoring service; Interpretive data (17 pages) available; test booklets, tapes, and answer sheets are to be returned to Software, Inc.

Time: 60(65) minutes.

Comments: Also called AATG National Standardized Testing Program; formerly called AATG German Test and National German Contest for High School Students; tests administered annually in December and January under auspices of high school guidance departments and administration; test is new each year.

Author: American Association of Teachers of German.

Publisher: American Association of Teachers of German, Inc.

Cross References: For reviews by Gilbert C. Kettelkamp and Theodor F. Naumann of an earlier edition, see 6:382.

[1718]
National Institute for Personnel Research Normal Battery.

Purpose: "Designed as a selection device for use mainly with Bantu clerks in various industrial and government organizations."

Population: South African Standards 6–10 and job applicants with 8–11 years of education.

Publication Dates: 1960–1973.

Subtests, 5: Mental Alertness, Reading Comprehension, Vocabulary, Spelling, Computation.

Administration: Group.

Price Data: Price information available from publisher for test materials including manual (1969, 129 pages).

Author: S. M. A. Waterhouse (manual).

Publisher: Human Sciences Research Council [South Africa].

Cross References: See T2:1085 (2 references) and 6:779.

[1719]
National Police Officer Selection Test.

Purpose: Measures skills critical to the successful performance of entry-level officers.

Population: Police officer candidates.

Publication Dates: 1991–1992.

Acronym: POST.
Partial Batteries: POST III or POST IV.
Administration: Group.
Restricted Distribution: Available to authorized police personnel only.
Price Data: Price information available from publisher for administration guide (1991, 12 pages), examiner's manual (1992, 13 pages; required with first purchase), and study guide.
Comments: Test may be self-scored or scored by Stanard & Associates, Inc.
Author: Stanard & Associates, Inc.
Publisher: Stanard & Associates, Inc.
a) POST III.
Scores, 4: Mathematics, Reading Comprehension, Grammar, Total.
Price Data: Price information available from publisher for 1-250 POST III (scored by publisher) and 1–250 POST III (self-scored).
Time: 66 (71) minutes.
b) POST IV.
Scores, 5: Mathematics, Reading Comprehension, Grammar, Incident Report Writing, Total.
Price Data: Price information available from publisher for 1-250 POST IV (scored by publisher) and 1–250 POST IV (self-scored).
Time: 83 (88) minutes.
Cross References: See T5:1763 (1 reference); for reviews by Jim C. Fortune and Abbot Packard and by Kurt F. Geisinger, see 12:253.

[1720]
National Spanish Examinations.

Purpose: Designed as a motivational extracurricular contest for students of members of the American Association of Teachers of Spanish and Portuguese (AATSP) and chapters.
Population: Second semester of 1, 2, 3, 4–6 year Spanish students.
Publication Dates: 1957–2002.
Acronym: NSE.
Scores: Total score only.
Administration: Group.
Levels, 6: 01, 1, 2, 3, 4, 5 (3, 4, and 5 include a Bilingual/Native Supplement).
Manual: Directions for Administering, 2002, 10 pages (revised annually).
Restricted Distribution: Available only to current members of AATSP.
Price Data: Available from publisher.
Time: 60 minutes.
Comments: New form constructed annually for administration in February and March at local secondary schools or centers established by local chapters of the AATSP; summary of results of top three scorers in each level published in Hispania in September following the completion of the testing program; now available as online test only (no paper copies).
Author: Test Development Committees, American Association of Teachers of Spanish and Portuguese.
Publisher: National Spanish Exam.
Cross References: See 8:168 (2 references); for a review by Walter V. Kalfers of earlier forms, see 7:323 (1 reference); see also 6:428 (8 references).

[1721]
National Survey of Student Engagement.

Purpose: Designed to provide colleges and universities information about the student experience and institutional performance to use to improve undergraduate education, inform accountability and accreditation efforts, and facilitate national and sector benchmarking efforts.
Population: Bachelor's degree-seeking undergraduate students at 4-year colleges and universities.
Publication Dates: 2000–2005.
Acronym: NSSE.
Scores, 7: Level of Academic Challenge, Active and Collaborative Learning, Student Interactions with Faculty Members, Enriching Educational Experiences, Supportive Campus Environment, Background Information, Consortium Questions.
Administration: Group.
Price Data, 2002: $300 institutional participation fee and $3,375 to $7,500 student sampling fee (includes customized institutional report with means and frequency distribution by item, along with sector and national comparisons, response rates and sampling error, student response data on a CD-ROM, national report and institutional benchmarks of effective educational practice, and a sample presentation); $7.50 each for paper oversampling; $1.50 each for web-only mode oversampling; $2 for locally administered oversampling; additional fees for participating in consortium or special analyses; $35 per Technical and Norms Report (2001, 290 pages); fees for special peer comparison reports that compares institution against a elect group of 6–10 other participating institutions.
Time: (10–15) minutes.
Authors: George D. Kuh (test and technical report); J. C. Hayek, R. M. Carini, J. A. Oimet, R. M. Gonyea, and J. Kennedy (technical report).
Publisher: Indiana University Center for Postsecondary Research.
Cross References: For reviews by William I. Sauser, Jr. and Eugene P. Sheehan, see 16:160.

[1722]
Naturalistic Action Test.

Purpose: Designed to "assess errors of action in the performance of routine activities of daily living."
Population: Adults.

Publication Dates: 2002–2003.

Acronym: NAT.

Scores, 8: Accomplishment Score, Error Score, Naturalized Attention Test (NAT) Score for Task 1: Toast and Coffee, NAT Score for Task 2: Present, NAT Score for Task 3: Lunchbox and Schoolbag, Total NAT Score, Comprehensive Error Score, Lateralized Attention Score.

Administration: Individual.

Price Data, 2006: £319.50 per complete kit including manual (2002, 22 pages), 25 scoring sheets, work space template, 2 master score sheets, bell, doll, plastic lunchbox, flask, paper bags, and cardboard boxes; £41.50 per 50 scoring sheets.

Time: (30-40) minutes.

Comments: Adaptation of Multi-Level Action Test.

Authors: Myrna F. Schwartz, Laurel J. Buxbaum, Mary Ferraro, Tracy Veramonti, and Mary Segal.

Publisher: Harcourt Assessment [England].

[1723]

Neale Analysis of Reading Ability: Second Revised British Edition.

Purpose: Designed to measure reading accuracy, comprehension and rate and to provide diagnostic information about children's reading difficulties.

Population: Ages 6-0 to 12-11.

Publication Dates: 1958–1997.

Acronym: NARA II.

Scores, 3: Comprehension, Accuracy, Rate; plus 4 supplementary diagnostic scores (Discrimination of Initial and Final Sounds, Names and Sounds of the Alphabet, Graded Spelling, Auditory Discrimination and Blending).

Administration: Individual.

Forms, 3: 1, 2, Diagnostic Tutor Form (not norm referenced).

Price Data: Available from publisher.

Time: (20) minutes.

Comments: Revision includes new norms and larger standardization sample.

Authors: Marie D. Neale (test and manual); Second Revised British Edition and standardization by Chris Whetton, Louise Caspall, and Kay McCulloch.

Publisher: NFER-Nelson Publishing Co., Ltd. [England].

Cross References: For reviews by Marie Miller-Whitehead and Elizabeth Kelley Rhoades, see 16:161; see also T5:1765 (36 references) and T4:1714 (7 references); for reviews by Cleborne D. Maddux and G. Michael Poteat of an earlier edition, see 11:257 (41 references); see also T3:1567 (13 references) and T2:1683 (7 references); for reviews by M. Alan Brimer and Magdalen D. Vernon, and an excerpted review, see 6:843.

[1724]

Neale Analysis of Reading Ability, 3rd Edition [Australian Standardisation].

Purpose: Designed to "assess reading progress objectivity [and] to obtain structured diagnostic observations of an individual's reading behaviour."

Population: Ages 6 to 12.

Publication Dates: 1958–1999.

Scores, 3: Accuracy, Comprehension, Rate.

Administration: Individual.

Forms, 2: 1, 2.

Price Data, 2006: A$38.50 per test booklet; A$1.95 per individual record standardised test (specify form); A$1.95 per individual record diagnostic tutor (specify form); A$54.95 per manual (1999, 141 pages); A$99.95 per specimen set including test booklet, 1 each individual record standarised test Form 1 and 2, 1 each individual record diagnostic tutor Form A and B, and manual; A$149.95 per specimen set plus video; A$49.95 per video; A$21.95 per audio cassette.

Time: Administration time not reported.

Comments: Includes six supplementary diagnostic tests (Discrimination of Initial and Final Sounds, Names and Sounds of the Alphabet, Graded Spelling, Auditory Discrimination and Blending, Word Lists, and Silent Reading/Writing).

Authors: Marie D. Neale, Michael McKay, and John Barnard.

Publisher: Australian Council for Educational Research Ltd. [Australia].

Cross References: For reviews by Valentina McInerney and Bruce G. Rogers, see 15:173.

[1725]

NEEDS Survey.

Purpose: Designed "to provide a concise but comprehensive profile of an individual's functioning" relative to the treatment of substance abuse.

Population: Adults.

Publication Date: 1994.

Acronym: NEEDS.

Scores, 10: Test Taking Attitude, Basic Problem Solving and Reading, Emotional Stability, Substance Abuse, Employment, Personal Relationship and Support System, Physical Health, Education, Criminal History, Overall "Needs."

Administration: Individual or group.

Price Data: Available from publisher.

Time: (26) minutes.

Comments: Self-administered; computer-scored, IBM compatible with either DOS or Windows required; provides DSM-IV classification for alcohol and drug abuse and ASAM patient placement criteria for treatment recommendations; available in English or Spanish.

Authors: ADE Incorporated.

Publisher: ADE Incorporated.
Cross References: For reviews by Anita M. Hubley and Paul M. Mastrangelo, see 14:253.

[1726]
Nelson-Denny Reading Test CD-ROM Version 1.2.

Purpose: "To provide a trustworthy assessment of student ability in three areas of academic achievement: vocabulary, reading comprehension, and reading rate."
Population: Grades 9–16 and adults.
Publication Dates: 1929–2000.
Scores, 4: Vocabulary, Comprehension, Total, Reading Rate.
Administration: Group.
Forms, 2: G and H.
Price Data, 2005: $20 per Manual for Scoring and Interpretation; $6.61 per administration for 25 to 499 test administrations; quantity discounts available for administrations.
Time: 35(56) minutes.
Comments: Requires Windows 95, 98, NT, or 2000; extended time of 9 minutes for Vocabulary subtest and 12 minutes for Comprehension subtest available to meet the needs of special populations, such as students with English as a second language or as a foreign language, or returning adults; creates reports including the Individual Narrative, Individual Longitudinal, Group Longitudinal, Group Longitudinal Summary, List of Student Scores, and the Group Summary; a computerized alternative identical in content to paper-pencil Forms G and H and considered by the publisher to be parallel forms.
Authors: James I. Brown, Vivian Vick Fishco, and Gerald S. Hanna.
Publisher: Riverside Publishing.
Cross References: See T5:1767 (9 references); for reviews by Mildred Murray-Ward and Douglas K. Smith of Forms G and H, see 13:206 (52 references); see also T4:1715 (30 references); for reviews by Robert J. Tierney and James E. Ysseldyke of Forms E and F, see 9:745 (12 references); see also T3:1568 (38 references); for reviews by Robert A. Forsyth and Alton L. Raynor of Forms C and D, see 8:735 (31 references); see also T2:1572 (46 references); for reviews by David B. Orr and Agatha Townsend and an excerpted review by John O. Crites of Forms A and B, see 6:800 (13 references); for a review by Ivan A. Booker, see 4:544 (17 references); for a review by Hans C. Gordon, see 2:1557.

[1727]
Nelson-Denny Reading Test, Forms G and H.

Purpose: "To assess student achievement and progress in vocabulary, comprehension, and reading rate."
Population: Grades 9–16 and adult.
Publication Dates: 1929–1993.

Scores, 4: Vocabulary, Comprehension, Total, Reading Rate.
Administration: Group.
Price Data: Available from publisher.
Time: 35 minutes; 56 minutes for extended time administration.
Comments: Computer-administered version is available on CD-ROM in Windows format.
Authors: James I. Brown, Vivian Vick Fishco, and Gerald S. Hanna.
Publisher: Riverside Publishing.
Cross References: See T5:1767 (9 references); for reviews by Mildred Murray-Ward and Douglas K. Smith, see 13:206 (52 references); see also T4:1715 (30 references); for reviews by Robert J. Tierney and James E. Ysseldyke of Forms E and F, see 9:745 (12 references); see also T3:1568 (38 references); for reviews by Robert A. Forsyth and Alton L. Raynor of Forms C and D, see 8:735 (31 references); see also T2:1572 (46 references); for reviews by David B. Orr and Agatha Townsend and an excerpted review by John O. Crites of Forms A and B, see 6:800 (13 references); for a review by Ivan A. Booker, see 4:544 (17 references); for a review by Hans C. Gordon, see 2:1557.

[1728]
NEO-4.

Purpose: Designed as a four-factor version of the Revised NEO Personality Inventory.
Population: Ages 17 and older.
Publication Date: 1998.
Scores, 28: Extraversion (Warmth, Gregariousness, Assertiveness, Activity, Excitement-Seeking, Positive Emotions, Total); Openness to Experience (Fantasy, Aesthetics, Feelings, Actions, Ideas, Values, Total); Agreeableness (Trust, Straightforwardness, Altruism, Compliance, Modesty, Tender-Mindedness, Total); Conscientiousness (Competence, Order, Dutifulness, Achievement Striving, Self-Discipline, Deliberation, Total).
Administration: Group or individual.
Forms, 2: Form S (self-reports), Form R (observer ratings).
Price Data, 2006: $202 per introductory kit including NEO-4 manual supplement (19 pages), 10 each Form S and Form R reusable item booklets, 25 hand-scorable answer sheets, 25 profile forms, 25 style graph booklets, and 25 Your NEO-4 summary forms.
Time: [25–35] minutes.
Comments: Questionnaire items, scoring keys, and scale norms are identical to those found in the Revised NEO Personality Inventory (NEO PI-R; 1729) for the four factors of Extraversion, Openness to Experience, Agreeableness, and Conscientiousness and users are encouraged to consult the professional manual for the NEO PI-R.

Authors: Paul T. Costa and Robert R. McCrae.
Publisher: Psychological Assessment Resources, Inc.
Cross References: For reviews by Theresa M. Bahns and Carlen Hennington, see 14:254.

[1729]
NEO Personality Inventory—Revised.

Purpose: Designed to "obtain a comprehensive and detailed assessment of adult personality based on the Five Factor Model of personality."
Population: Ages 17 and older.
Publication Dates: 1978–1992.
Administration: Individual or group.
Price Data, 2006: $245 per NEO-PI-R comprehensive kit including professional manual, 10 each of reusable Form S and Form R booklets (5 women and 5 men), 25 each of the hand-scorable answer sheets (Form S and Form R), 25 adult profile forms, and 25 Your NEO Summary feedback sheets; $555 per NEO Software System with NEI PI-R and NEO-FFI modules (CD-ROM) including unlimited interpretive reports and 5 free on-screen administrations of either the PI-R or FFI.
Comments: Previously listed as Revised NEO Personality Inventory.
Authors: Paul T. Costa, Jr. and Robert R. McCrae.
Publisher: Psychological Assessment Resources, Inc.
a) REVISED NEO PERSONALITY INVENTORY.
Acronym: NEO PI-R.
Forms, 2: Form S (self-reports), Form R (observer ratings).
Scores, 35: 30 facets in 5 domains: Neuroticism (Anxiety, Angry Hostility, Depression, Self-Consciousness, Impulsiveness, Vulnerability, Total), Extraversion (Warmth, Gregariousness, Assertiveness, Activity, Excitement-Seeking, Positive Emotions, Total), Openness (Fantasy, Aesthetics, Feelings, Actions, Ideas, Values, Total), Agreeableness (Trust, Straightforwardness, Altruism, Compliance, Modesty, Tender-Mindedness, Total), Conscientiousness (Competence, Order, Dutifulness, Achievement Striving, Self-Discipline, Deliberation, Total).
Time: [35–45] minutes.
Comments: Form R has two parallel versions: male and female.
b) NEO FIVE-FACTOR INVENTORY.
Acronym: NEO-FFI.
Scores, 5: Neuroticism, Extraversion, Openness, Agreeableness, Conscientiousness.
Time: (10-15) minutes.
Comments: Shortened version of Form S.
Cross References: See T5:2218 (135 references); for reviews by Michael D. Botwin and Samuel Juni, see 12:330 (50 references); see also T4:2263 (49 references); for reviews by Allen K. Hess and Thomas A.

Widiger of an earlier edition see 11:258 (5 references); for a review by Robert Hogan of an earlier edition of a, see 10:214 (6 references).

[1730]
Neonatal Behavioral Assessment Scale, 3rd Edition.

Purpose: Designed to evaluate an infant's behavioral and neurological status.
Population: Ages 3 days through 2 months.
Publication Dates: 1973–1995.
Acronym: NBAS.
Scores, 53: (Each item represents a score) in 3 domains: Behavioral (28 items), Supplementary (7 items), Reflex (18 items).
Administration: Individual.
Price Data: Available from publisher.
Time: (20–30) minutes.
Comments: Previous version entitled Brazelton Neonatal Behavioral Assessment Scale-380; a 53-item rating scale of infant behavior and reflexes; not for use with infants recovering from illness or premature birth; to be administered by clinicians trained in neonatal behavior.
Authors: T. Berry Brazelton and J. Kevin Nugent.
Publisher: Cambridge University Press.
Cross References: For reviews by Carol M. McGregor and Hoi K. Suen, see 14:255; see also T5:1770 (17 references), T4:321 (9 references), 9:157 (9 references), and T3:311 (31 references); for a review by Anita Miller Sostek of an earlier edition, and an excerpted review by Stephen Wolkind of an earlier edition, see 8:208 (15 references).

[1731]
NEPSY: A Developmental Neuropsychological Assessment.

Purpose: "Designed to assess neuropsychological development."
Population: Ages 3–12.
Publication Date: 1998.
Acronym: NEPSY.
Scores, 32: Attention/Executive (Tower, Auditory Attention and Response Set, Visual Attention, Statue, Design Fluency, Knock and Tap, Total), Language (Body Part Naming, Phonological Processing, Speeded Naming, Comprehension of Instructions, Repetition of Nonsense Words, Verbal Fluency, Oromotor Sequences, Total), Sensorimotor (Fingertip Tapping, Imitating Hand Positions, Visuomotor Precision, Manual Motor Sequences, Finger Discrimination, Total), Visuospatial (Design Copying, Arrows, Block Construction, Route Finding, Total), Memory and Learning (Memory for Faces, Memory for Names, Narrative Memory, Sentence Repetition, List Learning, Total).
Administration: Individual.
Forms, 2: Ages 3–4, Ages 5–12.

Price Data, 2002: $575 per complete kit including manual (464 pages), 10 record forms for both Ages 3–4 version and Ages 5–12 version, 10 response booklets for both Ages 3–4 version and Ages 5–12 version, scoring templates and manipulables packaged in a bright nylon bag; $26 per 25 Ages 3–4 response booklets; $32 per 25 Ages 5–12 response booklets; $29 per 25 Ages 3–4 record forms; $34 per 25 Ages 5–12 record forms; $96 per manual; $112 per stimulus booklet; $96 per tower (with 3 balls).
Time: (45–60) minutes for preschool-aged children; (65–120) minutes for school-aged children.
Comments: Also includes optional qualitative behavioral observations and supplemental scores.
Authors: Marit Korkman, Ursula Kirk, and Sally Kemp.
Publisher: PsychCorp, A brand of Harcourt Assessment, Inc.
Cross References: For reviews by Sandra D. Haynes and Daniel C. Miller, see 14:256.

[1732]
Network Analyst Staff Selector.

Purpose: To evaluate essential skills needed for the network analyst.
Population: Candidates for technical network positions.
Publication Date: 1992.
Acronym: NETAL.
Scores: Total Score, Narrative Evaluation, Ranking, Recommendation.
Administration: Group.
Price Data, 2001: $340 per candidate; quantity discounts available.
Time: (150) minutes.
Comments: Scored by publisher; must be proctored.
Author: Bruce A. Winrow.
Publisher: Walden Personnel Performance, Inc. [Canada].

[1733]
Network Technician Staff Selector.

Purpose: To measure network knowledge and analytical skills.
Population: Candidates for the position of network technician.
Publication Date: 1992.
Acronym: NETECH.
Scores: Total Score, Narrative Evaluation, Ranking, Recommendation.
Administration: Group.
Price Data, 2001: $340 per candidate.
Time: (107) minutes.
Comments: Scored by publisher; must be proctored.
Author: Bruce A. Winrow.
Publisher: Walden Personnel Performance, Inc. [Canada].

[1734]
Neurobehavioral Functioning Inventory.

Purpose: "Designed to measure the frequency of neurobehavioral problems associated with traumatic brain injury and other neurological disorders."
Population: Patients ages 17 and older.
Publication Date: 1999.
Acronym: NFI.
Scores, 6: Depression, Somatic, Memory/Attention, Communication, Aggression, Motor.
Administration: Individual or group.
Price Data, 2002: $137 per complete kit including manual (120 pages), 25 Family record forms, and 25 Patient record forms; $79 per manual; $39 per 25 record forms (Family or Patient).
Time: (30) minutes.
Comments: Self-scoring self-report forms.
Authors: Jeffrey S. Kreutzer, Ronald T. Seel, and Jennifer H. Marwitz.
Publisher: PsychCorp, A brand of Harcourt Assessment, Inc.
Cross References: For reviews by Raymond S. Dean and John J. Brinkman, Jr., and by Thomas McKnight, see 16:162.

[1735]
Neuropsychological Assessment Battery.

Purpose: "Developed for the assessment of a wide array of cognitive skills and functions in adults with known or suspected disorders of the central nervous system."
Population: Ages 18–97.
Publication Dates: 2001–2003.
Forms, 2: Form 1, Form 2 (equivalent forms).
Price Data: Available from publisher.
Time: Administration time not reported.
Comments: Modules may be administered individually; NAB Training Program on DVD is included with each module; software portfolio available for use on CD-ROM.
Authors: Robert A. Stern and Travis White.
Publisher: Psychological Assessment Resources, Inc.
  a) SCREENING MODULE.
    Scores, 6: Attention, Language, Memory, Spatial, Executive Function, Total.
    Comments: May be used to determine whether more in-depth, followup examinations are necessary.
  b) ATTENTION MODULE.
    Scores, 12: Digits (2), Dots, Numbers & Letters (7), Driving Scenes, Total.
  c) LANGUAGE MODULE.
    Scores, 6: Oral Production, Auditory Comprehension, Naming, Writing, Bill Payment, Total.
  d) MEMORY MODULE.
    Scores, 5: List Learning, Shape Learning, Story Learning, Daily Living Memory, Total.

e) SPATIAL MODULE.

Scores, 5: Visual Discrimination, Design Construction, Figure Drawing, Map Reading, Total.

f) EXECUTIVE FUNCTIONS.

Scores, 5: Mazes, Judgment, Categories, Word Generation, Total.

Cross References: For reviews by Timothy J. Makatura and by Wilfred G. Van Gorp and Jason Hassenstab, see 16:163.

[1736]
The Neuropsychological Impairment Scale.

Purpose: Designed to screen for "neuropsychological symptoms."

Population: Ages 18–88 years.

Publication Date: 1994.

Acronym: NIS.

Scores, 14: Defensiveness, Affective Disturbance, Response Inconsistency, Subjective Distortion Index, Global Measure of Impairment, Total Items Circled, Symptom Intensity Measure, Critical Items, Cognitive Efficiency, Attention, Memory, Frustration Tolerance, Learning-Verbal, Academic Skills.

Administration: Group.

Forms, 3: Self-Report, Observer Report, Senior Interview.

Price Data, 2006: $148.50 per complete kit including 25 self-report AutoScore™ answer forms, 25 observer-report AutoScore™ answer forms, and manual (71 pages) with Senior Interview Supplement and Response Card; $46.50 per 25 self-report AutoScore™ answer forms; $46.50 per 25 observer-report AutoScore™ answer forms; $61.50 per manual; $98 per Senior Interview kit including 25 Senior Interview AutoScore™ answer forms, 1 manual with Senior Interview Supplement and Response Card; $46.50 per 25 Senior Interview AutoScore™ answer forms; $155 per 10-use disk for use with self report, observer report, and senior interview; $16.50 per PC Answer Sheet in packages of 100.

Time: (15–20) minutes.

Comments: Self-Report form and Observer-Report form both utilize the 14 scores listed above, Senior Interview provides Global Measure of Impairment and scores for Defensiveness, Affective Disturbance, and Inconsistency.

Authors: William E. O'Donnell, Clinton B. DeSoto, Janet L. DeSoto, and Don McQ. Reynolds.

Publisher: Western Psychological Services.

Cross References: For a review by Robert A. Leark, see 14:257; see also T5:1775 (3 references).

[1737]
Neuropsychological Status Exam.

Purpose: Designed to organize data useful in neuropsychological assessment.

Population: Neuropsychological patients.

Publication Date: 1983.

Acronym: NSE.

Scores: Checklists in 13 areas: Patient Data, Referral Data, Tentative Findings, Neuropsychological Symptom Checklist, Premorbid Status, Physical Status, Emotional Status, Cognitive Status, Test Administration, Results of Neuropsychological Testing, Diagnostic Comments, Effects on Patient Functioning, Treatment Recommendations.

Administration: Individual.

Price Data, 2005: $59 per complete kit including 25 NSE and 25 NSC (Checklist) forms and manual (13 pages).

Time: Administration time not reported.

Author: John A. Schinka.

Publisher: Psychological Assessment Resources, Inc.

[1738]
Neuropsychology Behavior and Affect Profile.

Purpose: Designed to assess psychological changes in personality that accompany selective neurological disorders.

Population: Brain-impaired individuals ages 15 and over.

Publication Dates: 1989–1994.

Acronym: NBAP.

Scores, 5: Indifference, Inappropriateness, Pragnosia, Depression, Mania.

Administration: Individual.

Forms, 2: Form S, Form O.

Price Data: Available from publisher (www.mindgarden.com).

Time: Administration time not reported.

Comments: Form S is self-administered by patients judged capable of accurate self-report; Form O is filled out by significant other when Form S is deemed inappropriate.

Authors: Linda Nelson, Paul Satz, and Louis F. D'Elia.

Publisher: Mind Garden, Inc.

Cross References: For a review by Surendra P. Singh, see 14:258.

[1739]
New Jersey Test of Reasoning Skills—Form B.

Purpose: Assesses elementary reasoning and inquiry skills.

Population: Reading level grade 5 and over.

Publication Dates: 1983-1985.

Scores: 22 skill areas: Converting Statements, Translating into Logical Form, Inclusion/Exclusion, Recognizing Improper Questions, Avoiding Jumping to Conclusions, Analogical Reasoning, Detecting Underlying Assumptions, Eliminating Alternatives, Inductive Rea-

soning, Reasoning with Relationships, Detecting Ambiguities, Discerning Causal Relationships, Identifying Good Reasons, Recognizing Symmetrical Relationships, Syllogistic Reasoning (Categorical), Distinguishing Differences of Kind and Degree, Recognizing Transitive Relationships, Recognizing Dubious Authority, Reasoning with 4-Possibilities Matrix, Contradicting Statements, Whole-Part and Part-Whole Reasoning, Syllogistic Reasoning (Conditional).
Administration: Group.
Manual: No manual.
Price Data, 2001: $2.40 per test booklet.
Time: (30-45) minutes.
Author: Virginia Shipman.
Publisher: Institute for the Advancement of Philosophy for Children.
Cross References: See T4:1723 (1 reference); for reviews by Arthur S. Ellen and Rosemary E. Sutton, see 11:259 (1 reference).

[1740]
New Standards Reference Examinations: English Language Arts.

Purpose: Designed to assess student performance "in the areas of reading and writing."
Population: Elementary, middle, and high school students.
Publication Dates: 1996–2003.
Acronym: NSRE: English Language Arts.
Scores, 4: Reading: Basic Understanding, Reading: Analysis and Interpretation, Writing: Effectiveness, Writing: Conventions.
Administration: Group.
Levels, 3: Elementary, Middle, High School.
Forms, 2: E, F.
Price Data: Available from publisher.
Time: Three 55-minute sessions.
Comments: Scoring service provided by publisher.
Author: National Center on Education and the Economy; Learning Research and Development Center, University of Pittsburgh.
Publisher: Harcourt Assessment, Inc.
Cross References: For a review by Dorothy M. Singleton, see 16:164.

[1741]
New Standards Reference Examinations: Mathematics.

Purpose: Designed to assess student performance in mathematics.
Population: Elementary, middle, and high school students.
Publication Dates: 1996–2003.
Acronym: NSRE: Mathematics.
Scores, 3: Skills, Concepts, Problem Solving.
Administration: Group.

Levels, 3: Elementary, Middle, High School.
Forms, 2: C, D.
Price Data: Available from publisher.
Foreign Language Edition: Spanish edition available.
Time: Three (55–65) minute sessions.
Comments: Scoring service provided by publisher.
Author: National Center on Education and the Economy; Learning Research and Development Center, University of Pittsburgh.
Publisher: Harcourt Assessment, Inc.
Cross References: For reviews by Maria del R. Medina-Diaz and Carol S. Parke, see 16:165.

[1742]
The New York Longitudinal Scales Adult Temperament Questionnaire.

Purpose: Measures the nine NYLS dimensions of temperament in adulthood.
Population: Adults ages 17-40.
Publication Dates: 1995–2003.
Scores, 9: Activity, Rhythmicity, Adaptability, Threshold, Approach, Distractibility, Intensity, Persistence, Mood.
Administration: Group.
Price Data, 2003: $69.95 per complete kit including test manual (2003, 28 pages), user's guide, and 25 questionnaires including scoring and profile slides; $49.95 per 25 questionnaire refills including scoring and profile sheets; $34.95 per 25 questionnaire refills only; quantity discounts available.
Time: (10–15) minutes.
Comments: Self-report ratings of 54 items plus 9 general impressions of temperament; scoring and report software available for online administration; details are available at www.b-di.com.
Authors: Stella Chess and Alexander Thomas.
Publisher: Behavioral-Developmental Initiative.
Cross References: For reviews by James A. Athanasou and Stephen N. Axford, see 16:166.

[1743]
NewGAP.

Purpose: Constructed to assess reading comprehension using Cloze technique.
Population: Grades 2-5; ages 7 through 12.
Publication Date: 1990.
Scores: Total score only.
Administration: Group or individual.
Forms, 2: I, II.
Price Data, 2006: $55 per complete kit including 25 each of Forms I and II, scoring template, and manual (39 pages); $22 per 50 test forms (25 each Form I and II); $6 per scoring template; $24 per manual; $24 per specimen set.
Time: 15(20) minutes.

Comments: Norm-referenced.
Authors: John McLeod and Rita McLeod.
Publisher: Academic Therapy Publications.
Cross References: For reviews by Terry A. Ackerman and Ruth Johnson, see 12:254.

[1744]
Nims Observational Checklist.

Purpose: Constructed to assist in child custody evaluations.
Population: Parents and children.
Publication Dates: 1994–1995.
Acronym: NOC.
Scores, 6: Safety/Environment, Behavior to Child, Teaching/Training, Control, Child Initiated Behavior, Total.
Administration: Individual.
Manual: No manual.
Price Data, 2006: $103 per complete kit including 25 booklets and 25 overall summary forms; $106 per 25 booklets; $14 per 25 summary forms.
Time: Administration time not reported.
Comments: Ratings by clinicians.
Author: Jerry P. Nims.
Publisher: Multi-Health Systems, Inc.

[1745]
901 Correctional Facility First-Line Supervisor Test.

Purpose: Designed "to assist correctional facilities … in promoting qualified candidates to the supervisory level."
Population: Candidates for promotion to the correctional facility first-line supervisory position.
Publication Dates: 2002-2006.
Scores: 6 knowledge areas: Concepts of Supervision, Correctional Facility Operation, Concepts for Writing and Reviewing Reports and Paperwork, Concepts of Evaluating Subordinate Performance, Concepts of Training, Concepts of Administration.
Administration: Individual or group.
Price Data: Available from publisher.
Time: 150 minutes.
Comments: A reading list is available to help candidates prepare for the test.
Author: International Public Management Association for Human Resources.
Publisher: International Public Management Association for Human Resources (IPMA-HR).

[1746]
19 Field Interest Inventory.

Purpose: Measures vocational interests in 19 broad vocational areas.
Population: Standards 8–10 in South African school system and college and adults.
Publication Dates: 1970–1971.
Acronym: 19FII.
Scores, 21: Fine Arts, Performing Arts, Language, Historical, Service, Social Work, Sociability, Public Speaking, Law, Creative Thought, Science, Practical-Male, Practical-Female, Numerical, Business, Clerical, Travel, Nature, Sport, Work-Hobby, Active-Passive.
Administration: Group.
Price Data: Available from publisher.
Time: (45) minutes.
Authors: F. A. Fouche and N. F. Alberts.
Publisher: Human Sciences Research Council [South Africa].
Cross References: For additional information, see 7:1027.

[1747]
NOCTI Experienced Worker Assessments.

Purpose: "Designed to measure an individual's knowledge of higher-level concepts, theories, and applications in the related occupation."
Population: Career and technical education teachers, potential teachers, and journey workers.
Publication Dates: 1993–2002.
Scores: Duty category scores and total scores are reported for 52 Written and Performance tests: Advertising and Design, Air Cooled Gas Engine Repair, Appliance Repair, Architectural Drafting, Audio Visual Communications Technology, Automotive Technician, Building and Home Maintenance Services, Building Construction Occupations, Building Trades Maintenance, Cabinetmaking and Millwork, Carpentry, Collision Repair, Collision Repair/Refinishing Technology, Computer Programming, Computer Technology, Cosmetology, Diesel Engine Repair, Diesel Mechanics, Drafting Occupations, Early Child Care and Education, Electrical Construction, Electrical Installation, Electromechanical Technology, Electronic Product Servicing, Electronics Communications, Electronics Technology, Graphic Imaging Technology, Heating/Ventilation & Air Conditioning (HVAC), Heating/Ventilation/Air Conditioning & Refrigeration (HVAC/R), Heavy Equipment Mechanics, Hospitality Management—Food & Beverage, Hospitality Management—Lodging, Industrial Electrician, Industrial Electronics, Industrial Technology, Marine Mechanics, Masonry, Materials Handling, Metalworking Occupations, Motorcycle Mechanics, Painting and Decorating, Plumbing, Precision Machining, Quantity Food Preparation, Quantity Foods, Refinishing Technology, Retail Commercial Baking, Retail Trades, Sheet Metal, Technical Drafting, Tool and Die Making, Welding.
Administration: Group.
Parts, 2: Written, Performance.
Price Data, 2005: $180 per complete test including written and performance parts, instructions for admin-

istration, scoring and reporting services and certificates of competence, if applicable.

Time: (180) minutes for all written tests; (1.5–6) hours for performance tests.

Comments: The National Occupational Competency Testing Institute (NOCTI) is a not-for-profit organization with a primary mission to serve all levels of the career-technical education field and to assist in developing a world-class workforce. NOCTI's assessment services include customization of assessments to better meet client needs. Assessments are designed to meet psychometric standards that utilize the psychomotor, cognitive, and affective domains of learning to assess competence. Most standardized assessments have both written (cognitive) and performance (psychomotor) components.

Authors: National Occupational Competency Testing Institute.

Publisher: National Occupational Competency Testing Institute/The Whitener Group.

Cross References: For a review of an earlier version of the NOCTI program, see 8:1153 (6 references). Reviews and references for previous separate NOCTI TOCT tests: Appliance Repair: For reviews by Geneva D. Haertel and Cyril J. Sadowski, see 13:208; for a review by Richard C. Erickson, see 10:227; Architectural Drafting: See 9:776 (1 reference); for a review by Gary E. Lintereur, see 8:1131; Audio-Visual Communications Technology: For reviews by JoEllen V. Carlson and Anne L. Harvey, see 11:262; for reviews by Patricia A. Bachelor and Connie Kubo Della-Piana, see 13:209; Auto Body Repair: For reviews by Robert J. Drummond and Dale P. Scannell, see 13:210; see also 9:777 (1 reference); Automotive Technician: For reviews by Dale P. Scannell and George C. Thornton III, see 13:211; see also 9:778 and T3:1595 (1 reference); for a review by Charles W. Pendleton, see 8:1133; Brick Masonry: For a review by Thomas S. Baldwin, see 10:229; Building and Home Maintenance Services: For a review by Gary E. Lintereur, see 10:230; Cabinet Making and Millwork: See 9:782 (1 reference); for a review by Gary E. Lintereur, see 8:1134; Carpentry: See 9:783 (1 reference); for a review by Daniel L. Householder, see 8:1535; Child Care and Guidance: For reviews by Patricia B. Keith and by Jean Powell Kirnan and Jennifer DeNicolis, see 12:255; Commercial Art: For a review by Gary E. Lintereur, see 10:231; Diesel Engine Repair: See 9:786 (1 reference); for a review by Charles W. Pendleton, see 8:1138; Electrical Installation: See 9:788 (1 reference) and T3:1601 (1 reference); for a review by Alan R. Suess, see 8:1139 (1 reference); Electronics Communications: See 9:789 (1 reference); for a review by Emil H. Hoch, see 8:1140; Industrial Electrician: See 9:792 (1 reference); for a review by Alan R. Suess, see 8:1141; Industrial Electronics: See 9:793 (1 reference); for a review by Emil H. Hoch, see 8:1142; Machine Drafting: See 9:794 (1 reference); for a review by Tim L. Wentling, see 8:1143; Machine Trades: For a review by Thomas S. Baldwin, see 10:239; see also 9:795 (1 reference) and 8:1144 (1 reference); Masonry: See 9:797 (1 reference); Mechanical Technology: For reviews by Bruce K. Alcorn and David O. Anderson, see 12:256; Microcomputer Repair: For reviews by Kurt F. Geisinger and David O. Herman, see 12:257; Plumbing: See 9:801 (1 reference); for a review by Richard C. Erickson, see 8:1147; Quantity Food Preparation: See 9:804 (1 reference); Scientific Data Processing: For reviews by Jim C. Fortune and Myra N. Womble, see 13:212; for a review by William M. Bart, see 11:263; Sheet Metal: See 9:807 (1 reference) and T3:1612 (1 reference); for a review by Daniel L. Householder, see 8:1150; Small Engine Repair: See 9:808 (1 reference); for a review by Kenneth E. Poucher, see 8:1151; Welding: See 9:809 (1 reference); for a review by Richard C. Erickson, see 8:1152.

[1748]

NOCTI Job Ready Assessments.

Purpose: "Designed to measure an individual's knowledge of basic processes including the identification and use of terminology and tools."

Population: Students in career and technical education programs.

Publication Dates: 1983–2005.

Scores: Duty category and total scores are reported for 85 Written and Performance tests: Accounting, Administrative Assisting, Advertising and Design, Agriculture Mechanics, Air Cooled Gas Engine Repair, Appliance Repair, Architectural Drafting, Audio-Visual Communications, Auto Diesel Mechanics, Automotive Technician, Building Construction Occupations, Building Trades Maintenance, Business and Information Processing, CAD/CAM, Cabinetmaking, Carpentry, Clothing and Textiles Management and Production, Collision Repair, Collision Repair/Refinishing Technology, Commercial Foods, Computer Networking Fundamentals, Computer Programming, Computer Repair Technology, Computer Technology, Construction Electricity, Construction Masonry–Blocklaying, Construction Masonry—Bricklaying, Construction Masonry–Stone, Cosmetology, Criminal Justice, Dental Assisting, Dental Lab Technology, Diesel Engine Mechanics, Early Childhood Care & Education, Electrical Construction, Electrical Occupations, Electronic Product Servicing, Electronic Technology, Electronics, Floriculture, Food Production Management and Services, Forestry Products and Processing, General Drafting and Design, Graphic Communications Tech, Health Assisting, Heating/Ventilation & Air Conditioning, Heating/Ventilation/Air Conditioning & Refrigeration, Heavy Equipment Maintenance and Repair, Home Health Aide, Horticulture-Land-

scaping, Horticulture—Olericulture, Hospitality Management—Food & Beverage, Hospitality Management—Lodging, Industrial Electricity, Industrial Electronics, Industrial Maintenance Mechanic, Manufacturing Technology, Marine Mechanics, Medical Assisting, Metalworking and Fabrication, Motorcycle Mechanics, Nursing Assisting, Painting and Decorating, Plumbing, Practical Nursing, Pre-Engineering/Engineering Technology, Precision Machining, Production Agriculture, Refinishing Technology, Retail Commercial Baking, Retail Trades, Robotics Technology, Technical Drafting, Television Broadcasting, Truck and Bus Mechanics, Visual Communications, Warehousing Services, Welding, Workplace Readiness.
Administration: Group.
Parts, 2: Written, Performance.
Price Data, 2005: $20 per complete online test (Written and Performance) including instructions for administration, scoring and reporting services, and certificates of completion, if applicable; $17.50 if purchased separately (Written only or Performance only); $25 per complete paper/pencil test combination; $23 if purchased separately.
Time: (180) minutes for most Written tests; (1–5) hours for Performance tests.
Comments: The National Occupational Competency Testing Institute (NOCTI) is a not-for-profit organization with a primary mission to serve all levels of the career-technical education field and to assist in developing a world-class workforce. NOCTI's assessment services include customization of assessments to better meet client needs. Assessments meet psychometric standards that utilize the psychomotor, cognitive, and affective domains of learning to assess competence. Most standardized assessments have both written (cognitive) and performance (psychomotor) components. Assessments are reviewed for revision every 2 years.
Authors: National Occupational Competency Testing Institute.
Publisher: National Occupational Competency Testing Institute/The Whitener Group.

[1749]
Noncognitive Variables and Questionnaire.
Purpose: To aid in admission decisions and advising regarding minority college student applicants.
Population: Minority college student applicants.
Publication Dates: 1978–1998.
Acronym: NCQ.
Scores, 8: Positive Self-Concept or Confidence, Realistic Self-Appraisal, Understands and Deals with Racism, Prefers Long-Range Goals to Short-Term or Immediate Needs, Availability of Strong Support Person, Successful Leadership Experience, Demonstrated Community Service, Knowledge Acquired in a Field.
Administration: Group.

Manual: No manual.
Price Data: Available from publisher.
Time: [20] minutes.
Author: William E. Sedlacek.
Publisher: University of Maryland, University Counseling Center [No reply from publisher; status unknown].
Cross References: For reviews by Gregory J. Marchant and Lisa F. Smith, see 14:259.

[1750]
Non-Reading Intelligence Tests, Levels 1–3.
Purpose: Measures "aspects of language and thinking that are not fully represented in the earlier stages of learning in reading and mathematics."
Population: Ages 6-4 to 8-3, 7-4 to 9-3, 8-4 to 10-11.
Publication Dates: 1989–1992.
Acronym: NRIT.
Scores, 5: Total score for each of four subtests (A, B, C, D), Grand Total.
Administration: Group.
Levels: 3 overlapping levels.
Price Data, 2002: £16.99 per specimen set including manual (1989, 48 pages) and one copy each of the three test forms; £11.99 per manual; £7.99 per 20 Level 1, Level 2 or Level 3 test sheets; £5.99 per marking template.
Time: (60) minutes for Levels 1 and 2; (45–60) minutes for Level 3.
Comments: Incorporates the Non-Readers Intelligence Test (9:811) as Level 1 and the Oral Verbal Intelligence Test (8:197) as Level 3, along with a newer intermediate test as Level 2.
Author: Dennis Young.
Publisher: Hodder & Stoughton Educational [England].
Cross References: For reviews by Carole M. Krauthamer and Esther E. Diamond, see 12:258; see also T4:1816 (1 reference). For a review by A. E. G. Pilliner of the Oral Verbal Intelligence Test, see 8:197; for reviews by Calvin O. Dyer and Steven I. Pfeiffer of the Non-Readers Intelligence Test, Third Edition, see 9:811.

[1751]
Nonverbal Form.
Purpose: Measures general learning ability independent of language and reading skills.
Population: Measures general learning ability independent of language and reading skills.
Publication Dates: 1946–1986.
Scores: Total score only.
Administration: Individual or group.
Price Data: Available from publisher.
Time: 10 minutes.

Comments: Previously listed as SRA Nonverbal Form.
Authors: Robert N. McMurray and Joseph E. King.
Publisher: Pearson Performance Solutions [No reply from publisher; status unknown].
Cross References: See T2:449 (12 references); for a review by W. D. Commins, see 4:318; for an excerpted review, see 3:261 (incorrectly listed under 3:260 in the first printing of The Third Mental Measurements Yearbook).

[1752]
Nonverbal Personality Questionnaire and Five-Factor Nonverbal Personality Questionnaire.

Purpose: Designed to "measure normal personality characteristics" with the use of pictures instead of words.
Population: Ages 18 and over.
Publication Date: 2004.
Administration: Group or individual.
Price Data, 2005: $20 per manual (72 pages).
Comments: Tests can be administered together and use the same manual; can be used in research, counseling, and business settings.
Authors: Sampo V. Paunonen, Douglas N. Jackson, and Michael C. Ashton (manual).
Publisher: Sigma Assessment Systems, Inc.

a) NONVERBAL PERSONALITY QUESTIONNAIRE.
Acronym: NPQ.
Scores, 17: Achievement, Affiliation, Aggression, Autonomy, Dominance, Endurance, Exhibition, Thrill-Seeking, Impulsivity, Nurturance, Order, Play, Sentience, Social Recognition, Succorance, Understanding, Deviation.
Price Data: $40 per handscorable examination kit including manual, picture booklet, 5 answer sheets, and 5 profile sheets; $50 per 10 picture booklets; $62.50 per 25 answer sheets; $40 per 25 profile sheets.
Time: (20–35) minutes.
Authors: Sampo V. Paunonen and Douglas N. Jackson.

b) FIVE-FACTOR NONVERBAL PERSONALITY QUESTIONNAIRE.
Acronym: FF-NPQ.
Scores, 5: Extraversion, Agreeableness, Conscientiousness, Neuroticism, Openness to Experience.
Price Data: $40 per examination kit including manual, picture booklet, 5 answer sheets, and 5 profile sheets; $50 per 10 picture booklets; $50 per 25 answer sheets; $32 per 25 profile sheets.
Time: (10–15) minutes.
Authors: Sampo Paunonen, Douglas N. Jackson, and Michael C. Ashton.

[1753]
Nonverbal Reasoning.

Purpose: "To measure the capacity to reason logically as indicated by solutions to pictoral problems."
Population: Individuals in a variety of occupations.
Publication Dates: 1957–1986.
Scores: Total score only.
Administration: Individual or group.
Price Data, 2002: $94 per start-up kit including 25 test booklets, score key, and interpretation and research manual; $58 per 25 test booklets (quantity discounts available); $20 per score key; $28 per interpretation and research manual.
Time: No limit (approximately 20 minutes).
Author: Raymond J. Corsini.
Publisher: Pearson Performance Solutions [No reply from publisher; status unknown].
Cross References: See T4:1817 (1 reference) and T2:414 (2 references); for reviews by James E. Kennedy and David G. Ryans, see 6:478.

[1754]
Non-Verbal Reasoning Test Series.

Purpose: Designed to assess "a pupil's ability to recognise similarities, analogies and patterns in unfamiliar designs."
Population: Ages 7.3-15.3.
Publication Date: 1993.
Scores: Total score only.
Administration: Group.
Levels, 3: Age 8 and 9; Age 10 and 11; Ages 12–14.
Price Data: Available from publisher.
Time: (40–45) minutes.
Authors: Pauline Smith and Neil Hagues.
Publisher: NFER-Nelson Publishing Co., Ltd. [England].
Cross References: For reviews by Sally Kuhlenschmidt and Julia Y. Porter, see 16:167.

[1755]
Norris Educational Achievement Test.

Purpose: Designed to assess educational ability.
Publication Dates: 1991–1992.
Acronym: NEAT.
Administration: Individual.
Forms, 2: A, B.
Price Data, 2002: $128.50 per complete kit including 10 test booklets (5 Form A, 5 Form B), administration and scoring manual (1992, 234 pages), and technical manual (1992, 86 pages); $38.50 per 25 test booklets (select Form A or B); $65 per administration and scoring manual; $49.95 per technical manual.
Authors: Janet Switzer and Christian P. Gruber (manuals).
Publisher: Western Psychological Services.

a) READINESS.
Population: Ages 4-0 to 6-11.
Scores, 4: Fine Motor Coordination, Math Concepts, Letters, Total.
Time: (10–15) minutes.
b) ACHIEVEMENT.
Population: Ages 6-0 to 17-11.
Scores, 4-6: Word Recognition, Spelling, Arithmetic, Total plus 2 supplemental scores (Oral Reading and Comprehension, Written Language).
Time: (20–30) minutes for basic battery; (30–40) minutes for entire battery.
Cross References: See T5:1802 (1 reference); for reviews by A. Harry Passow and Michael S. Trevisan, see 12:260.

[1756]
Novaco Anger Scale and Provocation Inventory.

Purpose: "Designed to assess anger as a problem of psychological functioning and physical health and to assess therapeutic change."
Population: Ages 9–84 years.
Publication Date: 2003.
Acronym: NAS-PI.
Administration: Individual or group.
Price Data, 2006: $92 per complete kit including 25 AutoScore test forms and manual (64 pages); $53 per manual; $43.50 per 25 AutoScore test forms (bulk discounts available); Computerized Components: $125 per 25-use Computer Scoring CD for Windows; $16.50 per 100 PC answer sheets.
Comments: Can be administered as a whole or as two separate parts.
Author: Raymond W. Novaco.
Publisher: Western Psychological Services.
a) THE NOVACO ANGER SCALE.
Purpose: Designed to assess "how an individual experiences anger."
Scores: Cognitive, Arousal, Behavior, NAS Total, Anger Regulation.
Time: (10-20) minutes.
b) THE PROVOCATION INVENTORY.
Purpose: Designed to identify "the kinds of situations that lead to anger."
Scores: PI Total.
Time: (5-15) minutes.

[1757]
NPF [Second Edition].

Purpose: "To assess stress tolerance and overall adjustment."
Population: Ages 16-adult.
Publication Dates: 1955-1992.
Acronym: NPF.

Scores, 3: Validity Scores (Uncertainty, Good Impression), Total Adjustment.
Administration: Group or individual.
Price Data, 2005: $30 per introductory kit including manual (1992, 10 pages), 20 test booklets, and scoring key; $26 per 20 test booklets; $10 per manual.
Time: (5-10) minutes.
Comments: Previously listed as a subtest of the Employee Attitude Series of the Job-Tests Program (T3:1219).
Author: Samuel E. Krug.
Publisher: Industrial Psychology International Ltd.
Cross References: For reviews by Charles D. Claiborn and Howard M. Knoff, see 12:261.

[1758]
NSight Aptitude/Personality Questionnaire.

Purpose: A "method for measuring a person's work-related characteristics ... [that can be used] for hiring and promoting people who are similar to those already successful in the job."
Population: Adults.
Publication Dates: 1990–2002.
Acronym: NAPQ.
Scores, 26: 3 Cognitive Characteristics (Verbal Reasoning/Comprehension, Numerical Reasoning, Word Knowledge); 1 Achievement Characteristic (Visual Perception); 19 Personality Characteristics measured along 6 subtopics: Thinking Style (Emotional Decision Maker, Analytical Thinker, Logical Thinker, Practical), Drives (Security Oriented, Cooperative, Rule Bound), Stress (Anxious, Tolerant, Apprehensive), Communication (Serious, Reserved, Assuming), Leadership (Passive, Submissive, Suspicious), Reliability (Indifferent, Changeable, Expedient); 3 Validity Scales (Lie, Faking Bad, Faking Good).
Administration: Group.
Price Data, 2002: $168 per assessment including 11-page report and telephone consultation; quantity discounts available.
Time: (120) minutes for Cognitive Characteristics Inventory; Personality Inventory untimed.
Author: Stephen Overcash.
Publisher: Directional Insight International, Inc.
Cross References: For a review by John S. Geisler, see 15:174.

[1759]
Number Test DE.

Purpose: "To provide a measure of the child's understanding of the four number processes (addition, subtraction, multiplication and division)."
Population: Ages 10-6 to 12-6.
Publication Date: 1965.
Scores: Total score only.
Administration: Group.

Price Data: Available from publisher.
Time: (50–60) minutes.
Comments: Formerly called Number Test 1.
Author: E. L. Barnard.
Publisher: NFER-Nelson Publishing Co., Ltd. [England].
Cross References: See T3:1652 (1 reference).

[1760]
Numeracy Impact Tests.

Purpose: "Designed to assess the impact of intervention strategies which are intended to raise the level of achievement of pupils who are working on the borderline between levels 3 and 4 in mathematics."
Population: Ages 10–11.
Publication Date: 2000.
Scores: Total score only.
Administration: Group.
Forms: 2 tests: A, B.
Price Data, 2003: £18.90 per 10 test booklets; £16.80 per evaluation pack.
Time: (30) minutes.
Authors: Tandi Clausen-May, Helen Claydon, and Graham Ruddock.
Publisher: NFER-Nelson Publishing Co., Ltd. [England].
Cross References: For reviews by Dixie McGinty and Georgette Yetter, see 16:168.

[1761]
Nurse Entrance Test.

Purpose: "Designed ... as a diagnostic instrument to assist nursing programs evaluate the academic and social skills of new applicants to their programs."
Population: Adult applicants to nursing schools.
Publication Dates: 1998–2001.
Acronym: NET.
Scores, 28: 7 Essential Math Skills scores (Whole Numbers, Number System Conversions, Algebra Equations, Percentage Operations, Decimal Operations, Fraction Operations, Essential Math Skills), 3 Reading Comprehension scores (Reading Rate, Reading Rate Placement, Reading Comprehension), 3 Critical Thinking Appraisal scores (Main Idea of Passage, Inferential Reading, Predicting of Outcomes), Testtaking Skills score, 2 Social Interaction Profile scores (Passive, Aggressive), 5 Stress Level Profile scores (Family, Social, Money/Time, Academic, Work Place), 6 Learning Styles (Auditory Learner, Solitary Learner, Visual Learner, Social Learner, Oral Dependent Learner, Writing Dependent Learner), Composite Percentage.
Administration: Group.
Price Data, 2002: $17 per test by computer; $10.50 per test; $8 per answer sheet; $27.50 per Study Guide.
Time: (150) minutes.
Comments: Generates a Diagnostic Report including NET Group Report, individual Student Reports;

Group Report provides group-level mean percentages and normative comparisons for the 28 scores; optional Study Guide offers testtaking strategy tips and practice tests.
Author: Michael D. Frost.
Publisher: Educational Resources, Inc.
Cross References: For reviews by Mark A. Albanese and Patricia A. Bachelor, see 16:169.

[1762]
O*NET Career Interests Inventory: Based on the "O*NET Interest Profiler" developed by the U.S. Department of Labor.

Purpose: To allow users to rank six career interest areas and relate them to specific careers.
Population: Youth and adults.
Publication Date: 2002.
Scores: 6 interest categories: Realistic, Investigative, Artistic, Social, Enterprising, Conventional.
Administration: Group or individual.
Price Data, 2006: $29.95 per 25 inventories including copy of administrator's guide (8 pages).
Time: (20–60) minutes.
Comments: Twelve-panel foldout; a compact, shorter, and less expensive version of the Department of Labor's "O*NET Interest Profiler"; based on the "O*NET Interest Profiler" developed by the U.S. Department of Labor.
Authors: JIST Publishing, Inc.
Publisher: JIST Publishing, Inc.
Cross References: For reviews by Mark Pope and Eleanor E. Sanford, see 16:172.

[1763]
O*NET Career Values Inventory: Based on the "O*NET Work Importance Locator" developed by the U.S. Department of Labor.

Purpose: To allow users to rank six work values and relate them to specific careers.
Population: Youth and adults.
Publication Date: 2002.
Scores: Achievement, Independence, Recognition, Relationships, Support, Working Conditions.
Administration: Group or individual.
Price Data, 2006: $29.95 per 25 inventories including administrator's guide (8 pages).
Time: (20–60) minutes.
Comments: Twelve-panel foldout; a compact, shorter, and less expensive version of the Department of Labor's "O*NET Work Importance Locator"; based on the "O*NET Work Importance Locator" developed by the U.S. Department of Labor.
Authors: JIST Publishing, Inc.
Publisher: JIST Publishing, Inc.
Cross References: For reviews by Kathy Green and Richard E. Harding, see 16:173.

[1764]
O*NET Interest Profiler.

Purpose: "Provides ... self-knowledge about [one's] ... vocational personality type ... [and] fosters career awareness."

Population: Age 14 and older.

Publication Dates: 1985–2000.

Acronym: IP.

Scores, 11: Interest Areas (Realistic, Investigative, Artistic, Social, Enterprising, Conventional), Job Zones (Little or No Preparation Needed, Some Preparation Needed, Medium Preparation Needed, Considerable Preparation Needed, Extensive Preparation Needed).

Administration: Group.

Price Data: Available from publisher.

Time: (20–60) minutes.

Comments: Replaces the Job Search Inventory (T5:1351); self-administered and self-scored; pencil-and-paper format; Computerized Interest Profile is administered and scored on computer; part of the O*NET Career Exploration Tools; intended for career exploration, planning, and counseling purposes only; results should not be used for employment or hiring decisions.

Author: U.S. Department of Labor, Employment and Training Administration.

Publisher: U.S. Department of Labor, Employment and Training Administration.

Cross References: For reviews by Michael B. Brown and William B. Michael, see 16:174; for reviews by Ralph O. Mueller and Sheldon Zedeck of the Job Search Inventory, see 13:163.

[1765]
O*NET Work Importance Locator.

Purpose: "Helps users identify what is important to them in a job."

Population: Ages 16 and older.

Publication Date: 2000.

Acronym: WIL.

Scores, 6: Achievement, Independence, Recognition, Relationships, Support, Working Conditions.

Administration: Group.

Price Data: Available from publisher.

Time: (15–45) minutes.

Comments: Available in paper-and-pencil format only; related Work Importance Profiler is administered and scored on computer; part of O*NET Career Exploration Tools; intended for career exploration, planning, and counseling purposes only; results should not be used for employment or hiring decisions.

Author: U.S. Department of Labor, Employment and Training Administration.

Publisher: U.S. Department of Labor, Employment and Training Administration.

Cross References: For reviews by Karl N. Kelley and William B. Michael, see 16:175.

[1766]
The OAD Survey.

Purpose: "Measures seven work-related personality traits and seven perceptions of how an individual believes he/she must behave in his/her job."

Population: Employees.

Publication Dates: 1990-2002.

Acronym: OAD.

Scores, 7: Autonomy, Extroversion, Patience, Detail, Versatility Level, Emotional Control, Creativity.

Administration: Individual and group.

Restricted Distribution: Completion of a 3-day seminar is required for a participant to administer and use the survey within their organization.

Price Data: Available from publisher.

Foreign Language Editions: Available in 10 languages.

Time: Not timed.

Comments: Web-based scoring process is available.

Author: Michael J. Gray.

Publisher: Organization Analysis and Design LLC.

[1767]
OARS Multidimensional Functional Assessment Questionnaire.

Purpose: Designed to assess individual functioning in the elderly.

Population: Ages 65 and over.

Publication Dates: 1975–1988.

Acronym: OARS MFAQ.

Scores: One of 6 ratings (Excellent, Good, Mildly Impaired, Moderately Impaired, Severely Impaired, Totally Impaired) for 5 scales: Social Resources, Economic Resources, Mental Health, Physical Health, Activities of Daily Living.

Administration: Individual.

Price Data: Price data for test materials including manual (1988, 191 pages) available from publisher.

Time: (45) minutes.

Comments: Orally administered to the subject or to someone who knows the subject well.

Author: Center for the Study of Aging and Human Development.

Publisher: Center for the Study of Aging and Human Development, Duke University Medical Center.

Cross References: See T5:1808 (3 references) and T4:1855 (9 references); for reviews by Keith S. Dobson and Bruce R. Fretz, see 9:847 (4 references); see also T3:1659 (1 reference).

[1768]
Oaster Stressors Scales.

Purpose: Designed to index an individual's level of stressors by using derived trait scales.

Population: Adults.

Publication Date: 1983.

Scores: 4 profiles: Classic/Overload Stressor Pattern of Type A Behavior, Overload Stressor Pattern, Underload Stressor Pattern/Goal-Blocked Type A, Type B Behavior Pattern.
Administration: Group.
Price Data: Available from publisher.
Time: Administration time not reported.
Author: Thomas R. Oaster.
Publisher: Thomas R. Oaster.

[1769]
Object-Oriented Programmer Analyst Staff Selector.

Purpose: To measure knowledge of object-oriented terminology and C++.
Population: Candidates for the position of object-oriented programmer analyst.
Publication Date: 1994.
Acronym: OOPS.
Scores: Total Score, Narrative Evaluation, Ranking, Recommendation.
Administration: Group.
Price Data, 2001: $350 per candidate; quantity discounts available.
Time: (120) minutes.
Comments: Scored by publisher.
Author: Bruce A. Winrow.
Publisher: Walden Personnel Performance, Inc. [Canada].
Cross References: For reviews by Dennis Doverspike and Matthew E. Lambert, see 16:170.

[1770]
Observation Ability Test for the Police Service.

Purpose: As a supplement for other testing instruments for police jobs, such as Investigator and Detective, and other jobs with high observational requirements.
Population: Candidates for police entry-level and promotional positions.
Publication Date: 1993.
Scores, 1: Observation Ability.
Administration: Group.
Restricted Distribution: Distribution restricted to civil service commissions and qualified municipal officials.
Price Data: Available from publisher.
Time: (45) minutes.
Author: McCann Associates, Inc.
Publisher: Vantage McCann Associates.

[1771]
Observation of Type Preference.

Purpose: Designed to provide a view of MBTI® type from others who work with an executive.
Population: Executives in leadership positions.
Publication Date: 1995.

Acronym: OTP.
Scores, 8: Introversion, Extraversion, Intuitive, Sensate, Thinking, Feeling, Judging, Perceiving.
Administration: Group.
Manual: Manual not available.
Price Data, 2005: $49 per complete set including questionnaires and answer sheets; $50 per report for an additional paper report.
Time: [30] minutes.
Comments: Assessment is administered online via Lore's Assessment Center; results are emailed to participant and additional paper report may be requested for additional charge; complements the Myers-Briggs Type Indicator (MBTI; 1710) and helps executives understand how others view their operating style, which is useful in coaching when executives' own operating style preferences differ significantly from how they are perceived.
Author: Lore International Institute.
Publisher: Lore International Institute.

[1772]
Observational Assessment of Temperament.

Purpose: Assesses temperamental characteristics, primarily in industrial/organizational settings.
Population: Higher level specialized and managerial personnel.
Publication Dates: 1979–1996.
Acronym: CAT.
Scores: 3 behavior factors: Extroversive/Impulsive vs. Introversive/Reserved, Emotional/Responsive vs. Nonemotional/Controlled, Self-Reliant/Individually Oriented vs. Dependent/Group Oriented.
Administration: Group.
Price Data, 2002: $54 per 25 tests (including background research, scoring iinstructions, and norms).
Time: (10) minutes.
Comments: Can be used as a self-assessment or for the assessment of the observed behavior of others; assesses the three behavior factors measured by the Temperament Comparator (2559).
Author: Melany E. Baehr.
Publisher: Pearson Performance Solutions [No reply from publisher; status unknown].
Cross References: For reviews by Stephen J. DePaola and David J. Pittenger, see 15:175.

[1773]
Observational Emotional Inventory—Revised.

Purpose: "Provides a stucture for observing and rating overt emotional behaviors which interfere with educational or vocational potential."
Population: Students and adults.
Publication Date: 1986.
Acronym: OEI-R.

Scores, 8: Impulsivity-Frustration, Anxiety, Depression-Withdrawal, Socialization, Self-Concept, Aggression, Reality Disorientation, Total Score.
Administration: Group.
Price Data, 2006: $44 per package of 25 inventories.
Time: 120 minutes each day for 5 days.
Comments: Problems checklist.
Authors: Lawrence T. McCarron and Jack G. Dial.
Publisher: McCarron-Dial Systems.
Cross References: For a review by Joseph G. Ponterotto, see 11:266.

[1774]
Occupational Aptitude Survey and Interest Schedule—Third Edition.

Purpose: To assist in career development.
Population: Grades 8–12 and adults.
Publication Date: 1983–2002.
Acronym: OASIS-3:AS.
Administration: Group or individual.
Price Data, 2006: $51 per machine score kit.
Time: (30–45) minutes per survey.
Comments: Machine scoring is available.
Author: Randall M. Parker.
Publisher: PRO-ED.
 a) APTITUDE SURVEY.
 Acronym: OASIS-3:AS.
 Scores, 6: General Ability, Verbal Aptitude, Numerical Aptitude, Spatial Aptitude, Perceptual Aptitude, Manual Dexterity.
 Price Data: $170 per complete kit including 10 student test booklets, 50 handscorable answer sheets, 50 profile sheets, and examiner's manual (2002, 45 pages); $45 per 10 student test booklets; $45 per 50 handscorable answer sheets; $28 per 50 profile sheets; $60 per examiner's manual.
 b) INTEREST SCHEDULE.
 Acronym: OASIS-3:IS.
 Scores, 12: Artistic, Scientific, Nature, Protective, Mechanical, Industrial, Business Detail, Selling, Accommodating, Humanitarian, Leading-Influencing, Physical Performing.
 Price Data: $174 per complete kit including 25 student test booklets, 50 handscorable answer sheets, 50 profile sheets, 50 scoring forms, and examiner's manual (2002, 53 pages); $40 per 25 student test booklets; $28 per 50 handscorable answer sheets; $28 per 50 profile sheets; $28 per scoring forms; $56 per examiner's manual; $56 per Interpretation Workbook.
Cross References: For reviews by Michael B. Bunch and William B. Michael, see 16:171; for reviews by Laura L. B. Barnes and Thomas E. Dinero of an earlier version of the Aptitude Survey, see 12:263 (2 references); see also T4:1862 (2 references). For reviews by Robert J. Miller and Donald G. Zytowski of an earlier

version of the Interest Schedule, see 12:264; see also T4:1863 (2 references); for reviews by Christopher Borman and Ruth G. Thomas of an earlier edition, see 20:244 (1 reference).

[1775]
Occupational Interest Inventories.

Purpose: Interest assessment to be used in career guidance, placement, selection, and counseling.
Population: Adults.
Publication Date: 1982.
Administration: Group.
Price Data: Available from publisher.
Time: (25–45) minutes per inventory.
Authors: Ruth Holdsworth and Lisa Camp (manual and user's guide).
Publisher: SHL Group plc [United Kingdom].
 a) GENERAL OCCUPATIONAL INTEREST INVENTORY.
 Population: Adults of average educational level.
 Acronym: GOII.
 Scores, 18: Medical, Welfare, Personal Services, Selling Goods, Selling Services, Supervision, Clerical, Office Equipment, Control, Leisure, Art and Design, Crafts, Plants, Animals, Transport, Construction, Electrical, Mechanical.
 b) ADVANCED OCCUPATIONAL INTEREST INVENTORY.
 Population: Adults of above average educational level.
 Acronym: AOII.
 Scores, 19: Medical, Welfare, Education, Control, Commercial, Managerial, Administration, Legal, Financial, Data Processing, Information, Media, Art and Design, Biological Sciences, Physical Sciences, Process, Mechanical, Electrical/Electronic, Construction.

[1776]
Occupational Interests Card Sort.

Purpose: To identify and rank occupational interests.
Population: Adults.
Publication Dates: 1993–2002.
Scores: Interests Summary Sheet.
Administration: Group or individual.
Price Data: Available from publisher.
Time: (20–30) minutes.
Author: Richard L. Knowdell.
Publisher: CareerTrainer.
Cross References: For reviews by Michael B. Bunch and Donald Thompson, see 13:213.

[1777]
Occupational Personality Assessment.

Purpose: Designed as a "computer simulation of a vocational assessment."

Population: Individuals seeking vocational counseling.
Publication Date: 1993.
Acronym: OPA.
Administration: Individual.
Price Data: Available from publisher.
Time: Administration time not reported.
Comments: Self-administered computerized test requires IBM or compatible Windows for administration.
Authors: Don Schaeffer and Joyce Schaeffer.
Publisher: Measurement for Human Resources.
a) INTEREST TEST.
Purpose: "Designed to assess what kinds of things a person would enjoy doing."
Scores, 3: Interest Profile, Experience Profile, How Much Interest and Experience Match.
Comments: Scores are based on Holland's RIASEC occupational codes.
b) COMMERCIAL ORIENTATION.
Purpose: Designed to measure "skills and attitudes related to commercial business."
Scores, 4: Focus on Making Money, Tactical Orientation, Reading Business Tables, Total.
c) MOTIVATION.
Purpose: Constructed to assess "motivational preferences."
Scores, 8: Personal Motives (Peaceful, Sensory, Acquisitive, Work Driven), Work Motives (Intellect, Beauty, Independent Authority, Pleasing Others).
d) MANAGEMENT.
Purpose: Designed to assess "management style."
Scores, 7: Aggressiveness, Field Independence, Toughness, Determination, Fluctuating Salary, Fluctuating Income Tolerance, Management Style Preference.
Cross References: For a review by Peter F. Merenda, see 13:214.

[1778]
Occupational Stress Inventory—Revised Edition.

Purpose: Designed as a "measure of three dimensions of occupational adjustment: occupational stress, psychological strain, and coping resources."
Population: Age 18 years and over.
Publication Dates: 1981–1998.
Acronym: OSI-R.
Scores, 14: Occupational Roles Questionnaire (Role Overload, Role Insufficiency, Role Ambiguity, Role Boundary, Responsibility, Physical Environment); Personal Strain Questionnaire (Vocational Strain, Psychological Strain, Interpersonal Strain, Physical Strain); Personal Resources Questionnaire (Recreation, Self-Care, Social Support, Rational Cognitive Coping).
Administration: Individual or group.

Price Data, 2006: $172 per introductory kit including professional manual, 25 reusable item booklets, 50 rating sheets, 50 gender-specific profile forms, and 50 generic profile forms.
Time: (30) minutes.
Comments: Self-administered.
Author: Samuel H. Osipow.
Publisher: Psychological Assessment Resources, Inc.
Cross References: For reviews by Patricia K. Freitag and Robert Wall, see 14:260; see also T5:1825 (7 references) and T4:1870 (4 references); for reviews by Mary Ann Bunda and Larry Cochran of an earlier edition, see 11:269 (1 reference).

[1779]
Occupational Test Series-Basic Skills Tests.

Purpose: Designed for the "assessment of current levels of skill in comprehension, writing and dealing with numbers."
Population: New trainees and employees.
Publication Date: 1988.
Scores, 7: Literacy (Reading Comprehension and Information-Seeking, Writing [optional], Total), Numeracy (Calculating, Approximating, Problem-Solving, Total).
Administration: Group.
Price Data: Price information available from publisher for Reference Set, reusable Literacy Newspapers, Literacy Administration pack, Numeracy Administration pack, and reusable Numeracy Question Booklets.
Time: 35(45) minutes for Literacy Test (both sections); 20(30) minutes for Reading section of Literacy Test; (35) minutes for Numeracy Test.
Authors: Pauline Smith and Chris Whetton.
Publisher: NFER-Nelson Publishing Co., Ltd. [England].
Cross References: For reviews by Phyllis Kuehn and Mark Pope, see 12:267.

[1780]
Occupational Test Series: General Ability Tests.

Purpose: "Assessing persons without previous work experience; selection for supervisory and similar management posts."
Population: Employees and candidates for employment.
Publication Date: 1988.
Scores: 4 tests: Verbal, Non-Verbal, Numerical, Spatial.
Administration: Group.
Price Data: Price information available from publisher for Reference Set, test booklet (specify Verbal, Non-Verbal, Numerical, or Spatial), Administration Pack (specify Non-Verbal, Numerical, or Spatial), and Test Taker's Guide.
Time: 25(30) minutes for Verbal; 30(35) minutes for each (Non-Verbal, Numerical, Spatial).

Comments: Tests may be administered separately.
Authors: Pauline Smith and Chris Whetton.
Publisher: NFER-Nelson Publishing Co., Ltd. [England].
Cross References: For reviews by Philip G. Benson and Michael S. Trevisan, see 11:270.

[1781]
Oetting Michaels Anchored Ratings for Therapists.

Purpose: Designed for use by supervisors to rate therapists in training.
Population: Graduate students and interns in counseling and clinical training.
Publication Date: 1989.
Acronym: OMART.
Scores: Developmental ratings on 34 dimensions of therapist effectiveness: Interviewing (Relationship with the Client, Dealing with Therapist Identification Issues, Personal Style, Exploration of Client Goals, Exploration of Issues, Exploration of Feelings, Time During the Interview, Responsiveness to Nonverbal Cues, Use of Language), Conceptualization of Therapy (Knowledge of Personality Theory, Applying Psychotherapy Theory, Knowledge of DSM III, Ability to Analyze Course of Therapy, Treatment Plans), Reaction to Supervision (Interaction During Supervision, Openness to Feedback, Confidence, Self Evaluation), Sensitivity to Client Issues (Dealing with Dependency, Dealing with Client/Therapist Sexual Feelings, Awareness of Environmental Influences, Sensitivity to Cultural Differences, Sensitivity to Sex-Role Stereotypes, Handling of Conflicts of Client/Therapist Values), Trainee Issues (Management of Personal Stress, Interference Because of Therapist's Adjustment Problems, Self-Direction of Professional Development), Other (Dealing with Ambiguity, Therapist's Attitudes to Authority, Writing Reports, General Test Interpretation, Intellective Assessment, Appropriate Handling of Sexual Material).
Administration: Individual.
Price Data: Available from publisher (license to reproduce provided for Ph.D.s or Ed.D.s).
Time: [20–30] minutes.
Comments: Completed by supervisor.
Authors: E. R. Oetting and Laurie Michaels.
Publisher: E. R. Oetting, Colorado State University.
Cross References: For a review by John S. Geisler, see 14:262.

[1782]
Oetting's Computer Anxiety Scale.

Purpose: Developed "to provide a general measure of computer anxiety."
Population: Entering college freshmen.
Publication Date: 1983.
Acronym: COMPAS.
Scores, 8: Hand Calculator, Trust, General Attitude, Data Entry, Word Processing, Business Operations, Computer Science, Total; Total score only for short form.
Administration: Group.
Price Data: License to reproduce for Ph.D.s or Ed.D.s available from publisher.
Time: [15] minutes.
Author: E. R. Oetting.
Publisher: E. R. Oetting, Colorado State University.
Cross References: For reviews by Benjamin Kleinmuntz and Steven L. Wise, see 10:245.

[1783]
Offer Self-Image Questionnaire for Adolescents, Revised.

Purpose: Designed to measure the self-image of adolescents.
Population: Ages 13–19.
Publication Dates: 1971–1992.
Acronym: OSIQ-R.
Scores, 13: Emotional Tone, Impulse Control, Mental Health, Social Functioning, Family Functioning, Vocational Attitudes, Self-Confidence, Self-Reliance, Body Image, Sexuality, Ethical Values, Idealism, Total Self-Image.
Administration: Group or individual.
Price Data, 2006: $109.50 per complete kit including manual (1992, 75 pages), 2 reusable administration booklets, and 5 WPS Test Report prepaid mail-in answer sheets; $35.75 per 10 reusable administration booklets; $49.50 per manual; $17.50 per mail-in answer sheet; $260 per 25-use WPS Test Report IBM Microcomputer scoring disk; $16.50 per 100 answer sheets for use with Microcomputer disk; $10.50 per FAX scoring.
Time: 30 minutes.
Comments: Computer scored via disk or prepaid mail-in answer sheet.
Authors: Daniel Offer (test/manual), E. Ostrov (manual), K. I. Howard (manual), and S. Dolan (manual).
Publisher: Western Psychological Services.
Cross References: See T5:1832 (17 references); for reviews by Sarah J. Allen and by Michael Furlong and Mitchell Karno, see 12:268 (9 references); see also T4:1877 (6 references); for reviews of an earlier edition by Robert Hogan and Roy P. Martin, see 9:855 (5 references); see also T3:1673 (1 reference) and 8:633 (10 references).

[1784]
Office Arithmetic Test—Form CA.

Purpose: "Evaluate the ability to perform basic computations at various levels of difficulty."
Population: Adults.

Publication Dates: 1990-2005.
Scores: Total score only.
Administration: Group.
Price Data, 2006: $12 per test administration with scoring key provided; $24.95 per manual (1997).
Time: (30) minutes.
Author: Roland T. Ramsay.
Publisher: Ramsay Corporation.
Cross References: For reviews by Frederick Bessai and Anita Tesh, see 13:255.

[1785]
Office Proficiency Assessment and Certification [OPAC System].

Purpose: "Assess[es] the knowledge, skills, and abilities of ... job candidates [and students]" "for both the corporate and educational environments."
Population: Ages 18 and over.
Publication Dates: 1994–2002.
Acronym: OPAC System.
Scores, 41: 28 office skills scores [Computer Applications (Windows, Editing/Formatting from a Rough Draft, Spreadsheet, Intermediate Excel, Database, PowerPoint), Keyboarding Skills (Keyboarding, 10-Key, Data Entry—Vendor, Data Entry—Inventory, Data Entry—Invoice), Clerical Skills (Formatting a Letter, Transcription, Alphabetic Filing, Minutes Composition, Numeric Filing, Proofreading 1, Proofreading 2, Content Proofreading Practice), Financial Skills (Bank Deposit, Bank Reconciliation, Petty Cash, Basic Math), Professional Skills (Legal and Medical Keyboarding, Legal and Medical Proofreading, Legal and Medical Terminology, Legal and Medical Transcription)]; 13 Hogan Personality Inventory scores [7 primary scale scores (Intellectance, Adjustment, Ambition, Sociability, Likeability, Prudence, School Success), 6 occupational scale scores (Service Orientation, Stress Tolerance, Reliability, Clerical Potential, Sales Potential, Managerial Potential)].
Administration: Individual or group.
Price Data, 2002: $2,295 per Single-User OPAC including CD-ROM, administrator manual (2001, 200 pages), candidate manual (2001, 92 pages), one test station packet per station, and 3 dictation cassette tapes; $4,295 per Multi-User OPAC (up to 5 test stations); $6,295 per Multi-User OPAC (up to 10 test stations, plus $200 for each test station over 10); all packages include one year OPAC Plus Customer Support offering unlimited technical support, free updates, and free upgrades; $50 per administrator manual; $30 per Test Station Pack; price information available from publisher for additional site licenses and OPAC Plus subscriptions available.
Time: Time limits for OPAC tests set by user; (15–20) minutes for Hogan Personality Inventory.
Comments: Computer administered; System requirements: Windows 95, 98, or ME (16 MB additional RAM, 32 MB recommended), Windows 2000, XKP, NT 4.0 (128 MB RAM, 256 MB recommended), 16-bit color SVGA monitor, Pentium 133 or higher; self-administered, self-scored; user selects tests to be administered; test writer provides custom test development inhouse enabling user to create additional tests in other content areas; assists user in determining cutoff scores and examining content validity; includes Hogan Personality Inventory (HPI).
Author: International Association of Administrative Professionals.
Publisher: Biddle Consulting Group Inc.

[1786]
Office Reading Test—Form G.

Purpose: "Measures the ability to read, comprehend, and answer questions based on a printed passage."
Population: Adults.
Publication Dates: 1990–1999.
Scores: Total score only.
Administration: Group.
Price Data, 2006: $12 per test administration with scoring key provided; $24.95 per manual (1999, 15 pages).
Time: (30) minutes.
Author: Roland T. Ramsay.
Publisher: Ramsay Corporation.
Cross References: For reviews by Laura L. B. Barnes and Steven J. Osterlind, see 13:256 (1 reference).

[1787]
Office Skills Achievement Test.

Purpose: Constructed to assess office skills.
Population: Office employees.
Publication Dates: 1962–1963.
Scores, 7: Business Letter, Grammar, Checking, Filing, Arithmetic, Written Directions, Total.
Administration: Group.
Price Data: Available from publisher.
Time: 20(25) minutes.
Author: P. L. Mellenbruch.
Publisher: Psychometric Affiliates.
Cross References: For reviews by Douglas G. Schultz and Paul W. Thayer, see 6:1043.

[1788]
Office Skills Assessment Battery.

Purpose: Designed to "provide objective information to aid in your hiring and placement decisions."
Population: Administrative support and clerical position applicants.
Publication Date: 1991.
Acronym: OSAB.
Administration: Individual or group.
Forms, 5: Quanta Touch Test, Quanta Software for Windows—administration and scoring, Quanta Software for Windows—scoring only, RLH Online, Mail-in Scoring.

Price Data, 2002: $18 per 25–99 each Quanta Touch Test, Quanta Software for Windows—administration and scoring (no booklets), Quanta Software for Windows—scoring only (one booklet for every coupon ordered), RLH Online, OSAB-S, OSAB-A, OSAB-S&A; volume discounts available.
Author: London House.
Publisher: Pearson Performance Solutions [No reply from publisher; status unknown].
  a) OFFICE SKILLS ASSESSMENT BATTERY—SKILLS.
  Acronym: OSAB-S.
  Scores, 9: Number Comparison, Checking, Filing, Grammar, Office Vocabulary, Spelling, Punctuation/Capitalization, Career Development, Office Skills Index.
  Time: (50–70) minutes for battery; 3(8) minutes for Sessions 1, 2, and 4; 5(10) minutes for Session 3.
  b) OFFICE SKILLS ASSESSMENT BATTERY—ATTITUDES.
  Acronym: OSAB-A.
  Scores, 12: Work Conduct, Work Accountability, Work Performance, Office Practices, Tenure, Energy Level, Stress Tolerance, Career Interests, Background/Education/Work Experience, Office Attitudes Index, Candidness, Accuracy.
  Time: [10–20] minutes.

[1789]
Office Skills Tests.

Purpose: Designed for measurement of aptitudes for twelve on-the-job skills.
Population: Applicants for clerical positions.
Publication Dates: 1977–1984.
Acronym: OST.
Scores: Total score only for each of 12 tests: Checking, Coding, Filing, Forms Completion, Grammar, Numerical Skills, Oral Directions, Punctuation, Reading Comprehension, Spelling, Typing, Vocabulary.
Administration: Individual or group.
Forms, 2: A, B for each test.
Price Data, 2002: $93 per start-up kit including 25 test booklets, scoring stencil, and examiner's manual (specify test; $126 per start-up kit including Oral Directions audiocassette; $56 per 25 test booklets (specify test; quantity discounts available); $20 per scoring stencil (specify test); $28 per examiner's manual; $37 per Oral Directions audiocassette.
Time: (3–10) minutes.
Author: Science Research Associates.
Publisher: Pearson Performance Solutions [No reply from publisher; status unknown].
Cross References: See T5:1836 (1 references); for reviews by Benjamin Shimberg and Paul W. Thayer, see 9:857.

[1790]
Official GED Practice Test.

Purpose: To help candidates determine their readiness to take the full-length GED tests.
Population: Candidates preparing for the full-length GED.
Publication Dates: 1979–1983.
Scores, 5: Writing Skills, Social Studies, Science, Reading Skills, Mathematics.
Administration: Group.
Forms, 2: A, B.
Price Data: Not available.
Foreign Language Edition: Spanish edition available.
Time: 202.5(227.5) minutes for complete test.
Comments: Suggested standards of mastery for full length GED given for each state.
Author: American Council on Education.
Publisher: Prentice Hall [No reply from publisher; status unknown].

[1791]
The Ohio Penal Classification Test.

Purpose: Developed to assess mental abilities of penal populations.
Population: Penal institutions.
Publication Dates: 1952–1954.
Acronym: OPCT.
Scores, 5: Block Counting, Digit-Symbol, Number Series, Memory Span, Total.
Administration: Group.
Price Data: Available from publisher.
Time: (25–30) minutes.
Comments: Also available for industrial use under the title Ohio Classification Test (1957).
Authors: DeWitt E. Sell, Robert W. Scollay, and Leroy N. Vernon (manual for industrial edition).
Publisher: Psychometric Affiliates.
Cross References: See T2:418 (2 references); for a review by Norman Eagle, see 5:358.

[1792]
Older Persons Counseling Needs Survey.

Purpose: To assess the needs of older persons and their desires for counseling.
Population: Ages 60 and over.
Publication Date: 1993.
Scores, 3: Needs, Desires, Total.
Administration: Group or individual.
Price Data: Available from publisher (www.mindgarden.com).
Time: (10–15) minutes.
Author: Jane E. Myers.
Publisher: Mind Garden, Inc.
Cross References: For reviews by Dennis C. Harper and Lawrence J. Ryan, see 14:264.

[1793]
Oliver Organization Description Questionnaire.

Purpose: Describes occupational organizations along four dimensions.
Population: Adults.
Publication Date: 1981.
Acronym: OODQ.
Scores, 4: H (Hierarchy), P (Professional), T (Task), G (Group).
Administration: Group.
Price Data, 2002: $30 per 50 tests with scoring sheets; $5 per scoring guide (1981, 13 pages).
Time: (15–20) minutes.
Author: John E. Oliver, Jr.
Publisher: Organizational Measurement Systems Press.
Cross References: For a review by Peter Villanova and H. John Bernardin, see 11:271.

[1794]
OMNI Personality Inventory and OMNI-IV Personality Disorder Inventory.

Purpose: "Comprehensive self-report instruments for measuring normal and abnormal personality traits."
Population: Ages 18–74 years.
Publication Date: 2001.
Administration: Individual or group.
Price Data, 2006: $172 per OMNI introductory kit including OMNI professional manual (75 pages), 25 OMNI test booklets, OMNI CD-ROM software system with on-screen manual, and 5 free on-screen administrations of the OMNI; $150 per OMNI-IV Introductory kit including OMNI professional manual (75 pages), 25 OMNI-IV test booklets, OMNI-IV CD-ROM software system with on-screen manual, and 5 free on-screen administrations of the OMNI-IV.
Comments: Paper-and-pencil and computer administration available; computer-scored only (cannot be hand-scored); CD-ROM based scoring software generates interpretive report.
Author: Armand W. Loranger.
Publisher: Psychological Assessment Resources, Inc.
a) OMNI PERSONALITY INVENTORY.
  Acronym: OMNI.
  Scores, 44: 2 Validity Scales: Variable Response Inconsistency (VRIN), Current Distress (CD); 25 Normal Scales: Aestheticism (AE), Ambition (AM), Anxiety (AN), Assertiveness (AS), Conventionality (CO), Depression (DE), Dutifulness (DU), Excitement (EC), Exhibitionism (EH), Energy (EN), Flexibility (FL), Hostility (HS), Impulsiveness (IM), Intellect (IT), Irritability (IR), Modesty (MD), Moodiness (MO), Orderliness (OR), Self-Indulgence (SI), Sincerity (SN), Sociability (SO), Self-Reliance (SR), Tolerance (TO), Trustfulness (TR), Warmth (WR); 10 Personality Disorder Scales: Paranoid (PAR), Schizoid (SCH), Schizotypal (SCT), Antisocial (ANT), Borderline (BOR), Histrionic (HIS) Narcissistic (NAR), Avoidant (AVD), Dependent (DEP), Obsessive-Compulsive (OBC); 7 Personality Factor Scales: Agreeableness (AGRE), Conscientiousness (CONC), Extraversion (EXTR), Narcissism (NARC), Neuroticism (NEUR), Openness (OPEN), Sensation-Seeking (SENS).
  Time: (60–90) minutes.
  Comments: 375-item self-report inventory; measure both normal and abnormal personality traits as specified in DSM-IV.
b) OMNI-IV PERSONALITY DISORDER INVENTORY.
  Acronym: OMNI-IV.
  Scores, 12: 2 Validity Scales: Variable Response Inconsistency (VRIN), Current Distress (CD); 10 Personality Disorder Scales: Paranoid (PAR), Schizoid (SCH), Schizotypal (SCT), Antisocial (ANT), Borderline (BOR), Histrionic (HIS), Narcissistic (NAR), Avoidant (AVD), Dependent (DEP), Obsessive-Compulsive (OBC).
  Time: (35–45) minutes.
  Comments: 210 items taken from the OMNI; assesses personality disorders as specified in DSM-IV.
Cross References: For a review by Kevin Lanning, see 15:177.

[1795]
An Online Computerized Adaptive Placement Exam in Spanish, French, German, Russian, and ESL.

Purpose: Designed to assist appropriate placement into college-level beginning Spanish, French, German, Russian, and ESL courses.
Population: College students.
Publication Dates: 1986–1996.
Acronym: WebCAPE (S, F, G, R, or E).
Scores: Total score only.
Administration: Individual.
Price Data: Available from publisher.
Time: (20–25) minutes.
Comments: Tests taken online (creativeworks.byu.edu/hrc).
Authors: Jerry W. Larson, Kim L. Smith, Don Jensen, Randall L. Jones, Marshall Murray, and Diane Strong-Krause.
Publisher: Brigham Young University, Humanities Technology and Research Support Center.
Cross References: For reviews by G. Gage Kingsbury and Steven L. Wise, see 12:364.

[1796]
Opinions About Deaf People Scale.

Purpose: To measure hearing adults' beliefs about the capabilities of deaf adults.
Population: Adults.
Publication Date: Undated.
Scores: Total score only.
Administration: Group.
Price Data: Price information available from publisher for development and validation manual (127 pages), administration guide including reproducible copy of the scale, and disk of both.
Time: Administration time not reported.
Authors: Paul James Berkay, J. Emmett Gardener, and Patricia L. Smith.
Publisher: National Clearinghouse of Rehabilitation Training Materials.
Cross References: For reviews by Jeffery P. Braden and by Vincent J. Samar and Ila Parasnis, see 14:265.

[1797]
OPQ32.

Purpose: "Designed to give information on individual styles or preferences at work."
Population: Employees and employee candidates.
Publication Dates: 1984–1999.
Acronym: OPQ32.
Scores: 32 scales: Relationships with People (Persuasive, Controlling, Outspoken, Independent Minded, Outgoing, Affiliative, Socially Confident, Modest, Democratic, Caring), Thinking Style (Data Rational, Evaluative, Behavioural, Conventional, Conceptual, Innovative, Variety Seeking, Adaptable, Forward Thinking, Detail Conscious, Conscientious, Rule Following), Feelings and Emotions (Relaxed, Worrying, Tough Minded, Optimistic, Trusting, Emotionally Controlled, Vigorous, Competitive, Achieving, Decisive).
Administration: Group.
Forms, 2: OPQ32n, OPQ32i.
Price Data: Available from publisher.
Time: Untimed; administration time not reported.
Comments: May be administered via Palm-top (PSION) Personal Questionnaire Administrator, personal computer, booklet and answer sheet, or on the internet; previous version was listed as Occupational Personality Questionnaire.
Author: SHL Group plc.
Publisher: SHL Group plc [United Kingdom].
Cross References: See T5:1822 (7 references); for a review by Thomas M. Haladyna of the earlier edition, see 11:267.

[1798]
Optometry Admission Testing Program.

Purpose: "Designed to measure general academic ability and comprehension of scientific information."
Population: Optometry school applicants.
Publication Dates: 1987-2006.
Acronym: OAT.
Scores, 8: Academic Average, Quantitative Reasoning, Reading Comprehension, Physics, Biology, General Chemistry, Organic Chemistry, Total Science.
Administration: Group.
Price Data: Available from publisher.
Time: 245(285) minutes.
Comments: Administered via computer.
Author: Optometry Admission Testing Program.
Publisher: Optometry Admission Testing Program.
Cross References: For reviews by Alan C. Bugbee, Jr. and James E. Carlson, see 12:269; for a review by Penelope Kegel-Flom of the Optometry College Admission Test, see 8:1104 (3 references).

[1799]
OQ-10.2 [A Brief Screening & Outcome Questionnaire].

Purpose: "Designed as a brief screening instrument … intended to alert the physician to the possibility that the patient was experiencing enough psychological distress to consider follow-up with other specific diagnostic tests or interviews."
Population: Ages 17-80 years.
Publication Dates: 1998-2000.
Acronym: OQ-10.2.
Scores: Total score only.
Administration: Individual or group.
Restricted Distribution: Requires licensure from American Professional Credentialing Services LLC.
Price Data, 2006: Licensing cost available from publisher; $25 per administration and scoring manual (1998, 10 pages); $25 per test.
Foreign Language Editions: English, Spanish, and French editions available.
Time: (1-5) minutes.
Authors: Michael J. Lambert, Arthur M. Finch, John Okishi, Gary M. Burlingame (manual only), Celeste McKelvey (manual only), and Curtis W. Reisinger.
Publisher: OQ Measures LLC.

[1800]
OQ-30.1 [Outcome Questionnaire for Adults].

Purpose: Designed to "measure patient progress following psychological and medical interventions."
Population: Ages 17-80 years.
Publication Dates: 2001-2003.
Acronym: OQ 30.1.
Scores: Total score only.
Administration: Individual or group.
Restricted Distribution: Requires licensure from American Professional Credentialing Services LLC.

Price Data, 2006: Licensing cost available from publisher; $25 per administration and scoring manual (2003, 18 pages); $25 per test.
Foreign Language Editions: English, Spanish, and French editions available.
Time: (2-15) minutes.
Comments: Test can be administered orally.
Authors: Michael J. Lambert, Derek R. Hatfield, David A. Vermeersch (manual only), Gary M. Burlingame, Curtis W. Resinger, and G. S. (Jeb) Brown (manual only).
Publisher: OQ Measures LLC.

[1801]
OQ-45.2 (Outcome Questionnaire).

Purpose: Designed to measure "patient progress in therapy."
Population: Adult therapy patients.
Publication Dates: 1996–2004.
Scores, 4: Symptom Distress, Interpersonal Relations, Social Role, Total.
Administration: Individual.
Price Data: Price data for manual (2004, 54 pages), questionnaire, and scoring services available from publisher.
Foreign Language Editions: Spanish, German, French, Dutch, Swedish, Norwegian, Hebrew, and Japanese editions available.
Time: (5–15) minutes.
Comments: Designed for repeated administration over the course of therapy; computer scoring available; may be administered orally.
Authors: Michael J. Lambert, Jared S. Morton, Derick Hatfield, Cory Harmon, Stacy Hamilton, Rory C. Reid, Kenichi Shumokawa, Cody Christopherson, and Gary Burlingame.
Publisher: OQ Measures LLC.
Cross References: For reviews by William E. Hanson and Brad M. Merker and by Steven I. Pfeiffer, see 16:176.

[1802]
Oral and Written Language Scales: Listening Comprehension (LC) and Oral Expression (OE) Scales.

Purpose: Assesses receptive and expressive oral language.
Population: Ages 3–21.
Publication Date: 1995.
Acronym: OWLS LC/OE.
Scores, 3: Listening Comprehension, Oral Expression, Oral Composite.
Administration: Individual.
Price Data, 2005: $229.99 per complete kit, including manual (212 pages), Listening Comprehension Easel, Oral Expression Easel, and 25 record forms;

$34.99 per 25 record forms; $34.99 per 25 response booklets; $199.99 per AGS Computer ASSIST™ for OWLS LC/OE (Windows or Macintosh).
Time: (5–15) minutes for LC; (10–25) minutes for OE.
Author: Elizabeth Carrow-Woolfolk.
Publisher: Pearson Assessments (originally published by AGS Publishing, acquired by Pearson in 2005).
Cross References: For reviews by Steve Graham and Koressa Kutsick Malcolm, see 14:266.

[1803]
Oral and Written Language Scales: Written Expression (WE) Scale.

Purpose: Constructed as an "assessment of written language."
Population: Ages 5–21.
Publication Date: 1996.
Acronym: OWLS WE.
Scores, 2: Written Expression, Language Composite (when used with OWL Listening Comprehension and Oral Expression Scales).
Administration: Individual or group.
Price Data, 2005: $124.99 per complete kit, including manual (255 pages), 25 response booklets, 25 record forms, and 1 Administration Card; $34.99 per 25 response booklets; $29.99 per 25 record forms; $79.99 per manual; $199.99 per AGS Computer AS-SIST™ for OWLS WE (Windows or Macintosh).
Time: (10–40) minutes.
Comments: May be used alone or in combination with OWLS Listening Comprehension and Oral Expression (1802).
Author: Elizabeth Carrow-Woolfolk.
Publisher: Pearson Assessments (originally published by AGS Publishing, acquired by Pearson in 2005).
Cross References: For reviews by C. Dale Carpenter and Koressa Kutsick Malcolm, see 14:267.

[1804]
Oral English/Spanish Placement Test.

Purpose: A measure of bilingualism to aid in placing children properly for efficient instruction.
Population: Ages 4–20.
Publication Dates: 1974–1976.
Acronym: OE/SPPT.
Scores: Total score and grade level equivalents.
Administration: Individual.
Tests, 2: English, Spanish.
Price Data, 2006: $20 per packet (includes manual and 1 English and 1 Spanish rating/answer sheets); permission to copy answer sheets is included.
Time: (1–2) minutes for children with little or no proficiency; (2–5) minutes for children with slightly better proficiency.
Comments: Performance rated by examiner; no reading by examinees.

Author: Steve Moreno.
Publisher: Moreno Educational Co.
Cross References: For a review by Stephen Powers, see 9:902.

[1805]
Oral-Motor/Feeding Rating Scale.

Purpose: Constructed to assess "oral-motor movement/feeding dysfunction."
Population: Ages 1 and over.
Publication Date: 1990.
Scores: Item scores only.
Administration: Individual.
Price Data, 2002: $40 per complete kit including 25 progress charts and manual (26 pages); $23 per 25 progress charts.
Time: (60) minutes or less.
Comments: Ratings by professional.
Author: Judy Michels Jelm.
Publisher: Harcourt Assessment, Inc.
Cross References: For reviews by Glen E. Ray and Donna Spiker, see 12:271.

[1806]
Oral Speech Mechanism Screening Examination, Third Edition.

Purpose: "To provide the speech-language pathologist and other professionals with a method for assessing the adequacy of the oral mechanism for speech and related functions."
Population: Age 5 through adults.
Publication Dates: 1981–2000.
Acronym: OSMSE-3.
Scores: 9 areas: Lips, Tongue, Jaw, Teeth, Hard Palate, Soft Palate, Pharynx, Breathing, Diadochokinesis.
Administration: Individual.
Price Data, 2006: $101 per complete kit; $30 per 50 scoring forms; $20 per audio cassette; $56 per examiner's manual.
Time: (10–15) minutes.
Authors: Kenneth O. St. Louis and Dennis M. Ruscello.
Publisher: PRO-ED.
Cross References: For a review by Roger L. Towne, see 14:268; see also T5:1852 (6 references) and T4:1900 (4 references); for reviews by Charles Wm. Martin and Malcolm R. McNeil of an earlier edition, see 11:272.

[1807]
Organic Dysfunction Survey Schedules.

Purpose: To assist in discovering psychological and medical factors that may contribute to treatment.
Population: Adult clients.
Publication Date: 1981.
Acronym: ODSS.

Scores: 22 survey schedules: Arthritis, Asthma, Cancer, Cardiac, Covert Thermal, Cues for Tension and Anxiety, Dysmenorrhea, Gastrointestinal, Guidelines for Cardiac Rehabilitation, Headache, Hypertension, Nutrition, Organic Dysfunction-Medical, Organic Dysfunction-Psychological, Pain, Physical Complaint, Reactions Toward Illness, Renal Failure, Seizure, Stress, Stroke, Vomiting.
Administration: Group or individual.
Manual: No manual.
Price Data, 2001: $79.95 per set of schedules.
Time: Administration time not reported.
Author: Joseph R. Cautela.
Publisher: Cambridge Center for Behavioral Studies.
Cross References: See T5:1853 (1 reference); for reviews by Julian Fabry and George N. Prigitano, see 9:909.

[1808]
Organizational and Team Culture Indicator.

Purpose: Measures unconscious archetypal stories based on an aggregate assessment and relates these to an organization's or team's values and strengths; interpretative results also gauge the relative balance of attention to building stable systems, achieving results, creating and sustaining community, and fostering learning and growth; is intended to help an organization optimize customer service, support employee satisfaction and communication, and generate strong brand identity.
Population: Adults.
Publication Dates: 2003–2004.
Acronym: OTCI.
Scores: 12 Archetypes: Creator, Everyperson, Hero, Caregiver, Innocent, Magician, Jester, Lover, Sage, Ruler, Explorer, Revolutionary.
Administration: Individual or group.
Restricted Distribution: Distribution of Professional Report is restricted to persons who have completed the publisher's or author's training course.
Price Data, 2004: $45 per manual (2004, 141 pages); $18 per Basic Report (print version) including 1 instrument, 1 self-scorable report form, and 1 Understanding Archetypes in Your Organization (2003, 49 pages); $15 per Basic Report (online version); prices for administering the OTCI in the aggregrate format using the OTCI Professional Report for intepretation available from publisher.
Time: Administration time not reported.
Comments: Results are available in either Basic or more comprehensive Professional Report Format; Basic Report is available for online or self-scored administration and Professional Report format is available only through qualified professionals.
Authors: Carol S. Pearson (test and manual) and Allen L. Hammer (manual).

Publisher: Center for Applications of Psychological Type.
Cross References: For a review by Stephen B. Johnson, see 16:178.

[1809]
Organizational Assessment Survey.
Purpose: Designed to help businesses identify problems leading to low productivity and employee dissatisfaction.
Population: Adult.
Publication Date: 1985.
Acronym: OAS.
Scores, 4: Accomplishment, Recognition, Power, Affiliation.
Administration: Group or individual.
Price Data, 2005: $49.50 per OAS Report Kit including manual, reusable test booklets, and processing of 2 reports; $15.75–$21 each per individual report; $8.50–$12 each per group report.
Time: Untimed.
Authors: Larry A. Breskamp and Martin L. Maehr.
Publisher: MetriTech, Inc.

[1810]
Organizational Behavior Profile.
Purpose: Designed to detect signs of codependency in organizations.
Population: Organizations.
Publication Date: 1993.
Acronym: OBP.
Scores, 4: Closed/Open, Denial/Collusion, Excessive Changes/Crisis Management/Confusion, Excessive Promises.
Administration: Group.
Price Data: Available from publisher.
Time: Administration time not reported.
Comments: Self-scored inventory; completed by members to measure the organization.
Authors: Jeanette Goodstein and Earnie Larsen.
Publisher: Jossey-Bass, A Wiley Company.

[1811]
Organizational Beliefs Questionnaire.
Purpose: "Intended to give concerned managers a deeper understanding of their own organization's culture."
Population: Organizations.
Publication Date: 1997.
Acronym: OBQ.
Scores, 10: Work Can Be As Much Fun As Play, Seek Constant Improvement, Accept Specific And Difficult Goals, Accept Responsibility For Your Actions, Care About One Another, Quality Is Crucially Important, Work Together To Get The Job Done, Have Concern For Measures Of Our Success, There

Must Be Hands-On Management, A Strong Set Of Shared Values And Beliefs Guide Our Actions.
Administration: Group.
Price Data: Available from publisher.
Time: Administration time not reported.
Comments: Computerized interpretive information provided by publisher, including scale summaries and individual item analyses.
Author: Marshall Sashkin.
Publisher: HRD Press, Inc.
Cross References: For reviews by Cynthia A. Larson-Daugherty and Mary Roznowski, see 14:269.

[1812]
Organizational Change-Readiness Scale.
Purpose: Constructed "to analyze the ability of an organization to manage change effectively and to plan improvement actions."
Population: Employees.
Publication Date: 1996.
Acronym: OCRS.
Scores: 5 scales: Structural Readiness, Technological Readiness, Climatic Readiness, Systemic Readiness, People Readiness.
Administration: Group.
Price Data, 1996: $6.50 per assessment inventory; $24.95 per facilitator's guide (24 pages).
Time: (20) minutes.
Comments: Redevelopment of Organizational Change-Readiness Survey.
Authors: John E. Jones and William L. Bearley.
Publisher: HRD Press, Inc.
Cross References: For reviews by Gary J. Dean and Eugene P. Sheehan, see 14:270.

[1813]
Organizational Climate Exercise II.
Purpose: Assesses the current climate within an organization/department versus how one thinks it should be.
Population: Work groups.
Publication Dates: 1991–1993.
Acronym: OCE.
Scores, 12: Actual Organizational Climate and Ideal Organizational Climate on 6 dimensions: Flexibility, Responsibility, Standards, Rewards, Clarity, Team Commitment.
Administration: Group or individual.
Price Data, 2006: $79 per complete kit including 10 questionnaires and 10 profiles and interpretive notes (11 pages); $29 per 10 Feedback Version questionnaires; $25 per Trainer's Guide (1993, 31 pages) hardcopy or free electronic version.
Foreign Language Editions: French and Spanish editions available.
Time: [30] minutes.

Comments: Self-scored instrument; publisher recommends Pulse Surveys as an alternative on-line version.
Author: Hay Group.
Publisher: Hay Group.
Cross References: For reviews by Mary Anne Bunda and Erich P. Prien, see 13:217.

[1814]
Organizational Culture Inventory.

Purpose: Designed to measure an organization's current and ideal norms and expectations.
Population: Organizational members.
Publication Dates: 1987–1989.
Acronym: OCI.
Scores: 12 culture styles: Constructive Cultures (Achievement, Self-Actualizing, Humanistic-Encouraging, Affiliative), Passive/Defensive Cultures (Approval, Conventional, Dependent, Avoidance Style), Aggressive/Defensive Cultures (Oppositional, Power, Competitive, Perfectionistic).
Administration: Group or individual.
Forms, 2: OCI Ideal, OCI Current.
Price Data: Price information available from publisher for test materials including Leader's Guide (1989, 74 pages).
Time: [15-20] minutes.
Authors: Robert A. Cooke and J. Clayton Lafferty.
Publisher: Human Synergistics International.
Cross References: See T5:1862 (2 references); for reviews by Charlene M. Alexander and Gargi Roysircar Sodowsky, see 12:272 (1 reference).

[1815]
Organizational Description Questionnaire.

Purpose: Designed to "measure how often each member of the organization perceives the culture of their unit/department/organization to be using a full range of specific leadership factors."
Population: Organizations.
Publication Date: 1992.
Acronym: ODQ.
Scores, 2: Transactional, Transformational.
Administration: Group.
Price Data: Available from publisher (www.mindgarden.com).
Time: (20–25) minutes.
Comments: Web-based administration and reporting available.
Authors: Bernard M. Bass and Bruce J. Avolio.
Publisher: Mind Garden, Inc.

[1816]
Organizational Effectiveness Inventory.

Purpose: Determines the impact of organizational, group, and job level factors on organizational effectiveness.
Population: Organization members.
Publication Date: 1997.

Acronym: OEI.
Scores: 41 Outcomes and Causal Factors: Mission and Philosophy (Articulation of Mission, Customer-Service Focus), Structures (Empowerment, Employee Involvement), Systems (Selection /Placement, Training and Development, Respect for Members, Fairness of Appraisals, Use of Rewards, Use of Punishment, Goal Clarity, Goal Challenge, Participative Goal Setting, Goal Acceptance), Technology (Autonomy, Skill Variety, Feedback, Task identity, Significance, Interdependence), Skills/Qualities (Upward Communication, Downward Communication, Communication for Learning, Interaction Facilitation, Task Facilitation, Goal Emphasis, Consideration, Personal Bases of Power, Organizational Bases of Power), Individual Outcomes—Positive Indices (Role Clarity, Motivation, Satisfaction, Intention to Stay), Individual Outcomes—Negative Indices (Role Conflict, Job Insecurity, Stress), Group Outcomes (Intra-Unit Cooperation, Inter-Unit Coordination, Departmental—Level Quality), Organizational Outcomes (Organizational—Level Quality, External Adaptability).
Administration: Individual or group.
Price Data: Available from publisher.
Time: Administration time not reported.
Author: Robert A. Cooke.
Publisher: Human Synergistics International.

[1817]
Orleans-Hanna Algebra Prognosis Test, Third Edition.

Purpose: Designed to "determine algebra readiness" and as a predictor of student success in first-year algebra.
Population: Grades 7–11.
Publication Dates: 1928–1998.
Scores: Total score only.
Administration: Group.
Price Data, 2005: $85 per 25 test booklets and manual (1998, 55 pages); $35 per 25 hand-scorable answer documents including class record; $21 per key to use with hand-scorable answer documents; $30 per 25 student report forms; $35 per 25 machine-scorable answer documents.
Time: 35(40) minutes.
Author: Gerald S. Hanna.
Publisher: Harcourt Assessment, Inc.
Cross References: See T4:1910 (3 references); for reviews by Dietmar Küchemann and Charles Secolsky of an earlier edition, see 9:912 (1 reference); see also T2:688 (11 references); for reviews by W. L. Bashaw and Cyril J. Hoyt of an earlier edition, see 7:510 (3 references); for reviews by Harold Gulliksen and Emma Spany, see 4:396 (1 reference); for a review by S. S. Wilks, see 2:1444 (4 references).

[1818]

OSOT Perceptual Evaluation.

Purpose: Designed to identify perceptual impairment in adults.

Population: Adults.

Publication Date: 1991.

Scores, 19: Scanning, Spatial Neglect, Motor Planning, Copying 2 Dimensional Designs, Copying 3 Dimensional Designs, Body Puzzle, Draw-a-Person, Right/Left Discrimination, Clock, Peg Board, Draw-a-House, Shape Recognition, Colour Recognition, Size Recognition, Figure Ground Discrimination, Proprioception, Stereognosis R, Stereognosis L, Total.

Administration: Individual.

Price Data, 2005: $859 per test kit; $37.70 per English manual (included in kit, 60 pages), $36.70 per French manual.

Time: Administration time not reported.

Authors: Pat Fisher, Marian Boys, and Claire Holzberg.

Publisher: Nelson, A Thomson Company [Canada].

Cross References: For a review by Raoula Arreola, see 12:274.

[1819]

Otis-Lennon School Ability Test®, Seventh Edition.

Purpose: "Designed to measure abstract thinking and reasoning ability."

Population: Grades K–12.

Publication Dates: 1977–1996.

Acronym: OLSAT®.

Scores, 3: Verbal, Nonverbal, Total.

Administration: Group.

Levels, 7: A, B, C, D, E, F, G.

Forms, 3: 1, 2, 3.

Price Data, 2002: $25.50 per examination kit including one test booklet and directions for administering (Form 3, Levels A-G); $95 per 25 Type 1 machine-scorable test booklets including 1 directions for administering (Form 3, Levels AD); $70 per 25 test booklets (specify reusable or hand scorable, and level); $29 per 25 Type 1 machine-scorable answer documents; $29 per 25 hand-scorable answer documents; $70 per technical manual; $14.50 per separate directions for administering; $49 per side-by-side keys for hand-scorable test booklets; $25 per stencil keys for hand-scorable answer documents; $25 per overlay keys for Type 1 machine-scorable answer documents; $6 per response keys (Form 3, specify level); $14.50 per 25 practice tests, including 1 directions for administering (Form 3, specify level); $6 per separate directions for administering practice tests; $75 per norms book (specify spring or fall); $6.50 per class records (Form 3, specify level).

Comments: Originally titled Otis-Lennon Mental Ability Test.

Authors: Arthur S. Otis and Roger T. Lennon.

Publisher: Harcourt Assessment, Inc.

a) LEVEL A.

Population: Grade K.

Time: (70) minutes over 2 sessions.

Comments: Orally administered.

b) LEVEL B.

Population: Grade 1.

Time: Same as *a* above.

Comments: Orally administered.

c) LEVEL C.

Population: Grade 2.

Time: Same as *a* above.

Comments: Partially self-administered.

d) LEVEL D.

Population: Grade 3.

Time: (60) minutes.

Comments: Self-administered.

e) LEVEL E.

Population: Grades 4–5.

Time: Same as *d* above.

Comments: Self-administered.

f) LEVEL F.

Population: Grades 6–8.

Time: Same as *d* above.

Comments: Self-administered.

g) LEVEL G.

Population: Grades 9–12.

Time: Same as *d* above.

Comments: Self-administered.

Cross References: For reviews by Lizanne DeStefano and Bert A. Goldman, see 14:271; see also T5:1866 (45 references) and T4:1913 (8 references); for reviews by Anne Anastasi and Mark E. Swerdlik of an earlier edition, see 11:274 (48 references); for reviews by Calvin O. Dyer and Thomas Oakland of an earlier edition, see 9:913 (7 references); see also T3:1754 (64 references); 8:198 (35 references), and T2:424 (10 references); for a review by John E. Milholland and excerpted reviews by Arden Grotelueschen and Arthur E. Smith of an earlier edition, see 7:370 (6 references).

[1820]

Our Class and Its Work.

Purpose: "To measure those teaching behaviors believed to contribute to student achievement in the classroom."

Population: Grades 3–12.

Publication Date: 1983.

Acronym: OCIW.

Scores, 9: Didactic Instruction, Enthusiasm, Feedback, Instructional Time, Opportunity to Learn, Pacing, Structuring Comments, Task Orientation, Total.

Administration: Group.

Price Data: Available from publisher.

Time: Administration time not reported.

Comments: Self-report instrument.
Authors: Maurice J. Eash and Hersholt C. Waxman.
Publisher: Maurice J. Eash [No reply from publisher; status unknown].
Cross References: See T4:1914 (1 reference); for reviews by James R. Barclay and F. Charles Mace, see 10:269 (1 reference).

[1821]
Outcomes: Planning, Monitoring, Evaluating.

Purpose: "A tool for monitoring student progress toward selected goals."
Population: Grades K–12.
Publication Date: 2002.
Acronym: PME.
Scores: 11 categories: Concern Description, Goals and Benchmarks, Benchmark Sealing, Social-Validation Criteria, Intervention Planning, Progress-Monitoring Procedures, Progress Chart, Progress Analysis, Evaluation of Outcomes, Next-Step Strategies, Special Education Considerations.
Administration: Individual.
Price Data, 2002: $85 per complete kit including manual (2002, 139 pages), binder, and 25 record forms; $50 per manual; $40 per 25 record forms.
Time: Untimed.
Comments: Provides a framework for documenting education professionals' problem-solving efforts; helps identify concerns, describe context of problem, rate baseline performance, operationalize goals, plan intervention, monitor and graph student progress, evaluate intervention outcomes, plan next steps.
Authors: Karen Callan Stoiber and Thomas R. Kratochwill.
Publisher: PsychCorp, A brand of Harcourt Assessment, Inc.
Cross References: For a review by Gypsy M. Denzine, see 15:178.

[1822]
Overeating Questionnaire.

Purpose: Designed to measure "key habits, thoughts, and attitudes related to obesity."
Population: Ages 9–98 years.
Publication Date: 2004.
Acronym: OQ.
Scores, 12: 2 Validity scores (Inconsistent Responding, Defensiveness), 6 Eating-Related Habits and Attitudes scores (Overeating, Undereating, Craving, Expectations About Eating, Rationalizations, Motivation to Lose Weight), 4 general Health Habits and Psychosocial Functioning scores (Health Habits, Body Image, Social Isolation, Affective Disturbance).
Administration: Group or individual.

Price Data, 2006: $93.50 per complete kit including 25 AutoScore answer sheets and manual (51 pages); $42.50 per 25 AutoScore answer sheets (bulk discounts available); $55 per manual; Computerized components: $280 per 25-use computer disk for Windows; $16.50 per 100 PC answer sheets.
Time: 20 minutes.
Comments: Written for individuals with a fourth-grade reading level and higher.
Authors: William E. O'Donnell and W. L. Warren.
Publisher: Western Psychological Services.

[1823]
P-BDQ Police Officer Background Data Questionnaire.

Purpose: Assesses backgrounds and personal characteristics of entry-level police officer candidates.
Population: Candidates for entry-level police officer positions.
Publication Dates: 1999-2000.
Acronym: P-BDQ.
Scores: 5 biodata subtypes: Background, Lifestyle, Interest, Personality, Ability.
Administration: Individual or group.
Price Data: Available from publisher.
Time: 30 minutes.
Comments: "It is recommended that this test be used in conjunction with one of IPMA-HR's other entry-level police officer tests."
Authors: International Public Management Association for Human Resources & Bruce Davey Associates.
Publisher: International Public Management Association for Human Resources (IPMA-HR).

[1824]
P-Det 1.0 and 2.0 Police Detective Tests.

Purpose: Developed "to assist law enforcement departments … in promoting qualified candidates to the detective position."
Population: Candidates for promotion to the police detective position.
Publication Dates: 2004-2006.
Acronym: P-Det 1.0, P-Det 2.0.
Scores: 3 knowledge areas: Police Investigation Procedures, Laws Related to Police Work, Concepts for Writing and Completing Reports/Records and Paperwork.
Administration: Individual or group.
Forms, 2: P-Det 1.0, P-Det 2.0.
Price Data: Available from publisher.
Time: 120 minutes per test.
Comments: P-Det 1.0 and P-Det 2.0 are comparable forms; reading lists are available to help candidates prepare for the tests.
Author: International Public Management Association for Human Resources.

Publisher: International Public Management Association for Human Resources (IPMA-HR).

[1825]
P-1SV and P-2SV Police Officer Tests.

Purpose: Developed to "assess the competencies that new police officers need to perform successfully on the job."
Population: Candidates for entry-level police officer positions.
Publication Dates: 2003-2006.
Acronym: P-1SV, P-2SV.
Scores: 5 job dimensions: Ability to Learn and Apply Police Information, Ability to Observe and Remember Details, Verbal Ability, Ability to Follow Directions, Ability to Use Judgment and Logic.
Administration: Individual or group.
Forms, 2: P-1SV, P-2SV.
Price Data: Available from publisher.
Time: 130 minutes per test.
Comments: P-1SV and P-2SV are parallel forms; no prior training or experience as a police officer is assumed of candidates taking the tests.
Author: International Public Management Association for Human Resources.
Publisher: International Public Management Association for Human Resources (IPMA-HR).

[1826]
Paced Auditory Serial Attention Test.

Purpose: "To evaluate the capacity for sustained attention and rate of information processing."
Population: Ages 9–69.
Publication Date: 1998.
Acronym: PASAT.
Scores, 16: Response Type Summary, Total Correct Responses, Total Incorrect Responses, Total No-Responses, Total Correct Strings, Longest Correct String, Suppression Failures, Suppression Failure Index, Reaction Time Summary (Average [mean] Correct Responses, Average [mean] Incorrect Responses, Average [mean] Suppression Failures, Average [mean] Total Responses, Median Correct Responses, Median Incorrect Responses, Median Suppression Failures, Median Total Responses).
Administration: Individual.
Price Data: Available from publisher.
Time: Administration time not reported.
Comments: Test is a software package and can be administered as standard, revised, abbreviated, children's, or customized version.
Author: The Psychological Corporation.
Publisher: PsychCorp, A brand of Harcourt Assessment, Inc.

[1827]
Pain Assessment Battery, Research Edition.

Purpose: Constructed as "a comprehensive assessment tool for evaluating and documenting the physical, experiential, behavioral, and psychological dimensions of chronic pain."

Population: Patients with chronic pain.
Publication Dates: 1993–1999.
Acronym: PAB-RE.
Scores: 7 tests: Pain History and Status Interview, Pain Imagery Interview, Pain Experience Scale, Pain Coping Interview—Research Edition, Stress Symptoms Checklist, Coping Style Profile, Interview Behavior Checklist.
Administration: Individual.
Price Data, 2002: $400 per test.
Time: (10–120) minutes.
Comments: Research instrument; computer-administered (DOS version only).
Authors: Bruce N. Eimer and Lyle M. Allen, III.
Publisher: CogniSyst, Inc.
Cross References: For reviews by M. Allan Cooperstein and F. Felicia Ferrara, see 14:272.

[1828]
Pain Patient Profile.

Purpose: "Designed to identify patients who are experiencing emotional distress associated with primary complaints of pain and assess the severity of distress in comparison to community and pain patient population national sample."
Population: Pain patients aged 17–76.
Publication Dates: 1992–1995.
Acronym: P-3®.
Scores, 4: Depression, Anxiety, Somatization, Validity Index.
Administration: Group.
Price Data, 2006: $55 per Q Local interpretive starter kit including manual (1995, 89 pages) and 3 answer sheets with test items to conduct and receive 3 Q Local administrations (starter kits with 10 or 30 Q Local administrations available); $63 per mail-in scoring starter kit including manual and 3 answer sheets with test items to conduct and receive 3 interpretive reports; $92.50 per 50 hand-scorable answer sheets; $10.25 per Q Local interpretive report; $13.25 per mail-in interpretive report including answer sheet with test items; $33 per manual; quantity discounts available for the reports; price information for Spanish materials available from publisher.
Foreign Language Edition: Spanish materials available.
Time: (10–15) minutes.
Authors: C. David Tollison and Jerry C. Langley.
Publisher: Pearson Assessments.
Cross References: For reviews by Gregory J. Boyle and Ronald J. Ganellen, see 14:273.

[1829]
Pair Attraction Inventory.

Purpose: "Designed to measure both complementarity and symmetry in pair relationships."
Population: College and adults.
Publication Dates: 1970–1971.

Acronym: PAI.
Scores, 7: Mother-Son, Daddy-Doll, Bitch-Nice Guy, Master-Servant, Hawks, Doves, Person-Person.
Administration: Individual.
Price Data: Available from publisher.
Time: (20-30) minutes.
Author: Everett L. Shostrom.
Publisher: EdITS/Educational and Industrial Testing Service.
Cross References: For a review by James R. Clopton, see 8:349 (10 references).

[1830]
Panic and Agoraphobia Scale.

Purpose: "Determine[s] the severity of panic disorder with or without agoraphobia and … monitor[s] treatment efficacy."
Population: Age 16 and older.
Publication Date: 1999.
Acronym: PAS.
Scores, 5: Panic Attacks, Agoraphobic Avoidance, Anticipatory Anxiety, Disability, Worries About Health.
Administration: Individual and group.
Forms, 2: Observer-rated, self-rated.
Price Data, 2006: $79.50 per kit including manual (88 pages), 50 observer-rated scales, and 50 patient questionnaires; $14.50 per 50 patient questionnaires; $12 per 50 observer-rated scales; $49 per manual; $4 per folder.
Time: (5–10) minutes for observer-rated scale.
Comments: Self-administered; computerized version of self-rated scale in preparation; compatible with DSM-IV and ICD-10 classifications.
Author: Borwin Bandelow.
Publisher: Hogrefe & Huber Publishers.
Cross References: For reviews by C. G. Bellah and by James Donnelly and Scott T. Meier, see 15:179.

[1831]
Paper and Pencil Games.

Purpose: Constructed to measure "figural, quantitative and verbal skills closely related to scholastic achievement."
Population: Pupils in their second, third and fourth years in South African school system.
Publication Date: 1996.
Acronym: PPG.
Administration: Group.
Levels, 2: 2, 3.
Price Data, 2002: R5.13 per test booklet (specify level); R3.99 per Level 2 short version test booklet; R1.14 per practice test; R39.90 per manual (90 pages) (English only); R28.50 per directions for administration (specify language).
Foreign Language Editions: Available in Afrikaans, Ndebele, Northern Sotho, Swati, Southern Sotho, Tsonga, Tswana, Venda, Xhosa, and Zulu.

Time: (150–180) minutes including 20-minute break.
Author: N. C. W. Claassen.
Publisher: Human Sciences Research Council [South Africa].
a) LEVEL 2.
Population: School years 2–3.
Scores, 5: Classification, Verbal and Quantitative Reasoning, Figure Series, Comprehension, Pattern Completion.
b) LEVEL 3.
Population: School years 3–4.
Scores, 5: Figure Series, Verbal and Quantitative Reasoning, Pattern Completion, Comprehension, Number Series.
Cross References: For a review by Gary L. Marco, see 14:274.

[1832]
PAR: Proficiency Assessment Report.

Purpose: Developed to identify proficiency in 22 abilities associated with effective management.
Population: Supervisors and managers.
Publication Date: 1989.
Scores, 24: 22 Ability Scores, 2 Style Scores.
Administration: Group or individual.
Manual: No manual.
Price Data: Available from publisher.
Time: (30) minutes.
Comments: Ratings by manager and self; administered prior to training program and then discussed in pairs.
Author: Training House, Inc.
Publisher: Training House, Inc.
Cross References: For reviews by Stephen F. Davis and S. Alvin Leung, see 12:276.

[1833]
Parallel Spelling Tests, Second Edition.

Purpose: Designed to help "chart children's progress in spelling."
Population: Ages 6 to 13 years.
Publication Dates: 1983–1998.
Scores: Total score only.
Administration: Group.
Price Data, 2002: £16.99 per test booklet/manual (1998, 40 pages).
Time: (20) minutes per test.
Comments: Teachers create tests from two banks of items: A (for ages 6 to 10) and B (for ages 9 to 13).
Author: Dennis Young.
Publisher: Hodder & Stoughton Educational [England].
Cross References: For reviews by Theresa G. Siskind and Lisa F. Smith, see 14:275; for reviews by Steven R. Shaw and Mark E. Swerdlik and by Claudia R. Wright of an earlier edition, see 12:277.

[1834]
A Parent-Adolescent Communication Inventory.

Purpose: "Designed to measure the parent's perceived communication with the adolescent."
Population: Parents and adolescents.
Publication Dates: 1968–1979.
Acronym: PACI.
Scores: Total score only.
Administration: Group.
Price Data: Price information available from publisher for parent or adolescent form and user's guide (1969, 4 pages).
Time: (20) minutes.
Author: Millard J. Bienvenu.
Publisher: Millard J. Bienvenu, Northwest Publications.
Cross References: See T5:1876 (1 reference) and T4:1929 (1 reference); for a review by Mark W. Roberts, see 9:916 (12 references); see also T3:1761 (2 references) and T2:1310 (1 reference); for a review by David B. Orr of an earlier edition, see 7:119 (3 references).

[1835]
Parent-Adolescent Communication Scale.

Purpose: Designed to assess "the views of adolescents and their parents regarding their perceptions and experience of communication with each other."
Population: Adolescents and their parents.
Publication Date: 1982.
Scores, 3: 2 subscale scores (Open Family Communication, Problems in Family Communication), Total Communication.
Administration: Individual and group.
Price Data, 2006: $30 per manual (16 pages) including scale; unlimited duplication allowed.
Time: 10-15 minutes.
Authors: Howard Barnes and David H. Olson.
Publisher: Life Innovations, Inc.
Cross References: See T5:1877 (2 references); for reviews by Allen Jack Edwards and Steven Ira Pfeiffer, see 12:278 (7 references); see also T4:1930 (3 references).

[1836]
Parent As A Teacher Inventory [Revised].

Purpose: "Intended to help mothers and fathers of preschool and primary grade children ... recognize their favorable qualities and identify realms in which further personal growth is needed."
Population: Mothers and fathers of children ages 3–9.
Publication Dates: 1984-1995.
Acronym: PAAT.
Scores, 6: Creativity, Frustration, Control, Play, Teaching/Learning, Total.

Administration: Group or individual.
Price Data, 2005: $58.95 per starter set including manual (1995, 29 pages), 20 inventory booklets/identification questionnaires, and 20 profiles (specify English or Spanish); $22.95 per 20 inventory booklets/identification questionnaires; $22 per 20 profiles; $18.85 per inventory manual; $20.90 per sample set.
Foreign Language Edition: Spanish edition available.
Time: (30–45) minutes.
Author: Robert D. Strom.
Publisher: Scholastic Testing Service, Inc.
Cross References: See T5:1878 (1 reference); for reviews by Alice J. Corkill and Ralph F. Darr, Jr., see 13:218 (4 references); see also T4:1922 (6 references); for a review by Elizabeth A. Robinson of an earlier edition, see 9:917 (1 reference).

[1837]
Parent Awareness Skills Survey.

Purpose: Constructed to identify strengths and weaknesses in a parent's sensitivity to typical child care situations.
Population: Parents involved in custody decisions.
Publication Dates: 1990–2002.
Acronym: PASS.
Scores, 18: 6 categories (Awareness of Critical Issues, Awareness of Adequate Solutions, Awareness of Communicating in Understandable Terms, Awareness of Acknowledging Feelings, Awareness of the Importance of Relevant Aspects of a Child's Past History, Awareness of Feedback Data) for each of the following conditions (Spontaneous Level, Probe Level One, Probe Level Two).
Administration: Individual.
Price Data, 2002: $189 per complete kit including 8 booklets, 8 scoring summaries, answer pen, updates, and manual and scoring guide; $99 per 8 booklets; $159 per 16 booklets; $199 per 24 booklets; $129 per manual and scoring guide.
Time: [30–60] minutes.
Comments: Orally administered.
Author: Barry Bricklin.
Publisher: Village Publishing.
Cross References: For reviews by Lisa G. Bischoff and Debra E. Cole, see 12:279.

[1838]
Parent Behavior Form.

Purpose: "Designed to assess ... dimensions of perceived parent behavior."
Population: Parents; ratings by ages 8–12, 12–18 and adults.
Publication Date: No date.
Acronym: PBF.
Scores, 15: Acceptance, Active Involvement, Egalitarianism, Cognitive Independence, Cognitive-Under-

standing, Cognitive Competence, Lax Control, Conformity, Achievement, Strict Control, Punitive Control, Hostile Control, Rejection, Inconsistent Responding, Social Desirability.
Administration: Group or individual.
Forms, 5: PBF, PBF-S, PBF Elementary, Form A, Form C-B.
Price Data: Available from publisher.
Time: Administration time not reported.
Comments: Ratings of parent behavior by their children; form for parent self-rating available.
Authors: Leonard Worell and Judith Worell.
Publisher: Judith Worell, Ph.D.
Cross References: See T5:1881 (3 references) and T4:1925 (1 reference); for reviews by JoEllen V. Carlson and Stephen Olejnik, see 11:277 (1 reference).

[1839]
Parent-Child Communication Inventory.

Purpose: "To better understand how parents and their children communicate."
Population: Children and parents.
Publication Date: 1974.
Acronym: PCCI.
Scores, 2: Total Child, Total Parent.
Administration: Group.
Manual: No manual.
Price Data: Price information available from publisher for child form, parent form, and guide.
Time: Administration time not reported.
Author: Millard J. Bienvenu.
Publisher: Millard J. Bienvenu, Northwest Publications.

[1840]
Parent-Child Relationship Inventory.

Purpose: "Assesses parents' attitudes toward parenting and toward their children."
Population: Parents of 3–15-year-old children.
Publication Date: 1994.
Acronym: PCRI.
Scores, 9: 7 content scales (Parental Support, Satisfaction With Parenting, Involvement, Communication, Limit Setting, Autonomy, Role Orientation), 2 validity indicators (Social Desirability, Inconsistency).
Administration: Group.
Price Data, 2006: $99 per complete kit including manual (57 pages) and 25 AutoScore™ answer sheets; $47 per 25 AutoScore™ answer sheets; $58 per manual; $17.50 per each mail-in computer scored and interpreted answer sheet; $329 per 25-use disk (PC with Microsoft Windows); $16.50 per 100 microcomputer answer sheets; $13 each for FAX service scoring.
Time: (15) minutes.
Comments: Self-report; microcomputer edition available.

Author: Anthony B. Gerard.
Publisher: Western Psychological Services.
Cross References: See T5:1883 (1 reference); for reviews by Roger A. Boothroyd and Gregory J. Marchant, see 13:220.

[1841]
Parent/Family Involvement Index.

Purpose: "Measure of the extent to which parents are involved in their child's special education program."
Population: Parents with children in special education programs.
Publication Dates: 1984–1985.
Acronym: P/FII.
Scores, 13: Contact with Teacher, Participation in the Special Education Process, Transportation, Observations at School, Educational Activities at Home, Attending Parent Education/Consultation Meetings, Classroom Volunteering, Involvement with Administration, Involvement in Fund Raising Activities, Involvement in Advocacy Groups, Disseminating Information, Involvement Total, Total.
Administration: Group.
Price Data: Price information available from publisher for index and mimeographed paper (1985, 21 pages).
Time: (12–15) minutes.
Comments: Ratings by teachers.
Authors: John D. Cone, David D. DeLawyer, and Vicky V. Wolfe.
Publisher: John D. Cone.
Cross References: For reviews by Marilyn Friend and Koressa Kutsick, see 10:270.

[1842]
Parent Opinion Inventory, Revised Edition.

Purpose: Designed "to provide the school personnel or administrator(s) with the opinions of parents in regard to how they believe the school is meeting the needs of students."
Population: Parents of school children.
Publication Dates: 1976–2003.
Scores: 4 subscales: Parent/School/Community Relations, Quality of the Instructional Program, Support for Student Learning, School Climate/Environment for Learning.
Administration: Group.
Parts, 2: A (Likert-scale items), B (customize up to 20 local questions).
Price Data, 2006: $25 per 25 inventories; administrator's manual may be downloaded free from publisher webpage.
Foreign Language Edition: Available in Spanish.
Time: Untimed.
Author: National Study of School Evaluation.
Publisher: National Study of School Evaluation.

[1843]
Parent Perception of Child Profile.

Purpose: Designed to elicit a parent's knowledge and understanding of a child.
Population: Parents.
Publication Dates: 1991–2002.
Acronym: PPCP.
Scores, 13: Interpersonal Relations, Daily Routine, Health History, Developmental History, School History, Fears, Communication Style, Depth of Knowledge, Scope of Knowledge, Emotional Tone, Value/Philosophy, Areas Needing Attention, Recall.
Administration: Individual.
Price Data, 2002: $189 per comprehensive starting kit including directions (1991, 11 pages), 8 Q-books, 8 recall worksheets, 8 summary forms, "answer" pen (black), "other source" pen (red), and updates; $99 per 8 Q-books with recall worksheets and summary sheets; $159 per 16 Q-books with recall worksheets and summary sheets; $199 per 24 Q-books with recall worksheets and summary sheets; $109 per directions.
Time: (60) minutes.
Comments: Self- or evaluator-administered.
Authors: Barry Bricklin and Gail Elliot.
Publisher: Village Publishing.
Cross References: For reviews by Robert W. Hiltonsmith and Mary Lou Kelley, see 12:280.

[1844]
Parent Success Indicator.

Purpose: Designed to identify "favorable qualities of parents and aspects of their behavior where education seems warranted."
Population: Parents of children ages 10 to 14.
Publication Dates: 1984–1998.
Acronym: PSI.
Scores, 6: Communication, Use of Time, Teaching, Frustration, Satisfaction, Information Needs.
Administration: Group or individual.
Forms, 2: Parent, Child.
Price Data, 2005: $73.90 per starter set including manual (1998, 58 pages), 20 parent inventory booklets, 20 child inventory booklets, and 20 profiles; $15.80 per manual; $63.35 per additional forms package including 20 parent inventory booklets, 20 child inventory booklets, and 20 profiles; $20 per sample set.
Foreign Language Edition: Spanish edition available (manual in English only).
Time: (15–20) minutes.
Comments: Parents report self-impressions; children report observations of the parent.
Authors: Robert D. Strom and Shirley K. Strom.
Publisher: Scholastic Testing Service, Inc.
Cross References: For reviews by C. Ruth Solomon Scherzer and Suzanne Young, see 16:179.

[1845]
Parent/Teacher Conference Checklist.

Purpose: Designed "to provide a self-evaluation of the teacher's role in the parent/teacher conference."
Population: Teachers.
Publication Date: 1988.
Scores: Not scored.
Administration: Individual.
Manual: No manual.
Price Data, 2002: $10 per 25 forms.
Time: [5–10] minutes.
Comments: Self-report inventory; title on checklist is Parent Conference Evaluation Form.
Author: Academic Consulting & Testing Service.
Publisher: Academic Consulting & Testing Service.

[1846]
The Parenthood Questionnaire.

Purpose: Designed to obtain information from youth concerning their opinions and knowledge of parenting and child development.
Population: Youth who are prospective parents or who may work with children in the future.
Publication Dates: 1977–1978.
Scores: 9 subsections: Opinions About Marriage and Having Children, Feelings About Parenthood, Feelings About Myself, Opinions About Children, Understanding of Children, Child Care Skills, Before Birth, Family Life Situations, Knowledge and Opinions About Sex.
Administration: Group.
Price Data: Available from publisher.
Foreign Language Edition: Spanish version available.
Time: Administration time not reported.
Comments: Intended for use in parent-training or child care training programs; manual title is Education for Parenthood: A Program, Curriculum, and Evaluation Guide.
Authors: James C. Petersen, Jean M. Baker, Larry A. Morris, and Rachel Burkholder.
Publisher: The Assessment and Development Centre.
Cross References: For reviews by Sarah J. Allen and Cynthia A. Rohrbeck, see 15:180.

[1847]
Parenting Alliance Measure.

Purpose: "Measures the strength of the perceived alliance between parents of children ages 1 to 19 years"; and "reflects the parents' ability to cooperate with each other in meeting the needs of the child."
Population: Parents of children ages 1–19 years.
Publication Dates: 1988–1999.
Acronym: PAM.
Scores: Total score only.
Administration: Group.

Price Data, 2006: $119 per introductory kit including professional manual and 50 hand-scorable test forms.
Time: (5–15) minutes.
Authors: Richard R. Abidin (test) and Timothy R. Konold (manual and test).
Publisher: Psychological Assessment Resources, Inc.
Cross References: For reviews by Cindy I. Carlson and Mary M. Clare, see 15:181.

[1848]
Parenting Satisfaction Scale™.

Purpose: Designed to assess "parents' attitudes toward parenting."
Population: Adults with dependent children.
Publication Date: 1994.
Acronym: PSS.
Scores, 3: Satisfaction with Spouse/Ex-Spouse Parenting Performance, Satisfaction with the Parent-Child Relationship, Satisfaction with Parenting Performance.
Administration: Group.
Price Data, 2002: $119 per comprehensive kit including manual (47 pages) and 25 ReadyScore® answer documents; $37 per 25 ReadyScore® answer documents; $87 per manual.
Time: (30) minutes.
Authors: John Guidubaldi and Helen K. Cleminshaw.
Publisher: PsychCorp, A brand of Harcourt Assessment, Inc.
Cross References: For reviews by Ira Stuart Katz and Janet V. Smith, see 14:276; see also T5:1888 (1 reference).

[1849]
Parenting Stress Index, Third Edition.

Purpose: To identify stressors experienced by parents that are related to dysfunctional parenting.
Population: Parents of children ages 1 month to 12 years.
Publication Dates: 1983–1995.
Acronym: PSI.
Scores, 15: Child Domain (Adaptability, Acceptability, Demandingness, Mood, Hyperactivity and Distractibility, Reinforces Parent), Parent Domain (Depression, Attachment, Restrictions of Role, Sense of Competence, Social Isolation, Relationship with Spouse, Parental Health), Life Stress, Total Score.
Administration: Group.
Forms, 2: Full Length, Short Form.
Price Data, 2006: $158 per introductory kit including manual, 10 reusable item booklets, and 25 hand-scorable answer sheet/profile forms; $595 per PSI Software Portfolio including unlimited scoring/reporting software for hand-administered forms, 10 PSI software test booklets, 10 PSI software short form test booklets, and 5 free on-screen administrations.

Time: (20–30) minutes.
Comments: PSI Software Portfolio (CD-ROM) allows for on-screen administration and scoring, or scoring of hand-entered item responses from either PSI form.
Authors: Richard R. Abidin, and PAR Staff (Software Portfolio).
Publisher: Psychological Assessment Resources, Inc.
Cross References: See T5:1889 (20 references); for reviews by Julie A. Allison and by Laura L. B. Barnes and Judy J. Oehler-Stinnett, see 13:221 (51 references); see also T4:1933 (22 references); for reviews by Frank M. Gresham and Richard A. Wantz of an earlier edition, see 10:271 (2 references).

[1850]
Parents' Evaluation of Developmental Status.

Purpose: Designed to help "identify children at risk for school problems and those with undetected developmental and behavioral disabilities"; "helps providers decide when to refer, reassure, advise, wait and see versus screen."
Population: Birth–8 years.
Publication Dates: 1997–1998.
Acronym: PEDS.
Scores, 3: Low Risk, Medium Risk, High Risk.
Administration: Individual.
Price Data: Available from publisher.
Foreign Language Edition: Spanish version available.
Time: (2–5) minutes.
Comments: Questionnaire for parents about children; can be administered as an interview or in paper and pencil form.
Author: Frances Page Glascoe.
Publisher: Ellsworth & Vandermeer Press, Ltd.
Cross References: For reviews by Lisa Bischoff and Mark W. Roberts, see 14:277.

[1851]
Parents' Observation of Study Behaviors Survey.

Purpose: To measure students' improvement in study habits and behaviors.
Population: Grades 6–13.
Publication Date: 1991.
Scores, 4: Positive Attitudes, Useful Work Habits, Efficient Learning Tools, Effective Test Taking.
Administration: Individual.
Price Data, 2001: $3 per survey.
Time: Administration time not reported.
Comments: Ratings by parents.
Author: The Cambridge Stratford Study Skills Institute.
Publisher: The Cambridge Stratford Study Skills Institute.

[1852]
Parents' Observations of Infants and Toddlers.

Purpose: "Designed to identify young children with potential problems who may be in need of further diagnostic assessment."
Population: Ages 2-36 months.
Publication Date: 2006.
Acronym: POINT.
Scores, 4: Being Healthy & Early Moving Skills, Thinking/Talking & Early Learning Skills, Feelings/ Learning About Others & Everyday Skills, Total.
Administration: Individual.
Levels, 6: Level 1 (2-6 months), Level 2 (6-9 months), Level 3 (9-12 months), Level 4 (12-18 months), Level 5 (18-24 months), Level 6 (24-36 months).
Price Data, 2006: $175 per complete basic kit including manual (2006, 112 pages), 12 record forms for each level in choice of Spanish or English, 1 set of record forms in the other language, 1 set of transparent scoring masks for each level, 1 set duplication masters of POINT Parent Conference Plan form, and the POINT Report Card in English and Spanish; $205 per complete bilingual kit including manual, 12 record forms for each level in both English and Spanish, 1 set of transparent scoring masks for each level, 1 set of duplication masters of the POINT Parent Conference Plan form and POINT Report Card in English and Spanish; $22.50 per POINT Portfolio; $30 per 12 record forms for each level in English or Spanish; $10 per 24 record forms for one level; $25 per 6 sets of transparent scoring masks; $6 per set of 3 Conference Plan and Report Card duplication masters.
Foreign Language Editions: Spanish version available; standardized in Spanish and English.
Time: (15-20) minutes.
Comments: Test to be completed by one or two parents/guardians and/or one or two caregivers.
Authors: Carol D. Mardell and Dorothea S. Goldenberg.
Publisher: Master Publishing, Inc.

[1853]
Parker Team Player Survey.

Purpose: "Helps individuals identify their primary team player styles."
Population: Employees.
Publication Date: 1991.
Acronym: PTPS.
Scores, 4: Contributor, Collaborator, Communicator, Challenger.
Administration: Group or individual.
Time: (15) minutes.
Comments: Self-scored.
Author: Glenn M. Parker.
Publisher: CPP, Inc.

a) PARKER TEAM PLAYER SURVEY.
Price Data, 2001: $9 per test booklet/manual (23 pages).
b) PTPS: STYLES OF ANOTHER PERSON.
Price Data: $6.75 per test booklet/manual (12 pages).
Cross References: For reviews by Gary J. Dean and Richard B. Stuart, see 13:222 (1 reference).

[1854]
A Partial Index of Modernization: Measurement of Attitudes Toward Morality.

Purpose: Designed to measure attitudes toward morality issues.
Population: Children and adults.
Publication Date: 1972.
Scores: Total score only.
Administration: Group.
Manual: No manual.
Price Data, 2005: $2 per scale.
Time: [8] minutes.
Comments: Supplementary article available.
Author: Panos D. Bardis.
Publisher: Donna Bardis.
Cross References: See 8:464 (1 reference).

[1855]
Participative Management Survey.

Purpose: To assess the extent to which a leader provides opportunities and support for employee involvement.
Population: Individuals involved in a leadership capacity with others.
Publication Date: 1988.
Acronym: PMS.
Scores, 5: Basic Creature Comfort, Safety, Belonging, Ego-Status, Actualization.
Administration: Group or individual.
Price Data, 2001: $8.95 per instrument (17 pages).
Time: Administration time not reported.
Author: Jay Hall.
Publisher: Teleometrics International, Inc.

[1856]
Partners in Play: Assessing Infants and Toddlers in Natural Contexts.

Purpose: Designed "for the identification and follow-up of infants and toddlers ... who might be eligible for early intervention services."
Population: Ages 1-36 months.
Publication Date: 2007.
Acronym: PIP.
Scores, 5: Neuromotor Domain, Sensory-Perceptual Domain, Cognitive Domain, Language Domain, Social-Emotional Behavior.
Administration: Individual.

Parts, 5: Initial Caregiver Interview, Caregiver Report of Child Development, Unstructured Caregiver-Child Play, Unstructured Examiner-Child Play, Structured Examiner-Child Play.
Price Data, 2006: $19.95 per book including assessment (219 pages).
Authors: Gail L. Ensher, Tasia P. Bobish, Eric F. Gardner, Carol L. Reinson, Deborah A. Bryden, and Daniel J. Foertsch.
Publisher: Thomson Delmar Learning.
   a) CAREGIVER FORMS/INTERVIEWS.
   Time: (30-45) minutes.
     1) *Initial Caregiver Interview.*
     Scores: Not scored.
     2) *Caregiver Report of Child Development.*
     Scores, 5: Neuromotor Skills, Sensory-Perceptual Skills, Cognitive Domain, Language Skills, Social-Emotional Skills.
   b) PLAY INTERACTIONS.
Comments: It is preferable to conduct all play interactions in one session; if they need to be broken up into two sessions, complete both unstructured interactions in one session, and schedule another session within 5 days to conduct the structured interaction.
   1) *Unstructured Caregiver-Child Play.*
   Scores: 5 scales, 13 subscales: Language Domain (Strategies for Communication, Communication of Needs/Intent, Understanding of Language Communication [3-36 months], Vocalized Turn-Taking [1-18 months], Joint Referencing with Caregiver), Social-Emotional Behavior (Quality of Social Interaction with Caregiver [1-36 months only], Emotional Stability), Cognitive Domain (Play Strategies Observed [5-36 months]), Sensory-Perceptual Domain (Moving/Maneuvering in the Environment [3-36 months], Skill in Eating [1-18 months], Skill in Drinking), Neuromotor Domain (Picking Up Finger Food/Self-Feeding [9-24 months], Self-Feeding with Eating Utensils [11-36 months]).
   Time: (20-30) minutes.
   2) *Unstructured Examiner-Child Play.*
   Scores: 5 scales, 15 subscales: Language Domain (Response to Common Sounds in the Environment, Intelligibility of Speech and Language [1-36 months]), Imitation Skills [5-36 months]), Social-Emotional Behavior (Quality of Interaction with Unfamiliar People, Attentiveness to Play Activities, Attention-Gaining Behaviors Observed [5-36 months]), Neuromotor Domain (Quality of Movement [3-36 months], Large Motor Milestones [5-36 months], Hand Skills Observation [3-36 months], Body Symmetry, Transition Into/Out of Various Positions [9-36 months], Protec-

tive Responses [5-12 months]), Sensory-Perceptual Domain (Response to Touch), Cognitive Domain (Purposeful Behavior in Play [7-36 months], Problem-Solving Skills [11-36 months]).
   Time: (20-30) minutes.
   3) *Structured Examiner-Child Play.*
   Scores: 5 scales, 15 subscales: Neuromotor Domain (Play with Rattles [3-12 months], Play with Balls [7-36 months]), Sensory-Perceptual Domain (Tracking, Play with Bubble Tumbler [13-36 months], Undressing/Dressing [9-36 months]), Cognitive Domain (Attention to Faces/Designs [1-18 months], Response to Hidden Objects [5-12 months], Early Understanding of Cause/Effect [5-24 months], Play with Blocks/Shape Sorter [9-36 months], Play with Pictures and Point [5-36 months], Advanced Doll Play [13-36 months], Problem-Solving [13-36 months]), Language Domain (Response to Bell, Early Social Games [3-18 months]), Social Emotional Behavior (Adaptability [11-36 months]).
   Time: (30-40) minutes.

[1857]
PASAT 2000 [Poppleton Allen Sales Aptitude Test].
Purpose: "Designed to measure those personality attributes which have a direct relevance to success in sales roles."
Population: Adults.
Publication Date: 1999.
Acronym: PASAT 2000.
Scores: 11 scales: Motivational, Emotional, Social, Adaptability, Conscientious, Emotional Stability, Social Control, Self-Assurance, Attentive Distortion, Adaptive Distortion, Social Distortion.
Administration: Group.
Price Data: Available from publisher.
Time: (20) minutes.
Authors: Steve Poppleton and Peter Jones.
Publisher: The Test Agency Limited [England] [No reply from publisher; status unknown].
Cross References: For reviews by Richard E. Harding and John Tivendell, see 15:182; for reviews by Larry Cochran and David O. Herman of an earlier edition of the Poppleton Allen Sales Aptitude Test, see 10:285.

[1858]
Pathways to Independence, Second Edition.
Purpose: Assess skills that contribute to personal and social independence.
Population: Disadvantaged school-aged children and mentally and otherwise handicapped teenagers and adults and rehabilitating brain-damaged and geriatric patients.

Publication Dates: 1982–1998.
Scores: Checklists for recording behavior in 11 areas: Eating and Drinking, Domestic Tasks, Cleanliness and Health, Clothing, Giving Information, Use of Information, Time, Money, Freedom of Movement, Use of Amenities, Leisure.
Administration: Individual.
Manual: No manual.
Price Data, 2002: £22.99 per 10 checklists, including instructions and profile sheet; £4.99 per specimen copy.
Time: Administration time not reported.
Authors: Dorothy M. Jeffree and Sally Cheseldine.
Publisher: Hodder & Stoughton Educational [England].
Cross References: See T5:1897 (1 reference) and T4:1940 (2 references).

[1859]
The Patterned Elicitation Syntax Test with Morphonemic Analysis.

Purpose: Designed to determine "whether a child's expressive grammatical skills are age appropriate."
Population: Ages 3–0 to 7–6.
Publication Dates: 1981–1993.
Acronym: PEST.
Scores, 13: Articles, Adjectives, Auxilaries/Modals/Copulas, Conjunctions, Negatives, Plurals, Possessives, Pronouns, Questions, Verbs, Subject/Verb Agreement, Embedded Elements, Total.
Administration: Individual.
Price Data: Price information available from publisher for complete kit including manual (1993, 18 pages), stimulus picture book, and 10 data form booklets.
Time: (15–20) minutes.
Comments: Previously titled The Patterned Elicitation Syntax Test.
Authors: Edna Carter Young and Joseph J. Perachio.
Publisher: Harcourt Assessment, Inc.
Cross References: For reviews by Clinton W. Bennett and Sheila R. Pratt, see 13:223 (2 references); for a review by Carolyn Peluso Atkins of an earlier edition, see 9:921.

[1860]
Paulhus Deception Scales: Balanced Inventory of Desirable Responding Version 7.

Purpose: Designed to measure the tendency to give socially desirable responses to tests.
Population: Ages 16 and older.
Publication Dates: 1998–1999.
Acronym: PDS.
Scores, 2: Impression Management, Self-Deceptive Enhancement.
Administration: Group.
Price Data, 2006: $67 per complete kit including 25 QuikScore™ forms and manual; $33 per 25 QuikScore™ forms; $47 per manual.

Time: (5–7) minutes.
Comments: Self-report; computerized version for Windows™ available on CD.
Author: Delroy L. Paulhus.
Publisher: Multi-Health Systems, Inc.
Cross References: For reviews by Kwong-Liem Karl Kwan and Romeo Vitelli, see 15:183; see T5:1898 (1 reference).

[1861]
P.C. User Aptitude Test.

Purpose: To evaluate the practical and analytical skills required for the effective use of microcomputers.
Population: Applicants for positions involving the use of microcomputers.
Publication Date: 1986.
Acronym: WMICRO.
Scores: Total Score, Narrative Evaluation, Ranking, Recommendation.
Administration: Group.
Price Data, 2001: $235 per candidate; quantity discounts available.
Foreign Language Edition: French edition available.
Time: 75 minutes.
Comments: Graded by publisher; must be proctored; previously listed as Microcomputer User Aptitude Test.
Author: Richard Label.
Publisher: Walden Personnel Performance, Inc. [Canada].
Cross References: For a review by Robert Fitzpatrick, see 11:473.

[1862]
PDD Behavior Inventory.

Purpose: Designed to assist in the assessment of children who have been diagnosed with a pervasive developmental disorder.
Population: Ages 1-6 to 12-5.
Publication Dates: 1999-2005.
Acronym: PDDBI.
Scores, 51: 29 Approach/Withdrawal Problems scores: Approach/Withdrawal Problems Composite, Receptive/Ritualistic/Pragmatic Problems Composite, Sensory/Perceptual Repetitive Approach Behaviors (Visual Behaviors, Non-Food Taste Behaviors, Touch Behaviors, Proprioceptive/Kinesthetic Behaviors, Receptive Manipulative Behaviors), Ritualism/Resistance to Change (Resistance to Change in the Environment, Resistance to Change in Schedules/Routines, Rituals), Social Pragmatic Problems (Problems with Social Approach, Social Awareness Problems, Inappropriate Reactions to the Approaches of Others), Semantic/Pragmatic Problems (Aberrant Vocal Quality When Speaking, Problems with Understanding Words, Verbal Pragmatic Deficits), Arousal Regulation Problems

(Kinesthetic Behaviors, Reduced Responsiveness, Sleep Regulation Problem [extended form only]), Specific Fears (Sadness When Away From Caregiver/Other Significant Figure/or in New Situation, Anxious When Away From Caregiver/Other Significant Figure/or in New Situation, Auditory Withdrawal Behaviors, Fears and Anxieties, Social Withdrawal Behaviors [extended form only]), Aggressiveness (Self-Directed Aggressive Behaviors, Incongruous Negative Affect, Problems When Caregiver or Other Significant Figure Returns From Work/an Outing/or Vacation, Aggressiveness Toward Others, Overall Temperament Problems [extended form only]); 22 Receptive/Expressive Social Communication Abilities scores: Receptive/Expressive Social Communication Abilities Composite, Expressive Social Communication Abilities Composite, Social Approach Behaviors (Visual Social Approach Behaviors, Positive Affect Behaviors, Gestural Approach Behaviors, Responsiveness to Social Inhibition Cues, Social Play Behaviors, Imaginative Play Behaviors, Empathy Behaviors, Social Interaction Behaviors [parent/caregiver form only], Social Imitative Behaviors), Expressive Language (Vowel Production, Consonant Production at the Beginning/Middle/and End of Words, Diphthong Production, Expressive Language Competence, Verbal Affective Tone, Pragmatic Conversational Skills), Learning/Memory/Receptive Language (General Memory Skills, Receptive Language Competence [extended form only]), Autism Composite, SOCPP-SOCAPP Discrepancy Score, SEMPP-EXPRESS Discrepancy Score.
Administration: Individual or group.
Forms, 4: Parent/Guardian or Teacher, Standard or Extended.
Price Data, 2006: $230 per complete kit including professional manual (2005, 545 pages), 25 Parent Rating forms, 25 Teacher Rating forms, 25 Parent Score Summary sheets, 25 Teacher Score Summary sheets, and 50 Profile forms; $75 per professional manual; $60 per 25 Parent Rating forms; $60 per 25 Teacher Rating forms; $15 per 25 Parent Score Summary sheets; $15 per 25 Teacher Score Summary sheets; $25 per 50 Profile forms; $225 per unlimited use PDDBI Scoring Program software CD.
Time: (30-45) minutes for Extended forms; (20-30) minutes to Standard forms.
Comments: Ratings from both parents and multiple teachers/school personnel is desirable.
Authors: Ira L. Cohen and Vicki Sudhalter.
Publisher: Psychological Assessment Resources, Inc.

[1863]
PDI Employment Inventory and PDI Customer Service Inventory.

Purpose: Designed to identify job applicants most likely to display positive employee traits.
Population: Job applicants.

Publication Dates: 1985–1993.
Administration: Group.
Price Data: Available from publisher.
Time: (30) minutes.
Comments: Paper and pencil inventories of attitudes and self-descriptions; oral instructions; computer-scored.
Authors: George E. Paajanen, Timothy L. Hansen, and Richard A. McLellan.
Publisher: Personnel Decisions, Inc.
  a) PDI EMPLOYMENT INVENTORY.
  Purpose: Designed to identify job applicants who will be likely to be productive and to stay on the job at least 3 months.
  Publication Dates: 1985–1993.
  Acronym: PDI-EI.
  Scores, 2: Performance, Tenure.
  Foreign Language and Special Editions: Foreign and bilingual editions available include American Spanish/English, French-Canadian English, Mexican Spanish, British English, and Vietnamese/English.
  b) PDI CUSTOMER SERVICE INVENTORY.
  Purpose: Designed to identify job applicants most likely to exhibit helpful and positive behaviors in interacting with customers.
  Publication Dates: 1991–1993.
  Acronym: PDI-CSI.
  Score: Customer Service Knowledge and Skills (Total).
  Foreign Language Edition: Spanish-English edition available.
Cross References: For reviews by Gordon C. Bruner II and Annie W. Ward, see 14:278.

[1864]
Peabody Developmental Motor Scales—Second Edition.

Purpose: Designed "to assess gross motor skills and fine motor skills."
Population: Birth to 72 months.
Publication Dates: 1983–2000.
Acronym: PDMS-2.
Scores, 9: Reflexes, Stationary, Locomotion, Object Manipulation, Grasping, Visual-Motor Integration, Gross Motor, Fine Motor, Total Motor.
Administration: Individual.
Price Data, 2006: $445 per complete kit including examiner's manual (2000, 234 pages), 25 profile/summary forms, 25 examiner record booklets, administration guide, motor activities program manual, black-and-white motor development chart, 25 black-and-white motor development parent charts, and manipulatives; $331 per complete test including everything in complete kit except the motor activities program; $70 per 25 examiner record booklets; $30 per 25 profile/summary forms; $81 per motor activities program; $51 per object kit; $10 per shape cards/

BLM kit; $92 per administration guide; $81 per examiner's manual; $20 per 25 black-and-white motor development parent charts; $19 per full-color parent chart; $112 per software CD (PC; Windows 95/98).
Time: (45–60) minutes.
Authors: M. Rhonda Folio and Rebecca R. Fewell.
Publisher: PRO-ED.
Cross References: For reviews by Linda K. Bunker and Peggy Kellers and by Donald Lee Stovall, see 15:184; see T5:1901 (19 references) and T4:1943 (3 references); for a review by Homer B. C. Read, Jr. of an earlier edition, see 9:922.

[1865]
Peabody Individual Achievement Test—Revised [1997 Normative Update].

Purpose: Designed to measure academic achievement.
Population: Grades K–12; ages 5-0 through 21-11.
Publication Dates: 1970–1998.
Acronym: PIAT-R/NU.
Scores, 9: General Information, Reading Recognition, Reading Comprehension, Total Reading, Mathematics, Spelling, Total Test, Written Expression, Written Language.
Administration: Individual.
Levels: 2 for Written Expression subtest (Level I: Grades K–1; Level II: Grades 2–12).
Price Data, 2006: $385.99 per complete kit including 4 easels, 50 combined test record and written expression response booklets, and NU manual (1998, 271 pages); $87.99 per 50 combined test record/written expression response booklets; $112.99 per manual; $199.99 per software package (Windows or Macintosh).
Time: (60) minutes.
Comments: This test (PIAT-R/NU [1998 Normative Update]) is the same as the PIAT-R (1989) but with new norms.
Author: Frederick C. Markwardt Jr.
Publisher: Pearson Assessments (originally published by AGS Publishing, acquired by Pearson in 2005).
Cross References: For reviews by Lawrence H. Cross and Jennifer J. Fager, see 14:279; see also T5:1902 (103 references) and T4:1944 (33 references); for reviews by Kathryn M. Benes and Bruce G. Rogers of an earlier version, see 11:280 (125 references); see also 9:923 (39 references), T4:1944 (33 references), and T3:1769 (67 references); for excerpted reviews by Alex Bannatyne and Barton B. Proger of the original edition, see 8:24 (36 references); see also T2:26 (2 references); for a review by Howard B. Lyman of the original edition, see 7:17.

[1866]
Peabody Picture Vocabulary Test—Third Edition.

Purpose: Designed to measure receptive vocabulary and can also be used as a screening test of verbal ability.

Population: Ages 2.5–90+.
Publication Dates: 1959–1997.
Acronym: PPVT-III.
Scores: Total score only.
Administration: Individual.
Forms, 2: IIIA, IIIB.
Price Data, 2005: $299.95 per complete kit, including PicturePlates for Forms IIIA and IIIB, 2 Norms Booklets (1997, 48 pages), 2 examiner's manuals (1997, 68 pages), 25 Performance Records for Form IIIA, and 25 Performance Records for Form IIIB; $174.99 per PPVT-IIIA Test Kit; $174.99 per PPVT-IIIB Test Kit; $34.99 per 25 Performance Records; $199.99 per AGS Computer ASSIST™ for the PPVT-III (Windows or Macintosh); $49.99 per Technical References to the PPVT-III.
Time: (10–15) minutes.
Comments: Orally administered, norm-referenced test; only for use with standard-English-speaking individuals.
Authors: Lloyd M. Dunn, Leota M. Dunn, Kathleen T. Williams (technical supplement), and Jing-Jen Wang (technical supplement).
Publisher: Pearson Assessments (originally published by AGS Publishing, acquired by Pearson in 2005).
Cross References: For reviews by Frederick Bessai and Orest Eugene Wasyliw, see 14:280; see also T5:1903 (585 references) and T4:1945 (426 references); for reviews by R. Steve McCallum and Elisabeth H. Wiig of an earlier edition, see 9:926 (117 references); see also T3:1771 (301 references), 8:222 (213 references), T2:516 (77 references), and 7:417 (201 references); for reviews by Howard B. Lyman and Ellen V. Piers, see 6:530 (21 references).

[1867]
Pearson-Marr Archetype Indicator.

Purpose: Designed to help people discover the stories that define the personal archetypal journey in professional and personal lives; provides a unique perspective that facilitates the understanding of life patterns and how they affect a person's choices, behaviors, and future vision.
Population: Adolescent—adult.
Publication Dates: 1989–2003.
Acronym: PMAI.
Scores: 12 archetypes: Innocent, Orphan, Warrior, Caregiver, Seeker, Lover, Destroyer, Creator, Ruler, Magician, Saga, Jester.
Administration: Group.
Price Data, 2003: $18 per Introduction to Archetypes (2003, 64 pages), questionnaire, and individualized scoring sheet; $15 per online administration; $35 per manual (2003, 103 pages).
Time: Administration time not reported.
Comments: Self-administered and self-scored; can also be administered and scored online.
Authors: Carol S. Pearson and Hugh K. Marr.

Publisher: Center for Applications of Psychological Type, Inc.

Cross References: For reviews by Carl Isenhart and William E. Martin, Jr., see 16:180.

[1868]
Pediatric Early Elementary Examination (PEEX2)

Purpose: Designed to "enable health care and other professionals to derive an empirical description of a child's development and functional neurologic status."

Population: Ages 6–9.

Publication Dates: 1983–1996.

Acronym: PEEX-2.

Scores, 6: Fine Motor/Graphomotor Functions, Attention Checkpoints, Language Functions, Gross Motor Functions, Memory Functions, Visual Processing Functions.

Administration: Individual.

Price Data, 2006: $111.30 per complete set including all materials except observer's guide and video; $18.60 per manual (1998, 65 pages); $74.05 per record form and response book; $21.75 per stimulus book; $38.10 per observer's guide; $23.55 per specimen set including observer's guide, record form, and examiner's manual; $54.30 per clinician's training video tape; quantity discounts available.

Time: (60) minutes.

Comments: Recommended for use as part of a multifaceted assessment process.

Authors: Developed under the direction of Melvin D. Levine and Adrian D. Sandler.

Publisher: Educators Publishing Service, Inc.

Cross References: For reviews by Denise M. DeZolt and Carl J. Dunst of an earlier edition, see 13:224 (1 reference); for reviews by J. Jeffrey Grill and Neil H. Schwartz of another earlier edition, see 10:272.

[1869]
Pediatric Evaluation of Disability Inventory.

Purpose: Designed as a "comprehensive clinical assessment instrument that samples key functional capabilities and performance."

Population: Ages 6 months to 7.5 years.

Publication Date: 1992.

Acronym: PEDI.

Scores, 9: Self-Care (Functional Skills, Caregiver Assistance, Modification Frequencies), Mobility (Functional Skills, Caregiver Assistance, Modification Frequencies), Social Function (Functional Skills, Caregiver Assistance, Modification Frequencies).

Administration: Individual.

Price Data: Available from publisher.

Time: (45–60) minutes.

Comments: Should be completed by the person or group of persons familiar with the child's typical performance in the domains surveyed; software program (IBM-compatible) available for data entry, scoring, and generation of individual summary score profiles.

Authors: Stephen M. Haley, Wendy J. Coster, Larry H. Ludlow, Jane T. Haltiwanger, and Peter J. Andrellos.

Publisher: Health and Disability Research Institute, Boston University.

Cross References: For a review by Billy T. Ogletree, see 14:281.

[1870]
Pediatric Examination of Educational Readiness at Middle Childhood.

Purpose: Constructed to "survey neurodevelopmental areas that may be associated with academic difficulties."

Population: Ages 9 to 15.

Publication Dates: 1984–1996.

Acronym: PEERAMID-2.

Scores: 6 major sections: Fine Motor/Graphomotor Function, Attention Checkpoints, Language Functions, Gross Motor Functions, Memory Functions, Visual Processing Functions.

Administration: Individual.

Price Data, 2006: $131.80 per complete kit including manual (1996, 80 pages), stimulus booklet, PEERAMID 2 kit, 12 record forms, and 12 response booklets; $86.40 per 12 record forms and 12 response booklets; $21.75 per stimulus booklet; $5.50 per PEERAMID 2 kit including cup and ball; $18.60 per examiner's manual (1996, 80 pages); $23.55 per specimen set including observer's guide, record form, and examiner's manual; $42.85 observer's guide; $54.30 per clinician's training video; quantity discounts available.

Time: (60) minutes.

Comments: Publisher suggests should only be used as a part of a multifaceted evaluation.

Author: Melvin D. Levine.

Publisher: Educators Publishing Service, Inc.

Cross References: For reviews by Joseph C. Kush and Robert G. Morwood, see 14:282; see also T5:1908 (1 reference); for reviews by Cathy W. Hall and Jan N. Hughes of the original edition, see 10:273.

[1871]
Pediatric Examination of Educational Readiness (PEER).

Purpose: "A combined neurodevelopmental, behavioral, and health assessment "that generates descriptive observations to be used in planning health, education, and developmentally oriented services."

Population: Ages 4-6.

Publication Dates: 1982–1988.

Acronym: PEER.

Scores: 27 or 28 rating scores: Developmental Attainment (Orientation, Gross Motor, Visual-Fine Motor, Associated Observations, Sequential, Linguistic,

Preacademic Learning), Associated Observations (Selective Attention/Activity, Processing Efficiency, Adaptation), Neuromaturation (Associated Movements, Other Minor Neurological Signs), Other Physical Findings (General Physical Examination, Neurological Examination, Auditory and Vision Testing, Dressing and Undressing [optional]), Task Analysis (Visual, Verbal, Sequential, Somesthetic, Total, Short-Term Memory, Experiential Acquisition, Total, Fine Motor, Motor Sequential, Verbal Sequential, Verbal Expressive, Total).

Administration: Individual.

Price Data, 2006: $104.15 per complete set including examiner's manual, stimulus booklet, PEER kit, and 24 record forms; $40.15 per 24 record forms; $15.55 per stimulus booklet; $19.40 per PEER kit including ball, plastic sticks, wooden blocks, key, and rubber band; $29.50 per examiner's manual (80 pages); $30.25 per specimen set including record form and examiner's manual; quantity discounts available.

Time: (40-50) minutes excluding physical examination.

Authors: Developed under the direction of Melvin D. Levine and Elizabeth A. Schneider (manual).

Publisher: Educators Publishing Service, Inc.

Cross References: See T4:1947 (1 reference).

[1872]
Pediatric Extended Examination at Three (PEET).

Purpose: "To aid in the early detection and clarification of problems with learning, attention, and behavior in three- to four-year-old children."

Population: Ages 3-4.

Publication Date: 1986.

Acronym: PEET.

Scores, 20: Developmental Attainment (Gross Motor, Language, Visual-Fine Motor, Memory, Intersensory Integration), Assessment of Behavior Rating Scale (Initial Adaptation, Reactions during Assessment), Global Language Rating Scale, Physical Findings (General Physical Examination, Neurological Examination, Auditory and Vision Testing), Task Analysis (Reception, Discrimination, Sequencing, Memory, Fine Motor Output, Gross Motor Output, Expressive Language, Instructional Output, Experiential Application).

Administration: Individual.

Price Data, 2006: $151.80 per complete kit including 24 record booklets, PEET kit (ball, target, key, wooden blocks, plastic sticks, car, crayon, doll, buttoning strip, checkers, and objects for stereognosis task), stimulus booklet (40 pages), and examiner's manual (64 pages); $32.95 per 24 record forms; $21.75 per stimulus booklet; $16.65 per examiner's manual; $81.45 per PEET kit; $17.60 per specimen set including examiner's manual and record form; quantity discounts available.

Time: Administration time not reported.

Authors: James A. Blackman, Melvin D. Levine, and Martha Markowitz.

Publisher: Educators Publishing Service, Inc.

Cross References: For reviews by William B. Michael and Hoi K. Suen, see 11:281.

[1873]
PEEK—Perceptions, Expectations, Emotions, and Knowledge About College.

Purpose: "Designed to assess prospective student's expectations about what college will be like."

Population: Prospective college students.

Publication Date: 1995.

Acronym: PEEK.

Scores, 3: Academic Expectations, Personal Expectations, Social Expectations.

Administration: Group or individual.

Price Data, 2006: $2 per publisher-scored form; $1.50 per internet form (volume discounts available).

Time: (15–25) minutes.

Comments: Self-report questionnaire; can be machine scored by publisher or locally via the internet.

Authors: Claire E. Weinstein, David R. Palmer, and Gary R. Hanson.

Publisher: H & H Publishing Co., Inc.

Cross References: For reviews by David Gillespie and Daniel L. Yazak, see 14:283.

[1874]
Peg Board.

Purpose: Developed to measure manual dexterity.

Population: Applicants for electrical and light engineering assembly jobs.

Publication Date: 1983.

Scores, 4: Preferred Hand, Non-Preferred Hand, Both Hands, Assemblies.

Administration: Group.

Price Data: Available from publisher.

Time: 3 minutes and 50 seconds (7 minutes).

Author: Educational & Industrial Test Services Ltd.

Publisher: Educational & Industrial Test Services Ltd. [England].

[1875]
Penna Assessor Adaptive Ability Tests.

Purpose: "For use in the selection, training, and career development of personnel in the UK."

Population: Junior school–adult.

Publication Dates: 1988–1990.

Administration: Individual.

Price Data: Available from publisher.

Time: [15] minutes per subtest.

Comments: All subtests are computer administered; previously listed as Selby MillSmith Adaptive Ability Tests.

Author: Selby MillSmith Ltd.

Publisher: Penna Assessment [England] [No reply from publisher; status unknown].

a) NUMERIC ABILITY TEST.

Purpose: "To assess basic numeracy and numerical skills at all levels of the organisation."

Scores: Total score only.

b) LANGUAGE ABILITY TEST.

Purpose: "Assesses the individual's range and clarity in the use of vocabulary."

Scores: Total score only.

c) ADMINISTRATIVE ABILITY TEST.

Purpose: "To assess the speed and accuracy of an individual's administrative capabilities."

Scores, 3: Numbers, Addresses, Codes.

Cross References: For reviews by Colin Cooper and Glen Fox, see 13:279.

[1876]
Penna Assessor Values Indices.

Purpose: "A measure of personal values associated with work and the working environment."

Population: Adults.

Publication Dates: 1985–1991.

Administration: Individual or group.

Editions, 2: Management Values Index, Supervisory Values Index.

Price Data: Available from publisher.

Comments: Test may be paper-and-pencil or computer administered; previously listed as Selby MillSmith Values Indices.

Author: Adrian W. Savage.

Publisher: Penna Assessment [England] [No reply from publisher: status unknown].

a) MANAGEMENT VALUES INDEX.

Purpose: "For selection, assessment and training and development at managerial and senior levels within an organisation."

Population: Managers.

Acronym: MVI.

Scores, 27: Core Scales [Achievement Values (Work Ethic, Responsibility, Risk Taking, Task Orientation, Leadership, Activity, Need for Status, Self Esteem), Expertise Values (Need for Mental Challenge, Innovation, Analysis, Attention to Detail), Consolidation Values (Need for Stability, Need for Structure, Career Development), Interpersonal Values (Sociability, Inclusion, Personal Warmth, Tactfulness, Tolerance)], [Second Order Indices (Executive Index, Stability Index, Conscientiousness Index, Expert Orientation Index, Team Orientation Index, Empathy Index, Motivational Distortion Index)].

Time: (30–45) minutes.

b) SUPERVISORY VALUES INDEX.

Purpose: "For selection, assessment and training and development at supervisory and 'A' level standard."

Scores, 26: Core Scales [Achievement Values (Work Ethic, Responsibility, Risk Taking, Task Orientation, Leadership, Activity, Need for Status, Self Esteem), Expertise Values (Need for Mental Challenge, Innovation, Analysis, Attention to Detail), Consolidation Values (Need for Stability, Need for Structure, Career Development), Interpersonal Values (Sociability, Inclusion, Personal Warmth, Tactfulness, Tolerance)], Second Order Indices (Initiative Index, Team Orientation Index, Stability Index, Enquiry Index, Conscientiousness Index, Motivational Distortion Index).

Time: (30–45) minutes.

Cross References: For reviews by Peter Miles Berger and Gerald R. Schneck, see 14:343.

[1877]
People Performance Profile.

Purpose: Designed to determine how employees perceive their organization, their work team, and themselves.

Population: Organization members.

Publication Date: 1985.

Acronym: PPP.

Scores, 20: Organizational Performance (Planning, Management Procedures, Motivational Climate, Physical Environment, Organizational Stress Factors), Work-Team Performance (Supervision, Role Clarity, Communications, Conflict Management, Problem Solving, Meeting Effectiveness, Job Satisfaction, Group Productivity), Personal Fitness (Health, Exercise, Nutrition, Alcohol and Drug Use, Interpersonal Support, Time Management, Personal Stress Management).

Administration: Group.

Price Data: Available from publisher.

Time: Administration time not reported.

Authors: Bob Crosby, John Scherer (survey, leader's guide), and Gil Crosby (work-team guide).

Publisher: Jossey-Bass, A Wiley Company.

Cross References: For reviews by Seymour Adler and Larry Cochran, see 10:274.

[1878]
The People Process.

Purpose: Designed to help determine personalities and assist in relating to people "of the same or different personality traits."

Population: Adults.

Publication Date: 1992.

Scores: 4 processes: Energy, Information, Decisions, Actions.

Administration: Group.

Price Data: Available from publisher.

Time: (120–240) minutes.

Author: Pam Hollister.

Publisher: Jossey-Bass, A Wiley Company.

[1879]
People Smarts: Behavioral Profiles.

Purpose: Designed to reveal perceptions of behavioral styles in the workplace.
Population: Adults.
Publication Date: 1994.
Scores: 4 profiles: Relater, Socializer, Thinker, Director.
Administration: Group.
Price Data: Price information available from publisher for trainer's package including trainer's guide (100 pages), 1 self-assessment, 1 observer assessment, 1 scoring matrix, 1 reminder card, 1 45-minute videocassette, and 1 People Smarts book (224 pages); participant's package including 1 workbook, 1 self-assessment, 1 scoring matrix, and 5 observer assessments; 1 self-assessment or 1 observer assessment; scoring matrix; reminder card; participant workbook; People Smarts book.
Time: Administration time not reported.
Author: Tony Alessandra.
Publisher: Jossey-Bass, A Wiley Company.

[1880]
Per-Flu-Dex Tests.

Purpose: Developed to test "a variety of abilities to cope with the needs for effective performance."
Population: High school and college and industry.
Publication Date: 1955.
Administration: Group.
Price Data: Available from publisher.
Time: 7(25) minutes; 1(5) minutes for any one test.
Author: Frank J. Holmes.
Publisher: Psychometric Affiliates.
a) PER-SYMB TEST.
Purpose: Symbol number substitution.
b) PER-VERB TEST.
Purpose: Letter perception and counting.
c) PER-NUMB TEST.
Purpose: Number counting and perception.
d) FLU-VERB TEST.
Purpose: Word completion and verbal fluency.
e) FLU-NUMB TEST.
Purpose: Arithmetic computation.
f) THE DEX-MAN SCALE.
Purpose: Manual speed of movement.
g) DEX-AIM TEST.
Purpose: Aiming accuracy and speed.
Cross References: See T2:2286 (2 references); for reviews by Andrew L. Comrey and John W. French, see 5:901.

[1881]
Perception-Of-Relationships-Test.

Purpose: Constructed to measure the degree to which a child seeks psychological "closeness" with each parent; and the types of behaviors the child has had to develop to permit or accommodate interaction with each parent.
Population: Children age 3 and over.
Publication Dates: 1964–2002.
Acronym: PORT.
Scores: No scores.
Administration: Individual.
Price Data, 2002: $199 per complete kit including 8 test/scoring booklets, handbook (1990, 179 pages); pen, eraser, and updates; $99 per 8 test/scoring booklets; $159 per 16 test/scoring booklets; $199 per 24 test/scoring booklets; $149 per handbook; $198 per IBM computer scoring profile (3.5-inch disk).
Time: [30] minutes.
Comments: Projective test for use in custody decisions.
Author: Barry Bricklin.
Publisher: Village Publishing.
Cross References: For reviews by Janet F. Carlson and Judith Conger, see 12:283.

[1882]
Perceptions of Parental Role Scales.

Purpose: "To measure perceived parental role responsibilities."
Population: Parents.
Publication Date: 1982.
Acronym: PPRS.
Scores: 13 areas in 3 domains: Teaching the Child (Cognitive Development, Social Skills, Handling of Emotions, Physical Health, Norms and Social Values, Personal Hygiene, Survival Skills), Meeting the Child's Basic Needs (Health Care, Food/Clothing/Shelter, Child's Emotional Needs, Child Care), Family as an Interface With Society (Social Institutions, the Family Unit Itself).
Administration: Group.
Price Data: Available from publisher.
Time: (15) minutes.
Comments: Self-administered.
Authors: Lucia A. Gilbert and Gary R. Hanson.
Publisher: Lucia A. Gilbert, Ph.D.
Cross References: For reviews by Cindy I. Carlson and Mark W. Roberts, see 11:282.

[1883]
Perceptual-Motor Assessment for Children & Emotional/Behavioral Screening Program.

Purpose: "Designed for screening visual, auditory and haptic perception; fine and gross motor abilities; and perceptual memory in children."
Population: Ages 4-0-15-11.
Publication Date: 1988.
Acronym: P-MAC/ESP.
Scores, 12: 3 scores for the Perceptual Memory Task-Abbreviated (PMT-A): Spatial Relations, Audi-

tory-Visual Colors Recognition, Auditory-Visual Colors Sequence; 3 scores for Haptic Visual Discrimination Test-Abbreviated (HVDT-A): Shape, Size, Texture; 6 scores for McCarron Assessment of Neuromuscular Development-Abbreviated (MAND-A): Beads in Box, Finger Tapping, Nut and Bolt, Hand Strength, Standing on One Foot, Finger-Nose-Finger.
Subtests, 3: PMT-A, HVDT-A, MAND-A.
Administration: Individual.
Price Data, 2006: $2,075 per P-MAC including P-MAC battery, computer program, manual (219 pages), 25 Protocol/Data Entry Forms, and 5 GEM volumes; $250 per ESP including 25 Behavioral Checklists for Students, computer program, and manual; $2,075 per combined P-MAC & ESP; $46.75 per each of 5 GEM volumes; $44.50 per 25 P-MAC Protocol/Data Entry Forms; $32 per 25 Behavioral Checklists for Students; $65 per P-MAC manual; $26.50 per separate ESP manual.
Time: (45) minutes.
Comments: P-MAC battery consists of selected subtests from the MAND, HVDT, and PMT; 5 age-specific volumes of Guides for Educational Management (GEM) that provide expanded recommendations and functional implications; computer software included; Behavioral Checklist for Students for ESP program.
Authors: Jack G. Dial (P-MAC and ESP), Lawrence McCarron (P-MAC), and Garry Amann (P-MAC and ESP).
Publisher: McCarron-Dial Systems.
Cross References: See T5:1919 (1 reference); for reviews by Barbara A. Rothlisberg and E. W. Testut, see 12:284.

[1884]
Perceptual Speed (Identical Forms).

Purpose: Designed to assess "the ability to rapidly compare visual configurations and identify two figures as similar or identical or to identify some particular detail that is buried in distracting material."
Population: Visual inspectors, proofreaders, clerical personnel.
Publication Dates: 1984–1996.
Scores: Total score only.
Administration: Group or individual.
Price Data, 2002: $51 per 25 tests; $28 per interpretation and research manual (1959, 10 pages); $20 per score key.
Time: 5 minutes.
Comments: Primarily used in industry and governmental organizations (norms provided to these personnel).
Authors: L. L. Thurstone and T. E. Jeffrey.
Publisher: Pearson Performance Solutions [No reply from publisher; status unknown].
Cross References: For reviews by John W. Fleenor and Paul M. Mastrangelo, see 15:185.

[1885]
[Performance Review Forms].

Purpose: To provide a format to accomplish an appraisal of managerial performance in relation to accountability and personal characteristics.
Population: Employees, managers.
Publication Dates: 1960-1961.
Scores: Ratings in 3 areas: Accountability, Performance, Developmental Program.
Administration: Individual.
Author: Seymour Levy.
Publisher: Martin M. Bruce, Ph.D.
a) COUNSELING INTERVIEW SUMMARY.
Purpose: For summarizing a performance review interview.
Population: Employees, managers.
Publication Date: 1960.
Forms, 2: Employee, Management.
Price Data, 2006: $6.25 per employee forms; $3.50 per employee specimen set; $8.25 per management forms; $4.95 per management specimen set; $9.75 per guide to counseling.
Time: (10) minutes.
b) MANAGERIAL PERFORMANCE REVIEW.
Purpose: Ratings by supervisors preparatory to performance review interview.
Population: Managers.
Publication Date: 1961.
Price Data: $52 per forms; $27 per specimen set.
Time: (40-50) minutes.

[1886]
Performance Series.

Purpose: A computer-adaptive assessment of student performance and progress, modified to measure the different academic objectives of individual state standards.
Population: Grades 2-10.
Publication Dates: 2002-2006.
Scores, 21: Reading (Vocabulary, Fiction, Nonfiction, Long Passages, Total), Mathematics (Number & Operations, Algebra, Geometry, Measurement, Data Analysis & Probability, Total), Language Arts (Capitalization, Parts of Speech, Punctuation, Sentence Structure, Total), Science (Ecology, Science Processes, Living Things, Total), Total.
Administration: Group.
Price Data, 2006: $12-$15 per student annual subscription cost.
Time: (60) minutes per subject area.
Comments: Web-administered, computer-adaptive instrument for Windows or Macintosh platforms; bookmarking allows students to take assessments over more than one test period.
Author: Scantron Corporation.
Publisher: Scantron Corporation.

[1887]
Performance Skills Leader.
Purpose: Designed to identify "leadership strengths and developmental needs."
Population: Employees in leadership positions.
Publication Date: 1996.
Acronym: PS Leader.
Scores, 24: Strategic Focus (Vision, Business Knowledge, Change Management), Business Focus (Quality Centered, Planning and Executing, Budgeting, Technology Management and Application), Work Force Focus (Coaching, Team Leadership, Creativity and Innovation, Commitment to Work Force Diversity, Human Resource Management), Interpersonal Focus (Interpersonal Skills, Oral Communication, Influencing, Writing, Conflict Resolution and Negotiation), Personal Focus (Self-Development, Action Orientation, Results Focus, Flexibility, Problem Solving and Decision Making, Role Modeling, Time Management).
Administration: Group.
Price Data: Available from publisher.
Time: Administration time not reported.
Author: Human Technology, Inc.
Publisher: HRD Press, Inc.
Cross References: For reviews by Trenton R. Ferro and George C. Thornton III, see 14:284.

[1888]
Personal Achievement Formula.
Purpose: Constructed to identify an individual's managerial strategy and his/her view of the organizational culture.
Population: Managers.
Publication Dates: 1976–1997.
Scores: 4 scores (Personal Achievement Formula, Organizational Culture, Group Achievement Formula, Group Assessment of Organization) each falling in one of 4 domains (Human Relations Specialist, Low Achiever, Average Achiever, High Achiever).
Administration: Group.
Price Data, 2001: $8.95 per instrument.
Time: Administration time not reported.
Author: Jay Hall.
Publisher: Teleometrics International, Inc.

[1889]
Personal Assessment of Intimacy in Relationships [Revised].
Purpose: "Measures the expected (ideal) versus the realized (perceived) degree of intimacy" in a relationship.
Population: Couples.
Publication Dates: 1981-2005.
Acronym: PAIR.
Scores: 6 types of intimacy: Emotional, Social, Sexual, Intellectual, Recreational, Conventionality.

Administration: Individual, couples, or group.
Price Data, 2006: $50 for complete package and unlimited duplication; package includes item booklets, answer sheets, scoring template, couple feedback sheet, and procedure manual (14 pages).
Time: (20–30) minutes.
Comments: Self-report, hand-scored measure; forms may be photocopied after obtaining permission by submitting Abstract on Proposed Study.
Authors: David H. Olson and Mark T. Schaefer.
Publisher: Life Innovations, Inc.
Cross References: See T5:1927 (9 references) and T4:1966 (2 references); for a review by Richard M. Wolf of an earlier edition, see 11:283.

[1890]
Personal Audit.
Purpose: Assess individual personality characteristics.
Population: Individuals in a variety of professional occupations.
Publication Dates: 1941–1992.
Administration: Individual or group.
Price Data: Available from publisher.
Authors: Clifford R. Adams and William M. Lepley.
Publisher: Pearson Performance Solutions [No reply from publisher; status unknown].
    a) FORM SS (SHORT FORM).
    Scores, 6: Seriousness, Firmness, Frankness, Tranquility, Stability, Tolerance.
    Time: No limit (approximately 40 minutes).
    b) FORM LL (LONG FORM).
    Scores, 9: 6 scores listed in a above plus Steadiness, Persistence, Contentment.
    Time: No limit (approximately 50 minutes).
Cross References: See T2:1314 (4 references) and P:192 (6 references); for a review by William Seeman, see 4:75 (3 references); for a review by Percival M. Symonds, see 3:64 (10 references).

[1891]
Personal Characteristics Inventory™.
Purpose: Used for selection and developmental purposes; designed to gauge individual standing on the "Big Five" primary dimensions of personality to predict important work, education, and life outcomes and to help organizations identify promising candidates more effectively and provide feedback to individuals regarding strengths and areas where improvement is necessary.
Population: Ages 15 and over.
Publication Dates: 1995–2005.
Acronym: PCI.
Scores, 26: Conscientiousness (Dependability, Achievement Striving, Efficiency, Total), Stability (Even Temperament, Self-Confidence, Total), Extraversion (Sociability, Need for Recognition, Leadership Orien-

tation, Total), Agreeableness (Cooperation, Consideration, Total), Openness (Abstract Thinking, Creative Thinking, Total), Occupational Score (Manager, Sales, Clerical, Production, Driver), Teamwork, Integrity, Learning Orientation, Commitment to Work.
Administration: Group or individual.
Price Data: Available from publisher.
Foreign Language Editions: French and Spanish editions available.
Time: 25–30 minutes.
Comments: Online administration available.
Authors: Michael K. Mount, Murray R. Barrick, and Wonderlic Consulting.
Publisher: Wonderlic, Inc.
Cross References: For reviews by Susan M. Brookhart and Mark L. Pope, see 16:181.

[1892]
Personal Creativity Assessment.

Purpose: Designed "to allow individuals to determine how they measure up in the realm of creativity."
Population: Age 18 and above.
Publication Date: 1999.
Acronym: PCA.
Scores, 2: Enabler, Barrier.
Administration: Group or individual.
Price Data, 2001: $29.95 per Creativity by Design leader's guide (73 pages).
Time: (20–25) minutes.
Author: Alexander Watson Hiam.
Publisher: HRD Press, Inc.

[1893]
Personal Directions®.

Purpose: An executive coaching tool designed to aid in the structured exploration of an individual's personal choices regarding life balance issues, career planning, feelings of satisfaction and security, and opportunities for growth and development.
Population: Adults.
Publication Dates: 1997–2001.
Scores: 46 dimensions: Types of Emotional Satisfaction (Giving, Receiving, Belonging, Expressing, Gaining Stature, Entertaining, Creating, Interpreting, Excelling, Enduring, Structuring, Maneuvering, Winning, Controlling, Stability, Independence, Irreproachability), Areas of Emphasis (Career, Economic, Community, Interpersonal, Recreation, Travel, Nature, Palate, Arts, Practical Arts, Home, Romance, Family, Intellectual, Ideological, Physical, Emotional, Spiritual), World Outcomes (Level of Satisfaction, Level of Dissatisfaction, Level of Security, Level of Insecurity, Level of Growth, Balance of World, Level of Present Support, Internal Focus of World, External Focus of World, Flexibility of Boundaries, Level of Public Success).
Administration: Group.

Price Data: Available from publisher.
Foreign Language Editions: Available in English (American), English (British), Danish, Dutch, French, German, Italian, and Swedish.
Time: (45) minutes.
Comments: Purchase and use requires training by publisher.
Authors: James T. Mahoney, Joan W. Chadbourne (test), and Robert I. Kabacoff (manual).
Publisher: Management Research Group.

[1894]
Personal Dynamics Profile.

Purpose: Designed to measure "personality characteristics relevant to success," and "to assist organizations in hiring the best available applicants and developing employees to their potential," and to "assist individuals in achieving career success and personal contentment."
Population: Current personnel and potential employees.
Publication Dates: 1995–1998.
Acronym: PDP.
Scores, 26: Assessment Validity (Objectivity, Accuracy), Interpersonal Traits (Sociability, Recognition, Conscientiousness, Exhibition, Trust, Nurturance); Organizational Traits (Alertness, Structure, Order, Flexibility, Creativity, Responsibility); Dedication Traits (Ambition, Endurance, Assertiveness, Boldness, Coachability, Leadership); Self-Control Traits (Self-Confidence, Composure, Tough-Mindedness, Autonomy, Contentment, Control).
Administration: Individual or group.
Price Data, 1998: $195 per report including participant's report, manager's report, executive profiles, position compatibility report, group profiles, subgroup profiles, group profile overlays, success profile overlays, and position analyses report; group discounts available.
Time: [60] minutes.
Authors: Denis Waitley, Lem Burnham, Charles C. Kaufman, J. Michael Priddy, Joan L. Francis, Thomas A. Tutko, Bruce C. Ogilvie, and Leland P. Lyon.
Publisher: Winslow Research Institute.

[1895]
Personal Effectiveness Inventory.

Purpose: Provides insights into attitudes, beliefs, and behavior, and increases skills for effectiveness.
Population: Adults.
Publication Date: 1996.
Acronym: PEI.
Scores, 15: Self-Development (Self-Image, Control, Approval, Amicability), Relationship Building (Trust, Cooperation, Interpersonal, Inclusion), Goal Achievement (Satisfaction, Directedness, Expectations, Effectiveness), Time Orientation (Past, Present, Future).

Administration: Individual.
Price Data: Price data for test materials including Self-Development Guide (70 pages) available from publisher.
Time: Administration time not reported.
Author: Human Synergistics International.
Publisher: Human Synergistics International.

[1896]
Personal Experience Inventory.

Purpose: "Assesses all forms of substance abuse plus related psychosocial problems and personal risk factors."
Population: Ages 12–18.
Publication Dates: 1988–1989.
Acronym: PEI.
Scores: 45 scores/screens: Chemical Involvement Problem Severity Section: Basic Scales (Personal Involvement with Chemicals, Effects from Drug Use, Social Benefits of Drug Use, Personal Consequences of Drug Use, Polydrug Use), Clinical Scales (Social-Recreational Drug Use, Psychological Benefits of Drug Use, Transsituational Drug Use, Preoccupation with Drugs, Loss of Control), Validity Indicators (Infrequent Responses, Defensiveness, Pattern Misfit), Drug Use Frequency/Duration/Age of Onset (Alcohol, Marijuana, LSD, Psychedelics, Cocaine, Amphetamines, Quaaludes, Barbiturates, Tranquilizers, Heroin, Opiates, Inhalants); Psychosocial Section: Personal Risk Factor Scales (Negative Self-Image, Psychological Disturbance, Social Isolation, Uncontrolled, Rejecting Convention, Deviant Behavior, Absence of Goals, Spiritual Isolation), Environmental Risk Factor Scales (Peer Chemical Environment, Sibling Chemical Use, Family Pathology, Family Estrangement), Problem Screens (Psychiatric Referral, Eating Disorder, Sexual Abuse, Physical Abuse, Family Chemical Dependency, Suicide Potential), Validity Indicators (Infrequent Responses, Defensiveness).
Administration: Group.
Parts, 2: Chemical Involvement Problem Severity Section, Psychosocial Section.
Price Data, 2006: $165 per kit for mail-in computer scoring including 5 prepaid mail-in answer booklets for computer scoring and interpretation and manual (1989, 103 pages); $132 per kit for on-site computer scoring including 5-use disk (PC with Windows), 5 PC answer booklets, and manual; $55 per manual; $26.95 per mail-in answer booklet; $329 per 25-use disk (PC with Windows); $24.75 per 10 PC answer booklets; $13.00 per FAX service scoring.
Time: 45 minutes.
Authors: Ken C. Winters and George A. Henly.
Publisher: Western Psychological Services.
Cross References: See T5:1931 (1 reference) and T4:1971 (2 references); for reviews by Tony Toneatto and Jalie A. Tucker, see 11:284.

[1897]
Personal Experience Inventory for Adults.

Purpose: Designed to yield "comprehensive information about an individual's substance abuse patterns and problems."
Population: Age 19 and older.
Publication Dates: 1995–1996.
Acronym: PEI-A.
Scores, 37: Problem Severity Scales (Personal Involvement with Drugs, Physiological Dependence, Effects of Use, Social Benefits of Use, Personal Consequences of Use, Recreational Use, Transsituational Use, Psychological Benefits of Use, Preoccupation, Loss of Control, Infrequency—1, Self-Deception, Social Desirability—1, Treatment Receptiveness), Psychosocial Scales (Negative Self-Image, Psychological Disturbance, Social Isolation, Uncontrolled, Rejecting Convention, Deviant Behavior, Absence of Goals, Spiritual Isolation, Peer Drug Use, Interpersonal Pathology, Estrangement in the Home, Infrequency—2, Social Desirability—2), Problem Screens (Suicide Risk, Work Environment Risk, Past Family Pathology, Other Impulse-Related Problems, Significant Other Drug Problem, Sexual Abuse Perpetrator, Physical Abuse Perpetrator, Physical/Sexual Abuse Victim, Need for Psychiatric Referral, Miscellaneous).
Administration: Group.
Parts, 2: Problem Severity Scales, Psychosocial Scales.
Price Data, 2006: $165 per kit for mail-in computer scoring including 5 prepaid mail-in answer booklets and manual (1996, 100 pages); $132 per kit with disc for on-site computer scoring including 5-use disk, 5 PC answer booklets, and manual; $132 per kit with CD for on-site computer scoring including 5-use CD, 5 PC answer booklets, and manual; $26.95 or less per mail-in answer booklet; $329 or less per 25-use (PC with Windows) scoring disk; $329 or less per 25-use (PC with Windows) scoring CD; $25 or less per 10 PC answer booklets for use with computer disk; $55 per manual.
Time: (45–60) minutes.
Comments: Untimed self-report inventory; computer scored only.
Author: Ken C. Winters.
Publisher: Western Psychological Services.
Cross References: For reviews by Mark D. Shriver and Claudia R. Wright, see 13:225.

[1898]
Personal Experience Screening Questionnaire.

Purpose: "Designed as a brief screening tool to aid . . . in the identification of teenagers likely to need a drug abuse assessment referral."
Population: Adolescents.
Publication Date: 1991.

Acronym: PESQ.
Scores, 3: Infrequency, Defensiveness, Problem Severity.
Administration: Group.
Price Data, 2006: $91 per complete kit including 25 AutoScore™ test forms and manual (30 pages); $41 per 25 AutoScore™ test forms; $53 per manual.
Time: (10) minutes.
Author: Ken C. Winters.
Publisher: Western Psychological Services.
Cross References: For reviews by Stuart N. Hart and Richard W. Johnson, see 12:286 (1 reference).

[1899]
Personal Experience Screening Questionnaire for Adults.

Purpose: Designed to "screen for the abuse of alcohol and other drugs by adults."
Population: Ages 19 and over.
Publication Date: 2003.
Acronym: PESQ-A.
Scores, 2: Problem Severity, Defensiveness.
Administration: Individual or group.
Price Data, 2006: $91 per kit including Autoscore™ test forms and manual; $41 per 25 Autoscore™ test forms; $53 per manual; volume discount available.
Time: (10) minutes.
Comments: Self-report behavior inventory.
Author: Ken C. Winters.
Publisher: Western Psychological Services.
Cross References: For reviews by Jody L. Kulstad and William E. Martin, Jr., see 16:182.

[1900]
Personal History Checklist for Adolescents.

Purpose: To obtain historical information during routine intake procedures.
Population: Adolescent clients of mental health services.
Publication Date: 1989.
Scores: Item scores only.
Administration: Individual.
Manual: No manual.
Price Data, 2006: $50 per package of 25.
Time: Administration time not reported.
Comments: Can be completed by client or clinician.
Authors: Edward H. Dougherty and John A. Schinka.
Publisher: Psychological Assessment Resources, Inc.

[1901]
Personal History Checklist for Adults.

Purpose: To obtain historical information during routine intake procedures.
Population: Adult clients of mental health services.
Publication Date: 1989.
Scores: Item scores only.

Administration: Individual.
Manual: No manual.
Price Data, 2006: $50 per package of 25.
Time: Administration time not reported.
Comments: Checklist can be completed by client or clinician.
Author: John A. Schinka.
Publisher: Psychological Assessment Resources, Inc.
Cross References: For a review by Thomas A. Widiger, see 11:285.

[1902]
Personal Inventory of Needs.

Purpose: Designed as a self-assessment tool to identify the strengths of basic needs.
Population: Employees.
Publication Date: 1990.
Scores, 3: Achievement, Affiliation, Power.
Administration: Group or individual.
Price Data: Price information available from publisher for complete kit including 20 inventories, 20 response sheets, and 20 interpretation sheets.
Time: [30] minutes administration; [30] minutes interpretation.
Comments: Self-administered, self-scored; based on David McClelland's research at MIT.
Author: Training House, Inc.
Publisher: Training House, Inc.
Cross References: For reviews by Gary J. Dean and Trenton R. Ferro, see 12:287.

[1903]
Personal Opinion Matrix.

Purpose: Surveys the impressions and reactions of those who are managed.
Population: Employees.
Publication Dates: 1977-1983.
Scores, 2: Managerial Review, Climate.
Administration: Group.
Manual: No manual.
Price Data, 2001: $7.95 per instrument.
Time: Administration time not reported.
Comments: Self-administered survey.
Author: Jay Hall.
Publisher: Teleometrics International, Inc.
Cross References: For a review by Gregory H. Dobbins, see 10:276 (7 references).

[1904]
Personal Orientation Dimensions.

Purpose: Designed to "measure attitudes and values in terms of concepts of the actualizing person."
Population: High school, college, and adults.
Publication Dates: 1975–1977.
Acronym: POD.
Scores, 13: Orientation (Time Orientation, Core Centeredness), Polarities (Strength, Weakness, Anger,

Love), Integration (Synergistic Integration, Potentiation), Awareness (Being, Trust in Humanity, Creative Living, Mission, Manipulation Awareness).
Administration: Group.
Price Data: Available from publisher.
Time: Administration time not reported.
Comments: A refinement and extension of concepts first measured by the Personal Orientation Inventory (1905); self-administering.
Author: Everett L. Shostrom.
Publisher: EdITS/Educational and Industrial Testing Service.
Cross References: For reviews by Gloria Maccow and Claudia R. Wright, see 14:285; see also T5:1938 (1 reference) and T4:1977 (1 reference).

[1905]
Personal Orientation Inventory.
Purpose: Designed as a "measure of values and behavior seen to be of importance in the development of the self-actualizing person."
Population: High school, college, and adults.
Publication Dates: 1962–1996.
Acronym: POI.
Scores, 12: Time Ratio, Support Ratio, Self-Actualizing Value, Existentiality, Feeling Reactivity, Spontaneity, Self-Regard, Self-Acceptance, Nature of Man, Synergy, Acceptance of Aggression, Capacity for Intimate Contact.
Administration: Group.
Price Data: Available from publisher.
Time: (30–40) minutes.
Comments: Self-administered.
Author: Everett L. Shostrum.
Publisher: EdITS/Educational and Industrial Testing Service.
Cross References: See T5:1939 (15 references), T4:1978 (42 references), 9:943 (24 references), and T3:1789 (98 references); for an excerpted review by Donald J. Tosi and Cathy A. Lindamood, see 8:641 (433 references); see also T2:1315 (80 references); for reviews by Bruce Bloxom and Richard W. Coan, see 7:121 (97 references); see also P:193 (26 references).

[1906]
Personal Problems Checklist—Adult.
Purpose: "To facilitate the rapid assessment of an individual's problems as seen from that person's point of view."
Population: Adults.
Publication Date: 1985.
Scores: 13 areas: Social, Appearance, Vocational, Family and Home, School, Finances, Religion, Emotions, Sex, Legal, Health and Habits, Attitude, Crises.
Administration: Individual or group.
Manual: No manual.

Price Data, 2006: $50 per package of 25.
Time: (10) minutes.
Author: John A. Schinka.
Publisher: Psychological Assessment Resources, Inc.
Cross References: See T5:1941 (1 reference); for a review by Harold R. Keller, see 10:278.

[1907]
Personal Problems Checklist for Adolescents.
Purpose: "To identify relevant problems, establish rapport, and provide written documentation of presenting problems consistent with community standards of care."
Population: Adolescents.
Publication Dates: 1985–1989.
Acronym: PPC.
Scores: 13 problem areas: Social and Friends, Appearance, Job, Parents, Family and Home, School, Money, Religion, Emotions, Dating and Sex, Health and Habits, Attitudes and Opinions, Crises.
Administration: Individual or group.
Manual: No manual.
Price Data, 2006: $50 per package of 25.
Time: (10–20) minutes.
Comments: Adolescent version of the Personal Problems Checklist (1906).
Authors: John A. Schinka.
Publisher: Psychological Assessment Resources, Inc.
Cross References: See T5:1942 (1 reference); for reviews by Brian K. Martens and Toni E. Santmire, see 10:279.

[1908]
Personal Profile System.
Purpose: "Helps people identify their behavioral style and pinpoints what they might do to become more effective and successful people."
Population: Employees.
Publication Dates: 1977-1983.
Scores: Behavioral Patterns (Work).
Administration: Group.
Price Data: Available from publisher.
Time: (60-360) minutes depending on preferred program format.
Comments: Self-report instrument.
Author: Performax Systems International, Inc.
Publisher: Inscape Publishing.
Cross References: For a review by Ellen McGinnis, see 10:280.

[1909]
Personal Reaction Index.
Purpose: Assesses how people feel regarding the aspects of their work environment.
Population: Employees.
Publication Dates: 1974-1995.
Scores, 6: Degree of Participation, Feelings of Satisfaction, Feelings of Responsibility, Feelings of Com-

mitment, Feelings of Frustration, Perceived Decision Quality.
Administration: Group.
Manual: No manual.
Price Data, 2001: $2.95 per instrument.
Time: Administration time not reported.
Comments: Self-administered survey.
Author: Jay Hall.
Publisher: Teleometrics International, Inc.
Cross References: For reviews by Ralph M. Alexander and Daniel G. Spencer, see 9:946.

[1910]
Personal Relationship Inventory.

Purpose: "Designed to assess one's capacity to develop and sustain intimate interpersonal relationships."
Population: Ages 15 and over.
Publication Dates: 1988–2006.
Acronym: PRI.
Scores, 13: Compassion, Friendship, Intimacy, Masculine/Feminine, Primitive Self, Psychological Adjustment, Romantic Love, Self-Respect, Sensitivity, Spirituality, Trust, Love Capacity (Total), Persona.
Administration: Individual.
Price Data: Price information is available from the publisher for group discounts and research projects; now immediately scored and processed online; downloads for A Guide to Using The Love Factor are available at www.ronmann.com and free partial results are also available.
Time: (15-20) minutes.
Comments: Comments: Originally published as the Love Factor Inventory.
Author: Ronald L. Mann.
Publisher: Ronald L. Mann, Ph.D.
Cross References: For reviews by Bradley Elison and William K. Wilkinson, see 12:288.

[1911]
Personal Resource Questionnaire.

Purpose: Provides information about adults' social networks and perceived levels of social support.
Population: Ages 18–80.
Publication Dates: 1981–1987.
Acronym: PRQ-85.
Scores: Part I, 3 scores: Size of Network, Number of Problems Experienced, Degree of Satisfaction with Help Received; Part II, total score only.
Administration: Group.
Parts, 2: I, II.
Manual: No manual.
Price Data: Price information available from publisher for instructions and Questionnaire; additional copies may be photocopied locally.
Time: (10–15) minutes.

Comments: May be self-administered; Parts I and II can be administered independently of each other.
Authors: Patricia Brandt and Clarann Weinert.
Publisher: Patricia Brandt and Clarann Weinert.
Cross References: See T5:1947 (8 references); for a review by Esther E. Diamond, see 11:286.

[1912]
Personal Stress Assessment Inventory.

Purpose: A self-assessment instrument designed to identify those who would most likely benefit from participation in stress-management training.
Population: Adults.
Publication Dates: 1981–1993.
Acronym: PSAI.
Scores, 6: Predisposition, Resilience, Sources of Stress, Overall Stress Factor, Health Symptoms, Personal Reactions.
Administration: Group or individual.
Price Data, 2002: $8.95 per inventory; minimum of 20 (volume discounts available).
Time: (20–30) minutes.
Comments: Self-administered; self-scored.
Author: Herbert S. Kindler.
Publisher: The Center for Management Effectiveness, Inc.
Cross References: For reviews by E. Scott Huebner and Norman D. Sundberg, see 14:286.

[1913]
Personal Stress Navigator.

Purpose: "Samples the magnitude and types of stress [and stress symptoms] experienced by the respondent and assesses relative vulnerability to stress."
Population: Adults.
Publication Dates: 1983-1987.
Scores, 16: Situational (Family, Individual Roles, Social Being, Environment, Financial, Work/School), Symptom (Muscular System, Parasympathetic Nervous System, Sympathetic Nervous System, Emotional, Cognitive System, Endocrine, Immune System), Vulnerability, Total Situational Stress, Total Symptoms.
Administration: Group.
Price Data: Available from publisher.
Time: [20-30] minutes.
Comments: Self-administered; v5.0 is available in paper-and-pencil format (optically scannable for computer scoring and interpretation), PC format (computer administration, scoring, and interpretation), and on the World Wide Web (http://www.bbinst.org/); entitled Stress Audit on previous listing.
Authors: Lyle H. Miller, Alma Dell Smith, and Bruce L. Mehler (manual only).
Publisher: Stress Directions, Inc.
Cross References: For a review by Rolf A. Peterson, see 10:347.

[1914]
Personal Style Assessment.

Purpose: To assess an individual's personal style of communication.
Population: Adults.
Publication Dates: 1980–1987.
Scores, 4: Thinker, Intuitor, Sensor, Feeler.
Administration: Group.
Manual: No manual.
Price Data: Price information available from publisher for tests and interpretation sheets.
Time: (15–25) minutes.
Comments: Self-administered, self-scored.
Author: Training House, Inc.
Publisher: Training House, Inc.
Cross References: For reviews by Cathy W. Hall and Gerald L. Stone, see 11:287.

[1915]
Personal Style Assessment, Jung-Parry Form.

Purpose: To assess an individual's relative strength on Jung's four personal styles, or "psychological types."
Population: Adults.
Publication Date: 1992.
Scores, 4: Thinker, Intuitor, Sensor, Feeler.
Administration: Group or individual.
Manual: No manual.
Price Data: Price information available from publisher for set including tests, answer sheets, and interpretation folder.
Time: (20–30) minutes.
Comments: Self-administered; self-scored.
Author: Scott B. Parry.
Publisher: Training House, Inc.
Cross References: For a review by Vicki S. Packman, see 13:227.

[1916]
Personal Style Indicator [Revised].

Purpose: Designed to increase mutual understanding, acceptance, and communication among people and to increase self-awareness.
Population: Ages 15 years–adults.
Publication Dates: 1988-2006.
Acronym: PSI.
Scores, 4: Behavioral/Action, Cognitive/Analysis, Interpersonal/Harmony, Affective/Expression.
Administration: Individual or group.
Price Data, 2006: $13.95 per test booklet (2006, 20 pages); $14.95 per In-Depth Interpretations booklet (2006, 28 pages); $26.95 per access code for online version; $69.95 per Professional's Guide (2006, 64 pages); $35 per Trainer's Guidelines (1996, 70 pages); $159.95 per PSI Power Point CD and binder (2006, 116 slides); $23.95 per participant workbook Building Relationships With Style (2006, 68 pages); $22.95 per Why Aren't You More Like Me? book second edition (1994, 226 pages); $109.95 per CRG Models Master Handouts binder and CD for PSI-color PDFs (2005, 26 pages).
Foreign Language Editions: Available online in English, French, and German, and in print in English, French, Japanese, Dutch, and Spanish; the In-Depth interpretations booklet is available in English, Japanese, Dutch, Spanish, and French.
Time: [90] minutes; [180-720] minutes advanced.
Comments: Self-administered and self-scored.
Authors: Ken Keis, Terry D. Anderson, and Everett T. Robinson.
Publisher: Consulting Resource Group International, Inc.
Cross References: For reviews by James T. Austin and Kusum Singh of an earlier edition, see 13:228.

[1917]
Personal Styles Inventory [PSI-120] [1999 Revision].

Purpose: Provides a comprehensive assessment of normal personality characteristics.
Population: Adults.
Publication Dates: 1990–2005.
Acronym: PSI-120.
Scores, 24: Styles of Expressing Emotions (Sympathetic, Enthusiastic, Expansive, Confronting, Self-Willed, Reserved, Modest, Patient), Styles of Doing Things (Agreeing, Sociable, Excitement-Seeking, Venturing, Restless, Self-Directed, Self-Motivated, Organizing), Styles of Thinking (Traditional, Dedicated, Imaginative, Inquiring, Individualistic, Analytical, Practical, Focused).
Administration: Group or individual.
Price Data: Available from publisher.
Time: (20–30) minutes.
Comments: Computerized interpretation report is available.
Authors: Joseph T. Kunce, Corrine S. Cope, and Russel M. Newton.
Publisher: Educational & Psychological Consultants, Inc.
Cross References: See T5:1954 (1 reference); for reviews by Paul A. Arbisi and Mary Henning-Stout of an earlier edition, see 13:229 (2 references); see also T4:1993 (4 references).

[1918]
Personal Success Profile.

Purpose: Designed "to measure the personality characteristics of individuals, to assist organizations in hiring the best available applicants and developing current employees to their potential, and to assist individuals in achieving career success and personal contentment."
Population: Current personnel and potential employees.

Publication Dates: 1968–1996.
Scores, 16: Assessment Validity (Objectivity, Accuracy), Competitiveness Traits (Drive, Assertiveness, Determination, Leadership), Self-Control Traits (Self-Confidence, Emotional Control, Mental Toughness), Dedication Traits (Coachability, Conscientiousness, Responsibility, Trust), Composite Traits (Competitiveness, Self-Control, Dedication), Ambition.
Administration: Individual and group.
Price Data, 1998: $95 per report including participant's report, manager's report, executive profiles, group profiles, sub-group profiles, and group profile overlays; group discounts available.
Time: (45) minutes.
Comments: Derivation of the Athletic Motivation Inventory (219).
Authors: Denis Waitley, Lem Burnham, Charles C. Kaufman, J. Michael Priddy, Linda G. Griggs, Joan L. Francis, Thomas A. Tutko, Leland P. Lyon, and Bruce C. Ogilvie.
Publisher: Winslow Research Institute.
　a) PERSONAL SUCCESS SURVEY.
　Publication Dates: 1990–1995.
　Scores, 3: Ambition, Self-Confidence, Mental Toughness.
　Price Data: Available from publisher.
　Time: (10) minutes.
　Comments: Shortened version of the Personal Success Profile; derivation of the Athletic Motivation Inventory (219).

[1919]
Personal Values Inventory [Personal Strengths Publishing].

Purpose: Designed to facilitate self-discovery of personal style of approaching tasks, conflicts, decision-making, and relationships.
Population: Adolescents and adults with sixth grade or above reading levels.
Publication Dates: 1973–1997.
Acronym: PVI.
Scores: 7 Motivational Values (a set of values that helps a person decide how to act when things are going well); 13 scores reflecting predictable progressive responses to conflict and opposition.
Administration: Group or individual.
Editions, 2: Personal Values Inventory; Mirror Edition of the Personal Values Inventory.
Price Data, 2001: $10 per self-scorable inventory; $30 per manual (1996, 146 pages).
Time: (20–40) minutes.
Comments: Highest scores represent motivational values and valued relating style for an individual; self-scorable; for corporate (e.g., training workshops), and clinical (e.g., individual and group counseling) uses; can be self-administered, but trained administrators and interpreters recommended; Mirror Edition uses self-ratings and ratings from a significant other person.
Authors: Elias H. Porter and Sara E. Maloney.
Publisher: Personal Strengths Publishing.

[1920]
Personal Values Questionnaire.

Purpose: Measures individuals' "values related to achievement, affiliation, and power."
Population: Adults.
Publication Date: 1993.
Acronym: PVQ.
Scores, 3: Achievement, Affiliation, Power.
Administration: Individual.
Price Data, 2006: $69 per complete kit including 10 questionnaires and 10 profiles and interpretive notes (11 pages).
Time: [30] minutes.
Comments: Self-scored profile; also available online.
Author: Hay Group.
Publisher: Hay Group.
Cross References: For reviews by Brian F. Bolton and Gary J. Dean, see 13:230.

[1921]
Personality Adjective Check List.

Purpose: "Developed primarily as a self-report instrument for measuring personality in counseling clients and normal adults."
Population: Ages 16-adult.
Publication Dates: 1987-1991.
Acronym: PACL.
Scores, 9: Introversive, Inhibited, Cooperative, Sociable, Confident, Forceful, Respectful, Sensitive, PI (indicator of potential personality problems).
Administration: Group.
Price Data, 2001: $79 per start-up kit including manual (92 pages), scoring keys, 50 test sheets, and 50 profile sheets; $30 per manual; $30 per 50 test sheets; $25 per 50 profile sheets; $15 per scoring key set; $425 per WinPACL and AutoPACL software with narrative interpretations.
Time: (10-15) minutes.
Comments: Conceived as a tool for measuring the personality styles outlined by Theodore Millon among counseling clients and normal adults.
Author: Stephen Strack.
Publisher: 21st Century Assessment.
Cross References: See T5:1958 (1 reference); for reviews by Allen K. Hess and Howard M. Knoff, see 12:289 (1 reference); see also T4:1996 (3 references).

[1922]
Personality Advantage Questionnaire.

Purpose: Designed to "identify personality strengths, and set those strengths in a work context."

Population: Employees.
Publication Date: 1998.
Acronym: PAQ.
Scores, 5: Communication Style, Emotions, Drive and Determination, Relationships with People, Thinking Style.
Administration: Individual.
Manual: No manual.
Price Data, 2001: $14.95 per diskette.
Time: Administration time not reported.
Author: Human Resource Development Press.
Publisher: HRD Press, Inc.

[1923]
Personality Assessment Inventory.

Purpose: Designed to provide information relevant to clinical diagnosis, treatment planning, and screening for psychopathology.
Population: Ages 18–adult.
Publication Date: 1991.
Acronym: PAI.
Scores, 53: Inconsistency, Infrequency, Negative Impression, Positive Impression, Somatic Complaints (Conversion, Somatization, Health Concerns, Total), Anxiety (Cognitive, Affective, Physiological, Total), Anxiety-Related Disorders (Obsessive-Compulsive, Phobias, Traumatic Stress, Total), Depression (Cognitive, Affective, Physiological, Total), Mania (Activity Level, Grandiosity, Irritability, Total), Paranoia (Hypervigilance, Persecution, Resentment, Total), Schizophrenia (Psychotic Experiences, Social Detachment, Thought Disorder, Total), Borderline Features (Affective Instability, Identity Problems, Negative Relationships, Self-Harm, Total), Antisocial Features (Antisocial Behaviors, Egocentricity, Stimulus-Seeking, Total), Alcohol Problems, Drug Problems, Aggression (Aggressive Attitude, Verbal Aggression, Physical Aggression, Total), Suicidal Ideation, Stress, Nonsupport, Treatment Rejection, Dominance, Warmth.
Administration: Individual or group.
Price Data, 2006: $254 per comprehensive kit including professional manual (193 pages), 2 reusable item booklets, 2 administration folios, 25 Form HS (handscorable) answer sheets, 25 adult profile forms, and 25 critical items forms; $695 per PAI Software Portfolio CD-ROM with PAI, PAS, and APAI-IE modules, 25 PAI software item response booklets, 25 PAS software item response booklets, and 5 bonus on-screen administrations of both the PAI and PAS.
Time: [50–60] minutes.
Comments: Self-report inventory of adult psychopathology; PAI Law Enforcement, Corrections and Public Safety Selection Report Module, and PAI Interpretive Report for Correctional Settings are also available from publisher.
Author: Leslie C. Morey.

Publisher: Psychological Assessment Resources, Inc.
Cross References: See T5:1959 (8 references); for reviews by Gregory J. Boyle and Michael G. Kavan, see 12:290 (8 references); see also T4:1997 (3 references).

[1924]
Personality Assessment Screener.

Purpose: "Designed to identify individuals in need of further assessment for emotional problems, behavioral problems, or both."
Population: Ages 18 and older.
Publication Dates: 1991–1997.
Acronym: PAS.
Scores, 11: Negative Affect, Acting Out, Health Problems, Psychotic Features, Social Withdrawal, Hostile Control, Suicidal Thinking, Alienation, Alcohol Problem, Anger Control, Total.
Administration: Individual or group.
Price Data, 2006: $85 per complete kit including manual (1997, 69 pages) and 25 hand-scorable response forms.
Time: (5) minutes.
Comments: Screening version of the Personality Assessment Inventory (1923).
Author: Leslie C. Morey.
Publisher: Psychological Assessment Resources, Inc.
Cross References: For a review by Matthew Burns, see 14:288.

[1925]
Personality Disorder Interview-IV: A Semistructured Interview for the Assessment of Personality Disorders.

Purpose: Constructed to "facilitate reliable and valid interview assessments of DSM-IV personality disorders."
Population: Ages 18 and older.
Publication Date: 1995.
Acronym: PDI—IV.
Scores, 21: 12 Personality Disorder Scores (Antisocial, Avoidant, Borderline, Dependent, Histrionic, Narcissistic, Obsessive-Compulsive, Paranoid, Schizoid, Schizotypal, Depressive, Passive-Aggressive); 9 Thematic Content Area Scores (Attitudes Toward Self, Attitudes Toward Others, Security/Comfort with Others, Friendships and Relationships, Conflicts and Disagreements, Work and Leisure, Social Norms, Mood, Appearance and Perception).
Administration: Individual.
Price Data, 2006: $145 per introductory kit including hardcover manual (1995, 277 pages), 2 of each Interview Booklet, 10 score summary booklets, and 10 profile booklets.
Time: [120] minutes.
Comments: Corresponds with DSM—IV Personality Disorder diagnosis criteria.

Authors: Thomas A. Widiger, Steve Mangine, Elizabeth M. Corbitt, Cynthia G. Ellis, and Glenn V. Thomas.

Publisher: Psychological Assessment Resources, Inc.

Cross References: For reviews by Samuel Juni and Paul Retzlaff, see 14:289.

[1926]
Personality Inventory for Children, Second Edition.

Purpose: "Assesses both broad and narrow dimensions of behavioral, emotional, cognitive, and interpersonal adjustment."

Population: Ages 5–19 years (Kindergarten–Grade 12).

Publication Dates: 1977–2001.

Acronym: PIC-2.

Administration: Group.

Forms, 2: Standard Form, Behavioral Summary.

Price Data, 2002: $175 per kit including 2 reusable administration booklets, 50 answer sheets, 1 set of scoring templates, 25 Behavioral Summary AutoScore forms, 50 Standard Form profile sheets, manual (2001, 212 pages), 25 Behavioral Summary profile sheets, and 50 Critical Items summary sheets; $50 per manual; $25 per reusable administration booklet, quantity discount available; $19.50 per 5 Spanish translation administration booklets, quantity discount available; $19.50 per 100 answer sheets; $32.50 per set of scoring templates.

Foreign Language Editions: Spanish editions available for both forms.

Comments: Complete revision and restandardization of Personality Inventory for Children, Revised (PIC-R); old edition no longer available; coordinates with Personality Inventory for Youth (PIY, 1927) and Student Behavior Survey (SBS, 2460).

Authors: David Lachar and Christian P. Gruber.

Publisher: Western Psychological Services.

a) STANDARD FORM.

Scores, 33: 9 Adjustment Scales and 21 Adjustment Subscales: Cognitive Impairment (Inadequate Abilities, Poor Achievement, Developmental Delay), Impulsivity and Distractibility (Disruptive Behavior, Fearlessness), Delinquency (Antisocial Behavior, Dyscontrol, Noncompliance), Family Dysfunction (Conflict Among Members, Parent Maladjustment), Reality Distortion (Developmental Deviation, Hallucinations and Delusions), Somatic Concern (Psychosomatic Preoccupation, Muscular Tension and Anxiety), Psychological Discomfort (Fear and Worry, Depression, Sleep Disturbance/Preoccupation with Death), Social Withdrawal (Social Introversion, Isolation), Social Skill Deficits (Limited Peer Status, Conflict With Peers), 3 Response Validity Scales (Defensiveness, Dissimulation, Inconsistency).

Price Data: $19.50 per 100 Standard Form profiles or 100 Critical Items summary sheets.

Time: (40) minutes.

Comments: Hand-scored; computer scoring option will be available 2003 and will include mail, fax, or computer disks; system requirements DOS 3.0 or above, 512K memory, 286 processor, 1 MB free disk space, 3.5-inch high-density floppy drive.

b) BEHAVIORAL SUMMARY.

Scores, 12: 8 Short Adjustment Scales (Impulsivity and Distractibility—Short, Delinquency—Short, Family Dysfunction—Short, Reality Distortion—Short, Somatic Concern—Short, Psychological Discomfort—Short, Social Withdrawal—Short, Social Skill Deficits—Short), 3 Composite Scales (Externalization—Composite, Internalization—Composite, Adjustment—Composite), Total Score.

Price Data: $29.95 per 25 Behavioral Summary AutoScore answer forms, quantity discount available; $19.50 per 100 Behavioral Summary profiles.

Time: (15) minutes.

Comments: "A quick screening version of the Standard Form; focuses on current behavior that can support the development of a treatment plan; can be administered using standard PIC-2 test materials"; hand-score only.

Cross References: For reviews by Radhika Krishnamurthy and Susana Urbina, see 16:183; see T5:1962 (23 references) and T4:1998 (21 references); for a review by Howard M. Knoff of an earlier edition, see 10:281 (20 references); for reviews by Cecil R. Reynolds and June M. Tuma of an earlier edition, see 9:949 (5 references); see also T3:1796 (5 references).

[1927]
Personality Inventory for Youth.

Purpose: "Assesses emotional and behavioral adjustment, family character and interaction, and school adjustment and academic ability."

Population: Ages 9–19.

Publication Date: 1995.

Acronym: PIY.

Scores, 37: Validity, Inconsistency, Dissimulation, Defensiveness, Cognitive Impairment (Poor Achievement and Memory, Inadequate Abilities, Learning Problems, Total), Impulsivity and Distractibility (Brashness, Distractibility and Overactivity, Impulsivity, Total), Delinquency (Antisocial Behavior, Dyscontrol, Noncompliance, Total), Family Dysfunction (Parent-Child Conflict, Parent Maladjustment, Marital Discord, Total), Reality Distortion (Feelings of Alienation, Hallucinations and Delusions, Total), Somatic Concern (Psychosomatic Syndrome, Muscular Tension and Anxiety, Preoccupation with Disease, Total), Psychological Discomfort (Fear and Worry, Depression, Sleep Disturbance, Total), Social Withdrawal (Social Introversion, Isolation, Total), Social Skill Deficits (Limited Peer Status, Conflict with Peers, Total).

Administration: Group.

Price Data, 2006: $247.50 per complete kit including administration and interpretation guide, technical guide, 100 answer sheets, 1 set of scoring templates, 100 profile forms (male and female), 100 critical items summary sheets (male and female), 2 reusable administration booklets, and audiotape; $27.50 per reusable administration booklet; $24.75 per Spanish Research Edition reusable administration booklet; $26.50 per 100 answer sheets; $26.50 per 100 profile forms; $26.50 per 100 critical items summary sheets; $20.50 per mail-in answer sheet; $329.50 per 25-use disk (PC with Microsoft Windows); $12 per FAX service scoring charge; $35.75 per set of scoring templates; $16.50 per audiotape; $52.25 per administration and interpretation guide; $54.50 per technical guide.

Time: (45) minutes.

Authors: David Lachar and Christian P. Gruber.

Publisher: Western Psychological Services.

Cross References: For reviews by Lizanne DeStefano and by Gregory J. Marchant and T. Andrew Ridenour, see 13:231.

[1928]
Personality Research Form, 3rd Edition.

Purpose: Designed as an "extensively validated comprehensive measure of normal personality."

Population: Grade 6-college, adults.

Publication Dates: 1964-1997.

Acronym: PRF.

Administration: Group or individual.

Forms, 5: A, B, AA, BB, and E (Form E sent out unless specified; contact publisher for availability and prices of other forms).

Price Data, 2006: $80 per examination kit including manual (1984, 72 pages), 5 test booklets, 5 handscorable answer sheets, 5 profile sheets, scoring template, and one machine-scorable answer sheet and coupon for an Extended Report; $33 per test manual; $50 per 25 test booklets; $40 per 25 hand-scorable answer sheets; $40 per 25 profile sheets; $17 per scoring template; $85–$95 (depending on volume) per 10 machine-scorable answer sheets and coupons for Mail-in Extended Report; $58–$65 (depending on volume) per 10 machine-scorable answer sheets and coupons for Mail-in Basic Report; $30 per audio presentation cassette tape; $105 per software package including disks, software manual for Windows, test manual, and 10 coupons for computer reports; $14 per online password; volume discounts available.

Foreign Language Editions: Available in Spanish and French (Form E test booklets only).

Comments: Cassette tape available for audio presentation of Form E; the PRF is available for online scoring at www.sigmatesting.com.

Author: Douglas N. Jackson.

Publisher: Sigma Assessment Systems, Inc.

a) FORM A.

Population: Ages 16-adult.

Publication Dates: 1965-1985.

Scores, 15: Achievement, Affiliation, Aggression, Autonomy, Dominance, Endurance, Exhibition, Harmavoidance, Impulsivity, Nurturance, Order, Play, Social Recognition, Understanding, Infrequency.

Time: (30-45) minutes.

b) FORM B.

Comments: Parallel form to Form A.

c) FORM AA.

Population: College students.

Publication Dates: 1965-1985.

Scores, 22: Same as Form A and Form B plus Abasement, Change, Cognitive Structure, Defendence, Sentience, Succorance, Desirability.

Time: (40-70) minutes.

d) FORM BB.

Comments: Parallel form to Form AA.

e) FORM E.

Population: Grade 6-adult.

Publication Dates: 1974-1987.

Scores, 22: Same as Form AA.

Comments: Cassette tape available for administration to individuals with limited verbal skills.

Time: 45 minutes.

Cross References: See T5:1965 (86 references) and T4:2000 (45 references); for reviews by Robert Hogan and Jerry S. Wiggins, see 10:282 (68 references); see also 9:950 (42 references) and T3:1798 (116 references); for a review by Robert Hogan of an earlier edition, see 8:643 (132 references); see also T3:1322 (23 references); for reviews by Anne Anastasi, E. Lowell Kelly, and Jerry Wiggins, and excerpted reviews by John O. Crites, Lonnie D. Valentine, Jr., and Ruth Wessler with Jane Loevinger of an earlier edition, see 7:123 (27 references); see also P:201 (13 references).

[1929]
Personality Self-Portrait [Revised].

Purpose: Designed to illustrate "the wide range of normal personality styles that combine to create each individual's unique personality profile and demonstrates how each personality style influences relationships, work and home life."

Population: Ages 18 and over.

Publication Dates: 1995–1996.

Acronym: PSP.

Scores, 14: Vigilant, Solitary, Idiosyncratic, Adventurous, Mercurial, Dramatic, Self-Confident, Sensitive,

Devoted, Conscientious, Leisurely, Aggressive, Self-Sacrificing, Serious.
Administration: Individual.
Price Data, 2006: $155 per complete kit including the New Personality Self-Portrait book (1995, 463 pages), 5 reusable item booklets, 20 Quikscore forms, and 20 interpretation guides; $90 per 10 reusable item booklets; $26 per 20 Quikscore forms; $94 per 20 interpretive guides, $5.50 per web-based profile report (minimum purchase of 20).
Time: [30] minutes.
Comments: Self-report questionnaire; online administration available.
Authors: John M. Oldham and Lois B. Morris.
Publisher: Multi-Health Systems, Inc.
Cross References: For reviews by Gregory J. Boyle and Sandra D. Haynes, see 16:184.

[1930]
Personalized Achievement Summary System.

Purpose: Designed to provide information useful for monitoring academic progress, selecting curriculum and evaluating and planning instructional programming in home school settings.
Population: Grades 3–8.
Publication Dates: 1981–1993.
Acronym: PASS.
Scores, 20: Reading (Word Meaning, Literal Comprehension, Interpretive Comprehension, Evaluative Comprehension, Total); Mathematics (Numeration and Number Systems, Fractions, Decimals/Percent/and Currency, Geometry and Measurement, Graphs/Charts/and Statistics, Word Problems and Problem Solving, Computation, Total); Language Usage (Grammar, Capitalization, Punctuation, Composition, Study Skills, Spelling, Total).
Administration: Individual.
Price Data, 2006: $27 plus shipping/handling per complete test.
Time: (210–330) minutes.
Comments: Items taken from the Portland Achievement Level Tests (PALT).
Author: Hewitt Research Foundation.
Publisher: Hewitt Homeschooling Resources.
Cross References: For reviews by Douglas F. Kauffman and Michael S. Trevisan, see 16:185.

[1931]
Personalysis®.

Purpose: Constructed "to inventory personality characteristics of individuals at five different levels" yielding information on "how to maximize personal, interpersonal, and group effectiveness in the work place."
Population: Leaders, employees, families, individuals.
Publication Dates: 1975–2001.
Scores, 32: Preferred Style—Rational Self (Authoritative, Democratic, Structured, Self Directed), Communication Expectations—Socialized Self (Direction, Involvement, Methodology, Input), Motivational Needs—Instinctive Self (Authority, Influence, Control, Understanding), Defensive Self (Coerce, Provoke, Resist, Reject), Irrational Self (Hostile, Rebellious, Stubborn, Withdrawn); Act, Adapt, Analyze, and Assess scores for Preferred Style—Rational Self, Back-Up Style—Socialized Self, and Functional Stress—Instinctive.
Administration: Individual or group.
Price Data: Available from publisher.
Time: Untimed.
Comments: Self-administered.
Author: James R. Noland.
Publisher: Personalysis Corporation.
Cross References: For reviews by Jack Gebart-Eaglemont and S. Alvin Leung, see 16:186; for reviews by George Engelhard, Jr. and L. Alan Witt of an earlier edition, see 12:291.

[1932]
Personnel Assessment Form.

Purpose: To measure mental ability and intelligence for employee selection and placement planning.
Population: Ages 16 and older.
Publication Date: 2004.
Acronym: PAF.
Scores: Verbal Subtest Score, Quantitative Subtest Score, Total Score.
Subtest: Verbal Subtest, Quantitative Subtest.
Administration: Group.
Forms, 2: A, C.
Price Data, 2006: $15 per manual (24 pages); $17 per report; volume discounts available.
Time: 14 minutes.
Comments: Norms are linked to the Multidimensional Aptitude Battery—II (1688); the PAF is available through fax-in scoring and online administration at www.sigmatesting.com.
Author: Douglas N. Jackson.
Publisher: Sigma Assessment Systems, Inc.

[1933]
[Personnel Interviewing Form].

Purpose: Designed to help business and industry to obtain various information from interviewees.
Population: Business and industry.
Publication Dates: 1956-1984.
Administration: Individual.
Manual: No manual.
Time: (20-30) minutes.
Authors: Judd-Safian Associates.
Publisher: Martin M. Bruce, Ph.D.
   a) INITIAL INTERVIEW TABULATION.
   Scores: For recording ratings in 10 areas: Appearance, Voice and Speech, Poise, Health, Education, Manner, Responsiveness, Experience, Job Stability, Motivation.

Price Data, 2006: $5.40 per specimen set; $9.35 per package of forms.

b) DEPTH INTERVIEW PATTERN.

Scores: For interviewing in 5 areas: Work Evaluation, Educational and Social Evaluation, Economic Evaluation, Personality Evaluation, Ambitions Evaluation.

Price Data: $14.50 per specimen set; $27.00 per package of forms.

c) EMPLOYMENT REFERENCE INQUIRY.

Purpose: For securing employee evaluation from previous employers.

Price Data: $4.75 per specimen set; $9.35 per package of forms.

[1934]
Personnel Reaction Blank.

Purpose: A personality-based integrity test to help in hiring trustworthy, dependable employees.
Population: Ages 15 to adult.
Publication Dates: 1972–2003.
Acronym: PRB.
Scores, 5: Personality Reliability Index, which is a composite of 4 subscales: Prosocial Background, Compliance with Social Norms, Sense of Well-Being, Conventional Occupational Preferences.
Administration: Group or individual.
Price Data: Available from publisher.
Time: (15) minutes.
Comments: In addition to the scores, the report produces a narrative statement for each score that describes typical behavior of low scorers and high scorers; the summary page of the report provides item responses, raw scores, standard scores, and number of missing responses for each scale.
Authors: Harrison G. Gough, Richard Arvey, and Pamela Bradley.
Publisher: Institute for Personality and Ability Testing, Inc. (IPAT).
Cross References: For a review by Donna L. Sundre of an earlier version, see 13:232.

[1935]
Personnel Relations Survey [Revised].

Purpose: "Designed to assess the understanding and behavior of managers in their interpersonal relationships."
Population: Managers.
Publication Dates: 1967–2000.
Acronym: PRS.
Scores, 6: Relationships with Employees (Exposure, Feedback); Relationships with Colleagues (Exposure, Feedback); Relationships with Superiors (Exposure, Feedback).
Administration: Group.
Manual: Leader's Guide available.
Price Data, 2006: $9.95 per instrument.

Time: Administration time not reported.
Comments: Self-administered, self-scored; based on the Johari Window Model of interpersonal relationships.
Authors: Jay Hall and Martha S. Williams.
Publisher: Teleometrics International, Inc.
Cross References: For a review by Matthew E. Lambert, see 14:29.

[1936]
Personnel Selection Inventory.

Purpose: Helps identify job applicants who are likely to be honest and have positive attitudes toward work, safety and customer service and provides a valid, fair, and cost effective means of identifying applicants who are likely to be productive and responsible.
Population: Job applicants.
Publication Dates: 1975–1980.
Acronym: PSI.
Scores: 21 scales: Honesty, Supervision Attitudes, Tenure, Drug Avoidance Scale, Nonviolence Scale, Employee/Customer Relations Scale, Risk Avoidance Scale, Stress Tolerance Scale, Safety Scale, Work Values Scale, Math Scale, Responsibility, Productivity, Customer Service Aptitude Scale, Customer Service Attitude Scale, Sales Aptitude Scale, Customer Service Index, Candidness Validity Scale, Employability Index, Detailed Personal and Behavioral History.
Administration: Individual or group.
Forms: 20 versions available including non-integrity test versions.
Price Data: Available frm publisher.
Time: Varies based on version.
Comments: Previously listed as London House Personnel Selection Inventory.
Author: London House.
Publisher: Pearson Performance Solutions [No reply from publisher; status unknown].
Cross References: See T5:1972 (1 reference) and T4:1478 (1 reference); for a review by William I. Sauser, see 9:631; see also T3:1339 (2 references).

[1937]
Personnel Test Battery.

Purpose: Designed to assess numerical skills, language proficiency, and perceptual accuracy.
Population: Office and sales groups.
Publication Dates: 1979–1981.
Acronym: PTB.
Subtests: Available as separates.
Administration: Group.
Levels, 2: 1, 2.
Restricted Distribution: Restricted to persons who have completed the publisher's training course or members of the Division of Occupational Psychology of the British Psychological Society.

Price Data: Available from publisher.
Authors: Peter Saville, Gill Nyfield, Roger Holdsworth (test), and Ruth Holdsworth (manual).
Publisher: SHL Group plc [United Kingdom].
a) LEVEL 1.
Comments: "Basic skills and comprehension"; 3 tests plus 2 optional tests for Levels 1 and 2.
1) *Verbal Usage.*
Acronym: VPI.
Time: 10(15) minutes.
2) *Numerical Comprehension.*
Acronym: NP2.
Time: 7(12) minutes.
3) *Checking.*
Acronym: CP3.
Time: 7(12) minutes.
4) *Basic Checking.*
Acronym: CP7.
Time: 5(10) minutes.
Comments: Optional test for Levels 1 and 2.
5) *Audio Checking.*
Acronym: CP8.
Time: (15) minutes.
Comments: Optional test for Levels 1 and 2; test administered by cassette tape.
b) LEVEL 2.
Comments: "Higher-order reasoning skills"; 3 tests plus 2 optional tests for Levels 1 and 2.
1) *Classification.*
Acronym: CP4.
Time: 7(12) minutes.
2) *Verbal Meaning.*
Acronym: VP5.
Time: 10(15) minutes.
3) *Numerical Reasoning.*
Acronym: NP6.
Time: 10(15) minutes.

[1938]
Personnel Tests for Industry.

Purpose: To assist in the selection, placement, training, and promotion of individuals in industrial settings.
Population: Trade school and adults
Publication Dates: 1945–1995.
Acronym: PTI.
Scores: Total score only.
Administration: Group or individual.
Publisher: PsychCorp, A brand of Harcourt Assessment, Inc.
a) PTI-VERBAL TEST.
Publication Dates: 1952–1969.
Acronym: PTI-V.
Forms, 2: A, B.
Price Data, 2006: $50 per examination kit including all forms of Verbal and Numerical booklets and manual; $100 per 25 test booklets (manual,

booklets, key) (specify Form A or B); $285 per 100 test booklets (includes manual, booklet, key).
Time: 5(15) minutes.
Author: Alexander G. Wesman.
b) PTI-NUMERICAL TEST.
Publication Dates: 1952–1969.
Acronym: PTI-N.
Forms, 2: A, B.
Price Data: Same as for *a* above.
Time: 20(25) minutes.
Author: Jerome E. Doppelt.
c) PTI-ORAL DIRECTIONS TEST.
Publication Dates: 1945–1995.
Acronym: PTI-ODT.
Author: Charles R. Langmuir.
Cross References: See T5:1974 (1 reference), T4:2008 (5 references), T3:1808 (3 references), T2:433 (5 references), and 7:373 (3 references); for a review by Erwin K. Taylor, see 5:366; see also 4:309 (1 reference); for reviews by Charles D. Flory, Irving Lorge, and William W. Turnbull on the Oral Directions Test, see 3:245.

[1939]
Personnel Tests for Industry-Oral Directions Test [Second Edition].

Purpose: A test of general ability designed to "assess an individual's ability to follow directions presented orally" and as a selection tool "to predict performance in a variety of vocational and technical training settings."
Population: Adolescents and adults.
Publication Dates: 1974-1995.
Acronym: PTI-ODT.
Scores: Total score only.
Administration: Individual or group.
Forms, 2: S, T.
Price Data, 2006: $185 per complete set including recording, manual (1995, 67 pages), script, key, 100 answer documents, directions for administering, and cassette tape Form S or T; $50 per examination kit including scripts and answer documents for both forms and manual.
Time: (15) minutes.
Comments: Tape-recorded administration; one of three subtests of Personnel Tests for Industry (1938).
Author: Charles R. Langmuir.
Publisher: Harcourt Assessment, Inc.
Cross References: For information for Personnel Tests for Industry, see T5:1974 (1 reference), T4:2008 (5 references), T3:1808 (3 references), T2:433 (5 references), and 7:373 (3 references); for a review by Erwin K. Taylor, see 5:366; see also 4:309 (1 reference); for reviews by Charles D. Flory, Irving Lorge, and William W. Turnbull of the Oral Directions Test, see 3:245.

[1940]
Pervasive Developmental Disorder in Mental Retardation Scale [Second Revised Edition].

Purpose: "A simple classification and screening instrument designed for the identification of Pervasive Developmental Disorders in persons with mental retardation/intellectual disability."

Population: Ages 2-70.

Publication Dates: 1990-2006.

Acronym: PDD-MRS.

Scores: Total score only.

Administration: Individual.

Price Data, 2006: EURO123,40 (U.S. $148.08) per starter set including manual (2006, 53 pages) and 75 record forms; EURO49,50 (U.S. $59.40) per manual; EURO73,90 (U.S. $88.68) per 75 record forms.

Foreign Language Editions: First published in Dutch; English, German, and Italian versions are available.

Time: (10-20) minutes.

Comments: Norms of the scale are based on data of 1,230 children, adolescents, and adults in the profound, severe, moderate, and mild ranges of mental retardation.

Author: D. W. Kraijer.

Publisher: PITS: Psychologische Instrumenten Tests en Services [The Netherlands].

[1941]
Pervasive Developmental Disorders Screening Test, Second Edition.

Purpose: Designed as "a clinical screening tool for autism (autistic disorder)/AD and other pervasive developmental disorders, such as pervasive developmental disorder, not otherwise specified (PDD-NOS) and Asperger's Disorder."

Population: Ages 12 to 48 months.

Publication Date: 2004.

Acronym: PDDST-II.

Scores: Total score only.

Administration: Individual.

Forms, 3: Stage 1—Primary Care Screener, Stage 2—Developmental Clinic Screener, Stage 3—Autism Clinic Severity Screener.

Price Data, 2004: $125 per complete kit including manual (42 pages) and record forms; $30 per 25 Stage 1 record forms; $30 per 25 Stage 2 record forms; $30 per 25 Stage 3 record forms.

Time: (10–20) minutes.

Comments: Parent-report screening measure.

Author: Bryna Siegel.

Publisher: PsychCorp, A brand of Harcourt Assessment, Inc.

[1942]
Pharmacy College Admission Test.

Purpose: Developed to measure the abilities, aptitudes, and skills that pharmacy schools have deemed essential for success in basic pharmacy curricula.

Population: Pharmacy school applicants.

Publication Dates: 1974– 2006.

Acronym: PCAT.

Scores, 7: Verbal Ability, Biology, Reading Comprehension, Quantitative Ability, Chemistry, Composite, Writing.

Administration: Group.

Restricted Distribution: Distribution restricted and test administered at testing centers; details may be obtained from publisher.

Price Data: Available from publisher.

Time: 235 minutes.

Comments: Paper-and-pencil; national test dates.

Author: Harcourt Assessment, Inc.

Publisher: PsychCorp, A brand of Harcourt Assessment, Inc.

Cross References: For reviews by Mark Albanese and Leo M. Harvill, see 13:233.

[1943]
Phelps Kindergarten Readiness Scale.

Purpose: Constructed to assess the academic strengths and weaknesses of children prior to enrolling in kindergarten or shortly after starting school.

Population: Pre-kindergarten and early kindergarten.

Publication Dates: 1991–1997.

Acronym: PKRS.

Scores, 4: Verbal Processing, Perceptual Processing, Auditory Processing, Total Readiness.

Administration: Individual.

Price Data: Available from publisher.

Time: (15) minutes.

Author: LeAdelle Phelps.

Publisher: Psychology Press Inc.

Cross References: For a review by Theresa H. Elofson, see 12:292.

[1944]
Phonemic-Awareness Skills Screening.

Purpose: "The PASS is a quick screening that pinpoints" three "specific areas of phonological weakness": to identify students with problems, to determine strengths and weaknesses, to document progress.

Population: Grades 1–2.

Publication Date: 2000.

Acronym: PASS.

Scores: 8 subtests: Rhyming, Sentence Segmentation, Blending, Syllable Segmentation, Deletion, Phoneme Isolation, Phoneme Segmentation, Substitution, Total.

Administration: Individual.
Price Data, 2006: $30 per complete kit including examiner's manual (16 pages) and 25 record forms; $20 per 25 record forms; $13 per examiner's manual.
Time: (15) minutes.
Comments: Can be administered by a teacher or assistant, requires "no specialized training in testing"; subtests may be administered separately.
Authors: Linda Crumrine and Helen Lonegan.
Publisher: PRO-ED.
Cross References: For reviews by Steven Long and by Vincent J. Samar and Ricki Korey Birnbaum, see 15:187.

[1945]
Phonics-Based Reading Test.

Purpose: "Designed to assess reading skills" and "To measure an individual's ability to apply phonics concepts when reading single words and connected text."
Population: Ages 6-0 through 12-11.
Publication Date: 2002.
Acronym: PRT.
Scores, 4: Decoding, Fluency, Comprehension, Total Reading Standard Score.
Administration: Individual.
Price Data, 2006: $82 per test kit including manual (109 pages), stimulus book, and 25 student test booklets; $25 per stimulus book; $27 per 25 student test booklets; $30 per manual.
Time: (20–30) minutes.
Comments: Norm- and criterion-referenced.
Author: Rick Brownell.
Publisher: Academic Therapy Publications
Cross References: For reviews by Karen Mackler and Annita Marie Ward, see 16:187.

[1946]
Phonological Abilities Test.

Purpose: "A screening test for the identification of children at risk of reading difficulties and as a diagnostic test to assess the nature and extent of phonological difficulties in older children with recognized reading problems."
Population: Ages 5–7.
Publication Date: 1997.
Acronym: PAT.
Scores, 8: Rhyme Detection, Rhyme Production, Word Completion—Syllables, Word Completion—Phonemes, Phoneme Deletion—Beginning Sounds, Phoneme Deletion—End Sounds, Speech Rate, Letter Knowledge.
Administration: Individual.
Price Data, 2006: £90 per complete kit including examiner's manual (45 pages), stimulus manual, alphabet cards, and record forms in carrying case; £29.50 per 25 record forms; £36.50 per examiner's manual; £44.50 per stimulus manual; £21.50 per alpahabet cards.

Time: 30 minutes.
Comments: Normed in the U.K.; tests can be given individually or in combination; normative data are also available for 4-year-olds.
Authors: Valerie Muter, Charles Hulme, and Margaret Snowling.
Publisher: Harcourt Assessment [England].
Cross References: For a review by Annita Marie Ward, see 15:188.

[1947]
Phonological Assessment Battery [Standardised Edition].

Purpose: Designed to identify "those children who need special help by providing an individual assessment of the child's phonological skills."
Population: Ages 6–15.
Publication Date: 1997.
Acronym: PLAB.
Scores: 6 tests: Alliteration, Naming Speed, Rhyme, Spoonerisms, Fluency, Non-Word Reading.
Administration: Individual.
Price Data, 1998: £75 per complete set including 10 record booklets and manual (130 pages); £10 per 10 record booklets; sample sheets are free.
Time: (30–40) minutes.
Comments: Is also appropriate for children whose first language is not English.
Authors: Norah Frederickson, Uta Frith, and Rea Reason.
Publisher: NFER-Nelson Publishing Co., Ltd. [England].
Cross References: For a review by Claudia R. Wright, see 15:189.

[1948]
The Phonological Awareness Skills Program Test.

Purpose: "Designed to provide a means for placing students at the appropriate entry points in the Phonological Awareness Skills Program Curriculum."
Population: Ages 4 to 10.
Publication Date: 1999.
Acronym: PASP Test.
Scores: Total score only.
Administration: Individual.
Price Data, 2006: $83 per complete kit including 25 record forms, curriculum manual, and instrument manual (24 pages); $16 per 25 record forms.
Time: (2–4) minutes.
Author: Jerome Rosner.
Publisher: PRO-ED.
Cross References: For a review by Janet Norris, see 15:190.

[1949]

Phonovisual Diagnostic Tests [1975 Revision].

Purpose: "Designed to test phonetic skills as taught by the Phonovisual Method."
Population: Grades 3–12.
Publication Date: 1975.
Scores: Total score only.
Administration: Group.
Tests: 6 tests consisting of 24 words each.
Price Data, 2001: $9.50 per set of tests and instructions.
Time: Administration time not reported.
Authors: Edna B. Smith and Mazie C. Lloyd.
Publisher: Phonovisual Products, Inc.
Cross References: For reviews by Charles M. Brown and George D. Spache of an earlier edition, see 6:829.

[1950]

Photo Articulation Test, Third Edition.

Purpose: Constructed as a "systematic method for eliciting speech sounds from children and identifying errors in articulation."
Population: Ages 3–8.
Publication Dates: 1969–1997.
Acronym: PAT-3.
Scores: Total score only.
Administration: Individual.
Price Data, 2006: $180 per complete kit; $45 per summary/response forms; $45 per examiner's manual; $65 per photo album picture book; $35 per picture card deck.
Time: (20) minutes.
Authors: Barbara A. Lippke, Stanley E. Dickey, John W. Selmar, and Anton L. Sodor.
Publisher: PRO-ED.
Cross References: For a review by David P. Hurford, see 14:291; see also T5:1982 (15 references), T4:2017 (12 references), 9:957 (2 references), and T3:1814 (5 references); for a review by Lawrence D. Shriberg of an earlier edition, see 8:969 (1 reference); see also 7:962 (2 references).

[1951]

PHSF Relations Questionnaire.

Purpose: Constructed "to measure … the personal, home, social and formal relations of high school pupils, students and adults, in order to determine the level of adjustment."
Population: Standards 6–10 in South African school system, college, and adults.
Publication Dates: 1969–1971.
Acronym: PHSF.
Scores, 12: Personal (Self-Confidence, Self-Esteem, Self-Control, Nervousness, Health), Home (Family Influences, Personal Freedom), Social (Sociability-Group, Sociability-Specific Person, Moral Sense), Formal Relations, Validity Scale.
Administration: Group.
Price Data: Available from publisher.
Time: (30) minutes.
Comments: Test materials in both English and Afrikaans.
Authors: F. A. Fouche and P. E. Grobbelaar.
Publisher: Human Sciences Research Council [South Africa].

[1952]

Pictographic Self Rating Scale.

Purpose: Designed to assess pupils' attitudes toward their academic subjects and classroom activities.
Population: High school and college.
Publication Dates: 1955–1957.
Scores: Total score only.
Administration: Group.
Price Data: Available from publisher.
Time: (35) minutes.
Author: Einar R. Ryden.
Publisher: Psychometric Affiliates.
Cross References: For reviews by Stanley E. Davis and John D. Krumboltz, see 6:701 (2 references).

[1953]

Pictorial Reasoning Test.

Purpose: Assesses general learning ability independent of language and reading skills.
Population: Entry-level positions in a variety of occupations.
Publication Dates: 1966–1994.
Acronym: PRT.
Scores: Total score only.
Administration: Individual or group.
Price Data: Available from publisher.
Time: 15 minutes.
Comments: Previously listed as SRA Pictorial Reasoning Test.
Authors: Robert N. McMurry and Phyllis D. Arnold (test), and Bruce A. Campbell (manual).
Publisher: Pearson Performance Solutions [No reply from publisher; status unknown].
Cross References: For reviews by Raymond A. Katzell and John E. Milholland, and an excerpted review by John L. Horn, see 7:381.

[1954]

The Pictorial Scale of Perceived Competence and Social Acceptance for Young Children.

Purpose: Measures "perceived competence and perceived social acceptance" in young children.
Population: Preschool through second grade.
Publication Dates: 1980–1983.
Scores, 4: Cognitive Competence, Peer Acceptance, Physical Competence, Maternal Acceptance.

Administration: Individual.
Forms, 2: Preschool/Kindergarten, First/Second Grade.
Price Data: Available from publisher.
Time: Administration time not reported.
Comments: Downward extension of the Perceived Competence Scale for Children.
Authors: Susan Harter and Robin Pike in collaboration with Carole Efron, Christine Chao, and Beth Ann Bierer.
Publisher: Susan Harter, University of Denver.
Cross References: See T5:1987 (23 references) and T4:2022 (6 references); for reviews by William B. Michael and Susan M. Sheridan, see 11:292 (9 references).

[1955]
Pictorial Test of Intelligence, Second Edition.

Purpose: Designed to "identify children who are significantly below their peers in important abilities and to identify children among these who are physically disabled who are more able to think and reason than their traditional communication skills support."
Population: Ages 3–8.
Publication Dates: 1964–2001.
Acronym: PTI-2.
Scores, 4: Verbal Abstractions, Form Discrimination, Quantitative Concepts, Pictorial Intelligence Quotient.
Administration: Individual.
Price Data, 2006: $143 per kit including examiner's manual (2001, 87 pages), picture book, and 25 profile/examiner record booklets; $40 per 25 record booklets; $45 per manual; $61 per picture book.
Time: (15–30) minutes.
Author: Joseph L. French.
Publisher: PRO-ED.
Cross References: For reviews by Michelle Athanasiou and by Dawn P. Flanagan and Leonard F. Caltabiano, see 15:191; see T3:1823 (3 references); for an excerpted review by Thomas A. Smith, see 8:223 (11 references); see also T2:517 (1 reference); for reviews by Philip Himelstein and T. Ernest Newland, see 7:418 (17 references); see also 6:531 (2 references).

[1956]
Picture Identification Test.

Purpose: "Designed to measure judgments, attitudes, sex-of picture differences, organizing principle strength, and need ego relationships associations pertaining to 22 needs based on the Murray need system."
Population: 12 years and older.
Publication Dates: 1959–1979.
Acronym: PIT.
Scores: 4 scores (Judgment Problem, Ego Problem, Organizing Principle, Sex-of-Picture) for each of 22 needs (Abasement, Achievement, Affiliation, Aggres-sion, Autonomy, Blame Avoidance, Counteraction, Deference, Dependence, Dominance, Exhibition, Gratitude, Harm Avoidance, Inferiority Avoidance, Nurturance, Order, Play, Rejection, Sentience, Sex, Succorance, Understanding), plus scores for 3 need dimensions (Combative, Personal-Social, Competitive), 6 Dimension Confusion scores, 3 Dimension Weight scores, 9 Sex-of-Picture Dimension Attitude score, scores for 10 need clusters (Friendliness, Intimacy, Inhibition, Competition, Dominance, Sociability, Independence, Aggression, Performance, Failure Avoidance), 10 Cluster Problem scores, 10 Combative Dimension Cluster Problem scores, 10 Persona-Social Dimension Cluster Problem scores, 10 Competitive Dimension Cluster Problem scores, 20 Combative Dimension Cluster Conflict score, 9 Personal-Social Dimension Cluster Conflict scores, 10 Competitive Dimension Cluster Conflict scores, 13 Averaged Set Problem scores, 1 General Motivation System Function score.
Administration: Group or individual.
Price Data: Available from publisher.
Time: [40] minutes.
Author: Jay L. Chambers.
Publisher: Jay L. Chambers.
Cross References: See T4:2026 (2 references), T3:1825 (3 references), T2:1490 (2 references), and P:463 (17 references).

[1957]
Piers-Harris Children's Self-Concept Scale, Second Edition.

Purpose: Designed to aid in the "assessment of self-concept in children and adolescents."
Population: Ages 7–18.
Publication Dates: 1969–2002.
Acronym: Piers-Harris 2.
Scores, 7: Behavioral Adjustment, Intellectual and School Status, Physical Appearance and Attributes, Freedom From Anxiety, Popularity, Happiness and Satisfaction, Total.
Administration: Group or individual.
Price Data, 2006: $119 per complete kit including 20 AutoScore™ answer forms, manual (2002, 135 pages); $43.50 per 20 AutoScore™ answer forms; $60.50 per manual; $19.25 per 20 Spanish answer forms; $20.50 per mail-in answer sheet; $291.50 per 25-Use Disk (PC with Windows); $16.50 per 100 PC answer sheets; $11 per fax scoring.
Foreign Language Edition: Spanish answer forms available.
Time: (10–15) minutes.
Authors: Ellen V. Piers (test and manual), David S. Herzberg (test and manual), and Dale B. Harris (test).
Publisher: Western Psychological Services.
Cross References: For reviews by Mary Lou Kelley and Donald P. Oswald, see 16:188; see also T5:1991

(108 references) and T4:2030 (123 references); for reviews by Jayne H. Epstein and Patrick J. Jeske of an earlier edition, see 9:960 (38 references); see also T3:1831 (107 references), 8:646 (95 references); and T2:1326 (10 references); for a review by Peter M. Bentler of an earlier edition, see 7:124 (8 references).

[1958]
A Pill Scale.
Purpose: Designed to measure attitudes toward oral contraception.
Population: Adults.
Publication Dates: 1969–1988.
Scores: Total score only.
Administration: Group.
Manual: No manual.
Price Data, 2005: $2 per scale.
Time: [10] minutes.
Comments: Supplementary article available.
Author: Panos D. Bardis.
Publisher: Donna Bardis.
Cross References: See 8:350 (3 references).

[1959]
PIM 8–12.
Purpose: Designed "to assess the extent to which children have acquired the mathematical skills and concepts covered by each year's curriculum."
Population: Ages 8–12.
Publication Dates: 1983–1985.
Scores, 5: Understanding, Computation, Application, Factual Recall, Total.
Administration: Group.
Levels, 5: Mathematics 8, Mathematics 9, Mathematics 10, Mathematics 11, Mathematics 12.
Price Data: Price information available from publisher for test booklets (specify Mathematics 8, 9, 10, 11, or 12), Teacher's Guide, and specimen set including 1 each of 8–12 test booklets, teacher's guide, and group record sheet.
Time: (60–80) minutes for each level.
Authors: Alan Brighouse, David Godber, and Peter Patilla.
Publisher: NFER-Nelson Publishing Co., Ltd. [England].

[1960]
PIP Developmental Charts, Second Edition.
Purpose: Assess behaviors to establish several developmental levels.
Population: Mentally handicapped children birth to age 5.
Publication Dates: 1976–1998.
Scores: Profile of 5 areas of development: Physical, Social, Eye-Hand, Development of Play, Language.
Administration: Individual.

Manual: No manual (instructions for administration and scoring included on test).
Price Data, 2002: £12.99 per 10 charts; £3.99 per specimen copy.
Time: Administration time not reported.
Authors: Dorothy M. Jeffree and Ray McConkey.
Publisher: Hodder & Stoughton Educational [England].
Cross References: For reviews by Joan F. Goodman and Robert L. Slonaker, see 9:961.

[1961]
PL-1 and PL-2 Police Administrator Tests (Lieutenant).
Purpose: Developed as knowledge-based tests suitable for the command level and to assist police departments in promoting qualified candidates to a higher rank.
Population: Candidates for promotion to the police administrator position.
Publication Dates: 1998-2006.
Acronym: PL-1, PL-2.
Scores: 4 knowledge areas: Police Procedures: Patrol and Investigation, Laws Related to Police Work, Concepts of Supervision, Concepts of Administration.
Administration: Individual or group.
Forms, 2: PL-1, PL-2.
Price Data: Available from publisher.
Time: 150 minutes per test.
Comments: PL-1 and PL-2 are comparable forms; reading lists are available to help candidates prepare for the tests.
Author: International Public Management Association for Human Resources.
Publisher: International Public Management Association for Human Resources (IPMA-HR).

[1962]
PLAN.
Purpose: Measures knowledge and skills attained early in secondary education in four curriculum areas: English, mathematics, reading, and science. Serves as a predictor of success on the ACT, an early indicator of college readiness, and a tool to help students explore careers that match their interests.
Population: Grade 10.
Publication Dates: 1989-2005.
Administration: Group.
Price Data: Available from publisher.
Time: 115 minutes for 4 academic tests; (60-70) minutes for student information, Interest Inventory, Study Power Assessment, and High School Course information.
Comments: Formerly called P-ACT+; special testing with extended time and alternate test formats are available for students who receive special accommodations in school due to professionally diagnosed and documented disabilities.

Author: ACT, Inc.
Publisher: ACT, Inc.

a) PLAN ENGLISH TEST.
Purpose: Measures understanding of the conventions of standard written English.
Scores, 7: Usage/Mechanics (Punctuation, Basic Grammar, Sentence Structure), Rhetorical Skills (Strategy, Organization, Style), Total.
Time: 30 minutes.

b) PLAN MATHEMATICS TEST.
Purpose: Measures student's mathematical reasoning skills.
Scores, 5: Algebra (Pre-Algebra, Elementary Algebra), Geometry (Coordinate Geometry, Plane Geometry), Total.
Time: 40 minutes.

c) PLAN READING TEST.
Purpose: Measures reading comprehension as a product of referring and reasoning skills.
Scores: Total score only.
Time: 20 minutes.

d) PLAN SCIENCE TEST.
Purpose: Measures scientific reasoning skills.
Scores: Total score only.
Time: 25 minutes.

Cross References: See T5:1997 (1 reference); for reviews by Martha Blackwell and Mary Henning-Stout, see 12:296.

[1963]
Plane Geometry: National Achievement Tests.

Purpose: To measure students' knowledge of plane geometry.
Population: High school.
Publication Dates: 1958–1960.
Scores: Total score only.
Administration: Group.
Forms, 2: A, B.
Price Data: Available from publisher.
Time: 40(45) minutes.
Authors: Ray Webb and Julius H. Hlavaty.
Publisher: Psychometric Affiliates.
Cross References: For a review by Dorothy L. Jones, see 7:540.

[1964]
Plane Trigonometry: National Achievement Tests.

Purpose: To measure students' knowledge of plane trigonometry.
Population: Grades 10–16.
Publication Dates: 1958–1960.
Scores: Total score only.
Administration: Group.
Forms, 2: A, B.

Price Data: Available from publisher.
Time: 40(45) minutes.
Authors: Ray Webb and Julius H. Hlavaty.
Publisher: Psychometric Affiliates.

[1965]
Planning, Organizing, & Scheduling Test, Revised Edition.

Purpose: Designed to measure an individual's "ability to plan, organize the actions and resources of, and schedule events around an activity."
Population: Adults.
Publication Date: 2004.
Acronym: POST.
Scores: Total score only.
Administration: Individual or group.
Manual: No manual.
Price Data: Available from publisher.
Time: 20(25) minutes.
Authors: Erich P. Prien and Leonard D. Goodstein.
Publisher: HRD Press, Inc.

[1966]
The Play Observation Scale [Revised].

Purpose: To assess the social and cognitive levels of children's play behaviors in natural settings.
Population: Preschool to elementary school children.
Publication Dates: 1989-2001.
Acronym: POS.
Scores: 28 possible ratings: 7 Non-Play (Transition, Unoccupied, Onlooker, Aggression, Rough-and-Tumble, Teacher Conversation, Peer Conversation); 15 Play, 5 cognitive ratings (Functional, Exploratory, Constructive, Dramatic, Games) in each of 3 social areas (Solitary, Parallel, Group); 3 Affective (Positive, Negative, Neutral).
Administration: Individual.
Price Data: Price available from publisher for complete kit including manual (20 pages).
Time: (3) minutes per observation.
Author: Kenneth H. Rubin.
Publisher: Kenneth H. Rubin, Ph.D. (the author).
Cross References: For reviews by Denise M. DeZolt and Mark H. Fugate of an earlier edition, see 13:234.

[1967]
Police Promotion Tests—Complete Service [Revised].

Purpose: "Custom-made test to fit duties and responsibilities for promotion of Police Officers."
Population: Police officers.
Publication Dates: 1979–2002.
Scores: 6 subtests: Technical Police Knowledge, Investigative Knowledge, Legal Knowledge, Supervisory and Managerial Knowledge, Administrative Knowledge, Comprehension Ability, Total.

Administration: Group.
Restricted Distribution: Distribution restricted to civil service commissions and qualified municipal officials.
Price Data: Available from publisher.
Time: (210) minutes.
Comments: Candidate study guide available.
Author: McCann Associates, Inc.
Publisher: Vantage McCann Associates.

[1968]
Police Selection Test.

Purpose: "Designed to measure abilities important for successful performance in training and on-the-job" as a police officer.
Population: Police officer applicants.
Publication Dates: 1989–2005.
Acronym: PST.
Scores: Total score only.
Administration: Group or individual.
Forms, 3: A, A-1, B-1.
Price Data: Price information available from publisher for test material including Technical manual (1990, 17 pages), Technical Report Addendum: The Development of PST Short Forms A-1 & B-1 (2005, 9 pages), User's Manual (2005, 10 pages), Study Guide and sample questions (1990, 21 pages).
Time: 120(125) minutes for long form; 60(65) minutes for short forms.
Comments: Measures reading comprehension, quantitative problem solving, data interpretation, writing skills, and verbal problem solving.
Author: Psychological Services, Inc.
Publisher: Psychological Services, Inc.
Cross References: For reviews by Jim C. Fortune and Deniz S. Ones, see 14:292.

[1969]
Polish Proficiency Test.

Purpose: "Designed to assess the general proficiency in listening and reading comprehension attained by English-speaking learners of Polish."
Population: Postsecondary to adult.
Publication Date: 1992.
Acronym: PPT.
Scores, 3: Listening Comprehension, Reading Comprehension, Structure.
Administration: Group.
Price Data, 2005: $25 per test; quantity discounts available; $6 per official score report.
Time: 120 (150) minutes.
Comments: Machine-scorable.
Author: Center for Applied Linguistics.
Publisher: Center for Applied Linguistics.
Cross References: For a review by Jack Gebart-Eaglemont, see 16:189.

[1970]
Polyfactorial Study of Personality.

Purpose: Developed "to offer diagnostic profiles approximating those which would be obtained with projective instruments."
Population: Adults.
Publication Dates: 1959-1984.
Acronym: PSP.
Scores, 11: Hypochondriasis, Sexual Identification, Anxiety, Social Distance, Sociopathy, Depression, Compulsivity, Repression, Paranoia, Schizophrenia, Hyperaffectivity.
Administration: Group.
Price Data, 2006: $54.50 per test package; $59 per IBM answer sheet/profile sheet package; $39 per set of IBM scoring stencils; $41.50 per manual (1959, 11 pages) and manuals supplement (1984, 17 pages); $53.50 per specimen set.
Time: (45-50) minutes.
Authors: Ronald H. Stark and Martin M. Bruce.
Publisher: Martin M. Bruce, Ph.D.
Cross References: For reviews by Bertram D. Cohen and Donald R. Peterson and an excerpted review by Edward S. Bordin, see 6:160.

[1971]
Portable Tactual Performance Test.

Purpose: Designed to assess the speed of movement, tactile perception, and problem-solving ability.
Population: Ages 5 to adult.
Publication Date: 1984.
Acronym: P-TPT.
Scores, 3: Dominant Hand, Non-dominant Hand, Both Hands.
Administration: Individual.
Price Data, 2006: $415 per introductory kit including 50 recording forms, 6-hole and 10-hole form boards in case, and manual (8 pages).
Time: (10-15) minutes per trial (three trial limit).
Comments: A portable alternative to the original Tactual Performance Test for use with the Halstead-Reitan Neuropsychological Test Battery (1137).
Author: Psychological Assessment Resources, Inc.
Publisher: Psychological Assessment Resources, Inc.
Cross References: For a review by Calvin P. Garbin, see 11:296.

[1972]
Porteus Mazes.

Purpose: "Designed to examine the individual's ability or ... tendency to use planning capacity, prudence and mental alertness in a new situation of a concrete nature."
Publication Dates: 1914–1965.
Scores, 2: Quantitative, Qualitative.
Administration: Group.

Price Data, 2002: $19 per 100 score sheets; $56 per manual (1965, 324 pages).
Comments: Formerly called The Porteus Maze Test.
Author: S. D. Porteus.
Publisher: PsychCorp, A brand of Harcourt Assessment, Inc.

a) VINELAND REVISION.
Population: Ages 3–12, 14, adult.
Price Data: $225 per basic set including mazes and 100 score sheets.
Time: Administration time not recorded.
b) PORTEUS MAZE EXTENSION.
Population: Ages 7–12, 14, adult.
Price Data: $165 per basic set including mazes and 100 score sheets.
Time: [25] minutes.
Comments: For use only as a practice-free re-test of *a*.
c) PORTEUS MAZE SUPPLEMENT.
Population: Ages 7–12, 14, adult.
Price Data: $155 per basic set including 100 each of 8 mazes.
Time: [25] minutes.
Comments: For use only as a third retest after *a* and *b*.
Cross References: See T5:2010 (24 references), T4:2051 (25 references), 9:965 (19 references), T3:1853 (34 references), 8:224 (25 references), and T2:518 (52 references); for reviews by Richard F. Docter and John L. Horn, and excerpted reviews by William D. Altus, H. B. Gibson, D. C. Kendrick, and Laurance F. Shaffer, see 7:419 (67 references); see also 6:532 (38 references) and 5:412 (28 references); for reviews by C. M. Louttit and Gladys C. Schwesinger, see 4:356 (56 references).

[1973]
Portland Digit Recognition Test [Revised].

Purpose: "Designed for neuropsychological assessment of exaggeration and malingering."
Population: Adults.
Publication Dates: 1989-2001.
Acronym: PDRT.
Scores, 3: Easy Items, Hard Items, Total.
Administration: Individual.
Price Data, 2006: $149 per complete kit.
Time: (40) minutes.
Author: Laurence M. Binder.
Publisher: Laurence M. Binder, Ph.D. (the author).
Cross References: For reviews by Charles J. Long and Stephanie Western and by Orest E. Wasyliw of an earlier version, see 12:297 (1 reference); see also T4:2052 (1 reference).

[1974]
Portland Problem Behavior Checklist—Revised.

Purpose: "Developed to aid school and mental health personnel to identify problem behaviors, make classification or diagnostic decisions, and evaluate counseling, intervention, or behavior consultation procedures."
Population: Grades K–12.
Publication Dates: 1980–1992.
Acronym: PPBC-R.
Administration: Individual.
Price Data, 2001: $45 per complete kit; $20 per 25 male or female forms.
Time: Untimed.
Comments: Respondents are professionals working with children; scoring form also includes opportunity to report on "other" problems (those not specifically included as a subscale).
Author: Steven A. Waksman.
Publisher: Enrichment Press.

a) FORM FOR FEMALES, GRADES K–6.
Scores, 4: Conduct Problems, Peer Problems, Personal Problems, Total.
b) FORM FOR FEMALES, GRADES 7–12.
Scores, 5: Academic Problems, Personal Problems, Conduct Problems, Anxiety Problems, Total.
c) FORM FOR MALES, GRADES K–6.
Scores, 5: Conduct Problems, Academic Problems, Anxiety Problems, Peer Problems, Total.
d) FORM FOR MALES, GRADES 7–12.
Scores, 6: Academic Problems, Anxiety Problems, Peer Problems, Conduct Problems, Personal Problems, Total.
Cross References: For reviews by Thomas McKnight and Robert Spies, see 14:293; for reviews by Terry A. Stinnett and John G. Svinicki of an earlier edition, see 10:287 (1 reference).

[1975]
Portrait of Overdone Strengths.

Purpose: Designed to demonstrate how one may "overdo or misapply" personal strengths, thereby contributing to unwarranted conflict in relationships.
Population: Adults.
Publication Dates: 1973–1996.
Scores, 3: Profile, Most Overdone Strengths, Least Overdone Strengths.
Administration: Group or individual.
Price Data, 2001: $5.50 per test booklet; $100 per facilitation guide.
Time: (20–40) minutes.
Comments: To be used with the Strength Deployment Inventory (2436); self-report using Q_Sort; Feedback Edition of the Portrait of Overdone Strengths

uses self-ratings and ratings from a significant other person.
Author: Personal Strengths Publishing.
Publisher: Personal Strengths Publishing.

[1976]
Portrait of Personal Strengths.

Purpose: "Designed to help you see how you use your strengths when things are going well in your relationships."
Population: Adults.
Publication Dates: 1973–1996.
Scores, 3: Profile, Top Strengths (6), Least Deployed Strengths (6).
Administration: Group or individual.
Price Data, 2001: $5.50 per test booklet; $100 per facilitation guide.
Time: (20–40) minutes.
Comments: To be used with the Strength Deployment Inventory (2436); self-report by Q Sort; Feedback Edition of the Portrait of Personal Strengths uses self-rating and ratings from a significant other person.
Author: Personal Strengths Publishing.
Publisher: Personal Strengths Publishing.

[1977]
Position Analysis Questionnaire.

Purpose: Constructed to analyze "jobs in terms of work activities and work-situation variables."
Population: Business and industrial jobs.
Publication Dates: 1969–1989.
Acronym: PAQ.
Scores: 45 dimensions in 7 divisions: Information Input, Mental Processes, Work Output, Relationships with Other Persons, Job Context, Other Job Characteristics, Overall Dimensions.
Administration: Individual.
Price Data: Available from publisher.
Time: Administration time not reported.
Comments: Ratings by 2 or more analysts; also provides estimates of selected employment tests useful for personnel selection and job evaluation points.
Authors: Ernest J. McCormick, Robert C. Mecham, and P. R. Jeanneret.
Publisher: PAQ Services, Inc.
Cross References: See T5:2016 (2 references); for reviews by Ronald A. Ash and George C. Thornton III, see 12:299 (2 references); see also T4:2054 (17 references) and T3:1855 (12 references); for a review by Alan R. Bass, see 8:983 (17 references).

[1978]
Position Classification Inventory.

Purpose: Designed "as an inventory for classifying positions and occupations" to assess the demands, rewards, and opportunities of work environments.
Population: Adults.

Publication Date: 1991.
Acronym: PCI.
Scores, 6: Realistic, Investigative, Artistic, Social, Enterprising, Conventional.
Administration: Individual or group.
Price Data, 2006: $85 per introductory kit including manual, 25 reusable item booklets, and 25 answer sheets/profile forms; $25 per manual; $33 per 25 reusable item booklets; $33 per 25 answer sheets/profile forms.
Time: (5-15) minutes.
Authors: Gary D. Gottfredson and John L. Holland.
Publisher: Psychological Assessment Resources, Inc.

[1979]
Positive and Negative Syndrome Scale.

Purpose: "Designed to assist in the assessment of schizophrenia."
Population: Psychiatric patients.
Publication Dates: 1986–2005.
Acronym: PANSS.
Scores: Standard Model: Positive, Negative, Composite Index, General Psychopathology, Anergia, Thought Disturbance, Activation, Paranoid/Belligerence, Depression, Supplemental; Pentagonal Model: Positive, Negative, Activation, Dysphoric Mood, Autistic Preoccupation.
Administration: Individual.
Price Data, 2006: $207 per complete kit including manual (2005, 88 pages), 25 QuikScore™ forms, 25 Structured Clinical Interview forms, and 25 Informant Questionnaire forms; $47 per manual; $44 per 25 QuikScore™ forms; $79 per 25 SCI-PANSS Structured Clinical Interview forms; $71 per 25 IQ-PANSS Informant Questionnaire forms.
Time: (30-40) minutes.
Comments: Completed by clinician.
Authors: Stanley R. Kay, Lewis A. Opler, and Abraham Fiszbein.
Publisher: Multi-Health Systems, Inc.
Cross References: See T5:2017 (17 references); for reviews by Barbara J. Kaplan and Cecil R. Reynolds, see 12:300 (15 references); see also T4:2055 (1 reference).

[1980]
Post-Assault Traumatic Brain Injury Interview and Checklist.

Purpose: "Designed to assist in treatment planning for neuropsychological and neurological evaluation, treatment, and rehabilitation."
Population: Assault victims.
Publication Date: 1997.
Acronym: P-TBI-IC.
Scores: 13 symptom areas: Hallmarks of Brain Injury Alertness, Prosody, Memory, Sensorimotor Functions, Speech, Academic Abilities, Cognitive Problem Solving, Organic Depression, Organic Anxiety, Organic Impulsivity, Laterality, Treatment Problems.

Administration: Group or individual.
Price Data, 2002: $75 per complete kit including manual (11 pages), and 10 test booklets; $50 per 10 test booklets; $30 per manual; student, volume, and research discounts available.
Time: Administration time not reported.
Comments: Ratings by health care professionals, shelter personnel, sexual assault center personnel, and from data obtained from client, significant others, and other health care professionals.
Authors: Martha E. Banks and Rosalie J. Ackerman.
Publisher: ABackans DCP, Inc.
Cross References: For reviews by James C. Reed and by Wilfred G. Van Gorp and Colleen A. Ewing, see 15:192.

[1981]
Postpartum Depression Screening Scale.

Purpose: Designed to assess the presence, severity, and type of postpartum depression symptoms.
Population: New mothers ages 14–49.
Publication Date: 2002.
Acronym: PDSS.
Scores, 10: Inconsistent Responding Index, Sleeping/Eating Disturbances, Anxiety/Insecurity, Emotional Lability, Mental Confusion, Loss of Self, Guilt/Shame, Suicidal Thoughts, Short Total Score, Total Score.
Administration: Group.
Price Data, 2005: $72.50 per kit including manual (59 pages) and 25 AutoScore™ test forms; $32.50 per 25 AutoScore™ test forms; $45 per manual; $17.50 per 10 test forms in Spanish.
Time: (5–10) minutes; (1–2) minutes for short form.
Comments: May be orally administered; allows for detection of women in need of psychiatric evaluation; short form consists of just 7 items and yields a short total score.
Authors: Cheryl Tatano Beck and Robert K. Gable.
Publisher: Western Psychological Services.
Cross References: For reviews by Paul A. Arbisi and Delores D. Walcott, see 16:190.

[1982]
Posttraumatic Stress Diagnostic Scale.

Purpose: "Designed to aid in the diagnosis of posttraumatic stress disorder."
Population: Ages 17–65.
Publication Date: 1995.
Acronym: PDS.
Scores, 5: Symptom Severity Score, Number of Symptoms Endorsed, Symptom Severity Rating, Level of Impairment in Functioning, PTSD Diagnosis.
Administration: Group.
Price Data, 2006: $57 per hand scoring starter kit including manual (54 pages), 10 answer sheets, 10 scoring worksheets, and 1 scoring sheet; $130 per hand scoring reorder kit including 50 answer sheets, 50 scoring worksheets, and 1 scoring sheet; $21 per 25 Q Local answer sheets; $5.75 per Q Local profile report; $34 per manual; $47.50 per Q Local starter kit including manual, answer sheets, and materials for 3 assessments.
Time: (10–15) minutes.
Author: Edna B. Foa.
Publisher: Pearson Assessments.
Cross References: For reviews by Stephen N. Axford and Beth Doll, see 14:294; see also T5:2018 (1 reference).

[1983]
Posture and Fine Motor Assessment of Infants.

Purpose: Designed to identify motor delays in infants and to monitor progress in the first year of life.
Population: Ages 2–12 months.
Publication Date: 2000.
Acronym: PFMAI.
Scores, 2: Posture, Fine Motor.
Administration: Individual.
Levels, 2: PFMAI-I (2–6 months), PFMAI-II (6–12) months.
Price Data, 2001: $55 per manual (99 pages).
Time: (25–30) minutes.
Authors: Jane Case-Smith and Rosemarie Bigsby.
Publisher: Harcourt Assessment, Inc.
Cross References: For reviews by Linda K. Bunker, B. Ann Boyce, and Gregory Hanson, and by John J. Venn, see 16:191.

[1984]
Power and Performance Measures.

Purpose: Battery of nine aptitude and ability tests designed to measure both potential and achievement in a wide range of occupational settings.
Population: Ages 16 and over.
Publication Dates: 1990–1996.
Acronym: PPM.
Scores: Verbal Reasoning, Verbal Comprehension, Perceptual Reasoning, Spatial Ability, Numerical Reasoning, Numerical Computation, Mechanical Understanding, Clerical Speed and Accuracy, Applied Logic.
Administration: Group or individual.
Price Data, 2001: £55 per technical handbook (1996, 54 pages); £6.50 per question booklet; £2.75 per answer sheet; £133 per specimen set.
Time: (3–12) minutes.
Author: James S. Barrett.
Publisher: The Test Agency Ltd. [England] [No reply from publisher; status unknown].
Cross References: For a review by Kurt F. Geisinger, see 16:192.

[1985]
Power Base Inventory.
Purpose: Assesses the techniques individuals use to influence others.
Population: Work team members, leaders, managers, supervisors.
Publication Dates: 1985–1991.
Acronym: PBI.
Scores, 6: Information, Expertise, Goodwill, Authority, Reward, Discipline.
Administration: Group or individual.
Price Data, 2001: $8.50 per inventory.
Time: (15) minutes.
Comments: Self-scored.
Authors: Kenneth W. Thomas and Gail Fann Thomas.
Publisher: CPP, Inc.
Cross References: For a review by Judy L. Elliott, see 13:235.

[1986]
Power Management Inventory.
Purpose: "Designed to assess a manager's characteristic management of influence dynamics; that is, how a given manager prefers to handle situations calling for the exercise of power and authority."
Population: Managers.
Publication Dates: 1981–2000.
Acronym: PMI.
Scores, 4: Power Motive (Personalized, Socialized, Affiliative), Power Style.
Administration: Group.
Manual: No manual.
Price Data, 2001: $8.95 per instrument.
Time: Administration time not reported.
Comments: Self-administered survey; companion to Power Management Profile (1987).
Authors: Jay Hall and James Hawker.
Publisher: Teleometrics International, Inc.
Cross References: For reviews by Philip G. Benson and William A. Owens, see 9:967.

[1987]
Power Management Profile.
Purpose: Assesses "the methods and reasons which most characterize your manager's handling of power situations."
Population: Managers.
Publication Dates: 1981–1995.
Acronym: PMP.
Scores, 5: Power Motive (Personalized, Socialized, Affiliative), Power Style, Moral.
Administration: Group.
Manual: No manual.
Price Data, 2001: $8.95 per instrument.
Time: Administration time not reported.

Comments: Self-administered survey; companion to Power Management Inventory (1986).
Authors: Jay Hall and James Hawker.
Publisher: Teleometrics International, Inc.
Cross References: For a review by Rhonda L. Gutenberg, see 9:968.

[1988]
The Power of Influence Test.
Purpose: Designed as an instrument that "records the attitudes of pupils toward each other and tells which pupils have friendship capacity."
Population: Grade 5 and over.
Publication Date: No date.
Scores: Total score only.
Administration: Group.
Price Data: Available from publisher.
Time: (5) minutes.
Comments: Also referred to as The Sociometric Test.
Authors: Roy Cochrane and Wesley Roeder.
Publisher: Psychometric Affiliates.
Cross References: For reviews by Salvador Hector Ochoa and Jeffrey K. Smith, see 15:193.

[1989]
Power Reading Assessment Kit.
Purpose: Created to "determine a student's reading level and best entry level into the Power Reading Program."
Population: Students.
Publication Date: 2005.
Scores, 3: Reading Accuracy, Comprehension, Fluency.
Administration: Individual.
Levels, 24: Reading levels from Primer (.3) to 10th grade (10.8).
Price Data, 2006: $129.95 per Reading Assessment Kit including teacher's guide (191 pages), 24 leveled, recorded Power Reading stories on 24 audiotapes or CDs with line-by-line word counts for fluency assessment, story cards for comprehension assessment, examiner worksheets, record-keeping charts, graphs, and timer.
Time: (5-10) minutes.
Author: Marie Carbo.
Publisher: National Reading Styles Institute, Inc.

[1990]
Practical Adolescent Dual Diagnostic Interview.
Purpose: "To elicit information relevant to the identification and diagnosis of mental health and substance use disorders in adolescents."
Population: Ages 12–18.
Publication Date: 2000.

Acronym: PADDI.
Scores, 17: Major Depressive Episode, Manic Episode, Mixed Episode, Psychotic Symptoms, Panic Attacks, Anxiety and Phobias, Posttraumatic Stress Disorder, Obsessions/Compulsions, Conduct Disorder, Oppositional Defiant Disorder, Personality Disorders, Paranoid Personality Traits, Dependent Personality Traits, Sexual Orientation, Substance Abused Disorders, Dangerousness to Self or Others, Child Abuse—Victimization.
Administration: Individual.
Price Data: Available from publisher.
Time: (20–40) minutes.
Comments: A structured diagnostic interview compatible with the DSM-IV diagnostic criteria; can be administered by paraprofessionals as a screening device.
Authors: Todd W. Estroff and Norman G. Hoffmann.
Publisher: Change Companies.
Cross References: For reviews by C. G. Bellah and Michael G. Kavan, see 16:193.

[1991]
Pragmatic Language Skills Inventory.

Purpose: Designed to help identify children "who have pragmatic language disabilities."
Population: Ages 5-12.
Publication Date: 2006.
Acronym: PLSI.
Scores: 3 subscales: Classroom Interaction, Social Interaction, Personal Interaction; Pragmatic Language Index.
Administration: Individual.
Price Data, 2006: $95 per complete kit including examiner's manual (59 pages) and 25 summary/response forms; $55 per manual; $45 per 25 summary/response forms.
Time: (5-10) minutes.
Comments: Appropriate raters include teachers, parents, teacher assistants, or other qualified persons who work closely with the child and are well acquainted with the child's language characteristics.
Authors: James E. Gilliam and Lynda Miller.
Publisher: PRO-ED.

[1992]
The Praxis Series: Professional Assessments for Beginning Teachers.

Purpose: Includes tests that correspond to two key milestones in the development as a teacher entering a teacher training program and obtaining a license to teach.
Population: Beginning teachers.
Publication Dates: 1993–1998.
Administration: Group.
Restricted Distribution: Secure instruments administered at centers established by the publisher.

Comments: Tests administered 7 times annually; earlier versions previously available as NTE Programs (1940–1992).
Author: Educational Testing Service.
Publisher: Educational Testing Service.
a) PRAXIS I: ACADEMIC SKILLS ASSESSMENTS.
Purpose: Designed to be taken early in a student's college career to measure reading, writing and mathematical skills.
Price Data, 2006: PPST tests: $35 per test; CPPST tests: $75 for one test, $110 for two tests, $145 for three tests; $125 for CPPST combined test.
Time: PPST tests: 60 minutes per test; PI-CBT tests: 120 minutes per test.
Comments: Includes the paper-based Pre-Professional Skills Test (PPST®) and the Praxis I Computer-Based Tests (PI-CPPST) in Reading, Writing, and Mathematics.
b) PRAXIS II: SUBJECT ASSESSMENTS.
Purpose: Measures a student's content knowledge of subjects he or she will teach.
Price Data: $60 each per 1-hour Multiple-Choice tests; $75 each per 1-hour Constructed-Response tests; $75 each per 2-hour Multiple-Choice tests; $190 each per 2-hour Constructed-Response tests; $85 each per 2-hour Multiple-Choice and Constructed-Response tests; $115 each per Principals of Learning and Teaching test.
Comments: Includes: Subject Assessments/Specialty Area test, 1-hour Multiple-Choice tests, 1-hour Constructed-Response tests, 2-hour Multiple-Choice tests, 2-hour Constructed-Response tests, and Principals of Learning and Teaching (PLT) test.
c) PRAXIS III: CLASSROOM PERFORMANCE ASSESSMENT.
Comments: Developed to assess teachers' classroom performance for licensure needs of some states. To determine whether required in a particular state, please contact that state's department of education.
Cross References: For information on earlier editions of the NTE Core Battery, see T4:1824 (5 references), T3:1624 (1 reference), and 8:382 (2 references). For information on earlier editions of the Pre-Professional Skills Test, see T4:2071 (6 references); for reviews by Don B. Oppenheim and Edys S. Quellmalz of an earlier edition, see 9:975.

[1993]
Predictive Ability Test, Adult Edition.

Purpose: Measures "the ability to predict" as the basis for determining intelligence.
Population: Ages 17 and over.
Publication Date: 1974.
Acronym: PAT.
Scores: Overall performance score.

Administration: Group.
Price Data: Available from publisher.
Time: [30-40] minutes.
Author: Myles I. Friedman.
Publisher: Myles I. Friedman.
Cross References: For a review by Arthur R. Jensen, see 9:971.

[1994]
Pre-Kindergarten Screen.

Purpose: Designed "to be a quick screening instrument for children between the ages of 4 years 0 months and 5 years 11 months who may be at risk for early academic difficulty."
Population: Ages 4 through 6.
Publication Date: 2000.
Acronym: PKS.
Scores, 10: Gross Motor Skills, Fine Motor Skills, Following Directions, Block Tapping, Visual Matching, Visual Memory, Imitation, Basic Academic Skills, Delayed Gratification, Total.
Administration: Individual.
Price Data, 2006: $65 per test kit including manual (56 pages), 50 record forms, and test plates; $25 per 50 record forms; $18 per test plates; $22 per manual.
Time: [15] minutes.
Authors: Raymond E. Webster and Angela Matthews.
Publisher: Academic Therapy Publications.
Cross References: For reviews by Mary M. Chittooran and Mary Lou Kelley, see 15:194.

[1995]
PreLAS® 2000.

Purpose: Designed to "assess oral language proficiency and preliteracy skills in young children"; the PreLAS2000 "assesses receptive language and expressive language, which requires all the processing capacities of comprehension plus cognitive organization and the performance of appropriate motor behavior to make the requisite speech sounds"; helps measure the language development of first- and second-language students in both English and Spanish.
Population: Ages 4–6.
Publication Date: 1998.
Scores, 12: Oral Language Component (Simon Says, Art Show, Say What You Hear, Human Body, Story #1, Story #2); Pre-Literacy Component (Letters, Numbers, Colors, Shapes, Reading, Writing).
Administration: Individual.
Parts, 2: Oral Language Component, Pre-Literacy Component.
Price Data, 2006: $216 per examiner's kit including manual (79 pages); $34 per technical report.
Time: (15–25) minutes.
Authors: Sharon E. Duncan and Edward A. De Avila.

Publisher: CTB/McGraw-Hill.
Cross References: For reviews by Sheila Pratt and Annita Marie Ward, see 15:195.

[1996]
Preliminary SAT/National Merit Scholarship Qualifying Test.

Purpose: "Measures reasoning, math problem-solving, and writing skills generally associated with academic achievement in college—for guidance in grades 10-11 and entry to scholarship programs in grade 11."
Population: Grades 10-11.
Publication Dates: 1959-1998.
Acronym: PSAT/NMSQT.
Scores, 4: Verbal, Mathematical, Writing Skills, Section Index (for scholarship consideration by NMSC).
Administration: Group.
Price Data: Available from publisher.
Special Editions: Braille, cassette, script, and large-type editions available.
Time: [140] minutes.
Comments: A shortened version of SAT I; administered in October at participating secondary schools; testing accommodations available for students with disabilities.
Author: Administered for the College Board and National Merit Scholarship Corporation by Educational Testing Service.
Publisher: Educational Testing Service.
Cross References: See T5:2031 (11 references), T4:2067 (6 references), and T3:1866 (7 references); for reviews by Jerome E. Doppelt and J. Thomas Hastings, see 8:199 (15 references); see also T2:436 (4 references) and 7:375 (10 references); for a review by Wayne S. Zimmerman of earlier forms, see 6:487 (2 references).

[1997]
Preliminary Test of English as a Foreign Language.

Purpose: Designed to evaluate the English language skills of nonnative speakers of English at the beginning levels of study.
Population: College and other institutional applicants, grade 11 and over, from non-English-language countries.
Publication Dates: 1983–1989.
Acronym: Pre-TOEFL®.
Scores, 4: 3 section scores for Listening Comprehension, Structure and Written Expression, Reading Comprehension and Vocabulary, and a Total score.
Administration: Group.
Price Data: Price information available from publisher for examination fee per institution per administration; fee includes machine scoring by publisher, test results, and use of booklets and administrative materials which must be returned to publisher.

Time: 70 minutes.
Comments: A shorter test measuring the same components of language proficiency as the regular TOEFL; 2 forms per year; Pre-TOEFL is offered only through the TOEFL Institutional Testing Program.
Authors: Jointly sponsored by College Entrance Examination Board, Graduate Record Examination Board, and Educational Testing Service.
Publisher: Educational Testing Service.
Cross References: For reviews by Roger A. Richards and Charlene Rivera, see 11:298. For reviews by Brenda H. Loyd and Kikumi K. Tatsuoka of the Test of English as a Foreign Language, see 9:1257 (1 reference); see also T3:2441 (9 references), 8:110 (15 references), and T2:238 (4 references); for reviews by Clinton I. Chase and George Domino of the TOEFL, see 7:266 (10 references).

[1998]
Pre-Literacy Skills Screening.

Purpose: Provides a quick look at the reading readiness skills of children beginning school.
Population: Kindergarten.
Publication Date: 1999.
Acronym: PLSS.
Scores, 11: Rhyme, Sentence Repetition, Naming Accuracy, Naming Time, Blending, Sentence Segmentation, Letter Naming, Syllable Segmentation, Deletion, Multisyllabic Word Repetition, Overall Score.
Administration: Individual.
Price Data, 2006: $51 per complete kit including 25 record forms, and examiner's manual (30 pages); $20 per 25 record forms; $33 per examiner's manual.
Time: (15) minutes.
Authors: Linda Crumrine and Helen Lonegan.
Publisher: PRO-ED.
Cross References: For reviews by Carol E. Kessler and Koressa Kutsick Malcolm, see 15:196.

[1999]
A Premarital Communication Inventory.

Purpose: "To help counselors assess the marriageability of a couple."
Population: Premarital couples.
Publication Dates: 1968-1982.
Acronym: PCI.
Scores: Total score only.
Administration: Group.
Price Data, 1993: $.75 per inventory; $2.50 per manual (1982, 6 pages).
Time: (20) minutes.
Author: Millard J. Bienvenu.
Publisher: Millard J. Bienvenu, Northwest Publications.
Cross References: For a review by James R. Clopton, see 8:351.

[2000]
PREPARE/ENRICH.

Purpose: Designed as a series of tests for use in assessing couples' relationships.
Population: Premarital and married couples.
Scores: 17 scores common to all four tests: Idealistic Distortion, Personality Issues, Communication, Conflict Resolution, Financial Management, Leisure Activities, Sexual Expectations, Role Relationship, Spiritual Beliefs, Couple Closeness, Couple Flexibility, Family Closeness, Family Flexibility, Self-Confidence, Assertiveness, Avoidance, Partner Dominance.
Administration: Individual or group.
Price Data, 2006: $150 per training in day workshop, which includes Counselor's Manual and 5 couple inventories including PREPARE, PREPARE-MC (Marriage with Children), PREPARE-CC (Cohabiting Couples), ENRICH, and MATE; $195 per self-training option for professional counselors including the above materials and the day workshop on a 3 DVD set; online version available.
Time: (30-45) minutes.
Comments: Counselor Computer Report (15 pages) and Building Strong Marriage Booklet for Couple (25 pages) with six couple exercises are available; additional information is available at www.prepare-enrich.com.
Publisher: Life Innovations, Inc.

a) PREMARITAL PERSONAL AND RELATIONSHIP EVALUATION.
Purpose: Designed to help couples getting ready for marriage (who do not have children) assess their relationship.
Population: Couples planning to marry who do not have children.
Publication Dates: 1978–1998.
Acronym: PREPARE.
Scores, 20: 17 scores common to all 5 tests plus Marital Expectations, Children and Parenting, Family and Friends.
Authors: David H. Olson, David G. Fournier, and Joan M. Druckman.

b) PREMARITAL PERSONAL AND RELATIONSHIP EVALUATION—MARRIED WITH CHILDREN.
Purpose: Designed to help couples who are planning to marry (and who already have children) assess their relationship and identify important issues.
Population: Couples planning to marry who have children.
Publication Dates: 1981–1998.
Acronym: PREPARE-MC.
Scores, 20: Same as *a* above.
Authors: David H. Olson, David G. Fournier, and Joan M. Druckman.

c) ENRICHING RELATIONSHIP ISSUES, COMMUNICATION AND HAPPINESS.

Purpose: Designed to assess relationship strengths and areas for growth.

Population: Married couples or couples who have cohabitated for 2 or more years.

Publication Dates: 1981–1998.

Acronym: ENRICH.

Scores, 19: 17 scores common to all 5 tests plus: Marital Satisfaction, Children and Parenting.

Authors: David H. Olson, David G. Fournier, and Joan M. Druckman.

d) MATURE AGE TRANSITION EVALUATION.

Purpose: Designed to help mature couples who are preparing for marriage assess their relationships.

Population: Couples over 50 planning marriage.

Publication Dates: 1995–1998.

Acronym: MATE.

Scores, 20: 17 scores common to all 5 tests plus: Life Transitions, Intergenerational Issues, Health Issues.

Authors: David H. Olson and Elinor Adams.

e) PREPARE FOR COHABITING COUPLES.

Purpose: Designed to help couples who are living together and are planning to marry.

Acronym: PREPARE CC.

Cross References: For reviews by Corine Fitzpatrick and Jay A. Mancini, see 14:295; see also T5:2034 (7 references).

[2001]
Pre-Reading Inventory of Phonological Awareness.

Purpose: "Designed to assess phonological awareness in young students."

Population: Ages 4.0–6.11.

Publication Dates: 2000–2003.

Acronym: PIPA.

Scores, 6: Rhyme Awareness, Syllable Segmentation, Alliteration Awareness, Sound Isolation, Sound Segmentation, Letter–Sound Knowledge.

Administration: Individual.

Price Data, 2004: $135 per complete kit including manual (2003, 82 pages), stimulus book, and 25 record forms; $40 per 25 record forms; $100 per stimulus book; $75 per manual.

Time: (25–30) minutes.

Authors: Barbara Dodd, Sharon Crosbie, Beth McIntosh, Tania Teitzel, and Anne Ozanne.

Publisher: PsychCorp, A brand of Harcourt Assessment, Inc.

[2002]
Pre-Referral Intervention Manual-Third Edition.

Purpose: To provide appropriate intervention strategies for learning and behavior problems.

Population: Grades K-12.

Publication Dates: 1988-2006.

Acronym: PRIM-3.

Scores: Not scored.

Administration: Individual.

Price Data, 2006: $105 per complete kit including manual (2006, 570 pages), 50 checklist forms, and 50 intervention strategies documentation forms; $40 per manual; $35 per 50 learning and behavior problem checklists; $30 per 50 intervention strategies documentation forms; $225 per Pre-Referral Intervention Manual (WIN).

Time: Administration time not reported.

Comments: Intervention strategies in 13 areas: Memory/Abstractions/Generalizations/Organizations, Listening, Speaking, Reading, Writing, Spelling, Mathematical Calculations, Academic Performance, Interpersonal Relationships, Depression and Motivation, Inappropriate Behavior Under Normal Circumstances, Rules and Regulations, Group Behavior.

Authors: Stephen B. McCarney and Kathy Cummins Wunderlich.

Publisher: Hawthorne Educational Services, Inc.

Cross References: For reviews by Anthony W. Paolitto and Gabriele van Lingen of an earlier form, see 13:236.

[2003]
Preschool and Kindergarten Behavior Scales, Second Edition.

Purpose: "Designed for use in evaluating social skills and problem behaviors of preschool and kindergarten-age children."

Population: Ages 3–6.

Publication Dates: 1994–2002.

Acronym: PKBS-2.

Scores, 12: Social Skills (Social Cooperation, Social Interaction, Social Independence, Total), Problem Behavior (Externalizing Problems, Internalizing Problems, Total), Supplemental Problem Behavior Subscales (Self-Control/Explosive, Attention Problems/Overactive, Antisocial/Aggressive, Social Withdrawal, Anxiety/Somatic Problems).

Administration: Group.

Price Data, 2006: $110 per complete kit including examiner's manual (2002, 103 pages) and 50 profile/record forms (specify English or Spanish); $71 per examiner's manual; $41 per 50 record forms (specify English or Spanish).

Foreign Language Edition: Spanish version available.

Time: (8–12) minutes.

Comments: Ratings by home-based raters or school-based raters; Supplemental Problem Behavior Subscales can be used to identify more specific symptoms of emotional and behavioral problems.

Author: Kenneth W. Merrell.
Publisher: PRO-ED.
Cross References: For reviews by Doreen Ward Fairbank and Ronald A. Madle, see 16:194; see also T5:2036 (1 reference); for reviews by David MacPhee and T. Steuart Watson of an earlier edition, see 13:237.

[2004]
Preschool and Kindergarten Interest Descriptor.

Purpose: "Identify children with attitudes and interests usually associated with preschool and kindergarten creativity."
Population: Ages 3-6.
Publication Date: 1983.
Acronym: PRIDE.
Scores: 4 dimension scores: Originality, Imagination-Playfulness, Independence-Perseverance, Many Interests.
Administration: Group.
Price Data, 2005: $120 per complete set including manual (10 pages) and 30 scales; $15 per specimen set.
Time: (20-35) minutes.
Comments: Downward extension of the Group Inventory for Finding Creative Talent (1121); scale for rating by parents.
Author: Sylvia B. Rimm.
Publisher: Educational Assessment Service, Inc.
Cross References: For reviews by Gloria A. Galvin and Sue White, see 10:289.

[2005]
Preschool and Primary Inventory of Phonological Awareness.

Purpose: "Designed to identify children who have poor phonological awareness" and are at risk for literacy problems.
Population: Ages 3 years to 6 years, 11 months.
Publication Date: 2000.
Acronym: PIPA.
Scores: 6 subtests: Syllable Segmentation, Rhyme Awareness, Alliteration Awareness, Phoneme Isolation, Phoneme Segmentation, Letter Knowledge.
Administration: Individual.
Price Data, 2006: £92 per complete kit including record forms, stimulus manual, and manual (54 pages).
Time: (25–30) minutes; (5) minutes per subtest.
Comments: A version with U.S. norms, the Pre-Reading Inventory of Phonological Awareness (2003), is available from Harcourt Assessment (USA) and will be reviewed in the *Seventeenth Mental Measurements Yearbook*.
Authors: Barbara Dodd, Sharon Crosbie, Beth McIntosh, Tania Teitzel, and Anne Ozanne.
Publisher: Harcourt Assessment [England].
Cross References: For reviews by Carlos Inchaurralde and Gene Schwarting, see 16:195.

[2006]
Pre-School Behavior Checklist.

Purpose: "To help identify children with emotional and behavioral problems by providing a tool for the systematic and objective description of behavior."
Population: Ages 2 through 5.
Publication Date: 1988.
Acronym: PBCL.
Scores: Total score only.
Administration: Group.
Price Data, 2006: ATP prices: $67 per test kit including 25 recording forms, scoring acetate, 50 Developmental Activities Checklist forms, and manual; $20 per 25 recording forms; $10 per scoring acetate; $15 per 50 Developmental Activities Checklist forms; $22 per manual; $22 per specimen set including manual and sample forms; NFER-Nelson prices: Available from publisher.
Time: (8–10) minutes.
Comments: Behavior checklist.
Authors: Jacqueline McGuire and Naomi Richman.
Publisher: NFER-Nelson Publishing Co., Ltd. [England]; licensed to Academic Therapy Publications.
Cross References: See T5:2038 (5 references); for reviews by Roger D. Carlson and Gary Stoner, see 11:299.

[2007]
The Preschool Behavior Questionnaire.

Purpose: Designed as a screening tool to identify emotional/behavioral problems in children.
Population: Ages 3-6.
Publication Date: 1974.
Acronym: PBQ.
Scores, 4: Hostile-Aggressive, Anxious-Fearful, Hyperactive-Distractible, Total.
Administration: Group.
Price Data, 2005: $25 per 50 questionnaires, 50 scores sheets, and manual (16 pages).
Time: [5-10] minutes.
Comments: Modification of Michael A. Rutter's 1967 unpublished Children's Behavior Questionnaire; available in English and Spanish.
Authors: Lenore Behar and Samuel Stringfield.
Publisher: Lenore Behar (the author).
Cross References: See T5:2039 (24 references) and T4:2077 (15 references); for a review by Robert A. Fox, see 9:978 (6 references).

[2008]
Preschool Child Observation Record, Second Edition.

Purpose: Designed to create a "picture of children's development and abilities."
Population: Ages 2-6 to 6-0 years.
Publication Dates: 1992-2003.

Acronym: COR.
Scores: 7 areas: Initiative, Social Relations, Creative Representation, Movement/Music, Language and Literacy, Mathematics/Science, Total.
Administration: Indivdual or group.
Price Data, 2006: $174.95 per complete kit including 2 Observation Items manuals (2003, 45 pages), user's guide, What's Next? Planning Children's Activities Around Preschool Child Observations Guide, 25 Child Anecdotes booklets, 25 Parent Guide booklets (includes Spanish version), 1 Class Summary form, 25 Child Information and Developmental Summary forms, 50 Parent Report forms (includes Spanish version), Preschool COR poster, High/Scope Preschool Key Experiences poster, 2 complete desk posters, and 2 sets of COR category tabs; $14.95 per 2 Observation Items manuals; $15.95 per user's guide; $16.95 per What's Next? Planning Children's Activities Around Preschool Child Observations Guide; $39.95 per 25 Child Anecdotes booklets; $39.95 per 25 Parent Guide booklets (includes Spanish version); $11.95 per 1 Class Summary form and 25 Child Information and Developmental Summary forms; $16.95 per 50 Parent Report forms (includes Spanish version); $5.95 per Preschool COR poster; $5.95 per High/Scope Preschool Key Experiences poster; $8.95 per 2 complete desk posters.
Foreign Editions: Parent Guide booklets (2003) and Parent Report forms available in Spanish.
Time: Untimed.
Comments: This test is to be completed by teachers and parents/guardians; previous version was entitled High/Scope Child Observation Record for Ages 2 1/2—6.
Author: High/Scope Educational Research Foundation.
Publisher: High/Scope Educational Research Foundation.
Cross References: For reviews by Glen P. Aylwood and Mary Mathai Chittooran of an earlier version, see 14:167.

[2009]
Preschool Development Inventory.

Purpose: A brief screening inventory "designed to help identify children with developmental, behavioral, or health problems."
Population: Ages 3–6.
Publication Dates: 1984–1998.
Acronym: PDI.
Scores: General Development Score, Possible Problems List (24); 4 ratings: Child Description, Special Problems or Handicaps, Parent's Questions/Concerns, Parent's Functioning.
Administration: Individual.
Price Data, 2005: $12.50 per manual (1998, 25 pages); $12.50 per 25 parent questionnaires.

Time: (15) minutes.
Comments: Parent-completed questionnaire; replaces the Minnesota Preschool Inventory (aka Minnesota PreKindergarten Inventory) (9:720) and the Preschool Developmental Inventory (10:291) and publisher now recommends using Child Development Review Parent Questionnaire (455) over this.
Author: Harold Ireton.
Publisher: Child Development Review - Behavior Science Systems, Inc.
Cross References: For reviews by Lena R. Gaddis and Diane J. Sawyer, see 13:238; see also T4:2079 (1 reference); for a review by R. A. Bornstein of an earlier edition, see 10:291.

[2010]
Preschool Developmental Profile.

Purpose: "Designed to write an individualized education program and to serve as a way of measuring a child's developmental progress."
Population: Children who function at the 3–6-year developmental age.
Publication Dates: 1977–2006.
Scores, 10: Perceptual/Fine Motor, Cognition (Classification, Number, Space, Seriation, Time), Speech and Language, Social Emotional, Self-Care, Gross Motor.
Administration: Individual.
Price Data: Available from publisher and at www.press.umich.edu.
Time: (50–60) minutes.
Comments: See Early Intervention Developmental Profile (884) for developmental ages of 0 to 36 months.
Authors: Diane B. D'Eugenio, Martha S. Moersch, Sara L. Brown, Judith E. Drews, B. Suzanne Haskin, Eleanor Whiteside Lynch, and Sally J. Rogers.
Publisher: University of Michigan Press.
Cross References: For reviews by Doreen Ward Fairbank and David MacPhee, see 13:239.

[2011]
Preschool Evaluation Scale.

Purpose: Designed to assess behavior related to developmental delays.
Population: Birth–72 months.
Publication Dates: 1991–1992.
Acronym: PES.
Scores, 6: Large Muscle Skills, Small Muscle Skills, Cognitive Thinking, Expressive Language Skills, Social/Emotional, Self-Help Skills.
Administration: Individual.
Levels, 2: Birth–35 months, 36–72 months.
Price Data, 2006: $180 per complete kit including school and home technical manuals ($15 each), 50 School Version birth–35 months rating forms, 50 Home Version birth–35 months rating forms, 50 School Ver-

sion 36–72 months rating forms, 50 Home Version 36–72 months rating forms (each pkg. [50] $35; forms also available in Spanish); $35 per computerized quick score (WIN).
Time: (20–25) minutes.
Comments: Ratings by parents or child care providers.
Author: Stephen B. McCarney.
Publisher: Hawthorne Educational Services, Inc.
Cross References: For reviews by Mary Mathai Chittooran and Lena R. Gaddis, see 13:240.

[2012]
Preschool Language Assessment Instrument—Second Edition.

Purpose: Designed to test "children's discourse abilities" in "aspects of early educational exchanges."
Population: Ages 3-0 to 5-11.
Publication Dates: 1978–2003.
Acronym: PLAI-2.
Administration: Individual.
Forms, 2: Age 3 years, Ages 4–5 years.
Price Data, 2006: $197 per complete kit including examiner's manual (2003, 71 pages), picture book, 25 profile/examiner record booklets—3-year-olds, and 25 profile/examiner record booklets—4/5-year-olds; $52 per examiner's manual; $77 per picture book; $40 per 25 profile/examiner's record booklets for 3-year-olds; $40 per 25 profile/examiner's record booklets for 4/5-year-olds.
Time: (30) minutes.
Comments: Includes nonstandardized procedures for analyzing adequacy of response and interfering behaviors.
Authors: Marion Blank, Susan A. Rose, and Laura J. Berlin.
Publisher: PRO-ED.
   a) AGES 3 YEARS.
   Scores, 6: Discourse Ability (Matching, Selective Analysis, Reordering and Reasoning, Receptive, Expressive, Total).
   b) AGES 4–5 YEARS.
   Scores, 7: Discourse Ability (Matching, Selective Analysis, Reordering, Reasoning, Receptive, Expressive, Total).
Cross References: For reviews by Koressa Kutsick Malcolm and Rebecca McCauley, see 16:197; see also T5:2044 (6 references) and T4:2083 (2 references); for reviews by William O. Haynes and Kenneth G. Shipley of a previous edition, see 9:979.

[2013]
Preschool Language Scale, Fourth Edition.

Purpose: Designed to "identify children who have a language disorder or delay."
Population: Ages birth to 6-11.
Publication Dates: 1969–2002.
Acronym: PLS-4.

Scores, 4: Auditory Comprehension, Expressive Communication, Total Language, Articulation.
Administration: Individual.
Price Data, 2003: $235 per English basic kit with manipulatives including examiner's manual (2002, 287 pages), picture manual, 15 record forms, and 23 manipulatives; $185 per English basic kit without manipulatives including examiner's manual, picture manual, and 15 record forms; $60 per examiner's manual; $109 per picture manual; $37 per 15 English record forms; $59 per set of manipulatives.
Foreign Language Edition: Spanish edition available.
Time: (20–45) minutes.
Comments: Fourth edition adds supplemental subtests and norms based on 2000 U.S. Census figures.
Authors: Irla Lee Zimmerman, Violette G. Steiner, and Roberta Evatt Pond.
Publisher: Harcourt Assessment, Inc.
   a) ARTICULATION SCREENER.
   Purpose: Designed to evaluate articulation in single words.
   Population: Ages 2-6 to 6-11.
   Scores: Total score only.
   Time: (2) minutes.
   Comments: "Criterion-referenced" optional subtest.
   b) LANGUAGE SAMPLE CHECKLIST.
   Purpose: Designed to evaluate spontaneous speech.
   Population: Ages 1 to 6-11.
   Scores: No scores.
   Time: (15–60) minutes.
   Comments: Supplemental checklist allows validation of information obtained from the Expressive Communication subscale.
   c) CAREGIVER QUESTIONNAIRE.
   Purpose: Designed to "enable parents/caregivers to provide information about the child's communication behaviors" at home or preschool.
   Population: Ages birth to 2-11.
   Scores: Not scored.
   Time: (15–20) minutes.
   Comments: Supplemental questionnaire; may be administered as an interview.
Cross References: For reviews by Terri Flowerday and Hoi K. Suen, see 16:198; see also T5:2045 (6 references); for reviews by J. Jeffrey Grill and Janet A. Norris of a previous edition, see 13:241 (26 references); see also T4:2084 (24 references); for an excerpted review by Barton B. Proger of a previous editions, see 8:929 (3 references); see also T2:2024 (1 reference); for a review by Joel Stark and an excerpted review by C. H. Ammons, see 7:965.

[2014]
Preschool Motor Speech Evaluation & Intervention.

Purpose: To assess oral motor and motor speech abilities of children from 18 to 60 months who are exhibiting significant speech delays.
Population: Ages 18–60 months.
Publication Date: 2000.
Scores: No scores.
Administration: Individual.
Price Data, 2006: $59 per complete kit including spiral-bound soft cover manual with an assessment form and several reproducible pages.
Time: (75–160) minutes.
Comments: Parent interview/observation.
Author: Margaret M. Earnest.
Publisher: PRO-ED.

[2015]
Preschool Program Quality Assessment, Second Edition.

Purpose: "Designed to evaluate the quality of early childhood programs and identify staff training needs."
Population: Center-based early childhood education settings.
Publication Dates: 1998-2003.
Acronym: PQA.
Administration: Individual or group.
Forms, 2: A, B.
Price Data, 2006: $25.95 per complete kit including administration manual (2003, 32 pages), Form A-Classroom Items, Form B-Agency Items, and set of Index Tabs; $12.95 per administration manual; $6.95 per Form B-Agency items; $6.95 per Form A-Classroom Items; $1.95 per index tab set.
Time: Administration time not reported.
Comments: "Based on classroom observations and interviews with teaching and administrative staff."
Author: High/Scope Educational Research Foundation.
Publisher: High/Scope Educational Research Foundation.
   a) FORM A-CLASSROOM ITEMS.
   Scores, 5: Learning Environment, Daily Routine, Adult-Child Interaction, Curriculum Planning/Assessment, Classroom Score.
   b) FORM B-AGENCY ITEMS.
   Scores, 4: Parent Involvement/Family Services, Staff Qualifications/Development, Program Management, Agency Score.
Cross References: For reviews by Michael B. Bunch and William J. Sauser, Jr. of an earlier version, see 15:198.

[2016]
Preschool Screening Instrument.

Purpose: Designed to identify potential learning problems in prekindergarten children.
Population: Ages 3-0 to 5-3.
Publication Date: 1979.
Acronym: PSSI.
Scores, 6: Human Figure Drawing, Visual Motor Perception/Fine Motor, Gross Motor, Language Development, Speech, Behavior.
Administration: Individual.
Price Data, 2005: $90 per complete kit including 25 student record forms, 25 parental questionnaires, story card, manipulatives, and manual (40 pages); $30 per 25 student record forms; $20 per 25 parental questionnaires; $23 per manual.
Time: (5–8) minutes.
Author: Stephen Paul Cohen.
Publisher: Stoelting Co.
Cross References: For a review by Gene Schwarting, see 9:981.

[2017]
Preschool Screening System.

Purpose: For identifying children with special needs.
Population: Ages 2-6 to 5-9.
Publication Date: 1980.
Acronym: PSS.
Scores: Child Record Form: 7 skills areas: Body Awareness and Control Skills, Visual-Perceptual-Motor Skills, Language Skills, Imitation, Learned Skills, Behavioral Characteristics, Total; Parental Questionnaire: 3 area profiles: Developmental History, Medical History, Behavioral History.
Administration: Individual.
Parts: Child Record Form; Parental Questionnaire.
Price Data: Available from publisher.
Time: 20(25) minutes.
Authors: Peter K. Hainsworth and Marion L. Hainsworth.
Publisher: ERISys [No reply from publisher; status unknown].
Cross References: See T4:2086 (1 reference).

[2018]
The Pre-School Screening Test.

Purpose: To screen children for special educational needs.
Population: 3 years 6 months to 4 years 5 months.
Publication Date: 2001.
Acronym: PREST.
Scores, 14: PREST 1 (Rapid Naming, Bead Threading & Paper Cutting, Digits & Letters, Repetition, Shape Copying, Corsi Frog, At-Risk Total), PREST 2 (Balance, Phonological Discrimination, Digit Span, Rhyme, Sound Order, Teddy and Form Matching, At-Risk Total).

Administration: Individual.
Price Data, 2006: £97 per complete kit including manual (98 pages), score keys, sample permission letter, test cards, beads, cord, sound order tape, frog pond card and frog, 50 double-sided record forms, and training video in a bag; £29 per manual; £38.50 per 50 record forms.
Time: (10–30) minutes.
Authors: Angela Fawcett, Rod Nicholson, and Ray Lee.
Publisher: Harcourt Assessment [England].
Cross References: For reviews by Sherry K. Bain and Young Ju Lee and by Gene Schwarting, see 16:196.

[2019]
Preschool Skills Test.

Purpose: "Designed to assess the [developmental] skills of preschool-aged, early elementary or mentally handicapped children."
Population: Age 2 through Grade 2 level children.
Publication Dates: 1983–1993.
Scores: 7 developmental areas: Fine Motor, Personal/Social, Visual, Visual Identification, Number Concepts, Discrimination/Matching, Readiness/Academic.
Administration: Individual.
Price Data: Available from publisher.
Time: [20–30] minutes.
Comments: Previous edition entitled Preschool Screening Test.
Author: Carol Lepera.
Publisher: Preschool Skills Test.
Cross References: For reviews by Doreen Ward Fairbank and Mark E. Swerdlik, see 14:296; for a review by Ruth Tomes of an earlier edition, see 12:303.

[2020]
Present State Examination.

Purpose: Clinical interview questionnaire for ratings of psychiatric symptoms reported by patient during preceding month.
Population: Adult psychiatric patients.
Publication Dates: 1967–1974.
Acronym: PSE.
Scores: 38 syndrome scores and various derived scores.
Administration: Individual.
Price Data: Available from publisher.
Time: (45–60) minutes.
Comments: No scoring instructions except description of computer scoring program.
Authors: J. K. Wing, J. E. Cooper, and N. Sartorius.
Publisher: Cambridge University Press.
Cross References: See T5:2050 (142 references), T4:2091 (237 references), 9:985 (71 references), and T3:1883 (70 references); for a review by Jack Zusman, Isabel C. A. Moyes, Clive A. Sims, and David Goldberg, see 8:649.

[2021]
The Press Test.

Purpose: Measures how well an individual performs tasks when experiencing stress.
Population: Managers and high-level professionals.
Publication Dates: 1959–1987.
Scores, 5: Reading Speed, Color-Naming Speed, Color-Naming Speed With Distraction, Difference Between Color-Naming Speed With and Without Distraction, Difference Between Reading Speed and Color-Naming Speed.
Administration: Individual or group.
Price Data: Available from publisher.
Time: (6–10) minutes.
Authors: Melany E. Baehr and Raymond J. Corsini.
Publisher: Pearson Performance Solutions [No reply from publisher; status unknown].
Cross References: For a review by Robert P. Vecchio, see 9:986; see also T3:1884 (2 references), T2:1333 (1 reference), and P:213 (1 reference); for reviews by William H. Helm and Allyn Miles Munger, see 6:163.

[2022]
The Prevocational Assessment and Curriculum Guide.

Purpose: Designed to "assess and identify the prevocational training needs of handicapped persons."
Population: Mentally retarded individuals.
Publication Dates: 1978–1993.
Acronym: PACG.
Scores: 9 categories: Attendance/Endurance, Independence, Production, Learning, Behavior, Communication, Social Skills, Grooming/Eating, Toileting.
Administration: Individual.
Price Data, 2005: $12 per complete kit including 10 inventories, summary profile sheets, curriculum guides, and one manual (6 pages); $8 per set of 10 additional forms.
Time: [15–20] minutes.
Comments: Ratings by professional acquainted with individual; title on test is PACG Inventory.
Authors: Dennis E. Mithaug, Deanna K. Mar, and Jeffrey E. Stewart.
Publisher: Exceptional Education.
Cross References: For reviews by Richard A. Wantz and Jean M. Williams, see 12:304.

[2023]
Prevocational Assessment Screen.

Purpose: "Designed to assess a student's motor and perceptual abilities in relation to performance requirements within a local vocational training program."
Population: Grades 8-12.
Publication Dates: 1985–2000.
Acronym: PAS.

Scores, 16: Time and Error scores for 8 modules: Alphabetizing, Etch A Sketch Maze, Calculating, Small Parts, Pipe Assembly, O Rings, Block Design, Color Sort.
Administration: Individual.
Price Data, 2002: $1,195 per complete kit including manual (50 pages) and computer software for use in scoring and reporting.
Time: (50) minutes.
Author: Michele Rosinek.
Publisher: Piney Mountain Press, Inc.
Cross References: For reviews by Stephen L. Koffler and James B. Rounds, see 12:305.

[2024]
Primary Measures of Music Audiation.

Purpose: To assess basic music aptitudes.
Population: K-3.
Publication Date: 1979.
Acronym: PMMA.
Scores, 3: Tonal, Rhythm, Composite.
Administration: Group.
Price Data, 2006: $100 per complete kit including 1 tonal and rhythm compact disc, 100 total answer sheets and 100 rhythm answer sheets, 1 set of scoring masks, 100 profile cards, 4 class record sheets, and test manual (107 pages); $25 per CD ; $41.50 per 100 tonal or rhythm answer sheets; $5 per set of scoring masks; $15.50 per 100 profile cards; $2 per 10 class record sheets; $20 per manual.
Time: (20) minutes per tonal tape and (20) minutes per rhythm tape.
Comments: For upward extension, see Intermediate Measures of Music Audiation (1260); test administered by CD.
Author: Edwin E. Gordon.
Publisher: GIA Publications, Inc.
Cross References: See T4:2099 (2 references); for reviews by Paul R. Lehman and Walter L. Wehner, see 9:988; see also T3:1891 (1 reference).

[2025]
Primary Test of Cognitive Skills.

Purpose: Designed to "measure verbal, spatial, memory, and conceptual abilities."
Population: Grades K–1.
Publication Date: 1990.
Acronym: PTCS.
Scores, 5: Spatial, Memory, Concepts, Verbal, Total.
Administration: Group.
Price Data: Price information available from publisher for test materials including manual (70 pages), norms book (82 pages), and technical bulletin (23 pages); scoring service available from publisher.
Time: Untimed, (30) minutes per subtest; (120) minutes total test.

Authors: Janellen Huttenlocher and Susan Cohen Levine.
Publisher: CTB/McGraw-Hill.
Cross References: For reviews by Sherry K. Bain and Laura L. B. Barnes and David E. McIntosh, see 12:307.

[2026]
Principles of Adult Mentoring Inventory.

Purpose: Designed "to provide a self-assessment instrument for those who have assumed the role of mentor in their contact with adult learners."
Population: Adults.
Publication Date: 1998.
Acronym: PAMI.
Scores, 7: Relationship Emphasis/Trust, information Emphasis/Advice, Facilitative Focus/Alternatives, Confrontive Focus/Challenge, Mentor Model/Motivation, Employee Vision/Initiative, Total.
Administration: Individual.
Price Data, 2001: $39.95 per leader's guide (51 pages); $4.95 per critique form.
Time: Administration time not reported.
Author: Norman H. Cohen.
Publisher: HRD Press, Inc.
Cross References: For reviews by L. Carolyn Pearson and Trey Martindale and by Cecil R. Reynolds, see 15:197.

[2027]
PrinTest—Forms A-C and B-C.

Purpose: "Select or develop entry-level production or maintenance employees where the reading of prints and drawings is required."
Population: Adults.
Publication Dates: 1990–2001.
Acronym: RCJS-PrinTest.
Scores: Total score only.
Administration: Group.
Price Data, 2006: $20 per consumable self-scoring test booklet; $24.95 per manual (1998).
Time: (35) minutes.
Comments: Self-scoring instrument.
Author: Roland T. Ramsay.
Publisher: Ramsay Corporation.
Cross References: For reviews by James W. Pinkney and Nambury S. Raju, see 13:258.

[2028]
Prison Inmate Inventory.

Purpose: "Designed for inmate risk assessment and needs identification."
Population: Prison inmates.
Publication Date: 1996.
Acronym: PII.
Scores: 10 scales: Truthfulness, Violence, Antisocial, Adjustment, Self-Esteem, Alcohol, Drugs, Judgment, Distress, Stress Coping Abilities.

Administration: Group.
Price Data: Available from publisher.
Time: (35) minutes.
Comments: Available in English and Spanish; both computer version and paper-pencil format are scored on IBM-PC compatibles.
Author: Risk & Needs Assessment, Inc.
Publisher: Risk & Needs Assessment, Inc.
Cross References: For reviews by R. J. DeAyala and John A. Mills, see 14:297.

[2029]
Problem Behavior Inventory [Adult & Adolescent Screening Forms].

Purpose: Designed to help "clinicians structure and focus the diagnostic interview."
Population: Adults and adolescents.
Publication Date: 1991.
Scores: No scores.
Administration: Group.
Forms, 2: Adult, Adolescent.
Price Data, 2006: 42.50 per 25 forms (specify Adult or Adolescent).
Time: (10-20) minutes.
Author: Leigh Silverton.
Publisher: Western Psychological Services.

[2030]
Problem Experiences Checklist.

Purpose: Developed for use prior to the initial intake interview to identify potential problems for further discussion.
Population: Adolescents, adults.
Publication Date: 1991.
Scores: No scores.
Administration: Individual.
Editions, 2: Adolescent, Adult.
Manual: No manual.
Price Data, 2006: $27.50 per 25 checklists (specify Adult or Adolescent).
Time: [10-15] minutes.
Author: Leigh Silverton.
Publisher: Western Psychological Services.
Cross References: For reviews by Mark H. Daniel and Michael J. Sporakowski, see 12:309.

[2031]
Problem-Solving Decision-Making Style Inventory.

Purpose: Provides feedback on one's perception of problem-solving and decision-making styles of self or others.
Population: High school and college and adults in organizational settings.
Publication Date: 1982.
Scores, 4: Delegative, Facilitative, Consultative, Authoritative.

Administration: Group.
Forms, 2: Self, Other.
Manual: No manual (administrative and scoring directions included in instrument).
Price Data: Price information available from publisher.
Time: Administration time not reported.
Comments: Self-administered ratings questionnaire.
Authors: Paul Hersey and Walter E. Natemeyer.
Publisher: Jossey-Bass, A Wiley Company.
Cross References: For reviews by David N. Dixon and Paul McReynolds, see 10:295.

[2032]
The Problem Solving Inventory.

Purpose: "To assess an individual's perceptions of his or her own problem-solving behaviors and attitudes."
Population: Age 16 and above.
Publication Date: 1988.
Acronym: PSI.
Scores, 4: Problem-Solving Confidence, Approach-Avoidance Style, Personal Control, Total.
Administration: Group and individual.
Price Data, 2001: $31.25 per 25 test booklets; $13.50 per scoring key; $32 per manual (23 pages); $47 per preview kit including manual, test booklet, and scoring key.
Time: (10-15) minutes.
Comments: Self-ratings scale.
Author: P. Paul Heppner.
Publisher: CPP, Inc.
Cross References: See T5:2065 (35 references) and T4:2108 (26 references); for reviews by Cameron J. Camp and Steven G. LoBello, see 11:303 (11 references).

[2033]
Process Assessment of the Learner: Test Battery for Reading and Writing.

Purpose: "Designed for assessing the development of reading and writing processes in children in kindergarten through grade 6."
Population: Grades K–6.
Publication Date: 2001.
Acronym: PAL.
Administration: Individual.
Levels, 3: Kindergarten, Grades 1–3, Grades 4–6.
Price Data, 2002: $260 per complete kit in a box including examiner's manual (180 pages), 2 stimulus booklets, 25 record forms, 25 response forms, stylus-wood, word card, audiotape, and shield; $285 per complete kit in a bag including examiner's manual, 2 stimulus booklets, 25 record forms, 25 response forms, stylus-wood, word card, audiotape, and shield; $150 per PAL Scoring Assistant for Windows (CD ROM or 3.5-inch diskette); $64 per manual; $48 per 25 record

forms or response forms; $80 per stimulus book (specify Book 1 or Book 2); $11 per word card and audiotape; PAL Test Battery Training Video available (contact publisher for price information); quantity discounts available.

Time: (30–60) minutes if all subtests for a specific grade are administered; (1–6) minutes per subtest.

Comments: Subtests may be administered separately; PAL Scoring Assistant for Windows available.

Author: Virginia Wise Berninger.

Publisher: PsychCorp, A brand of Harcourt Assessment, Inc.

a) KINDERGARTEN.
Scores, 10: Alphabet Writing, Receptive Coding—Tasks A and B, Rapid Automatized Naming—Letters, Rapid Automatized Naming—Digits, Rhyming—Tasks A and B, Syllables, Phonemes—Tasks A and B, Story Retell, Finger Sense, Copying—Task A.

b) GRADES 1–3.
Scores, 14: Alphabet Writing; Receptive Coding—Tasks A, B, and C; Rapid Automatized Naming—Letters; Rapid Automatized Naming—Words; Rapid Automatized Naming—Digits; Rapid Automatized Naming—Words and Digits; Syllables; Phonemes—Tasks A, B, and C; Rimes—Task A; Word Choice; Pseudoword Decoding; Finger Sense; Sentence Sense; Copying—Tasks A and B.

c) GRADES 4–6.
Scores, 17: Alphabet Writing; Receptive Coding—Tasks C, D, and E; Expressive Coding—Tasks A, B, and C; Rapid Automatized Naming—Letters; Rapid Automatized Naming—Words; Rapid Automatized Naming—Digits; Rapid Automatized Naming—Words and Digits; Note-Taking—Task A; Syllables; Phonemes—Task D; Rimes—Task B; Word Choice; Pseudoword Decoding; Finger Sense; Sentence Sense; Copying—Tasks A and B; Note-Taking—Task B.

Cross References: For a review by Karen E. Jennings, see 16:199.

[2034]
Productive Practices Survey.

Purpose: "To assess, describe, and pinpoint specific practices of the manager which support—or fail to support—organizational productivity."

Population: Managers.

Publication Dates: 1987–1996.

Acronym: PPS.

Scores, 12: Dimension I (Management Values, Support Structure, Managerial Credibility, Total), Dimension II (Impact, Relevance, Community, Total), Dimension III (Task Environment, Social Context, Problem Solving, Total).

Administration: Group.

Price Data, 2001: $8.95 per instrument.

Time: (30-35) minutes.

Comments: Based on model of organizational functioning called Competence Theory; self ratings; self scored.

Author: Jay Hall.

Publisher: Teleometrics International, Inc.

[2035]
Productivity Assessment Questionnaire.

Purpose: Assesses an employee's opinions about productivity in the organization in which they work.

Population: Employees.

Publication Date: 1984.

Scores: 11 areas: Policy, Leadership, Objectives, Inputs, Performance, Technology, Work Procedures, HRD, Work Quality, Managerial Skills, Quality of Work Life.

Administration: Group.

Price Data, 2006: $40 per 10 questionnaires; quantity discounts available.

Time: (10-12) minutes.

Comments: Self-administered and self-scored; can be made available for electronic administration.

Author: Robert C. Preziosi.

Publisher: Preziosi Partners, Inc.

Cross References: For a review by Robert M. Guion, see 10:297.

[2036]
Productivity Environmental Preference Survey.

Purpose: Identifies "how adults prefer to function, learn, concentrate and perform in their occupational or educational activities."

Population: Adults.

Publication Dates: 1979–1996.

Acronym: PEPS.

Scores, 20: Sound, Light, Temperature, Design, Motivated/Unmotivated, Persistent, Responsible, Structure, Learning Alone/Peer-Oriented Learner, Authority-Oriented Learner, Several Ways, Auditory Preferences, Visual Preferences, Tactile Preferences, Kinesthetic Preferences, Requires Intake, Evening/Morning, Late Morning, Afternoon, Needs Mobility.

Administration: Group or individual.

Price Data, 2006: $22.50 per 10 answer sheets for adults (includes scoring); $7.50 or less per group and subscale summary available from publisher only in addition to individual profiles; $.60 per individual interpretative booklet; $9 per manual (1996, 66 pages); $395 per computerized self-administered inventory program with 100 administrations (multi-language version $495) ($60 per 100 additional administrations) (Windows); $495 for Scanwin program permitting schools and businesses to

scan and profile forms on site, includes multi-language capability; $.60 per answer form to use with Scanwin.
Time: (20–30) minutes.
Comments: PC compatible computer required for (optional) computerized administration; NCS Pearson Optical Mark Reader with dual pencil reader; Scrantron 8000, 8200, 8400, or SCANMARK 2550, 2660, 2800, 4000, or 5500 Scanner with dual pencil read for Scanwin; online administration available at www.learningstyle.com.
Authors: Gary E. Price, Rita Dunn, and Kenneth Dunn.
Publisher: Price Systems, Inc.
Cross References: See T5:2069 (3 references); for reviews by Javaid Kaiser and Thaddeus Rozecki, see 13:242 (6 references); see also T4:2114 (2 references); for reviews by Craig N. Mills and Bertram C. Sippola of an earlier edition, see 11:306 (9 references).

[2037]
Professional and Managerial Position Questionnaire.
Purpose: Constructed for use in analyzing professional and managerial jobs.
Population: Professional and managerial jobs.
Publication Dates: 1980–1992.
Acronym: PMPQ.
Scores: 3 categories: Job Functions, Personal Requirements, Other Information.
Administration: Group.
Price Data: Available from publisher.
Time: Administration time not reported.
Authors: J. L. Mitchell, E. J. McCormick, S. Morton McPhail (manual), P. Richard Jeanneret (manual), and Robert C. Mecham (manual).
Publisher: PAQ Services, Inc.
Cross References: For reviews by Mary Anne Bunda and William I. Sauser, Jr., see 12:311; for reviews of an earlier edition by Gregory H. Dobbins and George Thornton, see 9:993.

[2038]
Professional Employment Test.
Purpose: Designed to measure reading comprehension, reasoning, quantitative problem solving, and data interpretation for use in selecting personnel for professional, administrative, and managerial occupations.
Population: Potential managerial, administrative, and professional employees.
Publication Dates: 1986–2004.
Acronym: PET.
Scores: Total score only.
Administration: Group or individual.
Forms, 8: A, B, C, D, A-1, B-1, C-1, D-1.
Price Data: Price information available from publisher for test material including Technical Manual

(2004, 40 pages), Supplemental Technical Manual for Form A-1 (1988, 9 pages), Supplemental Technical Manual for Forms C, D, C-1, and D-1 (2004, 11 pages), and User's Manual (2004, 19 pages).
Time: 80(85) minutes for long form; 40(45) minutes for short form.
Comments: Computerized versions available.
Authors: William W. Ruch, Richard H. McKillip, and Ricki Buckly.
Publisher: Psychological Services, Inc.
Cross References: For reviews by Gregory J. Cizek and Jayne E. Stake, see 12:312.

[2039]
Profile of Aptitude for Leadership.
Purpose: To measure an individual's relative strength in each of four leadership styles (or types of leader).
Population: Adults.
Publication Date: 1991.
Acronym: PAL.
Scores, 4: Manager (Administrator), Supervisor (Coach), Entrepreneur (Leader), Technician (Specialist).
Administration: Group or individual.
Manual: No manual.
Price Data: Price information available from publisher for test, answer sheet, and interpretation folder.
Time: (20) minutes.
Comments: Self-administered; self-scored.
Author: Training House, Inc.
Publisher: Training House, Inc.
Cross References: For reviews by Jack E. Gebart-Eaglemont and Neal Schmitt, see 13:243.

[2040]
Profile of Mood States.
Purpose: "Developed to measure mood or affective states."
Population: College and psychiatric outpatients.
Publication Dates: 1971–2003.
Acronym: POMS.
Scores, 6: Tension-Anxiety, Depression-Dejection, Anger-Hostility, Vigor-Activity, Fatigue-Inertia, Confusion-Bewilderment.
Administration: Individual or group.
Price Data, 2006: $44 per POMS Standard Kit (technical manual and 25 POMS standard Quikscore forms); $32 per technical manual; $30 per 25 Standard QuikScore forms.
Time: (5-10) minutes.
Comments: Earlier experimental forms called Lorr Outpatient Mood Scale and Psychiatric Outpatient Mood Scale; self-administering.
Authors: Douglas M. McNair, Maurice Lorr, and Leo F. Droppleman.
Publisher: Multi-Health Systems, Inc.
Cross References: See T5:2076 (187 references) and T4:2122 (191 references), 9:998 (46 references),

and T3:1904 (84 references); for reviews by William J. Eichman and Thaddeus E. Weckowicz, see 8:651 (33 references); see also T2:1337 (17 references).

[2041]
Profile of Mood States, Bi-Polar Form.

Purpose: Developed to measure mood dimensions in terms of six bipolar affective states.
Population: Ages 18–adult.
Publication Dates: 1984–2003.
Acronym: POMS-BI.
Scores, 6: Composed—Anxious, Elated—Depressed, Agreeable—Hostile, Energetic—Tired, Clearheaded—Confused, Confident—Unsure.
Administration: Group.
Price Data, 2006: $55 per POMS Bipolar Kit (POMS technical manual, POMS bipolar supplement, & 25 POMS bipolar quikscore forms); $39 per POMS technical manual and POMS bipolar supplement; $17 per POMS bipolar supplement; $30 per 25 POMS bipolar quikscore forms.
Time: (5-10) minutes.
Authors: Maurice Lorr, Douglas M. McNair, and W. P. Heuchert.
Publisher: Multi-Health Systems, Inc.
Cross References: See T5:2077 (9 references).

[2042]
Profile of Nonverbal Sensitivity.

Purpose: "Designed to measure ability to decode nonverbal cues conveyed by the face, body, and tone of voice."
Population: Grades 3-16 and adults.
Publication Date: 1979.
Acronym: PONS.
Scores: Total score only.
Administration: Group.
Price Data: Price information available from publisher for manual (1979, 90 pages), 50 question sheets, and 50 child's version question sheets.
Authors: Robert Rosenthal, Judith Hall, Dane Archer, Robin DiMatteo, and Peter Rogers.
Publisher: Irvington Publishers, Inc.
   a) THE FULL PONS TEST.
   Purpose: Matching facial expressions, body movements, and tone of voice to situations.
   Price Data: Price information available from publisher for VHS video cassette.
   Time: 45(50) minutes.
   b) AUDIO CASSETTE VERSION.
   Purpose: To test sensitivity to tone of voice.
   Price Data: Price information available from publisher for audio cassette.
   Time: 60(65) minutes.
   Comments: Cassette tape includes the audio sections of the Full PONS, male, female, and child speakers.
   c) FACE AND BODY PONS.
   Price Data: Price information available from publisher for VHS video cassette.
   Time: 8(13) minutes.
   Comments: Visual-only-no-sound test; contains 20 face-only and 20 body-only items from the Full PONS test.
   d) BRIEF EXPOSURE PONS.
   Price Data: Price information available from publisher for VHS video cassette.
   Time: 8(13) minutes.
   Comments: Contains same 40 items as c but the exposure times are shortened to from 2 seconds to 1/24, 3/24, 9/24, and 27/24 seconds.
   e) NON-VERBAL DISCREPANCY TEST.
   Purpose: Measures how well the viewer detects discrepant audio versus visual signals.
   Price Data: Price information available from publisher for VHS video cassette.
   Time: 30(35) minutes.
Cross References: See T5:2078 (7 references) and T4:2124 (7 references).

[2043]
ProfileXT Assessment.

Purpose: "Multi-purpose assessment that is used for selection, coaching, training, promotion, managing, and succession planning."
Population: Present and potential employees.
Publication Dates: 1999-2005.
Scores: 21 scores in 4 subgroups: Thinking Style Scale (Learning Index, Verbal Skill, Verbal Reasoning, Numerical Ability, Numeric Reasoning), Behavioral Trait Scales (Energy Level, Assertiveness, Sociability, Manageability, Attitude, Decisiveness, Accommodating, Independence, Objective Judgment), Occupational Interests Scales (Enterprising, Financial/Administrative, People Service, Technical, Mechanical, Creative), Distortion Scale.
Administration: Group or individual
Forms, 2: Online, Paper and Pencil.
Price Data: Available from publisher.
Time: (50-70) minutes.
Comments: Web-based administration available; 8 result reports: Placement Report, Coaching Report, Individual Report, Succession Planing Report, Candidate Matching Report, Job Profile Summary Report, Job Summary Graph, and Job Analysis Report.
Author: Profiles International, Inc.
Publisher: Profiles International, Inc.

[2044]
Program for Assessing Youth Employment Skills.

Purpose: Measures attitudes concerning job-holding skills and supervision, self-confidence, cognitive measures, and vocational interest for persons with low verbal skills.

Population: Adolescents and young adults with low verbal skills.
Publication Dates: 1967–1979.
Acronym: PAYES.
Scores: 7 subtests: Job-Holding Skills, Attitudes Toward Supervision, Self-Confidence, Job Knowledge, Job-Seeking Skills, Practical Reasoning, Vocational Interest Inventory.
Administration: Group.
Forms: 1 form in 3 booklets: Booklet 1 (1979, 18 pages), Booklet 2 (1979, 31 pages), Booklet 3 (1979, 11 pages).
Price Data: Not available.
Time: (75) minutes.
Comments: May be orally administered.
Author: Simon & Schuster Higher Education Group.
Publisher: Prentice Hall [No reply from publisher; status unknown].
Cross References: For reviews by Shirley A. White and Dan Zakay, see 9:1001.

[2045]
Program Self-Assessment Service.

Purpose: "To assist colleges and universities that are carrying out departmental or program reviews at the undergraduate level."
Population: Faculty members, students majoring in the department, and recent graduates.
Publication Date: 1986.
Acronym: PSAS.
Scores, 16: Environment for Learning, Scholarly Excellence, Quality of Teaching, Faculty Concern for Students, Curriculum, Departmental Procedures, Available Resources, Student Satisfaction With Program, Internship/Fieldwork/Clinical Experiences, Resource Accessibility, Employment Assistance, Faculty Work Environment, Faculty Program Involvement, Faculty Research Activities, Faculty Professional Activities, Student Accomplishments.
Administration: Group.
Forms, 3: Faculty, Student, Alumni.
Price Data: Available from publisher.
Time: (30-45) minutes.
Author: Educational Testing Service.
Publisher: Educational Testing Service.
Cross References: For a review by Darrell L. Sabers, see 10:298.

[2046]
Programmer Analyst Aptitude Test [One-Hour Version].

Purpose: To evaluate the candidate's aptitude and potential for programming and analyzing business problems.
Population: Entry-level and experienced applicants for programmer analyst positions.
Publication Date: 1997.
Acronym: PROGANI.

Scores: Total Score, Narrative Evaluation, Ranking, Recommendation.
Administration: Group.
Price Data, 2001: $235 per person; quantity discounts available.
Foreign Language Edition: Available in French.
Time: (60) minutes.
Comments: Available in booklet and Internet versions; scored by publisher; must be proctored.
Author: Bruce A. Winrow.
Publisher: Walden Personnel Performance, Inc. [Canada].
Cross References: For a review by Suzanne Young, see 16:200.

[2047]
Programmer Analyst Aptitude Test [Two-Hour Version].

Purpose: "To evaluate the candidate's aptitude and potential for programming and analyzing business problems."
Population: Applicants for programmer analyst positions.
Publication Date: 1984.
Acronym: PAAT.
Scores: Programming, Analytical, Total, Narrative Evaluation, Ranking, Recommendation.
Administration: Group.
Price Data, 2001: $350 per candidate; quantity discounts available.
Time: (120) minutes.
Comments: Tests scored by publisher only; must be proctored.
Author: Bruce Winrow.
Publisher: Walden Personnel Performance, Inc. [Canada].
Cross References: For reviews by Frederick Bessai and Ralph F. Darr, Jr., see 11:308.

[2048]
Programmer Aptitude Battery.

Purpose: Designed to assess aptitude for programming.
Population: Adults naive to programming task.
Publication Date: 1988.
Acronym: PAB.
Scores, 4: Procedures, Matrices I, Matrices II, Grand Total.
Administration: Group.
Price Data: Available from publisher.
Foreign Language Edition: Test printed in both English and Afrikaans.
Time: 100(135) minutes.
Author: T. R. Taylor.
Publisher: Human Sciences Research Council [South Africa].

[2049]

Programmer Aptitude Series.

Purpose: Assess skills needed in the data processing environment.
Population: Computer programming personnel.
Publication Dates: 1979–1983.
Acronym: PAS.
Administration: Group or individual.
Restricted Distribution: Distribution restricted to persons who have completed the publisher's training course or members of the Division of Occupational Psychology of the British Psychological Society.
Price Data: Available from publisher.
Comments: Consists of tests from within the Advanced, Personnel, and Technical Test Batteries; subtests available as separates.
Authors: Peter Saville (VA1, NA2, manual), Gill Nyfield (CP7, manual), Roger Holdsworth (VA3, NA4), David Hawkey (DA5, ST7, DT8, ST9), Sue Bawtree (CP7), Steve Blinkhorn (VA3), and Alan Iliffe (NA4).
Publisher: SHL Group plc [United Kingdom].

a) LEVEL 1.
Publication Dates: 1979–1981.
Purpose: Basic programming.

1) *Number Series.*
Publication Date: 1980.
Acronym: NA2.
Time: 15(20) minutes.

2) *Diagramming.*
Publication Date: 1980.
Acronym: DA5.
Time: 20(25) minutes.

3) *Verbal Concepts.*
Publication Date: 1980.
Acronym: VA1.
Time: 15(20) minutes.

4) *Basic Checking.*
Publication Dates: 1980–1981.
Acronym: CP7.
Time: 10(15) minutes.

5) *Spatial Recognition.*
Publication Dates: 1980–1981.
Acronym: ST9.
Time: 15(20) minutes.

b) LEVEL 2.
Publication Dates: 1979–1983.
Purpose: Complex programming skills.

1) *Number Series.*
Details same as for Level 1.
2) *Diagramming.*
Details same as for Level 1.
3) *Verbal Critical Reasoning.*
Publication Date: 1983.
Acronym: VA3.
Time: 30(35) minutes.

4) *Basic Checking.*
Details same as for Level 1.
5) *Special Reasoning.*
Publication Dates: 1979–1981.
Acronym: ST7.
Time: 20(25) minutes.

c) LEVEL 3.
Publication Dates: 1979–1983.
Population: Systems analysts and management.

1) *Verbal Concepts.*
Details same as for Level 1.
2) *Number Series.*
Details same as for Level 1.
3) *Verbal Reasoning.*
Details same as for Level 2.
4) *Numerical Critical Reasoning.*
Publication Dates: 1979–1983.
Acronym: NA4.
Time: 35(40) minutes.
5) *Diagrammatic Reasoning.*
Publication Dates: 1979–1981.
Acronym: DT8.
Time: 15(20) minutes.

[2050]

Progress Assessment Chart of Social and Personal Development.

Purpose: Constructed to assess progress in social development.
Publication Dates: 1966–1982.
Administration: Individual.
Price Data: Available from publisher.
Foreign Language Editions: Dutch, French, German, Portuguese, and Spanish editions available.
Time: Administration time not reported.
Comments: Behavior checklist.
Author: H. C. Gunzburg.
Publisher: SEFA (Publications) Ltd. [England].

a) PRIMARY PROGRESS ASSESSMENT CHART OF SOCIAL DEVELOPMENT, FORM P.
Population: Young mentally handicapped children, severely handicapped young children, and profoundly handicapped adults, very young normal children.
Acronym: P-PAC.
Scores: 4 areas: Self-Help, Communication, Occupation, Socialisation.

b) PROGRESS ASSESSMENT CHART OF SOCIAL AND PERSONAL DEVELOPMENT, FORM 1.
Population: Handicapped children and adolescents.
Acronym: PAC-1.
Scores: 5 areas: Same as a above plus Personal Assessment.

c) PROGRESS ASSESSMENT CHART OF SO-CIAL AND PERSONAL DEVELOPMENT, FORM A1.
Population: Same as *b* above.
Acronym: A-PAC1.
Scores: Same as *b* above.
Comments: Extension of PAC-1.
d) PROGRESS ASSESSMENT CHART OF SO-CIAL AND PERSONAL DEVELOPMENT, FORM 2.
Population: Mentally handicapped adolescents and adults.
Acronym: PAC-2.
Scores: Same as *b* above.
e) PROGRESS ASSESSMENT CHART OF THE SOCIAL DEVELOPMENT OF CHILDREN WITH DOWN'S SYNDROME, FORM 1.
Population: Mentally handicapped children with Down's Syndrome.
Acronym: M-PAC1.
Scores: Same as *a* above.
Authors: H. C. Gunzberg and Janice Sinson.
f) ELEMENTARY PROGRESS ASSESSMENT CHART, FORM S/E.
Population: Profoundly and severely handicapped persons.
Acronym: S/E PAC.
Scores: Same as *a* above.
g) PROGRESS ASSESSMENT CHART S1 OF SOCIAL AND PERSONAL DEVELOPMENT, FORM S1.
Population: Same as *f* above.
Acronym: S-PAC1.
Scores: Same as *b* above.
h) PROGRESS ASSESSMENT CHART OF SO-CIAL AND PERSONAL DEVELOPMENT, FORM S2.
Population: Same as *f* above.
Acronym: S-PAC2.
Scores: Same as *b* above.
Cross References: See T5:2088 (1 reference); for reviews by Betty N. Gordon and Joel Hundert, see 9:1003; see also T3:1908 (1 reference), T2:1338 (3 references), 7:125 (1 reference), and P:216 (5 references).

[2051]
Progress in English 5–14.
Purpose: Designed as "a comprehensive standardized English test series that assesses reading and writing skills."
Population: Ages 4.0–15.05.
Publication Dates: 1994–2001.
Acronym: PiE 5–14.
Administration: Group.
Price Data: Available from publisher.
Comments: Assessments linked to curriculum guidelines for England and Wales, Scotland and Northern Ireland.

Publisher: NFER-Nelson Publishing Co., Ltd. [England].
a) PROGRESS IN ENGLISH 5.
Population: Ages 4.0–6.03.
Scores, 3: Initial Literacy, Understanding of Whole Text, Total.
Time: (40) minutes.
Authors: Lynn Howard, Anne Kispal, and Neil Hagues, National Foundation for Educational Research.
b) PROGRESS IN ENGLISH 6.
Population: Ages 5.0–7.05.
Scores, 5: Early Reading, Early Reading-Spelling, Understanding of Whole Text, Understanding Language in Context.
Time: (40-45) minutes.
Authors: Anne Kispal, and Neil Hagues, National Foundation for Educational Research.
c) PROGRESS IN ENGLISH 7.
Population: Ages 6.0–8.05.
Scores, 5: Understanding of Whole Text, Understanding Language in Context, Grammar, Spelling, Total.
Time: (60) minutes.
Authors: Anne Kispal, and Neil Hagues, National Foundation for Educational Research.
d) PROGRESS IN ENGLISH 8.
Population: Ages 7.0–9.5.
Scores, 5: Spelling, Grammar, Understanding of Whole Text, Understanding Language in Context, Total.
Time: (60) minutes.
Authors: Anne Kispal, Neil Hagues, and Graham Ruddock, National Foundation for Educational Research.
e) PROGRESS IN ENGLISH 9.
Population: Ages 8.0–10.05.
Scores, 6: Same as *d* above.
Time: (60) minutes.
Authors: Anne Kispal, Neil Hagues, and Graham Ruddock, National Foundation for Educational Research.
f) PROGRESS IN ENGLISH 10.
Population: Ages 9.0–11.05.
Scores, 6: Spelling, Grammar, Understanding of Whole Text, Vocabulary(Frequency and Spelling), Style, Total.
Time: (60) minutes.
Authors: Anne Kispal, Neil Hagues, and Graham Ruddock, National Foundation for Educational Research.
g) PROGRESS IN ENGLISH 11.
Population: Ages 10.0–12.05.
Scores, 6: Same as *f* above.
Time: (60) minutes.

Authors: Anne Kispal, Neil Hagues, and Graham Ruddock, National Foundation for Educational Research.
h) PROGRESS IN ENGLISH 12.
Population: Ages 11.0–13.05.
Scores, 6: Same as *f* above.
Time: (60) minutes.
Authors: Anne Kispal, Neil Hagues, and Graham Ruddock, National Foundation for Educational Research.
i) PROGRESS IN ENGLISH 13.
Population: Ages 12.0–14.05.
Scores, 6: Same as *f* above.
Time: (60) minutes.
Authors: Annc Kispal, Neil Hagues, and Graham Ruddock, National Foundation for Educational Research.
j) PROGRESS IN ENGLISH 14.
Population: Ages 13.0–15.05.
Scores, 6: Same as *f* above.
Time: (60) minutes.
Authors: Anne Kispal, and Neil Hagues, National Foundation for Educational Research.
Cross References: For reviews by Andrew A. Cox and Natalie Rathvon, see 16:201.

[2052]
Progressive Achievement Test of Mathematics [2006].
Purpose: To assist classroom teachers in determining the mathematics skills of their students.
Population: Ages 8-14.
Publication Dates: 1974-2006.
Acronym: PAT Mathematics.
Scores: Total score only.
Administration: Group.
Levels, 7: Individual tests for 7 year levels.
Price Data, 2006: NZ $4.50 per test booklet; NZ $1.80 per 10 answer sheets; NZ $22.50 per teacher's manual (2006); NZ $2.70 per marking key; price data for specimen sets for split year levels available from publisher.
Time: (35-45) minutes.
Comments: Electronic marking service available to generate specific reports for each child/classroom/year level.
Author: Charles Darr.
Publisher: New Zealand Council for Educational Research [New Zealand].
Cross References: For reviews by Linda E. Brady and Suzanne Lane of an earlier edition, see 12:313; see also T3:1911 (1 reference); for a review by Harold C. Trimble of an earlier edition, see 8:288; for reviews by James C. Impara and A. Harry Passow of an earlier Australian edition, see 11:309.

[2053]
Progressive Achievement Tests in Mathematics—3rd Edition.
Purpose: Designed "to provide information to teachers about the level of achievement attained by their students in the skills and understanding of mathematics."
Population: Australian students in years 3-10.
Publication Dates: 1983–2005.
Acronym: PATMaths 3rd edition.
Scores: Total score only.
Administration: Group.
Price Data, 2005: A$6.50 per test booklet; A$149.95 per specimen set including one of each test booklet, teacher's manual, answer sheet, and CD-ROM; A$50 per 10 answer sheets–OMR or non-OMR available.
Time: (45) minutes.
Author: Australian Council for Educational Research Press.
Publisher: Australian Council for Educational Research Ltd. [Australia].
a) LEVEL 1.
Population: Years 4–6.
b) LEVEL 2.
Population: Years 6–9.
c) LEVEL 3.
Population: Years 7–9.
Cross References: For reviews by Kevin D. Crehan and Cindy M. Walker of an earlier edition, see 15:199; see T5:2091 (5 references); for reviews by James C. Impara and A. Harry Passow of an earlier edition, see 11:309 (2 references). For information on the New Zealand edition, see T3:1911 (1 reference); for additional information and a review by Harold C. Trimble, see 8:288.

[2054]
Progressive Achievement Tests in Reading: Comprehension and Vocabulary—Third Edition.
Purpose: "Tests designed to assist teachers in their assessment of students' reading comprehension skills and vocabulary knowledge."
Population: Years 3-9 in Australian school system.
Publication Dates: 1973–2001.
Acronym: PAT-R.
Scores, 2: Reading Comprehension, Reading Vocabulary .
Administration: Individual or group.
Parts, 2: PAT-R: Comprehension, PAT-R: Vocabulary.
Levels, 4: 4 levels for Comprehension and for Vocabulary: Test Form 1 (Years 3–5), Test Form 2 (Years 4–6), Test Form 3 (Years 6–8), Test Form 4 (Years 7–9).
Price Data, 2006: A$130 per specimen set including revised teacher's manual with score keys (2001, 79

pages), Comprehension test forms 1–4 (reusable), Comprehension answer sheets (10 each for Forms 1–4), Vocabulary test forms 1–4 (reusable), Vocabulary answer sheets (10 each for Forms 1–4); $85 per revised manual with score keys; $6.30 per Comprehension test form (any of Levels 1–4); $3.85 per Vocabulary test for (any of Levels 1–4); $11 per 10 Comprehension answer sheets or 10 Vocabulary answer sheets (any of Levels 1–4).

Time: 40(55) minutes (Comprehension); 25 minutes (Vocabulary).

Comments: Developed especially, but not exclusively, for use in Australian schools; hand- or machine-scorable; machine scoring performed by publisher; two types of reports available (PAT-R Report, PAT-R Diagnostic Report).

Author: Australian Council for Educational Research, Ltd.

Publisher: Australian Council for Educational Research Ltd. [Australia]

Cross References: For a review by Mark H. Fugate, see 15:200; for information on an earlier edition, see T5:2092 (4 references); for reviews by Paul C. Burnett and Richard Lehrer of an earlier edition, see 11:310 (4 references); see also T3:1912 (4 references); for a review by Douglas A. Pidgeon of an earlier edition, see 8:738 (1 reference); see also T2:1579 (1 reference); for excerpted reviews by Milton L. Clark and J. Elkins, see 7:699.

[2055]
Progressive Achievement Test of Listening Comprehension [Revised].

Purpose: "Intended … to assist teachers in determining levels of development attained by their students in the basic skills of listening comprehension."

Population: Ages 7–14.

Publication Dates: 1971–1994.

Acronym: PAT: Listening Comprehension.

Scores: Total score only.

Administration: Group.

Levels: 8 overlapping levels labeled Parts 1–8: Primary: Parts 1–4 (Standards 1–4); Intermediate: Parts 5–6 (Forms 1–2); Secondary: Parts 7–8 (Forms 3–4).

Price Data, 2001: NZ$1.80 per Primary, Intermediate, or Secondary test booklet; $4.50 per Primary, Intermediate, or Secondary teacher's script; $.99 per scoring key; $1.44 per 10 answer sheets; $9 per Intermediate audiotape; $9.90 per Secondary audiotape; $9 per teacher's manual (1994, 32 pages).

Time: (55) minutes.

Comments: 2 forms (A & B) available (Form A is used in odd-numbered years and Form B is used in even-numbered years); this test was specifically developed for use in New Zealand schools.

Authors: Neil A. Reid, Ian C. Johnston, and Warwick B. Elley.

Publisher: New Zealand Council for Educational Research [New Zealand].

Cross References: For a review by Sherwyn Morreale and Philip Backlund, see 13:245 (1 reference); see also T4:2140 (2 references) and T3:1910 (1 reference); for a review by Roger A. Richards of an earlier edition, see 8:453 (2 references).

[2056]
Progressive Achievement Tests of Reading [Revised].

Purpose: Designed to assess the skills and abilities of the students in reading with a view to providing instruction adapted to their present stages of development.

Population: Ages 8–14.

Publication Dates: 1969–1991.

Scores, 2: Reading Comprehension, Reading Vocabulary.

Administration: Group.

Levels, 3: Primary, Intermediate, Secondary.

Forms, 2: A, B.

Price Data: Available from publisher.

Time: 45 minutes for Comprehension part, 30 minutes for Vocabulary part.

Comments: Raw scores convert to the Level scores (1–10), age percentile rank, and class percentile rank.

Authors: Neil A. Reid and Warwick B. Elley.

Publisher: New Zealand Council for Educational Research [New Zealand].

Cross References: See T5:2094 (3 references); for a review by Herbert C. Rudman, see 12:314 (3 references); see also T4:2141 (7 references) and T3:1912 (2 references); for a review by Douglas A. Pidgeon, see 8:738 (1 reference); see also T2:1579 (1 reference); for excerpted reviews by Milton L. Clark and J. Elkins, see 7:699.

[2057]
Project Implementation Profile.

Purpose: To identify and measure behavioral variables that may be related to project success.

Population: Project managers and team members.

Publication Date: 1992.

Acronym: PIP.

Scores, 11: Project Mission, Top Management Support, Project Schedule, Client Consultation, Personnel, Technical Tasks, Client Acceptance, Monitoring and Feedback, Communication, Trouble-Shooting, Overall Performance.

Administration: Group.

Price Data: Available from publisher.

Time: (20) minutes.

Authors: Jeffrey K. Pinto and Dennis P. Slevin.

Publisher: Innodyne, Inc.

Cross References: For reviews by Sally Kuhlenschmidt and Kimberly A. Lawless, see 13:246.

[2058]
Project Leader Skills Evaluation.
Purpose: To assess essential skills needed for the position of Project Leader.
Population: Candidates for Project Leader position.
Publication Date: 1993.
Scores: Total Score, Narrative Evaluation, Ranking, Recommendation.
Administration: Group.
Price Data, 2001: $235 per candidate; quantity discounts available.
Foreign Language Edition: Available in French.
Time: [60] minutes.
Comments: Scored by publisher; available in booklet and Internet versions; must be proctored.
Author: Bruce A. Winrow.
Publisher: Walden Personnel Performance, Inc. [Canada].
Cross References: For reviews by Laura L. B. Barnes and Alan D. Moore, see 16:202.

[2059]
Project Management Competency Assessment.
Purpose: Designed to assess project manager competencies.
Population: Project managers.
Publication Date: 1996.
Scores, 18: Project Definition, Organization Awareness, Team Leadership, Time Management, Resource Management, Lost Management, Quality Management, Risk Management, Team Facilitation, Managing Conflict, Negotiating Changes, Communication Management, Project Integration, Receiving Feedback, Results Focus, Goal Pressure, Delegation, Recognition.
Administration: Group.
Manual: No manual.
Price Data: Available from publisher.
Time: Administration time not reported.
Comments: Ratings by self and/or coworkers; can be used alone or in conjunction with Project Management Knowledge & Skills Assessment (14:298).
Author: Clark L. Wilson.
Publisher: The Clark Wilson Group for the exclusive use of Educational Services Institute.

[2060]
Projective Storytelling Cards.
Purpose: "This is neither a test nor a technique, but a carefully designed system of card pictures, characters, and potential themes that serve as the basis for endless interactive assessment and treatment uses."
Population: Children and adolescents.
Publication Dates: 1993–2000.
Scores: No scores.
Administration: Individual.
Price Data, 2000: $35 per 35-card set including user's manual (2000, 67 pages); $40 per 12-card Child Exploitation Series; $165 per 35-card set and 12-card set; $17.50 per Court Preparation Set including 5 cards plus booklet of "Chris Tells the Truth."
Time: Administration time not reported.
Comments: Projective nontest, up to 47 different cards; cards are available in minority sets, nonminority sets, and racially mixed sets.
Authors: Kent R. Caruso and Richard J. Pulcini.
Publisher: Northwest Psychological Publishers, Inc.

[2061]
Proof-Reading Tests of Spelling.
Purpose: Constructed to measure a child's ability to discriminate between words spelled correctly and incorrectly in the context of meaningful paragraphs.
Population: Ages 8–13.
Publication Date: 1981.
Acronym: PRETOS.
Scores, 2: Production, Recognition.
Administration: Group.
Levels, 5: Test 2, Test 3, Test 4, Test 5, Test 6.
Price Data: Available from publisher.
Time: 30 minutes.
Authors: Cedric Croft, Alison Gilmore, Neil Reid, and Peter Jackson.
Publisher: New Zealand Council for Educational Research [New Zealand].
Cross References: See T4:2146 (2 references); for a review by Sally Anita Whiting, see 9:1009.

[2062]
Prospector: Discovering the Ability to Learn and to Lead.
Purpose: "Designed to assess openness to learning from experience."
Population: Managers and executives.
Publication Date: 1996.
Scores, 11: Seeks Opportunities to Learn, Has the Courage to Take Risks, Seeks Broad Business Knowledge, Adapts to Cultural Differences, Acts with Integrity, Is Committed to Making a Difference, Brings Out the Best in People, Is Insightful: Sees Things from New Angles, Seeks and Uses Feedback, Learns from Mistakes, Is Open to Criticism.
Administration: Group.
Price Data, 2006: $225 per set including an unlimited number of questionnaires (Prospector is only available online), feedback reports, one learning guide, and one facilitators guide (96 pages); quantity discounts are available.
Time: [10–15] minutes.
Authors: Morgan W. McCall, Gretchen M. Spreitzer, and Joan Jay Mahoney.
Publisher: Center for Creative Leadership.
Cross References: For reviews by Theodore L. Hayes and Neil P. Lewis, see 14:299.

[2063]
PSACS Public Safety Assessment Center System for Police Sergeant.

Purpose: Designed "to help assess the promotional potential of police officers for the position of police sergeant."

Population: Candidates for promotion to the police sergeant position.

Publication Date: 2006.

Acronym: PSACS.

Scores: 7 competencies: Problem Identification and Analysis, Decision Making/Decisiveness, Oral Communication, Written Communication, Interpersonal and Community Relations, Planning and Supervising, Applied Technical Knowledge.

Administration: Individual or group.

Price Data: Available from publisher.

Time: 2 days.

Comments: Part of Public Safety Assessment Center System; modifications for rank structure or job title for sheriff's departments can be made; system includes subordinate role play exercise, video-based technical exercise, and an in-basket exercise; the system contains multiple simulation exercises, some of which are automated; also includes educational and training materials for jurisdictions to administer the assessment center without incurring the added cost of hiring a consultant; exercises vary by rank and are updated every other year.

Author: International Public Management Association for Human Resources.

Publisher: International Public Management Association for Human Resources (IPMA-HR).

[2064]
PSB Aptitude for Practical Nursing Examination.

Purpose: Designed as a "method of selection, placement, guidance and counseling of incoming practical/vocational nursing students."

Population: Applicants for admission to practical/vocational nursing schools.

Publication Dates: 1961-2006.

Scores, 8: Academic Aptitude (Verbal, Arithmetic, Nonverbal, Total), Spelling, Information in the Natural Sciences, Judgment and Comprehension in Practical Nursing Situations, Vocational Adjustment Index.

Administration: Individual or group.

Price Data, 2006: $15 per electronic test.

Time: (135) minutes.

Comments: Electronic tests available at www.psbtests.com.

Authors: Anna S. Evans, Phyllis G. Roumm, and George A. W. Stouffer, Jr., with technical assistance from Psychological Services Bureau, Inc.

Publisher: Psychological Services Bureau, Inc.

Cross References: For reviews by Mark Albanese and Anita Tesh of the Revised PSB Aptitude for Practical Nursing Examination, see 13:264.

[2065]
PSB Health Occupations Aptitude Examination.

Purpose: Measures "abilities, skills, knowledge, and attitudes important for successful performance of students in the allied health education programs."

Population: Candidates for admission to programs of study for the allied health occupations.

Publication Dates: 1978–1999.

Scores, 8: Academic Aptitude (Verbal, Arithmetic, Nonverbal, Total), Spelling, Reading Comprehension, Information in the Natural Sciences, Vocational Adjustment Index.

Administration: Group or individual.

Price Data, 2006: $15 per electronic test.

Time: (135) minutes.

Comments: Electronic tests available at www.psbtests.com.

Authors: Psychological Services Bureau, Inc. with consultant contributions.

Publisher: Psychological Services Bureau, Inc.

Cross References: For reviews by Betty Bergstrom and Hilda Wing of the Revised PSB Health Occupations Aptitude Examination, see 13:265; for reviews by Stephen B. Dunbar and Lawrence M. Rudner of an earlier edition, see 11:312.

[2066]
PSB Reading Comprehension Examination.

Purpose: To reveal the examinee's comprehension or understanding of what is read.

Population: Secondary and postsecondary students applying or enrolled in terminal vocational or occupational programs, general population.

Publication Dates: 2000-2006.

Scores: Total score only.

Administration: Group or individual.

Price Data, 2006: $15 per electronic test.

Time: (60) minutes.

Comments: Electronic tests available at www.psbtests.com.

Authors: Psychological Services Bureau, Inc., with consultant contributions.

Publisher: Psychological Services Bureau, Inc.

Cross References: For reviews by Ray Fenton and Felice J. Green of the Revised PSB–Reading Comprehension Examination, see 13:267; for reviews by Joseph C. Ciechalski and by Brandon Davis and John A. Glover of an earlier edition, see 11:314.

[2067]
PSB Registered Nursing School Aptitude Examination.

Purpose: Predicts "readiness or suitability for specialized instruction in a school/program of professional nursing."

Population: Prospective nursing students.

Publication Dates: 1978-2006.

Scores, 8: Academic Aptitude (Verbal, Arithmetic, Nonverbal, Total), Spelling, Reading Comprehension, Information in the Natural Sciences, Vocational Adjustment Index.

Administration: Individual or group.

Price Data, 2006: $15 per electronic test.

Time: (105) minutes.

Comments: Electronic tests available at www.psbtests.com; previously listed as PSB Nursing School Aptitude Examination (RN).

Authors: Anna S. Evans, Phyllis G. Roumm, and George A. W. Stouffer, Jr.

Publisher: Psychological Services Bureau, Inc.

Cross References: For reviews by Mark H. Daniel and William B. Michael of the Revised PSB–Nursing School Aptitude Examination (R.N.), see 13:266; for reviews by Kurt F. Geisinger and James C. Impara of an earlier edition, see 11:313.

[2068]
PSC-Survey ADT.

Purpose: "Evaluates a job applicant's attitudes toward companies, business, work and trust attitudes."

Population: Job applicants.

Publication Date: 1987.

Scores, 4: Alienation, Trustworthiness, Total, False Positives.

Administration: Group or individual.

Price Data: Available from publisher.

Time: (15–20) minutes.

Comments: On-site scoring available.

Authors: Alan L. Strand and Mark L. Strand.

Publisher: Predictive Surveys Corporation.

Cross References: For a review by Chantale Jeanrie, see 13:247.

[2069]
PSC Survey-SA.

Purpose: "Measures attitudes toward the position of supervisor for selection or promotion."

Population: Job applicants or current employees.

Publication Date: 1987.

Scores, 6: Attitudes Toward Companies and Business, Attitudes Toward Managers and Executives, Attitudes Toward Peers and Associates, Attitudes Toward Being a Supervisor, Attitudes Toward Subordinates, Total.

Administration: Group or individual.

Price Data: Available from publisher.

Time: (10–15) minutes.

Authors: Alan L. Strand and Mark L. Strand.

Publisher: Predictive Surveys Corporation.

Cross References: For reviews by L. Carolyn Pearson and E. Lea Witta, see 13:248.

[2070]
PSI Basic Skills Tests for Business, Industry, and Government.

Purpose: "Designed to assess abilities and skills that are important for clerical, Administrative, and customer service positions."

Population: Prospective administrative, customer service, and clerical employees.

Publication Dates: 1981–1984.

Acronym: BST.

Scores: 15 subtest scores: Language Skills, Reading Comprehension, Vocabulary, Computation, Problem Solving, Decision Making, Following Oral Directions, Following Written Directions, Forms Checking, Reasoning, Classifying, Coding, Filing Names, Filing Numbers, Visual Speed and Accuracy.

Administration: Group or individual.

Price Data: Price information available from publisher for test material including User's Manual (2005, 59 pages), Technical Manual (2001, 61 pages), Technical Report Addendum: Meta-Analysis of the Validity of the Basic Skills Tests (2002, 14 pages), Validation Report (1982, 93 pages).

Time: 1.5-10(5-15) minutes for each test.

Comments: Tests available separately; computerized versions available; transportability procedure available.

Authors: William W. Ruch, Allen N. Shub, Sheryl M. Moinat, and David A. Dye.

Publisher: Psychological Services, Inc.

Cross References: See T5:2105 (1 reference); for reviews by Michael J. Stahl and Sheldon Zedeck, see 9:1010.

[2071]
PST-100SV and PST-80SV Public Safety Telecommunicator Tests.

Purpose: Designed to assess critical abilities required for entry-level public safety telecommunicator positions.

Population: Candidates for entry-level public safety communicator positions.

Publication Date: 1995.

Acronym: PST-80SV, PST-100SV.

Scores: 5 knowledge areas: Listening Skills, Reading Comprehension, Ability to Learn and Apply Information, Reasoning Ability, Ability to Use Situational Judgment.

Administration: Individual or group.

Forms, 2: PST-80SV, PST-100SV.

Price Data: Available from publisher.
Time: 144 minutes for PST-100SV; 120 minutes for PST-80SV.
Comments: The two versions contain exactly the same questions with the exception of the Listening Skills subtest, which has an audio component and so the PST-80SV version of the exam is available for those jurisdictions that do not have the audio equipment needed to administer the Listening Skills subtest.
Author: International Public Management Association for Human Resources.
Publisher: International Public Management Association for Human Resources (IPMA-HR).

[2072]
PSUP 1.1, 2.1, and 3.1 Police Supervisor Tests (Corporal/Sergeant).

Purpose: Designed as "a promotional test for first-line police supervisor."
Population: Candidates for promotion to the police supervisor or corporal/sergeant position.
Publication Dates: 2003-2006.
Acronym: PSUP 1.1, PSUP 2.1, PSUP 3.1.
Scores: 5 knowledge areas: Laws Related to Police Work, Police Field Operations, Investigative Procedures, Supervisory Principles and Concepts & Reports, Records and Paperwork.
Administration: Individual or group.
Forms, 3: PSUP 1.1, PSUP 2.1, PSUP 3.1.
Price Data: Available from publisher.
Time: 150 minutes per test.
Comments: PSUP 1.1, PSUP 2.1, PSUP 3.1 are comparable forms; reading lists are available to help candidates prepare for the tests.
Authors: International Public Management Association for Human Resources & Bruce Davey Associates.
Publisher: International Public Management Association for Human Resources (IPMA-HR).

[2073]
PsychEval Personality Questionnaire.

Purpose: "Measures both normal personality and pathology-oriented traits to provide a multidimensional profile of the individual."
Population: Ages 16 and over; adults.
Publication Dates: 2002-2003.
Acronym: PEPQ.
Administration: Individual or group.
Price Data, 2006: $61 per interpretation introductory kit including manual (2003, 144 pages), test booklet, answer sheet, and pre-paid mail-in processing certificate; $58 per manual; $20 per 10 reusable test booklets; $18 per 25 answer sheets; publisher scoring rate varies by quantity ($19.50 to $30 per report); $61 per Protective Services Report Plus introductory kit including manual (2003, 62 pages), questionnaire, an-

swer sheet, and pre-paid mail-in report processing certificate; $58 per Protective Services Report manual; $19.50 to $30 per Protective Services Report (volume discounts available).
Time: (75-90) minutes.
Comments: Computer administration and scoring available; Protective Services Report Plus available for post-offer selection and fitness for duty evaluations for personnel in high-risk, public safety professions.
Authors: Raymond B. Cattell, A. Karen S. Cattell, Heather E. P. Cattell, Mary T. Russell, and Scott Bedwell.
Publisher: Institute for Personality and Ability Testing (IPAT), Inc.
a) NORMAL PERSONALITY SCALES.
Scores: 21 factors: Abstractedness, Anxiety, Apprehension, Dominance, Emotional Stability, Extraversion, Independence, Liveliness, Openness to Change, Perfectionism, Privateness, Reasoning, Rule-Consciousness, Self-Control, Self-Reliance, Sensitivity, Social Boldness, Tension, Tough-Mindedness, Vigilance, Warmth.
Comments: Items and norms from the 16PF Fifth Edition (2346).
b) PATHOLOGY-ORIENTED SCALES.
Scores, 12: Anxious Depression, Apathetic Withdrawal, Attention and Perceptual Distortion, Health Concerns, Low Energy State, Obsessional Thinking, Paranoid Ideation, Psychological Inadequacy, Self-Reproach, Suicidal Thinking, Threat Immunity, Thrill-Seeking.
c) PROTECTIVE SERVICES REPORT PLUS.
Purpose: Assesses the personal qualities that are relevant in protective services settings, and explores implications of these qualities for high-risk occupations.
Population: Adults.
Acronym: PSR Plus.
Scores: Same as *a* and *b* above plus Protective Services Dimensions (Emotional Adjustment, Integrity/Control, Intellectual Efficiency, Interpersonal Relations), plus 3 composite indices.

[2074]
Psychiatric Content Analysis and Diagnosis.

Purpose: "For measuring the magnitude of various psychological states and traits from the content analysis of verbal behavior."
Population: Children and adults.
Publication Dates: 1993–2000.
Acronym: PCAD.
Scores, 13: Anxiety Scale, Hostility Scales (Hostility Directed Outward, Hostility Directed Inward, Ambivalent Hostility), Social Alienation—Personal Disorganization Scale, Cognitive and Intellectual Impairment Scale, Depression Scale, Hope Scale, Health-Sickness

Scale, Achievement Striving Scale, Human Relations Scale, Dependency Strivings Scale, Quality of Life Scale.
Administration: Individual or group.
Price Data, 2005: $299.95 per software license including media and manual (2000, 83 pages).
Time: (5) minutes; more if multiple speakers.
Comments: Earlier version listed in previous Buros publications as Psychologic and Neuropsychiatric Assessment Manual.
Authors: Louis A. Gottschalk and Robert Bechtel.
Publisher: GB Software LLC.
Cross References: For a review by William M. Reynolds, see 14:300.

[2075]
Psychiatric Diagnostic Screening Questionnaire.

Purpose: "Designed to screen for the DSM-IV (Diagnostic and Statistical Manual of Mental Disorders, Fourth Edition) Axis I disorders most commonly encountered in medical and outpatient mental health settings."
Population: Adult psychiatric patients.
Publication Date: 2002.
Acronym: PDSQ.
Scores, 14: Major Depressive Disorder, Posttraumatic Stress Disorder, Bulimia/Binge-Eating Disorder, Obsessive-Compulsive Disorder, Panic Disorder, Psychosis, Agoraphobia, Social Phobia, Alcohol Abuse/Dependence, Drug Abuse/Dependence, Generalized Anxiety Disorder, Somatization Disorder, Hypochondriasis, Total.
Administration: Individual.
Price Data, 2006: $114.50 per test kit including manual, 25 test booklets, 25 summary sheets, and CD containing 13 follow-up interview guides (one for each disorder); $49.50 per manual; $43.50 per 25 test booklets; $29.00 per 100 summary sheets; volume discounts available.
Time: (15–20) minutes.
Comments: Self-report questionnaire.
Author: Mark Zimmerman.
Publisher: Western Psychological Services.
Cross References: For reviews by Michael G. Kavan and Sean P. Reilley, see 16:203.

[2076]
Psychiatric Evaluation Form.

Purpose: Designed "to record scaled judgments of a subject's functioning during a one week period" on dimensions of psychopathology.
Population: Psychiatric patients and nonpatients.
Publication Dates: 1967-1968.
Acronym: PEF.
Scores, 28: 20 psychopathological scores in Part I (Narcotics-Drugs, Agitation-Excitement, Suicide-Self Mutilation, Grandiosity, Somatic Concerns, Anti-Social Attitudes-Acts, Speech Disorganization, Halluci-

nations, Social Isolation, Belligerence-Negativism, Disorientation-Memory, Alcohol Abuse, Anxiety, Inappropriate, Suspicion-Persecution, Daily Routine-Leisure Time, Denial of Illness, Depression, Retardation-Lack of Emotion, Overall Severity of Illness), 3 occupational roles and 2 social roles; 3 admission scores (Duration, Stress, Reason for Admission).
Administration: Individual.
Price Data, 2001: $3.50 per booklet including score sheet; $1 per instruction manual; $4 per teaching tape/key; additional price data available from publisher.
Time: (20-40) minutes.
Authors: Robert L. Spitzer, Jean Endicott, Alvin Mesnikoff, and George Cohen.
Publisher: Department of Research Assessment and Training.
Cross References: See T5:2108 (5 references) and T4:2153 (9 references); for reviews by Goldine C. Gleser and Jerome D. Paulker, see 7:126 (1 reference); see also T3:1922 (15 references) and T2:1339 (4 references).

[2077]
Psychiatric Self-Assessment & Review.

Purpose: "To assist psychiatrists in keeping abreast of new knowledge and scientific developments in the field of psychology."
Population: Physicians.
Publication Date: 1999.
Acronym: PSA-R.
Scores: Total score only.
Administration: Individual.
Price Data: Available from publisher.
Time: Administration time not reported.
Comments: Self-administered and self-scored; information regarding obtaining Continuing Medical Education credit for this examination available from publisher.
Authors: American Psychiatric Association.
Publisher: American Psychiatric Association.

[2078]
The Psychiatric Status Schedule: Subject Form, Second Edition.

Purpose: Designed to evaluate social and role functioning as well as mental status.
Population: Psychiatric patients and nonpatients.
Publication Dates: 1966-1968.
Acronym: PSS-2.
Scores, 43: 18 symptom scores (Inappropriate Affect—Appearance—Behavior, Interview Belligerence—Negativism, Agitation—Excitement, Retardation—Lack of Emotion, Speech Disorganization, Grandiosity, Suspicion—Persecution—Hallucinations, Reported Overt Anger, Depression—Anxiety, Suicide—Self-Mutilation, Somatic Concerns, Social Isolation, Daily Routine—Leisure Time Impairment, Antisocial Impulses or Acts, Alcoholic Abuse, Drug Abuse, Disorientation Memory, Denial or

Illness), 5 role functioning scores (Wage Earner, House-keeper, Student or Trainee, Mate, Parent), 5 summary symptom and role scales (Subjective Distress, Behavioral Disturbance, Impulse Control Disturbance, Reality Testing Disturbance, Summary Role), 20 supplemental scores (Anxiety, Auditory Hallucinations, Catatonic Behavior, Conversion Reaction, Delusions—Hallucinations, Depression—Suicide, Disassociation, Elated Mood, Guilt, Lack of Emotion, Obsessions—Compulsions, Persecutory Delusions, Phobia, Psychomotor Retardation, Sex Deviation, Silliness, Somatic Delusions or Hallucinations, Visual Hallucinations, Miscellaneous, Validity Check).
Administration: Individual.
Price Data: Available from publisher.
Time: (30-50) minutes.
Comments: Most sections dealing with signs and symptoms of psychiatric disorder are from Mental Status Schedule.
Authors: Robert L. Spitzer, Jean Endicott, and George M. Cohen.
Publisher: Department of Research Assessment and Training.
Cross References: See T5:2109 (1 reference), T4:2154 (14 references), T3:1923 (18 references), and T2:1340 (6 references); for a review by Hans H. Strupp, see 7:127 (5 references).

[2079]
Psycho-Epistemological Profile.

Purpose: "Designed to provide a profile of an individual's epistemological hierarchy."
Population: College and adults.
Publication Dates: 1968–1980.
Acronym: PEP.
Scores, 3: Metaphoric, Rational, Empirical.
Administration: Group.
Price Data: Available from publisher.
Foreign Language Edition: French edition available.
Time: (20–30) minutes.
Comments: Experimental form.
Authors: J. R. Royce and L. P. Mos.
Publisher: Psychometric Affiliates.
Cross References: See T5:2112 (1 reference) and T4:2157 (2 references); for reviews by Bruce A. Bracken and Thomas J. Kehle, see 9:1013; see also 8:653 (2 references).

[2080]
Psychoeducational Profile: TEACCH Individualized Psychoeducational Assessment for Children with Autism Spectrum Disorders—Third Edition.

Purpose: Designed as a measure of autism and related developmental disabilities.
Population: Ages 6 months to 7 years 5 months.

Publication Dates: 1979-2005.
Acronym: PEP-3.
Administration: Individual.
Price Data, 2006: $450 per complete kit including examiner's manual, guide to item administration, picture book, 10 examiner scoring/sumary booklets, 10 response booklets, 10 caregiver report forms, and object kit; $61 per examiner's manual; $41 per guide to item administration; $41 per picture book; $28 per 10 examiner scoring/summary booklets; $19 per 10 response booklets; $19 per 10 caregiver report forms; $266 per object kit.
Time: (45-90) minutes.
Comments: Includes a norm-referenced scale and parent/caregiver scale; caregiver "must be an adult who is familiar with the behavior of the child being evaluated."
Authors: Eric Schopler, Margaret D. Lansing, Robert J. Reichler, and Lee M. Marcus.
Publisher: PRO-ED.
a) PERFORMANCE PART.
1) *Developmental Abilities.*
Scores: 6 subscales: Cognitive Verbal/Preverbal, Expressive Language, Receptive Language, Fine Motor, Gross Motor, Visual-Motor Imitation.
2) *Maladaptive Behaviors.*
Scores: 4 subscales: Affective Expression, Social Reciprocity, Characteristic Motor Behaviors, Characteristic Verbal Behaviors.
3) *Composites.*
Scores: 3 subscales: Communication, Motor, Maladaptive Behaviors.
b) CAREGIVER REPORT.
1) *Clinical Sections.*
Scores: 2 subscales: Child's Current Developmental Level in Several Areas, Degree of Problems in Different Diagnostic Categories.
Subtests, 3: Problem Behaviors, Personal Self-Care, Adaptive Behavior.
Cross References: See: T5:2111 (2 references); for reviews by Pat Mirenda and Gerald Tindal of an earlier edition, see 12:316 (2 references); for reviews by Gerald S. Hanna and Martin J. Wiese of the original edition, see 11:317.

[2081]
Psycholinguistic Assessments of Language Processing in Aphasia.

Purpose: Designed as "an assessment of language processing in adult acquired aphasia."
Population: Adults with aphasia.
Publication Date: 1992.
Acronym: PALPA.
Scores: Available from publisher.
Administration: Individual.
Price Data, 2001: $397 per box file including 60 tests.

Time: Administration time not reported.
Authors: Janice Kay, Ruth Lesser, and Max Coltheart.
Publisher: Psychology Press.

[2082]
Psychological Processing Checklist.

Purpose: Designed to "measure psychological processing difficulty."
Population: Kindergarten–Grade 5.
Publication Date: 2003.
Acronym: PPC.
Scores, 7: Auditory Processing, Visual Processing, Visual Motor Processing, Social Perception, Organization, Attention, Total.
Administration: Individual.
Price Data, 2006: $76 per complete kit including technical manual (96 pages), and 25 QuikScore™ forms; $57 per technical manual; $39 per 25 QuikScore™ forms.
Time: (15) minutes, plus 10–15 minutes for scoring.
Comments: Teacher-completed rating scale.
Authors: Mark E. Swerdlik, Peggy Swerdlik, and Jeffrey H. Kahn.
Publisher: Multi-Health Systems, Inc.
Cross References: For reviews by Bruce A. Bracken and Keith F. Widaman, see 16:204.

[2083]
Psychological Screening Inventory.

Purpose: Developed to screen for mental health problems.
Population: Ages 16 and over.
Publication Dates: 1973-1978.
Acronym: PSI.
Scores, 5: Alienation, Social Nonconformity, Discomfort, Expression, Defensiveness.
Administration: Group or individual.
Price Data, 2006: $70 per examination kit including manual (1978, 44 pages), 5 question-and-answer sheets, 5 profile sheets, and set of scoring templates; $22 per test manual; $45 per set of scoring templates; $50 per testing kit (including 25 question-and-answer sheets and 25 profile sheets).
Foreign Language Edition: Available in Spanish (question and answer sheets only).
Time: 15 minutes.
Author: Richard I. Lanyon.
Publisher: Sigma Assessment Systems, Inc.
Cross References: See T5:2115 (6 references), T4:2159 (20 references), 9:1015 (2 references), and T3:1931 (18 references); for a review by Stephen L. Golding, see 8:654 (32 references); see also T2:1342 (7 references).

[2084]
Psychometric Behavior Checklist.

Purpose: For recording unusual test taking behavior.
Population: Adults.
Publication Date: 1960.
Acronym: PBC.
Score: Total score only.
Administration: Group.
Price Data: Available from publisher.
Time: Administration time not reported.
Comments: Also called Maryland Test Behavior Checklist.
Authors: Bernard G. Berenson, Kathryn C. Biersdorf, Thomas M. Magoon, Martha J. Maxwell, Donald K. Pumroy, and Marjorie H. Richey.
Publisher: University of Maryland, University Counseling Center [No reply from publisher; status unknown].
Cross References: See 6:166 (1 reference).

[2085]
Psychopathic Personality Inventory-Revised.

Purpose: Designed to help "assess psychopathic personality traits."
Population: Ages 18-86.
Publication Date: 2005.
Acronym: PPI-R.
Scores, 15: 8 Content scores (Machiavellian Egocentricity, Rebellious Nonconformity, Blame Externalization, Carefree Nonplanfulness, Social Influence, Fearlessness, Stress Immunity, Coldheartedness), Total, 4 Validity scores (Virtuous Responding, Deviant Responding, Inconsistent Responding 15, Inconsistent Responding 40), 3 Factor scores (Self-Centered Impulsivity, Fearless Dominance, Coldheartedness).
Administration: Individual or group.
Price Data, 2006: $199 per introductory kit including professional manual (166 pages), 25 item booklets, 25 response forms, and 25 scoring summary forms; $70 per professional manual; $45 per 25 response forms; $55 per 25 reusable item booklets; $45 per 25 scoring summary forms.
Time: (20-30) minutes.
Comments: "PPI-R scores and profiles should not be used as the sole basis for diagnostic and treatment decisions that require the integration of information from varying sources."
Authors: Scott O. Lilienfeld and Michelle R. Widows.
Publisher: Psychological Assessment Resources, Inc.

[2086]
Psychosocial Adjustment to Illness Scale.

Purpose: "Designed to assess the quality of a patient's psychosocial adjustment to a current medical illness or its residual effects."
Population: Medical patients or their immediate relatives.
Publication Date: 1983.
Acronym: PAIS and PAIS-SR.
Scores, 8: Health Care Orientation, Vocational Environment, Domestic Environment, Sexual Relation-

ship, Extended Family, Social Environment, Psychological Distress, Total.
Administration: Individual.
Editions, 3: Interview, Self-Report, Caretaker version.
Price Data, 2006: $3 per reusable booklet (interview); $1.30 per self-report booklet; $.50 per score/profile sheet (select edition); $.25 per score sheet; $29 per manual (56 pages).
Time: (20–30) minutes.
Comments: Scoring is available online, $1.50 per scoring, at www.derogatis-tests.com.
Author: Leonard R. Derogatis.
Publisher: Clinical Psychometric Research, Inc.
Cross References: See T5:2117 (5 references) and T4:2161 (3 references); for a review by Cabrini S. Swassing, see 10:299.

[2087]
Psychosocial Evaluation & Threat Risk Assessment.

Purpose: Designed to "assist school personnel in … determining the nature and degree of violence risk among students."
Population: Ages 11-18.
Publication Date: 2005.
Acronym: PETRA.
Scores, 15: 4 Domain scores (Psychological Domain, Ecological Domain, Resiliency Problems Domain, Total Domain), 8 Cluster scores (Depressed Mood, Alienation, Egocentricism, Aggression, Family/Home, School, Stress, Coping Problems), 2 Response Style Indicator scores (Social Desirability, Inconsistency), PETRA Threat Assessment Matrix score.
Administration: Individual or group.
Price Data, 2006: $115 per introductory kit including professional manual (2005, 5 pages), 25 rating forms, and 25 score summary/profile forms; $50 per professional manual; $50 per 25 rating forms; $25 per 25 score summary/profile forms.
Time: (10-15) minutes.
Author: Jay Schneller.
Publisher: Psychological Assessment Resources, Inc.

[2088]
Psychosocial Pain Inventory [Revised].

Purpose: "Provides a standardized method of evaluating psychosocial factors important in maintaining and exacerbating chronic pain problems."
Population: Adults with chronic pain.
Publication Dates: 1980–1985.
Acronym: PSPI.
Scores: Item scores only.
Administration: Individual.
Price Data, 2006: $115 per introductory kit including manual (1985, 38 pages) and 50 forms.
Time: [60-120] minutes.

Authors: R. K. Heaton, R. A. W. Lehman, and C. J. Getto.
Publisher: Psychological Assessment Resources, Inc.
Cross References: For reviews by Julie A. Allison and Dennis C. Harper, see 14:301; see also T4:2162 (1 reference).

[2089]
Psychotherapy Outcome Kit (Including Quality of Emotional Life Self-Report).

Purpose: Designed to assist mental health care providers in collecting treatment outcome data.
Population: Age 15 and under, age 16 and older.
Publication Date: 1994.
Scores: Total score only.
Administration: Individual.
Price Data: Available from publisher (www.mindgarden.com).
Time: Administration time not reported.
Author: David P. Isenberg.
Publisher: Mind Garden, Inc.
  a) CHILD VERSION.
    Population: Age 15 and under.
    Comments: Child Version QELSR completed by parent/guardian.
  b) ADULT VERSION.
    Population: Age 16 and older.
    Comments: Adult Version QELSR completed by patient.
Cross References: For reviews by Matthew Burns and George Domino, see 14:302.

[2090]
Psypercept-170.

Purpose: "Designed to measure work-related personality and interest variables among managers."
Population: Managers.
Publication Date: 1996.
Acronym: Psypercept-170.
Scores, 17: Directive, Inclusive, Expressive, Persuasive, Persistent, Accommodating, Calming, Inventive, Discerning, Aspiring, Urgent, Materialistic, Numerical, Altruistic, Technological, Artistic, Procedural.
Administration: Individual or group.
Price Data, 2001: $300 per assessment set including 5 reusable test booklets, 50 answer sheets, 50 data summary sheets, 1 set of hand-scoring keys, and manual (66 pages); $75 per 5 reusable test booklets; $75 per 50 answer sheets; $50 per 50 data summary sheets; $60 per set of hand-scoring keys; $75 per manual.
Time: (35–45) minutes.
Comments: A 170-item self-administered questionnaire; "For use in assessing and developing the talents of executives, managers, and supervisors."
Author: Joseph Hartman.
Publisher: Joseph Hartman, Ph.D.

Cross References: For reviews by Patricia A. Bachelor and William I. Sauser, Jr., see 15:201.

[2091]
The Pupil Rating Scale Revised: Screening for Learning Disabilities.

Purpose: To identify students with deficits in learning.
Population: Grades K–6.
Publication Dates: 1971–1981.
Scores, 8: Verbal (Auditory Comprehension, Spoken Language, Total), Nonverbal (Orientation, Motor Coordination, Personal-Social Behavior, Total), Total.
Administration: Individual.
Price Data, 2002: $53 per 50 record forms; $49 per manual (1981, 84 pages).
Time: (10–15) minutes.
Comments: Ratings by teachers.
Author: Helmer R. Myklebust.
Publisher: PsychCorp, A brand of Harcourt Assessment, Inc.
Cross References: See T5:2123 (1 reference) and T4:2165 (2 references); for a review by Shavaun M. Wall, see 9:1019 (3 references); see also T3:1934 (8 references); for a review by Nicholas J. Anastasiow of an earlier edition and an excerpted review by Barton B. Proger, see 8:439 (5 references).

[2092]
Purdue Interest Questionnaire.

Purpose: To help students identify an appropriate specialization within or outside of engineering.
Population: Freshmen engineering students.
Publication Dates: 1976–1980.
Acronym: PIQ.
Scores: 18 scale scores: 11 engineering, 5 transfer, 2 general.
Administration: Group.
Price Data: Available from publisher.
Time: Administration time not reported.
Comments: Separate answer sheets (machine scored) must be used.
Authors: William K. LeBold and Kevin D. Shell (manual).
Publisher: Purdue Research Foundation [No reply from publisher; status unknown].
Cross References: See T4:2167 (1 reference) and 9:1020 (1 reference).

[2093]
Purdue Pegboard.

Purpose: Measures an individual's ability to move hands, fingers, and arms (gross movement) and to control movements of small objects (finger tip dexterity).
Population: Assembly, general factory and various industrial positions and vocational rehabilitation.

Publication Dates: 1941–1992.
Scores, 5: Right Hand, Left Hand, Both Hands, Right plus Left plus Both Hands, Assembly.
Administration: Individual or group.
Price Data, 2002: $346 per start-up kit including 100 profile sheets, pegboard with complete set of washers, collars, and pegs, and examiner's manual; $70 per 100 profile sheets (quantity discounts available); $47 per replacement set of pegs, washers, and collars; $28 per examiner's manual.
Time: (3–9) minutes.
Author: Purdue Research Foundation.
Publisher: Pearson Performance Solutions [No reply from publisher; status unknown].
Cross References: See T5:2125 (30 references), T4:2168 (34 references), T3:948 (13 references), T2:2234 (51 references), and 6:1081 (15 references); for a review by Neil D. Warren, see 5:873 (11 references); see also 4:751 (12 references); for reviews by Edwin F. Ghiselli, Thomas W. Harrell, and Albert Gibson Packard, see 3:666 (3 references).

[2094]
The Purpose in Life Test.

Purpose: To detect "existential vacuum."
Population: Adults.
Publication Dates: 1962–1981.
Acronym: PIL.
Scores: Total score only.
Administration: Individual or group.
Price Data: Available from publisher.
Time: (10–15) minutes.
Comments: 1976 form identical to 1969 version except for minor format changes; 1981 manual identical to 1969 version.
Authors: James C. Crumbaugh and Leonard T. Maholick.
Publisher: Psychometric Affiliates.
Cross References: See T5:2126 (16 references), T4:2169 (17 references), 9:1021 (9 references), T3:1960 (21 references), 8:656 (54 references), and T2:1350 (4 references); for reviews by John R. Braun and George Domino, see 7:130 (7 references).

[2095]
Putney Auditory Comprehension Screening Test.

Purpose: Designed to "assess auditory comprehension in severely physically disabled patients."
Population: Adults.
Publication Date: 2002.
Acronym: PACST.
Score: Total score only.
Administration: Individual.
Price Data, 2006: £62 per complete kit including manual (23 pages) and 25 questionnaire/scoring sheets; £33 per 50 questionnaire/scoring sheets.

Time: Untimed.
Comments: Requires only the ability to provide verbal or nonverbal "yes" or "no" responses.
Authors: J. G. Beaumont, Julia Marjoribanks, Sarah Flury, and Tracey Lintern.
Publisher: Harcourt Assessment [England].

[2096]
The Pyramid Scales.

Purpose: "Assesses adaptive behavior in handicapped persons of all ages."
Population: Handicapped persons ages birth to 78.
Publication Date: 1984.
Scores, 20: Sensory (Tactile Responsiveness, Auditory Responsiveness, Visual Responsiveness), Primary (Gross Motor, Eating, Fine Motor, Toileting, Dressing, Social Interaction, Washing/Grooming, Receptive Language, Expressive Language), Secondary (Recreation/Leisure, Writing, Domestic Behavior, Reading, Vocational, Time, Numbers, Money).
Administration: Individual.
Price Data: Available from publisher.
Time: (30–45) minutes.
Comments: "Criterion-referenced"; behavior checklist for measuring adaptive behavior by directly observing client or by interviewing adult informant.
Author: John D. Cone.
Publisher: John D. Cone.
Cross References: See T5:2127 (2 references) and T4:2170 (1 reference); for a review by John G. Svinicki, see 10:300.

[2097]
The Pyramids and Palm Trees Test.

Purpose: Designed "to assess a person's ability to access detailed semantic representations from words and from pictures."
Population: Ages 18-80.
Publication Date: 1992.
Scores: Total score only.
Administration: Individual.
Price Data, 2006: £96.50 per complete kit including manual, 50 scoring sheets, word card, and stimulus book; £12.50 per 50 scoring sheets.
Time: Administration time not reported.
Authors: David Howard and Karalyn Patterson.
Publisher: Harcourt Assessment [England].

[2098]
The Q-Tags Test of Personality.

Purpose: "Designed to enquire into the self-development influences."
Population: Ages 6 and over.
Publication Dates: 1967–1969.
Acronym: Q-TTP.
Administration: Group or individual.

Price Data, 2005: $22 per 25 answer sheets; $44 per specimen set (including 4 series of 54 tags, 4 paper boards, manual [1969, 27 pages], list of directions, and 25 answer sheets).
Time: (60–80) minutes in 2 sessions.
Comments: Self-administering.
Authors: Arthur G. Storey and Louise I. Masson.
Publisher: Institute of Psychological Research, Inc. [Canada].
  a) [BIOGRAPHICAL FORM].
  Population: Ages 6 and over.
  Scores, 13: 6 factor scores (Affective, Assertive, Effective, Hostility, Reverie, Social) in each of 2 areas (He or She Is, He or She Should Be), Correlation of Self and Ideal Self.
  b) [AUTOBIOGRAPHICAL FORM].
  Population: Ages 12 and over.
  Scores, 13: 6 factor scores (same as *a* above) in each of 2 areas (I Am, I Wish I Were), Correlation of Self and Ideal Self.
Cross References: See T4:2171 (1 reference) and T2:1351 (2 references); for a review by Joan Preston, see 7:131 (2 references); see also P:225 (5 references).

[2099]
Quality Culture Assessment.

Purpose: Designed to assess and evaluate organizational practices, policies, and procedures.
Population: Managers and personnel.
Acronym: QCA.
Administration: Group.
Manual: No manual.
Price Data: Available from publisher.
Time: Administration time not reported.
Authors: Juran Institute and Teleometrics International.
Publisher: Teleometrics International, Inc.
  a) QUALITY POTENTIAL ANALYSIS.
  Publication Dates: 1982–1995.
  Acronym: QPA.
  Scores, 2: As It Is Now, As I Would Like It To Be.
  b) QUALITY CULTURE ANALYSIS.
  Publication Date: 1995.
  Acronym: QCA.
  Scores, 9: Quality Values (Senior Leadership, Goals and Objectives, Rewards and Recognition), Empowered Employees (Self-Control, Recovery, Participation), Customer Focus (Individual Customer Focus, Managerial Customer Focus, Organizational Customer Focus).

[2100]
Quality of Life Enjoyment and Satisfaction Questionnaire.

Purpose: Designed to measure the "degree of enjoyment and satisfaction experienced by subjects in various areas of daily functioning."

Population: Adults with mental or medical disorders.
Publication Date: 1990.
Acronym: Q-LES-Q.
Scores, 9: 6 scores (Physical Health, Subjective Feelings, Leisure Time Activities, Social Relationships, General Activities, Overall Life Enjoyment and Satisfaction); 3 optional scores (Work, Household Duties, School/Coursework).
Administration: Group.
Forms, 2: Regular Form, Short Form.
Price Data, 2001: $1.50 per regular form; $.50 per short form; $1.50 per summary scale scores.
Time: Regular Form: [5–15] minutes; Short Form: [3–5] minutes.
Comments: Self-report measure.
Author: Jean Endicott.
Publisher: Department of Research Assessment and Training.
Cross References: For reviews by John C. Caruso and Mary Lou Bryant Frank, see 14:303.

[2101]
Quality of Life Inventory.

Purpose: Developed to provide a measure of a person's quality of life and their satisfaction with life.
Population: Ages 18 and over.
Publication Date: 1994.
Acronym: QOLI®.
Scores: 17 scales: Health, Self-Esteem, Goals-and-Values, Money, Work, Play, Learning, Creativity, Helping, Love, Friends, Children, Relatives, Home, Neighborhood, Community, Overall Quality of Life.
Administration: Group or individual.
Price Data, 2006: $98 per hand-scoring starter kit including manual (84 pages), 50 answer sheets, and 50 worksheets; $95 per Q Local starter kit including 25 answer sheets to conduct and receive 25 Q Local profile reports; $75 per hand-scoring reorder kit including 50 answer sheets and 50 worksheets; $21 per Q Local answer sheets; $2.25 per Q Local profile report; $40 per manual; quantity discounts available for the reports.
Time: (5) minutes.
Comments: Useful for outcomes measurement as well as individual counseling.
Author: Michael B. Frisch.
Publisher: Pearson Assessments.
Cross References: For reviews by Laura L. B. Barnes and Richard W. Johnson, see 14:304.

[2102]
Quality of Life Questionnaire.

Purpose: "Designed to assess the relationship between the quality of an individual's life and other behaviors and afflictions, such as physical health, psychological health, and alcohol or substance use."
Population: Ages 18 and over.

Publication Date: 1989.
Acronym: QLQ.
Scores, 17: Material Well-Being, Physical Well-Being, Personal Growth, Marital Relations, Parent-Child Relations, Extended Family Relations, Extramarital Relations, Altruistic Behavior, Political Behavior, Job Characteristics, Occupational Relations, Job Satisfiers, Creative/Aesthetic Behavior, Sports Activity, Vacation Behavior, Social Desirability, Total Quality of Life.
Administration: Group.
Price Data, 2006: $69 per complete kit including 25 QuikScore™ answer forms, 10 question booklets, and manual (43 pages); $25 per 10 reusable question booklets; $25 per 25 QuikScore™ answer forms; $33 per manual; $35 per QLQ Online Report Kit including manual and 3 QLQ reports.
Time: (30) minutes.
Comments: Self-report; MS-DOS computer software program available for administration, scoring, and to generate narrative report.
Authors: David R. Evans and Wendy E. Cope.
Publisher: Multi-Health Systems, Inc.
Cross References: See T5:2132 (4 references) and T4:2172 (1 reference); for reviews by Gary B. Seltzer and Richard B. Stuart, see 11:318.

[2103]
Quality Potential Assessment.

Purpose: "Designed to provide information about an organization, such as data on its policies, practices, and logistics, and the degree to which the data contribute to encouraging staff to give their best to the organization."
Population: Adults.
Publication Dates: 1992–1995.
Acronym: QPA.
Scores: Actual and Desired ratings in 10 areas: Collaboration (Management Values, Support Structure, Managerial Credibility, Climate), Commitment (Impact, Relevance, Community), Creativity (Task Environment, Social Context, Problem Solving).
Administration: Group.
Price Data: Available from publisher.
Time: Administration time not reported.
Author: Jay Hall.
Publisher: Teleometrics International, Inc.
Cross References: For reviews by Theodore L. Hayes and Michael J. Zickar, see 14:305.

[2104]
Qualls Early Learning Inventory.

Purpose: Designed to provide a diagnostic review of six key developmental aras of learning that are important for success in school.
Population: Grades K–1.
Publication Date: 2003.
Acronym: QELI.

Scores, 6: General Knowledge, Oral Communication, Written Language, Math Concepts, Work Habits, Attentive Behavior.
Administration: Individual or group.
Price Data, 2006: $30 per 25 Inventories and 1 Teacher's Directions and Interpretive Guide; Score Reports: $.60 per student and $.36 for extra copy per student for Profile Narrative, $.75 per student and $.36 for extra copy per student for Class Diagnostic Report, and $.47 per student and $.24 for extra copy per student for Class, Building, and System Summary.
Time: (10) minutes per student.
Comments: Teacher-completed rating scale; observation of individual students; computer scoring and individual and group score reports available through Riverside Scoring Service; test was previously listed as Iowa Early Learning Inventory.
Authors: A. L. Qualls, H. D. Hoover, S. B. Dunbar, and D. A. Frisbie.
Publisher: Riverside Publishing.
Cross References: For reviews by Leslie Eastman Lukin and Carol M. McGregor, see 16:115.

[2105]
Questionnaire Measure of Trait Arousability (Or Its Converse, Stimulus Screening).

Purpose: Designed to measure individual differences in positive and/or negative emotionality, emotional sensitivity, or emotional reactivity.
Population: Ages 15 and older.
Publication Dates: 1976–1994.
Scores: Total score only.
Administration: Group or individual.
Price Data: Available from publisher for specimen set including manual (1994, 8 pages) and literature review.
Time: (10–15) minutes.
Comments: Previously known as Questionnaire Measure of Stimulus Screening and Arousability.
Author: Albert Mehrabian.
Publisher: Albert Mehrabian.
Cross References: For a review by Robert A. Leark, see 13:249; for a review by James J. Jupp of the earlier edition, see 9:1025.

[2106]
QUESTS: A Life-Choice Inventory.

Purpose: To assess outcomes of substance abuse prevention education.
Population: Grades 9–12.
Publication Dates: 1974–1976.
Acronym: QUESTS.
Scores, 6: Needs Recognition, Values Classification, Adaptive Autonomy, Perception of Reality, Self-Worth, Total.
Administration: Group.
Price Data: Available from publisher.

Time: (23–30) minutes.
Comments: Scoring must be done by publisher.
Authors: Norman J. Milchus, Omar D. Numey, and David N. Rodwell.
Publisher: Norman Milchus (the author).

[2107]
QUIC Tests.

Purpose: Designed "to establish or verify the functional level of proficiency in the areas of either mathematics or the communicative arts."
Population: Grades 2–12.
Publication Dates: 1989–2006.
Scores, 8: Mathematics (Computation, Concepts, Problem Solving, Total), Communicative Arts (Reading, Reference Skills, Language Arts, Total).
Administration: Individual or group.
Forms, 2: G, H.
Price Data, 2005: $66.55 per self-scoring starter set including 20 tests (specify content area of Mathematics or Communicative Arts and Form G or H), 20 response forms, and examiner's manual; $35.90 per 20 response forms; $17.60 per examiner's manual; $28 per sample set including 1 test and response form for each of content areas and examiner's manual; $66.55 per machine-scorable starter set including 20 tests (specify content area of Mathematics or Communicative Arts and Form G or H), 20 answer sheets, 1 interpretive manual; $4 per additional manual (specify Mathematics or Communicative Arts); $18.50 per additional package of 20 answer sheets; $13.50 per additional interpretive manual; scoring service $2.10 per student (minimum scoring service is $43.65).
Time: (35) minutes or less.
Comments: Self-administered; competency-based interpretation.
Author: Scholastic Testing Service, Inc.
Publisher: Scholastic Testing Service, Inc.
Cross References: For a review by Delwyn L. Harnisch, see 11:320.

[2108]
Quick Informal Assessment [Third Edition].

Purpose: Designed to quickly and informally "assess a student's proficiency level in English."
Population: Grades K-12.
Publication Dates: 1997-2006.
Acronym: QIA.
Scores: Total score only.
Administration: Individual.
Forms: 6 alternate forms: A-F.
Price Data, 2006: $130 per complete set including English and Spanish examiner's manuals, test picture book, and 50 class profile forms.
Foreign Language Editions: Available in Spanish and English.

Time: (5) minutes.
Comments: Students classified into one of five levels of language proficiency: beginning, early intermediate, intermediate, early advanced, advanced; leveled score system.
Author: Constance O. Williams.
Publisher: Ballard & Tighe, Publishers.
Cross References: For reviews by Alan Garfinkel and Alfred P. Longo of an earlier edition, see 13:250.

[2109]
Quick Language Assessment Inventory.

Purpose: Designed to provide information about student's English and Spanish language background.
Population: Grades K–6.
Publication Date: 1974.
Scores: Total score and grade level equivalents.
Administration: Individual.
Price Data: Available from publisher.
Time: (1–2) minutes.
Comments: Designed for children suspected of needing English as a second language; parents or guardians provide information about child's English and Spanish background.
Author: Steve Moreno.
Publisher: Moreno Educational Co.
Cross References: For reviews by Giuseppe Costantino and Beth L. Evard, see 9:1026.

[2110]
Quick Neurological Screening Test II.

Purpose: "Designed to assess areas of neurological integration as they relate to learning."
Population: Ages 5 through 18.
Publication Dates: 1974-1998.
Acronym: QNST-II.
Scores, 15: Hand Skill, Figure Recognition and Production, Palm Form Recognition, Eye Tracking, Sound Patterns, Finger to Nose, Thumb and Finger Circle, Double Simultaneous Stimulation of Hand and Cheek, Rapidly Reversing Repetitive Hand Movements, Arm and Leg Extensions, Tandem Walk, Standing on One Leg, Skipping, Left-Right Discrimination, Behavioral Irregularities.
Administration: Individual.
Price Data, 2006: $95 per test kit including manual (93 pages), 25 scoring forms, 25 geometric form reproduction sheets, 25 remedial guideline forms, and cue cards; $35 per manual; $20 per 25 scoring forms; $10 per 25 geometric form reproduction sheets; $12 per 25 remedial guideline forms; $18 per directions for administration and scoring printed on 20 cue cards; $35 per specimen set including manual and sample forms.
Time: (20-30) minutes.
Comments: Screening for early identification of learning disabilities; 1998 edition provides extensive litera-

ture reviews, clarified directions for administration, and reformatted test protocol sheets.
Authors: Margaret C. Mutti, Harold M. Sterling, Nancy A. Martin, and Norma V. Spalding.
Publisher: Academic Therapy Publications.
Cross References: For a review by Edward E. Gotts, see 14:306; see also T5:2141 (1 reference) and T4:2183 (3 references); for a review by Russell L. Adams of an earlier edition, see 9:1027.

[2111]
Quick Phonics Survey.

Purpose: Designed to "assess a child's understanding of sound/symbol relationships, transfers, and associations."
Population: Grades 1- 7.
Publication Date: 1976.
Acronym: QPS.
Scores: Total score only.
Administration: Individual.
Manual: No manual.
Price Data, 2006: $15 per plasticized stimulus card and 50 recording forms with directions.
Time: Administration time not reported.
Comments: Criterion-referenced.
Author: John Arena.
Publisher: Academic Therapy Publications.
Cross References: For reviews by Beth D. Bader and Dawn P. Flanagan, see 12:318.

[2112]
Quick Quizzes for U.S. History Classes.

Purpose: To be used as pre- or post-tests, self-tests, or study guides for 52 U.S. History topics.
Population: Grades 6–12.
Publication Date: 1989.
Scores: Total score only.
Administration: Group.
Manual: No manual.
Price Data: Price information available from publisher for 52 blackline master quiz forms and answer booklet.
Time: Administration time not reported.
Authors: E. Richard Churchill and Linda R. Churchill.
Publisher: Walch Publishing.

[2113]
Quick Spelling Inventory.

Purpose: To "identify the grade level at which a student can function in spelling."
Population: Grades 2-8.
Publication Date: 1988.
Acronym: QSI.
Scores: Total score only.
Administration: Group or individual.
Manual: No manual.
Price Data, 2006: $15 per 50 recording forms and plasticized word list with directions.

Time: Administration time not reported.
Author: John Arena.
Publisher: Academic Therapy Publications (High Noon Division).
Cross References: For reviews by Kevin D. Crehan and Dale P. Scannell, see 11:322.

[2114]
Quick Style Indicator.
Purpose: Designed to help identify "personal style as it relates to people, tasks, time and situations."
Population: Adults and teenagers.
Publication Dates: 1996-2006.
Acronym: QSI.
Scores, 4: Behavioral/Action, Cognitive/Analysis, Interpersonal/Harmony, Affective/Expression.
Administration: Individual or group.
Price Data, 2006: $11.95 per test booklet (2006, 12 pages); $14.94 per In-Depth Interpretations booklet (2006, 48 pages).
Time: (30) minutes; (90-180 minutes program options).
Comments: Shorter version of Personal Style Indicator (1916); self-administered and self-scored.
Authors: Ken Keis, Terry D. Anderson, Marilyn Hamilton, and Everett T. Robinson.
Publisher: Consulting Resource Group International, Inc.

[2115]
The Quick Test.
Purpose: Designed to assess intelligence based on verbal-perceptual performance.
Population: Ages 2 and over.
Publication Dates: 1958-1962.
Acronym: QT.
Scores: Total score only.
Administration: Individual.
Forms, 3: 1, 2, 3.
Price Data: Price data available from publisher for complete kit including 3 plates, 100 record sheets, instruction card, and item card, and provisional manual (1962, 54 pages).
Time: (3-10) minutes.
Authors: R. B. Ammons and C. H. Ammons.
Publisher: Psychological Test Specialists.
Cross References: See T5:2146 (20 references), T4:2191 (44 references), 9:1028 (19 references), T3:1969 (44 references), 8:225 (33 references), and T2:522 (15 references); for excerpted reviews by Peter F. Merenda and B. Semeonoff, see 7:422 (30 references); for reviews by Boyd R. McCandless and Ellen V. Piers, see 6:534 (3 references).

[2116]
Quickview Social History.
Purpose: Assists in the collection and reporting of client information.

Population: Ages 16 and older.
Publication Dates: 1983–1992.
Administration: Group or individual.
Price Data, 2006: $83 per Q Local starter kit including user's guide (1992, 33 pages), hardcover test booklet, 3 answer sheets, and 3 assessments; $58 per hardcover test booklet; $47 per 10 reusable soft cover test booklets; $12.25 per Q Local report.
Time: (30–45) minutes
Author: Ronald A. Giannetti.
Publisher: Pearson Assessments.
   a) BASIC REPORT.
   Scores: 9 areas of inquiry: Demographic Data, Developmental History, Family of Origin, Educational History, Marital History, Occupational History/Financial Status, Legal History, Military History, Symptom Screen.
   Comments: The report also has a follow-up summary that includes contradictory responses, indeterminate responses, and client-requested follow-up sections.
   b) CLINICAL SUPPLEMENT.
   Scores: Includes 8 areas of inquiry listed in Basic Report, plus Physical and Psychological Symptom Screens including: Adult Problems (Substance Use, Psychotic Symptoms, Mood Symptoms, Anxiety Disorders, Somatoform Symptoms, Psychosexual Disorders, Sleep and Arousal, Antisocial Personality, Other Current or Past Potential Adult Problems/Stressors), Developmental Problems (Activity Level/Lability, Conduct Problems, Anxious/Avoidant, Eating/Weight, Tic/Elimination/Sleep, Other Disorders/Delays, Other Potential Developmental Problems/Stressors).
Cross References: For reviews by David N. Dixon and Edward R. Starr, see 13:251.

[2117]
Racial Attitude Survey.
Purpose: Measures attitudes toward an examiner-selected group of people using a generic semantic differential method.
Population: Adults.
Publication Dates: 1989–1996.
Scores, 9: Physical, Ego Strength (Dominance, Control, Anxiety, Ethics, General Social, On-the-Job), Social Distance, Casual Contact.
Administration: Individual or group.
Manual: No manual.
Price Data: Available from publisher.
Time: Administration time not reported.
Comments: Previously entitled Racial Attitude Test; technical information provided is from thesis by Cynthia Lewis.
Author: Thomas J. Rundquist.
Publisher: Nova Media, Inc.

Cross References: For a review by Deborah L. Bandalos, see 16:206.

[2118]

Rahim Organizational Conflict Inventories.

Purpose: "Designed to measure three independent dimensions of organizational conflict: Intrapersonal, Intragroup, Intergroup" (ROCI-I) and "designed to measure five independent dimensions that represent styles of handling interpersonal conflict: Integrating, Obliging, Dominating, Avoiding, and Compromising" (ROCI-II).
Population: Managers, employees, supervisors.
Publication Date: 1983.
Acronym: ROCI.
Administration: Group.
Price Data, 2006: $25 per manual (70 pages).
Comments: Self-administering; separate answer sheets must be used.
Author: M. Afzalur Rahim.
Publisher: Center for Advanced Studies in Management.

    a) RAHIM ORGANIZATIONAL CONFLICT INVENTORY I.
    Acronym: ROCI-I.
    Scores: 3 subscales: Intrapersonal, Intragroup, Intergroup.
    Price Data: $150 per permission to make 300 copies for institutional or funded projects; $75 per permission to make 300 copies for individual or unfunded projects; quantity discounts available.
    Time: (10–12) minutes.
    b) RAHIM ORGANIZATIONAL CONFLICT INVENTORY II.
    Acronym: ROCI-II.
    Scores, 5: Integrating, Obliging, Dominating, Avoiding, Compromising.
    Price Data: $170 per permission to make 300 copies for institutional or funded projects; $100 per permission to make 300 copies for individual or unfunded projects; quantity discounts available.
    Time: (10–12) minutes.
Cross References: See T5:2149 (5 references) and T4:2195 (1 reference); for a review by George C. Thornton III, see 10:303 (3 references).

[2119]

RAND-36 Health Status Inventory.

Purpose: Designed to assess "general health status."
Population: Adults.
Publication Date: 1998.
Acronym: R-36 HSI.
Scores, 10: Physical Functioning, Role Limitations Due to Physical Health Problems, Pain, General Health Perceptions, Emotional Well-Being, Role Limitations Due to Emotional Problems, Social Functioning, Energy/Fatigue/Physical Health Composite, Mental Health Composite, Global Health Composite.
Administration: Group or individual.
Forms, 2: RAND-36, RAND-12 (a short form).
Price Data, 2002: $60 per complete kit including manual (126 pages), 25 question/answer sheets, and 25 hand-scoring worksheets; $8 per 25 question/answer sheets; $8 per 25 hand-scoring worksheets; $8 per 25 RAND-12 HSI question/answer sheets; $50 per manual.
Time: Administration time not reported.
Comments: Paper-and-pencil or computer administered; hand-scoring forms also available.
Author: Ron D. Hays.
Publisher: PsychCorp, A brand of Harcourt Assessment, Inc.
Cross References: For reviews by Corine Fitzpatrick and Richard I. Frederick, see 14:307.

[2120]

Randt Memory Test.

Purpose: Designed "as a global survey and evaluation of patients' complaints concerning their memory."
Population: Ages 20-90.
Publication Dates: 1983-1989.
Acronym: RMT.
Scores, 10: Acquisition Recall (Five Items Acquisition, Paired Words Acquisition, Short Story Verbatim, Digit Span, Incidental Learning), Delayed Recall (Five Items Recall, Paired Words Recall, Picture Recall, General Information), Memory Index.
Administration: Individual.
Forms, 5: Alternative forms for repeated measures.
Price Data, 2001: $95 per complete test including 10 administration booklets, 5 sets of picture cards, and manual (1989, 36 pages); $45 per 50 administration booklets.
Time: (20-25) minutes.
Authors: C. T. Randt and E. R. Brown.
Publisher: Life Science Associates.
Cross References: See T5:2159 (4 references) and T4:2204 (2 references); for a review by Joseph D. Matarazzo, see 10:304 (1 reference).

[2121]

Rapid Automatized Naming and Rapid Alternating Stimulus Tests.

Purpose: "Designed to estimate an individual's ability to see a visual symbol … and name it accurately and rapidly."
Population: Ages 5-0 to 18-11.
Publication Date: 2005.
Acronym: RAN/RAS.
Scores, 6: Rapid Automatized Naming (Objects, Colors, Numbers, Letters), Rapid Alternating Stimulus (2-Set Letters and Numbers, 3-Set Letters/Numbers and Colors).

Administration: Individual.
Price Data, 2006: $130 per complete kit including examiner's manual (112 pages), 50 record forms, and set of 6 cards; $60 per examiner's manual; $50 per 50 record forms; $25 per set of 6 cards.
Time: (5–10) minutes.
Authors: Maryanne Wolf and Martha Bridge Denckla.
Publisher: PRO-ED.

[2122]
Raven's Progressive Matrices.

Purpose: Constructed as a nonverbal assessment of perception and thinking skills.
Publication Dates: 1938–2000.
Acronym: RPM.
Scores: Total score only.
Price Data: Available from publisher.
Comments: Formerly called Progressive Matrices; may be used with Crichton Vocabulary Scale (730) or Mill Hill Vocabulary Scale (1621).
Authors: J. C. Raven, J. H. Court (manual), and J. Raven (manual).
Publisher: Oxford Psychologists Press, Ltd. [England].
a) STANDARD.
Population: Ages 6–65.
Acronym: SPM.
Administration: Group.
Time: (45) minutes.
Comments: Includes Classic, Parallel, and Plus Versions.
b) COLOURED.
Population: Ages 5–11 and people with mental defects and elderly people.
Acronym: CPM.
Administration: Individual.
Forms, 2: Board, Book.
Time: (15–30) minutes.
c) ADVANCED.
Population: Ages 11 and over with average or high intellectual ability.
Acronym: APM.
Administration: Group.
1) *Set I.*
Time: (10) minutes.
2) *Set II.*
Time: 40(45) or 60(65) minutes.
Cross References: See T5:2163 (356 references), T4:2208 (260 references), 9:1007 (67 references), T3:1914 (200 references), 8:200 (190 references), T2:439 (122 references), and 7:376 (194 references); for a review by Morton Bortner, see 6:490 (78 references); see also 5:370 (62 references); for reviews by Charlotte Banks, W. D. Wall, and George Westby, see 4:314 (32 references); for reviews by Walter C. Shipley and David Wechsler of the 1938 edition, see 3:258 (13 references); for a review by T. J. Keating, see 2:1417 (8 references).

[2123]
Reading and Arithmetic Indexes.

Purpose: "Measures level of development in reading and math." "Assesses proficiency levels in reading and math."
Population: Age 14–adult applicants for entry level jobs and special training programs.
Publication Dates: 1968–1996.
Administration: Group.
Forms, 2: Reading Index, Arithmetic Index.
Price Data, 1998: $53 per 25 tests (specify Arithmetic Index or Reading Index); $19.75 per examiner's manual.
Author: Science Research Associates.
Publisher: Pearson Performance Solutions [No reply from publisher; status unknown].
a) READING–ARITHMETIC INDEX.
Purpose: "Measures level of development in reading and math."
Acronym: RAI.
Scores, 11: Reading Index (Picture-Word Association, Word Decoding, Comprehension of Phrases, Comprehension of Sentences, Comprehension of Paragraphs, Total), Arithmetic Index (Addition and Subtraction of Whole Numbers, Multiplication and Division of Whole Numbers, Basic Operations Involving Fractions, Basic Operations Involving Decimals and Percentages, Total).
Time: (25) minutes per Index.
b) READING AND ARITHMETIC INDEXES (12).
Purpose: "Assesses proficiency levels in reading and math."
Acronym: RAI-12.
Scores, 14: Reading Index (Picture-Word Association, Word Decoding, Comprehension of Phrases, Comprehension of Sentences, Comprehension of Paragraphs I, Comprehension of Paragraphs II, Total), Arithmetic Index (Addition and Subtraction of Whole Numbers, Multiplication and Division of Whole Numbers, Basic Operations Involving Fractions, Basic Operations Involving Decimals and Percentages, Basic Operations Involving Square Roots and Powers, Basic Operations Involving Geometry and Word Problems, Total).
Time: (35) minutes per Index.
Cross References: For reviews by D. Joe Olmi and Jay R. Stewart, see 15:202; for a review by Dorothy C. Adkins of an earlier edition, see 7:20. See T4:2538 (1 reference) and 8:813 (3 references) for information regarding the Reading Index. See T5:171 (2 references) and 8:307 (3 references) for information regarding the Arithmetic Index.

[2124]

Reading Comprehension Battery for Aphasia, Second Edition.

Purpose: "Designed to provide systematic evaluation of the nature and degree of reading impairment in adolescents and adults with aphasia."

Population: Pre-adolescent to geriatric aphasic people.

Publication Dates: 1979–1998.

Acronym: RCBA-2.

Scores, 19: Word–Visual, Word–Auditory, Word–Semantic, Functional Reading, Synonyms, Sentence–Picture, Paragraph–Picture, Paragraph–Factual, Paragraph–Inferential, Morpho–Syntax, Overall Score of Core Subtests, Letter Discrimination, Letter Naming, Letter Recognition, Lexical Decision, Semantic Categorization, Oral Reading: Words, Oral Reading: Sentences, Overall Score of Supplemental Subtests.

Administration: Individual.

Price Data, 2006: $180 per complete kit including examiner's manual (1998, 38 pages), picture book, supplementary picture book, and 25 profile/summary record forms; $30 per examiner's manual, $55 per picture book or supplementary picture book; $45 per 25 profile/summary record forms.

Time: (30) minutes.

Comments: Instrument is criterion-referenced.

Authors: Leonard L. LaPointe and Jennifer Horner.

Publisher: PRO-ED.

Cross References: For reviews by Candice Haas Hollingsead and Robert Wall, see 14:308; see also T5:2172 (1 reference), T4:2220 (5 references), and 9:1033 (1 reference).

[2125]

Reading Evaluation Adult Diagnosis, Fifth Edition.

Purpose: Designed for assessing existing reading competencies.

Population: Illiterate adult students.

Publication Dates: 1972–1999.

Acronym: READ.

Scores: 3 parts, 21 scores: Sight Words (List 1, List 2, List 3, List 4), Word Analysis Skills (Letter Sound Relationships, Letter Names [Upper-Case], Letter Names [Lower-Case], Reversals, CVC, CV[CC], Final Digraphs, Initial Digraphs, Final Blends, Initial Blends, Multi-Syllabic Words, Silent Letters, Soft C & G, Suffixes), Reading/Listening Inventory (Word Recognition, Reading Comprehension, Listening Comprehension).

Administration: Individual.

Price Data, 2005: $15 per test booklet/manual (1999, 51 pages); $6.50 per answer pad.

Time: Administration time not reported.

Authors: Original test by Ruth J. Colvin and Jane H. Root; 1999 revision by Kathleen A. Hinchman and Rebecca Schoultz.

Publisher: ProLiteracy Worldwide.

Cross References: For reviews by Howard Margolis and Timothy Shanahan, see 14:309; for reviews by Mary E. Huba and Diane J. Sawyer of an earlier edition, see 11:326 (1 reference).

[2126]

Reading Fluency Indicator.

Purpose: A brief, individually administered test of oral reading fluency that measures rate, accuracy, comprehension, and prosody.

Population: Grades 1–12.

Publication Date: 2004.

Acronym: RFI.

Scores: Total Reading Time, Total Miscues, Total Comprehension Passage Level, Words Read per Minute, Miscue Descriptive Analysis (Addition, Omission, Provided Word, Repetition, Reversal, Substitution), Prosody Rating System, Comprehension Descriptive Analysis (Literal Comprehension Questions, Inferential Comprehension Questions).

Administration: Individual.

Levels, 10: P, K, 1–6, M, H.

Price Data, 2006: $154.99 per starter set including manual (42 pages), passage book, and 30 progress record forms; $82.99 per passage book; $30.99 per 20 progress record forms; $82.99 per manual.

Time: (5–10) minutes.

Comments: May be used as supplement to the Group Reading Assessment and Diagnostic Evaluation (1127); "criterion-referenced."

Author: Kathleen T. Williams.

Publisher: Pearson Assessments (originally published by AGS Publishing, acquired by Pearson in 2005).

[2127]

Reading-Free Vocational Interest Inventory: 2.

Purpose: "To measure the vocational interest of the special needs student/adult and regular classroom students."

Population: Ages 12 to 69.

Publication Dates: 1975–2000.

Acronym: RFVII:2.

Scores: 11 scales: Automotive, Building Trades, Clerical, Animal Care, Food Service, Patient Care, Horticulture, Housekeeping, Personal Service, Laundry Service, Materials Handling, plus 5 cluster scores: Mechanical, Outdoor, Mechanical—Outdoor, Food Service—Handling Operations, Clerical—Social Service.

Administration: Individual.

Price Data, 2005: $104.50 per complete kit including 20 test booklets, manual (2000, 123 pages), and

Occupational Title Lists 2 (2001, 42 pages); $54.75 per sample set including 10 test booklets and manual; $40.00 per examination set including 1 test booklet and manual; $39.50 per 20 test booklets (discounts available for orders of 40 or more); $39 per manual.

Time: 20(30) minutes.

Comments: Revision of Reading-Free Vocational Interest Inventory; earlier edition listed as AAMD-Becker Reading-Free Vocational Interest Inventory; self-administered; hand-scorable only.

Author: Ralph L. Becker.

Publisher: Elbern Publications.

Cross References: For reviews by Zandra S. Gratz and Mark Pope, see 15:203; for information on an earlier edition, see T4:2177; for a review by Robert J. Miller of an earlier edition, see 11:327; see also T3:1996 (2 references); for reviews by Esther E. Diamond and George Domino of an earlier edition, see 8:988 (6 references).

[2128]
Reading-Level Indicator.

Purpose: Designed "to identify individual reading at a second-to-sixth-grade level and functional nonreaders."

Population: Upper elementary to college students.

Publication Dates: 2000-2002.

Scores, 5: Sentence Comprehension Score, Vocabulary Score, Total Raw Score, Instructional Reading Level, Independent Reading Level.

Administration: Group or individual.

Forms, 2: Blue Form, Purple Form.

Price Data, 2006: $73.99 per starter Set including manual, 1 package (25) Purple forms, 1 package (25) Blue forms; $26.99 per 25 forms (specify Purple or Blue); $26.99 per manual; $73.99 per Spanish Companion.

Foreign Language Edition: Spanish translation available.

Time: (4–20) minutes.

Comments: Designed to work with Group Reading Assessment and Diagnostic Evaluation (GRADE; 1127), a diagnostic reading test.

Author: Kathleen T. Williams.

Publisher: Pearson Assessments (originally published by AGS Publishing, acquired by Pearson in 2005).

Cross References: For reviews by Elizabeth Kelley Boyles and Robert E. Wall, see 15:204.

[2129]
Reading Progress Tests.

Purpose: Designed to "provide a continuous measure of individual and group progress in reading comprehension."

Population: Ages 5-0 to 12-2.

Publication Dates: 1996–1997.

Acronym: RPT.

Scores: Total score only.

Administration: Group.

Price Data, 2002: £12.99 per Stage One manual (1996, 48 pages); £13.50 per Stage Two manual (1997, 47 pages); £14.99 per Stage One specimen set; £16.99 per Stage Two specimen set.

Time: (20) minutes per test.

Authors: Denis Vincent, Mary Crumpler, and Mike de la Mare.

Publisher: Hodder & Stoughton Educational [England].

a) STAGE ONE.

   1) *Literacy Baseline.*

   Purpose: "To provide a 'baseline' from which to measure subsequent progress."

   Population: Children in first term of their first year of compulsory schooling (ages 5-0 to 6-4).

   Price Data: £6.99 per 10 copies.

   2) *RPT Test 1.*

   Purpose: Constructed to "assess developing reading skills."

   Population: Year 1 (ages 5-8 to 7-2).

   Price Data: £6.99 per 10 copies.

   Time: (45–50) minutes.

   3) *RPT Test 2.*

   Population: Year 2 (ages 6-8 to 8-1).

   Price Data: £6.99 per 10 copies.

b) STAGE TWO.

   1) *RPT Test 3.*

   Population: Year 3 (ages 7-8 to 9-2).

   Price Data: £6.99 per 10 copies; £11.50 per 10 Test 3 broadsheets.

   2) *RPT Test 4.*

   Population: Year 4 (ages 8-8 to 10-2).

   Price Data: £6.99 per 10 copies; £11.50 per 10 Test 4 broadsheets.

   3) *RPT Test 5.*

   Population: Year 5 (ages 9-8 to 11-2).

   Price Data: £6.99 per 10 copies; £11.50 per 10 Test 5 broadsheets.

   4) *RPT Test 6.*

   Population: Year 6 (ages 10-8 to 12-2).

   Price Data: £6.99 per 10 copies; £11.50 per 10 Test 6 broadsheets.

[2130]
Reading Skills Diagnostic Test III, Level 4.

Purpose: Assesses "three areas in encoding/decoding" of reading including content, processes, and basic capacity.

Population: Grades 2.5–12.

Publication Dates: 1967–1983.

Acronym: RSDT-III.

Scores, 12: Letter Writing, Short Term Memory—Letters, Simple Phonics, Open Syllable Writing, Syllable Writing, Word Writing, Short Term Memory—Words, Long Vowels, Consonant Diphthongs, Vowel

Diphthongs, Sight Word Writing (2 parts), Context Clues.
Administration: Group.
Price Data: Available from publisher.
Time: (40–60) minutes.
Author: Richard H. Bloomer.
Publisher: Brador Publications, Inc. [No reply from publisher; status unknown].
Cross References: For reviews by Ira E. Aaron and Edward R. Sipay, see 8:772; see also T2:1644 (1 reference).

[2131]
Reading Style Inventory 2000.

Purpose: Designed to identify "the way each student learns best then (match) those strengths to the most effective reading methods, materials and strategies."
Population: Grade 1 to adults.
Publication Dates: 1980–2000.
Acronym: RSI.
Scores: 52 elements: Global Tendencies, Analytical Tendencies, Perceptual Strengths (Auditory Strengths, Visual Strengths, Tactile Strengths, Kinesthetic Strengths), Reading Methods (Carbo Recorded-Book Method, Fernald Method, Individualized Method, Modeling Methods, Language-Experience Method, Orton-Gillingham Method, Phonics Method, Whole-Word Method, Recorded Books, Computers), Preferred Reading Environment (Quiet—No Talking, Quiet—No Music, Dim Light, Warm Temperatures, Informal Design, Highly Organized), Emotional Profile (Peer Motivated, Adult Motivated, Self-Motivated, Persistent, Responsible), These Students Prefer (Choices, Direction, Work Checked), Sociological Preferences (Read to a Teacher, Read with Peers, Read Alone, Read with Peers/Teacher, Read with One Peer), Physical Preferences (Intake While Reading, Read in the Morning, Read in Early Afternoon, Read in Late Afternoon, Read in Evening, Mobility), Reading Materials (Audio-Visuals, Basal Reader Phonics, Basal Reader Whole-Word, Computers, Fernald Materials, Reading Activities, Orton-Gillingham Materials, Reading Kits, Recorded-Books, Tradebooks, Newspapers, etc.; Workbooks and Worksheets).
Administration: Individual and group.
Forms, 3: Primary, Intermediate, Adult.
Price Data, 2006: Price per administration varies by volume.
Time: Administration time not reported.
Comments: Available online only at www.nrsi.com.
Author: National Reading Styles Institute.
Publisher: National Reading Styles Institute, Inc.
Cross References: For reviews by Alice Corkill and by Thomas Emerson Hancock and Kathleen Allen, see 16:207; see also T5:218 (2 references); for reviews by Jeri Benson and Alice J. Corkill of a previous edition, see 11:328 (1 reference).

[2132]
Reading Test (Comprehension and Speed): Municipal Tests: National Achievement Tests.

Purpose: Measures reading comprehension and speed.
Population: Grades 3–6, 6–8.
Publication Dates: 1938–1957.
Scores, 5: Following Directions, Sentence Meaning, Paragraph Meaning, Reading Speed, Total.
Administration: Group.
Price Data: Available from publisher.
Time: (32) minutes.
Comments: Subtest of Municipal Battery; 2 forms: A, B.
Authors: Robert K. Speer and Samuel Smith.
Publisher: Psychometric Affiliates.
Cross References: For a review by Larry A. Harris, see 8:741. For reviews of the complete battery, see 5:18 (1 review), 4:20 (1 review), and 2:1191 (2 reviews).

[2133]
Reading Test SR-A & SR-B.

Purpose: "Designed to provide a means of estimating the reading attainment of primary school children."
Population: Ages 7-6 to 11-11.
Publication Dates: 1970–1982.
Scores: Total score only.
Administration: Group.
Editions, 2: SR-A, SR-B.
Price Data: Price information available from publisher for test booklets and manual (1971, 17 pages).
Time: 20(25) minutes.
Authors: Brian Pritchard and the National Foundation for Educational Research in England and Wales.
Publisher: NFER-Nelson Publishing Co., Ltd. [England].
Cross References: For reviews by Robert C. Calfee and Marian Jean Dreher, see 10:311.

[2134]
Reading Tests EH 1-2.

Purpose: Provides a measure of reading ability.
Population: Ages 11-0 to 15-1.
Publication Dates: 1961–1966.
Scores: 2 tests: Vocabulary, Comprehension.
Administration: Group.
Price Data: Price information available from publisher for test booklets (specify EH1 [Vocabulary] or EH2 [Comprehension]) and for manual.
Time: (15–20) minutes for EH1; (40–45) minutes for EH2.
Author: S. M. Bate.
Publisher: NFER-Nelson Publishing Co., Ltd. [England].
Cross References: See T3:2004 (1 reference).

[2135]
Ready to Learn: A Dyslexia Screener.

Purpose: Designed as a screening instrument for underlying early learning and prereading skills "so that children at risk for developing reading problems can be identified early."
Population: Ages 3-6 to 6-5.
Publication Dates: 1996-2004.
Scores: 16 subscale scores: (Rapid Naming, Bead Threading and Paper Cutting, Corsi Frog, Balance, Phonological Discrimination, Digit Span, Rhyming, Sound Order, Teddy & Form Matching, Vocabulary, Shape & Letter Copying [optional for ages 3-6 to 4-5], Repetition [optional for ages 3-6 to 4-5], Digit Naming [optional for ages 3-6 to 4-5], Letter Naming [optional for ages 3-6 to 4-5], First Letter Sound [ages 4-6 to 6-5], Postural Sound [ages 4-6 to 6-5]), Risk Index [one score for each of the above scale scores].
Administration: Individual.
Price Data, 2006: $250 per complete kit including manual (2004, 109 pages), 25 record forms, audio CD, stimulus book, set of manipulatives, and soft case; $110 per manual; $43 per 25 record forms; $12 per audio CD; $80 per stimulus book; $43 per set of manipulatives; $18 per Balance Test manipulative; $6.50 per CORSI Frog manipulative; $18 per 13 beads and a cord manipulative.
Time: (30-45) minutes.
Comments: This test can be completed in two sessions if necessary.
Authors: Angela J. Fawcett, Rod I. Nicolson, and Ray Lee.
Publisher: PsychCorp, A brand of Harcourt Assessment, Inc.

[2136]
Reality Check Survey.

Purpose: Assesses "how managerial actions serve employee needs."
Population: Adults.
Publication Dates: 1989–1995.
Acronym: RCS.
Scores: Total score only.
Administration: Group.
Price Data, 2001: $7.95 per instrument.
Time: Untimed.
Comments: Self-administered survey.
Author: Jay Hall.
Publisher: Teleometrics International, Inc.
Cross References: For reviews by S. Alvin Leung and Sheldon Zedeck, see 12:322.

[2137]
Receptive-Expressive Emergent Language Test, Third Edition.

Purpose: Designed to identify babies or young children with delayed language acquisition, to determine discrepancy between receptive and expressive processes of emergent language and to document intervention effects.
Population: Ages 0–36 months.
Publication Dates: 1971–2003.
Acronym: REEL-3.
Scores, 3: Receptive Language Ability, Expressive Language Ability, Language Ability.
Administration: Individual.
Price Data, 2003: $88 per complete kit including examiner's manual (2003, 98 pages) and 25 profile/examiner record booklets; $55 per examiner's manual; $39 per 25 profile/examiner record booklets.
Time: (20–30) minutes.
Comments: Informants knowledgeable about child's language behavior are interviewed; first edition titled The Bzoch-League Receptive Expressive Emergent Language Scale: For the Measurement of Language Skills in Infancy.
Authors: Kenneth R. Bzoch, Richard League, and Virginia L. Brown.
Publisher: PRO-ED.
Cross References: For reviews by David P. Hurford and Gabrielle Stutman, see 16:208; see also T5:2189 (7 references); for reviews by Lyle F. Bachman and Lynn S. Bliss of a previous edition, see 12:323 (2 references); see also T4:2238 (3 references) and T3:338 (5 references); for excerpted reviews by Alex Bannatyne, Dale L. Johnson, and Barton B. Proger of the first edition, see 8:956 (5 references); see also T2:2067 (2 references).

[2138]
Receptive One-Word Picture Vocabulary Test—Spanish-Bilingual Edition.

Purpose: Designed to provide "an assessment of an individual's combined Spanish and English hearing vocabulary."
Population: Ages 4.0–12.11.
Publication Date: 2001.
Acronym: ROWPVT-SBE.
Scores: Total score only.
Administration: Individual.
Price Data, 2006: $140 per test kit including manual (92 pages), test plates, and 25 Spanish-Bilingual record forms in portfolio; $38 per manual; $27 per 25 Spanish-Bilingual record forms; $75 per book of test plates (uses same plate booklet as English edition)
Time: (15–20) minutes.
Comments: Co-normed with the Expressive One-Word Picture Vocabulary Test—Spanish-Bilingual Edition (985) to allow for comparisons of an individual's expressive and receptive vocabulary.
Author: Rick Brownell.
Publisher: Academic Therapy Publications
Cross References: For reviews by S. Kathleen Krach and Maria del R. Medina-Diaz, see 16:209.

[2139]
Receptive One-Word Picture Vocabulary Test [2000 Edition].

Purpose: Designed to assess an individual's English hearing vocabulary.
Population: Ages 2–0 through 18–11.
Publication Dates: 1985–2000.
Acronym: ROWPVT.
Scores: Total score only.
Administration: Individual.
Price Data, 2006: $145 per kit including manual (2000, 110 pages), 25 record forms, and test plates; $30 per 25 record forms; $75 per test plates; $40 per manual.
Time: (10–15) minutes.
Comments: Lower and upper levels have been combined into this edition.
Authors: 1985 edition by Morrison F. Gardner; 2000 edition prepared by Rick Brownell.
Publisher: Academic Therapy Publications.
Cross References: For reviews by Doreen W. Fairbank and Sheila Pratt, see 15:205; see T5:2190 (9 references); T4:2239 (1 reference); for reviews by Janice A. Dole and Janice Santogrossi of an earlier edition, see 10:312; for reviews by Laurie Ford and William D. Schaffer of an earlier edition of the upper level, see 11:329.

[2140]
Recognition Memory Test.

Purpose: Allows clinicians to quickly distinguish between right- and left-hemisphere brain damage.
Population: Adult patients referred for neuropsychological assessment.
Publication Date: 1984.
Acronym: RMT.
Scores, 2: Words, Faces.
Administration: Individual.
Price Data, 2006: $185 per kit including 1 reusable test booklet and word card, 25 record forms. and manual (16 pages); $32.50 per 100 record forms; $38.50 per manual.
Time: (15) minutes.
Author: Elizabeth K. Warrington.
Publisher: Western Psychological Services.
Cross References: See T5:2193 (59 references) and T4:2241 (12 references); for a review by Russell L. Adams, see 10:313 (1 reference).

[2141]
Recovery Attitude and Treatment Evaluator.

Purpose: Intended for use after diagnosis of alcohol or other drug dependency to determine the "patient's level of resistance to treatment and other important information" to be considered in treatment planning.
Population: Adults.
Publication Dates: 1987–1996.
Acronym: RAATE–CE; RAATE–QI.

Scores: 5 dimensions: Resistance to Treatment, Resistance to Continuing Care, Acuity of Biomedical Problems, Acuity of Psychiatric/Psychological Problems, Social/Family Environmental Status.
Administration: Individual.
Forms, 2: Clinical Evaluation, Initial Questionnaire.
Price Data: Available from publisher.
Time: (30–45) minutes for Clinical Evaluation; [20–30] minutes for Initial Questionnaire.
Authors: David Mee-Lee, Norman G. Hoffmann, and Maurice B. Smith (manual).
Publisher: Change Companies.
Cross References: For reviews by Philip Ash and Tony Toneatto, see 14:311.

[2142]
REHAB: Rehabiliation Evaluation Hall and Baker.

Purpose: "Designed to assess people with a major psychiatric handicap."
Population: Psychiatric patients who live in residential care.
Publication Dates: 1984–1994.
Acronym: REHAB.
Scores, 8: Deviant Behaviour, General Behaviour (Social Activity, Speech Disturbance, Self Care, Community Skills, Overall Rating), Speech Skills.
Administration: Individual.
Price Data, 2005: $405 (£215) per complete set including 50 assessment forms, 5 rater guides, 1 scoring key, 25 score sheets, 25 individual presentation sheets, 25 group presentation sheets, manual (1994, 136 pages), and carrying case; $33 (£17.50) per 25 assessment forms; $44 (£23) per 5 raters guides; $34 (£17.50) per scoring key; $19.50 (£10.50) per 25 score sheets; $27.50 (£14.50) per 25 individual presentation sheets; $46 (£26) per 25 group presentation sheets; $88 (£45.50) per manual; $105 (£60) per carrying case.
Time: (1) week.
Comments: A multipurpose behavior rating scale requiring observation of the target client over a period of one week; raters can include any direct care staff.
Authors: Roger Baker and John N. Hall.
Publisher: Dr. Baker Partnership [England].
Cross References: For reviews by James P. Choca and Pamilla Morales, see 14:312; see also T5:2195 (2 references).

[2143]
Rehabilitation Checklist.

Purpose: Designed to help determine the needs of clients recovering from serious and soft-tissue physical injuries, cognitive impairment (mild to moderate brain injury), and related psychological adjustment and/or trauma.
Population: Adults.

Publication Dates: 1998–1999.
Acronym: RCL.
Scores: 7 scales (Physical, Cognitive, Emotional Psychosocial, Employability, Job), plus Total and Total Rehabilitation subscale.
Administration: Group.
Price Data, 2006: $108 per complete kit including 25 QuikScore™ forms and manual (1998, 54 pages); $63 per 25 QuikScore™ forms; $63 per manual.
Time: (15) minutes.
Comments: Self-report.
Author: J. Douglas Salmon, Jr.
Publisher: Multi-Health Systems, Inc.
Cross References: For reviews by Michael G. Kavan and Carolyn Mitchell Person, see 15:206.

[2144]
Rehabilitation Compliance Scale.

Purpose: Intended to provide a measurement of compliance to a rehabilitation program in the severely injured musculoskeletal patient.
Population: Severely injured patients ages 17–85 years.
Publication Date: 1994.
Administration: Group.
Price Data: Available from publisher (www.mindgarden.com).
Time: Administration time not reported.
Author: Neil W. Rheiner.
Publisher: Mind Garden, Inc.
 a) REHABILITATION COMPLIANCE SCALE.
 Acronym: RHAB.
 Scores, 3: Appointment Compliance, Participation in Therapy, Progress in Therapy.
 Forms, 2: A, B.
 b) PATIENT EXPERIENCE QUESTIONNAIRE.
 Score: Total score only.
Cross References: For reviews by Michael P. Gamache and Robert A. Leark, see 14:313.

[2145]
Rehabilitation Survey of Problems and Coping.

Purpose: Intended for use as a symptom rating and disability management tool.
Population: Age 14 and over.
Publication Date: 2002.
Acronym: R-SOPAC.
Scores, 12: Overall Total, Problem Total, Coping Total, Emotional Overall, Emotional Problem, Emotional Coping, Physical Overall, Physical Problem, Physical Coping, Cognitive Overall, Cognitive Problem, Cognitive Coping.
Administration: Group.
Parts, 2: Survey of Problems, Survey of Coping.

Price Data, 2006: $89 per complete kit including technical manual (124 pages) and 25 QuikScore forms™; $72 per technical manual; $41 per 25 QuikScore™ forms.
Time: (10–15) minutes.
Comments: One of several measures comprising a broad battery of rehabilitation-oriented instruments together entitled the Rehabilitation Assessment Series (RAS).
Authors: J. Douglas Salmon and Marek Celinski.
Publisher: Multi-Health Systems, Inc.
Cross References: For reviews by Theodore L. Hayes and Nambury S. Raju, see 16:210.

[2146]
Reiss-Epstein-Gursky Anxiety Sensitivity Index.

Purpose: To measure the fear of anxiety in order to "identify patients with high anxiety sensitivity" and "to obtain information relevant to the diagnosis of panic disorder or posttraumatic stress disorder; to evaluate treatment outcomes; to assess soldiers at risk to panic under stress."
Population: Adults and adolescents.
Publication Date: 1987.
Acronym: ASI.
Scores: Total Anxiety Sensitivity.
Administration: Individual or group.
Price Data: Available from publisher.
Time: [5] minutes.
Comments: Translated into 18 languages: Catalan, Chinese, Dutch, Farsi, French, German, Greek, Icelandic, Italian, Japanese, Polish, Portuguese, Russian, Spanish, Swedish, Turkish.
Authors: Steven Reiss and Rolf A. Peterson.
Publisher: IDS Publishing Inc.
Cross References: See T5:2199 (14 references) and T4:2244 (2 references); for a review by Harrison G. Gough, see 11:330.

[2147]
A Religion Scale.

Purpose: Measures attitudes toward religion.
Population: Adolescents and adults.
Publication Date: 1961.
Scores: Total score only.
Administration: Group.
Manual: No manual.
Price Data, 2005: $2 per scale.
Time: [10] minutes.
Comments: Supplementary article available.
Author: Panos D. Bardis.
Publisher: Donna Bardis.
Cross References: See 8:465 (2 references).

[2148]
The Renfrew Bus Story.

Purpose: Designed as a "test of narrative recall."

Population: Ages 3.6–7.0.
Publication Date: 1994.
Scores, 4: Information, Sentence Length, Complexity, Independence.
Administration: Individual.
Price Data, 2001: $45 per complete kit including manual (56 pages), 15 record forms, and story booklet; $10 per 15 record forms.
Time: Administration time not reported.
Comments: American adaptation of original British version.
Authors: Judy Cowley and Cheryl Glasgow.
Publisher: Centreville School.
Cross References: For reviews by Sherry K. Bain and Robert R. Haccoun, see 14:314.

[2149]

Repeatable Battery for the Assessment of Neuropsychological Status.

Purpose: Designed to measure "attention, language, visuospatial/constructional abilities, and immediate and delayed memory."
Population: Ages 20–89.
Publication Date: 1998.
Acronym: RBANS.
Scores, 18: Immediate Memory (List Learning, Short Memory, Total), Visuospatial/Constructional (Figure Copy, Line Orientation, Total), Language (Picture Naming, Semantic Fluency, Total), Attention (Digit Span, Coding, Total), Delayed Memory (List Recall, List Recognition, Story Memory, Figure Recall, Total), Total.
Administration: Individual.
Forms, 2: A, B.
Price Data, 2002: $149 per primary form kit including manual, record form A, stimulus book A, and coding scoring template A; $125 per alternative form kit including 25 record form B, stimulus book B, and coding scoring template B; $44 per 25 record forms (specify form); $81 per stimulus book (specify form); $13 per coding scoring template (specify form); $37 per manual.
Time: (20–30) minutes.
Author: Christopher Randolph.
Publisher: PsychCorp, A brand of Harcourt Assessment, Inc.
Cross References: For reviews by Stephen J. Freeman and Timothy J. Makatura, see 14:315.

[2150]

Report Completion Exercise for Firefighter, Police Officer, and Correctional Officer.

Purpose: "Video-based test designed to assess observation and listening skills as well as written communication skills."
Population: Candidates for entry-level firefighter, police officer, and correctional officer positions.
Publication Date: 2005.

Scores: Total score only.
Administration: Individual or group.
Price Data: Price data available from publisher (administration fee is waived if ordered with another testing product).
Time: 30 minutes.
Comments: Departments choosing to administer one of the tests must develop their own scoring criteria; administered via videos; joint technical report available for all three tests.
Author: International Public Management Association for Human Resources.
Publisher: International Public Management Association for Human Resources (IPMA-HR).
   a) FIREFIGHTER REPORT COMPLETION EXERCISE.
   Population: Entry-level firefighter candidates.
   Publication Date: 2005.
   Acronym: F-RCE.
   b) POLICE OFFICER REPORT COMPLETION EXERCISE.
   Population: Entry-level police officer candidates.
   Publication Date: 2005.
   Acronym: P-RCE.
   c) CORRECTIONAL OFFICER REPORT COMPLETION EXERCISE.
   Population: Entry-level correctional officer candidates.
   Publication Date: 2005.
   Acronym: C-RCE.

[2151]

Research Personnel Review Form.

Purpose: Designed "to provide a means for the periodic review of scientific, engineering, and technical personnel, and the environment in which they work."
Population: Research and engineering and scientific firms.
Publication Dates: 1959–1960.
Acronym: RPRF.
Scores: No scores.
Administration: Group.
Price Data: Available from publisher.
Time: Administration time not reported.
Author: Morris I. Stein.
Publisher: The Mews Press.

[2152]

Responsibility and Independence Scale for Adolescents.

Purpose: Measures adolescents' adaptive behaviors.
Population: Ages 12.0–19.11.
Publication Date: 1990.
Acronym: RISA.
Scores, 3: Responsibility, Independence, Adaptive Behavior Total.

Subscales, 9: Self-Management, Social Maturity, Social Communication, Domestic Skills, Money Management, Citizenship, Personal Planning, Transportation Skills, Career Development.
Administration: Individual.
Price Data, 2006: $210.50 per complete kit including test book, examiner's manual (176 pages), 25 response forms; $76.50 per examiner's manual, $46 per 25 response forms.
Time: (30–45) minutes.
Comments: Administered in a standardized interview format to a respondent who is familiar with the adolescent.
Authors: John Salvia, John T. Neisworth, and Mary W. Schmidt.
Publisher: Riverside Publishing.
Cross References: For reviews by D. Joe Olmi and James P. Van Haneghan, see 13:325 (2 references).

[2153]
Retail Management Applicant Inventory.

Purpose: Designed for "personnel selection and placement and the identification of strengths and areas to improve" in the field of retail management.
Population: Retail management applicants.
Publication Dates: 1994–1998.
Acronym: RMAI.
Scores, 13: Validity (Candidness, Accuracy), Management Focus (Background and Work Experience, Management and Leadership Interest), Motivation and Attitudes (Management Responsibility, Customer Service, Energy Level, Management Orientation), Job Knowledge (Managerial Arithmetic, Understanding Management Procedures and Practices), Stability and Risk (Business Ethics, Job Stability), Management Potential Index.
Administration: Individual or group.
Forms, 5: Quanta Touch Test, Quanta Software for Windows—administration and scoring, Quanta Software for Windows—scoring only, RLH Online, Mail-in Scoring.
Price Data, 2005: $32 per 25–99 each Quanta Touch Test, Quanta Software for Windows—administration and scoring (no booklets), Quanta Software for Windows—scoring only (one booklet for every coupon ordered), RLH Online; volume discounts available.
Time: [40–60] minutes.
Author: London House.
Publisher: Pearson Performance Solutions [No reply from publisher; status unknown].

[2154]
Retail Sales Skills Test.

Purpose: To evaluate the knowledge necessary for successful performance as a retail salesperson.
Population: Candidates for the position of retail salesperson.
Publication Date: 1994.
Acronym: RETSALES.

Scores: Total Score, Narrative Evaluation, Ranking, Recommendation.
Administration: Group.
Price Data, 2001: $150 per candidate; quantity discounts available.
Time: (70) minutes.
Comments: Scored by publisher; must be proctored.
Author: Walden Personnel Performance, Inc.
Publisher: Walden Personnel Performance, Inc.

[2155]
Retail Store Manager Staff Selector.

Purpose: To evaluate the knowledge necessary for successful performance in retail store management.
Population: Candidates for the position of store manager or assistant manager.
Publication Date: 1996.
Acronym: RSALES.
Scores: Total Score, Narrative Evaluation, Ranking, Recommendation.
Administration: Group.
Price Data, 2001: $500 per candidate; quantity discounts available.
Time: (255) minutes.
Comments: Scored by publisher; must be proctored.
Author: Walden Personnel Performance, Inc.
Publisher: Walden Personnel Performance, Inc. (Canada).

[2156]
Retirement Activities Card Sort Planning Kit.

Purpose: "To introduce a new perspective on adult development and a model of understanding the process of change as it relates to retirement; to stimulate personal thinking on handling retirement; and to assist participants to identify and begin planning for avenues of new growth or expanded satisfaction in retirement living."
Population: Retired adults or adults who plan to retire.
Publication Dates: 1992–1994.
Scores: Item scores only.
Administration: Group or individual.
Price Data: Available from publisher.
Time: (75–120) minutes.
Comments: 8 supplementary activities included.
Author: Richard L. Knowdell.
Publisher: CareerTrainer.
Cross References: For reviews by M. Allan Cooperstein and Robert B. Frary, see 13:262.

[2157]
Retirement Descriptive Index.

Purpose: Designed to measure satisfaction with facets of retirement.
Population: Retirees.
Publication Dates: 1969–1993.
Acronym: RDI.

Scores, 4: Present Work and Activities, Financial Situation, Present Health, People You Associate With.
Administration: Group or individual.
Price Data, 2006: $50 per 100 test booklets.
Time: 5 minutes.
Comments: Previously listed with the Job Descriptive Index (1313).
Authors: Patricia C. Smith, Lorne M. Kendall, and Charles L. Hulin.
Publisher: Bowling Green State University.
Cross References: For reviews by Charles K. Parsons and Norman D. Sundberg of the Job Descriptive Index and Retirement Descriptive Index, see 12:199 (33 references); see also T4:1312 (63 references).

[2158]
Revised Behavior Problem Checklist [PAR Edition].

Purpose: Developed to "rate problem behaviors observed in adolescents and young children."
Population: Ages 5–18.
Publication Dates: 1979–1987.
Acronym: RBPC.
Scores, 6: Conduct Disorder, Socialized Aggression, Attention Problems-Immaturity, Anxiety-Withdrawal, Psychotic Behavior, Motor Tension-Excess.
Administration: Individual.
Price Data, 2006: $182 per introductory kit including professional manual, 50 test booklets, and 50 profiles.
Time: 20 (30) minutes.
Comments: Ratings by teachers, parents, and child care staff.
Authors: Herbert C. Quay and Donald R. Peterson.
Publisher: Psychological Assessment Resources, Inc.
Cross References: See T5:2211 (52 references) and T4:2254 (45 references); for reviews by Denise M. Dezolt and by Edward S. Shapiro and Stewart M. Shear, see 11:332 (80 references); for a review by Anthony A. Cancelli, see 9:1043 (31 references); see also T3:2012 (6 references).

[2159]
Revised Children's Manifest Anxiety Scale.

Purpose: "Designed to assess the level and nature of anxiety in children and adolescents."
Population: Ages 6–19.
Publication Date: 1985.
Acronym: RCMAS.
Scores, 5: Physiological Anxiety, Worry/Oversensitivity, Social Concerns/Concentration, Total Anxiety, Lie scale.
Administration: Group.
Price Data, 2006: $126.50 per kit including 50 AutoScore™ answer forms and manual (106 pages); $42.50 per 25 AutoScore™ answer forms; $54.50 per manual; $68 per Spanish language kit including 15 test forms, scoring key, and manual (all in Spanish); $22.50

per 15 Spanish test forms; $12 per scoring key for Spanish test forms; $52.50 per Spanish manual.
Foreign Language Edition: Spanish version available.
Time: (10) minutes.
Comments: Revision and published version of the Children's Manifest Anxiety Scale (CMAS).
Authors: Cecil R. Reynolds and Bert O. Richmond.
Publisher: Western Psychological Services.
Cross References: See T5:2214 (140 references) and T4:2257 (47 references); for a review by Frank M. Gresham, see 10:314 (7 references).

[2160]
Revised Evaluating Acquired Skills in Communication.

Purpose: Constructed to assess communication skills in the areas of semantics, syntax, morphology, and pragmatics.
Population: Children 3 months to 8 years with severe language impairments.
Publication Dates: 1984-1991.
Acronym: EASIC.
Scores: Ratings in 10 areas: Labels/Nouns and Pronouns, Verbs and Action Commands, Comprehension of Three-Word Phrases, Affirmation and Negation, Prepositional Location Commands, Comprehension of Singular and Plural, Adjectives and Attributes, Money Concepts, Categorization and Association, Interrogatives.
Administration: Individual.
Price Data: Price data available from publisher for complete kit including manual (1991, 54 pages).
Time: Administration time not reported.
Author: Anita Marcott Riley.
Publisher: Harcourt Assessment, Inc.
Cross References: For reviews by William O. Haynes and John H. Kranzler, see 12:329; for reviews by Barry W. Jones and Robert E. Owens, Jr. of an earlier edition, see 10:109.

[2161]
Revised Hamilton Rating Scale for Depression.

Purpose: Designed as a clinician-rated scale for evaluating individuals already diagnosed with depressive illness.
Population: Depressed individuals.
Publication Date: 1994.
Acronym: RHRSD.
Scores, 22: General Screening, Depressed Mood, Feelings of Guilt, Suicide, Insomnia, Nocturnal Waking, Early Morning Waking, Work and Activities, Sexual Symptoms, Loss of Insight, Retardation, Agitation, Worry, Somatic Anxiety, Gastrointestinal Somatic Symptoms, General Somatic Symptoms, Hypochondriasis, Loss of Weight, Diurnal Variation,

Obsessive-Compulsive Symptoms, Paranoid Symptoms, Depersonalization/Derealization.

Administration: Individual.

Price Data, 2006: $115.50 per kit including 10 AutoScore™ clinican forms, 10 AutoScore™ self-report problem inventories, manual (62 pages); $42.50 per 25 AutoScore™ clinician forms; $42.50 per 25 AutoScore™ self-report problem inventories; $55 per manual; $220 or less per 20-use IBM scoring interpretive software; $16.50 per 100 microcomputer answer sheets; $10.75 each per FAX report service.

Time: (5–10) minutes.

Comments: A self-report scale is also provided.

Author: W. L. Warren.

Publisher: Western Psychological Services

Cross References: For reviews by Paul C. Burnett and Barbara J. Kaplan, see 13:263 (382 references); see also T4:2261 (10 references).

[2162]
Revised Minnesota Paper Form Board Test, Second Edition.

Purpose: "Designed to measure aspects of mechanical ability requiring the capacity to visualize and manipulate objects in space."

Population: Grade 9 and over.

Publication Dates: 1934–1995.

Acronym: RMPFBT.

Scores: Total score only.

Administration: Group.

Forms, 4: Series AA, BB, MA, MB.

Price Data, 2006: $60 per examination kit including test booklets for 4 forms and manual; $95 per 25 Form AA or BB test booklets for booklet scoring; $120 per 25 test booklets for Forms MA and MB for use with scannable or hand-scorable answer document; $10 per key for Forms AA and BB; $50 per key for hand scoring scannable answer document for Forms MA and MB; $75 per 50 scannable answer documents for use with Form MA or MB; $45 per manual.

Foreign Adaptations: Australian edition: 1981; revised edition prepared by J. Jenkinson; Australian Council for Education Research [Australia]; British norms supplement: 1978; Gil Nyfield, NFER-Nelson Publishing Co. [England].

Time: 20(40) minutes.

Authors: Rensis Likert and W. H. Quasha.

Publisher: PsychCorp, A brand of Harcourt Assessment, Inc.

Cross References: For reviews by L. Carolyn Pearson and Michael J. Roszkowski, see 14:316; see also T5:2217 (3 references) and T4:2262 (2 references); for a review by Paul W. Thayer of an earlier edition, see 9:1045 (2 references); see also T3:2015 (19 references), T2:2266 (37 references), 7:1056 (19 references), and 6:1092 (16 references); for a review by D. W. McElwain, see

5:885 (29 references); for reviews by Clifford E. Jurgensen and Raymond A. Katzell, see 4:763 (38 references); for a review by Dewey B. Stuit, see 3:677 (48 references); for a review by Alec Rodger, see 2:1673 (9 references).

[2163]
Revised Pre-Reading Screening Procedures [1997 Edition].

Purpose: Designed to "find among children of average to superior intelligence the ones who show difficulties in Auditory, Visual, and/or Kinesthetic modalities that often indicate Specific Language Disability (SLD)."

Population: First grade entrants.

Publication Dates: 1968–1997.

Scores: 7 areas: Visual, Visual-Kinesthetic-Motor, Auditory, Auditory-Visual, Auditory-Visual-Kinesthetic-Motor, Language, Letter Knowledge.

Administration: Group.

Price Data, 2006: $65.65 per test booklet (32 pages) including 12 Teacher Observation/Summary sheets, 12 Practice Pages, and 12 cardboard markers; $21.75 per Teacher's Manual (1997, 94 pages) including instructions plus detachable key; $24.45 per Teacher's Cards and Chart (2 sets of 5 x 10 cards and 2 copies of a wall chart used in giving the tests); $23.55 per specimen set including Teacher's Manual and 1 test booklet; quantity discounts available.

Time: Administration time not reported.

Authors: Beth H. Slingerland and Marty Aho.

Publisher: Educators Publishing Service, Inc.

Cross References: For a review by Maurine A. Fry of an earlier edition, see 9:1046; see also T2:1721 (1 reference); for reviews by Colleen B. Jamison and Roy A. Kress of an earlier edition, see 7:732 (1 reference).

[2164]
The Revised Sheridan Gardiner Test of Visual Acuity.

Purpose: To measure visual acuity.

Population: Age 5 and over.

Publication Dates: 1970–c1993.

Scores, 2: Distance Vision, Near Vision.

Administration: Individual.

Manual: No manual.

Price Data, 2001: $36 per test.

Time: Administration time not reported.

Authors: Mary D. Sheridan and Peter A. Gardiner.

Publisher: Keeler Instruments Inc. (U.S. Distributor).

Cross References: See T2:1926 (1 reference).

[2165]
Revised Token Test.

Purpose: Designed as a quantitative and descriptive test for "auditory disorders associated with aphasia and brain damage."

Population: Preliminary normative data based on the following standardization samples: non-brain-damaged, left hemisphere brain-damaged, right hemisphere brain-damaged.
Publication Date: 1978.
Acronym: RTT.
Scores, 22: 10 Subtest mean scores, Overall mean score, 11 Linguistic Element mean scores.
Administration: Individual.
Price Data, 2006: $153 per complete kit including 25 scoring forms, 25 profile forms, administration manual, 24 tokens, and manual (118 pages); $35 per profile forms; $35 per administration manual and scoring forms; $37 per tokens; $50 per manual.
Time: Administration time varies with condition.
Comments: Reconstruction of the Token Test.
Authors: Malcolm Ray McNeil and Thomas E. Prescott.
Publisher: PRO-ED.
Cross References: See T5:2225 (21 references) and T4:2270 (5 references); for reviews by Michael D. Franzen and Charles J. Golden and by Thomas Hammeke, see 9:1048; see also T3:2017 (5 references).

[2166]
Rey Auditory Verbal Learning Test: A Handbook.

Purpose: Designed to measure "verbal learning and memory."
Population: Ages 7–89.
Publication Date: 1996.
Acronym: RAVLT.
Scores, 3: Learning, Recall, Recognition.
Administration: Individual.
Price Data, 2006: $87.95 per complete kit including handbook (148 pages) and 25 record sheets and score summaries; $27.50 per 25 record sheets and score summaries; $64 per handbook.
Time: (15) minutes.
Author: Michael Schmidt.
Publisher: Western Psychological Services.
Cross References: For reviews by Karen Mackler and Steven R. Shaw, see 14:317; see also T5:2226 (42 references).

[2167]
Rey Complex Figure Test and Recognition Trial.

Purpose: Designed to assess "visuospatial constructional ability and visuospatial memory."
Population: Ages 6–89.
Publication Dates: 1995–1996.
Acronym: RCFT.
Scores, 9: Immediate Recall, Delayed Recall, Recognition Total Correct, Copy, Time to Copy, Recognition True Positives, Recognition False Positives, Recognition True Negatives, Recognition False Negatives.

Administration: Individual.
Price Data, 2006: $252 per introductory kit including manual (1995, 126 pages), 25 test booklets, stimulus card, and supplemental norms for children and adolescents (1996, 21 pages).
Time: (45) minutes, including a 30-minute delay interval.
Authors: John E. Meyers and Kelly R. Meyers.
Publisher: Psychological Assessment Resources, Inc.
Cross References: For reviews by D. Ashley Cohen and Deborah D. Roman, see 14:318; see also T5:2227 (62 references).

[2168]
Reynell Developmental Language Scales [U.S. Edition].

Purpose: Developed to measure verbal comprehension and expressive language skills.
Population: Ages 1 to 6.
Publication Dates: 1977–1990.
Acronym: RDLS.
Scores, 2: Verbal Comprehension, Expressive Language.
Administration: Individual.
Price Data, 2006: $549 per complete kit including a set of stimulus materials, 10 record forms, and manual (1990, 91 pages) in carrying case; $54.50 per 25 record forms; $66 per manual.
Time: (30) minutes.
Comments: Two Verbal Comprehension scales available to accommodate simple oral responses or pointing responses; British version available.
Authors: Joan K. Reynell and Christian P. Gruber.
Publisher: Western Psychological Services.
Cross References: See T5:2229 (16 references); for reviews by Dawn P. Flanagan and Rebecca J. McCauley, see 12:331 (3 references); see also T4:2272 (2 references); for reviews by Doris V. Allen and Diane Nelson Bryen of the British version, see 9:1049 (5 references); see also T3:2018 (16 references); for reviews by Katharine G. Butler and Joel Stark of the British version, see 8:974 (3 references); see also T2:2025 (3 references).

[2169]
Reynolds Adolescent Adjustment Screening Inventory.

Purpose: Designed as "a screening measure of adolescent adjustment."
Population: Ages 12–19.
Publication Dates: 1998–2001.
Acronym: RAASI.
Scores, 5: Antisocial Behavior, Anger Control Problems, Emotional Distress, Positive Self, Adjustment Total Score.
Administration: Individual or group.

Price Data, 2006: $140 per introductory kit including 50 test booklets and professional manual (2001, 134 pages).

Time: (5) minutes.

Author: William M. Reynolds.

Publisher: Psychological Assessment Resources, Inc.

Cross References: For reviews by Lynn Lakota Brown and Kevin M. Jones, see 15:207.

[2170]
Reynolds Adolescent Depression Scale—2nd Edition.

Purpose: Designed "to assess the severity of depressive symptomatology in adolescents in school and clinical settings."

Population: Ages 11–20.

Publication Dates: 1986–2002.

Acronym: RADS-2.

Scores, 5: Dysphoric Mood, Anhedonia/Negative Affect, Negative Self-Evaluation, Somatic Complaints, Depression Total.

Administration: Individual or group.

Price Data, 2006: $134 per introductory kit including professional manual (2002, 172 pages), 25 hand-scorable test booklets, and 25 summary/profile forms.

Time: (5–10) minutes.

Comments: Self-report measure; hand scored; may be administered aloud; test booklet is titled "About Myself."

Author: William M. Reynolds.

Publisher: Psychological Assessment Resources, Inc.

Cross References: For reviews by Kimberly A. Blair and Janet F. Carlson, see 16:211; see also T5:2230 (21 references) and T4:2274 (11 references); for reviews by Barbara J. Kaplan and Deborah King Kundert of an earlier edition, see 11:333 (6 references).

[2171]
Reynolds Bully-Victimization Scales for Schools.

Purpose: Designed to evaluate "school-related violence and its impact on students."

Publication Date: 2003.

Acronym: RBVSS.

Administration: Individual or group.

Levels, 3: Bully-Victimization Scale, Bully-Victimization Distress Scale, School Violence Anxiety Scale.

Price Data, 2003: $160 per complete kit including manual (181 pages), 30 Bully-Victimization Scale forms, 30 School Violence Anxiety Scale forms, 30 Bully-Victimization Distress forms, Bully-Victimization Scale scoring key—English/Spanish, and Bully-Victimization Distress Scale scoring key—English/Spanish; $65 per manual; $30 per 30 Bully-Victimization Scale (specify English or Spanish); $30 per 30 School Violence Anxiety Scale (specify English or Spanish); $30 per 30 Bully-Victimization Distress Scale (specify English or Spanish); $10 per Bully-Victimization Scale scoring key—English/Spanish; $10 per Bully-Victimization Distress Scale scoring key—English/Spanish.

Foreign Edition: Spanish edition available.

Time: (5–10) minutes per scale.

Comments: Scales may be used individually or as a battery; automated group testing available.

Author: William Reynolds.

Publisher: PsychCorp, A brand of Harcourt Assessment, Inc.

a) BULLY-VICTIMIZATION SCALE.

Purpose: "Designed to measure bullying behavior and victimization among peers in or near school settings."

Population: Grades 3–12.

Acronym: BVS.

Scores, 2: Bullying, Victimization.

b) BULLY-VICTIMIZATION DISTRESS SCALE.

Purpose: Designed to "evaluate the dimensions of students' psychological distress specific to being bullied."

Population: Grades 3–12.

Acronym: BVDS.

Scores, 3: Total Distress (Externalizing, Internalizing, Total).

c) SCHOOL VIOLENCE ANXIETY SCALE.

Purpose: Designed to "measure student anxiety about schools as unsafe or threatening environments."

Population: Grades 5–12.

Acronym: SVAS.

Scores: Total score only.

Cross References: For reviews by Christopher A. Sink and Cher I. Edwards and by Susan M. Swearer and Kelly Brey Love, see 16:212.

[2172]
Reynolds Child Depression Scale.

Purpose: Provides screening for and a measure of depressive symptomatology.

Population: Grades 3–6.

Publication Dates: 1981–1989.

Scores: Total score only.

Administration: Group or individual.

Price Data, 2006: $132 per introductory kit including professional manual (189, 55 pages), 50 test hand-scorable answer sheets, and scoring key.

Time: (10-15) minutes.

Comments: Test booklet title is About Me; self-ratings.

Author: William M. Reynolds.

Publisher: Psychological Assessment Resources, Inc.

Cross References: See T5:2231 (7 references) and T4:2275 (3 references); for reviews by Janet F. Carlson and Cynthia A. Rohrbeck, see 11:334 (1 reference).

[2173]
Reynolds Depression Screening Inventory.
Purpose: Constructed as a "self-report measure of the severity of depressive symptoms."
Population: Ages 18–89.
Publication Date: 1998.
Acronym: RDSI.
Scores: Total score only.
Administration: Individual or group.
Price Data, 2006: $71 per introductory kit including manual (64 pages) and 25 booklets.
Time: (5–10) minutes.
Authors: William M. Reynolds and Kenneth A. Kobak.
Publisher: Psychological Assessment Resources, Inc.
Cross References: For reviews by Michael H. Campbell and Rosemary Flanagan, see 14:320.

[2174]
Reynolds Intellectual Assessment Scales and the Reynolds Intellectual Screening Test.
Purpose: Designed to assess verbal and nonverbal intelligence and memory.
Population: Ages 3–94.
Publication Dates: 1998–2003.
Administration: Individual.
Price Data, 2006: $385 per RIAS/RIST combination kit including 3-volume set of stimulus books, 25 RIAS record forms and 25 RIST record forms, and professional manual (2003, 267 pages) in a softsided attache case; $165 per RIAS scoring program software on CD-ROM including unlimited use software for scoring and report generation of RIAS and RIST.
Authors: Cecil R. Reynolds and Randy W. Kamphaus.
Publisher: Psychological Assessment Resources, Inc.
   a) REYNOLDS INTELLECTUAL SCREENING TEST.
   Purpose: Designed to identify quickly those who need a more comprehensive intellectual assessment.
   Acronym: RIST.
   Scores, 3: Guess What, Odd-Item Out, Total RIST Index.
   Time: (10–15) minutes.
   Comments: Brief screening test comprising two RIAS subtests.
   b) REYNOLDS INTELLECTUAL ASSESSMENT SCALES.
   Purpose: Designed to measure intellectual level.
   Acronym: RIAS.
   Scores, 10: Verbal Intelligence Index (Guess What, Verbal Reasoning), Nonverbal Intelligence Index (Odd-Item Out, What's Missing), Composite Intelligence Index, Composite Memory Index (Verbal Memory, Nonverbal Memory).
   Time: (30–35) minutes.
Cross References: For reviews by Bruce A. Bracken and Gregory Schraw, see 16:213.

[2175]
Rhode Island Test of Language Structure.
Purpose: "Provides a measure of English language development—a profile of the child's understanding of language structure—and assessment data."
Population: Hearing-impaired children ages 3-20, hearing children ages 3-6.
Publication Date: 1983.
Acronym: RITLS.
Scores: Measures syntax response errors for 20 sentence types, both simple and complex, including Relative and Adverbial Clauses, Subject and Other Complements, Reversible and Nonreversible Passives, Datives, Deletions, Negations, Conjunctives, Embedded Imperatives.
Administration: Individual.
Price Data, 2006: $143 per complete kit including 10 analysis sheets, 10 response sheets, test booklet, and manual (114 pages); $30 per 10 response and 10 analysis sheets; $67 per test booklet; $51 per manual.
Time: (25-35) minutes.
Authors: Elizabeth Engen and Trygg Engen.
Publisher: PRO-ED.
Cross References: See T5:2233 (4 references) and T4:2276 (1 reference); for reviews by Lynn S. Bliss and Joan I. Lynch, see 10:315.

[2176]
The Riley Articulation and Language Test, Revised.
Purpose: To identify children in need of speech therapy.
Population: Grades K–2.
Publication Dates: 1966–1971.
Acronym: RALT.
Scores, 3: Language Proficiency and Intelligibility, Articulation Function, Language Function.
Administration: Individual.
Price Data, 2006: $58 per complete kit including 25 tests and manual (1971, 7 pages); $29 per 25 tests; $33 per manual.
Time: (3–5) minutes.
Author: Glyndon D. Riley.
Publisher: Western Psychological Services.
Cross References: For reviews by Ralph L. Shelton and Lawrence D. Shriberg, see 8:975 (1 reference); for a review by Raphael M. Haller of the original edition, see 7:967 (1 reference).

[2177]
Risk-Sophistication-Treatment Inventory.
Purpose: Designed to assess juvenile offenders' risk for dangerousness, sophistication-maturity, and amenability to treatment.
Population: Juvenile offenders ages 9–18.
Publication Dates: 1998–2004.
Acronym: RSTI.

Scores, 12: Risk for Dangerousness (Violent and Aggressive Tendencies, Planned and Extensive Criminality, Psychopathic Features, Total), Sophistication-Maturity (Autonomy, Cognitive Capacities, Emotional Maturity, Total), Treatment Amenability (Psychopathology-Degree and Type, Responsibility and Motivation to Change, Consideration and Tolerance of Others, Total).
Administration: Individual.
Price Data, 2006: $170 per introductory kit including professional manual (2004, 109 pages), 25 interview booklets, and 25 rating forms.
Time: (50–65) minutes for semistructured interview; [15–20] minutes for rating form.
Comments: Semistructured interview and rating scale.
Author: Randall T. Salekin.
Publisher: Psychological Assessment Resources, Inc.

[2178]
Risk Taking Inventory & Guide.

Purpose: Designed to "help respondents see the filters through which they assess risk" and "also guides them in improving the likelihood of gains while reducing uncertainty and the likelihood of losses."
Population: Managers.
Publication Date: 1997.
Scores, 3: Risk-Preference Pattern, Risk-Avoidance Pattern, Risk-Neutral Pattern.
Administration: Group.
Manual: No manual.
Price Data, 2002: $8.95 per inventory and guide; minimum of 20 (volume discounts available).
Time: [15] minutes including self-scoring.
Author: Herbert S. Kindler.
Publisher: The Center for Management Effectiveness, Inc.

[2179]
Rivermead Assessment of Somatosensory Performance.

Purpose: "Designed to provide therapists and doctors with a brief, quantifiable and reliable assessment of somatosensory functioning after neurological disorders such as stroke, MS, peripheral neuropathies, head injury and spinal cord injury."
Population: Age 18 and over.
Publication Date: 2000.
Acronym: RASP.
Scores: Total score only.
Subtests, 7: Sharp/Dull Discrimination, Surface Pressure Touch, Surface Localization, Temperature Discrimination, Movement, Direction Proprioception Discrimination, Sensory Extinction, Two-Point Discrimination.
Administration: Individual.
Price Data, 2006: £184 per complete kit including manual (19 pages), 25 scoring sheets, reference card, 2 aesthesiometers/neurometers, 2 neurotemps, two-point discriminator/neurodisk, and 30 neurotips; £35 per 50 scoring sheets.
Time: (25–35) minutes.
Authors: Charlotte E. Winward, Peter W. Halligan, and Derick T. Wade.
Publisher: Harcourt Assessment [England].

[2180]
The Rivermead Behavioural Memory Test-Extended Version.

Purpose: Designed "to predict everyday memory problems in people with acquired, non-progressive brain injury and monitor change over time."
Population: Ages 16-65.
Publication Dates: 1985-1999.
Acronym: RBMT-E.
Scores, 12: First Names, Second Names, Belongings and Appointments, Picture Recognition, Story (Immediate), Story (Delayed), Face Recognition, Route (Immediate), Route (Delayed), Messages (Immediate), Messages (Delayed), Orientation and Date.
Administration: Individual.
Forms: 2 versions: A, B.
Price Data, 2006: £295.50 per complete kit including manual (1999, 20 pages), 25 scoring sheets, 2 stimulus books, picture cards, and timer.
Time: (25-30) minutes.
Authors: Barbara A. Wilson, Linda Clare, Janet M. Cockburn, Alan D. Baddeley, Robyn Tate, and Peter Watson.
Publisher: Harcourt Assessment [England].

[2181]
The Rivermead Behavioural Memory Test [Second Edition].

Purpose: "Developed to detect impairment of everyday memory functioning and to monitor change following treatment for memory difficulties."
Publication Dates: 1985–2003.
Acronym: RBMT-II.
Administration: Individual.
Price Data: Available from publisher.
Time: (25-30) minutes.
Publisher: Harcourt Assessment [England].
a) THE RIVERMEAD BEHAVIOURAL MEMORY TEST.
Population: Brain-damaged persons, ages 16-96 years.
Publication Dates: 1985–2003.
Scores, 2: Screening Score, Standardized Profile Score.
Comments: For multiple administrations with the same subject, four parallel versions available.
Authors: Barbara Wilson (test, manual, supplementary manual 2), Janet Cockburn (test, manual,

supplementary manuals 2 and 3), and Alan Baddely (test, manual, supplementary manual 2).
b) THE RIVERMEAD BEHAVIOURAL MEMORY TEST FOR CHILDREN.
Population: Brain-damaged children, ages 5–11 years.
Publication Date: 1991.
Score: Standardized Profile Score.
Comments: Separate test; materials from adult version used for most subtests, but some additional materials needed.
Authors: Barbara A. Wilson (test and manual), Rebecca Ivani-Chalian (test and manual), and Frances Aldrich (manual).
Cross References: For reviews by Anthony M. Paolo and by Goran Westergren and Ingela Westergren, see 14:321; see also T5:2239 (35 references).

[2182]
Roberts-2.
Purpose: Designed to provide an "assessment of a child's or adolescent's level of social cognitive understanding."
Population: Ages 6-18 years.
Publication Dates: 1982-2005.
Scores, 28: 2 Theme Overview scales (Popular Pull, Complete Meaning), 6 Available Resources scales (Support from Self-Feeling, Support from Self-Advocacy, Support from Other-Feeling, Support from Other-Help, Reliance on Other, Limit Setting), 5 Problem Identification scales (Recognition, Description, Clarification, Definition, Explanation), 5 Resolution scales (Simple Closure or Easy Outcome, Easy and Realistically Positive Outcome, Constructive Resolution, Constructive Resolution of Feeling and Situation, Elaborated Process with Possible Insight), 4 Emotion scales (Anxiety, Aggression, Depression, Rejection), 4 Outcome scales (Unresolved Outcome, Nonadaptive Outcome, Maladaptive Outcome, Unrealistic Outcome), 2 Unusual or Atypical Responses scales (Unusual-Refusal/No Score/Antisocial, Atypical Categories).
Administration: Individual.
Editions, 3: Set of Test Pictures Featuring White Children and Adolescents, Set of Test Pictures Featuring Black Children and Adolescents, Set of Test Pictures Featuring Hispanic Children and Adolescents.
Price Data, 2006: $140 per complete kit including manual (2005, 171 pages), Set of Test Pictures Featuring White Children and Adolescents, and 25 record forms; $49.95 per manual; $59.95 per Set of Test Pictures Featuring White, Black, or Hispanic Children and Adolescents; $34.50 per 25 record forms; $33 per Continuing Education Questionnaire and Evaluation Form.
Time: (30-40) minutes.
Comments: Previous version entitled Roberts Apperception Test for Children.

Authors: Glen E. Roberts and Chris Gruber.
Publisher: Western Psychological Services.
Cross References: For reviews by Merith Cosden and Niels G. Waller of an earlier version, see 14:322; see also T5:2242 (8 references) and T4:2285 (5 references); for a review by Jacob O. Sines of an earlier edition, see 9:15054.

[2183]
Rockford Infant Developmental Evaluation Scales.
Purpose: Developed as a developmental checklist offering an informal assessment of developmental function.
Population: Birth-4 years.
Publication Date: 1979.
Acronym: RIDES.
Scores, 5: Personal-Social/Self-Help, Fine Motor/Adaptive, Receptive Language, Expressive Language, Gross Motor.
Administration: Individual.
Price Data, 2005: $50.50 per starter set including manual (150 pages) and 20 checklists; $29.85 per additional manual; $23.20 per 20 additional checklists.
Time: Administration time varies; author recommends administration in several sessions in one week.
Comments: 3 ways of administering items: ask parents for information, observe spontaneous actions and informal play, present specific tasks or set up situation that will elicit a particular kind of response.
Authors: Developed by PROJECT RHISE, Children's Development Center, Rockford, IL.
Publisher: Scholastic Testing Service, Inc.
Cross References: See T5:2243 (1 reference); for a review by Dennis C. Harper, see 9:1055.

[2184]
Roeder Manipulative Aptitude Test.
Purpose: Measures manual and finger dexterity and hand-eye coordination.
Population: Elementary school to adult.
Publication Date: 1967.
Scores, 1 to 3: Left Hand Dexterity (optional), Right Hand Dexterity (optional), Total.
Administration: Group.
Price Data: Available from publisher.
Time: 5(10) minutes.
Author: Wesley S. Roeder.
Publisher: Lafayette Instrument.
Cross References: For reviews by Jean Powell Kirnan and Shauna Faltin and by Suzanne Lane, see 12:333.

[2185]
Rogers Criminal Responsibility Assessment Scales.
Purpose: "To quantify essential psychological and situational variables at the time of the crime and to

implement criterion-based decision models for criminal responsibility."
Population: Adults.
Publication Date: 1984.
Acronym: R-CRAS.
Scores: 5 scales: Patient Reliability, Organicity, Psychopathology, Cognitive Control, Behavioral Control.
Administration: Individual.
Price Data, 2006: $104 per introductory kit including professional manual and 50 examination booklets.
Time: Administration time not reported.
Comments: "Criterion-referenced."
Author: Richard Rogers.
Publisher: Psychological Assessment Resources, Inc.
Cross References: See T4:2288 (1 reference); for a review by Robert J. Howell and R. Lynn Richards, see 10:316.

[2186]
Rokeach Value Survey.

Purpose: Constructed to identify values of importance to the respondent.
Population: Ages 11 and over.
Publication Dates: 1967–1983.
Scores: No scores.
Administration: Group.
Price Data, 2001: $67 per 25 test booklets; $32.95 per manual (322 pages).
Time: (10-20) minutes.
Comments: Rankings of 18 terminal values ("end-states of existence") and 18 instrumental values ("modes of behavior"); manual title is Understanding Human Values.
Author: Milton Rokeach.
Publisher: CPP, Inc.
Cross References: See T5:2246 (14 references); for reviews by Susan M. Brookhart and Eleanor E. Sanford, see 12:334 (14 references); see also T4:2290 (28 references), 9:1058 (17 references), and T3:2029 (49 references); for reviews by Jacob Cohen and Tom Kitwood, see 8:660 (155 references); see also T2:1355 (39 references).

[2187]
Rorschach.

Purpose: A projective technique for clinical assessment and diagnosis.
Population: Ages 5 and over.
Publication Dates: 1921–1998.
Scores: Many variations of scoring and interpretation are in use with no single method generally accepted.
Administration: Individual.
Price Data, 2006: $75 per set of 10 plates; $17 per 100 recording sheets; $32 per set of 5 location charts; $54 per manual (1998, 228 pages).
Time: (20–30) minutes.

Comments: Variously referred to by such titles as Rorschach Method, Rorschach Test, Rorschach Psychodiagnostics.
Author: Hermann Rorschach.
Publisher: Hogrefe & Huber Publishers.
Cross References: For a review by Allen K. Hess, Peter Zachar, and Jeffrey Kramer, see 14:323; see also T5:2247 (136 references), T4:2292 (273 references), 9:1059 (79 references), and T3:2030 (155 references); for reviews by Richard H. Dana and Rolf A. Peterson, see 8:661 (360 references); see also T2:1499 (376 references); for reviews by Alvin G. Burstein, John F. Knutson, Charles C. McArthur, Albert I. Rabin, and Marvin Resnikoff, see 7:175 (455 references); see also P:470 (719 references); for reviews by Richard H. Dana, Leonard D. Eron, and Arthur R. Jensen, see 6:237 (734 references); for reviews by Samuel J. Beck, H. J. Eysenck, Raymond J. McCall, and Laurance F. Shaffer, see 5:154 (1078 references); for a review by Helen Sargent, see 4:117 (621 references); for reviews by Morris Krugman and J. R. Wittenborn, see 3:73 (452 references); see also 2:1246 (147 references).

[2188]
Ross Information Processing Assessment—Geriatric.

Purpose: A clinical instrument designed to identify, describe, and quantify cognitive-linguistic deficits in the geriatric population following traumatic brain injury.
Population: Geriatric patients.
Publication Date: 1996.
Acronym: RIPA-G.
Scores, 12: Immediate Memory, Recent Memory, Temporal Orientation, Spatial Orientation, Orientation to Environment, Recall of General Information, Problem Solving and Abstract Reasoning, Organization of Information, Auditory Processing and Comprehension, Problem Solving and Concrete Reasoning, Naming Common Objects, Functional Oral Reading.
Administration: Individual.
Price Data, 2006: $235 per complete kit; $55 per examiner's manual (77 pages); $60 per 25 response record forms; $30 per 25 profile summary forms; $55 per picture book; $45 per Geriatric Treatment Manual.
Time: (45–60) minutes.
Comments: 10 core subtests, 2 supplemental subtests.
Authors: Deborah Ross-Swain and Paul T. Fogle.
Publisher: PRO-ED.
Cross References: For reviews by Surendra P. Singh and Wilfred G. Van Gorp, see 14:324.

[2189]
Ross Information Processing Assessment—Primary.

Purpose: Designed to "assess information processing skills in children ages 5-0 through 12-11 who have acquired or developmental problems involving the brain."

Population: "Ages 5-0 through 12-11 who have acquired or developmental problems involving the brain."
Publication Date: 1999.
Acronym: RIPA-P.
Scores, 12: 8 subtests (Immediate Memory, Recent Memory, Recall of General Information, Spatial Orientation, Temporal Orientation, Organization, Problem Solving, Abstract Reasoning); 4 composite scores (Memory, Orientation, Thinking and Reasoning, Information Processing).
Administration: Individual.
Price Data, 2006: $130 per complete kit including manual (61 pages), 25 record booklets, and 25 profile forms; $59 per manual; $45 per 25 record booklets; $30 per 25 profile forms.
Time: (45) minutes for complete battery.
Comments: Certain subtests not administered to younger children.
Author: Deborah Ross-Swain.
Publisher: PRO-ED.
Cross References: For reviews by Dawn P. Flanagan and Leonard F. Caltabiano and by Matthew E. Lambert, see 15:208.

[2190]
Ross Information Processing Assessment, Second Edition.

Purpose: Designed to assess "cognitive-linguistic deficits following traumatic brain injury."
Population: Ages 15–90.
Publication Dates: 1986–1996.
Acronym: RIPA-2.
Scores, 20: 10 Subtest scores (Immediate Memory, Recent Memory, Temporal Orientation [Recent Memory, Remote Memory], Spatial Orientation, Orientation to Environment, Recall of General Information, Problem Solving and Abstract Reasoning, Organization, Auditory Processing and Retention); 10 Diacritical scores (Errors, Perseveration, Repeat Instructions/Stimulus, Denial/Refusal, Delayed Response, Confabulation, Partially Correct, Irrelevant, Tangential, Self-Corrected).
Administration: Individual.
Price Data, 2006: $150 per complete kit including examiner's manual (1996, 68 pages), 25 record forms, and 25 profile/summary forms in storage box; $55 per 25 record forms; $35 per 25 profile/summary forms; $65 per examiner's manual.
Time: (60) minutes.
Author: Deborah Ross-Swain.
Publisher: PRO-ED.
Cross References: For a review by Stephen R. Hooper, see 14:325; see also T4:2294; for a review by Jonathan Ehrlich of an earlier edition, see 11:337.

[2191]
Rothwell-Miller Interest Blank.

Purpose: Designed to assess vocational interests.
Population: Ages 12 and over.
Publication Date: 1986.
Acronym: RMIB.
Scores, 12: Outdoor, Mechanical, Computational, Scientific, Persuasive, Artistic, Literary, Musical, Social Service, Clerical, Practical, Medical.
Administration: Group.
Price Data: Available from publisher.
Foreign Language Edition: Test printed in English and Afrikaans.
Time: 30(40) minutes.
Authors: B. A. Hall, M. E. Halstead, and T. R. Taylor.
Publisher: Human Sciences Research Council [South Africa].

[2192]
Rothwell Miller Interest Blank (Revised).

Purpose: "Designed primarily to give an assessment of vocational interests as an aid to a career interview . Other applications include company selection and promotion, and clinical and rehabilitation counselling."
Population: Ages 13 and over.
Publication Dates: 1958–1994.
Acronym: RMIB.
Scores, 12: Outdoor, Mechanical, Computational, Scientific, Persuasive, Aesthetic, Literary, Musical, Social Service, Clerical, Practical, Medical.
Forms, 3: A, B, and C.
Administration: Individual or group.
Price Data: Available from publisher.
Foreign Language and Special Editions: Culturally adapted editions (English language): Australian, New Zealand, Philippine, Singapore, South African editions; Foreign language editions: French and Greek language editions available (Afrikaans, German, Hungarian, Icelandic, and Romanian editions in progress).
Time: (15–30) minutes.
Comments: In addition to main task of ranking occupations in order of preference, there is an opportunity for free choice responses; can be used in conjunction with the complementary measure Rothwell Miller Values Blank (2193).
Authors: J. W. Rothwell (original test), K. M. Miller (original test and revision), and B. Tyler (1994 revision).
Publisher: Miller & Tyler, Limited [England].
Cross References: For reviews by Richard E. Harding and William K. Wilkinson, see 13:269; for reviews by A. W. Heim and Clive Jones of an earlier edition, see 7:1034 (2 references).

[2193]
Rothwell Miller Values Blank.

Purpose: "Designed as a measure of work related values to be used primarily in career guidance, in conjunction with an occupational interests measure. Other applications include company selection (with school leavers or older basic level staff) and clinical and rehabilitation counselling."
Population: Ages 15 and older.
Publication Dates: 1968–1994.
Acronym: RMVB.
Scores, 5: Rewards, Interest, Security, Pride in Work, Autonomy.
Administration: Individual or group.
Price Data: Available from publisher.
Foreign Language Editions: French and Greek language editions available; Afrikaans, German, Hungarian, Icelandic, and Romanian editions in progress.
Time: [10–20] minutes.
Comments: Previously entitled Choosing a Career; developed as a complementary measure to be used with the Rothwell Miller Interest Blank (2191).
Authors: J. W. Rothwell, K. M. Miller, and B. Tyler.
Publisher: Miller & Tyler, Limited [England].
Cross References: For reviews by John S. Geisler and William I. Sauser, Jr., see 14:328.

[2194]
Rotter Incomplete Sentences Blank, Second Edition.

Purpose: Primarily used "as a screening instrument of overall adjustment."
Population: College students, adults, high-school students.
Publication Dates: 1950–1992.
Acronym: RISB.
Score: Index of Overall Adjustment.
Administration: Individual or group.
Forms, 3: College, Adult, High School.
Price Data, 2002: $34 per 25 response sheets or $127 per 100 response sheets(specify High School, College, or Adult; $82 per manual (1992, 256 pages).
Time: (20–40) minutes.
Authors: Julian B. Rotter, Michael I. Lah, and Janet E. Rafferty.
Publisher: PsychCorp, A brand of Harcourt Assessment, Inc.
Cross References: See T5:2258 (6 references); for reviews by Gregory J. Boyle and Mary J. McLellan, see 12:335 (3 references); see also T4:2300 (11 references), T3:2037 (11 references), 8:663 (21 references), T2:1501 (48 references), P:472 (35 references), 6:239 (17 references), and 5:156 (18 references); for reviews by Charles N. Cofer and William Schofield of an earlier edition and an excerpted review by Adolf G. Woltmann, see 4:130 (6 references).

[2195]
Ruff Figural Fluency Test.

Purpose: Developed with the "aim of providing clinical information regarding nonverbal capacity for fluid and divergent thinking, ability to flexibly shift cognitive set, planning strategies, and executive ability to coordinate this process."
Population: Ages 16–70.
Publication Dates: 1988–1996.
Acronym: RFFT.
Scores, 3: Unique Designs, Perseverative Errors, Index of Planning Efficiency (Error Ratio).
Administration: Individual.
Price Data, 2006: $118 per introductory kit including 25 test booklets and professional manual (1996, 43 pages).
Time: 5 minutes.
Comments: Especially useful in neuropsychological applications.
Author: Ronald M. Ruff.
Publisher: Psychological Assessment Resources, Inc.
Cross References: For reviews by Raymond S. Dean and John J. Brinkman, Jr. and by Vincent J. Samar, see 15:209.

[2196]
Ruff-Light Trail Learning Test.

Purpose: "To assess visuospatial learning and memory."
Population: Ages 16–70.
Publication Date: 1999.
Acronym: RULIT.
Scores, 7: Learning (Total Correct, Total Step Errors, Trials to Completion), Immediate Memory (Trial 2 Correct, Trial 2 Errors), Delayed Memory (Delayed Correct, Delayed Errors).
Administration: Individual.
Price Data, 2006: $130 per introductory kit including professional manual, 50 test booklets, and stimulus cards.
Time: (5–15) minutes with a 60-minute delay.
Comments: Two alternate versions of a 15-step trail; long-term memory is evaluated by having the respondent retrace the trail after a 60-minute delay.
Authors: Ronald M. Ruff and C. Christopher Allen.
Publisher: Psychological Assessment Resources, Inc.
Cross References: For reviews by D. Ashley Cohen and Joseph G. Law, Jr., see 15:210.

[2197]
Ruff Neurobehavioral Inventory.

Purpose: Designed to measure cognitive, emotional, physical, and psychosocial problems both before and after a specified event—usually an injury or neuropsychiatric illness.
Population: Ages 18 and older.

Publication Date: 2003.

Acronym: RNBI.

Scores, 26: Inconsistency, Infrequency, Negative Impression, Positive Impression, Cognitive Composite, Emotional Composite, Physical Composite, Quality of Life Composite, Attention & Concentration, Executive Functions, Learning & Memory, Speech & Language, Anger & Aggression, Anxiety, Depression, Paranoia & Suspicion, Posttraumatic Stress Disorder, Substance Abuse, Neurological Status, Pain, Somatic Complaints, Abuse, Activities of Daily Living, Psychosocial Integration & Recreation, Vocation & Finance, Spirituality.

Administration: Individual or group.

Price Data, 2006: $158 per introductory kit including 25 reusable item booklets, 25 answer booklets, 25 profile booklets, and professional manual (123 pages).

Time: [30–45] minutes.

Authors: Ronald M. Ruff and Kristin M. Hibbard.

Publisher: Psychological Assessment Resources, Inc.

Cross References: For reviews by Andrew S. Davis and W. Holmes Finch and by Wilfred G. Van Gorp and Jason Hassenstab, see 16:214.

[2198]
Ruff 2 & 7 Selective Attention Test.

Purpose: Developed to "measure two overlapping aspects of visual attention: sustained attention, and selective attention."

Population: Ages 16–70 years.

Publication Dates: 1995–1996.

Acronym: 2 & 7 Test.

Scores, 11: Automatic Detection Speed, Automatic Detection Errors, Automatic Detection Accuracy, Controlled Search Speed, Controlled Search Errors, Controlled Search Accuracy, Total Speed, Total Accuracy, Speed Difference, Accuracy Difference, Total Difference.

Administration: Individual.

Price Data, 2006: $155 per introductory kit including manual and 50 test booklets.

Time: (5) minutes.

Authors: Ronald M. Ruff and C. Christopher Allen.

Publisher: Psychological Assessment Resources, Inc.

Cross References: For a review by Daniel C. Miller, see 15:211.

[2199]
Rust Advanced Numerical Reasoning Appraisal.

Purpose: Measures the ability to recognize, understand, and apply mathematical and statistical reasoning abilities.

Population: Adults.

Publication Dates: 2001–2002.

Acronym: RANRA.

Scores: Total score only.

Administration: Group or individual.

Price Data, 2006: £195 per complete kit.

Time: 20 minutes.

Author: John Rust.

Publisher: Harcourt Assessment [England].

Cross References: For reviews by Cederick O. Lindskog and Eleanor E. Sanford, see 16:215.

[2200]
Rust Inventory of Schizotypal Cognitions.

Purpose: For assessment of risk of schizotypal symptoms

Population: Age 16 and over.

Publication Date: 1989.

Acronym: RISC.

Scores: Total score only.

Administration: Individual.

Price Data, 2006: £67.50 per complete kit including record forms and manual (57 pages).

Time: (10) minutes.

Author: John Rust.

Publisher: Harcourt Assessment [England].

Cross References: For reviews by Gregory J. Boyle and George Domino, see 13:270 (3 references); see also T4:2303 (3 references).

[2201]
The Rutgers Drawing Test.

Purpose: A nonverbal "test of perception through motor response."

Population: Ages 4–6, 6–9.

Publication Dates: 1961–1973.

Scores: Total score only.

Administration: Group.

Price Data, 2005: $24 per specimen set; $44 per 25 test forms (specify Form A or Form B).

Time: Administration time not reported.

Author: Anna Spiesman Starr.

Publisher: Institute of Psychological Research, Inc. [Canada].

    a) FORM A.

    Population: Ages 4–6.

    b) FORM B.

    Population: Ages 6–9.

Cross References: For a review by Melvyn I. Semmel, see 7:446 (6 references); see also 6:559 (2 references).

[2202]
Safran Student's Interest Inventory, Third Edition.

Purpose: Developed to identify occupational interests.

Population: Grades 5-9, 8-12.

Publication Dates: 1960-1985.

Scores, 7: Economic, Technical, Outdoor, Service, Humane, Artistic, Scientific.

Administration: Group.

Levels, 2: 1 (grades 5-9), 2 (grades 8-12).
Price Data, 2005: $74.50 per 35 test booklets (select level); $44.10 per 35 students' manuals (1985, 8 pages); $41.30 per counsellor's manual (1985, 39 pages); $42.40 per preview kit.
Time: (40) minutes.
Comments: Self-administered.
Authors: Carl Safran, Douglas W. Feltham, and Edgar N. Wright.
Publisher: Nelson, A Thomson Company [Canada].
Cross References: For reviews by Albert M. Bugaj and Caroline Manuele-Adkins, see 12:336; for a review by Thomas T. Frantz of an earlier edition, see 7:1035; see also 6:1069 (1 reference).

[2203]
Sales Achievement Predictor.

Purpose: Constructed to assess "characteristics that are critical for success in sales."
Population: Adults.
Publication Date: 1995.
Acronym: Sales AP.
Scores, 21: Validity Scores (Inconsistent Responding, Self-Enhancing, Self-Critical), Special Scores (Sales Disposition, Initiative-Cold Calling, Sales Closing), Basic Domain Scores (Achievement, Motivation, Competitiveness, Goal Orientation, Planning, Initiative-General, Team Player, Managerial, Assertiveness, Personal Diplomacy, Extroversion, Cooperativeness, Relaxed Style, Patience, Self-Confidence).
Administration: Group.
Price Data, 2006: $165 per kit including manual (73 pages), 2 mail-in answer sheets; $54.50 per mail-in answer sheet; $60.50 per manual; $430 per 10-use computer CD (PC with Windows); $16.50 per 100 PC answer sheets; $38.50 per FAX service scoring.
Time: 20 minutes.
Comments: Microsoft Windows 3.1 or above required for computer scoring.
Authors: Jotham G. Friedland, Sander I. Marcus, and Harvey P. Mandel.
Publisher: Western Psychological Services.
Cross References: For reviews by Gordon C. Bruner II and Brent W. Roberts, see 14:329.

[2204]
Sales Aptitude Test.

Purpose: "To measure an individual's sales aptitude."
Population: Sales people and sales managers.
Publication Dates: 1993–1996.
Scores: Total score only.
Administration: Group.
Price Data, 2002: $106 per start-up kit including 25 test booklets and examiner's manual (1996, 11 pages); $91 per 25 tests; $28 per examiner's manual; price information for Quanta scoring software available from publisher.

Time: (30) minutes.
Comments: Paper-and-pencil or computer administration available.
Author: Science Research Associates.
Publisher: Pearson Performance Solutions [No reply from publisher; status unknown].
Cross References: For reviews by Deniz S. Ones and Sheldon Zedeck, see 15:212.

[2205]
Sales Attitude Check List.

Purpose: To measure attitudes toward selling and habits in the sales situation.
Population: Applicants for sales positions.
Publication Dates: 1960–1992.
Acronym: SACL.
Scores: Total score only.
Administration: Individual or group.
Price Data, 2002: $97 per start-up kit including 25 test booklets and examiner's manual; $81 per 25 test booklets (quantity discounts available); $28 per examiner's manual.
Time: No limit (approximately 10–15 minutes).
Author: Erwin K. Taylor.
Publisher: Pearson Performance Solutions [No reply from publisher; status unknown].
Cross References: For reviews by Walter C. Borman and Stephan J. Motowidlo, see 9:1066 (1 reference); for a review by John P. Foley, Jr., see 6:1177.

[2206]
Sales Competency Inventory.

Purpose: Designed to measure the frequency with which respondents display certain competencies associated with effective sales performance.
Population: Salespeople.
Publication Date: 1996.
Scores, 5: Achievement Orientation, Customer Service Orientation, Impact and Influence, Initiative, Interpersonal Understanding.
Administration: Individual or group.
Price Data, 2006: $69 per 10 Profile and Interpretive Notes (22 pages) and 10 questionnaires; $29 per 10 Employee Version questionnaires; $55 per 10 Development Assistant booklets.
Time: [30–40] minutes.
Comments: Self-scoring and interpretive information provided.
Author: Hay Group.
Publisher: Hay Group.

[2207]
Sales Comprehension Test.

Purpose: "Designed to aid in the appraisal of sales ability and potential."
Population: Sales applicants and employees.
Publication Dates: 1947-1994.

Acronym: SCT.
Scores: Total score only.
Administration: Group.
Price Data, 2006: $119.50 per test; $3.75 per key; $36.50 per profiles; $53 per manual (1976, 20 pages), manual supplement (1984, 17 pages), manual supplement (1985, 4 pages), and norms supplement (1994, 4 pages); $4.50 per norms supplement (1988, 1 page); $56.95 per specimen set.
Foreign Language Editions: Spanish, Dutch, French, German, and Italian editions available.
Time: (15-20) minutes.
Comments: Revision of the Aptitudes Associates Test of Sales Aptitude.
Author: Martin M. Bruce.
Publisher: Martin M. Bruce, Ph.D.
Cross References: See T2:2406 (3 references) and 6:1178 (7 references); for a review by Raymond A. Katzell, see 5:947 (10 references).

[2208]
Sales Effectiveness Survey.

Purpose: Designed as a 360° measure of more than 70 competencies and personality traits that are common among the most successful salespeople.
Population: Sales and business development professionals.
Publication Date: 1996.
Scores, 7: Overall Sales Effectiveness, Comparative Sales Effectiveness, Personal Sales Characteristics, Basic Sales Skills, Selling Skills, Account Management Skills, Opportunity Management Skills.
Administration: Group.
Manual: No manual.
Price Data, 2005: $49 per set including questionnaires and answer sheets for 1 self-assessment, 6 others, 6 customers, and 1 feedback report; $50 fee for additional paper report.
Time: [30] minutes.
Comments: Assessment is administered online via Lore's Assessment Center; assessment results are emailed to participant; a paper report may be requested for an additional fee; the group report, available separately, summarizes the results for an entire sales group without identifying the individuals and enables the sales manager to look at the strengths and developmental needs of the group as a whole.
Author: Lore International Institute.
Publisher: Lore International Institute.

[2209]
Sales Motivation Inventory, Revised.

Purpose: Designed for "assessment of interest in, and motivation for, sales work."
Population: Prospective and employed salespeople.
Publication Dates: 1953-1988.

Acronym: SMI.
Scores: Total score only.
Administration: Group.
Price Data, 2006: $119.50 per test package; $52.65 per manual/manuals supplement; $4.50 per norms supplement; $36.50 per profile sheet package; $3.75 per scoring key; $55.95 per specimen set.
Foreign Language Edition: French edition also available.
Time: (20-30) minutes.
Author: Martin M. Bruce.
Publisher: Martin M. Bruce, Ph.D.
Cross References: For a review by Leo M. Harvill, see 11:338; for reviews by Robert M. Guion and Stephan J. Motowidlo of an earlier edition, see 9:1067; see also T2:2408 (5 references); for a review by S. Rains Wallace, see 5:948 (2 references).

[2210]
Sales Motivation Survey.

Purpose: Designed to assess the kinds of needs and values salespeople see as important considerations in making decisions about their work.
Population: Salespeople.
Publication Dates: 1972–1995.
Scores, 5: Basic Creative Comfort, Safety and Order, Belonging and Affiliation, Ego-Status, Actualization and Self-Expression.
Administration: Group.
Price Data, 2001: $7.95 per instrument.
Time: Administration time is not reported.
Comments: Self-administered; self-scored.
Authors: Jay Hall and Norman J. Seim.
Publisher: Teleometrics International, Inc.
Cross References: For reviews by Leslie H. Krieger and Sheldon Zedeck, see 14:330.

[2211]
Sales Performance Assessment™.

Purpose: Designed to identify an individual's strengths and weaknesses in the area of sales.
Population: Salespeople.
Publication Dates: 1985-2005.
Acronym: SPA.
Scores, 25: Market Awareness, Technical, Strategic, Structure, Sales Focus, Prospecting, Entrepreneurship, Communication, Outgoing, Optimistic, Excitement, Persuasive Negotiation, Insight, Aggressiveness, Tactical, Empathy, Customer Identification, Team Player, Persistence, Production, Management Focus, Idealism, Ego Drive, Materialism, Exaggeration.
Administration: Group.
Price Data: Available from publisher.
Foreign Language Editions: Available in English (American), English (British), Dutch, French, and German.

Time: (45) minutes.
Comments: Purchase and use requires training by publisher; test previously listed as Sales Effectiveness Analysis.
Authors: James T. Mahoney (test) and Management Research Group Staff (manual).
Publisher: Management Research Group

[2212]
Sales Personality Questionnaire.

Purpose: Developed to assess personality characteristics necessary for sales success.
Population: Sales applicants.
Publication Dates: 1987–1990.
Acronym: SPQ.
Scores, 12: Interpersonal (Confidence, Empathy, Persuasive), Administration (Systematic, Conscientious, Forward Planning), Opportunities (Creative, Observant), Energies (Relaxed, Resilient, Results Oriented), Social Desirability.
Administration: Group.
Price Data: Available from publisher.
Time: (20-30) minutes.
Author: Saville & Holdsworth Ltd.
Publisher: SHL Group plc [United Kingdom].
Cross References: For reviews by Wayne J. Camara and Michael J. Roszkowski, see 12:337.

[2213]
Sales Potential Inventory.

Purpose: "Designed to help select top sales performers and determine the sales ability levels of current employees in any external or internal sales position."
Population: Job applicants and employees in sales positions.
Publication Dates: 2000–2001.
Acronym: S.P.I.
Scores, 2: S.P.I. score, Deception Scale score.
Administration: Group.
Price Data, 2005: $79.99 per starter kit including administrator's manual (2001, 28 pages), 5 tests, and 1 test log; $9.29 per 10 tests (volume discount available); $9.29 per 10 test logs for the online test version (volume discount available); $29.99 per administrator's manual.
Time: (15–20) minutes.
Comments: Online and paper-and-pencil versions of test are available; online version includes interpretive reports and follow-up interview questions.
Author: J. M. Llobet.
Publisher: G. Neil.

[2214]
Sales Professional Assessment Inventory.

Purpose: Designed "to assess the individual's interest, motivation and skills needed for success in the sales profession."

Population: Salespeople.
Publication Dates: 1989–1992.
Acronym: SPAI.
Scores, 15: Validity (Candidness, Accuracy), Sales Motivation (Sales/Work Experience, Sales Interest, Sales Responsibility, Sales Orientation, Energy Level, Self Development), Sales Readiness (Sales Skills, Sales Understanding, Sales Arithmetic, Customer Service), Dependability (Business Ethics, Job Stability), Overall Index (Sales Potential).
Administration: Group or individual.
Price Data: Price information for Quanta Touch Test administration and scoring and for Windows administration and scoring available from publisher.
Time: (45) minutes.
Author: London House.
Publisher: Pearson Performance Solutions [No reply from publisher; status unknown].

[2215]
Sales Relations Survey.

Purpose: Designed to assess the interpersonal practices and customer orientation of salespeople.
Population: Salespeople.
Publication Dates: 1972–1995.
Scores, 2: Exposure, Feedback.
Administration: Group.
Price Data, 2001: $8.95 per instrument.
Time: Administration time not reported.
Comments: Self-administered; self-scored.
Author: Jay Hall.
Publisher: Teleometrics International, Inc.

[2216]
The Sales Sentence Completion Blank.

Purpose: "Designed to aid in the selection of competent sales personnel."
Population: Applicants for sales positions.
Publication Dates: 1961-1982.
Acronym: SSCB.
Scores: Total score only.
Subtest: Total score only.
Administration: Group.
Price Data, 2006: $65.95 per test package; $19.50 per manual (1961, 25 pages); $28.05 per specimen set.
Time: (20-35) minutes.
Author: Norman Gekoski.
Publisher: Martin M. Bruce, Ph.D.
Cross References: For a review by William E. Kendall, and an excerpted review by John O. Crites, see 6:1181.

[2217]
Sales Skills Test.

Purpose: Designed "to evaluate the knowledge, skills, and abilities for a sales position."
Population: Adult sales position applicants.
Publication Dates: 2001–2002.

Scores, 6: Sales Principles, Sales Terms, Vocabulary, Sales Comprehension, Sales Situations, Math/Logic & Attention to Detail.
Administration: Individual.
Price Data: Available from publisher.
Time: (65) minutes.
Comments: Scoring available by mail, courier service, fax service, telephone, or "super-fast" fax service.
Author: Bruce Winrow.
Publisher: Walden Personnel Testing and Consulting, Inc. [Canada].
Cross References: For reviews by JoEllen V. Carlson and Paul M. Muchinsky, see 16:216.

[2218]
Sales Staff Selector.

Purpose: "Evaluates the suitability of candidates of all levels of experience for the position of Sales Representative."
Population: Candidates for sales representative positions.
Publication Date: 1984.
Scores: Total score, Narrative Evaluation, Ranking, Recommendation.
Administration: Group.
Price Data, 2001: $150 per candidate; quantity discounts available.
Foreign Language Edition: French edition available.
Time: (65) minutes.
Comments: Scored by publisher; available in booklet and internet versions.
Author: Walden Personnel Performance, Inc.
Publisher: Walden Personnel Performance, Inc. [Canada].
Cross References: For reviews by Philip G. Benson and Richard W. Johnson, see 10:319.

[2219]
Sales Style Indicator [Revised].

Purpose: Designed to help an individual identify their preferred selling style and "assist individuals and teams to increase their sales and customer service performance."
Population: Sales personnel, sales managers, and customer service representatives.
Publication Dates: 1991-2006.
Acronym: SSI.
Scores, 4: Behavioral/Action, Cognitive/Analysis, Interpersonal/Harmony, Affective/Expression.
Administration: Individual or group.
Price Data, 2006: $13.95 per test booklet (2006, 20 pages); $14.95 per In-Depth Interpretations Booklet (2006, 48 pages); $26.95 per code for online version, which includes assessment and in-depth interpretations; $159.95 per SSI Power Point CD and binder

(2006, 143 Slides); $23.95 per Why Don't You Sell That Way That I Buy? participant workbook (2006, 80 pages); $38 per Trainer's Guidelines (1996, 24 pages).
Foreign Language Editions: Available online in English, French, and German, and in print in English, French, and Spanish; the In-Depth interpretations booklet is available in English and French.
Time: 15 minutes to administer; 90-180 minutes for short program; up to 2 days for the full program.
Comments: Test can be self-administered, self-scored, and self-interpreted; full 1-2-day training program available using "Why Don't You Sell The Way That I Buy?" workbook and SSI Power Point as support.
Authors: Ken Keis, Terry D. Anderson, and Bruce Wares.
Publisher: Consulting Resource Group International, Inc.
Cross References: For reviews by Wayne J. Camara and Gerald A. Rosen of an earlier edition, see 13:271.

[2220]
Sales Transaction Audit.

Purpose: Intended as an assessment of sales style and its impact on salesperson-customer transactions.
Population: Salespeople.
Publication Dates: 1972–1980.
Acronym: STA.
Scores, 3: Parent, Adult, Child.
Administration: Group.
Manual: No manual.
Price Data, 2001: $8.95 per instrument.
Time: Administration time not reported.
Authors: Jay Hall and C. Leo Griffith.
Publisher: Teleometrics International, Inc.
Cross References: For a review by Chantale Jeanrie, see 14:331; for a review by Stephen L. Cohen of an earlier edition, see 8:1127.

[2221]
SalesMax System Internet Version.

Purpose: Designed as a pre-employment assessment for the selection of top performing sales people for professional, consultative sales positions.
Population: Potential employees for consultative sales positions.
Publication Date: 1998.
Scores, 25: Sales Personality (Energetic, Follows Through, Optimistic, Resilient, Assertive, Social, Expressive, Serious-Minded, Self-Reliant, Accommodating, Positive About People), Sales Knowledge (Prospecting/Pre-qualifying, First Meetings/First Impressions, Probing/Presenting, Overcoming Objections, Influencing/Convincing, Closing), Sales Motivations (Recognition/Attention, Control, Money, Freedom, Developing Expertise, Affiliation, Security/Stability, Achievement).

Administration: Group or individual.

Price Data, 2002: $995 per one-time purchase of the web-based system including units for 10 administrations; subsequent report costs vary from $74 to $98 depending on volume purchase.

Time: (90) minutes.

Comments: Administered via the web.

Author: Bigby, Havis & Associates, Inc.

Publisher: Bigby, Havis & Associates, Inc.

Cross References: For reviews by Gerald r. Schneck and Michael Spangler, see 15:213.

[2222]
Salford Sentence Reading Test (Revised).

Purpose: To assess level of oral reading achievement.

Population: Ages 6-0 to 10-6.

Publication Dates: 1976–2000.

Acronym: SSRT (R).

Scores: Reading Age.

Administration: Individual.

Forms, 2: X and Y.

Price Data, 2002: £8.99 per set of 2 test cards (X and Y); £8.99 per manual (2000, 16 pages); £6.99 per 20 record sheets; £17.99 per specimen set including one each of test cards X and Y, record sheet, and manual.

Time: [2–3] minutes.

Authors: G. E. Bookbinder; revision by Denis Vincent and Mary Crumpler.

Publisher: Hodder & Stoughton Educational [England].

Cross References: See T4:2320 (1 reference); for a review by J. Douglas Ayers of an earlier edition, see 8:791.

[2223]
SAQ-Adult Probation III.

Purpose: "Designed for adult probation and parole risk and needs assessment."

Population: Adult probationers and parolees.

Publication Dates: 1985–1997.

Acronym: SAQ.

Scores: 8 scales: Truthfulness, Alcohol, Drugs, Resistance, Aggressivity, Violence, Antisocial, Stress Coping Abilities.

Administration: Group.

Price Data: Available from publisher.

Time: (30) minutes.

Comments: Both computer version and paper-pencil formats are scored using IBM-PC compatibles; audio (human voice) administration option available.

Author: Risk & Needs Assessment, Inc.

Publisher: Risk & Needs Assessment, Inc.

Cross References: For reviews by John R. Hays and by Robert Spies and Mark Cooper, see 14:332; for a review by Tony Toneatto of an earlier edition, see 12:338.

[2224]
SAQS Chicago Q Sort.

Purpose: Developed to "describe people to be sorted out in terms of continuum of applicability about self or others" to obtain a measure of similarity.

Population: College and adults.

Publication Dates: 1956–1957.

Acronym: SAQS.

Scores: Total score only.

Administration: Group.

Price Data: Available from publisher.

Time: (10–15) minutes.

Author: Raymond Corsini.

Publisher: Psychometric Affiliates.

Cross References: See T2:1358 (5 references) and P:232 (2 references); for reviews by William Stephenson and Clifford H. Swenson, Jr., see 5:103 (2 references).

[2225]
SASB [Structural Analysis of Social Behavior] Intrex Questionnaires.

Purpose: Designed to measure the patient's perceptions of self and others, based on trait x state x situational philosophy and Structural Analysis of Social Behavior.

Population: Psychiatric patients and normals.

Publication Dates: 1980–2000.

Acronym: SASB Intrex.

Scores: Pattern Coefficient Scores, cluster profiles, and weighted affiliation and autonomy scores for each of 3 areas: Interpersonal Transitive-Focus on Other, Interpersonal Intransitive-Focus on Self, Intrapsychic Introjection; 3 forms (short, medium, long), 6 subtests: Self (Best, Worst), He/I Present Tense (Best, Worst), She/I Present Tense (Best, Worst), Mother/I Past Tense, Father/I Past Tense, Mother with Father/Father with Mother Past Tense.

Administration: Individual or group.

Price Data, 2000: $120 (research use) or $160 (clinical use) per questionnaire and coding software package including all 3 forms of Intrex questionnaire (short, medium, long), electronic forms, questionnaire user's manual (2000, 56 pages), SASBWorks coding programs (Process, Content, Complex, Markov), and coding reference manual (2000, 59 pages); $80 (research use) or $120 (clinical use) per all 3 forms of Intrex questionnaire with electronic forms and questionnaire user's manual; $80 per all 4 SASBWorks coding programs with coding reference manual; $.20 (research use, $10 minimum) or $2 (clinical use, $20 minimum) royalty fee per administration; $25 per questionnaire user's manual; $15 per coding reference manual; miscellaneous specialized SASB coding programs also available (contact intrex@psych.utah.edu for details).

Time: (60) minutes for complete battery, short form.

Comments: PC systems with DOS or Windows 95/98/2000 and Microsoft Access2000, Excel (1997 version or later), and Word necessary to process SASBWorks coding programs. Information and updates available online at: http://www.psych.utah.edu/benjamin/sasb/
Author: Lorna Smith Benjamin.
Publisher: University of Utah, Department of Psychology.
Cross References: For reviews by Dennis Doverspike and Thomas P. Hogan, see 15:214; see T5:1298 (1 reference); for a review by Scott T. Meier of an earlier edition, see 12:192; see also T4:1258 (2 references).

[2226]
SAT On-Campus Program (Institutional SAT Reasoning Test and SAT Subject Tests).

Purpose: To place students at the appropriate level of study in college, and/or to help determine admission status.
Population: Entering college freshmen.
Publication Dates: 1962–2005.
Scores: SAT Reasoning Test provides a Verbal, Mathematics, and Writing score on the College Board 200 to 800 scale. SAT Subject Tests provide total test scores on the College Board's 200 to 800 score scale, except for the English Language Proficiency Test that is on a score scale from 901 to 999. Some SAT Subject Tests also provide subscores.
Tests: SAT Reasoning Test and SAT Subject Tests. Subject Tests include: English Language Proficiency; Literature; Writing; Mathematics Levels I and Mathematics 2; Biology E/M (Ecological/Molecular); Chemistry, Physics; Reading Language Tests in French, German, Modern Hebrew, Italian, Latin, and Spanish; and Reading and Listening Language Tests in Chinese, French, German, Japanese, Korean, and Spanish.
Administration: Group or individual.
Price Data: Available from publisher.
Comments: Available for local administration and scoring by higher educational institutions. The Institutional SAT tests are offered through the College Board's SAT On-Campus Testing Program. Institutional SAT Reasoning test answer sheets are scored locally with MicroScore software; Institutional SAT Subject test answer sheets are scored using clear scoring templates. The Institutional SAT Subject Tests were previously known as the College Placement Tests and the One-Hour Achievement Tests. The Institutional SAT Reasoning Test was previously known as the Scholastic Aptitude Test and SAT.
Author: Educational Testing Service.
Publisher: The College Board.

Cross References: See T5:1274 (2 references) and T3:507 (2 references); for a review by John R. Hills of the College Placement Tests, see 7:665.

[2227]
Scale for Assessing Emotional Disturbance.

Purpose: Designed to assist in "the identification of children who qualify for the federal special education category of emotional disturbance."
Population: Students ages 5-0 to 18-11.
Publication Date: 1998.
Acronym: SAED.
Scores, 7: Inability to Learn, Relationship Problems, Inappropriate Behavior, Unhappiness or Depression, Physical Symptoms or Fears, Socially Maladjusted, Overall Competence.
Administration: Individual.
Price Data, 2006: $100 per complete kit; $55 per manual (66 pages); $50 per 50 S/R forms.
Time: (10) minutes.
Comments: Should be "completed … by teachers or other school personnel who have had substantial contact with the student."
Authors: Michael H. Epstein and Douglas Cullinan.
Publisher: PRO-ED.
Cross References: For reviews by Sandra J. Carr and Gretchen Owens, see 14:333.

[2228]
Scale for the Assessment of Negative Symptoms.

Purpose: To assess negative symptoms of schizophrenia.
Population: Psychiatric inpatients and outpatients of all ages.
Publication Dates: 1981-1984.
Acronym: SANS.
Scores: 25 behavioral rating scores within 5 areas: Affective Flattening or Blunting, Alogia, Avolition-Apathy, Anhedonia-Asociality, Attention.
Administration: Individual.
Price Data: Available from publisher.
Foreign Language Editions: Available in Spanish, French, Italian, German, Portuguese, Japanese, Chinese, and Greek.
Time: [15-30] minutes.
Comments: May be used in conjunction with the Scale for the Assessment of Positive Symptoms (SAPS; 2229).
Author: Nancy C. Andreasen.
Publisher: Nancy C. Andreasen.
Cross References: See T5:2288 (85 references); for reviews by Suzanne King and Niels G. Waller, see 12:339 (75 references); see also T4:2325 (37 references); for information on an earlier edition, see 9:1069 (2 references).

[2229]
Scale for the Assessment of Positive Symptoms.

Purpose: "Designed to assess positive symptoms, principally those that occur in schizophrenia."
Population: Psychiatric inpatients and outpatients of all ages.
Publication Date: 1984.
Acronym: SAPS.
Scores: 35 behavior ratings within 5 areas: Hallucinations, Delusions, Bizarre Behavior, Positive Formal Thought Disorder, Inappropriate Affect.
Administration: Individual.
Price Data: Available from publisher.
Time: [15-30] minutes.
Comments: Intended to serve as a complementary instrument to the Scale for the Assessment of Negative Symptoms (SANS; 2228).
Author: Nancy C. Andreasen.
Publisher: Nancy C. Andreasen.
Cross References: See T5:2289 (69 references); for reviews by John D. King and Suzanne King, see 12:340 (44 references); see also T4:2326 (24 references).

[2230]
Scale for the Assessment of Thought, Language, and Communication.

Purpose: Designed to assess clinical and pathological characteristics of language behavior.
Population: Manics, depressives, and schizophrenics.
Publication Date: 1980.
Acronym: TLC.
Scores: 19 ratings: Poverty of Speech, Poverty of Content of Speech, Pressure of Speech, Distractible Speech, Tangentiality, Derailment, Incoherence, Illogicality, Clanging, Neologisms, Word Approximations, Circumstantiality, Loss of Goal, Perseveration, Echolalia, Blocking, Stilted Speech, Self-Reference, Global Rating.
Administration: Individual.
Price Data: Price data for materials including manual (19 pages) available from publisher.
Time: [45-60] minutes.
Author: Nancy C. Andreasen.
Publisher: Nancy C. Andreasen.
Cross References: See T5:2290 (2 references) and T4:2327 (4 references).

[2231]
Scale of Feelings and Behavior of Love: Revised.

Purpose: Designed to "identify the patterns of behavior and feelings people exhibit and experience in their love relationships."
Population: College and adults.

Publication Dates: 1973-1992.
Scores, 8: Verbal Expression of Affection, Self-Disclosure, Toleration of Loved Ones' Bothersome Aspects, Moral Support/Encouragement and Interest, Feelings Not Expressed, Material Evidence of Affection, Total Love Scale, Love Scale Index.
Administration: Group.
Price Data: Available from publisher.
Time: (30) minutes.
Comments: Separate answer sheets may be used; current edition now included in Innovations in Clinical Practice: A Source Book (Vol. II).
Authors: Clifford H. Swensen, Michele Killough Nelson, Jan Warner, and David Dunlap.
Publisher: Clifford H. Swensen.
Cross References: See T4:2328 (1 reference); for a review by H. Thompson Prout of an earlier edition, see 9:1072.

[2232]
Scale of Job-Related Social Skill Performance.

Purpose: Designed to assess the strengths and weaknesses of a student's social skill performance in various work settings.
Publication Date: [Undated].
Administration: Individual.
Price Data: Price data available from publisher for complete kit including teaching guide and script, response form, and interpretation/scoring guide.
Authors: Michael Bullis, Vicki Nishioka-Evans, H. D. Bud Fredericks, and Cheryl D. Davis.
Publisher: James Stanfield Co., Inc.
a) SCALE OF JOB-RELATED SOCIAL SKILLS KNOWLEDGE.
Population: Ages 15–25.
Acronym: SSSK.
Scores: Total score only.
Time: (45) minutes.
Comments: Administered using a verbal role playing method.
b) SCALE OF JOB-RELATED SOCIAL SKILL PERFORMANCE.
Population: Ages 14–21.
Acronym: SSSP.
Scores: 6 scales: Positive Social Behaviors, Self Control, Personal Issues, Body Movements, Personal Appearance, Negative Social Behaviors.
Time: Administration time not reported.

[2233]
Scale of Marriage Problems: Revised.

Purpose: Designed to measure marital conflicts.
Population: Couples.
Publication Dates: 1975–1992.
Scores, 7: Problem-Solving, Childrearing, Relatives, Personal Care, Money, Outside Relationships, Total.

Administration: Group.
Price Data: Available from publisher.
Time: Administration time not reported.
Comments: Current edition now included in Innovations in Clinical Practice: A Source Book (Vol. II).
Authors: Clifford H. Swensen, Michele Killough Nelson, Jan Warner, and David Dunlap.
Publisher: Clifford H. Swensen.
Cross References: For reviews by Cindy Carlson and Delores D. Walcott, see 14:334.

[2234]
Scaled Curriculum Achievement Levels Test.

Purpose: Assesses individual and group achievement in mathematics computation, reading, and language usage.
Population: Grades 3–8.
Publication Date: 1992.
Acronym: SCALE.
Administration: Group.
Levels: 9 levels in each of 3 subtests: Mathematics Computation (M1-M9), Reading (R1-R9), Language Usage (L1-L9).
Price Data, 2006: $109.50 per complete kit including 6 reusable administration booklets (2 each for Mathematics Computation, Reading, and Language Usage), 10 class placement/record sheets, 30 answer forms (10 each for Mathematics Computation, Reading, and Language Usage), and manual (135 pages); $16.50 per 100 class placement/record sheets; $52 per manual.
Authors: Victor W. Doherty and Gale H. Roid.
Publisher: Western Psychological Services.
a) MATHEMATICS COMPUTATION.
Scores: Total score only.
Price Data: $28.50 per 10 reusable administration booklets; $17.50 per 10 AutoScore™ answer forms.
Time: (20–25) minutes.
b) READING.
Scores: Same as *a* above.
Price Data: $41 per 10 reusable administration booklets; $17.50 per 10 AutoScore™ answer forms.
Time: Same as *a* above.
c) LANGUAGE USAGE.
Scores: Sames as *a* above.
Price Data: $36 per 10 reusable administration booklets; $17.50 per 10 AutoScore™ answer forms.
Time: (15–20) minutes.
Cross References: For reviews by Russell N. Carney and Robert K. Gable, see 12:341.

[2235]
Scales for Diagnosing Attention-Deficit/ Hyperactivity Disorder.

Purpose: "To help identify children and adolescents who have attention-deficit/hyperactivity disorder (ADHD)."

Population: Ages 5-0 through 18-11.
Publication Date: 2002.
Acronym: SCALES.
Scores, 4: Inattention, Hyperactivity, Impulsivity, Total.
Administration: Individual.
Forms, 2: Summary/School Rating Scale Form (SRS), Home Rating Scale Form (HRS).
Price Data, 2006: $95 per complete kit including examiner's manual (78 pages), 25 summary/school rating forms, and 25 home rating forms; $51 per examiner's manual; $30 per 25 summary/school rating forms; $20 per 25 home rating forms.
Time: 15–20 minutes.
Comments: Completed by parents and teachers of target child; designed as part of a comprehensive ADHD assessment; identifies specific behavioral targets for intervention; allows for ratings on DSM-IV-TR criterion for ADHD.
Authors: Gail Ryser and Kathleen McConnell.
Publisher: PRO-ED.
Cross References: For a review by Joseph G. Law, Jr., see 15:215.

[2236]
Scales for Identifying Gifted Students.

Purpose: "Designed to assist school districts in the identification of students as gifted."
Population: Ages 5-18 years.
Publication Date: 2004.
Acronym: SIGS.
Scores: 7 areas: General Intellectual Ability, Language Arts, Mathematics, Science, Social Studies, Creativity, Leadership.
Administration: Individual.
Forms, 2: Home Rating Scale, School Rating Scale.
Price Data, 2006: $150 per complete kit including manual (57 pages), 25 Home Rating Scale forms, 25 School Rating forms, and 25 Summary forms; $65 per manual; $35 per 25 Home Rating Scale forms; $35 per 25 School Rating Scale forms; $20 per 25 Summary forms.
Foreign Language Edition: Available in a Spanish-speaking version.
Time: (10-15) minutes.
Comments: This test "is designed to be completed by a teacher, counselor, or other professional who has an opportunity to observe the student for an extended period of time."
Authors: Gail R. Ryser and Kathleen McConnell.
Publisher: Prufrock Press Inc.

[2237]
Scales for Rating the Behavioral Characteristics of Superior Students.

Purpose: Designed to aid teachers in the identification of gifted children.

Population: Population unspecified, developed from research with students in Grades 4–6.
Publication Date: 1976.
Acronym: SRBCSS.
Scores, 10: Learning, Motivational, Creativity, Leadership, Artistic, Musical, Dramatics, Communication (Precision, Expressiveness), Planning.
Administration: Group.
Price Data: Available from publisher.
Time: Administration time not reported.
Comments: Scales for rating by teachers.
Authors: Joseph S. Renzulli, Linda H. Smith, Alan J. White, Carolyn M. Callahan, and Robert K. Hartman.
Publisher: Creative Learning Press, Inc.
Cross References: See T5:2295 (9 references); for reviews by Edward N. Argulewicz and James O. Rust, see 9:1073 (1 reference).

[2238]
Scales of Cognitive Ability for Traumatic Brain Injury.

Purpose: To "provide a systematic method of assessing cognitive deficits associated with traumatic brain injury."
Population: Patients with acquired brain damage.
Publication Date: 1992.
Acronym: SCATBI.
Scores, 46: Perception and Discrimination (Sound Recognition, Shape Recognition, Word Recognition [no distraction], Word Recognition [with distraction], Color Discrimination, Shape Discrimination, Size Discrimination, Discrimination of Color/Shape/Size, Discrimination of Pictured Objects, Auditory Discrimination [real words], Auditory Discrimination [nonsense], Total); Orientation (Premorbid Questions, Postmorbid Questions, Total); Organization (Identifying Pictured Categories, Identifying Pictured Category Members, Word Associations, Sequencing Objects [size], Sequencing Words [alphabetical], Sequencing Events [time of year], Sequencing Events [pictured task steps], Sequencing Events [recall task steps], Total); Recall (Memory for Graphic Elements, Naming Pictures, Immediate Recall of Word Strings, Delayed Recall of Word Strings, Cued Recall of Words, Cued Recall of Words in Discourse, Word Generation, Immediate Recall of Oral Directions, Recall of Oral Paragraphs, Total); Reasoning (Figural Reasoning: Matrix Analogies, Convergent Thinking: Central Theme, Deductive Reasoning: Elimination, Inductive Reasoning: Opposites, Inductive Reasoning: Analogies, Divergent Thinking: Homographs, Divergent Thinking: Idioms, Divergent Thinking: Proverbs, Divergent Thinking: Verbal Absurdities, Multiprocess Reasoning: Task Insight, Multiprocess Reasoning: Analysis, Total).
Administration: Individual.
Price Data, 2006: $277 per complete kit; $56 per 25 record forms; $57 per stimulus card set; $71 per stimulus manual; $71 per examiner's manual; $30 per audiocassette.
Time: Administration time not reported.
Authors: Brenda Adamovich and Jennifer Henderson.
Publisher: PRO-ED.
Cross References: For reviews by Charles J. Long and Faith Gunning and by Deborah D. Roman, see 13:273.

[2239]
Scales of Early Communication Skills for Hearing-Impaired Children.

Purpose: "Designed to evaluate speech and language development of hearing-impaired children between the ages of two and eight years."
Population: Ages 2-0 to 8-11.
Publication Date: 1975.
Acronym: SECS.
Scores, 4: Receptive Language Skills, Expressive Language Skills, Nonverbal Receptive Skills, Nonverbal Expressive Skills.
Administration: Individual.
Price Data, 2002: $14.95 per manual (42 pages); $12 per 25 rating forms.
Time: [60] minutes (through observation).
Comments: Ratings by teachers.
Authors: Jean S. Moog and Ann E. Geers.
Publisher: Central Institute for the Deaf.
Cross References: See T5:2298 (3 references); for reviews by Vincent J. Samar and Marc Marschark and by E. W. Testut, see 12:342.

[2240]
Scales of Independent Behavior—Revised.

Purpose: "Designed to measure functional independence and adaptive functioning in school, home, employment, and community settings."
Population: Infants to adults, with or without developmental disabilities.
Publication Dates: 1984–1996.
Acronym: SIB-R.
Scores, 24: Full Scale (Gross-Motor Skills, Fine Motor Skills, Social Interaction, Language Comprehension, Language Expression, Eating and Meal Preparation, Toileting, Dressing, Personal Self-Care, Domestic Skills, Time and Punctuality, Money and Value, Work Skills, Home/Community Orientation), Maladaptive Behavior Scale [optional] (Hurtful to Self, Unusual or Repetitive Habits, Withdrawal or Inattentive Behavior, Socially Offensive Behavior, Uncooperative Behavior, Hurtful to Others, Destructive to Property, Disruptive Behavior).
Administration: Individual.
Forms, 3: Full Scale, Short Form, Early Development.
Price Data, 2006: $240.50 per complete kit including interview book, comprehensive manual (1996, 306

pages), 15 full scale response booklets with IPRs, 5 short form response booklets with IPRs, and 5 early development form response booklets with IPRs; $86 per comprehensive manual; $61 per 25 full scale response booklets with IPRs; $38.50 per 25 short form response booklets with IPRs; $38.50 per 25 early development form response booklets with IPRs; $52.50 per 25 short form for the visually impaired response booklets.

Time: (45–60) minutes for Full Scale; (15–20) minutes for Short Form; (15–20) minutes for Early Development.

Comments: SIB-R in conjunction with the Wood-cock-Johnson® Psychoeducational Battery—Revised can be used as a comprehensive diagnostic system for measuring adaptive behavior, problem behavior, cognitive ability, language proficiency, and achievement; can be administered either via interview or checklist; short and early development forms available as part of test kit; computerized scoring system available in Windows or Macintosh; visually impaired short form also available.

Authors: Robert H. Bruininks, Richard W. Woodcock, Richard F. Weatherman, and Bradley K. Hill.

Publisher: Riverside Publishing.

Cross References: For reviews by Gloria Maccow and Leland C. Zlomke, see 14:337; see also T5:2299 (7 references) and T4:2335 (6 references); for reviews by Bonnie W. Camp and Louis J. Heifetz of the earlier version, see 10:321.

[2241]
SCAN-A: A Test for Auditory Processing Disorders in Adolescents and Adults.

Purpose: Used to identify adolescents and adults who have auditory processing disorders and who may benefit from intervention.

Population: Ages 12 to 50.

Publication Dates: 1986–1994.

Acronym: SCAN-A.

Scores, 6: Filtered Words, Auditory Figure-Ground, Competing Words, Competing Sentences, Total Test, Competing Words Ear Advantage.

Administration: Individual.

Price Data, 2002: $129 per audiocassette complete kit including examiner's manual (1994, 69 pages), test audiocassette, and 12 record forms; $19 per 12 record forms; $60 per examiner's manual; $80 per test audiocassette; $129 per CD-ROM complete kit including examiner's manual, Test CD-ROM, and 12 record forms; $80 per Test CD-ROM; $160 per Scanware™-A 5.0.

Time: (20–25) minutes.

Comments: SCAN-A requires an audiocassette player, two sets of stereo headphones, and a "Y" adapter.

Author: Robert W. Keith.

Publisher: PsychCorp, A brand of Harcourt Assessment, Inc.

Cross References: For reviews by William R. Merz, Sr., and Jaclyn B. Spitzer, see 13:275.

[2242]
SCAN-C: Test for Auditory Processing Disorders in Children—Revised.

Purpose: Designed to identify children who have auditory processing disorders.

Population: Ages 5-0 to 11-11.

Publication Dates: 1986–1999.

Acronym: SCAN-C.

Scores, 5: Filtered Words, Auditory Figure-Ground, Competing Words, Competing Sentences, Composite.

Administration: Individual.

Price Data, 2002: $149 per kit including 25 record forms, compact disc in a vinyl album, and examiner's manual (2000, 129 pages); $34 per 25 record forms; $58 per examiner's manual.

Time: (30) minutes.

Comments: Formerly called SCAN: A Screening Test for Auditory Processing Disorders.

Author: Robert W. Keith.

Publisher: PsychCorp, A brand of Harcourt Assessment, Inc.

Cross References: For reviews by Annabel J. Cohen and by Jaclyn B. Spitzer and Abbey L. Berg, see 16:217; see also T5:2300 (1 reference); for a review by Sami Gulgoz of an earlier edition, see 11:341 (2 references).

[2243]
The Scenotest: A Practical Technique for Understanding Unconscious Problems and Personality Structure.

Purpose: A projective instrument intended "to help very quickly assess emotional problems in children."

Population: Children and adolescents.

Publication Dates: 1971–1998.

Scores: Score information available from publisher.

Administration: Individual.

Price Data, 2006: $980 per complete test kit and manual (1998, 110 pages).

Time: Administration time not reported.

Comments: Material in the test kit consists of flexible human figures and accessories including animals, trees, symbolic figures, and items from everyday life.

Authors: G. von Staabs (original edition) and Joseph A. Smith (translated from the German edition and adapted).

Publisher: Hogrefe & Huber Publishers.

Cross References: For reviews by Joseph C. Kush and Paul Retzlaff, see 15:216.

[2244]
Schaie-Thurstone Adult Mental Abilities Test.

Purpose: Designed to "measure the mental abilities of adults."

Population: Ages 22-84.

Publication Dates: 1985-1998.

Acronym: STAMAT.

Scores: 7 scale scores: Recognition Vocabulary (V), Figure Rotation (FR), Object Rotation (OR, Form OA only), Letter Series (LS), Word Series (WS, Form OA only), Number Addition (N), Word Fluency (W).

Administration: Group.

Forms, 2: Form A (for "Adult," essentially the Thurstone Primary Mental Abilities Test Form II-17 (PMA) with new adult norms), Form OA (for "Older Adult," large-type version of the original plus two additional scales for adults over age 55).

Price Data: Price information available from publisher for Form OA expendable test booklets, Form A booklets, Form A answer sheets, Form A scoring key, profiles for both OA and A, manual (86 pages), and specimen set.

Time: (50–60) minutes.

Comments: Norms updated in 1998.

Author: K. Warner Schaie.

Publisher: K. Warner Schaie (the author).

Cross References: See T5:2304 (4 references) and T4:2339)3 references); for a review by Eric F. Gardner, see 10:322.

[2245]

Schedule for Affective Disorders and Schizophrenia, Third Edition.

Purpose: "To record information regarding a subject's functioning and psychopathology."

Population: Adults.

Publication Dates: 1977-1988.

Acronym: SADS.

Administration: Individual.

Price Data, 2001: $.50 per SADS/SADS-L suggested procedures; $2.50 per SADS/SADS-L instructions and clarifications (1985, 24 pages).

Time: [30–120] minutes.

Authors: Robert L. Spitzer, Jean Endicott, Jo Ellen Loth (SADS-LB, SADS-LI), Patricia McDonald-Scott (SADS-LI), and Patricia Wasek (SADS-LI).

Publisher: Department of Research Assessment and Training.

a) SCHEDULE FOR AFFECTIVE DISORDERS AND SCHIZOPHRENIA.

Scores, 24: Current Syndromes (Depressive Mood/Ideation, Endogenous Features, Depressive-Associated Features, Suicidal Ideation/Behavior, Anxiety, Manic Syndrome, Delusions-Hallucinations, Formal Thought Disorder, Impaired Functioning, Alcohol or Drug Abuse, Behavioral Disorganization, Miscellaneous Psychopathology, GAS [worst period], Extracted Hamilton); Past Week Functioning (Depressive Syndrome, Endogenous Features, Manic Syndrome, Anxiety, Delusions-Hall-Disorganization, GAS rating, Extracted Hamilton, Miscellaneous Psychopathology); Past Other than Diagnosis (Social Functioning, Suicidal Behavior).

Price Data: $3 per SADS booklet; $.50 per SADS score sheet; $1.50 per SADS summary scales scores; $.50 per editing and coding instructions; $2.50 per instructions/clarifications.

b) SCHEDULE FOR AFFECTIVE DISORDERS AND SCHIZOPHRENIA LIFETIME (VARIOUS VERSIONS).

1) *SADS-L.*

Purpose: To record information regarding a subject's functioning and psychopathology; includes current disturbance.

Price Data: $2 per SADS-L booklet; $.50 per SADS-L score sheet.

2) *SADS-LB.*

Purpose: To record information regarding a subject's functioning and psychopathology; includes current disturbance and additional items related to bipolar affective disorder.

Price Data: $2 per SADS-LB booklet; $.50 per SADS-LB score sheet.

3) *SADS-LI.*

Purpose: To record information regarding a subject's functioning and psychopathology; specifies follow-up interval.

Price Data: $2 per SADS-LI booklet; $.50 per SADS-LI score sheet.

Cross References: See T5:2305 (248 references); for reviews by Paul A. Arbisi and James C. Carmer, see 12:343 (414 references); see also T4:2340 (152 references).

[2246]

Schedule for Nonadaptive and Adaptive Personality.

Purpose: "Designed to assess trait dimensions in the domain of personality disorders."

Population: Ages 18 and older

Publication Date: 1993.

Acronym: SNAP.

Scores: 34 scales: Trait (Mistrust, Manipulativeness, Aggression, Self-harm, Eccentric Perceptions, Dependency, Exhibitionism, Entitlement, Detachment, Impulsivity, Propriety, Workaholism), Temperament (Negative Temperament, Positive Temperament, Disinhibition), Diagnostic (Paranoid, Schizoid, Schizotypal, Antisocial, Borderline, Histrionic, Narcissistic, Avoidant, Dependent, Obsessive-Compulsive, Passive-Aggressive, Sadistic, Self-Defeating), Validity (Variable Response Inconsistency, True Response Inconsistency, Desirable Response Inconsistency, Deviance, Rare Virtues, Invalidity Index).

Administration: Individual or group.

Price Data, 2006: $55 per starter kit including 10 test booklets, 100 answer sheets, set of scoring keys, 25 profile forms, and manual for administration, scoring, and interpretation (92 pages); $10 per 10 test booklets;

$15 per 100 answer sheets; $35 per set of 34 scoring keys; $5 per 25 profile forms (specify diagnostic scales or validity trait, and temperament scales); $15 per manual for administration, scoring, and interpretation; price data for scoring disks available from publisher.
Time: 45 minutes.
Author: Lee Anna Clark.
Publisher: University of Minnesota Press.
Cross References: For reviews by Lizanne DeStefano and Niels G. Waller, see 14:338; see also T5:2306 (1 reference) and T4:2341 (1 reference).

[2247]
A Schedule of Adaptive Mechanisms in CAT Response.

Purpose: "Designed to aid in qualitative evaluation of C.A.T. stories."
Population: Children.
Publication Date: [ca. 1963].
Scores: 12 categories: Defense Mechanisms (Reaction-Formation, Undoing and Ambivalence, Isolation, Repression and Denial, Deception, Symbolization, Projection and Introjection, Fear and Anxiety, Regression, Controls Weak or Absent), Identification (Adequate/Same-Sex, Confused/or Opposite Sex).
Administration: Individual.
Manual: No manual.
Price Data, 2001: $9 per 30 forms.
Time: Administration time not reported.
Comments: See Children's Apperception Test (465).
Author: Mary Haworth.
Publisher: C.P.S., Inc.

[2248]
The Schedule of Growing Skills: Second Edition.

Purpose: Designed as an assessment of child development.
Population: Ages 0–5 years.
Publication Dates: 1987–1996.
Acronym: SGS II.
Scores, 9: Passive Postural, Active Postural, Locomotor, Manipulative, Visual, Hearing and Language, Speech and Language, Interactive Social, Self-Care Social.
Administration: Individual.
Price Data, 1998: £120 per starter set including 10 child records, 50 profiles, user's guide (1996, 109 pages), and all stimulus materials; £40 per conversion kit including user's guide, picture book, shape formboard, fish formboard, pegboard and pegs, STYCAR distant vision card B and key card, pom pom, and baby rattle; £65 per 10 record forms; £40 per 50 profiles; £30 per reference manual.
Time: (20) minutes.
Authors: Martin Bellman, Sundara Lingam, and Anne Aukett.

Publisher: NFER-Nelson Publishing Co., Ltd. [England].
Cross References: For reviews by Carol M. McGregor and Leah M. Nellis, see 15:217; see T5:2308 (1 reference); for reviews by Michelle M. Creighton and Scott R. McConnell and by Donna Spiker of an earlier edition, see 11:342.

[2249]
Schedules for Clinical Assessment in Neuropsychiatry, Version 2.0.

Purpose: "Aimed at assessing, measuring and classifying the psychopathology and behavior associated with the major psychiatric syndromes of adult life."
Population: Adults.
Publication Dates: 1982-1995.
Acronym: SCAN.
Scores: Item scores only.
Administration: Individual.
Parts, 3: Present State Examination, Item Group Checklist, Clinical History Schedule.
Price Data, 2006: $34.95 per manual; $32.50 per Glossary; $28.50 per recording booklets.
Foreign Language Editions: Contact publisher for information regarding availability of foreign language editions.
Time: Administration time not reported.
Comments: Computer administration and scoring available for DOS and Windows.
Author: World Health Organization.
Publisher: American Psychiatric Publishing, Inc.
 a) PRESENT STATE EXAMINATION.
 Acronym: PSE10.
 Subtests, 2: Part One, Part Two.
 Comments: Part One covers somatoform, dissociative, anxiety, depressive, and bipolar disorders and problems associated with basic bodily functions and use of alcohol and other substance use. Part Two covers psychotic and cognitive disorders and observed abnormalities of speech, affect, and behavior.
 b) ITEM GROUP CHECKLIST.
 Acronym: IGC.
 Comments: 40 Item Groups cover disorders in subchapters F2 (psychotic disorders), F3 (affective disorders), and F40-42 (neurotic disorders) of ICD10.
 c) CLINICAL HISTORY SCHEDULE.
 Acronym: CHS.
 Comments: Includes broader clinical and social history data.

[2250]
Scholastic Abilities Test for Adults.

Purpose: "Designed to be a general measure of scholastic accomplishment."

Population: Ages 16 through 70.
Publication Date: 1991.
Acronym: SATA.
Scores: 9 subtest scores: Verbal Reasoning, Nonverbal Reasoning, Quantitative Reasoning, Reading Vocabulary, Reading Comprehension, Math Calculation, Math Application, Writing Mechanics, Writing Composition, and 9 composite scores: Scholastic Abilities, General Aptitude, Total Achievement, Verbal, Quantitative, Reading, Mathematics, Writing, Achievement Screener.
Administration: Group.
Price Data, 2006: $164 per complete kit including 10 test books, 25 response booklets, 25 profile/examiner record forms, and examiner's manual (102 pages); $53 per 10 test books; $40 per 25 response booklets; $25 per 25 profile/examiner record forms; $51 per examiner's manual.
Time: (60-120) minutes.
Authors: Brian R. Bryant, James R. Patton, and Caroline Dunn.
Publisher: PRO-ED.
Cross References: See T5:2309 (2 references); for reviews by Nambury S. Raju and Douglas K. Smith, see 12:344.

[2251]
School-Age Care Environment Rating Scale.
Purpose: Designed to assess the quality of center-based child care for school-aged children.
Population: Child care programs.
Publication Dates: 1980–1996.
Acronym: SACERS.
Scores, 7: Space and Furnishings, Health and Safety, Activities, Interactions, Program Structure, Staff Development, Total.
Administration: Group.
Price Data, 2006: $15.95 per rating scale (1996, 44 pages); $8.95 per 30 scoring sheets.
Time: (120) minutes.
Comments: An adaptation of the Early Childhood Environment Rating Scale (880); for use with center-based care (not family child care homes); respondents cue evaluators of the child-care environment; "Also includes a set of 6 supplementary items for centers that include children with special needs."
Authors: Thelma Harms, Ellen Vineberg Jacobs, and Donna Romano White.
Publisher: Teachers College Press.
Cross References: For reviews by Patricia B. Keith and Hillary Michaels, see 14:339.

[2252]
School Archival Records Search.
Purpose: "Designed to overlay existing school records so that they can be coded and quantified systematically."
Population: Grades 1–12.

Publication Date: 1991.
Acronym: SARS.
Scores: 11 archival variables: Demographics, Attendance, Achievement Test Information, School Failure, Disciplinary Contacts, Within-School Referrals, Certification for Special Education, Placement Out of Regular Classroom, Receiving Chapter I Services, Out-of-School Referrals, Negative Narrative Comments.
Administration: Group.
Price Data, 2002: $35 per complete kit including user's guide, technical manual (86 pages), and 50 instrument packets.
Time: Administration time varies.
Authors: Hill M. Walker, Alice Block-Pedego, Bonnie Todis, and Herbert H. Severson.
Publisher: Sopris West.
Cross References: For reviews by John Crawford and Robert Fitzpatrick, see 13:275 (1 reference).

[2253]
School Assessment Survey.
Purpose: "Designed to measure schoolwide characteristics."
Population: Elementary through senior high school teachers and administrators.
Publication Date: 1985.
Acronym: SAS.
Scores, 9: Goal Consensus, Facilitative Leadership, Centralization of Influence: Classroom Instruction, Centralization of Influence: Curriculum and Resources, Vertical Communication, Horizontal Communication, Staff Conflict, Student Discipline, Teaching Behavior.
Administration: Group.
Price Data, 2001: $9.99 per kit including manual (69 pages).
Time: [30-40] minutes.
Authors: Bruce L. Wilson and William A. Firestone.
Publisher: Research for Better Schools, Inc.
Cross References: See T5:2312 (1 reference); for reviews by LeAnn M. Gamache and by Dean Nafziger and Joanne L. Jensen, see 12:345 (1 reference); see also T4:2355 (1 reference).

[2254]
School Effectiveness Questionnaire.
Purpose: Assesses variables that have an impact on school effectiveness.
Population: Students, teachers, parents.
Publication Date: 1993.
Acronym: SEQ.
Scores, 11: Effective Instructional Leadership, Clear and Focused Mission, Safe and Orderly Environment, Positive School Climate, High Expectations, Frequent Assessment/Monitoring of Student Achievement, Emphasis on Basic Skills, Maximum Opportunities for Learning, Parent/Community Involvement, Strong Pro-

fessional Development, Teacher Involvement in Decision Making.
Administration: Group.
Forms, 4: Level 1 Students (Elementary), Level 2 Students (High School), Teachers, Parents.
Price Data, 2002: $13 per 10 reusable questionnaires (Teacher Form); $33 per 10 reusable questionnaires (Level 1, Level 2, Parent Forms); $18 per manual (45 pages); $85 per 100 Type 2 machine-scorable answer documents; $22 per examination kit including manual, one each of all four questionnaires, and one answer document.
Time: (15–20) minutes.
Comments: Optional data analysis software available from publisher.
Authors: Lee Baldwin, Freeman Coney III, Diane Färdig, and Roberta Thomas.
Publisher: PsychCorp, A brand of Harcourt Assessment, Inc.
Cross References: For reviews by Robert Fitzpatrick and Michael Harwell, see 13:276.

[2255]

School Environment Preference Survey.

Purpose: "Designed to measure the student's commitment to the set of attitudes, values and behaviors that have been characteristically fostered and rewarded in traditional school environments."
Population: Grades 4–12.
Publication Date: 1978.
Acronym: SEPS.
Scores, 5: Self-Subordination, Traditionalism, Rule Conformity, Uncriticalness, Structured Role Orientation.
Administration: Group.
Price Data: Available from publisher.
Time: (10–15) minutes.
Author: Leonard V. Gordon.
Publisher: EdITS/Educational and Industrial Testing Service.
Cross References: See T5:2315 (1 reference) and T4:2360 (1 reference); for a review by Joan Silverstein, see 10:324.

[2256]

School Function Assessment.

Purpose: Designed to "measure a student's performance of functional tasks that support his or her participation in the academic and social aspects of an elementary school program."
Population: Grades K–6.
Publication Date: 1998.
Acronym: SFA.
Scores, 26: Participation, Task Supports (Physical Tasks Assistance, Physical Tasks Adaptations, Cognitive/Behavioral Tasks Assistance, Cognitive/Behavioral Tasks Adaptations), Activity Performance (Travel,

Maintaining and Changing Positions, Recreational Movement, Manipulation with Movement, Using Materials, Setup and Cleanup, Eating and Drinking, Hygiene, Clothing Management, Up/Down Stairs, Written Work, Computer and Equipment Use, Functional Communication, Memory and Understanding, Following Social Conventions, Compliance with Adult Directives and School Rules, Task Behavior/Completion, Positive Interaction, Behavior Regulation, Personal Care Awareness, Safety).
Administration: Individual.
Price Data, 2002: $149 per complete kit including 25 record forms with 3 rating scale guides and user's manual (136 pages); $59 per 25 record forms with 3 rating scale guides.
Time: Untimed; (5–10) minutes per scale.
Comments: Ratings to be completed by an educational and therapeutic professional who is familiar with the child's typical performance.
Authors: Wendy Coster, Theresa Deeney, Jane Haltiwanger, and Stephen Haley.
Publisher: Harcourt Assessment, Inc.
Cross References: For reviews by Wayne C. Piersel and William D. Schafer, see 14:340.

[2257]

The School Leadership Series.

Purpose: Consists of two assessments developed to provide states with assessments to use as part of the licensure process for principals, superintendents, and school leaders.
Population: Prospective school principals, superintendents, and school leaders.
Publication Date: 1998.
Scores: Total score only.
Administration: Group.
Restricted Distribution: Secure instruments administered three time annually at centers established by the publisher.
Price Data, 2006: $425 per School Leaders Assessment; $250 per School Superintendent Assessment.
Time: 360 minutes in three 120-minute modules.
Comments: State department of education for a particular state should be consulted to determine whether the School Leaders Licensure Assessment or the Superintendent Assessment is required.
Author: Educational Testing Service.
Publisher: Educational Testing Service.

[2258]

School Readiness Checklist.

Purpose: Designed "to involve the parent in planning the child's educational program."
Population: Kindergarten entrants.
Publication Date: 1989.
Scores: Not scored.
Administration: Individual.
Manual: No manual.

Price Data, 2002: $10 per 25 checklists.
Time: [5–10] minutes.
Comments: Ratings by parents.
Author: Academic Consulting & Testing Service.
Publisher: Academic Consulting & Testing Service.

[2259]
School-Readiness Evaluation by Trained Teachers.

Purpose: To screen all school entrants to identify different levels of school-readiness.
Population: South African school beginners.
Publication Date: 1984.
Acronym: SETT.
Scores, 9: Language and General Development (Basic Level, Potential Level, Total), Physical Motor Development (Motor Ability, Integration, Total), Emotional Social Development (Sociability, Emotionality, Total).
Administration: Individual.
Price Data: Available from publisher.
Time: (30) minutes.
Comments: Parent Questionnaire for the Evaluation of School-Readiness and Nursery-School Questionnaire for the Evaluation of School-Readiness may be used in conjunction with this test.
Author: Marianne Joubert.
Publisher: Human Sciences Research Council [South Africa].

[2260]
School Readiness Test.

Purpose: Designed to test the student's readiness for first grade academics.
Population: End of kindergarten through first 3 weeks of Grade 1.
Publication Dates: 1974–2004.
Acronym: SRT.
Scores, 9: Vocabulary, Identifying Letters, Visual Discrimination, Phonemic Awareness, Comprehension and Interpretation, Mathematical Knowledge, Developmental Spelling Ability, Optional Handwriting Assessment, Total.
Administration: Group.
Price Data, 2005: $68.85 per 35 test booklets, scoring key, class summary report, class record sheet, and manual (2004, 35 pages); $7.50 per scoring key; $15.75 per manual; $2.70 per class record sheet; $2.70 per additional class summary report; $24 per sample set.
Time: (80) minutes.
Comments: Subtest scores convert to Individual Readiness Ratings of adequate, marginal, and low; Total score converts to Overall Readiness Ratings of high, above average, average, marginal, not ready without special attention, and not ready without much special attention.
Authors: O. F. Anderhalter and Jan Perney.
Publisher: Scholastic Testing Service, Inc.

Cross References: For reviews by Esther Stavrou Toubanos and Larry Weber, see 12:346; for a review by Thorsten R. Carlson of an earlier edition, see 8:808.

[2261]
School Situation Survey.

Purpose: Designed to measure "school-related student stress."
Population: Grades 4-12.
Publication Date: 1989.
Acronym: SSS.
Scores, 7: Sources of Stress (Teacher Interactions, Academic Stress, Peer Interactions, Academic Self-Concept), Manifestations of Stress (Emotional, Behavioral, Physiological).
Administration: Group.
Price Data: Available from publisher.
Time: (10-15) minutes.
Authors: Barbara J. Helms and Robert K. Gable.
Publisher: Mind Garden, Inc.
Cross References: For reviews by Theodore Coladarci and LeAdelle Phelps, see 12:347; see also T4:2368 (1 reference).

[2262]
School Social Behavior Scales, Second Edition.

Purpose: Designed to evaluate social competence and antisocial behavior of children and youth in Grades K-12 (ages 5-18).
Population: Grades K–12.
Publication Dates: 1993–2002.
Acronym: SBSS-2.
Scores, 8: Social Competence Scale (Peer Relations, Self-Management/Compliance, Academic Behavior, Social Competence Total), Antisocial Behavior Scale (Hostile/Irritable, Antisocial/Aggressive, Defiant/Disruptive, Antisocial Behavior Total).
Administration: Individual.
Price Data, 2006: $36 per 25 rating forms; $49 per user's guide (2002, 114 pages).
Time: (8–10) minutes.
Comments: Companion to Home & Community Social Behavior Scales (1189); rated by teachers or other school personnel.
Author: Kenneth W. Merrell.
Publisher: Assessment-Intervention Resources.
Cross References: For reviews by Rosemary Flanagan and by Michael J. Furlong and Alicia Soliz, see 16:218; for reviews by Stephen R. Hooper and Lesley A. Welsh of a previous edition, see 13:277 (2 references); see also T4:2369 (1 reference).

[2263]
School Social Skills.

Purpose: Developed to assess social skills exhibited in a school setting.

Population: Elementary school and junior high school and high school.
Publication Date: 1984.
Acronym: S3.
Scores: Ratings in 4 categories: Adult Relations, Peer Relations, School Rules, Classroom Behaviors.
Administration: Individual.
Price Data, 2002: $58 per complete kit including manual (25 pages); $38 per 50 rating scales; $25 per manual.
Time: (10) minutes.
Comments: Ratings by teachers.
Authors: Laura J. Brown, Donald D. Black, and John C. Downs.
Publisher: Slosson Educational Publications, Inc.
Cross References: For reviews by Beth D. Bader and William K. Wilkinson, see 12:348; see also T4:2370 (1 reference).

[2264]
Schubert General Ability Battery.

Purpose: Developed as a test of an individual's ability to understand and think in terms of words, numbers, and ideas.
Population: Grades 12–16 and adults.
Publication Dates: 1946–1965.
Acronym: SGAB.
Scores, 5: Vocabulary, Analogies, Arithmetic Problems, Syllogisms, Total.
Administration: Group.
Price Data, 2005: $72.75 per complete kit including 25 tests and manual (1965, 24 pages); $41 per 25 tests.
Time: 16(25) or 32(40) minutes.
Authors: Herman J. P. Schubert and Daniel S. P. Schubert (test).
Publisher: Slosson Educational Publications, Inc.
Cross References: See 7:386 (1 reference); for a review by William B. Schrader, see 5:382.

[2265]
SCID Screen Patient Questionnaire and SCID Screen Patient Questionnaire Extended.

Purpose: "An Axis I symptoms and disorders screening tool."
Population: Psychiatric or general medical patients ages 18 or older.
Publication Dates: 1991–1999.
Acronyms: SSPQ, SSPQ-X.
Scores, 6: Mood Disorders, Anxiety Disorders, Substance Use Disorders, Somatoform Disorders, Eating Disorders, Schizophrenia and Other Psychotic Disorders.
Administration: Individual.
Price Data, 2006: $427 per SSPQ unlimited-use software program; $535 per SSPQ-X unlimited-use software program; $50 per SSPQ software preview version (3 uses); $50 per SSPQ-X software preview version.

Time: (20) minutes SSPQ; (30–45) minutes for SSPQ-X.
Comments: SSPQ is an abbreviated computer-administered screening version of the Structured Clinical Interview for DSM-IV (SCID-I) and an adaptation of the MiniSCID for DSM-IIIR; SSPQ-X is an extended adaptation of the SSPQ; System requirements: Pentium, 120 MB hard drive, VGA or SVGA color monitor, 16 MB RAM, 3.5-inch floppy disk drive, CD-ROM drive, Windows 95 or higher.
Authors: Michael B. First, Miriam Gibbon, Janet B. W. Williams, and Robert L. Spitzer.
Publisher: Multi-Health Systems, Inc.; American Psychiatric Association.
Cross References: For reviews by Mark H. Stone and Peter Zachar, see 15:218; for reviews by Paul D. Werner and Thomas A. Widiger of the clinician version, see 14:373 (9 references); see also T5:2519 (56 references).

[2266]
Science Assessment Series 1 and 2.

Purpose: Designed to assist teachers in "checking children's understanding of the science taught" during primary and secondary education.
Population: Ages 5–9, Ages 8–13.
Publication Date: 2001.
Administration: Group.
Levels, 2: Series 1, Series 2.
Price Data: Available from publisher.
Comments: Designed to correspond to the national curricula of England and Wales, Northern Ireland, and Scotland.
Authors: Terry Russell and Linda McGuigan.
Publisher: NFER-Nelson Publishing Co. Ltd. [England].
 a) SCIENCE ASSESSMENT SERIES 1.
 Population: Ages 5–9.
 Scores: 5 subtest units: Humans and Other Animals, Planets, Materials, Light and Sound, Electricity and Forces.
 Time: (45) minutes per unit.
 b) SCIENCE ASSESSMENT SERIES 2.
 Population: Ages 8–13.
 Scores: 8 subtest units: Humans and Other Animals, Planets, Living Things in the Environment, Materials, Changing Materials, Electricity, Light and Sound, Forces and the Earth and Beyond.
 Time: (45) minutes per unit.
Cross References: For reviews by Bruce G. Rogers and William D. Schafer, see 16:219.

[2267]
Scientific Orientation Test.

Purpose: "Designed to measure a range of affective outcomes for students of science or science-related subjects."

Population: Students in school years 5 to 12.
Publication Date: 1995.
Acronym: S.OR.T.
Scores, 4: Interest in Science, Scientific Attitude, Attitude to School Science, Total.
Administration: Group or individual.
Price Data: Available from publisher.
Time: (40) minutes.
Comments: Includes 5 subtests yielding 13 subscores; formerly titled A Test of Interests.
Author: G. Rex Meyer.
Publisher: GRM Educational Consultancy [Australia].
Cross References: For reviews by Bruce G. Rogers and Herbert C. Rudman, see 14:341.

[2268]
SCL-90 Analogue™.

Purpose: A brief rating scale "for collecting observer data on a patient's psychological symptomatic distress."
Population: Adults and adolescents.
Publication Date: 1976.
Scores, 10: Primary Dimensional Scales (Somatization, Obsessive Compulsive, Interpersonal Sensitivity, Depression, Anxiety, Hostility, Phobic Anxiety, Paranoid Ideation, Psychoticism), Global Psychopathology Scale.
Administration: Group.
Price Data, 2006: $45.25 per 100 forms.
Time: (1–3) minutes.
Comments: Designed for use by health professionals without in-depth training or knowledge of psychopathology.
Author: Leonard R. Derogatis.
Publisher: Pearson Assessments.
Cross References: See T5:2326 (3 references).

[2269]
Screening Assessment for Gifted Elementary and Middle School Students, Second Edition.

Purpose: "Used to identify students who are gifted in academics and reasoning."
Population: Ages 5–14.
Publication Dates: 1987–2001.
Acronym: SAGES-2.
Scores, 3: Mathematics/Science, Language Arts/Social Studies, Reasoning.
Administration: Group.
Price Data, 2006: $215 per kit including 10 K–3 mathematics/science student response booklets, 10 K–3 language arts/social studies student response booklets, 10 K–3 reasoning student response booklets, 10 4–8 mathematics/science student response booklets, 10 4–8 language arts/social studies student response booklets, 10 4–8 reasoning response booklets, manual (2001, 128 pages), 50 K–3 profile/scoring sheets, 50 4–8 profile/response sheets, and a 4–8 scoring transparency; $20 per 10 K–3 mathematics/science student response booklets; $20 per 10 K–3 language arts/social studies student response booklets; $20 per 10 K–3 reasoning student response booklets; $15 per 10 4–8 mathematics/science student response booklets; $15 per 10 4–8 language arts/social studies student response booklets; $15 per 10 4–8 reasoning student response booklets; $51 per manual; $30 per 50 K–3 profile/scoring sheets; $30 per 50 4–8 profile/response sheets; $10 per 4–8 scoring transparency.
Time: (30–45) minutes.
Comments: This edition replaces both the earlier Screening Assessment for Gifted Elementary Students (T5:2328) and the Screening Assessment for Gifted Elementary Students—Primary (T5:2329).
Authors: Susan K. Johnsen and Anne L. Corn.
Publisher: PRO-ED.
Cross References: For reviews by Carolyn M. Callahan and Howard M. Knoff, see 15:219; see T5:2328 (1 reference); for reviews by Lewis R. Aiken and Susana Urbina of an earlier edition, see 12:349; for a review by E. Scott Huebner of an earlier edition, see 10:327.

[2270]
Screening Kit of Language Development.

Purpose: Assesses preschool language development in order to identify language disorders/delays.
Population: Ages 2–5.
Publication Dates: 1983–2002.
Acronym: SKOLD.
Scores, 6: Vocabulary, Comprehension, Story Completion, Individual and Paired Sentence Repetition with Pictures, Individual Sentence Repetition without Pictures, Comprehension of Commands.
Administration: Individual.
Editions, 2: Standard English, Black English.
Price Data, 2002: $93 per complete kit including manual (37 pages), stimulus book, and 1 set of standard English scoring forms or 1 set of Black English scoring forms; $42 per 25 standard English scoring forms; $42 per 25 Black English scoring forms; $30 per stimulus materials and scoring guidelines; $26 per examiner's manual.
Time: (15) minutes.
Authors: Lynn S. Bliss and Doris V. Allen.
Publisher: Slosson Educational Publications, Inc.
Cross References: See T4:2381 (1 reference).

[2271]
Screening Test for Developmental Apraxia of Speech—Second Edition.

Purpose: Developed "to screen for the potential presence of developmental apraxia of speech in children."
Population: Ages 4-0 to 12-11.
Publication Dates: 1980–2001.
Acronym: STDAS-2.
Scores, 3: Prosody, Verbal Sequencing, Articulation.
Administration: Individual.

Price Data, 2006: $95 per complete kit including examiner's manual (2001, 37 pages) and 50 profile/examiner record forms; $45 per 50 profile/examiner record forms; $55 per examiner's manual.
Time: (10–15) minutes.
Author: Robert W. Blakeley.
Publisher: PRO-ED.
Cross References: For reviews by Rebecca McCauley and Janet Norris, see 15:220; see T5:2332 (2 references) and T4:2383 (3 references); for a review by Ronald K. Sommers of an earlier edition, see 11:347.

[2272]
Screening Test for Educational Prerequisite Skills.

Purpose: Developed to screen for skills needed for beginning kindergarten.
Population: Ages 4–5 years.
Publication Dates: 1976–1990.
Acronym: STEPS.
Scores: 5 areas: Motor Skills, Intellectual Skills, Verbal Information Skills, Cognitive Strategies, Attitudes.
Administration: Individual.
Price Data, 2006: $165 per complete kit including test materials (pictures, bears, pencil), 25 AutoScore™ forms, 25 AutoScore™ home questionnaires, and manual (1990, 68 pages); $42 per set of test materials; $54.95 per 25 AutoScore™ forms; $36 per 25 AutoScore™ home questionnaires; $48.50 per manual.
Time: (8–10) minutes.
Author: Frances Smith.
Publisher: Western Psychological Services.
Cross References: For reviews by John Christian Busch, M. Elizabeth Graue, and Jeffrey K. Smith, see 12:351.

[2273]
Screening Test for the Luria-Nebraska Neuropsychological Battery: Adult and Children's Forms.

Purpose: Screening tests for "predicting which individuals would probably show 'normal' or 'clinical' patterns if they were administered the appropriate form of the full Luria-Nebraska Neuropsychological Battery."
Population: Ages 8–12, 13 and older.
Publication Date: 1987.
Acronym: ST-LNNB.
Scores: Cutoff score only.
Administration: Individual.
Forms, 2: Children's Form, Adult Form.
Price Data, 2006: $157 per complete set including 25 administration and scoring booklets for children, 25 administration and scoring booklets for adults, set of stimulus cards adult and children, and manual for adult and children; $32.50 per 25 administration and scoring booklets (specify adult or children's form); $58 per set of stimulus cards; $53 per manual.

Time: (20) minutes.
Comments: For screening purposes only.
Author: Charles J. Golden.
Publisher: Western Psychological Services.
Cross References: For reviews by Arlene Coopersmith Rosenthal and W. Grant Willis, see 11:348.

[2274]
Screening Test of Adolescent Language.

Purpose: Designed to identify adolescents at risk of having language disorders.
Population: Junior and senior high school.
Publication Date: 1980.
Acronym: STAL.
Scores, 5: 4 subtests (Vocabulary, Auditory Memory Span, Language Processing, Proverb Explanation), Total.
Administration: Individual.
Price Data, 2006: $69 per kit, including manual (24 pages), mini-screen, 50 tests, and administration and scoring card and scoring instructions; $27.50 per 50 test forms; $42.50 per manual.
Time: (7) minutes.
Authors: Elizabeth M. Prather, Sheila Van Ausdal Breecher, Marimyn Lee Stafford, and Elizabeth Matthews Wallace.
Publisher: Western Psychological Services.
Cross References: See T4:2387 (1 reference); for a review by Ronald K. Sommers, see 9:1086 (1 reference).

[2275]
Search Institute Profiles of Student Life: Attitudes and Behaviors.

Purpose: Designed to "assist … communities in measuring 40 developmental assets related to youth well-being."
Population: Grades 6–12.
Publication Dates: 1989–1996.
Scores: Total score only.
Administration: Group.
Price Data, 2001: $55 per 25 copies of survey; $700 per 80-page report.
Time: (50) minutes.
Author: Search Institute.
Publisher: Search Institute.
Cross References: For reviews by George Engelhard, Jr. and Carol M. McGregor, see 15:221; for reviews by Ernest A. Bauer and Sharon Johnson-Lewis of an earlier edition, see 11:350.

[2276]
Secondary Level English Proficiency Test.

Purpose: "A measure of ability in two primary areas: understanding spoken English and understanding written English."
Population: Grades 7-12.

Publication Dates: 1980-2003.
Acronym: SLEP.
Scores, 3: 2 section scores for Listening Comprehension and Reading Comprehension, and a Total score.
Administration: Individuals or group.
Forms, 3: 1, 2, 3.
Price Data: Available from publisher.
Time: 85(90) minutes.
Comments: Can be administered in a single session or in two separate sessions.
Author: Educational Testing Service.
Publisher: Educational Testing Service.
Cross References: See T4:2393 (2 references); for reviews by Brenda H. Loyd and Michael J. Subkoviak, see 9:1090.

[2277]
Secondary-School Record.

Purpose: "Designed to present a summary of the student's academic record and summarize ratings by several teachers."
Population: Grades 9–12.
Publication Dates: 1941–1964.
Acronym: SSR.
Price Data: Available from publisher.
Time: Administration time not reported.
Comments: Transcript form only still available.
Author: National Association of Secondary School Principals.
Publisher: National Association of Secondary School Principals.
Cross References: See 4:516 (1 reference).

[2278]
Secondary Screening Profiles.

Purpose: Designed to help "identify pupils' individual strengths and weaknesses upon entry to secondary school (junior high)," and also as a "standardised basis for screening special education needs."
Population: Junior high students, ages 10–13 years.
Publication Dates: 1995–1999.
Acronym: SSP.
Scores, 3: Reasoning, Reading, Mathematical.
Administration: Group.
Forms, 6: Reading, Forms A and B; Mathematics, Forms A and B; Reasoning, Forms A and B.
Price Data, 2002: £12.99 per 20 test forms; £16.99 per manual; £16.99 per specimen set.
Time: (20–40) minutes for each form.
Author: Centre for Research on Learning and Instruction, University of Edinburgh.
Publisher: Hodder & Stoughton Educational [England].
Cross References: For reviews by John O. Anderson and Susan J. Maller, see 15:222.

[2279]
The Seeking of Noetic Goals Test.

Purpose: Constructed "to measure the strength of motivation to find life meaning."
Population: Adolescents and adults.
Publication Date: 1977.
Acronym: SONG.
Scores: Total score only.
Administration: Group.
Price Data: Available from publisher.
Time: (10) minutes.
Comments: Complementary scale to the Purpose in Life Test.
Author: James C. Crumbaugh.
Publisher: Psychometric Affiliates.
Cross References: For reviews by Brenda Bailey-Richardson and Kevin L. Moreland, see 9:1092, see also T3:2124 (1 reference).

[2280]
Seguin-Goddard Formboards.

Purpose: Designed for testing spatial perception and motor coordination.
Population: Age 4 to adult.
Publication Date: [1911].
Scores: No scores.
Price Data, 2005: $185 per "flush" formboard; $340 per "raised" formboard.
Time: [5-10] minutes.
Comments: Used in the Halstead-Reitan Neuropsychological Test Battery (1137), Merrill-Palmer Scale of Mental Tests (1601), and Arthur Point Scale of Performance Tests (T5:182).
Authors: E. Seguin, H. H. Goddard, and N. Norsworthy.
Publisher: Stoelting Co.
Cross References: See T4: 2397 (1 reference), T3:2125 (1 reference), and T2: 578 (25 references).

[2281]
SELECT Associate Screening System—Internet Version.

Purpose: Designed to assist organizations in making effective employee selection decisions at the associate level.
Publication Dates: 1995–2002.
Acronym: SELECT.
Administration: Individual or group.
Price Data, 2002: $489 per one-time purchase of Initial System including units for 10–12 surveys, SELECT software, and user's guide (1998, 90 pages); $8–$22 per report.
Time: (20–45) minutes depending on survey.
Comments: A software platform that combines 17 screening tools validated for specific jobs or industries; web-based administered, scored, and interpreted; reports

include results, recommendations, and interview questions.

Author: Bigby, Havis, & Associates, Inc.

Publisher: Bigby, Havis, & Associates, Inc.

a) SELECT FOR CONVENIENCE STORES.

Purpose: Designed to "measure characteristics and abilities important in most convenience store jobs."

Population: Applicants for positions in convenience stores.

Scores, 3: Provides Overall Performance, Integrity, and Retail Math indices with recommended ranges; subscale results for Energy, Frustration Tolerance, Self-Control, Accommodation to Others, Acceptance of Diversity, Positive Service Attitude; also includes self-report of Counterproductive Work Behaviors, Willingness to Do Common C-Store Tasks.

b) SELECT FOR CUSTOMER SERVICE.

Purpose: Designed as an associate-level pre-employment test for positions in customer service.

Population: Job Applicants for customer service positions.

Scores, 2: Provides Overall Performance and Integrity indices with recommended ranges; subscale results for Energy, Frustration Tolerance, Accommodation to Others, Acceptance of Diversity, and Positive Service Attitude; optional modules available for Counterproductive Behaviors, Retail Math.

c) SELECT FOR HEALTH CARE.

Purpose: Designed to "measure characteristics important in most health care provider jobs."

Population: Applicants for health care positions.

Scores, 2: Provides Overall Performance and Integrity indices with recommended ranges; subscale results for Energy, Frustration Tolerance, Accommodation to Others, Acceptance of Diversity, Positive Service Attitude, Accountability, Rapport, Empathy, Multi-Tasking.

d) SELECT FOR PRODUCTION AND DISTRIBUTION.

Purpose: Designed to "measure characteristics important to team-oriented manufacturing and distribution jobs."

Population: Applicants for production and distribution positions.

Scores, 2: Provides Overall Performance and Integrity indices with recommended ranges; subscale results for Energy, Frustration Tolerance, Acceptance of Diversity, Self-Control, Acceptance of Structure, Productive Attitude; optional module is available for Counterproductive Behaviors.

e) SELECT FOR ADMINISTRATIVE SUPPORT.

Purpose: Designed "as a personality-based survey for measuring characteristics that have been found to predict job effectiveness in administrative or clerical positions."

Population: Applicants for administrative support positions.

Scores, 2: Provides Overall Performance and Integrity indices with recommended ranges; subscale results for Energy, Multi-Tasking, Attention to Detail, Self-Reliance, Task Focus, Interpersonal Insight, Criticism Tolerance, Acceptance of Diversity, Self-Control, Productive Attitude.

f) SELECT FOR PERSONAL SERVICES.

Purpose: Designed "as a personality-based survey for measuring characteristics that have been found to predict job effectiveness for those employed in personal-care-type positions."

Population: Applicants for personal services positions (i.e., hairstylists/photographers).

Scores, 2: Provides Overall Performance and Integrity indices with recommended ranges; subscale results for Energy, Frustration Tolerance, Accommodation to Others, Acceptance of Diversity, Socially Outgoing, Positive Service Attitude.

g) SELECT FOR CALL CENTERS—INBOUND SERVICE.

Purpose: Designed to help screen applicants for inbound service positions at call centers.

Population: Applicants for inbound service positions at call centers.

Scores, 2: Provides Overall Performance and Integrity indices with recommended ranges; subscale results for Energy, Frustration Tolerance, Accommodation to Others, Acceptance of Diversity, Positive Service Attitude.

h) SELECT FOR CALL CENTERS—INBOUND SALES.

Purpose: Designed to help screen applicants for inbound sales positions at call centers.

Population: Applicants for inbound sales positions at call centers.

Scores, 2: Provides Overall Performance and Integrity indices with recommended ranges; subscale results for Energy, Frustration Tolerance, Accountability, Preference for Structure, Influence, Social Comfort, Productive Attitude.

i) SELECT FOR CALL CENTERS—OUTBOUND SALES.

Purpose: Designed to help screen applicants for outbound sales positions at call centers.

Population: Applicants for outbound sales positions at call centers.

Scores, 2: Provides Overall Performance and Integrity indices with recommended ranges; subscale results for Energy, Multi-Tasking Ability, Accountability, Assertiveness, Social Comfort, Diplomacy, Acceptance of Diversity, Frustration

Tolerance, Criticism Tolerance, Productive Attitude.

j) SELECT FOR HELP DESK AGENTS.
Purpose: Designed to help screen applicants for help desk agents.
Population: Applicants for help desk agent positions.
Scores, 2: Provides Overall Performance and Integrity indices with recommended ranges; subscale results for Energy, Problem Solving, Multi-Tasking, Accountability, Assertiveness, Collaboration, Frustration Tolerance, Criticism Tolerance, Acceptance of Diversity.

k) SELECT FOR CONVENIENCE STORE MANAGERS.
Purpose: Designed to help identify people who will manage a small team of associates to serve and sell to customers in convenience stores and gas stations.
Population: Applicants for convenience store management positions.
Scores, 3: Provides Overall Performance, Integrity, and Retail Math indices with recommended ranges: subscale results for Positive Sales Attitude, Leadership, Persuasiveness, Energy, Good Judgment, Organization and Attention to Detail, Frustration Tolerance.

l) SELECT FOR RETAIL SALES ASSOCIATES.
Purpose: Designed to help identify people who enjoy selling and dealing with customers in a retail store.
Population: Applicants for retail sales positions in a retail store.
Scores, 3: Provides Overall Performance, Integrity, and Retail Math indices with recommended ranges; subscale results for Positive Sales Attitude, Persuasiveness, Energy, Initiative, Good Judgment, Frustration Tolerance.

m) SELECT FOR RETAIL CLERK/CASHIERS.
Purpose: Designed to help identify people who enjoy serving others in a retail store in positions where active selling is not required.
Population: Applicants for clerk or cashier positions in a retail store.
Scores, 3: Provides Overall Performance, Integrity, and Retail Math indices with recommended ranges; subscale results for Energy, Frustration Tolerance, Accommodation to Others, Acceptance of Diversity, Positive Service Attitude.

n) SELECT FOR ENTRY LEVEL RETAIL MANAGERS.
Purpose: Designed to help identify people who can manage associates to serve and sell in small format stores or department managers in large format stores.
Population: Applicants for entry level retail management positions.

Scores: Provides Overall Performance, Integrity, and Retail Math indices with the recommended ranges; subscale results for Energy, Positive Sales Attitude, Leadership, Persuasiveness, Good Judgment, Organization and Attention to Detail, Frustration Tolerance.

o) SELECT FOR HOSPITALITY.
Purpose: Designed to help identify people who have a positive and engaging service attitude.
Population: Applicants for wait staff or host positions in restaurants, hotels, and other hospitality positions.
Scores, 2: Provides Overall Performance and Integrity indices with recommended ranges; subscale results for Energy, Frustration Tolerance, Accommodation to Others, Acceptance of Diversity, Positive Service Attitude, Socially Outgoing.

p) SELECT FOR LEASING AGENTS.
Purpose: Designed to help identify people who will be positive service providers and are able to influence people to lease or rent apartments.
Population: Applicants for leasing agent positions.
Scores, 3: Provides Overall Performance, Integrity, and Leasing Agent Math indices with recommended ranges; subscale results for Energy, Assertiveness, Positive Sales Attitude, Social Comfort, Accommodation to Others, Frustration Tolerance, Criticism Tolerance, Self-Reliance, Acceptance of Diversity.

q) SELECT FOR RECEPTIONISTS.
Purpose: Designed to identify people who are socially engaging and enjoy serving the needs of the customer.
Population: Applicants for receptionist positions.
Scores, 2: Provides Overall Performance and Integrity indices with recommended ranges; subscale results for Energy, Frustration Tolerance, Accommodation to Others, Acceptance of Diversity, Positive Service Attitude, Socially Outgoing.

Cross References: For reviews by James T. Austin and Vicki S. Packman, see 14:344.

[2282]
[Selection Interview Forms].

Purpose: Designed to help interviewers obtain appropriate and valid information from job applicants.
Population: Business and industry.
Publication Date: 1962.
Scores: Ratings in 8 areas (Motivation for the Job, Adequacy of Work Experience, Supervisory Experience and Ability, Achievements at School, Vocational Adjustment, Family Background and Personal Adjustments, Wife's and Family's Role, Health) plus Total.
Administration: Individual.
Author: Benjamin Balinsky.
Publisher: Martin M. Bruce, Ph.D.

a) SELECTION INTERVIEW FORM.
Price Data, 2006: $13.75 per specimen set; $26.40 per package of forms.
Time: [60-90] minutes.
b) INTERVIEW RATING FORM.
Price Data: $10.45 per specimen set; $19.80 per package of forms.
Time: [15] minutes.

[2283]
Self-Appraisal Questionnaire.

Purpose: "Multi-dimensional self-administered questionnaire designed to predict violent and non-violent offender recidivism among correctional/forensic populations and to assist with the assignment of these populations to appropriate treatment/correctional programs and different institutional security levels."
Population: Male offenders, age 18 and older.
Publication Date: 2005.
Acronym: SAQ.
Scores, 8: Criminal Tendencies, Antisocial Personality Problems, Conduct Problems, Criminal History, Alcohol/Drug Abuse, Antisocial Associates, Anger, Total.
Administration: Individual or group.
Price Data, 2006: $75 per complete kit including technical manual (80 pages) and 25 QuikScore forms; $52 per technical manual; $38 per 25 QuikScore forms.
Time: (10–15) minutes.
Comments: Can be administered verbally.
Author: Wagdy Loza.
Publisher: Multi-Health Systems Inc.

[2284]
Self-Assessment in Writing Skills.

Purpose: Developed as a self-assessment tool to assess writing skills.
Population: Clerical, managerial, and sales employees.
Publication Date: 1990.
Scores, 3: Content and Style, Organization and Format, Total.
Administration: Group or individual.
Price Data: Price information available from publisher for complete kit including 20 inventories, 20 scoring sheets for part 1, and 20 scoring sheets for part 2.
Time: [90–120] minutes.
Comments: Self-administered, self-scored.
Author: Training House, Inc.
Publisher: Training House, Inc.
Cross References: For reviews by Gabriel M. Della-Piana and Stephen Jurs, see 12:352.

[2285]
Self-Awareness Profile.

Purpose: "This self-assessment provides insight into the basic personality attributes that influence the way we behave."
Population: Industry.

Publication Dates: 1980–1987.
Scores, 4: Dominance, Influence, Conformity, Evenness.
Administration: Individual or group.
Price Data: Price information available from publisher for complete sets including 16-item inventory, interpretation sheet, planning sheet, and 20 sets of cards containing profiles on 10 different personalities, to be sorted by participants ("most like me, next most," etc.).
Time: (80–100) minutes.
Author: Scott B. Parry.
Publisher: Training House, Inc.
Cross References: For a review by Timothy M. Osberg, see 11:353.

[2286]
The Self-Concept and Motivation Inventory: What Face Would You Wear?

Purpose: To assess motivation and academic self-concept.
Population: Age 4–kindergarten, grades 1–3, 3–6, 7–12.
Publication Dates: 1967–1977.
Acronym: SCAMIN.
Administration: Group.
Price Data: Available from publisher.
Authors: Norman J. Milchus, George A. Farrah, and William Reitz.
Publisher: Norman Milchus (the author).
a) PRE-SCHOOL/KINDERGARTEN FORM.
Population: Age 4–kindergarten.
Scores, 14: Motivation (Goal and Achievement Needs, Achievement Investment, Self-Concept), Total (optional).
Time: (25–30) minutes.
b) EARLY ELEMENTARY FORM.
Population: Grades 1-3.
Scores, 5: Motivation (Goal and Achievement Needs, Achievement Investment), Self-Concept (Role Expectations, Self-Adequacy), Total (optional).
Time: (25–30) minutes.
c) LATER ELEMENTARY FORM.
Population: Grades 3–6.
Scores, 10: Same as *b* above plus 6 optional Sources of Support Climate scores (Parents, Teachers, Peers and Siblings, Academic Self, Academic Activity Climate, School Climate), Total (optional).
Time: (30–35) minutes.
d) SECONDARY FORM.
Population: Grades 7–12.
Scores, 20: Same as *b* above plus 16 optional scores: Sources of Support Climate (Parents, Teachers, Peers, Academic Self, Physical and Social Self,

Adults and Counselors, Academic Activity Climate, School Climate), Immediate-Intrinsic Orientation (Evaluated Competition, Tasks and Projects, Discovery and Creativity, Skills), Fulfillment Orientation (Aspiration, Cooperation and Conformity, Responsibility, Acceptance and Praise).

Time: (40) minutes.

Cross References: See T5:2355 (3 references) and T4:2408 (3 references); for a review by Lorrie Shepard, see 8:670 (4 references).

[2287]
Self-Description Questionnaire—I, II, III.

Purpose: To measure aspects of self-concept.
Population: Ages 5–12, 13–17, 16–Adult.
Publication Dates: 1987–1992.
Acronym: SDQ.
Administration: Group.
Price Data: Available from publisher.
Comments: Self-report measures.
Author: Herbert W. Marsh.
Publisher: SELF Research Centre [Australia].

a) SELF-DESCRIPTION QUESTIONNAIRE—I.
Population: Ages 8–12.
Scores, 11: Academic (Mathematics, Reading, General—School, Total), Non-Academic (Physical Abilities, Physical Appearance, Peer Relations, Parent Relations, Total), Global (General—Self, Total—Self).
Time: (15–20) minutes.

b) SELF-DESCRIPTION QUESTIONNAIRE—II.
Population: Ages 13–17.
Scores, 12: Academic (Mathematics, Verbal, General—School), Non-Academic (Physical Abilities, Physical Appearance, Same Sex Peer Relations, Opposite Sex Peer Relations, Parent Relations, Emotional Stability, Honesty/Trustworthiness), Global (General—Self, Total—Self).
Time: (20–25) minutes.

c) SELF-DESCRIPTION QUESTIONNAIRE—III.
Population: Ages 16–Adult.
Scores, 14: Academic (Mathematics, Verbal, Problem-Solving, General—Academic), Non-Academic (Physical Abilities, Physical Appearance, Same Sex Peer Relations, Opposite Sex Peer Relations, Parent Relations, Spiritual Values/Religion, Honesty/Trustworthiness, Emotional Stability), Global (General—Self, Total—Self).
Time: (20–25) minutes.

Cross References: See T5:2358 (17 references); for reviews by Jeffrey A. Atlas, Robert K. Gable, and Steven Isonio, see 13:280 (42 references); see also T4:2412 (10 references).

[2288]
Self-Directed Learning Readiness Scale/Learning Preference Assessment.

Purpose: The SDLRS/LPA is designed to measure attitudes, abilities, and characteristics that comprise readiness to engage in self-directed learning.
Population: Ages 7-14, age 14 and over.
Publication Dates: 1977-2005.
Acronym: SDLRS.
Scores: Total score only.
Administration: Individual or group.
Price Data, 2006: $4.95 each scale; quantity discounts available.
Foreign Language Editions: The adult form has been translated into Spanish, French, German, Italian, Korean, Chinese, Japanese, Finnish, Greek, Portuguese, Afrikaans, and Lithuanian.
Time: [25] minutes.
Comments: A self-scoring form, entitled the Learning Preference Assessment, is available for use in workshops; an elementary form is available for Grades 3–7.
Authors: Lucy M. Guglielmino (all forms) and Paul J. Guglielmino (self-scoring form).
Publisher: Guglielmino & Associates.
Cross References: See T5:2359 (2 references).

[2289]
Self-Directed Search, 4th Edition [Forms R, E, CE, and CP].

Purpose: A vocational inventory designed to identify "a person's particular activities, competencies, and self-estimates compared with various occupational groups."
Population: Ages 12 and above.
Publication Dates: 1970–1997.
Acronym: SDS.
Scores, 6: Realistic, Investigative, Artistic, Social, Enterprising, Conventional.
Administration: Group.
Editions, 4: Form R (Regular), Form E (Easy), Form CP (Career Planning), Form CE (Career Explorer).
Price Data, 2006: $186 per SDS Form R Comprehensive Kit including manuals, 25 booklets and occupational finders, 25 "You and Your Career" booklets, 10 leisure activity finders, and 10 educational opportunities finders; $99 per SDS software portfolio (CD-ROM) including unlimited scoring and report generation for Form R and 5 free on-screen administrations.
Foreign Language Editions: "Adaptations available in the following countries/continents: Australia, Canada, China, Finland, France, Greece, Guyana, Hungary, Indonesia, Israel, Italy, Japan, Netherlands, New Zealand, Nigeria, Norway, Poland, Portugal, Russia, Saudi Arabia, Slovenia, South Africa, South

America, Spain, Switzerland"; English-Canadian, Spanish, Vietnamese, and Braille editions also available.
Time: (30–50) minutes.
Comments: Self-administered, -scored, and -interpreted; computer software available; based on the Holland typology of vocational preferences.
Authors: John L. Holland (test and manuals), Amy B. Powell (manuals), and Barbara A. Fritzsche (manuals).
Publisher: Psychological Assessment Resources, Inc.
Cross References: For a review by Michael B. Brown, see 14:345; see also T5:2360 (13 references); for reviews by Joseph C. Ciechalski and Esther E. Diamond of an earlier edition, see 13:281 (48 references); see also T4:2414 (23 references); for reviews by M. Harry Daniels and Caroline Manuele-Adkins, see 10:330 (19 references); for a review by Robert H. Dolliver, see 9:1098 (12 references); see also T3:2134 (55 references); for a review by John O. Crites and excerpted reviews by Fred Brown, Richard Seligman, Catherine C. Cutts, Robert H. Dolliver, and Robert N. Hanson, see 8:1022 (88 references); see also T2:2211 (1 reference).

[2290]
Self-Directed Search—Revised 2001 Australian Edition.

Purpose: Designed as an instrument "for students and adults wishing to explore their career options."
Population: Ages 15 and over.
Publication Dates: 1970–2006.
Acronym: SDS.
Scores: 4 scales: Activities, Competencies, Occupations, Summary.
Administration: Group or individual.
Price Data, 2006: A$30.80 per 10 assessment booklets; $39.95 per 10 Occupations finder; $16.50 per 10 "You and Your Career"; $5.95 per Alphabetical Occupations Finder; $60.50 per manual; $70.40 per specimen set.
Foreign Language and Special Editions: Spanish, Vietnamese, French, and Braille editions available.
Time: (50) minutes.
Authors: John L. Holland, Meredith Shears (Australian Manual), and Adrian Harvey-Beavis (Australian Manual).
Publisher: Australian Council for Educational Research Ltd. [Australia].
Cross References: For a review by Nancy L. Crumpton, see 15:223.

[2291]
Self-Esteem Index.

Purpose: "Designed to measure the way individuals perceive themselves."
Population: Ages 7-0 to 18-11.
Publication Dates: 1990-1991.

Acronym: SEI.
Scores, 5: Familial Acceptance, Academic Competence, Peer Popularity, Personal Security, Self-Esteem Quotient.
Administration: Group.
Price Data, 2006: $128 per complete kit including 50 student response booklets, 50 profile/record forms, and manual (1991, 51 pages); $40 per 50 student response booklets; $40 per 50 profile/record forms; $51 per examiner's manual.
Time: (30-35) minutes.
Authors: Linda Brown and Jacquelyn Alexander.
Publisher: PRO-ED.
Cross References: See T5:2361 (4 references); for reviews by E. Scott Huebner and by Ralph O. Mueller and Paula J. Dupuy, see 11:354.

[2292]
The Self-Esteem Inventory.

Purpose: Developed to examine an individual's self-esteem.
Population: Adolescents and adults.
Publication Date: 1995.
Scores: Total score only.
Administration: Group.
Manual: No manual.
Price Data: Available from publisher.
Time: Administration time not reported.
Author: Millard J. Bienvenu.
Publisher: Millard J. Bienvenu, Northwest Publications.

[2293]
Self-Esteem Questionnaire.

Purpose: Measures self esteem and satisfaction with self esteem.
Population: Ages 9 and over.
Publication Dates: 1971–1976.
Acronym: SEQ.
Scores, 2: Self-Esteem, Self-Other Satisfaction.
Administration: Group.
Price Data: Not available.
Time: (15–20) minutes.
Author: James K. Hoffmeister.
Publisher: Test Analysis & Development Corporation.
Cross References: See T4:2416 (3 references).

[2294]
The Self Image Profiles.

Purpose: To quickly assess self image and self esteem in children and adolescents.
Publication Date: 2001.
Acronym: SIP.
Administration: Group or individual.
Price Data, 2006: £73.50 per complete kit including Adolescent Profiles, Child Profiles, 25 SIP-C record forms, 25 SIP-A record forms, and manual (43) pages.

Author: Richard J. Butler.
Publisher: Harcourt Assessment [England].
   a) THE SELF IMAGE PROFILE FOR CHILDREN.
   Population: Ages 7–11.
   Acronym: SIP-C.
   Scores, 11: Positive Self Image, Negative Self Image, Sense of Difference, Self Esteem, Aspects of Self (Behaviour, Social, Emotional, Outgoing, Academic, Resourceful, Appearance).
   Time: (12–25) minutes.
   b) THE SELF IMAGE PROFILE FOR ADOLESCENTS.
   Population: Ages 12–16.
   Acronym: SIP-A.
   Scores, 14: Positive Self Image, Negative Self Image, Sense of Difference, Self Esteem, Aspects of Self (Expressive, Caring, Outgoing, Academic, Emotional, Hesitant, Feel Different, Inactive, Unease, Resourceful).
   Time: (9–17) minutes.
Cross References: For a review by Jayne E. Stake, see 15:224.

[2295]
Self-Motivated Career Planning Guide.

Purpose: To help the individual develop vocational objectives through self-administered exercises.
Population: High school and college and adults.
Publication Dates: 1978–1984.
Acronym: SMCP.
Scores: 7 pencil/paper exercises (Personal Orientation Survey, Education Summary, Career Experience Summary, Personal Career Life Summary, Career Strengths and Interests, Next Career Steps, Personal Development Summary) plus a 16PF personality assessment and interpretive report (Personal/Career Development Profile).
Administration: Group or individual.
Price Data, 2005: $25 per self-motivated Career Planning Guide (1984, 88 pages); testing materials and report purchased separately.
Time: (50–120) minutes per exercise.
Authors: Verne Walter and Melvin Wallace.
Publisher: Institute for Personality and Ability Testing, Inc. (IPAT).
Cross References: For reviews by Larry Cochran and Samuel Juni, see 11:355; for reviews by Robert H. Dolliver and Kevin W. Mossholder of an earlier edition, see 9:1099.

[2296]
Self Observation Scales.

Purpose: Designed as a measure of self-concept.
Population: Grades K–3, 4–6, 7–9, 10–12.
Publication Dates: 1974–1979.
Acronym: SOS.

Administration: Group.
Forms: 1 or 2 for each of 4 levels.
Price Data: Available from publisher.
Time: (20–30) minutes.
Comments: Publisher recommends use of local norms; self-report; interactive computer version of the SOS available.
Authors: A. Jackson Stenner and William G. Katzenmeyer.
Publisher: NTS Research Corporation [No reply from publisher; status unknown].
   a) PRIMARY LEVEL.
   Population: Grades K–3.
   Scores: 4 scales: Self Acceptance, Self Security, Social Maturity, School Affiliation.
   Forms, 2: A, C.
   Comments: Orally administered.
   b) INTERMEDIATE LEVEL.
   Population: Grades 4–6.
   Scores: 7 scales: Same as *a* above plus Social Confidence, Teacher Affiliation, Peer Affiliation.
   Forms, 2: A, C.
   c) JUNIOR HIGH LEVEL.
   Population: Grades 7–9.
   Scores: 7 scales: Same as *a* above except include Self Assertion in place of Social Maturity.
   d) SENIOR HIGH LEVEL.
   Population: Grades 10–12.
   Scores: 7 scales: Same as *c* above.
Cross References: See T4:2418 (2 references); see 9:1100 (3 references).

[2297]
Self-Perception Profile for College Students.

Purpose: To measure college students' self-concept.
Population: College students.
Publication Date: 1986.
Scores: 13 domains: Creativity, Intellectual Ability, Scholastic Competence, Job Competence, Athletic Competence, Appearance, Romantic Relationships, Social Acceptance, Close Friendships, Parent Relationships, Finding Humor in One's Life, Morality, Global Self-Worth.
Administration: Group.
Price Data: Available from publisher.
Time: 30(40) minutes.
Authors: Jennifer Neemann and Susan Harter.
Publisher: Susan Harter, University of Denver.
Cross References: See T5:2369 (12 references); for reviews by Robert D. Brown and Stephen F. Davis, see 11:357 (1 reference).

[2298]
Self-Perceptions Inventory [2006 Revision].

Purpose: To describe "the present affective dimensions of children and adults primarily in regard to themselves and in their relationships with others."

Population: Grades 1–12, adults, student teachers, instructors, nurses, nursing students, administrators and coordinators.
Publication Dates: 1965–2006.
Acronym: SPI.
Administration: Group.
Price Data, 2006: $30 per 25 forms; $30 per separate test manual (specify for Student Forms, Adult Forms, Teacher Forms, Nursing Forms, or Educational Leadership Forms [2006]); $60 per composite manual (2006).
Time: (5–20) minutes per test.
Authors: Louise M. Soares and Anthony T. Soares.
Publisher: Castle Consultants.

a) STUDENT FORMS.
Population: Grades 1–12.
Scores: 11 scales: Self Concept, Ideal Concept, Reflected Self/Classmates, Reflected Self/Friends, Reflected Self/Teachers, Reflected Self/Parents or Guardians, Reflected Self/Others, Perceptions of Others/Males, Perceptions of Others/Females, Student Self, Perceptions of Others/Students, Reflected Self of Mothers Alone or Fathers Alone.

b) ADULT FORMS.
Population: Grades 9–12 and adults.
Scores: 11 scales: Self Concept, Ideal Concept, Reflected Self/Friends, Reflected Self/Teachers/Professors, Reflected Self/Parents, Reflected Self/Partners, Reflected Self/Others, Perceptions of Others, Student Self, Perceptions of Others/Students, Reflected Self of Mothers Alone or Fathers Alone.

c) TEACHER FORMS.
Population: Student teachers and other instructors.
Scores: 8 scales: Self as a Teacher, Ideal as a Teacher, Self as a College Professor, Self as a Student Teacher, Self as an Intern, Reflected Self of Administrators/Classroom Aides/Colleagues/Community/Department Heads/Parents/Students/Supervisors, Perceptions of Others/Teachers.

d) NURSING FORMS.
Population: Nurses and nursing students.
Scores: 6 scales: Self Concept, Self as a Nurse, Ideal as a Nurse, Reflected Self by Administrators/Colleagues/Instructors/Nurses' Aides/Patients/Physicians' Assistants/Students/Supervisors, Perceptions of Others/Nurses.

e) EDUCATIONAL LEADERSHIP.
Population: Administrators and coordinators.
Scores: 9 scales: Self Concept, Self as an Educational Leader, Ideal Educational Leader, Self as an Educational Manager, Reflected Self/Leader, Reflected Self/Manager, Perceptions of Others/Leaders, Perceptions of Others/Managers [Community/Parents/Peers/School Board/Students/Supervisors/Teachers], Ideal Educational Manager.

Cross References: For reviews by Mary M. Clare and Aimin Wang of the 1999 Revision, see 15:226; see T4:2421 (1 reference); for a review by Janet Morgan Riggs of an earlier edition, see 9:1101; for a review by Lorrie Shepard of an earlier edition, see 8:673 (2 references). For reviews by Gerald E. DeMauro and Michael R. Harwell of an earlier edition of the Nursing forms, see 11:356.

[2299]
Self Worth Inventory.
Purpose: "Helps respondents increase their understanding of self-worth and how it is developed."
Population: Adults and teenagers.
Publication Dates: 1990-2006.
Acronym: SWI.
Scores, 8: Self, Family, Peers, Work, Projected Self, Self-Concept, Self-Esteem, Self-Worth.
Administration: Individual and group.
Price Data, 2006: $13.95 per inventory (1990, 8 pages); $13.95 per access code online version; $38 per SWI Trainer's Guidelines (1996, 24 pages).
Time: 60 minutes (short program); 120-180 minutes (longer program).
Comments: May be self-administered.
Author: Everett Robinson.
Publisher: Consulting Resource Group International, Inc.
Cross References: For reviews by Jayne E. Stake and Norman D. Sundberg, see 13:282.

[2300]
The Senior Apperception Technique [1985 Revision].
Purpose: A projective instrument to gather information on forms of depression, loneliness, or rage in the elderly.
Population: Ages 65 and over.
Publication Dates: 1973–1985.
Acronym: S.A.T.
Scores: No scores.
Administration: Individual.
Price Data, 2001: $22 per manual (1985, 12 pages) and set of picture cards.
Time: Administration time not reported.
Author: Leopold Bellak.
Publisher: C.P.S., Inc.
Cross References: For reviews by Paul A. Arbisi and Michael G. Kavan, see 13:283; see also T3:2148 (2 references); for a review by K. Warner Schaie of an earlier edition, see 8:676 (1 reference).

[2301]
Senior Aptitude Tests.
Purpose: Constructed "to measure a number of aptitudes of pupils . . . for the purpose of guidance and selection."

Population: Standards 8–10 in South African schools, college, and adults.
Publication Dates: 1969–1970.
Acronym: SAT.
Scores, 12: Verbal Comprehension, Numerical Fluency, Word Fluency, Visual Perception Speed, Reasoning (Deductive, Inductive), Spatial Visualization (2 Dimensional, 3 Dimensional), Memory (Paragraphs, Symbols), Psychomotor Coordination, Writing Speed.
Administration: Group.
Price Data: Available from publisher.
Time: 88(120) minutes.
Comments: Test materials in English and Afrikaans.
Authors: F. A. Fouche and N. F. Alberts.
Publisher: Human Sciences Research Council [South Africa].
Cross References: See T5:2373 (1 reference) and T4:2430 (1 reference).

[2302]
Senior South African Individual Scale—Revised.

Purpose: Measures general intelligence.
Population: Ages 7-0 to 16-11.
Publication Dates: 1964–1991.
Acronym: SSAIS-R.
Scores: 11 tests: Verbal (Vocabulary, Comprehension, Similarities, Number Problems, Story Memory, Memory for Digits), Nonverbal (Pattern Completion, Block Designs, Missing Parts, Form Board, Coding).
Administration: Individual.
Price Data: Available from publisher.
Time: Tests 1–9: (75) minutes; Tests 10–11: (10) minutes; Tests 3, 4, 7, and 8 (Abbreviated Scale): (45) minutes.
Comments: Developed for Afrikaans-speaking and English-speaking South African students.
Author: Human Sciences Research Council.
Publisher: Human Sciences Research Council [South Africa].
Cross References: See T3:2153 (1 reference) and 7:413 (1 reference).

[2303]
Sensory Evaluation Kit.

Purpose: "Designed to increase functional performance through the primary use of smell."
Population: Ages 2 to adult.
Publication Date: 1991.
Scores, 20: Motor, Tactile, Visual, Auditory, Olfactory, Gustatory, Problem Solving, Attention Span, Directions (2-Step, No Cuing), Interpretation of Signs/Symbols, Memory, Body Scheme (Body Parts, R/L

Discrimination), Motor Planning, Stereognosis, Figure/Ground, Color Perception, Form Constancy, Position in Space.
Administration: Individual.
Price Data: Available from publisher.
Time: Administration time not reported.
Author: Bonnye S. Klein.
Publisher: Maddak Inc.
Cross References: For reviews by J. Jeffrey Grill and Ellen Weissinger, see 13:284.

[2304]
Sensory Integration and Praxis Tests.

Purpose: Designed to assess several practic abilities, various aspects of sensory processing status, and behavioral manifestations of deficits in integration of sensory inputs from these systems.
Population: Ages 4–8.11.
Publication Date: 1989.
Acronym: SIPT.
Scores: 17 tests: Space Visualization, Figure-Ground Perception, Standing and Walking Balance, Design Copying, Postural Praxis, Bilateral Motor Coordination, Praxis Verbal Command, Constructional Praxis, Postrotary Nystagmus, Motor Accuracy, Sequencing Praxis, Oral Praxis, Manual Form Perception, Kinesthesia, Finger Identification, Graphesthesia, Localization of Tactile Stimuli.
Administration: Individual.
Price Data, 2002: $1,15 per set for mail-in scoring including all test materials, 25 copies of each consumable test form, 10 complete sets of all 17 computer-scored answer sheets with 10 transmittal sheets, manual (307 pages), and carrying case; $1,150 per set for PC scoring including all test materials, 25 copies of each consumable test form, 1 disk, 10 PC answer booklets, manual, and carrying case; $29.50 per one each of 17 test answer sheets and 1 transmittal sheet; $14.50 per transmittal sheet; $3.90 per individual test answer sheet; $255 per 10-use disk (PC with Microsoft Windows) with 10 PC answer booklets; $18.50 per 25 test booklets (specify Design Copying, Motor Accuracy, or Kinesthesia); $70 per manual; $132.50 per training administration video (VHS); $179.50 per training administration 2 CD-ROM set.
Time: (10) minutes or less per individual test.
Comments: Extension and revision of the Southern California Sensory Integration Tests (SCSIT) and the Southern California Postrotary Nystagmus Test (SCPNT); computer-scoring only; stopwatch capable of recording 1/10 seconds needed (available from publisher).
Author: A. Jean Ayres.
Publisher: Western Psychological Services.
Cross References: See T5:2377 (4 references); for a review by James E. Ysseldyke, see 12:353 (18 refer-

ences); see also T4:2433 (9 references). For a review by
Byron P. Rourke of the SCPNT, see 9:1157 (20 references); for information on the SCSIT, see 9:1158 (5
references) and T3:2244 (21 references); for reviews by
Homer B. C. Reed, Jr. and Alida S. Westman of the
SCSIT, see 8:875 (5 references); see also T2:1887 (18
references).

[2305]
Sensory Integration Inventory—Revised for Individuals with Developmental Disabilities.
Purpose: "Designed to screen for [occupational
therapy] clients who might benefit from a sensory
integration treatment approach."
Population: Developmentally disabled occupational
therapy clients school aged to adults, including autism
spectrum and PDD.
Publication Dates: 1990–1992.
Acronym: SI Inventory.
Scores: Item scores in each of 4 sections interpreted
individually: Tactile, Vestibular, Proprioception, Gen-
eral Reactions.
Administration: Individual.
Price Data: Available from publisher.
Time: Administration time not reported.
Comments: A semistructured interview of a person
who works/lives closely with the client (e.g., parent or
therapeutic staff member); space also provided for quali-
tative comments.
Authors: Judith E. Reisman and Bonnie Hanschu.
Publisher: P.D.P. Press, Inc.
Cross References: For a review by William Verdi,
see 14:346.

[2306]
Sensory Profile.
Purpose: "To measure a child's sensory processing
abilities."
Publication Dates: 1999–2002.
Administration: Individual or group.
Levels, 2: Infant/Toddler Sensory Profile—Clinical
Edition, Sensory Profile.
Price Data, 2002: $150 per software kit including
user's manual (1999, 146 pages), e-record forms, and 1-
year subscription; $105 per software stand-alone in-
cluding 1-year subscription for e-record forms; $65 per
manual; $45 per e-record forms including subscription
renewal for 1-year.
Foreign Language Edition: Available in Spanish.
Comments: Profiles completed by child's caregiver;
can be administered and scored electronically using
personal computer or PDA (Windows and Palm OS),
contact publisher for details.
Publisher: PsychCorp, A brand of Harcourt Assessment, Inc.

a) INFANT/TODDLER SENSORY PROFILE—
CLINICAL EDITION.
Population: Birth to 36 months.
Publication Date: 2002.
Scores, 6: General Processing, Auditory Pro-
cessing, Visual Processing, Tactile Processing, Ves-
tibular Processing, Oral Sensory Processing.
Price Data: $119 per Infant/Toddler Sensory
Profile complete kit including user's manual (2002,
21 pages), 25 English caregiver questionnaires,
and 25 summary score sheets; $75 per user's manual;
$31.50 per 25 caregiver questionnaires (English or
Spanish); $16.50 per 25 summary score sheets.
Time: 15(25) minutes.
Comments: Ages birth to 6 months: 5 scores
(General Processing, Auditory Processing, Visual
Processing, Tactile Processing, Vestibular Pro-
cessing).
Author: Winnie Dunn.
b) SENSORY PROFILE.
Population: Ages 3–10.
Forms, 2: Sensory Profile, Short Sensory Pro-
file.
Scores, 23: 6 Sensory Processing categories
(Auditory Processing, Visual Processing, Vestibu-
lar Processing, Touch Processing, Multisensory
Processing, Oral Sensory Processing); 5 Modulation categories (Sensory Processing Related to En-
durance/Tone, Modulation Related to Body Position and Movement, Modulation of Movement
Affecting Activity Level, Modulation of Sensory
Input Affecting Emotional Responses, Modulation of Visual Input Affecting Emotional Responses and Activity Level); 3 Behavioral and Emotional Responses categories (Emotional/Social
Responses, Behavioral Outcomes of Sensory Processing, Items Indicating Thresholds for Response);
9 Factor Scores (Sensory Seeking, Emotionally Reactive, Low Endurance/Tone, Oral Sensitivity, Inat-
tention/Distractibility, Poor Registration, Sensory
Sensitivity, Sedentary, Fine Motor/Perceptual).
Price Data: $119 per Sensory Profile complete
kit including user's manual, and 25 each of each of
caregiver questionnaires, short sensory profiles,
and summary score sheets; $65 per user's manual;
$32 per 25 caregiver questionnaires (English or
Spanish); $15 per 25 short sensory profiles (En-
glish or Spanish); $19 per 25 summary score sheets
(English or Spanish).
Time: (15–30) minutes.
Comments: 125-question profile.
Author: Winnie Dunn.
c) SHORT SENSORY PROFILE.
Purpose: "To help service providers in screening
settings quickly identify children with sensory processing difficulties."

Population: Ages 5–10.
Acronym: SSP.
Scores, 8: Tactile Sensitivity, Taste/Smell Sensitivity, Movement Sensitivity, Underresponsive/ Seeks Sensation, Auditory Filtering, Low Energy/ Weak, Visual/Auditory Sensitivity, Total.
Time: (10) minutes.
Authors: Daniel N. McIntosh, Lucy Jane Miller, Vivian Shyu, and Winnie Dunn.
Cross References: For reviews by Doreen W. Fairbank and John J. Vacca, see 16:220.

[2307]
Sentence Completion Series.

Purpose: Designed to "identify underlying concerns and specific areas of distress."
Population: Adolescents and adults.
Publication Dates: 1991–1992.
Acronym: SCS.
Scores: No scores.
Administration: Individual or group.
Forms, 8: Adult, Adolescent, Family, Marriage, Parenting, Work, Illness, Aging.
Price Data, 2006: $108 per introductory kit including manual and 15 of each of 8 forms.
Time: [10–45] minutes.
Comments: Forms may be administered alone or in any combination; clinicians evaluates responses.
Authors: Larry H. Brown and Michael A. Unger.
Publisher: Psychological Assessment Resources, Inc.
Cross References: For reviews by Kevin L. Moreland and Paul D. Werner, see 14:347.

[2308]
Sentence Completion Tests.

Purpose: "These tests provide a projective technique for individuals to express in their own way their own unique feelings, behaviors, attitudes, assets, needs, problems, thoughts, opinions of self, relationships, likes, dislikes, moods, frustrations, inhibitions, fantasies, backgrounds, responses from others, desires, mistakes, habits, secrets, idiosyncrasies, dreams, attitudes toward the test, etc."
Publication Dates: 1989-1995.
Administration: Group.
Price Data, 2001: $10 per 20 tests; $95 for 2 copies of all tests and Lifetime License to copy for personal or institutional use.
Time: Administration time not reported.
Comments: Master List includes sentence completion stems and alternatives used in the development of all the tests.
Author: Allan Roe.
Publisher: Diagnostic Specialists, Inc.
a) GENERAL INCOMPLETE SENTENCES TEST.
Population: General including college, clinical, hospitalized, and private practice adults.

Acronym: GIST.
Foreign Language Edition: Spanish GIST is available.
b) SHORT INCOMPLETE SENTENCES.
Population: Adult and adolescent clients.
Acronym: SIS.
c) FULL INCOMPLETE SENTENCES TEST.
Purpose: To be used for courts, custody, and diagnostic decisions.
Acronym: FIST.
d) FULL I AM TEST.
Purpose: "Helpful for eliciting identity problems."
Acronym: FIAT.
e) KIDS INCOMPLETE SENTENCES TEST.
Population: Ages 5-12.
Acronym: KIST.
f) TEENAGE SENTENCE COMPLETION.
Population: Ages 13-19.
Acronym: TASC.
g) MARRIAGE INCOMPLETE SENTENCES TEST.
Population: Married couples.
Acronym: MIST.
h) RELATIONSHIP INCOMPLETE SENTENCES TEST.
Population: Any relationship.
Acronym: RIST.
i) FULL LENGTH ALCOHOL SENTENCE COMPLETION.
Population: Alcohol users.
Acronym: FLASC.
j) DRUG INQUIRY SENTENCE COMPLETION.
Population: Drug users.
Acronym: DISC.
k) TALKING HONESTLY AND OPENLY ABOUT OUR RELATIONSHIP.
Population: Sex offenders.
Acronym: THOR.
l) SEXUAL ABUSE SURVIVOR'S TEST.
Population: Sex abuse victim.
Acronym: SAST.

[2309]
Sequenced Inventory of Communication Development, Revised Edition.

Purpose: Designed as a diagnostic assessment to evaluate the communication abilities of normal and retarded children.
Population: Ages 4 months through 4 years.
Publication Dates: 1975–1984.
Acronym: SICD-R.
Administration: Individual.
Price Data, 2006: $435 per complete kit (includes all test materials in a sturdy carrying case, 50 record/ booklet/profiles, 1 instruction manual, and 1 test

manual); $54.95 per 25 record booklet/profile forms; $36 per instruction manual; $36 per test manual.

Foreign Language Editions: Cuban-Spanish edition available; Spanish translation included in test manual and separate Spanish-language forms with pictures are available.

Time: (30–75) minutes.

Comments: Some test accessories (e.g., paper, coins, and picture book) must be assembled locally.

Authors: Dona Lea Hedrick, Elizabeth M. Prather, and Annette R. Tobin, with contributions by Doris V. Allen, Lynn S. Bliss, and Lillian R. Rosenberg.

Publisher: Western Psychological Services.

a) RECEPTIVE SCALE.

Scores, 3: Awareness, Discrimination, Understanding.

b) EXPRESSIVE SCALE.

Scores, 4: Imitating, Initiating, Responding, Verbal Output.

Cross References: See T5:2382 (40 references) and T4:2438 (21 references); for reviews by Carol Mardell-Czudnowski and Mary Ellen Pearson, see 10:331 (6 references); for reviews by Barbara W. Hodson and Joan I. Lynch of the earlier edition, see 9:1109 (4 references); see also T3:2159 (4 references).

[2310]
Service Ability Inventory.

Purpose: Designed "to select job applicants who have a service orientation … to determine the service skill levels of current employees."

Population: Current and prospective employees.

Publication Dates: 1999–2004.

Acronym: SAI.

Scores, 7: Service Orientation, Interpersonal Skills, Tolerance for Stress, Team Skills, Patience, Coping Skills, Deception Scale.

Administration: Individual or group.

Price Data: $79.99 per starter kit including 5 tests, administrator's manual (2004, 32 pages), and 1 test log.

Time: (20–25) minutes.

Comments: Online and paper-and-pencil versions of test are available; online version includes interpretive reports and follow-up interview questions.

Author: J. M. Llobet.

Publisher: G. Neil.

[2311]
Service Animal Adaptive Intervention Assessment.

Purpose: Constructed for "evaluating predispositions to and outcomes of service animal use."

Population: Occupational, physical, and recreational therapists, assistive technology professionals, and animal assisted therapy specialists.

Publication Date: 1998.

Acronym: SAAIA.

Scores, 5: Knowledge and Experience of Animals, Typical Activities/Skills, Personal/Social Characteristics, Requirements of Service Animal Compared to Resources of Person, Total Predisposition Score.

Administration: Group or individual.

Price Data, 2001: $29.95 per complete kit including all assessments as masters for photocopying and manual (10 pages).

Time: (90–120) minutes.

Comments: Ratings by professionals; also includes qualitative information.

Author: Susan A. Zapf.

Publisher: The Instute for Matching Person & Technology, Inc.

Cross References: For reviews by Ronald A. Berk and Judith A. Rein, see 15:227.

[2312]
ServiceFirst.

Purpose: Constructed to measure "customer service orientation or potential."

Population: Employees in service-oriented positions.

Publication Dates: 1990–2001.

Scores, 5: Active Customer Relations, Polite Customer Relations, Helpful Customer Relations, Personalized Customer Relations, Total.

Administration: Group.

Price Data, 2006: $30 per test kit including sample test booklet, sample answer sheet, test manual (2001, 47 pages), administration and scoring manual, and demonstration administration and scoring manual; $10 per administrator's manual; $10 per reusable test booklet; scoring service $11.50 to $15 per applicant.

Time: (20) minutes.

Comments: Internet-based administration and scoring is available at www.peoplefocus.com; paper-and-pencil and PC administration also available with scoring via telephone or fax by publisher, or onsite with a computer disk.

Author: Larry Fogli.

Publisher: People Focus.

Cross References: For reviews by Michael B. Bunch and Mary A. Lewis, see 14:348.

[2313]
701 and 702 Fire Supervisor Tests (Lieutenant).

Purpose: Designed to measure knowledge in the firefighting field as promotional tests for fire department first-line supervisors.

Population: Candidates for promotion to the fire supervisor or lieutenant position.

Publication Date: 2001-2006.

Scores: 9 knowledge areas: Fire Behavior and Fire Service, Firefighting Tactics and Procedures, Rescue

and Safety, Firefighting Equipment and Apparatus, Building Construction, Supervisory Practices, Fire Prevention and Fire Safety, Hazardous Materials, Emergency Medical Care (Test 701 only).
Administration: Individual or group.
Forms, 2: 701, 702.
Price Data: Available from publisher.
Time: 120 minutes per test.
Comments: Reading lists are available to help candidates prepare for the tests.
Authors: International Public Management Association for Human Resources & Bruce Davey Associates.
Publisher: International Public Management Association for Human Resources (IPMA-HR).

[2314]
Severe Cognitive Impairment Profile.
Purpose: Designed to "measure and track impairment of cognitive abilities in adults with primary progressive dementia."
Population: Ages 42–90 and older.
Publication Dates: 1995–1998.
Acronym: SCIP.
Scores, 9: Comportment, Attention, Language, Memory, Motor, Conceptualization, Arithmetic, Visuospatial, Total.
Administration: Individual.
Price Data, 2005: $399 per introductory kit including professional manual (1998, 67 pages), 25 record forms, and manipulative materials to administer subtests, all packaged in sturdy briefcase.
Time: (30–45) minutes.
Author: Guerry M. Peavy.
Publisher: Psychological Assessment Resources, Inc.
Cross References: For reviews by Joan C. Ballard and Lawrence J. Ryan, see 14:349.

[2315]
The Severe Impairment Battery.
Purpose: Designed "to assess severe dementia in the elderly."
Population: Ages 51-91.
Publication Date: 1993.
Acronym: SIB.
Scores, 7: Attention, Orientation, Language, Memory, Visual-Spatial Ability, Construction, Total.
Administration: Individual.
Price Data, 2006: £200 per complete kit including manual (16 pages), 25 scoring sheets, stimulus cards, plastic shapes, spoon, cup, and full distractor pack in bag; £107.50 per 50 score sheets.
Time: 20 minutes.
Comments: Test takes into account specific behavioral and cognitive deficits associated with severe dementia; provides an assessment of social interaction skills abstracted from the Communication Activities of Daily Living (635).

Authors: J. Saxton, K. L. McGonigle, A. A. Swihart, and F. Boller.
Publisher: Harcourt Assessment [England].

[2316]
The Severity and Acuity of Psychiatric Illness Scales—Adult Version.
Purpose: Designed to assess the severity and acuity of psychiatric illness in adult mental health service recipients.
Population: Adults.
Publication Date: 1998.
Scores, 6: Severity (Complexity Indicator, Probability of Admission, Total), Acuity (Clinical Status, Nursing Status, Total).
Administration: Individual.
Price Data, 2002: $75 per starter kit including training manual (52 pages), 10 reusable Severity item booklets, 25 Severity scale rating sheets, 10 reusable Acuity item booklets, and 25 Acuity scale rating sheets; $18 per 10 Severity scale item booklets; $15 per 25 Severity scale rating sheets; $18 per 10 Acuity scale item booklets; $15 per 25 Acuity scale rating sheets; $120 per training manual.
Time: (5) minutes.
Comments: Computer versions available; two scales (Severity and Acuity) can be used separately or together; results to be used as an "integrated outcomes-management and decision-support system for assisting treatment decision-making"; ratings are done by caregivers about clients/patients.
Author: John S. Lyons.
Publisher: PsychCorp, A brand of Harcourt Assessment, Inc.
Cross References: For reviews by Mark J. Atkinson and Roger A. Boothroyd, see 14:350.

[2317]
Sex-Role Egalitarianism Scale.
Purpose: "Developed to measure attitudes toward the equality of men and women."
Population: High school to adult.
Publication Date: 1993.
Acronym: SRES.
Scores, 6: Marital Roles, Parental Roles, Employment Roles, Social-Interpersonal-Heterosexual Roles, Educational Roles, Total.
Administration: Group or individual.
Price Data, 2006: $50 per examination kit including manual (1993, 58 pages), 5 Form B question-and-answer documents, and 5 profile sheets; $32 per test manual; $50 per 25 Form B question-and-answer documents; $35 per 25 Form K Research Forms; $40 per 25 profile sheets; $40 per 25 Short Form BB or KK question-and-answer sheets; $45 per researcher's kit including manual, one Form K question-and-answer

document, and one each of Form BB and KK Short Forms.
Time: 25 minutes.
Comments: Two full forms, B and K; two abbreviated forms, BB and KK.
Authors: Lynda A. King and Daniel W. King.
Publisher: Sigma Assessment Systems, Inc.
Cross References: See T5:2389 (1 reference); for a review by Carol Collins, see 13:285.

[2318]
Sexometer.
Purpose: Designed to measure one's sex information.
Population: Adolescents and adults.
Publication Dates: 1974–1988.
Scores: Total score only.
Administration: Group.
Manual: No manual.
Price Data, 2005: $2 per scale.
Time: [20] minutes.
Comments: Supplementary article available.
Author: Panos D. Bardis.
Publisher: Donna Bardis.
Cross References: See 8:353 (1 reference).

[2319]
Sexual Adaptation and Functioning Test.
Purpose: Designed "as an aid in the planning of psychotherapeutic intervention techniques and to gain insight into an individual's sexual adaptation and sexual functioning."
Population: White adults ages 16 and over.
Publication Dates: 1985–1986.
Acronym: SAFT.
Scores: Total score only.
Administration: Individual.
Restricted Distribution: Distribution restricted to psychologists registered with the South African Medical and Dental Council.
Price Data: Available from publisher.
Foreign Language Edition: Afrikaans edition available.
Time: (90–100) minutes.
Comments: Projective test; self-administered using audiotaped instructions.
Author: Louise Olivier.
Publisher: Human Sciences Research Council [South Africa].

[2320]
Sexual Adjustment Inventory.
Purpose: "Designed to identify sexually deviate and paraphiliac behavior."
Population: People accused or convicted of sexual offenses.
Publication Date: 1991.
Acronym: SAI.

Scores: 13 scales: Test Item Truthfulness, Sex Item Truthfulness, Sexual Adjustment, Child Molest, Sexual Assault, Exhibitionism, Incest, Alcohol, Drugs, Violence, Antisocial, Distress, Judgment.
Administration: Group.
Forms, 2: Adult, Juvenile.
Price Data: Available from publisher.
Time: (35–40) minutes.
Comments: Both computer version and paper-pencil format are scored using IBM-PC compatibles.
Author: Risk & Needs Assessment, Inc.
Publisher: Risk & Needs Assessment, Inc.
Cross References: For reviews by Richard F. Farmer and Sheila Mehta, see 14:351.

[2321]
Sexual Communication Inventory.
Purpose: Designed to help couples develop their skills for communicating about sexual matters in their relationship.
Population: Premarital and marital counselees.
Publication Date: 1980.
Acronym: SCI.
Scores: Overall score.
Administration: Group.
Price Data, 1993: $.75 per inventory; $2 per manual (6 pages).
Time: (20) minutes
Author: Millard J. Bienvenu.
Publisher: Millard J. Bienvenu, Northwest Publications.
Cross References: For a review by Richard B. Stuart, see 9:1118.

[2322]
Sexual Violence Risk-20.
Purpose: Designed as a "method" (not a test or scale) of assessing an individual's risk for committing sexual violence.
Population: Individuals suspected to be at-risk for committing sexual violence.
Publication Dates: 1997–1998.
Acronym: SVR-20.
Scores: Not scored; ratings in five areas: Psychosocial Adjustment, Sexual Offenses, Future Plans, Other Considerations, Summary Risk Rating.
Administration: Individual.
Price Data: Available from publisher.
Time: Administration time not reported.
Comments: "Designed to assist evaluations of risk for sexual violence"; administration and coding by trained professionals only; rating done by the professional about a client/offender.
Authors: Douglas P. Boer, Stephen D. Hart, P. Randall Kropp, and Christopher D. Webster.

Publisher: British Columbia Institute Against Family Violence [Canada].

Cross References: For reviews by Rita M. Budrionis and Paul Retzlaff, see 15:228.

[2323]
Sexuality Experience Scales.

Purpose: To be used in sex counseling as an aid in interviewing, diagnosis of sexual dysfunction, and evaluation of therapy, as well as in research.

Population: Adults.

Publication Date: 1981.

Acronym: SES.

Scores: 4 scales: Sexual Morality, Psychosexual Stimulation, Sexual Motivation, Attraction to Marriage.

Administration: Group.

Editions, 2: Female, Male.

Price Data: Available from publisher.

Time: Administration time not reported.

Authors: J. Frenken and P. Vennix.

Publisher: Harcourt Assessment [England].

Cross References: See T5:2396 (1 reference) and T4:2449 (2 references).

[2324]
SF-36 Health Survey.

Purpose: Designed as a "survey of general health concepts."

Population: Ages 14 and older.

Publication Dates: 1989–2005.

Acronym: SF-36.

Scores: 8 scales: Physical Functioning, Role-Physical, Bodily Pain, General Health, Vitality, Social Functioning, Role-Emotional, Mental Health, plus 2 summary component scores.

Administration: Group.

Price Data: Available from publisher; administration and scoring software available from various vendors authorized by the publisher.

Foreign Language Editions: Translated into 60+ languages.

Time: Administration time not reported.

Comments: Permissions to use the SF-36 are granted through a combined licensing program of Medical Outcomes Trust, QualityMetric Incorporated, and Health Assessment Lab. The program itself is administered by QualityMetric, on behalf of the three organizations. Additional information is available at www.qualitymetric.com and www.sf-36.org.

Author: John E. Ware, Jr.

Publisher: Medical Outcomes Trust.

Cross References: For reviews by Ashraf Kagee and Nathaniel J. Pallone, see 14:352; see also T5:2397 (1 reference).

[2325]
Shapes Analysis Test.

Purpose: Designed as a test of spatial perception.

Population: Ages 14 and over.

Publication Date: 1972.

Acronym: SAT.

Scores, 3: 2-Dimensional, 3-Dimensional, Total.

Administration: Group.

Price Data, 2001: £21 per 19 booklets; £35 per 50 answer sheets; £10 per manual (20 pages); £15 per specimen set.

Time: 25(35) minutes.

Authors: A. W. Heim, K. P. Watts, and V. Simmonds.

Publisher: The Test Agency Limited [England] [No reply from publisher; status unknown].

Cross References: For a review by Charles T. Myers, see 8:1046 (2 references).

[2326]
Shapiro Control Inventory.

Purpose: Designed to "categorize, refine, and articulate a person's state of consciousness regarding control."

Population: Ages 14–88.

Publication Date: 1994.

Acronym: SCI.

Scores, 9: General Domain (Overall Sense of Control, Positive Sense of Control, Negative Sense of Control), Modes of Control (Positive Assertive, Positive Yielding, Negative Assertive, Negative Yielding), Domain-Specific Sense of Control, Overall Desire for Control.

Administration: Group or individual.

Price Data: Available from publisher.

Foreign Language Editions: Spanish, Japanese, and Polish editions under development.

Time: (20–30) minutes.

Author: Deane H. Shapiro, Jr.

Publisher: Behaviordata, Inc.

Cross References: See T5:2399 (1 reference); for reviews by Wesley E. Sime and Claudia R. Wright, see 13:286.

[2327]
Ship Destination Test.

Purpose: Constructed to measure "general reasoning."

Population: Grades 9 and over.

Publication Dates: 1955–1956.

Scores: Total score only.

Administration: Group.

Price Data: Available from publisher.

Time: 15(20) minutes.

Authors: Paul R. Christensen and J. P. Guilford.

Publisher: Charlotte Mackley [No reply from publisher; status unknown].

Cross References: See T5:2401 (1 reference) and T2:457 (13 references); for a review by William B. Schrader, see 6:500 (8 references); for a review by C. J. Adcock, see 5:383.

[2328]
Shipley Institute of Living Scale.

Purpose: "Designed to assess general intellectual functioning in adults and adolescents and to aid in detecting cognitive impairment in individuals with normal original intelligence."
Population: Ages 14 and over.
Publication Dates: 1939–1986.
Acronym: SILS.
Scores, 6: Vocabulary, Abstraction, Combined Total, Conceptual Quotient, Abstraction Quotient, Estimated WAIS or WAIS-R IQ.
Administration: Group.
Price Data, 2006: $126.50 per complete kit including 100 test forms, hand-scoring key, 2 AutoScore™ test forms, and manual (1986, 100 pages); $21.95 per hand-scoring key; $53 per 100 test forms; $48 per 25 AutoScore™ test forms; $52.50 per manual; $286 per 25-use IBM Shipley microcomputer disk (PC with DOS).
Time: 20 minutes.
Comments: Formerly called Shipley-Hartford Retreat Scale for Measuring Intellectual Impairment and Shipley-Institute of Living Scale for Measuring Intellectual Impairment.
Authors: Walter C. Shipley (test and original manual) and Robert A. Zachary (revised manual).
Publisher: Western Psychological Services.
Cross References: See T5:2402 (71 references) and T4:2453 (63 references); for a review by William L. Deaton, see 11:360 (56 references); see also 9:1122 (13 references), T3:2179 (64 references), 8:677 (39 references), and T2:1380 (34 references); for a review by Aubrey J. Yates, see 7:138 (21 references); see also P:244 (38 references), 6:173 (13 references), and 5:111 (23 references); for reviews by E. J. G. Bradford, William A. Hunt, and Margaret Ives, see 3:95 (25 references).

[2329]
Shoplifting Inventory.

Purpose: "Designed to evaluate people charged or convicted of shoplifting."
Population: Shoplifting offenders.
Publication Date: 1995.
Acronym: SI.
Scores: 9 scales: Truthfulness, Entitlement, Shoplifting, Antisocial, Peer Pressure, Self-Esteem, Impulsiveness, Alcohol, Drugs.
Administration: Group.
Price Data: Available from publisher.
Time: (35) minutes.
Comments: Both computer version and paper-pencil format are scored on IBM-PC compatibles.

Author: Risk & Needs Assessment, Inc.
Publisher: Risk & Needs Assessment, Inc.
Cross References: For reviews by G. Gage Kingsbury and Kwong-Liem Karl Kwan, see 14:353.

[2330]
Shorr Imagery Test.

Purpose: "Designed to elicit and score the degree of conflict in the visual images projected by the subject."
Population: College students and adults.
Publication Dates: 1974–1977.
Acronym: SIT.
Scores, 6: Item scores in 5 areas (Human, Animal, Inanimate, Botanical, Others) plus Total score for Conflict.
Administration: Individual.
Price Data: Available from publisher.
Time: (15-40) minutes.
Comments: For information for Group Shorr Imagery Test, see 1130.
Author: Joseph E. Shorr.
Publisher: Institute for Psychoimagination Therapy.

[2331]
Short Category Test, Booklet Format.

Purpose: A sensitive indicator of brain damage measuring an individual's ability to solve problems requiring careful observation, development of organizing principles, and responsiveness to feedback.
Population: Ages 20 and over.
Publication Dates: 1986–1987.
Scores: Total score only.
Subtests, 5: 1, 2, 3, 4, 5.
Administration: Individual.
Price Data, 2006: $192.50 per complete kit including 100 answer sheets, set of stimulus cards, and manual (1987, 40 pages); $126.50 per set of stimulus cards, 5 booklets (1986, 20 cards per booklet); $27.50 per 100 answer sheets; $49.50 per manual.
Time: (15–30) minutes.
Comments: Revision of the Halstead-Reitan Category Test.
Authors: Linda Wetzel and Thomas J. Boll.
Publisher: Western Psychological Services.
Cross References: See T5:2405 (1 reference); for reviews by Scott W. Brown and Hope J. Hartman, see 11:361.

[2332]
Short Employment Tests, Second Edition.

Purpose: "Measures verbal, numerical, and clerical skills."
Population: Adults.
Publication Dates: 1951–1993.
Acronym: SET.
Scores, 4: Verbal, Numerical, Clerical, Total.
Administration: Group or individual.

Forms: 2 forms of each subtest (Verbal, Numerical, Clerical Aptitude).
Price Data, 2006: $249 per starter kit, including 25 each of the Verbal, Numerical, and Clerical Aptitude test booklets, scoring key, and manual; $95 per package of 25 test bookets (specify version and Form 1 or 2); $320 per package of 100 test booklets (specify version and Form 1 or 2); $30 per combination scoring key; $45 per manual.
Time: 5(10) minutes.
Comments: Distribution of Form 1 restricted to banks that are members of the American Banking Association.
Authors: George K. Bennett and Marjorie Gelink.
Publisher: Harcourt Assessment, Inc.
Cross References: For reviews by Caroline Manuele-Adkins and by Bert W. Westbrook and Michael C. Hansen, see 13:287; see also T4:2456 (3 references); for reviews by Samuel Juni and Ronald Baumanis and by Leonard J. West of an earlier edition, see 9:1124 (1 reference); see also T3:2180 (1 reference); for reviews by Ronald N. Taylor and Paul W. Thayer, see 8:1037 (4 references); see also T2:2151 (6 references); for a review by Leonard W. Ferguson, see 6:1045 (9 references); for a review by P. L. Mellenbruch, see 5:854 (16 references).

[2333]
Short Tests of Clerical Ability.

Purpose: Designed to measure aptitudes and abilities in tasks common to various office jobs.
Population: Applicants for office positions.
Publication Dates: 1959–1997.
Acronym: STCA.
Administration: Individual or group.
Price Data, 2002: $73 per start-up kit including 25 test booklets and examiner's manual (specify Arithmetic, Business Vocabulary, Checking, Coding, Directions—Oral and Written, Filing, or Language); $54 per 25 test booklets (specify test; quantity discounts available); price information available from publisher for Quanta Computer Administration and Scoring software (Windows); $73 per Quanta start-up kit including examiner's manual, 25 administrations and scoring, and oral directions sheet (does not include Quanta software)
Author: Science Research Associates.
Publisher: Pearson Performance Solutions [No reply from publisher; status unknown].
a) ARITHMETIC.
Scores, 3: Computation, Business Arithmetic, Total.
Time: 6 minutes.
b) BUSINESS VOCABULARY.
Time: 5 minutes.
c) CHECKING.
Time: 5 minutes.
d) CODING.
Time: 5 minutes.
e) DIRECTIONS—ORAL AND WRITTEN.
Time: 5 minutes.
f) FILING.
Time: 5 minutes.
g) LANGUAGE.
Time: 5 minutes.
Cross References: For reviews by Lorraine D. Eyde and Dean R. Malsbary, see 8:1039 (1 reference); for reviews by Philip H. Kriedt and Paul W. Thayer, see 6:1046.

[2334]
Shortened Edinburgh Reading Test.

Purpose: Designed as a survey measure of children's reading skills in the upper primary school, and as a screening instrument to detect children who might need remedial help in reading.
Population: Ages 10-0 to 11-6.
Publication Date: 1985.
Scores, 5: Vocabulary, Syntax, Comprehension, Retention, General Reading Quotient.
Administration: Group.
Price Data, 2002: £15.99 per 20 test booklets; £16.99 per manual; £15.99 per specimen set.
Time: (40–45) minutes.
Author: The Godfrey Thomson Unit, University of Edinburgh.
Publisher: Hodder & Stoughton [England].
Cross References: For reviews by Douglas K. Smith and Betsy Waterman, see 14:354.

[2335]
Sigma Survey for Police Officers.

Purpose: "Designed to identify job applicants possessing the cognitive skills necessary to use sound practical judgement in police situations, and to write meaningful and credible police incident reports."
Population: Ages 18 and over.
Publication Dates: 2001–2002.
Acronym: SSPO.
Scores, 6: Incident Report Writing (Spelling, Grammar, Vocabulary, Total), Police Problem Solving, Total.
Administration: Individual or group.
Price Data, 2006: $15 per manual; $20 per report; volume discounts available.
Time: 35 minutes.
Comments: Fax-in scoring service available through publisher; available in Canadian format and American format; publisher recommends use of the SSPO in conjunction with the Employee Screening Questionnaire (945).
Author: Douglas N. Jackson.
Publisher: Sigma Assessment Systems, Inc.
Cross References: For reviews by Thomas M. Dunn and Chockalingam Viswesvaran, see 16:221.

[2336]
Sigma Survey for Sales Professionals.

Purpose: Designed to analyze "the strengths and weaknesses of sales and sales manager job candidates on 28 dimensions of expected job performance."

Population: 18 and over.

Publication Dates: 2002–2003.

Acronym: 3SP.

Scores, 28: Technical Orientation, Creativity, Thoroughness, Risk Taking, Open Mindedness, First Impression, Interpersonal Relations, Sensitivity, Social Astuteness, Communication, Formal Presentation, Persuasiveness, Negotiation, Listening Skill, Achievement and Motivation, Self-Discipline, Flexibility, Independence, Self Esteem, Emotional Control, Dependability, Ambition, Organizational Spokesperson, Assuming Responsibility, Vision, Short-Term Planning, Strategic Planning, Productivity.

Administration: Group.

Price Data, 2006: $15 per test manual; $55 per administration; volume discounts available.

Time: 40 minutes.

Comments: Publisher scoring services available via internet or fax-in.

Author: Douglas N. Jackson.

Publisher: Sigma Assessment Systems, Inc.

Cross References: For reviews by Martha E. Hennen and Stephen B. Johnson, see 16:222.

[2337]
Sigma Survey for Security Officers.

Purpose: Designed as a "test for screening job applicants for the position of security officer."

Population: Ages 18 and over.

Publication Dates: 1996–2003.

Acronym: SSSO.

Scores, 5: Security Officer Problem Solving, Incident Report Writing Aptitude (Spelling, Grammar and Punctuation, Total), Overall Score.

Administration: Individual or group.

Parts, 2: Security Problem Solving, Incident Report Writing.

Price Data, 2006: $15 per test manual; $17 per administration; volume discounts available.

Time: 30 minutes.

Comments: Fax-in scoring services available through publisher; recommended by publisher for use in conjunction with the Employee Screening Questionnaire (945).

Author: Douglas N. Jackson.

Publisher: Sigma Assessment Systems, Inc.

Cross References: For reviews by James T. Austin and Erich C. Fein and by David J. Pittenger, see 16:223.

[2338]
Signposts Early Assessment System.

Purpose: Designed to provide an integrated set of measures with an emphasis on literacy development focusing on prereading and reading skills.

Population: Grades K–3.5.

Publication Dates: 2000–2001.

Scores: Total score only.

Subtests: 4 components: Early Literacy Battery, Pre-DRP Tests, Performance Tasks, Informal Assessments.

Administration: Group (individual for some components).

Levels, 5: SA-1 (Grades K–K.5), SA-2 (Grades K.5–1.4), SA-3 (Grades 1.0–1.9), SA-4 (Grades 1.7–2.7), SA-5 (Grades 2.5–3.5).

Price Data, 2006: $50 per examination set including 1 test booklet of each level, administration procedures, handbook (2001, 68 pages), and norms book (2001, 31 pages); $99 per classroom set including 25 test booklets (specify level) including administration procedures, a class record, handbook, and norms book; $72 per 25 test booklets (specify level) including administration procedures and a class record sheet; $10 per scoring key (specify level); $24 per handbook; $20 per norms book.

Time: (110–165) minutes.

Comments: Scoring keys must be purchased separately.

Author: Touchstone Applied Science Associates, Inc.

Publisher: Touchstone Applied Science Associates (TASA), Inc.

Cross References: For reviews by Thomas P. Hogan and Judith A. Monsaas, see 16:224.

[2339]
Singer-Loomis Type Deployment Inventory.

Purpose: Designed to assess "personality factors that may help an individual in self-understanding and in utilizing skills, talents, and abilities, so as to better deal with interactions between oneself and the environment."

Population: High school and college and adults.

Publication Dates: 1984–1997.

Acronym: SL-TDI.

Scores: Profile of 8 scores: Introverted, Extroverted for each of 4 functions (Thinking, Feeling, Sensing, Intuition), plus Extraversion, Introversion, Judging, Perceiving.

Administration: Group.

Price Data: Available from publisher.

Time: (30–40) minutes.

Comments: Self-report type profile based on Jung's typology.

Authors: June Singer, Mary Loomis, Elizabeth Kirkhart (revision), and Larry Kirkhart (revision).

Publisher: Moving Boundaries, Inc.

Cross References: For reviews by Joni R. Hays and Kevin Lanning, see 14:356; for a review by Richard B. Stuart of the earlier edition, see 10:334 (1 reference).

[2340]
SIPOAS: Styles in Perception of Affect Scale.

Purpose: "A personality scale measuring the ability to respond to the subtle, changing physical cues arising from the body's response to perceptions, memories and associations, and to integrate them into optimal emotional and behavioral response."
Population: Age 18 to adult.
Publication Date: 1995.
Acronym: SIPOAS.
Scores: 3 styles: BB (Based on Body), EE (Emphasis on Evaluation), LL (Looking to Logic).
Administration: Individual or group.
Price Data, 2002: $20 per 25 copies of questionnaire including scoring template with scoring criteria (can be mechanically reproduced); $22.50 per complete research report (203 pages); $14.25 per administration/interpretation manual.
Time: [20–30] minutes.
Comments: Paper-and-pencil test; may be completed by the individual or administered by an assistant to an individual or group. Can be used to determine predominant styles, which is helpful for selecting the optimal psychotherapeutic modality and for predicting therapy outcome. Also has application in marital therapy and in personnel and organizational decision making, and may have application in legal justice settings such as jury selection, witness coaching, child custody and probation/parole issues.
Author: Michael Bernet.
Publisher: Institute for Somat Awareness.
Cross References: For reviews by Brian F. Bolton and S. Alvin Leung, see 14:357.

[2341]
Situational Attitude Scale.

Purpose: "Measures the attitudes of whites toward blacks."
Population: College and adults.
Publication Dates: c1969–1972.
Acronym: SAS.
Scores, 11: 10 situation scores, Total.
Administration: Group.
Forms, 2: A, B.
Price Data: Available from publisher.
Time: Untimed.
Authors: William E. Sedlacek and Glenwood C. Brooks, Jr.
Publisher: University of Maryland, University Counseling Center [No reply from publisher; status unknown].

Cross References: See T5:2413 (1 reference) and T4:2466 (2 references); for reviews by Ralph Mason Dreger and Marvin E. Shaw, see 8:678 (1 reference); see also T2:1381 (3 references).

[2342]
Situational Confidence Questionnaire.

Purpose: Designed to help clients identify high-risk drinking relapse situations.
Population: Adult alcoholics.
Publication Dates: 1987–1988.
Administration: Group.
Editions, 2: Computerized, print.
Authors: Helen M. Annis and J. Martin Graham.
Publisher: Centre for Addiction and Mental Health [Canada].
a) SITUATIONAL CONFIDENCE QUESTIONNAIRE.
Acronym: SCQ-39.
Scores, 9: Unpleasant Emotions/Frustrations, Physical Discomfort, Social Problems at Work, Social Tension, Pleasant Emotions, Positive Social Situations, Urges and Temptations, Testing Personal Control, Average.
Price Data, 2002: C$14.75 per 25 questionnaires; C$13.50 per user's guide (1988, 49 pages); C$25 per specimen set including user's guide and 25 questionnaires.
Time: (10–15) minutes.
b) ALCOHOL CONFIDENCE QUESTIONNAIRE.
Acronym: ACQ-16.
Scores: Total score only.
Time: Administration time not reported.
Comments: Brief version of the Situational Confidence Questionnaire; test items listed in SCQ user's guide.
Cross References: See T5:2414 (7 references); for reviews by Merith Cosden and Cecil R. Reynolds, see 13:288 (4 references); see also T4:2467 (1 reference).

[2343]
Situational Leadership®.

Purpose: Designed to identify successful leaders as "those who can adapt their behavior to meet the demands of their own unique situation."
Population: Managers, leaders, administrators, supervisors, and staff.
Publication Dates: 1973–1998.
Acronym: SL.
Administration: Group.
Manual: No manual.
Price Data: Available from publisher.
Time: Administration time not reported.
Comments: Related programs, Situational Leadership Simulator and Situational Leadership: Leveraging

Human Performance, and Situational Leadership One-Day, also available.

Authors: Paul Hersey and Ron Campbell.

Publisher: Leadership Studies, Inc.

a) LEADER EFFECTIVENESS AND ADAPT-ABILITY.

Publication Dates: 1973–1998.

Acronym: LEAD.

Comments: Ratings of self and others.

Forms, 2: LEAD Self, LEAD Other.

b) READINESS STYLE MATCH.

Publication Date: 1979.

Acronym: RSM.

Scores: Ratings in 4 areas: Major Objectives, Readiness, Integration of Style and Readiness, Readiness Style Match Matrix.

Forms, 2: Staff Member Rating Form, Manager Rating Form.

c) READINESS SCALE.

Publication Date: 1977.

Acronym: MS.

Scores: 2 scores (Task Readiness, Psychological Readiness) for each of 5 major objectives or responsibilities.

Forms, 2: Self Rating Form, Manager Rating Form.

d) POWER PERCEPTION PROFILE.

Publication Dates: 1979–1998.

Acronym: PPP.

Scores, 7: Coercive, Connection, Expert, Information, Legitimate, Referent, Reward.

Forms, 2: Perception of Self, Perception of Other.

e) LEADERSHIP SCALE.

Publication Dates: 1980–1997.

Acronym: LS.

Scores: 2 scores (Total Task-Behavior, Total Relationship-Behavior) for each of 5 major objectives or responsibilities.

Forms, 2: Staff Member Form, Manager Form.

Cross References: For reviews by Bruce J. Eberhardt and Sheldon Zedeck, see 9:1133.

[2344]
Situational Preference Inventory.

Purpose: "Designed to assess individual styles of social interaction."

Population: Grades 9-16 and adults.

Publication Dates: 1968-1973.

Acronym: SPI.

Scores, 3: Cooperational, Instrumental, Analytic.

Administration: Group.

Price Data: Available from publisher.

Time: (10-15) minutes.

Comments: Self-administered.

Author: Carl N. Edwards.

Publisher: Carl N. Edwards.

Cross References: See T2:1382 (2 references).

[2345]
Six Factor Personality Questionnaire.

Purpose: Designed as a measure of six personality dimensions or broad factors.

Population: Adults.

Publication Date: 2000.

Acronym: SFPQ.

Scores, 6: Extraversion, Agreeableness, Independence, Openness to Experience, Methodicalness, Industriousness.

Administration: Individual or group.

Price Data, 2006: $70 per examination kit including manual on CD (2000, 68 pages), 5 quick score answer sheets, 5 profile sheets, and one machine-scorable answer sheet for a Mail-in Basic Report; $15 per test manual on CD; $50 per 25 test booklets; $55 per Quick Answer Score sheets; $40 per 25 profile forms; $58–$65 (depending on volume) per 10 machine-scorable answer sheets and coupons for Mail-in Basic Report; $105 per SigmaSoft SFPQ for Windows Software package including disks, software manual for Windows, test manual, and 10 coupons for computer reports; $14 per online password; volume discounts available.

Time: 20 minutes.

Comments: Available for online administration at www.sigmatesting.com.

Authors: Douglas N. Jackson, Sampo V. Paunonen, and Paul F. Tremblay.

Publisher: Sigma Assessment Systems, Inc.

Cross References: For a review by Jeffrey A. Jenkins, see 15:229.

[2346]
Sixteen Personality Factor (16PF®) Questionnaire, Fifth Edition.

Purpose: Designed to measure personality traits.

Population: Ages 16 and over.

Publication Dates: 1949–2002.

Acronym: 16PF.

Scores, 24: 16 primary factor scores: Warm vs. Reserved (A), Abstract-Reasoning vs. Concrete-Reasoning (B), Emotionally Stable vs. Reactive (C), Dominant vs. Deferential (E), Lively vs. Serious (F), Rule-Conscious vs. Expedient (G), Socially Bold vs. Shy (H), Sensitive vs. Utilitarian (I), Vigilant vs. Trusting (L), Abstracted vs. Grounded (M), Private vs. Forthright (N), Apprehensive vs. Self-Assured (0), Open to Change vs. Traditional (Q1), Self-Reliant vs. Group-Oriented (Q2), Perfectionistic vs. Tolerates Disorder (Q3), Tense vs. Relaxed (Q4); 5 global factor scores: Extraverted vs. Introverted (EX), High Anxiety vs. Low Anxiety (AX), Tough-Minded vs. Receptive (TM), Independent vs. Accommodating (IN), Self-Controlled vs. Unrestrained

(SC); 3 response style indices: Impression Management (IM), Infrequency (INF), Acquiescence (ACQ).

Administration: Group or individual.

Price Data, 2005: $120 per complete kit including 10 test booklets, 25 answer sheets, 25 individual record forms, scoring keys, administrator's manual (2002, 162 pages), and one prepaid processing certificate for a Basic Interpretive Report (BIR); $20 per 10 test booklets; $28 per scoring keys and norms table; $18 per 25 answer sheets; $10 per 25 individual record forms; $44 per administrator's manual; $47 per trial packet including test booklet, answer sheet, administrator's manual, and certificate for a Basic Interpretive Report (BIR); $11.50–$30 for Basic Interpretive Report including profiles, scores, and descriptive comments; $8–$30 per Basic Score Report (includes scores only); $65 per technical manual (2002, 279 pages).

Time: (35–50) minutes.

Comments: Computer administration, interpretive reports, and scoring available.

Authors: Raymond B. Cattell, A. Karen S. Cattell, and Heather E. P. Cattell.

Publisher: Institute for Personality and Ability Testing, Inc. (IPAT).

a) 16PF BASIC SCORE REPORT.

Comments: Most concise 16PF report.

b) 16PF DATA SUMMARY REPORT.

Comments: Developed to provide standard output for researchers providing profiles on individual test takers as well as group average profile.

c) 16PF BASIC INTERPRETIVE REPORT.

Comments: A multipurpose, computerized interpretation of the 16PF providing the basic 16 personality scores and other information about characteristics relevant to personal and vocational counseling.

d) 16PF TEAMWORK DEVELOPMENT REPORT.

Comments: Intended to evaluate personality implications for performance in teamwork settings, for development of either individual and/or teams.

e) 16PF PERSONAL CAREER DEVELOPMENT PROFILE.

Comments: Facilitates consulting with clients on how their personal strengths can lead to personal and career success.

f) 16PF HUMAN RESOURCE DEVELOPMENT REPORT.

Comments: Assesses leadership and management potential by analyzing the personality dimensions associated with success in a broad range of managerial settings, and projecting how the examinee might be expected to function.

g) 16PF CATTELL COMPREHENSIVE PERSONALITY INTERPRETATION.

Comments: Provides 8–10 pages of comprehensive narrative covering a number of diverse areas of functioning and offering multi-trait combinations and interactions to provide an in-depth understanding of the client's whole personality. The narrative also discusses therapeutic considerations and approaches.

h) 16PF KARSON CLINICAL REPORT.

Comments: Provides 2–3 pages of descriptive narrative intended for professional use only. Contains sections describing basic areas of functioning, including: emotional adjustment, interpersonal issues, self-control, cognitive style, and areas to explore in couseling.

i) 16PF COUPLE'S COUNSELING REPORT.

Comments: A computer-interpreted report for paired 16PF profiles that examines the personality organization of two people, and compares the profiles; uses 16PF items plus additional questions about relationship history and satisfaction.

j) 16PF INDIVIDUALIZED STRESS MANAGEMENT PROGRAM.

Comments: An assessment and training package using 16PF data plus a stress evaluation inventory to yield a computer-generated, book-length report providing an individualized prescription plan for participants in a stress management program.

k) 16PF LEADERSHIP COACHING REPORT.

Comments: Designed to facilitate the developmental process of individuals desiring to become more effective leaders by increasing awareness/understanding of their personal behavioral traits, identifying areas for development, and providing individualized developmental strategies to increase leadership effectiveness.

Cross References: See T5:2417 (43 references); for reviews by Mary J. McLellan and Pamela Carrington Rotto, see 12:354 (38 references); see also T4:2470 (140 references); for reviews of an earlier edition by James N. Butcher and Marvin Zuckerman, see 9:1136 (67 references); see also T3:2208 (182 references); for reviews by Bruce M. Bloxam, Brian F. Bolton, and James A. Walsh, see 8:679 (619 references); see also T2:1383 (244 references); for reviews by Thomas J. Bouchard, Jr. and Leonard G. Rorer, see 7:139 (295 references); see also P:245 (249 references); for a review by Maurice Lorr, see 6:174 (81 references); for a review by C. J. Adcock, see 5:112 (21 references); for reviews by Charles M. Harsh, Ardie Lubin, and J. Richard Wittenborn, see 4:87 (8 references).

[2347]

16PF Adolescent Personality Questionnaire.

Purpose: Designed to "measure normal personality of adolescents, problem-solving abilities, and preferred work activities," and to identify problems in areas known to be problematic to adolescents.

Population: Ages 11–22.

Publication Date: 2001.

Acronym: APQ.

Scores: 21 normal personality scales: Primary Personality Factor Scales (Warmth, Reasoning, Emotional Stability, Dominance, Liveliness, Rule-Consciousness, Social Boldness, Sensitivity, Vigilance, Abstractedness, Privateness, Apprehension, Openness to Change, Self-Reliance, Perfectionism, Tension), Global Factor Scales (Extraversion, Anxiety, Tough-Mindedness, Independence, Self-Control); plus a ranking of Work Activity Preferences (Manual, Scientific, Artistic, Helping, Sales/Management, and Procedural), Personal Discomfort (Discouragement, Worry, Poor Body Image, Overall Discomfort), "Getting in Trouble" (Anger or Aggression, Problems with Authority, Alcohol or Drugs, Overall Trouble), Context (Home or School), Coping/Managing Difficulty, Impression Management, Missing Responses, Central Responses, Predicted Grade Point Average.

Administration: Group or individual.

Price Data: Available from publisher.

Time: (54–65) minutes (untimed).

Comments: Computerized scoring and interpretive reports available (APQ Guidance Report and APQ Psychological Report); optional Life's Difficulties section provides an opportunity for the youth to indicate particular problems in areas known to be problematic for adolescents, making the APQ appropriate for screening and for introducing sensitive topics in a counseling setting.

Author: J. M. Schuerger.

Publisher: Institute for Personality and Ability Testing, Inc. (IPAT).

Cross References: For reviews by William M. Reynolds and by Susan C. Whiston and Jennifer C. Bouwkamp, see 15:230.

[2348]
16PF® Human Resource Development Report.

Purpose: Assesses an individual's management potential and style, provides insights into the individual's personality, and focuses on five management dimensions frequently identified in research on successful managers.

Population: Managerial candidates.

Publication Dates: 1982–1997.

Acronym: HRDR.

Scores: 5 management dimensions: Leadership, Interaction with Others, Decision-Making Abilities, Initiative, Personal Adjustment; 16 primary factor scores; 5 global factor scores.

Administration: Group or individual.

Price Data, 2006: $33 per introductory kit including test booklet, answer sheet, prepaid processing form to receive Human Resource Development Report, and user's guide (1997, 55 pages); $20 per 10 reusable test booklets; $18 per 25 machine-scorable answer sheets;

$30 per user's guide; $16.50 to $30 per Human Resource Development Report available from publisher scoring service.

Time: 35–50 minutes.

Comments: Based on the Sixteen Personality Factor Questionnaire (2346); mail-in, fax, on-site software, and Net Assess internet delivery options available; can be generated from 4th or 5th edition of 16PF questionnaire.

Author: IPAT staff.

Publisher: Institute for Personality and Ability Testing, Inc. (IPAT).

Cross References: For reviews by S. Alvin Leung and Mary A. Lewis, see 11:169.

[2349]
16PF Select.

Purpose: A shorter version of the 16PF Fifth Edition personality measure, which was designed for personnel selection.

Population: Ages 16 and over.

Publication Date: 1999.

Acronym: 16PF Select.

Scores, 12: Warmth, Calmness, Dominance, Liveliness, Rule-Consciousness, Social Boldness, Trust, Imagination, Self-Assuredness, Openness, Self-Reliance, Organization.

Administration: Individual or group.

Price Data, 2006: $58 per introductory kit including manual (1999, 75 pages), dimension specification form, questionnaire/answer sheet booklet and prepaid mail-in report processing certificate; $30 per manual; $30 per 10 questionnaire/answer sheet booklets; $15.50 to $30 per report.

Time: (20) minutes (untimed).

Comments: A shorter version of the 16PF Fifth Edition (2346).

Authors: Raymond B. Cattell, A. Karen S. Cattell, Heather E. P. Cattell, and Mary L. Kelly.

Publisher: Institute for Personality and Ability Testing, Inc. (IPAT).

Cross References: For reviews by Paul A. Arbisi and Stephen E. Trotter, see 15:231; for information about the complete 16PF see T5:2417 (43 references); for reviews of an earlier edition of the 16PF by Mary J. McLellan and Pamela Carrington Rotto, see 12:354 (38 references); see also T4:2470 (140 references); for reviews by James N. Butcher and Marvin Zuckerman, see 9:1136 (67 references); see also T3:2208 (182 references); for reviews by Bruce M. Bloxam, Brian F. Bolton, and James A. Walsh, see 8:679 (619 references); see also T2:1383 (244 references); for reviews of an earlier edition by Thomas J. Bouchard, Jr. and Leonard G. Rorer, see 7:139 (295 references); see also P:245 (249 references); for a review by Maurice Lorr, see 6:174 (81 references); for a review by C. J. Adcock, see 5:112 (21 references); for reviews by Charles M.

Harsh, Ardie Lubin, and J. Richard Wittenborn, see 4:87 (8 references).

[2350]
Skills and Attributes Inventory.

Purpose: Assesses the relative importance of job-related skills and attributes for a position as well as the degree to which an individual possesses those skills and attributes.
Population: Non-management positions.
Publication Dates: 1976–1979.
Acronym: SAI.
Scores, 13: General Functioning Intelligence, Visual Acuity, Visual and Coordination Skills, Physical Coordination, Mechanical Skills, Graphic and Clerical Skills, General Clerical Skills, Leadership Ability, Tolerance in Interpersonal Relations, Organization Identification, Conscientiousness and Reliability, Efficiency Under Stress, Solitary Work.
Administration: Individual or group.
Price Data, 2002: $101 per start-up kit (specify Importance or Ability) including 25 test booklets, 25 score sheets, and interpretation and research manual; $54 per 25 test booklets (specify Importance or Ability); $31 per 25 score sheets; $28 per interpretation and research manual.
Time: No limit (approximately 30–45 minutes).
Author: Melany E. Baehr.
Publisher: Pearson Performance Solutions [No reply from publisher; status unknown].
Cross References: For a review by Lenore W. Harmon, see 9:1137.

[2351]
Skills Assessment Module.

Purpose: To assess a student's affective, cognitive, and manipulative strengths and weaknesses in relation to vocational skills required in various training programs within a school system.
Population: Average, handicapped, and disadvantaged vocational training school students ages 14-18.
Publication Dates: 1985–2000.
Acronym: SAM.
Scores, 13: Digital Discrimination, Clerical Verbal, Motor Coordination, Clerical Numerical, Following Written Directions, Finger Dexterity, Aiming, Reading a Ruler (Measurement), Manual Dexterity, Form Perception, Spatial Perception, Color Discrimination, Following Diagrammed Instructions.
Administration: Individual in part.
Price Data, 2002: $2,995 for complete test including all subtests.
Time: (90-150) minutes.
Comments: Module includes Career Development ITEP software, Basic Skills Locater Test (262), Learning Styles Inventory (1439), Auditory Directions Screen, Voc-Ties Interest Survey, and 13 hands on performance work samples.

Author: Michele Rosinek.
Publisher: Piney Mountain Press, Inc.
Cross References: For reviews by Jean Powell Kirnan and Wilbur L. Layton, see 11:364.

[2352]
Skills Inventory for Teams.

Purpose: To aid early intervention practitioners to "evaluate their ability to work as part of a team."
Population: Early intervention practitioners.
Publication Dates: 1978–1992.
Acronym: SIFT.
Scores, 12: Clarity of Purpose, Cohesion, Clarity of Roles, Communication, Use of Resources, Decision Making/Problem Solving, Responsibility Implementation, Conflict Resolution, View of Family Role, Evaluation, External Support, Internal Support.
Administration: Group.
Price Data: Price information for administration guide and inventory (1992, 66 pages) available from publisher.
Time: Administration time not reported.
Comments: Previously called Skills Inventory for Teachers; self-administered inventory.
Authors: Corinne Garland, Adrienne Frank, Deana Buck, and Patti Seklemian.
Publisher: Child Development Resources.
Cross References: For reviews by Robert Johnson and E. Lea Witta, see 13:289.

[2353]
SKILLSCOPE®.

Purpose: Assesses managerial strengths and developmental needs from managers' and coworkers' perspectives.
Population: Managers.
Publication Dates: 1988-1997.
Scores: 15 Skill Areas: Getting Information, Communication, Taking Action, Risk Taking, Administration, Conflict Management, Relationships, Selecting/Developing, Influencing, Flexibility, Knowledge of Job, Energy/Drive, Time Management, Coping With Pressure, Self-Management.
Administration: Group.
Price Data, 2006: $155 per set including 9 survey instruments, a feedback report, a development planning guide, and a facilitators's guide (2006, 63 pages); $195 per group profile; quantity discounts available.
Time: [20–30] minutes.
Comments: SKILLSCOPE questionnaires can be returned to the Center for Creative Leadership for confidential scoring or the questionnaires can be completed on-line; managers are rated by self and by coworkers.
Author: Robert E. Kaplan.
Publisher: Center for Creative Leadership.
Cross References: For a review by Linda F. Wightman, see 12:355.

[2354]

Slingerland Screening Tests for Identifying Children with Specific Language Disability

Purpose: "To screen from among a group of children those with potential language difficulties and those with already present specific language disabilities who are in need of special attention."

Population: Grades 1–2.5, 2.5–3.5, 3.5–4, 5–6

Publication Dates: 1962–2005.

Subtests, 8 or 9: Copying-Chart, Copying-Page, Visual Perception-Memory, Visual Discrimination, Visual Perception-Memory with Kinesthetic Memory, Auditory Recall, Auditory Sounds, Auditory Association, Orientation (Form D only); plus individual Echolalia test.

Administration: Group (Echolalia test individually administered).

Author: Beth H. Slingerland.

Publisher: Educators Publishing Service, Inc.

a) FORMS A, B, C, REVISED EDITION.

Population: Grades 1–2.5, 2.5–3.5, 3.5–4.

Publication Dates: 1962-2005.

Scores, 13: (8 tests) Visual Copying Far Point, Visual Copying Near Point, Total, Visual Perception-Memory, Visual Discrimination, Visual Perception-Memory with Kinesthetic Memory, Auditory Recall (Letters, Numbers, Spelling), Auditory Discrimination of Sounds, Auditory-Visual Association, Total Errors (excluding Visual Copying), Total Errors plus Self-Corrections and Poor Formations.

Price Data, 2006: $33 per 12 tests (A, B, or C); $20 per cards and charts (A, B, or C); $17.80 per teacher's manual (2005, 172 pages); $20.80 per specimen set including manual and one each of above tests; quantity discounts available.

Time: 56(66) minutes in 2 or 3 sessions.

Authors: Revisions by Beth H. Slingerland and Alice S. Ansara.

1) *Form A.*
Population: Grades 1–2.5.
2) *Form B.*
Population: Grades 2.5–3.5.
3) *Form C.*
Population: Grades 3.5–4.

b) FORM D.

Population: Grades 5–6.

Publication Date: 1974.

Scores, 14: (9 tests) Visual Copying Far Point, Visual Copying Near Point, Total, Visual Perception-Memory, Visual Discrimination, Visual Perception-Memory with Kinesthetic Memory, Auditory Recall (Letters, Numbers, Spelling), Auditory Discrimination of Sounds, Auditory-Visual Association, Auditory Perception and Individual Orientation, Total Errors (excluding Visual Copying), Total Errors and Confusions.

Price Data: $24.80 per 12 tests and 12 summary sheets; $22.75 per cards and charts including directions for administration and scoring; $14.20 per teacher's manual; $15.20 per specimen set including teacher's manual, Form D test, summary sheet, and list of material needed; quantity discounts available.

Time: (110-125) minutes in 2 sessions.

Cross References: See T4:2478 (2 references); for reviews by Martin Fujiki and Elisabeth H. Wiig, see 9:1141 (4 references); see also T3:2214 (2 references); for an excerpted review by Barton B. Proger, see 8:446 (3 references); see also T2:989 (4 references); for reviews by Evelyn Deno and Joseph M. Wepman of a, see 7:969 (3 references).

[2355]

Slosson Articulation, Language Test with Phonology.

Purpose: Measures the communicative competence of a child by combining into a single score the assessment of articulation, phonology and language.

Population: Ages 3-0 to 5-11.

Publication Date: 1986.

Acronym: SALT-P.

Scores, 4: Consonants + Vowels/Diphthongs, Phonological Processes, Language Errors, Composite Score.

Administration: Individual.

Price Data, 1992: $50 per complete kit; $14 per examiner's manual (12 pages); $20 per 50 scoring forms; $18 per test book/picture plates; $70 per video tape.

Time: (7-10) minutes.

Comments: Instructional video tape with taped administration of test available.

Author: Wilma Jean Tade.

Publisher: Slosson Educational Publications, Inc.

Cross References: For reviews by Clinton W. Bennett and Robert A. Reineke, see 12:357.

[2356]

Slosson Full-Range Intelligence Test.

Purpose: Constructed as a "quick estimate of general cognitive ability."

Population: Ages 5–21.

Publication Dates: 1988–2002.

Acronym: S-FRIT.

Scores, 8: General Cognition (Full-Range Intelligence Quotient, Rapid Cognitive Index, Best g Index), Cognitive Subdomains (Verbal Index, Abstract Index, Quantitative Index, Memory Index, Performance Index).

Administration: Individual.

Forms, 2: Item Profiles/Score Summaries Form, Brief Score Form.

Price Data, 2002: $110 per complete kit including examiner's manual (1994, 80 pages), normative/technical manual (1994, 93 pages), picture book, 50 motor

response forms, 50 brief score forms, and 50 item profiles/score summaries: $38 per 50 forms (specify Motor response, brief score, or item profiles/score summaries); $70 per examiner's manual; $40 per normative/technical manual; $26.50 per picture book.
Time: (20–35) minutes.
Authors: Bob Algozzine, Ronald C. Eaves, Lester Mann, H. Robert Vance, and Steven W. Slosson (Brief Score Form).
Publisher: Slosson Educational Publications, Inc.
Cross References: For reviews by Gerald S. Hanna and Gerald Tindal, see 14:359.

[2357]
Slosson Intelligence Test 3rd [2002 Edition].
Purpose: Designed for use as a "quick estimate of general verbal cognitive ability."
Population: Ages 4-65 and over.
Publication Dates: 1961–2002.
Acronym: SIT-R3.
Scores: Total score only.
Administration: Individual.
Price Data, 2005: $110.25 per complete kit including 50 test forms, manual (1991, 45 pages), and norms tables/technical manual (1991, 39 pages); $27 per 50 test forms; $47 per norms tables/technical manual; $47 per manual.
Time: (10-20) minutes.
Authors: Richard L. Slosson, Charles L. Nicholson (revision), and Terry H. Hibpshman (revision).
Publisher: Slosson Educational Publications, Inc.
Cross References: See T5:2432 (33 references); for reviews by Randy W. Kamphaus and T. Steuart Watson, see 12:358 (16 references); see also T4:2482 (43 references); for reviews by Thomas Oakland and William M. Reynolds of an earlier edition , see 9:1142 (11 references); see also T3:2217 (82 references), 8:227 (62 references), and T2:524 (12 references); for reviews by Philip Himelstein and Jane V. Hunt, see 7:424 (31 references).

[2358]
Slosson Oral Reading Test—Revised.
Purpose: Designed as a "quick estimate to target word recognition levels for children and adults."
Population: Preschool–adult.
Publication Dates: 1963–2002.
Acronym: SORT-R.
Scores: Total score only.
Administration: Individual.
Price Data, 2002: $60 per complete kit; $40 per manual (1990, 38 pages); $26 per 50 score sheets; $14 per spiral-bound word lists; $7 per large print word lists.
Special Editions: Large print edition available for individuals with visual handicaps.
Time: (3-5) minutes.

Comments: Grade equivalent (GE) and age equivalent (AE) scores are also available.
Authors: Richard L. Slosson and Charles L. Nicholson.
Publisher: Slosson Educational Publications, Inc.
Cross References: See T5:2433 (4 references); for reviews by Steven R. Shaw and Carol E. Westby, see 12:359 (4 references); see T4:2483 (16 references), T3:2218 (15 references), T2:1688 (5 references), and 6:844.

[2359]
Slosson Test of Reading Readiness.
Purpose: "Designed to identify children who are at risk of failure in programs of formal reading instruction."
Population: Latter kindergarten-grade 1.
Publication Date: 1991.
Acronym: STRR.
Scores, 12: Visual Skills (Recognition of Capital Letters, Recognition of Lower Case Letters, Matching Capital and Lower Case Letters, Visual Discrimination-Matching Word Forms, Total), Auditory Skills (Auditory Discrimination-Rhyming Words, Auditory Discrimination and Memory—Recognition of Beginning Sounds, Total), Cognitive Skills (Sequencing, Opposites, Total), Total Inventory.
Administration: Individual.
Price Data, 1992: $48 per complete kit; $18 per manual (24 pages); $12 per test stimulus booklet; $16 per 50 scoring booklets; $6 per 50 letter to parent.
Time: (15) minutes.
Authors: Leslie Anne Perry and Gary J. Vitali.
Publisher: Slosson Educational Publications, Inc.
Cross References: For reviews by Gerald S. Hanna and Diane J. Sawyer, see 12:360.

[2360]
Smedley Hand Dynamometer.
Purpose: Developed to "measure the muscular torque (grip) of the hand and forearm."
Population: Ages 6–18.
Publication Dates: [1920–1953].
Scores: Total score only.
Administration: Individual.
Price Data, 2005: $215 per hand dynamometer.
Time: Administration time not reported.
Author: F. Smedley.
Publisher: Stoelting Co.
Cross References: See T2:1901 (10 references).

[2361]
Smell Identification Test™ [Revised].
Purpose: Designed to measure an individual's ability to "identify a number of odorants at the suprathreshold level."
Population: People 5 years and up with suspected olfactory dysfunction.
Publication Dates: 1981–1995.

Acronyms: SIT; UPSIT.
Scores: Total score only.
Administration: Individual.
Price Data: Available from publisher.
Time: [10–15] minutes.
Comments: A 40-item forced-choice questionnaire; also known as University of Pennsylvania Smell Identification Test; for use only by individuals "professionally engaged in the scientific or medical evaluation of smell function"; related versions include the Pocket Smell Test, the Cross-Cultural Smell Identification Test, and the Picture Identification Test (equivalent to the SIT except stimuli are pictures rather than odors).
Author: Richard L. Doty.
Publisher: Sensonics, Inc.
Cross References: For a review by Ralph G. Leverett, see 14:360; see also T5:2437 (4 references).

[2362]
Smit-Hand Articulation and Phonology Evaluation.

Purpose: Designed to assess a child's level of phonology.
Population: Ages 3–9.
Publication Date: 1997.
Acronym: SHAPE.
Scores, 11: Total, Weak Syllable Deletion, Final Consonant Deletion, Reduction of /lrw/ Clusters, Reduction of /s/ Clusters, Stopping of Initial Fricatives, Voicing of Initial Voiceless Obstruents, Fronting of Velars, Depalatalization, Gliding of Liquid Singletons, Vocalization of Liquids.
Administration: Individual.
Price Data, 2006: $146 per kit including 10 record booklets, 10 autoscore answer forms, manual (63 pages), and 1 picture set; $32.50 per 10 record booklets; $21.50 per 10 autoscore forms; $38.50 per manual; $71.50 per picture set.
Time: (30) minutes.
Authors: Ann B. Smit and Linda Hand.
Publisher: Western Psychological Services.
Cross References: For reviews by David P. Hurford and Ralph G. Leverett, see 14:361.

[2363]
Smoker Complaint Scale.

Purpose: Designed to measure changes in physiological/emotional/craving states as a function of smoking cessation.
Population: Persons quitting smoking.
Publication Date: 1984.
Acronym: SCS.
Scores: Total score and item scores only.
Administration: Individual or group.
Manual: No manual.
Price Data: Instrument now available without charge from publisher.

Foreign Language Editions: Translations available in Danish, Dutch, English for Australia, German, Italian, and Norwegian.
Time: (1-5) minutes.
Comments: Self-administered; also available online at www.proqolid.org.
Author: Nina G. Schneider.
Publisher: Nina G. Schneider, Ph.D.
Cross References: See T5:2440 (1 reference).

[2364]
Snijders-Oomen Non-Verbal Intelligence Test—Revised.

Purpose: Developed as an untimed, nonverbal test of intelligence.
Publication Dates: 1939–1997.
Administration: Individual.
Price Data: Available from publisher.
Foreign Language Editions: Dutch and German editions available.
Comments: Administered in pantomime (for hearing impaired) or orally.
Publisher: Hogrefe & Huber Publishers.
a) SNIJDERS-OOMEN NON-VERBAL INTELLIGENCE SCALE FOR YOUNG CHILDREN.
Population: Dutch children ages 2-6 to 7-0.
Acronym: SON-R 2 1/2-7.
Scores, 6: Sorting, Mosaic, Combination, Memory, Copying, Total.
Time: (45–50) minutes.
Comments: Also called Non-Verbal Intelligence Scale S.O.N. 2 1/2-7.
Authors: J. T. Snijders and N. Snijders-Oomen.
b) SON-R.
Population: Dutch children ages 5-6 to 17-0.
Acronym: SON-R 5 1/2-17.
Scores, 8: Categories, Mosaics, Hidden Pictures, Patterns, Situations, Analogies, Stories, Total.
Time: (60–120) minutes.
Comments: Revised version of the SON-'58 and SSON; older versions out-of-print.
Authors: J. T. Snijders, P. J. Tellegen, J. A. Laros, N. Snijders-Oomen (test), and M. A. H. Huijnen (test).
Cross References: See T5:2441 (2 references) and T4:2491 (2 references); for reviews by Douglas K. Detterman and Timothy Z. Keith of an earlier edition, see 9:1146; see also T3:2221 (1 reference) and T2:512 (5 references); for a review by J. S. Lawes of the 1958 edition, see 6:529 (2 references).

[2365]
Social Adjustment Scale—Self Report.

Purpose: Designed to assess "the ability of an individual to adapt to, and derive satisfaction from, their social roles."

Population: Age 17 and older.
Publication Date: 1999.
Acronym: SAS-SR.
Scores: 7 areas: Work, Social and Leisure Activities, Relations with Extended Family, Primary Relationship, Parenthood, Family Life, Economic.
Administration: Group.
Price Data, 2006: $142 per complete kit including 10 question booklets, 25 QuikScore™ forms, and manual; $39 per 10 question booklets; $54 per 25 QuikScore™ forms; $76 per manual.
Foreign Language Editions: Available in Afrikaans, Cantonese, Czech, Danish, Dutch, Finnish, Flemish, French (European), French-Canadian, German, Greek, Hebrew, Hungarian, Italian, Japanese, Korean, Mandarin, Norwegian, Portuguese, Russian, Spanish (European), Spanish (South American), and Swedish.
Time: (15–20) minutes.
Author: Myrna Weissmann.
Publisher: Multi-Health Systems, Inc.
Cross References: For reviews by Julie A. Allison and Romeo Vitelli, see 15:232.

[2366]
Social Behavior Assessment Inventory.
Purpose: Assesses social skill levels in students.
Population: Grades K–9.
Publication Date: 1978–1992.
Acronym: SBAI.
Scores, 30: Environmental Behaviors (Care for the Environment, Dealing with Emergencies, Lunchroom Behavior, Movement Around Environment), Interpersonal Behaviors (Accepting Authority, Coping with Conflict, Gaining Attention, Greeting Others, Helping Others, Making Conversation, Organized Play, Positive Attitude Toward Others, Playing Informally, Property: Own and Others), Self-Related Behaviors (Accepting Consequences, Ethical Behavior, Expressing Feelings, Positive Attitude Toward Self, Responsible Behavior, Self-Care), Task-Related Behaviors (Asking and Answering Questions, Attending Behavior, Classroom Discussion, Completing Tasks, Following Directions, Group Activities, Independent Work, On-Task Behavior, Performing Before Others, Quality of Work).
Administration: Individual or group.
Price Data, 2006: $140 per introductory kit including Social Skills in the Classroom–2nd ed., manual (1992, 34 pages), and 25 rating booklets.
Time: (30–45) minutes.
Comments: Observations made by teacher or trained paraprofessional.
Authors: Thomas M. Stephens and Kevin D. Arnold.
Publisher: Psychological Assessment Resources, Inc.
Cross References: See T5:2444 (1 reference); for reviews by Kathryn A. Hess and David MacPhee, see 12:361; see also T4:2493 (1 reference); for a review by

Ronald S. Drabman of an earlier edition, see 9:1148; see also T3:2226 (1 reference).

[2367]
Social Competence and Behavior Evaluation, Preschool Edition.
Purpose: "Designed to assess patterns of social competence, affective expression, and adjustment difficulties."
Population: Children aged 30 months to 76 months (2 1/2 to 6 years).
Publication Date: 1995.
Acronym: SCBE.
Scores: 8 Basic scales (Depressive-Joyful, Anxious-Secure, Angry-Tolerant, Isolated-Integrated, Aggressive-Calm, Egotistical-Prosocial, Oppositional-Cooperative, Dependent-Autonomous); 4 Summary scales (Social Competence, Internalizing Problems, Externalizing Problems, General Adaptation).
Administration: Group.
Price Data, 2006: $92.50 per complete kit including 25 AutoScore™ forms and manual (67 pages); $44 per 25 AutoScore™ forms; $53 per manual.
Time: (15) minutes.
Comments: Ratings by teachers or other child care professionals.
Authors: Peter J. LaFreniere and Jean E. Dumas.
Publisher: Western Psychological Services.
Cross References: For reviews by Ronald A. Madle and G. Michael Poteat, see 14:362.

[2368]
Social-Emotional Dimension Scale—Second Edition.
Purpose: "Designed to provide school personnel ... with a means for rating student behavior problems that may interfere with academic functioning."
Population: Ages 6.0-18.11.
Publication Dates: 1986–2004.
Acronym: SEDS-2.
Administration: Individual.
Price Data, 2006: $149 per complete kit: $45 per examiner's manual; $40 per 25 comprehensive forms; $41 per 50 screener forms; $41 per 50 screener summary forms.
Comments: Norm-referenced behavior rating scale.
Authors: Jerry B. Hutton and Timothy G. Roberts.
Publisher: PRO-ED.
  a) SCREENER FORM.
  Scores: Total score only.
  Time: (5–8) minutes.
  b) COMPREHENSIVE FORM.
  Scores, 8: Externalizing Behavior (Interpersonal Relationships, Conduct Problems, Total), Internalizing Behavior (Inappropriate Behavior, Depression, Anxiety/Inattention, Total), Overall Social-Emotional Disturbance.
  Time: (15–20) minutes.

c) FUNCTIONAL ASSESSMENT INTERVIEW.
Scores: Not scored.
Time: (30) minutes.
Cross References: For a review by Mark D. Shriver, see 16:226; for a review by Jean Powell Kirnan of the earlier edition, see 11:368.

[2369]
Social Phobia and Anxiety Inventory.

Purpose: Constructed for assessment of the "somatic, cognitive and behavioral aspects of social phobia."
Population: Ages 14 and older.
Publication Date: 1996.
Acronym: SPAI.
Scores, 3: Social Phobia, Agoraphobia, Difference.
Administration: Individual or group.
Price Data, 2006: $85 per complete kit including manual and 25 QuikScore™ forms; $42 per 25 QuikScore™ forms; $59 per manual.
Time: (15) minutes.
Comments: Self-report.
Authors: Samuel M. Turner, Deborah C. Beidel, and Constance V. Dancu.
Publisher: Multi-Health Systems, Inc.
Cross References: For reviews by George Engelhard, Jr. and Delores D. Walcott, see 14:363.

[2370]
Social Phobia & Anxiety Inventory for Children.

Purpose: "Assesses the frequency and range of social fears and anxiety in children and adolescents."
Population: Ages 8–14.
Publication Date: 1998.
Acronym: SPAI-C.
Scores: Total score only.
Administration: Group or individual.
Price Data, 2006: $85 per complete kit including manual and 25 QuikScore™ forms; $42 per 25 QuikScore™ forms; $59 per manual (1998, 50 pages).
Time: (20–30) minutes.
Comments: Self-report; also available as a Windows compatible computer program with a decremented counter; "has been translated into several languages."
Authors: Deborah C. Beidel, Samuel M. Turner, and Tracy L. Morris.
Publisher: Multi-Health Systems, Inc.
Cross References: For reviews by Sarah J. Allen and Loraine J. Spenciner, see 15:233.

[2371]
Social Problem-Solving Inventory—Revised.

Purpose: Designed to measure people's "ability to resolve problems of everyday living."
Population: Ages 13 and over.
Publication Dates: 1990–2002.

Acronym: SPSI-R.
Administration: Individual.
Price Data, 2006: $112 per complete kit including technical manual (2002, 114 pages), 25 long forms, and 25 short forms; $59 per technical manual; $42 per 25 long QuikScore™ forms; $40 per 25 short QuikScore™ forms.
Foreign Editions: Also available in French-Canadian, German, Russian, Spanish, and Turkish.
Authors: Thomas J. D'Zurilla, Arthur M. Nezu, and Albert Maydeu-Olivares.
Publisher: Multi-Health Systems, Inc.
  a) LONG VERSION.
  Acronym: SPSI-R: L.
  Scores, 9: Positive Problem Orientation, Negative Problem Orientation, Rational Problem Solving (Problem Definition and Formulation, Generation of Alternative Solutions, Decision Making, Solution Implementation and Verification), Impulsivity/Carelessness Style, Avoidance Style.
  Time: (15–20) minutes.
  b) SHORT VERSION.
  Acronym: SPSI-R: S.
  Scores, 4: Positive Problem Orientation, Negative Problem Orientation, Impulsivity/Carelessness Style, Avoidance Style.
  Time: (10) minutes.
Cross References: For reviews by Pam Lindsey and Gretchen Owens, see 16:227.

[2372]
Social Responsiveness Scale.

Purpose: Designed to help "establish the diagnosis of autism spectrum conditions."
Population: Ages 4-18 years.
Publication Date: 2005.
Acronym: SRS.
Scores, 6: Social Awareness, Social Cognition, Social Communication, Social Motivation, Autistic Mannerisms, Total.
Administration: Group or individual.
Price Data, 2006: $91 per complete kit including 15 Parent AutoScore forms, 15 Teacher AutoScore forms, and manual (69 pages); $50 per manual; $38.50 per 25 Parent AutoScore forms; $38.50 per 25 Teacher AutoScore forms, bulk discounts available; Computerized components: $88 per 25-use Windows SRS scoring CD, bulk discounts available; $16.50 per 100 PC answer sheets; $22 per Continuing Education Questionnaire and Evaluation Form.
Time: (15-20) minutes.
Comments: This test is to be completed by a parent, teacher, or other custodial caretaker.
Authors: John N. Constantino and Christian P. Gruber.
Publisher: Western Psychological Services.

[2373]

Social Reticence Scale.

Purpose: To assess an individual's shyness.
Population: High school and college and adults.
Publication Date: 1986.
Acronym: SRTS.
Scores: Total score only.
Administration: Individual or group.
Price Data: Available from publisher (www.mindgarden.com).
Time: (5-10) minutes.
Authors: Warren H. Jones and Stephen Briggs.
Publisher: Mind Garden, Inc.
Cross References: See T4:2499 (1 reference); for reviews by Owen Scott, III and William K. Wilkinson, see 11:370 (1 reference).

[2374]

Social Skills Inventory, Research Edition.

Purpose: "To assess basic social communication skills."
Population: Ages 14 and over reading at or above the eighth grade level.
Publication Date: 1989.
Acronym: SSI.
Scores, 7: Emotional Expressivity, Emotional Sensitivity, Emotional Control, Social Expressivity, Social Sensitivity, Social Control, Total.
Administration: Group and individual.
Price Data, 2006: $40 per sampler set including manual (21 pages); $120 per 150-copy duplication set; quantity discounts available for bulk permissions; $10 per individual report for web-based version.
Time: (30–45) minutes.
Comments: Test booklet title is Self-Description Inventory; self-administered; web version is available.
Author: Ronald E. Riggio.
Publisher: Mind Garden, Inc.
Cross References: See T5:2451 (4 references) and T4:2501 (4 references); for reviews by Judith C. Conger and Susan M. Sheridan, see 11:371 (3 references).

[2375]

Social Skills Rating System.

Purpose: Designed to obtain information on the social behaviors of children and adolescents from teachers, parents, and the students themselves.
Population: Ages 3 to 18.
Publication Date: 1990.
Acronym: SSRS.
Administration: Individual or group.
Price Data, 2006: $129.99 per preschool/elementary levels starter set including 10 copies of each form and level questionnaires, 10 assessment-intervention records, and manual (207 pages); $110.99 per secondary level starter set; $33.99 per 30 hand-scored questionnaires (select level and form); $46.99 per 30 scannable questionnaires (select level and form; $45.99 per 30 assessment-intervention records; $21.99 per 25 scannable header sheets; $85.99 per manual; $249.99 per ASSIST Kit for Individual Scoring and Reporting (Macintosh/Windows); $999.99 per ASSIST Kit for Individual and Group Scanning and Reporting (Windows CD-ROM).
Time: (15-25) minutes.
Comments: Ratings by teachers and parents as well as student self-ratings; expanded version of the Teacher Ratings of Social Skills; hand scored or computer scores; computer-scored report options: individual or group summary reports, teacher and parent letters, suggested intervention activities.
Authors: Frank M. Gresham and Stephen N. Elliott.
Publisher: Pearson Assessments (originally published by AGS Publishing, acquired by Pearson in 2005).
  a) PRESCHOOL.
  Population: Ages 3-0 to 4-11.
  Scores, 6: Social Skills, Cooperation, Assertion, Problem Behaviors, Internalizing, Externalizing.
  Forms, 2: Parent, Teacher.
  b) ELEMENTARY.
  Population: Grades K–6.
  Scores, 11: Social Skills, Cooperation, Assertion, Responsibility, Empathy, Self-Control, Problem Behaviors, Externalizing, Internalizing, Hyperactivity, Academic Competence.
  Forms, 3: Student, Parent, Teacher.
  Comments: Forms for all grades completed by parent and teacher; those for Grades 3–6 also completed by student.
  c) SECONDARY.
  Population: Grades 7–12.
  Scores, 3: Same as *b* above except no Hyperactivity subscale.
  Forms, 3: Same as *b* above.
Cross References: See T5:2452 (24 references); for reviews by Kathryn M. Benes and Michael Furlong and by Mitchell Karno, see 12:362 (10 references); see also T4:2502 (4 references).

[2376]

Social Skills Training: Enhancing Social Competence with Children and Adolescents.

Purpose: Designed to measure social skills problems and help design appropriate intervention programs to develop social competence.
Population: Ages 5–18.
Publication Date: 1995.
Administration: Individual.
Forms, 3: Parent, Teacher, Pupil.
Price Data, 2004: Price data for user's guide (267 pages) photocopiable resource book, 8 photo cards, and research and technical supplement (37 pages) available from publisher.

Time: Administration time not reported.
Comments: Assessments are incorporated in Social Skills Training: Enhancing Social Competence with Children and Adolescents program.
Authors: Susan H. Spence.
Publisher: NFER-Nelson Publishing Co. Ltd. [England].
    a) SOCIAL COMPETENCE WITH PEERS QUESTIONNAIRE.
    Forms, 3: Parent, Teacher, Pupil.
    Scores, 3: Total score for each form.
    b) SOCIAL WORRIES QUESTIONNAIRE.
    Forms, 3: Parent, Teacher, Pupil.
    Scores, 3: Total score for each form.
    c) SOCIAL SITUATION CHECKLIST.
    Scores, 1: Total score only.
    d) SOCIAL SKILLS QUESTIONNAIRE.
    Forms, 3: Parent, Teacher, Pupil.
    Scores, 3: Total score for each form.
    e) ASSESSMENT OF PERCEPTION OF EMOTION FROM FACIAL EXPRESSION.
    Scores: Total score only.
    f) ASSESSMENT OF PERCEPTION OF EMOTION FROM POSTURE CUES.
    Scores: Total score only.
Cross References: For reviews by Kathleen M. Johnson and Caroline Manuele-Adkins, see 16:228.

[2377]

Social Styles Analysis.

Purpose: Constructed to identify a person's social style of presentation and interaction.
Population: Adults.
Publication Date: 1989.
Scores: 4 categories: Analytical, Driver, Amiable, Expressive.
Administration: Group.
Editions, 2: Self, Other.
Manual: No manual.
Price Data: Price information available from publisher for package for self analysis (5.25-inch or 3.5-inch diskette); package for other analyses (5.25-inch or 3.5-inch diskette).
Time: Administration time not reported.
Comments: IBM microcomputer necessary for scoring.
Author: Wilson Learning Corporation.
Publisher: Jossey-Bass, A Wiley Company.
Cross References: For a review by C. Dale Carpenter, see 11:372.

[2378]

Socio-Sexual Knowledge and Attitudes Assessment Tool—Revised.

Purpose: Designed to assess sexual knowledge and attitudes of individuals with developmental disabilities.

Population: Developmentally disabled adults (ages 16-71), can be used with other adults.
Publication Dates: 1976–2003.
Acronym: SSKAAT-R.
Scores, 8: Anatomy, Women's Bodies and Women's Knowledge of Men, Men's Bodies and Men's Knowledge of Women, Intimacy, Pregnancy/Childbirth and Child Rearing, Birth Control and STDs, Sexual Boundaries, Total.
Administration: Individual.
Price Data, 2005: $295 per complete kit including easel, stimulus cards, 20 record forms, and manual (2003, 47 pages); $55 per 20 record forms; $75 per training video (DVD format).
Time: Untimed.
Authors: Dorothy Griffiths and Yona Lunsky.
Publisher: Stoelting Co.
Cross References: For a review by Mary M. Clare, see 16:229; for a review by Edward S. Herold of an earlier edition, see 9:1152; see also T3:2237 (1 reference).

[2379]

Softball Skills Test.

Purpose: "To improve teaching and evaluation of softball skills."
Population: Grades 5-12 and college.
Publication Date: 1991.
Scores, 4: Batting, Fielding Ground Balls, Overhand Throwing, Baserunning.
Administration: Individual.
Price Data, 2001: $14 per manual (64 pages).
Time: Administration time not reported.
Author: Roberta E. Rikli, Editor.
Publisher: American Association for Active Lifestyles and Fitness.
Cross References: For a review by Don Sebolt, see 12:363.

[2380]

Solid Geometry: National Achievement Tests.

Purpose: To measure achievement in solid geometry.
Population: High school students.
Publication Dates: 1958–1960.
Scores: Total score only.
Administration: Group.
Forms, 2: A, B.
Price Data: Available from publisher.
Time: 40 minutes.
Comments: No specific manual; combined manual (1958, 12 pages) for this test and following tests: Plane Trigonometry (T6:1918), Plane Geometry (T6:1917), and First Year Algebra Test (T6:1003).
Authors: Ray Webb and Julius H. Hlavaty (manual).
Publisher: Psychometric Affiliates.
Cross References: For a review by Sheldon S. Myers, see 6:653.

[2381]
Sources of Stress Scale [2006 Revision].

Purpose: Designed as "an instrument to identify origins of perceived and current anxiety, to quantify the intensity of such stresses, and to determine the pattern of such perceptions for predictions and subsequent interventions."
Population: High school and adults.
Publication Dates: 1986-2006.
Acronym: S.O.S.S.
Administration: Group.
Price Data, 2006: $30 per 25 scales; $.40 per answer sheet; $30 per test manual (2006, 37 pages); $.30 per scoring scale; $.50 per answer sheet; $.25 for profile charts.
Time: [5-15] minutes per scale.
Comments: Self-rating scale.
Authors: Louise M. Soares and Anthony T. Soares.
Publisher: Castle Consultants.

a) CORPORATE EXECUTIVE FORM.
Scores: 12 categories: Daily Issues, Professional Issues, Internal Personnel, Outside Influence, Changes, Finances/Money, The Future, Health, My Personal Life, Myself, Personal Relationships, Time Management.

b) GRADUATE STUDENT FORM.
Scores: 12 categories: Campus Life, Academic Activities, Field Experiences, College Personnel, plus last 8 categories from *a* above.

c) CORPORATE EXECUTIVE FORM.
Scores: 12 categories: Daily Issues, Professional Issues, Internal Personnel, Outside Influence, Changes, Finances/Money, The Future, Health, My Personal Life, Myself, Personal Relationships, Time Management.

d) HIGH SCHOOL FORM.
Scores: 12 categories: Extracurricular Activities, Academic Activities, Life at School, High School, plus last 8 categories from *a* above.

e) NURSING FORM.
Scores: 12 categories: Same as *a* above.

f) PARENT FORM.
Scores: 12 categories: Children, Family Issues, Spouse/Partner, Work/Job/Occupation, plus last 8 categories from *a* above.

g) POLITICIAN FORM.
Scores: 12 categories: Same as *a* above.

h) SCHOOL ADMINISTRATOR FORM.
Scores: 12 categories: Instructional Leadership, Organizational Issues, Legal & Political Issues, Resource Allocation, plus last 8 categories from *a* above.

i) SENIOR CITIZEN FORM.
Scores: 12 categories: Same as *f* above but including Quality of Life Issues and excluding Work/Job/Occupation.

j) TEACHER FORM.
Scores: 12 categories: Classroom Issues, Professional Issues, School Issues, plus last 9 categories from *a* above.

k) YOUNG ADULTS FORM.
Scores: 12 categories: Same as *f* above.
Cross References: For reviews by JoAnn Murphey and Wesley E. Sime of an earlier edition, see 15:235.

[2382]
The Southern California Ordinal Scales of Development.

Purpose: To provide "differential assessment of educational needs and abilities."
Population: Multihandicapped, developmentally delayed, and learning disabled children.
Publication Dates: 1977–1985.
Acronym: SCOSD.
Scores: 6 scales: Cognition, Communication, Social-Affective Behavior, Practical Abilities, Fine Motor Abilities, Gross Motor Abilities.
Administration: Individual.
Price Data, 2002: $130 per complete instrument.
Time: (60–120) minutes per scale.
Comments: A Piagetian-based assessment system.
Authors: Donald I. Ashurst, Elaine Bamberg, Julika Barrett, Ann Bisno, Artice Burke, David C. Chambers, Jean Fentiman, Ronald Kadish, Mary Lou Mitchell, Lambert Neeley, Todd Thorne, and Doris Wents.
Publisher: Foreworks.
Cross References: See T5:2459 (1 reference); for reviews by Cameron J. Camp and Arlene C. Rosenthal, see 10:338.

[2383]
Space Relations (Paper Puzzles).

Purpose: Developed as an assessment of mechanical aptitude.
Population: Ages 17 and over.
Publication Dates: 1984–1996.
Scores: Total score only.
Administration: Group.
Price Data, 2002: $91 per start-up kit including 25 test booklets, score key, and interpretation and research manual; $54 per 25 tests; $28 per interpretation and research manual; $20 per score key.
Time: (9) minutes.
Authors: L. L. Thurstone and T. E. Jeffrey.
Publisher: Pearson Performance Solutions [No reply from publisher; status unknown].
Cross References: For reviews by Phillip L. Ackerman and Mark A. Albanese, see 15:236.

[2384]
Space Thinking (Flags).

Purpose: To measure the ability to visualize a stable figure, drawing or diagram when it is moved into different positions.
Population: Industrial employees.
Publication Dates: 1959–1984.
Scores: Total score only.

Administration: Individual or group.
Price Data, 2002: $91 per start-up kit including 25 test booklets, score key, and interpretation and research manual; $54 per 25 test booklets (quantity discounts available); $20 per score key; $28 per interpretation and research manual.
Time: 5 minutes.
Authors: L. L. Thurstone and T. E. Jeffrey.
Publisher: Pearson Performance Solutions [No reply from publisher; status unknown].
Cross References: See T4:2515 (1 reference), T3:898 (1 reference), and T2:2245 (1 reference); for a review by I. MacFarlane Smith, see 6:1086.

[2385]
Spadafore ADHD Rating Scale.

Purpose: Designed "to examine the wide range of behaviors that are frequently associated with ADHD symptoms."
Population: Ages 5 through 19.
Publication Date: 1997.
Acronym: S-ADHD-RS.
Scores, 4: Impulsivity/Hyperactivity, Attention, Social Adjustment, ADHD Index.
Administration: Individual.
Price Data, 2006: $80 per test kit including manual (80 pages) 25 scoring protocols, 25 observation forms, and 25 medication tracking forms; $25 per 25 scoring protocols; $15 per 25 observation forms; $15 per 25 medication tracking forms; $25 per manual.
Time: Untimed.
Comments: Rating scale to be completed by classroom teachers about a child; also included in kit: behavioral observation form and medication monitoring form; previously listed as Spadafore Attention Deficit Hyperactivity Disorder Rating Scale.
Authors: Gerald J. Spadafore and Sharon J. Spadafore.
Publisher: Academic Therapy Publications.
Cross References: For reviews by Scott T. Meier and Judy Oehler-Stinnett, see 14:364.

[2386]
Spadafore Diagnostic Reading Test.

Purpose: Constructed to assess decoding and comprehension skills in reading.
Population: Grades 1–12; ages 6 through adults.
Publication Date: 1983.
Acronym: SDRT.
Scores, 15: 3 performance levels (Independent, Instructional, Frustration) for each of 5 subtests (Decoding [Word Recognition, Oral Reading], Comprehension [Oral Reading, Silent Reading, Listening]).
Administration: Individual.
Price Data, 2006: $65 per complete kit including manual (60 pages), test plates, and 10 test booklets; $28 per set of test plates; $15 per 10 test booklets; $22 per manual; $22 per specimen set.

Time: (30–60) minutes.
Comments: Criterion-referenced.
Author: Gerald J. Spadafore.
Publisher: Academic Therapy Publications.
Cross References: See T4:2516 (1 reference); for a review by James R. Sanders and Blaine R. Worthen, see 9:1159.

[2387]
Spanish Assessment of Basic Education, Second Edition.

Purpose: "Designed to measure achievement in the basic skills … with students for whom Spanish is the language of instruction."
Population: Grades 1.0–1.9, 1.6–2.9, 2.6–3.9, 3.6–4.9, 4.6–6.9, 7.0–8.9.
Publication Dates: 1991–1994.
Acronym: SABE/2.
Administration: Group.
Price Data, 2006: $24 per 35 practice tests (select level); $63 per 100 student diagnostic profiles (select level); $24 per 35 parent reports (select level); $3.15 per class record sheet; $23 per examiner's manual (1991, 41–57 pages) (select level); $27 per user's guide (1991, 64 pages); $31 per technical report (1994, 43 pages); $23 per norms book (1994, 159 pages); scoring service available from publisher.
Author: CTB Macmillan/McGraw-Hill.
Publisher: CTB/McGraw-Hill.
   a) LEVEL 1.
Population: Grades 1.0–1.9.
Scores, 11: Word Attack, Vocabulary, Reading Comprehension, Mechanics, Expression, Mathematics Computation, Mathematics Concepts and Applications, Total Reading, Total Mathematics, Total Language, Total Battery.
Price Data: $228 per 35 scannable test books.
Time: (205) minutes.
   b) LEVEL 2.
Population: Grades 1.6–2.9.
Scores: Same as *a* above.
Price Data: Same as *a* above.
Time: (219) minutes.
   c) LEVEL 3.
Population: Grades 2.6–3.9.
Scores: Same as *a* above.
Price Data: Same as *a* above.
Time: (255) minutes.
   d) LEVEL 4.
Population: Grades 3.6–4.9.
Scores, 12: Vocabulary, Reading Comprehension, Spelling, Mechanics, Expression, Mathematics Computation, Mathematics Concepts and Applications, Study Skills, Total Reading, Total Mathematics, Total Language, Total Battery.

Price Data: $179 per 35 reusable test books; $68 per 50 answer sheets (for CompuScan® or handscoring); $72 per set of 3 handscoring stencils.
Time: (249) minutes.
e) LEVEL 5.
Population: Grades 4.6–6.9.
Scores: Same as *d* above.
Price Data: Same as *d* above.
Time: (260) minutes.
f) LEVEL 6.
Population: Grades 7.0–8.9.
Scores: Same as *d* above.
Price Data: Same as *d* above.
Time: (259) minutes.
Cross References: For reviews by Maria Prendes Lintel and Emelia C. Lopez, see 13:291.

[2388]
Spanish/English Reading Comprehension Test [Revised].

Purpose: Designed to "determine the degrees of bilingualism."
Population: Grades 1–6.
Publication Dates: 1974–1993.
Scores: Total score and grade level equivalents.
Administration: Group or individual.
Forms, 2: English, Spanish.
Price Data, 2006: $20 per packet including manual (1993, 42 pages) and 1 English and 1 Spanish rating/answer sheet (permission to copy answer sheets is included).
Time: (30) minutes.
Comments: Spanish Reading based on Mexican curriculum materials; English Reading based on U.S.A. curriculum materials; English Reading Comprehension Test is translated from the Spanish version; pretesting and posttesting used.
Author: Steve Moreno.
Publisher: Moreno Educational Co.
Cross References: For reviews by Jorge E. Gonzalez and Craig S. Shwery and by Salvador Hector Ochoa, see 15:237; for reviews by Esteban L. Olmedo and David T. Sanchez, see 9:1161.

[2389]
Spanish Reading Inventory.

Purpose: To help teachers and other professionals determine a student's reading proficiency in Spanish.
Population: Grades 1–4+.
Publication Date: 1997.
Scores, 7: Independent, Instructional, Frustration, Word Recognition in Isolation, Word Recognition in Context, Comprehension-Oral, Comprehension-Silent.
Administration: Individual.
Forms, 2: A, B.

Price Data, 2003: $52.95 per complete kit (specify Form A or Form B); $32.95 per performance booklets (specify Form A or Form B).
Time: Administration time not reported.
Author: Jerry L. Johns.
Publisher: Kendall/Hunt Publishing Company.
Cross References: For a review by Salvador Hector Ochoa, see 16:230.

[2390]
Spanish Structured Photographic Expressive Language Test.

Purpose: Assessment of "the monolingual or bilingual child's generation of specific morphological and syntactical structures."
Population: Ages 3-0 to 5-11, 4-0 to 9-5.
Publication Date: 1989.
Acronym: SPELT.
Scores: Item scores only.
Administration: Individual.
Time: Administration time not reported.
Comments: The design of the Spanish SPELT tests is patterned after the original SPELT-II and SPELT-P (9:1198), however, it is not a direct translation of them. Many of the grammatical structures in the English edition were not able to be translated into Spanish. When necessary, to allow for differences in the two languages, grammatical structures were either deleted or added.
Authors: Ellen O'Hara Werner and Janet Dawson Kresheck.
Publisher: Janelle Publications, Inc.
a) SPANISH STRUCTURED PHOTOGRAPHIC EXPRESSIVE LANGUAGE TEST-II.
Population: Ages 4-0 to 9-5.
Acronym: SPELT-II.
Price Data: Price information available from publisher forr 10 response forms, 50 color photographs, and manual (1989, 39 pages).
b) SPANISH STRUCTURED PHOTOGRAPHIC EXPRESSIVE LANGUAGE TEST-PRESCHOOL.
Population: Ages 3-0 to 5-11.
Acronym: SPELT-P.
Price Data: Price information available from publisher for 10 response forms, 37 color photographs, and manual (1989, 34 pages).
Cross References: For a review by Ronald B. Gillam and Linda S. Day, see 11:373; for a review by Joan D. Berryman of the original SPELT, see 9:1198 (2 references).

[2391]
SPAR Spelling and Reading Tests, Third Edition.

Purpose: Designed as a "group test of literacy."
Population: Ages 7-0 to 12-11 years.

Publication Dates: 1976–1998.
Acronym: SPAR.
Scores, 2: Reading Total Score, Spelling Total Score.
Administration: Group.
Parts, 2: Reading Test, Spelling Test.
Price Data, 2002: £7.99 per 20 For A or Form B; £9.99 per manual (1976, 32 pages) including photocopiable version of spelling test; £4.99 per scoring template (A or B); £11.99 per specimen set including 1 copy each of Test Forms A and B, and manual.
Time: 13 minutes for Spelling Test; (20–25) minutes for Reading Test.
Comments: Reading Test is available in parallel Forms (A and B); Spelling Test is created from three parallel banks of items found in the manual.
Author: Dennis Young.
Publisher: Hodder & Stoughton Educational [England].
Cross References: For reviews by Timothy Z. Keith and Brenda A. Stevens, see 14:365; see also T5:2467 (1 reference); for reviews by Cleborne D. Maddux and William R. Merz of the second edition, see 12:365 (2 references); see also T4:2520 (3 references); for reviews by J. Douglas Ayers of earlier editions of the Spelling Test and the Reading Test, see 8:76 and 8:742.

[2392]
Spatial Awareness Skills Program Test.

Purpose: Constructed to identify "children whose spatial awareness skills are developing more slowly than expected" and provide "information about how to remedy a deficit."
Population: Ages 4 to 10.
Publication Date: 1999.
Acronym: SASP Test.
Scores: Total score only.
Administration: Individual.
Price Data, 2006: $104 per complete kit including curriculum manual, instrument manual, 25 student response booklets, and scoring transparency; $41 per 25 student response booklets.
Time: (5) minutes.
Comments: Previously titled Test of Visual Analysis Skills (T5:2721); designed to be used with the Spatial Awareness Skills Program (SASP) Curriculum; criterion-referenced.
Author: Jerome Rosner.
Publisher: PRO-ED.
Cross References: For reviews by Connie T. England and Robert M. Thorndike, see 15:238.

[2393]
Spatial Reasoning.

Purpose: Designed to assess "a pupil's ability to manipulate shapes and patterns."
Population: Ages 5.4–15.5.

Publication Date: 2002.
Scores: Total score only.
Administration: Group.
Levels, 4: Age 6 and 7; Age 8 and 9; Age 10 and 11; Ages 12–14.
Price Data: Available from publisher.
Time: 20(35–40) minutes for Age 6 and 7; 27(40–45) minutes for Age 8 and 9; 28(45) minutes for Age 10 and 11; 33(45–50) minutes for Ages 12–14.
Comments: Designed to complement the publisher's Verbal (2701) and Non-Verbal Reasoning (1754) series of tests.
Authors: Pauline Smith and Thomas R. Lord.
Publisher: NFER-Nelson Publishing Co., Ltd. [England].
Cross References: For reviews by Kathy Bohan and Beth Doll, see 16:231.

[2394]
Speaking Proficiency English Assessment Kit.

Purpose: "To assess the English speaking proficiency of people who are not native speakers of English."
Population: Nonnative speakers of English.
Publication Date: 1996.
Acronym: SPEAK.
Scores: Total score only.
Administration: Individual or group.
Price Data: Available from publisher.
Time: (20) minutes.
Comments: Produced by the Test of English as a Foreign Language Program; provides a measure of an individual's speaking ability at the intermediate to advanced levels for English language programs, international teaching assistant training programs, and businesses.
Author: Educational Testing Service.
Publisher: Educational Testing Service.

[2395]
Speech and Language Evaluation Scale.

Purpose: "Designed for in-school screening and referral of students with speech and language problems."
Population: Ages 4.5-18.
Publication Dates: 1989-1990.
Acronym: SLES.
Scores, 6: Speech (Articulation, Voice, Fluency), Language (Form, Content, Pragmatics).
Administration: Individual.
Price Data, 2006: $135 per complete kit including 50 pre-referral checklist forms, 50 pre-referral intervention strategies documentation forms, technical manual (1989, 47 pages), 50 rating forms, and Speech and Language Classroom Intervention Manual (1990, 206 pages); $30 per 50 pre-referral checklist forms; $30 per 50 intervention strategies documentation forms; $15 per technical manual; $35 per 50 rating forms; $25 per

Speech and Language Intervention Manual; $25 per computerized quick score (WIN).
Time: (15-20) minutes.
Comments: Ratings by teachers.
Authors: Diane R. Fressola, Sandra Cipponeri-Hoerchler, Jacquelyn S. Hagan, Steven B. McDannold, Jacqueline Meyer (manual), and Stephen B. McCarney (technical manual).
Publisher: Hawthorne Educational Services, Inc.
Cross References: For reviews by Katharine G. Butler and Penelope K. Hall, see 12:367.

[2396]
Speech-Ease Screening Inventory (K–1).
Purpose: "Designed to screen the articulation, language development," and auditory comprehension of kindergartners and first-graders.
Population: Grades K–1.
Publication Date: 1985.
Scores: Item scores only in 5 areas (Articulation, Language Association, Auditory Recall, Vocabulary, Basic Concepts) and in 4 optional areas (Auditory, Similarities and Differences, Language Sample, Linguistic Relationships) plus 5 observational ratings (Voice Quality, Fluency, Syntax, Oral-Peripheral, Hearing).
Administration: Individual.
Price Data, 2006: $115 per complete kit; $32 per 100 screening forms; $27 per 50 summary sheets (specify kindergarten or first grade); $41 per manual (32 pages).
Time: (7-10) minutes.
Authors: Teryl Pigott, Jane Barry, Barbara Hughes, Debra Eastin, Patricia Titus, Harriett Stensel, Kathleen Metcalf, and Belinda Porter.
Publisher: PRO-ED.
Cross References: For reviews by Kris L. Baack and Eleanor E. Sanford, see 12:368.

[2397]
Speech Evaluation of the Patient with a Tracheostomy Tube.
Purpose: Designed to help speech-language pathologists "assess the potential of an adult patient with an artificial airway to use a device that promotes phonation."
Population: Adults with artificial airways.
Publication Dates: 1994–1997.
Scores: 6 evaluative areas: Current Airway Assessment Information, Ventilation Status, Nutritional and Swallowing Status, Clinical Observations/Assessment, Patient Goals, Recommendations.
Administration: Individual.
Price Data, 2006: $61 per kit including manual (1997, 124 pages) and reproducible diagrams and laminated evaluation report form.
Time: Administration time not reported.
Comments: Not a standardized test but author provides clinical recommendations based on the information provided on a patient's report form.

Author: Nancy Conway.
Publisher: PRO-ED.

[2398]
Speech Perception Instructional Curriculum and Evaluation.
Purpose: "Designed to provide a guide for developing listening skills in severely and profoundly deaf children."
Population: Hearing-impaired individuals ages 3–12.
Publication Date: 1995.
Acronym: SPICE.
Scores: Rates total of 16 goals within 4 categories: Detection (Detects Speech, Indicates Onset and Termination of Speech), Suprasegmental Perception (Discriminates between 2 Stimuli Differing in Duration/Stress/and/or Intonation, Identifies Among 3 Stimuli Differing in Duration/Stress/and/or Intonation, Identifies Among 4 Stimuli Differing in Duration/Stress/and/or Intonation, Differentiates Stimuli With Similar Duration but Differing in Stress and/or Intonation; Identifies Among Sentences Differing Only in Duration of Key Words, Vowels and Consonants (Identifies Among Six Sounds, Identifies Words of Similar Duration and Differing in Vowels and/or Consonants, Identifies Monosyllables With the Same Consonants and Differing Vowels; Engages in Discussion About a Familiar Topic, Engages in Connected Discourse Tracking), Connected Speech (Identifies Key Words in the Context of Sentences, Practiced Sentences, Converses Using Picture Context, Engaged in Discussion About a Familiar Topic, Engages in Connected Discourse Tracking.
Administration: Individual.
Price Data, 2001: $350 per complete kit including manual (221 pages), rating forms, box of 16 toys for listening activities, 374 illustrated word and sentence cards, auditory training screen, instructional videotape.
Time: Administration time not reported.
Comments: Informally documents present auditory skill level, helps identify instructional objectives; instructional videotape contains 18 teaching segments; can be adapted for individuals over age 12 through adult.
Authors: Jean S. Moog, Julia J. Biedenstein, and Lisa S. Davidson.
Publisher: Central Institute for the Deaf.

[2399]
The Speed and Capacity of Language Processing Test.
Purpose: "Designed to provide a wholistic measure of the efficacy of language comprehension."
Population: Ages 16–65.
Publication Date: 1992.
Acronym: SCOLP.
Scores, 2: The Speed of Comprehension Test, The Spot-the-Word Test.
Administration: Individual.

Price Data, 2006: £92 per complete kit including manual (16 pages), 3 acetates, and 6 packs of 25 scoring sheets; £18 per 25 scoring sheets (specify Speed of Comprehension Test A, Speed of Comprehension Test B, Speed of Comprehension Test C, Speed of Comprehension Test D, Spot-the-Word Vocabulary Test A, or Spot-the-Word Vocabulary Test B).
Time: Untimed.
Comments: Each subtest comes with different versions for the purpose of retesting: The Speed of Comprehension Test has 4 versions (A, B, C, D) and The Spot-the-Word Test has 2 versions (A, B).
Authors: Alan Baddeley, Hazel Emslie, and Ian Nimmo-Smith.
Publisher: Harcourt Assessment [England].

[2400]
Spelling Test: National Achievement Tests.
Purpose: Assesses achievement in the spelling of common words.
Population: Grades 3–4, 5–8, 7–9, 10–12.
Publication Dates: 1936–1957.
Scores: Total score only.
Administration: Group.
Manual: No manual.
Price Data: Available from publisher.
Time: (25) minutes.
Comments: 1956–1957 tests identical to tests copyrighted 1939.
Authors: Robert K. Speer and Samuel Smith.
Publisher: Psychometric Affiliates.
Cross References: For a review by James A. Fitzgerald, see 5:230; for a review by W. J. Osburn, see 1:1161.

[2401]
Spiritual Well-Being Scale.
Purpose: "Developed as a general indicator of the subjective state of religious and existential well-being."
Population: Adults.
Publication Dates: 1982-1991.
Acronym: SWBS.
Scores, 3: Religious Well-Being, Existential Well-Being, Total Spiritual Well-Being.
Administration: Individual or group.
Price Data, 2001: $20 per specimen set including scale, manual (1991, 6 pages), bibliography, and scoring and research information; $2.25 or less per scale; volume discounts and student discounts available.
Time: (10-15) minutes.
Comments: Even-numbered items produce Existential Well-Being Scale (EWB); odd-numbered items produce Religious Well-Being Scale (RWB).
Authors: Craig W. Ellison and Raymond F. Paloutzian.
Publisher: Life Advance, Inc.

Cross References: See T5:2474 (1 reference); for reviews by Ayres D'Costa and Patricia Schoenrade, see 12:369 (1 reference); see also T4:2529 (1 reference).

[2402]
Sports Emotion Test.
Purpose: "Designed to show how an athlete responds affectively to a competition."
Population: High school through adult athletes.
Publication Dates: 1980-1983.
Acronym: SET.
Scores, 24: 4 scores (Intensity, Concentration, Anxiety, Physical Readiness) for 6 different points in time (24 Hours Before, At Breakfast, Just Before, After Start, At Peak, Something Wrong).
Administration: Group.
Price Data: License to reproduce for Ph.Ds and Ed.D.s available from publisher.
Time: (10-20) minutes.
Authors: E. R. Oetting and C. W. Cole (profile).
Publisher: E. R. Oetting, Colorado State University.
Cross References: For reviews by Robert D. Brown and Robert P. Markley, see 10:339.

[2403]
Spousal Assault Risk Assessment Guide.
Purpose: "Helps criminal justice professionals predict the likelihood of domestic violence."
Population: Individuals suspected of or being treated for spousal or family-related assault.
Publication Date: 1999.
Acronym: SARA.
Scores: Total score only.
Administration: Individual.
Price Data, 2006: $74 per complete kit including 25 checklist forms, 25 assessment forms, and manual; $31 per 25 assessment forms; $21 per 25 checklist forms; $40 per manual.
Time: Administration time not reported.
Comments: Completed by clinician/rater (criminal justice professional) after all available sources of information from suspect/offender, victim, etc. are gathered.
Authors: P. Randall Kropp, Stephen D. Hart, Christopher D. Webster, and Derek Eaves.
Publisher: Multi-Health Systems, Inc.
Cross References: For reviews by Ira S. Katz and Michael J. Scheel, see 15:239.

[2404]
Standard Progressive Matrices, New Zealand Standardization.
Purpose: Designed as a measure of nonverbal reasoning skills.
Population: New Zealand children ages 8–15 and adults.
Publication Date: 1985.

Acronym: SPM.
Scores: Total score only.
Administration: Group.
Price Data: Available from publisher.
Time: 30 minutes.
Authors: J. Raven (manual), J. C. Raven (manual), J. H. Court (manual), and New Zealand Council for Educational Research.
Publisher: New Zealand Council for Educational Research [New Zealand].
Cross References: See T5:2478 (2 references); for information on all editions of the Progressive Matrices, see 9:1007 (67 references), T3:1914 (200 references), 8:200 (190 references), T2:439 (122 references), and 7:376 (194 references); for a review by Morton Bortner, see 6:490 (78 references); see also 5:370 (62 references); for reviews by Charlotte Banks, W. D. Wall, and George Westby, see 4:314 (32 references); for reviews by Walter C. Shipley and David Wechsler of the 1938 edition, see 3:258 (13 references); for a review by T. J. Keating, see 2:1417 (8 references).

[2405]
The Standard Timing Model.

Purpose: "Designed to simulate the motions, functions and operations of automatic production machines" for use in selection, evaluation, and training of employees.
Population: Mechanics, electricians, and operators.
Publication Date: 1971.
Scores: 4 tasks.
Administration: Individual.
Price Data: Available from publisher.
Time: [60] minutes.
Author: Scientific Management Techniques, Inc.
Publisher: Scientific Management Techniques, Inc.
Cross References: For reviews by Sami Gulgoz and Gary L. Marco, see 12:370.

[2406]
Standardized Bible Content Tests, Forms I and J.

Purpose: Intended for "assessment of biblical knowledge (Bible/Theology/World View)."
Population: College freshman and seniors.
Publication Dates: 1956-1996.
Acronym: SBCT.
Scores: Total score only.
Administration: Group or individual.
Restricted Distribution: This test is "for the exclusive use of institutions of higher learning, such as Bible colleges, liberal arts colleges, and seminaries."
Price Data, 2005: $1 per test; $.10 per answer sheet; $2 per scoring key; bulk discount pricing is available.
Time: (35-45) minutes.
Comments: Formerly Major Bible Tests A and B.

Author: Commission on Professional Development of the Accrediting Association of Bible Colleges.
Publisher: The Association for Biblical Higher Education.
Cross References: See 7:651 (1 reference).

[2407]
Standardized Reading Inventory, Second Edition.

Purpose: "Designed primarily to assess children's independent, instructional, and frustration reading levels in word recognition and comprehension skills."
Population: Ages 6-0 to 14-6.
Publication Dates: 1986–1999.
Acronym: SRI-2.
Scores, 4: Passage, Comprehension, Word Accuracy, Vocabulary in Context, Reading Quotient.
Administration: Individual.
Forms, 2: A, B.
Price Data, 2006: $268 per complete kit including manual (1999, 134 pages), story book, 25 each Forms A and B vocabulary sheets, 25 each Forms A and B record booklets, and 50 profile scoring forms; $20 per 25 vocabulary sheets (specify form); $55 per 25 record booklets (specify form); $25 per 50 profile scoring forms; $50 per story book; $50 per examiner's manual.
Time: (30–90) minutes.
Comments: Second Edition is norm-referenced.
Author: Phyllis L. Newcomer.
Publisher: PRO-ED.
Cross References: For reviews by Alan Solomon and Brenda A. Stevens, see 14:366; for reviews by Kenneth W. Howell and Cleborne D. Maddux of the original edition, see 10:340.

[2408]
Standardized Test of Computer Literacy and Computer Anxiety Index (Version AZ), Revised.

Purpose: To measure general computer literacy and identify students who have computer-related anxieties.
Population: Students in introductory computer literacy courses.
Publication Date: 1984.
Acronym: STCL and CAIN.
Administration: Group.
Price Data: Available from publisher.
Authors: Michael Simonson, Mary Montag (manual and achievement test), and Matt Maurer (manual and anxiety survey).
Publisher: Iowa State University Research Foundation, Inc. [No reply from publisher; status unknown].
  a) STANDARDIZED TEST OF COMPUTER LITERACY (VERSION AZ), REVISED.
  Purpose: Measures achievement in computer literacy.

Scores, 3: Computer Systems, Computer Applications, Computer Programming.
Time: 90(105) minutes.
Comments: May be administered in one session or in separate sessions for each of 3 sections.
b) COMPUTER ANXIETY INDEX.
Time: Administration time not reported.
Comments: Test booklet title is Computer Opinion Survey.
Cross References: For reviews by Ron Edwards and Kevin L. Moreland, see 10:341.

[2409]
Stanford Achievement Test—Abbreviated Version—8th Edition.

Purpose: "Measures student achievement in reading, mathematics, language, spelling, study skills, science, social science, and listening."
Population: Primary (1.5–4.5), Intermediate (4.5–7.5), Advanced (7.5–9.9), TASK (9.0–12.9).
Publication Dates: 1989–1992.
Administration: Group.
Price Data, 2002: $52 per examination kit (for preview only) including complete battery test booklet, directions for administering, practice test with directions (Primary 1 through Advanced 2 only), and hand-scorable answer document (Primary 3 through TASK 3 only); $29 per 25 complete/partial battery hand-scorable test booklets; $21 per copy of directions for administration (specify level); $7.50 per copy of class records; $64 per fall or spring national norms booklet (1988), and $103 per SAT abbreviated national norms booklet (1991).
Comments: For fall testing, the publisher recommends the use of the previous grade level test.
Author: The Psychological Corporation.
Publisher: PsychCorp, A brand of Harcourt Assessment, Inc.

a) PRIMARY 1.
Population: Grades 1.5–2.5.
Scores, 12: Word Study Skills, Word Reading, Reading Comprehension, Total Reading, Language/English, Spelling, Listening, Concepts of Number, Mathematics Computation, Mathematics Applications, Total Mathematics, Environment.
Price Data: $156 per 25 complete battery Type 2 machine-scorable test booklets; $129 per 25 hand-scorable test booklets; $39.80 for keys for hand scoring (hand scoring requires Norms Booklets) complete/partial battery hand-scorable test booklets (Primary 1–Primary 3).
Time: 167 minutes for Partial battery; 187 minutes for Basic battery; 210 minutes for Complete battery.
b) PRIMARY 2.
Population: Grades 2.5–3.5.
Scores, 12: Word Study Skills, Reading Vocabulary, Reading Comprehension, Total Read-

ing, Language/English, Spelling, Listening, Concepts of Numbers, Mathematics Computation, Mathematics Applications, Total Mathematics, Environment.
Price Data: Same as *a* above.
Time: 160 minutes for Partial battery; 180 minutes for Basic battery; 203 minutes for Complete battery.
c) PRIMARY 3.
Population: Grades 3.5–4.5.
Scores, 16: Word Study Skills, Reading Vocabulary, Reading Comprehension, Total Reading, Language Mechanics, Language Expression, Total Language, Study Skills, Spelling, Listening, Concepts of Number, Mathematics Computation, Mathematics Applications, Total Mathematics, Science, Social Science.
Price Data: $156 per 25 complete battery machine-scorable test booklets; $129 per 25 complete battery hand-scorable test booklets; $156 per 25 Type 2 partial battery machine-scorable test booklets; $129 per 25 partial battery hand-scorable test booklets; $129 per 25 complete battery reusable test booklets; $129 per 25 partial battery reusable test booklets; $117 per 100 complete/partial battery Type 2 machine-scorable answer folders; $29 per 25 Form J complete/partial battery hand-scorable answer folders; $46 per keys for hand scoring complete battery hand-scorable answer folders (Primary 3–TASK 3).
Time: 152 minutes for Partial battery; 197 minutes for Basic battery; 233 minutes for Complete battery.
d) INTERMEDIATE 1–3.
Population: Grades 4.5–7.5.
Scores, 15: Reading Vocabulary, Reading Comprehension, Total Reading, Language Mechanics, Language Expression, Total Language, Study Skills, Spelling, Listening, Concepts of Numbers, Mathematics Computation, Mathematics Applications, Total Mathematics, Science, Social Science.
Price Data: $129 per 25 complete battery reusable test booklets; $128 per 25 partial battery reusable test booklets; $117 per 100 complete/partial battery Type 2 machine-scorable answer folders; $29 per 25 Form J complete/partial battery hand-scorable answer folders; $46 per keys for hand scoring complete battery hand-scorable answer folders (Primary 3–TASK 3); see c above for additional price information.
Time: 142 minutes for Partial battery; 187 minutes for Basic battery; 223 minutes for Complete battery.
e) ADVANCED 1–2.
Population: Grades 7–8.
Scores, 15: Reading Vocabulary, Reading Comprehension, Total Reading, Language Mechanics,

Language Expression, Total Language, Study Skills, Spelling, Listening, Concepts of Numbers, Mathematics Computation, Mathematics Applications, Total Mathematics, Science, Social Science.

Price Data: Same as *d* above.

Time: 142 minutes for Partial battery; 186 minutes for Basic battery; 222 minutes for Complete battery.

f) TASK 1–3.

Population: Grades 9–12.

Scores, 9: Reading Vocabulary, Reading Comprehension, Total Reading, Language/English, Study Skills, Spelling, Mathematics, Science, Social Science.

Price Data: $118 per 25 complete battery reusable test booklets; $117 per 100 complete/partial battery Type 2 machine-scorable answer folders; $29 per 25 Form J complete/partial battery hand-scorable answer folders.

Time: 95 minutes for Partial battery; 119 minutes for Basic battery; 155 minutes for Complete battery.

Cross References: See T5:2483 (1 reference); for reviews by Stephen N. Elliott, James A. Wollack, and Kevin L. Moreland, see 12:371.

[2410]
Stanford Achievement Test, Tenth Edition.

Purpose: Measures student achievement in reading, language, spelling, study skills, listening, mathematics, science and social science.

Population: Grades K.0–12.9.

Publication Dates: 1923–2003.

Acronym: Stanford 10.

Administration: Group.

Forms, 4: A, B, D, E.

Levels, 13: Stanford Early School Achievement Test 1, Stanford Early School Achievement Test 2, Primary 1, Primary 2, Primary 3, Intermediate 1, Intermediate 2, Intermediate 3, Advanced 1, Advanced 2, Stanford Test of Academic Skills 1, Stanford Test of Academic Skills 2, Stanford Test of Academic Skills 3.

Price Data: Available from publisher.

Comments: A variety of assessment options are available including full-length and abbreviated multiple-choice batteries; large-print and Braille editions are available.

Author: Harcourt Assessment, Inc.

Publisher: Harcourt Assessment, Inc.

a) STANFORD EARLY SCHOOL ACHIEVEMENT TEST 1.

Population: Grades K.0–K.5.

Acronym: SESAT 1.

Forms, 2: Basic Battery, Complete Battery.

Scores, 6: Reading (Sounds and Letters, Word Reading, Total), Mathematics, Listening to Words and Stories, Environment.

Time: (105) minutes for Basic Battery; (135) minutes for Complete Battery.

b) STANFORD EARLY SCHOOL ACHIEVEMENT TEST 2.

Population: Grades K.5–1.5.

Acronym: SESAT 2.

Forms, 2: Basic Battery, Complete Battery.

Scores, 7: Reading (Sounds and Letters, Word Reading, Sentence Reading, Total), Mathematics, Listening to Words and Stories, Environment.

Time: (140) minutes for Basic Battery; (170) minutes for Complete Battery.

c) PRIMARY 1.

Population: Grades 1.5–2.5.

Forms, 4: Basic Battery, Complete Battery, Abbreviated Battery, Language.

Scores, 11-12: Reading (Word Study Skills, Word Reading, Sentence Reading, Reading Comprehension, Total), Mathematics (Mathematics Problem Solving, Mathematics Procedures, Total), Language, Spelling, Listening (not available in Abbreviated Battery), Environment.

Time: (295) minutes for Basic Battery; (325) minutes for Complete Battery; (212) minutes for Abbreviated Battery.

d) PRIMARY 2.

Population: Grades 2.5–3.5.

Forms, 4: Same as *c* above.

Scores, 10-11: Reading (Word Study Skills, Reading Vocabulary, Reading Comprehension, Total), Mathematics (Mathematics Problem Solving, Mathematics Procedures, Total), Language, Spelling, Listening (not available in Abbreviated Battery), Environment.

Time: (265) minutes for Basic Battery; (295) minutes for Complete Battery; (189) minutes for Abbreviated Battery.

e) PRIMARY 3.

Population: Grades 3.5–4.5.

Forms, 4: Same as *c* above.

Scores, 11-12: Reading (Word Study Skills, Reading Vocabulary, Reading Comprehension, Total), Mathematics (Mathematics Problem Solving, Mathematics Procedures, Total), Language, Spelling, Listening (not available in Abbreviated Battery), Science, Social Science.

Time: (280) minutes for Basic Battery; (330) minutes for Complete Battery; (203) minutes for Abbreviated Battery.

f) INTERMEDIATE 1.

Population: Grades 4.5–5.5.

Forms, 4: Same as *c* above.

Scores, 11-12: Same as *c* above.

Time: (280) minutes for Basic Battery; (330) minutes for Complete Battery; (201) minutes for Abbreviated Battery.

g) INTERMEDIATE 2.
Population: Grades 5.5–6.5.
Forms, 4: Same as *c* above.
Scores, 10-11: Reading (Reading Vocabulary, Reading Comprehension, Total), Mathematics (Mathematics Problem Solving, Mathematics Procedures, Total), Language, Spelling, Listening (not available in Abbreviated Battery), Science, Social Science.
Time: (260) minutes for Basic Battery; (310) minutes for Complete Battery; (187) minutes for Abbreviated Battery.
h) INTERMEDIATE 3.
Population: Grades 6.5–7.5.
Forms, 4: Same as *c* above.
Scores, 10-11: Same as *g* above.
Time: (260) minutes for Basic Battery; (310) minutes for Complete Battery; (187) minutes for Abbreviated Battery.
i) ADVANCED 1.
Population: Grades 7.5–8.5.
Forms, 4: Same as *c* above.
Scores, 10-11: Same as *g* above.
Time: (260) minutes for Basic Battery; (310) minutes for Complete Battery; (186) minutes for Abbreviated Battery.
j) ADVANCED 2.
Population: Grades 8.5–9.9.
Forms, 4: Same as *c* above.
Scores, 10-11: Same as *g* above.
Time: (260) minutes for Basic Battery; (310) minutes for Complete Battery; (185) minutes for Abbreviated Battery.
k) STANFORD TEST OF ACADEMIC SKILLS 1.
Population: Grades 9.0–9.9.
Acronym: TASK 1.
Forms, 4: Same as *c* above.
Scores, 8: Reading (Reading Vocabulary, Reading Comprehension, Total), Mathematics, Language, Spelling, Science, Social Science.
Time: (180) minutes for Basic Battery; (230) minutes for Complete Battery; (160) minutes for Abbreviated Battery.
l) STANFORD TEST OF ACADEMIC SKILLS 2.
Population: Grades 10.0–10.9.
Acronym: TASK 2.
Forms, 4: Same as *c* above.
Scores, 8: Same as *k* above.
Time: Same as *k* above.
m) STANFORD TEST OF ACADEMIC SKILLS 3.
Population: Grades 11.0–12.9.
Acronym: TASK 3.
Forms, 4: Same as *c* above.
Scores, 8: Same as *k* above.
Time: Same as *k* above.

Cross References: For reviews by Russell N. Carney and David T. Morse, see 16:232; see T5:2484 (15 references); for reviews by Ronald A. Berk and Thomas M. Haladyna of an earlier edition, see 13:292 (80 references); for reviews of the Stanford Achievement Test-Abbreviated-8th Edition by Stephen N. Elliott and James A. Wollack and by Kevin L. Moreland, see 12:371; for information on an earlier edition of the Stanford Achievement Test, see T4:2551 (44 references); for reviews by Frederick G. Brown and Howard Stoker, see 11:377 (78 references); for reviews by Mark L. Davison and by Michael J. Subkoviak and Frank H. Farley of the 1982 Edition, see 9:1172 (19 references); see also T3:2286 (80 references); for reviews by Robert L. Ebel and A. Harry Passow and an excerpted review by Irvin J. Lehmann of the 1973 edition, see 8:29 (51 references); see also T2:36 (87 references); for an excerpted review by Peter F. Merenda of the 1964 edition, see 7:25 (44 references); for a review by Miriam M. Bryan and an excerpted review by Robert E. Stake (with J. Thomas Hastings), see 6:26 (13 references); for a review by N. L. Gage of an earlier edition, see 5:25 (19 references); for reviews by Paul R. Hanna (with Claude E. Norcross) and by Virgil E. Herrick, see 4:25 (20 references); for reviews by Walter W. Cook and Ralph C. Preston, see 3:18 (33 references). For reviews of subtests, see 9:1173 (1 review), 9:1174 (1 review), 9:1175 (1 review), 8:291 (2 reviews), 8:745 (2 reviews), 7:209 (2 reviews), 7:537 (1 review), 7:708 (1 review), 7:802 (1 review), 7:895 (1 review), 6:637 (1 review), 5:656 (2 reviews), 5:698 (2 reviews), 5:799 (1 review), 4:419 (1 review), 4:555 (1 review), 4:593 (2 reviews), 3:503 (1 review), and 3:595 (1 review); for a review of the Stanford Test of Academic Skills [1982 Edition] by John C. Ory, see 9:1182; see also T3:2298 (3 references); for reviews by Clinton I. Chase and Robert L. Thorndike of an earlier edition, see 8:31.

[2411]
Stanford-Binet Intelligence Scales, Fifth Edition.

Purpose: Designed to assess "intelligence and cognitive abilities."
Population: Ages 2-0 to 89-9.
Publication Dates: 1916–2003.
Acronym: SB5.
Scores, 13: Nonverbal Fluid Reasoning, Verbal Fluid Reasoning, Nonverbal Knowledge, Verbal Knowledge, Nonverbal Quantitative Reasoning, Verbal Quantitative Reasoning, Nonverbal Visual-Spatial Processing, Verbal Visual-Spatial Processing, Nonverbal Working Memory, Verbal Working Memory, Nonverbal IQ, Verbal IQ, Full Scale IQ.
Subtests: Subtests and Partial Batteries: Abbreviated Battery (Nonverbal Fluid Reasoning and Verbal Knowledge).

Administration: Individual.
Price Data, 2006: $937 per complete kit including examiner's manual (336 pages), 3 item books, technical manual, 25 test records, child card, layout card, and manipulatives in a storage case all in a canvas bag; $113.50 per examiner's manual; $113.50 per technical manual; $56.50 per 25 test records.
Time: (45–75) minutes; (15–20) minutes for Abbreviated Battery.
Author: Gale H. Roid.
Publisher: Riverside Publishing.
Cross References: For reviews by Judy A. Johnson and Rik Carl D'Amato and by Joseph C. Kush, see 16:233; for information on an earlier edition, see T5:2485 (245 references) and T4:2553 (120 references); for reviews by Anne Anastasi and Lee J. Cronbach, see 10:342 (89 references); see also 9:1176 (41 references), T3:2289 (203 references), 8:229 (176 references), and T2:525 (428 references); for a review by David Freides, see 7:425 (258 references); for a review by Elizabeth D. Fraser and excerpted reviews by Benjamin Balinski, L. B. Birch, James Maxwell, Marie D. Neale, and Julian C. Stanley, see 6:536 (110 references); for reviews by Mary R. Haworth and Norman D. Sundberg of the second revision, see 5:413 (121 references); for a review by Boyd R. McCandless, see 4:358 (142 references); see also 3:292 (217 references); for excerpted reviews by Cyril Burt, Grace H. Kent, and M. Krugman, see 2:1420 (132 references); for reviews by Francis W. Maxfield, J. W. M. Rothney, and F. L. Wells, see 1:1062.

[2412]
Stanford-Binet Intelligence Scales for Early Childhood, Fifth Edition.

Purpose: Designed to assess intelligence and cognitive abilities.
Population: Ages 2 years to 7 years, 3 months.
Publication Date: 2005.
Acronym: Early SB5.
Scores, 14: Full Scale IQ (Nonverbal IQ, Verbal IQ), Nonverbal IQ (Nonverbal Fluid Reasoning, Nonverbal Knowledge, Nonverbal Quantitative Reasoning, Nonverbal Visual-Spatial Processing, Nonverbal Working Memory); Verbal IQ (Verbal Fluid Reasoning, Verbal Knowledge, Verbal Quantitative Reasoning, Verbal Visual-Spatial Processing, Verbal Working Memory); Abbreviated Battery IQ (Nonverbal Fluid Reasoning, Verbal Knowledge).
Administration: Individual.
Price Data, 2006: $355 per complete package including examiner's manual (282 pages), Item Book 1, Item Book 2, 25 record forms, manipulatives kit, child card, layout card, and carrying case; $49.50 per 25 record forms; $54.50 per examiner's manual.
Time: (15–50) minutes.

Comments: Adaptation of Stanford-Binet Intelligence Scales, Fifth Edition (2411).
Author: Gale H. Roid.
Publisher: Riverside Publishing.

[2413]
Stanford Diagnostic Mathematics Test, Fourth Edition.

Purpose: Designed to measure "competence in the basic concepts and skills that are prerequisite to problem solving in mathematics."
Publication Dates: 1976–1996.
Acronym: SDMT.
Administration: Group.
Parts, 2: Multiple Choice, Free Response.
Forms: 1 for Red, Orange, and Green levels; 2 (J, K) for Purple, Brown, and Blue levels.
Price Data, 2002: $37.50 per examination kit including multiple-choice test booklet and free-response test booklet (specify level) and directions for administering for each, answer document, practice test and practice test directions for administering, and ruler/marker; $17 per 25 practice tests and directions (specify level); $112 per 25 machine-scorable multiple-choice test booklets (specify Red, Orange, or Green level); $76 per 25 hand-scorable multiple-choice test booklets (specify Red, Orange, or Green level), directions for administering, and class record; $76 per 25 free-response test booklets (specify Red, Orange, or Green level) and directions for administering; $112 per hand-scorable multiple-choice/free-response combination kit including 25 hand-scorable multiple-choice test booklets and directions for administering, 25 free-response test booklets and directions for administering, and class record (specify Red, Orange, or Green level); $139 per machine-scorable multiple-choice/free response combination kit including 25 machine-scorable multiple-choice test booklets and directions for administering and 25 free-response test booklets and directions for administering (specify Red, Orange, or Green level); $76 per 25 reusable multiple-choice test booklets and directions for administering (specify Purple, Brown, or Blue level and Form J or K); $76 per 25 free response test booklets and directions for administering (specify Purple, Brown, or Blue level and Form J or K); $112 per reusable multiple-choice/free-response combination kit including 25 reusable multiple-choice test booklets and directions for administering and 25 free-response test booklets and directions for administering (specify Purple, Brown, or Blue level and Form J or K); $15 per set of response keys for multiple-choice tests (specify level and form); $16 per side-by-side keys for hand-scorable test booklets including blackline master of student record form (specify Red, Orange, or Green level); $15.50 per scoring guide for free-response tests including blackline master of student record form (specify level and form);

$22 per stencil keys for hand-scorable answer documents (specify Purple, Brown, or Blue level and Form J or K); $30 per 25 hand-scorable answer documents with blackline master of student record form and class record (specify Purple, Brown, or Blue level); $38 per 25 Purple/Brown/Blue level machine-scorable answer documents type I; $6.50 per 25 ruler/markers; $52 per Fall (1996, 166 pages) or Spring (1996, 166 pages) multilevel norms booklet; $22 per teacher's manual for interpreting (specify Level Red/Orange [1996, 61 pages], Green/Purple [1996, 64 pages], or Brown/Blue [1996, 63 pages]); $10 per directions for administering (specify multiple-choice or free-response, and Level Red, Orange, Green, or Purple/Brown/Blue); $6.50 per practice test directions for administering (specify Red, Orange, Green, Purple, or Brown Level); $6.50 per class record (specify Red, Orange, Green, or Purple/Brown/Blue level); price information for various scoring services available from publisher.

Author: Harcourt Brace Educational Measurement.

Publisher: Harcourt Assessment, Inc.

a) RED LEVEL.

Population: Grades 1.5–2.5.

Scores, 9: Concepts and Applications (Number Systems and Numeration, Patterns and Functions, Graphs and Tables, Problem Solving, Geometry and Measurement, Total), Computation (Addition of Whole Numbers, Subtraction of Whole Numbers, Total).

Time: 65 minutes for multiple choice; 90 minutes for free response.

b) ORANGE LEVEL.

Population: Grades 2.5–3.5.

Scores, 9: Same as for Red level.

Time: Same as for Red level.

c) GREEN LEVEL.

Population: Grades 3.5–4.5.

Scores, 11: Concepts and Applications (Number Systems and Numeration, Patterns and Functions, Graphs and Tables, Problem Solving, Geometry and Measurement, Total), Computation (Addition of Whole Numbers, Subtraction of Whole Numbers, Multiplication of Whole Numbers, Division of Whole Numbers, Total).

Time: Same as for Red level.

d) PURPLE LEVEL.

Population: Grades 4.5–6.5.

Scores, 12: Concepts and Applications (Number Systems and Numeration, Statistics and Probability, Graphs and Tables, Problem Solving, Geometry and Measurement, Patterns and Functions [free response only], Total), Computation (Addition of Whole Numbers, Subtraction of Whole Numbers, Multiplication of Whole Numbers, Division of Whole Numbers, Total).

Time: 65 minutes for multiple choice; 80 minutes for free response.

e) BROWN LEVEL.

Population: Grades 6.5–8.9.

Scores, 15: Concepts and Applications (Number Systems and Numeration, Patterns and Functions [free response only], Statistics and Probability, Graphs and Tables, Problem Solving, Geometry and Measurement, Total), Computation (Addition and Subtraction of Whole Numbers, Multiplication of Whole Numbers [multiple choice only], Division of Whole Numbers [multiple choice only], Multiplication and Division of Whole Numbers [free response only], Operations with Fractions and Mixed Numbers, Operations with Decimals and Percents, Equations, Total).

Time: Same as Purple level.

f) BLUE LEVEL.

Population: Grades 9.0–13.0.

Scores, 12: Concepts and Applications (Number Systems and Numeration, Patterns and Functions [free response only], Statistics and Probability, Graphs and Tables, Problem Solving, Geometry and Measurement, Total), Computation (Operations with Whole Numbers, Operations with Fractions and Mixed Numbers, Operations with Decimals and Percents, Equations, Total).

Time: Same as Purple level.

Cross References: See T5:2486 (3 references); for reviews by Irvin J. Lehmann, Philip Nagy, and G. Michael Poteat, see 13:293; see also T4:2554 (5 references); for reviews by Bruce G. Rogers and Lorrie A. Shepard of an earlier edition, see 9:1177 (2 references); see also T3:2291 (1 reference); for reviews by Glenda Lappan and Larry Souder, see 8:292.

[2414]
Stanford Diagnostic Reading Test, Fourth Edition.

Purpose: "Intended to diagnose students' strengths and weaknesses in the major components of the reading process."

Publication Dates: 1978–1996.

Acronym: SDRT4.

Administration: Group.

Forms, 2: J, K (for Purple, Brown, and Blue levels).

Price Data, 2002: $37.50 per examination kit including multiple-choice test booklet and directions for administering, practice test and directions for administering, answer document, class record form, Reading Questionnaire, Reading Strategies Survey, Story Retelling (Story and Response Form), and directions for each (specify level); $17 per 25 practice tests and directions for administering (specify Red, Orange, Green, Purple, or Brown level); $111 per 25 machine-scorable test booklets type 1 and directions for administering (specify Red, Orange, or Green level); $76 per 25 hand-scorable test booklets, directions for administering, and class record (specify Red, Orange, or Green level); $76 per 25 reusable test booklets and directions for administering (specify level and form); $37.50 per 25 Reading Questionnaires and directions for administering (specify level and form); $37.50 per 25 Reading Strategies Surveys and directions for administering (specify Level Red/Orange, Green/Purple, or Brown/Blue); $44.50 per Story Retelling manual (1995, 15 pages) and 25 Story and Response forms (specify Level Red/Orange, Green/Purple, or Brown/Blue); $37.50 per 25 machine-scorable answer documents type 1 (for Purple/Brown/Blue levels); $30 per 25 hand-scorable answer documents with blackline master of student record form and class record (for Purple/Brown/Blue levels); $15 per side-by-side keys for hand-scorable test booklets including blackline master of student record form (specify Red, Orange, or Green level); $15 per response keys (specify Purple, Brown, or Blue level and Form J or K); $22 per stencil keys for hand-scorable answer documents (specify Purple, Brown, or Blue level and Form J or K); $6.50 per class record (specify Level Red, Orange, Green, or Purple/Brown/Blue); $6.90 per 25 row markers; $52 per Fall or Spring Multilevel norms booklet (1996, 103 pages); $22 per teacher's manual for interpreting (specify Level Red/Orange [1996, 67 pages], Green/Purple [1996, 68 pages], or Brown/Blue [1996, 62 pages]); $10 per test directions for administering (specify Level Red, Orange, Green, or Purple/Brown/Blue); $6.50 per practice test directions for administering (specify Level Red, Orange, Green, Purple, or Brown); $6.50 per Reading Questionnaire directions for administering; $6.50 per Reading Strategies Survey directions for administering; $9 per Story Retelling manual; price information for scoring services available from publisher.

Authors: Bjorn Karlsen and Eric F. Gardner.
Publisher: Harcourt Assessment, Inc.

a) RED LEVEL.
Population: Grades 1.5–2.5.
Scores, 19: Phonetic Analysis (Consonants-Single, Consonants-Blends, Consonants-Digraphs, Consonants Total, Vowels-Short, Vowels-Long, Vowels Total, Total), Vocabulary (Word Reading, Listening Vocabulary, Nouns, Verbs, Others, Total), Comprehension (Sentences, Riddles, Cloze, Total), Paragraphs with Questions.
Time: 105(110) minutes.

b) ORANGE LEVEL.
Population: Grades 2.5–3.5.
Scores, 19: Phonetic Analysis (Consonants-Single, Consonants-Blends, Consonants-Digraphs, Consonants Total, Vowels-Short, Vowels-Long, Vowels Total, Total), Vocabulary (Listening Vocabulary, Reading Vocabulary, Synonyms, Classification, Total), Comprehension (Cloze, Total),

Paragraphs with Questions, Recreational Reading, Textual Reading, Functional Reading.
Time: 100(105) minutes.

c) GREEN LEVEL.
Population: Grades 3.5–4.5.
Scores, 25: Phonetic Analysis (Consonants-Single, Consonants-Blends, Consonants-Digraphs, Consonants Total, Vowels-Short, Vowels-Long, Vowels-Other, Vowels Total, Total), Vocabulary (Listening Vocabulary, Reading Vocabulary, Synonyms, Classification, Word Parts, Content Area Words, Total), Comprehension, Paragraphs with Questions, Recreational Reading, Textual Reading, Functional Reading, Initial Understanding, Interpretation, Critical Analysis and Reading Strategies.
Time: 100(105) minutes.

d) PURPLE LEVEL.
Population: Grades 4.5–6.5.
Scores, 16: Vocabulary (Reading Vocabulary, Synonyms, Classification, Word Parts, Content Area Words, Total), Comprehension, Paragraphs with Questions, Recreational Reading, Textual Reading, Functional Reading, Initial Understanding, Interpretation, Critical Analysis, Reading Strategies, Scanning.
Time: 85(90) minutes.

e) BROWN LEVEL.
Population: Grades 6.5–8.9.
Scores, 16: Same as Purple Level.
Time: 85(90) minutes.

f) BLUE LEVEL.
Population: Grades 9.0–12.9.
Scores, 16: Same as Purple Level.
Time: 85(90) minutes.

Cross References: See T5:2487 (19 references); for reviews by George Engelhard, Jr. and by Mark E. Swerdlik and Jayne E. Bucy, see 13:294 (9 references); see also T4:2555 (24 references); for reviews by Robert J. Tierney and James E. Ysseldyke of an earlier edition, see 9:1178 (7 references); see also T3:2292 (15 references); for a review by Bryon H. Van Roekel, see 8:777 (13 references); see T2:1651 (2 references); for a review by Lawrence M. Kasdon of Levels 1–2 of an earlier edition, see 7:725 (3 references).

[2415]
Stanford Early School Achievement Test, Third Edition.

Purpose: Measures school achievement.
Population: Grades K.0–K.5, K.5–1.5.
Publication Dates: 1969–1991.
Acronym: SESAT.
Administration: Group.
Forms, 2: J, L.
Price Data, 2002: $185 per 25 machine-scorable tests (Type 1, Form J; Type 2, Form L) (scored by

publisher) (select level); $23.90 per 25 practice tests and one directions for administering (select level); $7.50 per class record form; $35.50 per 25 previews for parents (select level); $21 per administration directions (select level and form); $7.50 per administration directions for practice test (select level); $67.50 per norms booklet (1988, Form J Only; 1991, Forms J and L) (select level); $47 per coordinator's handbook; $51.50 per examination kit including test booklet, administration directions, and practice test with directions (select level and form).
Comments: Downward extension of the Stanford Achievement Test Series.
Author: The Psychological Corporation.
Publisher: PsychCorp, A brand of Harcourt Assessment, Inc.

a) LEVEL 1.
Population: Grades K.0–K.5.
Scores, 8: Sounds and Letters, Word Reading, Total, Mathematics, Listening to Words and Stories, Total for Basic Battery, Environment, Total for Complete Battery.
Price Data: $185 per 25 machine-scorable test booklets (Type 1, Form J; Type 2, Form L); $119 per 25 hand-scorable test booklets (select form); $175 per set of scoring keys (select form).
Time: (190) minutes over 9 sessions.

b) LEVEL 2.
Population: Grades K.5–1.5.
Scores, 9: Sounds and Letters, Word Reading, Sentence Reading, Total, Mathematics, Listening to Words and Stories, Basic Battery Total, Environment, Complete Battery Total.
Price Data: $185 per 25 machine-scorable test booklets (Type 1, Form J; Type 2, Form L); $126 per 25 hand-scorable test booklets (select form); $175 per set of scoring keys (select form).
Time: (225) minutes over 9 sessions.
Cross References: See T5:2488 (10 references) and T4:2556 (2 references); for reviews by Phillip L. Ackerman and C. Dale Carpenter, see 11:378 (8 references); for a review by Mary J. Allen of an earlier edition, see 9:1179 (1 reference); see also T3:2293 (9 references); for a review by Courtney B. Cazden of an earlier edition, see 8:30 (6 references); see also T2:38 (1 reference); for reviews by Elizabeth Hagen and William A. Mehrens of Level 1, see 7:28.

[2416]
Stanford English Language Proficiency Test.
Purpose: Designed to evaluate "the listening, reading, writing, speaking, and comprehension skills" of English language learners.
Population: Grades K-12.
Publication Date: 2005.
Acronym: Stanford ELP.

Administration: Individual or group.
Forms, 3: A, B, C.
Levels, 5: Preliteracy, Primary, Elementary, Middle Grades, High School.
Restricted Distribution: Distribution is restricted to accredited schools and school districts.
Price Data, 2006: $104 per Ready-to-Test package-Form A, B, or C-Primary Level; $125 per Ready-to-Test package-Form A, B, or C-Elementary, Middle Grade, or High School Level; $42 per Exam kit including Test Booklet, Directions for Administering, Screening Test, Screening Test Directions, Response Booklet (Elementary-High School), Practice Test, and Practice Test Directions; $6.50 per Practice Test Directions for Administering; $11.50 per 10 Practice Test packs; $13.50 per 5 Screening tests; $6.50 per Screening Test Directions for Administering; $40 per cassettes; $12 per Directions for Administering; $36.50 per 10 machine-scorable test packs (Form A-Preliteracy [Listening/Speaking or Early Reading/Early Writing]); $36.50 per 10 machine-scorable test packs (Form A, B, or C-Primary); $26 per 10 machine-scorable record forms (Form A-Readiness); $26 per 10 machine-scorable response booklet packs (Form A, B, or C-Elementary, Middle Grade, or High School Level); $10.50 per Speaking booklet (Form A, B, or C-Primary); $44 per 10 reusable test packs (Form A, B, or C-Elementary, Middle Grade, or High School Level); $7 per class record; $31.50 per Readiness/Preliteracy Training CD; $22 per response keys (Form A, B, or C); $31.50 per Speaking/Writing Training Manual; $42 per technical report/manual (2005, 191 pages).
Foreign Language Edition: Stanford Spanish Language Proficiency Test edition available.
Comments: Test requires the use of a cassette player.
Author: Harcourt Assessment, Inc.
Publisher: Harcourt Assessment, Inc.

a) PRELITERACY.
Population: Grade K.
Subtests, 2: Listening, Speaking.
Scores: 3 scales: 2 Content scales (Listening, Speaking), 1 Communication scale (Social [Listening, Speaking]).
Time: (35-45) minutes.

b) PRIMARY.
Population: Grades K-2.
Subtests, 5: Listening, Speaking, Reading, Writing Conventions, Writing.
Scores: 8 scales: 5 Content scales (Listening, Speaking, Reading, Total Writing [Writing conventions, Writing], Comprehension [Listening and Reading]), 3 Communication scales (Social [Listening, Speaking], Academic [Reading, Writing Conventions, Writing], Productive [Speaking, Writing]).
Time: (85-95) minutes.

c) ELEMENTARY.
Population: Grades 3-5.
Subtests: Same as Primary.
Scores: Same as Primary.
Time: Same as Primary.
d) MIDDLE GRADES.
Population: Grades 6-8.
Subtests: Same as Primary.
Scores: Same as Primary.
Time: (95-105) minutes.
e) HIGH SCHOOL.
Population: Grades 9-12.
Subtests: Same as Primary.
Scores: Same as Primary.
Time: Same as Middle Grades.

[2417]
Stanford Writing Assessment Program, Third Edition.

Purpose: Provides for the direct assessment of written expression in four modes: Descriptive, Narrative, Expository, and Persuasive.
Population: Grades 3–12.
Publication Dates: 1982–1997.
Scores: 4 writing modes: Descriptive, Narrative, Expository, Persuasive.
Administration: Group.
Levels, 9: Primary 3, Intermediate 1, Intermediate 2, Intermediate 3, Advanced 1, Advanced 2, TASK 1, TASK 2, TASK 3.
Forms, 2: S, T (Form T is a secure form).
Price Data, 2002: $25.50 per 25 writing prompts, 25 response forms, and Directions for Administering (specify Descriptive, Narrative, Expository, or Persuasive); $8 per Directions for Administering (specify Descriptive, Narrative, Expository, or Persuasive); $11 per writing exam kit including 1 prompt each of Descriptive, Narrative, Expository and Persuasive, 1 Directions for Administering, 1 response form, and Reviewer's Edition; $75 per norms book; $22 per manual for interpreting (1997, 70 pages) (all forms and levels); scoring prices available from publisher.
Time: (50) minutes.
Comments: Holistic and analytic scoring available; computer scoring available; Form T is a secure form; Third edition provides information about student strengths and weaknesses, which can assist in instructional planning.
Author: Harcourt Brace Educational Measurement.
Publisher: Harcourt Assessment, Inc.
Cross References: For reviews by Linda Crocker and Sharon H. deFur, see 14:367; for reviews by Philip Nagy and Wayne H. Slater of an earlier editions, see 13:295.

[2418]
The Stanton Profile.

Purpose: Designed to provide "pre-employment personality and attitudinal assessments."
Population: Employment applicants.
Publication Dates: 1987–1995.
Scores, 6: 4 content scores (Work Motivation, Adaptability/Flexibility, Service Orientation, Trustworthiness), 2 validity checks (Social Desirability Bias, Infrequent Response Patterns).
Administration: Group or individual.
Manual: No manual.
Price Data: Available from the publisher.
Time: Untimed, generally requiring approximately 20 minutes.
Author: William G. Harris.
Publisher: ChoicePoint.

[2419]
The Stanton Survey and the Stanton Survey Phase II .

Purpose: Provides indications of previous counterproductive work behavior and attitudes toward honesty.
Population: Applicants for employment.
Publication Dates: 1964–1995.
Scores: Total score only.
Administration: Individual or group.
Price Data: Available from publisher.
Time: Untimed.
Comments: Available in hard copy or via telephonic IVR.
Authors: Carl S. Klump, Homer B. C. Reed, Jr., and Sherwood Perman.
Publisher: ChoicePoint.
  a) THE STANTON SURVEY.
  b) THE STANTON SURVEY PHASE II.
Cross References: For reviews by H. C. Ganguli and Kenneth G. Wheeler, see 9:1185. (An additional review by William G. Harris is available electronically from the Buros Institute national database: available from Ovid and EBSCO, and from Tests Reviews Online via the Buros webpage.)

[2420]
STAR Early Literacy®.

Purpose: A computer-adaptive, progress-monitoring assessment designed to assess the early literacy skills of beginning readers.
Population: Prekindergarten–Grade 3.
Publication Dates: 2001-2006.
Scores, 8: Graphophonemic Knowledge, General Readiness, Phonemic Awareness, Phonics, Comprehension, Structural Analysis, Vocabulary, Scaled Score.
Administration: Group.
Price Data, 2006: First year: $1,299, which includes software, manual, installation guide, testing in-

structions, support plan, remote installation & setup, plus $.39 per student. Subsequent years: $.39 per student ($50 minimum per school), which includes continued support plan and all upgrades/updates.

Time: (10) minutes.

Comments: Reports criterion-referenced scores; software includes report capabilities (e.g., diagnostic reports); capable of sharing databases with other Renaissance Learning software; data may be maintained on-site or hosted by the publisher; may be administered 2-10 times per year at monthly intervals. Minimum requirements (Windows and Macintosh): Internet Explorer 5.01, Netscape 7, Firefox 1.0, or Safari 1.0; 300-MHz processor; Windows 98SE or OS9; 32 MB Ram (128 for some components); 250 MB hard drive memory available; 800x600 resolution monitor with 256 colors; printer; information regarding complete system requirements available at http://renlearn.com/.

Author: Renaissance Learning, Inc.

Publisher: Renaissance Learning, Inc.

Cross References: For reviews by Theresa Graham and Sandra B. Ward, see 15:240.

[2421]
STAR Math®.

Purpose: A computer-adaptive, progress-monitoring assessment designed to assess students' mathematical abilities and overall mathematics achievement.

Population: Grades 1–12.

Publication Dates: 1998–2006.

Scores: Total score only.

Administration: Group.

Price Data, 2006: First year: $1,299, which includes software, manual, installation guide, testing instructions, support plan, remote installation & setup, plus $.39 per student. Subsequent years: $.39 per student ($50 minimum per school), which includes continued support plan and all upgrades/updates.

Time: (15) minutes.

Comments: Reports norm-referenced (percentile ranks, normal curve equivalents, grade equivalents) and criterion-referenced (math instructional levels) scores; software includes report capabilities (e.g., diagnostic reports); capable of sharing databases with other Renaissance Learning software; data may be maintained on-site or hosted by the publisher; may be administered 2-10 times per year at monthly intervals. Minimum requirements (Windows and Macintosh): Internet Explorer 5.01, Netscape 7, Firefox 1.0, or Safari 1.0; 300-MHz processor; Windows 98SE or OS9; 32 MB Ram (128 for some components); 250 MB hard drive memory available; 800x600 resolution monitor with 256 colors; printer; information regarding complete system requirements available at http://renlearn.com/.

Author: Renaissance Learning, Inc.

Publisher: Renaissance Learning, Inc.

Cross References: For reviews by Mary L. Garner and G. Michael Poteat, see 16:234; for reviews by Joseph C. Ciechalski and Cindy M. Walker of an earlier version, see 15:241.

[2422]
STAR Reading®.

Purpose: A computer-adaptive, progress-monitoring assessment designed to assess students' reading comprehension and overall reading achievement.

Population: Grades 1–12.

Publication Dates: 1996–2005.

Scores: Total score only.

Administration: Group.

Price Data, 2006: First year: $1,299, which includes software, manual, installation guide, testing instructions, support plan, remote installation & setup, plus $.39 per student. Subsequent years: $.39 per student ($50 minimum per school), which includes continued support plan and all upgrades/updates.

Time: (10) minutes.

Comments: Reports norm-referenced (percentile ranks, normal curve equivalents, grade equivalents) and criterion-referenced (instructional reading levels) scores; software includes report capabilities (e.g., diagnostic reports); capable of sharing databases with other Renaissance Learning software; data may be maintained on-site or hosted by the publisher; may be administered 2-10 times per year at monthly intervals. Minimum requirements (Windows and Macintosh): Internet Explorer 5.01, Netscape 7, Firefox 1.0, or Safari 1.0; 300-MHz processor; Windows 98SE or OS9; 32 MB Ram (128 for some components); 250 MB hard drive memory available; 800x600 resolution monitor with 256 colors; printer; information regarding complete system requirements available at http://renlearn.com/.

Author: Renaissance Learning, Inc.

Publisher: Renaissance Learning, Inc.

Cross References: For reviews by Lori Nebelsick-Gullett and by Betsy B. Waterman and David M. Sargent, see 15:242; for reviews by Theresa Volpe-Johnstone and Sandra Ward of the original edition, see 14:368.

[2423]
STAR Supplementary Tests of Achievement in Reading.

Purpose: "Designed to supplement the assessments that teachers make about their pupils' progress and achievement in reading.

Population: Ages 7–13.

Publication Dates: 2000–2003.

Administration: Group.

Levels, 3: STAR Test (Year 3), STAR Test (Years 4–6), STAR Test (Years 7–9).

Forms, 2: A, B.

Price Data, 2006: NZ$38.70 per specimen set (specify level) including teacher's manual (2001, 35 pages), 1 test booklet each of Forms A and B, 1 set answer keys each of Forms A and B; NZ$9.90 per 10 test booklets (specify Form A or B, specify level); NZ$9 per photocopiable masters answer key (Level 3, 4–6, specify Form A or B); NZ$9 per photocopiable masters marking key (Level 7–9, specify Form A or B).
Comments: Normed on children living in New Zealand.
Author: Warwick B. Elley.
Publisher: New Zealand Council for Educational Research [New Zealand].

> *a)* STAR TEST (3)
> **Scores, 4:** Word Recognition, Sentence Comprehension, Paragraph Comprehension, Vocabulary Range.
> *b)* STAR TEST (4–6).
> **Scores, 4:** Word Recognition, Sentence Comprehension, Paragraph Comprehension, Vocabulary Range.
> **Time:** 20(35) minutes.
> *c)* STAR TEST (7–9).
> **Scores, 6:** Word Recognition, Sentence Comprehension, Paragraph Comprehension, Vocabulary Range, The Language of Advertising, Reading Different Genres or Styles of Writing.
> **Time:** 30(45) minutes.

Cross References: For a review by John W. Young, see 15:243.

[2424]
START—Strategic Assessment of Readiness for Training.

Purpose: Designed to diagnose adults' learning strengths and weaknesses for workplace application.
Population: Adults.
Publication Date: 1994.
Acronym: START.
Scores, 8: Anxiety, Attitude, Motivation, Concentration, Identifying Important Information, Knowledge Acquisition Strategies, Monitoring Learning, Time Management.
Administration: Group or individual.
Price Data, 2006: $4.95 per assessment (volume discounts available).
Time: (15) minutes.
Authors: Claire E. Weinstein and David R. Palmer.
Publisher: H & H Publishing Co., Inc.
Cross References: For reviews by Phillip L. Ackerman and Patricia A. Bachelor, see 14:369.

[2425]
State-Trait Anger Expression Inventory-2.

Purpose: "Designed to measure the experience, expression, and control of anger for adolescents and adults."

Population: Ages 16 and over.
Publication Dates: 1988–1999.
Acronym: STAXI-2.
Scores, 12: State Anger Scale (Feeling Angry, Feel like Expressing Anger Verbally, Feel like Expressing Anger Physically, Total), Trait Anger Scale (Angry Temperament, Angry Reaction, Total), Angry Expression and Anger Control Scales (Anger Expression—Out, Anger Expression—In, Anger Control—Out, Anger Control—In), Anger Expression Index.
Administration: Group or individual.
Price Data, 2006: $226 per introductory kit including professional manual, 25 reusable item booklets, 50 rating sheets, and 50 profile forms; $445 per interpretive report software (CD-ROM) with unlimited scoring and interpretive reports.
Time: (12–15) minutes.
Author: Charles D. Spielberger.
Publisher: Psychological Assessment Resources, Inc.
Cross References: For reviews by Stephen J. Freeman and Beverly M. Klecker, see 15:244; see T5:2496 (6 references); for reviews by David J. Pittenger and Alan J. Raphael of the Revised Research Edition, see 13:296 (52 references); see also T4:2562 (12 references); for reviews by Bruce H. Biskin and Paul Retzlaff of the STAXI-Research Edition, see 11:379 (8 references).

[2426]
State-Trait Anxiety Inventory.

Purpose: Designed to assess anxiety as an emotional state (S-Anxiety) and individual differences in anxiety proneness as a personality trait (T-Anxiety).
Population: Grades 9-16 and adults.
Publication Dates: 1968-1984.
Acronym: STAI.
Scores, 2: State Anxiety, Trait Anxiety.
Administration: Group.
Forms, 2: X, Y.
Parts, 2: 2 parts for each form labeled Form 1 (State), Form 2 (Trait).
Price Data: Available from publisher (www.mindgarden.com).
Foreign Language Edition: Spanish edition available; many researcher translations available.
Time: (10-20) minutes.
Comments: Title on test is Self-Evaluation Questionnaire.
Authors: Charles D. Spielberger; Form Y and manual prepared in collaboration with R. L. Gorsuch, R. Lushene, P. R. Vagg, and G. A. Jacobs.
Publisher: Mind Garden, Inc.
Cross References: See T5:2497 (680 references), T4:2563 (646 references), 9:1186 (158 references), and T3:2300 (277 references); for reviews by Ralph Mason Dreger and Edward S. Katkin, see 8:683 (268 references); see also T2:1391 (45 references) and 7:141 (20 references).

[2427]

State-Trait Anxiety Inventory for Children.

Purpose: Designed to measure anxiety in children; distinguishes between a general proneness to anxious behavior rooted in the personality and anxiety as a fleeting emotional state.

Population: Upper elementary through junior high school children.

Publication Dates: 1970-1973.

Acronym: STAIC.

Scores, 2: State Anxiety, Trait Anxiety.

Administration: Group.

Price Data: Available from publisher (www. mindgarden.com).

Time: (20) minutes.

Comments: Downward extension of State-Trait Anxiety Inventory (2426); title on test is "How-I-Feel Questionnaire"; self-administering; can be administered verbally to younger children.

Authors: Charles D. Spielberger, C. Drew Edwards, Robert E. Lushene, Joseph Montuori, Denna Platzek.

Publisher: Mind Garden, Inc.

Cross References: See T5:2498 (78 references), T4:2564 (58 references), and T3:2301 (15 references); for a review by Norman S. Endler, see 8:684 (19 references); see also T2:1392 (2 references).

[2428]

State Trait-Depression Adjective Check Lists.

Purpose: "To measure both state and trait depression mood and feelings."

Population: Ages 14 and over.

Publication Dates: 1967–2002.

Acronym: ST-DACL.

Scores, 6: State-Positive Mood, State-Negative Mood, State Mood-Total, Trait-Positive Mood, Trait-Negative Mood, Trait Mood-Total.

Administration: Group.

Forms, 4: 1, 2, A-B, C-D.

Price Data: Price information available from publisher for introductory kit including manual (2002, 83 pages), 25 forms 1 & 2, 25 forms C-D, and 25 profile forms.

Time: (4–8) minutes per list.

Comments: Developed from the Depression Adjective Check List.

Author: Bernard Lubin.

Publisher: EdITS/Educational and Industrial Testing Service.

Cross References: See T5:2499 (1 reference); for reviews by Andres Barona and by Janet F. Carlson and Betsy Waterman of an earlier edition, see 13:297 (21 references); see also T4:742 (79 references), 9:315 (21 references), T3:681 (46 references), 8:536 (20 references), and T2:1154 (2 references); for reviews of the earlier edition by Leonard D. Goodstein and Douglas M. McNair, see 7:65 (3 references); see also P:57 (4 references).

[2429]

Station Employee Applicant Inventory.

Purpose: Designed to help "assess a potential employee's willingness to contribute to team efforts, practice safe work habits, handle cash and merchandise with complete trustworthiness, stay on the job once hired" and "follow company policies."

Population: Service station applicants.

Publication Date: 1997.

Acronym: SEAI.

Scores, 9: Validity/Candidness, Honesty, Interpersonal Cooperation, Drug Avoidance, Applied Arithmetic, Skills and Abilities, Safety, Tenure, Employability Index.

Administration: Individual or group.

Forms, 2: Paper and pencil, computer.

Price Data, 2005: $24 per 1–999 each Quanta Touch Test, Quanta Software for Windows—administration and scoring (no booklets), Quanta Software for Windows—scoring only (one booklet for every coupon ordered), RLH Online; volume discounts available.

Foreign Language Edition: Available in Spanish.

Time: (45–60) minutes.

Author: London House.

Publisher: Pearson Performance Solutions [No reply from publisher; status unknown].

[2430]

Stephens Oral Language Screening Test.

Purpose: To screen children "for potential problems in syntax and/or articulation associated with their production of standard American English dialects."

Population: Prekindergarten-grade 1.

Publication Date: 1977.

Acronym: SOLST.

Scores, 2: Syntax, Articulation.

Administration: Individual.

Price Data: Available from publisher.

Time: (9) minutes.

Author: M. Irene Stephens.

Publisher: Interim Publishers [No reply from publisher; status unknown].

Cross References: See 9:1193 (2 references).

[2431]

The Stieglitz Informal Reading Inventory: Assessing Reading Behaviors from Emergent to Advanced Levels.

Purpose: Designed to provide educators with information about students' reading behaviors.

Population: Grades 1–9.

Publication Date: 1992.
Acronym: SIRI.
Scores, 7: Graded Words in Context (Independent, Instructional, Frustration), Graded Reading Passages (Word Recognition, Oral Comprehension, Prior Knowledge, Interest).
Administration: Individual.
Price Data: Available from publisher.
Time: (20–30) minutes.
Author: Ezra L. Stieglitz.
Publisher: Pearson Allyn & Bacon.
Cross References: For reviews by Koressa Kutsick Malcolm and Stephanie Stein, see 13:298.

[2432]
Stirling Eating Disorder Scales.

Purpose: Developed as a comprehensive measure of anorexia and bulimia.
Population: Adolescents and adults.
Publication Dates: 1995–1996.
Acronym: SEDS.
Scores: 8 scales: Anorexic Dietary Cognitions, Anorexic Dietary Behavior, Bulimic Dietary Cognitions, Bulimic Dietary Behavior, Perceived External Control, Low Assertiveness, Low Self-Esteem, Self-Directed Hostility.
Administration: Individual.
Price Data, 2006: £74 per complete kit including 25 record forms, 25 profile sheets, and manual (1995, 33 pages).
Time: (30) minutes.
Authors: Gwenllian-Jane Williams and Kevin Power.
Publisher: Harcourt Assessment [England].
Cross References: For reviews by Jeffrey A. Atlas and Ronald A. Berk, see 16:235.

[2433]
Stoelting Brief Nonverbal Intelligence Test.

Purpose: Designed as a nonverbal, nonlanguage measure of cognitive functions.
Population: Ages 6-0 to 20-11.
Publication Date: 1999.
Acronym: S-BIT.
Scores, 7: Figure Ground, Form Completion, Sequential Order, Repeated Patterns, S-BIT IQ, Visualization, Fluid Reasoning.
Administration: Individual.
Price Data, 2005: $295 per complete kit including 20 record forms, examiner's manual (1999, 191 pages), easel book, and response cards; $20 per 20 record forms; $50 per examiner's manual; $170 per easel book; $35 per carrying case; $70 per response cards.
Time: (25) minutes.
Authors: Gale H. Roid and Lucy J. Miller.
Publisher: Stoelting Co.
Cross References: For reviews by Russell N. Carney and Susana Urbina, see 15:245.

[2434]
Stokes/Gordon Stress Scale.

Purpose: Developed to measure stressors in healthy individuals over age 65.
Population: Healthy individuals over age 65.
Publication Date: 1987.
Acronym: SGSS.
Scores: Total stress score.
Administration: Group.
Price Data: Available from publisher.
Time: (15–30) minutes.
Comments: Self-administered in person or by mail.
Authors: Shirlee A. Stokes and Susan E. Gordon.
Publisher: Lienhard School of Nursing.
Cross References: For a review by Sharon L. Weinberg, see 13:299; see also T4:2572 (1 reference).

[2435]
Strategic Decision Making Inventory.

Purpose: Designed as a guide to business managers to help them think strategically in their decision making process (deciding how to decide).
Population: Business managers.
Publication Date: 1983.
Scores, 2: Flexibility, Appropriateness.
Administration: Group.
Price Data, 2002: $8.95 per inventory; minimum of 20 (volume discounts available).
Time: [15–20] minutes.
Comments: Self-administered; self-scored.
Author: Herbert S. Kindler.
Publisher: The Center for Management Effectiveness, Inc.

[2436]
Strength Deployment Inventory.

Purpose: Designed to assess "personal strengths in relating to others" under two conditions: when things are going well, and when there is conflict.
Population: Adults.
Publication Dates: 1973–1996.
Acronym: SDI.
Scores: 7 Motivational Values Systems: (Altruistic-Nurturing, Assertive-Directing, Analytic-Autonomizing, Flexible-Cohering, Assertive-Nurturing, Judicious-Competing, Cautious-Supporting); 13 scores reflecting progression through stages of conflict.
Administration: Group or individual.
Price Data, 2001: $22 per Premier Edition including Standard Edition of the Strength Deployment Inventory, interpretive cards, and 2 exercises; Portrait of Personal Strengths and Portrait of Overdone Strengths; $5.50 per either Portrait available separately; $10 per Standard Edition; $14 per Component Edition including interpretive cards; $30 per manual (1996, 146 pages).

Foreign Language Editions: Standard Edition available in French, Swedish, and Spanish; Premier Edition available in Swedish and Dutch.
Time: (20–40) minutes for Standard Edition; (20–40) minutes per exercise in Premier Edition.
Comments: Self-scorable; for corporate (e.g., team building), clinical (e.g., relationship counseling), and career development (e.g., outplacement and welfare-to-work) uses; Feedback Edition uses self-rating and ratings of a significant other person.
Author: Elias H. Porter.
Publisher: Personal Strengths Publishing.
Cross References: For a review by Frederick T. L. Leong, see 14:371.

[2437]
Stress in General Scale.

Purpose: To measure job stress.
Population: Employees
Publication Date: 1992–2002.
Acronym: SIG.
Scores, 2: Pressure, Threat.
Administration: Individual or group.
Price Data, 2006: $10 per 100 test booklets.
Time: 3-5 minutes.
Comments: Previously listed with the Job Descriptive Index (1313).
Authors: Jeffrey M. Stanton, William K. Balzer, Patricia C. Smith, Luis Fernando Parra, and Gail H. Ironson.
Publisher: Bowling Green State University.
Cross References: For reviews by Christopher G. Bellah and by Leonard Handler and Amanda Jill Clemence, see 15:246.

[2438]
Stress Index for Parents of Adolescents.

Purpose: Designed to "identify stressful areas in parent-adolescent interactions."
Population: Parents of adolescents ages 11–19 years.
Publication Date: 1998.
Scores, 11: Adolescent Domain (Moodiness/Emotional Lability, Social Isolation/Withdrawal, Delinquency/Antisocial, Failure to Achieve or Persevere), Parent Domain (Life Restrictions, Relationship with Spouse/Partner, Social Alienation, Incompetence/Guilt), Adolescent-Parent Relationship Domain, Life Stressors, Total Parenting Stress.
Administration: Individual.
Price Data, 2006: $120 per introductory kit including 25 reusable item booklets, 25 hand-scorable answer sheet/profile forms, and professional manual (70 pages).
Time: (20) minutes.
Authors: Peter L. Sheras and Richard R. Abidin.
Publisher: Psychological Assessment Resources, Inc.
Cross References: For reviews by Elizabeth L. Jones and Susan M. Swearer, see 14:372.

[2439]
Stress Indicator & Health Planner [Revised].

Purpose: Designed to help an individual assess their current levels of stress, health, and wellness.
Population: Adults.
Publication Dates: 1990-2006.
Acronym: SIHP.
Scores, 10: Physical Distress, Psychological Distress, Behavioral Distress, Total Distress, Interpersonal Stress Assessment, Nutritional, Health Assessment, Total Wellness Assessment, Time-Stress Assessment, Occupational Stress Assessment.
Administration: Individual or group.
Parts, 5: Personal Distress Assessment, Interpersonal Stress Assessment, Wellness Assessment, Time-Stress Assessment, Occupational Stress Assessment.
Price Data, 2006: $14.95 per test booklet (2006, 24 pages); $38 per Professional/Trainer's Guidelines (1993, 15 pages); $14.95 per online version code.
Time: [30-60] minutes for basic; [180-360] minutes for facilitated/advanced.
Comments: Test can be self-administered and self-scored and includes a health planner.
Authors: Ken Keis, Terry D. Anderson, and Gwen Faulkner.
Publisher: Consulting Resource Group International, Inc.
Cross References: For reviews by Dennis C. Harper and Barbara L. Lachar of an earlier edition, see 13:300.

[2440]
Stress Management Questionnaire [Revised].

Purpose: Identifies how one responds to life stressors and copes with stress.
Population: Adults and adolescents.
Publication Dates: 1980–1999.
Acronym: SMQ.
Scores, 11: Warning Signs (Hostility/Anger, Perfectionism, Time Orientation, Disappointment, Negative Mood, Underachievement, Tension), Stress Effects (Physical, Live Work Satisfaction), Stressors (Life Events, Hassles)
Administration: Group or individual.
Forms, 2: Participant, Companion.
Price Data, 2001: $14 per questionnaire (discounts available).
Time: (20–25) minutes.
Comments: Manual title is "Stressmaster Trainer's Manual"; questionnaire completed by self and by a close companion; self-scored.
Author: James C. Petersen.
Publisher: The Assessment and Development Centre.
Cross References: For a review by Jayne E. Stake of an earlier version, see 10:348.

[2441]
Stress Processing Report.

Purpose: Enables individuals to identify, understand and change their reactions to stress, thereby improving their receptivity to organizational change.
Population: Adults.
Publication Date: 1994.
Acronym: SPR.
Scores: 19 domains: Self (Self-Image, Past View, Control, Approval, Growth, Effectiveness), Others (Inclusion, Interpersonal, Intimacy, Trust), Process (Receptiveness, Synergy, Cooperation, Time Orientation, Time Utilization), Goals (Satisfaction, Directedness, Expectations, Future View).
Administration: Individual or group.
Price Data: Price data for test materials including Self-Development Guide and Leader's Guide available from publisher.
Time: Administration time not reported.
Author: Human Synergistics International.
Publisher: Human Synergistics International.

[2442]
Stress Profile.

Purpose: "Developed to provide a brief yet comprehensive stress and health risk assessment."
Population: Adults.
Publication Date: 1999.
Scores, 16: Stress, Health Habits, Exercise, Rest/Sleep, Eating/Nutrition, Prevention, ARC Item Cluster, Social Support Network, Type A Behavior, Cognitive Hardiness, Coping Style, Positive Appraisal, Negative Appraisal, Threat Minimization, Problem Focus, Psychological Well-Being.
Administration: Group.
Price Data, 2006: $110 per kit including 25 AutoScore™ forms, manual (63 pages), and 1 reusable administration booklet; $46.75 per 25 AutoScore™ forms to be used with administration booklet; $54.50 per manual; $29 per 25 disposable administration booklets; $61 per 5 reusable administration booklets (quantity discounts available); $18 for WPS Test Report mail-in answer sheet; $260 per 25-use disk; $10.50 for FAX service.
Time: (20–30) minutes.
Comments: Can be administered and scored by hand or by computer.
Author: Kenneth M. Nowack.
Publisher: Western Psychological Services.
Cross References: For reviews by Carl Isenhart and Kevin J. McCarthy, see 15:247.

[2443]
Stress Resiliency Profile.

Purpose: Designed to identify some ways individuals unintentionally contribute to their own stress levels.
Population: Employees.

Publication Date: 1992.
Acronym: SRP.
Scores, 3: Deficiency Focusing, Necessitating, Skill Recognition.
Administration: Group or individual.
Price Data, 2001: $8.50 per test booklet/manual (23 pages).
Time: (15) minutes.
Comments: Self-administered and self-scored.
Authors: Kenneth W. Thomas and Walter G. Tymon, Jr.
Publisher: CPP, Inc.
Cross References: For reviews by John A. Mills and William R. Merz, Sr., see 13:301.

[2444]
Stromberg Dexterity Test.

Purpose: "Developed as an aid in choosing workers for jobs which require speed and accuracy of arm and hand movement."
Population: Trade school and adults.
Publication Dates: 1945–1981.
Acronym: SDT.
Scores: Total score only.
Administration: Individual.
Price Data, 2006: $700 per complete set including all necessary equipment and manual in case; $45 per manual.
Time: (5–10) minutes.
Author: Eleroy L. Stromberg.
Publisher: Harcourt Assessment, Inc.
Cross References: See T3:2317 (2 references) and T2:2235 (8 references); for a review by Julian C. Stanley, see 4:755 (1 reference).

[2445]
Strong Interest Inventory® [1994].

Purpose: Designed to "identify general areas of interests as well as specific activities and occupations" for further exploration.
Population: Ages 16 and over.
Publication Dates: 1927–1994.
Acronym: Strong.
Scores, 267: 6 General Occupational Themes: Realistic, Investigative, Artistic, Social, Enterprising, Conventional; 25 Basic Interest Scales: Realistic (Agriculture, Nature, Military Activities, Athletics, Mechanical Activities), Investigative (Science, Mathematics, Medical Science), Artistic (Music/Dramatics, Art, Applied Arts, Writing, Culinary Arts), Social (Teaching, Social Service, Medical Service, Religious Activities), Enterprising (Public Speaking, Law/Politics, Merchandising, Sales, Organizational Management), Conventional (Data Management, Computer Activities, Office Services); 211 Occupational Scales: Accountant (female, male), Actuary (f, m), Advertising Executive (f, m),

Agribusiness Manager (m), Architect (f, m), Artist/ Commercial (f, m), Artist/Fine (f, m), Art Teacher (f, m), Athletic Trainer (f, m), Audiologist (f, m), Auto Mechanic (f, m), Banker (f, m), Biologist (f, m), Bookkeeper (f, m), Broadcaster (f, m), Business Education Teacher (f, m), Buyer (f, m), Carpenter (f, m), Chef (f, m), Chemist (f, m), Child Care Provider (f), Chiropractor (f, m), College Professor (f, m), Community Service Organization Director (f, m), Computer Programmer/Systems Analyst (f, m), Corporate Trainer (f, m), Credit Manager (f, m), Dental Assistant (f), Dental Hygienist (f), Dentist (f, m), Dietitian (f, m), Elected Public Official (f, m), Electrician (f, m), Elementary School Teacher (f, m), Emergency Medical Technician (f, m), Engineer (f, m), English Teacher (f, m), Farmer (f, m), Flight Attendant (f, m), Florist (f, m), Food Service Manager (f, m), Foreign Language Teacher (f, m), Forester (f, m), Gardener/Groundskeeper (f, m), Geographer (f, m), Geologist (f, m), Hair Stylist (f, m), High School Counselor (f, m), Home Economics Teacher (f), Horticultural Worker (f, m), Housekeeping & Maintenance Supervisor (f, m), Human Resources Director (f, m), Interior Decorator (f, m), Investments Manager (f, m), Lawyer (f, m), Librarian (f, m), Life Insurance Agent (f, m), Marketing Executive (f, m), Mathematician (f, m), Mathematics Teacher (f, m), Medical Illustrator (f, m), Medical Records Technician (f, m), Medical Technician (f, m), Medical Technologist (f, m), Military Enlisted Personnel (f, m), Military Officer (f, m), Minister (f, m), Musician (f, m), Nurse/Licensed Practical (f, m), Nurse/Registered (f, m), Nursing Home Administrator (f, m), Occupational Therapist (f, m), Optician (f, m), Optometrist (f, m), Paralegal (f, m), Parks and Recreation Coordinator (f, m), Pharmacist (f, m), Photographer (f, m), Physical Education Teacher (f, m), Physical Therapist (f, m), Physician (f, m), Physicist (f, m), Plumber (m), Police Officer (f, m), Psychologist (f, m), Public Administrator (f, m), Public Relations Director (f, m), Purchasing Agent (f, m), Radiologic Technologist (f, m), Realtor (f, m), Reporter (f, m), Research & Development Manager (f, m), Respiratory Therapist (f, m), Restaurant Manager (f, m), School Administrator (f, m), Science Teacher (f, m), Secretary (f), Small Business Owner (f, m), Social Science Teacher (f, m), Social Worker (f, m), Sociologist (f, m), Special Education Teacher (f, m), Speech Pathologist (f, m), Store Manager (f, m), Technical Writer (f, m), Translator (f, m), Travel Agent (f, m), Veterinarian (f, m), Vocational Agriculture Teacher (f, m); 4 Personal Style Scales: Work Style, Learning Environment, Leadership Style, Risk Taking/Adventure; 27 Administrative Indexes: Total Response, Infrequent Response, Response Percentages (Like, Indifferent, Dislike) for each of 8 inventory sections (Occupations, School Subjects, Activities, Leisure Activities, Types of People, Characteristics, Preferences: Activities, Preferences: Work), Total for all parts.

Administration: Group.

Price Data, 2001: $75 per 10 prepaid profile combined item booklet/answer sheets; $235 per 10 prepaid interpretive report combined item booklet/answer sheets; $72 per Strong Applications and Technical Guide (1994, 425 pages); $18.95 per Strong Profile preview kit including prepaid profile item booklet/answer sheet and client booklet; $23.10 per Strong interpretive report preview kit including prepaid interpretive item booklet/answer sheet and client booklet; $40 per 10 client booklets; $163 per 10 prepaid professional report combined item booklet/answer sheets; $26.50 per Strong Professional report preview kit including prepaid professional item booklet/answer sheet and booklet; $75 per 10 prepaid Strong Profile, High School Edition combined item booklet/answer sheets; $10.75 per Strong Profile, High School Edition preview kit including prepaid High School profile item booklet/answer sheet and client booklet; $75 per 10 prepaid Strong college item booklet/answer sheets; $10.75 per Strong college preview kit.

Time: (35–40) minutes.

Comments: Scoring options: Prepaid (mail-in) and CPP software system (price data available from publisher); administration also available via CPP software system and the internet: Strong Interest Inventory and Skills Confidence Inventory, Strong and MBTI Career Report, and Strong and MBTI Entrepreneur Report also available from publisher.

Authors: Edward K. Strong, Jr. (original inventory), David P. Campbell (test and manual revision), Lenore W. Harmon (applications and technical guide), Jo-Ida C. Hansen (applications and technical guide), Fred H. Borgen (applications and technical guide), and Allen L. Hammer (applications and technical guide).

Publisher: CPP, Inc.

Cross References: For reviews by Kevin R. Kelly and Eugene P. Sheehan, see 15:248; see T5:1790 (19 references); for reviews by John Christian Busch and by Blaine R. Worthen and Perry Sailor of the Fourth Edition, see 12:374 (43 references); see also T4:2581 (64 references); for reviews by Wilbur L. Layton and Bert W. Westbrook, see 9:1195 (17 references); see also T3:2318 (99 references); for reviews by John O. Crites, Robert H. Dolliver, Patricia W. Lunneborg, and excerpted reviews by Richard W. Johnson, David P. Campbell, and Jean C. Steinhauer, see 8:1023 (289 references, these references are for SVIB-M, SBIV-W, and SCII). For references on the Strong Vocational Interest Blank For Men, see T2:2212 (133 references); for reviews by Martin R. Katz and Charles J. Krauskopf and excerpted reviews by David P. Campbell and John W. M. Rothney, see 7:1036 (485 references); for reviews by Alexander W. Astin and Edward J. Furst, see 6:1070 (189 references); see also 5:868 (153 references); for reviews by Edward S. Bordin and Elmer D. Hinckley, see 4:747 (98 references); see also 3:647 (102 references); for reviews by Harold D. Carter, John G. Darley, and N. W. Morton, see 2:1680 (71 references); for a review by John G. Darley, see 1:1178. For references on the Strong Vocational Interest Blank For Women, see T2:2213 (30 references); for reviews by Dorothy M. Clendenen and Barbara A. Kirk, see 7:1037 (92 references); see also 6:1071 (12 references) and 5:869 (19 references); for a review by Gwendolen Schneidler Dickson, see 3:649 (38 references); for a review by Ruth Strang, see 2:1681 (10 references); for a review by John G. Darley, see 1:1179.

[2446]
The Strong Narrative Assessment Procedure.
Purpose: Designed to "evaluate language and narrative skills of students with diverse impairments such as language, learning, and cognitive challenges."
Population: Grades K-8.
Publication Date: 1998.
Acronym: SNAP.
Scores, 56: Awareness of Story Structure (Setting Includes Place and Time, Identification of Central Characters), Major Plot Episodes (Statement of Problem, Statement of Plan to Solve Problem, Statement of Problem Resolution), Use of Stylistic Devices (Formal Beginning of Story, Formal Conclusion), Coherence (Logical Story Consequence, Correct Sequence of Events, Use of Transition Terms), Total Story Retelling, Responses to Comprehension Questions (Factual, Inferential), Length (Number of C-units, Number of Words), Syntax (Average Words per C-unit, Total Number of Clauses, Number of Subordinate Clauses, Number of Clauses per C-unit, Number of Adverbial Clauses, Number of Nominal Clauses, Number of Relative Clauses, Complex Subordination, Cohesion (Number of Incomplete/Erroneous Reference Cohesion Ties, Number of Complete Reference Cohesion Ties, Total Reference Cohesion Ties, Percentage of Incomplete/Erroneous Reference Ties, Successful Revisions of Reference Ties, Total Number of Conjunction Cohesion Ties, Number of Additive Ties, Number of Temporal Ties, Number of Causal Ties, Number of Adversative Ties, Percentage of Additive Ties, Percentage of Temporal Ties, Percentage of Causal Ties, Percentage of Adversative Ties, Examples of Types of Conjunction Cohesion Ties, Examples of Conjunction Cohesion Ties Used Erroneously, Story Grammar (Total Number of Story Grammar Components, Number of Settings, Percentage of Settings, Number of Initiating Events, Percentage of Initiating Events, Number of Internal Responses, Percentage of Internal Responses, Number of Plans, Percentage of Plans, Number of Attempts, Percentage of Attempts, Number of Consequences, Percentage of Consequences, Number of Reactions, Percentage of Reactions, Number of Complete Episodes, Results of Story Retelling Questionnaire).

Administration: Individual or group.
Price Data, 2006: $99 per complete kit including manual (221 pages), 4 Mercer Mayer books, and 2 audiocassettes (1 story per side).
Time: 45(40-60) minutes per battery.
Comments: This test requires the use of a cassette tape player; 4 picture books/stimulus stories include: A Boy, A Dog and A Frog; Where Are You?; One Frog Too Many; Frog Goes to Dinner.
Author: Carol J. Strong.
Publisher: Thinking Publications.

[2447]
Stroop Color and Word Test [Adult and Children's Versions, Revised].
Purpose: Designed to test "the ability of the individual to separate the word and color naming stimuli."
Publication Dates: 1978-2003.
Scores, 4: Word, Color, Color-Word, Interference.
Administration: Individual or group.
Forms, 2: Children's Version, Adult Version.
Price Data, 2006: $85 per complete kit including manual and 25 test booklets (specify Children's or Adult Version); $35 per manual (specify Children's [2003, 35 pages] or Adult Version [2002, 72 pages]); $55 per 25 test bookets (specify Children's or Adult Version); $25 per computerized scoring; $80 per Spanish test booklet; $40 per Spanish manual.
Foreign Language Edition: Spanish version available.
Time: (5-15) minutes.
Publisher: Stoelting Co.
   a) CHILDREN'S VERSION.
   Population: Ages 5-14 years.
   Authors: Charles J. Golden, Shawna M. Freshwater, and Zarabeth Golden.
   b) ADULT VERSION.
   Population: Ages 15 years and older.
   Authors: Charles J. Golden and Shawna M. Freshwater.
Cross References: See T5:2516 (122 references) and T4:2582 (40 references); for reviews by James R. Evans and George W. Hynd of an earlier edition of the adult version, see 9:1196 (15 references); see also T3:2319 (1 reference).

[2448]
Stroop Neuropsychological Screening Test.
Purpose: Provides "an efficient and sensitive neuropsychological screening measure based on the Stroop procedure."
Population: Ages 18 and over.
Publication Date: 1989.
Acronym: SNST.
Scores, 2: Color, Color-Word.
Administration: Individual.

Price Data, 2006: $126 per introductory kit including manual, 25 Form C stimulus sheets, 25 Form C-W stimulus sheets, and 50 record forms.
Time: 4 minutes (timed).
Authors: Max R. Trenerry, Bruce Crosson, James DeBoe, and William R. Leber.
Publisher: Psychological Assessment Resources, Inc.
Cross References: See T5:2517 (8 references) and T4:2583 (3 references); for reviews by Manfred J. Meier and Cecil R. Reynolds, see 11:382 (1 reference).

[2449]
Structure of Intellect Learning Abilities Test.
Purpose: "Designed to assess a wide variety of cognitive abilities or factors of intelligence in children and adults."
Population: Preschool–adult.
Publication Dates: 1975–1985.
Acronym: SOI-LA.
Administration: Group or individual.
Price Data, 2006: $236.50 per complete kit including 10 standard test booklets (5 Form A and 5 Form B), set of scoring keys, set of stimulus cards, 10 worksheets/profiles, and manual (1985, 165 pages); $28.50 per 5 standard test booklets (specify Form A or B); $44 per scoring keys for Forms A, B, and G; $86 per manual (1985, 165 pages).
Authors: Mary Meeker, Robert Meeker, and Gale H. Roid (manual).
Publisher: Western Psychological Services.
 a) FORM A.
  Population: Grade 2–adult.
  Scores: 26 subtests in 5 test areas: Cognition (Cognition of Figural Units, Cognition of Figural Classes, Cognition of Figural Systems, Cognition of Figural Transformations, Cognition of Symbolic Relations, Cognition of Symbolic Systems, Cognition of Semantic Units, Cognition of Semantic Relations, Cognition of Semantic Systems), Memory (Memory of Figural Units, Memory of Symbolic Units—Visual, Memory of Symbolic Systems—Visual, Memory of Symbolic Units—Auditory, Memory of Symbolic Systems—Auditory, Memory of Symbolic Implications), Evaluation (Evaluation of Figural Units, Evaluation of Figural Classes, Evaluation of Symbolic Classes, Evaluation of Symbolic Systems), Convergent Production (Convergent Production of Figural Units, Convergent Production of Symbolic Systems, Convergent Production of Symbolic Transformations, Convergent Production of Symbolic Implications), and Divergent Production (Divergent Production of Figural Units, Divergent Production of Semantic Units, Divergent Production of Symbolic Relations) yielding 14 general ability scores: Cognition, Memory, Evaluation, Convergent Production, Divergent Production,

Figural, Symbolic, Semantic, Units, Classes, Relations, Systems, Transformations, Implications.
  Time: (150–180) minutes.
 b) FORM B.
  Purpose: Alternative to Form A.
 c) GIFTED SCREENING FORM (FORM G).
  Population: Grade 2–adult.
  Subtests, 12: From Form A which best predict gifted status.
  Price Data: $26 per 5 test booklets.
  Time: (60–90) minutes.
 d) PRIMARY FORM (FORM P).
  Population: Grades K–3.
  Subtests, 11: Similar to Form A, 5 measuring figural abilities, 3 measuring symbolic abilities, and 3 measuring semantic abilities.
  Price Data: $27.50 per 5 test booklets; $45 per scoring key.
  Time: (60–90) minutes.
  Comments: Formerly called Process and Diagnostic Screening Test.
Cross References: See T5:2518 (4 references); for reviews by Jack A. Cummings and Dianna L. Newman, see 10:349 (5 references); for reviews by William E. Coffman and Donald A. Leton of an earlier form, see 9:1197 (2 references); see also T3:2320 (2 references).

[2450]
Structured Clinical Interview for DSM-IV Axis I Disorders: Clinician Version.
Purpose: Constructed as "a semistructured interview for making the major DSM-IV Axis I diagnoses."
Population: Psychiatric or general medical patients ages 18 or older.
Publication Date: 1997.
Acronym: SCID-CV.
Scores, 6: Mood Episodes, Psychotic Symptoms, Psychotic Disorders, Mood Disorders, Substance Use Disorders, Anxiety and Other Disorders.
Administration: Individual.
Price Data, 2006: $116 per complete kit including user's guide (138 pages), administration booklet (84 pages), and 5 score sheets; $45.50 per packet of 5 score sheets; $52 per user's guide; $48.95 per administration booklet.
Time: (45–90) minutes.
Comments: Shortened, clinician version of the Structured Clinical interview for DSM-IV Axis I Disorders: Research Version.
Authors: Michael B. First, Robert L. Spitzer, Miriam Gibbon, and Janet B. W. Williams.
Publisher: American Psychiatric Publishing, Inc.
Cross References: For reviews by Paul D. Werner and Thomas A. Widiger, see 14:373; see also T5:2519 (56 references).

[2451]
Structured Clinical Interview for DSM-IV Axis II Personality Disorders.

Purpose: Designed as "a semistructured diagnostic interview for assessing the 10 DSM-IV Axis II personality disorders as well as Depressive Personality Disorder and Passive-Aggressive Personality Disorder."

Population: Adults receiving psychiatric or general medical care.

Publication Date: 1997.

Acronym: SCID-II.

Scores, 13: Avoidant, Dependent, Obsessive-Compulsive, Passive-Aggressive, Depressive, Paranoid, Schizotypal, Schizoid, Histrionic, Narcissistic, Borderline, Antisocial, Not Otherwise Specified.

Administration: Individual.

Price Data, 2006: $84 per complete kit including user's guide and packet of 5 interviews and questionnaire; $45.50 per 5 interviews and questionnaires; $53 per user's guide.

Time: Administration time not reported.

Comments: Also includes optional, self-report SCID-II Personality Questionnaire.

Authors: Michael B. First, Miriam Gibbon, Robert L. Spitzer, Janet B. W. Williams, and Lorna Smith Benjamin.

Publisher: American Psychiatric Publishing, Inc.

Cross References: For reviews by Paul A. Arbisi and Suzanne G. Martin, see 14:374; see also T5:2520 (25 references).

[2452]
Structured Clinical Interview for DSM-IV Dissociative Disorders—Revised.

Purpose: "Can be used to assess dissociative symptoms and disorders in subjects with a variety of psychiatric illnesses."

Population: Adults with psychiatric illnesses.

Publication Date: 1994.

Acronym: SCID-D-R.

Scores, 5: Amnesia, Depersonalization, Derealization, Identity Confusion, Identity Alteration.

Administration: Individual.

Price Data, 2006: $69 per Interviewer's Guide (168 pages); $45.50 package of 5 interviews; $97 per Interviewer's Guide and package of 5 interviews.

Time: Administration time not reported.

Comments: Composed of both closed- and open-ended questions and does not provide quantitative information regarding a subject; can be used as part of an overall battery of psychiatric diagnostic instruments, or can be administered independently.

Author: Marlene Steinberg.

Publisher: American Psychiatric Publishing, Inc.

[2453]
Structured Interview for the Five-Factor Model of Personality.

Purpose: Designed to "assess both normal and abnormal personality functioning" using the Five-Factor Model.

Population: Ages 18 and above.

Publication Date: 1997.

Acronym: SIFFM.

Scores, 35: Neuroticism (Anxiety, Hostility, Depression, Self-Consciousness, Impulsiveness, Vulnerability, Total), Extraversion (Warmth, Gregariousness, Assertiveness, Activity, Excitement-Seeking, Positive Emotions, Total), Openness to Experience (Fantasy, Aesthetics, Feelings, Actions, Ideas, Values, Total), Agreeableness (Trust, Straightforwardness, Altruism, Compliance, Modesty, Tender-Mindedness, Total), Conscientiousness (Competence, Order, Dutifulness, Achievement-Striving, Self-Discipline, Deliberation, Total).

Administration: Individual.

Price Data, 2006: $128 per introductory kit including 25 interview booklets and professional manual (85 pages).

Time: (60) minutes.

Authors: Timothy J. Trull and Thomas A. Widiger.

Publisher: Psychological Assessment Resources, Inc.

Cross References: For reviews by Paul M. Mastrangelo and Susana Urbina, see 15:249.

[2454]
Structured Interview of Reported Symptoms.

Purpose: Designed to "assess malingering and feigning of psychiatric symptoms."

Population: Ages 18 and over.

Publication Dates: 1986–1992.

Acronym: SIRS.

Scores, 13: Primary Scales (Rare Symptoms, Symptom Combinations, Improbable and Absurd Symptoms, Subtle Symptoms, Blatant Symptoms, Severity of Symptoms, Selectivity of Symptoms, Reported vs. Observed Symptoms), Supplementary Scales (Direct Appraisal of Honesty, Defensive Symptoms, Symptom Onset and Resolution, Overly Specified Symptoms, Inconsistency of Symptoms).

Administration: Individual.

Price Data, 2006: $249 per introductory kit including manual (1992, 47 pages) and 25 interview booklets.

Time: [45–60] minutes.

Authors: Richard Rogers, R. Michael Bagby, and Susan E. Dickens.

Publisher: Psychological Assessment Resources, Inc.

Cross References: For reviews by David N. Dixon and Ronald J. Ganellen, see 12:375.

[2455]
Structured Inventory of Malingered Symptomatology.

Purpose: Designed as a screening measure of malingering to assess symptoms of both feigned psychopathology and cognitive function.
Population: Ages 18 and over.
Publication Date: 2005.
Acronym: SIMS.
Scores, 6: Neurologic Impairment, Affective Disorders, Psychosis, Low Intelligence, Amnestic Disorders, Total.
Administration: Individual.
Price Data, 2006: $115 per complete kit including professional manual (46 pages) and 25 response forms; $65 per professional manual; $59 per 25 response forms.
Time: (10-15) minutes.
Comments: This test can be self-administered.
Authors: Glenn P. Smith and Michelle R. Widows.
Publisher: Psychological Assessment Resources, Inc.

[2456]
Structured Photographic Articulation Test II Featuring Dudsberry.

Purpose: Designed to assess children's articulation and phonological skills.
Population: Ages 3-0 through 9-11 years.
Publication Dates: 1989–2001.
Acronym: SPAT-D II.
Scores: Total score only.
Administration: Individual.
Price Data: Available from publisher.
Time: Administration time not reported.
Comments: Forty photographs are used to assess 59 singleton consonants and 10 consonant blends; revision of the Structured Photographic Articulation Test Featuring Dudsberry (SPAT-D).
Authors: Janet I. Dawson and Patricia J. Tattersall.
Publisher: Janelle Publications, Inc.
Cross References: For reviews by Mildred Murray-Ward and Roger L. Towne, see 16:236; for reviews by Clinton W. Bennett and Susan Felsenfeld of the earlier edition, see 12:376.

[2457]
Structured Photographic Expressive Language Test.

Purpose: Designed "to assess ... production of expressive morphology and syntax."
Publication Date: 1983.
Acronym: SPELT II.
Scores: Total score only.
Administration: Individual.
Comments: Includes a system of alternative response structures for assessment of the Black population.

Authors: Ellen O'Hara Werner and Janet Dawson Kresheck.
Publisher: Janelle Publications, Inc.
a) STRUCTURED PHOTOGRAPHIC EXPRESSIVE LANGUAGE TEST—PRESCHOOL.
Population: Ages 3-0 to 5-11.
Acronym: SPELT-P.
Price Data: Price information available from publishe for complete kit including 37 color photos, 10 response forms, and manual (27 pages).
Time: (3–10) minutes.
b) STRUCTURED PHOTOGRAPHIC EXPRESSIVE LANGUAGE TEST—II.
Population: Ages 4-0 to 9-5.
Acronym: SPELT-II.
Price Data: Price information available from publisher for complete kit including 50 color photos, 10 response forms, and manual (51 pages).
Time: (15–25) minutes.
Cross References: See T5:2524 (13 references) and T4:2588 (1 reference); for a review by Joan D. Berryman, see 9:1198 (2 references).

[2458]
Student Adaptation to College Questionnaire.

Purpose: "Designed to assess how well a student is adapting to the demands of the college experience."
Population: College freshmen.
Publication Date: 1989.
Acronym: SACQ.
Scores, 5: Academic Adjustment, Social Adjustment, Personal Emotional Adjustment, Attachment, Full Scale.
Administration: Group or individual.
Price Data, 2006: $98.50 per complete kit including 25 hand-scorable questionnaires and manual (76 pages) $47 per 25 hand-scorable questionnaires; $55 per manual; $14.50 per computer-scored mail-in answer sheet (quantity discounts available).
Time: 15 to 20 minutes.
Authors: Robert W. Baker and Bohdan Siryk.
Publisher: Western Psychological Services.
Cross References: See T5:2525 (13 references) and T4:2590 (9 references); for a review by E. Jack Asher, Jr., see 11:383 (4 references).

[2459]
Student Adjustment Inventory.

Purpose: Designed as "an instrument for identifying common affective-social problems."
Population: Upper elementary, junior high, senior high, and beginning college students.
Publication Dates: 1975–1989.
Acronym: SAI.

Scores, 7: Self-Esteem, Group Interaction, Self-Discipline, Communication, Energy/Effort, Learning/Studying, Attitude Towards Learning Environment.
Administration: Group or individual.
Price Data, 2005: $34 per report kit including manual (1989, 23 pages), 2 reusable test booklets, 5 answer sheets, and processing of 5 mail-in reports; $10 per 10 reusable test booklets; $8 per 50 answer sheets; $10 per manual; $5.45-$6.35 per mail-in report; $225 per SAI microcomputer version per 50 administrations (IBM 3.5-inch disk).
Time: (20–30) minutes.
Comments: Available in pencil and paper or microcomputer versions.
Author: James R. Barclay.
Publisher: MetriTech, Inc.
Cross References: For reviews by Philip Ash and Mark J. Benson, see 12:377.

[2460]
Student Behavior Survey.

Purpose: A multidimensional assessment to rate behavior and classroom performance to reflect the presence of problems in emotional and behavioral adjustment.
Population: Ages 5–18.
Publication Date: 2000.
Acronym: SBS.
Scores: 11 scales: Academic Performance, Academic Habits, Social Skills, Parent Participation, Health Concerns, Emotional Distress, Unusual Behavior, Social Problems, Verbal Aggression, Physical Aggression, Behavior Problems.
Administration: Individual.
Price Data, 2006: $95 per introductory kit including 25 AutoScore™ answer/profile forms and manual (72 pages); $40 per 25 AutoScore™ answer/profile forms; $59.50 per manual.
Time: Untimed.
Comments: Ratings by teachers.
Authors: David Lachar, Sabine A. Wingenfeld, Rex B. Kline, and Christian P. Gruber.
Publisher: Western Psychological Services.
Cross References: For reviews by Stephen N. Axford and by Michael J. Furlong and Renee Pavelski, see 15:250.

[2461]
Student Developmental Task and Lifestyle Inventory.

Purpose: "Assisting students in understanding their own development and establishing goals and plans to shape their own futures."
Population: College students ages 17–24.
Publication Date: 1987.
Acronym: SDTLI.

Scores, 12: Establishing and Clarifying Purpose Task (Educational Involvement Subtask, Career Planning Subtask, Life Management Subtask, Lifestyle Planning Subtask, Cultural Participation Subtask), Developing Mature Interpersonal Relationships Task (Peer Relationships Subtask, Tolerance Subtask, Emotional Autonomy Subtask), Academic Autonomy Task, Salubrious Lifestyle Scale, Intimacy Scale, Response Bias Scale.
Administration: Group.
Price Data: Not available.
Time: (30-40) minutes.
Comments: Revision of the Student Developmental Task Inventory, Revised, Second Edition.
Authors: Roger B. Winston, Jr., Theodore K. Miller, and Judith S. Prince.
Publisher: Student Development Associates, Inc. [No reply from publisher; status unknown].
Cross References: See T5:2527 (17 references) and T4:2592 (9 references); for reviews by Mary Henning-Stout and Willam D. Porterfield, see 11:384 (13 references); for reviews by Fred H. Borgen and Steven D. Brown of the Second Edition, see 9:1199 (5 references).

[2462]
Student Instructional Report II.

Purpose: Designed to objectively capture students' evaluations of faculty performance.
Population: College faculty and administrators.
Publication Dates: 1971–2006.
Acronym: SIR II.
Scores: 45 item scores plus up to 10 optional locally prepared items.
Administration: Group.
Price Data: Available from publisher at www.ets.org/SIRII.
Time: (10–15) minutes.
Comments: Students anonymously answer questions covering multiple dimensions of their college instruction; the informed feedback and timely responses are intended to be helpful to faculty who are experimenting with new classroom practices and teaching methods; a Distance Learning Version is also available (e-SirII).
Author: Educational Testing Service.
Publisher: Educational Testing Service.
Cross References: See T5:2531 (3 references), T4:2597 (1 reference), and T3:2334 (3 references); for reviews by Frank Costin and William C. McGaghie of the earlier edition, see 8:398 (16 references); see also T2:894 (1 reference).

[2463]
Student Opinion Inventory, Revised Edition.

Purpose: To assess students' opinions concerning many facets of the school and to "solicit students' recommendations for improvement."
Population: Grades 5–12.
Publication Dates: 1974–2003.

Scores: 4 subscales: Quality of the Instructional Program, Support for Student Learning, School Climate/Environment for Learning, Student Activities/Intervention in School.
Administration: Group.
Parts, 2: A (Likert-scale items), B (customize up to 20 local questions).
Price Data, 2006: $25 per 25 inventories; administrator's manual may be downloaded free from publisher website.
Time: (35–40) minutes.
Author: National Study of School Evaluation.
Publisher: National Study of School Evaluation.
Cross References: See T3:2335 (1 reference).

[2464]
Student Rights Scales.

Purpose: Designed to determine student and teacher perceptions of student rights in junior and senior high school.
Population: Grades 7–12.
Publication Dates: 1982–1986.
Acronym: SRS.
Scores, 5: General Rights, Due Process, Academic Self Determination, Freedom of Expression, Personal Conduct.
Administration: Group.
Price Data: Available from publisher.
Time: Administration time not reported.
Comments: For research use only.
Author: Thomas R. Oaster.
Publisher: Thomas R. Oaster.
Cross References: For reviews by Steven W. Lee and David Moshman, see 10:351.

[2465]
Student Self-Concept Scale.

Purpose: An individually or group-administered multidimensional measure of self-concept.
Population: Grades 3–12.
Publication Date: 1993.
Acronym: SSCS.
Scores, 13: Self-Confidence (Self-Image, Academic, Social, Lie, Composite), Importance (Self-Image, Academic, Social, Lie), Outcome Confidence (Self-Image, Academic, Social, Composite).
Administration: Group or individual.
Levels, 2: Grades 3–6, grades 7–12.
Price Data, 2006: $46.99 per 25 record booklets (specify Level 1 or Level 2); $64.99 per manual (82 pages).
Time: (20–30) minutes.
Authors: Frank M. Gresham, Stephen N. Elliott, and Sally E. Evans-Fernandez.
Publisher: Pearson Assessments (originally published by AGS Publishing, acquired by Pearson in 2005).
Cross References: For reviews by Jeri Benson and Frederick T. L. Leong, see 13:303.

[2466]
Student Styles Questionnaire™.

Purpose: "Designed to detect individual differences students display in their preferences, temperaments, and personal styles."
Population: Ages 8–13.
Publication Date: 1996.
Acronym: SSQ.
Scores, 8: Extroverted, Introverted, Practical, Imaginative, Thinking, Feeling, Organized, Flexible.
Administration: Group or individual.
Price Data, 2002: $98 per starter kit including manual (241 pages), classroom applications booklet, 5 Ready Score™ answer documents, and question booklet; $66 per 25 question booklets; $35 per 25 Ready Score™ answer documents; $18 per 25 record forms; $75 per manual; $22 per classroom applications booklet; $107 per microcomputer kit including 3.5-inch diskette, user's guide, and 25 record forms (Windows only).
Time: (30) minutes.
Authors: Thomas Oakland, Joseph Glutting, and Connie Horton.
Publisher: PsychCorp, A brand of Harcourt Assessment, Inc.
Cross References: For reviews by Gregory Schraw and Jay R. Stewart, see 14:375.

[2467]
Student Talent and Risk Profile.

Purpose: To identify talented students as well as students "at-risk" for counseling, guidance, and special teaching strategies.
Population: Grades 5–12.
Publication Date: 1990.
Acronym: STAR Profile.
Scores, 7: Academic Performance, Creativity, Artistic Potential, Leadership, Emotional Maturity, Educational Orientation, At Risk.
Administration: Group.
Price Data: Available from publisher.
Time: (60–65) minutes.
Comments: Revision of Biographical Inventory Form U.
Author: Institute for Behavioral Research in Creativity.
Publisher: Institute for Behavioral Research in Creativity.
Cross References: For reviews by Barbara Kerr and John W. Shepard, see 12:378; for reviews by Christopher Borman and Courtland C. Lee of Biographical Inventory Form U, see 9:150.

[2468]
Student-Teacher Relationship Scale.

Purpose: "Provides a quantitative self-report assessment of the relationship between a teacher and a specific student."

Population: Teachers of preschool through Grade 3 students.
Publication Date: 2001.
Acronym: STRS.
Scores, 4: Conflict, Closeness, Dependency, Total.
Administration: Group or individual.
Price Data, 2006: $96 per introductory kit including professional manual (58 pages), and 50 response forms.
Time: (5–10) minutes per individual; (10–15) minutes per group.
Comments: Intended to inform consultation and intervention efforts as part of the Student, Teachers, and Relationship Support (STARS) program.
Author: Robert C. Pianta.
Publisher: Psychological Assessment Resources, Inc.
Cross References: For reviews by Gerald Giraud and by Jorge E. Gonzalez and Chris Gonzalez, see 15:251.

[2469]
Study Attitudes and Methods Survey [Revised Short Form].

Purpose: "Developed to measure non-cognitive factors associated with success in school."
Population: Junior high, high school, college.
Publication Dates: 1972–1985.
Acronym: SAMS.
Scores, 6: Academic Interest-Love of Learning, Academic Drive-Conformity, Study Methods, Study Anxiety, Manipulation, Alienation Toward Authority.
Administration: Group.
Price Data: Available from publisher.
Time: (20–25) minutes.
Authors: William B. Michael, Joan J. Michael, and Wayne S. Zimmerman.
Publisher: EdITS/Educational and Industrial Testing Service.
Cross References: For reviews by Robert G. Harrington and Kenneth A. Kiewra, see 14:376; see also T5:2538 (1 reference), T4:2604 (6 references), and T3:2340 (2 references); for reviews by Allen Berger and John W. Lombard of an earlier edition, see 8:818 (6 references); see also T2:1766 (4 references).

[2470]
Stuttering Prediction Instrument for Young Children.

Purpose: Designed to "measure severity and predict chronicity."
Population: Ages 3-8.
Publication Date: 1981.
Acronym: SPI.
Scores, 5: Reactions, Part-Word Repetitions, Prolongations, Frequency, Total.
Administration: Individual.

Price Data, 2006: $105 per complete kit including 50 tests, picture plates, and manual (45 pages); $50 per 50 test forms; $60 per manual with picture plates.
Time: Administration time not reported.
Comments: Information taken from parent interview, observation and tape recording of the child's speech, and analysis of the tape recording.
Author: Glyndon D. Riley.
Publisher: PRO-ED.
Cross References: See T5:2542 (2 references) and T4:2612 (1 reference).

[2471]
Stuttering Severity Instrument for Children and Adults, Third Edition.

Purpose: "Measures stuttering severity for both children and adults."
Population: School-age children and adults.
Publication Dates: 1980–1994.
Acronym: SSI-3.
Scores, 8: Frequency, Duration, Physical Concomitants (Distracting Sounds, Facial Grimaces, Head Movements, Movements of the Extremities, Total), Total.
Administration: Individual.
Forms, 2: Reading, Nonreading.
Price Data, 2006: $110 per complete kit; $50 per 50 test record and frequency computation forms; $65 per examiner's manual (1994, 48 pages) and picture plates.
Time: Administration time not reported.
Comments: Tape recorder necessary for speech sample.
Author: Glyndon D. Riley.
Publisher: PRO-ED.
Cross References: See T5:2543 (3 references); for reviews by Ronald B. Gillam and Rebecca McCauley, see 13:304 (21 references); see also T4:2613 (5 references).

[2472]
Style of Learning and Thinking.

Purpose: To indicate a student's learning stategy and brain hemisphere preference in problem solving.
Population: Grades K–5, 6–12.
Publication Date: 1988.
Acronym: SOLAT.
Scores, 3: Whole Brain, Left Brain, Right Brain.
Administration: Group.
Forms, 2: Elementary, Youth.
Price Data, 2005: $48.15 per starter set including administrator's manual (46 pages) and 35 questionnaires (specify form); $33.90 per 35 questionnaires (specify form); $16.15 per administrator's manual; $19.50 per sample set including manual and 1 each of Elementary and Youth Form questionnaires.
Time: [30-40] minutes.
Comments: Self-scored.

Author: E. Paul Torrance.
Publisher: Scholastic Testing Service, Inc.
Cross References: See T5:2545 (6 references); for reviews by Kenneth A. Kiewra and Damian McShane and by Donald U. Robertson and Virginia L. Brown, see 11:390 (2 references).

[2473]
Styles of Leadership Survey.
Purpose: Assesses individual leadership skills under a variety of conditions.
Population: Adults.
Publication Dates: 1968-1995.
Scores, 5: Philosophy, Planning and Goal Setting, Implementation, Performance and Evaluation, Total.
Administration: Group.
Price Data, 2001: $8.95 per instrument.
Time: Untimed.
Comments: Self-administered survey.
Authors: Jay Hall, Jerry B. Harvey, and Martha S. Williams.
Publisher: Teleometrics International, Inc.
Cross References: See T5:2547 (1 reference); for reviews by Kenneth N. Anchor and Norman Sundberg, see 12:379 (1 reference); see T3:2351 (1 reference); for a review by Abraham K. Korman of [Styles of Leadership and Management], see 8:1185 (8 references).

[2474]
Styles of Management Inventory.
Purpose: Assesses individual management style under a variety of conditions.
Population: Adults.
Publication Dates: 1964-2000.
Scores, 5: Philosophy, Planning and Goal Setting, Implementation, Performance Evaluation, Total.
Administration: Group.
Price Data, 2001: $8.95 per instrument.
Time: Untimed.
Comments: Self-administered survey.
Authors: Jay Hall, Jerry B. Harvey, and Martha S. Williams.
Publisher: Teleometrics International, Inc.
Cross References: For reviews by Richard W. Faunce and Linda F. Wightman, see 12:380; see T3:2351 (1 reference); for a review by Abraham K. Korman of [Styles of Leadership and Management], see 8:1185 (8 references).

[2475]
Styles of Teamwork Inventory.
Purpose: Assess individual feelings about working in teams and the behaviors one typically employs in work-team situations.
Population: Individuals whose work responsibilities require work-team cooperation.

Publication Dates: 1963-1995.
Acronym: STI.
Scores, 5: Synergistic, Compromise, Win-Lose, Yield-Lose, Lose-Leave.
Administration: Group.
Price Data, 2001: $8.95 per instrument.
Time: Administration time not reported.
Comments: Based on Team Behaviors Model of analysis of individual behaviors in a team setting; self ratings; self scored; formerly called Group Encounter Survey (T3:1014).
Author: Jay Hall.
Publisher: Teleometrics International, Inc.
Cross References: See 8:1048 (2 references).

[2476]
Substance Abuse Life Circumstance Evaluation.
Purpose: "Designed to assess alcohol and drug use/abuse behavior, as well as the role that attitude and stress may play in this use/abuse."
Population: Adults.
Publication Date: 1988.
Acronym: SALCE.
Scores, 6: Test-Taking Attitude, Life Circumstance Evaluation, Drinking Evaluation Category, Alcohol Addiction Evaluation, Drug Use Evaluation, Summary Score.
Administration: Individual or group.
Price Data: Available from publisher.
Time: (20) minutes.
Comments: Self-administered; computer scored, IBM compatible with Windows required; provides both DSM-IV classification and ASAM patient placement criteria.
Author: ADE Incorporated.
Publisher: ADE Incorporated.
Cross References: For a review by Anita M. Hubley, see 14:377.

[2477]
Substance Abuse Relapse Assessment.
Purpose: Designed to help "develop relapse prevention goals and monitor treatment progress."
Population: Adolescents and adults.
Publication Date: 1993.
Acronym: SARA.
Scores: 4 parts: Substance Abuse Behavior, Antecedents of Substance Abuse, Consequences of Substance Abuse, Responses to Slips and Relapses.
Administration: Individual.
Price Data, 2006: $130 per introductory kit including 25 interview record forms, 25 each of 3 relapse prevention planning forms, and manual (31 pages) with stimulus card.
Time: (60) minutes.
Authors: Lawrence Schonfeld, Roger Peters, and Addis Dolente.

Publisher: Psychological Assessment Resources, Inc.
Cross References: For reviews by Michael G. Kavan and Jeffrey S. Rain, see 13:306.

[2478]
Substance Abuse Screening Test.

Purpose: "Designed to screen-out those students who are unlikely to have a substance abuse problem."
Population: Ages 13–adult.
Publication Date: 1993.
Acronym: SAST.
Scores: Total Level of Risk.
Administration: Group.
Forms, 2: Response Form, Observation Report.
Price Data, 2002: $56 per complete kit including 50 Response Forms, 50 Observation Reports, and manual (34 pages); $21 per 50 Response Forms; $21 per 50 Observation Reports; $29 per manual.
Time: (5) minutes.
Authors: Terry Hibpshman and Sue Larson.
Publisher: Slosson Educational Publications, Inc.
Cross References: For reviews by Mary Lou Kelley and Mariela C. Shirley, see 13:307.

[2479]
The Substance Abuse Subtle Screening Inventory—3.

Purpose: Designed to "identify individuals who have a high probability of having a substance dependence disorder."
Population: Ages 18–73.
Publication Dates: 1983–1997.
Acronym: SASSI-3.
Scores: 10 subscales: Face Valid Alcohol, Face Valid Other Drugs, Symptoms, Obvious Attributes, Subtle Attributes, Defensiveness, Supplemental Addiction Measure, Family vs. Controls, Correctional, Random Answering Pattern.
Administration: Individual or group.
Price Data: Available from publisher.
Time: [15] minutes.
Comments: May be administered as paper-and-pencil instrument with hand scoring or scoring by optical scanning, computer administered, or via audiotape for people with special needs regarding vision or literacy.
Author: Flenn A. Miller.
Publisher: The SASSI Institute.
Cross References: For reviews by Ephrem Fernandez and David J. Pittenger, see 15:252; see T5:2553 (6 references); for reviews by Barbara Kerr and Nicholas A. Vacc of an earlier edition, see 12:381 (1 reference); see also T4:2623 (1 reference).

[2480]
Substance Use Disorders Diagnostic Schedule-IV.

Purpose: "Designed to elicit information related to the diagnosis of substance use disorders."
Population: Adults suspected of abusing alcohol or drugs.
Publication Dates: 1995–2001.
Acronym: SUDDS-IV.
Scores: Number of Current Dependence Symptoms in Past Year, Number of Current Dependence Categories, Number of Current Abuse Symptoms in Past Year, Number of Current Abuse Categories for 10 Substance Categories (Alcohol, Marijuana, Cocaine, Sedatives/Tranquilizers, Stimulants, Heroin/Other Opioids, Hallucinogens, PCP, Inhalants, Other/Mixed), DSM-IV Psychoactive Substance Use Disorder Diagnosis Codes (Dependence, Abuse), Ratings for Stress, Depression and Anxiety Screens.
Administration: Individual.
Price Data: Available from publisher.
Time: (30–45) minutes.
Comments: Structured diagnostic interview; also available as a computer-administered interview; designed primarily to provide comprehensive diagnostic information for substance use disorders according to DSM-IV criteria; provides information for patient placement according to American Society of Addiction Medicine criteria.
Authors: Norman G. Hoffmann and Patricia Ann Harrison.
Publisher: Change Companies.
Cross References: For reviews by Tony Cellucci and Mark H. Stone, see 15:253; for reviews by Andres Barona and Steven I. Pfeiffer of an earlier edition, see 13:308 (2 references).

[2481]
Subsumed Abilities Test.

Purpose: Designed "to determine an individual's or group's ability to learn or to use a previously learned written language, system of mathematics, coding system, or other visual symbol system."
Population: Ages 9 and over.
Publication Dates: 1957-1984.
Acronym: SAT.
Scores, 5: Recognition, Abstraction, Conceptualization, Total (Demonstrated Abilities), Potential Abilities.
Administration: Individual or group.
Price Data, 2006: $69 per test package; $39.50 per manual (1963, 12 pages) and manual supplement (1984, 17 pages); $29 per key-tabulation sheet package; $46.50 per specimen set.
Time: 30(40) minutes.
Comments: Subtitle on manual is A Measure of Learning Efficiency.
Author: Joseph R. Sanders.
Publisher: Martin M. Bruce, Ph.D.
Cross References: See T2:582 (2 references); for a review by Naomi Stewart, see 6:560.

[2482]
Suffolk Reading Scale 2.

Purpose: Designed to assess "reading ability."
Population: Ages 6.0 to 14.11.
Publication Dates: 1986–2002.
Acronym: SRS2.
Scores: Total score only.
Administration: Individual or group.
Levels, 3: 1 (Ages 6.0 to 8.11), 2 (Ages 8.0 to 11.11), 3 (Ages 10.0 to 14.11).
Forms, 2: A, B.
Price Data: Available from publisher.
Time: (50) minutes.
Author: Fred Hagley.
Publisher: NFER-Nelson Publishing Co., Ltd. [England].
Cross References: For reviews by Jennifer N. Mahdavi and Howard Margolis, see 16:237; see also T5:2556 (3 references); for reviews by Robert B. Cooter, Jr. and Richard Lehrer of an earlier edition, see 11:392.

[2483]
Suicidal Ideation Questionnaire.

Purpose: Designed to "screen for suicidal ideation in adolescents."
Population: Grades 7–9 (SIQ), 10–12 (SIQ-JR).
Publication Dates: 1987–1988.
Acronym: SIQ.
Scores: Total Suicidal Ideation.
Administration: Individual or small group.
Levels, 2: SIQ (senior high school), SIQ-JR (junior high school).
Price Data, 2006: $148 per introductory kit including manual (1988, 47 pages), 25 each SIQ and SIQ-JR hand-scorable answer sheets, and scoring keys for SIQ and SIQ-JR.
Time: (5–10) minutes.
Author: William M. Reynolds.
Publisher: Psychological Assessment Resources, Inc.
Cross References: See T5:2556 (11 references) and T4:2627 (1 reference); for reviews by James C. Carmer and Collie W. Conoley, see 11:393 (2 references).

[2484]
Suicide Intervention Response Inventory [Revised].

Purpose: Designed to assess "the paraprofessional's ability to select an appropriate response to the self-destructive client."
Population: Mental health paraprofessionals.
Publication Dates: 1980–1997.
Acronym: SIRI.
Scores: Total score only.
Administration: Group.
Price Data: Available from publisher.
Time: (15) minutes.
Author: Robert A. Neimeyer.
Publisher: Robert A. Neimeyer, Ph.D.
Cross References: See T5:2558 (3 references).

[2485]
Suicide Probability Scale.

Purpose: Designed to "measure an individual's self-reported attitudes and behaviors which have a bearing on suicide risk."
Population: Ages 14 and over.
Publication Date: 1982.
Acronym: SPS.
Scores, 5: Hopelessness, Suicide Ideation, Negative Self-Evaluations, Hostility, Total.
Administration: Group or individual.
Price Data, 2006: $121 per kit including 25 tests, 25 profiles, and manual (73 pages plus test and profile); $43.50 per 25 tests; $42 per 100 profiles; $49.50 per manual; $10 per FAX Service scoring charge.
Time: (5–10) minutes.
Authors: John G. Cull and Wayne S. Gill.
Publisher: Western Psychological Services.
Cross References: See T5:2559 (13 references) and T4:2629 (6 references); for a review by Stephen L. Golding, see 9:1210.

[2486]
Super's Work Values Inventory—Revised.

Purpose: Assesses relative importance of selected attributes of occupations and jobs.
Population: Middle school through adult.
Publication Date: 2001.
Acronym: WVI-R.
Scores, 12: Achievement, Co-Workers, Creativity, Income, Independence, Lifestyle, Mental Challenge, Prestige, Security, Supervision, Work Environment, Variety.
Administration: Individual or group.
Price Data: Available from publisher.
Time: (15–20) minutes.
Comments: Online administration; instant scoring; with Kuder Career Search (1379) and Kuder Skills Assessment (1382), plus the Kuder Electronic Career Portfolio, constitutes the Kuder Career Planning System.
Authors: Donald E. Super; revised by Donald G. Zytowski.
Publisher: National Career Assessment Services, Inc. [No reply from publisher; status unknown].
Cross References: See T4:2998 (9 references) and T3:2567 (17 references); for an excerpted review by Frederick Brown of an earlier edition, see 8:1030 (52 references); see also T2:2221 (12 references); for reviews by Ralph F. Berdie and David V. Tiedeman, and an excerpted review by John W. French, see 7:1042 (33 references).

[2487]

SuperSelect.

Purpose: Designed to "assess the work related attitudes, opinions, and behaviors of job applicants for the supermarket bagger, cashier, and courtesy clerk positions."
Population: Age 18 and over.
Publication Date: 2001.
Acronym: BCCC.
Scores, 13: Customer Service, Interpersonal Skills, Communication, Productivity, Work Conduct, Integrity, Drug Avoidance, Adaptability, Candidness, Accuracy, Performance Index, Dependability Index, Overall Composite Index.
Administration: Individual or group.
Price Data: Available from publisher.
Time: Administration time not reported.
Author: Reid London House.
Publisher: Pearson Performance Solutions [No reply from publisher; status unknown].

[2488]

Supervisory Behavior Description Questionnaire.

Purpose: "Designed to measure the behavior patterns of supervisory and management personnel on two major dimensions of leadership: 'Consideration' and 'Structure.'"
Population: Supervisors and prospective supervisors.
Publication Dates: 1970–1996.
Acronym: SBD.
Scores, 2: Consideraton, Structure.
Administration: Group.
Price Data: Available from publisher.
Time: (20) minutes.
Comments: Paper-and-pencil or computer administration available.
Author: Edin A. Reishman.
Publisher: Pearson Performance Solutions [No reply from publisher; status unknown].
Cross References: For reviews by Albert M. Bugaj and Michael J. Roszkowski, see 15:254.

[2489]

Supervisory Inventory on Communication.

Purpose: Designed to assess supervisor's knowledge of certain principles, facts, and techniques of communication.
Population: Supervisors and prospective supervisors.
Publication Dates: 1965-1979.
Acronym: SIC.
Scores: Total score only.
Administration: Group.
Price Data, 2001: $40 per 20 SIC tests and answer booklets; $5 per instructor's manual (1979, 11 pages); $10 per specimen set (including test, answer booklet, manual and leader's guide).
Time: (20) minutes.

Author: Donald L. Kirkpatrick.
Publisher: Donald L. Kirkpatrick (the author).
Cross References: For a review by Joyce L. Carbonell, see 9:1211; see also 7:1152 (1 reference).

[2490]

Supervisory Inventory on Human Relations.

Purpose: Designed to assess supervisors' knowledge of human relations principles, facts, and techniques.
Population: Supervisors and prospective supervisors.
Publication Dates: 1960-1982.
Acronym: SIHR.
Scores: Total score only.
Administration: Group.
Price Data, 2001: $40 per 20 tests and answer booklets; $5 per instructor's manual (1982, 12 pages); $10 per specimen set (including test, answer booklet, and manual).
Time: (15-20) minutes.
Authors: Donald L. Kirkpatrick and Earl Planty (test).
Publisher: Donald L. Kirkpatrick (the author).
Cross References: See T2:2463 (1 reference); for a review by Seymour Levy of the original edition, see 6:1193 (1 reference).

[2491]

Supervisory Practices Test, Revised.

Purpose: "Designed to aid in appraising supervisory ability and potential."
Population: Supervisors.
Publication Dates: 1957-1984.
Acronym: SPT.
Scores: Total score only.
Administration: Group.
Price Data, 2006: $58.95 per specimen set; $119.50 per test package; $53.00 per manual (1974, 14 pages), manual supplement (1984, 17 pages), and norms supplement; $36.50 per profile sheet package; $3.75 per key.
Foreign Language Editions: French, German, and Spanish editions available.
Time: (20-30) minutes.
Author: Martin M. Bruce.
Publisher: Martin M. Bruce, Ph.D.
Cross References: See T3:2363 (1 reference), T2:2466 (2 references), and 6:1194 (4 references); for reviews by Clifford E. Jurgensen and Mary Ellen Oliverio, see 5:955.

[2492]

Supervisory Simulator.

Purpose: "Designed to assess supervisory skills of first-level supervisors, forepersons and/or team leaders independent of any particular job title or organization; may be used for selection and/or career development."
Population: First-level supervisors, forepersons, or team leaders.

Publication Dates: 1991–2006.
Acronym: SupSim.
Scores, 3: Leadership/Decision Making, Team Relations, Total .
Administration: Group or individual.
Forms, 5: Public and private sector forms include Blue-Collar Teams, Office/Clerical Teams, Police, Fire, Transportation.
Restricted Distribution: Clients may be required to pay a nominal one-time overhead/sign-up fee.
Price Data, 2006: $235 per candidate for rental/scoring and a detailed Career Development Report that identifies strengths, weaknesses, and developmental needs with specific learning objectives, for each of the two factors measured by the test.
Time: (75) minutes.
Author: Richard C. Joines.
Publisher: Management & Personnel Systems, Inc.

[2493]
Supervisory Skills Inventory.

Purpose: Developed to assess a supervisor's day-to-day, on-the-job behavior as seen by self and collectively by five other people.
Population: First-line supervisors.
Publication Date: 1982.
Acronym: SSI.
Scores: 2 scores (Self, Other) in 12 supervisory skill areas: Setting Goals, Planning and Organizing, Directing and Delegating, Solving Problems, Enforcing Work Rules, Relating to and Supporting Staff, Maintaining and Controlling Materials and Equipment, Building Teams, Assuring Safety, Evaluating Performance, Training and Coaching, Reacting to Stress, plus 5 summary perception scores.
Administration: Group.
Forms, 2: Self-Description, Description by Others.
Price Data: Available from publisher.
Comments: Administered to supervisor and 4 or 5 workers.
Author: Human Synergistics International.
Publisher: Human Synergistics International.

[2494]
Support Staff Opinion Inventory.

Purpose: Designed to measure general perceptions about the school from support staff.
Population: School support staff.
Publication Date: 2005.
Scores: 4 subscales: Quality of the Instructional Program, Support for Student Learning, School Climate/Environment, School Organization and Administration.
Administration: Group.
Parts, 2: A (Likert-scale items), B (customize up to 20 local questions).

Price Data, 2006: $25 per 25 inventories; administrator's manual may be downloaded free from publisher webpage.
Foreign Language Edition: Available in Spanish.
Time: (15) minutes.
Author: National Study of School Evaluation.
Publisher: National Study of School Evaluation.

[2495]
Supports Intensity Scale.

Purpose: Designed to help service providers "understand the support needs of people with intellectual disabilities (i.e., mental retardation) and closely related developmental disabilities."
Population: Individuals ages 16–72 with intellectual or closely related developmental disabilities
Publication Date: 2004.
Acronym: SIS.
Scores, 9: Home Living, Community Living, Lifelong Learning, Employment, Health and Safety, Social, Support Needs Index, Exceptional Medical Needs, Exceptional Behavioral Needs.
Administration: Individual.
Price Data, 2006: $125 per complete set including user's manual (128 pages) and 25 interview forms; $95 per user's manual; $38.75 per 25 interview forms; $375 per Electronic Scoring Program on CD-ROM; Pricing for SISOnline, web-based scoring application determined on case-by-case basis available from publisher (www.siswebsite.org).
Time: Administration time not reported.
Comments: Semistructured, multiple informant interview format.
Authors: James R. Thompson, Brian R. Bryant, Edward M. Campbell, Ellis M. Craig, Carolyn M. Hughes, David A. Rotholz, Robert L. Schalock, Wayne P. Silverman, Marc J. Tassé, and Michael L. Wehmeyer.
Publisher: AAMR American Association on Mental Retardation
Cross References: For reviews by Sandra A. Loew and David J. Pittenger, see 16:238.

[2496]
SUP'R Star Profiles.

Purpose: Designed to identify an individual's dominant personality type.
Population: Adults.
Publication Date: 1994.
Scores: 4 personality types: Self-Reliant, Upbeat, Patient, Reasoning.
Administration: Group.
Price Data: Available from publisher.
Time: (15–20) minutes.
Author: James H. Brewer.
Publisher: Associated Consultants in Education.

Cross References: For reviews by Jeffrey B. Brookings and Carol Collins, see 13:309.

[2497]
Survey Ballot for Industry.

Purpose: Designed "specifically as the psychological measuring instrument for economical assessment of job satisfaction levels of worker groups."
Population: Employee groups.
Publication Date: No date.
Scores, 11: Job Security, Welfare Interest, Supervision, Working Conditions, Co-Workers, Pay, Freedom of Communication, Management Good Intent, Management Good Judgment, Company Effect on Happiness, Total Satisfaction.
Administration: Group.
Price Data, 2001: $4 per specimen set.
Time: Administration time not reported.
Author: W. A. Kerr.
Publisher: Psychometric Affiliates.

[2498]
Survey of Employee Access.

Purpose: Measures effective managerial behavior.
Population: Adults.
Publication Dates: 1989–2000.
Acronym: SEA.
Scores, 5: Access to the Problem, Access to People, Access to Information and Resources, Access to Emotional/Procedural Supports, Access to Solution.
Administration: Group.
Price Data, 2001: $7.95 per instrument.
Time: Untimed.
Comments: Self-administered survey.
Author: Jay Hall.
Publisher: Teleometrics International, Inc.
Cross References: For reviews by Marcia J. Belcher and Robert Fitzpatrick, see 12:383.

[2499]
Survey of Functional Adaptive Behaviors.

Purpose: To assess an individual's skill level of adaptive behavior.
Population: Ages 16 and over.
Publication Date: 1986.
Acronym: SFAB.
Scores, 5: Residential Living Skills, Daily Living Skills, Academic Skills, Vocational Skills, SFAB Total Score.
Administration: Individual.
Manual: No manual.
Price Data, 2006: $54.50 per 25 surveys.
Authors: Jack G. Dial, Carolyn Mezger, Theresa Massey, Steve Carter, and Lawrence T. McCarron.
Publisher: McCarron-Dial Systems.
Cross References: For reviews by Steven W. Lee and Steven I. Pfeiffer, see 11:404.

[2500]
Survey of Goals for Student Learning.

Purpose: "Designed to help schools assess the extent of students' achievement of essential goals for their learning and the level of priority that should be assigned to each goal."
Population: Teachers and administrators.
Publication Date: 1997.
Scores: 2 subscales: Level of Student Achievement, Level of Priority for Improvement.
Administration: Group.
Price Data, 2006: $25 per 25 inventories; administrator's manual may be downloaded from publisher webpage.
Time: (30) minutes.
Comments: Ten additional goals for student learning can be added to both parts of the survey.
Author: National Study of School Evaluation.
Publisher: National Study of School Evaluation.

[2501]
Survey of Influence Effectiveness.

Purpose: Designed as a 360° assessment to measure an executive's influence skills and interpersonal effectiveness; a multidimensional survey that identifies how effectively an individual influences others by comparing self-perceptions to the perceptions of others.
Population: Executives in leadership positions.
Publication Date: 1994.
Administration: Group.
Forms, 2: Self, Other.
Manual: No manual.
Price Data, 2005: $49 per set including questionnaires and answer sheets for 1 self-assessment, 6 others, 6 customers, and 1 feedback report; $50 per additional paper report.
Time: [30] minutes.
Comments: Assessment is administered online via Lore's Assessment Center; results are emailed to participant; a paper report may be requested for an additional fee; the SIE is based on an influence framework that features 10 positive influence tactics, 4 negative tactics, and 10 sources of power.
Author: Lore International Institute.
Publisher: Lore International Institute.

    a) SELF FORM.
    Scores, 4: Influence Tactic Frequency, Influence Tactic Appropriateness, Influence Tactic Skills and Effectiveness, Source of Power.
    Comments: 10 Influence tactics are measured and reported.
    b) OTHER FORM.
    Scores, 7: Positive Influence Tactic Frequency, Negative Influence Tactic Frequency, Influence Tactic Appropriateness, Influence Tactic Skills

and Effectiveness, Overall Influence Assessment, Sources of Power Recommendations.

Comments: A 128-item rating form.

[2502]

Survey of Instructional and Organizational Effectiveness.

Purpose: Designed "to help schools identify the strengths and limitations of the effectiveness of the instructional practices and organizational conditions of their school."

Population: Teachers and administrators.

Publication Date: 1997.

Scores: 2 subscales: Indicators of Quality Instructional Systems, Indicators of Quality Organizational Systems.

Administration: Group.

Price Data, 2006: $25 per 25 inventories; administrator's manual may be downloaded from publisher webpage.

Time: (30) minutes.

Author: National Study of School Evaluation.

Publisher: National Study of School Evaluation.

[2503]

Survey of Interpersonal Values.

Purpose: Designed to measure certain values involving an individual's relationships with others.

Population: Individuals in a variety of occupations and job levels.

Publication Dates: 1960–1993.

Acronym: SIV.

Scores, 6: Support, Conformity, Recognition, Independence, Benevolence, Leadership.

Administration: Individual or group.

Price Data, 2002: $163 per start-up kit including 25 test booklets, 100 profile sheets, scoring stencil, and examiner's manual; $64 per 25 test booklets (quantity discounts available); $70 per 100 profile sheets; $20 per scoring stencil; $28 per examiner's manual.

Time: No limit (approximately 15 minutes).

Author: Leonard V. Gordon.

Publisher: Pearson Performance Solutions [No reply from publisher; status unknown].

Cross References: See T5:2581 (3 references), T4:2653 (3 references), and T3:2366 (14 references); for reviews by John D. Black and Allan L. LaVoie, see 8:688 (51 references); see also T2:1407 (78 references) and P:261 (48 references); for reviews by Lee J. Cronbach, Leonard D. Goodstein, and John K. Hemphill and an excerpted review by Laurence Siegel, see 6:184 (12 references).

[2504]

Survey of Management Practices.

Purpose: To assess a manager's organizational practices, and whether they enhance employee productivity.

Population: Subordinates of managers.

Publication Dates: 1987–1995.

Acronym: SMP.

Scores, 12: Dimension I (Management Values, Support Structure, Managerial Credibility, Total), Dimension II (Impact, Relevance, Community, Total), Dimension III (Task Environment, Social Context, Problem Solving, Total).

Administration: Group.

Price Data, 2001: $7.95 per instrument.

Time: Administration time not reported.

Comments: Manager behavior rated by subordinates.

Author: Jay Hall.

Publisher: Teleometrics International, Inc.

[2505]

Survey of Organizational Climate.

Purpose: To assess an individual's opinion of his/her organizational climate.

Population: Employees.

Publication Dates: 1977–1985.

Scores, 12: Clarity of Goals, Job Interest and Challenge, Rewards and Satisfactions, Standards of Excellence, Degree of Responsibility, Personal Development, Working Relationships, Advancement/Mobility, Job Security, Management's Credibility, Personnel Policies and Procedures, Self-Confidence.

Administration: Group or individual.

Manual: No manual.

Price Data: Price information available from publisher for kit including 20 copies of survey, 20 answer sheets, and 20 interpretation sheets.

Time: (20) minutes.

Comments: Self-scored.

Author: Training House, Inc.

Publisher: Training House, Inc.

Cross References: For a review by Charles K. Parsons, see 11:406.

[2506]

Survey of Organizational Culture.

Purpose: Identification of organizational purpose and mission, perception of customers, and interrelationships of organization members.

Population: Employees of organizations.

Publication Dates: 1987–1989.

Acronym: SOC.

Scores: 15 scales: Culture (Orientation to Customers, Orientation to Employees, Orientation to Stakeholders, Impact of Mission, Managerial Depth, Decision Level/Autonomy, Communication/Openness, Human Scale, Incentive/Motivation, Cooperation/Competition, Organizational Congruence, Behavior Under Pressure, Theory-S/Theory-T, 13 Scales Aggregated), Job Characteristics (Job Satisfaction, Organizational Commitment).

Administration: Group.
Editions, 2: Select Items, Professional.
Manual: No manual.
Price Data: Available from publisher.
Time: (20–25) minutes.
Authors: Robert W. Tucker and Walt J. McCoy.
Publisher: Human Services Resource Group [No reply from publisher; status unknown].
Cross References: For a review by Bertram C. Sippola, see 11:407.

[2507]
Survey of Personal Values.

Purpose: To "measure certain critical values that help to determine the manner in which individuals cope with the problems of everyday living."
Population: Individuals in a variety of occupations, high school and college students.
Publication Dates: 1964–1992.
Acronym: SPV.
Scores, 6: Practical Mindedness, Achievement, Variety, Decisiveness, Orderliness, Goal Orientation.
Administration: Individual or group.
Price Data, 2002: $163 per start-up kit including 25 test booklets, 100 profile sheets, scoring stencil, and examiner's manual: $64 per 25 test booklets (quantity discount available); $70 per 100 profile sheets; $20 per scoring stencil; $28 per examiner's manual.
Time: No limit (approximately 15 minutes).
Author: Leonard V. Gordon.
Publisher: Pearson Performance Solutions [No reply from publisher; status unknown].
Cross References: For reviews by William P. Erchul and Rodney L. Lowman, see 10:354; see also T3:2370 (5 references) and T2:1409 (5 references); for a review by Gene V Glass, see 7:148 (6 references); see also P:263 (3 references).

[2508]
Survey of Student Assessment of Study Behaviors.

Purpose: Designed to help students understand their current study behaviors.
Population: Grades 6–13.
Publication Date: 1991.
Scores, 6: Positive Attitudes, Useful Work Habits, Efficient Learning Tools, Good Comprehension, High Performance Writing, Effective Test Taking.
Administration: Individual.
Price Data, 2001: $3 per survey.
Time: Administration time not reported.
Comments: Self-report survey.
Author: The Cambridge Stratford Study Skills Institute.
Publisher: The Cambridge Stratford Study Skills Institute.

[2509]
Survey of Teenage Readiness and Neurodevelopmental Status.

Purpose: "Provides an overview of an adolescent's own perceptions of his or her functioning and performance strategies across a variety of neurocognitive and psychosocial domains."
Population: Ages 13–19.
Publication Date: 2001.
Acronym: STRANDS.
Scores, 13: Attention, Memory, Sequencing, Language, Visual Processing, Motor Functions, Organization and Strategies, Higher-Order Cognition, School Skills, School Life, Social Life, School and Work Preferences, Reasons.
Administration: Individual.
Price Data, 2006: $86.95 per complete set including manual for administration, scoring and interpretation (114 pages), 12 student questionnaires (15 pages), 12 student interview booklets (30 pages), and 12 profile sheets; $23.45 per specimen set including manual for administration, scoring, and interpretation, 1 student questionnaire, and 1 student interview booklet; $21.20 per manual; $73.60 per 12 pair of student questionnaires and student interview booklets; $6.20 per 12 profile sheets (quantity discounts available).
Time: (40) minutes for Student Interview; (20) minutes for Student Questionnaire.
Comments: Examines the relationship between metacognitive knowledge and actual strategic behavior; consists of 2 parts: structured clinical student interview (closed- and open-ended questions), student-completed questionnaire.
Authors: Melvin D. Levine and Stephen R. Hooper.
Publisher: Educators Publishing Service, Inc.
Cross References: For a review by Scott T. Meier, see 16:239.

[2510]
Survey of Work Styles.

Purpose: A "measure of six components of the Type A behavior pattern."
Population: Adults.
Publication Dates: 1987–1998.
Acronym: SWS.
Scores, 8: Impatience, Anger, Time Urgency, Work Involvement, Job Dissatisfaction, Competitiveness, Scale A, Total.
Administration: Group or individual.
Price Data, 2006: $60 per research test kit including manual, 2nd edition (1993, 22 pages), 5 hand-scorable question-and-answer documents, 5 scoring sheets, and one set of templates; $15 per test manual on CD; $35 per 25 question-and-answer documents; $25 per 25 scoring sheets; $17 per set of scoring templates; $15 per machine-scorable question-and-answer docu-

ment for a Mail-in Developmental Report; $10 per machine-scorable question-and-answer document for a Mail-in Basic Report; $105 per software package including disks, software manual for Windows, test manual, and 10 coupons for computer reports; $14 per online password; volume discounts available.
Time: 15 minutes.
Comments: Available for online scoring at www.sigmatesting.com.
Authors: Douglas N. Jackson and Anna Mavrogiannis Gray.
Publisher: Sigma Assessment Systems, Inc.
Cross References: See T5:2592 (1 reference); for a review by Peggy A. Hicks, see 13:311 (1 reference); see also T4:2664 (1 reference).

[2511]
Survey of Work Values, Revised, Form U.
Purpose: To measure work values.
Population: Employees.
Publication Dates: 1975-1976.
Scores, 6: Social Status, Activity Preference, Upward Striving, Attitude Toward Earnings, Pride in Work, Job Involvement.
Administration: Group or individual.
Manual: No manual.
Price Data, 2006: $10 per 100 test booklets.
Time: 15 minutes.
Author: Bowling Green State University.
Publisher: Bowling Green State University
Cross References: For reviews by Julie A. Allison and by H. John Bernardin and Donna K. Cooke, see 12:383 (1 reference); see also T4:2665 (1 reference).

[2512]
Surveys of Research Administration and Environment.
Purpose: Designed "to gather both facts and opinions on a variety of factors related to the jobs of scientists, engineers, and technicians."
Population: Research and engineering and scientific firms.
Publication Dates: 1959–1960.
Scores: No scores.
Administration: Group.
Price Data: Available from publisher.
Author: Morris I. Stein.
Publisher: The Mews Press.
a) STEIN SURVEY FOR ADMINISTRATION.
Population: Supervisors and administrators.
Comments: Also part of Technical Personnel Recruiting Inventory.
Time: (30–40) minutes.
b) STEIN RESEARCH ENVIRONMENTAL SURVEY.
Population: Research and technical personnel.
Time: (90–120) minutes.

[2513]
Swallowing Ability and Function Evaluation.
Purpose: "Designed for evaluating and treating dysphagia."
Population: Ages 30 and over.
Publication Date: 2003.
Acronym: SAFE.
Scores, 3: Physical Examination, Oral Phase, Pharyngeal Phase.
Administration: Individual.
Price Data, 2006: $117 per complete kit including examiner's manual (37 pages), Treatment and Resource Manual (235 pages), and 50 profile/examiner record forms; $51 per examiner's manual; $42 per Treatment Manual; $28 per 50 profile/examiner record forms.
Time: (20–25) minutes.
Authors: Peggy Kipping and Deborah Ross-Swain.
Publisher: PRO-ED.
Cross References: For a review by Carolyn Mitchell Person, see 16:240.

[2514]
Swanson-Cognitive Processing Test.
Purpose: Designed to assess "different aspects of mental processing ability and potential."
Population: Ages 5 to adult.
Publication Date: 1996.
Acronym: S-CPT.
Scores: 11 subtest scores: Rhyming Words, Visual Matrix, Auditory Digit Sequence, Mapping and Directions, Story Retelling, Picture Sequence, Phrase Recall, Spatial Organization, Semantic Association, Semantic Categorization, Nonverbal Sequence; 3 composite scores: Semantic, Episodic, Total; 4 component scores: Auditory, Visual, Prospective, Retrospective; 4 supplementary scores: Strategy Efficiency Index, Processing Difference Index, Instructional Efficiency Index, Stability Index.
Administration: Individual.
Price Data, 2006: $215 per complete kit including manual (183 pages), 25 profile/examiner record booklets, picture book, card decks, and strategy cards in storage box; $70 per 25 profile/examiner record booklets; $60 per manual; $30 per picture book; $51 per card deck; $20 per strategy cards.
Time: (120) minutes.
Author: H. Lee Swanson.
Publisher: PRO-ED.
Cross References: See T5:2596 (1 reference); for reviews by Carolyn M. Callahan and Ralph F. Darr, Jr., see 13:312.

[2515]
Symbol Digit Modalities Test.
Purpose: Designed as an early screening of cerebral dysfunction.
Population: Ages 8 and over.

Publication Date: 1973.
Acronym: SDMT.
Scores: Total score only.
Administration: Group or individual.
Forms, 2: Written, Oral.
Price Data, 2006: $91 per complete kit including 25 WPS AutoScore™ test forms and manual (10 pages plus test); $46.50 per 25 AutoScore™ test forms; $48.50 per manual.
Time: 1.5(10) minutes.
Author: Aaron Smith.
Publisher: Western Psychological Services.
Cross References: See T5:2599 (43 references), T4:2671 (20 references), and T3:2380 (2 references); for reviews by Brad S. Chissom and James C. Reed, see 8:878; see also T2:1889 (4 references).

[2516]
Symbolic Play Test, Second Edition.

Purpose: Developed to assess early concept formation and symbolization based on a child's spontaneous non-verbal play.
Population: Ages 1–3.
Publication Dates: 1976–1988.
Scores: Total score only.
Administration: Individual.
Price Data, 1999: £145 per complete set including toys, 25 record forms, and manual (1988, 39 pages); £14.50 per 25 record forms; £25 per manual.
Time: (10–15) minutes.
Authors: Marianne Lowe and Anthony J. Costello.
Publisher: NFER-Nelson Publishing Co., Ltd. [England].
Cross References: See T5:2601 (3 references); for reviews by Anthony W. Paolitto and Harvey N. Switzky, see 12:384; see also T4:2673 (2 references) and T3:2383 (1 reference).

[2517]
Symptom Assessment—45 Questionnaire.

Purpose: "Designed as a brief yet comprehensive general assessment of psychiatric symptomalogy."
Population: Ages 13 and over, reading at the 6th grade level or higher.
Publication Dates: 1996–1998.
Acronym: SA-45.
Scores, 11: 9 subscales (Anxiety, Depression, Hostility, Interpersonal Sensitivity, Obsessive-Compulsive, Paranoid Ideation, Phobic Anxiety, Psychoticism, Somatization), 2 composite scores (Global Severity Index, Positive Symptom Total).
Administration: Group.
Price Data, 2006: $75 per complete kit including technical manual and 25 Quikscore forms; $39 per 25 Quikscore forms; $51 per technical manual.
Time: (10–15) minutes.

Comments: Derived from the original Symptom Checklist—90 (SCL-90; 2518); self-report inventory.
Authors: Strategic Advantage, Inc. and Mark Marush.
Publisher: Multi-Health Systems, Inc.
Cross References: For reviews by William M. Reynolds and Chockalingam Viswesvaran, see 14:378.

[2518]
Symptom Checklist-90-Revised.

Purpose: "Designed primarily to reflect the psychological symptom patterns of psychiatric and medical patients," as well as nonpatients.
Population: Adults and adolescents age 13 and older.
Publication Date: 1975.
Acronym: SCL-90-R®.
Scores: 9 primary symptom dimensions: Somatization, Obsessive-Compulsive, Interpersonal Sensitivity, Depression, Anxiety, Hostility, Phobic Anxiety, Paranoid Ideation, Psychoticism; plus 3 indices of distress: Global Severity Index, Positive Symptom Distress Index, Positive Symptom Total.
Administration: Group or individual.
Price Data, 2006: $57.25 per Q Local starter kit with interpretive reports including manual and 3 answer sheets with test items to conduct and receive 3 Q Local administrations; $26 per 25 Q Local answer sheets; $10 per Q Local interpretive reports; $4.15 per Q Local profile reports; $65 per mail-in scoring service starter kit with interpretive reports including manual, softcover test booklet, and 3 answer sheets to conduct and receive 3 administrations using the mail-in scoring service; $13 per mail-in interpretive reports; $7.15 per mail-in profile reports; $100 per hand-scoring starter kit including manual, 50 answer sheets with test items, 50 profile forms, 2 worksheets, and answer keys (specify Nonpatient Adult, Nonpatient Adolescent, Outpatient Psychiatric, Inpatient Psychiatric); $52.50 per hand-scoring answer sheets with test items; $24.50 per 50 profile forms and 2 worksheets (specify Nonpatient Adult, Nonpatient Adolescent, Outpatient Psychiatric, Inpatient Psychiatric); $24.75 per answer keys; $34 per manual; $10.25 per 5 test booklets; $51.50 per compact disc; quantity discounts available for the reports; price data for Spanish materials available from publisher.
Foreign Language Edition: Spanish materials available.
Time: (12–15) minutes.
Comments: Self-report test; companion clinician and observer rating forms also available.
Author: Leonard R. Derogatis.
Publisher: Pearson Assessments.
Cross References: See T5:2603 (593 references) and T4:2674 (318 references); for reviews by Jerome D. Pauker and Robert W. Payne, see 9:1082 (61 references); see also T3:2100 (13 references).

[2519]
System for Testing and Evaluation of Potential.

Purpose: "To evaluate managerial and professional personnel."

Population: Managerial and professional personnel.

Publication Dates: 1986–1995.

Acronym: LH-STEP.

Administration: Group or individual.

Price Data, 2002: $287 per job analysis kit including 10 job analysis questionnaires, computer scoring, individual and composite reports, and a recommendation regarding which LH-STEP battery to use.

Author: Human Resources Center, The University of Chicago.

Publisher: Pearson Performance Solutions [No reply from publisher; status unknown].

a) LH-STEP (STANDARD REPORT).

Scores: 6 ratings: Potential Estimates (Executive, Middle Manager, Supervisors and Nonsupervisory Professionals), Job Skills (Executive, Middle Manager, Supervisors and Nonsupervisory Professionals); 39 scores: Predictor Profile: (School Achievement, Drive, Vocational Satisfaction, Financial Responsibility, General Family Responsibility, Leadership, Relaxation Pursuits, Non-Verbal Reasoning, Word Fluency, Vocabulary, Closure Flexibility, Creative Potential, Sales Aptitude, Personal Insight, Extroversion, Emotional Responsiveness, Self-Reliance, Ability to Work Under Pressure, Level of Stress Response, Internal Adjustment, External Adjustment, Social Adjustment, General Adjustment), Job Skills: Organization (Setting Organizational Objectives, Financial Planning and Review, Improving Work Procedures and Practices, Interdepartmental Coordination), Leadership (Developing and Implementing Technical Ideas, Judgment and Decision Making, Developing Group Cooperation and Teamwork, Coping With Difficulties and Emergencies, Promoting Safety Attitudes and Practices, Communications), Human Resources (Developing Employee Potential, Supervisory Practices, Self-Development and Improvement, Personnel Practices), Community (Promoting Community/Organization Relations, Handling Outside Contacts).

Price Data: $230 or less per battery.

Time: (190–210) minutes.

b) LH-STEP (EXTENDED REPORT).

Scores: 6 ratings: same as LH-STEP Standard Report; 63 scores: same as LH-STEP Standard Report, plus Calm, Cautious, Composed, Decisive, Demonstrative, Even-Tempered, Persevering, Seeks Company, Self-Confident, Serious, Steady Worker, Talkative, Reaction Time to Verbal Stimuli, Reaction Time to Color Stimuli, Dominance, Independence, Autonomous Work Environment, Pressure Performance, Energy Level, Speed of Reaction, Ideational Spontaneity, Theoretical Interests, Artistic Interests, Mechanical Interests; 12 tests: Managerial and Professional Job Functions Inventory for Ability, Experience and Background Inventory, Word Fluency, Temperament Comparator, Vocabulary Inventory, Non-Verbal Reasoning, Sales Inventory, Cree Questionnaire, The Press Test, Closure Flexibility, EMO Questionnaire, Management Style Questionnaire.

Price Data: $230 or less per battery.

Time: (190–210) minutes.

[2520]
System of Multicultural Pluralistic Assessment.

Purpose: Designed as "a comprehensive system for assessing the level at which children function in cognitive abilities, perceptual motor abilities, and adaptive behavior."

Population: Ages 5–11.

Publication Dates: 1977–1978.

Acronym: SOMPA.

Administration: Individual.

Price Data, 2002: $327 per basic kit including parent interview manual (1977, 150 pages), 25 parent interview record forms, 6 ABIC scoring keys, student assessment manual (1978, 125 pages), 25 student assessment record forms, 25 profile folders, and technical manual (1979, 164 pages).

Foreign Language Edition: Spanish edition available.

Authors: Jane R. Mercer and June F. Lewis.

Publisher: PsychCorp, A brand of Harcourt Assessment, Inc.

a) STUDENT ASSESSMENT.

Population: Ages 5–11.

Publication Date: 1978.

Scores: 6 instruments: Physical Dexterity Tasks, Bender Visual Motor Gestalt Test, Weight by Height, Visual Acuity (Snellen Test), Auditory Acuity (audiometer), WISC-R (WPPSI for children under 6 years).

Price Data: $209 per SOMPA student assessment kit including 25 record forms, 25 profile folders, and manual.

Time: (60) minutes, several test sessions should be scheduled.

Comments: The following instruments are not available in the SOMPA test kit and must be obtained by the tester: Bender Gestalt, Snellen Test, audiometer, WISC-R, or WPPSI.

b) PARENT INTERVIEW.
Population: Parents.
Publication Date: 1977.
Scores: 3 instruments: Sociocultural Scales, Adaptive Behavior Inventory for Children (ABIC), Health History Inventory.
Price Data: $265 per SOMPA parent interview kit including 25 record forms, 25 profile folders, and manual.
Cross References: See T5:2606 (5 references) and T4:2676 (11 references); for reviews by Lloyd G. Humphreys, Cecil R. Reynolds, and Jonathan Sandoval, see 9:1222 (6 references).

[2521]
Systematic Screening for Behavior Disorders.
Purpose: To screen and identify students at risk for developing serious behavior problems.
Population: Grades K–6.
Publication Dates: 1990–1992.
Acronym: SSBD.
Administration: Individual and group.
Price Data, 2002: $195 per complete kit including technical manual (1992, 80 pages), user's guide (1992, 151 pages), observer training manual (1992, 136 pages), videotape, and 25 sets of classroom screening forms.
Authors: Hill M. Walker and Herbert H. Severson.
Publisher: Sopris West.
   a) STAGE I.
Scores: 2 rankings: Internalizing, Externalizing.
Time: (30–45) minutes.
Comments: Rankings by teacher.
   b) STAGE II.
Scores, 6: 3 scores: Total Critical Events, Total Adaptive Behavior, Total Maladaptive Behavior in two areas: Internalizing, Externalizing.
Time: (30–45) minutes.
Comments: Ratings by teachers.
   c) STAGE III.
Scores, 11: Academic Engaged Time (Total); Peer Social Behavior (Social Engagement, Participation, Parallel Play, Alone, No Code, Social Interaction, Negative Interaction, Positive Interaction, Total Positive Behavior, Total Negative Behavior).
Administration: Individual and group.
Time: (60–90) minutes.
Comments: Observations by trained staff member.
Cross References: See T5:2607 (1 reference); for reviews by Mary Lou Kelley and by Leland C. Zlomke and Robert Spies, see 13:313.

[2522]
Systems Analysis Aptitude Test.
Purpose: "Measures aptitude for business systems design using a real-life problem."
Population: Applicants for computer systems analyst position.
Publication Date: 1973.
Acronym: SAAT.
Administration: Group.
Restricted Distribution: Restricted to employers of systems analysts, not available to school personnel.
Price Data, 2001: $465 per candidate.
Time: (240) minutes.
Comments: Detailed report on system designed by each candidate.
Author: Jack M. Wolfe.
Publisher: Rose Wolfe Family Partnership LLP [Canada].

[2523]
Systems Programming Aptitude Test.
Purpose: "To evaluate the aptitude and potential of systems programming candidates of all experience levels, for work in all types of systems programming tasks."
Population: Systems programmers.
Publication Date: 1979.
Acronym: SPAT.
Administration: Group.
Price Data, 2001: $440 per person.
Time: Untimed.
Comments: Detailed report provided on each candidate.
Author: Jack M. Wolfe.
Publisher: Rose Wolfe Family Partnership LLP [Canada].
Cross References: For reviews by Samuel Juni and David Marshall, see 10:356.

[2524]
T.A. Survey.
Purpose: "Evaluates an individual's trust attitudes which predict trust performance."
Population: Employees.
Publication Dates: 1970–1981.
Scores: Total score only.
Administration: Group or individual.
Price Data: Price information available from publisher for surveys and yearly license fee.
Time: (15) minutes.
Comments: Also called Trustworthiness Attitude Survey.
Authors: Alan L. Strand and others.
Publisher: Predictive Surveys Corporation.
Cross References: For reviews by John K. Butler, Jr. and Denise M. Rousseau, see 9:1223.

[2525]
Tapping Students' Science Beliefs: A Resource for Teaching and Learning.
Purpose: Designed to "assess the belief students have about certain natural phenomena and permits appropriate learning experiences to be planned."

Population: Primary grade level students.
Publication Date: 1993.
Acronym: TSSB.
Scores, 5: Skateboard News, What Happened Last Night, The Day We Cooked Pancakes in School, Children's Week, Our School Garden.
Administration: Group.
Price Data, 2006: A$43.95 per complete kit including manual (77 pages), 5 unit tests with 1 student score sheet and 1 group profile sheet per unit; A10.95 per manual.
Time: (30) minutes per unit.
Authors: Brian Doig and Ray Adams.
Publisher: Australian Council for Educational Research Ltd. [Australia]
Cross References: For reviews by Jerrilyn V. Andrews and James P. Van Haneghan, see 13:314.

[2526]
The Tapping Test: A Predictor of Typing and Other Tapping Operations.

Purpose: Measures the student's ability to learn typing.
Population: High school.
Publication Dates: 1959–1970.
Acronym: TARC.
Scores: Total score only.
Administration: Group.
Price Data: Available from publisher.
Time: [30] minutes.
Authors: John C. Flanagan, Grace Fivars (manual), Shirley A. Tuska (manual), and Carol F. Hershey (manual).
Publisher: Grace Fivars.
Cross References: See T2:796 (3 references); for reviews by Ray G. Price and Henry Weitz, see 6:52 (2 references).

[2527]
Target Mathematics Tests.

Purpose: Designed "to provide achievement tests which reflect the content of the National Curriculum in Mathematics" in Great Britain.
Population: Levels 2–5, 2–6.
Publication Date: 1993.
Scores: Total score only.
Administration: Group.
Forms, 2: Test 4, Test 5.
Price Data, 2002: £9.99 per 20 test booklets (specify test); £9.99 per manual; £10.99 per specimen set.
Time: [30] minutes.
Author: D. Young.
Publisher: Hodder & Stoughton Educational [England].
Cross References: For reviews by Kevin D. Crehan and Gerald E. DeMauro, see 14:380.

[2528]
Tasks of Emotional Development Test.

Purpose: Assesses "the emotional and social adjustment of children" by means of projective techniques.
Population: Ages 6-11, 12-18.
Publication Dates: 1960-1971.
Acronym: T.E.D.
Scores: LATENCY: 5 scores: (Perception, Outcome, Affect, Motivation, Spontaneity) in each of 12 areas (Peer Socialization, Trust, Aggression Toward Peers, Attitudes For Learning, Respect For Property of Others, Separation From Mother Figure, Identification With Same-Sex Parent, Acceptance of Siblings, Acceptance of Need-Frustration, Acceptance of Parents' Affection to One Another, Orderliness and Responsibility, Self-Image); ADOLESCENCE: 5 scores in each of 13 areas: Same as for Latency plus Heterosexual Socialization.
Administration: Individual.
Levels, 2: Latency (Ages 6-11); Adolescence (Ages 12-18).
Price Data: Available from publisher.
Time: [30-40] minutes.
Authors: Haskel Cohen and Geraldine Rickard Weil.
Publisher: Massachusetts School of Professional Psychology/T.E.D. Test.
Cross References: See T5:2614 (2 references) and T4:2686 (1 reference); for excerpted reviews by Edward Earl Gates and by C. H. Ammons and R. B. Ammons, see 8:691 (7 references); see also T2:1517 (2 references) and P:481 (1 reference).

[2529]
TAV Selection System.

Purpose: Constructed to measure "interpersonal reactions" for use in vocational selection and counseling.
Population: Adults.
Publication Dates: 1963-1968.
Acronym: TAV.
Administration: Group.
Price Data: Available from publisher.
Time: (180) minutes for the battery, (15-20) minutes for any one test.
Comments: Self-administered.
Author: R. R. Morman.
Publisher: TAV Selection System.
　　a) TAV ADJECTIVE CHECKLIST.
　　Scores, 3: Toward People (T), Away from People (A), Versus People (V).
　　b) TAV JUDGMENTS.
　　Scores, 3: Same as *a* above.
　　c) TAV PERSONAL DATA.
　　Scores, 3: Same as *a* above.
　　d) TAV PREFERENCES.
　　Scores, 3: Same as *a* above.
　　e) TAV PROVERBS AND SAYINGS.
　　Scores, 3: Same as *a* above.

f) TAV SALESMAN REACTIONS.

Scores, 3: Same as *a* above.

g) TAV MENTAL AGILITY.

Scores, 3: Follow Directions and Carefulness, Weights and Balances, Verbal Comprehension.

Cross References: For a review by Robert G. Demaree, see 8:986 (1 reference); see also T2:2113 (3 references); for an excerpted review by John O. Crites, see 7:983 (1 reference); see also P:263A (11 references).

[2530]

The Taylor-Helmstadter Pair Comparison Scale of Aesthetic Judgment.

Purpose: Constructed to assess aesthetic judgment.

Population: Ages 4 and over.

Publication Dates: 1973–1976.

Scores: Total score only.

Administration: Group.

Price Data: Available from publisher.

Time: [20–30] minutes.

Comments: Two carousel slide projectors necessary for administration.

Author: Anne P. Taylor.

Publisher: Anne P. Taylor.

Cross References: See T3:2395 (1 reference).

[2531]

Taylor-Johnson Temperament Analysis® [2006 Edition]

Purpose: Designed to "measure a number of ... personality variables or attitudes and behavioral tendencies which influence personal, social, marital, parental, family, scholastic, and vocational adjustment."

Population: Ages 11 and up.

Publication Dates: 1941–2006.

Acronym: T-JTA®.

Scores, 11: Nervous vs. Composed, Depressive vs. Light-Hearted, Active-Social vs. Quiet, Expressive-Responsive vs. Inhibited, Sympathetic vs. Indifferent, Subjective vs. Objective, Dominant vs. Submissive, Hostile vs. Tolerant, Self-Disciplined vs. Impulsive, Test-Taking Attitude, Total Mids; computer scoring software includes 8 additional scales: Overall Adjustment, Emotional Stability, Alienating, Interpersonal Effectiveness, Self-Esteem, Outgoing/Gregarious, Industrious/Persevering, Consistency (validity scale).

Administration: Individual or group.

Forms, 4: Regular Edition (criss-cross and self-report forms); Form "S" for Adolescents (criss-cross and self-report).

Price Data, 2006: $279 per complete kit (for handscoring and computer software scoring); $249 per complete kit (for scoring using computer software); $149 per complete kit (for online administration and scoring); $179 per computer scoring package (for use with mail-in scoring service); $135 per test manual; $52 per handbook.

Foreign Language Editions: Available in Spanish, German, French, Portuguese, Japanese, Chinese, Korean, and Danish; norms for Chinese, Spanish, and German editions only.

Time: Untimed.

Comments: Can be used as a self-report questionnaire or as a tool for obtaining perceptions of another person (criss-cross form); Form S can be used with adolescents or with adults with poor reading skills; 2002 Edition based upon new 2002 norms.

Authors: Original edition by Roswell H. Johnson, revision by Robert M. Taylor, Lucile P. Morrison (manual), W. Lee Morrison (statistical consultant), and Richard C. Romoser (statistical consultant).

Publisher: Psychological Publications, Inc.

Cross References: For reviews by Stephen N. Axford and Gregory J. Boyle, see 16:241; for reviews by Michael J. Sporakowski and Stephen E. Trotter of the 1996 Edition, see 14:381; for reviews by Jeffrey A. Jenkins and Barbara J. Kaplan of an earlier edition, see 13:315; see also T4:2690 (3 references); for reviews by Cathy W. Hall and Paul McReynolds, see 10:357; see also T3:2396 (1 reference) and T2:840 (3 references); for a review by Robert F. Stahmann, see 8:692 (18 references); for a review by Donald L. Mosher of an earlier edition, see 7:572 (1 reference); see also P:264 (3 references) and 6:130 (10 references); for a review by Albert Ellis of the original edition, see 4:62 (6 references); for a review by H. Meltzer of the original edition, see 3:57.

[2532]

TD (Tardive Dyskinesia) Monitor.

Purpose: "Measures the presence and severity of the tardive dyskinesia movements."

Population: Patients receiving chronic neuroleptic maintenance.

Publication Date: 1992.

Acronym: TD Monitor.

Scores: Total score only.

Administration: Individual.

Price Data, 2005: $100 per complete kit (manual, 25 modified AIMS QuikScore Forms, 25 modified Webster QuikScore Forms, and 25 TD Monitor History Forms); $50 per manual; $26 per 25 TD Monitor Modified AIMS QuikScore Forms; $26 per 25 TD Monitor Modified Webster QuikScore Forms; $39 per 25 TD Monitor History Forms.

Time: Administration time not reported.

Comments: Includes the Modified Webster Scale of Parkinsonism and centers around the Modified Abnormal Involuntary Movement Scale.

Author: William M. Glazer.

Publisher: Multi-Health Systems, Inc.

Cross References: For reviews by Timothy J. Makatura and Anthony M. Paolo, see 15:255.

[2533]
Teacher Assessment of Grammatical Structures.

Purpose: "Developed to evaluate a child's understanding and use of the grammatical structures of English and to suggest a sequence for teaching these structures."

Population: Ages 2–4, 5–9, 9 and over.

Publication Date: 1983.

Acronym: TAGS.

Scores: 3 ratings: Imitated, Prompted, Spontaneous Production.

Administration: Individual.

Price Data, 2005: $19.95 per manual (203 pages) for all 3 levels; $12 per 25 rating forms (specify TAGS-P, Pre-Sentence Level; TAGS-S, Simple Sentence Level; or TAGS-C, Complex Sentence Level).

Time: Administration time not reported.

Comments: Ratings are based on informal administration in classroom or therapy setting.

Authors: Jean S. Moog and Victoria J. Kozak.

Publisher: Central Institute for the Deaf.

  a) TAGS-P, PRE-SENTENCE LEVEL.

  Population: Ages up to 6 years for hearing-impaired children, ages 2–4 for language-impaired children.

  Comments: Assesses receptive and expressive skills.

  b) TAGS-S, SIMPLE-SENTENCE LEVEL.

  Population: Ages 5–9 years for hearing-impaired children, ages 3 and over for language-impaired children.

  Comments: Assesses expressive skills.

  c) TAGS-C, COMPLEX SENTENCE LEVEL.

  Population: Ages 8 and over for hearing-impaired children, ages 3.5 and over for language-impaired children.

Cross References: See T5:2620 (1 reference) and T4:2691 (1 reference); for reviews by Elizabeth M. Prather and Kenneth G. Shipley, see 10:358 (1 reference).

[2534]
Teacher Observation Scales for Identifying Children with Special Abilities.

Purpose: Designed as an assessment instrument for identifying gifted children, tailored to be culturally appropriate for use in New Zealand.

Population: Junior and middle primary school.

Publication Date: 1996.

Scores, 5: Learning Characteristics, Social Leadership Characteristics, Creative Thinking Characteristics, Self-Determination Characteristics, Motivational Characteristics.

Administration: Individual.

Price Data, 2001: NZ$12.60 per 20 observation scales; $12.60 per teacher's handbook (9 pages).

Time: Administration time not reported.

Authors: Don McAlpine and Neil Reid.

Publisher: New Zealand Council for Educational Research [New Zealand].

Cross References: For reviews by Ira Stuart Katz and Kenneth A. Kiewra, see 14:382.

[2535]
Teacher Opinion Inventory, Revised Edition.

Purpose: To assess teachers' opinions concerning many facets of the school, to "compile teachers' recommendations for improvement," and to provide "data to guide the school's professional staff in decision making relative to program development."

Population: Elementary and secondary school teachers.

Publication Dates: 1975–2003.

Scores: 4 subscales: Quality of the Instructional Program, Support for Student Learning, School Climate/Environment for Learning, School Organization and Administration.

Administration: Group.

Parts, 2: A (Likert-scale items), B (customize up to 20 local questions).

Price Data, 2006: $25 per 25 inventories; administrator's manual may be downloaded free from publisher website.

Time: Untimed.

Author: National Study of School Evaluation.

Publisher: National Study of School Evaluation.

[2536]
Teacher Performance Assessment [2006 Revision].

Purpose: "Developed to provide both an objective assessment and a self-assessment of classroom instructional activities from individuals who work in different roles and who make different contributions to the schools."

Population: Teachers, student teachers, interns, classroom assistants.

Publication Dates: 1991–2006.

Acronym: TPA.

Scores, 3: Performance Assessment, Self-Assessment, Reflected Self-Assessment.

Administration: Group.

Forms, 8: Classroom Teachers, Substitute Teachers, Field Associates, Internship I, Internship II, Student Teachers, Classroom Aides, Residents; plus supervisor forms for each (each form provides two formats—categories of teaching competencies and categories with related cluster performances).

Price, 2006: $30 per 25 scales (specify form); $.50 per answer sheet; $.50 per customized booklet; $30 per manual (2006); $.40 per scale for scoring.

Time: (15) minutes.

Authors: Louise M. Soares and Anthony T. Soares.
Publisher: Castle Consultants.
Cross References: For reviews by Raoul A. Arreola and Samuel Hinton of an earlier edition, see 15:256.

[2537]
Teacher Values Inventory.

Purpose: Measures "teacher's preferences and opinions."
Population: Teachers.
Publication Dates: 1980–1981.
Acronym: TVI.
Scores, 6: Theoretical, Economic, Aesthetic, Social, Political, Religious.
Administration: Group.
Price Data: Available from publisher.
Foreign Language Edition: Hindi version available.
Time: Administration time not reported.
Authors: Harbhajan L. Singh and S. P. Ahluwalia.
Publisher: National Psychological Corporation [India] [No reply from publisher; status unknown].

[2538]
Teaching Resource and Assessment of Critical Skills.

Purpose: Designed to assist decision making about an individual's skills and potential to live in an unsupervised setting.
Population: People with special needs.
Publication Date: 1989.
Acronym: TRACS.
Scores: Unscored.
Administration: Individual.
Price Data, 1998: $124 per program including resource, assessment and skill log booklets, user's guide (49 pages), master forms, and audio tape.
Time: Administration time not reported.
Authors: Lauren Meiklejohn and Mark Rice.
Publisher: Program Development Associates (Distributor).

[2539]
Team Competency Assessment.

Purpose: Designed to "evaluate the level at which a team is performing on ten team competencies."
Population: Team members.
Publication Date: Not dated.
Scores, 11: Committing to a Team Approach, Communicating Effectively Within Teams, Utilizing Team Member Abilities, Resolving Team Conflicts, Creating a Shared Team Purpose, Planning for Results, Making Meetings Work, Evaluating Team Process and Performance, Making Team Decisions by Consensus, Solving Team Problems, Climate.
Administration: Group.

Price Data: Available from publisher.
Time: Administration time not reported.
Comments: A 65-item questionnaire; can be computer administered, scored, and interpreted (requiring IBM Windows compatible) or available in pencil-paper format; can be used separately or as one component of a team skills workshop.
Author: Human Technology, Inc.
Publisher: HRD Press, Inc.

[2540]
Team-Development Inventory.

Purpose: "A means by which work-team members can give each other feedback concerning how they are working together."
Population: Work-team members.
Publication Date: 1982.
Acronym: TDI.
Scores, 8: Each team member rank orders all members on 8 dimensions: Participation, Collaboration, Flexibility, Sensitivity, Risk Taking, Commitment, Facilitation, Openness.
Administration: Group.
Price Data: Price information available from publisher for kit including 10 instruments, 10 handouts, and facilitator's guide (16 pages).
Time: (35–50) minutes.
Author: John E. Jones.
Publisher: Jossey-Bass, A Wiley Company.

[2541]
Team Effectiveness Survey.

Purpose: Designed to assess process issues associated with team dynamics.
Population: Team members.
Publication Dates: 1968-1996.
Acronym: TES.
Scores: 4 scores for each team member: Exposure, Feedback, Defensive, Supportive, plus Total Team Effectiveness score.
Administration: Group.
Price Data, 2001: $8.95 per instrument.
Time: Administration time not reported.
Author: Jay Hall.
Publisher: Teleometrics International, Inc.
Cross References: For reviews by Gregory H. Dobbins and Harrison G. Gough, see 12:388; for a review by William G. Mollenkopf of an earlier version, see 8:1055.

[2542]
The Team Leadership Practices Inventory.

Purpose: Focuses on the behaviors and actions of high-performing teams and self-directed work groups.
Population: Managers.
Publication Date: 1992.
Acronym: LPI.

Scores, 15: 3 scores: Self-Average, Team-Average, Total in each of 5 areas: Challenging the Process, Inspiring a Shared Vision, Enabling Others to Act, Modeling the Way, Encouraging the Heart.
Administration: Group.
Price Data: Price information available from publisher for trainer's package including 3 booklets, self-assessment, and observer and trainer's manual (47 pages); deluxe trainer's package including the leadership challenge, self-assessment and analysis, and trainer's manual; IBM scoring program including manual (12 pages); instrument and participant's manual.
Time: (20–140) minutes.
Comments: Self-scored inventory.
Authors: James M. Kouzes and Barry Z. Posner.
Publisher: Jossey-Bass, A Wiley Company.
Cross References: For reviews by Jeffrey B. Brookings and William J. Waldron, see 13:317.

[2543]
Team Process Diagnostic.

Purpose: To analyze and classify group processes according to their implications for member and team effectiveness.
Population: Individuals whose work responsibilities require work-team cooperation.
Publication Dates: 1974–1989.
Scores: 9 clusters in 3 modes: Problem Solving (Integrative, Content-Bound, Process-Bound), Fight (Perceptual Difference, Status-Striving, Frustration), Flight (Fear, Indifference, Powerlessness).
Administration: Group.
Price Data: Price information available from publisher for instrument (1989, 21 pages).
Time: Administration time not reported.
Comments: Team associate ratings, self ratings, self scored.
Author: Jay Hall.
Publisher: Teleometrics International, Inc.
Cross References: For a review by Lawrence A. Aleamoni, see 11:416.

[2544]
Team Skills (Form A-C).

Purpose: To evaluate a candidate's ability to work as a member or leader of a team.
Population: Applicants and incumbents for jobs requiring knowledge of team principles.
Publication Dates: 1998–2001.
Scores: Total score only covering 7 areas: Conflict Resolution, Group Dynamics, Team Decision Making, Productivity and Motivation, Communication Skills, Leader & Member Skills, Interpersonal Skills.
Administration: Group.
Price Data, 2006: $13 per consumable self-scoring test booklet (minimum order of 20); $24.95 per manual (2001, 13 pages).

Time: (60) minutes.
Comments: Self-scoring instrument.
Author: Roland T. Ramsay.
Publisher: Ramsay Corporation.

[2545]
Teamness Index.

Purpose: To "survey … conditions of work and the array of feelings that might exist among two or more people as they seek to work together."
Population: Individuals whose work responsibilities require work-team cooperation.
Publication Dates: 1988–1995.
Scores: Item scores only.
Administration: Group.
Price Data, 2001: $8.95 per instrument.
Time: Administration time not reported.
Comments: Self-ratings; self-scored.
Author: Jay Hall.
Publisher: Teleometrics International, Inc.
Cross References: For reviews by Barbara Lachar and Frederick T. L. Leong, see 11:417.

[2546]
Teamwork Appraisal Survey.

Purpose: To assess "an associate's feelings about working in teams and the behaviors he or she employs in work-team situations."
Population: Individuals whose work responsibilities require work-team cooperation.
Publication Date: 1987.
Acronym: TAS.
Scores, 5: Synergistic, Compromise, Win-Lose, Yield-Lose, Lose-Leave.
Administration: Group.
Price Data: Price information available from publisher for instrument (24 pages).
Time: Administration time not reported.
Comments: Based on Team Behaviors Model of analysis of individual behaviors in a team setting; work associates rate each other's behavior.
Author: Jay Hall.
Publisher: Teleometrics International, Inc.

[2547]
Teamwork-KSA Test.

Purpose: Designed to "measure the essential knowledge, skills, and abilities that are predictive of working effectively in teams."
Population: Adults (industry).
Publication Date: 1994.
Scores: 7 subscales: Conflict Resolution, Collaborative Problem Solving, Communication, Interpersonal Skills, Goal Setting and Performance Management, Planning and Task Coordination, Self-Management Skills, plus Overall Score.
Administration: Group or individual.

Price Data, 2002: $127 per 10 tests; $28 per examiner's manual (1994, 23 pages); price data for scoring software available from publisher.
Time: [30–40] minutes.
Comments: Paper-and-pencil or computer administered.
Authors: Michael J. Stevens and Michael A. Campion.
Publisher: Pearson Performance Solutions [No reply from publisher; status unknown].
Cross References: For reviews by Patricia A. Bachelor and Patricia H. Wheeler, see 15:257.

[2548]
Technical Personnel Recruiting Inventory.

Purpose: Intended for use in research and development within industrial organizations; also for use in hiring.
Population: Research, engineering, and scientific firms.
Publication Dates: 1959–1960.
Scores: Item scores only.
Administration: Group.
Price Data: Available from publisher.
Author: Morris I. Stein.
Publisher: The Mews Press.
  a) INDIVIDUAL QUALIFICATION FORM.
  Population: Supervisors.
  Comments: For description of available position.
  b) PERSONAL DATA FORM FOR SCIENTIFIC, ENGINEERING, AND TECHNICAL PERSONNEL.
  Population: Job applicants.
  c) STEIN SURVEY FOR ADMINISTRATORS.
  Population: Administrators.
  Time: (30-40) minutes.
  Comments: Description of company's research environment; also part of Surveys of Research Administration and Environment (2512).
Cross References: For additional information, see 6:1167.

[2549]
Technical Support Staff Selector.

Purpose: To measure knowledge and aptitude for technical support positions.
Population: Candidates for the position of technical support.
Publication Date: 1994.
Acronym: TECHSUP.
Scores: Total Score, Narrative Evaluation, Ranking, Recommendation.
Administration: Group.
Price Data, 2001: $400 per candidate; quantity discounts available.
Time: (80) minutes.
Comments: Scored by publisher; must be proctored.

Author: Bruce A. Winrow.
Publisher: Walden Personnel Performance, Inc.

[2550]
Technical Test Battery.

Purpose: "Designed for occupational selection and placement."
Population: Technical job applicants and incumbents entry level to professional.
Publication Date: 1990.
Acronym: TTB.
Scores: Total score only for each of 9 tests.
Administration: Individual or group.
Price Data: Available from publisher.
Comments: Subtests available as separates.
Author: Saville & Holdsworth Ltd.
Publisher: SHL Group plc [United Kingdom].
  a) FOLLOWING INSTRUCTIONS (VTS1).
  Time: 20(25) minutes.
  b) NUMERICAL COMPUTATION (NT2).
  Time: 10(15) minutes.
  c) MECHANICAL COMPREHENSION (MT4).
  Time: 15(20) minutes.
  d) NUMERICAL ESTIMATION (NTS2).
  Time: 10(15) minutes.
  e) MECHANICAL COMPREHENSION (MTS3).
  Time: 15(20) minutes.
  f) FAULT FINDING (FTS4).
  Time: 20(25) minutes.
  g) DIAGRAMMATIC THINKING (DTS6).
  Time: 20(25) minutes.
  h) SPATIAL REASONING (ST7).
  Time: 20(25) minutes.
  i) DIAGRAMMATIC REASONING (DT8).
  Time: 15(20) minutes.
Cross References: For a review by Sami Gulgoz, see 11:419.

[2551]
Technical Test Battery [British Edition].

Purpose: Assess vocational skills and abilities.
Population: Apprentice and technical personnel.
Publication Dates: 1979–1982.
Acronym: TTB.
Administration: Group.
Restricted Distribution: Persons who have completed the publisher's training course or members of the Division of Occupational Psychology of the British Psychological Society.
Price Data: Available from publisher.
Comments: Subtests available as separates.
Authors: David Hawkey, Peter Saville, Robert Page (MT4), and Gill Nyfield (manual).
Publisher: SHL Group plc [United Kingdom].
  a) LEVEL 1.
  Purpose: "Basic skills and comprehension."
  Publication Dates: 1979–1981.

1) *Verbal Comprehension.*
Acronym: VT 1.
Time: 10(15) minutes.
2) *Numerical Computation.*
Acronym: NT 2.
Time: 10(15) minutes.
3) *Visual Estimation.*
Acronym: ET 3.
Time: 10(15) minutes.
4) *Mechanical Comprehension.*
Acronym: MT 4.
Time: 15(20) minutes.
b) LEVEL 2.
Purpose: "Higher order reasoning and analytical skills."
Publication Dates: 1979-1981.
1) *Verbal Reasoning.*
Acronym: VT 5.
Time: 10(15) minutes.
2) *Numerical Reasoning.*
Acronym: NT 6.
Time: 10(15) minutes.
3) *Spatial Reasoning.*
Acronym: ST 7.
Time: 20(25) minutes.
4) *Diagrammatic Reasoning.*
Acronym: DT 8.
Time: 15(20) minutes.
5) *Spatial Recognition* (optional test for Levels 1 and 2).
Acronym: ST 9.
Time: 15(20) minutes.

[2552]
Technology and Internet Assessment.

Purpose: Designed to determine strengths and weaknesses in eight areas related to computer, Internet, and information skills.
Population: Middle school, high school, and college students, potential and existing employees.
Publication Date: 1999.
Acronym: TIA.
Scores, 8: Use of Technology, Specific Computer Skills, Acquisition of Technology Knowledge, Basic Internet Knowledge, Internet Information Skills, Adapting to Technological Change, Impact of Technology, Ethics of Technology.
Administration: Individual or group.
Price Data, 1999: $3 per test (100 copies or less); $2.50 per test (over 100 copies); user's manual free.
Time: (20–30) minutes.
Comments: Administration and results via World Wide Web.
Author: Michael Ealy.
Publisher: H & H Publishing Co., Inc.

[2553]
Teele Inventory for Multiple Intelligences.

Purpose: Designed to examine the dominant intelligences of individuals from the age of 3 to adults to identify the dominant ways individuals learn and process information.
Population: Age 3 to adult.
Publication Dates: 1992–1997.
Acronym: TIMI.
Scores, 7: Linguistic, Logical-Mathematical, Musical, Spatial, Bodily-Kinesthetic, Intrapersonal, Interpersonal.
Administration: Individual or group.
Price Data, 2006: $250 per complete kit including 35 pictorial inventories, 35 answer sheets, 1 scoring transparency and a teacher's manual (1997) plus postage; $25 per single set, includes one inventory, 35 answer sheets, and 1 scoring transparency; $10 per 35 scoring sheets plus transparency; $325 per test kit, includes 35 pictorial inventories, 35 answer sheets, 1 scoring transparency plus set of 25 rigid polished vinyl overhead transparencies for presentations.
Time: (15-20) minutes.
Comments: A spatial, forced-choice pictorial inventory that does not require the English language to complete.
Author: Sue Teele.
Publisher: Sue Teele & Associates.
Cross References: For reviews by Allen K. Hess and Sally Kuhlenschmidt, see 16:242.

[2554]
Telemarketing Applicant Inventory.

Purpose: "Provides a standardized measure of telemarketing potential and is an ideal instrument for selecting inbound and outbound telemarketing professionals" and is "ideal for personnel selection and placement, as well as identification of basic training needs."
Population: Applicants for telephone sales and service positions.
Publication Dates: 1992–2003.
Acronym: TMAI.
Scores, 13: Candidness, Accuracy, Sales Interest/Skill, Sales Responsibility, Productivity, Confidence/Influence, Interpersonal Orientation, Stress Tolerance, Job Stability, Job Stimulation Rating, Communicator Competence, Applied Verbal Reasoning, Readiness Index.
Administration: Individual.
Price Data: Available from publisher.
Time: (40–50) minutes.
Author: NCS Pearson, Inc.
Publisher: Pearson Performance Solutions [No reply from publisher; status unknown].

[2555]
Telemarketing Staff Selector.
Purpose: To evaluate the necessary knowledge and skills needed for the position of telemarketing representative.
Population: Candidates for the position of telemarketing representative.
Publication Date: 1997.
Scores: Total Score, Narrative Evaluation, Ranking, Recommendation.
Administration: Group.
Price Data, 2001: $150 per candidate; quantity discounts available.
Time: (81) minutes.
Comments: Scored by publisher; must be proctored.
Author: Walden Personnel Performance, Inc.
Publisher: Walden Personnel Performance, Inc.

[2556]
Telephone Interview for Cognitive Status.
Purpose: Designed to serve as a "brief test of global cognitive functioning" for administration over the telephone.
Population: Ages 60–98.
Publication Dates: 1987–2003.
Acronym: TICS.
Scores: Total score only.
Administration: Individual.
Price Data, 2006: $70 per introductory kit including manual (2003, 31 pages) and 50 record forms.
Time: (10) minutes.
Authors: Jason Brandt and Marshal F. Folstein.
Publisher: Psychological Assessment Resources, Inc.
Cross References: For reviews by Ronald J. Ganellen and Robert M. Thorndike, see 16:243.

[2557]
TEMAS (Tell-Me-A-Story).
Purpose: A culturally revelant apperception test for children.
Population: Ages 5–18.
Publication Dates: 1986–1988.
Acronym: TEMAS.
Scores, 34: Quantitative Scales (Cognitive Functions [Reaction Time, Total Time, Fluency, Total Omissions], Personality Functions [Interpersonal Relations, Aggression, Anxiety/Depression, Achievement Motivation, Delay of Gratification, Self-Concept, Sexual Identity, Moral Judgment, Reality Testing], Affective Functions [Happy, Sad, Angry, Fearful]), Qualitative Indicators (Affective Functions [Neutral, Ambivalent, Inappropriate Affect], Cognitive Functions [Conflict, Sequencing, Imagination, Relationships, Total Transformations, Inquiries, Omissions and Transformations scores for each of the following: Main Character, Secondary Character, Event, Setting]).

Administration: Individual.
Forms, 2: Short, Long.
Versions, 2: Minority, Nonminority.
Price Data, 2006: $291.50 per complete kit including nonminority stimulus cards (1986, 36 cards), minority stimulus cards (1986, 36 cards), 25 record booklets, administration instruction card, and manual (1988, 166 pages); $98 per set of stimulus cards; $24.75 per 25 record booklets; $13 per administration instruction card; $68.75 per manual.
Time: (45) minutes (short form); (120) minutes (long form).
Authors: Giuseppe Costantino, Robert G. Malgady (manual and record booklet), and Lloyd H. Rogler (manual).
Publisher: Western Psychological Services.
Cross References: See T5:2647 (2 references) and T4:2716 (1 reference); for a review by William Steve Lang, see 11:422.

[2558]
Temperament and Atypical Behavior Scale.
Purpose: Designed to measure temperament and dysfunctional behavior.
Population: 11–71 months.
Publication Date: 1999.
Acronym: TABS.
Scores, 5: Detached, Hyper-Sensitive/Active, Underreactive, Dysregulated, Temperament and Regulatory Index.
Administration: Individual.
Price Data, 2003: $85 per complete set including manual (122 pages), screener with 50 forms, and 30 assessment tools; $25 per 50 screener forms; $30 per 30 assessment tool forms; $40 per manual.
Time: (5) minutes for screener; (15) minutes for assessment tool.
Comments: Ratings by parents, surrogates, or other professionals.
Authors: John T. Neisworth, Stephen J. Bagnato, John Salvia, and Frances M. Hunt.
Publisher: Brookes Publishing Co., Inc.
Cross References: For reviews by Harold R. Keller and Loraine J. Spenciner, see 16:244.

[2559]
Temperament Comparator.
Purpose: "Designed to assess the relatively permanent temperament traits which are characteristic of an individual's behavior."
Population: Managers, supervisors, salespeople, and other higher-level professionals.
Publication Dates: 1958–1996.
Acronym: TC.
Scores, 15: Trait Scores (Calm, Cautious, Decisive, Demonstrative, Composed, Even-Tempered, Persever-

ing, Seeks Company, Self-Confident, Serious, Steady Worker, Talkative), Factor Scores (Extroversive/Impulsive vs. Introvertive/Cautious, Emotionally Responsive vs. Non-Emotionally Controlled, Self-Reliant/Self-Oriented vs. Dependent/Group Oriented).
Administration: Individual or group.
Price Data, 2002: $99 per start-up kit including 25 test booklets, 25 score sheets, and interpretation and research manual; $54 per 25 test booklets (quantity discounts available); $29 per 25 score sheets; $28 per interpretation and research manual.
Time: No limit (approximately 15 minutes).
Author: Melany E. Baehr.
Publisher: Pearson Performance Solutions [No reply from publisher; status unknown].
Cross References: See T5:2648 (1 reference); for reviews by Paul M. Muchinsky and Aharon Tziner, see 9:1234; see also T2:1413 (1 reference); for reviews by Lawrence J. Stricker and Robert L. Thorndike, see 6:187 (1 reference).

[2560]
Temperament Inventory.

Purpose: Designed to measure a set of four genetically determined temperaments.
Population: College and adults.
Publication Dates: 1977–1980.
Acronym: TI.
Scores, 4: Phlegmatic, Sanguine, Choleric, Melancholy.
Administration: Individual or group.
Price Data, 2005: $1.75 per test booklet; $7.99 per scoring templates; $3.99 per guide book.
Foreign Language Editions: Test booklets are available in English, French, German, and Spanish.
Time: Administration time not reported.
Comments: Includes 80 yes-or-no questions. The guide book, Understanding Your Temperament, is available for self-administering, self-scoring, and self-interpreting the scores from a Christian viewpoint; scoring templates are available (specify English or international) for efficient scoring.
Authors: Robert J. Cruise and W. Peter Blitchington.
Publisher: Andrews University Press.
a) [GROUP EDITION].
Publication Date: 1977.
b) UNDERSTANDING YOUR TEMPERAMENT.
Publication Date: 1979.
Cross References: For reviews by Allan L. Lavoie and Paul McReynolds, see 9:1235 (1 reference); see also T3:2411 (1 reference).

[2561]
Tennessee Self-Concept Scale, Second Edition.

Purpose: Designed as a multidimensional self-concept assessment instrument.

Population: Ages 7 to 90.
Publication Dates: 1964–1996.
Acronym: TSCS: 2.
Scores, 15: Validity scores (Inconsistent Responding, Self-Criticism, Faking Good, Response Distribution); Summary scores (Total Self-Concept, Conflict); Self-Concept scales (Physical, Moral, Personal, Family, Social, Academic/Work); Supplementary scores (Identity, Satisfaction, Behavior).
Administration: Group.
Price Data, 2006: $110 per complete kit including 24 AutoScore™ answer forms (12 for adults and 12 for children) and manual (1996, 141 pages); $46.75 per 25 AutoScore™ forms (specify Adult of Child); $16.50 per 10 Spanish Research edition answer sheets (specify Adult or Child); $14.85 per mail-in answer sheet (specify Adult or Child); $295 per 25-use disk (PC with Windows; specify Adult or Child form); $16.50 per 100 answer sheets for use with disk; $10.20 per FAX Service Scoring; $65.50 per manual.
Time: (10–20) minutes.
Comments: Self-administered; WPS TEST REPORT Service available for computerized scoring and test interpretation.
Authors: William H. Fitts and W. L. Warren.
Publisher: Western Psychological Services.
a) TSCS:2 ADULT FORM.
Population: Ages 13 and older.
b) TSCS:2 CHILD FORM.
Population: Ages 7–14.
c) TSCS:2 SHORT FORM.
Population: Adults (13 and older); child (7–14).
Comments: The Short Form consists of the first 20 items on the adult and child forms.
Cross References: See T5:2652 (12 references); for reviews by Ric Brown and John Hattie, see 13:320 (41 references); see also T4:2723 (32 references); for reviews by Francis X. Archambault, Jr. and E. Thomas Dowd, see 11:424 (89 references); see also 9:1236 (60 references), T3:2413 (120 references), 8:693 (384 references), and T2:1415 (80 references); for reviews by Peter M. Bentler and Richard M. Suinn and an excerpted review by John O. Crites of an earlier edition, see 7:151 (88 references); see also P:266 (30 references).

[2562]
Tennis Skills Test Manual.

Purpose: Designed to assess essential skills needed to play tennis.
Population: High school and college.
Publication Date: 1989.
Scores, 3: Ground Stroke, Serve, Volley.
Administration: Individual.
Price Data, 2001: $14 per manual (50 pages).
Time: Administration time not reported.

Authors: Larry Hensley, Graham Hatcher, Gloria Hook, Paul Hook, Carolyn Lehr, and Jacqueline Shick.
Publisher: American Association for Active Lifestyles and Fitness.
Cross References: For reviews by Claude A. Sandy and William A. Stock, see 12:390; see also T4:2724 (1 reference).

[2563]
TerraNova, The Second Edition.

Purpose: "A comprehensive, modular series offering multiple measures of both English- and Spanish-language student achievement."
Population: Grades K-12.
Publication Dates: 1997-2002.
Administration: Group.
Levels, 12: 10 (Kindergarten), 11 (Grade 1), 12 (Grade 2), 13 (Grade 3), 14 (Grade 4), 15 (Grade 5), 16 (Grade 6), 17 (Grade 7), 18 (Grade 8), 19 (Grade 9), 20 (Grade 10), 21/22 (Grades 11, 12).
Forms, 2: C, D (2 forms of the Plus Tests also available).
Price Data, 2006: $61 per Teacher's Guide to TerraNova, The Second Edition (2000, 320 pages), quantity discount available; $61 per Technical Bulletin (2002, 310 pages), CD-ROM version only; $7.80 per Assessment Accommodations Supplement (17 pages); $3.33 per class record sheet for hand scoring; $54 per norms book.
Foreign Language and Special Editions: Available in English and Spanish editions (Supera); Braille and large print editions available.
Time: Administration time varies by test and level.
Comments: Also called California Achievement Test, Sixth Edition (CAT6); total remake of the TerraNova (T5:2654) including all new items and thematic content, new norms; TerraNova, The Second Edition, Forms C and D are designed as parallel test forms to the Comprehensive Tests of Basic Skills (CTBS; 1997) Forms A and B; Basic Battery, Basic Multiple Assessments measure only Reading, Language, Mathematics; Survey, Complete Battery, Multiple Assessments measure Reading, Language, Mathematics, Science, Social Studies; Plus Tests measure additional skills (Word Analysis, Vocabulary, Language Mechanics, Spelling, Mathematics Computation); tests may be administered alone or in any combination; full-service scoring available through publisher; reports and data available on CD-ROM; electronic report delivery available; information regarding numerous customized and packaged scoring and reporting services available from publisher; optional locator tests available to assist teachers in identifying appropriate testing level for individual students; optional practice activities available to help familiarize students with test-taking mechanics, item formats, test design elements; website (www.ctb.com) provides additional information on reports and pricing.

Author: CTB/McGraw-Hill.
Publisher: CTB/McGraw-Hill.
a) TERRANOVA, THE SECOND EDITION SURVEY AND SURVEY WITH PLUS.
Purpose: Designed to "yield norm-referenced and some curriculum-referenced information in a minimum of testing time."
Price Data: $135 per 25 consumable Survey test books (Levels 12–13, specify level) including manipulatives, and Test Directions for Teachers; $55 per 25 consumable Plus test books for use with Survey (Levels 12–13, specify level) including manipulatives, and Test Directions for Teachers; $122 per 25 reusable Survey test books (Levels 14–21/22, specify level); $48 per 25 reusable Plus test books for use with Survey (Levels 14–21/22, specify level); $57 per 50 Survey CompuScan answer sheets (Levels 14–21/22) including Plus answer grid; $1,408 per 1,250 continuous form (Trans-Optic) answer sheets for precoding (Levels 14–21/22) including Plus answer grid; $794 per 2,500 student information sheets; $9.98 per 30 Level 12–13 and $15.80 per 50 Level 14–22 Survey or Survey with Plus acetate scoring stencils; $22 per Test Directions for Teachers (Levels 12–22, specify level); Basic Service scoring: $4.53 per Basic Survey book (Levels 12–13); $2.64 per Survey answer sheet (Levels 14–21/22); $5.02 per Survey with Plus book (Levels 12–13); $3.13 per Survey with Plus answer sheet; $76 per Survey accommodation kit (Levels 12–22, specify level).
Comments: Provides norm-referenced scores; all items use selected-response format.
Time: Varies by level; Reading and Language Arts: 60–80(70–90) minutes; Mathematics: 35–40(45–50) minutes; Science, Social Studies: 20–25(30–35) minutes each; 135–170(155–190) minutes total; 215–235(260–280) minutes total with Plus tests.
1) Levels 12–13.
Population: Grades 2–3.
Scores: 5 Survey scores (Reading, Language, Mathematics, Science, Social Studies); 5 Plus scores (Vocabulary, Language Mechanics, Spelling, Mathematics Computation, Word Analysis).
2) Levels 14–21/22.
Population: Grades 4–12.
Scores: 5 Survey scores (Reading, Language, Mathematics, Science, Social Studies); 4 Plus scores (Vocabulary, Language Mechanics, Spelling, Mathematics Computation).
b) TERRANOVA, THE SECOND EDITION COMPLETE BATTERY AND COMPLETE BATTERY PLUS.
Purpose: "Generates norm-referenced achievement scores and a full complement of objective-mastery scores."

Price Data: $174 per 25 consumable Complete Battery test books (Levels 10–13, specify level); $179 per 25 consumable Complete Battery Plus test books (Levels 11–13, specify level); $135 per 25 reusable Complete Battery test books (Levels 14–21/22, specify level); $146 per 25 reusable Complete Battery Plus test books (Levels 14–21/22, specify level); $57 per 50 complete Battery CompuScan answer sheets (Levels 14–21/22) including Plus grid; $1,408 per 1,250 continuous form (Trans-Optic) answer sheets for precoding (Levels 14–21/22) including Plus answer grid; $794 per 2,500 student information sheets; $75 per 3 Complete Battery Plus acetate scoring stencils (Levels 14–21/22); $9.98 per 30 Battery ancillary pieces additional manipulatives (Levels 12–13); $15.80 per 50 Battery ancillary pieces additional manipulatives (Levels 14–21/22); $22 per additional Test Directions for Teachers (Levels 10–21/22, specify level); Basic Service scoring: $4.53 per Complete Battery book (Level 10–13); $2.64 per Complete Battery answer sheet (Levels 14–21/22); $3.89 per Complete Battery Plus book (Levels 10–13); $3.13 per Complete Battery Plus answer sheet; $76 per Complete Battery accommodation kit (Levels 10–22, specify level).

Comments: Combines Survey items with additional selected-response items; yields detailed diagnostic information; provides norm-referenced scores.

Time: Varies by level; Reading and Language Arts: 55–100(65–110) minutes; Mathematics: 40–70(50–80) minutes; Science, Social Studies: 20–40(30–50) minutes each; 95–250(115–270) minutes total; 95–315(140–360) minutes total with Plus tests.

1) *Level 10.*
Population: Kindergarten.
Scores: 3 Complete Battery scores (Reading, Language, Mathematics); 2 Plus scores (Language Mechanics, Spelling).
2) *Level 11.*
Population: Grade 1.
Scores: 5 Complete Battery scores (Reading, Language, Mathematics, Science, Social Studies); 2 Plus scores (Language Mechanics, Spelling).
3) *Levels 12 and 13.*
Population: Grades 2–3.
Scores: 5 Complete Battery scores (Reading, Language, Mathematics, Science, Social Studies); 5 Plus scores (Language Mechanics, Spelling, Vocabulary, Mathematics Computation, Word Analysis).
4) *Levels 14–21/22.*
Population: Grades 4–12.

Scores: 5 Complete Battery scores (Reading, Language, Mathematics, Science, Social Studies); 4 Plus scores (Language Mechanics, Spelling, Vocabulary, Mathematics Computation).

c) TERRANOVA, THE SECOND EDITION BASIC BATTERY AND BASIC BATTERY PLUS.
Purpose: Designed to "provide the same information as the Complete Battery, targeting the basic areas of reading, language arts, and mathematics."
Price Data: $131.45 per 25 consumable Basic Battery test books (Levels 11–13, specify level) including manipulatives, and Test Directions for Teachers; $42.95 per 25 consumable Plus test books for use with Basic Battery (Levels 11–13, specify level) including manipulatives, and Test Directions for Teachers; $134 per 25 reusable Basic Battery test books (Levels 14–21/22, specify level); $48 per 25 reusable Plus test books for use with Basic Battery (Levels 14–21/22, specify level); $57 per 50 Basic Battery CompuScan answer sheets (Levels 14–21/22) including Plus answer grid; $1,125 per 1,408 continuous form (Trans-Optic) answer sheets for precoding (Levels 14–21/22) including Plus answer grid; $794 per 2,500 student information sheets; $75 per 3 Basic Battery or Basic Battery with Plus acetate scoring stencils (Levels 14–21/22); $9.98 per 30 ancillary pieces additional manipulatives (Levels 12–13); $15.80 per 50 ancillary pieces additional manipulatives (Levels 14–21/22); $22 per additional Test Directions for Teachers (Levels 10–21/22, specify level); Basic Service scoring: $4.53 per Basic Battery book (Levels 10–13); $2.64 per Basic Battery answer sheet (Levels 14–21/22); $5.02 per Basic Battery Plus book (Levels 11–13); $3.13 per Basic Battery Plus answer sheet.

Comments: Reading/Language Arts and Mathematics tests same as for Complete Battery.
Time: Varies by level; 55–100(65-110) minutes for Reading and Language Arts, 40–70(50–80) minutes for Mathematics, 95–170(140–215) minutes total; 170(215) minutes total with Plus tests.
1) *Levels 10 and 11.*
Population: Kindergarten–Grade 1.
Scores: 3 Basic Battery scores (Reading, Language, Mathematics); 2 Plus scores (Language Mechanics, Spelling).
2) *Levels 12 and 13.*
Population: Grades 2–3.
Scores: 3 Basic Battery scores (Reading, Language, Mathematics); 5 Plus scores (Language Mechanics, Spelling, Vocabulary, Mathematics Computation, Word Analysis).
3) *Levels 14–21/22.*
Population: Grades 4–12.

Scores: 3 Basic Battery scores (Reading, Language, Mathematics); 4 Plus scores (Language Mechanics, Spelling, Vocabulary, Mathematics Computation).

d) TERRANOVA, THE SECOND EDITION MULTIPLE ASSESSMENTS AND MULTIPLE ASSESSMENTS WITH PLUS.

Purpose: Designed "to provide data on students' problem solving and reading skills."

Price Data: $181 per 25 consumable scannable Multiple Assessments test books (Levels 11–21/22, specify level); $55 per 25 consumable Plus test books for use with Multiple Assessments (Levels 11–13, specify level); $48 per 25 reusable Plus test books for use with Multiple Assessments (Levels 14–21/22, specify level); all test book sets include manipulatives and Test Directions for Teachers; $122 per Multiple Assessments scoring guide (CD-ROM, Levels 11–21/22); $25 per 30 Multiple Assessments ancillary pieces additional manipulatives (Levels 11–21/22); $22 per additional Test Directions for Teachers (Levels 11–21/22, specify level); Basic Service scoring: $15.30 per Multiple Assessment (all levels); $15.80 per Multiple Assessment with Plus (all levels); $76 per Multiple Assessments accommodation kit (Levels 11–22, specify level).

Comments: Combines selected-response items from Survey with constructed-response items allowing students to produce their own short and extended responses; constructed-response items scanned electronically, hand scored by publisher; produces norm-referenced and curriculum-referenced scores.

Time: Reading and Language Arts: 100–120(110–130) minutes; Mathematics: 50–90(60–100) minutes; Science: 45–60(55–70) minutes; Social Studies: 45–65(55–75) minutes; 240–335(280–375) minutes total; 290–400(355–465) minutes total with Plus tests.

1) *Level 11.*
Population: Grade 1.
Scores: 5 Multiple Assessments scores (Reading, Language, Mathematics, Science, Social Studies); 3 Plus scores (Vocabulary, Mathematics Computation, Word Analysis).

2) *Levels 12 and 13.*
Population: Grades 2–3.
Scores: 5 Multiple Assessments scores (Reading, Language, Mathematics, Science, Social Studies); 5 Plus scores (Vocabulary, Mathematics Computation, Language Mechanics, Spelling, Word Analysis).

3) *Levels 14–21/22.*
Population: Grades 4–12.
Scores: 5 Multiple Assessments scores (Reading, Language, Mathematics, Science, Social Studies); 4 Plus scores (Vocabulary, Mathematics Computation, Language Mechanics, Spelling).

e) TERRANOVA, THE SECOND EDITION BASIC MULTIPLE ASSESSMENTS AND BASIC MULTIPLE ASSESSMENTS PLUS.

Price Data: $145 per 25 consumable test books (Levels 11–21/22).

Time: Varies by level; 150–210(195–255) minutes total; 200–275(245–320) minutes total with Plus tests.

Comments: Includes both selected-response and constructed-response items; selected-response items scored electronically; constructed-response items hand scored by publisher; Reading/Language Arts and Mathematics tests same as for Complete Multiple Assessments.

1) *Level 11.*
Population: Grade 1.
Scores: 3 Basic Multiple Assessment scores (Reading, Language Arts, Mathematics); 3 Plus scores (Vocabulary, Mathematics Computation, Word Analysis).

2) *Levels 12–21/22.*
Population: Grades 2–12.
Scores: 3 Basic Multiple Assessment scores (Reading, Language Arts, Mathematics); 5 Plus scores (Vocabulary, Mathematics Computation, Language Mechanics, Spelling, Word Analysis).

f) TERRANOVA ALGEBRA ASSESSMENT SYSTEM.

Purpose: A comprehensive system designed to help identify students with the necessary skills for Algebra I placement, to monitor thier growth during Algebra 1 courses, and to assess their mastery of Algebra 1 content at course end.

Population: Students in grades 7–12.

Scores: Available from publisher.

Price Data: $6.50 per student per administration for Pre-Algebra Survey online administration and reporting; $8.50 per student for Formative Assessments online administration and reporting (12 formative tests and item bank); $8.50 per student per administration for Proficiency Exam online administration and reporting; price information for paper-and-pencil options available from publisher.

Time: Varies by component.

g) SUPERA.

Purpose: "The Spanish-language version of the assessment series, offering multiple measures of student achievement."

Population: Grades K–10.

Levels, 10: 10, 11, 12, 13, 14, 15, 16, 17, 18, 19/20.

Scores: 3 Supera scores (Reading, Language Arts, Mathematics); 5 Plus scores (Word Analysis, Vocabulary, Language Mechanics, Spelling, Mathematics Computation).

Price Data: $48 per Teacher's Guide; $23 per Norms Book (specify Fall or Spring); $56 per Test Coordinator's Handbook; $26 per Supera Technical Report disk; $14.80 per Handbook of Instructional Objectives (specify Survey, Multiple Assessments, or Plus Edition).

Comments: Uses Spanish "common to all dialects"; designed as a parallel test form of English TerraNova tests; separate norms "allow comparison with either Spanish- or English-speaking peers"; Custom Assessments (Evaluaciones Desarolladas a su Preferencia) and Multiple Assessments also available.

1) *SUPERA Survey (Evaluaciones Esenciales) and Survey Plus.*

Price Data: $198 per 30 consumable test books (Levels 10–13, specify level); $156 per 30 reusable test books (Levels 14–19/20, specify level); $45.35 per 50 CompuScan answer sheets (Levels 14–20); $44 per 25 SCOREZE answer sheets (Levels 14–20); $2,930 per 2,500 continuous form answer sheets (Levels 14–20); $53 per scoring stencil (Levels 14–20, specify level); $54 per 30 Supera Plus consumable test books (Levels 11–13, specify level); $54 per 30 Supera Plus reusable test books (Levels 14–20, specify level); $59 per 50 CompuScan Plus answer sheets (Levels 14–20); $1,480 per 1,250 continuous form Plus answer sheets (Levels 14–20); $44 per 25 Supera Plus SCOREZE answer sheets (Levels 14–20, specify level).

Time: Reading/Language Arts test: 110–160(155–205) minutes; Mathematics test: 70–100(115–145) minutes; Supera Plus tests: 25–30 minutes for Word Analysis, 20–40 minutes for Vocabulary tests, 25–35 minutes for Language Mechanics tests, 20–25 minutes for Spelling tests, 25–30 minutes for Mathematics Computation tests.

2) *SUPERA Multiple Assessments (Evaluaciones Multiples) and Multiple Assessments Plus.*

Price Data: $126.35 per 30 consumable scannable test books (specify level); $16.20 per scoring guide (specify level).

h) PERFORMANCE ASSESSMENTS.

Purpose: "Available for educators who wish to use extended open-ended assignments."

Population: Grades 3–12.

Levels, 6: 13/14, 14/15, 16/17, 17/18, 19/20, 21/22.

Scores, 10: 6 Communication Arts strands (Establish Understanding, Explore Meaning, Ex-tend Meaning and Examine Strategies, Evaluate Critically, Write Effectively, Write Fluently); 4 Mathematics Competencies (Problem Solving, Communication, Reasoning, Data and Information Processing).

Comments: Open-ended response items require students to "move through a series of activities culminating in a final product or summative activity."

Price Data: $88 per 30 consumable test books including test directions (Communication Arts or Mathematics, specify level); $6.35 per scoring guide (Communication Arts or Mathematics, specify level); $10.60 per additional copy of test directions (Communication Arts or Mathematics, specify level); $36.55 per 30 test materials and accessories for practice activities (Communication Arts or Mathematics, specify level); $79.50 per Communication Arts video cassette (specify level).

i) TERRANOVA ONLINE.

Purpose: Online version to provide immediate, actionable results to help teachers target instruction.

Population: Grades 3–10.

Publication Date: 2005.

Levels, 7: 13 (Grade 3), 14 (Grade 4), 15 (Grade 5), 16 (Grade 6), 17 (Grade 7), 18 (Grade 8), 19/20 (Grades 9/10).

Forms, 1: B.

Price Data: $10.50 per student administration (includes a test administration, reports, and training materials).

Comments: Both online and paper-and pencil administration available; both norm-referenced and objective information.

Cross References: For reviews by Gregory J. Cizek and Robert L. Johnson, see 16:245; for reviews by Judith A. Monsaas and Anthony J. Nitko of an earlier edition, see 14:383; for information on the Comprehensive Tests of Basic Skills, see T5:665 (95 references); see also T4:623 (23 references); for reviews by Kenneth D. Hopkins and M. David Miller of the CTBS, see 11:81 (70 references); for reviews by Robert L. Linn and Lorrie A. Shepard of an earlier form, see 9:258 (29 references); see also T3: 551 (59 references); for reviews by Warren G. Findley and Anthony J. Nitko of an earlier edition, see 8:12 (13 references); see also T2:11 (1 reference); for reviews by J. Stanley Ahmann and Frederick G. Brown and excerpted reviews by Brooke B. Collison and Peter A. Taylor (rejoinder by Verna White) of Forms Q and R, see 7:9. For reviews of subtests of earlier editions, see 8:721 (1 review), 8:825 (1 review), 7:685 (1 review), 7:514 (2 reviews), and 7:778 (1 review).

[2564]
Test Anxiety Profile.

Purpose: Constructed to measure "how much anxiety a person generally experiences in different types of testing situations."
Population: Grades 9–12 and college.
Publication Date: 1980.
Acronym: TAP.
Scores, 12: 2 anxiety scores (Feeling of Anxiety, Thought Interference) for 6 different situations (Multiple Choice Test, Time-Limit Test, "Pop" Quiz, Essay Test, Giving Talk, Math Test).
Administration: Group.
Price Data: License to reproduce for Ph.D.s or Ed.D.s available from publisher.
Time: (20) minutes.
Authors: E. R. Oetting, C. W. Cole (test), and J. L. Deffenbacher (manual).
Publisher: E. R. Oetting, Colorado State University.
Cross References: See T4:2725 (2 references); for reviews by Steven D. Brown and John P. Galassi, see 9:1237.

[2565]
Test Attitude Inventory.

Purpose: "Developed to measure individual differences in test anxiety as a situation-specific personality trait."
Population: High school and college students.
Publication Dates: 1977–1980.
Acronym: TAI.
Scores, 3: Worry, Emotionality, Total.
Administration: Group.
Price Data: Available from publisher (www.mindgarden.com).
Time: (5–10) minutes.
Comments: Self-report inventory of test anxiety; title of manual is Test Anxiety Inventory.
Author: Charles D. Spielberger.
Publisher: Mind Garden, Inc.
Cross References: See T5:2656 (25 references) and T4:2726 (16 references); for reviews by John P. Galassi and Thomas R. Knapp, see 9:1238 (3 references); see also T3:2417 (2 references).

[2566]
Test for Auditory Comprehension of Language—Third Edition.

Purpose: Designed as a measure of receptive spoken vocabulary, grammar, and syntax.
Population: Ages 3-0 to 9-11.
Publication Dates: 1973–1999.
Acronym: TACL-3.
Scores, 4: Vocabulary, Grammatical Morphemes, Elaborated Phrases and Sentences, Total.
Administration: Individual.

Price Data, 2006: $275 per complete kit; $81 per manual (1999, 117 pages); $155 per picture book; $45 per 25 profile/examiner record booklets.
Time: (15–25) minutes.
Author: Elizabeth Carrow-Woolfolk.
Publisher: PRO-ED.
Cross References: For reviews by Ramasamy Manikam and Christine Novak, see 14:384; see also T5:2657 (37 references) and T4:2727 (20 references); for reviews by Nicholas W. Bankson and William O. Haynes of an earlier edition, see 10:363; see also T3:2472 (25 references); for reviews by John T. Hatten and Huberto Molina of an earlier edition, see 8:454 (6 references); see also T2:997A (2 references).

[2567]
Test for Colour-Blindness.

Purpose: To identify congenital color vision deficiency.
Population: Ages 4 and over.
Publication Dates: 1917–1970.
Scores: Total score only.
Administration: Individual.
Price Data: Available from distributor.
Time: Administration time not reported.
Author: Shinobu Ishihara.
Publisher: Graham-Field (U.S. Distributor) [No reply from distributor; status unknown].
Cross References: See T5:2658 (2 references), T4:2729 (3 references), T3:2419 (1 reference), T2:1932 (29 references), 7:882 (13 references), and 6:962 (58 references).

[2568]
Test for Creative Thinking—Drawing Production.

Purpose: "Meant to be a screening instrument which allows for a first rough, simple, and economic assessment of a person's creative potential."
Population: Age 4–adult.
Publication Date: 1996.
Acronym: TCT-DP.
Scores, 15: Continuations, Completions, New Elements, Connections Made with Lines, Connections that Contribute to a Theme, Boundary-Breaking Being Fragment—Dependent, Perspective, Humour/Affectivity/Emotionality/Expressive Power of the Drawing, Unconventionality A—Uncovential Manipulation, Unconventionality B—Symbolic/Abstract/Fictional, Unconventionality C—Symbol-Figure-Combinations, Unconventionality D—Nonstereotypical Utilization of Given Fragments/Figures, Speed, Total.
Administration: Group.
Forms, 2: A, B.
Price Data: Available from publisher.
Time: (30) minutes.

Authors: Klaus K. Urban and Hans G. Jellen.
Publisher: Harcourt Assessment [England].
Cross References: For reviews by Alice J. Corkill and William Steve Lang, see 14:385.

[2569]
Test for Examining Expressive Morphology.
Purpose: "Developed to help clinicians evaluate expressive morpheme development with children whose language skills range from three to eight years of age."
Population: Ages 3-0 to 8-12.
Publication Date: 1983.
Acronym: TEEM.
Scores, 7: (6 morphemes plus 1 age level approximation): Present Progressives, Plurals, Possessives, Past Tenses, Third-Person Singulars, Derived Adjectives, Total.
Administration: Individual.
Price Data: Price information available from publisher for complete kit including manual (43 pages), test booklet, and 25 scoring forms.
Time: (5-7) minutes.
Authors: Kenneth G. Shipley, Terry A. Stone, and Marlene B. Sue.
Publisher: Harcourt Assessment, Inc.
Cross References: See T5:2660 (4 references) and T4:2730 (1 reference); for reviews by Doris V. Allen and Janice A. Dole, see 10:364.

[2570]
Test for the Reception of Grammar.
Purpose: "Designed to assess understanding of grammatical contrasts in English."
Population: Ages 4–12 years and also dysphasic adults.
Publication Dates: 1983–1989.
Acronym: TROG.
Scores, 21: Noun, Verb, Adjective, Two Element Combination, Negative, Three Element Combination, Singular/Plural Personal Pronoun, Reversible Active, Masculine/Feminine Personal Pronoun, Singular/Plural Noun Inflection, Comparative/Absolute, Reversible Passive, In and On, Postmodified Subject, X But Not Y, Above and Below, Not Only X But Also Y, Relative Clause, Neither X nor Y, Embedded Sentence, Total.
Administration: Individual.
Price Data: Available from publisher.
Time: (10–20) minutes.
Comments: An 80-item, orally administered, multiple-choice test; "suitable for American as well as British subjects."
Author: Dorothy Bishop.
Publisher: Dorothy Bishop [England].
Cross References: For a review by Roger L. Towne, see 15:258, see T5:2662 (8 references).

[2571]
Test Lessons in Primary Reading, Second Enlarged and Revised Edition.
Purpose: "Designed to evaluate students' reading progress and thinking skills."
Population: Children.
Publication Date: 1980.
Scores: Item scores only.
Administration: Group.
Price Data, 2006: $5.95 per lesson booklet; $2.95 per teacher's manual/answer key (17 pages).
Time: Administration time not reported.
Authors: William A. McCall and Mary Lourita Harby.
Publisher: Teachers College Press.

[2572]
Test of Academic Achievement Skills— Reading, Arithmetic, Spelling, and Listening Comprehension.
Purpose: Measures a child's reading, arithmetic, spelling, and listening comprehension skills.
Population: Ages 4-0 to 12-0.
Publication Date: 1989.
Scores, 6: Spelling, Total Reading (Letter/Word Identification, Listening Comprehension, Total), Arithmetic, Total.
Administration: Individual.
Price Data: Not available.
Time: (15–25) minutes.
Author: Morrison F. Gardner.
Publisher: Psychological & Educational Publications, Inc.
Cross References: For reviews by C. Dale Carpenter and Steve Graham, see 13:321.

[2573]
Test of Academic Performance.
Purpose: Developed to assess achievement in four curriculum areas: Mathematics, Spelling, Reading, and Writing.
Population: Grades K–12.
Publication Date: 1989.
Acronym: TOAP.
Scores, 6: Basic subtests (Mathematics, Spelling, Reading Recognition, Reading Comprehension), Optional subtests (Written Composition, Copying Rate).
Administration: Individual and group.
Price Data, 2002: $119 per complete set including examiner's manual (182 pages), 25 student response forms, 25 record forms, and package of four reading stimulus cards; $75 per examine's manual; $43 per 25 student response forms and record forms.
Time: (20–45) minutes.
Authors: Wayne Adams, Lynn Erb, and David Sheslow.

Publisher: PsychCorp, A brand of Harcourt Assessment, Inc.

Cross References: For reviews by Steve Graham and Cleborne D. Maddux, see 13:222.

[2574]
Test of Adolescent/Adult Word Finding.

Purpose: Developed to assess word finding skills.

Population: Ages 12-80.

Publication Date: 1990.

Acronym: TAWF.

Scores: 5 sections (Picture Naming: Nouns, Sentence Completion Naming, Description Naming, Picture Naming: Verbs, Category Naming) yielding 4 scores: Accuracy, Comprehension, Item Response Time, Word Finding Profile.

Administration: Individual.

Forms, 2: Complete, Brief.

Price Data, 2006: $300 per complete kit including test book, 25 response booklets, examiner's manual (204 pages), and technical manual (121 pages); $45 per 25 response forms; $150 per test book; $60 per examiner's manual; $60 per technical manual.

Time: (20-30) minutes for complete test; [10] minutes for brief test.

Comments: Upward extension of the Test of Word Finding (2627); speed can be measured in actual or estimated Item Response Time; tape recorder and stopwatch required on Section 1 only when using Actual Item Response Time Option.

Author: Diane J. German.

Publisher: PRO-ED.

Cross References: See T5:2667 (1 reference); for reviews by Ronald B. Gillam and Richard E. Harding, see 12:391.

[2575]
Test of Adolescent and Adult Language, Third Edition.

Purpose: Designed "(a) to identify adolescents and adults whose scores are significantly below those of their peers and who might need interventions designed to improve language proficiency; (b) to determine areas of relative strength and weakness across language abilities; (c) to document overall progress in language development as a consequence of intervention programs; and (d) to serve as a measure for research efforts designed to investigate language characteristics of adolescents and adults."

Population: Ages 12-0 to 24-11.

Publication Dates: 1980–1994.

Acronym: TOAL-3.

Scores, 8: 8 subtest scores (Listening/Vocabulary, Listening/Grammar, Speaking/Vocabulary, Speaking/Grammar, Reading/Vocabulary, Reading/Grammar, Writing/Vocabulary, Writing/Grammar); 10 composite scores (Listening, Speaking, Reading, Writing, Spoken Language, Written Language, Vocabulary, Grammar, Receptive Language, Expressive Language).

Administration: Individual and group.

Price Data, 2006: $210 per complete kit including 50 answer booklets, 10 test booklets, 50 summary/profile sheets, and examiner's manual (1994, 111 pages); $65 per 50 answer booklets; $45 per 10 test booklets; $50 per 50 summary/profile sheets; $59 per examiner's manual; $79 per IBM software scoring system.

Time: (60–180) minutes.

Authors: Donald D. Hammill, Virginia L. Brown, Stephen C. Larsen, and J. Lee Wiederholt.

Publisher: PRO-ED.

Cross References: See T5:2668 (7 references); for reviews by John MacDonald and Roger A. Richards, see 13:323 (6 references); see also T4:2738 (9 references); for reviews by Allen Jack Edwards and David A. Shapiro of an earlier edition, see 10:365; for a review by Robert T. Williams of an earlier edition, see 9:1243.

[2576]
Test of Articulation in Context.

Purpose: Designed to "examine a student's phonological abilities in the contest of spontaneous conversation, and can be used to screen, predict change, diagnose and assess a student's phonological progress following treatment."

Population: Preschool through elementary-school-aged children.

Publication Date: 1998.

Acronym: TAC.

Scores, 4: Sound Production, Speech Mechanism, Intelligibility, Adverse Effect on Educational Performance.

Administration: Individual.

Price Data, 2006: $133 per kit including 25 response forms, 4 laminated test boards, manual (45 pages), and canvas carrying bag; $51 per 25 response forms.

Time: Untimed.

Author: Teresa Lanphere.

Publisher: PRO-ED.

Cross References: For a review by Thomas W. Guyette, see 14:386.

[2577]
Test of Attitude Toward School.

Purpose: To assess a student's attitude toward school.

Population: Boys in grades 1, 3, 5.

Publication Dates: 1973–1984.

Acronym: TAS.

Scores, 2: Scholastic Attitude Score, Evaluation by the Teacher

Administration: Individual.

Price Data, 2005: $22 per set of 16 drawings; $54.95 per 25 teacher questionnaires (1984, 3 pages); $19.80 per manual (1984, 116 pages).

Time: Administration time not reported.
Comments: Projective test.
Authors: Guy Thibaudeau, Cathy Ingram-LeBlanc (translation from French), and Michael Dewson (verification of technical terms).
Publisher: Institute of Psychological Research, Inc. [Canada].
Cross References: For a review by Bert A. Goldman, see 11:425.

[2578]
Test of Auditory Analysis Skills.

Purpose: Constructed to assess "a child's auditory perceptual skills."
Population: Ages 5-8.
Publication Dates: 1975–1993.
Acronym: TAAS.
Scores: Total score only.
Administration: Individual.
Manual: No manual (directions on each form).
Price Data, 2006: $16 per 50 test forms.
Time: Administration time not reported.
Comments: Criterion-referenced; may be used in conjunction with the Test of Visual Analysis Skills; test is reproduced from author's book Helping Children Overcome Learning Difficulties (1993, Walker Publishing Company, New York).
Author: Jerome Rosner.
Publisher: Academic Therapy Publications
Cross References: See T5:2671 (3 references); for reviews by Allan O. Diefendorf and Kathy S. Kessler and by Rick Lindskog of the earlier edition, see 11:426.

[2579]
Test of Auditory Comprehension.

Purpose: Designed to be used for the selection of auditory training objectives and measurement of progress in comprehension.
Population: Hearing impaired ages 4–17.
Publication Dates: 1976–1981.
Acronym: TAC.
Scores, 10: Linguistic vs. Nonlinguistic, Linguistic/Human Nonlinguistic/Environmental, Stereotypic Messages, Single Element Core Noun Vocabulary, Recalls Two Critical Elements, Recalls Four Critical Elements, Sequences Three Events, Recalls Five Details, Sequences Three Events With Competing Message, Recalls Five Details With Competing Message.
Administration: Individual.
Price Data: Publisher advises in April 2006 that test is now out of print although support materials (score sheets, tapes, curriculum, etc.) will remain available for several years.
Time: (30) minutes.
Comments: Test administered by cassette tape.

Authors: Audiologic Services and Southwest School for the Hearing Impaired, Office of the Los Angeles County Superintendent of Schools.
Publisher: Foreworks.
Cross References: See T5:2672 (2 references) and T4:2741 (7 references); for a review by James R. Cox, see 9:1246.

[2580]
Test of Auditory-Perceptual Skills, 3rd Edition.

Purpose: "To measure a child's functioning in various areas of auditory perception."
Population: Ages 4–0 through 18-0.
Publication Dates: 1985-2006.
Acronym: TAPS-3.
Scores, 9: Word Discrimination, Phonological Segmentation, Phonological Blending, Numbers Forward, Numbers Reversed, Word Memory, Sentence Memory, Auditory Comprehension, Auditory Reasoning.
Administration: Individual.
Price Data: Available from publisher.
Foreign Language Edition: Spanish version is available.
Time: (15–25) minutes.
Authors: Nancy A. Martin (TAPS-3); earlier editions by Morrison F. Gardner.
Publisher: Academic Therapy Publications.
Cross References: For reviews by Annabel J. Cohen and by Anne R. Kessler and Jaclyn B. Spitzer of an earlier edition, see 13:324 (2 references).

[2581]
Test of Creativity.

Purpose: To gain a quick measure of a person's creativity.
Population: Adolescents and adults.
Publication Date: 1994.
Scores: Total score only.
Administration: Group.
Manual: No manual.
Price Data: Price information available from publisher for tests including self-assessment, answer sheet and feedback, and Types of Creativity.
Time: 35(40) minutes.
Comments: Self-administered, self-scored.
Author: Training House, Inc.
Publisher: Training House, Inc.

[2582]
Test of Early Language Development, Third Edition.

Purpose: Designed to measure the early development of spoken language in the areas of receptive and expressive language, syntax, and semantics.
Population: Ages 2-0 to 7-11.
Publication Dates: 1981–1999.

Acronym: TELD-3.
Scores, 3: Receptive Language, Expressive Language, Spoken Language Quotient.
Administration: Individual.
Forms, 2: A, B.
Price Data, 2006: $272 per complete kit; $76 per manual (1999, 159 pages); $66 per Picture Book; $40 each per profile/Examiner Record booklet; $56 per manipulatives.
Time: (15–40) minutes.
Authors: Wayne P. Hresko, D. Kim Reid, and Donald D. Hammill.
Publisher: PRO-ED.
Cross References: For reviews by Sherwyn P. Morreale and Hoi K. Suen, see 14:388; see also T5:2680 (19 references) and T4:2749 (6 references); for reviews by Javaid Kaiser and David A. Shapiro of an earlier edition, see 12:393 (4 references); for reviews by Janice Arnold Dale and Elizabeth M. Prather of an earlier edition, see 9:1250 (1 reference).

[2583]
Test of Early Mathematics Ability, Third Edition.

Purpose: Designed as a test of early mathematical ability.
Population: Ages 3-0 to 8-11.
Publication Dates: 1983–2003.
Acronym: TEMA-3.
Scores: Math Ability Score.
Administration: Individual.
Forms, 2: A, B.
Price Data, 2006: $265 per complete kit including examiner's manual (2003, 71 pages), picture book Form A, picture book Form B, 25 examiner record booklets Form A, 25 examiner record booklets Form B, 25 worksheets Form A, 25 worksheets Form B, assessment probes, 5"x8" cards, 20 blocks, 20 tokens, and mesh bag; $51 per picture book A or B; $25 per 25 Form A or Form B examiner record booklets; $19 per 25 Form A or Form B worksheets; $35 per Assessment Probes manual (2003, 82 pages); $48 per examiner's manual; $19 per objects kit.
Time: Untimed.
Authors: Herbert P. Ginsburg and Arthur J. Baroody.
Publisher: PRO-ED.
Cross References: For reviews by Kevin D. Crehan and Judith A. Monsaas, see 16:246; see also T5:2681 (2 references); for a review by Jerry Johnson and Joyce R. McLarty of an earlier edition, see 11:428 (1 reference); for a review by David P. Lindeman, see 9:1252.

[2584]
Test of Early Reading Ability—Deaf or Hard of Hearing.

Purpose: Designed to measure "children's ability to attribute meaning to printed symbols, their knowledge

of the alphabet and its functions, and their knowledge of the conventions of print."
Population: Deaf and hard of hearing children ages 3-0 to 13-11.
Publication Date: 1991.
Acronym: TERA-D/HH.
Scores: Total score only.
Administration: Individual.
Forms, 2: A, B.
Price Data, 2006: $190 per complete kit including picture book, 25 Form A and 25 Form B profile/examiner record forms, and manual (49 pages); $65 per picture book; $40 per 25 profile/examiner record forms (select Form A or B); $50 per manual.
Time: (20–30) minutes.
Comments: Adaptation of the Test of Early Reading Ability-2 (2585).
Authors: D. Kim Reid, Wayne P. Hresko, Donald D. Hammill, and Susal Wiltshire.
Publisher: PRO-ED.
Cross References: For reviews by Barbara A. Rothlisberg and Esther Stavrou Toubanos, see 12:394.

[2585]
Test of Early Reading Ability, Third Edition.

Purpose: Designed to "assess children's mastery of early developing reading skills."
Population: Ages 3-6 to 8-6.
Publication Dates: 1981–2001.
Acronym: TERA-3.
Scores, 3: Alphabet, Conventions, Meaning.
Administration: Individual.
Forms, 2: A, B.
Price Data, 2006: $265 per complete kit including examiner's manual (2001, 127 pages), 2 picture books (Form A and Form B), 25 Form A profile/examiner record forms, and 25 Form B profile/examiner record forms; $81 per examiner's manual; $56 per picture book (specify Form A or Form B); $30 per 25 profile/examiner record forms (specify Form A or Form B).
Time: (30) minutes.
Authors: D. Kim Reid, Wayne P. Hresko, and Donald D. Hammill.
Publisher: PRO-ED.
Cross References: For reviews by Sharon H. deFur and Lisa F. Smith, see 15:259; see also T5:2682 (13 references) and T4:2751 (2 references); for reviews by Michael D. Beck and Robert W. Hiltonsmith of an earlier edition, see 11:429 (1 reference); for reviews by Isabel L. Beck and Janet A. Norris of the original edition, see 9:1253.

[2586]
Test of Early Written Language, Second Edition.

Purpose: "Measures early writing ability in children."
Population: Ages 3–0 to 10–1.

Publication Dates: 1988–1996.
Acronym: TEWL-2.
Scores, 3: Basic Writing, Contextual Writing, Global Writing.
Administration: Individual or group.
Forms, 2: A, B.
Price Data, 2006: $190 per complete kit including manual (1996, 116 pages), 10 each Form A and Form B student workbooks, 10 each Form A and Form B profile/record booklets in storage box; $45 per 10 student workbooks (specify Form A or B); $25 per 10 profile/record booklets (specify Form A or B); $60 per manual.
Time: (30–45) minutes.
Authors: Wayne P. Hresko, Shelley R. Herron, and Pamela K. Peak.
Publisher: PRO-ED.
Cross References: For reviews by David P. Hurford and Michael S. Trevisan, see 13:326; for a review by Patricia Wheeler of an earlier edition, see 11:430

[2587]
Test of Economic Knowledge, Second Edition.

Purpose: Measures knowledge of economic concepts.
Population: Grades 7–9.
Publication Date: 1987.
Acronym: TEK.
Scores: Total score only.
Administration: Group.
Forms, 2: A, B.
Price Data, 2001: $19.95 per 25 test booklets (specify Form A or B); $14.95 per examiner's manual (61 pages).
Time: (40) minutes.
Comments: "Designed to replace the Junior High School Test of Economics."
Authors: William B. Walstad and John C. Soper.
Publisher: National Council on Economic Education.
Cross References: For reviews by William A. Mehrens and Anthony J. Nitko, see 11:431.

[2588]
Test of Economic Literacy, Third Edition.

Purpose: Designed to "evaluate a student's performance and make decisions about economics instruction at the senior high school level."
Population: Grades 11–12.
Publication Dates: 1978–2001.
Acronym: TEL.
Scores: Total score only.
Administration: Group.
Forms, 2: A, B.
Price Data, 2001: $22.95 per 25 test booklets (specify Form A or B); $17.95 per examiner's manual (2001, 75 pages), which includes scoring keys and a model answer sheet (may be duplicated locally).

Time: (40-50) minutes.
Authors: William B. Walstad and Ken Rebeck.
Publisher: National Council on Economic Education.
Cross References: For a review by John W. Young, see 15:260; see T5:2686 (2 references); for reviews by Jennifer J. Fager and Dan Wright of an earlier edition, see 12:395; for a review by Anna S. Ochoa, see 9:1256; see also T2:1968 (19 references); for reviews by Edward J. Furst and Christine H. McGuire, and an excerpted review by Robert L. Ebel, see 7:901 (10 references).

[2589]
Test of English for International Communication (TOEIC).

Purpose: To evaluate the English proficiency of those whose native language is not English.
Population: Adult nonnative speakers of English.
Publication Dates: 1980–1999.
Acronym: TOEIC.
Scores, 3: Listening Comprehension, Reading Comprehension, Total.
Administration: Group.
Price Data: Price varies for Secure and Institutional Programs; price data available from publisher for ICS Program, 5 test booklets and answer sheets, audiocassette, and test administration manual (1998, 26 pages); volume discounts available.
Time: (120) minutes.
Comments: Secure Program administered on set dates and scored by TOEIC program office; Institutional and ICS Program administered by the client on-site and/or by TOEIC representative; one-half of test (100 questions) administered by audiocassette tape recording; separate answer sheet.
Author: Educational Testing Service.
Publisher: The Chauncey Group International.
Cross References: For reviews by Dan Douglas and Roger A. Richards, see 11:432.

[2590]
The Test of Everyday Attention.

Purpose: To measure "selective attention, sustained attention and attentional switching."
Population: Ages 18–80.
Publication Date: 1994.
Acronym: TEA.
Scores, 9: Map Search, Elevator Counting, Elevator Counting with Distraction, Visual Elevator, Elevator Counting with Reversal, Telephone Search, Telephone Search While Counting, Lottery, Total.
Administration: Individual.
Forms, 3: A, B, C.
Price Data, 2006: £269.50 per complete kit including manual (32 pages), 25 scoring sheets, cue book, stimulus cards and maps, 3 CDs, and 1 videotape; £41.50 per 50 scoring sheets.

Time: (45–60) minutes.
Authors: Ian H. Robertson, Tony Ward, Valerie Ridgeway, and Ian Nimmo-Smith.
Publisher: Harcourt Assessment [England].

[2591]
The Test of Everyday Attention for Children.

Purpose: To measure "selective attention, sustained attention and attentional switching."
Population: Ages 6–16.
Publication Date: 1998.
Acronym: TEA-ch.
Scores: 9 subtests: Sky Search, Score!, Creature Counting, Sky Search DT, Map Mission, Score DT, Walk/Don't Walk, Opposite Worlds, Code Transmission.
Administration: Individual.
Forms, 2: A, B.
Price Data, 2006: £355.50 per complete kit including manual, 25 scoring sheets, cue book, stimulus cards and maps, and 2 audiotapes; £81 per 50 scoring sheets.
Time: (55–60) minutes.
Authors: Tom Manly, Ian H. Robertson, Vicky Anderson, and Ian Nimmo-Smith.
Publisher: Harcourt Assessment [England].

[2592]
Test of Gross Motor Development—Second Edition.

Purpose: To "measure gross motor abilities that develop early in life."
Population: Ages 3–10.
Publication Dates: 1985–2000.
Acronym: TGMD-2.
Scores, 2: Locomotor, Object Control.
Administration: Individual.
Price Data, 2006: $105 per kit including 50 profile/examiner record booklets, and examiner's manual (2000, 69 pages) in a sturdy storage box; $55 per 50 profile/examiner record booklets; $55 per manual.
Time: (15–20) minutes.
Author: Dale A. Ulrich.
Publisher: PRO-ED.
Cross References: For reviews by Libby G. Cohen and G. Michael Poteat, see 15:261; see T5:2689 (2 references) and T4:2762 (2 references); for reviews by Linda K. Bunker and Ron Edwards of an earlier edition, see 10:370.

[2593]
Test of Inference Ability in Reading Comprehension.

Purpose: "Designed to provide diagnostic information about the inference ability of students."
Population: Grades 6–8.
Publication Dates: 1987–1989.
Scores: Total score only.
Administration: Individual or group.
Forms, 2: Multiple-choice, Constructed-response.

Price Data: Price information available from publisher for tests (specify multiple-choice or constructed-response), manual (1989, 24 pages), and technical report (1989, 58 pages).
Time: (40–45) minutes per form.
Authors: Linda M. Phillips (constructed-response format and multiple-choice format) and Cynthia C. Patterson (multiple-choice format).
Publisher: Linda Phillips (the author).
Cross References: For reviews by Douglas K. Smith and Robert Wall, see 13:327.

[2594]
Test of Interpersonal Competence for Employment.

Purpose: Designed to assess social interaction skills necessary for job tenure for mentally retarded adults.
Population: Mildly retarded adolescents and adults.
Publication Date: 1986.
Acronym: TICE.
Scores, 6: Handling Criticism and Correction, Requesting Assistance, Following Instructions, Cooperative Work Behavior, Handling of Teasing and Provocation, Resolving Personal Concerns.
Administration: Group.
Price Data: Price data available from publisher for set including teaching guide and script (56 pages).
Time: (60) minutes.
Authors: Gilbert Foss, Doug Cheney, and Michael Bullis.
Publisher: James Stanfield Co., Inc.
Cross References: For reviews by Sharon H. deFur and Lawrence J. Ryan, see 15:262.

[2595]
Test of Kindergarten/First Grade Readiness Skills.

Purpose: "To assess a child's readiness for kindergarten or for first grade."
Population: Ages 3–6 through 7–0.
Publication Date: 1987.
Acronym: TKFGRS.
Scores, 3: Reading, Spelling, Arithmetic.
Administration: Individual.
Price Data, 2006: $60 per test kit including manual, 25 record booklets, and 8 stimulus cards.
Time: (20–25) minutes.
Author: Karen Gardner Codding.
Publisher: Academic Therapy Publications.
Cross References: For reviews by D. Joe Olmi and J. Steven Welsh, see 13:328.

[2596]
Test of Language Competence—Expanded Edition.

Purpose: "To evaluate delays in the emergence of linguistic competence and in the use of semantic, syntactic, and pragmatic strategies."

Population: Ages 5 through 18.
Publication Date: 1989.
Acronym: TLC-Expanded.
Scores: 5 subtest scores: Ambiguous Sentences, Listening Comprehension: Making Inferences, Oral Expression: Recreating Speech Acts, Figurative Language, Remembering Word Pairs (supplemental subtest for Level 2 only), plus 4 composite scores: Expressing Intents, Interpreting Intents, Screening Composite, TLC-Expanded Composite.
Administration: Individual.
Price Data, 2006: $459 per complete kit with briefcase including 25 Level 1 & 2 record forms, Level 1 & 2 stimulus manuals, administration manual (1989, 311 pages), and technical manual (1989, 98 pages); $399 per complete kit without briefcase; $55 per 25 Level 1 or Level 2 record forms.
Time: (60) minutes.
Authors: Elisabeth H. Wiig and Wayne Secord.
Publisher: PsychCorp, A brand of Harcourt Assessment, Inc.
  a) LEVEL 1.
  Population: Ages 5 through 9.
  Price Data: $55 per 25 record forms.
  b) LEVEL 2.
  Population: Ages 10 through 18.
  Price Data: $55 per 25 record forms.
Cross References: See T5:2693 (10 references); for reviews by Dolores Kluppel Vetter and Carol E. Westby, see 11:435 (1 reference).

[2597]
Test of Language Development—Intermediate, Third Edition.
Purpose: To determine strengths and weaknesses in language skills.
Population: Ages 8-0 to 12-11.
Publication Dates: 1977–1997.
Acronym: TOLD-I:3.
Scores, 12: General Intelligence/Aptitude Quotient, Spoken Language Quotient (SLQ), Listening Quotient (LiQ), Speaking Quotient (SpA), Semantics Quotient (SeQ), Syntax Quotient (SyQ), Sentence Combining (SC), Picture Vocabulary (PV), Word Ordering (WO), Generals (GL), Grammatic Comprehension (GC), Malapropism (MP).
Administration: Individual.
Price Data, 2006: $185 per complete kit; $45 per profile/examiner record forms; $75 per examiner's manual; $70 per picture book; $98 per PRO-SCORE system (Mac or Windows).
Time: (30–60) minutes.
Comments: Primary edition also available.
Authors: Donald D. Hammill and Phyllis L. Newcomer.
Publisher: PRO-ED.

Cross References: For reviews by David P. Hurford and Pat Mirenda, see 14:389; see also T5:2694 (27 references) and T4:2767 (7 references); for reviews by Rebecca McCauley and Kenneth G. Shipley of the TOLD-I:2, see 11:436 (5 references). For a review by Doris V. Allen of an earlier version of the entire Test of Language Development, see 9:1261 (5 references).

[2598]
Test of Language Development—Primary, Third Edition.
Purpose: To determine children's specific strengths and weaknesses in language skills.
Population: Ages 4-0 to 8-11.
Publication Dates: 1977–1997.
Acronym: TOLD-P:3.
Scores: 15 subtests (Picture Vocabulary, Relational Vocabulary, Oral Vocabulary, Grammatic Understanding, Sentence Imitation, Grammatic Completion, Word Discrimination [Optional], Phoenemic Analysis [Optional], Word Articulation [Optional]); Composites (Listening, Organizing, Speaking, Semantics, Syntax, Spoken Language).
Administration: Individual.
Parts, 2: Subtests, Composites.
Price Data, 2006: $256 per complete kit; $60 per profile/examiner record forms; $85 per examiner's manual; $115 per picture book; $98 per PRO-SCORE systems (Mac or Windows).
Time: (60) minutes.
Comments: Intermediate edition also available; orally administered; examiners need formal training in assessment; PRO-SCORE Computer Scoring System available for Macintosh, Windows, and DOS (1998).
Authors: Phyllis L. Newcomer and Donald D. Hammill.
Publisher: PRO-ED.
Cross References: For reviews by Ronald A. Madle and Gabrielle Stutman, see 14:390; see also T5:2695 (72 references) and T4:2768 (21 references); for reviews by Linda Crocker and Carol E. Westby of a previous edition, see 11:437 (20 references).

[2599]
Test of Mathematical Abilities for Gifted Students.
Purpose: "Designed to identify students who have talent or giftedness in mathematics."
Population: Ages 6–12.
Publication Date: 1998.
Acronym: TOMAGS.
Scores: Total score only.
Administration: Group or individual.
Levels, 2: Primary, Intermediate.
Price Data, 2006: $175 per complete kit including manual (53 pages), 25 each Primary Level and Interme-

diate Level student booklets, and 25 each Primary Level and Intermediate Level profile/scoring sheets; $45 per 25 student booklets (specify level); $20 per 25 profile/scoring sheets (specify level); $56 per manual.
Time: (30–60) minutes.
Authors: Gail R. Ryser and Susan K. Johnsen.
Publisher: PRO-ED.
Cross References: For reviews by Robert B. Frary and Delwyn L. Harnisch, see 14:391.

[2600]
Test of Mathematical Abilities, Second Edition.

Purpose: "A measure of math ability."
Population: Ages 8-0 to 18-11.
Publication Dates: 1984–1994.
Acronym: TOMA-2.
Scores, 6: Vocabulary, Computation, General Information, Story Problems, Attitude Toward Math, Total.
Administration: Group.
Price Data, 2006: $92 per complete kit including 25 profile/record forms and examiner's manual (1994, 51 pages); $45 per 25 profile/record forms; $48 per examiner's manual.
Time: (120–130) minutes.
Authors: Virginia L. Brown, Mary E. Cronin, and Elizabeth McEntire.
Publisher: PRO-ED.
Cross References: For reviews by Delwyn L. Harnisch and Rosemary Sutton, see 13:329 (1 reference); for a review by Mark L. Davison of the earlier edition, see 9:1263.

[2601]
Test of Mechanical Concepts.

Purpose: "Designed to measure an individual's ability to visualize and understand basic mechanical relationships."
Population: Applicants for industrial positions.
Publication Dates: 1976–1995.
Scores, 4: Mechanical Interrelationships, Mechanical Tools and Devices, Spatial Relations, Total.
Administration: Individual or group.
Forms, 2: A, B.
Price Data, 2002: $106 per start-up kit including 25 test booklets (specify Form A or Form B) and examiner's manual; $91 per 25 test booklets (quantity discounts available; specify Form A or Form B); $28 per examiner's manual.
Time: No limit (approximately 35–45 minutes).
Author: Science Research Associates.
Publisher: Pearson Performance Solutions [No reply from publisher; status unknown].
Cross References: See T5:2700 (1 reference); for reviews by Lorraine D. Eyde and Lyle F. Schoenfeldt, see 8:1045.

[2602]
Test of Memory and Learning.

Purpose: For "evaluating children or adolescents referred for learning disabilities, traumatic brain injury, neurological diseases, serious emotional disturbance, Attention Deficit-Hyperactivity Disorder."
Population: Ages 5 to 19.
Publication Date: 1994.
Acronym: TOMAL.
Scores, 25: 9 Verbal subtest scores (Memory for Stories, Word Selective Reminding, Object Recall, Digits Forward, Paired Recall, Letters Forward, Digits Backward, Letters Backward, Total); 7 Nonverbal subtest scores (Facial Memory, Visual Selective Reminding, Abstract Visual Memory, Visual Sequential Memory, Memory for Location, Manual Imitation, Total); 4 composite scores (Verbal Memory Index, Nonverbal Memory Index, Composite Memory Index, Delayed Recall Index); 5 Delayed Recall scores (Memory for Stories, Facial Memory, Word Selective Reminding, Visual Selective Reminding, Total).
Administration: Individual.
Price Data, 2006: $270 per complete kit including examiner's manual (105 pages), picture book, 25 record forms and administration booklets, 25 supplementary analysis forms, facial memory picture book, 15 facial memory chips, visual selective reminding test board, and a set of delayed recall cue cards; $51 per examiner's manual; $76 per picture book; $55 per 25 record forms and administration booklets; $25 per 25 supplementary analysis forms; $40 per facial memory picture book; $9 per visual selective reminding test board; $20 per delayed cue card set.
Time: (40–45) minutes.
Authors: Cecil R. Reynolds and Erin D. Bigler.
Publisher: PRO-ED.
Cross References: For reviews by Karen Geller and Susan J. Maller, see 13:330 (1 reference).

[2603]
Test of Memory Malingering.

Purpose: "To assist neuropsychologists in discriminating between true memory-impaired patients and malingerers."
Population: Ages 16 to 84.
Publication Date: 1996.
Acronym: TOMM.
Scores: Total score only.
Administration: Individual.
Price Data, 2006: $144 per complete kit including manual (55 pages), 25 recording forms, and 1 set of stimulus booklets; $33 per 25 recording forms; $86 per set of 3 stimulus booklets; $61 per manual; $20 per Research Monograph; $67 per Computer Program for Windows™ including user's manual, software manual, and 3 uses.

Time: (15–20) minutes.
Comments: Self-completed; Windows™ computer software available on CD or 3.5-inch disk to administer, score, and report results of TOMM.
Author: Tom N. Tombaugh.
Publisher: Multi-Health Systems, Inc.
Cross References: For reviews by M. Allan Cooperstein and Romeo Vitelli, see 14:392.

[2604]
Test of Minimal Articulation Competence.
Purpose: Assesses articulation performance in children and adults.
Population: Ages 3 to adult.
Publication Date: 1981.
Acronym: T-MAC.
Scores, 3: Vowel/Diphthong, Consonant, Total.
Administration: Individual.
Parts, 3: Complete Test, Screening Test, Rapid Screening Test.
Price Data, 2002: $119 per complete program including Examiner's Manual and 25 record forms; $46 per 25 record forms; $80 per examiner's manual including administration, scoring, and interpretation information.
Time: Administration time not reported.
Author: Wayne Secord.
Publisher: PsychCorp, A brand of Harcourt Assessment, Inc.
Cross References: See T5:2703 (2 references); for a review by Barbara W. Hodson, see 9:1264.

[2605]
Test of Narrative Language.
Purpose: Designed to measure "children's ability to understand and tell stories."
Population: Ages 5-0 to 11-11.
Publication Date: 2004.
Acronym: TNL.
Scores, 3: 2 subtests: Narrative Comprehension, Oral Narration, plus Narrative Language Ability Index.
Administration: Individual.
Price Data, 2006: $160 per complete kit including examiner's manual (119 pages), picture book, and 25 examiner record booklets; $60 per examiner's manual; $65 per picture book; $45 per 25 examiner record booklets.
Time: (15–20) minutes.
Authors: Ronald B. Gillam and Nils A. Pearson.
Publisher: PRO-ED.
Cross References: For reviews by Abigail Baxter and Gabriele Van Lingen, see 16:247.

[2606]
Test of Nonverbal Intelligence, Third Edition.
Purpose: "Developed to assess aptitude, intelligence, abstract reasoning, and problem solving in a completely language-free format."

Population: Ages 6-0 through 89-11.
Publication Dates: 1982–1997.
Acronym: TONI-3.
Scores: Total score only.
Administration: Individual.
Price Data, 2006: $275 per complete kit including manual (1997, 160 pages), picture book, and 50 each Form A and Form B answer booklets and record forms; $45 per 50 answer booklet and record forms (specify Form A or B); $120 per picture book; $73 per manual.
Time: (15–20) minutes.
Authors: Linda Brown, Rita J. Sherbenou, and Susan K. Johnsen.
Publisher: PRO-ED.
Cross References: For a review by Jeffrey A. Atlas, see 14:393; see also T5:2704 (47 references) and T4:2775 (10 references); for reviews by Kevin K. Murphy and T. Steuart Watson of the Second Edition, see 11:439 (9 references); for reviews by Philip M. Clark and Samuel T. Mayo of the original edition, see 9:1266.

[2607]
Test of Oral Structures and Functions.
Purpose: "Assesses oral structures and motor integrity during verbal and nonverbal oral functioning."
Population: Ages 7–adults.
Publication Dates: 1986–2002.
Acronym: TOSF.
Scores, 16: Speech Survey (Articulation, Rate/Prosody, Fluency, Voice, Total); Verbal Oral Functioning (Resonance, Balance, Sequenced Syllables, Mixed Syllable Sequence, Sequenced Vowels, Sequenced Syllable Rates, Total); Nonverbal Oral Functions (Isolated Functioning, Sequenced Functioning); Survey of Orofacial Structures; History-Behavioral Survey.
Administration: Individual.
Price Data, 2002: $85 per complete kit including manual (36 pages), 25 test booklets, finger cots, tongue blades, penlight, and balloons; $35 per examiner's manual; $40 per 25 test booklets; $8 per oroscope penlight.
Time: (20) minutes.
Author: Gary J. Vitali.
Publisher: Slosson Educational Publications, Inc.
Cross References: See T5:2706 (2 references); for reviews by Ronald B. Gillam and Roger L. Towne, see 12:397.

[2608]
Test of Phonological Awareness in Spanish.
Purpose: To assess phonological awareness in children whose first language is Spanish.
Population: Ages 4-0 to 10-11.
Publication Date: 2004.
Acronym: TPAS.
Scores, 5: Phonological Awareness Ability, Initial Sounds, Final Sounds, Rhyming Words, Deletion.

Administration: Individual.
Price Data, 2006: $84 per complete kit; $49 per examiner's manual; $39 per examiner record booklets.
Time: (10–15) minutes.
Authors: Cynthia A. Riccio, Brian Imhoff, Jan E. Hasbrouck, and G. Nicole Davis.
Publisher: PRO-ED.
Cross References: For reviews by Carlos Inchaurralde and Vincent J. Samar, see 16:248.

[2609]
Test of Phonological Awareness—Second Edition: PLUS.

Purpose: Designed to measure "young children's ability to isolate individual phonemes in spoken words and their knowledge of relationships between letters and phonemes in English."
Population: Ages 5–8.
Publication Dates: 1994–2004.
Acronym: TOPA-2+
Scores: 2 subtests: Phonological Awareness, Letter Sounds.
Administration: Individual or group.
Levels, 2: Kindergarten, Early Elementary.
Price Data, 2006: $210 per complete kit including examiner's manual (2004, 78 pages), 50 Kindergarten summary forms, 50 Early Elementary summary forms, 25 student booklets for Kindergarten, and 25 student booklets for Early Elementary; $72 per examiner's manual; $30 per 50 Kindergarten summary forms; $30 per 50 Early Elementary summary forms; $47 per 25 Kindergarten student booklets; $47 per 25 Early Elementary student booklets.
Time: (15–30) minutes for Early Elementary version.
Authors: Joseph K. Torgesen and Brian R. Bryant.
Publisher: PRO-ED.
Cross References: For a review by Ray Fenton, see 16:249; for reviews by Steven H. Long and by Rebecca McCauley of a previous edition, see 13:333 (3 references).

[2610]
Test of Phonological Awareness Skills.

Purpose: Designed to "measure varied aspects of phonological awareness."
Population: Ages 5-0 to 10-11.
Publication Date: 2003.
Acronym: TOPAS.
Scores, 5: Rhyming, Incomplete Words, Sound Sequencing, Phoneme Deletion, Phonological Awareness.
Administration: Individual.
Price Data, 2006: $110 per complete kit; $49 per examiner's manual: $39 per 25 examiner record booklets; $14 per Block kit; $16 per audio cassette.
Time: (20–30) minutes.

Authors: Phyllis L. Newcomer and Edna Barenbaum.
Publisher: PRO-ED.
Cross References: For a review by Catherine P. Cook-Cottone and Jennifer Piccolo, see 16:250.

[2611]
Test of Pragmatic Language.

Purpose: Designed "to provide an in-depth screening of the effectiveness and appropriateness of a student's pragmatic, or social, language skills."
Population: Ages 5-0 to 13-11.
Publication Date: 1992.
Acronym: TOPL.
Scores, 3: Listening Skills, Speaking Skills, Total.
Administration: Individual.
Price Data, 2006: $160 per complete kit; $55 per examiner's manual (35 pages); $61 per picture book; $50 per 25 profile/examiner record forms.
Time: (45) minutes.
Authors: Diana Phelps-Terasaki and Trisha Phelps-Gunn.
Publisher: PRO-ED.
Cross References: For reviews by Salvador Hector Ochoa and William K. Wilkinson, see 12:398.

[2612]
Test of Pretend Play.

Purpose: To assess symbolic play, conceptual development, and use of symbols.
Population: Ages 1–6.
Publication Dates: 1997–1998.
Acronym: ToPP.
Scores: Scores for 4 sections (Self With Everyday Objects, Toy and Non-representational Material, Representational Toy Alone, Self Alone), and Total Score.
Administration: Individual.
Price Data, 2006: £356.50 per complete kit including 25 record forms, manipulables, and manual (1997, 58 pages).
Time: (45) minutes.
Authors: Vicky Lewis and Jill Boucher.
Publisher: Harcourt Assessment [England].
Cross References: For reviews by Pam Lindsey and Louise M. Soares, see 15:263.

[2613]
Test of Problem Solving 3: Elementary.

Purpose: Designed to assess children's critical thinking and problem solving skills.
Population: Ages 6.0-12.11.
Publication Dates: 1984-2005.
Acronym: TOPS 3.
Scores, 7: Making Inferences, Sequencing, Negative Questions, Problem Solving, Predicting, Determining Causes, Total.
Administration: Individual.

Price Data: Available from publisher.
Time: (35-40) minutes.
Authors: Linda Bowers, Rosemary Huisingh, and Carolyn LoGiudice.
Publisher: LinguiSystems, Inc.
Cross References: See T5:2710 (8 references).

[2614]
Test of Reading Comprehension, Third Edition.

Purpose: Designed to "quantify the reading comprehension ability of individuals."
Population: Ages 7-0 to 17-11.
Publication Dates: 1978–1995.
Acronym: TORC-3.
Scores: 9 subtests: General Vocabulary, Syntactic Similarities, Paragraph Reading, Sentence Sequencing, Supplementary (Mathematics Vocabulary, Social Studies Vocabulary, Science Vocabulary, Reading the Directions of Schoolwork), Reading Comprehension Quotient.
Administration: Group or individual.
Price Data, 2006: $189 per complete kit including 10 student booklets, 50 answer sheets and subtest 8, 50 profiles, and manual (1995, 91 pages) in storage box; $45 per 10 student booklets; $50 per 50 answer sheets and subtest 8; $50 per 50 profiles; $60 per manual.
Time: (60) minutes.
Authors: Virginia L. Brown, Donald D. Hammill, and J. Lee Wiederholt.
Publisher: PRO-ED.
Cross References: See T5:2712 (1 reference); for reviews by Felice J. Green and Carole Perlman, see 13:334 (3 references); see also T4:2785 (3 references); for reviews by James A. Poteet and Robert J. Tierney of an earlier edition, see 10:372 (4 references); for reviews by Brendon John Bartlett and Joyce Hood of the original edition, see 9:1270; see also T3:2456 (1 reference).

[2615]
Test of Sensory Functions in Infants.

Purpose: Developed to measure "sensory processing and reactivity in infants."
Population: Infants ages 4-18 months.
Publication Date: 1989.
Acronym: TSFI.
Scores, 6: Reactivity to Tactile Deep Pressure, Adaptive Motor Functions, Visual-Tactile Integration, Ocular-Motor Control, Reactivity to Vestibular Stimulation, Total.
Administration: Individual.
Price Data, 2006: $192.50 per complete kit including set of test materials, 100 administration and scoring forms, and manual (45 pages) in carrying case; $29 per 100 administration and scoring forms; $42.50 per manual.
Time: (20) minutes.

Authors: Georgia A. DeGangi and Stanley I. Greenspan.
Publisher: Western Psychological Services.
Cross References: See T5:2715 (1 reference); for a review by Mark Albanese, see 11:441.

[2616]
Test of Silent Contextual Reading Fluency.

Purpose: Designed as a quick and accurate method of assessing silent reading ability.
Population: Ages 7 to 18 years.
Publication Date: 2006.
Acronym: TOSCRF.
Scores: Total score only.
Administration: Group or individual.
Forms: 4 equivalent forms: A, B, C, D.
Price Data, 2006: $200 per complete kit including examiner's manual (98 pages), 25 Student record Forms A, 25 Student record Forms B, 25 Student record Forms C, and 25 Student record Forms D; $55 per examiner's manual; $45 per 25 Student record forms.
Time: (10) minutes.
Authors: Donald D. Hammill, J. Lee Wiederholt, and Elizabeth A. Allen.
Publisher: PRO-ED.

[2617]
Test of Silent Word Reading Fluency.

Purpose: Measures the ability to recognize printed words accurately and efficiently.
Population: Ages 6-6 to 17-11.
Publication Date: 2004.
Acronym: TOSWRF.
Scores: Total score only.
Forms, 2: A, B.
Price Data: 2006; $135 per complete kit including examiner's manual, 50 student record forms A, and 50 student record forms B; $55 per examiner's manual; $45 per 50 student record forms (specify Form A or B); $73 per 100 student record forms (specify A kit or B kit).
Time: 3 minutes per form.
Authors: Nancy Mather, Donald D. Hammill, Elizabeth A. Allen, and Rhia Roberts.
Publisher: PRO-ED.
Cross References: For reviews by Michael D. Beck and John W. Young, see 16:251.

[2618]
Test of Social Insight.

Purpose: Designed to "appraise the characteristic mode of reaction the individual uses in resolving interpersonal (social) problems."
Population: Grades 6-12, 13-16 and adults.
Publication Dates: 1959-1984.
Acronym: TSI.
Scores, 6: Withdrawal, Passivity, Cooperation, Competition, Aggression, Total.

Administration: Group.

Levels, 2: Youth Edition, Adult Edition.

Price Data, 2006: $95 per test package; $57.50 per manual (1963, 19 pages) and manual supplement (1984, 19 pages); $85 per IBM answer sheet/profile sheet package; $45 per set of IBM scoring stencils; $61.50 per specimen set.

Time: [20-25] minutes.

Author: Russell N. Cassel.

Publisher: Martin M. Bruce, Ph.D.

Cross References: See T3:2461 (1 reference) and T2: 1419 (3 references). For reviews by John D. Black and John Pierce-Jones, and an excerpted review by Edward S. Bordin, see 6:190 (4 references).

[2619]
Test of Spoken English.

Purpose: Measures the ability of nonnative speakers of English to communicate orally in English.

Population: Nonnative speakers of English.

Publication Dates: 1979–2006.

Acronym: TSE.

Scores: Total score only.

Administration: Group.

Price Data: Examination fee per candidate available from publisher.

Time: (20–25) minutes.

Comments: Because TOEFL iBT will assess all four language skills (listening, reading, writing, and speaking), using integrated tasks to evaluate communicative competency in English for nonnative speakers, ETS will discontinue TSE as a stand-alone testing program in areas where TOEFL iBT is being delivered.

Author: International Language Programs, Educational Testing Service.

Publisher: Educational Testing Service.

Cross References: See T5:2717 (1 reference); for reviews by Michael J. Subkoviak and Kikumi K. Tatsuoka, see 9:1273.

[2620]
Test of Supervisory Skills.

Purpose: Designed to measure an individual's understanding of "the roles and responsibilities of a first-line supervisor."

Population: Business supervisors and potential business supervisors.

Publication Date: 2004.

Acronym: TOSS.

Scores, 8: Management of Performance Quality, Staffing/Personnel Actions, Communications, Interpersonal Relations, Problem Analysis/Resolution, Project Planning, Direct Supervision, Total.

Administration: Individual or group.

Price Data, 2005: $29.95 per technical and administrative manual; $50 per 10 question booklets; $75 per 25 answer sheets.

Time: (30–45) minutes.

Comments: Available in paper-and-pencil and Web-based versions.

Authors: Erich P. Prien and Leonard D. Goodstein.

Publisher: HRD Press, Inc.

[2621]
Test of Understanding in College Economics, Third Edition.

Purpose: To measure college students' understanding of college economics.

Population: Introductory economics students.

Publication Dates: 1967–1991.

Acronym: TUCE III.

Scores: Total score only.

Administration: Group.

Editions, 2: Microeconomics, Macroeconomics.

Price Data, 2001: $19.95 per 25 test booklets (specify Macroeconomics or Microeconomics); $14.85 per examiner's manual (1991, 46 pages), which includes scoring keys.

Time: (45) minutes per test.

Author: Phillip Saunders.

Publisher: National Council on Economic Education.

Cross References: For reviews by Joseph C. Ciechalski and Jennifer J. Fager, see 13:335; see also T2:1970 (10 references); for a review by Christine H. McGuire of an earlier edition, see 7:902.

[2622]
Test of Variables of Attention (Version 7.03).

Purpose: "Developed to assess attention and impulse control."

Population: Ages 4–80.

Publication Dates: 1988–1996.

Acronym: TOVA.

Administration: Individual.

Price Data: Available from publisher.

Time: (21.6) minutes.

Comments: Computer administered via separate or combined software; IBM and Macintosh versions available.

Authors: Lawrence M. Greenberg, Clifford L. Corman, and Carol L. Kindschi.

Publisher: Universal Attention Disorders, Inc.

a) T.O.V.A. VISUAL.

Scores, 4: Commission, Omission, Response Time, Response Time Variability and Signal Detection.

b) T.O.V.A. AUDITORY.

Scores: Same as *a* above.

Cross References: For reviews by Sandra Loew and by Susan C. Whiston and Harrison Kane, see 14:394; see also T5:2720 (2 references); for reviews by Rosa A. Hagin and Peter Della Bella and by Margot B. Stein of an earlier edition, see 13:336 (1 reference).

[2623]
Test of Visual-Motor Skills—Revised.

Purpose: To assess a child's visual-motor functioning.
Population: Ages 2–0 through 13-11.
Publication Dates: 1986-1995.
Acronym: TVMS-R.
Scores: Total score plus 8 error scores.
Administration: Group or individual.
Price Data, 2006: $90 per test kit including manual, 15 test booklets, 15 scoring forms, and protractor; $28 per manual; $34 per 15 test booklets; $25 per scoring-criterion forms; $3 per protractor.
Time: (3-5) minutes.
Author: Morrison F. Gardner.
Publisher: Academic Therapy Publications.
Cross References: For reviews by Deborah Erickson and Janet E. Spector of an earlier edition, see 13:337 (2 references); see also T4:2791 (1 reference).

[2624]
Test of Visual-Motor Skills—Upper Level.

Purpose: To assess a child's visual-motor functioning.
Population: Ages 2–0 through 13-11.
Publication Dates: 1986-1995.
Acronym: TVMS.
Scores: Total score plus 8 error scores.
Administration: Group or individual.
Price Data, 2006: $70 per test kit including manual, 25 test booklets, 25 scoring forms, and protractor; $17 per manual; $44 per test booklets, $3 per protractor; $6 per 25 scoring sheets.
Time: (3-5) minutes.
Author: Morrison F. Gardner.
Publisher: Academic Therapy Publications.

[2625]
Test of Visual-Perceptual Skills (Non-Motor), 3rd Edition.

Purpose: Constructed to "determine a child's visual-perceptual strengths and weaknesses."
Population: Ages 4-0 through 18-11.
Publication Dates: 1982-2006.
Acronym: TVPS-3.
Scores: 7 subtests: Visual Discrimination, Visual Memory, Visual-Spatial Relationships, Visual Form Constancy, Visual Sequential Memory, Visual Figure-Ground, Visual Closure, Total Score; 3 Composite Indices.
Administration: Individual.
Price Data, 2006: $150 per test kit including manual, test plates, and 25 record forms; $40 per manual; $80 per test plates; $30 per 25 record forms.
Time: (15-25) minutes.
Authors: Nancy Martin (TVPS-3); earlier editions by Morrison F. Gardner.
Publisher: Academic Therapy Publications.

Cross References: See T5:2724 (13 references); for reviews by Nancy A. Busch-Rossnagel and Joseph W. Denison of an earlier edition, see 9:1276.

[2626]
Test of Word Finding in Discourse.

Purpose: Designed to assess children's word-finding skills in discourse.
Population: Ages 6-6 to 12-11.
Publication Date: 1991.
Acronym: TWFD.
Scores, 2: Productivity Index, Word-Finding Behaviors Index.
Administration: Individual.
Price Data, 2006: $120 per complete test including manual (173 pages) and 25 test record forms; $40 per 25 test record forms; $81 per manual.
Time: (15-20) minutes.
Author: Diane J. German.
Publisher: PRO-ED.
Cross References: For reviews by James Dean Brown and Rebecca J. Kopriva, see 12:399; see also T4:2800 (1 reference).

[2627]
Test of Word Finding, Second Edition.

Purpose: Designed as a diagnostic tool for the assessment of children's word finding skills.
Population: Ages 4–12.
Publication Dates: 1986–2000.
Acronym: TWF-2.
Scores, 11: 8 scores for Standardized Assessment (Picture Naming: Nouns, Sentence Completion Naming, Picture Naming: Verbs, Picture Naming: Categories, Comprehension Check for Picture Naming: Nouns, Comprehension Check for Sentence Completion Naming, Comprehension Check for Picture Naming: Verbs, Comprehension Check for Picture Naming: Categories); 5 scores for Informal Assessment (Delayed Response Procedure, Secondary Characteristics Tally, Phonemic Cueing Procedure, Imitation Procedure, Response Analysis for Nouns).
Administration: Individual.
Levels, 3: Preprimary, Primary, Intermediate.
Forms, 2: Standardized Assessment, Informal Assessment.
Price Data, 2006: $388 per complete kit including examiner's manual (2000, 194 pages), picture books 1 and 2, 10 preprimary profile/examiner record forms, 10 primary profile/examiner record forms, and 10 intermediate profile/examiner record forms; $15 per 10 preprimary profile/examiner record forms; $20 per 10 profile/examiner record forms (specify primary or intermediate); $81 per examiner's manual; $150 per picture book 1; $110 per picture book 2.
Time: (20–30) minutes.
Author: Diane J. German.

Publisher: PRO-ED.

Cross References: For a review by D. Joe Olmi, see 15:264; see T5:2725 (10 references); for reviews by Sharon L. Weinberg and Susan Ellis Weisman of an earlier edition, see 11:443 (1 reference); for reviews by Mavis Donahue and Priscilla A. Drum of an earlier edition, see 10:373.

[2628]
Test of Word Knowledge.

Purpose: Developed to "assess a student's skill in the reception and expression of ... semantics."

Population: Ages 5–17.

Publication Date: 1992.

Acronym: TOWK.

Scores, 11: Expressive Vocabulary, Receptive Vocabulary, Word Opposites, Word Definitions, Synonyms, Multiple Contexts, Figurative Usage, Conjunctions and Transition Words, Receptive Composite, Expressive Composite, Total.

Administration: Individual.

Levels, 2: Ages 5–8, Ages 8–17.

Price Data, 2006: $195 per complete kit including stimulus manual, examiner's manual (118 pages), and 12 record forms; $40 per 12 record forms.

Time: (25) minutes for Level 1; (65) minutes for Level 2.

Authors: Elisabeth H. Wiig and Wayne Secord.

Publisher: PsychCorp, A brand of Harcourt Assessment, Inc.

Cross References: See T5:2727 (1 reference); for a review by Rick Lindskog, see 13:338 (3 references).

[2629]
Test of Word Reading Efficiency.

Purpose: Constructed as a "measure of an individual's ability to pronounce printed words accurately and fluently."

Population: Ages 6-0 to 24-11.

Publication Date: 1999.

Acronym: TOWRE.

Scores, 3: Sight Word Efficiency, Phonemic Decoding Efficiency, Total Word Reading Efficiency.

Administration: Individual.

Forms, 2: A, B.

Price Data, 2006: $178 per complete kit including manual (115 pages), 25 each Forms A and B record booklets, and 1 each Forms A and B word cards; $35 per 25 record booklets (specify form); $25 per word cards (specify form); $65 per manual.

Time: (5–8) minutes.

Authors: Joseph K. Torgesen, Richard K. Wagner, and Carol A. Rashotte.

Publisher: PRO-ED.

Cross References: For reviews by Gerald Tindal and John J. Vacca, see 15:265.

[2630]
Test of Written Expression.

Purpose: Constructed as a "norm-referenced test of writing."

Population: Ages 6-6 to 14-11.

Publication Date: 1995.

Acronym: TOWE.

Scores, 2: Items, Essay.

Administration: Individual or group.

Price Data, 2006: $145 per complete kit including manual (58 pages), 25 profile/examiner record forms, and 25 student booklets in storage box; $45 per 25 student booklets; $50 per profile/examiner record forms; $57 per examiner's manual.

Time: (60) minutes.

Authors: Ron McGhee, Brian R. Bryant, Stephen C. Larsen, and Diane M. Rivera.

Publisher: PRO-ED.

Cross References: For reviews by Mildred Murray-Ward and Carole Perlman, see 13:339 (1 reference).

[2631]
Test of Written Language—Third Edition.

Purpose: Designed to "(a) identify students who perform significantly more poorly than their peers in writing and who as a result need special help; (b) determine a student's particular strengths and weaknesses in various writing abilities; (c) document a student's progress in a special writing program; and conduct research in writing."

Population: Ages 7-6 to 17-11.

Publication Dates: 1978–1996.

Acronym: TOWL-3.

Scores: 8 subtest scores (Vocabulary, Spelling, Style, Logical Sentences, Sentence Combining, Contextual Conventions, Contextual Language, Story Construction) plus 3 composite scores (Contrived Writing, Spontaneous Writing, Overall Writing).

Administration: Individual or group.

Forms, 2: A, B.

Price Data, 2006: $210 per complete kit including manual (1996, 134 pages), 25 student response booklets Form A, 25 student response booklets Form B, and 50 profile/story scoring forms in storage box; $50 per 25 A or B student response booklets; $45 per 50 profile/story scoring forms; $70 per manual; $98 per Windows or Macintosh PRO-SCORE System; $89 per IBM DOS PRO-SCORE System.

Time: (90) minutes.

Authors: Donald D. Hammill and Stephen C. Larsen.

Publisher: PRO-ED.

Cross References: See T5:2731 (8 references); for reviews by Joe B. Hansen and by Jayne E. Bucy and Mark E. Swerdlik, see 13:340 (16 references); see also T4:2804 (2 references); for reviews by Stephen L. Benton and Joseph M. Ryan of an earlier edition, see 11:444 (6 references); for reviews by Edward A. Polloway and Robert T. Williams of the original edition, see 9:1278.

[2632]
Test of Written Spelling, Fourth Edition.

Purpose: Designed to assess students' spelling abilities.

Population: Ages 6-0 to 18-11.

Publication Dates: 1976–1999.

Acronym: TWS-4.

Scores: Total score only.

Administration: Group.

Price Data, 2006: $85 per complete kit including manual (1999, 59 pages) and 50 answer sheets; $50 per examiner's manual; $40 per 50 answer sheets.

Time: (15) minutes.

Authors: Stephen C. Larsen, Donald D. Hammill, and Louisa C. Moats.

Publisher: PRO-ED.

Cross References: For a review by Gerald E. DeMauro, see 15:266; see T5:2732 (2 references); for reviews by Alfred P. Longo and Hoi K. Suen of an earlier edition, see 13:341 (5 references); see also T4:2805 (4 references); for reviews by Deborah B. Erickson and Ruth M. Noyce of an earlier edition, see 10:374; for reviews by John M. Bradley and Deborah B. Erickson of an earlier edition, see 9:1279.

[2633]
Test on Appraising Observations.

Purpose: Designed to test one aspect of critical thinking: judging credibility.

Population: Grade 10 to adult.

Publication Dates: 1983–1990.

Administration: Group.

Price Data: Available from publisher.

Authors: Stephen P. Norris (multiple-choice format and constructed-response format) and Ruth King (multiple-choice format).

Publisher: Faculty of Education, Memorial University of Newfoundland [Canada].

a) MULTIPLE-CHOICE FORMAT.
Publication Date: 1983.
Scores: Total score only.
Parts, 2: A, B.
Time: (40–45) minutes.
b) CONSTRUCTED-RESPONSE VERSION.
Publication Date: 1986.
Scores, 2: Answer-Choice, Justification.
Time: (40–45) minutes.

Cross References: For reviews by Michael Kane and Jeffrey K. Smith, see 13:342; see also T4:2806 (1 reference).

[2634]
Tests of Achievement and Proficiency™, Forms K, L, and M.

Purpose: Designed to "provide a comprehensive and objective measure of students' progress in a high school curriculum."

Population: Grades 9–12.

Publication Dates: 1978–1996.

Acronym: TAP™.

Administration: Group.

Forms, 3: K, L, M; 2 batteries: Complete and Survey.

Levels, 4: 15, 16, 17, 18.

Price Data: Available from publisher.

Special Editions: Braille and large-print editions available.

Authors: Dale P. Scannell, Oscar M. Haugh, Brenda H. Loyd, and C. Frederick Risinger.

Publisher: Riverside Publishing.

a) COMPLETE BATTERY.
Scores, 15: Vocabulary, Reading Comprehension, Written Expression, Math Concepts and Problem Solving, Math Computation [optional], Social Studies, Science, Information Processing, Reading Total, Math Total, Core Total, Composite, plus Advance Skills Scores for reading, language, and mathematics.
Time: (255) minutes; (275) minutes with optional test.
b) SURVEY BATTERY.
Scores, 10: Reading (Vocabulary, Comprehension, Total), Written Expression, Math Concepts and Problem Solving, Math Computation [optional], Total, plus Advanced Skills Scores for reading, language, and mathematics.
Time: (90) minutes; (100) minutes with optional test.

Cross References: For reviews by Susan M. Brookhart and Darrell L. Sabers, see 14:396; see also T5:2735 (1 reference), T4:2810 (1 reference), and 11:445 (4 references); for a review by Elaine Clark of Forms G and H, see 10:375 (2 references); for reviews by John M. Keene, Jr. and James L. Wardrop of an earlier form, see 9:1282.

[2635]
Tests of Achievement in Basic Skills: Mathematics.

Purpose: To assess mathematics achievement.

Population: Preschool-kindergarten, Grades 1, 2, 3–4, 4–6, 7–9, 10–adult.

Publication Dates: 1970–1976.

Acronym: TABS-M.

Administration: Group.

Price Data: Available from publisher.

Time: (45–70) minutes.

Comments: May be used separately or as part of instructional Individualized Mathematics Program (IMP); "criterion-referenced tests"; 18-69 item scores, each item measuring a specific objective, and part and total scores; separate answer sheets (Digitek) must be used with Levels B-D.
Authors: James C. Young and Robert R. Knapp (Level C manuals).
Publisher: EdITS/Educational and Industrial Testing Service.

a) LEVEL K.
Population: Preschool-kindergarten.
Publication Date: 1974.
Scores: 18 item scores in 3 areas: Arithmetic Skills, Geometry-Measurement, Modern Concepts.
b) LEVEL 1.
Population: Grade 1.
Publication Date: 1974.
Scores: 36 item scores in 3 areas: same as *a* above.
c) LEVEL 2.
Population: Grade 2.
Publication Date: 1974.
Scores: 41 item scores in 3 areas: same as *a* above.
d) LEVEL A.
Population: Grades 3–4.
Publication Date: 1973.
Scores: 49 item scores in 3 areas: same as *a* above.
e) LEVEL B.
Population: Grades 4–6.
Publication Dates: 1972–1973.
Scores: 73 items and total scores in 3 areas: same as *a* above, plus Total.
f) LEVEL C.
Population: Grades 7–9.
Publication Dates: 1970–1971.
Scores: 68 items and total scores in 3 areas: same as *e* above.
g) LEVEL D.
Population: Grades 10-12.
Publication Dates: 1972–1976.
Scores: 47 items and total scores in 2 areas: Arithmetic Skills, Arithmetic Application, plus Total.
Cross References: For reviews by James Braswell and C. Alan Riedesel, and an excerpted review by Barton B. Proger, see 8:293 (2 references); see also 7:492 (1 reference).

[2636]
Tests of Adult Basic Education, Forms 9 & 10.
Purpose: "Designed and developed to provide achievement scores that are valid for most types of adult education decision-making."

Population: Adults.
Acronym: TABE.
Subtests, 4-11: Pre-Reading (Level L), Reading, Mathematics Computation, Applied Mathematics, Language, Language Mechanics (optional), Vocabulary (optional), Spelling (optional), Science/Social Studies (Level A), Algebra/Geometry (Level A), Writing (Level A).
Administration: Individual or group.
Editions, 2: Complete Battery, Survey.
Forms, 2: 9, 10.
Price Data, 2006: $36 per 25 hand-scored SCOREZE answer sheets; $31 per 50 CompuScan answer sheets; $16 per 25 Individual Diagnostic Profiles; $32 per review materials; $19 per test directions book; $27 per 25 examinee books; $4 per group record sheet; $19 per norms book; $21 per Technical Report CD (116 pages printed); $24.50 per 25 Getting to Know TABE Workbooks; $60 per Guide to Administering TABE 9 & 10 book; $40 per TABE Teacher's Guide for Reading and Language: Linking Assessments to Learning book; $40 per TABE Teacher's Guide for Mathematics: linking Assessments to Learning book; $46 per 10 consumable test books; $46 per 10 reusable test books; $35 per audio tape; $19 per large print test directions; $58 per large print test book; $57 per 25 large print SCOREZE answer sheets; $8 per online test administration (bulk discounts available).
Special Editions: Form 9 is available in Large Print, Braille, and Audio.
Comments: Both forms available online.
Author: CTB/McGraw-Hill.
Publisher: CTB/McGraw-Hill.

a) COMPLETE BATTERY.
Purpose: Designed to "assess skill levels and help determine appropriate career or training programs."
Publication Dates: 1957-2004.
Levels, 4-5: L (Limited Literacy), E (Easy), M (Medium), D (Difficult), A (Advanced).
Scores, 4: Total Mathematics (Mathematics Computation, Applied Mathematics), Total Battery (Pre-Reading/Reading, Total Mathematics, Language).
Price Data: $101 per 25 Complete Battery test books; $42 per Complete Battery scoring stencils; $236 per Braille Complete Battery Test book; $48 per Writing test book; $16 per Writing Assessment and scoring manual; $72 per Science/Social Studies test book; $13 per Science/Social Studies test directions; $32 per 25 Science/Social Studies SCOREZE answer sheets; $23.50 per 50 Science/Social Studies CompuScan answer sheets; $21.25 per Science/Social Studies scoring stencils; $72 per Algebra/Geometry test book; $13 per Algebra/Geometry test directions; $32 per 25 Algebra/Geometry SCOREZE answer sheets; $23.50 per

50 Algebra/Geometry CompuScan answer sheets; $21.25 per Algebra/Geometry scoring stencils; $16 per Science/Social Studies and Algebra/Geometry tables book.

1) *Pre-Reading.*
Scores, 4: Match Letters, Recognize Letters, Recognize Beginning/Ending Sounds, Middle Sounds.
Levels: Level L only.
Time: 13(23) minutes.

2) *Reading.*
Scores, 4-5: Interpret Graphic Information, Words in Context, Recall Information, Construct Meaning, Evaluate/Extend Meaning [Levels E-A only].
Time: 32(42) minutes for Level L; 50(60) minutes for Levels E-A.

3) *Mathematics Computation.*
Scores, 2-6: Add Whole Numbers [Levels L-M], Subtract Whole Numbers [Levels L-M], Multiply Whole Numbers [Levels E-D], Divide Whole Numbers [Levels E-D], Decimals [Levels E-A], Fractions [Levels M-A], Integers [Levels D, A], Percents [Levels D, A], Order of Operations [Level A], Algebraic Operations [Level A].
Time: 15(25) minutes for Level L; 24(34) minutes for Levels E-A.

4) *Applied Mathematics.*
Scores, 6-9: Number & Number Operations, Computation in Context, Estimation [Levels E-A], Measurement, Geometry & Spatial Sense, Data Analysis, Statistics & Probability [Levels E-A], Patterns/Functions/Algebra, Problem Solving & Reasoning [Levels E-A].
Levels: Level L only.
Time: 45(55) minutes for Level L; 50(60) minutes for Levels E-A.

5) *Language.*
Scores, 6: Usage, Sentence Formation, Paragraph Development, Capitalization, Punctuation, Writing Conventions.
Levels: Levels E-A only.
Time: 55(65) minutes.

6) *Vocabulary.*
Scores, 3: Word Meaning, Multi-Meaning Words, Words in Context.
Levels: Levels E-A only.
Time: 14(24) minutes.
Comments: This subtest is optional.

7) *Language Mechanics.*
Scores, 2: Sentences/Phrases/Clauses, Writing Conventions.
Levels: Levels E-A only.
Time: 14(24) minutes.
Comments: This subtest is optional.

8) *Spelling.*
Scores, 3: Vowel, Consonant, Structural Unit.
Levels: Levels E-A only.
Time: 10(20) minutes.
Comments: This subtest is optional.

9) *Science/Social Studies.*
Scores: Scores not presented.
Level: Level A only.
Time: Administration time not reported.
Comments: This subtest is optional.

10) *Algebra/Geometry.*
Scores: Scores not presented.
Level: Level A only.
Time: Administration time not reported.
Comments: This subtest is optional.

11) *Writing.*
Scores: Scores not presented.
Level: Level A only.
Time: 45(55) minutes.
Comments: This subtest is optional.

b) SURVEY.
Purpose: Provides a skill snapshot for placement information.
Publication Dates: 1987-2004.
Levels, 4: Same as Complete Battery except for omission of Level L.
Scores, 2: Same as Complete Battery.
Price Data: $101 per Survey test book; $42 per Survey scoring stencils; $212 per Braille Survey test book.

1) *Reading.*
Scores, 5: Same as Complete Battery.
Time: 25(35) minutes.

2) *Mathematics Computation.*
Scores, 5-6: Same as Complete Battery.
Time: 15(25) minutes.

3) *Applied Mathematics.*
Scores, 9: Same as Complete Battery.
Time: 25(35) minutes.

4) *Language.*
Scores, 6: Same as Complete Battery.
Time: 25(35) minutes.

5) *Language Mechanics.*
Scores, 3: Same as Complete Battery.
Time: 14(24) minutes.
Comments: This subtest is optional.

6) *Vocabulary.*
Scores, 3: Same as Complete Battery.
Time: 14(24) minutes.
Comments: This subtest is optional.

7) *Spelling.*
Scores, 3: Same as Complete Battery.
Time: 10(20) minutes.
Comments: This subtest is optional.

c) LOCATOR TEST.
Purpose: Designed to "help teachers in assigning the level of the TABE test to administer."

Subtests, 4: Reading, Mathematics Computation, Applied Mathematics, Language.
Scores: Total score only.
Price Data: $58 per 2 Practice Exercise and Locator Test books; $21 per Practice and Locator Test scoring stencils; $130 per Braille Practice Exercise and Locator Test books.
Time: 37(47) minutes for Complete Battery; 35(45) minutes for Survey.
d) WORD LIST.
Scores: Total score only.
Price Data: $26 per Word List Test book; $58 per large print word list.
Time: 15(25) minutes.
e) PRACTICE EXERCISE.
Scores: Not scored.
Price Data: Same as *c* above.
Time: 20(30) minutes.
Cross References: For reviews by Michael D. Beck and Bruce G. Rogers of an earlier edition, see 13:343; for reviews by Robert W. Lissitz and Steven J. Osterlind of an earlier edition, see 11:446 (2 references); for reviews by Thomas F. Donlon and Norman E. Gronlund of an earlier edition, see 8:33 (1 reference); for a review by A. N. Hieronymus and an excerpted review by S. Alan Cohen of an earlier edition, see 7:32.

[2637]
Tests of Adult Basic Education Work-Related Foundation Skills.

Purpose: "To provide pre-instructional information about an examinee's level of achievement on basic skills, … to identify areas of weakness … measure growth, … and involve the examinee in appraising his or her learning needs to assist … [in preparing] an instructional program to meet the examinee's individual needs."
Population: Adults in vocational/technical programs, students in adult basic education programs 2-year colleges, and secondary school ROP & JTPA programs.
Publication Dates: 1994–1996.
Acronym: TABE WF.
Scores, 6: Reading, Math Computation, Applied Math, Total Mathematics (Math Computation and Applied Math), Language, Total Battery.
Administration: Group.
Forms, 4: General, Business/Office, Health, Trade/Technical.
Price Data, 2002: $33.65 per review kit including general test book, trade/technical test book, health test book, business/office test book, examiner's manual (1994, 30 pages), and individual diagnostic profile; $54 per manual and 25 locator tests; $83.40 per manual and general trade technical, health, or business/office test book; $24.50 per 25 locator test SCOREZE answer sheets; $29 per general trade/technical, health, or business/office SCOREZE answer sheets; $28.80 per 50 CompuScan answer sheets; $23.95 per 50 Scantron Opt. 2 answer sheets; $12.75 per 25 individual diagnostic profiles; $17.40 per handscoring stencil; $2.85 per group record sheet; $15.80 per examiner's manual; $15.30 per norms book; $14.25 per technical bulletin; $14.25 per technical report (1996, 33 pages) for use with this test and the TABE Work-Related Problem Solving available from publisher.
Time: 120(160) minutes.
Author: CTB Macmillan/McGraw-Hill.
Publisher: CTB/McGraw-Hill.
Cross References: For reviews by Kurt F. Geisinger and Jeffrey A. Jenkins, see 13:344.

[2638]
Tests of Adult Basic Education Work-Related Problem Solving.

Purpose: "Designed to help employers, educators, and training professionals diagnose how an examinee deals with the different aspects of problem solving."
Population: Students in secondary schools, vocational education programs, adult basic education programs, and junior colleges, and employees in industry.
Publication Dates: 1994–1996.
Acronym: TABE-PS.
Scores, 5: Competency scores (Employs Reading and Math Skills to Identify and Define a Problem, Examines Situations Using Problem-Solving Techniques, Makes Decisions About Possible Solutions, Evaluates Outcomes and Effects of Implementing Solutions), Total Number Correct Score.
Administration: Group.
Forms, 2: 7, 8.
Price Data, 2006: $23 per review kit including examiner's manual/scoring guide (1994, 56 pages), and test book; $67 per 25 test books with 1 manual; $40 per 25 practice exercise test book; $32 per 25 scannable answer sheet; $21 per examiner's manual/scoring guide.
Time: 70(75) minutes for Form 7; 60(65) minutes for Form 8.
Comments: May be administered alone or in conjunction with other TABE materials; test includes a Practice Exercise which was included in the norming studies and so should be administered along with the test; includes Individual Diagnostic Profile, and Interview/Interest Questionnaire.
Author: CTB/McGraw-Hill.
Publisher: CTB/McGraw-Hill.
Cross References: For reviews by Gale M. Morrison and Jerry Tindal, see 13:345.

[2639]
Tests of General Educational Development [the GED Tests].

Purpose: To "assess skills representative of the typical outcomes of a traditional high school education" for the purpose of awarding a secondary school level (GED) diploma.

Population: Candidates for high school equivalency diplomas.

Publication Dates: 1944–1998.

Acronym: GED Tests.

Scores, 6: Writing Skills, Social Studies, Science, Interpreting Literature and the Arts, Mathematics, Total.

Administration: Group or individual.

Forms: 17 U.S. English Operational (secure) full-length forms available; 8 U.S. English forms available of Official GED Practice test (7 nonsecure half-length test, 1 nonsecure full-length test).

Price Data, 1998: Operational (secure) forms not available for purchase and are available only to and administered at Official GED Testing Centers; Official GED Practice Tests half-length (available from Steck-Vaughn Co., (800) 531-5015): $37.50 per 10 test batteries; $15.98 per set of 50 universal machine-scorable answer sheets; $12.98 per set of 10 self-scoring answer sheets (for use with half-length practice test U.S. English Form CC only); full-length U.S. English practice test: $36 per set of 5; $14.91 per set of 25 corresponding answer sheets; $24.20 per administrator's set including teacher's manual (1989, 203 pages), scoring materials, and conversion tables, available in U.S. English half-length, U.S. English full-length, Spanish, or French; $40.50 per 10 Spanish-language edition batteries (or $.88 for one test and one universal answer sheet); $15.98 per 50 Spanish-language universal answer sheets; $40.50 per 10 French-language edition batteries (or $4.88 for one test and one universal answer sheet); $15.98 per 50 French-language universal answer sheets; $13.80 per 1 Large Print practice test (U.S. English only) and universal answer sheet; $47.87 per 1 audio-cassette practice test (U.S. English only) with large print reference copy. Canadian English practice test batteries (2 forms) available from Gage Publishing Ltd., (416) 293-8141: C27.50 per 10 batteries (avalable singly at C$4.98 each); C$13.68 per 50 Canadian English universal answer sheets; C$25.99 per Canadian English administrator's set. U.S. English (4 forms) and Canadian English (2 forms) computer-delivered practice tests available on CD-ROM through NTC/Contemporary Publishing, (800) 621-1918; outside the U.S., Canada, and their territories through Sylvan Learning Systems (800) 627-4276.

Foreign Language and Special Editions: Operational (secure) full length GED batteries: Canadian English (6 forms), Spanish (3 forms), French (2 forms), and U.S. English large print (3 forms), audiocassettte (2 forms), and Braille (2 forms) available. Computer-delivered U.S. English-language tests available only outside U.S., Canada, and their territories. Official GED Practice Tests: Canadian English, Spanish, French, U.S. English large print, and audiocassette.

Time: 120 minutes for Writing Skills, 85 minutes for Social Studies, 95 minutes for Science, 65 minutes for Interpreting Literature and the Arts, 90 minutes for Mathematics [all times are for Operational (secure) forms) of the tests and do not include time required to give and clarify verbal test-taking instructions].

Comments: Tests administered throughout the year at official GED centers; tests originated in 1942 for granting high school/college credit for veterans, in mid-1950s GED program extended to all non-high school graduates; extensive 1988 revisions include addition of essay component to Writing Skills test and increased emphasis on higher order cognitive skills (e.g., application, analysis/evaluation, and math problem solving) throughout the battery.

Author: General Educational Development Testing Service of the American Council on Education.

Publisher: General Educational Development Testing Service of the American Council on Education.

Cross References: See T4:2816 (2 references); for reviews by Bruce G. Rogers and Michael S. Trevisan, see 11:447 (2 references); for reviews by J. Stanley Ahmann and A. Harry Passow, see 9:1284 (1 reference); see also T3:2485 (2 references), 8:35 (20 references), and 7:34 (21 references); for a review by Robert J. Solomon of earlier forms, see 5:29 (39 references); for a review by Gustav J. Froehlich, see 4:26 (27 references); for reviews by Herbert S. Conrad and Warren G. Findley, see 3:20 (11 references). For reviews by Charlotte W. Croon of an earlier form of the expression subtest, see 3:122; for reviews by W. E. Hall and C. Robert Pace of an earlier form of the social studies reading subtest, see 3:528.

[2640]
Tests of Reading Comprehension, Second Edition.

Purpose: "They aim at assessing the extent to which readers are able to obtain meaning from text."

Population: Grades 3–7, 6–10, and individuals with special needs.

Publication Dates: 1987–2003.

Acronym: TORCH.

Scores, 14: Grasshoppers, The Bear Who Liked Hugging People, Lizards Love Eggs, Getting Better, Feeding Puff, Shocking Things/Earthquakes!, The Swamp-creature, The Cats, A Horse of Her Own, Iceberg Towing, The Accident, The Killer Smog of London, I Want to be Andy, The Red Ace of Spades.

Administration: Individual or group.

Price Data, 2006: A$109.95 per complete kit including reading booklet, one of each answer sheet, and manual; A$89.95 per manual; A$8.95 per test booklet; A$11 per pack of 10 answer sheets for each of 12 levels.

Time: (30) minutes, untimed.

Comments: "Content-referenced" and/or "norm-referenced."
Authors: Leila Mossenson, Peter Hill, and Geoffrey Masters.
Publisher: Australian Council for Educational Research Ltd. [Australia].
Cross References: See T5:2743 (3 references) and T4:2817 (1 reference); for reviews by Robert B. Cooter, Jr. and Diane J. Sawyer of the earlier edition, see 11:448.

[2641]
TestWell: Health Risk Appraisal.

Purpose: "Designed to provide an awareness of how current behaviors and physical health measurements impact health risks."
Population: Adults ages 18–60 with a minimum of 10th grade education.
Publication Date: 1992.
Scores, 5: Appraised Age, Achievable Age, Positive Lifestyle Behaviors, Top 10 Risks of Death, Suggestions for Improvement.
Administration: Group.
Manual: No manual.
Price Data: Available from publisher.
Time: (20) minutes.
Comments: Scoring by National Wellness Institute; individual and group reports available.
Author: National Wellness Institute, Inc.
Publisher: National Wellness Institute, Inc.
Cross References: For reviews by Barbara L. Lachar and Steven G. LoBello, see 13:346.

[2642]
TestWell: Wellness Inventory for Windows.

Purpose: Designed to promote awareness of wellness.
Population: Adults with a minimum of 10th grade education.
Publication Date: 1992.
Scores, 11: Physical Fitness and Nutrition, Social Awareness, Medical Self-Care, Spirituality and Values, Emotional Management, Intellectual Wellness, Environmental Wellness, Safety, Occupational Wellness, Sexuality and Emotional Awareness, Total.
Administration: Group.
Manual: No manual.
Price Data: Available from publisher.
Time: (20) minutes.
Comments: Requires IBM or compatible computer hardware.
Author: National Wellness Institute, Inc.
Publisher: National Wellness Institute, Inc.
Cross References: For reviews by William W. Deardorff and Theodore L. Hayes, see 13:347; see also T4:2821 (1 reference).

[2643]
TestWell: Wellness Inventory for Windows—College Version.

Purpose: "Designed to address lifestyle choices facing today's college students."
Population: College students.
Publication Date: 1993.
Scores, 11: Physical Fitness, Nutrition, Social Awareness, Self-Care and Safety, Emotional and Sexuality, Intellectual Wellness, Environmental Wellness, Emotional Management, Occupational Wellness, Spirituality and Values, Total.
Administration: Group.
Price Data: Available from publisher.
Time: (20) minutes.
Author: National Wellness Institute, Inc.
Publisher: National Wellness Institute, Inc.
Cross References: For reviews by David L. Bolton and Richard E. Harding, see 13:348.

[2644]
Thanatometer.

Purpose: Measures attitudes concerning death.
Population: Adults.
Publication Date: 1986.
Scores: Total score only.
Administration: Group or individual.
Manual: No manual.
Price Data, 2005: $2 per scale.
Time: [5-10] minutes.
Comments: Supplementary article available.
Author: Panos D. Bardis.
Publisher: Donna Bardis.

[2645]
Thematic Apperception Test.

Purpose: "A method of revealing to the trained interpreter some of the dominant drives, emotions, sentiments, complexes and conflicts of a personality."
Population: Ages 4 and over.
Publication Dates: 1935–1943.
Acronym: TAT.
Scores: Total score only.
Administration: Individual.
Price Data: Available from publisher.
Time: 100(200) minutes in 2 sessions 1 day apart.
Author: Henry A. Murray.
Publisher: Harvard University Press.
Cross References: See T5:2749 (87 references), T4:2824 (107 references), 9:1287 (51 references), and T3:2491 (105 references); for a review by Jon D. Swartz, see 8:697 (241 references); see also T2:1519 (231 references); for a review by Richard H. Dana and Leonard D. Eron, see 7:181 (297 references); see also P:484 (339 references); for a review by C. J. Adcock, see 6:245 (287 references); for reviews by Leonard D. Eron and Arthur

R. Jensen, see 5:164 (311 references); for a review by Arthur L. Benton, see 4:136 (198 references); for reviews by Arthur L. Benton, Julian Rotter, and J. R. Wittenborn and an excerpted review, see 3:103 (102 references).

[2646]
Theological School Inventory.

Purpose: Assesses motivation for entering the ministry.
Population: Incoming seminary students.
Publication Dates: 1962–1972.
Acronym: TSI.
Scores, 12: Definiteness, Natural Leading, Special Leading, Concept of the Call, Flexibility, Acceptance by Others, Intellectual Concern, Self-Fulfillment, Leadership Success, Evangelistic Witness, Social Reform, Service to Persons.
Administration: Group.
Price Data: Available from publisher.
Time: Administration time not reported.
Authors: James E. Dittes, Frederick Kling, Ellery Pierson, and Harry DeWire.
Publisher: Ministry Inventories.
Cross References: See T2:1028 (7 references) and P:273 (5 references).

[2647]
Therapy Attitude Inventory.

Purpose: Provides ratings of parental satisfaction with parent training interventions for child behavior problems.
Population: Parents.
Publication Date: 1974.
Scores: Total score only.
Administration: Individual.
Price Data, 1994: No charge for first copy; may photocopy for research or clinical use.
Time: (5) minutes.
Author: Sheila M. Eyberg.
Publisher: Sheila M. Eyberg (the author).
Cross References: See T5:2752 (2 references) and T4:2827 (1 reference); for a review by Terry B. Gutkin, see 9:1289 (2 references); see also T3:2494 (1 reference).

[2648]
Thinking Creatively in Action and Movement.

Purpose: Designed to sample creative thinking abilities of preschool children with limited verbal and drawing skills.
Population: Ages 3–6.
Publication Date: 1981.
Acronym: TCAM.
Scores, 3: Fluency, Originality, Imagination.
Administration: Individual.

Price Data, 2005: $43.20 per 20 tests and manual/scoring guide (34 pages); $23.40 per manual; $23.15 per sample set.
Time: (10–30) minutes.
Author: E. Paul Torrance.
Publisher: Scholastic Testing Service, Inc.
Cross References: See T5:2754 (5 references) and T4:2829 (2 references); for reviews by Joseph S. Renzulli and James O. Rust, see 9:1290.

[2649]
Thinking Creatively With Sounds and Words.

Purpose: Developed to assess creative thinking through response to sound and words.
Population: Grades 3–12, adults.
Publication Dates: 1973-1990.
Acronym: TCSW.
Scores, 2: Sounds and Images, Onomatopoeia and Images.
Administration: Group.
Levels, 2: I, II.
Forms, 2: A, B.
Price Data, 2005: $37.65 per complete kit including 20 test booklets (specify level and form) and manual/scoring guide (20 pages); $23.40 per cassette; $15.25 per manual/scoring guide; $15.30 per norms/technical manual (65 pages); $18 per sample set (specify form).
Time: (30–35) minutes for each test.
Authors: E. Paul Torrance, Joe Khatena, and Bert F. Cunnington (except technical manual).
Publisher: Scholastic Testing Service, Inc.
Cross References: See T5:2755 (2 references) and T4:2830 (5 references); for a review by Lynn H. Fox, see 9:1291 (3 references); see also T3:2496 (5 references); for reviews by Philip M. Clark and Mary Lee Smith, see 8:248 (6 references); see also T2:587 (17 references).

[2650]
Thomas Concept Inventory of Core Strengths.

Purpose: "To identify eight patterns of human strengths."
Population: Managers and adults in organizational settings.
Publication Dates: 1977– 2006.
Acronym: TCICS.
Scores: Core Strengths.
Administration: Individual.
Forms, 2: Self-report (1977, 2 pages, for self-ratings), B (1977, 2 pages, for ratings by up to 5 others).
Restricted Distribution: Personal Guide and Relationship Guide available to general public; Analysis of Strengths restricted to Thomas Concept Certified Professionals.

Price Data, 2006: Scoring service, $12.95 per Personal Guide; $24.95 per Relationship Guide; $49.95 per Analysis of Strengths (includes Personal and Relationship Guides); online printing only.
Time: (10) minutes.
Comments: Forms available only at www.oppositestrengths.com.
Authors: J. W. Thomas, Clyde C. Mayo (manual), and T. J. Thomas (interpretive materials).
Publisher: Thomas Concept.

[2651]
Thomas-Kilmann Conflict Mode Instrument.

Purpose: Designed to assess "an individual's behavior in conflict situations."
Population: Managers.
Publication Date: 1974.
Acronym: TKI.
Scores, 5: Competing, Collaborating, Compromising, Avoiding, Accommodating.
Administration: Group or individual.
Price Data, 2001: $9 per instrument (16 pages including test and general information).
Time: [15] minutes.
Comments: Self-administered, self-scored, online at skillsone.com.
Authors: Kenneth W. Thomas and Ralph H. Kilmann.
Publisher: CPP, Inc.
Cross References: See T5:2756 (2 references); for reviews by Richard E. Harding and Ronn Johnson, see 10:377 (4 references).

[2652]
Thurstone Temperament Schedule.

Purpose: Measures personality traits related to job performance.
Population: Variety of occupations from entry-level to management.
Publication Dates: 1949–1991.
Acronym: TTS.
Scores, 6: Active, Impulsive, Dominant, Stable, Sociable, Reflective.
Administration: Individual or group.
Price Data, 2002: $75 per start-up kit including 25 test booklets and examiner's manual; $56 per 25 test booklets (quantity discount available); $28 per examiner's manual.
Time: No limit (approximately 15–20 minutes).
Comments: Administered via paper and pencil; hand-scored carbon format.
Author: L. L. Thurstone.
Publisher: Pearson Performance Solutions [No reply from publisher; status unknown].

Cross References: See T5:2757 (1 reference), T4:2833 (6 references), T3:2499 (2 references), T2:1423 (32 references), P:277 (20 references), and 6:192 (17 references); for a review by Neil J. Van Steenberg, see 5:118 (12 references); for reviews by Hans J. Eysenck, Charles M. Harsh, and David G. Ryans, and an excerpted review by Laurance F. Shaffer, see 4:93.

[2653]
Thurstone Test of Mental Alertness.

Purpose: Measures general mental ability to learn and comprehend.
Population: Wide variety of occupations
Publication Dates: 1943–1998.
Acronym: TMA.
Scores, 3: Quantitative, Linguistic, Total.
Administration: Individual or group.
Forms, 2: A, B.
Price Data, 2002: $86 per start-up kit including 25 test booklets and examiner's manual (specify Form A or Form B); $68 per 25 test booklets (quantity discounts available; specify Form A or Form B); $28 per examiner's manual; price data available from publisher for Quanta computer administration and scoring software (Windows); $86 per Quanta start-up kit including examiner's manual, 25 administrations and scoring (does not include Quanta software).
Time: 20 minutes.
Authors: Thelma Gwinn Thurstone and L. L. Thurstone.
Publisher: Pearson Performance Solutions [No reply from publisher; status unknown].
Cross References: See T5:2758 (1 reference) and T2:469 (5 references); for a review by Robert D. North, see 7:392 (4 references); for a review by Joshua A. Fishman, see 5:391; see also 4:326 (3 references); for reviews by Anne Anastasi and Emily T. Burr of an earlier edition, see 3:265.

[2654]
Tiffany Control Scales.

Purpose: Designed to evaluate personality problems related to one's experience of control across different situations.
Population: Adolescents and adults.
Publication Dates: 1985–1999.
Acronym: TCS.
Scores, 16: Control from Self/Internal, Control over Self, Control over the Environment, Control from the Environment, Coping Index, Passive/Assertive/Aggressive Index, Extratensive/Intratensive Index, Repression, Expressive, Self-Directed, Non-Self-Directed, and 5 other measures.
Administration: Individual or group.
Editions, 2: Paper and pencil, computer administered.

Price Data, 2001: $12.50 per 25 paper and pencil tests; $495.95 per computer edition, unlimited use; $50 per limited use edition (5 uses); demo and sample report are free; $25 per test for mail-in scoring; $19.95 per manual (1999, 83 pages).
Time: [20] minutes for Standard TCS; varies when customized.
Comments: For research or clinical use or in employment screening; may be customized to fit examiner's needs; self-rating instrument; scoring and interpretation by computer.
Authors: Donald W. Tiffany and Phyllis G. Tiffany.
Publisher: Psychological Growth Associates, Inc.
Cross References: For a review by Brian F. Bolton, see 14:397.

[2655]
The Time of Your Life.

Purpose: Constructed as a self-assessment tool to provide "insight" into time management.
Population: Employees.
Publication Date: 1988.
Scores: Total score only.
Administration: Group or individual.
Price Data: Price available from publisher for complete kit including 20 inventories and 20 scoring and interpretation sheets.
Time: [30] minutes.
Comments: Self-administered, self-scored.
Author: Training House, Inc.
Publisher: Training House, Inc.
Cross References: For reviews by Ralph F. Darr, Jr. and Richard W. Faunce, see 12:400.

[2656]
Timed Typings for Holidays.

Purpose: To measure typing skill growth, develop fluency, and help reach for new speed goals.
Population: Students in typing classes.
Publication Date: 1988.
Scores: Total score only.
Administration: Group.
Manual: No manual.
Price Data: Price information available from publisher for blackline masters.
Time: (1–5) minutes per writing.
Authors: Berkley H. Rudd and Carol R. Scott.
Publisher: Walch Publishing.

[2657]
TMJ Scale.

Purpose: "Designed to measure the [clinical significance of] symptom patterns of dental patients with temporomandibular joint disorders and orofacial pain."
Population: TM [temporomandibular] dental patients ages 13 and over.
Publication Dates: 1984–1987.

Scores, 10: Physical Domain (Pain Report, Palpation Pain, Perceived Malocclusion, Joint Dysfunction, Range of Motion Limitation, Non-TM Disorder), Psychosocial Domain (Psychological Factors, Stress, Chronicity), Global Scale.
Administration: Individual.
Price Data, 1994: $20 per specimen set including question booklet, manual (1987, 86 pages), and sample report.
Time: (10–15) minutes.
Comments: Self-administered; self-report.
Authors: Stephen R. Levitt, Tom F. Lundeen, and Michael W. McKinney.
Publisher: Pain Resource Center, Inc.
Cross References: For a review by William W. Deardorff, see 12:402; see also T4:2842 (3 references).

[2658]
Toddler and Infant Motor Evaluation.

Purpose: Designed to be used for "diagnostic, comprehensive assessment of children who are suspected to have motor delays or deviations, the development of appropriate remediation programs, and treatment efficacy research."
Population: Ages 4 months to 3.5 years.
Publication Date: 1994.
Acronym: TIME.
Scores: 5 Primary Subtests: Mobility, Stability, Motor Organization, Social-Emotional, Functional Performance; 3 Clinical Subtests: Quality Rating, Component Analysis Rating, Atypical Positions.
Administration: Individual.
Price Data, 2002: $451 per complete kit including manual (324 pages), 10 record forms, timer, rattle, 2 balls, squeak toy, toy car, 3 containers, toy telephone, 2 shoelaces, 6 blocks, and nylon tote bag; $37.50 per 10 record forms; $137 per manual.
Time: (15–40) minutes.
Comments: Diagnostic assessment tool designed to be used by licensed/highly trained physical and occupational therapists, or appropriately trained adaptive physical educators, special education teachers, or others with expertise in the motor domain; administered utilizing a partnership between parent(s) or caretaker(s) and a trained examiner.
Authors: Lucy J. Miller and Gale H. Roid.
Publisher: Harcourt Assessment, Inc.
Cross References: For reviews by Larry M. Bolen and William R. Merz, Sr., see 14:399.

[2659]
The Toglia Category Assessment.

Purpose: Designed "to examine the ability of adults with brain injury or psychiatric illness to establish categories and switch conceptual set."
Population: Adults 18 and over who have neurological impairment.

Publication Date: 1994.
Acronym: TCA.
Scores: Total score only.
Administration: Individual.
Price Data: Price data for "Dynamic Assessment of Categorization TCA: The Toglia Category Assessment" (1994, 43 pages), score sheets, and manipulatives available from publisher.
Time: (10–20) minutes.
Authors: Joan Toglia assisted by Naomi Josman.
Publisher: Maddak Inc.
Cross References: For reviews by Thomas McKnight and by Scott A. Napolitano and Courtney Miller, see 16:252.

[2660]
The Token Test for Children.

Purpose: Designed to assess receptive language dysfunction.
Population: Ages 3-12.
Publication Date: 1978.
Scores: Total score only.
Administration: Individual.
Parts, 5: I, II, III, IV, V.
Price Data, 2006: $125 per complete kit including 50 scoring forms, 20 tokens, and manual (63 pages); $45 per 20 tokens; $45 per 50 forms; $41 per manual.
Time: (8) minutes.
Author: Frank DiSimoni.
Publisher: PRO-ED.
Cross References: See T5:2768 (43 references) and T4:2846 (24 references); for reviews by William M. Reynolds and John Salvia, see 9:1295 (9 references); see also T3:2509 (1 reference).

[2661]
Tooze Braille Speed Test: A Test of Basic Ability in Reading Braille.

Purpose: "A speed test which seeks to give a quick appraisal of the child's ability to read Braille characters."
Population: Students (Ages 7-13) in Grades 1 or 2 Braille.
Publication Date: 1962.
Scores: Total score only.
Administration: Individual.
Price Data: Available from publisher.
Time: 1(5) minutes.
Author: F. H. G. Tooze.
Publisher: Association for the Education and Welfare of the Visually Handicapped [England] [No reply from publisher; status unknown].

[2662]
Torrance Tests of Creative Thinking.

Purpose: To identify and evaluate creative potential through words (verbal forms) and pictures (figural forms).

Population: Grades K through adult.
Publication Dates: 1966–2006.
Acronym: TTCT.
Administration: Individual and group.
Price Data, 2005: $48.60 per 20 scoring worksheets, class record sheet, and directions manual/scoring guide (specify Form A or B and Figural or Verbal); $24 per sample set including Figural and Verbal booklets and manual (specify Form A or B); $6.45 per student for scoring service of Figural; $7.70 per student for scoring service of Verbal.
Author: E. Paul Torrance.
Publisher: Scholastic Testing Service, Inc.
  a) VERBAL TEST.
  Scores: 3 for equivalent Forms A and B: Fluency, Flexibility, Originality.
  Administration: Individual for Grades K to 3.
  Price Data: $34 per examiner's kit (required); $17.45 per manual for scoring and interpreting results (49 pages; specify Form A or B).
  Time: 45(60) minutes.
  Comments: Test booklet is titled Thinking Creatively With Words.
  b) FIGURAL TEST.
  Scores: 4 for equivalent Forms A and B: Fluency, Flexibility, Originality, Elaboration.
  Price Data: $17.45 per directions manual (43–48 pages; specify Form A or B); $34.55 per streamlined scoring guide for Forms A and B (74 pages).
  Time: 30(45) minutes.
  Comments: Test booklet is titled Thinking Creatively with Pictures.
Cross References: See T5:2771 (45 references) and T4:2849 (33 references); for reviews by Clinton I. Chase and Donald J. Treffinger, see 9:1296 (20 references); see also T3:2512 (107 references), 8:249 (229 references), and T2:589 (88 references); for reviews by Leonard L. Baird and Robert L. Thorndike, and excerpted reviews by Ralph Hoepfner, John L. Holland, and Michael A. Wallach, see 7:448 (243 references).

[2663]
Tower of London—Drexel University: 2nd Edition.

Purpose: A neuropsychological instrument "designed to assess higher-order problem solving—specifically, executive planning abilities—in children and adults."
Population: Ages 7–80.
Publication Dates: 1999–2005.
Acronym: TOLDX 2nd Ed.
Scores, 8: Total Move Score, Total Correct Score, Total Time Violation, Total Rules Violation, Total Initiation Time, Total Execution Time, Total Problem-Solving Time, Total Stimulus-Bound.
Administration: Individual.
Forms, 2: Adult, Child.

Price Data, 2006: $278 per complete kit including technical manual (2005, 104 pages), 2 peg boards with beads, 25 child record forms, and 25 adult record forms; $87 per technical manual; $42 per 25 child or adult record forms.
Time: (10–15) minutes.
Comments: Special instructions for mentally challenged populations.
Authors: William C. Culbertson and Eric A. Zilmer.
Publisher: Multi-Health Systems, Inc.
  a) CHILD.
  Population: Ages 7–15.
  b) ADULT.
  Population: Ages 16 and older.
Cross References: For reviews by Carolyn M. Callahan and James P. Van Haneghan of the previous edition, see 15:267.

[2664]
Trade Aptitude Test Battery.

Purpose: "To select prospective pupils for admission to technical institutes and colleges."
Population: First-year South African students in the technical fields.
Publication Dates: 1981–1983.
Acronym: TRAT.
Scores, 16: Dexterity, Co-ordination, Patterns, Components, Classification, Assembly, Computations, Inspection, Graphs, Mechanical Insight, Mathematics, Spatial Perception/2-D, Vocabulary, Figure Series, Woordeskat, Spatial Perception/3-D.
Administration: Group.
Price Data: Available from publisher.
Time: 288(293) minutes.
Comments: Test materials in both English and Afrikaans.
Authors: J. J. Taljaard and J. W. von Mollendorf (test).
Publisher: Human Sciences Research Council [South Africa].

[2665]
Trainer's Assessment of Proficiency (TAP).

Purpose: Constructed as a "self-assessment exercise that measures relative strengths in twelve instructional skills."
Population: Trainers.
Publication Date: 1991.
Acronym: TAP.
Scores, 12: Assessing Needs and Entering Behavior, Setting Objectives and Terminal Behavior, Analyzing Participants and Situations, Eliciting Relevant Responses and Testing, Applying Classroom Facilitation Skills, Forming Questions and Probes Effectively, Maintaining Adult Relationships, Giving Feedback and Reinforcement, Building Toward Transfer of Training, Getting All Learners to Participate, Managing Class-room Time Effectively, Displaying Good Flow/Logic/Organization.
Administration: Group.
Forms, 2: Long, Short.
Price Data: Available from publisher.
Time: (60) minutes for Short form; (180) minutes for Long form.
Comments: Videocassette recorder necessary for administration of inventory.
Author: Scott B. Parry.
Publisher: Training House, Inc.
Cross References: For reviews by Mark W. Roberts and Daniel E. Vogler, see 12:403.

[2666]
Trait Evaluation Index.

Purpose: "Designed to elicit comprehensive, multi-dimensional appraisals of 'normal' personality dimensions."
Population: College and adults.
Publication Dates: 1967-1984.
Acronym: TEI.
Scores: 29 scores (Social Orientation, Compliance, Benevolence, Elation, Ambition, Motivational Drive, Self-Confidence, Dynamism, Independence, Personal Adequacy, Caution, Self-Organization, Responsibility, Propriety, Courtesy, Verbal Orientation, Intellectual Orientation, Perception, Self-Control, Fairmindedness, Adaptability, Sincerity) plus 4 general supplementary scores (Overall Adjustment, Masculinity, Femininity, Consistency) and 3 supplementary scores for engineers (Employment Stability, Productivity-Creativity, Job Satisfaction).
Administration: Group.
Price Data, 2006: $94.20 per test package; $83.40 per IBM answer/profile sheet package; $46 per set of IBM scoring stencils; $56.40 per manual (1968, 38 pages) and manual supplement (1984, 17 pages); $75.50 per specimen set; $137.45 per German edition test package.
Foreign Language Edition: German edition available.
Time: (30-50) minutes.
Author: Alan R. Nelson.
Publisher: Martin M. Bruce, Ph.D.
Cross References: See T2:1424 (1 reference); for reviews by Harold Borko and Jacob Cohen, see 7:155 (1 reference).

[2667]
The Trait Pleasure-Displeasure Scale.

Purpose: One of three fundamental dimensions of temperament in Mehrabian's Temperament Model; provides a general assessment of psychological adjustment-maladjustment.
Population: Ages 15 and older.
Publication Dates: 1978–1994.
Scores: Total score only.

Administration: Group or individual.
Price Data: Available from publisher for complete kit including scale, scoring directions, norms, manual (1994, 10 pages), and literature review.
Time: (10–15) minutes.
Author: Albert Mehrabian.
Publisher: Albert Mehrabian (the author).
Cross References: For reviews by Thaddeus Rozecki and Chockalingam Viswesvaran, see 13:351 (1 reference).

[2668]
Transdisciplinary Play-Based Assessment, Revised Edition.

Purpose: Constructed as a multidimensional approach to identifying service needs, to developing intervention plans, and to evaluating progress in children.
Population: Children developmentally functioning between infancy and 6 years of age.
Publication Date: 1993.
Acronym: TPBA.
Scores: 4 domains: Cognitive, Social-Emotional, Communication and Language, Sensorimotor Development.
Administration: Individual.
Price Data, 2002: $44 per manual (352 pages).
Time: (60–90) minutes.
Comments: Ratings by transdisciplinary team.
Author: Toni W. Linder.
Publisher: Paul H. Brookes Publishing Co., Inc.
Cross References: For reviews by Terry Overton and Gary J. Stainback, see 13:352.

[2669]
Transition Behavior Scale—Second Edition.

Purpose: "Developed to be an educational-relevant measure of predicted success in employment and independent living based upon school personnel's observation of a student's behavior or skills."
Population: Ages 12–18.
Publication Dates: 1989–2000.
Acronym: TBS-2.
Scores, 3: Work-Related, Interpersonal Relations, Social/Community Expectations.
Administration: Group or individual.
Price Data, 2006: $125 per complete kit including 50 school version rating forms, 50 self-report rating forms, school version technical manual (2000, 41 pages), self-report technical manual (2000, 36 pages), and IEP and intervention manual (2000, 188 pages); $35 per 50 school version rating forms; $35 per 50 self-report rating forms; $15 per school version technical manual; $15 per self-report technical manual; $25 per IEP and intervention manual.
Time: (15–20) minutes.
Authors: Stephen B. McCarney and Paul D. Anderson.

Publisher: Hawthorne Educational Services, Inc.
Cross References: For reviews by Susan K. Green and Michael S. Trevisan, see 16:253; for reviews by Martha Blackwell and David O. Herman of the original edition, see 12:404.

[2670]
Transition Competence Battery for Deaf and Hard of Hearing Adolescents and Young Adults.

Purpose: To measure work and social skills necessary to successfully work and live in the community for persons who are deaf and hard of hearing to successfully work and live in the community.
Population: Deaf and hard of hearing adolescents and young adults.
Publication Date: 1993.
Acronym: TCB.
Scores, 6: Job-Seeking Skills, Work Adjustment Skills, Job-Related Social and Interpersonal Skills, Money Management Skills, Health and Home Skills, Community Awareness Skills.
Administration: Group.
Price Data: Price data for complete set available from publisher.
Time: (180) minutes.
Comments: In addition to the written form, a video form is also available in which the test is presented in sign language.
Authors: John Reiman, Michael Bullis, and Cheryl Davis.
Publisher: James Stanfield Co., Inc.
Cross References: For a review by Connie T. England, see 15:268.

[2671]
Transition Planning Inventory (Updated Version).

Purpose: Designed to help identify "preferences and interests and areas of transition strength and needs."
Population: Students with disabilities who desire to plan for the future.
Publication Dates: 1997-2006.
Acronym: TPI-UV.
Scores: Ratings in 9 areas: Employment, Further Education, Daily Living, Leisure Activities, Community Participation, Health, Self-Determination, Communication, Interpersonal Relationships.
Administration: Group or individual.
Forms, 5: Student, Home, School, Profile and Further Recommendations, Modified Form for Students with Significant Disabilities.
Versions, 2: Paper and pencil, Computer.
Price Data, 2006: $190 per complete kit including Administration and Resource Guide (2006, 184 pages), 25 Profile and Further Assessment Recommendation

forms, 25 School forms, 25 Home forms, 25 Student forms, Informal Assessments for Transition Planning resource, and Case Studies in Transition Planning book; $40 per Administration and Resource Guide; $30 per 25 Profile and Further Assessment Recommendation forms; $30 per 25 School forms; $30 per 25 Home forms; $25 per 25 Student forms.

Foreign Language Editions: Home forms available in Spanish, Chinese, Japanese, and Korean.

Time: (15-30) minutes per form.

Comments: The Home and Student forms can be administered independently, individually (assisted), in small groups, or orally; Student, Home, School, and Profile and Further Recommendations forms should all be used when working with students without significant disabilities.

Authors: Gary M. Clark and James R. Patton.

Publisher: PRO-ED.

Cross References: For reviews by Robert K. Gable and by Rosemary E. Sutton and Theresa A. Quigney of an earlier form, see 14:400.

[2672]
Transition-to-Work Inventory.

Purpose: Designed to "measure a person's leisure interests in order to help him or her turn these interests into possible employment opportunities in a full- or part-time job, small business enterprise, or home-based business."

Population: Job seekers.

Publication Date: 2004.

Acronym: TWI.

Scores, 14: Arts/Entertainment/Media, Science/Math/Engineering, Plants/Animals, Law/Law Enforcement/Public Safety, Mechanics/Installers/Repairers, Construction/Mining/Drilling, Transportation, Industrial Production, Business Detail, Sales/Marketing, Recreation/Travel/Other Personal Services, Education/Social Sciences, General Management/Support, Medical/Health Services.

Administration: Individual or group.

Price Data, 2006: $34.95 per complete kit including 25 test booklets and administrator's guide (4 pages).

Time: (20-30) minutes.

Comments: This test can be self-administered and self-scored.

Author: John Liptak.

Publisher: JIST Publishing, Inc.

[2673]
Transition-to-Work Inventory: A Job Placement System for Workers with Severe disAbilities.

Purpose: "Designed to assist employers, supported employment counselors, and other transition professionals in identifying the best match between the skills of an individual with disabilities and the requirements of the job."

Population: Individuals with severe disabilities.

Publication Dates: 1995–1996.

Acronym: TWI™.

Scores, 3: Job Analysis Rating, Worker Analysis Rating, Difference Score.

Administration: Individual.

Parts, 2: Job Analysis Scale, Worker Analysis Scale.

Price Data, 2006: $105 per starter kit including user and accommodation manual, 10 job analysis booklets, 25 worker analysis booklets, and 25 profile sheets; $23 per 10 worker analysis booklets; $41 per 25 job analysis booklets; $22 per individual profile sheets; $68 per manual and accommodation guide.

Time: (30–35) minutes per scale.

Comments: Ratings by transition professionals.

Authors: Lee Friedman, Carl Cameron, and Jennifer Fletcher.

Publisher: Harcourt Assessment, Inc.

Cross References: For reviews by Chantale Jeanrie and Erich P. Prien, see 14:401.

[2674]
Trauma and Attachment Belief Scale.

Purpose: Measures beliefs related to five need areas that are sensitive to the effects of traumatic experiences.

Population: Ages 9–18, 17–78.

Publication Date: 2003.

Acronym: TABS.

Scores, 11: Self-Safety, Other-Safety, Self-Trust, Other-Trust, Self-Esteem, Other-Esteem, Self-Intimacy, Other-Intimacy, Self-Control, Other-Control, Total.

Administration: Group.

Forms, 2: Profile Sheet, Profile Sheet for Youth.

Price Data, 2006: $109.50 per kit including 25 Adult AutoScore™ test/profile forms, 25 Youth AutoScore™ test/profile forms, and manual (52 pages); $43.50 per 25 AutoScore™ test/profile forms; $53 per manual.

Time: (10–15) minutes.

Comments: Previously known as Traumatic Stress Institute (TSI) Belief Scale.

Author: Laurie Anne Pearlman.

Publisher: Western Psychological Services.

Cross References: For reviews by Eugene V. Aidman and Adrienne Garro, see 16:254.

[2675]
Trauma Assessment Inventories.

Purpose: "Designed to screen for Posttraumatic Stress Disorder" and designed to assess "Cognitive and emotional aspects of guilt associated with a specific traumatic event."

Population: Ages 18 years and older.

Publication Date: 2004.

Administration: Individual.

Price Data, 2006: $192.50 per complete kit including Screening Kit and Treatment Kit; Computerized

Components: $68.50 per 20-use Windows DISK for Computer Scoring Only; $40 per 25 AutoScore forms (specify screening or treatment); $16.50 per 100 computerized answer sheets (specify screening or treatment).
Author: Edward S. Kubany.
Publisher: Western Psychological Services.

a) SCREENING KIT.
Purpose: "Designed to screen for Posttraumatic Stress Disorder."
Price Data: $109 per complete screening kit including 25 AutoScore forms, 25 test forms, and screening manual (47 pages); $44 per screening manual.
Time: (10-20) minutes.
Comments: This test can be abbreviated if time constraints are an issue.

1) *Traumatic Life Events Questionnaire.*
Acronym: TLEQ.
Scores, 3: Count of Events, Count of Events Associated with Fear or Hopelessness, Occurrences.
Price Data: $29 per 25 test forms.

2) *PTSD Screening and Diagnostic Scale.*
Acronym: PSDS.
Scores, 7: Criterion A, Criterion B, Criterion C, Criterion D, PSDS Symptom Score, Criterion E, Criterion F.

b) TREATMENT KIT.
Purpose: Designed to assess "Cognitive and emotional aspects of guilt associated with a specific traumatic event."
Price Data: $88 per complete treatment kit including 25 AutoScore forms, 25 test forms, and treatment manual (59 pages); $52 per treatment manual.
Time: Administration time not reported.

1) *The Trauma-Related Guilt Inventory.*
Acronym: TRGI.
Scores, 6: Global Guilt, Distress, Guilt Cognitions (Wrongdoing, Insufficient Justification, Hindsight-Bias/Responsibility).
Comments: This test is written at a 5th-grade reading level.

[2676]
Trauma Symptom Checklist for Children.
Purpose: Designed "to measure acute and chronic posttraumatic stress and related psychological symptomatology."
Population: Ages 8–16.
Publication Date: 1996.
Acronym: TSCC.
Scores: 8 scales: Underresponse, Hyperresponse, Anxiety, Depression, Anger, Posttraumatic Stress, Dissociation, Sexual Concerns.
Administration: Group or individual.

Price Data, 2006: $146 per introductory kit including professional manual, 25 test booklets, 25 male profile forms, and 25 female profile forms; $275 per software portfolio (CD-ROM) including unlimited scoring, reports, and profiles.
Time: (15–20) minutes.
Author: John Briere.
Publisher: Psychological Assessment Resources, Inc.
Cross References: For reviews by Gregory J. Boyle and Chockalingam Viswesvaran, see 15:269.

[2677]
Trauma Symptom Checklist for Young Children.
Purpose: Designed "to measure acute and chronic posttraumatic stress and related psychological symptomatology."
Population: Ages 3–12 years.
Publication Dates: 1999–2005.
Acronym: TSCYC.
Scores, 11: Validity scales (Response Level, Atypical Response), Clinical scales (Anxiety, Depression, Anger/Aggression, Posttraumatic Stress-Intrusion, Posttraumatic Stress-Avoidance, Posttraumatic Stress-Arousal, Posttraumatic Stress-Total, Dissociation, Sexual Concerns).
Administration: Group.
Price Data, 2006: $180 per introductory kit including professional manual (2005, 61 pages), 25 item booklets, 25 hand-scorable answer sheets, 25 profile forms (Male & Female Ages 3–4 Years), 25 profile forms (Male & Female Ages 5–9 Years), and 25 profile forms (Male & Female Ages 10–12 Years; $275 per scoring program (CD-ROM) including unlimited scoring, reports, and profiles.
Time: (15–20) minutes.
Comments: Instrument is answered by the child's parents and/or caretakers.
Author: John Briere.
Publisher: Psychological Assessment Resources, Inc.

[2678]
Trauma Symptom Inventory.
Purpose: Designed for the "evaluation of acute and chronic posttraumatic symptomatology."
Population: Ages 18 and older.
Publication Date: 1995.
Acronym: TSI.
Scores, 13: Validity Scales (Response Level, Atypical Response, Inconsistent Response); Clinical Scales (Anxious Arousal, Depression, Anger/Irritability, Intrusive Experiences, Defensive Avoidance, Dissociation, Sexual Concerns, Dysfunctional Sexual Behavior, Impaired Self-Reference, Tension Reduction Behavior).
Administration: Group.
Price Data, 2006: $189 per introductory kit including manual (67 pages), 10 item booklets, 25 hand-

scorable answer sheets, and 25 each of male and female profile forms; $275 per Scoring Program including unlimited scoring reports.

Time: (20) minutes.

Comments: Computer scoring system available from publisher.

Author: John Briere.

Publisher: Psychological Assessment Resources, Inc.

Cross References: For reviews by Ephrem Fernandez and Jack E. Gebart-Eaglemont, see 14:402; see also T5:2782 (3 references).

[2679]
Treatment Intervention Inventory.

Purpose: Designed for intake, referral and post-treatment comparisons of adult counseling clients.

Population: Ages 12–18; Adult counseling clients.

Publication Dates: 1991–1997.

Acronyms: TII; TII-J.

Scores, 9: Truthfulness, Anxiety, Depression, Self-Esteem, Distress, Family, Alcohol, Drug, Stress Coping Abilities.

Administration: Group.

Levels, 2: Adult, Juvenile.

Price Data: Available from publisher.

Time: (35) minutes Adult; (25–30) minutes Juvenile.

Comments: "A computerized, self-report assessment"; administration by paper and pencil or by computer; computer scored.

Author: Behavior Data Systems Ltd.

Publisher: Behavior Data Systems Ltd.

Cross References: For reviews by Janice G. Murdoch and Linda J. Zimmerman, see 14:403.

[2680]
Triadal Equated Personality Inventory.

Purpose: To measure personality variables.

Population: Adult males.

Publication Dates: 1960–1963.

Acronym: TEPI.

Scores, 22: Dominance, Self-Confidence, Decisiveness, Independence, Toughness, Suspiciousness, Conscientiousness, Introversion, Restlessness, Solemnity, Foresight, Industriousness, Warmth, Enthusiasm, Conformity, Inventiveness, Persistence, Sex Drive, Recognition Drive, Cooperativeness, Humility-Tolerance, Self-Control.

Administration: Group.

Price Data: Available from publisher.

Time: (50–120) minutes.

Author: Research Staff, United Consultants.

Publisher: Psychometric Affiliates.

Cross References: For a review by Jacob Cohen, see 7:156.

[2681]
Triage Assessment for Addictive Disorders.

Purpose: "Designed to cover diagnostic information for current dependence or abuse of alcohol and drugs."

Population: Adults.

Publication Dates: 1995–2000.

Acronym: TAAD.

Scores, 2: Abuse, Dependence.

Administration: Individual.

Price Data: Available from publisher.

Time: (10) minutes.

Comments: Structured interview; screens for DSM-IV diagnostic criteria, providing an estimate of the likelihood that an individual meets the criteria for abuse or dependency; covers current problems only; can be administered by paraprofessionals; scores indicate number of positive symptoms and criteria for alcohol abuse and dependence specifically, and number of positive symptoms and criteria for drug abuse and dependence collectively.

Author: Norman G. Hoffmann.

Publisher: The Change Companies.

Cross References: For reviews by JoAnn Murphey and by Wendy Naumann and Robin Rix, see 15:270.

[2682]
Tutor Evaluation and Self-Assessment Tool.

Purpose: "A structured profile that evaluates tutors' effectiveness … to improve growth and development."

Population: Tutors of all subjects and grade levels.

Publication Date: 1996.

Acronym: TESAT.

Scores, 12: Greeting, Identification of Task, Breaking the Task into Parts, Identification of Thought Process, Setting Agenda, Addressing the Task, Tutee Summary of Content, Tutee Summary of Underlying Process, Confirmation, What Next?, Arranging and Planning Next Session, Closing.

Administration: Group.

Price Data, 2001: $198 per 100 TESATs, quantity discount available; $64.95 (+$3.50 shipping) per Tutor Trainer's Manual (64 pages); $85 per transparency set, $23.95 per Master Tutor Guidebook (124 pages) (quantities up to 29); $16.95 per Master Tutor Guidebook (quantities of 30 or more); Orders of 100 or more Master Tutor Guidebooks include free Tutor Trainer's Manual, transparency set, and 100 tests.

Time: Untimed.

Comments: Administered in paper-and-pencil format only using carbonated compilation and scoring sheets; ranks tutors into one of four skill categories (outstanding, proficient, adequate, needs improvement) for each of 12 steps of the "Tutor Cycle," based on the author's tutoring model; can be completed by tutor for self-assessment or by other evaluator.

Author: Ross B. MacDonald.
Publisher: The Cambridge Stratford Study Skills Institute.

[2683]

Typing 5.

Purpose: Assesses typing skills.
Population: Administrative assistants, secretaries, and any position requiring typing ability.
Publication Date: 1975.
Scores, 2: Speed, Accuracy.
Administration: Individual or group.
Price Data, 1998: $70.50 per start-up kit (specify Form A, B, or C) including 25 test booklets, 25 practice sheets, and examiner's manual; $44 per 25 test booklets (specify Form A, B, or C; quantity discounts available); $14.75 per 25 practice sheets (quantity discounts available); $19.75 per examiner's manual.
Time: 5 minutes per test.
Comments: Previously listed as SRA Typing 5.
Author: Science Research Associates.
Publisher: Pearson Performance Solutions [No reply from publisher; status unknown].
    a) FORM A—TYPING SPEED.
    b) FORM B—BUSINESS LETTER.
    c) FORM C—NUMERICAL.
Cross References: For reviews by Charles J. Cranny and Lawrence W. Erickson, see 8:1035.

[2684]

The Uncritical Inference Test.

Purpose: "Helps students learn to distinguish between observations (or facts) and inferences, assumptions, beliefs, and judgments."
Population: Adolescents and adults.
Publication Dates: 1955–1982.
Scores: Total score only.
Administration: Group.
Manual: No manual.
Price Data, 2006: $1 per test (minimum order of 10 paper tests); electronic delivery via email attachment or download in PDF format (from www.time-binding.org/store.htm) includes license for multiple usages at $.75 per use.
Time: Administration time not reported.
Author: William V. Haney.
Publisher: Institute of General Semantics.

[2685]

Understanding and Managing Stress.

Purpose: Assesses stress level and health-related behaviors.
Population: Adults.
Publication Date: 1989.
Scores: Continuum of risk scores (low, medium, high) for each of 22 areas: Changes on the Job/Total, Changes on the Job/High-Impact, Changes in Personal Life/Total, Changes in Personal Life/High-Impact, Chronic Stressful Conditions on the Job, Chronic Stressful Conditions in Personal Life, Strain Response, Psychological Outlook, General Lifestyle/Importance to Health, General Lifestyle/Present Effectiveness, Social Support, Nutritional Habits and Awareness/Total, Physical Exercise Habits and Awareness, Drinking Habits, Behavioral Habits, Tobacco, Systolic Blood Pressure Reading, Diastolic Blood Pressure Reading, Total Cholesterol, High-Density Lipoprotein (HDL) Level, Ratio of Total Cholesterol to HDL, Triglyceride Level.
Administration: Group.
Price Data: Price information available from publisher for handbook (64 pages).
Time: Administration time not reported.
Comments: Self-administered, self-scored.
Author: John D. Adams.
Publisher: Jossey-Bass, A Wiley Company.
Cross References: For reviews by William J. Waldron and by William K. Wilkinson and Christopher P. Migotsky, see 12:405.

[2686]

Understanding Communication.

Purpose: Developed "to measure comprehension of verbal material in the form of short sentences and phrases."
Population: Variety of occupations.
Publication Dates: 1959–1992.
Scores: Total score only.
Administration: Individual or group.
Price Data, 2002: $91 per start-up kit including 25 test booklets, score key, and interpretation and research manual; $54 per 25 test booklets (quantity discounts available); $20 per score key; $28 per interpretation and research manual.
Time: 15 minutes.
Author: Thelma Gwinn Thurstone.
Publisher: Pearson Performance Solutions [No reply from publisher; status unknown].
Cross References: See T4:2864 (1 reference) and T2:1747 (1 reference); for reviews by C. E. Jurgensen and Donald E. P. Smith, see 6:840.

[2687]

Uniform Child Custody Evaluation System.

Purpose: Constructed as a "uniform child custody evaluation procedure."
Population: Professionals involved in custody evaluation.
Publication Date: 1994.
Acronym: UCCES.
Scores: No scores.
Administration: Individual.
Forms, 25: General Data and Administrative Forms (UCCES Checklist, Initial Referral Form, Chrono-

logical Record of all Case Contacts Form, Case Notes Form, Consent for Psychological Services to Child(ren) Form, Authorization to Release Information Form, Suitability for Joint Custody Checklist, Collateral Interview Form, Consent for Evaluation of Minor(s) Form, UCCES Summary Chart), Parent Forms (Parent's Family/Personal History Questionnaire, Parent Interview Form, Parenting Abilities Checklist, Suitability for Joint Custody Interview, Analysis of Response Validity Checklist, Behavioral Observations of Parent-Child Interaction Form, Home Visit Observation Form, Agreement Between Parent and Evaluator Form, Explanation of Custody Evaluation Procedures for Parents and Attorneys), Child Forms (Child History Questionnaire, Child Interview Form, Child Abuse Interview Form, Abuse/Neglect Checklist, Child's Adjustment to Home and Community Checklist, Parent-Child Goodness of Fit Observation Form and Checklist).

Price Data, 2006: $180 per introductory kit including manual (47 pages), 2 sets of Parent Forms, 2 sets of Child Forms, and 1 set of Administrative and Data Forms.

Time: Administration time varies.

Authors: Harry L. Munsinger and Kevin W. Karlson.

Publisher: Psychological Assessment Resources, Inc.

Cross References: For a review by Steven Zucker, see 13:353.

[2688]
Universal Nonverbal Intelligence Test™.

Purpose: "Designed to provide a … fair measure of the general intelligence and cognitive abilities of children and adolescents … who may be disadvantaged by traditional verbal and language-loaded measures."

Population: Ages 5 years through 17 years, 11 months.

Publication Date: 1998.

Acronym: UNIT™.

Scores, 11: Symbolic Memory, Cube Design, Spatial Memory, Analogic Reasoning, Object Memory, Mazes, Memory Quotient, Reasoning Quotient, Symbolic Quotient, Nonsymbolic Quotient, Full Scale IQ.

Administration: Individual.

Forms: Abbreviated Battery, Standard Battery, Extended Battery.

Price Data, 2006: $635 per complete test kit including examiner's manual, 2 stimulus books, 16 response chips, response grid, 9 cubes, response mat, 10 symbolic memory cards, 25 record forms, 25 mazes response booklets, black pencil, red pencil, and Administration at a Glance all in a canvas carrying case; $92 per examiner's manual; $48.50 per 25 record forms; $54 per mazes response booklets.

Time: (10–15) minutes, Abbreviated Battery; (30) minutes, Standard Battery; (45) minutes, Extended Battery.

Authors: Bruce A. Bracken and R. Steve McCallum.

Publisher: Riverside Publishing.

Cross References: For a review by Deborah L. Bandalos, see 14:404.

[2689]
University Residence Environment Scale [Revised].

Purpose: Designed to "assess the social climate of university student living groups."

Population: University students and staff.

Publication Dates: 1974–1988.

Acronym: URES.

Scores, 10: Involvement, Emotional Support, Independence, Traditional Social Orientation, Competition, Academic Achievement, Intellectuality, Order and Organization, Student Influence, Innovation.

Administration: Group.

Forms, 4: Real (R), Ideal (I), Expectations (E), Short (S).

Price Data: Available from publisher (www.mindgarden.com).

Time: Administration time not reported.

Comments: Part of the Social Climate Scales (T5:2445); focuses on student-student and student-staff relationships and the organizational structure of a living group; for use in student living groups and in program evaluation and counseling; can also be completed by observers and other nonresidents, such as parents and student visitors; provides information about student living groups and encourages staff to become involved in program planning and design.

Author: Rudolf H. Moos.

Publisher: Mind Garden, Inc.

Cross References: For reviews by Barbara A. Rothlisberg and Theresa G. Siskind, see 14:405; see also T4:2865 (8 references) and T3:2534 (3 references); for reviews by Fred H. Borgen and James V. Mitchell, Jr. of an earlier edition, see 8:700 (12 references).

[2690]
Useful Field of View.

Purpose: Designed as a "computer-administered and computer-scored test of visual attention," which may be used to help predict the degree to which a person may perform some everyday activities, such as driving a motor vehicle, safely.

Population: Adults.

Publication Date: 1998.

Acronym: UFOV.

Scores, 3: Central Vision and Processing Speed, Divided Attention, Selective Attention.

Administration: Individual.

Price Data, 1998: $130 per complete kit including user's manual (106 pages), reference card, CD, and use counter.

Time: (15) minutes.
Comments: Microsoft Windows 95 required with video card and CD ROM drive; not for use with laptops.
Authors: Karlene K. Ball and Daniel L. Roenker.
Publisher: PsychCorp, A brand of Harcourt Assessment, Inc.
Cross References: For reviews by Gregory Schraw and James P. Van Haneghan, see 15:271.

[2691]
Utah Test of Language Development, Fourth Edition.

Purpose: Designed to "identify children who are significantly below their peers in language proficiency."
Population: Ages 3-0 to 9-11.
Publication Dates: 1958–2003.
Acronym: UTLD-4.
Scores, 8: Picture Identification, Word Functions, Morphological Structures, Sentence Repetition, Word Segmentation, Total Language Composite, Content Composite, Form Composite.
Administration: Individual.
Price Data, 2006: $140 per complete kit including examiner's manual, picture book, and 25 profile/examiner record booklets, all in a sturdy storage box; $50 per examiner's manual; $60 per picture book; $35 per 25 profile/examiner record booklets.
Time: (15–30) minutes.
Comments: Earliest edition of this test was called the Utah Verbal Language Development.
Author: Merlin J. Mecham.
Publisher: PRO-ED.
Cross References: For reviews by David P. Hurford and Judith R. Johnston, see 16:255; see also T5:2801 (3 references) and T4:2872 (1 reference); for a review by Lynn S. Bliss of the third edition, see 11:454 (2 references); for reviews by Joan I. Lynch and Michelle Quinn of an earlier edition, see 9:1306 (3 references); see also T3:2541 (5 references) and T2:2097 (4 references); for reviews by Katharine G. Butler and William H. Perkins of an earlier edition, see 7:973.

[2692]
Validity Indicator Profile.

Purpose: "Designed to evaluate an individual's motivation and effort to assess whether the results of cognitive, neuropsychological or other types of testing should be considered representative of an individual's overall capacities."
Population: Ages 18–69.
Publication Date: 1997.
Acronym: VIP.
Scores, 2: Nonverbal Subtest Response Style, Verbal Subtest Response Style.
Administration: Individual.

Price Data, 2006: $39 per test booklet; $21 per 25 answer sheets; $42 per manual; $18.25 per interpretive report and $13.75 per profile report (Q Local™ scoring); $21.25 per interpretive report and $16.75 per profile report (mail-in scoring); $117-$123 per starter kit including manual, test booklet, 3 answer sheets, and 3 interpretive reports (specify Q Local™ scoring or mail-in scoring); quantity discounts available for the reports.
Time: (50) minutes for both subtests; (20) minutes for verbal subtest and (30) minutes for nonverbal subtest.
Comments: Instrument must be scored by computer.
Author: Richard I. Frederick.
Publisher: Pearson Assessments.
Cross References: For reviews by Jack E. Gebart-Eaglemont and Stephen H. Ivens, see 14:406.

[2693]
Valpar Test of Essential Skills.

Purpose: Designed to "help examinees demonstrate in a relatively short period of time important basic English and math skills required of workers in most of the occupations or training programs in the United States and Canada."
Population: Ages 15 and over.
Publication Dates: 1998–1999.
Acronym: VTES.
Administration: Individual or group.
Price Data, 2006: $30 per manual (1998, 76 pages), $75 per 25 answer sheets; $50 per 10 math test booklets (specify Form A or Form B); $50 per 10 English booklets (specify Form A or Form B); $50 per Evaluation Kit including 1 manual, 10 answer sheets, 2 math test booklets, 2 English test booklets, and scoring software.
Comments: Time limited; criterion-referenced; computer scoring only; requires IBM PC or compatible, 486 or higher; "percent correct" scores provided for all subtests and totals for English and Math; test booklets are reusable.
Authors: Bryan B. Christopherson and Alex Swartz.
Publisher: Valpar International Corporation.
  a) VTES ENGLISH.
  Scores, 6: Vocabulary/Grade Level, Spelling/Grade Level, Usage/Grade Level, Reading/Grade Level, Total/Grade Level, Total/General Educational Development-L (GED-L).
  Forms, 2: Alternate Forms: Form A and Form B.
  Time: (60) minutes.
  b) VTES MATH.
  Scores, 6: Computation/Grade Level, Usage/Grade Level, Total/Grade Level, Computation/General Educational Development-M (GED-M), Usage/General Educational Development-M (GED-M), Total/General Educational Development-M (GED-M).

Forms, 2: Alternate Forms: Form A and Form B.

Time: (60) minutes.

Cross References: For reviews by Arthur S. Ellen and by Shawn Powell and Michelle A. Butler, see 16:256.

[2694]
Values Preference Indicator [Revised].

Purpose: Provides respondents with the tools to examine their values and priorities for the purpose of self-learning, group discussion, team development, and gaining insight into corporate culture.

Population: Adults.

Publication Dates: 1990-2006.

Acronym: VPI.

Scores, 21: Accomplishment, Acknowledgment, Challenge, Cooperation, Creativity, Expertise, Friendship, Honesty, Independence, Instruction, Intimacy, Organization, Pleasure, Quality, Recognition, Responsibility, Security, Spirituality, Tranquility, Variety, Wealth.

Administration: Individual or group.

Price Data, 2006: $13.95 per test booklet (2006, 12 pages); $13.95 per code for online version; $38 per Trainer's Guidelines (1996, 22 pages).

Time: [30-45] minutes to administer; 90-180 for program.

Comments: Test can be self-administered and self-scored.

Authors: Ken Keis and Everett T. Robinson.

Publisher: Consulting Resource Group International, Inc.

[2695]
The Values Scale, Second Edition.

Purpose: "A cross-cultural measure of values in various life roles."

Population: Junior high school to adult.

Publication Dates: 1986–1989.

Acronym: VS.

Scores, 21: Ability Utilization, Achievement, Advancement, Aesthetics, Altruism, Authority, Autonomy, Creativity, Economic Rewards, Life Style, Personal Development, Physical Activity, Prestige, Risk, Social Interaction, Social Relations, Variety, Working Conditions, Cultural Identity, Physical Prowess, Economic Security.

Administration: Group.

Price Data, 2001: 470 per preview kit including item booklet, prepaid answer sheet, and manual; $62 per 25 reusable test booklets; $38 per 25 non-prepaid answer sheets; $38 per 25 report forms; $59.40 per manual.

Time: (30–45) minutes.

Authors: Dorothy D. Nevill and Donald E. Super.

Publisher: CPP, Inc.

Cross References: See T5:2805 (3 references); for reviews by Kathy E. Green and Patricia Schoenrade, see 13:355 (4 references); see also T4:2876 (1 reference); for reviews by Denise M. Rousseau and Robert B. Slaney of an earlier edition, see 10:379.

[2696]
Vasectomy Scale: Attitudes.

Purpose: To measure attitudes toward vasectomy.

Population: Adults.

Publication Dates: 1974–1988.

Scores: Total score only.

Administration: Group.

Manual: No manual.

Price Data, 2005: $2 per scale.

Time: [10] minutes.

Comments: Supplementary article available.

Author: Panos D. Bardis.

Publisher: Donna Bardis.

[2697]
Verb and Sentence Test.

Purpose: "Developed to investigate disorders affecting the production and comprehension of verbs and sentences."

Population: People with aphasia, aged 18–80 years.

Publication Date: 2002.

Acronym: VAST.

Scores: 10 subtests: Verb Comprehension, Sentence Comprehension, Grammaticality Judgement, Action Naming, Verb Finite, Verb Infinitive, Sentence Construction, Anagrams Without Picture, Anagrams With Picture, Wh-Anagrams.

Administration: Individual.

Price Data: Available from publisher.

Time: (180) minutes for complete battery.

Comments: Subtests may be administered individually.

Authors: Roelien Bastiaanse, Susan Edwards, and Judith Rispens.

Publisher: Harcourt Assessment [England].

[2698]
Verbal Form.

Purpose: Designed to measure general ability to learn and comprehend.

Population: Employees in a wide variety of occupations.

Publication Dates: 1946–1984.

Scores, 3: Quantitative, Linguistic, Total.

Administration: Individual or group.

Forms, 2: A, B.

Price Data, 2002: $78 per start-up kit including 25 test booklets (specify Form A or Form B) and examiner's manual; $60 per 25 test booklets (quantity discounts available; specify Form A or Form B); $28 per examiner's manual; price data available from publisher for Quanta computer administration and scoring software (Windows); $78 per Quanta start-up kit including examiner's manual, 25 administrations, and scoring (does not include Quanta software).

Time: 15 minutes.

Comments: Previously listed as SRA Verbal Form.

Authors: Thelma Gwinn Thurstone and L. L. Thurstone.

Publisher: Pearson Performance Solutions [No reply from publisher; status unknown].

Cross References: See T4:2542 (3 references), T3:2276 (3 references), T2:452 (1 reference), and 7:383 (2 references); for reviews by W. D. Commins and Willis C. Schaefer, see 4:319.

[2699]
Verbal Motor Production Assessment for Children.

Purpose: "Designed to aid in the systematic assessment of the neuromotor integrity of the motor speech system in children … [with] speech production disorders."

Population: Speech-disordered children ages 3–12.

Publication Date: 1999.

Acronym: VMPAC.

Scores, 8: Global Motor Control, Focal Oromotor Control, Sequencing, Connected Speech and Language Control, Speech Characteristics, Auditory, Visual, Tactile.

Administration: Individual.

Price Data, 2005: $115 per complete kit including examiner's manual (206 pages), 11 stimulus cards, 15 record forms, and training videotape (45 minutes); $80 per examiner's manual; $32 per 15 record forms; $32 per stimulus cards; $43 per training videotape.

Time: (30) minutes.

Authors: Deborah Hayden and Paula Square.

Publisher: PsychCorp, A brand of Harcourt Assessment, Inc.

Cross References: For a review by Katharine Snyder, see 16:257.

[2700]
Verbal Reasoning.

Purpose: To measure the capacity to reason logically based on verbal problems.

Population: Wide variety of occupations and vocational counseling.

Publication Dates: 1958–1961.

Scores: Total score only.

Administration: Individual or group.

Price Data, 2002: $92 per start-up kit including 25 test booklets, score key, and interpretation and research manual (1961, 20 pages); $55 per 25 test booklets (quantity discounts available); $20 per score key; $28 per interpretation and research manual (1961, 20 pages).

Time: 15 minutes.

Authors: Raymond J. Corsini and Richard Renck.

Publisher: Pearson Performance Solutions [No reply from publisher; status unknown].

Cross References: See T3:2553 (1 reference); for reviews by James E. Kennedy and David G. Ryans, see 6:509.

[2701]
Verbal Reasoning Tests.

Purpose: Designed to "assess a pupil's verbal skills."

Population: Ages 7.3–10.3; Ages 9.3–12.3; 11.3–14.3.

Publication Date: 1993.

Scores, 5: Vocabulary, Relationships, Sentences, Reasoning, Symbol Manipulation.

Administration: Group.

Levels, 3: 8 and 9, 10 and 11, 12 and 13.

Price Data: Available from publisher.

Authors: Neil Hagues and Denise Courtenay.

Publisher: NFER-Nelson Publishing Co. Ltd. [England].

a) VERBAL REASONING 8 and 9.

Population: Ages 7.3–10.3.

Time: (40) minutes.

b) VERBAL REASONING 10 and 11.

Population: Ages 9.3–12.3.

Time: (45) minutes.

c) VERBAL REASONING 12 and 13.

Population: Ages 11.3–14.3.

Time: (50) minutes.

Cross References: For reviews by Hoi K. Suen and by Rosemary E. Sutton and Jeremy Genovese, see 16:258.

[2702]
Versant.

Purpose: Measures speaking and listening skills over the telephone and measures facility in spoken English and Spanish, which includes the ease and immediacy in understanding and producing basic conversational English and Spanish.

Population: Ages 8–79.

Publication Dates: 2000–2006.

Scores, 5: Overall Score, Sentence Mastery, Vocabulary, Fluency, Pronunciation.

Administration: Individual.

Forms, 3: 5 minutes, 10 minutes, 15 minutes.

Price Data, 2005: $24 per 5-minute test; $40 per 10-minute or 15-minute test.

Time: (5–15) minutes.

Comments: Test administered via telephone or PC; previously titled Ordinate Spoken English Test.

Authors: Ordinate Corporation and Harcourt Assessment.

Publisher: Harcourt Assessment, Inc.

Cross References: For reviews by Dennis Doverspike and Alan Garfinkel, see 16:177.

[2703]
VESPAR: A Verbal and Spatial Reasoning Test.

Purpose: "Designed to measure fluid intelligence in neurological patients."
Population: People "who have suffered physical or cognitive impairments as a result of neurological illness."
Publication Date: 1995.
Acronym: VESPAR.
Scores: Available from publisher.
Administration: Individual.
Price Data, 2001: $198 per multi-part test.
Time: Administration time not reported.
Authors: Dawn W. Langdon and Elizabeth K. Warrington.
Publisher: Psychology Press.

[2704]
Victoria Symptom Validity Test.

Purpose: Designed to "assess possible exaggeration or feigning of cognitive impairments."
Population: Ages 18 and over.
Publication Date: 1997.
Acronym: VSVT.
Scores, 6: Total Items Correct, Easy Items Correct, Difficult Items Correct, Easy Items Response Latency, Difficult Items Response Latency, Right-Left Preference.
Administration: Individual.
Price Data, 2006: $99 per introductory kit including unlimited use software (CD-ROM) for administering, scoring, and reports, with professional manual (93 pages).
Time: 18-25 minutes.
Authors: Daniel Slick, Grace Hopp, Esther Strauss, and Garrie B. Thompson.
Publisher: Psychological Assessment Resources, Inc.
Cross References: For reviews by Stephen J. Freeman and Linda J. Zimmerman, see 14:407.

[2705]
VIEW: An Assessment of Problem Solving Style.

Purpose: Designed to assess "problem-solving styles."
Population: Ages 12 years and older.
Publication Dates: 2002-2004.
Acronym: VIEW.
Scores, 3: Orientation to Change, Manner of Processing, Ways of Decoding.
Administration: Individual or group.
Price Data, 2006: $25 per manual (70 pages); $165 per complete kit including facilitator's guide (219 pages) and 10 paper copies of VIEW (required for all first-time orders); $90 per 10 paper copies; $50 per set-up fee for on-line access; $90 per 10 on-line uses; discounts available for nonprofit schools, religious organizations, college and university faculty, and researchers.
Foreign Editions: Information regarding translated tests available from publisher.
Time: (10-15) minutes.
Comments: Available in online and print versions.
Authors: Edwin C. Selby, Donald J. Treffinger, Scott G. Isaksen, and Kenneth J. Lauer (technical manual only).
Publisher: Center for Creative Learning.

[2706]
ViewPoint.

Purpose: An assessment of work attitudes designed for use in employee selection.
Population: Applicants for nonexempt or entry-level positions in industries.
Publication Dates: 1998–2003.
Scores: 10 scales: WorkView Total, ServiceView Total, Conscientiousness, Trustworthiness, Managing Work Pressure, Getting Along with Others, Drug/Alcohol Avoidance, Safety Orientation, Carelessness, Faking.
Administration: Group or individual.
Price Data, 2005: Available from publisher for test materials including Technical Manual (1999, 62 pages), Technical Report Addendum: A Meta-Analysis of the Validity of ViewPoint (2001, 13 pages), and User's Manual (2005, 56 pages).
Comments: Published in five different forms, each one covering a different combination of work and service attitudes; computerized versions are available.
Authors: W. M. Gibson, M. L. Holcom, S. W. Stang, and W. W. Ruch.
Publisher: Psychological Services, Inc.
a) WORKVIEW 6.
Acronym: W6.
Time: (15–20) minutes.
b) WORKVIEW 4.
Acronym: W4.
Time: (10–15) minutes.
c) SERVICEVIEW.
Acronym: SV.
Time: (10–15) minutes.
d) WORKVIEW 6 + SERVICE.
Acronym: W6SV.
Time: (20–30) minutes.
e) WORKVIEW 4 + SERVICE.
Acronym: W4SV.
Time: (20–25) minutes.
Cross References: For a review by Robert Fitzpatrick, see 16:259.

[2707]
Vigil Continuous Performance Test.

Purpose: Designed to "measure a person's ability to concentrate on a simple or relatively complex task over time."
Population: Ages 6 to 90.

Publication Dates: 1996–1998.

Scores, 4: Errors of Omission, Errors of Commission, Hit Rate, Reaction Time.

Administration: Individual.

Price Data, 2003: $545 per complete kit including Windows Version Binder and three 3.5-inch disks.

Time: [8] minutes.

Comments: Test is computer administered and scored; requires IBM compatible 386 or 486 20 MB hard drive, 3.5-inch disk drive, Windows 3.1, mouse, color V6A or Super V6A, monitor, and Sound System compatible with Sound Blaster Pro Deluxe Soundboard.

Author: The Psychological Corporation.

Publisher: PsychCorp, A brand of Harcourt Assessment, Inc.

Cross References: For a review by Joseph C. Kush, see 16:260.

[2708]
Vineland Adaptive Behavior Scales.

Purpose: To "assess personal and social sufficiency of individuals from birth to adulthood."

Population: Birth through age 18-11 and low-functioning adults, ages 3 through 12-11.

Publication Dates: 1935–1985.

Scores, 13: 3 Communication scores (Receptive, Expressive, Written), 3 Daily Living scores (Personal, Domestic, Community), 3 Socialization scores (Interpersonal Relationships, Play and Leisure Time, Coping Skills), 2 Motor Skills scores (Gross, Fine), Adaptive Behavior Composite, Maladaptive Behavior (optional for Survey and Expanded Forms only).

Administration: Individual.

Foreign Language Edition: Spanish edition available.

Comments: Revision of the Vineland Social Maturity Scale; semistructured interview for Survey and Expanded Forms.

Publisher: Pearson Assessments (originally published by AGS Publishing, acquired by Pearson in 2005).

a) INTERVIEW EDITION, SURVEY FORM.

Purpose: General assessment of adaptive strengths and weaknesses.

Population: Birth through age 18-11 and low-functioning adults.

Publication Dates: 1935–1984.

Price Data, 2002: $49.95 per 25 record booklets; $19.95 per 25 reports to parents; $16.95 per Interview Training Audiocassette; $56.95 per manual (1984, 313 pages); $84.95 per starter set including 10 record booklets, manual, and 1 report to parents; $199.95 per scoring and reporting software (DOS version for PCs).

Time: (20–60) minutes.

Authors: Sara S. Sparrow, David A. Balla, and Domenic V. Cicchetti.

b) INTERVIEW EDITION, EXPANDED FORM.

Purpose: Comprehensive assessment of adaptive behavior for program planning.

Population: Birth through age 18-11 and low-functioning adults.

Publication Dates: 1935–1984.

Price Data: $84.95 per 25 item booklets and 25 score summary and profile reports; $19.95 per 25 reports to parents; $30.95 per 25 program planning reports; $116.95 per starter set including 10 item booklets, 10 score summary and profile reports, 1 program planning report, 1 report to parents and manual (1984, 334 pages); $199.95 per scoring and reporting software (DOS version for PCs).

Time: (60–90) minutes.

Authors: Sara S. Sparrow, David A. Balla, and Domenic V. Cicchetti.

c) CLASSROOM EDITION.

Purpose: Assessment of adaptive behavior in the classroom.

Population: Ages 3 through 12-11.

Publication Date: 1985.

Price Data: $46.95 per 25 questionnaire booklets; $19.95 per 25 reports to parents; $54.95 per starter set including 10 questionnaire booklets, manual (1985, 186 pages), and 1 report to parents; $199.95 per scoring and reporting software (DOS version for PCs).

Time: (20) minutes.

Authors: Sara S. Sparrow (test and report), David A. Balla (test and report), Domenic V. Cicchetti (test and report), and Patti L. Harrison (manual).

Cross References: See T5:2813 (156 references) and T4:2882 (62 references); for a review by Jerome M. Sattler, see 10:381 (9 references); for a review by Iris Amos Campbell of the Survey Form and Expanded Form, see 9:1327 (8 references); see also T3:2557 (38 references), 8:703 (23 references), T2:1428 (50 references), P:281 (21 references), 6:194 (20 references), and 5:120 (15 references); for reviews by William M. Cruickshank and Florence M. Teagarden of an earlier edition, see 4:94 (21 references); for reviews by C. M. Louttit and John W. M. Rothney and an excerpted review, see 3:107 (58 references); for reviews by Paul H. Furfey, Elaine F. Kinder, and Anna S. Starr, see 1:1143.

[2709]
Vineland Social-Emotional Early Childhood Scales.

Purpose: Designed to assess the social and emotional functioning of young children.

Population: Birth to age 5-11.

Publication Date: 1998.

Acronym: SEEC.

Scores, 4: Interpersonal Relationships, Play and Leisure Time, Coping Skills, Composite.
Administration: Individual.
Price Data, 2006: $71.99 per complete kit; $32.99 per 25 record forms; $199.99 for reporting software (Early Childhood Assessment ASSIST).
Foreign Language Edition: Spanish edition available.
Time: (15–25) minutes.
Comments: Administered as a structured oral interview; interviewee should be the person with the most knowledge of the child's social and emotional functioning (e.g., parent, grandparent, legal guardian).
Authors: Sara S. Sparrow, David A. Balla, and Dominic V. Cicchetti.
Publisher: Pearson Assessments (originally published by AGS Publishing, acquired by Pearson in 2005).
Cross References: For reviews by Joseph C. Kush and Donald Lee Stovall, see 14:408.

[2710]
A Violence Scale.

Purpose: Designed to measure attitudes toward violence.
Population: Adolescents and adults.
Publication Date: 1973.
Scores: Total score only.
Administration: Group.
Manual: No manual.
Price Data, 2005: $2 per scale.
Time: [10] minutes.
Comments: Supplementary article available.
Author: Panos D. Bardis.
Publisher: Donna Bardis.
Cross References: See 8:704 (1 reference).

[2711]
Visual Analog Mood Scales.

Purpose: Designed to "assess internal mood states in neurologically impaired adults and in patients in medical and psychiatric settings."
Population: Ages 18 and over.
Publication Dates: 1996–1997.
Acronym: VAMS.
Scores: 8 scales: Afraid, Confused, Sad, Angry, Energetic, Tired, Happy, Tense.
Administration: Group or individual.
Price Data, 2006: $122 per introductory kit including 25 response booklets, professional manual (1997, 48 pages), and metric ruler.
Time: 5 minutes.
Comments: Self-administered or administered by examiner.
Author: Robert A. Stern.
Publisher: Psychological Assessment Resources, Inc.

Cross References: For reviews by S. Alvin Leung and William E. Martin, Jr., see 15:272.

[2712]
Visual Association Test.

Purpose: "Designed to detect anterograde amnesia and certain brain disorders it is connected with."
Population: Ages 16–94.
Publication Date: 2003.
Acronym: VAT.
Scores, 12: Form A: Trial 1 & 2, Trial 3 (optional), Delayed Reproduction (optional); Parallel Form B: idem; Long Form (Form A + B): idem.
Administration: Individual.
Forms, 3: Form A, Form B, Long Form (Form A + B).
Price Data: Available from publisher (www.pits-online.nl/en).
Foreign Language Editions: Dutch, English, and German editions available.
Time: 5-15 minutes (depending on the form chosen).
Comments: Based on the Visual Association Method; manual includes section for each language.
Authors: J. Lindeboom and B. Schmand.
Publisher: PITS: Psychologische Instrumenten Tests en Services [The Netherlands].
Cross References: For a review by Stephen J. Freeman, see 16:261.

[2713]
The Visual Aural Digit Span Test.

Purpose: Intended as a "standardized test of intersensory integration and short-term memory for school-age children."
Population: Ages 5-6 to 12.
Publication Date: 1977.
Acronym: VADS Test.
Scores, 11: Aural-Oral, Visual-Oral, Aural-Written, Visual-Written, Aural Input, Visual Input, Oral Expression, Written Expression, Intrasensory Integration, Intersensory Integration, Total.
Subtests, 4: Aural-Oral, Visual-Oral, Aural-Written, Visual-Written.
Administration: Individual.
Price Data, 2002: $61 per examination kit including 1 package of stimulus cards, Directions for Administering, and 100 visual scoring forms; $34 per 100 visual scoring forms; $83 per manual (1977, 216 pages).
Time: [10–15] minutes.
Author: Elizabeth M. Koppitz.
Publisher: PsychCorp, A brand of Harcourt Assessment, Inc.
Cross References: See T5:2816 (1 reference) and T4:2884 (1 reference); for reviews by H. Lee Swanson and Robert H. Zabel, see 9:1329 (2 references); see also T3:2560 (2 references).

[2714]
Visual Functioning Assessment Tool.

Purpose: "Assessment of a student's visual functioning in the educational setting."
Population: Visually impaired in grades preschool and over.
Publication Date: 1980.
Acronym: VFAT.
Scores: No scores.
Administration: Individual.
Price Data, 2005: $95 per complete kit; $38 per reproducible recording booklet; $65 per manual (123 pages).
Time: Untimed.
Authors: Kathleen Byrnes Costello, Patricia Pinkney, and Wendy Scheffers.
Publisher: Stoelting Co.

[2715]
Visual Motor Assessment.

Purpose: "Designed to identify visual-motor problems in children and adults."
Population: Ages 6 and older.
Publication Dates: 1962-2006.
Acronym: ViMo.
Scores, 5: Total Rotation Score, T-Score, Total SPCD (Separation of the Circle-Diamond Figure), Total DCD (Distortion of the Circle-Diamond Figure), Total DD (Distortion of the Dot Figure).
Administration: Individual.
Price Data, 2006: $100 per complete kit including technical manual (104 pages), 25 record forms, and 2 sets of test cards; $60 per technical manual; $37 per 25 record forms.
Time: (5-15) minutes.
Comments: Formerly known as the Minnesota Percepto-Diagnostic (MPD) Test.
Author: Gerald B. Fuller.
Publisher: Multi-Health Systems, Inc.
Cross References: For information on the Minnesota Percepto-Diagnostic Test, see T5:1699 (2 references), T4:1647 (6 references), 9:719 (3 references), 8:872 (22 references), T2:1485 (17 references), and P:475 (19 references); for reviews by Richard W. Coan and Eugene E. Levitt of the original edition of the Minnesota Percepto-Diagnostic Test, see 6:231 (2 references).

[2716]
The Visual Object and Space Perception Battery.

Purpose: Designed to assess visual object and space perception.
Population: Adults.
Publication Date: 1991.
Acronym: VOSP.
Scores: 9 tests: Shape Detection Screening Test, Incomplete Letters, Silhouettes, Object Decision, Progressive Silhouettes, Dot Counting, Position Discrimination, Number Location, Cube Analysis.
Administration: Individual.
Price Data, 2006: £162 per complete kit including manual (20 pages), 25 scoring sheets, and 3 stimulus books; £39.50 per 50 scoring sheets.
Time: Untimed.
Comments: Tests may be administered separately, in groups, or as a complete battery.
Authors: Elizabeth K. Warrington and Merle James.
Publisher: Harcourt Assessment [England].

[2717]
Visual Patterns Test.

Purpose: Designed to measure "short term visual memory."
Population: Ages 18 and over.
Publication Date: 1997.
Acronym: VPT.
Score: Total score only.
Administration: Individual.
Forms: 2 parallel forms: A, B.
Price Data, 2006: £70 per complete kit including manual (12 pages), stimulus cards, and response sheet; £35 per 50 scoring sheets.
Time: [10] minutes.
Authors: Sergio Della Sala, Colin Gray, Alan Baddeley, and Lindsay Wilson.
Publisher: Harcourt Assessment [England].

[2718]
Visual Search and Attention Test.

Purpose: Constructed to "measure attentional processes commonly disrupted in acute and chronic brain damage or disease."
Population: Ages 18 and over.
Publication Dates: 1987–1990.
Acronym: VSAT.
Scores, 3: Left, Right, Total.
Administration: Individual.
Price Data, 2006: $156 per introductory kit including 50 test booklets and manual (1990, 18 pages).
Time: 6 minutes.
Authors: Max R. Trenerry, Bruce Crosson, James DeBoe, and William R. Leber.
Publisher: Psychological Assessment Resources, Inc.
Cross References: See T5:2820 (1 reference); for reviews by Stephen R. Hooper and Wilfred G. Van Gorp, see 12:407.

[2719]
Visual Skills Appraisal.

Purpose: "Developed to assist teachers and other educators, who may not have specialized training in

visual skills assessment, to identify visual inefficiencies that affect school performance."
Population: Grades K–4; ages 5 through 9.
Publication Date: 1984.
Acronym: VSA.
Scores: 6 subtests: Pursuits, Scanning, Aligning, Locating, Eye-Hand Coordination, Fixation Unity.
Administration: Individual.
Price Data, 2006: $85 per complete kit including manual (112 pages), stimulus cards, 25 design completion forms, 25 red/green trail forms, 25 score sheets, and red/green glasses; $12 per stimulus cards; $12 per 25 design completion forms, 25 red/green trail forms, or 25 score sheets; $10 per red/green glasses; $27 per manual.
Time: (10–15) minutes.
Comments: Criterion-referenced.
Authors: Regina G. Richards and Gary S. Oppenheim in consultation with G. N. Getman.
Publisher: Academic Therapy Publications.
Cross References: See 11:456 (1 reference).

[2720]
Voc-Tech Quick Screener.
Purpose: Designed to identify job interests.
Population: Non-college bound high school students and adults.
Publication Dates: 1984–1990.
Acronym: VTQS.
Scores, 14: Administrative Support/Clerical, Agriculture/Animals and Forestry, Construction Trades, Design/Graphics and Communication, Food/Beverage Services, Health Services, Health Technicians, Industrial Production Trades, Marketing/Sales, Mechanical/Craftsmanship Trades, Personal Services, Protective Services, Science/Engineering Technicians, Transportation/Equipment Operators.
Administration: Group.
Price Data: Available from publisher.
Time: (20–25) minutes.
Authors: Robert Kauk and Robert Robinett.
Publisher: CFKR Career Materials.
Cross References: For reviews by Albert M. Bugaj and Del Eberhardt, see 12:411.

[2721]
Vocabulary Test: National Achievement Tests.
Purpose: Measures the student's vocabulary and judgment in the choice of effective words.
Population: Grades 3–8, 7–12.
Publication Dates: 1939–1957.
Scores: Total score only.
Administration: Group.
Price Data: Available from publisher.
Time: (15) minutes.
Authors: Robert K. Speer and Samuel Smith.

Publisher: Psychometric Affiliates.
Cross References: For a review by Clifford Woody, see 3:168.

[2722]
Vocational Assessment and Curriculum Guide.
Purpose: "Designed to assess and identify skill deficits in terms of competitive employment expectations; to prescribe training goals designed to reduce identified deficits; to evaluate program effectiveness by reassessing the worker after training."
Population: Mentally retarded employees.
Publication Dates: 1982–2003.
Acronym: VACG.
Scores, 10: Attendance/Endurance, Independence, Production, Learning, Behavior, Communication Skills, Social Skills, Grooming/Eating, Reading/Writing, Math.
Administration: Group.
Price Data, 2002: $12 per complete kit including manual (5 pages), 10 test booklets, curriculum guides, and summary profile sheets; $8 per set of 10 extra forms.
Time: (15–20) minutes.
Authors: Frank R. Rusch, Richard P. Schutz, Dennis E. Mithaug, Jeffrey E. Stewart, and Deanna K. Mar.
Publisher: Exceptional Education.
Cross References: For reviews by Hinsdale Bernard and Gerald R. Schneck, see 13:356; see also T4:2898 (1 reference).

[2723]
Vocational Decision-Making Interview, Revised Edition.
Purpose: Designed to improve the vocational decision making of people with learning and other disabilities.
Population: People with learning and other disabilities, including vision impairments, limited academic skills, limited English-language proficiency, or with displaced workers and people in substance abuse programs.
Publication Dates: 1993–1999.
Acronym: VDMI.
Scores, 3: Decision-Making Readiness, Employment Readiness, Self-Appraisal.
Administration: Individual.
Price Data, 2006: $26.95 per 10 assessments; a Tips booklet included free with each 10 assessments; price information for administration manual available from publisher.
Time: (20–40) minutes.
Comments: Not self-administered or self-scored; six-panel foldout; consumable; no other components needed.
Authors: Thomas Czerlinsky and Shirley K. Chandler.
Publisher: JIST Publishing, Inc.
Cross References: For reviews by Karen T. Carey and Donald W. Tiffany of an earlier version, see 14:409.

[2724]
Vocational Interest, Experience and Skill Assessment (VIESA), 2nd Canadian Edition.

Purpose: Designed to stimulate career exploration.
Population: Grades 8-10, 11-adults.
Publication Dates: 1985–1992.
Acronym: VIESA, 2nd Canadian Edition.
Scores: Scores for Interests, Skills, and Experiences in 4 areas: People, Data, Things, Ideas.
Administration: Group or individual.
Levels, 2: 1 (grades 8-10), 2 (grade 11-adult).
Price Data, 2005: $68.50 per 25 guide books and job family charts (specify level); $36.60 per preview kit Level 1 & 2; $35.40 per user's handbook.
Time: (40-45) minutes.
Comments: Self-scored inventory of career-related interests, experiences, skills and values, with supporting materials for counselors; adapted from VIESA, U.S. Edition.
Author: ACT Career Planning Services.
Publisher: Nelson, A Thomson Company [Canada].
Cross References: For reviews by David J. Bateson and Brenda H. Loyd; see 12:409; for information for VIESA, 2nd Edition, see 9:1338; for a review by Charles J. Krauskopf of an earlier edition, see 8:1025.

[2725]
Vocational Interest Inventory and Exploration Survey (Voc-Ties).

Purpose: Designed to "assess a student's interest in school based training programs" and provide "information about the training area."
Population: Vocational education students.
Publication Dates: 1991–2000.
Scores: 15 vocational training interest areas: Auto Mechanics, Business and Office, Construction, Cosmetology, Drafting, Electromechanics, Electronics, Family and Consumer Science, Food Service, Graphic Arts, Health Services, Horticulture/Agriculture, Marketing, Metals, Technology Education.
Home Economics, Technology Education.
Administration: Individual or group.
Price Data, 2002: $595 per media kit including guide, video cassette, software, and answer sheets; $195 per single station version; $495 per multi-station version; $995 per Network version.
Time: (15-20) minutes.
Authors: Nancy L. Scott and Charles Gilbreath.
Publisher: Piney Mountain Press, Inc.
Cross References: For reviews by Larry Cochran and Kevin R. Murphy of an earlier edition, see 12:408.

[2726]
Vocational Interest Survey for Australia.

Purpose: Designed to "assist Australians facing career decisions by providing an assessment of their vocational interests."
Population: Job applicants.
Publication Dates: 1989–1995.
Acronym: VISA.
Scores, 8: Caring, Culture, Service, Managing, Clerical, Science, Practical, Environmental.
Administration: Group or individual.
Price Data, 2006: A$173.05 per complete test.
Time: 20 minutes.
Author: Robert Pryor.
Publisher: Harcourt Assessment Australia and New Zealand [Australia].
Cross References: For reviews by Eugene V. Aidman and Neroli Sawyer and by Robert Fitzpatrick, see 15:273.

[2727]
Vocational Opinion Index.

Purpose: Constructed to measure "an individual's attitudes, perceptions and motivations that impact on his/her ability to get and/or hold a job."
Population: Disadvantaged trainees in vocational skills programs.
Publication Dates: 1973-1976.
Acronym: VOI.
Scores, 13: Attractions to Work (Overall, Benefits to Children, Benefits to Worker, Better Life Style, Independence), Losses Associated with Work (Overall, Personal Freedom, Time for Family), Barriers to Employment (Medical, Child Care and Family, New Situation and People, Ability to Get and Hold a Job, Transportation).
Administration: Group.
Forms, 2: A, B.
Price Data: Available from publisher.
Foreign Language Edition: Spanish edition available.
Time: (20-40) minutes.
Author: Associates for Research in Behavior, Inc.
Publisher: ARBOR, Inc.

[2728]
Vocational Preference Inventory, 1985 Edition.

Purpose: Designed to "assess career interests."
Population: High school and college and adults.
Publication Dates: 1953–1985.
Acronym: VPI.
Scores: 11 scales: Realistic, Investigative, Social, Conventional, Enterprising, Artistic, Self-Control, Masculinity-Femininity, Status, Infrequency, Acquiescence.
Administration: Individual or group.
Price Data, 2006: $99 per introductory kit including 50 test booklet/answer sheet/profile combinations and manual (1985, 36 pages).
Time: (15–30) minutes.
Author: John L. Holland.

Publisher: Psychological Assessment Resources, Inc.
Cross References: See T5:2835 (28 references) and T4:2910 (9 references); for reviews by John W. Shepard and Nicholas A. Vacc, see 10:382 (17 references); for reviews by James B. Rounds and by Nicholas A. Vacc and James Pickering of an earlier edition, see 9:1342 (19 references); see also T3:2581 (45 references); for an excerpted review by W. Bruce Walsh of an earlier edition, see 8:1028 (175 references); see also T2:1430 (48 references); for reviews by Joseph A. Johnston and Paul R. Lohnes, see 7:157 (39 references); see also P:283 (31 references); for reviews by Robert L. French and H. Bradley Sagen of an earlier edition, see 6:115 (13 references).

[2729]
A Voice Assessment Protocol For Children and Adults.
Purpose: "Assesses five parameters of the voice: pitch, loudness, quality, breath features, and rate/rhythm."
Population: Children and adults.
Publication Date: 1987.
Scores: 5 assessments: Pitch, Loudness, Quality, Breath Features, Rate/Rhythm.
Administration: Individual.
Price Data, 2006: $75 per complete kit including 25 protocols, audiocassette, and manual (24 pages); $35 per 25 protocols; $15 per audiocassette; $30 per manual.
Time: Administration time not reported.
Author: Rebekah H. Pindzola.
Publisher: PRO-ED.
Cross References: See T5:2837 (1 reference); for a review by Maynard D. Filter, see 11:459.

[2730]
Vulpe Assessment Battery—Revised.
Purpose: Designed as "a comprehensive, process-oriented, criterion-referenced assessment that emphasizes children's functional abilities."
Population: Children functioning between full term birth to six years of age.
Publication Date: 1994.
Acronym: VAB-R.
Scores: 8 scales: Basic Senses and Functions, Gross Motor, Fine Motor, Language, Cognitive Processes and Specific Concepts, Adaptive Behaviors, Activities of Daily Living, Environmental Assessment.
Administration: Individual or group.
Price Data, 2002: $109 per complete kit including manual (1994, 480 pages) and 50 record sheets; $21 per 50 record sheets.
Time: Administration time not reported.
Comments: Ratings by person familiar with the child.
Author: Shirley German Vulpe.
Publisher: Slosson Educational Publications, Inc.

Cross References: For reviews by Theresa Graham and Diane J. Sawyer, see 14:411.

[2731]
W-APT Programming Aptitude Test.
Purpose: To evaluate the aptitude and potential for computer programming work at all levels of experience.
Population: Programmers and general population.
Publication Date: 1984.
Acronym: W-APT.
Scores: Total score only.
Administration: Group.
Price Data, 2001: $190 per candidate.
Time: (60) minutes.
Comments: Detailed report provided on each candidate.
Author: Jack M. Wolfe.
Publisher: Rose Wolfe Family Partnership LLP [Canada].

[2732]
Wagner Enneagram Personality Style Scales.
Purpose: Designed "to measure the nine personality styles described by Enneagram."
Population: Ages 18 years and over.
Publication Date: 1999.
Acronym: WEKPSS.
Scores: 9 scales: The Good Person, The Loving Person, The Effective Person, The Original Person, The Wise Person, The Loyal Person, The Joyful Person, The Powerful Person, The Peaceful Person.
Administration: Group or individual.
Price Data, 2006: $154 per kit including 25 autoscore forms, manual (114 pages), 100 glossary sheets, 100 brief guides to WEPSS results, ; $54.50 per 25 answer forms; $60.50 per manual; $21.50 per glossary sheet; $21.50 per brief guide to WEPSS results; $16.50 per mail-in answer form; $280 per 25-use PC scoring disk; $16.50 per 100 PC answer sheets; $10.50 per FAX service.
Time: (20–40) minutes.
Comments: Paper-and-pencil or computer administration available.
Author: Jerome P. Wagner.
Publisher: Western Psychological Services
Cross References: For reviews by Frank M. Bernt and Johnnie A. Brown, see 15:274.

[2733]
WAIS-R NI.
Purpose: Constructed as a "process approach to neuropsychological assessment of cognitive functions."
Population: Ages 16–74.
Publication Date: 1991.
Scores, 14: Verbal (Information, Comprehension, Arithmetic, Similarities, Digit Span, Vocabulary, Total), Performance (Digit Symbol, Picture Completion,

Block Design, Picture Arrangement, Object Assembly, Total), Total.
Administration: Individual.
Price Data, 2002: $541 per complete kit including manual (153 pages), stimulus booklet, sentence arrangement booklet, 25 response booklets, 25 record forms, 3 puzzles/boxes, spatial span board, object assembly layout shield, and 3 Koh's blocks; $1,155 per combination kit including WAIS-R NI complete kit, WAIS-R complete set and attaché case; $31 per 25 digit symbol response booklets; $110 per 25 record forms.
Time: Administration time varies by number of supplemental subtests administered.
Comments: It is necessary to have the Wechsler Adult Intelligence Scale—Revised (WAIS-R; T4:2937) complete set in order to administer WAIS-R NI.
Authors: Edith Kaplan, Deborah Fein, Robin Morris, and Dean C. Delis.
Publisher: PsychCorp, A brand of Harcourt Assessment, Inc.
Cross References: For reviews by Keith Hattrup and David C. S. Richard, see 14:412.

[2734]
Waksman Social Skills Rating Scale.
Purpose: "Developed to assist psychologists, educators, and other clinicians to identify specific and clinically important social skill deficits in children and adolescents."
Population: Grades K-12.
Publication Dates: 1983-1992.
Acronym: WSSRS.
Scores, 3: Aggressive, Passive, Total.
Administration: Individual.
Price Data, 2001: $45 per complete kit including 50 each of male and female forms, and manual (1992, 10 pages); 420 per 25 male or female forms.
Time: 10 minutes.
Author: Steven A. Waksman.
Publisher: Enrichment Press.
Cross References: See T5:2841 (1 reference) and T4:2915 (2 references); for reviews by Harold R. Keller and Ellen McGinnis, see 10:383.

[2735]
Walden Structured Analysis and Design Concepts Proficiency Test.
Purpose: "Evaluates candidate's knowledge of structured analysis and design methodology, as well as commonly used tools and techniques."
Population: Candidates for EDP systems analysts/designers.
Publication Date: 1983.
Scores: Total Score, Narrative Evaluation, Ranking, Recommendation.
Administration: Group.

Price Data, 2001: $140 per candidate.
Time: (45) minutes.
Comments: Scored by publisher; must be proctored; test previously listed as Wolfe-Winrow Structured Analysis and Design Concepts Proficiency Test.
Author: Bruce A. Winrow.
Publisher: Walden Personnel Performance, Inc. [Canada].
Cross References: For reviews by David O. Anderson and Cynthia Ann Druva-Roush, see 11:474.

[2736]
Ward Atmosphere Scale [Third Edition].
Purpose: Designed to evaluate treatment program social climates in health care settings.
Population: Patients and staff members.
Publication Dates: 1974–1996.
Acronym: WAS.
Scores, 10: Involvement, Support, Spontaneity, Autonomy, Practical Orientation, Personal Problems Orientation, Anger and Aggression, Order and Organization, Program Clarity, Staff Control.
Administration: Group.
Forms, 3: Real, Ideal, Expectations.
Price Data: Available from publisher (www.mindgarden.com).
Foreign Language Editions: Translations available in Danish, Dutch, Finnish, French, German, Hebrew, Italian, Norwegian, Spanish, and Swedish.
Time: Administration time not reported.
Comments: Used to describe, plan for, and monitor change or improvements in treatment programs by examining patient and staff social climate perceptions.
Author: Rudolph H. Moos.
Publisher: Mind Garden, Inc.
Cross References: For reviews by Ronald A. Berk and Mary Anne Bunda, see 14:413; see also T5:2850 (3 references), T4:2925 (17 references), and T3:2587 (16 references); for a review by Earl S. Taulbee of an earlier edition, see 8:706 (31 references). For a review of the Social Climate Scales, see 8:681.

[2737]
Warehouse/Plant Worker Staff Selector.
Purpose: To assess the intellectual skills needed for the position of plant worker.
Population: Applicants for plant work.
Publication Date: 1991.
Acronym: PLANT.
Scores: Total Score, Narrative Evaluation, Ranking, Recommendation.
Administration: Group.
Price Data, 2001: $95 per candidate; quantity discounts available.
Time: (60) minutes.
Comments: Scored by publisher.

Author: Walden Personnel Performance, Inc.
Publisher: Walden Personnel Performance, Inc. [Canada].

[2738]
Washer Visual Acuity Screening Technique.
Purpose: To assess visual acuity for near and far vision in very young children and mentally challenged or low functioning individuals.
Population: Mental ages 2.5-adult.
Publication Date: 1984.
Acronym: WVAST.
Scores, 6: Farpoint (Both Eyes, Right Eye, Left Eye), Nearpoint (Both Eyes, Right Eye, Left Eye).
Administration: Individual.
Price Data, 2006: $87.85 per starter set including manual (15 pages), 20 screening records, symbol cards, stimulus cards, and set of equipment; $14.70 per additional manual; $11.70 per 20 screening records; $76.90 per additional set of equipment; $22 per sample set.
Time: Administration time not reported.
Comments: Criterion-referenced scores.
Author: Rhonda Wiczer Washer.
Publisher: Scholastic Testing Service, Inc.

[2739]
The Watkins-Farnum Performance Scale: A Standardized Achievement Test for All Band Instruments.
Purpose: Designed to measure performance and progress on a musical instrument.
Population: Music students.
Publication Dates: 1942–1962.
Scores: Total score only.
Administration: Individual.
Forms, 2: A, B.
Price Data: Available from publisher.
Time: [20-30] minutes.
Authors: John G. Watkins and Stephen E. Farnum.
Publisher: Hal Leonard Publishing Corporation [No reply from publisher; status unknown].
Cross References: See T2:216 (4 references); for a review by Herbert D. Wing, see 5:253 (2 references); for related reviews, see 3:1228 (4 excerpts).

[2740]
Watson-Barker Listening Test.
Purpose: To measure adult interpersonal listening abilities.
Population: Adults in business, professions, and college.
Publication Dates: 1984–1994.
Scores, 6: Evaluating Message Content, Understanding Meaning in Conversations, Understanding and Remembering Information in Lectures, Evaluating

Emotional Meanings in Messages, Following Instructions and Directions, Total.
Administration: Group.
Forms, 3: A (pre-test), B (post-test), Short Form (for demonstration and listening awareness).
Price Data: Available from publisher.
Time: (40) minutes.
Comments: Administered by video tape.
Authors: Kittie W. Watson and Larry L. Barker with Charles Roberts and Patrice Johnson.
Publisher: Jossey-Bass, A Wiley Company.
Cross References: For a review by James R. Clopton, see 10:384.

[2741]
Watson-Barker Listening Test—High School Version.
Purpose: "Designed to assess overall listening ability."
Population: Grades 7–12.
Publication Dates: 1985–1991.
Acronym: HS-WBLT.
Scores, 6: Evaluating Message Content, Understanding Meaning in Conversations, Understanding and Remembering Information in Lectures, Evaluating Emotional Meanings in Messages, Following Instructions and Directions, Total.
Administration: Group.
Forms, 2: A (pre-test) and B (post-test).
Price Data: Price information available from publisher for Form A and B package (including video tape, facilitator's guide [1991, 42 pages], and 20 answer sheets per group [A & B]).
Time: 40 minutes.
Comments: May be self-scored for awareness training; VHS video tape player and 17-inch (minimum size) color TV monitor needed; high school version of Watson-Barker Listening Test (2740).
Authors: Kittie W. Watson, Larry L. Barker, and Charles V. Roberts.
Publisher: SPECTRA Incorporated, Publishers.
Cross References: For reviews by Michael R. Harwell and by Carol Kehr Tittle and Deborah Hecht, see 11:461; for reviews by James R. Clopton and Joseph P. Stokes of the adult version, see 10:384.

[2742]
Watson-Glaser Critical Thinking Appraisal.
Purpose: Constructed to assess critical thinking abilities related to reading comprehension.
Population: Grades 9-12 and college and adults.
Publication Dates: 1942-1980.
Acronym: WGCTA.
Scores, 6: Inference, Recognition of Assumptions, Deduction, Interpretation, Evaluation of Arguments, Total.
Administration: Group or individual.

Forms, 2: A, B.
Price Data, 2006: $195 per starter kit including 10 test booklets, 25 answer documents, score key, and manual; $115 per set of 10 test booklets; $175 per set of 25 test booklets; $65 per 25 answer documents; $35 per hand scoring key; $45 per manual.
Time: (40–60) minutes.
Comments: Revision of Form YM and ZM.
Authors: Goodwin Watson and Edward M. Glaser.
Publisher: Harcourt Assessment, Inc.
Cross References: See T5:2856 (13 references) and T4:2933 (5 references); for reviews by Allen Berger and Gerald C. Helmstadter, see 9:1347 (4 references); see also T3:2594 (15 references), 8:822 (49 references), and T2:1775 (35 references); for excerpted reviews by John O. Crites and G. C. Helmstadtler, see 7:783 (74 references); see also 6:867 (24 references); for reviews by Walker H. Hill and Carl I. Hovland of an earlier edition, see 5:700 (8 references); for a review by Robert H. Thouless and an excerpted review by Harold P. Fawcett, see 3:544 (3 references).

[2743]
Watson-Glaser Critical Thinking Appraisal, Short Form.

Purpose: Designed to help "select employees for any job requiring careful, analytical thinking."
Population: Adults with at least a ninth grade education.
Publication Date: 1994.
Acronym: WGCTA-S.
Scores: Composite score derived from following content areas: Inference, Recognition of Assumptions, Deduction, Interpretation, Evaluation of Arguments.
Administration: Group or individual.
Price Data, 2006: $175 per starter kit including 10 test booklets, 25 answer document, scoring key, and manual (87 pages); $95 per 10 test booklets; $145 per 25 test booklets; $60 per 25 answer documents; $35 key for hand scoring key; $45 per manual; also available for online administration.
Time: (30–45) minutes.
Comments: Developed as a shorter version of the WGCTA Form A; Form S norms are developed from norms of original WGCTA (2742).
Authors: Goodwin B. Watson and Edward M. Glaser.
Publisher: Harcourt Assessment, Inc.
Cross References: See T5:2857 (1 reference); for reviews by Kurt F. Geisinger and Stephen H. Ivens, see 13:358. For information on the original edition of the WGCTA, see T4:2933; for reviews by Allen Berger and Gerald C. Helmstadter, see 9:1347 (4 references); see also T3:2594 (15 references), 8:822 (49 references), and T2:1775 (35 references); for excerpted reviews by John O. Crites and G. C. Helmstadtler, see 7:783 (74 references); see also 6:867 (24 references); for reviews by Walker H. Hill and Carl I. Hovland of an earlier edition, see 5:700 (8 references); for a review by Robert H. Thouless and an excerpted review by Harold P. Fawcett, see 3:544 (3 references).

[2744]
Ways of Coping Questionnaire.

Purpose: "To identify the thoughts and actions an individual has used to cope with a specific stressful encounter."
Population: Adults.
Publication Date: 1988.
Scores, 8: Confrontive Coping, Distancing, Self-Controlling, Seeking Social Support, Accepting Responsibility, Escape-Avoidance, Planful Problem-Solving, Positive Reappraisal.
Administration: Group.
Price Data: Available from publisher (www.mindgarden.com).
Time: (10-15) minutes.
Comments: Self-administered.
Authors: Susan Folkman and Richard S. Lazarus.
Publisher: Mind Garden, Inc.
Cross References: See T5:2858 (129 references) and T4:2936 (25 references); for reviews by Judith C. Conger and Kathryn D. Hess, see 11:462 (16 references).

[2745]
Wechsler Abbreviated Scale of Intelligence.

Purpose: Designed as a "short and reliable measure of intelligence"; serves as a quick measure of an individual's verbal, nonverbal, and general cognitive functioning in any setting.
Population: Ages 6–89.
Publication Date: 1999.
Administration: Individual.
Price Data, 2006: $250 per complete kit; $62 per 25 record forms; $235 per 100 record forms; $130 per stimulus book; $130 per manual (238 pages).
Author: The Psychological Corporation.
Publisher: PsychCorp, A brand of Harcourt Assessment, Inc.
   a) TWO SUBTEST FORM.
   Scores, 3: Verbal (Vocabulary), Performance (Matrix Reasoning), Full Scale IQ.
   Time: (15) minutes.
   b) FOUR SUBTEST FORM.
   Scores, 7: Verbal (Vocabulary, Similarities), Performance (Block Design, Matrix Reasoning), Verbal IQ, Performance IQ, Full Scale IQ.
   Time: (30) minutes.
Cross References: For reviews by Timothy Z. Keith and by Cederick O. Lindskog and Janet V. Smith, see 14:414.

[2746]
Wechsler Adult Intelligence Scale—Third Edition.

Purpose: Designed to assess the intellectual ability of adults.
Population: Ages 16–89.
Publication Dates: 1939–1997.
Acronym: WAIS-III.
Scores, 22: Verbal (Vocabulary, Similarities, Arithmetic, Digit Span, Information, Comprehension, Letter-Number Sequencing [supplementary], Total), Performance (Picture Completion, Digit Symbol, Block Design, Matrix Reasoning, Picture Arrangement, Symbol Search [supplementary], Object Assembly [optional], Total), Verbal Comprehension Index, Perceptual Organization Index, Working Memory Index, Processing Speed Index, Full Scale IQ.
Administration: Individual.
Price Data, 2006: $925 per complete set in attaché or soft case; $875 per complete set in box; $62 per 25 response books; $235 per 100 response books; $99 per 25 record forms; $365 per 100 record forms; $130 per administration and scoring manual (1997, 217 pages); $85 per technical manual (1997, 370 pages).
Time: (60–90) minutes for VIQ, PIQ, & FSIQ scores. (65-95) minutes for IQ and Index Scores.
Author: David Wechsler.
Publisher: PsychCorp, A brand of Harcourt Assessment, Inc.
Cross References: For reviews by Allen K. Hess and Bruce G. Rogers, see 14:415; see also T5:2860 (1422 references) and T4:2937 (1131 references); for reviews by Alan S. Kaufman and Joseph D. Matarazzo of the revised edition, see 9:1348 (291 references); see also T3:2598 (576 references), 8:230 (351 references), and T2:529 (178 references); for reviews by Alvin G. Burstein and Howard B. Lyman of the original edition, see 7:429 (538 references); see also 6:538 (180 references); for reviews by Nancy Bayley and Wilson H. Guertin, see 5:414 (42 references).

[2747]
Wechsler Individual Achievement Test—Second Edition.

Purpose: "A ... measurement tool useful for achievement skills assessment, learning disability diagnosis, special education placement, curriculum planning, and clinical appraisal for preschool children through adults."
Population: Ages 4–85 years.
Publication Dates: 1992–2001.
Acronym: WIAT-II.
Scores, 21: 9 subtests (Word Reading, Pseudoword Decoding, Reading Comprehension, Math Reasoning, Numerical Operations, Listening Comprehension, Oral Expression, Spelling, Written Expression), 4 composite scores (Reading Composite, Written Language Composite, Mathematics Composite, Oral Language Composite), Total Composite, 7 supplemental scores: Reading (Reading Comprehension, Target Words, Reading Speed), Written Expression (Alphabet Writing, Word Fluency, Word Count), Oral Expression (Word Fluency).
Administration: Individual.
Price Data, 2002: $321 per complete kit including stimulus book 1, stimulus book 2, 25 record forms, 25 response booklets, examiner's manual (2001, 193 pages), Scoring and Normative supplement for Grades PreK–12, Scoring and Normative Supplement for College Students and Adults, word cards, audiotape, and bag; $59 per 25 combination record forms/response booklets; $86 per stimulus book 1 or 2; $11 per word card, pseudoword card, and audiotape; $96 per examiner's manual, Scoring and Normative Supplement for Grades PreK–12, and Scoring and Normative Supplement for College Students and Adults; $50 per administration training video (CD-ROM Windows or Videotape); $125 per WIAT-II Scoring Assistant (CD-ROM Windows); $150 per WISC-III/WIAT-II Scoring Assistant (CD-ROM Windows or Macintosh); $150 per WAIS-III/WMS-III/WIAT-11 Scoring Assistant (CD-ROM Windows); $399 per WIAT-II Kit with WIAT-II Scoring Assistant (CD-ROM Windows); $449 per WIAT-II Kit with WISC-III/WIAT-II Scoring Assistant (CD-ROM Windows); $449 per WIAT-II Kit with WAIS-III/WMS-III/WIAT-II Scoring Assistant (CD-ROM Windows); $398 per WISC-III/WIAT-II Writer or WAIS-III/WMS-III/WIAT-II Writer (CD-ROM Windows); all software also available in 3.5-inch diskettes.
Time: Comprehensive Battery: (45) minutes for Grades PreK–K; (90) minutes for Grades 1–6; (90–120) minutes for Grades 7–16.
Comments: Subtests may be given individually; includes norms for 2-year and 4-year college students; standardized with Wechsler Intelligence Scale for Children-III, Wechsler Preschool and Primary Scale of Intelligence—Revised, Wechsler Adult Intelligence Scale—Third Edition, and the Process Assessment of the Learner: Test Battery for Reading and Writing; complete battery is composed of fewer tests for Grades PreK and K; manual or computer scoring; 3 software scoring programs available; WIAT-II Scoring Assistant software generates standard scores and error analyses using raw scores; WISC-III/WIAT-II Scoring Assistant (revision of the Scoring Assistant for the Wechsler Scales) includes all capabilities of WIAT-II Scoring Assistant and computes ability-achievement discrepancy analysis using the WISC-III; WAIS-III/WMS-III/WIAT-II Scoring Assistant software (revision of the Scoring Assistant for the Wechsler Scales for Adults) includes all capabilities of WIAT-II Scoring Assistant, computes ability-achievement discrep-

ancy analysis using the WAIS-III, and generates reports; WISC-III/WIAT-II Writer software (revision of the WISC-III Writer) summarizes results, displays results in tabular and graphic formats, generates interpretive report; WAIS-III/WMS-III/WIAT-II Writer software scores and interprets results; system requirements for all software: Windows 95/98/2000/ME/NT 4.0 Workstation, 100 MHz Pentium processor, 32 MB RAM, 2 MB video card capable of 800 x 600 resolution (256 colors), 20 MB free hard disk space, 3.5-inch floppy drive, 50 MB temporary disk space; WIAT-II PDA Pocket Norms software available, system requirements Palm OS Personal Digital Assistant.

Author: The Psychological Corporation.

Publisher: PsychCorp, A brand of Harcourt Assessment, Inc.

Cross References: For reviews by Beth J. Doll and by Gerald Tindal and Michelle Nutter, see 15:275; see T5:2861 (4 references); for reviews by Terry Ackerman and Steven Ferrara of a previous edition, see 13:359 (17 references).

[2748]
Wechsler Individual Achievement Test— Second Edition Abbreviated.

Purpose: "Identif[ies] and track[s] basic academic skills and intervention needs in children and adults."

Population: Grades K–16; ages 6–85 years.

Publication Date: 2001.

Acronym: WIAT-II-A.

Scores, 4: 3 subtests (Word Reading, Numerical Operations, Spelling), Composite Score.

Administration: Individual.

Price Data, 2003: $130 per test kit including manual (206 pages), combination record forms/response booklets, 2 word cards, and bag; $55 per manual; $48 per 25 combination record forms/response booklets; $15 per set of 2 word cards.

Time: (15–25) minutes.

Comments: Subtests are taken from the WIAT-II (2747); can be used with Wechsler Abbreviated Scale of Intelligence (2745) for a brief cognitive and achievement battery.

Author: The Psychological Corporation.

Publisher: PsychCorp, A brand of Harcourt Assessment, Inc.

Cross References: For a review by Kathleen M. Johnson, see 15:276.

[2749]
Wechsler Intelligence Scale for Children— Fourth Edition.

Purpose: Designed to assess "the cognitive ability of children"; provides four index scores that reflect different abilities, important in the expression of intelligent behavior in the classroom and beyond.

Population: Ages 6-0 to 16-11.

Publication Dates: 1971–2003.

Acronym: WISC-IV.

Scores, 15 to 20: Verbal Comprehension (Similarities, Vocabulary, Comprehension, Information [supplemental], Word Reasoning [supplemental], Total), Perceptual Reasoning (Block Design, Picture Concepts, Matrix Reasoning, Picture Completion [supplemental], Total), Working Memory (Digit Span, Letter-Number Sequencing, Arithmetic [supplemental], Total), Processing Speed (Coding, Symbol Search, Cancellation [supplemental], Total), Full Scale IQ.

Administration: Individual.

Price Data, 2006: $925 per Basic Kit in hard or soft case including administration manual (2003, 282 pages), technical manual, stimulus book #1, 25 record forms, 25 response booklet #1, 25 response booklet #2, block design set, symbol search scoring key, coding scoring key with coding recall [for use with both WISC-IV and WISC-IV Integrated], and cancellation scoring templates; $875 per Basic Kit in box; $1049 per Basic Kit with Scoring Assistant in box; $1099 per Basic Kit with Scoring Assistant in hard or soft case; $1,249 per Basic Kit with Writer in soft case; $99 per 25 record forms; $62 per 25 response booklet #1, $62 per 25 response booklet #2; $365 per 100 record forms; $235 per 100 response booklet #1; $235 per 100 response booklet #2; $210 per scoring assistant; $425 per writer; $250 per scoring assistant upgrade to writer.

Time: Core subtests (65–80) minutes; Supplemental: (10–15) minutes.

Author: David Wechsler.

Publisher: PsychCorp, A brand of Harcourt Assessment, Inc.

Cross References: For reviews by Susan J. Maller and Bruce Thompson, see 16:262; see also T5:2862 (740 references); for reviews by Jeffrey P. Braden and Jonathan Sandoval of an earlier edition, see 12:412 (409 references); see also T4:2939 (911 references); for reviews by Morton Bortner, Douglas K. Detterman, and by Joseph C. Witt and Frank Gresham of an earlier edition, see 9:1351 (299 references); see also T3:2602 (645 references); for reviews by David Freides and Randolph H. Whitworth, and excerpted reviews by Carol Kehr Tittle and Joseph Petrosko, see 8:232 (548 references); see also T2:533 (230 references); for reviews by David Freides and R. T. Osborne of the original edition, see 7:431 (518 references); for a review by Alvin G. Burnstein, see 6:540 (155 references); for reviews by Elizabeth D. Fraser, Gerald R. Patterson, and Albert I. Rabin, see 5:416 (111 references); for reviews by James M. Anderson, Harold A. Delp, and Boyd R. McCandless, and an excerpted review by Laurance F. Shaffer, see 4:363 (22 references).

[2750]
Wechsler Intelligence Scale for Children—Fourth Edition Integrated.

Purpose: "Designed to assess the cognitive ability and problem-solving process of children"; provides a comprehensive measure of learning strengths and difficulties.

Population: Ages 6-0 to 16-11.

Publication Dates: 1971–2004.

Scores, 47: Verbal Comprehension Scale (Similarities, Vocabulary, Comprehension, Information [supplemental], Word Reasoning [supplemental], Index), Perceptual Reasoning Scale (Block Design, Picture Concepts, Matrix Reasoning, Picture Completion [supplemental], Index), Working Memory Scale (Digit Span, Letter-Number Sequencing, Arithmetic [supplemental], Index), Processing Speed Scale (Coding, Symbol Search, Cancellation [supplemental], Index), Full Scale IQ, Process Subtests (Similarities Multiple Choice, Vocabulary Multiple Choice, Picture Vocabulary Multiple Choice, Comprehension Multiple Choice, Information Multiple Choice, Block Design No Time Bonus, Block Design Multiple Choice, Block Design Multiple Choice No Time Bonus, Block Design Process Approach, Elithorn Mazes, Elithorn Mazes No Time Bonus, Digit Span Forward, Digit Span Backward, Visual Digit Span, Spatial Span Forward, Spatial Span Backward, Letter Span Nonrhyming, Letter Span Rhyming, Letter-Number Sequencing Process Approach, Arithmetic With Time Bonus, Arithmetic Process Approach-Part A, Arithmetic Process Approach-Part A With Time Bonus, Arithmetic Process Approach-Part B, Written Arithmetic, Cancellation Random, Cancellation Structured, Coding Recall, Coding Copy).

Administration: Individual.

Price Data, 2006: $1099 per complete basic kit in hard or rolling case including administration and scoring manual (2004, 487 pages), technical and interpretive manual (2004, 343 pages), WISC-IV stimulus booklet 1, WISC-IV Integrated stimulus booklets 2 and 3, block design set, 25 WISC-IV record forms, 10 WISC-IV Integrated record forms, 25 WISC-IV response booklet 1, 25 WISC-IV response booklet 2, 10 WISC-IV Integrated response booklet 3, Block Design Process Approach Grid Overlays, Visual Digit Span Card and Sleeve, Spatial Span Board, Symbol Search scoring key, Coding Scoring Key with Coding Recall, and Cancellation Scoring templates; $160 per integrated administration and scoring manual; $160 per technical and interpretive manual; $55 per 10 record forms; $37 per 10 response booklets 3; $499 per integrated writer; $299 per integrated scoring assistant software.

Time: (65–80) minutes for the 10 core subtests; additional time required for supplemental subtests; time for Process subtests varies by number of subtests administered.

Comments: Combination of the Wechsler Intelligence Scale for Children—Fourth Edition (2749) and the Wechsler Intelligence Scale for Children—Third Edition as a Process Instrument; guidelines are provided for administering test to children who are deaf or hard of hearing.

Authors: David Wechsler, Edith Kaplan, Deborah Fein, Joel Kramer, Robin Morris, Dean Delis, and Arthur Maelender.

Publisher: PsychCorp, A brand of Harcourt Assessment, Inc.

Cross References: For reviews by Susan J. Maller and Bruce Thompson of the WISC-IV, see 16:262; see also T5:2862 (740 references); for reviews by Jeffrey P. Braden and Jonathan Sandoval of an earlier edition, see 12:412 (409 references); see also T4:2939 (911 references); for reviews by Morton Bortner, Douglas K. Detterman, and by Joseph C. Witt and Frank Gresham of an earlier edition, see 9:1351 (299 references); see also T3:2602 (645 references); for reviews by David Freides and Randolph H. Whitworth, and excerpted reviews by Carol Kehr Tittle and Joseph Petrosko, see 8:232 (548 references); see also T2:533 (230 references); for reviews by David Freides and R. T. Osborne of the original edition, see 7:431 (518 references); for a review by Alvin G. Burnstein, see 6:540 (155 references); for reviews by Elizabeth D. Fraser, Gerald R. Patterson, and Albert I. Rabin, see 5:416 (111 references); for reviews by James M. Anderson, Harold A. Delp, and Boyd R. McCandless, and an an excerpted review by Laurance F. Shaffer, see 4:363 (22 references).

[2751]
Wechsler Memory Scale–Third Edition.

Purpose: Designed to "provide a detailed assessment of clinically relevant aspects of memory functioning" including measures of immediate and delayed memory, auditory and visual memory, learning, and working memory.

Population: Ages 16–89 years.

Publication Dates: 1945–1997.

Acronym: WMS-III.

Scores: 11 subtests: 6 primary (Logical Memory I and II, Verbal Paired Associates I and II, Letter-Number Sequencing, Faces I and II, Family Pictures I and II, Spatial Span); and 5 optional (Information and Orientation, Word Lists I and II, Mental Control, Digit Span, Visual Reproduction I and II); Primary and Optional Subtests combined yield 12 primary subtest scores, 27 supplemental subtest scores, and 2 optional subtest scores; Index/Composite scores: 8 primary index scores, 4 supplementary auditory processing composites.

Administration: Individual.
Price Data, 2006: $549 per complete kit including administration/norms manual, technical manual, 25 record forms, 25 visual reproduction response booklets, stimulus booklet 1, stimulus booklet 2, and spatial span board; $62 per 25 record forms; $235 per 100 record forms; $37 per 25 visual reproduction response booklets; $125 per 100 visual reproduction response booklets; $85 per WAIS-III/WMS-III technical manual update (2002 update, 1997 normative data); $115 per WAIS-III/WMS-III training video; $235 per WAIS-III/WMS-III/WIAT-II scoring assistant software (CD-ROM windows); $425 per WAIS-III/WMS-III/WIAT-II writer.
Time: (30–35) minutes for primary subtests.
Comments: "When used in conjunction with the WAIS-III, it is possible to compute ability-memory difference scores"; WAIS-III/WMS-III Writer interpretive report software available for use with IBM or compatible PC with at least 486 processor.
Author: David Wechsler.
Publisher: PsychCorp, A brand of Harcourt Assessment, Inc.
Cross References: For reviews by Rik Carl D'Amato and Cecil R. Reynolds, see 14:416; see also T5:2863 (431 references) and T4:2940 (117 references); for reviews by E. Scott Huebner and Robert C. Reinehr of an earlier edition, see 11:465 (166 references); see also 9:1355 (49 references); T3:2607 (96 references); 8:250 (36 references), T2:592 (70 references), and 6:561 (9 references); for reviews by Ivan Norma Mensh and Joseph Newman of the original version, see 4:364 (6 references); for a review by Kate Levine Kogan, see 3:302 (3 references).

[2752]
Wechsler Memory Scale—Third Edition Abbreviated.

Purpose: Designed to quickly assess adult memory function; to survey auditory and visual immediate and delayed memory; provides an estimate of general memory functioning when extended memory testing is not indicated or feasible.
Population: Ages 16–89.
Publication Dates: 1997–2003.
Acronym: WMS-III Abbreviated.
Scores, 11: Total Memory Composite, Delayed Memory Composite, Immediate Memory Composite, Logical Memory I, Family Pictures I, Logical Memory II, Family Pictures II, Logical Memory I—Family Pictures I, Logical Memory II—Family Pictures II, Immediate Memory Composite—Delayed Memory Composite, Predicted WMS-III General Memory Index Score.
Administration: Individual.
Price Data, 2006: $178 per complete kit including technical manual (2002, 207 pages), stimulus book, and

25 record forms; $43 per 25 record forms; $87 per stimulus book.
Time: 15–20 minutes.
Comments: Abbreviated adaptation of the Wechsler Memory Scale—Third Edition (T6:2695); provides statistics for comparing Total Memory with WAIS-III (IQ) and Serial Assessment.
Author: David Wechsler.
Publisher: PsychCorp, A brand of Harcourt Assessment, Inc.
Cross References: For reviews by Ronald K. Hambleton and by Joyce Meikamp and Carolyn H. Suppa, see 16:263.

[2753]
Wechsler Objective Language Dimensions.

Purpose: Designed to assess language skills.
Population: Ages 6 years to 16 years, 11 months.
Publication Date: 1996.
Acronym: WOLD.
Scores, 4: Listening Comprehension, Oral Expression, Written Expression, Total Composite Score.
Administration: Individual.
Price Data, 2006: £150.50 per complete kit including manual (209 pages), stimulus booklet, and 50 record forms; £52 per 50 record forms; £59.50 per manual; £59.50 per stimulus booklet.
Time: 30 minutes.
Author: David Wechsler.
Publisher: Harcourt Assessment [England].
Cross References: For reviews by Judith R. Johnston and Dolores Kluppel Vetter, see 16:264.

[2754]
Wechsler Objective Numerical Dimensions.

Purpose: Intended to assess a child's progress in acquiring fundamental numeracy skills.
Population: Ages 6 years to 16 years, 11 months.
Publication Date: 1996.
Acronym: WOND.
Scores, 3: Composite Score, Mathematics Reasoning, Numerical Operations.
Administration: Individual.
Price Data, 2006: £150.50 per complete kit including manual (134 pages), stimulus booklet, and 50 record forms; £52 per 50 record forms.
Time: 30 minutes.
Author: David Wechsler.
Publisher: Harcourt Assessment [England].
Cross References: For reviews by Mary L. Garner and Jerry Johnson, see 16:265.

[2755]
Wechsler Objective Reading Dimensions.

Purpose: Designed to assess literacy skills.
Population: Ages 6–16 years.
Publication Dates: 1990–1993.

Acronym: WORD.
Scores, 4: Basic Reading, Spelling, Reading Comprehension, Total Composite Score.
Administration: Individual.
Price Data, 2006: £150.50 per complete kit including manual (1993, 157 pages), stimulus booklet, and 50 record forms; £52 per 50 record forms.
Time: (20) minutes.
Author: David Wechsler.
Publisher: Harcourt Assessment [England].
Cross References: For reviews by Thomas Emerson Hancock and Alfred P. Longo, see 16:266.

[2756]
Wechsler Preschool and Primary Scale of Intelligence—Third Edition.

Purpose: Developed "for assessing the intelligence of young children."
Population: Ages 2-6 to 3-11, ages 4-0 to 7-3.
Publication Dates: 1949–2002.
Acronym: WPPSI-III.
Administration: Individual.
Price Data, 2006: $850 per complete box kit including all necessary stimulus and manipulative materials, administration and scoring manual (2002, 267 pages), technical and interpretive manual (2002, 228 pages), 25 record forms for ages 2-6 to 3-11, 25 record forms for ages 4-0 to 7-3, and 25 response booklets; $899 per complete kit including materials listed above (specify attaché or soft-sided case); $999 per complete kit with WPPSI-III Scoring Assistant in box; $1050 per complete kit with WPPSI-III Scoring Assistant in attaché or soft-sided case; $1225 per complete kit in soft-sided case with WPPSI-III Writer; $155 per complete manual including both administration and scoring manual and technical and interpretive manual; $130 per administration and scoring manual; $130 per technical and interpretive manual; $130 per stimulus booklet (specify 1 or 2); $62 per 25 response booklets; $235 per 100 response booklets; $62 per 25 record forms for ages 2-6 to 3-11; $235 per 100 record forms for ages 2-6 to 3-11; $99 per 25 record forms for ages 4-0 to 7-3; $365 per 100 record forms for ages 4-0 to 7-3; $210 per WPPSI-III Scoring Assistant (CD-ROM); $425 per WPPSI-III Writer including a comprehensive user's manual; $299 per WPPSI-III Scoring Assistant to Writer Upgrade including a CD-ROM and comprehensive user's manual.
Author: David Wechsler.
Publisher: PsychCorp, A brand of Harcourt Assessment, Inc.

a) 2:6–3:11 AGE BAND.
Population: Ages 2-6 to 3-11.
Scores, 7 to 9: Verbal (Receptive Vocabulary, Information, Picture Naming [supplemental], Total), Performance (Block Design, Object Assembly, Total), Global Language Composite [supplemental], Total.
Time: (30–45) minutes.
b) 4:0–7:3 AGE BAND.
Population: Ages 4-0 to 7-3.
Scores, 10 to 19: Verbal (Information, Vocabulary, Word Reasoning, Comprehension [supplemental], Similarities [supplemental], Receptive Vocabulary [optional], Picture Naming [optional], Total), Performance (Block Design, Matrix Reasoning, Picture Concepts, Picture Completion [supplemental], Object Assembly [supplemental], Total), Global Language Composite [optional], Total.
Cross References: For reviews by Ronald A. Madle and by Merilee McCurdy and Lynae A. Johnsen, see 16:267; see also T5:2864 (146 references) and T4:2941 (38 references); for reviews by Bruce A. Bracken and Jeffery P. Braden of an earlier edition, see 11:466 (118 references); for a review by B. J. Freeman, see 9:1356 (33 references); see also T3:2608 (280 references), 8:234 (84 references), and T2:538 (30 references); for reviews by Dorothy H. Eichorn and A. B. Silverstein, and excerpted reviews by C. H. Ammons and by O. A. Oldridge and E. E. Allison, see 7:434 (56 reference).

[2757]
Wechsler Test of Adult Reading.

Purpose: Developed as an assessment tool for estimating premorbid (pre-injury) intellectual functioning and to predict a person's pre-injury IQ and memory abilities.
Population: Ages 16–89.
Publication Date: 2001.
Acronym: WTAR
Scores: Total score only,
Administration: Individual.
Price Data, 2006: $125 per complete kit including manual, 25 record forms, word card, and audiotape; $45 per 25 record forms.
Time: [5–10] minutes.
Comments: Co-normed with the Wechsler Adult Intelligence Scale—Third Edition (2746) and the Wechsler Memory Scale—Third Edition (2751); U.K. norms available.
Author: The Psychological Corporation.
Publisher: PsychCorp, A brand of Harcourt Assessment, Inc.
Cross References: For reviews by Nora M. Thompson and Sandra Ward, see 16:268.

[2758]
Weidner-Fensch Speech Screening Test.

Purpose: Designed "to be used in screening out children with speech difficulties from those who have normally developed speech."

Population: Grades 1–3.
Publication Date: No date.
Scores: Item scores only.
Administration: Individual.
Forms, 2: A, B.
Price Data, 2001: $4 per specimen set.
Time: (5–10) minutes.
Authors: William E. Weidner and Edwin A. Fensch.
Publisher: Psychometric Affiliates.
Cross References: For a review by Kris L. Baack, see 16:269.

[2759]
Weiss Comprehensive Articulation Test.

Purpose: "For making a thorough diagnosis of articulation and its associated parameters."
Population: All ages.
Publication Dates: 1978–1980.
Acronym: WCAT.
Scores, 5: Articulation, Articulation Age, Intelligibility, Stimulability, Number of Misarticulations.
Administration: Individual.
Forms, 2: Nonreading Subjects, Reading Subjects.
Price Data, 2006: $125 per complete kit including picture cards, sentence card, 50 picture response forms, 50 sentence response forms, and manual (1980, 32 pages); $40 per 100 picture response forms; $40 per 100 sentence response forms.
Time: [20] minutes.
Author: Curtis E. Weiss.
Publisher: PRO-ED.
Cross References: See T5:2866 (5 references) and T4:2942 (2 references); for a review by Richard J. Schissel, see 9:1357.

[2760]
Weld Test—Form A C.

Purpose: To "select and develop journey-level, industrial welders."
Population: Welding job applicants.
Publication Dates: 1984–1998.
Scores: 7 areas: Print Reading, Welding/Cutting Torch and Arc Air Cutting, Welder Maintenance and Operation, Tools/Machines/Material and Equipment, Mobile Equipment and Rigging, Production Welding Calculations, Total.
Administration: Group.
Price Data, 2006: $20 per consumable self-scoring test booklet; $24.95 per manual (1998, 16 pages).
Time: (60) minutes.
Comments: Self-scoring instrument.
Author: Roland T. Ramsay.
Publisher: Ramsay Corporation.
Cross References: For reviews by John Peter Hudson, Jr. and David C. Roberts, see 13:360.

[2761]
Wellness Evaluation of Lifestyle [2004 Update].

Purpose: Designed to help respondents make healthy lifestyle choices based on their responses to each of the five life tasks and subtasks defined in the Wheel of Wellness; the life tasks of spirituality, self-direction, work & leisure, friendship, and love interact with a variety of life forces and global events.
Population: Ages 18 and over.
Publication Dates: 1994–2004.
Acronym: WEL.
Scores: Spirituality, Self-Direction, Sense of Worth, Sense of Control, Realistic Beliefs, Emotional Awareness and Coping, Intellectual Stimulation, Problem Solving and Creativity, Sense of Humor, Nutrition, Exercise, Self-Care, Stress Management, Gender Identity, Culture Identity, Work, Leisure, Friendship, Love, Total Wellness, Perceived Wellness.
Administration: Group or individual.
Price Data: Available from publisher.
Time: (15–20) minutes.
Comments: Web-based administration and reporting available (www.mindgarden.com).
Authors: Jane E. Myers, Thomas J. Sweeney, and J. Melvin Witmer.
Publisher: Mind Garden, Inc.
Cross References: For reviews by Richard F. Farmer and Trenton R. Ferro, see 16:270; for reviews by Andrew A. Cox and Ashraf Kagee of a previous edition, see 15:277.

[2762]
Welsh Figure Preference Test.

Purpose: A nonverbal approach to personality measurement and research incorporating the Barron-Welsh Art Scale.
Population: Ages 6 and over.
Publication Date: 1959-1980.
Acronym: WFPT.
Scores, 27: Like, Don't Like, Repeat, Conformance, Origence, Intellectence, Female Response, Movement, Figure Ground, Shading, Black, Anxiety, Repression, Conformity, Neuropsychiatric, Consensus Like, Female-Male, Children, Figure Ground Reversal, Sex Symbol (male and female).
Administration: Group or individual.
Price Data: Available from publisher (www.mindgarden.com).
Time: (50) minutes.
Comments: For research use only; self-administering.
Author: George S. Welsh.
Publisher: Mind Garden, Inc.
Cross References: See T5:2869 (1 reference) and T4:2945 (5 references); for a review by Julien Worland,

see 9:1360 (1 reference); see also T3:2613 (4 references), T2:1437 (34 references), and P:287 (24 references); for a review by Harold Borko and an excerpted review by Gordon V. Anderson, see 6:197 (20 references); for information for Barron-Welsh Art Scale, see T3:243 (15 references).

[2763]
Wepman's Auditory Discrimination Test, Second Edition.

Purpose: Measures children's ability to hear spoken English accurately, specifically to "discriminate between commonly used phonemes in the English language."
Population: Ages 4-8 years.
Publication Dates: 1958–1987.
Acronym: ADT.
Scores: Total score yielding Qualitative score, Standard score, Percentile rank.
Administration: Individual.
Forms, 2: 1A, 2A.
Price Data, 2006: $109.50 per complete kit including 200 tests (100 each of Forms 1A and 2A) and manual (1987, 58 pages); $40 per 100 tests (specify form); $44 per manual.
Time: 5 minutes.
Authors: Joseph M. Wepman (test) and William M. Reynolds (manual).
Publisher: Western Psychological Services.
Cross References: See T5:2870 (5 references) and T4:2946 (1 reference); for a review by Mary Pannbacker and Grace Middleton, see 11:467 (5 references); see also T3:226 (31 references), 8:932 (74 references), and T2:2028 (82 references); for a review by Louis M. DiCarlo of the original edition, see 6:940 (2 references).

[2764]
Wesman Personnel Classification Test.

Purpose: Developed to measure verbal reasoning and numerical ability.
Population: Grades 10-12 and applicants and employees.
Publication Dates: 1946-1965.
Acronym: PCT.
Scores, 3: Verbal, Numerical, Total.
Administration: Group or individual.
Forms, 3: A, B, C.
Price Data, 2006: $90 per starter kit, including 25 test booklets (specify form) and manual (1965, 28 pages).
Time: 28 minutes.
Author: Alexander G. Wesman.
Publisher: Harcourt Assessment, Inc.
Cross References: See T5:2871 (4 references), T4:2947 (5 references), T3:2614 (4 references), and

T2:480 (2 references); for a review by Arthur C. MacKinney, and an excerpted review by Jack C. Merwin, see 7:400 (7 references); see also 5:399 (8 references); for reviews by John C. Flanagan and Erwin K. Taylor, see 4:331 (3 references); for an excerpted review, see 3:253.

[2765]
The Wessex Head Injury Matrix.

Purpose: "Designed to assess and monitor recovery in patients after severe head injury."
Population: Ages 16 and over.
Publication Date: 2000.
Acronym: WHIM.
Scores: Not scored.
Administration: Individual.
Price Data, 2006: £69 per complete kit including manual and 25 scorint sheets; £71 per 50 scoring sheets.
Time: Untimed.
Authors: Agnes Shiel, Barbara A. Wilson, Lindsay McLellan, Sandra Horn, and Martin Watson.
Publisher: Harcourt Assessment [England].

[2766]
Western Aphasia Battery.

Purpose: "To evaluate the main clinical aspects of language function" as well as nonverbal skills.
Population: Adolescents and adults with language disorders.
Publication Dates: 1980–1982.
Acronym: WAB.
Scores: 17 obtained subscores which form 7 major scores: Spontaneous Speech, Comprehension, Repetition, Naming, Reading and Writing, Praxis, Construction (optional), plus 2 derived scores: Aphasia Quotient, Cortical Quotient (optional).
Administration: Individual.
Price Data, 2002: $120.50 per complete kit including 25 test booklets, manual (1980, 3 pages), and stimulus cards; $28 per 25 test booklets; $94 per stimulus cards; $20 per manual; $10 each per Koh's blocks (each two-color block: four blocks are required for testing); $31 per 50 answer documents; $360 per Raven's test booklets.
Time: [60–70] minutes.
Comments: Other test materials (e.g., cup, comb, flower) must be supplied by examiner; a computerized record form (1993) is also available (hardware requirements—DOS-based PC/4.0 or higher, 640K RAM, one hard or floppy drive).
Author: Andrew Kertesz.
Publisher: PsychCorp, A brand of Harcourt Assessment, Inc.
Cross References: See T5:2873 (74 references) and T4:2949 (33 references); for a review by Francis J. Pirozzolo, see 9:1362 (1 reference).

[2767]
The Western Personality Inventory.

Purpose: Combines the Manson Evaluation and the Alcadd Test to predict the likelihood of alcoholic addiction or abuse.
Population: Adults.
Publication Dates: 1963–1988.
Acronym: WPI.
Scores, 14: Anxiety, Depressive Fluctuations, Emotional Sensitivity, Resentfulness, Incompleteness, Aloneness, Interpersonal Relations, Total, Regularity of Drinking, Preference for Drinking over Other Activities, Lack of Controlled Drinking, Rationalization of Drinking, Excessive Emotionality, Total.
Administration: Individual or group.
Manual: No manual; use manuals for The Manson Evaluation and The Alcadd Test.
Price Data, 2006: $104.50 per complete kit including 5 AutoScore test forms, 2 prepaid mail-in answer sheets for computer scoring and interpretation, Manson Evaluation Manual, and Alcadd Manual; $49.50 per Manson Evaluation Manual or Alcadd Manual; $11.55 per mail-in answer sheet.
Time: 10 to 20 minutes.
Comments: Combination of The Manson Evaluation (1527) and The Alcadd Test (135).
Author: Morse P. Manson.
Publisher: Western Psychological Services.

[2768]
The WH Question Comprehension Test: Exploring the World of WH Question Comprehension for Students With an Autism Spectrum Disorder.

Purpose: Designed to indicate a student's competence in WH question form comprehension through appropriate match of question form and response.
Population: Ages 3 and up with cognitive impairments.
Publication Dates: 2002-2004.
Scores: 6 areas: Who, What, Where, When, Why, How.
Administration: Individual.
Price Data, 2006: $25 per combination test booklet/manual (2004, 175 pages).
Time: (20-30) minutes.
Comments: Test can be administered in multiple sessions if necessary.
Author: Beverly Vicker.
Publisher: Indiana Resource Center for Autism.

[2769]
What Do You Say?

Purpose: Designed as a self-assessment tool to identify communication style and relate it to two basic types of human interactions: parent-child (McGregor's Theory X) and adult-adult (Theory Y).
Population: Employees.
Publication Dates: 1986–1991.
Scores, 4: Empathic, Critical, Searching, Advising.
Administration: Group or individual.
Price Data: Price available from publisher for complete kit including 20 inventories, 20 answer sheets, and 20 interpretation booklets.
Time: [20] minutes administration; [10] minutes scoring; [30-60] minutes interpretation.
Comments: Self-administered, self-scored.
Author: Training House, Inc.
Publisher: Training House, Inc.
Cross References: For reviews by William L. Deaton and Gerald L. Stone, see 12:413.

[2770]
Whisler Strategy Test.

Purpose: "To discover how effective the individual is in drawing on his abilities and knowledges to demonstrate his general competence."
Population: Business and industry.
Publication Dates: 1955–1961.
Scores, 6: 4 direct scores (Number Circled-Boldness, Number Attempted-Speed, Number Right-Accuracy, Net Strategy), and 2 derived scores (Caution, Hypercaution).
Administration: Group.
Price Data: Available from publisher.
Time: (25) minutes.
Comments: Measures "intelligence action" or strategic ability.
Author: Laurence Whisler.
Publisher: Psychometric Affiliates.
Cross References: See T5:2877 (1 reference) and T2:2292 (1 reference); for reviews by Jean Maier Palormo and Paul F. Ross, see 6:1110 (1 reference).

[2771]
The Whitener Group Industrial Assessments.

Purpose: "Designed to measure an individual's knowledge of competencies related specifically to industrial occupations. These assessments consist of only a written portion; intended for evaluating individuals with a combination of education, training, and work experience. " Suggested uses include: selecting skilled workers (worry free); giving promotions based on objective, verifiable standards; providing blueprints for employee development; analyzing job requirements; and developing precise job descriptions, training curriculum, performance analysis charts, objective performance appraisals, valid interview protocol, and career paths.
Population: Industrial and potential industrial employees.
Publication Dates: 1996–2002.

Scores: Duty support scores and total scores are reported for 23 tests: Die Making, Electricity/Electronics, Electrical/Electronics Maintenance, General Industrial/Mechanical, General Maintenance, General Technical Skills, Industrial Maintenance Technician, Instrumentation and Control, Industrial Mechanic, Instrumentation and Electrician Technician, Lead Maintenance, Machine Repair, Maintenance, Maintenance Mechanic, Maintenance and Repair Mechanic, Maintenance Technician, Manufacturing Technician, Master Machine Repair, Mechanical Systems, Mechanical and Fluid Power Maintenance, Mechanical Maintenance, Pipefitter, Toolmaker.
Administration: Group.
Price Data, 2005: $75 per standardized industrial test, online or paper/pencil administration, including instructions for administration, scoring, and reporting services; contact publisher for pricing information on customized assessment services.
Time: (180) minutes per test.
Comments: Previously listed as NOCTI Industrial Assessments.
Authors: National Occupational Competency Testing Institute/The Whitener Group.
Publisher: National Occupational Competency Testing Institute/The Whitener Group.

[2772]
Who Am I?

Purpose: Assesses "a child's readiness for particular types of learning experiences and identifies the levels that children have reached in their understanding and use of conventional symbols and relevant early learning skills."
Population: Preschool–Year 2 in Australian school system.
Publication Date: 1999.
Scores, 4: Copying, Symbols, Drawing, Total.
Administration: Group or individual.
Price Data, 2006: A$59.95 per specimen set including task booklet, assessment manual (36 pages), and administration instructions; A$27.50 per 10 task booklets; A$44.95 per assessment manual; A$9.95 per administration instructions.
Time: (10–20) minutes.
Authors: Marion de Lemos and Brian Doig.
Publisher: Australian Council for Educational Research Ltd. [Australia].
Cross References: For reviews by G. Michael Poteat and Donald L. Stovall, see 15:278.

[2773]
Wide Range Achievement Test—Expanded Early Reading Assessment.

Purpose: Designed to measure "pre-reading and beginning reading skills."
Population: Ages 4.6–7.11.

Publication Date: 2003.
Acronym: ERA.
Scores, 7: Pre-Reading Skills (Letter/Word Discrimination, Letter-Sound Discrimination, Total), Reading Skills (Word Reading, Sentence Reading, Total), Total.
Administration: Individual.
Price Data, 2006: $210 per complete kit including manual (112 pages), flipbook, and 25 record forms.
Time: (35) minutes.
Author: Gary J. Robertson.
Publisher: Psychological Assessment Resources, Inc.
Cross References: For reviews by Leslie Eastman Lukin and Patrick P. McCabe, see 16:271.

[2774]
Wide Range Achievement Test—Expanded Edition.

Purpose: An achievement test battery "designed to assess the core curricular domains of reading, mathematics, and oral and written language."
Population: Grades 2–12; Ages 5–24.
Publication Dates: 2001—2002.
Comments: Designed to complement the WRAT-3.
Author: Gary J. Robertson.
Publisher: Psychological Assessment Resources, Inc.
a) WRAT-EXPANDED GROUP ASSESSMENT (FORM G).
Population: Grades 2–12.
Scores, 5: Reading (Basic Reading, Reading Comprehension), Mathematics, Nonverbal Reasoning.
Administration: Group.
Levels, 5: G-1 (Grade 2), G-2 (Grades 3–4), G-3 (Grades 5–6), G-4 (Grades 7–9), G-5 (Grades 10–12).
Price Data, 2006: $250 per WRAT—Expanded Group Assessment (Form G) comprehensive package including 10 booklets and scoring forms for each level, manuals for each level (2001, 71–75 pages each), and technical supplement (2001, 80 pages).
Time: (125–135) minutes.
b) WRAT-EXPANDED INDIVIDUAL ASSESSMENT (FORM I).
Population: Ages 5–24.
Scores, 5: Reading, Mathemaics, Listening Comprehension, Oral Expression, Written Language.
Administration: Individual.
Time: [30] minutes.
Cross References: For reviews by George Engelhard, Jr., and by Bo Zhang and Cindy M. Walker, see 16:272.

[2775]
Wide Range Achievement Test 3.

Purpose: To measure the skills needed to learn reading, spelling, and arithmetic.

Population: Ages 5-75.
Publication Dates: 1940–1993.
Acronym: WRAT3.
Scores: 3 subtests: Reading, Spelling, Arithmetic.
Administration: Individual in part.
Forms: 2 equivalent forms: Blue, Tan.
Price Data, 2002: $165 per starter set including 25 Blue test forms, 25 Tan test forms, 25 profile/analysis forms, set of 2 plastic cards for Reading/Spelling, and manual (1993, 188 pages) in soft side carrying case; $149 per scoring progam (on 3.5" floppy disk) including unlimited scoring and reports.
Time: (15–30) minutes.
Authors: Gary S. Wilkinson.
Publisher: Psychological Assessment Resources, Inc.
Cross References: See T5:2879 (237 references); for reviews by Linda Mabry and Annie W. Ward, see 12:414 (111 references); see also T4:2956 (121 references); for reviews by Elaine Clark and Patti L. Harrison, see 10:389 (161 references); for reviews by Paula Matuszek and Philip A. Saigh of an earlier edition, see 9:1364 (103 references); see also T3:2621 (249 references), 8:37 (117 references), and T2:50 (35 references); for reviews by Jack C. Merwin and Robert L. Thorndike of an earlier edition, see 7:36 (49 references); see also 6:27 (15 references); for reviews by Paul Douglas Courtney, Verner M. Sims, and Louis P. Thorpe of the 1946 edition, see 3:21.

[2776]
Wide Range Assessment of Memory and Learning, Second Edition.

Purpose: Designed for use in "clinical assessments of memory including evaluation of immediate and/or delay recall as well as differentiating between verbal, visual or more global memory deficits."
Population: Ages 5–90.
Publication Dates: 1990–2003.
Acronym: WRAML2.
Scores: 25: Verbal Memory (Story Memory, Verbal Learning, Total), Visual Memory (Design Memory, Picture Memory, Total), Attention/Concentration (Finger Windows, Number Letter, Total), General Memory; Optional scores: Working Memory (Verbal Working Memory, Symbolic Working Memory, Total), Verbal Recognition (Story Recognition, Verbal Learning Recognition, Total), Visual Recognition (Design Recognition, Picture Memory Recognition, Total), General Recognition, Sound Symbol, Sentence Memory, Story Memory Recall, Verbal Learning Recall, Sound Symbol Recall
Administration: Individual.
Price Data, 2006: $475 per complete kit including administration and technical manual (2003, 245 pages), 25 examiner forms, 25 Picture Memory response forms, 2 Picture Memory Recognition forms, 2 china markers,

25 Design Memory response forms, 25 Design Memory Recognition forms, 4 Picture Memory plates, 5 Design Memory cards, 1 Finger Windows board, 2 Symbolic Working Memory boards, and soft canvas briefcase. $195 per scoring software (CD-ROM) including unlimited scoring and reports.
Time: [60] minutes.
Authors: David Sheslow and Wayne Adams.
Publisher: Psychological Assessment Resources, Inc.
Cross References: For reviews by Thomas M. Dunn and Sandra D. Haynes, see 16:273; see also T5:2880 (7 references); for reviews by Richard M. Clark and Frederic J. Medway of a previous edition, see 11:470.

[2777]
Wide Range Assessment of Visual Motor Abilities.

Purpose: A standardized assessment of visual-motor, visual-spatial, and fine motor skills.
Population: Ages 3–17 years.
Publication Date: 1995.
Acronym: WRAVMA.
Scores, 4: Fine Motor, Visual-Spatial, Visual-Motor, Visual-Motor Integration Composite.
Administration: Individual.
Price Data, 2006: $260 per introductory kit including manual (151 pages), 25 drawing forms, 25 visual matching forms, 25 examiner record forms, pegboard and pegs, pencils, markers, and sharpener, all in a soft-side canvas attaché case.
Time: (15–30) minutes; (5–10) minutes per subtest.
Comments: Best results when "integrated with data from other standardized tests and clinical observations"; test should be interpreted by "those with graduate or equivalent professional training in cognitive assessment."
Authors: Wayne Adams and David Sheslow.
Publisher: Psychological Assessment Resources, Inc.
Cross References: For reviews by Linda K. Bunker and Keith F. Widaman, see 14:418.

[2778]
Wide Range Intelligence Test.

Purpose: "Designed to measure an individual's cognitive abilities."
Population: Ages 4–85.
Publication Date: 2000.
Acronym: WRIT.
Scores, 7: Verbal (Verbal Analogies, Vocabulary, Total), Visual (Matrices, Diamonds, Total), Total.
Administration: Individual.
Price Data, 2006: $275 per regular introductory kit including test manual, Matrices and Diamonds easel stimulus book, 25 examiner forms, and set of 21 Diamond Chips, all packaged in a canvas carrying case.

Time: (20–30) minutes.
Authors: Joseph Glutting, Wayne Adams, and David Sheslow.
Publisher: Psychological Assessment Resources, Inc.
Cross References: For reviews by Terry A. Stinnett and Keith F. Widaman, see 15:279.

[2779]
Wide Range Interest and Occupation Test, Second Edition.

Purpose: Designed to provide participants "with a better understanding of themselves, the types of occupations they prefer, their pattern of likes and dislikes among work-related activities, and the intensity and consistency of their response pattern."
Population: Ages 9–80.
Publication Dates: 1970–2003.
Acronym: WRIOT2.
Scores, 39: Occupational Cluster (Art, Music, Drama, Sales, Management, Clerical–Office, Personal Service, Food Service, Cleaning Service, Protective Service, Social Service, Science, Health Care, Build and Repair, Factory and Assembly Line, Heavy Equipment and/or Machine Operation, Plants and Animals); Interest Cluster (Spoken Words, Numbers, People, Things, Perceived Ability, Income, Leadership, Strenuous, Outdoors, Risk, Creative, Routine, Likes, Dislikes, Occupational Clarity, Inconsistency) Holland Type Cluster (Realistic, Investigative, Artistic, Social, Enterprising, Conventional).
Administration: Individual.
Price Data: Available from publisher.
Time: (30) minutes.
Comments: A nonverbal measure of occupational interest; previous edition called the Wide Range Interest-Opinion Test.
Authors: Joseph J. Glutting and Gary S. Wilkinson.
Publisher: Harcourt Assessment, Inc.
Cross References: For reviews by Albert M. Bugaj and Caroline Manuele-Adkins, see 16:274; see also T4:2959 (1 reference); for reviews by Louis M. Hsu and Caroline A. Manuele of a previous edition, see 9:1366; for a review by Donald G. Zytowski, see 8:1029.

[2780]
The Wiesen Test of Mechanical Aptitude.

Purpose: Designed to measure mechanical aptitude for purpose of personnel selection.
Population: Applicants (18 years and older) for jobs requiring mechanical aptitude.
Publication Dates: 1997–1999.
Acronym: WTMA.
Scores, 12: Total Score and 11 research scores: Basic Machines, Movement of Simple and Complex Objects, Center of Gravity and Gravity, Basic Electricity/Electronics, Transfer of Heat, Basic Physical Properties of Matter and Materials, Miscellaneous, Academic, Kitchen Objects, Non-Kitchen Objects, Other Everyday Objects.
Administration: Individual or group.
Price Data, 2005: $215 per introductory kit including manual, 10 item booklets, 25 answer sheets, and 1 scoring key.
Time: 30 minutes.
Comments: A 60-item multiple-choice objective test.
Author: Joel P. Wiesen.
Publisher: Psychological Assessment Resources, Inc.
Cross References: For reviews by John M. Enger and Nambury S. Raju, see 14:419.

[2781]
Wife's or Husband's Marriage Questions.

Purpose: Designed as "a comprehensive marriage analysis system."
Population: Husbands, wives.
Publication Date: 1994.
Administration: Individual or group.
Forms, 2: Wife's Marriage Questions, Husband's Marriage Questions.
Manual: No manual.
Price Data, 2001: $10 per 20 forms (specify Husband or Wife).
Time: Administration time not reported.
Author: Allan Roe.
Publisher: Diagnostic Specialists, Inc.

[2782]
Wiig Assessment of Basic Concepts.

Purpose: "Designed to evaluate a child's understanding and use of basic word opposites and related concepts."
Publication Date: 2004.
Acronym: WABC.
Scores, 10: Scores in 7 areas (Color/Shape, Size/Weight/Volume, Distance/Speed/Time, Quantity/Completeness, Location/Direction, Condition/Quality, Sensation/Emotion/Evaluation), Receptive raw score, Expressive raw score, Total raw score.
Administration: Individual.
Price Data, 2006: $179 per complete kit including Level 1 and Level 2 Storybooks, 50 Level 1 record forms, 50 Level 2 record forms, clipboard with calculator, Puppy Bank reinforcer with 30 Doggy Dog tokens, 75 WABC stickers, and tote bag; $29.96 per 50 Level 1-A Day at the Zoo record forms; $29.96 per 50 Level 2-A Day at the Park record forms; $4.95 per 75 WABC stickers; $14.95 per clipboard.
Time: (10-15) minutes.
Author: Elisabeth H. Wiig.
Publisher: Super Duper Publications.
  a) LEVEL 1: A DAY AT THE ZOO.
  Population: Ages 2-6 to 5-11 years.

b) LEVEL 2: A DAY AT THE PARK.
Population: Ages 5-0 to 7-11 years.

[2783]
Wiig Criterion Referenced Inventory of Language.

Purpose: "Designed to assist speech-language pathologists and special and regular educators in the diagnosis of children with language disorders and language delays."
Population: Ages 4 through 13.
Publication Date: 1990.
Acronym: Wiig CRIL.
Scores: 4 modules: Semantics, Morphology, Syntax, Pragmatics.
Administration: Individual.
Price Data, 2006: $299 per complete kit including Professional's Guide (63 pages), all 4 stimulus manuals, and 10 each of all four record forms; price information for the module package (specify Semantics, Morphology, Syntax, or Pragmatics) including stimulus manual and 10 record forms available from publisher; $49 per 20 record forms (specify Semantics, Morphology, Syntax, or Pragmatics).
Time: Untimed.
Author: Elisabeth H. Wiig.
Publisher: PsychCorp, A brand of Harcourt Assessment, Inc.
Cross References: For reviews by Clinton W. Bennett and Judith R. Johnston, see 13:361.

[2784]
Wilson Driver Selection Test.

Purpose: Constructed to measure aptitudes related to safe driving.
Population: Prospective motor vehicle operators.
Publication Dates: 1961-1984.
Scores, 7: Visual Attention, Depth Visualization, Recognition of Simple Detail, Recognition of Complex Detail, Eye-Hand Coordination, Steadiness, Total.
Administration: Group.
Price Data, 2006: $149.40 per test package; $3.75 per key; $54.60 per manual (1961, 28 pages) and manual supplement (1984, 17 pages); $59.95 per specimen set.
Time: 26(50) minutes.
Author: Clark L. Wilson.
Publisher: Martin M. Bruce, Ph.D.
Cross References: For reviews by Willard A. Kerr and D. H. Schuster, see 6:1200.

[2785]
The Wilson Syntax Screening Test.

Purpose: Analyzes a child's expressive ability on five grammatical constructions "to quickly screen large numbers of children to identify those who ought to undergo more extensive language evaluations."
Population: Ages 4:0 to 5:11.
Publication Date: 2000.
Scores, 3: Elicited Spontaneous Score, Mastery Score, Total.
Administration: Individual.
Price Data: Available from publisher.
Time: (2–4) minutes.
Author: Mary Sweig Wilson.
Publisher: PsychCorp, A brand of Harcourt Assessment, Inc.

[2786]
Wisconsin Behavior Rating Scale.

Purpose: "A least biased adaptive behavior scale" to "provide adequate assessment, intervention, and evaluation" of severely and profoundly retarded individuals and of persons functioning below the developmental level of 3 years.
Population: Persons functioning below the developmental level of 3 years.
Publication Dates: 1979-1991.
Acronym: WBRS.
Scores, 12: Gross Motor, Fine Motor, Expressive Language, Receptive Language, Play Skills, Socialization, Domestic Activity, Eating, Toileting, Dressing, Grooming, Total.
Administration: Group.
Price Data, 2005: $20 per 25 scales; $70 per 100 scales (1991, 12 pages); $6 per specimen set including scale and manual (1983, 30 pages).
Time: (10-15) minutes.
Comments: "The assessment is performed by interviewing informants who are most familiar with the behavior of the person being evaluated."
Authors: Agnes Song, Stephen Jones, Janet Lippert, Karin Metzgen, Jacqueline Miller, and Christopher Borreca.
Publisher: Central Wisconsin Center for the Developmentally Disabled.
Cross References: For reviews by Pat Mirenda and Harvey N. Switzky, see 11:472 (1 reference).

[2787]
Wisconsin Card Sorting Test.

Purpose: "Developed ... as a measure of abstract reasoning among normal adult populations" and "has increasingly been employed as a clinical neuropsychological instrument."
Population: Ages 6.5–89.
Publication Dates: 1981–1993.
Acronym: WCST.
Scores, 11: Number of Trials Administered, Total Number Correct, Total Number of Errors, Perseverative Responses, Perseverative Errors, Nonperseverative Errors, Conceptual Level Responses, Number of Categories Completed, Trials to Complete First Category, Failure to Maintain Set, Learning to Learn.

Administration: Individual.
Price Data, 2006: $325 per introductory kit including manual (1993, 234 pages), 2 decks of cards, and 50 record booklets; $640 per WCST Computer Version Research Edition software (CD-ROM)including unlimited on screen administration, scoring, and reports with 25 record forms; $450 per WCST Scoring Program Research Edition software (CD-ROM) including unlimited scoring and reports with 25 record forms.
Time: (20–30) minutes.
Comments: Additional materials necessary for testing include a pen or pencil and a clipboard.
Authors: Robert K. Heaton, Gordon J. Chelune, Jack L. Talley, Gary G. Kay, and Glenn Curtiss.
Publisher: Psychological Assessment Resources, Inc.
Cross References: For reviews by Elaine Clark and Deborah D. Roman, see 14:420; see also T5:2892 (309 references) and T4:2967 (96 references); for reviews by Byron Egeland and Robert P. Markley of an earlier edition, see 9:1372 (11 references).

[2788]
Wisconsin Card Sorting Test—64 Card Version.

Purpose: "Developed … as a measure of abstract reasoning among normal adult populations" and "has increasingly been employed as a clinical neuropsychological instrument."
Population: Ages 6.5–89.
Publication Dates: 1981–2000.
Acronym: WCST-64.
Scores, 10: Total Number Correct, Total Number of Errors, Perseverative Responses, Perseverative Errors, Nonperseverative Errors, Conceptual Level Responses, Number of Categories Completed, Trials to Complete First Category, Failure to Maintain Set, Learning to Learn.
Administration: Individual.
Price Data, 2006: $250 per introductory kit including manual (1993, 234 pages), 50 record booklets, and 1 card deck; $540 per Computer Version 2 software (CD-ROM)including unlimited on-screen administration, scoring, and reports, with 25 record forms; $315 per Computer Version 2 Scoring Program software (CD-ROM) including unlimited scoring and reports with 25 record forms.
Time: Untimed.
Comments: Abbreviated form of the standard 128-card version of the Wisconsin Card Sorting Test (2787).
Authors: Susan K. Kongs, Laetitia L. Thompson, Grant L. Iverson, and Robert K. Heaton.
Publisher: Psychological Assessment Resources, Inc.
Cross References: For a review by Michael S. Trevisan, see 15:280; for information on the Wisconsin Card Sorting Test, Revised and Expanded, see T5:2892 (309 references) and T4:2967 (96 references); for re-

views by Byron Egeland and Robert P. Markley of an earlier edition, see 9:1372 (11 references).

[2789]
WJ III® Diagnostic Reading Battery.

Purpose: "Measures important dimensions of phonological awareness, phonics knowledge, reading achievement, and related oral language abilities."
Population: Ages 2–90+.
Publication Date: 2004.
Acronym: WJ III DRB.
Scores, 8: Basic Reading Skills, Reading Comprehension, Phonics Knowledge, Phonemic Awareness, Oral Language Comprehension, Brief Reading, Broad Reading, Total Reading.
Subtest: 10: Letter-Word Identification, Passage Comprehension, Word Attack, Reading Vocabulary, Reading Fluency, Spelling of Sounds, Sound Awareness, Sound Blending, Oral Vocabulary, Oral Comprehension.
Administration: Individual.
Price Data, 2006: $382 per complete kit with carrying case including test book, audio CD package, comprehensive manual (197 pages), software package, and 25 test records and subject response booklets; $59 per 25 test records and subject response booklets; $64.50 per comprehensive manual; $140.50 per scoring and reporting program (Windows/Mac).
Time: (50-60) minutes.
Comments: Composed of 8 tests from the WJ III Tests of Achievement and 2 tests from the WJ III Tests of Cognitive Abilities (see Woodcock-Johnson® III; 2795); includes software for scoring and printing reports.
Authors: Fredrick A. Schrank, Nancy Mather, and Richard W. Woodcock.
Publisher: Riverside Publishing.

[2790]
The Wolfe Computer Operator Aptitude Test.

Purpose: Used "to evaluate a candidate's potential for work as a computer operator."
Population: Applicants for computer training or employment.
Publication Dates: 1979–1982.
Acronym: WCOAT.
Scores: Total score only.
Administration: Group.
Price Data, 2001: $165 per candidate.
Foreign Language Edition: French edition available.
Time: (90) minutes.
Comments: Detailed report provided on each candidate.
Author: Jack M. Wolfe.
Publisher: Rose Wolfe Family Partnership LLP [Canada].

[2791]
Wolfe-Spence Programming Aptitude Test.

Purpose: Designed as a screening test to identify persons who should receive further consideration for hiring or training for programming.
Population: Applicants in computer programming.
Publication Date: 1970.
Scores: Total score and percentile.
Administration: Group.
Price Data, 2001: $180 per candidate.
Time: (120) minutes.
Authors: Jack M. Wolfe and Richard J. Spence.
Publisher: Rose Wolfe Family Partnership LLP [Canada].

[2792]
Wonderlic Basic Skills Test.

Purpose: Designed to measure individual language and math skills; intended to serve in the selection and placement of individuals into suitable jobs that match identified skills, and the selection and placement of individuals into appropriate educational programs.
Population: Intended for high school students and adults.
Publication Dates: 1994–2003.
Acronym: WBST.
Scores, 24: Test of Verbal Skills (Word Knowledge, Sentence Construction, Information Retrieval, Verbal GED Level 1, Verbal GED Level 2, Verbal GED Level 3, Verbal GED Level Achieved, Verbal Grade Level Equivalent, Verbal Total), Test of Quantitative Skills (Explicit, Applied, Interpretive, Quantitative GED Level 1, Quantitative GED Level 2, Quantitative GED Level 3, Quantitative GED Level Achieved, Quantitative Grade Level Equivalent, Quantitative Total), Skills Composite (Skills Composite GED Level 1, Skills Composite GED Level 2, Skills Composite GED Level 3, Skills Composite GED Level Achieved, Skills Composite Grade Level Equivalent, Total Skills Composite).
Subtests, 2: Test of Verbal Skills, Test of Quantitative Skills.
Administration: Group or individual.
Forms: 2 equivalent forms for each subtest: VS-1, VS-2 for Test of Verbal Skills; QS-1, QS-2 for Test of Quantitative Skills.
Price Data: Available from publisher.
Time: (20) minutes for each subtest.
Comments: Designed for use in both education and business environments. The Verbal and Quantitative Skills subtests may be administered together or separately, and are available as separate booklets; an online version is available for administration in proctored settings. The WBST has been approved by the U.S. Department of Education for use in qualifying postsecondary students for Title IV Federal financial assistance. Schools using the WBST for this purpose must follow special procedures and guidelines published in the WBST User's Manual for Ability-to-Benefit Testing.
Authors: Eliot R. Long, Victor S. Artese, and Winifred L. Clonts.
Publisher: Wonderlic, Inc.
Cross References: For reviews by Thomas F. Donlon and Gerald S. Hanna, see 13:362.

[2793]
Wonderlic Personnel Test and Scholastic Level Exam.

Purpose: Designed for use by businesses and educational institutions to measure general cognitive ability; designed to determine whether an individual possesses the cognitive ability that is necessary to learn, be trained quickly, and solve problems at the level of complexity that is required.
Population: Ages 15 and up.
Publication Dates: 1937–2005.
Acronym: WPT and SLE.
Scores: Total score only.
Administration: Individual or group.
Forms: 6 alternate forms of the WPT, and 4 alternate forms of the SLE.
Price Data: Available from publisher.
Foreign Language and Special Editions: Chinese, French, Korean, Puerto Rican, Spanish, Swedish, U.K., Metric, large print, braille, and audio editions.
Time: 12 minutes.
Comments: An online version is available for administration in proctored settings.
Author: Wonderlic, Inc.
Publisher: Wonderlic, Inc.
Cross References: For reviews by Kurt F. Geisinger and Gregory Schraw, see 14:421; see also T5:2899 (20 references) and T4:2972 (11 references); for a review by Marcia J. Belcher of an earlier edition, see 11:475 (10 references); for reviews by Frank L. Schmidt and Lyle F. Schoenfeldt, see 9:1385 (8 references); see also T3:2638 (24 references), and T2:482 (10 references); for reviews by Robert C. Droege and John P. Foley, Jr., see 7:401 (28 references); for reviews by N. M. Downie and Marvin D. Dunnette, see 6:513 (17 references); see also 5:400 (59 references); for reviews by H. E. Brogden, Charles D. Flory, and Irving Lorge, see 3:269 (7 references); see also 2:1415 (2 references).

[2794]
Woodcock Diagnostic Reading Battery.

Purpose: "Provides a diagnostic test that assesses reading achievement and important related abilities."
Population: Ages 4 to 90+.
Publication Date: 1997.

Acronym: WDRB.
Scores, 17: Letter-Word Identification, Word Attack, Reading Vocabulary, Passage Comprehension, Incomplete Words, Sound Blending, Oral Vocabulary, Listening Comprehension, Memory for Sentences, Visual Matching, Total Reading, Broad Reading, Basic Reading Skills, Reading Comprehension, Phonological Awareness, Oral Comprehension, Reading Aptitude.
Administration: Individual.
Price Data, 2006: $374.50 per complete test kit including test book, examiner's manual (162 pages), norms tables, and 25 test records; $51 per package of 25 test records; $61 per examiner's manual.
Time: (50–60) minutes.
Comments: Battery comprises selected tests from the Woodcock-Johnson® Psycho-Educational Battery—Revised (2795); for educational, clinical, or research purposes; optional to use any combination of the subtests that are relevant to individual subjects.
Author: Richard W. Woodcock.
Publisher: Riverside Publishing.
Cross References: For reviews by D. Joe Olmi and Herbert C. Rudman, see 14:422.

[2795]
Woodcock-Johnson® III.

Purpose: Designed "to provide a co-normed set of tests for measuring general intellectual ability, specific cognitive abilities, scholastic aptitude, oral language, and academic achievement."
Population: Ages 2-90+.
Publication Dates: 1977–2001.
Acronym: WJ III®.
Administration: Individual.
Parts, 2: Tests of Cognitive Abilities, Tests of Achievement.
Price Data, 2006: $509.50 per Achievement Battery (Form A or B) including Achievement Standard and Extended test books, examiner's manual, audio cassette, 25 test records, 25 response booklets, CompuScore® and Profiles Program version 1.1b (Windows and Macintosh), technical manual, and scoring guides; $599.50 per Achievement Battery with leather carrying case (Form A or B); $70 per 25 Achievement test records and subject response booklets (Form A or B; $690 per Tests of Cognitive Abilities Battery including Cognitive Standard and Extended test books, examiner's manual, audio cassette, 25 test records, 25 response booklets, 5 Brief Intellectual ability Test Records, CompuScore® and Profiles Program version 1.1b (Windows and Macintosh), technical manual, and scoring guides; $779.50 per Tests of Cognitive Abilities Battery with leather carrying case; $70 per 25 Cognitive test records and subject response booklets; $32 per 25 Brief Intellectual Ability Test Records.

Comments: Tests can be administered separately; previous edition was entitled Woodcock-Johnson Psycho-Educational Battery—Revised; can be scored only with the Compuscore® software included or optional Report Writer; minimum system requirements: Microsoft Windows 95/98/NT 4.0/2000/Me/XP, PC with 486 processor, VGA monitor, 16 MB of RAM, 5MB of free hard disk space, Windows-supported printer (Windows System) or Apple system 7.5.5–9.1, Macintosh computer with 68020 processor, Macintosh-compatible printer (Macintosh System), 16 MB RAM, 10MB of free hard disk space; 1989 edition still available.
Authors: Richard W. Woodcock, Kevin S. McGrew, Nancy Mather; and Fredrick A. Schrank (Compuscore® and Profiles Program).
Publisher: Riverside Publishing.
  a) TESTS OF ACHIEVEMENT.
  Scores: 11 Standard Battery (Form A or B) test scores: Letter-Word Identification, Reading Fluency, Passage Comprehension, Story Recall, Understanding Directions, Calculation, Math Fluency, Applied Problems, Spelling, Writing Fluency, Writing Samples, and 3 Standard Battery Supplemental test scores: Story Recall—Delayed, Handwriting Legibility Scale, Writing Evaluation Scale, plus 6 Standard Battery cluster scores derived from combinations of the above test scores: Broad Reading, Oral Language-Standard, Broad Math, Math Calculation Skills, Broad Written Language, Written Expression, and 4 Supplementary Battery cluster scores: Academic Skills, Academic Fluency, Academic Applications, Total Achievement; 7 Extended Battery (Form A or B) test scores: Word Attack, Reading Vocabulary, Picture Vocabulary, Oral Comprehension, Quantitative Concepts, Editing, Academic Knowledge, and 3 Extended Battery Supplemental test scores: Spelling of Sounds, Sound Awareness, Punctuation & Capitalization, plus 9 Extended Battery cluster scores derived from combinations of standard and extended battery tests: Basic Reading Skills, Reading Comprehension, Oral Language—Extended, Oral Expression, Listening Comprehension, Math Reasoning, Basic Writing Skills, Academic Knowledge, Phoneme/Grapheme Knowledge.
  Forms, 2: A, B.
  Time: Approximately (5) minutes per test; (55–65) minutes for Standard Battery.
  b) TESTS OF COGNITIVE ABILITIES.
  Scores: 10 Standard Battery test scores: Verbal Comprehension, Visual-Auditory Learning, Spatial Relations, Sound Blending, Concept Formation, Visual Matching, Numbers Reversed, Incomplete Words, Auditory Working Memory, Visual-Auditory Learning—Delayed, plus 3 Stan-

dard Battery cluster scores: Verbal Ability, Thinking Ability, Cognitive Efficiency, and 10 Extended Battery test scores: General Information, Retrieval Fluency, Picture Recognition, Auditory Attention, Analysis—Synthesis, Decision Speed, Memory for Words, Rapid Picture Naming, Planning, Pair Cancellation plus 3 Extended Battery cluster scores: Verbal Ability, Thinking Ability, Cognitive Efficiency; 16 factor cluster scores: Comprehension—Knowledge, Long-Term Retrieval, Visual-Spatial Thinking, Auditory Processing, Fluid Reasoning, Processing Speed, Short-Term Memory, Quantitative Knowledge, Reading-Writing Ability, Phonemic Awareness, Working Memory, Broad Attention, Cognitive Fluency, Executive Processes, Delayed Recall, Knowledge.
Time: Approximately (5) minutes per test; (35–45) minutes per Standard Battery; (90–115) minutes per Extended Battery.
Cross References: For reviews by Gregory J. Cizek and Jonathan Sandoval, see 15:281; see T5:2901 (140 references); for reviews by Jack A. Cummings and by Steven W. Lee and Elaine Flory Stefany of the 1991 edition, see 12:415 (56 references); see also T4:2973 (90 references); for reviews by Jack A. Cummings and Alan S. Kaufman of the 1977 edition, see 9:1387 (6 references); see also T3:2639 (3 references).

[2796]
Woodcock Language Proficiency Battery—Revised.

Purpose: Intended to measure abilities and achievement in oral language, reading, and written language as well as English language competence.
Population: Ages 2–90+.
Publication Dates: 1980-1991.
Acronym: WLPB-R.
Scores, 25: Oral Language (Memory for Sentences, Picture Vocabulary, Oral Vocabulary, Listening Comprehension, Verbal Analogies), Reading (Letter-Word Identification, Passage Comprehension, Work Attack, Reading Vocabulary), Written Language (Dictation, Writing Samples, Proofing, Writing Fluency), Punctuation and Capitalization, Spelling, Usage, Handwriting, Oral Language, Broad Reading, Basic Reading Skills, Reading Comprehension, Broad Written Language, Basic Writing Skills, Written Expression, Broad English Ability.
Administration: Individual.
Price Data, 2006: $381.50 per complete kit in English or Spanish including test book, audio cassette, 25 test records and 25 subject response booklets, examiner's manual (238 pages), and norms tables; $66 per 25 test records and 25 subject response book-

lets; $70.50 per examiner's manual; $56 per norms tables.
Foreign Language Edition: Spanish edition available.
Time: (20-60) minutes.
Comments: Battery is a subset of the tests included in the Woodcock-Johnson® Psycho-Educational Battery—Revised (2795).
Authors: Richard W. Woodcock (English Form); Richard W. Woodcock and Ana F. Muñoz-Sandoval (Spanish Form).
Publisher: Riverside Publishing.
Cross References: See T5:2902 (5 references); for reviews by Irvin J. Lehmann and G. Michael Poteat, see 12:416 (3 references); see also T4:2974 (1 reference); for reviews by Ruth Noyce and Michelle Quinn, see 9:1388.

[2797]
Woodcock-Muñoz™ Language Survey–Revised.

Purpose: Designed "to provide a broad sampling of proficiency in oral language, language comprehension, reading, and writing."
Population: Ages 2–90+.
Publication Dates: 1993-2005.
Acronym: WMLS-R.
Scores, 7: Picture Vocabulary, Verbal Analogies, Letter Word Identification, Dictation, Understanding Directions, Story Recall, Passage Comprehension.
Administration: Individual.
Forms, 3: English A, English B, and Spanish.
Price Data, 2006: $299.50 per English complete kit including test book, 25 test records and 25 dictation worksheets, manual (174 pages), audio CD, and a scoring and reporting program; $299.50 per Spanish complete kit including test book, 25 test records and 25 dictation worksheets, manual (174 pages), audio CD, and a scoring and reporting program; $36 per package of 25 test records and 25 dictation worksheets; $90 per manual, $23 per audio CD; $118.50 per scoring and reporting program (Windows).
Foreign Language Edition: Also available in Spanish.
Time: (45-55) minutes for complete; (25) minutes for screening.
Comments: There is a computer program for scoring and generating narrative reports for any combination of tests from the test.
Authors: R. W. Woodcock, A. F. Muñoz-Sandoval, M. L. Ruef, and C. G. Alvarado.
Publisher: Riverside Publishing.
Cross References: For reviews by Linda Crocker and Chi-Wen Kao of an earlier edition, see 13:364.

[2798]
Woodcock Reading Mastery Tests—Revised [1998 Normative Update].

Purpose: To measure reading readiness, basic skills, and comprehension.

Population: Grades K through postsecondary; ages 5-0 through 75+.

Publication Dates: 1973–1998.

Scores, 11: Readiness Cluster (Visual-Auditory Learning, Letter Identification, Total), Basic Skills Cluster (Word Identification, Word Attack, Total), Reading Comprehension Cluster (Word Comprehension, Passage Comprehension, Total), Total Reading—Full Scale, Total Reading—Short Scale, plus a Supplementary Letter Checklist.

Administration: Individual.

Forms, 2: G, H (includes Reading Achievement tests only).

Price Data, 2005: $443.99 per Form G and Form H combined kit including Form G and Form H test books, 25 Form G and 25 Form G test records, sample NU Forms, G and H summary record form, pronunciation guide cassette, sample report to parents, examiner's manual (1998, 214 pages), and carrying bag; $550.99 per combined kit with ASSIST scoring software; $303.99 per Form G complete kit including materials in combined kit for Form G only, and G and H summary record form; $298.99 per Form H complete kit including materials in combined kit for Form H only, and G and H summary record form; $404.99 per Form H kit with ASSIST scoring software; $50.99 per 25 test records (specify Form G or Form H); $35.99 per 25 Form G and H summary record forms; $25.99 per 25 reports to parents; $199.95 per ASSIST scoring software (Windows or Macintosh).

Time: (40–45) minutes for entire battery; (15) minutes for Short Scale.

Comments: Test same as 1987 edition but with 1998 norms for grades K–12 and ages 5–22.

Author: Richard W. Woodcock.

Publisher: Pearson Assessments (originally published by AGS Publishing, acquired by Pearson in 2005).

Cross References: For reviews by Linda Crocker and Mildred Murray-Ward, see 14:423; see also T5:2905 (123 references) and T4:2976 (34 references); for reviews by Robert B. Cooter, Jr. and Richard M. Jaeger of an earlier edition, see 10:391 (38 references); see also T3:2641 (17 references); for reviews by Carol Anne Dwyer and J. Jaap Tuinman, and excerpted reviews by Alex Bannatyne, Richard L. Allington, Cherry Houck (with Larry A. Harris), and by Barton B. Proger of the 1973 edition, see 8:779 (7 references).

[2799]
Word Fluency.

Purpose: Measures ability to produce appropriate words rapidly for fluency in verbal expression.

Population: Positions requiring sharp verbal communication skills.

Publication Dates: 1959–1961.

Scores: Total score only.

Administration: Individual or group.

Price Data, 2002: $73 per start-up kit including 25 test booklets and interpretation and research manual (1959, 30 pages); $54 per 25 test booklets (quantity discounts available); $28 per interpretation and research manual.

Time: 10 minutes.

Author: Human Resource Center, The University of Chicago.

Publisher: Pearson Performance Solutions [No reply from publisher; status unknown].

Cross References: See T5:2907 (9 references), T4:2979 (6 references), T3:2645 (1 reference), and T2:594 (2 references); for a review by James E. Kennedy, see 6:562.

[2800]
Word Identification and Spelling Test.

Purpose: Designed to "assess a student's fundamental literacy skills."

Population: Ages 7.0–18.11.

Publication Date: 2004.

Acronym: WIST.

Scores, 4: Word Identification, Spelling, Sound-Symbol Knowledge, Fundamental Literacy Ability Index.

Administration: Individual.

Levels, 2: Elementary, Secondary.

Price Data, 2006: $235 per complete kit including examiner's manual (142 pages), 25 Elementary examiner record booklets, 25 Secondary examiner record booklets, 50 Spelling response forms, word card-Regular Words, word card-Irregular Words, word card-Letter/Pseudo Words, Elementary Spelling card, Secondary Spelling card, and Irregular Spelling card; $65 per examiner's manual; $40 per 25 examiner's record booklets (specify Elementary or Secondary); $15 per 50 Spelling response forms; $15 per word card (specify Regular, Irregular or Letter/Pseudo Words); $15 per Spelling card (specify Elementary or Secondary).

Time: (40) minutes.

Authors: Barbara A. Wilson and Rebecca H. Felton.

Publisher: PRO-ED.

Cross References: For reviews by W. Joel Schneider and Kathryn E. Hoff and by John T. Willse, see 16:276.

[2801]
Word Identification Scale.

Purpose: Designed as "an informal reading survey that allows a teacher to quickly identify" a student's readability level in terms of "decoding and word recognition skills."
Population: Students in Grades 1–12.
Publication Dates: 1988–1999.
Acronym: WIS.
Scores: Total score only.
Administration: Individual.
Manual: No manual.
Price Data, 2006: $15 per complete set including plasticized word card with instructions and 50 recording forms.
Time: (5–10) minutes.
Author: John Arena.
Publisher: Academic Therapy Publications.

[2802]
The Word Memory Test.

Purpose: Designed for symptom validity testing—detecting malingering and feigning in comparison to cases of true brain injury and amnesia.
Population: Adults.
Publication Dates: 1995–2000.
Acronym: WMT.
Scores, 5: Immediate Recognition, Delayed Recognition, Multiple Choice, Paired Associates, Free Recall.
Administration: Individual.
Forms, 2: Oral, Computerized.
Price Data: Available from publisher.
Time: (15) minutes.
Comments: Computerized form (C-WMT) self-administered.
Authors: Paul Green, Kevin Astner, and Lyle M. Allen.
Publisher: Green's Publishing [Canada].
Cross References: For reviews by M. Allan Cooperstein and Michael P. Gamache, see 14:424.

[2803]
Word Recognition and Phonic Skills.

Purpose: "Designed to give the teacher two assessments of a child's word recognition ability."
Population: Ages 5.0 to 8.6.
Publication Date: 1994.
Acronym: WRaPS.
Scores: Word Recognition.
Administration: Group.
Price Data, 2002: £6.99 per 10 test booklets; £10.99 per diagnostic scoring template; £10.99 per manual (31 pages); £10.99 per specimen set including one copy of test form and manual.
Time: (30) minutes.

Authors: Clifford Carver and David Moseley.
Publisher: Hodder & Stoughton Educational [England].
Cross References: For reviews by Robert G. Harrington and Joyce R. McLarty, see 14:425; see also T5:2910 (1 reference).

[2804]
The Word Test 2: Elementary.

Purpose: Designed to assess expressive vocabulary and semantics.
Population: Ages 6.0-11.11.
Publication Dates: 1981-2004.
Scores, 7: Associations, Synonyms, Semantic Absurdities, Antonyms, Definitions, Multiple Definitions, Total.
Administration: Individual.
Price Data: Available from publisher.
Time: (30) minutes.
Authors: Linda Bowers, Rosemary Huisingh, Carolyn LoGiudice, and Jane Orman.
Publisher: LinguiSystems, Inc.
Cross References: See T5:2911 (6 references) and T4:2983 (2 references); for reviews by Mavis Donahue and Nambury S. Raju of the original edition, see 9:1393.

[2805]
Wordchains: A Word Reading Test for All Ages.

Purpose: Designed to "screen for specific learning difficulties" and to help teachers "identify individual pupils with poor reading skills."
Population: Ages 7 and over.
Publication Date: 1999.
Scores, 2: Letterchains, Wordchains.
Administration: Individual or group.
Price Data: Available from publisher.
Time: (15) minutes.
Author: Louise Miller Guron.
Publisher: NFER-Nelson Publishing Co., Ltd. [England].
Cross References: For reviews by Colin Cooper and Steven R. Shaw, see 16:278.

[2806]
Work Adjustment Inventory.

Purpose: "Designed to evaluate adolescents' and young adults' temperament toward work activities, work environments, other employees, and other aspects of work."
Population: Adolescents and young adults.
Publication Date: 1994.
Acronym: WAI.
Scores, 7: Activity, Empathy, Sociability, Assertiveness, Adaptability, Emotionality, WAI Quotient.
Administration: Group or individual.

Price Data, 2006: $105 per complete kit; $50 per 50 record forms; $59 per manual.
Time: (15–20) minutes.
Author: James E. Gilliam.
Publisher: PRO-ED.
Cross References: For reviews by Mark J. Benson and Wayne J. Camara, see 13:365.

[2807]
Work Aspect Preference Scale.

Purpose: "Constructed to assess the qualities of work that individuals consider important to them."
Population: Grades 10–12 and college and adults.
Publication Dates: 1983-1999.
Acronym: WAPS.
Scores: 13 scales: Independence, Co-Workers, Self-Development, Creativity, Money, Life Style, Prestige, Altruism, Security, Management, Detachment, Physical Activity, Surroundings, plus 3 second order dimensions: On-Work Orientation, Human/Personal Concern, Freedom.
Administration: Group.
Price Data, 2005: A$2.50 per question/answer booklet; $1.05 per profile; $75.60 per manual (41 pages).
Time: (10-20) minutes.
Author: Robert Pryor.
Publisher: Australian Council for Educational Research Ltd. [Australia].
Cross References: See T5:2915 (8 references) and T4:2987 (1 reference).

[2808]
Work Attitudes Questionnaire (Version for Research).

Purpose: "Designed to differentiate the 'workaholic' or the Type A personality from the highly committed worker."
Population: Managers.
Publication Dates: 1980–1981.
Acronym: WAQ.
Scores, 3: Work Commitment, Psychological Health, Total.
Administration: Group.
Price Data: Available from publisher (now free of charge).
Time: Administration time not reported.
Authors: Maxene S. Doty and Nancy E. Betz.
Publisher: Nancy E. Betz, Ph.D.
Cross References: For a review by Mary L. Tenopyr, see 9:1395.

[2809]
Work Environment Scale, Second Edition.

Purpose: Developed to "measure the social environment of different types of work settings."
Population: Employees and supervisors.

Publication Dates: 1974-1989.
Acronym: WES.
Scores, 10: Involvement, Peer Cohesion, Supervisor Support, Autonomy, Task Orientation, Work Pressure, Clarity, Control, Innovation, Physical Comfort.
Administration: Group.
Forms, 3: Real (R), Ideal (I), Expected (E).
Price Data, 2001: $35.50 per 25 test booklets (Form R); $49.75 per 25 test booklets (select Form I or E); $19.25 per 25 answer sheets; $44 per 25 self-scorable answer sheets; $17 per set of scoring stencils; $8.50 per 25 profiles; $37.50 per 25 interpretive report forms; $48.80 per manual (57 pages); $13.20 per preview kit (nonprepaid).
Time: [15–20] minutes.
Comments: A part of the Social Climate Scales (T5:2445).
Authors: Rudolf H. Moos and Paul N. Insel (tests).
Publisher: CPP, Inc.
Cross References: See T5:2917 (5 references); for reviews by Ralph O. Mueller and Eugene P. Sheehan, see 12:417 (6 references); see also T4:2989 (19 references); for a review by Rabindra N. Kanungo, see 9:1398 (1 reference); see also T3:2652 (2 references) and 8:713 (3 references). For a review of the Social Climate Scales, see 8:681.

[2810]
The Work Experience Survey.

Purpose: Designed as a "structured interview protocol for identifying barriers (and possible solutions) to career maintenance" for a disabled person.
Population: "Individuals with disabilities who are either employed or about to begin employment."
Publication Date: 1995.
Acronym: WES.
Scores: Not scored.
Administration: Individual.
Price Data: Available from publisher.
Time: (30–60) minutes.
Comments: Administered in a face-to-face or telephone interview.
Authors: Richard T. Roessler (survey and manual), Cheryl A. Reed (manual), and Phillip D. Rumrill (manual).
Publisher: The National Center on Employment & Disability.
Cross References: For reviews by Albert M. Bugaj and Lawrence H. Cross, see 14:426.

[2811]
Work Information Inventory.

Purpose: Designed to assess employee morale by utilizing the direction of perception techniques.
Population: Employee groups in industry.
Publication Date: 1958.

Acronym: WII.
Scores: Total score only.
Administration: Group.
Price Data: Available from publisher.
Time: (15) minutes.
Author: Raymond E. Bernberg.
Publisher: Psychometric Affiliates.
Cross References: For additional information and a review by Albert K. Kurtz, see 8:1057.

[2812]
Work Keys Assessments.

Purpose: A job skills assessment system that measures "real world" skills.
Population: Grades 9 to adult.
Publication Dates: 1992–1994.
Administration: Individual or group.
Price Data: Available from publisher.
Author: ACT, Inc.
Publisher: ACT, Inc.
a) READING FOR INFORMATION ASSESSMENT.
Purpose: "Measures the learner's skill in reading and understanding work-related instructions and policies."
Scores: Total score only.
Levels: 5 reading skill levels.
Time: (45) minutes.
b) APPLIED MATHEMATICS ASSESSMENT.
Purpose: "Measures the learner's skill in applying mathematical reasoning to work-related problems."
Scores: Total score only.
Levels: 5 mathematics skill levels.
Time: (45) minutes.
c) LISTENING ASSESSMENT.
Purpose: "Measures the learner's skill at listening to and understanding work-related messages."
Scores: Total score only.
Levels: 5 listening skill levels.
Time: [40] minutes.
Comments: Constructed-response; administered via audiotape; hand-scored by ACT.
d) WRITING ASSESSMENT.
Purpose: "Measures the learner's skill at writing work-related messages."
Scores: Total score only.
Levels: 5 writing skill levels.
Time: [40] minutes.
Comments: Constructed-response; administered via audiotape; hand-scored by ACT.
e) LOCATING INFORMATION ASSESSMENT.
Purpose: "Measures the learner's skill in using information taken from workplace graphics such as diagrams, floor plans, tables, forms, graphs, charts, and instrument gauges."

Scores: Total score only.
Levels: 4 information skill levels.
Time: (45) minutes.
f) TEAMWORK ASSESSMENT.
Purpose: "Measures the learner's skill in choosing behaviors and/or actions that simultaneously support team interrelationships and lead toward the accomplishment of work tasks."
Parts: 2.
Scores: Total score only.
Levels: 4 teamwork skill levels.
Time: (62) minutes.
Comments: Administered via videotape.
g) APPLIED TECHNOLOGY ASSESSMENT.
Purpose: "Measures the learner's skill in solving problems of a technological nature."
Scores: Total score only.
Levels: 4 applied technology levels.
Time: (45) minutes.
h) OBSERVATION ASSESSMENT.
Purpose: "Measures the learner's skill in paying attention to instructions and demonstrations, and in noticing details."
Scores: Total score only.
Levels: 4 observation levels.
Time: (60) minutes.
Comments: Administered via videotape.

[2813]
[Work Motivation].

Purpose: Assesses assumptions and practices characterizing attempts to motivate employees, and evaluate employee motivational needs and values.
Population: Managers, employees.
Publication Dates: 1967–2000.
Scores, 5: Basic-Creature Comfort, Safety and Order, Belonging and Affiliation, Ego-Status, Actualization and Self-Expression.
Administration: Group.
Manual: No manual.
Price Data, 2001: $7.95 per instrument.
Time: [15-30] minutes.
Comments: Self-administered inventory.
Authors: Jay Hall and Martha Williams.
Publisher: Teleometrics International, Inc.
a) MANAGEMENT OF MOTIVES INDEX.
Purpose: Assesses assumptions and practices characterizing attempts to motivate employees.
Acronym: MMI.
b) WORK MOTIVATION INVENTORY.
Purpose: Evaluate employee motivational needs and values.
Acronym: WMI.
Cross References: See T3:2655 (4 references) and 8:1189 (3 references).

[2814]
Work Motivation Inventory: A Test of Adult Work Motivation.

Purpose: Measures the importance people place on four major goals or values related to career development decisions.
Population: Ages 16-Adult.
Publication Dates: 1985–1987.
Acronym: WMI.
Scores, 5: Bias, Accomplishment, Recognition, Power, Affiliation.
Administration: Group or individual.
Time: (10-15) minutes.
Comments: Self-administered survey; mail-in to publisher for narrative report processing.
Authors: Larry A. Braskamp and Martin L. Maehr.
Publisher: MetriTech, Inc.
  a) WMI NARRATIVE REPORTS.
  Price Data, 2005: $34 per narrative report kit including manual, processing of 5 reports, and 5 pre-paid test booklets; $5.25-$8.25 per narrative report including processing and answer sheets.
  Comments: Oriented to the test taker and features extensive interpretive information and guidelines for applying the test results to the test taker's career and life planning; based on parent program SPECTRUM.
  b) WMI/PC MICROCOMPUTER VERSION.
  Price Data: $49 per introductory kit including manual and 5 report demo disk; $105 per 10 administration disks; $237.50 per 25 administration disks; $400 per 50 administration disks; $14 per manual; $27 per 50 test booklets/answer sheets; $18 per 50 decision model worksheets.
  Comments: Supports both on-line and off-line testing; IBM version only.
Cross References: For reviews by Cyril J. Sadowski and Terry A. Stinnett, see 12:366.

[2815]
Work Orientation and Values Survey.

Purpose: Identifies and categorizes 32 work values, reflecting survey taker's approach to world of work.
Population: Adult and teenage job seekers and career planners.
Publication Date: 2002.
Acronym: WOVS.
Scores, 8: Earnings and Benefits, Working Conditions, Time Orientation, Task Orientation, Mission Orientation, Coworker Relations, Supervisor Relations, Managing Others.
Administration: Group or individual.
Price Data, 2006: $24.95 per 25 inventories including copy of administrator's guide (8 pages).
Time: (15–20) minutes.

Comments: Self-administered and self-scored.
Author: Robert P. Brady.
Publisher: JIST Publishing, Inc.

[2816]
Work Performance Assessment.

Purpose: Designed to assess "work-related social/interpersonal skills."
Population: Job trainees.
Publication Dates: 1987–1988.
Acronym: WPA.
Scores: 19 supervisory demands: Greet Each Trainee, Direct Trainee to Work Station and Explain Nature of Work, Provide Vague Instructions, Explain Supervisory Error, Provide Detailed Instructions, Observe Trainees Working, Stand Next to Trainee, Create a Distraction, Show New Way to Work, Introduce Time Pressure, Criticize Trainee's Work, Compliment Trainee's Work, Ask Trainees to Switch Tasks, Ask Trainees to Socialize, Direct Trainees to Work Together, Ask Trainees to Criticize Each Other, Ask Trainees to Compliment Each Other, Observe Trainees Completing the Task Together, Socialize with Each Trainee, yielding a Total Score.
Administration: Group.
Price Data: Available from publisher.
Time: (60–70) minutes.
Comments: Ratings by supervisor.
Authors: Richard Roessler, Suki Hinman, and Frank Lewis.
Publisher: The National Center on Employment & Disability.
Cross References: For reviews by Caroline Manuele-Adkins and Gerald R. Schneck, see 13:367.

[2817]
Work Personality Index.

Purpose: "Designed to identify personality traits that directly relate to work performance."
Population: High school to adult.
Publication Date: 2001.
Acronym: WPI.
Scores, 17: Teamwork, Concern for Others, Outgoing, Democratic, Attention to Detail, Rule-Following, Dependability, Ambition, Energy, Persistence, Leadership, Innovation, Analytic Thinking, Self-Control, Stress Tolerance, Initiative, Flexibility, and 5 factors: Achievement, Conscientiousness, Social Orientation, Practical Intelligence, Adjustment.
Administration: Group or individual.
Price Data: Available from publisher.
Foreign Language Editions: Available in English and French.
Time: (20–40) minutes.
Comments: May be administered via paper and pencil or on the internet.

Authors: Donald Macnab and Shawn Bakker.
Publisher: Psychometrics Canada Ltd. [Canada].
Cross References: For reviews by Janet F. Carlson and Joseph G. Law, Jr., see 16:279.

[2818]
Work Personality Profile.

Purpose: Designed to "assess fundamental work role requirements that are essential to achievement and maintenance of suitable employment."
Population: Vocational rehabilitation clients.
Publication Date: 1986.
Acronym: WPP.
Scores, 16: Acceptance of Work Role, Ability to Profit from Instruction or Correction, Work Persistence, Work Tolerance, Amount of Supervision Required, Extent Trainee Seeks Assistance from Supervisor, Degree of Comfort or Anxiety with Supervisor, Appropriateness of Personal Relations with Supervisor, Teamwork, Ability to Socialize with Co-Workers, Social Communication Skills, Task Orientation, Social Skills, Work Motivation, Work Conformance, Personal Presentation.
Administration: Individual.
Price Data: Price available from publisher for complete set including manual (40 pages), diskette, and 50 tests.
Time: (5–10) minutes.
Comments: Observational ratings by vocational evaluators; to be administered after one week (20-30 hours) in evaluation setting; available on diskette.
Authors: Brian Bolton and Richard Roessler.
Publisher: The National Center on Employment & Disability.
Cross References: See T5:2924 (4 references) and T4:2994 (1 reference); for a review by Ralph O. Mueller and Paula J. Dupuy, see 11:476.

[2819]
Work Potential Profile.

Purpose: "Developed as a tool for the initial descriptive assessment of long-term unemployed individuals."
Population: Ages 16 and older.
Publication Date: 1997.
Scores, 25: Coping (General Satisfaction, Stress and Anxiety, Self-image, Self-Discipline, Time Sense/Use, Total), Freedom from Major Barriers (Preoccupation with Health, Agitation/Aggression, Depression/Resentment, Pervasive Distrust/Delusions, Total), Social Resources (Attitude Towards Others, Social Skills, Total), Abilities (Communication and Literacy, Technology Use, Numeracy, Problem Solving, Total), Motivation (Work Motivation, Intrinsic Motivation, Extrinsic Motivation, Need for Status, Total), Physical Abilities.
Administration: Group.

Price Data, 2006: A\$149.50 per complete set; \$59.95 per manual; \$19.95 per 10 questionnaire; \$19.95 per 10 answer booklets; \$19.95 per 10 group record forms;\$19.95 per 10 individual record forms; \$39.95 per set of 9 score keys.
Time: (10–30) minutes.
Author: Helga A. H. Rowe.
Publisher: Australian Council for Educational Research Ltd. [Australia].
Cross References: For reviews by JoEllen V. Carlson and Robert Fitzpatrick, see 15:282.

[2820]
Work Preference Match: A Career Exploration Tool.

Purpose: Designed to "help career decision makers identify priorities and evaluate career or job choices based on those priorities."
Population: Career decision makers.
Publication Date: 2006.
Acronym: WPM.
Scores: No formal scores.
Administration: Individual or group.
Price Data, 2006: \$39.95 per complete kit including 25 booklets and 1 administrator's guide (8 pages); bulk discounts available.
Time: Untimed.
Comments: This is a "structured self-exploration tool."
Author: Lynn R. Dowd.
Publisher: JIST Publishing, Inc.

[2821]
Work Preference Questionnaire.

Purpose: To determine preferred job activities.
Population: Business and industry.
Publication Date: 1982.
Scores: Weighted combinations of 150 items into 16 dimensions of work: Making Decisions/Communicating and Having Responsibility, Operating Vehicles, Using Machines-Tools-Instruments, Performing Physical Activities, Operating Keyboard and Office Equipment, Monitoring and/or Controlling Equipment and/or Processes, Working Under Uncomfortable Conditions, Working With Art-Decor Entertainment, Performing Supervisory Duties, Performing Estimating Activities, Processing Written Information, Working With Buyers-Customers-Salespersons, Working Under Hazardous Conditions, Performing Paced and/or Repetitive Activities, Working With Aerial and Aquatic Equipment, Catering/Serving/Smelling/Tasting.
Administration: Group.
Price Data: Available from publisher.
Time: Administration time not reported.
Comments: Also known as Work Activity Questionnaire.

Authors: Robert C. Mecham, Alma F. Harris (test), Ernest J. McCormick (test), and P. R. Jenneret (test).
Publisher: PAQ Services, Inc.

[2822]
Work Profile Questionnaire.

Purpose: "Designed to look at work preference, and identify situations in which people are most likely to flourish and be effective."
Population: Job applicants.
Publication Date: 2001.
Acronym: WPQ.
Scores, 5: Communication Style, Emotions, Drive and Determination, Relationships with People, Thinking Style.
Administration: Individual.
Price Data, 2001: £22 per completed questionnaire.
Time: (5) minutes.
Author: Allan Cameron.
Publisher: The Test Agency Limited [England] [No reply from publisher; status unknown].

[2823]
Work Profile Questionnaire: Emotional Intelligence.

Purpose: "Designed to measure emotional intelligence ... and also identifies respondents' preferred [work] team role."
Population: Adults.
Publication Date: 1999.
Acronym: WPQei.
Scores, 8: Self-Awareness, Empathy, Intuition, Emotions, Motivation, Innovation, Social Skills, Emotional Intelligence.
Administration: Group.
Price Data, 2001: £37.50 per technical manual; £85 per 10 self-scoring questionnaire/answer sheet/profile set; £25 per computer-based WPQei Administrator and Narrative Report Generator.
Time: Untimed.
Comments: Based on the Belbin model of work team functioning; can be administered in paper-and-pencil or personal computer format; requires IBM-compatible PC running Microsoft Windows 95/98/NT, 800x600 resolution display with 256 colors, recommends Pentium processor at 90 Mhz or more, 8 Mb RAM.
Author: Allan Cameron.
Publisher: The Test Agency Limited [England] [No reply from publisher; status unknown].
Cross References: For reviews by Mark Pope and Larissa Smith, see 15:283.

[2824]
Work Readiness Profile.

Purpose: "Developed as a criterion-referenced tool for the initial descriptive assessment of individuals with disabilities."
Population: Older adolescents and adults with disabilities.
Publication Date: 1995.
Scores, 14: Physical Effectiveness (Health, Travel, Movement, Fine Motor Skills, Gross Motor Skills and Strength, Total Average), Personal Effectiveness (Social and Interpersonal, Work Adjustment, Communication Effectiveness, Abilities and Skills, Literacy and Numeracy, Total Average), Hearing, Vision.
Administration: Group.
Price Data, 2006: A$77 per set including manual (64 pages), 10 answer books, 10 group record forms, and 10 individual record forms; A$16.50 per 10 answer books; A$6.60 per 10 group record forms; A$6.60 per 10 individual record forms; A$49.50 per manual.
Time: (10–15) minutes.
Comments: Self-administered or ratings by informant.
Author: Helga A. H. Rowe.
Publisher: Australian Council for Educational Research Ltd. [Australia].
Cross References: For reviews by Jean Powell Kirnan and S. Alvin Leung, see 14:427.

[2825]
Work Skills Series Production.

Purpose: Designed to measure the ability to understand instructions, work with numbers, and accurately check machine settings visually.
Population: Manufacturing and production employees and prospective employees.
Publication Date: 1990.
Acronym: WSS.
Scores: Total score only for each of 3 tests: Understanding Instructions (VWP1), Working with Numbers (NWP2), Visual Checking (CWP3).
Administration: Individual or group.
Price Data: Available from publisher.
Time: 12 minutes for VWP1; 10 minutes for NWP2; 7 minutes for CWP3; 29(40) minutes for complete battery.
Author: Saville & Holdsworth Ltd.
Publisher: SHL Group plc [United Kingdom].
Cross References: For reviews by Brian Bolton and Wayne J. Camara, see 12:418.

[2826]
Work Team Simulator.

Purpose: "Designed to identify individuals who have the attitude and skills needed to be an effective member of a work team; test requires candidates to respond in narrative fashion to a series of job-related situations in order to determine likely real world choices and methods of operating."

Population: Team members.

Publication Dates: 1991–2006.

Acronym: WTS.

Scores, 3: Group Decision Making, Team Relations, Total.

Administration: Group or individual.

Forms, 5: Private and public sector forms: Blue Collar, Clerical/Office, Police Officer, Fire Fighter, Transportation Agency Blue Collar.

Restricted Distribution: Clients may be required to pay a nominal one-time overhead/sign-up fee.

Price Data, 2006: $150 per candidate for rental/scoring and feedback report.

Time: 75 minutes.

Author: Richard C. Joines.

Publisher: Management & Personnel Systems, Inc.

[2827]
Work Temperament Inventory.

Purpose: Identifies "personal traits" of the worker that are then matched to suitable occupations.

Population: Workers.

Publication Date: 1993.

Acronym: WTI.

Scores: 12 scales: Directive, Repetitive, Influencing, Variety, Expressing, Judgments, Alone, Stress, Tolerances, Under, People, Measurable.

Administration: Group.

Price Data: Available from publisher.

Time: (15–20) minutes.

Authors: Brian Bolton and Jeffrey Brookings.

Publisher: The National Center on Employment & Disability.

Cross References: For reviews by Peter F. Merenda and Alan J. Raphael, see 13:368.

[2828]
Working—Assessing Skills, Habits, and Style.

Purpose: "Designed to assess personal habits, skills, and styles that are associated with a positive work ethic."

Population: High school and college students and potential employees.

Publication Date: 1996.

Scores: 9 competencies: Taking Responsibility, Working in Teams, Persisting, Having A Sense of Quality, Life-Long Learning, Adapting to Change, Problem Solving, Information Processing, Systems Thinking.

Administration: Group or individual.

Price Data, 2006: $4 each (quantity discounts available); technical and applications manuals available upon request (price information available from publisher); user's manual free with each order.

Time: (30–35) minutes.

Comments: Inventory for self-rating; can be self-administered and self-scored, or assessed online with automatic scoring.

Authors: Curtis Miles (test and user's manual), Phyllis Grummon (test, user's manual, and technical manual), and Karen M. Maduschke (technical manual).

Publisher: H & H Publishing Co., Inc.

Cross References: For reviews by Wayne Camara and Joyce Meikamp, see 14:429.

[2829]
Working Memory Test Battery for Children.

Purpose: To evaluate working memory in children and young adolescents.

Population: Ages 5–15.

Publication Date: 2001.

Acronym: WMTB-C.

Scores: 9 subtests: Digit Recall, Word List Matching, Word List Recall, Block Recall, Nonword List Recall, Listening Recall, Counting Recall, Mazes Memory, Backward Digit Recall.

Administration: Individual.

Price Data, 2006: £275.50 per complete battery including forms, stimulus books, and manual (183 pages).

Time: (60) minutes.

Authors: Susan Pickering and Sue Gathercole.

Publisher: Harcourt Assessment [England].

Cross References: For a review by Rayne A. Sperling and Daniel L. McCollum, see 16:280.

[2830]
Workplace Skills Survey.

Purpose: Designed to provide "information regarding basic work ethics and employment skills."

Population: Job applicants and employees.

Publication Date: 1998.

Acronym: WSS.

Scores, 7: Communication, Adapting to Change, Problem Solving, Work Ethics, Technological Literacy, Teamwork, Composite.

Administration: Individual or group.

Price Data, 2005: $40 per introductory kit including 5 reusable test booklets, 20 answer/score sheets, and technical manual (9 pages); $30 per 20 answer/score sheets; $18 per 10 reusable test booklets.

Time: 20 minutes.

Author: Industrial Psychology International Ltd.

Publisher: Industrial Psychology International Ltd.

[2831]
Workplace Skills Survey—Form E.

Purpose: Designed to assess students' work place readiness and employment skills.

Population: Students in school-to-work and vocational programs
Publication Date: 2000.
Acronym: WSS-Form E.
Scores, 9: Career Planning, Job Attainment, Communication, Adapting and Coping with Change, Problem Solving, Work Ethics, Technological Literacy, Teamwork, Overall.
Administration: Individual or group.
Price Data, 2005: $8 per assessment per student; $6 per manual (4 pages); $45 per 25 reusable test booklets.
Time: 50 minutes.
Comments: Scoring and analysis provided by publisher.
Author: Industrial Psychology International Ltd.
Publisher: Industrial Psychology International Ltd.

[2832]
World Government Scale.
Purpose: Measures attitudes toward world government.
Population: Students.
Publication Date: 1985.
Scores: Total score only.
Administration: Group.
Manual: No manual.
Price Data, 2005: $2 per scale.
Time: [12] minutes.
Comments: Supplementary article available.
Author: Panos D. Bardis.
Publisher: Donna Bardis.

[2833]
World of Work Inventory.
Purpose: "Designed to assist clients in thinking about themselves in relation to their total environment" in relation to their personal career development.
Population: Ages 13–65+.
Publication Dates: 1970–2006.
Acronym: WOWI.
Scores: 35: Career Interest Activities (17 scores: Public Service, The Sciences, Engineering & Related, Business Relations, Managerial, The Arts, Clerical, Sales, Service, Primary Outdoor, Processing, Machine Work, Bench Work, Structural Work, Mechanical & Electrical Work, Graphic Arts, Mining); Job Satisfaction Indicators (12 scores: Versatile, Adaptable to Repetitive Work, Adaptable to Performing Under Specific Instructions, Dominant, Gregarious, Isolative, Influencing, Self-Controlled, Valuative, Objective, Subjective, Rigorous); Aptitude/Achievement (6 scores: Verbal, Numerical, Abstractions, Spatial-Form, Mechanical/Electrical, Organizing Skill).
Administration: Individual or group.

Price Data, 2004: Online administration: $13 per single profile report with summary; $19.50 per profile report with interpretative report, and $189 online site license fee; Paper-and-pencil administration: $7 per test booklet and $19.95 per interpretation manual (2001, 70 pages).
Time: (60) minutes for online version; (90) minutes for paper-and-pencil short form.
Authors: Robert E. Ripley, Gregory P. M. Neidert, and Nancy L. Ortman.
Publisher: World of Work, Inc.
Cross References: For reviews by Jeffrey A. Jenkins and Eugene P. Sheehan, see 16:281.

[2834]
Worley's ID Profile.
Purpose: Designed to identify temperament.
Population: Ages 6 and over.
Publication Dates: 1995–2000.
Acronym: WIDP.
Scores, 8: 3 profile scores: Social, Leadership, Relationship; 5 behavior scores: Introverted Sanguine, Sanguine, Phlegmatic, Melancholy, Choleric.
Administration: Individual or group.
Forms, 2: Adult and Youth (Ages 6 to 16).
Price Data: Available from publisher.
Foreign Language Editions: Available in English, Spanish, and Portuguese.
Time: (10) minutes.
Author: John W. Worley.
Publisher: Worley's Identity Discovery Profile, Inc.
Cross References: For reviews by Eugene V. Aidman and Frederick T. L. Leong, see 15:284.

[2835]
Writing Process Test.
Purpose: "Measures the quality of students' written products."
Population: Grades 2–12.
Publication Dates: 1991–1992.
Acronym: WPT.
Scores, 14: Development [First Pass (Purpose/Focus, Audience, Vocabulary, Style/Tone, Total), Second Pass (Support/Development, Organization/Coherence, Total)], Fluency [Third Pass (Sentence Structure/Variety, Grammar/Usage, Capitalization/Punctuation, Spelling, Total)], Total.
Administration: Group.
Editions, 2: Individual, Classroom.
Price Data, 2006: $179 per complete kit including test manual (1992, 144 pages), technical manual (1992, 40 pages), 25 analytic scales, 25 Form A first draft booklets, and 25 revision booklets; $57 per test manual; $19 per 25 analytic record forms; $21 per 25 first draft booklets; $14 per 25 revision booklets; $17

per scorer folder; $36 per technical manual; $57 per scoring videotape.
Time: [45] minutes (+30 minutes for revision).
Authors: Robin Warden and Thomas A. Hutchinson.
Publisher: PRO-ED.
Cross References: For reviews by Ernest W. Kimmel and Sandra Ward, see 13:369 (1 reference).

[2836]
The Written Expression Test.

Purpose: To "measure written expression objectively."
Population: Grades 1 to 6.
Publication Dates: 1979-1982.
Acronym: WET.
Scores, 5: Productivity, Mechanics, Handwriting, Maturity, Composite.
Administration: Individual or group.
Price Data: Not available.
Time: (30) minutes.
Authors: Clark Johnson and Sharon Hubly.
Publisher: McClain [No reply from publisher; status unknown].
Cross References: See T5:2934 (1 reference); for reviews by Noel Gregg and Lyn Haber, see 10:396.

[2837]
Written Language Assessment.

Purpose: Assesses writing ability.
Population: Grades 3–12.
Publication Date: 1989.
Acronym: WLA.
Scores, 5: General Writing Ability, Productivity, Word Complexity, Readability, Written Language Quotient.
Administration: Group.
Price Data, 2006: $80 per complete kit including manual (111 pages), 25 each of 3 writing record forms, 25 scoring/profile forms, and hand counter; $25 per 25 each of 3 writing record forms; $15 per 25 scoring/profile forms; $25 per manual; $15 per hand counter; $25 per specimen set.
Time: (45–60) minutes.
Authors: J. Jeffrey Grill and Margaret M. Kirwin.
Publisher: Academic Therapy Publications.
Cross References: See T5:2935 (2 references); for reviews by Stephen Jurs and Mary Ross Moran, see 11:477.

[2838]
Written Language Syntax Test.

Purpose: Designed as a "screening instrument used to provide information on student performance in written language syntax."
Population: Ages 10–17 hearing-impaired.
Publication Date: 1981.
Acronym: WLST.
Scores: Total score only.

Administration: Group or individual.
Levels, 3: 1, 2, 3.
Price Data: Price information available from publisher for tests (specify Level 1, 2, or 3), screening tests, individual data folders, and administrator's package including manual (33 pages) and one copy of each item.
Time: (10–20) minutes for screening test, (40-60) minutes per test.
Comments: Contains "Screening Test" to determine appropriate level for administration.
Author: Sharon R. Berry.
Publisher: Gallaudet University Press.
Cross References: For reviews by Michael W. Casby and Judith R. Johnston, see 9:1404.

[2839]
Y-OQ-SR 2.0 [Youth Outcome Questionnaire-Self Report].

Purpose: Designed to "assess behavior change as the adolescent clients themselves perceive it."
Population: Ages 12-18 years.
Publication Dates: 1999-2005.
Acronym: Y-OQ-SR 2.0.
Scores, 7: Intrapersonal Distress, Somatic, Interpersonal Relations, Social Problems, Behavioral Dysfunction, Critical Items, Total.
Administration: Individual or group.
Restricted Distribution: Requires licensure from American Professional Credentialing Services LLC.
Price Data, 2006: Licensing cost available from publisher; $25 per administration and scoring manual (1999, 15 pages); $25 per test.
Foreign Language Editions: English, Spanish, and French editions available.
Time: (7-15) minutes.
Authors: M. Gawain Wells, Gary M. Burlingame, Paul M. Rose (manual only), and Michael J. Lambert (test only).
Publisher: OQ Measures LLC.

[2840]
Y-OQ-30.1 [Youth Outcome Questionnaire-Omni Version].

Purpose: Designed to measure "the treatment process for children and adolescents receiving any form of behavioral health treatment including psychoactive medications."
Population: Ages 12-18 years.
Publication Dates: 1998-2002.
Acronym: Y-OQ-30.1.
Scores: Total score only.
Administration: Individual or group.
Restricted Distribution: Requires licensure from American Professional Credentialing Services LLC.

Price Data, 2006: Licensing cost available from publisher; $25 per administration and scoring manual (2003, 21 pages); $25 per test.
Foreign Language Editions: English, Spanish, and French editions available.
Time: (2-15) minutes.
Comments: Test can be parent-reported and self-reported.
Authors: Gary M. Burlingame, Bruce W. Jasper (manual only), Gary Peterson (manual only), M. Gawain Wells, Curtis W. Reisinger, G. S. (Jeb) Brown (manual only).
Publisher: OQ Measures LLC.

[2841]
Young Children's Achievement Test.

Purpose: Designed to help determine early academic abilities.
Population: Ages 4-0 to 7-11.
Publication Date: 2000.
Acronym: YCAT.
Scores, 6: General Information, Reading, Mathematics, Writing, Spoken Language, and Early Achievement Composite.
Administration: Individual.
Price Data, 2006: $210 per complete kit including examiner's manual (154 pages), picture book (48 pages), 25 student response forms, and 25 profile/examiner record booklets; $65 per examiner's manual; $70 per picture book; $30 per 25 student response forms; $50 per 25 profile/examiner record booklets.
Time: (25-45) minutes.
Authors: Wayne P. Hresko, Pamela K. Peak, Shelley R. Herron, and Deanna L. Bridges.
Publisher: PRO-ED.
Cross References: For reviews by Russell N. Carney and Susan J. Maller, see 15:285.

[2842]
Youth Level of Service/Case Management Inventory.

Purpose: Designed for use in "assessing risk, need, and responsibility factors" in young offenders.
Population: Juvenile Offenders, ages 12-17.
Publication Date: 2002.
Acronym: YLS/CMI.
Scores: 9 Risk Ratings: Offenses and Dispositions, Family Factors, Education and Employment, Peer Relations, Substance Abuse, Leisure/Recreation, Personality/Behavior, Attitudes/Orientation, Total.
Administration: Individual.
Parts, 7: Assessment of Risks and Needs, Summary of Risk/Need Factors, Assessment of Other Needs/Special Considerations, Your Assessment of the Client's General Risk/Need Level, Contact Level, Case Management Plan, Case Management Review.

Price Data, 2006: $160 per complete kit including user's manual (56 pages), 25 interview guides, 25 QuikScore™ forms, and 25 case management forms; $52 per user's manual; $65 per 25 interview guides; $38 per 25 QuikScore™ forms; $22 per 25 case management forms; $57 per specimen set including user's manual, 3 interview guides, 3 QuikScore™ forms, and 3 case management forms; software version also available.
Time: [30–40] minutes.
Comments: Risk assessment checklist completed on the bases of semistructured interview and record review; derived from the Level of Service Inventory—Revised.
Authors: Robert D. Hoge and D. A. Andrews.
Publisher: Multi-Health Systems, Inc.
Cross References: For reviews by Pam Lindsey and Stephen E. Trotter, see 16:282.

[2843]
Youth Outcome Questionnaire (Y-OQ-2.01).

Purpose: Designed as a "measure of treatment progress for children and adolescents receiving psychological or psychiatric treatment."
Population: Ages 4–17.
Publication Dates: 1996-2005.
Acronym: Y-OQ-2.0.
Scores, 7: Intrapersonal Distress, Somatic, Interpersonal Relations, Critical Items, Social Problems, Behavioral Dysfunction, Total.
Administration: Individual.
Price Data: Price data for manual (1996, 27 pages) and questionnaires available from publisher.
Time: (7–20) minutes.
Comments: Behavior rating scale completed by parent or "significant adult figure."
Authors: Gary M. Burlingame (test and manual), Michael J. Lambert (test and manual), M. Gawain Wells (manual), Matthew J. Hoag (manual), Carolen A. Hope (manual), R. Scott Nebeker (manual), Kimberly Konkel (manual), Pamela McCollam (manual), Gary Peterson (manual), Mark Latkowski (manual), and Curtis W. Reisinger (manual).
Publisher: OQ Measures LLC.
Cross References: For reviews by Susan K. Green and John Hattie, see 16:283.

[2844]
Youth Program Quality Assessment.

Purpose: "Designed to evaluate the quality of youth programs and identify staff training needs."
Population: Youth-serving programs.
Publication Date: 2005.
Acronyms: Youth PQA.
Administration: Individual or group.
Forms, 2: A, B.

Price Data, 2006: $39.95 per complete kit including administration manual (35 pages), Form A-Program Offering Items, and Form B-Organization Items; $19.95 per administration manual; $10.95 per Form A-Program Offering Items; $10.95 per Form B-Organization Items.

Comments: This test is based on observations and interviews by either "independent raters or as a self-assessment."

Author: High/Scope Educational Research Foundation.

Publisher: High/Scope Educational Research Foundation.

a) FORM A-PROGRAM OFFERING ITEMS.
Purpose: "Focuses on youth experiences during a program offering."
Scores, 5: Safe Environment, Supportive Environment, Interaction, Engagement, Total.
Time: (120) minutes.
b) FORM B-ORGANIZATION ITEMS.
Purpose: "Assesses the organization's infrastructure."
Scores, 4: Youth Centered Policies/Practices, High Expectations for All Students/Staff, Access, Total.
Time: (60) minutes.

[2845]
Youth Risk and Resilience Inventory.

Purpose: Designed "to identify individual assets or resilience factors" and "screen for the presence of risk factors such as teasing, intimidation, bullying, physical abuse, violence, and victimization; to identify signs of emotional stress; and to assess their impact on the individual."

Population: Ages 10 to 17.
Publication Date: 2006.

Acronyms: YRRI.
Scores, 2: Risk Factor, Resilience Factor.
Administration: Individual or group.
Price Data, 2006: $23.95 per complete kit including 25 test booklets and administrator's guide (8 pages); bulk discounts are available.
Time: Administration time not reported.
Comments: There is an optional "My Journal" section at the end of the test; this option does not affect the numeric scores.
Author: Robert P. Brady.
Publisher: JIST Publishing, Inc.

[2846]
Youth's Inventory—4.

Purpose: Designed to determine "the extent to which the adolescent patient is aware of his or her symptoms" (of adolescent psychopathology), as determined by self-report.
Population: Ages 12–18.
Publication Date: 1999.
Acronym: YI-4.
Scores, 11: AD/HD Inattentive, Hyperactive–Impulsive, Combined, Oppositional Defiant Disorder, Conduct Disorder, Generalized Anxiety Disorder, Major Depressive Disorder, Dysthymic Disorder, Sepration Anxiety Disorder, Eating Problems, Bipolar Disorder.
Administration: Individual.
Price Data, 2006: $75 per deluxe kit including 50 checklists, 50 symptom count score sheets, 50 symptom severity profile score sheets, and manual (1999, 170 pages); $52 per 50 checklists.
Time: [15] minutes.
Authors: Kenneth D. Gadow and Joyce Sprafkin.
Publisher: Checkmate Plus, Ltd.
Cross References: For reviews by Harold R. Keller and John J. Vacca, see 15:286.

INDEX OF
MMY TEST REVIEWERS

This record of Mental Measurements Yearbook *test reviewers lists all individuals reviewing in the 16 editions of the* MMY *series. The numbers after the names represent the* Mental Measurements Yearbooks *in which their reviews appeared.*

Based on the recommendation of our National Advisory Committee, the Buros Institute of Mental Measurements is now making special recognition of the long-term contributions of reviewers to the Mental Measurements Yearbook *series. To receive the "Distinguished Reviewer" designation, an individual must have contributed to six or more editions of this series beginning with* The Ninth Mental Measurements Yearbook. *By virtue of their long-term service, these reviewers exemplify an outstanding dedication in their professional lives to the principles of improving the science and practice of testing. Individuals receiving awards as Distinguished Reviewers as of the publication of* The Sixteenth Mental Measurements Yearbook *(2005) are indicated with an asterisk (*) below.*

Harold H. Abelson, 3
Murray Aborn, 4
Shawn K. Acheson, 15-16
*Phillip L. Ackerman, 11-16
Terry A. Ackerman, 12-13
Fred L. Adair, 8
Carol Adams, 9
Clifford R. Adams, 6
Elizabeth C. Adams, 4
Georgia S. Adams, 7-8
Gerald R. Adams, 9
Mary Friend Adams, 8
Russell L. Adams, 9-10
Susan F. Adams, 12
C. J. Adcock, 5-7
Dorothy C. Adkins, 3-7
Dan L. Adler, 5
Seymour Adler, 10
Janet G. Afflerbach, 5
Lois G. Afflerbach, 5
Frederick B. Agard, 3

J. Stanley Ahmann, 6-9
Eugene V. Aidman, 14-16
Lewis R. Aiken, 9, 12
Mary D. Ainsworth, 5
Peter W. Airasian, 8-10
*Mark A. Albanese, 11-16
Lewis E. Albright, 6-8
Norma A. Albright, 2
Bruce K. Alcorn, 11-12
Felito Aldarondo, 15
John Charles Alderson, 8
Lawrence M. Aleamoni, 8-9, 11-12
Charlene M. Alexander, 12
Ralph A. Alexander, 9
Bob Algozzine, 9
Henry A. Alker, 7-8
Doris V. Allen, 9-10
Kathleen Allen, 15
Lawrence Allen, 9
Mary J. Allen, 9
Nancy L. Allen, 11

Robert M. Allen, 8
Sarah J. Allen, 11-12, 15
Richard L. Allington, 9-10
Julie A. Allison, 12-15
John C. Almack, 1-2
William D. Altus, 4
Jean D. Amberson, 4
Sueann Robinson Ambron, 8
Vera M. Amerson, 3
Anne Anastasi, 1-11
Nicholas Anastasiow, 7-8
Kenneth N. Anchor, 12
Charles V. Anderson, 8
David O. Anderson, 11-13
Howard R. Anderson, 1-7
Irving H. Anderson, 1, 3
James M. Anderson, 3-4, 6
John O. Anderson, 11-12, 14-16
Kenneth E. Anderson, 4, 6
Robert P. Anderson, 8-9
Louanne Andersson, 15
Jerrilyn. V. Andrews, 11-13
Lawrence Andrus, 2
Harvey A. Andruss, 3
Charles J. Ansorge, 9
Edgar Anstey, 6
Paul A. Arbisi, 12-16
Francis X. Archambault, Jr., 9, 11-12
Robert P. Archer, 11
Joyce A. Arditti, 12
Edward N. Argulewicz, 9
James A. Armentrout, 8
Christian O. Arndt, 2
Dwight L. Arnold, 4-5
Gwen F. Arnold, 4
Edward Aronow, 12
Raoul A. Arreola, 12-15
Judith A. Arter, 9
F. Marion Asche, 12
Philip Ash, 11-14
Ronald A. Ash, 9, 12
E. Jack Asher, Jr., 11
Theodore A. Ashford, 3, 5
Lear Ashmore, 8-9
Alexander W. Astin, 6-7
Michelle Athanasiou, 15-16
James Athanasou, 15-16
Carolyn Peluso Atkins, 9
Samuel D. Atkins, 1-2
Mark J. Atkinson, 14-15
Deborah H. Atlas, 12
*Jeffrey A. Atlas, 11-16
Kathryn Hu-Pei Au, 9
Mark W. Aulls, 9
James T. Austin, 9, 11-14, 16
Mary C. Austin, 6
*Stephen N. Axford, 11-16

Frederic L. Ayer, 3-4
George W. Ayer, 8
J. Douglas Ayers, 6-8, 11
Glen P. Aylward, 11-14, 16
Kris L. Baack, 12, 16
James C. Babcock, 2
*Patricia A. Bachelor, 11-16
Lyle F. Bachman, 11-12
Philip A. Backlund, 13-14
Ellen H. Bacon, 10-11
Beth D. Bader, 12
Andrew R. Baggaley, 5-6
Stephen J. Bagnato, 9
Theresa M. Bahns, 14
Sherry K. Bain, 12, 14, 16
Leonard L. Baird, 7
Janet Baldwin, 12
Thomas S. Baldwin, 7-8, 10
Benjamin Balinsky, 4-5
Rachel S. Ball, 2
Joan C. Ballard, 14-16
Warren R. Baller, 4-5
Irol W. Balsley, 6
Deborah L. Bandalos, 12, 14, 16
K. Denise Bane, 11
Charlotte E. K. Banks, 4-5
Nicholas W. Bankson, 8-11
Allan G. Barclay, 7
James R. Barclay, 9-10
Benjamin D. Barker, 14
*Laura L. B. Barnes, 11-16
Walter Barnes, 1
Janet Barnes-Farrell, 14
David W. Barnett, 10-12
Rita M. Barnett, 12
W. Leslie Barnette, Jr., 8
Andrés Barona, 11, 13
A. S. Barr, 3
Rebecca C. Barr, 7-8
Richard S. Barrett, 6
Thomas C. Barrett, 6
Frank Barron, 5
William M. Bart, 11-12
Brendan John Bartlett, 9
W. L. Bashaw, 7
Alan R. Bass, 8
David J. Bateson, 12
Donald H. Baucom, 9
Ernest A. Bauer, 11-12
Robert H. Bauernfeind, 5-8
Sheri Bauman, 15
Ronald Baumanis, 9
Deborah N. Bauserman, 9
Abigail Baxter, 16
Brent Baxter, 3-5
Ernest Edward Bayles, 1
Nancy Bayley, 2-3, 5

Kenneth L. Bean, 5-6
Robert M. Bear, 3-4
Harold P. Bechtoldt, 4-7
Isabel L. Beck, 9
Michael D. Beck, 11-13, 16
Roland L. Beck, 2-3
Samuel J. Beck, 2, 5
Wesley C. Becker, 6
Ralph C. Bedell, 3, 5
H. R. Beech, 6
Martha C. Beech, 9
Fred S. Beers, 1
Isaac I. Bejar, 8
Marcia J. Belcher, 11
John E. Bell, 4-6
Peter Della Bella, 13
C.G. Bellah, 15-16
Camilla Persson Benbow, 11
Kathryn M. Benes, 11-12
James K. Benish, 13-15
Albert A. Bennett, 2-3
Clinton W. Bennett, 12-13
George K. Bennett, 3-7
Jeri Benson, 11, 13
Mark J. Benson, 12-13
Nicholas Benson, 13
Philip G. Benson, 9-12, 16
Marsha Bensoussan, 13, 16
Peter M. Bentler, 6-7
Arthur L. Benton, 3-4, 7
Sheryl Benton, 16
Stephen L. Benton, 11-12, 16
H. E. Benz, 2
Ralph F. Berdie, 3-7
Abbey L. Berg, 16
Harry D. Berg, 3-8
Paul Conrad Berg, 7
Allen Berger, 7-9
Michael Berger, 8
Peter Miles Berger, 14-15
Jennifer M. Bergeron, 16
Betty Bergstrom, 13
*Ronald A. Berk, 9, 12-16
Hinsdale Bernard, 12-13
H. John Bernardin, 9-12
Rita Sloan Berndt, 9-10
Jean-Jacques Bernier, 11-12
Robert G. Bernreuter, 1-4
Frank M. Bernt, 12-16
Joan D. Berryman, 9
Frederick Bessai, 11-14
Emmett A. Betts, 6
William Betz, 1, 3
Charles L. Bickel, 2
John Biggs, 9
Marion A. Bills, 3
Walter V. Bingham, 1

William C. Bingham, 6, 8
L. B. Birch, 6-7
Ricky Korey Birnbaum, 15
Herbert G. W. Bischoff, 9, 14
Lisa G. Bischoff, 11-15
Bruce H. Biskin, 11-12
Reign H. Bittner, 3-4
Harold H. Bixler, 3-4
Ake Bjerstedt, 5-6
Donald B. Black, 6-7
Hillel Black, 6
John D. Black, 5-6, 8-9
J. M. Blackburn, 2
James H. Blackhurst, 1
E. G. Blackstone, 3
Martha Blackwell, 12
Kimberly Ann Blair, 15-16
C. B. Blakemore, 6
Emery P. Bliesmer, 6
Lynn S. Bliss, 10-12
Sonya Blixt, 12
Jack Block, 8
Martin E. Block, 12
Paul J. Blommers, 3-6
Benjamin S. Bloom, 3-5, 7
Lisa A. Bloom, 12-13
Bruce M. Bloxom, 7-9
Milton L. Blum, 3-4
James A. Blumenthal, 9
Cynthia R. Bochna, 16
Jack L. Bodden, 7-9
Ann E. Boehm, 9
Kathy J. Bohan, 16
Larry M. Bolen, 14
Carol A. Boliek, 11
Joan Bollenbacher, 5
Nancy B. Bologna, 12, 14
*Brian F. Bolton, 8-9, 11-15
David L. Bolton, 12-13
Guy L. Bond, 2
Stephen J. Boney, 12
Mike Bonner, 15-16
Sarah Bonner, 16
Gwyneth M. Boodoo, 9
Ivan A. Booker, 1-4
Daniel R. Boone, 7-8
Roger A. Boothroyd, 12-16
Edward S. Bordin, 3-5
Fred H. Borgen, 7-9
William Borgen, 9
Harold Borko, 6-7
Christopher Borman, 9-10
Walter C. Borman, 8-9
John R. Bormuth, 7
Robert A. Bornstein, 9-12
Morton Bortner, 6, 8-9
Michael D. Botwin, 12

Thomas J. Bouchard, Jr., 7-8
William R. Boulton, 9
Nicholas G. Bountress, 9
Jennifer C. Bouwkamp, 15
John E. Bowers, 6
B. Ann Boyce, 16
*Gregory J. Boyle, 11-16
J. David Boyle, 12
Elizabeth Kelley Boyles, 15
Bruce A. Bracken, 9-12, 16
Jeffrey P. Braden, 11-12, 14, 16
E. J. G. Bradford, 3-4
John M. Bradley, 9
Robert H. Bradley, 9
Thomas B. Bradley, 9
Francis F. Bradshaw, 1
John C. Brantley, 11
Marla R. Brassard, 9
James Braswell, 7-8
John R. Braun, 7-9
Arthur H. Brayfield, 4-6
W. C. Brenke, 3
Ann Brewington, 3
Ann Brickner, 7
Robert G. Bridgham, 7
M. Alan Brimer, 5-7
Elizabeth L. Bringsjord, 13
John J. Brinkman, Jr., 15-16
Frank W. Broadbent, 9
Stanley L. Brodsky, 8
Linda E. Brody, 10, 12
Hubert E. Brogden, 3-4
Susan M. Brookhart, 12-14, 16
Jeffrey B. Brookings, 13
Nelson Brooks, 1-6
M. Eustace Broom, 2
R. A. Brotemarkle, 3
W. Dale Brotherton, 13
Diane Browder, 10
Alfred S. Brown, 3
Andrew W. Brown, 2
Charles M. Brown, 6
Clara M. Brown, 1-2
Douglas T. Brown, 9-10
Frederick G. Brown, 7-9, 11
James Dean Brown, 11-13, 16
Lynn L. Brown, 14-15
Michael B. Brown, 13-14, 16
Ric Brown, 9, 12-14, 16
Robert D. Brown, 9-11, 13-14
Scott W. Brown, 11-12
Steven D. Brown, 9
Virginia L. Brown, 11
William A. Brownell, 1-5
Richard Brozovich, 11-12
Leo J. Brueckner, 1-4
Gordon C. Bruner, II, 14

Roger S. Bruning, 9-10
Bethany A. Brunsman, 15-16
Jennifer A. Brush, 13
James E. Bryan, 5-8
Miriam M. Bryan, 4, 6-8
N. Dale Bryant, 5-8
Diane Nelson Bryen, 9
Aaron D. Buchanan, 8
Jayne E. Bucy, 13
Karen S. Budd, 11
Rita M. Budrionis, 15
William D. Buffington, 8
Albert M. Bugaj, 12-16
Alan C. Bugbee, Jr., 12-13, 16
Eric S. Buhs, 15
Norman A. Buktenica, 9
*Michael B. Bunch, 11-16
Mary Anne Bunda, 11-14
*Linda K. Bunker, 9-12, 14-16
Robert L. Burch, 4
Kenneth E. Burchett, 8
Thomas C. Burgess, 6
Carolyn L. Burke, 7
Paul C. Burnett, 11, 13
R. Will Burnett, 4
Donald G. Burns, 4
Matthew Burns, 14-16
Emily T. Burr, 3
Alvin G. Burstein, 6-7
Cyril Burt, 3, 5
Nancy W. Burton, 7
John Christian Busch, 12
Nancy A. Busch-Rossnagel, 9-10
Brenda R. Bush, 10-11
Ray R. Buss, 9
R. T. Busse, 11
Guy T. Buswell, 2
H. J. Butcher, 7
James N. Butcher, 8-9
Katharine G. Butler, 7-8, 10-12
John K. Butler, Jr., 9
Michelle A. Butler, 16
Dorcas Susan Butt, 8-9
Margaret C. Byrne, 7-9
Leonard S. Cahen, 7-8
G. P. Cahoon, 3-4
James R. Caldwell, 7
Kathryn Hoover Calfee, 8
Robert C. Calfee, 8-10
Carolyn M. Callahan, 12-16
Leroy G. Callahan, 8
Leonard F. Caltabiano, 15
Wayne J. Camara, 12-14, 16
Bonnie W. Camp, 9-10
Cameron J. Camp, 10-11, 13
David P. Campbell, 6-8
Donald T. Campbell, 4-6

Dugal Campbell, 6
Hank Campbell, 10
Iris Amos Campbell, 9
J. Arthur Campbell, 6, 8-9
Joel T. Campbell, 6-7
Michael H. Campbell, 14-16
Thomas F. Campbell, 13
Vincent N. Campbell, 7
Anthony A. Cancelli, 9
Gary L. Canivez, 14, 16
Joyce L. Carbonell, 9
Karen T. Carey, 11-14, 16
Cindy I. Carlson, 11, 14-15
James E. Carlson, 12
*Janet F. Carlson, 11-16
*JoEllen V. Carlson, 11-16
Kenneth A. Carlson, 8
Roger D. Carlson, 11
Thorsten R. Carlson, 7-8
James C. Carmer, 11-12
Arlene E. Carney, 12
Russell N. Carney, 12-13, 15-16
*C. Dale Carpenter, 9-14, 16
Sandra J. Carr, 14
W. L. Carr, 2
David J. Carroll, 8-9
John B. Carroll, 4-8
L. Ray Carry, 7
Harold D. Carter, 1-4
Launor F. Carter, 4
W. H. Cartwright, 3
Heidi M. Carty, 15
John C. Caruso, 14-15
J. Manuel Casas, 9-10
Michael W. Casby, 9
Thomas F. Cash, 9
Frank P. Cassaretto, 5
Linda Castillo, 16
Burton M. Castner, 2
Robert S. Cathcart, 5
Psyche Cattell, 1, 3
Raymond B. Cattell, 2
Darrell N. Caulley, 12
Courtney B. Cazden, 7-8
Stella Center, 1
Tony Cellucci, 14-16
Edward J. Cervenka, 8
Robert W. Ceurvorst, 9
Hester Chadderdon, 1-2, 4
Robert C. Challman, 4, 6-7
E. G. Chambers, 3-5
Carolyn Chaney, 11
Laura H. Chapman, 8
Clinton I. Chase, 7-10
Henry Chauncey, 3, 6
Maurice Chazan, 7
Henry M. Cherrick, 9

Kathleen Barrows Chesterfield, 9
Brad S. Chissom, 7-8
Mary Mathai Chittooran, 13-16
James P. Choca, 13-14
Andrew Christensen, 9
Sandra L. Christenson, 11
Robert Christopher, 14
Edmund P. Churchill, 3
Ruth D. Churchill, 3, 5
*Joseph C. Ciechalski, 11-16
*Gregory J. Cizek, 11-16
Charles D. Claiborn, 9, 12
Mary M. Clare, 15-16
Cherry Ann Clark, 5
D. F. Clark, 7
Elaine Clark, 10, 12-15
Gale W. Clark, 5
J. F. Clark, 5
John L. D. Clark, 7-8
John R. Clark, 2
Kenneth E. Clark, 4
Philip M. Clark, 8-9
Richard M. Clark, 9, 11
Willis W. Clark, 6
H. Harrison Clarke, 4
Glen U. Cleeton, 3
W. V. Clemans, 6
Amanda Jill Clemence, 15
Dorothy M. Clendenen, 5-7
Jeanette N. Cleveland, 9
Victor B. Cline, 7
James R. Clopton, 8-10
Richard W. Coan, 6-8
Harriet C. Cobb, 9
Larry R. Cochran, 9-12
Charles N. Cofer, 3-5
William E. Coffman, 3, 5-9, 11
Andrew D. Cohen, 12
Annabel J. Cohen, 12-13, 16
Ashley Cohen, 14, 16
Bertram D. Cohen, 6, 8
D. Ashley Cohen, 15
Jacob Cohen, 6-8
John Cohen, 3
Libby G. Cohen, 14-15
S. Alan Cohen, 7
Stephen L. Cohen, 8
Sanford J. Cohn, 9, 14
Theodore Coladarci, 12, 14, 16
Nicholas Colangelo, 10
Debra E. Cole, 12
Nancy S. Cole, 7-9
Thomas R. Coleman, 9
Roberta R. Collard, 7
Carol J. Collins, 13-14
Deborah Collins, 12
Richard Colwell, 7-10

W. D. Commins, 1-4
Andrew L. Comrey, 5, 7-8
Judith C. Conger, 11-12
Collie W. Conoley, 11-13, 16
Jane Close Conoley, 14
Clinton C. Conrad, 2
Herbert S. Conrad, 1-4
Norman A. Constantine, 11-12
Alicia Skinner Cook, 9, 11
John Cook, 7-9
Walter W. Cook, 2-3, 5
Catherine P. Cook-Cottone, 16
Donna K. Cooke, 12
Norma Cooke, 9
William W. Cooley, 6
Clyde H. Coombs, 3
Colin Cooper, 13-16
Mark Cooper, 14-15
M. Allan Cooperstein, 13-15
Robert B. Cooter, Jr., 10-11
Mary Kay Corbitt, 9
Stephen M. Corey, 1-2
Virginia E. Corgan, 10
Alice J. Corkill, 11-14, 16
Ethel L. Cornell, 1
Merith Cosden, 11-14
Giuseppe Costantino, 9-10
William C. Cottle, 5
Stuart A. Courtis, 1, 4
Douglas Courtney, 3-4
John A. Courtright, 9-10
Andrew A. Cox, 14-16
James R. Cox, 9
Marion Monroe Cox, 1, 3
Richard C. Cox, 8
John A. Cox, Jr., 5
Hazel M. Crain, 9
Rick Crandall, 8
A. Garr Cranney, 8
Charles J. Cranny, 8
Albert B. Crawford, 2
Douglas H. Crawford, 9
John Crawford, 13
William R. Crawford, 6-7
*Kevin D. Crehan, 11-16
Michelle M. Creighton, 11
Diana Crespo, 13
William J. E. Crissy, 4
R. Lenox Criswell, 2
John O. Crites, 6-9
Linda M. Crocker, 9-11, 13-14
Lysle W. Croft, 3-4
Lee J. Cronbach, 3-10
Lawrence A. Crosby, 9
Lawrence H. Cross, 12-14
Susan L. Crowley, 12
Douglas P. Crowne, 6

William M. Cruickshank, 4
Nancy L. Crumpton, 15
Thomas J. Cullen, Jr., 14
Thomas E. Culliton, Jr., 6
Jack A. Cummings, 9-10, 12, 14
Oliver W. Cummings, 9
Rhoda Cummings, 14
Bert P. Cundick, 9-10
Edward E. Cureton, 1-2, 4
Louise W. Cureton, 4
Thomas K. Cureton, 3
William L. Curlette, 11-12
William Curr, 5
Francis D. Curtis, 1-2
Mary E. Curtis, 9
Michael J. Curtis, 9
Stephanie L. Cutlan, 13
Peter A. Dahl, 8
W. Grant Dahlstrom, 4-6, 8
John T. Dailey, 4-5
Edgar Dale, 3
Reginald R. Dale, 5
Edward J. Daly III, 15
Fred L. Damarin, 8-9
Rik Carl D'Amato, 11-12, 14-16
Larry G. Daniel, 12
Mark H. Daniel, 12-14
John C. Daniels, 5
M. Harry Daniels, 9-10
John G. Darley, 1-2
Richard E. Darnell, 8-9
Ralph F. Darr, Jr., 11-13
J. P. Das, 9-10
Jane Dass, 8
John H. Daugherty, 3
James M. Daum, 9
Charles Davidshofer, 9
Andrew S. Davis, 15-16
Brandon Davis, 11, 13
Charlotte Croon Davis, 3-6, 8
D. Russell Davis, 4-5
Edwin W. Davis, 3
Frederick B. Davis, 1-5, 7
Paul C. Davis, 6
Robert A. Davis, 3
Stanley E. Davis, 6
Steven F. Davis, 11-14
Parker Davis, Jr., 3
Mark L. Davison, 9
Helen C. Dawe, 3
Robyn M. Dawes, 8
Carolyn Dawson, 8
Linda S. Day, 11
Ayres G. D'Costa, 11-15
Gary J. Dean, 12-15
Raymond S. Dean, 9, 14-16
Lester W. Dearborn, 6

William W. Deardorff, 12-13
William L. Deaton, 11-12
R. J. De Ayala, 14
David A. Decoster, 10
James Deese, 5
Sharon H. deFur, 14-15
Frank P. DeLay, 2
Connie Kubo Della-Piana, 13-14
Gabriel M. Della-Piana, 6, 11
Vincent J. Dell'Orto, 8
Dennis J. Deloria, 7-9
Harold A. Delp, 4
Robert H. Deluty, 9
George J. Demakis, 16
Randy Demaline, 8
Robert G. Demaree, 4, 7-8
*Gerald E. DeMauro, 11-16
Marilyn E. Demorest, 10
George D. Demos, 6
Jennifer Denicolis, 12
Joseph W. Denison, 9
Evelyn Deno, 7
Gypsy M. Denzine, 15-16
Stephen J. DePaola, 15
Susan K. Deri, 3
Mayhew Derryberry, 3
Lawrence G. Derthick, 5
Harry R. DeSilva, 2
Lizanne Destefano, 11-12, 14
Douglas K. Detterman, 9
M. Vere DeVault, 7
Edward F. deVillafranca, 8
Anthony J. DeVito, 9
Joseph C. Dewey, 1-2
Michael L. Dey, 9
Robert E. Deysach, 10
Denise M. DeZolt, 11-13
Esther E. Diamond, 8-9, 11-13
Joseph O. Prewitt Diaz, 14
Phil Diaz, 16
Louis M. DiCarlo, 6
Charles F. Dicken, 6
Gwendolen S. Dickson, 1, 3
Paul B. Diederich, 1-2, 7
Allan O. Diefendorf, 11-12
John S. Diekhoff, 3-5
Stephen Dilchert, 16
Thomas E. Dinero, 12
Jonathan G. Dings, 12
Robert L. Dipboye, 8
James Clyde DiPerna, 14-16
Jean Dirks, 9
David N. Dixon, 9-13
Faith Gunning-Dixon, 13-14
Gregory H. Dobbins, 9-10, 12
Keith S. Dobson, 9
Richard F. Docter, 7

Leland K. Doebler, 9
R. Anthony Doggett, 15-16
Janice A. Dole, 9-10
Kathleen A. Dolgos, 15
*Beth Doll, 10, 12-16
Robert H. Dolliver, 7-9
George Domino, 7-10, 12-14
Mavis L. Donahue, 9-10
Hei-Ki Dong, 9
Thomas F. Donlon, 8, 13
James Donnelly, 15
Jerome E. Doppelt, 4-8
Dan Douglas, 11
Harl R. Douglass, 2-3
Dennis Doverspike, 15-16
E. Thomas Dowd, 9, 11-14
N. M. Downie, 6
John Downing, 8
Kenneth O. Doyle, Jr., 8
Vincent R. D'Oyley, 7
Ronald S. Drabman, 9
Raleigh M. Drake, 2-5
Richard M. Drake, 2-3
Penelope W. Dralle, 12
Ralph Mason Dreger, 8
Arnold Dresden, 1
Paul L. Dressel, 3-8
James Drever, 2
Philip H. Dreyer, 8-9
Laura A. Driscoll, 8
Robert C. Droege, 7
Lee Droegemueller, 14
Priscilla A. Drum, 8-10
Robert J. Drummond, 11-15
Cynthia Ann Druva-Roush, 11-12
Judy R. Dubno, 9, 13
Linda M. DuBois, 9
Philip H. DuBois, 3, 6-7
John H. Duckitt, 9
Curtis Dudley-Marling, 9
Gerald G. Duffy, 7
Anthony T. Dugbartey, 15
Lydia A. Duggins, 5
Stanley G. Dulsky, 2-3
Stephen B. Dunbar, 11
Harold B. Dunkel, 2-6
Jack W. Dunlap, 1-3
James A. Dunn, 7
S. S. Dunn, 5-6
Thomas M. Dunn, 16
Marvin D. Dunnette, 6
Carl J. Dunst, 9-10, 13
Daniel R. Dupecher, 8
Mary M. Dupuis, 9
Paula J. Dupuy, 11
Richard P. Duran, 9
Walter N. Durost, 4-8

Amy Finch-Williams, 10
Diane Billings Findley, 11
Warren G. Findley, 2-8
Stefan R. Fink, 8
Louis J. Finkle, 9
Carmen J. Finley, 11-12
Martin A. Fischer, 13
Seymour Fisher, 6
Wayne D. Fisher, 6
Joshua A. Fishman, 5
John L. Fisk, 9
Donald W. Fiske, 5
James A. Fitzgerald, 5
Colleen Fitzmaurice, 10
Anne R. Fitzpatrick, 11
Corine Fitzpatrick, 14-16
*Robert Fitzpatrick, 7-16
Dawn P. Flanagan, 12, 15
John C. Flanagan, 1, 3-4, 6
Rosemary Flanagan, 14-16
Stephen G. Flanagan, 11
*John W. Fleenor, 11-16
Lisa Fleisher, 9
C. M. Fleming, 4
W. G. Fleming, 6
Charles D. Flory, 1, 3
Terri Flowerday, 16
Joseph J. Foley, 8
John P. Foley, Jr., 5-7
Mary O. Folsom, 7
Janet H. Fontaine, 14
Marie C. Fontana, 8
Thomas G. Foran, 1
Donna Ford, 12
Laurie Ford, 11-12
Rex L. Forehand, 9
Bertram R. Forer, 6
Frank J. Fornoff, 6, 8-9
Elaine Forsyth, 3
Robert A. Forsyth, 7-8
Tomlinson Fort, 2
Jim C. Fortune, 11-14
Judson W. Foust, 2
Hanford M. Fowler, 4-5
Raymond D. Fowler, Jr., 7-8
Charles Fox, 2
Glen Fox, 13-14
Hazel M. Fox, 10
Lynn H. Fox, 8-9
Robert A. Fox, 9
Austin C. Frank, 8
Mary Lou Bryant Frank, 14
Thomas T. Frantz, 7-8
Michael D. Franzen, 9
Stephen L. Franzoi, 9
Robert B. Frary, 9, 12-14
Barry J. Fraser, 9

Elizabeth D. Fraser, 5-6
Richard I. Frederick, 14
Wayne A. Frederick, 5
Norman Frederiksen, 3-8
Norman Fredman, 12
B. J. Freeman, 9
Frank S. Freeman, 4-5
Stephen J. Freeman, 14-16
David Freides, 7-8
J. Joseph Freilinger, 8
Patricia K. Freitag, 13-14
Brian F. French, 16
John W. French, 3-8
Joseph L. French, 7
Robert L. French, 6
Sidney J. French, 3
Bruce R. Fretz, 9
Benno G. Fricke, 5-6
Marilyn Friend, 10
David A. Frisbie, 8-9
Clifford P. Froehlich, 4-5
Gustav J. Froehlich, 3-6
Benjamin Fruchter, 5
Edward B. Fry, 6-8
Maurine A. Fry, 9
Douglas H. Fryer, 3
Verne C. Fryklund, 2
Douglas Fuchs, 10
Lynn S. Fuchs, 9-10
Mark H. Fugate, 12-13, 15
Martin Fujiki, 9-10
Solomon M. Fulero, 12, 14
Paul H. Furfey, 1
Michael Furlong, 12-16
Elaine Furniss, 12
Edward J. Furst, 6-8
Robert K. Gable, 9, 11-14
Lena R. Gaddis, 11-13
N. L. Gage, 4-5
Eugene L. Gaier, 5
Rosslyn Gaines, 7
John P. Galassi, 9
Peggy E. Gallaher, 13
Gloria A. Galvin, 10-11
Leann M. Gamache, 12
Michael P. Gamache, 14
Bessie Lee Gambrill, 2
Ronald J. Ganellen, 12-16
H. C. Ganguli, 9
Calvin P. Garbin, 11
Eugene E. Garcia, 9-10
Y. Evie Garcia, 15
Eric F. Gardner, 4-10
Sol L. Garfield, 7
Alan Garfinkel, 8-9, 11, 13-14, 16
Mary E. Garner, 16
Ruth Garner, 9

Edgar R. Garrett, 7
Henry E. Garrett, 1-5
Adrienne Garro, 16
Jack E. Gebart-Eaglemont, 13-16
Ann L. Gebhardt, 2
Karl W. Gehrkens, 2
Kurt F. Geisinger, 11-14, 16
John Geisler, 13-16
Kenneth E. Gell, 2
Karen Geller, 13
Glenn B. Gelman, 14
Jeremy Genovese, 16
Judy Lynn Genshaft, 9
J. Raymond Gerberich, 2-6
Kathryn Clark Gerken, 9-10
Joanne C. Gersten, 8
Maribeth Gettinger, 10
Esther Geva, 9
John J. Geyer, 7-8
Edwin E. Ghiselli, 3
Cecil A. Gibb, 5-7
Mark J. Gierl, 16
H. H. Giles, 1-2
Ronald B. Gillam, 11-13
David Gillespie, 14
Jerry S. Gilmer, 12
Gerald Giraud, 15
John W. Gittinger, 5
Gene V Glass, 7-8
Hugh W. Glenn, 14
James R. Glennon, 6
Goldine C. Gleser, 6-9
John A. Glover, 11
Joshua M. Gold, 15
Lewis R. Goldberg, 7-8
Charles J. Golden, 9
Stephen L. Golding, 8-9
Bert A. Goldman, 6-7, 11-15
Leo Goldman, 6
Ronald Goldman, 8
Steven H. Goldman, 9
Marcel L. Goldschmid, 7
Diane Goldsmith, 12
Keith Goltry, 2
Chris Gonzales, 15
Jorge E. Gonzales, 15
Ronald H. Good, III, 11
Elizabeth J. Goodacre, 7
Florence L. Goodenough, 2-3
Joan F. Goodman, 9
Clarence J. Goodnight, 7
Leonard D. Goodstein, 6-8
William L. Goodwin, 8
Rodney K. Goodyear, 9
Betty N. Gordon, 9
Edwin Gordon, 7
Hans C. Gordon, 2-3

Leonard V. Gordon, 6-8
John B. Gormly, 9
Elliot L. Gory, 9, 11
Edward Earl Gotts, 9, 14
Harrison G. Gough, 4-9, 11-12
Neil Gourlay, 5
C. Ray Graham, 8
Grace Graham, 1-2
John R. Graham, 11-12
Steve Graham, 9, 11-14
Theresa Graham, 14-16
Susan L. Graham-Clay, 9
Larry B. Grantham, 12
Vicki, Gratopp, 12
Zandra S. Gratz, 15-16
M. Elizabeth Graue, 12
Carol A. Gray, 9
William S. Gray, 1, 3-4
Felice J. Green, 13-14
Kathy E. Green, 12-13, 16
Russel F. Green, 6-7
Susan K. Green, 16
Edward B. Greene, 3-5
Harry A. Greene, 2-3
Jeffrey H. Greenhaus, 9
Noel Gregg, 10
Patrick Grehan, 16
Frank M. Gresham, 9-13
Konrad Gries, 4-5
*J. Jeffrey Grill, 8-14
Arnold B. Grobman, 7
Hulda Grobman, 7-8
Martin G. Groff, 9
Norman E. Gronlund, 8
Richard E. Gross, 5-8
Fred M. Grossman, 9-10
Foster E. Grossnickle, 1-4
William R. Grove, 3-4
Melissa M. Groves, 13
Wilson H. Guertin, 5-6
Richard E. Guest, 11
Walter S. Guiler, 4
J. P. Guilford, 1-5
Robert M. Guion, 8-10, 12-14
Sami Gulgoz, 11-12
Arlen R. Gullickson, 7-8, 12
R. Gulliford, 7
Harold Gulliksen, 1-2, 4
John Flagg Gummere, 2
John W. Gustad, 5
Rhonda L. Gutenberg, 9-10
George M. Guthrie, 8-9
John T. Guthrie, 7-8
Barbara Lapp Gutkin, 10
Terry B. Gutkin, 9, 14
Thomas W. Guyette, 9-10, 12, 14
Natasha Gwartney, 12

David K. Heenan, 5-6
Lloyd H. Heidgerd, 6
Louis J. Heifetz, 10
Edith S. Heil, 10
Louis M. Heil, 2
Alfred B. Heilbrun, Jr., 5-10
Nancy Heilman, 11
Alice W. Heim, 4-7
Harry Heller, 2
William H. Helme, 6
G. C. Helmstadter, 7, 9
John K. Hemphill, 6-7
Carlen Henington, 13-15
V. A. C. Henmon, 1
Martha E. Hennen, 14, 16
James J. Hennessy, 10, 14-16
Mary Henning-Stout, 10-13
Edwin R. Henry, 4
Stephan A. Henry, 10
William E. Henry, 4-5
William Hered, 6
David O. Herman, 12-13
Patricia Herman, 9
Edward S. Herold, 9
Edwin L. Herr, 9-10
Virgil E. Herrick, 4-5
*Allen K. Hess, 9-16
Brian Hess, 15
Kathryn D. Hess, 11-12
Robert M. Hess, 12
John R. Hester, 11
William L. Heward, 9
Julia A. Hickman, 10
Peggy A. Hicks, 13
Elfrieda H. Hiebert, 9
A. N. Hieronymus, 5-7
A. Dirk Hightower, 10
E. H. C. Hildebrandt, 3
Scott Kristian Hill, 14
Walker H. Hill, 5
John R. Hills, 6-9
Robert W. Hiltonsmith, 9, 11-13, 16
Philip Himelstein, 7
Elmer D. Hinckley, 4
C. B. Hindley, 6
Laura Hines, 9
J. Scott Hinkle, 11
Samual Hinton, 15
Michael D. Hiscox, 9
Marshall S. Hiskey, 6-7
Jean Hoard, 2
James R. Hobson, 2-5
Emil H. Hoch, 8
Elton Hocking, 3-4
James O. Hodges, 8
James M. Hodgson, 16
Barbara W. Hodson, 9

Kathryn E. Hoff, 15-16
James V. Hoffman, 9
Robert Hogan, 7-10, 16
Thomas P. Hogan, 8, 14-15
Dorothy E. Holberg, 3
Raymond H. Holden, 7
Candice Haas Hollingsead, 14
Warren S. Holmes, 2
Robert R. Holt, 4
Wayne H. Holtzman, 5, 7
Charles Holzwarth, 2
Susan P. Homan, 9
L. Michael Honaker, 11
Charles H. Honzik, 4
Marjorie P. Honzik, 6-7
Albert B. Hood, 8
Joyce E. Hood, 8-9
Stephen B. Hood, 8
Stephen R. Hooper, 10-14
Kenneth D. Hopkins, 6-9, 11
John L. Horn, 7
Thomas D. Horn, 7-8
John E. Horrocks, 5-6
Clark W. Horton, 2-5
Daniel L. Householder, 8
Charles Houston, 12
Carl I. Hovland, 3-5
Robert W. Howard, 2
Edgar Howarth, 8
George W. Howe, 9
Kenneth W. Howell, 9-10
Robert J. Howell, 10
Duncan Howie, 5
Monica M. Hoye, 3
Cyril J. Hoyt, 4-7
Kenneth B. Hoyt, 6
Louis M. Hsu, 9
Te-Fang Hua, 13
Mary E. Huba, 11
Carl J. Huberty, 7-9
Anita M. Hubley, 13-16
Edith M. Huddleston, 4
John Peter Hudson, Jr., 13
E. Scott Huebner, 10-11, 13-14
Mildred H. Huebner, 7-8
Jan N. Hughes, 10-11
Selma Hughes, 11-12
Violet Hughes, 2
Doncaster G. Humm, 2
Lloyd G. Humphreys, 3-6, 9
Joel Hundert, 9
John D. Hundleby, 6
Stephen Hunka, 6
Albert L. Hunsicker, 4
E. Patricia Hunt, 2
Jane V. Hunt, 7-8
Thelma Hunt, 3

William A. Hunt, 3
George W. Hunter, 1-2
Archer W. Hurd, 1
David P. Hurford, 13-16
Sylvia M. Hutchinson, 10
Robert R. Hutzell, 9
George W. Hynd, 9
Ludwig Immergluck, 3
James C. Impara, 11
Henry A. Imus, 3
Carlos Inchaurralde, 14, 16
Mario Iona, 8
Carl Isenhart, 13-16
Steven Isonio, 13
Stephen H. Ivens, 12-14
Annette M. Iverson, 11-12
Margaret Ives, 3
Edward F. Iwanicki, 8-9
Douglas N. Jackson, 7-9
Joseph F. Jackson, 2-3
Robert W. B. Jackson, 5
Richard M. Jaeger, 8-10
Alice N. Jameson, 3
Colleen B. Jamison, 7
Marc Janoson, 15
Patsy Arnett Jaynes, 11
Frank C. Jean, 1
Chantale Jeanrie, 13-15
*Jeffrey A. Jenkins, 11-16
Jill Ann Jenkins, 14-16
John R. Jennings, 5
Karen E. Jennings, 15-16
Arthur R. Jensen, 5-7, 9
Joanne L. Jensen, 12
Patrick J. Jeske, 9
Carl F. Jesness, 7
Richard Jessor, 5
Frank B. Jex, 6
James E. Jirsa, 9
Lynae A. Johnsen, 16
A. Pemberton Johnson, 5
Cecil D. Johnson, 5
Christopher Johnson, 15-16
Dale D. Johnson, 8
Jacqueline Johnson, 15
Jerry Johnson, 11, 16
Judy A. Johnson, 16
Kathleen M. Johnson, 15-16
Laura B. Johnson, 2
Leland P. Johnson, 4
Marjorie S. Johnson, 8
Palmer O. Johnson, 1-5
Richard T. Johnson, 6-8
Richard W. Johnson, 8-10, 12-14
Robert Johnson, 13
Robert L. Johnson, 15-16
Ronn Johnson, 10

Ruth Johnson, 12
Stephen B. Johnson, 16
Sylvia T. Johnson, 11
Wayde Johnson, 11
Sharon Johnson-Lewis, 11
Joseph A. Johnston, 7
Judith R. Johnston, 9, 13, 16
Barry W. Jones, 9-10
Carleton C. Jones, 1-2
Christina Finley Jones, 14
Clive Jones, 7
David Jones, 7
Dorothy L. Jones, 7
Edward S. Jones, 1-2
Elizabeth L. Jones, 12, 14
H. Gwynne Jones, 6
Harold E. Jones, 1-4
James A. Jones, 12
Katherine S. Jones, 12
Kenneth J. Jones, 6
Kevin M. Jones, 12-15
Ll. Wynn Jones, 2
Randall L. Jones, 8
Randall M. Jones, 9
Robert A. Jones, 5
Worth R. Jones, 5-6
A. M. Jordan, 2
Richard H. Jordan, 3
Helen L. Jorstad, 8
Gerald A. Juhnke, 13
Lee N. June, 9
Ehud Jungwirth, 8
*Samuel Juni, 9-14
James J. Jupp, 9
Clifford E. Jurgensen, 3-6
Stephen Jurs, 11-12
Joseph Justman, 5
Ashraf Kagee, 14-16
Javaid Kaiser, 11-13
Paul E. Kambly, 4
*Randy W. Kamphaus, 9-14
Harrison Kane, 14-16
Michael Kane, 13-14
Rabindra N. Kanungo, 9-10
Chi-Wen Kao, 13
David E. Kapel, 11
Barbara J. Kaplan, 11-13
David M. Kaplan, 14
Robert M. Kaplan, 10
Stuart A. Karabenick, 9
Harry W. Karn, 4
M. Ray Karnes, 4
Mitchell Karno, 12
Lawrence M. Kasdon, 7-9
Walter Kass, 5
Edward S. Katkin, 8
Walter Katkovsky, 6, 11

Ira Stuart Katz, 14-15
Martin R. Katz, 5-8
Raymond A. Katzell, 3-8
Douglas, F. Kauffman, 16
James M. Kauffman, 9
Alan S. Kaufman, 8-10, 13-14
Nadeen L. Kaufman, 9, 13-14
Walter V. Kaulfers, 1-7
Kenneth A. Kavale, 10
*Michael G. Kavan, 11-16
Michael J. Kavanagh, 8
T. J. Keating, 2
J. A. Keats, 5-6
John M. Keene, Jr., 9
J. Ward Keesling, 9
Thomas J. Kehle, 9-10
Jerard F. Kehoe, 11
Gertrude Keir, 4
Patricia B. Keith, 12-14
*Timothy Z. Keith, 9-10, 12, 14-16
Thomas Kellaghan, 8
Harold R. Keller, 10, 14-16
Peggy Kellers, 15
Karl N. Kelley, 16
*Mary Lou Kelley, 9-16
Truman L. Kelley, 2
Theodore E. Kellogg, 4-5
E. Lowell Kelly, 3-7
Kevin R. Kelly, 15-16
William E. Kendall, 6
Katherine G. Keneally, 4
James E. Kennedy, 6-7
Patricia H. Kennedy, 9
Kathryn W. Kenney, 10, 12
Douglas T. Kenny, 5
Leonard Kenowitz, 9
Grace H. Kent, 2-3
Barbara K. Keogh, 8-9
Robert E. Keohane, 2
Newell C. Kephart, 7
Barbara A. Kerr, 9-10, 12
Nancy Kerr, 9
Willard A. Kerr, 3-4, 6-7
Anne R. Kessler, 13
Carol E. Kessler, 14-15
Kathy S. Kessler, 11-12
Sandra M. Ketrow, 14
Gilbert C. Kettelkamp, 6
Thomas E. Kieren, 8
Kenneth A. Kiewra, 11-14
Edward Kifer, 9
Jeremy Kilpatrick, 7-8
Ernest W. Kimmel, 11, 13-14
Elaine F. Kinder, 1
Glen D. King, 8
John D. King, 12, 16
Joseph E. King, 3

Suzanne King, 12
Forrest A. Kingsbury, 2
G. Gage Kingsbury, 12, 14
Albert J. Kingston, 6-8
Lucien B. Kinney, 2, 4
Richard T. Kinnier, 13
John R. Kinzer, 3
Wayne K. Kirchner, 6
Barbara A. Kirk, 7
*Jean Powell Kirnan, 11-16
Karyll Kiser, 12
Philip M. Kitay, 6-7
Helen Kitchens, 13-14
Tom Kitwood, 8
Paul M. Kjeldergaard, 6
Seymour G. Klebanoff, 4
Beverly M. Klecker, 14-15
Benjamin Kleinmuntz, 6-10
Milton V. Kline, 6
Paul Kline, 7-8
William E. Kline, 7-8
Martin Kling, 7-8
Robert R. Knapp, 7
Samuel J. Knapp, 9
Thomas R. Knapp, 9, 13
Catharine C. Knight, 12
*Howard M. Knoff, 9-15
John F. Knutson, 7
William R. Koch, 11-12
Stephen L. Koffler, 12-13
Kate L. Kogan, 3-4
William S. Kogan, 4
Timothy R. Konold, 14
David Kopel, 1-2
Rebecca J. Kopriva, 12
Abraham K. Korman, 8
Stephen M. Koziol, Jr., 8
Ernest J. Kozma, 11
S. Kathleen Krach, 16
Jack J. Kramer, 9
Jeffrey Kramer, 14
John H. Kranzler, 12, 14
David R. Krathwohl, 5
Thomas R. Kratochwill, 9
Charles J. Krauskopf, 7-8
Carole M. Krauthamer, 12
Roy A. Kress, 7-9
A. C. Krey, 1
Philip H. Kriedt, 6
Leslie H. Krieger, 14
Radhika Krishnamurthy, 14, 16
S. David Kriska, 12
Russell P. Kropp, 5
Damon Krug, 13
Morris Krugman, 3-5
John D. Krumboltz, 6
David J. Krus, 9

Dietmar Kuchemann, 9
Frederic Kuder, 2-3
Jay Kuder, 11
Phyllis Kuehn, 12
Sally Kuhlenschmidt, 13-14 16
F. Kuhlmann, 2
Jody L. Kulstad, 15-16
Deborah King Kundert, 10-12
Antony John Kunnan, 13, 16
Dana G. Kurfman, 7-8
Albert K. Kurtz, 4-6, 8
Joseph C. Kush, 14-16
Koressa Kutsick, 10
W. C. Kvaraceus, 3-4
Kwong-Liem Karl Kwan, 13-15
Lou LaBrant, 2
Barbara Lachar, 11, 13
David Lachar, 11
Eleanor M. Ladd, 8
Robert Lado, 7
Linda A. Lagomarsino, 9
Matthew E. Lambert, 11, 13-16
Nadine M. Lambert, 9
Elaine L. La Monica, 8
W. Elmer Lancaster, 2
Daniel Landis, 7
Herbert A. Landry, 2
Edward Landy, 5
Frank J. Landy, 8
Suzanne Lane, 11, 15-16
William Steve Lang, 11-14
Theos A. Langlie, 1
Aimée Langlois, 12, 14, 16
Charles R. Langmuir, 3-6
Gerald V. Lannholm, 3-5
Kevin Lanning, 14-15
Richard I. Lanyon, 7-9, 11-12
Luis M. Laosa, 8
Glenda Lappan, 8-9
Peter A. Lappan, Jr., 6-8
William S. Larson, 2-6
Cynthia A. Larson-Daugherty, 14
Julian J. Lasky, 7
Robert L. Lathrop, 7
Kelly Laugle, 16
Allan L. LaVoie, 8-9
*Joseph G. Law, Jr., 11-16
J. S. Lawes, 6-7
Kimberly A. Lawless, 13
C. H. Lawshe, Jr., 3
Gary W. Lawson, 9
Martha E. Layman, 4
Wilbur L. Layton, 4-11
Robert A. Leark, 13-16
Steven B. Leder, 12, 14
Herbert Lederer, 8
Richard Ledgerwood, 1

James Ledvinka, 9
Courtland C. Lee, 9
J. Murray Lee, 1, 5
S. G. Lee, 6-7
Steven W. Lee, 10-13
Young Ju Lee, 16
D. Welty Lefever, 1-6
Sue M. Legg, 12
Paul R. Lehman, 7-10
Irvin J. Lehmann, 6-13
Richard Lehrer, 11
Roger T. Lennon, 4-5
Theodore F. Lentz, 3
Francis E. Lentz, Jr., 9-10
J. Paul Leonard, 2-3
*Frederick T. L. Leong, 11-16
Richard Lesh, 9
Donald A. Leton, 7-9
*S. Alvin Leung, 11-16
Ralph G. Leverett, 13-14, 16
Eugene E. Levitt, 6-8
Philip M. Levy, 6
Seymour Levy, 6
Mary A. Lewis, 11-14
Neil P. Lewis, 14
Roy D. Lewis, 5
Lester M. Libo, 7-8
Peter D. Lifton, 9
John Liggett, 5-6
Glynn D. Ligon, 9
Paul M. Limbert, 1
David P. Lindeman, 9
Steven J. Lindner, 14
E. F. Lindquist, 5
Mary Montgomery Lindquist, 8-9
Pam Lindsey, 15-16
*Rick Lindskog, 11-14, 15-16
C. Mauritz Lindvall, 7-8
W. Line, 2
James C. Lingoes, 6
James B. Lingwall, 8
Robert L. Linn, 8-10
Maria Prendes Lintel, 13-14
Gary E. Lintereur, 8, 10
Richard Lippa, 9
Robert W. Lissitz, 11
William M. Littell, 7
Orrel E. Little, 3
Wei-Ping Liu, 13
Alice K. Liveright, 2
Howard A. Lloyd, 14
John Wills Lloyd, 9
Steven G. LoBello, 11-13
Aileene S. Lockhart, 7
Jane Loevinger, 4, 8
Sandra Loew, 14-16
R. Duane Logue, 8

Paul R. Lohnes, 6-8
Walter F. W. Lohnes, 7
Paul S. Lomax, 3
John W. Lombard, 7-8
Charles J. Long, 12-14
John A. Long, 3
Louis Long, 3
Steven H. Long, 11-13, 15-16
Andrew Longacre, 2
Alfred P. Longo, 13, 15-16
Frank M. Loos, 4
Emilia C. Lopez, 13-14
Peter G. Loret, 6
Irving Lorge, 2-3, 5
Margaret F. Lorimer, 6
Maurice Lorr, 5-8
C. M. Louttit, 1-4
Kelly Brey Love, 16
Kenneth Lovell, 6-7
Benson P. Low, 9
Jerry M. Lowe, 14
Rodney L. Lowman, 9-10
Brenda H. Loyd, 9, 12
S. Ruben Lozano, 9
Ardie Lubin, 4
William H. Lucio, 6
William H. Lucow, 5
Leslie Eastman Lukin, 13-14, 16
James Lumsden, 5, 8
Robert W. Lundin, 5-7
Clifford E. Lunneborg, 7-8
Patricia W. Lunneborg, 8-9
David T. Lykken, 6-8
Howard B. Lyman, 6-7
Joan I. Lynch, 9-10
Hugh Lytton, 8
Henry S. Maas, 3
Linda Mabry, 12
Gloria Maccow, 13-14
John MacDonald, 13-14
F. Charles Mace, 9-10
Gordon N. MacKenzie, 3-4
Arthur C. MacKinney, 6-8
Karen Mackler, 14, 16
Saunders MacLane, 6
David MacPhee, 11-13
George F. Madaus, 8-9
Faith Madden, 4
*Cleborne D. Maddux, 10-16
Ronald A. Madle, 14-16
Thomas W. Mahan, Jr., 6
Jennifer N. Mahdavi, 16
Roderick K. Mahurin, 11-12
James Mainwaring, 5
Timothy J. Makatura, 14-16
Koressa Kutsick Malcolm, 11, 13-16
Julius B. Maller, 1-2

Susan J. Maller, 13-16
George G. Mallinson, 6-8
Jacqueline V. Mallinson, 6-8
Berenice Mallory, 2
Margaret E. Malone, 13-14
Dean R. Malsbary, 8
Jay A. Mancini, 14
Milton M. Mandell, 4
Joseph R. Manduchi, 14
Kenneth J. Manges, 14
Ramasamy Manikam, 14
Lester Mann, 7-9
M. Jacinta Mann, 5
John Manning, 5, 7
Winton H. Manning, 6
Herschel T. Manuel, 2-5
Caroline Manuele-Adkins, 9-10, 12-13, 16
Gregory J. Marchant, 12-14
Gary L. Marco, 11-14
Carol Mardell-Czudnowski, 10
Howard Margolis, 14, 16
Suzanne Markel-Fox, 12
Robert P. Markley, 9-10
Howard J. Markman, 9
Melvin R. Marks, 6
Marc Marschark, 12
Herbert W. Marsh, 9
David Marshall, 10
Brian K. Martens, 10-11
Charles Wm. Martin, 11
Roy P. Martin, 9
Suzanne G. Martin, 14
William E. Martin, Jr., 13-16
Trey Martindale, 15
Manuel Martinez-Pons, 16
Stanley S. Marzolf, 3
Bertram B. Masia, 6
Carolyn E. Massad, 8
M. Mastrangelo, 15
Paul Mastrangelo, 14
Joseph D. Matarazzo, 9-10
Johnny L. Matson, 9
Ross W. Matteson, 4
Paula Matuszek, 9
Francis N. Maxfield, 1-2
James Maxwell, 3-5
Susanna Maxwell, 9
Samuel T. Mayo, 6-9
Arthur B. Mays, 2
James J. Mazza, 10
Dawn Mazzie, 16
Charles C. McArthur, 7
Patrick P. McCabe, 16
John N. McCall, 7
Raymond J. McCall, 5
W. C. McCall, 2
William A. McCall, 2

James M. McCallister, 3
R. Steve McCallum, 9
Susan McCammon, 10
Boyd R. McCandless, 4, 6-7
James J. McCarthy, 7-9
Kevin J. McCarthy, 12, 14-15
James Leslie McCary, 8
Robert L. McCaul, 2-3
Clara J. McCauley, 2
*Rebecca J. McCauley, 11-16
Erin McClure, 12
Daniel L. McCollum, 16
Scott R. McConnell, 11
Andrew J. McConney, 14
Richard J. McCowan, 14
Sheila C. McCowan, 14
Robert R. McCrae, 9
David McCone, 15
R. W. McCulloch, 5
Constance M. McCullough, 2-3, 5, 7
Merilee McCurdy, 14, 16
S. P. McCutchen, 1-2
Hiram L. McDade, 9
Arthur S. McDonald, 6
D. W. McElwain, 4-5
William C. McGaghie, 8
Ellen McGinnis, 10
Dixie McGinty, 16
Carol M. McGregor, 14-16
Kevin S. McGrew, 10
Christine H. McGuire, 5-8
Valentina McInerney, 15
David E. McIntosh, 12
Robert M. McIntyre, 9
Michael G. McKee, 7
William T. McKee, 10
Margaret G. McKim, 3-4
Thomas McKnight, 14-16
Joyce R. McLarty, 11, 14
Kenneth F. McLaughlin, 6
John McLeish, 4, 7
Mary J. McLellan, 12-14
Jonathon C. McLendon, 6
John McLeod, 8
Robert J. McMahon, 9
Robert F. McMorris, 9-13
Douglas M. McNair, 7-8
Michael McNamara, 12
Sharon McNeely, 12
Malcolm R. McNeil, 10-14
Jeanette McPherrin, 2
John V. McQuitty, 3-4
Louis L. McQuitty, 4
Douglas J. McRae, 11-13
Leija V. McReynolds, 8
Paul McReynolds, 7-10
Damian McShane, 11

Richard A. Meade, 5
Arthur W. Meadows, 5
David J. Mealor, 9-11
I. G. Meddleton, 5
Albert E. Meder, Jr., 5
Maria Del R. Medina-Diaz, 13-14, 16
Frederic J. Medway, 11, 13, 16
Paul E. Meehl, 3
Sheila Mehta, 14
Edwin I. Megargee, 7-8
Howard D. Mehlinger, 7-8
William A. Mehrens, 7-9, 11-13
Sheila Mehta, 13
Manfred J. Meier, 7-9, 11
Norman C. Meier, 2
Scott T. Meier, 12-16
Joyce Meikamp, 14-16
William B. Meldrum, 1, 3
P. L. Mellenbruch, 5
Gary B. Melton, 9-10, 12
Richard S. Melton, 6, 8
H. Meltzer, 3
David M. Memory, 9
Gerald A. Mendelsohn, 6
Kevin Menefee, 11-12
Robert J. Menges, 8
Ivan N. Mensh, 4
Gerald M. Meredith, 7
Peter F. Merenda, 11-14
Brad M. Merker, 15-16
Philip R. Merrifield, 6
Jack C. Merwin, 6-8
William R. Merz, Sr., 12-14
Bernadine Meyer, 5
Donald L. Meyer, 6
John H. Meyer, 3
C. Edward Meyers, 8
Marcee J. Meyers, 9
Joan J. Michael, 7
*William B. Michael, 4-13, 15-16
Hillary Michaels, 14
William J. Micheels, 4-5
Grace Middleton, 11
Christopher P. Migotsky, 12
T. R. Miles, 5-6, 8
John E. Milholland, 5-8
C. Dean Miller, 9
Courtney Miller, 16
Daniel C. Miller, 14-16
Gloria E. Miller, 10
J. Monroe Miller, 16
John K. Miller, 9
Jon F. Miller, 9
Lovick C. Miller, 7-8
M. David Miller, 11-12, 14
Robert B. Miller, 14
Robert J. Miller, 11-14

Victor H. Noll, 1-7
Patricia Noller, 9
Claude E. Norcross, 4
Warren T. Norman, 5-7
*Janet A. Norris, 9-15
Raymond C. Norris, 5
Robert D. North, 5-7
Paul A. Northrop, 1-2
Christine Novak, 12, 14
Ruth M. Noyce, 9-10
Edward S. Noyes, 2-3
Jum C. Nunnally, 7
Michelle Nutter, 15
Thomas Oakland, 8-9
C. A. Oakley, 2-3
C. O. Oakley, 3
Thomas C. O'Brien, 7-8
John E. Obrzut, 9, 11
Anna S. Ochoa, 8-9
Salvador Hector Ochoa, 12-16
Charles W. Odell, 1-3
*Judy Oehler-Stinnett, 10-14, 16
Lynn R. Offermann, 13
Billy T. Ogletree, 13-14
Kevin E. O'Grady, 9-10
Stephen Olejnik, 11-12, 14
Artruro Olivarez, Jr., 16
Donald W. Oliver, 6
Mary Ellen Oliverio, 5, 7-8
Esteban L. Olmedo, 9
*D. Joe Olmi, 11-16
Carl J. Olson, 7
Thomas R. O'Neill, 16
Deniz S. Ones, 14-16
Albert C. Oosterhof, 12-13
Don B. Oppenheim, 9
Pedro T. Orata, 2
Michael D. Orlansky, 9
Jacob S. Orleans, 2-6
David B. Orr, 6-7
John C. Ory, 9
Timothy M. Osberg, 11
Agnes E. Osborne, 3
Alan Osborne, 7-8
R. T. Osborne, 7
Worth J. Osburn, 1-2, 4
Stuart Oskamp, 7-8
Alton O'Steen, 2
Steven J. Osterlind, 11-13
Nicki N. Ostrom, 9
Donald P. Oswald, 13, 15-16
Jay L. Otis, 3-4
Sandye M. Ouzts, 16
Terry Overton, 11-14
Steven V. Owen, 11-14
Gretchen Owens, 14-16
William A. Owens, 6, 8-9

Robert E. Owens, Jr., 9-10
Heidi K. Paa, 15
C. Robert Pace, 3-8
Abbot Packard, 12, 14
Albert G. Packard, 3
Vicki S. Packman, 14
Ellis Batten Page, 6-9
Kathleen D. Paget, 9-10, 13-14
Nathaniel J. Pallone, 14-16
Ian C. Palmer, 12
Orville Palmer, 5
Osmond E. Palmer, 5-7
Jean M. Palormo, 6
Josephine B. Pane, 7
Mary Pannbacker, 11
Anthony W. Paolitto, 12-14
Anthony M. Paolo, 14-15
Ila Parasnis, 14
Gino Parisi, 7
Carol S. Parke, 16
Jayne A. Parker, 9
Anna Parsek, 2
Charles K. Parsons, 9-12, 16
A. Harry Passow, 4, 8-9, 11-12
Thanos Patelis, 15-16
Donald G. Paterson, 2-4
Gerald R. Patterson, 5
Willard W. Patty, 4
Walter Pauk, 7
Jerome D. Pauker, 6-9
Sharon E. Paulson, 13
Renee Pavelski, 14-15
David A. Payne, 6-7
Douglas S. Payne, 9
Frank D. Payne, 9
Joshua W. Payne, 16
Robert W. Payne, 6-9
William G. Peacher, 4
L. Carolyn Pearson, 13-15
Mary Ellen Pearson, 9-11
John Gray Peatman, 2
Elazar J. Pedhazur, 8-9
E. A. Peel, 4-5
Charles W. Pendleton, 8
Douglas A. Penfield, 12
John P. Penna, 8
L. S. Penrose, 3
William H. Perkins, 7
Carole Perlman, 13
Kathleen N. Perret, 5
Barbara Perry-Sheldon, 10
Carolyn Mitchell Person, 14, 16
Michael Persampieri, 15
Charles C. Peters, 1
Jerry L. Peters, 10
Charles A. Peterson, 9-10, 12-14
Christopher Peterson, 9

Donald R. Peterson, 6
Francisca Esteban Peterson, 14
Gary W. Peterson, 9
Harold A. Peterson, 7-10
Norman G. Peterson, 9
Reece L. Peterson, 9
Rolf A. Peterson, 8, 10
Shailer Peterson, 3
Julia Pettiette-Doolin, 10
*Steven I. Pfeiffer, 9-16
Susanna W. Pflaum, 9
LeAdelle Phelps, 10, 12-13
Roger P. Phelps, 7-8
Gary W. Phillips, 9
Iris Phillips, 15
S. E. Phillips, 9-10
Theodore G. Phillips, 5-7
Nick J. Piazza, 10
Jennifer Piccolo, 16
Eugene (Geno) Pichette, 13
James Pickering, 9
Hale C. Pickett, 3
Douglas A. Pidgeon, 5-9
John Pierce-Jones, 5-6
Ellen V. Piers, 6
Wayne C. Piersel, 9-10, 13-14
Myrtle L. Pignatelli, 2
Len Pikaart, 7-8
A. E. G. Pilliner, 5-8
Paul Pimsleur, 6
James W. Pinkney, 9-10, 12-13, 15
Rudolf Pintner, 1
Francis J. Pirozzolo, 9
David J. Pittenger, 13-16
Barbara S. Plake, 9
Gus P. Plessas, 6-9
Lynnette B. Plumlee, 3, 5-7
John Poggio, 14
Joseph G. Ponterotto, 11
Marcel O. Ponton, 13
Robert C. Pooley, 2-7
Mark Pope, 11-12, 14-16
Donald B. Pope-Davis, 12
Mary S. Poplin, 9
Julia Y. Porter, 14, 16
Lyman W. Porter, 6
James M. Porter, Jr., 3
William D. Porterfield, 11
Stanley D. Porteus, 2
C. Dale Posey, 10
Winifred L. Post, 4-5
*G. Michael Poteat, 10-16
James A. Poteet, 9-10
Kenneth E. Poucher, 8
Shawn Powell, 15-16
Thomas E. Powell, 11
Stephen Powers, 9

Elizabeth M. Prather, 9-11
Michael W. Pratt, 9
Sheila R. Pratt, 13-16
Norman T. Pratt, Jr., 1-2
Daniel A. Prescott, 1
Joan Preston, 7
Ralph C. Preston, 3-4
H. Vernon Price, 5
Jack Price, 7
Ray G. Price, 3, 6-7
Roy A. Price, 2-3
Erich P. Prien, 13-14
Kristin O. Prien, 14
Hugh F. Priest, 7
George P. Prigatano, 9
M. L. Kellmer Pringle, 4-7
Barry M. Prizant, 11
Glen W. Probst, 7
Barton B. Proger, 8-9
H. Thompson Prout, 9
Richard C. Pugh, 12-13
Earl V. Pullias, 2
Alan C. Purves, 7-8
Joan E. Pynes, 10
Fred Pyrczak, 8
M. Y. Quereshi, 7-8
Theresa A. Quigney, 14
Michelle Quinn, 9
Albert I. Rabin, 4-5, 7
S. Rachman, 6
John A. Radcliffe, 5-6
Rudolf E. Radocy, 12-13
Jeffrey S. Rain, 12-13
*Nambury S. Raju, 9, 11-16
Pamilla Ramsden, 15-16
Bikkar S. Randhawa, 11-14
John F. Randolph, 3
Earl F. Rankin, 7-8
Alan J. Raphael, 13-14
Evelyn Raskin, 4
Leslie T. Raskind, 10
Natalie Rathvon, 16
Michael M. Ravitch, 9
Glen E. Ray, 12
Alton L. Raygor, 6, 8
S. A. Rayner, 5
Mark D. Reckase, 9
James C. Reed, 7-9, 12-14
Michael L. Reed, 9
Homer B. C. Reed, Jr., 8-9
Edwin H. Reeder, 3-4
Amy M. Rees, 16
Jeff Reese, 14
Ronald E. Reeve, 9
William R. Reevy, 6
Barbara A. Reilly, 11-12
David H. Reilly, 9

Sean P. Relly, 16
Judith A. Rein, 15-16
Robert C. Reinehr, 11-14
Robert A. Reineke, 11-12
Richard J. Reisboard, 8
Ralph M. Reitan, 6-7
Willard E. Reitz, 7
H. H. Remmers, 1, 3, 5
K. Ann Renninger, 9
Joseph S. Renzulli, 9
Harvey Resnick, 9
*Paul Retzlaff, 11-16
*Cecil R. Reynolds, 9, 11-15
Maynard C. Reynolds, 5
Sharon B. Reynolds, 10
William M. Reynolds, 9, 14-15
Marvin Reznikoff, 7
Elizabeth Kelley Rhoades, 16
James A. Rice, 8
Gilbert J. Rich, 3
David C. Richard, 14
R. Lynn Richards, 10
Roger A. Richards, 5-9, 11, 13-14
T. W. Richards, 4
James M. Richards, Jr., 7-8
J. A. Richardson, 5
M. W. Richardson, 1-2
S. C. Richardson, 5
Bert O. Richmond, 9
James H. Ricks, Jr., 4-6, 8
T. Andrew Ridenour, 13
Paul R. Rider, 2
Stanley E. Ridley, 9
C. Alan Riedesel, 6-8
William Rieman, III, 3-4
Michelle L. Ries, 14
Edward G. Rietz, 5
Henry L. Rietz, 1
Janet Morgan Riggs, 9
Seymour Rigrodsky, 7
Alice R. Rines, 8
Henry D. Rinsland, 1-4
Charlene Rivera, 11
Harry N. Rivlin, 4-5
Robin Rix, 15
James P. Rizzo, 6
Oscar H. Roberts, 7
Brent W. Roberts, 14
David C. Roberts, 13
Holland Roberts, 2-6
Mark W. Roberts, 9, 11, 14
Donald U. Robertson, 11
Gary J. Robertson, 9-10, 13
Elizabeth A. Robinson, 9
Eric Robinson, 12
G. Edith Robinson, 7
H. Alan Robinson, 6-8

Helen M. Robinson, 4-7
Richard D. Robinson, 8
Alec Rodger, 2-4
David A. Rodgers, 7
Ronald C. Rodgers, 9
*Bruce G. Rogers, 9-16
Carl R. Rogers, 2
Cyril A. Rogers, 5
Frederick R. Rogers, 2
Margaret R. Rogers, 12
Virginia M. Rogers, 7
W. Todd Rogers, 7
Cynthia A. Rohrbeck, 11, 13-16
Samuel Roll, 10
Deborah D. Roman, 12-14
Thomas A. Romberg, 7-8
Leonard G. Rorer, 7
Carl L. Rosen, 7-9
Ephraim Rosen, 4
Gerald A. Rosen, 13
Marvin Rosen, 8
John H. Rosenbach, 7-9
Robert L. Rosenbaum, 8
Jennifer A. Rosenblatt, 13
Sylvia Rosenfield, 9-10
Arlene Coopersmith Rosenthal, 9-11
Nancy L. Roser, 8-9
Benjamin Rosner, 5-7
Jerome Rosner, 7
Alan O. Ross, 6
C. C. Ross, 2-3
Charles S. Ross, 4-5
Paul F. Ross, 6
Myron F. Rosskopf, 5
*Michael J. Roszkowski, 9-10, 12-15
Rodney W. Roth, 11
Harold F. Rothe, 4
Robert D. Rothermel, 9
Barbara A. Rothlisberg, 11-14
John W. M. Rothney, 1, 3-7
Julian B. Rotter, 3
Pamela Carrington Rotto, 12
James B. Rounds, 9-10, 12
Byron P. Rourke, 9
Denise M. Rousseau, 9-10
Harold L. Royer, 6
Arthur B. Royse, 5-6
Thaddeus Rozecki, 13
Ronald H. Rozensky, 11
Mary Roznowski, 14
Donald L. Rubin, 11
Stanley I. Rubin, 6
Floyd L. Ruch, 3-4, 6
Giles M. Ruch, 2
Herbert C. Rudman, 9, 12-14
Lawrence M. Rudner, 11-12
Robert Rueda, 10

C. H. Ruedisili, 3
Mabel E. Rugen, 3
David L. Rule, 10
Edward A. Rundqust, 3
William H. Rupley, 9
David H. Russell, 2-4
Harry J. Russell, 2-3
Michael Lee Russell, 13-14
James O. Rust, 9-10
John Rust, 12
Leo P. Ruth, 8
Roger A. Ruth, 7-8
Joseph M. Ryan, 11
Lawrence J. Ryan, 14-15
Michael Ryan, 9-10
David G. Ryans, 3-4, 6
Jane A. Rysberg, 9-10
Richard Rystrom, 7-8
*Darrell L. Sabers, 8-16
Donna S. Sabers, 13
Everett B. Sackett, 1, 6
Paul R. Sackett, 9
Cyril J. Sadowski, 12-13
H. Bradley Sagen, 6-7
Philip A. Saigh, 9
Perry Sailor, 12
Kenneth Sakauye, 12
Rachel Salisbury, 2
John Salvia, 9
Vincent J. Samar, 11-12, 14-16
David T. Sanchez, 9
Daryl Sander, 9
C. Sanders, 5
James R. Sanders, 9
*Jonathan Sandoval, 9-10, 12-15
Claude A. Sandy, 12
*Eleanor E. Sanford, 11-16
Dixie D. Sanger, 9
Toni E. Santmire, 9-10
Janice Santogrossi, 10
H. J. Sants, 6
Bert R. Sappenfield, 5-6
Irwin G. Sarason, 6
Theodore R. Sarbin, 4
Timothy Sares, 16
David M. Sargent, 15
Helen Sargent, 4
I. David Satlow, 5
George A. Satter, 3-4
Jerome M. Sattler, 8-10
Richard A. Saudargas, 10
Aulus W. Saunders, 2
David M. Saunders, 11
David R. Saunders, 5
*William I. Sauser, Jr., 9-16
Jean-Guy Savard, 7
*Diane J. Sawyer, 9-14

Neroli Sawyer, 15
Gilbert Sax, 8
Peter Scales, 9
Dale P. Scannell, 9, 11-13
Douglas E. Scates, 1, 3, 5
William L. Schaaf, 4
Willis C. Schaefer, 4
William D. Schafer, 11-14, 16
Joyce Parr Schaie, 8
K. Warner Schaie, 8-9
Michael J. Scheel, 15
Susan J. Schenck, 9-10
Johann H. Schepers, 6
C. Ruth Solomon Scherzer, 16
Alvin W. Schindler, 1-2, 4
Steven P. Schinke, 10, 12
Richard F. Schmid, 9
Frank L. Schmidt, 8-9, 13, 16
John F. Schmitt, 9
Neal Schmitt, 9, 12-13
Gerald R. Schneck, 13-15
Arnold E. Schneider, 3
W. Joel Schneider, 16
Leroy H. Schnell, 2-3
Lyle F. Schoenfeldt, 7-10
Patricia Schoenrade, 12-13
Wiliiam Schofield, 4-6
Fred J. Schonell, 2, 4-5
Richard V. Schowengerdt, 14
William B. Schrader, 4-6
H. E. Schrammel, 1
Fredrick A. Schrank, 9-10
Gregory Schraw, 12, 14-16
Robert L. Schreiner, 8
Herbert Schueler, 3-6
Douglas G. Schultz, 4, 6-7
Geoffrey F. Schultz, 11
Harold A. Schultz, 4, 6
Dale H. Schunk, 9
Richard Schupbach, 8
Donald H. Schuster, 6-7
Richard E. Schutz, 6-9
Joseph J. Schwab, 3
*Gene Schwarting, 9, 12-16
Neil H. Schwartz, 9-10
Mariette Schwarz, 6
Dean M. Schweickhard, 2
Gladys C. Schwesinger, 4
Craig S. Scott, 8
Louise B. Scott, 5
Owen Scott, III, 11
May V. Seagoe, 4
Carl E. Seashore, 2
Harold G. Seashore, 3-6
Virginia Seavey, 3
Don Sebolt, 12
Charles Secolsky, 9

William Seeman, 4
Stanley J. Segal, 6
David Segel, 1, 3-4
Esther F. Segner, 2
S. B. Sells, 5-7
R. B. Selover, 3
Gary B. Seltzer, 11
Boris Semenonoff, 6
Melvin I. Semmel, 7
Trevor E. Sewell, 9
Robert E. Shafer, 9
Laurance F. Shaffer, 3-6
Marcia B. Shaffer, 9-12
Timothy Shanahan, 9, 14, 16
Spencer Shank, 1
Gregory A. Shannon, 11
David A. Shapiro, 10-12
Edward S. Shapiro, 10-11
Stephen Sharp, 8
Marvin E. Shaw, 8
Steven R. Shaw, 12-16
Carleton B. Shay, 7-8
Marion F. Shaycoft, 5-6
Steward M. Shear, 11
Cynthia M. Sheehan, 9
Eugene P. Sheehan, 12-16
Eugene C. Sheeley, 7-9
Linda Jensen Sheffield, 9-10
Kenneth L. Sheldon, 9-10
William D. Sheldon, 4
Sylvia Shellenberger, 9
Ralph L. Shelton, 7-8
John W. Shepard, 10
Lorrie A. Shepard, 8-9
June Ellen Shepherd, 11
Carl J. Sherperis, 16
James W. Sherbon, 12, 16
Susan M. Sheridan, 11
Bruce Shertzer, 9-10
John C. Sherwood, 6-9
Benjamin Shimberg, 3-4, 6-7, 9
Stanley L. Shinall, 8
Agnes E. Shine, 12
Richard E. Shine, 7
Kenneth G. Shipley, 9-11, 13
Walter C. Shipley, 3
Mariela C. Shirley, 13
Amy H. Shively, 11
Sidney W. Shnayer, 8
Edwin S. Shneidman, 5
Edward J. Shoben, Jr., 4
J. Harlan Shores, 4
Louis Shores, 4
Lawrence D. Shriberg, 8
Mark D. Shriver, 13-14, 16
Evan D. Shull, 7
David Shum, 15

L. K. Shumaker, 2
Craig S. Shwery, 13, 15
Mark E. Sibicky, 14
Sylvia Sibley, 10
Edward A. Silver, 9
Arthur B. Silverstein, 7-11
Joan Silverstein, 10
Wesley E. Sime, 13, 15
Jeanne Simental, 16
Richard L. Simpson, 9
Esther Sinclair, 10
Jacob O. Sines, 8-9
Harry Singer, 7-8
Kusum Singh, 12-13
Surendra P. Singh, 14-15
Dorothy M. Singleton, 14, 16
Christopher A. Sink, 16
Edward R. Sipay, 7-8
Bertram C. Sippola, 11-12
Theresa G. Siskind, 14
Rodney W. Skager, 7
Edgar P. Slack, 3
Robert B. Slaney, 9-10
Patrick Slater, 3
Wayne H. Slater, 13-14
William Sloan, 4-5
Robert L. Slonaker, 9
Alfred L. Smith, Jr., 12
C. Ebblewhite Smith, 2
Corinne Roth Smith, 9-10
Donald E. P. Smith, 5-6
Douglas K. Smith, 10, 12-14
Everett V. Smith, Jr., 14
Fred M. Smith, 7
Gerald R. Smith, 9
Henry P. Smith, 4
I. Macfarlane Smith, 4-6
J. Philip Smith, 8
Jane E. Smith, 7
Janet V. Smith, 13-14, 16
*Jeffrey K. Smith, 9-10, 12-16
Kenneth J. Smith, 7-9
Larissa Smith, 15
Lisa F. Smith, 14-16
Lyman J. Smith, 7
Mary Lee Smith, 8
Michael D. Smith, 9
Nick L. Smith, 8
Nila Banton Smith, 4
Percival Smith, 2
Philip L. Smith, 9
Sharon L. Smith, 9
William L. Smith, 8
Alfred L. Smith, Jr., 11
Charles D. Smock, 7
Daniel W. Snader, 3
Jeffrey H. Snow, 11-12

Brooke Snyder, 12
Katharine Snyder, 14-16
William U. Snyder, 3
Louise M. Soares, 15-16
Gargi Roysircar Sodowsky, 11-12
David C. Solly, 11
Alicia Soliz, 16
Alan Solomon, 14
Rhonda H. Solomon, 14
Robert J. Solomon, 5-6
Ronald K. Sommers, 8-9, 11
Anita Miller Sostek, 8
Larry Sowder, 8
George D. Spache, 3-7
Steven D. Spaner, 12
Emma Spaney, 4-5
Michael Spangler, 15
C. Spearman, 2
Donald Spearritt, 5
Janet E. Spector, 13-14
Robert K. Speer, 2
Daniel G. Spencer, 9
Douglas Spencer, 2-3
Loraine J. Spenciner, 14-16
Peter L. Spencer, 2
Rayne A. Sperling, 16
Charles D. Spielberger, 8
Robert Spies, 13-14
Donna Spiker, 11-12
Stephen A. Spillane, 14
Susan K. Spille, 12
Herbert F. Spitzer, 3-4
Jaclyn B. Spitzer, 9, 11, 13, 16
Gilbert M. Spivack, 9
Bernard Spolsky, 6
Michael J. Sporakowski, 12, 14
Scott Spreat, 12
Otfried Spreen, 6
Mark A. Staal, 15
Barrie G. Stacey, 9
Michael J. Stahl, 9-10
Steven A. Stahl, 11, 14
Robert F. Stahmann, 8
Gary J. Stainback, 11, 13-14
*Jayne E. Stake, 9-13, 15
Robert E. Stake, 6
John M. Stalnaker, 1-2, 4-6
Roy W. Stanhope, 5
Julian C. Stanley, 4-6
Charles W. Stansfield, 8-10, 14
Joel Stark, 7-8
E. P. Starke, 4
Stanley Starkman, 9
Anna S. Starr, 1
Edward R. Starr, 13
Russell G. Stauffer, 5-6
John E. Stecklein, 6

Elaine Flory Stefany, 12
Leslie P. Steffe, 7-8
Harry L. Stein, 5-6
Jack M. Stein, 6-7
Margot B. Stein, 13-14
*Stephanie Stein, 11-16
Wendy J. Steinberg, 10, 15-16
Hugh Stephenson, 15
William Stephenson, 4-6
F. E. Sterling, 9
Robert J. Sternberg, 9
Brenda A. Stevens, 14
Jay R. Stewart, 13-15
Krista J. Stewart, 9-10
Naomi Stewart, 4-6
Sheldon L. Stick, 9-10
Charles A. Stickland, 4
Harlan J. Stientjes, 11-12
*Terry A. Stinnett, 10-15
William A. Stock, 11-12
Howard Stoker, 11
Joseph P. Stokes, 9-10
Clarence R. Stone, 2
Gerald L. Stone, 9-13
L. Joseph Stone, 4-5
Mark Stone, 9, 15
Gary Stoner, 11
Janet M. Stoppard, 9
Donald Lee Stovall, 14-15
Phillip S. Strain, 9
David Strand, 10
Ruth M. Strang, 1-2, 5
Richard K. Stratton, 12
Christine F. Strauss, 12
Lois T. Strauss, 11
Lawrence J. Stricker, 6, 8
Ruth Strickland, 5
Douglas C. Strohmer, 9
Stanley R. Strong, 8-9
Charles R. Strother, 3-5
J. B. Stroud, 3
Hans H. Strupp, 7
*Richard B. Stuart, 9-13, 15
Dewey B. Stuit, 3-4
George W. Sturrock, 5
Gabrielle Stutman, 12-16
Frederick H. Stutz, 3, 5
Michael J. Subkoviak, 9, 11-13
Richard R. Sudweeks, 13
*Hoi K. Suen, 11-16
Alan R. Suess, 7-8, 10
Richard M. Suinn, 7
Gail M. Sullivan, 11
Patricia M. Sullivan, 9
W. L. Sumner, 4
Norman D. Sundberg, 5-9, 11-14
Donna L. Sundre, 12-13

Yong H. Sung, 9
Donald E. Super, 3-6, 8
Carolyn H. Suppa, 16
J. P. Sutcliffe, 5
John Sutherland, 5-6
Rosemary E. Sutton, 11-14, 16
Marilyn N. Suydam, 7-9
John G. Svinicki, 10
Edward O. Swanson, 6
H. Lee Swanson, 9
Richard A. Swanson, 7-8
Robert M. Swanson, 8
Robert S. Swanson, 8
Jon D. Swartz, 8-9
Jody L. Swartz-Kulstad, 14
Cabrini S. Swassing, 10
Susan M. Swearer, 14, 16
*Mark E. Swerdlik, 9, 11-16
Harvey N. Switzky, 9, 11-12
Percival M. Symonds, 2-5
Hilda Taba, 1-2, 4
Wendi L. Tai, 16
Harold Takooshian, 12
Xuan Tan, 16
Abraham J. Tannenbaum, 6
Kikumi K. Tatsuoka, 9, 11
Maurice Tatsuoka, 11
Earl S. Taulbee, 8
Calvin W. Taylor, 5
Cie Taylor, 9
Erwin K. Taylor, 3-7
Howard R. Taylor, 3-4
Hugh Taylor, 7
John M. Taylor, 10
Ronald N. Taylor, 8
Wallace W. Taylor, 2-3
Florence M. Teagarden, 2-5
Lorene Teegarden, 2
Phyllis Anne Teeter, 9
Auke Tellegen, 8-9
Cathy Fultz Telzrow, 9-10, 12
Mildred C. Templin, 4
Edward A. Tenney, 2
W. Wesley Tennyson, 5
Mary L. Tenopyr, 9-10
James S. Terwilliger, 11-12
Anita S. Tesh, 12-13
E. W. Testut, 11
James B. Tharp, 2, 4
Paul W. Thayer, 6, 8-10
Herbert A. Thelen, 3
William N. Thetford, 6
C. L. Thiele, 2-3
Charles S. Thomas, 1-2
Cleveland A. Thomas, 5
Ruth G. Thomas, 9-10
Albert S. Thompson, 1-2, 4-6

Anton Thompson, 4
Bruce Thompson, 14, 16
Donald Thompson, 12-16
John H. Thompson, 1
Nora M. Thompson, 11-13, 15-16
Richard A. Thompson, 8
Edith I. M. Thomson, 3
Godfrey H. Thomson, 2
Robert L. Thorndike, 2-8
Robert M. Thorndike, 8, 15-16
George C. Thornton III, 9-10, 12-14
Robert H. Thouless, 3
Pamela S. Tidwell, 12
David V. Tiedeman, 4-8
Ernest W. Tiegs, 1-3
Robert J. Tierney, 9-10
Donald W. Tiffany, 14
Joseph Tiffin, 1
James A. Till, 8
Murray H. Tillman, 8
Gerald Tindal, 11-15
Miles A. Tinker, 4
William C. Tirre, 14-15
C. Alan Titchenal, 10
Carol Kehr Tittle, 7, 9, 11-12
John Tivendell, 15
Hazel M. Toliver, 3
Robert Tolsma, 9
Ruth E. Tomes, 11-12, 14
Gail E. Tompkins, 9-10
Kathleen T. Toms, 11
Tony Toneatto, 11-12, 14
Barry W. Tones, 10
Herbert A. Tonne, 1, 3, 5
Herbert A. Topps, 3
T. L. Torgerson, 3
Joseph Torgesen, 9
Michelle T. Toshima, 10
Esther Stavrou Toubanos, 12
Roger L. Towne, 11-12, 14-16
Agatha Townsend, 3, 5-6
Marion R. Trabue, 1-2
Ross E. Traub, 12, 14
Kenneth J. Travers, 7
Robert M. W. Travers, 3-5
Arthur E. Traxler, 1-7
Donald J Treffinger, 9
*Michael S. Trevisan, 11-16
Carolyn Triay, 11
Frances O. Triggs, 3
Harold C. Trimble, 6-8
Marie E. Trost, 2
Stephen E. Trotter, 14-16
Maurice E. Troyer, 3
R. M. Tryon, 1-2
Robert C. Tryon, 2
Jalie A. Tucker, 11

Larry Weber, 12
Harold Webster, 5-6
William J. Webster, 7, 9
David Wechsler, 2-3
Thaddeus E. Weckowicz, 8
M. O'Neal Weeks, 9
Zona R. Weeks, 9
Walter L. Wehner, 8-9
Charles C. Weidemann, 1-2
David P. Weikart, 7
Sharon L. Weinberg, 9, 11-13
Annette B. Weinshank, 9
Sheldon A. Weintraub, 7-8
David L. Weis, 9
Susan Ellis Weismer, 11
David J. Weiss, 7-8
Ellen Weissinger, 12-13
Henry Weitz, 3-8
R. A. Weitzman, 9
Carolyn M. Welch, 3
Wayne W. Welch, 8
A. T. Welford, 4
Beth L. Wellman, 3
F. L. Wells, 1-3
J. Steven Welsh, 11, 13
Lesley A. Welsh, 13
Charles Wenar, 9
Tim L. Wentling, 8
Joseph M. Wepman, 7
Emmy E. Werner, 6-7
Paul D. Werner, 13-14
Edgar B. Wesley, 1-4
Alexander G. Wesman, 4-7
Leonard J. West, 7-9
Bert W. Westbrook, 7-9, 11-13
Carol E. Westby, 11-13
George Westby, 4-6
Goran Westergren, 14
Ingela Westergren, 14
Stephanie Western, 12
Alida S. Westman, 8-9, 11-12
Frederick L. Westover, 4
Harry G. Wheat, 2
D. K. Wheeler, 5
Kenneth G. Wheeler, 9
Patricia H. Wheeler, 11-12, 14-15
Susan C. Whiston, 14-16
Edward M. White, 8
Howard R. White, 4
Karl R. White, 9
Kenneth V. White, 11
Shirley A. White, 9
Sue White, 9-10
Sally Anita Whiting, 9
Dean K. Whitla, 6
Carroll A. Whitmer, 2-3
Richard G. Whitten, 13

Randolph H. Whitworth, 8
Lillian A. Whyte, 9
Keith F. Widaman, 14-16
Thomas A. Widiger, 9, 11, 14
J. Lee Wiederholt, 8-9
Margaret Rogers Wiese, 11
Martin J. Wiese, 12, 14
James D. Wiggins, 9
Jerry S. Wiggins, 6-7, 10
Linda F. Wightman, 11-12
Elisabeth H. Wiig, 9
Richard L. Wikoff, 9-10
Katherine W. Wilcox, 3
Terry M. Wildman, 12
*William K. Wilkinson, 10-16
S. S. Wilks, 1-2
Haydn S. Williams, 5
J. Robert Williams, 6
Janice G. Williams, 11-13
Jean M. Williams, 12
John M. Williams, 11
Robert T. Williams, 9-13
David M. Williamson, 13
Edmund G. Williamson, 1-2
Warren W. Willingham, 6
Carl G. Willis, 7-8
Margaret Willis, 2
W. Grant Willis, 11-12
John M. Willits, 3, 5
John T. Willse, 16
Victor L. Willson, 8-10, 12
J. Richard Wilmeth, 6
David R. Wilson, 9
Guy M. Wilson, 1-3
James W. Wilson, 7
Robert M. Wilson, 9
Marlene Wadsworth Winell, 9
Herbert D. Wing, 4-6
Hilda Wing, 11-14
Harris Winitz, 8
William L. Winnett, 7
George P. Winship, Jr., 6-7
R. Winterbourn, 5
Carrie L. Winterowd, 14
Robert D. Wirt, 6-7
Steven L. Wise, 9-10, 12
Emory E. Wiseman, 7
Stephen Wiseman, 3, 5
Ernest C. Witham, 2
E. Lea Witla, 13
Joseph C. Witt, 9-10, 12-13
L. Alan Witt, 11–12
J. Richard Wittenborn, 3-4
Donna Wittmer, 12
Paul A. Witty, 3
Gregory C. Wochos, 16
David L. Wodrich, 9, 14

Kristen Wojcik, 13
Richard M. Wolf, 8-9, 11-14
Dael L. Wolfle, 1-2, 4
Leroy Wolins, 6
James A. Wollack, 12, 14
Myra N. Womble, 13
E. F. Wonderlic, 3
Hugh B. Wood, 2
Michelle Wood, 13
Ray G. Wood, 3
Clifford Woody, 1, 3
D. A. Worcester, 2-4
Edward A. Workman, 9
Julien Worland, 9
Blaine R. Worthen, 7-9, 12-13
F. Lynwood Wren, 3
C. Gilbert Wrenn, 1-2, 5
Benjamin D. Wright, 9
*Claudia R. Wright, 11-16
Dan Wright, 9-12
Logan Wright, 11-12
Robert L. Wright, 7
William J. Wright, 8
J. Wayne Wrightstone, 1-3, 5
Jack Wrigley, 5
Thomas A. Wrobel, 11
Michael K. Wynne, 12
Kaoru Yamamoto, 8
Alfred Yates, 5
Aubrey J. Yates, 7

Daniel L. Yazak, 14
Albert H. Yee, 7
Frank R. Yekovich, 9
Tamela Yelland, 12
Georgette Yetter, 16
Dale Yoder, 4
John W. Young, 12, 14-16
Suzanne Young, 16
*James E. Ysseldyke, 8-12, 14, 16
William Yule, 8
Robert H. Zabel, 9
Peter Zachar, 13-16
Louis C. Zahner, 2-3, 5
Dan Zakay, 9
O. L. Zangwill, 3
John A. Zarske, 9-10
Bo Zhang, 16
*Sheldon Zedeck, 8-9, 11-15
Paul F. Zelhart, 10
Michael J. Zickar, 14
Edwin Ziegfeld, 2-4
Linda J. Zimmerman, 14
Wayne S. Zimmerman, 6-7
Fred Zimring, 9
Joseph E. Zins, 9
Leland C. Zlomke, 10-14
Steven Zucker, 13
Marvin Zuckerman, 9
Donald G. Zytowski, 7-9, 12

INDEX OF TITLES

This title index includes a comprehensive listing of tests currently in print and included in this volume as well as out-of-print (or status unknown) tests that were listed in Tests in Print VI *and* The Fifteenth *and* Sixteenth Mental Measurements Yearbooks. *Numbers without colons refer to in-print tests included in this volume. Numbers with colons refer to out-of-print tests not listed in this volume; readers interested in these tests are referred to the last volume listing the tests. For example, T6:1826 refers to test 1826 in* Tests in Print VI; *15:399 refers to test 399 in* The 15th MMY. *Superseded titles are listed with a cross reference to the present title. All numbers refer to test entries, not to page numbers.*

Personal History Checklist for Adults, 1901
Personal Inventory of Needs, 1902
Personal Opinion Matrix, 1903
Personal Orientation Dimensions, 1904
Personal Orientation Inventory, 1905
Personal Problems Checklist, see Personal Problems Checklist—Adult, 1906
Personal Problems Checklist—Adult, 1906
Personal Problems Checklist for Adolescents, 1907
Personal Profile System, 1908
Personal Questionnaire Rapid Scaling Technique, T6:1864
Personal Reaction Index, 1909
Personal Relationship Inventory, 1910
Personal Resource Questionnaire, 1911
Personal Skills Map, T6:1868
Personal Stress Assessment Inventory, 1912
Personal Stress Inventory, T6:1870
Personal Stress Navigator, 1913
Personal Style Assessment, 1914
Personal Style Assessment, Jung-Parry Form, 1915
Personal Style Indicator [Revised], 1916
Personal Styles Inventory [PSI-120] [1999 Revision], 1917
Personal Success Profile, 1918
Personal Values Inventory [Personal Strengths Publishing], 1919
Personal Values Questionnaire, 1920
Personality Adjective Check List, 1921
Personality Advantage Questionnaire, 1922
Personality Assessment Inventory, 1923
Personality Assessment Screener, 1924
Personality Disorder Interview-IV: A Semistructured Interview for the Assessment of Personality Disorders, 1925
Personality Inventory for Children, Second Edition, 1926
Personality Inventory for Youth, 1927
Personality Research Form, 3rd Edition, 1928
Personality Self-Portrait [Revised], 1929
Personalized Achievement Summary System, 1930
Personalysis®, 1931
Personnel Assessment Form, 1932
Personnel Assessment Selection System, T6:1887
[Personnel Interviewing Form], 1933
Personnel Performance Problems Inventory, T6:1889
Personnel Reaction Blank, 1934
Personnel Relations Survey [Revised], 1935
Personnel Selection Inventory, 1936
Personnel Test Battery, 1937
Personnel Tests for Industry, 1938
Personnel Tests for Industry—Oral Directions Test [Second Edition], 1939
Pervasive Developmental Disorder in Mental Retardation Scale [Second Revised Edition], 1940
Pervasive Developmental Disorders Screening Test, Second Edition, 1941
Pharmacy College Admission Test, 1942

Phelps Kindergarten Readiness Scale, 1943
Philadelphia Head Injury Questionnaire, T6:1897
Phonemic-Awareness Skills Screening, 1944
PhonePass Spoken English Test, see Versant, 2702
Phonics-Based Reading Test, 1945
Phonological Abilities Test, 1946
Phonological Assessment Battery [Standardised Edition], 1947
The Phonological Awareness Skills Program Test, 1948
Phonovisual Diagnostic Tests, [1975 Revision], 1949
Photo Articulation Test, Third Edition, 1950
PHSF Relations Questionnaire, 1951
Picha-Seron Career Analysis, T6:1905
Pictographic Self Rating Scale, 1952
Pictorial Reasoning Test, 1953
The Pictorial Scale of Perceived Competence and Social Acceptance for Young Children, 1954
Pictorial Test of Intelligence, Second Edition, 1955
Picture Identification Test, 1956
Picture Test A, T6:1911
Picture Vocational Interest Questionnaire for Adults, T6:1912
Piers-Harris Children's Self-Concept Scale, Second Edition, 1957
A Pill Scale, 1958
PIM 8–12, 1959
PIP Developmental Charts, Second Edition, 1960
PL-1 and PL-2 Police Administrator Tests (Lieutenant), 1961
PLAN, 1962
Plane Geometry: National Achievement Tests, 1963
Plane Trigonometry: National Achievement Tests, 1964
Planning, Organizing, & Scheduling Test, Revised Edition, 1965
Plant Worker Staff Selector, see Warehouse/Plant Worker Staff Selector, 2737
The Play Observation Scale [Revised], 1966
Police Promotion Tests—Complete Service [Revised], 1967
Police Selection Test, 1968
Polish Proficiency Test, 1969
Politte Sentence Completion Test, T6:1923
Polyfactorial Study of Personality, 1970
The Poppleton Allen Sales Aptitude Test, see PASAT 2000 [Poppleton Allen Sales Aptitude Test], 1857
Portable Tactual Performance Test, 1971
The Porteus Maze Test, see Porteus Mazes, 1972
Porteus Mazes, 1972
Portland Digit Recognition Test [Revised], 1973
Portland Problem Behavior Checklist—Revised, 1974
Portrait of Overdone Strengths, 1975
Portrait of Personal Strengths, 1976
Position Analysis Questionnaire, 1977
Position Classification Inventory, 1978
Positive and Negative Syndrome Scale, 1979
Post-Assault Traumatic Brain Injury Interview and Checklist, 1980

INDEX OF RECENTLY
OUT-OF-PRINT TESTS

The Index of Recently Out-of-Print Tests is a cumulative listing of tests that appeared in Tests in Print III *through* The Sixteenth Mental Measurements Yearbook *but that do not appear in* Tests in Print VII. *The publishers of most of these tests have advised that the tests are now out of print. For some others, status has been unknown for over 10 years and the last known publisher is no longer in business and the tests are not published by a different publisher so out-of-print status has been assumed. Those tests in this index that appeared in* Tests in Print VI *and/or* The Fifteenth *and* Sixteenth Mental Measurements Yearbooks *but are not in* Tests in Print VII *are also integrated into the Index of Titles. All numbers refer to test entries, not page numbers. For example, T4:233 refers to test 233 in* Tests in Print IV, *12:121 refers to test 121 in* The 12th MMY, *and 15:301 refers to test 301 in* The 15th MMY.

INDEX OF ACRONYMS

This Index of Acronyms refers the reader to the appropriate test in Tests in Print VII. *In some cases tests are better known by their acronyms than by their full titles, and this index can be of substantial help to the person who knows the former but not the latter. Acronyms are only listed if the author or publisher has made substantial use of the acronym in referring to the test, or if the test is widely known by the acronym. A few acronyms are also registered trademarks (e.g., SAT); where this is known to us, only the test with the registered trademark is referenced. There is some danger in the overuse of acronyms, but this index, like all other indexes in this work, is provided to make the task of identifying a test as easy as possible. All numbers refer to test numbers, not page numbers.*

LCT: Listening Comprehension Test, 1464

LDDI: Learning Disabilities Diagnostic Inventory, 1426

LDES: Learning Disability Evaluation Scale (Renormed), 1427

LDR: Leadership Development Report, 1408

LDS: Lexington Developmental Scales, 1452

LEA: Leadership Effectiveness Analysis™, 1409

LEAD: Situational Leadership®, 2343

LEADR: Law Enforcement Assessment and Development Report, 1397

LEAI: Law Enforcement Applicant Inventory, 1396

Leiter-R: Leiter International Performance Scale—Revised, 1447

LET-II: Learning Efficiency Test-II (1998 Revision), 1428

LHS: The Clark Wilson Group Multi-Level Feedback Instruments and Development Programs, 492

LH-STEP: System for Testing and Evaluation of Potential, 2519

LII: Leisure Interest Inventory, 1445

LISRES-A: Life Stressors and Social Resources Inventory—Adult Form, 1455

LISRES-Y: Life Stressors and Social Resources Inventory—Youth Form, 1456

LIST: The Listening Skills Test, 1466

LLQ: Leatherman Leadership Questionnaire [Revised], 1443

LLT: Location Learning Test, 1470

LMDMI: The Kirkpatrick Management and Supervisory Skills Series, 1369

LNNB: Luria-Nebraska Neuropsychological Battery: Forms I and II, 1480

LNNB-C: Luria-Nebraska Neuropsychological Battery: Children's Revision, 1479

LOCI-2R: Adult Level of Care Index–2R, 91

LOCO: LOCO (Learning Opportunities Coordination): A Scale for the Assessment of Coordinated Learning Opportunities in Living Units for People with a Handicap, 1471

LOCS: Leisure to Occupations Connection Search, 1446

LOPP: Learning Organization Practices Profile, 1429

LOQ: Leadership Opinion Questionnaire, 1411

LOTCA: Loewenstein Occupational Therapy Cognitive Assessment, 1472

LPD: Levine-Pilowsky [Depression] Questionnaire, 1451

LPI: Leadership Practices Inventory, 1412

LPI: The Team Leadership Practices Inventory, 2542

LPI-IC: Leadership Practices Inventory—Individual Contributor [Second Edition], 1413

LPQ: Learning Process Questionnaire, 1430

LPT 3: Language Processing Test 3: Elementary, 1392

LPTS: Language Proficiency Test Series, 1393

LQST: The Leadership Q-Sort Test (A Test of Leadership Values), 1414

LRS: Light's Retention Scale [Revised Edition 2006], 1460

LS/CMI: Level of Service/Case Management Inventory: An Offender Assessment System, 1448

LS: Situational Leadership®, 2343

LSAT: Law School Admission Test, 1401

LSAT-3: Language Sampling, Analysis, and Training—Third Edition, 1394

LSC: The Lake St. Clair Incident, 1386

LS-E: Woodcock-Muñoz™ Language Survey–Revised, 2797

LSI: Leadership Skills Inventory [Revised] [Consulting Resource Group International, Inc.], 1415

LSI: Learning Style Indicator [Revised], 1432

LSI: Learning Style Inventory [Price Systems, Inc.], 1433

LSI: Learning Styles Inventory [Educational Activities, Inc.], 1438

LSI: Learning Styles Inventory, 1437

LSI: Life Styles Inventory, 1458

LSI3: Learning Style Inventory, Version 3.1, 1434

LSI-III: Learning Styles Inventory, Version III, 1440

LSI-O: Leadership Skills Inventory [Revised] [Consulting Resource Group International, Inc.], 1415

LSI-R: The Level of Service Inventory—Revised [2003 Norms Update], 1450

LSI-R:SV: Level of Service Inventory—Revised: Screening Version, 1449

LSI-S: Leadership Skills Inventory [Revised] [Consulting Resource Group International, Inc.], 1415

LSP: Leadership Skills Profile, 1416

LSP: Leadership Spectrum Profile, 1417

LSP: Learning Skills Profile, 1431

LSP: Learning Style Profile, 1435

LSQ: Learning Style Questionnaire, 1436

LSQ: Life Style Questionnaire, 1457

LS-S: Woodcock-Muñoz™ Language Survey–Revised, 2797

LTI: Learning Tactics Inventory, 1441

MAACL-R: Multiple Affect Adjective Check List—Revised, 1701

MAB: Multidimensional Aptitude Battery-II, 1688

MAC II: Maculaitis Assessment of Competencies II, 1483

MACH: Measure of Achieving Tendency, 1563

MACI: Millon Adolescent Clinical Inventory, 1636

MAE: Multilingual Aphasia Examination, Third Edition, 1697

MAI: Mathematics Attitude Inventory, 1545

MAND: McCarron-Dial System, 1555

MAP: Managerial Assessment of Proficiency MAP™, 1518

MAP: Miller Assessment for Preschoolers, 1623

MAPI: Millon Adolescent Personality Inventory, 1637

MAPP: MAPP: Motivational Appraisal of Personal Potential, 1529

MAPP: The Multidimensional Addictions and Personality Profile, 1685

CLASSIFIED SUBJECT INDEX

The Classified Subject Index classifies all tests included in Tests in Print VII *into 18 major categories: Achievement, Behavior Assessment, Developmental, Education, English and Language, Fine Arts, Foreign Language, Intelligence and General Aptitude, Mathematics, Miscellaneous, Neuropsychological, Personality, Reading, Science, Sensory-Motor, Social Studies, Speech and Hearing, and Vocations. Each category appears in alphabetical order and tests are ordered alphabetically within each category. The Miscellaneous category has 15 subcategories with tests ordered alphabetically within the subcategories. Each test entry includes test title, population for which the test is intended, and the test entry number in* Tests in Print VII. *All numbers refer to test entry numbers, not to page numbers. Brief suggestions for the use of this index are presented in the introduction. Revised definitions of the categories were effective with the* Fourteenth Mental Measurements Yearbook. *Most tests in TIP VII have been classified using the revised definitions, which are provided below.*

Achievement

Tests that measure acquired knowledge across school subject content areas. Included here are test batteries that measure multiple content areas and individual subject areas not having separate classification categories. (Note: Some batteries include both achievement and aptitude subtests. Such batteries may be classified under the categories of either Achievement or Intelligence and Aptitude depending upon the principal content area.)

See also Fine Arts, Intelligence and General Aptitude, Mathematics, Reading, Science, and Social Studies.

Behavior Assessment

Tests that measure general or specific behavior within educational, vocational, community, or home settings. Included here are checklists, rating scales, and surveys that measure observer's interpretations of behavior in relation to adaptive or social skills, functional skills, and appropriateness or dysfunction within settings/situations.

Developmental

Tests that are designed to assess skills or emerging skills (such as number concepts, conservation, memory, fine motor, gross motor, communication, letter recognition, social competence) of young children (0-7 years) or tests which are designed to assess such skills in severely or profoundly disabled school-aged individuals. Included here are early screeners, developmental surveys/profiles, kindergarten or school readiness tests, early learning profiles, infant development scales, tests of play behavior, social acceptance/social skills; and preschool psychoeducational batteries. Content specific screeners, such as those assessing readiness, are classified by content area (e.g., Reading).

See also Neuropsychological and Sensory-Motor.

Education

General education-related tests, including measures of instructional/school environment, effective schools/teaching, study skills and strategies, learning styles and strategies, school attitudes, educational programs/curriculae, interest inventories, and educational leadership.

Specific content area tests (i.e., science, mathematics, social studies, etc.) are listed by their content area.

English and Language

Tests that measure skills in using or understanding the English language in spoken or written form. Included here are tests of language proficiency, applied literacy, language comprehension/development/proficiency, English skills/proficiency, communication skills, listening comprehension, linguistics, and receptive/expressive vocabulary. (Tests designed to measure the mechanics of speaking or communicating are classified under the category Speech and Hearing.)

Fine Arts

Tests that measure knowledge, skills, abilities, attitudes, and interests within the various areas of fine and performing arts. Included here are tests of aptitude, achievement, creativity/talent/giftedness specific to the Fine Arts area, and tests of aesthetic judgment.

Foreign Languages

Tests that measure competencies and readiness in reading, comprehending, and speaking a language other than English.

Intelligence and General Aptitude

Tests that measure general acquired knowledge, aptitudes, or cognitive ability and those that assess specific aspects of these general categories. Included here are tests of critical thinking skills, nonverbal/verbal reasoning, cognitive abilities/processing, learning potential/aptitude/efficiency, logical reasoning, abstract thinking, creative thinking/creativity, entrance exams and academic admissions tests.

Mathematics

Tests that measure competencies and attitudes in any of the various areas of mathematics (e.g., algebra, geometry, calculus) and those related to general mathematics achievement/proficiency. (Note: Included here are tests that assess personality or affective variables related to mathematics.)

Miscellaneous

Tests that cannot be sorted into any of the current MMY categories as listed and defined above. Included here are tests of handwriting, ethics and morality, religion, driving and safety, health and physical education, environment (e.g., classroom environment, family environment), custody decisions, substance abuse, and addictions. (See also Personality.)

Neuropsychological

Tests that measure neurological functioning or brain-behavior relationships either generally or in relation to specific areas of functioning. Included here are neuropsychological test batteries, questionnaires, and screening tests. Also included are tests that measure memory impairment, various disorders or decline associated with dementia, brain/head injury, visual attention, digit recognition, finger tapping, laterality, aphasia, and behavior (associated with organic brain dysfunction or brain injury).

See also Developmental, Intelligence and General Aptitude, Sensory-Motor, and Speech and Hearing.

Personality

Tests that measure individuals' ways of thinking, behaving, and functioning within family and society. Included here are projective and apperception tests, needs inventories, anxiety/depression scales; tests assessing substance use/abuse (or propensity for abuse), risk taking behavior, general mental health, emotional intelligence, self-image/-concept/-esteem, empathy, suicidal ideation, schizophrenia, depression/hopelessness, abuse, coping skills/stress, eating disorders, grief, decision-making, racial attitudes; general motivation, attributions, perceptions; adjustment, parenting styles, and marital issues/satisfaction.

For content-specific tests, see subject area categories (e.g., math efficacy instruments are located in Mathematics). Some areas, such as substance abuse, are cross-referenced with the Personality category.

Reading

Tests that measure competencies and attitudes within the broadly defined area of reading. Included here are reading inventories, tests of reading achievement and aptitude, reading readiness/early reading ability, reading comprehension, reading decoding, and oral reading. (Note: Included here are tests that assess personality or affective variables related to reading.)

Science

Tests that measure competencies and attitudes within any of the various areas of science (e.g., biology, chemistry, physics), and those related to general science achievement/proficiency. (Note: Included here are tests that assess personality or affective variables related to science.)

Sensory-Motor

Tests that are general or specific measures of any or all of the five senses and those that assess fine or gross motor skills. Included here are tests of manual dexterity, perceptual skills, visual-motor skills, perceptual-motor skills, movement and posture, laterality preference, sensory integration, motor development, color blindness/discrimination, visual perception/organization, and visual acuity. (Note: See also the categories Neuropsychological and Speech and Hearing.)

Social Studies

Tests that measure competencies and attitudes within the broadly defined area of social studies. Included here are tests related to economics, sociology, history, geography, and political science, and those related to general social studies achievement/proficiency. (Note: Also included here are tests that assess personality or affective variables related to social studies.)

Speech and Hearing

Tests that measure the mechanics of speaking or hearing the spoken word. Included here are tests of articulation, voice fluency, stuttering, speech sound perception/discrimination, auditory discrimination/ comprehension, audiometry, deafness, and hearing loss/impairment. (Note: See Developmental, English and Language, Neuropsychological, and Sensory-Motor.)

Vocations

Tests that measure employee skills, behaviors, attitudes, values, and perceptions relative to jobs, employment, and the work place or organizational environment. Included here are tests of management skill/ style/competence, leader behavior, careers (development, exploration, attitudes); job- or work-related selection/admission/entrance tests; tests of work adjustment, team or group processes/communication/ effectiveness, employability, vocational/occupational interests, employee aptitudes/competencies, and organizational climate.

See also Intelligence and General Aptitude, and Personality and also specific content area categories (e.g., Mathematics, Reading).

ACHIEVEMENT

Academic Competence Evaluation Scales; Grades K–12, Grades 6–12, 2- or 4-year college, see 12

ACER Tests of Basic Skills—Orchid Series; Students, year 4 to 6 in Australian school system, see 31

Achievement Test for Accounting Graduates; Accounting job applicants or employees, see 38

Adult Basic Learning Examination, Second Edition; Adults with less than 12 years of formal schooling, see 89

Ann Arbor Learning Inventory [1996 Edition]; Grades K–1, Grades 2–4, Grades 5–8, see 164

Aprenda®: La prueba de logros en español—Segunda edición.; Grades K.5–12.9, see 173

Basic Achievement Skills Individual Screener; Grades 1–12 and post high school, see 250

Basic Achievement Skills Inventory; Grades 3 & 4, 5 & 6, 7 & 8, 9–12, and ages 8 to 80, see 251

BRIGANCE® Diagnostic Comprehensive Inventory of Basic Skills, Revised; Pre K–Grade 9 (Criterion Testing); Grades 1–6 (Readiness Standardized Testing), see 351

BRIGANCE® Diagnostic Inventory of Essential Skills; Grade 6-adult, see 354

BRIGANCE® Diagnostic Life Skills Inventory; Grades 2–8, see 355

California Achievement Tests, Fifth Edition; Grades K–12, see 378

Canadian Achievement Survey Tests for Adults; Adults, see 397

Canadian Achievement Tests, Third Edition; Grades 1.6–postsecondary, see 398

Canadian Tests of Basic Skills, Forms K and L; Grades K–2, 3–8, and 9–12, see 402

Closed High School Placement Test; Eighth grade students., see 555

College Basic Academic Subjects Examination; College students having completed the general education component of a college curriculum, see 576

Collegiate Assessment of Academic Proficiency; Freshmen–Seniors in college, see 627

Comprehensive Testing Program 4; Grades 1–2, 2–3, 3–4, 4–5, 5–6, 6–7, 7–8, 8–9, 9–10, 10–11, see 668

Criterion Test of Basic Skills [2002 Edition]; Ages 6 through 11-11, see 731

Developing Skills Checklist; Ages 4–6, see 792

Diagnostic Achievement Battery, Third Edition; Ages 6-0 to 14-0, see 816

Diagnostic Achievement Test for Adolescents, Second Edition; Ages 12–0 to 18–11, see 817

Diagnostic Screening Test: Achievement; Grades K–12, see 825

Diagnostic Test of the New Testament; Ages 17 and older, see 831

Differential Ability Scales; Ages 2-6 to 17-11, see 833

Differential Aptitude Tests—Australian and New Zealand Editions [Forms V and W]; Grades 8–12, see 834

Differential Aptitude Tests, Fifth Edition; Grades 7–9, grades 10–12 and adults, see 835

Differential Aptitude Tests for Personnel and Career Assessment; Adult, see 836

English Test: Municipal Tests: National Achievement Tests; Grades 3-8, see 952

Essential Skills Assessments: Information Skills; Ages 9–14, see 963

Evaluation of Basic Skills; Ages 3 to 18, see 970

BEHAVIOR ASSESSMENT

DEVELOPMENTAL

EDUCATION

ENGLISH AND LANGUAGE

FINE ARTS

FOREIGN LANGUAGES

INTELLIGENCE AND GENERAL APTITUDE

Morrisby Profile; Age 14–adults, see 1670

Multidimensional Aptitude Battery-II; Ages 16 and over, see 1688

Naglieri Nonverbal Ability Test; Grades K–12, see 1712

Naglieri Nonverbal Ability Test—Individual Administration; Ages 5-0 to 17-11, see 1713

New Jersey Test of Reasoning Skills—Form B; Reading level grade 5 and over, see 1739

Non-Reading Intelligence Tests, Levels 1–3; Ages 6-4 to 8-3, 7-4 to 9-3, 8-4 to 10-11, see 1750

Non-Verbal Reasoning Test Series; Ages 7.3-15.3, see 1754

Nonverbal Form; Measures general learning ability independent of language and reading skills, see 1751

Nonverbal Reasoning; Individuals in a variety of occupations, see 1753

The Ohio Penal Classification Test; Penal institutions, see 1791

Otis-Lennon School Ability Test, Seventh Edition; Grades K–12, see 1819

Paper and Pencil Games; Pupils in their second, third and fourth years in South African school system, see 1831

Peabody Picture Vocabulary Test—Third Edition; Ages 2.5–90+, see 1866

Penna Assessor Adaptive Ability Tests; Junior school–adult, see 1875

Perceptual-Motor Assessment for Children & Emotional/Behavioral Screening Program; Ages 4-0-15-11, see 1883

Personal Creativity Assessment; Age 18 and above, see 1892

Pictorial Reasoning Test; Entry-level positions in a variety of occupations, see 1953

Pictorial Test of Intelligence, Second Edition; Ages 3–8, see 1955

Porteus Mazes; Ages 3–adult, see 1972

Power and Performance Measures; Ages 16 and over, see 1984

Predictive Ability Test, Adult Edition; Ages 17 and over, see 1993

Preliminary SAT/National Merit Scholarship Qualifying Test; Grades 10-11, see 1996

Preschool and Kindergarten Interest Descriptor; Ages 3-6, see 2004

Primary Test of Cognitive Skills; Grades K–1, see 2025

Psycho-Epistemological Profile; College and adults, see 2079

Psychological Processing Checklist; Kindergarten–Grade 5, see 2082

The Pyramids and Palm Trees Test; Ages 18-80, see 2097

The Quick Test; Ages 2 and over, see 2115

Randt Memory Test; Ages 20-90, see 2120

Raven's Progressive Matrices; Ages 6–65, see 2122

Receptive One-Word Picture Vocabulary Test [2000 Edition]; Ages 2-0 through 18-11, see 2139

Receptive One-Word Picture Vocabulary Test—Spanish-Bilingual Edition; Ages 4.0–12.11, see 2138

Recognition Memory Test; Adult patients referred for neuropsychological assessment, see 2140

Reynolds Intellectual Assessment Scales and the Reynolds Intellectual Screening Test; Ages 3–94, see 2174

Scales for Identifying Gifted Students; Ages 5-18 years, see 2236

Schaie-Thurstone Adult Mental Abilities Test; Ages 22-84, see 2244

Scholastic Abilities Test for Adults; Ages 16 through 70, see 2250

Schubert General Ability Battery; Grades 12–16 and adults, see 2264

Screening Assessment for Gifted Elementary and Middle School Students, Second Edition; Ages 5–14, see 2269

Senior Aptitude Tests; Standards 8–10 in South African schools, college, and adults, see 2301

Senior South African Individual Scale—Revised; Ages 7-0 to 16-11, see 2302

Ship Destination Test; Grades 9 and over, see 2327

Shipley Institute of Living Scale; Ages 14 and over, see 2328

Slosson Full-Range Intelligence Test; Ages 5–21, see 2356

Slosson Intelligence Test 3rd [2002 Edition]; Ages 4-65 and over, see 2357

Snijders-Oomen Non-Verbal Intelligence Test—Revised; Dutch children ages 2-6 to 7-0, Dutch children ages 5-6 to 17-0, see 2364

Space Thinking (Flags); Industrial employees, see 2384

Standard Progressive Matrices, New Zealand Standardization; New Zealand children ages 8–15 and adults, see 2404

Stanford-Binet Intelligence Scales, Fifth Edition; Ages 2-0 to 89-9, see 2411

Stanford-Binet Intelligence Scales for Early Childhood, Fifth Edition; Ages 2 years to 7 years, 3 months, see 2412

Stoelting Brief Nonverbal Intelligence Test; Ages 6-0 to 20-11, see 2433

Structure of Intellect Learning Abilities Test; Preschool–adult, see 2449

Subsumed Abilities Test; Ages 9 and over, see 2481

Swanson-Cognitive Processing Test; Ages 5 to adult, see 2514

Teacher Observation Scales for Identifying Children with Special Abilities; Junior and middle primary school, see 2534

Technical Test Battery [British Edition]; Apprentice and technical personnel, see 2551

Teele Inventory for Multiple Intelligences; Age 3 to adult, see 2553

Telephone Interview for Cognitive Status; Ages 60–98, see 2556

MATHEMATICS

MISCELLANEOUS

ADJUSTMENT/ADAPTIVE FUNCTIONING

cap; Residents of any type of living units where people with a handicap live with the assistance of care givers, see 1471

OARS Multidimensional Functional Assessment Questionnaire; Ages 65 and over, see 1767

The Prevocational Assessment and Curriculum Guide; Mentally retarded individuals, see 2022

Survey of Functional Adaptive Behaviors; Ages 16 and over, see 2499

Transition Competence Battery for Deaf and Hard of Hearing Adolescents and Young Adults; Deaf and hard of hearing adolescents and young adults, see 2670

Vineland Adaptive Behavior Scales; Birth through age 18-11 and low-functioning adults, ages 3 through 12-11, see 2708

ALCOHOL AND SUBSTANCE USE

Addiction Severity Index—Multimedia Version; Adults seeking substance abuse treatment, see 66

Adolescent American Drug and Alcohol Survey with Prevention Planning Survey; Grades 6–12, see 75

Adolescent Diagnostic Interview; Ages 12–18, see 80

Adult Level of Care Index–2R; Adults, see 91

Alcohol Use Disorders Identification Test; Adults, see 137

The American Drug and Alcohol Survey; Schools and school districts, see 149

ASIST: A Structured Addictions Assessment Interview for Selecting Treatment; Adults, see 190

Assessment of Chemical Health Inventory; Adolescents, adults, see 200

Drug Abuse Screening Test; Clients of addiction treatment, see 858

Drug-Taking Confidence Questionnaire; Clients of addiction treatment, see 859

Drug Use Screening Inventory—Revised; Ages 10 to 16; 17 and over, see 860

Inventory of Drinking Situations; Ages 18 to 75, see 1275

Inventory of Drug-Taking Situations; Drug or alcohol users, see 1276

Michigan Alcoholism Screening Test; Adults, see 1609

Personal Experience Screening Questionnaire for Adults; Ages 19 and over, see 1899

Practical Adolescent Dual Diagnostic Interview; Ages 12–18, see 1990

QUESTS: A Life-Choice Inventory; Grades 9-12, see 2106

Situational Confidence Questionnaire; Adult alcoholics, see 2342

Substance Abuse Relapse Assessment; Adolescents and adults, see 2477

Substance Abuse Screening Test; Ages 13–adult, see 2478

The Substance Abuse Subtle Screening Inventory–3; Ages 18–73, see 2479

Substance Use Disorders Diagnostic Schedule-IV; Adults suspected of abusing alcohol or drugs, see 2480

Triage Assessment for Addictive Disorders; Adults, see 2681

BLIND

Lorimer Braille Recognition Test: A Test of Ability in Reading Braille Contractions; Students (ages 7-13) in grade 2 Braille, see 1477

Tooze Braille Speed Test: A Test of Basic Ability in Reading Braille; Students (Ages 7-13) in Grades 1 or 2 Braille, see 2661

BUSINESS EDUCATION AND RELATIONSHIPS

Alleman Leadership Development Questionnaire; Mentors and proteges, see 140

Alleman Mentoring Activities Questionnaire; Mentors and proteges, see 141

Alleman Relationship Value Questionnaire; Mentors and proteges, see 142

Diagnosing Organizational Culture; Adults, see 815

Dissemination Self-Inventory; Organizations, see 845

Group Environment Scale, Third Edition; Group members and leaders; clinicians, consultants, and program evaluators, see 1120

I-SPEAK Your Language™: A Survey of Personal Styles; Employees, see 1211

Influence Strategies Exercise; Managers and employees, see 1241

Inventory for Client and Agency Planning; Infant to adult, see 1272

Kilmann-Saxton Culture-Gap Survey [Revised]; Work team members, employees, see 1361

Kipnis-Schmidt Profiles of Organizational Influence Strategies; Organizational members, see 1368

Management of Differences Inventory; Business managers, see 1505

Mentoring Skills Assessment; Mentors, coaches, and mentees, see 1599

Mentoring Style Indicator™; Mentors and proteges, see 1600

Organizational Climate Exercise II; Work groups, see 1813

Organizational Culture Inventory; Organizational members, see 1814

Project Implementation Profile; Project managers and team members, see 2057

Watson-Barker Listening Test; Adults in business, professions, and college, see 2740

Watson-Barker Listening Test—High School Version; Grades 7-12, see 2741

Whisler Strategy Test; Business and industry, see 2770

Work Environment Scale, Second Edition; Employees and supervisors, see 2809

Home Observation for Measurement of the Environment; Birth to age 3, early childhood, middle childhood, early adolescent, see 1191

Home Screening Questionnaire; Birth to age 3, ages 3–6, see 1192

Home-Visit Kit; Families involved in child custody situations, see 1193

How Am I Doing? A Self-Assessment for Child Caregivers; Caregivers of children with disabilities, see 1198

The Infant-Toddler and Family Instrument; Families with infants and toddlers 6–36 months, see 1237

Infant/Toddler Environment Rating Scale—Revised Edition; Infant/toddler day care centers, see 1239

Marital Evaluation Checklist; Married couples in counseling, see 1531

MATE [Marital ATtitude Evaluation]; Couples, see 1542

Miller Marriage Satisfaction Scale; Individuals who are dating, living together or who are married, see 1631

Mirror-Couple Relationship Inventory; Engaged and married couples, see 1658

Pair Attraction Inventory; College and adults, see 1829

Parent Perception of Child Profile; Parents, see 1843

Parent-Adolescent Communication Scale; Adolescents and their parents, see 1835

Parent-Child Communication Inventory; Children and parents, see 1839

Parent/Family Involvement Index; Parents with children in special education programs, see 1841

Parent Success Indicator; Parents of children ages 10 to 14, see 1844

The Parenthood Questionnaire; Youth who are prospective parents or who may work with children in the future, see 1846

Parenting Alliance Measure; Parents of children ages 1–19 years, see 1847

Parenting Satisfaction Scale™; Adults with dependent children, see 1848

Perceptions of Parental Role Scales; Parents, see 1882

Personal Assessment of Intimacy in Relationships [Revised]; Couples, see 1889

Personal Relationship Inventory; Ages 15 and over, see 1910

A Pill Scale; Adults, see 1958

The Power of Influence Test; Grade 5 and over, see 1988

A Premarital Communication Inventory; Premarital couples, see 1999

PREPARE/ENRICH; Premarital and married couples, see 2000

Scale of Marriage Problems: Revised; Couples, see 2233

Sex-Role Egalitarianism Scale; High school to adult, see 2317

Spousal Assault Risk Assessment Guide; Individuals suspected of or being treated for spousal or family-related assault, see 2403

Uniform Child Custody Evaluation System; Professionals involved in custody evaluation, see 2687

Vasectomy Scale: Attitudes; Adults, see 2696

Wife's or Husband's Marriage Questions; Husbands, wives, see 2781

HEALTH AND
PHYSICAL EDUCATION

The ANSER System-Aggregate Neurobehavioral Student Health and Educational Review [Revised 1997]; Children ages 3+, suspected of having learning difficulties, see 165

The Arizona Battery for Communication Disorders of Dementia; Alzheimer's patients, see 184

Behavioral Assessment of Pain Questionnaire; Subacute and chronic pain patients, see 297

Coitometer; Adults, see 573

Comprehensive Sex History; Adults, see 663

Cornell Index—Form N2; Ages 14 and over, see 714

Derogatis Interview for Sexual Functioning; Adults, see 783

Eating Inventory; Ages 17 and older, see 900

Erotometer: A Technique for the Measurement of Heterosexual Love; Adults, see 961

Fast Health Knowledge Test, 1986 Revision; High school and college, see 1009

Five Factor Wellness Inventory; Elementary, high school, and adults, see 1031

Functional Fitness Assessment for Adults over 60 Years, Second Edition; Adults over age 60, see 1054

Health and Daily Living Form, Second Edition; Students ages 12-18, Adults, see 1156

Health Problems Checklist; Adults, see 1163

Health Status Questionnaire 2.0; Ages 14 and older, see 1164

Katz Adjustment Scales—Relative Report Form; Adults with psychiatric, medical, or neurological disorders, see 1340

Krantz Health Opinion Survey; College, healthy adults, and chronic disease populations, see 1377

The LAW-PSI Sexual History Questionnaire; Adults, see 1400

Matching Assistive Technology & CHild; Children with disabilities, ages 0–5, see 1539

Medical Ethics Inventory; First year medical students, see 1589

Menometer; Adolescents and adults, see 1594

MILCOM Patient Data Base System; Medical patients, see 1619

Multidimensional Health Profile; Ages 18–90, see 1689

Organic Dysfunction Survey Schedules; Adult clients, see 1807

Overeating Questionnaire; Ages 9–98 years, see 1822

Pain Assessment Battery, Research Edition; Patients with chronic pain, see 1827

HANDWRITING

LEARNING DISABILITIES

PHILOSOPHY

PSYCHOLOGY

RECORD AND REPORT FORMS

SOCIO-ECONOMIC STATUS

TEST PROGRAMS

NEUROPSYCHOLOGICAL

PERSONALITY

Abortion Scale; Older adolescents and adults, see 6

Abuse Risk Inventory for Women, Experimental Edition; Women seeking medical or mental health services, see 8

Academic Perceptions Inventory [2000 Revision]; Grades K–16, see 15

ACDI-Corrections Version and Corrections Version II; Troubled youth between the ages of 12 and 18 years in juvenile probation, parole, and corrections programs, see 22

Achievement Motivation Profile; Ages 10 to 14 for AMP Juniors; 14 years and older in high school, junior college, and college, see 37

Adaptability Test; Job applicants, see 58

The Adjective Check List; High school and over, see 71

Adolescent Apperception Cards; Ages 12–19, see 78

Adolescent Coping Scale; Ages 12–18, see 79

Adolescent Dissociative Experiences Scale; Ages 11–17, see 81

Adolescent Drinking Index; Ages 12–17, see 82

Adolescent Psychopathology Scale; Ages 12–19, see 84

Adolescent Psychopathology Scale—Short Form; Ages 12–19 years, see 85

Adolescent Separation Anxiety Test; Ages 11-18, see 86

Adolescent Symptom Inventory—4; Ages 12–18, see 87

The Adult Manifest Anxiety Scale; Ages 19–59, college students, ages 60 and over, see 92

Adult Personality Inventory [Revised]; Ages 16–adult, see 93

Adult Self Expression Scale; Adults, see 95

Adult Suicidal Ideation Questionnaire; Ages 18 and over, see 96

Age Projection Test; Adults, see 128

Aggression Questionnaire; Ages 9–88, see 131

The Alcadd Test, Revised Edition; Adults, see 135

Alcohol Dependence Scale; Problem drinkers, see 136

Alcohol Use Inventory; Adults and adolescents suspected of problem drinking, see 138

Anger Disorders Scale; Ages 18 and over, see 163

Antisocial Process Screening Device; Ages 6–13, see 166

Appraise Your World™; Adults, see 171

The APT Inventory; Adults, see 174

Arousal Seeking Tendency Scale; Ages 15 and older, see 188

The Assertiveness Skills Inventory; Adults, see 192

Assessment of Core Goals; High school and over, see 205

The Assessment of Personal Goals; Adults, see 211

Assessment of Qualitative and Structural Dimensions of Object Representations, Revised Edition; Adolescents and adults (patients and normals), see 213

Assessor Occupational Type Profile; Adults, see 217

Association Adjustment Inventory; Normal and institutionalized adults, see 218

Athletic Motivation Inventory; Male and female athletes ages 13 and older and coaches, see 219

The Attentional and Interpersonal Style Inventory; Adults and adolescents, see 225

Attitudes Toward Working Mothers Scale; Adults, see 226

Attitudes Towards Guns and Violence Questionnaire; Ages 6–29, see 227

The Awareness of Social Inference Test; Ages 14–60, see 238

The Balanced Emotional Empathy Scale; Ages 15 and older, see 241

Bar-Ilan Picture Test for Children; Ages 4–16, see 245

BarOn Emotional Quotient-360; Ages 16 and over, see 246

Basic Personality Inventory; Adult and adolescent, see 259

BASIS-A Inventory [Basic Adlerian Scales for Interpersonal Success—Adult Form]; Adults, see 264

Battery for Health Improvement 2; Ages 18–65, individuals who are being treated for a physical injury, see 268

BDI-FastScreen for Medical Patients; Ages 12–82, see 273

Beck Anxiety Inventory [1993 Edition]; Adults and adolescents ages 17 and over, see 274

Beck Depression Inventory—II; Ages 13 and over, see 275

Beck Hopelessness Scale [Revised]; Adolescents and adults ages 17 and over, see 276

Beck Scale for Suicide Ideation; Adults and adolescents ages 17 and over, see 277

Beck Youth Inventories of Emotional & Social Impairment; Ages 7–14, see 278

Behavior Rating Scale; Grades K–8, see 294

Behaviour Problems: A System of Management; Problem behavior children in a classroom situation, see 301

Bell Object Relations and Reality Testing Inventory; Ages 18 and older, see 306

Bem Sex-Role Inventory; High school and college and adults, see 307

The Benziger Thinking Styles Assessment; Working adults, aged 18 or older, see 314

BEST Instruments; Adults, see 316

Biographical Inventory Form U; Grades 7–12, see 323

READING

SCIENCE

SENSORY-MOTOR

SOCIAL STUDIES

SPEECH AND HEARING

VOCATIONS

PUBLISHERS DIRECTORY AND INDEX

This directory and index gives the names and test entry numbers of all publishers represented in Tests in Print VII. *Current addresses are listed for all publishers for which this is known. Those publishers for which a current address is not available are listed as "Address Unknown." This directory and index also provides telephone and FAX numbers and e-mail and Web page addresses for those publishers who responded to our request for this information. Please note that all test numbers refer to test entry numbers, not page numbers. Publishers are an important source of information about catalogs, specimen sets, price changes, test revisions, and other details.*

AAMR American Association on Mental Retardation
444 North Capitol Street, NW, Suite 846
Washington, DC 20001-1512
Tests: 2495

ABackans DCP, Inc.
1700 West Market Street
Dept. RD301
Akron, OH 44313
Telephone: 330-745-4450
FAX: 330-745-4450
E-mail: ABackans@abackans.com
Web: abackans.com
Tests: 40, 1980

Academic Consulting & Testing Service
P.O. Box 1883
Lake Oswego, OR 97035
Telephone: 503-639-3292
FAX: 503-639-3292
E-mail: HEDSbyACTS@aol.com
Tests: 220, 805, 1425, 1845, 2258

Academic Therapy Publications
20 Commercial Boulevard
Novato, CA 94949-6191
Telephone: 800-422-7249
FAX: 415-883-3720
E-mail: atp@aol.com
Web: www.academictherapy.com/
Tests: 164, 229, 248,731, 852, 962, 985, 986, 1327, 1428, 1460, 1677, 1678, 1743, 1945, 1994, 2110, 2111, 2113, 2138, 2139, 2385, 2386, 2578, 2580, 2595, 2623, 2624, 2625, 2719, 2801, 2837

ACS DivCHED Examinations Institute
UW Milwaukee
Chemistry Department
3210 North Cramer Street
Milwaukee, WI 53211
Tests: 42, 43, 44, 45, 46, 47, 48, 49, 50, 51, 52, 53, 54, 55

ACT, Inc.
500 ACT Drive
P.O. Box 168
Iowa City, IA 52243-0168
Telephone: 319-337-1000
FAX: 319-341-2335
Web: www.act.org
Tests: 56, 57, 424, 627, 983, 1962, 2812

ADE Incorporated
P.O. Box 660
Clarkston, MI 48347
Telephone: 800-334-1918
Tests: 1337, 1725, 2476

Adult Self Expression Scale c/o John P. Galassi
CB #3500
Peabody Hall
University of North Carolina
Chapel Hill, NC 27599-3500
Tests: 95

AdvisorTeam, Inc.
340 Brannan Street, Suite 402
San Francisco, CA 94107-1891
Tests: 1351

AGS Publishing
Acquired by Pearson in 2005
See Pearson Assessments
Tests: 249, 283, 366, 467, 656, 802, 895, 987, 1082,
    1083, 1124, 1127, 1150, 1341, 1342, 1343, 1345,
    1347, 1348, 1349, 1355, 1358, 1543, 1681, 1802,
    1803, 1865, 1866, 2126, 2128, 2375, 2465, 2708,
    2709, 2798

AJA Associates
c/o Marchman Psychology
720 South Dubuque
Iowa City, IA 52240
Tests: 1697

American Association for Active Lifestyles and Fitness
1900 Association Drive
Reston, VA 22091
Telephone: 800-213-7193
FAX: 703-476-9527
E-mail: AAALF@AAHPERD.ORG
Web: www.aahperd.org/aapar/
Tests: 1054, 2379, 2662

American Association of Teachers of German, Inc.
112 Haddontowne Court, #104
Cherry Hill, NJ 08034-3668
Telephone: 856-795-5553
FAX: 856-795-9398
E-mail: headquarters@aatg.org
Web: www.aatg.org
Tests: 1717

American Dental Association
211 East Chicago Avenue, 6th Floor
Chicago, IL 60611-2678
Telephone: 312-440-7465
FAX: 312-587-4105
E-mail: kramerg@ada.org
Web: www.ada.org
Tests: 400, 772

American Management Association
Address Unknown
Tests: 148

American Psychiatric Association
1000 Wilson Blvd., Suite #1625
Arlington, VA 22209-3901
Tests: 2077, 2265

American Psychiatric Publishing, Inc.
1000 Wilson Blvd., Suite #1825
Arlington, VA 22209
Telephone: 800-368-5777
FAX: 703-907-1091
E-mail: appi@psych.org
Web: www.appi.org
Tests: 473, 2249, 2450, 2451, 2452

Dr. Nancy C. Andreasen
Department of Psychiatry
MHCRC, 2911 JPP
200 Hawkins Drive
Iowa City, IA 52242-1057
Telephone: 319-356-1553
FAX: 319-353-8300
E-mail: luann-godlove@uiowa.edu
Web: iowa-mhcrc.psychiatry.uiowa.edu/
Tests: 657, 2228, 2229, 2230

Andrews University Press
Sutherland House
Berrien Springs, MI 49104-1700
Telephone: 269-471-6915
FAX: 269-471-6224
E-mail: aupress@andrews.edu
Web: www.andrews.edu/universitypress/
Tests: 2560

AOTA Press
The American Occupational Therapy Association, Inc.
4720 Montgomery Lane
Bethesda, MD 20814-3425
Tests: 156, 1374

ARBOR, Inc.
ARBOR Corporate Center
One West Third Street
Media, PA 19063
Tests: 2727

ASEBA Research Center for Children, Youth, and
    Families
1 South Prospect Street
Burlington, VT 05401-3456
Telephone: 802-264-6432
FAX: 802-264-6433
E-mail: mail@ASEBA.org
Web: www.ASEBA.org
Tests: 33, 429

The Assessment and Development Centre
6890 E. Sunrise Drive, #120-382
Tucson, AZ 85750
Telephone: 520-299-5501
FAX: 520-299-5348
E-mail: stressmaster@qwest.net
Web: www.stressmaster.com
Tests: 1846, 2440

The Assessment and Qualifications Alliance (AQA)
Stag Hill House
Guildford, Surrey GU2 7XJ
England
Telephone: +44 1483 506506
FAX: +44 1483 300152
E-mail: gboyden@aqa.org.uk
Web: www.aqa.org.uk
Tests: 263

Assessment Enterprises
925 Hayslope Drive
Knoxville, TN 37919
Telephone: 865-690-4498
E-mail: MSTAHL@UTK.EDU
Tests: 1312

Assessment Resource Center
University of Missouri—Columbia
College of Education
2800 Maguire Blvd.
Columbia, MO 65211
Telephone: 800-366-8232
FAX: 573-822-8937
E-mail: umcarck-12@missouri.edu
Web: www.arc.missouri.edu
Tests: 576, 1661

Assessment Systems International, Inc.
544 East Ogden Avenue, Suite 700–391
Milwaukee, WI 53202
Telephone: 414-224-1400
FAX: 414-224-1401
E-mail: cspeck@execpc.com
Web: www.asi-intl.com
Tests: 1493

Assessment-Intervention Resources
2285 Elysium Avenue
Eugene, OR 97401-4903
Telephone: 541-338-8736
FAX: 541-338-8736
E-mail: info@assessment-intervention.com
Web: www.assessment-intervention.com
Tests: 1189, 2262

Associated Consultants in Education
P.O. Box 501
Niceville, FL 32588
Tests: 316, 2496

Association for Biblical Higher Education
5575 S. Semoran Blvd., Suite 26
Orlando, FL 32822-1781
Telephone: 407-207-0808
FAX: 407-207-0840
E-mail: exdir@abhe.org
Web: www.abhe.org
Tests: 831, 2406

Association for the Education and Welfare of the
    Visually Handicapped
ATTN: Mrs. S. A. Clamp, Deputy Head
St. Vincent's School for the Blind
Yew Tree Lane, West Derby
West Derby, Liverpool L12 9HN
England
Tests: 1477, 2661

Association of American Colleges and Universities
1818 "R" Street, NW
Washington, DC 20009
Tests: 965

Association of American Medical Colleges
2501 "M" Street, NW, Lobby 26
Washington, DC 20037-1300
Tests: 1588

Athletic Success Institute
2308 Crystal Court
Antioch, CA 94509
Tests: 219

Australian Council for Educational Research Ltd.
19 Prospect Hill Road
Camberwell,
Melbourne, Victoria 3124
Australia
Telephone: +61 3 9835 7411
FAX: +61 3 9835 7499
E-mail: power@acer.edu.au
Web: www.acer.edu.au
Tests: 23, 25, 26, 27, 28, 29, 30, 31, 32, 79, 176, 194, 332, 333, 628, 707, 799, 800, 819, 824, 834, 951, 1208, 1210, 1356, 1430, 1533, 1534, 1546, 1724, 2053, 2054, 2290, 2525, 2640, 2772, 2807, 2819, 2824,

Australian Department of Immigration and Multicultural Affairs
Benjamin Offices
Chan St.
Belconnen, ACT 2617
Australia
Tests: 233

AVIAT
c/o Denison Consulting
121 West Washington, Suite 201
Ann Arbor, MI 48104
Tests: 1126

Ballard & Tighe Publishers
P.O. Box 219
Brea, CA 92822-0219
Telephone: 800-321-4332
FAX: 714-255-9828
E-mail: info@ballard-tighe.com
Web: www.ballard-tighe.com
Tests: 1215, 1216, 1295, 2108

The Barber Center Press, Inc.
136 East Avenue
Erie, PA 16507
Telephone: 814-453-7661
FAX: 814-455-1132
E-mail: gabcmain@drbarbercenter.org
Web: www.drbarbercenter.org
Tests: 797

Donna Bardis
2533 Orkney Drive
Toledo, OH 43606
Telephone: 419-535-6146
E-mail: PBARDIS@POP3.UTOLEDO.EDU
Tests: 6, 335, 573, 758, 961, 996, 1007, 1106, 1245, 1297, 1594, 1854, 1958, 2147, 2318, 2644, 2696, 2710, 2832

Barrett & Associates, Inc.
1772 State Road
Cuyahoga Falls, OH 44223
Telephone: 330-762-2323
FAX: 330-928-2768
E-mail: gbarrett@barrett-associates.com
Web: www.barrett-associates.com
Tests: 230

The Basic Skills Agency
Commonwealth House
1-19 New Oxford Street
London WC1A 1NU
England
Tests: 1010

Bay State Psychological Associates
225 Friend Street
Boston, MA 02114
Telephone: 800-438-2772
FAX: 617-367-5888
E-mail: jerry@eri.com
Web: www.eri.com
Tests: 943

James R. Beatty
College of Business Administration
San Diego State University
San Diego, CA 92182
Tests: 1251

Lenore Behar
1821 Woodburn Road
Durham, NC 27705
Telephone: 919-489-1888
FAX: 919-489-1832
E-mail: lbehar@nc.rr.com
Web: www.lenorebehar.com
Tests: 2007

Behavior Data Systems, Ltd.
P.O. Box 44256
Phoenix, AZ 85064-4256
Tests: 857, 2679

Behavioral-Developmental Initiatives
14636 North 55th Street
Scottsdale, AZ 85254
Telephone: 800-405-2313
FAX: 602-494-2688
E-mail: BDI@TEMPERAMENT.COM
Web: www.b-di.com
Tests: 430, 1742

Behaviordata, Inc.
20833 Stevens Creek Blvd., Suite 100
Cupertino, CA 95014-2154
Tests: 2326

The Ber-Sil Co.
3412 Seaglen Drive
Rancho Palos Verdes, CA 90275-6140
Tests: 315

Nancy E. Betz, Ph.D.
104 Townshend
1885 Neil Ave Mall
The Ohio State University
Columbus, OH 43210
Telephone: 614-292-4166
FAX: 614-292-4537
E-mail: betz.3@osu.edu
Web: faculty.psy.ohio-state.edu/betz/
Tests: 413, 2808

Biddle Consulting Group Inc.
195 Blue Ravine Rd., Suite 270
Folsom, CA 95630-4760
Telephone: 800-999-0438 x 242
FAX: 916-563-7557
E-mail: blane@opac.com
Web: www.opac.com
Tests: 1785

Millard J. Bienvenu, Ph.D.
Northwest Publications
710 Watson Drive
Natchitoches, LA 71457
Tests: 192, 1265, 1274, 1280, 1530, 1834, 1839, 1999,
    2292, 2321

Bigby, Havis, & Associates, Inc.
12750 Merit Drive, Suite 660
Dallas, TX 75251
Telephone: 972-233-6055
FAX: 972-233-3154
E-mail: kcapelle@bigby.com
Web: www.bigby.com
Tests: 193, 221, 2281

Bilingual Educational Services, Inc.
2514 South Grand Avenue
Los Angeles, CA 90007-9979
Telephone: 213-749-6213
FAX: 213-749-1820
Tests: 724, 739

Laurence M. Binder, Ph.D.
4900 SW Griffith Dr.
Suite 244
Beaverton, OR 97005
Telephone: 503-626-5246
FAX: 503-626-1686
E-mail: pdxlarry@aol.com
Tests: 1973

Biofeedback Certification Institute of America
10200 W. 44th Avenue, Suite 304
Wheat Ridge, CO 80033-2840
Tests: 322

Birkman International, Inc.
3040 Post Oak Blvd., Suite 1425
Houston, TX 77056
Telephone: 800-215-2760
FAX: 713-963-9142
E-mail: sales@birkman.com
Web: www.birkman.com
Tests: 324

Dr. Dorothy Bishop
c/o TROG Research Fund
Age and Cognitive Performance Research Centre
University of Manchester
Manchester M13 9PL
England
Tests: 2570

Sidney J. Blatt
Yale University School of Medicine
Department of Psychiatry
25 Park Street
New Haven, CT 06519
Telephone: 203-785-2090
FAX: 203-785-7357
E-mail: sidney.blatt@yale.edu
Tests: 213, 781

Bowling Green State University
JDI Office
Department of Psychology
Bowling Green, OH 43403
Telephone: 419-372-8247
FAX: 419-372-6013
E-mail: JDI_RA@bgnet.bgnet.bgsu.edu
Web: www.bgsu.edu/departments/psych/JDI
Tests: 1313, 2157, 2437, 2511

Brador Publications, Inc.
Address Unknown
Tests: 327, 2130

Brain Technologies Corporation
P.O. Box 260886
Plano, TX 75026
Telephone: 972-769-2012
FAX: 972-867-0364
E-mail: order@braintechnologies.com
Web: www.braintechnologies.com
Tests: 341, 721, 1559, 1644

BrainTrain
727 Twin Ridge Lane
Richmond, VA 23235
Telephone: 804-320-0105
FAX: 804-320-0242
E-mail: info@braintrain.com
Web: www.braintrain.com
Tests: 1301

Branden Publishing Co.
P.O. Box 812094
Wellesley, MA 02482
Telephone: 781 235-3634
FAX: 781 790-1056
E-mail: branden@brandenbooks.com
Web: www.brandenbooks.com
Tests: 320

Brandon House, Inc.
P.O. Box 240
Bronx, NY 10471
Tests: 128, 911

Patricia Brandt, Ph.D.
Parent Child Nursing
School of Nursing
University of Washington
Seattle, WA 98195
Tests: 1911

Brigham Young University
Humanities Technology and Research Support Center
Foreign Language Testing
Provo, UT 84602
Tests: 1795

British Columbia Institute Against Family Violence
802-207 West Hastings Street
Vancouver, British Columbia V6B 1H7
Canada
Telephone: 604-669-7055
FAX: 604-669-7054
E-mail: resource@bcifv.org
Tests: 2322

Brookes Publishing Co., Inc.
P.O. Box 10624
Baltimore, MD 21285-0624
Telephone: 800-638-3775
FAX: 410-337-8539
E-mail: custserv@brookespublishing.com
Web: www.brookespublishing.com
Tests: 129, 130, 433, 484, 636, 1237, 2558, 2668

Brougham Press
P.O. Box 2702
Olathe, KS 66063-0702
Telephone: 800-360-6244
FAX: 913-782-1116
E-mail: CISE@BroughamPress.com
Web: www.BroughamPress.com
Tests: 475

Brown and Benchmark Publishers, A division of Wm.
    C. Brown Communications
2460 Kerper Blvd.
Dubuque, IA 52001
Tests: 497

Martin M. Bruce, Ph.D.
22516 Caravelle Circle
Boca Raton, FL 33433-5909
Telephone: 561-393-2428
FAX: 561-362-6185
E-mail: BRUCEPUBL@adelphia.net
Tests: 178, 218, 365, 374, 411, 535, 941, 1666,1885,
    1933, 1970, 2207, 2209, 2216, 2282, 2481, 2491,
    2618, 2666, 2784

Arnold R. Bruhn and Associates
7910 Woodmont Avenue, Suite 1300
Bethesda, MD 20814
Tests: 889

C.P.S., Inc..
P.O. Box 345
Englewood, NJ 07458
Telephone: 201-947-2002
FAX: 201-947-2002
E-mail: CPSPSYCH1@aol.com
Tests: 465, 909, 2247, 2300

California Counseling Center
22797 Barton Road, Suite 200
Grand Terrace, CA 92324
Telephone: 909-885-1000
FAX: 909-885-0500
E-mail: sblphdmpapsy@linkline.com
Tests: 1398, 1399, 1400, 1402

Callier Center for Communication Disorders
University of Texas at Dallas
1966 Inwood Road
Dallas, TX 75235
Tests: 390

Cambridge Center for Behavioral Studies
Publications Department
336 Baker Avenue
Concord, MA 01742
Telephone: 978-369-2227
FAX: 978-369-2227
E-mail: center@behavior.org
Web: www.behavior.org
Tests: 295, 1807

The Cambridge Stratford Study Skills Institute
8560 Main Street
Williamsville, NY 14221
Telephone: 800-466-2232
FAX: 716-626-9076
E-mail: cambridges@aol.com
Web: www.cambridgesTraTford.com
Tests: 1851, 2508, 2682

Cambridge University Press
100 Brook Hill Drive
West Nyack, NY 10994-2133
Tests: 1373, 1571, 1730, 2020

Camelot Unlimited
c/o Michael Lavelli
5757 N. Sheridan Road, Suite 13B
Chicago, IL 60660
Tests: 462

Canadian Test Centre
Educational Assessment Services
85 Citizen Court, Suites 7 & 8
Markham, Ontario L6G 1A8
Tests: 397, 398, 401

CareerTrainer
10725 Ellis Avenue, #D
Fountain Valley, CA 92708
Telephone: 800-888-4945
FAX: 714-965-7697
E-mail: customerservice@CAREERTRAINER.COM
Web: WWW.CAREERTRAINER.COM
Tests: 428, 1671, 1776, 2156

CASAS
5151 Murphy Canyon Road, Suite 220
San Diego, CA 92123-4339
Telephone: 858-292-2900
FAX: 858-292-2910
E-mail: bwalsh@casas.org
Web: WWW.CASAS.ORG
Tests: 648

Castle Consultants
111 Teeter Rock Road
Trumbull, CT 06611
Telephone: 203-375-5353
FAX: 203-375-2999
E-mail: cassie@castleconsultants.us
Web: www.castleconsultants.us
Tests: 15, 2298, 2381, 2536

Center for Advanced Studies in Management
1574 Mallory Court
Bowling Green, KY 42103
Tests: 2118

Center for Applications of Psychological Type, Inc.
2815 Northwest 13th Street, Suite 401
Gainesville, FL 32609
Tests: 1808, 1705, 1867

Center for Applied Linguistics
4646 40th Street, NW
Washington, DC 20016-1859
Telephone: 202-362-0700
FAX: 202-363-7204
E-mail: info@cal.org
Web: www.cal.org
Tests: 179, 256, 317, 483, 1969

Center for Architecture and Urban Planning Research
P.O. Box 413
University of Wisconsin—Milwaukee
Milwaukee, WI 53201-0413
Tests: 882

Center for Creative Leadership
One Leadership Place
P.O. Box 26300
Greensboro, NC 27438-6300
Telephone: 336-288-7210
FAX: 336-282-3284
E-mail: info@leaders.ccl.org
Web: www.ccl.org
Tests: 310, 1357, 2062, 2353

Center for Creative Learning
4921 Ringwood Meadow
Sarasota, FL 34235
Telephone: 941-342-9928
FAX: 941-342-0064
E-mail: info@creativelearning.com
Web: www.creativelearning.com
Tests: 2705

The Center for Management Effectiveness, Inc.
P.O. Box 1202
Pacific Palisades, CA 90272
Telephone: 310-459-6052
FAX: 310-459-9307
E-mail: info@cmeinc.org
Web: www.cmeinc.org
Tests: 1505, 1912, 2178, 2435

Center for the Study of Aging and Human Development
Box 3003
Duke University Medical Center
Durham, NC 27710
Telephone: 919-660-7500
FAX: 919-686-8569
E-mail: betty.ray@duke.edu
Web: www.geri.duke.edu
Tests: 1767

Center for the Study of Ethical Development
University of Minnesota
206 Burton Hall
178 Pillsbury Drive, SE
Minneapolis, MN 55455
Telephone: 612-624-0876
FAX: 612-624-8241
E-mail: tich0016@tc.umn.edu
Tests: 765

Center for the Study of Higher Education
The University of Memphis
308 Browning Hall
Memphis, TN 38152
Telephone: 901-678-2775
FAX: 901-678-4291
E-mail: ccseqlib@cc.memphis.edu
Web: www.memphis.edu/cshe
Tests: 640

Central Institute for the Deaf
Publications Department
4560 Clayton Avenue
St. Louis, MO 63110
Telephone: 314-977-0133
FAX: 314-977-0016
E-mail: dgushleff@cid.wustl.edu
Web: www.cid.wustl.edu
Tests: 487, 488, 897, 1104, 2239, 2398, 2533

Central Wisconsin Center for the Developmentally Disabled
ATTN: Psychology Department
317 Knutson Drive
Madison, WI 53704
Telephone: 608-301-9227
FAX: 608-301-9423
E-mail: kesligp@dhfs.state.wi.us
Tests: 2786

Centre for Addiction and Mental Health
Marketing Services
33 Russell Street
Toronto, Ontario M5S 2S1
Canada
Telephone: 416-595-6059
FAX: 416-593-4694
E-mail: marketing@camh.net
Web: www.camh.net
Tests: 136, 190, 858, 859, 1275, 1276, 2342

Centreville School
6201 Kennett Pike
Wilmington, DE 19807
Telephone: 302-571-0230
FAX: 302-571-0270
E-mail: language4@home.com
Tests: 2148

CERAD Administrative Core
Box 3203
Duke University Medical Center
Durham, NC 27710
Telephone: 919-286-6406
FAX: 919-286-9219
E-mail: stric007@mc.duke.edu
Web: cerad.mc.duke.edu
Tests: 439, 440

Vicentita M. Cervera, Ed.D.
13 Miller Street
San Francisco Del Monte
Quezon City 1105
Philippines
Telephone: (632) 374-8320
FAX: (632) 373-3715
E-mail: vcervera@mavec.com.ph
Web: www.mavec.com.ph
Tests: 1021

CFKR Career Materials
P.O. Box 99
Meadow Vista, CA 95722-0099
Tests: 186, 416, 984, 1173, 1314, 1475, 1488, 2720

Jay L. Chambers, Ph.D.
160 Kendal Dr. , #205
Lexington, VA 24450-1790
Telephone: 540-462-3874
E-mail: ibis@alexres.kendal.org
Tests: 1956

The Change Companies
5221 Sigstrom Drive
Carson City, NV 89706
Telephone: 888-889-8866
FAX: 775-885-0643
E-mail: info@changecompanies.net
Web: www.changecompanies.net
Tests: 91, 300, 1990, 2141, 2480, 2681

The Chauncey Group International
Educational Testing Service
P.O. Box 6604
Princeton, NJ 08541-6604
Tests: 2589

Checkmate Plus, Ltd.
P.O. Box 696
Stony Brook, NY 11790-0696
Telephone: 800-779-4292
FAX: 631-360-3432
E-mail: info@checkmateplus.com
Web: www.checkmateplus.com
Tests: 69, 87, 458, 881, 2846

Child Development Centers of the Bluegrass, Inc.
465 Springhill Drive
Lexington, KY 40503
Tests: 1452

Child Development Resources
P.O. Box 280
Norge, VA 23127-0280
Tests: 1198, 2352

Child Development Review - Behavior Science Systems, Inc.
P.O. Box 19512
5905 Elliot Avenue South
Minneapolis, MN 55419-9998
Telephone: 612-850-8700
FAX: 360-351-1374
E-mail: heidi@childdevrev.com
Web: www.childdevrev.com/
Tests: 454, 455, 877, 1236, 2009

Child Welfare League of America
Headquarters
440 First Street, NW, Third Floor
Washington, DC 20001-2085
Tests: 459, 741, 998

ChoicePoint
P.O. Box 49429
Charlotte, NC 28277-2712
Telephone: 888-310-2558
FAX: 888-286-5724
Tests: 2418, 2419

Chronicle Guidance Publications, Inc.
66 Aurora Street
Moravia, NY 13118-3569
Telephone: 800-622-7284
FAX: 315-497-3359
E-mail: CustomerService@ChronicleGuidance.com
Web: www.ChronicleGuidance.com
Tests: 486

The Clark Wilson Group, Inc.
4900 Nautilus Court N., Suite 220
Boulder, CO 80301-3242
Telephone: 800-537-7249
FAX: 303-581-9326
E-mail: info@clarkwilsongroup.com
Web: www.clarkwilsongroup.com
Tests: 492, 2059

Clinical Psychometric Research, Inc.
1228 Wine Spring Lane
Towson, MD 21204
Telephone: 800-245-0277; 410-321-6165
FAX: 410-321-6341
E-mail: mdero@aol.com
Web: www.derogatis-tests.com
Tests: 782, 783, 785, 786, 2086

CNS Vital Signs
1829 East Franklin Street, Bldg. 500
Chapel Hill, NC 27514
Telephone: 919-933-2000
FAX: 919-933-2830
Tests: 559

CogniSyst, Inc.
3937 Nottaway Road
Durham, NC 27707
Telephone: 919-489-1000
FAX: 919-489-0607
E-mail: lyleallen@nc.rr.com
Web: www.cognisyst.com
Tests: 674, 1827

CogScreen LLC
4910 Mass. Ave.
Washington, DC 20016
Tests: 572

The College Board
45 Columbus Avenue
New York, NY 10023-6992
Telephone: 212-713-8000
Web: WWW.COLLEGEBOARD.com
Tests: 21, 98, 99, 100, 101, 102, 103, 104, 105, 106,
107, 108, 109, 110, 111, 112, 113, 114, 115, 116,
117, 118, 119, 120, 121, 122, 123, 124, 125, 577,
578, 579, 580,581, 582, 583, 584, 585, 586, 587,
588, 589, 590, 591, 592, 593, 594, 595, 596, 598,
599, 600, 601, 602, 603, 604, 605, 606, 607, 608,
609, 610, 611, 612, 613, 614, 615, 616, 617, 618,
619, 620, 2226

Combined Program in Education and Psychology
University of Michigan
1406 School of Education
610 East University Avenue
Ann Arbor, MI 48109-1259
E-mail: cpep@umich.edu
Tests: 1672

John D. Cone
Department of Psychology & Family Studies
United States International University
10455 Pomerado Road
San Diego, CA 92131
Tests: 1841, 2096

Consulting Resource Group International, Inc.
P.O. Box 8000, PMB 386
Sumas, WA 98295-8000
Telephone: 604-852-0566
FAX: 604-850-3003
E-mail: info@crgleader.com
Web: www.crgleader.com
Tests: 958, 1250, 1321, 1415, 1432, 1916, 2114, 2219,
2299, 2439, 2694

Corporate Mentoring Solutions® Inc.
Corporate Head Office
Unit A — 6822 Veyanness Road
Saanichton
British Columbia V8M 2A8
Canada
Telephone: 800-877-955-0314
FAX: 250-652-6853
E-mail: wgray@mentoring-solutions.com
Web: www.mentoring-solutions.com
Tests: 1600

CPP, Inc.
1055 Joaquin Road, 2nd Floor
Mountain View, CA 94043
Telephone: 800-624-1765
FAX: 650-969-8608
E-mail: custserve@cpp.com
Web: www.cpp.com
Tests: 71, 385, 410, 417, 1027, 1361, 1362, 1419, 1538,
1708, 1710, 1711, 1853, 1985, 2032, 2186, 1443,
2445, 2651, 2695, 2809

Creative Learning Press, Inc.
P.O. Box 320
Mansfield Center, CT 06250
Tests: 494, 726, 1257, 1440, 2237

Creatrix
135 Black Oaks Lane
Wayzata, MN 55391
Telephone: 952-925-1757
E-mail: team@creatrix.com
Web: www.creatrix.com
Tests: 728

The Critical Thinking Co.
P.O. Box 1610
Seaside, CA 93955-1610
Telephone: 800-458-4849
FAX: 831-393-3277
E-mail: info@criticalthinking.com
Web: www.criticalthinking.com
Tests: 713, 1305

CTB/McGraw-Hill
20 Ryan Ranch Road
Monterey, CA 93940-5703
Telephone: 831-393-0700
Web: www.ctb.com
Tests: 90, 240, 378, 383, 384, 740, 492, 1042, 1043,
1044, 1285, 1388, 1389, 1390, 1391, 1716, 1995,
2025, 2387, 2563, 2636, 2637, 2638

Curriculum Associates, Inc.
153 Rangeway Road
P.O. Box 2001
North Billerica, MA 01862-0901
Telephone: 800-225-0248
FAX: 800-366-1158
E-mail: info@cainc.com
Web: www.curriculumassociates.com
Tests: 351, 352, 353, 354, 355, 356, 357, 358, 359, 650, 651, 652, 653

Dansk Psykologisk Forlag
Kongevejen 155
2830 Virum
Copenhagen, Denmark
Telephone: +45 3538 1655
FAX: +45 3538 1665
E-mail: dk-psych@dpf.dk
Web: www.dpf.dk
Tests: 245

Delaware County Reading Council
c/o Delaware County Intermediate Unit #25
200 Yale Avenue
Morton, PA 19070
Tests: 769

Denver Developmental Materials, Inc.
P.O. Box 371075
Denver, CO 80237-5075
Telephone: 800-419-4729
FAX: 303-355-5622
E-mail: sales@denverii.com
Web: www.denverii.com
Tests: 775, 776, 777, 778, 779, 1192

Department of Research Assessment and Training
1051 Riverside Drive, Unit 123
New York, NY 10032
Telephone: 212-543-5536
FAX: 212-543-5386
E-mail: je10@columbia.edu
Tests: 947, 1080, 2076, 2078, 2100, 2245

Development Associates, Inc.
2300 Wilson Blvd., #300
Arlington, VA 22201-3308
Telephone: 703-276-0677
FAX: 703-276-0432
E-mail: azehler@DEVASSOc1.COM
Tests: 94

Developmental Therapy Institute, Inc.
P.O. Box 5153
Athens, GA 30604-5153
Tests: 807

The Devine Group, Inc.
10200 Alliance Road, Suite 310
Cincinnati, OH 45242
Tests: 814

Diagnostic Counseling Services, Inc.
P.O. Box 6178
Kokomo, IN 46904-6178
Tests: 1685

Diagnostic Specialists, Inc.
1170 North 660 West
Orem, UT 84057
Telephone: 801-225-7698
FAX: 801-229-1944
E-mail: allanroe@earthlink.com
Web: www.psychstuff.com
Tests: 450, 649, 663, 664, 2308, 2781

Directional Insight International, Inc.
1111 McKinley Street
Ft. Worth, TX 76126
Telephone: 800-852-2001
FAX: 817-249-6266
E-mail: test@nsightsuccess.com
Web: www.nsightsuccess.com
Tests: 1758

Rodney L. Doran, Ph.D., Professor of Science Education
State University of New York at Buffalo
Department of Learning and Instruction
593 Baldy Hall
Buffalo, NY 14260
Tests: 1589

Dr. Baker Partnership
10 Elgin Rd.
Bournemouth BH4 9NL
United Kingdom
Telephone: 011-44-1202-763836
FAX: 011-44-1202-761766
Tests: 2142

Dragon Press
127 Sycamore Avenue
Mill Valley, CA 94941-2821
Tests: 466

Drake Beam Morin, Inc.
58 South Service Road, Suite #130
Melville, NY 11747
Telephone: 631-752-3789
FAX: 631-756-2571
E-mail: maureen_sullivan@dbm.com
Web: www.dbm.com
Tests: 1211

Dr. Maurice J. Eash, Director
Institute of Learning and Teaching
University of Massachusetts—Boston
Harbor Campus
Boston, MA 02125-3393
Tests: 1820

Eckstein Bros., Inc.
5601 West Slauson Avenue, Suite 170
Culver City, CA 90230-6534
Tests: 901

Ed & Psych Associates
210 West Hamilton Avenue, Suite #122
State College, PA 16801-5218
Telephone: 814-235-9115
FAX: 814-235-9115
Tests: 72

EdITS/Educational and Industrial Testing Service
P.O. Box 7234
San Diego, CA 92167
Tests: 404, 420, 421, 422, 423, 431, 676, 677, 678, 710,
    840, 990, 991, 1014, 1332, 1490, 1701, 1829, 1904,
    1905, 2255, 2428, 2469, 2635

Education Associates
P.O. Box 23308
Louisville, KY 40223
Telephone: 800-626-2950
FAX: 502-244-9144
E-mail: stw@educationassociates.com
Web: www.educationassociates.com
Tests: 1316

Educational Activities Software
Attn: Alan Stern
P.O. Box 754
Baldwin, NY 11510
Telephone: 1-800-645-2796
FAX: 516-379-7429
E-mail: achieve@ea-software.com
Web: www.ea-software.com
Tests: 180, 1243, 1438

Educational & Industrial Test Services, Ltd.
83 High Street
Hemel Hempstead,
Hertfordshire HP1 3AH
England
Telephone: +44 (0) 1442 215521
FAX: +44 (0) 1442 240531
E-mail: POST@MORRISBY.DEMON.CO.UK
Web: WWW.MORRISBY.com
Tests: 1022, 1244, 1528, 1874

Educational & Psychological Consultants, Inc.
1715 West Worley Street, Suite #A
Columbia, MO 65203-2603
Telephone: 573-446-6232
E-mail: kuncej@missouri.edu
Tests: 1917

Educational Assessment Service, Inc.
W6050 Apple Road
Watertown, WI 53098-3937
Telephone: 920-261-1118
FAX: 920-261-6622
E-mail: order@sylviarimm.com
Web: www.sylviarimm.com
Tests: 34, 35, 1115, 1121, 1122, 2004

Educational Publications
532 E. Blackridge
Tucson, AZ 85705
Tests: 1323

Educational Records Bureau
220 East 42nd Street, Suite 100
New York, NY 10017-5006
Telephone: 212-672-9800
FAX: 212-370-4096
E-mail: info@erbtest.org
Web: www.erbtest.org
Tests: 668, 960, 1227

Educational Resources, Inc.
8910 West 62nd Terrace
P.O. Box 29160
Shawnee Mission, KS 66201
Telephone: 1-800-292-2273
FAX: 913-362-4627
E-mail: testing@eriworld.com
Web: www.eriworld.com
Tests: 1162, 1177, 1761

Educational Testing Service
Publication Order Services
P.O. Box 6736
Princeton, NJ 08541-6736
Telephone: 609-921-9000
FAX: 609-734-5410
E-mail: etsinfo@ets.org
Web: www.ets.org
Tests: 126, 498, 499, 500, 501, 502, 503, 504, 505, 506,
    507, 508, 509, 510, 522, 512, 513, 514, 515, 516,
    517, 518, 519, 520, 521, 522, 523, 524, 525, 526,
    527, 528, 529, 530, 531, 622, 861, 1038, 1093,
    1094, 1095, 1096, 1097, 1098, 1099, 1100, 1101,
    1102, 1103, 1371, 1487 1715, 1992, 1996, 1997,
    2045, 2257, 2276, 2394, 2462, 2619

Educators Publishing Service, Inc.
P.O. Box 9031
Cambridge, MA 02139-9031
Telephone: 800-225-5750
FAX: 888-440-2665
E-mail: cpsbooks@epsbooks.com
Web: www.epsbooks.com
Tests: 165, 308, 1868, 1870, 1871, 1872, 2163, 2354, 2509

Carl N. Edwards, Ph.D.
P.O. Box 279
Dover, MA 02030
Telephone: 774-200-0201
FAX: 508-785-2526
E-mail: cedwards@socialaw.com
Tests: 2344

Ekman, Paul
Address Unknown
Tests: 993

Elbern Publications
P.O. Box 9497
Columbus, OH 43209
Telephone: 614-231-1950
FAX: 614-237-2637
E-mail: ebecker@insight.rr.com
Tests: 279, 2127

Dr. John Eliot
Institute for Child Study
University of Maryland
College Park, MD 20742
Tests: 924

Ellsworth & Vandermeer Press, Ltd.
P.O. Box 68164
Nashville, TN 37206
Tests: 1850

Patricia B. Elmore, Ph.D.
College of Education and Human Services, Dean's Office
Mail Code 4624
Southern Illinois University—Carbondale
Carbondale, IL 62901
Telephone: 618-453-2415
FAX: 618-453-1646
E-mail: pbelmore@siu.edu
Web: www.siu.edu/~epse1/elmore/
Tests: 294, 445, 1405

Endeavor Information Systems, Inc.
1317 Livingston Street
Evanston, IL 60201
Tests: 946

English Language Institute
University of Michigan
TCF Building, Suite 350
401 East Liberty Street
Ann Arbor, MI 48104-2298
Telephone: 734-764-2416
FAX: 734-763-0369
E-mail: melabelium@umich.edu
Web: www.lsa.umich.edu/eli/
Tests: 950, 973, 974, 1464, 1610, 1611, 1612, 1613

Enhanced Performance Systems, Inc.
1010 University Avenue, Suite 265
San Diego, CA 92103
Telephone: 619-497-0156
FAX: 619-497-0820
E-mail: sagal@enhanced-performance.com
Web: www.enhanced-performance.com
Tests: 225

Robert H. Ennis, Ph.D.
3904 Trentwood Place
Sarasota, FL 34243
Telephone: 941-358-0906
E-mail: rhennis@uiuc.edu
Web: faculty.ed.uiuc.edu/rhennis
Tests: 955

Enrichment Press
5441 SW Macadam Avenue, #206
Portland, OR 97239
Telephone: 503-222-4046
FAX: 503-222-9989
Tests: 1974, 2734

Enterprise Management Ltd.
4531 Roanoak Way
Palm Harbor, FL 34685
Telephone: 727-934-9810
E-mail: mlippitt@enterprisemgt.com
Web: www.enterprisemgt.com
Tests: 1417

ERISys
Box 1635
Pawtucket, RI 02862
Tests: 2017

Exceptional Education
P.O. Box 15308
Seattle, WA 98155
Telephone: 206-262-9538
FAX: 206-262-9538
Tests: 2022, 2722

Sheila M. Eyberg, Ph.D.
Department of Clinical & Health Psychology
Box 100165
University of Florida
Gainesville, FL 32610
E-mail: seyberg@phhp.ufl.edu
Web: www.pcit.org
Tests: 866, 2647

Faculty of Education
Memorial University of Newfoundland
St. John's, Newfoundland A1B 3X8
Canada
Tests: 2633

Dr. Charles G. Fast, Publisher
15265 Whimsy Trail
Novinger, MO 63559-3013
Tests: 1009

Grace Fivars
Psychometric Techniques Associates
5701 Centre Avenue, #511
Pittsburgh, PA 15206-3707
Tests: 551, 2526

Foreworks
Box 33493
Portland, OR 97292
Telephone: 503-653-2614
E-mail: eric@foreworks.com
Web: www.foreworks.com
Tests: 2382, 2579

Myles I. Friedman
College of Education
University of South Carolina
Columbia, SC 29208
Tests: 1993

Functional Resources
3905 Huntington Drive
Amarillo, TX 79019-4047
Telephone: 806-353-1114
FAX: 806-353-1114
E-mail: webmaster@winfssi.com
Web: www.winfssi.com
Tests: 1057

G. Neil
720 International Parkway
P.O. Box 450939
Sunrise, FL 33345-0939
Telephone: 800-999-9111
FAX: 954-846-0777
E-mail: hrassessments@gneil.com
Web: www.gneil.com
Tests: 170, 536, 2213, 2310

Gallaudet University Press
800 Florida Avenue, NE
Washington, DC 20002-3695
Telephone: 800-621-2736
FAX: 800-621-8476
Web: gupress.gallaudet.edu
Tests: 2737

GB Software LLC
4607 Perham Road
Corona del Mar, CA 92625
Tests: 2074

Ruth M. Geiman, Ph.D.
8184 Crete Ln.
Blacklick, OH 43004
Telephone: 937-901-1809
E-mail: rgeiman@wideopenwest.com
Tests: 1068

General Educational Development Testing Service of
the American Council on Education
One Dupont Circle, NW, Suite 250
Washington, DC 20036-1163
Telephone: 202-939-9490
E-mail: GED@ACE.NCHE.EDU
Web: WWW.GEDTEST.ORG
Tests: 2639

Gerontology Center
College of Health and Human Development
The Pennsylvania State University
135 E. Nittung Ave., Suite 405
State College, PA 16801
Telephone: 814-865-1710
FAX: 814-863-9423
E-mail: GERO@psu.edu
Web: geron.psu.edu
Tests: 1591

The Gesell Institute
310 Prospect Street, 2nd Floor
New Haven, CT 06511
Telephone: 203-777-3481
FAX: 203-776-5001
E-mail: gesell.inst@att.net
Web: www.gesellinstitute.org
Tests: 1070, 1071

GIA Publications, Inc.
7404 South Mason Avenue
Chicago, IL 60638
Telephone: 708-496-3800
FAX: 708-496-3828
E-mail: custserv@giamusic.com
Web: www.giamusic.com
Tests: 97, 147, 1149, 1252, 1260, 1293, 1707, 2024

Lucia A. Gilbert
Office of the Executive Vice President & Provost
Main 201 (G1000)
University of Texas at Austin
Austin, TX 78712
Telephone: 512-232-3310
FAX: 512-471-0577
E-mail: lucia@mail.utexas.edu
Web: www.utexas.edu/student/connexus/lucia/
    instruments.html
Tests: 1882

Golden Educational Center
857 Lake Blvd.
Redding, CA 96003
Telephone: 800-800-1791
FAX: 530-244-5939
E-mail: info@goldened.com
Web: www.goldened.com
Tests: 1256

Gordian Group
P.O. Box 1587
Hartsville, SC 29550
Tests: 860

Gordon Systems, Inc.
P.O. Box 746
DeWitt, NY 13214
Telephone: 315-446-4849 (#2) or 1-800-550-2343
FAX: 315-446-2012
E-mail: info@gsi-add.com
Tests: 105

Robert S. Goyer
Department of Communication
Arizona State University
Tempe, AZ 85287
Tests: 1088

Graham-Field Health Products, Inc.
2935 Northeast Parkway
Atlanta, GA 30360
Telephone: 800-347-5678
FAX: 800-726-0601
E-mail: cs@grahamfield.com
Web: www.grahamfield.com
Tests: 2567

Green's Publishing
201, 17107-107 Ave.
Edmonton, Alberta T5S 1G3
Canada
Telephone: 780-484-5550
FAX: 780-484-5631
E-mail: paulgreen@shaw.ca
Web: www.wordmemorytest.com
Tests: 2802

Gregorc Associates, Inc.
15 Doubleday Road
P.O. Box 351
Columbia, CT 06237
Telephone: 860-228-0093
FAX: 860-228-0093
Web: www.gregorc.com
Tests: 1111

GRM Educational Consultancy
P.O. Box 154
Beecroft, New South Wales 2119
Australia
Tests: 2267

Guglielmino & Associates
7339 Reserve Creek Drive
Port St. Lucie, FL 34986
Telephone: 772-429-2425
FAX: 772-429-2423
E-mail: guglielmino@rocketmail.com
Web: www.guglielmino734.com
Tests: 2288

Guilford Publications, Inc.
72 Spring Street
New York, NY 10012
Telephone: 212-431-9800
FAX: 212-966-6708
Web: www.guilford.com
Tests: 68

H&H Publishing Company, Inc.
1231 Kapp Drive
Clearwater, FL 33765-2116
Tests: 1423, 1424, 1873, 2424, 2552, 2828

Harcourt Assessment Australia and New Zealand
30–52 Smidmore Street
Marrickville, New South Wales 2204
Australia
Telephone: 61 2 9517 8958
FAX: 61 2 9517 8981
E-mail: customerservice@harcourt-au.com
Web: www.harcourt-au.com
Tests: 231, 232, 834, 2726

Harcourt Assessment [England]
Procter House
1 Procter Street
London WC1V 6EU
United Kingdom
Telephone: +44 (0)20 7911 1960
FAX: +44 (0)20 7911 1961
E-mail: info@harcourt-uk.com
Web: www.harcourt-uk.com
Tests: 236, 238, 242, 302, 303, 304, 391, 481, 646, 720,
851, 863, 871, 873, 875, 994, 1041, 1079, 1090,
1154, 1466, 1470, 1617, 1680, 1722, 1946, 2005,
2018, 2095, 2097, 2179, 2180, 2181, 2199, 2200,
2294, 2315, 2323, 2399, 2432, 2568, 2590, 2591,
2612, 2697, 2716, 2717, 2753, 2754, 2755, 2765,
2829

Harcourt Assessment, Inc.
19500 Bulverde Road
San Antonio, TX 78259-3701
Telephone: 800-211-8378
FAX: 877-576-1816
Tests: 162, 173, 312, 532, 679, 694, 86, 876, 1065,
1078, 1081, 1087, 1142, 1200, 1233, 1235, 1250,
1324, 1327, 1604, 1605, 1649, 1650, 1679, 1712,
1740, 1741, 1805, 1817, 1819, 1859, 1939, 1983,
2013, 2160, 2256, 2332, 2410, 2413, 2414, 2416,
2417, 2444, 2569, 2658, 2673, 2702, 2742, 2743,
2764, 2779

Susan Harter, Ph.D.
University of Denver
Department of Psychology
2155 South Race Street
Denver, CO 80208-0204
Tests: 1954, 2297

Joseph Hartman, Ph.D.
P.O. Box 37485
Raleigh, NC 27627-7485
Telephone: 919-851-9825
E-mail: jhartman611@nc.rr.com
Tests: 2090

Harvard University Press
79 Garden Street
Cambridge, MA 02138
Tests: 2645

Dr. Robert J. Harvey
1030 S. Jefferson Forest Lane
Blacksburg, VA 24060-8984
Tests: 634

Hawthorne Educational Services, Inc.
ATTN: Adina Laird, Dir. of External Relations
800 Gray Oak Drive
Columbia, MO 65201
Telephone: 800-542-1673
FAX: 800-442-9509
E-mail: adina_laird@hes-inc.com
Web: www.hes-inc.com
Tests: 60, 88, 221, 222, 285, 286, 287, 878, 879, 926,
930, 1074, 1427, 2002, 2011, 2395, 2669

Hay Group
Hay Resources Direct
116 Huntington Avenue
Boston, MA 02116-5712
Telephone: 800-729-8074
FAX: 617-927-5008
E-mail: Haytrg@haygroup.com
Web: www.hayresourcesdirect.haygroup.com
Tests: 65, 561, 928, 1241, 1407, 1431, 1434, 1509,
1521, 1524, 1813, 1920, 2206

Health and Disability Research Institute
Boston University
53 Bay State Road
Boston, MA 02215
Telephone: 617-353-1295
FAX: 612-358-1355
E-mail: smhaley@bu.edu
Web: www.bu.edu/hdr/
Tests: 1869

Health Prisms, Inc.
Address Unknown
Tests: 705

Mary J. Heppner, Ph.D.
Career Center
305 Noyes Hall
University of Missouri
Columbia, MO 65211
Tests: 427

Herrmann International
794 Buffalo Creek Road
Lake Lure, NC 28746
Telephone: 828-625-9153
FAX: 828-625-1402
E-mail: dorothy@hbdi.com
Web: www.hbdi.com
Tests: 1170

Hester Evaluation Systems, Inc.
2410 SW Granthurst Avenue
Topeka, KS 66611-1274
Telephone: 800-832-3825
FAX: 785-357-4041
E-mail: hester@inlandnet.net
Web: www.hestertesting.com
Tests: 1665

Hewitt Homeschooling Resources
P.O. Box 9
2103 B Street
Washougal, WA 98684
Telephone: 800-890-4097
FAX: 360-835-8697
E-mail: info@hewitthomeschooling.com
Web: www.hewitthomeschooling.com
Tests: 1930

High/Scope Educational Research Foundation
600 North River Street
Ypsilanti, MI 48198-2898
Telephone: 734-485-2000
FAX: 734-485-0704
E-mail: info@highscope.org
Web: www.highscope.org
Tests: 887, 922, 2008, 2015, 2844

Higher Education Research Institute
UCLA Graduate School of Education
405 Hilgard Avenue
3005 Moore Hall
Los Angeles, CA 90024-1521
Tests: 700

Hilson Research, Inc.
P.O. Box 150239
82-28 Abingdon Road
Kew Gardens, NY 11415-0239
Tests: 1179, 1180, 1181, 1182, 1286, 1287

Hodder & Stoughton Educational
Hodder Headline PLC
338 Euston Road
London NW1 3BH
England
Telephone: 0207 873 6000
FAX: 0207 873 6299
E-mail: chas.knight@hodder.co.uk
Web: www.hoddertests.co.uk
Tests: 257, 258, 539, 558, 886, 902, 903, 990, 991,
    1072, 1089, 1091, 1123, 1125, 1128, 1546, 1750,
    1833, 1858, 19600, 2129, 2222, 2278, 2334, 2391,
    2527, 2803

Hogan Assessment Systems, Inc.
2622 East 21st Street
Tulsa, OK 74144
Tests: 1185,1186, 1676

Hogrefe & Huber Publishers
875 Massachusetts Avenue
7th Floor
Cambridge, MA 02139
Telephone: 800-228-3749
FAX: 425-823-8324
E-mail: HH@HHPUB.COM
Web: WWW.HHPUB.COM
Tests: 36, 754, 760, 1006, 1296, 1830, 2187, 2243,
    2364

Home Inventory LLC
c/o Lorraine Coulson
2627 Winsor Drive
Eau Claire, WI 54703-1778
Telephone: 715-835-4393
Tests: 1191

Houghton Mifflin Company
College Division, Education
222 Berkeley Street
Boston, MA 02116-3764
Telephone: 617-351-5000
FAX: 617-351-1134
E-mail: college_educ@hmco.com
Web: education.college.hmco.com
Tests: 369

Howdah Press
c/o Priscilla S. Hill, Ph.D.
3530 Damien #117
LaVerne, CA 91750
Tests: 1178

HRD Press, Inc.
22 Amherst Road
Amherst, MA 01002–9709
Telephone: 800-822-2801
FAX: 413-253-3490
E-mail: info@hrdpress.com
Web: www.hrdpress.com
Tests: 442, 644, 685, 793, 1036, 1242, 1336, 1404,
1436, 1494, 1497, 1553, 1586, 1811, 1812, 1887,
1892, 1922, 1965, 2026, 2539, 2620

Edwina E. Hubert, Ph.D.
313 Wellesley Dr., SE
Albuquerque, NM 87106-1421
Tests: 1445

Nancy Hughes, Ph.D.
University of Kansas
Psychological Clinic
315 Fraser Hall
Lawrence, KS 66045
Tests: 1203

Human Sciences Research Council [South Africa]
Distributed by Mindmuzik Media
P O Box 2904 Brooklyn Square
Pretoria, Gauteng 0075
South Africa
Telephone: +27 (0)12-346-6008
FAX: +27 90) 346 4773
E-mail: frikkie@mindmuzik.com
Tests: 177, 328, 1020, 1171, 1172, 1234, 1267, 1330,
1335, 1718, 1746, 1831, 1951, 2048, 2191, 2259,
2301, 2302, 2319, 2664

Human Services Resource Group
College of Business Administration
University of Nebraska—Omaha
Omaha, NE 68182-0048
Tests: 2506

Human Synergistics International
39819 Plymouth Road, C-8020
Plymouth, MI 48170-8020
Telephone: 800-622-7584
FAX: 734-459-5557
E-mail: info@humansynergistics.com
Web: www.humansynergistics.com
Tests: 148, 1131, 1410, 1458, 1478, 1498, 1814, 1816,
1895, 2441, 2493

Humanics Learning
12 S. Dixie Hwy, Ste. 2000
Lake Worth, FL 33460-3737
Telephone: 404-874-2176
FAX: 404-874-1976
E-mail: humanics@mindspring.com
Web: www.humanicslearning.com
Tests: 453, 464, 1207, 1474

I-MED Instructional Materials & Equipment Distributors
1520 Cotner Avenue
Los Angeles, CA 90025
Tests: 872

The IDEA Center
211 South Seth Child Road
Manhattan, KS 66502-3089
Telephone: 800-255-2757
FAX: 785-532-5725
E-mail: IDEA@KSU.EDU
Web: WWW.IDEA.KSU.EDU
Tests: 1212, 1213, 1214, 1217

IDS Publishing Corporation
P.O. Box 389
Worthington, OH 43085
Telephone: 614-885-2323
FAX: 614-885-2323
Web: www.idspublishing.com
Tests: 2146

Illinois Critical Thinking Project; Department of Educational Policy Studies
University of Illinois at Urbana-Champaign
360 Education Bldg.
1310 South Sixth Street
Champaign, IL 61820
Tests: 711, 712

Indiana Resource Center for Autism
Indiana Institute on Disability and Community
2853 East Tenth Street
Bloomington, IN 47408-2696
Tests: 2768

Indiana University Center for Postsecondary Research
1900 East Tenth Street
Eigenmann Hall, Suite 419
Bloomington, IN 47406-7512
Telephone: 812-856-5824
FAX: 812-856-5150
E-mail: nsse@indiana.edu
Web: www.iub.edu/~cseq or www.iub.edu/~nsse
Tests: 623, 624, 1721

Industrial Psychology International, Ltd.
4106 Fieldstone Road
P.O. Box 6479
Champaign, IL 61826-6479
Telephone: 800-747-1119
FAX: 217-398-5798
E-mail: iPI@METRITECH.COM
Web: WWW.METRITECH.COM
Tests: 723, 1294, 1757, 2830, 2831

Innodyne, Inc.
734 Orchard Hill Drive
Pittsburgh, PA 15238
Telephone: 412-963-6701
FAX: 412-963-6751
Web: www.innodyneinc.com
Tests: 2057

INQ Educational Materials, Inc.
640 Davis Street, No. 28
San Francisco, CA 94111
Tests: 1246

Inscape Publishing
6465 Wayzata Blvd., Suite 800
Minneapolis, MN 55426
Tests: 842, 843, 1908

Insight Assessment—The California Academic Press
   LLC
217 La Cruz Avenue
Millbrae, CA 94030
Telephone: 650-697-5628
FAX: 650-692-0141
E-mail: info@insightassessment.com
Web: www.insightassessment.com
Tests: 381, 382

Institute for Behavioral Research in Creativity
4455 South 700 East, Suite 305
Salt Lake City, UT 84107
Telephone: 801-487-3209
FAX: 801-262-1739
Web: www.ibric.net
Tests: 323, 906, 2467

The Institute for Matching Person & Technology, Inc.
486 Lake Road
Webster, NY 14580
Telephone: 585-671-3461
FAX: 585-671-3461
E-mail: impt97@aol.com
Web: members.aol.com/IMPT97/MPT.html
Tests: 1539, 1541, 2311

Institute for Personality and Ability Testing, Inc. (IPAT)
P.O. Box 1188
Champaign, IL 61824-1188
Telephone: 217-352-4739
FAX: 217-352-9674
E-mail: custserv@ipat.com
Web: www.ipat.com
Tests: 477, 540, 647, 742, 893, 929, 978, 1158, 1174,
   1397, 1934, 2073, 2295, 2346, 2347, 2348, 2349

Institute for Psycho-Imagination Therapy
c/o Dr. Joseph E. Shorr
179 South Barrington Place
Los Angeles, CA 90049
Telephone: 310-472-3061
E-mail: info@psychoimagination.org
Web: www.psychoimagination.org
Tests: 1130, 2330

Institute for Somat Awareness
Michael Bernet, Ph.D.
1270 North Avenue, Suite 1-P
New Rochelle, NY 10804
Telephone: 914-633-1789
FAX: 914-633-3152
E-mail: mBernet@aol.com
Web: www.somats.com
Tests: 2340

Institute for the Advancement of Philosophy for Children
Montclair State University
Upper Montclair, NJ 07043
Telephone: 973-655-4277
FAX: 973-655-7834
E-mail: MATKOWSKI@SATURN.MONTCLAIR.
   EDU
Tests: 1739

The Institute of Conflict Analysis
Wilburton Inn
P.O. Box 468
257 Wilburton Drive
Manchester Village, VT 05254
Telephone: 802 362 3568
FAX: 802 362 1107
E-mail: moralscience@hotmail.com
Web: www.ArtToScience.org
Tests: 682

Institute of General Semantics
2260 College Avenue
Fort Worth, TX 76110
Telephone: 817-922-9950
FAX: 871-922-9903
E-mail: igs@time-binding.org
Web: www.time-binding.org
Tests: 2684

Institute of Psychological Research, Inc.
34 Fleury Street West
Montreal, Quebec H3L 1S9
Canada
Telephone: 514-382-3000
FAX: 514-382-3007
E-mail: info@i-r-p.ca
Tests: 403, 2098, 2201, 2577

Institute of Rehabilitation Medicine
New York University Medical Center
400 East 34th Street
New York, NY 10016
Tests: 1053

Interim Publishers
3900 Scobie Road
Peninsula, OH 44264
Tests: 2430

International Assessment Network
7400 Metro Blvd. Suite #350
Edina, MN 55439
Tests: 1529

International Public Management Association for Human Resources (IPMA-HR)
1617 Duke Street
Alexandria, VA 22314
Telephone: 800-381-8378
FAX: 703-684-0948
E-mail: assessment@ipma-hr.org
Web: testing.ipma-hr.org
Tests: 1, 73, 239, 376, 377, 753, 912, 1745, 1823, 1824, 1825, 1961, 2063, 2071, 2072, 2150, 2313

International Training Consultants, Inc.
1838 Park Oaks Street
Kemah, TX 77565-8135
Telephone: 281-557-9372
FAX: 281-557-9223
E-mail: itc@trainingitc.com
Web: www.trainingitc.com
Tests: 1443

Iowa State University Research Foundation, Inc.
Child Development Department
101 Child Development Building
Research Laboratories
Ames, IA 50011
Tests: 1289, 1290, 2403

Irvington Publishers, Inc.
R. R. 1, Box 85-1
Lower Mill Road
North Stratford, NH 03590
Tests: 2042

Israel Science Teaching Center
Hebrew University
Jerusalem 91904
Israel
Tests: 633

James Stanfield Co., Inc.
P.O. Box 41058
Santa Barbara, CA 93140
Telephone: 800-421-6534
FAX: 805-897-1187
E-mail: orderdesk@stanfield.com
Web: www.stanfield.com
Tests: 639, 2232, 2594, 2670

Janelle Publications, Inc.
P.O. Box 811
1189 Twombley Road
DeKalb, IL 60115
Tests: 2390, 2456, 2457

JIST Publishing, Inc.
8902 Otis Avenue
Indianapolis, IN 46216-1033
Telephone: 800-648-5478
FAX: 800-547-8329
E-mail: info@jist.com
Web: www.jist.com
Tests: 247, 406, 425, 626, 849, 1134, 1230, 1317, 1318, 1322, 1446, 1762, 1763, 2672, 2723, 2815, 2820, 2845

Jossey-Bass, A Wiley Company
989 Market Street
San Francisco, CA 94103
Tests: 196, 305, 405, 562, 638, 762, 815, 848, 939, 954, 966, 1270, 1311, 1326, 1368, 1412, 1413, 1420, 1429, 1441, 1463, 1467, 1674, 1810, 1877, 1878, 1879, 2031, 2377, 2540, 2542, 2685, 2740

C. G. Jung Institute of San Francisco
2040 Gough Street
San Francisco, CA 94109
Telephone: 415-771-8055 x 206
E-mail: jungmail@sfjung.org
Tests: 1331

Jerome Kagan
Harvard University
33 Kirkland Street
1510 William James Hall
Cambridge, MA 02138
Tests: 1540

Kaplan Early Learning Company
1310 Lewisville-Clemmons Road
Lewisville, NC 27023-0609
Tests: 434, 811, 812, 1421

Karl Albrecht International
3120 Old Bridgeport Way, #100
San Diego, CA 92111
Test: 1418, 1643

KBA, LLC
P.O. Box 3673
Carbondale, IL 62902
Tests: 314

Warren Keegan Associates Press
350 Theodore Fremd
Rye, NY 10580
Telephone: 914-967-9421
FAX: 914-967-8179
E-mail: wkeegan@keeganandco.com
Web: www.keeganandco.com
Tests: 1350

Keeler Instruments Inc.
456 Parkway
Broomall, PA 19008
Telephone: 610-353-4350
FAX: 610-353-7814
Web: www.keelerusa.com
Tests: 490, 2164

The Ken Blanchard Companies
125 State Place
Escondido, CA 92029
Tests: 1403

Kendall/Hunt Publishing Company
4050 Westmark Drive
P.O. Box 1840
Dubuque, IA 52004-1840
Telephone: 800-228-0810
FAX: 800-772-9165
E-mail: orders@kendallhunt.com
Web: WWW.KENDALLHUNT.COM
Tests: 260, 2389

KIDS, Inc.
1156 Point Vista Road
Corinth, TX 76210
Tests: 1363, 1364

Dr. Donald L. Kirkpatrick
842 Kirkland Court
Pewaukee, WI 53072
Telephone: 262-695-5851
E-mail: dleekirk1@aol.com
Tests: 1369, 1500, 1501, 1502, 1503, 1504, 2489, 2490

Marjorie H. Klein, Ph.D.
Department of Psychiatry
6001 Research Park Blvd.
Madison, WI 53717
Telephone: 608-263-6066
FAX: 608-265-4008
E-mail: mhklein@falstaff.wisc.edu
Tests: 982

Kolbe Corp
3421 N. 44th Street
Phoenix, AZ 85018
Telephone: 602-840-9770
FAX: 602-952-2706
E-mail: info@kolbe.com
Web: www.kolbe.com
Tests: 1376

David S. Krantz
Department of Medical and Clinical Psychology
University of the Health Sciences
4301 Jones Bridge Road
Bethesda, MD 20814-4799
E-mail: krantz@bob.usuhs.mil
Tests: 1377

Krieger Publishing Company
P.O. Box 9542
Melbourne, FL 32902-9542
Tests: 86

Ramanath Kundu
Department of Psychology
University of Calcutta
92, Acharya Prafulla Chandra Road
Calcutta 700009
India
Tests: 1384, 1385

Lafayette Instrument
P.O. Box 5729
3700 Sagamore Parkway North
Lafayette, IN 47904-5729
Telephone: 765-423-1505
FAX: 765-423-4111
E-mail: info@lafayetteinstrument.com
Web: www.lafayetteinstrument.com
Tests: 1114, 1653, 2184

Laurent Clerc National Deaf Education Center
KDES PAS-6
Gallaudet University
800 Florida Avenue, NE
Washington, DC 20002
Telephone: 202-651-5340
FAX: 202-651-5708
Web: clerccenter.gallaudet.edu
Tests: 1562

Law School Admission Council, Inc.
Box 40
Newtown, PA 18940-0040
Tests: 1401

Leadership Studies, Inc.
230 West Third Avenue
Escondido, CA 92025
Tests: 2343

Hal Leonard Publishing Corporation
7777 West Bluemound Road
P.O. Box 13819
Milwaukee, WI 53213
Tests: 1008, 2739

Lienhard School of Nursing
Pace University
Pleasantville/Briarcliff Campus
Bedford Road
Pleasantville, NY 10570
Tests: 2434

Life Advance, Inc.
81 Front Street
Nyack, NY 10960
Telephone: 845-358-2539
E-mail: craig.ellison@nyack.edu
Tests: 2401

Life Innovations, Inc.
P.O. Box 190
Minneapolis, MN 55440-0190
Telephone: 651-635-0511
FAX: 651-636-1668
E-mail: dolson@prepare-enrich.com
Tests: 552, 992, 1005, 1835, 1889, 2000

Life Science Associates
One Fenimore Road
Bayport, NY 11705-2115
Telephone: 631-472-2111
FAX: 631-472-8146
E-mail: lifesciassoc@pipeline.com
Web: lifesciassoc.home.pipeline.com
Tests: 2120

LIMRA International
P.O. Box 208
Hartford, CT 06141-0208
Tests: 198, 425

LinguiSystems, Inc.
3100 4th Avenue
East Moline, IL 61244-9700
Telephone: 800-776-4332
E-mail: testing@linguisystems.com
Tests: 1392, 2613, 2804

Lore International Institute
P.O. Box 1287
1130 Main Avenue
Durango, CO 81301
Telephone: 970-385-4955
FAX: 970-385-7804
E-mail: assessmentcenter@lorenet.com
Web: www.lorenet.com
Tests: 560, 1476, 1771, 2208, 2501

Pamela S. Ludolph, Ph.D.
311 Awixa Road
Ann Arbor, MI 48104-1811
Tests: 822

James B. Maas
The Center for Improvement of Undergraduate Education
115 Rand Hall
Cornell University
Ithaca, NY 14850
Tests: 715

Charlotte Mackley
948 South 2350 E
Springville, UT 84663
Tests: 144, 692, 1473, 2327

Jean D'Arcy Maculaitis, Ph.D.
P.O. Box 3056
Sea Bright, NJ 07760
Tests: 1481

Maddak Inc.
6 Industrial Road
Pequannock, NJ 07440-1993
Tests: 169, 1472, 2303, 2659

Madison Geriatric Research, Education, and Clinical
    Center
VA Medical Center
2500 Overlook Terrace
Madison, WI 53705
Tests: 209

Management & Personnel Systems, Inc.
2717 North Main Street, #2
Walnut Creek, CA 94597
Telephone: 800-576-7455
FAX: 925-977-8200
E-mail: mpscorp@value.net
Web: www.mps-corp.com
Tests: 750, 1066, 2492, 2826

Management Research Group
14 York Street, #301
Portland, ME 04101-4556
Telephone: 207-775-2173
FAX: 207-775-6796
E-mail: info@mrg.com
Web: www.mrg.com
Tests: 171, 1229, 1409, 1893, 2211

Management Research Institute, Inc.
11304 Spur Wheel Lane
Potomac, MD 20854
Tests: 1035

Ronald L. Mann, Ph.D.
17219 Palisades Circle
Pacific Palisades, CA 90272
Telephone: 310-454-3463
E-mail: mannr@ronmann.com
Web: www.ronmann.com
Tests: 1910

Massachusetts School of Professional Psychology
T.E.D. Test
221 Rivermoor Street
Boston, MA 02132
Telephone: 617-327-6777
FAX: 617-327-4447
E-mail: ce@mspp.edu
Tests: 2528

Master Publishing, Inc.
6125 West Howard Street
Niles, IL 60714-3401
Telephone: 847-763-0916
FAX: 847-763-0918
E-mail: TROTTER@FIRSTPOINTKIDS.COM
Web: www.firstpointkids.com
Tests: 1852

MAT
Boston University
School of Music
855 Commonwealth Avenue
Boston, MA 02215
Tests: 1706

Mathematical Association of America, American Math-
    ematics Competitions
Steven R. Dunbar, Director
University of Nebraska—Lincoln
1740 Vine Street
Lincoln, NE 68588-0658
Telephone: 800-527-3690; 402-472-2257
FAX: 402-472-6087
E-mail: amcinfo@unl.edu
Web: www.unl.edu/amc
Tests: 151, 153, 154, 1544

McCarron-Dial Systems, Inc.
P.O. Box 45628
Dallas, TX 75245
Telephone: 214-634-2863
FAX: 214-634-9970
E-mail: mds@mccarrondial.com
Web: mccarrondial.com
Tests: 39, 63, 206, 927, 1555, 1561, 1773, 1883, 2499

McClain
10 Blue Grouse Ridge Road
Littleton, CO 80127-5704
Tests: 1836

Measurement for Human Resources
83 Rouge Au Avenue
Winnipeg, Manitoba R2C 3X5
Tests: 1777

Medical Outcomes Trust
235 Wyman Street, Suite 130
Waltham, MA 02451
Telephone: 781-890-4884
FAX: 781-890-0922
E-mail: info@outcomes-trust.org
Web: www.outcomes-trust.org
Tests: 2324

Albert Mehrabian, Ph.D.
1130 Alta Mesa Road
Monterey, CA 93940
Telephone: 831-649-5710
FAX: 831-372-6829
E-mail: am@kaaj.com
Web: www.kaaj.com/psych/scales
Tests: 188, 241, 456, 1563, 1564, 1566, 1573, 1574, 1575, 2105, 2667

Mental Health, Law, and Policy Institute
Simon Fraser University
8888 University Drive
Burnaby, British Columbia V5A 1S6
Canada
Telephone: 604-291-4554
FAX: 604-268-6695
E-mail: roesch@sfu.ca
Web: www.sfu.ca/~mhlpi/
Tests: 1155

Meta Development LLC
4313 Garnet Street
Regina, Saskatchewan S4S 6J8
Canada
Tests: 1624, 1625, 1626, 1628, 1629, 1630, 1631, 1632, 1633, 1634, 1635

Meta-Visions
5076 Queen Victoria Lane
Kalamazoo, MI 49009-7799
Telephone: 616-353-7111
FAX: 616-353-9577
E-mail: JWalkerMI@aol.com
Tests: 1602

MetriTech, Inc.
4106 Fieldstone Road
Champaign, IL 61822
Telephone: 800-747-4868
FAX: 217-398-5798
E-mail: mtinfo@metritech.com
Web: www.metritech.com
Tests: 67, 93, 1249, 1993, 1809, 2459, 2814

The Mews Press
Box 2052
Amagansett, NY 11930
FAX: 212-475-2428
Tests: 2151, 2512, 2548

Norman Milchus
468 Essex Drive
Rochester Hills, MI 48307-3504
Tests: 968, 2106, 2286

MILCOM Systems
A Division of Hollister, Inc.
2000 Hollister Drive
Libertyville, IL 60048
Tests: 1619

Miller & Tyler Limited
Psychological Assessment and Counselling
96 Greenway
London N20 8EJ
England
Telephone: 44-020-8445-7463
FAX: 44-020-8445-0143
Tests: 2192, 2193

Mind Garden, Inc.
855 Oak Grove Ave., Suite 215
Menlo Park, CA 94025
Telephone: 650-322-6300
FAX: 650-322-6398
E-mail: info@mindgarden.com
Web: www.mindgarden.com
Tests: 8, 205, 211, 265, 307, 379, 386, 444, 496, 554, 643, 701, 704, 717, 718, 794, 868, 956, 1001, 1031, 1046, 1119, 1120, 1152, 1156, 1222, 1542, 1547, 1599, 1620, 1693, 1694, 1695, 1738, 1792, 1815, 2089, 2144, 2261, 2373, 2374, 2426, 2427, 2565, 2689, 2736, 2744, 2761, 2762

Ministry Inventories
ATTN: Richard A. Hunt, Ph.D.
Fuller Graduate School of Psychology
180 N. Oakland Avenue
Pasadena, CA 91101
Tests: 1281, 1658, 2646

MKM
401 3rd Street, Suite 1
Rapid City, SD 57701
Tests: 1662, 1663, 1664

Monaco & Associates Incorporated
4125 Gage Center Drive, Suite 204
Topeka, KS 66604
Telephone: 785-272-5501
FAX: 785-272-5152
E-mail: greg@monacoassociates.com
Web: www.monacoassociates.com
Tests: 1673

Moreno Educational Co.
P.O. Box 19329
San Diego, CA 91259-0329
Tests: 1804, 2109, 2388

The Morrisby Organisation
Focus 31 North
Cleveland Road
Hemel Hempstead,
Hertfordshire HP2 7EY
England
Telephone: 01442 215521
FAX: 01442 240531
E-mail: info@morrisby.com
Web: www.morrisby.com
Tests: 722, 1670

Moving Boundaries, Inc.
1375 SW Blaine Court
Gresham, OR 97080
Tests: 2339

Multi-Health Systems, Inc.
P.O. Box 950
North Tonawanda, NY 14120-0950
Telephone: 800-456-3003
FAX: 888-540-4484
E-mail: CUSTOMERSERVICE@MHS.COM
Web: www.mhs.com
Tests: 163, 166, 246, 309, 436, 471, 493, 553, 563,
  675, 686, 687, 688, 689, 690, 691, 703, 708, 750,
  823, 865, 932, 933, 034, 999, 1018, 1145, 1146,
  1147, 1148, 1159, 1187, 1221, 1261, 1306, 1307,
  1422, 1448, 1449, 1450, 1454, 1552, 1593, 1687,
  16900, 1744, 1860, 1929, 1979, 2040, 2041, 2082,
  2102, 2143, 2145, 2265, 2283, 2365, 2369, 2370,
  2371, 2403, 2517, 2532, 2603, 2663, 2715, 2842

Multiple Intelligences Research and Consulting, Inc.
1316 South Lincoln Street
Kent, OH 44240
Telephone: 330-677-8534
E-mail: sbranton@kent.edu
Web: WWW.miresearch.org
Tests: 1615

Munroe-Meyer Institute for Genetics & Rehabilitation
University of Nebraska Medical Center
985450 Nebraska Medical Center
Omaha, NE 68198-5450
Telephone: 402-559-7467
FAX: 402-559-5737
Web: www.unmc.edu/mmi
Tests: 1618

National Association of Secondary School Principals
1904 Association Drive
Reston, VA 20191-1537
Telephone: 703-860-0200
Tests: 654, 655, 1435, 2277

National Career Assessment Services, Inc.
601 Visions Parkway
P.O. Box 277
Adel, IA 50003
Telephone: 800-314-8972
FAX: 515-993-5422
E-mail: ncasi@ncasi.com
Web: www.ncasi.com or www.kuder.com
Tests: 1379, 1380, 1381, 1382, 2486

The National Center on Employment & Disability
P.O. Box 1358
Hot Springs, AR 71902
Tests: 936, 1319, 2810, 2816, 2818, 2827

National Clearinghouse for Rehabilitation Training
  Materials
6524 Old Main Hill
Utah State University
Logan, UT 84322-6524
Tests: 1796

National Communication Association
1765 N Street, NW
Washington, DC 20036
Tests: 195, 645, 698

National Council on Crime and Delinquency
NCCD Headquarters
1970 Broadway, Suite 500
Oakland, CA 94612
Telephone: 510-208-0500
FAX: 510-208-0511
Web: nccd-crc.org
Tests: 719, 1338

National Council on Economic Education
1140 Avenue of the Americas
New York, NY 10036
Telephone: 212-730-7007
FAX: 212-730-1793
E-mail: econed@ncee.net
Web: www.ncee.net
Tests: 254, 2587, 2588, 2621

National Occupational Competency Testing Institute/
  The Whitener Group
500 N. Bronson Avenue
Big Rapids, MI 49307-2737
Telephone: 800-334-6283
FAX: 231-796-4699
E-mail: nocti@nocti.org
Web: www.nocti.org
Tests: 1747, 1748, 2771

National Psychological Corporation
4/230, Kacheri Ghat
AGRA-4
India
Tests: 2537

National Reading Styles Institute, Inc.
P.O. Box 737
Syosset, NY 11791-0737
E-mail: nick@nrsi.com
Tests: 630, 1989, 2131

National Spanish Exam
2051 Mt. Zion Drive
Golden, CO 80401-1737
Telephone: 303-278-1021
FAX: 303-278-6400
E-mail: martha.quiat@mho.net
Web: viking.valpo.k12.in.us/~cessna/nse/index.htm
Tests: 1720

National Study of School Evaluation
1699 E. Woodfield Road, #406
Schaumburg, IL 60173-4958
Tests: 642, 923, 1282, 1842, 2463, 2494, 2500, 2502, 2535

National Wellness Institute, Inc.
1300 College Court
P.O. Box 827
Stevens Point, WI 54481-2962
Tests: 1459, 2641, 2642, 2643

Robert A. Neimeyer, Ph.D.
Department of Psychology
Memphis State University
Memphis, TN 38152
Telephone: 901-678-4680
FAX: 901-678-2579
E-mail: neimeyer@memphis.edu
Tests: 2484

Nelson, A Thomson Company
1120 Birchmount Road
Toronto, Ontario M1K 5G4
Canada
Telephone: 416-752-9448
FAX: 416-752-9646
E-mail: inquire@nelson.com
Web: www.nelson.com
Tests: 399, 402, 1059, 1818, 2202, 2724

C. H. Nevins Printing Co.
311 Bryn Mawr Island
Bayshore Gardens
Bradenton, FL 34207
Tests: 1117, 1118

New Zealand Council for Educational Research
Education House West
178-182 Willis Street
Box 3237
Wellington 6000
New Zealand
Telephone: 00 64 4 384 7939
FAX: 00 64 4 384 7933
E-mail: karyn.dunn@nzcer.org.nz
Web: www.nzcer.org.nz
Tests: 24, 370, 963, 2052, 2055, 2056, 2061, 2404, 2423, 2534

NFER-Nelson Publishing Co., Ltd.
The Chiswick Centre/9th Floor
414 Chiswick High Road
London W4 5TF
England
Tests: 132, 133, 203, 235, 301, 360, 361, 362, 371, 446, 870, 898, 1002, 1003, 1129, 1132, 1196, 1247, 1334, 1352, 1395, 1465, 1548, 1572, 1603, 1616, 1723, 1754, 1759, 1760, 1779, 1780, 1947, 1959, 2006, 2051, 2133, 2134, 2248, 2266, 2376, 2393, 2482, 2516, 2701, 2805

Nichols & Molinder Assessments
437 Bowes Drive
Fircrest, WA 98466-7047
Tests: 1700

Noel-Levitz
2101 ACT Circle
Iowa City, IA 52245-9581
Telephone: 319-337-4700
FAX: 319-337-5274
E-mail: info@noellevitz.com
Web: www.noellevitz.com
Tests: 625

Norland Software
P.O. Box 84499
Los Angeles, CA 90073-0499
Telephone: 310-825-9689
FAX: 310-825-9689
E-mail: emiller@ucla.edu
Web: www.calcaprt.com
Tests: 380

Northern California Neurobehavioral Group, Inc.
909 Hyde Street, Suite #620
San Francisco, CA 94109-4835
Tests: 564

Northwest Psychological Publishers, Inc.
P.O. Box 494958
Redding, CA 96049-4958
Tests: 2060

Nova Media, Inc.
1724 N. State
Big Rapids, MI 49307-9073
Telephone: 231-796-4637
FAX: 231-796-4637
E-mail: trund@nov.com
Web: www.nov.com
Tests: 2117

NTS Research Corporation
209 Markham Drive
Chapel Hill, NC 27514
Tests: 2296

Dr. Thomas R. Oaster
School of Education—Educational Research & Psy-
    chology
University of Missouri—Kansas City
5100 Rockhill Road
Kansas City, MO 64110-2499
Tests: 1768, 2464

The Occupational Research Centre
"Cornerways"
Cardigan Street
Newmarket, Suffolk CB8 8HZ
England
Tests: 1370

E. R. Oetting, Ph.D.
Psychology Department
Colorado State University
Fort Collins, CO 80523
Telephone: 970-491-1615
FAX: 970-491-0527
E-mail: goetting@lamar.colostate.edu
Tests: 1781, 1782, 2402, 2564

Optometry Admission Testing Program
211 East Chicago Avenue, 6th Floor
Chicago, IL 60611-2678
Telephone: 312-440-2684
FAX: 312-587-4105
E-mail: kramerg@ada.org
Tests: 1798

OQ Measures LLC
P.O. Box 521047
Salt Lake City, UT 84152-1047
Telephone: 1-888-647-2673
Tests: 1799, 1800, 1801, 2839, 2840, 2843

Organization Analysis and Design LLC
168 High Street
Norwell, MA 02061
Tests: 1766

Organizational Measurement Systems Press
P.O. Box 70586
Eugene, OR 97401
Telephone: 541-484-2715
FAX: 541-465-1602
E-mail: barb_john_miner@msn.com
Tests: 1645, 1793

Oxford Psychologists Press, Ltd.
Lambourne House
311-321 Banbury Road
Oxford OX2 7JH
United Kingdom
Tests: 730, 1621, 2122

P.D.P. Press, Inc.
1137 N. McKusick Rd. Lane
Stillwater, MN 55082
Tests: 2305

Pain Assessment Resources
3312 S. McCarran Blvd., #309
Reno, NV 89502
Telephone: 800-782-1501 or 775-828-2955
FAX: 775-828-4275
E-mail: office@painassessmentresources.com
Web: www.painassessmentresources.com
Tests: 297

Pain Resource Center, Inc.
P.O. Box 2836
Durham, NC 27715
Tests: 485, 2657

PAQ Services, Inc.
11 Bellwether Way, Suite 107
Bellingham, WA 98225
Tests: 1308, 1977, 2037, 2821

Pearson Allyn & Bacon
Department 894
160 Gould Street
Needham Heights, MA 02194-2310
Tests: 914, 2431

Pearson Assessments
5601 Green Valley Drive
Bloomington, MN 55437
Telephone: 800-627-7271 or 952-681-3232
FAX: 800-632-9011 or 952-681-3299
Web: www.pearsonassessments.com
Tests: 138, 251, 268, 282, 343, 344, 346, 347, 394, 407,
    408, 784, 1063, 1164, 1218, 1283, 1636, 1637,
    1638, 1639, 1640, 1641, 1654, 1655, 1828, 1982,
    2101, 2116, 2268, 2518, 2692

Pearson Early Learning
P.O. Box 2500
145 South Mt. Zion Road
Lebanon, IN 46052
Tests: 892, 894

Pearson Performance Solutions
One North Dearborn, Suite 1600
Chicago, IL 60602
Tests: 58, 168, 169, 252, 393, 395, 396, 534, 556, 557,
    672, 673, 729, 737, 748, 749, 751, 925, 942, 944,
    981, 1033, 1034, 1254, 1271, 1396, 1411, 1496,
    1507, 1512, 1517, 1580, 1582, 1751, 1753, 1772,
    1788, 1789, 1884, 1890, 1936, 1953, 2021, 2093,
    2123, 2153, 2204, 2205, 2214, 2333, 2350, 2383,
    2384, 2429, 2487, 2488, 2503, 2507, 2519, 2547,
    2554, 2559, 2601, 2652, 2653, 2683, 2686, 2698,
    2700, 2799

Pearson VUE
5601 Green Valley Dr.
Bloomington, MN 55437-1099
Telephone: 952-681-3000
FAX: 952-681-3899
Web: www.pearsonvue.com
Tests: 1092

Penna Assessment
Address Unknown
Tests: 215, 216, 217, 1875, 1876

People Focus
Pleasant Hill Executive Park
391 Taylor Blvd., Suite 110
Pleasant Hill, CA 94523-2275
Telephone: 925-676-6265
FAX: 925-676-0519
E-mail: lfogli@peoplefocus.com
Web: www.peoplefocus.com
Tests: 2312

Perfection Learning Corporation
1000 North Second Avenue
P.O. Box 500
Logan, IA 51546-0500
Tests: 1468

Personal Strengths Publishing
P.O. Box 2605
Carlsbad, CA 92018-2605
Telephone: 800-624-7347
FAX: 760-602-0087
E-mail: mail@PersonalStrengths.com
Web: www.PersonalStrengths.com
Tests: 979, 980, 1015, 1016, 1017, 1659, 1919, 1975,
    1976, 2436

Personalysis Corporation
5847 San Felipe, Suite 650
Houston, TX 77057-3008
Telephone: 713-784-4421
FAX: 713-784-9909
E-mail: info@personalysis.com
Web: www.personalysis.com
Tests: 1931

Personnel Decisions, Inc.
2000 Plaza VII Tower
45 South Seventh Street
Minneapolis, MN 55402-1608
Tests: 1863

Dr. Linda Phillips
Director, Centre for Research on Literacy
Faculty of Educacion
University of Alberta
Edmonton, Alberta T6G 2G5
Canada
Telephone: 780-492-4250
FAX: 780-492-0113
Tests: 2593

Phonovisual Products, Inc.
18761 North Frederick
Gaithersburg, MD 20879
Telephone: 800-283-4888
FAX: 240-358-0228
E-mail: Phonovisual@aol.com
Web: www.phonovisual.com
Tests: 1949

Dr. Issy Pilowsky
University of Sydney
Department of Psychological Medicine
Camperdown
New South Wales 2006
Australia
E-mail: ipilowsk@mail.usyd.edu.au
Tests: 1220, 1451

Piney Mountain Press, Inc.
P.O. Box 333
Cleveland, GA 30528
Telephone: 800-255-3127
FAX: 800-905-3127
E-mail: cyberguy@alltel.net
Web: www.pineymountain.com
Tests: 262, 1439, 1442, 2023, 2351, 2725

PITS: Psychologische Instrumenten Tests en Services
Postbus 1084
2302 BB Leiden
The Netherlands
Telephone: ++ (0)71-5318786
FAX: ++ (0)71-5728165
E-mail: info@pits-online.nl
Web: www.pits-online.nl
Tests: 157, 1940, 2712

Predictive Surveys Corporation
5802 Howard Avenue
LaGrange, IL 60525
Telephone: 708-246-1271
E-mail: markstrand@prodigy.net
Tests: 2068, 2069, 2524

Prentice-Hall
College Book Division
200 Old Tappan Rd.
Old Tappan, NJ 07675
Tests: 964, 1225, 1226, 1469, 1536, 1790, 2044

Preschool Skills Test
c/o Carol Lepera
P.O. Box 1246
Greenwood, IN 46142
Tests: 2019

Preziosi Partners, Inc.
9441 Hollyhock Court
Ft. Lauderdale, FL 33328
Tests: 2035

Price Systems, Inc.
Box 1818
Lawrence, KS 66044-8818
Telephone: 785-843-7892
FAX: 785-843-0101
E-mail: learn@learningstyle.com
Web: www.learningstyle.com
Tests: 1433, 2036

PRO-ED
8700 Shoal Creek Blvd.
Austin, TX 78757-6897
Telephone: 800-897-3202
FAX: 800-397-7633
E-mail: info@proedinc
Web: WWW.PROEDINC.COM
Tests: 2, 3, 61, 76, 83, 167, 172, 184, 191, 197, 199, 207, 208, 223, 234, 243, 244, 261, 280, 281, 293, 296, 326, 336, 337, 349, 435, 565, 635, 660, 662, 665, 666, 669, 680, 727, 743, 755, 780, 789, 790, 791, 795, 796, 798, 803, 806, 808, 816, 817, 855, 856, 885, 975, 1030, 1037, 1045, 1049, 1050, 1056, 1073, 1076, 1077, 1107, 1108, 1109, 1140, 1183, 1184, 1219, 1365, 1378, 1394, 1426, 1462, 1647, 1668, 1691, 1774, 1806, 1864, 1944, 1948, 1950, 1955, 1991, 1998, 2003, 2012, 2014, 2080, 2121, 2124, 2137, 2165, 2175, 2188, 2189, 2190, 2227, 2235, 2238, 2250, 2269, 2271, 2291, 2368, 2392, 2396, 23997, 2407, 2470, 2471, 2513, 2514, 2566, 2574, 2575, 2576, 2582, 2583, 2584, 2585, 2586, 2592, 2597, 2598, 2599, 2600, 2602, 2605, 2606, 2608, 2609, 2610, 2611, 2614, 2616, 2617, 2626, 2627, 2629, 2630, 2631, 2632, 2660, 2671, 2691, 2729, 2759, 2800, 2806, 2835, 2841

Professional Picture Framers Association
3000 Picture Place
Jackson, MI 49201
Telephone: 517-788-8100
FAX: 517-788-8371
E-mail: ppfa@ppfa.com
Tests: 441

Profiles International, Inc.
Profiles Office Park
5205 Lake Shore Drive
Waco, TX 76710-1732
Tests: 2043

Program Development Associates
P.O. Box 2038
Syracuse, NY 13220-2038
Tests: 2538

ProLiteracy Worldwide
1320 Jamesville Avenue
Syracuse, NY 13210
Telephone: 315-422-9121 Ext. 353
FAX: 315-422-6369
E-mail: corpcom@proliteracy.org
Web: www.proliteracy.org
Tests: 949, 2125

Prufrock Press Inc.
P.O. Box 8813
Waco, TX 76714-8813
Telephone: 800-998-2208
FAX: 800-240-0333
E-mail: info@prufrock.com
Web: www.prufrock.com
Tests: 2236

Psych Press
Level 4 398 Lonsdale Street
Melbourne
VIC 3000
Australia
Telephone: +61 3 9670 0590
FAX: +61 3 9642 3577
E-mail: info@psychpress.com.au
Web: www.psychpress.com
Tests: 977

PsychCorp, A brand of Harcourt Assessment, Inc.
19500 Bulverde Road
San Antonio, TX 78259-3701
Telephone: 800-211-8378
FAX: 800-232-1223
E-mail: customer_care@harcourt.com
Web: www.PsychCorp.com
Tests: 12, 14, 19, 20, 38, 59, 62, 66, 74, 89, 143, 146,
   228, 250, 270, 271, 272, 273, 274, 275, 276, 277,
   278, 313, 318, 319, 329, 330, 331, 339, 340, 363,
   364, 368, 375, 387, 388, 419, 438, 461, 469, 476,
   479, 480, 491, 495, 547, 548, 549, 550, 569, 631,
   658, 725, 770, 810, 813, 820, 821, 833, 835, 836,
   854, 862, 864, 867, 874, 888, 890, 891, 900, 907,
   1026, 1029, 1051, 1075, 1084, 1086, 1110, 1135,
   1188, 1224, 1255, 1277, 1300, 1339, 1551, 1556,
   1557, 1606, 1607, 1614, 1622, 1623, 1669, 1696,
   1713, 1731, 1734, 1821, 1826, 1848, 1938, 1941,
   1942, 1972, 2001, 2033, 2091, 2119, 2135, 2149,
   2162, 2171, 2194, 2241, 2242, 2254, 2306, 2316,
   2409, 2415, 2466, 2520, 2573, 2596, 2604, 2628,
   2690, 2699, 2707, 2713, 2733, 2745, 2756, 2747,
   2748, 2749, 2750, 2751, 2752, 2756, 2757, 2766,
   2783, 2785

Psychological Assessment Resources, Inc.
16204 N. Florida Avenue
Lutz, FL 33549-8119
Telephone: 800-331-8378
FAX: 800-727-9329
E-mail: custsupp@parinc.com
Web: www.parinc.com
Tests: 70, 77, 82, 84, 85, 96, 145, 289, 290, 291, 292,
   334, 338, 348, 350, 409, 412, 426, 447, 457, 463,
   468, 470, 478, 542, 543, 544, 545, 546, 567, 568,
   571, 574, 575, 629, 293, 296, 706, 771, 787, 801,

838, 899, 931, 938, 971, 989, 1047, 1139, 1163,
1195, 1197, 1228, 1262, 1263, 1273, 1320, 1354,
1455, 1456, 1531, 1576, 1592, 1596, 1597, 1598,
1627, 1648, 1686, 1689, 1692, 1702, 1728, 1729,
1735, 1737, 1778, 1794, 1847, 1849, 1862, 1900,
1901, 1906, 1907, 1923, 1924, 1925, 1971, 1978,
2085, 2087, 2088, 2158, 2167, 2169, 2170, 2172,
2173, 2174, 2177, 2185, 2195, 2196, 2197, 2198,
2289, 2307, 2314, 2366, 2425, 2438, 2448, 2453,
2454, 2455, 2468, 2477. 2483, 2556, 2676, 2677,
2678, 2687, 2704, 2711, 2718, 2728, 2773, 2774,
2775, 2776, 2777, 2778, 2780, 2787, 2788

Psychological & Educational Publications, Inc.
P.O. Box 520
Hydesville, CA 95547-0520
Tests: 2572

Psychological Growth Associates, Inc.
Products Division
3813 Tiffany Drive
Lawrence, KS 66049
Telephone: 785-841-1141
FAX: 785-749-2190
E-mail: 73204.303@compuserve. com
Tests: 2654

Psychological Publications, Inc.
P.O. Box 3577
Thousand Oaks, CA 91359-0577
Telephone: 800-345-8378
FAX: 805-527-9266
E-mail: tjta@aol.com
Web: www.tjta.com
Tests: 1004, 2531

Psychological Services Bureau, Inc.
2774 Hydraulic Road, Suite 101
Charlottesville, VA 22901
Telephone: 877-932-8378
FAX: 434-293-5885
E-mail: info@psbtests.com
Web: www.psbtests.com
Tests: 2064, 2065, 2066, 2067

Psychological Services, Inc.
2950 N. Hollywood Way, Suite 200
Burbank, CA 91505-1072
Tests: 937, 1024, 1025, 1968, 2038, 2070, 2706

Psychological Test Publications
Scamp's House
107 Pilton Street
Barnstaple, Devon
England
Tests: 1112, 1444

Psychological Test Specialists
Box 7922
Missoula, MT 59807
Telephone: 406-728-1710
E-mail: saisbell@ammonsscientific.com
Web: www.ammonsscientific.com
Tests: 2115

Psychology Press
270 Madison Avenue
New York, NY 10016
Telephone: 212-216-7800
FAX: 212-643-1430
Web: www.psypress.com
Tests: 325, 392, 437, 972, 2081, 2703

Psychology Press, Inc.
P.O. Box 328
Brandon, VT 05733-0328
Telephone: 802-247-8312
FAX: 802-247-8312
E-mail: info@great-ideas.org
Web: www.great-ideas.org
Tests: 1943

Psychometric Affiliates
118 Oakcrest Road
Huntsville, AL 35811-9072
Telephone: 256-859-2441
Tests: 10, 11, 13, 139, 150, 152, 155, 181, 182, 533,
    621, 641, 681, 738, 744, 745, 746, 841, 910, 919,
    935, 952, 953, 967, 969, 995, 997, 1011, 1012,
    1013, 1028, 1055, 1064, 1067, 1069, 1116, 1143,
    1157, 1160, 1161, 1165, 1176, 1206, 1284, 1309,
    1333, 1414, 1453, 1523, 1549, 1565, 1568, 1569,
    1570, 1578, 1675, 1787, 1791, 1880, 1952, 1963,
    1964, 1988, 2079, 2094, 2132, 2224, 2279, 2380,
    2400, 2497, 2680, 2721, 2758, 2770, 2811

Psychometrics Canada Ltd.
7125 - 77 Avenue
Edmonton, Alberta T6B 0B5
Canada
Telephone: 1-800-661-5158
FAX: 780-469-2283
E-mail: info@psychometrics.com
Web: www.psychometrics.com
Tests: 1231, 1232, 2817

Psytec Inc.
P.O. Box 564
DeKalb, IL 60115
Tests: 451

Donald K. Pumroy, Ph.D.
4006 Oliver Street
Hyattsville, MD 20782
Telephone: 301-864-8935
FAX: 301-864-8935
E-mail: dpumroy@earthlink.net
Tests: 1537

Purdue Research Foundation
Engineering and Administration Building
Purdue University
West Lafayette, IN 47907
Tests: 2092

Ramsay Corporation
Boyce Station Offices
1050 Boyce Road
Pittsburgh, PA 15241-3907
Tests: 134, 449, 632, 853, 915, 917, 918, 921, 1253,
    1482, 1484, 1485, 1486, 1577, 1579, 1581, 1583,
    1584, 1585, 1587, 1682, 1683, 1684, 1784, 1786,
    2027, 2544, 2760

Rehabilitation Research and Training Center on Blind-
    ness and Low Vision
Mississippi State University
P.O. Drawer 6189
Mississippi State, MS 39762
Telephone: 662-325-2001
FAX: 662-325-8989
E-mail: rrtc@ra.msstate.edu
Web: www.blind.msstate.edu
Tests: 920

Reitan Neuropsychology Laboratory/Press
P.O. Box 66080
Tucson, AZ 85728-6080
Telephone: 520-577-2970
FAX: 520-577-2940
E-mail: REITANLABs@AOL.COM
Tests: 1137

Renaissance Learning, Inc.
P.O. Box 8036
Wisconsin Rapids, WI 54495-8036
Telephone: 800-656-6740
FAX: 877-279-7642
E-mail: answers@renlearn.com
Web: www.renlearn.com
Tests: 2420, 2421, 2422

Renovex Corporation
1421 Jersey Avenue, N
Minneapolis, MN 55427
Tests: 200

Research Concepts
1368 East Airport Road
Muskegon, MI 49444
Telephone: 231-739-7401
 Tests: 1151

Research for Better Schools, Inc.
112 North Broad Streeet
Philadelphia, PA 19102-1510
Telephone: 215-574-9300
FAX: 215-574-0133
E-mail: maguire@rbs.org
Web: www.rbs.org
Tests: 204, 214, 839, 2253

Research Press
P.O. Box 9177
Champaign, IL 61826
Telephone: 800-519-2707
FAX: 217-352-1221
E-mail: rp@researchpress.com
Web: www.researchpress.com
Tests: 299, 452, 1040, 1199, 1387, 1698

Richmond Products, Inc.
4400 Silver Avenue, SE
Albuquerque, NM 87108
Telephone: 505-275-2406
FAX: 810-885-8319
E-mail: Lloydpo@aol.com
Web: www.RichmondProducts.com
Tests: 1201

Risk & Needs Assessment, Inc.
P.O. Box 44828
Phoenix, AZ 85064-4828
Telephone: 602-234-3506
FAX: 602-266-8227
E-mail: skarca@bdsltd.com
Web: www.riskandneeds.com
Tests: 22, 764, 860, 1304, 2028, 2223, 2320, 2329

Riverside Publishing
Attn: Rob Elsey
425 Spring Lake Drive
Itasca, IL 60143-2079
Telephone: 800-323-9540
FAX: 630-467-7192
Web: www.riversidepublishing.com
Tests: 253, 266, 267, 284, 311, 321, 448, 566, 756, 761, 818, 830, 1060, 1238, 1258, 1272, 1288, 1291, 1292, 1550, 1646, 1726, 1727, 2104, 2152, 2240, 2411, 2412, 2634, 2688, 2789, 2794, 2795, 2796, 2797

Rocky Mountain Behavioral Science Institute, Inc.
305 West Magnolia St., #291
Fort Collins, CO 80521
Telephone: 800-447-6354
FAX: 970-221-0595
E-mail: info@rmbsi.com
Web: www.rmbsi.com
Tests: 75, 149

Rose Wolfe Family Partnership LLP
c/o Walden Personnel Performance, Inc.
4115 Sherbrooke, W — #100
Montreal, Quebec H3Z 1K9
Canada
Telephone: 514-989-9555
FAX: 514-989-9934
E-mail: tests@waldentesting.com
Web: www.waldentesting.com
Tests: 175, 2522, 2523, 2731, 2790, 2791

Kenneth H. Rubin, Ph.D., Director
Center for Children, Relationships & Culture
Department of Human Development, 3304 Benjamin
    Building
University of Maryland
College Park, MD 20742-1131
Tests: 1966

SAGE Publications
2455 Teller Road
Thousand Oaks, CA 09320
Tests: 1699

Dr. Shoukry D. Saleh
Chairman, Department of Management Sciences
University of Waterloo
Waterloo, Ontario N2L 3G1
Canada
Tests: 1310

The SASSI Institute
201 Camelot Lane
Springville, IN 47462
Telephone: 800-726-0526
FAX: 800-546-7995
E-mail: sassi@sassi.com
Web: WWW.SASSI.COM
Tests: 2479

Scantron Corporation
110 West A Street, Suite 800
San Diego, CA 92101
Telephone: 800-722-6876
FAX: 619-615-0522
E-mail: marjorie—reynolds@scantron.com
Web: www.scantron.com
Tests: 1886

Dr. K. Warner Schaie
Penn State Gerontology Center
135 E. Nittany Ave., Suite 405
State College, PA 16801
Telephone: 814-863-9735
FAX: 814-863-4776
Web: geron.psu.edu
Tests: 2244

Ronald R. Schmeck, Ph.D.
Department of Psychology
Southern Illinois University at Carbondale
Carbondale, IL 62901-6502
Tests: 1278

Nina G. Schneider, Ph.D.
Greater LA VA Healthcare, Nicotine Research Unit
Bldg. 210, 2nd Floor, 11301 Wilshire Blvd.
Mail Code: 691/B151D
Los Angeles, CA 90073
Telephone: 310-268-3059
FAX: 310-268-4125
Tests: 2363

Scholastic Testing Service, Inc.
480 Meyer Road
Bensenville, IL 60106-1617
Telephone: 1-800-642-6787
FAX: 630-766-8054
E-mail: stesting@email.com
Web: www.ststesting.com
Tests: 4, 555, 659, 702, 883, 904, 1105, 1136, 1175, 1205, 1266, 1359, 1360, 1383, 1567, 1836, 18744, 2107, 2183, 2260, 2472, 2648, 2649, 2662, 2738

Scientific Management Techniques, Inc.
Towne Square Complex
12 Parmenter Road, Unit A-5
Londonderry, NH 03053
Telephone: 603-421-0222
FAX: 603-421-1881
E-mail: scibos@aol.com
Web: www.scientific-management.com
Tests: 2405

Search Institute
The Banks Building
615 First Avenue NE, Suite 125
Minneapolis, MN 55413
Telephone: 800-888-7828
FAX: 612-376-8956
E-mail: si@search-institute.org
Web: www.search-institute.org
Tests: 2275

SEFA (Publications) Ltd.
"The Globe"
4 Great William St.
Stratford-upon-Avon CV37-6RY
England
FAX: +43-2236-29554
E-mail: admin@sefa.org.uk
Tests: 1471, 2050

SELF Research Centre
University of Western Sydney
Bankstown Campus
Locked Bag 1797
Penrith South DC
New South Wales 1797
Australia
Tests: 2287

Melvin Selzer, M.D.
6967 Paseo Laredo
La Jolla, CA 92037
Telephone: 619-459-1035
Tests: 1609

Sensonics, Inc.
125 White Horse Pike
Haddon Heights, NJ 08035
Tests: 2361

SHL Group plc
The Pavillion
1 Atwell Place
Thames Ditton, Surrey KT7 0NE
England
Tests: 127, 237, 736, 959, 1492, 1499, 1775, 1797, 1937, 2049, 2212, 2550, 2551, 2825

The Sidran Institute
200 East Joppa Road, Suite 207
Towson, MD 21286
Tests: 81, 846, 847

SIGMA Assessment Systems, Inc.
511 Fort Street, Suite 435
P.O. Box 610984
Port Huron, MI 48061-0984
Telephone: 800-265-1285
FAX: 800-361-9411
E-mail: SIGMA@SigmaAssessmentSystems.com
Web: www.SigmaAssessmentSystems.com
Tests: 189, 259, 414, 432, 699, 945, 1302, 1303, 1408, 1416, 1688, 1752, 1928, 1932, 2083, 2317, 2335, 2336, 2337, 2345, 2510

Silverwood Enterprises, LLC
P.O. Box 363
Sharon Center, OH 44273
Telephone: 330-239-1646
FAX: 330-239-0250
E-mail: silverasoc@aol.com
Tests: 140, 141, 142, 1166

Jacob O. Sines
207 Black Springs Circle
Iowa City, IA 52246
Tests: 1190, 1660

SLACK Incorporated
6900 Grove Road
Thorofare, NJ 08086-9447
Tests: 1642

Slosson Educational Publications, Inc.
P.O. Box 544
East Aurora, NY 14052-0544
Telephone: 888-756-7766
FAX: 800-655-3840
E-mail: slosson@slosson.com
Web: www.slosson.com
Tests: 5, 158, 185, 482, 667, 825, 826, 827, 828, 829,
    837, 913, 1366, 2263, 2264, 2270, 2355, 2356,
    2357, 2358, 2359, 2478, 2607, 2730

SOI Systems
45755 Goodpasture Road
P.O. Box D
Vida, OR 97488
Tests: 773, 774, 1590

Sopris West
4093 Specialty Place
Longmont, CO 80504-5400
Telephone: 800-547-6747
FAX: 303-776-5934
E-mail: WWW.SOPRISWEST.COM
Tests: 832, 896, 1052, 1269, 2252, 2521

Southwest Educational Development Laboratory
211 East Seventh Street, Suite 400
Austin, TX 78701-3281
Tests: 845

SPECTRA Inc.
1004 Palmyra Drive
Tega Cay, SC 29706-8539
Tests: 2741

Stanard & Associates, Inc.
309 West Washington Street, Suite 1000
Chicago, IL 60606
Tests: 1719

Stoelting Co.
620 Wheat Lane
Wood Dale, IL 60191-1164
Telephone: 630-860-9700
FAX: 630-860-9775
E-mail: psychtests@stoeltingco.com
Web: www.stoeltingco.com/tests
Tests: 7, 288, 489, 1048, 1144, 1279, 1315, 1329, 1344,
    1346, 1372, 1375, 1447, 1461, 1601, 1667, 2016,
    2280, 2360, 2378, 2433, 2447, 2714

Stress Directions, Inc.
2464 Massachusetts Avenue, Suite 315C
Cambridge, MA 02140
Telephone: 617-547-3499
FAX: 617-547-3498
E-mail: lmiller@stressdirections.com
Web: www.stressdirections.com
Tests: 1913

Student Development Associates, Inc.
Address Unknown
Tests: 9, 2461

Super Duper Publications
P.O. Box 24997
Greenville, SC 29616-2497
Telephone: 800-277-8737
FAX: 800-978-7379
E-mail: custserv@superduperinc.com
Web: www.supeduperinc.com
Tests: 541, 2782

Clifford H. Swensen
Department of Psychological Sciences
Purdue University
1364 Psychological Sciences Building
West Lafayette, IN 47907-1364
Telephone: 765-496-6977
FAX: 765-496-2670
E-mail: cswensen@psych.purdue.edu
Tests: 2231, 22233

TAV Selection System
12807 Arminta Street
North Hollywood, CA 91605
Telephone: 818-765-1884
Tests: 2529

Anne P. Taylor
9 Tumble Weed, NW
Albuquerque, NM 87120-1823
Tests: 2530

Taylor & Francis
7625 Empire Drive
Florence, KY 41042-2919
Tests: 224

Taylor & Francis
Rankine Road
Basingstoke, Hampshire RG24 8PR
England
Tests: 1133

Teachers College Press
1234 Amsterdam Avenue
New York, NY 10027
Telephone: 212-678-3929
FAX: 212-678-4149
E-mail: tcpress@tc.columbia.edu
Web: www.teacherscollegepress.com
Tests: 212, 570, 880, 1000, 1061, 1239, 1554, 2251, 2571

Sue Teele & Associates
P.O. Box 7302
Redlands, CA 92375
Telephone: 909-793-1916
FAX: 909-793-1916
E-mail: scandsteele@msn.com
Tests: 2553

Teleometrics International, Inc.
4567 Lake Shore Drive
Waco, TX 76710
Telephone: 800-527-0406
FAX: 254-772-9588
E-mail: teleo.info@teleometrics.com
Web: www.teleometrics.com
Tests: 17, 443, 683, 684, 747, 940, 1223, 1406, 1495, 1506, 1508, 1511, 1514, 1515, 1519, 1520, 1522, 1714, 1855, 1888, 1903, 1909, 1935, 1986, 1987, 2034, 2099, 2103, 2136, 2210, 2215, 2220, 2473, 2474, 2475, 2498, 2504, 2541, 2543, 2545, 2546, 2813

The Test Agency Ltd.
Burgner House
4630 Kingsgate
Oxford Business Park South
Oxford OX4 2SU
England
Telephone: +44 (0) 1865 402900
FAX: +44 (0) 1865 402888
E-mail: info@testagency.com
Web: www.testagency.com
Tests: 908, 916, 1113, 1209, 1457, 1513, 1525, 1560, 1857, 1984, 2325, 2822, 2823

Test Analysis & Development Corporation
2400 Park Lake Drive
Boulder, CO 80301
Telephone: 303 666-8651
FAX: 303 665-6045
E-mail: jimh@testanalysis.com
Tests: 2293

Toby J. Tetenbaum
Fordham University
113 West 60th Street, Room 1119
New York, NY 10023
Tests: 226

Thinking Publications
424 Galloway Street
P.O. Box 163
Eau Claire, WI 54702-0163
Tests: 201, 695, 2446

Thomas Concept
P.O. Box 160220
Austin, TX 78716-0220
Telephone: 512-327-2656
FAX: 512-857-0998
E-mail: service@oppositestrengths.com
Web: www.oppositestrengths.com
Tests: 2650

Thomson Delmar Learning
Executive Woods
5 Maxwell Drive
P.O. Box 8007
Clifton Park, NY 12065-2919
Tests: 1856

Touchstone Applied Science Associates (TASA), Inc.
4 Hardscrabble Heights
P.O. Box 382
Brewster, NY 10509-0382
Web: WWW.TASA.COM
Tests: 767, 768, 1483, 2338

Training House, Inc.
22 Amherst Road
Pelham, MA 01002-9745
Tests: 161, 174, 2002, 637, 709, 1510, 1518, 1832, 1902, 1914, 1915, 2039, 2284, 2285, 2505, 2581, 2655, 2665, 2769

TRT Associates, Inc.
1579 Monroe Drive, Suite F510
Atlanta, GA 30324
Telephone: 404-406-8781
FAX: 404-873-3959
E-mail: trtbasis@hotmail.com
Web: www.mindspring.com/~trtbasis
Tests: 264

Trust Tutoring
8115 Fenton Street, #304
Silver Spring, MD 20910
Telephone: 800-301-3131
FAX: 301-589-0733 *51
E-mail: HAVIS@EROLS.COM
Web: trusttutoring.com
Tests: 970

Twenty-First Century Assessment
P.O. Box 608
South Pasadena, CA 91031–0608
Telephone: 800-374-2100
FAX: 626-441-0614
Web: www.21stcenturyassessment.com
Tests: 1921

U.S. Department of Labor
Division Chief for Evaluation and Skill Assessment
Office of Policy and Research
200 Constitution Avenue, NW
Washington, DC 20210
Tests: 1764, 1765

United States Military Entrance Processing Command
ATTN: Operations Directorate
2500 Green Bay Road
North Chicago, IL 60064-3094
Tests: 187

Universal Attention Disorders, Inc.
4281 Katella Avenue, #215
Los Alamitos, CA 90720
Telephone: 800-729-2886
FAX: 714-229-8782
E-mail: info@tovatest.com
Web: www.tovatest.com
Tests: 2622

University of Maryland
University Counseling Center
Shoemaker Hall
College Park, MD 20742
Tests: 1749, 2084, 2341

University of Michigan Press
839 Greene Street
Ann Arbor, MI 48104
Telephone: 734-764-4388
FAX: 734-615-1540
E-mail: um.press.bus@umich.edu
Web: www.press.umich.edu
Tests: 885, 2010

University of Minnesota Press
Test Division
Mill Place, Suite 290
111 Third Avenue South
Minneapolis, MN 55401-2520
Tests: 1654, 1655, 2246

University of Utah
Department of Psychology—SBS
390 South 1530 East
Salt Lake City, UT 84112-0251
Tests: 2225

Valpar International Corporation
P.O. Box 5767
Tucson, AZ 85703-5767
E-mail: valparbbc@aol.com
Tests: 2693

Vantage McCann Associates, Inc.
110 Terry Drive
Newtown, PA 18940-1850
Telephone: 267-759-1197
FAX: 215-579-8391
Web: www.vantagemccann.com
Tests: 732, 733, 734, 735, 788, 1023, 1770, 1967

Variety Child Learning Center
47 Humphrey Drive
Syosset, NY 11791-4098
Telephone: 516-921-7171
FAX: 516-921-8130
E-mail: jfriedman@vclc.org
Web: www.vclc.org
Tests: 1032

Village Publishing
73 Valley Drive
Furlong, PA 18925
Telephone: 800-553-7678
FAX: 215-794-3386
E-mail: VP@custody-vp.com
Web: www.custody-vp.com
Tests: 16, 210, 342, 844, 1193, 1837, 1843, 1881

Vocational and Rehabilitation Research Institute
3304 - 33rd Street, NW
Calgary, Alberta T2L 2A6
Tests: 64

Vocational Psychology Research
N657 Elliott Hall
University of Minnesota—Twin Cities
75 East River Road
Minneapolis, MN 55455-0344
Telephone: 612-625-1367
FAX: 612-626-0345
E-mail: vpr@tc.umn.edu
Web: www.psych.umn.edu/psylabs/vpr
Tests: 1652, 1652, 1646, 1657

VORT Corporation
P.O. Box 60880
Palo Alto, CA 94306
Tests: 298, 1168, 1169

Walch Publishing
40 Walch Drive
P.O. Box 658
Portland, ME 04104-0658
Tests: 1019, 2112, 2656

Walden Personnel Performance, Inc.
4115 Sherbrooke W, Suite #100
Montreal, Quebec H3Z 1K9
Telephone: 514-989-9555
FAX: 514-989-9934
E-mail: tests@waldentesting.com
Web: www.waldentesting.com
Tests: 18, 159, 160, 255, 372, 273, 289, 537, 538, 670, 671, 697, 752, 757, 976, 1167, 1298, 1299, 1516, 1732, 1733, 1769, 1861, 2046, 2047, 2058, 2154, 2155, 2217, 2218, 2549, 2555, 2735, 2737

Arthur Weider and James Weider
552 Laguardia Pl.
New York, NY 10012-1459
Telephone: 212-777-7303
FAX: 212-388-0001
E-mail: AWEIDER2000@msm.com
Tests: 714, 716

Western Psychological Services
12031 Wilshire Blvd.
Los Angeles, CA 90025-1251
Telephone: 310-478-2061
FAX: 310-478-7838
Web: www.wpspublish.com

Tests: 37, 41, 78, 80, 92, 131, 135, 183, 227, 306, 345, 367, 460, 472, 474, 763, 766, 804, 948, 988, 1039, 1062, 1138, 1141, 1194, 1202, 1204, 1259, 1264, 1268, 1328, 1340, 1353, 1367, 1386, 1437, 1479, 1480, 1489, 1491, 1526, 1527, 1532, 1535, 1558, 1595, 1608, 1703, 1704, 1709, 1736, 1755, 1756, 1783, 1822, 1840, 1896, 1897, 1898, 1899, 1926, 1927, 1957, 1981, 2029, 2030, 2075, 2140, 2159, 2161, 2166, 2168, 2176, 2182, 2203, 2234, 2272, 2273, 2274, 2304, 2309, 2328, 2331, 2362, 2367, 2372, 2442, 2449, 2458, 2460, 2485, 2515, 2557, 2561, 2615, 2674, 2675, 2732, 2763, 2767

Winslow Research Institute
1933 Windward Point
Discovery Bay, CA 94514
Tests: 1894, 1918

Wintergreen/Orchard House, Inc.
425 Spring Lake Drive
Itasca, IL 60143-2076
Tests: 418, 905, 1058

Wonderlic, Inc.
1795 N. Butterfield Road, Suite 200
Libertyville, IL 60048-1238
Telephone: 800-323-3742
FAX: 847-680-9492
E-mail: sales@wonderlic.com
Web: www.wonderlic.com and www.wonderlic-education.com
Tests: 661, 957, 1153, 1891, 2792, 2793

Judith Worell, Ph.D.
Educational & Counseling Psychology
245 Dickey Hall
University of Kentucky
Lexington, KY 40506-0017
Telephone: 859-254-0239
FAX: 859-254-0239
E-mail: jpwphd@aol.com
Tests: 1838

World Health Organization
Management of Substance Dependence
Dr. Maristela Monteiro
CH-1211
Geneva 27
Switzerland
Telephone: 41-22-791-4791
FAX: 41-22-791-4851
E-mail: monteirom@who.int
Web: www.who.int
Tests: 137

World of Work, Inc.
410 West 1st Street, Suite #103
Tempe, AZ 85281-2574
Tests: 2833

Worley's Identity Discovery Profile, Inc.
190 Bishop Road
Fitchburg, MA 01420-2993
Telephone: 978-448-2047
FAX: 978-448-3910
E-mail: WIDP@worleyid.com
Web: www.worleyid.com
Tests: 2834

INDEX OF NAMES

This index indicates whether a citation refers to authorship of a test or of a test review for a specific test in a previous Mental Measurements Yearbook. *Numbers refer to test entries in* Tests in Print VII, *not to pages. The abbreviations and numbers following the names may be interpreted as follows: "test, 73" indicates authorship of test 73; "rev, 86" is based on information listed in the cross references for a test and indicates authorship of a previous review of test 86.*

Aaron, I. E.: rev, 497, 2130
Aarons, M.: test, 235
Aase, D.: test, 695
Aasland, O. G.: test, 137
Abbott-Shim, M. S.: test, 453
Abell, E. L.: rev, 378
Abidin, R. R.: test, 1228, 1847, 1849, 2438
Abraham, J. A.: test, 1334
Academic Consulting & Testing Service: test, 1425, 1845, 2258
Academic Consulting and Testing Service: test, 220
Academic Freedom Committee, Illinois Division, American Civil Liberties Union: test, 13
Achenbach, T. M.: test, 33, 429
Acheson, S. K.: rev, 146, 1047, 1146, 1339
Achterberg, J.: test, 1158
Ackerman, M. J.: test, 41
Ackerman, P. L.: rev, 225, 537, 754, 929, 1348, 1544, 2383, 2415, 2424
Ackerman, R. J.: test, 40, 1980
Ackerman, T.: rev, 2747
Ackerman, T. A.: rev, 791, 1743
ACS DivCHED Examinations Institute: test, 42, 43, 44, 45, 46, 47, 48, 49, 50, 51, 52, 53, 54, 55
ACT Career Planning Services: test, 2724
ACT, Inc.: test, 56, 57, 424, 627, 983, 1962
Adamovich, B.: test, 2238
Adams, C.: test, 203
Adams, C. R.: test, 1890

Adams, E.: test, 2000
Adams, G. R.: rev, 743
Adams, J. D.: test, 2685
Adams, K. L.: test, 1644
Adams, M. F.: rev, 254
Adams, R. L.: rev, 1480, 2110, 2140
Adams, R.: test, 2525
Adams, W.: test, 574, 2573, 2776, 2777, 2778
Adcock, C. J.: rev, 1034, 1174, 1645, 2327, 2346, 2349, 2645
Adcock, D.: test, 652, 653
Addiction Research Foundation: test, 190
ADE Incorporated: test, 1337, 1725, 2476
Adkins, D. C.: rev, 937
Adkinson, D. R.: test, 1264
Adler, S.: rev, 1877
Adrian, M.: test, 1054
Ahluwalia, S. P.: test, 2537
Ahmann, J. S.: rev, 2563, 2639
Aho, M.: test, 2163
Ahrens, J. B.: test, 411
Ahsen, A.: test, 128, 911
Aidman, E. V.: rev, 225, 345, 1079, 2674, 2726, 2834
Aiken, L. R.: rev, 31, 57, 2269
Airasian, P. W.: rev, 378, 1291
Albanese, M.: rev, 1942, 2064, 2615
Albanese, M. A.: rev, 145, 422, 1153, 1648, 1761, 2383
Alberts, N. F.: test, 1746, 2301
Albrecht, K.: test, 1418, 1643

Albright, L. E.: rev, 1651, 1656
Alcorn, B. K.: rev, 1460, 1747
Aldarondo, F.: rev, 1262
Alden, L. E.: test, 1277
Alderman, N.: test, 302
Aldous, C.: test, 819
Aldrich, F.: test, 2181
Aleamoni, L. A.: rev, 939, 1131, 2543
Alessandra, T.: test, 1879
Alexander, C. M.: rev, 1814
Alexander, J.: test, 2291
Alexander, R. M.: rev, 1909
Algozzine, B.: test, 2356
Alker, H. A.: rev, 1655
Alleman, E.: test, 140, 141, 142
Allen, C. C.: test, 2196, 2198
Allen, D. V.: rev, 2168, 2569, 2597; test, 2270, 2309
Allen, E. A.: test, 2616, 2617
Allen, K.: rev, 239, 1397, 2131
Allen, L. M.: test, 2802
Allen, L. M., III: test, 674, 1827
Allen, M. J.: rev, 1638, 2415
Allen, N. L.: rev, 654
Allen, S. J.: rev, 293, 1040, 1783, 1846, 2370
Allington, R. L.: rev, 2798
Allison, E. E.: rev, 2756
Allison, J. A.: rev, 215, 1001, 1629, 1849, 2088, 2365, 2511
Allman, T.: test, 1169
Almond, P. J.: test, 234
Alnot, S. D.: test, 1292
Alpern, G.: test, 804
Alpine Media Corporation: test, 1351
Altus, W. D.: rev, 1972
Alvarado, C. G.: test, 321
Alvarado, G. G.: test, 266
Amabile, T. M.: test, 1357
Aman, M. G.: test, 5
Amann, G.: test, 1883
American Association of Teachers of German: test, 1716
American College Testing: test, 2812
American Council on Education: test, 1790
American Institute of Certified Public Accountants: test, 20
American Institutes for Research: test, 1588
American Mathematical Association of Two Year Colleges: test, 151, 153, 154
The American Occupational Therapy Association, Inc: test, 156
American Psychiatric Association: test, 2077
American Statistical Association: test, 151, 153, 154
Ames, L. B.: test, 1071
Ammer, J. J.: test, 326, 1140
Ammons, C. H.: rev, 3, 646, 1556, 2013, 2528, 2756; test, 2115
Ammons, R. B.: rev, 3, 646, 1556, 2528; test, 2115

Amori, B.: test, 1295
Amori, B. A.: test, 1215, 1216
Amundson, N.: test, 1232
Anastasi, A.: rev, 58, 477, 566, 790, 1084, 1342, 1819, 1928, 2411, 2653
Anastasiow, N. J.: rev, 2091
Anastopoulos, A. D.: test, 68
Anchor, K. N.: rev, 1515, 2473
Anderhalter, O. F.: test, 904, 2260
Anderson, D. O.: rev, 1025, 1577, 1747, 2735
Anderson, G. V.: rev, 2762
Anderson, H. R.: rev, 593, 601
Anderson, I. H.: rev, 809, 1607, 2749, 2750
Anderson, J. O.: rev, 397, 398, 399, 402, 468, 1175, 2278
Anderson, K. E.: rev, 44, 55
Anderson, P. D.: test, 88, 1074, 2669
Anderson, R. G.: test, 1383
Anderson, R. P.: rev, 659
Anderson, T. D.: test, 958, 1250, 1321, 1415, 1916, 2114, 2219, 2439
Anderson, V.: test, 2591
Andersson, L.: rev, 662
Andreasen, N. C.: test, 657, 2228, 2229, 2230
Andrellos, P. J.: test, 1869
Andrew, D. M.: test, 1649
Andrews, D.: test, 1449
Andrews, D. A.: test, 1448, 1450, 2842
Andrews, J. V.: rev, 260, 817, 2525
Annis, H. M.: test, 859, 1275, 1276, 2342
Ansley, T. N.: test, 1288, 1292
Ansorge, C. J.: rev, 566
Anthony, J.: test, 1002, 1003
Anton, W. D.: test, 575, 938
Antoni, M.: test, 1638
Apfel, N. H.: test, 1237
Arbisi, P. A.: rev, 275, 1155, 1700, 1917, 1981, 2245, 2300, 2349, 2451
Archambault, F. X., Jr.: rev, 1691, 2561
Archer, D.: test, 711, 2042
Archer, P.: test, 779
Archer, R. P.: rev, 1655; test, 1654
Arditti, J. A.: rev, 41
Arena, J.: test, 2111, 2113, 2801
Argulewicz, E. N.: rev, 2237
Arick, J. R.: test, 234, 1378
Arlin, P. K.: test, 185
Armstrong, J.: test, 81
Arnold, G. F.: rev, 1447
Arnold, K. D.: test, 2366
Arnold, P. D.: test, 1953
Aronow, E.: rev, 128
Arreola, R.: rev, 1818
Arreola, R. A.: rev, 1217, 1376, 1600, 1629, 2536
Artese, V. S.: test, 2792
Arthaud, T. J.: test, 222, 286, 287, 926, 930
Arthur, W., Jr.: test, 230

Beringer, M. L.: test, 315

Berk, R. A.: rev, 358, 1166, 1526, 1592, 2311, 2410, 2432, 2736; test, 766

Berkay, P. J.: test, 1796

Berke, S.: test, 537

Berlin, L. J.: test, 2012

Berna, J. M.: test, 1709

Bernard, H.: rev, 640, 2722

Bernardin, H. J.: rev, 1403, 1492, 1524, 1793, 2511

Bernberg, R. E.: test, 1206, 2811

Berndt, D. J.: test, 1703, 1704

Berndt, R. S.: rev, 337, 635

Bernet, M.: test, 2340

Bernier, J. J.: rev, 402, 816

Berninger, V. W.: test, 2033

Bernstein, D. P.: test, 461

Bernt, F.: rev, 1532

Bernt, F. M.: rev, 440, 444, 457, 803, 1631, 2732

Bernthal, J. E.: test, 243

Berntson, B.: test, 200

Berry, S. R.: test, 2838

Berryman, J. D.: rev, 2390, 2457

Bers, S. A.: test, 781

Bessai, F.: rev, 684, 987, 1695, 1784, 1866, 2047

The Best Plus Development Team: test, 317

Betz, N. E.: test, 413, 1547, 2808

Betz, W.: rev, 1333

Beukelman, D. R.: test, 207

Beukes, D. P. M.: test, 1171

Beyer, F. S.: test, 214, 839

Biedenstein, J. J.: test, 2398

Bienvenu, M.: test, 192

Bienvenu, M. J.: test, 1265, 1274, 1280, 1530, 1834, 1839, 1999, 2292, 2321

Bierer, B. A.: test, 1954

Biersdorf, K. C.: test, 2084

Bigby, Havis, & Associates, Inc.: test, 193, 2221, 2281

Biggs, J.: rev, 248, 1437; test, 1430

Bigler, E. D.: test, 546, 2602

Bigsby, R.: test, 1983

Bilder, R.: test, 977

Billingslea, F. Y.: rev, 311

Bills, M. A.: rev, 11, 58, 533, 1284

Binder, L. M.: test, 1973

Biofeedback Certification Institute of America: test, 322

Birch, L. B.: rev, 402, 2411

Bird, E.: test, 959

Birkman, R. W.: test, 324

Birnbaum, R. K.: rev, 1944

Bischoff, H.: rev, 137

Bischoff, H. G. W.: rev, 840

Bischoff, L.: rev, 1006, 1850

Bischoff, L. G.: rev, 367, 453, 882, 1198, 1837

Bishop, D.: test, 2570

Biskin, B. H.: rev, 2425

Bisno, A.: test, 2382

Bittner, R. H.: rev, 1153, 1578

Bjerstedt, A.: rev, 907

Black, D. D.: test, 2263

Black, J. D.: rev, 2503, 2618

Blackman, J. A.: test, 1872

Blackwell, M.: rev, 1962, 2669

Blackwell, M. W.: rev, 284, 1424

Blair, K. A.: rev, 191, 326, 1032, 2170

Blakeley, R. W.: test, 2271

Blakemore, C. B.: rev, 311

Blalock, G.: test, 1109

Blanchard, K.: test, 1403

Blank, M.: test, 2012

Blatt, S. J.: test, 213, 781

Blinkhorn, S.: test, 127, 2049

Bliss, L. S.: rev, 243, 2137, 2175, 2691; test, 2270, 2309

Blitchington, W. P.: test, 2560

Blixt, S.: rev, 1435

Bloch, J. S.: test, 1032

Block, J.: rev, 991; test, 379, 386

Block, M. E.: rev, 797

Block-Pedego, A.: test, 2252

Bloom, B. S.: rev, 622

Bloom, L.: rev, 810, 900

Bloom, L. A.: rev, 293

Bloomer, J.: test, 269

Bloomer, R. H.: test, 327, 2130

Bloxom, B.: rev, 1027, 1905

Bloxam, B. M.: rev, 2346, 2349

Blum, L. H.: test, 631

Blum, M.: test, 1499

Blumenthal, J. A.: rev, 1377

Bly, L.: test, 1679

Boatwright, B. S.: test, 542, 543

Bobish, T. P.: test, 1856

Bochna, C. R.: rev, 1043

Bock, S. J.: test, 191

Bodden, J. L.: rev, 407, 408, 1386

Boder, E.: test, 329

Bodey, W.: test, 799

Boehm, A. E.: rev, 358; test, 330, 331, 570

Boer, D. P.: test, 2322

Boggs, S. R.: test, 866

Bohan, K.: rev, 2393

Bohan, K. J.: rev, 1650

Bolen, L. M.: rev, 1680, 2658

Boliek, C. A.: rev, 311, 1647

Boll, T.: test, 469, 804

Boll, T. J.: test, 2331

Boller, F.: test, 2315

Bologna, N. B.: rev, 696, 809, 1677, 1697

Bolser, C.: test, 652

Bolton, B.: rev, 93, 156, 279, 385, 1286, 2825; test, 936, 2818, 2827

Bolton, B. F.: rev, 1633, 1920, 2340, 2346, 2349, 2654

Bolton, D. L.: rev, 410, 1249, 1360, 2643

Bond, D.: test, 333
Bond, G. L.: rev, 862
Bond, N. A., Jr.: test, 868
Bonner, M.: rev, 278, 544, 1349
Bonner, S.: rev, 12, 311
Bonta, J.: test, 1449
Bonta, J. L.: test, 1448, 1450
Bookbinder, G. E.: test, 2222
Booker, G.: test, 332, 333
Booker, I. A.: rev, 1726, 1727
Boone, D. R.: rev, 337
Booth, S. B.: test, 1207
Boothroyd, R. A.: rev, 347, 493, 704, 787, 1105, 1340, 1673, 1840, 2316
Bordin, E. S.: rev, 907, 218, 1284, 2445, 2618
Borgen, F. H.: rev, 365, 1222, 2461, 2689; test, 1652, 2445
Borko, H.: rev, 2666, 2762
Borman, C.: rev, 323, 1774
Borman, W. C.: rev, 1508, 2205
Bornstein, R. A.: rev, 766, 771, 1647, 2009
Borofsky, G. L.: test, 943
Borreca, C.: test, 2786
Borstelmann, L. J.: rev, 1070
Bortner, M.: rev, 3, 730, 1621, 2122, 2404, 2749, 2750
Botwin, M. D.: rev, 128, 1729
Bouchard, T. J., Jr.: rev, 265, 835, 2346, 2349
Boucher, J.: test, 2612
Bountress, N. G.: rev, 1462
Bouwkamp, J. C.: rev, 989, 2347
Bowers, J. E.: rev, 600
Bowers, L.: test, 2613, 2804
Bowling Green State University: test, 2511
Boyatzis, R.: test, 928
Boyatzis, R. E.: test, 65, 1431
Boyce, B. A.: rev, 129, 1983
Boyle, G. J.: rev, 188, 268, 1262, 1310, 1370, 1458, 1828, 1923, 1929, 2194, 2200, 2531, 2676
Boyle, J.: test, 886
Boyle, J. D.: rev, 1132, 1706
Boyles, E. K.: rev, 348, 2128
Boys, M.: test, 1818
Braaten, S.: test, 299, 1387
Bracken, B. A.: rev, 489, 2079, 2082, 2174, 2756; test, 339, 340, 542, 543, 544, 545, 1691, 2688
Braden, J. P.: rev, 229, 1342, 1796, 2749, 2750, 2756
Bradford, E. G.: rev, 1041
Bradford, E. J. G.: rev, 2328
Bradley, J. M.: rev, 2632
Bradley, P.: test, 385, 1934
Bradley, R. H.: rev, 1070; test, 1191
Bradley-Johnson, S.: test, 197;, 565
Brady, M.: test, 1315
Brady, R. P.: test, 849, 2815;, 2845
Bramson, R. M.: test, 1246
Brandt, J.: test, 1195, 2556
Brandt, P.: test, 1911

Brannigan, G. G.: test, 311
Braskamp, L. A.: test, 1249, 1809, 2814
Braswell, J.: rev, 2635
Braun, J. R.: rev, 2094
Bray, G. B.: test, 1291
Brayfield, A. H.: rev, 841
Brazelton, T. B.: test, 1730
Breecher, S. V. A.: test, 2274
Bresnick, B.: test, 779
Brewer, J. H.: test, 316, 2496
Brickenkamp, R.: test, 754
Bricker, D.: test, 129, 130
Bricklin, B.: rev, 911; test, 16, 342, 844, 1193, 1837, 1843, 1881
Bridges, A. F.: test, 1161
Bridges, D.: test, 2841
Briere, J.: test, 568, 787, 1273, 1702;, 2676, 2677, 2678
Brigance, A.: test, 354
Brigance, A. H.: test, 351, 352, 353, 355, 356, 357, 358, 359
Briggs, K. C.: test, 1710, 1711
Briggs, S.: test, 2373
Briggs-Gowan, M. J.: test, 1300
Brighouse, A.: test, 1959
Brimer, M. A.: rev, 1723
Bringsjord, E. L.: rev, 378, 1401
Brinkman, J. J., Jr.: rev, 172, 1339, 1734, 2195
Britton, G.: test, 1709
Brody, L. E.: rev, 2052
Brogden, H. E.: rev, 2793
Brookhart, S. M.: rev, 682, 1291, 1891, 2186, 2634
Brookings, J.: test, 2827
Brookings, J. B.: rev, 2496, 2542
Brooks, G. C., Jr.: test, 2341
Browder, D.: rev, 1057
Brown, A. S.: rev, 52
Brown, C. E.: test, 74
Brown, C. M.: rev, 1949
Brown, D. T.: rev, 1303, 1636
Brown, E. R.: test, 2120
Brown, F.: rev, 2289, 2486
Brown, F. G.: rev, 1381, 2410, 2563
Brown, G.: test, 963
Brown, G. K.: test, 273, 275
Brown, G. S.: test, 1800, 2840
Brown, J. A.: rev, 131, 2732
Brown, J. D.: rev, 179, 949, 1216, 1464, 2626
Brown, J. F.: test, 1438
Brown, J. I.: test, 1726, 1727
Brown, L.: test, 61, 293, 2291, 2606
Brown, L. H.: test, 2307
Brown, L. J.: test, 2263
Brown, L. L.: rev, 737, 834, 1370, 2169
Brown, M. B.: rev, 409, 696, 1459, 1764, 2289
Brown, R.: rev, 195, 246, 638, 816, 1088, 1370, 1438, 1659, 2561; test, 908
Brown, R. D.: rev, 9, 624, 1430, 2297, 2402

Craig, J. R.: test, 1685
Craig, P.: test, 1685
Cramp, L.: test, 1499
Crane, B. J.: test, 724, 739
Cranny, C. J.: rev, 2683
Crase, S. J.: test, 1289, 1290
Crawford, D. H.: rev, 1125
Crawford, D. M.: test, 725
Crawford, J.: rev, 2252
Crawford, J. E.: test, 725
Crawford, W. R.: rev, 48, 55
Crehan, K. D.: rev, 180, 258, 818, 1089, 1439, 1456, 2053, 2113, 2527, 2583
Creighton, M. M.: rev, 2248
Crespo, D.: rev, 454
Crimmins, D. B.: test, 1673
Critchlow, D. D.: test, 852
Crites, J. O.: rev, 385, 937, 1086, 1313, 1726, 1727, 1928, 2216, 2289, 2445, 2529, 2561, 2742, 2743
Crocker, L.: rev, 83, 495, 548, 2417, 2598, 2797, 2798
Crocker, L. M.: rev, 547
Croft, C.: test, 24, 370, 963, 2061
Cronbach, L. J.: rev, 385, 600, 2411, 2503
Cronin, M. E.: test, 1140, 2600
Cronkite, R. C.: test, 1156
Croon, C. W.: rev, 2639
Crosbie, S.: test, 2001, 2005
Crosby, B.: test, 1877
Crosby, G.: test, 1877
Crosby, L. A.: rev, 1092
Cross, L. H.: rev, 1291, 1314, 1865, 2810
Crosson, B.: test, 2448, 2718
Crow, L. D.: test, 1064, 1067, 1069, 1157
Cruickshank, W. M.: rev, 2708
Cruise, R. J.: test, 2560
Crumbaugh, J. C.: test, 2094, 2279
Crumpler, M.: test, 362, 2129
Crumpton, N. L.: rev, 1108, 2290
Crumrine, L.: test, 1944, 1998
Crutchley, A.: test, 203
Cryer, D.: test, 880, 1239
CTB Macmillan/McGraw-Hill: test, 378, 740, 792, 2387, 2637
CTB/McGraw-Hill: test, 383, 384, 1042, 1043, 1044, 1285, 1390, 1391, 2563, 2636, 2638
Cull, J. G.: test, 2485
Cullbertson, W. C.: test, 2663
Cullen, T. J., Jr.: rev, 554, 571
Cullinan, D.: test, 2227
Cummings, J. A.: rev, 199, 266, 399, 986, 1224, 2449, 2795, 2795
Cummings, R.: rev, 355, 1463
Cummins, J.: test, 321
Cundick, B. C.: rev, 346, 347
Cundick, B. P.: rev, 1188, 1367
Cunnington, B. F.: test, 2649
Cureton, E. E.: rev, 1153

Curlette, W. L.: rev, 135, 683, 906; test, 264, 705
Curtis, F. D.: rev, 1069
Curtis, J. W.: test, 738, 744, 745, 746
Curtis, M. J.: rev, 1120
Curtiss, G.: test, 2787
Cutlan, S. L.: rev, 1614
Cutler, A.: test, 416, 1314, 1488
Cutts, C. C.: rev, 2289
Czerlinsky, T.: test, 2723

D'Amato, R.: rev, 687
D'Amato, R. C.: rev, 93, 302, 760, 1159, 1170, 2411, 2751
D'Costa, A. G.: rev, 67, 425, 1201, 1315
D'Costa, A.: rev, 417, 1610, 2401
D'Elia, L. F.: test, 470, 629, 1738
D'Eugenio, D. B.: test, 884, 2010
D'Zurilla, T. J.: test, 2371
Dabul, B. L.: test, 172
Dahl, P. A.: rev, 47
Dahl, T. A.: rev, 330
Dahlstrom, W. G.: rev, 218, 925; test, 1655
Daiger, D.: test, 1708
Dailey, J. T.: rev, 600, 1098, 1622
Dale, J. A.: rev, 2582
Dalton, E. F.: test, 1215, 1216, 1295
Dalton, M.: test, 1441, 2353
Daly, E. J., III: rev, 212
Damarin, F.: rev, 271, 438, 727
Dana, R. H.: rev, 2187, 2645
Dancu, C. V.: test, 2369
Dander, D.: rev, 835
Daniel, L. G.: rev, 486, 1674
Daniel, M. H.: rev, 26, 397, 1560, 1608, 2030, 2067, 2289
Danzer, V. A.: test, 755
Darkin, L.: test, 799
Darley, J. G.: rev, 2445
Darnell, R. E.: rev, 809
Darr, C.: test, 2052
Darr, R. F., Jr.: rev, 1511, 1836, 2047, 2514, 2655
Das, J. P.: rev, 1205; test, 756
Davidshofer, C.: rev, 1303
Davidson, J.: test, 759
Davidson, L.S.: test, 2398
Davis, A. S.: rev, 470, 687, 760, 2197
Davis, B.: rev, 270, 892, 2066
Davis, C.: test, 2670
Davis, C. C.: rev, 531, 595
Davis, C. D.: test, 2232
Davis, C. S.: test, 1275
Davis, D. R.: rev, 975
Davis, E. E.: rev, 1556
Davis, F. B.: rev, 595, 600, 1383
Davis, G. A.: test, 1122
Davis, G. N.: test, 2608
Davis, M. S.: test, 130

Davis, R.: test, 1636, 1639
Davis, S. E.: rev, 1952
Davis, S. F.: rev, 202, 644, 696, 958, 1493, 1832, 2297
Davison, M.: test, 765
Davison, M. L.: rev, 2410, 2600
Dawes, R. M.: rev, 1120
Dawis, R. V.: test, 1651, 1652, 1656, 1657
Dawson, J. I.: test, 2456
Day, L. S.: rev, 2390
De Ayala, R. J.: rev, 2028
de la Fuente, J. R.: test, 137
de la Mare, M.: test, 2129
de Lemos, M.: test, 1210, 2772
de Lemos, M. M.: test, 32, 834
de Villiers, J.: test, 820, 821
de Villiers, P. A.: test, 821
Dean, E.: test, 1603
Dean, G. J.: rev, 205, 1021, 1513, 1675, 1812, 1853, 1902, 1920
Dean, R. S.: rev, 172, 334, 838, 1137, 1339, 1372, 1734, 2195; test, 761
Deardorff, W. W.: rev, 230, 2642, 2657
Deaton, W. L.: rev, 814, 2328, 2769
DeAvila, E. A.: test, 90, 1388, 1389, 1995
DeBoe, J.: test, 2448, 2718
DeBoer, A.: test, 1269
DeBruin-Parecki, A.: test, 887
Decker, S. L.: test, 311
Decoster, D. A.: rev, 624
Deen, C. C.: test, 1452
Deeney, T.: test, 2256
Defense Activity for Non-Traditional Education Support: test, 861
Deffenbacher, J. L.: test, 2564
DeFilippis, N. A.: test, 334
deFur, S. H.: rev, 807, 2417, 2585, 2594
DeFuria, G. L.: test, 1270
DeGangi, G. A.: test, 1240, 2615, 766
Dehne, P.: test, 1618
DeLawyer, D. D.: test, 1841
Delis, D.: test, 2750
Delis, D. C.: test, 387, 388, 770, 2733
Della Sala, S.: test, 2717
Della-Piana, C. K.: rev, 198, 1476, 1747
Della-Piana, G. M.: rev, 198, 1061, 1255, 2284
Dellarosa, D. M.: test, 876
Deloria, D. J.: rev, 1623
Delp, H. A.: rev, 2749, 2750
Deluty, R. H.: rev, 1566
Demakis, G. J.: rev, 686
Demaree, R. G.: rev, 676, 1014, 2529
DeMauro, G. E.: rev, 297, 817, 1247, 1370, 1701, 2298, 2527, 2606, 2632
Demorest, M. E.: rev, 1562
Denckla, M. B.: test, 2121
DeNicolis, J.: rev, 1747
Denison, J. W.: rev, 2625

Deno, E.: rev, 2354
Denzine, G. M.: rev, 843, 1247, 1821
DePaola, S. J.: rev, 546, 1772
Department of Testing Services: test, 400, 772
Dermen, D.: test, 1371
Derogatis, L. R.: test, 344, 346, 347, 782, 783, 784, 785, 786, 2086, 2268, 2518
DeSoto, C. B.: test, 1535, 1736
DeSoto, J. L.: test, 1535, 1736
DeStefano, L.: rev, 1819, 1927, 2246
Detterman, D. K.: rev, 2364, 2749, 2750
Developmental Therapy Institute, Inc.: test, 807
DeVillafranca, E. F.: rev, 48
Devine, D. W.: test, 814
DeVito, A. J.: rev, 1710, 1711
DeVries, R.: rev, 678
DeWire, H.: test, 2646
Dewson, M.: test, 2577
Deysach, R. E.: rev, 136, 822
DeZolt, D. M.: rev, 447, 894, 1868, 1966, 2158
Dial, J. G.: test, 927, 1555, 1773, 1883, 2499
Diamond, E. E.: rev, 428, 570, 904, 1750, 1911, 2127, 2289; test, 1381
Diaz, J. O. P.: rev, 173, 806
Diaz, P.: rev, 286, 1189
Dibenedetto, B.: test, 763
DiCarlo, L. M.: rev, 975, 2763
DiCerbo, P. A.: test, 94
Dicken, C. F.: rev, 1087
Dickens, S. E.: test, 2454
Dickey, S. E.: test, 1950
Dickson, G. S.: rev, 2445
Diefendorf, A. O.: rev, 1184, 1603, 2578
Diekhoff, J. S.: rev, 105
DiGiuseppe, R.: test, 163
Dilchert, S.: rev, 929, 1079
Dill, S.: test, 832
DiMatteo, R.: test, 711, 2042
Dinero, T. E.: rev, 789, 1774
Dings, J. G.: rev, 848
DiPerna, J. C.: rev, 69, 283, 458, 566; test, 12, 14
DiSimoni, F.: test, 2660
Disorbio, J. M.: test, 268
Dittes, J. E.: test, 2646
Division of Testing and Certification: test, 1613
Dixon, D. N.: rev, 683, 1532, 1703, 2031, 2116, 2454
Dobbins, G. H.: rev, 1608, 1903, 2037, 2541
Dobson, B.: test, 1613
Dobson, K. S.: rev, 1767
Docter, R. F.: rev, 1972
Dodd, B.: test, 2001, 2005
Dodds, J.: test, 779
Doebler, L. K.: rev, 25
Doggett, R. A.: rev, 208, 291, 933, 1539
Doherty, V. W.: test, 2234
Doig, B.: test, 30, 31, 824, 1210, 2525, 2772

Esonis, S.: test, 1040
Espenschade, A.: rev, 366, 1461
Espey, L.: test, 1492
Espy, K. A.: test, 291
Estroff, T. W.: test, 1990
Ethington, C. A.: test, 640
Euhardy, R.: test, 209
Evans, A. S.: test, 2064, 2067
Evans, D. R.: test, 2102
Evans, J.: test, 731
Evans, J. J.: test, 302, 391; rev, 2447
Evans-Fernandez, S. E.: test, 2465
Evard, B. L.: rev, 2109
Ewing, C. A.: rev, 40, 1980
Exner, J. E., Jr.: rev, 386
Eyberg, S. M.: test, 866, 989, 2647
Eyde, L. D.: rev, 73, 2333, 2601
Eysenck, H. J.: rev, 385, 1188, 1444, 1655, 2187, 2652; test, 990, 991
Eysenck, S. B. G.: test, 990, 991, 1332

Fabry, J.: rev, 1596, 1699, 1807
Facione, N. C.: test, 381
Facione, P. A.: test, 381, 382
Fad, K. M.: test, 39
Fager, J. J.: rev, 1217, 1595, 1865, 2588, 2621
Fairbank, D. W.: rev, 235, 286, 288, 802, 2003, 2010, 2019, 2139, 2306
Falender, C. A.: test, 1564, 1575
Faltin, S.: rev, 2184
Fandal, A. W.: test, 1192
Fanjiang, G.: test, 1648
Fardig, D.: test, 2254
Farley, F. H.: rev, 2410
Farmer, R. F.: rev, 810, 275, 2320, 2761
Farnum, S. E.: test, 1008, 2739
Farr, B.: test, 1255
Farr, J. M.: test, 1134
Farr, M.: test, 406
Farr, R.: test, 1255
Farrah, G. A.: test, 2286
Farrell, J.: test, 129
Farrell, R. J., II: rev, 473, 475
Farrell-Holtan, J.: test, 209
Fasiska, E. J.: test, 957
Fassbinder, W.: rev, 1697
Fast, C. G.: test, 1009
Fastenau, P. S.: test, 988
Faulkner, G.: test, 2439
Faunce, R. W.: rev, 1492, 2474, 2655
Fauth, J.: rev, 956
Fawcett, A. J.: test, 873, 875, 2135
Fawcett, A.: test, 871, 2018
Fawcett, H. P.: rev, 2742, 2743
Fawkes, D.: test, 1305
Fay, K.: rev, 1198
Feil, E. G.: test, 896

Fein, D.: test, 2733, 2750
Fein, E. C.: rev, 1162, 2337
Feinburg, H.: rev, 790
Feiring, C.: rev, 1353
Feldt, L. S.: rev, 531; test, 1292
Felsenfeld, S.: rev, 2456
Feltham, D. W.: test, 2202
Felton, R.: test, 2800
Fensch, E. A.: test, 2758
Fentiman, J.: test, 2382
Fenton, R.: rev, 388, 2066, 2609
Ferguson, G. A.: rev, 132
Ferguson, L. W.: rev, 2332
Fernandez, E.: rev, 388, 1139, 2479, 2678
Ferrara, F. F.: rev, 675, 981, 1170, 1827
Ferrara, S.: rev, 206, 263, 2747
Ferraro, M.: test, 1722
Ferro, T. R.: rev, 685, 1111, 1634, 1887, 1902, 2761
Ferry, F.: test, 416, 1314, 1488
Fewell, R. R.: test, 795, 1864
Field, J. A., Jr.: rev, 123
File, Q. W.: test, 1200
Filter, M. D.: rev, 876, 2729
Finch, A. J., Jr.: test, 474
Finch, A. M.: test, 1799
Finch, W. H.: rev, 470, 2197
Finch-Williams, A.: rev, 83
Findley, D. B.: rev, 1420
Findley, W. G.: rev, 57, 126, 378, 622, 1604, 2563, 2639
Fink, J. J.: test, 1920
Fink, L.: test, 461
Fink, S. R.: rev, 505
Finley, C. J.: rev, 1355, 1604
Finney, J. W.: test, 1156
Firestone, G.: test, 1264
Firestone, L. A.: test, 1026
Firestone, R. W.: test, 1026
Firestone, W. A.: test, 2253
First, M. B.: test, 2265, 2450, 2451
Fischer, M. A.: rev, 21, 1325
Fishco, V. V.: test, 1726, 1727
Fisher, D. J.: test, 1126
Fisher, H. B.: test, 1030
Fisher, J. P.: test, 1208
Fisher, K. A.: test, 1126
Fisher, P.: test, 1818
Fishman, J. A.: rev, 2653
Fiske, D. W.: rev, 907
Fiszbein, A.: test, 1979
Fitts, W. H.: test, 2561
Fitzgerald, J. A.: rev, 2400
Fitzmaurice, C.: rev, 330
Fitzpatrick, A. R.: rev, 89, 263
Fitzpatrick, C.: rev, 74, 289, 2000, 2119
Fitzpatrick, R.: rev, 365, 535, 1063, 1316, 1538, 1861, 2252, 2254, 2498, 2706, 2726, 2819

Fivars, G.: test, 551, 2526
Flage, D.: test, 1305
Flanagan, D. P.: rev, 1341, 1955, 2111, 2168, 2189
Flanagan, J. C.: rev, 2764; test, 551, 1033, 1034, 2526
Flanagan, R.: rev, 33, 81, 458, 1273, 2173, 2262
Flanagan, S. G.: rev, 1703
Flanagan, S.: test, 238
Fleenor, J. W.: rev, 628, 815, 1046, 1148, 1214, 1288, 1317, 1553, 1710, 1711, 1884
Fleishman, E.: test, 1411
Fleishman, E. A.: test, 1035, 2488
Fletcher, J.: test, 2673
Fletcher, R.: test, 490
Flett, G. L.: test, 1690
Floden, R. E.: rev, 250
Flory, C. D.: rev, 1938, 1939, 2793
Flowerday, T.: rev, 648, 2013
Fluharty, N. B.: test, 1037
Flury, S.: test, 2095
Foa, E. B.: test, 1982
Foertsch, D. J.: test, 1856
Fogle, P. T.: test, 2188
Fogli, L.: test, 2312
Foley, J.: test, 391
Foley, J. P., Jr.: rev, 1656, 2205, 2793
Folio, M. R.: test, 1864
Folkman, S.: test, 1152, 2744
Folstein, M. F.: test, 1648, 2556
Folstein, S. E.: test, 1648
Fontaine, J. H.: rev, 426
Fontana, M. C.: rev, 1030
Ford, D.: rev, 80
Ford, J. S.: test, 937
Ford, L.: rev, 1348, 2139
Ford, M. E.: test, 211
Forer, B. R.: rev, 218, 1188; test, 1039
Forest, C.: test, 653
Forest, R. G.: test, 650, 651
Fornoff, F. J.: rev, 44, 47, 48, 49, 55
Forster, M.: test, 799, 800
Forsyth, D.: test, 1403
Forsyth, R. A.: rev, 1726, 1727; test, 1292
Forth, A. E.: test, 1148
Fortune, J.: rev, 905
Fortune, J. C.: rev, 1719, 1747, 1968
Foss, G.: test, 2594
Foster, C.: test, 1466
Foster, F. M.: test, 138
Fouche, F. A.: test, 1746, 1951, 2301
Fournier, D. G.: test, 2000
Fox, E. E.: test, 1231
Fox, G.: rev, 306, 1185, 1875; test, 722
Fox, L. H.: rev, 1285, 2649
Fox, R. A.: rev, 2007
Francis, J.: test, 1918
Francis, J. L.: test, 1894
Frank, A.: test, 2352

Frank, A. C.: rev, 1136
Frank, M. L. B.: rev, 1532, 2100
Frankenburg, W. K.: test, 775, 776, 777, 778, 779, 1192
Fransella, F.: test, 1112
Frantz, T. T.: rev, 2202
Franzen, M. D.: rev, 2165
Franzoi, S. L.: rev, 1264
Frary, R. B.: rev, 266, 852, 1088, 1622, 2156, 2599
Fraser, E. D.: rev, 2411, 2749, 2750
Fraser, S. L.: test, 751
Frattali, C.: test, 635
Frederick, R. I.: rev, 2119; test, 2692
Frederick, R.: rev, 368
Fredericks, H. D. B.: test, 2232
Frederickson, N.: test, 1947
Frederiksen, N.: rev, 835, 1033
Freeberg, N. E.: test, 964
Freeman, B. J.: rev, 33, 2756
Freeman, F. S.: rev, 330
Freeman, S. J.: rev, 1593, 2149, 2425, 2704, 2712
Freides, D.: rev, 2411, 2749, 2750
Freitag, P. K.: rev, 648, 1778
French, B. F.: rev, 689, 1713
French, J. L.: test, 1955
French, J. W.: rev, 868, 1284, 1880, 2486; test, 1371
French, R. L.: rev, 1098, 2728
French, S. J.: rev, 44
Frenken, J.: test, 2323
Freshwater, S. M.: test, 2447
Fressola, D. R.: test, 2395
Fretz, B. R.: rev, 416, 1767
Frey, P. W.: test, 946
Frick, P. J.: test, 166, 658
Fricke, B. G.: rev, 599, 1087, 1165
Fridlund, A. J.: test, 387
Friedland, J. G.: test, 37, 2203
Friedlander, J.: test, 640
Friedman, J. L.: test, 1032
Friedman, L.: test, 2673
Friedman, M. I.: test, 554, 1993
Friedman, P. H.: test, 1046
Friedrich, W. N.: test, 457
Friend, M.: rev, 1841
Friesen, W. V.: test, 993
Frintrup, A.: test, 36
Frisbie, D. A.: rev, 126, 622; test, 1291, 2104
Frisch, M. B.: test, 2101
Frisell, W. R.: rev, 43
Fristad, M. A.: test, 473
Fristoe, M.: test, 1082, 1083
Frith, U.: test, 1947
Fritzsche, B. A.: test, 2289
Froehlich, G. J.: rev, 1292, 2639
Froemel, E. C.: test, 981
Fromm, D.: test, 635
Frost, M. D.: test, 1162, 1761

Gilmer, J. S.: rev, 772
Gilmore, A.: test, 370, 2061
Gilmore, E. C.: test, 1078
Gilmore, G.: rev, 1660
Gilmore, J. V.: test, 1078
Gimpel, G. A.: test, 70
Ginsburg, H. P.: test, 2583
Gioia, G. A.: test, 289, 290, 291, 292
Giraud, G.: rev, 2468
Gittens, T.: test, 235
Glascoe, F. P.: test, 351, 353, 356, 357, 359, 1850
Glaser, E. M.: test, 2742, 2743
Glasgow, C.: test, 2148
Glass, G. V: rev, 2507
Glazer, W. M.: test, 2532
Glenister, J. M.: test, 1208
Glenn, H. W.: rev, 222, 249
Gleser, G. C.: rev, 95, 692, 1141, 2076
Glock, M. D.: rev, 155
Glover, J. A.: rev, 2066; test, 654
Glover, M. E.: test, 1421
Glutting, J.: test, 574, 2466, 2778
Glutting, J. J.: test, 1135, 2779
Gnagey, P. A.: test, 158, 825, 826, 828
Gnagey, T. D.: test, 158, 825, 826, 827, 828, 829
Godber, D.: test, 1959
Goddard, H. H.: test, 2280
The Godfrey Thomson Unit, University of Edinburgh: test, 902, 903, 2334
Goff, K.: test, 4
Gold, J. M.: rev, 1277
Goldberg, D.: rev, 2020
Goldberg, E.: test, 977
Goldberg, L. R.: rev, 385, 1302
Golden, C. J.: rev, 2165; test, 1479, 1480, 2273, 2447
Golden, S. B., Jr.: test, 1012
Golden, Z.: test, 2447
Goldenberg, D. S.: test, 802, 1852
Golding, E.: test, 1617
Golding, S. L.: rev, 2083, 2485
Goldman, B.: test, 1116
Goldman, B. A.: rev, 287, 318, 415, 565, 566, 1063, 1131, 1819, 2577
Goldman, R.: test, 1082, 1083
Goldschmid, M. L.: rev, 566; test, 678
Goldstein, A. D.: test, 777
Goleman, D.: test, 928
Gonyea, R. M.: test, 1721
Gonzalez, C.: rev, 2468
Gonzalez, J. E.: rev, 2388, 2468
Good, K. C.: test, 1011, 1012, 1013, 1565, 1568, 1569, 1570, 1675
Good, L. R.: test, 1011, 1012, 1013, 1565, 1568, 1569, 1570, 1675
Good, R. H., III: test, 832
Goodenough, F. L.: test, 1084
Goodglass, H.: test, 337

Goodman, J. F.: rev, 1960
Goodstein, J.: test, 1810
Goodstein, L. D.: rev, 1119, 2428, 2503; test, 1494, 1586, 1965, 2620
Goodwin, W. L.: rev, 454
Gorall, D.: test, 992
Gordon, B. N.: rev, 2050
Gordon, E. E.: test, 97, 147, 1149, 1252, 1260, 1293, 1707, 2024
Gordon, H. C.: rev, 1726, 1727
Gordon, L. V.: test, 1669, 2255, 2503, 2507
Gordon, M.: test, 1085, 1086, 1087
Gordon, S. E.: test, 2434
Gorham, D. R.: test, 1188
Gormly, J. B.: rev, 1574
Gorsuch, R.L.: test, 2426
Gory, E. L.: rev, 279, 353
Gottesman, R. L.: test, 913
Gottfredson, G. D.: test, 409, 1978
Gottfried, A.: test, 463
Gotts, E. E.: rev, 327, 674, 2110
Gottschalk, L. A.: test, 2074
Gough, H. G.: rev, 477, 728, 910, 2146, 2541; test, 71, 385, 444, 718, 1934
Goyer, R. S.: test, 1088
Grace, J.: test, 1047
Graduate Management Admission Council: test, 1092
Graduate Record Examination Board: test, 1997
Graham, C. R.: rev, 319
Graham, J. M.: test, 1275;, 2342
Graham, J. R.: rev, 1420; test, 1654, 1655
Graham, S.: rev, 360, 1802, 2572, 2573
Graham, T.: rev, 331, 357, 806, 1210, 2420, 2730
Grant, M.: test, 137
Grantham, L. B.: rev, 986
Gratz, Z. S.: rev, 253, 260, 1543, 2127
Graue, M. E.: rev, 2272
Gray, A. M.: test, 2510
Gray, C.: test, 2717
Gray, C. A.: rev, 806
Gray, H.: test, 1331
Gray, M. J.: test, 1766
Gray, W. A.: test, 1600
Green, C. J.: test, 1637
Green, F. J.: rev, 369, 767, 2066, 2614
Green, K.: rev, 1763
Green, K. E.: rev, 247, 475, 1194, 2695
Green, S. K.: rev, 2669, 2843
Green, W. P.: test, 2802
Greenberg, G. D.: test, 1221
Greenberg, L. M.: test, 2622
Greene, E. B.: rev, 374
Greene, H. A.: rev, 953
Greene, R. W.: test, 1228
Greenspan, S. I.: test, 1110, 2615
Gregg, N.: rev, 1434, 2836
Gregorc, A. F.: test, 1111

Grehan, P.: rev, 481
Greig, M. E.: test, 904
Greis, A. B.: test, 1452
Gresham, F.: rev, 857, 1376, 2749, 2750
Gresham, F. M.: rev, 797, 1849, 2159; test, 2375, 2465
Gries, K.: rev, 587, 613
Griffin, J. R.: test, 872
Griffith, C. L.: test, 1514, 2220, 747
Griffith, F.: rev, 1607
Griffiths, D.: test, 2378
Griffiths, R.: test, 1113
Griggs, L. G.: test, 1918
Grill, J. J.: rev, 5, 287, 76, 659, 802, 896, 926, 1868, 2013, 2303; test, 2837
Grimsley, G.: test, 937
Grobbelaar, P. E.: test, 1951
Groff, P.: rev, 1128
Grognet, A.: test, 256
Gronlund, N. E.: rev, 1604, 2636
Groot, Y.: test, 391
Gross, A. B.: test, 1217
Gross, R. E.: rev, 530
Grossman, F. M.: rev, 872
Grossman, S.: test, 1636, 1638, 1639, 1641
Grossnickle, F. E.: rev, 181
Grote, K.: test, 848
Grotelueschen, A.: rev, 1819
Groves, M. M.: rev, 1238
Gruber, C.: test, 1491, 2182
Gruber, C. P.: test, 1755, 1926, 1927, 2168, 2372, 2460
Grummon, P.: test, 2828
Grundin, H. U.: test, 1209
Gryskiewicz, S. S.: test, 1357
Gudjonsson, G. H.: test, 1133
Guertin, W. H.: rev, 969, 2746
Guest, R. E.: rev, 721
Guglielmino, L. M.: test, 2288
Guglielmino, P. J.: test, 2288
Guidubaldi, J.: test, 267, 1848
Guilford, A. M.: test, 83
Guilford, J. P.: rev, 1098, 1622; test, 144, 692, 868, 1473, 2327
Guion, R. M.: rev, 410, 932, 943, 1087, 1307, 1656, 2035, 2209
Gulati, A.: test, 1312
Gulgoz, S.: rev, 2242, 2405, 2550
Gullickson, A. R.: rev, 824
Gulliksen, H.: rev, 1288, 1817
Gunderson, J. G.: test, 822
Gunning, F.: rev, 2238
Gunning-Dixon, F.: rev, 564
Gunzburg, A. L.: test, 1471
Gunzburg, H. C.: test, 1471, 2050
Guron, L. M.: test, 2805
Gustad, J. W.: rev, 907

Gutenberg, R. L.: rev, 1987
Guthrie, A. M.: test, 640
Guthrie, G.: rev, 540
Gutkin, T. B.: rev, 1426, 2647
Guy, S. C.: test, 289, 292
Guyette, T. W.: rev, 1389, 1392, 2576
Guzzetta, J.: test, 712
Gwartney, N.: rev, 1279
Gynther, M. D.: rev, 385, 1655

Haber, L.: rev, 1388, 1392, 2836
Habicht, M. H.: rev, 871
Haccoun, R. R.: rev, 550, 2148
Hachimi, A.: rev, 179
Hacker, B. J.: test, 433
Hackett, G.: test, 1547
Hadjistavropoulos, T.: test, 553
Haertel, E. H.: rev, 1604
Haertel, G. D.: rev, 561, 1175, 1747
Hafner, H.: test, 1296
Hagan, J. S.: test, 2395
Hagen, E. P.: test, 399, 566
Hagen, E.: rev, 577, 602, 2415
Hagin, R. A.: rev, 15
Hagin, R. A.: rev, 342, 477, 2622
Hagiwara, M. P.: rev, 108, 109, 504
Hagley, F.: test, 2482
Hagues, N.: test, 1465, 1754, 2051, 2701
Hahn, M. E.: rev, 178, 1062
Haines, J.: test, 1071
Hainsworth, M. L.: test, 2017
Hainsworth, P. K.: test, 2017
Hakstian, A. R.: test, 647
Haladyna, T. M.: rev, 17, 1639, 1797, 2410
Halderson, C.: test, 654
Haley, S.: test, 2256
Haley, S. M.: test, 1869
Halinski, R. S.: test, 254
Hall, A. E.: rev, 516, 1119
Hall, B. A.: test, 2191
Hall, C. W.: rev, 1430, 1870, 1914, 2531
Hall, J. N.: test, 2142
Hall, J. W.: rev, 89
Hall, J.: test, 17, 443, 683, 684, 711, 747, 940, 1223, 1406, 1495, 1506, 1508, 1511, 1514, 1515, 1519, 1520, 1714, 1855, 1888, 1903, 1909, 1935, 1986, 1987, 2034, 2042, 2103, 2136, 2210, 2215, 2220, 2473, 2474, 2475, 2498, 2504, 2541, 2543, 2545, 2546, 2813
Hall, L. G.: test, 1136
Hall, P. K.: rev, 183, 2395
Hall, V. C.: rev, 678
Hall, W. B.: rev, 935
Hall, W. E.: rev, 2639
Hallam, G.: test, 393
Haller, R. M.: rev, 183, 1053, 2176
Halligan, P.: test, 304

Halligan, P. W.: test, 2179
Halpern, H.: rev, 1053
Halstead, M. E.: test, 2191
Haltiwanger, J.: test, 2256
Haltiwanger, J. T.: test, 1869
Hambleton, R. K.: rev, 12, 312, 835, 1604, 2752; test, 1403
Hamil, W. L.: rev, 883
Hamilton, M.: test, 1444, 2114
Hamilton, S.: test, 1801
Hamlett, C.: test, 867, 1668
Hammeke, T.: rev, 2165
Hammeke, T. A.: rev, 334; test, 1480
Hammer, A. L.: test, 704, 1710, 1711, 1808, 2445
Hammer, E.: test, 1057
Hammer, E. F.: test, 1202
Hammill, D.: test, 1678
Hammill, D. D.: test, 261, 293, 662, 665, 789, 790, 791, 809, 1049, 1140, 1219, 1426, 1677, 2575, 2582, 2584, 2585, 2597, 2598, 2614, 2616, 2617, 2631, 2632
Hamsher, deS.: test, 1697
Hanawalt, N. G.: rev, 313
Hanburg, H. G.: test, 86
Hancock, T. E.: rev, 2131, 2755
Hand, L.: test, 2362
Handler, L.: rev, 708, 2437
Handley, P.: test, 1248
Handley, R.: test, 246
Hanes, B.: test, 1143
Hanes, K. R.: rev, 277, 559, 889
Haney, W. V.: test, 2684
Hanna, G. S.: rev, 767, 835, 1726, 1727, 1817, 2080, 2356, 2359, 2792
Hanna, L. A.: rev, 1292
Hanna, P. R.: rev, 2410
Hannafin, M. J.: rev, 1460
Hannavy, S.: test, 1616
Hanner, M. A.: test, 1392
Hanschu, B.: test, 2305
Hansen, J. B.: rev, 740, 2631
Hansen, J. C.: test, 2445
Hansen, M. C.: rev, 2332
Hansen, T. L.: test, 1863
Hanson, G.: rev, 1983
Hanson, G. R.: rev, 1092; test, 1873;, 1882
Hanson, R. N.: rev, 2289
Hanson, W. E.: rev, 347, 375, 1801
Harby, M. L.: test, 2571
Harcourt Assessment: test, 2702
Harcourt Assessment, Inc.: test, 1622, 1942, 2410, 2416
Harcourt Brace Educational Measurement: test, 1081, 2413
Harcourt Brace Educational Measurement, a division of The Psychological Corporation: test, 2417
Harcourt Educational Measurement: test, 1605

Harden, L.: test, 78
Harding, R. E.: rev, 314, 1763, 1857, 2192, 2574, 2643, 2651
Hardy, E.: test, 280
Hardy, L. H.: test, 1201
Hare, R. D.: test, 166, 1145, 1146, 1147, 1148
Hargrove, D. S.: rev, 1397, 1538
Haring, T. G.: rev, 63, 1696
Harkin, G. L.: test, 434
Harman, H. H.: test, 1371
Harmon, C.: test, 1801
Harmon, L. W.: rev, 373, 412, 1502, 2350, 2445
Harms, T.: test, 880, 1000, 1239, 2251
Harnisch, D. L.: rev, 31, 576, 1089, 1606, 2107, 2599, 2600
Harper, D. C.: rev, 795, 804, 1792, 2088, 2183, 2439
Harrell, A. V.: test, 82
Harrell, M.: test, 571
Harrell, T. W.: rev, 2093
Harriman, P. L.: rev, 1202
Harrington, R. G.: rev, 3, 165, 1085, 1428, 2469, 2803
Harrington, T. F.: test, 1150
Harris, A. F.: test, 1308, 2821
Harris, A. J.: rev, 1078
Harris, D. B.: rev, 1002, 1003, 1660; test, 1084, 1957
Harris, L. A.: rev, 1291, 2132, 2798
Harris, N. G. S.: test, 338
Harris, W. G.: rev, 2419; test, 2418
Harrison, A. F.: test, 1246
Harrison, P. A.: test, 2480
Harrison, P. L.: rev, 2, 87, 844, 930, 1018, 1460, 1716, 2775; 59, 895, 2708
Harrison, R.: test, 815
Harsh, C. M.: rev, 312, 2346, 2349, 2652
Hart, K.: test, 898
Hart, S. D.: test, 1147, 1155, 2322, 2403
Hart, S. N.: rev, 451, 462, 552, 1898
Hart, V.: rev, 1289, 1681
Harter, S.: test, 1954, 2297
Harting-McChesney, J.: rev, 799
Hartman, B. W.: rev, 186
Hartman, H. J.: rev, 2331
Hartman, J.: test, 2090
Hartman, R. K.: test, 2237
Hartman, R. S.: test, 1151
Hartnett, R. T.: rev, 56
Hartshorne, T. S.: rev, 763, 1563
Hartsough, C.: test, 467
Hartsough, C. S.: rev, 86
Harvey, A. L.: rev, 962, 1747
Harvey, J. B.: test, 1495, 1511, 1515, 2473, 2474
Harvey, R. J.: test, 634
Harvey-Beavis, A.: test, 2290
Harvill, L. M.: rev, 1442, 1942, 2209
Harwell, M.: rev, 260, 2254
Harwell, M. R.: rev, 723, 1313, 1604, 2298, 2741
Hasbrouck, J. E.: test, 2608

Maholick, L. T.: test, 2094
Mahoney, J. J.: test, 2062
Mahoney, J. T.: test, 171, 1229, 1409, 1893, 2211
Mahurin, R. K.: rev, 673, 1114, 1138
Maitlen, B. R.: test, 1230
Majors, M. S.: test, 1711
Makatura, T. J.: rev, 568, 686, 1735, 2149, 2532
Malcolm, K. K.: rev, 232, 331, 713, 914, 1169, 1802, 1803, 1998, 2012, 2431
Malgady, R. G.: test, 2557
Maller, S. J.: rev, 401, 2278, 2602, 2749, 2750, 2841
Mallinson, G.: test, 904
Mallinson, G. G.: rev, 529
Mallinson, J.: test, 904
Malloy, P. F.: test, 1047
Maloney, S. E.: test, 1919
Malsbary, D. R.: rev, 2333
Management Research Group Staff: test, 2211
Mancini, J. A.: rev, 1001, 2000
Mandel, H. P.: test, 37, 2203
Mandell, M. M.: rev, 1200
Manduchi, J. R.: rev, 655
Manges, K. J.: rev, 999
Mangine, S.: test, 1925
Manikam, R.: rev, 81, 2566
Manly, T.: test, 2591
Mann, L.: rev, 287, 809; test, 2356
Mann, R. L.: test, 1910
Mansfield, R.: test, 1920
Manson, M. P.: test, 135, 1527, 2767
Manuele, C. A.: rev, 2779
Manuele-Adkins, C.: rev, 1150, 2202, 2289, 2332, 2376, 2779, 2816
Mar, D. K.: test, 2022, 2722
March, J.: test, 1687
March, J. S.: test, 690
Marchant, G. J.: rev, 978, 1749, 1840, 1927
Marchese, A. C.: test, 551
Marco, G. J.: rev, 1447, 1831, 2405
Marcus, L. M.: test, 2080
Marcus, S. I.: test, 37, 2203
Mardell, C. D.: test, 1852
Mardell-Czudnowski, C.: rev, 2309; test, 802
Margolis, H.: rev, 767, 2125, 2482
Maria, K.: test, 1060
Marjoribanks, J.: test, 2095
Markel-Fox, S.: rev, 709
Markley, R. P.: rev, 2402, 2787, 2788
Markos, J. R.: test, 1019
Markowitz, M.: test, 1872
Markwardt, F. C., Jr.: test, 1865
Marlett, N. J.: test, 64
Marr, H. K.: test, 1867
Marr, M. B.: rev, 914
Marschark, M.: rev, 2239
Marsden, D. B.: test, 894
Marsh, H. W.: test, 2287

Marshall, C. W.: test, 189
Marshall, D.: rev, 2523
Marston, N. C.: test, 72
Martens, B. K.: rev, 691, 1907
Martin, A. W.: test, 208
Martin, C. W.: rev, 183, 1806
Martin, D. G.: rev, 1188
Martin, F.: test, 1534
Martin, N.: test, 2625
Martin, N. A.: test, 2110, 2580
Martin, R. P.: rev, 1783
Martin, S. G.: rev, 2451
Martin, W. E., Jr.: rev, 575, 759, 1026, 1196, 1459, 1867, 1899, 2711
Martindale, T.: rev, 2026
Martinez-Pons, M.: rev, 292, 481
Marting, M. S.: test, 704
Marush, M.: test, 2517
Marwitz, J. H.: test, 1734
Maryolf, S. S.: rev, 1383
Maschka, P.: test, 779
Maslach, C.: test, 1538
Massey, T.: test, 927, 2499
Masson, L. I.: test, 2098
Masters, G.: test, 799, 800, 2640
Mastrangelo, P.: rev, 1725
Mastrangelo, P. M.: rev, 1710, 1711, 1884, 2453
Matarazzo, J. D.: rev, 1352, 1589, 2120
Mathematical Association of America: test, 151, 153, 154
Mathematics Assessment Resource Service: test, 240
Matheny, K. B.: test, 705
Mather, N.: test, 266, 830, 1219, 1550, 2617, 2789, 2795
Mathieu, P. L.: test, 982
Matthews, A.: test, 1994
Mattis, S.: test, 771
Matuszek, P.: rev, 354, 2775
Mauger, P. A.: test, 1264
Maurer, K.: test, 1296
Maurer, M.: test, 2408
Maxfield, F. W.: rev, 2411
Maxwell, J.: rev, 862, 2411
Maxwell, K. L.: test, 212
Maxwell, M. J.: test, 2084
Maxwell, S.: rev, 462
Maydeu-Olivares, A.: test, 2371
Mayer, J. D.: test, 1552
Mayo, C. C.: test, 2650
Mayo, S. T.: rev, 904, 2606
McAlpine, D.: test, 2534
McArthur, C. C.: rev, 2187
McArthur, R.: test, 1204
McBer and Company: test, 561, 1241, 1524
McCabe, P. P.: rev, 1060, 2773
McCall, J. N.: rev, 1086, 1380
McCall, M. W.: test, 2062
McCall, R. J.: rev, 1188, 2187

Mecham, M. J.: test, 2691
Mecham, R. C.: test, 1308, 1977, 2037, 2821
Medelovits, J.: test, 799
Medina-Diaz, M.: rev, 173
Medina-Diaz, M. D. R.: rev, 852, 1741, 2138
Medoff-Cooper, B.: test, 430
Medway, F. J.: rev, 1198, 1460, 1709, 2776
Meeker, M.: test, 773, 774, 1590, 2449
Meeker, R.: test, 773, 774, 2449
Mee-Lee, D.: test, 91, 300, 2141
Megargee, E. I.: rev, 1306, 1701
Mehler, B. L.: test, 1913
Mehlinger, H. D.: rev, 498
Mehrabian, A.: test, 188, 241, 456, 1563, 1564, 1566, 1573, 1574, 1575, 2105, 2667
Mehrens, W. A.: rev, 790, 861, 904, 1292, 2415, 2587
Mehta, S.: rev, 345, 1573, 2320
Meier, M. J.: rev, 337, 341, 1137, 2448
Meier, S. T.: rev, 685, 956, 1552, 1573, 1830, 2225, 2385, 2509
Meikamp, J.: rev, 565, 756, 989, 2752, 2828
Meiklejohn, L.: test, 2538
Meisels, S. J.: test, 894
Meisgeier, C.: test, 1705
Melamed, L. E.: test, 1354
Melchior, L. A.: test, 135
Meldrum, W. B.: rev, 42
Melinger, J.: test, 729
Mellenbruch, P. L.: rev, 2332; test, 1309, 1787
Melton, G. B.: rev, 41, 451, 1401, 1589
Melton, R. S.: rev, 745
Meltzer, H.: rev, 2531
Mendelsohn, G. A.: rev, 1710, 1711
Menefee, K.: rev, 894, 1548
Mengeling, M. A.: test, 1291
Mensh, I. N.: rev, 313, 2751
Merbler, J. B.: test, 299
Mercer, J. R.: test, 62, 2520
Mercier, L.: test, 1678
Merenda, P. F.: rev, 193, 196, 931, 1777, 2115, 2410, 2827
Merker, B. M.: rev, 1635, 1801
Merrell, K. W.: test, 70, 1189, 2003, 2262
Merrifield, P. R.: test, 144, 692
Merten, T.: test, 157
Merwin, J. C.: rev, 378, 835, 2764, 2775
Merwood, P.: test, 1465
Mery, M.: rev, 678
Merz, W. R.: rev, 2391
Merz, W. R., Sr.: rev, 32, 1107, 1128, 2241, 2443, 2658
Mesibov, G.: test, 76
Mesnikoff, A.: test, 2076
Messick, S.: test, 900
Metcalf, K.: test, 2396
MetriTech, Inc.: test, 1249, 1393
Metzgen, K.: test, 2786

Meyer, D. L.: rev, 1028
Meyer, G. R.: test, 2267
Meyer, H. D.: test, 1608
Meyer, J.: test, 2395
Meyers, J.: test, 737
Meyers, J. E.: test, 2167
Meyers, K. R.: test, 2167
Mezger, C.: test, 927, 2499
MHS Staff: test, 688, 689, 823
Michael, J. J.: test, 840, 2469
Michael, L. D.: test, 1662, 1663, 1664
Michael, W. B.: rev, 382, 778, 795, 1033, 1383, 1441, 1623, 1646, 1764, 1765, 1774, 1872, 1954, 2067; test, 840, 2469
Michaels, H.: rev, 2251
Michaels, L.: test, 1781
Michaelson, R. B.: test, 1004
Middleton, G.: rev, 2763
Miedaner, J.: test, 1618
Migotsky, C. P.: rev, 2685
Miguel, S. A.: test, 803
Milchus, N. J.: test, 968, 2106, 2286
MILCOM Systems, A Division of Hollister, Inc.: test, 1619
Miles, C.: test, 2828
Milholland, J. E.: rev, 742, 1292, 1819, 1953
Milianti, F. J.: test, 1183
Millar, G.: test, 1567
Miller, C.: rev, 689, 2659
Miller, C. D.: rev, 1437
Miller, D. C.: rev, 838, 988, 1051, 1647, 1731, 2198; test, 1363, 1364
Miller, E. N.: test, 380
Miller, G. A.: test, 2479
Miller, G. E.: rev, 1290
Miller, H. J.: test, 1624, 1625, 1626, 1627, 1628, 1629, 1630, 1631, 1632, 1633, 1634, 1635
Miller, J.: test, 2786
Miller, J. A.: test, 553
Miller, J. F.: rev, 547
Miller, J. K.: rev, 624
Miller, J. M.: rev, 624
Miller, K. M.: test, 1089, 1546, 2192, 2193
Miller, L.: test, 1991
Miller, L. C.: rev, 3, 893, 1660
Miller, L. H.: test, 1913
Miller, L. J.: test, 1029, 1447, 1623, 2306, 2433, 2658
Miller, M. A.: test, 1363, 1364
Miller, M. D.: rev, 299, 624, 717, 793, 1134, 1153, 1214, 1343, 2563
Miller, P.: test, 721
Miller, R. J.: rev, 67, 223, 1218, 1774, 2127
Miller, S.: test, 721
Miller, T. K.: test, 2461
Miller-Whitehead, M.: rev, 890, 1108, 1393, 1723
Millis, S. R.: test, 157
Millman, J.: test, 713

Sabers, D. L.: rev, 12, 282, 311, 414, 668, 802, 844, 1081, 1109, 1233, 1567, 2045, 2634
Sackett, P. R.: rev, 1308
Sadowski, C. J.: rev, 198, 1747, 2814
Safran, C.: test, 2202
Sagen, H. B.: rev, 265, 2728
Sagris-Desmond, A.: test, 1533
Saigh, P. A.: rev, 354, 2775; test, 479
Sailor, P.: rev, 2445
Sakauye, K.: rev, 184, 1699
Saleh, S. D.: test, 1310
Salekin, R. T.: test, 2177
Salkind, N. J.: test, 1540
Salmon, J. D.: test, 2145
Salmon, J. D., Jr.: test, 2143
Salovey, P.: test, 1552
Salvia, J.: rev, 2660; test, 2152;, 2558
Samar, V. J.: rev, 487, 488, 548, 1796, 1944, 2195, 2239, 2608
Sampers, J. L.: test, 1601
Sampson, J. P., Jr.: test, 426
Sanchez, D. T.: rev, 2388
Sanchez, J. I.: test, 751
Sanchez, P.: rev, 724
Sander, D.: rev, 1488
Sanders, C.: rev, 23, 24
Sanders, J. R.: rev, 2386; test, 2481
Sandford, J. A.: test, 1301
Sandler, A. D.: test, 1868
Sandman, R. S.: test, 1545
Sandor, J. A.: test, 9
Sandoval, J.: rev, 283, 461, 879, 1538, 2520, 2749, 2750, 2795; test, 467
Sands, E. S.: test, 281
Sandy, C. A.: rev, 2562
Sanford, A. R.: test, 1421
Sanford, E. E.: rev, 537, 970, 1135, 1140, 1303, 1646, 1762, 2186, 2199, 2396
Sanger, D. D.: rev, 548
Santa-Barbara, J.: test, 999
Santmire, T. E.: rev, 185, 1907
Santogrossi, J.: rev, 2139
Sares, T.: rev, 830
Sargent, D. M.: rev, 2422
Sargent, H.: rev, 2187
Sarmousakis, G.: rev, 911
Sarno, M. T.: test, 1053
Sartorius, N.: test, 2020
Sashkin, M.: test, 685, 1242, 1404, 1553, 1811
Satter, G. A.: rev, 312, 534
Sattler, J. M.: rev, 311, 1349, 1372, 1556, 2708
Satz, P.: test, 470, 629, 1738
Saudargas, R. A.: rev, 496
Saunders, D. E.: test, 426
Saunders, D. M.: rev, 1499
Saunders, J.: test, 137
Saunders, P.: test, 2621

Saunders, S. M.: test, 1159
Sauser, W. I., Jr.: rev, 416, 978, 1021, 1134, 1319, 1721, 2037, 2193, 2015, 2090; rev, 1232, 1936
Savage, A. W.: test, 1876
Saville & Holdsworth Ltd.: test, 1492, 2212, 2550, 2825
Saville, P.: test, 127, 736, 1937, 2049, 2551
Sawyer, D. I.: rev, 1243
Sawyer, D. J.: rev, 1050, 1128, 1353, 2009, 2125, 2359, 2640, 2730
Sawyer, N.: rev, 2726
Saxton, J.: test, 2315
Saxton, M. J.: test, 1361
Scannell, D. P.: rev, 204, 1747, 2113; test, 402, 2634
Scantron Corporation: test, 1886
Schacter, H.: rev, 1453
Schaefer, M. T.: test, 1889
Schaefer, W. C.: rev, 2698
Schaeffer, D.: test, 1777
Schaeffer, J.: test, 1777
Schafer, D. S.: test, 884
Schafer, R. E.: rev, 829
Schafer, W. D.: rev, 360, 419, 648, 673, 1292, 1349, 2256, 2266
Schaffer, B.: test, 76
Schaffer, C. E.: test, 213, 781
Schaffer, W. D.: rev, 2139
Schaie, K. W.: rev, 539, 1352, 2300; test, 2244
Schalock, R. L.: test, 2495
Schaufeli, W. B.: test, 1538
Scheel, M. J.: rev, 1635, 2403
Scheffers, W.: test, 2714
Schein, E. H.: test, 405
Schelfhout, S.: test, 695
Schepers, J. M.: rev, 1041
Scherer, J.: test, 1877
Scherer, M. J.: test, 1539, 1541
Scherzer, C. R. S.: rev, 1844
Schindler, A. W.: rev, 378
Schinka, J. A.: test, 478, 801, 1163, 1596, 1597, 1598, 1737, 1900, 1901, 1906, 1907
Schinke, S.: rev, 149, 899
Schinke, S. P.: rev, 462, 1156
Schissel, R. J.: rev, 2759
Schlebusch, D.: test, 1267
Schlieve, P. L.: test, 660
Schmand, B.: test, 157, 2712
Schmeck, R. R.: test, 1278
Schmid, R. F.: rev, 1545
Schmidt, M. M.: test, 1259
Schmidt, F.: rev, 316, 945
Schmidt, F. L.: rev, 1524, 2793
Schmidt, J. P.: test, 1422
Schmidt, M.: test, 2166
Schmidt, M. W.: test, 2152
Schmidt, S. M.: test, 1368
Schmitt, J. F.: rev, 1326

Schmitt, N.: rev, 835, 1321, 2039; test, 654
Schmuckler, J.: rev, 48
Schneck, G. R.: rev, 28, 1263, 1876, 2221, 2722, 2816
Schneider, E. A.: test, 1871
Schneider, N. G.: test, 2363
Schneider, W. J.: rev, 296, 458, 1593, 2800
Schneidmann, N. V.: rev, 438
Schnell, L. H.: rev, 182
Schneller, J.: test, 2087
Schoen, H. L.: test, 1288
Schoendorf, K.: test, 41
Schoenfeldt, L. F.: rev, 2601, 2793
Schoenrade, P.: rev, 1458, 2401, 2695
Schofield, W.: rev, 313, 2194
Scholastic Testing Service, Inc.: test, 555, 1175, 2107
Schonfeld, L.: test, 2477
Schopler, E.: test, 76, 460, 2080
Schowengerdt, R. V.: rev, 72
Schrader, W. B.: rev, 10, 11, 1622, 2264, 2327
Schram, M.: test, 209
Schrank, F. A.: rev, 186, 329, 414; test, 266, 830, 2789, 2795
Schraw, G.: rev, 289, 1136, 1360, 1428, 1667, 2174, 2466, 2690, 2793
Schretlen, D.: test, 348
Schroeder, L. C.: test, 1554
Schubert, D. S. P.: test, 2264
Schubert, H. J. P.: test, 2264
Schueler, H.: rev, 583
Schuerger, J. M.: test, 2347
Schuler, H.: test, 36
Schulte, A. C.: test, 1424
Schultz, D. G.: rev, 1580, 1787
Schultz, G. F.: rev, 35
Schur, S.: test, 1057
Schuster, D. H.: rev, 2784
Schuster, J. W.: test, 212
Schutz, R. E.: rev, 250, 835
Schutz, R. P.: test, 2722
Schutz, W.: test, 1027, 1542
Schwarting, G.: rev, 340, 803, 818, 880, 1466, 1869, 2005, 2016, 2018
Schwartz, M. F.: test, 1722
Schwartz, N. H.: rev, 1868
Schweigert, P.: test, 162
Schwesinger, G. C.: rev, 742, 1972
Science Research Associates: test, 672, 673, 1789, 2123, 2204, 2333, 2601, 2683
Science Research Associates, Inc.: test, 1716
Scientific Management Techniques, Inc.: test, 2405
Scolley, R. W.: test, 1791
Scott, C. R.: test, 2656
Scott, N. L.: test, 2725
Scott, O., III: rev, 2373
The Scottish Education Department: test, 903
Search Institute: test, 2275
Seashore, H.: rev, 1102, 1103

Seashore, H. G.: test, 834, 835, 836
Sebolt, D.: rev, 2379
Secolsky, C.: rev, 1817
Secord, W.: test, 549, 2596, 2604, 2628
Secord, W. A.: test, 541, 547, 548, 550
Sedlacek, W. E.: test, 1749, 2341
Seel, R. T.: test, 1734
Seeman, W.: rev, 1890
Segal, M.: test, 1722
Segel, D.: rev, 1288, 1383
Seguin, E.: test, 2280
Seifert, K.: test, 452
Seim, N. J.: test, 1223, 2210
Seklemian, P.: test, 2352
Selby MillSmith Ltd.: test, 215, 216, 217, 1875
Selby, E. C.: test, 2705
Seligman, R.: rev, 2289
Sell, D. E.: test, 967, 1791
Sells, S. B.: rev, 716
Selmar, J. W.: test, 1950
Selover, R. B.: rev, 1649
Seltzer, G. B.: rev, 2102
Selzer, M. L.: test, 1609
Semel, E.: test, 547, 548, 549, 550
Semeonoff, B.: rev, 1002, 1332, 2115
Semmel, M. I.: rev, 3, 2201
Severson, H. H.: test, 896, 2252, 2521
Sewell, K. W.: test, 971
Sewell, T. E.: rev, 701
Seymour, H. N.: test, 820, 821
Shaffer, J. C.: test, 949
Shaffer, L. F.: rev, 385, 465, 864, 907, 975, 1087, 1294, 1447, 1972, 2187, 2652, 2749, 2750
Shaffer, M. B.: rev, 158, 342, 465, 1141, 1150, 1598
Shallice, T.: test, 1154
Shanahan, T.: rev, 329, 369, 832, 2125
Shanker, J. L.: test, 914
Shannon, G. P.: test, 1291
Shapiro, D. A.: rev, 548, 2575, 2582
Shapiro, D. H., Jr.: test, 2326
Shapiro, E.: test, 14
Shapiro, E. S.: rev, 369, 1353, 2158
Shapiro, H.: test, 779
Shapiro, J. P.: test, 227
Shaw, J. H.: test, 1160
Shaw, M. E.: rev, 2341
Shaw, S. R.: rev, 208, 348, 564, 890, 1345, 1833, 2166, 2358, 2805
Shaycoft, M. F.: rev, 555
Shear, S. M.: rev, 2158
Shearer, C. B.: test, 1615
Shearer, M.: test, 804
Shears, M.: test, 2290
Sheehan, E. P.: rev, 1303, 1311, 1497, 1500, 1721, 1812, 2445, 2809, 2833
Sheeley, E. C.: rev, 1083
Sheldon, K. L.: rev, 1562

Stuberg, W.: test, 1618
Stuit, D. B.: rev, 2162
Stunkard, A. J.: test, 900
Stutman, G.: rev, 440, 656, 1243, 2137, 2598
Subkoviak, M. J.: rev, 743, 1080, 1292, 2276, 2410, 2619
Sudhalter, V.: test, 1862
Sudweeks, R. R.: rev, 914
Sue, M. B.: test, 2569
Suen, H. K.: rev, 262, 805, 927, 1705, 1730, 1872, 2013, 2582, 2632, 2701
Suess, A. R.: rev, 1747
Sugden, D. A.: test, 1680
Suinn, R. M.: rev, 2561
Sundberg, N.: rev, 2473
Sundberg, N. D.: rev, 275, 1313, 1361, 1710, 1711, 1912, 2157, 2299, 2411
Sundre, D. L.: rev, 1249, 1595, 1934
Super, D. E.: rev, 1649, 1670; test, 2486, 2695
Suppa, C. H.: rev, 59, 2752
Sutton, R.: rev, 2600
Sutton, R. E.: rev, 640, 765, 1366, 1739, 2671, 2701
Suydam, M. N.: rev, 258
Svinicki, J.: test, 267
Svinicki, J. G.: rev, 1974, 2096
Swain, C.: test, 660
Swanson, D.: test, 765
Swanson, H. L.: rev, 2713; test, 2514
Swart, D. J.: test, 177
Swartz, A.: test, 2693
Swartz, J. D.: rev, 188, 1286, 2645
Swartz-Kulstad, J. L.: rev, 78, 1337
Swassing, C. S.: rev, 899, 2086
Swearer, S. M.: rev, 436, 1261, 2171, 2438
Sweeney, T. J.: test, 1031, 2761
Swensen, C. H.: rev, 213; test, 2231, 2233
Swenson, C. H., Jr.: rev, 2224
Swerdlik, M. E.: rev, 296, 351, 805, 1060, 1593, 1819, 1833, 2019, 2414, 2631; test, 2082
Swerdlik, P.: test, 2082
Swihart, A. A.: test, 2315
Switzer, J.: test, 1755
Switzky, H. N.: rev, 60, 298, 796, 2516, 2786
Sykken, D. T.: rev, 386
Symonds, P. M.: rev, 1039, 1890
Szczepanski, M.: test, 883

Tade, W. J.: test, 2355
Tafrate, R. C.: test, 163
Taggart, B.: test, 1205
Taggart, W.: test, 1205
Tai, W. L.: rev, 1231
Taljaard, J. J.: test, 2664
Talley, J. L.: test, 468, 2787
Tamir, P.: test, 633
Tan, X.: rev, 888
Tannenbaum, A. J.: rev, 742

Tarter, R. E.: test, 860
Tasse, M. J.: test, 2495
Tate, R.: test, 2180
Tatsuoka, K. K.: rev, 1997, 2619
Tattersall, P. J.: test, 2456
Taulbee, E. S.: rev, 2736
Taylor, A. P.: test, 2530
Taylor, E. K.: rev, 937, 1649, 1938, 1939, 2764; test, 2205
Taylor, E. M.: rev, 1070
Taylor, H. F.: test, 705
Taylor, H. R.: rev, 403
Taylor, K. M.: test, 413
Taylor, P. A.: rev, 2563
Taylor, R. A.: test, 1452
Taylor, R. L.: test, 199
Taylor, R. M.: test, 1004, 2531
Taylor, R. N.: rev, 1514, 2332
Taylor, T. R.: test, 1020, 1172, 1234, 2048, 2191
Teagarden, F. M.: rev, 438, 2708
Tearnan, B. H.: test, 297
Teele, S.: test, 2553
Teeter, P. A.: rev, 71, 1346
Teitzel, T.: test, 2001, 2005
Teleometrics International: test, 2099
Tellegen, A.: rev, 990, 991; test, 1654, 1655
Tellegen, P. J.: test, 2364
Telzrow, C.: rev, 895
Telzrow, C. F.: rev, 791, 880, 1329
Tenopyr, M. L.: rev, 1381, 2808
Terborg, J. R.: test, 1522
Terwilliger, J. S.: rev, 57
Tesh, A.: rev, 1784, 2064
The Test Agency Ltd.: test, 916, 1560
Test Development Committees, American Association of Teachers of Spanish and Portuguese: test, 1720
Test Development Unit of the Foundation for Educational Research in England and Wales: test, 1548
Testing and Certification Division, English Language Institute, University of Michigan: test, 950
Testut, E. W.: rev, 1883, 2239
Tetenbaum, T. J.: test, 226
Thayer, P. W.: rev, 1787, 1789, 2162, 2332, 2333
Thetford, W. N.: rev, 1188
Thibaudeau, G.: test, 2577
Thoma, S.: test, 765
Thomas, A.: test, 1742
Thomas, G. F.: test, 1985
Thomas, G. V.: test, 1925
Thomas, J. W.: test, 2650
Thomas, K. W.: test, 1985, 2443, 2651
Thomas, R.: test, 2254
Thomas, R. G.: rev, 1303, 1649, 1774
Thomas, T. J.: test, 2650
Thompson, B.: rev, 1285, 1550, 2749, 2750
Thompson, D.: rev, 486, 756, 1380, 1776

Winrow, B.: test, 2217

Winrow, B. A.: test, 159, 160, 372, 373, 389, 538, 670, 671, 1298, 1732, 1733, 1769, 2046, 2047, 2058, 2549, 2735

Winston, R. B.: test, 9

Winston, R. B., Jr.: test, 2461

Winterowd, C. L.: rev, 1541

Winters, K. C.: test, 80, 1896, 1897, 1898, 1899

Winward, C. E.: test, 2179

Wirt, R. D.: rev, 465, 477, 1332

Wirtz, P. W.: test, 82

Wise, S. L.: rev, 1782, 1795

Wiseman, S.: rev, 1292

Wiske, M. S.: test, 894

Wiswell, R.: test, 1054

Witkin, H. A.: test, 1119

Witmer, J. M.: test, 2761

Witt, J. C.: rev, 283, 293, 330, 1052, 1668, 2749, 2750

Witt, L. A.: rev, 1517, 1931

Witta, E. L.: rev, 2069, 2352

Wittenborn, J. R.: rev, 2187, 2346 2349, 2645

Witty, P. A.: rev, 378

Wnek, L.: test, 267

Wochos, G. C.: rev, 1159

Wodrich, D. L.: rev, 1556, 2019

Woff, I. R.: test, 26

Woff, I.: test, 30

Wojcik, J. V.: test, 1159

Wojcik, K.: rev, 1311

Wolf, M.: test, 2121

Wolf, R. M.: rev, 1256, 1604, 1889

Wolfe, J. M.: test, 175, 2522, 2523, 2731, 2791

Wolfe, J. W.: test, 2790

Wolfe, V. V.: test, 1841

Wolf-Schein, E. G.: test, 288

Wolkind, S.: rev, 1730

Wollack, J. A.: rev, 355, 1355, 2409, 2410

Wolpe, J.: test, 1014

Woltmann, A. G.: rev, 465, 1084, 2194

Womble, M. N.: rev, 1561, 1747

Women's Studies Program, Duke University: test, 965

Womer, F.: rev, 378

Wonderlic Consulting: test, 1891

Wonderlic Inc.: test, 661, 957, 2793

Wonderlic, E. F.: rev, 533, 1649

Wood, H. B.: rev, 1604

Wood, M.: rev, 33; test, 1027

Wood, M. M.: test, 807

Woodcock, R. W.: test, 266, 761, 830, 1083, 1272, 1550, 1646, 2240, 2789, 2794, 2795, 2796, 2797, 2798

Woodford, P. E.: rev, 724

Woody, C.: rev, 2721

Worcester, D. A.: rev, 790

Worell, J.: test, 1838

Worell, L.: test, 1838

Workman, E.: rev, 288

Worland, J.: rev, 2762

World Health Organization: test, 2249

Worley, J. W.: test, 2834

Wormith, J. S.: test, 1448

Worth, M. J.: test, 1231

Worthen, B. R.: rev, 914, 2386, 2445

Wozniak, J.: test, 1353

Wright, B. D.: rev, 360

Wright, C. R.: rev, 151, 195, 666, 1243, 1323, 1538, 1833, 1897, 1904, 1947, 2326

Wright, D.: rev, 358, 1121, 2588

Wright, E. N.: test, 399, 2202

Wright, L.: rev, 80, 883, 1279

Wrightstone, J. W.: test, 10, 11, 533, 1284, 1453, 1578

Wrobel, T. A.: rev, 1644

Wu, M.: test, 1356

Wunderlich, K. C.: test, 286, 2002

Wylie, E.: test, 233

Wynne, M. K.: rev, 1184, 1603

Yamamoto, K.: test, 964

Yanico, B.: test, 412

Yates, A. J.: rev, 2328

Yazak, D. L.: rev, 655, 1873

Yegidis, B. L.: test, 8

Yelland, T.: rev, 259, 1246

Yetter, G.: rev, 1307, 1760

Yockelson, S.: test, 130

Yorkston, K. M.: test, 207

Young, A.: test, 966, 994

Young, D.: test, 558, 1125, 1128, 1750, 1833, 2391, 2527

Young, E. C.: test, 1859

Young, J. C.: test, 2635

Young, J. W.: rev, 1074, 1128, 1343, 1592, 2423, 2588, 2617

Young, S.: rev, 1844, 2046

Youniss, R. P.: test, 1268

Ysseldyke, J. E.: rev, 282, 339, 817, 875, 1661, 1726, 1727, 2304, 2414

Ysseldyke, J.: rev, 688, 1072; test, 1052

Zabel, R. H.: rev, 2713

Zachar, P.: rev, 699, 1302, 1351, 1640, 2187, 2265

Zachary, R. A.: test, 2328

Zakay, D.: rev, 2044

Zangwill, O. L.: rev, 1667

Zapf, S. A.: test, 2311

Zarit, J. M.: test, 1591

Zarit, S. H.: test, 1591

Zarske, J. A.: rev, 71, 1701

Zedeck, S.: rev, 310, 419, 1315, 1517, 1651, 1652, 1676, 1764, 2070, 2136, 2204, 2210, 2343

Zehler, A. M.: test, 94

Zehrbach, R. R.: test, 659

Zeisloft-Falbey, B.: test, 1169

SCORE INDEX

This Score Index lists all the scores, in alphabetical order, for all the tests included in Tests in Print VII. Because test scores can be regarded as operational definitions of the variable measured, sometimes the scores provide better leads to what a test actually measures than the test title or other available information. The Score Index is very detailed, and the reader should keep in mind that a given variable (or concept) of interest may be defined in several different ways. Thus the reader should look up these several possible alternative definitions before drawing final conclusions about whether tests measuring a particular variable of interest can be located in TIP VII. If the kind of score sought is located in a particular test or tests, the reader should then read the test descriptive information carefully to determine whether the test(s) in which the score is found is (are) consistent with reader purpose. Used wisely, the Score Index can be another useful resource in locating the right score in the right test. As usual, all numbers in the index are test numbers, not page numbers.

Awareness Score: 694
Away from People (A): 2529

B-expectation: 1437
Babbling: 234
Back F (FB): 1655
Back-Up Style-Parent: 1931
Background: 376, 1823
Background and Work Experience: 1396, 2153
Background/Education/Work Experience: 1788
Background Information: 623, 624, 1721
Background Knowledge: 1536
Background Noise: 1083
Backward: 476
Backward Digit Recall: 2829
Backward Digit Span Accuracy: 572
Backward Parachute: 1618
Backwards Digit Span: 875
Backwards Parachute: 1235
Backwards Span: 871
Bad Impression: 93
Balance: 366, 1188, 1301, 1707, 2018, 2135, 2607
Balance Between Personal Life And Work: 310
Balance of World: 171, 1893
Balance Responses: 1601
Balanced Cohesion: 992
Balanced Flexibility: 992
Balanced Judgment: 751
Ball Handling Skills: 1203
Ball Skills: 1680
Balloon Portraits and Story: 682
Bank Deposit: 1785
Bank Manager: 394, 407
Bank Reconciliation: 1785
Bank Teller: 407, 408
Banker: 2445
Banking and Accounting: 414
Barber/Hairstylist: 407, 408
Barbiturates: 1896
Bargain: 1505
Bargaining: 685, 1241, 1368
Barrier: 1188, 1892
Barriers: 1708
Barriers to Employment: 2727
Basal Left: 314
Basal Reader Phonics: 2131
Basal Reader Whole-Word: 2131
Basal Right: 314
Basal Vocabulary: 763
Based on Body: 2340
Baserunning: 2379
Basic: 1506
Basic AC & DC Theory: 1486
Basic AC/DC Theory: 918
Basic AC/DC Theory and Electrical Maintenance: 915
Basic AC/DC Theory/Power Distribution and Electrical Maintenance: 1683

Basic Academic Skills: 1994
Basic Academics: 796
Basic Algebra: 627
Basic Calculations: 660
Basic Care: 1000
Basic Checking: 1937, 2049
Basic Communication Skills: 1642
Basic Concepts: 63, 330, 549, 656, 1355, 2396
Basic Creative Comfort: 1223, 2210
Basic Creature Comfort: 940, 1855
Basic-Creature Comfort: 2813
Basic Electricity/Electronics: 2780
Basic Encoding Skills: 337
Basic Facts Screening: 1696
Basic Filing Skills: 73
Basic Grammar: 1962
Basic Information: 190, 570, 789, 790
Basic Interest Area Scales: 408
Basic Interest Scales: 414
Basic Internet Knowledge: 2552
Basic Level: 2259
Basic Machines: 2780
Basic Math: 1785
Basic Math Calculations: 73
Basic Math Computation: 1668
Basic Mathematical Ability: 30
Basic Neurological Functions/Intactness: 270
Basic Number Skills: 833
Basic Operations Involving Decimals and Percentages: 2123
Basic Operations Involving Fractions: 2123
Basic Operations Involving Geometry and Word Problems: 2123
Basic Operations Involving Square Roots and Powers: 2123
Basic Oral Word Reading: 337
Basic Physical Properties of Matter and Materials: 2780
Basic Problem Solving and Reading: 1725
Basic Process Scores: 827
Basic Reading: 1668, 2755, 2774
Basic Reading Skills: 2789, 2794, 2795, 2796
Basic Sales Skills: 2208
Basic Senses and Functions: 2730
Basic Sight Phrases: 914
Basic Sight Words: 914
Basic Skills: 555, 904, 1646
Basic Skills and Concepts: 1057
Basic Skills Cluster: 2798
Basic Speech and Hearing Processes: 495
Basic Spelling: 1668
Basic Story Words: 1060
Basic Symbol Recognition: 337
Basic Task Areas: 198
Basic Training Conditions: 1471
Basic Vocabulary and Grammatical Structures: 949
Basic Word Discrimination: 337

Personal Style: 1529, 1781
Personal Superstitious Thinking: 693
Personal Traits: 1529
Personal Values: 492
Personal Warmth: 1876
Personality: 376, 1202, 1658, 1669, 1823
Personality/Behavior: 2842
Personality Disorder Domain: 84
Personality Disorder Factor: 84
Personality Disorder Scores: 1925
Personality Disorders: 1990
Personality Evaluation: 1933
Personality Functions: 2557
Personality Issues: 2000
Personality Mediators: 786
Personality-Pain Coping Style: 485
Personality Patterns: 1636
Personality Primary Factor Scores: 1397
Personality Reliability Index: 1934
Personality Scores: 93
Personality Traits: 957
Personality Type: 957
Personalized: 1986, 1987
Personalized Customer Relations: 2312
Personnel: 2057
Personnel and Human Resources: 1035
Personnel and Training: 1499
Personnel Management: 1213, 1214
Personnel Manager: 407, 408
Personnel Policies: 1310
Personnel Policies and Procedures: 2505
Personnel Practices: 1517, 2519
Perspective: 2568
Perspectives on Technologies: 1541
Persuader: 1269
Persuading: 1499
Persuading/Influencing Employees: 1443
Persuasion: 1035, 1418
Persuasive: 395, 414, 1062, 1380, 1409, 1715, 1797, 2090, 2191, 2192, 2212, 2417
Persuasive/Interactive: 316
Persuasive Interest: 324
Persuasive Negotiation: 2211
Persuasiveness: 425, 492, 1416, 1602, 2281, 2336
Pervasive Developmental Problems: 33, 429
Pervasive Distrust/Delusions: 2819
Pessimism: 1703, 1704
PETRA Threat Assessment Matrix score: 2087
Petty Cash: 1785
Pharmacist: 407, 2445
Pharmacy Technician: 407, 408
Pharmacy: 905
Pharyngeal Control: 876
Pharyngeal Phase: 2513
Pharyngeal Stage: 876
Pharyngeal State: 280
Pharynx: 1806

Philosophy: 443, 1406, 1495, 1511, 1515, 2473, 2474
Philosophy and Religion: 905
Philosophy and Theology: 1035
Phlegmatic: 2560, 2834
Phlegmatic vs. Excitable: 477
Phobia: 709, 2078
Phobias: 1923
Phobias–Social: 823
Phobias–Specific: 823
Phobic Anxiety: 344, 346, 784, 2268, 2517, 2518
Phobic Feeling: 86
Phobic Personality: 1286
Phonation: 869
Phoneme Awareness: 260
Phoneme Deletion: 2610
Phoneme Deletion–Beginning Sounds: 1946
Phoneme Deletion–End Sounds: 1946
Phoneme/Grapheme Knowledge: 2795
Phoneme-Grapheme Correspondence: 1127
Phoneme Isolation: 1944, 2005
Phoneme Reversal: 666
Phoneme Segmentation: 260, 1944, 2005
Phoneme Segmentation Fluency: 832
Phonemes: 890, 1388, 2033
Phonemes in Spoken Words: 862
Phonemic Analysis: 816, 2598
Phonemic Awareness: 229, 887, 1043, 1216, 1363, 1944, 2420, 2789, 2795
Phonemic Awareness and Decoding: 358
Phonemic Decoding Efficiency: 2629
Phonemic-Initial Sounds: 1295
Phonemic Recoding: Bridging to Written Words: 194
Phonemic Segmentation: 871, 875
Phonetic Analysis: 1107, 2414
Phonetic Skills: 1949
Phonic Patterns: 763
Phonic Spelling of Words: 862
Phonic Words: 763
Phonics: 337, 829, 1043, 1216, 2420
Phonics-Initial Blends and Digraphs: 1295
Phonics Knowledge: 2789
Phonics Method: 2131
Phonics Patterns: 731
Phonics/Sight Ratio: 828
Phonics Written: 829
Phonograms: 862, 914
Phonological Awareness: 548, 549, 666, 887, 890, 1044, 1107, 1349, 1948, 2609, 2610, 2794
Phonological Awareness Ability: 2608
Phonological Blending: 2580
Phonological Discrimination: 873, 2018, 2135
Phonological Memory: 666
Phonological Processes: 2355
Phonological Processes Composite: 243
Phonological Processing: 891, 1731
Phonological Recoding Skills: 1534
Phonological Segmentation: 2580

Total Auditory Memory: 1428
Total Battery: 2636
Total Behavior: 956
Total Child: 1839
Total Cholesterol: 2685
Total Cognition: 956
Total Communication: 1835
Total Competence: 33
Total Composite: 2747
Total Composite Score: 2753, 2755
Total Composite Severity Rating: 569
Total Comprehension: 1243
Total Comprehension Passage Level: 2126
Total Correct: 674
Total Correct Responses: 1826
Total Correct Score: 2663
Total Correct Strings: 1826
Total Critical Events: 2521
Total Difference: 2198
Total Displacement Score: 1470
Total Distress: 2171
Total Emotional Behavioral Checklist: 927
Total EQ: 932, 933, 934
Total Error Score: 228
Total Errors: 230, 838
Total Execution Time: 2663
Total Expectation: 1437
Total Extroversion: 723
Total Family Satisfaction: 1005
Total Family Violence Score: 1007
Total General Conceptual Ability: 833
Total/General Educational Development-L (GED-L): 2693
Total/General Educational Development-M (GED-M): 2693
Total/Grade Level: 2693
Total Growth Chart Score: 1110
Total Incorrect Responses: 1826
Total Index: 1339
Total Initiation Time: 2663
Total Interaction: 269
Total Intrinsic: 1310
Total Intrusions: 468, 1592
Total Involvement: 1003
Total Items Circled: 1736
Total Items Correct: 2704
Total Language: 353, 826, 2013, 2387, 2409
Total Language Composite: 820, 2691
Total Left: 313
Total Level of Risk: 2478
Total Life Change Unit: 563
Total Love Scale: 2231
Total Maladaptive Behavior: 2521
Total Mathematics: 173, 1604, 2387, 2409, 2410, 2636, 2637
Total Mathematics Self-Efficacy Score: 1547
Total Memory Composite: 2752

Total Mids: 2531
Total Miscues: 2126
Total Motor: 353, 1864
Total Move Score: 2663
Total Naturalized Attention Test Score: 1722
Total Negative: 1576
Total Negative Behavior: 2521
Total Negative Emotions: 238
Total No-Responses: 1826
Total Number Correct: 2787, 2788
Total Number Correct Score: 2638
Total Number of Clauses: 2446
Total Number of Conjunction Cohesion Ties: 2446
Total Number of Errors: 2787, 2788
Total Number of Story Grammar Components: 2446
Total Occurrences of Major Phonological Deviations: 1184
Total Omissions: 2557
Total Parent: 1839
Total Parenting Stress: 2438
Total Pathology: 931
Total Pegs Correctly Placed: 1114
Total Percentile Rank: 88, 221, 878, 879
Total Physical Child Abuse: 451
Total PMT: 206
Total Positive: 1576
Total Positive and Negative Emotions: 238
Total Positive Behavior: 2521
Total Positive Emotions: 238
Total Predisposition Score: 2311
Total Problem-Solving Time: 2663
Total Problems: 33
Total Protective Factors: 811
Total Psychological Distress: 1689
Total Quality of Life: 2102
Total Raw Score: 2128
Total Readiness: 1943
Total Reading: 173, 1604, 1865, 2387, 2409, 2410, 2572, 2789, 2794
Total Reading Standard Score: 1945
Total Reading Time: 2126
Total Reading–Full Scale: 2798
Total Reading–Short Scale: 2798
Total Recall: 350, 694, 1048, 1195
Total Recognition Discriminability: 388
Total Reference Cohesion Ties: 2446
Total Rehabilitation: 2143
Total Relationship-Behavior: 2343
Total Resolution: 1576
Total Response: 2445
Total Right: 313
Total RIST Index: 2174
Total Rules Violation: 2663
Total Satisfaction: 2497
Total Scaled Score: 4
Total Scholastic Aptitude: 835
Total Science: 1798